THE
NEW ENGLAND
HISTORICAL AND GENEALOGICAL
REGISTER

INDEX OF PERSONS

VOLUMES 51 - 148

I - Q

THE
NEW ENGLAND
HISTORICAL AND GENEALOGICAL
REGISTER

INDEX OF PERSONS

VOLUMES 51 - 148

I - Q

Jane Fletcher Fiske, Editor

New England Historic Genealogical Society

Boston

1995

Library of Congress Catalog Number 94-73898

ISBN 0-88082-038-1

Published by

New England Historic Genealogical Society

Printed by Picton Press, Camden, Maine

INDEX OF PERSONS

IASIGI Amy Gore **78** 205
  82 126 247 497
  Annie Walker **82** 497
  Eulalie Lois **82** 497
  Joseph **82** 497
  Nora **82** 497
  Oscar **82** 497
  Oscar (Mrs.) **77** 155 **78** 205
IBBOTSON Ibbitson
  Esther **117** 294
  Henry **117** 294
  Jane **117** 286
  Levi **117** 286
  Robert **72** 159
  Sheila J. **117** 293
IBERT Matthew **65** 230
IBROOK —— **57** 337 **121**
  24 116
  Elizabeth **131** 125
  Ellen **121** 10 **131** 125
  John **131** 316
  Margaret **92** 192 **102** 307
  121 11
  Peter **55** 302
  Rebecca **55** 302 **121** 3
  Richard **131** 316
  Robert **92** 192
IBSEN Henrik **65** 3
ICHINGHAM
  Edward **98** 278
  Mary **98** 278
ICKS Gertrude Genevieve
  (Duel) **114** 161 **118** 79
  120 235
  Robert J. **114** 161 **118** 79
  120 235
IDDENDEN
  Agnes **95** 262 263
  Anne **68** 188
  Christian **68** 187-189
  Edmund **70** 349
  Edward **68** 187
  Elizabeth **68** 187
  George **95** 262 263
  James **95** 262 263
  Jane **68** 187
  Joan **68** 187
  John **68** 187-189
  Katharine **68** 187 189
  Margaret **68** 187
  Mary **68** 186 187 189
  75 225

IDDENDEN cont'd
  Nathan **95** 262 263
  Richard **68** 187
  Stephen **70** 349
  Thomas **68** 187
  Thomasine **68** 187
  William **68** 187 188
IDDINGS Mary **74** xlv
IDE —— **100** 57
  — Lieut. **62** 371
  Abigail **57** 225 **87** 263
  Amanda (Bishop) **114** 285
  Amos **96** 260
  Benjamin **96** 260
  Betsey **114** 285
  Catherine **115** 124
  Charles **93** 341
  Clarissa **57** 190
  Corinne **63** 49
  Daniel **96** 269 270
  Eliza Ann **81** 187
  Elizabeth **96** 269
  Elizabeth (Cooper) **96** 269
  Elpalet **114** 285 287
  Experience **96** 269
  Ezra **57** 225 **96** 401 **105** 281
  114 285 287
  George **66** 22
  Gregory **57** 190
  Hannah (Carpenter)
  96 270
  Herbert C. **53** 133 **60** 185
  Jacob **54** lxxxi **59** 232
  96 260
  Jane **96** 255
  John **66** 21 22 24 **96** 260
  99 94 97 98 108
  Jonathan **114** 285 287
  Joseph **81** 187
  Josiah **96** 269 **98** 327
  Lemuel **135** 302
  Lucy **96** 264
  Lydia **114** 285
  Lydia (Newman) **96** 263
  Martha **96** 260 263 **98** 175
  Martha (Bliss) **96** 260
  98 234
  Mary **96** 269 **98** 234 **146**
  339 340
  Mary (Perrin) (Ormsbee)
  96 260
  Mary A. **126** 21

IDE cont'd
  Nathaniel **96** 260 263 **114**
  285 287
  Nehemiah **96** 401
  Nicholas **53** 133 **60** 185
  62 237 347-349 **96** 260
  262 265-269 **97** 319 **98**
  172 234 **99** 94 97 105
  238
  Patience **96** 260 **98** 172
  Rachel **95** 299 **96** 269 270
  Richard **51** 390
  Sally **114** 285 287-289
  Sally I. **114** 287
  Sarah **96** 260 **114** 285 287
  288
  Sarah (Perry) **96** 260
  Sarah (Wilmarth) (French)
  114 288
  Susan **82** 490
  Timothy **62** 347 348 **96**
  262 268 270 353 **97** 319
  98 170 174 240 325 **99**
  108 **141** 349
  William **114** 285 287-289
Ieffs *see* Jeffs
IENE John **128** 62
  Timothy **128** 62
IFFLAND Arthur Beecher
  (Mrs.) **96** 160
IGGLEDEN
  — Widow **65** 185
  Agnes **65** 174-178
  Alexander **65** 183
  Alice **65** 175 177 179 180
  185 186
  Alicia **65** 174
  Ambrose **65** 184 185
  Ann **65** 186 187
  Anna **65** 185
  Bartholomew **65** 179 183
  Benjamin **65** 184 185
  Cecily **65** 183
  Daniel **65** 185
  Denise **65** 181 182
  Dionysos **65** 184 186
  Elizabeth **65** 179 180 182
  184-187 **75** 220 225
  Francis **65** 185
  Hannah **65** 184 185 187
  Helen **65** 184
  Isabel **65** 176

IGGLEDEN *cont'd*
James **65** 176 179-181 183-186
Jane **65** 187 **75** 220
Joan **65** 175 176 178 179 183 184 186
John **65** 174-186 326 **75** 220
Joseph **65** 179 182-185
Josias **65** 185 186
Julian **65** 174-177 179
Katharine **65** 176
Lettice **65** 180 183-186
Lydia **65** 184
Margaret **65** 180 182-186
Margery **65** 184
Marie **65** 182 185 186
Martha **65** 185
Mary **65** 184-187
Mercy **65** 184
Moses **65** 183
Peaceable **65** 186
Phebe **65** 185
Richard **65** 174 175 177-179 182 184-187
Ruth **65** 183 185 187
Sarah **65** 182-187 **75** 220
Stephen **65** 180-187 **75** 225
Susan **65** 182 183 185 186
Susanna **65** 186
Thomas **65** 174-176 182 184 186 290
Thomasine **65** 184 185
Warham **65** 184
William **65** 175 180 181 183 186
IGLEHART E. **122** 18
Elizabeth **73** 226
Florence (Barton) **107** 211
Jemima **73** 229
John **73** 262
Levi **73** 264
Lucinda **78** 327
Mary **78** 327
Michael **78** 327
Susanna **73** 148
William **73** 140 **107** 211
IGOU Mary A. **80** 160
Merala **80** 160
Silas **80** 160
IHILER Jacob **140** 156
Pamelia (Osgood) **140** 156
Simeon **140** 156
Thomas G. **140** 156
IJAMS
Burch (Mrs.) **82** 198
Frank Burch **121** 155
Helen Pauline **82** 198
Isaac **73** 220
J. Horton (Mrs.) **101** 251
Margaret Seton (Porter) **101** 251
IKELING
Gal. de **102** 298
IKERD Kenneth Glenham (Mrs.) **107** 133
ILBERD Ilbierd
Christian **147** 143
Edmund **147** 143 145
Joan **96** 186

ILBERD *cont'd*
Lydia **141** 321 **147** 143
Martha **147** 143
Martha (Moulton) **141** 320 321 **147** 138 143
Mary **147** 143
Robert **147** 143
Thomas **69** 343-345 **147** 143
ILCHESTER
— Earl of **142** 239
ILE Barbara **132** 47
ILEMENSTRE
John de **145** 6
ILES — Mrs. **51** 112
Deborah **99** 122
Grace **99** 119 122 **101** 54
Grace (Stringer) **100** 242
Joan **66** 252
John **99** 119
Thomas **93** 391 **97** 297 **99** 119 122 **100** 242 **101** 54 **110** 262 **147** 30
Timothy **93** 384
ILL Edward J. **90** 97
ILLIG Elise **84** 294
ILLINGWORTH
W. **116** 171
ILLMAN George **60** 400
ILLSLEY Ilsley Illsleye Ilsey
—— **53** 39
— Mr. **83** 306 **127** 169
Almira **72** 84
Charles P. **120** 13
Charlotte **133** 303 305
Elizabeth (Smith) **133** 303 305
Elizabeth L. **52** 383
Enoch **72** 84 **133** 303 305
Hannah (Pike) **121** 164
Henry **121** 164
Isaac **72** 85
Jonas **118** 230
Jonathan **134** 215
Lucy A. N. **83** 182
Lydia (Foot) **120** 13
Mary **84** 29 **90** 216 **133** 305
Parker **133** 303 305
Randal **64** 323
Rebecca **90** 277
Robert **61** 145
Sarah J. **83** 298 299
Theodora **77** 156 **78** 203
William **73** 75 76
Wingate N. **84** 29
Illsleye *see* Illsley
Ilsey *see* Illsley
ILSLER Joshua **78** 111
Ilsley *see* Illsley
ILVERD John **65** 323
IMBERT
Harriet **100** 186
Harriet (Myrick) **100** 186
Lewis B. **100** 186
IMBRIE
Addison Murray **108** 236
Andrew C. **100** 179
Boyd Vincent **108** 236
James **108** 236

IMBRIE *cont'd*
Schuyler Van Rensselear **92** 223
IMGRABEN
August **81** 408
Frederike B. **81** 408
Otto **81** 408
IMHOFF
Daniel L. **99** 147
IMLAY — Mrs. **79** 405 **80** 55
Adelaide **79** 167
Mary **79** 169
William **79** 167 169 **80** 55
IMONDI Nancy Hancock (Baylies) **113** 226
Rizziero (Mrs.) **113** 226
IMPEY —— **143** 149
Joan **143** 145
John **143** 145
IMPSON Ben **105** 240
Elias **105** 240
Maria **105** 239
Maria H. **105** 240
Melinda **105** 240
Minerva **105** 240
William **105** 240
IMSON David P. **109** 316
INASH Almy **127** 222
INCE Jonathan **89** 175
Mary **68** 360 361
Thomas **52** 106 108 109 117
INCELL Artis **114** 185
John **114** 185
Mary **114** 185
INCH Agnes (Commins) **100** 240
James **100** 240
INCHES —— **140** 46
—— (Boit) **140** 41
Betsey **84** 371
Charles **140** 41
Elizabeth **79** 303 **84** 260
Elizabeth (Brimmer) **84** 272 **97** 6
Hannah (Weems) **97** 6
Henderson **84** 260 262 268 272 371 379 **91** 354 **94** 293 **97** 6
Henderson (Mrs.) **91** 354
John Chester **56** xiv xli **59** lxvii
Sarah **84** 268 **91** 354
Sarah (Jackson) **84** 262 268 **97** 6
Susan Brimmer **73** xlii **98** 289
Thomas **56** 189 **58** 68 **97** 6 **146** 347
INCLEDON
Benjamin **58** 93
INDAIN Jenny **140** 177
Indicott *see* Endicott
INDROF Edward **91** 326
INDRUK
Gustave C. **107** 176
INDYE — Fr. **64** 243
Ines *see* Innes
INESON
Elizabeth **144** 313

INESON *cont'd*
Emeline (Wilson) **144** 313
George **144** 313
Samuel **144** 313
INFIELD
Elizabeth **71** 327
Ingaham *see* Ingham
INGALLS Ingall Ingals
Ingel Ingell Ingels
Ingles Ingols
—— **51** 201 **53** 133 **58**
lxxx **64** 119 **74** 209 **109**
231 **111** 213 **116** 12 119
— Senator **59** 128
— Widow **138** 25
____ (Brazer) **140** 44
Abiathar **51** 497
Abigail **74** 209 **84** 446
117 281
Abigail (Baker) **115** 292
Abigail (Fuller) **111** 146
Abigail (Stocker) **111** 146
Abijah **54** 187
Abner **111** 146
Albert S. (Mrs.) **84** 293
Amanda Jane **67** 350
69 38
Amarilla **115** 294
Andrew Stewart **104** 161
Ann **78** 316 **111** 146
Anna **85** 233
Anne (Collins) **111** 146
Annie Davenport **92** 222
Annis **116** 70
Barnard **145** 259
Benjamin **52** 274 **67** 375
138 25-28 31 **143** 255
Benjamin S. **115** 292
Bertha Mae **104** 161
Blaney **96** 57
Caleb **142** 380
Caroline Bass **77** 291
Catherine **111** 145
Catherine (Mayo) **125** 216
Charles B. **116** 119
Charles Edward **92** 222
Charles W. **116** 63
Charlotte Jane (White)
104 161
Chester **66** 136 137
116 114
Claire **104** 146 **106** 123
Cynthia Briggs **92** 222
Daniel **61** 167
David O. **115** 292
David S. (Mrs.) **101** 166
Dorcas (Chase) **87** 256
Dorothy **68** 97
Ebenezer **138** 25 27-30
Edmond **139** 42
Edmund **58** lxxx **60** 185
61 237 **84** 465 **87** 256
111 146 **138** 25 27-29
Elizabeth **65** lviii **92** 80
137 326
Elizabeth (Bump) **116** 63
Elizabeth (Cloon) **85** 100
Elizabeth (Ditson) **91** 267
Elizabeth Amanda **85** 100
Elizabeth C. **68** 154
Ella (Ford) **120** 50 **137** 48

INGALLS *cont'd*
Ella (Gordon) **111** 145
Ella (Northup) **115** 292
Ella Francis (Jordan)
92 222
Emeline E. **89** 399
Emily Cutter **88** 341
Emma Frances (Renton)
111 145
Ephraim **85** 100 **97** 264
Eugene Herbert **92** 222
Eunice **70** 227
Florence Mary **76** 99
Frances **60** 297
Francis **58** lxxx **68** 195-197
84 465
Francis Bernard **92** 222
George **74** 209
George S. **116** 210
George Torrey **92** 222
Gilman **67** 350 **117** 281
Hannah **51** 466 **52** 274 **68**
154 **74** 206 **86** 141 **88**
381 **102** 25 **105** 313 **116**
137
Hannah (Fellows) **86** 141
Hannah (Manning)
97 264
Hannah (Warden)
111 146
Harvey **120** 50
Havy **63** 87
Henry **52** 102
Hildegarde **111** 146
Horace **116** 119
Horace H. **115** 292
Horatio Burdett **92** 222
Ida (Cramer) **115** 292
Isabella Cornelia **92** 222
J. **115** 292
Jacob **59** 221
James **77** 234 **125** 100
Jane Ellison (Taft) **84** 293
Jerome **111** 145 146
John **62** 180 **64** 123 **67** 373
74 206 **91** 326 **105** 313
111 146 **116** 7 119
John S. **91** 326
Jonathan **51** 497
Joseph **67** 375 **111** 146
120 49 50 **138** 27-29
Josiah **58** 19
Josiah E. **68** 97
Josiah S. **68** 97
Kenneth **92** 222
Laura A. **116** 119
Laura L. **75** 319
Laura Lettice **68** 97
Leander **115** 292
Leonard **115** 292 **116** 119
Louie Bell **62** xxxix
Louisa **51** 319
Louise (Harkness)
101 166
Louise Steele **92** 222
Lucina **124** 63
Luther **89** 399
Lycaonia **63** 87
Lydia **68** 196 **95** 361 **115**
292 **116** 119

INGALLS *cont'd*
Mabel Morgan (Satterlee)
101 167
Margaret **107** 319
Marguerite Griswold
116 227
Martha **55** 394 **58** lxxix
Mary **58** lxxiii **59** 221 **61**
167 237 **67** 373 375 **68**
196 **85** 400 **90** 355 **111**
150 **116** 119
Mary (Bump) **115** 292
Mary (Winchip) **116** 63
Mary A. **115** 207
Mary J. **64** 123
Mary Louise **92** 222
Mary Waterman **76** 99
Maud **74** 209
Mehitable **67** 373
Moriah (Potter) **123** 240
Nancy **88** 284
Nathaniel **83** 145 **91** 267
111 146
Newton S. **91** 326
Olive **58** 19 **91** 267 **116** 119
Olive (Lee) **115** 292
Orrilla **81** 273
Pamelia **66** 137
Phebe (Chapman)
116 114
Phebe (Doty) **116** 114
Polly **58** 18 **66** 136
Polly (Beals) **125** 100
Rebecca **67** 373 **77** 320 **78**
398 **142** 380
Rebecca (Collins) **111** 146
Rebecca (Leighton)
97 260
Reuben **115** 292 **116** 114
Robert **97** 260 **105** 19 **111**
146 **142** 264
Rosamund **111** 145
Rubie J. **116** 114
Ruth **89** 267 **137** 326
Ruth (Knight) **137** 326
Ruth E. **87** 395
Sally **116** 119 **120** 49
Sally (Woodell) **115** 292
Samuel **76** 99 **86** 141 **137**
326 **138** 29 30
Sarah **66** 99 **67** 350 375 **74**
206 **89** 399 **91** 266 **97**
260 264 **101** 64 **105** 313
Sarah (Abbott) **120** 49 50
Sarah (Bullock) **115** 292
Sarah (Harker) **111** 146
Sarah Ballard (Bancroft)
96 57
Sarah Eaton **92** 222
Satchell C. **68** 154
Simeon **70** 227 **116** 119
Sophia **58** lxxxvi **86** 95
Sophia (Shurtleff) **86** 95
Sophia B. **87** 26
Stephen **67** 373 **78** 308
Susan **64** 123
Susan Longaker **142** 186
381 382
Sylvia **66** 136 137
Tabitha **101** 70
Theophilus **111** 146

INGALLS *cont'd*
Thomas **58** lxxxvi **86** 95
Timothy E. **117** 281
Ursula **111** 146
Walter Renton **84** 465
  90 136 **111** 61 145 146
William **61** xxx **74** 206
  92 222 **99** 8 **125** 216
  140 44
William L. **116** 63
Winslow Lewis **92** 222
Ingalsbe *see* Ingoldsby
Ingam *see* Ingham
INGBY
Ann **99** 120
Anne (Newman) **100** 239
Ezekiel **99** 120 **100** 239
William **142** 153
INGE Thomas **94** 339
INGEBRETSEN
Ingerbert **68** 136
Ingel *see* Ingalls
Ingell *see* Ingalls
Ingels *see* Ingalls
INGEMANSEN
—— **148** 188
Ingepenne *see* Ingpen
INGERBERTSEN
Annie **83** 306
INGERFIELD
Paul **145** 302 303
Peter **65** 370 **79** 42 **145** 303
  302 303
Silence (Swift) **145** 294
INGERSOLL Ingersol
Ingersull Ingesoll
—— **82** 42 **90** 92 **105** 263
  122 294 **140** 156
—— (Littlefield) **105** 263
—— (Norton) **140** 156
Abby **76** lxxxvii
Abiah **136** 328
Abigail **56** 318 **68** 22
  122 293
Abraham **99** 280
Agnes **54** 343 **55** 110
Agnes (Langley) **90** 92
  109 163
Albert Converse (Mrs.)
  86 197
Alice **90** 92
Alta Dierexa (Fitch) **98** 82
Alvan Hyde **98** 82 **136** 325
Ann **99** 280
Ann (Langley) **109** 163
Anne **59** 366 **130** 311
  134 147
Annie R. (Batson) **125** 142
Azubah **60** 80 **72** 74
Bathsheba **62** 335 **90** 92
Bathshua **53** 37 **55** 196
Benjamin **140** 156
Bethiah **76** 244
Bethiah (Gardner) **110** 143
Betsey **90** 174
Catherine Jackson
  (Seeley) **83** 330
Catherine L. (Talcott)
  136 325
Charles **140** 156
Cornelia Howard **98** 82

INGERSOLL *cont'd*
Cornelia Howard
  (Saunders) **98** 81 82
Cynthia **70** 329 335
Daniel **65** 371 **78** 403 **84**
  153 **140** 145 156 238
Daniel Gridley **140** 156
David **98** 82 **136** 325
David Spear **125** 109
Deborah **82** 290 297
Deliverance **86** 76
Deliverance (Littlefield)
  86 76
Dolly **86** 227
Dorothy **123** 259
Edna D. **125** 142
Edward Payson **61** 217
Eleanor Houghton
  78 102
Elijah **116** 103
Elisa (Field) **125** 109
Eliza **80** 127 **122** 294
Elizabeth **54** 343 **55** 147 **68**
  22 **80** 127 **122** 293 294
  130 69 **135** 123
Elizabeth (Knowles) **122**
  292 293
Elvina S. **80** 129
Esther (Broom) **130** 69
Eunice **120** 96
Eunice (West) **120** 95
George **65** 147 **82** 42 **90** 92
  93 304 **100** 66 **116** 129
  138 **140** 145 156
George Goldthwait **140**
  145 156
George Lyman **98** 81 82
  136 325
Hannah **66** 333 **67** 118 **72**
  216 **89** 180 **125** 142
Hannah (Lyman) **98** 82
  136 325
Harriet Voorhees **83** 330
Henry **134** 147
Homer Austin **92** 41
Howard Lyman **88** 169
  98 81 82 **88** 152 205
James **80** 127 **86** 76 **122**
  293 294
Jared **57** 140
Jno **123** 259
Joanna **53** 37 **83** 259 **90** 92
John **54** 94 410 **56** 318 **67**
  120 **68** 22 **72** 216 **79** 193
  90 92 **98** 81 205 **134** 147
  140 156
John Avery (Mrs.) **78** 102
John S. **77** 232
Jonathan **51** 466 **62** 364 **74**
  81 **79** 160 **83** 330 **110**
  143
Joseph **67** 117 **84** 153 **99**
  280 **134** 147 **140** 156
Lois **67** 115 **74** 204
Lorenzo Will **125** 142
Lovina A. (Rich) **125** 142
Lucy **122** 292 **125** 107
Lucy (Day) **134** 147
Lurton Dunham **64** 63
Lydia **98** 82
Lydia (Child) **98** 82

INGERSOLL *cont'd*
Lydia (Ingersoll) **98** 82
Lydia L. **80** 127
Marcella Caroline (Wass)
  125 142
Margaret **111** 313
Margaret M. **80** 127
Marie **54** 94
Marion A. (Crary) **90** 184
Martha **74** 42 **87** 286
Martha (Goldthwait)
  140 145 156
Martha P. (Dorr) **125** 142
Mary **51** 466 **54** 94 **66** 46
  67 369 **68** 22 **80** 127 **82**
  290 298 **89** 311 **104** 168
  110 143 **112** 150 **119** 5
  122 292-294 **125** 141
  127 240 **140** 145 156
Mary (Barlow) **116** 103
Mary (Brewer) **134** 147
Mary (Hunt) **98** 82
Mary (Perry) **116** 103
Mary (Smith) **124** 12
Mary (Strout) **125** 142
Mary A. (Dorr) **125** 142
Mary Augusta **136** 325
Mary Hodges **112** 150
Mehitable **67** 116 **89** 296
Moses **120** 95 96
Nancy **86** 339
Nathan **116** 103
Nathaniel **80** 127 **90** 92
  110 143 **112** 150 **122**
  293 294 **125** 141
Nathaniel Merritt **125** 142
Nehemiah **68** 22 **140** 156
Nehemiah (Mrs.) **85** 121
Patty G. **140** 145
Perkins **66** 333
Polly **116** 103
Polly (Perry) **116** 103
Prudence **80** 127
Rachel **90** 174
Raymond Vail (Mrs.)
  90 184
Rebecca **70** 335 **85** 88 **101**
  107 **122** 292 **128** 211
Rebecca (Parker) **128** 211
Rebecca A. (Batson)
  125 142
Richard **54** 94 343 **55** 110
  60 80 **64** 91 **67** 115-118
  120 **72** 74 **83** 259 **90** 92
  98 81 **125** 141
Royal Eason (Mrs.)
  110 160
Samuel **61** 145 **70** 335 **77**
  131 **80** 127 **122** 293 294
  134 147
Sarah **63** 290 **77** 131 **80** 127
  82 42 **90** 92 **109** 163
  122 292-294 **134** 147
  140 156 238
Sarah (Ashley) **98** 82
  123 262
Sarah (Parker) **122** 292
  125 141
Sarah (Parsons) **98** 82
  136 325
Sarah A. **125** 142

INGERSOLL *cont'd*
Sarah S. (Kelley)
  (Plummer) **125** 142
Sargent **90** 87 **130** 69
Sukey **122** 294
Susan **80** 127 129 **122** 294
Susanna **80** 127 **90** 277
  134 147
Thomas **67** 115 **72** 74 **80**
  127 **98** 82 **122** 294 **123**
  262 **124** 10 12 **125** 141
  142 **140** 156
Tryphena (Wines) **126** 80
William **80** 127 129 **82** 42
  290 298 **98** 82 **122** 292-
  294 **125** 141 142
William (Mrs.) **122** 292
Winchester Fitch **98** 82
Winifred Katharine **92** 41
Zipporah **67** 115-118 120
  216
INGERSON Ingirson
Abigail **97** 85 **109** 299
Bert L. **89** 120
Cordelia Maria **109** 233
Deliah (Arey) **87** 19
Eliza **86** 302
Elnora Etta (Lazell)
  89 120
Jennie M. **123** 97
John **109** 299
Lucy M. **76** 38
Mary (Henny) **114** 291
Richard **65** 112 **109** 163
  114 291
Sarah **91** 248 **109** 163
Susanna (Perkins)
  116 129
Willard **87** 19
INGGS
Mary (Beale) **121** 193
Samuel **121** 193 194
INGHAM Ingaham Ingam
  —— **54** 50
Abigail **99** 25 26
Agnes **68** 266 272
Alexander **52** 308 **110** 241
Alice Martha **117** 107
Alpheus **72** 102
Angeline **76** 276
Anne **68** 272
Beulah **72** 102
Catherine **123** 200
Charles S. **88** 305
Clarence **117** 113
Eleanor Mary **117** 113
Elizabeth (Graves)
  110 241
Ella Prendergast
  (Triscott) **117** 113
Ellen **65** 50
George D. **97** 215
Geraldine Marion
  117 107
Gertrude **117** 107
Gertrude (Penrose) **117**
  107 113
Gertrude Katharine
  117 113
Harold **117** 288
Henry Laurance **86** 197

INGHAM *cont'd*
James Geoffrey Penrose
  117 113
James Penrose **117** 107
James Taylor **117** 107 113
Joan de **109** 277
John **57** 178 **62** 334 **85** 140
John Oliver **117** 113
Jonathan **117** 235
Joseph **53** 209 **88** 305
Joshua **117** 107
Julia Lucretia (Larrabee)
  97 215
Lancelot Gordon **117** 113
Louisa Geraldine **117** 113
Louisa Pettitot
  Fitzgerald **117** 107
Margaret Nancy (Waring)
  117 113
Mary **62** 334 **73** 213 **120** 5
  147 60
Mary Ann **79** 154
Mary Elizabeth (Penrose)
  117 107 113
Mary Helen (Cooper)
  117 113
Matilda Jane **117** 107
Nevill Robert **117** 113
Norman W. **112** 119
North **99** 25 26
Oliver de **109** 277
Oliver Edward Uniacke
  117 113
Priscilla Beatrice **117** 113
Rebecca **132** 42
Richard **65** 50
Robert Benjamin Fuller
  117 113
Robert John Fitzgerald
  117 113
Robert Wood **117** 107 113
Ruth **52** 308 **135** 75
Samuel **52** 308 **88** 305
Sarah **53** 209 **57** 85 **59** 133
  64 190
Sarah (Chandler) **85** 140
Susanna **99** 26
Susanna Mary **117** 113
Thomas **57** 85 178 182
  110 241
Wilfred Rawdon **117** 113
Zelda Raney (Dalrymple)
  117 113
Zubella L. **123** 200
Ingirson *see* Ingerson
Ingland *see* England
Inglande *see* England
Ingleby *see* Inglesby
INGLEE Betsey (Stetson)
  125 104
Caroline Bass **76** xxxvi
Lemuel **125** 104
Martha **55** 166
Nancy **78** 308
Timothy **55** 166
Waitstill **55** 166
INGLEFIELD
Ann **116** 254
John **116** 254
Ingles *see* Ingalls
Inglesby *see* Ingoldsby

INGLET Sarah **52** 128
INGLIS Inglishe - *see also*
  English
  —— **54** 127
Alexander **82** 290 302
  144 204 206
Anna **82** 290 302
Charles **67** 111
Christopher **94** 9
Elizabeth (Callender)
  144 204
George **127** 13
John **118** 44 54
Margaret **67** 111
Marion **60** 238
Robert **52** 320
INGOLDE John **71** 22
INGOLDSBY Ingalsbe
  Ingleby Inglesbee
  Inglesby Ingoldesby
  —— **104** 279 **116** 63
A. **115** 292
Aaron **115** 292
Adaline (Norton) **115** 292
Alfred S. **116** 63
Alma **75** 267
Anna **77** 25
Artemas **115** 292
Belus **115** 292
Bethiah **92** 52
Camilla **116** 114
Carrie M. **115** 292
Charlott **115** 292
Dency **115** 292
Ebenezer **77** 23-27
Eddie R. **116** 63
Elizabeth **115** 292
Elmer M. **116** 63
Eunice **77** 26
Fanny **116** 113 114
Frances **142** 7
Henriette **103** 58
Homer **116** 63
James **103** 58 **116** 113 114
James R. **116** 63
John **77** 23 **104** 278
Joseph **77** 24 **115** 292
L. L. **115** 292
Laura Ann **116** 114
Laura B. **115** 292
Lewis **115** 292
Mabel **116** 63
Marie A. **116** 63
Mary **116** 68
Molly **77** 25
Myra L. **116** 63
Nancy **116** 63
Nancy Jane **103** 58
Nancy M. (Austin) **116** 63
Nancy R. (Jacobs) **116** 63
Phebe Ann **115** 292
Polly **115** 292
Rawlyn **98** 114
Rebecca **75** 267 **116** 114
Reuben **115** 292
Royal **116** 63
Sally **115** 292
Sarah **55** 162 **78** 16
Silas **75** 267 **116** 114
Susie J. M. **101** 216
Thomas **120** 172 174

INGOLDSBY *cont'd*
Zaccheus **115** 292
Ingols *see* Ingalls
INGPEN Ingepenne
—— **52** 262
Adrian **52** 262
Arthur Robert **65** 8/
67 305
William **52** 262
INGRAHAM Ingram
—— **53** 143 146 **58** 145
62 288 353 **63** 35 **119** 49
54 127 **139** 31-33 43 46
47
— Mr. **71** 139
— Mrs. **55** 442 **119** 50 57
58 **129** 383
— Widow **71** 139
___ (Wilson) **144** 328
Aaron **111** 228 **112** 174
115 64
Aaron S. **83** 158 160
Abby **125** 239 244
Abel **70** 58-61 136 **81** 265
Abel A. **81** 265
Abigail **56** 159 **61** 76 **65** 40
78 239 **105** 221 **111** 230
115 64 **142** 165 166 **143**
310
Abigail (Howe) **120** 5
Abigail (Trask) **126** 144
Abijah **76** 134 136
Abraham **111** 228
Agnes (Morse) **120** 5
Alice **114** 130
Alice Maud **78** 238
Allen **60** 17 18
Andrew **87** 255
Anna **111** 256
Anne **115** 65 214
Anne (Pearce) **111** 256
Annie Beautina (Hill)
113 155
Arthur **67** 70 71 73
Arthur K. (Mrs.) **112** 148
Benjamin **53** 146 **56** 74
57 142 **62** 285 **65** 40 41
76 134-137 **96** 260 **105**
114 **127** 306
Benjamin R. **83** 160
Bethiah (Preble) **111** 230
114 131
Bethiah (Young) **111** 228
Betsey **61** 76 **78** 241
Betsey (Davis) **126** 79
Calvin C. **91** 326
Candace **63** 341
Catherine B. **135** 250
136 79
Catherine P. **123** 123
Chloe **57** 142 **65** 40 **83** 359
Clarence **87** 108
D. **91** 326
D. Phoenix (Mrs.) **85** 242
Deane Martin (Mrs.) **106**
125 **107** 240
Diademia **111** 256 **119** 53
Dorothy **85** 152
Duncan **53** 249 **78** 415 **84**
377 **85** 6 20 **140** 233
Edward **67** 264 **79** 11 **112**

INGRAHAM *cont'd*
25 217 218 **114** 133 **115**
140 **134** 252 **147** 30
Eleanor (Ennis) **126** 79
Eleanor (Hartshorn)
112 148
Elenia **83** 359
Eliza (Cunningham)
126 68
Elizabeth **58** 145 **61** 391 **81**
265 **112** 25 218 **115** 137
133 322
Elizabeth (Dolbeare)
112 174
Elizabeth (Moulton)
141 327
Emeline **88** 339
Emeline Thomas **135** 250
136 79
Emma **82** 12
Emma Elvira **79** 11
Ephraim **86** 379
Ernest Edward **102** 123
Erskine Bronson **81** 107
219 **114** 70
Ethelinda **61** 76
Ezra **61** 76
Francis **61** 76 **125** 104
135 250 **136** 79
Frederick William **92** 120
Garrat **65** 62 65 66
George **111** 230 **114** 131
Gerard **139** 25 26 29 46 47
49
Grace Bernon **78** 207
Hannah **53** 465 **76** 135 **77**
283 **88** 397 **93** 374 **97** 91
111 256 **115** 63
Hannah (Bumstead)
140 312
Hannah (Norton) **126** 79
Hannah (Sprague) **132** 42
Helen **113** 155
Henry **55** 141 **101** 212
111 228 **112** 174 **114**
128 **132** 41
Henry L. **126** 144
Henry Lawton **135** 250
136 79
Hepzibah **111** 256 **144**
207 328 **145** 43
Ira **55** 425 **78** 241
Isaac **63** 53 **70** 61 136
Isabella **73** 85
Jacob **115** 56
James **77** 268 **83** 359
James Wilmot **113** 155
Jane **80** 30 **92** 119
Jane (Salter) **93** 262
Jane Terry **80** 264
Jared **63** 131 331 **97** 326
Jarrett **62** 347 **96** 267 **97**
320 **98** 171
Jemima **65** 40
Jeremiah **97** 326 **120** 5
124 170 178 **129** 381
Joanna **84** 98 **91** 367
Job **140** 312
John **62** 360 **63** 334 **66** 248
70 61 136 **82** 289 290
104 250 **129** 381 **141**

INGRAHAM *cont'd*
327
John H. **94** 35
John Van Ness **67** 194
91 98
Jonathan **55** 443 **63** 334
120 5
Joseph **53** 249 302 **56** 349
86 52 **92** 119 120 **111**
256 **132** 42
Joseph (Mrs.) **93** 262
Joseph Holt **112** 25
Joseph Sprague **73** 85
Josiah **111** 228 **125** 203
Judah **65** 40
Judith **75** 202
Katey **82** 289 290
Kenneth C. **112** 154 233
Lewis **65** 40
Lodema **119** 56-58 128
129 132 133
Lois **65** 40
Lucretia **61** 76
Lucy **86** 52 **93** 138
Lucy (Hubbard) **104** 250
Lydia **60** 18 157 **61** 76 **82**
290 297 **87** 383 **111** 256
112 25 217 **115** 61
Lydia (Dowse) **112** 174
Lydia (Holt) **112** 25
Lydia M. **83** 158 160
Mabel Heath **82** 12
Marelia J. **83** 160
Margaret **99** 108 **112** 152
Marilla Sophia **104** 250
Martha **61** 76
Martha M. (Arey) **87** 108
Martha S. **145** 136
Mary **53** 249 **60** 18 **63** 334
70 82 **71** 218 **77** 229 **78**
68 269 270 **111** 256 **112**
25 **115** 217 **120** 5
Mary (Miner) **101** 212
Mary Little **81** 476
Mary Miner (Huntley)
101 212
Mary Preble **111** 230
Mehitable **111** 256
Miriam **70** 59-61 136
Moses **111** 256
Nancy **80** 177
Nathan **83** 160
Nathaniel **55** 343
Norton **125** 37
Obadiah **98** 325
Parnel **61** 76
Patience **127** 225
Patience (Ide) **96** 260
Phebe **119** 129
Philip **119** 45
Polly **85** 131
Priscilla **88** 280
Priscilla (Gray) **135** 250
Priscilla Gray (Oliver)
125 104 **136** 79
R. **111** 53
R. H. **53** 133
R. M. **111** 53
Rachel **111** 228
Raffe **86** 421
Rebecca **65** 63 65 66 **139** 29

INGRAHAM *cont'd*
Rhoby Anna **80** 30 264
Rhoda (Chase) **87** 255
Richard **65** 66
Robert **58** 398 **80** 30
Robert Crossman **80** 264
Ruth **83** 160 **86** 379 **89** 55
   112 25
Ruth Lena **103** 116
Sally **60** 18 **65** 40 **104** 118
Samuel **55** 343 **61** 76 **76**
   137 **111** 256
Samuel Gilbert (Mrs.)
   109 129
Sarah **63** 35 **65** 92 **92** 100
Sarah (Bill) **132** 41
Silence **84** 223
Simeon **127** 303 **129** 382
Sophia **79** 151
Susan C. **116** 199
Susanna **53** 249 **132** 325
Susanna (Greenleaf)
   84 377
Thomas **70** 59 61 136
Timothy **101** 299 **123** 192
   127 140 164 **144** 328
Welthy B. **83** 160
Will **64** 31
William **57** 142 **64** 21 **65**
   63 66 **71** 136 **79** 378 **97**
   320 325 **99** 240 **103** 256
   112 25 **123** 193 **139** 49
William Hammond
   82 12
Zilpha **102** 142
INGSBY — Mrs. **101** 274
INGWERSEN
John Arthur **108** 151
Marion (Bradt) **108** 151
INKEEP
Delilah **80** 46 237
Gertrude **80** 241
James **80** 242
Mary A. **80** 242
INKPEN Emma **120** 77
INLOES
Aberrilla **127** 120
Aquila **127** 120
Elizabeth **127** 120
Joseph Leanneau **127** 120
William **127** 120
INLOW Ruby **117** 129
INMAN Inmann
  —— **51** 186 **56** 210 **59** 165
   136 283 **138** 123
Abigail (Chase) **87** 318
Abraham **128** 62 **137** 282
Alce / Elsie **134** 171
Alonzo **113** 159
Arthur Crew **77** xxviii 77
   81 220 **118** 159
Asa **138** 120 121
Caroline (Waiste) **113** 157
Carrie **74** xxx
Catherine Adams **57** 394
Charles G. **113** 159
David **128** 62
Deborah **80** 181
Dora Ellen **113** 159
Edward **52** 208 212 **87** 323
Elijah **87** 318

INMAN *cont'd*
Elisha **128** 62
Elizabeth (Chase) **87** 323
Elizabeth (Murray)
   (Campbell) (Smith)
   112 273 274
Elizabeth (Smith) **84** 271
Emma (Chamberlain)
   89 116
Enos **138** 121
Esten **138** 121
Euphemia (Bowker)
   89 116
Ezekiel **137** 282
Francis Henry **138** 115
George **55** 422 **84** 380
   144 265
Gerald (Mrs.) **124** 84
Hannah **77** 297
Hannah Rowe **81** 462
Henry **138** 120
Ida A. **89** 116
Isaiah **87** 317
Israel **128** 62
Jeremiah **129** 383
Joanna **52** 208 **84** 445 **87**
   248 **123** 253 **138** 125
John **84** 366 **128** 62
   138 119
Joseph **80** 181 **105** 277
Julia **138** 118
Lois **109** 319
Marjorie **138** 115
Martha **138** 119
Mary Ann **55** 422 **78** 247
Mercy (Chase) (Wixon)
   87 317
Mowry **138** 123
Obadiah **128** 62 **136** 185
Ozial **128** 62
Peleg **137** 282
Phebe **138** 119
Rachel **58** 244
Ralph **57** 280 **58** 68 **84**
   271 360 366 **112** 212 274
Ralph (Mrs.) **112** 204 212
   268 272 273 **113** 4 7 10
   89
Royal **128** 62
Rufus **105** 277
Sally **84** 366
Sally (Haskins) **84** 366
Samuel **128** 62
Sarah **128** 56 **137** 74
Seth **57** 394
Stephen **129** 383
Sukey **84** 360
Susanna **103** 148
Uriah **89** 116
Welcome **138** 120
Willard A. **138** 123
William **135** 50
INNES —— **56** 56
Alexander **82** 456 **118** 54
Anne Bevier (Hasbrouck)
   108 307
Archelaus **67** 271
Asa **59** 35
Betsey **59** 35
Catherine **105** 62 **143** 335
Charles Stuart **112** 245

INNES *cont'd*
Clark **59** 35
Cosmo **52** 13
Eleanor **59** 35
Eleanor S. **67** 271
Eliza **59** 35 **78** 72
Elizabeth **59** 35 **67** 271
George **108** 307 **118** 44-
   47 50 53-56 **119** 238 **121**
   316
George Henry **61** 217
Hannah **78** 308
Harry **104** 175
Helen **118** 54
James **118** 54 **145** 249
Jessie MacQueen **119** 238
   121 316
John **59** 35 **118** 54 **140** 156
Josias **106** 113
Lavinia **59** 35
Louisa **107** 231
Lydia **59** 35
Margaret **59** 35
Margaretann S. **116** 141
Martha **86** 200 **108** 307
Milly **59** 35
Parnel (Ellis) **120** 118
Robert **63** 17 **104** 175
Robert Stuart **125** 163
Simon **64** 20
Stephen **100** 186 **120** 117
   118
Thomas **114** 239
William **118** 54
William E. **82** 429
INNOCENT III Pope
   71 236
INSKEEP
Abigail L. **82** 128
L. D. **82** 128
INSLEE
Edith M. **69** 30
Edward **69** 30
Elizabeth **121** 176
Experience **98** 48 **145** 195
Grace (Moores) **98** 48
Jonathan **98** 48
Lodemia **69** 30
Nathaniel **121** 176
INSLEY
Andrew **106** 318
Frederick **140** 157
Rebecca Ann **106** 318
William Quinn **106** 318
INSON William **78** 410
INSTANCE
Deborah **52** 371
INSTANT Mary **113** 73
INSTON Eliza **68** 241
Robert **68** 241
INSULA John de **112** 310
INTOSS — Mr. **74** 292
INYON John **128** 134
IOOR John **113** 66
IOYS Christian **124** 253
IRANDE Martha **110** 83
IRBY Ireby
  —— **52** 128
Adam de **96** 314
Alice Armitice **78** 322
Frances **136** 316

IRBY *cont'd*
Juliana de **96** 314
IREDALE Rachel B. **83** 432
84 21
IREDELL James **53** 465
IRELAND —— **53** 380 **92**
55 **99** 252
— Miss **98** 183
Abigail **53** 246 **75** 210
136 50
Abraham **53** 246 **57** 149
Alice **52** 106
Aloise **82** 486
Anna May (Brown)
105 62
Anne **52** 106
Catherine (Inness) **105** 62
Christian **64** 163
David E. (Mrs.) **121** 56
Edith (Bancroft) **97** 73
Elizabeth **52** 106 108 114
129 **53** 339 **83** 202 **92** 57
105 62
Elizabeth (Losee) **105** 62
Emeline **75** 210
Francis **58** 139
Frederick **105** 62
George **64** 33 **68** 341 **101**
14 **105** 62
Gordon **82** 513 **83** 123 232
93 381 **103** 157 **104** 239
105 62 132 **145** 301
Hannah (Norton) **105** 62
Helen Nelson (Maynard)
105 62
Henry **66** 252 **75** 210
Hester **52** 106 109 117
Isabell **92** 301
Isaiah **92** 57
Jacob **66** 233
James **73** 262
James D. **106** 64
Janet **141** 385
Jeannie (Gordon) **105** 62
Jere R. **137** 220
Joan **92** 177
Johanna **82** 486
John **52** 105 106 109 115
117 129 **53** 245 246 **57**
149 **75** 210 **83** 202 **98**
285 **105** 62 **112** 172 173
132 256 **144** 44
John B. **83** 201 202
John Lawrence **83** 202
Jonathan **75** 210 **92** 57 **125**
290 **136** 360 **145** 350
Joseph **55** 80 **105** 62
Kate B. (Hanna) **88** 169
Louisa **75** 210
Lucinda **75** 210
Margaret **68** 341 **105** 174
144 298
Marjorie **101** 11
Mark Lorin **95** 94 146
102 121 **118** 68
Martha **75** 210
Mary **52** 106 108
Mary (Abrahams) **105** 62
Mary (Floyd) **83** 202
Mary C. **83** 299 301

IRELAND *cont'd*
Mary Esther (Wood)
83 202
Mercy (Carlton) **125** 290
Mercy (Pollard)
(Carleton) **136** 360
Norma Olin **107** 249
Olive **55** 80 **63** 272
Oscar Brown **105** 62
Paulina **91** 388
Philip **112** 172 173
R. **97** 73
Richard **64** 33 **66** 245
Robert **66** 245 253 **101** 11
12
Robert Livingston **73**
236 **74** xxiv **82** 254 **83**
201 235
Samuel **145** 319
Sarah **51** 462 **53** 245 246 **75**
210 **95** 293 **105** 62 **136**
360
Sarah (Shepard) **98** 285
Shadrach **65** 381
Stephen **92** 96
Susanna **92** 57 **94** 328
101 12
Thomas **52** 106 **64** 107 **82**
513 **92** 55 **101** 11 12 **105**
62
Thomas Saxton **82** 486
125 164
Tobye **52** 106 114
Walter Hamlin **84** 341
85 195
William **52** 197 **61** 118
64 33 **106** 33 34 **118** 46
IREMONGER
Martha **63** 164
Richard **63** 164
IRENAEUS —— **59** 16
IRESON
Betsey **126** 207
Floyd **60** 310
Flud **61** xix
Sarah **122** 292
IRETON Henry **131** 7
IRICK — Mrs. **125** 36
IRISH Iris Irishe
—— **104** 62 **136** 211
— Mr. **62** 356
Abigail **104** 291 **118** 310
125 245
Abigail (Wilbor)
(Gifford) **137** 154 155
Alanson **68** 329
Albert **122** 214 299
Alice **113** 297
Alice Leigh (More)
113 297
Asa **87** 337
Benjamin **104** 134 291
122 106 214 **127** 142
Betsey **104** 60 **108** 285
114 182
Blanche May **95** 186
Charles **56** 410 **95** 186
127 13
Content **127** 256 **130** 138-
140 286
David **127** 221 **130** 138 139

IRISH *cont'd*
Deborah **68** 167 **70** 327
Desire More **113** 297
147 69
Edmund **110** 191
Edward **56** 295 296 **127** 12
Elias **63** 229 **122** 106 214
Elizabeth **81** 164 **113** 297
116 55
Elizabeth (Simmons)
125 174
Eunice **89** 274
Frank E. **107** 317
George **62** 356 **122** 106
214 215 299 **125** 174 181
127 142
Gilbert Henry **100** 111
H. Mary (Bailey) **125** 178
Hannah **87** 121 **122** 106
Henry **62** 122
Henry T. **122** 214 **125** 178
Hiram **62** 127
Holmes **125** 240
Ichabod **68** 167 **70** 271
113 297
Isaac **118** 310 **127** 145
James **95** 305 **104** 60 62
105 210 **108** 285 **122**
106
James R. **65** 153
Jane L. **104** 60
Janette **68** 329
Jedediah **122** 106 214
Jesse **104** 80
Job **122** 105
John **54** 181 **55** 76 **57** 154
63 229 230 **68** 167 **73**
295 **94** 241 **97** 311 **102**
13 **109** 314 **113** 297 **115**
172 **116** 55 **119** 74 **122**
106 214 243 **130** 138
Joseph **113** 297 **122** 106
Joshua **127** 13
Lily A. **125** 113
Lois **56** 296
Lois (Shaw) **113** 297
Louisa **104** 291
Lucy (Stover) **104** 134
Lydia **87** 250 **115** 172 **116**
122 **122** 105
Lydia (Chase) **87** 337
Margaret (Woodward)
(Cogan) **110** 191
Marion **104** 59
Martha **62** 122 **122** 106
Martha (Nelson) **130** 138
140
Mary **56** 410 **57** 154 **93** 206
101 330 **102** 13 **122** 105
106 **125** 181 **126** 20
Mary (Bailey) **125** 178
Mary Ann **68** 329
Mary H. **122** 214
Mary Holmes **125** 240
Mary J. (Hawks) **107** 317
Miriam **104** 59
Nancy **115** 172 **122** 214
Nicholas **62** 356
Oliver Shaw **113** 297
Orvilla **62** 126
Patience **122** 106 214 215

IRISH *cont'd*
Patty **87** 123
Peggy **87** 121
Perry C. **122** 214
Phebe **81** 164 **122** 106
  125 173
Phebe (Falkner) **125** 180
Polly **113** 297
Priscilla **54** 181 **130** 139
  140 286
Rebecca **63** 229
Rebecca (Doty) **122** 243
Reuben **78** 405
Richard **110** 198
Ruth **130** 139
Samuel **127** 221
Samuel T. **115** 172
Sarah **122** 106 298
Sarah Ann **122** 214
Sarah Jane **62** 122
Sarah June (Dunham)
  113 297
Sarah L. **120** 6
Sarah Loring (Mitchell)
  113 297
Sintha **108** 285
Southwick **125** 180
Statira **108** 285
Statiry B. **104** 60
Stella Bertha (Putnam)
  119 74
Stella P. **109** 79
Susan E. **122** 215
Susanna **86** 222 **123** 40
Thankful **68** 167 **89** 23
Thankful (Wilbor) **102** 13
  113 297
Thomas **127** 221
William **89** 274 **122** 214
William C. **122** 214 299
  125 174
William Mitchell **84** 111
  185 **112** 220 **113** 297
Willis Luther **109** 80 314
  119 74
Willis Luther (Mrs.) **109**
  129 320
IRISK John **82** 57
IRLAME William **82** 193
IRONMONGER Elizabeth
  Hogg **117** 155
IRONS Arthur **86** 379
Charles **110** 119
Harry Stuart **66** 192
Horatio Needham
  110 119
Jeremiah **128** 62
Lucy **82** 181
Mary **86** 379
Mary A. **86** 379
Nancy **96** 76
Nellie (Needham) **110** 119
Owen **106** 45
Penelope (Freeman)
  106 45
Resolved **128** 62 **147** 69
Samuel **60** 130 **128** 62
Sarah **60** 130 **106** 45 **112** 79
Sophronia **144** 120
Stephen **128** 62
Thomas **106** 45 49 **128** 62

IRONS *cont'd*
Timothy **106** 45
Titus **106** 45
Vergil **82** 181
Waite **54** 251
William **110** 119 **128** 62
IRONSIDE
Edmund **106** 52 53
IRONWOOD
Alexander **143** 31
IRRIBARREN Maria
  Felisa Ossandon **109**
  285 288
Paula Ossandon **109** 285
  287
IRVIN Abigail **77** 220
Alex **62** 171
Andrew **91** 39
B. B. (Mrs.) **83** 248
Benjamin Screven **95** 341
Benjamin Screven (Mrs.)
  84 186 **95** 341 **96** 87 163
Charlotte **62** 79
Elizabeth (Joiner) **95** 341
Isaiah Tucker **95** 341
James **62** 247 **78** 318
  92 114
Jane **92** 114
Jeannette E. **66** lxxxiv
Jessie **118** 244
John **62** 79
Joseph **117** 51
Margaret **73** 230
Mary **91** 389
Mary Baine (Brewer)
  95 341
Mary Margaret **92** 114
Mildred Screven **95** 341
Natalie **124** 196
Sarah (Tracy) **91** 38
  111 153
Sarah Elizabeth **117** 51
Sarah M. (Tracy) **91** 38
Theodosia (Welles)
  117 51
William (Mrs.) **111** 163
IRVINE
—— **56** 192 **112** 289
Adam **65** 118
Charles A. Hood **68** 30
Christopher **112** 289
Dorcas (Montgomery)
  112 289
Elizabeth **65** 118
Ella Eliza **68** 30
Henry **120** 17
Hood **68** 30
James **56** 192 334
Jane **120** 15
John **120** 15 17
John Frogley (Mrs.)
  93 137
Martha **120** 17
Mary **91** 389 **112** 289 **120**
  15 17
Mary Ann **120** 15
Mary Ann (Baker) **120** 15
Mary Jane **120** 17
Matilda Edith **68** 30
Sherry **148** 296
William **120** 15

IRVINE *cont'd*
William (Mrs.) **109** 157
  110 155
William Ferguson **51** 235
  54 115 348 349
William Galbreath (Mrs.)
  104 144
William Struthers **68** 30
IRVING —— **67** 85
Charlotte Van Wart
  90 69 70
Ebenezer **90** 70
Elizabeth (Kip) **90** 70
Emily **77** 264
George **129** 104
Gertrude **108** 136
Harriet **145** 248
Helen Grant **104** 143
Henry **66** lxxii **78** 120
Jean **91** 352
John **91** 352 **129** 104
  140 252
John G. S. **88** 337
Letitia **68** 256
Mary **91** 352
Mary Jane **85** 323
Nancy (Hill) **88** 337
Nathaniel **58** 68
Peyton **77** 264
Washington **52** 388 **90** 70
  99 24
IRWIN Irwyn
Albert Fracker **124** 196
Albert James (Mrs.) **103**
  119 **104** 323
Alvin B. **78** 50
Ann **60** 348
Annie Mary **60** lxv
Caroline (Addoms)
  112 316
David Duryea (Mrs.)
  82 364
Dorcas **112** 300
Dorothea Clifford **82** 364
Dorothy (Fracker)
  124 196
Dudley Marvin **92** 305
E. K. **91** 326
Edward **60** 348 **92** 169
Elizabeth **97** 183 **98** 341
Elizabeth Jane **68** 150
Gerard **112** 301
Harry Thomas (Mrs.)
  98 147
Huldah L. (Johnson)
  92 169
J. M. **112** 316
James **112** 290 300
Jane **81** 339
John **79** 327 **81** 339
John Rice **118** 167
Joseph **80** 156
Letitia **81** 339
Lydia **79** 327
Mabel Vernell **97** 120
Margaret **112** 301
Martha Teller **92** 305
Mary **60** 348
Mary A. **80** 242
Mary J. **78** 50
Myra **97** 392

IRWIN *cont'd*
Natalie **124** 196
Octavia Olivia **80** 156
Patrick **60** 348
Rebecca **80** 156
Richard B. **64** 69
Robert **124** 196
Sarah Hill (Coe) **116** 312
William **91** 326 **92** 305
William Alexander
97 120
William P. **60** lxv
Irwyn *see* Irwin
ISAAC Isaack Isaacke
Isaacs Isaacks Isacke
Isake Izacke
——— **59** 291 294-297
Aaron **54** 210 430 432
Abraham **59** 219
Allen **117** 319
Amelia **117** 319
Ann **73** 270
Benjamin **144** 241
Caroline M. **73** 219
Catherine **54** 430 **122** 267
Clarissa **54** 210
Daniel **93** 362
Edward **102** 6 9 248 253
103 18 **147** 10
Elias **117** 319
Elijah **117** 319
Elisha **117** 319
Elizabeth **110** 274 **117** 319
Esther **54** 210
Frances **87** 192 **91** 326
Frances Maria **54** lvii
Godfrey **117** 319
Grace **79** 264
Hannah **73** 141 266 **78** 235
Isaac **108** 279 281
Isabel **122** 270
Jacob **127** 9
Jane **117** 319
Joanna **122** 267 270
John **63** 280 **78** 235 **93** 362
117 319 **139** 141 **143**
329 330
John Hedges **54** 432
Jos. **62** 245
Joseph **73** 276 **108** 281
Joseph Gray **108** 281
Mahala **117** 319
Margery (Wheathill)
103 18
Margery (Whetehill)
102 6 9 **147** 10
Martha Ann **73** 277
Mary **54** 430 432 **55** 206
73 261 **93** 362 **102** 5 6 9
109 318 **117** 319 **119** 4
120 242 **121** 190 **141** 99
147 3-5 9 10
Mary E. **125** 240
Mercy Gray **108** 281
Miranda **73** 278
Moses **127** 6
Nancy **117** 319
Nancy (Bradford) **130** 70
Parsons **116** 235
Polly **117** 319
Rachel **73** 220 268 **117** 319

ISAAC *cont'd*
Richard **73** 269 **85** 75
111 10
Rugg **137** 90
Samuel **58** 190 **65** 236
110 274 **117** 319
Sarah **73** 148
Thomas **93** 362 **122** 267
270
Wiley **73** 276
William **65** 251 **93** 362
108 281 **147** 10
ISABELLA I of Spain **77** 93
ISABELLA of Castile
141 101
ISABELLE Queen of
England **104** 270
Isabelle *see* Isbell
Isacke *see* Isaac
Isake *see* Isaac
ISAN
Molly (Gaines) **85** 54
ISBELL Isabelle Isbel
Isbelle Isbells Isbyll
Edmund (Mrs.) **148** 140
Elizabeth **141** 117
Fanny (Carmon) **89** 317
Hannah **105** 269
John **69** 343 **142** 262
Lydia **78** 40
Lyman **89** 317
Mary **56** 263 **114** 307
Mary Frances **89** 317
Patty **59** 256
Peruda **114** 307
Robert **105** 269 **141** 318
Sally **71** 12
Sarah **60** 334
William **78** 40
ISBERG
Louise Von **78** 49
ISBISTER ——— **71** 368
ISBURGH
Alexander **82** 350
Charles H. **82** 349 350
Donald **82** 350 382 **83** 229
120 148
Grace **82** 350
Ida Josephine **82** 349
Karl **74** 157 **75** xxii **82**
248 253 349 350 382 **83**
229
Marion Van Buren **82** 350
Mary A. **82** 350
Isbyll *see* Isbell
ISDAHL C. Bors (Mrs.) **70**
liv **80** 100
ISDELL Susanna **114** 212
ISELIN
Adrian **86** 336 337
Arthur **106** 4
Caroline Lydia **78** 205
Charles Oliver **75** xxiii 64
86 236 336 337 **87** 176
Edith Hope **86** 336
Edith Hope (Goddard)
86 336
Eleonora **86** 336
Eleonora (O'Donnell)
86 336
Emilie (Roulet) **86** 336

ISELIN *cont'd*
Ethel May **85** 232
Fannie Garner **86** 337
Frances (Garner) **86** 336
Isaac **86** 336 **112** 247
John Henry **85** 232 **106** 4
John Henry (Mrs.) **77** 323
78 205
Mary Philipse
(Gouverneur) **85** 232
O'Donnell (Mrs.) **86** 449
ISELY
Jeter Allen **101** 336
ISERSON Abraham S. **73**
317 **74** xxiv
ISGATE
Abigail **59** 274
Eleazer **59** 88-90 154 274
361 362 364
Gershom **59** 362
Martha **59** 364
Rachel **59** 89 90 154 274
361 362 364
Rejoice **59** 88
ISGRIG Ann **113** 152
ISHAM — Lady **97** 100
— Professor **52** 211
— Rev. Mr. **62** 275
A. Olney **100** 333
Abel **59** 209
Abigail **56** 348 **72** 130 **73**
39 **83** 99
Albert Keep **92** 82
Alfoy Olney **111** 133
Alfred **81** 50
Alice **121** 257
Allen **73** 39
Allena C. **76** 99
Amanda H. **76** 86 87
Anna **56** 350 **59** 99
Anna (Lambert) **92** 81
Anna Jane **76** 87 99
Anne **94** 331
Asa Brainerd **64** 69
Asahel **76** 87
Ashur **59** 99-101 209 416
60 73 204 **73** 39
Bertha M. **74** 316
Betsey A. **76** 87
Calista (Chapman) **100**
333 **111** 133
Catherine **79** 155
Charles **97** 100
Charles (Mrs.) **81** 247
Chester **59** 99
Chester C. **73** 39
Clara A. **74** 316
Clara Augusta **76** 87 99
D. C. **74** 316
Daniel **91** 197
David B. **100** 333
David Bliss **111** 133
Delia (Snell) **92** 81 82
Dimice **74** 168
Dorothy (Foote) **92** 81
Edward Swift **81** 245
Eleanor **97** 99
Elizabeth **80** 350 367
Ella Agnes **76** 86 87 99
Ephraim **55** 282 **56** 354
356

ISHAM *cont'd*
Eunice **76** 87 97
Euseby **94** 254 331 **97** 144
Eva Newton **111** 133
Frank Newton **111** 133
George **51** 268 270
Gurdon **72** 130 **73** 39
Hannah **76** 87
Harriet A. **72** 130
Henry **97** 101 **98** 199
   107 110
Henry Spencer **76** 87 97
Isaac **92** 81
J. Rollo **76** 99
Jane **53** 248 **74** 316 **77** 262
Jane (Parker) **92** 81 **112**
   195 196 **113** 257
Jane Elliot **76** 86 87 99
Jeanie **97** 122
Jeannette **73** 39
Jennie L. **76** 87 97
John **53** 248 **81** 50 **92** 81 82
   97 100 **112** 195 258 **139**
   328
John W. **73** 39
Joseph **123** 59
Judith (Lewin) **97** 100
Justinian **97** 100 101
Katharine Ellen (Snow)
   92 81
Laure **81** 50
Lee Clifford **74** 316
Lincoln **81** 247
Lois **81** 50
Louisa **94** 252 **97** 99
Lucretia **68** 332
Lucy G. (Keep) **92** 82
Madelon Burbeck **93** 399
Martha Jane Eleanor
   (Wilson) **97** 99
Mary **81** 247 **89** 68 **91** 208
   115 282
Mary (Jerrod) **109** 39
Mary Ann T. **74** 316
Mary L. **111** 133
Mary Louise (Otis) **92** 82
Mehitable Hammond
   83 359
Miriam **72** 74
Molly (Thomas) **91** 197
Nelson **92** 81
Nelson W. **74** 316
Nelson William **76** 86 87
   99
Noah **56** 349 **92** 81
Norman **80** 74
Norman Morrison **68**
   xxxiv **76** 154 **77** xxiii **90**
   128
Obed **83** 359
Oliver K. **72** 74
Ralph **74** 156 **75** xxiii **92**
   81 82 90 118
Ralph Nelson **92** 81 82
Rebecca **83** 99
Robert **97** 99 100 **102** 244
Rosa E. **111** 133
Rosannah **59** 101
Sarah **55** 282 **56** 354 356
   124 220
Simon **63** 279

ISHAM *cont'd*
Sophia **83** 99
Susan **51** 268 270
Susanna (Swift) **123** 59
Thankful **59** 411 **122** 61
Thankful (Lumbert)
   92 81
Thomas **80** 350 367 **109** 39
Timothy **56** 164 348 350
   83 99
Tryphena **73** 39
Tryphena Easson **59** 100
Vere **94** 252 **97** 100
Warren Spencer **74** 316
   76 87 99
William **79** 155
ISHERWOOD
Delia (Noble) **95** 188
John W. **117** 293
William **65** 50 **95** 188
ISLEIB
Andrew **85** 313
   86 320
Andrew F. **86** 320
Anna Catherine **85** 313
   314
Emma M. B. **85** 313
Eva N. **85** 313
Henry A. **85** 313
Henry R. **85** 313
Jessie D. **85** 313
John **85** 313
John P. **85** 313
Johnnie **86** 320
Katharine **85** 313
Katie **86** 320
Leon R. **85** 313
Louisa **86** 321
Lucy **85** 313
Margaretha **86** 321
Margie R. **86** 321
Martha Kothe **85** 314
Martin **85** 313 **86** 321
Sarah J. Little **85** 313
Valentine **85** 313 314
ISLES Mary **106** 320
ISLEY Islley Issely
Anne **52** 432
Frances **89** 199
Henry **74** 75
Richard **52** 432
ISMOND D. V. **105** 153
ISOM Herbert **107** 133
ISRAEL Isriel
Anna **66** 20
Charles Cushing **83** 172
Edward H. **108** 304
Eunice (Reed) **147** 270
Jennie (Merrill) **83** 299
   300
Joseph **62** 250 320
Josephine **83** 172
Josie **83** 299 300
Kate **83** 172 299 300
Margaretta Alberta
   (Kenney) **108** 304
Martin **66** 20
Mary **83** 172
Mary L. **83** 299 301
Mary Lewis **83** 172

ISRAEL *cont'd*
Mary S. (Cushing)
   83 179 182
Mary Sheafe **84** 29
Orrin **66** 20
Peter **62** 250 320
Robert W. **83** 172 179 182
Thomas **66** 20
Warner **66** 20
William **62** 250 320 **66** 20
William P. **83** 299 300
William Pusey **83** 172
ISSAACSON
Edward L. **117** 126
Lillie Delia (Rutherford)
   117 126
ISSELY *see* Isley
ISTED Thomas **51** 412
ISWELL —— **53** 379
ITHELL
Dorothy **114** 115
John **117** 103
Thomas **54** 449
ITURBIDE
Agustin de **122** 180
Agustin Jeronimo de
   122 180
Iunius *see* Junius
IVANOFF —— **79** 300
Ive *see* Ives
Ivens *see* Ivins
IVERS —— **102** 34
Anna **100** 140
Charles **99** 120 **101** 270
Edward **99** 27
Elizabeth **92** 13 **100** 137
Gregory **92** 11 13 **94** 294
Hannah **78** 300 **88** 279 **100**
   140 **136** 324 **140** 332
Hannah (Trecothick)
   140 332 333
James **84** 154 **85** 125 **99** 27
   140 34 157 332 **144** 267
Jane **77** 291 **85** 8 **99** 27 28
   118 120 **100** 135 137 140
   101 51 275 276 **102** 32
   140 34 332
Jane (Barber) **100** 239
John **99** 28 **101** 51
Lucy Jane **77** 148
Mary **65** 10 **78** 302 **140** 45
Nancy **79** 39 **140** 45
Polly (Cutler) **85** 125
Samuel **92** 11
Sarah **100** 29 **101** 275
Thomas **84** 154 **85** 8 **99**
   118 **100** 135 137 140-142
   101 275 276 **102** 32 **140**
   45
Trecothick **140** 332
William **76** lviii **99** 28
   118 120 **100** 29 239 **101**
   51 247 275
William H. **77** 148
IVERSON
John **71** xlv 284 285
Nancy (Thomas) **71** xliv
   xlv 284 285 **88** 280
Ivery *see* Ivory
IVES Ive
   —— **58** 411 **129** 315

IVES *cont'd*
— Miss **58** 412
— Mr. **71** 143
— Mrs. **71** 118
____ (Amory) **140** 31
Abigail **75** 90 **104** 288
  136 325
Abigail (Burroughs)
  136 325
Abraham **56** 138 **147** 326
Alethea **148** 267
Alma Cornelia **53** 398
Ann **66** 201 **70** 263 **77** 130
  79 449
Ann Brooks **75** 93
Anna **53** 398 **59** 72
Annabella **79** 93
Anne **71** 27
Anne (Derby) **104** 288
Annie Maude (Downing)
  96 33
Arthur Coon **86** 197
  87 209
Arthur Coon (Mrs.) **109**
  129 **113** 81
Arthur S. **56** 324 **60** 185
Barbara **56** 138
Beatrice **136** 333
Beatrix **63** 285
Benjamin **66** 113 116 120
  123 124 **77** 130 **79** 449
  104 288 289
Carnelia Ann (Warren)
  135 337
Charles Edward **136** 319
Charles H. **147** 259
Charles James **53** 398
Charles Pomeroy (Mrs.)
  103 119
Clarence W. **87** 92
David **71** 279
David Perkins **62** 213
Deborah **63** 285
Dwight Foster **53** 398
Edwin **135** 337
Elanthan **64** 206
Elihu **108** 245
Eliza **62** 97
Eliza H. **72** 74
Elizabeth **63** 285 **72** 74 **77**
  130 **79** 449 **95** 113 **104**
  288
Elizabeth (Buttery)
  147 326
Elizabeth (Newhall)
  83 471
Elmira E. (Jones) **87** 92
Eunice **71** 279
George Edward **136** 319
George H. **53** 398
George White **136** 319
Gideon **136** 325
Hannah (Royce) **136** 319
Harriet **53** 398
Harriet Bowen (Amory)
  120 85
Hope (Brown) **133** 306
Isaac **115** 19 **136** 319
James **53** 398
James E. **97** 53
James S. **53** 398

IVES *cont'd*
Jane **51** 138 **63** 285 **100** 133
Joel **70** 81
Joel S. **54** 360
John **51** 113 **61** 22 **63** 285
  286 **67** 49 **81** 126 **92** 182
  104 289 **123** 320 **136**
  319
Joseph **61** 118 **66** 330
Jotham **136** 325
Levi Stillman (Bp. of N.C.)
  64 297
Lizzie C. **125** 182
Lois **56** 288 **67** 49 **70** 74
Lucy (Whittemore)
  108 245
Lydia **55** 370
Margaret **92** 182 **104** 289
Marie **71** 27
Martha **54** 26 396 **104** 288
  112 227
Mary **53** 398 **66** 330 **73** 15
  78 185 **104** 288
Mary (Combs) **135** 337
Mary (Hall) **136** 319
Mary (Royce) **136** 325
Mary Elizabeth (Parmelee)
  136 319
Matthew **144** 106
Michael **51** 138
Miles **51** 138 **54** 396 397
Mineas **135** 337
Molly (Gaines) **85** 54
Nathaniel **56** 288 **72** 74
Nicholas **51** 253 **86** 413
  133 306
Noah **75** 90
Polly **67** 223
Prudence **115** 19
Rachel **59** 72
Rebecca **66** 328 **67** 224
  90 361
Reuben **62** 383
Robert **64** 350 **69** 22 **87** 92
  140 31
Robert Hale **95** 114
Robert Hall **120** 85
Ross **102** 102
Ruth F. **53** 398
Sarah **54** 396 **56** 288 **61** 118
  70 81 **112** 227
Sarah (Bray) **95** 114
Sarah Amelia (White)
  136 319
Sarah Hotchkiss (Wilcox)
  136 319
Stephen **56** 288
Stephen B. **62** lxxvi
Susan **71** 27
Susanna **53** 398 **115** 19
  123 320
Thomas **53** 398 **58** 412 **63**
  285 286 **64** 125 **66** 201
  328 **71** 27 **77** 130 **79** 449
  83 322 **100** 133
Thomas P. **96** 57 **133** 308
Whiting **67** 224
William **56** 324 **60** 185
  66 345 **81** 126 **84** 71
  112 227 **125** 34
Zachariah **70** 74

IVES *cont'd*
Zerviah **56** 288
IVEY Ivie Ivy Ivye Jvey
— Mr. **55** 342
Jesse C. **69** xxx
John **55** 73
Joseph Henry **61** 105
Lucy Abbie **64** xxxiii
Mary **55** 73
Thomas **52** 47 **138** 225
Thomasine **52** 47
Iviens *see* Ivins
IVINGTON Ann **73** 227
IVINS Ivens
Mary **128** 171
William M. **76** lxxxii
IVITT — Widow **84** 306
Edward **84** 308
IVORY Ivery Ivroy
——— **67** 337 339
— Dea. **69** 221
Abigail **67** 336 342
Agnes **67** 331 340
Alice **67** 330 340
Angel **67** 336
Ann **67** 334 341 **83** 121
Anne **67** 333 335 340
Annis **67** 330 332 340
Benjamin **132** 39
Betty **69** 9
Bynah **69** 12
Charlestown **69** 123
Charlotte A. (Hall) **91** 227
Christian **67** 339
Deborah **57** 281 **113** 305
Deborah Tobie **132** 39
Dorcas **67** 335 342 343
Dorothy **67** 335
Edmund **67** 333 334 337-
  339 341
Edward **67** 335
Elizabeth **61** 398 **67** 330-
  336 338-342
Faith **67** 330 335 339
Joan **67** 332 339 340
John **57** 75 **61** 398 **67** 331-
  334 336 337 339-342 **69**
  9 10 13-17 120 121 123
  124 126 222-224 295 298
  300 303-306 **70** 13 14 17
  18 137 140
John (Mrs.) **69** 11 **70** 16
  19 137
Joseph **67** 332 333 335
  338 339 341 342
Katharine **67** 331 332 335
  336 340 341
Lois **67** 341 **74** 200 **83** 121
Lucy **57** 75
Luke **60** 312 **67** 332-336
  338 339 341 342
Margery **67** 330 339
Martha **78** 417
Mary **52** 430 **67** 333 336
  341 342
Rebecca **67** 335 336 341
Richard **67** 330-335 340
Robert **67** 330-337 339-342
  94 274
Roger **67** 330 336 339
Ruth **61** 398 **67** 341

IVORY cont'd
Sally **70** 17
Sarah **57** 75 **67** 333 334
  336 341 342
Susan **67** 332 333 335 336
  338 339 341 342
Susanna **67** 335
Thomas **57** 75 **67** 330-335
  340 341 **69** 15 **83** 121
William **67** 331-335 337
  338 340-343
Ivy see Ivey
Ivye see Ivey
IWALT
Elizabeth B. **126** 207
IWARDBY Elizabeth **118**
  252 **119** 314
John **118** 252
IWICK Jane **55** 103
IYENAGA
Toyokichi **70** 288
Izacke see Isaac
IZANT Martha **72** 292
Sarah Luella **72** 292
Silas **72** 292
Walter **72** 292
IZARD — Mr. **55** 275
IZOD
Anne (Gunne) **84** 290
Henry **84** 290
IZQUIERDO Elena
  (Trumbull) **109** 291
Guillermo **109** 291

JABIN Jabine
—— **61** 110
Nicholas **79** 300
JACIE Henry **114** 84
JACK —— **143** 366
— Mr. **71** 135 **74** 149
Ada **83** 182 186
Albert **125** 240
Alexander **127** 6
Andrew **125** 261
Annie C. **68** lxxv
Annis **100** 143
Calvin **72** 15
Charles Walter **89** 225
D. L. **145** 255
D. R. **145** 71
David **125** 291
David Russell **55** 233 359
  56 xxxii **58** xlv lxi **59**
  xliv **60** xxxvi **61** xxxiv
  62 xxxvii **64** xxxi **66**
  xlix **67** 305 **68** xxx
  xxxiii xlii lxxv lxxvi
Dorianna (Hartling)
  125 261
E. C. **56** 324 **145** 371
Elizabeth **84** 423 **114** 186
Elizabeth (Bowering)
  125 291
Elizabeth Margaret
  (Kress) (Huger) **95** 172
Frances G. **125** 178
Frances G. (Thompson)
  125 240
Gertrude Lazell (Emery)
  89 225

JACK cont'd
Hannah (Tibbetts)
  100 148
Harriet **125** 260
Henry **68** lxxv
Hugh **112** 286
I. Allen **55** 123
James **77** 218 **87** 125
James R. **91** 299 **92** 142
Jane **114** 186
Jessie June **93** 138
John **112** 285 **119** 21 **125**
  260 261
Joseph **100** 148
Joseph L. **64** 155
Julia **78** 329
Louise M. **68** lxxvi
Margaret **77** 140
Marion Elizabeth
  68 lxxvi
Mary **114** 186 190
Mary A. P. **64** 155
Mary Ann **64** 155
Matthew **114** 186
Molly **51** 492
Polly **114** 186
Richard **114** 186
Sallie (Cushman) **72** 15
Samuel **114** 186
Samuel J. C. **125** 240
Sarah (Esty) **100** 148
Sophia (Baker) **125** 261
T. C. **56** 324 **145** 371
Walter **100** 143
William **114** 186
Jackes see Jacks
JACKIM Jacob **65** 169
JACKINS Anna **111** 115
Christopher **111** 40
Josiah Nason **111** 40
Kendall S. **75** 255
Lizzie E. **75** 255
Patty **66** 110
Ruth **111** 40
JACKLER Robert **52** 234
JACKLIN Jackline Jackling
—— **83** 445
Louisa **115** 292
Samuel **55** 141
William T. **115** 292
JACKMAN —— **54** 362
Abigail **85** lxiv
Agnes (Collman) **141** 56
Alice **141** 56
Ambrose **141** 56
Ann **57** 317
Chloe (Jackson) **86** 303
Dorothy W. **60** 294
  126 141
Edward **57** 316 317
Elizabeth **141** 56 **147** 257
Elizabeth Ann **64** 212
Eunice **141** 56
Faith **141** 56
Frederick E. **140** 133
Freeman Tilton (Mrs.)
  83 217 **84** 189
George W. **60** 185 **63** 374
  64 156
James **53** 36 37 **60** 185
  61 313

JACKMAN cont'd
Joan **141** 56
Joanna **53** 37
John **52** 105 **57** 316 **125** 29
  141 56
Joseph **103** 58
Julia **69** 143
Julia A. (Gordon) **140** 133
Julia Ann **140** 133
Lois Belle (Cole) **86** 303
Lorinda Adalade **103** 58
Louisa **103** 58
Lucretia Ann **63** 374
  64 156
Lucy Day **86** 306
Lyman **64** 134
Margaret **141** 56
Margaret (Bumstead)
  141 56
Mary **134** 67
Mary (Day) **86** 306
Mary M. **91** 41
Mary W. **126** 65
Moses **86** 303 306
Nancy **67** 351
Orville **86** 303
P. A. **61** 313
Panoncha **141** 56
Parmenio Adams **60** 185
Permelia **109** 182
Rachel **53** 36 37
Richard **66** 259
Rose (Hart) **141** 56
Sarah **125** 217
Susanna **68** 205
Thomas R. **91** 202
Unice **141** 56
William **66** 249
JACKS see also Jackson
Agnes **144** 34-37
Agnes (Prouce) **144** 36
Alice **144** 34-36
Annis **144** 36
Bartholomew **144** 36
Daniel **144** 35 36
Dewnes / Dionis **144** 35
Edward **144** 36
Elizabeth **144** 35
Frances (Lidston) **144** 35
George **144** 36
Helen **144** 36
Hugh **144** 35
James **63** 234
Joan **144** 34-36
Joan (Cann) **144** 35
John **144** 34-36
Joys **144** 36
Judith **144** 35
Marie **144** 36
Marie (Trend) **144** 35 36
Mary **144** 35 36
Matthew **144** 36
Millicent (Hore) **144** 35
Rose **144** 36
Sarah **144** 36
Sarah (Palmer) **144** 36 37
Simeon **144** 36
Thomas **144** 34-36
Thomsine **144** 36
William **144** 36

JACKSON Jackston - *see also* Jacks
— Capt. **65** 338 362
— Col. **65** 337 341 **85** 131 **112** 205 206
— Dr. **58** 33 34 137
— Goodman **64** 7
— Judge **56** 300
— Lieut. **84** 388
— Mr. **65** 370 **69** 372 **70** 187 **74** 149 **81** 316 **92** 20
— Mrs. **54** 411 **65** 367 **83** 33 193 **92** 314
— Rev. Mr. **65** 362 **67** 112
— Widow **83** 33 **101** 270
____ (Avery) **140** 34 35 157
____ (Callender) **140** 48
____ (Seward) **144** 34
A. **91** 326
A. H. **91** 326
Aaron **56** 39 **57** 106 262 **66** 35 **71** 343 **86** 60 70 71 153 303
Abby Crocker (West) **89** 56
Abby E. **73** 179
Abel **65** 113
Abigail **55** 147 **57** 103 259 **59** 92 93 **62** 373 **66** 84 **71** 148 343 346 350 **73** 102 **75** 145 **76** 218 **78** 302 **81** 427 **97** 4 **100** 186 **114** 181 **124** 7 238 **144** 324
Abigail (Bancroft) **103** 63
Abigail (Callender) **144** 324-327 330
Abigail (Cleaveland) **100** 186
Abigail (Drew) (Ellins) **144** 34
Abigail (Moody) **84** 426
Abigail (Tupper) **99** 127 **120** 102
Abigail (West) **124** 7
Abigail C. **144** 327
Abraham **55** 420 **68** 232 **71** 342 343 **89** 56 **100** 303
Ada Lillian **117** 126
Ada May **86** 370
Adam **144** 30
Adele M. **71** lxii
Adeline **93** 216
Adeline Zoa **86** 153 311
Agnes **91** 347 348 **97** 3
Agnes Washburn **106** 157
Albert Brown (Mrs.) **108** 134
Albert R. **73** 102
Alden **73** 166 **88** 63
Alexander **73** 144 168 **88** 332 **113** 297
Alfred Andrew **93** 220 221 **94** 167
Alfred Joseph **93** 220
Alice **117** 290 **131** 127 **144** 30-32
Alice F. **106** 157
Allen **89** 57
Almeda German **93** 217

JACKSON *cont'd*
Amanda Jane (Cole) **86** 153
Amasa **73** 14 **79** 161 **93** 304 **100** 66 **125** 42
Amelia **76** 206 **78** 314
Amelia Lee **76** 206 **84** 214 **104** 314 **136** 319
Amnies **144** 30
Amos B. **147** 272
Amy **99** 209 281 282 **100** 139 **144** 31
Andrew **51** 144 **53** 153 **54** 113 133 456 **62** xxi 92 **63** 158 **67** 326 **68** 71 **70** 307 308 **72** 7 **77** 215 219 222 244 252 **89** 349 **90** 47 **103** 63 **133** 155 **136** 67 **137** 227
Andrew D. **69** 162
Andrew F. **91** 195
Andrew Hayden **93** 221
Andrew Vaughn **78** 176
Andrew W. **100** 213
Angell **144** 30
Ann **51** 461 **52** 65 **83** 22 24 25 **91** 352 **100** 236 **119** 183 **125** 290
Ann (Lockman) **122** 188
Ann (Potter) **88** 332
Ann I. C. **74** 298
Ann-Louisa T. (Nelson) **90** 54
Anna **62** 372 374 **71** 126 346 **73** 115 **78** 180 **82** 42 286 290-292 **98** 180 **111** 305
Anna Maude **79** 135
Anne **91** 345 349 350 **93** 221 **119** 183 **124** 6 7 **144** 32
Anne (Barnes) **89** 56
Anne (Thomas) **124** 6
Anners **57** 220
Annis **97** 158 **144** 37
Annis Maria **93** 215
Anstis **107** 31
Ansyl **91** 195
Arlotta **66** 186
Artemas **124** 7
Arthur Loring (Mrs.) **76** 85 **83** 332
Arthur Obed **86** 153
Artsimmon **125** 108
Asa **71** 343
Asahel **124** 7
Atwood **73** 179
Austin **73** 170
Azubah **122** 197
Barbara (Bassett) **125** 9 **126** 238
Barnabas **145** 352
Barnard **78** 89
Bart **127** 15
Bartlett **83** 146
Bathsheba **56** 202 **78** 89
Benjamin **58** 237 **61** 360 **63** 243 **82** 42 290 **83** 143 **87** 233 235 **89** 349 **93** 214 215 **111** 304 **147** 261 263

JACKSON *cont'd*
Benjamin Bixby Murry **88** 240
Benjamin Franklin **93** 184
Bertha H. **84** 29
Bessie Emily **74** xxix
Betsey **65** 113 **68** 168 **73** 166 **78** 358 405 **80** 308 **114** 307 **115** 27 **124** 7 **125** 108
Betsey (Hall) **89** 56
Betsey (Pringle) **94** 280
Bettina **106** 157
Betty **82** 42
Betty (Wade) **136** 39
Beulah **57** 282 **124** 6 7
Beulah (Stearns) **124** 6 14
Blake S. **109** 129
Blanche **111** 300
Bleazer **98** 105
Briggs C. **73** 184
C. **75** 12
Caddie **100** 213
Caleb **54** 224 **62** 372 373 **93** 214 **124** 6 7 14
Caroline **88** 282 **124** 8
Caroline Keith (Fobes) **98** 75
Caroline M. **108** 278
Carynthaphuch **147** 189-191
Catherine **65** 113 **66** 13 **76** 31 **91** 195 **114** 307 **125** 294
Catherine (Newton) **95** 315
Catherine Cabot **90** 70
Catherine E. **88** 335
Cecil C. **97** 396
Charity **88** 338 **144** 31 32
Charity (Hellier) **144** 31
Charity (Lemons) **88** 330
Charles **60** lxviii 224 **63** 95 **76** 206 208 **78** 44 **91** 310 326 **93** 214 215 **104** 314 **124** 7 141
Charles Addison **93** 215
Charles Ambray **93** 217
Charles Cabot **59** xlvii **81** 468
Charles Hervey (Mrs.) **85** 90
Charles Selvin **67** xxi 86
Charles Tracy **81** 465
Charlotte **125** 287
Charlotte (Beech) **120** 14
Charlotte (Landress) **90** 47
Charlotte Sanford (Cheeseman) **112** 223
Chester **93** 214 216
Chloe **86** 70 303 **87** 283 **93** 214
Christian (Furneis) **144** 32 33
Christopher **58** 299 **66** 84 **94** 263 **144** 30-32
Cicely **144** 30
Clara **73** 176

JACKSON *cont'd*
Clara Rose (Jaedicke)
  94 281
Clarissa **73** 102 183 **88** 158
Clarissa (Clark) **100** 10
Clark **100** 287
Clement **82** 412 **84** 253
  92 19 **97** 3 4 6 9 **142** 143
  144 37 38
Clinton **93** 219
Clinton Ellis **93** 221
Clinton Waitt **93** 221
Corinne Lucy **93** 220
Cornelia **69** 162
Cynthia **65** 370
Cynthia Diadema **115** 27
Cyrene (Hall) **87** 231 233
Daniel **51** 45 **56** 93 **62**
  373 374 **65** 113 **81** 427
  444 **82** 26 42 43 290 292
  298 **88** 158 249 **89** 274
  93 111 **95** 380 **100** 66
  127 305 **140** 265
Daniel Magnus **100** 235
Darius **89** 349
David **60** 75 76 **62** 373 **71**
  343 **84** 136 **86** 70 **87** 5
  92 49 50 **101** 203
David F. **84** 136
Deborah **53** 444 **59** 85
  112 142 **124** 5 6
Deborah (Baker) **99** 127
Deborah (Fifield) **124** 5
Deborah (Prentice)
  147 272
Deidama (Dunham)
  94 280
Derius Merrill **88** 240
Dexter **142** 61
Dolly **89** 349
Doris **93** 220
Dorothy **81** 427 **83** 446
  84 14 **88** 231 **144** 34 37
Dorothy (Quincy) **103** 75
Dorothy Edna **93** 219
Dorothy Q. **103** 76
E. **70** 294
E. H. **123** 123
E. J. **112** 284
Earl P. **93** 218
Eben **81** 444
Ebenezer **70** 220 **82** 43 **94**
  280 **107** 155 **115** 26 27
  124 7 8
Edith **81** 427 **82** 290 295
Edith L. **111** 300 305
Edmund **51** 173 **52** 218
  54 cl **59** 215
Edmund Francis **93** 220
Edna **78** 324
Edward **51** 132 133 **55** 396
  57 103 280 388 **58** 68 **59**
  86 **62** 223 225 **64** 307 **65**
  238 243 362 **66** 84 **68**
  284 285 **70** 54 **71** 343 **84**
  159 **86** 62 68 **88** 337 **90**
  400 **92** 16 19 20 22 23
  93 217 263 **96** 279 **97** 6
  99 79 **103** 75 **133** 308
  140 157 **142** 133 142
  143

JACKSON *cont'd*
Edward C. **78** 304
Edward Evarts **58** xlv **59**
  87 105 153 216 269 360
  60 41 **61** xxxiv **63**
  xxxiv **64** xxi xxxi
Edward G. **66** 84
Edward Lawrence
  93 214 217
Edward Lefevre **93** 217
Edwin **94** 285
Edwin M. **73** 102
Effie Adella **93** 217
Elbridge Gary **83** 111
Eleanor **81** 444 **82** 43 290
  291 293 **93** 221 **104** 39
Eleanor (Gray) **95** 251
Eleanor (Milcome) **144** 33
  34
Eleanor (Praytor) **144** 32
Eleanor O. **75** 39
Eleanor W. **100** 213
Eleazer **53** 444 **65** 367 **78**
  400 **93** 214 **98** 105 **141**
  195
Eli **65** 112 **70** 153
Elijah Marcy **93** 215 219
Elisha **51** 169 173 **60** 75
  82 26 290 291 **95** 372
Elisha Tucker **98** 75
Elixie **93** 218
Eliza **68** 155 **73** 102 **78** 305
  79 46 **88** 333 **127** 62
Eliza (Briggs) **127** 62
Eliza Ann **91** 195
Eliza Ann Nichols
  114 238
Eliza Jane B. (Long)
  90 105
Elizabeth **51** 133 **52** 141 **55**
  148 **58** 68 337 **62** 372-
  375 **65** 162 352 **66** 84 **70**
  153 **71** 343 **73** 169 184
  76 218 **77** 307 **78** 308
  79 321 **81** 427 444 **82** 43
  288 290 293 420 **83** 306
  84 423 **86** 70 447 **89** 186
  91 195 350 **92** 20 **93** 221
  99 127 209 **100** 186 **106**
  143 **112** 142 **113** 274
  120 10 **125** 92 **130** 236
  140 157 **142** 143 **144** 31
  32
Elizabeth (Baker) **103** 75
Elizabeth (Cahoon)
  127 117
Elizabeth (Litchfield)
  144 31
Elizabeth (Nile) **125** 288
Elizabeth (Seaman)
  123 85
Elizabeth A. (Duroe) **112**
  55 57
Elizabeth Ann **80** 307
Elizabeth Davidson
  91 301
Elizabeth Fales **120** 10
Elizabeth Fales (Diman)
  120 5
Elizabeth Lee **76** 206

JACKSON *cont'd*
Elizabeth Mae (Clark)
  93 185
Elizabeth O. (Lake) **88** 336
Elizabeth P. **90** 50
Elizabeth Virginia **94** 281
Ellen **93** 217 218
Elmira **69** 144 **73** 166
Elsey **62** 374
Elvira **86** 157 311
Emelia (Livingston)
  133 308
Emeline A. (Veber) **111**
  305 308
Emily Jane (Andrews)
  103 75
Emma Caroline **85** 187
  95 74 149 **98** 75
Emma J. **108** 301
Emma M. **108** 278
Emma M. (Babson)
  140 265
Enoch **71** 343
Ephraim **51** 45 **56** 202 **57**
  106 200 257-259 69 296
  70 214-216 **78** 89 **81**
  427 444 **83** 21 24 **88** 343
  93 397 **100** 63 **117** 315
Esther **68** 93 **71** 343 **80** 332
  82 348 **84** 186 **89** 79 134
  90 68 **91** 195 **93** 214
  103 76 **107** 129
Esther (Abbot) **93** 213
Esther (Nash) **88** 283
Ethel Louise **94** 139
Ethel May **101** 122 **116** 71
Eugene Bailey **116** 53
Eunice **68** 284 285 **73** 168
  169 174 **90** 68
Eunice (Willis) **132** 76
Eva **68** 155
Eva Frances **78** 176
Eva Miriam **93** 219
Experience **71** 261 **88** 63
Ezra **71** 343
F. Nevill (Mrs.) **81** 214
Faith **52** 215
Fannie (Maverick) **97** 63
Fannie (Oslin) **146** 390
Fannie Louise **95** 315
Fanny (Cabot) **91** 310
Fanny Cabot **81** 331 **98** 85
Fanny Polk **78** 176
Fanny Roberts **107** 129
Florence **98** 147
Francena A. **89** 357
Frances **64** 341 **66** 84 **76**
  206 **90** 108
Frances Elizabeth **93** 220
Francis **53** 43 114 216 **55**
  420 **57** 102 63 309 **65** 15
  71 258 **76** 235 **78** 24
  128 254 **141** 292 298
  299
Francis Bradford **93** 220
Francis E. **98** 314
Frank **86** 379
Frank P. **93** 218
Frank R. **93** 219
Frank Warren **93** 218
Frank Will (Mrs.) **74** xxix

JACKSON *cont'd*
Fred Kinney **86** 197 **94**
   399 **99** 257
Frederick **93** 217
Frederick Elijah **93** 221
Frederick Wendell **53** 149
Freelove (Chase) **87** 315
G. R. **79** 160
G. W. **79** 38
Gabriel **144** 30-32
George **54** 413 **55** 330 **57**
   317 **60** 153 **63** 95 **72** 58
   78 407 **81** 427 444 **82** 26
   42 43 291 297 299 **108**
   278 **109** 253 256 **125**
   215 **144** 30 32
George A. **60** 105
George Andrew **120** 17
George Anson **60** xxxiv
   61 321 **62** xlviii lxvii
   lxviii
George Cleo **60** 185
George Coulter **76** xxii
   76 **93** 83 142 **94** 280
George E. **73** 184
George Frederick **94** 281
George H. **125** 53
George H. (Mrs.) **99** 153
George Jeremiah **93** 217
   219 220
George Moore **78** 164
George T. **117** 42
George W. **89** 357
George Washington **59**
   civ **93** 215
George West **59** xlvii **78**
   266 267 269 **89** 56 80
   137
George West (Mrs.)
   90 136
George Winfield **93** 220
Gershom **71** 343
Gertrude **93** 218 **115** 114
Giles **124** 6 7
Gladstone **78** 109
Gladys Starr **93** 185
Glaskey **145** 363
Godfrey **87** 231 233
Grace **76** 12 **99** 281 **144** 30
Grace (Gray) **128** 17
Grace Irving (Whiting)
   89 57
Grace Isabelle **93** 221
Hall **93** 222 **94** 65 167 **97**
   4 5 7 8 **118** 313 **134** 260
   265 266 268 270 272 275
Hannah **52** 218 **53** 444 **58**
   231 337 392 393 **62** 372
   373 **63** 76 **65** 113 **67** 286
   71 263 343 **72** 286 **73**
   168 169 172 **76** 206 208
   80 241 **81** 427 **82** 26 290
   292 **83** 21 24 **87** 65 122
   89 267 **91** 367 **92** 51
   100 241 302 **107** 226
   110 231 **123** 284 **124** 8
   130 216 **142** 61 **145** 308
Hannah (Avery) **84** 167
   97 9
Hannah (Barton) **83** 21
Hannah (Bonney) **83** 137

JACKSON *cont'd*
Hannah (Brewer) **124** 7
Hannah (Johnson) **144** 34
Hannah (Osborne)
   113 297
Hannah (Smith) **86** 60 70
   153 303
Hannah (Swett) **103** 75
Hannah (Tracy) **103** 75
Hannah (Wheelock)
   124 7
Hannah (Woodworth)
   89 56
Hannah Allen **88** 158
Hannah B. **93** 111
Hannah E. **73** 102
Hannah L. **63** 95 **74** 32
Hannah Lowell **89** 65
Hannah S. **69** 141
Harriet **73** 266 **83** 143
   140 157
Harriet C. (Jenkins)
   90 115
Harriet Elizabeth **93** 217
Harriet Elliot **89** 262
Harriet F. **84** 136
Harriet Starr **93** 185
Harriet Susan **93** 217
Harry **92** 25 117
Harry M. **116** 55
Helen A. (Payn) **97** 396
Helen Lucy **93** 220
Helen Maria (Fiske)
   (Hunt) **136** 319 330
Helen Viola **101** 124
Helene Eliza **67** xxxiv
Henrietta **118** 131
Henrietta (Johnson)
   88 343
Henrietta (Lang) **86** 71
Henry **51** 223 461 **55** 367
   65 59 60 107-110 113
   115 147 149 222 225 226
   255 257 260 262 366 **69**
   224 **72** 55 **73** 85 179 **76**
   215 **78** 190 315 **82** 43 **85**
   124 **88** 63 95 382 **97** 6
   99 113 **100** 10 **102** 217
   103 75 **122** 188 **125** 12
   32 **130** 155 **142** 197
Henry (Mrs.) **112** 96
Henry Chester **122** 188
Henry Clay **56** xxxiv **57**
   xxxvi **77** xxxvi **78** 89
Henry Clinton **93** 219 220
Henry G. **115** 168
Henry Harold **108** 134
Henry J. **140** 157
Henry T. **104** 96
Henry Welstead **91** 354
   92 25 117 **94** 296
Herbert **93** 215
Herbert W. **95** 146
Hester **65** 322
Hezekiah **120** 5 10
Hiram **68** 155
Hopestill (Briant) **147**
   261 263
Howell E. **77** 142
Hugh **60** 24 **94** 251
Huldah **124** 8

JACKSON *cont'd*
I. H. **93** 301
Ida Bardwell **130** 72
Ida Valeria **92** 37
Irene **86** 60
Isaac **62** 374 **86** 71 239
   114 216
Isabel **94** 307 **101** 163
Isabella **63** 141
Isabella Dove **76** 215
Israel **80** 332
Israel M. **73** 273
J. **70** 142 299
J. C. **88** 342 **128** 263
Jabez T. **89** 349
Jackson **51** 255
Jacob **125** 288 **141** 195
James **54** 224 **56** 209 **58**
   231 **65** 125 **73** 166 **77**
   lxvii 215 **78** 304 **80** 115
   308 **85** 367 **90** 68 **91** 199
   326 **93** 214 **97** 334 338
   98 75 **99** 127 **112** 55 57
   113 274 **117** 290 **124** 7
   127 294
James (Mrs.) **84** 342 **85**
   195 **94** 88
James A. **73** 179
James Chadwick **124** 8
James H. **64** xxxi
James Henry **92** 353
James L. **52** 464
James Robert **64** 231
Jane **73** 168 169 175 **78** 164
   83 23 24 **85** 62 **100** 235
   144 32
Jane (Frothingham) **83** 23
Jane (Grant) **90** 106
Jane (Saunders) **99** 127
Jane Catherine **92** 353
Jane Delphin **82** 43
Japhet **72** 286
Jasper **91** 326
Jeffery **81** 427
Jemima **87** 233 236
Jemima (Orton) **124** 7
Jemima (Sampson)
   141 207
Jemima Deuel **80** 331 332
Jemina **120** 283
Jenett **84** 14
Jenny **92** 22
Jeremiah **52** 215 218 **90**
   115 **93** 214 **94** 167
Jerome **93** 218
Jerusha **82** 290 298 412
Jesenthie Roseboom
   115 114
Jesse **71** 343 **115** 79
Joan **90** 310 **144** 32
Joan (Lurfete) **144** 33 34
Joan (Palmer) (Deering)
   97 3
Joanna **80** 115 **81** 298 427
   82 290 291 **98** 361
Job H. **78** 316
John **51** 45 121 **52** 128 **59**
   85-8 11 14 **129** 359 **136**
   39 **140** 35 157 **141** 35
   142 143 **144** 29-34 37 46
John Armstead **78** 176

JACKSON *cont'd*
John Barnard Swett
  103 75
John D. **66** 226
John F. **66** 226 **93** 220
John Gardner **84** 372
  91 352
John Henry **59** xlvii
John M. **117** 290
John P. **108** 278
John W. **71** 355
John William (Mrs.)
  109 129
Johnson **58** 337 **84** 99 377
  85 121 **140** 157
Jonas **71** 343 352 **86** 68 70
Jonathan **54** cv **56** 93 **57**
  280 388 **62** 372-375 **76**
  193 206 208 **79** 48 **84**
  158 **103** 75 **104** 242 **113**
  62 **121** 247 **123** 284 **131**
  45 **140** 153
Joseph **52** 77 **55** 146 147
  56 318 **58** 137 337 **62**
  373 374 **63** 191 **64** 155
  71 148 151 **73** 102 168
  170 **77** 318 **81** 427 444-6
  9 **99** 127 **100** 236 **103**
  299 **106** 160 **109** 153
  114 292 **116** 110 **120** 5
  10 14 102 **129** 220 **130**
  137 **140** 157 **142** 143
  144 38 **145** 47
Joseph A. **73** 166
Joseph Anthony **93** 220
Joseph Bradford **93** 217
Joseph C. **67** xxxi
Joseph Green **55** 147
Joseph Riggs **73** xix 160
Josephine **52** 397
Joshua **56** 142 **57** 151 **62**
  373 374 **78** 397 **82** 291
  292 **87** 229 233 **107** 269-
  271 **144** 222
Josiah **95** 315 **107** 271
Judith **55** 396 **78** 312 **97** 63
  118 33
Judith Jean **97** 396
Julia A. **89** 349
Julia T. (Flanagan) **90** 68
Juliet **73** 266
Julius Dunham **94** 280
Katharine **82** 43 **148** 319
  321
Katharine Seymour
  90 136
Laban **87** 315 **142** 61 78
Laura **81** 458 **89** 349
Laura J. **89** 352
Laura M. **88** 240
Laura Wolcott **145** 313
Leavitt Taylor **89** 56
Leila **93** 218
Leila Maria **71** 42
Lemuel **120** 283 **126** 58
  136 38 39 **141** 207
Leonard **89** 57
Leonice **88** 158
Letitia E. **75** 39
Levi **90** 106
Levina **93** 214

JACKSON *cont'd*
Lewis W. **109** 269 **114** 307
Lidian **84** 220
Lidy **121** 199
Lillian **93** 221
Lois **69** 372 **71** 352 **86** 71
  144 302 304 **1-5** 320 **105**
  320 **110** 72 **130** 137
Loraine **88** 188
Lorenzo **90** 54
Lorinda **73** 179
Lottie Vennetta **103** 117
Louis D'Aquilar **52** 187
Louisa **59** civ **92** 347
Lovicia Wyman **52** 464
Lovina **86** 303
Lovisa **124** 8
Lucia (Cole) **86** 68
Lucinda **73** 184
Lucius F. **75** 39
Lucretia **93** 215
Lucy **60** 339 **62** 374 **63** 95
  69 372 **72** 285 **78** 89 **88**
  275 **95** 372
Lucy (Buell) **124** 7
Lucy A. **80** 308
Lucy Ann (Forbush) **86**
  70 157 303
Lucy Cabot **91** 307 310
Lucy Tracy (Burdick)
  94 167
Lucy W. **76** 215
Lusina **89** 355
Lydia **56** 202 **59** 286 **62**
  372-374 **71** 148 **72** 285
  73 169 **88** 231 275 **93**
  215 **94** 356 **124** 141
Lydia (Barrows) **114** 216
Lydia Ann **114** 188
Lydia R. **84** 136
Lydia Yeaton **82** 43
Lyman **94** 280
M. **96** 55
M. Carrie **83** 299 300
Mabel **93** 218
Madeline **76** 218
Manus **131** 126
Marcia Ann **93** 217
Marcia Ann (Gavit) **85** 90
Marcy (Godfrey) **127** 41
Margaret **52** 478 **66** 84
  71 263 343 **73** 166 173
  183 **82** 291 297 **83** 193
  113 235 **114** 185 **142** 78
  144 34
Margaret (Lumberdey)
  144 32
Margaret (Pinkham)
  99 127
Margery **144** 32
Maria **110** 24
Maria Amanda **78** 89
Marion **73** 179
Marion Frances **79** 103
  202
Martha **55** 264 310 **59** 215
  62 373 **64** 257 **71** 264
  343 **72** 85 **81** 427 **82** 43
  78 291 296 **120** 10 **128**
  98
Martha (Hyde) **86** 67 70

JACKSON *cont'd*
Martha Bennett **72** 16
Martha Cheney **93** 218
Martin **125** 40
Mary **51** 45 169 173 **53** 336
  54 cv 224 413 **55** 49 50
  106 264 **56** 33 38 39 209
  318 **57** 106 258 262 282
  58 228 299 392 393 **59**
  civ **60** 292 **61** xlviii 256
  62 372-374 **63** 191 **65**
  367 **66** lxv **67** 181 **70** 71
  71 264 343 **72** 58 **73** 14
  165 168-170 173 181 263
  76 208 **78** 176 308 328
  403 408 **81** 126 427 444
  466 **82** 43 285 291 293
  299 **83** 21 24 479 **84** 60
  151 152 158 159 424 **87**
  202 233 239 **88** 249 282
  89 180 **90** 310 **93** 89 214
  215 218 263 **96** 190 **97** 3
  4 98 361 **109** 66 **122** 53
  124 8 **125** 222 **126** 142
  140 157 **142** 61 143 **144**
  33 46 **145** 57 **148** 311
  312
Mary (Averill) **93** 214
Mary (Brooks) **83** 21
Mary (Cazneau) **97** 6 **142**
  133 142 143
Mary (Cole) **86** 62
Mary (Duncan) **127** 294
Mary (Fitz Randolph)
  (Thorne) **97** 334
  335 338
Mary (Gifford) **129** 223
Mary (Mitchell) **100** 303
Mary (Salter) **103** 75
Mary (Spring) **95** 325
Mary (Whittemore)
  106 33
Mary A. **114** 307
Mary A. (Simpson)
  125 301
Mary Ann **78** 44 **108** 278
  142 78
Mary Ann (Coulter)
  94 280
Mary Ann (Elderkin)
  (Clark) **124** 7
Mary Ann (Ford) **117** 42
Mary Anne **87** 283
Mary Augusta **79** 142
Mary B. **68** lviii 100
Mary B. Wilson **104** 96
Mary Doe **83** 111
Mary E. **117** 290
Mary Eliza **78** 176
Mary Elizabeth **97** 9
Mary Emma **83** 111
Mary Emma (Jocelyn)
  93 184
Mary Jane **93** 215
Mary Louisa **79** 337
Mary Louise **78** 176
  85 192
Mary Sophia (Tupper)
  120 17
Mary Stuart **66** lxv
Mary Susanna **84** 98 99

JACKSON *cont'd*
Mary T. (Nash) **87** 233 235
Mary W. (Childs) **88** 342
Mary Waitt **93** 220 221
Mary Waldo (Nowell)
    84 99
Matilda (Fotherly) **88** 330
Matthew **62** 374
Matthew Murray **93** 214
Mehitable **61** 355 **62** 373
    88 63 **120** 73
Melinda (Gregory) **109**
    253 256
Mercy **76** 218 **81** 298 **82**
    43 420 **124** 5-8 **145** 47
Mercy (Chadwick) **124** 5-
    7 14
Mercy P. **147** 272
Meribah **67** 181
Merrill S. **93** 219
Merrill W. **71** 42
Merrill Walter **93** 218
Meta Ora **77** 257
Michael **65** 28 78 79 257
    260 262 338 **72** 285 287
    93 214 **94** 280 317 **95**
    112 **135** 102 **141** 14 **145**
    45
Miles **66** 84
Minerva **109** 269
Minnie Adela **93** 218
Miriam **73** 33
Miriam (Cole) **86** 70
Molly **71** 343 **89** 274
    107 269
Molly (Dalling)
    (Wentworth) **97** 7
Monroe **93** 215
Moses **57** 258 **71** 343 **86** 70
    157 303
Moses H. **88** 343
Nabby (Starr) **125** 108
Nancy **60** 338 **73** 90 169
    88 284 287 **92** 353 **93** 60
    215
Nancy (Boardman)
    93 326
Nancy (Lemoyne)
    125 222
Nancy Carolyn **93** 221
Nancy Niles **88** 283
Nancy S. **124** 7
Nathan **57** 257 **62** 373 **69**
    364 372 **71** 343 **93** 214
    215 **124** 7 8
Nathaniel **51** 46 173 **52**
    478 **59** 93 **73** 168 **82** 43
    88 263 **89** 56 **111** 305
    120 10 **126** 58 **144** 222
Nathaniel B. **111** 308
Nathaniel Curtis **92** 124
Nathaniel P. **143** 158
Nathaniel Starr **93** 185
Nehemiah **93** 213 214 216
    94 167
Nellie Jane **93** 217
Nettie Snow (Leigh)
    94 167
Newark **99** 209 281 282
Nicholas **62** 372-375 **65**
    176 **86** 78 249 **93** 214

JACKSON *cont'd*
144 30
Olive **55** 55 **68** 168 **73** 170
    81 154 497 **84** 60 **124** 7
    134 116 117
Oliver **57** 282
Onliker **106** 33
Oren **83** 146
Orinda (Goodell) **93** 215
Orrington **73** 168
Orynthia **72** 16
Otis **93** 215
Otis Eugene **93** 220
Otis Goodwin **93** 220
P. **116** 152
Palmyra **109** 269
Patience **69** 378 **71** 148
Patrick **112** 286
Patrick Tracy **83** 122 232
    92 358 **93** 253 **95** 251
    114 69
Patten **116** 53
Patty **71** 343
Paul W. **78** 89
Pauline Fay (Stone) **76** 85
    83 332
Peggey **88** 158
Peletiah **83** 143
Peregrine **93** 215
Peres **72** 285
Peter **64** 257 **72** 184
Phebe **97** 338 **98** 46
Phebe (Murray) **93** 214
Phebe (Pinkham) **98** 223
Phebe A. **89** 349
Phebe Ann (Bowen)
    88 341
Phebe J. (Bush) **125** 53
Pheriba Anne **136** 330
Philip **54** 94 **125** 9 **126** 238
    144 32
Philip Andrew **93** 220
Philippa (Peratt) **144** 32
Phineas **73** 170
Polly **55** 49 50 **72** 285 **74**
    176 **115** 292 **124** 7
Polly (Nowell) **140** 157
Polly H. **98** 257 258
Polly Hollen **88** 158
Priscilla **88** 158 **132** 40
Priscilla (Grafton) **96** 360
Prudence **86** 78 248
    141 195
Prudence (Marche)
    86 249
Prudence (Smith) **109** 152
Prudence Smith **109** 153
Rachel **73** 168 169 175 **77**
    lxvii 252 **82** 291 293 **141**
    195
Rachel (Alexander)
    130 155
Ralph **51** 137 **74** 32
Ralph Dighton **100** 102
    101 119
Ralph Temple **83** 123
Ralph Temple Cushman
    83 232 **101** 124
Ransom **113** 257 **114** 216
Rawson **86** 8
Rebecca **52** 127 128 140

JACKSON *cont'd*
141 218 **59** 93 **67** liii **69**
    296 **71** 149 **73** 102 169
    82 358 **83** 137 **109** 152
    153 **113** 274 **131** 126
    147 127 261 263 264
Rebecca (Hallett) **97** 334
    338
Rebecca (Huntley)
    101 203
Relief (Beard) **95** 372
Remember (Marton)
    89 56
Remembrance (Jackson)
    130 137
Reuben **88** 158 **89** 349
    93 399
Rhoda **109** 149
Richard **51** 478 **65** 50 **72**
    58 **73** 115 **88** 384 **93** 221
    111 249 250 252 **125** 94
    131 127 **144** 30 31 33 34
Robert **60** 185 348 **63** 241
    242 **65** 45 **68** 168 **84** 60
    100 235 106 157 **107** 33
    109 242 **110** 182 183
    112 210 213 **113** 92 **124**
    309 **147** 110 111
Robert C. **91** 195
Robert Charles **103** 119
Robert F. **78** 182 **91** 195
Robert Fletcher **78** 176
Robert S. **91** 195
Robert Smith **112** 223
Robert Tracy **59** xlvii 229
    60 xxxiv **61** xxxvi **67**
    xxx **90** 125 **103** 75 76 78
    126
Roberta **78** 234
Roger Sessions **93** 219
Rosalinda **113** 297
Rosanna (Hall) **88** 280
Rowena **93** 214 **120** 51
Roy Foster **78** 176
Russell Leigh **68** xxxi **71**
    xxiii **79** 193 **90** 129 **92**
    400 **93** 213-5 173 260
    353 **98** 163 **112** 121 **115**
    168 **142** 143 **144** 29
Ruth **51** 302 **58** 183 **85** 333
Ruth (Godfrey) **87** 231
    233
Ruth (Jenney) **89** 56
Ruth A. **71** 42
Sally **84** 262 362 **88** 63 278
    93 214 **97** 268 **124** 7 8
Sally (Pierce) **125** 215
Salome **144** 34
Sambo **140** 67
Samson **144** 34
Samuel **51** 45 169 173 223
    52 165 **58** 68 237 **59** 369
    62 372-374 **65** 322 **66**
    lxv 37 **71** 352 **73** 166 168
    169 179 181 **77** 320 **82**
    43 291 293 **88** 330 **91**
    195 **92** 286 317 **99** 127
    103 82 **111** 305 **124** 7
    125 92 94 102 **127** 224
    132 76 **139** 308 **142** 61
    145 355

JACKSON *cont'd*
Samuel Dalling **97** 9
Samuel Waters **73** 166 179
Sarah **56** 210 **62** 372-375
65 34 **71** 148 149 343
349 352 **73** 168 176 183-
6 9 **101** 273 **108** 170 171
120 319 **123** 85 **124** 7
142 143
Sarah (Atwood) (Orton)
124 6
Sarah (Brown) **100** 303
Sarah (Cobb) **87** 5
Sarah (Cole) **86** 70
Sarah (Cummings)
87 229 233
Sarah (Faunce) **113** 257
114 216
Sarah (Hall) **97** 3 **144** 38
Sarah (Lane) **86** 70
Sarah (Leavitt) **97** 4
Sarah (Merrill) **124** 8
Sarah (Palmer) **97** 3
Sarah (Saunders) **88** 337
Sarah (Stephens) **124** 7
Sarah (Taylor) **89** 56
Sarah A. **71** 355
Sarah A. (Wilson) **90** 51
Sarah Ann **71** 52
Sarah C. **73** 98
Sarah Cabell **78** 164
Sarah E. **73** 166 **93** 334
108 278
Sarah Frances **93** 221
Sarah H. **98** 314
Sarah Moore **77** 215
78 161
Sarah S. **118** 317
Sarah Spring **95** 325
Sargent **81** 444
Sebas **71** 148 346
Silence **75** 264
Silva **87** 230 233
Simon **65** 333 **95** 325
142 197
Solomon **124** 8
Sophia **86** 71 **91** 195
127 294
Sory **142** 61
Stanford **82** 43 412
Stanford (Mrs.) **82** 412
Stephen **65** 127 **67** 300
73 115 **80** 307 308 **115**
292
Stonewall **118** 165
Sukey **125** 291
Sukey (Whitmarsh)
125 102
Susan **59** 369 **60** 153 **66**
84 226 **71** 53 **78** 70 **84**
210 **90** 114 **93** 253 **142**
78
Susan G. (Hayden) **88** 343
Susan Loring **95** 251
Susan Mary (Loring)
92 358
Susanna **52** 77 **55** 111 **62**
374 **65** 116 **78** 414 **97** 4
6 7 **110** 281 **117** 290 **130**
155 **140** 157 **142** 61 143
Susanna (Gray) **97** 5

JACKSON *cont'd*
142 143
Susanna (Wilcoxson)
94 280
Susie E. **81** 458
Symm **144** 30
T. M. **54** 351
Temperance P. **80** 26
Thaddeus **58** 236 **71** 343
350
Thankful **72** 287
Thankful Elizabeth
112 223
Theodore **97** 9
Theophilus **107** 33
Thomas **51** 45 **52** 237 **55**
264 **57** 280 **58** 68 337
392 393 **62** 291 **63** 351
64 19 114 259 **65** 25 162
172 **66** 35 **75** 221 **76** 218
80 384 **82** 43 190 291
293 **84** 362 372 **89** 56 **91**
345 347-350 352 354 **96**
360 **97** 271 **99** 79 **100**
303 **114** 181 **117** 279
290 **127** 224 **128** 17 **131**
189 **140** 48 244 **144** 30
31 34 324 327
Thomas (Mrs.) **91** 354
97 271
Thomas Jefferson **72** 16
Thomas Jonathan **65** 101
78 167
Thomas Manning
55 xxxv
Thomas Waitt **93** 221
Thomasin **144** 32 34
Timothy **62** 122 **71** 148
78 24
Tom **91** 347
Trumbull Starr **93** 185
Tryphena **126** 22
Ursula (Brummett)
126 65
Vashti **124** 7
Velma Lorraine **117** 42
Vesta **98** 108
Vestie **87** 110
Walter **65** 367 **67** 181 **71**
341 **93** 215 217 **125** 222
Walter Delmont (Mrs.)
89 132
Walter P. **65** 367
Ward **60** 339 **88** 336
Warren **73** 170
Wayne **103** 119
Will **80** 447
Willard **93** 214
William **55** 432 **57** 200
58 xliii **60** 338 **61** 360
64 316 343 **65** 130 245
66 lx lxv 93 **67** 73 181
68 73 **71** 343 **72** 52 85
73 102 150 168 169 267
76 31 **78** 24 **81** 427 **83**
306 446 **84** 14 159 426
85 122 128 **86** 153 311
88 63 158 231 280 330
89 56 349 **90** 105 310 **91**
326 **92** 353 **93** 60 184
217 326 **95** 396 **97** 6 **98**

JACKSON *cont'd*
361 **99** 127 **101** 270 **109**
152 153 **112** 142 **117** 15
122 89 **127** 117 **129** 250
144 30 **147** 360
William A. **95** 263
William B. **73** 268
William C. **88** 341
William Chester **93** 217
William E. **93** 219
William F. **84** 136
William Francis **89** 56
William H. **93** 334
William Henry **93** 220
William Hunking **82** 43
William John **73** 149
William Otis **93** 215
William P. **84** 136
William Purnell **80** 101
206
William Starr **74** 237 **75**
xxiii **92** 148 199 **93** 136
184
Wilmot **144** 30 32
Winfield Scott **93** 220
Winifred **64** 155
Winifred Williams **100**
102 **101** 119
Xena **124** 6 14
Yerley **91** 326
Zebedee **88** 249 **89** 055 057
Zebediah **87** 123
Zipporah (Whipple)
(Tower) **106** 160
Zulema **73** 176 184
Zulerna **73** 102
JACKSTRAW ——— **63** 224
Jacob *see* Jacobs
JACOBENS
Brechje **96** 397
JACOBIE Cora M. **79** 30
JACOBS Jacob
——— **52** 32 **57** 140 224 **58**
261 266 **89** 383 384 **94**
403 **117** 64 **119** 297 298
121 109 278 281 **135**
306 **145** 168
— Capt. **143** 251
— Mrs. **127** 16
Aaron **76** 110 **116** 139
Abigail **51** 408 **55** 328 329
56 70-72 **60** 180 **86** 127
121 213
Abigail (Faunce) **114** 213
Abigail (Phillips) **116** 139
Abner **92** 332
Abraham **71** 249
Adeline **89** 340
Adolphus **138** 118
Adonijah **83** 47 **115** 37
Albert Cutts **96** 178
Alcut **116** 139
Alice **73** 148
Almeda Ellen (Munroe)
100 91
Alpheus M. **84** 139
Amy Cushing **61** 58
Andrew **85** 111
Ann **79** 432
Anna **89** 150
Anna Forsdick **59** 255

JACOBS *cont'd*
Anna L. **77** 318
Anne **90** 280
Anthony D. **93** 238
Archelaus **99** 193
Aretes L. **100** 91
B. C. **91** 326
Bela **80** 30
Bela Tower **61** 59
Benjamin **60** 40 391 **68** 318
319 **75** 51 **76** 109 110
179 185 192 194 **79** 15
85 53 **114** 294 **116** 221
304 305 **121** 110 200 206
Benjamin Hearsy **60** 272
Benjamin J. **89** 340
Bessie Louise (Cornell)
100 91
Betsey **61** 175 **82** 345
Betsey (Gaines) **85** 53
Betsey (Snelling) **105** 55
Betsey Turner **61** 57
Braddock **60** 272-274
Bridget **91** 358
Carl **113** 62
Caroline Nicholson
120 76
Carrie **100** 91
Carrie Holmes Varney
90 127 200
Catherine (Chase) **87** 331
Charles **105** 55 **108** 185
Charles (Mrs.) **119** 79
Charles A. **93** 238
Charles F. **103** 112
Charles J. **102** 5 **112** 134
135 222 314 **113** 61 148
149 233 293
Charles Juan **114** 70 140
142 228 309 **115** 68 145
146 229 313 **116** 73 144
145 227 306 **117** 73 149
151 231 312 **118** 69 160
161 246 324 **119** 72 150
151 236 312 **120** 56 150
151 233 310 **121** 75 150
151
Charles Juan Stephen
Richard **122** 95
Charles S. **103** 75
Charles Sumner (Mrs.)
103 75 78 124
Charles T. **84** 140
Charles Walter **110** 229
Claaske **128** 167
Clarence Houghton
(Mrs.) **103** 119
Clarissa **60** 272 **67** 123 215
Comfort (Billings) **96** 178
Cynthia (Stearns) **125** 289
Daniel **74** 16 **76** 102
115 35
David **58** 88 171 **59** 76 **77**
233 **78** 315 **83** 47 48 **85**
53 **87** 84 **88** 126 **99** 193
107 99 **121** 277 **140** 327
143 44
David H. **116** 114
David Richmond **61** 290
Deborah **60** 62 338 **75** 112
76 109 **88** 360 **101** 66

JACOBS *cont'd*
108 189 **121** 16 115 195
196 200 **129** 170 **143**
139
Deborah Richmond
60 273
Delia W. **89** 340
Desire **93** 279
Dexter **61** 291
Ealcy (Webber) **126** 142
Ebenezer **74** 259 **76** 106
247
Edward **61** 58 **93** 108
Edward A. **93** 238
Eliakim **99** 193
Elias **75** 112 **76** 108-110
182 186 188 189 259 **85**
53 **87** 207
Elijah **67** 379
Eliphalet **89** 383 384
Elisha **59** 21 138 **61** 59
68 319
Eliza **89** 340
Eliza (Akins) **125** 217
Eliza (Chase) **88** 126
Eliza (Perkins) **116** 304
305
Eliza Jane **109** 173
Eliza Jane (Cushman)
109 269
Elizabeth **51** 329 408 **57**
179 **58** 25 **67** 350 **71** 249
74 259 **76** 193 **83** 47 **91**
86 **95** 362 **96** 178 **106**
306 **111** 20 **121** 21 271
135 300
Elizabeth (Briggs) **126** 30
Elizabeth (Ferris) **89** 29
Elizabeth (Snelling)
108 185
Elizabeth (Starr) (Com-
stock) **96** 378
Elizabeth (Turner)
110 229
Elizabeth M. **69** 291
Ellen **55** 213
Ellen A. **96** 178
Elmira S. **92** 332
Elnathan **85** 53
Emily (Blanchard)
(Kidder) **110** 229
Emily Martin **110** 229
Emma L. **93** 238
Esther **69** 57
Eunice **59** 312
Ezra **108** 85
Ferris **89** 29
Foster **61** 58 59
Francis Burdell (Mrs.)
95 146
Frank Elmer (Mrs.) **101**
124 **119** 148
Franklin **62** 383
Frederic C. **89** 340
Freeman **61** 291
Garrie (Holmes) (Varney)
67 xxxiv **72** 245 **103** 75
George **65** 113 **70** 66 **71**
106 **75** 50-53 110 112
113 120 121 312 313 **76**
102 104 106 113 187 190

JACOBS *cont'd*
247 249 250 254 257 260
78 37 **109** 173 269 **111**
19 **114** 133 **124** 228
George C. **88** 335
George F. **125** 217
George M. **110** 229
George W. **100** 91
George Ward **61** 290
Grace (Learned) **125** 106
H. B. (Mrs.) **123** 98 225
Hannah **59** 310 **60** 274 338
61 173 175 **67** 279 **75** 44
120 **76** 109 110 179 185
190 192 **82** 282 291 **84**
323 **92** 55 332 **93** 238
115 137 220 306 **116**
114 **117** 143 144 **121** 12
107 **125** 214 **143** 135
136 138
Hannah (Allen) **88** 360
Hannah (Banks) **114** 294
Hannah (Bosworth) **142**
277 278
Hannah (Cousins) **111** 19
Hannah (Moody) **119** 287
Hannah (Perkins) **117**
143 144
Hannah (Tolman) **108**
185 **110** 229
Hannah (Whittemore)
108 85
Hannah B. **121** 160
Hannah Bailey **141** 48
Hannah Banks **76** 179
Hannah E. (McLane)
88 331
Hannah Jane **92** 332
Hannah Waterman
60 274
Harry M. **100** 91
Hazel Christine **108** 135
Henry **85** 10 **95** 46 **114** 189
143 212
Henry B. **123** 96 225 306
Hepzibah **65** 113 **76** 113
187 247 249 250 254 260
Hiram **91** 326 **113** 78
Huldah **61** 175 291 **76** 186
86 15 **118** 154
Ichabod R. **62** 383
Isaac **116** 251
Isaac P. **84** 140
Isabell **84** 140
Isabella **78** 37
J. **89** 383
J. A. **75** 217 **79** 108 **92** 366
367
Jabez **76** 110
Jacomyntie **102** 142
Jael **88** 264 **121** 215
James **59** 388 **92** 331 332
117 172 **122** 215
James A. **123** 226
Jane **121** 115
Jason K. **67** 350
Jemima **73** 141
Jennie (Parcher) **96** 178
Joanna **60** 274
John **51** 408 **52** 67 **53** 429-
431 **54** 194 **55** 213 **56**

JACOBS *cont'd*
399 **57** 224 399 **59** 138
61 173 **63** 75 **70** 262 **75**
53 112 312 **76** 108 193
77 119 **84** 276 **85** 135
86 417 **89** 29 **92** 332 341
108 185 **110** 229 **114**
189 213 290 **116** 114 139
121 104 106 109 118 121
124 127 198 200 205 280
283 **123** 7 **125** 106 **129**
261 **130** 178 **143** 45 139
257 346 **145** 356
John D. (Mrs.) **89** 132
John E. **92** 332
John Knickerbocker
99 193
John R. **88** 331
John W. **83** 424 432
John Y. **123** 124
Johnnie **78** 177
Jonathan **93** 238 **111** 20
119 287
Joseph **51** 329 **57** 401 **58**
88 **59** 138 140 310 313
388 390 **60** 62 64 65 176
178 180 182 272 **61** 173
76 250 **82** 282 291 **87** 75
96 178 **115** 217 **118** 245
319 **121** 18 193 196 200
206 282 **142** 278 **144**
206 **148** 334
Joshua **59** 76 135 138 140
312 388 **60** 64 274 336
340 **61** 55-59 173 288-
290 292 373 **78** 312 **110**
229 **129** 261
Joshua William **70** 331
335
Josiah **76** 110 **121** 15 160
145 362
Judith **94** 219 397-399 **110**
223 **143** 41
Julia (Cushing) **89** 340
Julia A. **84** 140
Juliaette **115** 292
Juliana (Briggs) (Calvin)
126 268
Keziah **72** 220
Lemuel **60** 272 **61** 175
Leonard **84** 140
Lizzie J. **93** 108
Lois **75** 313
Loring **62** 383
Louise Hickman **102** 122
Lovina (Gaines) **85** 53
Lucia **89** 29
Lucretia **78** 401
Lucretia L. **93** 238
Lucy **60** 64 337 **76** 192
115 122 220
Lucy Clapp **61** 58
Lydia **53** 442 **59** 388 **60**
273 339 **75** 52 80 263
119 123 **121** 208 289
143 43 45
Maartgen **128** 163
Margaret **76** 67 71 **116** 143
Margaret (Cavanagh)
125 72

JACOBS *cont'd*
Margaret (McGlathry)
89 340
Margery (Eames) **130** 178
Maria **128** 165
Maria (Penrose) **117** 64
Marietta (Stoddard)
110 229
Martha **68** 333
Martha (Appleton) **94** 399
Mary **51** 329 463 **52** 76 **53**
428 **55** 437 **57** 91 179 **59**
76 135 138 140 310 312
313 388 390 **60** 62 64 65
178 340 **61** 373 66 262
70 159 **75** 110 112 113
120 121 312 313 **76** 102
104 106 108-110 182 186-
188 195 257 **78** 180 **83**
46 47 **84** 383 **88** 31 292
97 93 **117** 228 229 **119**
37 **121** 111 216 **129** 261
143 136
Mary (Chase) **87** 331
Mary (Dinley) (Goold)
143 44 45
Mary (Gilman) **143** 135
Mary (James) **110** 229
Mary (Russell) **143** 45 139
Mary (Webb) **121** 160
Mary Ann **61** 56
Mary Ann (Marshall) **88**
335 **124** 228
Mary Ann (Owen) **99** 193
Mary Elizabeth (Howe)
85 111
Mary Elizabeth (Hyde)
89 29
Mary Elizabeth (Wilson)
121 144 145
Mary Elizabeth (Wright)
89 29
Mary P. (Blair) **85** 111
Mercy **66** 198
Michael **62** 383
Mildred J. (Campbell)
83 424 432
Molly **83** 47
Mordecai **73** 150 276
Moses **65** 117 **76** 110 **117**
143 144
Nancy **60** 272 **118** 196
Nancy (Lazell) **89** 29
Nancy Agnes **92** 332
Nancy R. **116** 63
Naomi **89** 383
Nathaniel **60** 64 65 **61**
173 292 **87** 331 **94** 399
96 378 **121** 212 **127** 227
303
Nathaniel P. **138** 124
Nehemiah P. M. **92** 33
Nicholas **51** 329 **55** xii
57 224 **87** 218 **121** 107
126 268 **139** 131 **143**
135 136
Obed **93** 238
Olcut **76** 109
Olive **127** 305
Orpah I. / L. **83** 203
Palmyra **109** 269

JACOBS *cont'd*
Penelope **60** 30
Perez **60** 273 338 **135** 44
Peter **88** 360 **121** 281 **126**
142 **143** 261
Phebe (Jenkins) **113** 78
Piam **61** 289
Policarpus **60** 339
Polly **70** 159
Polly (Clark) **123** 124
Priscilla **75** 50 **76** 189
Rachel **138** 118
Rebecca **78** 188 **135** 44
Rebecca (Penrose)
116 251
Relief **59** 140 **60** 338
Relief (Bowker) **135** 44
Rhoda (Gaines) **85** 53
Rhoda S. **93** 238
Richard **63** 33 **72** 188 **73**
135 **94** 399 **110** 83 84
Robert **79** 425 **144** 339
Robert J. **89** 340
Rosetta E. **75** 97
Rowland Turner **110** 229
Ruby **69** 258 **81** 327
Ruth **57** 140 **83** 47 48
Ruth (Tupper) **99** 193
Ruth (Wilson) **135** 306
Sally **79** 15
Sally (Hubbard) **118** 319
Samuel **60** 30 **63** 25 **75** 110
89 340 **92** 332 **111** 20
121 283
Sarah **58** 88 **59** 313 **61** 175
373 **67** 350 **70** 331 **76**
188 189 259 **79** 15 **84**
140 **88** 360 **94** 284 106
71 72 **121** 107 201 **125**
107 108 **129** 165 **130**
178
Sarah (Brown) **106** 71
Sarah J. **109** 173
Sarah S. **51** 86 **56** 106
Sarah T. **70** 335
Seth **60** 30 **67** 379
Sibyl Narcissa **70** 335
Simon **143** 255 340
Solomon **69** 57
Sophia **96** 344 **119** 145 224
Stephen **84** 140
Sukey **116** 305
Sukey (Fluent) **116** 221
Susan **78** 416 **123** 93
Susan E. **92** 332
Susanna **60** 30 **75** 121 **76**
254 **123** 93
Sylvester **125** 289
Tabitha **76** 185 **115** 226
Temperance **118** 319
Theodore **76** 249
Theodosia **116** 295
Theophilus **61** 57
Thomas **64** 106 **106** 71
143 13
Thomas W. **136** 147
Thomas White **70** 331 335
Tillie **79** 25
Timothy Lasell **89** 29
Tristram Billings **96** 178
Truman **59** 255 **70** 159

JACOBS *cont'd*
Udney Hay **67** 350
Walter **61** 56 57 175
  110 229
Walter Ballou **84** 340
  85 182
Warren **78** 187 **85** 111
Whitman **79** 245
William **55** 328 **56** 70-72
  60 40 **68** 318 **79** 412 420
  432 **87** 221 **91** 326 357
  358 **127** 224
William Austin **126** 30
William Cushing **61** 288
William J. **91** 326
William T. **121** 144 145
William W. **78** 397
Woodman **76** 104
Zalmon L. **72** 130
Zurviah **67** 123 215 219
JACOBSON Jacobsen
  Jakobson
— Capt. **84** 168
Alma **86** 309
Amund **106** 53
Ane **72** 130
Anna E. M.S. **98** 289
Annie **102** 123
Benjamin F. **76** 21
Carma Erika **98** 289
  99 337
Catherina **128** 175
Edna **108** 16
Edna L. **107** 20
Erika S. **99** 337
Eve **115** 108
J. Larry **122** 79
Jacob **115** 108
Jacob Melchior **85** 70 71
John **128** 175
John Theodore (Mrs.)
  88 197
Joseph **115** 108
Lily May **97** 157
Maria (Norden) **86** 309
Martha Cecilia **76** 21
Mary Louisa **107** 295
Minnia **85** 219
Priscilla (Chase) **88** 197
Sophia **125** 287
Susanna **85** 70
Susanna (Talemann)
  85 71
T. Harold A. **98** 289 **99** 337
William **86** 309
JACOBSZOON
  Jan Paets **89** 304
JACOBUS Antje (Doremus)
  125 3
Donald Lines **59** xliv 67
  167 227 **60** xxxvi 101
  66 15 197 308 327 **67** 48
  123 223-5 55 233 265
  127 167 **129** 397 **132**
  140 145 **136** 320 **141** 24
  46 95 99 105 259 **142** 46
  176 253 323-327 329 330
  333-337 339 344 346 **143**
  24 47 109 240-246 250
  251 302-306 338 368 **144**
  4 6 19 359 **145** 3 40 72

JACOBUS *cont'd*
  127 174 198 317 322 325
  378 **146** 370 383 **147** 20
  54 68 153 241 242 **148**
  28 220 222 240 241
Fransyntje (Ricke) **125** 3
Geertruyt / Gertrude
  (Buys) **125** 3
Harriet Amanda (Aber)
  125 3
Henry Oliver **125** 3
Ida Wilmot (Lines) **76**
  130 **125** 3 **136** 320
Jannetje **125** 3
Jans **125** 3
Johannes **125** 3
John Ira **125** 3 **136** 320
Mary (Aber) **125** 3
Roelof **125** 3
Saertje (Bruyn) **125** 3
JACOBY
  Bartholomew **111** 323
  Helen Eaton **89** 130
    111 323
  Jeannette Helen **83** 110
JACOCKS Ann (Hufftan)
  112 313
Charles West **102** 123
  112 222 312 313
Elizabeth (Collins)
  112 313
Elizabeth Bryan (Hill)
  112 313
Emily Baker (Nicholls)
  112 312
Gertrude Rivers
  (Sessoms) **112** 313
Gertrude Sessoms
  112 313
Jonathan **112** 313
Jonathan Joseph **112** 312
Martha Ann (Mullen)
  112 313
Thomas **112** 313 320
William Picard **112** 320
  120 149
Jacqua *see* Jaqua
Jacques *see* Jaques
Jacquis *see* Jaques
Jacquity *see* Jaquith
JAEDICKE
  Clara Rose **94** 281
  Frederick William **94** 281
  Ottile Julia (Kessler)
    94 281
JAEGER Elizabeth Mary
  (Wilson) **105** 218
  Philip **105** 218
JAFFE Irma B. **141** 108
JAFFIA George **148** 35
Jaffray *see* Jeffrey
JAGARD Jagar Jaggard
— **57** 336
Ann **111** 282
Caroline Septemia
  (Brown) **94** 24
James **111** 282
Susan Bliss (Merrill)
  94 24
Thomas **111** 282
William **54** 91 **111** 282

Jaggar *see* Jagger
Jaggard *see* Jagard
JAGGER Jaggar Jaggers
— **54** lvii
___ (Ferris) **101** 105
Abigail **55** 206
Anna **101** 108
Benjamin **100** 332
Beverly Robinson
  101 108
Charles Ludwig
  Augustus **94** 24
Elizabeth **60** 367 **100** 332
  101 104 105 108
Francis **101** 104
Hannah **100** 332 **101** 105-
  108
Hannah (Cross) **100** 332
  101 105
Harry G. **100** 333 **101** 104
Isabella **60** 167
Jeremiah **89** 175 **94** 97
  100 332 333 **101** 104-
  108
Jeremy **60** 367 **78** 288
Joanna (Holly) **101** 107
John **60** 167 **94** 97 **100**
  331-333 **101** 105-108
John Carl **94** 24
Jonathan **100** 332 333
  101 105 106
Joshua Reuben **101** 107
Lydia **100** 332
Martin Bernard (Mrs.)
  101 124
Mary **78** 288 **100** 332 **101**
  105 106
Mercy A. (Gager) **94** 203
Nathan **101** 108
Nathaniel **101** 107 108
Nemiah **101** 107
Noah **101** 108
Phebe **101** 107 108
Polly **101** 108
Rebecca **101** 107 108
Rebecca (Holmes) **100**
  332 **101** 106
Rebecca (Ingersoll)
  101 107
Reuben **101** 107
Robert **101** 108
Samuel **100** 332 **101** 256
Sarah **100** 332 **101** 105 107
Sarah (Maltby) **101** 106
Seth Ransom **94** 203
Susanna **100** 332
Thomas **101** 107
William **55** 206 **101** 104
Zerviah **101** 256
JAGNER Ralph **71** 316
JAHN Mary Virginia (Cate)
  105 128 233
  William Frederick **105**
  128 233
JAKEMAN
  Benet **118** 253
  Richard **65** 50
JAKINS
  Alvah H. **100** 209
  Charles **100** 209
  Charles W. **100** 209

JAKINS *cont'd*
E. Henry **100** 209
Eleanor **100** 209
Frederick **100** 209
Harrie M. **100** 209
Mary **100** 209
Mary J. **100** 209
Jakobson *see* Jacobson
JAKWAY Jackways
Jakways
Albina H. **116** 206
Archie **116** 207
Asenath **116** 206
Catherine **127** 6
Clara **116** 206
Elisha **116** 206
Emma **116** 206
George **116** 206
Georgiana A. (Wood)
116 206
Harriet **116** 206 207
Harriet E. (Waller)
116 206
Henry **116** 206
Israel **116** 206
John **116** 206 **117** 17
Jonathan **116** 205 206
Louise **116** 206
Lucretia (Wells) **116** 206
Lydia **116** 206
Mary **116** 206
Philena **116** 206
Sarah **116** 206
Simeon **116** 206
Spink **116** 206
Thomas **116** 206
Waller **116** 206
JALON
Alice (Thing) **95** 88
Daniel **95** 88
JAMES I King of England
51 125 404 **53** 94 131
461 **54** 283 **55** 211 212
416 **56** 309 **57** 42 43 **59**
53 338 **61** 147 **64** 58 169
65 87 **66** xix **71** 248 **74**
121 **129** 4 **134** 184 185
138 10 183 **139** 187 **140**
5 6 **142** 110 **143** 248 **144**
129 249 261 **145** 117 118
JAMES II King of England
53 293 **54** 142 **55** 380
60 31 **133** 105 **136** 12
186 **142** 126
JAMES The Apostle
143 223
JAMES Jamis
—— **52** 470 **56** 409 **57** 85
59 xxx 182 **60** 337 **62**
360 **63** 231 **91** 303 **100**
186 **102** 152 **121** 12 **126**
251
— Dr. **51** 400
— Mr. **52** 58 94 **71** 136
82 43 **94** 39
— Widow **74** 36
____ (Carter) **91** 303
____ (Jennison) **140** 157
158
____ (Wilcox) **127** 37
Aaron Rathburn **126** 254

JAMES *cont'd*
Abby C. **127** 37
Abby F. **127** 36
Abby Ruhannah **102** 225
Abby S. (Ennis) **127** 87
Abby W. **73** 115
Abigail **60** 96 **63** 89 **102**
291 **125** 288 **126** 251
252 254 **127** 31 35 90
Abigail (Partelou)
147 346
Abigail (Phillips) **127** 32
Ada Blanche **103** 180
Addie J. (Carter) **101** 217
103 181
Agnes **63** 165 166 **138** 40
Agnes T. **101** 216
Albert **61** 291
Albert Greene **127** 34
Alice **63** 164 **103** 58 **126**
251 **127** 31
Alice (Potter) **127** 31
Alma Lewis **90** 209 401
Almeda **103** 58
Almeda (Campbell)
126 254
Almira **61** 57
Alverado Grant **102** 225
Amanda **68** 198
Amanda Keziah **81** 458
459
Amos **68** 198
Amos Davis **67** 280
Amy **127** 32 36 87
Amy (Kenyon) **127** 36
Amy (Sherman) **127** 87
Amy Grace **91** 90
Amy K. **91** 89 90
Amy Uranah (Harris) **90**
94 **91** 88-90
Andrew **52** 264 **88** 119
Andrew D. **87** 350
Angelina T. **102** 291
Angie T. **101** 216
Ann **63** 241 73 152 **74** 46
75 xc **77** 234 **81** 444 **83**
63 **92** 95 **118** 81 **126** 248
133 193 235 **147** 335
337 338 350
Ann (Taylor) **126** 248
147 333 343 345 346 348
Ann E. **127** 91
Ann Eliza **127** 33
Anna **63** 48 **86** 144 **116** 274
126 251 **127** 31 32 **131**
126
Anna (Bell) (LeMoyne)
101 179
Anna (Taylor) **126** 248
Anna Elizabeth **127** 88
Anna Margarethe **81** 460
Anne **55** 208 **72** 232 **74** 45
107 114 **126** 249 251
147 343 346
Anne (Barber) **127** 31
Anne (Lord) **92** 95
Anne Appleton **61** 291
Annie **98** 208
Annie D. (Lewis) **127** 35
Annis **59** 37
Anthony **127** 33

JAMES *cont'd*
Anthony John **81** 460
Armamilla Ruggles
(Dwight) **91** 80
Arnold **125** 180
Arthur Curtiss **74** ix xxiv
84 185 231 **87** 166 **95**
353 354 356 357 **96** 87
162 163
Arthur W. **117** 155
Avis **63** 165
Barrett **91** 90
Benedict K. **127** 36
Benjamin **58** 137 168 **59**
140 **76** 24 **77** 234 **90** 396
397 **126** 247-250 254
127 11 30 31 36 37 87
129 263 **133** 287 **134**
141 **140** 157 **147** 333
341 343 345 347-354 **148**
66
Benjamin F. **77** 146
Benjamin Franklin **103**
100 179
Bennett **127** 218
Bessie **105** 298
Betsey **60** 271 **61** 173 **82** 43
89 206 **126** 254
Betsey (Eastman) **126** 254
Betsey (Ingersoll) **90** 174
Betsey Ann **127** 90 91
Blanche **81** 254
Brinton **127** 32
Bushrod Washington
76 242
C. P. **91** 89 90
C. R. (Mrs.) **110** 148
Caleb **147** 349 350
Caleb Barber **127** 90
Caroline **58** 62 **76** 212
Caroline A. (Gordon)
127 35
Caroline Matilda **92** 350
94 39
Carrie Cecelia **102** 291
Cassimer P. **91** 89
Catherine **57** 225 **74** 46
92 95 **127** 31 **134** 127
Catherine (Cunningham)
57 225
Celia **127** 34
Celia (Downie) **127** 34
Charles **61** 57 **63** 16 **100**
186 **124** 160 297 **127** 34
147 351-353
Charles Anthony **102** 291
Charles H. **91** 89
Charles Henry **57** 340 **90**
94 95
Charles Tillinghast
127 35
Charlotte **90** 106 **101** 217
102 225
Charlotte (Cooley) **90** 58
Charlotte (Davis) **101** 33
Charlotte Mary (Mosher)
91 379
Christian **68** 198 **143** 226
Christine Catherine
(Wright) **127** 89
Christopher **78** 405

JAMES *cont'd*
147 353
Clara Bell 103 100 179
Clara Loveland 85 166
Clarisa C. 103 58
Clarissa 65 lxii
Clement 63 164
Colin 114 158 115 150
Colin (Mrs.) 116 76
Colin Dew 81 458 459
Constance 58 377
Content 58 262 126 248
Cora Dell 77 xliii
Cordelia 124 160
Cynthia (Russell) 126 254
Daniel 63 165 64 326 73
135 90 174 95 356 127
31 32 89 146 347
Daniel N. 100 186
Daniel Willis 95 354 356
Daphne (Bemis) 103 62
David 78 412 126 254
127 31 32
David W. 127 36
Davis 127 32
Deborah 115 274 126 251
127 31
Deborah (Baker) 126 254
Deborah (Bates) (Stodder)
91 80
Deborah (Packard)
126 251
Deborah (Tefft) 127 32
Delila (Woodmansee)
127 87
Deliverance Ann (Card)
127 36
Delonzo 89 379
Diana 126 254
Dolly (Walker) 126 254
Donald 90 95
Donald W. 147 329 148 66
Dora B. 103 100
Dorcas 126 253
Dorcas (Perry) 126 254
E. 58 62
Earl Dewey 103 181
Ebenezer 145 160
Eber S. 127 88
Edmund 57 317 58 139
63 164-166
Edmund J. 51 77 244
52 397 399
Edmund James 74 xxiv
156 80 102 205 216 81
458-460
Edna 101 215 127 91
Edna L. E. 69 280
Edna Vina 103 181
Edward 52 263 63 165 68
332 74 278 279 90 396
126 249 252 147 343
Edward Fendall 89 92
Edward Holton 80 335 81
221 136 312
Edward N. 68 332
Edward W. 51 238 385
53 371 54 xxxviii
Edward Wilson 55 xxxi
Edwin 100 186
Edwin Clarke 127 89 91

JAMES *cont'd*
Edwin Herman 103 181
Eleanor 74 36 45 92 95
Eleanor F. 91 89
Eleazar 58 60 62
Elisha 58 171 59 389 60
336 61 173 74 45 90 396
92 95 116 274 129 252
374 137 73
Elisha B. R. 126 254
Eliza 61 58 91 89 100 149
Eliza (Huntress) 126 141
Eliza (White) 91 89
Eliza (Whitford) 127 90
Eliza A. 91 90 127 86
Eliza J. (Sisson) 127 37
Eliza P. 127 88
Elizabeth 56 91 63 165 66
67 67 287 68 107 75 lx
81 458 94 400 100 301
102 224 103 100 121
110 123 303 126 256
127 25 30-35 90 91 128
20 131 126 133 100 143
115 145 160 147 342
353 354 148 66
Elizabeth (Barber) 127 30
Elizabeth (Bennit) 147 347
350-352
Elizabeth (Card) 127 89
Elizabeth (Forest) 127 37
Elizabeth (Greene) 127 33
Elizabeth (Kenyon)
126 250
Elizabeth (Lyman) 91 80
Elizabeth (Milton) 56 91
Elizabeth (Reynolds)
126 249
Elizabeth (Sabens) 127 32
Elizabeth (Smith) 147 351
Elizabeth (Wilcox) 127 87
Elizabeth Devereux
74 207
Elizabeth G. 127 35
Elizabeth S. (Locke) 127
89 90
Elizabeth Woodbridge
(Phelps) 90 174 95 356
Ella K. 112 316
Ella Nora 91 90
Ellen Elizabeth 136 316
Ellen Fendall 89 92
Ellen Stebbins (Curtiss)
95 354 356
Elmer Merton 103 181
Elnathan 79 168
Emily 61 290
Emily Jane 77 184
Emily Lovene (Atwood)
90 94
Enoch 60 96 78 74 91 80
140 157 158 329
Ephraim O. 52 378
Esther 126 251
Esther (Denison) 126 251
Esther (Greene) 127 34
Ethel Rohana 103 181
Eunice 57 398 58 87 88
168 170 171 174 60 63
129 165 145 160
Eunice (Stetson) 134 114

JAMES *cont'd*
Eunice (Stilson) 110 229
Evan 65 23
Evelyn 78 37 40
Evelyn Marie 90 95
Everett Clayton 103 181
Ezekiel 126 252 253 127
30 86 87
Ezekiel Samuel 127 87
Fanny Rebecca 102 291
Fidelia Maria 80 247
136 333
Florence 90 95 136 320
Florence Carlotta 90 94
Florence Crowell 81 254
Frances 77 261 116 62
121 19 20 113 119 124
215 126 253 254
Frances (Jones) 113 220
Frances C. 91 89 90
Frances Elizabeth 127 89
Francis 56 91 66 67 68
107 108 88 257 90 396
91 79 100 186 101 179
121 120 127 116 139
132 140 157
Francis Hickman 89 92
Frank Barrett 91 90
Franklin 125 180
Franklin Freeman
102 291
Fred E. 69 286
Frederic Henan 102 291
Freelove A. (Hudson)
147 353
Freeman 73 115 102 152
225
Galen Clapp 60 271
Gardner 127 32 37 90
Gaudy 131 126
George 54 336 63 16 64
111 74 277 88 276 124
160 296 125 106 126
250 127 30 37
George Abbott 79 231
George F. 103 58 127 37
George S. 127 86
George W. 91 199 127 33
86
Gertrude 106 228
Gholson 55 51
Giles 127 35
Gordon 90 95
Grace 91 60
Grace Fidelia 91 79 148
Grace Porter 91 90
H. B. 96 54
Hannah 55 207 208 60 68
271 61 173 175 65 349
68 253 71 38 74 36 46
193 78 295 92 95 100
141 103 297 105 59 124
60 160 126 247-249 251
254 127 8 32 35 86 135
303 147 280 281 343 350
Hannah (Bailey) 126 252
Hannah (Barney) 147
333 334 336-339
Hannah (Clarke) 127 90
Hannah (Crandall)
126 253

JAMES *cont'd*
Hannah (Evans) **100** 302
Hannah (Scofield)
  124 160
Hannah C. **58** 28 **127** 36
  90
Hannah F. G. **127** 89
Harriet **55** 51
Harriet C. (Clark) **127** 87
Harriet Eddy (Parsons)
  84 185 231 **95** 353 357
  96 87 163
Harriet Eliza **81** 254
Harriet Frances (Grinnell)
  127 91
Harriet L. **91** 90
Harris L. **91** 89 90
Hart **56** 91
Hartly **103** 58
Harvey **102** 152 **126** 254
Harvey R. **102** 152
Hazard **127** 33
Heart (Bird) **56** 91
Helen **61** 29 **90** 95 **91** 211
  216
Helen Dickson **81** 460
Helen Eliza (Field) **91** 79
Helen Lois **90** 95
Henrietta **65** 130
Henry **73** 115 **79** 139 **80**
  247 **108** 292
Herbert Foster **84** 29
Herman Edgar **103** 181
Herman Gerlach **80** 205
  81 460 **115** 66
Hester Ann **103** 58
Hester Ann (Munson)
  101 33
Hickman **89** 92 93
Horace **60** 272 **75** lx
  125 36
Horace P. **127** 88
Horatio N. **101** 214 **103**
  100 179
Hosea Stevens **103** 100
  179
Howard K. **126** 247 254
Hugh **63** 165
Ida Kate **91** 89
Ida Louise **91** 90
Ira **58** 38
Isaac **74** 319
Isabel **63** 164 165
Ivory **87** 350
J. **144** 339
J. G. **74** 207
Jabez **58** 139
James **76** 24 **91** 326 **126**
  249 251 252 **127** 32 **147**
  343
James B. **127** 33
Jane **68** 107 108 198 **81** 254
  92 226 **100** 164 **116** 152
  121 116
Jane (Andrews) **127** 34
Jane (Hazard) **127** 87
Jane C. (Chase) **88** 119
Jane Emerson **146** 324 334
Jane M. Hoskins
  (Crandall) **127** 88
Jane S. (King) **125** 180

JAMES *cont'd*
Jeannette Barber **76** 209
Jeffrey W. **127** 37
Jemima **52** 134
Jesse **72** 74
Jesse Reynolds **127** 31
Jessie M. **103** 100 179
Jessie May **102** 291
Joan **60** 287 **63** 164-166
  143 115 **147** 347 349
  350
Joanna **73** 115 **127** 37 87
  147 333
Joanna (Smith) **88** 276
Joanna (Webb) **127** 87
Joe **91** 303
John **51** 423 **57** 34 182 398
  399 401 403 **58** 85 87 88
  168 170 171 174 **59** 78
  310 312 314 389 391 **60**
  63 65 175-177 179 271
  272 274 283 338 **61** 57
  58 174 288 372 **62** 181
  356 **63** 144 164-166 **67**
  190 **70** 264 **71** 139 **74** 45
  77 321 **79** 49 **81** 254 444
  82 43 **84** 306 **87** 200 398
  89 206 **90** 396 **91** 80 89
  92 95 **104** 20 **110** 229
  114 189 **124** 102 **126**
  248 249 251 **127** 17 31
  35 89 **129** 252 **134** 141
  147 333 340 342-346 348
  350-352
John Card **127** 89
John G. **127** 90
John K. **126** 254
John Oscar **127** 89
John P. **103** 160
John Paul **102** 123
John W. **127** 87 89 90
  140 157
Jonah **101** 33 **103** 58
Jonathan **59** 37 **100** 186
  125 180 **126** 249 250
  253 254 **127** 31-33 86
  147 343
Jonathan A. **126** 254
Joseph **61** 57 **63** 165 **68**
  180 **76** 24 **89** 92 **100** 186
  124 102 **126** 247-249
  251 253 **127** 30-34 **128**
  297 **147** 332-338 341 342
  344
Joseph Webb **127** 87
Joshua **61** 175 290-292 **91**
  216 326
Josiah **60** 271
Josiah Russell **126** 254
Josiah Stephens **81** 254
Judith (Phillips) **127** 32
Julia Ann **103** 277
Julia Elizabeth **103** 181
Julia Florence **102** 225
Juliet E. **72** 74
Julieta **103** 58
Kate **91** 90
Kate (Casey) **91** 89
Kate V. **91** 90
Katharine **55** 298 **63** 165
Katharine (Blux) **105** 59

JAMES *cont'd*
Lena May **103** 180
Leta Clark **103** 181
Levi **102** 224 291
Levi Leslie **102** 291
Levitt **60** 271
Lewis **63** 165
Lilles A. **87** 350
Lillian E. **68** 332
Lillian M. (Larkin) **127** 87
Lizzic B. **75** lx
Lizzie M. **103** 180
Lizzie M. (Clark) **101** 317
Lizzie Ruth **103** 181
Lois **127** 34 35
Lois (Beals) **91** 80
Lois (Matteson) **127** 35
Lois A. **127** 36
Loring Josephine **127** 91
Lottie May **103** 181
Louis **89** 206
Louisa **136** 312 328
Louisa (Gage) **126** 209
Lucinda (Waite) **127** 35
Lucretia E. (Giles) **90** 44
Lucy **60** 177 274 **126** 254
  127 34
Lucy (Reynolds) **127** 90
Lucy E. (Potter) **127** 35
Lydia **57** 34 401 **58** 170
  60 65 176 271 **61** 372 **69**
  280 **74** 46 92 95
Lydia (Capwell) **127** 36
Lydia (Door) **92** 95
Lydia (Peckham) **126** 248
  147 333 344-346 351
Lydia (Turner) **87** 200
  110 229
Lydia M. **69** 280
Lydia Whitman
  (Sherman) **127** 87
Lyman Dwight **91** 79 80
Mabel **96** 160
Mabel H. (James) **127** 89
Mabel Viola **103** 181
Mable (Samuelson) **90** 95
Maggie W. (Clark)
  101 214
Malachi **91** 80
Malinda **127** 90
Marcia **116** 273
Marcy **90** 396 **129** 263
Margaret **100** 142 **127** 31
  135 142 **143** 115
Margaret (Clark) **103** 100
Margaret (Eldredge)
  126 253
Margaret (Fendall)
  89 92 93
Margaret (Stringer)
  127 31
Margaret A. H. **94** 34
Margaret W. **103** 179
Margery **63** 166
Maria **127** 34
Mariam **126** 253
Marietta Edna **102** 225
Marion **90** 95
Marion A. **91** 89 90
Marion Eleanor **90** 95
Martha **117** 65 **127** 37

JAMES *cont'd*
143 115 **147** 351-353
Martha (Worden) **127** 37
Martha Esther **103** 100 179
Martha Hicks **77** 261
Martin **57** 34 **126** 248
  147 347
Marvel **127** 33 35 86
Marvel (James) (Stanton)
  127 33
Marvel (Perkins) **127** 34
Mary **55** 208 **58** 85 **61** 173
  288 **63** 164 **64** 284 **74** 45
  104 **78** 67 **81** 444 **82** 43
  89 92 **90** 396 **92** 95 **105**
  59 316 **110** 229 **113** 294
  116 273 274 **120** 8 **126**
  249 250 252 253 **127** 33
  34 88 **147** 333 340 341
Mary (Barber) **126** 250
  127 87 90
Mary (Emms) **90** 174
Mary (Parsons) **143** 114
  115
Mary (Whipple) **127** 36
Mary A. (Barber) **127** 87
Mary A. (Morgan)
  126 254
Mary Abbie (Browning)
  127 87
Mary Ann **112** 316 **147**
  353 **148** 66
Mary Ann (Nichols) **127**
  87 89
Mary Ann (Thomas)
  126 254
Mary Bradford (Rollins)
  127 87
Mary C. **73** 115 **127** 91
Mary Cenar (Cottrell)
  127 90
Mary E. **87** 350 **127** 87
Mary Eliza **127** 35
Mary Elizabeth **127** 89
Mary Elizabeth
  (Holberton) **127** 87
Mary Ella (Beverly)
  127 87
Mary Jane **89** 92
Mary Jenison **58** 62
Mary L. **91** 89
Mary Louisa (Cushing)
  136 312
Mary Lucinda (Holton)
  67 xxxiv **136** 312
Mary Maria **58** 60
Mary R. **61** 176
Mary Randall **61** 291
Matida S. (Greene) **127** 89
Matilda **133** 52
Matthew **140** 157
Maurice Clifford **103** 181
May (Titus) **89** 379
Mayetta **102** 225
Mehitable **127** 33 **133** 100
Mehitable (Webb)
  126 253
Melissa **105** 298
Mercy **59** 140 **90** 396 **126**
  252 **127** 34 35 **134** 141

JAMES *cont'd*
Mercy (Stockbridge)
  134 141
Mercy Ann **127** 36
Minerva **103** 58
Minerva (Titus) **89** 379
Minnie Beatrice **88** 93
Miriam **56** 90 **126** 249 254
  147 343
Molly **60** 273
Moses B. **127** 33
Nancy **102** 152 224 **125** 219
  221 **127** 32 34
Nancy (Bell) (LeMoyne)
  101 179
Nancy (Cook) **126** 251
Nancy C. (Shepard) **123**
  90 306
Nancy M. **77** xliii
Nancy / Anna (Bell)
  (LeMoyne) **101** 179
Nathan **126** 254
Nathan Tucker **127** 89
Nathaniel **51** 423 **55** 208
  105 58 59
Nathaniel E. **90** 174 **95** 356
Nellie May **103** 181
Noah **90** 44 57
Norman **91** 379
Norman B. **89** 379
Olive **59** 412 **63** 177
Olive B. **103** 236
Olivia Phelps **75** xxii **90**
  139 174 199
Orella **102** 225
Oscar F. **89** 379
Oscar Lowell **102** 291
Otis Martin **103** 180
Owen **110** 169
Pamela (Moore) **126** 254
Patience **58** 262 **60** 338
  61 174 **74** 45 **92** 95 **126**
  250 254 **127** 30
Patience (Cottrell)
  126 250
Patience (Tower) (Farrow)
  91 80
Patrick **132** 75
Paul **126** 253
Peggy **70** 230
Penelope **127** 88
Percy Chatham (Mrs.)
  90 136
Peregrine **127** 34
Perry Greene **127** 34
Peter **62** 289 356 **63** 165
  166
Phebe **67** 280 **127** 90
Phebe (Miller) **132** 75
Phebe (Rogers) **127** 31
Phebe (Tillinghast)
  127 35
Phebe Ann **100** 186 **127** 34
Phebe G. (Davis) **116** 274
Philip **91** 79 **121** 272
Phineas **59** 412
Phyla (Carpenter) **91** 118
Polly **59** 37 **60** 271 **90** 396
  126 251 254 **127** 34 **133**
  307 308
Polly (Abbey) **126** 254

JAMES *cont'd*
Prudence **59** 310 312 314
  389 391 **60** 63 65 176
Prudence (Stanton)
  129 252
Pruella **74** 319
R. J. **91** 376
Rachel **52** 134 **102** 224
Rachel (Ingersoll) **90** 174
Ralph **73** 115
Randall **67** 287 **126** 250
Randall Cottrell **127** 88
Raymond Wesley
  103 180
Reana **88** 384
Rebecca **64** 200 **100** 156
  126 248
Rebecca (Woodman)
  147 333 347 348 350
Rebecca Fidelia **89** 379
Remington **126** 254
Remington K. **126** 254
Reuben **90** 95
Reynolds **127** 31
Rhoda **58** 38 **59** 78 314
  126 254
Rhoda (Butler) **124** 160
Rhoda (Kenyon) **126** 254
Rhoda (Reynolds) **127** 31
Richard **63** 165 166 **93** 359
  143 114 115
Robert **126** 251 **127** 31 89
Robertson **136** 312
Rodman **70** 230 **71** 38
  127 31 90
Rowland B. **100** 186
Roxanna **127** 91
Roxie Elizabeth **127** 91
Ruhamah **127** 32 **134** 127
Ruhamah (Bentley) **126**
  251 252
Russell **127** 31 32 90
Ruth **55** 208 **60** 336 **61** 173
  74 205 **105** 56-60 **106**
  27 28 **120** 5 8 **127** 90
  306
Ruth (Barber) **127** 33
Ruth (Carter) **147** 353 354
  148 66
Ruth (Jones) **105** 57
Ruth (Kenyon) **127** 86
Ruth (Perry) **127** 31
Ruth A. (Sherman) **127** 87
Ruth E. **127** 33
Ruth Evangeline **90** 95
Sally **59** 37 **61** 175 **90** 396
  127 32 **140** 149
Sally (Griggs) **126** 254
Samantha (Stone) **126** 254
Samuel **63** 165 **67** 280 **68**
  108 **82** 43 **116** 273 274
  121 198 **126** 253 **127** 37
  304
Samuel Carter **103** 181
Samuel Gibbs **143** 226
Sarah **53** 248 **55** 208 **57** 190
  63 164 **74** 46 **77** 146 **82**
  43 **87** 381 **89** 379 **91** 216
  92 95 **96** 27 **101** 31 **105**
  59 **106** 229 **112** 191 **121**
  113 **124** 102 **125** 179

JAMES *cont'd*
183 **126** 248 249 251 253
127 31-36 86 88 90 **147**
333 338 339 342 343
Sarah (Holmes) **90** 396
397 **134** 142
Sarah (James) **91** 216
Sarah (Lillibridge) **127** 87
Sarah (Perry) **127** 86
Sarah (Peterson) (Clarke)
127 88
Sarah (Reynolds) **127** 31
Sarah (Saunders) **127** 86
Sarah (Sisson) **127** 30
Sarah (Warren) **137** 73
Sarah (Watson) **127** 88
Sarah (Wilcox) **127** 30
Sarah A. (Johnson) **127**
89 91
Sarah Ann **127** 31
Sarah Caroline **148** 66
Sarah Catherine
(Sherman) **127** 87
Sarah Elizabeth **127** 89 91
Sarah Elizabeth Susan
127 87
Sarah G. (Sweet) **127** 33
Sarah Stanton **127** 87
Sarah Wales **90** 396
Silas **126** 253 **127** 34-36
Simeon **126** 251
Simeon Clarke **127** 89 90
Solomon **69** 296
Spain N. **77** xliii
Stanton **59** 310
Stephen **112** 316 **124** 160
126 250 **127** 31 **128** 128
Susan **57** 34 **127** 86 87
147 353
Susan A. **127** 89
Susan E. (Holloway)
127 89
Susan Luette **67** 279 280
Susanna **58** 35 139 **126**
248 249 251 **127** 31 **147**
338 340 343 347 352
Susanna (Mallett) **125** 106
Susanna (Martin) **126** 247
147 329-333 338 347-
349 **148** 66
Susanna (Sherman)
127 86
Susanna (Stevens) **132** 75
Susanna (Wilcox) **126** 251
Sydney V. **118** 145
Sylvester **127** 30 89 91
Tacy **127** 36
Taliaferro **77** 261
Thankful (Dye) **126** 250
Thankful (Hoxsie) **127** 31
Thomas **51** 422 423 **53** 62
54 306 **55** 200 207 208
298 **56** 91 **57** 197 **58** 262
60 179 283 287 **63** 164-
166 **68** 108 **76** 79 **91** 79
96 252 **98** 208 **100** 141
156 302 **101** 33 217 **102**
224 225 **103** 181 **105** 57
59 **106** 27 **117** 155 **118**
53 **121** 125 **124** 93 102
126 249-251 253 254

JAMES *cont'd*
127 36 **131** 9 12 13 16
126 **132** 75 **136** 94 **140**
203 **141** 95 98 100 105
144 46 **147** 341-343
Thomas A. **103** 58
Thomas Austin **103** 181
Thomas Fendall **89** 92
Thomas H. B. **105** 298
Thomas W. **118** 44 51 54
Tirzah **109** 67
Varnum **127** 87
Velonia Abbie **102** 291
Vivian **90** 95
Waity **127** 31
Walker **126** 82
Walter Freeman **103** 181
Waterman **127** 34
Webster **127** 304
Wellington **102** 225
Wellington Carroll
103 181
Wellington J. **101** 217
103 180
Welthea **61** 175
Welthea Alden **61** 292
William **57** 34 225 315 **59**
391 **60** 271 273 **61** 173
177 291 292 **63** 164 165
64 284 **66** 113 117 123
73 115 **74** 104 **76** 24 **79**
138 139 **80** 247 **81** 444
491 **82** 43 **91** 89 90 326
98 246 **113** 220 **119** 16
123 90 306 **126** 141 247-
249 251 252 254 **127** 31
32 36 90 **128** 296 **133**
100 **135** 272 **136** 216
147 329-334 336 337 340-
343 347-353 **148** 66
William A. **97** 210
William B. **81** 458
William Crandall **127** 89
William D. **89** 379
William F. **127** 36
William H. **76** 50
William Henry **61** 291
William Lewis **89** 92
William R. **69** 280
William Reynolds **127** 91
William Russell **127** 91
William S. **126** 209
William Vincent **90** 94 95
91 88-90
Winfield Scott **102** 291
Zacharius **102** 225
Ziphorah **58** 174
Zoe **59** 37 **74** 319
JAMESON Jamieson
Jamison Jamsen
—— **111** 52
Abigail (Cook) **90** 90
Agnes **85** 225
Alexander **100** 31 **112** 269
120 142
Anna Belle **89** 111
Archibald **100** 31
Arthur Orcutt **57** lxix
B. **91** 326
Benedict **73** 221

JAMESON *cont'd*
Caroline Cogswell
57 lxix
Catherine **100** 31
Charles D. **55** 351
Charles Davis (Mrs.)
91 177
Charlotte A. **76** 275
Clara **134** 334
Daniel **57** lxviii
David **53** 452 **55** 351
64 189
Dorothy Henderson
101 337
E. O. **54** 357 **55** 351 **61** 259
124 172
Ebenezer **105** 286
Edward A. **105** 73
Eleanor **62** 66
Elizabeth **96** 397 **111** 180
Elizabeth (Seavey) **90** 92
Elizabeth M. **77** 189
Ella N. (Marston) **83** 432
435
Elsie **97** 133
Ephraim Orcutt **51** 93 95
99 **53** 253 452 **56** xxx
57 xxxi xlii lxviii lxix
51 53-55 185 **65** 14 **145**
209
Esther **109** 129 **115** 27
117 318
Esther (Martin) **115** 27
Evaline J. (Stoning)
139 295
George **112** 18
Hannah **57** lxviii **61** 273
62 66 **81** 371 **117** 143
144
Hannah (Cook) **90** 89
Harry Downs **115** 317
Helen (Kernochan)
111 52
Hugh **51** 493 **57** lxviii
Isaac **83** 375
Isabella **61** 243
J. F. **55** 451 **106** 245
J. Franklin **52** 396 **54** 242
James **53** 452 **62** 66 244
301 **64** 165 **71** 220 **76** 47
78 187 **90** 92 **91** 326
115 27 **120** 142 **134** 334
Jane **57** lxviii **86** 224
Jane (Crosly) **117** 66
Jeanne **134** 334
Jeremiah **83** 375
Jerome **139** 295
John **55** 351 **56** 149 **64** 324
90 90 **107** 155 **111** 206
115 27 **117** 66 **120** 142
Joseph **86** 135
Joseph William **85** 195
Katharine Strong **57** lxix
Laura **86** 361
Leonidas **91** 326
Lole **90** 90
Louis **125** 251
Luciana **83** 486
Margaret **94** 198 **117** 66
136 313
Maria **90** 89

JAMESON *cont'd*
Martin **105** 286
Mary **51** 493 **55** 351 **57**
lxviii lxix **71** 219 **90** 91
115 177 **134** 254
Mary (Knowlton) **86** 135
Mary Joanna **57** lxviii
Mary O. (Sparrow)
102 286
Myrtle Hill **93** 138
Nathan Cleaves **62** 113
Oswald **73** 232
Paul **90** 89
Phebe **61** 387
Rachel **90** 91
Robert **83** 375 **120** 142
Ruth **93** 215
Sally **90** 89
Samuel **66** 366
Sarah **64** 12 **90** 89 **111** 206
Seth **93** 215
Sophia **73** 202
T. C. **123** 68
Thomas **51** 469 **55** 67 **61**
243 **65** 47 **83** 432 435 **97**
233
Thomas Henry **62** 113
Thurston W. **83** 375
Tryphosa Colton
(Freeman) **125** 251
Wallace Crawford **97** 158
Watey **90** 91
William **53** 452 **64** 12 **71**
220 **77** 189 **83** 375 **90** 89
95 132 **111** 210 **115** 177
William Cogswell
57 lxix
Willie **102** 286
Jamis *see* James
Jamison *see* Jameson
JANDIN John **58** 70
JANDINE Martha **145** 127
JANDIS J. W. **91** 326
JANDRELL
Ann E. **76** 52
John **76** 52
JANE Jayne
____ (Matthews) **82** 261
100 250
Catherine **128** 33
Charlotte (Huntley)
101 208
Daniel **128** 33
Elizabeth **59** xcvii **60** 290
82 261
Henry LaBarre **59** xcvii
82 261 **100** 250
Holder (Chase) **88** 123
Isaac **128** 33
Isabel (Sinclare) **128** 33
Mary **88** 24
Nancy (Adlington)
100 187
P. **66** 11
Peter **66** 12 **78** 188 **101** 208
Rebecca **128** 33
JANEKIN
John **113** 57 94
Katharine **113** 57
JANES —— **54** 371
A. P. **55** 224

JANES *cont'd*
Abel **74** 113
Adaline **100** 326
Adaline (Root) **100** 326
Adrian **100** 326 327
Albon **110** 36
Alfred **100** 326 327
Alfred William **90** 355
Alice **100** 326
Alice (Cross) **100** 326
Alvin **100** 326
Annis (Munroe) **100** 9
Arvilla B. **62** 122
Benjamin **71** 201
Benjamin Franklin **100**
326 327
Betsey **100** 9
Caroline Augusta
(Furness) **91** 398
Charles **91** 41
Clarissa (Fuller) **148** 266
Clementina **94** 289
Ebenezer **57** 189 **103** 89
Elias **126** 86
Eliza **100** 326
Frederic **144** 324
Hannah **103** 89
Henry **100** 326
Hopy **100** 326
Hopy (Cook) **100** 326
Horace **91** 398
Irene **71** 201
Irene (Watkins) **100** 326
Israel **74** 113
James **100** 9
James Olives **144** 324
Joseph **55** 224 **59** 331
60 185
Levi **110** 121
Lewis Almeron **100** 326
Liberty **148** 266
Lucretia **58** 345 **92** 123
Lucretia F. **144** 324
Lucretia Richardson
136 317
Lucy C. **74** 172
Lydia **55** 224
Marcus T. **67** 300
Mary **55** 224 **74** 113 **92** 123
111 88
Mary (Lumbard) **110** 121
Mary Abigail (Schultz)
90 355
Mary D. **91** 236
Mary Jane (Leigh)
100 326
Michael **55** 224
Mildred Evelyn
(Hannum) **91** 41
Minnie Lawrence
63 xxxiii
Nancy **100** 326
Nancy (Mulks) **100** 326
Nancy E. **110** 121
Polly **100** 326
Polly (Warren) **100** 326
Roxanna (Field) **144** 324
Ruth **90** 190
Samuel **91** 236 **92** 123
94 376
Sarah **57** 189 **110** 36

JANES *cont'd*
Sarah (Deman) **100** 326
Susanna (Stotle) **100** 326
Thomas **91** 326 **118** 42
Thomas W. **118** 42
Walter Scott **58** 345
Wheaton B. **100** 326
William **55** 224
JANEWAY Anna Eaton
(Ebrick) **90** 279
Carrie Lucille **90** 279
Elizabeth Ayers Mellick
(Bulkley) **83** 339
George Harold (Mrs.)
85 437
Henry H. (Mrs.) **83** 339
Mary Louise (Davis)
85 437
William Francis **90** 279
JANIGON James **106** 113
JANING Alice **69** 248
Jeffrey **69** 248
JANNE Mary **78** 71
JANNEY
Caroline **88** 93
Edgar **77** 189
George **88** 93
Helen Mary **83** 231
Mary Brown **77** 189
Rebecca Ann (Betts) **88** 93
JANNOOTAS —— **63** 231
JANNYNG
William **141** 236
JANOCK Joshua **55** 301
JANS Agneta **106** 7
Anneke **57** 415 **79** 116
106 168
Annetje **51** 373
Josijntje **128** 165
Lysbeth **86** 223
Maartje **128** 164
Reymerig **111** 75
Sara **128** 169
Sarah **66** 17
JANSDOCHTER
Maartgen **128** 168
JANSEN Janseens Janson
Janssen
—— **63** 188
Anna Barbara **93** 278
Cornelius **100** 99
Dirk **107** 49
Elizabeth **62** 232
Gerrit **128** 167
Govert **128** 164
H. Q. **143** 201
Jacob **96** 396
Jane **83** 23 24
John B. **97** 59
Maria **128** 167
Marie **99** 57
Mary Ann **83** 24 27
Mary Emily **94** 187
Michael **52** 315
Sophia **107** 49
Thomas E. **109** 129
JANSZ Gerrit **128** 163
Philip **128** 164
Januarin *see* Janvrin
JANUARY Derick
Algernon **83** 336

JANUARY *cont'd*
  Isabel Valle **88** 5
  Janet **83** 336
  Julia (Churchill) **83** 336
Janverin *see* Janvrin
JANVIER
  Thomas A. **64** 379
JANVRIN Januarin
  Janverin Jeanverin
  — Miss **83** 193
  — Mrs. **83** 193
  — Widow **73** 197
  Abigail **82** 291 296
  Dorothy **53** 163
  Elizabeth **58** 250
  Elizabeth Mendum **82** 43
  Frances Henrietta **69** xlix
  George **53** 163 **81** 444 **82**
    43 291 296 412 **83** 22 24
  Jane **53** 163
  Jean **88** 255 256
  John **53** 163 **68** 141 **82** 43
    99 79
  Joseph **53** 165 **97** 358
  Joshua **132** 325
  Katharine (Hutchinson)
    (Bartholomew)
    145 264
  Louis B. **83** 432 436
  Marion F. (Merrill)
    83 432 436
  Martha **82** 291 294
  Martha Moulton **82** 43
  Mary **56** 38 **99** 245
  Mary (French) **132** 325
  Mary Moulton **82** 43
  Mendum **81** 444 **82** 43 291
    294
  Molly **53** 165
  Nabby **82** 43
  Nancy **82** 420 **83** 22 24
  Nancy (Fall) **83** 22
  Richard **145** 264
  Sarah E. **51** 248
  Thomas **82** 43
JAQUA Jacqua Jayqua
  Aaron **61** 203 **99** 301 302
    305 **117** 239
  Betty **99** 305
  Daniel **56** 347
  Eleanor (Campbell)
    117 239
  Gamaliel **117** 239
  Hannah **62** 63 **99** 301
  John **62** 63
  Mary **62** 360 **81** 291
  Parthenia **83** 48 **99** 302
  Polly **105** 313
  Rebecca (House) **99** 302
    305 **117** 239
  Ruth (Hanchet) **105** 313
  Ruth (House) **99** 301
  Samuel **62** 63
  Simon **105** 313
  Stephen **125** 44
JAQUELIN
  Edward **63** 102 103
JAQUES Jacques Jaquess
  Jacquis
  —— **52** 333 **144** 34
  — Maj. **77** 81

JAQUES *cont'd*
  — Mr. **53** 309
  Abigail **64** 157 **66** 274
    275 278 **125** 215
  Alice **92** 197
  Alonzo P. **66** 278
  Amos **72** 130
  Amos W. **72** 130
  Ann **52** 68 **64** 157 **66** 278
  Anna **52** 68 **64** 157
  Anna (Knight) **92** 196
  Apphia **63** 373 376 **64** 75
    66 274-276 279
  Augustus **115** 231
  Benjamin **53** 39 **63** 373 376
    64 75 157 **66** 274 275
    279 **110** 286 **115** 59
  Betsey **64** 75 **66** 278 279
  Betsey E. **66** 278
  Betty **64** 75
  Betty (Farnam) **115** 59
  Caroline Louisa
    (Merriam) **61** lxiii
    92 196
  Carrie Ella **81** 395
  Charles **66** 275 278 **78** 189
  Charles M. **66** 278
  Cynthia **66** 275 278 279
  Daniel **64** 157
  Deborah **63** 373 376 **64**
    75 157 **66** 275 279 **137**
    254
  Deborah (Plumer) **92** 196
  Dorothy **53** 39
  Edgar R. **114** 64
  Edith **52** 68
  Edna **63** 373 376 **64** 75 **66**
    274 275 299 **134** 215
  Edna May (Aulls) **114** 64
  Edwin **92** 62
  Eleanor **52** 68 **63** 139
  Eliphalet **64** 75
  Elizabeth **63** 373 376 **64**
    157 **66** 274 275 **75** 262
    133 156 233 **134** 215
  Ellen Maria **66** 278
  Emma **66** 278
  Ethel **96** 161
  Everett L. **92** 62
  Francis **92** 196 197
  Frank Mortimer **81** 395
  Fred William **81** 395
  George **52** 68
  Grace **52** 68
  Hannah **64** 157 **66** 275 278
    128 125
  Hannah Eliza **66** 278
  Harriet **66** 278 **147** 212 213
  Harriet (Whittemore)
    108 247
  Harry **92** 62
  Hattie B. (Stanton) **92** 62
  Helen **61** lviii
  Helen Louise **85** 190 **92**
    99 196 **93** 141
  Henry **52** 68 **61** lxiii **64**
    157 **92** 196 **108** 247 **140**
    207 208 **147** 213
  Jacob **63** 376 **66** 275
  James **107** 305 **128** 129
  Joanna **67** 74

JAQUES *cont'd*
  John **52** 68 **63** 242 **64** 75
    67 74
  John Maxwell **136** 78
  John Thurston **75** 262
  Jonathan **128** 126
  Joseph **63** 139 **66** 275 278
    128 128
  Joseph C. **66** 278
  Judith **66** 275
  Julia Ann **61** 235
  Kate S. **75** 262
  Katharine **52** 68
  Keziah **78** 402
  Keziah (Thompson)
    92 196
  Laura A. **116** 258
  Louisa **147** 213
  Lucy **75** 262
  Lydia **53** 40
  Lydia (Pike) **92** 196
    121 168
  Mabel Lyles **98** 146
  Margaret **77** 232
  Maria **66** 278
  Mary **51** 466 **53** 39 **63** 373
    376 **64** 157 **66** 274 275
    278 279 **72** 130 **81** 395
    114 294
  Mary (Baldwin) **115** 231
  Mary (Harmon) **110** 286
    114 46
  Mary Caroline **75** 262
  Mary N. **66** 275 278
  Mary Orr **88** 341
  Maude **52** 68
  Mildred Noyes **108** 134
  Miriam **110** 286 **114** 228
  Moody **66** 274 275 278
  Morris **92** 62
  Moses **63** 373 376 **64** 75 **66**
    274 275 278 279 **134** 215
  Nathan **128** 130
  Olive **66** 275
  Parker **51** 466 **63** 373 376
    64 75 66 274 275 279
    134 215 218
  Paul **81** 428
  Peter **52** 68
  Phineas **66** 275
  Rebecca **66** 275 278 279
    81 428
  Rebecca A. **66** 278
  Richard **52** 68 **54** 337 **64**
    157 **77** 69 90 400 **110**
    286 **114** 46 **140** 157
  Robert **52** 68 **92** 62
  Romulus **66** 278
  Rosabell **81** 395
  Ruth **64** 157 **78** 309
  Ruth (Wyman) **92** 196
  Sally **66** 274 275
  Samuel **61** 354 **63** 373 376
    64 75 157 **66** 274 275
    279 **92** 196 **108** 247 **111**
    184 **121** 168 **128** 129
    134 215 218
  Sarah **64** 75 157 **66** 274
    275 278 279 **80** 44 **81**
    428

JAQUES *cont'd*
  Sarah (Whittemore) **92**
    196 **108** 247
  Sarah W. **66** 278
  Stephen **53** 39 **64** 75 157
    87 398 **92** 196 **134** 215
  Susan **66** 278
  Susan Jane (Milne) **136** 78
  Susanna **53** 39 **100** 246
    110 286 **113** 224 **114**
    294
  Thankful **53** 39 **64** 75
  Thomas **52** 68 **107** 214
  Vienna **147** 212 213
  William **63** 25 **75** 262
  William Pratt **81** 395
  William White **75** 262
JAQUET Jacquett Jaquett
  Jean Paul **69** 385 **87** 304
    106 14 **108** 33 35
  Josephine **119** 153
  Maria **69** 385
  Pierre **62** 206
JAQUITH Jacquith Jaqueth
  —— **53** 41
  Abigail **136** 56
  Abraham **55** 402 **56** 41
    61 151 **125** 295 **136** 55
    56 61 143 **137** 242
  Adford **137** 242
  Alice **55** 402
  Andrew **137** 78
  Annes **58** 48
  Benjamin **57** 355 **61** 252
    62 63 **111** 185 **136** 56
  Betsey **59** 340
  Betsey (Spaulding)
    131 317
  David **61** 252
  Deborah **136** 55
  Dolly **78** 314
  Ebenezer **67** 286 **136** 56
  Edwin **88** 341
  Elizabeth **89** 182 **101** 251
    136 56 136
  Esther **62** 153
  Florence **84** 188
  George **125** 295
  Hannah **55** 402 **56** 41 **57**
    355 **61** 252 **136** 56 **137**
    336
  Hannah (Farley) **136** 55 56
  Heath E. Benjamin
    131 317
  John **61** 252 **62** 62 **78** 304
    106 198
  Jonathan **59** 275 **62** 151
  Joseph **136** 56
  Josephine Romaine
    78 240
  Judith **111** 185
  L. E. **78** 240
  Lucy (Peters) **137** 78
  Lydia **59** 275 **64** 212 **67**
    286 **68** 95 **111** 184
  Margaret (Leman)
    137 241
  Mary **55** 402 **56** 41 **61** 151
    62 62 **88** 337 **136** 56
  Mary (Alexander) **88** 277
  Mary E. (Mace) **88** 341

JAQUITH *cont'd*
  Miriam **55** 402
  Moses **88** 277
  Nathan **62** 153
  Olive (Davis) **137** 242
  Phebe **62** 63
  Polly **131** 30
  Rebecca **61** 354 **136** 56
  Ruth **61** 153
  Sarah **61** 151 **88** 334 **108**
    167 **136** 56
  Sarah (Jones) **136** 56
    137 242
  Susanna **60** 296 **136** 144
  Tamsen **61** 252
  Thirza **62** 151
  Thomas **64** 212
  Timothy **55** 402 **136** 56
  William **78** 181
JARANT Ann **54** 218
  Robert **54** 218
JARBOE
  Cynthia M. **78** 354
  Walter S. **78** 354
JARDINE
  Elizabeth **101** 51
  Jenny Maxwell **82** 505
  John **55** 372 **82** 505 **83** 13
    148 **101** 51
  Olive **55** 372 **83** 13 148
  Olive (Haley) **83** 13
  Rishworth **74** 253
  Sarah **74** 253
JARE Mary (Palgrave)
    102 96
  William **102** 96
JARED Eli **117** 45
JARETZKI Sonia (Lasell)
    100 162
JARMAN
  Ann **73** 140 267
  Elizabeth **73** 152
  James **54** 193
  Joan **54** 219
  John **94** 264
  Margaret **135** 77
  Mary **54** 219
  Priscilla **55** 345
  William Charles **89** 132
    98 145
JARNEGAN
  Henry **144** 129
JARNETTE
  Eleanor de **105** 148
JARRAND
  Nathaniel **93** 298
JARRATT William **63** 243
JARRED Mary **80** 330
JARRELL
  Martha **102** 165
  Polly **105** 146
JARRETT Jarret
  Ann (Lukens) **117** 68
  Dorcas **100** 236
  Eleanor (Doughtery)
    106 151
  Elizabeth **65** 21
  Gainor (Penrose) **117** 68
  Grace **51** 285
  Hannah **117** 68
  Hannah (Mather) **117** 68

JARRETT *cont'd*
  James H. **53** 136 362
  John **66** 43
  Jonathan **117** 68
  Joseph **100** 236
  Lambert **106** 151
  Mary Gray (Thacher)
    88 330
  Mercy **100** 300
  Phebe **100** 236
  Return **51** 285
  Richard **117** 68
  Sarah Catherine **106** 151
  Susanna **66** 43
  William **117** 68
JARROLD —— **51** 374
  Anne **71** 329 334
  William **51** 85
JARROT
  Lewis F. A. **88** 330
JARSEY Sarah **125** 244
JARTSEY Robert **52** 253
JARUZELSKI John J. (Mrs.)
    124 319
JARVIE Isabella (New-
    begin) **83** 491
  James Newbegin **74**
    xxiv 78 **83** 491 **84** 107
    194
  Selina Huntington
    113 304
  William **83** 491
JARVIS Jervis - *see also*
    Gervis
  —— **65** 8 **92** 347 351
    101 270
  — Capt. **83** 193 **84** 161 255
  — Miss **83** 193
  — Mr. **83** 306
  Abigail **115** 16 18 19 21
    23 107 113 114
  Abigail A. **125** 222
  Abraham **145** 147
  Adeline (Rust) **85** 436
    93 194
  Alvah **147** 53
  Ann **90** 53 **140** 157
  Ann Jane **102** 313
  Anna **140** 45
  Anna Grace **81** 222 **85** 436
    86 108 205
  Asa **91** 326
  Asahel **115** 16 18 19 21 23
    107
  Benjamin **92** 345 **94** 380
    115 56 **140** 330
  Bessie **108** 214
  Caroline L. **74** 309
  Catherine **66** 58 **115** 109
    144 244 **145** 146 147
  Catherine (Raymond)
    145 147
  Charles **78** 306 **125** 23
    140 157 324
  Charles H. **90** 116
  Daphne **115** 113 114
  Delia **52** 275 **80** 98 **85** 132
    140 255
  Deliverance **80** 98
  Deming **92** 347 351 **94**
    380 **140** 45 157

JARVIS *cont'd*
Dwight **115** 16
Edwin **115** 19
Eglintine **92** 73
Elias **76** 219 **80** 98
Elizabeth **72** 216 **78** 310 **79**
154 **107** 213
Elizabeth (Bowman)
85 436
Elizabeth Miller (Hart)
93 363
Ellen H. **84** 29
Emma **83** 432 437
Emma (Wiley) **110** 53
Esther **72** 314 **115** 23
Esther Cranston **80** 151
Eugene LeBaron **110** 53
Francis Carr **110** 53
Frank **110** 213
George **65** 121 **93** 300
George A. **110** 49 **145** 147
George Murray **145** 147
George Willis **110** 213
Hannah **72** 216 **141** 258
Hannah (Seabury)
140 157
Hannah Owen **72** 216
Harriet **115** 107
Henry **110** 168
Herman Carty **115** 109
Helly Hart **93** 363
Ida Caroline **102** 126
Isaac **145** 74
Isabella **72** 216
J. J. **55** 364
James **63** 186
James Jackson **92** 351
James Lawrence **85** 436
James M. **84** 29
Joan **93** 384
John **58** 306 **72** 216 **73**
131 156 157 **76** 62 **77**
236 **85** 436 **93** 194 **123**
118 **125** 100 **140** 157
145 147
John Deming **92** 347
John Wesley **52** 275
Jonathan **73** 148
Joseph Russell **110** 52 53
Joseph Sidney **115** 23
Kent **115** 18
Lavinia **72** 216
Leonard **58** 68 **64** 118 **84**
267 **93** 261 **110** 49 50 53
140 158 322
Leonard Bradford **110** 53
Lorenzo Taylor **115** 114
Louisa (Post) (Gillet)
147 53
Lucinda (Knowles)
123 199
Lucretia (Cooper) **85** 436
Lucy **110** 213
Lulu Rhoda **91** 141
Lydia **68** 106
Margaret **74** 200
Martha **72** 216
Mary **72** 216 314 **101** 274
115 15 **137** 35
Mary A. P. **78** 408
Mary Ann **109** 265 **115** 21

JARVIS *cont'd*
Mary Ann Porter **92** 345
Mary Pepperell
Sparhawk **96** 71
Mary Putney **81** 381
Matilda **126** 142
May **78** 205
May (Tibbetts) **92** 304 **98**
57 132 215 293 **99** 52
110 244 323 **100** 34 144
Mercy **140** 158
Munson **72** 216
Naomi **72** 216
Nathaniel **77** 232 **79** 37
85 124
Philip **105** 209 210 **140** 330
Pierce L. **81** 381
Polly **72** 216 **104** 215
105 103
Rebecca **58** 306 **66** 333
Robert **84** 152
Rowling **80** 151
Sally (Cunningham) **85**
436 **125** 100
Sally Maria **115** 109
Samuel **68** 106 **72** 216
134 59 **140** 330
Samuel M. **115** 109
Sarah **72** 216 **73** 156 157
93 261
Sarah (Church) **110** 49
Sarah Ann **93** 194
Sarah Leonard (Bradford)
110 52
Sarah M. (Lambert)
90 116
Seymour **72** 216
Susan **110** 53
Susanna **110** 49
Susanna (Condy) **110** 49
Thankful (Mayo) **123** 118
Timothy **123** 199
Walter Chester (Mrs.) **77**
323 **78** 205
William **72** 216 314 **79** 154
93 363 **110** 49 **115** 15
113 **124** 177
William C. **115** 114
William Porter **92** 345
Zora Smith **118** 76
JASON David **137** 361
Meribah B. **137** 361
JASPER Jaspers
Ann **289 83** 81 284 286
288 289 294 **91** 308
Edward **65** 47
Elizabeth 284 288 **81** 250
82 225 **83** 284 286 288
88 383 384 **90** 70 71 **91**
307-310 **106** 310
John **54** 325
Lancelot **90** 71 **91** 308
Lois **90** 71
Margaret **54** 325
Marjory **125** 107
Mary (Vosa) **88** 338
Nancy (Crafford) **125** 218
Rose **83** 293 **90** 71 **91** 308
Samuel **88** 338 **125** 218
William **114** 191
JASPEY Nancy **125** 99

JASTRAM John **57** 142
Money **57** 142
JAUDON Daniel **51** 241
Francois **51** 241
Peter **51** 241
JAUNCEY Jauncye
James **107** 168
Thomas **143** 30 31
William **107** 168
JAURDIN
Abigail **83** 22 24
JAVES William **65** 236
JAVIS John **55** 322
Rebecca **55** 322
JAWNING Robert **70** 56
JAXION Abigail **121** 262
JAY Jaye
—— **53** 464 **107** 234
— Capt. **82** 98
— Dr. **76** 157
Agnes **86** 425
Anna **83** 80 488
Anna Marie **125** 238
Anne **83** 81 **86** 425
Annes **83** 72
Benjamin **120** 9
Beulah E. **84** 189 **119** 149
Bridget **83** 72 81 294
Cassius Milton **84** 354
85 242 **118** 248
Charles **62** 129
Daniel **83** 73 81 294
Delancey Kane (Mrs.)
88 77
Edmund **86** 431 **88** 146
Edward **86** 425
Edward G. (Mrs.) **84** 106
189 **119** 149
Elizabeth **52** 253 **83** 72 80
81 286 288 289 294
Elizabeth Sarah (Morgan)
88 77
Etta **89** 105
Frances **83** 72 294
Francis **83** 293
G. B. **77** 308
Henrietta Braisted
(Lawrence) **94** 83
Henrietta Florence **94** 83
Henry **57** 317 **83** 72 73 81
294 **86** 425
Jane **83** 81
Jeremiah **83** 81
Jeremy **83** 72 73 81 294
John **51** 158 **52** 388 **53** 372
54 359 **56** 329 **79** 166
83 73 81 294 **84** 241 **86**
425 **97** 58 **98** 121 **117** 3
12 **121** 247 **131** 42 **142**
144
John Hand **115** 118
Jonathan **83** 72 81 294
Joseph **83** 72 81 294
Joseph W. **115** 114 118
Josephine Margelia
Smith **94** 83
Launcelot **83** 72 80 81
284 286 288 293
Lois **115** 114
Lydia **83** 81 294
Maria **83** 72 81 294

JAY *cont'd*
Maria Caroline (Graves)
  94 83
Mary **83** 72 81 294
Mary (Swazey) **94** 83
Mary Ann **115** 118
Mary Serene (Donaldson)
  94 83
Mary Vestal **118** 248
Nathaniel **83** 72 81 294
Oscar **115** 118
Peter Augustus **84** 241
Rachel **83** 81 294
Rose **83** 72 73 81 293 294
Ruth **83** 81 294
Samuel **83** 81 294
Sarah **107** 234
Sarah (Wheeler) **107** 234
Silence **115** 114 118
Susan **83** 81 294
Thomas Henry **94** 83
William **80** 437 **83** 72 73
  80 81 278 293 294 **86**
  425 **89** 105 **97** 297 **118**
  248
William (Mrs.) **83** 81
William Henry Enoch
  92 146 **93** 277 **94** 83 143
William Thomas **94** 83
JAYES Robert **64** 343
Jayqua *see* Jaqua
JAZBERING
Paul **54** 347
Jeaffreson *see* Jefferson
JEAN Jeane
— Capt. de **64** 287
John **81** 322
Teresia de **64** 287
JEANBLANC Abel
Ferdinand (Mrs.) **84**
  465 **85** 195
JEANES Jeans
Henry S. **96** 196
Jacob **73** 274
Jenkinson **117** 15
Joseph Yerkes **94** 138
Lenette Ellison (Ford)
  94 138
Mary **73** 139 **123** 251
Susanna **73** 146
JEANETTE
Matilda R. **95** 285
JEANSACK —— **64** 287
Jeanverin *see* Janvrin
JEBBINGS —— **75** 294
JEDKINS
Leonard **105** 207
Nathaniel **102** 12
Jefferds *see* Jeffords
Jefes *see* Jefts
JEFF — Mr. **71** 134
JEFFAS Chester **147** 258
JEFFCOAT Q. P. **117** 291
Jefferies *see* Jeffries
JEFFERS *see also* Jeffords
— Capt. **84** 66
Aaron **55** 140
Annie Robinson (Tuttle)
  136 320
Betsey (Drew) **133** 307
Caroline B. **93** 216

JEFFERS *cont'd*
Charity **83** 475
Charles D. **130** 51
Elizabeth Catherine **112**
  229 230
George **140** 327
Hannah **62** 289
Hepzibah **100** 297
Jeffrey **63** 53
John **65** 147
John Robinson **136** 320
John Rufus **93** 216
Jos. **63** 55
Nancy **125** 178
Rebecca **63** 56
Robinson **136** 320
Samuel **133** 308
Susan E. (Brott) **130** 51
William **61** 269
William Hamilton
  136 320
JEFFERSON Jeaffreson
  Jepherson Jeptherson
Abigail Baldwin **92** 24 25
Alice (Twigden) **94** 325
Amos **59** 194
Amy Ann **82** 364
Benjamin **128** 135
Betsey (Clfflin) **110** 322
Christopher **140** 108
Cyra **145** 79
David **91** 326
Elizabeth **82** 278 **92** 24 25
Field **104** 323
George **51** 21 153
Hannah **68** 121
Ichabod **110** 322
James **114** 189
Jane **93** 326
John **52** 249 **143** 257
Joseph **55** 126 **78** 120 439
  82 364
L. C. (Mrs.) **141** 244
Martha **75** lxxxv **77** 299
Pablo Delano **109** 286
Patty (Pease) **145** 79
Raphe **94** 325
Rebecca **88** 20
Robert **62** 320 **63** 244 345
  92 24 25
Samuel **98** 272
Sarah **61** 346
Susanna **82** 364
Susanna (Burt) **110** 322
Thankful **134** 62
Thomas **51** 19-25 104 143
  153-158 323-328 426 509
  52 273 387 388 **53** 224
  54 123 237 **55** 125 272-
  276 381-384 **56** 54-56
  149-152 **57** 122 **60** 306
  61 221 **64** 182 266 361
  65 83 204 **70** 307 **72** 7
  75 lxiv lxxxv **77** 271 299
  79 106 82 278 **83** 132
  84 389 **88** 397 **93** 326
  374 **95** 399 **97** 92 101 **99**
  258 **101** 195 109 219
  112 52 **117** 132 133 **118**
  313 **129** 137 **130** 202
  203 **135** 109 114 118

JEFFERSON *cont'd*
  136 67 87 **137** 227 **144**
  56 168
Willard **110** 322
William **73** 276
Je^ffery *see* Jeffrey
Jefferye *see* Jeffrey
Jefferyes *see* Jeffrey
Jefferys *see* Jeffrey
Jeffes *see* Jefts
JEFFORDS Jeffard Jeffares
  Jefferd Jefferds Jefford -
  see also Jeffers
—— **58** 101
— Mr. **68** 197
Abigail **75** 121
Angelyn **96** 159 **105** 125
Anna **76** 104 107 114 182
  188 189 258 **93** 247 248
B. F. **91** 326
Bartholomew **55** 333
  75 112
Chloe **66** 241
Eleanor **63** 175
Eleanor (McCormach)
  108 124
Elizabeth **75** 115 314
George **75** 106 **76** 114 250
  93 247
Hannah **75** 311 314 **76**
  103 105 179 180 185 195
  250 251 254 **93** 103 247
Hannah Ann **93** 247
Isabel **96** 176 180
James **63** 175 **108** 124
John **102** 159
Joseph C. **81** 238
Joseph Crosby **82** 236
Mary **75** 119 **76** 254
Nathaniel **76** 105 111
Olive **76** 111 185 196
Ralph **76** 250 **93** 247
Rhoda **76** 188 **93** 247
Sally (Walker) **108** 190
Samuel **75** 42 43 56 57
  105-107 112 115 118-121
  311 314 **76** 103 105 179
  180 190 195 251 **87** 207
  90 400 **93** 247 248
Samuel M. **93** 247 248
Samuel McClure **76** 104
  250 251 254
Sarah **59** 366 **75** 105-107
  112 115 118 120 121 **76**
  180 189 193 195 **93** 247
Sarah Dobson (Fiske)
  94 138 **120** 232
Sarah E. **93** 248
Simon **75** 107 **76** 104 107
  114 182 188 189 250 258
  93 247 248
Susanna **75** 120
Vincent **88** 333
Walter Morrison **94** 138
  120 232
William **75** 107 311 **76**
  111 185 196 **87** 206 **108**
  190 **134** 222

JEFFREY Geoffrey
  Geofrey Jaffray Jaffrey
  Jeffres Jeffery Jefferye
  Jefferyes Jefferys
  Jeffress
—— **51** 418 **67** 249
— Mr. **51** 288 **61** 394
— Mrs. **127** 13
— Widow **127** 9
____ (Amory) **140** 32
____ (Wilks) (Haley)
  140 158
Abel **53** 23
Abigail **79** 71
Agnes **85** 218
Alice (Rogers) **85** 217
Angelina (Robinson)
  85 217
Ann (Worth) **85** 217
Ann Geyer (Amory)
  120 84
Archie Ransom **125** 163
Arminda Wood **123** 231
Arthur **106** 265
B. Joy **60** 226
Barbary **140** 172
Bartholomew **57** 316
Benjamin **71** 222 **84** 152
  108 189
Benjamin Berry **73** 152
Betsoy **108** 69
Betty (Emmons) **108** 189
C. P. Beauchamp **125** 171
Catherine (Coulter)
  106 228
Celia Celista (Harris)
  85 218
Charles **126** 255 **128** 18
Charles Ellsworth **96** 180
Charlotte Ross **104** 310
Clarence **115** 230
Clemence D'Espaigne
  102 231
Constant **64** 262
Cyprian **125** 92 94
David **51** 64 65 **53** 23 **67**
  211 313 **69** 362 **84** 252
  256 379 **85** 122 128 **87**
  398 **102** 231 **104** 242
  107 44 **119** 20 **140** 139
  165
Deborah **84** 252
Deborah (Lyde) **140** 165
Dorothy **53** 23 **69** 102
Ebenzer **108** 189
Edmund **107** 200
Edward **91** 326
Eleanor **107** 275 **108** 59 60
Elizabeth **53** 23 **81** 167 **108**
  80 **122** 10 14 16 **126** 22
  255 **128** 18
Elizabeth (Allen) **85** 217
Elizabeth A **96** 385
Ernest Irving **92** 363
Eusebe Soutiere dit la
  115 230
Florence **85** 218
Frances **108** 60
Francis **51** 145 **85** 217
  128 253 **129** 42
George **51** 44 **53** 188 292

JEFFREY *cont'd*
  293 **55** 187 **56** 189 **61**
  365 **69** 361 362 **79** 71 **84**
  262 **87** 398 **88** 255 **107**
  313 **127** 115
Giles **65** 355
Gregory **71** 124
Hannah (Winslow)
  84 256
Henry **103** 187
Henry Thomas **106** 228
Hester **53** 23
I. **91** 326
Isabel **96** 180 **108** 59
Isabella **96** 180
James **63** 351 **85** 217 **94**
  354 **107** 275 **108** 59 60
  114 186 **144** 323
James Freeman **95** 401
Jane **76** lxxiii **109** 145
Jeremiah **108** 59
Jerre A. **91** 200
Jesse **85** 217
Joan **51** 186 **52** 47 **55** 99
  100 **67** 345 347 **85** 397
  137 296
Joanna **65** 355
John **51** 186 **52** 47 **53** 72
  56 339 **57** 280 **71** 233
  78 221 **84** 259 **85** 132
  217 **102** 231 **114** 186
  120 84 **121** 247 **122** 10
  129 103 **140** 32 **143** 48
John Amory **102** 231
John Temple Lloyd **68**
  384 **69** xxxii **71** xxiii
Jonathan **108** 60 **127** 11
Joseph **53** 23 **58** 142 **108**
  59 **127** 8 13 **128** 218
Joseph A. **75** 316
Joseph Andrew **76** xxi
  79 81 **80** 231 **81** 62 **82**
  54 **83** 8 **84** 69 **85** 29 108
  203 217 **86** 59 **87** 39 **88**
  6 **89** 9 90 103 **91** 6 **92**
  29 **93** 47 **94** 19 **95** 89 **96**
  58 **97** 147 **98** 90 **99** 70
  101 278 **102** 196 **103** 20
  240 **104** 212 **105** 248
  106 181 **108** 313 **109**
  107 **110** 184 **111** 59 **114**
  114
Joseph Walter **85** 218
Josephine Ann **92** 363
Judith Webb **126** 156
Katharine **51** 419
Lucretia J. **128** 267
Mabel Florence **106** 228
Malcolm Douglas **85** 218
Margaret **131** 100
Mary **55** 99 **71** 61 **82** 291
  301 **85** 227 **127** 11 **131**
  127
Mary (Edwards) **100** 296
Minnie **85** 218
Nancy (Bishop) **108** 189
Nelley **108** 59
Nellie Estelle (Brandt) 363
  92 363
Nicholas **55** 99 **125** 173
  174

JEFFREY *cont'd*
  Olive **107** 200 **108** 59
  Oliver W. **125** 173
  Patrick **140** 158
  Phebe (Crocker) **126** 66
  R. B. **125** 174
  Reuben **56** 24 **126** 255
  Richard **114** 318
  Robert **96** 252 **101** 10 **131**
    16 127
  Robert Hutchins **85** 218
  Sarah **51** 288 **53** 23 **81** 122
    126 **102** 231 **123** 261
    140 139
  Sarah (Bishop) **122** 10
  Sarah (Goold) **143** 48
  Sarah M. (Bush) **125** 173
    174
  Stephen **55** 99 100
  Susan **114** 318
  Susan P. **78** 190
  Susanna **108** 59 188
  Thomas **64** 286 **73** lxiv
    81 122 126 **96** 381
  Walter Lloyd **99** 88 90
  William **51** 400 419 **52** 67
    73 lix 226 **82** 291 301 **85**
    217 **87** 265 **89** 280 **96**
    180 380 **107** 44 **120** 252
    129 35 36 **129** 42 **134**
    288
  William Augustus **67**
    xxx xxxiv **90** 127 **102**
    219 231 **103** 125
  William H. **64** 69
JEFFRIES Jeffereys Jefferis
—— **100** 218 223
— Capt. **113** 219
  Aaron **148** 18 21
  Anna Lloyd (Greene)
    102 231
  Anne Geyer (Armory)
    102 231
  Charity **83** 475
  Clemence (Eustis)
    102 231
  David **100** 221
  Desire **148** 21
  Elizabeth **108** 80 **148** 21
  Elizabeth (Usher) **100** 221
    102 231
  Giles **100** 296
  Hannah (Hunt) **102** 231
  John **136** 108
  Joseph **148** 21
  Joseph Andrew **100** 127
    113 130
  Katharine (Ayer) **102** 231
  Martha **114** 186
  Mary **85** 227 **148** 21
  Mary (Blackleach) **148** 14
    15 17 18 21
  Sarah **123** 261
  Sarah (Jaffrey) **102** 231
  Thomas **62** 290
  William **62** 328
Jeffs *see* Jefts
Jeffts *see* Jefts
JEFFUS Alexander McGee
  133 72
  Benjamin **133** 72

JEFFUS *cont'd*
Betsey (Nickilson) **133** 72
Dorecie **133** 72
James **133** 72
John **133** 72
Lamar **133** 72
Lucinda Sernia Roach
    (Pittman) **133** 72
Mary **133** 72
Matthew **133** 72
Samuel R. **133** 72
Sara Nevada **133** 72
JEFTS Jefes Jeffes Jeffs Jeffts
Abbie / Abby Susan **68**
    xxxiii **77** xxxvii ci **109**
    241
Agnes **82** 446 451
Ann **82** 451
Anne (Payson) **107** 98
Benjamin **54** 395 **77** ci
David **77** ci
Elizabeth **100** 301
Emily Susan **77** ci
Hannah **51** 308 **59** 245
Hannah (Births) **136** 43 44
Henry **51** 308 **54** 395 **59**
    245 **136** 43 45
James **107** 98
John **63** 289 **78** 410
Luman Thompson **77** ci
    109 241
Lydia **63** 289
Mary **54** 395 **59** 245
    126 204
Richard **82** 446 451
S. **136** 136
Sarah **107** 98
Thomas **54** 395 **114** 181
JEGGELL Agnes **52** 243
Alice **52** 243
Ambrose **52** 243
Daniel **52** 243 244 247
Elizabeth **52** 244
Francis **52** 243
Joan **52** 243
John **52** 243
Robert **52** 243
Susan **52** 243
Thomas **52** 243
Tobey **52** 243
William **52** 243 244
JEGGON Dorothy **105** 21
JEGOR John **54** 346
Jekill *see* Jekyll
JEKOON
Timothee **143** 262
JEKYLL Jekill Jekyl
—— **140** 176 178
John **57** 280 388
Nicholas **73** 27
Thomas **60** 34
Jeleson *see* Jellison
Jelff *see* Jelleff
Jelison *see* Jellison
JELKS Vivian Freddie
    104 144
JELLEFF Jeliffe
Frank Ronaldson **101**
    121 **116** 144
George **147** 32 34
Henrie **53** 432 467

JELLEFF *cont'd*
James **109** 364
Lydia (Blachley) **109** 264
Maria **109** 264
Ruth R. **122** 289
Thomas **122** 289
Jellerson *see* Jellison
Jelleson *see* Jellison
Jelliffe *see* Jelleff
JELLIKER — Miss **94** 42
JELLIMAN Martha **83** 255
    90 212
JELLISON Jelcson Jelison
    Jellerson Jelleson
—— **82** 86
Abel **90** 235 **91** 115 116
Abel Hersey **91** 116
Abial **97** 234
Abigail **55** 316 **74** 224 **82**
    95 205 210 211 316 **83**
    12 **90** 243 **91** 116 **117**
    227
Abigail (Carpenter)
    90 232 253
Abigail (Cook) **91** 119
Abigail (Hill) **90** 254 **91**
    118 **96** 248
Abigail (Lord) **90** 331
Abijah **90** 254 **91** 116
    96 248
Abram **91** 31
Agnes **90** 243
Alexander **55** 312 **74** 215
    82 84 320 322 324 510
    91 115 **119** 67
Alice **55** 314 **83** 9
Alice (Abbot) **83** 9
Alice (Kimbal) **119** 143
Anna **90** 335
Anna M. **123** 150
Asa **97** 18
Benjamin **90** 243
Benjamin B. **117** 139 141
Betsey **90** 331 **91** 21 25 115
    97 16 17
Betsey (Wadlin) **90** 252
Bridget **82** 83
Cadelia F. **123** 150
Caleb **91** 115 116
Caleb H. **91** 121
Charity **82** 208 **91** 116
Charles Adams **82** 320
    324
Charlotte **119** 226
Clara **83** 432 **84** 18
Cordelia F. **121** 71 73
    123 235
David **90** 232 243 252
    96 146
David W. **91** 26 32
David Washington
    90 243
Deborah **90** 243
Deborah (Preble) **115** 215
Diamond Cleaves **90** 243
Dimon C. **97** 223
Eleanor **116** 226
Eleanor (Junkins) **112**
    103 **115** 58
Elizabeth **55** 316 **66** 110 **82**
    84 317 **83** 12 **91** 116 **119**

JELLISON *cont'd*
    278 283 284 **123** 152
Elizabeth (Wadlen)
    91 115
Esther **90** 227 245 **91** 116
    112 102
Eunice **82** 324
Eunice (Smith) **90** 334
    91 23
Eveline **117** 223
George **82** 320 **91** 33 115
    116 **97** 232
George W. **90** 334
Hannah **74** 257 **91** 116
Hannah (Knight) **91** 26 32
Hezekiah **55** 314 **82** 83
    83 9
Huldah **116** 297
Ichabod **111** 92 **112** 103
    115 58 214
Isaiah **90** 243 328 **96** 344
Ivory **90** 334 **91** 23
James **82** 320 **90** 252 **91**
    115 119 123 **115** 220
Jane **59** 37 **82** 84 205
Jane (Roberts) **97** 234
Jedediah **82** 316
Job **66** 110 **112** 102 **114** 291
Joel **112** 103 **115** 223 225
John **82** 83 **91** 116 **119**
    144 145 **132** 271 **143** 18
Joseph **55** 316 **74** 257 **82**
    83 84 86 96 205 211 216
    314 317 319 **83** 12 **96**
    248 **115** 215
Joseph (Mrs.) **82** 211
Joseph L. **97** 17
Josephus **119** 143
Kate **91** 118
Loraine **118** 320
Lorenzo **91** 116
Lucinda **91** 116
Lucy **74** 250
Lydia **55** 314 **82** 211 **83** 10
    95 195
Lydia (Hutchins) **132** 271
Lydia A. (Libby) **91** 121
Mahala (Straw) **91** 33
    97 232
Margaret **55** 312 **74** 215
    82 322 510
Maria **119** 61
Marion L. **92** 332
Martha **76** 111 260 **118** 320
    123 233
Mary **82** 210 **91** 116 **95** 338
Mary (Brock) **90** 328
    96 344
Maum **90** 253
Mehitable **90** 282 **96** 248
    97 265
Mercy F. (Shaw) **119** 144
    145
Miriam **82** 84
Molly **55** 316 **83** 13
Moses **91** 115 116
Nahum **91** 115
Nancy **91** 33 **95** 88 190
    96 337
Nancy (Hodsdon) **90** 332
    91 22

JELLISON *cont'd*
  Nathan **90** 243 331
  Nathaniel **112** 102 **114** 290
  Naum **90** 232
  Nicholas **82** 83
  Olive **55** 316 **83** 12 **91** 115
    116 221
  Oliver **90** 243
  Patience **82** 211
  Peggy **96** 247
  Perkins **97** 225
  Philena **82** 207
  Polly **90** 237 243 **91** 116
  Polly (Lord) **90** 232 252
    96 146
  Rebecca **90** 233 236
  Rebecca (Peas) **90** 334
  Rebecca (Skillins) **96** 248
  Roseman (Abbot) **91** 31
  Sally **63** 177 **74** 257 259
    90 243 **96** 248
  Sally (Allen) **119** 67
  Samuel **74** 249 **82** 94
    112 102
  Samuel L. **90** 332 **91** 22
  Samuel Lord **90** 243
  Sarah **55** 313 **74** 249 250
    256 **82** 83 84 86 89 96
    314 511 **90** 233 235 **91**
    33 116 **96** 144 338 **97**
    223
  Sarah (Weymouth)
    97 223
  Sarah Jane (Harrigan)
    95 377
  Simon **90** 243
  Sophia (Hill) **96** 248
  Stephen **97** 17
  Susanna (Kinket) **112** 102
    114 291
  Tabitha **112** 102
  Tabitha (Staples) **117** 139
    141
  Thankful **111** 92
  Theda Ann **119** 279
  Thomas **74** 224 250 257
    82 84 94 95 205 207 210
    217 320 324 **96** 248
  Willard Rouse **112** 88
  William **76** 111
JELLOWS
  Joseph S. **131** 95
JELLS — Capt. **69** 228
JELLY Hugh **61** 351
  Marianna M. **79** 15
  William H. **64** 101
JELSON —— **127** 139
  Stephen **127** 224
JEM Richard **94** 340
JEMERSON Sally **90** 89
JEMMAT Ann **52** 134
  John **52** 134
  Nathaniel **52** 134
Jenckes *see* Jenks
Jencks *see* Jenks
Jenekes *see* Jenks
Jenekins *see* Jenkins
JENENS James **92** 52
Jener *see* Jenner
JENERY Sally **76** 268
  Simeon **62** 371

Jeneson *see* Jennison
JENIFER
  — Maj. **53** 304
  Daniel **73** 265
Jenison *see* Jennison
JENKINS Jenekins Jenkin
  —— **52** 98 **61** 374 **70** 146
    92 248 251 343 348 349
    99 126 127 **100** 187 **107**
    210 **118** 211 **120** 90 119
    121 214 **145** 46 49 162
  — Capt. **85** 20 **142** 145
  — Lieut. **62** 93
  — M. **84** 252
  — Mr. **65** 361 368 **80** 61
    83 306
  — Mrs. **52** 230 **53** 63
    101 248
  —— (Crowel) **108** 262
  Aaron **104** 117 **118** 75
  Abbie (Norris) **92** 203
  Abby P. **69** 315
  Abiah (Allen) **129** 339
  Abigail **51** 196 299 **52** 233
    58 61 **66** 269 271 273
    315 **76** 57 **92** 189 247
    116 32
  Abigail (Brown) **87** 111
  Abigail (Ingerson) **97** 85
  Abigail (Merrill) **129** 164
  Abigail (Perry) **116** 32
  Abigail (Whiston)
    112 195
  Abigail A. **69** 181
  Abner **120** 247 **134** 60
  Adah A. (Manning)
    130 53
  Agnes **76** 57 65 71 72
  Alice **76** 55 58 61 63 64 72
  Alice Abby **92** 203
  Alise **97** 144
  Ally **73** 228
  Alma Campbell **69** 315
  Alvin **120** 119
  Alzina E. **90** 116
  Amelia **126** 64
  Amelia Stiles **68** lxix
  Andrew Rayner **92** 348
  Angelina S. **88** 95
  Ann **73** 219 226 276 **76** 61
    71 **121** 268 **140** 158 **148**
    82
  Ann (Wells) **126** 206
  Ann Sarah **73** 278
  Anna **66** 270 320 **76** 63 66
    68 75 **107** 210 **119** 250
    121 268 **126** 257
  Anna Foote **68** lxx
  Anna M. **68** 94
  Anne **61** 256 **67** 181 **76** 66
  Apphia **98** 311 312
  Archibald **73** 276
  Arthur **82** 285 291
  Arvilla (Bray) **96** 73
  Asa **66** 319
  Augustine Littlefield
    95 38
  Aurelia **142** 33
  Austin **63** 22
  Austin Dickinson **68** lxx
  Bailey **61** 58 175 288-290

JENKINS *cont'd*
  Barbara **76** 58 59
  Barnabas E. **100** 187
  Barzillai **100** 187
  Bathsheba **135** 40
  Benjamin **61** 360 **66** 272
    273 317-321 **82** 43 **83** 33
    100 133 **104** 117 **117**
    189 **125** 95 **129** 61
  Benjamin Gilbert **96** 73
  Bethiah **120** 247
  Betsey **66** 320 **69** lxix **91**
    290 **92** 94 **114** 184 **127**
    224
  Betsey (Russell) **125** 218
  Betsey P. **84** 346
  Braley **103** 93
  C. W. **130** 49 50
  Caddie D. **107** 133
  Calvin **92** 94
  Caroline **92** 252
  Caroline A. **75** 207
  Caroline Mary **88** 394
  Carrie B. **130** 54
  Cassie L. **130** 53
  Catherine **66** 271 **73** 45
    76 67 **142** 33
  Cecille **76** 66
  Charity **130** 49 50
  Charles **68** lxix **69** 319 **100**
    187 **129** 51
  Charles Albert **87** 343
  Charles Coffin **92** 344
  Charles Edward **72** 270
  Charles Horace (Mrs.)
    80 102 208
  Charles M. (Mrs.) **108** 314
  Charles S. **129** 52
  Charles Trinder **96** 73
  Charles Weston **74** lxiv
    93 180
  Charlotte **87** 343 **113** 178
    114 138
  Chloris Ann **82** 278
  Clara **74** lxvii
  Clara Elizabeth (Upton)
    93 179
  Colmore **73** 277
  Content **72** 257 **73** 45
  Content C. **72** 258
  Cornelia **111** 125
  David **148** 82
  Delphine (Fielding)
    93 180
  Desire **148** 362
  Dorothy **96** 73 **123** 130
  Drusilla **73** 265
  E. **129** 52
  Ebenezer **92** 128 129 131
    248 252 343 348 349 **93**
    321 **94** 377 **113** 167 **120**
    119 **121** 138 **133** 295
  Ebenezer Curtis **92** 131
  Edith **98** 146
  Edson A. **100** 87
  Edward **57** 319 **66** 273 **72**
    264 272 **75** 218 **92** 247
    129 164 **133** 189
  Edward Cobb **69** 181
  Edward Henry **126** 141
  Eleanor **73** 228 **103** 225

JENKINS *cont'd*
Eleazer **72** 103
Electa **130** 51
Eli **120** 247 **126** 206
Eliab **66** 320
Elijah **72** 256 264 270 **104** 117
Elisha **108** 262
Eliza **72** 103 **138** 208
Eliza (Banford) **110** 121
Eliza Cody **80** 97
Eliza E. **70** 279 328 334
Eliza J. **129** 51
Eliza Jane **87** 343
Eliza Reed **92** 129
Elizabeth **51** 196 197 299 **52** 371 **56** 78 **57** 200 **63** 253 **65** 132 **66** 269 271 272 316 318-321 **67** 12 13 **68** 167 169 244 **69** 73 182 **72** 255 264 **73** 274 **82** 37 282 288 291 **92** 94 **99** 25 27 117 118 120 **100** 28 298 **101** 248 312 **114** 9 **128** 247
Elizabeth (Atkins) **111** 30 **124** 54
Elizabeth (Eldredge) **125** 130
Elizabeth (Manchester) **102** 12
Elizabeth (Nichols) **129** 164 **135** 40
Elizabeth (Robinson) **93** 180
Elizabeth (Upton) **93** 179
Elizabeth (White) **112** 195
Elizabeth S. **108** 134
Ellen **115** 124
Ellis **120** 119
Elsie **65** 351
Emeline **70** 279
Emeline Baker **92** 248
Emery **126** 257
Emily **78** 397 **92** 94 252
Emily (Howard) **90** 45
Emily Hart **103** 67
Enoch **66** 316
Estelle (Hannum) **91** 112
Estelle E. **129** 51
Esther **57** 201
Etta **82** 438
Eunice **66** 321 **92** 128 131 252 **93** 321 **126** 208
Eunice (Hopkins) **103** 93
Evan **93** 384 **110** 121
Experience **93** 375
Ezekiel **63** 249 253 257 **66** 268 269 271 273 319
Ezra **66** 273 319
Fanny **92** 94
Francis **73** 139
Frank **130** 50
Frank (Mrs.) **103** 119
Franklin Dow **69** 267
Fred S. **129** 52
Freeman Hopkins **103** 93
George **73** 273 **78** 314 **99** 120 **138** 30
George A. **87** 334
George Alfred **110** 121

JENKINS *cont'd*
George B. **129** 51
George H. **69** 181
George Henry **82** 274
George J. **112** 231
George Lindley **69** 181
George W. **123** 128 **130** 53 54
George Walker **88** 394
George Walker (Mrs.) **78** 205 **88** 394 **89** 80 136
Georgianna **81** 381
Gideon Hobby **70** 279
Grace Hartley **88** 394
Hannah **57** 183 **59** 411 **60** 298 **62** 152 202 **66** 269 316 319-321 **68** 167 381 **70** 330 334 335 **72** 26 **86** 395 **113** 20 **114** 321 **120** 247 248 **128** 247 **148** 347
Hannah (Barton) **107** 210
Hannah (Handy) **124** 284 **125** 130 135
Hannah H. **70** 279
Hannah O. (Smith) **100** 87
Hannah S. **72** 272
Harriet **57** 200 **80** 207
Harriet (Creech) **126** 64
Harriet C. **90** 115
Harriet H. **107** 210
Harry H. **87** 343
Harry Lawrence (Mrs.) **87** 174
Hartwell **70** 279
Hartwell Albert **70** 330 335
Helen **78** 205 **96** 300 **100** 168
Helen **96** 300 **100** 168
Helen (Hartley) **88** 394
Helen Elizabeth **93** 180
Helen Hartley **77** 323 **88** 394
Henry **56** 111 **69** 181 **70** 279 **91** 326 **100** 28 **101** 271
Henry Alonzo **70** 330
Henry S. **130** 51
Hepzibah **66** 272 273
Hervey Hatch **61** 290
Heta Blish **116** 32
Hodiah (Hinckley) **103** 93
Howard Cary **70** 279
Ida Powell **83** 514
Isaac **69** 73 **73** 148 **88** 282 **125** 218
J. G. **110** 251
Jabez **68** 167 169 244 246 248 **69** 73 81 181 182 315 **114** 9
Jackin **73** 144
James **79** 54 **92** 94 **93** 180 **129** 153 156 166 253 **133** 137 295
James G. **72** 258
James Green **95** 38
James Samuel **82** 278
Jane **100** 296
Jean **101** 271
Jedediah **55** 374 **83** 15

JENKINS *cont'd*
Jemima **66** 271 316 **72** 258 **73** 51
Jennie **69** 319
Jeremiah **127** 225
Jeremiah Fones **100** 31
Joanna **82** 274 **98** 311 312 **100** 304 **124** 284 **125** 130
Job **128** 256
Joel **57** 201 **61** 253 **66** 268-273 315-321 **67** 89 **93** 397 **100** 63 **117** 319 **129** 51 **130** 53 **143** 124
Johannah **98** 311 312
John **54** 93 **61** 199 **62** 251 **64** 26 **66** 67 271 316 317 319 320 **67** 181 **68** 108 109 **69** 358 **73** 232 **74** lxvi **78** 409 **80** 289 290 359 **82** 43 **91** 326 **93** 179 180 **97** 319 **99** 27 118 **100** 28 29 31 133 135 138 187 238 298 **104** 117 **108** 181 **112** 191 194- 196 199 260 **116** 189 **123** 130 **127** 226 306 **128** 244 247 249 **129** 31 37 339 **140** 158 **141** 351
John (Mrs.) **85** 121
John Albert **69** 181 315
John Francis **93** 180
John Holland **113** 80
John Holmes **113** 80
John Jay **103** 119
John L. **130** 53
John P. **129** 48
John S. **129** 48
John W. **107** 210
Jonathan **66** 318 320 **106** 47 **113** 131 **127** 225
Jonathan Leavitt **67** xxxiv **68** xliii lxix lxx
Joseph **51** 196 299 **52** 230 233 **59** 411 **60** 298 **62** 152 **64** 162 **66** 269 271- 273 317 318 321 **73** 44 139 **82** 43 282 291 **86** 395 **87** 343 **90** 53 **93** 180 **100** 187 **104** 117 **112** 195 257 259 **113** 115 **125** 130
Joseph A. **87** 343
Joseph H. **113** 162 **114** 160 **115** 158 **116** 156 **117** 158 **118** 169 **119** 158 **121** 158
Joseph Herschel **96** 300
Joseph R. **88** 285
Joseph S. **78** 69
Joseph Warren **104** 117
Joshua **63** 177 **72** 256 264 **73** 49-51 125 **75** 9-12 **82** 384 **125** 130 **126** 60 **128** 259
Joshua Brown **72** 270
Josiah **65** 341 **93** 397 **100** 63 **116** 32 **120** 119 **121** 138 **125** 38 **142** 31 33
Judah (White) **120** 119
Judith **51** 162

JENKINS *cont'd*
Julia M. **117** 213
Juliett (Henderson)
  116 212
Katharine Elizabeth
  (Rockwood) **96** 300
L. **60** 161
Laurence Waters **97** 158
Lavinia **68** 246 **69** 176 181
Lavinia J. **68** 248
Lawrence Waters **96** 73
  106 316 **109** 208 **115**
  229
Lawrence Waters (Mrs.)
  93 137 **95** 74 151 **96** 73
Leah (Jones) **113** 131
Lemuel **51** 196 198 299
  52 368 369 371 **53** 104
  66 268-271 273 315-319
  78 23 **124** 54
Leonard **73** 223 269
Leonard Abbot **74** xxiv
  lxvii **93** 83 139 179
Lewis **64** 158 164 261 **67**
  17 **104** 117
Lewis J. **130** 56
Lionel **94** 273
Lois **66** 273 319
Lonie (Hayward) (Burns)
  93 180
Lot **116** 32
Louisa **130** 53
Love **55** 374
Love (Butler) **83** 15
Lucy **66** 318 **103** 93 **106**
  237 **143** 336
Lydia **61** 203 **66** 269 270
  272 273 317 318 320 **70**
  279 **72** 257 **114** 10 **117**
  189 **120** 247 **126** 130
Lydia N. (Robinson)
  88 285
Mabel **92** 94
Mabel Julia (Belcher)
  110 121
MacGregor **68** lxx
Marcy (Berry) (Baker)
  114 80 161
Margaret **63** 249 **66** 270
  271 273 319 **73** 139 **78**
  412
Margaret (Niblo) **129** 51
Margaret (Snelling)
  108 181
Maria **66** 321 **115** 292 **120**
  119 **121** 139
Mariah (Ellis) **120** 119
  121 138
Marshall **51** 196 **52** 233
  369 371
Martha **66** 320 **68** 108 **77**
  xx **91** 188 **94** 222
Martha Ann (Stevens)
  126 206
Martha Neal **66** lxvii
Mary **51** 196 299 **52** 369
  371 **57** 288 391 **60** 128
  61 253 **66** 270-273 317-
  319 **67** 89 **68** 108 109
  169 246 248 **69** 81 141
  181 358 **70** 249 **72** 78

JENKINS *cont'd*
  270 **73** 219 262 **78** 23
  400 **79** 44 **82** 43 291 294
  384 438 **83** 33 **85** 157 **87**
  64 **91** 24 **92** 247 254 344
  93 322 **99** 118 **100** 135
  138 142 143 236 238 240
  101 51 **102** 31 **104** 117
  108 262 **112** 194 195
  199 **120** 119 247 **125** 31
  126 205 **130** 51 **142** 273
Mary (Barnard) **98** 135
Mary (Eles) **120** 119
Mary (Ewer) **93** 179
  112 195
Mary (Harnet) **117** 319
Mary (Hinckley) **120** 119
Mary (Hunt) **126** 257
Mary (Jones) (Lewis)
  143 124
Mary (Noble) **95** 38
Mary (Parker) **112** 194 195
Mary (Pilkinton) **108** 181
Mary (White) (Ellis) **120**
  119 **121** 138 139
Mary A. **119** 224
Mary Ann **69** 267
Mary B. (Murray) **123** 128
  130 53
Mary Dennis (Pierce)
  126 65
Mary E. **87** 111
Mary Eliza **90** 183
Mary Elizabeth **72** 270
Mary Freeman **116** 32
Mary Grace (Owen)
  93 180
Mary P. (Willis) **90** 53
Mary S. **90** 43
Mary Steele **102** 123
Mary Wheeler **92** 104
Massey M. **73** 220
Matilda Golden **77** 141
Matthew **100** 187
Matthias **99** 118
May Louise Rice **72** 79
Mehitable **72** 256 264 **73**
  128 **75** 6 9 **87** 343 **112**
  195 **119** 257
Mehitable (Blish) **117** 189
Mehitable Blish **116** 32
Mehitable Bunker **87** 343
Mercy **51** 299 **66** 269 270
  113 115
Mercy (Howland) **113** 115
Mercy Freeman **58** 59
Mercy (Winslow) (White)
  120 119
Micah **66** 320
Miles **51** 354
Mina Belle **82** 278
Miriam **63** 177 **72** 264
  73 49
Miriam (Bancroft) **97** 71
Molly **66** 320
Moses **68** 169 **69** 71 73 267
  70 306
Moses Cary **69** 267
Moses Noble **95** 38
Nabby **66** 320
Nancy **66** 317 **78** 310

JENKINS *cont'd*
Nancy (Brown) **126** 141
Nancy B. **68** 94
Naomi Kendall **66** 321
Nathan **66** 320 **72** 264
  73 51
Nathaniel **51** 299 **63** 253
  66 269 271 315 316 319
  73 44 **87** 343 **90** 37 **92**
  134 247 252 258 344 **93**
  322 **94** 378 **102** 12 **120**
  119 **127** 7 **140** 158 327
Nelle Morris **117** 158
Nellie **129** 51
Nelson **115** 292
Newell Owen **93** 180
Newell Sill **73** 318 **74** xxiv
  xxxvi lxvi **93** 139 179
  180
Nora Cornelia **74** lxvii
Obadiah **66** 268-270 272
  273 316-318 320 321 **92**
  47 **97** 300 **126** 130 **142**
  273 274 **143** 124
Olive **120** 119
Orville **130** 50
Osmore **81** 381
Palmer **66** 319
Patty **66** 320
Pauline Augusta **82** 274
Peggy **66** 320
Peter **100** 142 143 236
  102 31
Phebe **63** 253 **66** 273 315
  317 320 **72** 264 **73** 50 **74**
  lxvi **82** 285 291 **113** 78
  120 247
Phebe (Gifford) **134** 60
Phena **57** 201
Philip **77** 141 **112** 195
  120 247 **128** 135
Philomene Loretta **80** 208
Polly **66** 319 320 **129** 48
Polly S. **66** 321
Prince **103** 93
Priscilla **73** 136 147
Priscilla (Dorman)
  108 124
Priscilla (Hopkins)
  104 299
Priscilla Ann **73** 278
Prudence **100** 28 29 31 133
  142 33
Prudence (Taylor)
  100 298
Prudie **130** 51
Rachel **61** 58 175 **125** 130
Rachel L. **78** 185
Rachel Woodward **61** 289
Rebecca **61** 253 355 **66**
  272 273 317-320 **81** 329
  82 285 291 **102** 145 **113**
  262 **117** 319 **120** 73
Rebua **120** 247
Reliance (Davis)
  (Lawrence) **125** 130 135
  126 60
Rest (Snow) **125** 130
  134 60
Rhoda E. **72** 272
Richard **60** 128 **64** 26 **65**

JENKINS *cont'd*
32 **75** 221 **78** 183 **100**
218 **108** 181
Robert **58** 64 68 **67** 12 **94**
61 **99** 25 27 117 118 120
100 28 **101** 51 271 **102**
31
Robert Dalton **73** 264
Rollin L. **130** 51
Rowland **92** 94
Ruth **60** 143 **61** 173 **66** 316
67 17 **82** 291 295 **88** 330
112 195
Ruth (Lincoln) **129** 156
166
Ruth D. **96** 179
Rynold **72** 257
S. Lizzie **69** 315 316
Sally **66** 319 **73** 153 **78** 419
92 94
Sally (Child) **88** 282
Sally (Hunting) **126** 65
Sally A. **114** 184
Samuel **53** 266 **61** 355 **66**
272 273 315-317 319-321
82 43 **99** 117 **101** 51
106 23 **112** 195 **114** 184
120 119 **123** 130 **125**
130 **134** 60 **140** 327
Samuel B. **123** 130
Samuel Flint **66** 321
Sarah **51** 299 **53** 266 **55** 310
62 63 64 152 **63** 177 253
66 268-273 315 316 318
320 321 **67** 89 372 **68**
169 244 **69** 71 81 181
267 **72** 264 **73** 50 **78** 443
82 43 398 **87** 112 **96** 79
100 133 135 **104** 117
108 216 **112** 195 **115**
240 **117** 189 **118** 276
120 249 **132** 42 **133** 294
Sarah (Bailey) **119** 251
Sarah (Ellis) **122** 199
Sarah (Gilbert) **143** 124
Sarah Austin **95** 38
Sarah Barnes **66** 321
Sarah Eaton **68** lxx
Sarah F. **87** 343
Sarah Hunt **100** 236
102 31
Sarah Jane **70** 330 335
Sarah M. **66** 321
Sarah Maria **68** lxx **69** 267
Sarah N. **69** 181 315
Satia Jewett (Hyde) **93** 180
Seth **100** 187 **127** 227
Shadrach **104** 299
Sibyl **72** 264 **73** 49-51
129 48
Silas **68** 94 **129** 151 164
Simeon **103** 93
Simon Steven **72** 270
Sophronia L. (Olcott)
130 51
Stephen **66** 316 **68** 167 381
69 73 **70** 279 334 335 **72**
258 **73** 51 **75** 11 **82** 285
291 **104** 117 **125** 95
Stephen H. **70** 330
Stephen Waters **96** 73

JENKINS *cont'd*
Susanna **66** 316 318 319
92 247 **94** 379 **100** 28
238 **104** 117 **120** 247
128 247 **129** 339
Tabitha **103** 166
Temperance **120** 119
Theophilus **66** 269
Thomas **51** 162 **57** 183
318 319 **60** 335 **66** 271
316 **68** 108 **73** 148 **98**
135 **100** 143 **108** 124
116 212 **119** 251 **120**
119 **121** 138 **127** 225
Thomas Bailey **61** 58
Thomas H. **90** 45 **126** 206
Thomas Jefferson **66** 321
Thomas R. **68** 94 **114** 184
Thomas T. **70** 330
Timothy **58** 59 61 **116** 32
Timothy Walker **66** 321
Triffa **73** 262
Turner Hatch **61** 288
Virginia **106** 47
W. E. (Mrs.) **108** 134
W. LeRoy **129** 52
Walter C. **97** 71
Weston **74** lxvi **93** 180
William **51** 196 198 **52** 68
267 **56** 25 184 **59** 299 **61**
39 **62** 248 **64** 325 **65** 351
66 316 321 **69** 73 **72** 264
73 136 270 276 **78** 412
82 37 43 291 294 **83** 33
87 111 **93** 384 100 187
238 **129** 51 **132** 264 **138**
162 208
William Augustus **92** 349
William B. **92** 203
William H. **129** 51
William Henry **69** 267
William Williams **66** 321
William Woodward
61 58
Winifred **73** 218
Zachariah **128** 244 257
129 31 224 339
Zadok **73** 223
Zenas **126** 257
Zephaniah **114** 80 161 321
JENKINSON
Bernard **67** 208
Delilah **96** 75
Edward **51** 298
Hannah **96** 75
John **67** 209
Mary **67** 208 209
Nettie **104** 102
Rebecca **67** 209
Richard **59** 109
Sarah E. **104** 102
Thomas **104** 102
William **83** 444 **96** 75
104 102
JENKS Jencks Jenckes
—— **53** 460 **57** 159 **75** 215
93 116 117 **100** 187 **109**
64 **120** 205
— Capt. **124** 293
— Dr. **57** 50
— Gov. **96** 10 349

JENKS *cont'd*
— Mr. **80** 85
___ (Williams) **140** 262
Abigail **56** 170 **98** 358
100 187 **140** 303
Abigail (Bryant) **137** 331
Abigail (Seymour) **132**
190 191
Addie **73** 214
Adeline **73** 212
Agnes **110** 164 167 245
Albert Alvin **75** xxiii 155
77 xxxv cii civ **78** 202
100 170 **101** 127
Albert Ernest **110** 18
Alice (Bowdler) **110** 246
Alice (Wilson) **110** 248
Alicia **110** 164
Allen Brown **118** 141
Alley Rae **92** 231
Almira **79** 153 168 **81** 328
Alse T. **63** 275
Alvin **77** ciii civ
Alvin Cleveland **100** 170
Alvin Fales **77** ciii **100** 170
Ames **93** 117
Amos **129** 387 **132** 190 **137**
283 **140** 303
Amy (Savage) **132** 190
137 283
Anastasia Alice (Ahern)
109 64 134
Ancilles **73** 303
Ann **95** 349 **110** 165 171
Anna **81** 328
Anne **110** 163-167
Annie Amelia **85** 194
Annie Cleveland **77** civ
Annie Cleveland (Rice)
100 170
Annis **110** 167
Annis Allen (Brown)
118 141
Annis (Pullen) **51** 231
91 397
Anphillis **62** 282
Arthur **110** 10
Beatrix **110** 163
Benjamin **127** 217 **137** 331
Boomer **56** 170
C. P. **94** 124
Calvin **118** 141
Catherine **97** 22
Catherine Way **89** 109
Chad **98** 358
Charles **79** 168
Charles B. **63** 275
Charles Fitch **75** liii
Charles N. **110** 18
Charles W. **56** 43 **79** 162
401
Charles William **62** 69
157 **63** 73
Charlotte **70** 153
Chr. **111** 89
Christopher **146** 347
Clarissa **79** 166
Clarissa P. (Greenleaf)
94 124
Cornelia Hood **90** 116
Cynthia **54** 407

JENKS *cont'd*
Daniel **62** 231 232 **63** 150
69 98 **87** 335 **129** 386
387 **140** 158
Daniel Loring **118** 139-141
David **54** cxlvi **110** 247 248
David K. **76** 46
Deborah **54** cxlvi **111** 109
Delia **132** 191
Dolly (Loring) **118** 139 140
Dorothy **110** 164 167
E. A. **94** 124
E. M. **70** 153
Edith **75** xxii
Edmund **79** 356 **110** 247
Edward **110** 247
Edward M. **70** 153
Edwina Booth **78** 205 **79** 211 **81** 101
Eleanor **108** 153 **110** 88 **122** 168-170
Elezer Alley **94** 124
Elisha M. **79** 166
Eliza **73** 212 **77** ciii
Eliza H. **90** 108
Elizabeth **107** 57 **110** 12 167 248 249 **122** 169
Elizabeth (Berry) **111** 109 **132** 41 **148** 331 332
Elizabeth (Blunt) **110** 248
Elizabeth (Story) **94** 285 **98** 343
Elizabeth Alley **94** 124
Ellen **110** 14
Ellen (Hearne) **110** 250
Elvira Welden **85** 313 320
Emily C. (Jenks) **118** 141
Esther **110** 14
Ethel **92** 231
Ethel Linwood **80** 248
Eunice (Coffin) **100** 187
Fanny **57** 159
Frances **110** 10 163 167
Francis **93** 116 117 **94** 43 **110** 163 170 247 248
Francisca **110** 163 167
Frederick Angier **75** liii
Freelove **80** 182
George **110** 247-249
George F. **73** 212
Grenville Tudor **93** 116
H. F. **53** 253
H. W. **83** 255
Hannah **63** 152
Hannah (Razee) **137** 283
Hannah B. **76** 52
Hannah Howland **77** ciii
Harlan Walker **110** 9 **112** 75
Hawking **98** 358
Helen **110** 87 89 92
Henry **78** 304 **110** 163 166 167
Henry Angier **75** liii **77** 322 **78** 205 **81** 102
Henry Angier (Mrs.) **77** 322 **78** 205
Henry F. **51** 130

JENKS *cont'd*
Henry Fitch **54** vii xxviii xciv cvii **55** vii xx **56** vii xxiv 43 415 **57** xxxi **75** xxxiv lii **81** 102
Herbert **110** 247
Hiram **87** 255
Hugh **110** 163 164 167 247
Huldah **108** 267
Isaac **118** 139 140
Isaac Coffin **100** 187
J. E. **70** 153
J. M. **79** 156
Jane **110** 167
Jeremiah **129** 386
Joan **110** 12 14 164 167 171 249 254 **122** 169
Joan (Hearne) **110** 253
Joanna **96** 10
Johes **110** 92
John **57** 334 **65** 147 **78** 302 **89** 372 **91** 397 **98** 358 **107** 57 **110** 11 13 14 18 81 83 85-92 161-168 245-247 **111** 109 **122** 168-170 **129** 387 **132** 41 **140** 158 **148** 331 332
John Davis **57** 159
John Henry **56** 43 **75** lii **81** 102 **90** 108
Jonas **110** 86 91 161 162 165 166 168 171
Jonathan **54** 407 **137** 283 331 332 **140** 303
Joseph **51** 359 **54** 407 **65** 147 **66** 29 **69** 91 **76** 318 **77** ciii civ **80** 76 **83** 255 **96** 10 **100** 170 **110** 9-20 81 83 85-87 89-92 161-163 165 167 244 247-250 253 254 **122** 168-171 **129** 385 **136** 216 **146** 347
Josephus **110** 12
Joshua **110** 165 168
Josiah **110** 165 166
Josias **110** 171
Julia **132** 191
Julia Ann **89** 225
Julianna **110** 245
Katharine **62** 231
Laura **58** 319
Lavinia Hathaway **75** liii **81** 102
Lucretia W. **70** 153
Lucy **75** 252
Lucy (Whitney) **140** 303
Lucy Maria **132** 191
Lydia **80** 170 **100** 334 **132** 191
Lydia (Chase) **87** 255
Lydia G. **79** 50
Lydia May **96** 160
Marcien **84** 106 189
Marcy **110** 167
Margaret **110** 247 248
Margaret (Lutley) **110** 247
Margery **110** 166 245
Maria B. **76** 52
Marjorie **110** 162
Martha **80** 76 **129** 374

JENKS *cont'd*
133 230
Martha (Brown) **97** 22
Martha Ann **79** 165
Marvin Lee **109** 64
Mary **78** 186 **80** 85 185 **98** 358 **110** 12 **122** 169
Mary (Tervyn) **122** 168
Mary (White) **107** 57
Mary C. **79** 156
Mary E. **77** 180
Mary Edith **86** 336
Mary Elwell **55** lxxviii
Mary Esther (Mann) **90** 44
Mary Gardner **69** xxxv
Mary H. **98** 358
Mary Jane (Fuller) **108** 153
Mary Rand **56** 43 **75** lii **81** 102
Mary Rand (Fitch) **90** 108
Matthew **110** 11 163 166 167
Melvina Frances **92** 192
Mercy **63** 150
Michael **118** 139
Mildred **92** 231
Milla Jenette **118** 141
Minerva **79** 356
Nancy (Bellows) **89** 372
Nancy R. **89** 225 372
Nancy (Richardson) **118** 141
Naomi **58** 319
Nathan **58** 319
Nathaniel **77** ciii **100** 170 **127** 227
Nehemiah **81** 328
Olive A. **84** 101
Oliver **132** 190 191
Otis Dexter **118** 140
Patience **63** 148 149 **80** 185 **91** 267
Peter **98** 358
Peter Gordon **109** 64
Phebe **107** 57
Polly **79** 356
Priscilla **81** 444
Rachel **57** 334 **73** 212
Rachel Story **94** 285 **98** 343
Rebecca **125** 101 **126** 307
Rhoda **80** 171 **110** 10
Richard **110** 161-168 171 245 246 248
Richard Alvin **77** civ **100** 170 101 121
Richard Atherly **110** 248
Robert **110** 163 247
Robert C. (Mrs.) **124** 160
Robert Rice **77** civ **78** 202 **100** 103 170 **101** 121 127
Robert W. **100** 187
Roberta **100** 170
Rowland **110** 245 246
Ruth **55** 170 **87** 263 **118** 139 140
Ruth (Thresher) **100** 170
Sally **91** 397 **98** 358

JENKS *cont'd*
Samuel **63** 247 **73** 212
  100 187 **127** 312 **140**
  158
Samuel H. **56** 25 **100** 187
  140 262
Sarah **57** 159 **87** 321 **90** 51
  107 57 **110** 11 13 83 86
  89 90 **122** 169
Sarah (Baldwin) **126** 233
Sarah (Barton) **107** 57
Sarah (Fulwater) **122** 169
Sarah (Mygatt) **107** 57
Sarah J. **90** 50
Sarah Maria **118** 140
Sarah Peckham **57** 159
Sibyl (Chase) **87** 335
Stephen **77** ciii **100** 170
Sumner Walter **109** 64
Susan **78** 421 **79** 356
Tabitha **74** 192
Theodore **118** 140 141
Theodore Russell **90** 44
Thomas **73** 212 **98** 358 **107**
  57 **110** 163 166 245-248
Thomas Edward **109** 64
Thomas Leighton **54**
  xlvii cxlvi cxlvii
Tudor **68** 342
Wealthy **119** 259
Wilbur Leon **109** 64 134
William **54** 407 **56** 43 **62**
  282 **63** 148 149 **66** 103
  72 107 **75** lii **78** 111 **80**
  182 185 **81** 102 **90** 41
  104 **99** 9 **107** 57 **110** 12
  162-168 245-249 **114**
  259 **140** 158 **145** 205
  211 213 222 224 **146** 347
  148 331
William Francis **92** 231
William P. **98** 343
William Pearson **94** 285
Zelotes **70** 153
JENNER Genner Jennar
  — Mr. **85** 248
Abigail **98** 284
Abriel **73** 221
Aeltye **66** 18
Alice **55** 302 **81** 130
Anna **66** 18
Antje **66** 18
David **85** 454 **116** 110
  143 37 38
Edward **79** 160
Eleanor **143** 38
Elizabeth **55** 302 **67** 311
  136 269 **143** 37 38
Ellen **131** 127
Elsje **66** 18
Henry **51** 376
Jan **66** 18
Jannetye **66** 18
Jochim **66** 18
John **55** 302 **66** 18
Joseph **55** 302
Lambert **66** 18
Maria **66** 18
Mary **55** 302
Rebecca **143** 38
Rebecca (Trerise) **143** 38

JENNER *cont'd*
Robert **83** 71
Samuel **143** 38
Sarah **66** 18 **143** 38
Thomas **53** 84 **55** 302 **57**
  280 388 **67** 72 **81** 130 **91**
  269 **131** 127 **143** 38
William **64** 115 **66** 18
JENNERY Mary **85** 231
JENNESS Jennis Jennys
Abigail **55** 316 **65** 355 **76**
  37 **83** 12
Abigail (Drake) **141** 141
Ann **71** 66
Anna **82** 289 291 **105** 298
Anna St. Clair **83** 181 182
Annetta L. (Besson) **92** 78
Belinda **76** 37
Benjamin W. **68** 37
Benning W. **76** 33
Benning Wentworth
  68 253
Bessie A. **83** 424 432
Betsey **59** 288
C. E. **83** 193
Caroline **69** lxi
Caroline Elizabeth **83** 172
Caroline McC. **84** 29
Charles W. **68** 99
Clara H. **83** 181 182
Clarissa **141** 141
Clarissa (Jenness) **141** 141
Daniel L. **105** 298
Deborah **68** 253
Diantha E. **68** 98 99
Eliza **76** 34
Eliza A. **68** 99
Elizabeth **68** 99
Elizabeth (Goodwin)
  (Shapleigh) **95** 268
Esther **76** 38
Experience **114** 316
Francis **144** 34
Franklin P. **68** 98
George **83** 306
Hannah **65** 354 **68** 98
  69 326
Hannah J. **68** 99
Ira Huckins **68** 99
Isaac **76** 36
Isabel Eleanor **83** 295
James F. **84** 29
Job **65** 355
John **76** 36
John H. **120** 68
John J. **76** 37
John S. **83** 306
John Scribner **67** 237
Jonathan L. **105** 298
Josephine **69** xliii lxi **83**
  182 186
Joses **59** 287
Joshua **68** 99
Judith **76** 36
Lucy **126** 155
Lydia **65** 310 **76** 36
Lydia (Lucas) **132** 163
Mark **56** 409 **65** 355
Mary **65** 355 **67** 278 **68** 98
  89 259
Mary (Dow) **95** 268

JENNESS *cont'd*
Mary (Wedgewood)
  141 141
Mary C. **83** 302
Mary Ann **68** 99
Mary C. **83** 299 302 **88** 341
Mary Elizabeth **68** 99
Mary L. **76** 32
Mehitable **105** 298
Minerva Seavey **92** 78
Myra Jane **68** 253
Nancy Hill **68** 99 **69** 320
  326
Nancy W. **76** 33
Nathaniel **141** 141
Newall B. **105** 298
Olive (Shapleigh) **95** 268
Oliver **92** 78
Paul **65** 214 **75** 9 12
Peter **68** 99 **83** 306 **105** 298
  141 141
Phena **59** 287
Returah **65** 214
Richard **69** lxi **83** 306
  95 268
Ruth **87** 202
Ruth Moore (Badlam)
  (Cook) **141** 141
Sally **76** 29
Sally Natalie **83** 295
Salome (Jackson) (Wyatt)
  (White) **144** 34
Samuel **68** 98 **69** 326 **76** 29
  95 268 **141** 141
Samuel L. **68** 99
Sarah **65** 354 **67** 285 **84** 222
Sarah B. **135** 79
Sarah Louisa (Starkey)
  120 68
Seth **76** 38
Sidney Langdon (Seavey)
  92 78
Simon **95** 268
Stephen **76** 36
Susan **76** 36
Thomas **68** 253 **107** 237
Vera **83** 295
William **59** 288 **65** 354
  68 99
JENNETTE
Catherine **84** 223
JENNEY Jenny
Abbie (Bowers) **86** 341
Abigail **88** 80 **113** 24
Abigail (Spooner)
  115 285
Albert **126** 198
Alice **118** 201
Ann **92** 355
Annie **83** 503
Benjamin **117** 185
Bernard **86** 341 **92** 355
Betsey **78** 31
Caleb **52** 365 **117** 185
Calvin **115** 285
Catherine (Green)
  117 185
Charles Edwin **78** 339 **84**
  298 **90** 286
Charles Francis **69** xxx
  xxxv **77** 161 **78** 216 339

JENNEY *cont'd*
342 343 **84** 298 **89** 101
90 287 **141** 6
Charles Stoddard **86** 341
Chiron **115** 285
Clarence F. R. (Mrs.)
76 161
Cornelius **117** 185
Darah **84** 219
Deborah **115** 274
Deborah (Landers) (Perry)
115 274 **116** 44 **124** 53
Desire **117** 185
Edmund **98** 116
Edwin **90** 287
Edwin Clark **78** 340 **84**
106 189 **90** 286 **91** 57
147
Eleanor (Cole) (Young)
117 185
Elisha **57** 162 **66** 20
Elizabeth **57** 162 **59** 109
117 185
Elizabeth (Goodhue)
86 341
Elizabeth (Handy)
126 198
Elizabeth Bowers (Hedge)
86 340
Elsie **78** 339
Elvira Frances **78** 339
Elvira Frances (Clark)
84 298 **90** 286 287
Esther Gates **115** 285
Eunice (Perry) **116** 44
Experience **114** 316
Frazier **83** 503
Frederick G. **115** 233 235
Genevieve **70** 337
George **117** 301
Gideon **125** 221
Grace (Snow) **86** 341
Hannah **57** 34 38 162
115 284
Hannah (Perry) **115** 285
Hannah Perry **115** 285
Harry **125** 107
Henry **119** 234
Hiram **115** 285
Hix **115** 274 **116** 44 **124** 53
Ignatius **117** 185
Isaac **65** 378 **92** 355 **93** 65
94 42
Isaac Lothrop **93** 65
James Hunter **93** 65
Job **116** 44
John **61** 161 **78** 339 **90** 286
98 121 **115** 233 284 **119**
234 **124** 146 **129** 223
John H. **125** 109
Joseph **125** 222 289
Joseph H. **113** 172
Judith (Spencer)
(Lawrence) **100** 187
Justus **115** 285
Lettice **117** 185
Lora J. (Pattee) **90** 287
Lucretia **125** 222
Lucretia Perry **115** 285
Lucy (Wicker) **115** 285
Luther **127** 198

JENNEY *cont'd*
Lydia (Mendall) **123** 61
Martha (Johnson) **86** 341
Mabelle **78** 340
Mabelle Clark **84** 298
Malcolm **86** 341 **87** 174
Mark **123** 61 **130** 41
Martha (Gilbert) **115** 285
Mary **57** 39 162 **108** 115
110 160 **117** 185
Mary (Bassett) **115** 285
Mary (Mitchell) **117** 185
Mary E. **78** 339 340
Mary Frances (Coney)
86 341
Mary H. **70** 337
Matilda (Severance)
115 285
Mehitable **123** 60 **129** 223
Mildred **78** 340
Milicent **65** 378
Miriam (Parsons) **86** 341
Nathan **120** 111
Nathaniel **117** 185 **125** 186
Noah S. **70** 337
Patience **52** 365 **127** 198
Patience (Hall) **117** 185
Patience (Jenney) **127** 198
Patience (Standish)
117 185
Pemal **117** 185
Polly (Gifford) **134** 64
135 48
Reliance **117** 185
Reuben **134** 64 **135** 48
Richard **61** 257 **125** 92 95
96
Ruth **89** 56 **117** 185
Samuel **57** 38 **108** 115
117 185 **125** 95 127
Sarah **84** 219 **117** 185 **124**
146 **127** 94
Sarah (Bosmore) **90** 287
Sarah (Carey) **90** 287
Sarah (White) **86** 341
Sarah D. **125** 254
Seth Spooner **115** 285
Silence (French) (House)
117 185
Sophia **94** 42
Sophia Ann **93** 65
Sophia Cotton **92** 355
Sophronia (Paige)
115 285
Walter **65** xxi **86** 341
Walter (Mrs.) **86** 340 346
87 178
Walter Hedge **86** 341
Warren **70** 337
Wealthy H. **127** 198
JENNINGS Gennings
Jennins Jennynge
—— **52** 131 **57** 337 **63** 370
69 232 **83** 33 459 **102**
261 **122** 290 **140** 158
— Mr. **57** 294 **83** 33
84 164
— Mrs. **65** 361
___ (Gillett) **101** 283
Aaron **69** 46
Abigail **86** 450 **100** 32

JENNINGS *cont'd*
133 134 **122** 288
Abigail (Gould) **87** 198
Abner **119** 234
Abraham **96** 276
Abraham Gould **87** 198
Absalom **115** 41
Agnes **126** 208
Agnes (Bradford) **83** 457
458 459
Albert E. **68** 198
Albert Wellington
114 241
Alice **83** 33 **87** 174 **114** 241
Alice R. **128** 232
Althea **122** 286
Ambrose **51** 406 407
Andrew **88** 125 **122** 218
Ann **67** 40 **82** 200 **99** 121
122 **113** 271 **126** 256
128 20 **141** 253
Anna **66** 19 **68** 198 **70** 243
Anna B. **61** xxxiv
Anna M. **72** 47
Annah **69** 239
Anne **67** 43
Annie B. **145** 378
Annie (Burr) **73** 317 **74**
xxiv **87** 198 199 **94** 80 86
141 **148** 240
Appollina **69** 238
Ariana (Vanderheyden)
(Frisby) (Bordley) **145**
26 27
Arline **111** 191
Arthur (Mrs.) **117** 158
Asa Kempton **119** 234
Benjamin **65** 374 **69** 239
83 381 **100** 32 133 134
114 316 **140** 158 **145**
352 359
Benjamin Brewster
91 181
Bethiah **100** 136-139 141
Bethiah (Tucker) **100** 299
Betsey **83** 381 **122** 290
140 158
Betsey (Beals) **95** 290
Betsey (Hopkins) **102** 261
Bonella **109** 99
Burrit **69** 238
C. F. (Mrs.) **108** 239
Calvin **104** 216
Captivity **101** 46 283
Caroline (Sherwood)
114 321
Carson Gary **80** 151
Catherine **88** 281
Catherine (Channon)
141 29
Catherine (Hatch) **125** 289
Cecil Franklin (Mrs.)
108 134
Charity **113** 208
Charles **114** 241
Charles O. **122** 286
Charlotte **90** 53 **125** 102
Clarabella H. **117** 220
Constance **57** 199
Curtis Herman (Mrs.)
89 132

JENNINGS *cont'd*
Cynthia **101** 322
Daniel **78** 178 **100** 137
   102 3 **114** 241
David **69** 46 373 **72** 14
   115 119 **145** 352
David F. **111** 191
Deborah **99** 291 **127** 149
Desire **117** 185
Dillea (Laurens) **88** 275
E. **57** 293
Ebenezer **71** 185
Edmund **145** 26 27
Edna E. **121** 180
Edward **112** 181 **115** 56
   131 189
Elias **67** 122
Eliphalet **69** 239 **145** 352
Elise **82** 236
Eliza **79** 157
Elizabeth **53** 302 **70** 35 **100**
   133 **101** 312 **102** 15 **114**
   316
Elizabeth (Burbank)
   (Marsh) **102** 3
Elizabeth (Cousins) **102** 3
Ellen Cloutman **117** 79
Emeline **114** 241
Emma Brewster **78** 203
   97 78 162 383
Ephraim **65** 365 **67** 122
Esbos **114** 192
Esther **67** 117-119 **99** 291
   120 28
Esther Judson (Goodsell)
   87 198 **91** 181 **94** 86 **97**
   383
Eunice **63** 88 **67** 120 **70** 36
   114 316 **136** 136
Experience **67** 117 **114** 316
Faith **122** 288
Fanny M. **122** 286
Frances **136** 80
Francis **83** 381 **93** 384
Francis Mitchell **83** 381
George **62** 324 **65** 27 **67** 40
   43 **83** 381 **115** 45 **122**
   286
Gertrude J. **85** 353
Gladys **80** 151
Hannah **54** 225 **59** 396 **68**
   198 **71** 185 201 **114** 316
   119 234 **129** 41 **145** 74
Hannah (Dickinson)
   (Gillett) **101** 46
Hannah (Newcomb)
   (Sturges) **118** 202 212
Hannah Cornelia **111** 191
Harriet **83** 381 **122** 218
Harry **125** 107
Henrietta **119** 234
Henry **69** 373 **79** 312
   119 234
Herman **119** 234
Hezekiah **69** 378
Hiram D. **114** 241
Horace Newton **65** 383 **67**
   xxxiv
Inez **128** 233
Ira **122** 290
Isaac **77** 33 **81** 491 **82** 200

JENNINGS *cont'd*
   87 198 **114** 316 **120** 188
   127 149
Isabella **88** 278 **145** 38
J. T. **75** lix
Jabez **122** 286
James **116** 76
James Joseph (Mrs.)
   82 236 252
Jane **74** xxix **81** 364 **82**
   199 200 248 **114** 241
   115 41
Jane Beals **83** 381
Jean Pollock (Brown)
   87 199
Jeannette **87** 199
Jemima **71** 185
Jennet **83** 444
Jeremiah **56** 363
Jira Payne Thayer **134** 255
Joel **69** 46
John **68** 170 171 176 287 **69**
   46 235 **75** 305 **82** 43 **83**
   381 442-444 446 458 459
   461 **84** 14 **102** 181 **105**
   82 **114** 314 316 **118** 212
   141 253
Jonathan **71** 185 201
   72 130
Joseph **51** 351 **62** 249 **65**
   360 **68** 170 171 176 **69**
   232 **83** 261 381 **88** 275
   101 283 **122** 288
Joshua **87** 198 199 **91** 181
   94 86 **97** 383
Josiah **69** 46
Judson T. **55** 358
Julia (Thayer) **134** 255
Julia E. **122** 218
Justin **122** 218
Larinda **122** 286
Laurence Kirtland **91** 181
Lavinah **56** 34
Lavinia **68** 291 **69** 238
Lester D. **114** 241
Lettice **117** 185
Levi **69** 373 **83** 381 **84** 358
   363 **90** 87 **100** 136-139
   141 299 **119** 234 **140**
   158
Levi (Mrs.) **84** 363
Lois **63** 90 **114** 316
Loren B. **114** 241
Lucretia **100** 136 **125** 222
Lucy **126** 204
Lucy Adelia **103** 116
Lucy L. **114** 241
Lydia **103** 61 **118** 88 210
   121 224 **122** 286
Lydia (Claflin) **102** 3
Margaret **52** 247 **78** 405
Martha **51** 491
Mary **65** 356 **69** 46 371
   376 378 **70** 35 **71** 185 **82**
   43 **83** 382 **99** 121 **100**
   139 **114** 316 **128** 304
   132 162
Mary (Gray) **87** 198
Mary (Taylor) (Rich)
   83 261
Mary (Williams) **91** 181

JENNINGS *cont'd*
   94 86 **97** 383
Mary Ann **69** 373 **114** 241
Mary Dows (Brewster)
   91 181
Mary Emily (Dunn)
   88 344
Mary F. **68** 198
Mary F. (Wilson) **114** 241
Mehitable **65** 351
Mercy **102** 3 .
Mercy P. **83** 24 26
Meribah **119** 234
Mindwell **72** 130
Minnie T. **110** 54
Nancy Moores Watts
   117 158
Naomi **69** 378
Nathan **67** 117-120 122 219
   68 198 **71** 185
Nathaniel **82** 43
Nehemiah **69** 378
Nicholas **89** 175
Noble **122** 290
Olive **126** 206
Olive (Chase) **88** 125
Olive (Tupper) **99** 290
Oliver Burr **87** 198 199
   88 167 **91** 181 **94** 86 **97**
   383
Oliver G. **75** 316
Oliver Gould **76** xxi **87**
   199 **91** 147 176 181 **97**
   383
Orrin C. **114** 241
Patience **69** 378
Pauline **91** 195
Penelope **57** 34 39 **119** 191
Persis **57** 286
Peter **73** 218 **145** 27
Phebe **116** 76 **119** 234
   123 319
Phebe (Staples) **87** 198
Phila A. **70** 243
Philemon **69** 238
Philena (Knowlton)
   104 216
Polly **77** 32 **82** 491 **83** 381
   382 **95** 290
Polly (Clark) **114** 241
Rebecca **53** 128
Remember **105** 82 **118** 88
Remember (Smith)
   118 210
Remembrance **141** 253
Reuben **67** 122 219
Richard **57** 197 **105** 237
   138 104
Richard William **85** 353
Robert **75** 219
Rose **114** 316 **120** 188
Rose (Goodspeed) **114**
   316 **120** 188
Roswell **67** 122
Ruhamah **118** 202
Ruhamah (Turner) **114**
   314 **141** 253
Russell **114** 241
Sally (Joy) **125** 221
Samuel **68** 173 174 **69**
   189 371 **99** 290 291 **113**

JENNINGS *cont'd*
271 **115** 92 95 **116** 219
118 88 206 210 211 **119**
264 **120** 28 **121** 224 **123**
59
Sarah **51** 222 **56** 137 139 **68**
176 198 288 **69** 46 **70** 37
72 14 **91** 346 **94** 274
100 141 **113** 271 **141** 30
Sarah (Peaton) **141** 30
Sarah (Williams) **125** 107
Seth **57** 286 **68** 291 **69** 378
114 321
Solomon **92** 52 53 **99** 121
122
Stella **82** 237
Stephen **101** 46 289 **119**
234 **138** 28
Sumner **122** 218
Susan **69** 46 **111** 191
Susan A. **114** 241
Susanna **105** 82 **114** 314
Susanna (Day) **125** 109
Sylvius **69** 238
Tammy **63** 370
Temperance **79** 437
Thaddeus **68** 171 291
69 46 238
Thankful **77** 33
Theodore **65** 122
Thomas **85** 137 142 **115** 40
Tobias **141** 29
Triphena **67** 219
Virginia Lobdell **117** 158
Walter **73** 235 **74** xxiv **87**
161 198 199 **88** 167 171
91 181 **94** 86 **97** 383
William **67** 117 **68** 198
81 179 **82** 43 199 200 **83**
381 **95** 290 **100** 134 **131**
127 **140** 158
William H. **55** 445 **56** 95
70 243
William Henry **53** 128
133 **88** 344
Zebulon **53** 128
Jenninson *see* Jenison
Jennis *see* Jenness
JENNISON Gennison
Jeneson Jenison
Jennerson Jenninson
—— **69** 305 **71** 321 **106** 93
122 226 **140** 157 158
— Capt. **53** 48
— Mrs. **71** 119
— Widow **65** 363 **83** 379
Abigail **57** 200 **61** 261
125 105 129 376
Abijah **57** 412-414 **58** 55 56
Alfred **56** 46
Andrew Belcher **58** 55 336
Annamaria **57** 200
Annie Savage **68** 126
Asa **125** 217
Belsey **125** 101
Belsey (Jennison) **125** 101
Betsey (Fessenden)
125 214
Brooks **57** 412
Caroline (Dean) **125** 217

JENNISON *cont'd*
Charles Humphrey
78 350
Clara Ella **68** 126
Daniel **95** 369
David Warren **68** 126
Dorothy (Thomas) (Whit-
temore) **106** 93
Edwin **99** 246
Elias **84** 413
Eliza **78** 180
Elizabeth **94** 388 **111** 180
Emma **125** 216
Eula **93** 138
Eunice Miranda (Briggs)
126 122
Eunice Rebecca **78** 350
Fanny **59** 369
Fletcher **58** 55
Frances **58** 336
George B. **89** 91
H. L. **78** 112
Hannah **53** 350
Hannah (Twist) **84** 413
Helen Otis **68** 126
Hepzibah **56** 46
Herbert Warren **68** 126
Hopestill **58** 54 55
Isaac **111** 183
Isabel **57** 412
Israel **77** 290
James **83** 180 182 **125** 214
Jane **60** 392
Jerusha **144** 221
John **65** 250 **125** 108
John F. **77** 321
John Lucas **68** 232 **125** 101
Jonas **57** 200 **70** 146 214
219
Jonas L. **57** 200
Jonathan **56** 46 **58** 336
Josiah **57** 414
Judith **91** 364
Leander Warren **68** 126
Lemuel **128** 45
Lot **65** 363
Louisa **58** 336
Lucy **128** 41
Lydia **52** 426
Lydia (Upham) **125** 108
Margaret (Edgecomb) **83**
180 182
Marguerite **77** 290
Maria **57** 200
Mariette Dorothy
(Bullard) **89** 22
Martin **56** 46
Mary **51** 75 **58** 336 **77** 287
127 187
Mary Ann **58** 336 **125** 104
Mary Barker (Tibbetts)
99 246
Mary F. **83** 381 **118** 94
Mary E. B. **83** 146
Mary Emilia Elizabeth
58 335 336
Maverick **116** 186
Mercy **51** 75
Michael **92** 195 **120** 185
313
Minot Ripley **58** 59

JENNISON *cont'd*
Molly **95** 369
Moses **57** 200 **69** 213 **70**
140 144 146 214 218 219
300 **136** 269
Nancy **145** 36
Nathan **65** 360
Nathaniel **52** 193 **57** 412
58 55 **82** 43 **137** 95
Olive **82** 43 **84** 413
Peter **79** 48 **118** 183
Phebe A. (Snow) **123** 201
Phineas **59** 369
Polly **58** 55 **95** 369
Rebecca **61** 263
Rebecca (Hathorn)
125 101
Relief **66** 335 336
Rhoda **56** 46
Robert **65** 362 **78** 112 **86**
351 **106** 93 **120** 313
Robert R. **123** 201
Ruth **82** 288 297 **126** 180
Sally (Sanderson) **128** 45
Samuel **52** 163 426 **54** 45
57 413 **60** 391 **61** 42 263
68 232 **78** 309 **83** 376
85 454 **90** 400 **125** 101
126 122 **140** 157 158
144 265
Sanford **89** 22
Sarah **56** 33 **57** 200 **77** 230
82 26 **106** 66 **108** 307
133 121
Sarah (Longley) **136** 269
Sarah E. (Fisher) **116** 186
Sibyl **89** 64
Susan **88** 277
Susanna **59** 369 **79** 54
Thomas **57** 200 **64** 254 256
70 308
Timothy Lindall **58** 336
145 62
Tom **70** 304
Victory **58** 54
William **58** 336 **78** 405
83 378 **90** 400 **106** 93
199 **118** 183 **120** 313
131 127 **137** 244 **144**
265
William H. **78** 399
JENNITT Sarah **66** 65
Jennor *see* Jenner
Jenny *see* Jenney
Jennynge *see* Jennings
Jennys *see* Jenness
JENOUR
Richard **74** 136
Wiburga **74** 136
JENOWAY Robert **70** 366
JENSEN Jenson Jennsen
A. R. **147** 193
Adelaide Dorothea
Natalie **82** 270
Arel Isaac (Mrs.) **107** 133
C. S. (Mrs.) **121** 154
Camelia **88** 170
Elizabeth **92** 49
Erastus Nephi (Mrs.)
107 133

JENSEN *cont'd*
George Rulon (Mrs.)
102 123
Grady E. **129** 86
Hanna Maria **102** 238
Helen Lorraine (Fracker)
124 262
Henry **120** 247
Howard S. **124** 262
James Maurice (Mrs.)
109 129
Jans Thomsen **51** 343
Jens **51** 343
John Cornelius **82** 270
Katharine **82** 270
Katrina **51** 343
Martin LeRoy (Mrs.)
107 133
Mary **111** 156 **114** 149
Merrill **112** 322
Myrtle **93** 137
Norman Ramsey **82** 270
Peter Andrew **124** 262
Sophie **51** 343
Thoms **51** 343 344
William George (Mrs.)
106 125
JENT *see also* Gent
Priscilla **91** 350
JENYKIN John **113** 74
JENYVER June **111** 319
JEPHCOTE
Mary **71** 317 321
Samuel **71** 317 321
Jepherson *see* Jefferson
JEPSON Jeppson
— Capt. **62** 354
Abigail **72** 270 **73** 45 47 50
Abigail (Callender)
(Cushing) **145** 43
Abigail B. D. **70** 322
Abner **68** 168 248 **70** 277
320 334 **72** 262 **75** 5
Abraham **72** 270 **75** 10 11
Abram **73** 49 **93** 337
Almira P. **68** 248 **69** 314
Ann **126** 209
Ann R. **117** 164
Anna **72** 259
Anna (Cooper) **140** 313
315
Anne **140** 315
Apphia (Rolfe) **140** 316
Benjamin **68** 244 **69** 177
70 270 322 **78** 414 **84**
153 **92** 26 **125** 106 **140**
158
Benjamin F. **70** 323
Benjamin R. **70** 336
Betsey **125** 108
Carl (Mrs.) **100** 111
Charles **70** 279
Charles Henry **69** 314
70 327
Clara Ann **70** 327
Clara C. **69** 181 **70** 335
Clara R. **70** 331
Comfort **68** 168 248
70 277 334
Content **69** 181
Cynthia **72** 272

JEPSON *cont'd*
Cynthia W. **73** 49
Daniel **69** 177 **70** 270
Dorothy **93** 337
Eli **69** 181 **70** 279 331 335
Elijah **72** 270 **73** 127 **75** 9
Elijah D. **70** 323
Eliza **69** 175 **70** 322
Eliza C. **70** 329
Elizabeth **70** 320 **72** 262
272 **75** 5 51 54
Elizabeth B. **70** 279
Elizabeth Hart **92** 28
Ella Zimena **70** 322
Ellen Maria **70** 327
Emm (Coddington)
140 315
Flavilla **70** 279
George **69** 314 **70** 279
George Nathaniel **85** 188
117 148
Hannah (Cooper) **140** 315
Hannah P. **69** 317
Hannah R. **70** 336
Henry **69** 314
Henry A. **68** 248 **70** 277
Huldah **72** 270
Isaac **70** 270
Isaiah **70** 277
Isaiah Clarkson **70** 322
J. W. **93** 337
James **75** 54
Jedediah **68** 168 244 **69**
177 314 **70** 270 279 320
331 332 335 **72** 262 **75** 5
87 206
Jerusha **79** 246
John **68** 244 **69** 177 **70**
270 320 336 **72** 262 **73**
125 128 **78** 186 **84** 153
103 234 **140** 315 316
John A. **70** 322
John William **72** 272
Joseph **92** 27 **125** 38
144 209
Judith **70** 277 320 332 **72**
261 262 **75** 5
L. Maria **68** 248
Lois **70** 320 331 **72** 262
75 5
Lois Maria **70** 279
Lucy Ann **70** 279 336
Lydia **68** 244 **69** 177 **70**
270 320 336 **72** 262 270
272 **73** 49 **75** 5 **92** 22
144 209
Lydia (Callender) **144** 209
145 43
Lydia R. **70** 323
Margaret **68** 168 **70** 320
331 332 335 **72** 262 **75** 5
Margaret (Sumner)
144 209
Mary **70** 320 331 **72** 262
272 **73** 50 **75** 5 **79** 250
80 79 **140** 158
Mary (Call) **140** 48
Mary A. **76** 19
Mary F. **70** 279 **93** 337
Nancy Lowette **114** 278
Nathaniel **145** 43

JEPSON *cont'd*
Olive E. **93** 337
Oliver **68** 248 **70** 279 320
332 335 336 **72** 262 **75** 5
Patience **68** 244 **70** 322
Phebe C. **72** 272 **73** 47
93 337
Rebecca **68** 244 **69** 314
Rebecca Page (Campbell)
125 106
Rosamond **110** 182
Ruth **140** 315
Ruth (Gardner) **140** 315
316
Sally **125** 107
Samuel **69** 174 **70** 329 **72**
270 **73** 127 **79** 48 **92** 20
22 26-28 **94** 295 **140** 158
144 209 **145** 43
Samuel R. **70** 277 334
Sarah **69** 174 **70** 334 **72** 267
270 **73** 45
Sarah C. **70** 329
Sarah Jane **70** 327
Silas Frye **69** 314 **70** 277
327
Soviah **72** 272
Susanna **69** 177 **70** 320
72 262 **75** 5
Syrena B. **70** 279 332 335
336
Syrena P. **68** 248
Thomas **69** 175
Thomas Watson **70** 277
322
Timothy **72** 270
Webster Charles
64 xxxiii
William **70** 279 **72** 270 272
73 45 47 50 **75** 51 52 54
92 20 **93** 337 **110** 182
136 107 109 **140** 158
313 315 **144** 209
Jeptherson *see* Jefferson
JEQUIT Henry **51** 46
Jerald *see* Jerauld
JERARD
— Capt. **99** 283
Elias **99** 208 281 285
Elizabeth **99** 285
John **63** 346
Mary **99** 208
Samuel **99** 281
Sarah **99** 285
Sary **99** 281
JERAULD Jerald Jereld
Jerrold Jerrolds - *see*
also Gerald
—— **64** 56
Amy **129** 62
Bennett **69** 198
Dutee **102** 235 **129** 271
Gorton **129** 271
James **52** 77 **62** 369 **129**
274 **140** 67
Louis **51** 189
Lucile **106** 126
Mary Barnes **69** 198
Polly **72** 285
Susanna **140** 67
JERBYN Mabel **51** 186

Jereld *see* Jerauld
JERELON Joan **86** 415
  92 177 182
JEREMY Anne **54** 196
JERKYN Agnes **75** 287
  John **75** 287
JERLAND Isaiah **63** 76
JERMAIN
  Margaret **81** 330
  Margaret Pierson **81** 330
  Sylvanus P. **81** 330
JERMYN Jermin
  —— **57** 422 423
  Ambrose **75** 284
  Ambrosius **57** 312
  Annie E. **60** 47
  Anthony **57** 312
  George B. **60** 47 **94** 370
  John **147** 172
  Mary **71** 243
  Robert **54** 341 **75** 285 287
    288 **86** 417 **91** 363
  Thomas **54** 153 **57** 312 **134**
    288 **138** 88
  William **70** 262
JERNEGAN Jernigan
    Jernygan
  Abigail **59** 403 409
  Anne **107** 216
  Clementine C. C. **125** 177
  Elizabeth **59** 401
  Eunice **59** 301 307
  Henry **107** 216
  Huldah **59** 403
  Leonard **59** 401
  Mary **59** 203 207 410 411
  Sarah **59** 410
  Stanley Sharp (Mrs.)
    96 160
  Thomas **52** 370 **53** 102 106
    59 204 403
  William **59** 203 207 299-
    301 305 307 409-411
JEROME
  Amasa H. **72** 50
  Amelia Harrod **93** 66
  Ann **54** 273
  Caroline Andrews **93** 66
  Charles Guillaume Juste
    110 133
  Eugene Murray **112** 161
  George B. **52** 374
  Hope H. (Colgate) **99** 331
  Jason **52** 374 **72** 169
  Jennie **136** 87
  John **93** 66 **94** 46
  John J. **52** 374
  John Quincy Adams
    93 66
  Lucy **52** 374 **92** 74
  Lucy T. **72** 50 107
  Maria Louisa Burnham
    93 66
  Mary **51** 222 **90** 339
  Paul Frederick **105** 128
  Phebe **93** 66 **94** 46
  Roxy L. **72** 50
  Timothy **54** 273
  Timothy G. **72** 60
  Wealthy Ann **52** 374
  William S. **52** 374

JEROME *cont'd*
  William T. (Mrs.) **99** 331
JERRED
  Francis **100** 303
  Susanna (Ellis) **100** 303
JERROD Mary **109** 39
Jerrold *see* Jerauld
Jerrolds *see* Jerauld
JERRY James **61** 214
JERSEY Edward Stephen
    (Mrs.) **105** 128
  Henry **101** 53
  Mary de **57** 365
JERSEYS
  — Widow **127** 138
Jervis *see* Jarvis
JERVOISE —— **57** 128
Jesoppe *see* Jessop
JESS —— **60** 214
  Abigail **90** 159
  Ann **88** 12
  Charlotte **120** 15
  Charlotte (Bosdick)
    120 16
  Charlotte (Huntley)
    101 203
  Daniel **120** 16
  George **101** 203 **120** 15
  George Lewis **120** 16
  Leonora Inez **102** 123
  Mary Elisa (Lockhart)
    120 16
  Sarah **88** 12
  William **101** 203 **117** 86
JESSAMY Paul **66** 37
JESSE David **148** 28
  Elizabeth **72** 320
  John Heneage **121** 189
    190
  Mary (Wilson) **148** 28
JESSEE Nancy **124** 305
JESSELL Alice Winfred
    (Tucker) **95** 318
  Charles L. **95** 318
  Ida May **95** 318
JESSEMAN Jessemane
    Jessemen Jessemene
  Francis **78** 67
  James **79** 37
  Joseph **78** 185
  Mabel S. **117** 316
JESSON Jacob **102** 182
JESSOP Jesoppe Jessope
    Jessopp Jessup
  —— **53** 68 **108** 103
  Abraham **119** 240
  Aery **117** 62
  Ann **56** 122 123
  Antoinette (Quintard)
    109 192
  Augustus **70** 53
  Augustus Edward **103**
    249 253
  Charles L. **97** 201 203
  Clara Sophia **103** 249 253
  Ebenezer **58** xcvi
  Edith Newbold **81** 369
    89 361
  Edmonde **86** 427
  Edward **58** xcv xcvi **61**
    286 **144** 41 **148** 42

JESSOP *cont'd*
  Edward Peter **109** 192
  Elizabeth **69** 376
  Grace (Penrose) **117** 62
  Hannah **107** 294 **109** 185
    119 240
  Hannah Taber (Pratt) **97**
    201 203
  Henry **125** 39
  Henry Griswold **58** liv
    xcv-xcvii
  Jeremiah **61** 286
  John **75** 293 **143** 113 114
  John Colgate (Mrs.)
    98 186
  Joseph **79** 246
  Lois **79** 246
  Louise Knox (Foote)
    98 186
  Mary Hannah **58** xcv
  Morris Ketchum **58** xcvi
    62 213
  Richard **109** 20
  Robert **143** 113 114
  Samuel **109** 192
  Sarah **148** 62
  Sarah W. (Purdy) **109** 192
  Thomas **111** 250
  William **124** 116
  William (Mrs.) **107** 133
  William Henry **58** xcv
    xcvi
JESTER
  Annie Lash **115** 13
  Lewis T. (Mrs.) **113** 308
  Mary **80** 44
  Samuel **91** 326
JETHRO
  Abigail **100** 187
  Athearn **66** 80
JETT Jette
  — Mr. **84** 433
  Ann Delana **117** 41
  Asa H. **117** 41
  Elizabeth A. (Davis)
    117 41
  I. **145** 130
  Polly **92** 73
  Rene **145** 129
JEUDEVINE
  Mary **144** 202
JEUNE Jevne
  Virginia **110** 319
JEVAN
  Anne (Wilson) **101** 6
JEWELL Jewel Juell Julls
  —— **59** xxx **64** 213 **111** 8
  — Bp. **57** 60
  Aaron **129** 369
  Abi **98** 283
  Abigail **52** 433 **65** 113 **68**
    153 **71** 262
  Abraham **105** 206
  Aby **98** 283
  Ada Bertha **95** 187
  Albert **90** 52
  Alice **66** 254
  Amy **68** 250
  Ann **52** 428 **53** 165 276
  Anne **52** 434 **53** 163
  Anne Jane **134** 221

JEWELL *cont'd*
Archibald **85** 228
Asa **73** 65 71 74 76
Barnard **53** 282
Barnibury **91** 257
Benjamin **91** 258
Benoia **91** 258
Benoni **64** 213 **91** 257
Betsey **145** 46 166
Bradbury **118** 78
Catherine **69** 326
Charles (Mrs.) **96** 202
Charles H. **89** 349 **121** 309
Charles M. **76** 44
Charlotte **65** 113
Christian **72** 28
Clara (Cox) **134** 221
Clara Melissa **134** 221
Daniel **73** 76 **116** 266
  134 221
David **65** 113 **73** 69 **83** 52
  116 265 266 **123** 123
  200
Dolly **58** 19
Dorcas **64** 213 **114** 273
Dorothy **53** 163
E. D. **89** 274
Eben **86** 293
Edmund **66** 254
Edward **66** 254
Eleanor B. (Grant) **88** 337
Eliza J. (Atwood) **123** 123
  200
Elizabeth **52** 429 **66** 254 **72**
  28 **95** 92
Elizabeth (Lowe) **116** 265
Elizabeth (Marston) **95** 92
Elizabeth (Webster)
  129 369
Ella **98** 346
Elmina (Conger) **85** 227
  228
Fielder **73** 272
George **59** 256
Georgianna **97** 132
Grissell **51** 308 **56** 183
Grissell (Fletcher) **123** 173
Gurney A. **101** 258
Hannah **51** 466 **52** 429 430
  63 364 **85** 454 **95** 92
  110 229 **112** 159 **113**
  240 241 **121** 216
Hannah (Curtis) **129** 369
Hannah (Marston) **95** 92
Harriet **128** 265
Harvey **54** cxxvii **59** 41
Henry **66** 254
Henry Lunkester **52** 429
Hosea **88** 337
J. E. **89** 274
Jacob **53** 282
James **105** 206
Jane **87** 126
Joan **66** 254
Joel **116** 265
John **52** 433 **65** 113 **66** 254
  73 71 **145** 46 166
John A. **86** 293
Jonathan **53** 163 165 167
  168 276 282 **72** 22 28
  108

JEWELL *cont'd*
Joseph **52** 429 432 433 **53**
  165 167 **85** 228
Judith **52** 429 **53** 165
Junkins **71** x
Justus **85** 228
Laura **83** 299 302
Laura B. **59** 256
Lavinia (Silvester) **86** 293
Levi **95** 92
Lewis **95** 92
Louisa Jane (Silvester)
  86 293
Lucy **145** 46 166
Marcena **89** 274
Margaret A. **128** 97
Maria L. **76** 44
Mark **69** 326
Marshall **77** 166 167
Martha **91** 257
Martha (Knight) (Dutch)
  144 138 140 142
Mary **52** 429 433 **53** 168
  63 380 **64** 213 **106** 143
Mary (Cole) **140** 130
Mary (Dool) **128** 97
Mary (Morris) **85** 228
Mary (Robinson) **85** 228
Mary E. **75** xxiii **89** 349
Mary Elmina **85** 227 235
  86 201 **87** 168
Mary O. (Payne) **121** 309
Mercy **51** 308 **63** 380 381
  64 79 **85** 95
Miriam **52** 432
Molly **65** 113
Moses **85** 227 228 **140** 130
Nancy **69** 326
Nancy (Cox) **90** 52
Nathaniel **83** 53 **111** 161
  129 369
Paul **116** 271
Pliny **116** 265 **121** 150
Rachel **52** 432 **53** 282
Rebecca (Leonard) **85** 228
Richard **76** 57
Ruth **58** 47
Ruth (Badger) **116** 266
Sally **116** 265
Samuel **57** 65
Sarah **52** 429 **53** 165 167
  168 276 282 **108** 150
  116 265 266
Thomas **63** 364 **85** 227 228
  110 229 **113** 241 **116**
  266 **123** 173
Thomas Benjamin **91** 257
Timothy **58** 47
Walter Towner (Mrs.)
  98 147
William **144** 142
Zecharia **128** 97
JEWERS A. J. **59** 49
Anne (Bryden / Dryden)
  125 258
Arthur J. **55** 446 **148** 78
Elizabeth (Riley) **125** 259
Francis **118** 54 **125** 259
Frank **118** 54
George **118** 54
Henry **118** 54

JEWERS *cont'd*
J. **118** 53
James **118** 54
John **118** 53 54 57 **125** 198
  259
Mary **118** 54 **125** 259
Robert **118** 54
Sarah **125** 198
Solomon **125** 198
Unice **125** 198
William **118** 54 **125** 258
JEWETT Jowett Juatt
  —— **62** 50 **89** 340 **92** 347
  94 99 100 102 103 **98**
  221 **123** 96 **133** 308
  — Capt. **83** 415 420
  — Lieut. **61** 358
  — Mrs. **73** 73 **121** 111
  133 308 310
  — Widow **94** 102
Aaron **61** 352 **73** 74 75
  117 280
Abbie J. **57** 200
Abel **61** 341 345 **123** 281
Abigail **56** 256 **81** 302
  123 50 304 **128** 233 234
Abigail (Potter) **128** 233
Abigail Dorothy (Lazell)
  89 22
Abraham **94** 102 105
Adah **90** 45
Addie Villette **72** 295
Albert Henry Clay
  100 178
Alfred S. **57** xxxiii
Alice **101** 168
Alice (Hopkinson) **94** 101
Amanda **133** 233
Amos **55** 197 **115** 36 **128**
  234 **133** 249
Amos E. **119** 244
Amos Everett **68** xxxiv
  69 xxx **87** 306 **94** 105
  101 79 119 **147** 81 **148**
  130 134
Aner (Mawde) **94** 101
Ann **55** 197 **93** 193 **94** 102
  104
Ann (Allen) **94** 105
Ann (Field) **94** 102 105
Anna **127** 289 **136** 140
Anne **94** 102
Aquila **62** 373 **112** 130
  128 121
Arthur Star **72** 295
Asa **61** 384
Ashbury C. **68** 98
Austin **72** 74
Banja: **125** 92
Benjamin **59** 131 **89** 46
  95 86 87 **134** 87 **145** 364
Betsey **61** 384 **78** 381 **82** 8
  92 345 **94** 380 **103** 170
  104 206
Caleb **99** 196
Caroline **68** 98 **82** 508
Caroline (Wheeler) **123**
  52 306
Carrie Belle **77** xxviii 78
  90 276 294 **91** 147
Catherine B. **68** 98

JEWETT *cont'd*
Charles Augustus **92** 345
Charles Coffin **82** 5
 105 319
Charles Neil (Mrs.) **79** 202
Charlotte T. (Cross) **83** 19
Clarissa B. **78** 380
Daniel **61** 342 **82** 8 **88** 284
 90 42
David **60** 53 **72** 74 **78** 380
 90 276 **107** 313 **126** 225
David M. **78** 380
Deborah **78** 370 381
 115 35
Delia M. (Wheeler) **123** 96
Delvina Lena **89** 46
Dorcas **67** 343 **121** 254
Dorcas (Gates) **121** 254
Dorcas (Hovey) **90** 276
Dorcas Ann (Beard)
 88 284
Dorothy **82** 420
Dorothy (Abells) **89** 22
Dorothy (Wilson) **94** 101
Dummer **116** 110
E. R. **123** 52 306
Edgar Morton **83** 299 302
Edith **63** 257 260
Edith (Claxton) **94** 168
Ednah **93** 379
Edward **90** 276 **94** 99-104
 111 112 **103** 185 **113**
 229 **121** 254 **128** 233
 234
Eleanor (Cochran) **83** 415
Eleazer **89** 22 **108** 225
Eli **73** 76
Eliphalet **53** 205
Elisha Hanson **82** 508
 83 19
Elisha Payne **85** 332
Eliza **62** 50 121 126 **123** 307
Eliza (Cushing) **89** 340
Elizabeth **51** 466 **55** 71 **60**
 363 **61** 240 343 **68** 98 **72**
 74 **82** 508 **83** 150 152 **94**
 101 **123** 51
Elizabeth (Cummings)
 90 276 **94** 105 **145** 240
Elizabeth (How)
 (Chadwell) **94** 105
Elizabeth (Manning)
 90 42
Elizabeth (Phelps) **90** 276
Elizabeth Smith **93** 180
Ellen (Patterson) **94** 101
Ellen (Pell) (Boynton)
 94 104
Ellen D. **94** 102
Ellen M. (Carver) **89** 46
Eloisa S. (Merritt) **123** 52
Emerson **88** 284
Emily Mabel Adams **101**
 79 119 **148** 130
Enoch **90** 276
Enoch G. **68** 98
Ephraim H. **68** 98
Epps **68** 98
Esther **114** 287 288
Esther Jane **92** 308 309
Ethel Sargent **83** 432 437

JEWETT *cont'd*
Eunice **54** 134 **57** 80 **64**
 213 **103** 67
Everett D. **112** 237 **115** 156
 116 155 **117** 155 **118**
 165
Everett Douglas **108** 134
 110 155 **111** 163
Exercise (Pierce) **94** 106
Ezekiel **78** 27
Ezra **123** 281
Faith **88** 398 **92** 77 **94** 106
 107
Florence (Sise) **83** 299 302
Forestus A. **57** 200
Frances **94** 103
Frances (Pickard) **94** 101
Frances (Rawson) **94** 101
Frank **89** 22
Fred I. **94** 168
Frederic C. **89** 46
Frederic Clarke **148** 133
George **60** 53
George Anson **67** xxx
 xxxiv **70** 190
George Campbell **82** 508
George E. **90** 276
George K. **83** 182 184
Gibbons **81** 60 270
Gladys Douglas **94** 168
Grace **94** 105
Grace (Shawe) **94** 102
Grace D. **94** 102
Hannah **54** 260 **60** 53 193
 68 58 **71** 263 **81** 60 270
 302 **87** 387 **91** 255 **93** 10
 44 **94** 106 **109** 230 **113**
 229 **114** 74 **121** 207 212
 216
Hannah (Mann) **88** 284
Hannah (Moody /
 Mouday) **95** 86 87
Harriet **91** 393 **95** 115
Harriette Marie **52** 404
Hattie **75** 24
Haynes **62** 121
Helen Amanda **92** 347
Helen Augusta (Durrell)
 133 124
Helen Etheridge **80** 105
 208 **96** 160
Henry **56** 260
Henry H. **78** 380
Henry Moore **82** 508
Henry Steward **133** 124
Hepzibah **72** 295 **89** 286
Herbert Trull **133** 124
Homer Curtis **72** 295
Homer Lyon **89** 46
Ira **72** 74
Isaac **67** 343 **90** 276
Isabel (Brockden) **94** 102
Isabel (Jewett) **94** 101
Isabel (Pearson) **94** 101
Jacob **73** 64 66 **126** 225
James **62** 120 123 126 **71**
 52 **91** 262 326 **136** 144
 145 **139** 249 **145** 363
 147 82
James R. **72** 74
Jane **60** 193

JEWETT *cont'd*
Jared **133** 233
Jason **89** 22
Jay Marcus **89** 46
Jedediah **63** 257 **99** 79
Jemima **116** 19 **121** 244
Jennie E. **72** 74
Jeremiah **61** 240 **93** 33 **94**
 106 112
Jeremiah Peabody **64** 228
 67 277
Jeremy **94** 102 **140** 207
Jerusha **75** 190
Joanna **114** 277
Joel M. **57** 200
John **60** 53 **73** 72 **89** 22
 90 276 **94** 13 102 105
 121 212 **145** 240
John A. **68** 98
John G. **78** 380
John Lord **82** 508
John P. **51** 367
John R. **79** 159
Jonas **94** 102 **145** 363
Jonathan **60** 255 **73** 63 68
 73 **81** 302 **90** 111
Joseph **51** 317 **60** 53 **61**
 384 **62** 256 **63** 258 **64** 1
 68 58 98 211 **69** 245 **70**
 227 **93** 33 43 44 **94** 99
 100 102 104-109 112 **99**
 237 **101** 57 **103** 185 **107**
 152 **121** 103 **140** 206
 207 **148** 133
Joseph Scott **52** 404
Joshua **51** 317 **118** 313
Josiah **61** 240
Josias **94** 102 105
Judith **94** 102 105
Julia Ann **78** 330 337
 79 202
Julia Kellogg (Fiel)
 85 332
Katharine (Richardson)
 94 101
Katie F. **61** xxxiv
 62 xxxvii
Katy **66** 22
Lina **125** 54
Lord S. **78** 380
Louisa **123** 96
Lucian Henry **89** 46
Lucinda (Bigelow)
 133 124
Lucretia **64** 1 **72** 295 **89** 46
Lucretia (Richarson)
 89 46
Lucy **91** 106
Lucy (Dewey) **90** 276
Lucy (Farley) **136** 144
Lucy (Perry) **99** 125
 116 43
Lucy Ada **120** 75 **126** 49
Lucy J. **117** 280
Lura **94** 102
Luther **79** 44
Luthera **86** 360
Lydia **78** 27 **91** 262
Lydia Sophia **72** 295
Marcus Lyon **89** 46
Margaret **52** 428 **136** 145

JEWETT *cont'd*
Marget (McMaster)
   91 262
Maria L. (March) **83** 182
   184
Marie **94** 10 102
Marie (Denby) **94** 102
Mark **147** 81
Martha **60** 53 255 **80** 28
   82 8 **91** 394 **111** 116
   136 362
Martha A. **57** 200
Martha Caroline **69** xxxv
Martha Jane **72** 295
Mary **51** 317 **53** 203 **61**
   238 341 342 **62** 256 258
   373 **68** 58 **76** 15 **80** 26
   81 219 392 **89** 22 **91** 31
   94 100-105 107 108 **107**
   162 **121** 195 **123** 136
   134 87
Mary (Chute) **147** 81
Mary (Dearborn) **134** 87
Mary (Mallinson) **93** 44
   94 102 105 112 **148** 133
Mary (Tayler) **94** 100 101
   103 104 112
Mary E. **68** 98
Mary Elizabeth **82** 508
Mary H. (Kempton)
   125 288
Mary J. **68** 98
Mary Louise (Tippetts)
   98 221
Mary Shepard **95** 345
Maude **81** 109 **82** 253
   89 46
Maude Ione **81** 221 **83** 230
   108 61 139
Maximilian **93** 33 **94** 99
   100 102 104 106 **103** 185
   109 230
Mead **62** 120 125
Mehitable **147** 81-83
Mehitable (Durgin)
   90 331
Mehitable (Harris) **90** 276
Molly **62** 121
Moses **62** 120 125 **80** 26
Myron Holly **89** 22
Myron Star **72** 295
Myrtle **126** 155
Myrtle (Gunter) **126** 155
Naomi **78** 380
Nathan **64** l **78** 370 381 382
   90 331 **94** 102 105 **99**
   125 **116** 43 **145** 363
Nathaniel **53** 203
Nehemiah **56** 45 **94** 106
Nina **95** 146
Norman Victor **89** 46
Olive **82** 508 **83** 151 152
Oliver **55** 71
Othniel **123** 311 312
Patience **54** 260 **93** 44
   94 106
Peter **94** 102
Phebe **62** 120 122 **90** 111
Philena **56** 260
Philomela **85** 437
Pickard **103** 170

JEWETT *cont'd*
Polly **118** 315
Priscilla **64** 38
Prudence (Perry) **131** 76
Rebecca **61** 240
Rebecca Greene **82** 5
Rebecca P. **78** 380
Reform (Trescott)
   86 133 142
Rhoda **68** 328
Richard **94** 101-103
Rose Ann (Monaghan)
   85 377
Ruth **80** 27 **91** 262 **92** 307
   308 **97** 222 237 **123** 230
   136 145
Ruth (Wood) **94** 107
   123 230
Ruth Payson **85** 332
Sally **70** 227
Sally (Soule) **124** 153
Sally Orne **82** 508
Samuel **68** 98 **78** 382 **91**
   255 326 **92** 345 347 **94**
   380 **97** 395 **105** 210 **124**
   153 **139** 99 248
Samuel A. W. **68** 98
Samuel Walker **82** 508
Sarah **53** 205 **55** 372 **61** 342
   384 **62** 120 126 **69** 245
   78 380 **94** 100 102 105
   106 108 112 **107** 152
   116 18 **120** 256 **148** 133
Sarah (Dickinson) **94** 106
Sarah (Sherman) **108** 225
Sarah Ann **90** 51
Sarah E. **57** 200 **68** 98
Sarah Jane **74** 239
Sarah Louise **108** 225
Sarah Orne **63** 394 **105**
   82 211
Sarah Richards **90** 56
Sarah Townsley (Ward)
   90 276
Sexton Butler **89** 46
Solomon **56** 256 **125** 288
Sophronia **68** 98
Stephen **58** lxxxv **65** 147
   90 276
Susan **94** 102
Susan M. **68** 98
Susanna **88** 156
Susanna (Gilford)
   121 192
Susanna (Stevens) **90** 276
Sylvia **71** 52
Theodore **82** 508
Theodore F. **83** 151 152
Theodore F. (Mrs.) **83** 152
Thirza **56** 45
Thomas **82** 508 **83** 150 152
   85 378 **95** 115 **121** 192
   198 **131** 76
Thomas Dearborn **82** 508
Timothy **90** 276
Toh **121** 192
Tryphosa **73** xlvi
Wilbur F. **68** 98
Willard **121** 155
William **52** 66 **60** 193 **80**
   27 **94** 100-105

JEWETT *cont'd*
William Durham **82** 508
William O. L. **68** 98
Wilson F. (Mrs.) **81** 107
   219
Winnie May **72** 295
Zerviah (Carver) **89** 46
Zilphah **57** 368
JEWKES
   Lorus Dall **109** 130
JEWNESS Lucy **126** 155
JEYES Elizabeth **94** 326
JIGGLES Mercy **66** 285
   Sarah **97** 307
   Thomas **66** 285
JILLSON
   Abigail (Pray) **83** 12
   Achsah **88** 19
   Adelaide **104** 102
   Adelaide Woodworth
      104 102
   Anna **113** 135
   Annie K. **106** 108
   Arloine J. **104** 102
   Asa **80** 264
   Asa Windham **80** 38
   Betsey **116** 114
   Calvin G. **115** 292
   Camelia A. **80** 38
   Charles **104** 102
   Charlotte **116** 114
   David **54** 442 **86** 113
      120 20
   Deborah **141** 201 332 341
   Desire **120** 20
   Elizabeth **83** 12
   Emily **115** 292
   Enos **129** 387
   George **115** 292
   George P. **116** 114
   Hannah **115** 292
   Hannah (Peck) **140** 128
   Hannah Eldredge **80** 38
   Harriet **120** 20
   Henry O. **104** 102
   Isaac **141** 341
   John Hervey **86** 113
   Luke **129** 384
   Lydia **83** 10
   Martha **140** 128
   Mary **116** 158 **125** 183
   Mary E. (Coffin) **104** 102
   Molly **83** 13
   Myrtle M. **94** 97 **111** 77
      117 97 **118** 295 **143** 35
      148 239
   Myrtle Mae **92** 146
   Nancy **87** 320
   Nathan **115** 292 **129** 384
   Nathaniel **60** 210 **129** 384
      141 201 332 341
   Olive **83** 12
   Otis **141** 201 332 341
   Priscilla **80** 181
   Ruth **60** 210
   Samuel T. **106** 108
   Sarah Jane (Harrigan)
      95 377
   Stephen **116** 114 **140** 128
   Uriah **129** 384
   Vina Evelyn **86** 113

JINEY — Mr. **62** 22
Aba **62** 128
JINNET
Rebecca S. **77** li
JIRSA
Leo E. **83** 430 432
Margaret C. (Goodwin)
83 430 432
JOAN of Arc **60** 406
Joanes *see* Jones
Joans *see* Jones
JOB —— **53** 352
Benjamin **58** 142
Fannie **105** 128
Fanny **77** 263
Helen M. **144** 117
Jemima **127** 51
Joseph **70** 265
Mordica **70** 265
Temperance **62** 23
JOBIE Thomas **84** 307
JOBIN —— **61** 110
JOBO Marie **57** 330 **90** 301
JOBSON Ada **96** 134
Alice Elizabeth **96** 134
Job **85** 397
John **60** 59 **85** 399
William **96** 134
JOCELYN Harriet (Starr)
93 184
Maria Sophia **85** 324
Mary Emma **93** 184
JOCOT Richard **109** 22
JOEL of Totnes **57** 61
JOEL —— **120** 127 131
Dick **136** 39
Ezekiell **120** 26 27
Julia M. **81** 38
Richard **112** 27 **136** 39
JOENSSON Per **111** 100
JOFFRE Jofre
Joseph Jacques Césaire
72 xlv
Luisa **109** 290
JOGUES
Isaac **55** 119 132
JOHANNIS Davyd **110** 166
Johannot *see* Johonnot
JOHANSON Ann Elizabeth
(Lowd) **83** 183 184
Anna Caisa Catherine
147 218 225 226
Carl Johan **147** 225
Grace Ella (Arnold)
115 150
Kaisa (Bengtson) **147** 225
Matthew **83** 183 184
JOHGE Andrew **75** 278
Mary **75** 278
JOHN ERNEST Duke of
Saxe-Coburg-Saalfeld
88 101
JOHN FREDERICK
Elector of Saxony **88**
100 101
JOHN XXIII Pope **132** 253
JOHN Duke of Exeter **148** 165
JOHN King of England
56 271 **64** 99 **79** 374
140 221 222 **141** 96 105
142 239

JOHN of Gaunt **60** 58
JOHN Prior of Clattercote
145 11
JOHN The Divine **132** 102
JOHN — Bp. **75** 61
Anne **109** 23
Elizabeth **62** 272
Griffith **60** 101
Hugh **103** 105
Lewis **109** 21 23
Peter **66** 34
Porter **62** 272
JOHNE — Prof. **89** 369
Johnes *see* Jones
Johns *see* Jones
JOHNSON Jonson
—— **51** 190 **52** 145 295
333 **53** 122 356 385 463
54 lxxx 93 200 294 370
408 456 **55** 115 188 351
56 lxvii 151 214 327 333
57 160 335 350 **58** 51
101 **59** 115 182 **60** 203
61 149 401 **62** 59 **63** 200
66 xxv 47 **67** 178 **69** 299
71 52 218 **72** 104 **74** 141
76 153 170 173 285 **77**
221 **83** 34 193 **85** 55 **86**
43 91 400 **87** 338 **88** 352
376 **89** 343 **92** 258 279
353 380 **93** 66 **97** 137 **99**
284 **100** 230 **101** 94 229
246 341 **102** 261 **103** 89
105 109 **106** 211 **110** 1
111 256 **112** 186 **114** 29
117 14 **118** 119 304-306
119 45 **121** 110 **122** 70
123 17 23 **126** 255 **128**
269 **129** 395 **130** 234
235 **143** 259 **147** 60
— Capt. **58** 161 **65** 355
74 320 **85** 128 367 **89**
250 **99** 242 **101** 246 **143**
251
— Col. **147** 184
— Cornet **112** 291
— Dea. **71** 52
— Dr. **52** 262 **57** 45 **71** 276
85 13
— Gen. **86** 35
— Lieut. **54** 74
— Mother **146** 274
— Mr. **52** 223 460 463 **53**
420 **57** 418 **61** 313 **63**
383 **65** 119 167 **67** 30 **68**
135 **69** 17 **71** 51 **83** 193
306 **90** 35 **91** 302 **92** 353
93 122 **95** 43
— Mrs. **52** 112 **55** 433 **57**
418 **62** 106 285 **70** 309
83 34 193 **97** 269 272 **98**
302 **137** 19
— Widow **58** 402 **146** 273
____ (Edwards) **120** 295
____ (Soren) **140** 159
____ (Storer) **140** 249
____ (Young) **112** 215
A. **115** 239
Aafye **66** 17
Aaron **61** 22 **66** 241 242
73 89 **114** 41 204

JOHNSON *cont'd*
Aaron Gay **128** 277
Abbie Lizzie Grant **83** 144
Abby **100** 168
Abby Ann **89** 233
Abby Ledora **80** 448
Abby W. (Laighton)
83 299
Abel **59** 150 **66** 239 **68**
198 199 **72** 285 **86** 334
92 53
Abial **72** 201
Abial (Leavitt) (Lazell)
88 259
Abiathar **59** 146 276
Abiel **54** 200 292 **59** 275
Abigail **52** 223 **53** 408 **55**
52 369-371 **56** 135 138
139 158 168 170 297 298
57 192 352 **58** 129 178
282 **59** 72 81 82 84 85
143-146 148 151 153 188
276 278 281 282 **60** 249
360 **62** 271 **63** 290 **66**
228 235 237 239 240 242
67 29 115 68 143 144 **70**
319 345 **72** 201 **77** 202
315 **78** 259 **79** 310 **84**
140 **86** 306 **90** 355 **91** 81
267 297 **94** 162 **95** 358
106 211 **114** 28 **116** 135
118 320 **121** 274 **124** 80
125 214 128 218 **132**
323 **137** 325 **140** 309
147 227 231
Abigail (Bancroft) **95** 277
Abigail (Cooper) **91** 183
Abigail (Fry) (Willis)
114 275
Abigail (Gardner)
(Thompson) **140**
313 315
Abigail (Gilbert) **93** 366
Abigail (Goodnow)
114 29
Abigail (Hooper) **90** 238
Abigail (Johnson) **86** 306
124 80
Abigail (Leavitt) (Lazell)
115 193
Abigail (Oliver) **112** 152
Abigail (Parsons) **97** 343
Abigail (Perry) **116** 42
Abigail (Phillips) **116** 190
Abigail (Stansfull) (May)
146 275
Abigail (Waldo) **87** 211
Abigail (Willard) **110** 223
Abigail B. **74** 62
Abigail Brewster **76** 136
Abigail Butler **66** 243
Abigail K. **86** 380
Abigail R. **59** 282
Abijah **59** 149 150 279
Abner **55** 369-372 **88** 352
Abraham **53** 70 **55** 369
76 144 **90** 383 **97** 339
148 114
Acenith **142** 284
Achsah **59** 281 **66** 241
Achsah Washburn **66** 242

JOHNSON *cont'd*
Acton **111** 128
Adalia Lathrop **80** 42
Adaline Bourne (Bly)
  102 145
Adam **66** 241 **125** 16
Addie **100** 197
Adelaide **55** 371
Adelaide M. **68** 198
Adelia Melissa (Chase)
  87 259
Adeline **56** 133 **66** 243
Adeline (Richardson)
  125 291
Adeline (Thompson)
  88 392
Adeline Maria **128** 277
Adeline Newton **66** 243
Adeline T. **95** 37
Adelpha **88** 375
Adelpha (Lazell) **88** 376
Adyan **51** 112
Agnes **67** 171 **86** 131 **101**
  82 **146** 271 272
Agnes A. **88** 285
Agnes Amelia
  Livingston **82** 493
Agnes L. (Fowler) **92** 169
Agnes L. (Leslie) **83** 432
  434
Ahitable **61** 381
Aholiab **66** 40
Albert **91** 326
Albert H. **86** 317
Albert M. **111** 122
Albert N. **111** 127
Albert R. **80** 261
Albion **101** 234
Albion W. **83** 299
Aldred **76** 169
Alexander **73** 224 **76** 136
  138 139 141-143 145 **84**
  136 140 **90** 54 **96** 321
Alexander H. **90** 58
Alfred **66** 103 **67** xxxiv
  68 v vii-ix xv 287 **70** v
  vii viii x 43 86 90 9vii-xi
  xvii 76 **73** v vii viii xi
  74 v vii viii xi 82 159
  162 **75** v vii xi xviii 73
  163 225 315-317 **76** v
  vii x xvii 77 154 251 322
  77 v vii xv ciii 79 82 83
  155 238 241 321 326 **78**
  75 110 192 217 219 220
  444 **79** 104 105 114 187
  194 213 215 216 225 **80**
  196 219 221 222 334 **81**
  3 63 106 110 208 233 235
  82 10 221 248 250 251
  271 354 **83** 219 245 246
  84 205 **85** 214 **86** 214
  87 161 211 212 **88** 163
  173 **89** 343 **92** 169
Alfred Christian (Mrs.)
  107 133
Alfred Waldo **68** 145
Alice **59** 85 **67** 170 171 **76**
  224 **90** 248 **100** 29 **101**
  273 **130** 235 **131** 127
  146 270-273

JOHNSON *cont'd*
Alice (Briggs) **146** 273
Alice Cornelia **82** 365
Alice Everett **91** 183
Alice J. **98** 258
Alice Marion **94** 23
Alice Preston 432 **83** 431
  432
Alice Trevett **82** 365
Alitha **82** 420
Allen **76** 273 **129** 57
Allison Dyson **148** 82 84
  213 365
Alma **80** 46
Almena **104** 96
Almira **66** 241 **87** 19
  140 309
Almira (Capron) **143** 365
Almira C. **90** 56
Almira S. **93** 346
Almon **112** 57
Alonzo **92** 169
Alonzo G. **101** 234
Alpheus **66** 242
Alphoretta L. (Carlton)
  130 52
Alta **92** 332
Alta L. **81** 332
Alvin P. **111** 154
Alvin Page **51** 76 **81** 363
  82 234 **87** 209 **105** 158
  116 227
Amanda **82** 420 **84** 140
Amanda J. (Fernald) **119**
  69 **120** 68 **123** 75
Amandus **66** 96 **69** 385
Amariah **90** 383
Amela **56** 254
Amelia **54** 296 **90** 53
  126 209
America S. **84** 137
Amos **56** 138 139 **59** 150
  66 239 242 **67** 116 **70**
  345 **80** 69
Amy **59** 69 278 **71** 133 **75**
  12 **79** 71 **129** 67 **130** 232
Andrew **54** xlix 249 **56**
  lvii **59** lxiv lxv **70**
  xxxvii **77** 244 **80** 305 **81**
  247 **84** 137 **125** 214 **136**
  67 138 139 **146** 271
Andrew F. **83** 432 434
Angelina **66** 241
Angle **112** 296
Ann **56** 136 59 152 **60** 18
  67 170 172 **73** 265 278
  74 62 **79** 266 357 **80** 51
  99 283 **114** 185 **141** 343
  142 62
Ann (Arnold) **111** 122 127
Ann (Deering) **93** 60
  94 41
Ann (Maverick) **97** 60
Ann Delana (Jett) **117** 41
Ann E. **147** 231
Ann Eliza (Pike) **100** 204
Ann Elizabeth Agnew
  86 380
Ann Jane **128** 264
Ann Maria **69** 38

JOHNSON *cont'd*
Ann McGee (Willis)
  114 277
Ann S. (Briggs) **116** 257
Ann Sarah **68** 145
Anna **55** 369 **56** 140 298 **59**
  69 152 259 277 **60** 130
  66 16-18 241 243 328 **69**
  160 260 **70** 227 **72** 202
  73 39 **75** 303 **77** 202 203
  88 93 **98** 130 **102** 275
  141 355
Anna (Atkinson) **87** 212
Anna (Belcher) **142** 128
Anna (Hedges) **91** 180
Anna (Martin) **111** 133
Anna Augusta **72** xx **88**
  392 **89** 80 136
Anna Elizabeth **87** 17
Anna Louisa **59** cvii
Anna Maria **68** 145
Anna Maria (Taylor)
  98 342
Anna Moody **83** 203
Anna Pennock **79** 358
Anne **53** 311 **56** 137 **67** 53
  90 90 **91** 267 **96** 240
  100 140 **115** 212 220
  123 108 **146** 270-273
Anne (Cook) **126** 83
Anne (Downes) **146** 272
Anne (Gillford) **146** 273
Anne E. **147** 231
Annetje **66** 17
Annie (Taylor) **100** 40
Annie Elizabeth (King)
  94 23
Annie Elizabeth (Snow)
  75 xlix
Annie F. **74** 302
Annie M. **72** 130
Annie Penn **78** 325
Annie R. (Noble) **95** 378
Annis **146** 274
Ansel L. **111** 127
Anson **66** 241 **68** 144
  76 151
Anthony **52** 258
Antius F. **77** 58
Antje **66** 17 18
Apelton **129** 49
Arad (Mrs.) **121** 93
Aratas (Fitz Randolph)
  97 339
Arbella **75** 236 **84** 353 **99**
  227 **107** 41 **110** 276 **124**
  285
Arch **143** 62
Archibald **57** 140 **59** 64
Arnold **97** 137
Artemus W. **126** 220
Arthur F. **68** 250
Arthur Stoddard **54** xli 14
  55 xxxi **67** xxx **84** 181
  90 124 **93** 131 **96** 154
  99 139 162 **100** 124 **101**
  138 **102** 115 **112** 133
  152
Arthur Stoddard (Mrs.)
  77 156 **78** 205
Arvilla Lola **66** 243

JOHNSON *cont'd*
70 xxxiii
Asa **54** 84 **55** 383 **56** 347 **59**
  145 279 383 384 **66** 19
  240 **71** 85 **72** 202 **88** 227
  137 97 334 **148** 169
Asa S. **100** 313
Asach **57** 333
Asahel **54** 199 **76** 149 150
Ashbel **66** 237 239
Athina **57** 394
Atlen C. **111** 128
Augusta (Victor) **128** 170
Augusta E. (Hallenerentz)
  107 149
Augusta Virginia **64** 293
Augustus **55** 371 **64** 210
Aurelia **85** 295
Austin **71** 55 116 **88** 376
Ava T. **111** 128
Azariah **59** 143
Azel **59** 149 278
Azubah (Puffer) **114** 199
B. **59** 183
B. F. **53** 256 **54** xxxv
  130 51
Barbara **56** 138
Bartholomew **67** 171-173
Baruch **78** 378
Bathsheba **52** 468 **88** 356
  99 201
Belcher **55** 372
Belinda **147** 180
Ben **53** 369 **113** 147
Benajah **56** 297
Benjamin **52** 326 **54** 202
  227 **56** 79 136 137 140
  387 **57** 85 356 **58** 175 **59**
  82 83 85 86 144 149 150
  276 278 279 **62** 356 **63**
  290 **66** 17 18 240 243 **69**
  280 **72** 201 202 **73** 153
  78 409 **88** 64 **90** 113 **94**
  363 **107** 184 253 **109**
  211 **110** 284 **118** 313
  120 41 **121** 212 216 **125**
  203 **126** 251 **129** 61 67
  132 323 **136** 60 61 **140**
  315
Benjamin Anderson
  135 76
Benjamin F. **78** 317
Benjamin G. **83** 503
Benjamin Newhall **65** 201
Bennoney **84** 140
Bertha L. **69** 206
Bethiah **59** 80 81 83 **67** 173
  68 142 **72** 201 **125** 287
Bethiah (Hartwell)
  127 289
Bethiah (Martin) **86** 334
Bethiah (Newhall) **112** 152
Bethiah (Reade) **86** 334
  87 211
Betsey **57** 391 **59** 280 **63** 49
  64 151 **66** 243 **71** 56 **73**
  113 167 **83** 141 142 **88**
  29 349 **89** 104 105 **99**
  199-201 **101** 339 **104**
  284 **111** 123 **113** 113
  115 25 125 **125** 108 223

JOHNSON *cont'd*
Betsey (Clough) (Tibbetts)
  100 40
Betsey (Terry) **88** 29
Betsey Abigail
  (Richardson) **98** 365
Betsey B. **66** 112
Betsey S. **83** 142 143
Betty **59** 277 280 **66** 239
  67 219 **68** 143 **70** 345
  88 64 **113** 174 **124** 80
Betty (Bradstreet) **97** 262
Beulah **66** 237 239
Bia **84** 218
Billings **82** 181
Birdie E. **98** 365
Boardman **55** 368
Bracket **73** 74
Bradstreet **97** 262
Bretelle **98** 365
Burke **97** 137
Burren **51** 72
Byancy **97** 137
Byron Berkeley **63** 204
  68 xxxi 206 **69** xxxii 95
C. **68** 132 133
C. H. **100** 214
C. M. **91** 326
Caleb **52** 341 **55** 369 372
  57 302 **61** 217 **65** 376
  66 234-243 **67** 216 **125**
  287 **126** 83 **127** 191 **136**
  134
Caleb Albro **80** 448
Caleb Burbank **66** 243
Calvin **52** 341 **67** 122 **72**
  201 **83** 138 140-142 **84**
  448
Calvin Lester (Mrs.)
  107 133
Camillus Ridder **83** 143
Carl Edward **115** 150 151
Caroline **57** 391 **71** 116
  73 89 178 **74** 302 **79** 44
  81 265 **92** 258 **111** 127
  147 231
Caroline Emily
  (Rittberger) **100** 313
Caroline Esther (Rixford)
  64 xxix xxxiii
Caroline L. **86** 297
Caroline Priscilla **113** 83
Caroline S. **123** 179
Caroline Scribner **86** 240
Carpenter Burlingham
  88 356 **99** 201
Carrie Borden **87** 379
Carrie Lavina **116** 63
Carver **93** 273
Catherine **52** 197 **55** 271
  56 297 59 278 **66** 68 **67**
  169 172 176 **69** 154 **76**
  39 **88** 376 **100** 242 **113**
  311 **115** 53 **125** 216
Catherine (Clarke) **109** 79
Catherine (Hunter)
  95 305
Catherine (Skipper)
  (Maverick) **96** 239 240
Catherine C. **128** 262
Catherine Jewett **82** 201

JOHNSON *cont'd*
Caty (Mountfort) **125** 220
Caziah **56** 140
Cecil **141** 110
Celia **78** 188 **86** 197
Cephas **55** 371 **59** 281
Chandler **137** 361
Charity **55** 369 370 **56** 298
  57 88
Charity Betsey **55** 372
Charles **55** 370-372 **59** 282
  63 348 **66** 236 243 **72**
  182 **75** 181 **76** 47 **86** 379
  91 326 **93** 24 **97** 144
  100 204 **107** 149 **126**
  270 **128** 170
Charles Aug. **128** 175
Charles B. **109** 258
Charles Brayton **62**
  xxviii xxxvii
Charles C. P. **97** 21
Charles DeForest **100** 248
  102 65
Charles E. **89** 302
Charles Edward **94** 23
Charles F. A. **91** 326
Charles Fabian Herman
  101 121 **107** 124 131
  136 149
Charles H. **91** 304 **95** 378
Charles Henry (Mrs.)
  101 124
Charles Isaac **112** 246
Charles King **104** 117
Charles L. **82** 433
Charles Lincoln **80** 42
  138 133
Charles Musgrove
  102 123
Charles Owen **116** 81
Charles Robbins **93** 122
Charles S. **92** 332
Charles Samuel **74** 316
Charles Sweet **52** 397
  110 76
Charles Wendall **83** 143
Charlie **98** 194
Charlotte **54** 11 **60** liii **66**
  242 **109** 79 **125** 137
Charlotte (Chase) **87** 328
  88 26
Charlotte Abigail (Howe)
  54 cxxxiv 11 **74** lxiv **82**
  364 365 **112** 152
Charlotte Howe **82** 365
Charlotte P. **83** 142
Chauncy **126** 155
Chester **97** 137 **123** 19
Chloe **59** 64 **60** 332 **66** 241
  100 187
Christian **76** 116 121 127
Christiana O. **55** 371
Christina (Nordquist)
  128 172
Christina (Storm) **128** 170
Christine **79** 133 **105** 221
Christopher **146** 271
Cicely **146** 273
Cicely (Bawman) **146** 272
Cina **56** 255
Cinderilla Ann **76** 267

JOHNSON *cont'd*
Clara **80** 42 **86** 197
Clara Belle Lord **92** 332
Clara Esther (Cole) **86** 362
Clara Louise **89** 132
Clara M. **83** 299 303 **89** 302
Clare **54** 84 **56** 354 **146** 272
Clarendon **66** 241
Clarinda L. **83** 503
Clarissa **55** 283 **59** 281 282
  69 168 **79** 44 **82** 181 **83**
  234 **126** 66
Clarissa (Carver) **88** 227
Clarissa Austin (Crown)
  91 291
Clarissa F. **79** 310
Clarissa Louisa **68** 199
Clark **66** 239 240 242
  123 266
Clark Gerry **66** 243
Claus W. **128** 92
Clifton **54** 121 122
Clinton **86** 362
Clinton G. (Mrs.) **120** 236
Clistie B. **112** 324
Comfort **65** 377
Concurrence **56** 59
Content **72** 201
Cora Estella (Smith) **100**
  247 248 **102** 65
Cordelia (Haight) **107** 207
Cornelia **66** 243
Cornelius **52** 427 **53** 408
  56 140 **66** 17-19
Cressy **86** 14
Currence **137** 282
Cynthia Henrietta **68** lxiii
Cypress **137** 361
Cyrena **101** 94
Cyrus **59** 279 **62** 122 **83**
  503 **89** 12 **125** 238
Cyrus W. **125** 238
Damaris **56** 138
Dan **71** 202
Danford **73** 253
Daniel **55** 369-371 **56** 133
  135 137 138 297 298 **59**
  86 151 280 **64** 123 **66**
  235-240 242 243 **67** 53
  55 171 172 **72** 130 **76**
  145 151 **83** 160 **86** 287
  87 124 **88** 351 **90** 237
  238 **92** 378 **98** 302 **99**
  200 **104** 284 **105** 285
  108 315 **115** 20 **116** 42
  120 113 **125** 23 219 291
  294 **128** 218 277 **134**
  334 **142** 205 P**115** 27
Daniel C. **89** 302
Daniel Coffin **61** lvi
Daniel Hobbs **92** 378
Daniel John (Mrs.)
  108 134
Daniel T. **122** 218
Daniel W. **119** 281
David **55** 371 **56** 134 297
  298 **57** 413 **58** 16 **59** 151
  213 280 281 **65** 131 **66**
  238 240 241 **71** 321 **73**
  39 **75** 185 **81** 265 **83** 34
  503 **84** 136 **86** 123 **100**

JOHNSON *cont'd*
  40 **101** 94 **106** 211 **116** 7
  117 195 **119** 289 **121**
  279 **125** 257 **130** 53
David B. **108** 315
David E. **104** 284
David N. **61** 217
Davis B. **85** 195
Dayton **55** 370
De Witt Clinton **83** 143
Dearborn **92** 284
Debby (Webber) **125** 217
Deborah **53** 56 410 **59** 85
  276 **66** 227 235 236 **68**
  199 **70** 78 76 268 **78** 314
  79 49 **86** 379 400 **115**
  193 **121** 123 211 **134**
  255 **136** 80
Deborah (Arey) **86** 400
Deborah (Cole) **86** 69
Deborah (Preston) **86** 334
Deborah C. **90** 43 **126** 245
Delucia Sophia **103** 142
Dena **109** 261
Dennis **65** 113 **88** 350 351
  356 **99** 197-201 **104** 284
Desire **88** 350 **99** 197
  142 205
Dewitt Clinton **66** 243
Diadame **111** 115
Diah A. **98** 365
Diana **56** 298 **64** 257
Diantha **55** 372
Didymus **129** 21
Dillington **58** 280
Dinah Holbrook **57** 393
Diodate **77** 202 **81** 265
Dodicy **101** 234
Dole **59** 143
Dolly **59** 281 **66** 40
  148 169
Dolly (Bacheldor) **90** 237
Dominic **148** 318 321
Donald Coit **100** 311
Donald E. **120** 316
Dora **66** 242
Dorcas **54** 200 202 292 **67**
  115 **99** 282 **146** 271
Dorcas (Hooper) **91** 28 33
Dorcas (Nele) **146** 272
Dorman **120** 93
Dorothy **59** 143 **66** 235-
  238 **67** 169 171 **71** 256
  146 274
Dorris Davids (Mrs.)
  105 128
Dower **97** 339
Drusilla **73** 262
Duzenbury **76** 267
Dwight Henry **68** 199
Dyar C. **101** 234
Dyer **147** 216-218 230 231
Ebenezer **51** 45 **54** 199
  201 202 **55** 369 **56** 249
  57 412-414 **58** 62 393
  59 69 82 84 85 146-148
  275-278 **65** 351 **66** 328
  68 144 **69** 162 **70** 153
  72 202 **75** 176 181 **84**
  136 137 **86** 379 **91** 180
  93 346 **98** 302 **115** 25

JOHNSON *cont'd*
  129 66
Ebenezer B. **77** 80
Ebenezer Murray **68** 144
Ebenezer Oscar **91** 291
Eber **88** 376
Eber B. **77** 80
Edelbert M. **111** 127
Edith (Feeley) **97** 48
Edith Augusta Rooch
  (Nix) **115** 151
Edith L. **63** lviii
Edith M. **105** 155
Edith Mabel **100** 111
Edith Maude **97** 121
Edmund **93** 366 **109** 238
  113 157 **129** 67 **141** 328
Edmund Roe **109** 238
Edna **117** 124
Edward **51** 423 **53** 241
  412 415 **54** 199 **56** 139
  368 **57** 351 352 **59** 79-86
  143-152 275-282 **60** 101
  61 lvi 154 198 **62** 21 58
  63 204 238 289 290 **64**
  21 **65** 276 **66** xiii **67**
  170-173 177-179 **68** 142-
  145 206 **69** 158 287 **70**
  79 **71** 8 310 **74** 322 **75**
  221 225 **76** 236 **77** ci cii
  281 **80** 434 **82** 364 **85**
  454 **86** 334 349 **87** 211-
  213 216 **95** 305 **96** 373
  109 222 **112** 152 **124**
  189 190 **125** 151 **129** 11
  350 353 **131** 14 17 19
  127 **132** 6 7 13 16 **134**
  286 **136** 43 **137** 94 **139**
  60 321 322 324 **140** 313
  316 **143** 35 36 39
Edward (Mrs.) **83** 343
Edward Alonzo **93** 66
Edward Coke **82** 100
Edward Crosby **72** xx
  81 364 **82** 247 364 365
Edward Everett **82** 122
  236 **83** 144 **91** 183 298
  92 150
Edward F. **51** 377 378 381
  383 384 **52** 53 **57** 351 **58**
  49 52 53 127 **61** 105 **117**
  273 **141** 53 **143** 38
Edward Francis **59** 79
  143 275 **60** xxxiv 101
  67 170 **68** xxi **73** 3 **77**
  xxxviii ci cii **87** 215
Edward Hine **55** 370 371
Edward Moses **83** 141 144
Edward Robbins **109** 79
Edward Stearns **64** xxxiii
Edward Taft **62** 271
Edward W. **124** 34
Edwin Comstock **112** 317
Edwin H. **148** 173
Edwin M. **145** 256
Edwin R. **58** lxxix **120** 159
Edwin R. (Mrs.) **125** 72
Effie C. **109** 261
Egbert B. **107** 207
Eldridge Reeves **84** 110
  185 **100** 47 115 313

JOHNSON *cont'd*
Eldridge Reeves
  Fenimore **100** 313
Eleanor **52** 427 435 **55** 165
  65 352 **66** 233 234 **67**
  380 **77** ciii **85** 220 **88**
  275 375 **92** 269 **93** 24
  100 301 **129** 34 56
Eleanor (Frost) **108** 216
Eleanor (Hall) **137** 334
Eleanor (Norton) **93** 24
Eleanor (Twigden)
  94 330 335
Eleanor Foulke **100** 248
  102 65
Eleazer **59** 145 **61** lvi **78**
  306 **84** 271 272 **99** 207
  100 27 29 **101** 273 **115**
  103 **140** 67 158
Eleazer A. **61** lv lvi
Electa **83** 503
Eleo **100** 27
Eli **66** 242 243 **101** 94
Elias **62** 271
Elihu **56** 139 **73** 39 **100** 248
  102 65
Elijah **57** 414 **67** 122 **73** 187
  76 143 **80** 434 **99** 66
  100 303 **129** 271 274
Eliphalet **56** 297 **84** 137
  115 34
Elisha **52** 327 **56** 140 **58**
  139 **66** 242 **68** 198 199
  69 287 **79** 353 **80** 434
  93 366 **101** 94 234 **126**
  83 **129** 57 **147** 231
Elisha G. **89** 298 302
Elisha Moses **107** 79
Eliza **52** 74 **59** 282 **68** 199
  71 53 **85** 457 **91** 119 123
  92 378 **115** 38 **129** 395
  134 336
Eliza (Barlow) **125** 219
Eliza (Bunton) **120** 142
Eliza (Towne) **95** 378
Eliza Ann **72** 248
Eliza Anna **123** 285
Eliza C. **116** 260
Eliza J. (Gage) **107** 72
Eliza Jane **77** 224
Eliza Millett **83** 144
Eliza R. **116** 258
Eliza Shepherd (Harris)
  93 192
Elizabeth **53** 209 415 **55**
  271 369 371 372 404 **56**
  29 135 139 256 297 298
  58 cix 129 **59** 69 84-86
  144 145 147 148 151-153
  280 282 **60** 18 **62** 146
  147 261 **63** 290 291 **64**
  376 **65** 49 **66** 19 227 235-
  238 241 243 308 331 **67**
  55 117 170-173 285 **68**
  143 144 199 **69** 38 154
  155 **70** 79 **71** 8 366 **72**
  27 **73** 39 218 220 **74** 262
  75 176 179 181 **77** 202
  78 260 315 419 **79** 266
  81 408 **82** 116 **83** 140
  141 **84** 136 271 **90** 73 **92**

JOHNSON *cont'd*
  49 **96** 240 **97** 60 356 **98**
  348 **100** 3 300 **103** 142
  105 314 **106** 211 227
  108 239 **109** 208 **110**
  285 **111** 108 325 **112**
  102 215 **114** 184 290 293
  115 20 34 44 140 **116**
  256 **121** 53 **125** 289 **126**
  83 **136** 30 138 139 **139**
  323 **140** 68 **146** 270-273
  275 278 **148** 50
Elizabeth (Adams)
  110 284
Elizabeth (Barnes) **124**
  189 190
Elizabeth (Blake) **100** 248
  102 65
Elizabeth (Bushnell)
  106 211
Elizabeth (Chadderton)
  148 114 127
Elizabeth (Cutter) **125** 214
Elizabeth (Delloe) **146** 272
Elizabeth (Elliot) **110** 223
Elizabeth (Estol) **133** 232
Elizabeth (Gilbert) **91** 180
Elizabeth (Gwin) **146** 272
Elizabeth (Hamlin)
  102 65
Elizabeth (Haskins)
  121 245
Elizabeth (Longley)
  90 105
Elizabeth (Maverick) **96**
  239 **97** 60
Elizabeth (Patterson)
  83 138
Elizabeth (Porter) **90** 73
  91 180 **100** 247 **102** 65
  146 267 274 **148** 45 46
  49 50 57 65
Elizabeth (Portridge)
  (Hamlen) **91** 180
Elizabeth (Prosser)
  147 231
Elizabeth (Sanderson)
  128 43
Elizabeth (Sawyer)
  110 223
Elizabeth (Story) **110** 223
Elizabeth (Whitford)
  88 296
Elizabeth (Wilder) **83** 139
Elizabeth B. **108** 315
Elizabeth C. (Page)
  110 223
Elizabeth Chambers
  79 357
Elizabeth F. **77** 182 **90** 113
Elizabeth J. **142** 4
Elizabeth J. (Bartlett)
  90 58
Elkanah **65** 381 **129** 66
Ella **111** 188
Ella G. **89** 302
Ella Jeanette **82** 201
Ella Viola **107** 134
Ellen **70** 69 **81** 130 **114** 191
  146 271
Ellen (Cheney) **146** 275

JOHNSON *cont'd*
Ellen Ann **80** 43
Ellen S. **111** 125 127
Ellena **56** 297
Elmer David (Mrs.)
  103 119
Elmer M. **111** 128
Elmer Wiberg (Mrs.)
  98 147
Elmira **73** 39
Elsie A. **85** 166
Elsie Elizabeth **101** 122
Elsie L. **89** 302
Elsie Reeves (Fenimore)
  100 313
Elvira **76** 47 **112** 57
Elvira (Eaton) **112** 55 57
Emanuel **65** 124
Emeline **62** 122 **78** 375
  96 61 **97** 137
Emeline (Hall) **86** 334
Emeline (Leavitt) **83** 183
Emeline (McCollough)
  100 248 **102** 65
Emeline A. (Fayerweather)
  145 256
Emily **59** 282 **66** 243 **77**
  221 **79** 154 **82** 200 **88**
  340 **129** 49
Emily Allen **85** 166
Emily Frances **68** 199
Emma **66** 243 **82** 181
Emma E. **80** 434
Emma F. **98** 227
Emma G. **72** 107
Emory O. **124** 192
Enoch **56** 36 **59** cvi 143
  150 279 **130** 235 **135**
  158
Enoch Stafford **59** lv cvi
  cvii
Enos **55** 369 **67** 125
Ephraim **66** 239 **73** 88 89
  84 426 **87** 95 **128** 266
  136 138
Erastus **62** 271
Eri **111** 127
Eri H. **101** 234
Erick T. (Mrs.) **101** 124
Esdras **67** 173
Estella S. **77** 180
Esther **55** 370 372 **56** 138-
  140 **57** 192 352 **58** 128
  175 **59** 80-85 143-145
  148 151 **63** 290 292 **66**
  238 **68** 143 **70** 37 **71** 8
  269 **72** 201 **73** 89 **77** 281
  83 126 **84** 136 **87** 282
  92 321 **93** 185 **111** 296
  120 41
Esther (Sawtell) **126** 16
Esther (Wheadon)
  124 189
Esther Billings **92** 378
Esther E. **116** 67
Esther L. (Smith) **91** 384
Esther Whittemore
  (Wright) **91** 183
Ethel **84** 49
Etta **66** 243
Etta M. **98** 258

JOHNSON *cont'd*
Eunice **53** 315 **55** 369 **58**
  167 **59** 276 **66** 241 **67**
  115 117 **68** 199 **70** 122
  153 **76** 133 **100** 74 **104**
  284 **112** 228 **115** 130
  125 104 **129** 50
Eunice (Kellogg) **89** 324
Eunice (Linscot) **90** 328
Eunice (Merrick) **86** 334
Eunice (Stevens) **117** 227
Eunice Carrie (Dawson)
  100 312
Evan Lewis **98** 342
Evangeline **98** 365
Evelyn Herrick **83** 143
Everett B. **84** 40
Experience **59** 143 **70** 229
  73 88
Experience (Briggs)
  126 220
Experience Ann **73** 89
Ezekiel **59** 280 **62** 357
  129 66 315 **133** 232
Ezra **59** 70 **83** 141
Ezra Larence **83** 138
Ezra T. (Lillie) **129** 395
F. C. **54** 106 237 **55** xxix
  58 213
Fannie **116** 57
Fanny **59** 279 **85** 337
Fanny (Noble) **94** 363
Fenn **60** 78
Fern **100** 204
Fidelia **96** 61
Fidelia E. **90** 385 386
Fletcher W. **97** 121
Flora **79** 55
Florence **100** 311
Florence Esther **144** 116
Florence Ida **78** 322
Florence M. (Dickinson)
  100 311
Florence May **100** 113
Florence Pearl **116** 72
Frances **61** 172 **67** 173
  80 208
Frances (Skyngle)
  146 272
Frances A. (Edmonds)
  111 127
Frances A. (Kenniston)
  61 lvi
Frances Adams (Coit)
  100 311
Frances Decker **68** 145
Frances Elizabeth **91** 103
Frances Emily **68** 145
Frances H. **90** 204
Frances Miller **78** 290
  84 103
Frances S. **114** 311
Francis **58** 129 **59** 85 86
  151 281 282 **63** 35 300
  73 88 **78** 181 **92** 321
  103 43 **124** 92 254 **146**
  271-273
Frank **54** xxxviii **92** 332
  112 154
Frank Coit **75** x xxiii **99**
  134 145 150 **100** 311

JOHNSON *cont'd*
Frank G. **90** 383
Frank Leonard **78** 330
  79 202 **91** 148 176 180
  105 318
Frank N. **116** 63
Frank Thomas **74** 302
Franklin **93** 191 **130** 52
Franklin (Mrs.) **93** 125
  143 191
Franklin Russell (Mrs.)
  90 136
Fred **69** 137 **93** 329
  109 269
Fred F. **83** 299 300
Fred N. **116** 63
Frederick **59** 151 282 **63**
  49 **66** 239 **71** 118 **89** 324
  115 254
Frederick (Mrs.) **115** 254
Frederick Charles **54** xli
  55 369 370 **56** xxx 108
  59 xli **62** xxxv **65** 304
  66 xlviii **68** xlii lxiii
Frederick Green **68** lxiv
Frederick W. (Mrs.) **113**
  243 324
Fredericke **148** 113
Freelove **57** 412 **63** 56
Freelove (Manchester)
  102 17
Frida Charlotte **110** 227
Gabriel **63** 42
Garard **67** 169 170
Gardner **66** 241 **128** 127
Garrett **67** 131
Geneva Louise (Whitney)
  85 108
George **55** 372 425 **59** 80-
  82 **61** 237 **62** 245 **63** 113
  65 22 124 236 **66** 239
  242 243 **67** 170-172 177
  178 **68** 142 **73** 88 **75** 181
  221 **80** 40 **84** 217 **88** 376
  94 363 **100** 140 108 168
  113 311 **114** 199 **115** 16
  146 271 272
George Atkinson **68** 145
George B. **66** 227 **93** 274
George Blake **112** 152
George Clarke **109** 79
George D. **61** 109
George Dana **69** 287
George Francis (Mrs.)
  85 195
George Henry **63** xxxiii
  68 xxx 205 **81** 113
George James **56** 24
George L. **89** 302 **100** 208
George Merritt **83** 144
George N. (Mrs.) **103** 119
George P. **78** 416 **98** 365
George R. **78** 417
George Ransom **55** 370
George W. **51** 82 **57** 393
  126 141 **132** 302
George Washington
  110 76
George William **63** 314
  110 76
Georgia **68** lxiv

JOHNSON *cont'd*
Georgiana Parker (Miller)
  68 145 **87** 211
Gertrude Louise **87** 216
Gertrude Louise (Hall)
  115 144
Gideon **74** 253 **78** 259
  128 218
Giles **58** 129 **59** 85 151 282
  77 230 **103** 89 **105** 212
Giles M. **85** 166
Gladys **86** 362
Gladys Hanks **120** 236
Glennis **105** 130
Goldie Mildred **92** 332
Gorham **66** 277
Gorrel **81** 408
Gould **100** 312
Grace **71** 31 250 **79** 78
  116 63 **146** 271
Grace (Negus) (Fawer)
  146 274
Grace Ella / Etta (Arnold)
  115 150 151
Grace Rich (Treadwell)
  83 343
H. B. **91** 326 **98** 258
H. C. **147** 168
H. Earle **97** 398
H. Louise **86** 379
H. P. **72** 130
Halcyone Lenora **88** 169
Halle **84** 296
Hannah **51** 305 **53** 232 406
  55 222 372 **56** 36 134
  136 137 140 257 297 298
  57 89 **58** 180 337 345
  393 **59** 81-83 85 86 143
  146 150-152 280 281 **62**
  124 **64** 156 **65** 351 **66** 19
  40 234-236 240 241 **67**
  173 271 371 **68** 199 **70**
  75 79 227 **72** 283 **73** 193
  75 xlix 176 181 **76** 135
  142 **78** 180 262 315 **79**
  40 145 **81** 130 **82** 200 **83**
  138-141 **84** 137 352 **86**
  306 **88** 349 **91** 27 33 261
  99 199 **101** 323 **106** 35
  69 **108** 154 315 **110** 284
  285 **111** 115 **112** 215
  115 63 **118** 80 **119** 10
  121 282 **124** 11 **125** 216
  128 170 **133** 249 250
  302 **134** 171 333 **142**
  128 129 137 186 342 **144**
  34 **146** 271 275
Hannah (Barnard)
  126 142
Hannah (Chandler) **136**
  138 139
Hannah (Crosby) **119** 248
Hannah (Foulke) **100** 248
  102 65
Hannah (Guthrie) **144** 348
  354
Hannah (Harmon) **91** 16
Hannah (Hobbs) **108** 168
Hannah (James) **126** 251
Hannah (Lazell) (Turner)
  88 258

JOHNSON *cont'd*
Hannah (Ricker) **90** 238
Hannah (Robbins) **94** 318
Hannah (Sawyer) **126** 143
Hannah (Sperry) **91** 183
Hannah (Tenney) **110** 223
   126 5
Hannah (Young) **112** 102
   115 60
Hannah A. **100** 228
Hannah B. **104** 284
Hannah Brooks **85** 437
Hannah D. **89** 302
Hannah Edith **147** 217
   231 232
Hannah Maria
   (Lumsbury) **145** 309
Hannah P. (Warren)
   125 238
Hannah S. **83** 144
Harland Hills (Mrs.)
   97 158
Harmond **65** 285
Harold Burton **86** 367
Harold Pendexter **77** ciii
Harriet **66** 241 **67** 131 **68**
   250 **69** 280 **83** 497 **84**
   217 **90** 55 96 **91** 361 **92**
   172
Harriet (Brown) **88** 333
Harriet (Johnson) **84** 217
Harriet (Revere) **145** 309
Harriet C. **58** 345
Harriet D. (Clark) **120** 159
Harriet E. **66** 277
Harriet Elizabeth **102** 4
Harriet F. **111** 123
Harriet L. **80** 434
Harriet Louise **145** 309
Harriet Miller **79** 358
Harris **101** 234 **111** 302
   305 **126** 83
Harrison **77** 224 **126** 143
Harry **76** 225
Harvey **61** 196 **83** 99
Hasadiah **64** 147
Hattie E. **104** 284
Hattie Florence (Elliot)
   93 367
Haynes **110** 223 **124** 62
Haynes C. **68** 250
Health **72** 130
Helen **146** 272
Helen (Davis) **112** 152
Helen (Smith) **91** 180
Helen B. **81** 72
Helen Burroughs **68**
   xxxiv **97** 306
Helen J. **77** 175
Helen Lorraine (Fracker)
   (Jensen) **124** 262
Helen M. **66** 277
Helen P. **74** 302
Helen Randall **86** 379
Helen Sylvester (Woods)
   138 133
Helen V. **73** 39
Helen Wright **84** 189 232
Helene Vennum **82** 201
Hendrick **66** 17
Henri Lewis **65** xxxvi

JOHNSON *cont'd*
Henrietta **73** 154 **88** 343
   114 60
Henrietta (Bailey) **98** 265
Henrietta Colt **87** 216
Henrietta T. **108** 315
Henriette (Lazell) **89** 12
Henry **58** 68 **59** 83 86 **66**
   242 **75** 174 **83** 445 **84**
   140 **85** 123 **90** 105 **91**
   326 **100** 208 **114** 266
   129 66 **146** 271 272
Henry A. **51** 16
Henry Aaron **88** 341
Henry Elisha **62** xxxix
   74 xxviii **84** 180 **90** 124
   93 366 **94** 79 142
Henry Elliott **93** 367
Henry F. **54** xxxviii **55**
   xxxi **77** 180 **81** 113
Henry L. **85** 457
Henry P. **93** 210 **146** 373
Henry Poellnitz **117** 77
Henry Spring **66** 243
Hepzibah **66** 237
Hepzibah Hunt Page
   83 503
Herbert D. **80** 448
Herbert Fisk **101** 121
Herbert J. **86** 367
Hersford **64** 114
Hervy **56** 348
Hester **52** 123 **59** 80 82 **67**
   172 **76** 127 **146** 273
Hester (Gardner) **140**
   315 316
Hester Ann **68** 150
Hetty **114** 188
Hezekiah **55** 370-372 **59**
   143 **64** 215 **73** 115 279
   76 152 171 **93** 192
Hiram **121** 93 **126** 155 220
Holden P. **78** 308
Holman **114** 9 **128** 277
   145 361
Holton **102** 275
Homer **66** 242
Hope **55** 369
Horace **127** 33 **132** 323
Horace Newton **98** 265
Hosea **101** 234
Howard **112** 57
Howard M. **118** 327
Hugh **57** 220 **64** 238
   85 457
Hugh Andrew **85** 195
Hugh Moore **123** 284 285
Huldah **54** 271 **57** 89
   68 144
Huldah L. **92** 169
Humility **110** 285 **112** 215
Humphrey **57** 84-86 178
   79 266 **121** 121 202 **146**
   273 275
Ichabod **59** 84 145 152 **63**
   289 **132** 302
Ida (Nelson) **128** 92
Ida Christina **128** 175
Ida M. **92** 332
Ida May **68** 250
Ida Minette **80** 448

JOHNSON *cont'd*
Illathera B. **108** 315
Ira **101** 234 **111** 127
Irah **88** 286
Irene **78** 113
Irene E. **144** 348 354
Isa Wood **83** 144
Isaac **51** 188 **52** 468 **53** 69-
   71 **54** 179 **55** 369-371
   56 250 251 255 386 **57**
   264 **58** 68 281 **59** 72 151
   256 280 281 371 **61** lvi
   62 146 **63** 96 **65** 86 **66**
   240 **67** 115-117 122 219
   222 **68** 74 **69** 157 **72** 201
   73 253 **75** 236 **78** 93 264
   83 183 **85** 221 **86** 69 376
   379 **88** 259 263 355 **90**
   73 383 **91** 180 183 326
   92 378 **93** 62 211 **96** 236
   99 102 103 109 201 207
   208 227 279 **100** 27 247
   311 **102** 65 **106** 23 234
   235 **107** 46 **108** 168 **113**
   37 **114** 86 277 115 193
   121 121 **125** 289 294
   126 142 **128** 301 **129** 55
   67 **142** 120 270 279 342
   353 **143** 253 342 146
   261 267 273 274 **148** 45
   50 65 114 127
Isaac F. **86** 362
Isaac L. **104** 284
Isaac Lord **114** 277
Isabel **59** 148 **63** 75 **114**
   182 **146** 273
Isabella **51** 133 134 **68** 144
Isabelle **88** 394
Isaiah **54** 200 202 292 **56**
   384 387 **73** 89 **128** 277
Isaiah W. **116** 257
Israel **54** 271 **55** 369 370 **59**
   151 **66** 238 **76** 135 136
   83 141-143 146 147 **109**
   111 199
Israel W. **83** 141 143
Israel Wood **83** 144
Issacher **66** 238
Ivie **77** xxix
J. **92** 169 **129** 50
J. A.B. **108** 216
J. Clayton (Mrs.) **122** 80
J. G. (Mrs.) **99** 50
J. M. **90** 33
J. W. **87** 379
Jacob **54** 106 **55** 369-372
   389 **56** 134 **57** 333 **62**
   186 **64** 19 **65** 304 **66** 16-
   18 227 277 **68** lxiii 143-
   145 **70** 345 **73** 39 88 89
   87 211 **99** 208 **115** 20 45
   132 193
Jacob L. **91** 326
Jacobus **66** 16
James **51** 46 **54** 11 **55** 254
   56 136 137 **57** 190 **58**
   139 392 395 **59** 60 146
   147 149 276 277 **64** 260
   315 345 **65** 50 **66** 47 239
   67 116 **68** 199 **73** 142
   227 270 **74** 263 **75** 12 **76**

JOHNSON *cont'd*
37 127 **80** 261 **82** 364 **88**
392 **89** 326 **91** 326 **92**
280 **93** 366 **98** 104 194
100 41 **104** 131 **105** 288
112 152 **117** 318 **126** 83
133 323 **137** 361 **142**
389 **145** 364 **148** 262
James B. **93** 60 66 **94** 41
109 269 **120** 16
James Brown **66** 241
James C. **78** 380
James E. **120** 15
James Gerald (Mrs.)
101 124
James H. **66** 243
James Lathrop **86** 380
James M. **83** 503 **89** 302
James N. **137** 48
James Paul (Mrs.) **98** 147
James Riley **87** 95
James T. **117** 41
James Theodore **82** 181
James Theron **119** 316
James W. **86** 380 **103** 268
James Whitcomb **88** 351
James Wickhum **99** 199
Jan **66** 16-18
Jane **56** 79 **64** 252 **66** 235
72 202 **73** 88 166 **79** 35
115 315 **125** 247 257
128 264 **132** 323
Jane (Main) (Parker)
111 127
Jane (Robinson) **120** 39
Jane Margaret **77** 269
Jane T. **104** 284
Jared **101** 234
Jarvis **147** 230
Jasper G. **72** 130
Jasper Nichols **61** xxxiv
63 xxxiii **66** xlix **69**
xxxv
Jean (Robinson) **120** 39
Jeanette C. **78** 236
Jeanette Shirley **108** 136
Jedediah **68** 144 **70** 153
Jedidah (Ellis) **120** 113
Jehoida Pitt **55** 371
68 lxiii
Jemima **59** 148 **77** 224
137 94 99
Jemima (Austin) **130** 53
Jemima (Ball) **89** 106
Jemima (Munger) **110** 29
Jennetji (Wycoff) **101** 324
Jennette Ann (Huntoon)
86 106
Jennie **51** 189 **122** 218
136 324
Jennie Ambrosina **98** 365
Jennie E. (Murphy)
130 54
Jennie M. **78** 205 **89** 347
Jennie Maria (Blake)
112 152
Jennings **56** 138
Jeremiah **56** 133 134 297
66 15 327 **75** 176 **78** 260
81 126 **84** 137 140 **87**
328 **88** 26 **99** 283

JOHNSON *cont'd*
Jerrod **91** 326
Jerusha **56** 298 **59** 148 **86**
376 380 **101** 234
Jerusha K. **101** 234
Jess **59** 150
Jessamine **80** 208
Jesse **59** 153 280 **66** 19 **91**
183 **110** 76 223 **125** 94
127 115
Jessie **129** 50
Jessie A. **93** 249
Joab **89** 106 **98** 302
Joan **67** 169 171 **123** 249
143 215 **146** 270-272
274
Joan (Wattes) **146** 272
Joanna **55** 369 370 **59** 147
280 **66** 15-18 234 235 **73**
115
Job **58** 237 **128** 127 218
Joel **51** 495 **59** 149 278 **66**
237 **78** 375 **79** 71 **92** 123
94 376 **108** 25
Joel Grant **83** 144
Johanna Christina
128 175
Johanna Marie
(Anderson) **86** 106
John **51** 39 41 45 133 134
222 342 **52** 207 211 361
53 48 406 408 **54** 164
200 449 **55** 52 369 **56**
132-140 297 326 **57** 84
88 350 **58** 29 30 107 **59**
64 80-83 151 153 260
276 281 282 **60** 50 332
345 360 **61** 136 360 381
62 122 223 226 227 229
337 342 343 357-359 **63**
60 61 66 120 123 125 138
242 343 **64** 253 257 325
340 342 **65** 34 118 355
66 15-17 35 68 75 202
205 228 233-243 277 **67**
29 169-173 176 177 182
216 380 **68** 142-145 191
199 312 **69** 51 154 155
70 73 345 **71** 256 339 **72**
130 201 **73** 88 89 149
167 278 **74** 62 285 286
292 **75** 181 221 **76** 75
116 127 **77** ci cii **78** 69
252 **79** 71 80 39 **81** 126
130 455 **82** 200 **83** 179
183 **85** 454 **86** 106 334
349 **87** 119 211 **88** 351
89 175 **90** 383 **91** 180
326 **93** 41 **95** 102 382 **96**
97 239 240 **97** 60 319 **98**
302 **99** 97 197 206 **100**
40 247 **101** 265 324 **102**
65 66 **103** 18 **104** 102
105 318 **106** 23 24 30
109 164 **110** 223 285
112 102 215 241 **113** 86
93 309 **114** 146 **115** 60
117 4 **119** 244 248 **120**
113 141 142 **121** 36 177
195 206 **125** 34 94 115
239 **126** 16 83 **128** 170

JOHNSON *cont'd*
218 **129** 49 62 64 275
134 333 **137** 37 251 252
140 159 296 **141** 343
145 361 **146** 261-263
268 270-274 278 **148** 46
50
John B. **65** 9 **108** 315
John Benjamin **69** 163
John Bradford **80** 42
John C. **91** 326
John Chaloner **62** 272
John Dix **59** 281
John E. **76** 47
John Edgar **58** 109
John F. **98** 365
John French **54** xxxvi **55**
xxix **56** xxx 205 **60** 56
61 xlv lv lvi **115** 28 31
John H. **98** 365 **130** 53
John Jay **115** 20
John Oscar Emile **86** 106
John Oscar Emile (Mrs.)
85 190 195 **86** 106 109
203
John P. **86** 380
John S. **65** 376
John Victor (Mrs.) **98** 147
John W. **78** 375 **88** 296
John Wesley **148** 173
Johson **67** 31
Jonah **66** 238 **91** 16
Jonas **58** 59 **59** 145 150 278
66 240 **137** 99
Jonathan **58** 139 **59** 145
149 152 **62** 342 **63** 59 61
62 66 120 121 123 125
219 222 223 226 **66** 239
241 242 **73** 253 **74** 224
82 364 **86** 43 **88** 29 **90**
390 **92** 285 **96** 61 63 **100**
248 **102** 65 **110** 223 **112**
152 305 **114** 50 **115** 137
118 204 **121** 281 **129** 57
67 **135** 158 251 **145** 50
146 270 273
Jonathan C. **69** 330
Jonathan H. **67** 271
Jonathan H. E. **76** 40
Jonathan J. **66** 242
Joseph **52** 433 **55** 370 **56**
136 137 297 **57** 85 **58** 33
62 138 **59** 82-85 143 146-
148 276 277 **60** 95 130
249 **62** 120 **64** 25 65 **65**
124 **66** 108 233-235 **67**
129 68 143 330 **69** 38 **71**
202 316 **72** 201 73 225
76 46 127 136 137 174
78 401 **79** 37 **80** 42 **81**
265 **83** 138 140-142 144
84 137 140 **88** 64 395 **90**
237 **91** 180 262 267 **93**
274 366 **96** 339 **97** 269
98 265 **100** 247 **101** 324
102 17 65 **104** 117 284
106 165 **108** 315 **110**
223 **111** 325 **114** 184
115 33 123 127 **117** 227
121 198 **125** 109 **126** 5
83 **129** 67 **133** 111 **142**

JOHNSON *cont'd*
128 129 **144** 45 **146** 271-
275 **148** 50
Joseph B. **108** 315
Joseph F. **80** 434
Joseph G. **67** 274
Joseph H. **55** 372 **60** 187
91 326 **100** 187
Joseph Howard **74** 302
Joseph S. **78** 378
Joseph W. **83** 144
Joseph Warren **83** 143
Joseph Winfield **80** 43
Josephine **66** 243 **81** 482
483 **89** 324
Josephine C. **68** 199
Josephine Wells **82** 201
Josephus **59** 281
Joshua **55** 370 **56** 257 385
59 86 145 259 **66** 237
240 241 **79** 357 **80** 51 **92**
228 **95** 273 **97** 274 **103**
300 **115** 53 **116** 295 **121**
274 281 **146** 271
Joshua (Mrs.) **97** 274
Josiah **51** 305 **55** 165 **56**
256 **58** 132 **59** 82 85 150
151 279-282 **63** 289-291
75 304 **78** 302 **91** 180
107 313 **113** 37 **114** 122
116 190 **118** 80 **136** 61
Josiah F. **83** 141
Jotham **59** 152 **137** 97
Joyce **67** 171 **146** 271-273
Joyce (Cooper) **146** 272
Jozinah D. **111** 127 129
Judith **57** 555 **59** 145 149
276 280 **63** 74 **66** 16 17
68 143 **131** 127 **132** 275
135 158 251 **139** 294
Judith (Joy) **95** 382
Julia **101** 234 **109** 188
Julia A. **66** 227
Julia Ann **77** ci cii **80** 42
Julia Dean **98** 342
Julia Emerson **68** 145
Julia Etta (Rich) **84** 40
Julia H. **101** 234
Julia M. **83** 160 162
Juliette R. **68** 155
Justin **55** 370
Kate (Barton) **107** 113
Katharine **59** 80-82 148
61 22 **64** 238 **67** 172 **76**
79 **81** 482 483 **85** 137 **88**
293 **146** 271-273
Katharine Maria **65** 9
Katy (Dame) **113** 311
Keith A. **142** 395
Kenneth Simonds **77** ciii
Keziah **56** 140 **59** 149 150
61 22 **110** 284 **111** 22
114 48 204
Keziah (Bennet) **114** 41
204
Kimball **119** 316
L. **121** 55
L. A. **93** 249
Lambert **56** 139 140 **66**
15-18 **67** 380
Lamphire **66** 241

JOHNSON *cont'd*
Laura **52** 341 **78** 263
112 57
Laura (Fitts) **89** 102
Laura (Whiting) **110** 73
Laura Ann **80** 271
Laura R. **69** 137
Laura S. **83** 144
Laurence Ayres **108** 134
109 238 **117** 231
Laurence Henry Hitch
(Mrs.) **90** 77
Lavinia **97** 99
Lawrence **79** 78 **88** 401
128 18 **146** 271 272
Lawton **102** 17
Lazzie **128** 92
Leander T. **77** 178
Legrand **68** 199
Lemuel **66** 238 **73** 253
Lenna O. **92** 332
Leon C. (Mrs.) **122** 315
124 72
Leon Leslie **95** 146
Leona **105** 127
Leona Amy **109** 130
Leonard **83** 141 **91** 180
Leonora Polk **78** 325
Lester **101** 234
Levi **54** 83 56 348 **59** 276
280 **61** 194 196 **63** 68 **66**
241-243 **76** 150 **83** 99
140 **93** 366 **111** 133
Levi Lincoln **66** 242 243
70 xxxiii
Levina **123** 284 285
Levina (Powers) **123** 284
285
Levinah **66** 238 239
111 314
Lewis **51** 45 **66** 239 **69** 62
72 201 **76** 146 **90** 114
128 277
Lewis Cranston **80** 42
Lillian A. (Merriam)
86 367
Lillias Sanford Sheffield
(Moriarty) (Snow) **101**
229 **123** 5
Lily A. **83** 432 **84** 18
Linda **66** 243
Litna B. **111** 128
Liva **126** 83
Lodema **68** 143 **70** 226
Lois **55** 370 371 **58** 284
129 315
Lois (Hotchkiss) **58** 284
Lorana **120** 51
Lorand V. **96** 97
Lorinda (Williams)
86 362
Lot **53** 415
Lotta J. **68** 330
Lottie **100** 214
Lottie Irene **80** 42
Louis **117** 124
Louisa **55** 51 371 **66** 243
76 272 **90** 56 **144** 56
Louisa A. **101** 234
Louisa Abigail **68** 144
Louisa Catherine **136** 308

JOHNSON *cont'd*
Louisa F. **104** 284
Louisa Fuller **85** 234
Louisa Mathewson
85 428
Louise **96** 33
Louise H. **83** 432 434
Louise Miller **87** 216
Lovewell **75** 308
Lovilla **66** 243
Lovilla E. **67** 273
Loving **56** 297
Lucinda **55** 372 **64** 151 **66**
239 **70** 153 **83** 142 143
85 295
Lucinda (Bassett) **125** 16
Lucinda F. **104** 284
Lucius E. **125** 295
Lucretia **59** 277 280 **68** 330
104 284 **119** 298 304
Lucretia (Kilborn)
132 323
Lucretia (Ranney) **109** 188
Lucretia (Wheeler) **113** 83
Lucretia Taylor **86** 380
Lucy **56** 139 **59** 145 151 152
275 279 280 **61** 357 **62**
272 **66** 239 240 243 **68**
144 199 **70** 153 231 **79**
154 398 **83** 160 **94** 55
111 130 **125** 222 291
126 66
Lucy (Johnson) **125** 291
Lucy (Kent) **126** 141
Lucy (Temple) **100** 248
102 65
Lucy Amelia **86** 380
Lucy Ann **62** 122
Lucy D. **88** 295
Lucy Doty **81** 368
Lucy Emeline (Dauchy)
111 302 305
Lucy Jane **84** 140
Lucy Lane **66** 242
Lucy Noyes **115** 25
Lucy Perkins **86** 380
Lucy W. **98** 85
Luella Adelia **70** xxxiii
Luke **53** 302 **73** 89 **78** 414
Lulu **85** 196
Lulu Theodosia **88** 395
101 324 **102** 61 129 **103**
68
Lurandas **72** 130
Luther **54** 200 **59** 279 **66**
241 **67** 122 **92** 258
Lydia **54** 83 **55** 54 369-371
59 69 86 275 277 280
282 **62** 150 **66** 240-242
328 **67** 122 **68** 143 144
70 153 231 **73** 253 **76**
127 80 42 434 **83** 99 **85**
55 **88** 340 **90** 113 **97** 135
144 **98** 258 **112** 57 **130**
304 **136** 243
Lydia (Bancroft) **94** 318
Lydia (Cleaveland) **87** 211
Lydia (Gaines) **85** 55
Lydia (Hastings) **114** 277
Lydia (Hews) **126** 67
Lydia (Joyce) **89** 233

JOHNSON *cont'd*
Lydia (Payn) **97** 137
Lydia (Underwood)
  130 235
Lydia Ann (Parker)
  120 16
Lydia Caroline **54** cxxxix
Lydia Elizabeth **80** 42
Lydia Elizabeth
  (Chapman) **91** 183
Lydia Elizabeth Parker
  109 79
Lydia F. **111** 110 110'
Lydia M. **83** 141
Lyman **66** 19 **101** 234
Lyman D. **101** 234
Lyndon Baines **120** 141
  143 236 **121** 229
Mabel **56** 135-137 **66** 205
  68 278 **69** 160 **81** 495
  97 159 **115** 76
Mabel (Blais) **86** 367
Mabel A. (Libby) **83** 299
  300
Mabel Amanda Crown
  91 291
Mabel Atherton **89** 343
Mabel L. **65** 9
Magdalene **72** 54 **74** 141
Magee **114** 188
Maggie **80** 168
Maggie E. **74** 316
Mahala Almira **123** 285
Mahala Frances **64** 210
Mahlon **86** 240
Malinda **60** 346
Malinda Caroline **123** 285
Mamie E. (Mosher)
  130 53
Marcie F. **120** 309 **121** 70
Marcus **68** 199 **86** 334
Marcus Monroe **86** 334
Marcy **88** 64
Margaret **52** 246 **57** 86
  58 395 **59** 81 **60** 360 **65**
  124 355 **67** 173 **68** lxiv
  72 201 **76** 70 75 136 **77**
  153 **81** 313 **84** 97 137
  140 **93** 26 **94** 245 **102**
  123 **104** 246 **111** 148
  121 199 **125** 247 257
  127 307 **128** 36 42 **130**
  132 **134** 335 **139** 301
  144 348 354 **146** 271
  272
Margaret (Fitch) **120** 15
Margaret (Gardner)
  146 273
Margaret (Ingraham)
  112 152
Margaret (Morris)
  146 278
Margaret (Rule) (Page)
  104 178 **108** 180
Margaret Atherton
  (Nichols) **89** 343
Margaret L. (Davis)
  83 179 183
Margaret Laughton
  55 lxi
Margaret M. **65** 8

JOHNSON *cont'd*
Margaretta Lawrence
  (Paddock) **112** 317
Margery **51** 389 **52** 137
  56 298 **61** 286 **63** 278
  100 247 **102** 65 **146** 261
  270 274
Maria **66** 18 242 243 277 **73**
  89 **82** 100 **109** 79
Maria (Cutler) **125** 288
Maria (Gilbert) **137** 360
Maria (Prout) **91** 180
Maria A. **90** 56
Maria F. **123** 75
Maria Louisa **92** 87
Maria Louise **84** 333
Maria Marcy **111** 128
Marian Christine **100** 109
Marie **146** 271
Marie Agnes **80** 42
Marie Francoeur
  (Brewster) **90** 77
Marie Merrill **83** 144
Marietta Amelia (Lazell)
  89 102
Marietta E. **77** 58
Marion F. **77** 178
Marjorie E. **116** 63
Marjorie Walthal **117** 73
Marmaduke **71** 92 **104** 82
Maro **90** 136 **117** 72
Marquis **111** 187
Marquis A. **111** 128
Martha **51** 305 **56** 297 298
  58 280 **59** 81 85 150 151
  277 279-281 **61** 198 **62**
  58 **63** 138 379 **64** 124 **66**
  108 237 238 242 **67** 172
  374 **68** 142 **73** 88 **75** 221
  306 **78** 418 **82** 465 86
  341 380 **87** 124 **92** 332
  94 363 **95** 355 **97** 188
  99 201 203 **101** 234 **128**
  277 **130** 234 **134** 293
  146 271 273
Martha (Bailey) **147** 229
Martha (Barker) **108** 315
Martha (Dahlquist)
  115 151
Martha (Perkins) **100** 311
Martha (Roberts) **103** 43
Martha (Waller) **89** 343
Martha (Whitehouse)
  112 241
Martha (Whitemore)
  118 80
Martha A. **55** 52
Martha A. (Fracker)
  124 192
Martha Ann **80** 40 **86** 380
  108 315 **109** 131
Martha Ann (Mumford)
  86 380
Martha Tappan **72** xlii
Martin **90** 33 **110** 73
Martina Regina **110** 307
Mary **52** 140-142 207 211
  53 415 464 **54** 14 119
  352 **55** 225 369-371 376
  56 135 137 140 298 **57**
  178 333 355 356 394 **58**

JOHNSON *cont'd*
  281 **59** 70 81-83 85 86
  144-146 148-150 275-277
  279-281 **61** 339 **62** 186
  271 **63** 355 **65** 113 351
  381 **66** 17-19 40 227 234
  235 237 239 241 243 **67**
  125 129 171 173 216 375
  68 95 142-144 240 **70**
  153 **71** 279 **73** 141 184
  74 62 **76** 127 **77** 202 262
  280 **78** 68 265 378 418
  79 37 357 **80** 51 **82** 375
  433 **83** 18 **84** 445 **85** 227
  86 43 **88** 333 **90** 358 383
  92 123 **93** 329 **95** 290
  98 302 **99** 207 208 299
  100 293 **101** 234 248
  104 284 **106** 23 30 211
  243 **107** 180 **109** 12 228
  112 305 **113** 102 **114**
  181 189 **115** 59 140 141
  117 239 **120** 136 **121**
  132 277 **126** 83 **128** 265
  277 **129** 41 **137** 182 **142**
  203 **146** 261 270-274
  148 50 145-147
Mary (Ball) **137** 94
Mary (Bicknall) **125** 287
Mary (Bryant) **137** 249 251
Mary (Clark) **146** 272 273
Mary (Clerks) **146** 273
Mary (Coffin) **113** 113
Mary (Cook) **126** 83
Mary (Earley) **86** 334
Mary (Farley) **136** 138
Mary (Fowall) **115** 139
Mary (Fuller) **112** 152
Mary (Gates) **90** 54
Mary (Godfrey) **125** 16
Mary (Gustin) **114** 181
Mary (Guy) **85** 432
Mary (Harriman) **135** 158
Mary (Harris) **91** 180 **100**
  247 **102** 65 **148** 50
Mary (Heath) **146** 263
  268 270 272 274 275 **148**
  50
Mary (Johnson) **148** 146
Mary (King) **121** 245
Mary (Lyon) **125** 239
Mary (Magdalyn) **101** 324
Mary (McKean) **98** 364
  99 173 **100** 74
Mary (More) **128** 36
Mary (Newcomb) **102** 261
Mary (Porter) **100** 248
  102 65
Mary (Powell) **88** 341
Mary (Sage) **106** 211 215
Mary (Sawtell) **126** 5
Mary (Smith) **146** 278
  148 51
Mary (Stoddard) **112** 152
Mary (Stuart) **100** 303
Mary (Tallman) **147** 231
Mary (Tibbetts) (Gatchell)
  100 41
Mary (Tripe) **115** 137
Mary A. **54** cxxxiv **70** 198
  86 379 **91** 40 **101** 234

JOHNSON *cont'd*
  104 284 **110** 73 **129** 49
Mary A. (Smith) **110** 222
Mary Adelaide **110** 73
Mary Allura **80** 43
Mary Ann **61** lv **73** 226 **79**
  357 **80** 42 261 **91** 28 34
  101 94 **113** 257 **147** 218
  228-230
Mary Ann Chase **101** 94
Mary Ann Denison
  101 234
Mary Armstrong **61** 147
  84 448
Mary Ashercraft **67** 384
Mary B. **125** 223 **136** 78
Mary C. **103** 47
Mary Carlton **95** 246
Mary Caroline **134** 226
Mary Carrington **97** 186
Mary Chase **72** xlii
Mary Coffin **77** 324
Mary Cook **81** 203
Mary Cooper **94** 138
Mary D. (Weeks) **85** 457
  458
Mary Dean **100** 44 108
  115 312
Mary Dorothy **85** 458
Mary E. **100** 208 **141** 18
Mary E. (Billings) **93** 274
Mary E. (Palmer) **130** 53
Mary E. (Spensly) **90** 114
Mary Edith **98** 126
Mary Eleanor **97** 73
Mary Eliza **81** 324
Mary Elizabeth **77** ciii
  88 296
Mary Elizabeth
  (Gladding) **90** 280
Mary Fern **107** 134
  118 159
Mary Frances **80** 208 **84**
  107 187 **98** 248 265 **99**
  150
Mary Frothingham
  82 365
Mary Fry (Lewis) **91** 183
Mary G. **89** 326
Mary Gracie **82** 375
Mary H. **70** 158 **73** 89
Mary Hannah (Stoddard)
  65 xxxiii
Mary J. (Gray) **89** 302
Mary Jeanette **82** 201
Mary Josephine **102** 305
Mary L. (Moody) **119**
  284 285
Mary Louisa **68** 145
Mary Louise **92** 228
Mary Lovina (Shepard)
  109 258
Mary Luvanne Ayres
  (Trowbridge) **94** 90
Mary Stoddard **112** 152
Mary T. **88** 139
Mary Tufts (Stone) **97** 73
Maryett **80** 434
Matilda **66** 40 **79** 353
Matilda K. (Haeusen)
  107 149

JOHNSON *cont'd*
Matthew **57** 351 **59** 80 81
  83 85 86 150 152 **67** 172
  173 **68** 142 **75** 221 **85**
  454 **86** 349 **99** 299
Mattie **130** 234
Maud E. **78** 450
Maude (Linscomb)
  97 121
Maude Harriet (Hobbs)
  118 237
Maude Horne **118** 74 75
Maurice Flower (Mrs.)
  120 147
Mehitable **56** 135-137 **67**
  117 372 **71** 202 **79** 71
  106 108 **133** 282 **145** 50
Melinda **83** 141
Melville **78** 382
Melvin **89** 298
Melvin M. **69** 289 **70** 290
Melvin Maynard **92** 305
Menzo M. **101** 234
Mercy **56** 298 **59** 149 **73**
  253 **74** 224 253 **106** 211
  126 83
Mercy (Ellis) **121** 137
Meribah **59** 276
Micah **59** 149 **66** 237 240
  241
Michael **52** 223 **67** 67
  88 118
Mildred M. **130** 54
Mildred Noé **102** 145
Miles **53** 56 **55** 369 **59** 276
  95 277 279
Millard F. **104** 284
Miller **105** 281
Milly **59** 279
Milton **91** 183
Milton Harmon **91** 183
Mime **73** 253
Mindwell **55** 370
Minerva **66** 243
Minerva E. (Fleming)
  98 227
Minnie **82** 439
Miranda **68** 199
Miriam **56** 139 **62** 123 **76**
  149 **127** 8
Mitty **78** 380
Molly **52** 327 **59** 275
  66 239
Moody **57** 391 **91** 262
Mortimer L. **83** 299 301
  84 29
Morton **82** 100
Moses **52** 340 **56** 140 **62**
  120 125 **65** 357 **67** 271
  73 253 **79** 193 **82** 200
  85 437 **91** 260 261 **110**
  29 **125** 295 **126** 225 **130**
  235 **142** 284 **143** 260
Munson **59** 281
N. D. **91** 202
Nabby **73** 88 89
Nabby (Bancroft) **95** 277
  279
Nabby (Hooper) **90** 237
Nahum **89** 233
Nancy **59** 371 **66** 242 **68**

JOHNSON *cont'd*
  145 **73** 89 **74** 263 **83** 141
  142 **87** 124 **98** 286 **106**
  108 **116** 84 **122** 130
Nancy (Atkinson) **87** 212
Nancy (Gibbs) **125** 289
Nancy (Jackson) **88** 287
Nancy (Linscott) **112** 241
Nancy (Silvester) **86** 287
Nancy C. **106** 108
Nancy H. **67** 271
Naomi **76** 170 **91** 385
Napoleon B. **97** 73
Nathan **52** 433 **54** 201 **59**
  145 278 **65** 351 **66** 240
  243 **76** 147 **86** 306 **89**
  383 **105** 207 **112** 57 58
  125 295 **142** 203
Nathan Brooks **59** 281
Nathan Griffing **78** 380
Nathan P. **112** 55 57
Nathan R. **104** 284
Nathaniel **56** 297 298 **57**
  89 404 **59** 83 277 **61** 286
  62 146 147 343 **63** 61 66
  120 123 **66** 233-235 **67**
  375 **68** 143 **69** 57 **73** 88
  89 **76** 147 151 171 **77**
  202 **81** 413 **83** 138 **84**
  140 **98** 200 **99** 200 **104**
  284 **106** 211 **107** 189
  109 79 **112** 215 **114** 179
  121 119 **128** 277 299
  146 261 278 **147** 52 **148**
  51
Nathaniel P. **76** 267
Nathaniel Severs **100** 312
Nehemiah **73** 89 **141** 193
Nellie E. (Preston)
  83 299 301
Nellie P. **122** 280
Nellie W. **101** 307
Nelson **100** 187
Nettie **66** 243
Nettie Avon (Richardson)
  86 106
Nettie E. (Hudson) **112** 57
Nicholas **63** 162 163 **66** 34
  67 173 **76** 121 127 **108**
  320 **127** 140 **129** 61 **146**
  271 272
Noah **59** 82 83 144 145
  151 277 281 **63** 289 290
  292 **65** 113 **90** 328 **108**
  19
Norman Constant **89** 102
Norton **119** 284 285
Obadiah **59** 83 147 276 **60**
  392 **68** 142-145 311 312
  70 153 154 **87** 211 **100** 4
  101 94 **129** 66
Obadiah Elderkin
  70 231 345
Obed **59** 69
Olediah **57** 333
Olive **52** 341 **59** 148 153 **66**
  243 **68** 143 **87** 290 89
  298 **91** 121 124 **116** 63
Olive (Briggs) **126** 270
Olive E. **128** 267
Oliver **58** 345 **86** 380 **98**

JOHNSON *cont'd*
122 **100** 311 **104** 284
Oliver L. **86** 380
Oriannah **104** 284
Orin **66** 243
Oroon Datis **66** 243
Orpha (Lowder) **117** 124
Orris **73** 89
Orson Elworth (Mrs.)
  103 119
Orval **125** 16
Othniel **75** 303
Otis **59** cvi
Otis Russell **82** 200
Otis S. **59** cvii
Otis Wells **81** 107 207 219
  82 200 248
Otto **86** 317 **128** 172
Palmer White (Mrs.)
  90 136
Pamela **125** 293
Patience **55** 165 **56** 138
  58 122 **63** 378 **64** 375
  72 201 **87** 336 **126** 83
Patience (Faunce) **114** 122
  116 190
Patience (Tallman)
  137 361
Patrick **106** 108
Patten **80** 69
Patty **54** 294 **66** 239 242
  73 88 89
Paul Franklin **80** 102 206
  100 108 232 247 248
  101 122 127 **102** 65 **105**
  318
Pauline **148** 186
Pearl **78** 328
Peggy **72** 201 **76** 37
Peleg Pearl **80** 42
Peluna **105** 161
Perley W. **98** 365
Permelia **101** 179
Perry (Mrs.) **99** 147
Perseverance **131** 123
Persis Isabel (Swett) **73**
  xix **90** 131 **93** 191
Peter **58** 34 35 **66** 237 239
  240 **75** 176 181 **76** 150
  84 140 **95** 257 305 **101**
  324 **124** 80 **125** 217 220
  141 314 328 **144** 262
  148 173
Peter B. **113** 83
Phebe **54** 199 **56** 138 387
  57 264 **59** 66 279 **61** 30
  66 238 240-242 **68** 199
  78 380 **79** 71 **81** 272 **83**
  503 **88** 349 **99** 199 **111**
  325 **135** 158 251 337
  136 362 **147** 231 232
Phebe (Burton) **112** 152
Phebe (Grant) **86** 69
Phebe Ann **79** 353 **80** 41
Phebe Ann (Angell) **147**
  214 216-218 230-232
Phebe F. **89** 298
Phebe H. **79** 78
Phebe Maria **84** 217
Phila **101** 234
Phila E. **89** 346

JOHNSON *cont'd*
Philadelphia Borden
  87 379
Philena (Barlett) **121** 177
Philip **66** 238 **76** 79
  135 218
Philip Stanley **94** 138
  112 222
Philo **76** 144
Philomela (Jewett) **85** 437
Philura **59** 260
Phineas **58** 284 **113** 32 34
  40
Phyllis **57** 404 **68** 144
Pierpont **101** 229
Pierrepont E. (Mrs.)
  123 5
Pierrepont Edwards
  91 142
Pillsbury **66** 277
Platt **111** 244
Pleasant **104** 102
Polly **53** 57 **54** 85 **58** 402
  59 282 **66** 239 **71** 276
  75 304 **80** 434 **88** 350
  99 197 **112** 57 **113** 34
  122 256 **124** 10 **125** 106
  133 156
Polly (Bachelder) **96** 339
Polly (Bragdon) **117** 228
Polly (Farnum) **132** 302
Polly (Newcomb) **102** 261
Polly A. **113** 32 40
Polly Ann **147** 218 226-
  230
Porter **62** 272
Priscilla **59** 146 **112** 239
Priscilla (Fletcher) **97** 21
Priscilla (Storer) **91** 302
Prudence **55** 369 **59** 383
  384 **69** 62 **132** 242
Prudie (Jenkins) **130** 51
Rachel **55** 370 **56** 256 298
  57 220 **59** 72 **66** 18 241
  68 174 **70** 79 **77** 202 **78**
  415 **83** 138 **88** 118 **90**
  187 **98** 194 **99** 206 **111**
  115 **114** 188 **115** 38 127
  120 93 **125** 115 **133** 282
  141 332 343 355
Rachel (Church) **120** 93
Rachel (Tewksbury) **100**
  248 **102** 65
Ralph **68** 199 **91** 28 33
  146 272
Ralph Cross **57** 346 **68**
  145 **82** 10 **89** 343
Ralph E. **64** 292
Ralph Miller **87** 216
Ralph Walter **118** 74 75
Randolph **72** 130
Ransom **55** 371
Ray W. **116** 63
Raymond F. **92** 332
Rebecca **52** 326 **55** 369 370
  56 140 **57** 333 **59** 73 80
  81 83 85 86 143-145 147
  148 277 278 **60** 78 **63**
  293 **66** 18 104 111 241
  67 29 31 173 **68** 143 **70**
  73 **72** 285 **76** 153 **78** 307

JOHNSON *cont'd*
  83 140-142 **84** 137 **87**
  124 **90** 383 **109** 318 **111**
  180 **117** 38 117 **121** 214
  271 **128** 277 **141** 385
  146 271
Rebecca (Baines) **120** 141
Rebecca (Brooks) **87** 211
Rebecca (Donovan)
  125 290
Rebecca (Lawrence)
  83 138
Rebecca Baines **120** 141-
  143 236 **121** 230
Rebecca E. **80** 42
Rebecca R. **108** 263
Return **148** 146
Reuben **52** 428 **53** 410 **55**
  83 369 **59** 146 147 275
  66 240 **74** 316 **77** cii **78**
  70 **92** 279 **129** 67
Reverdy **73** 275 **84** 333
Reyne **66** 18
Reynolds **79** 71
Rhea Duryea **113** 321
Rhoda **59** 153 282 **72** 202
  88 350 356 **92** 286 **99**
  197-201
Rhoda (Abbot) **135** 158
  251
Rhoda M. **75** 12
Rhoda Moorman **81** 455
Richard **59** cvi **62** 271 **66**
  15 68 **67** 169 **68** 180 **73**
  277 **80** 315 **81** 123 126
  91 183 **96** 321 **97** 327
  100 248 **102** 65 270 **131**
  127 **146** 271-273
Richard Brigham **122**
  207 208 **123** 220 **124**
  264 **125** 213
Richard M. **83** 143
Rinaldo **73** 137
Robert **53** 70 **56** 132-139
  297 298 326 386 **61** 145
  62 80 **63** 26 **64** 361 366
  65 55 **67** 169 **71** 31 250
  75 258 **81** 126 135 **102**
  185 **104** 96 **105** 96 **112**
  186 **127** 79 89 **143** 204
  144 348 354 **146** 271-
  273
Robert B. **83** 183 187
Robert L. (Mrs.) **98** 80
Robert Noé **102** 145
Robert Noé (Mrs.) **95** 146
  102 113 129 145
Robert Powers **123** 284
  285
Robert Raves **84** 140
Robert Underwood
  85 175
Robert W. **84** 108 **118**
  237 323
Robert Winder **63** 303
  64 xxxi **88** 401
Robert Wood **84** 185
Roberta Wood **86** 198
Robie F. **92** 332
Rollin L. **130** 54
Rosalie Morris **63** 303

JOHNSON *cont'd*
Rosamond (Porter) **111**
  12 128 187
Rosan Knowlton **112** 240
Rosanna **69** 330
Rosanna K. **66** 277
Rosanna Knowlton **112**
  240 **114** 146
Rosannah (Williams)
  125 303
Rose **146** 271 272
Ross B. **124** 80 **129** 315
Rowena M. (Cook)
  83 426 432
Roxana **59** 151 **60** 333 **66**
  241 **68** 161
Roxana M. **69** 145
Royal **78** 131 **126** 308 **127**
  79 **128** 284
Ruby **83** 406
Ruby (McFarland)
  126 220
Ruel **59** 280
Rufus **59** 276 **66** 238 240
  72 130 **117** 228
Ruhama **96** 240 **126** 83
Ruhamah (Steevens)
  129 21
Russell **112** 57
Rutgert **66** 16 17
Ruth **52** 340 **55** 372 **56**
  135 138 158 298 **58** 167
  59 83 144 146-150 249
  280 **61** 355 **66** 331 **67**
  115 216 **68** lxiv 144 199
  338 **71** 92 **72** 130 201
  202 **76** 141 **87** 285 **91**
  260 **96** 240 **108** 167 **110**
  285 **115** 130 **121** 278
  125 203 **137** 334
Ruth (Chase) **87** 255
Ruth (Cole) **86** 367
Ruth (Moulton) **141** 314
  328 **144** 262
Ruth (Rugg) **86** 334
Ruth A. **104** 284
Ruth Ann **52** 203
Ruth E. (James) **127** 33
Ruth Miranda **77** lxxxviii
Ruthy **78** 304
S. **91** 326
S. Albert **55** 370
S. D. **91** 326
Sabin **101** 339 **136** 78
Sabin B. **83** 142
Sabra (Howland) **126** 67
Salina **69** 163
Sally **59** 276 **66** 242 277
  68 311 **70** 227 **73** 89 **74**
  62 262 **75** 261 **76** 171 **83**
  140 142 **89** 298 **97** 137
  101 94 316 **104** 284 **122**
  279 **125** 109 220 **134**
  173 **140** 247
Sally (Elwell) **125** 294
Sally (Johnson) **97** 137
Sally (Knowlton) **84** 426
  125 109
Sally (Lincoln) **124** 200
Sally (Wadsworth) **91** 183
Sally Banks **77** 202

JOHNSON *cont'd*
Sally C. (Hawks)
  (Pillsbury) **114** 146
Sally M. **132** 302
Salmon **112** 58
Salonna **62** 271
Sam Ealy (Mrs.) **104** 144
Samson **104** 32
Samuel **53** 209 **54** xlvi
  cxxxiv cxxxv 11-14 352
  373 409 456 461 **55** 22
  369 **56** lxxv 134 135 137
  138 158 250 297 298 **57**
  89 352 355 **58** 109 175
  395 **59** cvi 69 83 84 86
  145 146 152 153 275 276
  60 18 **61** 101 286 339 **62**
  146 252 260 261 371 **64**
  376 **66** 234 235 237 241
  328 **68** 143 199 **69** 160
  218 347 **72** 244 **73** 88 **76**
  134 144 146 268 **77** cii
  280 **81** 408 **82** 200 364
  365 **85** 120 **86** 69 **90** 383
  91 200 326 **94** 368 **106**
  211 218 296 **110** 282 284
  285 **111** 22 **112** 152 215
  115 37 44 **121** 137 245
  127 304 **128** 43 **129** 64
  67 **130** 279 **142** 65
Samuel A. **57** 391 **83** 503
Samuel Ealy **120** 141
Samuel Leonard **91** 180
Samuel Lewis **76** 144
Samuel Marshall **79** 358
Samuel Monson **93** 366
  367
Samuel P. **78** 325
Samuel Pennock **79** 357
Samuel W. **83** 426 432
  111 323
Samuel Willard **123** 284
  285
Samuel William **64** 101
Samuel Wistar **78** 328
Sanford **73** 39
Saphronia (Freethy)
  112 154
Sarah **51** 222 425 **52** 428 **53**
  56 **55** 197 369 370 372
  56 134-139 297 298 **57**
  140 352 362 **58** 129 131
  395 **59** 145-148 151-153
  188 256 275-280 282 **60**
  95 **61** 154 203 236 **62** 61
  63 174 289 290 300 **64**
  376 **65** 165 352 **66** 16-18
  237-243 308 327 331 **67**
  36 115 277 **68** 144 199
  69 154 **70** 69 **71** 8 11
  355 **72** 104 201 285 **73**
  39 115 142 **74** 62 224 **75**
  176 181 185 191 258 **76**
  136 138 **78** 182 413 **79**
  50 **80** 434 **82** 10 282 291
  83 503 **87** 122 **90** 383
  92 185 326 **96** 78 240 **98**
  302 **99** 206 279 **102** 65
  106 151 **109** 68 **110** 231
  282 284 **112** 305 **114** 41
  115 135 141 156 214

JOHNSON *cont'd*
  121 245 281 **122** 256
  125 115 **128** 18 277 **133**
  232 **134** 297 333 **135**
  253 **141** 343 **145** 246
  146 270-273 275 **148**
  173
Sarah (Archer) **146** 272
Sarah (Armstrong)
  84 448
Sarah (Ayers) **126** 66
Sarah (Babb) **90** 390
  114 50
Sarah (Barrett) **125** 294
Sarah (Burrell) **110** 285
Sarah (Clarke) **120** 113
Sarah (Clewley) **114** 303
Sarah (Cory) **148** 357
Sarah (Cross) **87** 212
  89 343
Sarah (Daniels) **93** 366
Sarah (Ford) **91** 267
Sarah (Foster) **129** 85 86
Sarah (Hall) **91** 183
Sarah (Hawkes) **133** 323
Sarah (Haynes) **110** 223
Sarah (Huntington)
  85 222
Sarah (Keaser) (Gilloway)
  96 240
Sarah (Mansfield) **112** 152
Sarah (McDonald)
  101 324
Sarah (Redington)
  109 164
Sarah (Sanderson)
  127 191
Sarah (Shawe) **146** 272
Sarah (Sperry) **91** 183
Sarah (Stone) **88** 286
Sarah (Van Buskirk)
  108 320
Sarah (Wales) **126** 308
Sarah A. **58** 345 **127** 89 91
Sarah A. (Hopkins)
  105 109
Sarah Ann **92** 351 **94** 380
Sarah Ann (Fuller)
  119 281
Sarah Ann (Trickey)
  83 183 187
Sarah D. **101** 234
Sarah E. **76** 40
Sarah E. (Van Valken-
  burgh) **92** 169
Sarah Eaton **66** 239
Sarah Elizabeth **78** 325
Sarah Ellen **79** 358
Sarah F. **98** 258
Sarah Forster **74** 302
Sarah G. **68** 198
Sarah J. **86** 317
Sarah J. (Grindle) **109** 111
Sarah Jane (Angell)
  (Tolman) **147** 230
Sarah M. **109** 79
Sarah Norwood **73** 265
Sarah Osgood **77** 149
Sarah Perkins **85** 221
Sarah R. **138** 127
Sarah T. (Northup) **116** 63

JOHNSON *cont'd*
Sarah Wales **78** 131
Sarah Winslow (Cushing)
  68 145 **89** 343
Sardis **62** 160
Seleah **88** 64
Seneca **83** 142 143
Serena **101** 234
Serena Hubbard **101** 234
Seth **59** 85 150 151 281 **60**
  204 392 **62** 150 **66** 238
  74 62 **116** 42 **128** 277
  284
Seth Herrin **74** 302
Seymour Foulke **100** 248
  101 122 **102** 65
Shemei **125** 29
Shubael **59** 149 278 279
Shuborn **55** 369
Sibyl **56** 139 **59** 148 **76** 127
Sigrid I. **99** 32
Silas **55** 369 **59** 150
  128 277
Silas Dean **100** 312
Simeon **51** 42 **56** 139 **67**
  277 **109** 188
Simon **135** 158 251
Sisle **67** 171
Smith **66** 228 **73** 115
Solomon **55** 370 371 **60**
  357 **62** 223 226-228 336
  339 341-344 **63** 59-61 65
  66 118 120 125 **66** 233-
  243 **138** 117
Solomon Rice **55** 371
Solomon Whittlesey
  55 371
Sophia **55** 372 **66** 243 **84**
  137 **112** 57-59 **120** 39
Sophia (Rockwell) **112** 58
Sophia H. (Hotchkiss)
  126 208
Sophronia Aurora
  69 lxviii
Sophronia M. **67** 294
Spile **62** 271
Stanley Victor **115** 151
Stella **81** 265
Stella Emeline **77** xxviii
  77 **86** 109 204 334
Stephen **55** 271 371 **56** 297
  58 77 **66** 238 **67** 286 **70**
  154 229 **73** 193 **76** 39 **77**
  202 203 208-210 **79** 384
  83 503 **88** 287 **106** 215
  115 139 **123** 19 **125** 303
  128 218 **140** 19
Stephen Hotchkiss
  55 372
Steven **123** 29
Stintie **66** 17
Stuart Holmes **99** 145
  100 311
Subbiear **93** 260
Submit **58** 77 **60** 333 **79**
  384 **142** 341 342
Submit (Riley) **87** 95 104
Sumner **78** 205 **81** 110 231
  82 100
Supply **59** 148
Susa **98** 302

JOHNSON *cont'd*
Susan **56** 297 **59** 80 81 **66**
  84 **67** 171 172 176-178
  180 **68** 142 **75** 221 225
  77 ci **80** 448 **96** 160 **97**
  48 **103** 44 **109** 217 **110**
  222 223 **146** 271-275
Susan (Comes) **146** 272
Susan (Munter) **86** 334
  87 211 **131** 127 **139** 322
  324
Susan (Porredge) **86** 334
  87 211 **139** 324
Susan (Tripp) **109** 240
Susan A. **104** 284
Susan E. **68** 155
Susan F. **95** 272
Susan L. **59** cvii **124** 208
Susanna **54** 449 **57** 160
  58 16 132 393 **59** 81 82
  84 145 146 150 151 280
  282 378 **61** lvi 154 **64**
  12 **65** 351 354 **66** 234
  238 241 **67** 182 286 **72**
  14 **75** 307 **88** 64 **111** 256
  309 **114** 132 **115** 40 123
  125 37 **127** 191 **136** 306
  141 199 349 **148** 143
  262
Susanna (Brown) **97** 262
Susanna (Manchester)
  102 17
Susanna (Silvester) **86** 91
Susanna (Waters) **148** 262
Susanna (White) **87** 119
Susanna Payson
  (Whittemore) **108** 168
Susie **92** 169
Swen **128** 175
Sydney Evans (Mrs.)
  103 119
Sylvan **67** 36
Sylvanus **57** 394
Sylvanus Elihu (Mrs.)
  84 234 **85** 195
Sylvester **87** 255 **129** 54
Sylvester (Mrs.) **90** 280
Sylvia **66** 243 **75** 306
Sylvia (Gibbs) **123** 266
T. **70** 295 **147** 75
Tabitha **54** 202 **57** 190
  61 237
Tamar **56** 139 297 **59** 145
Taphena K. Denison
  101 234
Thaddeus Harris **62** 272
Thankful **54** 179 **66** 236
  124 80
Thankful (Cowles)
  142 342
Thankful L. **90** 115
Thena (Robinson) **92** 169
Theo **91** 326
Theodore **92** 332 **119** 69
  120 68 **123** 75 **147** 229
Theodosia (Schofield)
  88 395 **101** 324
Theresa **101** 94
Thirza **61** 95 **66** 243
Thirza Maria **66** 243
Thomas **51** 389 **55** 271 432

JOHNSON *cont'd*
  56 132-138 297 321 326
  57 389 **59** 282 **61** 67 134
  62 336 **63** 146 **64** 12 158
  321 343 **65** 172 **66** 15
  238 239 **67** 29 172 173
  68 199 239 **70** 69 249 **71**
  341 355 **73** 253 **75** 176
  79 353 **81** 126 272 **83**
  445 **84** 252 438 **85** 390
  86 131 289 **90** 358 **91**
  326 **92** 54 **94** 363 **109**
  282 314 **110** 223 262
  114 275 **116** 7 **119** 246
  121 106 124 208 **125**
  116 288 **127** 115 **131** 42
  139 133 **140** 176 **144**
  204 **145** 364 **146** 267
  270-274 **147** 227
Thomas Boyd **75** xlix
Thomas Conn **92** 378
Thomas H. **94** 402 **98** 286
Thomas Jefferson
  100 187
Thomas W. **95** 378
Thomasine **67** 171
Tillie **128** 94
Timothy **56** 297 298 385
  58 167 **59** 85 148 **61** 172
  66 239 242 **71** 8 **76** 139
  77 202 **85** 432 **96** 240
  97 60 **106** 211
Tirzah **64** 123
Tirzah Adaline **84** 459
Truman **62** 122 **68** 199
Tryntie **66** 15 17
Tryphoza **89** 103 106
Turall **66** 241
Unity (Esty) **99** 66
Uri (Mrs.) **121** 94
Uriah **66** 239 **87** 118 119
  90 383
Uzal **79** 71
Valerie M. **142** 126
Vashti **57** 333
Velona E. **68** 198 199
Vera **107** 133
Vergerice **146** 271
Vesta **126** 142
Vickery L. **130** 53
Victor M. **78** 382
Viola Alice **84** 192
Virginia **59** cvi
Virginia Ann **148** 173
Virginia Voight **65** xxxiv
Virginia W. **88** 341
Virlinda **73** 141
W. Harvey (Mrs.) **113** 321
W. R. **109** 269
Walcott Howe **54** 14
Waldo **68** 144
Walter **56** 137 139 140 **58**
  345 **66** 15-18 **67** 380 **71**
  53 **98** 258 **127** 8
Walter F. **66** 227
Walter W. **69** xxxii
Walter Whitney **55** xxxv
Wanda Dakota **86** 362
Ward Mark **97** 48
Warren **55** 369 371 **73** 39
  89 **92** 169

JOHNSON *cont'd*
Warren Scott (Mrs.) **85**
195 **90** 80 151 **91** 158 **92**
162 **93** 153
Warren Seymour **100**
247 248 **102** 65
Wealthian **66** 240
Weintie **66** 16 17
Weltha **88** 64 **103** 151
Wesley **68** lxiii
Whittenton **114** 188
Wilbur Warren **62** 309
Wilder **83** 139-142
Wilford **62** 147
Wilfred **146** 273
Will. **146** 273
Willard **66** 240 243 **89** 102
115 127
Willard Cummings **110**
222 223
Willett **55** 371
William **51** 381 **52** 123
125 140 141 258 **53** 20
209 311 415 **54** 237 **55**
369-372 390 391 **56** li 29
132-135 138 139 297 298
57 268 351 **58** 49 280
282 **59** 21 79-85 143-152
275-282 **60** 185 **61** lvi
62 252 **63** 138 190 242
290 343 **64** 266 **65** 123
124 235 354 **66** 15 181
241-243 308 331 **67** 115-
117 169-173 176-178 180
216 **68** lxiii 142 143 199
240 285 338 **69** 154 **70**
226 345 **71** 8 56 116 **72**
202 **73** 167 **75** 221 225
76 127 **77** ci cii 203 239
241 320 **78** 380 **80** 226
81 126 134 498 **82** 364
514 **84** 147 169 **85** 454
466 **86** 43 270 334 349
87 122 211 **88** 98 258
333 349 351 352 355 **90**
238 **91** 122 124 125 183
254 260 **93** 26 401 **94**
330 335 **96** 97 240 **97**
262 **98** 227 286 **99** 79
198-201 **100** 74 140 248
101 324 **102** 65 **104** 102
284 **106** 78 211 **109** 211
222 **110** 76 223 **112** 152
113 113 318 **114** 226
116 63 **119** 21 **120** 39
121 41 **122** 256 **123** 177
125 295 **126** 155 **127**
289 **128** 36 **129** 57 63
131 127 **133** 232 **136** 11
137 251 **139** 324 **140**
316 **142** 205 **143** 36 **145**
141 309 **146** 271-274
147 122
William A. **87** 259 **107** 113
William Alfred (Mrs.)
82 219 **83** 232
William B. **54** cxxxix
William C. **68** 198 199
William D. **82** 375
William H. **78** 380 **79** 310
98 194 **124** 262 **128** 264

JOHNSON *cont'd*
William Henry **61** 321
141 48 **145** 309
William J. **80** 271
William L. **83** 146
William Lawrence **83** 138
William M. **83** 141
William Moore **108** 134
William Octavius **92** 353
William Otis **85** 460
William P. **55** 52 **68** 155
91 326
William Perry **106** 317
William Samuel **56** 137
298 **79** 158 **92** 97 **93** 400
97 199 **106** 211 **110** 316
William Stapleton **84** 103
William Treby **72** xlii
William Victor (Mrs.)
79 324 **80** 208
William W. **54** 368 **55**
xxxi **73** 39 **77** 269 **84** 137
William Walker **94** 90
William Wallace **51** 95
Williamson **114** 303
Willis **121** 92 94
Willis Fletcher **62** 106
Wingle **56** 138
Winnifret **66** 17
Wolcott Howe **67** 95
Wouter **66** 15 17
Wylmyn **67** 169
Wyman **59** 281
Wyntie **66** 18
Zaccheus **66** 239
Zachariah **125** 290 **143** 36
313
Zeba **105** 33
Zebediah **66** 236 238
94 318
Zebina **125** 291
Zeluma (Lindsey) **135** 76
Zeruiah **54** 199 201 202
66 238
Zeruiah (Van Gilder)
90 383
Ziba **124** 200
Zibiah **56** 249
Zibiah W. **83** 143 144
Zoeth **77** 28
Zurvilla G. **66** 242
JOHNSTON Johnstone -
see also Johnson
——— **57** 121 **60** 104 **101**
341 **116** 28 **128** 18 238
143 366
— Dr. **85** 460
— Gen. **57** 60
A. **92** 169
Abigail (Shaw) **116** 131
Adam **51** 372
Alexander **72** 245 **112** 300
Alice **69** 115
Alice (Grass) **111** 138
Allerton **99** 71
Amelia Elizabeth **69** 114
Andrew **79** 61 **111** 79
Ann **62** 170 **72** 245 **114** 188
Ann Jane **128** 264
Anna **110** 179
Annie C. **68** lxxv

JOHNSTON *cont'd*
Arthur **60** 161
Aug. **63** 52
Augusta **62** 189
Augusta M. **63** lvii
Augusta Mary **81** 482
86 29
Bapt **112** 300
Bathsheba **67** 314
Benjamin **110** 179 **112** 103
116 131 141
Benson Vaughan **90** 209
Bessie Florence **104** 234
Betsey **111** 117
Betsey C. **94** 22
C. E. **60** 188
Catherine **77** xlvi **118** 295
Celia (Everett) **111** 139
Charles **62** 170
Charles Erastus **85** 93
Charles Ernest **55** 227
Charlotte **95** 316
Christian **55** 149
Clarina **62** 190 **81** 482
Clarina (Bartow) **86** 29
Cornelia **62** 190 **70** 192
Coy K. **120** 314
Cyrus **96** 137 **142** 369 370
Daniel **105** 209 **110** 179
112 103 **114** 187 **115** 61
David **77** 239
Deborah (Morris) **133** 232
Deidamia **83** 114
Dorothy (Davis) **91** 291
Eleanor **111** 79
Eliza **106** 308
Eliza (Patterson) **106** 308
Elizabeth **66** lxvi **69** 113
114 **72** 245 **79** 61 **80** 54
84 397 399 **92** 169 **111**
79 **122** 107
Elizabeth (Billings)
94 49 50
Elizabeth (Sedgley)
116 130
Elizabeth Ann Taylor
118 293
Elizabeth Lichtenstein
92 79
Elnora **92** 169
Emma F. **91** 384
Eugene Egbert **84** 189 232
85 93 107 205
Eugenia Morris **78** 47
Euphena **115** 292
Eva (Davis) **97** 119
Ezekiel **133** 232
Frances **83** 346
Frances Tippetts **104** 144
Francis C. **72** 245
Frank **91** 326 **95** 316
Franklin **95** 316
G. **99** 42
George **84** 425 **133** 232
George W. **111** 138
Hannah (Ricke) **90** 236
Harriet **74** 208 **95** 316
Harriet Elizabeth **102** 4
Helen T. (Thompson)
99 168
Henry **104** 102

JOHNSTON *cont'd*
Henry A. **111** 139
Henry P. **54** 359 **113** 90
  117 100 **147** 51
Henry Phelps **64** 65
  69 288
Henry Poellnitz **119** 156
Hiram **97** 119
Hitty Wenzel (De Graff)
  95 316
Houston Watson **78** 175
Hugh **115** 292
Hugh B. **120** 314
Hugo Richards **99** 71
Hugo Richards (Mrs.)
  75 xxiii **97** 288 **98** 149
  99 71
Isabella **89** 8 **111** 79
J. A. **125** 43
J. Raymond C. **80** 54
James **53** 124 **69** 289 **94** 22
  110 180 **111** 70 206 **112**
  103 **114** 187 **119** 21 **125**
  30 **133** 232
James Knox **108** 134
James William **69** 114
  104 102
Jane (Huddleston) **111** 79
Janet **89** 361
Jessie (Porteous) **104** 234
Joanna **80** 99
John **61** 139 **62** 79 **64** 94
  130 **66** 37 **72** 245 **79** 8
  80 54 **84** 369 **86** 262 **92**
  169 **117** 15 **127** 307
John D. **84** 397
John Henry **78** 47
John James **104** 234
John Louis (Mrs.) **91** 291
John Lowther **132** 187
Jonathan **91** 229
Joseph E. **77** 256
Joseph Eggleston **66** 293
Joseph Sands **85** 93
Josephine **95** 316
Joshua **116** 142
Julia **87** 56
Julia (Howard)
  (Robinson) **142**
  369 370
Julia Martha **103** 137
Kate Allerton **75** 64
Katharine **95** 316
Laleah Peyton **69** 113
Lawrence **126** 255
Lewis **118** 41-43 50 52 54
Linda Lou **104** 102
Lucile **78** 206
Lucy **82** 99
Luke **133** 232
Lydia H. **96** 285
Marcus J. **125** 40
Margaret **112** 300
Marie **96** 30
Martha **53** 124
Martha (Hodgkins)
  84 425
Martha Ella (Shields)
  85 93
Martha Emeline **78** 47
Mary **60** 161 **72** 245 **112**

JOHNSTON *cont'd*
  103 **115** 220 **129** 41 **133**
  232
Mary (Anderson) **133** 232
Mary (Megill) **133** 232
Mary Barrett **72** 245
Mary Caroline **134** 226
Mary E. **96** 136
Mary Elizabeth **62** 189
  107 135
Mary Espy (Anderson)
  83 346
Mary Hannah Stoddard
  61 xxxvi
Mary L. **92** 169
Mary S. **80** 54
Matilda **84** 397
Matthew **78** 51
Maud Cyrene **97** 119
Mehitable (Freeman)
  (Hopkins) **103** 26
Mercy **102** 179
Michael **147** 83
Miriam **111** 138
Moses **143** 260
Nancy (Foster) **94** 22
Nora Kathleen **95** 344
Nora Knight **95** 344
Patience **90** 326 **91** 17
  118 154 155
Patience (Grant) **112** 103
  115 61
Patrick **66** 37
Patty (Spear) **84** 369
Prescott **69** 115
Rachel **55** 148
Rebecca **93** 182
Rhoda **110** 179
Richard **112** 300
Robert **61** 268 **66** 30 **94** 50
  112 300
Robert J. (Mrs.) **98** 290
Rosa **112** 300
Ruth **122** 107
Ruth Rayburn **104** 102
Samuel **68** 199 **81** 482 **86**
  29 **114** 187 **125** 30
Sarah **92** 169 185 **112** 103
  115 214 **124** 34 **125** 241
  126 255 **128** 18
Sarah (Bragdon) **110** 179
Sarah (Bush) **84** 397
Sarah (Hamilton) **95** 344
Sarah Elizabeth **86** 312
Sarah H. **116** 63
Sarah Hall **69** 194 386
Sarah Hallam **62** 189
Scarlet **128** 238
Simeon **105** 278
Sophia **112** 300
Stephen **62** 79 **111** 79
Stewart (Mrs.) **91** 142
Submit **122** 107
Susan **72** 242 245
Susanna **68** 199
Theodore **112** 103 **116** 130
Thomas **67** 12 **70** 192 **73**
  263 **74** 208 **112** 300 **118**
  295 **143** 262
Vanderburgh **99** 71
William **55** 119 **64** 218

JOHNSTON *cont'd*
  90 236 **106** 307 **111** 202
  114 188 **117** 15 **120** 314
  125 32 43 **127** 52 55 180
  203 208 270 274
William Henry **72** 245
William Martin **69** 113
  114
William Preston **83** 134
William Sage **62** 190 **81**
  482 **86** 29
Willie P. **78** 175
JOHNSTONBAUGH
John Jacob **105** 128
Johnstone *see* Johnston
JOHONNOT Johannot
  Johonet Johonnet
  Johonot
— **143** 365
Andrew **84** 373 378 **85** 6
Andrew E. **93** 253
Betsey **125** 99
Charlotte **84** 382
Daniel **57** 389 **77** 294
  85 124
Elizabeth **84** 369 **93** 253
Francis **57** 280 **85** 6 7
  140 159
Francis J. **140** 231
Gabriel **84** 251 371 381
  101 59 **105** 290 **143** 16
George **85** 124
Harriet Elizabeth **93** 253
Judith **84** 370
Judith (Cooper) **84** 251
  370
Katharine **84** 259 **85** 7
Katharine (Dudley)
  84 259
Marianne **77** 294
Mary **114** 181 **140** 159 231
Oliver **114** 181
Patty **84** 373
Peter **84** 259
Rachel **125** 102
Sally **81** 380
Sarah (Bradstreet) **84** 381
Sukey **85** 125
Susanna **84** 373 378
Thomas **143** 262
William **93** 397 **100** 63
  114 181
Zachariah **57** 280 **84** 369
  382
Joice *see* Joyce
JOILES — Mr. **71** 140
Joiner *see* Joyner
JOINT Lydia **115** 240
JOITEAU Lewis **65** 230
JOKCHERER Alexander
  Lewis **73** 221
JOLAS Molly **115** 41
JOLES Hiram **109** 269
Joliff *see* Jolliffe
Jolley *see* Jolly
JOLLIET Louis **64** 95
JOLLIFFE Joliff Jolliff
  Jollyffe Joyliff Joyliffe
  Anna **143** 343
  Edith **100** 111
  Elizabeth **72** 186

JOLLIFFE *cont'd*
  Humphrey **61** 278 **63** 33
    34 **72** 188
  Jno. **111** 15 **124** 101
  Joan **72** 185 189
  John **52** 32 **55** 142 **64** 33
    72 186 **96** 321 **101** 29
    139 305 **143** 343
  Martha **79** 432
  Susanna **72** 186
  Thomas **77** 118 **84** 285 435
  William **51** 105 **72** 185 190
JOLLISON
  Polly (Bean) **90** 235
JOLLS — Mrs. **129** 380
  Robert **97** 30 40 **129** 380
JOLLY Jolley Jollye
  Desire (Chase) **87** 336
  Edward **56** 403
  George **98** 117
  James **65** 27
  John **87** 144
  Margaret **116** 252
  Marie Gladys **78** 323
  Martin **65** 25
  William **58** 312 **87** 336
    105 8
Jolyffe *see* Jolliffe
JONAE Petins **118** 164
JONAH Eleanor **78** 311
  William H. **77** 236
JONAS —— **143** 202
JONATHAN
  Martha **55** 202
JONES alias NELSON
  Catherine (Parkhurst)
    113 136
JONES Joanes Joans
  Johnes Johns Jons
    —— **100** 146 **102** 80
    139 46
  — Capt. **57** 157 **58** 168
    63 142 **66** 122 **77** 95 **89**
    244 **98** 48 **101** 247 **105**
    119
  — Col. **74** 19 **85** 121
  — Dea. **92** 12
  — Dr. **91** 303
  — Mr. **51** 259 **52** 471 **63**
    230 **65** 282 366 **80** 66 **84**
    153 **92** 11 13
  — Mrs. **62** 286 **63** 142 **64**
    31 **82** 412 **129** 68
  — Widow **65** 294 **81** 127
  ____ (Alexander?) (Curtis)
    143 121
  ____ (Bicker) **140** 39 159
  ____ (Dawes) **140** 59
  ____ (Fanueil) **140** 159
  ____ (Goodman) **122** 305
  ____ (Lee) **84** 373 **140** 159
  ____ (Shaw) **113** 140
  A. Frances (Lambert)
    122 230
  A. L. **53** 431
  A. T. **70** 319
  A. W. **120** 158
  Aaron **57** 390 **59** 66 **60** 166
    61 354 358 **108** 281 **110**
    299 **113** 142 **128** 20
  Abbie C. **92** 333

JONES *cont'd*
  Abbot **61** 251
  Abby **77** 152 **80** 189 **89** 245
  Abby A. **89** 245
  Abel **61** 356 **62** 151 **68**
    166 246 **69** 177 **70** 271
    333-335 **76** 47 **119** 42
  Abi **62** 29 **110** 66
  Abial **91** 31
  Abiel **61** 254 357 **83** 183
    184
  Abigail **51** 73 **52** 308 **53** 59
    60 164 434 **55** 111 **58**
    122 125 378 379 **59** 77
    60 165-167 **61** 22 31 151-
    156 252 253 354 356 358
    62 25 64 151 152 **68** 217
    70 227 **74** 22 247 **78** 304
    314 433 **79** 50 **81** 428 83
    193 **86** 97 **89** 245 **90** 383
    91 26 31 **95** 345 **97** 336
    103 190 **105** 193 **106** 65
    113 43 52 132-135 138
    141 143 146 **124** 152
    127 191 **131** 38 237 **140**
    159 **147** 77
  Abigail (Atwater) **110** 72
  Abigail (Bolter) **133** 259
  Abigail (Browne) **113** 51
  Abigail (Carver) **88** 312
  Abigail (Cheney) **113** 143
  Abigail (Feathergail)
    100 300
  Abigail (Grindle) **110** 26
    104
  Abigail (Hewett) **113** 131
  Abigail (Hobbs) **127** 189
  Abigail (Holbrook)
    113 135
  Abigail (Jones) **113** 52 138
  Abigail (Leach) **124** 152
  Abigail (Rogers) **113** 132
  Abigail (Sumner)
    (Elithorp) **113** 43
    143 125
  Abigail (Thayer) **113** 145
  Abigail (Tirrell) **134** 293
  Abigail (Wise) **131** 127
  Abigail D. **62** 28
  Abigail H. **70** 320
  Abigail P. **62** 28
  Abigail Waters **61** 252 253
  Abijah **58** 401 403 **59** 96
    60 76 205 **79** 46 **83** 364
    126 32
  Abner **88** 109
  Abner Gates **80** 193
    89 250 251
  Abner W. **88** 120
  Abraham **51** 283 284 **53** 59
    58 42 57 58 393 **60** 60
    61 253 **68** 108 109 **72**
    306 **73** 228 275 **75** 303
    305 308 **76** 164 **81** 444
    82 43 **113** 33 42-45 47-
    52 131 134-139 143-146
    142 116 117 359 **143**
    123 125-129 131 132 138
    255 348
  Abram **81** 428
  Absolom **91** 326

JONES *cont'd*
  Achsah **102** 239 **104** 80
  Acilla **99** 45
  Ada (Lester) **83** 485
  Ada Isabell **85** 196
  Adaline (Freeman)
    108 238
  Adam **57** 34 **65** 361 364
    142 125
  Adam F. **61** 243
  Adams Fletcher **62** 25 26
  Addie Augusta **85** 94
  Adelaide Augusta **67** lix
  Adelaide Howard (Field)
    85 333
  Adelia **79** 349 **117** 128
  Adeline **74** 316 **76** 50
    91 122
  Adeline B. **64** 210
  Affe / Affey **87** 92 **88** 284
  Afton **95** 289
  Agnes **60** 284 286 **82** 55-
    57 62
  Agnes (Green) **109** 221
  Agnes Amelia **79** 349
  Agnes Murray **103** 142
  Agneta **82** 56
  Ahijah **63** 48
  Albert **78** 398 **85** 409
    91 326
  Albert Arnold Aldrich
    61 359
  Albert Dodge (Mrs.)
    87 174
  Albert F. **148** 170 174
  Albert L. **83** 183 187 306
  Albert Lunt **82** 420
  Albert Marshall (Mrs.)
    85 195
  Albert Smith **133** 72
  Albian **133** 72
  Alexander **64** 340 **72** 105
    73 167 **81** 488-490 **82**
    55-58 60-63 83 **113** 144
  Alexandria (Bond)
    125 221
  Alexandrine M. **61** 247
  Alfred **70** 275 **75** 303
  Alfred H. **61** 248 **70** 275
    330 334
  Algenon Sydney **60** 167
  Alice **58** 43 **60** 283 **68** 162
    163 **70** 335 **78** 49 **81** 488-
    490 **82** 2 55-57 63 **84**
    423 113 140 141 **131**
    127 **140** 68
  Alice (Ayers) **133** 267
  Alice (Rand) **124** 62
  Alice Lane **80** 141
  Alice M. **70** 336
  Alice May **109** 171 269
  Alice P. **109** 202
  Alice Potter **80** 141
  Alice R. **69** 311
  Allan **73** 167
  Allen **51** 283 284 **77** 251
  Allen W. **62** 31
  Alma Clara **148** 174
  Almeda (Torrey) **85** 229
  Almira **61** 249 358 **62** 30
    70 269 **75** 95 **79** 153 168

JONES *cont'd*
Almira (Grindle) **108** 279
Alney T. **70** 320
Aloan **125** 291 **147** 70
Alonzo **62** 26 **68** 161
Alonzo Franklin **133** 72
Altheda **113** 142
Alton P. **70** 328
Alvin Lincoln **121** 184
Alvina P. **68** 246 **70** 331
Alvon Speaks (Mrs.)
 105 128
Alvra Roscoe **110** 299
Amanda **72** 307 **148** 178
Amanda (Sanderson)
 95 288
Amanda Louise
 (Mattoon) **121** 183
Amasa **64** 41
Amelia Adeline **57** 294
Amelia F. **62** 28
Amia **82** 56 62
Amos **60** 166 **61** 355 358
 70 227 **74** 264 317 **76**
 114 **80** 189 **86** 126 **88**
 312 **89** 245 246 **120** 72
 73 **126** 256 **129** 56 **147**
 77
Amos Brooks **58** 129
 61 358
Amos Emery **104** 293
Amos Peaslea **70** 269 334
Amy **70** 274 334 **74** 225
 253 **75** 302 **82** 43 56 **100**
 280 **105** 116
Andrew **61** 253 **70** 335
 82 266 **104** 319
Andrew C. **125** 291
Andrew J. **109** 15
Andrew Jackson **110** 105
Ann **51** 152 283 284 289
 60 60 **61** 327 **64** 159 162
 68 245 **70** 275 **72** 215
 73 137 144 154 222 **79**
 337 **81** 138 146 **82** 43
 375 420 **88** 336 **99** 285
 106 23 **109** 306 **113** 42-
 44 137 145 219 **127** 91
 142 352 **143** 124-126
 146 369
Ann (Clewley) **114** 298
Ann (Dunn) **88** 279
Ann (Griggs) **123** 170
Ann (Hamilton) **117** 254
Ann (Scannell) **113** 145
Ann (Stone ?) **94** 388
Ann (Vassall) **109** 92
Ann (Weymouth) **126** 209
Ann G. **83** 25 172
Ann Greenleaf **82** 420 421
Ann Mariah **148** 178
Ann P. **83** 34
Ann Parry **83** 298 299
Ann Richards **73** 261
Ann S. **83** 183 184
Ann Simes **82** 420
Anna **51** 69 281 303 **60**
 166-168 **61** 246 250 252
 355 357 392 **62** 30 **65**
 354 **70** 272 **74** 228 250
 257 **78** 433 **80** 168 **81**

JONES *cont'd*
 428 **82** 56 57 83 412 **102**
 142 **107** 305 **108** 278
 109 93 **112** 312 **113** 46
 51 52 138 146 **123** 169
 124 154 **131** 127 **143**
 131 **146** 369 370
Anna (Bibble) **142** 273 274
Anna (Chase) (Clarm)
 88 109
Anna (Gates) **121** 220
Anna (Goodwin) **90** 330
 91 21
Anna (Lufkin) **113** 51 146
Anna (Sharp) **143** 54
Anna Adelaide **148** 178
Anna Eliza **109** 219
Anna J. **84** 213
Anna Louise **83** 429 432
Anna M. **72** 105
Anna Maria **120** 18
Anna Maria (Mills)
 133 232
Anna P. **140** 159
Anna Ticknor **51** 150
Anna Wing **80** 141
Anna Winslow **78** 205
Anna Wylly **68** 18
Annah **124** 273
Anne **53** 86 **58** 280 **59** 66
 60 243 **61** 247 250 253
 66 270 **73** 150 **77** 289
 82 55 **86** 441 **113** 218
 117 254 **139** 140 141
 142 357
Anne (Bibble) **143** 122 123
Anne (Bluet) **113** 217 221
Anne (Post) **146** 369
Anne Elizabeth (Starkie)
 94 138 **108** 219 **109** 134
 219
Anne Taylor **85** 189
Annette **148** 178
Annie L. **104** 80
Annie Lurana **102** 123
Annie M. **95** 334
Annie Stevens **101** 335
Annie Virginia **70** 336
Ansel **108** 264
Anstace **82** 56
Anthony **51** 69 **52** 167
 55 35
Antoinette S. **61** 247
 88 334
Aphia **115** 112
Apollos **68** 163 **69** 73
 120 239
Appia (Palmer) **111** 305
 306
Arathusa (Gates) **97** 75
Archelaus **113** 145
Archibald **61** 253 **73** 167
Ardan **61** 358
Arey **73** 145
Artemas **61** 248
Arthur **112** 294
Arthur Morse **59** xlvii
 60 209 **74** xxviii **90** 125
 97 288 **98** 150
Arthur W. **70** 330
Asa **61** 253 **69** 81 **70** 277

JONES *cont'd*
 332 336 **79** 245 **113** 140
 143 **116** 7 **144** 45
Asa Selden **57** 294
Asael **113** 140 141 **122** 110
Asahel **51** 291
Asenath (Baldwin)
 113 144
Aseny **113** 142
Asia **122** 280 281
Augusta **55** xlvi
Augusta E. **73** 194 **83** 178
 183
Augusta Thayer **85** 332
Augusta Victoria **62** 25
Augustine **52** 86 **58** xliii
 59 v xvi **64** xviii 77 **66**
 xlviii **71** 289
Augustine T. **70** 329
Augustus **85** 229 **92** 333
Augustus Appleton
 57 390
Augustus V. **62** 25
Aurelius S. **103** 267
Aurora **61** 247
Avis Keen **70** 269 334
Azubah **57** 289
Azubah (Fleming) **89** 90
 91
Azubah Caroline **57** 294
Azubah F. **89** 91
B. M. **78** 320
Barbara (Reineer) **113** 296
Barbara (Walters) **117** 202
Bartholomew **76** 111 185
 186 188 192
Barzillai **100** 187
Basil **60** 167
Bathsheba **53** 59 **57** 394
 78 141 **99** 295 **113** 46
 133 **143** 130 131 333
Bathsheba (Bosworth)
 143 122
Bathsheba (Drowne)
 113 133
Beatrice **117** 291
Belinda A. **121** 177
Belle **105** 113
Belle (Hills) **116** 63
Ben **95** 146 **121** 272 277
Benaiah **90** 383
Benia: **121** 111
Benjamin **52** 181-184 309
 420 **58** 381 **60** 60 133
 166 307 **61** 29 253 **64** 31
 65 95 **67** 384 **68** 109 **73**
 76 147 262 **74** 20 49 248
 266 **81** 428 **82** 26 291
 293 **86** 169 **88** 366 **103**
 266 **104** 182 **105** 115
 108 309 **110** 300 **113** 45
 48 49 131 133 134 140
 141 143 **121** 10 270 282
 123 192 **126** 123 272
 127 140 129 65 **142** 273
 357 **143** 121-124 127-
 130 333 348 **146** 367 370
Benjamin D. **106** 108
Benjamin F. **81** 418 **103**
 137 **110** 302

JONES *cont'd*
Benjamin Franklin **61**
  356 358 **75** 251 **78** 322
  83 23 24 **108** 281
Benjamin W. **74** 316
  108 281
Benjamin Worth **70** 275
Benoni **113** 134
Berta (Burr) **133** 232
Bertha May **133** 268
Bessie B. **110** 303
Bethany P. **91** 375
Bethiah **53** 59 103 **62** 25
  104 59 292 **105** 116 **110**
  21 23 110 **113** 133 **127**
  113
Bethiah (Robinson)
  127 196
Bethuel **80** 193 **89** 250
Betsey **57** 390 **61** 175 248
  358 380 **62** 293 **72** 315
  74 263 317 **75** 192 196
  307 **78** 262 **83** 160 **86**
  169 **104** 293 **105** 116
  108 279 281 **109** 200
  113 144 **122** 110 **125**
  288 **126** 268 **134** 69 **140**
  68 **147** 77 259 **148** 178
Betsey (Briggs) **122** 279
  126 268
Betsey (Clark) **133** 282
Betsey (Davis) **104** 182
Betsey (Jones) **125** 288
Betsey (Joslin) **94** 388
Betsey (Richardson)
  113 143
Betsey (Stover) **104** 57 58
Betsey (Varney) **83** 183
  188
Betsey Gould **134** 89
Betsey Kimble **108** 281
Betsey Lang **82** 43
Betsey Matilda **60** 200
Bettee **147** 128
Bettet **141** 189
Betty **52** 35 **58** 194 **59** 311
  60 79 181 **61** 246 **74** 22
  257 **75** 313 **76** 185 **112**
  156 **113** 138 **147** 128
Beula **61** 251
Beulah (Stratton) **128** 41
Billy **119** 52
Bini **73** 217
Binns **117** 255
Bluet **113** 219
Bowen **62** 27
Boynton **148** 178 179
Brace **99** 123
Bradley **62** 29
Bridget **61** 356 **78** 56 **113**
  50 135 **143** 129
Bruce Stevenson (Mrs.)
  107 133 160
Burr W. **106** 313
Burrington **60** 167
Butler **73** 151
C. Goodwin **120** 73
C. R. **120** 239 **122** 160 **123**
  160 **124** 216 **129** 315
Cadwallader **77** 251 253
  113 216-219 221

JONES *cont'd*
Cadwallader Ford **61** 355
Caesar **64** 46
Cal **101** 80
Caleb **52** 435 **53** 280 **58**
  300 **59** 387 **60** 165 166
  61 156 250 254 355 356
  68 166 **69** 177 **70** 269
  271 332 335 **120** 72 73
Caleb G. **120** 73
Calvin **73** 212 **77** 145
Calvin Gay **76** 111
Calvin M. **73** 212
Candace E. **62** 25
Carolina **124** 29
Caroline **52** 148 **74** 317
  75 101 **84** 319 **89** 12
  113 141 **124** 29 **133** 282
Caroline (Emery) **121** 177
Caroline (Lundes)
  133 267
Caroline A. **88** 212
Caroline Amelia **77** 186
Caroline E. **77** 257
Caroline M. **61** 248 **62** 25
Carrie **65** xxxvi
Carrie E. **110** 303
Carrie J. (Benchley)
  143 54
Carroll Brewster **100** 111
Carter **79** 332
Cassina May **72** xxi
Catherine **58** 175 **62** 29
  74 22 23 **78** 416 **88** 298
  90 383 **94** 137 **99** 55 326
  112 294 **115** 113 **121** 53
  122 110
Catherine (Bassett)
  125 105
Catherine (Caswell)
  88 359
Catherine (Lazell)
  (Flanders) **89** 228
Catherine (Niles) **85** 149
Catherine Bushnell
  94 389
Catherine R. S. (Benoist)
  86 380
Cecil Lister **83** 485
Celia **76** 186
Cereno Percy **60** xxxvi
Cereno Upham **59** 421
Charity **73** 146
Charity (Britton) **104** 309
Charity (Perkins) **113** 140
Charles **51** 150 **54** 149 **58**
  57 **60** 167 **61** 291 358 **62**
  31 383 **63** 347 **65** 232 **83**
  248 **70** 272 **74** 29 316 **83**
  183 188 **89** 90 **91** 326 **92**
  120 **101** 214 **104** 293
  109 15 **124** 27 **140** 159
Charles A. **119** 158
Charles B. **87** 10
Charles Bunker **70** 275
Charles C. **71** liv **112** 210
Charles Carlton **110** 209
Charles Colcock **54** lii-liv
  95 15
Charles Cotton **110** 209
Charles E. **92** 332 333

JONES *cont'd*
Charles Edwin **133** 267
Charles F. **62** 28 **86** 52
  110 303
Charles Francis **108** 309
Charles Furber **110** 209
Charles H. **68** 248 **69** 319
  148 179
Charles Hart **108** 238
Charles Henry **63** 391
  124 28 29
Charles Hopkins **83** 485
Charles J. **78** 49
Charles L. **73** 268
Charles M. **109** 202
  113 139
Charles Parkman **89** 90
  145 158
Charles Prentice **70** 224
Charles R. **122** 111
Charles Rice **92** 253
Charles W. **61** lvii **69** 32
  85 310 313
Charles William **91** 142
Charles Wisner **80** 141
Charlotte **61** 359 **81** 391
  87 292 **94** 161 **113** 53
Charlotte Anne **61** 359
Charlotte Helen **120** 72 73
Chauncey **61** 357
Chester **85** 160 166
Chester G. **148** 179
Chester Lloyd **94** 97
Chloe **51** 292 **100** 287
  113 143
Christabel **81** 491 **82** 56 63
Christian **112** 35
Christiana **76** 111 185
  186 188 196 **82** 57 58
Christina **82** 266
Christopher **61** 358 **70**
  337-341 **82** 55 57 **83** 251
  96 126 **146** 369 **147** 49
Christopher C. **77** 314
Christopher Paul **126** 267
Clara **83** 193 **85** 166
  133 267
Clara (Bogue) **85** 165
Clara Augusta **82** 420
Clara E. **87** 92
Clara F. **87** 93 **108** 281
Clara Lucinda **147** 221
Clarence W. **77** 56
Clariet **73** 273
Clarinda Rogers **133** 72
Clarine **86** 52
Clarine Mary **86** 52
Clarissa **61** 359 **62** 30 **90**
  367 **108** 281
Clarissa (Bolton) **108** 279
Clarissa (Howard)
  113 144
Clarissa (Meads) **126** 164
Clarissa Learned (Dick-
  inson) **126** 145
Clarissa M. B. **85** 456 457
Clarkson **68** 246 **69** 181
  70 275 331 336 337
Clement Rackliff **70** 278
Clementine (Parker)
  121 142

JONES *cont'd*
Clementine C. **92** 236
Clytie C. **110** 303
Comfort **68** 246 **70** 275
334 335 **85** 335
Consider **57** 26 **59** 310
Content **59** 137
Coolidge **61** 253
Cora L. **113** 53
Cora Maria **82** 399
Cordelia **61** 357
Cornelius **57** 289 **59** 387
90 383 **111** 305 306 **113**
135 141 **114** 187 **115**
112 **116** 110 **118** 202
119 22
Corydon **61** 247
Cotter **114** 189
Cushing **61** 291
Cynthia **61** 358 **62** 25 **63**
85 **70** 275 299 301 319
329 **113** 141 142 **117** 55
126 273 **147** 55
Cynthia (Hunt) **113** 143
Cynthia A. **70** 334
Cynthia M. **74** 171 317
Cyrus **61** 253 358 **70** 271
330
Cyrus Athern **89** 90 91
Cyrus Everet **70** 328
Cyrus R. **62** 26
Damon **115** 114
Damon Everett **113** 296
Daniel **52** 184 429 **53** 163
59 197 202 261 387 **60**
166 167 307 **61** 153 154
247 248 253 355 357 **62**
29 32 **65** 147 **66** 109 **70**
275 **76** 248 **79** 165 **80**
189 **82** 420 **83** 34 **84** 160
270 **89** 245 **90** 383 **91**
353 **92** 11 13 117 253
258 345 350 **93** 259 321
95 54 **100** 187 **104** 293
106 42 **108** 279-281 **113**
135 141 **118** 192 313
120 72 **126** 225 **146** 347
367
Daniel (Mrs.) **108** 281
Daniel A. **62** 27
Daniel G. **62** 28
Daniel Gates **61** 247
Daniel P. **62** 25
Daniel R. **70** 330
Daniel Winfield **55** xliv
xlvi xlvii
Darius **61** 358
Darius Bailey **61** 358
Davenport Augustus
90 57
David **51** 395 **53** 164 **55**
334 **58** 118 **61** 153 156
157 244 248 253 355-358
63 142 **65** 45 63 **66** 37
70 274 **73** 138 222 253
261 **74** 49 **78** 185 **82** 56
57 **88** 297 340 366 **90**
262 **92** 19 **105** 116 **108**
224 279 **110** 166 **113**
131 135-137 144 **120** 72
124 28 **140** 68 159 **142**

JONES *cont'd*
304
David C. **126** 205
David Cheney **113** 143
David DeL. **109** 320 **110**
80 158
David H. **121** 181
David L. **69** 198
David McGregor **61** 355
356
David Nelson **113** 144
David P. **61** 357
David R. **80** 157 **102** 79
David W. **122** 88
David Walter **124** 29
David Wasson **110** 297
David Wilder **61** 358
Davis **61** 254
De Los G. **121** 177
Deanes **81** 490 **82** 56 63
Dearing **113** 49 134 135
142 272
Deborah **53** 231 **59** 387
60 166 167 **61** 151 254
357 **70** 273 **74** 317 78
308 **80** 427 **87** 346 **99**
123 **111** 292 **146** 375
147 52
Deborah (Babb) **126** 145
Deborah (Foster) **113** 139
Deborah Champion
94 136
Delia (Seymour) **133** 32
Delia (Tuttle) **90** 367
Dency (Briggs) (Bowen)
126 219
Desire **71** 137
Diademia **71** 202
Dinah **58** 380 381
Diodate **60** 165 167 **81** 269
Dollie Elizabeth **133** 267
Dolly **61** 245 246 249 250
62 31 32 **87** 201 **108** 5
147 259
Dolly Head **71** lvii
Donald Edgar **122** 280
Donna Clara (Kelley)
113 143
Dorcas **54** 222 **61** 245 251
252 **62** 26 27 **70** 320 **74**
49 **91** 33 **98** 268 **101** 171
109 306
Dorothy **52** 32 429 **61**
245 249 250 356 **62** 27
82 62 289 291 **89** 369
100 240 **113** 145 218
221 **122** 240 **127** 78 79
Dorothy Frances (Gallup)
85 224
Dorothy Mae **121** 74 182
E. A. **112** 211 273 **113** 93
E. A. (Blake) **122** 280
E. Alfred **69** 383 **113** 14
117 18 **142** 143
E. C.B. **122** 17 **124** 100
E. M. **108** 281 **122** 280
E. Medora **108** 231
E. O. **73** 212
E. Pendleton **109** 295
Eaton **60** 167
Ebenezer **51** 440 **53** 59 55

JONES *cont'd*
375 **57** 26 402 **58** 230
379 381 **59** 75 77 135
138 263 310 **60** 39 166
61 152 155 156 244 251
360 **62** 60 62 **63** 172 **64**
72 **68** 216 218 220 223
313 **72** 215 **74** 22 212
216-218 225 229 258 **76**
38 **83** 17 **106** 177 **113**
133 140 143 **123** 260
125 201 **126** 145 **136** 33
34
Eda **57** 393
Edgar A. **110** 303
Edgar F. **62** 25
Edgar Mott **122** 280
Edgar S. **86** 155
Edith **87** 132
Edith Katharine **80** 141
Edith M. **70** 337
Edith Marion **101** 124
115 66
Edmond E. **110** 299
Edmund **82** 430 441 **129**
112 115
Edna Blanche **86** 155
Edson Salisbury **61** 99
63 109 **68** 370 **69** 64
Edward **52** 251 252 **55**
201 208 **60** 40 391 **61**
358 **64** 159 161 163 164
214 263 345 **69** 273 **70**
332 333 336 **73** 184 225
231 77 320 **78** 72 **82** 43
56 62 443 **83** 25 27 **85**
149 **95** 52 **100** 187 **113**
53 54 129 **123** 170 **125**
104 **131** 127 **140** 159
244
Edward Everett (Mrs.)
109 127
Edward F. **55** xxxi **59** xliv
111 137
Edward Franklin **70** 330
Edward Lewis **85** 333
Edward Milton **79** 349
Edward P. **81** 239 **92** 304
Edward Payson **93** 137
108 63 139 308 309
Edward T. **115** 79 **116** 76
Edward W. **68** 248
Edward Wright (Mrs.)
91 196
Edwin **61** 358 **70** 272 331
336
Edwin Pitkin **108** 308 309
Edwin Retiah **148** 174
Elam **61** 32
Elbridge **61** 356
Eldad **52** 409 **61** 356
83 364
Eleanor **53** 239 **55** 312 **75**
153 **82** 57 509 **100** 240
101 85 **102** 148 **103** 229
104 292 **110** 214 **140** 41
Eleanor Elizabeth **62** 367
Eleanor H. **77** 237 **93** 128
151 **94** 152 **95** 159 **96** 51
100 46
Eleanor Hooper **78** 205

JONES *cont'd*
120 232
Eleanor Mae **95** 289
Eleanor Robinson **62** 25
Eleanor Temperance
  (Ricks) **95** 289
Eleanora **82** 56 57
Eleazer **60** 307 **85** 314
Eli **54** 293 **57** 289 **69** 177
  70 271 319 333 335 336
  144 223
Eli Grellet **70** 319
Eli J. **74** 317
Elias **136** 270 **141** 350
  143 68
Elias Adam **109** 202
Elias W. **90** 109
Elihu **54** 259 **56** 353 **60** 78
Elijah **61** 22 **63** 46 **68** 216
  236 237 **69** 183 **73** 144
  105 279 **108** 309 **144**
  110 120 122 **148** 178
Elijah F. **61** 22
Elijah I. **60** 40
Eliphalet **74** 251 **79** 94
Eliphaz **56** 308
Elisha **51** 269 **55** 85 **57**
  127 294 **59** 137 311 **61**
  248 **67** 51 **70** 269 333
  334 **78** 186 **90** 383 **108**
  89 **113** 132 139 **120** 53
  122 258 **126** 218 219
  144 217
Elisha Franklin **70** 269
Elisha W. **108** 308
Elisha William **89** 259
Elishaba **52** 309
Elitheusa **61** 253
Eliza **55** 50 **61** 355 357 358
  62 367 **63** 48 **65** 133 **70**
  203 269 **73** 99 **77** 264 **78**
  359 **82** 282 289 291 **86**
  169 **88** 76 **106** 68 **110**
  299 **120** 72 73 **125** 289
  293 **147** 259
Eliza (Atkins) **87** 92
Eliza (Buck) **108** 264
Eliza (Fish) **120** 248
Eliza (Patch) (Woods) **120**
  72 73
Eliza (Temple) **113** 141
Eliza A. **103** 45
Eliza Ann **62** 367
Eliza B. **70** 329 **120** 73
Eliza Boynton **120** 72
Eliza C. **87** 92
Eliza Curtis **97** 72
Eliza E. **79** 156 **80** 59
Eliza Jane (Green) **126** 144
Eliza M. **61** 247
Eliza S. **79** 154
Eliza Tannahill **78** 49
Eliza W. **76** 35
Eliza Wedgewood **68** 251
Elizabeth **51** 69 **52** 167
  412 428 432 **53** 59 162
  239 414 441 **54** 325 328
  55 85 208 **57** 412 **58** 240
  280 300 **60** 79 165-168
  204 285 307 363 **61** 151
  153-157 245 249-251 253-

JONES *cont'd*
  255 344 355-357 **62** 27
  28 30 269 328 **63** 48 98
  266 292 378 **64** 123 162
  164 374 **66** 33 187 188
  68 196 218 237 **70** 226
  71 217 **72** 257 **73** 142
  147 173 212 225 253 274
  74 22 49 187 248 266 **75**
  12 **76** 110 112 113 248
  250 **78** 143 186 433 **79**
  71 331 **81** 491 **82** 56 57
  62 63 **83** 364 **85** 314 424
  86 101 **88** 334 **89** 132
  246 **90** 104 **92** 292 **94**
  269 **95** 15 16 **97** 133 **99**
  284 **100** 222 **101** 50 247
  103 69 **105** 115 145 **108**
  63 118 139 224 **112** 241
  113 44-46 49 131 133
  135 136 141 146 219 **114**
  189 190 **121** 113 211
  123 170 **126** 28 67 208
  284 **127** 112 113 **136**
  308 312 331 **140** 159
  142 304 335 357 **143**
  121-123 125 131 **146** 347
  148 170 174
Elizabeth (Bate) **113** 139
Elizabeth (Binns) **117** 255
Elizabeth (Borden)
  143 124
Elizabeth (Brownson)
  114 190
Elizabeth (Butler) **127** 113
Elizabeth (Cargill)
  117 255
Elizabeth (Chillson)
  113 135
Elizabeth (Clark) **95** 288
  113 219
Elizabeth (Creswick)
  (Hippisley) **113**
  218 219
Elizabeth (Cushing)
  (Loring) **113** 138
Elizabeth (Damon)
  113 296
Elizabeth (Deering) **113**
  49 146 **143** 123 128 129
Elizabeth (Gage) **113** 136
Elizabeth (Gale) **95** 288
Elizabeth (Graves) **112**
  236 **123** 261
Elizabeth (Gray) **125** 291
Elizabeth (Hazeltine)
  113 144
Elizabeth (Hunter) **124** 78
Elizabeth (Jennison)
  94 388
Elizabeth (Lambert)
  125 100
Elizabeth (Lobdell)
  113 135
Elizabeth (Loring)
  113 138
Elizabeth (Pitts) **113** 45
  121 194 **143** 126 129
  130 343
Elizabeth (Pratt) **113** 133

JONES *cont'd*
Elizabeth (Russell)
  117 273
Elizabeth (Sayres) **119** 193
Elizabeth (Smith) **113** 134
Elizabeth (Wild) **108** 309
Elizabeth A. **73** 39 **122** 280
Elizabeth Alice **111** 155
  114 149
Elizabeth Ann (Blake) **122**
  278 280 281
Elizabeth Ann (Mackey)
  108 224
Elizabeth Anne **80** 141
Elizabeth B. **89** 246
Elizabeth Brent **83** 485
Elizabeth C. **81** 150
Elizabeth Cargill **117** 255
Elizabeth Dodd **77** 225
Elizabeth E. **73** 276 **81** 418
Elizabeth E. Boice **77** 159
  94 399 **114** 38
Elizabeth Edwards **80** 141
Elizabeth J. **95** 16
Elizabeth K. **70** 336
Elizabeth M. **70** 330
Elizabeth Rhoda **89** 90
Elizabeth Russell **61** 253
Elizabeth S. **65** 133
Elizabeth Stokes **62** 367
Elizabeth Thayer **78** 294
Elizabeth W. **83** 183
Elizabeth Wyer **82** 421
Elkanah **90** 383
Ella **79** 136 137 **133** 267
Ella A. **86** 169
Ella Bancroft **79** 202
Ella Margaret **91** 51
Ella May **94** 97 **107** 133
Ellen **77** 266 **123** 235
  148 179
Ellen (Herbert) **95** 288
Ellen B. **86** 169
Ellen L. (Conn) **87** 88
Ellen Lunt **82** 421 **83** 34
Ellen May **148** 365
Ellen S. **62** 294
Ellis **63** 351
Elma M. **68** 248
Elma Maria **69** 273
Elmer L. **100** 212
Elmira **68** 161 **109** 15
Elmira E. **87** 92
Elmira Jones (Curtis)
  85 314
Elmo **93** 98
Elnathan **53** 59 **79** 153
  113 48 49 **143** 128
Elvina **74** 27
Elvina P. **69** 181
Elvira (Bushnell) **94** 388
Elvira (Hoisington)
  141 46
Elwood William **70** 330
Ely **90** 383
Emeline **74** 317 **77** 266
Emeline H. **70** 320
Emerson M. **70** 92
Emery **74** 27 **110** 214
Emily **61** 247 248 **62** 26
  73 167 **77** 146 **110** 303

JONES *cont'd*
133 72
Emily Eugenia 82 430
  441 442
Emily Farnum 83 172
Emily J. 133 72
Emma 78 240 110 22
Emma A. 55 xlvii 74 317
Emma Brewster 61 274
  97 140 143 47
Emma Cordelia Brewster
  53 132 58 95 60 83 63
  384 64 xxxi 114 318
  142 176
Emma F. 92 332 333
Emma Forbes 85 314
Emma Jane 69 261
Emma Taylor 133 268
Enoch 61 248 73 173 74 49
Enos 76 155
Ephra 121 194
Ephraham 124 226
Ephraim 52 438 53 59 55
  391 58 42-44 60 60 61
  245 355 62 25 26 70 272
  333 334 71 139 140 85
  110 103 152 111 155
  113 43-47 49-51 132 133
  137 138 145 146 114 149
  121 22 125 203 126 32
  140 68 143 121 125-127
  129 365 147 55 61
Erasmus 52 102
Erastus 54 258 74 23 75
  302 80 427
Ernest Lester 83 217 372
  485 84 189 196
Esther 53 224 55 202 205
  60 167 324 61 154 155
  249 62 27 367 69 81 283
  70 269 73 48 74 229 79
  352 103 255 109 202
  141 190
Esther Hill (Sherwood)
  108 309
Etha Lee 78 47
Ethel M. 83 426 432
Ethel Mercedes 103 120
Etta 133 72
Etta E. 100 212
Eulata 142 199
Eunice 54 292 293 55 429
  56 35 249 388 58 196 60
  166 167 61 254 357 63
  46 68 167 245 70 271
  272 319 333 335 73 173
  74 317 78 253 81 444
  82 43 83 343 92 253 345
  93 321 95 51 106 240
  112 78 113 52 138 115
  118
Eunice (Davis) 124 28
Eunice (Legg) 113 143
Eunice (Lillibridge)
  (Rockwell) 144 120 122
Eunice (Wingate) 98 224
Eunice E. 89 246
Eunice H. 70 272 275 320
  335
Eunice Hacker 70 275
Eunice M. 86 233

JONES *cont'd*
Eunice S. 75 27
Eva (Bartlett) 89 259
Eva Berrien 54 liv
Fva J 110 303
Evaline (Monroe) 100 87
Evan 61 356 65 50 104 225
  113 209
Eveline (Hall) 111 303 305
Evelyn Hunter 117 199
Experience 113 135
  123 261
Experience (Northam)
  90 383
Ezekiel Rice 92 350
Ezra 57 412 58 42-44 47
  280 63 98 64 123 80 427
  85 409 94 388 113 141
  120 248 146 369
Ezra F. 85 409
Ezra G. 115 16
Ezra T. 85 409
F. A. 81 97
Fannie Scarlett (Royall)
  109 295
Fanny 55 180 61 254 355
  62 30 70 92 73 173 77
  257 120 72
Fanny A. 70 92
Fanny B. 134 127
Fanny Congdon 87 391
Fanueil 140 159
Fidelia 60 147
Fidelia Diantha 57 294
Fletcher 62 25
Flora A. 122 280
Florence 70 203
Flossie M. 110 303
Fordyce 113 145
Foster 61 253
Frances 60 167 61 359 76
  47 79 331 332 83 429
  432 93 61 113 220 126
  79
Frances (Stringer)
  100 297
Frances Adelaide 62 367
Frances Ann 61 359 62
  367 94 90
Frances Augusta 62 30
Frances Elizabeth 78 44
Frances Ellen 65 lv
Frances Isabelle
  (Bronson) 108 309
Frances L. (Williams)
  126 145
Frances M. 121 178
Frances Tasker 79 331
Francis 51 46 291 68 81
  69 361 70 262 269 329
  334 79 224 80 189 89
  245 110 246 111 155
  113 46 140 141 114 149
  189 117 99 100 141 103
Francis A. 63 48
Francis B. 91 326 129 50
Francis E. 62 25
Francis Gerard (Mrs.)
  87 174
Francis Richard 94 138
Francisca 82 56

JONES *cont'd*
Frank 97 215 128 175
  133 268
Frank Gleason 122 280
Frank H. 87 92
Frank W. 84 29 92 331 333
Frank W. (Mrs.) 84 29
Franklin 62 25 26 128 175
Franklin Chappell 86 380
Franklin Pierce 105 220
Fred Dresser 110 297
Fred Howard (Mrs.)
  85 195
Fred P. 121 180
Frederick 52 148 67 94
  73 265 79 332 108 220
  109 202
Frederick A. 109 202
Frederick Alexander
  107 133 120 147
Frederick Alonzo 109 202
Frederick D. 70 331
Frederick Hall 94 138
  108 219 109 134 219
Frederick M. 70 203
Frederick P. 78 43
Frederick Sidney 62 25
Frederick William 55 356
Freeman 124 152
G. A.B. 105 74
Gabriel 82 57 58
Gardner 61 252
Gardner Irving 113 296
Gardner Irving (Mrs.)
  95 146 112 220 113 296
Genevieve 70 337 109 269
Geoffrey 53 414 82 58
George 54 325 328 60 382
  62 31 63 48 64 216 68
  18 69 32 183 70 279 73
  145 148 149 225 279
George B. 61 247 120 73
George C. 109 202
George D. 106 108
George E. 110 213
George F. 71 xxxix
George Farquhar 113
  144 145
George Fenwick 68 18
George G. 62 26
George Hacker 70 275
George Henry 70 328
George Janverin 82 421
George L. 69 319
George Macy 100 187
George Martin 77 225
George Noble 68 18
George R. 119 157
George Russell 67 384
  68 xxxi
George S. 70 269
George W. 61 274 62 28
  73 202 75 251 91 326
  126 142
Georgia (Westley)
  133 268
Georgianna (Hilden-
  brand) 97 133
Gershom 95 334 127 303
Gertrude Henriella
  101 124

JONES *cont'd*
Gertrude May **108** 136
Gertrude Tucker **80** 141
Gibson **147** 77
Gideon **54** 85 **59** 387
Gilbert **61** 248 **108** 281
Gilbert A. **117** 219
Gilbert John **61** 248
Giles **55** 109
Gilman **61** 253
Gladys Y. **141** 114
Grace **58** 240
Grace (Fitz Randolph)
97 280
Grace (Harris) **126** 256
128 20
Grace (Webber) **85** 215
86 215
Grace Angeline (Smith)
94 389
Grace D. **110** 297
Grace Guernsey **82** 266
Griffith **58** 379 381 **67** 175
108 228 **123** 259
Gurdon **90** 367
Gwyneth Mabel **109** 129
H. Elizabeth **69** 319
H. G. **117** 316
H. L. **86** 380
Hallie **119** 73
Hamill **63** 48
Hamilton Polk **77** 257
Hank **113** 241
Hannah **51** 69 463 **52** 225
428 429 **53** 59 86 279
280 **55** 50 401 **57** 140
390 401 **58** 174 260 266
318 388 390 393 402 **59**
75 106 **60** 21 164-167 **61**
151 153 214 215 219 254
355-358 395 **62** 26 28 29
120 125 268 **63** 167 **64**
161 **66** 320 **69** 283 **70**
227 274 332 334 **73** 87
74 22 90 217 316 **75** 31
78 320 433 **81** 269 428
82 43 **84** 363 **87** 132 **99**
123 168 207 208 **100** 235
102 31 **103** 192 254 **104**
319 **108** 220 280 281
109 220 **110** 72 **111** 30
113 44 47 51 52 131-133
135-138 141 144 216 219
220 **114** 127 **118** 202
119 192 **120** 72 **123** 170
124 13 **127** 79 **131** 317
136 36 **138** 322 **139** 46
143 124-128 **144** 167
168 227 **147** 128
Hannah (Blodgett) **110** 22
Hannah (Copeland)
113 51
Hannah (Darling)
113 135
Hannah (Dean) **113** 133
144
Hannah (Ewell) **113** 135
Hannah (Francis) **113** 220
144 166 167 **146** 382
Hannah (Heath) **146** 268
Hannah (Jones) **113** 51 52

JONES *cont'd*
Hannah (Nelson) **113** 143
Hannah (Paull) **126** 307
Hannah (Percival)
118 202
Hannah (Perry) **134** 291
Hannah (Pratt) **113** 135
Hannah (Read) **84** 363
Hannah (Richards) **113** 51
143 129
Hannah (Stannard)
90 383
Hannah (Stover) **108** 279
Hannah (Tupper) **99** 123
Hannah Amelia **74** xlvi
Hannah C. **126** 64
Hannah D. **93** 191
Hannah Delia **64** 373
Hannah Dow **70** 274
Hannah Frances **104** 292
Hannah H. **76** 38
Hannah Lincoln **71** liv
Hannah M. **89** 347
Hannah Sampson **70**
272 274 330 334
Harding **122** 101
Harold Boyer **100** 111
Harold E. **99** 174
Harold Johnson **122** 280
Harrie L. **110** 303
Harriet **58** 135 **60** 167 **61**
355 356 **62** 26 29 **68** 248
76 41 **79** 156 **106** 108
114 187 **119** 203 **137** 37
147 77
Harriet (Bragdon)
126 205
Harriet (Pettee) **113** 141
Harriet A. C. **120** 73
Harriet Ann **100** 187
Harriet B. **70** 274 334
Harriet Betsey **78** 352
Harriet E. **122** 280
Harriet H. **61** 247 **88** 337
Harriet Mildred 430
83 430 432
Harriet N. **62** 28
Harriet Newell **104** 309
Harris **60** 167
Harry **61** 357
Harry Villard **133** 268
Hatherly **53** 59 60 **113** 48
132 **143** 128
Hatta (Chadsey) **128** 36
Hattie F. **100** 212
Hattie M. **74** 317
Hattie Solders (Sinkey)
133 267
Hatton Middleton **73** 262
Hawks **73** 87
Hazel Parker **116** 313
Helen **79** 349 **82** 57 **83**
297 299 **90** 256
Helen (Steel) **94** 138
Helen E. **91** 384
Helen Folsom **62** xxxvii
Helen Maria **69** 166
75 254
Helen Sophia **93** 254
Henriette **127** 195
Henry **51** 508 **54** 257 411

JONES *cont'd*
60 167 **61** 253 **62** 30 330
63 50 **64** 164 **65** 237 **68**
220 **69** 81 **70** 269 **73** 141
184 275 **75** 147 **79** 154
81 488-490 **82** 55-60 62
85 409 **89** 90 91 **91** 326
92 124 **95** 288 **111** 252
126 145 273
Henry A. **62** 31 32
Henry Atwood **110** 297
Henry Augustus **80** 140
89 91
Henry B. **86** 169
Henry Brown **93** 254
Henry C. **62** 25
Henry Cranston **80** 141
Henry D. **90** 106
Henry Hope **92** 121 123
Henry S. **108** 281
Henry T. **64** 330
Henry Tandy **77** 225
Henry Z **144** 363
Hepzibah **55** 406 **56** 46
61 253 354 **111** 312 **113**
178 **123** 260
Hepzibah Chase **70** 278
Hepzibah H. **126** 209
Herbert F. **87** 88
Horman **61** 252
Hester **60** 167 **64** 345
Hezekiah **60** 167 **61** 251
356 **109** 219
Himes **68** 161
Hiram **57** 289 **61** 357 **78**
352 **94** 388 **104** 292
Hiram Thompson **61** 356
Hitty **84** 426
Hollet **90** 44
Homer Tilford **107** 133
Hope **68** 163 **69** 73
Hope (Peabody) **120** 239
Hopestill (Franklin)
122 23
Horace **75** 96
Horace Luther (Mrs.)
105 128
Horace W. **62** lviii
Horatio **62** 25
Hosea **61** 357
Howell **64** 345
Hugh **51** 73 **52** 413 **59** 412
60 79 **61** 149-156 244-
254 354-359 **62** 25-32
207 253 **64** 161 163 **66**
187 **68** 55 **78** 295 **81** 491
82 56 63 **83** 364 **89** 365
93 300 384 **101** 12 **117**
272 273 **125** 160 **131**
175 **143** 117
Hugo **66** 188
Huldah **68** 248 **89** 246
126 172 179
Hyrum Pidding (Mrs.)
103 119
I. **74** 62
I. Fitzroy **147** 251 252
Ichabod **61** 154 **85** 20 23
Ichabod Howland **80** 141
Ida Aline **111** 306
Ida C. **73** 212

JONES *cont'd*
Ida Emma **103** 116
Ida Louise **83** 432 **84** 18
Ida M. **76** 176
Indearing **113** 135 **147** 70
Ino **58** 68
Iram **91** 326
Irena **70** 274 334
Irene Bilyieu **128** 311
Irene Stuart **70** 269 333
Irenia **62** 31
Irvin Harvey **90** 136
Irving Washington
    61 357
Isaac **51** 69 **52** 196 419 **53**
    280 **57** 401 **58** 90 174
    260 266 388 390 **59** 106
    412 **60** 165-167 204 **61**
    31 252 **62** 367 **64** 373 **70**
    269 320 332 334 **75** 307
    76 112 **78** 253 **82** 291
    298 **100** 138 **101** 276
    111 292 **113** 48 52 131
    132 138 140 **119** 40 **127**
    189 **134** 291 **143** 128
    258 **144** 218 219 223 224
    146 268
Isaac Morley (Mrs.)
    94 138
Isaac Watts **147** 77
Isabel **51** 291 **65** 168 **80**
    140 141 **131** 157
Isabel (Gilmor) **113** 141
Isabel C. **64** 203
Isabell (Cogan) **111** 86
Isabella **60** 167 **79** 155
    90 374
Isabella C. **51** 152
Isabella L. **68** 248
Isabella P. **90** 374
Isaiah **70** 274 320 **108** 281
    110 26 104
Isaiah Randell **70** 269
Israel **60** 396 **61** 34 **64** 373
    70 273 **95** 88 **108** 309
    113 48 132 138 **133** 72
    143 128
Israel N. **89** 246
J. Albert **70** 330
J. Athearn **99** 8
J. P. **137** 47
J. Paul **111** 194
J. T. **79** 156 **80** 59 **89** 206
J. Wesley **118** 326
Jabez **61** 252 **80** 189 **89** 246
Jackson **110** 209
Jacob **51** 463 **52** 430 **60** 166
    61 155 156 251-253 **66**
    320 **86** 380 **95** 288 **100**
    287 **113** 48 49 132 134
    138 139 **127** 267 **128** 36
    143 128 **145** 349
James **53** 302 **58** 393 **60**
    166 **61** 157 252 253 **62**
    31 32 **63** 48 **64** 107 112
    65 32 **70** 274 334 **71** 202
    73 87 145 146 **74** 22 216
    253 316 317 **76** 248 **77**
    225 **81** 428 **82** 43 44 103
    83 34 **85** 124 **94** 84 **98**
    233 **99** 123 **103** 254 **104**

JONES *cont'd*
    117 **105** 32 116 **113** 132
    141 142 **114** 189 **116** 7
    117 202 **120** 263 **127**
    191 277 **146** 331
James (Mrs.) **97** 267
James A. **129** 47
James Alexander **74** 317
James Asa **85** 94
James Boyd **128** 36
James C. **62** 31 **76** 46
James Currier **62** 30
James Godfrey **73** 278
James Henry **110** 297
James Judson **70** 274
James Naylor **95** 288
James Parnell **70** 319 336
Jane **57** 402 **59** 75 77 135
    138 310 **60** 164 167 168
    61 245 **62** 30 **67** 126 182
    69 81 329 **73** 91 262 **74**
    253 **79** 331 **81** 488 490
    82 55-57 63 65 **83** 160
    92 13 **93** 123 300 **94** 159
    103 265 **105** 116 **109** 12
    113 145 220 **130** 52 **136**
    33 **142** 304 **147** 259
Jane (Binney) **113** 138
Jane (Bolter) **133** 267
Jane (Field) **113** 144
Jane (Madgwick) **113** 220
Jane (Murray) **90** 44
Jane (Ruble) **108** 224
Jane Amanda **73** 202
Jane D. **78** 427
Jane Emily **78** 43
Jane H. **97** 203
Jane M. **62** 25 28
Jane Wilson **113** 144
Janette Sarah **79** 27
Jardus **118** 166
Jared **61** 248
Jarvis **94** 269
Jedidiah **128** 11 247
Jefferson **62** 31 **111** 155
    114 149
Jefferson Winslow **111**
    155 **114** 149
Jeffrey **82** 57 61 **97** 333
Jehiel **121** 184
Jehu **133** 282
Jemima **60** 307 **61** 253 **82**
    291 297 **141** 350
Jemina (Clark) **108** 309
Jency **78** 44
Jennette **62** 31
Jennie **110** 299
Jennie (Hannum) **90** 262
Jenny **62** 283
Jepthah **61** 252
Jere **110** 206
Jeremiah **61** 357 **64** 254
    69 173 **76** 108 **85** 431
    104 292 **105** 113 116
    212 **107** 63 **108** 281 **109**
    15 **110** 297 299 **125** 38
    145 350
Jeremiah D. **75** 254
Jeremiah Pingree **52** 486
Jeremiah R. **68** 246 **70** 328
Jeremiah Rogers **70** 275

JONES *cont'd*
    335 336
Jerome **71** 172
Jerusha **54** 256 **61** 85 **113**
    141 **115** 41
Jesse **61** 244 355
Jesse Holman **75** 316 **76**
    xxi **79** 81 **80** 231 **81** 62
    82 54 **83** 8 **84** 69 **85** 29
    86 59 **87** 39 **88** 6 **89** 9
    90 103 **91** 6 **92** 29 **93** 47
    277 **94** 19 **95** 89 **96** 58
    97 147 **98** 90 **99** 70 **100**
    127 **101** 278 **102** 196
    103 20 240 **104** 212 **105**
    248 **106** 181 **108** 313
    109 107 **110** 184 **111** 59
    60 64 **113** 130 **114** 114
Jessie **122** 280
Jessie B. **122** 280
Jessie Fremont **71** liv
Jethro **56** 74
Jewett **61** 251
Joab **61** 252
Joan **52** 252 **70** 340 **82** 56-
    58 62
Joanath **110** 111
Joanna **58** 122 132 295 **59**
    96 **60** 265 **61** 155 156
    252 **62** 26 **74** 49 212 216-
    218 225 229 **78** 142 **81**
    126 161 444 **82** 57 **83**
    364 **99** 123 **113** 140 143
    120 71
Joanna (Caswell) **113** 132
Joanna (Drury) **113** 142
Joanne C. **86** 344 **87** 105
Joannes **82** 58
Joel **52** 413 **56** 308 **61** 253
    63 98 **79** 337 **113** 139
    140 68
Johanna **53** 96 **81** 444 **82**
    57 282 291
Johanna E. **63** 50
John **51** 69 223 281-284 289
    52 31 145 166 225 **53** 59
    197 **54** lii 51 81 245 246
    250 255-259 292 **55** 35
    36 141 345 **56** 33 35 39
    165 352 405 **57** 280 388
    393 394 **58** 64 68 122
    238 243 295 393 **59** 387
    60 22 60 164-167 181
    283 284-86 108 194 **108**
    84 230 **109** 92 202 306
    110 303 **111** 30 **113** 44-
    46 49 51 132 135-137
    139 141-143 145 146 216
    218 219 **115** 114 118
    117 255 **119** 20 **120** 18
    144 145 **121** 25 **122** 23
    125 92 221 270 **126** 98
    109 127 **113** 228 **128** 72
    133 267 **136** 257 **137**
    361 **138** 24 26-30 **139**
    140 141 239 246-248 **140**
    159 **142** 273 **143** 121-
    123 125-127 129 **144** 161
    162 166 227 234 235 **146**
    381 382
John (Mrs.) **101** 271 **104**

JONES *cont'd*
293 **109** 202
John A. **91** 326
John Alan (Mrs.) **105** 316
John B. **61** 247 **119** 198
John Benner **113** 52
John C. **65** 147 **93** 397
100 63
John Cargill **117** 255
John Christine **82** 266
John Clark (Mrs.) **77** 156
78 205
John Coffin **84** 373 **126**
225 **140** 37 159
John D. **70** 274
John David **52** 31
John E. **113** 53 **137** 361
John F. **121** 177 **124** 62
John Gilmore **113** 141
John H. **61** 401
John Hall (Mrs.) **96** 160
John I. **112** 161
John J. **62** 71 **92** 169
John Kimble **108** 281
John L. **61** 358 **70** 336
76 176
John Lemuel **69** 261
John M. **91** 326 **97** 133
John Madgwick **113** 220
John P. **55** xlvi **65** 61 **112**
147 148
John Paul **56** 70 **58** 107
221 233 409 **60** 404 405
61 95 **63** 13 **65** 257 258
260 334 **69** 243 **112** 52
115 81 168 **140** 68
John Percival **134** 27
John R. **88** 382
John Reymore **61** 359
John Sullivan **113** 145
John W. **92** 221
John Wesley **104** 293
Jonas **113** 144
Jonathan **52** 432 435 **53**
279 **59** 154 **61** 152-156
244 245 249 250 252-254
353-358 **62** 25 26 **73** 173
77 239 **83** 380 **89** 90 **91**
326 **92** 14 18 19 21 22
93 260 **104** 292 **110** 107
111 **113** 136 137 145
117 272 273 **120** 72 73
Jonathan Greene **81** 150
Jonathan Richardson
62 26
Jonathan W. **62** 25
Joseph **51** 180 181 283 284
52 23 430 435 **53** 59 280
281 **54** lii **58** 142 **60** 60
61 252 360 **62** 252 **65** 95
68 248 **70** 163 **73** 87 271
75 313 **76** 29 111 **77** 257
82 43 289 291 421 **83** 34
86 404 **95** 288 **97** 27
104 292 293 **106** 178
109 12 202 **113** 45 47-52
133 135-138 140 143-146
121 108 111 114 118 121
198 199 280 284 **124** 28
125 99 **129** 61 **133** 259
143 121-123 127-129

JONES *cont'd*
345 **145** 354 365 **147** 77
Joseph B. **65** 133
Joseph Bolles **62** 367
Joseph Bradley **62** 30
Joseph Davis **124** 29
Joseph G. **109** 111
Joseph Russell **119** 157
Joseph Strong **113** 144
Joseph W. **133** 72
Joseph William **62** 367
Josephine **128** 162
Josephine S. **122** 111
Joshua **58** 393 **61** 152 156
157 244-246 253 254 354
62 30 31 **75** 305 **81** 444
82 43 44 416 420 421 **83**
34 **90** 330 **91** 21 **116** 7
127 307 **147** 259
Joshua S. **77** 152
Josiah **58** 240 **59** 416 **60**
60 74 147 **61** 156 157
248 354 355 **63** 292 **68**
245 246 **70** 275 334-336
71 145 **77** 279 **83** 503
85 25 **88** 132 **94** 46 388
101 247 **102** 33 **105** 209
113 45 **120** 73 **127** 91
148 168
Josiah M. **65** xlvi
Josiah Moore **89** 65
Josiah Spring **92** 345
Josias **58** 195 **73** 145 232
129 55
Jotham **62** 25
Jude **61** 356
Judith **51** 289 **52** 429 435
61 358 **62** 29 **82** 56 **100**
187 **104** 292 **107** 305
Judith (Spaulding)
103 235
Judy **107** 64
Julette **146** 369
Julia **88** 289
Julia (Bourne) **119** 42
Julia A. **89** 345 **109** 60
Julia Ann **58** 96 **64** 373
76 318 **96** 305
Julia Clara **70** 202
Julia W. **61** 248
Juliana **100** 138 **101** 276
113 144
Juliann (Lymburner)
109 111
Julianna (Carpenter)
122 281
Julieta P. **70** 328 336
Julius **57** 289
Julyan **82** 57
Justus **61** 358
Kate **77** 266
Kate F. **75** 251
Katharine **51** 291 **55** 334
70 272 **74** 253 **82** 56 **93**
384 **97** 353
Katharine (Gates) **121** 53
Katharine (Wiggles-
worth) **97** 353
Katharine Richie **80** 141
Katie **61** 253 **74** 225
Katy (Leonard) **113** 141

JONES *cont'd*
Kendrick Leavitt **62** 28
Kenneth Ricks **95** 289
Keturah **147** 55
Keturah (Post) **147** 55 56
Keziah **113** 136 143 **134**
315 **146** 368
Keziah (Whitney) **113** 136
Knoful (Mrs.) **115** 79
L. Ann **106** 108
L. Maria **68** 248
Laban **113** 144
Lacitna **87** 93
Lafayette **62** 25
Laura **62** 26 **69** 32 **77** 266
113 229
Laura (Hoisington)
(Ferris) **141** 47
Laura Ann (Holman)
111 64
Laura Augusta **111** 155
114 149
Laura Hatch **110** 297
Laura Louise (Carpenter)
94 388
Laura Maxwell **77** 257
Laura W. **69** 330
Laura Williams **81** 465
Lavenia **110** 107
Lavias 220 **125** 220
Lavina **70** 320 332 334-336
Lavinia **69** 79 **110** 107 111
Lavinia H. **70** 320 336 337
Lawrence **64** 25
Layne Thomas **95** 289
Lazarus **76** 110 112 113 248
250
Leah **113** 131
Leander P. **61** 321
Leiger V. **109** 202
Lemuel **54** 259 **58** 195 **59**
412 **60** 382 383 **61** 85 87
88 **62** 88 90 **68** 248 **70**
322 **73** 48
Lemuel A. **70** 320
Lena **75** 98
Leonard **60** 201 **61** 357
82 416 **85** 166
Leonora **113** 141
LeRoy Reade (Mrs.)
106 125
Lester Warren **105** 128
Letitia **62** 31
Letitia (Gay) **111** 155
114 149
Levi **62** 28 30 31 **112** 156
113 143
Levina **56** 308 **61** 249 250
359 **146** 364
Levina Jane **61** 359
Lewellen **56** 149
Lewes **82** 56
Lewis **54** 245 **59** 421 **61**
327 **64** 337 **76** 273 **79**
337 **94** 388 **113** 236 237
Lewis B. **143** 54
Lewis Hampton **67** xxxi
94
Lewis Llewellyn **113** 237
Lewis M. **85** 314

JONES *cont'd*
Lilian Louise (Fuller)
  105 316
Lillian A. (Gilman)
  121 180
Lillian Chittenden
  103 121
Lillian Maude (Goode)
  (Hannum) **91** 53
Lillie Noble **68** 18
Lily **77** 266
Lindley F. **70** 331
Lindley H. **68** 248
Lindsey S. **69** 311
Lindsey W. **62** 25
Littey **73** 151
Livinia **112** 156
Lizette **133** 72
Lizzie A. **122** 280 **129** 47
Lizzie Eleanor **72** xx
Lizzie Elizabeth **117** 219
Lloyd Peniston **102** 155
Loftus **67** 113
Lois **67** 49 **70** 272 333
  113 134
Lois (Bruce) **113** 134
Lois Claflin **51** 69
Lois Olds **90** 385
Loren **61** 357
Lorenda A. **62** 293
Lorenzo **61** 250
Lorin F. **111** 165 246
Lorinda **61** 355
Lorinda A. **86** 169
Lot **69** 79 **70** 269 320 332
Lottie May **74** 317
Louis **51** 152
Louis C. **110** 153 **120** 76
Louis E. **86** 351
Louisa **58** 57 **61** 359 **73**
  274 **76** 30 272 **82** 421 **94**
  46 **115** 118
Louisa (Brooke) **94** 138
Louisa Elizabeth **82** 103
  94 84
Louisa T. **122** 280
Louise **133** 268
Louise (Raymond) **96** 340
Louise Wyman **114** 81
Lovey **61** 355
Lovina **61** 253
Lovina (Cook) **126** 179
Lovinia **108** 280 **110** 107
Lovinna **83** 496
Lucas **52** 409
Lucina Oresta **76** 20
Lucinda **56** 308 **73** 87 **92**
  313 **113** 144
Lucinda Sophronia
  113 144
Lucius Allen **89** 228
Lucius Polk **77** 266
Lucretia **52** 310 **59** 210 **60**
  77 205 **61** 87 **62** 84 88
  100 287 **113** 144
Lucretia (Partridge)
  99 123
Lucy **53** 86 314 **61** 22 248
  250 252 253 357 **63** 48
  75 303 **77** 312 **80** 140
  82 44 **83** 481 **108** 281

JONES *cont'd*
  109 15 **110** 106 210 **113**
  141 **126** 143 **144** 219
Lucy (Aiken) **125** 291
Lucy (Barree) **113** 52
Lucy (Boston) **117** 140
Lucy (Lane) **89** 91
Lucy (Sanderson) **99** 123
Lucy (Wasson) **110** 297
Lucy A. **74** 317
Lucy Ann **90** 394
Lucy Ann (Tilton) **90** 115
Lucy Ann Elizabeth
  83 25 28
Lucy B. (Knowles) **110**
  107 111
Lucy Binns (Cargill)
  117 255
Lucy Cadwallader **77** 253
Lucy Hall **82** 44
Lucy J. **110** 25 26 **123** 295
Lucy Jane (Wasson) **110**
  206 297
Lucy M. **61** 22
Ludora (Kratz) **133** 267
Luke **61** 248
Lulu Clarabelle **102** 122
Luman **61** 357
Luther **61** 358 359
Luther Otis **57** 360
Lydia **51** 69 **53** 59 164 **54**
  259 **59** 210 420 **60** 78
  166 **61** 151 244 246 252
  253 355 356 **62** 25 30 32
  383 **68** 246 **69** 181 **70**
  272 274 **71** 145 **73** 87 95
  74 225 249 317 **77** 279
  80 193 **89** 250 **97** 130
  103 261 **112** 156 **113** 45
  46 48-50 133 136 137
  142 145 **121** 105 **122**
  258 **124** 9 **126** 98 **128** 41
  143 128-131 340 343
  147 127
Lydia (Chase) **88** 30
Lydia (Davis) **121** 177
Lydia (Jonson) **88** 340
Lydia (Neale) **113** 48
  143 128
Lydia (Nichols) **87** 92
Lydia (Rockwood) **124** 9
Lydia (Rogers) **147** 124
  127
Lydia (Rutherford)
  133 267
Lydia (Sherman) **113** 143
Lydia (Treadway) **94** 388
Lydia Ann **62** 25 **124** 29
Lydia H. **126** 207
Lydia Jenkins **70** 335
Lydia Parker (Howland)
  113 117
Lydia R. **70** 329 331
Lydia T. **69** 319
Lydia V. **109** 202
Lydia Webber **110** 300
Lynds Eugene **133** 232
Lynds Lysander **133** 232
M. E. Ann (Carter)
  (Michie) **91** 303
M. W. **91** 53

JONES *cont'd*
Mabel Laighton **66** lii
Madison **62** 30
Mae (Heald) **86** 155
Magdalen **51** 280
Mahala **62** 28 **70** 277 332
  336 **98** 233
Malantha H. Weir **86** 169
Manley **62** 29
Marah **61** 152 **142** 279
Marcella **62** 25
Marcia **62** 25 **63** 48
Marcus L. **61** 359
Marcy **126** 267
Marcy (Briggs) **126** 267
Margaret **56** 308 **64** 259
  337 **65** 173 **73** 141 **74** 18
  22 33 87 **75** 221 **79** 14
  443 **81** 320 488-491 **82**
  55-58 61-63 65 291 295
  83 65 **90** 368 **93** 175
  100 234 **104** 71 **123** 166
Margaret (Fitz Randolph)
  98 47
Margaret (Williams)
  95 288
Margaret Adeline **117** 128
Margaret Ann **111** 155
  114 149
Margaret B. **68** 246
Margaret Belvin **100** 165
Margaret Eliza **110** 299
Margaret Elizabeth
  105 220
Margaret J. **98** 178
Margaret J. (Lear) **121** 177
Margery **81** 444 **82** 55 56
  284 291 294
Margetie **51** 187
Marguerite **113** 296
Maria **52** 148 **62** 25 **70** 329
  73 48 277 **75** 251 **82** 57
  58 **115** 26
Maria (Belcher) **113** 141
Maria (Harding) **113** 141
Maria Buckminster
  65 xlvi
Maria Buckminster
  (Bullard) **89** 65
Maria L. **70** 320
Maria Louisa **62** 25
Maria Louisa (Simes) **83**
  183 186
Maria Louise **84** 29
Maria S. (Wilson) **90** 54
Marian Douglas **85** 113
  333
Marie **53** 239
Marinda **105** 115
Marion Barr **80** 141
Mark **64** 373 **81** 490 **82** 55
  62
Marquis **126** 219
Marsey **143** 129
Marshall **70** 92 **119** 59
Marshall Branch **77** 266
Marshall S. **94** 161
Martha **51** 69 **52** 225 **58**
  302 **59** 387 **61** 156 248
  249 356 357 **64** 41 **67** 51
  206 **68** 108 **70** 92 272

JONES *cont'd*
334 **73** 135 173 253 268
74 255 264 **77** 213 251
79 385 **81** 32 **82** 56 57
83 380 **84** 256 **87** 92 **92**
102 **99** 208 **108** 187 **113**
219 220 **114** 187 **144**
167 168 **148** 178
Martha (Ewer) **122** 258
Martha (Ingraham)
146 369
Martha (Smith) **113** 219
144 166
Martha Ann **61** 248 **83** 23
24
Martha Ann (Goodhue)
83 23
Martha Carter **61** 356
Martha E. **103** 45 267
Martha E. (Robinson)
103 267
Martha Helenah **133** 72
Martha Maria **62** 367
Martha W. (Price) **113** 145
Martin **113** 141
Martin Cox **61** 250
Martin Parry **82** 421 **83**
183 186 306
Martin W. **92** 146
Mary **51** 180 440 **52** 181-
184 251 309 412 420 428
438 **53** 41 59 163 165
209 279 280 459 **54** lii
cxi 245 255 325 332 **55** 85
333 404 **56** lxxv 168 171
57 34 390 **58** 43 90 122
260 295 318 381 **59** 65
210 252 261 386 387 395
60 43 166-168 267 306
61 150-153 155-157 244
245 247 248 250-253 332-
335 **71** 145 **73** 138 151
170 173 184 212 222 224
74 22 29 33 184 249 **75**
146 147 204 206 313 **76**
185 **77** 251 **78** 295 398
79 399 **80** 140 189 **81**
269 428 **82** 26 44-52 131-
134 136 137 140-142 145
146 209 219 221 237 **115**
26 **119** 13 **120** 53 263
265 **121** 16 199 **122** 101
280 **125** 133 160 **126**
209 **129** 112 **134** 291
292 **135** 129 **136** 362
137 49 **139** 140 141 **142**
278 **143** 124 126-131 345
145 109 167 **147** 77
Mary (Adams) **113** 51
143 129
Mary (Baker) **142** 125
Mary (Ball) **113** 145
Mary (Bancroft) **95** 285
Mary (Barnes) **100** 240
Mary (Barnett) **105** 220
Mary (Bennet) **113** 51
Mary (Carter) **147** 77
Mary (Chapin) **113** 144
Mary (Coomes) (Vickery)
143 128 345
Mary (Copeland) **113** 137

JONES *cont'd*
143 129
Mary (Cross) **92** 169
Mary (Daggett) **113** 142
Mary (Dean) **113** 133
Mary (Farquhar) **113** 144
Mary (Finney) **113** 140
Mary (Gates) **120** 263
Mary (Jordan) **113** 131
Mary (Keef) **125** 216
Mary (Kent) **95** 88
Mary (King) (True)
133 267
Mary (Loring) **113** 47
143 127 138
Mary (Loud) **113** 139
Mary (Meacham) **108** 309
Mary (Murch) **90** 50
Mary (Naylor) **95** 288
Mary (North) **108** 309
Mary (Pattee) **147** 77
Mary (Perrigoe) **100** 240
Mary (Potbery) **113** 49
143 129
Mary (Pybern) **95** 288
Mary (Quincy) **125** 215
Mary (Randal) **113** 131
Mary (Raynsford)
(Rogers) **139** 306
Mary (Rockwood)
113 135
Mary (Sanderson)
128 122
Mary (Sayrl) **113** 134
Mary (Simmons) **88** 339
Mary (Smith) **106** 68
Mary (Smith) (Basset)
106 240
Mary (Speer) **113** 50 51
143 129
Mary (Spencer) **102** 187
Mary (Stephens) **113** 142
Mary (Stevens) **125** 287
Mary (Van Meter) **108** 224
Mary (Vickery) **113** 48
Mary (Whitney) **113** 136
137
Mary (Williams) **90** 57
113 139
Mary (Wing) **128** 11
Mary (Winsor) **113** 131
143 127
Mary (Worster) **97** 274
Mary A. **61** 247 **68** 246 **70**
275 336 **79** 53 **82** 375 **88**
332 **113** 53 **120** 73 **125**
160
Mary A. Virginia **101** 80
Mary Adelaide **70** 330
Mary Ann **69** 32 181 **73**
167 270 **79** 49 **82** 44 **83**
25 27 34 **86** 221 **89** 90
92 122 **97** 75 **115** 268
140 159
Mary Ann (Chaffee)
110 37
Mary Ann (Upham)
116 257
Mary Ann Rogers
(Prince) **83** 183 185
Mary Anne **61** 247 358

JONES *cont'd*
62 30 **70** 330 331
Mary B. **61** 248 **62** 31
Mary Battle (Robertson)
108 224
Mary Belle (Gibbs) **111** 64
Mary Benson **113** 134
Mary Buckminster **65**
xlvi **89** 65 **103** 146
Mary C. **68** 248 **70** 336
Mary Cabot (Newell)
124 29
Mary Caroline **88** 132
Mary Closson (Reed)
110 302
Mary Cornelia **75** 96
Mary Cross **92** 169
Mary Dewey **76** 17
Mary E. (Smith) **121** 181
Mary E. R. **59** 421
Mary Edwards **77** 225
Mary Eliza (Brown)
(Brown) **86** 391 **87** 10
Mary Elizabeth **54** 149
69 32 **98** 76 **129** 47
Mary Elizabeth (Locke)
85 94
Mary Elizabeth Ann
(Carter) **91** 303
Mary Emma D. **113** 237
Mary Ermina **57** 361
Mary F. **92** 169
Mary Foster **62** 29
Mary G. **70** 331 336
Mary Geddings (Coult)
108 308
Mary Gerrish **67** 113
Mary H. (Field) **85** 332
Mary Hope **96** 76
Mary J. **62** 28 **121** 182
Mary J. C. **62** 31
Mary Jane **62** 31 **108** 281
Mary L. **62** 25 28
Mary Louisa **61** lvii
Mary Martha (Hays) **108**
230 231
Mary Mather **115** 112
Mary Matilda **124** 29
Mary Noyes (Tyler)
109 219
Mary Polk **77** 253
Mary Rendell **70** 269 330
334
Mary Rogers **82** 421
Mary Rushworth
(Crossley) **97** 215
Mary S. (Seaward) **88** 382
Mary Soper **89** 90 91
Mary Sumner (Hawes)
113 236 237
Mary Susan **103** 43
Mary T. **89** 369
Mary Trifery **61** 355
Mary Tuck **58** lxxv
Mary Tuttle **70** 277 278
Mary U. **134** 240
Mary W. **70** 320 332
Mary W. (Gould) **134** 89
Mary W. (Storer) **83** 183
187
Mary W. B. **70** 329

JONES *cont'd*
Mary Wallace **68** 18
Mary Whitney **113** 145
Matilda **61** 357 **82** 56
   98 224
Matilda (Davis) **113** 142
Matilda H. **73** 276
Matt Bushnell **56** xxx
   xxxiv **59** xiii xxx xxxiv
   xli **61** xxxiii 142 212 **62**
   xxxv 98 333 **63** vii 196
   391 **64** vii xxix **65** vii
   xxxiii **66** vii 32 **67** vii
   68 vii **69** vii **70** vii **71**
   vii **72** vii **73** vi **74** 77 **79**
   330 **84** 354 **88** 167 **90**
   125 306 **93** 402 **94** 154
   388 389 **95** 73 150 **144**
   107
Matthew **73** 212 **85** 454
   107 160 **123** 170 **129**
   224
Matthias Stone **94** 388
Mattie (Seeke) **87** 92
Maud L. **110** 300
Maude **53** 239
Maurice **64** 337 **82** 59 61
May **80** 157
May A. **82** 430 441
Meady **78** 44
Mehitable **51** 69 **53** 279
   56 39 **58** 47 **61** 22 249
   355 357 **62** 32 **70** 228 **73**
   212 **86** 404 **109** 202 **113**
   49 **120** 72 73 248 **124** 11
   127 267 **133** 302 **146**
   367
Mehitable (Arey) **86** 404
Mehitable (Bowden)
   109 112
Mehitable (Garfield)
   94 388
Mehitable (Goodwin)
   120 73
Mehitable (Leach) **113** 140
Mehitable (Leonard)
   113 48
Mehitable (Wyman)
   89 365
Mehitable R. **73** 212
Melchesadeck **69** 67
Melinda **62** 25
Melinda (Harding)
   113 141
Melinda Ann **84** 188
Melinda Tilson **64** 373
Melvin E. **82** 384 **89** 96
   125 270 **143** 121 124
Melvin Elijah **83** 122 232
   85 176
Mercy **58** 379 **60** 133 **61**
   243 358 **62** 25-27 29 **64**
   72 **73** 212 **75** 147 **78** 178
   291 **113** 50 131 **123** 259
   142 273 **143** 124
Mercy (Bagg) **123** 260
Mercy (Bale) **86** 458
Mercy (Goodspeed)
   119 40
Mercy (Goodwin) **119** 40
Mercy (Gushee) **113** 139

JONES *cont'd*
Mercy (Hildrick) **137** 361
Mercy (Parkhurst)
   113 136
Mercy K. **134** 85
Mercy Richardson **62** 26
Meribah **55** 35 **56** 165
   75 304
Merrill **53** 163
Merritt C. **70** 203
Merriwether **51** 156 157
Michael **74** 22 **114** 54 **119**
   20 **134** 89
Miles **125** 39
Millard Chester **148** 174
Millicent Frances **87** 280
Milliken **73** 167
Milo J. **62** 26
Milton **61** 357
Milton H. **70** 330
Milton Ragan (Mrs.)
   103 119
Mima **55** 36
Minah **62** 29 **88** 282
Mindwell **60** 165 166
Minerva **64** 155 **78** 320
Minerva H. (Bridges)
   101 214
Minor **113** 141
Mira **128** 36
Miranda **61** 249 250
   105 115
Miriam **52** 432 433 **53** 279
   58 44 **61** 244 **63** 48 379
   70 229 **73** 173 **82** 282
   291 **100** 187 340
Miriam Austin **70** 275 334
Miry **109** 15
Mittie **58** 129
Molly **52** 435 **53** 162 164
   57 76 **58** 194 **61** 244 358
   63 172 **64** 123 **74** 225
   251 258 **75** 313 **77** 266
   99 326 **113** 135 138
Molly (Hazeltine) **113** 143
Molly (Pattee) **147** 77
Molly (Stannard) **146** 370
Monica **73** 140
Monica Semantha **57** 294
Monroe **85** 166
Morgan **52** 28-36 291 **82**
   56 57 **106** 83 **110** 169
   113 204
Moses **53** 279 280 **56** 249
   57 360 **58** 129 **60** 43 **61**
   358 **62** 325 **70** 298 304
   307 308 **73** 152 **74** 218
   77 lxxiii **79** 36 **106** 68
   113 137 145 146 **134**
   293
Moses L. **95** 15
Myra **109** 15
Myrion **115** 119
N. **58** 194
Nabby **61** 253 357 358 **71**
   202 **74** 225 229 249 **82**
   44
Nabby (Tirrell) **113** 145
Nabby Ann **82** 44
Nabby B. **122** 280
Nahum **56** xxxii **58** xlv

JONES *cont'd*
   90 50
Nancy **61** 22 248-250 252
   358 **62** 31 **66** 109 **70** 178
   269 332 334 **73** 173 263
   74 20 27 **75** 305 **76** 36
   83 380 **85** 166 **86** 169
   87 233 237 **88** 225 **89**
   239 **91** 34 **106** 80 **107**
   160 **108** 171 281 **113**
   144 **114** 180 **122** 280
   135 145 **147** 77
Nancy (Hunter) **113** 139
Nancy (Jaspey) **125** 99
Nancy (Jones) **91** 34
Nancy B. **62** 31 **73** 184
Nancy Caroline **62** 367
Nancy Clark **133** 282
Nancy Electa **62** 25
Nancy Elizabeth **103** 121
Nancy H. **70** 328 335
Nancy Jane **110** 214
Nancy M. **61** 22
Nancy Maria **70** 320
Nancy R. **62** 26 28
Nancy Randal **70** 320
Nancy Susan **57** 360
Naomi **52** 309 **113** 47 144
Naomi (Foster) **113** 47
   143 128
Naomi K. **88** 330
Nathan **53** 59 **58** 58 122
   194-197 401 **60** 204 **61**
   153-155 245 251 252 **62**
   27 28 **74** 171 317 **95** 61
   113 48 49 133 140 **143**
   128
Nathaniel **53** 204 **55** 236
   58 194 295 393 **59** 386
   387 **60** 164-166 **61** 153
   245 260 **62** 28-30 **63** 292
   78 433 **81** 444 491 492
   82 26 44 63 **88** 30 **97** 75
   353 **104** 293 **109** 112
   201 **110** 72 **113** 50 136
   142 144 **126** 145 **138**
   212 **143** 129 **146** 367
Nathaniel Allen **51** 69
Nathaniel V. **87** 10
Nehemiah **51** 292 **53** 59 **58**
   97 **61** 357 **62** 26 **65** 46
   48 **82** 83 **113** 133 139
   140 59
Nellie **122** 280
Nellie (Avery) **110** 303
Nellie P. (Johnson)
   122 280
Newman **61** 355
Nicholas **54** 345 **59** 108
   60 167 **63** 327 **78** 433
   111 86
Nina **95** 289
Nixon **51** 94
Noah **58** 280 **69** 79 **70** 269
   320 332 335 336 **113** 144
Noah Nichols **61** 291
Noble **125** 29
Noble Lovely **121** 184
Noble Wimberley **68** 18
Nona **95** 289
Norman **122** 110

JONES *cont'd*
Norton M. **91** 326
Obadiah **79** 71
Octavia Rowena **77** 145
Olive **58** 401 **59** 412 **60** 79
   61 246 359 **62** 27 29 31
   67 52 229 **84** 425 **106**
   141 **113** 144 **141** 190
Olive (Bates) **113** 143
Olive (Landers) **120** 239
   124 275
Olive (Leach) **120** 144
Olive E. (Main) **128** 175
Olive Louise (Hoyt) **106**
   313 315
Olive M. **109** 202
Olive T. **60** 297
Oliver **61** 246 **62** 31 32 **70**
   229 **75** 31 **97** 272 **108** 5
   113 141
Oliver B. **62** 293
Oliver M. **62** 31
Oliver O. **60** 406
Orren **62** 30 **86** 233
Orris Hyman **110** 299
Otis **57** 360 361
Otis G. **111** 155 **114** 149
Owen **61** 357 **64** 163 **65** 44
   91 326 **125** 100
Palmer **113** 53
Pamelia **63** 175 **68** 162 163
Parigreen **113** 142
Parker **62** 367 **70** 202
Patience **60** 167 **61** 29 **69**
   181 **70** 163 **73** 172 **88**
   359 **119** 30 40 **121** 274
   122 319
Patience (Little) **143** 122
Patrick Tracy **82** 44
Patty **84** 158 **113** 141
Patty (Bixby) **136** 270
Patty (Smith) **113** 146
Paul **55** 107 **57** 122 **65** 80
   81 338 340 **68** 162 163
   69 73
Paul (Mrs.) **96** 160
Paul B. **124** 262
Paul Ricks **95** 289
Paul V. B. **73** 82
Paulina **62** 30
Peace **68** 166 **70** 271 332
   335
Peggy **55** 375 **83** 17
Peggy (Goodwin) **83** 17
Pelatiah **55** xlvi **61** 250
   101 43
Percival **77** xxviii 77
Perry **73** 217
Persis **61** 247-250
Persis (Parks) **88** 212
Peter **51** 303 **61** 245 **62** 28
   31 **64** 159 257 **91** 326 **95**
   51 **114** 186
Peter B. **77** 266
Peter C. **62** 31
Peter Woodbury **62** 28
Phebe **61** 155 252 **68** 246
   69 173 **70** 273 322 **75**
   308 **86** 295 **91** 385 **113**
   146 **119** 196 200 **126**
   273

JONES *cont'd*
Phebe (Howland) **138** 205
Phebe Ann **61** 274 **115** 38
Phebe P. **70** 328 334
   110 209
Phebe Rebecca **117** 202
Phebe Worth **70** 275
Philander A. **77** 146
Philemon **73** 271
Philip **59** 411 **65** 31 **82** 57
   58 **117** 55 **136** 186
Philip C. **118** 131 **122** 280
Philip C. (Mrs.) **122** 278
   279 281
Phillis **108** **73** 232 **125** 108
Phineas **52** 413 **53** 85 86
   57 280 **58** 401 402 **59**
   412 **60** 79 202 **61** 237
   245 **62** 28 30 265 268
   269 **64** 12 **80** 126 **106**
   270 **121** 53 **148** 168
Pitman **115** 252
Pitt Harold **122** 280
Polly **51** 292 **55** 179 **58** 97
   59 197 **61** 245 248-250
   253 355 357-359 **62** 25
   30 **70** 229 **92** 22 **93** 263
   104 132 **113** 142 145
   115 114 **123** 47 **147** 127
Polly (Alden) **113** 139
Polly (Godson) **133** 307
Polly (Higley) **117** 55
Polly (Strong) **113** 144
Polly (Todd) **125** 289
Polly Strong **113** 144
Prescott **62** 29
Priscilla **74** 212 216 217
   225 227 228 253 255 317
   76 107 108 111 114 185
   259 **79** 253 **113** 136 **116**
   306
Priscilla (Corbett)
   113 136
Priscilla Alden **122** 49 51
   154 278
Prudence **62** 26 27 **78** 43
   113 145 146
Prudence (Briggs)
   126 123
Prudence (Godfrey)
   113 139
Prudence Whitney **76** 13
R. Bissell **105** 56
Rachel **59** 387 **61** 22 151
   156 245 246 251 252 **62**
   26 28 **68** 167 **70** 275 **72**
   315 **74** 227 254 **75** 303
   78 295 **80** 427 **81** 269
   93 198 **95** 324 **99** 327
   113 47 131 132 142 **143**
   127
Rachel (Beals) **113** 140
Rachel (Chapin) **113** 142
Rachel (Jones) **113** 131 132
Rachel (Kester) **95** 166
Rachel (Mastens) **125** 104
Rachel W. **70** 334
Rachie E. **100** 214
Ralph **118** 205 **123** 61 **130**
   7 9 **131** 316

JONES *cont'd*
Ralph Davis (Mrs.)
   107 133
Randall **73** 184 **82** 254
   83 227
Rebecca **51** 290 **59** 154 **60**
   165 167 **61** 151 250 253
   254 354 355 **62** 159 **66**
   272 **68** 290 **69** 370 **70** 39
   73 139 173 231 **77** 251
   86 404 **102** 278 320 **108**
   274 **113** 49 131 134 139-
   141 **120** 72 **126** 237 **127**
   267 **128** 36 **140** 303 **142**
   273 **143** 124 **148** 178
Rebecca (Arey) **86** 404
Rebecca (Beals) **125** 104
Rebecca (Benson) **113** 134
   142 272
Rebecca (Chenery)
   134 293
Rebecca (Cole) **126** 290
Rebecca (Epes) **107** 80
Rebecca (Farley) (Putnam)
   136 144
Rebecca (Hatch) **128** 11
Rebecca (Jenkins) **120** 73
Rebecca (Jones) **113** 131
Rebecca (McCoy) **126** 205
Rebecca (Snow) **113** 140
Rebecca (Wing) (Hatch)
   128 11 **130** 133
Rebecca B. **62** 26
Rebecca Edwards **77** 251
   253
Rebecca Maria **70** 336
Reese **88** 339 **104** 309
Reliah D. **148** 170 174
Relief **61** 253 **62** 26
Remer Young (Mrs.)
   98 147
Rensaleer **62** 293
Reuben **54** 291-293 **55** 429
   56 249 388 **60** 167 **61**
   251 **62** 29 **70** 334 **74** 216
   249 **112** 156 **113** 141
   118 202 **142** 48
Reuben A. **100** 214
Reuben T. **70** 334
Rhoda **52** 410 **60** 78 **61** 357
   62 27 29 **89** 90
Rhoda (Man) **128** 175
Rhoda (Soper) **89** 90
Rice **123** 170
Richard **51** 283 284 **53** 279
   55 67 69 70 **60** 162 **62**
   252 367 **64** 107 159 163
   216 254 336 337 **67** 182
   71 liii **73** 142 221 264 **74**
   17 18 22 23 **82** 44 56 57
   59 60 **95** 288 **100** 234
   104 281 **105** 96 **113** 140
   115 99 **117** 254 255 **119**
   20 **125** 104 **131** 127 **141**
   236 **143** 121
Richard (Mrs.) **124** 84
Richard Augustine
   70 319
Richard Edgarton
   109 221
Richard Lake **127** 113

JONES *cont'd*
Richard Mott **70** 272 319
  333 336 337 **79** 224 **95**
  166
Richard Philip **122** 280
Richmond L. **69** xxxii
Rispah (Briggs) **126** 272
Roba **75** 305
Robert **51** 283 **52** 145 **60**
  60 **61** 345 **62** 323 **64** 162
  164 218 **66** 188 270 **68**
  196 **70** 272 **74** 22 23 **77**
  213 **78** 56 **81** 488-492
  82 55-57 59 61 63 384
  83 160 **84** 77 **89** 96 **90**
  209 **97** 320 326 **108** 224
  112 199 **113** 42 53 **117**
  140 **121** 119 278 **127**
  222 **128** 218 264 **139** 25
  46 47 49 306 **142** 273
  274 357 **143** 121-124 365
Robert A. **116** 63 **126** 144
Robert Anderson **73** 230
Robert Elam **108** 224
Robert G. **125** 216
Robert Huhn **121** 238
Robin ap Cadwallader
  77 253
Robin ap Robin **77** 253
Robinson **82** 289 291
  105 114 **127** 113 **133** 56
Roderick **70** 92
Roderick Bissell **97** 134
  101 338 **104** 77 **105** 190
  242 272 **106** 15 **107** 127
  108 71 309 **143** 240-245
  148 39
Roger **61** 392 **67** 94
Roland **130** 233
Rolinda **122** 111
Rollin C. **62** 25
Rosa **139** 214
Rosalinda **73** 167
Rosamond **61** 250
Rosannah **59** 210
Rose Ellen **122** 280
Rosel **70** 227
Roseltha S. **86** 169
Rosemary **144** 59
Rowe **65** 251
Rowland **64** 160 **81** 490
  82 56 **133** 308
Roxanna **61** 357 **74** 22
Roxanna (Fuller) **128** 264
Roy E. **116** 63
Royal E. **122** 230
Ruby (Chase) **88** 120
Rufus **69** 177 **70** 271 319
  75 302
Russell **58** 401 **61** 252 356
  62 151
Ruth **60** 391 **61** 236 247
  248 254 354 392 **63** 73
  266 **64** 123 **69** 73 **74** 22
  251 **86** 85 **105** 57 **113** 48
  135 137 **121** 124 **125**
  293 **137** 76 **143** 128 **147**
  77
Ruth (Ackley) **108** 309
Ruth (Bowden) **109** 201
Ruth (Burrell) **113** 139

JONES *cont'd*
  120 53
Ruth (Goodwin) **91** 31
Ruth (Nelson) **113** 144
Ruth (Petty) **113** 132
Ruth (Vinton) **85** 110
  131 33
Ruth (Wheler) **85** 110
Ruth Berrien **54** liv
Ruth J. (Webb) **111** 137
Ruth Mary **89** 259
Ruth Mealy **70** 269
S. **91** 326
Sabra **108** 120 **142** 48
  148 179
Sabra Richardson **62** 26
Sabra Wyman **62** 32
  89 365
Sacharressa **95** 15
Sala **80** 189 **89** 246
Sally **60** 295 **61** 354 358
  62 31 **70** 230 308 **73** 167
  262 **74** 19 22 225 250 **75**
  305 **76** 147 **82** 44 **84** 270
  90 328 **91** 82 **99** 123
  100 187 **113** 141 142
  125 291 **134** 293 **147**
  127
Sally (Chapel) **113** 142
Sally (Hovey) **126** 142
Sally (Kindrick) **113** 142
Sally (Whittemore)
  108 84
Sally A. **61** 355 **143** 68
Sally Louisa **57** 294
Sally W. **61** 358
Saloma **63** 46 **144** 104
  110 120 122
Samuel **51** 69 73 283 284
  52 429 **53** 59 208 209
  279 280 **54** 83 **55** xlvi
  111 401 **59** 84 386 387
  60 39 165-167 **61** 22 31
  151-157 244 246 247 249-
  254 354 356-358 392 **62**
  33 **65** 20 **66** 62 **68** 217
  218 246 **70** 275 **71** 145
  73 149 227 270 **74** 49
  184 189 216 218 247 250
  317 **75** 101 147 **76** 113
  77 236 **78** 303 **80** 427
  81 269 444 **82** 43 44 55
  58 282 291 297 **83** 34 **95**
  15 **103** 189 255 **104** 293
  105 212 **108** 281 309
  110 302 **113** 49 131 134
  136 139 141 142 **115** 99
  113 **116** 313 **121** 220
  136 270 **142** 358 **146** 3
  365
Samuel (Mrs.) **109** 202
Samuel B. **61** 354 **84** 49
Samuel Cleaves **55** xlvii
Samuel Findley **61** 392
Samuel Lee **62** 29
Samuel Minot **77** 159
Samuel N. **75** 98
Samuel Sylvester **121** 142
Sarah **51** 69 223 460 **52**
  308-310 409 413 415 417
  418 429 430 **53** 59 162

JONES *cont'd*
  163 197 280 281 300 449
  57 393 394 **58** 42 118
  175 194 266 390 **59** 45
  137 311 387 415 **60** 43
  79 165-167 201 204 **61**
  51 151 153-155 237 246-
  249 254 260 355 356 358
  392 **62** 25-31 **63** 93 174
  177 **67** 374 **68** 18 109
  195 290 **69** 378 **70** 163
  306 **73** 135 152 167 173
  261 276 **74** 23 33 49 62
  75 147 **76** 34 **77** lxxiii
  56 176 251 318 **78** 363
  433 **80** 193 **81** 153 **82** 44
  83 291 293 **83** 364 380
  85 291 **89** 250 **92** 11 21
  93 259 94 355 **96** 337
  99 168 **101** 13 43 **102**
  152 **104** 225 226 292 309
  107 118 **108** 20 220 **109**
  255 **110** 21 111 **111** 155
  113 44-46 48 50 52 131-
  136 141-143 145 146 223
  114 149 186 **115** 26 **117**
  255 **121** 192 **122** 280
  123 170 **124** 28 29 **125**
  29 **126** 144 **129** 47 **136**
  56 **137** 242 **139** 137 **142**
  7 9 10 273 352 353 **143**
  121 122 124-131 133 **147**
  127 237 **148** 168
Sarah (Bancroft) **95** 61
Sarah (Bosworth) **143** 129
Sarah (Briggs) **125** 269
  270
Sarah (Church) **126** 255
  128 19
Sarah (Fay) **113** 46 146
Sarah (Fracker) **124** 28
Sarah (Gates) **120** 260
Sarah (Gibson) **113** 133
Sarah (Gooden) **113** 46
Sarah (Horsum) **113** 51
Sarah (Horton) **137** 37
Sarah (Lewis) **101** 12
Sarah (Lloyd) **113** 220
Sarah (Lobdell) **113** 49
  143 129
Sarah (Loring) **113** 138
Sarah (Moore) **127** 191
Sarah (Percival) **118** 202
Sarah (Sanford) **113** 141
Sarah (Sawtelle) **122** 281
  283
Sarah (Shaw) **113** 131
Sarah (Simpson) **130** 52
Sarah (Wheeler) **89** 90
Sarah (Whitman) **113** 44
  143 126 127 131
Sarah (Wilson) **133** 72
Sarah A. **61** 22 247 **88** 336
  100 187
Sarah Abigail **145** 158
Sarah Ann (Malarnee)
  95 288
Sarah Annis **61** 355
Sarah Aurelia (Everett)
  113 296

JONES *cont'd*
Sarah Blackman Alis **115** 179
Sarah C. **54** c
Sarah Campbell **68** 18
Sarah D. **86** 52 **110** 206
Sarah E. **57** 205
Sarah Edna **100** 112
Sarah Elizabeth **80** 241
Sarah Ellen **70** 278 336
    111 155 **114** 149
Sarah Ermina **70** 319
Sarah Fidelia **85** 229
Sarah Freeman **74** 31
Sarah H. **83** 24 25
Sarah Hatch **110** 297
Sarah Hubbard
    (Fayerweather)
    145 158
Sarah J. **69** 198 **109** 202
    111 155 **114** 149
Sarah Jakell **79** 331
Sarah Jane **62** 29 **148** 170
    174
Sarah Joanna **61** 359
Sarah Kimball **64** 373
Sarah L. **110** 206
Sarah M. **87** 261 **104** 77
Sarah Pamelia **64** 373
Sarah Parker **61** 358
Sarah Payson **77** lxxii
Sarah Polk **77** 253
Sarah Rachel **77** 253
Sarah Reed **113** 141
Sarah Reynolds (Kelsey)
    143 54
Sarah S. **56** 182 **61** 124
    110 206
Sarah T. **69** 183 **70** 279
    319 336
Sarah W. (Hemmenway)
    90 106
Sarah Wesson **108** 281
Sarepta Cordelia **94** 85
Scriven **65** 22
Sebrina R. **148** 179
Selden **80** 427
Selina **117** 291
Sephlinda **88** 26
Sereno U. **106** 206
Serjeant **126** 307
Serviah **62** 27
Seth **53** 59 60 **59** 310 **60**
    383 **95** 55 **113** 132 136
    142
Seth C. **87** 10
Seth Corbet **113** 142
Seviah **69** 183 **70** 279
Sewall **61** 357 **90** 54 115
    108 280
Shepard S. **61** 248
Shubael **128** 11 **130** 133
Sibyl **54** 216 217 **59** 65 **60**
    166 167 **63** 286 287 **69**
    177 **70** 272 319 333 335
    336 **82** 57
Sibyl Narcissa **70** 319 335
Silas **61** 154 155 249-251
    253 **66** 37 **69** 183 **70** 279
    333 **95** 285 **100** 187 **113**
    117

JONES *cont'd*
Silas N. **126** 179
Silence (Hewett) **113** 49
Simeon **59** 135 **61** 253 **70**
    178 224 **71** 139 **74** 22 33
    104 292 **108** 279 **109** 15
    110 37 **136** 36
Simon **53** 239 **87** 92
Simpson **51** 71 283 284
    62 371
Smith **128** 36
Solomon **53** 59 **61** 245 249
    250 253 **62** 29 **83** 160
    113 47 131-133 136 138
    140 142 144 **128** 41 **142**
    199 **143** 127
Solomon Bird **105** 116
Solomon Verrill **110** 22
Solon **61** 358
Sophia **61** 383 **62** 28 **63** 46
    70 269 334 **91** 293 **93**
    254 **110** 230 **113** 141
    144 110 120 122
Sophia (Weston) **147** 70
Sophia Eleanor **95** 166
Sophia G. **76** 33
Sophia Weston **92** 361
Sophronia **63** 46 **144** 104
    110 120 122
Stella (Blake) **122** 281
Stella B. **122** 280
Stephen **52** 180 183 308-
    310 408-410 412 413 415
    417 418 **53** 164 281 **58**
    401 **59** 413 **60** 38 39 73
    204 266 **61** 254 360 **68**
    167 218 **70** 275 334 **71**
    223 **73** 253 **74** 217 255
    75 147 **76** 30 **78** 363 **79**
    47 **83** 160 364 **85** 20 **92**
    102 **97** 280 **98** 224 **113**
    252 **117** 160 **122** 293
Stephen Alfred **70** 330
Stephen S. **73** 261 **76** 41
Stephen Warren **70** 275
Stewart **113** 218
Stillman **61** 357
Storer W. **55** xxxi
Submit **58** 129 **61** 358 **93**
    198 **113** 49 **143** 128
Sue **77** 266
Sukey **59** 258 263 **62** 73
Sukey P. **62** 159
Sullivan **61** 249 250 358
    128 122
Susan **68** 382 **70** 273 **76** 29
    78 33 **79** 55 **82** 57 **93**
    300 **97** 190 **108** 93 **110**
    209 **113** 140 **114** 269
Susan (Carlton) **110** 110
    209
Susan (Fisher) **113** 141
Susan (Tibbetts) **100** 148
Susan Amanda **72** 306
Susan Angeline (Reed)
    132 306
Susan Elizabeth **110** 209
Susan F. (Cotton) **110** 105
Susan Irene (Girardeau)
    95 15
Susan Jane **78** 322

JONES *cont'd*
Susan Louisa **92** 253
Susan M. (Merrill)
    83 183 184
Susan Marston **116** 105
Susan Osgood **82** 421
    83 183 188
Susan P. **79** 55
Susan R. **77** 257
Susan Taber **70** 319
Susan Williams **78** 322
Susanna **52** 434 **54** 81 255
    59 84 **60** 165 167 283
    396 **61** 31 154 155 245
    246 249 251 252 254 357
    62 25 30 150 157 **67** 126
    68 81 166 246 **69** 177
    352 361 **70** 271 272 333-
    335 **72** 306 **73** 225 231
    261 **75** 305 **81** 31 428 **82**
    103 291 298 **86** 380 **99**
    282 **105** 32 **113** 52 132
    136-140 143 220 **121** 274
    125 41 **126** 284 290 **127**
    113 196 277 **133** 214
    144 166-168 **148** 28
Susanna (Beale) **121** 270
Susanna (Collier) **113** 134
    142 358
Susanna (Goddard) **94** 84
Susanna (Hamilton)
    98 233
Susanna (Rowland)
    113 139
Susanna (Stone) **94** 388
Susanna (Walker)
    123 170
Susanna Budd **53** 460
Susanna G. (Springer)
    109 112
Susanne F. **81** 474
Suzanna **113** 219 220
Suzanna (Smith) **113** 219
Sylvanus **86** 404 **127** 113
    141 46
Sylvia (Bonney) **122** 281
Sylvilla **75** 304
T. **61** 34 **91** 326 **128** 97
T. R. (Mrs.) **102** 80
Tabitha **53** 444 **97** 335
    113 133 **122** 280 **126**
    272
Tabitha (Knapp) **113** 133
Tabitha (Leavitt) **122** 281
    126 272 273
Tabitha (Tirrell) **113** 138
Tacy **81** 490 **82** 55 56 62
Talitha **54** 83
Tamar **147** 56
Tamsin **52** 430
Tarzar **53** 163
Temperance **90** 383
    146 369
Thacher **96** 340
Thaddeus **78** 421
Thaddeus C. **62** 31
Thankful **80** 427 **104** 293
    119 35
Thankful (Cowles)
    108 309

JONES *cont'd*
Thankful Bangs (Rich)
84 49
Theodore **73** 276
Theodore F. **98** 206 **99** 307
Theodore Francis **75** xxvi
65 **79** 147
Theodosia **119** 192 193
Theophilus **60** 165 166
78 433
Theophilus Eaton
60 165 167
Theron **122** 111
Theziah **120** 52
Thirza (Adams) **86** 233
Thomas **51** 71 283 284 **52**
251 408 **53** 96 209 238
239 **55** 109 **56** 155 380
57 77 **58** 175 318 **59** 85
386 387 **60** 60 75 200
283 306 396 397 **61** 31
34 57 88 206 245 358 401
62 26 28 33 293 325 **63**
31 141 **64** 106 259 **65** 23
35 44 119 120 132 **66** 36
80 81 **67** 300 **68** 109 204
220 **69** 283 **70** 272 **73** 48
151 194 278 **76** 50 81
110 **79** 331 419 **80** 352
82 44 55 56 58 59 61 412
83 25 28 364 **85** 125 332
86 169 **87** 97 207 **88** 359
91 326 **92** 361 **93** 382-
384 387 **95** 288 **97** 395
100 240 287 **101** 85 163
105 115 172 193 **106**
199 **108** 281 309 **110**
207 316 **113** 42-47 49 51
52 131 138 229 **117** 18
290 **121** 12 109 194 205
123 261 **124** 9 78 **125**
289 **126** 255 **127** 113
196 303 **128** 19 **129** 47
130 52 **131** 127 **133** 137
137 315 **139** 140 141
142 116-118 122 269 352
359 **143** 48 121 123 125-
130 138 343 345 365 **144**
255 **145** 167 175 363
147 77 127
Thomas ap Thomas
79 331
Thomas C. **103** 235
Thomas Catesby **94** 138
Thomas Floyd **61** xxxiv
Thomas J. **61** 357 **62** 31
Thomas Jefferson (Mrs.)
83 125 232
Thomas K. **92** 119 122 123
93 263 **140** 39 59 159
Thomas Kilby **92** 12 117
120 121 **94** 296
Thomas Luke **109** 130
Thomas Morton **92** 119
140 159
Thomas R. **109** 269
Thomas Richards (Mrs.)
102 123
Thomas S. **86** 169
Thomas W. **76** 50
Thomas William **95** 73

JONES *cont'd*
146 151 288
Thomas William (Mrs.)
96 160
Tillman (Mrs.) **116** 313
Timothy **53** 59 280 **58** 42
60 166 167 **61** 154 155
245 249 250 383 **62** 27
28 69 72 73 157-159 **63**
75 **67** 126 **106** 65 **113** 48
131 132 137 145 **118** 313
119 193 **120** 239 **124**
275 **125** 96 **126** 32 **136**
144 336 **137** 37 **143** 128
144 265
Timothy B. **62** 27
Timothy Ellis **57** 293
Timothy L. **83** 193
Tobias **70** 274 332 **74** 257
100 32
Tristam **60** 391
Tryphena **60** 166 **70** 269
274 333 334
Tryphena S. **70** 269
Van Ranselear O. **86** 169
Velora E. **87** 92
Vienna **68** 161
Vincent L. **119** 78
Virginia **77** 266
Virginia Amelia (Fracker)
124 262
Virginia Brent (Fox)
83 485
Virginia Costello **70** 337
W. **82** 60 **89** 91
W. A. **55** 356
W. Northey **80** 226
W. P. **83** 306
Wait **70** 322
Waitstill **113** 138
Wallace **86** 351
Wallace Savage **68** 18
Walter **59** 142 **61** 253 **63**
85 **78** 221 **82** 56 58
Walter Alonzo **94** 388
Walter Edgarton **109** 221
Walter Edwin **70** 331
Walter Leland **94** 389
Warner **62** 30 **70** 299
Warren G. **86** 52
Warren N. **82** 375
Warwick **125** 288
Washington **73** 167
Watkins **93** 300
Watson **62** 293
Wayne Van Leer **77**
xxviii 78
Wealthy **57** 77 **133** 72
Wesley **62** 25
Whitney **113** 144
Wilbur T. **87** 92
Wilda Jane **69** 261
Willard **59** 275 **61** 253 356
69 166
William **51** 283 284 **52** 96
57 388 **58** 96 197 **59** 386
60 21 22 164-168 179
185 285 286 291 61 156
249 250 253 254 260 291
62 30-32 245 367 **63** 142
177 236 243 **64** 20 155

JONES *cont'd*
216 319 **65** 30 126 129-
131 **66** 34 272 **67** 49 229
68 199 236 245 **69** 181
70 189 303 **71** 202 **73**
152 167 217 269 273 **74**
22 184 186-188 **75** 221
302 303 **76** 272 318 **78**
44 307 331 433 434 **79**
57 202 247 344 352 **80**
30 138 140 141 232 337
370 449 **81** 124 126 129
428 444 488-492 **82** 44
55-63 65 420 421 **83** 24
25 34 172 193 464 **84**
240 363 **87** 74 80 **88** 212
215 311 **89** 34 90 91 **90**
297 **91** 34 326 **92** 18 121
124 **93** 254 384 **94** 66
297 **97** 395 **98** 47 **99** 285
100 187 235 287 297 300
102 31 **103** 192 193 195
196 254 257 265 **105** 114
115 **106** 162 172 **108**
281 **110** 110 209 **111**
292 305 **112** 245 **113** 46
51 52 146 218-220 **114**
186 298 **116** 257 **117**
253 319 **118** 102 **119** 20
120 260 **121** 115 **122** 87
123 175 **125** 105 215
287 **126** 28 205 **127** 303
129 47 **133** 267 **139** 129
141 350 **143** 31 **144** 166-
168 **145** 63 353 **147** 17
148 179
William (Mrs.) **83** 193
William A. **68** 246 **70** 330
331 336
William Alfred **70** 275
William Augustus
74 xxix
William Blair **107** 133
William Cranston **79** 349
William Edward **84** 114
William Ellis **53** 369 **54**
xxxviii **55** 359 **60** 111 **63**
211 **72** 80
William G. **62** 32
William H. **62** 32 **86** 380
133 72
William Haslet **141** 114
127 313 329 **142** 255 268
393 **144** 245-253 255 256
259-263 **147** 129 130 134
139 141
William Hasque **111** 64
William Henry **61** 274
89 90
William Linwood **70** 328
William Mosew **117** 236
William O. **73** 279
William P. **83** 183 185
111 303 306
William P. (Mrs.) **83** 193
William Palmer **115** 112
William Parker **61** 109
William Parry **82** 421
William Preble **83** 385
84 114 465 **134** 305
William Rosewell **60** 168

JONES *cont'd*
William S. **86** 169 **133** 32
William Thomas **93** 254
William Thompson
113 296
William Trowbridge
60 167
William Wurts **86** 380
Willie **101** 80
Wilton **91** 326
Windsor **60** 392
Winslow H. **70** 320
Wiser **68** 310
Wiswall **113** 145
Woodford Ransom (Mrs.)
102 143
Worthy **62** 30
Zach. **105** 113
Zachariah **121** 177 **143** 124
Zachariah Hard **60** 166
Zachary **142** 273
Zadock **61** 254
Zebadiah **61** 244 245 **62** 26
Zebina **81** 391
Zelma May **102** 125
Zenas **66** 22
Zerviah **61** 246
Zilpha **54** 85
Zophar **61** 359
JONGH
Wyntje Ariens de **98**
201 **107** 190
JONGHBLOETS
Jannetgen Jans
143 210
Jons *see* Jones
Jonson *see* Johnson
JONUS
Anna (Perry) **113** 143
JOPE John **61** 279
JOPLIN
Abigail **123** 50
Isham Bert (Mrs.) **103** 119
Joseph **78** 319
Matilda **78** 319
JOPP Hugh **63** 235
Kenneth B. **72** 245 **73** xvii
JORALEMON
Lydia Ann **95** 115
Teunis **54** lvii
JORDAN Jordain Jorden
Jordin Jordon
Jourdain
—— **104** 57
— Capt. **148** 152
— Lieut. **85** 19
— Miss **85** 449
— Mr. **71** 137 **96** 304
— Mrs. **117** 168
____ (Allen) **83** 509
A. P. **91** 326
Abial **89** 118
Abigail **63** 174 **71** 211
212 214 215 223 **89** 274
105 275 **108** 116 **120** 53
125 100
Abigail Ross **82** 362
84 445
Abner **142** 303
Abraham **128** 277 284
142 32

JORDAN *cont'd*
Ada E. **99** 133
Ada L. **89** 348
Addie **98** 189
Adelaide Amelia **64** 372
Adeline **148** 174
Albert **148** 173
Albert Hastings (Mrs.)
86 336
Alice (Broughton)
132 326
Alletta (Ward) **88** 288
Almira **107** 304
Almira Priscilla **79** 271
275
Amanda Ellen **89** 118
Amanda Jeanie **102** 125
Amasa **64** 372 **145** 311
Andrew **118** 53-55
Ann **59** 132 328 **62** 333
94 394
Ann (Bishop) **128** 24
Ann Maria **72** xliv
Anna **78** 312 **116** 252-254
Anna A. F. **98** 194
Anna M. **83** 207
Anne **77** li
Antoine **117** 271
Archibald **118** 41 44 55
Archibald Campbell
(Mrs.) **85** 195
Asa **103** 256
Augusta H. **107** 304
Baruch **56** 397 **129** 65
Beatrice Fairfax **97** 76
Benjamin **76** lvi **145** 162
Benjamin P. **148** 173
Benjamin Reudel **97** 365
Bertha Hessie **93** 218
Bethanai (Kingsley)
88 286
Betsey **66** 112 **105** 320
127 63
Bevan Page Yeates **77** li
Buckman **145** 46
C. F. **98** 194 195
Catherine **53** 211 **62** 334
63 196 **77** xlix **136** 167
146 369
Celestia **107** 304
Charity **108** 115
Charles **97** 200 **148** 173
Charles Downes **64** 372
Charles Ellison **148** 177
Charles L. **97** 200
Charlie **98** 194
Chester B. **55** xxxi
Christanesco **105** 275
Christian **125** 259
Christinies **105** 275
Christopher **125** 142
Clarissa M. **148** 173
Claudia Spofford **148** 174
Clement **83** 509
Clifford Moody (Hall)
88 288
Collins Hansberger
88 288
Cornelia (Gifford)
134 132

JORDAN *cont'd*
Cornelia Howard (Inger-
soll) **98** 82
Cornelius **109** 258
Curtis **90** 234
Cynthia (Woodman)
83 207
Cyrus **148** 173
D. E. **134** 132
Daniel **67** 30
Darius **98** 194
David **90** 48 **98** 194 **145** 46
David Jefferson **88** 288
David Starr **83** 513
136 320
Dayton DeForest **93** 218
Deborah **62** 333 **83** 25 30
148 173
Dennison Palmer **93** 218
Desdemona (Ringe)
90 48
Diana **113** 243 324
Domini **64** 8
Dominicus **76** lvi **133** 41
147 77 **148** 170
Dorcas **98** 260 **100** 139
145 47
Dorothy **52** 130 **62** 334
E. S. **98** 195
Eben **125** 142 **148** 175
Eben D. **52** 153
Ebenezer **71** 222 **105** 207
Ed **62** 289
Edmund **129** 63
Edna D. (Ingersoll)
125 142
Edward **105** 275 **107** 63
304 **132** 326
Edward M. **109** 269
Edwin **91** 326
Eleazer **124** 62
Elijah **56** 74 **145** 55 162
Elinda Monroe **109** 146
Eliphalet **142** 32
Eliza **90** 104 **98** 194 195
119 256
Eliza Jane (Taylor)
109 258
Elizabeth **51** 347 351 358
58 85 **62** 333 334 **71** 212
77 xlix l **82** 287 291 **95**
266 **100** 236 **111** 12 **138**
213 **148** 175
Elizabeth (Dorr) **126** 206
Elizabeth Ann **93** 95
Elizabeth E. **79** 142
Elizabeth Sophia **76** lvi
Ella Francis **92** 222
Elmira **107** 304
Emily **77** xlix l
Emily Eugenia **82** 429
440 441
Emma **148** 175
Emma A. **104** 221
Emma S. **98** 194
Emma Stewart (Bixby)
86 336
Emma Woodman **83** 207
Enoch Goodale **67** 30
Ephraim **148** 169
Erastus **98** 195

JORDAN *cont'd*
Ethel **76** lvii
Eunice **60** 335 **61** 173 **79**
  271 275 **128** 210 **145** 47
Eunice White **79** 271 275
Evaline E. **148** 171
Evelina **148** 173
Ezekiel **93** 95
Fountain **114** 193
Frances Claudia **82** 429
  440
Frances Isabella **148** 176
Francis **77** xlix l **97** 76 199
  120 318
Frank B. **98** 195
Frederick **77** xlix
Frederick W. **148** 172
Fritz Hermann **52** 379
  76 xxx lvi lvii
Gardner **148** 173
George **51** 358 **64** 372 **91**
  326 **100** 236
George D. **93** 95
George F. **98** 195
George Henry **148** 176
Geraldine **83** 233
Grace (Keney) **108** 116
Grace Edington **117** 76
Hannah **55** 312 **60** 49 **62**
  333 334 **64** 85 372 **67**
  206 **71** 128 216 224 **78**
  105 **82** 510 **88** 149 **98**
  194 **109** 312 **110** 97 **121**
  313 **142** 303 **148** 171
  175
Hannah (Deake) **93** 95
Hannah (Lazell) **88** 361
Hannah Abigail **93** 95
Hannah E. (Pike) **133** 41
Hannah I. **148** 174
Harriet **67** 30
Harriet (Brazier) **89** 199
Harriet (Ordway) **89** 118
Harriet Granger **67** 30
Harriet N. **89** 357
Harris Weeman **148** 174
Harry O. **98** 195
Hattie **89** 357
Hattie E. **98** 195
Hattie P. **98** 195
Helen **77** li
Helen L. **63** 14
Henry **105** 320
Henry C. **82** 429 440-442
Henry I. **97** 200
Henry Sylvester Rogers
  82 429 440 441
Hezekiah **145** 47
Hiram **136** 320
Holman **148** 173
Huldah Jane **148** 177
Huldah Lake (Hawley)
  136 320
Humphrey **142** 386
Ignatius **51** 358 **52** 93 **59**
  296 **109** 160 **111** 11 12
Imogene D. V. **148** 176
Isaac **105** 76
Isaiah **148** 173 174
Israel **78** 105 **83** 207 **93** 95
J. A. **71** xlviii **91** 326

JORDAN *cont'd*
J. H. **91** 326
J. T. **98** 195
J. W. **91** 326
James **62** 334 **63** 196 **77**
  105 **91** 327 **105** 207 320
  109 258 **126** 206 **148**
  174
James Horace **148** 177
James J. **98** 195
James M. **148** 173
Jane **61** 205 **65** 91 **70** 102
  71 215 **105** 320
Jane (Northrop) **97** 76
Jane (Wilson) **97** 199
  120 318
Jane M. **111** 137
Jedediah **110** 97
Jefferson **145** 46
Jemima Hathaway
  (Newell) **90** 56
Jeremiah **65** 353 **81** 428
Jianet **97** 69
Joan **55** 210 213 217
  94 393 394
Joanna **59** 328 **64** 372 **84**
  64 **115** 138 **142** 386
Joanna (Downes) **145** 311
John **51** 347 **52** 94 **58** 265
  59 132 328 **62** 333 334
  63 196 **65** 173 **68** 178
  70 263 **77** xlix l **81** 131
  84 64 76 **87** 218 219 **88**
  275 288 **90** 56 **97** 200
  104 58 134 **105** 113 275
  320 **109** 146 **116** 63 136
  119 21 256 **128** 24 **141**
  201 **143** 204 **145** 47
John C. W. **148** 176
John L. **148** 171 176
John Woolf **52** 96 **53** 374
  378 458 **54** xxxviii **55**
  xxxii 341 **59** xliv **63**
  xxxiii **71** 96 **77** xxviii
  xlix-li **78** 90 **99** 51
Johnson **129** 63
Johnson Henry **126** 123
Jonas **99** 131
Joseph **63** 170 **71** 215 **88**
  286 **108** 116 **128** 284
Joseph D. **93** 95
Joseph T. **98** 195
Joseph True **88** 239
Joshua **98** 194 195 **148**
  171 174
Joshua W. **93** 95
Josiah **88** 149 **105** 320
Julia **112** 155
Julia Ann (Cady) **88** 288
Julyann **105** 275
Kate **109** 258
Katharine **51** 358 **63** 196
Keziah (Hill) **133** 41
Laura Evelyn (Rowe) **83**
  433 **84** 18
Laura Porter **64** 372
  145 311
Lauretta **107** 304
Leonard G. **64** 129
Leroy W. **97** 200
Livonia **148** 168

JORDAN *cont'd*
Louisa (Shepherd) **92** 222
Lucinda **107** 63
Lucy **105** 320
Lucy (Briesler) **88** 275
Luther P. **98** 195
Lydia **58** 318 **88** 149 249
  89 356 **97** 199 **98** 195
  105 275 **142** 32 303
Lydia Ann **148** 168
Lydia S. **98** 195
Margaret **131** 129 **143** 36
  148 174
Mariah Titcomb **148** 174
Marilla **148** 168
Martha Ann **148** 175
Martha W. **119** 160
Mary **51** 358 **59** 132 328
  60 43 252 **62** 333 334 **63**
  168 170 196 **64** 371 **67**
  376 **69** 319 **71** 131 214
  216 224 **77** 262 **81** 428
  83 112 **86** 130 **89** 356
  93 95 **96** 304 **97** 200 365
  104 308 **105** 275 320
  107 304 **109** 258 **113**
  131 **126** 145 **134** 132
  142 206 **145** 55 162
Mary (Blake) **107** 63
Mary (Briggs) **126** 123
Mary (Lord) **90** 234
Mary (McFadden) **109** 160
Mary A. **90** 43 **98** 195
Mary Adeline **148** 174
Mary Amelia (Harding)
  97 76
Mary Ann **79** 36 **81** 312 **90**
  335 **148** 171 173
Mary E. **98** 195
Mary Ellen **148** 168
Mary Fernald **133** 41
Mary Fourguereau
  109 309
Mary Gilmer **124** 148
Mary Jane **107** 304
  109 254
Mary Louise (Scott)
  88 288
Mary Martha (Clark)
  100 38
Mehitable **105** 275
Mehitable (Mayo) **104** 58
Melatiah **59** lxxxiv **71** 214
Mercy **54** 399 **67** 30 31 **71**
  214 **118** 281 282 **148**
  169
Mercy (Bourne) **118** 283
Miles **51** 181 **59** 108
Minnie F. **98** 195
Miriam **64** 371 **97** 365
Moses Swett **89** 357
N. F. **98** 195
N. G. **98** 194
Nancy **100** 37 **105** 320
Nancy C. **107** 304
Nannie **123** 224
Nathaniel **60** 335 337 **61**
  173 **76** lvi **81** 428 **89**
  274 **97** 365 **98** 195 **105**
  112 **109** 312 **114** 290
Nellie (Fernald) **98** 195

JORDAN *cont'd*
Nicholas **55** 213
Nora **91** 103
O. W. **98** 194 195
Octavia W. **67** 351
Olive **71** 128 131 132 211
   216 217 222 225
Olive Ann **148** 168
Oliver **72** xliv
Orin Alando **148** 177
Patience **58** 265 **60** 176
Paul **82** 438
Peace **97** 365
Peleg **86** 89
Peter **118** 50 54 55 **125** 116
Phebe **87** 121 **88** 149
   145 46
Phebe (Gray) **147** 77
Polly **86** 122 **88** 149
Priscilla (Applewhite)
   105 320
Prolixana **91** 327
Putnam **78** 419 **105** 275
   125 107
R. **91** 327
Rachel **67** 83
Ralph Tristram **71** 215
   133 41
Rebecca **105** 320
Relief **86** 292
Richard **97** 200
Rishworth **63** 167 172 **71**
   128 211 212 214-216 226
   76 lvi **133** 41
Rispah (Silvester) **86** 89
Robert **51** 347 **66** 332 **67**
   83 **76** lvi **87** 143 **96** 303
   304 **97** 200 **102** 170 **132**
   326 **133** 41
Robert M. **97** 365
Rosanna **86** 123
Ruth **125** 142
Ruth Megquier **88** 239
S. Lewis **99** 133
Sally **59** lxxxiv **83** 470 **88**
   239 **128** 277 **148** 169
Sally (Brewer) **125** 107
Sally G. **83** 150 153
Sally Haynes **142** 386
Sally Merrell **88** 239
Samuel **58** 318 **63** 168 **65**
   20 **71** 128 130 131 214
   215 218 **79** 38 **81** 428 **88**
   149 249 **89** 356 **96** 304
   97 105 **100** 287 **108** 116
   109 312 **113** 318 **118**
   283 **133** 41
Samuel Warren **83** 433
   84 18
Sarah **51** 347 **52** 83 **63** 149
   151 **65** 353 **69** 34 **71** 128
   132 212 223 **81** 428 **88**
   149 **93** 95 **96** 161 **97** 200
   98 195 **105** 275 **108** 279
   115 211 **142** 303 **147** 77
Sarah (Bartlett)
   (Wentworth) **135** 101
Sarah (Staples) **97** 200
Sarah (Winter) **96** 304
Sarah Davis **82** 438
Sarah M. **148** 173

JORDAN *cont'd*
Scott **54** 356 **74** xxviii **84**
   180 **88** 87 173 288
Simeon **105** 275
Simon **92** 178 183
Solomon **92** 222 **97** 200
Sophronia **148** 176
Stephen **58** 318 **59** 242
   70 102 **94** 394
Steward **91** 327
Submit **141** 53
Sumner C. **88** 339
Susan **78** 104 105 **90** 44
   93 95 **105** 320 **125** 216
Susan (Oakes) **126** 67
Susan A. **116** 260
Susanna **54** 222 **61** 139
   65 241 **100** 236
Susanna (Bodge) **101** 101
Susanna (Merrill) **94** 394
Susanna Richardson
   73 283
Sylvia **58** 318
Sylvia (Stainton) **97** 76
Temperance **145** 46
Thankful **148** 173
Thomas **52** 130 **53** 208 **62**
   333 334 **63** 196 **65** 129
   78 416 **101** 101 **105** 288
   320 **135** 225 **142** 206
   148 173
Tristram **54** 99 **55** 312 **67**
   30 **71** 131 218 **82** 510 **83**
   509 **88** 361 **115** 224
Viola May **148** 177
Virginia N. (Burrows)
   88 339
Walter **148** 171
Walter M. **89** 357
Warren **148** 175
Washington **148** 173
Washington Irving
   79 271 275
Wentworth **142** 303
   148 168
Wilfred **77** li
Wilkisson **128** 49
William **59** 296 **64** 371
   65 20 **88** 149 239 **89** 199
   304 **139** 311 **145** 47 **148**
   174
William Beaumont
   88 288
William Churchill
   82 429 440
William F. **107** 304
William George **74** 242
William H. **148** 173 175
William Leonard **148** 174
William M. **79** 271 275
William Melvin **88** 239
William Morgrage
   79 271 275
Winter **148** 173
Winthrop Stanwood
   76 lvi
JORGENSEN
Engeborg M. **72** 129
Fern **108** 135
Kjersten **121** 316
Jos *see* Joss

JOSCELINE Bp. of Sarum
   75 61
JOSE Celinda (Goodwin)
   97 229
Damaris **81** 428
Dennis **81** 428 **82** 44
Ebenezer **81** 428 **82** 44
Eunice **97** 221
Hannah **51** 46 118 **81** 428
   124 288 289 293
Hannah (Martyn) **124** 288
Johanna **82** 44
John **54** 98
Mark L. **124** 153
Martin **65** 353 **81** 428
   97 229 233
Martin (Mrs.) **81** 428
Mary **81** 428
Mercy **65** 353 **81** 428
Michael **82** 44
Nancy Ann (Grant)
   97 233
Nathaniel **81** 428
Richard **51** 46 118 **81** 428
   82 81 83 **124** 288 289
Roxanna (Soule) **124** 153
Sclinda (Goodwin)
   97 233
Susanna **81** 428
Thomas **55** 105 **97** 233
Thomas L. **84** 29
Joselyn *see* Joslyn
JOSEPH —— **130** 154
Aaron C. **88** 336
Allen (Mrs.) **103** 161
Allen Franz (Mrs.)
   103 119
Anthony **66** 35
Betsey Rachel (Hopkins)
   104 297
Desire **90** 54
Elizabeth **75** 228 229 233
Eunice **51** 165
Francis (Seymoor) **88** 336
Manuel **51** 165 **104** 297
Maria **82** 170
Millerd **97** 319
Robert **75** 229 233
Samuel **89** 210
Wilkinson **129** 188
William Carr **133** 154 320
JOSIAH — Mr. **66** 365
Sarah **66** 365
JOSIAS Sachem of Nauset
   115 88
JOSLYN Joselyn Joslen
   Joslin Josling Josselyn
   —— **56** 274 **61** 374 401
   62 xxviii 18 129 **71** 229
   234 236 247 248 250 **136**
   33 34 36 39 234
   — Capt. **62** 20
   — Mr. **62** 21 **86** 44 **95** 133
   — Widow **71** 33
Abiah **79** 245
Abigail **57** 182 **71** 32 255
   113 53 **123** 50 **133** 192
   137 144 145
Abigail (Stockbridge)
   134 71 72
Abigail Nims **75** lv

JOSLYN *cont'd*

Abraham **51** 297 **52** 37
55 303 **56** 410 **57** 182
58 244 **71** 233 234 252-
255 **119** 108 117 **121** 22
132 277 **133** 192 **136** 33
35-37 **142** 275
Adam **93** 348
Addie Lucy **77** 187
Adeline **88** 287
Agnes **71** 20 32 33 241
242 245 250
Alice **64** 35 **71** 32 33 237
240 243 246 247
Allen L. **51** 409
Almira **69** liii
Alonzo **77** 149
Amanda **89** 16
Amaziah **59** 61 62
Ann **71** 32 255
Ann Mary **109** 262
Anna **71** 29 32 33 **77** 27
134 72
Anne **57** 318 **71** 20-24 27
30 32 33 231 238 241-
243 245 246 248-252 **133**
192
Annie (Knapp) **109** 262
Ann / Anna (Stockbridge)
133 193 **134** 71 291
Anthony **71** 23 25 27 28
246
Austin M. C. **88** 342
Beatrice **55** 303 **71** 237
240 254 255
Beatrice (Hampson) **133**
192 **142** 275 **143** 43
Beatrix **79** 393
Benjamin **70** 4 **71** 249
85 328
Bethiah (Bourne) **145** 300
Betsey **94** 388
Bridget **71** 249
C. J. **111** 191
Caroline A. **77** 149
Catherine **107** 224
Cecelia **71** 20
Celinda **109** 269
Charles **74** 26 **133** 192
Charlotte Elizabeth
63 214
Charlotte M. A. **78** 416
Christiana **86** 126
Christopher **71** 23-25 27
28 246
Cicely **71** 241
Constantine **71** 249
Cynthia S. **86** 126
Dana Israel **61** 321 **62**
xxviii xxxvii
Daniel **87** 394 **101** 206
Daniel D. **111** 303 305
David **132** 220
Deborah **118** 63 **134** 73
Deborah (Thurston)
132 277
Deidamia **111** 191
Denise **71** 20 21 243
Dolly **124** 13
Doris A. **111** 305
Dorothy **55** 302 **71** 20-23

JOSLYN *cont'd*

27 28 30 31 33 227 230
231 243 245 248-251 253
256 **75** lvi **77** 27
Dorothy (Paul) **133** 192
Ebenezer **71** 249 **119** 108
186
Edmund **72** 74
Edna **70** 203
Edward **71** 22 23 26-28
244 245 249
Edward Henry **72** 74
Egidius **71** 236
Eldora **93** 347
Eleanor (Snowman)
85 328
Eleazer **145** 300
Electa **86** 106
Eliza **71** 253
Eliza (Huntley) **101** 206
Eliza (Thornton) **85** 328
Eliza K. **67** 272
Elizabeth **55** 302 303 **59**
61 62 **71** 20 21 23 25 27
29 31-33 228 239 241
242 244-253 255 256
Elizabeth (Wiseman)
108 287
Elizabeth J. (Ware) **88** 342
Elizabeth Maria (Lincoln)
145 300
Emma R. (Denman) **111**
303 305
Enoch **132** 277
Esek **72** 130 131
Esther **71** 255 256
Esther (Hearsey) **119** 108
Eunice **58** 244 **86** 126
Fanny (Nichols) **90** 43
Fanny (Thatcher) **108** 265
Frances **58** 170 172 **71** 249
Frances (Yellings) **131**
236 **133** 192
Frances Revere (Lincoln)
145 300
Francis **71** 23 25 28 33
246 251 **136** 38 40
Frank A. **70** 203
Gabriel **71** 20 241
Geoffrey **71** 20 21 32 227
236
George **71** 20 232 240-242
85 328
George Henry (Mrs.)
108 134
Gilbert **71** 235 236
Grace **71** 23 30-32 246 250
251
Hannah **55** 399 **64** 34 **71**
252 255 256 **115** 34 **122**
214 **136** 34
Hannah (Oldham) **133**
192 **136** 34
Harriet **109** 269
Hattie **70** 203
Helen **71** 32 251
Helenora **71** 32 247
Henrietta **59** 62
Henry **55** 303 **57** 182 318
58 173 263 387 **60** 339
62 167 **70** 4 **71** 20 22-28

JOSLYN *cont'd*

233 236 237 245-249 253
255 **95** 182 **101** 18 **127**
147 **128** 298 **132** 277
133 191 192 **134** 72 **136**
34
Herbert Allyn **93** 347
Hope **65** 148 **129** 55
Humphrey **71** 23 245
Isaac **88** 112 **100** 187 **126**
261 **136** 35 41
Isaiah **121** 247 **134** 72
Israel **85** 328
Jabez **133** 192 **134** 136
James **61** 145 **71** 32 235
236 **137** 362
James T. **57** 235
James Thomas **56** xxxiv
57 xxxi
Jane **71** 20 27 31 237 242-
245 251 252
Jeffrey **71** 23 26 27 227
238-241 245 247
Jemima **133** 192
Jerusha **62** 17
Joan **71** 23-25 32 33 236
237 239 240 242 243 247
Joanna **71** 256 **79** 398
John **52** 121 **69** 157 **71** 19-
33 227-229 231-233 236
237 239-242 244-253 **76**
76 **86** 125 126 **96** 235
236 249 **108** 287 **122** 54
55 **125** 35 **128** 293 **134**
72
John Jay **70** 203
John Lincoln **56** 172
John Reed **86** 126
Jonas **129** 384
Jonathan **61** 75
Joseph **53** 409 **58** 263 **69**
283 **71** 29 30 33 230-232
234 235 250-252 255 **75**
lvi **98** 323 **119** 108 **121**
280 **133** 193 **136** 34 **137**
144
Joshua **105** 285
Joyce **71** 244
Katharine **71** 23 25 27 232
237 239-241 246
Keyte **71** 244
Keziah **58** 173 **133** 192
Leonard **71** 21 244
Leonard H. **67** 272
Lois **56** 246
Lois (Ramsdell) **126** 261
Lou **60** 339
Louisa **56** 172
Louise Edgell **75** lvi
Lucinda **93** 347
Lucy **105** 240
Lydia **70** 4 **124** 154
Lydia Colcord (Wadley)
132 220
Lydia S. **72** 130
Margaret **62** 167 **71** 22 23
27 28 32 238 239 241 245
247 249 **86** 129 **122** 54
125 245
Margaret Mary
(Coughlin) **103** 49

JOSLYN *cont'd*
Margery **71** 239
Martha **71** 244 256 **72** 74
  108 287
Martha (Chase) **88** 112
Martha (Enos) **111** 191
Marvel **72** 74
Mary **55** 302 303 **58** 86 170
  63 43 **71** 21 23-26 28-33
  227 231 243-245 247-254
  256 **77** 24 **133** 192 **137**
  146 **141** 247
Mary (Brown) **85** 328
Mary (Drummond)
  100 301
Mary Bard **93** 54
Mary Chamberlin **75** lvi
Mary E. **70** 203
Mary Emma **93** 184
Mary Sophia **85** 324
Mary Vinal (Lincoln)
  145 300
Maud **71** 237 238 241
Mehitable Place **74** 26
Mercy **71** 249
Minerva L. **72** 130
Myron Henry **103** 49
N. W. **113** 53
Nancy (Chase) **88** 112
Naomi **61** 145 **94** 388
Nathan **93** 347 **145** 300
Nathaniel **55** 302 303 **56**
  246 **58** 86 170 172 **63**
  223 **71** 29 30 33 230 244
  251 253 255 256 **75** lvi
  131 236 **133** 192 **141**
  247
Nehemiah **88** 112
Nicholas **71** 20 21 242 243
Olive **81** 330
Olive (Standish) **134** 72
Oppis **108** 265
Oswalda **71** 236
Otis **55** 399 **93** 347
Parmelia **88** 112
Patience (Barker) **134** 72
Persis **77** 26
Peter **64** 34 35 **71** 30 251
  256 **75** lvi **77** 24 26 27
  137 89 90 113
Philip **55** 303 **71** 20 21 33
  227 228 241-243 255 **121**
  23 **134** 73
Philippa **71** 239 241 242
  248
Polly **60** 200
Polly (Lincoln) **145** 300
Polly (Loring) **132** 277
Priscilla (Bourn) **136** 41
Priscilla (Reed) (Carter)
  (Richardson) **137** 362
Priscilla (Standish)
  134 72
Ralph **71** 20-25 27-33 227-
  233 237-245 247 250-254
Rebecca **55** 302 303 **56** 410
  62 101 **71** 30-32 227 252-
  256 **105** 190 **106** 22 **133**
  192 **142** 275 **143** 43 344
Rebecca (Tirrell) **119** 108

JOSLYN *cont'd*
Rebecca Lamyra (Wade)
  87 394
Richard **71** 21 22 25 29-31
  33 227 230 231 234 240
  243 244 247 250 251
Robert **71** 236 **85** 328
Roger D. **128** 311 **142** 3
  15 177 195 281 293 296
  355 371 385 396 **143** 38
  50 52 69 152 170 361 365
  367 369 **144** 60 170 273
  145 80 233 272 346 376
  380 **147** 288 **148** 142
  294
Roullin **60** 200
Roxana **72** 74
Ruth **134** 72
Ruth (Bates) **133** 193
Sage **86** 125
Sage (Sylvester) **86** 126
  134 72
Sally **77** 229 **124** 18
Samuel **71** 33 250
Samuel Russel **59** 61
Sarah **56** 246 **61** 75 **71** 30
  32 251 255 256 **119** 107
  108 **122** 55 **128** 293 **137**
  50
Sarah (Bayley) **85** 328
Sarah (Brown) **85** 328
Sarah (Ford) **119** 108
Sarah (Turner) **133** 192
Sarah Ann (Emerson)
  51 409
Sarai **53** 409
Seth **134** 72
Simeon Smith **93** 184
Simon **71** 22 25 27-30 32
  33 228 230 232 234 235
  245 247 248 250 251
Sprague Urana **72** 131
Stephen Perry **64** xxxiii
  75 xxxv lv lvi
Stockbridge **134** 72
Susan **71** 241
Susan A. **93** 347
Susanna **141** 247-250
Susanna (Robinson)
  85 328
Susanna J. **120** 220
Sylvester (Barker)
  133 193
Thankful **124** 80 **128** 312
Thankful (Matthews)
  86 44
Theba **71** 33 251
Theodora **71** 248 249
Theresa **74** xxiv
Theresa Brown **85** 328 345
  86 201
Thomas **55** lxii 302 303
  57 401 **58** 387 **60** 357
  71 20-26 29 30 32 227-
  233 236-250 252-255 **75**
  lvi **86** 264 **100** 301 **111**
  321 **129** 58 384 **132** 277
  133 193 **134** 72 291 **136**
  39 **141** 247
Thomas Hill **136** 38 40
Thomazine **71** 250

JOSLYN *cont'd*
Torrell **71** 248
Wilder **90** 43
William **71** 229 232 233
  236 239 **75** lv lvi **85**
  328 **109** 269 **111** 191
William Edwin **85** 328
William Edwin (Mrs.)
  73 318 **74** xxiv **85** 328
  345 **86** 201
William H. **109** 262
William Harry **85** 328
Winifred **71** 23 25 27 244-
  246
JOSON John **129** 380
JOSS Jos Josse
  Ada J. **79** 139
  Paulina K. (Lord) **97** 21
    238
  William **54** 219 **97** 21 238
    145 356
Josselyn *see* Joslyn
JOSSERA
  Eleanor **51** 465
  John **51** 465
JOST A. C. **112** 210
  Caroline M. (Rudolf)
    110 146
  Conrad **119** 71
  Henry Smith **110** 146
  Isabelle Josephine
    110 146
JOSTON Freben **129** 57
JOTT Prudence **90** 47
JOUBERT
  Augustin M. **106** 108
  Gretchen Marie **103** 117
  Jean-Baptiste **143** 12
  Juliann **106** 108
  Julie (Robichaux) **143** 12
  Madeleine (Renard)
    143 12
  Pierre **143** 12
Jourdain *see* Jordan
JOURN John **64** 321
JOURNAY Journey
  Grace **99** 50
  James **98** 48 50
  John **98** 48 50
  Margaret **73** 220
  Martha **98** 48 50
  Mercy (Fitz Randolph)
    98 47 48 50 **99** 50
JOUVET Elizabeth
    (Coggeshall) **125** 177
  Mary C. **125** 177
  Peter **125** 177
  Susan **93** 91
JOWERS Joshua **98** 241
Jowett *see* Jewett
JOWLER Henry **51** 415
  Julut **51** 415
JOY Joye
  —— **54** civ **57** 191 **82** 320
    92 243 248 **94** 355 **104** 3
    121 122 277
  — Mrs. **79** 298
  Abel **87** 257
  Abigail **58** 262 **74** 252 **82**
    207 **129** 258 **140** 159
  Abigail F. **88** 338

JOY *cont'd*
Ada (Furbush) **117** 140
Adaline **118** 318
Alexander **83** 155
Almira (Fitgerald) **120** 308
Almira (Joy) **123** 234
Almira A. **116** 185
Amos **58** 262
Ann (Pitts) **90** 67
Anna **121** 201
Anne **74** 70
Asa **119** 64
Augustus T. **90** 53
Beatrice **72** xlv
Benjamin **55** 406 **87** 331 **120** 6 9 **121** 199 **132** 193 **136** 360 **137** 74 **140** 34 36 **147** 264 266 275 362
Benjamin Cartwright **100** 187
Betsey **87** 346 **88** 334
Betsey (Davis) (Welch) **94** 355 **95** 382
Catherine **116** 224
Charles **87** 331 **132** 327
Charles (Mrs.) **84** 445
Charles Lowell **92** 243
Charlotte (Jennings) **90** 53
Christopher Gore **92** 243 **132** 327
David **87** 250 **98** 326 **100** 52 187 **115** 197 **118** 135 **119** 20 **121** 281
Deborah **104** 191 **121** 269
Deborah (Wathen) **148** 68-70 73 75
Desire (Beal) **134** 138
Donald Winslow **84** 340 **85** 195
Dorcas (Bragdon) **119** 64
Ebenezer **52** 232
Elida **63** 271
Elisha **88** 277
Eliza **82** 320
Eliza (Moulton) **118** 242
Elizabeth **55** 316 **71** 221 **72** 285 **83** 12 60 **84** 324 **87** 250
Elizabeth (Andruce) **121** 275
Elizabeth (Chase) **87** 257
Elizabeth (Chase) (Davis) **87** 331
Ella G. (Rich) **84** 125
Ella Hopkins **90** 68
Ella Tirzah **79** 142
Ellen Gertrude (Hopkins) **90** 68
Eloisa **55** 375 **83** 16
Eloisa (Nason) **83** 16
Enoch **95** 382
Ephraim **51** 68 **55** 115 **63** 169 **82** 75 76 95 207 209 216 314 318 321 330 502 **97** 221 **110** 287 **115** 304
Esther **60** 68
Ethel **75** 213
Eveline (Grant) **97** 221
Fanny **116** 142

JOY *cont'd*
Frances **82** 18
Frances E. **120** 306 **123** 233
Francis **100** 187
Franklin Lawrence **55** xxxii **59** xlvii **72** xxx xlv
Frederick D. **76** 41
Frederick R. **118** 190 **119** 314
Gilbert **100** 187
Gregory **52** 253
Hannah **55** 406 **71** 219 **82** 502 **87** 345 **95** 339 **120** 42
Hannah (Barrell) **140** 36
Hannah (Cram) **90** 67
Hannah S. **90** 105
Harriet **100** 187 **123** 152
Helen **113** 298
Helen Bourne **91** 84
Helen Hall (Newberry) **91** 84 **113** 298
Henry Bourne **85** 188 **91** 60 83 84 145 **113** 298
Henry Bourne (Mrs.) **100** 108 **113** 59 298
Henry L. **84** 125
Hugh **80** 358
Irene **95** 382
Ivory **117** 140
Jacob **87** 345 346 **90** 67 **116** 303
James **55** 315 **63** 344 **82** 216 **83** 11 **90** 67 **93** 336 **94** 97 **95** 382 **107** 237 **116** 220
James F. **109** 38 **113** 298
James Frederick **90** 67 **91** 83
James Richard **55** 115
Jane Straw **87** 346
Jeannie B. **72** xlv
Jeremiah **82** 314
Joan **74** 98
Joan (Gallop) **90** 67
Joanna **92** 243
John **85** 132 **96** 272 **98** 118 **121** 197 284 **140** 159
John D. W. **72** xlv
John H. **72** xlv
John Noble **94** 355 **95** 382 **119** 314
Jonathan **60** 391
Joseph **55** 115 **60** 68 **73** 220 **98** 326 **121** 120 122 126 192 193 206 275 278 **140** 159
Joseph B. **120** 308 **123** 234
Joseph E. **123** 234
Joseph F. **78** 401
Joseph Hicks **87** 346
Judith **95** 382 **100** 187
Katharine **63** 169
Katharine (Stevens) **115** 304
Levi **78** 415 **92** 243 248 **93** 321 **94** 378 **120** 6 **132** 327
Lewis **57** 191
Louis **95** 382

JOY *cont'd*
Louisa **63** 271
Lovey **87** 345
Lydia **74** 253 **82** 330 **85** 8 **100** 187 **116** 305 **121** 2/4 **134** 240
Lydia (Carter) **125** 291
Lydia Cartwright **100** 187
Marah (Eastman) **90** 67
Margaret **82** 318 **121** 126 192
Marie Louise **72** xx
Martha **74** 251
Martha (Reed) **109** 38
Martha A. **62** 157
Martha Ann **119** 314
Mary **71** 223 **82** 318 **110** 287 **114** 47 **121** 193
Mary (Bourne) **90** 67
Mary (Burley) **90** 67
Mary (Ford) **120** 42
Mary (Moore) **90** 68
Mary (Prince) **121** 120
Mary Ann **76** 41 **92** 248
Mary Ann (Blodgett) **103** 48
Mary Ann (Lougee) **118** 190
Mary Crosby (Libbie) **84** 445
Mary E. (Wilbur) (Donnell) **123** 234
Mary R. **114** 180
Mary R. (Clarkson) **114** 180
Mary Simon (Mullet) **88** 277
Matilda **123** 233
Matthew **100** 187
Mehitable **55** 315 **83** 11 **95** 382 **116** 224
Mehitable (Whitcher / Whittier) **83** 11 **107** 237
Melinda **72** 50
Mercy **120** 41
Mercy (Boston) **116** 303
Mercy (Ford) **120** 42
Michael **126** 225
Molly **118** 134
Molly (Russell) **118** 135
Moses M. **103** 48
N. Elizabeth **119** 314
Nabby (Green) **85** 132
Nancy **100** 187
Nancy (Waldron) **120** 6
Nathaniel **55** 375 **82** 85 316 318 323 **83** 16
Nehemiah **120** 42
Noah **119** 258 **120** 42
Obed **100** 187
Olive **117** 144
Patience **76** 196 **82** 318 323
Patience (Sargent) **116** 302
Persis **134** 279
Peter **77** 129
Phebe **100** 187
Phebe (Coffin) **87** 250
Polly **88** 277
Prince **58** 262 **121** 277

JOY *cont'd*
Reuben **65** 365 **116** 132
Rhoda **116** 226
Richard **95** 382
Richard Pickering **84** 234
 85 188 **90** 67 68 81 139
 91 83
Robert **63** 271
Ruth **121** 204 272
Ruth (Ford) **115** 197
Sally **95** 382 **99** 73 **116** 132
 120 6 **125** 221
Sally (Noble) **95** 382
Samuel **55** 115 **63** 271 **82**
 77 95 **90** 67 **100** 187 **116**
 142 **117** 193 **118** 242
 121 122 125 **125** 291
 145 358
Samuel West Shaw
 92 243
Sarah **55** 311 **56** 210 **63** 271
 74 98 251 **82** 75-77 82
 85 95 207 316 330 **115**
 197 **121** 207 **136** 78
Sarah (Cummings) **136**
 360 **137** 74
Sarah (Noble) **94** 355
Sarah (Pickering) **90** 67
Sarah Elizabeth **63** 314
Sarah Pickering **94** 97
Simon **121** 205
Stephen **71** 223 **93** 335
 95 382 **116** 302
Susanna **71** 219 **82** 75 330
 92 243 **125** 99 **134** 138
Temperance **92** 243
Thaddeus **100** 187
Thankful **51** 163
Thomas **55** 115 **74** 98 **82**
 76 **90** 67 **91** 83 **121** 21
 124 192 202 **134** 138
 140 102
Thomas Bourne **90** 68
Walter **79** 142 **148** 69 75
West **132** 327
William **74** 251 **82** 321
 92 243 **100** 187
William Moore **90** 68
JOYCE Joice Joies Joys
 Joysh
 —— **57** 25 **60** xvii 109
Abigail **133** 293
Abigail (Hopkins)
 126 286
Alford **76** 155
Alice M. (Hayes) **121** 181
Allston P. **54** xxxviii
Ann **66** 250
Anne **66** 251 **74** 70
Arthur Wellesley (Mrs.)
 96 80
Bathsheba **136** 21
Beatrice **63** 32
Charles W. **121** 181
Dorcas **52** 81 **105** 85 **125** 7
Dorothy **52** 81 **53** 301
 100 150
Elizabeth **82** 427 **85** 358 **87**
 382 **105** 85 **136** 21 **148**
 109 111 114 115 117

JOYCE *cont'd*
Elizabeth (Chipman)
 112 196
Gerald Stanley **95** 146
Hannah **66** 86
Hannah (Bassage)
 108 233
Helen Worrell (Lewis)
 96 80
Hosea **82** 427 **112** 196
Isabel F. **75** 37
Isabella Eleanor **52** 384
James **105** 207
Jennie Almira May
 82 169
Jeremiah **105** 85
John **52** 81 **53** 301 **66** 35
 87 49 **95** 367 **125** 7
John Warren **97** 158
 100 260
Jonathan **76** 155
Leander R. **81** 311
Lizzie **81** 311
Lorenzo **82** 170
Loring **82** 169
Lucretia **85** 358
Lucy **145** 242
Lydia **86** 85 **89** 233
 108 227
Martha **108** 233
Martha (Ryal) **108** 233
Mary **52** 81 358 **78** 42 **82**
 427 **105** 85 **112** 196
Mary (Bancroft) **95** 367
Mary Ann **65** 291 **81** 35
Mary Jane **82** 169
Mary Parker **82** 169
Matthias **61** 133 134
Minnie Elizabeth **82** 170
Nathan **108** 233
Nellie May **81** 311
Nicholas **55** 98
Peter **116** 202
Philip R. **91** 326
Polly Ann (Lacy) **145** 242
Rachel **126** 286
Robert **64** 336
Robert E. (Mrs.) **130** 157
Samuel C. **95** 367
Sarah **87** 130 **105** 85
 121 284
Sarah (Perry) **116** 202
Sarah M. **137** 47
Theophilus Stover **82** 169
Thomas **63** 32 **105** 85
Walter **85** 358 **136** 21
Walter W. **111** 76
William **55** 141 **66** 246 247
 90 63
William Beard **145** 242
Joye *see* Joy
Joyes *see* Joyce
Joyliff *see* Jolliffe
Joyliffe *see* Jolliffe
JOYLY Joseph **102** 37
JOYNER Joiner Joynor

JOYNER *cont'd*
Humphrey **80** 295 296
Jerusha **74** 316
Joan **70** 116
John **56** 86
Joseph **73** 226
Lucy **71** 279
Margaret **93** 195
Nason **104** 117
Robert **71** 279 **76** 53
Susanna **124** 12
William **74** 316
JOYNES E. S. **61** 315
Joys *see* Joyce
Joysh *see* Joyce
JOZEAR Sarah (Bodge)
 101 101
JUAREZ
Benito P. **76** xliv
Juatt *see* Jewett
JUBE Fannie **96** 73
JUCCY Mary **72** 154
JUCENT John **56** 312
JUCHES Henderson **90** 87
JUCK John **85** 166
JUDAH —— **109** 40
Hilel **127** 11
Jacob **70** 262
JUDD Jud
 —— **53** 358 405 **57** 268
 76 132 **111** 294 **118** 17
 304 **119** 132 217 **120**
 303
Abigail **115** 17 19 **144** 107
Albert G. **140** 132
Alice **104** 28
Allyn Southmayd **73** 16
Almira **115** 17
Althea **73** 16 **93** 205
Amelia **115** 116
Amon **140** 131 132
Amos **72** 220
Amy **71** 281
Amyrillis **89** 240
Andrew **104** 28 35 **105** 5
 18
Anna **73** 16
Anne **53** 58
Annys **104** 28
Anthony **72** 220 221
 73 15 18
Bathsheba **106** 215 **142** 346
Belinda (Howland)
 140 132
Benajah **76** 133
Benjamin **72** 220 **85** 62
 93 308 **106** 215 **143** 323
Benjamin Boyce (Mrs.)
 99 147
Betsey **72** 221 **126** 118
Betsey (Monroe) **140** 131
 132
Betsey B. **53** 58
Beulah Thayer **74** 297
Blanche Lydia **103** 121
Carl Arden **74** 297
Catherine **71** 121
Charles J. **109** 105
Charles Moseley **109** 105
Chauncy **67** 52 **115** 116
Chauncy P. **61** xxxiv

JUDD *cont'd*
Chloe **104** 298
Curtis A. **70** 154
Daniel **71** 116
Ebenezer **76** 131-133
Edwin **69** 208
Edwin Young **97** 117
Elizabeth **65** 148 **72** 220-
  222 **73** 16 **97** 117 **111**
  168 **136** 313 319 331
Elizabeth (Bryant) **97** 117
Ellen **79** 132
Ellen S. **69** 208
Enoch **72** 281
Esther **53** 405
Esther (Allen) **105** 79
Fanny **73** 16
Flora Agnes **109** 105
Florence E. **74** xxiv
Frances Jane **109** 105
Frank **79** 132
Frederick **73** 16
Gaylord **73** 16
Gerrit P. **77** 325
Hannah **52** 41 **55** 32 **72**
  221 281 **124** 80
Hannah (Howland)
  140 131
Harold Lee (Mrs.) **74** xxiv
  156
Helen P. **85** 166
Henry Clay **97** 117
Hope **53** 55 **55** 255
Ira **61** 307 **70** 154
Ira A. **70** 154
Isaac **72** 221 **115** 19
Isabel **74** 297
Isenath **68** 205
James **85** 166 **105** 79
Jane A. (Moseley) **109** 105
Jane Ann **109** 106
Jane M. **73** 16 **104** 96
Jean **97** 117
Jemima **142** 344
Jesse **136** 324
Joanna **73** 16 **93** 308
Job **72** 221
John **64** 59 **72** 220-222 **73**
  15 18 **104** 35 **109** 71 **142**
  344
John Bryant **97** 117
Jonathan **53** 58
Juliette **54** 402
Keziah **72** 220
Lucy **72** 220 **73** 16
Lydia **71** 11 **72** 220 **87** 254
  105 147
Mabel **67** 52 **72** 220
Marilla M. **70** 154
Martha **94** 384 **104** 27 28
  105 18
Mary **56** 308 **65** 138 **72** 220
  104 27 28 35 **105** 240
  106 80 **114** 185 **136** 311
  P**104** 30
Mary (Brown) **114** 185
Mary (Buell) **136** 324
Mary (Maltby) (Brown)
  111 294
Mary (Mathew) (Langton)
  104 27

JUDD *cont'd*
Mary (Peck) **97** 117
Mary C. **56** 58
Matthew **71** 11
Mehitable **72** 220
Melissa **72** 98 **73** 7
Mercy **72** 220
Mercy (Bronson) **142** 344
Milicent **73** 16
Molly **72** 220
Nancy **72** 46 89 183
  136 324
Naomi **72** 220 **80** 14
Nina **59** xliv
Norman **115** 116
Norton E. **90** 32
Olive **71** 282
Orrin **74** 297
Phebe Theresa **136** 331
Phineas **72** 220 221
Polly **72** 221 **73** 15 16
  124 319
Princess (Hannum)
  90 162
Rachel (Wendall) **125** 109
Rebecca **72** 221 **124** 11
Rebecca (Curtis) **124** 11
Reuben **71** 281 **75** 185
Rhoda **72** 219 221 **109** 65
Roland D. **120** 76
Root **72** 221
Ruth **72** 220 221
Ruth (Lee) **136** 324
S. F. **104** 96
Sadie Eva **103** 121
Sally **73** 16
Sally (Howland) **140** 131
Sally H. **69** 208
Samuel **72** 220 **73** 104
  125 109
Sarah **75** 178 185 **76** 131 **85**
  62 **121** 85 **126** 90 **142**
  336
Selah **72** 221
Seymour **72** 220
Silas **115** 17 19
Simeon **71** 274 281 282
Solomon **56** 308 **72** 98
  90 162
Statira **54** 85
Stephen **140** 131
Susanna **72** 220 221 **73**
  15 16 18
Susanna (North) **93** 308
  106 215
Susie **71** 274
Sylvester **59** 347 348 **60**
  110 **73** 294 **118** 3 4 272
  139 153 **141** 41 **142** 356
  143 320 321 **145** 320
  333 334 **148** 220
Tabitha **109** 71
Theodosia **71** 281
Thomas **55** 255 **72** 220 221
  73 15 16 18 **105** 177 **120**
  76 **137** 282
Timothy **73** 16
Uriah **72** 220 **126** 118
Walter F. **69** 208
William **53** 55 **55** 255 **73**
  16 **105** 175 177 **136** 324

JUDD *cont'd*
William Talcott **109** 105
JUDEN George
  Washington **134** 68
Margaret Sloan **134** 68
Mary Elizabeth (Coker)
  134 68
JUDGE
Annie (Lyman) **97** 53
Arthur H. **97** 53
Cyril Bathurst **97** 53
Frederica G. (Mathias)
  97 53
Hugh **56** 127
James **93** 175
William I. **83** 492
William Q. **82** 346
JUDKINS Judkin Judkyn
Abigail (Briggs) **126** 33
Abigail (Harriman)
  104 234
Abigail D. (Corson)
  90 114
Adelia M. (Crockett)
  104 234
Alice H. **89** 349
Alice Lucy **108** 134
Alma (Payson) **104** 234
Appa **88** 155
Benjamin **56** 20
Benjamin C. **90** 114
Benjamin L. **54** lxii
Bessie Florence
  (Johnstone) **104** 234
Betsey **88** 155
Clyde Hollingsworth
  76 159
Cyrena **89** 384
Cyrus F. **126** 33
Ebenezer H. **87** 233 241
Edith **104** 234
Edith F. **105** 128
Edward Hartshorn
  95 238
Elizabeth **52** 434 **54** lxii
Elizabeth (Leavitt)
  121 120
Elizabeth Littlefield
  116 313
Flora Belle **95** 39
Frances **134** 280
Hannah **104** 234 **113** 129
  142 268
Helen **104** 234
Henry **58** 124 125
Hill **145** 359
Horace **89** 384
Jennie Hester (Parmenter)
  95 238
Joann (Hayes) **89** 349
Job **104** 234 **116** 313 **125** 96
Joel **104** 234
John **52** 434 **94** 340 **116**
  264 **145** 354
Judith **52** 433 **100** 41
Leonard **54** lxii **101** 124
  104 234 237 **105** 132
Lorana S. (Bailey) **89** 349
Lorin **92** 221
Marcellus **89** 384

JUDKINS *cont'd*
Margery (Spencer)
  94 339
Mary **58** 124 125
Mary (Bean) **104** 234
Mary (Malone) **90** 114
Mary Anne **77** 184
Mehitable (Elkins)
  104 234
Moses **88** 155 **89** 349
  145 353
Obadiah **54** lxii
Peter **145** 351
Philip **104** 234
Polly (Cowen) **134** 334
Rebecca **58** 122
Rhoda **103** 235
Rosanna Robbins
  (Ackley) **104** 234
S. M. **91** 327
Sally F. (Wilbur) **87** 241
Samuel **104** 234 **121** 120
  276
Samuel Webb **104** 234
Sarah **54** lxii **99** 72 **104**
  234 **110** 309 **142** 271
Sarah (Colby) **104** 234
Sarah (Cram) **104** 234
Sarah (Wilbur) **87** 233 241
Stanley P. (Mrs.) **116** 313
Thomas **94** 258 339
Waldo B. **95** 238
Warren S. **90** 114
William B. **92** 221
Zaccheus **92** 221
Zachariah **134** 334
JUDSON — Mr. **60** 264
Abigail **115** 110
Abigail (Brown) **131** 115
Abraham **107** 155
Adoniram **76** x **131** 115
Amelia **52** 328
Andrew **63** 84-88
Andrew Thompson
  63 86
Ann **54** 386 **75** 179 190
  80 305
Ann H. **88** 139
Ann Hasseltine **55** 20
Anna **125** 235
Anne **75** 186
Annie **75** xxvi
Beach **107** 155
Benjamin **55** 256 **144** 332
Bette **137** 256
Catherine **69** 60
Chester **79** 156
David **65** 148
David William **79** 300
Deborah **54** 385
Diantha **57** 138
Edward **79** 300
Eliza **79** 300
Elizabeth **59** 68 **63** 86
  81 126 127
Ephraim **137** 131
Esther **98** 86 **148** 43
Grace **84** 64
Hannah **81** 126
Hannah S. **79** 156
Harriet **79** 300

JUDSON *cont'd*
Heaton **81** 126
Helen Louise **86** 464
Hemmas **115** 117
James **80** 304 305
Jeremiah **81** 127
Joseph **52** 39 **54** 385 **55**
  24 27 **63** 85 **81** 127 **107**
  155
Joshua **115** 117
Julia Ann (Bishop) **120** 17
Levina **75** 190
Lewis **75** 191
Lewis Birdsey **115** 27
Lydia **55** 256
Maria **71** 12
Mary **63** 86 **81** 126
Mary A. **122** 319
Mary E. **69** 208
Mary N. (Pearson) **88** 283
Mehitable **71** 12 **144** 332
Melancthon **63** 87
Mercy **105** 158
Mills **79** 300
Nabby **115** 27 110
Nancy **79** 300
P. **79** 300
Peter **72** 175
Phebe **107** 155
Philo **79** 300
Rebecca **66** 207 **80** 304
  109 263
Ruth **71** 15
Samuel **115** 27 110
Samuel H. **88** 283
Sarah **52** 39 **55** 24 **56** 159
  79 300 **110** 142 **136** 321
Sterling **79** 300
Sylvester Gilbert **63** 87
Thomas **64** 23
William **59** 68 **71** 288 **81**
  127 **86** 464 **115** 110 **140**
  120
William Legrand **71** 15
Zuinglius **63** 87
JUDY E. L. **106** 78
James **93** 171
Juell *see* Jewell
JUES
Joseph **81** 121 135
Mary **81** 135
JUGLET Sarah **52** 128
JUHLING
Florence E. **93** 138
JUHRING John Christo-
  pher **101** 121
JUHT
Ludwig **97** 79 154
Ludwig (Mme.) **97** 79 154
Juilliard *see* Julliard
JUKES David **63** 242
Sarah **52** 250
JULIEN Julian
Henry **84** 307
John **145** 103
John B. **78** 179
Joseph Francois Baptistan
  Denis **64** 379 **66** 95 194
  69 lxxiii
Julia Ann (Harris)
  136 318

JULIEN *cont'd*
Lilly **69** lxxiv
Magdalene **69** lxxiii
Matthew Cantine **51** 101
  230 **58** xliii 98 **64** 379
  65 xxxiii **66** xlviii **69**
  xliv lxxiii
JULLIARD Juilliard
Annette (Berlette) **92** 187
Augustus D. **92** 188
Charles Frederic **92** 187
Florence Isabelle **92** 188
Frederic Augustus **73** 317
  74 xxiv **92** 148 187 198
Jean Nicholas **92** 187
Pierre **92** 187
Sarah Ann (Chilton)
  92 187
Julls *see* Jewell
JULSE Julia Ann **83** 331
JULSS Sarah **108** 150
JULY Simon **140** 172
JUMEL — Mme **102** 62
Allen **56** xxxii
JUMPER Agnes J. (Davis)
  83 427 433
Anna **88** 63
Betsey **126** 272 274
Daniel **88** 55
Edward **88** 61 63
Elizabeth **88** 61
James **88** 61
John S. **83** 427 433
Joseph **70** 151 **88** 55
Mary **88** 55
Phebe Cummins **88** 63
Rebecca **88** 55
Ruth **88** 55
JUNDERLIN Charlotte
  (Martin) **125** 290
Jeffrey **125** 290
JUNE Stephen **66** 36
Thomas **108** 291
JUNGK Henrietta **86** 368
JUNGMAN
Anna S. B. **86** 22
JUNIPER Junipher
Adelaide **67** xxxiv
Daniel **142** 37
Mary **142** 37
JUNIUS — Fr. **143** 222
Junkens *see* Junkins
JUNKESENP **120** 26
JUNKINS Junkens
—— **113** 129
Abby F. **120** 309 **121** 71
  310 **122** 230
Abigail **112** 306 **113** 123
  115 227 **117** 229 **119**
  146
Abigail (Ingerson)
  109 299
Alexander **110** 286 287
  112 104 **113** 26 27 264
  114 51 **115** 61 217 218
  116 225 302 303 **119**
  144
Alice S. (Paul) **119** 225
Amelia S. **121** 304
Amelia Sarah **113** 195
Ann (Averill) **120** 219 220

JUNKINS *cont'd*
Ann Maria **119** 279
Anna (Lord) **115** 216
Annie E. (McIntire) **121**
  71 72
Barak **119** 225
Betsey **90** 229 250
Catherine **111** 23 **115** 214
Catherine (Bragdon)
  113 125 267 **119** 143
Charles **113** 125 **119** 281
  121 73 146
Charles H. **121** 309
Charles Horace **113** 125
  267
Charles W. **121** 71 72
Clarissa **117** 144 222
Daniel **57** lxvii **97** 271 **110**
  281 **111** 24 94 **112** 25
  103 **114** 133 **115** 141
  116 135 **117** 226 **119**
  283 285
Daniel (Mrs.) **97** 271
David **116** 136
Edward Payson **113** 195
Eleanor **63** 169 **90** 234
  110 281 **112** 103 **115** 58
  216 304 **119** 145
Eleanor (Came) **110** 281
Elias S. **119** 61
Elijah **112** 306 **117** 140
Eliphalet **90** 252 **115** 215
Eliza (Kingsbury)
  117 223
Eliza A. **120** 68
Eliza Ann **120** 67
Elizabeth **71** 221 **112** 104
  115 135
Elizabeth (Kingsbury)
  114 291
Elle **115** 310
Ellen M. **121** 144 146
Ellen Matilda **113** 195
Emma L. **121** 310
Emma Louza **113** 195
Esther **74** 255
Eunice **63** 169 **65** 113 **112**
  306 **115** 304 **119** 279
  120 223
Eunice (Lunt) **115** 305
Eunice (Young) **112** 306
Eunice K. (Varney) **117**
  223 **119** 227
George **117** 140
Hannah **63** 169 **65** 113 **90**
  231 248 249 **91** 28 34
  112 104 306 **113** 129
  115 142 306 **116** 130
  117 143 226 227 **118**
  318 319
Hannah (Bragdon)
  119 144
Hannah (Langton) **115**
  305 **116** 302 303
Hannah (Leach) **117** 140
Hannah (Littlefield) **121**
  73 146
Hannah (McIntire) **112**
  104 **114** 51
Hannah (Nowell) **116** 225
Hannah B. **61** 384

JUNKINS *cont'd*
Hannah J. **121** 71 73
Hannah M. (Carpenter)
  121 307
Hannah M. (Hanscom)
  118 154
Harriet W. **119** 147
Hattie A. **122** 229
Henry **61** 384
Hepzibah **113** 125 **118**
  242 317
Hepzibah (Kingsbury)
  113 124
Hepzibah (Preble)
  115 138
Hiram **118** 241
Ichabod **97** 274 **117** 223
Ida A. (Wentworth)
  121 309
Ivory **120** 136
James **90** 234 236 **110** 281
  114 291 **115** 140 310
  116 141
Jane (Staples) **119** 281
Jane F. **122** 71
Jerusha (Bradbury) **113**
  195 **119** 68
Joanna **113** 27 **116** 141
Joanna S. **119** 67
Joanna S. (Parsons)
  119 61
John **63** 169 **65** 113 **97** 267
  109 299 **111** 260 **112**
  104 218 306 **113** 123 264
  114 132 **115** 61 305 **116**
  131 **119** 61 62 **121** 144
  147
John Henry **120** 223
Jonathan **110** 281 **115** 216
  116 127 225
Joseph **55** 311 **97** 274 **109**
  299 **110** 286 **111** 23 **113**
  124 125 195 **114** 47 **115**
  63 307 **116** 134 **117** 223
  119 69
Joseph Howard **113** 125
  267
Joseph P. **118** 319 321
  120 136 139
Joseph Preble **113** 125
Josephine (Ramsdell)
  121 144 147
Jotham **115** 214
Julia A. (Higgins) **120** 223
Julia Maria **113** 125 267
Katharine (Stackpole)
  110 286
Leonard P. **120** 219 220
Loisa **65** 261
Lucy **115** 214
Luther **113** 125 195 **119** 68
  120 138 **121** 307 309
  122 153
Lydia **57** lxvii **74** 266 **110**
  281 **111** 94 **114** 50 **117**
  223
Lydia (Junkins) **115** 307
Lydia M. **121** 144 146
Lydia W. **119** 281
Mabel Florence **113** 195
Marchia Ann **120** 139

JUNKINS *cont'd*
Margaret **111** 260 **112** 218
  115 141
Maria **119** 279
Marian A. **76** 23
Marsha Ann **120** 138
Martha **110** 286 **112** 104
  114 126 **115** 217
Mary **110** 281 286 287 **111**
  260 **112** 25 104 **113** 26
  264 **114** 45 46 **115** 63 65
  116 135 136 **117** 223
  118 154 **119** 60 61
Mary (Baston) **120** 138
Mary (Cashman) (Frost)
  113 195 **121** 309
Mary (Curtis) **117** 224
Mary (Frost) **122** 153
Mary (Johnson) **120** 136
Mary (Nowell) **117** 140
Mary (Weare) **117** 144 222
Mary Abigail **119** 229 277
Mary Ann (Dixon) **119**
  283 285
Mary E. **119** 228
Mary H. **120** 215 216
Mercy **110** 286 **114** 133
  116 138
Nabby **116** 136 **117** 221
Nathan **118** 154
Nellie Mabel (Shapleigh)
  95 329
Noah **116** 137
Olive **63** 169 **90** 232 252
  113 264 **115** 304
Olive (Williams) **117** 224
  226
Patience **55** 311 **115** 65 141
Patience (Lord) **111** 23
Paul **71** 223 **112** 104 **115**
  211 **116** 294
Polina **119** 64
Priscilla **63** 176
Rebecca (Nowell) **117** 229
Rebecca (Winn) **117** 226
Robert **74** 255 **93** 97 **112**
  104 **144** 265
Sally **113** 124 **116** 299 302
  117 229 230
Sally L. (Varrell) **118** 241
Samuel **111** 23 **113** 124
  125 195 **115** 138 **116**
  128 **117** 144 222 224 226
Samuel W. **113** 125 **123**
  152 153
Samuel Washington
  113 267
Sarah **110** 281 **111** 24 260
  112 104 **114** 132 **115**
  308 **116** 130 **134** 226
Sarah (Grant) **90** 252
Sarah (Johnston) **115** 214
Sarah (Rogers) **115** 215
Sarah Ann (Cutts) **118**
  319 321
Sarah Elizabeth **119** 283
  284
Sarah Elizabeth (Keen)
  119 224
Statira (Waterman)
  90 234 236

JUNKINS *cont'd*
Susan (Carey) **119** 69
Susan (McIntire) **119** 62
Susan E. **120** 307
Susanna **112** 306 **115** 220
Susanna (McIntire)
119 61
Sylvester **95** 329 **119** 224
Tabitha **71** 225 **115** 216
Tabitha (Nowell) **115** 63
Thomas **63** 176 **117** 224
120 138
Washington **113** 125 267
119 143 **120** 135 140
215-225 304-308 **121**
147
William **63** 169 **112** 104
115 305 **117** 229
Wyman Bradbury
113 195
JUNUN John **56** 311
JUNY Domingo **110** 129
JUPP John **55** 271 **69** 122
220
John (Mrs.) **69** 221
Mary **55** 271 **69** 295
JURCKES
Antje **123** 108
Johannes **123** 108
JURDEN Humphrey **147** 25
JURGELA
Constantine R. **99** 257
JURIAEN —— **52** 313
JURIANSE
Kenira **66** 17
Laurens **66** 16 17
JURIEU
Matthew **96** 327
Pierre **96** 327
JURY Domingo **110** 129
Thomas **77** 306
JUSEE Mary **59** 155
Peter **59** 155
Rhoda **126** 32
Justen *see* Justin
JUSTICE Justis Justus
—— **117** 70
Alfred Rudolph **74** xvi
68 130 **75** xvi **79** 57 **113**
279 **117** 61 62 **141** 106
Allen Lloyd **93** 182
Alvirdo A. **111** 128
Anna Mabel **80** 53
Catherine Springer **80** 53
David **90** 344
Drusilla (Simmons)
(Hannum) **90** 344
E. **91** 327
Eleanor Cranston **80** 53
Elizabeth **115** 122
G. **91** 327
George **98** 44
Gustavus Adolphus
80 53
Hannah (Epley) **93** 182
Henrietta **83** 232
Henrietta (White) **82** 382
83 232 **92** 91 151 **93** 182
Henry **64** 346
Jacob **98** 44
James Cranston **80** 53

JUSTICE *cont'd*
James R. **93** 182
Justa Gostaffsin **80** 53
Leila (Parker) **85** 324
Margaret F. (Fitz
Randolph) **98** 44
Mary Cook **102** 147
Mary Elizabeth **80** 53
May **85** 324
Minor **142** 46
Miriam **142** 46
Phebe (Middleton) **98** 44
Robert C. **80** 53
Samuel **80** 53
Sterling **147** 69
Sterling A. **111** 128
Thurlow Weed **82** 382
83 232 **92** 91 151 **93** 182
William **115** 122
William Clive **85** 324
JUSTIN Justen
—— **56** 343
Andrew **78** 26
Charles **70** 315 **78** 26
Clarinda G. **86** 52
Elisha **86** 52
Hamblet **86** 389
Harris **89** 244 245
Ira **78** 26
Julia E. **86** 389
Mary E. **86** 52
Ruth C. **86** 389
Sarah **78** 26
Justis *see* Justice
Justus *see* Justice
JUTRAS
Elizabeth **128** 182
JUTTE Ida B. **95** 349
JUTTON Daniel **94** 65
Hannah Woodbridge
(Plumer) **94** 65
JUTZ Sarah **78** 319
JUXON —— **51** 417 **52**
111 115 120 125 135 372
— Bp. **52** 119 122
— Dr. **52** 122
— Mr. **52** 113
— Mrs. **52** 129
Agnes **52** 129
Albon **52** 106 113
Alice **52** 124
Ann **52** 121
Anne **51** 424 **52** 113 122
Arthur **51** 424 **52** 108-111
113 118 120 121 129
Christopher **51** 424
52 129
Elias **52** 106 113-116
Elizabeth **51** 249-251 **52**
100 108 109 113-115 118-
121 123-129 141 **55** 218
Ellio **52** 108 113 114
Francis **52** 119 122
George **52** 121-123 127 128
Gilbert **52** 125
Hannah **52** 128
Hester **52** 115
Joan **52** 115
John **51** 424 **52** 107-111
113 116-124 126 127 129
140

JUXON *cont'd*
Joseph **52** 109 124
Judith **52** 110 116 124
Margaret **52** 125
Mary **51** 424 **52** 106 114
129
Nicholas **52** 112 118 120
121 123 125-127
Ralph **51** 424 **52** 107 109
110 118 121 123 124 129
Rebecca **52** 106 114
Richard **52** 109 113 121 129
70 55
Rowland **51** 424 **52** 107
109
Samuel **52** 125
Sarah **51** 424 **52** 109 114
124 125 129 140
Susan **52** 116
Thomas **51** 250 424 **52**
105 106 109 113-116 118
121-126 128 129 141 142
William **52** 119 121-127
129 **138** 82-84 102
JUY'N John **141** 230
Jvy *see* Ivey
Jvye *see* Ivey

Kabbot *see* Cabot
KABELAC Edward (Mrs.)
111 326
Elizabeth (Lyon) **132** 297
KACHLER Sarah **125** 35
KAEGMELE
Margaretha **85** 166
KAEMMERLY Melissa
(Hazeltine) **97** 217
KAGEY Jean Alvina
(Bowers) **109** 64
William Francis **109** 64
KAHAILE Sarah **80** 29
KAHAO Ethel **81** 325
Martin J. (Mrs.) **81** 325
KAHL
William F. **124** 102
KAHLER Erich **118** 240
KAHN Blanche **93** 181
Cecelia (Weil) **93** 181
Emanuel **93** 181
KAHNIS —— **56** 15
Kahoun *see* Cahoun
KAIGHN
Juliana **80** 448
Peleg A. **80** 448
KAIL Henry **111** 287
KAILER —— **122** 29
KAILLY Adam de **75** 62
119 101
Mabilia de **75** 62
KAIME Robert **92** 276
Kaine *see* Kane
KAIR James **108** 285
Thomas **63** 240
KAISER
Anna Catherine **96** 396
Roland G. **117** 155
KALAY Edward **77** 186
Louisa **77** 186
KALB *see also* De Kalb
Adelyn **105** 53

KALB cont'd
George L. **55** 236
KALBACH
Margaret **68** 121
KALENS William **60** 240
KALIN Thomas **65** 124
KALISH Henry **121** 79
Lena **121** 79
Ruth Edith **121** 79
KALLOCH
Amariah **90** 92
Mehitable (Hussey) **90** 89
Moses **90** 89
KALLY David **67** 202
Michael **115** 292
KALTENBORN
Rudolph von **108** 34
KALTON
Katharine **76** 312
KALTZ Julia **96** 389
KAMENS Nancy **130** 236
KAMER C. **64** 193
KAMES
Ann Louisa **77** 179
George S. **77** 179
KAMEY Lawrence **64** 219
KAMINKOW Jack **119** 158
231 **122** 114
Marion J. **119** 159 231
121 158 **122** 114 **146**
391
KAMISIN Philip **99** 209
KAMLEN Eleazer **54** 45
KAMM
Amelia H. **85** 314
Caroline A. **80** 337
Gustav **85** 314
Henry **85** 314
Jacob (Mrs.) **80** 337
KAMMERER John **85** 314
Lucy **85** 314
Pauline **85** 314
KAMPER
Anna Alice **106** 125
Kanada see Kennedy
Kanady see Kennedy
Kandall see Kendall
KANDER Helen Frances
(Dennis) **84** 455
Louis Edward (Mrs.)
84 455
KANDRUP Bernice Emilie
113 316
Daniel Edward **113** 316
George William **113** 316
Ida Evelina (Dame)
113 316
Shirley Doris **113** 316
KANE Kaine - see also Cain
& Cane
Agnes **98** 109
Albert **98** 109
Charles **98** 109
Frederick **139** 214
George Philip **139** 214
Georgiana Maria **86** 444
Gertrude Margaret
139 214
Grace (Smith) **98** 109
Hannah **136** 81
John **61** 347 405 **73** 133

KANE cont'd
79 299 308
Joseph Lawrence **139** 213
Lawrence M. **139** 213
Margaret (Murphy)
139 213
Margaret Gertrude
139 214
Margaret L. **99** 147
Mark **125** 40
Mary **64** 373 **73** 133 **85** 226
Mary L. (Kennedy) **139**
212 213
Mary Margaret **139** 213
May R. **125** 236
Michael **66** 307
Philip **139** 213
Philip George **139** 214
R. Keith (Mrs.) **99** 73
Sibyl **73** 133
Thomas E. **99** 147
KANEM Emma **91** 53
KANLER John **102** 288
KANNEY Mary **68** 204
KANOUSE John **76** 269
Olive **76** 269
KANT Jane **100** 300
KAPLE Edward **61** 274
Mary Elizabeth **61** 274
KAPLER William **77** 312
KAPP Eleanor **74** 306
Elvira Ramsey **74** 306
Levi **74** 306
KAPPEL Philip **84** 354
KARACSONYI
Janos **96** 139-141
KARAJAN Florence
Winchester de **78** 248
Harriet Winchester de
78 248
Harriette Henchman de
78 248
Nicholas Theodore de
78 248
KARCHER John **126** 209
Vira Blanche **92** 146
KARDELL
Caroline Lewis **141** 57
251 254 361 **147** 281
KARDEY William **119** 21
KARDOYLE
Elizabeth **94** 206
John **94** 206
Kargill see Cargill
KARI Adam de **60** 317
62 307
KARKAR Sarah **91** 190
KARL Wilhelm **111** 102
KARLEE Margaret **78** 190
KARLIN Patrick **61** 267
KARLING Marva Vaunceil
100 113
KARLSEFNE
Thorfinn **52** 88
KARLSEN
Carol F. **144** 358-360
KARN Ann Fredericka
107 309
KARNAN
Henrietta **79** 34
Robert Wilson **79** 34

KARNER
Elizabeth **89** 110
Laura Justina **78** 353
Lucinda **89** 110
Karney see Carney
KAROLIK Martha
Catherine (Codman)
102 232
Maxim **102** 233 **103** 119
107 130
Maxim (Mrs.) **102** 219
232 233 **103** 123
KARR see also Carr
Betsey **98** 364
Margret **89** 202
Mary **71** 304
Moses **71** 154
William **71** 154
KARRANKY
William **125** 38
KARSTEDT
Edwin Stanton **91** 108
H. **91** 108
Louise **91** 108
Maude Elissa (Hannum)
91 108
KARTCHMER
Floy **100** 112
Karty see Carty
KARVYLL Robert **98** 37
KAS Mary E. **128** 263
KASKEY
Erastus **76** 273
Sarah L. **76** 273
KASPER
Lewis P. **100** 338
Rose **92** 221
KASSON Adam **147** 109
Archibald **129** 64
Benadam **81** 413
Joseph S. **70** 92
Josie B. **81** 413
Laura A. **81** 413
Laura E. **81** 413
Margaret **70** 92
William **147** 109
KAST ____ (Haskins)
140 151
Ann **100** 139
Frederic **140** 159
Mary **100** 28
Philip Godfrid **77** xxii
100 28 **140** 159
Thomas **84** 257 **100** 28 **126**
225 **140** 151 159 324
KASTNER
Charles **92** 333
Martha J. (Winn) **92** 333
93 57
KATASAROS
James **107** 162
KATE Edwin I **121** 147
Mary J. (Blaisdell) **121** 147
KATELY Ithail **66** 13
Parhurst **66** 13
KATERMAN
Mary **114** 187
Mary (Redman) **114** 187
KATES Richard **87** 117
KATHAN —— **58** 381 386
59 340

KATHAN cont'd
Alexander **58** 385
Daniel **126** 140
Esther **57** 308
Frances M. (Howe) **130** 52
Grace H. **130** 52
John **57** 303 308 309 **58** 382
384 385
Lois **57** 309
Mabel J. **130** 52
Margaret **57** 308 **58** 385
Martha **57** 303 **58** 382
Mary **58** 380 382 383 385
Molly **58** 385
Orange E. **130** 52
KATHERINS
E. A. **78** 302
KATING Sophia **142** 59
KATION
Frank A. **117** 291
Joseph M. **117** 291
Manuel **117** 291
KATNER Jane **118** 236
KATONA Louis **109** 313
KATSAROS
James **108** 10 13
KATTELLE Charles
Edward **84** 330
Charles Edward (Mrs.)
85 205
Maria (Merrick) **84** 330
Mary Catherine (Roby)
72 xx **84** 235 329
Noble **84** 330
Walter Roby **84** 330
KATTENBURIE
Margerie **55** 105
Thomas **55** 105
Kaufman see Kaufmann
Kauffmann see Kaufmann
KAUFHOLZ Charles
Frederick **104** 144 **105**
125 **106** 220 **110** 238
KAUFMANN Kauffman
Kauffmann Kaufman
Anna Wood **124** 32
Betsey Beecher **68** xxxi
Carl F. **109** 220
Carl Friedrich (Mrs.) **78**
108 **95** 145 **109** 121 220
Charles B. (Mrs.) **86** 197
Christian Heinrich
72 xxxv
Ed. G. **118** 248
Elizabeth **78** 108
Elizabeth (Cheney)
109 220
Francis Philips **124** 32
Frederick Grimm **124** 32
Freni Strausz **118** 248
Jessie (Christopher)
124 32
Jessie (Kennedy) **124** 32
Louisa **72** xxxv
Louise **124** 32
Mary **113** 323
Orrin Frederick (Mrs.) **84**
111 189
Peter **118** 248
Rudolph **124** 32
Samuel Kay **124** 32

KAUFMANN cont'd
Sarah Clark (Fracker)
124 32
Sophia **72** xxxv
Una (Libby) **90** 169
Victor **124** 32
KAUGHO Morris **63** 238
Kaul see Kaull
KAULBACK
Andrew **102** 225
John G. **102** 225
KAULL Kaul
Anstris **125** 172
Catherine **125** 172
John A. **125** 172 241 **126** 20
Kate (Kargill) **125** 241
126 20
KAUSMAN Jemira **81** 388
KAUTZ Albert **74** 244
KAUWERTZ
Frederick **98** 73
Marie **98** 73
Marie E. **98** 73
Kavana see Cavenaugh
Kavanagh see Cavenaugh
Kavanaugh see Cavenaugh
KAVAROVICS
Helen A. **109** 158
KAW John **125** 40
KAY De Kay Kaye
— Mrs. **82** 75
Ann **63** 135 **81** 154
Anne **131** 172
Arthur **61** 186 **80** 90 92
Beatrice **63** 32
Betsey **63** 176
Brian / Bryan **63** 135 137
Charles **64** 25
Charmy **82** 206
Della **77** 265
Dorothy **63** 135
Elizabeth **61** 186 **63** 32 135
80 92 **111** 275 276
Emma **77** 266
Grace **93** 198
Grisse **82** 74
Hannah **63** 135 169 **91** 397
I. **124** 100
Isabel **61** 187 **80** 93
J. S. **77** 265
Jacob **88** 115
James **61** 186 **80** 92 **91** 327
Jane **63** 32 135
Jeanne **134** 334
Joan **80** 90 92
John **80** 88 89 **82** 74 81 206
111 274 275 **113** 7
Jonie **61** 186
Katrina de **54** 419
Lawrence **80** 90
Margaret Nelson **108** 135
Mary **63** 32
Maurice **52** 128
Molly **63** 177
Nathan Aaron **95** 146
Nathaniel **96** 357
Ralph **80** 90
Richard **51** 133 **80** 89
Robert **63** 32 135 **93** 198
134 334
Roger **80** 89

KAY cont'd
Ruth Lincoln **122** 78 160
319 **123** 114 **126** 113
Sarah **63** 32 135
Sarah (Chase) **88** 115
Thomas **80** 88 89
Victor **63** 32
William **63** 135 176
KAYHAWLEY
David **73** 138
KAYLOR
Daniel Pringle
104 165
Elizabeth Pringle **104** 165
Sarah Whitfield
(McBryde) **104** 165
KAYNOR Dorothy (Van-
derwerker) **102** 165
Frank **102** 165
KAZEY — Mrs. **72** 175
Keable see Keble
KEADLE
Elizabeth **73** 143
John **73** 261
Mary **73** 154
Thomas **73** 144
William **73** 230
Wiseman **73** 148
KEADY Eleanor (Yates)
95 76
Martha Ann **95** 76
Samuel **95** 76
KEAFF
Cornealles **119** 21
KEAIS Keaise - see also
Case
Margaret **67** 286
Samuel **51** 45
William **67** 286 **87** 366
Kealer see Keeler
KEALLE Susan **51** 122
KEALLY Francis (Mrs.)
95 174
Mildred Fessenden
(Taber) **95** 174
KEALY John E. **69** xxxii
KEAN Keane - see also
Keene
Abel **52** 222
Edward Joseph **112** 153
Elisha **126** 273
Elizabeth (Sparrow)
(Penrose) **117** 108
Elizabeth Hazylin **78** 170
Florence Newcomb
(Huntley) **112** 153
Georgiana Isabella
117 114
Hamilton Fish (Mrs.) **78**
109 205 **86** 444
Hannah **106** 20
Jane **126** 204
John **52** 33 **106** 20
Julia **78** 434 435
Katharine **78** 205
Katharine (Winthrop)
86 444
Peter **78** 435
Richard **117** 108
Robert **52** 43 482
Sarah Sabina **78** 435

KEAN cont'd
 Sumner **112** 75
 Thomas **52** 44
 William L. **54** 238
  55 xxxii
KEAR Peter **121** 154
KEARFOOTE
 Margaret **64** 253
KEARL Lula Barzilla
  (Humphrey) **119** 316
KEARNEY Kearny
 —— **53** 460
 Andrew Jackson **98** 337
 Clara Evangeline **106** 125
 Graham **119** 192
 Mary **134** 329
 Philip **68** 209 **92** 97
 Stephen Watts **62** 311
  92 97
 Susan (Fitz Randolph)
  98 337
 Thomas **92** 97
KEARNS
 Anthony **66** 307
 Caleb **125** 220
 M. M. **115** 292
 Mary **73** 131
 Sarah (Neal) **125** 220
 Walter M. **59** xliv
Kearny see Kearney
KEARSE
 Hendrick **106** 175 178
KEARSLEY Jane **65** 195
 Jonathan **65** 195
Kearswell see Kerswell
KEASBEY
 Edward **95** 336
 Mary Anna (Griffith)
  95 336
 Mary Parry **95** 336
KEASER George **125** 24
 Sarah **96** 240
KEAST Lois J. **112** 141
KEAT John **66** xiii
KEATER William **64** 109
KEATES Richard **146** 381
KEATING Keatinge
 —— **61** 228
 —— (Storer) **140** 249
 Clare L. **74** xxiv
 Edward **126** 145
 Elizabeth W. **116** 141
 Ella P. Talcott **85** 166
 Francis Talfourd (Mrs.)
  74 ix xxiv **113** 59
 Hannah Wood **83** 193
 Jessie **96** 160 **100** 44 116
 Joseph M. **83** 99
 Martha **62** 92
 Michael **85** 166
 Nellie (Carpenter) **83** 99
 Oliver **87** 206 **115** 226
  140 42 249
 Richard **115** 219 **116** 140
  297
 Sally S. **116** 140
 Sarah (Linton) **126** 145
KEATLEY
 Vivien Bulloch **96** 209
KEATON
 C. C.Rose **101** 339

KEATON cont'd
 James **134** 222
 Jane (Newell) **134** 222
 Sarah Jane **134** 222
 William **65** 33
KEATOR Alfred Decker
  116 232
KEAY Keays - see also Kay
 — Mr. **71** 139
 Abby Jane **59** lxxv
 Alan Kent **96** 83
 Carol Seaver **96** 83
 Charles **119** 63
 Edith **106** 146
 Edythe Leonard **96** 83
 Fanny (Leonard) **96** 83
 Gladys **96** 83
 Grizzel **98** 219
 Hannah J. **121** 306
 Harriet Atwood **81** 148
 Hawley A. **98** 195
 John **98** 219
 Lizzie Lake **59** lxxv
 Louise (Kent) **96** 83
 Louise Nathalie **96** 83
 Lucy (Sawyer) **118** 241
 Mary **81** 148 158 **98** 219
 Mary (Farquahar) **106** 146
 Mary (Remick) **98** 195
 Matilda (McIntire) **119** 63
 Molly **98** 219
 Molly (Jones) **99** 326
 Nathaniel Seaver **96** 83
 Nathaniel Seaver (Mrs.)
  85 195 242 **96** 83 149
  166
 Nathaniel Washburn
  96 83
 Otis **118** 241
 Susan Woodworth
  (Seaver) **96** 83
 Thomas **96** 83
 Uriah **71** 135
 Warren **81** 148
 William Farquahar
  106 146
KEAYNE Anna **67** 107
 Anne **61** 41
 Benjamin **67** 107
 Robert **54** 217 **61** 41 **62**
  216 **67** 107 199
Keays see Keay
KEAZER
 Carrie **104** 214
 Rebecca **132** 245
 Sarah **104** 172
KEBLE Keable Kebel
  Kebell Kebill Keebe
  —— **56** 212
 Elizabeth **54** 193 **119** 162
 Grace (Riddlesdale)
  143 215
 Henry **65** 30
 Isabel **93** 171
 Joana (Ffyske) **87** 41
 John **54** 193 **68** 183 **71** 243
  143 209
 Katharine **105** 6
 Mary **71** 243
 Richard **143** 214 215
 Robert **75** 276

KEBLE cont'd
 Roger **64** 352
 Thomas **87** 41
 William **112** 257
KEBLER
 Anna Sophia **57** 382
 Emeline **57** 382
 Frederic **57** 382
KEBUR Robert **94** 264
KECKE Keck
 —— **84** 288
 Alice **80** 446
 Aloise **82** 486
 Caroline **110** 322
 George **107** 74
 Marie **80** 446 **84** 289
 Mary (Tomes) **84** 289
 Mary A. (Grant) **110** 322
 Reuben **110** 322
 Sarah Catherine **107** 74
 Thomas **80** 285 446
 William **80** 446 **84** 289
KEDAL —— **58** 199
 Bethiah **58** 199 **110** 277
 James **58** 236
 Mary **58** 318
 William **58** 318
KEDDER
 Christian **70** 263
KEDMAN Thomas **65** 27
KEDTON William **64** 22
KEE Abigail **66** 130 132 137
 Chloe **66** 136
 Daniel **66** 132 135 137
 Hannah **66** 135
 Jerusha **66** 132
 Joanna **66** 130 132
 John **66** 132
 Joseph **66** 132 **72** 283
 Mary **66** 132 **72** 283
 Pardon **66** 135
 Sarah **84** 221
 Shubael **66** 137
Keeble see Keble
KEEBY Dorcas (Galee)
  100 303
 William **100** 303
KEECH Abigail (Silvester)
  86 289
 Abraham **124** 78
 Anne Parker **84** 188
 Benjamin A. **142** 372
 Caroline Cordelia **61** 274
 Clarissa **73** 261
 Dorcas E. **93** 219
 Emily J. **142** 372
 George **116** 259
 George L. **142** 372
 George R. **124** 78
 Jane (Sweet) **116** 259
 Jeremiah **128** 59
 Jesse **128** 59
 Joan **67** 261
 Joanna **67** 261
 Joanna Manton
  (Benchley) **142** 371
 John **67** 261 **86** 289 **93** 218
  105 196
 John Everett **93** 219
 John R. **93** 219
 Joseph **128** 59

KEECH *cont'd*
Mabel Louise **112** 74
Mary Alice **55** xxxiv **59**
  v xvi **60** v xxv xxxiv **61**
  v **62** xvi **65** xliv lx
Mary Elizabeth **77** 188
Mary P. **142** 372
Mary Tibbetts **65** lx
Meribah (Ryan) **124** 78
Merrill H. **93** 218
Norman Wesley **61** 274
Olney **142** 371 372
Peter **87** 263
Rice **142** 372
Robert Nelson **93** 219
Sarah (Chase) **87** 263
Seth **128** 52
Stephen **128** 59
Sylvenus **128** 59
Walter Edmund **93** 219
William **65** lx **73** 139
William Walker **65** lx
Zephaniah **65** lx **128** 58
KEEFE Keef Keeffe
Alice (Connors) **84** 295
Alice Dunn **84** 295
David **78** 406
Harry J. **146** 383
John **84** 295
Mary **125** 216
Owen **64** 226
Polly **97** 372
Sally **97** 372
Thomas **97** 372
KEEFER Baltus **102** 70
Charlotte Frances
  (Woodworth) **102** 70
Christina (Muller) **102** 70
Edith C. **102** 70
Elizabeth (Hogan) **102** 70
Elizabeth (Louk) **102** 70
Emma Clarissa **109** 307
Fletcher Peter **102** 70
Hendrick **102** 70
Henry **102** 70
Johan William **102** 70
Josephine **85** 198 **102** 62
  70 129
Katharine B. **127** 160
Maria (Aergenbreg)
  102 70
Martha Maria (Hotaling)
  102 70
Peter **102** 70
Robert **90** 208
KEEGAN John **66** 36
KEEISE Robert **127** 144
KEEL Ann **104** 309
Aurora Calender **104** 309
Elizabeth (Chestnutwood)
  104 309
Ella **101** 125 **104** 309 **105**
  68 132
Joseph **104** 309
Joseph M. **104** 309
Mary Graves (McKenzie)
  104 309
KEELAND —— **101** 270
KEELE David Rue (Mrs.)
  109 130
KEELER —— **95** 405

KEELER *cont'd*
— Mr. **71** 45
Aaron **114** 184
Abigail **72** 312 **104** 117
Albert C. **111** 305 307
Alice Adell **93** 137
Andrew Jackson **105** 273
Angela Adalaide **102** 289
Anna **145** 74
Anna (Hubbell) **144** 237
Charlotte M. **69** 163
Cornelius P. **114** 184
Daniel M. (Mrs.) **118** 76
Eliza **62** 368
Elizabeth Klock (Whitin)
  89 31 **94** 290
Emily Frances **97** 187
Esther **72** 312
Etta D. **125** 54
Eugene (Mrs.) **90** 137
Evelyn Wood **94** 208
  95 78
Fanny **71** 121
Fanny (Carver) **88** 229
Floyd Yates **86** 197
Frederick **114** 184
Frederick Sterling
  89 392 393
Hannah **52** 39 **72** 312
Harriet (Hamlin) **109** 258
Henry **105** 273
Henry Hayden **136** 79
Herman **62** 368
Hezekiah **136** 79
Huldah **103** 230
James **104** 117
Jean Patricia **108** 134
Jeremiah **72** 312
Jessie Maud **89** 31
John **58** 358 **102** 288
Jonathan **105** 273
Julia (Lathrop) **89** 31
Julius A. **114** 184
Julius Melanchton **89** 31
Lawrence Murray **89** 31
Lawrence Murray (Mrs.)
  94 290
Mary **98** 229 **105** 273
  114 184
Mary Elizabeth **136** 78
Mehitable **58** 358
Mercy **59** 360
Nannie M. (Spaulding)
  111 305 307
Nathan **109** 258
Nathaniel **114** 184
Patrick **145** 74
Ralph **59** 357 **72** 312
Rebecca Budd
  (Van Amringe) **89**
  392 393
Rosannah **105** 273
Roy A. **111** 305
Rufus **59** 360
Ruth **118** 76
Sally **114** 184
Samuel **72** 312
Samuel Gardner **105** 273
Sara Louisa **102** 286
Sarah **59** 357 **69** 60 **72** 312
  121 251

KEELER *cont'd*
Sarah (Mosher) **123** 239
Seth **88** 229
Seth H. **82** 71
Thaddeus **72** 312
Thomas **116** 134 **145** 141
Timothy **72** 312
Urias **105** 273
Virginia Christensen
  118 76
William A. **114** 184
William Morford
  89 392-394
William Van Amringe
  89 393
KEELEY Julia **88** 192
KEELING Alice **94** 273
Bethiah (Cheever) **126** 281
Dora Janet **80** 158
Hope **64** 122
John **94** 273
Samuel **56** 37
Keen *see* Keene
KEENAN
Catherine **64** 293
Maria C. (Rice) **125** 243
Mary Lily **92** 190
Samuel **125** 243
Samuel R. **125** 243
William W. **125** 243
KEENE Keen - *see also*
Kean
—— **60** 338 **105** 49
— Widow **66** 364
—— (Swayne) **105** 50
Aaron **74** 220
Abdon W. **91** 384
Abel **120** 46
Abigail **60** 30 70 **84** 427
Abigail (Barnes) **88** 316
Abner **84** 423
Ada F. (Millett) **98** 195
Adeline S. **98** 195 196
Alexander **97** 206
Alford B. **98** 195
Alice (Jones) **84** 423
Almira **82** 22
Alpheus D. **98** 195 196
Amaziah **98** 195
Andrew **98** 195
Ann **81** 272
Anna **105** 49
Anna (Briggs) **126** 273
Anna (Genthner) **84** 424
Anne **94** 396
Appleton **97** 133
Arthur B. **73** 78
Ashton **105** 49
Benjamin **74** 220 **116** 188
Bessie (Robbins) **98** 195
Bethiah **60** 143 **91** 371
Betsey **95** 316 **118** 204
  121 135 **122** 257 258
Betsey D. **120** 115 116
Bonham **105** 50
Carrie E. (Cox) **91** 384
Charles **127** 226
Charles H. **98** 195
Charles L. **98** 195
Chloe R. **98** 195
Christiana **84** 424

KEENE *cont'd*
Christiana (Perry)
  116 107
Christopher **100** 220
Clawson **105** 50
Clifford Bonham **105** 49
Cora **105** 49 51
Cornelius **89** 41
Daniel **68** 163 **105** 49
Deborah **71** 92 **87** 290
Doris **105** 50
Ebenezer **53** 358
Edith (Rich) **84** 304
Edna S. **98** 195
Edward **54** 325 330 335
  65 235 **142** 296
Edwin Ames **82** 276
Eleanor **54** 325 335
Eleanor N. (Hodgdon)
  98 195
Elizabeth **56** 405 406 **74**
  230 258 **84** 425 **105** 49
  107 93 **119** 252
Elizabeth (Clawson)
  105 49
Elizabeth (Gosnold)
  105 14
Elizabeth (Stockbridge)
  (Turner) **134** 141
Elizabeth Read **85** 194
Ella (House) **105** 49
Ellen N. **98** 185 195
Elton C. **98** 195 196
Emily A. **98** 192
Emma **98** 195
Ephraim **63** 377 **64** 76 **66**
  362 **74** 220 **111** 246 **115**
  140 **116** 188 **122** 21
Eunice **114** 316
Eunice (Jennings)
  114 316
Eva H. **83** 430 433
Eveline **92** 333
Fanny **63** 378 **64** 375
Fhilena **98** 195
Flora M. (Hanscom)
  89 357
Frances (Blackler) **110** 222
Frances B. G. **110** 222
Frances Blackler Gerry
  110 222
Frank **98** 196
Frank A. **98** 195
Frencenia **92** 234
George **105** 49 **107** 188
George N. **98** 195
George T. **98** 195
Gerald L. B. **98** 195
Grace **136** 36
Gregory B. **66** 96
Gregory Bernard **105** 48
Hamden C. **123** 153
Hannah **53** 358 **105** 49
  195 196 **133** 193 **136** 35
Hannah (Whittemore)
  107 188
Hannah M. **61** 237 **98** 195
Harriet **75** 269
Harris Wesley **105** 49
Harry A. **98** 195
Harry N. **98** 195

KEENE *cont'd*
Hattie (Wilbur) **123** 153
Hattie Louise **97** 81
Henry **56** 405 **97** 207 224
  105 14
Herbert Beers (Mrs.) **96**
  160 **103** 79 125
Hira **98** 195 196
Horatio N. **84** 304
Ida **98** 195
Ida (Elliott) **97** 133
Ida Florence **98** 195
Isaac **115** 303
Isaac H. **98** 195
Isaiah **136** 35 37
Isetta **90** 42
Jacob **116** 188
Jacob B. **105** 49
Jacob William **105** 49
James **64** 112
Jane **126** 17
Jemima (Ellis) **116** 107
  121 134
Jerusha (Blake) **126** 273
Jesse **116** 188
Job **111** 246
John **82** 443 449 **87** 398
  97 206 **105** 49 195 196
  127 223 **134** 141
Jonas **116** 187 188
Jonathan **74** 220 221 230
  249
Joran **105** 48
Joseph **51** 361 **74** 220
  82 443
Joseph Ashton **105** 49
Joseph P. **123** 153
Joseph Swift **105** 48
Josephus **116** 107 **121** 134
Joshua **98** 195 196
Josiah **92** 234 333
Josiah F. **92** 333
Julia A. **99** 133
Julia A. (Brown) **119** 285
Julia Ursin (Niemcewicz)
  85 113
Katharine **105** 49 50
Laodamia **116** 188
Lemuel C. **98** 195 196
Linwood S. **98** 195
Lucy H. (Carver) **89** 41
Lulie V. **98** 195
Luther **63** 377 **64** 374
  66 365
Lydia **63** 377 **64** 374 **66**
  365 **98** 195 **116** 188
Mamie Luella **103** 122
Margaret **82** 449 **116** 188
  126 64
Margaret Orr **66** lxviii
Maria **73** liv **128** 281
Maria (Bonham) **105** 49
Maria (Freeman) **121** 134
Marie **105** 50
Mark E. **98** 195
Mark W. **93** 333
Martha (Freeman) **122**
  257 258
Martha A. **98** 195 196
Martha E. **98** 195 196
Mary **63** 379 **74** 214 220

KEENE *cont'd*
  221 230 249 **75** 213 **98**
  196 **99** 191 **105** 48 52
  116 188
Mary (Hall) **116** 187
Mary A. (Picoat) **123** 153
Mary Ann **119** 277
Mary Ann (Storm) **105** 49
Mary E. (Hatch) **98** 196
Mary M. **142** 296
Mary W. (Jackman)
  126 65
Mercy **63** 377 **64** 76 **66** 362
  111 246
Mercy (Allen) **111** 246
Mercy (Main) **115** 303
Miles Allen **111** 246
Moses **120** 116 **121** 134
  122 257
Myra L. **74** 309
Nancy **125** 293
Nancy (Carver) **89** 42
Nathaniel **98** 195 196
Neigh **66** 361
Nellie Caroline **95** 39
Olean Augusta **82** 276
Olive Frances **82** 276
Orrin S. **98** 195 196
Ozin G. **98** 195 196
Peter **105** 49
Phebe **116** 188
Phena M. **93** 333
Philena **98** 195
Philip **63** 378 **64** 375
Prince **127** 226
Priscilla **105** 48
R. A. **89** 357
Rebecca **116** 187 188
Rebecca (Barker) **134** 141
Robert **57** 311 312 **105** 49
Rollin A. **98** 196
Rose M. **98** 196
Rowena E. **98** 196
Ruth **122** 257 **136** 38
Ruth (Sprague) **136** 36
Sally **98** 195 196 **126** 68
Sam Ashton **105** 49
Samuel **63** 378 **64** 375
  116 107 **136** 36
Samuel M. **98** 196
Sarah **94** 396 **105** 49 50 **115**
  218 **127** 65 **142** 296 **148**
  187
Sarah (Hendrickson)
  105 49
Sarah (Yard) **105** 49
Sarah Elizabeth **119** 224
Seth **98** 195 196
Shadrach **134** 141
Sidney T. **98** 196
Simeon **89** 42 **105** 281
Sprague **98** 196 **136** 38
Susan **125** 289
Susan B. **101** 33
Susan C. **98** 196
Susan S. **98** 196
Susanna **60** 338 **63** 378
  64 375
Thaddeus **105** 49
Thomas **56** 405 **105** 14
Thomas Goodwin **74** 221

KEENE *cont'd*
Wealthy **87** 139
Wesley **105** 49
Wilfred **82** 276
William **60** 70 **64** 321 **66**
359 364 **84** 424 **88** 281
97 206 **105** 49 50 **107** 93
134 141
William B. **119** 285
William E. **98** 196
William G. **98** 196
William Gray Swett
110 222
William S. **99** 133
KEENEY Keeny
Aaron J. **85** 314
Adotia **83** 160
Agnes **53** 414
Amos **126** 255 **128** 18
Angeles M. **86** 169
Angie C **72** 65
Anna **72** 201
Anna (Rogers) **126** 255
Anson P. **72** 74
Asahel **82** 104
Betsey **79** 79 **83** 157 160
Belly **84** 140
Carolina A. Pease **85** 409
Caroline Wright **70** 240
Champion **127** 71
Charles **85** 314
Charles S. **83** 160
Charles W. **85** 314
Charlie **83** 160
Clarissa **85** 314
Delia Hyde **85** 314
E. Eliza **83** 160
Ebenezer **77** 80 **84** 140
Edith L. **83** 503
Edna **83** 160
Edson Fitch **83** 160
Edward P. **83** 160
Edwin **86** 169
Elizabeth **83** 99 **147** 42
Emma **85** 409
Emma Louisa **86** 335
Esther **85** 314 **124** 259 261
Eugenia **86** 169
Ezekiel **72** 74
Fanny **83** 160
Fanny Fitch **83** 160
Franklin **83** 99
George G. **147** 61
George S. **83** 160
Harrie Augustus **85** 314
Harriet J. **83** 503
Harriet Louisa (Lines)
82 353
Harriet Marilla (Post)
147 61
Hattie Louise **97** 81
Hephzibah **85** 52
Herbert H. **86** 169
Hiram G. **85** 409
Innes Spotts **80** 37
Isaac **83** 160
Isaac Patten **83** 160
James R. **86** 169
John **64** 188 **126** 19
Joseph **54** 257 **86** 335
Joseph N. **72** 74

KEENEY *cont'd*
Josiah **72** 201
Katie **83** 160
Katie E. **72** 74
Lester L. **83** 503
Lucy **84** 140
Luna W. **85** 409
Lydia (Rogers) **128** 18
M. G. **83** 160
Marilla M. **72** 74
Martha A. **86** 169
Mary **53** 414 **62** 294 **79** 79
Mary (Bishop) **86** 335
Mary Ann **82** 104
Mary M. **72** 66
Medad **77** 80
N. **83** 160
N. L. **83** 160
Nancy **72** 74 **83** 99 160
Nancy Hunt **83** 160
Naomi **79** 79
Nathaniel **83** 359
Nelson **83** 160
Oscar D. **85** 314
Perry **83** 160
Riley F. **86** 169
Robert **126** 19
Sally **79** 79
Samuel W. **83** 160
Sarah **85** 314 **86** 21
Sheldon **82** 353
Shubael **70** 240
Sirviller **83** 503
Susanna **64** 188
Theodosia **82** 104
Thomas **64** 188
Timothy **54** 257
Tryphena **83** 160
Viola **86** 169
W. P. **83** 160
William **64** 188 **79** 79 **83**
99 160
KEEP Keepe
Abner Newton **82** 369
Albert **61** 406 **92** 82
Almeyda **117** 264
Annie Bliss **68** lxvi
Austin B. **107** 13
Austin Baxter **67** 184 **68**
xix xxxi **74** 241
Caleb **114** 203
Chellis **117** 264
Elizabeth **53** 378 **61** 341
Experience **64** 149
Hannah **53** 378 **71** 46 49
116 **115** 33 **117** 264
Hannah (Woodbury)
117 264
Heber **53** 379
Helen E. **52** 480 **53** 450
54 353 **56** 92 **59** xliv **60**
184 277
Helen Elizabeth **60** 392
61 31
Jabez **53** 378 **64** 149
James **64** 321
John **53** 374 378 379 **58**
lxxii **123** 258 259 **148**
223
Josiah **117** 264
Leonard **70** 9

KEEP *cont'd*
Lester **53** 379
Lois **117** 264
Lucy Gunn **92** 82
Maranda **82** 369
Mary (Sylvester) **86** 461
Moses **117** 264
Nathan Cooley **58** lxxii
68 lxvi
Noble **117** 264
Phebe **61** 341 343
Rachel **61** 342
Ruth **61** 341 **64** 149
Sallie **82** 369
Samuel **53** 379 **71** 46
123 263
Sarah **53** 378 379 **61** 341
123 261 **148** 223
Sarah (Colton) **123** 263
Sarah (Leonard) **148** 223
Susan Haskell **58** lxxii
Susan Prentice **58** lxxii
Susan Prentiss **68** lxvi
Thomas **117** 264
KEEPAR Richard **101** 8
Keepe *see* Keep
KEEPERS
Adelaide A **84** 29
KEERL George H. **73** 275
KEESE Kees - *see also* Case
—— **143** 202
Chloe Bradish **77** 57
David **114** 186
Elizabeth Trimingham
54 152
Emily Bailie **77** 57
Foster DeForest (Mrs.)
109 130
George **114** 186
John Anton (Mrs.) **99** 147
Mary **107** 261
Peter **114** 186
Philip **114** 186
Robert E. **107** 209
Sarah **74** 267
Sarah K. (Barton) **107** 209
Sibyl **74** 14
Theodore **77** 57
William S. **106** 77
KEESEY Jane R. **79** 26
KEESLER
Laura Agnes **105** 128
KEET —— Widow **70** 248
Joel **117** 262
John **117** 262
Jonathan **117** 262
Mary **117** 262
Mary E. **78** 205
Reuben **117** 262
Ruth **117** 262
Sarah **117** 262
KEEZER
Alonzo **147** 367
Ambrose **147** 367
Bertie **147** 367
Charles **147** 367
David **147** 266 267 273
364-367
Delia **147** 367
Eliphaz **147** 365-367
Frank Merriam **147** 366

KEEZER cont'd
Hannah **147** 367
Henrietta C. (Merriam)
147 366
Jennie **147** 367
Julia (Oakes) **147** 367
Lavina **147** 367
Lizzie **147** 367
Mamie **147** 367
Marion **147** 366
Mary **147** 364 367 368
Mary (Rogers) **147** 265-
267 273 364 365
Rachel **84** 51
Sarah (Davis) **147** 366
Sarah B. (Merriam)
147 366
Susan **147** 273 274 366
KEFAUVER Webster
Albert (Mrs.) **109** 130
KEFFER John Poist **116**
233 **120** 155 158
KEGAN Hetty **93** 324
KEGLEY F. B. **92** 402
111 201
KEGRICE Peter **133** 72
Susan **133** 72
KEHALE Nancy **80** 26
KEHN
Dove (Mrs.) **130** 156
Olney Eugene **106** 125
KEHOE M. **58** cx
KEHR
Elizabeth D. **130** 56
Jacob H. **130** 56
KEHRT Jacob **60** 185
KEICKSER
Elnor Jane **128** 171
KEIF Francis Patrick (Mrs.)
82 122 236
Maud Emily **82** 236
KEIGHLY
Elizabeth **56** 38
John **55** 262 **57** 257
Lydia **55** 262
Sarah **57** 257
William **57** 257
KEIGWIN Cagwin
Jerusha (Gates) **120** 272
Thomas **120** 272
KEIL Ella **128** 268
KEILEY
Hannah **100** 142
John **100** 141 142
Mary **100** 142
KEILL —— **56** 343
KEILY
Alexander **125** 220
Elizabeth (Hill) **125** 101
Matthew **125** 101
KEIM —— **53** 265 267 379
380 466
DeB. Randolph **53** 265 374
54 xxxviii **55** xxxii
George DeBenneville
83 258 **85** 465 **86** 114
91 210
Jessie Isabel **84** 192
KEINATH
Elizabeth **68** 158

KEINE
Robert **67** 151 153
KEIPER
Christian Butz **113** 227
Elizabeth **113** 227
Francis Pitman **113** 227
Frank **113** 227
Frank (Mrs.) **102** 123 **113**
59 227
Katharine **113** 227
KEISER
Caroline R. **76** 276
David S. **122** 154
George W. **76** 276
KEISTER
Cecile M. **147** 179
KEIT
Elizabeth **59** 418
Joseph **59** 418
KEITH —— **53** 413 **62** 391
127 179
— Esq. **59** 240
— Mr. **126** 114
— Mrs. **103** 300 **126** 114
____ (Polley) **140** 237
Abby **84** 212
Abiah **114** 120
Abigail **55** 260 **56** 265 269
57 257 **65** l **72** 287 **77**
lxxx **82** 280 **89** 11 **125**
221 **136** 333
Abigail (Robinson)
84 212
Abijah **137** 219
Abner **86** 146 152 312
Achsah (Sawyer) **125** 289
Agatha (Bryant) **110** 309
Alanson **123** 303
Albert **62** 113
Albert Guy (Mrs.) **86** 197
Alexander **97** 183
Alfred **144** 100
Alice **109** 146
Almira Jane **123** 303
Amos **53** 434
Anfel **89** 206
Ann **126** 64
Ann C. **68** 245
Ann Maria **101** 164
Anna **101** 94 **136** 318
Anna (Turner) **134** 141
Anna Dickson **82** 236
Anne **60** 245 **72** 287
Arthur Leslie **84** 172 **85**
186 **97** 183 **98** 149
Bathsheba **78** 89
Bathsheba (Sproat)
141 211
Bertha A. **83** 428 433
Bethiah **136** 25
Bethuel **90** 57
Betsey **101** 94 **123** 307 308
126 204
Betty **72** 287
C. P. **116** 237
Caleb **72** 287 **89** 12
Caroline (Jones) **89** 12
Caroline M. **113** 253
Cassandra **142** 73
Charles Alexander (Mrs.)
81 364 **82** 236 **108** 62

KEITH cont'd
140
Charles C. **81** 364 **82** 229
Charles Leslie **97** 149
Charles P. **100** 132
Charles Penrose **117** 251
Charlotte (Lazell) **89** 12
Charlotte Amelia **89** 67
Charlotte Belle (Emerson)
108 306
Chester **80** 35
Christianna (Farfar)
97 183
Clarissa **86** 146
Clayton **71** 95
Collins **138** 124
Cyrus **141** 211
Cyrus R. **144** 100
Damaris Williams
66 lxviii
Daniel **56** 147 **57** 255 **126**
115 116
Daniel G. **68** 199
Deborah **57** 52 **77** lxxix
lxxx **111** 116 **126** 145
Deborah A. **88** 342
Duffina **117** 239
Duncan **65** 235
Ebenezer **88** 316
Edith M. **96** 132
Edson **62** liii
Edward **73** 217
Eileen (Rutherford)
117 129
Eleazer **72** 287
Elizabeth **79** 272 **101** 94
Elizabeth (Fobes) **136**
309 318 333
Elizabeth (Irwin) **97** 183
Elizabeth P. (Paine) **90** 57
Elmer Davenport **81** 477
82 100
Emma (Goodnow)
117 165
Ephraim **89** 37 **99** 79 **121**
247 **130** 236
Esther M. **101** 94
Eunice **55** 61 396
Eunice (Barton) **84** 410
Eunice (Benson) **86** 146
Evelyn Reed **96** 160
Frances (Potter) **125** 241
Francis G. **125** 241
George **54** 425 **79** 54 271
272 **111** 269
George Evitts **123** 303
Gerrard **73** 142
Gershom **130** 137
Grindal **55** 61 **84** 410
Hannah **57** 285 **89** 206
136 312
Hannah (Briggs) **125** 274
Hannah (Fobes) **136** 312
Hannah (Perry) **116** 202
Hannah Maria **81** 192
Hannah Thayer **81** 192
Harriet **138** 124
Harriet A. (Colgrove)
109 173 269
Helen Kenyon (Benchley)
142 281

KEITH *cont'd*
Henry **97** 183
Hepzibah (Perkins)
(Carver) **88** 316
Holman **72** 287
Horace Alden **68** xxxiv
90 128
Howard **117** 129
Huldah **65** 307
Huldah (Waid) **86** 152 312
Ichabod **53** 434 **65** 381
72 287
Isaac **72** 287
Isaac Newton **101** 94
Isaiah **51** 292
Israel **57** 52 **126** 225 **140**
160 324
James **55** 439 **56** 142 **57**
52 151 **64** lxviii 113 328
65 307 **72** 286 **77** lxxix
81 64 **93** 397 **94** 241
100 63 **109** 173 269 **118**
170
James Drances **89** 12
James G. **125** 241
Jane **72** 287 **123** 51 305
Jane (Faunce) (Finney)
114 120
Jared **89** 67
Jeremiah **110** 309
John **55** 260 **56** 141 142 144
146-148 265 269 **57** 151
153 253 255-257 **60** 245
65 148 **97** 183 **98** 105
112 291 **118** 170 **125**
274
John A. (Mrs.) **114** 190
John Lawson **97** 183
John Quincy **72** 287
Jonathan **97** 183
Joseph **72** 286 287 **118** 170
134 141 **136** 309 318
333
Joseph I. **125** 289
Josiah **118** 170 **123** 48 92
93 303 312 313
Julia **80** 35
Kinsley **101** 94
Lorrania **123** 303
Louisa **77** lxxix
Lucius **86** 146
Lucy **79** 271 272 **126** 144
Luke **89** 206
Luther **101** 94
Lydia **53** 434
Lydia (Nichols) **127** 179
Lydia (Richardson)
100 132
Lydia (Wyer) **106** 138 148
Lymus **127** 8
Mabelle Harding
(Homerick) **97** 183
Margaret **118** 170
Margaret (Harned)
97 183
Margaret C. **113** 253
Margaret Elizabeth
95 180
Maria **79** 271 272
Martha (Conant) **136** 119
Mary **55** 392 **57** 52 **64**

KEITH *cont'd*
lxviii 190 **72** 287 **77**
lxxix **85** 437 **94** 245 **118**
170 **126** 115 **136** 309
147 126
Mary (Smith) **130** 236
Mary (Taylor) **125** 220
Mary A. **86** 146
Mary Albertina Leland
92 145
Mary Ann **78** 401
Mary Ann (Meloney)
125 292
Mary Ann (Robertson)
97 183
Mary F. **81** 301
Mary R. **144** 100
Merton S. **54** 454
Minerva **123** 303
Mitchell **89** 12
Molly **126** 115
Nabby **72** 287
Nancy A. **109** 269
Nancy Teresa (Perry)
116 204
Naomi **131** 195
Nathaniel **125** 292
Oren **116** 202
Pamelia **90** 171
Paul **84** 332
Persis (Cole) (Somers)
86 146
Phineas **128** 59
Polly **51** 292 **102** 301
Priscilla Winship
(Whiston) **88** 281
Rachel **89** 12
Rebecca **73** 153 **77** lxxx
136 318
Rhoda **56** 146 148 269 **57**
253 256
Robert **113** 253 **117** 129
127 144
Robert Swan **81** 192
Roxana **128** 281
Royal **77** lxxix lxxx
Ruby (Inlow) **117** 129
Ruth **123** 48 303
Salome (Lazell) **89** 12
Samantha **84** 222
Samuel **118** 170
Sarah **53** 434 **72** 286 287 **89**
37 **91** 239
Sarah (Washburn) **89** 37
Scott **84** 212
Seth **72** 287
Sherman L. **109** 269
Simeon **77** lxxx **126** 115
Sophronia **116** 259
Stephen **79** 55 **123** 303
125 220
Stillman Otis **62** 213
Susan **81** 477 **82** 100
Susan Hardwick
(Lawson) **97** 183
Susanna **72** 286 287 **77**
lxxix **99** 73 **110** 309 **118**
170 **123** 59
Susanna (Field) **134** 141
Susanna (Mitchell) **89** 12
Susanna R. **101** 94

KEITH *cont'd*
Sylvia **51** 440 **72** 287
Thankful **72** 287
Thomas Mitchell **89** 12
Timothy **106** 148 **118** 170
136 312
William **72** 287 **88** 281
101 94 **133** 180 **140** 237
William Fuller **116** 204
William H. **101** 94
William P. **117** 165
William R. **79** 56
William T. **123** 94 307 308
Zenas **72** 287
Zephaniah **136** 119
KEITON Hannah (Welch)
115 217
William **115** 217
KEITT Carol Seaver (Keay)
96 83
George Wanamaker
(Mrs.) **96** 83
KEIZER Hannah **51** 176
KELANI Keola-o Hilo
(Prince of) **94** 195
KELAY
Ann (Coburne) **88** 3
John **88** 282
KELBY Margaret **53** 150
151 **77** 231
Mary V. **53** 151
Robert Hendre **60** 218
Thomas **53** 150 151
William **53** 150 151 269
70 265 **72** 250
Kelcey *see* Kelcy
KELCHER
Lina Nichols **77** 187
William Edwin **77** 187
KELCY Kelcey - *see also*
Kelsey
—— **105** 288
Eleanor Jennet **105** 223
Freelove **66** 229
Keturah **66** 229
Nathaniel **66** 229
Susan **66** 229
KELDAR George **61** 42
James **61** 42
KELGREN —— **65** lvi
KELHAM Mary **125** 108
Rebecca (Frost) **86** 65
KELKE
Christopher **111** 200
Elizabeth **148** 117
Johanna **111** 200
Sisly **95** 9
William **95** 9
KELKER Henry **125** 164
KELL
Carl (Mrs.) **96** 394
Emma St. Lize (Sise) **83**
433 **84** 19
Hannah **134** 41
Marcia (Rudd) **96** 394
Mary Jane **99** 45
William H. **83** 433 **84** 19
KELLAHORN —— **70** 264
KELLAM Amasa **104** 76
Ellen O. **98** 130
George **98** 127

KELLAM *cont'd*
Mary (Cunningham)
125 217
Phineas **117** 252
Sarah (Sanford) **104** 76
Sarah Ann **98** 127
Sarah M. **98** 127
KELLAR Elizabeth
(Cummings) **124** 40
John **91** 55
Katharine **94** 165 166
Minerva (Hannum) **91** 55
William **124** 40
KELLAWAY
Mary **60** 286 287
KELLÉGAN
Catherine **125** 39
KELLEHER David **86** 89
Jane (Silvester) **86** 89
John **86** 89
William **86** 89
KELLEN
Ella F. **81** 345
William Vail **52** 283
91 219
William Vail (Mrs.)
81 345
KELLER —— **95** 405
Carl Tilden **57** xxxv
Carl Tilden (Mrs.) **96** 160
Conrad **114** 193
Finley **87** 400
Frances E. **93** 272
Frederico Victorrio
Bonaparte (Mrs.)
100 111
George Meinhard (Mrs.)
99 147
Helen **54** 454 **103** 71
Henry **109** 15
Lillian Sophia **97** 158
Mabelle A. (Trask) **96** 330
Margaret **80** 207
Margaret (Westcott)
80 102 207
Margaret E. **112** 58
Marie **85** 295
Marion Virginia **86** 195
106 123
Mary Catherine **90** 346
Mary Young **87** 400
Merle Leiberum **84** 140
Orinda I. **77** 150
Owen Bullitt (Mrs.)
86 197
Peter Frederick **90** 47
Sarah (Mosher) **123** 239
Sarah (Vose) **90** 47
Theodore Christian (Mrs.)
83 249 **84** 189
William **84** 140
KELLERAN
Arthur F. **90** 91
Edward **60** 23
Julietta A. L. (Comery)
90 92
Mary (Norton) **90** 91
Mary Elizabeth **90** 92
William **90** 92
KELLERHOFER
—— **67** 101

KELLERMANN
Johann George **81** 290
Katharine Elizabeth
81 290
Oscar **81** 290
KELLESHULL
Richard de **109** 21
KELLET — Mr. **83** 119
**KELLEY alias OCHTER-
LONEY** —— **56** 190
KELLEY Killey - *see also*
Kelly
— Capt. **52** 230
— Mrs. **52** 231 **90** 83
A. L. **68** 209
Aaron **90** 291 **123** 67
Abbey Bates **100** 187
Abby (Barber) **90** 106
Abby Eliza **81** 37
Abiah **68** 255
Abiel **87** 206
Abigail **65** 355 **66** 136
67 282
Abigail (Tibbetts)
(Caldwell) **100** 40
Abigail Townsend **81** 37
Abra **76** 28
Abraham **59** 302
Adeline **81** 301
Agnes **97** 73
Albert B. **125** 160
Albert L. **78** 334
Albert Livingston **76** xlv
Alberta English **92** 41
Alexander **73** 131 **74** 24
79 42
Alfred **69** 209 210
Alice (Williams) **85** 91
Allen **100** 187 281
Amanda **76** xlvi
Amos **127** 97 **133** 230
Amy **119** 101
Amy (Harper) **96** 130
Ann **83** 205
Ann H. (Allen) **116** 257
Anna **55** lxiii 347 **73** 77
77 181 **125** 11
Anna (Chase) **87** 318
Anna J. **55** lxiv
Anne **77** 182
Anne Louise **97** 85
Anthony **87** 18 318
Arthur Willard **65** xxxvi
81 110 **90** 126 293 **92**
137 **94** 127 143 196
Asa **87** 318
Augusta Lewis
(Maverick) **102** 167
Barnabas **101** 218 **102** 291
Bathsheba **59** 207 303 308
Bathsheba (Crocker)
130 288
Benjamin **67** 275 **82** 211
104 117
Benjamin Franklin
90 291 292
Betsey (Batchelder)
135 159
Betsey (Tibbetts) **98** 295
Betsey Adams (Gifford)
137 152

KELLEY *cont'd*
Betty **121** 128
Bridget **89** 179
Caroline **76** xlv **78** 334
Carrie E. (De Kalb)
83 427 433
Catherine **117** 256 **130** 289
Catherine Van Allen
73 131
Charles **61** 347 **91** 327
Charles E. **92** 333
Charles N. **61** 345
Christopher **55** 391
116 309
Clarissa **66** 136
Clarissa Goves **145** 307
Clementine **77** 181
Content (Colby) **125** 112
Cook C. **110** 149
Daniel **55** 67 **66** 136 67
282 **104** 117 292 **127**
165 166
Daniel C. **67** 282
Darby **125** 96
David **97** 85 **113** 143 **130**
288 289
David Humiston **101**
109 110 **107** 279 287
110 38 40 **121** 28 232
233 **141** 92 94 **145** 268
Deborah (Page) **125** 112
Deborah (Stiles) **98** 295
Delphia **87** 18
Dennis **123** 88 89
Dennis Francis **89** 132
Derby **79** 46
Didamia (Chase) **87** 318
Donna Clara **113** 143
Dora (Carey) **96** 130
Dora J. **78** 321
Dorcas (Chase) **87** 316
Dorothy **93** 348
Dorothy (Colby) **125** 112
Dorothy Jean **96** 130
Dudley **135** 159
Duncan **52** 233
E. **102** 199
Ebenezer **98** 295
Edith **111** 128
Edith (Chase) **87** 317
Edmond **79** 71
Edna Watson **88** 141
Edward **66** 146 **96** 327
Edward A. **76** xlvi **83** 203
Edward F. **91** 327
Edward Frazee **92** 41
Eleanor (Foster) **103** 308
Eleazer **87** 330
Elihu **87** 318
Elijah **87** 18
Eliza A. **104** 52
Eliza A. (Reeves) **125** 53
Eliza L. **82** 275
Eliza W. **90** 326
Elizabeth **55** lxiii **68** 255
88 359 **100** 295 **102** 26
291 **124** 227 **128** 210
130 289
Elizabeth (Bridges)
101 218
Elizabeth (Chase) **87** 132

KELLEY *cont'd*
Elizabeth (Doody)
 136 361
Elizabeth (Ellis) **121** 128
Elizabeth (Gifford)
 130 288
Elizabeth (Rosbotham)
 127 165
Elizabeth Canning
 79 133
Elizabeth E. **68** 155
Ellen **82** 176
Emeline **100** 187
Emerson Crosby **92** 399
Emma L. **55** lxiv
Erskine Hawes **93** 348
Ervin F. **83** 427 433
Eunice **96** 53 **107** 134
 116 257
Eunice Earle **93** 347
Eunice L. **74** 314
Ezro **102** 285
F. R. (Mrs.) **91** 183
Fannie M. (Banks) **90** 292
Fanny Fuller **79** 142
Fitzroy **59** xlvii **76** xxix
 xlv xlvi
Florence **102** 167
Frances P. **68** 204
Francis **90** 32
Francis Chase **94** 196
Frank **125** 150
George **68** 255 **91** 327
George H. **55** lxiv
George W. **88** 141
George Waldron **111** 49
Georgiana **105** 103
Gertrude **72** 309
Gorden **143** 260
Grace **61** 248
H. S. **105** 302 306
Hall **125** 293
Hall J. **126** 145
Hannah **66** 142 144 300
 67 277 **68** 167 **83** 490
 125 112 188 189 **130**
 289
Hannah (Burgess)
 102 199
Hannah (Colby) **125** 112
Hannah (Parker) **128** 209
Hannah H. **76** 28
Hannah Moore (Farrell)
 111 241
Hannah Saunders **96** 334
Happy (Chase) **87** 323
Harriet **108** 301
Harriet (Saunders) **96** 334
Harriet (Trussell) **123** 126
Harriet L. **142** 385
Hattie L. **124** 34
Hattie Maria **122** 231
Hattie **68** 167
Helen **69** 209
Helen Augusta (Leeds)
 (Durrell) **133** 283
Henrietta Maria **55** lxiii
Henry C. **116** 257
Hepsibah (Chase) **87** 318
Herbert Laurence **78** 191
 79 202

KELLEY *cont'd*
Herman Alfred **52** 396
Holdrich **67** 277
Holdridg **73** 63
Hugh **61** 347
Ida A. **92** 172
Isaac **90** 327 **98** 135
Israel Webster **76** xlv
J. Frederick **102** 318
James **73** 67 **90** 37 107 **98**
 295 **125** 112 223 **126**
 156
James Blinn **85** 91
James D. **78** 321
James E. **52** 484
James Edward **76** ix xxii
 90 291 **91** 57 148 **107**
 127 130
James R. **104** 96
James Templeton **66** lii
Jane **59** 308 **69** 210 **72** 176
 73 221 **74** 18
Jane Page **110** 145
Janet Baldwin (English)
 92 41
Jay **93** 347
Jean **52** 233
Jeffry **69** 362
Joanna **51** 176 **66** 146
John **71** 81 164 280 **72** 39
 76 xlv 270 **81** 145 **87** 266
 88 282 **94** 196 **96** 334
 100 40 187 **101** 218 **111**
 240 **124** 34 287 292 293
 303 **125** 53 112 **127** 165
 129 66
John D. **96** 130
John H. **133** 24
John Inzer **105** 128
John Raymond **110** 145
John Sarson **59** 207
John W. **85** 379 **145** 359
Joseph **52** 396 398 **57** 66
 59 206 **68** 255 **73** 74 **77**
 189 **87** 132 317 318 **91**
 264 **100** 186 187 **104**
 117 **124** 227 **127** 165
 166 **147** 330 333
Joseph H. **95** 93
Josephine **78** 321
Joshua **125** 112
Josiah **102** 291
Judith (Pease) **111** 241
Kate **73** 68
Katharine Pease **111** 240
Kathie Marie **122** 231
Katie **83** 423 433
Katie Maria **122** 70
Keith **104** 96
Kit **104** 96
L. F. **93** 107
Laura E. **110** 149
Lavina (Couillard) **90** 105
Lawrence **65** 235
Lawrence E. **93** 107
Lemuel **59** 205 207 303 308
Leroy Fenton **94** 138
Lilly **87** 317
Lois **67** 277
Lois (Sargent) **96** 53

KELLEY *cont'd*
Louisa P. (Adams)
 90 291 292
Love **66** 300
Lucia W. (Bearce) **95** 93
Lucinda (Pear) **91** 45
Lucy A. **81** 37
Lydia **68** 255 **104** 96 262
 125 294
Lydia (Pettingale)
 125 223
M. G. **91** 327
Marcia M. **72** 131
Maren **111** 116
Margaret **63** 276 **66** 300
 73 136 **74** 24 89
Margaret Anna **74** 24
Maria **66** 52
Maria Catherine **72** 309
Marinda **111** 138
Mark **61** 270
Marshel **125** 96
Martha **82** 284 291
Martha Perrin **104** 96
Mary **55** lxiii **61** 134 270
 346 **67** 277 **88** 13 17 106
 91 259 **97** 277 **100** 86
 113 81 **125** 217 **126** 144
Mary (Baldwin) **125** 290
Mary (Lackey) **113** 143
Mary (Starbuck) (Coffin)
 98 135
Mary A. **84** 52 126
Mary Ann (Kimball)
 125 160
Mary Anne **77** 184
Mary L. (White) **85** 379
Mary S. **133** 230
Mary Seymour **69** 210
Mary Upham **52** 97
Mary W. **104** 299
Matilda J. **124** 34
Max **96** 130
Mehitable (Wing) **127** 24
Melinda (Hopkins)
 104 52
Micajah **137** 152
Micha **126** 145
Michael **66** 34
Mindwell **71** 81
Minnie **81** 41
Minnie C. **92** 333
Miriam (Johnston)
 111 138
Morris **69** 295 296 **81** 37
Morris A. **81** 37
Moses **74** 18 **76** xlv **93** 347
Moses Gilbert **77** 184
N. S. **93** 107
Nancy **55** lxiii **90** 236 238
 104 117
Nancy (Hancock) **126** 67
Naomi **127** 97
Natenis **105** 128
Nathan Spaulding
 76 xlvi
Nelson **111** 138
Nicholas **102** 167
Nina (Dwinell) **83** 203
O. B. **91** 327
Oscar **68** 255

KELLEY *cont'd*
Patrick **87** 316 318 **121** 128
Paul Judge **96** 130
Perry (Bradlee) **126** 145
Peter **91** 327
Phebe **76** 270 **87** 317 326
    90 83
Phebe H. **91** 386
Rachel **125** 188 189
Rebecca **76** xlv **100** 187
Rebecca (Chase) **87** 318
Reynald **119** 18
Rhoda **87** 318
Richard **78** 397 **94** 196
Robert **59** 194 **66** 52
    104 52
Robert John **74** 24 89
Robinson **127** 17
Roger **61** 309 **67** 277 **69**
    360 362 **72** 39
Roland R. **77** 181
Rose **87** 111
Rosella **85** 378
Rosie Richer **104** 96
Roxanna **89** 310
Russell **121** 93
Ruth **127** 97
Ruth (Chase) (Studley)
    87 318
Sabrina **111** 128
Sally **100** 186
Salome **87** 327
Samuel **76** 28 **82** 211 284
    291 **87** 318 **90** 291 **92**
    318 **119** 22 **123** 67
Samuel B. **90** 105
Sarah **59** 206 **67** 282 **82** 211
    84 210 **97** 386 **123** 67
Sarah (Chase) **87** 330
Sarah (Emery) **91** 126
Sarah (Lovejoy) **97** 85
Sarah (Lovewell) **91** 264
    124 227
Sarah (Porter) **133** 230
Sarah (Stone) **90** 291
Sarah (Vickery) **90** 291
    292
Sarah B. **88** 141
Sarah Effie Vinton **119** 75
Sarah Elizabeth **77** 189
Sarson **59** 203
Sears **87** 323
Seth **92** 97 **93** 347 **127** 24
    130 288
Shaun (Mrs.) **85** 335
Sophia S. **68** 155
Stephen **94** 196 **96** 53
    123 126
Susan **81** 160 **88** 332
    124 34
Susan (Chase) **87** 327
Susan A. **83** 299 303
Susanna **66** 142 300 301
Susanna (Martin) (James)
    147 330-333 338 347
Temperance **87** 316 327
Thankful Baker **87** 79
Thomas **51** 352 **55** lxiii
    61 136 **74** 24 89 **82** 211
    87 316 **119** 20 **123** 67
    135 159

KELLEY *cont'd*
Thomas Henry **74** 24
Truman Lee (Mrs.) **86** 197
Virgil **68** 255
W. J. **104** 96
Waldo **93** 347
Walter Edward **90** 292
Washington **87** 327
Wilfred F. **92** 209
William **55** lxiii **72** 309
    73 276 **78** 420 **104** 96
    117 **125** 23 188
William A. **91** 126
William A. (Mrs.) **101** 326
William Farrington
    133 283
William H. **111** 128
William Henry **55** xli
    lxiii lxiv
William J. **122** 315
William P. **92** 97 **93** 347
William Robinson
    55 lxiii
Wyzeman **68** 155
KELLIHER
Laura Blaisdell **115** 155
Laurel Blaisdell **112** 161
    113 159
KELLING Hannah (Lynde)
    (Trerise) **143** 39
James **143** 39
Matthew **65** 33
KELLISON
William **71** 327
KELLOCH
Finley **87** 400
Mary **90** 90
Mary Young **87** 400
Polly **90** 90
KELLOCK Alice **51** 332
Allyn S. **51** 330 331
Anne Pamela (Pollard-
    Lowsley) **117** 200
Bridget **51** 330-332
Daniel **51** 330-332
Elijah **51** 362
Elisha **51** 362
Jason **51** 362
Jemima **51** 362
John **51** 362
Joseph **51** 362
Lucy **51** 362
Mary **51** 362
Pliny **51** 362
Rebecca **51** 362
Stephen **51** 362
Susan **51** 362
KELLOGG Kellog
—— **55** 37 **56** 324 **57** 113
    91 327 **97** 220 **105** 108
    118 16 217 232 **119** 53
    136 137 214 291 301 304
    120 126 133 203 207 208
    210 212-214 296 299 300
    122 64 115 117 118 120
    121
— Capt. **118** 230 233 **119**
    55 56 128 140 220 289
    298 306 **120** 57 58 61
    129 131 204 209 213
— Dr. **118** 109

KELLOGG *cont'd*
— Lieut. **118** 23 110
— Miss **58** 412
— Mr. **62** 267
— Mrs. **80** 61 **118** 116 299
    119 212 **120** 61 **123** 303
— Rev. Mr. **62** 275
Aaron **59** 98 **71** 86 **83** 503
    504
Abigail **53** 460 **59** 414 **60**
    263 **62** 267 **83** 364 **101**
    234
Abigail (Terry) **106** 145
Abigail Olmstead **59** 209
Abigail Shelding **118** 24
Abraham **72** 318 **73** 8
    118 122 **119** 220
Abram **72** 318
Achsah Bates **80** 273
Adeline **72** 131
Adosha **146** 359
Alexander **108** 42
Alfred E. **142** 385
Alfred Hosea **78** 281
Alfred St. Claire **67** xxv
    xxxiv
Alithea **60** 267
Allyn **60** 267 **83** 503 504
Allyn S. **83** 504 **120** 185
    142 381
Allyne **59** 97
Amanda **103** 144
Amanda Elizabeth
    78 280 281
Amos **122** 78 160
Amy Stoughton (Dickin-
    son) **92** 100
Ann **52** 271 **54** 82 **61** 33
Ann Janette (Stanley)
    106 145
Anna **60** 395 **62** 214 **72** 145
    318 **90** 276 **110** 142
Anna A. **91** 381
Anna A. (Pike) **91** 381
Anna E. **83** 504
Anna L. S. **83** 504
Anna M. **96** 92
Anne **83** 54
Annie **82** 379
Armida **75** 28
Asa **54** 82 **129** 50
Augustus P. **72** 131
Bela **79** 168
Bella **122** 119
Benjamin **73** 253 **84** 94
    122 306 **123** 16 17 19 25
    26 29 30
Bertha **78** 207
Beth **106** 145
Bethiah **72** 145
Betsey **60** 264
Beulah **116** 33
Branton H. (Mrs.) **81** 337
Bridget (Bouton) **92** 300
Calista **68** 257
Caroline **72** lvii
Caroline Lavinia **72** lvii
Carrie (Staines) **106** 145
Catalina Parker **99** 76
Catherine **99** 76 **123** 114
    117

KELLOGG *cont'd*
Catherine G. **72** 131
Catherine R. (Edmands)
  88 336
Charity **136** 80
Charles **52** 411 412 417
  56 162 **59** 416 **78** 280
  83 99 **91** 381 **120** 20
  129 50
Charles A. **91** 381
Charles C. **91** 30
Charles D. **62** xxxvii
  83 504
Charles Frederic **91** 381
Charles Harvey **126** 113
Charles M. **68** 98 **72** 131
Charles W. **83** 504
Charles Wetmore **63** 394
Charles Wetmore (Mrs.)
  94 138
Chauncey Seymour **73** 8
Chester **72** 145
Clara Augusta **91** 381
Clarissa L. **73** 8
Cora M. **69** 165
Cornelia F. **125** 53
Dale C. **110** 238 **121** 77
Dale Cosnett **99** 147
Daniel **57** 420 **58** 194 **60**
  75 **97** 300 **121** 95
Daniel G. **83** 504
David Sherwood **65** xliv
  lxv
Delia Sophia **108** 266
Delight **110** 32
Dora **82** 379
Dora Zink **85** 239 **88** 209
Dorothy **123** 114-117 278
  279 **126** 15
Dorothy (Bissell) **123**
  114 278 279
Dorothy (Chester)
  111 315
Douglas E. **112** 229
E. Frank **72** 74
Ebenezer **58** 193-196 401
  59 95-98 100 208 209
  412 414-416 **60** 73-75 77
  201 205 263 264 **62** 295
  78 301 **83** 364 504 **85** 50
Ebenezer Noble **59** 211
Edgar Romeyn (Mrs.)
  85 195
Edith **117** 118
Edward **122** 77 111 159
  319 **123** 114-116 278 279
  126 15
Edward P. **72** 131
Eleanor **86** 97 **123** 114 117
Elihu **101** 234
Elijah **54** 117 **78** 111 **86** 122
  122 78 160 319 **123** 48
  142 206 207
Elisha **86** 52 53
Eliza **59** 212 **60** 266 267
  83 504 **95** 188 **104** 231
Eliza A. **96** 92 **101** 234
Eliza Maria **112** 58
Eliza Nash **83** 504
Eliza Noble **83** 504
Eliza W. **83** 504

KELLOGG *cont'd*
Eliza White **83** 503
Elizabeth **52** 271 **58** 401 **59**
  98 208 412 **60** 201 267
  67 124 **78** 280 281 **83**
  208 364 **109** 188 **113** 30
  34 37 41 **123** 19
Elizabeth (Drury)
  (Prentiss) **126** 113
Elizabeth Hosmer **106** 67
Elizabeth Sackett **80** 273
Elizabeth Stafford **65** lxv
Ella Osborn (Davis)
  106 145
Emeline **72** 131
Emily **86** 52 **137** 282
Emily B. **85** 314
Emily Benton **80** 273
Emily Louisa **76** xxi **78**
  214 280 281 **79** 81 **80**
  231 **81** 62 **82** 54 **83** 8 **84**
  69 **85** 29 **86** 59 **87** 39 **88**
  6 **89** 9 **90** 103 **91** 6 **92**
  29 **93** 47 **94** 19 **95** 89 96
  58 **97** 147 **98** 90 **99** 70
  100 127 **101** 278 **102**
  196 197 **103** 20 240 **104**
  212 **105** 248 **106** 181
  108 313 **109** 107 **110**
  184 **111** 59 **113** 130 **111**
  114
Ephraim **123** 114 115 117
  126 15
Esther **78** 280 **120** 94 134
  301 **121** 60 99 **142** 374
Esther (Kimberly)
  102 110
Eudosia **72** 145
Eunice **58** 196 **60** 199 **89**
  324 **142** 207
Eveline Charlotte **65** lxv
Ezekiel **60** 395 **61** 33 **83** 54
  113 37-39
Ezra **91** 229
F. C. (Mrs.) **85** 239
Fanny **60** 215 **72** 145 204
  82 379 380 **129** 50
Fanny E. **82** 379
Ferris **135** 50
Florence **83** 504
Frances **120** 94
Frances F. **82** 379
Francis Asbury **80** 273
Francis F. **65** lxv
Frank Gibson (Mrs.) **82**
  236 252
Frederick **60** 215
Gardner **104** 117 **106** 146
  120 205 297 **121** 57 64
  95 **122** 302 **123** 25
George **59** 97 211 212 **60**
  266 **83** 504
George B. **61** lxiv **86** 53
George Washington
  73 8
Giles Crouch **116** 110
  123 32
Gustavus **86** 53
H. **72** 131
Hannah **58** 195 **59** 98 208
  415 **60** 80 205 264 302

KELLOGG *cont'd*
  72 318 **83** 364 **120** 28
  123 48 **127** 283
Hannah (Smith) **106** 146
Hannah Barnard **80** 273
Hannah E. **83** 504
Hannah E. Wright **83** 503
Harriet **82** 379 **85** 314
Hattie Maybelle **79** 278
Hazel Jeannette **120** 147
Henry **52** 271 **59** 98 **60** 266
  267
Henry Clay **78** 280 281
Horace **72** 145 205 318
  84 94
Horace Dryden **73** 8
Hosea **78** 280 281
Hosmer **72** lvii
Howard **82** 379
Howard C. **82** 379
Hubbard **59** 99 **83** 504
Hudson **59** 99
Huldah **56** 92
Isaac **72** 318 **73** 8 **101** 159
Isadore **82** 379
Jabez **70** 152
James H. **82** 379
James Knowles **80** 273
Jane D. **68** 199
Jeannette Eliza **80** 273
Jemima **111** 315 **118** 26
Jemima (Bartlett) **122** 77
  159 319
Jerusha **72** 318 **118** 117
Joanna **106** 145 **110** 66 **118**
  219 305 **123** 114 116
Joel **118** 116 118 119 124
  224 227 **119** 139 216 292
  295 297 299 300 303 **120**
  58 60 63 124 131 132 205
  295
Joel (Mrs.) **118** 217
John **60** 334 **72** 318 **80** 273
  92 100 **112** 287 **118** 115
John (Mrs.) **121** 94
John Azor **92** 100
John Harvey **106** 145
John L. **106** 145
John Preston **106** 145 146
Jonathan **85** 147
Jos. **71** 86
Joseph **53** 142 145 458 460
  54 460 **57** 420 **58** 379
  380 **72** 318 **73** 8 253 **80**
  327 **84** 94 **85** 314 **88** 107
  93 273 **106** 145 **112** 58
  123 114 116
Joseph H. **82** 379
Joseph Mitchell **82** 382
  83 212
Joseph S. **92** 282
Josiah **106** 146 **121** 94
  123 17 19 21 22 24 27 29
Julia E. **82** 379
Julia Matilda **123** 303
Julia Selden **83** 504
Juliette **86** 53
Julius Conant **123** 303
Justin Perkins **52** 271 373
  53 142 358 458 460 **54**
  xxxviii 103 224 **55** xxix

KELLOGG *cont'd*
xxxiv 223 **84** 94
Karl H. **106** 145
Laura **73** 8 **109** 189
Leonard F. **82** 379
Louisa **142** 385
Louise Phelps **112** 14 88
Lovisa **71** 53 56
Lucia Hosmer (Andrews)
106 67
Lucy **73** 8 **110** 29 **119** 242
130 49
Lucy (Powell) **128** 80
Lucy C. **56** 323
Lucy Cutler **57** xxxiii 233
64 xxxi 95
Lucy Jane **64** 332
Lucy Mary **105** 128 **116** 83
135 152 **143** 63 **147** 263
265 **148** 259
Lydia **60** 398 **72** 105 145
73 9 **99** 125 **100** 166
116 43 **126** 15
Lydia (Sawtell) **126** 15
M. **72** 131
Mabel **60** 205
Margaret **83** 504
Margaret B. **83** 504
Maria **60** 266 **73** 8
Maria Ann **110** 142
Maria D. **99** 76
Maria L. Avery **83** 504
Marion Chedell **83** 504
Martha (Allis)
(Hammond) **106** 146
Martha A. **80** 273
Martin **52** 271 **57** 338 420
59 96 **60** 75 266 **73** 8 **78**
280 **83** 364 504 **110** 238
111 315 **112** 229 **113**
229 **129** 50
Martin Van Buren **79** 278
Mary **52** 271 **59** 329 **60** 263
72 204 **101** 234 **122** 117
123 22 114 117
Mary (Bartlett) **105** 108
Mary (Chase) **88** 107
Mary (Drake) **123** 278
Mary (Niles) **85** 147
Mary A. **72** 74
Mary Ann **73** 8
Mary B. **73** 8
Mary Elizabeth **86** 97
Mary Hubbard **83** 504
Mary J. **68** 98
Mary P. (Brumley)
142 385
Mary Potter **80** 273
Medad **72** 145
Meriam **118** 119
Merron **73** 8
Minnie **71** xxiv
Mirah **123** 29
Moses **84** 94 **101** 234 **118**
22 24 29 108 113 115 116
124 222 **119** 140 209
120 63 **123** 31 32
Nathaniel **52** 271 **53** 460
57 338 420 **78** 280 **80**
273 **84** 94 **106** 145 **122**
122 221 **123** 23-27 **129**

KELLOGG *cont'd*
50
Nathaniel Olmstead **59**
98 **60** 267 **83** 504
Nelson **65** lxv
Nicholas **78** 280
Norman **82** 379
Olive **73** 8 **78** 350 **144** 195
Olive C. **123** 306
Orinda **60** 75 **83** 364
Orpah **72** 318
Orsamus **102** 110
Paul Merrill (Mrs.) **116** 71
Philinda **54** 354
Philippe **78** 280
Polly **72** 145 **119** 140 213
122 117 **129** 50
Porter **72** 204
Preserved **122** 78 160 319
Prudence **78** 280 **80** 272
Rachel **60** 334 **83** 53 54
Ralph **73** 8
Ralph Phineas **73** 8
Rebecca **73** 8
Rebecca (Turner) **101** 260
Rebecca Dora Leona
Leotta **82** 236
Reuben **90** 32 **101** 234
Rhoda **72** 314 318
Rhoda E. **82** 379
Richard **52** 271 **123** 29
Robert **52** 271
Robert D. **65** lxv
Roxana (Mattoon) **92** 100
Russell **52** 412 **78** 280
Ruth Mary **81** 337
Sally **113** 34 38
Samuel **57** 420 **60** 302 **72**
318 **73** 8 **78** 280 **99** 76
113 34 39 **145** 335
Samuel B. **99** 76
Sarah **52** 417 **54** 83 **56** 352
60 302 **72** 318 **73** 8 253
78 280 **80** 273 327 **92**
300 **97** 386 **112** 58 **117**
266 **118** 127 **119** 220
123 22 25 **125** 54 **142**
382 **145** 335
Sarah (Boltwood) **106** 145
Sarah (Horton) **118** 135
Sarah (Preston) **106** 146
Sarah (Root) **145** 335
Sarah O. **57** 80
Sarah V. **112** 58
Sheldon **59** 100 416 **83** 364
Sheldon Ingalls **88** 336
Shilomith **109** 263
Shirley **72** 105
Sibyl **114** 207
Sibyl Woodbury **53** 460
Silas **73** 253 **112** 58
Solomon **101** 260
Sophia **72** 145
Sophia C. (Carll) **91** 30
Stephen Wright **106** 67
Steven **55** 343
Stillman **53** 460
Submit **123** 48
Susan **108** 271
Susan Coit **83** 504
Susanna **70** 152

KELLOGG *cont'd*
Sylvester **123** 17
Thankful (Chapin)
106 146
Theodosia **114** 313
Thomas **78** 280 **123** 114
115 117
Thomas Donald **117** 200
Thomas W. **59** 98 99 208
60 263 **83** 504
Thomas Wright **58** 196
Tirzah **72** 145
Truman **82** 380 **135** 50
Tryphena Ely **60** 215
Virgil **72** 318
Waitstill **123** 310
Warren **72** 318
Will Keith **80** 103 206
106 62 129 145 146
William S. **83** 504
KELLON John **91** 327
KELLOND Abigail **55** 378
102 185
Susanna **55** 378
Thomas **55** 378 **102** 185
KELLOW William **114** 190
KELLOWAY
Anna **77** 73 132
Margaret **56** 378
Mary **56** 378 **83** 466 467
106 19
Melcas **56** 378
Milcha **83** 467
Walter **56** 378
William **77** 73 132
Kellso *see* Kelso
KELLUM Amanda **69** 266
Edward Martin **119** 319
Ellen O. **98** 130
Elsie Reamer **74** 310
Ephraim **73** 104
James **136** 166
John **119** 319
Joshua **73** 104
Lewis **136** 166
Margaret (Dutton)
136 166
KELLWAY
Dorothea **138** 9
Edward **138** 9
KELLY Killy - *see also*
Kelley
—— **60** 220
Addi **134** 173
Agnes **97** 73
Albert Livingston
62 lxxi
Andrew **140** 160
Anna **106** 183
Anna (Kenniston)
134 173
Anner **106** 183
Annie Newhall **134** 277
Antoinette (Cole) **103** 308
Asenatha Angell **128** 189
B. **64** 111
Benjamin **106** 183 **134** 173
Betsey **58** 60
Betsey L. **114** 180
Beulah **132** 75
Bradley **138** 116

KELLY *cont'd*
Caroline **62** lxxi
Caty **134** 173
Charles Warren **134** 277
Charlotte **103** 239
Clarissa **58** 61
Daniel **56** 91 **58** 43 44 **70**
　263 **134** 173 **138** 117
David **62** 79
Delphia **87** 18
Edward **62** 252 **64** 20
Edward Albert **62** xlix
　lxxi lxxii
Eleazer **134** 330
Eliza **126** 65
Eliza Chase **134** 277
Elizabeth **58** 363 **100** 295
　108 261
Elizabeth (Crowell)
　128 210
Elizabeth (Emery) **94** 196
Elizabeth (Killy) **108** 261
Elizabeth Farley **62** lxxii
Emma B. (Leavitt) **120** 224
Emma Mathis **99** 167
Esther **134** 173
Eunice (Sargent) **94** 196
Fletcher Wyman **134** 277
Francis **60** 240
Fred **134** 277
George W. **134** 173
Georgiana **105** 103
Grace **58** 56
Hannah **58** 56 **60** 95 **62**
　lxxi **114** 129 **115** 29 **144**
　348 354
Hannah (Bartlett) **94** 196
Hannah M. **62** lxv
Hannah Reed **80** 52
Harriet P. **80** 52
Henry **143** 257
Hugh **60** 348
Isaac **103** 308
Isaac Amsden **58** 60
Isabella (Woods) **134** 277
Israel Webster **62** lxxi
Jacob **58** 45
James **60** 25 **64** 319 **114**
　186 **134** 173
Jane P. **110** 145
Jedidah (Wing) (Chase)
　87 316
Jeremiah **56** 22 **118** 57
　134 330
Jesse **103** 308
Joel **58** 57
John **54** 235 **56** 180 **58** 56
　57 60 61 **60** 160 **62** lxxi
　52 **99** 9 **128** 210
John H. **120** 224
Jonah **118** 301
Jonathan **134** 276 277
Joseph **80** 52 **134** 173
Judith Webb (Jeffry)
　126 156
Julia (Holmes) **126** 156
Kenneth L. **120** 155
Lakey **64** 217
Lemuel **53** 102 104
Levi **134** 173
Lois (Sargent) **94** 196

KELLY *cont'd*
Lucinda (Pear) **91** 45
Lucretia **54** cvii
Lydia **58** 45 **60** 55 **62** lxxi
Marcella Lucy (Brown)
　94 196
Margaret **60** 348
Marie (McCollum)
　110 145
Martha **106** 183
Mary **58** 43 44 **60** 55 **62** 79
　100 86 **140** 68
Mary (Ferris) **101** 218
Mary (Gilpatrick) **90** 327
Mary (Linsley) **123** 89
Mary Adams **62** lxxii
Mary Jane **112** 239
Moses **62** lxxi
Nancy **90** 236 238
Patrick **114** 186
Patty **58** 56
Phebe **134** 330
Phebe (Atkinson) **126** 145
Philip **70** 263
Polly **58** 60 363
Rebecca **56** 91 **62** lxxi
Relief **58** 60
Resign **58** 56
Richard **103** 192 **115** 29
Robert **62** lxxi **112** 269
Rose **87** 111
Roxanna **89** 310
Ruth **56** 172
Samuel **56** 225
Sarah **58** 30 **97** 386 **118** 329
Sarah (Chase) **134** 330
Sarah (Knight) **94** 196
Serena Amanda (Durrell)
　134 276 277
Stephen **145** 361
Susanna **106** 183
Sylvanus **128** 209
Thankful **109** 40
Thomas **103** 189
Timothy **103** 239
William **58** 44 **60** 55 163
William H. **99** 8
KELM Mary (Martin)
　125 103
Robert **125** 103
KELNAY Robert **139** 231
KELSDEN Joan **67** 36
KELSEY Kelsea
　—— **53** 379 **62** 360 391
　71 305 **85** 166 **98** 136
—— Mr. **71** 119
—— Mrs. **72** 179
Aaron **72** 307
Abigail **52** 467 **100** 173
　135 298
Abigail (Wheaton)
　108 275
Abigail Marion
　(Burleson) **116** 281 282
　118 315
Absalom **57** 90 **141** 113
Agnes **59** 284
Almira **63** 379
Andrew **109** 173 269
Andrew J. **65** 134

KELSEY *cont'd*
Ann Elizabeth (Chase)
　88 15
Anna **58** 359 **100** 173 275
Anna (Brown) **100** 173
Antoinette Cecilia **74** 299
　85 430
Asa **100** 173
Benjamin **65** 125 **141** 112
Bethiah (Hopkins)
　112 164
Betsey **57** 92 **67** 278 **90** 241
Betty **61** 388
Bridget (Williams)
　(Demeritt) **98** 136
C. R. **56** 323
Carrie (Cronk) **109** 173
　269
Charity **58** 359
Charles **88** 15
Charles C. **95** 317
Charles Edwin **116** 281
Charles T. **125** 53
Charlotte **145** 41
Clarence Eugene **85** 195
Clarence Hill **84** 111
Clarissa **56** 263
Cornelia **126** 307
D. S. **91** 327
Damaris **71** 270
Daniel **57** 201 **70** 15 142
　304
Daniel D. **109** 269 271 274
E. I. **103** 157
E. Jane (Toles) **109** 269 274
Earl Leland **141** 112
Edward **65** 133
Edwin **65** 134
Eleanor Jennet **105** 222
Eliza **95** 188
Elizabeth **56** 259 318 363
　59 45 **95** 307 **99** 267
　127 199 **136** 309
Elizabeth (Hammond)
　112 164
Elizabeth (Maskell) **148**
　232 234
Elizabeth Gardiner
　101 66
Ellen **72** 307
Emeline **111** 305
Ephraim **57** 92
Erastus Spencer **101** 66
Esther **72** 264
Eunice **91** 46 **123** 301
　146 376
Fanny Spencer **85** 166
Florence **85** 100
Francis **62** 178
G. P. **148** 285
Gamaliel **127** 199-201
　135 298
George **112** 164
George B. **92** 169
George S. **65** 134
George W. **101** 216
Giles **80** 150 **141** 113
Grace **109** 269
Hannah **53** 210 **56** 359 **62**
　178 **72** 307
Hannah (Andrus) **145** 41

KELSEY *cont'd*
Harriet **115** 30
Helen M. **83** 371
Helen Marian **84** 189
Hepsibah (Bellows)
  115 30
Hester **71** 278
Hezekiah **72** 174 180
I. M. **76** 50
Ira **115** 30
Isaac **53** 210
James **56** 318 **100** 173 **108**
  275 **118** 232
James Alexander **126** 307
James H. **90** 241
Jane **56** 361 **142** 281
Jane Porter **85** 166
Jeremiah **115** 30 **141** 111-
  113 **147** 54
Job **62** 176
Joel **70** 146
John **55** 152 **57** 201 264
  69 121 217 221 296-298
  302 **70** 9-11 13 16-18 21
  22 139-142 146 214 219
  303 306 **81** 31 **90** 231
  241 248 **126** 307 **148**
  351
John Henry **65** 134
John Henry (Mrs.) **87** 174
Jonas **118** 232 298
Joseph **148** 349 356 358
Julia **109** 308
Katharine McKinlay **67**
  xxxiv **90** 127
LaGrand **111** 128
Lois **78** 241 **141** 113
Lorenzo **74** 299
Lucinda **70** 141
Lucy **70** 145 **72** 5
Lydia **54** 48 **62** 367 **72** 102
  100 173
Marcy **57** 90
Margaret (Morris) **147** 54
Margaret Parsons **101** 66
Mark **112** 164
Martha **57** 201 **69** 121
  81 31
Martha (Townsend)
  125 53
Martin **91** 46
Mary **55** 152 **57** 201 **59**
  283 284 **90** 241 **100** 276
  115 30
Mary (Gray) **135** 298
Mary A. (Pope) **109** 269
  271
Mary Ann **72** 296
Mary E. **65** 134
Mary Ella (Swan) **101** 216
Mary Eunice **91** 46
Mehitable **62** 239
Mercy (Denison) **127** 199
Mercy (Evans) **148** 349-
  351
Minnie L. (Church) **111**
  124 128
Molly **81** 31
Molly (Roberts) **90** 231
  248
Moses **59** 283 **145** 41

KELSEY *cont'd*
Myra Agnes **98** 348 349
Myrta B. **109** 269
Nathan **56** 359 **65** 134
Oliver **72** 102
Oliver H. **65** 134
Orphana **65** 133
Patience **134** 123
Phebe **119** 80
Polly **59** 285 287 **70** 18
Polly (Goodwin) **115** 30
Preston **56** 263
Preston Telford (Mrs.)
  84 109 189
Priscilla **100** 276
Rebecca (Hoskins)
  112 164
Rhoda (Dye) **100** 173
Robert **59** 285 **100** 173 **118**
  36 **125** 93
Roswell **100** 173 **115** 30
  141 113
Roxana **80** 150
Ruth **112** 141 **141** 113
S. L. **111** 124
Sally **61** 243 **100** 173
Samuel **61** 388
Sarah **57** 201 **88** 312 **109**
  269 270
Sarah Reynolds **143** 54
Silas **100** 173
Silas L. **111** 128
Solomon **100** 173
Sophia **74** 299
Stephen **123** 301
Stephen Tomlinson **84**
  185 **117** 71
Susanna **56** 161 **90** 241
Tamer **61** 30
Temperance **55** 33
Thankful **55** 152
Thomas **148** 232 234
Thomas B. **85** 166
Thomas Olmstead **85** 166
Tryphena **71** 281
Vienna **100** 173
Will **70** 305
Willard **115** 30
William **59** 45 **71** 281 **98**
  349 **100** 275 276 **108**
  152 **111** 128 **112** 164
  141 112 **145** 323 **146**
  376
William Sylvester **101** 66
William Sylvester (Mrs.)
  100 103 **101** 65 66 129
Zachariah **72** 177
KELSO Kellso
—— **56** 210
— Mr. **65** 89
Andrew Foster **112** 237
Cora **97** 219
Henry **112** 291
Homer H. **91** 36
James **97** 219 **103** 63
Louise (Nye) **113** 249
Margaret **89** 232 **125** 104
Mari (Hannum) **91** 36
Patience (Bancroft) **97** 219
  103 63
Sarah **125** 105

KELSO *cont'd*
W. **56** 111
Kelssey *see* Kelsey
KELT Agnes **88** 341
James **88** 279
John **91** 327
Nancy (Stivart) **88** 279
KELTIE
Dorothy May **86** 450
George Ross **86** 450
John **86** 450
John Ross **86** 450
John Ross (Mrs.) **85** 195
  86 450 **87** 71 179
Katharine (Ross) **86** 450
Louise May (Potter)
  86 450
Ralph **86** 450
Ralph John **86** 450
KELTON
Adelaide **104** 140
Barnard **79** 246
Catherine **72** 273
Dorothy **78** 130
Dwight H. **63** 154
Edith R. Wills **67** xxxi
Edward **75** 154
Elock **58** 142
Enos **78** 130
Frances (Travelstead)
  130 156
Jane **71** 22 23 244 **75** 154
John Cunningham
  102 302
John Cunningham Rus-
  sell **83** 257
Lydia A. **79** 34
Margaretta Nataline
  102 302
Mary **75** 154 **79** 41
Mehitable **79** 246
Molly **56** 36
Pauline **130** 156
Richard **71** 22 244
Samuel **56** 36 **72** 273
  130 156
Sarah **75** 34
Sarah F. **77** 184
Thomas W. **77** 184
Travelstead **130** 156
KELTY Amelia **91** 40
KELVEDON Jane **98** 275
William **98** 275
KELVIN — Lord **58** 93
KEMANSON
Margery **101** 7
Kemball *see* Kimball
KEMBER Robert **84** 281
KEMBLE *see also* Kimball
—— **53** 150
Abigail **143** 38
Abigail (Bumstead)
  140 47
Elizabeth **124** 166 **143** 38
Elizabeth (Trerise) **143**
  37 38
Fanny **89** 162
John **89** 162 **143** 38
John R. **59** 105
Martha (Prince) **114** 185
Mary **87** 301 **128** 119

KEMBLE *cont'd*
Rebecca **143** 38
Sarah **84** 402 **124** 166 **143**
  37 38 364
T. H. **140** 47
Thomas **56** 188 **84** 402 **124**
  166 167 **143** 34 35 38
KEMBLIN
Aralin / Araten **91** 327
KEME
William **53** 223 224
KEMER Margaret **66** 258
KEMEYS Jenkin **51** 211
KEMGS Samuel **65** 20
KEMLIN Eleazer **54** 225
KEMLO William **90** 109
KEMMERER
Mary Magdalene
  110 224
KEMP Kempe
—— **51** 419 **52** 261 **59** 338
  60 212 **62** 74 387 **70** 220
— Mr. **52** 266
— Rev. **108** 232
Abigail **62** 159 **64** 209
  131 154
Abizer **121** 314
Albert S. **57** 201
Alvira **82** 172
Amy **52** 262
Ann **66** 358
Annabelle **119** 317
Asa **90** 50
Bartholomew **57** 316
Benjamin **64** 151
Betsey **72** 151 152
Biron **62** 266
Caleb **94** 101
Charity **88** 377
Daniel **121** 314
David **126** 129
Delbert Clinton (Mrs.)
  103 119
Dorothy Sims **108** 134
Ebenezer **104** 206 **145** 45
Edward **52** 262 266 **73** 317
  74 xxiv **81** 109 229 **82**
  103 104 219 **83** 229 **94**
  84 141
Edwin Augustine **75** 39
Edwin C. **104** 171
Effie **84** 133
Elijah **145** 45
Eliza (Bell) **98** 266
Elizabeth **52** 262 **57** 416
  417 **67** 201 **126** 132
Elizabeth (Kezar) **133** 321
Ellen Elizabeth **109** 73
Emma **56** 172
Esther **61** 168
Esther M. **75** 39
Eunice **126** 132
Flora (Clifford) **98** 266
Frances **52** 262 268 **65**
  288 318 **78** 274
Francis **52** 262 266 267
  78 274
Furber **125** 294
G. Austin (Mrs.) **113** 307
G. Ward **93** 400
George **77** 236 **82** 103

KEMP *cont'd*
100 98
George Edward **93** 400
Hannah **63** 300 **121** 314
Hannah (Kendall)
  125 294
Hannah (Sawtell) **126** 129
Hannah (Snow) **121** 313
Harriet E. **76** 7
Henry Morton **82** 172
Herbert Thomas **82** 172
Horace **98** 266
James **73** 262 **121** 314
Jason **63** 300
Jerusha **64** 310
Jessie Isabel **75** 39
Joan **66** 358
John **52** 262 265 **66** 358
  77 264 **95** 6 7 **116** 168
  121 314 **126** 225 **145**
  115
Jonathan **145** 45
Josephine **82** 103
Laura **133** 24
Lawrence **52** 341 **75** 303
Louisa Elizabeth (Jones)
  82 103 **94** 84
Louise May **78** 205 **82** 219
  83 229 **94** 79 84 141
Lucretia **78** 182
Lucy **137** 76
Lucy Mabel **82** 172
Lydia **56** 169 172 **64** 151
  145 45
Mabel **54** 151
Margaret **82** 103 **86** 410
  87 370
Margaret (Traver) **94** 84
Martha **65** 288 316 318
Mary **52** 262 **83** 168 **112**
  241 **145** 45
Mary Ann (Underwood)
  90 50
Mary Nettie (Mason)
  113 307
Matthew **52** 244
Mehitable **52** 341 **126** 129
Minnie **77** 264
Molly **97** 292
Nancy **77** 229
Nevell **65** 288 289 316 318
Nicholas **82** 188
Olivey P. **88** 286
Pasco **88** 377
Patience **57** 417
Patience (Nutting)
  126 129
Phineas A. **72** 151
Rachel **52** 341 **62** 266
Rebecca **78** 67
Richard **94** 341
Robert **52** 262 266 **86** 424
  88 377
Roxana Angeline **82** 172
Ruth **61** 170
Ruth (Atwood) **84** 133
Samuel **126** 129 132
  133 321
Samuel Halliday **82** 172
Samuel Thomas **82** 172
Sarah **121** 314

KEMP *cont'd*
Sarah (Lacy) **126** 129
Silas **55** 391
Susan **52** 244
Thomas **52** 262 268 **66** 358
  84 133
Thomas Jay **145** 176
Timothy **121** 313 314
Tobias **88** 377
Van Horne **82** 103 104
Wesley Calhoun **118** 170
William **56** 172 **57** 416 417
  82 103 **90** 155 **94** 84 **95**
  259 **126** 129
William Sumner **76** xxii
  76 **98** 248 266 **99** 151
KEMPER
Caroline **86** 195
Clarence Barton (Mrs.)
  101 124
Edward S. **125** 35
John Mason **110** 309
Sidney A. **82** 384
Sylvia Mayo (Pratt)
  110 309
Walter Young (Mrs.) **83**
  249 **84** 189
William Winton **100** 111
KEMPSTON
Agnes **94** 277
Anne **94** 277
James **94** 277
KEMPTE Kempt
—— **82** 412
Amy **142** 265
KEMPTHORN
Mary (Longe) **104** 38
Simon **104** 38
KEMPTIE
Lieut. **84** 150
KEMPTON Kimpton
—— **78** 356 **123** 100
Abigail **56** 383 **127** 276
Abigail (Carver) **88** 316
Abigail (Millard) **127** 276
Amy (Mayor) **89** 242
Ann **128** 117
Betsey (Chase) **88** 110
Catherine **56** 321
Charles **105** 208
David **99** 62 **127** 193
  130 141
David Bacon **93** 186
David Snow **127** 208
Ebenezer **89** 242
Edward S. **125** 43
Edwin **72** 74
Elijah **56** 321
Eliza L. **126** 206
Elizabeth **56** 397 **86** 53 **97**
  294 **99** 62 **122** 50 **127**
  271 **128** 34
Elizabeth (Dogget)
  127 122
Elizabeth (Gifford)
  130 141
Elizabeth (Tupper) **99** 62
Elizabeth Bacon **93** 186
Elsie **79** 202
Ephraim **57** 82-84 **60** 185
  88 110 **99** 62 **114** 120

KEMPTON *cont'd*
127 193 148 342-344
Ephraim W. 116 52
Esther 127 193
Eva Belle 148 342 343
Fanheus 72 183
Fear 126 100 127 53 122
208 268 271 276
Fear (Curtiss) 126 96
Francis 126 100 127 276
128 117
Harriet 86 53
Harriet (Nay) 126 80
Jacob 127 208
Jacob Curtis 126 100
127 271
Jerusha 56 397
Jerusha (Nay) 126 80
Joan 127 223 148 59
Joan (Goodman /
Manne) 148 58
Joanna 57 82 116 189 119
266 148 342 343
Joanna (Crowell) 127 271
Joanna (Rawlings) 148
342 343
Joanna (Wakefield) 99 62
John 56 397 105 281 120
277 125 73 150 126 100
127 208 148 58 59 344
John B. 86 28
Jonathan 127 271 135 311
Joseph 135 309
Julia (Adams) 123 100
Lemuel 86 28
Lois 79 246 80 119
Lydia 99 62 135 311
Manasseh 57 34 83 81 296
97 311 103 160 111 176
178 114 117 118 122 60
127 193 148 342 344
Margaret 88 313 127 271
Maria (Carder) 107 230
Martha 64 11
Mary 53 285 99 62 126 100
127 53 135 311
Mary (Hathaway) 99 62
127 193
Mary (Hillman) 99 62
Mary (Holmes) 88 313
Mary (Kempton) 99 62
Mary (Reeves) 148 344
Mary (Taber) 99 62
Mary Carolyn 95 339
Mary E. 103 48
Mary H. 125 288
Mary Hale (Hanks) 86 28
Mary Snow 127 208
Mellin G. 72 74
Mercy 59 93
Milford William 108 134
Mira 107 230
Nancy V. (Nightingale)
126 216
Obed 88 316
Patience 57 83 148 342 344
Patience (Faunce) 114 120
Paul 99 62
Phebe (Kirby) 93 186
Rebecca 126 100 127 268
271

KEMPTON *cont'd*
Richard 107 230 126 96
100 127 53 122 208 268
271 276
Rockwell M. (Mrs.) 78
331 79 202
Rufus 56 383
Ruth 57 84 148 342-344
Samuel 83 145
Sarah (Burton) 125 150
126 295
Sarah (Snow) 127 208
Sarah A. 72 74
Seth 91 327 105 290
Stephen 127 208 148 344
Sukey 127 208
Susan (Gifford) 135 309
Tabitha 103 160
Thomas 58 142 73 137 88
313 99 62 126 100 127
122 193 128 34 140 116
Thomas W. 116 52
William 53 285 127 276
Zaccheus 86 53
Zibah 127 271
Kenacut *see* Kennicut
KENBNER Matthew 66 36
KENCEY Ephraim 91 327
KENCH
Abigail 110 110
Abigail B. (Cousins)
110 26
Ada A. 110 110
Adaline 105 200 109 111
Addie 131 89
Anisan / Anissessem
Ann 105 200
Betsey 99 30
Bryant Morton 104 185
Clara A. 89 300
Elizabeth 89 30 104 184
185 109 200
Elizabeth Ann 110 110
Elizabeth Mary 105 200
Florence L. 89 300
George 104 185
Huldah 105 200 110 110
John 105 200 110 26 110
John E. 110 110
John Ellis Gray 104 185
Joseph 104 184 109 109
Laura A. 110 110
Lucy 104 184
Lucy B. 105 200
Lucy Maria 110 110
Margaret G. 105 200
Maria L. 110 110
Mary 104 184 185
Mary A. 89 300
Mary Ann (Howard)
108 286 109 109
Mehitable (Woodbridge)
104 61
Mercy 104 184 185
Mercy (Doar) 104 62
Nelson M. 89 300
Robert Hall 104 185
Russell 109 203
Russell Horton 104 185
Sarah Abigail 105 200
Sarah Angela 110 110

KENCH *cont'd*
Sarah J. 89 300
Stephen 89 300 104 184
108 286 109 15 109
Stillman S. 110 110
Thomas 104 184 105 200
109 203
Thomas E. 105 200
William 104 61 62 184 185
109 199
KENDALL Kandall
Kindal Kindall Kindell
— Miss 80 55
— Mrs. 58 18 61 307
69 280
— Widow 65 366
A. 56 lxiv
Abbie 61 22
Abbie M. (Stinson)
117 165
Abbie Vinal 95 55
Abel 52 148 385
Abiather 111 41
Abigail 51 318 320 57 285
59 145 152 153 61 379
64 38 69 280 80 250
109 162 228 137 251
139 315 141 223 245
247
Abigail (Locke) 90 360
Abigail B. 126 141
Abijah 101 32
Abraham 107 97
Abram 106 99
Achsah Hawes 52 149 385
Adaline Amanda 84 102
Alice 107 102 103
Alice (Temple) 107 99 102
136 58
Alice (Whittemore)
108 93
Alice M. (Parkhurst)
100 330
Almira 115 53
Alpheus 56 259
Amory Holman 93 253
Amos 68 309 69 280
88 372
Ann 57 149 65 34 126 113
206
Ann (Carter) 88 337
Ann Elizabeth 77 53
Anna 83 477
Anna (Farley) 136 57
Anne 56 265 266 57 104
151
Asa 147 259
Asaph 90 44
Benjamin 119 20 126 209
Bert G. 105 298
Betsey 63 215 64 207 70
345 89 381
Betsey (Colburn) 139 92
Betsey L. 56 257
Caleb 58 280
Caroline 66 24
Catherine 56 258 59 278
92 124 94 376
Charles Ezekiel 93 251
Charles Faulkner 52 149
385

KENDALL *cont'd*
Charles S. **88** 337
Charlotte **125** 290
Charlotte A. Towle
  105 298
Chrissa K. M. **88** 207
Christian **145** 103
Cordelia **52** 148 385
Cosen **147** 237
Dan (Mrs.) **121** 94
Daniel **61** 237 **62** 72 **69**
  280 **91** 263 **92** 272 276
  107 103 104
Daniel William **103** 45
David **111** 41
David Wolcott **62** xxxix
Deborah **59** 276 **107** 104
Deborah (Richardson)
  107 104
Delia M. **105** 229
Dorcas **72** 74
E. **139** 257
Ebenezer **63** 89 **72** 204 **108**
  93 **132** 42
Edith **74** 158 **75** xxv **87**
  286 296 **88** 173
Edith Stone **52** 149 385
Editha Penelope **82** 125
  236
Edward **136** 233
Eleanor / Nellie Marie
  (Fracker) **124** 256
Eleazer **55** 59 430 431
  56 256
Elias **69** 280
Eliphalet **139** 92
Elisha **72** 204 **92** 24
Eliza **85** 335 **94** 189
Eliza J. **142** 374
Eliza Jane **96** 132
Eliza Lorence (Preston)
  87 286
Eliza T. **125** 293
Elizabeth **53** 357 **55** 443 **56**
  244 **57** 111 114 223 **58**
  130 132 **59** 150 152 153
  61 201 **63** 89 **72** 204 221
  76 74 **78** 284 **94** 221 222
  96 28 **111** 41 118 **113** 30
Elizabeth (Adams) **57** 114
Elizabeth (Strenglits)
  (Harris) **106** 28
Emily P. **93** 253
Enoch **57** 201 **62** 152
Ephraim **54** 185 **56** 144
  57 153 355 **59** 145 146
  60 198 **65** 148 **87** 286
Erastus **69** 280 **77** 53
Esther **61** 239
Esther (Kellogg) **142** 374
Ethan **57** 309
Eunice **58** 51 **63** 85 88
  113 33 38 **115** 34
Ezekiel **93** 121 251
Ezra **94** 157
Fanny **72** 204 **95** 117 **97**
  217 **103** 44
Fanny (Senter) **105** 229
Filpah **56** 171
Frances **52** 246 **57** 389
  89 230

KENDALL *cont'd*
Frances A. (Carver)
  88 329
Frances C. **58** cix
Francis **52** 148 385 **55** 443
  57 351 **58** 51 **85** 455 **87**
  286 **132** 270 **136** 137
Fred Melvin (Mrs.) **108**
  134 **113** 233
G. A. **56** lxiv
G. W. **91** 327
George Augustus **52**
  148 149 385
George Frederick **72** xx
George Henry **83** 478
George Kimball **92** 130
Gertrude Everett
  (Horton) **81** 219 **83** 236
  248 478
H. P. **95** 8
Hannah **55** 431 **56** 144
  244 256 266 **57** 153 353
  59 152 **60** 364 **61** 342
  92 272 **94** 221 **108** 93
  115 33
Hannah (Cole) **125** 104
Hannah (Hassy) **132** 42
Hannah (Trask) **125** 287
Hannah Poor **82** 467 468
Harriet Gertrude **75** 261
Harry **131** 154
Hartwell **115** 53
Helen **78** 74
Helen E. P. **54** 251
Heman **132** 270
Henry **92** 280 284
Henry Augustus **87** 286
Henry John Broughton
  64 293 **65** xxxiv
Henry P. **87** 286
Henry Plimpton **106** 158
Hepsabah **97** 229
Hezekiah **88** 283 **136** 57
Hezekiah Smith **88** 333
Horace **92** 276
Hugh P. **95** 6
Huldah **111** 41
I. **89** 381
Irena **56** 259
Isaac **57** 353 **75** 256
  125 287
Isaac P. **57** 282
Isabel **67** 75
Iva **109** 128
Jacob **59** 150 278 **61** 236 **92**
  124 126 130 **107** 99 102
  103 **136** 58 **148** 239
James **57** 201 **58** 280
Jane **57** 104 **128** 122
Jeremiah **96** 132
Jerreb **64** 206
Jerusha **88** 372
Jesse **61** 239
Joanna **58** 134 **78** 184
John **51** 128 **54** 86 87 **58** 51
  68 309 **90** 360 **101** 103
  107 104 **112** 58 **125** 104
  287 **137** 183 **145** 103
John Colburn **61** 241
John Dickson (Mrs.)
  106 125

KENDALL *cont'd*
John Dwight **124** 195
John Gordon **137** 183
John T. **100** 330
Jonas **52** 148 385 **56** 244
  57 285 **89** 384
Jonathan **57** 389 **58** 134 **61**
  237 **87** 286 **105** 298 **124**
  199 **142** 140
Joseph **59** 148 276 277 **63**
  89 **137** 183
Joseph S. **69** 100
Joshua **53** 357 **54** 353 **56**
  142 144 265 266 **57** 104
  149 151 152 **59** 145 **61**
  380
Josiah **58** 133 **64** 153
  132 270
Judith **57** 355 **59** 145
Judith (Walker) **87** 286
Judith Peirce **93** 124
  94 150
Katharine **61** 242 **82** 435
Keziah **59** 150
Laura (Chamberlain)
  131 154
Laura (Sherwin) **103** 45
Laura M. **105** 298
Lemuel **63** 85
Levi **61** 22
Levi G. **61** 22
Lewis A. **124** 256
Lloyd **72** 204
Lois **69** 280 **112** 58
Louisa **66** 112
Lucy **64** 206 **88** 332
  142 140
Lucy (Ashby) **125** 287
Lydia **57** 201 **63** 256 **67** 31
  91 229
Lydia (Butman) **96** 132
Lydia (Emerson) **91** 229
  132 270
Lydia P. **66** 111
Lyman **52** 74
M. A. **128** 173
Mabel **87** 294 **100** 23
Margaret **77** xxviii 78 **84**
  111 186
Margaret Gray (Douglas)
  (Talent) **124** 195
Maria Eunice **64** 153
Marion A. **55** 317 345 **56**
  xxxii
Martha **93** 121 **94** 157
  133 139
Martha (Ingersoll) **87** 286
Martha Jane **93** 121
Martin **57** 282
Mary **55** 290 292 429 430
  56 388 **60** 198 **61** 380
  64 312 **72** 222 265 **77**
  317 **79** 182 269 **94** 221
  97 221 **107** 95 **123** 288
  134 231 **137** 236 237
Mary (Bancroft) **96** 331
Mary (Bodge) **101** 103
Mary (Doyle) **126** 209
Mary (Fairbanks) **132** 270
Mary (Locke) **94** 223
Mary (Tidd) **87** 286

KENDALL *cont'd*
Mary Ann (Holbrook)
  88 339
Mary B. (Merrill) **90** 44
Mary E. **88** 337
Mary Eliza (Andem)
  88 333
Mary Elizabeth **91** 229
Mary Jane (Wood) **83** 478
Mary Louisa **142** 374
Mary P. **61** 381
Mary Wright (Lathrop)
  137 183
Matilda Thomas **91** 305
Melissa Russell **64** 152
Mercy **69** 189
Meriam **125** 223
Milton T. **117** 165
Miranda **55** 357
Molly **63** 89
Nathan **56** 171 **61** 344 **91**
  229 **115** 34 **132** 270
Nathan M. **56** 257
Nathan O. **119** 277 278
Nathan Otis **91** 229
Nathaniel **59** 152 153 277
  66 21 24 **90** 360 **101** 103
Nehemiah **89** 383
Nellie (Fracker) **124** 256
Newton Jones **61** 22
Nicholas **51** 150 151
Obadiah **59** 280 **78** 418
Oliver **95** 282
Orilla Alice **100** 330
P. Redfield **54** 251
Patience **62** 152
Patty **61** 241
Pernie **107** 103
Persis **87** 294
Peter **70** 345
Phebe **63** 88
Phila **75** 256
Piezeis **91** 264
Polly **61** 239 **77** 228
  147 259
Polly K. **94** 156
Priscilla **137** 183
Prudence **57** 282
Ralph **111** 41 **119** 20
Ralph R. **91** 305
Rebecca **52** 81 **53** 357 **54**
  286 **61** 237 **115** 33 **136**
  222 **137** 236
Rebecca (Bodge) **101** 103
Rebecca (Pierce) **88** 283
Rebecca Pierce **59** 189
Reuben **69** 302 **78** 183
  145 362
Richard **87** 286 **127** 172
Robert de **96** 112 **100** 23
Robert R. **79** 6
Roger de **96** 124 125
Rufus **72** 74
Ruth **52** 74 **57** 354 356 **59**
  146 372 **62** 152 **92** 24
  107 97
Ruth (Blodget) **87** 286
Ruth (Eustis)
  (Whittemore) **107** 97
Ruth (Pierce) **87** 286
Sally **57** 201 **72** 286 **92** 130

KENDALL *cont'd*
125 105
Sally (Cole) **125** 100
Sally (Foster) **137** 183
Salina **64** 152
Samuel **51** 377 **52** 134
  148 385 **53** 357 **56** 37 **58**
  132 **59** 150 **79** 48 **89** 384
  93 253 **94** 156 223 **104**
  242 **113** 33 37-39 **132**
  270
Samuel E. **88** 339
Samuel Reed **91** 305
Samuel S. **66** 24
Samuel T. C. **77** 316
Sarah **52** 74 **54** 286 **56** 46
  256 **57** 104 **59** 148 277
  280 **61** 236 237 344 **63**
  88 89 **78** 312 **88** 280 344
  107 99 **111** 41 318 **115**
  33 34 **136** 133
Sarah (Cheever) **132** 38
Sarah (Foster) **137** 183
Sarah (Rhoades) **126** 206
Sarah (Richardson)
  91 263
Sarah E. **69** 264
Sarah Maria **91** 229
Sarah W. **94** 161
Sarah Williams **95** 282
Sarah Wyman **93** 251
Sewall **93** 124 251
Simeon M. **68** 199
Simon **53** 357 **57** 114
Smith **63** 89
Solomon **142** 374
Stephen **57** 201 **111** 116
  139 257
Susan **127** 190
Susan C. **61** 346
Susan E. (Lowe) **119** 277
  278
Susanna **56** 256 **58** 132
  59 145 150 **60** 197 198
  63 180 **75** 36 **77** 39 **107**
  106
Susanna (Lincoln)
  (Clapp) **124** 199
  142 140
Susanna (Perkins) **87** 286
Tabitha **104** 128 **107** 32
  111 312
Temple **108** 93
Thaddeus **61** 241 379
Thankful **57** 309
Theoda **53** 357
Thomas **52** 81 148 385 **54**
  286 **57** 104 354 **60** 364
  66 236 237 **77** 313 **87**
  286 **111** 312 **125** 100
  126 206 **132** 38 270 **137**
  236
Timothy **61** 239 **64** 312
  105 229
Tiny (Endell) **96** 331
Tryphena **54** 353 **57** 114
Uriah **111** 41
Waldo **96** 331
Walter Melvin **83** 478
Walter Melvin (Mrs.) **80**
  335 **81** 219

KENDALL *cont'd*
William **51** 127 **61** 343
  66 111 112 **67** 31 32 **79**
  182 269 **91** 358 **106** 28
  107 238 **109** 238 **111** 41
  116
William E. **104** 144
William P. **88** 329
William Sergeant **96** 28
William Tedstill **92** 126
Willis **96** 331
Winthrop **58** xlv
Winthrop Reed **68** xxxi
KENDIG
Amos Barr **97** 127 214
Annie **97** 127
Barbara **106** 312
Carrie **97** 127
Mary (Bancroft) **97** 127
Mary C. Edwards
  (Bancroft) **97** 214
KENDRICK Kindrick
  —— **52** 127 260 **59** 299
  70 264 **71** 339 341
— Mr. **57** 229
Abigail **58** 134
Abigail (Hawes) **102** 202
Alfred **102** 289
Alice **102** 286
Ann **107** 226
Anna **61** 238 **136** 135
Anne Elizabeth (Hopkins)
  136 310
Ansel A. **102** 202
Arthur W. **86** 367
Asa **120** 54
Asahel Clark **136** 310
Azubah **79** 382
Benjamin **61** 379
Catherine **104** 71
Daniel **62** 27 **91** 327 **97**
  231 232 **139** 99
David **108** 212
Deborah **132** 85 86
Diana **106** 311
E. **102** 290
Ebenezer **71** 263 **136** 135
Edmund S. **108** 217
Elijah **56** 32 **71** 263 **107** 226
Eliza **88** 284 **105** 34
Eliza Ann **106** 311
Elizabeth **53** 129 **62** 27 **97**
  39 **108** 302
Elizabeth (Kenney) **108**
  212 302 303
Elvira E. (Sparrow)
  86 367
English **81** 108 222
Ermina (Doane) **108** 213
Esther Ann **110** 33
Fidelia **100** 242
Frederick **102** 287
Frederick (Mrs.) **102** 286
George **53** 129 **62** 348 **96**
  254 255 257 268 **97** 319
  98 168 **99** 96
Georgiana **92** 322
Gladys Estelle **86** 367
Hannah **71** 263 **96** 263 **136**
  135 **139** 249

KENDRICK *cont'd*
Hannah (Horner) **108**
212 302
Hannah (Jackson)
107 226
Helen Mar (Cahoon)
108 217
Ida (Harsha) **104** 71
James **92** 322
Jane **70** 318
Jane (Ide) **96** 255
Jane Beals (Jennings)
83 381
Jason M. **56** 170
Jedidah (Crowell) **108** 213
Jemima **108** 212
John **52** 120 **71** 263 **90** 83
102 287 290 **108** 212
302 303 **118** 62 **120** 54
132 104
Jonathan **102** 257
Joseph **108** 212 302
Justin Smith **104** 71
Kate (Crosby) **102** 287
Keziah **120** 54
Levi **102** 202
Louise **119** 177
Louise Ensign **104** 145
Lydia **59** 299
Lydia (Covel) (Kenney)
108 303
Lydia (Smith) (Ford)
120 54 **137** 50
Marcia B. (Mayo) **102** 290
Margaret W. **77** 150
Mary **81** 35 **120** 318
Mary (Bassett) **126** 238
Mary (Farley) **136** 135
Mary F. **92** 400 **97** 302
Mary Isabella **90** 288
May (Erath) **118** 62
Mehitable **133** 236
Mercy **102** 202
Mira **56** 170
Nathan **71** 267
Nathaniel **136** 135
Polly **120** 318
R. **79** 382
Rachel **83** 476
Rachel Shepard **80** 97
Rebecca **52** 127 128 **61** 379
102 290
Richard **52** 127
Ruth **56** 32 **58** 384 385 **63**
176 **74** 258 **97** 40
Sallah **113** 142
Samuel **63** 176 **74** 258
Sarah **57** 55 **61** 381 **90** 83
Seth **108** 213
Stephen **80** 97
Susie **74** 303
Tabitha (Eldridge)
102 257
Thomas **97** 319 **99** 94 98
99 108 **139** 108
Tobias James (Mrs.)
81 222
W. H. **76** 46
Warren Anson **79** 382
William **81** 35 **91** 327
KENE *see also* Kean &

KENE *cont'd*
Keene
Dorothy **67** 154 **80** 395
Gilbert **80** 395
Jane **86** 417
Nathaniel **54** 408 409 **131**
251 252
Robert **54** 156 **67** 154
KENEBES —— **96** 271
KENERSON Kennerson
Edward Hibbard **78** 447
79 201
Eliza **82** 285 291
Hannah H. **77** 178
Hazel **103** 119
Keney *see* Kenney
KENFIELD John **139** 284
Kenison *see* Kennison
KENLY Anna H. **79** 329
Beatrice **100** 110
Davis L. **79** 329
George Tyson **79** 329
Robert Gordon **79** 329
KENMORE
Margaret **126** 209
KENMURE Gordon
William (Lord) **67** 213
KENN
—— **99** 121 **101** 55
Deborah **99** 206
Thomas **99** 207
KENNAMER
Willard Clifton **90** 137
KENNAN Florence (James)
136 320
George **136** 320
George Frost **136** 320 325
Kossuth Kent **136** 320
Loa (Brown) **136** 320
Mary (Tullar) **136** 320
Sarah (Lathrop) **136** 320
Thomas **136** 320
Thomas Lathrop **136** 320
Thomas Lathrop (Mrs.)
87 174 189 **88** 88 185 **89**
53 147
KENNARD
—— Capt. **130** 85
—— Mr. **53** 323 324
—— Mrs. **53** 323 **83** 193
Abigail **55** 310
Adam **97** 122
Alpheus S. **65** 336
Ann **81** 261 **111** 48
Ann (Parry) **91** 188
Ann Mary **82** 421 **83** 34
183 186
Anna Laura **78** 37
Annie Maude **110** 223
Arthur Norris **105** 186
106 125
Arthur Wood **69** lxix
Caroline Augusta (Smith)
91 188
Caroline Manning
82 421
Charles Fairchild **69** lxix
Charles Heywood **97** 122
Cyril George Heywood
97 122
Damon **97** 270

KENNARD *cont'd*
Damon (Mrs.) **97** 270
David Della Morgan
78 37
David Mitchell **78** 36
Deborah **51** 208
Dorothy **82** 291 293
Edward **51** 45 118 207 208
55 250 253 255 **81** 261
87 125 **88** 348 **91** 188
130 85
Eliza **80** 65 **81** 261
Eliza Adeline **78** 37
Elizabeth **51** 118 207 **81**
261 **111** 46 48
Elizabeth (March) **91** 188
Elizabeth (Martyn) **91** 188
Elizabeth (Tetherly)
91 188
Elizabeth Southwood
(Boyd) **95** 335
Frances **83** 306
Frances (Blunt) **83** 178 183
Frederic Hedge **87** 174
90 80 **91** 178 188 **92** 150
George **83** 193
Grace **69** lxix
Harrison Eisenbrey
91 188
Helen G. **93** 137
Helen Lucy (Stebbins)
66 xlviii lii **69** xliii
lxviii
Howard William **105** 186
James **82** 421 **83** 34 178
183 193 **88** 348 **91** 188
97 272
James Knox Polk **78** 37
Jane **111** 46
Jerusha **88** 277
John **51** 45 208 **87** 206
111 48
John Burton **95** 335
John Harold **91** 188
John Stebbins **69** lxix
Jonathan **51** 207 208
Katharine Marjory
69 lxix
Linda **85** 200
Manning **82** 421
Margaret **81** 261
Margaret Alice **91** 188
Martin Parry **91** 188
Mary **55** 310 **65** 336 **82** 421
83 34
Mary Cleveland
(Channing) **97** 122
Mary Elizabeth **78** 37
95 329
Mary Elizabeth (Frost)
95 329 **119** 61
Mary Gardner **102** 66
Mary R. **110** 223
Michael **54** 409 **55** 250
253 255 **78** 37 **91** 188
Molly **88** 348
Moses **88** 348
Nacy **97** 272
Nathaniel **81** 261 **83** 223
88 348 **97** 265
Oliver Parry **91** 188

KENNARD cont'd
Ophelia Elizabeth Hines
  (Polk) **78** 36
Philena **69** lxix
Rebecca Novaline **78** 37
Robert Martin Parry
  91 188
Ruth **81** 261
Sallie Foster **78** 37
Sampson **67** 170
Samuel **55** 250 253
Samuel M. **110** 223
Sarah Harrison
  (Eisenbrey) **91** 188
Simeon **82** 291 293
Solomon **51** 208
Susan **73** 193
Susanna **51** 208
Thomas **51** 208
Timothy **65** 336 **97** 272
Violet Elizabeth Grace
  97 122
Walter C. **84** 29
William Henry **69** lxix
William L. **119** 61
William Leighton **95** 329
William Manning **82** 421
KENNEAR David **71** 95
KENNEDY Kanada Kanady
—— **80** 79
— Capt. **54** 268 **71** 143
— Mr. **71** 136 **76** 138 **81**
  160 **83** 416
— Mrs. **85** 461
— Widow **73** 194
Abiel **73** 172 179
Abigail **63** 378 **64** 374
  73 184
Adrianna **75** 128
Agnes **117** 251
Agnes McClure **85** 225
Alden **73** 102
Alexander **63** 17 378 **64**
  374 **66** 277 **73** 184 **127**
  307
Algernon S. **79** 155
Alice Mary **88** 395
Almyra **86** 17
Amelia **71** 202
Amy Gertrude
  (Richardson) **98** 365
Andrew **111** 192 **131** 76
Ann (Colgate) **110** 222
Anne **73** xlv
Archibald **98** 201 **107** 189
Augusta (Ellis) **135** 78
Benjamin **104** 117
Bershua **72** 37
Betsey **74** 168
Betty **77** 263 264
Bridget (Murphy) **139**
  211-213 215
Calvin **73** 167
Caroline Bouvier **139** 221
Caroline J. (Melcher) **83**
  183 184
Caroline Melcher **83** 172
Catherine **76** 138
Catherine A. **147** 61
Catherine Ward **59** 257
Charles **66** 32 **93** 183

KENNEDY cont'd
Chauncey **111** 192
Chester **74** 168
Christopher **102** 29
Christopher George
  139 223
Clara **78** 205
Clarissa **70** 232
Clemence A. **89** 326
Crawford H. **120** 236
Cyrene **73** 171
Daniel **73** 170
Daniel Edwards **70** xix
David **73** 175 178 **111** 192
David Anthony **139** 223
Dennis **117** 9 15
Diademia **52** 311
Dicy A. **128** 262
Donald **73** xlv **110** 222
Dorcas **125** 221
Douglas Harriman
  139 223
Edith Golding **73** xlv
Edward **66** 31 **92** 169
Edward Moore **139** 221
  223 224
Eleanor **71** xlvi
Electa **79** 157
Eliza **73** 184
Eliza C. **81** 105
Eliza J. **73** 167
Elizabeth **56** 92 **73** 171
  172 176 179 **93** 286 **99**
  207 **106** 239 **112** 77
Elizabeth (Peck) **92** 169
Emelia **60** 241
Emily **104** 313
Emily Ruth (Black)
  139 222
Emma Bradley **85** 195
Estell **92** 169
Estelle Gale **78** 175
Ethel (Skakel) **139** 222
Ethel D. (Horner) **83** 433
Eunice Mary **139** 220
F. **91** 327
Fergus **112** 291
Frances B. **110** 222
Frances B. G. (Keene)
  110 222
Frances Blackler **110** 222
Francis Benedict **139** 217
Francis M. E. **93** 97
Francis Marion **75** 128
Freelove **111** 192
George **73** 175
George G. **59** 118
George Golding **67**
  xxxiv **73** xxvii xlv **110**
  222
George H. **135** 78
Geraldine **81** 33
Glenn Alvin **117** 237
Gordon **110** 222
H. B. **79** 155
Hannah **73** 168 170
Hannah E. **71** 38
Harriet **66** 277 **71** 202
Harriet W. (Harris)
  110 222
Harriet White **73** xlv

KENNEDY cont'd
110 222
Harris **65** xxxvii **73** xlv
  90 126 **107** 125 **108** 138
  110 222
Henrietta **86** 25
Henry **66** 277 **73** 171 179
  75 269
Henry Edwin **73** 172
Henry S. **73** 171
Herbert **83** 433 **84** 21
Horatio **62** 301
Hugh **64** 342 **84** 154 **134**
  126 **136** 109
Hugh A. Studdert (Mrs.)
  90 135
Isaac **71** 202 **123** 154
Isabel **109** 226
Jacqueline Lee (Bouvier)
  139 221
James **66** 31 **71** 202 **73**
  184 226 **90** 351 **92** 169
  120 318 **125** 43 **139** 207
James W. **92** 169
Jane **73** 102 **91** 353 **115** 315
  116 65 **117** 258 **125** 106
  257
Janet **122** 270
Jared **111** 192
Jean **141** 114 **144** 263
Jean Ann **139** 220
Jessie **124** 32
Jessie (Hannum) **90** 351
Jessie Ann **89** 254
Jessie Graddy **84** 187 232
Joanna L. **139** 212 214
Joel **128** 93 95 97
John **59** 257 **60** 242 **64** 111
  66 31 133 281 **70** 316 **73**
  102 170 171 184 **81** 339
  82 32 **83** 416 **91** 193 **93**
  397 **100** 63 **104** 117 **105**
  233 **119** 75 **125** 38 104
  139 215 **140** 160
John F. **71** 38
John Fitzgerald **120** 55
  125 163 **136** 312 **139**
  194 211 219 221
John T. **118** 325 326
Jonathan **59** 21
Joseph **73** 102 **112** 17
Joseph Patrick **139** 217-
  219 222
Joseph Walker (Mrs.)
  84 213
Josephine Morton Smith
  113 83
Joshua **70** 232
Judith (Dunton) **83** 416
Justus R. **73** 179
Juva Louise La Burtte
  93 183
Kara Anne **139** 224
Katharine Browne
  (Worcester) **84** 213
Kathleen **139** 219
Kathleen Hartington
  139 222
Kyle Frances **139** 223
Levi **104** 117
Lincoln **73** 171

KENNEDY *cont'd*
Lizzie A. P. (Treadwell)
  83 433 **84** 21
Louise **83** 418 421 433
Lucinda **73** 181 183
Luther **73** 167
Lydia **82** 291 300 **111** 192
Mabel Esme **67** 18
Malcolm Gerry **110** 222
Margaret **60** 241 **96** 71
Margaret Louise **139** 217
Margaret M. **139** 212 215
Margaret Madeleine
  Wentworth **108** 134
Marguerite **104** 233
Martha Frances **108** 221
Martha J. **73** 102
Mary **63** 349 **73** 167 **81** 339
  91 353 **92** 164 **115** 315
  117 256 **125** 257
Mary (McClure) **85** 226
Mary Ann **73** 172 179
Mary Anne **78** 234
Mary Augusta (Hickey)
  139 216
Mary C. (Schermerhorn)
  92 169
Mary Courtney **139** 223
Mary Elizabeth **74** 21
Mary Jane **73** 175
Mary Johanna **139** 211
Mary Kerry **139** 223
Mary L. **139** 212 213
Mary Loretta **139** 217
Mary Oswald **67** 18
Matthew **91** 353 **139** 207
Matthew Maxwell Taylor
  139 223
Matthew Rauch **139** 222
Mercy **70** 229
Michael **62** 331
Michael LeMoyne
  139 223
Mildred **73** xlv
Miriam **71** 202
Mollie (Neston) **90** 351
Nancy **73** 175 **139** 208
Nathaniel **73** 175 178
Nicholas **73** 166
Olive **75** 264
Olive C. **60** 353
Otis **73** 171
Patricia **139** 220
Patrick **66** 31 **101** 247
  104 118 **139** 211-214
Patrick Bouvier **139** 222
Patrick Joseph **139** 212
  213 216 217 224
Percy **78** 175
Peter **60** 241
Phebe **83** 416
Phebe Leonard **67** 218
Platt **83** 62 68
Polly **73** 178 179 184 **117**
  256 **123** 207
Rachel **73** 171 **81** 159 160
  91 92
Rebecca **73** 184
Rhoda (Judkins) **103** 235
Robert **66** 133 **72** 37 **87**
  323 **95** 55 **120** 318 **130**

KENNEDY *cont'd*
  313
Robert Francis **139** 220
  222 223
Robert L. **92** 169
Robert M. **118** 168 **121** 77
Robert Maxwell **88** 395
Rory Elizabeth Katharine
  139 223
Rose Elizabeth
  (Fitzgerald) **139**
  218 219
Rosemary **139** 219
Rosilla **73** 175
Roxana **70** 316
Ruth **66** 133 **74** 168
Sally **73** 166
Sally (Hall) **140** 160
Sally (Maben) **92** 169
Sally (Weeks) **84** 424
Salome (Viles) **131** 76
Samuel **52** 310 **71** 202 **73**
  102 167 **103** 235
Sarah **52** 310 **73** 184
  140 160
Sarah Jane **67** 18
Sarah Maria **75** 269
Semandel **73** 171
Sheila Brewster (Rauch)
  139 222
Sinclair **73** xlv **110** 222
Sukey **78** 314
Susan **66** 31
Susan A. **71** 38
Susan C. **60** 117
Susan Haskell **73** 184
Susan Pratt **86** 199
  114 141
Susanna **73** 166
Thankful (Chase) **87** 323
Thomas **52** 310 311 **62** 249
  66 281 **73** 166 179 **84**
  424 **95** 51 **99** 207 **117**
  232 **139** 208
Thomas (Mrs.) **77** 156 **78**
  205 **95** 51
Thomas B. **98** 365
Thomas W. **83** 172 183 184
Timothy **64** 319
Victoria Denise (Gifford)
  139 223
Virginia Joan (Bennett)
  139 223 224
William **57** 388 **60** 255
  64 220 **66** 277 281 **67** 18
  73 102 171 **83** 418 **85**
  226 **102** 29 **111** 192 **140**
  160
William Henry **73** 175
William L. **73** 279
William N. **73** 179
William Robert (Mrs.)
  97 158
Yvonne Odette **117** 237
KENNEEN David **91** 327
KENNEHAN
Anise **72** 300
Annie Belle **72** 300
James **72** 300
KENNELL
Eliza **125** 219

KENNELL *cont'd*
Henry **76** 273
Laura Ann **76** 273
Matilda **76** 273
KENNELLY John **63** 16
KENNEN Hugh **60** 160
KENNER
Benjamin **83** 21 25
Dorcas **83** 21 25
Dorcas (Amazeen) **83** 21
Mabel **83** 232
Kennerson *see* Kenerson
KENNETT
Anna **68** 96 **136** 76
Belinda **133** 122
Edith Frances **101** 121
  116 71
John **68** 96
Lucinda **68** 96
Sarah **68** 96
KENNEY —— **60** 377 380
  61 84 87
— Mr. **62** 85
— Mrs. **62** 85
Aaron **99** 54
Abiel **126** 101
Abigail **54** 84 **61** 191 **66**
  147 188 **74** 44 **93** 268
  108 115 117 212 300
  126 237
Abigail (Chubock)
  108 115
Abigail (Wingate)
  108 117
Abigail Robbins **108** 301
Abijah **61** 391
Abra **74** 39
Abraham Weston **108** 300
Achsa **61** 191
Ada Lulu (Wheaton)
  108 303
Adra (Cunningham)
  108 215 302
Agnes **108** 212
Albert **108** 215 302
Alexander **54** 84 **58** 195-
  197 401-403 **59** 412 **60**
  199 203
Alfred **108** 119 305
Alice Maud **108** 303
Alice Maude (Cook)
  108 214
Allen **108** 120 217
Almira **108** 211 214 215
Almira Antoinette
  108 211
Almira D. (McGray)
  108 304
Amelia (Harris) **108** 216
Amos **61** 84 **74** 39
Andrew Collins **108** 303
Andrew Freeman **108** 303
Andria Jane **108** 304
Ann **61** 87 89 **90** 45 **108**
  116 117
Ann (Kenny) **108** 116
Anna **58** 195 **61** 389 **108**
  213 215
Anna (Godfrey) **108** 302
Anna Marie **108** 237
Anne **66** 217 218 220 **74** 49

KENNEY *cont'd*
Anne (Billings) **108** 116
Ansel **62** 84 **108** 301
Archibald **108** 212
Arnetta Louise **108** 305
Arnold **86** 169
Artemas **137** 76
Arthur **108** 113 114
Arthur W. **108** 211
Asa **125** 287
Ashbel **61** 196
Augustus **58** 196
Aurilla **108** 305
Aurora **58** 403
Bartlett Freeman **108** 304
  305
Belinda (Copp) **127** 78
Benjamin **61** 195 **62** 193
  73 97 **74** 44 192 252 **108**
  114 301 302 **126** 101
Benjamin Butler **128** 277
Bertha (Doane) **108** 120
Bessie (Jarvis) **108** 214
Bessie Ann **108** 304
Betsey **62** 85 **76** 32 36
  108 119
Betsey A. **86** 169
Betty **66** 220 **93** 268
Catherine (Manning)
  108 217
Catherine Coffin **108** 215
Celestia Ann Lakewana
  108 211
Charity **60** 382
Charles A. **108** 217
Charlotte **88** 339
Chester **58** 402
Chloe **58** 196 401 **108** 116
Christopher **108** 113
Clarissa **108** 212 302
Corcoran **108** 214
Corintha **125** 20
Cynthia **62** 85
Daniel **58** 401 **61** 84 **73** 98
  82 314 **108** 114 115 119
  212
David **61** 389 **62** 197 **108**
  214 **126** 101
David Smith **108** 301
Deborah (Pinkham)
  108 215
Delight **62** 84
Delina **108** 216
Didamia (Spinney)
  108 302
Dorcas **60** 378 **108** 119
Eaton **108** 213
Eaton Crowell **108** 119
  216
Ebenezer **74** 44 **108** 245
Edith (Malcolm) **108** 305
Edith Kate Troop **108** 304
Edith Robena (Peters)
  108 304
Edmund **74** 44
Edmund Doane **108** 304
Edward **108** 114
Edwin B. **59** 40
Eleanor **108** 302
Eli **62** 85
Eliezer **61** 87

KENNEY *cont'd*
Elisha **110** 290 **114** 48 **119**
  21 **126** 101
Eliza **78** 305 **108** 216 302
  303 **125** 219
Eliza (Burns) **108** 303
Eliza (Frost) **108** 303
Eliza Ann **108** 215
Eliza Antoinette **108** 301
Eliza Jane **108** 215 304
Elizabeth **58** 195 **74** 39 188
  86 161 **92** 78 **108** 114
  115 117 119 211 212 215
  300 302 303 305
Elizabeth (Bennett)
  108 115
Elizabeth (Burges)
  108 114
Elizabeth (Carnes)
  108 114
Elizabeth (Crowder)
  114 303
Elizabeth (Doty) **108** 115
Elizabeth (Kendrick)
  108 302
Elizabeth (McLearn)
  108 304
Elizabeth (Nickerson)
  108 117
Elizabeth (Shaller)
  108 116
Elizabeth (Tibbetts)
  99 113
Elizabeth (Wilson)
  108 215
Elizabeth Annie **89** 199
Elizabeth Jane **108** 302
Elizur **60** 382
Ellen **85** 378
Elmira **95** 375 **108** 120
Elsie **108** 305
Elvira Louise **108** 304
Emeline **108** 302
Emeline (Covel) **108** 304
Emeline C. **108** 305
Emily **108** 215
Emma (Willhousen)
  108 214
Emma C. **108** 305
Ephraim **60** 378 **74** 179
Erastus **58** 196
Ernest Alfred **108** 304
Estella (Beckwith) **108** 304
Estelle **103** 116
Esther **60** 199 **108** 215
Esther (Coffin) **108** 215
Esther (Goodwin)
  108 119
Esther (Swim) **108** 305
Ethel D. (Horner) **83** 431
Eugenia (Hale) **86** 169
Eunice **60** 380 **74** 39 **96** 28
  108 116
Eunice (Hopkins)
  108 119
Eunice (Nickerson)
  108 217
Eunice (Wentworth)
  108 116
Experience (Ellis) **108** 115
Fanny **62** 85

KENNEY *cont'd*
Flavia **108** 303
Flavia (Coffin) (Doane)
  108 214
Florence Adna **108** 214
Frances Jane **108** 304
Frances Morton (Wilson)
  108 304
Frances R. **108** 211
Frank Lincoln **108** 304
Franklin Castro **108** 301
Fred Leroy **92** 230
Frederick Ithamar
  114 303
Gamaliel **60** 365 **103** 30
  108 118 214 215 305
George **59** 277 **108** 217
George H. **108** 300
George Wentworth
  108 301
Gladys **129** 395
Gladys A. **130** 70 155
Grace **108** 116
Grace (Liscom) **108** 115
Hannah **61** 191 390 391
  62 85 376 **74** 252 **78** 189
  108 114 115 117 154 301
  128 277
Hannah (Durant) **125** 101
Hannah (Whitehouse)
  108 303
Hannah B. **108** 301
Hannah Durkee **108** 301
Hannah E. **108** 300
Hannah Mariah **108** 214
Hansell **128** 277
Harriet Anna (Atwood)
  108 216
Harriet Newell **108** 301
Harriet Pinkham **108** 214
Harry E. **83** 431 433
Hattie S. **130** 48
Helen (Kimball) **108** 215
  302
Helen Barbara **92** 230
Heman **60** 364-366 **108**
  117-120 212-215 300 302
  303 305 **127** 40
Henry **60** 185 **81** 339 **87**
  228 235 **99** 113 **108** 115
  110 27
Hepzibah **64** 372 **75** 212
  108 116 **128** 184
Hepzibah (Blackman)
  108 114
Honor **60** 382 **61** 87
Ida **92** 115
Ina Maude **94** 140
Irene **108** 211 217
Isaac **60** 365 381 **62** 298
  108 118 119 213-215 300
  302 303 305 **126** 101
  127 40
Isaac Freeman **108** 304
Isaac Jones **108** 214
Isabella **108** 214
Israel **73** 97 **100** 178
Israel Doane **108** 303
Israel L. **95** 50
Ithamar **114** 303
J. **87** 83

KENNEY *cont'd*
Jack Raymond **108** 300
Jacob **76** 32 **108** 115 300
James **61** 87 89 190 389
  62 299 **64** 13 **74** 39 44
  124 188 **108** 213-216 304
  305 **127** 78 **140** 160
James Albert **108** 302 303
James Bond **108** 211
James Covel **108** 303
James E. **59** 40
James Mann **108** 303
James Rodman **108** 304
James Stewart **108** 303
Jane **73** 98 **108** 113 114
Jean **126** 101
Jedidah **61** 390 **86** 161
  108 213 216 302
Jemima **60** 378 379 **61** 87
  387 **93** 265 **108** 117
Jemima (Blackman)
  108 115
Jemima (Kendrick)
  108 212
Jerusha **54** 84 **59** 148 **61**
  389 **62** 84 **108** 114 216
Jerusha (Clap) **108** 114
Jesse **58** 402 **59** 412 **103** 31
  108 118 119
Jessie **108** 301
Jethro Covel **108** 305
Joanna **108** 214
Job **108** 300
Joel **58** 195 **95** 367
John **52** 451 **55** 391 **61** 84
  65 109 **66** 217 **67** 364
  70 262 **74** 39 44 180 188
  82 412 **87** 83 **93** 268
  103 28 **108** 113-115 117
  120 211 214 300 317 318
  110 191 **117** 15 **119** 180
  128 284 **145** 364
John Emerson **108** 300
John Jenkins **108** 304
John M. **92** 230
John Winslow **108** 214
Jona **108** 115
Jonathan **93** 265 **108** 114-
  116 **126** 101
Joseph **59** 40 **61** 84 **62**
  180 291 **74** 44 **81** 339
  108 114 115 212 213 216
  300 303
Joseph A. **59** 40
Joseph Ernest **108** 301
Joseph Godfrey **108** 303
Joseph N. **108** 300
Joseph Robbins **108** 301
Joseph W. **108** 300
Joshua **73** 97
Josiah **75** 213 **93** 265 **108**
  114 116 **125** 20
Judith **74** 129
Julia Chaney **108** 304
Kathryn (Gipe) **130** 55
Keturah (Doane)
  (Hopkins) **103** 28
Keziah **108** 119
Keziah (Knowles?)
  108 119
Lavina **108** 302

KENNEY *cont'd*
Lemuel **128** 277
Leonard **108** 119 217
Levi **108** 214
Lewis **128** 277
Lois (Knowles) **108** 119
  212 302
Lois Elizabeth **108** 301
Louis **74** 44
Louisa **73** xl **108** 213 303
  304
Louisa (Hopkins)
  108 305
Louisa R. **59** 40
Louise Elizabeth **108** 302
Lovinia **108** 302
Lovisa **108** 217
Lovisa Emily **108** 217
Lucy **60** 377
Lucy J. (Bancroft) **95** 367
Ludia Ann **108** 304
Lydia **69** 282 **74** 44 **108**
  117 211 214 300 301 303
  126 101
Lydia (Covel) **108** 303
Lydia (Grover) **110** 290
  114 48
Lydia (Smith) **108** 304
Lydia (Talyor) **108** 114
Lydia A. **108** 217
Lydia Ann **108** 304
Lydia Ann (Swaine)
  108 305
Lydia Jane **108** 303
M. **87** 83
Manley Corwin (Mrs.)
  86 197
Marah **62** 84
Marcy **60** 365
Margaret **100** 147 **108** 215
Margaret (Hill) **108** 115
Margaret (Leatherhead)
  108 114
Margaret (Redding)
  108 117
Margaret Cheyne (Smith)
  108 303
Margaretta Alberta
  108 304
Maria **108** 302 304
Maria Osborn (Crowell)
  108 215
Martha (Crowell) **108** 217
Martha Ann **108** 301
Martha Blanche **108** 303
Martin **54** 84
Mary **61** 270 **64** 13 157 **74**
  39 **82** 291 297 **91** 367
  108 114 115 117 119 212
  214 216 300
Mary (Atwood)
  (Nickerson) **108** 217
Mary (Briard) **127** 78
Mary (Hopkins) **103** 31
  108 119 214
Mary (Jenney) **108** 115
Mary (Perry) (Duncan)
  108 213
Mary (Richards) **108** 115
Mary (Smith) **108** 213
  216 303

KENNEY *cont'd*
Mary (Thorp) **108** 214
Mary Deborah **108** 214
Mary Elizabeth **108** 214
Mary Ellen Gardner
  108 303
Mary Goodsel (Duncan)
  108 214
Mary Jane **108** 119 216
Mary Jane (Kenney)
  108 216
Mary Lillian **108** 211
Mary Lucinda **108** 305
Mary W. (Orcutt) **114** 303
Matilda (Spears) **108** 214
Matilda Nickerson
  108 119
Matilda Weston **108** 302
Matthew **67** 364
Matthew Nathan **108** 301
Mehitable **108** 211 213 301
Mehitable Ann **108** 303
Mehitable Doane **108** 303
Mehitable Jane **108** 214
Melinda **108** 300
Melinda Rogers **108** 300
Mercy **62** 297 **108** 118 211
  212 215 217
Mercy (Hopkins) **103** 30
Mercy (Nickerson) **108**
  118 **127** 40
Mercy (Smith) **102** 320
  108 117
Miriam **108** 118 **122** 144
Moses **74** 39 **108** 114 317
Myrinda **60** 80
Nancy **108** 213 217
Nancy (Demerritt) **99** 54
Nancy Jane **108** 304
Nathan **102** 320 **108** 114
  117-120 210 211 301
Nathaniel **59** 40 **93** 264
  265 **108** 114-116
Nathaniel B. **108** 217
Nehemiah **108** 118 119
  212 216 217 300
Nettie **108** 217
Obadiah **126** 101
Olive (Doane) **108** 213
Olive Jane **108** 211
Orlanda **87** 83
Parnel (Pinkham)
  108 214
Patience (Cushman)
  108 115
Patience (Smith) **108** 215
Patience (Wing) **108** 115
Patrick **61** 350 **66** 147 217
  218 220
Patrick M. **78** 299
Patrick Moor **125** 101
Paul **74** 39 **105** 281
Pearl Durkee **108** 301
Peggy **58** 403
Penelope **74** 130
Penina (Smith) **108** 305
Persis (Getchell) **137** 76
Phebe **74** 44 **108** 211 215
Phebe (Arnold) **119** 180
Phebe Jane **108** 300
Polly **61** 190 **108** 120

KENNEY *cont'd*
Polly (Carriel) (Bancroft) **95** 368
Polly (Page) **87** 228 235
Porter **56** 348
Prince Doane **108** 212 213 302
Prince William **108** 301-303
Priscilla **74** 39
Priscilla (Howes) **108** 217
Priscilla (Nickerson) **108** 217
Rachel **126** 101
Rebecca **59** 340
Rebecca Knowles **108** 119
Reliance **108** 217
Relief **129** 396
Reuben **60** 378 379 382 **61** 87 387 **126** 101
Reuben Cahoon **108** 217 303
Rhoda **61** 391 **108** 116 215
Rhoda A. (Beck) **108** 305
Richard **56** 348 349 **58** 195 **62** 250 **74** 127 **105** 113
Richard Pinkham **108** 215 302
Robert **60** 380 **108** 95 113 114 212 302
Robert Simeon **108** 211
Rose **74** 44
Rufus **108** 300
Russell **61** 89 90 191 193 195 389
Ruth **52** 451 **61** 389 **74** 168 **75** 213 **108** 115 118 212 302 **128** 284
Ruth (Crowell) **108** 216
Ruth (Doane) **108** 118 212 303
Ruth (Kenney) **108** 212 302
Sabra (Nason) **97** 224
Sally (Cahoon) **108** 217
Sally C. **108** 217
Samuel **61** 390 **62** 85 **66** 188 **86** 161 **108** 114-117 214 **126** 101
Samuel Augustus **108** 211
Samuel B. **59** 40
Samuel Freeman **108** 214
Sanford **95** 368
Sarah **58** 195 **60** 79 **61** 89 90 191 193 195 389 **66** 218 **73** 97 **82** 289 291 **108** 114-119 212 213 215 244 303 304 **119** 180
Sarah (Ford) **119** 180
Sarah (Godfrey) **108** 119 213 **127** 40
Sarah (Harrington) **108** 212
Sarah (Kenney) **108** 115 119
Sarah (Nickerson) **108** 210
Sarah (Redman) **108** 116
Sarah A. **108** 119
Sarah Alice **108** 304

KENNEY *cont'd*
Sarah Ann **108** 214 216
Sarah Chapin **59** 40
Sarah Jane (Crowell) **108** 213 216
Sarah McGray **108** 304
Sarah Morton **108** 216
Senah **61** 89
Sharlot S. **108** 217
Shubal **61** 196
Silas **128** 277
Simeon **59** 148
Simeon Bartlett **108** 211 213
Simon **58** 195 **60** 377
Solomon **108** 120 214 305
Sophia **126** 142
Sophia (Crowell) **108** 212 215
Stephen **61** 87 **74** 213 **105** 281 **108** 300
Stephen H. **59** 40
Stephen V. **108** 301
Sukey **73** 98
Susan **114** 303
Susan (Walker) **108** 217
Susan Alice **108** 305
Susan H. **83** 298 299
Susan Jane (Nickerson) **108** 302
Susanna **74** 248 **108** 114 117 119 213 216 317 318 **133** 155 **142** 346
Susanna (Doane) **108** 302
Susanna (Tibbetts) **98** 215
Susanna Doane **108** 303
Susie Hammond **108** 211
Sylvia **108** 115
Tabitha **108** 216
Tamasine **108** 211
Thankful **108** 120
Thankful Bassett **108** 217
Thirza **108** 118
Thomas **62** 297 **73** 97 **74** 44 **81** 339 **108** 115 117 211 213
Thomas P. **108** 211
Thyrsa (Thompson) **125** 287
Timothy **108** 116 216
Tracy **108** 120
Tracy (Mrs.) **102** 285
Tristram Coffin **108** 215
Urecta **108** 119
Warren **58** 197
Warren S. **130** 55
Wentworth **108** 302
William **53** 237 **60** 380 **61** 191 390 **62** 376 **74** 44 **108** 212 216 217 301 302
William Albert **108** 301
William Halstead **108** 301
William Nelson **108** 214
William Payne **108** 302
William Sherard **108** 215
William Thomas **108** 214
William Wallace **108** 304
Zarah **61** 195
Zeruah **108** 116
Zilpha **108** 300

KENNICUT Kenacut
Kennicott Kennicutt
Amy **80** 49
Daniel **62** 363
Elizabeth **106** 35
G. Hermann (Mrs.) **80** 437
Hester **116** 203
Hiram Langdon **82** 125 **83** 232
John **62** 359
May Appleton **80** 437
Roger **106** 33
KENNING Kyenynge
Alice **98** 39
Richard **101** 83
KENNINGTON
Francis **82** 287 291
Mehitable **82** 287 291
KENNISH
Fanny Isabel **84** 188
KENNISON Kenison
Kinnison
Abby Jane **77** 186
Abigail **64** 10 **73** 72
Abigail (Tibbetts) **100** 146
Amy **74** 265
Ann **73** 68
Caroline (Durrell) (Parke) **134** 149
Charles E. **81** 256
David **59** 283
Dorcas **73** 67
Dorcas (Fuller) **125** 218
Dorothy **59** 288 **73** 65
Durban **74** 316
Edward **100** 146
Elijah **74** 265
Etta B. **69** 37
Fanny **81** 256
George **73** 74
George Washington **77** 186
Henry **73** 66 67 69
Huldah **59** 283
James **73** 72 **81** 256
Jane **59** 286 **69** 37
John **68** 93
John Kent **125** 218
John L. **80** 271
Joseph **69** 37
Judith **134** 65
Lois Huckins **68** 93
Lydia **55** 376 **83** 18
Margaret **68** 100 **94** 357
Maria C. **80** 271
Mary **55** 376 **83** 18
Mehitable **140** 130
Nathan **87** 125 **134** 65
Olive Augusta **81** 256
Rebecca **74** 261 316
Sally **59** 290
Samuel **64** 10 **73** 66
Sarah (York) **134** 65
Sarah D. (French) **126** 67
Sibyl W. **80** 271
Simeon **59** 290
Stephen Jackson **68** 93
Susan R. **74** 316
Waldron **74** 261
William H. **134** 149

KENNISTON Kinaston
Kinneston Kinniston
Kynnaston
—— **92** 283 284 **97** 141
— Mrs. **94** 357
— Widow **96** 222
Abigail **65** 352-354 **67** 380
Ann **65** 354
Anna **134** 173
Annie **99** 54
Apphia **58** 20 **74** 259
Asa **67** 380
B. F. **103** 53
Bathsheba **81** 428
Benjamin **65** 354
Bradbury **67** 277
Bridget **65** 352 **86** 70
Charles **92** 310
Christopher **51** 45
Daniel **76** 35
Dolly **51** 465
Dorothy **65** 353 **101** 8
Elizabeth **58** 125 **64** 116 **65**
352 **81** 253 **132** 274
Ezra Frank **114** 177
Frances A. **61** lvi
Francis **61** lvi **64** 116
George **58** 140
Hannah **58** 17
Hannah (Durrell) **132** 274
Hugh **97** 270
James **65** 352 **111** 290
Job **58** 125
John **58** 17 **64** 116 **105** 288
Jonathan **58** 17
Joseph **65** 352 **84** 423
Joshua **65** 353
Judith **67** 277
Leroy J. **67** 380
Lucy **76** 35
Luella **64** 116
Mabelle Wendell **97** 157
117 71
Martha (Linscot) **84** 423
Mary **64** 116 **88** 286 **97** 146
Mary Elizabeth **103** 53
Mary Jane **81** 254
Mary M. **122** 232
Molly **51** 463
Moses **51** 465
Nancy **86** 449
Nathan **132** 274
Rebecca **132** 274
Rebecca Madora (Titus)
114 177
Rhoda **76** 32
Rondulph **101** 12
Sally **64** 116 117
Samuel **64** 116 117 **65** 354
97 273
Sarah **58** 17 **61** lvi **65** 351
355 **113** 315
Suzanna (Lewis) **101** 12
Vivian Inez **98** 146 **115** 66
William **65** 351
Willis **64** 116
KENNON Lomira **86** 366
Richard **115** 11
William **115** 11
Kenny *see* Kenney
KENNYM Joseph **85** 10

KENNYRGE
Nicholas **94** 333
KENRICK Ann **126** 34
Anna (Atkins) **125** 9
Eliza **105** 34
Elizabeth **105** 199
George **123** 35 36
Hannah **105** 148
Jane **123** 35
John **126** 3 **141** 308
Jonathan **116** 257 **123** 199
125 9 **126** 238
Joseph **60** 365
Martha (Smith) **84** 44
Mary (Bassett) **125** 9
126 238
Mary H. (Dill) **116** 257
123 199
Oliver **126** 277
Samuel **84** 44
Sarah **90** 83 **141** 308 309
Solomon **60** 365
Sophia **123** 123
Thomas **125** 9
KENRIE —— **53** 369
KENROCK Evangeline
St. Clair **102** 221
KENSINGTON
— Mr. **66** 18 19
R. H. **91** 327
Thomas **77** 114
KENSLER
Christopher **125** 287
Louis (Botham) **125** 287
KENSLEY — Mr. **62** 320
KENT — Ens. **97** 258
— Mr. **57** 222 **72** 57
— Mrs. **91** 351
— Widow **85** 121
Abbie L. (Frost) **123** 153
Abbie W. **123** 222
Abby J. **79** 139
Abigail **58** 87 **61** 241 **63**
248 **64** 249 **85** 234 **129**
253
Abigail (Atherton) **89** 361
Abigail (Barnard) **111** 62
Ada **87** 174
Adaline P. **84** 29
Adelaide **106** 124
Albert **72** 299
Albert Emmett **72** 299
Alice Wellington **83** 371
84 187
Almira Lovisa **85** 329
Alvah B. **58** xxvii li
Amelia **72** 204
Ammy **110** 93
Amos **61** 241 **89** 361
Ann **82** 23 **91** 351
Ann (Cogan) **110** 192
Anna **56** 206 **88** 168 **89** 81
138 361 **91** 304 **112** 231
Anna (Jones) **113** 138
Anne **59** 361
Anne (Hall) **89** 361
Annie Benjanin (Hatch)
97 48
Anson **107** 299
Artemas **59** 231
Asa **56** 21

KENT *cont'd*
Asbury **97** 48
Barker **127** 319
Benjamin **58** 68 **84** 168 374
91 350 351 **92** 12 **99** 79
100 140 **105** 31 205 **132**
43 **140** 174
Berye **81** 89 **91** 371
Betsey **80** 35
C. H. **95** 299 **96** 256
123 222
Calista Young **125** 73
Carlton **125** 73
Caroline **64** 251
Charles **127** 319
Charles N. **55** 127 **64** 135
Charlotte **126** 141
Charlotte (Mellen) **92** 284
Charlotte (Vinall) **140** 256
Charlotte Appleton
60 340
Chauncey **72** 204 **73** 39
Chloe **72** 221
Claire Estelle **99** 145
Clara **91** 304 **112** 231
Clarissa **73** 39
Cornelius **53** 336
Cynthia **64** 249
Dan **123** 46
Daniel **53** 267 **54** xxxviii
350 **72** 131 322 **73** 272
134 217
Deborah **85** 452 **88** 311
Deborah (Redding)
111 64
Dorman Bridgman Eaton
65 xxxiv **70** 370 **71** xxiii
Dudley **53** 316
E. V. **125** 73
Eben **91** 304 **112** 231
Ebenezer **53** 267 **58** 68 87
78 420 **92** 314 **106** 201
140 256
Ed. **67** 334
Edward **51** 146 147 **65** 235
109 79
Edward E. **53** 265
Elain / Ela (Hamby) **145**
111 112
Elihu **54** 106
Elijah **96** 264 **111** 315
Elisha **82** 23 **102** 258
118 101
Elisha Warren **82** 23
Eliza **70** 357 **143** 259
Eliza A. **122** 110
Elizabeth **51** 285 **54** 106 **61**
385 **70** 186 **71** 278 **78**
398 **82** 23 **90** 278 **91** 350
Elizabeth (Hassy) **132** 42
Elizabeth (Watts) **132** 43
Elizabeth Ellms
(Dunham) **95** 291
Elmore Albert **72** 299
Emeline **63** 184
Esther (Tupper) **99** 194
Ethel May (Frothingham)
83 429 433
Etta Marion **82** 23
Eunice **77** 317
Eunice (Trask) **125** 104

KENT *cont'd*
Evelyn Warren **82** 23
Ezekiel **58** 86 **88** 311
Ezra **71** 278
Fanny (Leonard) **96** 83
Francis Perez (Mrs.)
    98 147
Frank M. **83** 429 433
Frank P. (Mrs.) **105** 240
Frank T. **123** 153
Frederic Houston **74** 158
    75 xviii
G. D. **128** 268
George **51** 253 **53** 433
    89 361
George Anson **125** 73
Guy **84** 300
Hannah **60** 340 **67** 204 **96**
    264 **114** 49 288 **129** 169
Hannah (Bartlett) **101** 286
Hannah (Gillett) **101** 286
Hannah (Gookins)
    (Carter) **91** 303 304
Hannah (Hodgkins)
    110 93
Hannah (Lightfoot) **96** 83
Hannah (Perrin) **96** 264
Hannah T. **90** 46
Hannah W. **126** 141
Hannah Williams **61** 56
Harriet **73** 274 **79** 155
Harriet E. (McIntosh)
    124 240
Henry **63** 18
Henry O. **54** 132
Henry Oakes **63** 314
Henry T. (Mrs.) **85** 242
Horatio Nelson **125** 73
Huldah (Whittemore)
    106 201
Humphrey **51** 286
Ira Rich (Mrs.) **86** 191
Isaac **63** 73
J. Horace **84** 29
J. V. **119** 192
Jacob **104** 118 **111** 62
Jael **102** 17
James **52** 388 **89** 361 **92**
    169 **107** 17 **110** 93
Jane (Moody) **89** 361
Jemima (Brown) **95** 88
Jemima (Kellogg)
    111 315
Joanna **90** 245
John **51** 253 254 355 **53** 265
    267 **58** 86 **64** 249 **76** 226
    83 415 **89** 361 **92** 313
    97 286 **105** 175 **110** 93
    191 **115** 230 **116** 81 **125**
    104 **145** 356
John A. **58** 371
John Harvey (Mrs.)
    104 144
Jonathan **107** 313 **111** 64
Joseph **51** 253 **53** 267 **55**
    390 **62** 94 **64** 249 **69** 28
    73 232 **77** 226 **86** 325
    89 361 **97** 326 **99** 194
    101 286 **104** 242 **105**
    164 174 175 **139** 33-36
Joseph Jackson **77** 226

KENT *cont'd*
Joshua **53** 267 **85** 120
    105 175
Josiah **95** 88 **96** 83
Justin **116** 81
Levi **105** 283
Lodovicus **119** 180
Louise **85** 195 **96** 83 149
    166
Lucia **82** 398
Lucinda **58** 371 **63** 338
    72 299
Lucinda (Starkweather)
    125 73
Lucinda Wilson **125** 73
Lucretia (Barnard) **89** 361
Lucy **122** 110 **126** 141
    127 319
Lucy (Ide) **96** 264
Lucy Morton **113** 227
Lydia **92** 169 **96** 164 **109**
    232 **125** 302 **135** 44
Mahlon **125** 73
Margaret **72** 299 **78** 166
    89 339
Margaret (Cogan)
    110 192
Margaret (Hill) **92** 319
Margery **68** 107
Maria (Barton) **107** 299
Mariah **53** 316
Martha (Allen) **123** 263
Mary **64** 249 250 **68** lxxiii
    179 **84** 131 **86** 27 93 191
    95 88 **103** 174 **126** 208
    146 335
Mary (Austin) **92** 314
Mary (Hawes) **84** 338
Mary (Hobbs) **89** 361
Mary (Page) (Putnam)
    105 31
Mary (Tuthill) **119** 180
Mary A. **123** 222
Mary Abby **72** 299
Mary Ann **90** 167
Mary B. **111** 64 **137** 29
Mary G. **125** 288
Mary H. (Grant) **123** 153
Mary White **63** lvi
Matthew **110** 191 192
Melissa **72** 74
Melvin Ernest (Mrs.)
    101 124
Moss **52** 388
Moss E. **123** 153
Nabby **85** 132
Nancy **125** 174
Nathaniel **113** 138
Noah Brooks **95** 291
Norton Adams **72** 299
Olivia Polk **77** 226
Phebe **57** 270
Priscilla **91** 350
R. D. **91** 327
Rachel **111** 315 **119** 41
Rebecca **53** 384 **57** 334
Rebecca Prentiss **73** xxxii
Remember **96** 264
Richard **53** 265 267 433
    54 216 217 **63** 283 **67**
    204 **81** 7 **85** 31 **89** 361

KENT *cont'd*
    91 304 **105** 278 **125** 92
    138 184
Robert **61** 360
Rudolphus **119** 180
Ruth **53** 316
Ruth (Baker) **127** 319
Sally **84** 374
Samuel **51** 355 **60** 340 **61**
    56 **72** 74 **79** 43 **105** 175
    119 319 **123** 263
Sarah **53** 433 **58** 86 **59** 219
    71 66 **81** 7 **95** 88 **111** 62
    119 319 **123** 259 263
Sarah (Greenleaf) **89** 361
Sarah (Woodman) **97** 286
Sarah Alice **103** 174
Sarah Elizabeth **82** 23
Sarah Elizabeth Ellms
    95 291
Sarah Roach **77** 226
Seth **63** 335 338
Sibyl **57** 269
Sophronia Kenworthy
    125 73
Stephen **68** 107 **87** 265
Steven **132** 42
Susan **63** 338 **69** 28 **78** 404
Susan (George) **105** 164
Susanna **63** 335
Susanna (George) **86** 325
    105 175
Susanna (Thompson)
    83 415
Susanna (Winslow)
    88 311
Susanna Hincks (Rich)
    84 300
Theodore **122** 110
Thomas **51** 253 **53** 35 36
    61 385 **66** 253 **91** 327
    96 83 **103** 174
Thomas W. **91** 327
Timothy **84** 338 **145** 111
    112
Tryphena **64** 249
Tryphosa **60** 306
W. A. **92** 284 314
W. H. **91** 327
Walter **82** 23
Wi **105** 196
Wilbur **82** 23
William **52** 388 **68** 179
    77 134 **78** 305 **92** 313
    101 26 **107** 17
William A. **92** 319
William H. **91** 327
KENTFIELD
Desire **95** 78
Eleanor **102** 239
Fanny **104** 56
KENTISH
Alice **141** 132
Ann **65** 242
John **141** 132
Richard **53** 23
KENTLIN
Thankful **127** 223
KENTNER
Conrad **121** 100-102
George **121** 101 102

KENTNER *cont'd*
Lovina **121** 100
KENTON Kinton
Ann **108** 276
Richard **104** 20
KENTZER Matthew **91** 327
KENWARD John **66** 61
KENWOOD
Peter **57** 280 388
Keny *see* Kenney
KENYON Kinyon Kinyoun
—— **67** 286 **130** 154
136 211
— Baron **86** 327
Abby **63** 45
Abby (Lillibridge) **127** 88
Abby J. **63** 50
Abigail **67** 286
Abigail (Champlin)
117 196
Alfred Whitman **127** 88
Alice **67** 297 **86** 196 **96** 61
Amy **70** 231 **127** 33 36
Amy (Barber) **127** 36
Amy (Hunt) **108** 66
Ann **88** 136
Anna **128** 218
Anna E. (Gifford) **125** 240
Anne **63** 49
Annie F. **93** 218
Augusta T. **86** 380
Barber **115** 292
Benedict **63** 49 **127** 36
Benedict J. **117** 196
Benjamin **128** 302
Benjamin Franklin
77 186
Caleb **80** 74
Celia (Knowles) (Stanton)
88 133
Charity **63** 49 **115** 292
Charles H. **125** 245
Charles Wesley **92** 363
Clark **63** 49
Corey **117** 196
Cynthia **63** 50
Daniel **64** 342 **128** 217
David **61** 80 **70** 232
Dency **115** 292
Earl Samuel **92** 363
Edith Crozier **130** 49
Edward C. **57** 383
Elise Chesebrough
(Rathbone) **88** 79
Elisha Reynolds Potter
88 135
Elisha S. **125** 245
Elizabeth **67** 287 **88** 131
126 250 **134** 129
Elizabeth (Leonard) **88** 78
Elizabeth Richardson
(Bradford) **95** 93
Ellen C. **117** 292
Ellis **82** 339
Esther **70** 230
Fannie E. **116** 63
Frances (James) **126** 254
Frederic George **75** 316
76 xx **108** 61 66 137
Gardner **63** 49 **126** 254
George **82** 189 **100** 173

KENYON *cont'd*
121 34 35 **128** 223 302
George C. **86** 380 **142** 295
George S. **86** 169
George T. **63** 49
Green **86** 382
Hannah **86** 382
Harry **116** 63
Harry C. **117** 218
Helen Augusta **143** 66
Howard N. **89** 401
Howard Nathaniel **98** 147
Hoxsie **127** 88
Hugh **82** 188
Isaac C. **142** 289
James **67** 286 **128** 301
136 216
James H. **130** 49
James N. **88** 133
James T. **88** 136
Jane A. **51** 51
Jane Gray (Knowles)
88 136
Jared **92** 65
Joel **115** 292 293 **116** 114
Joel M. **115** 292
John **67** 286 297 **86** 380
88 78 **128** 217 295 303
136 216
John Hoxsie **127** 88
John Robert **108** 66
John S. **100** 338
John T. **127** 88
Joram **128** 59
Joseph **128** 217
Joshua **116** 203 **128** 217
Julia **115** 293
Julia (Waterman) **88** 78
Kathleen Mary **108** 66
Keith Earl **92** 363
Kessie Ella (Sanders)
92 363
Larkin **128** 217
Lavarah M. **125** 240
Levi C. **115** 292
Lillian A. **117** 218
Lloyd **105** 182
Louisa **63** 49
Lowell H. **63** 50
Lucretia **116** 203
Lucy **61** 80 **70** 232 **128** 217
Ludowick **128** 217
Lydia **63** 49
Margaret C. (Rodman)
125 245
Martha **107** 225
Martin R. **125** 240
Mary **63** 47 49 **67** 286 297
86 380 **100** 173 **105** 173
126 254 **127** 32 **130** 155
Mary (Gardiner) **88** 136
Mary (James) **127** 88
Mary (Lillibridge) **127** 86
Mary (Ray) **86** 327 **105** 173
181 182
Mary (Strawn) (Penrose)
117 196
Mary A. **116** 114
Mary Ann (Knowles)
88 135
Mary Elizabeth **127** 87

KENYON *cont'd*
Mary Jane **86** 380
Mary Louisa **77** 183
Mercy **67** 286
Nathan **91** 251 **128** 217
Nathaniel **128** 295 303
Nora Gwendolen
Margaret **108** 66
Oliver **130** 154
Oliver S. **115** 292
Paine **128** 21
Payne **88** 78
Peleg **86** 380 **128** 299
Perry **134** 129
Peter **128** 299
Phebe **100** 173 **130** 154
Philip **71** 140 142
Phineas **128** 295
Rachel **93** 217
Ralph Watson **88** 78
Ralph Wood **79** 196 **80**
204 **81** 216 **82** 231 **84**
179 **88** 78 86 171
Reana **121** 34 35
Rebecca A. (Griswold)
143 66
Remington **63** 49 **127** 8
129 57
Reynolds **63** 50
Rhoda **126** 254
Roger **67** 296 297 **86** 262
327 **105** 173 181 182 261
Ruth **63** 49 **70** 230 **127** 86
Ruth (Hoxsie) **127** 88
Sally **88** 135 **93** 217 **127** 88
Samuel **128** 217 303
Sarah **67** 286 **77** 184 **91** 251
Sarah (Brownell) **134** 129
Sarah (Sweet) **130** 155
Sarah A. **70** 154
Silas **126** 254
Sprague **127** 86
Stephen **121** 34-36 **128** 300
Susan Basset **77** 186
Susan Melissa (Hoxsie)
127 88
Susanna **88** 135 137
Theda **88** 79
Theda R. (Howard) **88** 78
Thedia Redelia **84** 455 **97**
90 **98** 90
Theodia (Howard) **128** 21
Theresa **86** 380
Thomas **67** 286 296 **100**
173 **112** 29
Varnum S. **143** 66
Victor (Mrs.) **103** 119
Volney **51** 51
Waitey (Moon) (Barber)
117 196
Wealthy **91** 251
Whitman **63** 45 **127** 88
William **110** 123 **128** 217
129 59
William Clark **77** 183
William H. **117** 292
Zebulon **115** 292
KEOGH Chester Henry
74 158 **75** xxvi **81** 240
George **78** 305
Katharine Roselia **103** 119

KEOGH cont'd
  106 221 **107** 137
KEON Margaret **79** 271
KEONEOTT
  Margaret **93** 236
KEOUGH — Bp. **94** 302
KEOUS
  Margaret W. **117** 144
  William **126** 225
KEPAS Richard **90** 197
KEPHART
  — Lt. Col. **99** 243
  Adam **114** 189
  Barbara **54** 150
  Calvin **93** 402 **104** 78 **106**
  160 **117** 271
  Calvin I. **118** 77
  Cornelia **54** 150
  Elizabeth **114** 189
  George Stebbins **54** 150
  Horace **54** 150 **56** 216 **57**
  xxxiii
  John **114** 189
  Laura White **54** 150
  Leonard Mack **54** 150
  Lucy Wheeler **54** 150
  Margaret **54** 150
  Mary **114** 189
  Nora Rebecca **124** 261
  Peter **114** 189
KEPLER Annie **91** 110
  Guy Link (Mrs.) **104** 144
  Samuel **91** 193
KEPLINGER
  Genevieve **69** 328
KEPP John **88** 278
  Mary (Allen) **88** 278
KEPPEL
  Helen Marie **119** 155
KEPTON Richard **107** 230
KERAGAN Eleanor **99** 122
  101 54
  John **99** 119 122 **101** 54
  Margaret **99** 119
  Sarah **99** 119
  Sheba **99** 122 **101** 54
KERBER John **127** 9
Kerby see Kirby
KERCHER
  Ann Barbara **101** 318
KERCHEVAL Jane
  (Shapleigh) **96** 35
  Margaret **77** 227
  Royal D. (Mrs.) **100** 169
  Royal Dickson **96** 35
KERCHIN Ann **65** 172
KEREN Daniel **143** 259
KERFBIJL Jan **106** 10
KERGILL
  Martha **125** 115 116
KERIE Jane **124** 43
  Richard **124** 43
  Sarah **124** 44
KERIN John A. **109** 78
  Mary Ann (Carney)
  109 78
KERINGTON
  Rose **104** 113
KERISON Eleanor (Bressey)
  112 31
  John **112** 31

KERISON cont'd
  William **112** 29
KERKE Henry **51** 45
KERKENER
  Agnes **51** 389
  Catherine **51** 389
  Erasmus **51** 389
KERLIN
  Anderson **128** 96
  Charlott **128** 96
  Mary Jane (Willits)
  128 96
KERLING N. J.M. **110** 9
  122 171
KERLY Absalom **78** 40
  Alice **78** 57 60 61
  Anna **78** 40
  Charles **78** 40
  Charles Talant **78** 41 42
  Chloe **78** 40
  Clemond **78** 40
  Cumberland Polk **78** 41
  Cyrus Granville **78** 41
  Edmund **60** 60 **78** 39 40
  Edward **78** 40
  Elijah **78** 40
  Elizabeth **78** 40
  Emma Cornelia **78** 41 202
  Evelyn **78** 37 40
  George **78** 40
  Henry **62** 226 227 229 337
  341 342 **63** 61 66 120
  123 125 **78** 40
  Hiram **78** 37 40
  James **60** 24 **78** 40
  John **78** 40
  John Brackville **78** 41
  Joseph **78** 40
  Larkin **78** 39 40
  Louise Elizabeth **78** 39 41
  Lucretia **78** 39 40
  Lucy **78** 40
  Martha **78** 40
  Mary **78** 39 40
  Mary Jane **78** 41
  Mila Mangrum **78** 42
  Nancy **78** 40
  Newton Fleming **78** 41
  Polly **78** 40
  Rachel **78** 40
  Rebecca **71** 253 **78** 40
  Rhoda Jeannette **78** 42
  Ruth **78** 40
  Samuel Reyburn **78** 41
  Sarah **78** 40
  Solomon **78** 40
  William **55** 303 **60** 60 357
  62 223 226-228 337 341
  343 344 **63** 59 61 63-66
  118 120 123 125 219 **71**
  253 **78** 39 40 **142** 115
  121 269
  Wilmoth **78** 40
KERMET Barbara **65** 28
KERN Kerne - see also
  Kinnear
  — **91** 111
  Charles W. **143** 266
  Christianne **80** 273
  David **80** 273
  Emily Benton **80** 273

KERN cont'd
  Jacob **80** 273
  Lawrence Russell **107** 133
  Pauline **85** 409
  Thomas **118** 144
KERNAN
  Francis **108** 67
  Patrick **60** 24
KERNISH
  Grace Antoinette
  105 226
  William Sheldon **105** 226
KERNOCHAN Abby
  Townsend (Lansing)
  92 146
  Edward Learned **92** 146
  Helen **111** 52
  Robert R. **111** 52
  Sophia Jenie (Dame)
  111 52
KERNOHAN J. W. **67** 193
  112 276 **117** 244
KERNOUGHAN
  Francis **141** 198
KERNS Alice **124** 298
  Elizabeth **59** 394
  John **98** 289
  Mary Alice **124** 298
  Mary Clifford **87** 174
  William **59** 394
KEROUALLE Louise de
  104 173 **105** 187 **121**
  188
KERR Ker Kyrr
  Adam **127** 304
  Agnes **108** 191
  Andrew **114** 186
  Arthur S. (Mrs.) **128** 160
  Augustus Pomero **93** 371
  Caroline Mary **55** xlvii
  Catherine **114** 191
  Charles **100** 67 **112** 233
  137 306
  Daniel **114** 150 186
  David **60** 161 **65** 248
  Elizabeth **51** 443 **61** 266 **85**
  349 **112** 297
  Elizabeth (Magee)
  112 297
  Emma Roy **77** 186
  Frank Melville **69** xxv 87
  Grace **72** 37
  H. W. (Mrs.) **109** 127
  Hamilton **61** 265 **65** 143
  Hannah **60** 161 **86** 446
  Harold (Mrs.) **107** 133
  Harrison **128** 176
  Harry V. (Mrs.) **113** 221
  James **111** 202 214
  John **85** 96 **111** 204
  John Robert **77** 186
  Joseph **61** 265 **95** 401
  Josiah **61** 265
  Juliette A. (Spencer)
  126 79
  Lawrence H. **51** 443
  Lottie Isobelle **93** 371
  Lydia **127** 225
  Lydia B. **101** 257
  Margaret **111** 214
  Mark **100** 67 **112** 233

KERR *cont'd*
Mary **111** 211
Mary Louise Merritt
85 96
Nancy **78** 409
Nathan **55** 147
Prudence **70** 317
Robert **70** 223 317
Sarah **61** 266 **128** 176
Sarah (Morris) **125** 287
Thomas **75** 280
Walter **79** 62
William **60** 25 **72** 37 **111**
208 **125** 287
KERRELL Thirza **111** 148
KERREY Agnes **67** 47
KERRICH Kerrick
Agnes **75** 293 295 298 300
Alice **75** 293-295 298 301
Ann **75** 293 295 296
Annis **75** 290 293 298 299
Anthony **75** 293 294 296
300
Aylmer **75** 293
Barbara **75** 293
Charles **75** 295 300
Christian **75** 290 299
Christopher **75** 293 294
Daniel **75** 293
Dorothy **75** 295 301
Edmund **75** 293
Elizabeth **73** 138 **75** 290
291 293-296 298 301
Faith **75** 294 295
Frances **75** 298
Francis **75** 294-296 300
George **75** 293 294 296 300
Giles **75** 291-293 295-297
299-301
Hannah **75** 294 295
Isabel **75** 291 292 300 301
Jane **75** 294-296 298
Joan **52** 239 **75** 290 293-295
298 301
John **75** 290-301
Katharine **75** 293-295 301
Lawrence **75** 291 297 298
Margaret **75** 290-295 298-
301
Margery **75** 279 292 293
295 296 300 301
Martha **75** 293 294 298
Mary **75** 292-295 298-301
Miles **75** 290 291 294-298
Oliver **75** 293
Peter **75** 294
Philip **75** 295 301
Robert **75** 290-301
Rose **75** 274 275 279 290-
292 295 298-301 **105** 254
Samuel **75** 293 295 301
Simon **75** 294
Susan **75** 293 295 296 300
Thomas **52** 239 **75** 290-301
William **75** 279 290-301
105 254
Wolfran **75** 294 295
KERRIDGE
Samuel **80** 365
Susan **80** 365
Thomas **80** 365

KERRIDGE *cont'd*
William **80** 365
KERRINGTON
Ann **113** 185
Anne **113** 188
KERRY
Lydia B. **101** 257
William **52** 107
KERS Ebenezer **59** 353
KERSAINT — Capt. **77** 65
KERSELEY John **52** 68
Margaret **52** 68
KERSEY —— **52** 69
Joseph **145** 366
Thomas **65** 127
KERSEYMER
Zephron **125** 106
KERSHAW Kershawe
Charles H. **117** 288
Eda B. **117** 288
James **64** 262
John **58** 199
Mary **115** 116
Ralph **64** 341
Robert **82** 188
Thomas **115** 116
KERSHNER
Barbara **96** 396
Howard Eldred **85** 353
KERSLAKE John **111** 8
KERSO Mary **104** 181
KERSON
John **55** 413 **78** 409
Margaret **55** 413
KERSTEMANN
Abraham **55** 436
Ellen **55** 436
KERSUM
Esther H. **73** 193
KERSWELL Kearswell
Kerswall Kerswill
Abigail **66** 215 297
Abigail (Varrell) **116** 128
Amos **66** 147 212 295 296
298
Anne **66** 147 295-297 299
306
Armine **97** 141
Arthur **66** 147 215
Betsey **115** 305
Betty **66** 224 297
Eliza (Gutridge) **117** 228
Elizabeth **66** 223-235 295
297 **97** 270
Joanna **66** 224 225 295
297 299
John **66** 210 224 225 295
297 299 **103** 236
Joshua **97** 144
Lemuel Muchmore
66 299
Mark **63** 173
Martha **66** 210 212 213 215
Mary **63** 173 **66** 212 300
301 **118** 240-242
Mary (Holt) **116** 131
Mary E. (Raymond)
103 236
Mercy **66** 155
Molly **66** 295
Nabby **117** 143

KERSWELL *cont'd*
Nancy **115** 309
Nanny **66** 299
Olive **116** 135
Pelatiah **66** 147 214 295-
297 299 **116** 136
Rachel **66** 295
Rebecca **66** 147 295 296
298 306 **116** 141
Robert **66** 210 212 213
215 223-225 295 300
Samuel **66** 213 296
117 228
Sarah **66** 144 155 210 212
214 215 224 296 300 **115**
309 **116** 131
Sukey **116** 137
Susan **117** 224 226
Susan (Kerswell) **117**
224 226
Susanna **66** 147 **115** 224
Tamzine **66** 210
Tryphena **66** 297
William **66** 144 155 210
212 214 215 223 295 304
116 128 131 **117** 224
226
KERTON William **63** 19
KERTY Abner **103** 236
Rebecca (Chase) **103** 236
KERWIN —— **58** 207
KESAIG Grizzle **125** 196
KESEE
Allen Polk **78** 160
Sarah Gladys **78** 160
Susan Huntington
78 160
Thomas Woodfin **78** 160
Zelda Polk **78** 160
Kesler *see* Kessler
KESMIRE Okie **78** 44
KESSBERGER
A. W. **104** 299
August **104** 299
Christianna (Hagedorn)
104 299
Gussie Leona (Hopkins)
104 299
KESSLER Kesler
Emeline (Parker) **97** 81
Frederick **97** 81
Hannah **51** 449
Helen Koues (Roelker)
108 153
John Alexander **108** 153
Louisa (Whipple) **102** 313
Margaret (Even) **112** 246
Marietta **97** 81
Michel **112** 246
Nicholas **102** 313
Ottile Julia **94** 281
KESTER
Paul P. **134** 36 37
Rachel **95** 166
KESWICK
Henry I. **69** 318
KETCH Nancy **93** 216
Ketcham *see* Ketchum
KETCHELL
Joanna **115** 38
Joseph **79** 108

KETCHELL *cont'd*
Simon **79** 108
KETCHERELL
Joseph **75** 219
Simon **75** 219
KETCHIN Alice **51** 124
KETCHUM Ketcham
Adeline Elizabeth **87** 281
Alfred **66** 231
Ann (Forrester) **109** 186
Ann (Whitman) **96** 294
Ann Laetitia (Smith)
  109 187
Anna Maria **109** 186
Barnard **57** 106
Betsey **109** 186
Betty **95** 249
Blanche Elida Melvina
  109 186
C. H. **118** 238
Caroline Amelia **94** 187
Charles **109** 186
Charles Frederick **109** 187
Charles Henry **109** 186
Charles John **109** 187
Charlotte **97** 126
Chauncy **133** 119
Clara Louise **96** 81
D. **80** 33
Daniel Littleton **129** 42
David **129** 42
Deborah **109** 186 187 **144**
  244 **145** 150 153 155
Deborah (Cluckstone)
  109 186
Edith Seeley **109** 186
Edward H. **66** 231
Edward Le Baron **109** 186
Edwin **109** 186
Eleanor (Soule) **120** 320
Elida (Snider) **109** 186
Elisha **105** 153
Eliza Randolph **73** xlviii
Elizabeth **66** 231
Elizabeth (Dibble)
  109 186
Elizabeth (Head) **109** 150
  187
Elizabeth (Raymond)
  109 186
Emily (Myers) **109** 187
Enoch **73** xlviii
Esther (Gifford) **129** 42
Frances **109** 186
Frances Ann **109** 186
Frank Forrester **109** 186
George Forrester **109** 186
George Henry **109** 187
George William **109** 186
Gertrude J. (Wright) **65**
  89 **67** 303 **68** xxxi
Hannah **59** 358
Hannah (Quintard) **109**
  186 **145** 150
Isaac **109** 186 187
James **109** 186
Jane C. **122** 217
John Dibble **109** 187
Jonathan **109** 186 **144** 242
  145 150-152
Joseph **59** 358 **109** 186

KETCHUM *cont'd*
  120 320
Joshua **120** 320
Katharine **83** 482
Laurinda **133** 119
Lydia **107** 160
Lydia (Sweet) **107** 160
Margaret A. (Leavitt)
  109 186
Margaret Doughty
  (Cadman) **109** 187
Martha **55** 300 **96** 294
Mary **57** 106 **99** 300
  109 186
Mary (Williams) **109** 186
Mary Bettey **95** 249
Mary Elizabeth **109** 186
Mary Elizabeth
  (Fairweather) **109** 186
Phebe **104** 265
Phebe A. **77** 152
Phebe C. **66** 231
Philip **55** 300
Polly **72** 215
Rebecca **92** 300
Rebecca Kimball
  (Phillips) **109** 187
Roxanna **105** 153
Roxanna (Billings)
  (Saxton) **105** 153
Sally **125** 228
Samuel **109** 186 **145** 151
  152
Sarah **131** 213
Sarah (Jagger) **100** 332
  101 105
Susan Van Auken
  73 xlviii
T. J. **122** 217
Thomas **109** 186
Thomas Carleton Lee
  109 187
William **109** 186
William H. **109** 186
William Quintard **109**
  150 187
Zebulon **96** 294
KETELBY Abel **95** 21
KETLER
John Carl **62** 244
KETLEY John **98** 105
KETLIN Jane **73** 272
KETT Francis **68** 206
George **68** 206
L. Marion **69** xxxii
Richard **59** 418
Robert **68** 206
Thomas **61** 279 **68** 206
  76 56
William **68** 206
KETTELL Kettle
—— **53** 195 **64** 247 **75** 298
___ (Freeman) **140** 143
___ (Jackson) **140** 160
Abigail **59** 251 252
Alice **108** 171
Alma F. **80** 250
Amasa **140** 160
Andrew **59** 252 **78** 304
  125 41
Annie Jane **80** 249

KETTELL *cont'd*
Caroline Freeman **92** 260
Charles **80** 250
Charlotte **59** 252
Daniel G. **126** 204
Dorothy (Edmunds)
  (Hett) **143** 50
Ebenezer **59** 252
Edward **123** 230
Edward Henry **92** 350
Eliza **86** 144
Elizabeth **59** 250 **64** 244
  247 **92** 53
Elizabeth (Chase) **87** 333
Esther **59** 252 **91** 270
  100 304
Esther (Ward) **131** 127
Hannah **59** 248 252 **132** 95
Hannah (Eveleth) **134** 302
Hepzibah **59** 252
Jacob Quincy **88** 350
  99 200
James **51** 296 **52** 37 **59** 250
  88 350 **99** 200 **133** 308
James A. **79** 37
Jean **80** 249
Joan **66** 72
John **51** 100 294-297 **52**
  37 38 290 **53** 266 **59** 252
  60 310 **68** 69 **83** 77 **86**
  144 **92** 53 260 346 350
  94 158 380 **140** 143 160
John (Mrs.) **92** 123
John B. **140** 160
John B. (Mrs.) **92** 123
John Brooks **92** 346
Jonathan **59** 252 **86** 144
  92 53
Joseph **59** 194 252 **140** 160
  143 50
Katharine **118** 323
Libbie **80** 250
Livonia Green (Waid)
  86 144
Lucy **59** 252
Margaret **75** 290 298
Maria **59** 252
Mary **54** 449 **59** 252 **86** 97
  88 350 **99** 200 **107** 255
Nathan **134** 302
Polly (Quincy) **133** 309
Ralph **64** 161 166
Rebecca **59** 252 **80** 7 **110**
  230 **140** 252
Rebecca Austin **59** 252
Richard **53** 266 **131** 127
Ruth **59** 249 251 252
Ruth (Simpson) **132** 95
Sally Sherburn **99** 200
Samuel **110** 230
Sarah **59** 324 **78** 419
Sheldon S. **80** 249
Suky Nye (Freeman)
  92 123
Susan **94** 380
Susan (Freeman) **140** 160
Susan (Taylor) **126** 204
Susanna **59** 252 **123** 230
Thomas **59** 252 **92** 53
  140 160
Thomas Prentice **59** 252

KETTELL *cont'd*
Tilly **113** 12
William **59** 249 251 252
365 **64** 225 **87** 333 **132**
95 **140** 252
KETTELLE
Violet E. **134** 200
KETTERIDGE
—— **120** 128
KETTERING Charles
Franklin **88** 169
Kettle *see* Kettell
KETTLEBOROUGH
Elizabeth **114** 150
KETTLES Emelie Frances
(Parmelee) **105** 52
Evelyn M. **105** 52
Frank S. **105** 52
KETTOW
Edward **60** 127 128
Mercy **60** 128
KETTSON Anna **53** 254
KETZ Barnet **114** 188
Jacob **114** 188
Lewis **114** 188
Peter **114** 188
Rachel **114** 188
Sarah **114** 188
KEUREN
Floyd von **107** 178
KEVSKIE
Elaine Hart **103** 116
KEW John **68** 148
Samuel **129** 55
KEWS William **98** 106
KEY Abigail **74** 263
Almy **66** 139
Anna **70** 227 **78** 50
Betsey **74** 259 262 265
Betsey H. **74** lxxii
Betty **74** 251
C. F. **78** 412
Charity **74** 213 226 248
82 209
Daniel **74** 256 265 **82** 315
Ebenezer **70** 227
Edmund **73** 269
Elizabeth **61** 68 **74** 265
Francis **80** 90
Fred E. **78** 320
Grissel **82** 74 97
Hannah **64** 155 **74** 249 257
Hannah (Bartlet) **116** 222
Hiram **74** 266
Horatio Nelson **66** 139
Huchens **66** 139
Ignatius **73** 146
James **74** 226 **82** 74 209
91 327
James T. **108** 104
Jane **74** 226 253 263
Joanna **74** 257
John **52** 123 127 128 **64** 343
74 226 249 251 254 262
82 74 81 97 209 316
Katarina De **98** 183
Levi **82** 85
Lois **74** 264 **116** 297
Love **74** 255
Lucinda **113** 154
Lucretia Mott **82** 267

KEY *cont'd*
Lula Helen **78** 320
Lydia **74** 190 251 255 262
Mary **64** 155 **74** 50 249 250
82 74 209 315
Mehitable **74** 249
Molly **74** 254 255 259
Olive **74** 266
Otis **74** 257
Patience **74** 256
Peter **74** 125 190
Phealy **74** 261
Samuel **74** 261
Sarah **74** 248
Sarah Gladys **78** 160
Susan Cleveland (Falley)
108 104
Susanna **74** 260
Thomas **80** 87 **110** 190
William **74** 259 265
82 209 315
Winthrop **116** 222
KEYCO —— **141** 55
KEYES Keys
—— **56** 106 **70** 23 24 300
308 **143** 202
— Capt. **70** 297 298 **121** 98
— Mr **93** 259
Abel **133** 231
Abial **83** 166
Abigail **70** 240 **77** 18 19 21
90 42 **111** 239
Abijah **77** 20 **89** 62
Aline **75** lxxx
Almond **70** 232
Amasa **94** 55
Amaziah **89** 62
Anna **131** 48
Anna Hunt **104** 102
Asa **57** 284 **91** 87 **132** 243
Asa D. **123** 313
Azubah **137** 361
Benjamin **77** 30
Bertha H. **92** 333
Betsey **92** 273
Betsey Elizabeth
(Richardson) **108** 134
Betty **77** 29
Caroline **86** 307
Carrie L. **93** 327
Catherine **77** 20 33
104 122
Charles Evans **136** 274
Charles Washington
108 134
Chloe **66** 137
Cornelia **57** 405
Cyprian **77** 19 24-27 29 30
Danforth **63** 292
Daniel **77** 28 **83** 166
David **63** 85 **77** 24 29
120 48
Deborah **72** 111
Dinah **77** 20 24
Dolly (Mathewson)
121 179
Ebenezer **61** 304 **77** 26
Edward **63** 88
Eleanor **70** 232
Eli **77** 18-22 27 28 32
Elias **61** 303 304 **102** 320

KEYES *cont'd*
120 163 **127** 297
Eliphaz **61** 304
Eliza **62** 170 **63** 85 **66** 141
77 176
Eliza K. **67** 272
Elizabeth **51** 466 **60** 375 **63**
85 89 **72** 111 **77** 20 27
87 294 **126** 129 **137** 361
Elizabeth (Irwin) **98** 341
Ellen Douglas **132** 243
Emily B. (Eaton) **77** 322
78 205
Emma Frances (Pierce)
87 63
Ephraim **77** 26
Esther **77** 20
Esther (Smith) (Nichols)
133 231
Eunice **58** 280 **70** 240
75 264
Ezra **77** 22 27
Frances **63** 292
Frances (Grant) **91** 87
Francis **77** 28
Franklin L. **77** 176
French **64** 212
George Thomas **77** 322
78 205
Hannah **63** lxii **77** 32
136 221
Hannah J. **121** 306
Harlan **78** 362
Harriet **70** 240
Henry **77** 20 29 **87** 63
Hepzibah **56** 45 **77** 18
Hettie Britt (Wright)
136 274
Homer Eaton **78** 447
79 194
Horace **124** 79
Hugh **98** 341
Huldah **54** cx **124** 79
Idelle **57** xxxiii **58** xlviii
60 xxxiv 185 **62** xxxv
66 xlviii **69** 189 **72** 76
75 vii **76** vii **77** vii **78**
29 **79** 215 **80** 221 **81** 235
89 62 81 137
Ivory **77** 13
Jane **51** 447
Jane (Aldrich) **89** 62
Jemima **62** 253
Joanna **51** 448 **55** 401
84 440
Joel **77** 30
John **51** 466 **60** 185 **61** 304
63 329 **72** 111 **75** 264
77 19-21 23 24 26 **82** 88
83 154 **89** 62 **92** 49 **97**
37 **104** 102 **136** 221 **144**
111
John Brooks **96** 160
John S. **57** 127 **89** 375
Jonas **58** 280
Jonathan **77** 19-21 23-26
28
Joseph **51** 448 **55** 401 **59**
193 **71** 42
Judah **71** 42
Judith **51** 447

KEYES *cont'd*
Julia **63** 49
Keziah (Brigham) **102** 320
L. E. **93** 327
Laura L. **77** 178
Levina **77** 26 **93** 259
Lewis E. **92** 333 **93** 327
Lorrin Porter **61** 321
Love **63** lxii
Lucretia **58** 280
Lucy **57** 284 **70** 240 **71** 3
　77 30 31 **79** 319 **83** 166
　95 372 **110** 231 **135** 17
Lucy (Stearns) **93** 185
Lucy Anna **63** lxii
Lucy S. **93** 327
Lydia **77** 30
Marah **63** 88
Marcia **67** 272
Martha **77** 19 24 **126** 89
Martha Gertrude **87** 63
Mary **57** 284 **62** 255 **63** 292
　64 212 **77** 19 20 **89** 371
　102 320 **107** 261 **111**
　224
Mary (Eames) **136** 221
Mary Elizabeth **78** 362
Mary Sargent (Mahoney)
　91 87
Matthias **62** 253
Mehitable (Kemp)
　126 129
Meribah A. **71** 42
Miranda M. **137** 152
Miriam **63** 89 **77** 24 32
Moses **126** 129
Muriel Elaine Sargent
　(Clapp) **96** 160
Nancy (Crafts) **89** 62
Nancy S. **87** 343
Oliver **77** 19 20 **89** 62
Otis **87** 343
Patience **77** 18
Patty **77** 26
Peabody **77** 27
Penelope (Williams)
　121 64
Percey **63** 85 89 **70** 240
Persis **77** 19 24
Phebe **77** 18 20 30 33
Phebe (Smith) **91** 87
Phila **71** 42
Polly **63** 85 **80** 7
Priscilla **77** 19 22
Ralph **121** 179
Rebecca **77** 18
Rebecca (Patterson) **89** 62
Relief **77** 27
Rhoda **66** 137
Robert **58** 280 **61** 303 **62**
　254 **91** 87 **137** 361
Ruth **57** 284 **77** 18 19 22
Ruth (Whittemore)
　108 163
Ruth Lovering **134** 221
Sally **63** 85 **83** 166 **84** 318
　85 327 425 **92** 128 **93**
　315 **119** 133 **121** 62
Sally (Billings) **94** 55
Sampson **70** 240 241
Samson **63** 88

KEYES *cont'd*
Samuel **56** 74 **90** 51
　105 212
Samuel B. **69** 211
Sarah **51** 447 **57** 284 **58** 257
　61 236 304 **62** 254 **63**
　292 **69** 189 **77** 18 21 24
　27 30 **98** 341 **136** 326
Sarah (Blandford) **120** 163
Sarah (Danforth) **91** 87
Sarah (Harbough) **89** 62
Sarah (Jaquith) **108** 167
Sarah F. **92** 333
Seth **76** 48
Silas **61** 236
Simeon **57** 284 **77** 29
　108 163
Simon **67** 272
Solomon **51** 447 **58** 237
　61 154 **63** 85 292 **77** 23
　26 **91** 87 **121** 221
Stephen **72** 111 **77** 26 27
Submit **77** 30
Susan **126** 209
Susan H. **93** 327
Thankful (Lincoln) **91** 87
Thomas **62** 170 **77** 24 29
Timothy **58** 280
Wade **54** 103 **59** xli **68** 204
　82 121 234 **84** 180 **90**
　124 **91** 60 87 147
Willard **57** 405
William **87** 366
William Edward **89** 62
William Wallace **91** 87
Wilson **66** 141
Zebediah **83** 166
KEYGER Nora **127** 67
KEYLICH Anna **78** 45
Feodor **78** 45
Lila M. **78** 45
KEYMER William **63** 240
KEYMES Bridget (Spear-
　man) **137** 284
William **137** 284
KEYMESTER John **64** 22
KEYN
Arthur **126** 17-19
Elizabeth **126** 19
James **126** 18 19
Jane **126** 17 19
John **126** 17-19
Nathaniel **126** 19
Rachel **126** 19
Thomas **126** 18
William **126** 18 19
KEYNE Sarah **108** 114
KEYNER John **55** 449
KEYNES
Hawise **142** 235
Lettice **142** 235-237
Robert **51** 354
Robert de **142** 235
William **142** 235
Keys *see* Keyes
KEYSER Keysar
　—— **56** 331
Alice (Bolesworth) **147** 21
Alice (Walker) **108** 68
Amelia Louise **101** 121
　115 146

KEYSER *cont'd*
Dirck Gerritze **108** 68
Elhanan Winchester
　68 121
Elizabeth (Forte) **124** 193
Elizabeth (Holyoke)
　147 21
George **147** 21
Helen Linthicum **108** 68
Keturah Benson **124** 193
　194
Kirck **124** 193
Maria **68** 121
Natalie Whiting (Hunt)
　108 68
Richard **111** 85
Sally Ann **68** 121
William **124** 193
William J. **76** 53
William Wallace **108** 68
KEYSEY Ann **90** 381
KEYSOR Mary **106** 125
KEYT Amanda (Fracker)
　124 257 258
Amanda Priscilla **124** 257
Edwin Bush **124** 257
KEZAR Kezer
Abigail **56** 208 **69** 124
Apphia **56** 208
Calenda **57** 201
Charles **70** 336
Elizabeth **133** 321
Ellen **96** 132
George **57** 201
Glenola Isabelle **78** 207
Hannah **56** 208 **70** 336
Helen **123** 126
Jane **96** 132
Jane K. **96** 130
Jane R. **96** 130
John **56** 208 **70** 336
Jonathan **69** 124 219
Luther **70** 23
Mehitable **56** 208
Moses **57** 201 **69** 121
　70 297 306
Nathaniel **69** 214 305
　70 13
Olive **86** 365
Sarah **57** 201 **69** 154 **70** 336
Sarah E. **114** 317
KIBBE Kibbee Kibbey
　Kibbie Kibby
　—— **53** 26 **59** 104
　— Maj. Gen. **79** 154
Aaron **115** 40 42
Acksah **115** 119
Alice **58** 404 **59** 215
Alvan **72** 204
Alvin **73** 39
Amy **132** 114
Amy Sophronia **90** 277
Angeline E. **79** 278
Ann **55** 290 292
Austin **72** 204
Austin S. (Mrs.) **82** 116
Betty **54** 53
Beulah **54** 53
Charles **60** 80 307
Clarissa **61** 299
Deborah **60** 80

KIBBE *cont'd*
Dorothy **115** 129
Dorothy (Phelps) **123** 263
Edward **59** 244 **60** 307
  121 235 236 **123** 262
  263
Eldad **115** 195
Elisha **118** 215
Eliza J. G. **72** 204
Elizabeth **54** 53 **59** 244 245
Ellen **82** 406
Elvirus Sullivan **90** 277
Esther **57** 213
Gaius **80** 56
Gideon **115** 37
Grace **60** 307
Hannah **59** 244 **73** 39
Hannah (Phelps) **123** 264
Inez Medora **82** 406
Irving Leslie **82** 406
Isaac **137** 22
Israel **110** 29
Jacob **60** 307
James **55** 293 **59** 244 245
James Allen **59** 227 **64** 203
Jedediah **120** 53
Jennie Mary **82** 406
John **123** 264
Leslie Maynard **82** 406
Lewis Nathaniel **82** 406
Lodice (Corliss) **137** 49
Lodisa **120** 53 **137** 49
Lydia **56** 241 **58** 200
  72 204
Lyman **72** 204
Lyman A. **72** 204
Margaret **55** 347 **79** 409
Mary **59** 244 **60** 307 **72** 204
  107 134 **123** 265 **137**
  320
Mary Jane **128** 171
Mary Partridge **121** 236
Mary S. **72** 204
Molly **54** 53
Moses **110** 29 **133** 321
Nathan **110** 29
Orrin **72** 204
Persis **120** 53 **137** 49
Phebe (Burger) **90** 277
Prudence **76** 271
Rachel **115** 40 **118** 215 216
  136 316
Rachel (Cook) **118** 215
Rebecca **60** 307
Rebecca (Hadlock)
  123 262
Reuben **110** 29
Roxana S. **116** 258
Ruth **110** 29
Ruth (Butler) **133** 321
Ruth (Needham) **110** 29
Ruth (Woodsworth)
  110 29
Ruth Lewis **82** 116
Ruth S. **72** 204
Samuel **54** 53
Sarah **59** 243 245 **110** 29
  115 45
Sarah (Horton) **110** 29
Sarah N. **73** 39
Simeon **79** 300

KIBBE *cont'd*
Sophronia **79** 154
William **58** 404 **59** 22
  80 56
KIBBER Samuel **62** 33
Kibbey *see* Kibbe
Kibbie *see* Kibbe
Kibby *see* Kibbe
KIBLEE Hannah **125** 215
KIBLER Joel **138** 211
  John F. **138** 211
  Sarah Ann (Gifford)
    138 211
  Sophia (Gifford) **138** 211
KIBLING Sally **61** 307
KIBLINGER
  Eliza **84** 462
  Jacob **77** 289
  Sarah **77** 289
KICHAMOKIN **89** 281
KICHEN
  Christian **144** 46
KICKEY
  Louisa (Rich) **84** 60
KICKLE Samuel **143** 261
KIDBY Lewis **142** 277
KIDD Kidde Kydd
  ——— **51** 135 **53** 12 302
    54 338
  Agnes (Johnson) **86** 131
  Alfred Vinal **74** lxiv
  Benjamin **86** 131
  Elmira Vandora **63** 47
  Frances Ruth **136** 96
  Hannah **110** 230
  J. W. **63** 47
  Justinian **74** 272
  Marah **89** 311
  Martha **72** 308
  Mildred Manton **74** lxiv
  Nehemiah **60** 25
  Peter Shand **136** 96
  Rhoda C. **77** 151
  Sarah **70** xxxii
  William **71** 102 **83** 85
Kiddar *see* Kidder
Kidde *see* Kidd
KIDDER Kiddar Kider
  ——— **52** 188 **54** xxxii **59**
    xx liv **60** lv **62** xlvii **91**
    258 **93** 251
  — Capt. **101** 270
  — Mrs. **83** 381
  Aaron **55** 401 **76** lxxxi
    103 63 **104** 118
  Abigail **96** 220
  Alfred **93** 251
  Alfred Vincent **85** 195
    98 153 **106** 100
  Almon **54** 223 **55** xxxii
    56 xxxii **141** 38 40 50 54
  Amos **70** 154 156
  Andrew B. **72** 163
  Andrew Bradshaw **78** 91
  Andrew Marcellus **77**
    xxxviii **78** 91
  Ann **51** 448 **76** lxviii
    77 315
  Anna **71** 261 **80** 97
  Ann / Anna (Moore) **84**
    440 **93** 89

KIDDER *cont'd*
Arthur T. **78** 91
Benjamin **63** 74 293-295
  65 236 **104** 118
Benjamin Harrison
  64 101
Bennett **122** 147
Betsey (Fuller) **104** 118
Betty **61** 237 **93** 390
C. **91** 327
Camillus **76** lxxxi **84** 440
  441
Camillus George **76** xxx
  lxxxi lxxxii **84** 441
Caroline **98** 107
Caroline Whitmarsh
  (Archbald) **93** 89
Catherine Lewis **66** lxxiv
  94 291 **95** 289
Charles Archbald **77** 156
  78 205 **90** 76
Charles S. **116** 117
Charlotte **140** 304
Charlotte Augusta
  (Adams) **125** 219
Chloe (Whitney) **137** 51
Clarissa (Purkitt) **93** 89
Daniel **125** 221
David **104** 118 **137** 51
Delphia **137** 51
Dorothy **71** 261 262 **94**
  188 **102** 144
Edward **66** 109 **76** lxviii
Edward Hartwell **76** xxx
  lxviii lxix lxxxi
Elbridge **103** 45
Eliza (Morse) **84** 441
Elizabeth **79** 42 **84** 441
  141 221
Ellen **111** 186
Ellen (Cogan) **111** 186
Ellis **61** 379
Emily (Blanchard)
  110 229
Enoch **56** 370 **80** 97
Ephraim **78** 307 **104** 118
  125 293
Ezra T. **59** 189
Fannie Maude **102** 147
Francis **89** 230
Frederic **54** xlv **103** **55** xl
  56 xxvi xxxix 203 **57** xl
  108 **58** xvi liii 90 198
  61 xliii **62** lxxxvii **63**
  xiii lxxvi 288 290 **64** 98
  134 232 **71** 284 **74** xxxi
  238 **76** lxviii **97** 149 **99**
  14 **109** 57 **145** 210 218
  219 221
G. **91** 327
George Herrick Faber
  76 lxxxii
H. P. **97** 52
Hannah **61** 356 **66** 103 **75**
  23 **91** 258 263 **125** 102
Hannah M. **78** 397
Helen Arianna **96** 133
Henry Purkitt **93** 89
  140 33
Hiram **104** 118
Huldah (Putnam) **104** 118

KIDDER cont'd
Isaac **78** 411 **80** 97 **97** 395
Isabella E. **70** 156
Isaiah **76** lxviii
James **71** 93 261 **76** lxviii
 lxxxi **78** 91 **80** 97 **84** 440
 93 89 **97** 154 **129** 349
James Hathaway **76** lxix
Jerome Faber **76** lxxxii
Jerome Henry **84** 441
Joanna **55** 401 **78** 412
Joanna (Keyes) **84** 440
John **51** 448 **55** 443 **58** 236
 63 294 **76** lxviii lxxxi
 84 440 **93** 89 **147** 237
John P. **116** 117
Jonas **104** 118 **147** 85
Jonathan **61** 242 **116** 110
Joseph **55** 187 401 **66**
 lxxiii lxxiv **76** lxxxi **93**
 251 **94** 291 **95** 289 **105**
 279 **121** 247
Joseph F. **91** 327
Josephine **78** 205
Josephine (Burnett) **77**
 156 **78** 205 **90** 76
Josiah **83** 144 **139** 257
Katharine **147** 237
Larnard **141** 54
Lois (Crosby) **84** 440
Lois Faber **76** lxxxii
Louisa (Archbald) **140** 33
Louisa (Bennett) **103** 45
Lucy **66** 109
Lydia **51** 448 **55** 443 **63**
 294 **140** 68
Lydia (Parker) **84** 440
Lydia (Prentice) **93** 89
M. A. **102** 320
Madeline (Appleton) **85**
 195 **106** 100
Margaret (Lightle)
 122 147
Maria (Lazell) **89** 230
Mary **80** 97 **90** 51 **96** 74
 109 220
Mary (Heywood) **148** 239
Mary (Jackson) **93** 89
Mary (Swan) **96** 133
Mary Abby **59** 189
Mary Ann (Hoisington)
 141 54
Mary Grace **76** lxix
Mary Lincoln (Faber)
 76 lxix
Matilda Cushman
 76 lxxxii
Mercy **51** 162
Mercy (Nickerson)
 (Godfrey) **126** 237
 128 291
Mina S. **103** 48
Miriam **91** 264
Moses **80** 97 **83** 476
N. A. **91** 327
Nabby **66** 320
Nancy **66** 108
Nancy (Child) **125** 221
Nancy Jenkins (Homer)
 66 lxxiv **95** 289
Nathan **116** 110

KIDDER cont'd
Nathaniel **125** 23 **141** 54
Nathaniel Thayer **60**
 xxxviii **71** xviii **74** 160
 77 78 **90** 125 **93** 83 89
 141
Nellie Adelaide **79** 202
Noah **62** 33
Pamela (Johnson)
 125 293
Pamelia (Fuller) **104** 118
Phebe **53** 229 **62** 124
Rachel **71** 358 **91** 265
Rachel (Kendrick) **83** 476
Rachel Shepard **80** 97
Rebecca **88** 75
Reuben **55** 401 **76** lxviii
 lxxxi **84** 440 **107** 105
 125 96
Richard **66** 103 **76** lxviii
 lxxxi **84** 440
S. T. **110** 238
Sally **61** 240
Samuel **63** 74 **93** 89
 111 186
Samuel D. **116** 117
Sarah **56** 370 **62** 120 123 **63**
 294 **80** 97
Sarah (Griggs) **93** 89
Sarah Elizabeth **78** 91
Sarah J. **90** 116
Sarah Thompson
 (Herrick) **76** lxxxi
 84 441
Solomon **56** 44
Sophia **83** 476
Sophia Kendrick **80** 96 97
Sophronia **77** 176
Speedy (Whitmore)
 141 54
Stephen **51** 162 **126** 237
 128 291
Susan Blanchard **54**
 xviii xxxviii **55** xxxii
 56 xxxii
Susan H. **88** 337
Susanna **61** 242
Susanna (Burge) **84** 440
Tabitha **144** 330
Thomas **53** 229 **55** 401 **62**
 124 **76** lxviii lxxxi **84**
 440 **93** 89 **140** 68
William **64** 114 **80** 97
 105 286 **125** 219
William Lambert **66** 320
Zedekiah **84** 441
Zimri **96** 133
KIDMAN Thomas **65** 21
KIDNER
Katharine Clinton
 69 202
Reuben **69** 202 **82** 270
KIDSON
Cary **71** 313 320
Henry **56** 311
Ruth M. **110** 310
KIDSTON
Pearl **103** 117
William **118** 45 46
KIDWELL
— Mrs. **51** 417

KIDWELL cont'd
Catherine **73** 269
Edgar Elias **86** 197
Elizabeth **73** 221
George **73** 227 274
Harriet **73** 268
James **73** 152 **87** 400
John **73** 144 145
Joseph W. **73** 271
Josias **73** 226
Leona Eveline (Crounse)
 86 197
Leonard **73** 224
Margaret **73** 145
Martha **73** 277
Mary **73** 273
Matthew **73** 141
Newell **51** 417
Nicholas **55** 110
Pricey **73** 229
Sarah **73** 145
Sophia Mary **73** 142
Theodore **73** 225
Thomas **51** 414 **73** 140
Walter **51** 417
William **73** 274
Witticim **73** 142
KIEDASCH
Anna Rommel **85** 314
Georgie **85** 314
John G. **85** 314 319
KIEFFER
Andrew James **106** 67
Ernest **97** 138
Josephine (Mecham)
 104 144
Kathryn Clarke **106** 67
Louis C. **104** 144
Mary Isabelle (Clark)
 106 67
Olive D. (Payn) **97** 138
Thomas **97** 138
Virginia Ann **97** 138
KIEFT — Gov. **98** 68
William **55** 298
KIEHL Kiel
Herman Gottlieb **81** 114
Ralph A. **114** 78
KIELBLOCK Ann **51** 499
KIELEY
Bartholomew **78** 308
Lydia (O'Neil) **126** 67
KIELLE —— **59** xxx
KIEN
Johann Jacob **87** 35
KIEPURA
Genevieve Tylee
 141 104
KIER
Hepzibah **116** 303
Hepzibah (Bowden)
 116 222
John **116** 222
KIERSEY Munson **70** 121
 115 134
Permelia J. **115** 133
KIERSTEAD
Eleanor **108** 245
Eleanor (Collier) **108** 245
Henry **108** 245
Margaret (Gee) **108** 246

KIERSTEAD *cont'd*
Mary (Hooghlin) **108** 245
KIERSTEDE
Blandina **81** 193
Hans **81** 194
Sarah **81** 194
KIES Alpheus **89** 20
Elizabeth (Lazell) **89** 20
Joseph S. **89** 20
KIESS Carl C. **114** 78
Johann Friederich **114** 78
KIESSEL
William C. **104** 81
KIGDON Jos. **70** 265
KIGHT Kightt
Hannah **91** 32
Judith **58** 397
Thomas **58** 397
KIGHTLEY Henry **51** 400
Kightt *see* Kight
KIHART
Mary (Bird) **111** 168
KIKER Amelia Bessie
108 134
KILBORN Kilbarn
Kilbourn Kilbourne
Kilburn
—— **72** 40 **76** 132 **120** 211
121 62 **123** 26 **145** 317
— Miss **80** 66
— Mr. **60** 264
— Mrs. **122** 302
— Rev. Mr. **63** 98
Abagail Ann **112** 145
Abigail **58** 269 **135** 40
Abigail (Billings) **94** 57
Abigail Ann **112** 145
Abraham **60** 140 **85** 62 63
166
Adeline **82** 273
Agnes Clark **82** 274
Alanson **74** 312
Albert G. **134** 330
Ann **85** 62
Anna **61** 342 **100** 182
Anne **80** 317 324
Asa **116** 7
Austin **85** 166
Austin Stanwood
58 lxxxvii
Benjamin **52** 413 414 **53**
449 **54** 257 **56** 352 **58**
194 195 **60** 204 **76** 132
Bethiah **74** 312
Betsey **59** 95 **103** 256
Betty **60** 80
Charles **115** 80
Cheney **139** 92 257
Chloe **54** 49 **61** 389
Clarissa **74** 312
Cleopatra **58** 194 **60** 79
Cyrus **94** 57
Daniel J. **113** 53
David **70** 142 213 217 219
304 308 **100** 182 **140**
293 294
Deborah **101** 234 **109** 38
229
Delia Harmony **101** 234
Desire **120** 318
Desire (Collins) **103** 170

KILBORN *cont'd*
Don Volckert **101** 234
Dwight C. **64** 96
Ebenezer **61** 178 **100** 182
142 331
Eleanor (Blair) **94** 49
Electa **72** 74
Elijah **100** 182
Elisha **76** 133
Eliza **52** 414 **85** 166
103 170
Elizabeth **52** 413 **54** 82 273
57 405 **58** 321 **60** 198
263 **70** 204 **78** 303 **85** 42
166 **102** 300 **137** 256
Elizabeth (Gayden)
135 338
Elizabeth (Stillman) **109**
38 229
Elizabeth Howard
134 330
Eunice **61** 178
Eva Maria **72** 299
Frances **58** 321 **80** 317
319 324
Francis **58** 321 **113** 53 54
Francis S. **113** 53
Frederick D. **58** 321
Freeman **79** 160
George **58** 321 **143** 307
George Harris **82** 273 274
George Pratt **82** 273
Giles **54** 49 **113** 53
Grace **96** 384
Gustavus **58** 194 **59** 95
60 80 263
Hannah **58** 195 269 **80** 424
85 166 **90** 51 **100** 182
136 125
Hannah (Alden) **100** 182
Hannah (Pike) **97** 358
Hannah Pike **97** 358
Hiram **94** 49 50
Horace **85** 166
Isaac **64** 113
Ivory **103** 257 258
Ivory Augustus **103** 267
Jacob **100** 182 **142** 34
James **70** 204 **132** 88
James H. **90** 351
James Madison **77** 184
Jane J. (Skillin) **134** 330
Jefferson Gayden **135** 338
Jerusha (Shailer) **100** 182
Jesse **103** 170 **105** 309
120 318
John **58** 194 321 **61** 178
65 372 **85** 42 62 **102** 104
315 **103** 259 264 269
113 30 **125** 294 **127** 9
135 338 **139** 92 **142** 34
John Arthur **93** 137
John D. **108** 230
John Dwight **104** 144
Jonathan **53** 402 **54** 257
80 424
Jonathan B. **77** 189
Joseph **58** 269 **60** 140
85 62 166
Joseph Knight **134** 330

KILBORN *cont'd*
Joseph Williamson
82 273
Laura (Hannum) **90** 351
Lewis **115** 80
Lillian Warren **99** 147
Louisa R. **65** xlix
Lovisa (Perkins) **140** 293
Lucretia **52** 414 **132** 323
Lucy **90** 163
Lydia **58** 321
Margaret **58** 321 **80** 412
Maria **76** xlviii
Maria Elizabeth **94** 55
Martha **106** 213
Martha (Warner) **145** 335
Mary **58** 269 321 **60** 140
61 143 **75** 303 **76** 133
85 62 166 **86** 343 **87** 14
91 99 **103** 264 **104** 218
120 79 **142** 34
Mary (Proctor) **125** 294
Mary A. **77** 189
Mary Beatrice **82** 273
Mary Freeman **82** 273
Mehitable **105** 309
Minerva **101** 234
Mischel **85** 63
Naomi **61** 177 178 **85** 42
Ogden **85** 166
Onor **85** 166
Parmelia **58** lxxxvii
Payne Kenyon **65** 156
Rebecca Clark **82** 273
Rhoda **70** 204
Robert A. **90** 351
Ruth **94** 49 **102** 27
Ruth (Warner) **145** 335
Sally **125** 288
Samuel **70** 141 **100** 182
109 38 229 **112** 145 **139**
92 257
Samuel Sawyer
58 lxxxvii
Samuel Smith **58** xlix lv
lxxxvii
Sarah **58** lxxxvii **85** 63 **103**
258 **109** 166
Sarah (Billings) **94** 50
Sarah Sophia **77** 184
Sophia (Hannum) **90** 351
Susanna **56** 45 **65** 372
134 334
Thomas **58** 321 **60** 355 **61**
143 **80** 316 317 319 320
324 326 **81** 84 **91** 99 **97**
358 **105** 309 **112** 145
134 215
Truman **101** 234
Violet **72** 40 169
Warren Silver **58** lxxxvii
William **58** lxxxvii **70** 215
Zilpah **132** 105
KILBY —— **57** 337 415
Abigail (Cushing)
129 375
Achsah **115** 119
Charles **100** 29
Christopher **58** 70 **59**
193 194 **91** 343 **100** 29
104 257

KILBY cont'd
Cushing **129** 151 376
Desire **120** 318
Desire (Collins) **103** 170
Edward **71** 256
Eliza **103** 170
Elizabeth **71** 256
Elizabeth (Bates) **129** 169
Fanny **129** 376
Fanny (Lincoln) **129** 151 376
Hannah **92** 14
Hannah (Wade) **129** 169
Huldah (Orcutt) **129** 151 376
Jane **92** 16
Jesse **103** 170 **120** 318
John **54** cxxxix **129** 169 **131** 182
Katharine **55** 135
Lydia **54** cxxxix
Lydia Cushing (Wilder) **54** cxxxix
Mary **100** 29 **109** 72 75 **125** 106
Priscilla **129** 169
Priscilla (Litchfield) **129** 169 362
Quincy **78** 108 109 198
Richard **129** 169 268 376
Sarah **99** 208
Thomas **55** 135 **71** 60 **90** 400 **99** 208 **124** 29
William **91** 343 **92** 16 **109** 75
William Henry **64** 131
William Tyler **92** 14 16 **94** 294
KILCUP Dudson **57** 388
George **67** 201
Martha **101** 275
Mary **67** 201
KILE Chloe **72** 285
Ella **128** 268
James **128** 268
John **72** 285
Margaret (Linnvile) **128** 268
Nancy **76** 272
Orville M. **114** 157
KILESKI Frederic Greenhalge **91** 142 **94** 155 **95** 74 162
KILEY John **84** 123
Lena J. (Rich) (Lombard) **84** 123
Mark **119** 77
Sarah (Rich) **84** 49
Thankful **84** 124
KILGORE Kilgour
Abigail **55** 313 **82** 510
Abigail (Lord) **102** 303
Abigail (Page) **102** 303
Alice **82** 88 **134** 173
Amy **55** 313 **63** 167 **82** 511
Amy (Hamilton) **134** 173
Ashburn Cogswell **69** xxxv
Benjamin **55** 313 **82** 511 **111** 25 **134** 173
Betsey **74** 256

KILGORE cont'd
Catherine **115** 61
Charles Merrill **102** 303
Damon Young **102** 303
Elizabeth **74** 248 266 267
Esther **142** 303
Esther (Abbott) **134** 173
Hannah **74** 251 **134** 173
Harold Dustin **76** 318 **77** xxviii 78 **101** 113 130 **102** 303
Hattie Angeline (Dustin) **102** 303
Isabella **90** 111
James **102** 303
John **74** 248 267 **90** 111
Joseph **55** 311 312 **82** 84 88 322 510 **102** 303 **111** 25 95 **114** 295 **134** 173
Katharine **111** 25
Lucy Ann (Merrill) **102** 303
Lydia **126** 206
Margaret **74** 251 **134** 173
Marian Demings (Bishop) **102** 303
Marjorie Bishop **102** 303
Mary **74** 253 **77** 157 **82** 84 322
Mehitable (Stearns) **102** 303
Penelope **55** 311 **82** 84 **111** 95
Penelope (Treworgy) **111** 25 **134** 173
Sally **74** 107
Sally (Johnson) **134** 173
Selden Hinckley **84** 109 189
Trueworthy **134** 173
142 303
KILHAM see also Kellam & Killam
Abigail **56** 345 346 **61** 333 **83** 108
Abraham **103** 73
Albert D. **91** 229
Alice **52** 238 239 **56** 344 345 **83** 108
Aline **103** 74
Ann **52** 238 **56** 345 346
Anna **56** 346
Arthur L. **86** 52
Augustine **52** 239 **56** 344 **83** 108
Austin **52** 238 239 **56** 344-346 **91** 229 **103** 73
Austin D. **121** 236
Belle G. **86** 52
Benjamin **56** 345 346
Caroline **86** 52
Catherine Lane **79** 102
Charles Harrington **103** 73
Daniel **52** 238 239 **56** 345 346 **61** 331 333-335 338 **83** 108 **86** 65 **91** 229 **103** 73
Daniel Tappen **91** 229
Deborah **56** 345 346 **61** 332

KILHAM cont'd
Ebenezer **56** 346
Edward **79** 164 **103** 73
Edward Holden **86** 52
Edward J. **86** 53
Eliphalet **56** 345 **79** 309 407
Elizabeth **52** 430 **56** 345 346 **61** 331 333 335 **79** 102
Elizabeth (Groce) **103** 73
Elizabeth (Kimball) **103** 73
Elizabeth (Lovett) **103** 73
Elizabeth (Ramsdell) **103** 73
Elizabeth L. **91** 229
Emily **86** 52
Ephraim L. **91** 229
Eustis B. **79** 40
George **52** 132
Grace **56** 346
Hannah **56** 345 346 **61** 335
Harriet **56** 345 **79** 154 407
Harriet G. **86** 52
Henry **52** 238 239 **56** 344-346
Herburt D. **91** 229
J. **79** 403
James **56** 345 **79** 102 154 407 **86** 52
James (Mrs.) **79** 409
James L. **86** 52
Jane Moody (Houston) **103** 74
Jeannette **103** 74
John **56** 345 346 **61** 332 **83** 108 **91** 229
John Austin **91** 229
John Frost **91** 229
John W. **86** 53
Jonathan **125** 107
Joseph **52** 430 **56** 345 346 **61** 336 **91** 206
Joseph Elbridge **83** 108
Juliette **86** 53
Lawrence **103** 74
Lois **83** 108
Lot **56** 345
Lucinda **86** 53
Lyman S. **86** 53
Margaret **56** 346
Maria Frances (Ober) **103** 73
Martha **56** 346 **61** 334 335 **83** 108
Martha Jane **79** 123
Mary **52** 238 239 **56** 344 345 **61** 356 **79** 102 408 **125** 108
Mary (Safford) **103** 73
Mehitable **74** 247 **91** 229 **96** 339
Nancy **91** 229
Nathaniel **56** 346
Peter Houston **103** 74
Phineas **56** 346 **58** 166 **125** 217
Priscilla **56** 346 **83** 108
Priscilla (Perley) **125** 107
R. L. **91** 229

KILHAM cont'd
Rachel **61** 334
Rebecca **86** 65
Rebecca (Frost) **103** 73
Robert **52** 238 239 **56** 344
  79 123
Roger **52** 238
Ruth **56** 345
Ruth (Littlefield) **91** 229
Sally **79** 309
Samuel **56** 345 346 **61** 334
  83 108
Sarah **56** 345 346 **61** 331
  335 338 **65** 303 **83** 108
Sarah (Geare) **103** 73
Susan **61** 331
Susanna **61** 331
T. **125** 43
Teresa C. **103** 74
Thankful **56** 346 **58** 166
Thomas **56** 345 346 **61** 335
  83 108
Timothy **79** 309
W. **61** 333
Walter **86** 52
Walter H. **103** 81
Walter Harrington **103**
  73 74 77 119 125
William **56** 345 346 **61** 335
Wry **56** 346
Ziba Westcott **79** 102
KILHEAD
Andrew **143** 259
Charles N. **143** 75
Elizabeth (Gilbert)
  (Rayner) **143** 220
Henry **143** 220
John **143** 219 259
Mary (Riddlesdale)
  143 220
Mary Louise (Theis)
  143 75
Richard **143** 220
Ursual (Scott) **143** 220
KILHEATH
James **61** 136
Jane **61** 136
KILL Effie E. **116** 63
Milo J. **116** 63
KILLACUTT
Sarah **57** 201
Thomas **57** 201
KILLAM Killom Killum
  Kilom - see also
  Kellam & Kilham
  —— **57** 120
— Capt. **122** 62
— Mr. **70** 301
Abigail **62** 41 43 45 **66** 231
Anna **62** 40 **136** 313
Augustine **57** 196
Benjamin **62** 34 39
Charles **62** 43
Charles W. **62** 383
Cyprian **145** 143
Daniel **62** 36 38-41 43 45
Deborah **55** 177 **62** 37
Eliphalet **80** 59
Elizabeth **62** 42 45
Elsebeth **62** 35
Esther **55** 177

KILLAM cont'd
Hannah **62** 34 35 38 **64**
  250 **134** 89 255 **135** 252
Holly **135** 252
James **80** 55 57 59 **109** 26
Jesse **66** 231
John **55** 177 **62** 35 38 43
  64 250
Joseph **62** 35 36 41 44 **94**
  95 **100** 65
Lucy **55** 17 **70** 109
Martha **62** 34
Mary **75** 41
Meribah **55** 177
Nancy (Black) **145** 143
Nathaniel **62** 44
Phebe S. **62** 383
Rachel **51** 462 **62** 34
Ruth **62** 37 151
Samuel **62** 36 41 43-45 **66**
  20 272 **67** 89
Sarah **55** 177 **62** 34 39 46
  66 272 **67** 89
Solomon **51** 462
Susanna **120** 13
Thomas **62** 36 38 43
Timothy **80** 55
William **62** 34 41-44 46
  7. **120** 13
KILLAND
John **82** 285 291
Sarah **82** 285 291
KILLBRATH
Sally **87** 125
KILLCREASE
Holdy **99** 284
John **99** 284
Thomas **99** 284
KILLCUP
George **100** 300
Katharine (Everton)
  100 300
Martha **100** 300
KILLEEN
George Drake **122** 281
KILLERAN
— Capt. **84** 153
Bartholomew **90** 91
Elizabeth **90** 90
Elizabeth (Henderson)
  90 91
Sally **90** 91 **108** 90
Sarah **90** 91
KILLETT John **100** 293
KILLEY see also Kelley
  —— **109** 43
— Mr. **83** 377
— Widow **83** 378
Abigail **105** 203
Ames **108** 263
Benjamin **105** 203 308-312
  107 39 107
Betsey (Baker) **108** 262
Charlotte **71** 366
Daniel **129** 277
David **105** 202 **109** 43
  147 39
Davis **107** 38
Ebenezer **107** 291
Eliza (Covil) **108** 262
Elizabeth **105** 308 **108** 261

KILLEY cont'd
Hannah **72** 21 24 109 **94**
  300 **107** 291 **108** 109
  128 260
Hannah (Wing) **128** 260
Hannah (Woodmansee)
  147 39
Hatsell **128** 260
Hattil **71** 366 367
Isaac **71** 366 367 **72** 24 109
Isaiah **90** 107 **108** 109
Jeremiah **128** 260
John **72** 109 **109** 41
  128 260
Jonathan **105** 203 **108** 261
Joseph **129** 277 **147** 39
Judith **71** 366 **72** 21 24
Katharine **95** 172
Keziah **105** 311
Loira (Bassett) **108** 263
Mary **71** 366 367 **72** 24 28
  105 203
Mary Coffin **72** 109
Mercy O. **105** 202
Molly **107** 38 39
Polly Thacher **107** 39
Reuben **72** 21 24
Richard **108** 262
Roxana (Godfrey) **90** 107
Ruth **72** 24 **105** 312
Salome **105** 203
Samuel E. **108** 262
Sarah **105** 309
Seth **109** 42
Sophia **72** 24
Stephen **128** 59
Susan **108** 262
Susanna **105** 203 209 308
  310-312 **107** 107
Sylvanus **107** 291 **108** 109
Thacher **107** 291
Thankful **109** 40
Zena **109** 40
KILLICUTT
Dorcas **64** 212
Thomas **69** 295 296 298
  299
KILLIE
Isaac Lawrence **91** 108
Martha Elissa (Hannum)
  91 108
Mattie Mabel **91** 108
KILLIEAN Mary **63** 150
KILLIGREW Kyllygrew
— Lieut. Col. **56** 188
Elizabeth **121** 188
William **142** 366
KILLIGROVE
Henry **99** 26 28
Mary **99** 26 28 **101** 50
KILLING James **59** 288
Mehitable **59** 288
KILLINGBECK
Killingbecke
Robert **109** 7
Thomas **90** 196
KILLINGS T. P. **91** 327
KILLINGWORTH
Edward **66** 168
Mary **106** 43

KILLION Bridget (Donlan)
  132 326
  Catherine Lyons **132** 326
  Martin **132** 326
  Michael J. **132** 326
KILLIPS
  Lydia A. **100** 194
KILLMAN
  Abbie M. **117** 166
  Amber **117** 172
  David **117** 166
  Emily J. (Curtis) **117** 166
Killom *see* Killam
KILLORIN
  John Farrell **102** 124
  Mary Elizabeth
    (Robinson) **102** 124
KILLOUGH Henrietta
  Zahm **72** 298
  James **130** 54
  Mae **130** 54
Killpatrick *see* Kilpatrick
KILLROY Matthew **84** 264
KILLSA Sally **78** 405
Killum *see* Killam
KILLWORTH Kilworth
  Dorothy **74** 283
  Edmund **112** 180
  Elizabeth **112** 180
  Elizabeth (Dolbeare)
    112 180
  Matthew **112** 180
  Prothero **74** 283
  William **112** 179 180
Killy *see* Kelly
KILMAN Ed **109** 78
  Lucretia **77** 131
  Stephen **105** 280
  William **62** 244
KILMARTIN
  Mary **78** 177
KILMER Aldeane **78** 87
  Caroline A. **78** 87
  David H. **124** 160 320
  Kilburn **58** 321
  Richard P. **78** 87
KILMISTER
  Hannah **129** 41
KILMORE Henry **53** 398
  Laury **53** 398
KILMOREY Robert
  Needham (Viscount)
    76 309 311
Kilom *see* Killam
KILPATRICK Killpatrick
  Kilpatric
  Adelaide Davenport
    85 333
  Agnes **61** 239
  Betty **75** 121
  Christopher **75** 50
  David **85** 333
  Elizabeth **75** 105-107 109
    111 118
  Elmina A. **92** 168
  Isaac **75** 105
  James **75** 113 117 119-121
    315 **76** 257
  Jane E. **92** 171
  Jeremiah **75** 52
  John **75** 105-107 109 111

KILPATRICK *cont'd*
  118 **76** 193 **85** 332
  Joseph **71** 130
  Joshua **75** 111 113
  Judson **71** li
  Katharine Rachel **85** 333
  Leon **93** 217
  Margaret **75** 51 105
  Marian Douglas (Jones)
    85 113 333
  Mary **75** 54 118
  Nathaniel **75** 106
  Olive **75** 119 315
  Pearl Blanche **83** 433 436
  Rachel (Thompson)
    85 332
  Robert **92** 169
  Robert Jackson **80** 332
    81 219 **85** 113 236 332
    86 203
  Samuel **75** 109 **85** 332
  Sarah **75** 113 117 119-121
    315 **76** 193
  Sarah (Wallace) **85** 332
  Stella (Billings) **94** 60
  Thirza (Eaton) **92** 169
  Thomas **61** 351 **75** 50-52
    54 105 107 **95** 299
  William **71** 130
KILROE Edwin P. **107** 13
  108 14
KILSHAW Martha **64** 344
KILTON
  —— **57** 338 **63** 157
  Abigail **68** 236
  Alice (Chase) **88** 27
  Amos **88** 27
  Anna **53** 254
  Benjamin **58** 58
  Betty **68** 219
  Ebenezer **53** 184 **68** 226
    231 320 321
  Edward **57** 259 **68** 220
    221 223 321
  Elihu **68** 221 223 224 226
    228 229 231 233 236 310
    321
  Elijah **68** 228
  Elisha **68** 228
  Elizabeth **68** 218 220
  Elizabeth (Miller) **100** 302
  Enoch **138** 30
  George **73** 221
  James **68** 224-226 230 231
    235
  Jane **68** 215 223 224
  John **58** 58 **68** 222 226
    138 25-30
  John J. **129** 62
  Lemuel **57** 259
  Lois **68** 231
  Mary **68** 216 221 230
  Mary Amanda **81** 150
  Persis **77** 232
  Rebecca **68** 219
  Rosanna **68** 301
  Rufus **60** 40 **68** 233
  Sally Lucy **63** 157
  Samuel **57** 258 259 **68**
    217 229 301
  Sarah **84** 98

KILTON *cont'd*
  Solomon **60** 39 **68** 217 218
    222 225 228
  Thankful **68** 223
  Thomas **60** 39 **68** 216 235
    100 302
  Volney **81** 150
KILWELL Isabel **101** 338
Kilworth *see* Killworth
KILY Phebe (Richards)
    125 220
KIMBALL Kemball
  Kimbal Kimballs
  Kimbel Kimble
  Kimbol
  — Capt. **84** 256
  — Mr. **77** 27
  — Mrs. **77** 31
  — Widow **92** 280 283
  A. **91** 327
  A. L. **91** 327
  Aaron **77** lxxix **90** 230
    241 251 **97** 222 237 **109**
    53
  Abbie Ann **79** 271
  Abbie Curtis **135** 20
  Abby Rice Brown **77** lxxx
  Abel **125** 160
  Abel Webber **125** 158 161
  Abigail **52** 248 **55** 268 **58**
    122 269 **62** 36 39 **67** 375
    75 105 107-109 116 117
    76 40 179 194 252 253
    79 141 **86** 18 **90** 192 241
    276 393 **91** 229 **92** 282
    96 190 341 **108** 150 110
    175 **111** 40 315 **125** 157
    126 35
  Abigail (Farnum) **91** 229
    96 248
  Abigail (Kimball) **90** 393
  Abigail (Peabody)
    109 233
  Abigail (Robie) **125** 158
  Abigail F. **91** 226
  Abigail Jane (Elkins)
    95 346
  Abner F. **92** 333
  Abraham **62** 39 60 **65** 113
    75 109 111 **90** 233 235
    92 277 **96** 248 340 **125**
    154-156
  Abram **83** 417
  Adaline **125** 158
  Addie F. **125** 161
  Addie R. **68** 204
  Adeline **125** 158
  Agnes **52** 247
  Albert **120** 305 **123** 149 153
    124 78
  Albert H. **94** 113
  Alfred **108** 212
  Alice **76** 256 **119** 143
  Alice Cary **89** 323 **106** 231
  Alice M. **68** 250 **92** 333
  Almira **98** 364 **112** 234 **127**
    34 **147** 258
  Almira S. **112** 235
  Almira Sophia **112** 233
  Alonzo **56** 213 **57** 119
    91 327

KIMBALL *cont'd*
Alpheus **76** 108
Alvira C. (Leighton)
  97 234
Amos **114** 105 **129** 274
Amos H. **69** 259
Andrew **136** 320
Ann **61** 333
Ann Alice (Gheen)
  136 320
Anna **65** 311 **67** 376 **90** 228
  241 246 **92** 309 **93** 330
  100 70 **112** 234 **113** 32
  40
Anna (Ayer) **92** 283
Anna (Smith) **109** 230
Anna (Spalding) **136** 320
Anna (Whitten) **95** 194
  108 190
Anna Elizabeth **91** 302
Anna S. **112** 233
Anne **52** 248
Anne Anstice (Hosford)
  84 234 **85** 195
Annie **77** 291
Annie A. (Fowler)
  123 153
Annie C. **96** 180
Annie F. **93** 330
Asa **55** 268 **66** 25 **92** 274
  275 280 310 320 **95** 186
  104 118 **128** 59
Asa Foster **92** 285
Asenath **92** 333
Augusta **91** 187
Augusta (Blanchard)
  91 187
Augusta Ann **94** 283
Augustin Hibbard **96** 74
Axie **75** 15
Azadiah **75** 113
Barak **76** 110-113 185 260
  87 206 **94** 113
Baruch **75** 109
Bathsheba **90** 241
Beatrice **52** 247 **125** 161
Benjamin **60** 56 192 **62** 38
  41 60 **65** 113 338 **75** 52
  112-114 120 123 **76** 104-
  106 114 179 194 250 252
  261 **81** 190 **83** 136 **90**
  229 241 247 392 393 **92**
  271 274-276 283 285 310
  315 316 319 321 **93** 46
  95 200 **96** 146 **106** 153
  109 229 **112** 234 **116**
  110 **117** 143 144 **119** 64
  66 **120** 64 **125** 156 **127**
  34 **134** 294 **142** 54 **146**
  332
Benjamin Gage **54** 246
Benjamin W. **123** 150
Beriah **75** 109 110 112 113
  118 314
Bernice Honora **69** 259
Bert C. **83** 433 437
Bethiah **75** 114
Bethiah (Bragdon)
  110 175
Betsey **56** 258 **58** 18 **59** 41
  61 237 382 **65** 113 **66** 10

KIMBALL *cont'd*
  76 188 **83** 136 144 **90**
  392 393 **92** 275 **112** 233
Betsey (Durrell) **133** 44
Betsey (Jelleson) **90** 331
  91 21 25 **97** 16
Betsey (Kimball) **90** 392
Betsey (Trask) **83** 417
Betsey Chandler **70** xxxii
Betsey E. **66** 278
Betty **90** 227 245 **100** 70
Bridget **52** 248
C. **61** 333 **62** 40
C. Buchanan **91** 302
Caleb **61** 333 334 **62** 36 42
  43 **69** 190 **75** 45-50 52
  109 110 112-114 118 314
  76 110 **77** xciii **79** 115
  92 321 **95** 189 346 **110**
  204 **111** 258 **132** 269
  133 41 44 123 **142** 54
Caroline **92** 333 **93** 119
Caroline A. **119** 285
Caroline Durrell **133** 45
Caroline Evelyn **76** 101
Caroline Matilda **94** 46
Caroline Matilda
  (Roulstone) **92** 133
Carrie J. **92** 333
Carrie L. (Sears) **125** 160
Carrie Maria (Bancroft)
  95 283
Catherine **76** 257 **106** 225
  134 278
Catherine (Brown)
  137 337
Catherine (Cousins)
  132 122
Catherine (Larribee)
  132 122
Catherine A. **85** 195
Catherine Eveline **81** 190
Caty Jerome (Sweet)
  124 78
Celinda **80** 47
Charles **58** 280 **60** 192 **76**
  251 **91** 31 **100** 37
Charles C. **60** 404
Charles Clark **81** 153
Charles Dean **56** 212
  102 143
Charles E. **92** 333 **93** 330
Charles G. **125** 160
Charles H. **67** 351
Charles J. **91** 120 123 124
  97 230
Charles Lafayette **67** 351
Charles N. **141** 359
Charles Nathaniel **88** 169
  89 130 **115** 229
Charles Wakefield **62** 314
Charlotte **99** 149
Charlotte (Tibbetts)
  (Libby) **100** 37
Charlotte Chandler
  (Tenney) **109** 230
Charlotte Peabody **109**
  229 230
Charlotte Tenney **96** 305
Christopher **108** 150
  119 143

KIMBALL *cont'd*
Cicely **52** 247
Clara C. **134** 221
Clarence P. **93** 338
Clarenda (Eaton) **90** 393
Clarissa **59** 289 **92** 315 **93**
  193 **112** 234
Clark **114** 276 **139** 294
Clarriet **80** 237
Clifton P. **97** 131
Conrad Bryant **56** 326
Cynthia Elizabeth **66** 278
Daniel **54** 246 **57** 381 382
  62 35 43 154 **63** 46 **67**
  376 **72** 284 **73** 6 **74** 44
  75 110 **77** xciii 31 **83**
  136 141 144 **92** 323 **95**
  193 200 **96** 305 **97** 18
  238 **105** 210 **109** 230
  233 **112** 233 234 **135**
  127
Daniel (Mrs.) **92** 323
Daniel B. **109** 230
Daniel Winslow **125** 161
David **56** 336 **58** 122 280
  62 255 256 259 **76** 104
  248 251 253-256 **77** 79
  115 **90** 241 335 **91** 187
  301 302 **92** 274 280 333
  105 169 171 **108** 20 **111**
  40 **125** 151-154 **145** 161
David Brainard **61** 406
David P. **68** xlvii
David Tenny **112** 234
Day **100** 109 **109** 217 232
Dean **128** 50
Deborah **56** 208 **61** 334
  62 261 **75** 118 **93** 103
Deborah (Wells) **117** 224
Demas **83** 165 **137** 337
Dennison J. **91** 202
Dependence **93** 242
Dolly (Eastman) **92** 320
Dominicus **90** 233 253
Dorcas **76** 254 **92** 274
Dorcas (Tompson)
  96 144 337
Dorcas Foster **113** 307
Dorothy **58** 47 **62** 263
  108 20 **139** 294
Dorothy (Bragdon)
  117 144
Dorothy (Kimball) **108** 20
Dorothy (Tenney)
  109 229
Dorothy Arleen **110** 223
E. A. **53** 459 **54** xxxviii
E. E. **91** 302
Ebenezer **55** 396 **62** 36 42
  63 300 **65** 365 **66** 10 11
  76 111 113 **79** 271 **90**
  112 **100** 70 **116** 224
Edith Chase **55** 114
Edith H. C. **106** 125
Edmund **62** 38 **100** 69
  108 20
Edna B. **83** 422 433
Edward **65** 365 **89** 350
  112 234
Edward A. **92** 116
Edward Adams **81** 190

KIMBALL *cont'd*
95 146 99 69 139 145
101 25
Edward Dearborn
81 189 190
Edward Payson 91 302
Elbert Bridane 89 230
Elbridge 125 158
Elden 93 338
Eleanor 60 295 75 120 123
76 253-256 81 190 92
333
Eleanor (Dennet) 108 120
Eleanor (Erskine) 90 46
Eleazer 62 43 71 214 218
111 258 114 227
Electa 65 113
Elector 96 144 343
Eleonar 111 40
Elijah H. 75 lxviii
Eliphalet 72 285
Elisha 90 254
Eliza 91 294 95 197 96 341
124 78
Eliza (Barton) 107 299
Eliza (Goodwin) 126 64
Eliza (Peaslee) 90 393
Eliza E. 91 302
Eliza Epes (Carter) 91 301
Eliza J. 121 144 146
Eliza Withington 75 247
Elizabeth 52 248 58 280 61
332 333 62 42-44 255
256 259 66 166 67 351
354 71 214 75 120 76
185 248 252 78 419 81
190 251 90 241 93 46
334 100 69 70 103 73
108 312 112 234 115
116 119 319 120 78 125
155 138 322
Elizabeth (Kimball)
100 69
Elizabeth (Lewis) 123 74
Elizabeth (Sanborn)
123 150
Elizabeth (Tenney) 109
230 112 233
Elizabeth A. (Parker)
97 127
Elizabeth Bartlett
(Raymond) 97 122
Elizabeth C. 81 150
Elizabeth Guernsey
145 12
Elizabeth Seaver 89 72
Elizabeth Wheeler
146 332
Ella F. 93 330
Ella S. 79 26
Ellen Frances 67 351
Ellen M. (Noble) 95 186
Ellwood Davis 61 xxxvi
65 xxi 66 233 70 xxix
xxxii
Elmer E. 93 338
Elona Harvey 94 120
Elvira C. 92 333
Elvira Evelina 77 lxxx
Elwood D. 61 95

KIMBALL *cont'd*
Emily A. (Daggett)
103 235
Emma G. 93 338
Emma H. 89 350
Emma J. (Colby) 125 160
Emma L. 67 354
Enos 115 116
Ensign 90 241
Ephraim 61 331 62 37 42
77 lxxx 95 186 126 136
140 68
Estelle Hart 112 146
Esther 62 38 70 225 86 142
92 318 97 19 222 237
146 332
Esther (Kimball) 97 222
237
Eugenia 79 271
Eunice 76 185 285 87 233
234
Eunice (Bowen) 88 284
Eunice (Stone) 108 190
Eunice (Tripe) 95 191 194
Eureka 96 74
Eva (Poor) 110 222 223
Evelyn Louisa 77 lxxx
Evelyn M. 110 223
Evelyn Marion (Billings)
98 111
Evelyn Mary 110 223
Ezekiel 51 463 139 294
Ezra 62 39 155 75 114 76
196 91 229 95 194 197
198 104 312 108 190
Fannie P. (Moody) 123 74
Fanny 58 124 61 382
147 258
Fiske 95 153
Florence Amelia (Cutler)
125 160
Frances 67 278 77 xciv
Frances H. (Young)
125 160
Frances Lavinia Angier
57 415 77 xciii 79 115
116
Frances Lavinia Angier
(Hathaway) 87 69
Francis 88 284
Francis F. 123 74
Francis Newton 67 351
Francis Otis 125 160
Frank E. 93 330 94 118
Frank Edwin 81 254
Frank L. 123 74
Frank O. 92 333
Franklin 62 122
Franklin Reed 72 xx 79
211 81 189 190 85 195
Frederick M. 123 220
125 212 213
Frederick Milton 101 124
102 139 111 141-143
112 70 134-136 222 314
113 61 148-150 234 293
114 70 140 142 143 228
309 310 115 68 145 147
148 161 229 230 313 314
116 73 74 144 146 227
228 306 117 73 149 151

KIMBALL *cont'd*
152 231 232 312 118 69
160-162 246 324 119 72
78 150-152 236 312 120
56 150 152 233 310 121
75 150 151 122 207 208
124 264 265
Frederick Oberlin 91 302
Frederick P. 92 274
Frederick W. 96 189
G. F. 52 286 290 55 230 56
212 413 57 119 229
G. N.E. 83 20
Gardner 92 271
George 70 210 91 327 92
109 111 40 128 43 44
George A. 63 210
George Brundage 89 32
George Franklin 89 323
106 231
George H. 123 150
George Keith 61 321
George Lasell 89 32
George Rogers 89 32
George S. 95 283
George T. 89 350
George W. 123 153
125 160
George Washington
147 258
Georgianna Eliza 81 150
Gibenes / Gibeons
96 144 146
Gustavus Franklin 54
xxxviii 55 xxxii 56
xxxii 58 xlv
Hadassah 93 330
Hannah 52 429 54 421 55
lvii 58 124 60 192 314
61 334 62 40 122 63 369
69 328 71 214 72 284
73 286 75 111-114 119
120 76 195 252 78 364
87 233 238 90 241 91
347 92 333 96 145 248
338 341 97 303 111 40
125 155 126 64 133 41
124 140 40 146 332 147
258
Hannah (Clark) 114 276
Hannah (Cluff) 95 193 200
Hannah (Dollof) 96 146
Hannah (Hodson)
108 312
Hannah (Parker) 109 233
Hannah (Rumery) 96 338
Hannah (Shackley) (Lord)
132 269 133 41
Hannah (Whittemore)
139 294
Hannah Hathaway 57 415
67 xxxiv 68 xlvii 77
xciii 79 116 119 87 69 70
72 178
Hannah Jane (Webber)
119 64 66
Hannah P. 99 183
Harriet 92 283 320
Harriet (Griggs) 126 144
Harriet (Merriman)
125 160

KIMBALL *cont'd*
Harriet (Willis) **114** 276
Harriet Bancroft
  (Whitaker) **97** 131
Harriet M. **125** 161
Harriet R. **88** 282
Harriet S. **90** 108
Harry C. **125** 160
Hasadiah **65** 113 **76** 184
  260 **88** 362
Hattie Dinsmore **102** 303
Hattie Hastings (Young)
  (Wormwood) **92** 116
Hattie M. **93** 338
Hazen **90** 393 **92** 314 319
  125 35 38
Heber **75** 110 **76** 108 182
  183 185 186 259 **95** 197
Heber Chase **136** 320 331
Heber Parley **136** 331
Helen **108** 215 302
Helen (Paine) **97** 121
Helen (Thomas) **96** 189
Helen Frances **54** vi **55**
  vi xxi xxix **56** v-vii
  xxxiii **62** v-vii xxxv 102
  63 vi xiv xvi **64** vi xxix
  65 vi xvii xxi xxxiii **66**
  vi xxxiv xlviii **67** vi xix
  68 vii xlvii **74** xxvi 77
  77 xii xiii xciii **79** 115-
  119 **80** 215 **82** 394 **87** 69
  99 183
Helen Gertrude (Everest)
  (Gilly) **110** 71
Helen May **125** 161
Henrietta **97** 235
Henry **52** 247 248 **62** 255
  75 247 **79** 52 **85** 78 **95**
  219 **105** 171 **106** 19 **142**
  52 **145** 239
Henry Ames **73** 159
Henry H. **51** 379
Henry Martyn **91** 302
Henry Swift **73** 318
  74 xxiv
Hepzibah (Davis) **90** 254
Hepzibah Eames **82** 176
Hepzibah K. (Knight)
  91 31
Herbert Freeman **125** 160
Herbert Sawyer **77** lxxx
Herbert Wood **55** xxxii
  67 xxxiv **77** xxxvii
  lxxix lxxx
Hezekiah **95** 346
Hiram **68** 250 **124** 78
Hovey **62** 122
Howard **107** 158 **125** 160
Huldah **59** 41
Ida Elmina (Carnahan)
  89 323 **106** 231
Ida Josephine **82** 349
Ida May **81** 254
Ira **91** 198
Isaac **70** xxxiii **75** 112 **87**
  206 380 **90** 48 **101** 260
  338 **102** 79 **108** 120 192
  125 157 158 160 162
  132 269 **133** 44
Isaac J. **78** 335

KIMBALL *cont'd*
Isabel **93** 242
Isabella Graham **91** 302
Israel **60** 295 **62** 39 **75** 114
  108 120 **133** 44
Issachar **91** 225 226 229
  95 197 **96** 248
Ivory **99** 201
J. W. **90** 37
J. Wendall **96** 160 **109** 217
  110 222 223
Jabol **70** 225
Jacob **61** 382 **75** 113 **76** 248
  93 330 **107** 158
James **62** 37 **63** 178 **74** 44
  259 **75** 110 **83** 136 140
  87 206 207 **108** 190 **111**
  298 **124** 78 **147** 258
James Monroe **110** 222
James R. **120** 78
James Smith **112** 233
James V. **69** 259
James W. **62** 313 **64** 302
  66 288 **67** 304 **68** 305
  70 97 289 **71** 370 **73** 81
  242 **74** 322
Jane **68** 333 **87** 65 **112** 234
  125 156 157
Jean **91** 345
Jeanie Lawrence (Perkins)
  109 232
Jedidah (Kenney) **108** 302
Jemima **62** 257 **146** 332
Jemima (Gage) **146** 331
Jemima Clement **96** 97
Jennet L. **78** 335
Jenny **90** 248 **125** 157
Jeremiah **62** 45 **92** 280
Jerusha **62** 40
Jesse **90** 393 **95** 197 **97**
  222 234 237 **133** 123
Jessie Emma (Fifield)
  125 160
Joan **125** 157
Joanna **75** 314 **76** 184 **88**
  195 **95** 197 **96** 248 **118**
  94
Job **70** 310
Joel **90** 241
John **54** 87 **56** 208 209 **58**
  47 **60** 314 **61** 335 **62** 36
  38 45-47 259 **66** 262 **67**
  353 **72** 204 **74** 118 **75**
  105 76 114 **77** lxxix
  xciii **79** 115 271 **81** 150
  83 140 147 379 **90** 311
  393 **92** 282 283 333 **93**
  58 **95** 346 **96** 144 337 **97**
  17 **98** 361 362 **123** 32
  128 59 **133** 123 **138** 45
  139 293 **140** 160 **145**
  350 **147** 258
John Alfred **92** 321
John E. **68** lxxiv
John F. **91** 302 **92** 133 **93**
  119 **94** 46
John Francis **93** 119
John G. **136** 270
John Gardner **70** xxxii
  xxxiii
John H. (Mrs.) **100** 101

KIMBALL *cont'd*
John Horne **103** 44
John L. **89** 350
John Peverly **81** 150 254
John Russell **52** 360
John Sawyer **81** 190
Jonathan **60** 56 **62** 35 47
  48 **70** xxxiii **76** 105 **81**
  190 **90** 241 **93** 334 **108**
  165 **109** 229 **146** 332
Jonathan Lord **97** 357
Joseph **52** 433 **59** 146 289
  373 **60** 191 192 **62** 37 **67**
  351 353 354 **76** 104 251
  252 261 **88** 287 **90** 241
  93 103 **94** 119 **95** 86 87
  96 339 **109** 233 **116** 306
  117 141 142 224 **120**
  218 **121** 146 **123** 150
  127 311 **133** 44 123 **135**
  20
Joseph F. **123** 150
Joseph H. **119** 67
Joseph Moody **94** 120
Josephine **74** 27
Josephine A.
  (Constantine) **123** 150
Josephine Adelaide
  97 383
Josephine Eugenia
  97 357
Joshua **56** 208 **75** 49 112
  120 **76** 108 194 248 252
  259 **77** 313 **79** 141 **115**
  220
Josiah **62** 39 **76** 106
Juda **61** 240
Judith **53** 465 **78** 344 **125**
  154 156
Judith (Hall) **125** 154 155
Judith (Johnson) (Gould)
  139 294
Judith (Webber) **101** 260
  338 **102** 79 **125** 157 161
Judith Marie **125** 158
Juley B. (Alley) **97** 17
Julia **97** 229 233
Julia (Hudson) **136** 270
Julia Ann **94** 120
Julia DeKay **89** 92
June Chatfield **80** 46
Kate Maria **87** 379 380
Katharine **75** 107 108
  112 149
Kathrina Prescott **77** lxxx
Laura **69** 256
Laura Ann Smith **112** 233
Laura Lasell **89** 32
Lavinia **83** 136 145 **93** 332
Leona **97** 236
Leonard **52** 247 **58** 280 **77**
  lxxlx
Leroy N. **74** 27
Levi **61** 245 **68** 110 **90** 241
  124 60
Lewis **83** 136
Lewis B. **93** 338
Lewis E. **93** 338
Lizzie N. **93** 330
Lois **68** 382 **146** 332
Lois (Pattee) **146** 331

KIMBALL *cont'd*
Lorana **83** 136 144
Lorenzo **133** 45
Louisa **77** lxxix **94** 120
Louisa (Adams) **90** 393
Louisa Maria **112** 233
Lovel **71** 341
Lucinda **83** 141
Lucretia **93** 193 **95** 193
  197 198
Lucretia (Cousins)
  104 312
Lucy **52** 100 **55** 178 **62** 46
  94 63
Lucy (Booker) **118** 318
Lucy (Bryant) **137** 334
Lucy (Pearl) **92** 285
Lucy A. **109** 60 61
Lucy Carter **91** 302
Lucy Dolph **80** 46
Lucy Durrell **133** 45
Lucy S. (Carter) **91** 302
Lucy Young **75** lxviii
Lulu **77** xciii
Lulu Burton (Randall)
  83 433 **84** 17
Lulu Stacy **57** 415 **79** 116
  119
Luther **83** 140 **95** 191 194
Lydia **55** 396 **60** 192 **61**
  336 **62** 37 **65** 113 **66** 10
  11 **74** 44 **75** 112-114 120
  123 **76** 104-106 113 179
  188 189 192 248 256 **77**
  lxxix **81** 190 **92** 320 **93**
  332 **94** 120 **95** 195 197
  104 312 **111** 258 **123**
  126
Lydia (Adams) **94** 119 120
Lydia (Bowden) **111** 258
Lydia (Day) **109** 229
Lydia (Fairfield) **86** 65
Lydia (Livermore)
  123 126
Lydia (Loomis) **91** 198
Lydia (McIntire) **126** 278
Lydia (Peavy) **96** 144 338
Lydia A. **126** 70
Lydia A. (Plaisted) **120**
  305 **123** 149 153
Lydia A. (Winn) **119** 143
  120 64
Lydia H. **92** 333
Lydia Jane (Burbank)
  95 186
Marabah **93** 338
Marcus Morton **109** 232
  233
Margaret **52** 247 **57** 415
  60 352 **61** 80 **62** 259 **71**
  xxiii **77** xxxviii xciii **79**
  116 119 271 **87** 69
Margaret (Blaisdell)
  119 67
Margaret (Cole) (Dow)
  142 257 258
Margaret Ann **89** 118
Margaret Arnold **81** 190
Margaret Revelle
  (Freeman) **125** 160

KIMBALL *cont'd*
Margery (Crowell)
  108 212
Maria **75** 319
Maria L. **125** 158
Marion E. **93** 338
Martha **61** 333 **62** 34 36 37
  74 44 **77** 218 **83** 136 **85**
  336 **114** 185 **135** 127
Martha (Wentworth)
  135 127
Martha Ann **91** 225
Mary **51** 322 **53** 338 **55** 320
  59 368 **60** 209 **61** 245
  331 332 335 **62** 18 36 60
  63 255 263 **63** 46 178
  369 **65** 113 **68** 250 **70**
  309 **74** 44 205 259 **75** 47
  110 111 119 122 **76** 114
  182 184 250 252 257 260
  261 **77** lxxix **81** 190 **83**
  136 145 **85** 387 **87** 301
  88 127 331 **90** 392 393
  95 88 193 197 **97** 225
  100 289 **101** 68 **109** 51
  110 204 **111** 110 239
  112 234 **125** 155 **126**
  220 **133** 45 **135** 20 **139**
  55 294
Mary (Brickett) **87** 380
Mary (Cole) **86** 65
Mary (Doane) **108** 212
Mary (Eastman) **92** 275
  125 155
Mary (Howland) (Luther)
  138 45
Mary (Jones?) (Lazell)
  88 362
Mary (Lewis) (Doane)
  108 302
Mary (Little) **90** 392
Mary (Ober) **111** 110
Mary (O'Connell) **83** 433
  437
Mary (Pike) **95** 86 87
Mary (Schrier) **89** 32
Mary (Sharples) **96** 338
Mary (Smith) **109** 51 233
  110 203 204 **142** 51 54
  55
Mary (Stiles) **124** 60
Mary (Stone) (Sawtell)
  126 136
Mary (Taylor) **96** 74
Mary (Wilson) **125** 155
Mary (Witt) **141** 21
Mary A. **90** 112
Mary Alice **78** 332 **79** 202
  82 235 **95** 297 346 **96**
  164
Mary Amanda **81** 150
Mary Ann **62** 154 **63** 46 **67**
  351 **93** 252 **94** 161 **125**
  160
Mary Ann (Baker) **89** 72
Mary E. **93** 330
Mary Eliza **81** 150 254
Mary Elizabeth **73** 6
Mary F. **68** xxxi
Mary F. G. **91** 395
Mary Frances **81** 190

KIMBALL *cont'd*
Mary H. (Adams) **90** 48
Mary Hall **91** 229
Mary Jane **57** 382 **67** 351
  97 225 232 **125** 158
Mary L. **90** 393
Mary M. **67** 353 **93** 338
Mary Nason **133** 45
Mary O. **92** 333
Mary Olive **133** 123
Mary Reynolds (Packard)
  133 123
Mary Ward (Ross) **95** 346
Matilda (Joy) **123** 233
Mehitable **62** 42 258 259
  72 283 **76** 186 **83** 203
  93 90 **95** 194 376 **134**
  222 **146** 332
Mehitable (Beede) **95** 346
Mehitable (Foster) **92** 274
Melatiah **88** 127
Melinda **92** 315
Melissa (Ross) **95** 377
Mellen **92** 280 282 283
  315 320
Mercy **62** 44 **75** 116 **81** 190
  83 141
Mercy (Haseltine) **93** 46
  109 229
Mercy Carter **100** 70
Meribah **76** 110
Mildred Dodge **95** 314
Milton **112** 233
Milton Isaac **125** 160
Miriam **51** 463 **62** 36 **76**
  111-113 185 **92** 269 **139**
  294
Miriam (Collins) **125** 155
Molly **125** 156 157
Moses **54** xliv **55** xxxix
  56 xxxviii 84 326 335-
  340 **57** xxxix lxix 415
  58 lii **59** liii **60** xliv **61**
  xlii **62** xlvi lxxxviii **63**
  lxxvii **68** xv **75** 70 **77**
  xciii **79** 115 116 118 **87**
  69 **90** 241 **92** 310 **96** 97
  111 239 **145** 161
Moses Day **109** 233
Myra L. (Page) **112** 234
Myron Willis **125** 161
N. L. **91** 327
Nabby **76** 254 **77** 151
  125 104
Nahum Clough **125** 160
Nancy **56** 335 **72** 204 **79** 51
  147 258
Nancy (Lazell) **89** 32
Nancy Smith **112** 233
Nancy Wilder **64** 10
Naoma (Johnson) **91** 385
Naomi **94** 113
Narissa E. **83** 20
Narissa E. (Goodwin)
  (Knight) **83** 20
Nathan **65** 113 **76** 113 188
  189 248 249 254 260 **109**
  53 **125** 157 **126** 144
Nathaniel **62** 38 39 **71** 221
  75 45 105 107-109 116
  117 **76** 194 249 257 **77**

KIMBALL *cont'd*
xciii **79** 115 **81** 190 **87**
207 **90** 229 247 **93** 332
95 346 **109** 229 **112** 233
234 **116** 298 **123** 126
132 271 **146** 330
Nathaniel G. **66** 278
Nehemiah **62** 39 **74** 44
83 136
Nellie L. **81** 153
Nellie M. **125** 161
Nicholas **52** 247
Noah **118** 318
Norah B. **84** 29
Obadiah **90** 393 **145** 162
Olive **64** 123 **68** 94 **81** 255
92 333 **111** 40 **117** 225
141 54
Olive (Woolley) **136** 320
Olive Jane **120** 138
Oliver **92** 333 **111** 110
Orinda **57** 11
Pamela **86** 359
Parker **97** 127
Parnell **52** 247
Patience **127** 34
Patin / Patten **93** 338
Patty **77** lxxix
Paul **62** 40 **86** 65
Paul Wellington **84** 234
85 195
Paulina **119** 225
Paulina (Trafton) **117**
143 144
Pearl **92** 283 320
Peter **64** 116
Peter Cammett **89** 72
Phebe **65** 113 **96** 341
125 293
Phebe Theresa (Judd)
136 331
Philip **92** 272 274 282
Phineas **92** 273 283 285
313 **113** 32 40
Phineas Sawyer **77** lxxx
Pline (Cluff) **95** 200
Polly **61** 239 245 **62** 155
83 140 **90** 315 **125** 156
157 **147** 258
Polly (Carll) **96** 146
Polly (Kimball) **125** 157
Polly (Smith) **90** 229 247
Polly (Young) **90** 230 251
Porter **61** 382
Priscilla **62** 60 261 **74** 27
110 66
R. H. **122** 230 232
Rachel **92** 78 **97** 221 237
Rachel (Roberts) **90** 233
253
Ralph E. **93** 330
Ralph W. **93** 330
Rebecca **55** 179 **59** 373 **76**
108 182 183 185 186 259
79 271 **89** 107 **90** 230
241 247 **113** 33 41 **125**
102
Rebecca Jones (Goodwin)
125 160
Reuben **79** 46 **92** 269 280
281 316 **100** 228 **105**

KIMBALL *cont'd*
284 **119** 229 **125** 152
147 85
Rhoda (Stockbridge)
134 294
Richard **52** 247 248 **56** 335
59 41 **60** 185 **61** 335 338
62 35 42 44 46 257 258
263 **67** 375 **70** xxxiii **73**
115 238 **75** 45 52 107
108 111-114 119 120 **76**
193 257 **77** lxxix lxxx
xciii **79** 115 **81** 189 **87** 69
90 331 392 393 **91** 21 25
95 346 **96** 337 **97** 16 **98**
362 **105** 171 **108** 312
109 229 233 **110** 204
125 37 44 **126** 278 **132**
122 269 **133** 41 44 123
142 54 55 257 **146** 331
332
Richard Davenport
77 lxxx
Richard M. **79** 29
Robert **63** 293 **76** 248 **91**
385 **92** 272 273 **93** 338
94 119 120
Robert Arthur **94** 138
Robert C. **114** 276
Robert Moody **100** 123
Robert Smith **94** 120
Rosana **91** 26
Rose E. (Tower) **123** 150
Royal **75** 305
Ruth **61** 242 **62** 259 **81** 32
92 197 280 **105** 61 **124**
247 **125** 113
Ruth (Smith) **96** 338
Ruth (Whittemore)
108 20
Ruth Earl **79** 141
S. **61** 333 335
Sabrey (Hobbs) **90** 335
Sally **62** 155 **65** 113 **66** 11
Sally (Curtis) **133** 44
135 20
Sally (Jellison) **96** 248
Sally (Lord) **108** 192
Salome (Knight) **96** 342
Samuel **52** 429 **58** 18 **61**
331 333 334 338 **62** 34
41 43 259 **70** xxxiii **75**
50 111 **76** 250 **83** 136
145 **87** 207 **108** 189 212
302 **109** 230 **112** 233
234 **114** 276 **117** 141
141 21
Samuel Augustus
112 233
Samuel C. **90** 46
Samuel F. **123** 233
Samuel Hale **97** 122
Sarah **52** 430 433 **56** 208
209 213 **57** 119 **58** 280
61 333 **62** 34 47 48 255
258 260 **67** 353 **69** 259
74 118 **75** xci 48 120 **76**
194 **77** lxxix **81** 150 190
82 350 **83** 203 **86** 151
90 112 311 393 **92** 283
93 90 **94** 119 **95** 197 **96**

KIMBALL *cont'd*
247 339 **98** 361 362 **109**
53 54 **117** 222 **125** 156
Sarah (Copeland) **88** 287
Sarah (Day) **109** 233
Sarah (Downing) **108** 189
Sarah (Durrell) **132** 269
Sarah (Farnham) **117** 141
Sarah (Haggett) **125** 156
157
Sarah (Jellison) **90** 233 235
Sarah (Jullss) **108** 150
Sarah (Spofford) **109** 233
Sarah (Stone) **108** 120
132 269 **133** 44
Sarah (Wilson) **95** 346
Sarah (Wood) **109** 53
Sarah A. **96** 131 **99** 183
Sarah A. M. **88** 342
Sarah Abby **92** 333
Sarah Abigail Clarke
77 xii
Sarah Ann **62** 122
Sarah Ann (Davis)
97 222 237
Sarah Elizabeth **91** 302
Sarah J. (Clough) **125** 160
Sarah Jane **125** 160
Sarah L. **123** 149
Sarah Louise **52** 379 **56**
208 **83** 513
Sarah M. (Strout) **92** 333
Sarah Rebecca (Brooks)
125 161
Sarah Rollins (Philpot)
103 44
Sarah Sanborn **81** 150
Sarah Smith **94** 120
Sarah Smith (Safford)
97 357
Sarah W. (Little) **120** 218
123 150
Sargent **90** 241
Sear **78** 73
Selinda **72** 285
Selma **105** 35
Seth **74** 205
Seth W. **103** 235
Simeon **92** 316 320
Solomon **105** 208
Solomon Farnham
136 320
Sophia **58** 280 **112** 234
124 78
Sophia (Kimball) **112** 234
Sophia (Maltby) **111** 298
Spencer Woolley **136**
320 331
Stephen **52** 248 249 **92** 333
94 372 373 **127** 5 311
138 45 **142** 178
Sukey **92** 281
Susan **62** 154 **89** 119 199
Susan (Bean) **91** 123 124
97 230
Susan (Johnson) **96** 160
109 217 **110** 222 223
Susan (Tillinghast)
109 233
Susan (Trafton) **96** 339
Susan Lord **133** 45

KIMBALL *cont'd*
Susan Sawyer **81** 189 190
Susanna **59** 146 **63** 293
  75 46 47 50 117 **76** 108
  183 184 252 254 259 **81**
  190 **90** 246 247 250 **95**
  191 **97** 16 18 238 **105** 61
Susanna (Bean) **91** 120
Susanna (Hogkins)
  96 340
Susanna (Kimball) **90** 247
  97 16 18 238
Susanna (Scribner)
  90 229
Susanna (Trafton) **117**
  141 142
Susanna (Whittemore)
  108 165
Susanna C. **88** 332
Susanna Everett **112** 233
Sylvester **77** 151 **95** 346
T. **61** 335
Tabitha **92** 333
Tamar **63** 300
Tamerson **120** 272
Tamison (Poor) **90** 393
Tamson (Tibbetts) **99** 248
Tamzine **71** 341
Thatcher Raymond
  97 121
Theodora **90** 133
Theodore **117** 144
Thomas **52** 247 248 **54** 421
  56 258 **59** 41 **61** 332 334
  335 **62** 35-37 43 44 46
  261 **75** 110 111 122 **77**
  lxxx **84** 402 **88** 387 **91**
  345 347 **96** 321 **109** 51
  233 **110** 175 **131** 109
  137 184 **142** 55 **143** 36
Thomas J. **82** 350
Timothy **90** 392 393
  92 277
Truman Marshall **80** 46
Tryphena **126** 278
Ursula (Scott) **52** 248 **56**
  335 **70** xxxiii **77** lxxix
  xciii **81** 189 **95** 346 **109**
  229 233 **142** 55
Ursula Clarissa (Lazell)
  89 230
Vilatte (Murray) **136** 331
Viola M. **123** 233
Virtue (Willis) **114** 276
Walter G. **78** 109
Walter Gardner **79** 202
Walter Milton **125** 160
Warren **107** 299
William **53** 337 **86** 65 **90**
  393 **91** 302 **93** 393 **96**
  342 **99** 248 **125** 154-156
William A. **68** 382
William Chatfield **80** 46
William F. Durant **91** 302
William H. **125** 161
William K. **68** 382
William N. **74** 27
William Richey **112** 233
William S. **137** 334
William Wilder **92** 275
William Wirt **81** 373

KIMBALL *cont'd*
Willis G. C. **83** 433 **84** 17
Winifred **136** 331
Wyman **62** 122
KIMBER —— **144** 51
Abby Katharine **95** 346
  347
Henry **95** 347
Jean (Henry) **95** 347
Sidney Arthur **69** xiv **77**
  241 **108** 238
Thomas **77** 241
Walter L. **108** 238
KIMBERLY Kimberley
—— **61** 101
— Mrs. **62** 196
___ (Winscott) **102** 107
Abel **102** 108 111
Abel Burritt **102** 108
Abiah **55** l **102** 102 103
  105 106 315 **142** 339
  145 325 340
Abigail **53** 408 **62** 378 **63**
  71 **82** 380 **86** 170 **102**
  103 105 107-110 112 315
Abigail (Adams) **102** 106
Abigail (Fitch) **102** 104
Abigail (Scranton)
  102 110
Abigail (Woodruff)
  102 106
Abraham **102** 102-108
  110 111 315 316
Adah (Ward) **102** 109
Agnes **111** 148
Alice **102** 102
Amanda **102** 110
Amy (Smith) **102** 111
Ann **54** 81 **85** 63 **86** 161
  102 108
Ann (Tittle) **102** 110
Anna **85** 63 **102** 106
Anne **85** 63 **102** 106 111
Azel **102** 109 111 316
Barshua **102** 106
Bathsheba **102** 106
Benjamin **102** 107
Betsey **102** 112
Beulah **59** 66 **102** 111
Beulah (Morse) **102** 110
Chloe **61** 390
Clara (Smith) **102** 109
Clark **102** 108
Clarry (Hurd) **102** 108
Currence (Prindle)
  102 108
David **51** 242 **102** 111 316
David Robert **102** 111
Dennis **102** 109
Desire **84** 140
E. **56** 263
Edmund **102** 110
Eleazer **60** 140 **85** 63 **102**
  102-106 315 **145** 324
Eli **57** 405 **102** 111
Eliakim **102** 109 112
Elizabeth **54** 322 **56** 280 **57**
  405 **58** 282 **59** 65 **61** 388
  85 63 **102** 103 104 106-
  108 112 315
Elizabeth (Smith) **102** 112

KIMBERLY *cont'd*
Elizabeth (Webb) **102** 110
Erastus Coan **102** 111
Esther **102** 109 110
Esther (Smith) **102** 108
Eunice **102** 112
Eustace de **102** 102
Ezra **102** 109
Fitch **102** 106 108 316
  137 11
Francis **102** 109
George **59** 66 **102** 107
  110 111
Gideon **102** 105 109 315
Gilead **51** 242 **82** 380 **102**
  109 111
Gratia **102** 111
Hannah **102** 102 103 105
  107 109 112 315
Hannah (Candee) **102** 107
Hannah (Coan) **102** 111
Hannah (Downs) **102** 105
Hannah (Hill) **102** 107
Hannah (Russell) **102** 102
Hannah E. **102** 111
Hazard **102** 110
Henry **102** 110
Hetty **102** 109
Horace **102** 109 112
Hugh de **102** 102
Huldah (Kimberly) **102**
  109 112
Ichabod **102** 108
Ira **102** 110
Isaac Sherman **102** 107
Isabel **102** 108
Israel **84** 140 **102** 107-110
  316
Jacob **102** 107
James C. **100** 108 **102** 102
James Cheney **105** 77
  116 72
Jedediah **102** 106
Jedidiah **102** 315
Jerre **102** 111
Jerusha **102** 108
Jessie Aurelia **101** 169
John **60** 141 **62** 86 **85** 63
  86 161 **102** 102 106-112
  316
Josiah **102** 111
Justul **102** 111
Katharine **102** 107
Katharine (Howe)
  102 102
Lester **102** 109
Leverett **102** 111
Liberty **102** 109
Linus **102** 111
Lois (Tuttle) **102** 105
Louisa **102** 109
Lovisa **102** 112
Lucretia **102** 111 112
Lydia **102** 112
Lydia (Wise) **102** 109 110
Mabel **66** 207
Mabel (Thompson) **102**
  110 111
Marguerite **81** 475
Maria **102** 112
Maria (Kimberly) **102** 112

KIMBERLY *cont'd*
Martha **51** 242
Martha (Hitchcock)
  102 107
Mary **51** 242 **56** 263 280
  60 141 269 **85** 63 **86** 161
  102 102-110 315 316
  106 214
Mary (Brockett) **102** 111
Mary (Coan) **102** 107
Mary (Graves) **102** 112
Mary (Hubbard) **102** 108
Mary (Merrick) (Bradley)
  (Gill) **102** 111 112
Mary (Osborne) **102** 105
Mary (Robbins) **102** 103
Mary (Seabrook)
  (Preston) **102** 102
Mary (Shearman) **102** 107
Mary (Talcott) **102** 316
Mary (Tolles) **102** 109
Mary A. **67** 226
Merry **61** 392
Miriam **102** 103
Nathan **81** 125 132
Nathaniel **53** 408 **54** 322
  56 280 **66** 207 **81** 133
  102 102-107 109 110 112
  315 316
Nehemiah **102** 112
Pamel **102** 111
Philomela **84** 140
Pitman **102** 110
Polly **66** 207 **102** 111
Polly (Green) **102** 108
Prudence **102** 105 316
Rhoda **61** 389 **62** 378
Robert **102** 102 107 111
Ruth **61** 178 390 **85** 63 65
  102 104 106-108 315
Ruth (Curtis) **102** 103
Ruth (Hale) **102** 106
Sally **102** 112
Sally Ann **102** 108
Samuel **85** 63 **102** 106
  108 110 316
Sarah **53** 312 **56** 280 **61** 388
  102 103 105-110 315 316
Sarah (Smith) **102** 109 112
Sarah (Wheaton) **102** 107
Sherman **102** 107 111
Silas **102** 107 109 112
Sophia **102** 112
Susanna **102** 106 107
Tamar (Bennett) **102** 108
Thankful (Chittenden)
  102 110
Thomas **51** 240 242 **54** 81
  55 I **56** 280 **60** 140 **61**
  178 **81** 121-123 125-127
  133 134 **85** 63 65 **102**
  102 104-106 108 315 316
  142 331
Thompson **102** 110
Walter **61** 392
William **102** 102 112
William H. **102** 110
Zuriel **102** 105-107 316
Kimble *see* Kimball
KIMBLIN
Aralin / Araten **91** 327

Kimbol *see* Kimball
KIMBOUGH
J. L. **91** 327
KIMBROUGH Elizabeth
  Greene **81** 222
James Mobley (Mrs.) **81**
  108 222
KIME Elizabeth **96** 231
KIMEL Alonzo **128** 171
Catherine (Hartzell)
  128 174
Elnor Jane (Keickser)
  128 171
Emma A. (Peck) **128** 174
Henry **128** 174
J. T. **128** 171
John H. **128** 174
Loretta E. (Kline) **128** 171
KIMM Ezekiel **127** 146
Leanhart **89** 206
KIMME
Lodema Willis **92** 220
KIMMINS John **92** 365
Mary Ann **120** 319
Moses **92** 101
Sarah **65** 214 **92** 101
KIMPSON
Frances **76** 308
George **76** 308
Kimpton *see* Kempton
KIMZEY
Benjamin **101** 80
Herbert Bennett **100** 111
  101 80 339
Nancy (McClure) **101** 339
Thomas **101** 339
Kinaston *see* Kenniston
KINCAID Kincade Kincaide
—— **113** 243
A. **115** 203
Adelia A. **115** 302
Benjamin Jefferson
  91 142
Calenda Smith **86** 337
Caroline Chandler **75** 269
Clara Elizabeth (Greenley)
  103 227
Cynthia **102** 260
Elizabeth (Carey) **128** 96
Elizabeth (Smith) **103** 227
Frederic Llewellyn **75** 269
George **54** 196 **62** 301
  137 40
George W. **137** 39
Jacob **128** 96
James **70** 264 **91** 327
  115 293
Jane **91** 387
Jane Elizabeth (Smith)
  103 227
Jean **86** 337
Johannah Morris
  (Baldwin) **137** 40
John **98** 106 **102** 260 **103**
  227 **122** 96 **128** 96
John Edward **74** 160 **89**
  147 **90** 151 **91** 158 **92**
  162 **93** 84 **94** 81 **98** 88
  102 116 230 231 **103**
  125
John Smith **103** 227

KINCAID *cont'd*
Margaret **115** 293
Margaretta Onelia (Tuttle)
  103 227
Maria (Vandalsem)
  128 96
Marion **62** 301
Martha **115** 293
Ransom D. **115** 293
Samuel **73** 174
Sarah **102** 169
Sephrona L. **91** 386
Susanna **73** 166
Viola V. **115** 293
William **103** 227
William Wallace **75** ix
  xxiii **103** 78 123 227
Winifred Weld
  (Batchelder) (Lasell) **61**
  xxxvi **68** liii **70** viii **71**
  viii **74** 160 **75** 76 76 77
  77 viii **78** 220 **89** 147 **90**
  125 151 **91** 158 **92** 162
  93 84 **94** 81 **98** 88 **102**
  116 230 231 **103** 125
KINCH
Elizabeth **109** 185
Heth P. **124** 34
Ira T. **124** 34
Jonathan **56** 269 **57** 146
Lois **56** 37 **57** 147
Lucy **57** 30
Magdalene **124** 34
Mary E. **124** 34
Molly **57** 144
Ruth **124** 34
Sally **124** 34
Susanna **55** 260 **56** 31
Susanna (Alden) **107** 69
Thomas **56** 31 265 **57** 29
  30 144 146 147 149 **107**
  69
William **57** 29 **124** 34
KINCHELOE
Cornelius **101** 327
KINCHMAN
Robert **68** 182
KIND Rachel **126** 19
KINDER William **64** 262
KINDERSONE
Mary **128** 166
KINDLE — Mr. **62** 158
Joshua **144** 218
KINDLEMARSH
Andrew **56** 404
Anne **56** 403 404
Edmund **56** 404
Humphrey **56** 404
Jane **56** 404
Katharine **56** 404
Margaret **56** 404
Phillippe **56** 404
Richard **56** 404
Robert **56** 404
Thomas **56** 403 404
KINDON
John Augusts **63** 143
Kindrick *see* Kendrick
KINE John **113** 63
KINEARD Robert **60** 25
William **60** 25

KINELLA Maria **82** 177
KINEN Patrick **73** 263
Kiney *see* Kinney
KING alias RICE Abigail
 130 302-304
 Abigail (Clapp) **130** 302-304
 Adonijah **130** 302-304
 Edmund **130** 302-304
 Ezra **130** 302-304
 Jonas **130** 302 304
 Samuel **130** 302-304
 Silence (Rice) **130** 302-304
KING Kinge Kyng
 —— **51** 273 **52** 99 140 394
 53 334 448 464 **54** 72
 134 **55** 275 **56** lxii 214
 326 **57** 209 **58** 347 348
 408 **62** 206 **68** 42 **72** 216
 80 63 **86** 92 **88** 127 **109**
 295 **119** 218 **126** 214
 130 311 313 **143** 366
 148 284
 — Capt. **52** 19 **59** 213 **65**
 108 381
 — Dr. **70** 149
 — Mr. **51** 40 41 **60** 264
 62 129 355 **63** 54 **79** 301
 127 138
 — Mrs. **51** 289 **79** 405
 — Rev. Mr. **85** 450
 — Widow **72** 93 **92** 318
 98 121
 —— (Burbeck) **140** 47
 —— (Ingersoll) **140** 156
 Aaron **91** 386 **109** 105
 Abba **57** 320
 Abby Ann **118** 150
 Abby Ingalls **74** 209 295
 Abby M. (Young) **125** 173
 Abel **60** 306
 Abiah **51** 290 **53** 434 435
 59 238 **136** 332
 Abigail **51** 362 437 **52** 418
 53 334 414 435-437 447
 57 78 271 **58** 401 **59** 415
 60 77 **65** 355 **66** 44 126
 127 **70** 259 **72** 99 217
 221 222 **83** 365 **84** 85
 119 103 151-153 **125**
 287 **130** 302-304
 Abigail (Manchester)
 102 10
 Abigail (Seymour)
 132 143
 Abigail (Williams) **87** 3
 Abraham **63** 351 **64** 161
 107 233 234
 Abram **107** 233
 Absalom **53** 412 415
 Addie **139** 66
 Adilla **119** 256
 Adonijah **130** 302-304
 Agnes **58** 347 348 **127**
 169 263
 Agnes (Gregson) **127** 263
 Albert S. **83** 504
 Alexander **58** 400 **72** 222
 79 167
 Alexander M. **130** 47
 Alfred **59** 240 **118** 150

KING *cont'd*
 Alice **51** 260 437 **52** 183
 53 436 **59** 238 **60** 93 152
 74 209 **83** 78
 Alice (Dean) **87** 3
 Alice (Webster) **142** 268
 Alicia **58** 348
 Allie Leona **84** 192
 Alzada **137** 282
 Ama **72** 102
 Amajiah **129** 65
 Amanda F. **117** 209
 Amanda M. **116** 259
 Amasa **104** 102 **127** 179
 Amelia Roxana (Case)
 85 223
 Amos **72** 221 **76** 155
 Amos Harriman **74** 209
 Amy **72** 44
 Andrew **69** 254 **100** 242
 111 283
 Angeline (Marsters)
 120 17
 Ann **52** 413 414 417 **53** 22
 449 **60** 204 **64** 254 **70**
 231 **73** 137 **107** 233 **131**
 237 **134** 337
 Ann Day (Fowler)
 107 233
 Ann P. (Torpin) **126** 67
 Ann Ryckman **107** 233
 Anna **51** 152 **53** 434 **56** 73
 58 172 **59** 101 415 **60** 79
 74 209 253 **83** 365 **104**
 24 **108** 221 **109** 95 **118**
 150
 Anna Devereux **74** 209
 Anna Z. **83** 504
 Anne **51** 282 286-289 **52**
 107 **55** 201 **62** 167 **71**
 256 **81** 444 **87** 115
 Anne (Finney) **111** 172
 148 316 317 322 327
 Anne (Ingersoll) **130** 311
 Anne P. **77** 321
 Anne Purinton **78** 205
 92 136 **93** 142 279
 Annie **91** 385
 Annie Elizabeth **94** 23
 Appollos **125** 290
 Archibald Gracey **53** 464
 Arnold **53** 22
 Arthur Baldwin **94** 25
 Arthur Caswell **87** 4
 Arvilla **148** 286 287
 Arvilla B. (Stearns) **124** 63
 Asa **53** 415 416 435 **65** 192
 66 127 **128** 53
 Asa Francis **77** 188
 Asahel **61** 234
 Aspasio **124** 63
 Augusta O. **81** 413
 Augustus **76** 278
 Azubah (Nichols) **127** 179
 B. M. **80** 62
 Barnabas **58** lxxi
 Barnabie **148** 49
 Barnett **101** 80
 Barzelia **53** 435
 Barzillai **51** 292
 Basil (Mrs.) **78** 205

KING *cont'd*
 Bathsheba **51** 316 438 **52**
 180 **53** 436 437
 Bathsheba (Harrod)
 100 242
 Bathshua **53** 333 413 414
 Bazaleel **53** 333 334 413
 414
 Beala (Hubbard) **134** 329
 Benedict **127** 79
 Benjamin **51** 438 **53** 416
 434 435 **54** 107 **57** 402
 58 89 **59** 238 239 **69** 346
 347 349 **77** 203 **102** 10
 105 216 **114** 181 **118** 64
 127 216 **130** 313 **148**
 157
 Benjamin F. **114** 111
 Benjamin Trussel **69** 267
 Bennet **70** 264
 Bertha Florence **82** 279
 Bessie **101** 321 **107** 133
 Bethiah **72** 222
 Bethsaida **58** 195 **60** 80
 Betsey **57** 190 **61** 243 **90**
 316 **104** 102 **112** 58 **114**
 181 **125** 100
 Betsey (Patten) **125** 106
 Betsey (Sawdy) **148** 287
 Betty **52** 409 **59** 238 **60** 78
 79
 Bridget **63** 281
 Bridget (Loker) (Davis)
 143 330
 Calvin **83** 504 **114** 181
 Cameron Haight **58** 347
 408 **60** 185 **63** 303 **64**
 xxxi
 Caroline **61** 346 **84** 333
 117 209 **148** 185
 Caroline B. **98** 91
 Caroline B. (Hill) **98** 91
 Caroline L. (Morgan)
 137 362
 Caroline W. **93** 280
 Caroline Webster **81** 364
 82 236
 Carrie Eliza **99** 168
 Catherine **113** 65
 Catherine (Leonard) **87** 3
 Cathy Lynn **119** 316
 Celia **101** 80
 Charity **60** 77 205
 Charles **52** 309-311 409-
 411 413 414 416 **53** 447
 464 **58** 28 402 **59** 412
 413 **60** 79 204 **64** 226 **68**
 219 **83** 365 **91** 79 **107** 7
 110 132 **140** 160
 Charles Bird **125** 172
 Charles Daly **111** 77
 Charles G. **54** xcvi **69** 98
 Charles Goodrich **65** lv
 Charles Gregory **94** 25
 Charles Sumner **74** 209
 Charles Thomas **77** 182
 Charles W. **81** 413
 Charlie **83** 504
 Charlotte **76** 265 **148** 282
 284 287
 Chester **58** 402

KING *cont'd*
Chester A. **79** 26
Chesterfield **71** 276
Chloe **60** 75 **63** 182 **72** 221
  83 365
Christia **58** 347
Christopher **51** 282
  65 236
Clamania L. **98** 91
Clarence E. **101** 124 **108**
  155 317
Clarence Edwin **85** 463
Clarissa **58** 197 402 **60** 199
  83 365 504
Clarissa S. **83** 504
Clement **71** lxviii **87** 136
  243
Collins P. **89** 384
Content (Chase) **87** 136
  243
Cora **78** 48
Cora L. **74** 209
Cornelia A. **83** 504
Cornelius **118** 150
Cyntha **105** 216
Cyntha Filenda **59** 210
Cynthia **53** 416 **59** 210 **60**
  266 **72** 103 **148** 157
Cynthia P. **118** 150
Cyrus **58** cxii **126** 204
D. Webster **64** 94
Daisy Mildred
  (Ackerman) **92** 213
Daisy O. **130** 47
Dan **72** 221
Daniel **51** 73 282 362 **57**
  83 181 323 324 **58** 57 85
  87-89 401 **59** 416 **65** lv
  84 **66** 125-128 **74** 119
  78 402 **81** 352 **83** 78 365
  93 279 **113** 65 **135** 222
Daniel A. **98** 91
Daniel L. **91** 393
Daniel Putnam **93** 279
Daniel Webster **93** 279
  280
David **51** 437 **52** 414 **53**
  334 413 414 434 437 **55**
  46 **58** 197 400-403 **59** 95-
  97 99 **60** 78 202 **70** 231
  71 221 **73** 283 289 290
  80 270 **90** 237 **110** 309
  137 282 **142** 338
Deborah **53** 414 **57** 322
  399 **58** 168 170 174 261
  60 175 **107** 233 **117** 215
  118 150 **121** 203
Deborah (Bird) **125** 172
Deborah (Carver) **88** 221
Deborah (Greene)
  134 202
Deborah (Knapp) **109** 187
Deborah (Prince) **121** 201
Deborah (Smith) **107** 233
  234
Delcevare **97** 398
Delia **69** 267
Delight **72** 221
Deliverance **53** 435
Deloss **131** 237
Dennis **123** 308

KING *cont'd*
Dervello J. **61** li
Desire **51** 178
Dever **131** 237
Dezel **131** 237
Diadema Calvin **59** 210
Diana **90** 316 **91** 16
Dilly **119** 256
Dora **85** 295
Dora E. **120** 223
Dorcas **54** lxvii **84** 450
Dorothy **51** 261 **53** 413
  56 407 **68** 323 **69** 22-24
  93 279
Dorothy (Bates) **97** 158
Dwight **131** 237
Dwight E. **83** 504
E. C. **54** 106
E. L.S. **143** 26
E. W. **89** 395
Eben **58** 196 **59** 413 **83** 365
Ebenezer **51** 73 437 438
  55 388 **57** 320 **58** 28 **59**
  99 157 **72** 221 222 **115**
  159 **129** 64 **132** 143
Edey Haxton **132** 244
Edgar **131** 237
Edith Madeline (Tyler)
  96 191
Edith Sawyer **71** lvii
Edward **52** 107 350 **54**
  xciv **57** 180 **63** 345 **66** 44
  68 179 **75** 228 **84** 153
  90 166 **142** 268
Edward Everett **74** 209
Edward Mason **74** 209
Edward Thorp **88** 98
Effie (Flood) **101** 124
Eleanor **73** 142
Eleazar **54** xciv
Elfe **58** 195
Eli **53** 435 **126** 232
Elias **104** 102
Elijah **58** 195-197 401 402
  59 413 416 **60** 75 204
  265 **65** lv **83** 365 **88** 70
  277 **109** 79 **113** 144
Eliphalet **58** 348
Elisha **58** 175 **73** 226
  127 309
Eliza **59** 237 **95** 17 **101** 80
  110 132
Eliza Ann **79** 155
Eliza Barrington **109** 260
Elizabeth **51** 360 362 459
  52 84 247 **53** 336 415
  416 **54** 353 **55** 388 **56**
  206 **57** 271 323 **58** 87-89
  262 348 **60** 78 **61** 141
  393 **64** lvi 161 257 **65**
  84 352 **66** 125 126 128
  72 217 221 222 **73** 146
  147 230 **74** 209 **75** 294
  298 **78** 410 **81** 310 **83** 78
  85 223 **87** 38 **92** 48 **96**
  74 **103** 309 **111** 57 **114**
  181 **130** 302-304 313
  137 282 **144** 335 **145**
  264 **148** 157
Elizabeth (Bennett) **101** 80
Elizabeth (Bicknell) **94** 25

KING *cont'd*
Elizabeth (Bosson)
  100 303
Elizabeth (Bryant) **148** 327
Elizabeth (Fuller) **57** 115
Elizabeth (Goold) **143** 42
Elizabeth (Heath) **146**
  263 265
Elizabeth (Lothrop)
  100 302
Elizabeth (Neal) **125** 287
Elizabeth (Sanders) **84**
  336 **126** 65
Elizabeth (Townsend)
  102 55
Elizabeth Denning
  53 464
Elizabeth Goodale
  (Briggs) **126** 41
Elizabeth M. **76** 273
Elizabeth Washington
  89 30
Ella **113** 306
Ella Rose **90** 190
Ellen **70** 118 **137** 282
Ellen E. **118** 150
Ellen Holbrook **70** li
Ellen Jane **76** 278
Ellen M. **77** 181
Ellery **148** 157
Elsie **60** 80
Emeline **116** 259
Emeline S. **83** 504 **84** 85
Emery **59** 96 **83** 504 **84** 85
Emily **72** 93 176
Emma **125** 54
Emma C. **51** 72 73 **53** 357
  54 353 **57** 114
Emma J. **117** 209
Emma Jane **82** 399 **85** 376
Erastus **72** 43 90
Ervilla **148** 287
Erwin Miles (Mrs.)
  108 134
Esek Clarke **71** lxvii
Estelle C. **61** li
Esther **52** 274 **55** 32
  127 305
Esther (Whittemore)
  107 253
Esther Lucile **107** 135
Esther Manton (Young)
  (Foote) **77** 155 **78** 205
  102 62 129 144
Etta A. **68** 200
Eugene P. **65** 192
Eunice **52** 413 **59** 99 **60** 78
  61 141 232 234 398 **72**
  221-223 **109** 119 **148**
  157
Eunice (Boardman)
  142 338
Eunice (Dunton) **114** 111
Eunice (George) **134** 87
Eunice P. **84** 85
Evelina Wilhelmina
  95 340
Evelyn L. **91** 393
Everett Mason **74** 209
Everett Willard **74** 209
Experience **72** 222 **136** 315

KING *cont'd*
148 261
Ezekiel 76 265
Ezra 66 44 130 302-304
F. C. 74 238
Fairzina A. (Ovitt) 130 47
Fanny 77 262
Fanny (Tewksbury) 94 25
Fearenot 123 260
Florence May 74 209
Florence Wales (Dean)
    87 4
Floyd Ross 124 260
Frances 53 413 74 209 94
    25 100 236
Frances Ellen 65 lv
Frances Neilson 65 lv
Frances Olivia 59 240
Francis 52 416 58 402 60
    265 83 504
Francis Backus 59 210
Francis P. 59 240
Francisca 82 238
Frank Barnard 52 79
Frank C. 107 76
Frank Cecil 75 xxvi 105
    125 106 100 108 76
Franklin 54 xxix xciv xcv
    83 359 102 120
Frederick 76 278 104 102
    119 191
Frederick C. 83 427 433
Freelove 79 351
Freelove (Manchester)
    102 17
G. W. 104 102
Gaius 53 435
Gamaliel 104 172
Gedney 54 xcvi 140 47
Genevieve 76 xxii 78
George 51 152 208 282
    286 289 53 434 55 187
    57 319 399 58 168 170
    174 261 59 238 239 60
    175 62 167 64 315 326
    65 lv 70 115 117 71 83
    274-276 282 72 32 151
    74 20 82 44 94 336 109
    95 115 156 123 66 127
    115 311 129 38 395 134
    87 142 247
George Allen 57 lxi
George Arthur 69 xxxv
    79 104 187 213 215 80
    219 222 81 213 233 236
    82 221 223 228 251 83
    129 222 246 383 512 84
    174 181 205 237 349 350
    464 85 108 111 181 184
    185 214 238 463 86 190
    214 347 87 3 169 179 88
    163
George E. 88 344
George Everett 74 209
George Farquhar Jones
    62 xxxv xl 63 101 65
    xlv lv
George Gordon 52 379
George H. 132 244
George Harrison
    Sanford 110 152 155

KING *cont'd*
241 311 322 113 77 115
    158 118 240 120 237
George Morgan 103 119
George Oscar 130 303
George P. 51 459
George Phillips 74 209
George Pickens 87 3
George Rogers 66 128
George W. 76 lxxxi
    87 250
George William 82 44
Georgia A. 83 433 438
Gertrude 76 lxxxi
Gertrude (Heely) 76 lxxxi
Gideon 52 181 58 195-197
    60 77 204 205 61 234 72
    222
Godfrey 102 10 118 150
    127 216 148 277 281
Grace Abbott 127 79
Grace Lillian 74 209
Grace W. 93 280
Gregory 118 172
Hallelujah 80 85
Hannah 51 291 316 437
    53 334 413-415 435 436
    55 252 57 114 58 cxii
    57 86 59 310 60 306 66
    125 128 68 226 74 119
    84 215 95 176 100 331
    105 216 114 181 119
    197 123 66 126 207 148
    327
Hannah (Allen) 88 277
Hannah (Cleveland)
    148 276
Hannah (Missimer)
    124 240
Hannah B. 61 383
Hannah Maria 77 188
Hannah May 148 316
Hannah Spicer (Rose)
    90 191
Hanson 80 62
Harriet 63 378 64 375
    78 318
Harriet Josephine 57 lxi
Harvey 70 xix
Harvey B. 52 97
Harvey James 58 348
    64 xxxi
Hazadiah 51 292 53 435
Helen 70 117 318
Helen Hester 110 155
Helen Louise (Baxter)
    97 398
Henrietta 53 464 73 230
Henry 52 123 59 97 75 294
    298 79 160 163 173 174
    301 80 75 83 504 84 84
    85 125 53 127 79 129 64
    136 77 143 131 147 250
    251
Henry C. 76 39
Henry F. 117 209
Henry Melville 51 244
    54 121 122 58 106 59
    237 63 211 64 296 65
    xxxiv
Henry William 85 223

KING *cont'd*
Hepzibah 91 37
Herbert Thorn 96 191
Hetty 61 76 73 219
Hezekiah 52 180 183 413
    414 417 419 53 447 58
    194-197 59 99 60 204
    64 189 83 365 84 85
    107 253
Hiram Prince 82 399
Hopestill 117 90
Hophni 93 273
Hugh 114 188
Hugh E. 110 238
Ichabod 56 206 57 183 58
    86 88 70 119 269 123 66
    Ida A. 98 91
Ida Bertha 83 504
Irvin E. 105 128
Isaac 51 223 437 438 53 437
    54 xciv 58 402 59 416
    60 73 365 73 225 83 365
    504 109 79 118 150 125
    293 148 316 327
Isabel 83 472 95 320
    126 292
Isabel Frances (Boyd)
    83 472
Isabella 59 11
Isabella (Bragdon) 115 59
Isham 77 262
Isobel (Chamber) 95 70
    324
J. Frank 81 408
J. Q. 91 327
Jabez 51 73
Jabez Wood 74 209
Jacob 73 229 107 318
James 51 215 282 360 52
    84 53 336 414 56 206 57
    115 58 347 348 60 28
    160 185 62 251 63 303
    65 129 66 126-128 72
    221 222 73 274 80 270
    99 26 100 240 112 299
    128 59 135 106
James Clark 82 399
James E. 118 150
James Swann 73 227
James William 90 191
Jane 51 168 277 57 181 58
    28 86 60 80 61 76 68
    217 70 258 73 225 74
    297 83 504 84 84 137
    282
Jane (Teel) 122 79
Jane Maria (Hunt)
    128 181
Jane S. 125 180
Jared 59 96
Javan Irvine 124 261
Jefferson 118 66
Jemima 57 180
Jemima Darte 58 198
Jennie 86 333
Jennie Booth 65 192
Jennie Elizabeth 81 392
Jennie L. 98 91
Jennie Walker (Purinton)
    93 279
Jeremiah 61 76 128 54

KING *cont'd*
Jeremiah M. **118** 150
Jerusha **58** 168 **59** 97
Jesse **110** 160 **113** 65
Jessie (Woods) **94** 22
Joan **70** 117 **83** 77 78
   114 94
Joanna **51** 73 282 286 **58**
   348 **80** 270 **98** 252 **106**
   80 **114** 293 **131** 137
Job **53** 438 **55** 46 **127** 79
   129 35 **148** 157
Joel **52** 411 **59** 95 413 **60** 76
   201 **83** 365 504 **84** 90
John **70** 259
John **51** 168 437 438 459 **52**
   182 247-249 **53** 412 414
   415 436 **54** xciv **56** 131
   406 407 **57** 84 181 209
   324 399 **58** 28 59 86-89
   142 168 170 172 175 197
   262 **59** 135 140 238 309
   60 93 199 **62** 81 251 **63**
   241 299 **65** 128 **67** 35 **68**
   222 **71** 266 **72** 181 **73**
   135 137 152 218 **74** 187
   208 **79** 45 **80** 315 **81** 74
   82 44 **83** 78 81 **84** 438
   87 3 93 93 279 **95** 255
   96 285 **100** 302 303 **101**
   80 **104** 108 **109** 79 **111**
   283 **112** 92 **113** 65 144
   114 181 188 **118** 134
   125 106 **126** 144 **127** 79
   128 54 **129** 65 **130** 311
   136 19 309 315 324 331
   137 282 **140** 160 **143** 42
   146 263 265
John (Mrs) **79** 403
John A. (Mrs.) **109** 320
   115 80
John Alsop **55** 353
John Barnard **51** 496
John Couper **95** 15
John Devereux **74** 208
John E. **77** 181
John Fowler **107** 233
John J. **125** 293
John L. **125** 30 **148** 287
John M. **83** 504 **84** 85
John McKeen **59** 209
John O. **83** 504
John Sylvester **86** 351
Jonas **61** 398 **89** 30 **130**
   302-304
Jonathan **51** 437 **52** 181
   419 **53** 434 447 **56** 350
   59 212 **61** 32 76 **65** 381
   69 298 **72** 222 **79** 89 **80**
   85 **83** 160 161 365 **88**
   221 **122** 79 **128** 54 55
Joseph **54** 305 353 **56** 73
   198 **57** 114 209 **58** 88
   195 348 **59** 99 139 210
   310 **60** 263 306 **61** 76
   141 **63** 98 **72** 222 **85** 377
   87 327 **88** 276 **102** 17
   114 185 **118** 150 **125**
   287 **129** 395 **134** 87 **148**
   316 317 327
Joseph I. **82** 279

KING *cont'd*
Josephine **96** 209
Joshua **54** 353 **127** 307
   130 311
Josiah **51** 437 438 **52** 15
   87 263 **100** 299 **114** 181
   122 137 138 **125** 222
Judith **51** 282 359 437 **59**
   238 **110** 186
Judith (Bates) (Gibbs)
   123 66
Judith (Cogan) **110** 186
   111 172
Judith (Whitman) **87** 3
Judy **101** 80
Julia **59** 100 **79** 301 **113** 65
   137 282
Julia (Mackim) **132** 327
Julia Elizabeth **95** 16
Julia Elizabeth (Clay)
   95 16
Julia Rebecca **95** 15 16
Juliana **104** 172
Julianne (LaFond)
   123 308
Kate **78** 34
Katharine **51** 292 316 438
   53 412 415 **78** 92 432 **94**
   267 336 **104** 68
Katharine (Twigden) **94**
   325 336
Katharine Brinley
   Huntington **95** 164
L. E. **110** 160
L. U.P. **62** lviii
Laura **60** 201 **69** 267 **83**
   365 **106** 313
Laura H. **83** 504
Lauren Everett **109** 130
Leander **61** 76
Lemuel **58** 194 **59** 96-101
   209 210 **60** 75 80 203 **68**
   223 **79** 165 **83** 504 **84** 84
Lemuel Henry **84** 85
Lena May **127** 131
Leonard **61** 383 **73** 139
Leonard Reed **74** 209
Letitia **80** 251
Lewis **114** 181
Lillian **74** 209
Lois **56** 350 **83** 160
Lorinda Nancy **63** 185
Louisa **83** 504
Louisa (Briggs) **126** 41
Louise **56** 206
Louise (Baldwin) **94** 25
Lovina **132** 244
Lucia **79** 89
Lucinda **51** 292 **54** xciv
   109 65 **121** 266 267
Lucinda (Jones) **113** 144
Lucinda Sophronia
   108 250
Lucretia **61** 76
Lucy **72** 221 **73** 286 289
   80 98 **104** 102 **112** 58
Lucy (Hopkins) **102** 201
Lucy (Pickens) **87** 3
Lucy Ann **71** lxvii **73** 289
Lucy Catherine **87** 4
   89 132

KING *cont'd*
Lucy Jane **57** 201
Luetta **59** 240
Luria **91** 393
Luria J. (Roberts) **91** 393
Lydia **51** 208 **52** 410 **58**
   174 403 **59** 309 **60** 78 **66**
   58 127 128 **72** 218 **73** 13
   78 408 **82** 370 **83** 365
   87 25 **88** 293 **104** 80
   129 170 265
Lydia (Hopkins) **102** 259
Lydia (Wright) **125** 293
Lydia Ann **82** 399
Lydia F. **88** 338
M. A. **128** 176
M. Josephine **81** 240 **82**
   256 **84** 239 **85** 240 **86**
   240 **87** 209 **88** 208 **89**
   209 **90** 208 **91** 207 **92**
   208 **93** 208 **94** 208 **95**
   208 **97** 207 **98** 209 **99**
   176 **100** 177 **101** 176
   102 154
Mabel **72** 44 93
Malinda **101** 80
Marah **83** 365
Margaret **56** 206 **58** 347
   348 **60** 199 285 **68** 323
   69 22-25 **70** 250 255 **79**
   20 89 **81** 444 **82** 44 **83**
   78 283 287 **90** 70 **91** 308
   105 216 **146** 265
Margaret (Sawdy) **148**
   156 157
Margaret M. **74** 24
Margaret Penniman
   (Littlefield) **134** 329
Margaretta LeCompt
   (Myer) **125** 53
Marget **59** 98
Maria **63** 339 **66** 128 **114**
   181 **136** 132
Marian (Appleton)
   93 285
Marian A. **98** 91
Marion **112** 299
Mariya **83** 365
Mark **86** 349
Marquis Fayette **51** 191
   238 239 **53** 139 **54** 236
   55 vii 439 **56** vii xxxiv
   57 v xvii xxxi 221 241
   333 **58** xvi xliii 105 **59**
   xli lvi cvii 116 237-241
   422 **64** 132 **131** 254
Martha **59** 210 **64** lv **72**
   41 216 **83** 160 161 504
   84 85 **127** 79
Martha Ann **81** 392
Martha Jane (Hannam)
   88 344
Martha Osgood **74** 209
Martin Luther **136** 153
Mary **51** 73 168 215 **52**
   182 247 248 276 409 411
   413 416 419 **53** 412 414
   415 437 438 447 **55** 43
   337 **57** 182 271 **58** 28 87
   347 **59** 87 135 157 238
   309 **60** 74 204 **64** 340 **66**

KING *cont'd*
44 125-128 **68** 218 **69**
298 **71** 152 **72** 217 221
222 **73** 224 264 279 **74**
20 205 208 **75** 203 250
76 203 **78** 265 281 **83** 81
160 365 **86** 349 **88** 70 **90**
51 171 **93** 365 **97** 83 **98**
126 **99** 73 **100** 295 301
110 309 **113** 65 **114** 188
121 245 **122** 247 **127** 16
130 302-304 **131** 208
133 267 **136** 324 **143** 42
147 251
Mary (Ashley) **129** 35
Mary (Carver) **88** 229
Mary (Chase) **87** 263
Mary (Connor) **100** 299
Mary (Farlow) **123** 66
Mary (Fowler) **123** 260
Mary (Laskey) **125** 222
Mary (Lewis) **101** 14
Mary (Moseley) **109** 105
Mary (Proctor) **85** 437
Mary (Russell) **102** 10
148 157
Mary (Simonds) **88** 276
Mary (Webster) **136** 324
Mary A. **79** 157
Mary Alice **134** 329
Mary Ann **76** 267 **101** 80
Mary Ann (Benjamin)
131 237
Mary Ann (Mitchell)
114 188
Mary Caroline **58** cxii
80 270
Mary E. **118** 150
Mary Elizabeth (Gaskell)
94 25
Mary Fifield **61** xlix
Mary Jane **84** 85 **118** 66
Mary Jennie (Thrall)
94 25
Mary L. **57** 190
Mary Leonard (Kinnicutt)
87 3
Mary Lois **82** 399
Mary Manser **127** 79
Mary Sherman **74** 209
Mary Somes (Durrell)
(Rowell) **134** 68
Mary Sweet **106** 240
Matheus **107** 318
McLeond **95** 16
Mehitable **57** 209 **58** 89
76 39 **89** 223 **99** 26
Mehitable (Bryant)
148 327
Mehitable (Pomeroy)
136 315
Mehitable (Savell)
100 240
Mehitable (Sheldon)
124 7
Melatiah **58** 28
Melville **51** 101
Mercy **51** 437 438 **53** 434
77 276 **126** 180
Mercy (Harris) **100** 295
Michael **60** 152

KING *cont'd*
Mindwell **57** 209 **83** 341
Minerva **102** 22
Minnie **82** 279
Mira **59** 99
Miranda **58** 402 **72** 151
Miriam **71** 164 **136** 272
Miriam (Moulton) **141**
314 325 327
Molly **58** 197
Morehouse **110** 160
Moses **57** 190 **72** 46 90 **83**
161 **104** 102 **107** 249
108 13
Myrinda **60** 200
N. Augusta **79** 284
Nabby **51** 438 **71** 272
111 108
Nahum **79** 164
Nancy **58** 402 **84** 85 **118**
309 **148** 157
Nancy (Jones) **113** 144
Nathan **51** 438 **53** 437 **57**
201 **66** 128 **70** 304 **98**
126 **142** 247 248
Nathan W. **57** 201
Nathaniel **74** 205 **101** 80
Nathaniel M. **114** 188
120 17
Nellie **74** 209
Nicholas **115** 156
Nora Phila (Fracker)
124 261
O. H. **83** 504 **84** 85
Olfrey **148** 276
Olive (Brooks) **90** 237
Oliver **52** 409 **58** 402 403
59 95 **60** 75 262 **83** 365
84 85
Oliver H. **84** 85
Olphrey **127** 216
Orpha Elvira **79** 26
Ovelie **72** 32
Ozias **104** 24
Parnell **63** 337
Parthenia **52** 41
Patience **114** 49
Patty **66** 110 **83** 504
Paul **53** 333 414
Pauline **59** 11 **80** 204 **82**
362 **95** 96 139 146 162
208 305 398 **96** 96 208
305 400 **97** 155 157 **102**
120 **103** 115 135 136
104 158 159 **105** 122
124 142 143 **106** 119 121
139 140 **107** 146 147
108 148 149 **109** 143
144 **110** 138 139 **111**
143 **112** 71 136 137 223
315 **113** 62 150 234 294
114 71 143 229 310 **115**
68 69 147-149 230 314
116 74 146 147 228 306
307 **117** 73 74 151-153
232 312 **118** 69 70 161-
163 246 324 **119** 72 151-
153 236 312 **120** 56 151-
153 233 310 **121** 75 149
151 **122** 207 208 **123**
220 221 **124** 264 265

KING *cont'd*
125 213
Peace **118** 150
Peggy **114** 181
Penelope **102** 144
Percy L. **87** 271
Persis **59** 95
Persis Strong **59** 210
Peter **51** 168 **62** 223 227
228 337 **63** 120 123 125
378 **64** 375 **66** 44 **100**
295 **130** 303
Pexcel **107** 233
Phebe **53** 434 **88** 331 **113**
65 **127** 79 **141** 198
Phebe Hannah **91** 182
Phebe M. **83** 359
Philena Hephsibah
77 182
Philene **51** 73
Philinda **76** 87 **129** 395
Philip **51** 437 459 **52** 18 19
53 436 437 **55** 43 105 **59**
238 **62** 234 **63** 130 229
327 **64** 32 **87** 3 **113** 47
115 156 **118** 309
Philip Jacob **115** 156
Philipa **61** 50
Plato **58** 195
Polly **51** 316 **60** 199 **70** 202
83 359
Polly (Osburn) **137** 282
Polly (Sawdy) **148** 283 284
Proserpina **58** 197
Prosper **113** 65
Prudence **53** 436
Rachel **52** 310 **58** 196 **60** 78
199 **108** 136 **111** 283
118 150
Rachel (Evelith) (Howe)
135 106
Rachel (Parsons) **142** 247
248
Ralph **51** 362 **66** 125-128
76 203 **127** 312
Ralph Tewksbury **94** 25
Ralph Thrall **94** 25
Rebecca **53** 434 437 **55** 46
57 399 **58** 87-89 168 170
172 175 262 **59** 139 **83**
78 **84** 84 85 **88** 326 **107**
233 **129** 260 **133** 292
Rebecca (Benedict) **121** 90
Rebecca (Chase) **87** 250
Rebecca (Dean) **110** 309
Rebecca (Pickens) **87** 3
Rebecca (Simonds)
126 204
Rebecca C. (Hanson)
91 386
Reuben **58** 196-198 401-
403 **60** 78 205 263 **71**
275 307 **83** 365 **114** 185
124 7
Rhoda **52** 410 **53** 437 **58**
170 197 **60** 200 **75** 302
115 35 **118** 150
Richard **51** 362 **53** 14 22
333 413 414 **54** lxvii
408 409 **55** 249 337 **58**
cxii **59** 11 **62** 206 **66** 58

KING *cont'd*
125-128 **68** 323 324 **69**
22-25 **73** 152 219 **75** 228
77 111 **96** 219 **101** 80
115 59 212
Richard Bourne **94** 25
Richard Edwin **97** 158
Richard S. **118** 79
Robert **53** 434 **57** 97 **58**
88 347 **65** 31 **85** 81 **95**
321 322 **97** 177-179 **101**
80 **112** 299
Robert (Mrs.) **85** 81
Robert C. **70** li
Robert M. **61** 243
Robert R. **124** 153
Robert Ray **142** 291
Robina A. (Denley)
83 427 433
Roger **58** 348 **103** 92
Rogers **66** 126-128
Rosey **84** 85
Roswell **58** 196 **71** 162
95 15-17
Roxellana **52** 417
Roxy **58** 403 **60** 266
Roy Stevenson **69** xxxii
191
Royal **79** 270
Ruby **74** 209
Rufus **51** 73 **53** 331 413
54 lxvii **57** 335 **59** xliv
11 324 **60** 91 **65** 84 **74**
20 **79** 165 **82** 362 **84** 333
88 70 **95** 210 **99** 84 **141**
255
Rufus Swan **59** 210
Rufus Tilden **66** 128
Ruggles **59** 100
Russell **58** 402 **59** 210 **60**
74 266 267
Russell Selden **59** 210
Ruth **51** 437 438 **52** 414
60 76 79 **72** 222 **73** 148
83 365 **115** 35 **148** 157
Ruth (Chase) **88** 127
Ruth (Swihart) **105** 128
Ruth Leola **74** 209
S. **60** 74
Sabret **73** 217
Sadie **117** 121
Sally **59** 238 **77** 320 **78** 140
90 315 **94** 25 **114** 181
126 232
Sally (Blanchard) **125** 290
Salmon **58** 196 **60** 264 265
Saludia (Williams)
124 260
Samuel **51** 45 **52** 414 **53**
333 334 413-415 437 **55**
328 385 388 **59** 238 **60**
79 **65** 28 141 355 **66** 125
126 **69** 51 **76** 267 **78** 140
79 351 446 **93** 279 397
95 372 **100** 63 **102** 259
104 80 **106** 43 **110** 186
111 172 **112** 58 **114** 188
119 103 **123** 132 284
289 290 **124** 240 **127**
312 **129** 58 **131** 237 **134**
202 **141** 336 **148** 260

KING *cont'd*
316 317 322 327
Samuel Hall **59** 237 238
Samuel Thomas **86** 353
Samuel W. **79** 36
Sarah **51** 290 291 **52** 309-
311 409 411 414 416 **53**
435 **54** xcv 107 **57** 83
180 209 211 414 **58** 261
301 **60** 77 78 204 210 **62**
283 **63** 338 340 **66** 25 **68**
224 **71** 255 256 282 **73**
150 228 **74** 20 **81** 408 **82**
118 **83** 365 **88** 70 336 **99**
26 **107** 233 **111** 93 **121**
85 **123** 80 169 **125** 289
129 395 **130** 303 313
133 95 **134** 202-204 **136**
77 309 331 **142** 271 **148**
151 259-261 264
Sarah (Dunham) **148** 327
Sarah (Griggs) **123** 171
Sarah (Holton) **136** 309
315 324 331
Sarah (King) **129** 395
Sarah (Mather) **129** 395
134 87
Sarah (Melton) **143** 131
Sarah (Moore) **98** 126
Sarah (Torrey) **148** 260
Sarah (Turner) **107** 233
Sarah (Williams) **126** 144
Sarah A. (Bancroft) **95** 372
Sarah Coe **71** lxvii
Sarah F. **91** 393
Sarah Kellogg **52** 386
Selina **71** 225
Serena Ann **97** 392
Seth **52** 409-411 413 416
53 418 **58** 402 **59** 412
60 204 205 262 **83** 365
Sherman **121** 90
Sidney **133** 23
Silas **51** 291 438 **58** 196
60 205 **87** 3
Silas A. **81** 392
Silas S. **131** 237
Silence **63** 190 **130** 302-304
Silence (Rice) **130** 302 304
Simeon **88** 229
Simon **58** 196 **59** 98 100
414 **60** 199 263
Smith **83** 365
Solomon **66** 128 **100** 236
292 **113** 65 **115** 37
Sophia **82** 378
Sophia (Sawyer) **125** 293
Stafford James **82** 279
Stanley **109** 319
Stanton H. **78** 332
Stella **100** 113
Stephen **51** 291 316 **53** 435
58 197 198 402 **59** 415
60 78 202 **83** 365 **104**
118 **105** 216 124 22 **127**
216 **145** 380 **148** 155
157
Susan **51** 275 277 282 **58**
lxxi **72** 293 **83** 78 **88** 332
138 92

KING *cont'd*
Susan (Chase) (Kelley)
87 327
Susan (Tillotson) **110** 160
Susan Allen **79** 270
Susan Howard **70** 209
Susan S. **118** 309
Susanna **53** 334 414 **55**
310 **58** 165 401 **60** 75 78
201 205 264 265 **66** 44
67 286 **70** 116 **73** 138
150 224 **75** 25 **83** 365
107 233 **125** 214 **148**
157
Susanna (Sawdy) **148** 276
Susie May **124** 260
Sweet W. **127** 79
Sylvia **51** 73
Tabitha **51** 362 **66** 125
Tamar **96** 285
Tarrant Putnam (Mrs.)
93 285
Telly **73** 271
Temperance **80** 270
Terry Gaskell **94** 25
Thankful **51** 208 223 **59**
139 **68** 220 **72** 221 **111**
161
Thankful Owen **127** 79
Theodore **82** 44
Thomas **51** 282 **52** 107 **57**
82-84 180-183 319-321
58 170 348 **59** 140 **62**
220 223 224 226-228 252
336 337 339-342 **63** 59-
62 65 66 101 118 121 125
281 **65** lv 123 **66** 44 **70**
258 **71** 165 225 256 **73**
148 276 278 **83** 77 78
323 **84** 336 **85** 255 90
171 **93** 172 **94** 325 336
95 320 324 **127** 177 263
130 302-304 **133** 94 95
136 324 **141** 314 327
143 330
Thomas M. **73** 151
Thomas Starr **51** 446 **52**
155 **68** 44 **71** lvii **95**
384 **135** 150
Thomas William **95** 303
Thompson **101** 80
Thurston **148** 276
Tillotson **110** 160
Timothy **71** 162 164 165
272 273 275 302 309 **72**
41 93 173
Tryphena **54** 353 **57** 114
71 83 275 282
Uriel **102** 201
Valerie Daly **111** 77
Vincent **69** 191
W. A. **111** 53
W. H. **65** 109
Wallace Starr **101** 124
Walter **59** 240
Walter John **74** 209
Warren **83** 365
Warren Bicknell **94** 25
Warren C. **59** 240
Wealthy **84** 85
Wilbur Lewis **107** 318

KING *cont'd*
Willard Devereux **74** 209
Willard Everett **74** 209
William **51** 118 275 277
  52 181 318 **53** 333 334
  413-415 435 **54** lxvii **55**
  32 **57** 414 **58** 57 59 196
  348 **59** 238 **60** 39 **63** 190
  199 303 **64** 336 **66** 128
  259 **67** 286 **68** 217-220
  222-224 226 **70** 116 **72**
  93 133 221 222 **73** 221
  74 234 268 **78** 432 **81**
  398 **82** 156 **93** 279 **101**
  14 290 **109** 79 187 **111**
  172 **113** 65 **121** 201 **123**
  171 **127** 296 **128** 54 **129**
  65 **131** 237 **132** 327 **137**
  282 **140** 156
William Basil **77** 155 **102**
  62 129 144
William Fuller **85** 437
William Gracie **110** 132
William H. **59** 232 **125** 173
William Harrison **69** 191
William Jones **65** lv
William P. **78** 419 **137** 362
William Ross **92** 213
William Skilbeck **100** 236
William Vinton **83** 472
Willie Everett **118** 150
Winifred **66** 16 **144** 360
Woods **94** 25
Wyllys **79** 155
Zachariah **55** 388 **93** 279
  107 187
Zebulon **53** 438 **65** 148
  91 206 **125** 172
Zenas **51** 438
Zilpah **79** 351
Zina **58** 197 **60** 202 265
Zipporah **55** 46
KINGDOM
Mildred L. **126** 82
KINGDON
Edith M. **79** 88
Jane **61** 207
John **61** 206 207
Kinge *see* King
KINGED David **87** 346
KINGERBY Faith **74** 52
Katharine **74** 52
Richard **74** 51 52
Robert **74** 52
Thomas **68** 74 77 **74** 51-53
William **74** 51
KINGFISHER
Nancy (Ward) **112** 325
KINGHAM De Kyngham
Kynggam
  —— **83** 322
Hannah **89** 234
Margaret de **110** 123
Robert de **110** 123
KINGHORN Kinghorne
Anna **73** 131
David **73** 131
George **73** 131 **82** 44
James **82** 44
Jane Grant **73** 131
John **82** 44

KINGHORN *cont'd*
Sarah **82** 44 285 291
KINGLARD
Henry **143** 261
KINGLEY
Elizabeth **51** 320
KINGMAN — Widow **69**
  127 **105** 75
Abiah **51** 291
Abigail (Copeland)
  137 42
Abigail Cobb **80** 271
Achsah **73** 212
Alexander **51** 291 **130** 313
Alice **105** 24
Anne **105** 22-25
Austin **73** 212
B. **114** 217
Barzillai **122** 226 **125** 290
Benjamin **63** 158 **105** 75
Bethiah **59** lxxii **104** 164
Bradford **54** xxxvi **55** 440
  58 lv **59** xii lxxii
  lxxiii 107 **64** 333 **67** 190
  105 23 24 **111** 325 **115**
  84
Bridget **105** 23-25
Caleb **52** 451
Caroline **73** 212
Cassander **127** 59
Charles G. **127** 59
Charles S. **87** 346
Charlotte **84** 441
Clyde William **105** 128
Content (Packard)
  119 253
Daniel **137** 42
Deborah (Loring)
  136 122
Deliverance **59** 107
Dorcas Annette
  (Shapleigh) **95** 334
Eben **51** 240 242
Edmund **73** 212
Edward **93** 397 **100** 63
  105 22-25
Elizabeth **51** 499 **59** lxxii
  107
Eunice **126** 67
Ezra **84** 441
Francis **81** 428
Freelove **52** 451
Grace **56** 403
Hannah **89** 234 **120** 230
Hannah (Tirrell) **120** 231
Harriet **90** 261
Henry **59** lxxii 107 **65** 384
  67 190 **85** 229 **104** 164
  105 22-25 **110** 309 **119**
  9
Hosea **127** 59
Isaac **119** 253
James H. **83** 425 433
Jane **88** 330
Joan **105** 22
Joanna **59** lxxii **105** 23-25
John **56** 365 403 **58** 266 **59**
  lxxii 107 **73** 192 **81** 428
  87 346 **99** 241 **105** 22-
  25 **120** 231
Jonathan **136** 309

KINGMAN *cont'd*
Joseph **75** 153
Josiah Washburn **59** lxxii
Judith **59** lxxii
Lemuel **136** 122
LeRoy Wilson **65** 384 **66**
  xlix **105** 23-25
Levi **119** 253
Lydia Celia **87** 346
Lydia H. **87** 346
Margaret Wetherell
  (Briggs) **127** 59
Martha **136** 309
Martin **80** 271
Mary **52** 438 **58** 266 **59**
  lxxii **73** 192 **75** 265 **81**
  428
Mary (Keith) **136** 309
Mary Elizabeth (Briggs)
  127 59
Mary T. (Cheever)
  83 425 433
Mehitable **73** 212 **119** 254
  137 42
Melinda **63** 158
Mercy **119** 111
Miriam **53** 394
Molly **53** 246
Nancy (Robinson)
  130 313
Nathan **69** 122 126
Nelda (Ropp) **105** 128
Parthenia **119** 253
Phebe **80** 271
Polly **75** 153
Prescott B. **95** 334
Prudence **147** 383
Rebecca **105** 23-25
Robert **127** 59
Ruth **136** 122
Sally **91** 376 **125** 107
Samuel **59** 107 **119** 190
Sarah **99** 73 **110** 309 **136** 25
  117
Sarah (Sargent) **125** 290
Sarah (Sherman) **88** 367
Sarah Ann **87** 346
Seth **59** lxxii **140** 160
Sophronia M. **136** 311
Susan Bradford **59** lxxiii
Susanna **59** 107 **60** 43
Susanna (Whitman)
  84 441
Thomas **60** 43 **105** 22-25
  120 230
Willard **73** 212
William **69** 147 **81** 428
William Livermore
  105 23
KINGON Paine **126** 256
Theodora (Howard)
  126 256
KINGSBER
Jonathan **59** 216
Kingsberry *see* Kingsbury
KINGSBEY Elisha **100** 68
KINGSBURY Kingsberry
Kinsbury
  —— **54** 232 **57** 53 **58** 205
  60 396 **72** 171 **89** 350
  110 284 **112** 216 **127**

KINGSBURY *cont'd*
187
— Capt. **98** 105
— Col. **65** 363
— Dr. **54** 248
— Mr. **62** 85 **71** 141
81 143
— Mrs. **61** 76 **83** 306 419
— Rev. **133** 308
— Widow **70** 315 **71** 135
A. **79** 164 308 **80** 66 **91** 327
Aaron **56** 74 **141** 338 339
Abby P. **57** 381 382
Abiel **55** 260 **57** 27
Abigail **52** 409-411 420
55 259 393 400 **56** 144
57 153 **59** 115 **79** 28 **86**
381 **98** 86 **99** 204 **110**
179 284 **111** 260 **112** 25
114 290 **116** 142 **138** 37
Abigail Phillips **57** 376
377
Abijah **79** 28
Alathea Ruth (Scovill)
92 186
Alfred **63** 367 **73** 115 116
Alice **55** 260 **57** 22 24
Alice Cary (Bussing)
92 187
Alice F. **89** 209
Alice Eliza **73** 318 **74** xxiv
92 90 148 186
Allora **79** 139
Almira **57** 378 **81** 313 **108**
54 **116** 304 305
Alzira **65** 113 **118** 241
Alzirah F. **118** 241
Amelia **110** 118
Amos Plimpton **81** 313
Amy **138** 37
Amy B. **58** 345
Andrew **110** 118 **138** 36
Ann **52** 311 **127** 79
Ann Elizabeth **93** 341
Anna **61** 229 232 **73** 41
115 116 **109** 115
Anna C. **95** 41 **96** 157
143 338
Anna Chandler **57** xxxv
58 xliii **69** 91 **78** 450 **79**
336 **83** 136 **87** 91 **90** 125
96 154 158 **98** 86 89 150
Anne **73** 39 **86** 380 **116** 134
Ariel **85** 159
Arthur Murray **116** 233
Asa **53** 33 **57** 143 **70** 225
311 312 317 **86** 380 **121**
92 **136** 236 **143** 14
Augustus **57** 377
Becca **57** 260
Benjamin **55** 259 **65** 113
97 273 **112** 25 **115** 227
125 222
Benjamin Ellis **86** 380
Betsey **56** 35 **65** 113 **72** 273
73 39 **79** 152 164 **97** 142
Betsey (Goddard) **138** 37
Betsey Sumner **57** 382
Caleb **55** 260 **56** 38 142
144 145 148 **57** 105 151
153 253 255 **65** 362 **124**

KINGSBURY *cont'd*
195
Caroline Lovan **136** 238
Caroline Ray **86** 381
Carrie Alice **85** 314
Catherine **66** 112 **72** 273
130 210
Charles **86** 381
Charles Dennison **92** 186
Charles E. **83** 172
Charles Edwin **83** 177 183
Charles W. **138** 37
Charlotte Bond **57** 374
Charlotte Polly (Niles)
85 159
Chester **57** 377
Chloe **59** 115
Christopher **61** 76
Clara **86** 380
Clarence **96** 334
Clarissa **57** 382
Cynthia (Wing) **92** 186
Cynthia Baxter **85** 314
Cyrus **55** 399 **57** 376-379
395
Daniel **52** 410 **55** 395 **56**
207 **57** 53 185 380 **60**
398 **85** 314 **86** 380 381
Daniel Arthur **85** 314
David **55** 100 **57** 145 373
375 **70** 310 **86** 380
Deborah **52** 184 309 419
83 99
Deliverance **52** 309
73 115 116
Denizon **53** 448
Dennison **56** 207 **60** 396
Dorcas (Shaw) **119** 225
227
Eben **63** 265
Ebenezer **53** 448 **57** 258 63
367 **71** 42 **73** 116 **92** 186
108 89 **142** 64
Edith Leonard **75** 123
Edmund Winchester
78 249
Edward Lyman **98** 86
Eleazer **52** 310 311 **53** 448
55 259 392 **56** 38 39 141
143 146 147 268 270 **57**
23 147 150 151 253 255
356 **65** 356 360 **72** 74 **73**
39 **85** 11 **98** 86
Elijah **56** 142 **57** 23 151
88 333
Eliphalet **56** 34 141 142
144 145 147 148 270 **57**
22 150 151 153 253 255
256 258-261 **65** 361 **98**
86 **110** 179
Eliza **57** 381 **88** 334
117 223
Eliza (Leavenworth)
92 186
Eliza Ann **57** 378
Eliza Jane **57** 381
Eliza Maria **124** 195
Eliza Rosanna Thayer
86 380
Elizabeth **55** 393 399 **56**
31 33 37 39 148 **57** 27 53

KINGSBURY *cont'd*
185 255 256 375 378 **70**
225 **72** 74 **73** 147 **74** 94
83 99 **88** 333 **93** 310 **98**
211 **99** 66 **109** 164 **110**
62 179 **113** 297 **114** 291
120 263 **125** 83 84 **138**
36
Elizabeth (Fuller) **113** 297
Elizabeth (Milberry) **112**
105 **115** 62
Elizabeth Frances **145** 308
Elizabeth N. **118** 153 155
Elizzie **89** 350
Ellen **110** 118
Emily **55** 399 **112** 237
Emily Rebecca **57** 380
Emma J. **89** 350
Enoch **56** 141 **57** 150 **72**
101 **105** 281
Ephraim **56** 207 **70** 176
309 **78** 136 **86** 380 **147**
109
Erastus **110** 118
Esther **55** 260 392 398 **56**
31 144 145 267 **57** 153
253 375 **70** 176 310 **138**
37
Esther (Crowninshield)
88 333
Esther (Judson) **98** 86
Esther (Whitney) **138** 35
36
Eunice **52** 183 **56** 270 **63**
367 **116** 133 **118** 154
155
Ezekiel **99** 204 **125** 294
Fanny **66** 25
Fanny D. **119** 65 69
Fanny R. **72** 104
Fanny Winchester **78** 249
Flora Jane (Bush) **113** 79
Florence Winchester
78 249
Forrest A. **113** 79
Frances **88** 276
Frances (Hearl) **119** 146
Frances Estelle **85** 314
Frank Burnside **59** xliv
115 **68** xxxi 111 **70** 94
76 158 **126** 242
Frank Burnside (Mrs.)
74 x **75** xxvi
Frederick John **59** 333
60 xxxvi **92** 186
Frederick S. **89** 350
Freelove **52** 310 **72** 74
Freelove (Utley) **110** 118
Galen **79** 139
George **126** 213 **138** 37
George C. **102** 152
George Henry **78** 249
George Williamson
81 313
Guy M. **138** 37
Hannah **52** 184 408 415
418 419 **53** 384 **55** 259
260 395 **56** 32 38 207
209 269 **57** 144 146 147
59 115 **60** 80 393 396
397 **63** 175 **72** 47 106 **73**

KINGSBURY *cont'd*
116 **80** 400 **110** 118 179
284 **111** 255 **112** 25 **114**
132 **115** 65 227 **127** 186
Hannah (Donnell) **113** 25
Hannah (Harmon) **113** 25
116 223
Hannah (Millar) **108** 124
Hannah (Needham)
110 118
Hannah (Sanderson)
127 187
Hannah B. **117** 225 226
Hannah Brown **113** 79
Hannah H. (Grow)
119 225
Hannah J. **120** 222 **123** 72
Hannah Jane **120** 221 222
Harriet Maria **57** 281
Henry **52** 24 **53** 384 **54** 260
59 333 **62** 254 **92** 186
106 144 **114** 85 **116** 233
119 225 **121** 164
Hepzibah **110** 179 **112** 103
113 124 **114** 291 **116**
134
Hepzibah (Junkins) **118**
242 317
Hezekiah **56** 32 209 **57** 30
144
Horace P. **85** 167
Howard **92** 186
Howard Thayer **86** 193 **92**
90 145 148 186 187
Irene (Buck) **124** 195
Isabella Dodd **53** 384
J. **86** 381
J. B. **61** 76
Jabez **53** 447 **73** 39 41
110 118
Jacob **86** 380 **138** 36
James **56** 266 **57** 22-24 **70**
311 **89** 350
James Ray **86** 381
Jane **89** 350
Jedidah **55** 259
Jemima **55** 259 260 264
56 31 147 270 **57** 24 25
27-29 144 255 256
Jeremiah **55** 397 400
57 374-377
Jerusha **115** 110
Jesse **55** 265 **56** 142 269
57 144-148 151 **65** 359
Joanna **58** 150
Joel **57** 261
John **52** 183 184 309 310
409-411 419 **53** 384 450
54 98 **55** 254 **56** 32 **57**
22 380 382 **60** 396 397
65 113 **67** 377 **70** 310
316 **72** 168 177 183 273
73 39 **75** 51 **79** 185 **81**
313 **83** 99 **92** 186 **97** 142
266 **110** 62 179 284 **111**
229 255 258 260 **112** 25
113 297 **114** 294 **115**
221 **116** 134 138 **118**
242 317 **138** 35 36
John Crane **57** 382
John D. **56** 116

KINGSBURY *cont'd*
John Denison **63** 113
John H. **72** 273
John M. **72** 204
John R. **72** 273
Jonas **57** 28 148
Jonathan **55** 264 266 **56**
142 **57** 22 147 151
Jonathan A. **138** 37
Joseph **52** 224 311 409 412
53 447 **55** 267 392 **56** 37
142 143 207 **57** 151 333
58 205 **63** 175 367 **73**
115 116 **78** 408 **81** 368
86 380 381 **92** 186 **98** 86
108 54 124 **110** 179 **112**
25 103 105 216 **113** 25
115 62 140 **116** 223 **119**
146 **125** 39 83 87
Joseph B. **113** 79
Joshua **99** 204 **100** 28
138 37
Josiah **56** 148 **57** 22-24 28
144 256 378 **98** 86
Josiah B. **121** 92
Keziah **56** 34
Lemuel **52** 412 416 **53** 448
72 74 **83** 99 **138** 35-37
Leonard **53** 384 **55** 399
Lewis **89** 350
Lewis T. **89** 350
Lois **138** 36
Lois (Porter) **92** 186
Louisa Hewlett (Holland)
98 86
Louise **101** 126
Love **86** 381
Love (Ayer) **92** 186
Lucinda Orr **57** 382
Lucretia **73** xxx
Lucy **55** 395 396 **110** 179
115 136 285 **138** 37
Lucy Deming **57** 381
Lucy Emeline **85** 314
Lucy M. (Cone) **85** 314
Lurana **86** 380
Luther **57** 259
Lydia **52** 184 **55** 259 263
392 395 397 **56** 148 **57**
258 374 375 **67** 377 **78**
136 **126** 213
Lydia Frost **65** 113
Lydia Wilder (Briggs)
126 213
Lyman E. **98** 86
Mabel Hope **58** 16 205
62 xxviii xxxvii **75** xxvi
81 368
Madeline Florence
103 119
Marcia (Bronson) **92** 186
Marcy **62** 85
Margaret **63** 367 **72** 273
73 116
Margaret (Redington)
109 164
Margaret M. **66** 112
Maria **68** 200 **76** 90
124 195
Marian **106** 151
Marion **78** 249

KINGSBURY *cont'd*
Martha **86** 380 **100** 28
Martha (Starr) **125** 222
Martha Abba (Ackerman)
83 177 183
Martha Abby **83** 172
Martha Abigail **79** 28
Martha M. **102** 152
Martha Maria **79** 139
Martha R. **116** 202
Martha T. (Speed) **125** 294
Martin H. **121** 307 **122** 151
123 74
Mary **52** 412 418 419 **53**
449 462 **55** 265 267 399
56 33 37 38 366 **57** 22
148 258 259 **58** 16 **65**
113 **77** 54 **98** 86 **99** 204
110 179 284 **111** 229
112 25 105 **114** 127 129
115 217 221 **117** 223
125 87 **126** 208 **132** 140
136 167 **138** 37
Mary (Junkins) **119** 60
Mary (Nowell) **123** 72 74
Mary (Stickney) **110** 179
284
Mary (Whitney) **138** 35 37
Mary Amelia **85** 314
Mary Ann **115** 110
Mary Ann (Shedd) **98** 86
145 308
Mary C. Loomis **85** 314
Mary E. (Grover) **123** 74
Mary Laura (Hughes)
110 118
Maud Lincoln **78** 249
Mehitable **57** 373 **78** 124
99 204
Mercy **56** 33 **57** 151 **63** 72
93 179 **125** 87 201
Mercy E. (Shaw) **121** 307
122 151
Millicent **55** 259 **57** 24 **98**
86 **125** 83
Miriam **53** 384 450
108 190
Molly **115** 220 310
Moses **55** 395 **56** 31 32 **57**
27 29
Moses Garfield **57** 376
Nancy **57** 379 **117** 92 93
226 227
Nathan **55** 399 **57** 258 261
65 39 **141** 343
Nathaniel **52** 184 419 **55**
263 **56** 207 366 **57** 30 **59**
115 **60** 79 **70** 313 **73** 39
40 **86** 381 **92** 186
Nellie M. **117** 167
Noah **99** 204
Obadiah **73** 39 **86** 380 381
Olive **116** 130
Olive Atarah **81** 313
Olive Ward (Gifford)
96 334
Oliver **92** 186
Oliver Richmond **92** 186
Patience **53** 384 **112** 25
115 222 **116** 225
Patience (Came) **110** 179

KINGSBURY *cont'd*
Patience Tappan **56** 224
Patty **55** 399
Perez **73** 40
Phebe **70** 176
Philip **121** 93
Phineas **52** 414-416 420
  56 147 **57** 255 **60** 393
  396-398 **80** 400 **105** 281
Phylette **57** 395
Polly **65** 362 **81** 313
Priscilla **53** 447 **65** 361
  92 186
Priscilla (Kingsbury)
  92 186
Prudence **52** 311
Rachel **55** 395 **57** 260
  70 225
Ransom **68** 200
Rebecca **53** 384 **55** 398 **56**
  268 **57** 147 **113** 255
Rebecca (Haley) **113** 124
  126
Rebecca Garfield **57** 376
Reuben Newell **57** 382
Rhodes **72** 273
Rosetta B. **72** 204
Roxana **85** 329
Ruby **57** 380
Rufus **119** 60 **121** 309 **123**
  72 74
Ruth **52** 184 224 **55** 259
  56 207 **57** 21 **60** 344 393
  73 39 **77** 230 **86** 381
Ruth (Denison) **92** 186
Ruth Oliver **92** 187
S. **77** 54 **85** 314 **121** 92
S. P. **86** 381
Sally **73** 39
Sally (Marsh) **138** 37
Sally (Whittemore)
  108 89
Sally Palmer **86** 380
Samuel **51** 197 **52** 230
  233 368 370 **53** 384 **56**
  35 268 **57** 22 144 258
  259 **58** 16 150 345 **60**
  159 **62** 275 **65** 362 **70**
  315 **73** 39 **78** 124 **89** 350
  110 179 **113** 124 126
  115 140 **118** 313
Samuel R. **73** 39
Samuel Rust **59** 21
Sarah **51** 174 180 **53** 448 **54**
  85 **55** 261 263 265 266
  392 394-396 **56** 31 32 **57**
  27 146 333 374 **60** 79
  397 **63** 340 **65** 113 **73** 39-
  41 **75** 51 **78** 403 **80** 400
  81 143 **86** 380 381 **90**
  174 **102** 80 158 240 **110**
  179 284 **111** 258 **112** 25
  114 132 **115** 306 **116**
  304
Sarah (Carlile) **112** 25
  114 294
Sarah (Hill) **92** 186
Sarah (Milberry) **115** 140
Sarah B. **119** 226
Sarah Esther **65** 39
Sarah Hill **86** 381

KINGSBURY *cont'd*
Sarah M. **90** 49
Sarah Sabin **79** 185
Seth **143** 10
Sibyl **93** 341
Sidney C. **72** 273
Silence **57** 53
Simon **52** 309 408 **53** 447
Sophia **73** 40
Sophia Howard (Thayer)
  92 186
Stephen **57** 53 **70** 313
  138 36
Submit **55** 400
Sukey **55** 399 **57** 380
Sukey Fessenden **57** 376
Susan (Marsh) **138** 37
Susan G. (Davis) **121** 309
Susan M. **60** 323
Susanna **53** 38 **54** 260 **56**
  147 **57** 255 **106** 144 **116**
  128 **121** 164
Susanna (Mory) **98** 86
T. H.C. **86** 373 381
Tabitha **110** 179 **112** 25
  136 316
Tabitha Hill **86** 381
Talitha **52** 224
Theo **89** 350
Theodore **115** 110
Thomas **57** 382 **109** 164
Tilley **127** 79
Timothy **55** 259 263 **56**
  31 148 268 270 **57** 21 25
  27-29 144 145 148 258-
  261 **65** 113 **97** 266 **112**
  25
Timothy Daniel **57** 381
  382
Urania **121** 147 **122** 147
Uriah **52** 310
Warren **138** 37
Wayland Briggs **113** 79
Willard **138** 36
William **51** 276 **56** 145
  57 23 253 **93** 344 **113**
  126 **116** 133 **119** 225
  227 **138** 37
William Alden **98** 86
  145 308
William D. **57** 381
William E. **86** 381
William Hooper **57** 381
William How **86** 381
William Sanford **85** 314
Wilmot C. **72** 273
Zipporah **66** 130 132
Zolon Zelotes **57** 380
Kingseley *see* Kingsley
KINGSFIELD
  Elizabeth **54** 219
KINGSFORD
  Philip **65** 127
KINGSLAND Kyngeslond
  Amy **109** 127
  Hester **81** 99
  Hugh **75** 238
  Isabella **114** 237
  Nathaniel **114** 237
  Thomas **145** 13 14

KINGSLEY Kingseley
  Kingsly Kinsley
  —— **52** 386 **57** 415 **139**
  23 25 26 31-34 39 46 47
  — Dr. **71** 119
  — Mr. **71** 136
  — Widow **66** 265
Aaron **57** 162 **65** 381 **98**
  241 244 **138** 25-27 29-31
Abby Durfee **55** lviii
Abel **126** 272
Abigail **57** 269 **63** 327
  100 336
Adaline **116** 59
Adriel **54** 199 202 **56** 384
Albert **83** 65
Albert E. **83** 422 433
Alden **97** 264
Alice **83** 65 **139** 46
Ally **70** 226
Alpheus **86** 381
Alpheus Eugene **86** 381
Amelia **83** 65
Amos **117** 155
Andrew **107** 57
Ann **100** 30 33 133 **101**
  273 274
Asahel **85** 159 **122** 217 218
Augustus C. **73** 116
Benjamin **125** 189
Bethanai **88** 286
Bethiah (Baker) **94** 385
Betsey **88** 282
Blanche **83** 65
C. A. **86** 381
C. Daisy (Barrett) **83** 422
Caleb **88** 206 207
Caroline **72** 297
Charles **61** 95 **68** 61
  126 156
Charles A. **136** 80
Charles Bliss **72** 297
Charles Phelps **72** 297
Charlotte Polly (Niles)
  85 159
Chloe **57** 272
Chrissa **88** 206 207
Clarence **123** 226
Cynthia **127** 281
Daisy (Barrett) **83** 433
Daniel **125** 149
Daniel Webster **72** 294
Dorcas T. **144** 317
Dorothy **63** 368
E. **123** 97
Edward W. **54** cxliii
Eldad **58** 52 **74** 62 **97** 320
  326 **99** 96 **139** 46 49
Elisha **60** 71 **100** 68
  110 150
Eliza **84** 56
Elizabeth **63** 296 **104** 220
Elizabeth Caroline **72** 297
Emily **96** 288
Emma **122** 217 218
Emma C. (Smith) **136** 80
Enoch **52** 338 **77** 26
Enos **57** 269
Esther **57** 77 **76** 267
Eunice **86** 381

KINGSLEY *cont'd*
Eunice (Bingham)
  125 149
Eunice Hartshorn **86** 381
Eveline **72** 294
Experience **67** 374
Fanny (De Golyer) **90** 378
Flavel **132** 189
Frank Warner **72** 298
Frederick **127** 11
Georgeanna Manolt
  (Vogell) **85** 433
Hains **63** 180
Hale **87** 252
Hannah **134** 332
Hannah (Brackett) **93** 164
Hannah B. **86** 381
Harry Holman **72** 298
Hattie Noyes **86** 381
Helen Louise **72** 297
Henry **125** 292
Henry H. **86** 381
Henry Peck **60** 71
Henry W. **86** 381
Hezekiah **60** 71 **70** 28
Hope **70** 28
Ida **123** 224
J. S. **60** 186
Ja **70** 312
James **83** 65 **110** 150
  115 215
Jason W. **86** 381
Jemima **60** 71
Jerusha G. **86** 381
Joanna **125** 271
John **60** 186 **63** 327 372
  97 319 **99** 96 98 **111** 133
  117 155 **138** 25 26 29
  146 274
John B. **125** 149
John H. **120** 9 11
Jonathan **59** 216 **67** 374 **70**
  28 **80** 175 **128** 135 **138**
  25-27 29
Joseph **78** 136 **86** 381
Judediah **128** 135
Julia Anna **86** 381
Julia E. **86** 381
Lemuel **86** 381
Lepha M. **122** 218
Lewis **73** 16
Louis N. **73** 116
Lovinia **67** 228
Lucinda **78** 136
Lucretia Emeline **109** 311
Lucy **86** 381 **88** 206 303
Lucy Elizabeth **86** 381
Lucy Katharine (Stevens)
  85 434
Lula Belle (Besaw) **123** 226
Luther **60** 71
Lydia **51** 319 **70** 159 **86**
  381 **110** 150 **131** 108
Lydia (Bowen) **110** 150
Lydia Jane (Tucker)
  85 433
Lyman **93** 156
Mabel Durant **72** 298
Margaret **100** 301 **109** 130
  125 218
Marie **134** 88

KINGSLEY *cont'd*
Martha **106** 66 **108** 307
  126 272
Martha M. (Sneden)
  123 97
Martin **105** 290
Mary **53** 462 **57** 39 162 212
  70 28 **87** 378 **88** 206 207
  115 194 **123** 39
Mary (Johnson) (Mowry)
  146 274
Mary (Pratt) **125** 292
Mary (Whipple) **107** 57
Mary Ann **70** 179 **88** 285
  108 311
Mary Zahm **72** 298
Mattie Holman **72** 298
Mehitable **58** 51 52 **88**
  206 207 **139** 26 27
Mehitable (Nash) **88** 206
Minnie May **72** 294
Myrtie **123** 224
Nancy Harris **89** 250
Nancy P. **71** 120
Naomi **54** 199-202 292
  294 299 **55** 429 **56** 384
  388
Nathan **60** 71 **88** 283
Nathaniel **80** 175 **139** 42
Nellie Holman **72** 297
Nettie **83** 65
Obadiah **85** 433
Pardon **73** 116
Patience **57** 162 **80** 175
Patty **126** 272
Pegge (Peck) **97** 254
Peleg **97** 254
Phear **73** 116
Philanda **80** 175
Philip **58** lxvii
Phineas **60** 392
Polly **59** 36
R. **72** 287 **91** 327
Ralph **83** 65
Ralph N. **73** 116
Renewed **54** 213
Roxa W. **73** 116
Ruth Smith (Brown)
  97 264
Sabin **56** 384
Sally **86** 381
Salome **72** 287
Salome E. **122** 287
Samuel **53** 434 **93** 164
  100 30 33 133 **101** 273
  274 **115** 194 **125** 200
  128 135
Sapphira **54** 294
Sarah **52** 338 **77** 26 **87** 257
  125 149
Sarah (Chase) **87** 252
Sarah E. Huntington
  86 381
Sarah K. **86** 381
Sarie M. (Pratt) **89** 246
Sewel **66** 28
Silas Hartshorn **86** 381
Simon **86** 381
Sophia **53** 434 **88** 206 207
Stephen **61** 95 **62** 94 **67** li
  101 246 **114** 125 **134** 88

KINGSLEY *cont'd*
Susan **73** 116
Susan (Tibbet) **88** 283
Susanna **63** 180 **98** 367
  100 33 **101** 273
Sylvanus **54** 199-202 292
  294
Sylvanus Sabin **54** 200
Tabitha **60** 402 **90** 162
  134 88
Thomas **70** 28 **139** 45
W. G. **89** 246
W. L. **115** 254
Walter Childs **72** 298
Washington **90** 378
Willey Josiah Paschal
  85 433
Willey Lyon **80** 105 206
  85 433 **86** 108 203
William **100** 133 **101** 274
  109 228
KINGSMILL
Alice **141** 107
Robert **95** 23
Thomas **52** 67
KINGSNORTH Kingsnoth
Henry **56** 357
James **56** 57
Mary **56** 357
Richard **115** 75
KINGSTON Kingstone
—— **80** 408
Daniel **56** 65
Dorcas **100** 139
Elias **99** 280 283 **100** 295
Eliza Baker **68** 125
John **117** 15
Margaret **115** 127
Mary **99** 283
Nancy **99** 280
Sarah **99** 280 283
Sarah (Ballard) **100** 295
William **103** 7
KINGSWELL
Edward **51** 283
Jane **51** 282 283
KINGSWORTH
Henry **61** 284
Mary **61** 284
KINGTON Theodora
  (Howard) **126** 256
KINHAM Alice **105** 24
KINKEAD
George B. **91** 305
Jane **112** 22
Sarah **102** 169
KINKEL
Henry E. **96** 129
Lisette Everard **96** 129
Sarah L. (Pitts) **96** 129
KINKET John **112** 102
  145 363
Susanna **112** 102 **114** 291
KINMAN Isaac **58** 18
Polly **58** 18
Robert **62** 80
KINNAIRD
Lawrence **103** 320
Kinne *see* Kinney
KINNEAR Kerne
—— **62** 101

KINNEAR *cont'd*
Adelaide (Fayerweather)
    145 253 254
Elizabeth **129** 51
Marainer **145** 254
William **60** 186
Kinnecott *see* Kinnicut
KINNECUM
— Mrs. **69** 217
Kinnecut *see* Kinnicut
KINNELLMARCH
Katharine **105** 11
KINNER
Keziah **125** 301
Sarah **123** 319
Kinneston *see* Kenniston
KINNEY Kiney Kinne
    Kyne Kynne
—— **52** 420 **60** 140 **61** 85
    62 368 **91** 254 **134** 200
— Mr. **56** 312
Aaron **85** 167 **86** 53
Aaron W. **86** 53
Abiel **127** 125
Abigail **60** 248 **108** 300
    123 112
Abigail Robbins **108** 301
Achsah **68** lxxviii
Achsah Celina **68** lxxviii
Addie Hodge **68** lxxviii
Adeline (Ritche) **108** 301
Adeline Happy **81** 339
Alexander **59** 96-99 213
    415 **60** 80 202 203 **83**
    365
Alfred **98** 333
Alice **80** 242
Almira **108** 211
Almira Antoinette
    108 211
Alta **80** 248
Amelia **85** 167
Amos **68** lxxviii **91** 257
    263
Amy **60** 351 **126** 30
Andrew **80** 242 **81** 273
Ann **101** 177
Anna **61** 390 **70** 229
Basil E. **119** 316
Betsey **59** 100 **60** 351
    78 262
Bette **93** 268
Betty (Davis) **108** 245
Bradford **70** 228
Bridget **70** 229
Caroline **69** 260
Carrie (Dayley) **108** 301
Carrie C. (Scott) **108** 301
Celestia Ann Lakewana
    108 211
Celia (Crowell) **108** 300
Champion **127** 70
Charles H. **70** 154
Charles N. **80** 248
Charlotte **69** 162
Chauncy **59** 97
Chester **74** 316
Chloe **59** 213 **83** 365
Cordelia (Hemeon)
    108 300
David **55** 177 **70** 178 316

KINNEY *cont'd*
71 137 **86** 19
Dawn Luiska **78** 354
Dita M. (Hopkins)
    119 177
Drusilla (Giggey)
    111 137
Dwight D. **70** 154
E. L. (Dr.) **130** 231
E. M. **57** 417
Edith A. **70** 154
Edward G. **68** 124
Elbridge **70** 154
Eleanor Rickner **112** 224
Elijah **128** 277
Elisha **127** 54 125
Eliza (Magray) **108** 301
Eliza (Ritche) **108** 211
Eliza (Smith) **108** 211
Eliza Antoinette **108** 301
Eliza Evans **70** 154
Eliza Gibbs **81** 339
Elizabeth **60** 80 **61** 80 **70**
    230 **83** 365 **85** 453 **108**
    211 300
Elizabeth (Hathaway)
    134 200
Elizabeth (Houghton)
    108 211
Elizabeth (Perry) **108** 301
Ely Merrick **100** 111
Emeline **69** 260
Emma B. (Wyman)
    108 301
Emma J. (Jackson)
    108 301
Ephraim **61** 85
Erastus **70** 154
Esther Ann (Hanks) **86** 19
Esther T. (Bond) **137** 29
Ethel **91** 46
Eunice **70** 178 230 **71** 139
Ezra **118** 80 **127** 200
Fidelia **103** 227
Frances R. **108** 211
George **81** 339 **90** 33
George Whitefield **70** 222
Gertrude M. **70** 154
Gideon **86** 53
Gladys M. **83** 428 433
Grace **106** 311
H. Sadie **70** 154
Hannah **108** 301 **137** 183
Hannah (Dunlop)
    127 276
Hannah (Durkee) **108** 301
Hannah (Marsh) **91** 263
Hannah (Weston)
    108 300
Hannah B. **108** 301
Hannah E. **108** 300
Hannah S. **66** 49
Harriet (Kelley) **108** 301
Harriet P. **70** 154
Harriet R. **70** 154
Harriet Sophia (Miller)
    108 301
Harvey G. **75** 213
Helen **70** 154
Helen C. **100** 111
Heman **80** 120

KINNEY *cont'd*
Henry **68** lxxviii **95** 314
    101 177
Henry Clay **70** 154
Henry E. **70** 154
Irene **108** 211
Isabel Graves **83** 427 433
James **59** 21 **64** 12 **71** 137
Jane **126** 287 289 **127** 54
    125
Jemima **70** 222
Jennie **62** 368
Jeremiah **52** 74
Jerusha **55** 177
Joan **113** 230
John **64** 187 **69** 260 **71**
    136 139 **82** 446 449 **105**
    283 **119** 180 **142** 238
John Coddington **98** 48
John James **100** 111
John M. **70** 154
John Miller **68** lxxviii
John T. **70** 154
John Wakeman **78** 354
Joseph **70** 177 222 **81** 339
    97 55 **127** 200 **137** 183
Katharine **80** 248
Laura H. Stevens **86** 53
Laura Jane **75** 213
Lawrence M. **98** 358
Lawson **137** 29
Levi **71** 135
Lois **80** 120 **85** 298 **101** 169
Lois Elizabeth **108** 301
Louisa C. (Pinkney)
    108 301
Luther **68** lxxviii
Lydia **105** 66 **108** 211 301
    114 67
Lydia (Bartlett) **108** 211
Lydia A. (Hadley) **93** 203
Lyman C. **93** 203
M. (Hatfield) **108** 301
M. J. **122** 111
Manuel **70** 178 223 **71**
    133 138 139 144
Marcus H. **119** 177
Margaret **82** 446 449
    128 172
Margaret Ellen **68** lxxviii
Margarette (Raynard)
    108 300
Mark Henry **119** 177 178
Martha **113** 79
Martha Ann **108** 301
Martha W. (Strickland)
    86 53
Martin Van Buren **63**
    xxxiii **68** xliii lxxviii
Mary **64** 12 **70** 232 **98** 358
    108 119
Mary (Maynard) **115** 293
Mary (Robbins) **108** 211
Mary A. Cornwall **86** 53
Mary Adeliza (Smith)
    95 314
Mary Ann **63** 50 **86** 53
Mary Ann (Getty) **108** 301
Mary Ann T. **74** 316
Mary Anne (FitzRan-
    dolph) **98** 333

KINNEY cont'd
Mary B. (Williams) **127** 70
Mary L. **70** 154
Mary Lillian **108** 211
Mary Reed (Ritche)
 108 301
Matilda (Bancroft)
 108 300
Matilda (Langworthy)
 118 79
Melatiah **78** 262
Melinda **108** 300
Melinda Rogers **108** 300
Menzo **98** 358
Mercy **64** 187 **70** 227
 108 211
Milton **115** 293
Minerva **80** 248
Myra (Merry) **100** 111
Nathan **64** 187
Nathaniel **71** 137
Nellie Grace **68** lxxviii
Nelson **80** 249
Newcomb **81** 339 **95** 368
Olive (Doane) **108** 211
Olive Jane **108** 211
Orpha (Robbins) **108** 301
Oscar **106** 311
Pamelia **97** 382
Patrick **67** 237
Peabody **61** 80
Phebe **70** 107 **80** 120 **91**
 254 **108** 211 215
Phebe Jane **108** 300
Polly **52** 74 **103** 227
Prentice **70** 230
Rachel **59** 98 99 415
 126 287
Rebecca E. (Moulton)
 108 300
Reuben **61** 85 **62** 296
Robert **70** 223
Roxy **59** 96 **60** 80
Roxy (Churchill) **122** 111
Ruth **74** 168
Sally **70** 228
Sally A. (Taylor) **86** 53
Sally Ann **68** lxxviii
Samuel **60** 351 **127** 276
Samuel T. **86** 53
Sarah **70** 154 **91** 254 267
 108 244 **127** 200 276
Sarah (Blunt) **97** 55
Sarah (Churchill) **108** 301
Sarah (Denison) **127** 200
Sarah (Howard) **126** 289
Sarah (Wyman) **108** 300
Sarah Ann **108** 214
Sarah T. **70** 154
Sarah Wakman **68** 124
Spencer **71** 140 142
Tamasine **108** 211
Thomas **68** lxxviii
 91 254 257
Udavilla (Purdy) **108** 211
Walter A. **86** 53
Warren **59** 100
Wealthian **70** 222
William **70** 154 **78** 262
William P. **70** 154
William Z. **111** 137

KINNEY cont'd
Woodbury **70** 231
Zerviah **70** 231
Zilpha **108** 300
Zilpha (Bridget) **108** 300
KINNICUT Kinnecott
 Kinnecut Kinnicutt
Amanda **70** 29
Amy **70** 29
Anne **70** 28
Antony **127** 302
Augusta **70** 29
Benjamin Townsend
 87 3
Betsey **96** 377
Betty **87** 320
Caroline B. **70** 29
Catherine Amanda **70** 29
Edward **70** 29 **97** 109
Eliza (Dean) **87** 3
Eliza B. **70** 29
Elizabeth **60** 68 **70** 29 32
 135 40
Elizabeth (Dean) **126** 79
Elizabeth A. **70** 29
Hannah **54** 169 **70** 29
Hezekiah **70** 29
Joanna **60** 68 **113** 103
 148 326
Joanna (Shepardson)
 148 326
John **54** 169 **60** 68 **70** 28 29
 129 379
Lydia **70** 29
Mary **70** 29 **113** 103
Mary Leonard **87** 3
Polly **70** 29
Robert **70** 29
Roger **97** 326 **113** 103
 148 326
Sarah **70** 29 **129** 380
Seth **70** 29
Shubael **70** 29
Shubel **129** 379
Simon **70** 29
Susan B. **70** 29
Thomas **70** 29 32
William **70** 29
Kinnie see Kinney
Kinnison see Kennison
Kinniston see Kenniston
Kinsbury see Kingsbury
KINSEY Annabel
 (Mootrey) **108** 338
Elizabeth **97** 333
Elizabeth Adaline **93** 85
Frank Stewart **112** 162
 115 156
Grace (Hull) (Fitz
 Randolph) **97** 332-334
Jacob **91** 97
James **119** 196
Jessie **87** 175
Joanna **97** 334
John **97** 332-334
John M. **128** 135
Jonathan **97** 338
Joseph T. **88** 72
Mabel (Medbury) **99** 147
Mary Southerland **88** 72
Mootrey **97** 338

KINSEY cont'd
Rachel **79** 358 **98** 229
Roy Walter **99** 147
Sarah **128** 98
Sarah (Duckett) **88** 72
Sarah (Fitz Randolph)
 97 338
Susan **109** 230
William **91** 97
KINSI John **143** 260
KINSLE John **112** 158
Kinsley see Kingsley
KINSLOW Thomas **65** 27
KINSMAN Kinsmon
 —— **59** 337 **61** 315
— Mr. **71** 134
Aaron **70** 152
Abigail (Chase) **88** 10
Abigail (Evelith) **135** 106
Abigail P. **78** 30
Amos **88** 10
Benjamin **53** 338
Betsey **64** 117
Coles **114** 85
Daniel **57** 412 **99** 300
Dorcas **70** 230
Dorothy (Chase) **88** 12
Ebenezer **90** 229
Ebenezer P. **90** 227 **97** 375
Elizabeth **53** 338 **84** 426
Ephraim **147** 260
Ephraim (Mrs.) **147** 260
Ezekiel **88** 10
George W. **78** 30
Hannah **60** 53 **70** 152
Hannah F. J. **60** 44
Hannah Olivia (Chase)
 88 10
James **88** 12
James Perkins **88** 10
Jane **60** 53 191
Jennette C. **83** 426 433
Jeremiah **86** 389 **128** 237
Joanna **86** 389 **103** 222
John **57** 412 **86** 389
Jonathan **145** 356
Joseph **86** 389
Lucy Elizabeth **79** 13
Margaret Louisa
 (McPhail) **120** 13
Martha **84** 422 426 **103** 228
Mary **60** lxx **61** 201 **136**
 316 322
Mary (Chase) **88** 10
Mary (Knowlton) **84** 422
Michael **60** 53 191 **61** 201
 84 422
Nathaniel **60** 53 **88** 28
 135 106
Nathaniel W. **79** 13
Newport **70** 230
Peletiah **60** 53 191 **84** 422
Polly **86** 389
Priscilla **60** 53
Rachel **51** 462
Rebecca **86** 389
Rebecca (Chase) **88** 28
Rebecca (Tupper) **99** 300
Rhoda **57** 392
Robert **60** lxx **64** 298 **70**
 103 **86** 389 **109** 222

KINSMAN *cont'd*
Samuel **57** 392
Sarah **60** 191 **70** 231 **81** 444
86 389 **109** 222 245
Sarah (Harris) **128** 237
Sarah Lucinda **81** 276 282
Susanna **84** 422
Susanna (Frost) **90** 227
Thomas **86** 389 **120** 13
Timothy **62** 75 160
Wiliam **81** 276
KINSOLVING
James **86** 266
Wythe Leigh **90** 208
KINSON Daniel **116** 114
KINSTER —— **57** 314
KINSTON Anna **88** 78
Kinton *see* Kenton
KINTY George W. **91** 327
KINWORTHY
— Mr. **71** 118
Kinyon *see* Kenyon
KINZER Dean **83** 64
Emma **83** 64
Ernest **83** 64
Ethel **83** 64
Jessie **83** 64
Joseph **83** 64
Lawrence **83** 64
Lura **83** 64
Rawlin **83** 64
Verna **83** 64
Ward **83** 64
Kip *see* Kipp
KIPLING Rudyard **133** 9
136 87
William **58** 70
KIPP Kip
—— **57** 236
Adelaide A. (Deyo) **92** 169
Alpheus **92** 169
Benjamin **92** 169
Benona **92** 169
Charles E. **92** 169
Cornelia L. **98** 208
Corydon **92** 169
Elizabeth **90** 70
Ellen **82** 176
Emily Addams **112** 317
Emily Hustace (Addams)
112 317
Frances **136** 360
Frank **92** 169
Grace Lawrence **112** 317
Henry **98** 208 **112** 317
Herbert **92** 169
Isaac **92** 169
Jennie L. **92** 168
Jesse **113** 209
Johannes **106** 175 176
John Caswell **122** 298
Laroy **92** 169
Lovina **92** 176
Lucinda (Decker) **92** 169
Mary F. (Jones) **92** 169
Maud Matilda **82** 176
May **93** 205
Nancy (Van Housen)
92 169
Nellie **92** 169
Rozina **92** 163

KIPP *cont'd*
Sally **92** 169
Samuel **122** 298
Sarah **92** 169
Whitney **84** 29
Wilfred Augustine
82 176
KIPPAX Elizabeth (Grene)
(Otes) **124** 255
Richard **124** 255
KIPPING Kippen Kippin
Kippinge Kypping
Arthur **53** 50
Elizabeth **141** 126
John **83** 324 **84** 76 **100** 133
101 276
Richard **100** 133
Sarah **100** 133 **101** 276
KIPSHAVEN —— **56** 98
KIRALFY A. K. R. **147** 9
KIRBY Cirbey Curbey
Kirbe Kirbey Kyrbye
—— **57** lii **62** lxxiii 391
119 262
— Dea. **71** 44
— Mr. **57** 229
Abiah **102** 103
Abiah (Kimberly) **102** 103
Abigail **55** 303 **56** 58 206
58 366 **100** 297 **110** 160
Abraham **71** 47 **123** 85
Ann **56** 123
Anna **85** 450
Audrey (Gifford) **132**
214 216
Babe **127** 79
Benjamin **60** 365
Cassie (Rutherford)
117 119
Christopher **64** 21
Clifton T. **117** 119
Daniel **54** 179
David **148** 288
Delbert (Mrs.) **97** 158
E. P. **117** 119
Edward **144** 208
Elihu **132** 214
Eliza **127** 79
Elizabeth **55** 303 **57** 34 **58**
366 **68** 126 **93** 308 **106**
43 210 **130** 276 **131** 140
Elizabeth (Callender)
144 208
Elizabeth E. (Baker)
117 119
Ella Josephine **90** 345
Ephraim **65** 148 **107** 73
Ethelbert **77** 219
Eunice **134** 311
Experience **128** 248 250
Francis **73** 142 264
Furnie **90** 91
George **117** 119
Gladys Burrelll (Gifford)
85 195
Gustavus Town **93** 280
Hannah **106** 218
Hannah (Snow) **106** 218
Hannah A. **79** 157
Hannah McClure
62 lxxiv

KIRBY *cont'd*
Helen **107** 73
Helen McClure **62** lxxiv
Henry **129** 339 **135** 46
Horace **125** 42
Ichabod **73** 301 **129** 340
Increase **55** 303
Isaac **131** 140
Isabella **93** 25
James **56** 123 **68** 191 **90**
345 **99** 64 **117** 119 **127**
79
Jane **55** 303 **73** 294 **124** 43
44
Jean MacKewan **85** 197
Joan **64** 186 **76** 123
John **51** 352 **52** 467 **53** 88
55 303 **56** 58 **64** 186 65
298 299 **93** 308 **106** 210
218 **115** 91 **127** 79 **128**
248 250 **129** 235
John Andrew **127** 79
John B. **57** 405
John Baptist **73** 137
John E. **89** 242
Jonathan **57** 404
Joseph **71** 47 **75** 189
117 119
Julia B. **97** 158
Julia F. (Adams) **89** 242
Katharine **107** 73
Louise **127** 79
Lucy **53** 88 **57** 404 **106** 8 80
117 119
Margaret **75** 189 **137** 150
Marie Antoinette **97** 74
Martha (Rivers) **90** 91
Mary **61** 28 **75** 189 **90** 90
Mary (Barnes) **123** 85
Mary Ann Thomas
57 405
Nancy **77** 219
Nathaniel **58** 366 **132** 214
217 **137** 159
Nehemiah **61** 28
Overton **127** 79
Patience **55** 303 **73** 297
Patience (Gifford) **128**
250 **129** 340 **132** 214
Phebe **73** 301 **93** 186
Polly **90** 90
Rachel (Allen) **129** 340
Rebecca **88** 399 **127** 79
Rebecca (Mosher) **128** 250
Rebecca (Potter) **128** 250
Recompense **62** 181
Richard **52** 105 **55** 299 303
73 143 **108** 203 **119** 163
128 250 **129** 339 **131**
140 **132** 213 214 217
Richard Shelton **94** 306
Robert **55** 303 **128** 248 250
129 235 **132** 214 217
Robertson / Robinson
127 79
Rose (Smith) **127** 79
Ruhamah **131** 214
Sabra **88** 186
Sarah **54** 179 **55** 303 **69** 92
73 135 **93** 308 **124** 44
128 248 250

KIRBY cont'd
Sarah (Swift) **115** 91
Silas **58** 366 **72** 109
  131 140
Sis **127** 79
Susan **78** 46
Susanna **52** 467 **72** 109
  106 212
Sylvia **148** 288
Temperance **55** 303 **128**
  248 250
Tessie **127** 79
Thankful **72** 109 110
Thomas **127** 79 **129** 235
  236 **130** 90 94 102
Timanda S. **83** 468
Valentine **65** 117
Walter Scott **85** 195
Weston **132** 214 217
Wilhelmine Stewart
  Dunn (Claffin) **93** 280
William **62** lxxiv **72** 109
  79 157 **117** 119 **132** 214
  216 **148** 286
William A. **97** 74
William Henry **64** 132
KIRCHBAUM
Franklin N. **99** 33
Philip Thurston **99** 33
KIRCHNER
Catherine **82** 16
Chester **108** 320
Clyde Chester **108** 134
KIRCHOFF —— **80** 31
Martin (Mrs.) **93** 203
Kircomb see Kirkham
KIRK Kirke Kyrke
— Miss **77** 164
Abigail **110** 203
Agnes (Millington)
  120 25
Angus **118** 51 54 55
Anne **71** 318
Catherine **125** 257
Catherine (McDonald)
  125 197
Clarissa (Lane) **90** 50
David **96** 271
Diadema **92** 170
Didemia (Thompson)
  92 169
Edward **145** 256
Edward N. **56** lx **137** 220
Eleanor Hubbard **90** 137
Elisha **56** 124
Eliza **92** 169
Elizabeth **125** 197
Ellen Warner **59** 236
Eve **92** 169 170
Eveline **92** 170
Gabriella M. (Marion)
  114 191
H. **92** 170
Hazel **101** 124 **130** 71
Henry **92** 169 170 **102** 184
Janet (Glencross) **125**
  198 259
Jennie **105** 50
John **64** 161 **68** 110 **90** 50
  113 64 **118** 51 55 **125**
  197 259

KIRK cont'd
John Foster **59** 235 236
Judith **88** 189
Laura Jane **78** 323
Margaret **85** 340 **93** 185
  125 257 258
Margaret (Miller) **92** 170
Maria **92** 170
Mary **77** 157
Mary Alice **82** 400
Mary Catherine **125** 197
Mary Elizabeth **82** 400
Mary Jane **102** 301
Mary Virginia **78** 203
Mehitable **126** 208
Mima **84** 191
R. E. **142** 239
Richard **77** 157
Robert **142** 73
Roxaline **92** 170
Sally **92** 176
Sarah **52** 359 **100** 239
Sarah (Nowell) **100** 299
Sarah A. **92** 176
Thomas **82** 400 **100** 299
  113 64
Thomas C. **113** 64
William **92** 169 170 **118**
  45 55 **125** 116 197 257
William M. **92** 170
William P. **92** 170
KIRKBRIDE
Andrew **98** 54
David **134** 226
Ellen Allison
  (FitzRandolph) **98** 54
Emma **134** 226
Georgianna Sheldon
  (Tilney) **81** 238 **82** 237
Matthew **60** 186
William Howard **81** 238
William Howard (Mrs.)
  82 237
KIRKBY —— **67** 67
Ann **63** 145
Ann (Wilberfosse) **93** 23
Gibbon **93** 23 27 30
Isabel (Gibbon) **93** 30
John **63** 145
Richard **100** 21
Robert **109** 315
Roger **93** 7 25 28-30
Susan (Nicholson) **93** 23
Thomas **102** 242
William **93** 7
Kirke see Kirk
KIRKEET William **71** 123
  126 127
KIRKEHOUSE
Dorothy **93** 24
KIRKENER
Agnes **51** 391 395
Anne **51** 391
Erasmus **51** 391 395
Katharine **51** 391 395 406
Susanna **51** 391 406
KIRKER
Elizabeth **112** 281
Elizabeth (Montgomery)
  112 281
James **118** 45 48

KIRKET Robert **148** 152
KIRKETON
Gilbert de **96** 45 111
KIRKHAM Kircomb
  Kirkome Kirkum
  Kyrkham
Ann **64** 340
Anna **59** 255
Anna Forsdick **59** 255
Anne **83** 82 281 **111** 294
Augustus **59** 256
Austin Parker **59** 256
Bedad **59** 256
Bela Stone **59** 256
Benjamin **58** 362 **59** 66 255
  61 30
Benjamin Franklin
  59 256
Benjamin Mortimer
  59 256
Betsey **59** 256
Bille **58** 363
Caleb Evarts **59** 256
Calvin Crampton **59** 256
Caroline A. **59** 256
Catherine **59** 256
Catherine Ward **59** 257
Chloe **59** 256
Clarissa Griswold **59** 257
Daniel **59** 255 256 **111** 294
Daniel Erastus **59** 256
Daniel Maltby **59** 256
David **59** 61 255 256
Deborah **58** 302 **59** 63 256
Delany **59** 256
Dora Isabel (Trexler)
  99 147
E. Kay **114** 159 **123** 144 145
Eber **59** 66 255
Edward **62** 249
Eli **59** 255 257 **111** 294
Eli Maltby **59** 257
Elihu **59** 255 **111** 294
Elijah **59** 255
Eliza Ann **59** 256
Elizabeth **59** 255
Ellen Roselia **59** 256
Erastus Rodney **59** 256
Esther **59** 255 **60** 210
  111 294
Esther (Maltby) **111** 294
George **59** 256
George Albert **59** 256
George Anson **59** 256
George Harrison **59** 256
Guilford Montgomery
  59 256
Harriet Maltby **59** 257
Henrietta **59** 257
Henry **59** 254 255
Isaac Johnson **59** 256
James Mercer **101** 124
Jane **58** 361-363 **59** 61 254
  255
Jane Amorett **59** 257
Jane Eliza **59** 256
Joanna **59** 255
John **58** 361 **59** 255-257
  60 210 **85** 277 283 **111**
  294
John Bates **59** 256

KIRKHAM cont'd
John Harrison **59** 257
John Marion **99** 147
John S. **90** 32
Julia **59** 256
Juliette **78** 238
Laura B. **59** 256
Levi **59** 255 **111** 294
Lydia **59** 255
Marietta **59** 257
Martha **59** 255
Martha Ann **103** 119
Mary **53** 315 **59** 66 255 256
Mary Ann **59** 257
Mercy **58** 361 **59** 255
Nancy **59** 256
Nathaniel **59** 255
Nicholas **115** 249
Patience **53** 407 **59** 255
Patty **59** 256
Philemon **59** 255 256
    111 294
Rebecca **59** 255
Richard Monson **59** 256
Ruth **59** 66 254-256 **61** 30
Samuel **58** 301 361-363
    59 61 63 254-257 **60** 210
    111 294 **142** 327
Sarah **59** 255-257 **72** 213
Solomon **59** 255 **111** 294
Susan **59** 256
Susanna Collins **59** 257
Thomas **59** 254-257 **60** 210
    142 325 **145** 325
Wealthy **59** 255
William **58** 302 **59** 63 255
    256
William L. **59** 256
Zerviah **53** 315 **59** 255
    111 294
KIRKHUFF
Eldora **82** 237
Eldora Mindwell (Poole)
    81 364 **82** 237 **100** 109
    110 220 223
Hazel Mindwell **110** 223
Isaac **110** 223
William Isaac **81** 364 **82**
    237 **100** 109 **110** 220
    223
KIRKLAND
—— **62** 301 **121** 60 66 302
    122 66 308
— Dr. **57** 377 378
— Rev. Mr. **58** 156
Amelia M. **83** 101
Anna **62** 239
Anne **62** 365
Augusta Hayden **93** 182
Betsey **117** 320
Betsey (Williams) **117** 320
Caroline **76** xlviii
Charles II. **90** 260
Cornelia F. (Kellogg)
    125 53
Daniel **117** 320 **136** 312
    324
Dorothy **78** 430
Elizabeth (Hannum)
    90 260
Esther E. **83** 99

KIRKLAND cont'd
Gilbert **62** 365
Hannah **117** 55
Hannah (Davis) **117** 56
Hannah (Perkins)
    136 324
Jane **78** 430
Jerusha **100** 2 **136** 312
Jerusha (Bingham) **136**
    312 320
John **52** 112 **62** 239 **117**
    55 56
John L. **62** 239
John T. **119** 125 **136** 90
John Thornton **63** lii
    136 320
Joseph **76** xlviii **136** 323
    324
Louisa **117** 320 **136** 323
Louisa Wilkinson
    76 xlviii
Lucy **53** 316 **103** 236
Margaret **52** 112
Marian Phebe **86** 197
Martha **52** 56
Mary **117** 320
Mary (Perkins) **136** 312
    324
Mary Ann **62** 365
Mary Elizabeth **103** 120
Mary Ethelyn **101** 322
Moses **62** 301
Nathaniel **83** 78 **101** 243
Polly **117** 320
Polly (Manly) **93** 182
Samuel **120** 85 **136** 312
    320
Sarah **120** 85
Sarah (Backus) **136** 324
Susanna **60** 136
Theodosia Burr Davis
    (Wilkinson) **76** xlviii
Thomas **78** 430 **93** 182
Thomas J. **118** 168 **121** 77
William **52** 112
KIRKMAN Kyrkman
—— **101** 51
George **80** 90
George W. **51** 361
James **60** 27
KIRKOD — Miss **103** 190
Kirkome see Kirkham
KIRKPATRICK
A. E. **91** 327
Abraham **69** 191
Ann Eliza **78** 46
Elijah **91** 294
Elizabeth **86** 113
Eunice **98** 333
Helen Katharine **101** 124
Isaac Barber **116** 154
Jane **116** 153
Jean Douglas **103** 313
Jesse Baird **103** 119
John **82** 257 **86** 113
John Foster **116** 153
Lurilda **117** 120
Mary (Nevins) **91** 294
Mary Lee **91** 294
Nancy Jane **116** 153
Richard Darrow **102** 124

KIRKPATRICK cont'd
Silas Preston **116** 153
Solomon **116** 153
Solomon Snyder **116** 154
William **113** 160
KIRKSEY
Margaret M. **77** 265
W. S.A. **77** 265
KIRKUFF Jane (De Cou)
    110 223
Kirkum see Kirkham
KIRKWOOD Abby
    Dickinson **68** 242
Alexander **61** 257 **67** 206
    79 48
Anna Jane **145** 31
Carolyn (Neal) **83** 122 232
Elizabeth **140** 68
Elizabeth R. **92** 323
J. T. **121** 28
Mary **67** 206 **145** 31
Robert **65** 54
Robert Grant **83** 122 232
Samuel **78** 183
William **68** 242
KIRLIN Abbie **128** 267
David **128** 266 267
Edna D. **128** 266
M. A. (Myers) **128** 266 267
KIRMAN John **53** 46
KIRRELL —— **52** 109
Elizabeth **52** 110 117
Henry **52** 107 110 117 118
John **52** 107 110 111 117
    118 127
Joseph **52** 111
Lucie **52** 117 118
William **52** 117
KIRRILL John **51** 424
KIRSBY Joseph **102** 103
KIRSCHENMANN Johan
    Christian **112** 237
KIRTLAND Ann **102** 267
Diana (Hilyer) **111** 326
Elizabeth **102** 267
Grace **69** xxxv
Hester **146** 369
John **70** 107
John B. **125** 34
John C. **125** 53
Mary **102** 266 267 **146** 375
Mary Ann **92** 74
Mary Ethelyn **101** 322
Nathaniel **60** 186 **102** 266
    267
Parnell **71** 62 **96** 364
    102 266
Philip **102** 267
Priscilla **126** 52
Sarah **54** lv **61** 117 **71** 301
KIRTLEY Elizabeth
    (Hassall) **91** 185
George **91** 185
Mary Y. **125** 238
Sarah Ann **91** 185
KIRTON Jane **103** 19
Katharine **72** 153
Margaret (White) **139** 228
Marie (Sadler) **139** 236
Mary **81** 489 **139** 226 228
    236 237

KIRTON *cont'd*
Peron **110** 82
Stephen **139** 236
Thomas **139** 236
William **81** 489 491
KIRTZ Hannah (Nelson)
110 76
KIRVAN Laura P. **84** 29
KIRWAN Thomas **66** 193
KISE Sarah **80** 182
KISH Alga **70** 243
John **70** 243
Rose **70** 243
KISHNER
Charles **76** 277
Henry **76** 277
Mary Jane **76** 277
Susan **75** 249
Kisick *see* Kissick
KISLER
Catherine **114** 187
George **114** 187
Hetty **114** 187
John **114** 187
Peter **114** 187
KISLOW S. **128** 268
KISNER Mary Ann **91** 208
KISSAM Adrian **80** 58
Daniel E. **66** 228
Daniel W. **66** 226
Deborah (Field) **113** 210
Elizabeth **52** 79 **66** 226
H. S. **55** 445
Hannah **66** 228
Jane **66** 226
Joseph **113** 210
Julia M. **79** 156 **80** 58
Madeline **80** 58
Maria **66** 226
Maria Louisa **89** 262
Phebe **66** 226
Richard S. **79** 156 **80** 58 61
Sarah V. B. **66** 226
Seabury **66** 226
Seabury Webster **66** 226
William Aymar **66** 228
KISSEL Barbara Eldred
(Case) **98** 271
W. Thorn (Mrs.) **98** 271
KISSICK Kisick
Eliza **125** 287
Francis **78** 408
John **71** 223 **99** 119
Mary **81** 444
Nathan **71** 221
Sarah **99** 119
Thomas **99** 119
KISSINGER
Henry **145** 200
KIST Levi **125** 38
KISTLER
Andrew Milton **80** 333
81 219 **86** 203 236 **87**
377
Ann Elizabeth
(Woodling) **87** 377
Anna Dorothea **87** 377
Charles Edmund **87** 377
Charles Edwin **87** 377
Edith (Furber) **87** 377

KISTLER *cont'd*
Ernestine (Huebner)
87 377
Frank Emerson **80** 101
206
George **99** 82
Jacob **87** 377
John **128** 98
John Frederick **87** 377
John George **87** 377
John L. **114** 79
L. C. **128** 98
Lizzie **128** 96
Magadelena (Brobst)
87 377
Mary (Collett) **87** 377
Mattie **128** 98
May (Travis) **128** 98
Michael **87** 377
Nancy (Hannum) **91** 112
Noah **91** 112
Norman H. **91** 112
Stephen **87** 377
KITCHELL Kitchel
—— **112** 41
— Dr. **55** 94
Aaron **119** 195 197
Abraham **119** 116 182 196
Allen F. **65** 10
Ann **65** 10
Charity (Ford) **119** 182
196
Cornelius H. **55** 231
Cornelius P. **65** 10
Demas **119** 182
Elizabeth **119** 182
Elizabeth (McCarty)
119 182
Esther **67** 384
Eunice **119** 182
Farrand De Forest **65** 10
Flora McDonald **65** 10
Ford **119** 182
Grace **60** 21 **119** 196
137 38
Hannah (Darling)
119 199
Hannah (Day) **119** 182
Hannah (Tuttle) **119** 182
Harman **55** 214
Harvey D. **65** 10
Helen B. **65** 10
James **119** 182
Jane **119** 197
Jemima **119** 199
Joanna **55** 214 **85** 227 **97**
189 **109** 65 **110** 69
John **67** 384
Joseph **119** 182 196 **137** 38
Kelsey Percival **99** 146
Lewis **119** 182
Margaret **55** 213 214
Margaret (Sheafe) **137** 291
Rachel (Bates) **119** 182 196
Ralph T. **65** 10
Robert **54** 270 **55** 213 214
218 **56** 155 261 **62** 230
137 291
Samuel **55** 214 **60** 21
Sarah **55** 214 **119** 182
Stephen **119** 199

KITCHELL *cont'd*
Susan **92** 400
Susanna **119** 179 181
Thomas **55** 208
Walter Howard **104** 141
William Lloyd **90** 137
KITCHEN Kitchem
Kitchin Kytchen
Kytchin Kytchynam
Alonzo McCready **70** 326
Anna **70** 325
Bethiah **55** 330
Bethiah (Weld) **106** 40
Charles Andrew **70** 326
Daniel Wheeler **70** 326
David H. **70** 326
David P. **70** 326
Edward **70** 326 **106** 30 40
41
Eliza **70** 334
Eliza Jane **70** 325
Elizabeth **67** 167 **70** 326
334 **77** 312 **106** 39 40
Elizabeth (Grafton)
106 38
Elizabeth (Grafton)
(Saunders) **106** 40
Francis **52** 106
George B. **70** 326
Hannah Maria **70** 326
Harriet **69** 314
Honnour **100** 29
J. Martin **69** 314
Jackson **70** 325
James **70** 326 334
James Martin **70** 325
James William **70** 326
Jane **70** 326
Joanna **70** 326
John **77** 312 **106** 38 40
114 73
John H. **70** 326
John R. **70** 328 334
John Richardson **70** 325
John Warren **70** 326
Joseph **70** 326
Joseph Dobinson **70** 326
Lindley M. **70** 326
Mae Clyde **114** 80 82
Martha **70** 326
Mary **70** 326 **77** 312 **108**
177 **110** 143 232
Mary (Boardman) **106** 40
Mary Ann **70** 325 329 334
Mary Anna B. **70** 326
Matthew **100** 29
Mercy H. **70** 328
Priscilla **106** 38-41 43 44 46
47 **107** 127 **116** 231
Rachel **70** 325
Rhoda Elizabeth **70** 326
Robert **51** 407 **53** 11 **77**
312 **90** 400 **106** 38 40 41
110 232 **148** 26
Sally **125** 287
Sarah **70** 325 326
Sarah Anna **70** 328
William **64** 161 166 **70** 326
100 29
KITCHENMAN
— Capt. **77** 101 104

KITCHER Richard **65** 24
KITCHERELL Kitcherel
  Martha **61** 310 **65** 371
Kitchin *see* Kitchen
KITCHING Abby **68** 282
KITCHNOR
  Henry **82** 291 301
  Margaret **82** 291 301
KITE Hugh **99** 147
  Mary **77** 150
  Thomas **62** 332
Kiterage *see* Kittredge
KITHRELL
  Mary Hervey **51** 388
KITLEN John **114** 192
KITLEY
  Sarah **55** 394 395
  William **55** 394
KITNEY Joan (Johnson)
    146 272
  John **146** 272
Kitridge *see* Kittredge
KITSON Kittson Kytson
  —— **83** 34
  — Capt. **83** 34 193
  Anne **78** 151
  Elizabeth **83** 193
  Ella **124** 34
  Emma **74** 304
  Eugene **125** 54
  Hattie (Crisfield) **125** 54
  Julia Ann **124** 34
  Katharine **98** 30
  Margaret **83** 25 27 172 306
  Maud Beatrice **117** 203
  Minerva **124** 34
  Ophelia **124** 34
  Peter **94** 101
  Richard **51** 350 **78** 151
  Samuel James **61** 109
  Shadrach **124** 34
  Thomas **83** 25 27
  Thomas L. **83** 172
  William **109** 7 8 **124** 34
Kittel *see* Kittle
Kittell *see* Kittle
Kitteradge *see* Kittredge
KITTEREY
  Rebecca **78** 311
Kitteridge *see* Kittredge
KITTIER
  Henry **113** 220
  Jane **113** 220
KITTLE Kittel Kittell
  —— **55** 303
  Albert R. **73** 212
  Allen **73** 212
  Alvinza **73** 212
  Anna **73** 212
  Benjamin **73** 212
  Catherine Chubbuck
    89 26
  Catherine Eunice (Lazell)
    89 26
  Edward **129** 61
  Edwin Howard **89** 26
  Electa **73** 212
  Elizabeth **73** 212
  Elizabeth (Ward) **96** 359
  Esther **73** 212
  Eunice **73** 212

KITTLE *cont'd*
  George Chauncey **89** 26
  George W. **73** 212
  Hannah **126** 256 **128** 20
  John **65** 148 **96** 359
  Joseph **115** 142
  Leah Belle (Bouton) **89** 26
  Lena (Christ) **89** 26
  Lucy **73** 212
  M. **73** 212
  Mary **107** 166
  Mary R. **73** 212
  Rachel Maria **73** 212
  Samuel Lasell **89** 26
  Samuel Parker **89** 26
  Stephen **73** 212
  Stephen S. **73** 212
  Susan **73** 212
  Susanna **73** 212
  Theresa Corinne **89** 26
  William **73** 212
KITTLESDATTER
  Gunhild **86** 221
KITTO Kittow
  Ann Elizabeth **87** 281
  Mary **85** 426
KITTREDGE Kiterage
    Kitridge Kitteradge
    Kitteridge Kittrege
    Kittridge
  —— **119** 209 217
  — Dr. **83** 193
  — Miss **52** 464
  — Mrs. **83** 306
  — Prof. **62** 111 **95** 44
  Abel **57** 291-293 361 **89** 58
    95 360 **98** 226
  Abigail **63** liv **86** 233
    137 363
  Abigail (Dutton) **109** 221
  Alfred Beard **74** 162
  Almena **73** 286
  Alvah **57** lxv
  Amy (Barker) **98** 227
  Anna (Thorndike) **95** 360
    98 226
  Augusta **58** cx **81** 347
  Belinda **87** 396
  Benjamin F. **57** 358-361
  Benjamin Franklin
    57 292 296
  Benjamin Kendall **73** 282
  Benjamin Whiting **73** 285
    289 290
  Beulah (Baker) **95** 360
  Calvin **73** 283 284
  Carrie Louise (Stimpson)
    101 70
  Catherine H. (McAfee)
    109 221
  Catherine Waldo **57** 361
  Charles **73** 289 **101** 70
  Charles Henry **98** 226
  Charles J. **89** 58
  Charles James **57** 293 **82**
    254 **83** 232
  Charles Prentice **101** 70
  Charlotte Elizabeth
    73 290
  Chessman **107** 307 308
    108 131

KITTREDGE *cont'd*
  Clarissa **55** xcv
  Daniel **109** 220
  Deborah (Lewis) (Benson)
    95 360
  Dora **95** 361
  Dorothy Brayton
    (Gifford) **107** 307 308
    108 131
  E. H. **94** 214
  Edward Holmes **71** xxiii
    73 vi **74** vi xxviii 160
    75 vi **76** vi **77** vi **78** 218
    79 214 **80** 220 **81** 234
    89 82 144 146 **90** 129
    150 **91** 59 156 **92** 137
    159 160 162 **93** 151 152
    154 **94** 152 153 **95** 138
    139 160 **96** 174 **97** 172
    98 137 151 225-227
  Edward Lyman **95** 360
  Elijah **132** 272
  Elizabeth (Foster) **109** 220
  Elizabeth P. **83** 25 34
  Ella Eugenia Forstina
    (Fuller) **97** 380 **109** 220
  Ella Isabelle **90** 135 **97** 380
    108 125 138 **109** 220
  Ellen Judith **89** 58 79 134
  Ellen Morley **85** 314
  Emma Louise (Crimp)
    101 70
  Eri **109** 221
  Eunice **57** 291-293
  Eunice (Chamberlin) **57**
    292 359 **89** 58
  Fanny **61** 382
  Fanny (Marsh) **95** 282
  Frances Adelia **95** 282
  Frances Eveline (Gordon)
    95 361
  Frances Gordon **95** 361
  Frances Jannett **57** 359
  Frances M. (Burchard)
    89 58
  Francis **101** 70
  Frank Edward **54** 361 **55**
    xxxii
  Fred Anderson **101** 70
  Frederick Curtiss **57** 295
  George **57** 295 **73** 290
  George Albert **55** xcv
  George Lyman **84** 180
    90 124 **92** 138 **93** 131
    132 **95** 360 **96** 87 166
  George W. **68** 40 43
    85 314
  H. C. **103** 32
  Hannah **63** 289 **89** 67
    98 361 362
  Hannah (French) **89** 58
    101 70
  Harriet **57** 296 358-360
  Harriet Cornelia **57** 296
  Henrietta **92** 346
  Henry C. **93** 402
  Henry Crocker **80** 334
    81 214 **95** 361
  Hosea **73** 284
  Ingalls **58** cx **81** 347
  Irene **88** 280

KITTREDGE *cont'd*
J. B. **91** 202
James **55** xcv **95** 360
    98 225
James Burchard **57** 361
Jane **73** 290 291 **95** 360
    98 226
Jane (Kittredge) **95** 360
    98 226
Jane W. **73** 287
Jeremiah Chapman **54**
    xlvii **55** xcv xcvi
John **55** xcv **57** 295 296
    358 **63** 181 289 **67** 348
    73 285 291 **84** 238 **89** 58
    95 360 **98** 225 **101** 70
    109 220 221 **125** 295
John Putnam **57** 295
Jonathan **63** 289
Joseph **83** 126 **84** 189 238
    109 221
Joseph B. **98** 227
Joseph Walter Adam **97**
    380 **109** 220 221
Joshua **95** 360 **98** 226
Judith Shead **57** 292
Julia **92** 346 **93** 326
Julia Augusta **73** 289
Julia Livingston **92** 346
Julia Root **57** 358
Kendall **73** 289 290
Lucretia **109** 221
Lucy **77** 319
Lydia **73** 285 289-291
    101 70
Lydia (Kittredge) **98** 226
Mabel Thorndike
    (Hodges) **83** 126 **84**
    189 238
Marion Stimpson **82**
    219 237 **101** 24 70 130
Martha **73** 286 **108** 85
Martha A. **55** xcvi
Martha McElwain **57** 358
Mary **55** xcv **57** 295 296
    358 **59** 246 **67** 348 **91**
    266 **98** 227 **99** 314 **107**
    37
Mary (Littlefield) **89** 58
    95 360 **98** 225 **101** 70
    109 220
Mary (Newhall) **101** 70
Mary (Wright) **89** 58
Mary Ann **73** 285
Mary Elizabeth **57** 296
Mary Lizzie (Kittredge)
    98 226
Mary Worthington
    57 292 360
Mehitable (Russell)
    101 70
N---m **111** 116
Peter **60** 44 **145** 348
Philura Curtis **57** 358
Prudy (Fillebrown)
    98 226
Rebecca **98** 227
Rebecca (Shed) **89** 58
Rufus **82** 421 **83** 182 183
Ruth (Shed) **109** 220
Samuel **98** 226

KITTREDGE *cont'd*
Samuel Lucius **57** 295
Sarah **73** 282 289 291
Sarah (Fowle) **98** 225
Sarah (French) **109** 221
Sarah A. **58** cx
Sarah Augusta **81** 347
Sarah Marsh **57** 360
Solomon **101** 70
Sophia (Lyman) **95** 360
    98 226
Sophronia **57** 292
Stephen **101** 70
Susan P. L. (Haven)
    83 182 183
Tabitha (Ingalls) **101** 70
Theodore **83** 25
Thomas **55** xcv **95** 360
    98 226 **126** 225
Timothy **95** 282
William **73** 290 **89** 58 **92**
    346 **93** 326 **108** 85
KITTRELL
Mary Harvey **70** lvi
Kittridge *see* Kittredge
KITTS John Franklin
    81 109 222
Katharine (Wallace)
    81 109 222
Kittson *see* Kitson
KIVLAN Ethel Lillian
    104 145
KIZER George **125** 94
KJELLENBERG
Marion S. **115** 158
KLAIR
A. Francis **80** 52 264
Adeline **80** 52 264
Annie Laurie **80** 264
Egbert **80** 52
Elizabeth **80** 52
Ella **80** 52
Ella C. **80** 264
Evalina **80** 52 264
Evan **80** 52
Evan H. **80** 264
Ida F. **80** 264
KLANCAR
Anthony J. **129** 188
KLAPPER Ethel Marie
    (Hansen) **94** 138
Harry **94** 138
KLAPPERT
Ruth Tebbs **83** 234
KLAUMAN Edna (Sheldon)
    100 111
Louie Herman **100** 111
KLAVITTER
Emma **96** 129
KLEBE Barbara **94** 193
KLECKNER
Bertha Diana **95** 147
KLEE Hattie **85** 226 227
KLEEBLATT Adeline Edle
    Von **83** 489
KLEEBLATT-WAGNER
Antoine Victorine
    Von **83** 489
KLEES Warren G. **120** 77
KLEIN
Alice L. **81** 282

KLEIN *cont'd*
Joseph H. (Mrs.) **113** 76
Magdalen Louise **77** 322
    78 203
Matilda **99** 46
Nicholas **99** 302
KLEINFELD
Otto **85** 314
KLEINGINNA
Johannes **113** 241
KLEINHANS —— **143** 369
KLEINMAN Horesa (Lilly-
    white) **99** 147
Joseph Le Roy **99** 147
KLEINSICK Ida May
    (Bancroft) (Reming-
    ton) **96** 289
KLEISDORF
Adam **100** 177
KLEISER
Pearl **83** 124 231
KLEMM Agnes G. **92** 289
KLETT Guy S. **117** 105
KLEUGEL
Helen
Richardson **143** 247
KLEYENENBURG
Jannetje Goverts von
    128 164
KLIENGER Adam **85** 167
Augusta **85** 167
Pauline **85** 167
KLIMAS Petras **99** 257
KLINCK
Daisy Louise **92** 63
KLINE A. J. **128** 171
Anna Gwynn **118** 293
Catherine (Barton)
    107 114
Elizabeth C. (Chase)
    87 326
Grace (Dean) **144** 115
Harmon **107** 114
Isaac **107** 114
John **143** 261
Joseph **87** 326
Loretta E. **128** 171
Magdalen Louise **78** 203
Nlanon Nlan **128** 171
Rachel (Barton) **107** 114
Rebecca **78** 290
Richard W. **78** 290
Ruth **105** 128
Sarah (Tupper) **99** 302
Victoria (Cook) **118** 293
William Davis **118** 293
KLING Amos H. **77** 246
Florence **77** 246 248 249
KLINGER Klingler
Albert Grover **108** 134
    114 309
Bertha Marie (Quiggle)
    108 134 **114** 309
Elizabeth **126** 232
Joan **105** 49
John **105** 49
John Hamilton **105** 49
Katharine **105** 49
Katharine (Hamilton)
    105 49
Mary Jean **105** 49

KLINGER *cont'd*
  Michael **114** 186
  Nancy Lee **105** 49
  Peter **114** 186
  Philip **114** 186
  Samuel **114** 186
KLOCK Elroy **79** 133
  Emma A. **104** 46
  John **91** 246
  Lorenzo **104** 46
  Louana Emily **79** 133
  Margaretta **104** 46
  Mary **91** 246
  Phebe **91** 246
KLOTZ A. **107** 112
  Anna (Barton) **107** 112
  Otto **81** 465
KLOUS Bernhard Forbes
  68 xxxiv
KLUEGEL Harry A. **114**
  158 **115** 230 **116** 81 **117**
  156 **118** 249 **121** 156
  Helen (Richardson) **114**
  158 **116** 81 316 **117** 156
  118 249 **119** 75 **120** 154
  121 156
KLUEVER Herman
  Christof **113** 78
KLUMAN
  Amy (Ehrmann)
  93 181
  Karl Myers **93** 181
KLUMPH
  Richard Amidon
  116 233
  Zoe Leete **85** 239
KLUNKENFORT
  Mary **103** 138
KLYBERG
  Albert T. **119** 318
KLYCE
  Stephen Downing
  100 111 177
KLYNTON
  John de **142** 236
KNACHBULL
  Anne **55** 209
  Joan **55** 209
  Richard **55** 209
KNAEBEL S. **136** 233
KNAGGS
  Elizabeth **57** 229
  Elizabeth (Connor)
  95 355
  Elizabeth Poellen **109** 70
  Emma Van Poelien
  95 354 355
  George **57** 229
  James **57** 229
  John **83** 444
  Thomas **57** 229
  Thomas Jackson
  Van Poelien **95** 355
  Whitmore **57** 229
  Wiliam **57** 229
KNAPP Knap Knop Knopp
  — Capt. **77** 158
  — Goody **145** 378
  ____ (Davis) **140** 57
  ____ (Fairservice) **140** 140
  Aaron **93** 97 **94** 209 **95** 209

KNAPP *cont'd*
  96 209 **97** 208 328 329
  98 209 **99** 177 **100** 178
  101 177 **102** 155 **103**
  157 **104** 169 **105** 156
  106 158 **107** 158 **108**
  236 **109** 157 **110** 155
  111 163 **112** 162 **113**
  160 **114** 157 **115** 156
  116 155 **125** 81
  Abby (Ball) **88** 342
  Abby Leah (Packer)
  90 167
  Abiah **51** 291 **115** 22
  Abiel **79** 246 **126** 116
  Abigail **94** 64 **123** 66 **124** 9
  Abigail (Westcott)
  108 290
  Abijah Cady **115** 108
  Abram **101** 234
  Adam **97** 327
  Ag. **147** 320
  Agnes **93** 228 **109** 222
  Albert W. **145** 74
  Alexander **112** 45
  Alexander Horace **112** 45
  Alfred Averill **89** 132 **94**
  399 **101** 335 **102** 317
  107 79 **108** 157 **111** 77
  117 73 **145** 75
  Alfred Merrill **124** 18
  Alfred Metcalf **102** 240
  Alice **147** 319 320 322
  Alice (Howlat) **147** 317
  318 323
  Alicia **147** 319
  Alvah Edward **94** 209
  Amy **147** 320
  Ann **52** 259 **58** 384 **108** 256
  115 22 **147** 316 318 320
  321 323
  Ann (Randall) **147** 320
  Ann Alexander
  (Woodbury) **97** 264
  Anna **72** 211 **147** 319
  Anna C. **69** 205
  Anne **54** 338 **55** 318 **56** 305
  108 255 256 **133** 307
  308 **147** 315 317-319 326
  Anne (Huntley) **101** 204
  Annie **109** 262
  Anthony **97** 264 354
  Arietta M. **76** 270
  Arthur Mason **54** 230 **63**
  386 **74** lxxi
  Arvilla **110** 322
  Barnabe **147** 319
  Benjamin **103** 60 **144** 337
  338 **145** 156
  Benjamin S. **112** 45
  Betsey **75** 34 **77** 158
  115 114
  Betsey (Cook) **97** 264
  Beulah **71** 265
  Caleb **121** 319
  Caroline (Brothwell)
  145 74
  Catherine **140** 31 **145** 156
  Catherine (Brothwell)
  145 74

KNAPP *cont'd*
  Catherine (Munnings)
  147 320
  Chandler **110** 322
  Charity **145** 156
  Charles **115** 114 115
  140 160
  Charles L. **88** 342
  Charles P. **142** 289
  Charlotte (Brothwell)
  145 74
  Chester P. **76** 53
  Chloe **79** 246
  Clara L. **103** 63
  Clarissa **87** 192
  D. H. **116** 210
  Daniel **71** 265
  David **114** 283 **117** 15
  129 272 **137** 361
  David Edgar **84** 189 232
  Deborah **109** 187
  Dorcas **147** 320
  Dorothy **65** 382 **147** 321
  Dwight **116** 63
  Ebenezer **57** 25 **111** 257
  145 75 156
  Edna **91** 106
  Edward **74** 295
  Eleanor **54** 338
  Elihu **101** 204
  Elijah **126** 116 **137** 361
  Elizabeth **57** 159 **59** 326 **72**
  210 211 **97** 357 **108** 251
  255-257 **137** 361 **147**
  315-321 323 325-327
  Elizabeth (Fayerweather)
  (Wilson) **144** 337 338
  145 156
  Elizabeth (McRay)
  145 156
  Elizabeth (Reade) **108** 256
  147 317 318 327
  Elizabeth (Warren)
  147 327
  Elizabeth Dixon **74** lxxi
  Elizabeth R. **58** 94
  Ella **90** 167
  Ellen **54** 338 **147** 319
  Elnathan **102** 240
  Elsie M. **116** 63
  Emeline **145** 74 75
  Emeline (Knapp) **145** 75
  Emily **54** 407
  Emm **147** 320
  Emma (Rich) **84** 126
  Emma L. **116** 63
  Emma Thompson **89** 184
  Ephraim **55** 111
  Esther **56** 142 **61** 285
  Etta (Raymond) **136** 268
  Eunice (Carver) **88** 225
  Eunice (Morehouse)
  145 74
  Ezekiel **144** 47
  Ezra **124** 9
  Ezra Fred **82** 384 **94** 399
  F. N. **110** 48
  Fanny **147** 86
  Florence C. **133** 32
  Florence R. **116** 63
  Floyd **116** 210

KNAPP *cont'd*
Frederick **116** 63 **137** 361
George **53** 434 438 **107** 79
   136 268 270 **140** 160
   147 319 320 322 323
George Brown **54** vi **55**
   vi xxix **56** vi xxx **57** vi
   xxxi **58** xliii **59** vi xxiv
   xli **60** vi xviii xxxiv **61**
   vi xvii **62** vi xix xxxv
   63 vi xviii 386 **64** vi
   xvii xxix **65** xxxiii **66**
   xlviii **67** xxx **68** xxx **69**
   xxx **71** xviii **74** xxxvii
   lxxi
Halsey Wing **90** 167
Hannah **55** 111 **72** 211 **97**
   354 **104** 72 **109** 185 **115**
   42 **124** 199 **126** 79
Hannah (Ferris) **109** 185
   187
Hannah (Jennings)
   145 74
Hannah (Maltby) **112** 45
Hannah (Smith) **121** 319
Henry **147** 321
Henry E. **112** 45
Hiram **63** 386 **74** lxxi
   116 63
Horatio **100** 187
Huldah **71** 265
Huldah (Fuller) **126** 79
Isaac **114** 278
Isaac Newton **97** 264
Isaiah **52** 78
Israel **72** 211 **137** 361
Jacob **115** 22 108 109
James **63** 274 **66** 187 **74**
   lxxi **108** 255 256 **140** 130
   145 74 **147** 316 318-321
   323 325-327
James M. **83** 299 303
Jane **147** 319
Jedediah **145** 75
Jedidiah **55** 260 **56** 142
Jefferey **147** 320
Jerusha **115** 109 **139** 317
Jerusha (Owen) (Mason)
   126 79
Jesse **55** 263
Jesse Maltby **112** 45
Joan **147** 319 321
Job **65** 382 **107** 79
John **52** 257 259 532 **55** 172
   62 155 **66** 187 **71** 102
   350 **74** lxxi **85** 455 **108**
   255 256 292 **109** 185 187
   126 170 **129** 272 **140**
   160 **145** 74 **147** 316-321
   323-327
John R. **58** 94
Jonah **58** 384
Jonathan **70** 36
Joseph **88** 225 **125** 88
Joseph J. **88** 338
Joshua **55** 318 **72** 211
Josiah **55** 421 **91** 266 **140**
   60 61 140 160 166
Judith **65** 90 **96** 296 **108**
   256 **147** 316 317 326 327
Judith (Tue) **147** 318 319

KNAPP *cont'd*
   323 324 328
Justin Willis **97** 158
Justus **126** 170
Katharine **63** 386
Lathrop **147** 258
Leonard **76** 267
Lewis G. **145** 379 **148** 41
Lizzie L. (Weeks) **83** 299
   303
Lucia Alden (Bradford)
   110 48
Lucinda **115** 22 108 109
Lucinda (Mann) **136** 270
Lucinda (Mason) **86** 311
Lucretia **58** 384 **140** 160
Lucy (Wheeler) **95** 67
   103 60
Luke **115** 22
Lydia **53** 398 **56** 33
   108 290
Lydia (McDonald)
   102 240
Lydia F. (King) **88** 338
Mabel Fidelia (Hale)
   97 158
Mabel Warren (Brown)
   115 150
Margaret **108** 255 256
   147 316-318 321-323
   326 327
Margaret (Allen) **147** 319
Margaret (Brand) **147** 320
Margaret (Deane) **108** 256
   147 317 327
Margaret (Kingsley)
   109 130
Margaret D. **100** 94
Margery **147** 319 322
Marie **54** 338 **147** 319
Martha **55** 421 **72** 211
   147 258
Mary **52** 432 **66** 333 **70** 36
   71 343 350 **72** 211 **82**
   291 **88** 83 **100** 314 **109**
   192 **135** 297 **140** 160
   147 316 319 322 326
Mary (Brown) **145** 74
Mary (Cooke) **147** 321
Mary (Fairservice) **91** 266
Mary (Hanion) **137** 361
Mary (Morris) **121** 319
   122 160 **123** 239
Mary (Upcher) **147** 319
Mary Lenore **102** 317
Maturah (Campbell)
   145 75
May Isabel **84** 29
Melina (Wilson) **126** 170
Melinda **58** 94
Minerva B. (Benchley)
   142 289
Minetta **74** 295
Molly **89** 39
Moses **55** 171 **62** 234 **64** 29
   108 290 **125** 88 **143** 11
Muriel **99** 148
Nancy **63** 274
Naomi **51** 290
Nathan **81** 313 **145** 161
   147 258

KNAPP *cont'd*
Nathaniel Fairweather
   145 156
Nehemiah **128** 54
Newcomb **121** 319 **122**
   160 **128** 312
Nicholas **72** 211 **82** 384
   93 97 **94** 209 399 **95** 209
   96 209 **97** 208 **98** 209
   99 177 **100** 178 **101** 177
   102 155 **103** 157 **104**
   169 **105** 156 **106** 158
   107 158 **108** 157 236
   109 157 **110** 155 **111** 77
   163 **112** 162 **113** 160
   114 157 **115** 156 **116**
   155 **124** 18 **136** 112 **145**
   75 **147** 327
Oliver **51** 189 **140** 130
   147 258
Oren S. **78** 91
Oscar F. **76** 270
Oswald Greenwaye
   66 287
Patience **114** 283 284
Patience (Rhodes)
   114 283
Paul K. **119** 155
Peter **122** 154
Phebe **124** 8 **125** 88
Phebe (Rawson) **124** 8 9
Philip **53** 438
Polly (Morris) **121** 319
   122 160 **123** 239 **128**
   312
Polly (Smith) **126** 170
Polly A. **145** 74
Prudence **52** 78 **72** 211
   96 387
R. W. **84** 126
Rachel **109** 192 **147** 320
   321
Rachel Ann **69** 170
Ransom **115** 22
Rebecca **66** 333 **72** 211 **90**
   53 **134** 335 **137** 362
Rhoda (Howland)
   140 129
Robert **108** 255 256 **147**
   316 319 320 322 323
Roger **93** 97 **94** 209 **95** 209
   96 209 **98** 209 **99** 177
   100 178 **101** 177 **102**
   155 **103** 157 **104** 169
   105 156 **106** 158 **107**
   158 **108** 236 **109** 157
   110 155 **111** 163 **112**
   162 **113** 160 **114** 157
   115 156 **116** 155
Rosanna **69** 205
Rose **108** 255-257 **147** 316
   317 320 327
Ruth **65** 382 **91** 182
S. B. **116** 210
Sally **81** 313 **107** 227
   145 74
Salome **121** 266 267
   147 319
Samantha **101** 234
Samuel **55** 171-175 **58** 236
   82 291 **105** 278 **125** 90

KNAPP *cont'd*
 137 361
 Samuel Isaac **112** 45
 Samuel L. **140** 57
 Sarah **52** 432 **53** 434 438 **54**
  338 **55** 260 **71** 265 **83** 77
  96 377 **97** 354 **114** 48
 Sarah (Adams) **124** 9
 Sarah (Butler) **111** 257
 Sarah (Young) **147** 327
 Sarah C. **62** 155
 Sarah E. **141** 47
 Sarah Pierce **81** 312
 Shepherd **65** xxxiv
  101 335
 Sidney Mills **109** 130
 Sophronia **74** lxxi
 Su. **147** 320
 Submit **55** 263
 Sumner **110** 322
 Susan **89** 91
 Susanna **54** 338 **87** 328
  137 361
 Susie (Bourne) **116** 63
 Sylvia **143** 14
 Tabitha **53** 59 **113** 133
 Terza **115** 22
 Thomas **93** 228 **108** 255-
  257 **117** 316 **321 323 327**
 Timothy **72** 211 **106** 177
 Titus **109** 192
 Uzzal **52** 78
 W. C. **128** 269
 William **53** 398 **54** 338
  63 386 **65** 90 **69** 170 205
  74 lxxi **93** 97 **94** 209 **95**
  209 **96** 209 296 **98** 209
  99 177 **100** 178 **101** 177
  102 155 **103** 157 **104**
  169 **105** 156 **106** 158
  107 158 **108** 236 255-
  257 **109** 157 **110** 155
  111 163 **112** 162 **113**
  160 **114** 157 **115** 156
  116 155 **121** 267 **147**
  315-327
 William H. **56** 22
 William L. **58** 94
 William Roger **97** 208
 Zephaniah Mayhew
  115 108
 Zilpah **106** 302
KNAPPEN Asa **73** 212
 Eliza A. **73** 212
 John R. **73** 212
 Sally **73** 212
 Sherebiah **73** 212
KNAPS Elijah **127** 141
KNATCHBULL Knatchball
 — Lady **52** 137
 Elizabeth **137** 295
 Katharine **137** 294
 Richard **137** 294
KNAUT Ann **127** 277
 Benjamin **125** 277 **128** 34
 Frederick Thomas **128** 34
 John Philip **127** 277
 Lewis Voster **128** 34
 Lucy (Collins) **127** 277
 Lucy (Hopkins) **128** 34
 Mary Elizabeth **128** 34

KNAUT *cont'd*
 Philip **54** 45 **67** 112
 Philip Augustus **127** 277
KNAUTH Fanny Elizabeth
  (Steyer) **119** 5
 Franz Theodor **82** 156
  119 5
 Selma **119** 5
KNECHT
 Ora (Lee) **109** 130
 William Peter **99** 147
  109 130
KNEEBONE
 Elizabeth **139** 305
KNEELAND —— **57** 337
  118 20 308
 — Mrs. **119** 140
 — Rev. **100** 142
 ___ (Sewall) **85** 131
 Abigail **92** 19
 Addie C. (Herrick) **89** 350
 Alva Belle **71** lxv
 Amasa **140** 304
 Ann **75** 213
 Augustus **84** 85
 Bartholomew **85** 131 **92**
  276 **115** 218 **140** 68 160
 Benjamin **81** 269
 Charlotte (Kidder)
  140 304
 Christopher **125** 288
 Claribel **123** 224
 Cynthia **102** 260
 D. Benjamin **80** 427
 Delia Frye **71** lxv
 Dwight **84** 85
 Ebenezer **129** 20
 Edward **85** 7 **117** 165 172
  123 18 20 24 26 27 29
 Edward (Mrs.) **117** 170
 Eliza A. **117** 164
 Elizabeth **85** 121
 Elizabeth (Alden) **104** 84
 Elizabeth (Green) **104** 84
 Elizabeth (Sedgwick)
  (Stevens) (Taylor)
  129 20
 Ellen **140** 304
 Emily F. **84** 85
 Hannah (Cook) **126** 83
 Hannah E. **84** 85
 Henry **93** 119 **123** 29
 Henry Wilton **91** 142
  119 148
 Ianthe **81** 187
 Isaac **126** 83
 James O. **117** 165
 Jane Amanda (Curtis)
  91 142 **119** 148
 Jane B. **117** 167
 Jane S. (Carlile) **117** 165
 John **55** 149 **61** 42 **68** 218
  84 373 **92** 19 **93** 160 263
  94 294 **104** 83 **119** 20
  131 235 236 **140** 160
  144 162 165
 John S. **89** 350
 Jonas **85** 121
 Joseph **124** 239 **144** 163
 Juliana **93** 119 **94** 157
 Lucinda **79** 36

KNEELAND *cont'd*
 Lucretia **84** 271
 Lydia **84** 257
 Martha **93** 263
 Martha (Hall) **85** 24
  95 364
 Mary **95** 364
 Mary (Green) **104** 83
  131 235
 Nancy **52** 188
 Nancy (Bent) **93** 119
 Oressa **117** 172
 Orissa R. (Billado)
  117 165
 Rachel **52** 199 201 **80** 427
  81 269
 Rebecca A. **117** 164
 Richard **68** 218 **85** 24
  95 364
 Ruth (Hartwell) **124** 239
 Ruth (Thayer) **125** 288
 S. **93** 119
 Sally **135** 336
 Sally (Baxter) **85** 7
 Samuel **61** 42 235 **84** 162
  259 261 372 **93** 119 **94**
  157 96 358 **104** 83 84 87
  110 317
 Sarah **131** 236
 Solomon **84** 257
 Stillman Foster **104** 92
 Susanna **140** 160
 Susanna (Sewall) **92** 276
 Timothy **84** 271 372
 Tryphena J. **82** 130
 William **110** 317 **113** 24
  116 110
 William Henry **71** lxv
KNEELON
 Charity Betsey **55** 372
KNELL
 Christiana **82** 377
 John **69** 362
 Phebe (Nichols) **143** 251
KNELLER
 Godfrey (Sir) **53** 298
KNEPPER
 Orlo Smith **87** 174
KNET Francis **65** 27
KNEVET —— **141** 94
KNEWSTEAD
 Mary **99** 117
KNEWSTUBBE —— **51** 127
KNIBBS —— **61** lxiv
KNIBLOE
 —— **102** 258 259
 Ralph **80** 110
 Rosanna W. **80** 110
KNICKERBOCKER
 — Bp. **74** 300
 — Col. **134** 62
 A. Jackson **90** 384
 Abraham **99** 193
 Almira **90** 384
 Betsey **90** 384
 Caroline **79** 153 **80** 66
 Charles **81** 495
 Cornelius **90** 384
 Delia Ann **90** 384
 Eliza Ann **90** 384
 Elizabeth **85** 218 **112** 316

KNICKERBOCKER *cont'd*
Elizabeth (Stickle) **90** 384
Frank **90** 384
Herman **115** 280 **137** 160
Hiram **90** 384
James **90** 384
Jane **99** 193
Jerome **90** 384
Jocomynte (Freer) **99** 193
John **79** 153 403 **80** 66 **99** 193 **105** 73
John C. **90** 384
Mahala **81** 495
Mary Ann **90** 384
Molly **99** 193
Nancy **68** 106
Nellie J. **78** 345
S. **91** 327
Sarah M. **90** 384
Tamma E. **90** 384
Walter **90** 384
William H. **78** 345
KNIFFEN Kniffin Kniffon
Asenath (Hopkins) **103** 309
Elizabeth **78** 125
George **108** 289
Hannah **104** 55
Jane **134** 255 334
John **103** 309
Nathan **134** 255
Samuel **81** 134
KNIGHT Knyght
— Capt. **85** 23
— Dr. **70** 314
— Judge **54** 436
— Mr. **68** 239
— Mrs. **51** 413 **58** 253
— Widow **71** 135
____ (Hiller) **140** 156
A. **104** 46
Aaron **88** 242
Abbie Elizabeth **97** 182
Abbie J. **84** 29
Abel **115** 45
Abia (Coffin) **133** 218
Abiah **65** 113 341 **90** 317
Abiah H. **91** 30 35
Abial **90** 243 **97** 19 20
Abial W. **95** 53
Abigail **61** 272 **70** 178 **83** 142 143 **88** 242 **96** 337 **102** 18 **103** 235 **144** 142
Abigail (Leigh) **94** 63
Abigail (Philbrook) **90** 329
Abigail (Wilson) **144** 142
Abijah **66** 21
Abraham **88** 242 **142** 300
Abraham A. **98** 196
Adaline E. **98** 196
Adelaide **89** 362 **90** 135 **104** 134 147
Adele Cordelia **85** 196
Adeline **78** 364
Adeline E. **98** 196
Agnes **74** 264
Albert **83** 142
Albert D. **69** 280 **84** 85
Alexander **56** 378 **142** 52
Alfred **81** 238 **82** 237 **113**

KNIGHT *cont'd*
147 228
Alice **70** 117 **84** 29 **92** 48 **95** 265 **102** 74 **144** 142
Alice (Huyck) **111** 304 305
Alice W. (Knight) **98** 258
Allie W. **98** 196
Almira **91** 117 **110** 153
Almira (Hamilton) **90** 334 **91** 117
Alpheus **68** 200
Alvin **91** 33
Amaziah **92** 48
Amos **55** 145 **114** 81
Andrew **90** 242 **128** 52
Andrew Charles **90** 243
Ann **52** 276 487 **68** 178 **70** 312 **87** 266 267 **126** 204 **144** 138 140 141
Ann (Goodwin) **94** 64
Ann (Manchester) **87** 270
Ann Maria (Junkins) **119** 279
Anna **56** 66 **57** 289-291 **64** 157 **87** 266 **90** 232 243 252 318 **92** 48 196 **102** 68
Anna (Follett) **103** 236
Anna (Knight) **90** 232 252
Anna Louisa **57** 291
Anna Woodbury **58** 94
Anne **51** 273 285 **86** 420 **87** 267
Anne (Condry) **94** 64
Annie E. **77** 180
Anthony **60** 197 **90** 327
Ariel B. **91** 384
Artemas **128** 43
Asa **90** 357
Asa M. **90** 55
Ashur **87** 387
Austin Melvin **77** xxviii 78
Azubah **57** 365
B. F. **62** 135
Barnard **52** 45
Barzillia **128** 55
Bathshua **53** 37 **55** 196
Benjamin **62** 126 **73** 174 **87** 269 270 387 **90** 357 **113** 229 **128** 54
Benjamin F. **97** 230
Bethiah **59** 83 **68** 142
Betsey **65** 114 **73** 174 **86** 286 **90** 229 249 317 329 **91** 22
Betsey (Barber) **83** 417
Betsey (Roberts) **91** 34
Betty **105** 50
Bridget **61** 83 **65** 217 **95** 265 **102** 74
Bridget (Sloper) **95** 265 **102** 74
Caleb **57** 282 290-292
Caroline **142** 300
Caroline O. **81** 249
Charles **91** 31 **94** 63 64 **98** 78 **102** 74 **144** 138 140 141
Charles Backus **57** 289
Charles Condry **94** 64

KNIGHT *cont'd*
Charles Donor **91** 39
Charles Henry **93** 122
Charles R. **89** 350
Charlotte **88** 238 **141** 199
Christian **144** 138 140 142
Cora **111** 305
Cornelia Russell **92** 249
Cornelia Spaulding (Davis) **87** 387
Cynthia **86** 19
Daniel **54** 393 395 **55** 251 252 **57** 284 **58** 280 **62** 80 **63** 169 **64** 41 **70** 215 **73** 174 314 **83** 142 143 145 **90** 252 318 **95** 52 265 **96** 146 **102** 74 **115** 223 305 **137** 325
Daniel R. **127** 33
David **53** 443 **70** 175 178 **87** 266 267 269 387 **113** 229 **127** 307
Deborah **53** 38 **77** 316 **95** 265 **102** 74
Deborah (Coffin) **121** 169
Deliverance **87** 256 267
Deliverance (Rolph) **87** 267
Deon **71** 135
Dinah **51** 303 **83** 293 **120** 252 253
Dorcas **65** 113 **80** 172 **88** 67 **90** 243 315 317 **91** 16 **128** 50 **138** 322
Dorcas (Lunt) **116** 132
Dorothy **88** 67
Dulcenia (Fletcher) **105** 226
E. W. (Mrs.) **84** 234
Earnest L. **121** 182
Ebenezer **54** 396 **55** 143-145 **59** 86 **90** 357 **92** 48 **106** 195
Edith Corrie (Robinson) **84** 172 **85** 190 **105** 68 132
Edmund **51** 119 **88** 67 **94** 63
Edward **60** 284 **66** 316
Edward Boardman **90** 357
Edward E. **93** 108
Edward Everett **93** 120
Edward Joseph Dexter **89** 291 292
Edward Quintus **84** 172 **85** 190 **105** 68 132
Edward Wallace **85** 195
Elbridge G. **89** 350
Eleanor **82** 286 291 **87** 267 **131** 131
Eleanor (Hudson) **102** 18
Elijah **56** 394
Elijah W. **83** 143
Elisha **55** 144 **56** 63 **70** 216 217 **147** 54
Eliza **89** 205 206 **98** 196 **116** 134
Eliza (Bagley) **90** 330 **91** 21
Eliza (Munn) **89** 206

KNIGHT *cont'd*
Elizabeth **53** 20 37 **55** 196
56 63 368 **58** 129 130
298 **59** 56 **61** 83 **70** 226
74 209 **75** 31 **82** 291 292
298 302 **90** 185 **95** 265
102 74 142 **106** 92 **110**
30 114 **131** 121 **134** 253
142 110 **144** 141
Elizabeth (Conkey)
111 64
Elizabeth (Cutler) **137** 325
Elizabeth (Leach) **113** 229
Elizabeth (Shapleigh) **95**
265 **102** 73 74
Elizabeth Ann (Coates)
111 226
Elizabeth Jane **81** 249
Elizabeth Powers **94** 64
Elizabeth Russell (Chase)
94 63
Ella Joanna (Waters)
113 228
Ella Perley **82** 277
Ellen M. **90** 36
Ellen P **77** 146 **117** 286
Emily **103** 261
Emily H **90** 397
Emily Hanson **89** 291
Emily Jane **133** 218
Emma **105** 226 **131** 128
Emma C. **89** 204
Emma D. **83** 299 300
Emma Jane E. **69** 280
84 85
Emma Reed **89** 291
105 226
Enoch **83** 225 **136** 266
Enos **90** 357
Ephraim **59** 283 **114** 81
Ernest **117** 286
Esther **52** 276 **141** 199
Esther (Fairbanks)
137 325
Esther (Ross) **96** 344
Eunice **90** 329 **91** 19 30 35
118 118
Eunice (Carll) **90** 232 252
Ezekiel **52** 276
Ezra **129** 65
Faithful **75** 102
Fanny **59** 35 **94** 379
Flavilla **96** 179
Foster **91** 200
Frances **85** 193 **91** 117
Francis **121** 241
Francis Parkman **93** 119
Francis T. **77** 180
Fred Turner **107** 133
Frederic **94** 64
Frederic Irving **94** 64
Frederic William **92** 255
George **58** 94 298 **59** 56 **74**
209 **76** 176 **88** 238 **89**
274 **90** 237 **95** 265 **96**
344 **102** 74 **103** 260
George A. **98** 111
George Allen **92** 251
George C. **103** 45
George Everett **98** 258
George H. **54** 358 **104** 102

KNIGHT *cont'd*
George Perry **81** 249
George W. **98** 258
Gertrude Mary **117** 204
Gideon **55** 251 252
Giles **66** 191
Grace **67** 346 **98** 78
Grace Bayeux (Lazell)
89 325
Grifin **64** 107
Grindal **74** 212 213 **82** 83
324 **83** 155 **144** 142
H. (Cross) **83** 19
Hannah **53** 37 **55** 48 144
56 255 **65** 114 **66** 339
68 168 **73** 191 **75** 47 83
293 **85** 418 419 **87** 122
203 268 269 **88** 238 **90**
242 243 248 333 **91** 26
27 32 **102** 184 185 **103**
298 **142** 300
Hannah (Beaman) **114** 81
Hannah (Bryant) **137** 324
325
Hannah (Day) **95** 194 200
Hannah (Drown) **97** 19
20
Hannah (Jewett) **87** 387
113 229
Hannah (Nobel) **95** 191
Hannah (Teal) **116** 303 305
Hannah (Townsend)
(Hull) (Allen) **102** 177-
179 187 263
Hannah (Warren) **91** 33
Hannah E. **98** 196
Hannah Elizabeth (White)
90 357
Hannah Norris **73** 204
Hannah W. **98** 196
Harriet Helen **89** 182
Harriet Hieatt (Black)
113 229
Helen **103** 236
Helen L. **89** 205
Helen M. (Stowell) **103** 45
Henry **51** 261 **103** 268
128 54
Henry Potter **78** 364
Hepzibah **55** 197 **97** 14
Hepzibah K. **91** 31
Hiram **54** 126
Hudson **88** 67
Inez V. **121** 182
Irene **88** 168
Isaac **54** 216 **58** 280 **63** 286
65 148 **66** 338 **71** 139
142 143 **88** 238 **89** 274
Isaac Chandler **88** 240
Israel **127** 310
J. **57** 359 **58** 94
J. J. Howard **148** 250
Jacob **63** 235
James **60** lxix 36 **78** 111 **80**
308 **90** 234 236 317 **94**
64 **116** 303 305 **133** 218
James D. **114** 191
James R. **92** 249 251
94 379
Jane **51** 119 **65** 47 **90** 317
Jane (Carle) **90** 234 236

KNIGHT *cont'd*
133 218
Jane D. **115** 122
Jane F. **63** 50
Jennie **97** 358
Jennie (Hannum) **91** 39
Jennie Victoria **58** lxx
Jeremiah **128** 52
Jerusha **53** 443 **126** 180
Jesse **95** 399
Jesse William **95** 399
Jewell B. **103** 127
Jno **125** 94
Joan **148** 120
Joanna **53** 201 377 **59** 283
78 301
Job **128** 55
Joel **56** 255 **61** 22
John **51** 44 45 **52** 261 **53** 37
55 143 144 196 312 316
56 85 **57** 280 351 388 **58**
49 249-252 **60** 357 **61** 83
62 321 **63** 143 **64** 223
322 **67** 347 **70** 246 311
73 174 191 201 204 314
74 127 212 213 215 225
227 **82** 83 211 213 317
320 323 325 510 **83** 12
293 **84** 29 153 238 261
86 82 **87** 265-269 353
88 359 **91** 113 **92** 60 **95**
200 265 **100** 218 **102** 74
103 260 **105** 215 **111**
172 **114** 81 **115** 220 **124**
240 **126** 7 **133** 216 **141**
199 **142** 66 **144** 140-142
148 120
John A. **68** 168
John M **73** 225
Jonathan **59** 83 **65** 113 341
68 142 **87** 266-269 **90**
317 **128** 49 50 294 **133**
218 **145** 149
Joseph **52** 431 **53** 38 **54**
98 393-395 **55** 143 144
56 200 **57** 351 **58** 402
59 412 **60** 197 252 386
61 406 **63** xlvii **65** 114
70 263 **74** 215 253 83
365 **85** 12 **87** 269 387 **90**
397 **95** 194 200 **113** 229
114 81 **121** 169 125 92
127 312 137 325 **144**
142
Joseph R. **89** 292 **90** 397
92 255
Joseph Roberts **89** 291
292
Josephine **89** 291
Josephine Louisa
(Webster) **89** 362
Joshua **73** 314 **90** 334 **91**
117 229 **116** 7
Joshua Cree **58** 280
Josiah **88** 238
Josiah W. **122** 16
Judah **74** 227
Judith **53** 38 **98** 220 **121**
169 **133** 216
Julia **89** 206
Julia A. (Rider) **89** 206

KNIGHT *cont'd*
Julia Ann **89** 206
Julia M. **88** 342
Kate **98** 197
Keziah **68** 168
L. B. **98** 258 **120** 69 137 139
Laura (Jones) **113** 229
Laura M. **91** 38
Laura M. (Edson) **121** 182
Lawrence **73** 198
Lendall **98** 196
Levi **89** 205 206 **145** 168
Levi S. **89** 206
Lewis **142** 300
Lillie Blanch (Collum)
  107 133
Lizzie F. (Robbins) **91** 384
Lizzie W. **98** 258
Loice **119** 136
Lois (Hawke) **90** 357
Loren **111** 305
Louisa **57** 290
Louisa (Hobbs) **91** 32
Louisa Armistead
  (Appleton) **94** 64
Louisa Villiers Westcott
  (Tucker) **134** 89
Love **72** 5
Lucie Fisher **81** 221
Lucina Slocum
  (Comstock) **134** 89
Lucinda G. (Pitts) **91** 120
  124
Lucinda R. **88** 338
Lucy **78** 314 **90** 326 **91** 17
Lucy (Mills) **91** 113
Lucy A. (Post) **147** 54
Lucy Belle (Lazell) **89** 118
Lucy Blanchard **126** 143
Lucy D. (Eaton) **94** 64
Lurana **87** 269
Luther **114** 81
Luther B. **98** 258
Luther D. **98** 196
Lydia **63** 176 **73** 314 **74**
  259 264 **88** 238 **90** 243
  348 397
Lydia (Cleverly) **137** 326
Lydia (Goodhue) **97** 182
Lydia Elizabeth **89** 291
Lydia G. **90** 397
Lydia G. (Dexter) **89** 291
Lydia H. **68** 258
M. C. **88** 304 **114** 81
Mabel F. **87** 162 **88** 165
Mabel Frances **80** 333
  81 214
Magdalena **111** 74 75
Mamie C. **99** 246
Manassah **92** 358 **93** 60
  119 120 122 **94** 41 157
  140 156
Marcia W. **69** 280 **84** 85
Margaret **65** 351 **70** 178
  83 488 **132** 327 **144** 138
  140 142
Margaret (Emery) **90** 237
  138 321
Margaret (Peabody)
  90 357
Margery **96** 397 **131** 128

KNIGHT *cont'd*
Maria (Junkins) **119** 279
Marietta G. **84** 85
Mark **107** 317 **119** 279
Martha **114** 146 **144** 138
  140 142
Martha (Angell) **87** 268
Martha Cordelia (Clark)
  87 387
Martin **68** 200
Mary **51** 464 **52** 276 **53** 37
  54 xcvi xcvii 395 396 **55**
  143-145 316 **57** 353 **59**
  86 **60** 197 386 **61** 22 83
  63 xlvii **64** 41 **70** 231 **74**
  225 **78** 25 **82** 83 320 **83**
  12 **87** 269 270 **88** 240
  250 **89** 357 **90** 318 **92** 48
  93 365 **95** 265 **102** 74
  103 67 **114** 81 **117** 221
  222 **124** 240 **144** 138
  140-142
Mary (Adams) **87** 387
Mary (Bartoll) **144** 142
Mary (Bruce) **141** 247
Mary (Clark) **90** 237
Mary (Dana) **85** 195
Mary (Dugloss) **107** 317
Mary (Ford) **90** 237
Mary (Lord) **83** 12
Mary (Philbrick) **91** 32
Mary (Potter) **109** 195
Mary (Pray) **90** 325
Mary A. (Shannon)
  99 246
Mary Ann **110** 230
Mary Baker **89** 27
Mary Edith **83** 231 **87** 387
  88 87 176
Mary Ethel **83** 233 **89** 82
  137 **90** 357
Mary Hathorne **145** 298
Mary J. **104** 102
Mary Jane **89** 206
Mary Pratt (Frissell)
  87 387
Mary Ruth (Chandler)
  122 16
Mary T. **126** 22
Matthew **92** 48
Mehitable **90** 318 **91** 229
  112 143
Melinda (Adams) **90** 357
Melissa **91** 117
Mercy **55** 429
Mira Emma **105** 226
Miriam **90** 318
Miriam (Andrews) **90** 252
  96 146
Moody **98** 196 **142** 300
Moses **65** 352 **87** 125 **90**
  230 250 **115** 293
Nabby **102** 18
Nabuchodonizer **70** 115
  117
Nancy **75** lxxiii **93** 119
  94 157
Nancy (Hamilton) **91** 33
Nancy M. (Hersey) **90** 55
Narissa E. (Goodwin)
  83 20

KNIGHT *cont'd*
Nathan **51** 44 **55** 143 **58**
  249 393 **105** 286 287
Nathaniel **55** 368 **65** 353
  73 314 **83** 417 **84** 404
  90 232 252 329 **105** 285
  286
Needham **114** 81
Nehemiah **102** 18 **127** 5
  128 52
Nicholas **95** 265 **102** 74
Olive **55** 312 316 **65** 114 **74**
  100 215 225 227 **82** 323
  510 **83** 12 **86** 19 **90** 317
  325 **91** 16 229 **116** 134
  133 218 **138** 322
Olive (Hamilton) **133** 216
Olive E. **91** 30 35 **97** 228
Olive F. (Smith) **97** 230
Olive J. **89** 359
Olive Martha (Morton)
  89 119
Otis **98** 197
Pamelia Williams
  (Nutting) (Holbrook)
  89 291 292
Patience **63** 169
Patience (Gary) **115** 305
Patience (Smith) **95** 265
  102 74
Paul **53** 40
Peggy **65** 114
Persis **57** 365
Peter **67** 346
Phebe **73** 174 **74** 263
  88 242 276
Philip **57** 351 **90** 357 **128**
  50 **131** 128
Polly **57** 284 **65** 114 **68** 200
  73 174 **90** 242 317 326
  91 17 **99** 324
Polly (Clark) **96** 338
Porter **91** 120 124
Preston **105** 226
Priscilla **65** 353 **87** 266
  95 76
Prudence **73** 174
Rachel **66** 338 339 **87** 269
  142 66
Rebecca **51** 261 **54** 396 **55**
  144 **75** 151 **86** 335 **87**
  266 **115** 293
Rebecca E. (Rowe) **89** 350
Rebecca Willard **59** 369
Rena **105** 286
Reuben **58** 280 **99** 246
  128 55
Rhoda Lathrop **60** lxix
Rhoda May **60** lxix
Richard **56** 378 **60** 186 **68**
  178 **80** 449 **81** 444 **84**
  238 **85** 392 **87** 256 264-
  268 270 353 387 **94** 237
  102 179 184-186 188
  106 18 19 **113** 229 **117**
  204 **120** 252 253 **123** 35
  128 53 **143** 38
Richard F. **78** 178
Richard H. **122** 284
Richard Payne **92** 96
Robert **52** 276 **55** 310 **62**

KNIGHT *cont'd*
  322 **65** 32 **76** 237 **87** 268
  269 **89** 362 **96** 279 280
  109 195 **128** 49 52 **144**
  138-142
  Robert Cranmer **89** 325
  Robert Lippitt **89** 362
  Robert Whiting **144** 138
  Roger **61** 83
  Rosamond **65** 352
  Rosannah F. **126** 220
  Rose E. (Billings) **98** 111
  Rufus **91** 32
  Russell **55** 429 **56** 388
  141 246-248
  Ruth **55** 143 144 **60** 252
  85 33 **92** 48 **137** 326
  147 275
  Ruth (Gray) **142** 110
  Ruth (Hyde) **87** 387
  Ruth E. (James) (Johnson)
  127 33
  Ruthy **74** 209
  S. A. **98** 258
  Sally **55** 51 **74** 260 **87** 10
  90 243 317 **91** 26 31 **114**
  81 **127** 67 **142** 300
  Sally (Mills) **91** 31
  Sally E. **91** 31
  Salome **96** 342
  Samuel **61** 22 **66** 338 339
  73 174 **74** 264 **97** 182
  102 74 **111** 64
  Samuel B. **81** 249
  Sarah **54** 393-395 **55** 143
  144 197 **63** xlvii **66** 316
  338 **76** 192 **80** 26 **81** 190
  84 402 **87** 123 265 266
  268 269 **90** 317 326 **91**
  16 369 **92** 48 **94** 196 **95**
  265 **102** 74 **106** 92 144
  110 224 **111** 64 **115** 35
  293 **124** 166 167 **126** 18
  136 56 **137** 325 **138** 322
  144 141
  Sarah (Backus) **87** 269 387
  113 229
  Sarah (Hale) **94** 63
  Sarah (Kemble) **84** 402
  124 166 **143** 38 364
  Sarah (Lemon) **144** 141
  Sarah (Richardson)
  137 325
  Sarah (Rogers) **87** 264 387
  113 229
  Sarah (Sabin) **113** 229
  Sarah (Thompson) **95** 265
  102 74
  Sarah A. **98** 258 **106** 318
  Sarah Augusta **89** 291
  Sarah Hosmer **93** 119
  Sarah Jane **90** 335 **91** 24
  Sarah V. **89** 274
  Sarah Waldo **78** 205
  Sarah Waldo (Lippett)
  89 362 **90** 140
  Sarah Ward **118** 75
  Sewall **88** 238
  Sheldon C. (Mrs.) **118** 244
  Shem **90** 318
  Silas **62** 132

KNIGHT *cont'd*
  Simeon **65** 114 **90** 237 317
  91 32-34 **138** 321
  Simeon C. **97** 224
  Solomon **88** 238 240 250
  89 357 **103** 298 **145** 356
  Solomon (Mrs.) **103** 298
  Sophia Purkitt **94** 41
  Stephen **55** 144 **65** 114
  90 317 325 330 **91** 21
  116 138 **128** 55
  Susan E. (Camp) **93** 108
  Susanna **52** 431 **55** 144
  249 310 **59** 56 **74** 45 **76**
  176 **82** 78 **95** 265 **102** 74
  114 81 **136** 166
  Susanna (Barton) **84** 404
  Susanna (Chesley) **95** 265
  102 74
  Susanna (Lord) **144** 142
  Susanna (Maynard)
  114 81
  Susanna (Smith) **90** 230
  250
  Susie Maria (Rice)
  103 176
  Sylvester **134** 89
  Tabitha (Sanderson)
  128 43
  Temperance **102** 74
  Temperance (Pickering)
  95 265 **102** 74
  Thankful **74** 253
  Theloma **90** 243
  Thomas **55** 144 310 **56** 63
  58 130 **59** 194 **67** 343
  73 314 **79** 167 **85** 392
  90 232 242 243 252 **91**
  327 **95** 191 **97** 146 273
  100 218 **103** 12 **105** 285
  111 226 **113** 229 **114** 81
  Thomas B. **79** 42
  Thomas Benton **65** 201
  Toby **87** 266
  Truelove (Corbett)
  (Adams) **88** 359
  Uarda **101** 124
  Valentine **100** 218
  Vernon **113** 229
  W. L. **73** 212
  Walter **79** 445 **142** 110
  Walter Charles **102** 124
  Walter de **142** 236
  Walter Tracy **57** 289
  Warren **73** 174
  Webster **89** 362 **90** 140
  104 147
  Webster (Mrs.) **77** 323
  78 205 **83** 217 **84** 186
  89 362 **90** 79 135
  Wilhurta **100** 110
  William **52** 487 **53** 201 377
  70 245 263 **80** 410 **88**
  242 281 **100** 218 **102** 74
  113 229 **115** 56 **116** 132
  127 115 **128** 55 **131** 128
  137 325 **140** 160 **144**
  142 **145** 354
  William A. **77** 146
  William B. **59** 369
  William D. **111** 304 305

KNIGHT *cont'd*
  William Henry **113** 228
  229
  William Kirk **87** 387
  William L. **98** 196
  William Scott **89** 118
  Zachariah **145** 47
  Zebulon **90** 237 318 **105**
  114 **123** 74 75
  Zilpha **86** 448 **109** 195
KNIGHT-SMITH Alice
  Webb (Scott) **84** 453
  Reginald **84** 453
KNIGHTBRIDGE
  Jessie Mary **125** 165
KNIGHTERS
  William **52** 236
KNIGHTINGALL
  Berthya **106** 30
KNIGHTLEY Knightly
  Eleanor (Throckmorton)
  98 114
  John **51** 417
  Margaret **142** 230
  Margery **142** 229 232
  Richard **98** 114
  Valentine (Sir) **94** 339
KNIGHTON
  ⸺ **68** 361 **141** 97
  Elizabeth **94** 256 259 265
  332 338 340 341
  Elizabeth (Twigden) **94**
  254 256 259 324 332
  Jane Ann **147** 233
  Mabel **94** 254 265
  Mary **73** 232
  Richard **71** 325
  Samuel **73** 152 278
  Thomas **94** 254 255 257
  258 265 273 337 338 340
  Thompsey **73** 152
  Twigden **94** 254 265 272
  William **71** 327 **94** 254
  264 272 273 324 332 337
  340
KNIGHTS
  ⸺ Mr. **62** 22 24
  ⸺ Mrs. **62** 23
  Amanda **56** 249
  Amasa **56** 250
  Asahel **56** 249
  Betsey (Roberts) **97** 224
  Chloe **135** 73
  Eleanor (Pepper) **88** 281
  Elijah **54** 291 293 **56** 253
  Elisha **54** 294 **56** 249 250
  254
  Elizabeth **144** 215
  Hannah (Noble) **95** 191
  Harriet **126** 205
  Inez V. **121** 182
  Isaac **144** 218 219
  Judith **98** 220
  M. **62** 21
  Margery **96** 397
  Mary **92** 48 **93** 365
  Mercy **54** 291 293 **56** 253
  388
  Mercy (Tibbetts) **99** 247
  Nabby (Ford) **95** 200
  Olive (Hill) **90** 327

KNIGHTS cont'd
Olive (Tibbetts) **99** 247
Peter R. **142** 27 **147** 386
Phebe **54** 294 **56** 249 250
   254 **88** 276
Phebe Root **56** 249
Prince H. **62** 133
Ruth **147** 275
Silas **62** 24
Simeon **54** 293
William **88** 281
KNIGHTSBRIDGE
William **84** 309
KNIPE
Abby R. **125** 245
Amanda Elizabeth
   78 280 281
Conrad **78** 281
Elizabeth **78** 281
KNISKERN
Johann Peter **115** 76
Walter Hamlin **115** 76
KNISLEY Catherine (Nolte)
   113 323
George **113** 323
Mary (Kauffman) **113** 323
Samuel **113** 323
KNITTLE Walter Allen **91**
   210 **118** 177
KNIVETON
—— **141** 97 99
Ann (Dethick) **141** 100
Barbara **141** 100
Jane (Leeche) **141** 100
John **141** 100
Margaret (Montgomery)
   141 100
KNIVETT — Lady **141** 319
KNOBLACH
Mary Eva **80** 149
KNOBLOE —— **102** 259
KNOCK Knocke
Betty **123** 69
Elizabeth **55** 311
Hannah **90** 253
Henry **119** 109
Thomas **76** 240
Knocks see Knox
KNODLE Knodel
Benjamin **118** 57
Elizabeth **84** 373
Jacob **84** 373
KNOES — Mr. **54** 183
KNOKSTUBB Hugh **71** 21
KNOKYN Lucy Strange de
   111 198
Knoles see Knowles
KNOLL Thomas **143** 202
KNOLLENBERG
Bernhard **106** 238
KNOLLER
George **76** 68 71
Mary **76** 68 71
Knolles see Knowles
KNOLLIN Emily Hayman
   72 xxxvii
Knollys see Knowles
Knolton see Knowlton
KNONER R. C. **82** 375
KNOPF Alfred A. **106** 319
   108 78 **148** 184

Knopp see Knapp
KNOTT Knot Knotte
— Mr. **71** 190
Anne **51** 424 **94** 322
Celia Crocker Turner
   62 lxii
Clarence Blossom **62** lxii
Clement **73** 263
Dorothy **83** 119
Eleanor **74** 118
Elizabeth **73** 220 **74** 118
Eunice Blossom **62** lxii
Eustace R. **62** lxii
George **54** 354
George Washington
   106 125
Hannah **74** 116 118 220
James Edward **62** lxii
James Reynolds **62**
   xlviii lxi lxii
Jams **62** lxi lxii
Joan **131** 123
John **82** 191
John Henry **86** 150
Lillie (Uzzell) **106** 125
Louis Ernest **62** lxii
Margaret **51** 424
Marie **82** 189
Martha **62** lxii **115** 91
Martha Jane **86** 150
Mercy **51** 424
N. W.T. **62** lxii
Rachel Jane (Parker)
   86 150
Richard **74** 116 118 200
   83 119 **99** 103 **109** 206
Sarah **65** lxi
Thomas **51** 424 **52** 129 **60**
   400 **62** lxii
Thomas (Sir) **100** 15
Tina Spencer **109** 315
William **80** 403
KNOTTSFORD
Jane **93** 5 6
John **93** 5 6
KNOTTYNGESLEY
Isabel **109** 23
John **109** 23 28
KNOUS F. F. **59** xliv
KNOW Sarah (Perrin)
   96 267
William **88** 281
William B. **91** 327
KNOWER Knowhor
Abigail (Whittemore)
   107 180
Daniel **92** 51 54 **107** 180
Elizabeth **106** 33 **131** 128
George **106** 31 33 **131** 128
John **92** 49
Jonathan **92** 47 53 **107** 180
Mary **106** 33
Mary (Johnson) **107** 180
Noll **131** 128
Phebe **108** 87
Ruth Cornelia **108** 309
Sarah **106** 34 **108** 309
Thomas **92** 47 **131** 13 128
   143 28
KNOWLAND
Frederick **78** 92

KNOWLAND cont'd
James **127** 56
Josephine **78** 92
Margaret **127** 56
Patrick **127** 56
Peggy **127** 56
Sarah Cadwalader **78** 92
KNOWLDEN
Giles **65** 179
KNOWLE Nancy (Colby)
   125 112
KNOWLEN Elisa **120** 16
Henry **120** 16
KNOWLER
— Mr. **81** 428
John **75** 221
Mary **81** 428
Richard **81** 428
Sarah **81** 428
William **81** 428
KNOWLES Knoles
   Knolles Knollys
   Knowels Knowls
   Knowols
—— **52** 101 **54** lvii **59** 259
   84 133 **88** 38 129 133
   136 139 **89** 75 **91** 327 **92**
   284 **100** 187 **108** 211
   109 43 44 **143** 202
— Dr. **86** 399
— Mr. **73** 72 **80** 14
— Rev. Mr. **71** 190
— Widow **58** 29 36
   80 16 127
—— (Allen) **88** 37
—— (DeWolfe) **88** 38
—— (Lee) **88** 139
Abbie **88** 44 **123** 119
Abbie (Knowles) **123** 119
Abbie Frances **86** 96 197
   204
Abby **88** 44 45 131 135
Abby (Hazard) **88** 45
Abby F. **88** 140
Abiathar **80** 12 124 **105**
   290 **120** 238
Abigail **58** 36 **59** 191 **65**
   355 **75** 187 **80** 6-8 13 18
   19 21 22 121 123 124 127
   128 265 266 272 **88** 35
   36 **122** 105 **127** 98 **135**
   35
Abigail (Freeman) **86** 96
Abigail (Hall) **84** 42
Abigail (Seagar) **88** 35
Abigail (Smith) **88** 43
Abigail (Wilcox) **88** 41
Abigail D. **123** 120
Abigail M. **123** 122 200
Abigail W. (Kragman)
   123 203
Abner **80** 124 **87** 235
   145 365
Abraham **80** 16 127 **88** 42
   89 89
Abraham Remick **80** 16
   17
Achsah **80** 123 124
Adelaide F. **88** 137
Albert A. **88** 136
Albert Isaac **120** 238

KNOWLES *cont'd*
Albert S. **120** 238 239
Alexander **79** 287 288 **87**
359 **88** 135
Alfred **88** 44 139
Alice **79** 386 **80** 8 9 12 23
87 364 365 **88** 42 129
133
Alice (Doane) **123** 118
Alice (Fish) **87** 128 364
104 251
Alice Hall **103** 119 **113** 233
Alice Smith (Randall)
88 140
Allen H. **59** 160 **108** 261
123 199
Almania **123** 121
Almira **123** 198
Alonzo **88** 131
Amasa **80** 123 124 **91** 237
Amelia Chapman (Thorp)
88 296
Amos **58** 34 **79** 291 296
297 389 390 **80** 22 123
265 266 268-270 277 278
106 72 **143** 160
Amy **80** 128 **88** 36 140
Amy (Peck) **88** 139
Amy (Power) **88** 138
Amy Ann **88** 139
Ann **79** 287 379 380 **80** 6
7 17 19 **83** 394 **88** 35 36
38 43 133 **105** 34
Ann (Doane) **86** 96
Ann (Hull) **88** 34 **104** 251
Ann (Kenyon) **88** 136
Ann (Lyon) **88** 141
Ann (Power) **88** 138
Ann E. **88** 136
Ann Elizabeth (Clarke)
92 61
Anna **80** 10 14 18 **88** 39
41 42 139 **89** 89 **123** 120
Anna (Doane) **86** 96
Anna (Fisk) **89** 89
Anna (Kenney) **108** 215
Anna Almy **88** 131
Anna Deblois (Swift)
64 lxix
Anna F. **89** 89
Anna Freeman **80** 19
Anna Whitman **88** 132
Anne **80** 7 **93** 25
Anne Smith **88** 139
Annie **88** 130
Annie (Browning) **88** 36
Ansel **80** 16
Antis **88** 37
Antries **88** 37
Apphia **79** 293
Apphia (Bangs) **86** 96
Arabella (Mosher) **88** 129
Arnold **88** 39
Arthur T. **79** 286
Asa **80** 120 **88** 130 **89** 89
Augusta **83** 426 433
Augustus **88** 134
Augustus G. Hazard
88 45
Avis (Stanton) **88** 39
Azubah **79** 382 **80** 7 9 121

KNOWLES *cont'd*
122 **111** 156
Azubeth **123** 198
Barbara **79** 290 293
126 238
Barnabas Freeman **80** 22
124 271 **88** 131 **123** 119
Barney **88** 129
Bathsheba **80** 14 **88** 35 42
Bathsheba (Segar) **88** 41-
43 135 **104** 250
Benjamin **80** 6 8 9 22 23 **87**
334 **88** 38-40 131 141
123 118 204
Benjamin Franklin
88 131
Benjamin G. **88** 135
Benjamin Rodman **88** 43
Benjamin Stanton **88** 135
Bertram **88** 129
Bessie **88** 130
Bethiah **79** 381 **80** 8 14 20
21 23 119 **123** 117
Bethiah (Bangs) **123** 119
Betsey **61** 346 **78** 363 **80**
10 16 18 21 120 123 **88**
141 **123** 119
Betsey (Dimock) **88** 129
99 298
Betsey (Doane) **86** 96
123 121
Betsey (Gill) **123** 119
Betsey (Knowles) **123** 119
Betsey A. **78** 183
Betsey A. (Collins)
123 118
Betsey Atkins **80** 10
Betsey C. (Atwood)
123 203
Betsey C. (Higgins)
123 204
Betsey C. (Mayo) **123** 124
Betty **80** 7 8 **123** 117
Beulah **87** 225 233
Bial **109** 43
Bial (Marchant) **108** 262
C. S. **93** 376
Caleb **80** 18 **84** 42 **88** 135
Calvin **88** 131
Carl A. (Mrs.) **77** 323
Caroline **59** 160
Caroline (Brown) **123** 124
Caroline (Gill) **123** 202
Caroline (Pineo) **88** 38
Caroline D. **108** 261
Catherine **80** 15 16 **88** 38
131
Catherine E. (Collins)
88 131
Catherine Fry **88** 131
Catherine P. (Ingham /
Ingraham) **123**
123 200
Cecilia **117** 51
Celia **88** 133
Charles **65** 148 **70** 7 **79** 391
392 **80** 120 122 271-274
279 **87** 359 **88** 37 129
130 **91** 206 **94** 95 **100** 65
108 215 **132** 27-30
Charles Edwin **87** 66

KNOWLES *cont'd*
Charles F. **88** 137
Charles Hamilton **88** 129
Charles W. **88** 130
Charlotte **109** 183
Chester Lasell **89** 28 29
Chloe **80** 124
Christian **80** 15
Christopher Columbus
78 363
Church **88** 38
Clara Belle **112** 140
Clark **80** 16
Clifford Henry **88** 130
Comfort **88** 90 91
Comfort (Wallis) **88** 90
Concurrence **80** 13
Cornelius **79** 297 386 388
389 **80** 15 119 129 130
102 59 **114** 10 **126** 166
128 29
Cyrus Blake **84** 133
Daniel **80** 14 16 **87** 363-365
88 33 34 36 37 40 43 45
90 132 133 135 138 **89**
89 **128** 128
Daniel A. **104** 297
Daniel C. **91** 327
Daniel P. **88** 43
Daniel S. **88** 135
Daniel Wilber **88** 129
David **58** 17 **73** 232 **79** 390
80 10 21 272 **87** 66 **88**
40 130 **89** 89 **95** 92 **147**
8
David C. **76** 33
David Fisk **89** 89
David M. **119** 315 319
122 79
Deborah **80** 14 128 **88** 37
131
Deborah (Billings) **98** 7
Deborah (Carpenter)
88 40
Deborah (Palmer) **87** 66
Delia Collins **84** 295
Deliverance **65** 353 **80** 267-
269 **88** 37
Desire **80** 7
Diana **88** 44
Didamia **80** 10
Dilla **80** 13
Dorcas **80** 124 **88** 43 44
Dorcas (Gardiner) **88** 44
Dorcas (Northrup) **88** 43
Dorcas (Tillinghast)
88 132
Duncan **88** 38
Ebbie **88** 135
Ebenezer **88** 43 **128** 125
Ebenezer D. **88** 40
Edgar T. **88** 133
Edmund **64** 345
Edmund F. **123** 204
Edna Watson (Kelley)
88 141
Edward **79** 292 295 379-
381 **80** 6-9 11 19 266-
268 272 **86** 96 **87** 359 **88**
36 38 130 137 138 141
113 114 **123** 119 122

KNOWLES *cont'd*
200 **127** 224
Edward L. **88** 140
Edward Peck **88** 139 140
Edward Randall **88** 140
Edwin **88** 132
Edwin A. **88** 137
Edwin Clarke **88** 136
Edwin K. **88** 132
Eleanor **88** 128 **105** 34
Eleazer **144** 42
Eli **80** 19
Elijah **78** 307 **80** 8-11 21
124 **86** 96 **123** 118
Elijah E. **80** 10 **123** 123 200
Elimira **109** 183
Elisha **80** 13 14 130 270
106 72 **128** 29
Eliza **78** 362 **88** 43 133
123 118 121 123
Eliza (Bacon) **88** 130
Eliza (Crocket) **143** 160
Eliza (Neal) **109** 183
Eliza H. **88** 134
Elizabeth **51** 109 206 **70**
xix **74** xxvii **75** 187 **79**
287 296 379 383-385 388
390 **80** 6 10 11 13-15 17
20 21 24 120 127 129 130
272 **88** 33 34 39 40 43
128-132 135 136 **91** 367
106 61 72 128 **109** 240
116 97 **122** 292 293 **127**
274 **128** 29 **147** 58
Elizabeth (Burbank) **102**
59 **128** 29
Elizabeth (Miller) **104** 249
Elizabeth (Rice?) **120** 238
Elizabeth (Warner) **88** 33
Elizabeth Ann **88** 137
Elizabeth H. (Cowell)
88 140
Elizabeth L. **88** 135
Elizabeth Lombard (Rich)
84 133
Elizabeth Mary (Miller)
88 134
Elizabeth Reynolds
(Stanton) **88** 132
Elizabeth S. (Hopkins)
104 300
Elkanah **80** 12 130 **128** 29
Ella A. (Heaton) **88** 132
Ellen **89** 28
Ellen Britania
(Richardson) **87** 66
Ellen L. (Lewis) **88** 140
Elmira **109** 183
Else / Elsey **88** 42 139
Elsie M. (Withrow)
88 130
Elwell Preston **83** 433 434
Emeline L. **88** 135
Emeline S. (Nickerson)
123 203
Emily **88** 130
Emma **68** 250 **88** 129
104 133
Enos **79** 382 **80** 119-121
128 31
Ephraim F. **88** 40

KNOWLES *cont'd*
Ephraim T. **104** 217
Ernest Allen **81** 108 222
Esther **80** 14 122 123
88 131
Esther (Hoxie) **88** 130
Ethel **88** 130
Ethel (Stanwood) **104** 251
Eunice **80** 7 12 13 **88** 130
Everett **88** 141
Experience **80** 21 129 **88**
91 **102** 59 **107** 230 **126**
166
Experience (Chamberlin)
88 91
Ezekiel **87** 66 **88** 34 **109**
183 **123** 119
Fannie **88** 44
Fanny **80** 7-9 22
Ferdinando **55** 101
Florence McLean **85** 194
Frances **80** 7 **88** 138
Frances (Roberts) **87** 366
Frances A. (Stackpole)
88 132
Frances E. **88** 138
Francis **124** 254 **141** 95
Frank H. **88** 132
Franklin **80** 9 **123** 124
Frederick C. **88** 132
Frederick R. **88** 129
Freeman **79** 385 **80** 9 24
122 126-128 **83** 395 **105**
290 **123** 119 120 124 202
George **80** 8 **88** 38 40 45
105 290
George Brown **80** 266 267
George Clarke **88** 137
George G. **88** 137
George H. **88** 137
George Manning **88** 130
George Nathan **88** 129
George P. **88** 44
George Ranney **80** 16
Gertrude Newkirk
(Smith) **89** 28 29
Giles **80** 16
Gordon **88** 130
Grace **84** 133
Grace (Church) **88** 38
Grace (Sankford) **88** 38
Graves **79** 287
Gustavus Adolphus
88 128
Hannah **59** 283 **65** 355 **79**
380 386 **80** 8-12 15 16 18
20 22 23 120 121 123 124
128 **83** 400 **87** 365 **88** 33
34 42-45 131 135 **89** 89
95 92 **104** 301 **109** 183
123 117 118 121 123 199
Hannah (Browning)
87 365
Hannah (Carpenter)
88 40
Hannah (Dill) **123** 120 124
Hannah (Doane) **123** 119
Hannah (Hatch) **80** 8
Hannah (Hazard) **88** 36
Hannah (Hopkins)
105 33

KNOWLES *cont'd*
Hannah (Knowles) **88**
34 42 131
Hannah (Niles) **88** 43
Hannah (Pepper) **123** 118
Hannah (Pope) **88** 33
Hannah (States) **88** 141
Hannah H. **123** 122 124
198 201
Hannah L. **123** 202
Hannah Lyon **88** 141
Hansard **53** 69 **65** 269 **70**
184 **79** 287 **87** 359
Harding **80** 10 21 **123**
118 119
Harriet **57** 286 **80** 256 **88**
44 132 135 139 **123** 202
Harriet A. **145** 244 **146** 385
Harriet B. (Nickerson)
123 123 201
Harriet C. **88** 135
Harriet Lovina (Dimock)
88 130
Harrison **100** 86
Hatsel **80** 120 122
Hattie **102** 288
Hazard **86** 53 **88** 37 44 45
135-137 **127** 218 **144**
311
Hazard G. **88** 135
Hedley **88** 130
Helen Inez **87** 67
Helen Marjorie (Libby)
83 433 434
Helen Reece **80** 110
Henry **62** 283 **74** 321 **79**
287 **80** 6 7 10 19 124 **84**
238 **86** 96 **87** 359-366
88 33 36-38 40 42 44 **89**
89 **94** 254 331 **104** 250
251 **111** 156 **123** 199
139 235
Henry A. **88** 42
Henry L. **88** 135
Henry Swift **64** lxviii
Hepzibah **80** 130
Herbert Minot **88** 136
Honor (Bellinden) **88** 136
Horace Browning **88** 131
Horatio Nelson **88** 136
Huldah **80** 119
Huldah H. **89** 89
Ichabod **108** 259
Irving C. **88** 137
Isaac **79** 391 **80** 16 123 124
267 268 272 **88** 40 41 **89**
89 **118** 289 **120** 238 **126**
225
Isabel **88** 129
Isabel (Miller) **106** 72
Isabell H. **88** 128
Isaiah **80** 18
Isobell (Syme) **88** 129
Isobell McIntosh **88** 129
Israel **80** 267
Jacob **89** 89
James **79** 287-289 292 296
297 381 385 386 388 389
391 **80** 6 7 13 18 19 124
129 256 266 268 271-273
276-278 **86** 96 **88** 38 44

KNOWLES *cont'd*
90 91 **100** 225 **102** 59 60
103 161 **123** 119 **127**
274 **128** 29
James C. **88** 135
James D. **88** 140
James Davis **88** 139
James Freeman **80** 19
James H. **123** 200 201
James Hatch **80** 23
James Lyon **88** 141
James Munro **88** 128
Jane **80** 128 130 **88** 134
134 132
Jane (McLearn) **88** 128
Jane A. **88** 136
Jane F. **88** 135
Jane Gray **88** 136
Jemima **67** 79 **80** 18
Jemima (Asten) **87** 66
Jemima (Hoag) **89** 89
Jennie **88** 130
Jennie (Earl) **88** 140
Jeremiah **66** 27 **88** 44 141
Jeremiah Northup **88** 43
Jerry **105** 104
Jerusha **79** 382 **80** 12 119
123 124 **123** 120
Jesse **79** 381 **80** 11-13 120
83 399 401 **123** 118
Jim **88** 44
Jireh Mumford **88** 133
Joan **69** 18
Joanna **80** 7 269 270 **87**
366 **88** 39
Joanna (Hopkins)
104 217
Joanna F. (Smith) **123** 202
Joanna T. **125** 236 237
John **51** 109 **123 58** 31 **61**
lxviii **79** 287 288 290-297
380 381 386 387 389-392
80 6 9 11 13-15 18-22
119 120 129 130 266 268-
270 272 276 278 **83** 395
86 96 **87** 66 359 361-365
88 33 34 39 40 42 43 45
91 128 131 134 139 **93**
24 **98** 121 **100** 187 **102**
60 **103** 161 **104** 300 **105**
33 **106** 72 **113** 257 **116**
97 **119** 315 319 **120** 238
122 79 **123** 123 **126** 143
128 296 **138** 93 **143** 160
147 46 275 276
John Appleton **105** 128
John Courtland **88** 132
John Hazard **88** 45 136
John Hoxie **88** 131
John K. **144** 311
John P. **88** 44 **123** 124
John Power **88** 36 139 140
John Ross **88** 129
John Segar **88** 45 134 **104**
249 250
John Tillinghast **88** 132
John Warner **88** 130
Jon **88** 128
Jonathan **58** 33 34 **65** 355
80 22 120 123 **87** 223
231 359 **88** 36 38-41 128

KNOWLES *cont'd*
129 131 137 138 141 **92**
284 **105** 290 **123** 202
125 112 **127** 227
Jonathan G. **80** 16
Joseph **52** 317 **79** 381 **80**
20 **82** 292 295 **87** 233
240 **88** 34-36 41-43 45
132-134 **89** 89 **104** 250
251 **128** 128
Joseph B. **88** 140
Joseph Brown **88** 139
Joseph Croft **105** 223
Joseph D. **89** 89
Joseph F. (Mrs.) **75** xciii
Joseph M. **78** 416 **80** 23
Joseph Mumford **88** 41
132
Joseph R. **88** 43
Joshua **79** 380 381 **80** 9
11-13 18 22 270 **84** 295
296 **88** 40 128 129 **104**
300 301 **116** 257 **123**
118 122 199
Josiah **80** 11 12 22 **123**
121 198
Josiah M. **123** 202 204
Judith **80** 14
Julia **80** 272
Julia (Hazard) **88** 134
Julia Maria **80** 271
Juliette (Farrell) **88** 134
Kate **88** 133
Katharine **79** 287 **88** 42
131 141
Katharine (Barsley)
88 342
Katharine (Rodman)
88 130
Keziah **56** 34 **65** 351
108 119
Lafayette **143** 160
Lathrop **128** 29
Laura **80** 256
Laura (Baugh) **105** 222
Laura Pearl **105** 222 223
Lavinia **80** 13
Lemuel **84** 127
Lizzie **102** 285
Lizzie (Collins) **86** 96
Lizzie (Dennie) **88** 129
Lois **80** 119 120 **108** 119
212 302
Lois (Holmes) **108** 211
212
Lothrop **80** 130
Louis **88** 135
Louisa **80** 128 **88** 129
Louisa A. **88** 135
Louisa O. (Hopkins)
105 104
Louise **88** 139
Louise (Emerson) **88** 133
Lovey **80** 22 271
Lucia **80** 24 **123** 199
Lucia (Lazell) **89** 28 29
Lucinda **88** 129 **123** 199
Lucinda (Doane) **116** 257
123 122 199
Lucinda F. **123** 203
Lucretia **80** 19 **88** 41

KNOWLES *cont'd*
Lucretia (Rogers) **88** 40
Lucy **80** 11 15 16 18 272
88 141
Lucy (Mayo) **123** 119
Lucy Ann (Rodman) **88**
42 131
Lucy B. **110** 107 111
Lucy H. **61** 344
Lucy Stanley **88** 135
Lydia **79** 389 390 **80** 8 9
14-16 22 128 266 270
271 **88** 138 242 **109** 34
123 118 119 121 198 201
Lydia (Chaplin) **147** 276
Lydia (Hoxie) **88** 131
Lydia (Kinney) **108** 211
Lydia (Knowles) **123** 118
Lydia (Putnam) **88** 138
Lydia (Sheapherd) **88** 141
Lydia Ann **88** 40
Lydia Brainard **80** 14
Lydia D. **123** 204
Lydia Matthews **108** 259
Lyman **89** 28 29
M. Elizabeth **75** 13
Mabel Olivia **143** 160
Malatiah **79** 384
Mapa **80** 16
Marcy **57** 19 **88** 134
Margaret **66** 110 **67** 286
79 287 **87** 363-366 **88**
34 135 136 **125** 104
Margaret (Congdon) **88**
44 **144** 311
Margaret A. (Lindsay)
100 86
Margaret D. (Smith)
88 129
Margaret Douglass
88 129
Margery **80** 10 21 **123** 118
Margery (Knowles)
123 118
Maria **78** 137 **104** 303
Maria (Rogers) (Fletcher)
147 276
Marjorie **88** 141
Martha **79** 385 386 391 392
80 12 13 15 16 24 120
129 130 271 272 **86** 405
87 362 363 365 366 **88**
38 129 130 **102** 59 60
114 10 126 80 283
Martha (Bracket) **123** 201
Martha (Cobb) **127** 41
Martha B. (Wiley) **123**
121 198
Martha D. **80** 23
Martha Jones (Doyle)
88 132
Martin V. **88** 137
Mary **52** 317 **58** 77 **68** 106
76 33 **78** 430 443 **79** 287
292 379-381 383 384 387
80 6-9 12 14 16-19 21-23
122 124 125 128-130 265
272 **84** 295 296 **87** 128
362 363 365 366 **88** 34
37 42-45 90 91 129 131
132 135 137 138 **89** 362

KNOWLES *cont'd*
92 34 **95** 344 374 **104**
300 **105** 4 34 **116** 257
123 121 122 124 199
126 166 283 **128** 29 **144**
308 311 314 315
Mary (Bentley) **88** 44
Mary (Bowen) **88** 141
Mary (Brooks) **117** 51
Mary (Carpenter) **88** 43
133 **104** 250
Mary (Case) **87** 366
Mary (Edgecomb) **88** 129
Mary (Elva) **107** 133
Mary (Freeman) **83** 395
Mary (Hazard) **88** 134
Mary (Hobbs) **87** 66
Mary (Hopkins) **102** 59
114 10
Mary (Hoxsie) **88** 42 131
Mary (Jordan) **126** 145
Mary (Knowles) **88** 45
Mary (Libbey) **88** 90
Mary (McCloud) **116** 97
Mary (Smith) **88** 128
Mary (Wedgewood)
87 66
Mary (Winifred) **84** 127
Mary A. **88** 135
Mary A. (Horton) **123** 122
Mary A. (Manton) **88** 140
Mary Ann **80** 272 **88** 129
134 135 138 140
Mary Ann Power **88** 138
Mary B. **80** 267
Mary Bassett **80** 268
Mary Caroline (Jones)
88 132
Mary Delano **113** 257
Mary E. **88** 137
Mary E. (Howe) **123** 199
Mary E. (Jenckes) **88** 39
Mary Edith **88** 87
Mary Ellen **88** 128
Mary Elva **107** 133
Mary Everett **88** 140
Mary F. (Fry) **88** 140
Mary Freeman **83** 395
Mary Honor **88** 136
Mary Howland (Everett)
64 lxviii **88** 140
Mary J. **85** 156
Mary Jane **88** 128
Mary Keith **64** lxviii
Mary N. (Delano) **126** 143
Mary P. **88** 43
Mary T. (Johnson) **88** 139
Mary Welles **86** 53
Mary Welles (Hubbard)
86 53
Maryann (Horton)
123 200
Massa **80** 16
Matilda Levina (Rathbun)
88 130
Matilda Power **88** 139
Maude **88** 129
Mehitable **79** 290 293 **80**
11-14 16 123 266 **86** 338
123 120

KNOWLES *cont'd*
Mehitable (Rich) (Atkins)
83 399
Mehitable L. **102** 284
Mehitable P. **123** 121 124
Mercy **79** 295 296 380 384-
386 388 **80** 7 11 16 17 21
24 120 122 123 130 272
279 **83** 264 **88** 133 **108**
212 **126** 82 **127** 41 **128**
29 31
Mercy (Freeman) **83** 264
Mercy A. (Myrick)
123 200
Merton **126** 240
Mina Percelina (McDavitt)
87 67
Miriam **80** 14
Molly **80** 16 **88** 38 141
Molly (Williams) **88** 37
Morris **81** 108 222 **87** 66
67 72 179 **112** 140
Moses **58** 140
Mumford Gardiner
88 133
Muri **80** 272
N. H. **122** 79
Nabby **80** 24 **88** 44
123 119
Nancy **88** 138 **123** 120
Nancy (Stack) **88** 140
Nancy (Tilton) **106** 72
Nancy Bangs **80** 23
Nancy G. (Sisson) **88** 136
Nancy J. F. (Boyle)
105 128
Nathan **80** 10 16 **88** 38
Nathan H. **88** 135 **89** 89
Nathan S. **80** 9 **123** 124
Nathaniel **79** 288 296 297
382-384 **80** 7 12 119 120
122-126 267 272 **88** 342
98 6 **108** 211 212 215
120 238 **126** 145 **141**
202
Nathaniel Atwood **80** 21
Nathaniel Ingerson
80 128
Nehemiah **80** 19 **83** 395
Newton I. **80** 16
Nicholas A. **88** 43
Nicholas Paine **80** 271
Nicholas R. **123** 123 201
Obed **80** 8 23 **123** 119
Olive **80** 24 **123** 120
Olive Wentworth **75** liii
Pamela (Smith) **123** 204
Parker **80** 130 **128** 29
Patia **80** 123
Patty **80** 276
Patty (Mayo) **123** 119
Paul **79** 381 **80** 12 17-19
83 394
Paulina **123** 121 124
Penelope **88** 44
Peter **80** 266
Peter A. **88** 135
Phebe **54** 88 **78** 87 **80** 6 7
9 11 13 14 17 19 20 120
128 266 **83** 395 **123** 118
Phebe (Chase) **87** 334

KNOWLES *cont'd*
Phebe (Kinney) **108** 211
215
Phebe (Paine) **83** 394
Phebe (Rich) **83** 395
Phebe B. **116** 257 **123** 122
199
Polly **80** 128 **109** 183 **123**
118 **144** 308 311
Polly (Billings) **98** 6
Polly (Caverly) **87** 66
Polly F. **123** 123
Polly F. (Doane) **123** 118
Polly Freeman **80** 13
104 301
Porter **80** 272
Power **88** 138 139
Prince **80** 121 **126** 96
127 118
Priscilla **80** 13
Prudence **59** 259 **80** 16 127
271 272
Putnam D. **88** 138
Rachel **79** 386 387 391 **80**
17 22 270 271
Rachel (Horton) **116** 257
123 122 199
Rebecca **79** 287 295 297
380 384 386 387 389 390
80 7 10-12 21-24 123
124 266 269 270 **87** 365
88 129 130 **123** 118 121
124 202
Rebecca (Harding) **86** 96
Rebecca F. **123** 202 204
Rebecca F. (Knowles)
123 204
Remick **80** 16 17
Renewed **88** 135
Reuben **80** 123 **117** 51
Reynolds **88** 37 **92** 34
128 128
Rhoda (Tilson) **87** 233 240
Richard **54** 219 **64** lxviii
79 286-292 295 297 381
385 390 391 **80** 13 14
130 266 268 269 **86** 96
87 359 **91** 327 **124** 252
254 **125** 295 **127** 41 **128**
29 **143** 341
Robert **69** 362 **79** 287 **80**
22 266 **87** 359 363-366
88 33-37 39-44 130 131
135 **89** 89 **104** 251 **128**
127
Robert R. **88** 131
Robert W. **88** 43
Robert Winthrop **88** 296
Robey (Clarke) **88** 136
Robey (Hopkins) **88** 45
Robey Bowers **88** 136
Rodger **88** 40
Rose **87** 365
Rowland **88** 44
Rowland H. **88** 43
Roxanna **123** 118
Ruel **80** 14
Ruhamah **80** 16
Russell W. **117** 291
Ruth **69** 91 **79** 288 292
296 297 380 384 386 389

KNOWLES *cont'd*
390 **80** 10 12 14 15 18-21
23 120 122 123 **83** 395
88 131 **123** 117 **136** 360
143 341
Ruth (Bower) **86** 96
Ruth C. **89** 89
Ruth Doane (Knowles)
123 119
Ruth F. **123** 120
Ruth Freeman **80** 23
Ruth P. **88** 44
Sabra **88** 130
Sabra (Hamilton) **88** 129
Sabray **88** 38
Sally **58** 17 **80** 10 16 22 23
123 124 128 268 272 **88**
44 45 135 **100** 229 **123**
119
Sally (Freeman) **123** 200
Sally (Kenyon) **88** 135
Sally (Woodard) **88** 34
Sally Barber (Edgecomb)
88 40
Samuel **75** 187 **79** 290-
297 381 382 385 387 392
80 15 16 22 119 121 124-
128 130 271 279 **83** 264
88 33 34 39 41 91 129
102 104 108 **97** 352 **98** 7
103 29 **105** 34 **116** 97
122 293 **123** 118 **126** 96
144 42
Samuel E. **88** 40
Samuel Mumford **88** 132
Samuel Nathan **88** 129
Samuel Warner **88** 41
Samuel Watts **88** 129
Sarah **65** 355 **67** 79 **79** 292
379 386 **80** 7 8 11-13 15
16 18 21-23 119-121 123
126-128 268 270 **82** 292
295 **88** 34 35 38 39 43-45
91 129-133 135 141 **104**
217 250 **123** 200 **127**
195 **128** 31 **131** 317
Sarah (Babcock) **88** 39
Sarah (Barney) **88** 37
Sarah (Elkins) (Mayo)
86 96
Sarah (Elwell) **122** 293
Sarah (Green) **87** 66
112 140
Sarah (Hall) **87** 231 233
Sarah (Knowles) **88** 43
133
Sarah (Mumford) **88** 41
Sarah (Potter) **88** 43 133
135
Sarah (Rodman) **88** 44
Sarah (Stanton) **88** 135
Sarah (Walker) **83** 401
Sarah Amy **88** 139
Sarah Anne **84** 296
Sarah B. **123** 198
Sarah Elizabeth **104** 249
108 161
Sarah Elizabeth Mary **87**
360 **88** 134 **104** 250
Sarah H. **88** 40
Sarah Jackson **84** 323

KNOWLES *cont'd*
Sarah Jane **88** 128
Sarah T. **123** 121
Seth **64** lxviii **79** 381 382
80 8 10 12 14-16 19 23
24 120-123 265 **123** 203
Sibyl **80** 16 **87** 363 366
Silas **80** 17 18 **83** 395
Silence **80** 16 **88** 45 134
Simeon **80** 12 13
Simon **58** 30 **65** 353 **80** 14
105 286 **143** 160
Smith **83** 395
Solomon **80** 266
Solomon R. **88** 131
Sophia **80** 16 121 **127** 118
Sophronia (Story) **88** 40
Stephen **87** 366 **88** 45 132
Stephen C. **88** 137
Stephen D. **88** 135
Stephen M. **88** 140
Susan **88** 44 **123** 118 122
198
Susan (Hopkins) **104** 297
Susan (Snow) **123** 202
Susan Amy **88** 135
Susan Amy (Knowles)
88 137
Susan E. **88** 140
Susan E. (Langley) **88** 139
Susan S. **92** 74
Susanna **79** 287 **80** 9 12-
14 18 22 127 128 266 271
87 366 **88** 40 42 91 131
96 227
Susanna (Anthony) **88** 42
Susanna (Boss) **87** 366
Susanna (Crosby)
123 124
Susanna (Kenyon)
88 135 137
Susanna (Rodman)
88 42 131
Susanna (Wilcox) **88** 39
Sylvanus D. **123** 203
Sylvia **64** lxix **80** 266
Tabitha G. (Holbrook)
123 123 200
Tamzine **80** 123
Temperance **80** 23 24 269
270 **116** 257 **123** 118
122 199
Tempy S. (Hopkins)
123 199
Thankful **79** 389 **80** 9 10
16 19 21 24 128 269 270
123 119 121 124
Thankful M. **123** 204
Thankful Paine
(Hopkins) **104** 300 301
Theophilus **80** 12 **123** 119
Thomas **51** 206 **64** lxviii
75 187 **76** 140 **78** 430
79 287 288 380 **80** 6 7 9
10 18-20 23 130 **87** 359
88 128 **90** 63 64 **116** 257
123 122 123 199 **128** 29
139 229 **141** 95
Thomas Delos **88** 128
Thomas Henry **64** xliv
lxviii lxix

KNOWLES *cont'd*
Thomas Rodman **88** 131
Thomas S. **123** 200
Thomas Syme **88** 129
Thomasine **80** 19
Timothy Lasell **89** 28
Treat **80** 21
Tryphena **88** 91
Tryphena (Marsters)
88 130
Tupper **88** 129
Urania (Whitman)
88 139
Walker **80** 14
Warren **88** 44
Warren B. **88** 43
Warren Bradford **88** 133
Willard **64** lxviii **78** 443
79 294 381 **80** 11 15 16
20-22
William **79** 390 391 **80** 13-
16 21 23 120 **85** 75 **87**
128 359 361-365 **88** 34-
36 38-40 43 44 129 131-
133 135 137 138 141 **92**
61 281 **93** 24 **98** 24 **104**
251 **105** 34 **108** 259 262
109 43 44 **122** 105 **123**
203 **128** 128
William A. **88** 134
William C. **79** 286 **80** 13
William F. **80** 24 **123** 121
William Frederick
107 133
William G. **88** 135 137
William H. **88** 134
William Hazard **88** 45 135
William Henry **88** 129
135 136
William Henry Baldwin
88 38
William Manley **106** 72
William N. **88** 135
William P. **88** 44
William S. **88** 133
William T. **88** 39
Winslow Lewis **80** 23
Wylie **88** 38
Zaccheus **80** 18
Zerviah **80** 19 121 123
127 118
Zerviah (Atkins) **123** 123
Zerviah (Harding) **126** 96
KNOWLING Andrew **60**
207 **78** 338 339 390 **81**
136-138 **94** 256 258 260
264 268-271 326 335 338
97 101 196 **129** 107 110-
112 114 125 127
Ann **78** 388-390
Anne **81** 136-138 **94** 335
97 101 102
Anne (Thornton)
(Dickens) (Twigden)
94 256-258 326 **97** 101
102
George **94** 269
Hugh **94** 269
Jane **94** 338
John **54** 61
Robert **94** 269

KNOWLING *cont'd*
Thomas **94** 269
William **94** 269 270
KNOWLLON
Sarah Ann **122** 290
Sargent **122** 290
Knowls *see* Knowles
KNOWLSON
Deborah **78** 387
Joseph **78** 387
Richard J. **56** 209
KNOWLTON Knolton
— Capt. **86** 139
— Maj. **85** 117
— Major **56** 238
Aaron **117** 167
Abia **52** 413 415 417 **53** 449
Abiatha **60** 204
Abigail **51** 491 **56** 42 **62** 42
  86 133-135 138
Abigail (Dodge) **124** 239
  319
Abraham **51** 466 **61** 201
  65 114 **69** 340 341 **84**
  422 **86** 64 133 **135** 253
Ackley **120** 160
Adeline **57** 284
Alice (Hannum) **90** 258
Alice (Sherman) **120** 160
Almira **58** 280
Alone **58** 280
Alonzo **105** 298
Alonzo Frank **68** 251
Amaziah **86** 134
Ammi **86** 134 142 143
Amos **69** 340 341
Amos Arnold **83** 433 437
Amy **86** 134 135
Andrew **86** 132 133 135
  139 143 **105** 282
Ann (Billings) **116** 256
Anna **68** 145 **70** 241 **86** 134
  135 137 **87** 212 **93** 281
  108 296-299 **123** 125
Anna (Billings) **94** 58
Anna (Fellows) **86** 142
Anna (Hammon) **84** 424
Anna (Keyes) **131** 48
Anna (Pierce) **86** 134 142
Anna (Putnam) **86** 134
Anna Pierce **86** 140
Annie **60** 14
Annie Marie **110** 225
Arnon **69** 340 341
Asa **120** 16
Benjamin **61** 335 337 **62** 45
  71 357 358 **75** 303 **91**
  256 **98** 104 **108** 298 **123**
  259 **124** 239 319 **129**
  384 **141** 197 332 347
Bethiah **62** 43 **71** 358
Betsey **65** 218 **105** 298
Byron Oliver **65** xxxiv
Calista **69** 280 **110** 115
Calista Leonard **69** 340
Catherine **63** 95
Charles **58** 280
Charles Davison **60** 14
  62 xxxvii
Clarence S. **86** 143
Curtis **58** 280 **137** 282

KNOWLTON *cont'd*
Daniel **66** 14 **69** 280 340
  108 299 **119** 109 122
  120 17
Daniel H. **116** 256
Daniel M. **94** 58
David **51** 461
Deborah **95** 55 **108** 297
Dolly **114** 180
Dolly (Runlett) **118** 35
Dorcas (Shapleigh)
  95 268
Ebenezer **61** 336 337 **69**
  340 **78** 410 **86** 133 136-
  138 **125** 103
Edwin **69** 340
Elbridge H. **69** 280
Elbridge M. **69** 340
Elijah **62** 45
Elisha **80** 172 **108** 296 298
  299
Eliza **55** 344 **58** 280 **97** 145
Eliza (Stinchfield) **98** 258
  260
Eliza A. **69** 340
Eliza P. **98** 258
Elizabeth **61** 331 337 **62**
  35 39 **69** 280 **86** 93 133
  135 136
Elizabeth (Farnam)
  119 122
Elizabeth (Poland) **86** 136
Elizabeth (Presson)
  86 134
Ellen **74** 33
Emmerette E. **68** 160
Ephraim **62** 46
Esther **86** 139
Esther (Dane) **86** 134 135
  142
Eunice **71** 357 **84** 423
Experience (Hardy)
  92 285
Ezekiel **86** 142 **105** 288
  113 46
Fellows **86** 140
Fellows Stetson **86** 140
Frances L. **123** 100
Frank A. **91** 393
Frank Watson **91** 393
Fred **89** 228 **111** 139
Frederick **70** 241
George **58** 280
George Clinton **83** 232
  247
George H. **61** 201
George Henry **60** 186 **65**
  xxxiv
George W. **79** 6
Gideon **129** 397
Gilbert **105** 277
Hannah **65** 218 **69** 340
  70 241
Hannah (Allen) **110** 225
Hannah (Mirick) **123** 259
Hannah B. **68** 251
Harriet M. **69** 340
Harvey **74** 33
Havana **63** 88
Henry **69** 340 **98** 109
  117 167

KNOWLTON *cont'd*
Henry E. **69** 340 **90** 50
Henry Knowlton
  Swanville (Mrs.)
  117 167
Herbert C. **68** 154
Hosea **105** 295
Hosea C. **105** 298
Hosea M. **51** 499
Howard Atwood **122** 191
Israel **61** 201
J. **61** 335 **91** 327
Jacob **83** 413 **104** 248
  113 154
James **86** 140 **98** 258 260
  137 282
Jared **52** 145 413 417 **58**
  194 **60** 204
Jason **57** 284 **58** 280
Jemima (Clough) **126** 233
  137 282
Jennie Sinclair (Neil) **83**
  433 437
Jer. **66** 361 365
Jeremiah **84** 421 422 **86**
  132-135 139 140 142 143
  95 55
Jesse **58** 280
Joanna **86** 67
John **51** 491 **56** 60 **61** 330
  331 333 337 338 **62** 44
  63 378 **64** 374 **68** 154
  84 425 **86** 136 **92** 285
  95 268 **97** 145 **105** 282
  122 192 **126** 307
John C. **110** 225
John Elliot **84** 189 232
Jonathan **61** 334 337 **62**
  34 40 42-45 **68** 251 **69**
  340 341 **86** 134 135 137
  143 **126** 233 **137** 282
Jonathan W. **69** 340
Joseph **63** 377 379 **64** 374
  84 424 **86** 134 **91** 327
  92 319 **108** 296-299
Joseph Fellows **86** 140
Julia Ann **96** 400 **102** 38
Keziah **108** 299
Lavinia **116** 203
Leverett **137** 282
Lois **91** 255 **141** 348
Lucinda **70** 241
Lucy **58** 280 **86** 133
Lucy / Louie (Whipple)
  135 253
Luke **74** 150
Luthera **73** liii
Lydia **63** 378 379 **64** 374
  68 251 **86** 135 **108** 299
  140 124
Lydia (Tourtellotte)
  108 299
Lydia M. **69** 280
Marah **61** 152
Marcia (Rich) **84** 303
Marcus **69** 340
Marcy **84** 426
Marcy (Knowlton) **84** 426
Margaret **61** 335 **62** 36
  74 33
Margery **52** 413 **62** 48

KNOWLTON *cont'd*
Maria B. **61** 384
Maria J. **69** 340
Martha **51** 491 **55** 268 **61**
 337 **69** 280 **86** 18
Martha (Lanson) **135** 253
Martha (Pinder) **131** 48
Martha Marcy **69** 280
Martha Robinson **84** 421
Marvin **69** 280 340
Mary **51** 461 **58** 280 **60** 191
 61 152 201 330-332 334
 335 **62** 36 43 46 186 **80**
 172 **84** 422 **86** 135 **97**
 266 **108** 297-299 **111**
 130 **123** 264 **129** 397
 137 282
Mary (Blunt) (Oaks)
 86 134
Mary (Dodge) **86** 64
Mary (Smith) (Kimball)
 142 54
Mary (Wilson) **108** 297-
 299
Mary A. (Tilley) **111** 139
Mary Adelaide **68** 251
Mary Ann **69** 340
Mary C. (Fisher) **122** 192
Mary F. **69** 341
Mary J. (Billings) **98** 109
Mary Louise **122** 191
Mary Richards **58** 280
Mehitable **86** 139 140
Mehitable (Welch)
 125 103
Menta Belle **68** 154
Mercy **59** lxix **137** 282
Miner Rockwell **52** 98
Miriam **62** 35 **83** 207 **86** 64
Miriam (Cole) **86** 64
Molly **69** 341
Nabby **65** 218
Nancy **69** 340 341
Nancy P. **95** 315
Nathan **65** 218 **104** 216
 137 282
Nathaniel **86** 132 133 136-
 138 142 **92** 310
Nathaniel L. **69** 341
Olive **120** 17
Oliver **58** 280
Patience (Miller) **104** 216
Patrick **137** 282
Patty **84** 424
Paul **62** 45 **91** 255 **135** 253
Philena **104** 216
Polly **58** 280 **129** 397
Rachel **68** 154 **86** 135
Ralph H. **69** 341
Rebecca **69** 280
Rebecca F. Paul **69** 340
Reform **86** 133 142
Reform (Prescott) (Jewett)
 86 142
Reuben **105** 285
Rice **61** 335 **62** 34 41 43 46
 86 64
Richard **61** 332
Robert **61** 336 **62** 48 **86**
 133 **92** 278 323
Rosina C. D. Tufts **69** 340

KNOWLTON *cont'd*
Roxanna Irene (Rice)
 89 228
Ruth **52** 417 **62** 45 **108** 299
Ruth (Place) **108** 299
S. **123** 100
Sally **63** 88 **73** 89 **84** 426
 86 133 **125** 109
Sally (Dean) **84** 425
Sally (Woodbury)
 111 315
Sally Dean **84** 425
Salome **86** 133
Samuel **61** 331 333 337 338
 62 34 39 **84** 303 426 **86**
 132-143 **92** 285 **102** 38
 137 282
Sarah **51** 466 **61** 201 230 **62**
 44 63 376 **64** 76 **66** 361
 83 413 **84** 422 **86** 133-
 139 142 **91** 265 268 **97**
 75 **109** 116 **113** 154 **117**
 163 **137** 282
Sarah (Boyd) **137** 282
Sarah (Fellows) **86** 133
 134 138 140 141
Sarah (Ridlon) **86** 135
Sarah (Smith) **83** 413 **104**
 248 **113** 154
Sarah G. **69** 341
Sherburn **65** 218
Sophia (Taylor) **90** 50
Stephen **69** 340 341 **70** 241
 83 407 **105** 285
Susan **63** 376 377 **64** 76
 374 **66** 362 **69** 340 341
Susanna **58** 194 **61** 333
 335 337 **62** 34 35 45 **70**
 104 **90** 362 **108** 299 **140**
 124
Sylvester **137** 282
Thomas **53** 90 336 **61** 335
 337 **62** 36 45 186 **64** 65
 69 280 **70** 104 241 **92**
 319 **105** 285 **108** 296-
 299 **126** 307 **131** 48 **137**
 122 **140** 124 **142** 55
Timothy **61** 335 337 **62**
 36 45 46 **98** 104
W. S. **64** 132 **118** 131
Walter **58** 280
Walter F. **68** 251
Washington **63** 376 **64** 76
 66 362
William **62** 186 **86** 133 142
 105 283 **131** 48 **138** 125
Zerviah **69** 340 341 **120** 16
Knowols *see* Knowles
KNOWSLEY
 — Mr. **63** 137
Mary **55** 97
KNOX Knocks
 —— **55** 298 **59** 57 **65** 341
 74 225 226 **89** 379 **99**
 209 **126** 123 **145** 172
 — Gen. **99** 30 **142** 301
 143 171
 — Mrs. **88** 279
Abigail **74** 215 216 226
Ada Reynolds **116** 207
Adam **64** lv **85** 167 **91** 352

KNOX *cont'd*
Albert Franklin **102** 124
Alexander **99** 205
Almira (Perkins) **128** 173
Amariah **60** 266
Amaziah **60** 268
Amy **74** 230 264
Andrew **99** 207
Andrew G. **91** 327
Ann **64** lv **85** 167
Ann (Gyles) **97** 57
Ann Augusta (Colby)
 (Andrews) **125** 114
Anna **63** 171 **74** 257
Anna Leona (Arey)
 87 112
Annabel (Gordon) **98** 52
Anne **66** 144 **105** 150
Anne (Montgomery)
 (Logan) **112** 89 96 97
Archibald **91** 352 **124** 72
Asa **128** 173
Barnabas **125** 100
Barzillai **65** 334 **99** 53
Benjamin Hall **68** 126
Betsey **65** 256 341 **74** 262
Betty **74** 254
Caleb **90** 238 239
Catherine **111** 65
Charity **74** 263
Charles **74** 216
D. **91** 327
Daniel **74** 212 217 219 229
David **65** 114 334 **69** 282
Dolly **74** 254
Dorothy **74** 50
Dosia **65** 256
Drisko **74** 251
Ebenezer **73** 307 308 **74**
 50 129 198
Eleanor (Grange) **128** 312
Eleazer **74** 214 **99** 327
Eliza **64** lv **73** 189
Eliza (Hill) **87** 196
Elizabeth **64** 81 **73** 307 **74**
 50 129 215 226
Elizabeth (Barrett)
 140 160
Elizabeth (Messinger)
 135 302
Elizabeth (Titus) (Hoag)
 89 379
Elizabeth B. **128** 18
Ellen **128** 177
Emma Hannah Low
 68 126
Esther **73** 308 **74** 37 198
 90 231 247
Eunice **65** 256 **74** 252
 98 133
Eva Pray **73** 189
Fall **74** 217
Forrest S. (Mrs.) **117** 314
G. W. **73** 189
George **59** 194 **62** 301 **70**
 151 **99** 53
Grace Louise **144** 100 272
Hannah **65** 256 **74** 249
 252 255 261 263 **90** 233
 236 238 253 **96** 343
Henry **14** 77 **51** 147 504 **54**

KNOX *cont'd*
231 **55** 367 **57** 347 **58** ci
156 **60** xvi **65** 148 **67** 11
328 **74** 50 **78** 443 **79** 391
84 358 364 376 **88** 324
90 249 250 **99** 29 84 **101**
259 **105** 288 **112** 267
273 **129** 325 **130** 104
136 320 329 **147** 77
Huldah **79** 152
Isabelle (Briggs) **126** 123
Issachar **74** 50 **90** 252
James **57** 139 **77** 221 **91**
327 **96** 247 **112** 89 96
Jane **74** 250 **77** 221 **99** 207
209
Janet **97** 336
Jerusha **65** 114
Joan **84** 83
Joanna **77** 134
John **53** 231 **63** 389 **64** 80
81 **65** 114 **66** 38 **74** 215
85 455
John B. **124** 72
John Ballenger **111** 162
Jonathan **65** 256 341 **69**
282 **74** 213 219 254 **90**
239 245 **91** 31
Joseph **63** 171 **74** 214 217
225 257 263
Joshua **65** 341 **74** 192 213
215 219 226
Judith **73** 308 **74** 125 198
255 262
Katharine **96** 326
Leonard **65** 114 334
Lettes E. **128** 264
Lozette **69** 282
Lucy **67** 11
Lucy (Flucker) **84** 376
136 320 329
Lydia **65** 114 **69** 282 **73**
71 307 314 **74** 198 219
229 262 263 **90** 251
Margaret **51** 493 **74** 251
256 **91** 352 **135** 339
Margaret / Martha A.
(Vohond) **128** 173
Martha **64** lv **96** 247
Mary **65** 256 334 **73** 307
308 **74** 214 217 225 249
251 256 **84** 272 **88** 115
96 247 **97** 222 **128** 177
Mary (Jewet) **91** 31
Mary (Walker) **90** 326
91 17
Mary Eliza **84** 322
Mary F. **88** 336
Mercy **65** 114 334 **73** 311
74 41 182 251 **99** 247
Molly **65** 114
Moses **74** 250
Nancy **77** 134 135
Nancy (Hall) **90** 238 239
Nathan **74** 251 **90** 230 247
Nathaniel **74** 215 216 226
Nellie M. Starkey **117** 314
Nicholas **74** 114 252
Normand **79** 159 302
Olive **65** 256 **68** 94
Olivia Minerva **98** 186

KNOX *cont'd*
Orlando **91** 327
Patience **113** 225
Pauline **81** 257
Peg **70** 151
Priscilla **69** 282
Rachel (Tilton) **125** 100
Rainer **108** 101
Rebecca **73** 308 **74** 43
Reuben **73** 308
Richard **66** 144 **74** 219 **90**
228 230 246
Robert **99** 207 **140** 160
Robert Dale **87** 112
Roscoe C. **87** 112
Rufus **90** 326 335 **91** 17
Sadie Lucy (Barnes)
102 124
Sally **57** 139 **74** 250 **96** 247
Sally (Burnham) **97** 15
Samuel **66** 38 **68** 94 **74** 39
262 **90** 335 **91** 25 327 **96**
267 **125** 114 **140** 160
Sarah **63** 172 **73** 308 **74** 39
184 199 212 217 225 229
250-252 254 258 **90** 246
Sarah (Alley) **99** 327
Sarah (Randall) **90** 335
Sarah L. (Cousens) **90** 335
91 25
Sarah Lyons **68** 126
Sophia (Fowler) **108** 101
Stace Darling **74** 217
Sumner B. **128** 173
Susan (Roberts) **91** 27 31
97 222
Susanna **66** 38 **74** 262
Sylvanus **65** 256 **73** 308
74 124 181 **91** 27 31
Tamson (Tibbetts) **99** 327
Thomas **62** 301 **73** 308 **74**
181 182 184 190 250 262
78 73 **84** 83 **140** 160
William **62** 301 **65** 131
74 251 262 **81** 240 **84**
272 **85** 124 **99** 327
William H. **87** 347
Zachariah **74** 183 185 213
250 256 262
KNUDSON
Evelyn Fish **98** 209
Lucille **93** 137
Peter **76** 275
Knyght *see* Knight
KNYTHCOTE
Katharine **142** 228
Walter de **142** 228
KNYTS Robert **86** 411
KNYVET Knyvett
— **141** 94 102
Abigail **53** 114 115 250
Agnes **53** 250
Edmund **53** 115 250
Elizabeth (Neville)
(Strickland) (Burgh)
(Darcy) **96** 107
Jane **53** 250
Joan **53** 250
John **53** 115 250 **98** 69 120
138 319
Margaret **138** 319

KNYVET *cont'd*
Muriel **53** 115
Nicholas **65** 70
Thomas **53** 114 115 250
98 69 121
William **114** 53
KNYVETON
Maud **80** 390 391
William **80** 390 391
Knyvett *see* Knyvet
KOBACH Josephine
(Burcham) **113** 222
Michael **113** 222
KOCH Adrienne **119** 77
Rachel **133** 218
Raymond Joseph **85** 99
Virginia (Felt) **85** 99
William **115** 39
KOCKWOOD
Margaret S. **123** 199
KOEHLER Adelheid
(Droste) **89** 363
Edward **89** 363
Julius Balke **89** 363
Marie **87** 295
Rose (Balke) **89** 363
Rudolph Augustus **80**
106 206 **89** 363 **90** 79
140
KOELBERG Gustava
Wilhelmina **105** 228
Nils Gustav **105** 228
KOENIG Mabel Grace (Ely)
97 52
Robert F. **104** 246 **108** 77
KOENIGSBERGER
Rosa **85** 218
KOERNER
Bernhard **104** 50
Susan Catherine **136** 334
KOET
Abraham **128** 164 167
Ariaantje **128** 164
Denys **128** 164
Dirk **128** 164
Dorothea **128** 164 165 168
Francois **128** 164
Jacob **128** 164 165
Jacobus **128** 168
Jan **128** 165 168
Johannes **128** 164
Maria **128** 168
Marijtje **128** 164
Moses **128** 164
Neetje **128** 164 166
Petronella (Van Swieten)
128 165
Thomas **128** 162 163 165
168
KOETTERITZ
John B. **59** 420
KOGAN Patrick **61** 350
KOHL — **59** 235
Anthony Peter (Mrs.)
113 222
Eva Elizabeth **104** 286
Johann **104** 286
KOHLER
Abigail **51** 442
Abraham **51** 441 442
Albert **51** 445

KOHLER *cont'd*
Anna **51** 442 443 **86** 321
Anna Maria Barbara
87 36
Anne / Annie **51** 444 446
Austin **51** 201 445
Caroline **51** 445
Caroline Matilda **51** 445
Charles Henry **51** 446
Conrad **86** 321
Daniel **51** 445
Eliza **51** 445
Elizabeth **51** 442-444
Elizabeth Katharine
Whitford **51** 444
Ellen Augusta **51** 446
Emeline **51** 447
Emily **51** 445
Esther **51** 442
George **51** 441-445 **86** 321
George Albert **51** 447
George Cole **51** 445 447
George Gideon **51** 201
445 446
George Horatio **51** 201
445 447
George Wyser **51** 441 445
Grace **51** 204
Grace Lillian **51** 204 446
Hannah **51** 444 445
Horace **51** 447
Jacob **51** 201 441-447
John **51** 443 444 446 447
John Bradford **51** 446
John George **51** 204 442-
447
John Jacob **51** 441
John Michael **51** 442 445
Jonathan Christopher
137 306 311
Katharine **51** 444 445
Margaret **51** 441-443
Maria Margaretha **87** 36
Martha **51** 201 445
Martha Anne **51** 441 446
Mary **51** 442 443
Mary Frances **51** 446
Mary Rice **51** 445
Mary Roberts **51** 204
Mehitable **51** 442
Nancy **51** 445
Sarah **51** 442 444
William Putnam **51** 201-
204 384
KOHN Annie **139** 216
Betty **143** 166 167
Elizabeth **134** 330
S. Joshua **113** 162
KOHNE Elisa **114** 191
Elisa (Newfoille) **114** 191
KOHNER Bessie **118** 248
123 159
KOITS Curtis **128** 277
John **128** 277
KOKKE Adam **141** 216
KOKMAN Thomas **110** 188
KOLKHOFF
Charles **86** 321
Eva K. **86** 321
Louisa **86** 321
Martha **86** 321

KOLKHOFF *cont'd*
William **86** 321
KOLLBERG
Annette Barbara
111 101
KOLLER M. F. **104** 243
KOLLN
John Milton **86** 369
KOLLOCK —— **92** 373
Arthur Cornelius **62** 213
Cornelius **92** 374 **116** 82
142 66 **143** 11
Ebenezer **141** 340
Esther **81** 469
Jacob **92** 374
Lemuel **92** 374 **107** 155
125 41 **131** 41
Mary **92** 374
Susan Marion **83** 125 232
Susanna **141** 340
KOLM James **76** 132
John **76** 132
KOMAIKO Jean **122** 210
KONETZNY
Margaret M. **105** 125
KONIG Koning Koningh
Constantia **106** 6
David T. **141** 205
Heinrich **136** 77
Henry **136** 77
Jacob **106** 6 **107** 318
Matheus **107** 318
Mayke (Van Roon) **106** 6
KONKENTON
William **79** 48
KONNICK
Annetje **123** 103 104
KONTI Isadore **60** 322
KONVEYRE
Andre **110** 130
KOOGLER George **124** 312
KOOKEN Elizabeth (Work)
136 95
James **136** 95
KOONS Koon Koones -
see also Kuhn
Barbara A. **115** 162
Dana R. **115** 162
David **73** 265
Edith Lansing **109** 150
John C. **109** 150
Kate **80** 208
Maude (Powell) **109** 73
Nancy Moore (Williams)
109 150
Rebecca **70** 84
KOONTZ Ahava Harriet
(Hicks) **104** 144
Howard Deunham
104 144
KOOPMAN
Harry Lyman **63** 308
KOOTES Josias **93** 383 384
387
KOPPENHEFFER
Thomas **103** 161
KORBITZ
Ellen K. **113** 160
Norman D. (Mrs.)
113 160
KOREN John **77** 242

KORFFMANN
Johan Conrad **133** 181
KORINCK
William De **128** 162
KORNGIEBEL
Ada L. **86** 321
Daisy L. **86** 321
David **86** 321
Frederick **86** 321
Hannah M. **86** 321
Hannah M. Frey **86** 321
Hattie **86** 321
John **86** 321
Margaret **86** 321
Martha **86** 321
Martha Isleib **86** 321
Martin P. **86** 321
KORSWIG
Sarah D. **115** 267
Sigvard **115** 267
KORTRECHT Alexander
Humphreys **78** 326
Augusta **78** 326
Augustus **78** 326
Charles **78** 326
Charles Murray **78** 326
Evelyn Marshall **78** 326
Humphreys **78** 326
Mary Wilson **78** 326
KORTRIGHT Cornelis
Jansen **59** 419
KOSCIUSZKO
Thade **110** 130
KOSE Augusta **76** 274
Henry **76** 274
KOSSICLE
Richard **52** 262
KOSSUTH Louis **71** 196
KOSTER Fanny Leonard
69 xxxii 191
Max M. (Mrs.) **118** 74
Nancy Felton **118** 74
KOSZUL
Julien Pierre **145** 65
KOTHMAN Alpha
Katharine **78** 321
Corda Jane **78** 321
Emmett Floyd **78** 321
Howard Bert **78** 321
Katharine **78** 321
Louis William **78** 321
Maud **78** 321
Nellie Maude **78** 321
Olen Ross **78** 321
Raymond David **78** 321
Veda Bell **78** 321
William **78** 321
KOTT
Katharine
Elizabeth **81** 290
KOUES Anna Rossiter
108 153
George Ellsworth
108 153
Mary Parmly (Tobey)
108 153
KOUNTZE —— **59** 113
Harold **83** 210
Louise (Bulkley) **83** 210

KOUT
Andrew Louis (Mrs.)
81 222 237
Helen Lorraine **81** 222
KOUTS Mary **123** 240
KOVAROVICS
Helen **110** 157
KOWEN Jane **100** 241
KOWLES Charlotte
(Sherman) **108** 264
William **108** 264
KOZAK
Joseph Henry **93** 283
Katharine Lewis (von
Bichowsky) **93** 283
KRADER
Christina E. **124** 256
KRAETZER Edwin **97** 67
Emma **54** 151
Sarah W. (Bancroft) **97** 67
KRAFT
Dollie Leota (May)
117 128
Emma Wilma **117** 128
Hazel **104** 141
Herman A. **117** 128 129
Leta (May) **117** 129
Marie **117** 129
Minna **108** 270
KRAFTS
Margaretha **88** 188
KRAGMAN Abigail
(Higgins) **123** 201
Abigail W. **123** 203
Catherine F. **123** 199
Francis **123** 118 202
Joseph **123** 201
Lydia (Smith) **123** 202
Mary (Pepper) **123** 118
Sarah (Snow) **123** 199
Travius **123** 199
KRAISSL
Frederick (Mrs.)
85 242
KRAKE
Rachel **89** 315 316
KRAMER
Anna Helena **136** 331
John **82** 16
Katharine **82** 16
Sally Hauck **82** 16
KRANNERT
Herman C. **100** 108
KRAPPEN Frances **75** 190
KRASCHNEFSKI
Annie **85** 314
KRATZ
Bessie May **96** 128
Elizabeth (Deal) **96** 128
Henry Elton **96** 128
Ludora **133** 267
KRAUP —— **57** 338
KRAUSE Kraus
Michael **92** 209
Pauline **92** 229
Walter M. **95** 146
KRAUTHEIM
Elizabeth **89** 20
KRAVCHENKO
Victor **101** 177

KREBS Alexia Du Pont
(Ortiz) (Sharpless)
95 84
Edwin Philip **95** 146
Friedrich **108** 79
Henrik J. (Mrs.) **95** 84 144
John A. **86** 321
Max V. **110** 85
KRECHNIAK
Helen Bullard **120** 314
KREGEL Peter **97** 98
KREGER
Paulina T. **91** 393
William Robert **91** 393
KREHBIEL
Henry E. **107** 8
KREIDER
Abraham **107** 211
Mary Catherine **107** 211
Mary M. (Haupt) **107** 211
KREIGER Cornelia
Adriana (Van Casteel)
106 14
Johan D. **106** 207
Martin **106** 14
KREISLER Fritz **105** 82
KRELL Amanda Ellen
(Pemberton)
(Townsend) **85** 195
Daniel Frederick **85** 195
KREMER
Lillian Marie **70** 204
Russell Clarence **84** 109
189
KRESS Agatha (Sheehan)
95 171
Anna Elizabeth **87** 387
Catharina Margaret
95 171
Charles **95** 171
Claude Washington **84**
172 **85** 188 **95** 136 149
171
Elizabeth (Smith) **95** 171
Elizabeth Margaret
95 172
Frances **114** 63
Gertrude Gale (Greely)
90 9
Henry **95** 171
James M. **114** 63
Johann Carl **95** 171
Johann Peter **95** 171
John Franklin **95** 171
Margaret Dodson
(Connor) **95** 171
Maria Magdalene
(Corsbach) **95** 171
Philip Caspar **95** 171
Rosalind Elaine **95** 172
Ruth (Aulls) **114** 63
Samuel Henry **95** 171
Sarah (Kressler) **95** 171
KRESSLER Sarah **95** 171
KRETSCHMAR
Robert Salmon
103 119
KRICK Virginia **101** 337
KRISPE Robert **64** 243
KROAL Paul **120** 8

KROGER Alice Farrington
(Maher) **94** 187
Bernard H. **80** 104 206
Bernard Henry **93** 83 141
94 187 188
Chester Frederick **94** 188
Gretchen **94** 188
Helen **94** 188
John Henry **94** 187
Lucile **94** 188
Mary Emily (Jansen)
94 187
Mary Gertrude (Schlebe)
94 187
KROGMAN Samuel
Brown (Mrs.) **84**
106 189
KRON Albert Raymond
105 128
Helen (Clark) **105** 128
Kronenshelt see
Crowninshield
Kronkhite see Cronkhite
KROPF Lajos **96** 141
KROPFF
John Fredrick **92** 58
KROPINSKE
Wilhelmina **97** 119
KROPOTKIN Peter
Alexeievitch (Prince)
62 lv **70** xliii
Kross see Cross
KROUT
Caroline Virginia
108 158
John Allen **118** 72 78
Mary Hannah **108** 158
KROWLES David **73** 232
KRUA Theresia **112** 141
KRUG Harry L. **116** 155
KRUGER
A. **128** 262 265
Wilhelmina **89** 184
KRUISENGA Johanna
Arletta **92** 389
KRUM Krumm - see also
rum
Anna Gertrude **80** 154
Anny **101** 322
Carolyn Kirkland
(Sanborn) **76** xlviii
Carrie T. **80** 154
Chester Harding **89** 31
93 381
David **80** 154
Elizabeth **80** 154
Elizabeth Harrington
(Cutler) **89** 31 **93** 381
Henry Albert **80** 154
Mary Frances **89** 31 **93**
381 **100** 162
Morrow **76** xlviii
Walter C. **144** 235
KRUMBHAAR G. Douglas
(Mrs.) **109** 130
Hermann **75** lxx
Ruth S. (Cheney)
(Reynolds) **75** lxx
KRUONBHAAR
A. **116** 150

KRUSEN
Elizabeth **113** 304
KRUSI Hermann **62** 389
KRUSSELL
Carl Magnus **111** 100
Catherine (Ehrenpreus)
111 100
Catherine (Gyllenpalm)
111 100
Marta Eleanora
(Gyllensvard) **111** 100
Susanna (Lindebohm)
111 100
Virginia Eleanora
111 100
KRYTZER Caroline
Draper (Durrell)
134 68
Frances (Fraker) **134** 69
Isaac **134** 69
Milton **134** 68
KUCKER Robert **143** 257
KUEHL
Warren F. **115** 157
KUEHN Alfred Leonard
(Mrs.) **89** 132 **101** 122
KUENSTER
Albert **69** 266
Christine **69** 266
Herman **69** 266
Martha E. **69** 266
KUERDEN
—— **68** 345 346 363
368 369
KUGLAND William **138** 43
KUGLER
Catherine **109** 289
Daisy Alice Garcelon
(Hunton) **87** 174 **93** 83
143 189
Elizabeth Hetty
(Musselman) **93** 190
Harvey Roy **87** 174 **93** 83
143 189 190
John Jacob **93** 190
Lee K. **147** 281
KUHL Henrietta **99** 42
Henry **65** 56 148
KUHN Kuhns - *see also*
Koons
—— **92** 132 245 250 257
93 116 118 **147** 247
— Mrs. **94** 42
Abigail (Pike) **87** 38
Adam **78** 221
Albert **87** 38
Anna **87** 38 **94** 39
Anna Barbara **87** 35 38
Anna Margretha **87** 36
Anna Maria **87** 36
Anne **87** 38
Anne (Moody) **87** 38
C. Carroll **93** 208
Caroline Matilda **92** 257
94 46
Catherine **87** 38 **92** 245
94 46
Charles Henry **93** 118
Charlotte **135** 73
Daniel **78** 409 **92** 129
Elizabeth **63** 303 **93** 204

KUHN *cont'd*
Ellen Augusta **93** 116 121
Emeline (Chester) **87** 38
Emily **87** 38 **92** 127
Fanny **77** xlviii **85** 344
Frank **112** 246
George **87** 38 **140** 160 161
George Albert **87** 38
George Cole **87** 38 **92** 132
George H. **140** 160
George Horatio **96** 82
George Michael **87** 38
Hannah (Frost) **140** 161
Hans Michael **87** 36
Herbert Lewis **75** xxvi 65
Jacob **52** 98 99 101 **87** 35
37 38 **94** 39 42 **96** 82
140 160 161
Johann Friderich **87** 37
Johann George **87** 36 37
Johann Jacob **87** 35-37
Johann Michael **87** 35-37
John **87** 38 **92** 127 129 132
245 250 257 **93** 116 118
121 **94** 46 **140** 160 161
John Bradford **93** 116
John Francis (Mrs.)
96 160
John George **87** 36-38
John Jacob **87** 35 37
John Michael **87** 38
Katharine (Even) **112** 246
Lillie Belle **81** 38
Margaret **140** 68
Maria Barbara **87** 38
Martha (Frost) **96** 82
Martha Ann **96** 81 82
Mary **78** 311
Mary Ann **105** 33
Mary Francis **93** 116
Mary N. **93** 121
Mary Newell **94** 47
Mary Newell (Phipps)
87 38
Mary Rice **92** 250 **94** 46
Matthias **93** 208
Maude (Pinney) **98** 370
110 267 **147** 148 241
248 253
Mehitable (Stockman)
87 38
Michael **87** 37
Oscar **81** 38
Pansie Maynard **102** 124
Polly **140** 161
Rebecca **81** 38
Samuel **83** 255 **93** 208
Sarah **94** 46
Susan **90** 45
William **81** 38
William Putnam **96** 82
William Solyman **93** 208
KUHNLE Caroline **92** 37
KUJOLA Hedwick **92** 229
KUKAN Alexander **63** 236
KULCINSKI Bernice
(LaVerne) (Rohrer)
96 51
Louis **96** 160
KULICK Gary **142** 178

KULL
Helen Marie **90** 279
KULLIUS Hannah **62** 83
KULP George B. **144** 151
KUMBER William **62** 326
63 214
KUMLE Bernice **108** 135
KUMLERT Martin **65** 243
KUNBER William **63** 214
KUNBORN Carl **128** 170
KUNDI John **110** 16
KUNIN Polly **140** 161
KUNKEL
Beverly W. **106** 319
KUNTZ
Caroline Elizabeth
95 336
Matthias **83** 255
KUNZ
George Frederick **86**
236 **87** 170
KURATH Hans **95** 139 **96**
156 **104** 247
KURCK
Adam Julian **81** 403
KURKJIAN Maksoud **89**
283 **90** 132
KURTH Godefroid **101**
109-112
KURTS Curtis **128** 277
Elizabeth (Torey) **125** 218
John **125** 218 **128** 277
KURTZ
Elijah H. **118** 293
Emily Caroline (Lougee)
(Ainslie) **118** 293
Jeannette (Lindsay)
100 86
Joseph **95** 399
Stephen G. **121** 229
KUTZ
Erma Lenore **104** 142
KUWADA Gonpei **92** 209
KUYKENDALL
Ralph S. **103** 159
KUYPER
Harriet **110** 131
Peter **110** 131
KVENSKE Carl **76** 274
KVJOLA Hedwick **92** 229
KWELT Isabelle **85** 298
KYCHE Clement **79** 411
Kydd *see* Kidd
KYE Ann **82** 212
Charity **82** 90 92
Hannah **82** 217
James **82** 90
John **82** 90 92
Mary **55** 311 **82** 208 212
215
William **82** 208 212 215
217
KYEN Peter **55** 99
Kyenynge *see* Kenning
KYER Edward **82** 44
Mercy **82** 292 296
KYES Abigail T. (Davison)
90 51
Hannah **115** 119
John Fenderson **68** xxxiv
KYLE —— **54** lxvi

KYLE cont'd
Joseph **107** 43
Walter L. (Mrs.) **123** 79
KYLES William **130** 85
KYLL Forbes **63** 347
Kyllygrew see Killigrew
KYLYE Benett **97** 297
KYME De Kyme
Anthony **145** 106
Elizabeth **145** 103
Jane A. **145** 103
Lucy **145** 265
Philip **145** 265
Thomas **145** 103
William **116** 16 **145** 265
KYMER — Mr. **74** 148
William **52** 487
KYNDE Jane **126** 18
Sarah **126** 18
Kyne see Kinney
Kyng see King
Kyngeslond see Kingsland
Kynnaston see Kenniston
Kynne see Kinney
KYNOR Elizabeth (Lyon) **136** 361
John **136** 361
KYNSWELL Anne **70** 55
KYPLE Richard **65** 287
Kypping see Kipping
KYPPYR John **84** 76
Kyrbye see Kirby
Kyrke see Kirk
Kyrkham see Kirkham
Kyrr see Kerr
KYSOR Ruth A. (Carey) **108** 134
Willis Earl **108** 134
KYSTON
Katharine **98** 30
Thomas **98** 30
Kytchen see Kitchen
Kytchin see Kitchen
Kytchynam see Kitchen
KYTE —— **56** 114
KYTMER Frances **57** 95
KYTSFORD
Richard **110** 262
Willard Cummings **110** 222 223
William **110** 76 223
William Samuel **110** 316
Kytson see Kitson

LABADIE Pierre **107** 49
LABAREE
Benjamin W. **120** 231
Daniel M. **98** 298
Leonard W. **97** 394
Submit (Gatchell) **98** 298
LABARGE Anne (Coolidge) **95** 379
Edward **95** 379
Rose **95** 379
La Baron see Labarron
LABARRERA
Ottilia de **109** 290
LABARRON La Baron
La Barron
Alice **75** 18

LABARRON cont'd
Carl **81** 42
Flora J. **81** 42
H. G. **91** 327
Samuel **73** 104
LABATEAUX
Hannah **65** 148
LABATUT Andre J. **143** 235 366 **145** 292
LABAW George Warne **57** 236 **58** xlv **60** 279 **65** 303 **66** xlix
LABEAUME — de **53** 463
LABECHE
William de **109** 20
LA BELL
Cora Elmira **74** 317
Isabel A. **74** 317 319
Jesse Edward **74** 317
Joe **74** 319
Theophilus L. **74** 317
LABELLE
Percilia **145** 138
LABERTOUCHE
Peter Paul **93** 278
Sarah **93** 278
LABEY
Perronelle **88** 253
Thomas **88** 254
LA BLANCHE
Isabel **119** 98
LABODY Robert **60** 27
LABOISSIERE Alphonse Claude **112** 237
LA BOISSONADE
— Baron of **55** 47
LABONTA Leota (Marston) **115** 230
LABONTE Rosie **92** 337
LA BORDERIE
Arthur De **119** 99
LABOREE Laborie
Abigail (Blackleach) **148** 43
Anthony **148** 42
James **144** 41 **148** 43
Jeanne (Resseguie) **148** 43
John **148** 44
Mehitable (Leete) **148** 42 43
Peter **148** 43
LABORNE John **51** 354
LABOUISSE Frances Devereux **77** 257
Henry Richardson **77** 257
LABOUR
Abbie (Rich) **84** 125
Leslie J. **84** 125
LA BOYTEAUX
La Boyteaux
—— **101** 341
G. Brooks **101** 320
William Harvell **80** 104 206 **101** 116 320 **102** 127
LABREE Peter **88** 275
Sally (Stephens) **88** 275
LABRODEN Peter **66** 34
LABROSS Charles **55** 380
LABRYN —— **106** 12

LACASE
Florence **110** 230
LA CASSE
Margaret **91** 77
LACET Sarah **100** 301
Lacey see Lacy
LA CHAPELLE
Eva A. **69** 206
LACHMAN Mark **64** 107
LACHYNGDON
Margery **84** 80
Sibyl **84** 307 312
Sibyl (Lake) **84** 310 313
Thomas **84** 80 307 310 313
LACK Lacke
Edward **99** 117 283 **101** 271 273
John **65** 237
Martha **63** lx
Rebecca **99** 283
Thomas **99** 117 283 **101** 163
William Calvin **99** 117
LACKARY John **98** 128
Lacke see Lack
LACKEY Albert **90** 37
Albert A. **90** 37
Albert A. (Mrs.) **90** 37
Chloe **75** 305
Ellice **82** 292 293
Ellis **82** 44
Fobes **75** 306
Harriett Izella **99** 148 **120** 147
Jane **64** 261
Margaret **116** 206
Martha **100** 241 **145** 296
Mary **113** 143
Mary A. **90** 37
Olive E. (Legge) **89** 241
Rebecca **124** 15
Richard **64** 188
Samuel W. **89** 241
Sarah **72** 198
Waldo **90** 37
William **72** 198 **76** 47 **82** 292 293 **136** 52
LACKIN Marcy **79** 50
LACKINGTON
Nicholas **141** 119
LACKKES — Mr. **83** 379
LACLOCHE
James **54** xcvii
LACOE —— **55** 238
Ralph Dupuy **56** 332
LACOLOMBE Jean Pierre
Auge **110** 128
Lewis **110** 128
Louis Auge **110** 128
LACON Francis **103** 19
LA CORNE — Chevalier De **97** 111
LACOSSE
Ellen **100** 202
Francis Aaron **100** 202
Frank **100** 202
J. M. **100** 202
Massie Belle (Munroe) (Daffin) **100** 202
Melba Lee **100** 202
Norma Gene **100** 202

LACOSSE *cont'd*
Willie G. **100** 202
LACOTON
Arnold **59** 193
George **59** 193
LACOUNT
Azubah W. (Rich)
116 256
John **116** 256
LACOUR
Lewis Ambrose **65** 230
LA CROIX Lacroix
Alice Pervear **85** 196
Esther Humphrey **77**
lxxxviii
Frederick W. **109** 130
Morris Felton (Mrs.) **77**
lxxxviii
LACY Lacey
—— **123** 241
— Capt. **146** 368
— Mrs. **112** 299
Abigail **134** 226
Benjamin **145** 73
Betsey **55** 407
Charlotte **55** 407
Chloe **144** 238
David **55** 407 **130** 72
Edmund **145** 14
Edward **69** 377 **103** 66
Eleanor **93** 384
Eleazar **130** 72
Eli **130** 72
Elisha **130** 72
Elizabeth **130** 72
Elon **130** 72
Enoch **130** 72
Erastus **130** 72
Esther **70** 198 **130** 72
Eurial **130** 72
Ezra **130** 72
Georgianna (Thompson)
103 154 155
Henry **70** 198
Hugh de **116** 278 279
Isabell **90** 59 60
James **83** 329
John **51** 350 **83** 329 **86** 408
90 59 60 **95** 4 6 9 10 **103**
66
Josephine **70** 198
Josiah **70** 38
Lois (Handy) **126** 105
Lydia **99** 284 **100** 141
Lydia (Brumton) **100** 296
Margaret **95** 9
Margaret (Hall) **145** 73
Martha **76** 264
Mary **78** 252 **94** 276 **95** 8
145 73
Mary Ann **73** 264
Merritt **70** 198
Michael **112** 299
Mildred Brayton **103** 66
154
Molly **145** 73
Polly Ann **145** 242
Rebecca **69** 377
Richard **75** 287
Robert **83** 323
Ruth **70** 38

LACY *cont'd*
Samuel **103** 66
Sarah **126** 129
Stephen **100** 296 **126** 105
Stephen H. **76** 50
Stephen Henry **126** 105
Steven **99** 284
Thaddeus **105** 247
Thomas **84** 281 **90** 64
Thomas Jefferson Potter
103 66 154
William **122** 126
Lad *see* Ladd
LADBROOK
Robert **98** 123
LADD Lad Lade
A. H. **83** 193
Abigail **55** 316 **57** 395 **62**
258 **67** 286 **72** 74 **83** 12
22 25 **112** 77 **148** 147
Abigail (Hill) **83** 12
Abigail (Wright) **148** 147
Abigail Frances **132** 323
Adeline **83** 193
Adeline Haven **82** 421
89 198
Adella F. **73** 40
Ahijah **73** 40
Albert M. **110** 109
Alexander **58** 156 **82** 421
83 34 193 306 **89** 197
198
Alexander Hamilton **82**
421 **83** 34 172 173 183
89 198
Alexie May **110** 298
Alice **73** lx
Allen D. **123** 179
Alma **73** 40
Almaria **58** 402
Almira **84** 85
Alonzo B. **84** 85
Amanda **116** 114
Amelia **73** lx
Amoret C. **72** 74
Ann **62** 256 **83** 24 25 **92**
289 **133** 155
Ann Parry **83** 172
Anna **58** 198 **73** 40 **86** 382
118 35 **123** 223
Anna (Johnson) **98** 130
Anna M. **73** 40
Anna M. (Allen) **87** 396
Annett F. **91** 384
Annie L. (Chase) **117** 166
Annie P. **83** 299 303
Arathusa **58** 401
Ariel **73** 40
Arthur Eugene **89** 237
Asa A. **89** 252
Asa S. **80** 192
Austin **123** 179
Azail Polly **94** 246
Babson Savilian **73**
xxviii lx
Bathsheba **120** 50
Betsey **60** 200 **76** 29
Betty **94** 123
Bridget **56** 409
Caroline **86** 382
Caroline S. **83** 182 183

LADD *cont'd*
Caroline Sarah **82** 421
Celia **73** 40
Celia M. **73** 40
Charles **86** 382
Charles A. **84** 85
Charles Albert **83** 306
Charles Francis **94** 247
Charles Henry **82** 421
Charles Warner **58** 401
Charlotte **59** 95 **82** 421
Charlotte H. **83** 22 25
Charlotte Haven **82** 421
Clarinda **94** 247
Clarissa **58** 400 **60** 264
Cynthia **54** 406 407
Cyrus **117** 281
Daniel **58** 197 198 401 **60**
205 **62** 256 315 **73** lx **76**
46 **83** 24 25 **85** 372 **86**
382 **92** 289 **125** 94 **148**
143
Darius **90** 50
David **58** 403 **59** 95 96 414
60 79 **83** 365 **86** 382
110 22 24 109 298 306
Deborah **56** 28
Delle E. **73** 40
Dorcas **86** 382
Dorothy **117** 282
E. J. **121** 153
E. P. **86** 382
Easebia (Henry) **125** 215
Edith Eloise **89** 236
Edmond Orlando **94** 246
Edmund **94** 123
Edward **105** 207
Edward Johnson **83** 217
84 189 **103** 116 **119** 316
Eleanor Mary **71** xliv
Electa **59** 97
Eliab **73** 40 41
Eliphalet **55** 316 **83** 193
132 96
Elisha **58** 197 400-403 **59**
95 98 **60** 200 205 267
Eliza **54** 407
Eliza. **117** 282
Elizabeth **60** 134 **61** 230 **84**
306 **89** 240 **92** 289
Elizabeth (Head) **94** 123
Elizabeth (Redington)
109 117
Elizabeth Chauncey **82**
421 **89** 198
Elizabeth H. **83** 299 303
86 382
Elizabeth Hamilton
83 172
Elizabeth S. **73** 40
Elizabeth W. **83** 306
Elizabeth W. (Jones)
83 183
Ella Adelaide **86** 382
Ella Cora **89** lx
Emeline C. (Monroe)
116 259
Emily (Prescott) **90** 50
Emily Ann (Fitz
Randolph) **98** 130
Emily Appleton **82** 421

LADD *cont'd*
83 34 **89** 198
Emily James **68** lxxii
Ephraim **58** 197 400-402
  59 97-99 414 **60** 78 205
  73 40
Esther **58** 194
Esther Eliza **67** lvi
Eunice **58** 197 **60** 199
  86 382
Ezekiel **60** 78 205 **73** 40
Forest Filbrick **94** 247
Frances A. **84** 85
Frederick J. **126** 145
Fredus **86** 382 **89** 22
George **89** 236
George Edward **117** 166
George W. **83** 99
Gershom **117** 172
Gilbert **91** 201
Hannah **58** 17 **59** 286 **60**
  205 **73** 40 **86** 382 **93** 189
  99 290 **117** 282 **136** 36
Hannah (Clement) **97** 224
Hannah (Hurd) **132** 95
Harriet **80** 192 **89** 252
Harriet Almira **94** 247
Harriet E. **72** 204
Hattie **91** 248
Hattie G. **117** 167
Hattie M. **110** 109
Haven **82** 421 **89** 198
Hazen **86** 382
Henry **71** xliv **132** 95
  148 147
Henry G. **80** 192 **89** 252
Hepzibah **115** 197
Horace **59** 95
Horace Hall **54** 407
Horatio **58** 401
Horatio Oliver **61** 105
Hugh **110** 28
Irene **93** 186
Isaac **117** 282
Jackson A. **87** 395
James **59** 286 **98** 130 **123**
  234 **125** 95 **129** 58 **136**
  185
John B. **122** 215
John M. **73** 40
John Savilian **73** lx
John Tufton Mason **82**
  421 **83** 34 **89** 198
John Wood Brooks **73** lx
Jonathan **73** 40 **117** 282
Jonathan Arnold **54** 407
Jonathan T. **73** 40
Joseph **73** 40
Joseph E. **117** 166
Joseph P. **110** 109
Josephine **89** 237

LADD *cont'd*
Laura Emma **110** 298
Lewis **98** 130
Lewis W. **68** 200
Linnie Leontine **89** 237
Lois **59** 98 **60** 78 205
Louisa **117** 210 **126** 207
Love **58** 122
Lucinda **123** 179
Lucy **58** 403 **60** 79 81 205
  83 365
Lucy (Peck) **89** 22
Lucy A. **69** 138 **73** 40 **83** 99
Lucy Amanda **83** 183 187
Lucy P. **86** 382
Lura **59** 96 **73** 40
Lusalla **73** 40 41
Luther **73** 40
Lydia **60** 77 **62** 256 **73** 40
  184 **83** 365
Lydia A. **85** 105
Margaret **73** 40 **76** 59 70
  90 54
Margaretta **123** 179
Maria (Thayer) **126** 145
Maria A. **96** 179
Maria F. **82** 421
Maria Haven **83** 172
Maria T. **82** 421 **83** 34 193
Maria T. (Haven) **89** 197
Maria Tufton Mason **82**
  421 **89** 198
Mark Pitman **94** 247
Martha **68** lxxii
Martha B. (Southard)
  85 372
Martha Hastings **54** 407
Martin L. **116** 259
Mary **52** 55 **62** 258 **67** 286
  73 40 **86** 382 **99** 290
Mary (Woodward) **90** 44
Mary A. **84** 85
Mary Ann **73** lx 40
Mary Ann (Grant) **90** 44
Mary Ann (Gray) **110**
  298 306
Mary H. **83** 193
Mary Haven **82** 421
  83 173
Mary Larkin (Hurd)
  132 96
Mary May **85** 194
Mary Tufton Haven **83**
  173 297 299
Maud E. **110** 306
Mehitable **58** 124
Mercy **112** 77
Moses **94** 123
Moses Head **94** 123
N. **94** 246
Nabby **58** 18
Nancy **58** 197 **59** 98
  110 305
Nancy M. (Blake) **117** 166
Nancy Zelinda **110** 109
Nathaniel **71** 219 **73** lx
  94 246 **133** 155
Nicholas Easton **122** 215
Olive Snell (Carver) **89** 39
Parintha (Owen) **91** 248
Paulina **112** 77

LADD *cont'd*
Persis **58** 197 **60** 205
Phebe **95** 86
Phebe G. **134** 294
Rachel **86** 382
Rebecca **126** 280
Rebecca T. **73** 40
Rectyna B. **117** 281
Rhoda **86** 382
Richard **75** 227
Robert **56** 409
Rodolphus **58** 402
Roxy **58** 400 **59** 414 **60** 200
  73 40
Ruhamah (Benson) **110**
  22 24
Russell **58** 403
Ruth **73** 40
S. B. **94** 246
Sally **59** 290 **60** 149 **73** 285
Samuel **51** 95 98 **54** 406
  407 **58** 194 **61** 230 **73** 40
  86 382 **97** 224 **109** 117
Samuel Gray **115** 258
Sarah **60** 344 **115** 258
Sarah Bowman **94** 246
Sarah E. **116** 114
Sarah M. **72** 204
Sibyl **60** 78 79
Silas **110** 109 207
Sophia **132** 324
Sophia Catherine **82** 421
  83 193
Stephen **59** 290 **73** 40 **76**
  56 **116** 114
Stephen L. **116** 114
Susan **73** 40
Susanna **86** 382 **94** 123
Terrasha **117** 282
Theodore S. **73** 40
Thomas **76** 59 67 70
Timothy **90** 44 **105** 288
Urb **91** 248
Vincent **76** 59 70
Warham **72** 74
William **62** 356 **80** 72 192
  89 252 **90** 44 **94** 123
  115 258 **127** 221
William C. **72** 204
William Henry **68** lxxii
  89 39
William Jones **83** 173
LADER Eliza (Morse)
  125 222
Thomas **125** 222
La Despenser *see*
  espenser
LADEVEZE-ADLERCRON
  Rodolph **104** 173
LADIEU Curtis **60** 158
  Eliza Atwood **60** 158
  Rachel **60** 158
  Samuel **60** 158
LADIMORE Charitie
  (Cowes) **85** 386
  Richard **85** 386
Ladlaw *see* Laidlaw
LADUE Ladu
  Gladys **123** 301
  Oliver **69** 160
  Orra **73** 212

Jane Ellen **89** 22 23
Jennie **68** 200 **123** 179
Jeremiah **117** 172
Jesse **84** 85
Joel **73** 40
Johanna **89** 22
John **55** 66 **57** 395 **62** 258
  73 lx **76** 29 **105** 288 **112**
  77 **125** 215 **129** 270 274
  134 228 230 **136** 185

LADUE *cont'd*
  Phebe **69** 160
  Stephen **73** 212
LADYMAN
  Priscilla **73** 142
LADYMERE
  Elizabeth **73** 226
LAEBORNE Daniel **95** 135
LAERS Jacyna **128** 166
  Jan **128** 166
LA FANTASIE
  Glenn W. **143** 33 266
LAFAR Joseph **64** 19
LAFAUNT Alma Luella
  (Robison) **136** 327
  Harold Arundle **136** 327
  Lenore **136** 327
Lafavor *see* Lefavour
Lafavour *see* Lefavour
LAFAYETTE Layfet
  —— **99** 83 84 **133** 278
    148 292
  — Gen. **56** 70 329 **61** 77
    97 145 **109** 81 **141** 50
  Celina (Morcoux) **113** 299
  Flossie Irene **113** 299
  Helen (Delai) **113** 299
  Irma (McFarlane) **113** 299
  Jean Marie Francois
    (Marquis de) **51** 104
  John Baptiste **113** 299
  John Bartlett **113** 299
  Marie Jean Paul Roche
    Yves Gilbert Motier
    (Marquis de) **51** 89 145
    53 224 225 456 **54** 285
    379 381 **55** 92 361 **57**
    237 **58** lviii **60** 341 **63**
    317 **65** 346 **66** 316 **67**
    329 **77** 160 215 **86** 261
    270 **117** 4 178 179 **126**
    225 **130** 28-30 **145** 380
  Paul Gilbert **113** 299
  Pete Arthur **113** 299
  Pete Arthur (Mrs.) **113**
    59 299
  Phebe Cynthia (Bartlett)
    113 299
  Richard Alfred **113** 299
Lafebre *see* Lefebre
LAFETRA La Fetra
  Derentine **129** 49
La Fever *see* Lefever
LAFEY Catherine **55** 50
LAFFAN Robert **140** 161
LAFFERTY
  Bridget **139** 202
  Mary **126** 270
LAFFILLARD
  Peter **65** 231
LAFFIN James **72** 183
LAFFLINGE
  Elizabeth **141** 34
  Elizabeth (Waller) **141**
    34 35
  Thomas **141** 34 35
LAFITAN —— **52** 330
LAFLAM Hazel G. (Davis)
    98 362
LAFLAMME
  J. L.K. **64** 200

LAFLAN Robert **77** 230
LAFLER
  Hazel Kenerson
    103 160
  Herbert Alva (Mrs.) **103**
    119 **124** 79 **125** 72
  Sarah **76** 20
LA FLEUR Mattie Harper
    114 237
LAFLIN
  Agnes **63** 337 **78** 92
  Charles **63** 337 **76** 81 **78** 91
    92
  Clarissa **63** 338
  Elizabeth **63** 337
  Fanny **77** 3
  Florence **78** 92
  George Hinman **78** 91 92
  Georgiana **81** 290
  Heman **63** 338
  Henrietta Armenia **78** 92
    81 290
  Josephine **78** 92
  Katharine **78** 92
  Lawrence **78** 92
  Lloyd Alan **78** 92
  Louis Ellsworth **76** xxi
    77 81 **77** xxxvi **78** 91 92
    84 352
  Louis Ellsworth (Mrs.)
    84 352
  Louise Fanny **77** 3 **89** 58
  Lucy **78** 92
  Lydia **63** 338 **78** 92
  Mary Minerva **78** 91 92
  Matthew **63** 338 **78** 92
    81 290
  Samuel **59** 21
  Winthrop **77** 3
LAFOND
  Francoise **143** 9
  Julianne **123** 308
  Marguerite **145** 130
LAFORGE La Forge
  Frank (Mrs.) **85** 222
  L. **97** 384
  Margaret G. C. **65** 231
  Peter A. **65** 231
  Rachel **98** 335
LAFORME
  Joseph A. **58** lxxxiv
LA FOUNTAIN
  Marshall S. **129** 52
  Minnie **129** 52
LAFUNDER
  Peter **101** 273
LAGE Caleb **128** 59
LAGER
  Catherine **90** 278
  Catherine (Von Wehde)
    90 278
  Henry **90** 278
LAGG William **53** 97
LAGI
  Gilbert Fitz **95** 204
LAGRONE
  Millie May **98** 146
LAGROVES
  — Mrs. **71** 120
LAGROW *see also* Legrow
  Adelbert C. **74** 317

LAGROW *cont'd*
  Edna M. **74** 317
  Florence M. **74** 317
  Howard L. **74** 317
  Joel **74** 317
  Mary **74** 168 317
  Nellie **74** 317
  Norman B. **74** 317
  Rachel **74** 192
  Thomas L. **74** 317
LAHA Lahah
  Abraham **66** 300
  Azubah **87** 24
  Hannah **125** 100
  Isaac **87** 24
  Jane **66** 301
  Joseph **123** 307
  Lorania **87** 24
  Mary **77** 230 **126** 208
  Mary (LaMondo) **123** 307
LAHATT —— **102** 313
LAHAY
  Alexander **85** 167
  George Lewis **85** 167
  Margaret **85** 167
  Walter Albert **85** 167
LAHHEE Sarah **74** 187
LAHM Mary A. **94** 387
LA HUERTA Rosario
    Guerra de **109** 291
LAID William **63** 18
LAIDACKER Sam **95** 153
LAIDAIN
  Marie **121** 231
  Mary Ann **126** 206
LAIDLAW Ladlaw
  Henry Bell **87** 57
  James Lees **84** 186 232 **87**
    57 70 177
  Louise Burton **87** 57
  Robert **87** 57
  Stephen **60** 44
LAIDLEY Laidlie
  Archibald **85** 348
  Catherine **85** 348
  Margaret **98** 228
  Sarah **98** 228
  Thomas **98** 228
Laighton *see* Leighton
LAIKIE
  Archibald **64** 113
LAILER
  Alton Vesper **74** 89
  Arthur Clark **74** 89
  Frank H. **74** 89
  George Charles **74** 89
  Margaret Ellen **74** 89
  Mary Ann **74** 89
  Thomas S. **74** 89
LAIMBEER William **104**
    246 **143** 66
Lain *see* Lane
Laine *see* Lane
Laing *see* Lang
LAINHART Ann Smith
    142 126 148 **143** 168
    144 167 215 272
LAIR Amercia / Ameri-
    cus O. (Canum) **128**
    170
  Joseph B. **128** 170

LAIR *cont'd*
Sarah E. (Ross) **128** 170
W. W. **128** 170
LAIRD Alva **112** 79
Anne **76** 176
Annie Althea **77** 183
Clifford T. **113** 222
Edward **77** 183
Electra **112** 79
Erastus Sargent **76** 177
Ethel **91** 140
Eunice **76** 177
Frederick Jewell **58** xlv
George **60** 241
James **112** 79
Jean **141** 57
John **73** 222
Jonas **112** 79
Joseph **76** 176 177
Leonard Bentley (Mrs.)
   89 264
Lucy (Abernathy) **112** 79
Mary **60** 241
Rachel **60** 241
Robert **65** 148
Robert W. **111** 165 **112**
   164 **113** 162 **114** 160
   115 158 **116** 156 **117**
   159 **118** 169 **119** 158
   120 158 **121** 158
Rosa **104** 143
Samuel **60** 241 **97** 395
Thomas **141** 57
LAIREY — Mr. **83** 193
LAIS — Capt. **77** 67 109
LAISDELL Mary **83** 508
Mary (Allen) **83** 508
LAIT Jeremy **111** 40
William **140** 326
LAITHEWAITE
William **68** 364
LAJUS Adele **92** 75
LAKE Lak
—— **60** 186 **84** 312
— Goodwife **84** 311
— Mr. **62** 357
— Mrs. **83** 193
____ (Sumpter) **84** 314
Abby T. (Douglas) **126** 23
Abiah (Kimberly) **102** 105
Abigail **55** 61 63 64 **56** 389
   59 319 **102** 16 105
Abigail (Cooke) **125** 237
Abigail (Kimberly)
   102 105
Abigail (Sawtell) (Platts)
   126 135
Abner **117** 283
Abner D. **117** 209
Abraham **107** 157
Adeline (Wellington)
   99 303
Adoniram B. **118** 64
Albert Edward **64** xxxi 92
Alexander **90** 267 268 371
Alfred Peverly **81** 253
Almeric **84** 315
Almira **117** 20
Alvah **76** 14
Amariah **59** 320
Amy **75** 185

LAKE *cont'd*
Andrew Jackson **118** 65
Ann **75** 185 **84** 310 316 **86**
   244 **98** 332
Ann (Stratton) **135** 290
Ann Eliza **55** 63
Anna **84** 308 309 313
Anne **52** 275 **84** 308 314
   315
Anthony **117** 20
Arthur **84** 315
Arthur Crawford
   64 xxxi 92
Asa Howland **118** 65
Benjamin **107** 157 **126** 23
   148 278
Betsey **76** 145 **105** 217
Beverly S. **79** 144
Bibye **67** 107
Borden **117** 22 **148** 278
Bridgett **90** 267
Caleb **129** 337
Carrie **118** 310
Catherine Mary **107** 157
Charles **63** 238
Charles H. **117** 284
Clara P. **134** 333 **137** 182
Clarena (Van Dooren)
   126 142
Clarissa P. **134** 333
   137 182
Cynthia **117** 22
Cynthia (Taber) **148** 278
Daniel **125** 237 **127** 144
   148 278
David **64** 30 **66** 22 **76** 141
   104 227 **127** 26 144
David Minor **64** 92
Delia **118** 65
Dennis **107** 156
Devereux **92** 208
Edith B. **100** 10
Edmund **84** 311
Edward **52** 275 **84** 304
   311 312
Edward Mosher **118** 65
Eleanor T. **107** 157
Eliza **117** 284
Eliza A. **125** 177
Eliza Ann **126** 21
Elizabeth **54** 162 **66** 22 **76**
   14 **81** 253 **84** 306 307
   309-311 313 314 317 **88**
   334 **90** 267 **91** 390 **107**
   156
Elizabeth (Lone) **84** 310
   311
Elizabeth (Sandell) **84** 313
Elizabeth G. **118** 152
Elizabeth O. **88** 336
Elnathan **75** 185 **76** 139-
   141 144 145
Elvira **55** 64
Enos **126** 135
Ephraim **59** 171 **118** 310
Esther **118** 310
Eunice **127** 216
Everett Frank **81** 254
Everett J. **96** 77
Everett John **89** 308
George **58** 70 **107** 157

LAKE *cont'd*
George Edward **118** 65
Gershom **82** 351
Gertrude Imogene **67**
   xxxiv **81** 237 **82** 246 350
   351
Giles **127** 150
Hannah **59** 39 **60** 298 **80**
   97 **84** 304 316 **111** 150
Hannah (Salter) **102** 74
Hannah (Sawdy) **148** 278
Harriet **107** 156 157
   128 114
Harriet E. D. **117** 209
Harriet N. **116** 218
Harry Beaston (Mrs.)
   94 138
Henry **51** 351 **52** 225 **55** 61
   63 64 **123** 179
Hiram **82** 350 351 **118** 65
Hugh **54** 162
Huldah **88** 332
Huldah E. **77** 146
Isaac **118** 64 65
James **117** 283 284 **127** 216
James H. **91** 327
James S. **76** 263
Jane **90** 267 268 **107** 156
Jane Lawrence (Cooper)
   94 138
Jared **118** 152
Jemima **52** 225
Jessie Rebecca **92** 221
Joan **84** 310 313
Joanna **84** 310
Joanna (Butler) **127** 26
Job **117** 21 284 **127** 150
   148 278
Joel **104** 227 **127** 218
Johanna **84** 310
John **52** 275 **59** 39 319 **63**
   199 **70** 96 **81** 253 **82** 154
   84 304-316 **90** 61 263
   266-268 371 **94** 270 **100**
   229 **102** 74 105 **111** 150
   164 **112** 353 **113** 201
   236 **127** 26 **145** 364
John F. **118** 65
John Frank **81** 253
Jonathan **102** 16 **127** 143
   216
Joseph **52** 275 **82** 351
   97 264
Joseph A. **135** 249
Katharine **90** 266-268 371
Kirsopp **145** 197
Laban **82** 351
Lancelot **90** 195 265-268
   371 372 **93** 177
Levin **148** 278
Lilla May **81** 254
Louisa E. **100** 229 **105** 296
Lucy **63** 199 **66** 22 **113** 236
   117 20
Lucy (Brown) (Pillsbury)
   97 264
Luke **52** 275
Lydia Amanda **86** 438 439
Lydia Ann **118** 65
Margaret **59** 320 **84** 305
   309-311 313 314 **102** 16

LAKE *cont'd*
106 167 **111** 150 151
Margaret (Reade) **84** 113
304 315 316 **111** 150
Maria (Castle) **84** 310
Marie **84** 310
Martha **84** 304 310 316 317
111 151
Martin **118** 310
Mary 52 275 **59** 39 171 **61**
189 **69** 200 **84** 306 311
312 **90** 267 268 **113** 15
16 **124** 216 222-224 **125**
177 243 **126** 20 21 **137**
183
Mary (Castle **84** 311
Mary (Dyer) **86** 439
Mary (Landers) **124** 272
Mary (Parker) **113** 16
114 135 **124** 216 222
272
Mary (Ryder) **84** 314
Mary Aurelia (Fuller)
135 249
Mary Elizabeth **76** 14
Mary G. **117** 284
Mary J. **113** 315
Mary Jane **81** 253
Mary Prudence **97** 382
Mary W. **116** 218
Mercy (Heffernan)
148 278
Mercy J. **116** 218
Myra **81** 254
Nancy **125** 177 **135** 249
Nathaniel **52** 275
Nathaniel G. **117** 285
Nellie Delmont **79** 144
Nicholas **111** 164
Noah **87** 320 **127** 216
Olive Elizabeth **107** 157
Olive Fuller **82** 350 351
Otis **116** 218
Parnell **84** 310 314
Patience (Gifford)
129 337
Penelope **96** 50 **128** 114
Peter **84** 309 315
Philip H. **118** 65
Philip W. **118** 65
Polly **76** 130 263
Rebecca **52** 275 **84** 310
Reuben **76** 140
Rhoda **88** 125 **148** 278
Richard **84** 304 306-316
92 208 **106** 76 **114** 135
124 212 222 **127** 112
217 **133** 137
Robert **84** 306 310 312 **90**
267 268 371 **126** 142
Rodman **118** 151
Reuben **148** 278
Ruth **117** 21
Ruth (Rowell) **100** 229
Sally **56** 258
Salvina **135** 249
Samuel **84** 310 317 **117** 21
Samuel Albert **60** 298
Sarah **52** 275 **84** 310 312
104 227 **107** 157 **117**
284 **118** 152

LAKE *cont'd*
Sarah (Peet) **102** 105
Sarah E. **103** 67
Sarah Elizabeth **81** 253
Sibilla **84** 310
Sibyl **84** 306 309 310 313
314
Silas **117** 283
Sisbell (Hedendon)
84 310
Stephen **52** 275
Susan **84** 310 312 **117** 283
Susanna **85** 230 **125** 239
Susanna (Minard)
128 114
Susanna L. **118** 310
Tabitha **84** 308 312 313
Tabitha (Eliot) **97** 264
Tamsen **84** 308 313 314
Thomas **51** 417 **52** 275 **55**
347 **59** 106 **61** 189 **64** 92
67 309 **82** 154 **84** 304
305 308 309 311 313-316
85 131 **86** 244 **90** 267
268 371 **95** 390 **102** 105
118 152 **119** 19 **124** 101
Thomasine **84** 309 314
Unis **127** 216
Violet (Symons) **125** 105
Walker **76** 144
Weltha (Chase) (Grinman)
87 320
William **52** 275 **54** 219
56 124 **66** 22 162 **69** 200
84 312 **107** 157 **108** 33
125 105 **127** 14 26 110
147 **128** 114 **135** 290
William (Mrs.) **84** 307
William B. **86** 439
William Fletcher (Mrs.)
82 253 83 232
William Robert **128** 114
Willie L. **117** 209
Wolf **92** 221
LAKEIR
Sarah (Brown) **61** 118
William **61** 118
LAKEMAN Daniel **63** 17
Elizabeth **79** 54 **126** 67
Eunice **105** 154
Hannah **53** 338 **61** 240
Hannah W. **88** 283
Isaac **92** 318
John **56** 84 **78** 417 **79** 43
Joseph **61** 238
Lydia Ann **114** 182
Moses B. **61** 321 **90** 44
Pelatiah **78** 421
Peter **106** 28 29
Rebecca **61** 238
Sally **88** 32
Samuel **53** 338
Sibyl (Coburn) **90** 44
Thomas **114** 182
LAKEN — Sgt. **54** 188
LA KEUX Richard **116** 84
LAKIN Laking
Abigail **61** 73 **63** 319-322
324 326 **126** 15
Abraham **63** 319-322 326
Alice (Rowell) **138** 129

LAKIN *cont'd*
Ambrose **63** 325
Ann **63** 346
Anna **63** 324
Annis T. C. (Simpson)
88 331
Asa **70** 302
Benjamin **63** 319-324
88 331
Charles Gilford **103** 278
Charles Winslow **102** 64
David **63** 321 322 325
Dorothy **63** 325
Ebenezer **63** 321-324 326
Edna Maria **103** 180
Elizabeth **51** 448 **63** 291
319-325 **64** 145 **81** 27
108 243
Esther **63** 323
Esther (Sawtell) **126** 135
Eunice **63** 323 325 326 **64**
311 **81** 27
Flora E. (Laughton) **101**
217 **103** 180
Gabriel **63** 322 324 326
George **90** 55 106
Hannah **63** 321 322 325
64 311 312
Hannah J **68** 151
Harriet **101** 33
Harriet S. **102** 64
Ida Rebecca **103** 278
Isaac **63** 291 295 321 325
64 145
Jacob **63** 321-323 326
James **63** 321 324 325
Jane **63** 323
Jane (Arnold) **90** 106
Jemima **63** 324
Jerusha **63** 325
Joann **103** 278
Joanna (Smith) **101** 33
John **56** 44 **63** 318-326 364
81 27
Jonathan **63** 319-321 326
P 63 324
Joseph **63** 319 320 322
325 326 **108** 243
Joshua **63** 346
Josiah **63** 319 320 323 325
326
Lemuel **63** 324
Levi **63** 325 **64** 311
Lorenzo Judson **102** 64
Lucretia Laura **103** 278
Lucy **63** 323
Lucy Ellen **103** 278
Luther **101** 33 217 **102** 64
103 180 278
Lydia **56** 44 **63** 319-322 325
326 **81** 27 **106** 70 **126**
129
Martha **63** 321-323
Mary **63** 318-320 322-326
380 **97** 88 **104** 166
Mary Ann **90** 104
Miriam **63** 324
Nathaniel **63** 325 **69** 126
Oliver **63** 324
Phebe **63** 322 324 326
Priscilla **63** 324

LAKIN *cont'd*
Prudence **64** 311
Rachel **63** 323
Rebecca **63** 325 **102** 64
Robert Franklin **103** 278
Robinson **63** 325
Rosella **102** 64
Roxanna **102** 309
Ruth **63** 323
Samuel **63** 322
Sarah **63** 319 320 323 325
326 **64** 145
Sarah B. **78** 141
Sibyl **56** 44 **63** 324 325
Simeon **63** 325
Susan (Diman) **90** 55
Susanna **63** 325
Susie Mabell **103** 278
Sylvester **78** 141
Thomas **63** 320-322
Tryphosa **67** liv
William **51** 448 **63** 291 318-
326 **138** 129
Winslow **126** 135
LALANDE
Adolphe **69** 145
Henry Hector **69** 145
Winnie Leona **69** 145
Zulima **69** 145
LALER Simon **128** 115
LALLER M. **91** 327
LALLY John **125** 219
Margaret **121** 222
Sarah **95** 294
Susanna (Wier) **125** 219
LALONE
George Anderson
89 313
Martha Lemira (Williams)
89 313
LALOU Philippe **143** 202
LA LUZERNE
Anne Cesar de **116** 110
LALYNG
Agnes Wells **111** 311
LAMAM
Jacquemyne **143** 198
LAMAN
Charles F. **135** 79
Rachel (Pine) **135** 79
LAMAR Allen **73** 267
Christine **146** 135
Clarinda Huntington
(Pendleton) **95** 163
Elizabeth **52** 227 **73** 267
268
Francis **73** 263
James Sanford **95** 164
John W. **114** 186
Joseph Rucker **95** 163 164
Joseph Rucker (Mrs.)
89 306
Lucius Quintus
Cincinnatus **78** 159
Margaret (Anthony)
95 164
Marian T. **114** 186
Marion **114** 186
Martha (Urquhart) **95** 164
Mary **73** 268
Mary (Rucker) **95** 164

LAMAR *cont'd*
Mirabeau Buonaparte
78 159
Philip **95** 164
Philip R. **84** 172
Philip Rucker **85** 188 **95**
135 149 163
Priscilla **73** 150
Rachel **73** 144
Rebecca Evaline **78** 159
Richard **73** 152 **114** 186
Richard Melcom **73** 264
Robert **95** 164
Ruth (Davis) **95** 164
Sarah **73** 275
Sarah (Wilson) **95** 164
Susanna **73** 153
Thomas **95** 163 164
114 186
William **73** 231 **114** 186
William L. **114** 186
LAMARC John de **109** 21
LA MARE
William de **68** 358
LAMAS Abijah **95** 277
LAMAY Thomas J. **82** 442
LAMB Lambe
— Capt. **63** 374 375
— Col. **52** 452 **84** 384
104 195
— Dr. **95** 369
— Mr. **62** 131 132 **85** 6
— Mrs. **85** 6
____ (Dawes) **140** 59
____ (Eliot) **140** 161
Aaron **110** 66 **120** 160
Abiah **69** 187 334
Abial **57** 363 **62** 385 **99** 252
115 315
Abiel **84** 406 407 **109** 312
115 315 **116** 152
Abigail **57** 363 **66** 90 **70**
106 **123** 263
Abigail (Lewis) **110** 66
120 160
Adeline **68** 255 **110** 66
Aena (Garfield) **118** 79
Albert B. **88** 206
Alice **92** 37
Alpheus **112** 164
Ann **108** 41
Anna **108** 40 **109** 80
Asa **104** 118
Asena **69** 187
Avon **127** 299
Azubah **96** 286
Basil E. (Mrs.) **105** 154
Beckee **108** 41
Benjamin Waldo **140** 161
145 314
Bethiah **131** 156
Betsey **61** 300
Betsey (Lefebure) **84** 363
Betty **108** 41
Bryan **65** 235
Caleb **67** 373 375 **91** 66
99 308 313 314 **136** 311
321
Chancy **112** 164
Charles **60** 58 **77** 141
Charles Francis **84** 466

LAMB *cont'd*
Charles Francis (Mrs.)
78 332 **79** 202
Charles H. **147** 267 269
Charlotte M. **116** 62
Cynthia **60** 352
Daniel **62** lxxiii **87** 303
99 252
David **52** 312 **109** 312
121 260
Demaris **109** 147
Desire **91** 352 **145** 314
Desire (Swan) **142** 172
Desire (Thompson)
100 297
Dorothy **66** 236 **99** 104
134 52
Ebenezer **58** 163 **70** 106
99 252
Edward **54** 350 **108** 41 42
Edwin Travis **81** 108 219
115 228
Edwin Travis (Mrs.)
80 335
Elda Lohoma **101** 124
Eleanor **108** 41
Elijah **62** 270 **104** 118
Eliza **68** lxxvi **100** 89
137 29
Elizabeth **62** 385 **82** 463
108 41 **109** 312 **121** 258
123 264 **131** 156
Elizabeth (Curtis) **126** 142
Elizabeth (Gates) **121** 260
Elizabeth (Weld) **123** 294
Elizabeth A. **88** 334
Elizabeth Whitney **93** 138
99 69 152 252
Ella May **79** 202
Emeline **144** 109
Emery **116** 152
Emily Goddard **102** 144
Emory **101** 245 **105** 26
Emory C. **112** 164
Esau **131** 156
Esther **124** 188
Etta **117** 120
Eunice **108** 193
Experience **55** 177
Ezekiel **61** 373
Fannie Louvia (Wilson)
89 135
Florence Chase **98** 147
Frank Bird **59** xliv **60**
xxxviii 186 280 **62** 385
64 xxix **65** xxxiii **67** xxx
74 xxviii **80** 202 **82** 228
90 125 **96** 207 **102** 314
109 311 312 **110** 63
Fred M. **59** 331
Fred W. **54** 368 370 **55**
xxxii **58** 209 323 **60** 88
183 **62** 311
Fred William **58** xlv **59**
xliv **64** xxxi 97 **65** xxxiv
99 386 **66** xlix
Frederick **76** 265
Garrett D. **112** 164
George **58** xliii **59** 423
68 xliii lxxvi **71** 105 **89**
23 **114** 161 **140** 161

LAMB *cont'd*
George Clinton **68** lxxvi
Grace **59** 159
Grace Lucile **109** 311
Hannah **59** 159 **62** 200
Hannah Dawes (Eliot)
   86 102
Harriet **114** 182
Harriet Jane **109** 131
Helen **92** 37
Henry **62** 92 **86** 425
   131 156
Henry J. **90** 111
Henry W. **62** 218
Henry Whitney **62** xxi 92
Hilda **121** 190
Hiram **62** 270
Huldah **99** 313 314
Isaac **54** 370 **58** 209 **131**
   156 **132** 306
Jabez **90** 111
Jacob **131** 156
James **52** 264 **57** 403 **61**
   373 **84** 153 363 **86** 464
   91 352 **100** 297 **140** 161
   144 210 **145** 352
James G. **117** 235
James M. **117** 120
Jarius **109** 312
Jemima **59** 271 272
Joan **107** 215
Joanna **123** 260
Joel **109** 312
Joel Hall **109** 311 312
John **52** 77 **57** 297 **59** 88
   90 159 269-273 **62** 357
   359 **63** 242 351 **64** 165
   253 **65** 148 **71** 245 **77**
   239 **87** 303 **103** 38 **115**
   315 **123** 260 **138** 81 101
Jonathan **66** 238 **109** 312
   134 52
Joseph **59** 270 **65** 29 **126**
   142 **131** 156
Joshua **67** 297 **87** 398 **90**
   400 **92** 37 **97** 14 **99** 104
   105 286 287 **115** 293
Katharine (Lush) **100** 302
Lawrence **108** 79
Lemuel **142** 172
Lerotus **100** 89
Letitia **115** 112
Lisbon **87** 10
Louvisa **104** 118
Lovina **67** 378
Lucinda **94** 22
Lucy **79** 24 **112** 164
Lucy (Sanders) **127** 299
Luella A. M. **137** 31
Lurilda (Kirkpatrick)
   117 120
Luther **104** 118
Lydia **59** 88 270-273 **67** 373
   79 100 **123** 262
Lydia (Norton) **123** 262
Marcy **91** 198
Margaret **54** 350 **59** 159
   64 338
Margaret Eliot **86** 102
Maria (Bailey) **112** 164
Markes Graham **115** 112

LAMB *cont'd*
Marrett H. **112** 164
Martha **89** 23
Martin **115** 293
Mary **58** 163 **59** 159 **71** 22
   245 **90** 292 **104** 118 **112**
   141 **115** 293 **131** 156
   136 311 321 323
Mary (Alcock) **97** 14
Mary (Wise) **136** 311 321
Mary Putnam **51** 409
Michael **112** 286
Mildred Amanda
   (Payson) **109** 128
Nancy **108** 41
Nancy D. **104** 225
Nathan **69** 334 **84** 466
Nellie **108** 41
Olive **115** 293
Patience **57** 403 **61** 373
Peter **123** 294
Phebe **81** 96
Phineas **114** 161 **118** 79
Priscilla **76** 67 72
Rebecca **108** 41 **119** 14
Reuben **131** 156
Richard **108** 41 42
Robert **70** 184 **91** 352 **100**
   302 **113** 56 **140** 161
Rosanna **140** 161
Rosanna Duncan **145** 314
Rufus **72** 178 **74** 62
Ruth DeForest **104** 142
Sabrina **76** 266
Salem Towne **99** 252
Sally **108** 41 **115** 293
Sally B. (Munroe) **100** 89
Samuel **59** 269 **62** 200 **68**
   255 **108** 41 42
Sarah **59** 270 **62** lxxiii **68**
   255 **76** 265 **81** 170 173
   123 260 294
Sarah (Dean) **89** 23
Sarah (German) **92** 37
Sarah Dana **74** lx
Sarah Eleanor (Brown)
   87 10
Sarah German **92** 37
Sarah H. **74** 62
Sophia (Bailey) **112** 164
Stephen **107** 215
Stephen A. **69** 187 334
Susan **90** 367
Susanna **67** 297 375
Thankful **58** 160
Thomas **58** 160 **60** 186 **66**
   358 **68** 207 **83** 50 **85** 124
   86 102 **93** 304 **96** 207
   99 104 252 314 **109** 312
   115 315 **116** 152 **117**
   235 **131** 156 **138** 91 92
   140 59 161 **144** 210 **145**
   314
Tirza (Briggs) **126** 213
Tirzah **94** 22
Truxton German **92** 37
   111 323
Van Buren **86** 197 464
Warren **94** 22 **126** 213
William **51** 409 **64** 216
   82 334-336 **86** 420 **108**

LAMB *cont'd*
   41 42 **109** 26 **115** 112
   125 33 **131** 156
Lambard *see* Lombard
Lambarde *see* Lombard
LAMBDIN Lambden
   Lamdena
Ann **114** 189
Helen **81** 257
Nathaniel **62** 321
Phebe **81** 257
Sarah Ann **117** 259
William **81** 257
William McKendree
   81 257
Lambe *see* Lamb
Lamber *see* Lambert
Lamberd *see* Lambert
Lambersston *see*
   amberton
LAMBERT Lamber
   Lamberd
— Widow **82** 509
____ (Cunningham)
   140 55
A. Frances **122** 230
Abigail **83** 150 153 **97** 199
Abigail (Bumstead)
   140 312
Abishai **59** 405
Abraham **78** 414
Adeline Florence **83** 173
Alice **141** 358
Almira (Lenfest) **117** 163
Andrew **109** 270
Ann **99** 280
Anna **51** 389 **58** 387 **92** 81
Anna Jeannetta (Tebbs)
   105 50
Anne **51** 396 **126** 215
   148 134
Anthony **55** 103 **65** 22 28
   143 198
Antone **79** 283
Asenath **116** 198
Barbara **52** 262
Bartholinus **55** 103
Bartholomew **55** 102 103
Benjamin **55** 101 **66** 80
Betsey **147** 384
Caleb **58** 387
Carol Jean **105** 50
Catherine Cravath
   (Whitaker) **97** 131
Charles **67** 239
Charles Allen **68** 145
Charlotte **55** 309 **81** 282
Christian **97** 293
Constance **55** 102
Corliss Bancroft **97** 131
Daniel **110** 179 **111** 116
David **97** 131
Davis **140** 161
Deborah **52** 38 **53** 310 **59**
   259 **74** 88
Deborah (Gardner)
   134 332
Delia S. **117** 295
Donald Corliss **103** 225
Dorothy (Dill) **110** 179
E. **91** 327

LAMBERT *cont'd*
Ebbott **55** 102
Edward **56** 309 311 **78** 401
Edward Rodulphus
  79 223
Edward Whitney **55** lx
Elisha **84** 458
Elizabeth **51** 399 **55** 178 **56**
  309 311 **60** 153 **66** 148
  83 21 25 **91** 369 **110** 179
  125 100
Elizabeth (Beck) **83** 21
Elizabeth (Richardson)
  125 289
Elizabeth A. **83** 297 299
Elizabeth Augusta **83** 173
Elizabeth Hobson
  132 165
Elizabeth J. **73** 277
Elizabeth Sprague
  (Gould) **87 91 90** 47
Elizabeth V. (Brown)
  97 131
Ephraim **55** 101 **126** 215
  138 26 29 31
Ernestine **88** 396
Eunice (Norton) **84** 458
F. A. Heygate **51** 235
Flora May (Arey) **87** 16
Frances **122** 230
Frances Emily **68** 145
Francis **93** 185 **113** 259
  148 134
Frederic Nickerson
  83 173
Frederick D. (Mrs.)
  107 130
Frederick DeForest
  97 131
Friswith **99** 280 285 **100** 26
  139 **101** 248
Frizwell **99** 282
George **62** 243 **67** 239 **91**
  229 **99** 285
Georgia **123** 235
Gerard B. **84** 110 185
Gerard Barnes **136** 323
Gershom **105** 113
Harriet **54** 317 **55** 309
Hattie M. **109** 270
Henry **103** 225
Henry A. **97** 131
Henry Avalon **103** 225
Henry Clifford **83** 307
Henry S. **83** 299
Henry Siemers **83** 173
Hepsibah **53** 107 **59** 409
Herman Robert **79** 283
Hester Margaret **103** 225
Hickman **99** 122
Honora **144** 348 354
Howard Stanley (Mrs.)
  83 232 247
Huldah **60** 64
Ira C. **88** 305
Irene Florence (Gilbert)
  97 131
Iva **79** 283
James **57** 401 **58** 84 387
  59 75 76 78 135 138 309
  314 **60** 176 **62** 243 99

LAMBERT *cont'd*
  282
James B. **125** 38
James Franklin **118** 248
James L. **87** 91 **90** 47
Jane **61** 37
Jane Standish (Parker)
  (Colby) **113** 259
Jemima **136** 269
Jesse **52** 38 **53** 310 **64** 283
  79 223 **103** 225
Joan 454 **55** 103 **83** 454
Joan (Barker) **148** 134
Joanna **57** 401 **126** 215
John **55** 102 103 **57** 316
  58 260 265 387 **59** 140
  391 **60** 64 **84** 281 436 **91**
  229 230 **92** 69 **95** 14 16
  99 122 **100** 26 **125** 219
  289 **140** 161 312
John Albert **105** 50
John Ford **103** 225
John Warren **105** 50
John Wilson **87** 16
Joseph **59** 140 309 389
Joseph C. **141** 110
Joseph Elmer (Mrs.)
  109 130
Joshua **55** 101 **106** 86
  119 21
Julia **90** 393 394
Julia Emerson **68** 145
Julius N. **81** 282
Lewis **74** 88
Lizzie A. **83** 297 299
Lucy **55** 309 **59** 314
  106 141
Lucy A. (Laighton) **83** 299
Lucy Hill **82** 509
Luke **59** 78 **60** 43 **113** 134
Lurana **59** 391
Lydia **59** 138
Margery **55** 102 **92** 69
Marguerite **144** 208
Marguerite N. **144** 195
Marion J. **74** 88
Martha **81** 428
Mary **55** 103 **58** 260 **59** 135
  71 249 **78** 313 **81** 428
  84 436 **125** 104
Mary (Rees) **125** 219
Mary (Scanlon) **144** 348
  354
Mary (Woodward)
  125 102
Mary B. **88** 336
Mary Chapin **55** lx
Mary Davis **87** 228 233
Mary Hendee **83** 173
Mary Jane **74** 88
Matthias **134** 332
Mercy **53** 205
Nathan **53** 205
Nathaniel **68** 78 **117** 163
Nicholas **65** 230 **99** 280
  282 285 **100** 26 **101** 248
  271
Olive (Webber) **91** 229
Oliver **79** 426
Patricia Lee (Crutcher)
  97 131

LAMBERT *cont'd*
Phebe **141** 45
Porter **91** 229
Rachel **60** 43 316 **103** 230
Rachel Lowe **136** 322 323
Rachel Parkhill (Lowe)
  94 137 **136** 323
Richard **80** 316 **83** 193
  120 25 **144** 348 354
Richard Bowles **103** 225
Richard Holland **97** 131
Robert **79** 283 **110** 179 **113**
  56 **119** 21
Robert D. **97** 131
Roger **88** 305
Rose **80** 406
Ruby **97** 397
Ruth **58** 265 387 **88** 280
  136 361
Ruth (Lambert) **88** 280
Samuel **51** 249 251 252
  66 81 **92** 69 70
Sarah **51** 249-251 **52** 38 39
  53 310 **57** 401 **58** 84 **59**
  75 76 78 135 138 314 **60**
  176 **99** 122
Sarah Elizabeth **87** 91
Sarah G. (Corliss) **97** 131
Sarah M. **90** 116
Serene **72** 156 **106** 230
  143 234 235 **145** 292
Sherebiah **110** 179 **119** 21
Sibyl **122** 320
Susan **55** 103
Susanna **51** 291 **55** 101
  102 306 309
Thomas **51** 389 **52** 262 **55**
  102 178 **57** 86 280 401
  58 270 **65** 148 **66** 148
  67 58-62 132-134 262 **88**
  280 **93** 186
Thomas Ricker **93** 185
  186
Timothy **66** 81
Treat **81** 282
Tristram **72** 226
Wallace Corliss **92** 146
  103 77 125 225
Warren Charles (Mrs.)
  109 130
Wilhelmina Gertrude
  83 173
William **51** 250 **55** 103
  309 345 **57** 280 **58** 68 63
  351 **70** 264 **74** 88 **83** 21
  25 173 193 307 **93** 186
  119 246 **140** 55
William Boylston **83** 173
William Hofman **83** 295
William Perry (Mrs.)
  100 112
William Thomas **77** xxv
  79 196 **80** 204 **81** 215
  82 231 **84** 179 **89** 170
  90 123 **92** 136 **93** 141
  185 **113** 259
Willmote **55** 102 103
Zacheus **60** 339
Zipporah **60** 339
LAMBERTON Lambersston
  ——— **63** 56

LAMBERTON *cont'd*
— Capt. **65** 7
— Mr. **72** 97
Abigail **65** 7
Anna **92** 81
Deliverance **68** 283 284
Desire **68** 283 284
Dorothy (Harris) **106** 15
Elizabeth **68** 283 **109** 4
Eunice **106** 147
Francis Maria **72** 97
George **61** 189 **68** 273-
   276 283-285 **69** 52 53 **81**
   127 **109** 4 310
Hannah **68** 283 **80** 305
Henry **127** 179
Hope **68** 283 285 **109** 310
Margaret **61** 189 **68** 273
   283 **69** 53
Margaret (Dennis) **90** 172
Maria H. **72** 48
Mary **68** 283
Mercy **68** 273 275 283 284
   69 51-53 **71** 16
Obedience **68** 277 283 284
Parn **127** 178 179
Parn (Nichols) **127** 179
Stephen P. **72** 48
Thomas **106** 15 **141** 326
Lambes *see* Lambs
LAMBETH
Eliza **82** 289 292
Elizabeth **82** 44 292 297
Mary Weeks **112** 163
William H. (Mrs.) **112** 163
LAMBINET Emile **67** lvi
   95 327
LAMBING A. A. **53** 270
LAMBKINS Polly **89** 21
LAMBLY Patrick **115** 220
LAMBORD B. F. **84** 117
Belinda (Rich) (Snow)
   84 117
Elizabeth **77** 314
Ida (Dill) **84** 117
Isaiah Snow **84** 117
James Christie **84** 117
James Edwin **84** 117
John **78** 183
Luella (Hatch) **84** 117
Rebecca **126** 65
Thomas **79** 42
William **78** 301
Lamborn *see* Lambourne
LAMBORO
Benjamin F. **56** 21
LAMBOTH Philip **51** 46
LAMBOURNE Lamborn
Alice May **80** 167
Jane **75** 137
Joan **75** 137
Raymond M. **80** 167
William **75** 137
LAMBRIGHT Ann **95** 204
LAMBS Lambes
James **140** 49
Matthew **93** 384 387
Thomas **140** 49
LAMBSIELD Lambseild
Marena **134** 255
Martha **135** 252

Lambson *see* Lamson
Lamden *see* Lambdin
LAME — Capt. **62** 361
Annie W. (Stackpole)
   83 20
Joshua H. **83** 20
Lament *see* Lamont
Lamereaux *see* Lamoreaux
LAMES Abigail **73** 46
Huldah **73** 46
Nathaniel **73** 45 46
LAMEY Lany
Michael **117** 15
Lamfeer *see* Lamphear
LAMHAN Eliza **125** 177
LAMICIN
Ella (Allen) **130** 154
LAMIE Andrew **101** 72
LAMINGE Roger **76** 59
LAMIRE Jos. **70** 265
LAMKIN Claude Benjamin
   103 119
Mary **86** 68
LAMLEY
Elizabeth **69** 253
LAMM
Christina J. **73** 212
Etta N. **73** 212
LAMMAN Robert **76** 132
LAMMERS
Ed S. (Mrs.) **122** 18
LAMMIE Samuel **88** 304
LAMMON
Ainslee Seymour
   145 253
Alice Delilah **145** 253
Emma Letitia **145** 253
John Troup **145** 253
Mary Sophremia **145** 253
Patrick **145** 253
Phebe Emily
   (Fayerweather)
   145 253
Phebe Jane **145** 253
Sophia Amelia **145** 253
William Benjamin
   145 253
LAMMOND Mary **115** 41
LAMMOT Margaretta
Elizabeth **85** 228
LAMOLLIER
Henriette **112** 228
LAMON Andrew **66** 31
Charles **126** 145
Dacey (Cousins) **126** 145
Henry Leo (Mrs.) **109** 130
John **119** 54
Lydia (Alden) **100** 183
Samuel **100** 183
LAMONDO Mary **123** 307
LAMONT La Ment
Lament La Mont
— Capt. **58** 235 236
— Mrs. **61** 137
Alfred **145** 159
Anne L. **108** 65
Augusta **92** 170
Belle Eldredge **103** 319
Corliss **117** 155
Daniel **92** 170

LAMONT *cont'd*
Frances Georgiana
   82 367
George **92** 170
Hannah (Dunham)
   92 170
Hannah (Maben) **92** 170
Isaac **91** 327
John **145** 159
Justin **92** 170
Lucy **77** 57
Margaret **92** 170
Margaret (Smith) **92** 170
Martin J. **92** 170
Mary **94** 187 **145** 159
Mary Elizabeth (Wood)
   83 433 **84** 24
Mary Elizabeth Jean
   83 311
Mary Wood **83** 311 **84** 29
Mehitable **145** 159
Nancy **92** 170 **116** 65
Newman J. **92** 170
Polly L. **92** 165
Robert **83** 311
Robert Laurance **83** 433
   84 24
Sarah **92** 172
Solomon **92** 170
Thomas **70** 191 **77** 57
   117 155
Thomas William **70** 190
Walter M. (Mrs.) **82** 367
LAMONTA
George H. **91** 327
LAMORE
Charlotte A. **117** 280
Frank P. **117** 280
John **117** 280
Margrette **115** 131
LAMOREAUX Lamereaux
   Lamoreux Lamoureux
Clarissa Minerva **79** 125
David Albert (Mrs.)
   103 119
Domitille (Cyr) **145** 130
James **79** 125
Jessie **100** 197
Joseph **145** 130
Minerva **68** 95
LAMOS Abigail **98** 223
James **89** 84
Lora **105** 66
Phebe **105** 74
LAMOTHE Leon **111** 49
LA MOTTE
William **51** 450-452
Lamoureux *see* Lamoreaux
LAMOYN Nancy **65** 367
LAMPE Lamp
Estelle Avery **119** 76
Jeremy **100** 223
William P. **119** 76
LAMPEN
Elsett **144** 335
Matthew **65** 31
William **144** 335
Wilmott **144** 335
LAMPER
Eliza **83** 433 **84** 24

LAMPHEAR Lamfeer
  Lampher Lamphere
  Lamphier Lamphire
  Lanphear Lanpher
  Lanphere Lanphier
  Leanfear
  —— **59** 209
  — Mr. **71** 116
  — Rev. Mr. **80** 55
  Aaron **127** 6
  Abner **54** 82
  Abraham **128** 222
  Albert Henry **83** 218 244
    245
  Alwilda (Moore) **117** 165
  Ann **135** 300
  Anna **120** 20
  Anson **105** 283
  Benjamin **125** 214
  Catherine Broughton
    89 112
  Champlin **128** 222
  Champlin W. **117** 164
  Daniel **128** 223
  David **52** 418 **128** 223
  Desiah **117** 164
  Dorothy **82** 292 296
  Eady Esmina (Ellis)
    117 164
  Ebenezer **128** 299
  Edward Everett **114** 157
  Electa **83** 365
  Elias **128** 221
  Elisha **76** 263
  Eliza **108** 225
  Ella Minerva **79** 129
  Emily **76** 263
  Esmina **117** 171
  Estella **117** 165
  Eunice **62** 375 **77** 39
  Experience **135** 300
  Fanny **121** 252
  Francis D. **117** 165
  Francis P. **78** 113
  George Washington
    81 282
  Hannah **141** 45
  Harriet M. (Shattuck)
    141 54
  Harry **60** 202
  Henrietta **135** 249
  Hezekiah **52** 418 **135** 300
  Huldah **83** 365
  James **117** 166 **128** 19
  Jennie L. **103** 48
  Joanna **61** 256
  John **135** 300
  Jon. K. **81** 494
  Joseph **135** 300
  Joshua **128** 300 303
  June **117** 124
  Langworthy **105** 280
    117 165 **128** 220
  Lovina **78** 87
  Lucinda **74** 295 **81** 494
    83 365
  Lucy **63** 372
  Lucy (Dunlap) **117** 166
  Martha A. **73** 38
  Mary **55** 12 **125** 187
    135 300

LAMPHEAR *cont'd*
  Mary (Edes) **124** 78
  Mary (Palmer) **135** 338
  Matthew **124** 22 **137** 26
  Milo **59** 209 **60** 74
  Milow **83** 365
  Miriam (Falker) **89** 113
  Nathan **128** 222
  Nathaniel **76** 263
  Olive E. (Walker) **117** 166
  Oliver **135** 300
  Patty **60** 199
  Polly **63** 175 **76** 263
  Prudence **76** 264 **109** 308
    135 300
  Rachel **54** 82
  Raymond **124** 78
  Richard **120** 20
  Rowland **128** 300
  Samuel **63** 175
  Samuel Deering **89** 113
  Sarah **60** 202 268 **71** 348 **80**
    15 **135** 338
  Sarah A. **117** 164
  Sarah B. **88** 333
  Shadrack **135** 300
  Sibyl **54** 81
  Simon **83** 365
  Solomon **120** 48 **135** 300
    338
  Stephen **105** 283
  Susan (Bond) **124** 22
    137 26
  Susanna (King) **125** 214
  Truman **76** 264
  Wealthy (Coombs)
    135 249
  William **80** 15 **83** 365
    135 249
  William A. **79** 129
  William W. **117** 166
LAMPIER Clement **69** 362
LAMPKIN Lampkyn
  Amy **68** 188
  Deborah **136** 135
  Robert **68** 188
LAMPLEATH
  — Lady **91** 69
  George **91** 69 70
LAMPLIER
  Hannah **101** 339
LAMPLUGH Ruth
  (Barrington) **91** 70
LAMPMAN
  Abraham **121** 318
  Emeline **76** 271
  Jacob **121** 318
  Peter **121** 318
  Richard **76** 271
LAMPORT Martha **104** 261
LAMPRECHT Johann
  Bernhardt **87** 35
  Shirley (Adams) **125** 72
LAMPREY —— **92** 320
  — Mr. **58** 138
  A. S. **69** 97
  Aaron **92** 318 322
  Abigail **59** 38
  Agnes **55** 103 106
  Asa **81** 146
  Benjamin **58** 31 **66** 151

LAMPREY *cont'd*
  Celinda C. **68** 101
  Charles **55** 103
  Clara **68** 97
  Daniel **58** 30
  Deborah **68** 260
  Edith **91** 390
  Elizabeth **65** 355 **92** 318
    142 258
  Ella S. **68** 101
  Eme **55** 103
  Emmanuel **55** 103
  George **55** 103
  George W. **68** 101
  James **55** 103
  Joan **55** 103
  John **55** 103 **58** 138 **92** 320
    125 93
  Lucy **66** 99 **97** 263 353
  Margery **55** 103
  Marie **55** 103
  Mary **65** 355
  Mary F. **96** 89
  Maurice **65** 355
  Morris **58** 33 34 **59** 38
  Nancy **81** 146
  Nathaniel **58** 35
  Reuben **68** 97
  Richard **55** 103
  Ruth (Smith) **97** 264
  Samuel **97** 264
  Sarah **90** 54 **96** 89
  Simon **66** 151
  William **55** 103 106
LAMPSHIRE
  Abel **60** 331
LAMPSON *see also*
  Lamson
  Abigail **61** 332 **62** 37 42
  Alvira H. **103** 280
  Benjamin **62** 43
  Elizabeth **70** 69 **71** 6 **94**
    224 **95** 63 **112** 143
  Elizabeth (Bancroft)
    94 220 221
  Ephraim **100** 35
  Esther **61** 341
  Guy Clerson **103** 280
  John **61** 332 337 **62** 38 41
    70 69 **71** 5 **148** 144
  Jonathan **61** 236 **71** 6
  Joseph **103** 280
  Lydia **62** 45 **100** 34 **103** 64
  Martha **62** 39 45
  Mary **62** 45 **94** 315
  Mary (Nichols) **94** 221 224
  Miriam (Dyer) **87** 230
  Peter **62** 41
  Phebe (Tibbetts) **100** 35
  Rebecca **61** 236
  Samuel **61** 335 **62** 45 46
  Sarah **61** 236 335 **94** 224
  Serviah **62** 27
  Thomas **61** 335 **62** 42 43
    45 **71** 6
  William **61** 335 **62** 42 43
    45
LAMPTON Anna
  (Wheaton) **124** 258
  Laura Arnold (Fracker)
    124 58 258

LAMSEY Benjamin **91** 327
LAMSFIELD
  Martha **134** 89
LAMSLY Henry **108** 256
LAMSON *see also*
  Lampson
  —— **54** 72 **57** 337 **92** 347
    350 355 **93** 64 256 **116**
    194
  — Capt. **65** 18
  — Mr. **57** 378 **69** 234
    91 269
  Abigail **86** 64 **112** 68 **121**
    318 **137** 242
  Abigail (Bryant) **137** 241
    242
  Abigail (Chase) **95** 211
  Albert Henry **60** 86 186
    65 313 **66** liii **67** xxx
    72 v x **73** v vi xi **74** v
    vii xi 160 **75** v vii xi xvi
    317 **76** v vii x 76 77 154
    77 v vii xv 154 324 **78**
    109 192 217 219 224 **79**
    187 213 215 **80** 196 219
    221 **81** 208 233 235 364
    82 125 127 221 248 250
    84 174 203 205 **85** 177
    212 **86** 185 212 **87** 162
    186 **88** 161 183 **89** 123
    144 166 295 **90** 119 127
    148 **91** 130 155 **92** 95
    101 108 137 159 220 359
    93 128 150 **94** 129 152
    95 138 159 211 295 **96**
    152 164 **97** 151 155
  Amos **118** 313
  Ann **96** 73
  Annie Laura (Mangum)
    93 137
  Benjamin **92** 282
  Betsey **52** 372
  Caleb **95** 211 **107** 257 258
  Caroline Elizabeth **92** 350
  Charlena (Tidd) **86** 197
  Charles **93** 256
  Charles Allen **92** 108
  Charles Marshall **93** 256
  Charles Rhodes **92** 347
  Cyrene Dam (Eaton)
    95 211
  Daniel S. **55** xxxii
  Daniel Sanderson **93** 64
  Darius Francis **65** 13
  David **145** 362
  Donald Charles **92** 108
  Dorothea **92** 10-18
  Dorothy **106** 196
  Ebenezer **64** 201 **77** 282
    107 262 **112** 68
  Elizabeth **74** 265 **81** 127 **94**
    220 224 **95** 63 **112** 68
    143
  Elizabeth (Adams) **112** 68
  Elizabeth (Eaton) **137** 242
  Elizabeth (Rice) **112** 68
  Elizabeth (Sanderson)
    127 190
  Ephraim H. **74** 265
  Ernest Eugene **92** 108
  Esther **107** 262

LAMSON *cont'd*
  Eunice **79** 246
  Flora Mandana **54** xli
  Frank Bailey **64** xxxi 201
  Frank Bates (Mrs.) **93** 137
  Gertrude Eaton **92** 108
    95 213
  Grace M. **78** 109
  Hannah **112** 68
  Helen Lee (Little) (Page)
    95 213
  Herbert **85** 195
  Isaac **78** 305
  Joanna (Tuttler) **118** 34
  Johanna Powell **120** 70 71
  John **88** 331 **92** 347 350 355
    93 64 **94** 221 380 **95** 63
    211 **101** 281 **132** 39
  John A. **88** 286
  Jonathan **81** 127 **137** 242
  Joseph **59** 252 **78** 313 **95**
    211 **107** 260 **108** 243
    112 68
  Leveriah **106** 263
  Lydia **100** 34 **103** 64
    118 34
  Lydia (Porter) **95** 211
  Martha **79** 15 **88** 276
    148 144
  Martha (Perkins) **95** 211
  Martha Olivia (Perry)
    116 194
  Mary **56** 62 **91** 352 **94** 315
    112 68
  Mary (Bartlett) **101** 281
  Mary (Francis) **88** 286
  Mary Agnes **77** 184
  Mary Ann **68** 134
  Mary Ann (Ford) **88** 331
  Mary Ella **65** 313
  Mary Ella (Weeks) **95** 213
  Mary Jane (Butler) **95** 211
  Mehitable (Brintnal)
    132 39
  Mehitable (Holt) **137** 242
  Michael J. **123** 10
  Nathaniel **54** 71 **87** 230
    233 **106** 196 200 **107**
    256 **145** 361 362
  Nellie (Griggs) **92** 108
  Newton Webber (Mrs.)
    86 197
  O. E. **112** 68
  Otis Ephraim **64** 201
  Patience **107** 262
  Peter **91** 327
  Phebe **137** 242
  Phebe (Wyatt) **123** 10
  Rachel (Sanborn) **95** 211
  Rebecca **137** 242
  Rebecca (Collins) **140** 52
  Rebecca (Crosby) **137** 242
  Rufus **92** 108 **95** 211
  Rufus Edward **92** 108
    95 213
  Rufus William **92** 108 **95**
    211 212
  Ruth **135** 336
  Sally **88** 276
  Samuel **56** 61 62 **79** 46 **94**
    220 221 224 **107** 96 **127**

LAMSON *cont'd*
    190 **137** 242 **144** 224
  Sarah **78** 126 **94** 224 **95** 63
    137 242
  Sarah (Ayers) **95** 211
    114 319
  Sarah (Hartwell) **112** 68
  Seth Albert **92** 108
  Susan **65** lxiii **108** 243
  Susanna **59** 252
  Thomas **81** 127 **106** 180
  Timothy **107** 262
  W. J. **60** 186
  William **60** 186 **72** 162
    95 211 212 **114** 319 **118**
    34
  William George **92** 108
  William J. **95** 212
  William Judson **72** 162
  Zubah **81** 127
LAMUNYON Lamunion
  Lemunyon
  Arowit **118** 66 308
  H. **148** 157
  Howard **137** 77
  John **117** 283 **137** 77
  Lydia (Sawdy) **148** 280
  Nancy (King) **148** 157
  Phebe **118** 66
  Phebe (Sherman) **137** 77
    148 280
  Philip **65** 192 **127** 149
  Samuel **127** 149 **137** 77
    148 280
  Thomas **137** 77 **148** 280
LAMYRA Rebecca **87** 394
LAN Ida Mercy **63** 50
  William **63** 50
LANAHAN —— **98** 371
  Marisita R. **98** 77
LANAVAD John **66** 244
LANCASHIRE
  Henry **52** 137 138
  James **52** 137 138
  Rebecca **52** 137
  Susanna **52** 137
LANCASTER
  De Lancaster Lancester
  Lankester
  —— **59** 110 **85** 302
    112 233
  — Duke of **145** 12
  — Earl of **145** 9
  — Mrs. **103** 195
  — Rev. **103** 193
  — Widow **105** 280
  Abigail (Rowe) **91** 387
  Adelaide Maria (de Rieux)
    95 82
  Agnes **68** 323 324 **69** 26
    80 404
  Agnes Maria **82** 106
  Alston Howard **88** 401
  Angelett (Brown) **124** 229
  Annas **63** 358
  Annis **68** 325
  Apphia **56** 208
  Bartlett **95** 50
  Betsey **133** 324
  Catherine **135** 76
  Daniel **64** 229 **67** 182 270

LANCASTER *cont'd*
277 **68** 96 **90** 87 **118** 39
95 **119** 21
Daniel Moody **89** 48
David **97** 395
Dorothy **70** 168 **103** 191
Dorothy (Carew) **113** 221
Dorothy (Harvey)
133 232
Drusilla (Le Grand) **95** 82
Ebenezer **97** 395
Edmund (First Earl of)
141 94
Elihu **119** 21
Elizabeth **60** 18
Elizabeth Ann **89** 47 48 52
Esther **103** 258
Fidelia **133** 324
Flora Evelyn **81** 96
Francis M. **124** 229
Francis S. **91** 387
Geoffrey **95** 304
Gilbert **96** 104 309 318
104 271 **115** 47 48
Godith **103** 201
Harry Fred **60** 186
Hawis **95** 304
Helewise **96** 103 120 309-
312 **103** 202 **115** 48
Henretta **91** 386
Henry **58** 47 **63** 358 **68** 324
325 **69** 26 **70** 168 **89** 52
133 232 **135** 76
Hiram **114** 81
Jacob **90** 87 **98** 207
James Kimball **74** 304
Jane G. (Reed) **98** 207
Joan **113** 221
John **63** 348 **65** 48 166 170
171 **95** 50 52 82 **96** 308
317 **111** 58 **113** 221 223
John Alexander **95** 82
John Edward **81** 217 **82**
106 **120** 146
John Lord **95** 304
John of Gaunt (Duke of)
72 136
Jordan **96** 107 309
Joseph **88** 401 **119** 20
Joseph F. (Mrs.) **101** 321
Judith **58** 47
Levi **105** 289
Louisa Crosby **74** 304
Louisa Maria (Kimball)
112 233
Louise **82** 265
Margaret **80** 404 **95** 51
Mary **70** 168 **133** 324
135 76
Mary Louise **74** 304
Mary Maria (Ely) **95** 82
Matthew **51** 254
Mercy **60** 18 **95** 51
Narcissa (Reed) **98** 207
Nathan **90** 87
Nathaniel **95** 82
Nellie **69** 315
Phebe **117** 67
Polly **133** 324
Preston **69** 315
Rezin **81** 97

LANCASTER *cont'd*
Rhoda **81** 97
Richard **105** 289
Robert **60** 18
Robert Alexander **90** 135
199 **95** 73 82 148
Roger **95** 304 **96** 107 113
308 311
Roxanna D. **91** 387
Sally **135** 76
Samuel **60** 44
Sarah **79** 259 **85** 302 **111** 56
113 223
Sarah (Lee) **114** 81
Sarah (Stover) **85** 302
Sewall **103** 193
Stephen **83** 63
Thomas **60** 186 **63** 346 **64**
54 **86** 434 **98** 207 **103**
189 191 194 195 255 258
121 247 **135** 76
Valentine **91** 327
William **80** 362 **94** 345
95 396 **96** 93 94 103 307-
315 318 319 **97** 243 103
199 201 202 283 **105** 288
107 122 **115** 46 49 **116**
315 **117** 233 **135** 76
Zelotes **95** 51
LANCE
Jeremiah **83** 81 294
Mary **83** 81 294 **99** 282
Mary (Temple) **100** 296
Samuel **101** 162
Sarah **63** 173 **99** 282
Sarah (Hayden) **100** 302
Sarah Louisa **91** 76
Susan **83** 81 294
Thomas **100** 302
William **57** 280 **99** 282
100 296
LANCELOTT
Alice **142** 139
LANCEY Lancy - *see also*
elancey
Elizabeth **83** 167
Jane **63** 286
Mary (Jones) **126** 209
Samuel **83** 167
Samuel F. **126** 209
LANCHESTER
Jonathan **58** 19
Polly **58** 19
Lanckton *see* Langton
LANCOUR A. Harold **92**
210 **106** 203 **118** 158
169
Lancton *see* Langton
Lancy *see* Lancey
LAND —— **108** 269
Abigail (Wales) **90** 56
Anna (Keen) **105** 49
Aubrey C. **109** 318
Donna **105** 49
Elizabeth **74** 46 **109** 131
Faustus **105** 49
James **105** 49
Nicholas **90** 56
Priscilla **67** 335
Robert Herman (Mrs.)
109 130

LAND *cont'd*
William Goodfellow
87 174
LANDA Jose de (Mrs.)
89 372
LANDAIS Amelia Augus-
tine **51** 104
Louis **51** 104
LANDAUER
Bella C. **107** 171
LANDBERG
Annie A. **89** 351
J. L. **89** 351
Ray **89** 351
LANDBORG
Adolf **128** 265
Carrie (Parson) **128** 265
Hilda Caroline **128** 265
LANDCHARATS
— Mr de **125** 98
Landdon *see* Landon
LANDELL
George Albert **79** 329
Henrietta Maria **79** 329
Lydia **143** 140
Mabel **79** 329
Margaret (Cutts) (Pike)
121 171
Thomas **121** 171
LANDELS James **62** 301
Lander *see* Landers
LANDERKIN
Hannah **125** 291
LANDERS Lander
—— **63** 52
— Mr. **79** 305
—— (West) **140** 259
Abiel **124** 281
Abigail **113** 113 **124** 45
49 51 210-213 216 221
269 270 279 282-284
Abigail (Fish) **124** 282 283
Abigail (Gifford) **124** 215
129 41
Abigail (Hoxie) **124** 273
Abishai **124** 52 268 269
Abner **124** 281
Abraham **124** 215 216 273
274
Alice **124** 46
Almira **124** 279 280
Alvah **124** 279
Alvin **124** 269
Amos **124** 45 49-51 211-
213 267-270 281
Ann **124** 222 224
Anna **124** 48 210 275
Anna (Perry) **116** 42
Annah (Jones) **124** 273
Ansel **124** 281
Anselm **124** 282
Aquila **124** 220 275 276
Asahel **124** 223 224 279
Asenath (Fish) **124** 274
Aurelia **124** 279
Avis K. **124** 283
Benjamin **124** 47 48 56
220 222 283
Bethuel **124** 282
Caleb **73** 212 **124** 211 266
267 280

LANDERS *cont'd*
Caleb N. **124** 282
Caroline **88** 53 **124** 274
Charles W. **81** 282 **91** 199
Chloe **124** 274 281
Chloe (Hatch) **124** 281
Content **124** 52 53 210
   211 217 **129** 35
Content (Dexter) **124**
   209 210 **127** 252
Content (Nye) **115** 273
   120 288 **124** 52 53
Cynthia **124** 274
David **124** 218 **127** 256
David Y. (Mrs.) **120** 77
Davis **124** 283
Deborah **115** 95 273 274
   116 44 **119** 261 262 **124**
   46 48 217 221 275
Deborah (Dotey) **119** 173
   124 57 59
Deborah (Freeman) **119**
   261 262 **124** 46-48 55
Deborah (Ryder) **124**
   268 278
Delia J. **115** 132
Deliverance **124** 56 57
Desire **124** 278
Dotha (Bissell) **124** 278
Dura **88** 155
Ebenezer **124** 46 48 52 54-
   56 209 210 223 224 266
   276 277 **127** 252
Edmond **124** 281
Edmund **88** 53 155
Edward **126** 23 **140** 259
Edwin **124** 279
Electa **124** 279
Eliza Ann **124** 274
Elizabeth **117** 308 **119** 173
   124 56 57 213-215 217
   219 267 271-273 283 284
Elizabeth (Allen) **124** 272
Elizabeth (Bishop) **124** 57
Elizabeth (Carpenter)
   124 278
Elizabeth (Davis) **124**
   211 268 271 272 282 283
Elizabeth (Fuller) **124** 282
Elizabeth (Swift) **124** 267
   268 271 283
Elizabeth Ann (Brown)
   126 205
Elvira **124** 278 279
Erma Poston **120** 77
Esmond **124** 43
Esther B. **124** 51
Eunice **124** 282 283
Eunice (Soames) **124** 275
Experience **124** 211 267
   271
Experience (Robinson)
   124 211 270 271
Ezra **124** 273
Franklin **124** 280
Freeman **124** 52 211-213
   268 269 283
George **124** 274 279 280
   284
Gershom **124** 54 55 219
Hannah **88** 53 155 **124** 46

LANDERS *cont'd*
   211 213 214 220 267 271
   273
Harriet **124** 274 279 280
   283
Harriet M. **115** 132
Harrison **124** 274
Hasadiah **124** 45
Isaac **124** 221
Isaiah **124** 223 224 277 280
Jabez **116** 42 **124** 55 218
   275
James **124** 275 279 280
Jane **119** 262 **124** 43 44 49
   57 211-213 219 **128** 247
Jane (Hamblen) **124** 281
Jane (Kirby) **124** 43 44
Jean **124** 56 57
Jemima **124** 53
Jemima (Swift) **124** 283
Jerusha **113** 15 16 113
   124 216
Jerusha (Parker) **113** 16
   113 **114** 135 **124** 216
   217 222
Jesse **124** 275
Joanna **65** 130 **88** 53
John **63** 26 **64** 219 **112** 178
   115 273 **116** 43 **120** 288
   124 42 44 46 51-54 209
   211-213 215-217 223 224
   267-273 275 277 278 280
   282 823 **127** 17 **129** 41
   138 322
John M. **126** 205
Jonathan **66** 37 **124** 266
Joseph **115** 92 **116** 43 **119**
   173 **124** 44 45 47 48 51
   56 209 210 213 214 216
   220-224 271 273 274 277
   278 280 282 283 **127** 256
   128 258 259 **129** 37 235
Joshua **124** 221
Judith C. **124** 283
Keziah **124** 283
Ledy **124** 215
Lefe **88** 67
Levi **124** 270 272 282-284
Lot **88** 53 **124** 270 272 281
Love **124** 282
Love (Davis) **124** 282-284
Lucinda **124** 221
Lucretia (Butler) **124** 280
Lucy **124** 220 224 278
Lucy Maria **124** 280
Luke **124** 266
Lydia **73** 212 **108** 66 **117**
   194 **124** 52 56 57 214-
   216 219 267 272
Lydia (Baker) **124** 273
Lydia (Clifton) **124** 52
   214 215 272
Lydia (Sollows) **124** 275
Lydia (Weeks) **134** 239
Marcellus **124** 279 280
Marcy **88** 67 **124** 53
Margaret **124** 46 53
Maria **120** 288 **124** 53
Maritte (Hoyt) **124** 280
Marshall **124** 279
Martha **124** 44 217

LANDERS *cont'd*
Martha (Hatch) **124** 281
Mary **100** 239 **112** 178
   124 44 55 210 211 217
   220 221 224 266 272 273
   275 278 282 **133** 232
Mary (Fish) **120** 239
   124 274
Mary (Lake) **124** 222-224
Mary (Pitman) **124** 275
Mary (Pollard) **124** 278
Mary (Rowley) **124** 269
Mary (Willard) **138** 322
Mary A. **124** 266
Mary D. (Baker) **124** 274
Mary F. (Bodfish) **126** 23
Mehitable **124** 54 55 274
Mehitable (Bates) **124** 274
Mercy **124** 43 44 53 279
Mercy (Goodspeed)
   124 279
Merty **124** 44
Molly **124** 217
Moody **124** 274
Nathan **108** 66 **117** 194
   119 261 **123** 135 **124** 47
   48 55 56 210 219 276
Neal (Mrs.) **124** 218
Nicholas **124** 51 270 280
   281
Olive **120** 239 **124** 275 277
Olive (Osborne) **124** 276
Olivia **124** 218 219
Patience **124** 274
Patience (Bates) **124** 273
Peleg **124** 56 57 220 275
   276
Peter **51** 461 **124** 266
Phebe **124** 281
Philander **124** 280
Polly **124** 279
Polly (Farnsworth)
   124 280
Polly (Long) **124** 278
Prince **124** 211 213 267 269-
   272 281 283 284
Priscilla **88** 53
Prudence **124** 56
Prudence (Barlow) **124** 55
Rachel **124** 46 53 275
   126 291
Rachel (Freeman) **124** 45
   46
Rachel (Paris) **124** 266 275
Rebecca **51** 461 **124** 45
   210 284
Rebecca (Allen) **124** 45
Recompense **124** 52 213-
   215 270 272
Relief **124** 278
Remember **124** 221
Reuben **124** 211-213 267
   270 272 283
Richard **124** 44-46 49 211
   215 267 271-273 283 284
   129 224
Robinson **124** 269 270 281
   134 239
Rose **124** 213 267 270
Rosella **124** 274
Ruth **124** 219 220 282

LANDERS *cont'd*
Ruth (Benson) **124** 219
Ruth (Fish) **124** 273
Sally **124** 221
Samuel **64** 114 **114** 162
  124 266 281
Sarah **51** 465 **93** 60 **112** 178
  113 112 **114** 135 **124** 44
  45 52 211-213 215 220-
  224 266 **125** 135 **126** 60
  61
Sarah (Bates) **124** 217 275
Sarah (Crowell) **124** 218
Sarah (Freeman) **124** 49
  50 214
Sarah (Lovell) **124** 220
Sarah (Perry) **116** 43
Savery **124** 211 212 214
  215 270 272 284
Sealed **121** 133 **124** 55 217
  218 275 **125** 131
Seneca **88** 53
Seth **124** 221
Solomon **124** 277 278
Stephen **88** 67 **124** 210
  266 278
Susan **121** 240 **124** 221
Susanna **124** 281-283
Susanna (Perry) **116** 43
Tabitha **124** 44
Tabitha (Phinney)
  124 274
Temperance (Tobey)
  124 54
Thankful **124** 60 221 274
  275
Thankful (Handy) **124**
  218 **125** 131
Thankful (Hinckley)
  124 268
Thirza (Phelps) **124** 280
Thomas **113** 15 16 113
  114 177 **114** 135 **116** 43
  149 **119** 261 **120** 239
  123 141 **124** 42-47 50 53-
  55 58 59 146 209-211
  216 217 220 222 223 266
  267 273-275 277-280
  125 33 **127** 250
Thorndyke **116** 42
Timothy **124** 217 275
William **124** 42 43 268 275
William R. **126** 23
Zerviah (Burlingame)
  124 280
Zerviah (Warren) **124** 280
Zilpha **124** 221
LANDERSON
Sarah **88** 284
LANDES Aurelia **124** 279
LANDFIS John **105** 281
LANDIES
Peter **65** 80 264 340
LANDIMAN
William **125** 42
LANDINGHAM Susan
  (Harwood) **85** 199
LANDIS Dorothy Kathryn
  109 130
Henry Kinzer **94** 304
John **144** 55

LANDIS *cont'd*
Mary (Kelley) **113** 81
Peter **113** 81
LANDLEY
Mary D. **105** 299
LANDMAN — Mrs. **121** 98
  122 120
Edward **79** 39
James **55** 389
LANDON Landdon
— Mr. **71** 51
— Mrs. **122** 70
Abner **70** 76
Adaline (Hall) **145** 132
Addie **82** 174
Addie May **145** 132
Adelaide **103** 138
Adelaide (Denno) **145** 132
Alice M. **145** 132
Arthur **145** 132
Bethiah **53** 170 **65** 6
Betty **79** 330
Caroline Holmes **85** 104
Charles Griswold **103** 138
Charlotte **123** 94 227 305
  308
Charlotte (Hoyt) **123** 50
Charlotte L. **123** 223
Cynthia **73** 212
Daniel **73** 9
David **103** 138 **128** 48
David H. **145** 132
Deborah **53** 170
Dorcas **112** 243
Eleanor **103** 138
Elisha **123** 227 305
Elisha H. **123** 52
Emily Melissa (Clark)
  82 237 **93** 136
Eunice **70** 76 **73** 9
Ezra Hoyt **123** 227
Francis Griswold **86** 197
  102 116 **103** 124 138
Franklyn T. **145** 132
George **73** 212
George P. **145** 132
George Washington
  85 95
Glorianna **53** 171
Hannah **53** 170 **59** 66 **61**
  96 **62** 335 **65** 6
Hildreth (Chamberlain)
  145 132
Hoyt **123** 223
Hugh McKennan **85** 95
Hugh McKennan (Mrs.)
  84 110 185 **85** 95 189
  202 **89** 134 181
Isaac **76** 50
Isabella **115** 44
James **53** 171 **61** 96
Jared **53** 170
Jessie (Spalding) (Walker)
  85 106
Joanna (Shute) **139** 304
John **60** 341 **122** 48
Joseph **53** 171 **139** 304
L. **101** 291 292
Lydia **60** 341
Marcellus **145** 132
Margaret **53** 171

LANDON *cont'd*
Marianne **123** 95
Marianne F. **123** 45 225
Martha **53** 170 **73** 9 **126** 12
Mary **53** 171 **61** 96 **102** 124
  123 91 306
Mehitable **70** 76
Mills **123** 305
Mills J. **123** 98
Mills J. (Mrs.) **123** 98
Nathan **53** 170 171 **61** 96
  103 138
Nathaniel Ruggles
  103 138
Nelson **123** 306
Parnal **53** 170
Phebe (Phelps) **123** 306
Ralph **101** 124
Rebecca **115** 45
Richard **82** 174
Rose (Clark) **145** 132
Ruth **70** 122 **115** 33
Sally **73** 10
Samuel **53** 170 **59** 66 **62**
  335 **65** 6 **103** 138
Sara Catherine **123** 305
Sarah **82** 174
Seth **73** 9 10
Sylvia **85** 431
Thomas **65** 118
Tyla **122** 216
Walter F. **145** 132
Weston Miles (Mrs.) **81**
  363 **82** 237 **93** 136
William **105** 73
William Rufus **123** 227
LANDOR
Walter Savage **71** 70
LANDQUIST
Virginia **105** 49
LANDRESS
Charlotte **90** 47
LANDRETH
Lewis **128** 269
Mary **102** 122
Viola (Mardock) **128** 269
LANDRUM
Mary Ann **109** 310
Peter **109** 310
LANDRUS
Peter Paul **79** 302
LANDRY
Alexander **131** 96
Angelique **143** 9
Arthur E. **142** 176
Charlotte-Josephine
  (LeBlanc) **131** 97
Claude **64** 287
Elizabeth **64** 287
Jeanne (Robichaux) **143** 7
Joseph **143** 7
Joseph Raymond **131** 93
Josephine **131** 95
Josephine-Albina **131** 93
Leo Paul **118** 73
Leonie **131** 93
Louise **131** 93
Madeleine (Robichaux)
  143 5
Marguerite **143** 6
Marie **131** 93 **143** 8

LANDRY *cont'd*
Marilyn R. **143** 361
Marilyn Randall **142** 165
176 393
Perrine (Bourg) **143** 5
Pierre **143** 5
Rene **143** 5
Simon **131** 95 97
LANDSEER Edwin **62** 166
LANDSHEARE
Hercules **107** 61
Jonas **107** 61
LANE Lain Laine
— Capt. **58** 155 **120** 63 123
130 135 203 207 213 298
303 **121** 59 68 96 300
302 **122** 118 221
— Col. **52** 277 **80** 447
142 205
— Lieut. **52** 190
— Mr. **55** 331 **57** 228 229
79 330 **80** 241 **125** 39
— Mrs. **56** 387 **79** 309
119 216 **120** 302
____ (Brown) **140** 258
____ (Homer) **140** 154 161
____ (Spear) **140** 161
____ (Williams) **140** 42
262
Abby Frances **73** 62 63
Abial **55** 171 172
Abigail **54** 273 **55** xcii **58**
31 **59** 85 **61** 31 **63** 179
76 13 **99** 281 **121** 19 118
Abigail (Arey) **87** 9
Abigail (Burt) **136** 267
Abigail (Sibley) **125** 101
Abigail L. (Goss) **105** 298
Abner **105** 207
Abra **119** 227 228
Abraham **73** 64
Agnes **68** 73 **112** 288
Albert **88** 246 **98** 258
Albert H. **81** 282
Alexander H. (Mrs.)
119 115
Alexander Henry (Mrs.)
97 158
Alfred **93** 299
Alfred C. **78** 330
Alfred Church **58** xxxvii
xlv **75** 5 **79** 202 **84** 174
91 59 141 **102** 161-163
219 **103** 122
Alfred Church (Mrs.)
103 119
Alice **70** 62 **82** 309 **98** 258
105 298
Almira J. **105** 298
Alvin B. **91** 119 122
Alvin Valentine (Mrs.)
85 195
Amanda (Smith) **87** 6
Amanda J. (Mills) **128** 91
Ambrose **142** 120 **144** 33
Amelia **90** 44
Amelia (Carver) **89** 39
Amos **98** 246 **117** 49
Amos W. **77** 180
Andrew **51** 41 **63** 149 **83**
466 **96** 366 **105** 269 **119**

LANE *cont'd*
146 **121** 19 20 104 108
115 118 193 194 196 201
206 **132** 41
Andrew J. **89** 350
Ann **81** 322 **102** 167
Ann Berry **88** 242
Ann M. B. **120** 67
Ann Maria **77** 180 **83** 173
93 66 **120** 66
Anna **52** 198 **67** 107 **81** 104
88 325 327 **93** 366
Anna Elizabeth (Pidge)
132 242
Anna Mathes **73** 62
Anne **70** 152 **88** 325
Anne Warren (Foote) **97**
86 87
Annie Barclay **106** 231
Annie L. (Locke) **105** 298
Annie Maria **93** 90
Annis **131** 128
Annis K. **79** 120
Anthony **99** 117
Anthony Clopton **97** 86
Asa **121** 216
Asaph **83** 466
Augustine **60** 396 **61** 32
Augustus M. **98** 258
Barbara **73** 270
Barbara Susanna Parker
73 267
Barton George (Mrs.)
97 158
Bathsheba **58** 29
Beatrice **123** 160
Beja **88** 152
Ben P. **100** 257 258
Benjamin **56** 91 **60** 271-
274 **61** 57 **63** 74 **83** 467
87 9 **88** 63 246 **98** 258
105 206 **109** 40
Benjamin Boatright
115 79
Benjamin P. **97** 69
Benjamin Turner **60** 273
Bertha **77** 291 **82** 121 237
106 311 312 **107** 67 138
Bethiah **121** 206
Betsey **56** 91 **77** 236 **87** 18
105 298
Betsey (King) **90** 316
Betty **70** 119 **115** 132
132 114
Bridget **79** 94
Caleb **121** 107
Calvin **95** 371
Caroline **93** 124 **125** 39
Caroline (Davis) **98** 262
311
Caroline Eliza **93** 124
Caroline Elizabeth
(Lamson) **92** 350
Caroline Matilda **77** 291
Carrie **69** 166 **105** 298
Catherine **55** 403 **56** 371
79 102 **99** 117 **107** 300
Catherine (Atwood)
91 119 122
Charity **56** 210
Charles **61** 66 **73** 264 **74**

LANE *cont'd*
239 **88** 242 250 **89** 350
93 255 384 **105** 281 **128**
91 **135** 268 **145** 357
Charles Chester **66** lii
Charles John Hopkins
86 366
Charles L. **89** 350
Charlotte **88** 242 250 **89**
350 **93** 299 **106** 312 **127**
63
Chloe **62** 20 **142** 61
Christopher C. **106** 311
312
Clara **77** 226
Clarissa **90** 50 **126** 143
Clifford W. **121** 238
Clifford W. (Mrs.)
121 238
Columbia **98** 258
Conway **79** 39
Cynthia **98** 258
Cynthia (Clark) **106** 225
Cyrus **56** 210
Dan **56** 360
Daniel **51** 382 **53** 374 379
66 287 **93** 397 **100** 63
105 281 **106** 170 **132**
242
Daniel W. **96** 275
David **62** 73 158 **71** 82
272 281 **85** 120 **93** 124
116 110 **121** 279
David (Mrs.) **92** 350
Davis R. **78** 353
Deborah **60** 144 **63** 149
87 6 **102** 153 **105** 269
109 6 **121** 25 195
Deborah (Gill) **121** 192
Delila (Foster) **113** 78
Deliverance **59** 333
Dolly **88** 249
Dorothy **66** 271 273 **88**
152 **89** 350 **100** 249 **106**
15 **108** 227
Dorothy (Burton) **106** 16
E. H. **64** 235
E. Jennie **98** 258
Ebenezer **55** 171-173 175
403 **59** xxvi **70** 152 **83**
466 467 **105** 298 **106**
225 **121** 23 273 278 283
125 221 **141** 202
Edith Marie **80** 241
Edmund **76** 61 72 **116** 156
Edmund C. **126** 244
Edmund J. **73** 63
Edward **57** 339 **99** 281
Edwin **87** 9
Edwin Augustus **88** 242
Eleanor **73** 232
Eliab **62** 158 161
Eliab B. **62** 70
Elise Denison (Brown)
97 158 **109** 318
Eliz **91** 347
Eliza **98** 258
Eliza M. **107** 300
Elizabeth **52** 128 **54** 200 **55**
403 **56** 253 370 **58** 31
175 **61** 32 **62** 71 **64** 250

LANE *cont'd*
75 lxxxi **78** 308 **88** 246
90 47 70 **91** 345 **93** 253
96 382 **100** 299 **106** 19
107 212 **109** 66 **115** 79
121 197 **131** 165 **134**
137 **140** 38
Elizabeth (Gyles) **97** 57
Elizabeth (Loring)
134 297
Elizabeth (Russell) (Gid-
ding) **135** 278
Elizabeth (Selden) **97** 158
Elizabeth (Thaxter)
134 138
Elizabeth Bowie **73** 232
Elizabeth Ferrier **60** 403
Elizabeth O. **140** 161
Elizabeth S. **125** 173
Elizabeth W. **93** 255
Ellen **98** 258
Ellen Jeannette **83** 466
Emelina Augusta **88** 242
Emeline Winifred **78** 36
Emily **54** cxxii
Emma Amelia **97** 69
Emma Ann **78** 353
Enos **60** 396 397 **61** 31 33
136 58
Esther **52** 78 274 **70** 151
135 338
Eunice **65** 40
Evelyn C. **144** 270
F. Cole **140** 31
F. H. **91** 327
Faith **51** 401
Fanny **60** 273 **62** 75 160
Florence Amy **124** 192
Floyd Benjamin **109** 238
117 77
Fraisalette Cutler **111** 109
Frances **61** 378
Francis **77** 288
Francis Asbury **97** 86
Fred Athearn **140** 161
Frederic **140** 161 262
Frederick Chapin **102** 162
Frederick Kane **130** 52
Galen **62** 158 161
Gardner **89** 39
George **51** 382 **61** 42 57 **62**
160 **71** xlvi 253 **73** 62
63 73 77 **78** 443 **79** 94
83 466 467 **90** 42 **93** 253
255 386 387 **121** 11 14
17 118 200 274 **125** 37
134 137 138 **140** 154
155 161
George B. **56** 210 **57** 112
58 318 **60** 186
George W. **105** 298
Georgie A. **105** 298
Gershom Flagg **144** 220
Gorham **140** 303
Grace **67** 363 **100** 301
Grace Wilson
(Wilkinson) **86** 366
Gustavus **70** 361
Hannah **55** xcii 403 **56** 254
57 159 **58** 175 **59** 37 68

LANE *cont'd*
259 **69** 377 **82** 290 292
89 350 **102** 162 **113** 289
121 11 108 216 275 **141**
190 202 **147** 55
Hannah (Cunningham)
106 225
Hannah (Hersey) **121** 273
Hannah (Marston)
134 149
Hannah (Nason) **91** 27 34
Hannah (Reyner) **131** 165
Hannah H. **86** 89
Harriet (Robinson)
92 170
Harriet H. **94** 42
Harriet Houghton **93** 60
Harriet Page **102** 162
Harriet Robinson **92** 170
Helen (Bancroft) **95** 371
Henrietta **132** 221
Henry **51** 215 **70** 304 **71** 46
87 6 **91** 347 349 **93** 299
96 143 **125** 215 **135** 278
Henry F. **120** 221
Henry P. **81** 282
Hepzibah **77** 288 **141** 190
Hepzibah S. **88** 336
Herman **76** 50
Hester **96** 387
Hezekiah **105** 207
Hiram W. **60** 403
Huldah **105** 296
Hyrum V. **87** 9
Ida E. **128** 171
Isaac **58** 175 **88** 334
121 211
Isabella **142** 61
Isaiah L. **105** 298
Israel **54** 347
J. **136** 58 133
J. Allison **105** 298
J. Gregg **95** 401
J. P. **109** 32
Jabez **65** 78 79 109 114 **73**
62 63 69-73 77 **93** 397
100 63 **142** 38
Jacob **54** 160 **98** 258
106 312
James **57** 339 **59** 85 **63** 73
75 **73** 72 237 **78** 411 **86**
415 **92** 183 **106** 225 **119**
237
James B. **78** 402
James L. (Mrs.) **117** 79
119 237 **124** 160
James Pillsbury **73** 237
Jane **80** 447
Jane Maria **93** 88
Janie Warren
(Hollingsworth)
88 169
Jannetje (Rapalje) **113** 289
Jedediah **56** 210
Jedidiah **57** 112 225
Jemima (Richmond)
132 41
Jennie T. **63** 101 **66** xlix
71 369
Jeremiah **73** 77
Jerusha **141** 202

LANE *cont'd*
Jesse **141** 112 113
Joan **54** 280
Joanna **57** 112 **70** 151 **71**
219 **88** 237 **91** 347
Joanna Turner **60** 274
Job **52** 198 **55** 290 293 403
56 99 370 **57** 339 **62** 63
71 78 158 **64** 46 **65** 104
70 183 **85** 10 **102** 162
106 35 225 **131** 165 234
136 52 **137** 141
Joel **54** 368 370
Johanna (Sexton) **97** 119
John **51** 382 **52** 116 145
53 379 **54** cxxii **55** xcii
403 429 430 **56** 210 370
371 388 **57** 112 225 **60**
144 **61** xxx 32 209 **62**
248 **64** 223 322 **65** 353
69 377 **70** 56 **71** xlvi **72**
183 **73** 71 140 **78** 309
399 **79** 94 **83** 317 466
467 **87** 6 **88** 63 281 326
89 236 **92** 71 **99** 281
101 55 **102** 162 **106** 19
225 **108** 227 **111** 97 **121**
20 194 195 201 205 209
213 279-281 **125** 35 87
88 **128** 44 **136** 45 **140** 38
161 **145** 359 **148** 146
John Aloysius **97** 119
John F. W. **140** 161
John H. **77** 153 **89** 42
John Harold **92** 364
John Lindsay (Mrs.) **96**
160 **100** 116
John M. **51** 382 **78** 302
140 161
John Merrifield **71** xlvi
79 94 **93** 120
John S. **76** 13 **92** 170
John Thomas **97** 119
John W. **58** 29 136 **67** 61
Jonathan **55** 174 **62** 71 73
158-161 **65** 40 **89** 350
98 311 **102** 162 **121** 269
134 149 141 354 **142** 61
Jonathan Abbot **62** 73
102 161 162
Jonathan L. H. **88** 152
Joseph **54** 370 **55** 171 **74**
33 **87** 9 **88** 63 237 **98**
258 **105** 206
Joseph Hutchins **88** 237
Joseph J. **89** 350
Joseph Washington
140 303
Joshua **58** 29 **66** 221 **73**
64-66 74 **79** 301 **93** 366
105 298 **121** 104 202
Josiah **58** 29 **62** 71 **66** 221
83 466 467 **121** 14 126
127 192 196 205 214 272
281
Josiah S. **62** 71
Josie E. **89** 350
Jotham S. **114** 276
Judith **93** 299 **94** 335
98 258

LANE *cont'd*
Julian Carswell (Mrs.)
86 113 **88** 169
Katharine **90** 187
Lamnell **54** 160
Laura Ann **62** 78
Laura Augusta **90** 55
Laura Jennie **134** 149
Lauriat **102** 162
Lavina **77** 153
Leander **88** 244
Leavitt **134** 297
Lester A. **89** 350
Levi **56** 210 **57** 112 **65** 40
78 187 **97** 57 **140** 161
142 63
Living **90** 316
Lizzie June **96** 30
Lois **141** 202
Louisa M. **88** 287
Louisa Rebecca **91** 76
Lovicy **56** 210
Lucinda **74** lxi **76** 50 274
105 61
Lucius **69** 166
Lucius Page **57** xxxiii
Lucy **60** 272 338 **63** 75 76
66 239 **68** 383 **71** 82 272
281 **80** 140 **81** 282 **89** 91
91 146 **125** 51
Lucy (Church) **125** 51
Lucy (Jennings) **126** 204
Lucy A. (Dexter) **97** 69
Lucy Ann **71** xxxiv xlvi
79 93 94 **91** 187
Lucy M. (Dunn) **90** 42
Lucy N. **90** 107
Lucy Ware **97** 79 86 87 162
Luke John **126** 204
Lurina **61** 81
Lydia **55** 403 **56** 210 **73**
192 **134** 297
Lydia Jenison **88** 60
M. C. (Mrs.) **102** 320
Mae E. **83** 433 434
Mahala **87** 9 **109** 9
Malenda **88** 152
Margaret **76** 61 72 73
Margaret (Smith) **87** 6
Margaret Lucretia **90** 55
Margery **83** 317
Maria **61** 57
Maria Louisa **69** 166
Marjorie **79** 283 **92** 364
Marmaduke **52** 257
Martha **88** 286 **93** 235
Martha (Minot) **106** 225
Martha Ann **64** 6
Martha Jane **91** 370
Martin Herbert **97** 119
Mary **51** 215 **53** 24 374 379
56 360 370 378 **60** 396
61 33 66 **62** 161 **65** 353
71 xlvi **73** 68 **79** 94 102
83 466 **85** 250 436 **88** 60
244 **89** 236 **91** 349 **100**
37 328 **104** 37 **121** 19
103 196 209 277 **123** 234
127 320 **145** 36
Mary (Belknap) **88** 281

LANE *cont'd*
Mary (Chittenden)
125 221
Mary (Dunham) **125** 215
Mary (Emmons) **134** 253
Mary (Kelloway) **83** 467
Mary (Nowel) **111** 97
Mary A. **79** 45
Mary Ann **76** 13 **87** 6 **89**
350 **93** 299 **109** 6
Mary Ann (Spinner)
126 68
Mary Bogue (Alden)
96 185
Mary Bryant (Head)
97 119
Mary E. (Carver) **89** 42
Mary H. **61** 310
Mary J. **123** 234
Mary Jane **136** 132
Mary K. **126** l 244
Mary P. **90** 46
Mary Pollock **93** 60
Mary Thomas (Allen)
97 86
Mary Wellington **106** 224
225 **112** 142
Masena G. **89** 350
Matilda 187 **83** 183 187
Matthew **54** 200 **56** 253
79 102
Matthias **145** 356
Mehitable **83** 467 **106** 19
121 275
Mehitable (Hobart) **83**
467 **106** 19 **121** 195
Melatiah **65** 40 **83** 467
Melissa **74** 33
Mercy E. (Delano) **87** 10
Meribah **59** 38
Meribah T. **90** 57
Merton Chesleigh (Mrs.)
102 124 **115** 66
Milton A. **98** 311
Miranda **108** 265
Miriam **65** 40
Molly **62** 73 **141** 332
Molly (Knap) **89** 39
Murray **52** 93
Nancy **65** 40 **142** 61
Nancy (Allen) **97** 86
Nancy L. (Goss) **105** 298
Nathan **73** 104
Nathaniel **82** 290 292 **89**
274 **125** 41 **126** 211
Nehemiah **78** 190 **88** 63
237 **125** 101
Nelson A. **89** 350
Nicholas **86** 423
Noah **58** 137
Oliver **88** 63 **105** 207
Oliver W. **62** 78
Oliver Washington
140 161
Oliver Wellington
144 265
Orlistes **88** 237
Orville Wilbur **58** 412
66 xlix
Otice **88** 242
Patty **122** 224

LANE *cont'd*
Peggy **87** 6 **88** 326 **109** 6
Pela **119** 320
Penelope C. **70** 361
Peter **83** 466 **121** 106 275-
277 **134** 138
Phebe **56** 210 **57** 112 225
88 242 250 **89** 350 **115**
131
Phoenix **64** 250
Polly **88** 152 **89** 274
Priscilla **83** 466 **121** 205
141 197
Priscilla A. **91** 29 35
R. C. **98** 262 311
Rachel **73** 74 **121** 273
Ralph **66** 244 **67** 363
112 169
Ralph H. **110** 156
Rebecca **63** 73 **88** 63 237
98 311 **109** 9
Rebecca (Arey) **87** 6
88 326
Rebecca (Cobb) **126** 211
Rebecca (Jones) **140** 303
Rebecca C. (Lane) **87** 9
109 9
Reuben **144** 46
Reuben L. **73** 192
Rhoda **83** 178 183
Rhoda Ann **88** 237
Rhoda N. **89** 350
Richard **136** 267
Robert **51** 382 **53** 379 **56**
210 **57** 112 225 **60** 186
86 417 **92** 71 **93** 299
104 113 **145** 120
Rocksyllania T. **89** 350
Roger **56** 210 **62** 76 160
Rowland **142** 61
Rufus K. **91** 27 34
Ruhamah **62** 71 158
Ruth **57** 112 **97** 93 **121** 284
Ruth (Davis) **106** 225
Ruth (Sanderson) **128** 43
44
S. D. **73** 76
Sabra Jane **87** 6
Sally **65** 114 **88** 63 **98** 258
Sally (Weston) **106** 225
Sally P. **105** 298
Sampson **76** 317 **97** 86
Samuel **54** 273 **55** 403 **58**
31 **62** 73 159 **63** 75 64
250 **73** 62 63 67 68 72-77
79 **80** 327 **83** 466 **88** 60
152 242 249 250 **89** 350
106 225 **125** 93 95 **134**
253 **148** 185
Samuel M. **89** 350 **98** 258
Sarah **53** 379 **55** 289 290 **59**
37 167 **62** 74 **65** 40 114
78 443 **80** 327 **83** 467
86 70 **87** 109 **88** 242 250
93 347 **100** 295 **102** 145
121 10 209 213 280 282
125 88 210 **131** 165 234
141 190 354 **142** 61 123
143 137 343
Sarah (Beale) **83** 467
121 205

LANE *cont'd*
Sarah (Briggs) **125** 88
Sarah (Webster) **142** 268
Sarah Ann **77** 48
Sarah C. **94** 162
Sarah Carleton **93** 61
Sarah D. **89** 350
Sarah E. (Veasey) **105** 298
Sarah Goodrich **86** 106
Sarah M. **89** 350
Sarah Merritt **71** xlvi
  79 94
Sarah P. **105** 298
Sarah Perkins **105** 298
Sarah Turner **60** 273
  103 220
Semion **88** 152
Seth **55** 173 174 **60** 396 **88**
  152 **141** 202
Seth C. **88** 244
Seth Chandler **88** 242
Sibyl **77** 186
Simeon **88** 242 250 **89** 350
Simon **59** 37 38
Solomon **62** 74 **121** 281
Sophia **79** 53
Sophia Olive **94** 26
Stephen **62** 75 160
Stevens **56** 210
Susan (Douglas) **88** 334
Susan (Roberts) **87** 9
  109 9
Susan (Updike) **89** 236
Susan (Whitney)(Fincher)
  140 303
Susan Foster **75** 5
Susan M. **85** 325
Susan S. (Simpson)
  119 146
Susanna **55** 401 403 **59** 38
  62 60 **63** 76 **83** 317 **90**
  70 **93** 231 **103** 143 **121**
  17 277 **125** 222 **129** 168
  170
Susanna (Whipple)
  106 225
Susanna (Willis) **114** 276
Temperance **98** 97
Thomas **54** 194 **58** 70 **62**
  93 **89** 350 **95** 322 **97** 119
  121 214
Thomas H. **88** 152
Thomas Jefferson
  123 160
Thomas W. **54** xxxviii
  55 xxxii **56** xxxii **57**
  xxxiii **58** xlv **59** xv
Timothy **63** 73 **87** 6 **90** 42
  141 190
Triphane **63** 149 **105** 269
Turner **60** 338
Virginia Susanne
  (Clopton) **97** 86
W. C. **52** 404
W. H. **94** 42
Wallace S. **81** 282
Wallis **73** 206
Walter **93** 299
Walter E. **105** 298
Welthea (Bradford)
  134 138

LANE *cont'd*
William **51** 382 **56** 378
  57 408 409 **58** 29 137
  138 **62** 78 161 **64** 223 **65**
  42 63 66 **68** 73 **70** 62 **73**
  71 77 **76** 53 **83** 466 467
  87 9 **89** 39 **94** 335 **97** 86
  100 328 **104** 37 **106** 19
  112 75 **113** 289 **141** 190
  142 123 268 **143** 259
William C. **52** 282 **107** 17
William Coolidge **53** 148
  57 xxxiii 239 328 **58** xlv
  107 210 **60** 221 407 **61**
  xxxiv **65** 284 **77** 291 **80**
  138
William H. **93** 60 61 63
  66 117 120 **94** 162 **140**
  161
William Homer **77** 291
William Horner **93** 117
William Howes **93** 90
William R. **102** 149
William S. **87** 10
William Sanford **77** 186
Willie B. **98** 258
Winifred **89** 131
Zebulon **56** 84
Zenas **88** 63 246 **89** 351
  98 258
Ziba **61** 378
Zilpah **60** 43 **65** 40
Zilpha **142** 61
LANEBUT Nancy **73** 276
LANEFORD
  Leila **109** 295
LANES —— **145** 169
LANESBOROUGH
  —— **60** 218
LANETON George **87** 302
LANEY Aslack **54** 158
  Bass **67** 158
  Benjamin **54** 158
  Faith **54** 64
  James **54** 158
  Jane **54** 216
  John **54** 159 **67** 158
  Katharine **54** 64
  Maria Spencer **89** 40
  Richard **54** 64
  Sarah **95** 190
  Sylvia J. **121** 178
  Thomas **54** 158
LANFAIR Joshua **96** 63
LANG Laing Lange Layng
  —— **60** xxix **76** 280
  — Capt. **82** 26
  — Mrs. **82** 412
  Abiel **92** 312
  Abigail **52** 433 **81** 428
  Agnes **81** 428
  Agnes Barr (Means)
    111 311
  Agnes Wells **109** 221
    111 311
  Alfred **67** 280
  Alice (Patterson) **86** 369
  Alice B. **97** 44
  Alva **133** 24
  Angie M. (Mayne)
    111 128

LANG *cont'd*
Ann **73** 140
Ann Elmira **68** 246 247
  69 273 315
Anna **81** 428 **82** 292 296
  301
Anna Elmira **72** 271
Anna Margarethe **81** 460
Anna Maria **67** 280
Anne Margaret **72** xx
Antonie Wilhelmine
  81 460
Archie E. (Mrs.) **124** 240
August **82** 380
Augusta C. **69** 141
Benjamin **81** 428 445
Benjamin Johnson **63** 314
Benjamin Partridge **82** 44
Bert Charles **86** 310
Bridget W. **69** 140
Carrie Howard **124** 78
Catherine **73** 217 **82** 26
  89 180
Charity **81** 428
Charles Edward **97** 44
Christiana **84** 102
Daisy Mary **86** 369
Daniel **81** 428 444 445 **82**
  26 44 45 292 296 412 **88**
  282
Daniel (Mrs.) **81** 445
Data (Brown) **86** 71 147
David **73** 76 **98** 44
Deborah (Marston) **95** 92
Deliverance **81** 140 428
Dorothy **81** 428 **82** 44
Durward Ernest **86** 310
Edgar **98** 339
Edward **69** 146 147 **95** 92
Edward Henry **89** 180
Eldith Mae **86** 310
Eleanor **81** 444 **82** 292 295
Eliza **61** lix **81** 428 429
  82 26
Eliza (Wilkinson) **97** 44
Eliza K. **59** 190
Elizabeth **79** 13 **81** 260
  428 **82** 44 287 292
  98 44 129
Elizabeth Brown (Fitz-
  Randolph) **98** 339
Ella May (Cole) **86** 310
Emerson **86** 369
Emma **97** 128
Esther **81** 428
Ethel **92** 65
Eunice **81** 444
Fannie Louvia (Wilson)
  83 230 248 **88** 202
Felicia Livingston **89** 180
Frances E. **115** 298
Francis **86** 71 310
Francis M. **86** 147
Frank **92** 229 230
Franklin (Mrs.) **84** 234
  85 195
George N. **79** 327
George W. **77** 177
Gilbert Reed **82** 44
Grace **79** 220 **81** 428 444
  114 130

LANG *cont'd*
Guy **133** 24
Hannah **79** 218 220 **81**
  428 429 444 **82** 284 285
  292 **94** 358 **95** 36 **111** 48
Hannah (FitzRandolph)
  98 44
Hannah Frances M. **95** 92
Hannah G. **90** 56
Harold Holden **89** 180
Harriet **76** 216
Harriet Charity
  (Seymour) **133** 24
Henrietta **86** 71
Henry **61** 42 **81** 444 **82** 44
  292 301
Hester **74** 92
Hettie **73** li
Honor **85** 385
Huldah **98** 336
Immanuel **81** 429
Irany **72** 271
Isabel **97** 333
Iva Marguerite (Bryant)
  86 310
Jack **105** 74
Jacob **98** 46
James D. **109** 221
James D. (Mrs) **77** 322
  78 205
James Donly **111** 311
James Johnson **82** 44
Jane **81** 428 429 444 **82** 44
  288 292
Joanna **81** 429
John **51** 45 **58** 394 **60** 186
  73 138 **79** 220 **81** 428
  429 444 **82** 26 44 45 292
  301 412 **83** 34 **97** 333
  103 229 **105** 74
John A. **69** 315 **97** 182
John Alton **72** 271 **103** 229
John Andrew (Mrs.)
  100 111
John D. **68** 246 247 **69**
  273 315 **72** 271
John Dammon **103** 229
Jonathan **81** 444 **82** 44 45
  292 302
Joseph **81** 428 444
Joshua **81** 429
Joyce Julia **86** 310
Judith (Leaycraft) **98** 339
Julia Ann (Rowe) **86** 310
Julian **85** 386
Julian (Cowes) (Loring)
  85 386 387
Katharine **81** 428 429 444
  82 44 292 299 **92** 229
Laura (Kemp) **133** 24
Lester S. **111** 128
Lettis Bean **79** 327
Louisa **69** 273
Louisa L. **68** 246 **72** 271
Lowel **105** 286
Lucy **65** 354 **67** 278 **81**
  260 444 **82** 44 292 298
  299
Lucy S. **88** 338
Margaret **82** 26 44 292 302
  97 333 338

LANG *cont'd*
Martha **82** 44 **91** 16
Mary **53** 41 281 **81** 428 429
  82 26 44 291 292 298
  299 301 302 **94** 356
Mary Irany **72** 271
Mercy (FitzRandolph)
  98 46
Mesheck **92** 283
Michael **89** 180
Moses **81** 444 **82** 44
Nanny **82** 44
Nathaniel **51** 45 **81** 428
  429 **82** 44 412
Nellie **133** 24
Nicholas **62** 180 **63** 133
  97 327 **99** 240
Olive **82** 292 293
Patience **86** 149
Pauline **91** 388
Peter **133** 24 **148** 291
Phebe **105** 74
Phebe (Lamos) **105** 74
Phebe Ann **105** 74
Philip **118** 45
Priscilla **81** 429 445
R. R. (Mrs.) **125** 74
Rebecca **53** 282 **79** 123
Richard **81** 260 **82** 44
  85 385 386
Richard White **82** 45
Robert **51** 45 **53** 282 **60**
  186 **81** 140 428 429 444
  82 44 45 **85** 386
Roby (Tye) **88** 282
Ruth **53** 281 282 **58** 394
Sally **82** 45
Samuel **81** 444 **82** 26 44 45
  92 314 **103** 229
Sara D. **100** 207
Sara Drummond **82** 380
  83 232 **87** 224 **100** 336
  103 218 229 **104** 149
Sarah **53** 41 **81** 429 445 **82**
  45 **90** 328 **91** 19
Sarah Elmira **72** 271
Seymore **133** 24
Stephen **52** 433 **81** 428 429
  82 45 412 **92** 310 312
Susan E. **67** 280
Susan Goddard (Braid)
  97 44
Susan Helen **97** 44
Susanna **81** 428 429
Susy **82** 412
Theodate **68** 247 **69** 315
  72 271
Thomas **53** 41 **55** 209 **81**
  444 445 **82** 26 45 291
  292
Thomas S. **69** 315
Thomas Stackpole **72** 271
Vernona M. **78** 205
Veronica **92** 230
Virginia A. **77** 177
Wilhelm Roerich **81** 460
William **55** 141 **62** 202
  65 354 **81** 260 428 429
  444 445 **82** 44 45 **97** 44
  103 229
William A. **67** 280

LANG *cont'd*
William Andrew **118** 45
William Leaycraft **98** 339
LANGACRE Ethel **91** 48
LANGBAINE —— **57** 409
LANGBEHN
Doris M. **146** 383
LANGBERRY
Gregory **119** 17
LANGDALE
Edith Isabel **86** 199
LANGDELL
Charles **112** 286
Christopher Columbus
  61 109 **79** 235 **81** 17
John **65** 148 **91** 199
Langden *see* Langdon
LANGDICH
William **109** 19
LANGDON Langden
— Capt. **94** 354 **99** 328
  100 34
— Dea. **82** 45
— Mrs. **82** 412
— Rev. Dr. **84** 380 **85** 17
  88 91
Abby G. **120** 218 **122** 312
Abigail **124** 9
Abigail (Chase) **87** 304
Abigail (Greenwood)
  130 314
Abigail (Rockwood)
  124 9
Abigail Harris **130** 314
Abigail S. (Treadick)
  117 225
Alfred **91** 327
Alice Stowe Doud **123** 98
Amelia (Green) **97** 291
Amos **124** 9
Ann **58** 229 **82** 45 421 **83**
  25 28 34 **99** 118
Ann S. **79** 157
Anne Hurd **93** 325
  130 314
Benjamin Seaman **97** 291
Betsey **66** 110 **92** 23
Betty (Hickson) **113** 77
Blanche **96** 287
Caroline **58** 232
Caroline Bell **78** 109 203
  83 126 208 230
Caroline E. **83** 173
Caroline Laura **85** 104
Catherine Amelia **56** 222
  92 118
Catherine Clowes **97** 291
Catherine J. **97** 292
Chaney **123** 307
Charles J. **92** 189
Charles S. **97** 292
Charlotte **82** 274
Charlotte Augusta **92** 127
  94 39
Charlotte L. **83** 173
Chauncey **66** 22
Cortland Frederick
  107 133
Daniel **82** 274 **113** 77
David **67** 380
Dewit C. **97** 292

LANGDON *cont'd*
Dinah **81** 445
Edward **60** 186 **67** 379 380
  125 23 **128** 48
Edy Rich **82** 274
Electa J. **123** 98
Eliza **83** 34
Eliza (Field) **123** 307
Eliza Astor **84** 449
Elizabeth **58** 227 233 296
  297 **60** 292 **61** 83 **67** 379
  380 **71** 109 **72** 83 **81** 445
  82 26 45 282 292 354
  101 50 **115** 307 **125** 283
  140 139 **142** 148
Elizabeth (Eliot) **140** 139
Ellen F. **80** 59
Ellen Frances **79** 167
Emerson A. **123** 98
Ephraim **116** 110
Eugene Webster **82** 274
Flora **123** 100
Frances (Cutter) **92** 75
Frances A. **82** 421 **83** 193
Francis E. **83** 299
Francis Eustis **92** 75
Frank **82** 318
Franklin **85** 104
George **82** 421 **123** 154
  141 361
George D. **124** 113 137 146
  286
Gerherdus Clowes **97** 291
Grace **60** 186 **90** 207
Hannah **73** 206 **81** 429 **123**
  96 305
Hannah P. S. **123** 309
Harriet O. **83** 173
Hattie Theodora **85** 296
Helen **83** 307
Helen Bell (Haven) **83** 299
Helen Haven **81** 363 **82**
  237 **92** 75 92 150
Henry S. **82** 421 **133** 308
Henry S. (Mrs.) **82** 421
Henry Sherburne **92** 75
Hetty Green **97** 291
Honor **61** 83
Isaac **87** 334
J. G. **60** 186
James **67** 380
Jerusha (Sprague)
  123 307
Joanna **89** 368 **145** 298
John **51** 172 **53** 453 **56** 222
  58 227 233 **60** 186 **65** 29
  67 379 380 **71** 109 **73**
  204 **77** 129 **79** 228 **80** 98
  81 445 **82** 421 **84** 377
  85 125 **92** 22 23 26 27
  75 117 118 127 **93** 325
  356 **94** 39 295 **97** 290
  292-294 **101** 54 325 **128**
  48 **130** 314
John A. **97** 292
John Barton **97** 291
John S. **97** 292
John Walley **92** 22
Joseph **58** 229 252 **67** 379
  380 **71** 109 **81** 429 445
  82 45

LANGDON *cont'd*
Josiah **61** 22 **107** 99 **110**
  317 **121** 247 **125** 283
Jude **82** 45
Julia Olivia **92** 189
Katharine **65** 168
Katy S. **123** 98
Laura **123** 91
Lydia **67** 380
Margaret **84** 326
Maria **79** 156
Marion E. **123** 309
Mark **81** 445 **105** 114
Martha **95** 265 **100** 169
  106 229
Martha A. **123** 308
Mary **58** 230 **66** 110 **67**
  379 380 **71** 109 **79** 228
  81 429 **82** 26 292 296 **90**
  178 184 **92** 22 23 127 **93**
  318 **97** 190 291 **99** 118
  102 308 **145** 309
Mary (Hubbard) **95** 265
  106 229
Mary Ann **82** 421 **83** 183
  184 193
Mary H. **123** 305 309
Mary Huldana **123** 96
Mary Walley **130** 314
Michael J. **117** 211
Nabby **84** 377
Nancy Hurd **92** 27
Nanne / Nanny **81** 445
  82 45
Nathaniel **55** 389 **67** 379
  380
Noah **60** 186
Olive **97** 266
Paul **117** 225 **126** 225
  127 115
Peter **60** 186
Phebe **97** 290 292
Phebe (Seaman) **97** 290
Phebe Rowland **97** 291
Philip **56** 222 **60** 186
  128 48
Pierre C. **97** 292
Polly **92** 22
Reuben **79** 157
Richard **127** 115
Robert **56** 408
Robert Bruce **81** 240
  83 208
Robert Getty **60** 186
Roselle **56** 199
S. G. **79** 156
Sally **92** 26
Sally (Vans) **84** 271
Samuel **55** 147 **58** 324 **71**
  109 **73** 192 **79** 228 **81**
  429 **82** 25 26 45 **84** 377
  107 313 **127** 114 115
  130 278 **131** 192
Samuel Jones **97** 291 292
Sarah **58** 232 **67** 380 **78** 318
  82 292 298
Sarah (Smith) **83** 208
Sarah A. **73** 192
Sarah Allison **97** 291
Sarah S. **82** 421 **83** 24 25
Seth **81** 418 **123** 311

LANGDON *cont'd*
Shirley **123** 226
Sophia Ann **82** 421
Sophia Hill **82** 421 **83** 173
Sophic Eustis **78** 207
Susan **65** 10
Susanna **67** 380 **84** 326
Thomas **75** 176
Thomas Walley **92** 117
Timothy **67** 379 **84** 271
  121 247
Tobias **51** 43 44 **58** 227 230
  60 186 **61** 83 **92** 75 **95**
  265 **106** 229
Wallace W. **123** 307
Walter **58** 232
William **97** 292 **99** 118
William Coffin **67** 380
Woodberry **74** 187
Woodbury **58** 227 232
  82 292 298 **92** 75
Lange *see* Lang
LANGEATHY
Robert **70** 226
Susanna **70** 226
LANGEDON
John de **109** 21
LANGELL Abbie S.
  (Bragdon) **123** 232
Lewis L. **123** 232
Viola L. (Lucas) **123** 232
William A. **123** 232
LANGENBACHER
Anna Louisa **89** 233
Wilhelmena **89** 179
LANGER Langger
Agnes **83** 119
Margaret **53** 428 **130** 178
Richard **121** 111
Robert **83** 119
LANGERFELDT
Theodore Otto **61** 109
LANGESTER
John **63** 352
Langfellow *see*
  Longfellow
LANGFORD Lankford
Abraham **53** 433 **67** 367
  147 216
Arthur **140** 161
Barnum **70** 202
Celia Joy **107** 133
Charlotte Frances
  (Speaight) (Smith)
  113 295
Chloe **51** 209
Deborah **70** 151
Desire **56** 127
Edward **51** 354 **113** 295
Edward Vincent (Mrs.)
  100 112
Elizabeth **55** 51 **100** 32 **101**
  277 **135** 135
Elizabeth (Carter) **100** 298
Ellen Mabel **112** 220
  113 295
Ellen Marean (Priest)
  113 295
George **95** 146
Holdeby **128** 304
Isabella **97** 382

LANGFORD *cont'd*
J. L. **91** 327
John **56** 127 **60** 186 **122**
   43 44 **129** 53
John Thompson **113** 295
Jonas **67** 367
Joseph **129** 54
Julia **70** 202
Leila **109** 295
M. A.J. (Mrs.) **116** 163
Mary **62** 382 **78** 308 **97** 382
Michael **113** 295
Moroni B. **98** 147
Nicolas **100** 32
Phebe **147** 213
Richard **54** 219
Ruth **51** 347
Sarah (Husband) **113** 295
Thomas **62** 350 **63** 78 79
   93 384
William **64** 20 **100** 32 294
   113 295
Langger *see* Langer
LANGHAM
Elizabeth **52** 116 118
Francis **63** 363
George **52** 110 116 118
   123 124 126 128
Henry **52** 118
Joseph **101** 218
Lydia **63** 363
Mary **52** 128
Mary Ann **101** 218
Phebe **63** 363
Samuel **55** 438
Thomas **52** 118 123 128
   63 363
William **52** 118 **55** 438
LANGHOLME
William **116** 175
LANGHORN Langhorne
Cary D. **78** 287
Daniel **53** 116
John **53** 457
R. **54** 335
Terese **91** 399
William **51** 111 **53** 116
   78 274 275
Zaidee Forsyth **78** 287
Langiel *see* Langill
LANGIER Hannah (Minot)
   140 169
J. H. **140** 169
LANGILL Langiel Langille
—— **148** 188
Margaret **125** 116 120
Ross Alexander **104** 144
Ross Earl **104** 144 **108** 131
LANGINE —— **95** 132
Langis De *see* De Langis
LANGLADE
Charles **51** 245
LANGLE
Edward D. **104** 46
John **121** 118 119 193 199
   203 303
Jonathan **121** 269
Mary **121** 125 126
Nancy J. **104** 46
Nathaniel **121** 48
Samuel W. **104** 46

LANGLE *cont'd*
Sarah **121** 119 121 270
Susanna **121** 203
LANGLEY Langlee
   Langlie Langly
   Langlye
— Mr. **51** 399 **57** 316
— Mrs. **52** 420 **127** 138
Abigail **97** 377
Abigail Durrell **132** 276
Ada Leonore **90** 192
Ada Marie **86** 369
Agnes **54** 343 **55** 110 **83** 71
   90 92 **109** 163
Ann **90** 92 **109** 163
Ann (Hilton) **132** 276
Ann (Pendergast)
   132 275
Anne **52** 249
Anne M. **83** 183 185
Annie E. (Taylor) **90** 192
Benight **83** 71
Benjamin **82** 45
Berwick **69** 153
Bethiah **51** 168
Beulah **78** 19 20
Carl Edwin **95** 378
Caroline Amelia **77** 182
Charles (Mrs.) **77** xxviii
   154
Christopher **112** 255
Clara A. **144** 157
Comfort **103** 298
Cora Adelaide (Phipps)
   88 169
Cornelius **73** 274
Cyrena (Field) **118** 240
Daniel **100** 302
Daniel I. **91** 230
David **82** 285 292 **132** 276
Deborah **51** 169 **67** 273
   283
Dolly **97** 373
Ebenezer **68** 223
Edith **111** 91
Edith (McCormack)
   111 139
Edmund How **68** 238
Effie J. **82** 277
Elihu **82** 45
Eliza **61** 134
Eliza Ann **58** cv
Elizabeth **51** 169 **82** 285
   292 **83** 299 300 **100** 140
   127 9
Elizabeth (Lane) **90** 47
Elizabeth (Pettigrew)
   121 303
Elizabeth (Wheeler)
   109 249
Emily Adeline **81** 477
Emily Montague **81** 477
Emma **105** 300
Esther **82** 292 297
Francis **86** 254
George **51** 169 **93** 351
   103 297 **127** 16 **140** 161
George Swan (Mrs.)
   88 169
Grace May (Noble) **95** 378
Hannah **66** 48 **97** 372

LANGLEY *cont'd*
   132 276
Hannah (Jackson)
   100 302
Hannah (Runnells)
   132 276
Hannah (Thompson)
   132 163
Hannah (Vickery)
   143 342
Hannah Furbish **97** 377
Harriet (Walker) **132** 276
Harriet M. **82** 277
Hendrick **90** 47
Henry **73** 263
Isom P. **97** 381
J. B. **91** 327
James **73** 271 **91** 327 **100**
   140 **132** 276
James (Mrs.) **120** 147
James Henry **90** 192
James Towle **58** cv
Jane **68** 225
Joan Elizabeth **100** 40
John **51** 168 363 **63** 351
   68 221 223 228 **78** 19 20
   81 477 **92** 373 **93** 350
   111 139 **118** 240 **127** 16
   131 95 **143** 342
John C. **87** 350
John H. **109** 249
John S. **51** 168
John W. **95** 378
Jonathan **97** 373
Joseph **55** 389 **68** 221 223
   225 227 230 231 234 236
   238
Joseph Field **77** 182
Joshua H. **51** 168 **88** 139
Josiah **63** 351
Julia A. (Stearns) **91** 230
Laura Elizabeth **77** xxviii
Leaman **86** 369
Lee **51** 168 **127** 17
Lemuel **68** 227
Lessye Lee **97** 381
Levi **132** 276
Lizzie **83** 299 300
Lizzie D. **109** 249
Lucina D. **125** 240
Lucy (Grosvenor)
   132 276
Lydia **64** 40 **68** 221
Margaret **51** 169 **125** 178
   182
Maria (Grinnell) **125** 239
Marie **69** 153
Martina **73** 273
Mary **51** 168 169 **56** 80 **68**
   231 **69** 153 **87** 350 **125**
   242 **126** 23
Mary Ann **73** 278
Mary B. **90** 50
Mary E. **83** 182 183
Mary Eliza **58** cv
Mary Sumner (Williams)
   136 320
Mary W. **111** 305
Mary Williams **57** 338
Merle Francis **95** 378
Mildred **120** 147

LANGLEY *cont'd*
Nancy S. (Dunnells)
  95 378
Naomi **64** 40
Nathaniel **51** 168 363 **53**
  73 **64** 40 **75** 146
Nathaniel H. **125** 239
Nicholas Durrell **132** 276
Patience **51** 363
Peter **51** 168
Polly **134** 68
Ralph **65** 166
Rebecca **97** 372 373 377
Richard **51** 398 **69** 153
Roger **69** 153
Rosella (Kelley) **85** 378
Royal **51** 169
Sally (Hilton) **132** 276
Samuel **66** 48 **81** 477 **85**
  378 **111** 305 **132** 276
Samuel Pierpont **51** 510
  81 195 477 **90** 6 **136** 320
Sarah **51** 169 **60** 53 **61** 250
  68 221 **73** 261 **77** 131
  79 98 **97** 373 **143** 342
Sarah (Gill) **143** 342
Sarah A. **103** 235
Sarah A. H. **88** 205
Sarah Jane **87** 350
Sarah R. **51** 169
Sims **83** 365
Sophronia D. **85** 374 375
Susan **78** 319
Susan E. **88** 139
Susanna **75** 146
Thankful Evans **68** 234
Thomas **61** 360 **82** 292 297
  132 163
Timothy **63** 351 **135** 233
Virginia **131** 95
Volentine **97** 372 373 377
Walker **73** 231
Warren **87** 350
William **51** 168 **68** 228 230
  70 369 **73** 277 **82** 277
  85 30 **97** 373 **127** 141
William G. **125** 239
LANGLOIS Jean **131** 95
Marie Emily **83** 427 433
LANGMAID
— Mr. **54** 388
Ann Eliza **88** 338
Caroline Helen **134** 225
Charles A. **105** 299
Edward **105** 299
Ellen A. (Sanborn)
  105 299
Emma Catherine **134** 225
Frances **76** 37
George Alonzo **134** 224
Georgianna Prentiss
  134 225
Grace (Pousland) **105** 299
Hannah **76** 37
Henry **105** 113
Ina Maria **105** 299
Jacintha Maria **105** 299
John **134** 224
Josephine (Carpi) **105** 299
Margaret A. **77** 151
Maria J. **76** 41

LANGMAID *cont'd*
Marietta Amelia **134** 224
Mary **76** 43
Mary (Durrell) **134** 224
Mary M. **105** 299
Rachel (Chase) **134** 224
Samuel **105** 113
Samuel Prentiss **134** 224
Thomas **105** 299
Winthrop **76** 43
LANGMESSER
Frank P. **83** 433
Hedwig (Lanzindorf)
  83 433
LANGMUIR John Dean
  (Mrs.) **88** 291
Laura (Drake) **88** 291
LANGON
Jane (Brush) **97** 291
LANGRELL
Mary **120** 254
Thomas **116** 110
LANGRICE Peter **66** 36
LANGRIDGE
James **115** 131
LANGRISH
Martha **70** 61 136
Richard **70** 61
William **70** 59 61 136
LANGRUM
Rowland **135** 218
LANGSDALE
William **91** 327
LANGSDON Isaac **78** 37
Rebecca Novaline **78** 37
LANGSFORD Lanksford
Abigail **56** 319
Arthur **56** 319
Esther **127** 227
LANGSHAW
Albert Colburn
  101 252
Eunice **101** 252
John Pendlebury **101** 252
Richard **101** 252
Walter Hamer **74** xxiv 76
  101 248 252 **102** 126
Walter Seymour **101** 252
LANGSON
Nathaniel **54** 166
LANGSTAFF
Augustus **98** 336
John Brett **120** 79
Mary **73** 206
Rebecca (Fitz Randolph)
  98 336
Sarah **91** 365
LANGSTER
Henry **58** 249
LANGSTON —— **136** 102
A. L. **141** 102
Anne **139** 230
Anne (Raynsford)
  139 232
George **139** 231 232
J. N. **111** 162
Jane **71** 174 **75** 135
Joan **75** 135
John **71** 174 **75** 135
Thomas **71** 170 **74** 268
  139 232

LANGSTON *cont'd*
William **139** 231
LANGSTROTH
Clarissa **145** 155
Craven **145** 155
Frances **145** 155
Frances F. (Betts) **145** 155
Harriett (Dixon) **145** 155
Margaret Davison
  (Dixon) (Dodge)
  145 155
William **145** 155
LANGTON Lanckton
  Lancton Lankton
Abra **122** 311 **123** 72
Alice Marie **109** 130
Charles **67** 364
Cuthbert **109** 315
Ebenezer **56** 209
Eliza Jane **92** 223
Elizabeth **64** 248 **67** 364
  100 141 **112** 103
Elizabeth (Fernald)
  117 229
Ellen **52** 83
Esther **90** 158 159 **111** 152
George **60** 186 **87** 302 **90**
  158 159 207
Hannah **63** 169 **90** 158 159
  112 103 **115** 305 **116**
  302 303
Hannah (Bragdon) **112**
  103 **115** 61
Hester **87** 302
James **52** 312
Jane **104** 27 **109** 315
Joan **99** 335 **109** 315
Johanna **109** 315
Jonathan **117** 229
Joseph **112** 103 **115** 308
Katharine **67** 364
Lucy **112** 103 **115** 225
  119 66
Martha A. **123** 308
Mary **61** 96 **67** 364 **119** 69
Mary A. **123** 72 150
Mary Ann **77** 153
Rachel (Varney) (Cook)
  142 247 248
Ralph **109** 315
Richard **52** 83
Roxana **61** 141
Sally **116** 133
Samuel **63** 169 **64** 248 **82**
  325 326 **112** 103 **113**
  318 **115** 61-65 135-137
  142 212-217 227 228 303-
  307 **127** 115 **146** 361
Sarah **112** 103
Stephen **67** 364
Theodosia **117** 223
  123 233
Theodosia J. **120** 140
  123 72
Thomas **104** 27 **109** 315
Timothy **112** 103 **115** 310
Vincent **110** 194 **147** 251
  252
William **67** 364 **147** 17
LANGUAGE Elizabeth
Ann **116** 258

LANGWELL
James **145** 255
William **91** 327
LANGWORTHY
— Col. **126** 113 114
— Mr. **81** 358
Altana (Babcock) **91** 250
Amous **128** 300
Amy (Lewis) **91** 251
Andrew **95** 96 **136** 216
Anna (Dean) **133** 230
B. F. **91** 251
Belle Cosine **91** 250
Benjamin **59** 193 **128** 300
Betsey **115** 128
Bronson Lee **91** 251
Cleora Ella **71** 56
Content **91** 250
Daniel **59** 194
Daniel Avery **91** 250
Elias **148** 285
Eliza (Lewis) **91** 250
Elizabeth **81** 358
Emeline Ann **91** 251
Franklin **133** 230
George **71** 56
George Anson **133** 230
Harvey **133** 230
Isaac P. **120** 219
James **133** 230
James J. **133** 230
John **73** 104 **91** 250
John Avery **91** 250
John Erwin **133** 230
John Olin **91** 251
Joseph **128** 302
Laura Jane **133** 230
Lawrence **136** 216
Lois (Allen) (Crawford)
133 230
Lucretia Northup **91** 251
Mary Ann **71** 116
Mary Polly **133** 230
Matilda **118** 79
Maud (Bronson) **91** 251
Minerva **115** 127
Olin Lee **91** 251
Orthello S. **95** 96
Patience **103** 215
Phebe Ann **133** 230
Phebe P. C. **79** 76
Rachel (Hubbard) **95** 96
Ralph Carr **91** 251
Robert **73** 104
Samuel **128** 302
Sarah (Pendleton) **91** 250
Sarah Amanda **133** 230
Sarah Elizabeth **91** 250
Sarah Isabella (Cooke)
91 250
Walter **71** 117
William F. **90** 208 **91** 208
92 208 **93** 208 **94** 209
95 96 209 **96** 209
William Franklin **71** 369
95 96
LANHAM Lanhan
Ann **70** 284 **73** 151 232 274
100 236
Aquila **73** 149 274
Bartholomew **100** 236

LANHAM cont'd
Buford Monroe (Mrs.)
105 128
Camilla **81** 152
Catherine **73** 153
Charity **73** 135
Elizabeth **73** 146 262 273
George **73** 140 273
Hilliary **73** 143
Isott **70** 284
John **73** 226
Josias **73** 151
Layer **73** 148
Lucy **73** 274
Margaret **73** 231 **75** 295
Martha **81** 152
Mary **73** 150 152 273
100 236
Massey Ann **73** 143
Mildred **73** 219
Ruth **73** 272
Sally **73** 227
Sarah **73** 263 264 271
Sarah Ann **73** 138
Sarah Lee **73** 227
Solomon **73** 135
Stephen **73** 137
Susanna **73** 151
Thomas **81** 152
Virlinda **73** 141
William **73** 268 269 276
LANIER H. W. **107** 14
Henry Wysham **73** xix
Lucy **77** 260
Sarah **113** 230
Susie **78** 50
LANK William **91** 327
LANKEFORD
— Mr. **76** 122
Lankester see Lancaster
Lankford see Langford
Lanksford see Langsford
Lankton see Langton
LANMAN Charles **64** 68
112 88
Elizabeth (Ellis) **120** 99
James **93** 397 **100** 63
140 161
Lydia S. **86** 389
Marian Chandler **95** 349
Mary **86** 91 **88** 314
Mary G. **96** 28
P. **86** 389
Samuel **56** 397 **120** 99
William T. W. **74** 111
LANNING Lanninge
Edward **77** lxxv
John Tate **124** 100
John Wesley **116** 27
Lewis **122** 160
Robert **78** 55
Susie Carter **77** lxxv
LANNIVER
Tenessa **115** 37
LANNOM
J. R. (Mrs.) **113** 81
Lannoy De see Delano
Lanphear see Lamphear
Lanpher see Lamphear
Lanphere see Lamphear
Lanphier see Lamphear

LANSBERRY
Martha June **101** 124
LANSBURG
William **73** 230
LANSDALE Ann **73** 150
Catherine **73** 273
Cornelia **73** 232
Elizabeth **73** 219
Elizabeth M. **73** 265
Isaac **73** 153 218
John **108** 118
John W. **73** 270
Jonathan **65** 184
Margaret **65** 184 **73** 141
Violetta **62** 15
LANSDOWNE —— **59** 53
— Lord **60** 225
LANSE Laurens **143** 199
LANSING
Abby Townsend
92 146
Alexander **107** 166
Estella Maud **116** 73
Gerrit A. **51** 338
Grace Moffett **60** 188
Jane Anne **93** 368
Janetie **51** 337
John **136** 320
Magtel **51** 338
Maria Lay (Dodge)
136 320
Robert **78** 168 **136** 90 320
Ruth **51** 338
Sarah K. **81** 404
LANSINGER Harriett
(Walker) **113** 75
LANSINGLE
Gerrit **53** 120
LANSOME Robert **75** 291
LANSON
— Capt. **54** 186 187
Abigail (Faulkner)
135 253
Eliza T. (Kendall) **125** 293
John **125** 293 **139** 314
Martha **135** 253
Nabby **77** 320
Thomas **135** 253
LANTERSEE
Anne **62** 303
L'ANTIGUA
Paul A. **101** 178
LANTZ Alice **102** 122
Annie **83** 65
LANWARD —— **58** 322
Lany see Laney
LANYON
Edward Arthur **108** 34
Mary **82** 21
LANYS Robert **65** 174
LANZ Betty J. **92** 229
George **92** 229
Jerome L. **92** 229
Laura **92** 229
Leonard **92** 229
LANZINDORF
Hedwig **83** 433
LAPE Clara Elizabeth
109 225
Frederick Allen **109** 225

LAPHAM

Abbot Foster **82** 276
Abiah **61** 173
Abiah Joice **60** 273
Abigail **57** 324 **60** 182 **61**
 5**7 72** 21
Abigail (Brooks) **133** 292
Abigail (Joyce) **133** 293
Abner **129** 384
Abraham **72** 16 27
Adeline **80** 250
Albert **89** 324
Alice Augusta Yale
 80 250
Alice Gertrude **89** 132
Amos **58** 176 **59** 78
 133 292
Anne Grey (Soule) **84** 224
Arad **138** 125
Bathsheba **131** 136
Benjamin **59** 310 **61** 289
 72 21
Benjamin N. **66** 195
Catherine **58** 370
Charles **60** 273 274 338
 61 57 **80** 250
Charles Henry **61** 57
Charles Howard **92** 134
Charlotte **60** 274
Cornelius **82** 276
Cynthia **86** 89
Daniel **51** 444 **72** 16 27
 85 328
David **57** 402 **58** 86 **59** 75
 77 78 135 137 139 140
 310 **72** 16 23 27 **86** 87
 110 141 **129** 260 **133**
 292
Deborah **72** 16
Duty **138** 121
Elisha **129** 260 372
Elizabeth **58** 88 365 **59** 139
 72 16
Elizabeth (Arnold) **95** 287
Elizabeth (Griffith) **85** 328
Emily **85** 327 328 **95** 287
Emma Foster **82** 276
Emma R. **82** 276
Emory Delos **64** 377 **65**
 xxxvii **67** 189
Esther **72** 16 27
Eudora Cranston **80** 250
Frederick A. B. **82** 276
George **60** 271
George Bryant **84** 223
George D. **80** 250
George Henry **82** 276
Hannah **57** 324 **58** 85 88
 168 170 172 176 389 **72**
 16 24 **80** 82 **136** 309
Hannah (Rogers) **84** 223
Hannah (Sherman) **95**
 287 **136** 309
Henry G. **73** 317 **74** xxiv
 98 291 292
Henry G. (Mrs.) **98** 292
Henry George **85** 328 **94**
 127 141 **95** 144 286 287
Henry Griffith **95** 287
Humphrey **58** 370
Ira **72** 16 27

LAPHAM cont'd

Israel **60** 180 **61** 289
J. B. **91** 230
Jesse **95** 287 **133** 293
Jethro **128** 59
John **58** 365 **60** 186 **64** 377
 67 189 **72** 16 27 **80** 82
 95 286 287 **97** 311 **129**
 384 **131** 136 **136** 309
 317
John B. **74** 305
John Henry (Mrs.) **83** 471
John J. (Mrs.) **73** 317
 74 xxiv
John Jesse **85** 328 **95** 286
 287
John Jesse (Mrs.) **85** 176
 327 **86** 201
Jonathan **138** 212
Joseph **57** 83 324 **58** 365
 133 293
Josephine Margaret
 110 141
Joshua **58** 168 **59** 310 **72**
 16 24 **78** 309 **84** 223 **95**
 287 **136** 309
Jubaetta (Lazell) (Phillips)
 89 324
Judith **72** 16
Julie Edna (Capen) **83** 471
Katharyn Elizabeth
 95 287
Loring Cushing **60** 272
Luther **92** 134 **93** 318
 94 378
Lydia **57** 324 **58** 389 **60**
 340 **72** 27 **123** 66 142
 127 253
Lydia King **61** 290
M. G. **91** 230
Mary **51** 444 **58** 85 365 **59**
 310 **65** 331 **72** 21 **74** 305
 75 226 **80** 82 **115** 85
 136 39
Mary (Mann) **95** 287
Mary (Russell) **95** 287
 131 136 **136** 309 317
Mary (Tilden) **84** 223
Mary (Wood) **84** 223
Mary Elizabeth (Walker)
 74 xxiv **95** 286
Mercy **58** 170
Mercy (Randall) **133** 293
Micah **60** 272 339 340
 61 58
Minerva **82** 276
Nathan **72** 108 **95** 287
Nicholas **59** 28
Noah **59** 28 **87** 245
Patience **72** 16
Patience (Smith) **84** 223
Polly **60** 272
Rachel **59** 28
Rachel Clap **61** 289
Raymond W. **95** 144
Raymond White **95** 287
Rebecca **57** 82 402 **59** 75 77
 78 135 137 139 140 **60**
 271 **72** 16 **86** 85 **115** 83-
 85 **136** 317
Rebecca (King) **129** 260

LAPHAM cont'd

 133 292
Rebecca Bird (Lounsbery)
 95 287
Richard **67** 35
Ruth **60** 180 271 **72** 21
Ruth (Bryant) **84** 223
Sabrat **78** 180
Sally **61** 174 176 289
Sally (Randall) **125** 214
Samuel **57** 324 401 **58** 85
 86 88 168 170 172 176
 389 **59** 138 310 **79** 103
 202 **84** 174 223 224 **85**
 204 **124** 1 109
Samuel (Mrs.) **84** 340
 85 195
Sarah **51** 444 **59** 31 **60** 339
Sarah (Chase) **87** 245
Sarah R. (Warren) **110** 141
Savony **72** 27
Semantha (Vail) **95** 287
Solomon **128** 59
Sophia **93** 318
Sophie Greenleaf **74** 305
Stephen **51** 260 **59** 140
 60 182 **72** 27
Susan **126** 39 274
Susanna **93** 319 **126** 274
 138 126
Temperance **60** 338 **61** 58
Thankful **58** 172
Thomas **57** 82 83 324 **59**
 31 75 **60** 180 271-273 **61**
 57 173 174 289 290 **65**
 331 **75** 218 226 **84** 223
 85 262 **94** 174 **115** 84
 133 95 **146** 347
W. B. **59** 57
W. H. **98** 61
William **60** 273 **72** 16
 125 214 **138** 122 126
William B. **58** 132 **95** 299
 96 256 **114** 276 **121** 295
William Berry **64** 129
 130 132 **131** 250

LAPIER La Pier Lapiere

Alice (Gilman) **130** 48
Arvin F. **130** 47
Charles J. **130** 54
Charlie O. **130** 54
Clara M. **130** 54
Everett O. **130** 48
Jeane **88** 194
Judy M. **130** 54
Leah (Mosher) **130** 53
Lillian J. **130** 47
Louis **130** 53
Margaret **130** 49
Rickie L. **130** 54
Viola **130** 53
William Henry **130** 53

LAPINS James **60** 400
LAPIOLI Samuel Robert
 (Mrs.) **106** 125
LAPISH Robert **105** 114

LAPLACE

Caroline **78** 373
Jonathan **78** 373
Nancy E. **78** 373
Robert H. **78** 373

LAPLACE cont'd
Robert L. **78** 373
LAPLIME Amelia **145** 135
LA POMERAI
Henry de **119** 96
LAPORT
Antoni **121** 180
Marinda (Lear) **121** 180
LAPP Anna M. **73** 212
Anton **73** 212
Christia **58** 347 348
Conrad **73** 212
Elizabeth **73** 212
Isaac **104** 124
J. H. **122** 315
John **122** 315
Lizzie **73** 212
Martha E. **73** 212
Martha M. (Hopkins)
104 124
LAPPINGTON Hannah
(Morgan) **100** 302
Joshua **100** 302
LAPRADE
Emma Lou **78** 325
G. A. **78** 325
Peggy **78** 26 137
LAPSLEY —— **60** 104
G. T. **100** 307
Caillard **103** 286
LAPWORTH
John **100** 293
LAQUER
F. O. (Mrs.) **108** 134
Kathleen M. **108** 134
LARA James **145** 168
Mary **145** 168
Mary Oakes **125** 294
Larabe see Larrabee
Larabee see Larrabee
Laraby see Larrabee
LARAMORE
Vida C. **117** 197
Winnie E. (Shropshire)
117 197
LARAMS Henry **67** 334
Larance see Lawrence
LARAUT
Clintona A. **99** 251
LARAWAY Maria **133** 73
LARCHE
Mary Alice **100** 112
LARCHYN Alice **70** 117
LARCOM Larcombe
Larcum Larkham -
see also Larkin
— Rev. **101** 21
Abigail **61** 334 **62** 36
Amos **81** 408
Anna **81** 408
Elizabeth **62** 36
Fanny (Ellingwood)
77 lxxxv
Fanny Ellingwood **58**
cvi **77** lxxxv
George **51** 115 **94** 177
George D. **115** 293
George E. **70** 154
George H. **115** 293
Hannah **54** 290 **56** 253 **62**
40 44 **115** 293

LARCOM cont'd
Henry **77** lxxxv
J. C. **115** 290 293
Job **56** 387 **118** 206
John **54** 193 **62** 39
John Southey **75** xxiii 155
L. **115** 290
Lan **54** 193
Lucinda **116** 62
Lucy **105** 30
Martha **62** 37
Mary **61** 336 **62** 36 **118** 206
Melinda H. **115** 293
Mordecai **62** 36
Rebecca **62** 39
Sarah **115** 293 295
Sarah A. **70** 154
Thomas **51** 115 **115** 293
LARD — Lieut. **84** 382
Galen Carter **123** 305
James **61** 351
Jane **61** 351
L. Fayette Fillmore
123 305
Margaret **61** 351
Mary Nixon **123** 305
Sarah **61** 351
Stephen **59** 21
LARDER
Andrew **139** 233
Anne **139** 233 234
Constance **139** 233 234
Elizabeth **139** 233 234
Joyce **139** 233 234
Martha **139** 233 234
Martha (Raynsford) **139**
233 234
Walter **139** 233 234
LARDING Martha **55** 413
LARDNER
Hannah **54** 325
Mary **51** 113
Nathaniel **56** 377
R. **54** 325
Richard **56** 377
Samuel **51** 113
LAREAN Sarah A. **92** 333
LAREE John **71** 125
Morgan **71** 124 125
LAREL Joseph **60** 43
Susanna **60** 43
LAREW —— **62** 387
Larey see Lary
LARFAYTE Thomasyn
(Allen) **144** 33
William **144** 33
Larg see Large
LARGDOXE
Katheren **101** 91
LARGE Larg
—— **53** 460
Abraham **78** 320
Anne (Field) **113** 268
Benjamin **113** 269
Drusilla **78** 320
Ebenezer **113** 268
Eleanor **69** 326
Elizabeth **112** 120 **113** 269
Elizabeth (Field) **113** 269
Hannah **53** 210
Jacob **113** 269

LARGE cont'd
John **65** 185
Martha **52** 319 **65** 185
Prudence Piper **88** 283
Sarah Jane **78** 320
William **65** 185
L'ARGEAU —— **53** 307
LARGIN Alice **55** 378
Henry **55** 378 **140** 314
Joseph **55** 378
Laribee see Larrabee
Laribie see Larrabee
LARIMER Rachel
(McMasters) **105** 219
Rachel Hughey **105** 219
William **105** 219
LARIMORE Abigail **55** 328
56 70
James Taylor (Mrs.) **100**
71 112 **101** 80
Thomas **55** 328 **56** 70
LARISON
Eldon Lee (Mrs.) **76**
241 **77** xxviii
Jessie Ruth **77** xxviii
LARKE Lark
Agnes **84** 80
Alice (Heath) **146** 264 267
Annis **146** 267
Benjamin **146** 267
Elizabeth **146** 267
Frane C. **112** 78
John **146** 267
Joseph **146** 267
Mary **146** 267
Mary (Evans) **100** 240
Nathaniel **146** 264 267 270
Rebecca **146** 267
Robert **100** 240
Susanna **146** 267
Thomas **66** 345
Larken see Larkin
LARKES Peter **51** 390
Larkham see Larcom
LARKIN Larken Larking
Larkins Larkyn
Learkins Lorkin
Lorkyn - see also
Larcom
—— **70** 296
— Mr. **98** 13
—— (Rich) **84** 41
Abel **77** 52 **128** 221
Abiel **77** 231
Abigail **59** 252 **77** 28
Albert Chesebrough **76**
xxxix
Alfred Otis **72** xxx xxxvi
Alice E. **128** 177
Alice Sistare **72** xxxvi
Amos **133** 232
Amy **128** 301
Ann **64** 350 **108** 304
Anna **87** 357
Anna Cordelia **90** 365
Anne **64** 354 **142** 145
Arthur Staunton **98** 12
Azubah **77** 22
Barbara **57** 157
Benjamin **92** 28 117-119
94 296 **132** 94 **133** 232

LARKIN *cont'd*
140 161
Bethiah **133** 232
Catherine **140** 161
Cordelia (Fessenden)
  92 146
Cordelia Gertrude
  (Fessenden) **90** 365
Cristine **94** 77
Damaris **51** 347
Daniel Franklin **76** xxxix
David **88** 37 **128** 299
  133 232
Dorcas **88** 37
Ebenezer **72** xxxvi **77** 233
  79 47 **133** 307 308 **140**
  161
Edgar **128** 177
Edith **83** 387
Edmund **77** 27 28
Edward **63** 111 **66** 207 **84**
  352 **87** 354 355 357 **88**
  37 **90** 364 **107** 257 **131**
  128 **135** 158 **136** 216
Elisha **128** 217
Eliza **89** 249
Elizabeth **59** 252 **68** 326
Elizabeth (Crandall)
  90 364
Elizabeth (Hall) **87** 355
Ephraim **100** 90
Eunice **66** 207
Ezekias **71** 26
Frank **66** xxxvii **67** xxii
  76 xxxix
Frank Provost **76** xxxix
Gideon **88** 37
Hannah **61** 272
Hannah (Babcock) **87** 357
  90 364
Hannah (Taylor) **90** 364
Harriet Townsend **94** 156
Hazard **88** 37
Henry **64** 348
Hugh **83** 387
Isaac **140** 30
James **127** 142
Jane **92** 298
Jenny **78** 302
Jesse **88** 37
Jessie Chesebrough **65**
  xxi **68** xxi **71** xviii
Jessie Louise **76** xxxix
Jessie Noyes **64** xxxiii
  76 xxxi xxxix
Joan **92** 298 299
Joanna **81** 485 **83** 484 **89**
  371 **131** 132
Joanna (Hale) **131** 128
Joanna (Yorke) **133** 232
John **55** 389 **84** 80 **92** 118
  128 129 **140** 161 **59** 252
John Eliot **90** 365
John G. **61** 272
John S. **94** 156
Jonathan **90** 364
Joseph **83** 63 64 68 **92** 117
  127 305 **133** 232 **140**
  161
Joshua **133** 232

LARKIN *cont'd*
Katharine (Drisscol)
  100 300
Levi **56** 387
Lillian M. **127** 87
Lydia (Cook) **133** 232
Mabel E. **117** 292
Margaret A. **92** 205
Martha **76** xxxix
Mary **56** 246 **59** 252 **61** 134
  72 xxxvi **78** 406 **79** 394
  84 83 **132** 94 **140** 161
Mary (Harvell) **128** 238
Mary (Knowles) **88** 37
Mary (Landers) **133** 232
Mary (Munro) **133** 232
Mary Ann **100** 90
Mary Chilton **90** 365
Mary O. **84** 29
Moses **100** 300
Nabby **92** 119
Nabby (Clark) **140** 30
Nathan **128** 299
Oliver **88** 37
Oliver W. **111** 140
Peter **77** 22
Philip **79** 304 **105** 244
Polly **88** 37 **92** 28
Rachel Haven **72** xxxvi
Rebecca (Cook) (Pinkney)
  133 232
Rebecca C. **90** 364
Roger **87** 357 **90** 364
Ruth **59** 252
Ruth (Cook) **133** 232
Ruthy **133** 307
Sally **77** 43 52
Samuel **59** 252 **71** 26
  90 364
Sarah **59** 252 **76** 89 **77** 52
  90 364
Sarah (Larkin) **90** 364
Sarah (Sollows) **133** 232
Stella Emma (Pierce)
  90 364
Stephen **108** 300 **128** 124
  133 232
Sukey (Makepeace)
  140 161
Susan Makepeace **88** 282
Susanna **100** 90 **128** 224
Thankful **93** 350
Thomas **55** 389 **64** 189
  350-352
Thomas O. **78** 310
Thomas Oliver **72** xxxvi
Timothy **51** 347 **128** 301
William **84** 83 **108** 300
  133 232
William H. **62** 204 **63** 111
  68 111
William Harrison **62** xl
  90 126 364 365 **91** 58
  148
William Harrison (Mrs.)
  92 146
LARLEE
Daniel A. **111** 139
Harriet J. (Willett)
  111 139
Sarah Melvina **111** 139

LARLEY
Beatrice **90** 268 371
Margaret **121** 222
LARM
Margaret **82** 292 295
Peter **82** 292 295
LARMON Larman Larmond
John **70** 263 **119** 20
  126 144
Mercy Williams
  (McFarlane) **126** 144
Robert **60** 39
LARMOUR Jane **125** 109
LARMOYEUX
Pearl Duncan **115** 317
  117 318
Victor (Mrs.) **115** 317
LARN William **55** 141
Larnard *see* Learned
Larned *see* Learned
LARNELL
Benjamin **90** 400
LARNER John **64** 53 **118**
  41 45
LAROCCA Mary Brown
  143 3 23 364
LA ROCHE
Arthur William **105** 52
Barry Anderson **105** 52
Elizabeth **105** 52
Elizabeth Barry (Butler)
  105 52
LAROCK La Rock
  La Roque
Benjamin **74** 317
David **74** 317
Francis **74** 317
Isaac **74** 317
John **74** 317 **85** 167
Josie Sterling **104** 102
Julie **82** 16
Margaret **74** 317
Mary **74** 317 **85** 167
Peter **74** 317
Razilla **74** 317
William **104** 102 **122** 286
Wilma **104** 102
Zeb **74** 317
LAROUX — Mrs. **83** 34
LARPENT
Frederic de H. **70** 287
LARQUILHON Francis
  Alexander **65** 230
LARR John **51** 190
LARRABEE Larabe
  Larabee Laraby
  Larrabe Laribee
  Larraby Larribee
  Larribie
  —— **66** 279 **74** 317 **75** 193
  104 22
— Capt. **58** 68
Abigail **54** 199 **56** 253 **70**
  106 **99** 202
Abigail (Pitman) **132** 242
Abner **87** 322
Ada Perkins (Miller)
  94 138
Adelbert **74** 317
Albion K. P. **103** 261
Alice (Parke) **136** 313

LARRABEE *cont'd*
Alvin B. **103** 269 270
Ann **64** 153 **74** 88
Anna Cummings **97** 190
Anne **56** 384 387
Anthony **81** 429
Asenath **103** 270
B. F. **71** xxxvii
Benjamin **54** 199 **56** 253
  384 **64** 376 **87** 207 **88**
  284 **103** 192 196 254
  121 245
Betsey **99** 203
Betsey (Ford) **95** 199 201
Caroline (Taylor) **91** 192
Catherine **132** 122
Catherine (Ford) (Adams)
  132 122
Celina S. **74** 169
Clara (Nason) **86** 301
Cynthia **74** 169
Cynthia M. **64** 155
Daniel **61** 383 **103** 255
  256 259 265 267
Daniel Green **56** 290
David **70** 106
Dell **91** 192
Dorothy **98** 189
Ebenezer **70** 106 **99** 202
Edith **74** 317
Eleanor **54** 351
Eliza **81** 429
Eliza E. **83** 179 183
Elizabeth **63** 100 **67** 371
Elizabeth G. **88** 336
Enoch **70** 106
Ervette L. (Gammon)
  104 284
Esther **75** 47
Esther (Noble) **95** 32
Esther A. (Mayo) **83** 299
  300
Esther Adla (Hatch)
  86 301
Eunice **75** 193
Eunice (Hinman) **132** 122
Fannie **95** 378
Fanny (Bird) **88** 284
George **74** 169 **125** 37
George Edward **86** 301
George L. **86** 301
George West **56** 290
Greenfield **63** 100 **70** 106
  136 313
Hannah **61** 383 **81** 429 **95**
  190 **99** 116 **100** 145 **102**
  307 **103** 192 197 254
  110 230 **121** 313
Hannah (Ellis) **117** 164
Hannah Cooper (Beath)
  97 191
Harriet S. **103** 261
Helen Fairbanks **101** 71
Isaac **95** 199 201 **103** 193
  269 **142** 205
J. C. **83** 299 300
J. P. **83** 183 184
Jabez **70** 106
Jane **142** 205
Jane (Chase) **87** 322
Jesse **75** 111 **132** 121 122

LARRABEE *cont'd*
Joanna (Littlefield)
  132 122
Joel **75** 112 **132** 122
John **57** 149 **63** 100 **70**
  105 106 **84** 158 **100** 264
  103 257 261 262 270
  111 299
John S. **97** 215 **103** 265
  117 164
Jonathan **79** 36 **85** 51
Joseph **63** 100 **70** 106 **103**
  195 267 269
Joshua **95** 32
Judith **70** 106
Julia Lucretia **97** 215
Katharine **75** 47 117 119
Lawrence L. (Mrs.) **94** 97
Leonard W. **114** 158
Lois **57** 149
Lydia **70** 355 **75** 108 111
  112 116 117 119 122 **76**
  191 193 **133** 43
Lydia (Durrell) **132** 121
Lydia (Maltby) **111** 299
Lydia (Wakefield) **132**
  121 122
Lydia M. (Morrison) **83**
  183 184
Marcia Dean (Bancroft)
  97 215
Margaret **110** 230
Margaret (Wellington)
  85 51
Martha **57** 67 **61** 276 323
  99 203
Mary **54** 290 **56** 253 290
  385 **57** 149 201 **59** 57 **70**
  106 **75** 116 **103** 255 **126**
  255 **128** 18 **132** 122 **137**
  339
Mary (Gaines) **85** 51
Mary Jane **86** 155
Miriam (Lord) **132** 122
Molly (Merrill) **126** 275
Nancy **56** 65 **83** 114
Nathaniel **81** 162 **103** 189
  119 20
Pegge **55** 178
Phebe **63** 100 **94** 198 **103**
  269 270 **136** 313
Philip **103** 196 197
Polly **56** 65 290
Priscilla **86** 389 390
Ralph C. **119** 3
Ralph Clinton **61** xxxvi
Ralph Clinton (Mrs.)
  94 138
Rhoda **126** 275
Richard **70** 106
Robert **97** 191
Ruth **70** 106
Sally **56** 65 **87** 124 **94** 88
  108 163 **142** 205
Samuel **55** 429 **56** 290
  385 387 **57** 149 201 **87**
  123 **99** 203 **108** 20
Samuel H. **90** 37
Sarah **64** 376 **66** 280 **67** 224
  70 106 **75** 47 **81** 162 **87**
  62 **111** 130 **134** 232

LARRABEE *cont'd*
Sarah (Dyer) **110** 25
Sarah (Haskins) **121** 245
Sarah (Hatch) **122** 160
Sarah (Johnson) **121** 245
Seth **70** 106
Seth L. **103** 263
Silas **86** 390
Simeon **110** 25
Sophia **114** 317 **120** 189
Stephen **75** 47 108 111
  112 116 117 119 122 **76**
  194 **87** 206 **103** 195 255
  110 230 **126** 275 **132**
  121 122
Susanna **87** 125 **103** 260
Temperance (Walker)
  132 122
Teneriffe Temple **102** 317
Thankful **61** 22
Thomas **56** 65 **81** 429
  103 189
Timothy **65** 148
Westley G. **104** 284
William **56** 65 **61** 22 **75**
  108 **103** 194 262 **132**
  122
William Wellington
  85 51
Zerviah **70** 106
Larrance *see* Lawrence
LARRAUD
Marcelline **145** 131
LARREGNI
— Capt. **70** 261
LARREMERE
Jane **91** 327
Peter **91** 327
LARRET George **67** 156
Martha **67** 156
Larribee *see* Larrabee
LARRISON Mary **81** 162
L'ARROQUE
John **101** 53
LARROWE
Albertus **114** 59
Amelia (Chapin) **114** 59
Catherine **114** 59
Charlotte **114** 59
Elizabeth **86** 195 **114** 59
Elizabeth (Holmes)
  114 59
Fanny (Rose) **114** 59
Franklin B. **114** 59
Jacob **114** 49
James **114** 59
Jeanette (Aulls) **114** 59
Jeanette (Van Wormer)
  114 59
John **114** 59
Jonathan **114** 59
Lucretia (Coats) **114** 59
Mary J. **114** 59
Minerva **114** 59
Sarah A. **114** 59
William **114** 59
Larry *see* Lary
LARSELS
Charles **127** 225
Larsen *see* Larson

LARSLEY
Andrew **145** 108
William **145** 108
LARSON Larsen
Andrew **84** 85 **128** 262
Anna **128** 264
Axel **92** 229
C. Magnus **128** 98
Carl Christian (Mrs.)
101 124
Catherine C. (Johnson)
128 262
Charlotte Wilhelmina
111 101
Christine **86** 94
Dorothy **126** 240
Dorothy Frederick
(Anderson) **110** 227
Elie **107** 149
Elizabeth / Bess (Lee)
133 72
Emelia A. **91** 105
Emelie L. **115** 170
Emma M. **128** 262
Ernest Ludwig **110** 227
Katharine Marie **117** 129
Lars Victor **120** 234
Lawrence B. **107** 178
Lawrence M. **73** 82
Leonard Alfred (Mrs.)
109 130
Leverne I. **92** 229
Lewis **92** 229
Marian **82** 278
May Belle **107** 132
Nels **72** 204
Norma **102** 124
Pauline **89** 131
Roland (Mrs.) **101** 124
Sigurd Hialmar **85** 167
Stina Lisa (Abramsdotter)
128 98
Thelma Rebecca **91** 142
Violet M. **92** 229
Wadsworth (Mrs.)
113 226
Wallace H. (Mrs.) **108** 134
LART Charles E. **62** 390 **64**
199 **92** 399 401
LARUE De Larue La Rue
Abraham **122** 320
Anne **109** 235
Elias **109** 235
Elizabeth **109** 235
Fred **114** 68
Isaac **76** 81
Jacques **95** 399
John **109** 235
Margaret **78** 346
Philip **109** 235
Sibyl (Lambert) **122** 320
William **109** 235
LARWOOD
Agnes **141** 116
Bridgett **147** 143
Edmond **141** 321
Edmund **141** 118 **147** 143
Elizabeth **141** 117 118
Joan **141** 117 118
John **144** 258
Margaret (Ward) **141** 118

LARWOOD *cont'd*
Martha (Roo) **147** 143
Rebecca (Moulton) **141**
320 321 **147** 138 143
Thomas **141** 118 326 **142**
262 **147** 143
William **66** 182 **141** 117
118 **147** 143
LARY Larey Larry
— Mrs. **83** 34
— Widow **73** 69
Abby **76** xliii
Daniel **70** 264
Dinnis **111** 259 **114** 290
Eliza **59** 284
Hannah **55** 374 **81** 429
83 15
Hannah (Hubbard) **83** 15
James **111** 259
Jane **74** 250 **86** 151
John **55** 374 **83** 15 **98** 105
111 259 **115** 15 20
Jotham **86** 151
Lucy **115** 20
Margaret (Brown)
111 259
Margaret (Willson)
114 290
Mary **86** 153 **115** 20
Nella **115** 15
Olive **111** 259
Patric **103** 269
Polly **115** 15
Sally Durgin **100** 147
Sarah **98** 298
Sarah (Kimball) **86** 151
Thomas Jackman **86** 151
Velma Ellen Clytie (Cole)
86 151
William **105** 113
LARYMAN
George **51** 275 277
LA SALLE
Beatrice Franc **82** 17
Benjamin Franklin **82** 16
Clint Wood **82** 16
Francois **82** 16
Georgeanna Willitts
82 17
Julie **82** 16
Myra Mildred **82** 17
Robert Cavelier (Sieur de)
67 xi
Sarah Louisa **82** 16
LASATER Lois **102** 165
LASBURY
R. C. (Mrs.) **102** 147
LASCELLES
— Col. **112** 292
Mary **54** 68 **62** 357
LASCH
Christopher **132** 185
LASDEL
Ellison **105** 209
Hannah **95** 189
Joshua **105** 209
Mehitable (Ricker) **95** 86
Susanna (Adlington)
89 324
Lasell *see* Lazell
Laselle *see* Lazell

LASEY John **63** 19
LASH
___ (Wild) **140** 262
David Chapman **84** 173
85 195 **114** 157
Elizabeth **142** 130 134
Elizabeth (Skillen)
142 134
Ellen Jane **108** 223
Emma Shrives **114** 157
F. A. **95** 50
Margaret **73** 168
Mary **109** 68
Mary Ann (Stammers)
126 65
Nicholas **142** 134
Rebecca S. **78** 403
Robert **140** 262
LASHER ___ **58** 96 321
Francois **59** 225
Frederick **101** 205
James **101** 205
John **59** 225
Lucretia (Huntley)
101 205
Mariah **92** 165
Sebastian **59** 225
LASING
Phillippa **120** 23
LASINGBY
Benjamin **116** 110
LASKER
Albert Davis **88** 169
George F. **65** 92
LASKEY Abigail
(Wakeham) **99** 112
Alice **111** 106
Benjamin **111** 106
Elizabeth **79** 37
Jean **111** 106
Joanna **99** 112
John **99** 112
Margaret E. **138** 218
Mary **125** 222
Robert **111** 106
Sally **134** 149
Samuel **111** 106
Samuel Hendly **111** 106
Tabitha **111** 106
Tabitha (Coates) **111** 106
Thomas **111** 106
William **111** 106
LASKIN Edith **83** 387
LASLEE John **127** 15
LASON
Benjamin **116** 259
Charlotte (Whipple)
116 259
LASONBYE
William **116** 244
LASS
Anton Charles **89** 313
Friedrich **89** 313
Mary Ann (Lazell) **89** 313
Mine (Schonecker)
89 313
Thon Charles **89** 313
Lassel *see* Lazell
Lassell *see* Lazell
LASSEN
Christian **55** 362

LASSEY Sarah **67** 283
LASSINGH
  Pietre Pieterse **130** 209
LASSURE Betsey **126** 220
LAST John **100** 15
LASULL Martha **88** 259
LATANE — Rev. **91** 208
  Lucy Temple **91** 208
LA TAPPA Edward **83** 34
LATE Sarah **78** 184
Latemer see Latimer
LATERRIERE Peter de
  Sales **125** 23
LATEUR De Lateur
  Helen Katharine **92** 230
  Joseph Alphonse **92** 230
  Louise Albert **92** 230
  Oliver **104** 96
  Susan Lillebrant **104** 96
LATEWOOD
  William **65** 239
LATHAM Leatham
  Leathem
  —— **53** 142 144 146 **54**
    xliv **101** 301 **120** 207
  A. L. **62** 187
  Abigail **127** 58
  Abigail (Randol) **120** 46
  Abigail Haumer **82** 366
  Alexander **101** 301
  Alfred E. **79** 76
  Alice **79** 71 **80** 346
  Ann **103** 317
  Ann Elizabeth **79** 71
  Anna **66** 285
  Anna Mae **85** 198
  Anna Maria **66** lxviii
  Archibald **115** 18
  Arthur **146** 360
  Deriah **58** 246
  Betsey **115** 18
  Betsey (Chase) **89** 37
  Carrie **95** 147
  Cary **61** 385 **104** 187
  Catherine **61** 385
  Charles A. **66** xliii
  Chester Adelbert **72** xx
  Chilton **59** 107 **89** 37
    136 118
  Clarinda (Ford) **120** 46
  Cyrus **120** 46
  Deborah **58** 246
  Deborah (Hueitt) **100** 299
  Deliverance (Alger)
    136 37
  Drusilla **78** 320
  Ebenezer **85** 155
  Eliab **137** 49
  Eliza **79** 25
  Elizabeth **61** 385 **74** 132 **85**
    363 364 **91** 71 **100** 236
    102 47 **103** 72 **131** 156
  Elizabeth (Hanks) **86** 14
  Elizabeth (Masters) **91** 71
  Emma M. **72** 204
  Esther Gillett **108** 157
  Ethel Louisa **71** xxiii
  Eunice **102** 168
  Ezra B. **79** 76
  Fanny A. (Crowley)
    88 343

LATHAM cont'd
  Frances **60** 172 **74** 72 132
    79 57 248 **82** 156 **85** 417
    96 9 **103** 317 **141** 106
  George **89** 274 **100** 236
  Hannah **95** 358 **98** 84 **106**
    69 **144** 300
  Hannah (Morgan)
    136 313
  Harriet **101** 301
  Henry **105** 98-100 **115** 24
  Henry Bradford **101** 301
  Isaac **128** 271
  J. M. **80** 139
  James **136** 37
  Jane **61** 385
  John **61** 385 **63** 346 **64** 318
    101 301 **112** 286 287
    127 175 266
  Jonathan **85** 155
  Joseph **79** 71 **80** 77 80 **91**
    286 **96** 11 **101** 301 302
    128 222 **134** 141 **146**
    347
  Joseph B. **104** 77
  Keziah **115** 18 24
  L. B. **104** 77
  Lewis **74** 72 132 **79** 248
    103 317
  Lila **79** 25
  Lois **101** 302
  Lorenzo **115** 18
  Louis **80** 373
  Louis S. **110** 79 **116** 313
  Lucretia **87** 380
  Lucy **120** 53 **136** 313
    137 49
  Lucy (Niles) **85** 155
  Lucy Ann **79** 71
  Lydia **68** 302 **91** 286
  Marcus Austin **120** 46
  Margaret **59** 308 **100** 236
    128 173
  Mary **62** 187 320 **108** 223
  Mary (Post) **146** 360
  Mary A. K. **89** 274
  Mary Ann (Squire) **104** 77
  Mary E. **79** 76
  Mary Hannah **80** 139
  Mary Louise **105** 160
  Mercy D. **113** 295
  Monroe F. **104** 77
  Nancy **60** 149
  Nancy (Neff) **128** 271
  Nelson Avery **79** 71
  Nicholas **61** 385
  Paget **61** 385
  Paul Wheeler **101** 302
  Percy K. (Bullard) **104** 77
  Prudence **51** 278
  Rachel **101** 301
  Rachel (Bradford) **101** 301
  Richard **64** 339 **65** 50
  Robert **85** 364 **106** 69 **110**
    79 **112** 281 **146** 348
  Samuel **51** 278 **93** 99 **115**
    18 24 **126** 256
  Sarah **65** 1
  Sarah M. (Johns) **104** 77
  Sarah R. **104** 77
  Seth **86** 14

LATHAM cont'd
  Stanton **101** 301
  Stephen **82** 366
  Susanna **59** 107 **126** 275
    136 37
  Susanna (Winslow)
    106 69
  Thomas **58** 246 **63** 240 **66**
    285 **82** 333 **100** 299
  W. F. **72** 204
  William **55** xxxix **58** lii
    59 liii **60** xliv **61** xlii **80**
    346 **88** 343 **136** 313 **139**
    108 **147** 280
  William (Mrs.) **100** 264
  William Thayer **79** 25
  Williams **56** xxxviii **57**
    xxxix **62** xlvi lxxxviii
    63 lxxvii
  Woodward **137** 49
LATHBERRY Leota
  (Youtsey) **100** 87
  William **100** 87
LATHBRIDGE
  Dorothy **100** 303
  Jane **100** 304
LATHBURY Arthur **127**
    170 **128** 105
  Frances **127** 171
LATHE Anna **61** 343
  Eunice **61** 341
  Ezra **61** 341
  Francis **62** 36
  John **62** 37
  Marcia (Hanks) **86** 17
  Mary Ann **94** 286
  Sarah **124** 17
  Sylvanus B. **86** 17
LATHEMYT
  James **82** 334
LATHER William **91** 327
LATHERS
  Abby P. **125** 172 240
  Richard **62** 389 390
LATHLY
  Abigail **58** 176
  Margaret **83** 404
  Philip **58** 176
  William **58** 176
LATHROP —— **55** 449
    103 34 36 **130** 235 **140**
    55
  — Capt. **70** 110 **121** 197
  — Mr. **60** 377 **70** 249
  — Rev. Dr. **145** 305
  —— (Cordis) **140** 162
  —— (Hill) **105** 73
  Abial (Lazell) **88** 260
  Abigail **57** 335 **60** 145 **86**
    447 **102** 301 **115** 20 **142**
    123
  Abigail (Button)
    (Dudson) **145** 264
  Allathyna **58** 93
  Amanda Olive (Hill)
    98 91
  Anna M. **70** xlvii
  Arunah **98** 92
  Aurelia (Noble) **113** 304
  Azel **136** 326
  Barnabas **70** 108 **145** 264

LATHROP *cont'd*
Bathsheba **86** 456 457 **102**
    48 51
Benjamin **98** 92 **105** 73
    115 20
Caroline **133** 302
Caroline Brownson
    98 91
Caroline Cornelia
    (Brownson) **98** 92 93
Caroline Cushman
    136 326
Caroline Maria **98** 92 93
Charity **120** 266
Charity (Perkins) **120** 266
Charles **136** 315 **137** 182
Charles B. **123** 123
Charles Caldwell **58** 37
Clara **105** 73
Clara H. **98** 283
Clarisa H. **98** 283
Cornelia **58** 37 **105** 73
Cornelia C. **98** 92
Cornelia Clarissa **98** 92
    93
Cornelia Sterrett
    (Penfield) **93** 142
Daniel **51** 159
Daniel H. **137** 219
David **51** 159 160
Deborah **96** 382
Denison **136** 320
Dorcas **70** 108
Dyer **70** xlvii
Edward **51** 159-161 **140**
    68 161
Electa **115** 19
Eli B. **98** 93
Elisha **116** 7 **136** 320 325
Elizabeth **60** 148 **68** 106 **70**
    108 **140** 162
Elizabeth (Abell) **136** 326
Elizabeth (Hyde) **136** 326
Elizabeth (Waterman)
    136 320
Elizabeth Terry (Earle)
    98 343
Ella R. **113** 295
Erastus **136** 326
Ezra **70** 232
Fanny Bestow **57** 294
Flora (Crocker) **87** 25
Florence Wentworth
    136 325
Florrella G. **123** 51
Frank H. **98** 283
Frank William **98** 282
G. C. **108** 198
Gabos **116** 7
George Thomas **58** 37
Gilbert **93** 342
Hannah **62** 187 **70** 108
    123 65
Hannah (Hough) **136**
    320 325
Harriet Wadsworth
    136 315
Helen Earle **98** 343
Henry A. **109** 39
Henry Monroe (Mrs.)
    93 142

LATHROP *cont'd*
Henry Perkins **58** 37
Hubbel **98** 91-93 147 282-
    284 **105** 73
Ichabod **60** 145
Isaac **51** 159
Isaiah **58** 93
J. B. **98** 92
Jane **70** xlvii **140** 162
Jedediah Hyde **136** 325
Jedidiah **58** 37
Jennie (McGeachen)
    98 283
Joanna (Leffingwell)
    136 315
John **56** 136 **109** 311 **121**
    247 **126** 255 **130** 235
    136 326 **140** 153 162
    144 210 **145** 295 299
    148 324
John B. **98** 92 93 **105** 73
John Brownson **98** 92
Jonathan **51** 159
Joseph **60** 145 **115** 90 **121**
    139 **128** 258 **140** 162
Josiah **51** 159
Julia **89** 31
Justice **51** 34
Laura **98** 91 **105** 73
Laura (Brownson)
    98 282 283
Laura B. **98** 283 **105** 73
Lois (Huntington)
    136 325
Lucretia Jeanette **113** 304
Lucy **57** 294 **105** 73
Lucy C. **98** 93
Lucy Cornelia **98** 92
Lurancy (Hanks)
    (Winslow) **86** 21
Lydia **136** 315 317
Lydia (Abell) **136** 315 317
Lydia (Daniels) **126** 255
Maria **88** 287 **98** 350
Mariah **105** 73
Mariana (Bryan) **136** 325
Martha **96** 390 **127** 200
Mary **58** 37 **60** 150 **70** 232
    94 188 **127** 94 **136** 57
Mary (Emerson) **108** 306
Mary (Wheatley) **84** 268
Mary Wright **137** 183
Moses **130** 235
Nancy **115** 19 20
O. A. **98** 92
Olive Amanda **98** 93
Olive Amanda (Hill)
    98 91 92
Pamelia C. (Hill) **105** 73
    98 91 282 283
Polly (Bacon) **130** 235
Presinda **136** 334
Prudence **60** 145 151
Richard Tracy **58** 37
Rolland H. **98** 283
S. C. **128** 171
Samuel **51** 159 **126** 307
    136 320 325
Sarah **60** 145 **62** 188 **105** 73
    123 50 **136** 320
Sarah (Bailey) **136** 326

LATHROP *cont'd*
Sarah (Peck) **130** 235
Sarah B. (McAuley) **98** 93
Sarah Hubbard (Harris)
    136 320
Sarah P. **98** 283
Sarson **59** 198
Simon **58** 93 **108** 307
Sophronia **87** 25
Stephen P. **123** 50 53
Susanna (Hutchinson)
    137 182
Temperance **136** 319
Thomas **59** 200 **110** 27 **115**
    11 **136** 315 317
U. D. **128** 94 95 97 171
W. H. **98** 283
Warren (Mrs.) **98** 147
    103 79 127
William Edward **58** 37
William H. **98** 283 **105** 73
Zebediah **98** 343
Lathum *see* Latham
LATIMER Latemer
    Latimore Lattimer
—— **63** 72 **112** 187
— Col. **89** 258
— Dr. **84** 384 387
— Lord **114** 55
— Mr. **62** 196 **80** 187
Abigail **72** 47 97 180
    86 170
Abigail M. **72** 103
Addison **72** 291
Aholiab **62** 293 294 **63** 70
    71 **71** 161 277 **86** 161
    170
Alexander **71** 165
Alonzo Lyman **91** 105
Ann **123** 170 **142** 325
    145 321
Ann (Griggs) (Jones)
    123 170
Ann M. **81** 410 413
Anne **71** 279
Anson Herman **72** 93
Arthur R. **83** 426 433
Bedy **72** 101
Benjamin **81** 290
Betsey M. **72** 104
Bezaleel **56** 57 **60** 141 **71**
    158-162 164-166 301 308
    309 **72** 30 **86** 161
Bille **72** 30
Charles Edmund **81** 290
Chauncey **63** 72 **72** 180
Chauncey H. **86** 170
Christian **71** 160
Christopher **60** 239
Clara **71** 277
Clara Holman **72** 291
Clarissa **72** 96 101 106
Comfort **71** 163
E. Levi **72** 171
Ebenezer **71** 80 163-165
    280 301 **72** 42 87 90-93
    169 174-176 **79** 302
Ebenezer Whetmore
    71 164
Edith Siddell **91** 105
Eleanor **63** 72 **86** 170

LATIMER *cont'd*
Eleazer Curtis **72** 91
Elihu **71** 273 277 306 **72**
    46 95 96
Elihu Northe **71** 277
Elisha **71** 163 307 **143** 324
Eliza **72** 89 103
Elizabeth **60** 238 239 **71**
    77 81 158 164 280 **72** 40
    174 291 **123** 170 **142**
    325 **143** 306
Elizur **72** 104
Ellen A. **72** 107
Elois **62** 85
Emily Harriet **72** 291
Emily Susan **72** 91
Estella (Siddell) **91** 105
Eunice **71** 80 163 280 **72**
    42 90 102 **75** 78
Fanny **75** 78
Fidelia **72** 290
Fidelia Louisa **75** 78
Flora B. **81** 413
Foster **72** 47
Frances Cordelia **75** 78
G. **72** 179
George **71** 77 159
Giles **81** 413
Hannah **83** 55
Hannah A. **70** 120 **115** 132
Harriet S. **79** 151
Harvey **72** 87
Hector **72** 95 176
Henry **128** 19
Herman **72** 92 175
Hezekiah **71** 77 79 159
    160 162 163 165 271 273
    277 279 306 **72** 41 44 90
    101 171 177
Hiram **72** 95 290
Huldah **72** 290
Irene **86** 53
Isaac Newton **72** 291
Jacob **71** 166
James **73** 266
James Orson **72** 291
John **56** 57 **71** 163 **72** 180
    181 **82** 444 **87** 398 **142**
    325 332 **143** 306 **145**
    319-321
John I. **72** 103
John L. **72** 180 **89** 257
John Thrall **72** 90
Jonathan **56** 57 **84** 239
Josephine Adel **72** 291
Laura **71** 277 **72** 102
Laura Chapel **89** 257
Leicester Filley **72** 90
Lester **72** 47
Levi **62** 197 **63** 70 **71** 165
    72 42 89-91 172 **86** 161
Levi E. **72** 107
Lillian **69** 208
Lois **62** 293 **86** 161 170
Lucina **71** 163 308
Lucinda **72** 290
Lucretia **72** 95
Lurana Lamira **72** 290
Lyman **81** 410 413
Mabel Wilson **113** 304
Mahalah **72** 90 104

LATIMER *cont'd*
Margaret **70** 120 **114** 55
    115 132
Margaret (Speer) **113** 304
Maria **72** 89
Marilla **72** 182
Marion Millard (Mrs.)
    103 119
Mary **56** 57 **60** 239 **71** 80
    162 163 281
Mary Ann **72** 90 103
Mary Maria **72** 96
Mindwell **72** 44 177
Nabby **71** 165
Nancy **72** 89 102 **81** 410
Nancy C. **81** 413
Naomi **84** 466
Orrin **72** 87 90 169
Pamela **72** 90 171
Peter **75** 78
Peter Erskin **75** 78
Picket **75** 78
Prudence **71** 163
Rebecca **71** 77 277 **72** 41 42
    100
Robert **98** 116 **123** 170
    147 57
Roxie **71** 271 **72** 100
Ruth **71** 163
Sabra Emeline **72** 290
Saint **56** 57
Samuel **62** 197 **128** 20
Sarah **71** 308 **81** 413
Sibyl **71** 84
Solomon **71** 308
Sophia T. **81** 290
Submit **71** 163
Thomas Henry **113** 304
Tryphena **71** 79 159 279
    282
Wait **83** 55
Wealthian **71** 162
William **72** 290
Zeruah **81** 290
Ziba **81** 413
LATON — Mr. **56** 384
Eleanor **101** 218
Polly **78** 411
Polly (Barnes) **125** 104
Richard **58** 237 **96** 122
Thomas **125** 104
LATOUCHE
Robert **119** 100
LATOUR — Gov. **96** 271
— Mme **143** 32
Anne (Fulwater) **110** 84
Charles **96** 271 **140** 103
    104 110
Charles de **116** 8
Claude de **116** 8
Claude Sieur de **82** 136-
    138
Genevieve **110** 133
Hypolite **110** 133
Marie Adriane Pelagie
    110 133
Marie C. (Renaut) **110** 133
Martin **110** 133
Robert **110** 83 84
LATOURETTE
Lyman E. **110** 319

LATROBE Eliza Bradlee
    Winchester **78** 134
Osmun **78** 134
LATTA Agnes **107** 296
Lattamore *see* Lattimore
Lattemore *see* Lattimore
LATTIE Edith (Leeman)
    86 310
Frances Mildred **86** 310
James W. **86** 310
Lattimer *see* Latimer
LATTIMORE
Chauncey Hall **61** 297
Christopher **102** 180
Eleanor Harris **61** 297
Elizabeth **100** 266
Eloise **61** 297
George **61** 297
Henry **126** 255
Hepzibah **56** 254
Laura (Cooney) **83** 426
    433
Levi **56** 254 **61** 297
Mary **61** 138 **100** 266
Mediab **61** 297
Robert **100** 266
Solomon **59** 21
Timothy Robbins **61** 297
William **61** 138
LATTIN Abiah **115** 25
Cynthia **115** 27
Gideon **115** 27 110 117
Hannah **115** 27 110
Job **115** 115
Luke Blackman **115** 110
Luther **115** 117
Marius Clarke **115** 115
Mary **115** 117
Rosamond **115** 115
William **115** 25
LATTING
Charles **76** 267
Esther **99** 253
Jane E. **76** 267
LATTNEY
Mary **136** 304 306
LATTURE
Francis **65** 353
Susanna **65** 353
Sylvan Joseph **87** 174
LATTUWORTH
James de **109** 18
LATTY
Hannah G. **85** 372
Lucy Ann **85** 375
LAU Benjamin **145** 361
Kathryn **101** 126
LAUBER
Almon W. **93** 401
L. A. **52** 97
LAUBIN Gladys **90** 201
Reginald **90** 201
LAUCKS Anna Catherine
    (Kaiser) **96** 396
Barbara (Kershner)
    96 396
Blanche S. (Elliott) **96** 396
Caspar **96** 396
Elizabeth (Smyser) **96** 396
Elliott Forry **96** 396
George **96** 396

LAUCKS *cont'd*
Imilda Arabella (Wilt)
  96 396
Israel **96** 396
Mary (Lora) **96** 396
Peter **96** 396
Philip **96** 396
Samuel Forry **75** xxiii 65
  96 396 **97** 78 160
LAUD Lawd
Edward **82** 412
Martha A. **87** 375 376
William **52** 239 **53** 187 188
  54 313 342 **129** 4 6 107
  109 245 **130** 111 **132** 8
  138 79-93 96-98 103-105
  140 5 7
William (Abp. of
  Canterbury) **55** lxxxvi
  56 273 275 **57** 64 **60** 58
  59 **71** 252 **74** 139 **75** xlv
  78 116 **80** 134 **86** 256
  112 109 **134** 288 **135** 86
  91 **143** 27 248
LAUDER Edwin G. (Mrs.)
  84 332
Ethel Keith (Albee) **84** 332
George **136** 331
Katharine Morgan
  (Rowland) **136** 331
Mary Josephine **136** 331
LAUDERDALE
Annie M. **77** 224
Benjamin Winchester
  77 224
Frank **77** 224
Mary **77** 224
Mary Caroline **77** 224
Mary H. **77** 224
Samuel Holmes **77** 224
LAUER Philippe **99** 256
LAUERS Jacob **51** 45
LAUFMAN
Alberta Bond **84** 111
William Laburine (Mrs.)
  84 189
LAUGHIER
Hannah **78** 311
LAUGHLAND
Agnes **141** 57
LAUGHLIN
A. G. **104** 96
Alexander **105** 219
Alexander (Mrs.) **80** 102
  208
Alice Denniston **90** 137
Anne Irwin **84** 111 185
  102 61 127 **103** 137
Elizabeth **98** 178
F. B. **107** 20
F. C. **104** 96
Francis **96** 357
H. L. **104** 96
Harry Hamilton **72** xx
Henry **104** 96
Henry Alexander **103** 137
Hugh M. **66** 37
J. V. **104** 96
James **103** 137
James Laurence **60** lxviii
Julia Ann **87** 284

LAUGHLIN *cont'd*
Kendall **107** 238 **109** 238
Ledlie Irwin **84** 110 185
  95 153 **103** 137 **112** 173
  176 177 **116** 82
Lucy Hayes **69** 210
Margaret (Mellon)
  105 219
Mary **80** 208 **84** 189
Nancy **51** 190
Patrick **112** 287
Thomas **61** 138
Thomas McKennan
  69 210
Virginia **105** 128
Virginia E. **117** 238
LAUGHTERTON
Elizabeth **83** 119
LAUGHTON *see also*
  Lawton
Abby S. **122** 312
Abigail **126** 131
Abigail (Edwards)
  144 330
Anna F. **76** 16
Catherine **67** 17 188
Charles H. **76** 16 **84** 54
Charles Knox **103** 119
Elizabeth **140** 48 **144** 207
  324 329
Flora E. **101** 217
Henry **67** 188 **84** 152 366
  85 13
Hepzibah **108** 248
Isaac **76** 52
Isabell (Atwood alias Tay-
  lor) **147** 14
James **84** 426
John **55** 301 **62** 33 **88** 279
  97 395
Joseph **51** 91 **85** 124
  140 162
Katy **84** 366
Mary **61** 96 **121** 218
Nancy (Priest) **88** 279
Oliver **70** 219
Pamela **76** 16
Pamelia Gross (Rich)
  84 54
Peggy **85** 13
Sally **144** 324
Samuel **62** 33
Sarah **55** 301 **68** 196
Sarah (Wellman) **84** 426
Sarah E. **77** 149
Susanna **107** 306 **121** 222
Tabitha (Kidder) **144** 330
Thomas **62** 33 **68** 195 196
  107 306
William **144** 330
LAUGIER
— Baron de Tassy **140**
  162
Hannah (Minot) **140** 162
LAUIS William **55** 141
LAUMAN
— Brig. Gen. **80** 161
LAUN John de **85** 121
LAUNCE Mary **78** 443 **116**
  280 **119** 311

LAUNCH
Robert **100** 143
Sarah **100** 143
Thomas **100** 143
LAUNDELS John **109** 22
LAUNDER John **80** 357
Mary **61** 386
Launders *see* Landers
LAUNE
Gedeon de **110** 84
Gode de **110** 84
LAUNIUER
Margaret Agusta
  115 38
LAUNSDEN —— **55** 433
LAURE Marguerite **143** 8
LAUREN —Col. **84** 385
LAURENS
Dillea **88** 275
Henry **129** 133
John **54** 237
LAURENT
Francis **62** 330
James Francis **65** 230
LAURIAT Amelius
  Anselm **92** 191
Blanche **75** 5
Charles E. **54** xxxv
Charles Emelius **71** vi
  xxiii **72** vi **73** vi **75**
  xxxv xciii 3-5 **92** 191 192
Charles Emile **75** vi 5 155
  76 vi xxi **77** vi **78** 218
  79 214 **80** 220 **81** 234
  92 150 191 192 199
Emelius Anselm **75** 3
George Bullard **92** 192
Harriet Fidelia **75** 5
Lewis Anselm **92** 191
Louis Anselm **75** 3
Martha **75** 3
Natalie **92** 192
Sarah **75** 3
Susan / Susanna Foster
  75 5 **102** 162 **103** 119
LAURIE Harriet Westcott
  77 xii
James **118** 45
LAURIER Wilfred **54** 457
  91 101
LAURILL John **65** 165
Laurons *see* Lawrence
LAURY John L. **109** 14
Rosina (Billings) **98** 7
  109 14
LAUTENSCHLAGER
Mary Frances **125** 53
LAUTERBACH Amanda
  75 xxiii 64 **81** 109 230
  82 350
Edith **82** 350
Edward **82** 350
Edward (Mrs.) **75** xxiii
Mina **82** 350
Solon **82** 350
LAUTRIDGE —— **123** 23
LAUZUN Gontaut
  Armand Louis (Duc
  de) **84** 385
LAVAL De Laval
  — Sieur **119** 97

LAVAL *cont'd*
Emme **119** 100
Guy **119** 97 100
Hugh **96** 116
Katharine **96** 116
Margaret **96** 115 116
Maud **96** 116
Robert **96** 116
Walter **96** 116
William **96** 116
LAVALLE
Alice Cornelia **82** 365
Amalia de **81** 468
Eduardo Reyes **109** 287
John **82** 365
Maria Luisa (Foster) **109** 287
LAVAN John D. **76** 145
LAVEAU Ermine **75** xiv
LAVELL Amber **100** 188
John **63** 214
Lazarus **100** 188
LAVENDER
Abraham D. **148** 291
Allaine **127** 274
Ann Barba (Allaine) **127** 274
Harriet **127** 274
John **62** 322
Mary Jane **127** 274
Robert **127** 274
Sarah **118** 295
Simeon Leonard **127** 274
Susanna **127** 274
Susanna Richardson **127** 275
William Reed **127** 274
LAVENSALER
Jacob **105** 286
Stephen **105** 287
LAVEQUE Elizabeth Marie **125** 99
LAVER Judith **74** 38
Mary **74** 38
Molly **74** 184
Sarah **74** 39
Simon **91** 327
William **74** 39
LAVERDY Salome **74** 253
LAVERIDGE
Margaret **141** 25
LA VERNE
Bernice **96** 160
LAVEROCK Ann **68** 72
John **111** 263
LAVERS Jacob **69** 360
LAVERTY
Amelia **79** 306
Electa **109** 270 272
Eliza **60** 347
Esther Ann **79** 306
Henry **79** 306
William **109** 270 272
LAVERY Nellie **116** 64
LAVICOUNT
John **84** 255
Lucy (Vassall) **84** 255
LAVIGNE La Vigne
David E. **64** 200
Matilda **75** 24

LA VILLEBEUNE
Blanche Marie **82** 268
Jean Placid **82** 268
Lolitte **82** 268
LAVIN David **101** 215
Mary **101** 216
Mary Ann (Lynch) **101** 215
LAVINE
Sigmund A. **117** 79
LAVINSLEY
Margaret **64** 340
LAVISY Lavina **96** 300
Lavinia **96** 300
LAVOIE La Voie
Rosalie O. **83** 424 434
LAVOR
Elizabeth **110** 195
Joan **71** 167 169
LAVY Daniel **59** 290
Eliza **59** 290
LAW Lawe Llaw
—— **53** 12 20 302 **55** 433
Abigail **54** 387
Andrew **51** 40 41 **63** 235 **79** 259
Andrew Bonar **90** 168
Ann **98** 74
Anna **79** 3 4 **81** 28
Arthur James **61** xxxiv
Basil **66** 341
Betsey (Metcalf) **91** 197
Catherine **134** 92
Curtis **83** 193
Curtis (Mrs.) **83** 193
Daniel **60** 239 **126** 306
Desire **68** 276
Edward Morris **84** 295
Elizabeth **95** 16 **112** 69 125-127 129 130
Elizabeth (Tuttle) (Wood) **120** 270
Emma **80** 140
Francis **86** 256 **87** 307
Hannah **87** 337
Harriet **86** 222
Ida **85** 198
Isabel **66** 341
James **74** 99
Jane **145** 255
Joan (Hanson) **83** 453 **84** 11
John **83** 168 **97** 207 **112** 69 127 **118** 253 **120** 270
John Adger **91** 305
John S. **83** 193
Jonathan **54** 384 387 **57** 269 **58** 70
Joseph **64** 214 **91** 197 **107** 118
Joseph L. **95** 16
Joseph P. **95** 16
Laura (Jamison) **86** 361
Linn H. **86** 361
Lucy **86** 361
Lydia **83** 168
Lydia (Draper) **112** 69 127
Margaret **91** 263
Margery **66** 341
Martha **69** 262
Mary **120** 254

LAW *cont'd*
Mary (Barton) **107** 118
Mary (Langrell) **120** 254
Mary (Montgomery) **112** 289
Mary (Ordway) **126** 306
Mary Locke **83** 113
Mehitable **84** 295
Mertie Josephine (Rich) **84** 295
Nancy **83** 168 **126** 306
Nathaniel B. **80** 140
Patience **87** 338
Polly **127** 179
Polly (Barton) **107** 118
Richard **108** 23
Sally **83** 168
Saml. **147** 37
Samuel **112** 127 289 **120** 254
Sarah **54** 384 **57** 269 **67** 124
Sarah M. **95** 16
Stephen **83** 168
Thomas **52** 355 **65** 33 **72** 134 **83** 453 **84** 11
Thomas Graves **51** 246
William **56** 12 **63** 21 **67** 124 **84** 295
Zelotus **83** 168
LA WALL
Elbert William **79** 136
Grace **79** 136
Lawd *see* Laud
LAWDERBACK
Zacharias **143** 257
Lawe *see* Law
LAWES Mary **122** 275
LAWFORD Christopher Kennedy **139** 220
Jean Edith (Olsson) **139** 220
Martha **93** 246
May Somerville (Bunny) **139** 220
Patricia (Kennedy) **139** 220
Peter **139** 220
Robin Elizabeth **139** 220
Sydney Maleia **139** 220
Sydney Turing Barlow **139** 220
Victoria Francis **139** 220
William **93** 246
LAWLE Roger **83** 316
LAWLER Lawlor
Agnes **55** 179
Anna Elizabeth **82** 402
Annie Jay **72** 293
Clara **76** 90
Eleanor **72** 293
Francis Earl **104** 144
Henry E. **122** 108
James **122** 108
John **122** 108
John Joseph (Mrs.) **100** 112
Mary **63** 238 **100** 242 **101** 56 **122** 108
Mary Ann **64** 155
Susanna **69** 112
Thomas **64** 155 **69** 112 **101**

LAWLER *cont'd*
  56 **122** 108
  Thomas Bonaventure
    53 135
  Viola **105** 158-160 239 240
  William **72** 293
LAWLESS Lawles
  ___ (Courthope) **137** 303
  John **113** 4 5
  Katharine **145** 373
  Mehitable **77** 297 **144** 322
  Ray M. **119** 318
  Stella S. (Wilder) **83** 434
    84 23
  Tom **141** 385
  William **129** 381
  William E. **83** 434 **84** 23
LAWLEY Lawlye
  ——— **69** 123
  John **68** 92
  Susan **126** 68
LAWLIP Mary **82** 292
  Michael **82** 292
Lawlor *see* Lawler
LAWLOW — Capt. **101** 246
LAWMAN
  Eliza Ann **72** 292
  Henry **72** 292
  Jasper Holman **72** 292
  John **72** 292
  Lenore **72** 292
  Mary **72** 292
LAWN Ann (Griffith)
    96 188
  John **96** 188
  Susan **96** 188
LAWNDE — Mr. **51** 120
LAWNE Alice **75** 293
LAWQUAW
  Frederick **142** 59
  William **142** 59
Lawrance *see* Lawrence
LAWRELL Jonas **83** 76
LAWRENCE Laurance
  Laurence Larance
  Lawrance Laurons
  ——— **129** 396
  — Capt. **54** 185
  — Gov. **54** 166 **116** 4-6
    10 12 **117** 146 **118** 129
  — Lieut. **69** 296
  — Mr. **54** 199 **81** 388 390
  — Mrs. **62** 161 **79** 308
  — Widow **70** 313 **73** 64
  ___ (Boardman) **140** 41
    58
  ___ (Gurdon) **94** 369
  ___ (Richards) **140** 240
  A. G. **91** 327
  Abbie Laura (Pangborn)
    89 92
  Abbott **51** 104 203 **63** 207
    76 211 **89** 214 215 268
    269 **140** 32 148
  Abel **58** 371 **61** 276 277
    133 264 **134** 173 **136** 78
  Abel Lorenzo **61** 277
  Abigail **55** 346 403 **57** 141
    61 276 277 **62** 160 **66**
    127 128 **78** 304 **95** 172
  Abigail (Abbott) **96** 84

LAWRENCE *cont'd*
  Abigail (Chase) **87** 332
  Abigail (Hall) **84** 42
  Abigail (Parker) **120** 239
  Abigail (Snow) **124** 53
  Abigail (Tobey) **122** 257
  Abijah **74** 239
  Abner **58** 70
  Abraham **78** 187
  Ada Genevieve **77** xlix
  Adelia M. **92** 170
  Adeline C. **74** 28
  Adrianna **108** 250
  Aghrah M. **92** 170
  Agnes **112** 33
  Albina **135** 249
  Albion K. **89** 351
  Alexander A. **112** 210
    113 13
  Alice **60** 283 **69** 120 **71** 263
    116 192
  Alice Dean **87** 105
  Alida Louise **85** 192
  Alison Turnbull **89** 217
  Almina **124** 228
  Alvarus **74** 238 239
  Amelia M. **119** 158
  Amelia M. (Bancroft)
    103 63
  Amory Appleton **77** 300
    88 398
  Amos **51** 104 **55** 403 **58**
    323 **63** 215 **69** 13 **70** 23
    71 76 159 279 **72** 40 167
    76 159 **89** 212-216 **96**
    84 **140** 23 240 256
  Amos A. **84** 42 **96** 85
  Amos Abbott **61** 217
  Amos Adams **77** lxvi **85**
    5 103 344 **87** 304 **89** 215
    216 **96** 83 84
  Amy (Blodgett) (Whitney)
    138 35 37
  Andrew **69** 322 **135** 249
  Ann **60** 291 **67** 154 **75** 224
    122 301 **136** 268 **137**
    361
  Ann Maria **68** 125
  Anna **55** 263 **56** 79 **61** 70
    77 275 **94** 315 **108** 308
    136 360
  Anna (Fiske) **105** 29
  Anna (Landers) **124** 275
  Anna (Tarbell) **94** 315
    96 84
  Anna Eliza **122** 299
  Anna Koons **135** 249
  Anna Maria **51** 104
  Anne **51** 394 453 **64** 43 **67**
    251 257 **107** 268 **112** 33
  Anne (Erne) **112** 33
  Anstace **80** 351 363 369
  Anthony **62** 245 **63** 32
  Antoinette **69** 163
  Arthur **60** 218 **61** xxxiv
    105 **64** 101 **89** 217
  Asa **66** 127 128 **69** 212 **78**
    184 **95** 365 **105** 211
  Asa Farnsworth **79** 6
    95 365
  Audrey **94** 273

LAWRENCE *cont'd*
  Aurora Alice **77** xlix
  B. F. **120** 307 **121** 69
  Barbara **63** 32
  Bela Malcolm **87** 105
  Benjamin **61** 166 **64** 145
    66 112 **70** 24 **71** 55 **77**
    275 **95** 281 **101** 234 **107**
    52 **131** 116 200 **137** 335
  Bertha **92** 170
  Bessie A. **98** 196
  Bethiah **58** 166 **77** 232
  Betsey **65** 95 **81** 31 **127** 227
  Betsey G. **100** 188
  Bigelow **81** 413
  Caleb **51** 453 **89** 389
  Calvin **81** 384 413
  Carrie L. **72** 124
  Carrie Rebecca **66** lxxxi
  Catherine **135** 249
  Chancy **85** 298
  Charles **58** 335 **61** 277 **71**
    61 **78** 416 **100** 188 **138**
    253
  Charles A. **112** 140
  Charles Andrew **82** 434
  Charles E. **98** 196
  Charles Edward **71** xxiii
    74 xxviii **87** 161 280 **88**
    172
  Charles Willard **87** 280
  Charlotte **89** 389 **141** 144
  Chester A. **55** xxxii
  Chloe **84** 40 44
  Christiana **131** 128
  Christopher **75** 282
  Clarence George **74** 318
  Clarissa **78** 239 **87** 57
  Colon **104** 134
  Cora Belle (Smith)
    112 140
  Daniel **61** 277 **66** lxxx 129
    71 263 **75** 100 **99** 311
    105 285 **118** 132 269
    127 227
  Daniel W. **76** 15
  David **56** 369 **71** 43 **91**
    257 258 263 **103** 44 **106**
    95 97 **124** 52 **126** 13 60
    127 223
  Deborah **51** 302 320
    54 287
  Deborah Palmer
    (Quintard) (Ferris)
    109 192
  Delia Maria **74** 238 239
  Deliverance **115** 97
    118 209
  Delmond Wesley **85** 195
  Desire (Fuller) **123** 308
  Diademia **66** 128
  Dillea **88** 275
  Dorcas **78** 418
  Dorcas (Barret) **125** 103
  Dorcas (Bryant) **137** 334
  Dorothy **61** 276 277
  Dorothy (Chamberlain)
    134 175
  Dorothy Quincy **71** liv
  Ebenezer **54** 287 **57** 52 **78**
    308 **87** 226 233 **124** 53

LAWRENCE *cont'd*
Eber **125** 106
Edith **77** 300 **88** 398 **93** 291
Edith June **76** 159 242
Edmund **69** 14
Edward **60** lxxi **63** 17
Edward (Mrs.) **85** 195
Edward A. **98** 196
Edward J. **51** 194
Edward L. **74** 29
Edward Mercy **72** 33
Eleanor **96** 85 **122** 257
Eleanor (Handy) **124** 52
　125 135
Eleanor Maria **74** 239
Eleazar **104** 309
Elias **55** 263 **74** 176
Eliezer **81** 384
Elihu **71** 76 159 279 300
　301 **72** 33
Elisha **65** 148
Eliza **61** 277 **74** 243 244
　78 85 **140** 148
Eliza (Strong) **88** 282
Eliza (Swift) **115** 90
Elizabeth **51** 453 **53** 11 **54**
　338 **55** 404 **59** 148 **61**
　277 **63** 325 **66** lxxx 128
　70 74 76 211 **77** 83 **78**
　292 **83** 489 **87** 280 **89**
　211 389 **90** 283 **113** 209
　121 14 **135** 249 251 **136**
　360 **141** 97 345
Elizabeth (Barton)
　107 294
Elizabeth (Bates) **134** 252
Elizabeth (Castleman)
　141 144
Elizabeth (Crispe) **126** 8
Elizabeth (Kettleborough)
　114 150
Elizabeth (Martin)
　137 334
Elizabeth (Odell) **127** 88
Elizabeth (Tupper) **99** 63
Elizabeth Bigelow **79** 3 6
　95 365
Ellen **93** 20 39
Ellen B. **77** xlix
Ellen Sophia **58** lxxx
　112 226
Emily Fairfax (Silsbee) **77**
　300 **88** 398
Enoch **61** 396 **64** 38 **77**
　xlix **87** 280 **94** 83
Ephraim **66** 128
Esther **55** 403 **64** 38 **69** 324
　126 135 **147** 53
Esther (Warren) **128** 46
Eunice **61** 277 **71** 76 159
　279 300 301 **128** 46
Eunice A. **134** 334
Euphemia (Barton)
　107 52
Eva M. **92** 170
Evelyn Heath **77** xlix
Experience **64** 149
Ezekiel **61** 277
Fannie Blodgett **82** 180
Fannie I. **89** 351
Fanny **81** 197

LAWRENCE *cont'd*
Fanny D. **61** 277
Felix **112** 33 35 43
Fluvia **81** 390
Frances **66** 128
Frances Gordon **95** 365
Francis **64** 309 **74** 239
Francis S. **100** 188
Francis William **89** 217
Frankie A. **85** 314
Fred **85** 298
Frederic Cunningham
　96 85
Frederick **58** lxxx **112** 226
Frederick Koons **135** 249
Freelove **127** 226
Garret **115** 36
George **59** 304 **76** 81 **77** 83
　85 455 100 187 **113** 243
　126 8 **132** 75 **141** 144
George A. **73** 227
George Edmunds **89** 92
Gertrude **76** 211
Gideon **70** 312 **101** 234
Gillian **54** 338
Gladys **80** 208
Grace **77** 83
Guy **60** 291
H. Hooper **67** lxi
Hannah **51** 194 449 451-
　453 **52** 98 101 **57** 141 **58**
　lxxxv **59** 259 **67** 374 **71**
　263 **77** 295 **89** 389 **92** 24
　25 **99** 311 **126** 8 13 62
　135 249 **136** 360
Hannah (Chaddack) **124**
　52 **125** 135
Hannah (Chadwick)
　124 52
Hannah (Sawtell) **126** 13
Hannah (Tarbell) **96** 84
Hannah M. (Morse)
　92 170
Hannah Parker **64** 309
Harold Payne **61** 277
Harriet **75** 1 **81** 384
Harriett Dexter **85** 190 344
　115 67
Harriette White **76** 211
Harry Rheese **112** 140
Harry Rheese (Mrs.) **85**
　195 **112** 73 140
Hattie Louisa (Brown)
　89 237
Helen **76** 15
Helen Atherton **89** 220
Henrietta Braisted **94** 83
Henry **59** 96 **60** 203 66 128
　71 50 **77** xlix **80** 351
　369 **131** 128
Henry Edwin **74** 239
Henry Effingham **93** 291
Henry North **76** 159
Henry Otis **77** xlix
Hester **89** 389 **96** 159
Hetty Sullivan **85** 103
Hiram **69** 163
Horatio Gates **66** 128
I. D. Ryan **67** 136
Isaac **61** 166 277 **127** 88
　138 35 37 **147** 116

LAWRENCE *cont'd*
Isabel **107** 52
Isabel Cleaveland **89** 220
J. D. Ryan **67** 136
J. W. **69** 113
James **60** 284 **62** 161 321
　76 211 **119** 125 **120** 273
　121 36 261 **124** 275 **139**
　99 100 **148** 47
James Coffin **132** 75
James F. (Mrs.) **102** 66
James Hiram **115** 228
Jane **60** 252 **86** 98 **101** 331
　135 283-295 **141** 97
Jane Augusta (Young)
　103 44
Jane Cumings **61** 384
Jane Dennison (Frost)
　125 106
Jane Isabella (Smith)
　112 226
Jane Isabelle **58** lxxx
Jedidah **100** 191
Jennie Westfall (Rising)
　85 298
Jeremiah **64** 43
Joan **54** 338 **56** 312 **60** 287
　93 373
Joan (Antholus) **135** 283
　284 **141** 97
Joan (Cogan) **111** 88
Joanna **102** 303
John **51** 10 453 **57** 52 58
　323 **61** 70 276 277 **63** 98
　65 95 148 **67** 154 250
　251 257 **70** 14 18 215 **76**
　50 211 **77** xlix **82** 369
　86 424 427 **87** 280 **89**
　211 212 269 **90** 182 **94**
　78 315 **96** 83 84 235 **99**
　63 311 **106** 97 **107** 27
　268 **108** 25 111 88 **112**
　251 **113** 96 **114** 150 **116**
　231 242 **117** 126 **118**
　132-134 **120** 239 125
　108 **127** 110 **129** 396
　141 97 **144** 125 **145** 171
　147 172
John B. **51** 452 **108** 215
John C. **107** 294
John G. **105** 213
John S. **56** xxxii
John Sherman **89** 237
John Silsbee **79** 225
John Strachan **64** xxxi
　65 303 **66** xlix **67** xxxi
Jonas **62** 161
Jonathan **51** 495 **55** 404 **59**
　148 **91** 257 **124** 52 212
　214 215 **133** 135 **141**
　221
Joseph **51** 453 **58** 68 **70**
　176 312 **78** 304 **99** 311
　314 **106** 153 **116** 29 **120**
　37 **121** 261 **124** 52 **125**
　126 **127** 222 **136** 360
　137 334
Joseph H. **85** 314
Joseph W. **90** 57
Joseph Wilson **55** 233 **58**
　lvi lx

LAWRENCE *cont'd*
Joshua **113** 113 **115** 90
  116 192 **125** 103 289
Josiah **63** 325 **70** 220
Judith **57** 196 **83** 202 **92**
  388 **100** 187 **111** 4 **127**
  185
Judith (Coffin) **132** 75
Julia **55** 423 **96** 85
Julia (Cunningham)
  96 85
Julia A. **134** 60
Julian **54** 338
Katharine (Bancroft)
  95 72
Katharine (Bigelow) **89**
  215 **97** 211
Katharine (Forman)
  120 238
Katharine (Gurdon)
  95 72
Kimball W. **88** 283
Lambert Bigelow **60**
  xxxviii **77** xxxviii xlix
Laura Ann (Whitehouse)
  138 322
Laura E. (Gallup) **85** 298
Laura Emily (Heywood)
  87 105
Lelia **78** 52
Leonora (Hill) **86** 197
Levi **110** 322 **120** 238 239
Lillian Gorham **82** 434
Lovina **83** 146
Luann **80** 29
Lucille May **86** 195
Lucinda **82** 368
Lucinia (Granger) **136** 78
Lucy **55** 404 **63** 323 **74** 176
  101 234 **137** 334
Lucy Amanda **75** 267
Lucy Jane **80** 331
Lucy Jane (Marsters)
  137 219 223
Luther **51** 104 **70** 217 219
  89 214 **140** 33
Luther Lee **89** 92
Lydia **53** 460 **83** 138 **124**
  214 215 **133** 264
Lydia (Farnsworth)
  95 365
Lydia (Landers) **124** 52
  215
Lydia Hamilton **129** 396
Madeleine **69** xxxv **89** 220
Mahala **64** 313
Margaret **57** 196 **61** 276
  75 282
Margaret (Bennett)
  125 261
Margaret Anne (Rich)
  84 42
Margaret L. **90** 54
Maria **83** 473 **102** 158
Mariah (Ellis) **113** 243
Marian **85** 197 **96** 85
Marie **62** 387
Marion **112** 251 **113** 96
Martha **61** 277 **89** 389
  124 205 **127** 88 190
Martha Endicott **76** 211

LAWRENCE *cont'd*
Marvel **71** 43
Mary **51** 319 463 **52** 464
  465 **57** 52 **58** lxxxiv **61**
  166 277 **63** 278 325 **65**
  166 **69** 322 **70** 176 **71**
  279 **76** 15 **78** 68 292 **89**
  389 **90** 181 **91** 266 **93**
  370 **99** 311 **112** 140 251
  118 202 **125** 222 **127**
  110 **139** 99 **141** 97 **145**
  172
Mary (Coffin) **132** 75
Mary (Hallowell) **100** 302
Mary (Percival) **118** 202
Mary (Vandervoort)
  94 83
Mary (Wilbore) **112** 251
  113 96
Mary Ann **66** 112 **69** 322
Mary Ann (Bridges)
  90 107
Mary Anne Appleton
  94 390
Mary Augusta **74** 238
Mary Augusta Patch
  74 239
Mary E. **92** 170
Mary Elizabeth **88** 285
Mary F. (Patterson)
  112 140
Mary Frances **140** 261
Mary Helen **95** 365
Mary Louisa **74** 239
Mary Milnor **80** 331
Mary Philips (Munjoy)
  135 251
Mary W. (Clapp) **90** 57
Matthew **57** 196
Maul **106** 196
Maurice William **90** 107
Mercy **118** 133
Mercy (Hartshorne)
  113 275
Mercy (Reed) **98** 207
Meribah **130** 233
Micah **62** 276 **118** 313
Milicent **74** 239
Milla **131** 116
Millie A. **92** 170
Mollie (Rutherford)
  (Wilson) **117** 126
Moody **137** 334
Nancy **83** 144 **108** 166
  115 41 **126** 145
Nancy (Burt) **126** 67
Naomi **134** 173
Nathan **144** 126
Nathaniel **51** 68 302 **58**
  lxxxv 323 **60** 252 **61** 276
  277 **65** 297 **70** 20 **77**
  xlix **78** 308 **87** 280 **89**
  211-213 **96** 83 **99** 311
  105 27-29 **134** 175 **136**
  360
Nehemiah **55** 402 **138** 322
Nelson H. (Mrs.) **86** 197
Nicholas **52** 110 **59** 106
Olive **115** 190
Oliver **79** 429
Ozias **114** 161

LAWRENCE *cont'd*
P. B. **91** 327
Parker **77** xlix
Patty **125** 218
Paul William (Mrs.)
  80 208
Paul Willliam **79** 186
Peleg **118** 202 **139** 103 105
Persis **58** 371
Peter **61** 166 **110** 134
Phebe **94** 315 **95** 64
Phebe (Farr) **134** 173
Phebe (Russell) **118** 134
Philena **84** 125
Philomenia **66** 128
Polly **59** 96 **115** 33 **125** 101
  133 264 **134** 173
Polly (Dodge) **125** 108
Polly (Pratt)(Spaulding)
  137 335
Precinda **74** 176
Priscilla **77** 318
Rachel **56** 369 **57** 224 334
  81 384 **135** 249 **141** 336
Ralph **63** 166
Rebecca **64** 145 **74** 207 **83**
  138 **99** 311 **115** 41 **131**
  116
Rebecca (Dodge) **95** 281
Rebecca (Woods) **137** 335
Reliance (Davis) **124** 52
  125 130 135 **126** 60
Reuben **122** 257
Rhoda Benedict **101** 177
  102 155 **103** 157 **104**
  169
Richard **51** 453 **54** 333 338
  55 229 **63** 277 278 **87**
  280 **89** 389 **92** 296 **93**
  223 224 **94** 75 367 369
  95 71 72
Richard C. **137** 219 221 223
  234
Richard Charles **80** 331
Richard Rossman
  102 124
Robert **51** 352 **94** 236 **106**
  23 **113** 281 **115** 91 **116**
  149 **125** 191 **135** 251
Robert Means **58** xlviii
  323 **59** xli **66** 368 **67**
  viii xxx **68** vi **69** v vi x
  70 v **71** v 97 **72** xi **89**
  211 220 269 283 **90** 122
  140
Roderick **79** 308
Roger **105** 210
Rogers **66** 128
Rosamond **76** 211 **85** 190
  89 215 268 **90** 79 140
Rosman **121** 155 156
Roswell Newton **74** 239
Rowland **66** 128
Roxana **90** 57
Ruluf **71** 117
Ruth **89** 401 **91** 98 **96** 85
Ruth Amelia **82** 180
Sallie Ward **93** 137
Sally **61** 277 **64** 313
Sally (Philbrooke)
  125 289

LAWRENCE *cont'd*
Sally Ann **92** 221
Samuel **51** 319 **58** 323 **65**
  363 **66** 338 **67** 374 **70**
  139 **74** 243 **78** 301 **79** 92
  163 **81** 84 **89** 213 214
  217 269 **96** 84 **97** 293
  107 33 **118** 133 **124** 52
  215 **125** 261 **126** 60
Samuel C. **99** 92
Samuel Crocker **66** lix
  lxxx lxxxi **67** 95
Samuel Soden **93** 325
Samuel Warren **76** 15
Sara Tappan Doolittle
  58 xlv
Sarah **51** 302 **55** 380 **57** 52
  61 276 277 **65** 297 298
  69 246 **70** 176 177 180
  220 226 **71** 76 279 307
  72 40 167 **76** 159 211 **77**
  lxvi lxxxiv **79** 395 **85**
  223 **89** 212 389 **95** 281
  96 85 **97** 193 **99** 311
  105 27 28 **106** 95 96 **108**
  27 **111** 151 **114** 135 **121**
  16 **124** 52 **125** 135 **126**
  60
Sarah (Bailey) **134** 175
Sarah (Chamberlain)
  91 263
Sarah (Koons) **135** 249
Sarah (Landers) **124** 52
  215 **125** 135 **126** 60
Sarah (Morse) **96** 84
Sarah (Moss) **96** 84
Sarah (Nye) **127** 110
Sarah (Pinder) **88** 283
Sarah (Richards) **96** 84
Sarah (Whittemore)
  106 97
Sarah Ann **63** 238
Sarah Elizabeth
  (Appleton) **85** 5 **87** 304
  96 83 84
Sarah Frances **95** 365
Sarah Jane **74** 239 **79** 6
Sarah Jane (Bancroft)
  95 365
Sarah P. **69** 137
Schuyler **91** 382
Seth **92** 26 **120** 273 **121** 261
Shubael **120** 247
Sibyl **63** lxvii **97** 96
Simeon **87** 332
Solomon **129** 396
Sophia **81** 388 390
Sophrona J. **85** 314
Stephen **118** 133
Submit **121** 46
Susan **66** 51 **67** 154 157
  116 192
Susan A. **77** 152
Susan Mason **85** 5
Susanna **51** 461 **61** 70 **66**
  98 **74** 243 **91** 267 **97** 293
  102 259 **105** 29 **106** 97
  118 132 **123** 43
Susanna (Field) **113** 281
Susanna (Parker) **96** 84
Susanna (Prescott) **94** 315

LAWRENCE *cont'd*
95 64
Susanna (Turner) **123** 44
Thankful (Snow) **116** 192
Thomas **51** 100 394 **52**
  110 112 **54** 166 **55** 380
  56 312 **61** 277 **63** 25 144
  348 **64** 323 336 **67** 154
  70 140 180 220 311 **77**
  xlix **78** 292 **79** 43 395
  100 302 **108** 292 **112**
  251 **113** 94 96 **121** 105
  134 175 252 **135** 249
  382 **141** 97 **142** 161 164
Timothy **139** 255
Tryphena (Powers)
  141 221
Ursula **74** 294
Vernon **113** 243
Violetta **113** 282
Virginia Porter **83** 248
  84 189
W. S. **92** 170
Willard **87** 280
William **51** 452 **52** 110 236
  53 365 **54** 338 **55** 423
  56 311 312 **57** 129 **59**
  259 **60** 221 322 **61** 149
  199 277 **63** 163 **67** 296
  68 xix xxx **79** 139 196
  233 243 **80** 204 351 363
  369 **81** 25 216 **82** 231 **83**
  138 144 376 **84** 179 **87**
  304 **88** 282 **89** 213 215-
  217 **90** 123 **92** 24-26 **94**
  315 **95** 64 **96** 83 148 165
  98 207 **100** 188 **102** 28
  105 283 **106** 241 **109**
  192 311 **110** 317 **113**
  271 275 281 **140** 41 58
  141 97
William A. (Mrs.) **84** 461
William Appleton **96** 85
William E. **123** 225
William Richards **89** 211
  215-217
William S. **92** 170
William Savage **95** 365
Winthrop **120** 247
Zachariah **63** 323 **105** 285
Zadock **121** 93
Zeruiah **136** 360
LAWRENSON
Margerie **105** 96
LAWRIE James **63** 235
Mary Westcott **85** 192
LAWRY Benjamin **83** 375
  93 182
Edward **83** 375
Elizabeth **73** 227
Isaac **83** 375
Isabel Sabara **93** 181 182
John **83** 375 **98** 7
John L. **98** 7
Mary **88** 371
Mary (Wells) **110** 311
Rosina (Billings) **98** 7
LAWS Angelica **75** 36
Annie **59** xliv **60** 186
Calvin A **75** 36
Cecile Amelia **100** 113

LAWS *cont'd*
Charlotte **75** 36
Daniel **92** 170
Ebenezer **75** 36
Elizabeth **77** 135 **78** 40
Francis **54** 450
Henry **114** 193
Jeremiah **54** 450
John **54** 337 **77** 135
Mary **75** 36
Mary E. **75** 36
Mason P. **75** 36
Melinda **75** 36
Outten **106** 45
Polly **78** 40
Sarah (Pleasanton) **106** 45
Sarah A. **75** 36
Thomas **75** 36
Willard **75** 36
William **73** 144
LAWSELL John **64** 242
LAWSEY
Elizabeth **65** 291
James **65** 291
LAWSON — Mr. **57** 322
  323 **84** 152
Abby B. **69** 315
Ann **95** 83
Ann C. (Way) **126** 20
Anna **128** 174
Anne (Wentworth) **98** 17
Anthony **106** 318
Betsey **73** 287
C. C.P. **112** 210
Charles Robert **91** 248
Christopher **67** 66 **87** 265
  96 271 **98** 11 15-17 **119**
  19
David **58** 444 **75** 110 119
  76 193 **113** 31 37 **121**
  137
Deborah **66** 283 **102** 186
Deborah (Allen) **102** 191
Deodate **66** 283 **102** 186
  191 263 **121** 282
Douglas **103** 119
Edward **79** 174 **88** 336
Eleanor **58** 244
Eliza C. W. **126** 243
Elizabeth **66** 161 **67** 72 **73**
  229 276 **88** 124 **98** 11
  119 181
Elizabeth (Hughes)
  88 336
Ellen **68** 70
Eva Alberta (Pangburn)
  91 248
George **85** 373
Gertrude (Eells) **90** 359
Gretchen H. **77** xliv
Hannah **113** 31
Hannah D. (Mitchell)
  85 373
Harvey M. **58** 206
Harvey Merrill **59** 21 **60**
  xxxvi 99
Henry **65** 35
Ida L. **69** 315
J. Murray **54** xxxviii 237
Jennie Cornell
  (Hanscom) **83** 431 434

LAWSON *cont'd*
John **52** 168 **91** 350 **112**
   287 **124** 98 103
John (Mrs.) **90** 359
John Herrick **83** 434
Mabel **132** 46
Margaret **100** 301
Margaret Spottiswoode
   90 175
Martha **75** 119
Mary **73** 144 **83** 161
Mary (Bell) **126** 144
Miles B. **126** 20
Nancy (Foy) **88** 330
Nicholas **126** 144
Penelope **75** 110 119
   76 194
Publius Virgilius **58** 207
   59 xliv
Rhoda **124** 305
Robert **64** 257
Roger **67** 381
Rosa **77** xliv
Rossea **86** 333
Ruth **88** 277
Samuel **104** 20
Sarah **58** 244 **81** 98 **94** 88
Sarah A. (Taylor) **126** 20
Sarah Jane **85** 375
Sessions **83** 161
Suitliff **145** 348
Susan Hardwick **97** 183
Susanna **73** 272
Thankful **52** 370 371
Thomas **52** 232 371 **53** 108
   59 21 **73** 152 **98** 11 22
   102 191 **132** 46
Thomas E. **77** xliv
Thomas William
   62 xxxvii
Victor **86** 438
William **64** 164 **66** 161
   73 136 142 **88** 330 **93**
   297 **100** 63 **126** 20 **132**
   49 **145** 348
LAWTER
Anne **88** 145 272
Joseph **88** 145
Martha **88** 145
Mary **88** 145 265
Mary (Fiske) **88** 145 265
   272
Robert **86** 427 **88** 145 265
   272
LAWTON —— **92** 62
— Mr. **57** 228
Abby Perry **125** 177
Abigail **69** 91 **72** 28 **80** 144
   122 104 106 211 **134**
   118-120
Abigail (Lamb) **123** 263
Abigail (Spooner)
   125 178
Abner P. **122** 301
Adam **122** 211 **134** 118 120
Alida Allen **80** 31
Ama **114** 173
Andrew Almy **116** 54
Andrew H. **88** 106
Ann **114** 191 **122** 101 **123**
   40 **125** 239

LAWTON *cont'd*
Ann (Marsh) **125** 245
Ann (Stevens) **125** 177
Anna **81** 44
Anna G. **122** 295
Anne **80** 31 **123** 38 40
Anne Clow **80** 31
Arnold **86** 182 **125** 176
Arthur P. **117** 293
Benedick **60** 306
Benedicta **111** 248 **123** 261
Benjamin **125** 181 240
   127 8 **128** 297
Benjamin H. **125** 177
Benjamin I. **126** 24
Benjamin T. **125** 172 173
Betsey **67** 188
Betsey (Johnson) (Chase)
   88 29
Betsey (Paget) **125** 177
Charles **80** 31 **125** 180 240
Charles D. **89** 389
Charles F. **80** 31
Charlotte **126** 24
Comfort **141** 344
Cuff **127** 146
Daniel **66** 27 **105** 254
David **127** 10 145
Deborah **127** 147
Dorcas **127** 8
Dorothy Elsa **80** 31
E. W. **125** 178
Edward **88** 105 **128** 135
Elisha **127** 11
Eliza **80** 144 **81** 290
Eliza (Tuell) **125** 173
   126 20
Eliza B. **125** 172
Elizabeth **69** 91 **79** 254 **80**
   31 447 **102** 205 **105** 254
   113 102 **122** 104 211
   134 115 116 118-120
   142 17 24
Elizabeth (Gould) **126** 24
Elizabeth (Hazard)
   102 205
Elizabeth (Tallman) **85** 73
Elizabeth Bailey (Clarke)
   92 62
Elizabeth C. **54** 354
Elizabeth S. (Taylor)
   126 24
Elizabeth Wealthy **92** 62
Ellen Richardson (Vose)
   92 62
Ellin **111** 89
Elva **123** 40
Ernest Beattie **80** 31
F. C. **126** 22
Florence Dexter (Leach)
   92 62
Frances (Childs) **126** 22
Frances E. D. **144** 330
Frances M. (Brown) **90** 48
Frederick **55** 452
Frederick A. **122** 301
Frederick Tyler **109** 130
Freelove **57** 38 **122** 101
Freelove (Peckham)
   123 40
Gardner **123** 44

LAWTON *cont'd*
George **69** 91 **93** 194 **102**
   205 **105** 91 **127** 146 **136**
   216 **147** 339
George C. **81** 290
George W. **90** 48
Giles **122** 102 **127** 146
Giles Mumford **92** 62
Hannah **88** 21 **123** 40 43
   125 178
Hannah (Dickens) **86** 182
Hannah (Manchester)
   102 12
Hannah (Turner) **123** 40
   44
Henry **57** 280 **125** 180
Henry A. **126** 20
Herbert **86** 197
Ida May Frost **59** xlvii
   66 xxxvii **68** xxi
Isaac **56** 129 131 **67** 188
   85 73 **86** 182 **93** 194
   125 181 **126** 20 24 **127**
   144 **147** 350
James **64** 248 **80** 31 **123**
   263 **125** 173 177 181
   128 217
James E. **125** 172 182
James M. **125** 177
James Madison **80** 30 31
Jane **69** 92
Jane W. **57** 201
Jarvis **93** 194
Jeremiah **69** 91 **123** 40
   147 337
Joanna **51** 428
Joanna Snow **69** 91
Job **58** 142 **80** 37 **93** 194
   97 32 **122** 214 **125** 181
   147 338 339 350
Job H. **126** 22
Johanna T. (Knowles)
   125 237
John **51** 428 **60** 306 **102** 12
   127 6 12 147 **148** 151
John E. **125** 238
John Julian **88** 209
   124 143
John K. **57** xxxiii
John T. **126** 24
John Turner **123** 44
Jonathan **79** 254 **123** 40
   127 8 10
Joseph **64** 221 **81** 164
   128 301
Joseph H. **126** 22
Joshua **101** 313
Josiah **126** 24 **143** 230
Josias **125** 237 **128** 296
Kirke Brooks **115** 76
Leon J. **92** 62
Lewis D. **125** 245
Louisa M. (Chase) **88** 105
Louisa M. (Vailing)
   88 339
Lucinda **124** 193
Lucy **127** 9
Luther **87** 262
Lydia **126** 21
Margaret A. **125** 240

LAWTON *cont'd*
Margaret Jane (Wilson)
  144 316
Mark Anthony **66** lii **68**
  xxx **74** xxviii **90** 127 **93**
  125 141 194
Mark Anthony (Mrs.)
  80 332
Mark William **93** 194
Martha **122** 102
Martha (Manchester)
  101 313
Martha B. **125** 241
Mary **54** 407 **56** 129 **58** 280
  69 91 **85** 221 **96** 399
  107 317 **123** 261 **124**
  193 **125** 183 **127** 144
  129 225 **134** 118 **144**
  330
Mary (Collins) **126** 24
Mary (Gould) **147** 339
Mary (Hall) **123** 44
Mary (Hill) **123** 40
Mary Ann **57** 201 **122** 214
Mary Ann (Freeborn)
  125 181 **126** 20
Mary B. **116** 54
Mary C. **80** 31
Mary E. (Engs) **125** 178
Mary H. **125** 176 102 207
Mary Hall **123** 44
Mary L. **125** 175
Mary P. **57** 201
Matthew **127** 6
Maxwell Francis **80** 31
Mehitable **51** 459 **126** 24
Mercy **122** 102
Meribih B. (Jason)
  137 361
Moses **56** 129 **123** 44
Nancy **81** 164
Nancy (Stevens) **125** 181
Naomi **102** 265 277
Nathaniel **127** 146
Nina V. **92** 62
Oliver **57** 201 **128** 293
Patience Turner **123** 44
Peleg **125** 176 **127** 146
  144 316
Penelope (Brown)
  125 181
Phebe **123** 44
Polly (Chase) **87** 262
Prince **127** 14
Priscilla **69** 92 **105** 80
Rachel **57** 201
Rebecca **80** 37 179 **125** 243
  135 145
Rebecca (Cranston)
  125 181
Rebecca (Huddy) **125** 176
Rebecca Carpenter **69** 91
Rhoda (Cahoon) **125** 240
Rob **125** 181
Robert **63** 328 **123** 44 **125**
  238 **126** 20 **127** 12 **147**
  341 **148** 151
Robert S. **80** 31
Ruth **125** 244 **126** 20
Sabina G. **115** 169
Sadie **144** 316

LAWTON *cont'd*
Sadie S. **117** 293
Sally **122** 104 **134** 118 119
Sally (Freeborn) **125** 173
Samuel **57** 38 **58** 280 **80**
  144 **88** 339 **122** 104 **123**
  40 **125** 178 **127** 8 **134**
  118 119 **141** 344
Samuel H. **125** 245
Sarah **57** 201 **85** 230 343
  102 216 **122** 101 104
  123 38 40 **134** 119 120
Sarah (Anthony) **125** 238
  126 20
Sarah (Palmer) **144** 316
Sarah (Southworth) **134**
  115 119 120 **142** 24
Sarah (Thomas) **125** 180
Sarah (Trood) **147** 339 350
Sarah C. (Carver)
  (Winslow) **88** 106
Sarah Greene **80** 30
Sarah H. **122** 301
Sarah R. **125** 172
Sarah R. (Tilley) **125** 182
Seabury **93** 194
Sebray **69** 91
Shirley **127** 105
Stephen **69** 317
Susan A. **89** 390
Susan Amelia
  (Houghteling) **89** 389
Susanna **51** 219 **58** 280
  79 256 **122** 211
Theodore **116** 54
Thomas **58** 280 **69** 91 **87**
  361 **93** 194 **105** 91 **123**
  40 **128** 296 **136** 216 **141**
  344 **147** 12
Thomas Albert **65** xxi
  66 281
Thomas Albert (Mrs.)
  69 xxx
Thomas Clarke **92** 62
Thomas H. **125** 172 173
  126 20
Thomas S. **122** 301
Timothy **128** 296
W. H. **125** 172 182
Walter V. **92** 62
Wells A. **81** 290
Wilhelmine Alida **80** 31
William **54** 354 **80** 31 **88**
  29 **122** 104 **127** 146 **134**
  115 118-120 **141** 344
  142 24
William Cranston **80** 31
William F. **125** 181
William Hathaway **69** 91
William Hazard **144** 316
William L. **125** 173
William Orrin **144** 316
William T. **126** 20
LAWYER
— Gen. **109** 120
Anna **122** 296
Emma **104** 102
Madison **122** 296
Philip **104** 102
Ruth **122** 296
LAX Elizabeth **133** 56

LAXSON
Agnes (Cole) **86** 362
Albert Cole **86** 363
Clarice Emily **86** 363
Edith (Geil) **86** 363
Elizabeth (Martin) **86** 362
Ethel Laurice **86** 363
Hannah Emily **86** 363
James Peter **86** 362
Mabel Ettie **86** 363
Minnie Amelia (Brandt)
  86 363
William **86** 362
William James **86** 363
LAXTON
Mary Ann **109** 72
Richard **76** 279
LAY Laye
— Lord **89** 177
Aaron **62** 177
Abigail **62** 172 176 178
  238 240 **83** 112 **146** 370
Abner **61** 76 **62** 178
Albert Tracy **62** 241
Alfred French **62** 178
Amos **123** 46
Ann **62** 178
Ann Jeannette **62** 241
Anna **62** 137 176 178 238
  239 **146** 368
Anna Bull **62** 176
Anne **62** 176 238
Asa **62** 172 176 178 240 241
Asa Steuben **62** 241
Asa Wolcott **62** 178
Benjamin **62** 178
Bridgham **61** 76
Catherine **62** 178
Charles **62** 239
Charles Henry **62** 241
Chloe **62** 177
Christopher **62** 174 176
  178 **136** 320
Dana F. **117** 126
Daniel **62** 174 176-178
  240 241 365
De. **61** 76
Deborah **62** 174 176
Deborah (Post) **147** 51
Dense **146** 370
Desire **62** 177
Dorcas **145** 118
Dorothy **62** 173
E. E. **62** 172
Edward **52** 273 **61** 76 **62**
  172 **87** 74 **89** 175 **124**
  312
Edward Bliss **62** 178
Edward Tracy **62** 241
Elisha **61** 76
Elizabeth **61** 76 **62** 175
Elizabeth (Kelsey) **127** 199
Elizabeth (Roosevelt)
  124 240
Emily **62** 239
Emmie Elizabeth **62** 241
Enoch **61** 75 76
Ezra **61** 76 **62** 177 238 239
Fanny **62** 241
Francis T. **61** 76
George W. **52** 273

LAY *cont'd*
George Washington **62** 239 241
Gustavus **62** 240
Hannah **61** 75 77 **62** 175 177 178 239
Harriet **62** 239 241
Harriet Tracy **62** 239
Henry **62** 241
Horace **61** 76
Hubbell **61** 76
Huldah **62** 177
James **62** 172 176 178 240
Jared Cochran **62** 241
Jemima **62** 175 176 238
Jeremiah **62** 174 176
Jerusha **62** 178 240 364 365 **136** 320
John **52** 273 **60** 186 **61** 76 77 **62** 172-178 239 241 **124** 312 **147** 54
John Calvin **124** 240
John Foote **62** 241
Jonathan **53** 313 **62** 173 174 176 177 238 239 241
Joseph **61** 77
Juliette **62** 239
Keturah (Buckingham) **147** 51
Lee **61** 77 **125** 44
Lois **62** 177
Louis **62** 178
Louisa **61** 77
Lovina **62** 178
Lucretia **62** 176
Lucy **61** 76 **62** 177
Lucy Rebecca **62** 241
Lucy White **62** 178
Lydia **61** 76 77 **62** 174 175 177 **104** 193
Lydia Austin **62** 241
Margaret Weld **83** 231
Martha **62** 240
Martha Hubbard **62** 241
Mary **52** 57 **53** 211 **61** 76 77 **62** 172-177 238 239 241 **127** 198 199 **136** 309 320 329
Mary (Grinnell) **136** 320
Mary (Stanton) **127** 199 **136** 309 315 320 329
Mary Helen **62** 241
Matilda **62** 178
Mehitable **62** 239
Mercy **61** 77 **62** 177
Nancy **62** 178 238 **90** 95
Nathaniel **62** 178
Ninnie M. (Rutherford) **117** 127
Pauline **62** 240
Peter **61** 77
Phebe **53** 313 **54** cvii **61** 77 **62** 173-178 239 **146** 363 **147** 63
Polly **101** 212
Prudence **62** 176
Rhoda **61** 77
Richard **62** 137 178
Robert **52** 57 273 **54** cvii **61** 77 **62** 172-178 200 238-241 364 365 **124** 312

LAY *cont'd*
127 199 **136** 309 315 320 329 **145** 118
Samuel **62** 173 175 **147** 51
Sarah **54** cvii **61** 76 77 **62** 172 173 175 178 200 **101** 289 **128** 24
Sarah Ann **62** 241
Sibyl **62** 176
Sophia Maria **83** 343
Steuben **62** 172 178 240 241
Temperance **62** 173 175 **136** 315 324
Theodora **62** 178
Thomas **62** 173
Uru **62** 178
William **61** 77 **145** 118
Willoughby L. **61** 77
LAYCOCK Amy **93** 392
Amy (Clarke) **93** 392
Thomas **128** 245
LAYDEN Eunie M. **77** 189
Laye *see* Lay
LAYELL
Theodore Studley **54** xxii xli 226
LAYER —— **98** 120
Delia **80** 166
Elizabeth **98** 119
John **98** 119
Layfet *see* Lafayette
LAYFIELD Molly (Montgomery) **120** 239
William W. **120** 239
LAYFITE
Gilbert de **96** 106
William de **96** 106
LAYHA
Margaret N. **88** 286
LAYLAND Lucinda (Bourne) **120** 248
William **120** 248
LAYMAN —— **145** 121
Charles **52** 445 **108** 261 264
Griffith W. **83** 468
John **51** 421
Laura Amelia **83** 468 **104** 71
Margaret **51** 421 422
Nabby **52** 445
Nabby (Gorham) **108** 261
Patty Lewis (Taylor) **108** 264
Thomas **51** 421 422
Timanda S. (Kirby) **83** 468
LAYNE Jessie (Keating) (Newbert) **96** 160
Layng *see* Lang
LAYNOD Conrad **51** 39
LAYRWATHOLM
Adam de **96** 106
Christian de **96** 106
LAYSEY Thomas **55** 67
Layton - see Leighton
LAZARUS Amelie **93** 181
LAZCANO Mary (Delano) **109** 286

LAZCANO *cont'd*
Prudencio **109** 286
LAZDEE Benjamin **118** 98
LAZELL Lasell Lassell Lazel Lazelle
—— **120** 129
____ (Jones) **89** 110
____ (Smith) **88** 362
Abbie Ellen **89** 118
Abby **89** 22
Abby Ann **89** 233
Abby Hall **89** 325
Abby Jane **89** 120
Abby Maria **89** 104
Abial **88** 257 260
Abial (Leavitt) **88** 259
Abigail **88** 258 261 264 360 369-371 **89** 108
Abigail (Ames) **89** 14
Abigail (Bailey) (Allen) **88** 364
Abigail (Holbrook) **89** 107
Abigail (Leavitt) **115** 193 **121** 269
Abigail (Perkins) **88** 369
Abigail (Robinson) **89** 10
Abigail Dorothy **89** 22
Abigail Locock **89** 30
Abigail Louisa **89** 104
Abigail Mayo **89** 105
Abner **88** 263 364
Achsah (Lindsay) **89** 321
Achsah White **89** 310
Achsanna (Pease) **89** 318 **105** 153
Ada Adella **89** 322
Ada Laura **89** 230
Ada May **89** 315
Adaline **89** 20
Adam **88** 360
Addie (Gawn) **89** 310
Addie Amelia (Pond) **89** 316
Addie E. **89** 115
Addie Salome **89** 229
Addie Viola **89** 239
Adelaide **89** 112
Adelaide Madeline **89** 319
Adelia Jane (Rhoads) **89** 236
Adelia Neville **89** 319
Adeline **89** 20
Adeline Mahala **89** 18
Adelpha **88** 376
Adonijah **89** 23
Agnes (Burwell) (Story) **89** 236
Agnes (Prouty) **89** 106
Agnes Aurelia **89** 102 105
Agnes Fidelia **89** 25
Agnes Robinson (White) **89** 318
Albert **89** 21 225 317
Albert Coulson **89** 321
Albert Dwight **89** 28
Albert Elbridge **89** 230
Albert Eugene **89** 320
Alberta (Young) **89** 317
Alexander Hamilton **89** 111

LAZELL *cont'd*
Alice **89** 25 240
Alice Antoinette **89** 27
Alice Atwood **89** 103
Alice Cary (Kimball) **89**
  323 **106** 231
Alice Elizabeth **89** 235
Alice Elvira (Norton)
  89 316
Alice Frances **89** 230
Alice Leigh (Yeaton)
  89 32
Alice Lelia **89** 106
Alice Maria (Hyde) **89** 114
Alice Mary (Sears) **89** 114
Alice Page **89** 229
Alice Terry **89** 227
Allie **89** 319
Allison **105** 209
Almira **88** 375 376 **89** 238
Almira (Hawley) **89** 15
Almira (Luciver) (Luce)
  89 106
Almira Lucy (Shepard)
  (White) **89** 15
Almond **88** 372
Almus **89** 112
Althea **89** 322
Alvah **75** 308 **88** 365 **89**
  17 18 235 236
Alvah Danforth **89** 316
Alvah Skinner **89** 316
Alvilda Spaulding **89** 116
Amanda (Smith) **89** 228
Amanda Ellen (Jordon)
  89 118
Amanda Hawse **89** 325
Ambrose Pendleton
  89 120
Amelia De Ette **89** 236
Amos **88** 373
Amos Bangs **89** 240
Amy **88** 362 **107** 199 273
  108 122
Andra June **89** 311
Andrew **88** 262 362
  110 175
Angie Matilda **89** 233
Ann **88** 262
Ann (Wilkinson) **89** 13
Ann Aspasia (Mengous)
  (King) **89** 30
Ann Delight **89** 225
Ann E. (Eagan) **89** 111
Ann Elizabeth **89** 14
Ann Janette **89** 234
Ann Rebecca Gooding
  (Hollingsworth)
  89 228
Anna **88** 361 **89** 11 111 318
  108 120
Anna (Bailey) **88** 361
Anna (Poole) **88** 366
Anna (Powell) **89** 24
Anna Balch (Banker)
  89 314
Anna Laura **89** 317
Anna Maria **89** 314
Anne **89** 13
Annette (LeBaron) **89** 238
Annie **89** 319

LAZELL *cont'd*
Annie Adell **89** 240
Annie Duncan **89** 29
Annie E. **89** 225
Annie Lila **89** 117
Annie Warren **89** 108
Annis Frances **89** 319
Anthony Homer **89** 110
Araminta **89** 235
Archie Eugene **89** 117
Aristeen (Brown) **89** 238
Armenia **75** 308 **89** 18
Armenia Eliza **89** 19
Arthur **89** 23
Arthur Hamilton **89** 113
Asa **88** 362 370 371 **95** 86
  190
Asenath (Anthony) **89** 27
Aspasia **89** 30
Augusta Maria (Young)
  (Stevens) **89** 22
Aurelia (Phillips) **89** 102
Aurora F. (Sanford) **89** 24
Aylmer **89** 26 318 **105** 153
Azariah **89** 22
Bartholomew **88** 362 368
  107 270-272 274 **108** 55
  57 123 **115** 304
Barton Bassett **89** 238
Bathsheba **89** 111
Bathsheba (Patch) **89** 110
Bathsheba Ann **89** 110
Beatrice Palmerton
  89 321
Benjamin **89** 112
Benjamin Mason **89** 321
Bernard **89** 319
Bernard Ingraham **89** 117
Bertha **89** 115
Bertha (Miner) **89** 319
Bertha Marilla (Hero)
  89 228
Bertha Sarah (Sprague)
  89 104
Bertie **89** 226
Bessie **89** 312
Bessie Chamberlain
  89 230
Bethiah **88** 360 365 **89** 10
  11 15 **119** 89 90 187 **123**
  187
Bethiah (Alger) **88** 364
  119 187
Bethiah (Leonard) **89** 312
Bethiah (Woodward) **87**
  391 **88** 360
Betsey **83** 492 **88** 362 **89**
  10 11 16 17
Betsey (Ellis) **89** 108
Betsey Eveline (Bouton)
  89 232
Betsey Theresa **89** 239
Bingham **88** 367 **89** 21 24
  309
Biram **89** 19 235
Biram S. **89** 235
Blanche **89** 237
Blanche Augusta **89** 229
Blanche L. **89** 316
Burton Isabell **89** 317
Burton Robinson **89** 120

LAZELL *cont'd*
Burvillus Hilt **89** 119
Byantha Alexander **89** 118
Byantha Gordon **89** 119
Byram **88** 365 **89** 16
Caleb **65** 114 **88** 362 369
  370 **90** 329 **91** 19 **98** 296
Caleb Gannett **89** 233
Calista (Gove) **89** 25
Calista (Sherman)
  89 102 105
Calista Estella Anah
  89 107
Callie Hemenway **89** 118
Calvin **88** 365 **89** 19 20 240
Carleton Leslie **89** 103
Caroline **89** 13 25 238 313
  324 **145** 306
Caroline (Engelsbarger)
  89 110
Caroline Abigail **89** 109
Caroline Lucinda (Gates)
  89 27
Caroline Lydia **89** 314
Caroline Maria **89** 227
Caroline Marsh **89** 109
Caroline Meigs **89** 25
Caroline Olive (Patten)
  (Ford) **89** 120
Carrie **89** 117
Carrie Amelia (Hewes)
  89 117
Carrie Calista (Atwood)
  89 229
Carrie Lillian (Wing)
  89 227
Carrie Louise **89** 227
Catherine **75** xxiv **88** 361
  363 **89** 30 228
Catherine (Drown) **88** 262
Catherine (Danby)
  112 157
Catherine (Green) (Study)
  89 309
Catherine Broughton
  (Lanpher) **89** 112
Catherine Dorothy
  (Grant) **89** 25
Catherine Eunice **89** 26
Catherine Whitin **89** 31
  94 290 **95** 73 149 **108**
  226
Celestia (Crane) **89** 240
Celia **89** 236 322
Celia Almira (Taylor)
  89 314
Celina Spencer **89** 108
Cephas Clark **89** 312
Charles **77** 183 **89** 22 23
  25 225 228 313 325 326
Charles Albert **89** 324
Charles Allston **89** 116
Charles Atwood **89** 117
Charles Burvillus **89** 119
Charles C. **89** 228
Charles Clarence **89** 32
Charles Edward **89** 225
  311
Charles Franklin **89** 118
Charles Frederick **89** 234
Charles Fremont **89** 103

LAZELL *cont'd*
105
Charles Henry **89** 234
Charles Hobart **89** 24
Charles Horace **89** 228
Charles Israel **89** 117
Charles Lewis **89** 117
Charles M. **89** 115
Charles Thomas **89** 240
Charles Thurber **89** 109
Charles Wesley **89** 324
Charles Wilder **89** 120
Charlotte **88** 368 **89** 12 315
     107 271 272 274 **108** 55
     57
Charlotte (Caswell)
     89 229
Charlotte (Lazell) (Tisdale)
     89 12
Charlotte (Orne) **88** 368
     108 123
Charlotte Jones (Mitchell)
     89 116
Chauncey **88** 375 **89** 26
Chester **88** 367 **89** 23 28
     29 32 227 316 **93** 380 **94**
     290 **100** 162
Chester Harding **89** 31
     93 381
Chester Whitin **89** 31
Chloe **88** 262 365
Chloe (Millard) **88** 364
Chloe (Richardson) **89** 14
Chloe Ann **89** 21
Christiana (Gannett)
     89 233
Christine Towne
     (Stocker) **89** 289
Clara **89** 26
Clara (Poland) **89** 315
Clara Belle **89** 315
Clara Edith **89** 115
Clara May (Pierce) **89** 116
Clarence **89** 236
Clarence Delos **89** 105
Clarence Hamilton
     89 312
Clarissa (Sherburne)
     89 230
Claudius Buchanan **89** 30
Clemence A. (Kennedy)
     89 326
Clifford Julius **89** 105
Clifford Marshall **89** 317
Cloris Augusta
     (Masteller) **89** 115
Conant Leroy **89** 321
Content (Legg) **89** 111
Cora Ada **89** 117
Cora Alice **89** 316
Cora Jane **89** 234
Cordelia **89** 120
Cordelia K. **88** 372
Cordelia L. **89** 120
Cornelia (Merrill) **89** 235
Cornelia Annette **89** 320
Corra Edwin **89** 229
Cynthia **89** 33
Cynthia (Freeman) **89** 319
Cynthia (Morse) **89** 27
Cynthia C. **89** 120

LAZELL *cont'd*
Cynthia Maria **89** 105
Cynthia Merial **89** 103 106
Cyrene **89** 104
Cyrus **89** 10
Cyrus Martin **89** 10
Daisy (Williams) **89** 312
Dallas **89** 116
Daniel **88** 260 264 359 360
     365 368 **89** 16 19 20 106
     108 236 324 325
Daniel LeBaron **89** 238
Daniel Randall **89** 238
Daniel Webster **89** 232
Davenport **88** 372
David Philbrook **89** 115
David Zelotus **89** 119
Deane **89** 116
Deborah **88** 264 358 362
     363 **89** 10 11 13 325 **108**
     57 121
Deborah (Conant) **89** 12
     145 38 306
Deborah (Gillett) **89** 238
Deborah (Lincoln) **88** 260
     94 290
Deborah (Marsh) **88** 358
     106 230
Deborah (Thompson)
     88 368
Deborah Mary **89** 309 310
Deborah Melintha **89** 105
Delia **89** 230
Delilah (Spaulding)
     89 116
Della Jane **89** 119
Delphina Phidora Ella
     89 104
Desdemona **89** 33
Dewitt Clinton **89** 111
Diadama **88** 363
Diana (Stockwell) **89** 104
Didamia **88** 363
Donald King **89** 30
Donna Florence (Ordway)
     89 117
Dora Annette **89** 239
Dorcas **65** 114
Dorcas (Conant) **89** 319
Dorcas (White) **88** 369
     98 296
Dorothy (Brooks) **89** 22
Dorothy Maynard **89** 325
Ebenezer **88** 365 **89** 14
Eddie Freeman **89** 106
Eddie Jerome **89** 27
Edgar **89** 23
Edith **89** 103
Edith (Holmes) **89** 239
Edith Alice **89** 235
Edith F. S. (Congdon)
     89 117
Edith Isabelle (Brown)
     89 234
Edmond **119** 255
Edmund **88** 365 **89** 10
     119 187
Edna **89** 113
Edna Emily **89** 238 239
Edna Long (Maynard)
     89 325

LAZELL *cont'd*
Edna Maud **89** 120 316
Edrick **89** 120
Edward **88** 372 **89** 28 32
Edward Carson **89** 113
Edward Harper **89** 32
Edward Joshua **89** 224
Edward Lester **89** 318
Edward Russell **89** 24
Edward Tyler **89** 225
Edward Wilkins **89** 312
Edward William **89** 234
Edwin **88** 369 **89** 236
Edwin Bertram **89** 117
Edwin Quackenbush
     89 325
Edwin Roy **89** 102
Edwin Ward **89** 119
Eirene **89** 30
Eirene King **89** 30
Elbridge Bowdoin **89** 227
Elbridge Sherman **89** 225
Eleanor Folsom **89** 32
Electa **89** 20
Electa (Chubbuck) **89** 26
Electa (Gilmore) **89** 105
Electa Maud (Emerson)
     89 238
Elias **88** 367 368 **89** 23 24
     111
Elias C. **89** 111 112
Elias J. **89** 23
Elihu **88** 264
Elijah **89** 21 312
Elisa **90** 239
Eliza **88** 370 **89** 18 113
Eliza (Bard) **89** 18
Eliza (Flint) **89** 25
Eliza (Perry) **89** 23
Eliza (Richardson) **89** 112
Eliza (Slade) **89** 238
Eliza Angeline **89** 314
Eliza Ann **89** 19
Eliza Ann (Berry) **89** 118
Eliza Ann (Whittemore)
     89 228
Eliza Carleton **89** 119
Eliza Caroline **89** 310 311
Eliza Colvin **89** 325
Eliza Jane **89** 239
Elizabeth **88** 257-259 262
     264 361-363 366 370-372
     89 17-20 30 31 110 113
     115 235 238 326 **90** 315
     93 381 **108** 123 **110** 175
     121 108 198 210
Elizabeth (Ames) **121** 137
Elizabeth (Brown) **88** 361
Elizabeth (Cassady)
     89 325
Elizabeth (Dana) **88** 361
Elizabeth (Davenport)
     88 363
Elizabeth (Derry) **89** 115
Elizabeth (Gates) **88** 25
     257 **94** 290 **120** 163 **121**
     22
Elizabeth (Hatch) (Skiff)
     88 261
Elizabeth (Karner) **89** 110
Elizabeth (Mitten) **89** 309

LAZELL *cont'd*
Elizabeth (Packard)
    89 233
Elizabeth (Prince) (Ames)
    88 363 **121** 137
Elizabeth (Robinson)
    89 313
Elizabeth (Warner) **89** 17
Elizabeth Ann **89** 113
Elizabeth Breckinridge
    89 228
Elizabeth Catherine
    89 310
Elizabeth Comstock
    (Vaill) **89** 321
Elizabeth Cora **89** 231
Elizabeth Dorcas **89** 320
Elizabeth G. **88** 373
Elizabeth Graham
    (Campbell)
    (Crawford) **89** 320
Elizabeth H. **89** 111
Elizabeth Helen **89** 232
Elizabeth Jane **89** 108
Elizabeth L. **88** 373
Elizabeth Olive **89** 114
Elizabeth S. **89** 112
Elizabeth Susan
    (Williams) **89** 311
Elizabeth Washington
    (King) **89** 30
Elizur **89** 309
Elizur Bingham **89** 309
Ella **89** 112 227
Ella (Moore) **89** 104
Ella Eliza **89** 313
Ella Francelia **89** 229
Ella Frances (Hitman)
    89 316
Ella Mae / May **89** 25 317
Ella O. **88** 372
Ellen **89** 28 237
Ellen (Smith) **89** 225
Ellen Augusta **89** 312
Ellen Dorcas **89** 321
Ellen Douglas **89** 314
Ellen Frances **89** 16 234
Ellen Frances (Lazell)
    89 16
Ellen Jeanette **89** 111
Ellen Malissa (Hawkins)
    89 231
Ellen Olivia (Robinson)
    89 232
Ellen Sophia **89** 324
Ellen Thurber **89** 108
Ellery Douglas **89** 25
Ellis **89** 110
Ellis Draper **89** 323
    106 230
Ellis Warren **89** 323
Ellison **88** 262 362 363 371
    89 107
Ellsworth **89** 120
Ellura Frances **89** 313
Elmer Ellsworth **89** 117
Elmira (Tupper) **89** 230
Elnora Etta **89** 120
Else (Pendleton) **89** 231
Else Matilda **89** 231
Elsie **89** 117 312

LAZELL *cont'd*
Elsie Ellen **89** 312
Elsie Permelia **89** 106
Elvira (Popple) **89** 23
Emeline **89** 237 238
Emeline Dorcas (Cook)
    89 108
Emeline Mary **88** 370
    89 113
Emerson **89** 25
Emery **89** 225
Emily **89** 27 237 238
Emily (Mills) **89** 238
Emily (Snow) **89** 102
Emily (Warner) **89** 319
Emily Adelaide **89** 315
Emily Edith **89** 237
Emily Elizabeth (Russell)
    89 229
Emily Mary (Chester)
    89 227
Emily Snow (Gould)
    89 105
Emma **89** 23 237
Emma (Lyman) **89** 314
Emma (Quackenbush)
    89 325
Emma Amelia (Olin)
    89 315
Emma Ardell **89** 118
Emma Irene **89** 107
Emma Larane **89** 25
Emma Louisa **89** 231
Emma Taft **89** 324
Emmeagene (Stone)
    89 26
Emoret (Stocking) **89** 239
Emyra Seavey **89** 324
Enoch **88** 367 **89** 27
Enos Taylor **89** 235
Ephraim **89** 119 120
Erasmus **89** 235
Erasmus Darwin **89** 235
Erastus Otis **89** 108
Erastus Perkins **89** 317
Ernest Aylmer **89** 319
Ernest Chauncey **89** 321
Ernest Randolph **89** 316
Erwin Ensign **89** 25
Esther (Lichty) **89** 232
Esther (Pratt) **89** 19 234
Esto Ida (Crissey) **89** 235
Ethel Hilda **89** 30
Ethel May **89** 231
Etta (Jay) **89** 105
Etta Almira **89** 15
Etta Sincera **89** 228
Eugene Fremont **89** 114
Eunice **88** 261 362 364 365
    375
Eunice (Davenport)
    88 364
Eunice (Patterson) **88** 372
Eunice (Webb) **89** 25
Eunice Webb **89** 322
Eusebia Arnold (Billings)
    89 224
Eva C. (Hoffman) **89** 225
Eva M. (Hathaway) **89** 23
Eva May **89** 25 118
Evaline **89** 19

LAZELL *cont'd*
Evelina Robinson **89** 117
Everett Lowell **89** 116
Everett Pierce **89** 115
Ezra Stuart **89** 311
Ezra William **89** 312
Fannaye Louise
    (Parmalee) **89** 233
Fannie **89** 115
Fannie Berenice **89** 117
Fannie Ethel **89** 316
Fanny **89** 22 311
Flora **89** 312
Flora Amelia **89** 320
Florence **89** 19 113
Florence Belle **89** 227
Florence Celia **89** 106
Florence Delina (Wedge)
    89 321
Florence Mabel (Howard)
    89 24
Francelia Sarah (Morrow)
    89 320
Frances **89** 24 111
Frances (Sumner) **100** 162
Frances (Wilkins) **89** 230
Frances (Wood) **89** 112
Frances Ann **89** 227
Frances Augusta **89** 114
Frances Aurora **89** 24
Frances Catherine **89** 111
Frances Edwards
    (Pierpont) **89** 23
Frances Elizabeth (Parks)
    89 20
Frances Lorinda **89** 109
Frances Mahala (Bernard)
    89 319
Frances Medora (Monroe)
    89 232
Frances Octavia **89** 115
Frances Quackenbush
    89 325
Francilla M. **88** 373
Francis **89** 25
Francis Cobb **89** 112
Francis Emery **89** 311
Francis Marion **89** 115
    238
Francis Morton **89** 117
Francis William **89** 104
Frank **89** 112 119 226 238
Frank Chauncey **89** 321
Frank Elwell **89** 120
Frank Elwin **89** 235
Frank Grosvenor **89** 319
Frank I. **89** 326
Frank P. **89** 326
Frank Wilkins **89** 230
Franklin **89** 318
Franklin Eugene **89** 313
Fred **89** 115 225 226
Fred Norman **89** 317
Frederick **89** 32 119
Frederick Alfonzo **89** 316
Freeman Leon **89** 233
Geneva M. (Briggs)
    89 120
George **88** 371 **89** 17 20
    22 103 112 226 238 313

LAZELL *cont'd*
George Augustus
  Barlow **89** 110
George Boardman **89** 234
George Byram **89** 234
George C. **89** 228
George Carleton **89** 103
George Edgar **89** 315
George Elmer **89** 114
George Henry **89** 231
George Herbert **89** 117
George Kinner **89** 238
George Mason **89** 238
George Merrill **89** 316
George Perley **89** 112
George Sandford **89** 321
George Spaulding
  89 228
George Spear **89** 117
George Stanton **89** 235
George Thomas **89** 118
  240
George Washington
  89 310
Georgiana (Pray) **89** 113
Georgie (Staniels) **89** 228
Gertrude Mae / May
  89 116 233
Gertrude May (Welch)
  89 316
Gladys Ethelyne **89** 114
Glenn Raymond **89** 315
Glenn Saunders **89** 320
Grace **89** 108
Grace Bayeux **89** 325
Grace Hancock **89** 117
Grace May **89** 115 312
Grosvenor Gilbert
  89 320
Hamilton Alexander
  Clinton **89** 111
Hamilton Dennis **89** 236
Hannah **88** 258 259 262
  264 359 361 362 366 367
  369 371 372 **89** 12 21
  115 **90** 230 251 **95** 189
  191 **98** 296 **107** 272 **133**
  42
Hannah (Bingham)
  88 366
Hannah (Burbank) **88** 362
Hannah (Fearing)
  88 257 360
Hannah (O'Brien) **89** 119
Hannah (Turner) **89** 237
Hannah (Wood) (Soule)
  89 16
Hannah Brooks **89** 236
Hannah Crane **89** 117
Hannah Elizabeth **89** 18
Hannah Rebecca (Farwell)
  89 33
Harold Ernest **89** 112
Harold Laureston **89** 116
Harold Smith **89** 316
Harriet **89** 13 **108** 55
Harriet (Hinds) **89** 228
Harriet A. **89** 326
Harriet Aurelia **89** 102 104
  105
Harriet Belle **89** 317

LAZELL *cont'd*
Harriet Cordelia (Brooks)
  89 31 32
Harriet E. (Rich) **88** 372
Harriet Goulding **89** 229
Harriet Mainard **89** 325
Harriet Minerva **89** 240
Harriet Newell (Holman)
  89 323
Harriet White **89** 319
  102 231
Harriett Minerva **89** 240
Harris **89** 21 313 314
Harris James **89** 314 315
Harry **89** 32
Harry Raymond **89** 316
Harry Wentworth **89** 227
Harvey Barrell **89** 311
Haskell Smith **89** 316
Hattie Amanda **89** 321
Hattie Belle (Paul) **89** 317
Hattie Brown (Saunders)
  89 320
Hattie Delight **89** 225
Hattie Isadora **89** 117
Hattie Louise **89** 117
Hazel **89** 105
Hazel Ada **89** 228
Helen **89** 317
Helen (Moore) **89** 112
Helen Augusta (Maine)
  (Drew) (Willey) **89** 115
Helen E. (Thomas) **89** 32
Helen Elizabeth **89** 315
Helen Gladys **89** 22
Helen Howard **89** 24
Helen Maria **89** 109
Helen Phillips **89** 103
Helena Estella **89** 116
Henrietta Patch **89** 110
Henriette **89** 12
Henry **89** 24
Henry Arlington **89** 320
Henry Carlton **89** 231
Henry Daniel **89** 231
Henry E. **89** 225
Henry Ernest **89** 112
Henry Franklin **89** 234
Henry Haskell **89** 316
Henry Leonard **89** 27
Henry Lovewell **89** 317
Henry Martyn **89** 25 228
Henry Nathaniel **89** 312
Henry Patch **89** 111
Henry Robert **89** 316
Henry Rufus **89** 230
Henry Warren **89** 103
Hepzibah (Lovewell)
  89 315
Herbert Caleb **89** 234
Herbert F. **89** 326
Herbert Frank **89** 233
Herbert Ross **89** 321
Herbert Sumner **89** 102
Hermie Annis **89** 232
Herschel Bouton **89** 232
Hiland Hall **89** 325
Hildegarde **89** 31
Hiram **75** 308 **88** 365 **89**
  17-19 234 235
Hiram Mason **89** 238

LAZELL *cont'd*
Hollis Alvah **89** 316
Hollis William **89** 116
Horace **89** 228 **91** 201
Horace Gibbs **89** 229
Horace William **89** 113
Howland Augustus
  89 118
Hubert Harlan **89** 316
Huldah **88** 362 365 **89** 10
  19 21
Huldah (Leach) **88** 365
  89 19
Ida **89** 103
Ida A. (Inman) **89** 116
Ida E. **89** 117
Ida Eliza (Stratton) **89** 120
Ida Ethelind **89** 25
Ida May **89** 240
Idella M. (Seymour)
  89 120
Ina Eliza **89** 315
Ina Eva **89** 239
Ina Pearl **89** 240
Inez E. **89** 117
Inez Eliza **89** 105
Inez Floy **89** 106
Inez Madeline **89** 116
Inez Mary **89** 234
Ira Curtis **89** 104
Ira N. **89** 326
Irena (Smith) **89** 27
Irena Louisa **89** 106
Irene **89** 12
Isaac **88** 257-261 263 264
  358-360 364 365 368 373
  89 11 12 104 326 **106**
  230 **108** 185 **119** 187
  121 269 276 279
Isaac Hoyt **89** 22
Isaac Warren **89** 102 105
Isaac Watson **89** 105
Isabel **89** 110
Isabella (McLaren) **89** 230
Isabella (Worthing)
  89 113
Isabelle Thomas **89** 112
Israel **88** 257 258 260 263
  358 359 362 369 **106** 230
  121 127
J. M. **87** 190
Jacob **88** 263 363 364 372
  144 102 105
Jacob Hollingsworth
  Gaines **89** 229
Jael **88** 264
Jael (Cushing) **88** 264
  89 327
James **88** 258 261 360 361
  367 **89** 24 31-33 325
James Albert **89** 324
James Draper **89** 323
  106 231
James Duncan **89** 29
James Henry **89** 324
James Monroe **89** 113 114
James Myron **89** 315
James Otis **89** 325
James Thompson **89** 111
Jane **89** 11
Jane (McIntosh) **89** 33

LAZELL *cont'd*
Jane (Myram) **89** 11
Jane (Whitin) **89** 31
  94 290
Jane Bailey **89** 234
Jane E. (Fritts) **88** 372
Jane Elizabeth (Shepard)
  89 15
Jane Ellen (Ladd) **89** 22 23
Jane Pease **89** 319
Jane Wilson (Seavey) **89**
  323 **106** 231
Janette **89** 16
Janette (Wesley) **89** 16
Janette Leota **89** 113
Jared **89** 20 237
Jeanette **89** 111 112
Jeanette Maria (Tucker)
  89 229
Jennie (White) **89** 116
Jennie A. **89** 115
Jennie Belle (Munson)
  89 30
Jennie Frances **89** 229
Jennie Louisa **89** 316
Jennie Vennettie **89** 312
Jenny Leland **89** 31
Jeremiah **88** 262 361 372
  89 119 **110** 175
Jerusha (Kendall) **88** 372
Jerusha (Wales) (Cary)
  88 261
Jerusha Antoinette **89** 27
Jessie Erzela **89** 233
Jessie Maud (Keeler)
  89 31
Joanna **88** 263
Joanna (Tilson) (Wood)
  88 263
Joanna Victoria (Thomas)
  89 110
Johanna (Ladd) **89** 22
John **54** 226 **60** 186 **88**
  257 258 260-264 358 360
  361 363-368 370 371 373
  374 **89** 10 15 27 102 103
  106 112 224 226 230 309
  317 324 325 327 **90** 401
  93 380 **94** 290 **100** 162
  105 153 **106** 230 **113** 32
  115 193 **120** 163 **121** 22
  23 111 117 119 123 127
  138 **145** 306
John Adams **88** 368
  89 110 111
John Andrew **89** 231
John Ashley **89** 19
John Bertie **89** 320
John Bingham **89** 310
John Bouton **89** 232
John Byron **89** 315
John Foster **89** 310
John Francisco **89** 113
John Frank **89** 113
John M. **89** 115
John Milton **89** 110
John Powell **89** 25
John Quincy **89** 230
John Richardson **89** 112
John Samuel **89** 311
John Swinton **88** 362 371

LAZELL *cont'd*
  89 114
John W. **100** 162
John Wesley **89** 114
John Whitin **89** 31 **93** 381
  94 136 **100** 100 114 161
  162
John Willard **89** 118
Jonas King **89** 30
Jonathan **88** 260 360 362
  89 116
Jonathan Ellis **89** 109 111
  322 **106** 230
Joseph **88** 264 365 372 375
  89 14 15 20 227 **144** 105
Joseph Abner **89** 228
Joseph Monroe **89** 240
Joseph Turner **89** 237
Josephine **89** 237
Josephine (Dineen) **89** 32
Josephine (Johnson)
  89 324
Josephine Frances **89** 317
Josephine Orma (Potter)
  89 30
Joshia **136** 25
Joshua **88** 257-264 358
  359 361 363 364 366 368
  371-373 375 **89** 21 117
  224 326 **90** 390 93 380
  94 290 **100** 162 **105** 307
  106 230 **110** 175 **119** 85
  90 **121** 105 207 216 271
  273
Joshua Bradley **89** 112
Josiah **88** 257 259 264 265
  367 **89** 25 31 318 **93** 380
  381 **94** 290 **108** 226
Josiah M. **74** ix xxiv
Josiah Manning **89** 28 31
  93 380 **94** 79 136 141
  100 114 162
Jubaetta **89** 324
Judith **88** 362
Judith (Deering) **88** 362
Judson **89** 15
Julia **89** 14 32 120 **145** 38
Julia (Moore) **89** 226
Julia Ann (Draper) **89** 322
  106 230
Julia Ann (Thomas)
  89 118
Julia Draper (Cilley) **89**
  323 **106** 230
Julia Mae **89** 315
Juliet **88** 372
Kandase **89** 233
Karl Otto **89** 321
Kate (Fisher) **89** 116
Kate (Sheridan) **89** 113
Kate Fisher **89** 116
Katee (Quin) **89** 323
Katharine **88** 262 **89** 318
Katharine (Bowen) **89** 20
Katharine (Brown)
  110 175
Laban **88** 366 367 **89** 22
  315
Lacassard **89** 115
Lafayette **89** 110
Lanpher Dean **89** 113

LAZELL *cont'd*
Laura **89** 32
Laura (Williams) **89** 32
Laura Ann **89** 322
Laura Augusta **89** 106
Laura Crocker **89** 116
Laura Delphina (Miller)
  89 311
Laura Greeley **89** 226
Laura Louisa **89** 33
Laura Maria **89** 28 230
Laura Olivia **89** 103
Laura Whitman **89** 28
Laureston Robinson
  89 116
Lavern Charles **89** 235
Lavern Winsor **89** 235
Lavinia (Cook) **106** 230
Lawrence Hays **89** 104
Lelia Eunice (Perry)
  89 118
Lemuel **88** 366 **89** 22 317
Leona Adelle (Randall)
  89 238
Leroy Frederick **89** 320
Leslie **89** 116
Leslie Stillman **89** 105
Lester **89** 318
Lester Herbert **89** 24
Lester Norton **89** 316
Levantia **89** 235
Levantia (Warren) **89** 236
Levi **88** 364 373 375 376
  89 229 231 232
Levi Webster **89** 232
Levina **88** 368 **89** 107
Levina (Cook) **88** 368
Lewis **88** 368 **89** 109 226
Lewis Thurber **89** 108
Lida Samantha
  (Whitmore) **89** 320
Lilla Marion **89** 225
Lillian **89** 318
Lillian Edna **89** 227
Lillie (Striffler) **89** 235
Lina (Dunham) **89** 232
Linnie Lerena **89** 237
Lizzie M. **89** 117
Lizzie May (Cushman)
  89 114
Lizzie Spencer (Fernald)
  89 30
Lloyd **89** 240
Lloyd Munson **89** 30
Lloyd White **89** 30
Lois **88** 363
Lorenzo **89** 25
Lorenzo Harvey **89** 314
Lorinda **89** 109
Lorinda Irene **89** 107
Loron Marcellus **89** 316
Loron Wight **89** 316
Lottie (Chappell) **89** 233
Lottie May **89** 225
Lottie Viola **89** 316
Louis **89** 314 316
Louisa **89** 103 115 224-
  226 237
Louisa (Blunt) **89** 27
Louisa (Whitten) **88** 362
  89 114

LAZELL *cont'd*
Louisa Alice **89** 105 310
Louisa Almira **89** 315
Louisa Malzena **89** 116
Louisa Maria (Heald)
   89 22
Louise **89** 28 236
Louise Mary (Holt)
   89 229
Loville (Babcock) **89** 233
Lovinia **89** 110
Lovisa **88** 375 **89** 232
Lucia **89** 28 29
Lucia (Alvord) **89** 20
Lucia Parthenia **89** 20
Lucinda **88** 373 **89** 15 18
Lucinda (Karner) **89** 110
Lucinda (Stetson) **89** 15
Lucinda (Taylor) **89** 18
Lucretia (Temple) **88** 364
Lucy **88** 262 367 368 371 **89**
   10 11 15 17 18 21 114
   236
Lucy (Hitchcock) **89** 103
Lucy (Smith) **89** 119
Lucy (Stearns) (Sears) **89**
   103 106
Lucy (Wilson) **89** 104
Lucy Adelaide (Denison)
   89 106
Lucy Ann **89** 240
Lucy Ann (Nichols)
   89 232
Lucy Belle **89** 118
Lucy Irene **89** 105
Luella **89** 225
Luella Alberta **89** 316
Lula **89** 313
Lulu Blanche **89** 232
Lura **89** 226
Luther **88** 365 **89** 16 21
Luther Josiah **89** 314
Luther Robertson **89** 23
Lydia **57** liv **88** 259 261
   263 360 362 365 367 368
   371 373 374 **89** 13 19 23
   24 26 102 111 112 **107**
   199 273 **108** 122 **113** 32
   40 **121** 274
Lydia (Adams) **89** 102
Lydia (Bingham) **88** 367
   94 290
Lydia (Robertson) **89** 23
Lydia (Tinkham) **89** 234
Lydia Amelia **89** 102
Lydia Ann (Martin) **89** 25
Lydia Bingham **89** 30
Lydia Calderwood **89** 119
Lydia Margaret **89** 111
Lydia Maria (Fisk) **89** 314
Lydia R. **89** 24
Lydia Rowley **89** 309 311
Lydia Sylvester
   (Wynkoop) **89** 29
Lyman George **89** 314
Mabel **89** 238 312
Mabel Alida **89** 229
Mabel Ethel **89** 227
Malinda (Angle) **89** 105
Malinda (Metcalf) **89** 120
Marcella **89** 317

LAZELL *cont'd*
Marcellus **89** 229 317
Marcia **89** 26
Marcia Amanda **89** 28
Marcus **89** 27 321
Margaret **89** 289
Margaret (Cooke) **88** 262
Margaret Harding **89** 31
   93 381
Maria **89** 112 230
Maria (Perkins) **89** 112
Maria A. **88** 372
Maria Charity (Benedict)
   89 22
Maria Theresa **89** 22
Marianne Rhoda **89** 102
Mariel **88** 368
Marietta Amelia **89** 102
Marion Lucy **89** 105
Marion Murray **89** 31
Marius Warren **89** 236
Marshall **75** 308 **89** 17 18
   103 236
Marshall Milo **89** 316
Marston **89** 16 233 234
Martha **88** 259 264 366 367
   89 24 120 228 **121** 214
Martha (Harris) **88** 264
   94 290
Martha (Lamb) (Bennett)
   89 23
Martha (Malone) **88** 362
Martha (Persons) **89** 18
Martha (Wilson) **89** 311
Martha Ann **89** 25 317
Martha Ann (Palmerton)
   89 320
Martha Coburn **89** 324
Martha Lemira (Williams)
   89 313
Martha Saunders
   (Hubbard) **89** 310
Martha Thirza **89** 311
Martha Wynkoop **89** 30
Martin **89** 11 14 33
Martin Carroll **89** 229
Mary **65** 114 **88** 226 258
   259 262-265 360-363 365-
   367 371 373 **89** 10 15 16
   20 23 24 32 115 116 224
   310 311 318 326 **90** 300
   105 307 **110** 175 **147** 59
Mary (Allen) **88** 258
Mary (Bassett) **89** 232
Mary (Bowdoin) **89** 226
Mary (Burnap) **88** 260
Mary (Byram) **88** 365
Mary (Coburn) **89** 323
Mary (Culbertson) **89** 318
Mary (Ford) **89** 10 **119** 187
Mary (Fowler) **89** 22
Mary (Hudson) **88** 263
Mary (Jones) **88** 362
Mary (Lane) **89** 236
Mary (Lawry) **88** 371
Mary (Leet) **89** 320
Mary (Metcalf) **89** 120
Mary (Philbrook) **88** 371
Mary (Sawyer) **89** 237
Mary (Thomes) **89** 112
Mary (Wilbur) **89** 321

LAZELL *cont'd*
Mary A. (Fales) **89** 117
Mary A. (Green) **89** 117
Mary Adelia (Grosvenor)
   89 319
Mary Agnes **89** 106 107
Mary Angelina (Staples)
   89 228
Mary Ann **89** 24 227 313
Mary Ann (Buross)
   89 237
Mary Anne (Brooks)
   89 225
Mary Asenath (Crocker)
   89 115
Mary Augusta **89** 22
Mary Baker **89** 27
Mary Bessie **89** 228
Mary Caroline (Gilbert)
   89 33
Mary Chastina **89** 230
Mary Crowell **89** 30
Mary Duncan **89** 29
Mary E. **89** 113
Mary Eliza **89** 226
Mary Elizabeth
   (Willoughby) **89** 24
Mary Ella **89** 226 321 322
Mary Ellen **89** 120
Mary Ellen (Pierce)
   89 115
Mary Elma **89** 235
Mary Emma (Bolster)
   89 103
Mary Eunice **89** 320
Mary Evelyn **89** 117
Mary F. (Woodbridge)
   89 113
Mary Frances (Isbell)
   89 317
Mary Frances (Krum)
   89 31
Mary G. **89** 23 326
Mary G. (Johnson) **89** 326
Mary Hannah Hobbs
   (Taylor) (Simpson)
   89 114
Mary Irene **89** 233
Mary J. **88** 373
Mary Jane **89** 103 118 237
   324
Mary Jane (Martin)
   89 225
Mary Jane (O'Hara)
   89 120
Mary Jeanette **89** 24
Mary L. **89** 115
Mary Lavinia **89** 111
Mary Lucretia (Wilson)
   89 315
Mary Matlock (Reeves)
   89 31
Mary Myrtle **89** 312
Mary Porter **88** 370
Mary Pratt **89** 235
Mason **89** 26 319
Matilda **89** 28 32
Matilda Adaline
   (Leadbetter) **89** 118
Matthew **88** 262 362 370
   372 **89** 113 118 **90** 237

LAZELL *cont'd*
110 175
Maud (Bailey) **89** 317
Maud Eliza **89** 239
Maud Irene **89** 315
Maud J. **89** 316
May Lillian **89** 313
Mehbel (Ricker) **95** 190
Mehitable **88** 261 361 371
　89 115 **108** 122
Mehitable (Ricker) **88** 370
Mehitable (Smith) **88** 261
Melissa Rosina **89** 230
Mellie **89** 225
Mellie Eugenia **89** 225
Merrill Gilbert **89** 316
Merritt **89** 233
Mertie Carelton **89** 231
Mertie Carleton **89** 231
Merton **89** 321
Merton Sherman **89** 105
Mettie Aldoretta **89** 312
Mildred Marguerite
　89 104
Milo Galen **89** 316
Mina (Badgley) **89** 240
Minerva **88** 372
Minerva (Billings) **89** 229
Minerva (Richmond)
　89 239
Minnie **89** 311
Minnie LaVerne **89** 232
　233
Miriam **88** 361
Miriam K. (Sheldon)
　89 112
Moine **89** 311
Molly **88** 361 364 365 **108**
　121 **119** 187
Monvilla A. (Hazeltine)
　89 234
Myra Philinda (Lewis)
　89 19 235
Myron **89** 315
Myron Burvillus **89** 118
Myrtie Avanelle **89** 235
Nabby **89** 11
Nancy **88** 372 **89** 10 29 32
　325 **113** 33 40 **126** 64
Nancy (Conant) **89** 325
Nancy (Manning) **89** 28
　94 290
Nancy Ann **89** 312
Nancy Deborah (Taft)
　89 324
Nancy Ellen **89** 117
Nancy Jane **89** 116 319
Nancy M. **88** 374
Nancy Manning **89** 31
　93 381
Nancy W. (Bliss) (Root)
　89 226
Nathan **88** 365 368 **89** 12
　13 15 23 102 103 105 106
　109 323 **145** 38 306
Nathan Cicero **89** 231
Nathan Ellis **89** 324
Nathaniel **88** 261 **89** 29
　325
Nathaniel James **89** 325
Navillah **89** 116

LAZELL *cont'd*
Nehemiah **88** 369
Nell Eveline (Bingham)
　(Tompkins) **89** 232
Nellie **89** 226
Nellie (Dugan) **89** 316
Nellie Blanche **89** 116
Nellie Lovisa **89** 233
Nellie May (Parker)
　89 235
Nellie Vaill **89** 321
Nelson **89** 23 33
Nora (McCutcheon)
　89 318
Norman Azariah **89** 22 23
Odell Eugene **89** 33
Olive **88** 359 369 **89** 32
Olive (Aldrich) **89** 224
Olive (Brooks) **89** 236
Olive (Cadwell) **89** 19 235
Olive (Harrington)
　(Brooks) **89** 22
Olive (Taylor) **89** 20
Olive Elizabeth **89** 236
Olive Martha (Morton)
　(Knight) **89** 119
Olive Matilda (Bouton)
　89 232
Olive May **89** 114
Olive Metcalf **89** 120
Olive Swift (Foster)
　89 114
Oliver Milton **89** 110
Olivia **88** 373
Ophelia (Blumhardt)
　89 240
Ophelia Adelaide **89** 320
Ophelia Bard **89** 18
Orpha **89** 239
Oscar Adams **89** 102
Oscar Warren **89** 105
Othello Jay **89** 106
Othniel **88** 264 366
Otis Johnson **89** 106
Pamela **75** 307
Pamelia **89** 17 236
Pascall **89** 111 112
Patience **88** 261 262
Patience (Delano) **88** 261
Patience (Jones) **88** 359
Patty **88** 365
Patty Chellous (Bingham)
　89 312
Paul **89** 120
Pauline Lanpher **89** 113
Pearl A. **89** 115
Peggy **88** 366
Penelope **89** 110
Percy **89** 105
Perez F. **89** 115
Person Cheney **89** 319
　102 231
Phebe **88** 258 259 372
Phebe (Hall) **89** 325
Phebe Ann **89** 119
Phebe Jeanette (Parker)
　89 24
Philip **88** 365 **89** 17 18
Philip Bradford **89** 31
　93 381
Polly **88** 364 371 375 376

LAZELL *cont'd*
89 11
Polly (Lambkins) **89** 21
Polly (Phillips) **89** 236
Porter **89** 224 225
Prince **88** 363
Priscilla **88** 372 **89** 119 228
Priscilla Pendleton
　89 120
Prosher **89** 231
Prudence **88** 375
Rachel **88** 360 368 **89** 12
　108 185
Rachel (Lincoln) **88** 260
　106 230
Rachel (Stafford) **89** 231
Ralph **89** 22 23 316
Ralph W. **89** 316
Raymond Briggs **89** 120
Raymond Haskell **89** 316
Rebecca **89** 104 324
Rebecca (Haws) **89** 324
Reuben **88** 372 **89** 226
Reuben Aldrich **89** 225
Reuben Sherman **89** 224
Rhoda **89** 102
Richard **112** 157 **113** 236
Richard Bradford **89** 30
Richard Otis **89** 224 226
Robert **88** 365 371 **89** 17
　19 115 235 313
Robert Blaine **89** 314
Robert Carl **89** 103
Robert Deane **89** 320
Robert Elwell **89** 119
Roscoe David **89** 116
Roscoe Elwell **89** 119
Rosewel **108** 57
Rosilla Cross **89** 120
Rosilla Sophronia
　(Maker) **89** 117
Roxanna **75** 308 **89** 15 17
　18 227 236
Roxanna (Billings)
　(Saxton) (Ketcham)
　105 153
Roxanna (Coleman)
　89 227
Roxanna (Kelly) **89** 310
Roxanna (Pike) **89** 106
Roxanna Olinda **89** 18
Roy **89** 105
Royal Carter **89** 19
Ruby (McLain) **89** 105
Rufus **88** 364 373 **89** 230
Ruhamah (Philbrook)
　88 371
Russell **88** 372
Ruth **65** 114 **88** 258 362
　369 370 **89** 30 237 **90**
　316 **91** 16 **95** 199
Ruth (Lovett) **88** 361
Ruth (Nutter) **88** 369
Ruth (Whitman) **89** 28
Ruth Cordelia **89** 32
Ruth Field **89** 235
Rutha **88** 369
Ruthy **90** 316
Sabrina **89** 10
Sabrina Jane Noble
　(Greeley) **89** 114

LAZELL *cont'd*
Sally **88** 368 373 **89** 111 112
Sally (Morse) **89** 32
Sally (Sherman) **89** 224
Sally (Warren) **90** 237
Sally Hall **89** 240
Salome **89** 12
Samaria **89** 224 225
Samuel **88** 257 264 359 360 368
Samuel Crabtree **89** 120
Samuel Hubbard **89** 325
Samuel Mills **89** 29 30
Sanford Monroe **89** 119
Sarah **88** 258 259 263-265 360 366 373 375 **89** 13 20 110 115 120 **121** 280
Sarah (Alden) **88** 373
Sarah (Baker) (Freeman) **89** 120
Sarah (Bayley) **90** 390
Sarah (Duncan) **89** 29
Sarah (Hersey) **89** 16
Sarah (Hobbie) **88** 367
Sarah (Jacob) **88** 360
Sarah (Noble) **89** 112
Sarah (Payson) **89** 119
Sarah (Sherman) (Kingman) **88** 367
Sarah (Stocking) **89** 19
Sarah (Sweetland) **89** 117
Sarah (Warner) **89** 103
Sarah (Warren) **89** 113
Sarah Ann **89** 227
Sarah Ann (Skinner) **89** 316
Sarah Caroline **89** 310
Sarah E. (Crane) **89** 113
Sarah Elizabeth (Sickels) **89** 225
Sarah Ella **89** 118
Sarah Ellen **89** 19 225 235
Sarah Emma (Wight) **89** 316
Sarah Jane **89** 18 224-226
Sarah Jane (Cloud) **89** 311
Sarah Jane (Mitten) **89** 311
Sarah Jane (Neil) **89** 227
Sarah Jane (Sargent) **89** 316
Sarah Jane (Tuttle) **89** 315
Sarah Louisa **89** 237
Sarah Maria **89** 104 114
Sarah Maria (White) **89** 316
Sarah Marinda (Bradford) **89** 231
Selden Conant **89** 321
Sherrille Ellen **89** 313
Sidney Darrah **89** 30
Sidney Ephraim **89** 232
Sidney Locock **89** 30
Silas **88** 375
Silence **88** 359
Silence (Tower) **88** 359
Silvey **88** 361
Simon **88** 259 262 263 **121** 274

LAZELL *cont'd*
Sina Strobridge (Smith) **89** 234
Slade **89** 239
Smith **89** 316
Sophia **89** 237
Sophia Caton (Thurber) **89** 108
Sophia Caton Thurber **89** 109
Sophia Stone **89** 108
Sophia Willaims **89** 325
Spencer **89** 236
Stanley Parker **89** 24
Stephen **88** 257 259 **89** 24 **121** 106
Stephen Henry **89** 24
Stillman Harding **89** 102 105
Sullivan **89** 107
Sumner Curtis **89** 105
Sumner Wheelock **89** 315 317
Susan **89** 12 17 **91** 31
Susan (Burnham) **88** 370 **90** 329 **91** 19
Susan Adelaide **89** 118
Susan E. (Winkley) **89** 29
Susan Elizabeth **89** 25
Susan Ella (Whitten) **89** 115
Susan Jennette (Barrows) **89** 317
Susan Maria **77** 183
Susan Matilda **89** 27
Susan Sweetland **89** 119
Susanna **88** 358 366 373 **89** 11 16 **133** 41
Susanna (Adlington) **89** 327
Susanna (Pratt) **88** 373 **105** 307 **136** 25
Susanna (Swan) **88** 369
Susanna (Walden) **88** 366
Susie Irena **89** 27
Sylvanus **88** 365 **89** 10 11
Sylvia (Tremaine) **89** 314
Tabitha **88** 361 376
Tabitha (Chadwick) **89** 227
Tabitha (Warren) **88** 374
Terressa Elizabeth (Gillett) **89** 240
Thaddeus Pease **89** 319
Thankful (Irish) **89** 23
Theodore Franklin **89** 234
Theodore Lyman **89** 113 114
Theodore S. **56** 414 **60** 186 **92** 302 **94** 201 **142** 141
Theodore Studley **57** xxxi **59** vii **63** 185 **88** 257 358 **89** 10 102 224 309 323 **90** 124 401 **95** 74 **96** 150 154 **106** 222 230 **107** 138
Thirza (Campbell) **89** 309
Thirza Ann **89** 310
Thomas **88** 226 257 258 261 358 361 368 370 **89**

LAZELL *cont'd*
16 20 102 239 **119** 90 **121** 25
Thurber Houghton **89** 104
Timothy **89** 28 29
Tryphoza (Johnson) **89** 103 106
Uriah **89** 232
Uriah Ellis **89** 233
Ursula Clarissa **89** 230
Vermelia Agnes **89** 319
Viola Martha (Guiett) **89** 240
Virginia (DuComb) **89** 323
Virginia Rosa **89** 113
Vivian Gladys **89** 317
Waitstill (Dunham) **88** 361
Wallace Alphonzo **89** 315
Walter Alvin **89** 317
Walter Curtis **89** 105
Walter Raleigh **89** 33
Warren **88** 368 **89** 102 107 108 111 231 324
Warren Daniel **89** 232
Warren Ellis **89** 108 109
Warren Glenn **89** 105
Warren Henry **89** 228
Warren Mason **89** 319
Warren Nelson **89** 103
Warren Stuart **89** 310
Washburn **88** 372
Waterman **88** 375 **89** 233
Wealthy Ann (Winsor) **89** 235
Webster Stoughton **89** 320
Wheeler Adelmer **89** 118
Wilbert Bernard **89** 117
Wilfred H. **89** 120
Willard **89** 239
Willard Smith **89** 316
William **73** 131 **88** 263 364 371-373 375 **89** 14 24 25 116 239 **104** 160 **107** 271
William Arthur **89** 114 312
William Bradford **89** 32
William Duncan **89** 29
William Dupree **89** 227
William E. **89** 225
William Edwin **89** 229
William Franklin **89** 229
William Frederick **89** 234
William Hayden **89** 118
William Henry **89** 15 17 234 311
William Henry Harrison **89** 314
William Hixon **89** 227
William Hobart **89** 112
William Lewis **89** 118
William Marcellus **89** 119
William Nelson **89** 234
William Penn **89** 224 225
William Sears **89** 103
William Vaill **89** 321
Willis Edgar **89** 108

LAZELL *cont'd*
Winifred Weld
  (Batchelder) **89** 319 **102**
  116 230 **103** 125
Winnie Josephine **89** 317
Zachariah **89** 25
Zana **104** 160
Zenas **88** 364 374-376
LAZENBY
Bertha Mariah **90** 136
Charles **104** 175
Ellen (Penrose) **117** 207
Henry **117** 207
LAZINBY William **64** 114
LA ZOUCHE
Alan **108** 174
Dorothy **108** 177
Eudo **108** 174 **142** 232
Milicent **108** 175
Philip **142** 235 236
Richard **108** 177
William **108** 174
LE-HA Richard **122** 230
LEA —— **107** 154
____ (Fuller) **129** 86
____ (Woodworth) **133** 71
Ezra **144** 43
James Harold (Mrs.)
  107 133
James Henry **53** 130 **54**
  vii 116 188 325 336 **55**
  vii xxix 95 116 131 230
  231 239 331 432 **56** vii
  xxiii 84 181 196 213 308
  402 **59** x xxvii xli 48
  101 172 228 320 321 397
  60 xxxiv xliv **148** 59
John **107** 190
Katharine **110** 261
Mary (Mathers) **98** 345
Peter **107** 45
Robert **55** 96 **128** 69
Susanna **107** 241
William **129** 44
LEABERRY
Ann (White) **100** 299
William **100** 299
LEABORNE Hester **65** 93
LEACH Leache - *see also*
  Leech
—— **53** 28 **105** 150
  120 218
— Master **85** 25
— Mr. **54** 96 **56** 251
  71 117
— Widow **66** 257
____ (Bryant) **113** 140
A. E. **74** 318
Aaron A. **89** 206
Abbie J. (Bowden)
  123 153
Abigail **62** 47 **81** 429 **124**
  152 **131** 195
Abigail (Nichols) **109** 12
Abigail H. **131** 199
Abner **58** 142
Abraham **74** 62
Adoniram **124** 152
Adoniram Judson
  131 198
Agnes **66** 245 246

LEACH *cont'd*
Alice **53** 28 **63** 169 **65** 174
  102 240 **105** 150 **115**
  227 **119** 67
Alice (Freeman) **115** 65
Alice Belle **81** 96
Alice P. **122** 72 234
Alicia Minerva **82** 237
Almira **119** 229
Amos **74** 62
Andrew **89** 289 **122** 72
Andrew D. **123** 153
Andrew F. **123** 153
Ann **62** 38 **73** 262
Anna **88** 65 **137** 27
Anne **75** 142
Anne (Nokes) **105** 150
Anne E. **131** 197
Annie Adele **78** 91
Asa **122** 133
Augusta **83** 65
Augustin K. **131** 198
Backus **124** 152 153 **131**
  195 197 198
Beatrice Josie **105** 150
Benjamin **73** 141 **74** 318
  76 3 **82** 290 292 **94** 245
  288 **125** 202
Bethiah **74** 62
Bethiah (Hayward) **124**
  152 **131** 198
Betsey **60** 334
Betsey (Bray) **109** 12 109
Betsey (Humphrey)
  133 308
Betsey C. **114** 136
Betsey C. (Parker) **114** 137
Betsey Hill **74** 210
Caleb **53** 315
Caroline **131** 196
Caroline Alexandra
  (Phelps) **105** 150
Caroline Eastman **77** 241
Catherine **74** 210 **122** 133
  131 196
Catherine (Ellis) **122** 133
Charity **81** 429
Charles **78** 408 **133** 308
  140 162
Charles E. **72** 204
Charles W. **80** 110
Chloe (Shattuck) **105** 150
Chloe H. **131** 199
Clarissa **74** 62 **98** 108
  124 152
Clarissa (Leach) **124** 152
Clement **131** 199
Cordelia C. **131** 197
Cuthbert **94** 9 17 **111** 198
Daniel **80** 174
David **70** liii **116** 20
  134 141
Deborah **62** 42
Deborah (Bowman)
  89 289
Deborah (Webster)
  104 62
Dinah **51** 223
Donald Frederick **95** 116
Dorcas **88** 65 155 248
Dorothy **111** 198

LEACH *cont'd*
Dorothy Westgate
  142 397
Douglas Edward **113** 80
Draden **73** 231
Ebenezer **62** 46 **122** 133
Edith Emma **105** 150
Edmund S. **72** 204
Edward **74** 62 **98** 170 286
  111 198
Edward D. **131** 196
Edward H. **90** 234
Elijah **64** 212 **88** 65
Eliphalet **52** 368
Elisha **78** 379
Elisha Ely **78** 251
Eliza **78** 310 **81** 429 **82**
  287 292 301 **89** 206 **117**
  222
Eliza Ann **74** 298
Elizabeth **54** 351 **62** 37 **74**
  318 **81** 429 445 **82** 282
  292 **89** 206 **109** 227 **113**
  229 **121** 252
Elizabeth (Gates) **121** 252
Elizabeth Allen **100** 143
Elizabeth Cheever **76** 3 **81**
  455 **94** 288
Elizabeth Johnson **73** 228
Elizabeth M. **72** 204 **97**
  397 **98** 97
Elizabeth May **79** 203
Elizabeth R. **78** 91
Ella **72** 204
Ella H. Brace **89** 206
Ella Maria **132** 240
Emeline **117** 286
Emily A. **75** 103
Emma L. (Macmanimon)
  105 150
Enoch **124** 152 **131** 195
Ephraim **70** 166 **105** 150
  124 152 **131** 195-197
Esther **63** 174 **115** 215
Eugenia **77** 216
Eunice **81** 191 **88** 65
  122 133
Eva Mae **105** 128
Eveline Tuck **96** 394
F. **91** 327
F. Phelps **60** 183 186 190
  80 337 **88** 208
F. R. **95** 116
Fanny **94** 245
Fayette Phelps **76** ix xxi
  78 337 450 **79** 224 **105**
  117 132 149 150
Florence Dexter **92** 62
Frances M. **74** 296
Frank Willing **52** 79 374
  71 369 **116** 237
Fred P. **74** 318
Frederick I. **83** 434 **84** 20
Gaylord Platt **95** 116
George **97** 145
Giles **81** 356 **102** 240 **105**
  150 **128** 281
Gilson **60** 334
Grace **74** 208
Grace M. **117** 293
Granville **111** 272

LEACH *cont'd*
Hannah **51** 318 319 **56** 258
  61 333 334 **62** 35 36 41
  100 149 **105** 150 **117**
  140 **125** 292
Hannah (Raynsford)
  139 303
Hannah Maria **75** 207
Harold A. **117** 293
Harold Bancroft **95** 116
Harriet Byron **89** 289
Hart **80** 174
Hattie Frelove **89** 242
Hazel May **105** 150
Hendrick (Mrs.) **82** 125
  237
Henrietta (Baldwin)
  131 199
Henrietta M. (Smith) **83**
  434 **84** 20
Henry **74** 210 **90** 239 **91** 16
  138 321
Henry H. **131** 198
Hepzibah **78** 251
Hester **89** 206
Hester (Goodier) **89** 206
Hiram **109** 12 **110** 111
Horace Brayton **105** 149
  150
Horatio **131** 198
Hubbard **59** 287
Huldah **88** 365 **89** 19 **124**
  152 153 **131** 195 197 198
Ichabod **120** 135 **124** 152
  131 195-197
Ida Estelle **74** 309
Irene **78** 379
Irving L. **74** 309
Isaac **74** 62
Isaac B. **131** 196
Isabella **111** 189
Isobell McIntosh
  (Knowles) **88** 129
J. **95** 27
J. Granville **52** 358 **61** 225
  141 19
Jacob **89** 206 **109** 227
James **51** 60 **62** 287 **63** 28
  73 151 **81** 429 **88** 323
  95 317 **105** 211 **115** 65
  117 294 **131** 199
James Edward **62** 213
Jane **69** 206
Jane (Nichols) **110** 111
Janet W. **72** 204
Jemima Harris **89** 206
Jennie Richie **95** 317
Jerathmael **124** 152
  131 195
Jeremiah **88** 65
Jeremy **52** 137
Joan (Jacks) **144** 34
John **51** 465 **52** 14 **56** 60
  251 252 258 410 **57** 384
  60 331 **62** 34 36 40 **64**
  227 **73** 263 **74** 318 **76**
  116 122 127 **77** 84 **79**
  208 **80** 315 **81** 429 **82** 45
  287 292 **85** 33 314 **88** 65
  129 155 248 331 **97** 274
  98 107 286 **102** 240 **104**

LEACH *cont'd*
  202 203 **105** 112 150 211
  109 206 227 **115** 227
  140 162
John H. **131** 196
Jonathan Lyman **74** 62
Jos **75** 220
Joseph **56** 252 **62** 37 **65**
  148 **74** 62 63 **75** 104 **88**
  62 65 **97** 265 **105** 211
Joseph Smallidge **78** 89
Josiah **81** 445 **121** 252
Josiah F. **75** 207
Josiah Granville **53** 142
  56 412 **57** xxxi **58** 209
  409 **60** 214 **62** 388 **63**
  304 **65** xxxiii 92 **77**
  xxxviii **78** 89-91 **109** 113
  116 237
Josie L. (Brown) **105** 150
Julia **118** 245
Julia (Godfrey) **127** 101
Katharine **63** 173 **111** 198
Lancelott **111** 197
Laura **131** 199
Lawrence **60** 186 **78** 89
  450 **79** 224 **80** 337 **105**
  150 **109** 227 **131** 199
Leeman Robinson **95** 116
Lenny **75** 103
Lester **106** 108
Levi **74** 264
Lewis L. **131** 196
Libeus **94** 245
Lois **94** 245
Lorenzo D. **69** 206
Lottie E. (Martin) **105** 150
Lottie Lydia **105** 150
Louisa **121** 267
Lowena **74** 295
Lucina **79** 121
Lucius W. **74** 318
Lucy **82** 290 292 **116** 136
Luke **94** 245
Luna **74** 318
Lydia **56** 202 **57** 417 **74**
  264 318 **125** 288 **126**
  256 **128** 20
Lydia (Platt) **95** 116
M. Atherton **82** 229
Manasseh **78** 379 **128** 20
  131 199
Margaret **52** 135 **73** 136
  114 187
Margaret (Starr) **94** 245
Maria **54** cxli **92** 86
Maria (Black) **95** 317
Marie **111** 198
Mark **81** 445
Martha **62** 35 **76** 116 122
  127
Mary **51** 466 **56** 410 **57** 384
  61 332 334 **62** 34 36 37
  43 **63** 173 344 **73** 225 **74**
  63 173 **81** 445 **97** 129 **98**
  286 **101** 62 **109** 227 **111**
  197 **115** 320 **116** 141
  124 152 **131** 128
Mary (Keith) **94** 245
Mary (Powers) **89** 289
Mary (Starr) **94** 245

LEACH *cont'd*
Mary (Sumner) **124** 152
Mary Ann **76** lxxi **111** 314
Mary Atherton **100** 47
Mary E. **89** 206
Mary Eveline (Gaylord)
  95 116
Mary H. **125** 181
Mary Jane **108** 279
Mary K. **74** 173
Matilda **63** 89 **114** 206
  131 196 197
Matilda B. **131** 196
May Atherton **84** 105 106
  184 190 **100** 114 **101**
  165
Mehitable **113** 140
Mela **56** 252
Mercy **62** 35
Mercy (Bryant) **88** 365
Meredith Biddle **78** 91
Miles Strong **109** 227
Miraetta **131** 198
Myra **95** 331
N. W. **91** 327
Naamah **74** 128
Nathaniel **54** 408 409 **66**
  37 **105** 211 **140** 162
Nehemiah **88** 365 **113** 140
Nicholas **66** 257
Olive **63** 170 **75** 104 **82** 290
  292 **111** 230 **115** 305
  120 144
Olive (Carver) **88** 323
Olivia (Moulton) **89** 289
Orisa (Fanton) **105** 150
P. C. **75** 101
Palmer C. **74** 318
Paul **62** 38
Peletiah **105** 211
Penelope **124** 152 **131** 197
Penelope (Standish)
  (Cobb) **124** 152 **131** 195
Penelope Standish
  131 196
Philip **81** 429
Polly **59** 286 **78** 441 **103**
  239 **115** 320 **125** 221
Priscilla **72** 292
R. **61** 333
Rachel **81** 356 **104** 202-204
  148 339
Rachel (Chubbuck)
  131 198
Rachel A. (Butler) **123** 153
Rachel Gilbert **81** 355 356
Rebecca (Swan) **128** 281
Rebecca (Whiting) **88** 331
Rebecca S. **74** 63
Richard **61** 333 334 **62** 34
  41-44 46 47 **75** 142 **78**
  251 379 **109** 227 **125** 73
  136 361
Richard E. **99** 195
Robert **57** 384 **62** 47
  131 128
Robert H. (Mrs.) **81** 96
Robert K. **117** 290
Rosabella Almyra
  109 227
Rosanna (Alford) **124** 152

LEACH *cont'd*
Rosylind (Crane) **91** 387
Royal **74** 173
Rufus **91** 387
Ruth **57** 384 **62** 46 **88** 65
  248
Ruth M. **92** 333
S. Jane **75** 104
Sally **59** 287 **95** 274
Sally (Conant) **131** 195
Samuel **52** 137 **64** 301 **81**
  445 **82** 45 **117** 61
Sarah **53** 315 **57** 384 **62** 34
  46 **64** 212 **77** 84 **81** 429
  88 62 155 **100** 143
Sarah (Conant) **124** 152
  153
Sarah (Fuller) **125** 73
  136 361
Sarah (Talburt) **131** 199
Sarah Ann **119** 226 228
Sarah Ann (Hutchins)
  119 143
Seth **58** 142
Simon **83** 65
Solomon **105** 150
Sophia **78** 89
Sophia (Hawley) **105** 150
Stephen **82** 290 292
Susan (Cleever) **94** 288
Susan (Whipple) **98** 286
Susan Sophia **74** 309
  78 41
Susanna **51** 465 **73** 135
  79 339 **137** 218
Sylvanus **66** 20
Tabitha **73** 221
Terressa Chloe **131** 199
Tertius **105** 150
Tertius Hawley **105** 150
Thomas **58** 142 **72** 52 **73**
  150 261 **97** 265 272 **110**
  262 **117** 61 **131** 199 **140**
  162
Tobias **125** 96
Toby **58** 409
Tryphena (Grey) **98** 107
Virlinda **73** 150
Willfride **111** 198
William **52** 68 69 **66** 113
  123 124 **73** 266 **78** 316
  88 65 **94** 245 **100** 143
  104 62 202 203 **109** 12
  109 **116** 136 **119** 143
  120 144 **140** 162 **144** 34
William B. **79** 121
William Henry Harrison
  131 197
Willis E. **72** 204
Wilmon Whilldin **78** 91
Winifred **74** 208
Zachariah **81** 429 445
Zachery **54** 351
Zebulon **74** 318 **75** 103
Zenas C. **131** 196
Ziba (Cloyes) **131** 198
LEACHLAND Agnes **81**
  322 487 **82** 64
Alice **81** 320-323 **82** 64 65
Ambrose **81** 322 **82** 64
Ann **81** 322

LEACHLAND *cont'd*
Anne **81** 321 **82** 64
Annes **81** 322 323 **82** 64 65
Edward **81** 321 **82** 64
Eleanor **81** 321 322 **82** 64
Emme **81** 321
Frances **81** 321 486 **82** 64
Isabel **82** 63
Jane **81** 321 322 **82** 65
Joan **81** 321 322 487 **82** 63
  64
John **81** 322 486 487 **82** 63
  64
Lawrence **81** 322 323
  82 64
Lucy **81** 322 **82** 64
Margaret **81** 320-323 488
  491 **82** 57 63-65 **110** 270
Nicholas **81** 486 487 **82** 63
Robert **81** 322 **82** 64 65
Roger **81** 320-322 488 **82**
  57 63 65
Sarah **82** 65
Thomas **81** 320-323 487
  82 64 65 **110** 193
Walter **81** 487
William **81** 321 322 486
  82 64 65
LEACOCK
Arthur Gordner **97**
  158 **102** 113 **103** 124
LEAD
Elizabeth M. **116** 97
LEADAM I. S. **142** 233
  145 17
LEADBETTER Leadbeater
  Ledbetter Ledebetter
Benjamin F. **103** 235
Danville **70** 154
Deliverance **54** 213 **75**
  146 148 151 **93** 368
Ernest **147** 67
Eunice **103** 236
Evaline **103** 236
Hannah (Carver) (Smith)
  88 329
Henry **52** 339 **58** 28 **60** 38
  68 215 216 **75** 146 148
Increase **68** 217
Incress **144** 218
Jane **78** 398
John **105** 206
Lewis **89** 118
Lucinda (Heald) **103** 235
Luther **107** 231
Margaret (Tolman)
  89 118
Maria E. **107** 231
Mary **90** 336
Mary Ann **103** 235
Mary Jean **147** 64
Matilda Adaline **89** 118
Obadiah Swift **68** 216
Relief **52** 339
Reuben **88** 329
Roy C. **120** 76
Ruth **75** 145
Ruth (Litchfield) **147** 67
Sarah **58** 27 28 **75** 146 148
  151
Susanna **68** 215

LEADER —— **71** 89
Abigail **54** 350
John **51** 284 **54** 350
Rebecca **54** 350
Richard **94** 358 **100** 222
Robert Eadon **110** 85
Ruth **54** 350
Samuel **54** 350
Susan **67** 78
Thomas **54** 350 **67** 78
  68 72
LEADS Samuel **63** 83
LEAFIELD
Elizabeth **64** 344
Rob **64** 254
LEAFY — Mrs. **63** 280
LEAGER
Abraham **69** 354 355
Ann **69** 355
Ann (Blake) **134** 48 50
Anne **69** 356
Bethiah **69** 355 356 **134** 48
  50 51
Bethra **134** 48 50 51
Elizabeth **69** 355 356
Hannah **69** 355 356
Isaac **69** 354 355
Jacob **69** 354-357 **134** 48
  50 51 **143** 310
James **69** 354 355
Margaret **69** 354 355
Mary **69** 354 355
Sarah **69** 354 355
Sebastian **69** 355
Solomon **69** 356
LEAGET
Nathaniel **55** 141
LEAGUE
Charles **68** 255
Daisy **68** 255
Nellie **68** 255
LEAH — Mrs. **71** 181
— Rev. **102** 289
LEAHY
Alice Comack **90** 133
David **88** 330
Elizabeth (Thompson)
  88 330
Louisa **126** 80
LEAKE Leak
____ (Mountford) **112** 159
Agnes S. (Osborn)
  109 189
Andrew **112** 158
Anna (White) **109** 189
Anne **112** 158 159
Caroline Augusta
  (Richards) **109** 188
Catherine (Tillinghast)
  109 189
Catherine Yates **109** 189
Charles Tillinghast
  109 189
Christian **54** 142
Elizabeth **54** 142 **112** 158
Elizabeth C. **109** 189
Frederic D. **109** 188
Godfrey W. **109** 189
Hannah (Morrow)
  109 189

LEAKE *cont'd*
Hannah (Quintard)
 109 188
Horace **109** 189
Isaac Quintard **109** 188
 189
Joan **71** 167
John **54** 142 **71** 169
 109 188
John Shipman **109** 189
John W. **109** 188
Julia **109** 189
Julia (Johnson) **109** 188
Lucretia **109** 189
Lydia W. (Edmunds)
 109 189
Marie **112** 159
Mary **51** 134
Nathaniel **112** 158 159
Peggy **109** 188
Penelope **98** 41
Rebecca **112** 158 159
Robert (Earl Scarsdale)
 51 134
S. Martin **104** 258
Sarah **71** 167 169 **112** 159
Saray **112** 158
Simeon Johnson **109** 189
Stephen Martin **54** 142 **96**
 95 **104** 257
Thomas **143** 259
William D. **109** 189
LEAKYE John **82** 61
LEAL Elizabeth G. (Hoga-
 boom) **92** 170
J. **92** 170
Lealand *see* Leland
LEALER Patrick **60** 27
LEALON Margaret **115** 42
LEAMAN
 Catherine A. **128** 97
LEAMING
 Aaron **148** 345-347
 Christopher **148** 346
 Elizabeth **148** 347
 Elizabeth (Leaming)
 148 347
 Esther (Burnet) **148** 346
 George **133** 265
 Hester (Burnet) **148** 346
 Jane **57** 136
 Jeremiah **76** 131 **145** 142
 148 347
 Juliet (Mallery) **133** 264
 Lydia (Parsons) (Shaw)
 148 345-347
 Matthias **148** 347
 Thomas **148** 347
LEAMON
 James S. **143** 171
LEAN Betsey M. **72** 104
LEANEAU
 Margaret **126** 288
Leanfear *see* Lamphear
LEANORD *see also*
 Leonard
 Elizabeth (Lyman)
 123 261
 Hannah **123** 259
 Lidiah **123** 259
 Mary **123** 258 262

LEANORD *cont'd*
 Rebecca **123** 260
 Sarah **123** 260 263
 Sarah (Scot) **123** 260
Leanred *see* Learned
LEAP Ellen **51** 200
LEAPER Ellen **70** 117
 Melchizedek **70** 115 117
 Percy Faraday **122** 6
LEAR
 — Mrs. **82** 45 **83** 34
 Alexander **81** 445 **135** 126
 Ann **82** 45
 Anna **68** 81
 Benjamin **81** 429
 Benjamin F. **121** 178
 Calvin Davis **83** 426 434
 Catherine **126** 145
 David **128** 311
 Deborah **81** 445
 Deliverance **82** 292 299
 Dennis **121** 177
 Edward **107** 307
 Eliza **124** 62
 Elizabeth **58** 227 234 **61** 83
 81 141 429 445 **82** 27
 285 292 298
 Esther **82** 289 292
 Hannah **81** 429 **82** 45 290
 292 412 **124** 61
 Jesse **117** 16
 John **68** 80 81 **81** 429 **82** 45
 111 210 **121** 179
 Joseph **82** 27
 Laura A. (Emery) **121** 177
 Lydia Smith (Coleman)
 83 426 434
 Margaret J. **121** 177
 Marinda **121** 180
 Martha **90** 109
 Mary **78** 421 **81** 445 **82** 45
 285 292 298 299
 Mary P. (Maxfield)
 121 178
 Mira A. (Nelson) **121** 179
 Nathaniel **81** 141 **97** 269
 Perly H. **121** 182
 Peter **92** 60
 Robena A. (Loudon)
 121 182
 Sally **124** 60
 Samuel **81** 141 445
 82 285 292
 Samuel Peverly **81** 141
 Sarah **135** 126
 Temperance **81** 141
 Tobias **58** 227 234 **61** 83
 81 141 445 **82** 45 292
 299 412
 Venus **82** 45
 Walker **81** 445 **82** 27 45
 285 292
 Walter **105** 114
 William **82** 45 **96** 224
 William H. **78** 422
LEARCHER
 John **127** 303
LEARES — Col. **69** 361
Learkins *see* Larkin
LEARMONTH John **65** 54
LEARN Lydia **87** 377

LEARNED Larnard
 Larned Learnard
 Leanred - *see also*
 Leonard
 —— **103** l
 — Capt. **65** 359
 — Col. **95** 65
 — Lieut. **54** 72 73 **65** 367
 — Mr. **63** 191
 Abigail **57** 304 **61** 132
 112 155
 Abigail (Pisco) **91** 263
 Abijah **76** lii **91** 263
 100 130
 Amos **113** 36
 Anna **114** 42
 Asa **68** lxxiv
 Benjamin **61** 132
 Benoni **57** 104 **76** lii **77**
 277 **88** 385
 Bezaleel **83** 378
 Caleb **114** 42
 Cate **83** 137
 Catherine **84** 412 **113** 36
 42
 Catherine (Rice) **84** 412
 Charles **61** xxxiii 105 **68**
 xvii xlii lxxiv
 Charles William **64** 69
 Charlotte **81** 169
 Chloe **72** 305
 Cornelia M. **96** 54
 Cynthia P. **75** 38
 David **83** 379
 Derby **75** 38
 Dorothy **52** 73 **57** 363
 84 414
 Dorothy (Barton) **84** 414
 Ebenezer **56** 75 **81** 169 **84**
 406 414 **86** 37 **95** 278
 114 203 **124** 169 172
 Ebenezer Turell **84** 452
 Edward **57** 304 **61** 132
 Eli **115** 53
 Elisha **77** 316
 Elizabeth **53** 376 **57** 55 58
 239 240 **61** 132 **77** 284
 78 231
 Ellen Douglas **51** 496 **54**
 70 164 **55** 420 440 **58**
 203 206 **65** 159 **72** 140
 116 98 99 **119** 89 **123**
 188 **147** 108
 Eunice Williams **108** 64
 Fanny **75** 101
 Francis Mason **76** xxx lii
 Gearfield **90** 46
 Grace **125** 106
 Hannah **61** 261 **63** 290 **64**
 34 **71** 262 **79** 47 **84** 4 **91**
 296 **104** 131 **109** 151
 114 42
 Hannah (White) **114** 41
 Hannah B. **126** 205
 Harriet Lovenia **76** lii
 Henry **83** 377 378
 Hepzibah **115** 53
 Isaac **53** 376 **57** 55 **68** lxxiv
 76 lii **124** 169 **136** 46
 James **62** 21 **79** 27
 Jane **131** 128

LEARNED *cont'd*
Jane (Evans) **125** 292
Jedediah **78** 231
Jeremiah **84** 414
Joel **60** 193 **91** 392
John **60** 193 **64** 52 **72** 305
  125 102 **135** 340
John A. **75** 101 **76** 86
John K. **78** 302
Jonas **68** lxxiv
Jonathan **114** 41 42
Joseph **114** 42
Joseph Gay Eaton **53** 373
  376
Joshua **77** 284 **83** 377
Josiah **84** 412
Judith **131** 128
Juli Ann **115** 53
Larissa **68** lxxiv
Lavina **111** 326
Lucia I. **75** 101
Lucien S. **88** 338
Lucinda H. **72** 306
Lucretia **88** 334
Lucy **77** 293
Lucy S. (Lang) **88** 338
Lydia **60** 192 193 **67** 375
  78 415 **113** 38
Lydia (Haskell) **112** 155
Lyman **60** 193
Margaret **91** 392
Maria Lucinda Hoffman
  76 lii
Marion Dexter **63** 306
  64 201
Martha **52** 250 **125** 294
Martha / Patty
  (Townsend) **135** 340
Mary **52** 73 **57** 287 364 **60**
  193 **78** 231 407 **83** 376
  100 303 **111** 178 **125**
  107 **126** 221 **135** 340
Mary (Blake) **125** 102
Mary (Fanning) **88** 385
Mary Abby **79** 27
Mary Elizabeth **77** 181
Mary Jane (French) **90** 46
Mary Matilda (White)
  84 452
Mary White **84** 452
Merriam **126** 37
Miriam **83** 424
Miriam Ardelle **83** 424
  434
Moses **58** 241 **60** 192 193
  113 39
Nehemiah **113** 38
Oliver **79** 47
Oliver Sykes **72** 305 306
Parnel / Parney **114** 42
Patience **63** 88
Patty **56** 383
Prudence **83** 137 **112** 155
Rebecca **76** 86
Ruth **58** 241 **60** 192 193
  71 350
Samuel **60** 193 **77** 293 **79**
  41 **104** 131
Sarah **53** 376 **57** 55 104 **60**
  193 **69** 358 **79** 35 **131**
  121 **146** 368

LEARNED *cont'd*
Sarah Ball **72** 306
Sarah Miner **72** 305
Sarah Smith **81** 339
Silas **145** 353
Simon **93** 397 **100** 63
Sophia **115** 53
Susan **91** 392
Susanna **114** 42
Susanna (Willis) **114** 41
Tabitha **57** 104 105
Theophilus **63** 88
Thomas **60** 192 **76** lii **78**
  419 **114** 42
William **53** 373 376 **68**
  lxxiv **69** 358 **76** lii **83**
  137 **110** 148 **112** 155
  113 31 38 **114** 42 **125**
  292 **131** 19 128
William Law **53** 373 376
  54 xxxviii **69** 358 **114** 42
LEAROYD
Charles Henry **63** 214
John A. **86** 297
Sarah (Silvester) **86** 297
LEARSELL John **127** 304
LEARY — Widow **73** 312
Carrie M. **77** 179
Daniel **73** 312
Edmund O. **78** 186
Edward Francis (Mrs.)
  100 112
Evelyn **102** 124
George **75** xxiii 64 **97**
  287 382 **98** 145 149 **110**
  136
James **73** 312
James Daniel **97** 382
Jane **73** 312
John **74** 213
Julia Mary (Crofton)
  97 382
Katrine **68** 125
Mary A. (Lahm) **94** 387
Mary Cecelia (Fallon)
  97 382
Mary Jane **135** 159
Michael **61** 137
Minnie Frances **68** 125
Sarah **73** 312 **98** 298
Sydney **73** 312 **74** 185 187
Thomas **61** 137
LEAS Fay W. **86** 465
John **54** 190
LEASE
George I. **112** 281
Marian E. **124** 77
Rosa **77** xliv
LEASITER Adam **64** 340
John **64** 338
LEASK Alice **77** 57
LEASON Thomas **145** 362
Leath *see* Leathe
Leatham *see* Latham
LEATHBRIDGE
Jane **100** 304
LEATHE Leath
Eleanor **63** 246
Eleanor (Floyd) **132** 41
Elijah **58** 133
Francis **63** 246 **132** 40

LEATHE *cont'd*
Hepzibah **58** 133
James **58** 135
Jeptha **140** 68
John **63** 246 **132** 41
John W. **75** 211
Julia A. **72** 298
Mary **78** 301
Mary Jane **75** 211
Ruth **62** 150
Samuel **62** 150
Samuel H. (Mrs.) **73** 318
Sarah **63** 246 **94** 224
Sarah (Floyd) **132** 40
Sarah M. **75** 211
William M. **75** 211
Leathem *see* Latham
LEATHERBEE
Anna **90** 49
Charles W. **76** 13
Ella Duncan **66** lxxxiii
Ethel Brigham **59** xlvii **60**
  275 **62** 307
George Henry **66** lii lx
  lxxxiii
Harriet Gray **76** 13
Marjorie **85** 300
Mary Jane **66** lxxxiii
William Hault **66** lxxxiii
LEATHERGOUGH
John **64** 323
LEATHERHEAD
Margaret **108** 114
Rachel **108** 114
Zebulon **108** 114
LEATHERLAND
Sarah **53** 338
William **65** 174
LEATHERS
Abednego **61** 360 366
Abel **145** 363
Abigail **91** 304 **112** 230
Betsey (Rogers) **138** 322
Catherine **65** 219
Christian **144** 141
Edward **144** 141
Elijah **78** 399
Elizabeth **78** 184
Joanna B. **103** 43
Katharine **99** 54
Lucinda **76** 30
Mary **69** 222 **144** 141
Mary (Knight) **144** 138
  140 141
Miles **138** 322
Oliver **76** 30
Robert **144** 141
Rose Evalyn (Stephens)
  109 130
Sally **76** 32 **91** 16 **98** 136
Susanna **51** 461
William **144** 141
LEATHERWOOD
Mary (Stone) **135** 340
LEATHES
J. B. **117** 207
Margaret **117** 207
LEAVELL
Charlotte Henry
  112 320
Ullin W. (Mrs.) **112** 320

LEAVEN Hannah (Smith)
  97 223
Joseph **97** 223
LEAVENS Abel **51** 361
  Abigail **66** 129 339
  Barbara Briggs **102** 143
  Benjamin **107** 34
  Betsey **79** 139 **86** 32 45 46
  Calvin **64** 206
  Charles **106** 143 **134** 89
  Charles Henry **134** 89
  Clarissa **134** 281
  Darius **51** 361
  Dorothy **102** 143
  Elijah **78** 358 **106** 143
  Eliza Ann (Hyde) **134** 89
  Elizabeth **51** 361 **55** 224
    445
  Esther **66** 130 337
  Francis R. **79** 139
  George Davison **102** 143
  Hannah **52** 226
  Isaac **51** 361
  James **51** 361 **66** 339
  Jenny / Jennie Sherman
    (Briggs) **102** 62 129 143
  Jerusha **67** 373
  John **51** 361 **55** 224 445
    58 323 **65** 148 **86** 32
    106 143
  Joseph **65** 149 **69** 90
    106 143
  Judith **67** 373 **87** 202
  Louisa Ann **106** 143
  Lucy **64** 206
  Mary **67** 375
  Noah **106** 143
  Peter **51** 361
  Philo French **51** 361 **55**
    445 446 **58** 323 **59** xliv
  Rowland **52** 226
  Ruth **78** 358
  Sophia A. **79** 139
  Thomas **65** 50
  Zerviah **57** 364
LEAVENWORTH
  Abel **56** 161 **71** 355
  Abel E. **123** 99
  Abel E. (Mrs.) **123** 99
  Abigail **72** 78
  Alice **72** 78
  Andrew **145** 246
  Anna **71** 355
  Betsey **71** 353
  Burk **71** 355
  Calvin **75** 196
  Catherine **58** 184
  Charlotte **71** 355
  Clarence **123** 101
  Coman **116** 235
  David **72** 77
  Deborah **72** 78
  Dorman **71** 355 **72** 78
  E. S. **123** 101
  Ebenezer **84** 140
  Edmund **72** 78
  Elihu **72** 77
  Eliza **92** 186
  Franklin **80** 55
  Gideon **72** 77 78
  Grace **72** 78 **75** 177

LEAVENWORTH *cont'd*
  Harriet **79** 169
  Jesse **58** 184
  John **72** 78 **75** 177 **76** 149
  Lois **72** 78
  Lucy **71** 355
  Lydia **56** 161 **71** 355
  M. **110** 131
  Mark **58** 184
  Mark L. **79** 169
  Martin **72** 77
  Mary **72** 78 **102** 105
  Mary (Kimberly) **102** 105
  Meigs **71** 355
  Morse **72** 77 78
  Nathaniel **91** 206
  Olive **72** 77
  Phebe **72** 78 **75** 177
  Polly **84** 345 346
  Samuel Edgar **123** 101
  Sarah **72** 78
  Shelden **72** 77
  Sophia **75** 196
  Thomas **72** 78 **75** 177
    102 105
  Willie **123** 100
LEAVER Clarissa **91** 29 35
    134 281
  Damaris **62** 255
  James **90** 250 328 **91** 19
  Joseph **55** 375
  Judith **74** 254 **90** 250
  Lucy **55** 375
  Lydia **140** 210
  Mary **90** 333 **91** 27 **96** 147
    97 17 238 **106** 29
  Mary (Bean) **90** 328 **91** 19
  Olive **55** 376 **97** 20
  Olive (Hodsdon) **90** 315
  Orpha (Spears) **90** 250
  Prudence **62** 255 **87** 147
    102 306
  Sally **55** 375
  Sarah **74** 254 **97** 21 **142** 36
  Thomas **62** 255 **87** 147
  William **55** 376 **74** 254
    90 315 **142** 36
LEAVESLEY
  Thomas **60** 36
Leavett *see* Leavitt
LEAVEY
  Almira N. (Smith)
    101 32
  James E. C. **101** 32
LEAVIN Abigail **90** 315
LEAVITT Leavett Leavit
  — Col. **83** 34
  — Dr. **52** 118
  — Mr. **71** 117
  — Mrs. **78** 189
  — Widow **73** 67 68
  Abbie **121** 144
  Abiah **61** 340
  Abial **65** 355 **88** 259
  Abigail **59** 38 **61** 382 **65**
    114 341 **76** lxxxv **83** 34
    104 115 **115** 193 **121**
    269
  Abigail S. (Gilman)
    126 207
  Abigaill **121** 121

LEAVITT *cont'd*
  Abihail **72** 201
  Abijah **136** 33 37
  Abraham **103** 265 **121** 270
  Adeline **81** 153 263
  Albert **88** 150
  Alexander **90** 386
  Alice **59** 290
  Alice I. (Crowell) **86** 153
  Almira **81** 153 **86** 153
  Almira (Thompson)
    121 147
  Alpheus **97** 267 **118** 154
    155 **119** 226 **122** 72
  Alta Marie **93** 137
  Amelia Stiles **62** 270
    68 lxix
  Andrew **61** 382 **62** 27
  Ann **83** 23 25 **138** 111
  Ann (Brackett) **138** 110
    113
  Ann (Hussey) **138** 322
  Anna **59** 287 **73** 67 **111** 112
    115 **134** 294
  Anna (Stevens) **134** 294
  Anne M. **82** 171
  Annie **86** 154
  Aretas **90** 70
  Aretus **58** 33 **76** lxxxv
  Armina **119** 288
  Asa Sawyer **106** 108
  Asaph **60** 305 306 **121** 283
  Augustus **105** 299
  Azubah **77** 320
  Bathsheba **60** 305
  Bathshua (Hobart)
    121 116
  Benjamin **60** 296 **65** 82
    73 64 66 **76** lxxxv **91**
    126 327 **124** 290 291
  Benson **76** lxxxv
  Bersheba **111** 112
  Bert E. **81** 153
  Bert Elwin **86** 153
  Bethiah **115** 306
  Bethiah (Bragdon) **111** 19
  Betsey **65** 114 340 341 **90**
    227 **115** 309
  Betsey T. **105** 299
  Betty **63** 174 **90** 246
  Caleb **134** 279
  Caroline **91** 274
  Caroline (Sherman)
    91 274
  Caroline Elizabeth **91** 274
  Caroline Harriet **92** 40
  Caroline Sherman **91** 274
  Carr **92** 105
  Charles **73** 81
  Charles F. **83** 425 434
  Charles H. **71** 192 **100** 71
    327 340
  Charles Henry **91** 274 **99**
    147 **111** 76
  Charles M. **82** 171
  Charles W. **83** 183 186
  Christopher **76** 318
    87 360
  Church P. **103** 151
  Daniel **111** 19 112
  Daniel H. **122** 72 234

LEAVITT *cont'd*

Darel Noble (Mrs.) **109** 130

David **61** 340 **62** 147 **65** 148 **84** 97 **89** 186 **91** 274 **111** 112 148 **121** 277

David Charles **91** 274

David Franklin **91** 274

Dolle (McIntire) **115** 306

Dorothy **108** 154

Dorothy Frost **105** 299

Dudley **62** 277 **107** 313 **124** 291

Edgar **86** 153

Edmund **92** 281 314

Edward Webster **91** 275

Edwin Thomas **82** 171

Elijah **78** 400 **91** 274

Elise **91** 275

Elisha **85** 15 16 **93** 159

Eliza **58** 311 **124** 291

Eliza Payson **105** 299

Elizabeth **51** 460 **58** 138 338 **62** 27 **83** 231 **89** 186 **111** 19 316 317 **115** 60 **121** 17 120 273 **124** 291 **129** 85 **135** 74 **138** 110 111 113

Elizabeth (Atkinson) **97** 4

Elizabeth (Nelson) **135** 127

Elizabeth Hubbard **62** 272

Ella Gould **134** 279

Ellen Maria **91** 274

Elvira R. **105** 300

Emeline **81** 153 **83** 183

Emily Wilder **51** 307 447 **53** 129 **54** xxxvi 44 **55** xxix 114 131 448 **56** xxx **57** xxxi **58** xliii 323 **59** xli **60** xxxiv 102 188 **61** xxxiii **62** 96 200 306 **63** 14 **64** xxix **65** 95 **69** xxx **75** 185 **76** xxx lxxxv **77** xii **81** 371 **83** 280 290 **99** 183 **100** 79 **105** 199

Emma B. **120** 224

Ephraim **134** 232

Ephraim Merrill **105** 299

Eunice **82** 281

Everett J. **81** 153

Everett Joseph **86** 154

Fanny **81** 153 **86** 150 367

Fanny (Cole) **86** 153

Felix **60** 398

Foxwill **103** 264

Foxwill (Mrs.) **103** 264

Frances **81** 153

Frances (Hope) **111** 148

Frances Elizabeth (Tucker) **111** 148

Frances Hope (O'Brien) **111** 148

Francis **60** 308 **68** 74 77

Frank A. **114** 317

Franklin H. **91** 327

Franklin Samuel (Mrs.) **104** 144

Freegrace **61** 340 **62** 274

Gad **60** 339

LEAVITT *cont'd*

Gardiner Howland **75** xxiii 64 **81** 238 **82** 234 248 **84** 97

George B. **121** 147

George Edward **92** 40

George W. **90** 386

Georgia Ann (Sampson) **114** 317

Gideon **108** 154

Gladys (Carver) **83** 425 434

Grace **69** xxxv

Hannah **58** 122 **59** 289 **60** 306 **81** 153 **86** 116 154 **111** 112 116 118 **116** 138 **121** 11 109 115 213 **143** 138

Hannah (Seawards) **126** 144

Hannah P. **120** 140 215

Hannah Taylor **118** 191

Harriet **93** 346 **106** 108

Harriet (Bent) **91** 274

Harriet A. **91** 118

Hart **62** 272

Helen **106** 126

Helen L. **81** 153

Hezekiah **84** 254 **134** 138

Huldah **60** 339

Isaac **55** 26 29

Isabel **52** 28

Israel **58** 175 **63** 149 **105** 269 **106** 193 **121** 20 199 206

Jacintha **105** 299

Jacob **88** 150 **122** 281

Jael **121** 290

Jael (Hobart) **121** 287

Jairus **82** 280

James **58** 36 137 138 **65** 341 **71** 117 **81** 153 **97** 47 **117** 229 230 **138** 110 111 113

James O. **121** 144 145

Jane Huntington (Hatch) (Shepherd) **97** 47

Jane Whitney **90** 48

Jeremi **121** 216

Jeremiah **111** 19 40 **115** 140 **116** 132 295 **121** 18 287

Jeremy N. C. **105** 299

Jesse **88** 150

Joanna **125** 222

John **52** 28 **55** 26 29 **58** 29 34 124 **59** 286 **62** 295 **63** 174 **65** 355 **73** 72 **84** 97 **87** 97 **88** 259 **96** 97 **101** 55 **102** 234 **104** 246 **106** 108 **111** 148 **114** 48 **121** 19 113 116 121 201 278 **139** 131 **140** 68

John H. **59** xliv 229 **61** xxxiv **62** xxviii xxxii

John Lougee **118** 191

John S. **138** 322

Jonathan **57** 340 **58** 137-140 **59** 229 **62** 270-272 274 **68** lxix **73** 68 71 76 **79** 159 **90** 386 **92** 285

LEAVITT *cont'd*

295 **100** 254 **108** 154 **111** 116 **135** 127 **147** 182

Joseph **52** 434 **58** 32 **81** 153 **86** 153 154 **91** 327 **93** 345 346 **108** 154 **111** 19 **114** 48 **115** 59 306 **121** 208 287 **134** 294

Joseph Henry **79** 13

Joseph M. **58** 311

Joseph Melcher **71** 292

Joseph P. **126** 207

Josephine (Wells) **111** 149

Joshua **79** 309 **121** 271

Josiah **73** 64 65 **78** 67 **84** 97 **104** 242 246 **111** 148 **121** 103 199 204 **127** 190 **140** 162

Judith **105** 299

Judith (Hobart) **121** 287

Judith A. (Moulton) **121** 144 145

Julia **121** 19

Julia (Ellis) **91** 275

Julia M. (Cole) **86** 304

Katharine B. **81** 153

Katharine B. (Peverly) **86** 153 154

Katharine Peverly **81** 153

Laura M. **121** 307 **122** 150

Leonard **90** 386

Lester M. **83** 434 436

Lidy (Jackson) **121** 199

Loruhamah **58** 124

Louisa (Barnes) **86** 304

Louisa Augusta **71** 292 **76** xlvi

Lucy **82** 280 **111** 40

Lucy (Clark) **111** 148

Lucy Dunbar **82** 280

Lydia **55** 374 **63** 149 **83** 15 **105** 269 **116** 132 **118** 243 317

Lydia (Sanderson) **127** 190

Malvina **82** 171

Marden **86** 304

Margaret **55** 26 **82** 18 **86** 150 301 304 **121** 213

Margaret (Johnson) **111** 148 **121** 199

Margaret A. **109** 186

Margaret E. (Neal) **83** 434 436

Margery A. **85** 178 **95** 139 **96** 174 **97** 171-173 **98** 161-163 **99** 163-165 **100** 106

Margery Alberta **95** 146 160 162 **99** 145

Maria Clarissa (Lewis) **111** 148

Maria Holmes **62** 270

Maria Lewis **85** 199 **99** 254

Maria Osgood **79** 13

Martha **79** 36 **124** 300

Martin **88** 150 **144** 266

Mary **52** 434 **55** 25 26 29 **58** 175 **65** 114 **73** 76 **81**

LEAVITT *cont'd*
153 **82** 292 295 **90** 386
95 30 275 380 381 **110**
142 **114** 170 **115** 307
121 112 210 284 **134**
138 232 **136** 32
Mary (Baker) **134** 279
Mary (Beal) **134** 138
Mary (Emerson) **117** 229
230
Mary (Griswold) **111** 148
Mary A. **121** 310 **122** 229
Mary A. (Riley) **83** 183 186
Mary A. (Withers) **134** 92
Mary B. **111** 138
Mary E. **119** 147
Mary E. (Raitt) **122** 72 234
Mary E. (Rich) **84** 132
Mary S. **103** 151
Mehitable **81** 153 **86** 150
90 70
Mehitable (Marden)
86 150 153
Mehitable Clement
105 299
Melinda **60** 296
Mildred Evelyn **97** 155 **98**
147 **100** 126 **101** 140
102 139 **103** 136 **104**
159 **105** 143 **106** 140
107 147 **108** 149 **109**
144 **110** 139 **111** 143
112 137 **113** 150 **114**
143 **115** 148 **116** 147
117 152 **118** 162 **119**
152 **120** 152
Miles **73** 63
Molly **118** 33
Molly (Spencer) **115** 59
Moses **58** 35 **96** 97 **108** 154
121 23 **124** 291 **135** 127
Nancy **59** 286
Nathaniel **65** 114 **105** 299
106 153
Nathaniel Kimball
126 144
Nehemiah **111** 40 **121** 105
Nellie L. **81** 153
Nelson (Dam) **92** 105
Nina Malinda **102** 227
Olive **69** 37 **110** 311
Orion **88** 150
Peter **81** 153 **86** 150 153
Polly **65** 341 **84** 381 **90** 232
109 70 **111** 40
Rachel **62** 272
Ray B. (Mrs.) **107** 133
Rebecca (Camp) **111** 148
Rebecca (Hatch) **119** 226
Reuben **73** 65 66
Rhoda **88** 150
Richard **55** 26
Ruby Elmendorf **80** 209
Rufus **84** 97
Ruth S. **105** 299
Sala **121** 282
Sally **59** 289
Sally Catherine Birnard
62 272
Samuel **73** 67 **84** 97 **111** 19
121 13

LEAVITT *cont'd*
Sarah **52** 434 **55** 29 **81** 153
429 **88** 395 **97** 4 **111** 19
115 140 **121** 109 201
274
Sarah (Gilman) **88** 259
111 148
Sarah (Stockbridge)
135 127
Sarah A. **118** 191
Sarah E. **81** 254
Sarah Hooker **62** 270
Sarah Willets **84** 98
Sheldon **74** xxviii **90** 127
111 140 148 149
Shubel **91** 327
Silence **61** 340
Simeon **84** 132
Simon **59** 38
Solomon **86** 304 **121** 210
136 32 33
Stephen **111** 112
Sturgis E. **120** 237
Sukey (Kimball) **92** 281
Susan **74** 266 **79** 155
Susan (Hanscom) **119** 146
Susan Jane (Preble) **118**
154 155
Susanna **60** 296 **69** 256
73 71
Susanna (Harden) **136** 33
Sylvia Stevens **134** 294
Tabitha **122** 281 **126** 272
273
Tabitha (Crane) **136** 32
Thaddeus **79** 166
Thomas **52** 28 **54** 348 **58**
30 32 140 **59** 115 289 **60**
309 **68** 72 77 111 **69** 191
76 lxxxv **81** 153 **97** 4 **98**
288 **111** 19
Thomas Joseph **58** 311
Virginia (Lockwood)
86 154
Washington **74** 266
119 146
William **55** 26 31 **65** 114
340 341 **81** 153 **91** 327
111 40
William C. **59** 290
William G. **86** 304
William H. **57** 340 **59** 229
62 xxviii xxxii
William S. **123** 305
LEAVY John **74** 213
LEAYCRAFT
Judith **98** 339
LEAYES Hugh **54** 190
Jane **54** 190
LE BAILLY
Susanne **121** 231
LEBANON —— **101** 341
LE BAR
Margaret A. **65** 133
LE BARD Maud **109** 19
Simon **109** 19
LEBARON Lebaron
Lebarron
Almira **66** 84
Annette **89** 238
Bartlett **66** 85 **118** 313

LEBARON *cont'd*
Daniel **89** 238
Esther **66** 84
Francis **58** 209 **60** 388 **63**
115 **84** 96 **97** 364 **101**
323
Hannah **94** 190
Harriet **66** 84
Henry J. **130** 55
John **121** 40
John Francis **57** xxxiii
Lazarus **63** 115 **84** 358 378
86 8 **97** 361 **109** 314
121 312
Lucia **66** 84
Lucy **123** 214
Lydia **63** 115 **66** 85 **97** 360
103 121 **145** 301
Lydia (Bradford) **97** 360
361
Mary **58** 209
Nancy **66** 84
Nancy DeWolf **126** 308
Priscilla **97** 361
Sarah (Bartlett) **117** 188
Susanna **84** 378
Susanna (Johonnot)
84 378
Zeba **125** 39
LE BAUVIER
Marie **128** 178
LEBBALD George **73** 146
LEBBY Anna **83** 13
LEBERT Eugene Marie
(Mrs.) **96** 383 **98** 147
Florence Gladys (Avery)
96 383
LE BETTER
Daniel **77** 150
Elizabeth J. **77** 150
LE BLANC Leblanc
Anastasie (Babin) **131** 97
Angelique (Daigle)
131 93
Annie J. (Byers) **131** 89
Barbe **131** 97
Caroline-Elizabeth **131** 94
95 97
Charles-Edouard **131** 95
97
Charlotte **131** 95-97
Charlotte (Fougere) **131**
94 97
Charlotte (LeBlanc)
131 97
Charlotte-Josephine
131 97
Claude **143** 7
David **131** 97
Denis **131** 90
Esther **143** 11
Frederic **131** 95
Gaéton **131** 97
Hubert **131** 97
Isite **143** 7
Jean F. **95** 380
Jean-Maise **131** 93
Joseph **131** 91 93-95 97
Julie **131** 95-97
Louise (Landry) **131** 93
Lucie **131** 97

LE BLANC *cont'd*
Madeleine (Dugas) **143** 7
Magdeleine **128** 182
Maise-Jean **131** 93
Marguerite (Babin)
131 93
Marie **131** 93 96 97 **143** 6
Marie (Boucher) **131** 90
Marie (Landry) **131** 93
Marie-Anne **131** 93 96 97
Marie-Barbe (Theriault)
131 97
Marion-Edouard **131** 89
Martha **131** 92 93
Martha (Bellefontaine)
131 93
Monique (Robichaux)
143 6
Olivier **143** 6
Perpetue (Bellefontaine)
131 93
Sara-Genevieve **131** 95 97
Simon-Gaeton **131** 97
Victor **131** 93
LEBLOND
Alexander **84** 262
LEBOEUF
Alice **117** 289
Armand **117** 289
LEBOLD —— **143** 78
LE BORGNE
Marie **143** 7
LE BOSQUET Ebenezer
78 190 **92** 320
John **78** 74
Maurice **110** 154
Olivia K. (Chafee) **110** 154
Kate **110** 154
Rebecca **92** 320
LEBOURVEAU
Aaron **88** 285
Antoinette (Richards)
88 285
Lydia **126** 213
Sally **126** 213
Zenas **126** 213
LE BOUTILLIER Helen
Lincoln (Stephenson)
89 184
LEBOYTEAUX
—— **101** 341
LE BRET Reynold **96** 48
LE BRETON
Abbo **79** 369
Edmund Lewis **83** 487
Lucy Oliver (Prescott)
83 487
Mary Caroline **83** 487
95 76
LEBREUIL Louise-
Therese-Marie **145** 129
LEBROCKE
Bathshua **111** 242
LEBRUN Lebron Le Bron
Le Brun
Betsey **145** 131 135
Elizabeth Selden **92** 75
Leo **54** ciii
Maria Olivia **87** 400 **88** 96
89 96 291 303 390 399
90 388 **91** 90 **92** 144 **99**

LEBRUN *cont'd*
261 **107** 129
Maria Olivia (Steele)
92 150
Michel Moracin **59** 331 **61**
205 **63** 301 **92** 75
Michel Moracin (Mrs.) **77**
195 **78** 365 **79** 66 **80** 186
415 **81** 269 **84** 341 351
85 195 349 **92** 74 91 150
Morna Haines **54** ciii
Napoleon **92** 75
Olivia Adele **92** 75
Pierre Napoleon **92** 75
Richard **96** 44
Volance Martha **112** 232
LE CAIN Lecain
Benjamin **78** 20
Louisa **97** 75
Mary **78** 20
Thomas **101** 269
LECAROS Camela Alcalde
109 287
Lecester *see* Leicester
LECETER
Arthur **66** 245
Margaret **66** 245
LE CHAPEDELAIN
— Marquis **65** 148
LECHE William **141** 234
Lecheland *see* Lechland
LECHEMINANT Mary
Ellen (Hathaway)
105 128
LECHFORD Ann **54** 215
Eleanor **54** 215
Elizabeth **54** 215
Henry **54** 215
John **54** 215
Phebe **62** 200
Richard **54** 215
Susan **62** 200
Thomas **51** 105 114 251
52 295 **53** 48 **54** 215 **55**
214 298 **56** 184 **59** 423
62 200 **63** 161 162 **64** 84
66 359 **69** 356 358 **70**
258 **72** 51 **74** 142 143 **87**
272 **97** 393 **106** 32 **110**
269 **111** 11 **113** 64 **142**
111 275 **143** 29 30 50
144 6
William **54** 215
LECHLAND Lecheland
Alice **79** 412 413 421 422
443 447 **93** 175
Elizabeth **51** 137
Jane **79** 412
Joan **79** 413 422
Margaret **79** 411-413 421
422 443 447
Margaret (Jones) **93** 175
Roger **79** 411 412 415 443
93 175
Sarah **79** 415
Thomas **79** 412 413 415
421-423 447 **80** 357-362
93 175
William **79** 412
LECHMERE
—— **60** 223 **136** 283

LECHMERE *cont'd*
Anthony **110** 317
Mary **76** 202
Richard **76** 202 **84** 377
Thomas **57** 65 280 **58** 68
84 168 **96** 357 **107** 192
266
LECHNER Francis **85** 217
LECHYNDEN John **65**
174 175 177 178
Thomas **65** 178
LECKENBY Elizabeth
(Coates) **105** 221
John William **105** 221
Mary **105** 221
LECKEY Clara I. (Marden)
83 434 435 **84** 29
Elizabeth **84** 332 333
Howard L. **91** 207 305
LECKHAM Marie **100** 293
LECKIE James **52** 312
LECKINGER Belle
Charlotte (Bancroft)
(Price) **97** 126
Martin **97** 126
LECKLER
Catherine **72** 300
LECKOR Thomas **73** 145
LECKY Elizabeth **58** cvi
84 332
Howard L. **83** 125 232
John Hartpole **58** cv
Maria **58** cv
Thomas C. **83** 434 435
William Edward
Hartpole **58** liv cv cvi
LECLERCQ Leclerc Olivia
Le Clerc Leclerk
—— **56** 342
Augustin **65** 230 **143** 166
Jean **115** 70 106
Lena Theresa **117** 206
Lewis Peter **65** 230
Mary **143** 166 167
Peter **87** 218
Peter Francis Augustin
65 231
Peter Lewis **65** 230
LE COINT
Pacifique **131** 87
LE COMPTE Lecompt
Aime / Ayme **116** 236
Josephine **116** 236
Rezin **73** 227
LECONTE Le Conte
— Prof. **53** 134
Anne (Quarterman)
95 16
John **95** 14
Joseph **57** lviii **95** 14
Lewis / Louis **95** 14 16
LECOOTER Eleanor **99** 120
101 53
Eleanor (Bissel) **100** 241
John **99** 120 **100** 241
101 53
LECORNEE Joanna **108** 22
LECOUNT
Abigail (Rich) **84** 51
Azubah (Rich) **84** 51
John **84** 51

LECOUNT cont'd
Levin **84** 51
Samuel **65** 117
LECOUR Clotilde **84** 448
LE COUSTEUR
Elizabeth **88** 252 254
Isabelle **88** 254
Jean **88** 254
Jenne **88** 254
LECRAW Philip **110** 277
LECROIX
Andrew **65** 239
Mary (Phillips) **110** 277
LECUÑA Vicente **105** 319
LEDAIN Mary **100** 298
LEDAN Mary **120** 256
Ledbetter see Leadbetter
LEDDLE Henry **84** 379
LEDDRA
Elizabeth **67** 364 365
Grace **67** 364
Honor **67** 364
Jane **67** 364
John **67** 364
Martha **67** 365
Nathaniel **67** 364 365
William **54** 60 **67** 365
Leddyard see Ledyard
LEDÉ John **65** 180-182
Ledebeter see Leadbetter
Ledebeter see Leadbetter
LEDERER Inez (Stevens)
113 29
Max (Mrs.) **103** 119
LEDERMAN
Alice **117** 121
George **117** 121
Minnie (Abbott) **117** 121
LEDES
Margaret **116** 240
Robert **116** 172
Le Despenser see
Despenser
LEDFORD
Addie (King) **139** 66
Aley **139** 66
Burnam **139** 66
LEDGER Lettice **100** 240
LEDGERWOOD William
Lafayette (Mrs.)
106 125
LEDGETT
Elizabeth **144** 233
Lediard see Ledyard
LEDIN George A. **91** 327
LEDLAK Mary **133** 39
LEDLEE Robert **60** 400
LEDLIE Abby **79** 169
Joseph **116** 82
Rachel **135** 249
Samuel **79** 169
LEDOUX
Charles **74** 318
Jane **74** 318
LEDOYT James **114** 170
Margaret (Titus) **114** 170
LE DRAN Henri Francois
136 106
LE DRAPER
Joan **123** 244
John **123** 244

LEDUC Marie **93** 217
LEDWITH
Mary (Reed) **136** 271
LEDYARD Leddyard
Lyddiard Lydeard
Lydiard
— Col. **62** 240
Arabella **94** 288
Charles **61** 183
Deborah **73** 11
Earl **86** 317
Edna Gertrude **103** 120
Eunice **53** 328
Euphrasia **101** 318
George **80** 55
Gertrude P. **122** 301
Hephzibah **73** 10 11
Isaac **65** 148
Joan **138** 318
John **73** 11
L. **86** 317
Lewis Cass **122** 301
Lincklaen **116** 150
Lucretia **84** 449
Mary **62** 95 **73** 11 **81** 173
136 313
Mary (Avery) **136** 313
Nathaniel **73** 11
Nicholas **62** 95 **75** 50 52
Phebe **61** 183
S. **86** 317
Samuel **118** 41 46 48
133 27
Sarah **75** 52
Sophia **133** 27
Thomas **118** 42 43 56
138 318
Trustrum **94** 100
William **65** 154 **118** 48 50
56
Youngs **81** 174 **136** 313
Zachary **135** 293 296
LEE Lea - see also Leigh
— Capt. **51** 330 **57** 226
— Col. **65** 336
— Gen. **56** 54-56 151 220
84 377 **85** 20 21 126 **109**
295 **141** 136
— Maj. Gen. **113** 85
— Miss **83** 151 152 **84** 373
88 139
— Mme **83** 151
— Mr. **52** 133 **71** 117 251
98 76 **123** 191
— Mrs. **69** 147 **78** 241
79 406
— Rev. Mr. **79** 299
___ (Amory) **140** 31
Aaron **122** 79
Abbie A. (Rich) **85** 167
Abbie Little **94** 167
Abby **101** 35
Abby Katharine (Kimber)
95 346
Abby M. **78** 373
Abiah **76** 219 **79** 71
Abiah (Brown) **101** 205
Abiel **76** 219
Abigail **53** 53 54 58 **54** 178
56 357 **61** 77 310 **66** 23
70 92 **76** 201 203 219 **81**

LEE cont'd
445 **94** 63 164 **113** 223
123 262
Abigail (Russell) **118** 136
Abigail (Stanton) **111** 161
Abigail (Tully) **96** 364
Abigail Eliza **66** 23
Abner **60** 356 **77** 203 **78**
382 **120** 20
Abra **59** 284
Achsa **53** 57
Ada Elizabeth **79** 18
Ada Frances **84** 85
Adam **143** 261
Adele Hoes **85** 184
Adelfi **71** 117
Adeline **94** 164
Agnes **53** 56
Agustus **113** 237 238
Alexander **53** 58 **64** 319
Alexander Hamilton
53 58
Alfred **76** 202 **77** lxii
Alice **51** 249 389 **76** 215
Alice Del **68** 358
Alice Hathaway **76** 217
Alice Katharine
(Wentworth) **95** 238
Alonzo B. **135** 250
Alvan **53** 57
Amanda **53** 57 **60** 335
123 113
Amelia **76** 206
Amos **75** 5
Amos Little **93** 221
94 165 166
Amy **76** 215
Andrew **60** 24 **76** 269 **79**
18 **89** 396 **113** 223 **125**
23
Ann **53** 55 57 **70** 82 119
122 **115** 33 **124** 25 **133**
309 **147** 82
Ann Parker **124** 32
Ann Theresa Mary
Magdalen **76** 205
Anna **53** 54 58 **54** 48 **59**
213 285 **79** 71 **82** 292
294 **87** 141 **94** 62 64 **111**
192 **116** 288
Anna (Twigden) **94** 329
Anna Blackwell **69** lxxii
Anna Parker (Corkin)
121 141 142
Anna Sarah **94** 167
Anne **53** 315 **54** 49 **67** 251
252 257 **74** 75 **94** 322
114 29
Anne (Amory) (McLean)
120 82
Anne Collins **111** 66
Anne Wilson **76** 215
Annette Collins **111** 66
Annie (Renolds) **85** 298
Anstace **74** 13
Ardelle **87** 20
Arnold **138** 122
Arthur **60** 399 **64** 359 **65**
53 54 149 **78** 221 222
116 110
Arthur Howard **76** 216

LEE *cont'd*
Asa **78** 382 **83** 99
Ashabel **71** 118
Augustus **113** 238
Austin **80** 427
Avis Lucy **86** 364
Azariah **53** 57 **57** 112
58 318
Azubah **73** 131
B. **65** 149
Bane Arthur **94** 165
Barbara **94** 166 **105** 188
Basil **73** 272
Beatrice **77** 217
Benjamin **58** 371 **59** 284
60 211 355 **70** 313 **73**
273 **79** 78 **94** 60-62 64
164-166 **102** 30 31 **115**
164 168 **116** 78 **133** 232
Benjamin Chadburne
82 45
Benjamin Everett **94** 166
Benjamin Watkins **59** 121
Benoni **77** 28
Bertha **96** 332
Bess **133** 72
Bethiah (Driver) **122** 79
Betsey **53** 57 **76** 93-95
139 318
Betsey B. **53** 58
Betty (Wildes) **108** 189
Beulah **70** 84 **77** 28
Beulah Evelyn **94** 166
Boneta **94** 166
Bridget **58** 312
Caleb J. **86** 53
Campbell **79** 302
Caroline **94** 165 **104** 175
105 188
Caroline Haskell **76** 218
Caroline Jackson **110** 155
Caroline Watts **76** 217
Catherine **77** 144 **83** 64
111 297 **113** 237
Catherine (Forbes)
111 297
Catherine Eloise **81** 194
Catherine Stuart **104** 173
105 186
Catherine Williams **58** 61
143 155
Cazenove Gardner
112 238
Charles **53** 11 57 **55** 78 **59**
211 **60** xvi 265 **76** 206
84 85 265 **89** 296 **92** 152
94 337 **96** 332 **113** 6 8 9
14 **120** 89 **127** 223 **130**
273 **142** 145
Charles A. **77** 188 **85** 409
115 293
Charles E. **84** 85
Charles F. **84** 85
Charles Jackson **76** 212
Charles M. **106** 154
Charles Robert **94** 165
Charles W. **84** 85 **85** 409
Charles William (Mrs.)
105 128
Charlotte **53** 58 **65** lvi **70**
92 **94** 61 **112** 237

LEE *cont'd*
Charlotte Newell **113** 240
Chauncey **66** 23 **70** 84
111 161
Chauncey Graham **66** 23
111 161
Chloe **53** 58 **56** 258 **62** 50
Christopher **78** 365 378
Christopher H. **78** 378
Clara **76** 214
Clara Wetherill **113** 240
Clarissa **57** 141 **79** 155
113 237
Clarissa (Wetherill) **113**
237 240
Clarissa B. **115** 293
Clark **94** 165
Clemania **53** 58
Clement **94** 165
Clifford **116** 64
Cornelia Evelyn **77** 217
Curtis **94** 166
Cynthia **133** 232
D. **116** 115
D. Bernice **85** 298
Dan **77** 203 **78** 382
Dana F. **117** 126
Daniel **53** 54 57 **58** 318
70 36 **78** 382 **120** 37
Darby **66** 36
David **53** 56 57 **77** 203
David Booth **94** 165
Davis **53** 57
Deborah **53** 54 56 **76** 199
201 205 **77** 203 217 **88**
126
Diane Martindell **102** 156
Dorothy **51** 46 **80** 395
108 176
Dorothy B. (Winton)
85 298
Dudley **114** 190
Dwight Barlow **80** 104
206 **98** 150
Dwight Barton **98** 75
E. F. **77** 223
E. Lawrence **124** 99
Earle G. **113** 240
Earle Goodrich **113** 237
238
Ebenezer **53** 54-57 **59** 284
60 268 **109** 310 **141** 199
Eber **53** 56 **136** 312
Edith **113** 239
Edith Pearson **94** 168
Edmund **76** 48
Edna Mae **77** 263
Edward **53** 53-58 **56** 357
58 40 318 **61** 136 **68** 200
71 246 **95** 387 **101** 36
103 13 17 **104** 275
Edward Baker **75** xxiii 75
89 54 81 134
Edward Charles (Mrs.)
108 134
Edward Henry **104** 175
Edward William **53** 57
Edwin **82** 507 **89** 54
113 223
Edwin A. **116** 64
Edwin F. **89** 55

LEE *cont'd*
Eleanor **113** 237 238
114 29
Eleanor Selden **76** 216
Eleanor Wetherill **113** 239
Electa **76** 48
Electa (Guilford) **110** 159
Electa Ann **53** 58
Eli **53** 57 **61** 30
Elias **56** 258 **67** 115 216
68 200 334
Elijah **59** 211 **60** 74 266 **83**
359 **110** 322
Elisha **79** 71
Eliza **60** 333 **76** 203 206
Eliza (Hickman) **113** 237
Eliza Ann **53** 57
Eliza H. **113** 238
Eliza Polly **53** 57
Eliza W. **71** 36
Eliza Williams **61** 80
Elizabeth **51** 249 250 **53**
53-57 **56** 264 **57** 93 **58**
40 **61** 67 **62** 289 **67** 286
71 246 **72** 214 **74** 247
76 133 201 203-206 219-
221 **77** 144 203 **79** 71 **80**
191 **82** 284 292 302 **83**
119 **89** 253 **94** 61 **95** 16
100 303 **108** 64 **109** 310
112 99 **113** 239 **120** 24
125 219 **126** 282 **127**
171 **128** 110 **133** 72 **141**
199
Elizabeth (Crampton)
143 309
Elizabeth (Hotchkiss)
58 284
Elizabeth (Loomis)
136 324
Elizabeth (McDonald)
133 72
Elizabeth (Scrivens)
(Allen) **95** 16
Elizabeth (Shinnick) **113**
237 239
Elizabeth (Woodward)
123 262
Elizabeth Cabot **76** 209
Elizabeth Colclough
77 217
Elizabeth D. (Hubbard)
85 167
Elizabeth E. **78** 378
Elizabeth Hull **94** 165
Elizabeth Perkins **54** cv
76 212-214
Elizabeth Shelton **112** 99
Ellen **70** 357
Ellen (Smith) **89** 237
Ellen Salome **76** 215
Elliot Cabot **76** 214 **78** 287
Elma **98** 76
Elon **53** 55-57 **58** 284
Elsie P. **78** 104
Emily **59** 211 **79** 156 **111**
192 **136** 327
Emma **89** 237
Emma D. **95** 185
Emma F. **68** 155
Emma Florence **94** 167

LEE *cont'd*
Ephraim **61** 136
Erastus **53** 57 **78** 373
Ernest Emery **94** 165
Esther **67** 217 219 **76** 220
Eugene **89** 237
Eunice **53** 56 57 **57** 112
  58 284 **59** 285 **78** 251
  79 71 **102** 30 31
Eunice (Hotchkiss)
  58 284
Eunice Hall **113** 223
Eunice Whitman **102** 31
Eva Maria **76** 214
Evelyn **77** 203
Experience **53** 56
Ezekiel **59** 288
Ezra **57** 93 **59** 285 **77** 203
  79 159
Fannie (Eliot) **135** 250
Fitzhugh **81** 191 **93** 305
Florence **76** 214
Florence Lovina (Scoville)
  91 242
Florence / Flossie **133** 72
Frances **71** 318
Frances Elizabeth
  (Shepard) **133** 72
Frances Esther **107** 300
Frances M. **84** 85
Frances Read (Newell)
  113 239
Frances Trumbull
  69 lxxii
Francis **76** 207 220
Francis B. **59** 120 **101** 207
Francis Bazley **105** 48 59
Francis Henry **69** xliv
  xlviii **76** 210 212 **84** 326
Francis Henry (Mrs.)
  85 203
Francis L. **76** 197 209 215
Francis Lightfoot **73** 263
  265
Francis Marion **112** 99
Francis Wilson **76** 215
Frank S. **85** 167
Franklin Sheppard **113**
  239 240
Frederic William **53** 57
Frederick **53** 58 315
  82 284 292
Freelove **53** 56
G. **56** 151
Garrison Wentworth
  95 238
George **53** 54 **59** 211 **67**
  370 **76** 201 206 214 **81**
  50 **83** 64 **84** 85 **87** 256
  113 237 240
George Augustus **53** 57
George Cabot **76** 211
  217 218
George D. **120** 41
George Gardner **76** 205
  207
George Henry **58** 61
George Herbert **69** 113
George N. **119** 159
  120 318
George R. **85** 167

LEE *cont'd*
George W. **78** 373 **84** 85
  118 136
George Washington
  112 99
George Winthop **76** 216
Georgiana Gardner **76**
  207 208 **97** 120
Gertrude **76** 216
Gertrude T. **98** 76
Gilbert Miner **53** 57
Grace **53** 57 **71** 246 **75** lvii
  81 445 **89** 66 **113** 238
Grace Lawless **114** 245
Guy Hunter **76** 215
Hall Jackson **94** 64 65
  164 167
Hamon **94** 60
Hannah **51** 319 **59** 286 **70**
  84 **76** 133 **78** 181 **92** 249
  93 320 **94** 64 165 255 **97**
  279 **113** 240 **122** 19 **123**
  262 **136** 49 **146** 365
Hannah (Farley) **136** 48 50
Hannah (Pownall)
  113 240
Hannah (Russell) **118** 135
Hannah (Smith) **113** 240
Hannah (Tracy) **95** 346
Hannah (Twigden)
  94 255
Hannah D. **90** 377
Hannah Farnham **76** 207
Hannah Farnham
  (Sawyer) **97** 120
Hannah Greely **76** 211
Hannah T. **93** 320
Harriet **53** 57 58 **77** 203
  79 78 **82** 373
Harriet B. **125** 291
Harriet Clarissa **53** 57
Harriet Jackson **76** 209
Harriet Paine (Rose) **69**
  xlviii **76** 210 217 **77**
  lxxxiii **84** 326
Harriet Rose **76** 211
Harry **56** 149 **112** 140
Harry Arthur **94** 166
Harry Dale **85** 298
Helen (Joy) **113** 298
Helen (Steel) **113** 239
Helen Bourne (Joy) **91** 84
Helen Elizabeth (Hall)
  113 239 240
Helen L. **122** 79 **123** 98
Helen Maria (Amory)
  120 85
Helen Steel **113** 239
Henry **51** 78 382 **53** 58 **54**
  cv cvi **55** 227 **60** 215 **65**
  165 **69** lxxi 65 **70** 357
  73 141 **76** 197 201 202
  204 205 207-209 212-214
  78 241 **79** 301 **81** 466
  85 245 **95** 346 **113** 43
  121 188 **137** 313 **142**
  146
Henry A. **85** 167
Henry C. **84** 85
Henry D. **85** 137
Henry Foster **76** 216

LEE *cont'd*
Henry M. **81** 153 **86** 306
Henry Michael **86** 364
Henry Salem **53** 57
Hepzibah **57** 210 **77** 203
  79 78
Herbert N. **117** 288
Hester **70** 36
Hitty **59** 288
Hope **53** 55 **55** 255
Horace **53** 57 58 **79** 71
Horace Binney **105** 186
Hubbard Stone **53** 57
Hugh **53** 54
Huldah **53** 56 **61** 172
Huldah (Bishop) **136** 312
Humphrey **51** 268
Ida J. **92** 306
Idah H. **84** 85
Irene **113** 238 239
Irene Deborah **77** 217
Irene Graffin **113** 239
Irving Call **88** 208
Isaac **51** 159 **117** 69
Isaac N. **125** 31
Isaac P. **98** 345
Isabel **69** 65 **76** 220
Isabella **86** 53
Isabella Dove **76** 215
Isabella Mason **76** 218
Isannah Greely **92** 249
Isolda de **68** 358
Israel **82** 373
J. **143** 165
J. H. **104** 35 36
J. Henry **52** 44 98 101 321
  62 xi **95** 22 **99** 91 **105** 22
  148 59
J. Howard **85** 298
J. M. **79** 71
James **53** 56 **64** 217 **66** 107
  77 203 **79** 78 **110** 261
  114 164 **137** 361
James Burton **85** 298
James Edward **53** 57
James F. **77** 217
James Henry **51** 79 181
  348 **57** vii xi xxiii xxxi
  93 216 310 330 **58** x xxii
  xxx xxxi xliii 184 199
  285 288 311 349 396 **64**
  201 293 **66** 322 324 **67**
  155 **68** 146 **69** xliii lxxi
  70 340 **77** xi **78** 256 **99**
  180 181 220
James Jackson **76** 218
Jane **61** 116 117 **62** 199 **63**
  100 **68** 333 **76** 201 **78**
  182 **98** 333 334 **115** 315
Jane (Miller) **84** 267
Jane Ellis **112** 99
Jane M. **85** 167 **86** 156
Jane Smith
  (Montgomery)
  (Thompson) **112** 99
Jane Trumbull **69** lxxii
Jane Virginia **77** 223
Janet Norton **139** 221
Jason **79** 71 **101** 205
Jemima **57** 411 **141** 199
Jennie **53** 56 **78** 241

LEE *cont'd*
Jennie E. (Bancroft)
  96 332
Jeremiah **71** 192 **76** 202
  95 347 **117** 69
Jerusha **60** 342
Jesse **56** 20 **113** 237-239
Jezekiah **116** 35
Joan **61** 67 **67** 257 **71** 26
  33 247
Joanna **59** 288
Joanna (Raymond)
  95 346
Joel **53** 57 311 **138** 29 30
Joel Alvah **53** 57 **60** 335
John **51** 240 251 351 380
  382 389 **53** 53-58 **54** 148
  194 196 238 **56** 264 **57**
  112 **58** 300 318 371 **59**
  285 287 **60** 372 **62** 325
  64 218 350 **66** 36 **69**
  lxxi **76** 197 198 207 218
  220-223 **77** 239 **79** 71
  168 405 **80** 60 **81** 465 **82**
  334 **85** 298 304 **87** 198
  91 342 344 **94** 346 **95**
  213 229 230 346 **96** 364
  98 202 **102** 251 **103** 16
  104 188 324 **105** 209
  210 **111** 192 **114** 29 **115**
  56 **118** 135 **123** 260 **126**
  216 **131** 189 **133** 72 **135**
  51 **136** 86 99 324 **138** 25
  27 28 **142** 147 248 **143**
  308 309 **145** 294
John B. **148** 271
John Baker **82** 508
John C. (Mrs.) **85** 342
John Clarke **69** xlviii **76**
  208-210 216 **77** lxxxiii
  81 466 **84** 326 **93** 198
John Elliott **85** 167
John Fletcher **53** 57
John Francis **68** 200
John H. C. **91** 328
John James **133** 72
John M. **77** 144 **79** 71
John Newmarch
  Cushing **94** 167
John Rose **63** 214 **76** 210
  216
John William **77** 189
Jonas (Mrs.) **93** 317
Jonathan **53** 54 55 57 58
  54 48 49 **55** 255 **56** 160
  57 91 141 **70** 84 **83** 48
  87 198 **108** 64 **114** 29
  124 223
Jonathan Trumbull **53** 58
Joseph **52** 468 **53** 54 55 57
  54 cv 57 280 **58** 78 **59**
  418 **61** 77 **68** 333 **76** 201
  206 214 215 221 **79** 71
  81 167 168 **84** 377 378
  91 353 **94** 255 272 329
  99 79 **105** 213 **106** 173
  174 178 290 **113** 237-240
  114 29 **121** 247 **126** 225
  129 386 **135** 250 **141**
  199 **142** 147 **143** 309
Joseph E. **81** 194

LEE *cont'd*
Joseph L. **110** 134
Josephine Rose **76** 212
  93 198
Joshua **76** 197
Josiah **53** 55 **67** 219 **68** 200
  94 227
Joyce **67** 257 **102** 251
Judith **61** 358 **62** 29 **76** 204
  78 300
Judith Colman **76** 205
Julia **53** 58 **113** 238 239
  126 182
Julia Davis **113** 239
Julia McCalla (Davis)
  113 239
Julius A. **78** 373
Justin **53** 57
Kate **113** 237
Kate (Wallace) **113** 237
Katharine **57** 413 **67** 251
  252 257 **82** 192 **94** 337
  110 261
Keturah **113** 237 240
Keziah **68** 200
Lathrop **110** 322
Launcelot **51** 46
Laura Williams **81** 465
Lawrence Lamont **133** 72
Lelia C. **81** 51
Lemira A. **78** 373
Lemuel **53** 54 55 **83** 273
Leonard **51** 240 251 380 **54**
  238 **55** xxxii **118** 135
Leslie Alexander **62** 314
Levi **53** 56
Lewis **53** 54 **86** 53
Lewis Shinnick **113** 238
  239
Lilla Belle **78** 173
Lillian (Minor) (Cole)
  86 306 364
Lillian Howard **76** 216
Linus **53** 57 **58** 318
Lizzie (McDonald) **133** 72
Lois **53** 55 57 **60** 201 76
  201 203 204 **126** 107 108
Lois (Pond) **143** 309
Lora **59** 211
Lot **115** 293
Louisa **76** 204 207
Louisa Jane **69** lxxi
Louisa Sewall **81** 193 194
Louise **59** 285
Lovina **133** 233
Lucinda **57** 286
Lucinda (Dake) **135** 250
Lucius **136** 166
Lucretia **78** 382 **83** 59
Lucretia C. **78** 378
Lucy **52** 468 **53** 55-57 **54**
  271 **56** 264 **57** 112 **58** 61
  122 318 **59** 211 285 **60**
  266 **67** 115 **70** 312 **77**
  203 **78** 365 **81** 306
Lucy Ann (Roberts)
  86 147 306
Lucy E. (Shepard) **106** 74
Lucy Howard **76** 216
Lucy Maria **76** 216
Luranna **77** 203

LEE *cont'd*
Lydia **53** 56-58 **59** 211 213
  284 285 **61** 30 77 **71** 27
  247 **76** 207 **79** 156 **104**
  193
Lydia (Allen) **122** 79
Lydia (DeWolf) **120** 4
Lydia (Girdler) **122** 79
Lydia Gerry **76** 207
Lyman **53** 57
Mabel **53** 58 **58** 77 **70** 84
Madeline **76** 218
Maggie A. (Rodgers)
  113 238
Marah **101** 61
Marcia **94** 62 **114** 175
Margaret **51** 465 **76** 214
  77 217
Margaret Ann (Rodgers)
  113 239
Margaret Copley **76** 214
Margaret Elizabeth
  113 239
Margery **65** 320 321
  76 214
Maria **53** 57 **77** 158 **79** 406
  114 175
Maria A. **84** 58
Marion Glidden **76** 215
Marianne Cabot **76** 210
  89 269
Marie **76** 214
Marie Louise **76** 216
Marion **77** 255
Martha **53** 54 57 **59** 420
  76 132 198 199 201 204
  82 45 508 **83** 11 16
Martha (Montgomery)
  112 91 99
Martin **79** 159 **111** 192
  128 20
Mary **51** 168 319 **53** 54-58
  197 300 311 440 **54** cv
  56 160 284 319 **58** 78 **59**
  284 285 287 289 **60** 372
  61 117 **64** 260 347 **66**
  106 **71** 25-27 245 246 **76**
  197 201 208 215 219-221
  266 **77** 217 **78** 382 **79** 78
  155 **80** 427 **81** 160 168
  466 **82** 45 **91** 82 **93** 24
  40 **94** 17 60 61 63 **95**
  346 **96** 32 159 **99** 205
  102 30 **110** 219 **112** 99
  113 237 238 240 **114** 29
  115 164 **116** 78 **133** 72
  147 279
Mary (Cobb) **142** 147
Mary (Hart) **136** 99
Mary (Huntley) **100** 271
Mary (Lemon) **95** 346
Mary (Perry) **116** 35
Mary (Smith) **126** 216
Mary (Stevens) **133** 232
Mary (Tarring) **95** 346
Mary A. **77** 203
Mary Ann **57** 93 **60** 224 **75**
  16 **76** 208 212 **78** 378 **89**
  14 **91** 328 **113** 238 **145**
  306

LEE *cont'd*
Mary Ann (Davis) **113** 237
Mary Anna **76** 207 208
Mary B. **59** 290
Mary Cabot **74** 163 164
  76 208 **81** 466 **89** 267
  136 319
Mary Catherine **94** 166
Mary E. **68** 200 **84** 85 **113**
  238 239
Mary Eleanor **113** 238 239
Mary Elizabeth **81** 201
Mary Helen (Shirer)
  95 347
Mary Jane **84** 85
Mary Little **94** 65 167
Mary Lucinda **126** 182
Mary P. **85** 167
Mary Williston **94** 167
Matilda **53** 57
May **106** 74
Mehitable **71** 114
Melissa E. **81** 276
Mercy **53** 11 **66** 106 **76**
  203 218 219 **137** 79
Mercy Gilbert (Huntley)
  101 207
Michael **54** 335
Michael H. **86** 147 306
Miles **52** 69 **61** 391
Milo **81** 413
Milton Elwood (Mrs.)
  99 147
Mindwell **53** 54 58 **57** 81
Minerva (Scott) **101** 36
Minerva (Tenney)
  120 318
Miranda **85** 298
Miriam **53** 55 **58** 284
  66 329
Molly **79** 71
Molly (Perry) **116** 35
Moses **108** 239 **110** 159
  114 240
Myrta Ann **53** 57
Nabby **78** 382
Nabby (Russell) **118** 136
Nancy **53** 57 **76** 207 **78** 373
  82 509 **83** 149 151 152
  109 310
Nancy (Chase) **87** 256
Nancy (James) **125** 219
Nannie **78** 164
Nathan **53** 57 **59** 285
  66 106 107
Nathaniel **53** 54-56 58 **94**
  272 273 **101** 28 29 **122**
  79 **138** 25 27 28
Nathaniel Cabot **60** 224
  76 206 208
Nehemiah **59** 284
Nelson Borland **76** 218
  94 138
Nettie Snow **93** 221
  94 167
Nevada B. (Rising) **85** 298
Nicholas **61** 67 **67** 286
Nina **147** 182
Norman Arthur **86** 53
Norman L. **70** 92

LEE *cont'd*
Olive **70** 84 **96** 180 **115** 292
Oliver **59** 285
Oliver I. **77** 203
Ora **109** 130
Orib **136** 312
Orinda Ann **76** 269
Orrin **70** 92
Orrit **53** 56
Ozias **59** 213
Pamelia Penn **112** 99
Patty **59** 287
Percie E. **110** 234
Peter **110** 261
Peter Wallace **113** 240
Phebe **53** 56 **61** 116 117
  62 199 239 **63** 100 **77**
  203 **78** 251 **79** 71
Phebe S. **77** 188
Philemon **133** 248
Philip **67** 251 257
Phineas **53** 55 56
Pier **77** 253
Polly **53** 57 58 **59** 285 **80**
  427 **82** 45 **101** 205 212
  112 92
Priscilla **81** 167 168
Prudence **59** 285
Purchase **66** 106
Quartus **68** 200
R. L. **119** 102 **121** 191
R. M. (Mrs.) **105** 186
R. W. **60** 342 **91** 328
Rachel **53** 54 55 **65** 9
  81 445
Ralph **67** 171 **89** 237
  103 16
Raymond **140** 31
Rebecca **52** 328 **53** 55-57
  59 284 **76** 202 207 218
  219 **77** 229 **87** 56 **144**
  233
Rebecca (Chase) (Gardner)
  88 23
Rebecca (Marsters) **95** 346
Rebecca W. **95** 326
Reuben **53** 57 **113** 237-240
  126 107 108
Rhoda **53** 55 **94** 384
Rhoda (Hack) **137** 361
Rhoda W. (Brown)
  136 166
Richard **51** 398 **52** 116 **56**
  60 149 **64** 347 **71** 315 **73**
  138 **74** 75 **76** 197 **77** 203
  78 382 **86** 265 **95** 21 22
  101 13 81 **108** 176 **113**
  63 **138** 25 27 28 **139** 229
  143 212 **144** 339
Richard H. **112** 91 **140** 182
Richard Henry **51** 89 **52**
  387 **64** 273 **112** 99
Robert **51** 251 **61** 68 **64**
  319 **67** 251 257 **71** 25 26
  33 245-247 **82** 189 **94** 60
  62 64 164 **104** 191 **127**
  181 **128** 170 **146** 379
Robert E. **51** 234 366 **54**
  113 **55** lxvii **61** 213 315
  62 lvii **74** 299 **103** 246
  106 142 **109** 219 **116** 23

LEE *cont'd*
Robert E. (Mrs.) **104** 174
Robert Edward **64** 105
  69 lvi **70** xl **79** 106 **81**
  197 244 **101** 124 **117**
  150
Robert Ives **95** 346
Robert Meldrum **105** 186
Robert Wilson **76** 216
Roland **79** 163 301
Rosalind **53** 58
Rose **71** 247 **76** 217
Rose Smith **76** 211 **77**
  lxxxii lxxxiii
Roxana **68** 200
Roy A. **116** 64
Ruth **53** 56 57 **54** 179 **60** 22
  70 177 **76** 218 **114** 28 29
  136 324
Ruth Kline **121** 237
Ruth Webb **109** 135
Sadie L. **85** 167
Sally **83** 359 **87** 12 **96** 203
Salome Baker **82** 508
Sam **117** 127
Samuel **51** 283 **52** 328 **53**
  53 54 56 **54** 179 **57** 413
  414 **58** 55 142 **60** 22 63
  239 **70** 84 **71** 202 **73** 131
  76 197 222 **87** 198 **91**
  344 **95** 346 **96** 252 **113**
  138 **118** 135 **124** 162
  125 219 **142** 280 **143**
  203 **144** 233 **145** 219
Samuel Orlando **88** 208
Sarah **53** 54-58 **57** 189 **59**
  211 286 **60** 202 266 268
  61 96 117 **67** 216 251
  257 **68** 334 **71** 202 **76**
  221 222 **79** 71 **80** 102
  217 **81** 167 445 465 466
  85 409 **90** 378 **91** 342
  353 **94** 64 **101** 29 289
  111 192 **114** 81 **122** 60
  136 79
Sarah (Parsons) **142** 248
Sarah (Penrose) **117** 69
Sarah (Pixley) **123** 260
Sarah Ann **70** 92 **77** 203
  111 192
Sarah Eliza **53** 57
Sarah Elizabeth **80** 159
  126 182
Sarah Fiske **51** 380 **56** xxx
  57 xxxi **69** 289 **71** 357
  84 181 **87** 161 198 **88**
  172 **118** 135
Sarah Jackson **94** 65
Sarah Jane **77** 189
Sarah Louise **99** 183
Sarah M. **79** 155 **83** 99
Sarah Maria **137** 73
Sarah Marsh **51** 380 381
Sarah Mary Ann **76** 215
Sarah Parsons **76** 207
Sarah Polk **77** 253
Sarah White **77** xii
Savilion **79** 71
Selah **53** 55 58
Seth **57** 93
Seth T. **78** 378

LEE *cont'd*
Seth Washburn **59** 211
Shelomith **59** 213
Sherebiah **57** 411
Sherman S. **81** 413
Sibyl **61** 391
Sibylla (Breck) (Calleteau)
145 294
Sidney **51** 227 **141** 95
147 33
Silas **61** 77 **77** 203 **82** 362
Silas Pearson **94** 65
Simeon **53** 56 58
Simon **60** 132 **70** 247
Simone **76** 215
Sisle **67** 171
Solomon **78** 251 **79** 71
Sophia **79** 169
Sophia Edgell (Willson)
69 xlix **70** xix **76** 212 **84**
173 325
Sophia Penn **112** 99 100
Sophronia **62** 187
Sophy C. (Haynes)
113 238
St. George Tucker **76** 216
Statira **53** 58
Statira Lodocia **112** 99
Stephen **53** 55 57 **58** 318
59 213 **61** 77 **76** 133
111 297 **123** 262 **138** 29
30
Submit **53** 58
Susan **58** 61 **59** 287 **65** 44
66 107
Susan Dove **76** 215
Susan M. **78** 378
Susan Mary **76** 215
Susan Parkman **82** 509
Susan Pendleton **53** 256
Susanna **53** 54 **55** 225 **57**
414 **76** 201 220-222 **77**
217 **81** 50 **98** 127
Susanna (Palfrey) **142** 146
Tabitha **136** 98
Temperance **53** 55 56
Thankful (Barnes)
124 187
Thankful (Mayo) (Rich)
83 273
Theadore Stanton **133** 73
Theodia Dinsdall **58** 55
Theodora **60** 132
Theodore **66** 23 **79** 71
Theresa **77** 217
Thomas **51** 46 **52** 112 **53**
54 55 **54** cv **55** 225 **56**
319 **57** 280 389 **58** 68 60
238 **61** 67 116 117 **62**
199 289 **63** 100 **65** 321
71 246 **76** 132 133 197-
206 216 218-220 **79** 71
72 160 301 **80** 191 **82** 45
507-509 **83** 11 149 151
152 **84** 267 **88** 208 **89** 54
253 **90** 400 **94** 60 337 **96**
32 **99** 205 **104** 324 **108**
189 **111** 120 **113** 240
119 74 **134** 337 **136** 49
50 **138** 24 27 28
Thomas Amory **68** vi

LEE *cont'd*
xxxiv **69** v vii x xiii xxx
70 xii **71** 192 **76** 197 **77**
lxxxiii **84** 326 **90** 128 **95**
297 346 **96** 164
Thomas Eldred **110** 155
Thomas Virgil **77** 263
Thomas Zanslaur **63** 392
64 301 **71** 97 **78** 114
Timothy **53** 56-58
Uriah **53** 58
Ursula **81** 413
Velma **89** 237
Vene **53** 57
Vesta **116** 65
Virgie **78** 173
Virginia **77** 217
W. Asa **59** 285
W. B. **91** 328
W. Simmes **145** 127
Wallace Rodgers **113** 239
Walter **57** 210 **58** 371 **113**
238 239
Walter S. **68** 333
Wetherill **113** 237-239
William **51** 168 502 **52** 58
53 55 57 **57** 189 388 **58**
284 **61** 109 **64** 23 226 **65**
34 **68** 61 **70** 122 **71** 114
74 70 **76** 198 200 201
218-220 **77** 203 **80** 427
81 465 **84** 258 **89** 237
94 272 **101** 83 84 **105**
186 **108** 254 **111** 275
277 **113** 237 240 **114** 29
190 **115** 33 **120** 82 **127**
139 303 **142** 145 146
William (Mrs.) **114** 94
William A. **81** 50
William Augustine **58** 61
William C. **78** 318
William Colman **76** 205
William De **68** 358
William de **101** 266
William Edward **105** 128
William Fleming **112** 99
William H. **54** 240
William Hooker **109** 310
William Marcy **85** 314
William Montgomery
112 99
William Noble **119** 159
120 318
William Otis **88** 23
William P. **95** 238
William Paine **76** 211
William R. **92** 249 **93** 320
William R. H. **77** 203
William Raymond **60**
407 **76** 197 213 **95** 346
347 **120** 85
William S. **81** 51
William T. **79** 155
William Wallace **52** 102
65 155
Willoughby **70** 82
Winifred **95** 169
Winthrop Howard
76 216
LEE-MORTIMER
Sara White **72** 76

LEE-WARNER Philip H.
(Mrs.) **69** lxxv
William **69** lxxv
LEECH Leeche - *see also*
Leach
— Mr. **55** 431
Alice **139** 304
Ann **93** 368
Anna **107** 275 **108** 55 58
Anne **86** 3
Asa **108** 55
Deborah **108** 164
E. Bosdin **127** 229
Edward **93** 384
Elizabeth **139** 304
Hannah **86** 348 349 **108** 56
127 229 **139** 304
Hannah (Raynsford)
139 302 304
J. Granville **55** 71
James **108** 58 **127** 229
Jane **141** 100
John **55** 141 431 **107** 307
127 229
John A. **108** 211
Jotham **108** 55
Julius C. **127** 101
Lydia **126** 256
Manasah **126** 256
Margaret **55** 345
Mary Jane **108** 279
Molly **108** 55
Nathaniel **107** 275 **108** 55
56
Peter **139** 304
Phebe (Penrose) **117** 61
Richard **53** 50 **86** 348 349
93 368
Ruth **127** 229
Sarah **67** 372 **127** 229
Stephen **127** 311
Susanna **139** 304
Thomas **127** 229
William **112** 315
LEED Lawrence **63** 35
LEEDALL Alice **52** 356
Ann **52** 356
Bridget **52** 356
George **52** 356
Isabel **52** 356
Richard **52** 356
LEEDS Leede Leedes
Abigail **59** 317 **68** 223 237
Alexander **60** 40 **68** 237
Alice Maud (Marshall)
113 300
Alice Shapleigh **96** 31
Alice Whittlesey **113** 300
Amasa Jordan **64** 371
Amy Lee (Shapleigh)
96 31
Andrew **64** 165
Ann **68** 226 230
Anne **94** 272
Annie (Stuart) **86** 197
B. F. **51** 380
B. Frank **52** 97
Benjamin **84** 110 **94** 322
Benjamin Bass **68** 230 **75**
lvii **76** lxxi

LEEDS *cont'd*
Benjamin Ingersoll **83**
 493 **113** 300
Bridget Osborne
 (Duchess of) **81** 320
Caroline (Hills) **68** xxxiv
 69 xxx **83** 493 **84** 107
 195
Cary **108** 292
Charles **68** 313
Charles T. **83** 493
Charles Tileston **96** 31
Christopher **82** 187
Consider **60** 38 **68** 216
 112 175
Daniel **60** 40 **68** 228-230
 75 lvii **76** lxxi **78** 415
 113 300 **121** 247
David **68** 228 **113** 318
Edmund Ingersoll **67**
 viii xxxiv 87 **69** 88 **74**
 160 **76** viii 169 **77** viii
 78 219 220 **79** 216 **80**
 222 **81** 236 **82** 251 **83**
 493 **90** 127 **91** 59 60 **92**
 136 **95** 74 **112** 243 **113**
 59 300
Edmund Ingersoll (Mrs.)
 76 169
Edward **68** 315 321
 94 272 322
Edward Stow **64** 371 **68**
 226 315 316 318 319 321
Eleanor Huse **96** 31
Elizabeth **75** 146 **76** 169 **95**
 355 **99** 286 **124** 17 77
 188
Elizabeth (Merwin) **96** 31
Elizabeth Chandler **96** 31
Elizabeth Huse **113** 300
Elizabeth Tileston **68** 316
Elizabeth Trip **68** 321
Ellen **65** 170
Ellis **68** 310
Esther **68** 219
Ezekiel **68** 224 **112** 176
Frances **68** 221 225
George **60** 40 **64** 371
 68 321
Hannah **68** 230 **75** 203
 206 208 **85** 355 **102** 150
 112 176 **136** 314
Helen Augusta **133** 283
Hopestill **75** lvii **76** lxxi
 113 300
Isaac **68** 230 **108** 274
Isaiah **53** 72 **64** 371 **68**
 216 217 219 220 222 226
 228 230 **78** 300
James **60** 40 **68** 310
Japhet **59** 317
Jerusha **68** 237 **125** 293
Joan **65** 320 **76** lxxi
John **60** 40 **68** 237 310 **75**
 228 **94** 272 322 **112** 176
 145 112
John Kean **88** 169 **90** 304
Jonathan **60** 39 **68** 228-
 230 232 235 237 310 311
 75 206 208
Joseph **75** lvii 147 **76** lxxi

LEEDS *cont'd*
 113 300 **128** 277 **136**
 321
Josiah **68** 217 219 221 223-
 226 228 234 316
Juda **100** 304
Judith (Allen) **100** 301
Katharine **94** 272 322
Lydia **125** 218
Magdalen **145** 112
Margaret **112** 175 **116** 240
Margaret (Dolbeare)
 112 175
Martha Knapp (Huse)
 113 300
Mary **54** 106 **58** 119 **59** 317
 64 371 **68** 315 **75** 147
 96 300 **112** 175 **126** 204
Mary (Cotter) **126** 64
Mary (Tileston) **83** 493
Mary Ann **76** lxxi
Mary Eliza **76** lxxi
Mary Prentice (Rice)
 133 283
Mehitable **58** 18
Miriam **75** 147
Miriam (Cooke) **136** 321
Molly **56** 36 **68** 217 **76** 27
Nancy **64** 127 **68** 237 318
 319 **125** 214
Nathan **58** 18 **68** 219 311
 313 316 318
Nathaniel **68** 236 311 **100**
 301 **124** 225 **128** 277
 284
Norton Ingersoll **113** 300
Patience **68** 219 232 235 **75**
 206 208
Peregrine Osborne
 (Duke of) **81** 320
Phebe **64** 261
Polly **68** 311 320 **128** 277
 134 86
Priscilla **68** 216 220
Rebecca **59** 317 **64** 371 **68**
 217 315 **112** 175 **136**
 321
Richard **59** 106 **68** 224 **75**
 lvii **76** lxxi **90** 304 **113**
 300 **114** 23
Richard Clark **133** 283
Robert **59** 317
Samuel **58** 119 **68** 217
 219 229 230 232 236 310
 321 **75** 147 **94** 322 **113**
 300
Sarah **68** 229 **136** 324
Sarah Hannah **75** lvi lvii
Solomon **59** 317
Susanna **68** 216 217 224
 237 **112** 176
Theodore Churchill
 76 lxxi
Theodore Edward **76**
 xxx lxxi
Thomas **51** 383 **54** 106 **60**
 39 **68** 319-321 **86** 263
 112 176
Unity **128** 284
Ursula **94** 322
William **68** 228

LEEDS *cont'd*
William Bateman (Mrs.)
 86 197
LEEHE Elizabeth **51** 35
LEEK Leeke
 Abigail **55** 201
 Alice **55** 291 **89** 333-337
 91 7-9
 Alice (Bartram) **91** 8
 Benjamin **55** 84
 Charity **55** 84
 Daniel **55** 203-205
 Ebenezer **55** 201 **81** 127
 Elias **55** 84
 Ella Dora **89** 21
 Ellen **89** 335 **91** 9
 Hannah **55** 201 204 **76** 132
 Ichabod **55** 201
 Jemima **73** 232
 Johanna **81** 127
 John **62** 244 **64** 158 **76** 132
 89 333-339 **90** 372 **91** 7-
 10 14 15 282 **93** 178 359-
 361 **94** 72
 Katharine **89** 334-336 **91**
 8-10 **93** 358-360 **94** 71
 72
 Margaret **89** 335 **91** 9
 Martha **66** 31
 Mary **81** 127
 Nicholas **51** 416
 Penelope **76** 132
 Philip **81** 127 133
 Philo **81** 124
 Recompense **55** 201
 Rezin B. **73** 271
 Richard **89** 335 **91** 9
 Robert **89** 335 **91** 9 **94** 264
 Samuel **91** 328
 Sarah **55** 202
 Stephen **55** 201
 Thomas **81** 127 **89** 333 334
 91 7 8
 Timothy **66** 331
LEEKENBER
 Thomas **65** 167
LEEM Agnes **93** 79
 Hugh **93** 76
 John **93** 76
 Rose **93** 76
LEEMAN Leemans
 —— **51** 319
 Abel **63** 273
 Abigail **83** 418
 Amelia A. **69** 260
 Anna **95** 188
 Caroline **63** 271 **80** 28
 Cyrus P. **69** 260
 Daniel **83** 417 418 **110** 97
 Ebenezer **110** 97 **119** 22
 Edith **86** 310
 Elezab **110** 97
 Eliza J. **91** 384
 Elizabeth (Tukesbury)
 125 103
 Hannah **110** 97
 John **63** 272 **110** 97 **119** 22
 125 103
 Kate **69** 260
 Lize E. (Cudworth) **91** 384
 Louisa **63** 271

LEEMAN *cont'd*
Margaret **134** 332
Martha **56** 76
Martha G. **63** 273
Martin **91** 384
Mary **110** 97 223
Matthew D. **115** 177
Nathaniel **83** 418 **110** 97
Nettie M. **91** 384
Patty **83** 417
Patty (Gorham) **83** 417
Polly **83** 418
Samuel **80** 28 **106** 153
  110 97
Sarah **51** 319
Susan **63** 272
William **83** 419 420
LEEMONT
Benjamin Dodd **94** 247
Francis W. **94** 247
Mary Ann **94** 247
Nancy **94** 247
Thomas **94** 247
LEENDERTSE —— **53** 152
Josiah **53** 72
LEEPER James **100** 338
LEER Leere - *see also* Von
  Leer
Alice (Jackson) **144** 31
Corday **87** 173
Polly **125** 221
LEERTOUWER
Diederick **140** 156
LEES Leese
Charles **97** 98
Columbia (Willis)
  114 274
Eliza **92** 388
Elizabeth **117** 288
Elizabeth A. **109** 130
Emma **117** 289
John **84** 140
Katharine **65** 314 317
Lawrence **97** 98
Matthew **84** 347
Newton **84** 140
Samantha **84** 140
Samuel **114** 274
Thomas **65** 317
LEESAW George **89** 384
Leese *see* Lees
LEESON Eleazer **67** 122
  123 218
Esther **67** 123 218
Hannah **95** 293
Lana **104** 102
Nellie **104** 102
Samuel **67** 122
Sarah **67** 122
Smith **104** 102
William **91** 328
LEETE
—— **60** 352 **61** 207
Abigail **53** 311 **55** 152 **57**
  137 **58** 300 363 **62** 333
  68 250
Abraham **59** 63
Abram **58** 361
Absalom **65** 134
Adam Reynor **81** 387
Amasa **58** 361

LEETE *cont'd*
Ambrose **58** 302 304
  59 63 66
Amos **58** 362
Amy **60** 352 **68** 250
Andrew **54** 47 **57** 135 137
  58 358 **62** 333 334
Ann **58** 361 **61** 284
Anna **54** 272 **59** 62
Anne **59** 46 66
Anne / Anna (Raynsford)
  139 237 238
Belinda **81** 388
Benjamin C. **59** 256
Bethiah **54** 272 **58** 301 **59**
  62 63 66
Caleb **58** 300 301 **62** 333
  81 127
Catherine Olivia **82** 178
Charity **54** 272 **59** 62 65
Charles **68** 250
Charles F. **62** 241
Charles N. **54** xxxviii
Clara I. **65** 133
Clarissa **81** 388
Cora Caroline **81** 388
Daniel **54** 272 **58** 300 304
  361 **59** 62 65
Deborah **58** 300 302
Dorothy **59** 46 64 **62** 333
Eber **58** 360
Eddy Moss **82** 179
Edward L. **148** 42
Elijah **57** 89 **58** 361
Elizabeth **58** 360 **59** 66 **62**
  333 334 **72** 282
Elizabeth H. **65** 133
Elizabeth Ives **98** 148
Elvira Leanora **81** 387
Esther **58** 358
Frederick DeLand **98** 96
George Washington **81**
  387 **82** 178
Gideon **55** 152
Hannah **54** 272 **56** 261 **58**
  300 302 **59** 66
Horace **59** 256
Imogene B. **82** 179
James **58** 360 **59** 66 256
Jane **59** 64
Jared **58** 302
Jemima **59** 66
Jerusha **60** 333
Joel **59** 62
John **61** 284 **118** 53 55 56
  148 42
Jordan **58** 360 361 **59** 64
Joseph **61** 207 **62** xxxvii
Joseph A. **65** 133
Joshua **54** 47 178 **60** 333
Julia **59** 256
Juliana **57** 139
Justin O. **59** 256
Laura B. **59** 256
Leah **54** 178 **57** 89
Levi **58** 282 301
Linus **53** 315
Lucina **81** 387 **82** 178
Lucy **56** 159 **58** 302 **59** 65
Lucy Ann **65** 134
Lydia **52** 469 **58** 282 301

LEETE *cont'd*
  360-362
Lynn Tell **82** 179
Margaret **61** 286
Martha **59** 62
Martha Addie **81** 387
  82 178
Martha Hubbard **62** 241
Mary **54** 47 178 **57** 135 **83**
  334 **89** 320
Mary (Bartlett)
  (Crittenden) **126** 53
Mary (Chittenden) **148** 42
Mehitable **59** 64 **148** 42 43
Mercy **58** 300 **59** 64 **62** 333
Miner **59** 63
Miranda **59** 63 66
Nathan **58** 361
Noah **58** 360
Orpha Ada **82** 179
Orphana Kelsey **65** 133
Pelatiah **52** 469 **53** 311 **54**
  272 **58** 300 301 360-362
  59 62 63 66 **148** 42
Pharez **58** 362
Polly **81** 387 389 **82** 178
Rachel **59** 64
Rebecca **58** 360 361 **59** 64
Reuben **56** 159 **81** 387 **82**
  178 **126** 53
Reuben Warren **82** 179
Rhoda **53** 315 **58** 300 304
  361 **59** 65
Richard **68** 325
Ruth **59** 62 66 **126** 53
Sally **65** 134
Samuel **56** 261 **58** 300 302
  59 64 **62** 333 **94** 337 338
  139 238
Sarah **59** 256 **82** 179
Sarah Pamelia **82** 179
Seth Penn **82** 178
Sibyl **59** 64
Simeon **54** 272 **58** 361
Solomon **54** 272 **58** 303
  304 360-363 **59** 66
Tapher **81** 387
Temperance **70** 74
Thomas **54** 272 **58** 304
  59 66
Timothy **58** 301 302 **59** 62
Wealthy **59** 63
William **53** 208 **55** 150
  56 155 **57** 135 263 **58** 39
  281 **59** 46 **61** 284 286 **62**
  333 **81** 127 388 **85** 239
  86 268 **103** 252 **113** 64
William (Mrs.) **81** 127
Zerviah **54** 272
Zipporah **58** 303 304 360-
  363
LEETH
William de **83** 251
LEFABRE Betsey **85** 130
LEFAVOUR Lafavor
  Lafavour Lefaver
  Lefaveur Lefavor
  Le Favor
Caroline Thompson
  82 364
Daniel **129** 382

LEFAVOUR cont'd
Edna Jane **82** 364
Elizabeth **100** 29 **126** 206
  208
Elizabeth (Hubbard)
  100 298
Eunice **126** 208
Francis **100** 29
Hannah **103** 195
Henry **60** xxxviii **61** 204
  64 xix **74** xxviii **90** 125
  100 316 **101** 24
Jerusha **52** 218
John **52** 218
Lucy **60** 293
Mollie T. **83** 434 **84** 19
Nathaniel **60** 293 **103** 195
Peter **125** 109
Philip **100** 29 298
Rebecca **52** 218
Richard Merritt **82** 364
Roxbery (Gardner)
  125 109
Thomas **52** 218 **100** 316
Thomas Hovey **100** 316
LEFEBVRE DE CHEVERUS
Jean **60** 216
Lefebvre see Lefever
LEFECHYLD
Johane **86** 409
LEFEVER La Fever
  Lefebvre
— Capt. **67** 101
Betsey **84** 363
Catherine **81** 457
Fannie Helen **85** 192
Franklin D. **107** 159
George Newton **107** 159
Georges **102** 156
Isaac **81** 457
Mary **119** 125
LEFFERTS Anna **53** 316
Grace P. **111** 305
Marshall Clifford **61** 207
  62 xxxvii
Mary **53** 316 **61** 207
Samuel **53** 316
LEFFINGWELL
  Leffingwall
  Lefingwell
  Liffingwell
— Dea. **71** 141
Albert **52** 285
Alfred **52** 285
Ambrose **86** 382
Ann **53** 212
Bela **60** 18
Benajah **81** 169 **97** 188
Betsey **91** 40
Catherine Beatty (Alsop)
  97 188 189
Charity **60** 18
Charles Wesley **52** 285
Christopher **65** 148 **97**
  189 **136** 315 329
Christopher Starr **97** 188
  189
Douglas **84** 341 **85** 195
  97 148 163 188
E. H. **57** 48
Eliphalet Wright **66** 136

LEFFINGWELL cont'd
Elizabeth **136** 308 326
Elizabeth (Coit) **97** 189
  136 315 329
Eunice **60** 18 **70** 107
Hannah (Gifford) **136** 308
Harriet H. **60** 18
Jeremiah **66** 136 **70** 175
  177 316
Joanna **81** 169 **136** 315
Joanna (Christophers)
  97 188
John **136** 326
Lucius Wooster **97** 189
Lucretia **81** 169
Lucy **60** 18
Lydia **136** 329
Lydia Tracy **113** 223
Mary **53** 210 211 **59** 109
  60 18 **81** 169 **134** 292
Mary (Bushnell) **97** 188
Matthew **60** 18
Michael **85** 455
Nola Estelle **108** 225
  109 129
Olive Douglas (Starr)
  97 189
Prudence **60** 18
Rachel **94** 87
Sally Maria **62** 189
Samuel **136** 308
Sarah **66** 136 **70** 106 **136**
  311 317
Sarah (Abell) **136** 326
Sarah Maria (Beers)
  97 189
Silas Weaver **108** 225
Simeon **60** 18
Thomas **52** 285-287 **53**
  210 211 **81** 169 **85** 455
  97 188 **113** 223 **142** 254
William **62** 189 **79** 170
  97 189
William M. **130** 158 314
Zerviah **53** 212 **113** 223
LEFFLER Lefler
Ada Lovisa **111** 99
Ada Virginia **111** 101
Anders **111** 99 101 102
Anders Peter **111** 101
Andrew **111** 101 102
Bror Knut **111** 102
Carl Erik **111** 102
Conrad **65** 193
Ebba Augusta **111** 101
Elfrida Maria **111** 101
Ella Jane **85** 296
Erik Gustaf **111** 102
Fanny Amalia **111** 101
Hanna (Stuxberg)
  111 102
Hugh T. **124** 103
Johan Hakan **111** 101
Johannes August **111** 101
Lars August **111** 101
Lars Wilhelm **111** 101
Louisa Ulrika **111** 101
Magnus **111** 101
Magnus Gerhard **111** 101
Maria Lovisa (Brink)
  111 100 101

LEFFLER cont'd
Martha Eleanor **111** 102
Martin Birger **111** 101
Oscar Abraham **111** 101
Sophia Elizabeth **111** 101
Sophie Catharina
  (Blidberg) **111** 101
Sven Albrecht **111** 102
Sven Emil **111** 102
Lefingwell see Leffingwell
LE FLEMING ____ (de
  Stuteville) **96** 314
Christian (de Stainton)
  96 314
Eleanor **96** 312 314
Erneburga **96** 314
M. G. Hughes **96** 101
Lefler see Leffler
LEFORT
Robert **110** 290 291
LEFOSS Amos **95** 39
George E. **95** 39
Rose Ann (Noble) **95** 39
LE FOUNT Mary **64** 221
LE FOURNER
William **83** 393
LEFRIENE
Joseph **115** 130
LEFROY
— Maj. Gen. **53** 359
J. H. **105** 236
LEFSLEY Robert **63** 20
LEFTWICH
Alla Mae **102** 123
LEFURGEY
Dennis **133** 27
Jacob **132** 188
Leg see Legg
LEGA-WEEKES
Ethel **60** 218 **61** 212 309
  62 xxxviii 207 211 384
  64 xxxii
LEGAL Chapin **89** 317
Charles **89** 317
Harriet Belle (Lazell)
  89 317
Jacob **89** 317
Mary (Yeager) **89** 317
LEGALL
Catherine (White)
  88 216
LEGALLEY Legalais
David **57** 280 **58** 68
LEGALLIS Sarah **118** 282
LEGARD Joseph **64** 106
William **56** 408
LEGARDERE
Anne **67** 321
LEGARE Le Gare
—— **53** 134
— Mme **102** 270
— Mrs. **102** 271
Anne **102** 267 268 270 271
Daniel **102** 267 270-272
Elizabeth (Kirtland)
  102 267
Francis **102** 267
Hugh Swinton **102** 279
John **54** 197
Julia M. **98** 258
Mary **102** 191 267 268 270-

LEGARE cont'd
272
Peter **98** 258
Ruth (Bass) **102** 271
Samuel **54** 197
Solomon **102** 279
LEGATT Legat Legate
Bert **89** 313
Catherine **67** 382
Catherine (White) **88** 216
George **67** 344 382 **88** 216
Grace **71** 32 250
John **67** 344 **98** 116
101 244
Robert **91** 348
Stella (Newell) **89** 313
Thomas **67** 290 **78** 300 303
144 102
LEGENDRE
Harriet **78** 360
Leufroy **78** 360
Mary Ann **78** 360
LEGER Jacob **51** 173
Leget see Leggett
Legett see Leggett
LEGG Leg Legge
—— **118** 100
— Gov. **116** 12
A. E.E. **111** 49
Abigail **92** 388 **141** 194
Abigail (Patten) **100** 296
Carlton **140** 304
Catherine (Lougee)
118 100
Charlotte **57** 394
Christopher Augustus
Sackville **125** 165
Content **89** 111
Daniel **93** 384 386-388
Elizabeth **53** 391 **54** 278 **85**
48 **92** 286 **113** 75 **138** 14
Eunice **113** 143
Flora Almeda **111** 239
Francis **67** 289
Hannah **63** 94
Henry B. **78** 72
Isaac **70** 262
Jane **70** 57
Joan **82** 59
John **53** 391 **54** 278 **58** 64
82 59 **87** 398 **93** 384 387
99 229 **100** 196 **101** 161
274 **139** 325
Mary **51** 402
Olive E. **89** 241
Polly (Shays)(Tracy)
140 304
Richard **63** 40 **72** 227
Robert **51** 402
Roxana **140** 304
Samuel **105** 195 244 245
106 23
Sarah **101** 161
Thomas **51** 433 **147** 243
244 252 253
William (Lord
Dartmouth) **129** 137
138 141 142 146 171
LEGGETT —— **55** 229
— Mr. **82** 434
Allen **82** 434

LEGGETT cont'd
Allie E. **82** 434
Bernard H. **118** 46
Charles **113** 78
Clara **82** 434
Clara Jane **82** 434
Elisa (Rogers) **113** 78
Eliza **92** 121
Frelove (Frost) **104** 54
Guy M. **82** 434
Jessie B. **82** 434
John **118** 46 **125** 256
John Churchill **82** 434
John Churchill (Mrs.)
82 434
Linda **82** 434
Linda L. **82** 434
Lydia (Hopkins) **104** 54
Margaret **126** 145
Marion **82** 434
Morris **104** 54
Penny **104** 226
Rhoda **114** 187
Roy **82** 434
William **92** 121 122 **94** 297
William L. **104** 54
William T. **54** cxlvii
Woodson **82** 434
Leghton see Leighton
LEGOREE Daniel **121** 274
LEGORGE
Elizabeth **64** 189
LEGOT Thomas **70** 141
LEGOUX
Henriette **114** 244
LEGRAND Le Grand
—— **108** 230
Ann Marie **114** 186
Drusilla **95** 82
Martha Esther **68** 258
Peter **142** 131
Sibyl (Ford) **137** 42
William **110** 234
LEGRIGE DIT LAPLANTE
Rose **145** 130
LEGRIS DIT LEPINE
Angelique **143** 13
LEGRIS John **64** 351 352
LEGRO Legroe Legros
Le Gros Legrove Le
Grove Legrow
Abigail **73** 314 **98** 133
Arnold **79** 369
Betty **69** 283
Daniel **69** 282 **97** 145
David **69** 282 283 **73** 314
95 334 **98** 133
Dorcas (Goodwin) **98** 133
Esther Ann **95** 334
Eunice **69** 331
Eunice (Knox) **98** 133
Giroie **79** 369
Gisela **79** 369
Hildegarde **79** 369
Joanna **69** 282
John **62** 40 **69** 331 **73** 314
82 79 **98** 133
Judith **62** 42
Lizzie J. **73** 195
Lydia **69** 282
Martha **63** 172 **74** 258

LEGRO cont'd
Mary **62** 40 **82** 79
Philip **66** 35
Rachel **98** 132
Samuel **63** 172 **73** 314 **74**
258 **98** 133
Sarah **73** 314
Sarah (Randall) **98** 133
Susanna **86** 63
Thomas **73** 314 **98** 133
LEGYNGHAM
William **98** 116
LEHA Mary N. (McDonald)
121 310 **122** 230
Richard **121** 310
LE HARDY
William **84** 466
LEHMAN —— **53** 142
Clara **82** 267
Lilli **102** 302
Myrtle V. **82** 236
Peter **117** 237
Samuel A. **90** 209
LEHMANN-HAUPT
Hellmut **95** 402
LEHMER
Helen Mitchell **96** 159
LEHNHERR Earl Rudolph
(Mrs.) **93** 137
Katharine (Sutton) **93** 137
LEHR Lehre
— Mr. **85** 120
Helen A. **89** 53
Mary **132** 162
Thomas **114** 191
LEIA
John de **95** 123 124
LEIB
Catherine (Schmitt)
134 150
Fred **134** 150
Louise **134** 150
LEIBHART
Hazel Ripley **110** 240
LEIBY
Adrian C. **119** 77 318
Emorie A. **119** 318
LEICESTER Lecester
—— **51** 395 **54** 218
— Earl of **143** 200
George V. **51** 364
Jo **109** 94
John **101** 12
Leonard **84** 278 280
Robert (Earl of) **84** 289
Robert de Beaumont (Earl
of) **95** 123 124
Thomas **54** 345
Thomas William Coke
(Earl of) **77** 91
William **101** 12
LEICH
Christiann **109** 67
LEIDIUS
— Dominie **53** 119
LEIDS Dolly **134** 86
Jane **58** 404 **89** 72
LEIDY —— **55** lxxxvi
Allwin Franck **95** 250
Allwina Franck **95** 250
Ann (Harden) **95** 250

LEIDY cont'd
Joseph **95** 250
LEIFESTE
Charles P. D. **78** 321
Corda Jane **78** 321
Harry **78** 320
Lala **78** 320
Robert A. **78** 320
Ruby Isadora **78** 320
LEIGH see also Lee
—— **58** 223
Abbie Little **94** 167
Abigail **51** 466 **94** 63 164
Abigail (Little) **94** 64 165
Abigail (Peirce) **94** 61
  97 261
Adda S. (Hathaway)
  100 253
Adeline **94** 164
Amos Little **97** 5
Amy Augusta (Williston)
  94 167
Andrew L. **100** 253 254
Anna **97** 261
Benjamin **51** 460 466 **97** 5
  261 **100** 143 234 235
Caroline **94** 165
Charles E. **100** 253
Charlotte **100** 234
Cyrus **100** 271
Dwight Barlow **97** 288
Earl Frank (Mrs.) **100** 112
Edith Pearson **94** 168
Edward **100** 143 235
Elizabeth **100** 143 235 303
Elizabeth Hull **94** 165
Emma Florence **94** 167
Eunice **100** 234 235
Eunice Floyd (Pearson)
  (Lloyd) **94** 167
Eunice Whitman **100** 235
Francis **54** 341
George Asa **100** 253
George Gardner **97** 120
Georgiana Gardner
  97 120
Gladys Douglas (Jewett)
  94 168
Hall J. **97** 5
Hannah **55** 102 103 106
  94 64 165 **97** 279
Harriett Emily (Newell)
  94 166
Harry Whipple **100** 254
Humfrey **100** 293
Jane **115** 315 **125** 260
Jay N. **100** 253
John **142** 145 147 **148** 308
Maersje (Bant) **94** 60
  97 261
Marcia **94** 62
Margaret **125** 261
Martha **55** 275 315 **83** 16
  152
Martha (Chadbourn)
  83 11
Martha (Wilt) **94** 165
Martin **100** 76
Mary **51** 460 **94** 60 61 63
  100 143 **116** 78 **138** 278
Mary (Booth) **94** 164

LEIGH cont'd
Mary (Martin) **94** 166
Mary (Newmarch) **94** 61
Mary Adelaide (Benfield)
  94 166
Mary Anna **97** 121
Mary B. (Mitchell) **94** 165
Mary Catherine **94** 166
Mary Jane **100** 326
Mary Little **94** 65 167
Mentor Garfield **100** 254
Mercy Higgins (Snow)
  94 166
Minnie Augusta **100** 253
Nathan Evan **100** 254
Nellie Boneta (Shover)
  94 166
Nettie Snow **94** 167
Phebe A. **100** 254
Phebe A. (Hathaway)
  100 253
Phebe Adella **100** 253 254
Reuben Harrington **100**
  253 254
Reuben Henry **100** 253
  254
Richard **55** 96 100 102 103
  106
Robert **97** 261
Robert E. **97** 101
Sally (Long) **94** 166
Sarah **94** 64
Sarah (Davenport) **94** 65
  97 5
Sarah Jackson (Pearson)
  94 65 **97** 5
Silas Pearson **97** 5
Susan **55** 100 103 106
Susanna **55** 103
Thomas **51** 275 **55** 315 **100**
  268 **148** 308
Thomas (Baron) **94** 337
William Edson **100** 254
LEIGHMAN Paul **64** 158
LEIGHT Winifred **95** 169
LEIGHTON Laighton
  Layton Leghton
  Leiton - see also
  Layton
—— **53** 249 **54** 230 359
  62 363 **70** 12 20 **71** 124
  83 34 193 **137** 346
— Mrs. **54** 389 **63** 52 53
  83 307
A. E. **69** 318
Abby W. **83** 299
Abigail **64** 14 **76** 31 **82** 45
  84 456 **91** 230 **115** 310
Abigail (Frost) **91** 230
Abigail Blunt **82** 421
Albert **83** 181 183 298 299
  84 29
Albert (Mrs.) **83** 306
Alexander **55** liv **82** 416
Alfred Kendall **98** 182
Alfred Parker **75** xxiii 64
  98 182 248 **99** 150
Alfred S. **83** 306
Alice **82** 452 **105** 81 82
Alvira C. **97** 234
Ann **51** 80 **93** 88 **107** 307

LEIGHTON cont'd
Ann H. **83** 21 25
Ann Ham **82** 421
Anna **59** 290 **71** 350 **77** 298
  78 73
Anna (Chase) (Mills)
  88 29
Anna Louise **83** 173
Anne **74** 93
Annie L. **83** 299 301
Annie M. **83** 301
Arthur **82** 45 **83** 306
Augustus **91** 328
Benjamin **83** 306
Bethiah C. **91** 388
Betsey **90** 248 **127** 114
Betsey (Rich) **84** 40
Betsey Ann **91** 120 124
Bridget **75** 292
Caleb Rodney **106** 47
Caleb S. **106** 47
Caroline S. **98** 182
Caroline Stanard
  (Rogers) **98** 182
Catherine Hall **83** 173
Charles **82** 45
Charles E. **68** 141 **83** 299
  301 **84** 29 **98** 182
Charles E. (Mrs.) **83** 193
Charles Edward **82** 45
Charles M. **53** 453 **83** 299
  301
Charles Mills **98** 182
Daniel **60** 51 **90** 46
Daniel J. **106** 47
David **84** 40
Deborah **54** cxlvi **82** 45
  412
Dellen A. **83** 186
Dolly (Chase) **88** 284
Dorothy **106** 126
Ebenezer **105** 287
Edward **82** 45
Edward J. **83** 193
Eleanor **101** 218
Elisha **63** 55
Elisha P. **90** 45
Eliza **73** 192 **83** 24 25 34
  91 52
Elizabeth **53** 379 **55** liii
  63 28 **65** 214 **82** 76 **88**
  196 332 **89** 192 193 195
  365 **98** 63 **102** 226
Elizabeth C. (Littlefield)
  103 236
Elizabeth H. **83** 297 299
Elizabeth Howe **83** 173
Ellen A. **83** 183 186
Emeline L. **83** 296 299
Emeline Lincoln **83** 295
Emily A. **77** 149
Emily S. **84** 29 **98** 182
Emma A. **83** 183 187
Emmie **127** 131
Ephraim **87** 124 **135** 76
Esther **110** 285
Esther (Tibbets) **135** 76
Ethel S. **83** 424 434
Eunice **104** 68 162
Ezekiel **60** 51 **74** 93
Fanny **74** 264 **85** 377

LEIGHTON *cont'd*
Florence (Goodrich)
83 298 299
Florence Sullivan
(Peduzzi) **83** 299 301
98 182
Frances (Usher) (Parsons)
132 270
Frances E. **83** 298 299
Frances Elizabeth **83** 173
Frances S. **83** 173
Frances Seabury (Hall)
98 182
Frances Usher **132** 270
Frances Usher (Parsons)
91 230
Francis **53** 379 **55** 401 **60**
51 **63** 28 **75** 292 **107** 307
G. H. **83** 193
George **63** 56
George B. **75** 82
George Frost Blunt
91 230
Halstead **106** 47
Hannah **55** 401 **60** 51 **74**
49 93 **82** 45 **84** 355 **110**
285 **116** 224
Hannah (Grover) **110** 285
Hannah Ann **86** 307
Hannah Anna **86** 306 307
Hannah E. **76** 32
Harriet Ann **66** 52
Hateville **128** 211
Helen **109** 130
Helen M. (Goodrich) **83**
181 183
Isaac **63** 52 **76** 36 **99** 115
Isabel (Strout) **91** 387
Isabell **84** 437
James **71** 127 **82** 45 **91** 328
James H. **81** 384
Jane Ann W. **83** 183 184
Jemima **135** 128
Joanna **63** 170
Joanna (Donnell) **115** 305
Job **63** 329
John **54** 408-410 **55** 250
253 254 401 **59** 290 **60**
51 **61** 202 **63** 28 170 **71**
124 126 127 **76** 31 **82** 45
80 **83** 24 25 29 34 298
299 **84** 236 **87** 342 **88** 29
282 **91** 230 **95** 266 **97**
143 268 270 300 **110** 285
115 305 **117** 16 **120** 238
123 79 **125** 95 **145** 17
John Barns **82** 46
John E. **76** 35
Jonathan **81** 444 **103** 236
105 288 **135** 128
Joseph **66** 52 **71** 350 **100**
139 **101** 277 **127** 114
Joshua James **83** 173
Katharine **95** 268 270
L. Lee **106** 47
Levi **64** 131
Littleton M. **84** 29
Lois **76** 32
Louisa C. **83** 173
Lovicey **99** 115
Lucinda **76** 33

LEIGHTON *cont'd*
Lucy (Place) **135** 128
Lucy A. **83** 299
Lucy Almena **83** 173
Lucy Ann (Gardner)
88 337
Luke M. **82** 45 412 416
Luke Mills **82** 45
Lydia **55** 401 **76** 34 **81** 444
Lydia F. (Fernald) **90** 45
Mae **104** 144
Margaret Elizabeth
95 146
Maria **76** 36
Maria Louise **83** 307
Maria Louise (Penhallow)
83 299 301
Mark **128** 211
Martha **60** 51 **71** 126
Martha E. **113** 241
Martha Emma **106** 125
Martha R. **83** 183 184
Mary **55** 310 **63** 170 **79** 220
82 45 76 292 294 421 **83**
25 29 34 **95** 266 **97** 145
127 114
Mary (Bane) **95** 268
114 294
Mary (Worster) **99** 115
Mary A. **76** 42
Mary Ann **83** 297 299 **87**
289 **127** 80
Mary C. **84** 29 **118** 131
Mary D. **83** 307
Mary E. (Haley) **83** 298
299
Mary S. **83** 299 301
Mary W. **83** 298 299
Matilda (Harwell) **145** 17
Melinda **76** 36
Mercy **127** 114
Minerva Ann **97** 19
Miriam **67** liv **96** 395
116 133
Nancy **76** 34 **82** 75
Nancy (Newell) **86** 306
Nathaniel **91** 328
Olive B. **83** 25 28
Olive Bourn **82** 421
Olive J. **83** 183 188
Pamelia **128** 211
Paul **79** 220 **82** 45 292 294
83 34 193
Paul DeBlois **98** 182
Perley **141** 215
Permelia **128** 211
Phebe **76** 31 **127** 114
Philander W. **91** 328
Philip D. **84** 29
Pillsbury **91** 387
Plummer **73** 223
Robecca **73** 140 **82** 24 83
24 25 **97** 260
Rebecca (Scribner)
90 228 245
Rebecca (Walker) **88** 284
Relief **88** 340
Reuben **107** 307 **113** 241
Richard **88** 337
Robert **55** liv **63** 329
127 226

LEIGHTON *cont'd*
Robert R. **106** 47
Sally **113** 29
Samuel **54** 446 **60** 51 **65**
108 115 336 **82** 45 **83**
193 **91** 223 230 **95** 266
97 143 271 300 **120** 318
122 292 **132** 270
Samuel B. **88** 284
Samuel Ham **82** 46
Sarah **55** 311 **60** 51 **68** 253
76 34 **86** 148 **95** 273
100 139 147 **101** 277
115 63 **127** 114
Sarah (Chase) **88** 282
Sarah (Hutchins) **90** 46
Sarah (Ingersoll) (Rolf)
122 292
Sarah (Martin/Mirtin)
90 228 246
Sarah F. **76** 35
Sarah Jane **76** 40
Sarah Rebecca **81** 384
Stephen **76** 37
Susan **76** 37 41
Susan W. **84** 29
Thankful (Godfrey) **120**
238 **123** 79
Thomas **55** liii **58** 249 **60**
51 186 **64** 215 **65** 214 **73**
261 **84** 437 **85** 30 31 **89**
61 **91** 78 **105** 91 **108** 94
113 241 **127** 114 **128**
211
Thomas B. **73** 192
Thomas Plummer **73** 228
Timothy A. **69** 318
Tobias **90** 228 246 **107** 238
Valentine **114** 180
Walter L. **94** 400
Walter Leatherbee **88** 169
89 123 145 **90** 149 **91**
155 **92** 137
William **54** 410 **55** 250
253 255 311 **60** 51 **71** 90
73 228 **82** 45 80 **83** 307
86 148 306 **88** 284 **90**
228 245 **91** 230 **95** 268
97 145 271 300 **113** 29
114 294 **127** 114
William P. **76** 31
LEIGHTWTY
Francis **75** 229
LEIGNADIER Jean Jules
Alexander **110** 132
LEIHFIELD
Joseph **97** 266
LEIJONHUFVUD Martha
Ida Margaretha
(Baroness) **103** 249
LEIPER Agnes Mary
(Mitchell) **112** 313
Ellen (Wasson) **112** 313
George Neville **94** 138
112 222 313
Gertrude Mitchell
112 313
James **112** 313
James Gerhard **112** 313
James W. **112** 313
Jane **112** 313

LEIPER cont'd
Mary Belle (Fleming)
112 313
Mary Smith (Harper)
112 313
Sarah **112** 313
Thomas **51** 21 24 153 158
LEIRMOUTH
Elizabeth **56** 191
LEISCOMB Sarah **51** 291
LEISER Ida **90** 351
LEISIIMAN ——— **140** 245
James **118** 54 56-58
LEISLER
——— **54** 232 **55** 127
Jacob **52** 476 **105** 252
133 108
LEITER Levi Zeigler
76 lxxix
LEITH
Edward Porter **51** 497
LEITHFIELD
Ann **64** liii
LEITHOLD
Esther Moreland
100 177
LEITNER Catherine
(Spertsell) **95** 236
Catherine (Wenzel)
(Wakefield) **95** 236
George **95** 236
Leiton *see* Leighton
LEITTELBERYE
John **71** 24
Leivsay *see* Livesey
LE JEUNE
Edouard **131** 90
LE KEU Adam **80** 380
LEKEUX
Richard **114** 162 241
LEKVE Anna
Brynildsdatter
86 21 221
LELAM
Amy **94** 257 258 335
Amy (Chibnall) **94** 335
Anne **94** 259 335
Dorothy (Twigden) **94**
257 259 324 335
Edward **94** 335 336
Mary **94** 335 336
Mary (Symonds) **94** 335
Percival **94** 324 335
Robert **94** 335
Thomas **94** 335
LELAND Lealand
— Mr. **57** 288
Aaron **141** 143
Abigail **57** 186 **58** 159 240
124 17
Abigail (Gale) **124** 17
Adam **66** 14 **105** 315
Amanda **103** 172
Amory **92** 185
Anna **111** 156
Artemas **79** 281
Asaph **57** 185
Azubah **56** 401
Belle **58** xcii
Benjamin **124** 17
Betsey **71** 122 **85** 349

LELAND cont'd
Beulah **116** 80
Caleb **136** 322
Caleb W. **126** 142
Catherine Haven **89** 31
93 380 **94** 290
Charles **58** xci
Charles F. (Mrs.) **77** 155
Charles Frothingham
(Mrs.) **78** 205 **84** 234
357 **85** 187 **86** 189
Charles Godfrey **58** liv
xci xcii
Charlotte **59** xcvi
Charlotte (Clark) **126** 142
Clara Olivia **110** 228
Cynthia **54** 407
Daniel **57** 188 **105** 315
Deborah **105** 159
Deliverance **124** 16
Dinah **57** 186
Dorcas **54** lxvii
Dorcas (King) **84** 450
E. **91** 328
Ebenezer **91** 201 **105** 159
205 **136** 322
Edwin C. **123** 79
Eleonona **132** 239
Eliza **79** 281
Elizabeth **57** 185 **80** 99 **86**
146 **88** 307 **135** 17
Elizabeth Carter **92** 185
94 138
Elizabeth Rives **79** 185
Elizabeth S. **70** 208
Ella Abby **68** xxxiv
Ellen Elizabeth **59** xcv
Ellen Maria **79** 281
Experience **57** 392
Florence **89** 342
Frances **89** 341
Frances Eugenia (Adams)
89 342
Fred **71** 122
George Adams **79** 337
Grace Adams (Rogers)
91 148
Hannah **57** 56 **105** 314 315
136 322
Harriet **52** 278 **54** lxvii
Harriet (Ethridge) **126** 64
Henry **73** 285 **77** 277 **105**
159 315 **137** 320
Herbert Messinger **69**
386 **76** 322
Hope **55** 317
Hopestill **58** xci 159
105 315
Howard Thorndike
89 342
Hugh **64** 161
Isaac **102** 3 **116** 80
Jane Moore **84** 450
Jemima **95** 236
Jerusha **85** 101
Joanna **134** 292
John **57** 289-291 **58** xci
64 158 253
Joseph **54** lxvii **59** xcvi
84 450
Joseph Daniels **80** 99

LELAND cont'd
92 185
Joseph Daniels (Mrs.)
85 195 **91** 58 148 **92** 184
Joshua **56** 382
Judith (Morse) **136** 322
K. W. **83** 64
Keziah **116** 80
Leonora **132** 239 240
Lewis **55** 397 **77** 236
Lois **56** 401
Lucretia Wheeler Wood
100 318 319
Luther **70** 208
Lydia **101** 31
Margaret **58** 243
Margaret L. (Conant)
101 35
Margaret Leland
(Roberts) **124** 17
Margaret Waters **78** 205
Marine **110** 64 **111** 309
112 221 **114** 69
Martha **116** 194
Martha (Fairbanks)
136 322
Mary **63** 93 95 **77** 277
102 3
Mary (Derth) **105** 315
Mary (Hunt) **102** 3
Mary Louisa **83** 64
Mehitable **56** 382 **57** 56
Mercy (Jennings) **102** 3
Nancy **88** 307 **124** 17
Oliver **58** xci
Ophelia **88** 86
Orrison **132** 240
Oscar Hopestill **62** xxxvii
P. K. **91** 201
Pardon **83** 64
Patty **55** 397
Phineas **78** 21
Polly **79** 54
R. M. **91** 328
Rachel **56** 383 **57** 188
Rebecca **77** lxxx
Rebecca (Parker) **124** 17
Reuben **89** 342
Royal **124** 17
Ruth **58** 239 **105** 315
Ruth (Woodbury) **124** 17
Sally Davis **132** 240
Samuel **57** 186 **124** 17
Samuel Prescot **124** 17
Sarah **78** 21 **126** 142
Sherman **52** 148 **116** 80
123 79
Sibyl **66** 126
Simon **57** 56
Solomon **56** 401
Tabitha **124** 17
Thomas **54** 407
Thomas L. **101** 35
William **56** 382 **57** 56
65 45
LELIE Edward **125** 200
LELLYSDEN
Alice **66** 60
Elizabeth **66** 55 60
Joan **66** 55 56 60
Thomas **66** 55 60

LE LOCQ Peter **140** 162
LE LONGE John **113** 246
LELY Peter **53** 298 461
LEM Amy **76** 226
Lemahieu *see* Mayhew
LEMAIRE Anne Francoise
  110 133
  Etienne Francois **110** 133
  Jean Louis Pierre **110** 133
  Marie A. F. **110** 133
  Marie Anne **110** 133
  Therese Francoise
    110 133
LE MAISTRE
  Jean **88** 256
  John **88** 256
LE MAITRE Mary **108** 231
LEMAN Abigail **70** 122
  Abigail C. (Norcross)
    88 330
  Abraham **137** 242
  Abria (Hovel) **88** 268
  Amy (Morse)(Wheeler)
    137 242
  Catherine **114** 186
  Charity **88** 330
  Ebenezer **88** 330
  Eliza E. **83** 296 299
  Elizabeth **137** 242
  Elizabeth (Hastings)
    137 242
  Hannah **137** 242
  John **86** 422 **88** 286
  Love (Wheeler) **137** 242
  Margaret **137** 241
  Margaret (Hutchison)
    137 241
  Margaret T. (Grose)
    88 286
  Mary **95** 109 **110** 223 **114**
    131 **137** 242
  Mary (Bryant) **137** 241
  Nathaniel **137** 242
  Olive (Davis) (Jaquith)
    137 242
  Roger **69** 21
  Samuel **61** 70 **137** 241 242
  Sarah **137** 242
  Willey **114** 190
LE MAR
  Harold Dihel **96** 97
LEMAS Joseph **77** 319
LEMASTER Lemasters
  Abraham **116** 76
  Howard M. **116** 76
  John M. **117** 43
LEMAY
  Alice Alma **82** 275
  Ann **81** 148
  Bertha **92** 333
  C. Freeland **92** 333
  Charles **92** 333 **94** 372
  Herbert Hezeltine **82** 275
  Joseph **82** 275
  Le May **82** 275
  Lucy Ann **82** 275
  Margaret Williamson
    82 275
  Perry Heseltine **82** 275
LEMBERSTON
  Thomas **141** 326

LEMBERT
  Johanan **127** 227
LEME Hugh **92** 386
  John **92** 386 387
  Rose **92** 386
LEMERCIER Andrew **84**
  164 **114** 251
LEMEREE Joanna **126** 206
LEMEST Edward **60** 40
  Hannah **68** 318
  John **60** 39 **68** 315 318 319
    321
  William **68** 319
  William King **68** 321
LEMING
  Elizabeth (Tharp)
    136 29
  Joan **74** 52
  John **136** 29
  Robert **63** 139
  Sam K. **103** 158
  Thomas **62** 246
LEMIR Andrew **55** 70
LEMKE Theodor **107** 251
LEMLEY
  Conrad Braun **112** 141
  Cordelia Elizabeth
    (Rutherford) **117** 118
  Edna **117** 118
  Robert Davis **117** 118
  Ruth Peck (Piatt) **112** 141
  Wilbur **117** 118
LEMMAN Richard **54** 347
LEMMEX Mary **78** 315
LEMMIS John **68** 316
LEMMON —— **59** lxv
  Abiel **105** 107
  Abigail **115** 130
  C. **91** 334
  Caroline (Patterson)
    105 107
  Doratha **115** 34
  George **91** 328
  Jane **119** 40
  Joseph **91** 269 **104** 242
  Louise Caroline **105** 107
  Mary **136** 314
  Mary Ann **105** 148
LEMMOTT Juda **79** 54
LEMOINE Lemoyne
  —— **63** 234 **136** 191
  Anna (Bell) **101** 179
  B. D. **81** 282
  Charles **93** 111
  Coresta **81** 282
  Harriet Mary **67** lii
  James MacPherson **67**
    xlii lii
  John Julius **65** 230
  Julia Ann **67** lii
  Lewis Augustin **65** 230
  Louis **67** lii
  Marie **109** 3
  Mary (Dean) **125** 215
  Nancy **125** 222
  Nancy (Bell) **101** 179
  Robert **67** lii
  Thomas **101** 179 **125** 215
LEMOLLIER
  Henriette **112** 228

LEMON
  Alfred Lee **78** 320
  Angeline **129** 47
  Annie I. (Samuel) **112** 142
  Cora Elma **74** lxxii
  Edward Prescott **74** lxxii
  Edward Rivers **68** xxxiv
    74 xxxviii lxxi lxxii
  Eleanor **117** 51
  Elizabeth **74** 204 **77** 318
  Elizabeth (Hosington)
    141 46
  Elizabeth Gage **74** lxxi
  Eva Frank **77** 258
  Henrietta **129** 47
  James **74** lxxi
  John **74** lxxi **136** 134
    141 46
  John W. **129** 47
  Letitia Todd **112** 142
  Lydia **78** 346
  Marcy **78** 189
  Margaret **71** lvi
  Mary **95** 109 346 **144** 141
  Mary Ann **105** 148
  Robert **129** 47 **144** 141
  Sarah **78** 52 **144** 141
  Stella Maud **78** 320
  Thomas **78** 346
  William **67** 366 **74** lxxi
    96 362
LE MOND Celia (Johnson)
    86 197
  John Wellington (Mrs.)
    86 197
LEMONS
  Charity **88** 330
  Jerusha **72** 101
  Samuel **72** 101
LEMONT Jane **64** 155
  John **132** 76
  Levi P. **64** 130 131
  Mary (Robinson)
    Simonton) **132** 76
  Samuel R. **64** 155
  William **93** 397 **100** 63
LEMONY Anna (Crosby)
    100 295
  John **100** 295
Lemoyne *see* Lemoine
LEMPERT
  Leon Henry **100** 147
LEMPRIERE
  —— **54** xcvii
  Clement **88** 256
Lemunyon *see* Lamunyon
LE MYRE
  Louye **115** 256
  Matthias **115** 256
LENAHAN —— **98** 371
Lenard *see* Leonard
LENARTH Peter **65** 298
LENAWAY
  Charlotte **73** 227
LENBROUGH
  John De **120** 170
LENEHAN
  Benjamin **119** 22
  Clarke **119** 22
  Daniel **119** 22
  Joseph **119** 22

Lenekin *see* Lincoln
LE NEVE John **51** 200
  Peter **118** 172
LENEVEU Lewis **63** 347
L'ENFANT
  — Major **53** 225
LENFEST Lenfast Lenfist
  Abram **91** 328
  Almira **117** 163
  Elizabeth (Culmar)
    88 282
  Harriet B. (Clark) **88** 340
  Judith **63** 269
  Lydia **63** 269 **117** 163
  Solomon **88** 282
  Thomas H. **88** 340
LENG John **60** 36
L'ENGLEYS
  Christian **96** 112 113
  Robert **96** 113
  William **96** 112 113
LENHAM Dorothy **51** 417
LENICKE
  Hester **98** 123
  John **98** 119 122
LENIHAN Elizabeth Anna
    (Cleary) **82** 381 **83** 231
LENING Elizabeth **73** 38
LENK
  Walter S. **114** 255
  Walter S. (Mrs.) **114** 265
LENMAN Elisha **85** 431
  Isobel H. **73** 317
  Isobel Hunter **74** xxiv
    85 236 431 **86** 201
  John Thomas **85** 431
  William **85** 431
Lennakin *see* Lincoln
LENNAN Betsey **80** 28
  Content **80** 26
  James **80** 28
  Nancy **74** 293
LENNARD Leah **98** 45
LENNI LENAPE
  Tribe **55** 131
LENNON Lenon
  John Strother **112** 142
  Letitia Todd **112** 142
  Robert **107** 170
LENNORE
  Cornelius **102** 35
LENNOX Lenox Linnex
  Abigail **107** 98
  Alexander E. **91** 328
  Alexander Erskine **74** 96
  Alfred **74** 93 **86** 356
  Ann **74** 93
  Anna **100** 303
  Annie **74** 94
  Charles **74** 93 **121** 188
  David **107** 98
  Edwin Sewall **74** 96
  Eliza **74** 93
  Esmé Stuart (Duke of)
    74 139
  Frances **74** 94
  Frances Georgiana Trott
    (Erskine) **74** 96
  George Erastus **74** 96
  Harriet **74** 93 96
  Helen **74** 93

LENNOX *cont'd*
  Henry **74** 93
  James **66** xii xvii
  John **60** 160
  John Erskine **74** 93
  John M. **88** 343
  Louisa (Ceasar) **88** 343
  Lucinda Holmes **74** 96
  Lucretia **74** 93
  Margaret **74** 93 96
  Mary **74** 93 95 **106** 35
  Mary Eliza **74** 96
  May H. **74** 96
  Nancy **74** 93
  Nancy Jane **74** 93
  Parkman **95** 53
  Patrick **74** 93 96
  Peter **117** 12 16
  Robert **74** 93
  Sarah **74** 93
  Sarah E. **74** 96
  Sophia **74** 93
  Thomas **74** 93 95 **95** 53
  Thomas Parkman **74** 96
  William Patrick **74** 93
LENOIR Le Noir
  Charles Owen (Mrs.) **83**
    124 232 **99** 195
  Lavinia Bradford **99** 148
  Sarah John **78** 169
Lenon *see* Lennon
LENORD
  Joseph **123** 260
  Marcy **87** 233
  Mary **99** 62
  Rebecca (Dumbleton)
    123 263
  Rice **99** 96
Lenox *see* Lennox
LENS Judith (Countess)
    112 62
Lensey *see* Linsey
LENT Albert Jackson
    125 301
  Barbara (Croft) **125** 301
  Bethiah **81** 351
  Elizabeth (Colton) **134** 86
  John **125** 301
  John L. **125** 301
  Lucy **69** 163
  Lucy (Thacher) **125** 301
  Mary A. (Simpson)
    125 301
  Nancy **134** 86
  Robertalee **120** 317 **121** 77
  Tobias **125** 301
  William **134** 86
LENTHALL Lenthal
  —— **58** 208
  Anna **90** 358
  John **113** 221
  Mary (Jones)
    (Stonehouse) **113** 221
  Robert **85** 249 **140** 11
  William **113** 221
LENTNER Jennie **108** 74
LENTON
  Catherine **130** 212
  Elizabeth **52** 254 **138** 319
  Elizabeth (Shepherd)
    118 259

LENTON *cont'd*
  John **113** 236 **118** 259
    138 319
  Mary **73** 144
  Robert **112** 286
  Thomas **138** 319
LENTORPE
  Laurence **98** 115
LENTROOPE
  Thomas **85** 267-269
LENZ
  David Harold **96** 129
  Florence Inez (Morrison)
    96 129
  Harold B. **96** 129
LEO XIII Pope **59** 338
LEONARD Lenard - *see*
    also Leanord &
    Learned
  — Capt. **97** 322
  — Col. **125** 268
  — Mr. **51** 122 **79** 299
    80 55
  — Mrs. **94** 156
  — Widow **58** 197
  Abby **78** 267
  Abel **63** 335 **80** 26
  Abiah **53** 434 **59** 238
  Abiel **58** 197 **62** 275
    118 313
  Abigail **51** 315 316 **53**
    233 435 **54** 17 **55** 42 421
    59 81 **63** 327 **65** 381 **70**
    228 **78** 268 270 **81** 160
    100 6 **111** 128 **125** 86
    136 59 **141** 197
  Abigail (Clark) **89** 312
  Abigail (Morse) **119** 313
  Abigail (Wood) **144** 25 26
  Abijah **144** 224
  Abner **83** 56
  Adelaide King **75** lxix
  Adeline **75** 38
  Adeline Swift (Marston)
    113 307
  Alice L. **93** 274
  Alpheus **84** 215
  Alta L. **81** 332
  Alvah **53** 233
  Ann (Keith) **126** 64
  Ann Bradford **78** 269
    89 56
  Anna **53** 435 **54** 18 20 **63**
    378 **64** 375 **103** 266 **124**
    198 200 **136** 122
  Anna (Perry) **122** 259
  Anna Margaret **81** 331
    332
  Anna Rebecca **51** 94 97
    54 vi **55** vi xxix 440 **56**
    vi 70 xxvii lv
  Anna Sarah **55** 41
  Anne **52** 266
  Annie Wilbur **81** 332
  Apollo **126** 37
  Apollos **53** 435 **54** 17 **78**
    268 **121** 247
  Apollos Bradford **78** 269
    271
  Arnold **54** 20
  Artemas **51** 315 **55** 41

LEONARD *cont'd*
77 294
Arthur W. 93 345 346
Aserph 111 116
B. A. 60 87
Benjamin 63 129 327 113
  307 123 260 125 87 126
  220
Benjamin Savelle 96 294
Bernard Ammidown 69
  384 70 lvi
Bethiah 51 290 291 53 435
  54 17 55 47 89 312
Betsey 64 151 65 xlvii 77
  294 79 299
Bettie Ingalls 55 422
Boadicea (Thomson)
  96 83
Bradford 78 269
Brunswick W. 62 367
Caleb 68 243 145 359
Calvin 75 302
Camilla (Davis) 84 215
Candice 83 56
Cara Waterston 73 xx
Carlton 115 26
Caroline 54 17
Carrie 102 260
Catherine 87 3 135 159
Catherine M. 143 154
Charles 64 122 79 39
  116 45
Charles Reginald 96 295
Charles Webster 73 318
  74 xxiv 96 88 162 294
Christian 52 266
Christiana Nelson 75 lxix
Clarence Etienne 61
  xxxiv 77 324
Clarissa 55 43
Collister 93 274
Constance (Dewey)
  86 132
Cornelia 115 26
Cuff 90 110
Cynthia 55 47 60 201
  101 43
Daniel 55 321 63 191 73 8
  84 263 377 85 6 103 266
  118 313 129 103
David 54 18 20 70 lvi
  125 210 294
Deborah 59 290 78 411
Delia (Revere) 145 315 316
Demas 54 20
Diademia 119 39 40 313
Dorcas 54 18
Doris B. 111 63
Dorothy 58 371
Dorothy (MacLure)
  104 146
Dorus 53 233
Drusilla 53 461
E. N. 60 188 114 37
Ebenezer 55 111 81 160
Edgar Welch 96 295
Edmund 51 440 54 18
Eliakim 55 47
Elijah 51 292 54 20 55 41
  65 381 82 21 106 79
Eliphalet 52 449 84 215

LEONARD *cont'd*
Elisha C. 57 78 82 95 304
Elisha Clark 58 404
  113 307
Eliza 77 221
Eliza (Marsh) 125 294
Eliza Fales 89 268
Elizabeth 51 316 70 329 75
  214 76 27 88 78 93 175
  114 242 119 40 118 123
  203 144 224
Elizabeth (Farley) 136 58
  59
Elizabeth Bourne (Ellis)
  113 307
Elizabeth Frances 57
  xxxiii 59 xliv 61 xxxiv
  62 xxxvii 64 xxxi
Elkanah 51 456 64 32 125
  88 133 290
Ella Maria 62 367
Ellen 118 268
Ellen D. 118 273 120 185
Ellen H. 77 189
Ellen Maria 69 201
Ellis 64 211
Elmira 80 26
Elvira 113 35
Emeline Thacher (Welch)
  96 295
Emerett (Raymore)
  112 165
Emily Rebecca 82 24
Emma 93 175
Enoch 136 24
Ephraim 54 18 125 208
Ermina Newton 69 384
  143 325 330
Esther Elizabeth 101 68
Esther L. (Smith) 96 294
Esther Rowe 77 55
Ezra 51 316 54 17 89 312
Ezra Stiles 75 lxix
Fanny 51 316 55 43 96 83
Florence M. 113 162
Francis 52 266
Fred 90 354
G. B. 95 16
Gamaliel 53 436 55 47
  65 381
George 70 120 197 71 48
  76 219 98 246 107 104
  113 307 318 115 134
  123 204 125 88 209 273
  126 215 129 166 255
  131 89 145 142
George Henry 76 xxxi
  xxxiv xxxv
George Marston 94 399
  95 146 108 155 113 232
  307
George O. 102 260 103 46
George Walthour 95 16
Georgianna 122 258 259
Gilbert 122 49
Gustavus 51 315
Gwendolin 76 xxxv
Hannah 51 315 497 53
  435 436 54 17 18 20 55
  41 168 63 327 64 122 71
  355 73 84 75 211 260 85

LEONARD *cont'd*
  258 113 48 115 222 123
  259 124 198 200 125 73
  131 154
Hannah (Walley) (Stone)
  84 215
Hannah Tinkham (Clark)
  113 307
Hannah Wilbur 131 154
Hannum 90 354
Harriet 75 xxvi 132 245
Harrison 52 74
Hattie E. 65 10
Hazadiah 54 15
Helen 90 354
Helen (Fougere) (Doucet)
  131 89
Henry 58 364 64 72 80 110
  123 35
Hiram 128 284
Honour 70 197
Hopestill 96 255 106 149
Horace 64 151
Horatio 55 43 423
Huldah 54 18 58 197 60 79
  109 228
Ichabod 51 178 125 206
  126 272
Ida Delphine (Wade) 86
  96 87 393
Ida Wade 87 394
Isaac 54 20 55 41 63 331
  124 171 144 224
J. 52 19
Jacob 51 179 58 165 70 lvi
  91 206 371 92 347 349
  93 160
Jacob Low 92 349
James 51 497 53 436 54 17
  58 364 62 203 236 63
  130 327 64 32 69 191 75
  143 84 215 85 258 89 38
  90 45 94 399 97 280 328
  329 104 4 105 171 108
  155 113 307 115 196
  197 116 36 135 159
James T. 108 264
Jane 54 20 60 160 117 58
Jane (Coston) 132 245
Jedediah 59 213
Jedidiah 60 205
Jemima 53 230 54 19
Jennie 102 260
Jennie (Martin) 113 307
Jenny 95 188
Jeremiah Milton 82 24
Jerusha 52 453 120 125-
  127 132 133 203 205 212
  293 295 297 303 121 95
Jerusha (Haynes) 114 108
Jessie 101 234
Joanna 114 29
Job 54 20
John 52 276 53 378 58
  lxxii 73 293 90 110 113
  48 123 258 259 136 19
  143 115 145 316
Jonas 59 81
Jonathan 53 435 54 17
Jones 58 371
Joseph 63 327 70 lvi 97

LEONARD *cont'd*
328 **113** 307 **123** 260
261 263 **125** 222 **126**
220
Joseph N. **90** 261
Josephine **111** 128
Joshua **51** 315 316 **53** 435
54 20 **55** 41 **78** 268 **132**
245
Josiah **54** 17 **123** 260
Judith **51** 439 **54** 18 **87** 321
Julia **102** 260
Julia Ann (Myrick)
102 260
Julia Elma **69** 207
Katharine **51** 291 **53** 435
55 47 **84** 215
Katy **113** 141
Keziah **51** 291 **54** 20 **55** 47
64 251
Lawrence **90** 354
Leah **98** 45
Lecie Norwood **77** 221
Levi **54** 20 **125** 206
Levi Washburn **64** 229
Levinus Lamson **55** 321
Lillian Burbank **103** 119
Livona Maria (Eaton)
103 46
Lizzie Leonard **72** xx
Lois **55** 321
Lois Ann (Sawyer) **88** 335
Lot **98** 45
Louis Sanborn **87** 393
Louis Sanborn (Mrs.)
86 96
Louisa (Newcomb)
108 265
Lucia **61** 142
Lucinda **106** 79 **114** 108
Lucinda (Hannum)
90 261
Lucius **77** 221
Lucy **55** 321 **57** 413 **68** 243
115 26 **126** 144 207
Lucy M. **88** 285
Lurana **53** 233
Lydia **52** 271 **54** 17 18 **55**
319 320 346 **72** 213 **81**
160 **120** 287 **123** 259
126 65 **136** 26
Lydia (Chase) **87** 131
Lydia (Gulliver) **84** 215
Lydia D. (Knowles)
123 204
Madeleine Stickney
(Baker) **113** 307
Manning **51** 94 97 99 **52**
100 **70** lv lvi
Marcy **87** 231 233
Margaret **55** 319 320
63 327
Margaret (Knight)
132 327
Margaret (Martin) **84** 215
Margaret Elizabeth
(Keith) **95** 180
Margery **55** 320 **93** 175
113 251
Maria F. **93** 345
Marsha **123** 258

LEONARD *cont'd*
Marshall **54** 20
Marston Stickney
113 307
Martha **73** 293 **76** 53 **84**
215 **123** 259
Martha (Lyon) **133** 119
Martha E. **85** 375
Martha I. **85** 376
Mary **51** 308 440 **52** 276
53 435 436 **54** 17 18 20
55 318 320 321 392 423
58 197 **63** 183 335 **64**
lvi **77** liv **78** 422 **80** 352
365 **83** 161 **86** 132 **91** 99
93 68 69 270 341 **99** 62
101 43 **115** 183 **123** 35
258 262 **125** 210 **126**
117 **127** 120 **143** 154
Mary (Allen) **113** 307
Mary (Briggs) **125** 210
Mary (Doane) **126** 288
Mary (Gardner) **125** 293
Mary (Haven) **94** 156
Mary (Richmond)
113 307
Mary (Weld) **128** 24
Mary A. **70** 198 **90** 56
Mary Adams **95** 180
Mary Ann **55** 321
Mary Ann Vassall **92** 349
Mary C. **55** 321
Mary E. **65** xlvii
Mary Ellen **82** 24 **84** 55
Mary Ellen (Colby)
125 113
Mary Fisher **70** lv
Mary Hall **62** 107
Mary Jane **95** 16
Mary Jane (Stevens) **95** 16
17
Mary M. (Hannum)
90 354
Mary S. **92** 347
Mary Salisbury **64** 122
Mary Skinner **132** 245
Matilda **82** 358
Matilda (Parker) **125** 222
Matilda J. **85** 376
Mehitable **113** 48 **115** 196
Melansa **54** 20
Mercy Maria (Parker)
113 254
Merrill D. (Mrs.) **75** xxvi
76
Merron **73** 8
Miriam **55** 111 385
Molly **55** 47 **93** 160
Molly Wales **51** 292
Moses **58** 371 **63** 378 **64**
375 **71** 355 **86** 132
Moses Grant **55** 226 317
Nabby **55** 43 **78** 267
Nancy **64** 211 **83** 173 **106**
73 **108** 134 **142** 69
Nancy (Bailie) **90** 45
Nancy (Durgen) **126** 66
Nancy (Reed) **84** 215
Nathan **53** 435 **54** 18
Nathaniel **52** 453 **53** 435
54 17 45 **62** 273 **89** 37

LEONARD *cont'd*
90 400 **93** 341 **96** 294
101 43 **104** 206 **120** 191
121 289 **123** 62
Nehemiah **113** 307
125 288
Nicholas **54** 17
Noah **57** 413
Noahdiah **57** 199
Norman Curtis **55** 321
O. C. **93** 274
Olive **51** 316 **55** 41 **64** 72
Oliver **105** 278
Oliver B. **60** 86
Ozias **55** 321
Patric **103** 266
Paul **54** 17
Peggy **79** 299 **80** 55
Persis / Peirces **120** 213
214 302
Peter **60** 24 **127** 120
Peyton Randolph **54** 20
Phebe **53** 434-436 **54** 17
55 47 **76** 53 **83** 409 **88**
291 **115** 26
Philip **54** 17 18 **55** 168 **87**
131 **113** 307
Polly **51** 291 **57** 199 **89** 39
93 156 **122** 49
Portius **52** 74
Preserved **64** 250
Priscilla E. **113** 41
Prudence **53** 435 **54** 17
Rachel **55** 318-320 **125** 86
202 207 269 **129** 166 250
Reana **55** 226
Rebecca **53** 436 **54** 18 **63**
327 **85** 228 **123** 260
Reuben **54** 18
Rice **62** 183 **63** 83 **96** 255
97 319 **98** 167
Robert **55** 317 **60** 160 **61**
267 **115** 26
Robert Jarvis **96** 295
Robert Woodward **75**
xxiii 64 **84** 194 215 232
Rosalie E. **114** 82
Rowland **95** 16 **123** 272
Rowland S. **95** 16
Rufus **111** 128
Ruth **52** 449
Ruth (Carver) **88** 318
Ruth (Fenno) **84** 215
Ruth Josephine **101** 126
Ruth S. **89** 98
Ruth Shaw **86** 197
S. **91** 328
Sally **72** xlvii **78** 268 271
90 191
Sally (Hamock) **84** 263
Sally Richardson **55** 321
Samuel **51** 438 **52** 271 **53**
59 435 436 **54** 17-20 **55**
317 318 320 321 **60** 201
72 290 **78** 268 304 **81**
160 **113** 49 **114** 108 **128**
254 **129** 42 **144** 26
Sandford **115** 27
Sarah **51** 438 **52** 276 **53** 378
436 **54** 17 18 **55** 317-319
57 210 **58** 197 **59** 412

LEONARD cont'd
79 38 89 58 98 72 110
54 115 183 118 276 122
49 123 260 263 125 190
148 223
Sarah (Barnum) 125 288
Sarah (Hanks) 86 11
Sarah (Heald) 143 115
148 222
Sarah (Thrasher) 113 307
Sarah Maria Smith 86 382
Sebury 54 20
Seth 54 18 75 308 146 348
Seth C. 122 259
Silas 53 436 54 17 20
86 382
Silence 53 435 55 319 320
Silence (Howard) 84 215
Simeon 51 291 54 18 20
55 47 96 83 119 313
Simeon Lewis 113 254
Simeon W. 65 xlvii
Sirus 91 328
Solomon 51 94 97 99 52
271 54 18 70 lvi 86 11
94 241 115 183
Sophia 51 440 77 140
88 275
Sophia Caroline 55 321
Sophronia 72 290
Sorannus 55 41
Spencer 53 461
Stephen 52 266
Susan 68 243 70 322
Susanna 55 319 58 165
69 174
Susanna (Savelle) 96 294
Susanna (Spencer)
111 116
Susie 102 260
Sylome 55 318
Sylvia 88 282 90 110
Tabitha 51 438 52 295
Tamar 101 43
Thaddeus 133 119
Thankful 55 320 64 206
84 362
Thankful (Hubbard) 84
267 362
Theodosia 72 291
Thomas 51 291 52 22 23
276 53 436 54 17 18 55
47 333 345 57 332 333
59 107 108 325 62 179
232 234-236 63 82 130
233 327 64 30 32 33 66
36 84 267 270 362 97
328 329 109 228 111
116 113 48 123 34 125
80 293 126 117 225
Tirza 58 197
Uriah 63 129 327 125 83
136 58 59
Wealthy (Hannum)
90 261
Wells 83 161
Wetherell 54 20
Whitehead 97 280
Wilbur Wheeler 81 332
William 55 174 176 61 346
64 218 66 34 77 55 78

LEONARD cont'd
268 80 351 365 93 175
95 180 124 198 200 132
327
William Andrew 68 xxxi
William Augustus 55 42
43
William B. 88 318
William Francis (Mrs.)
104 144
William Henry 84 215
William W. 88 335
Williams 122 49
Zenas Lockwood 70 lvi
Zephaniah 51 315 316 440
53 435 436 54 17 18 55
42 43 421 78 267 268
112 202 113 48 118 313
129 63
Zeth 53 434
Zipporah 121 255
LEONAS Maryetta 85 293
LEOPOLD I King of
Belgium 88 99 101 102
LEOPOLD II King of
Belgium 88 99 102
LEOPOLD III King of
Belgium 88 104
LEOPOLD Owen 118 144
LEPEAN Abigail 92 258
93 324
Albert Augustus 92 258
Almira Caroline 92 258
Alonzo Joseph 92 258
Anna Cecelia 92 258
Elizabeth A. 92 348
Elizabeth Augusta 92 348
Francis William 92 258
John 92 258 348 357
LEPER Isaac 98 335
LE PEYTEVIN
Hamo 108 53
LEPHIEW Adelle
(Gardiner) 122 79
Michael 122 79
LEPIERE
Andrew 84 151 153
LEPINGWELL
Isabel 93 168
Michael 57 351 93 168
Tabitha 93 168
LE PLA Margriete (de
Lannoy) 143 199
Olivier 143 199
Ollie 143 198
LEPLEY Rhoda 97 118
LEPO John 65 22
LE PON Mary 143 199
LEPORT Michael 56 74
LEPP James 59 194
LEPPARD Elizabeth
(Colby) 83 418
James 83 418
LEPPINGTON
Elizabeth 78 405
Henry 57 94
Rebecca 132 93
LEPPINGWELL
Hannah 88 392
LEPRACK John 52 311
LEPRINCE Jean 55 31

LE PROUST
Charlotte 128 179
LEPSIE Oliver 91 328
LEPTON John 76 279
LERABY Margaret (Pain)
132 39
Steven 132 39
LERBY Robert 55 415
LERCH Annie (Kepler)
91 110
Harvey E. 91 110
Margaret Louise
(Hannum) 91 110
Rush Tilghman 91 110
LE REMAN
Rebecca 61 379
LERFENDORFER
Mary 128 92
LERLYNG
Robert 93 77 78
LERMOND
Alexander 95 300
James 95 300
Lois (Lazell) 88 363
William 88 363
LERNON
James McK. 119 177
LERNOULT
Richard B. 51 450
LERON
Alexander 125 223
Drusilla Noble (Eaton)
125 223
LEROUX Charles 109 187
LEROY Le Roy Leroy Le
Roys
Betsey 135 74
Caroline 80 72 82 203
Charles 77 146
Cornelia 82 204
Elizabeth Nicoll 82 203
Emily R. 115 78
Esther 145 264
Helen Otis 90 172
Henry Wyckoff 82 204
Herman 80 72 82 203
Jacob 82 203
Julia Edgar 81 111 231
82 203
Juliet 82 203
Mary 79 287
Pauline 96 86
Pauline (Bridge) 96 86
Phebe 81 493
Sarah Ann 77 146
Simeon 81 493
Stuyvesant 96 86
William Edgar 82 203
LERREBE
Mary (Came) 114 44
William 114 44
LERSELS Ralph 127 225
LE RUS Alice 142 242
Catherine 142 209
George 142 209
Mark 142 209
William 142 209
LERVIA Eunice 77 203
Harriet 77 203
James 77 203
John Henry 77 203

LERVIA *cont'd*
Lewis **77** 203
Margaret **77** 203
LESCE Thomas **83** 444
LESCELL Lesceell
Mary (Daniel) **100** 241
William **100** 241
LES DERNIER De Les
Derniers
Anne Maria **71** 61
Cynthia **62** lxxv
Elizabeth **71** 61
Harriet **71** 61
Peter Francis Christian
71 61
LESE —— **86** 434
LESESNER Laura M. (Gage)
107 72
Leseuer *see* Lesieur
Leseure *see* Lesieur
LESH
Balthaser **69** 191
Charles Perry (Mrs.) **77**
xxviii 78 **115** 86
Ora **77** xxviii
Susanna Phillipina
69 191
William Williams **69**
xxxii 191
LESHER
Emilie Theresa **78** 85
Emily Sniffen **75** xxvi
77 xxxviii **78** 85
Jessie E. **105** 128
John Charles (Mrs.)
101 124
Louisa **79** 134
Martha Ellen **92** 363
Stephen Rosson **78** 85
LESIEUR Leseuer Leseure
Lessieur Lessure Le
Sueur Lesure
Amasa **137** 160 161
Bebbe S. **126** 220
Betsey **72** 16
Christiana Spear **77** 183
Dorothea **117** 115
Elizabeth **72** 114
Francois **58** 321
Francoise (Moreau) **143** 8
J. W. **107** 54
James Warren **85** 195
Jannet **58** 321
John **117** 115 **126** 145
John B. **77** 183
Madeleine **143** 8
Margaret (Leggett)
126 145
Mary (Gifford) **137** 160
161
Miriam **72** 114
Philip **120** 79
Pierre **143** 8
Polly **126** 220
Simeon **72** 114
Simon **137** 160
Temperance **120** 79
LESINGHAM
John **109** 283
LESKONBY Thomas **64** 345

LESLIE Lesley
—— **88** 376
— Col. **58** 82 **85** 6 7
— Lieut. Col. **53** 178-180
— Mrs. **83** 193
Agnes L. **83** 432 434
Alice B. (Lang) **97** 44
Alice Cushing **55** xxxv
84 181 **90** 124
Alice Cushing
(Mansfield) **93** 142 **94**
82 83
Andrew **53** 237
Annie **97** 44
Annie G. **85** 195 **103** 78
125
Catherine **112** 284 288
Catherine (Johnson)
88 376
Charles **63** 17
Daniel **104** 118
David **64** 24
Edgar S. **105** 299
Edmund Norman **59** xliv
Edward Rice **94** 83
Elizabeth **60** 150
Elizabeth Buchanan
111 164
Ellis E. **97** 44
Frank **58** 331 **65** 4
Frank (Mrs.) **82** 495
Frederick Charles **94** 83
Frederick Charles (Mrs.)
92 136 **93** 142 **94** 82
George **112** 284 288 300
113 318
Harold Frederick **94** 83
Irville Irwin **94** 83
J. Fred **68** 207
Ja **119** 179
James **77** 312 **147** 258
James Henry **83** 122 232
John **112** 288
Lucy **104** 266 267
Margaret **112** 284 288
Margaret Leslie
(Montgomery)
112 284
Maria (Rice) **94** 83
Mary **79** 65
Mollie **121** 182
Perley (Mrs.) **85** 195 **103**
78 125
Robert **112** 301
Robert C. **76** 53
Robert H. **97** 44
Ruth Cleveland **111** 164
S. I. **112** 266
Samuel **61** 137
Sarah **93** 199
Susan J. **56** 332
William **61** 137 **128** 161
William Robert **111** 164
LESS Richard **98** 117
Sarah **63** 89
LESSEPS
Ferdinand de **62** vii
LESSER Harry **80** 105 206
100 44 115 245 246
Julius **100** 245 246
Marjorie May **100** 246

LESSER *cont'd*
Robert Charles **100** 246
LESSEY
Elsie Taylor **105** 128
LESSIE Sarah **57** 197
William **57** 197
Lessieur *see* Lesieur
LESSING —— **59** 19
Lessley *see* Leslie
Lesslie *see* Leslie
Lessly *see* Leslie
LESSNER
Elizabeth **74** 34
Frank H. **74** 34
Henry **74** 34
Margaret **74** 34
Mary **74** 34
Thomas Columbus **74** 34
Lessure *see* Lesieur
LEST Jacob **91** 328
LESTER —— **118** 293
— Mr. **71** 137
Ada **83** 485
Amos **98** 287
Andrew **81** 323 **147** 41
Ann **81** 158
Anna (Clarke) **147** 41
Anna (Colfax) **126** 256
128 20
Betsey **70** 199 229-231
Charles **63** 18
Charles Henry **98** 288
Claud Frederick **77** xxviii
77 **79** 212 **81** 323
Daniel **58** 381 **81** 323
102 80
Daniel Mason **80** 142
David **71** 259
Deborah **113** 176
Ebenezer **126** 256 **128** 20
Edith **58** 316
Edward Kinney **70** 199
Eliphalet **126** 256
Eliza Ann **80** 192 **89** 252
Elizabeth **70** 154 178 224
79 76 **81** 173 **102** 80
Elizabeth Kinney **70** 199
Emily **77** 266
Enoch **79** 76
Erastus **70** 178 199 231
Esther **70** 230
Eva Melinda **81** 323
Fanny **70** 232
Farrol **65** 24
Florinda B. **70** 154
Frances **98** 288
Frances C. **98** 287
Francis **64** 115 **127** 92
Frank S. **83** 434 **84** 17
Fred Volney **81** 323
George **70** 199 **117** 294
George B. **75** 316 **76** xxi
Georgie M. (Ramsdell)
83 434 **84** 17
Grace A. **80** 142
Hannah **135** 300 **147** 37
41 42
Hart **89** 264
J. William **92** 305
James **145** 361

LESTER *cont'd*
James Dowd (Mrs.)
94 289
James William **81** 240
John **70** 229 **80** 427 **126**
233 **135** 129
Jonathan **81** 323 **113** 176
126 233
Joseph **59** 194 **70** 60 230
71 135
Joseph P. **70** 154
Julia A. (Parmele) **118** 293
Keziah Price **79** 319
Lucy **70** 231
Lydia **64** 373 **70** 230 **79** 79
Lydia Crosby **70** 199
Maria P. (Luce) **126** 65
Martha **58** 381
Mary **53** 328 **70** 179 224
232 **80** 142
Mary (Allyn) **126** 233
Mary (Wells) **102** 80
Mary A. **79** 76
Mary Elizabeth **98** 288
Mary Ellen (Reed) **98** 287
Mary J. **89** 286
Mary Jane **81** 323
Mehitable **60** 136 **70** 228
98 288
Mehitable Morgan
(Beebe) **98** 287
Mordecai **144** 203
Nancy **125** 217
Noah **79** 79
Patty **58** 381
Phebe **58** 316
Polly **70** 229 **79** 76 **80** 427
Priscilla **71** 259
Rebecca (Crocker) **98** 287
S. P. **77** 266
Sarah **58** 128 **70** 154 **147** 37
41 42
Sarah (Rundlett) **135** 129
Sarah (Streeter) **94** 289
Sarah E. **68** 93
Sarah Maria **70** 199
Sessions **70** 230 232 **71**
135 138 140 142
Susan E. **70** 154
Thomas **58** 155 **81** 323
143 259
Timothy **60** 136 **70** 179
199 229 **71** 141 **147** 41
Volney **81** 323
William **65** 250 **70** 154
William Andros **70** 199
L'ESTRANGE Lestrange
Le Strange
——— **56** 343
Anne (Mountford) **121** 29
H. **141** 120 315
Hamon **51** 416
Hawise **140** 227
Jane Anne **67** 18
Joan (de Ingham) **109** 277
John **111** 159 **140** 227
Nicholas **111** 159
Roger **144** 213
Thomas **121** 29
Le Sueur *see* Lesieur
Lesure *see* Lesieur

LE TABLER Guy **75** 62
Isabel **75** 62
Thomas **75** 62
LETAILLEUR
John Baptist **65** 230
LETCHER John **111** 210
LETCHMAN
Mary **100** 293
LETCHWELT
Mary **73** 222
LETCHWORTH
John **73** 224
Joseph **73** 263
Martha **73** 261
Susanna **73** 231
LETFORD Roxanna **95** 114
LETHAM Leteham
— de **96** 107
Chetel de **115** 47
Christian de **96** 45 105
106 111 117 311 **113** 74
115 48-50
Janet (Urquhart) **110** 79
John de **115** 50
Ketel de **113** 75 **115** 47 50
LETHBERRIE
John **64** 339
Thomas **64** 339
LETHBRIDGE
Hopestill **141** 196
Roper **110** 271
Samuel **141** 195 198 336
340
LETHER
Martin **51** 261 262
LETHERBE Letherbay
Letherbie
Benjamin **121** 313
Ebenezer W. **77** 317
Hannah **121** 313
Sarah **65** 352
Thomas **51** 45
LETHERED
— Capt. **80** 372
LETHERLAND
Susanna **93** 20
LETHERMAN
I. John **96** 97
LETOMBE
Philip Joseph **140** 162
LETON Richard **108** 289
LETSCH William **96** 194
LETSON
Ednamary **92** 146
Ephraim **129** 65
Jeremiah **129** 65
John **129** 58
Mary **127** 216
Michael **129** 66
LETTENHOVE ——— **68** 361
LETTICE
Ann **91** 182 **114** 288
Dorothy **57** 32 **101** 309
114 288 **135** 299 **143**
136
Elizabeth **79** 91 **91** 182
Thomas **91** 182 **114** 288
Walter **99** 236
LETTLE
Fortunatus **88** 282
Rebecca (Freeman) **88** 282

LETTS Hatty **125** 53
M. **121** 231
Nehemiah **61** 205
LETTSOM
John Coakley **121** 247
LE TUBELIN Letubelin
Clement **88** 253
Jeanne (Gavey) **88** 253
Marie (Gavey) **88** 253
Thomas **88** 253
LETWOOD J. **125** 40
Leucas *see* Lucas
LEUCHARS
Orabella de **112** 64
LEUER Margery **58** 404
LEUERECH
— Mr. **62** 141
LEUET James **51** 45
LEUIN
Elizabeth **126** 285
Sarah **126** 285
Leuis *see* Lewis
LEUKHART
Cora **129** 316
Leuther *see* Luther
LEVAKE Esther **72** 215
John **108** 71
Lydia **108** 71
LE VALLEY Levallu
Levalley Levelly
Alice Minetta **71** lx
Almy **129** 274
Elizabeth **102** 17
Eunice **100** 61
Henry Jenckes **71** lx
John **100** 12 **129** 273 274
Marcey **134** 202
Mary **102** 17
Mary (Holman) **115** 61
Mercy **134** 202
Michael **134** 202
Patience H. **70** 46
Peter **102** 17 **129** 274
Rebecca Josephine **71** lx
Seraphine **100** 12
Seraphine B. **100** 12
Stephen **134** 206
Susanna **77** xliv
Thomas **115** 61
William **70** 46 154 **134** 201
LEVAN Charles W. **52** 90
LE VANNER Henry **110**
123 181 182
Joan **110** 180 181
Joan (Hansard) **110** 123
180-182
LEVARAS
——— **62** 285 353
— Mrs. **62** 288
LEVAREZ ——— **63** 52
LEVARNE Levarn
Casper L. **112** 76
Daniel **123** 224
Daniel (Mrs.) **123** 224
Frank **123** 224
Julia **123** 225
Louis **123** 224
LEVATT Thomas **51** 42
LE VAVASSEUR
____ (Gavey) **88** 253
Henry **88** 253

LE VEE —— **136** 76
LEVELY
Mary Catherine **59** 34
Susan B. **59** 34
LEVEN Alexander Leslie
(Earl of) **79** 65
Rachel **58** 126
LEVENDELL
Mary **66** 349
William **66** 349
Levengston *see* Livingston
LEVENS
Alice de **96** 112
Benedict de **96** 110
Dorothy **124** 252
John de **96** 110 112
Joseph **124** 232
Ketel de **96** 311 312
Mary **72** 282
Peter **72** 282
Thomas **124** 252
Thomas de **96** 110 112 312
LEVENSALER
Caleb **90** 91
Harriet (Gilchrist) **90** 91
Harriette **114** 304
LEVENTHORPE
Leventhorp
Leventhrop
Alice **71** 245
Anna **148** 166
Anne **148** 162
Edward **74** 140 **85** 277
Elizabeth **103** 105 106
120 246
Elizabeth (Brandon)
(Cavendish) **103** 106
John **103** 105 106 **109** 31
148 166
Margaret **74** 140
Thomas **85** 271 274 276
281 **120** 246
LEVENWORTH
Polly **84** 345 346
LEVER Adelaide M.
(Anson) **89** 242
Ashton **65** 126
Edmund **52** 247
James **54** 194
John **89** 242
John W. **90** 388
Joseph **83** 16
Lucy **83** 16
Lucy (Hodsdon) **83** 16
Mary **90** 253
Rebecca **53** 301
Richard **80** 90
Sally **83** 17
LEVERETT Leveret
— Dep. Gov. **87** 275
95 107
— Gov. **99** 101 **101** 178
— Miss **76** 64
Abigail **84** 372
Ann **87** 385 **144** 151
Anna **82** 291 292
Anne **67** 257 **70** 184
Benjamin **82** 46
Charles Warren **110** 143
144
Charlotte **72** xlix

LEVERETT *cont'd*
Daniel **72** xlix
Dorothy Christena (Park)
98 179
Ebenezer **110** 144
Ebenezer Turner **98** 179
110 144
Elisha **70** 184 185
Elizabeth **56** 38
F. P. **54** cxxvi
Fidelia Wellman **82** 112
Flotilla V. (Biddle)
110 143
Frances Evelyn (Gibson)
98 179
Francis Baker **82** 46
Frank **98** 137 147 152 179
George Haven **82** 46
George Vasmer **55** 135
65 xxi **66** xxxvii **67** xxii
72 xxx xlix l
Gideon **134** 173
Hannah **64** 284 **84** 255 **133**
308 **142** 394
Hannah (Leverett)
133 308
Hannah Gray **82** 46
Hudson **64** 189 **98** 179
134 173
Israel **70** 184 185
Jabesh **70** 184 185
James **70** 184
Jane **70** 184 185
John **51** 220 **52** 344 **53** 290
54 404 **63** 118 119 **64**
284 **65** 63 67 85 **67** 108
70 184 185 **82** 112 **84**
358 **85** 128 **87** 385 **94** 61
92 **97** 13 345 **98** 179 **104**
77 **109** 207 **121** 203 **131**
183 **132** 83 **133** 308 **134**
173 **142** 394 **143** 137
144 11 151 **148** 333
Joseph **98** 179 **110** 144
Knight **104** 86
Letha Pearl **105** 127 **110**
135 143
Lydia **55** 397
Lydia (Fuller) **98** 179
110 144
Lydia Marshall **82** 46
Margaret (Rogers) (Berry)
104 77
Maria **68** lviii 100
Marie **70** 184 185
Mary **60** 196 **82** 412
Mary (Turner) **98** 179
110 144
Mary B. **68** lviii 100
Mary E. L. **72** 1
Mary G. (Griffin) **134** 173
Mary Yeaton **82** 46
Nathaniel **70** 184 185
Rachel (Watts) **98** 179
110 144
Rebecca **104** 86
Rowena (Houston) **98**
179 **110** 144
Sarah **65** 67 **70** 184 185 **83**
34 **143** 137
Sarah (Black) **134** 173

LEVERETT *cont'd*
Sarah (Crisp) (Harris)
104 77
Sarah (Payton) **134** 173
Sarah Gano **103** 314 315
Susan **68** 100
Thomas **56** 341 344 **64**
184 284 **65** xix **70** 184
185 **82** 112 **84** 255 85
133 **134** 173 **144** 11 232
William **55** 397 **68** lviii
100 **82** 46 **98** 179 **103**
314 **106** 19 **110** 144 **134**
173
William Augustus **82** 46
LEVERICH Leveritch
Leverych Lyveryche
—— **118** 85
John **113** 216 **141** 228 230
Rebecca (Wright) **87** 376
Susanna (Field) (Sackett)
113 216
Thomas **65** 70
William **52** 33 **95** 48 **113**
204 **132** 173 **138** 104
LEVERICK
Deborah **69** 44
Gabriel **69** 44 **70** 37
Hannah **68** 294 **69** 44
Leveritch *see* Leverich
LEVERLAND
— Dr. **143** 207
B. N. **143** 197 198
Levermore *see* Livermore
LEVERN Harriet (Smith)
97 231
Joseph **97** 231
LEVERONI Frank **92** 209
LEVERSEDGE
Margaret **112** 37
LEVERSTON Ann **64** 227
Leverych *see* Leverich
Levesey *see* Livesey
LEVESON
Nicholas **139** 236
LEVESTON —— **92** 51
LEVET Levett - *see also*
Leavitt
Abigail **67** 80
Abigail Maria **67** 354
Agnes **67** 74 75
Alison **67** 75
Ann **67** 73 80
Anne **67** 67 68 72 74 76
Aretas **67** 79 80
Catherine **67** 68 74
Charles **67** 75 76
Christopher **67** xxii xxiii
67 70 71 75-77
Constance **67** 75
Deliverence **67** 80
Dudley **67** 77
E. H. **67** 354
Edith **67** 76
Elizabeth **67** 67-69 73 74 76
78 80
Ellen **67** 75 76
Emily Wilder **67** 371
Florence **67** 76
Frances **66** xxiii **67** 68 74
76

LEVET *cont'd*
Francis **67** 66-68 73 75
Gertrude **67** 68
Grace **67** 76
Guy **67** 75
Hamond de **67** 67
Hannah **67** 80
Henry **67** 75
Henry T. **67** 354
Hezron **51** 63 **67** 79 80
Isabel **67** 75-79
J. W. **67** 354
James **67** 67 76 78-81
Jane **67** 68 69 73 74
Jane Whitney **90** 48
Jeremiah **67** 76 **145** 350
Joan **67** 76
Joanna **67** 74
John **67** 67-77 79 80
Jonathan **145** 352
Judith **67** 73
Katharine **67** 74-76
Luther **67** 80
Lydia **51** 63 **67** 80
Margaret **67** 68 70 76
Marie **67** 74
Martha **67** 80
Mary **67** 67-69 71 76 80
Matthew **67** 75 76
Mehitable **67** 80
Mercy **67** 76
Moses **67** 80
Nicholas **67** 68 73 74
Nicholas de **67** 67
Percival **67** 75 76
Peter **67** 68 69 73 75
Polly **90** 232
Ralph **67** 66-69 72-75 78
Rebecca **67** 76
Richard **67** 67 75 76
Robert **67** 67 68 73-76
Rudderforth **67** 76
Ruth **67** 80
Sarah **67** 76 77 80 81
Sheldon **67** xxxiv 77
Thomas **67** 66-81
William **67** 67-69 73-76
Levey *see* Levy
LEVEY Sarah / Sally
(Briggs) **127** 158
LEVI Hester **63** 355
Moses **63** 355
Rachel S. **117** 292
LEVICK Hannah **68** 121
Jeannette **68** 121
Lewis J. **66** 191
Robert **68** 121
LEVIER Diente Denise
Laura **121** 159
James **121** 159
LEVILLAIN
—— **110** 291
L. **107** 279
Leon **110** 43 44 **114** 296
LEVIN
Alexandra Lee **115** 157
LEVING
Lettice **72** 133-135 137
Thomas **72** 134 135 137
LEVINGS
Edward **115** 56

Levingstone *see*
Livingston
LEVINGTON
Adam de **103** 200
LEVINS
Elizabeth **52** 119
Humphrey **52** 119
LEVINUS Thomas **66** 36
LEVIS — Duc de **60** 50
Nellie W. **90** 388
LEVITT Deliverance
(Whittemore) **106** 193
Philip **145** 356
LEVOWS Thomas **93** 228
LEVY Levey
Aaron **105** 239
Alfred **82** 345
Austin T. **74** ix xxiv
Babette May **99** 338
Betsey **82** 345
Edward **105** 114
Elizabeth **82** 209
Etta **82** 345
Hannah **58** 181
Helen **108** 151
Hyan **127** 13
Jacob **127** 158
James **105** 114
John **82** 209 **105** 114
Joseph M. **77** 182
Julius **75** 316 **76** xxi **79** 81
80 231 **81** 62 363 **82** 54
248 345 **83** 8 434 **84** 69
85 29 **86** 59 **87** 39 **88** 6
89 9 **90** 103 **91** 6 **92** 29
93 47 **94** 19 **95** 89 **96** 58
97 147 **98** 90 **99** 70 **100**
127 **101** 278 **102** 196
103 20 240 **104** 212 **105**
248 **106** 181 **108** 313
109 107 **110** 184 **111** 59
113 130 **114** 114
Lillian Verteen (Lunt)
83 434
Margaret Bispham **86** 197
Mary I. **77** 182
Mary / Polly (Pearce)
145 28
Maurice A. **70** 97
Michael S. **82** 345
Moses **127** 14 **145** 28
Rachel **58** 181
William **82** 345
Willy **75** 157 **76** xxi **108** 61
138
LEWAN Phebe **78** 74
LEWANDOWSKA Amelie
Eugenie **83** 215
LEWCE John **65** 236
LEWDEN Joseph **77** 236
LEWELLEN
Morris **148** 111
LEWENHAUPT
Claes C. **103** 250 251
LEWES Ann **86** 395
Ann (Weeks) **86** 395
Anna (Lothrop) **97** 277
Bathsheba **86** 395
Deborah **86** 396
Denise (Forman) **96** 79
Edward **56** 405

LEWES *cont'd*
Lydia (Morse) **83** 282
Margaret **127** 172
Mary **90** 250
Mary (Lumbard) **86** 395
Mary M. **51** 45
Patience (Woodward)
90 238
Sarah **86** 395
Sarah (Arey) **86** 395
Susanna (Cook) **90** 251
Thankful (Crowell)
86 396
LEWEY Susanna **72** 286
LEWIN Lewyn
— Mr. **71** 136
Abby J. **63** 50
Anne **97** 100
Clifford Erroll (Mrs.)
108 134
Cranson **71** 139
Dorothy **65** 285
Elizabeth **51** 187 **52** 51
Hannah (Chase) **87** 251
Jemima **87** 255
John **94** 332 **127** 206 271
John E. **87** 251
Judith **97** 100
Justinian **94** 260 **97** 100
Margaret **61** 189 **68** 273
283 **69** 53
Mary E. (Wheeler) **110**
63 68
Polly **93** 282
Rachel **79** 354
Rebecca **127** 206
Robert **104** 277
Sarah **79** 354 **83** 465 **88** 28
127 206 270 271
Sarah (Eastabrooks)
83 466
Thomas **65** 285
William **51** 274 **79** 354
83 465 466 **147** 30
William Henry **110** 68
William Henry (Mrs.)
104 144 **110** 63 68
LEWIS Leuis Llewis
—— **90** 326 **148** 326
— Capt. **51** 157 **76** 174
— Col. **52** 62
— Dea. **79** 77
— Lieut. **76** 131
— Miss **85** 121 **90** 326
— Mr. **51** 255 **58** 171 **60**
66 **82** 218 **84** 387
— Mrs. **61** 237 **83** 34 307
85 121
A. **118** 216
A. F. **59** xliv 231 **60** xxxvi
Aaron **76** lvii **79** 35 **120** 7
131 291
Abba B. **83** 18
Abba B. (Smith) **83** 18
Abby Altana **91** 251
Abby Catherine **69** xxxv
76 xxxi lxxxix
Abel **109** 35
Abel Frankling **116** 285
Abi **64** 150
Abigail **57** 189 **58** 128 **60**

LEWIS *cont'd*
239 **75** 190 200 **78** 443
80 22 **82** 21 **90** 232 253
96 79 **98** 221 **100** 35
102 309 **106** 299 300
302 303 **107** 55 58 236
108 210 **110** 66 **111** 19
112 216 **114** 90 130 **115**
138 **116** 183 **118** 283
120 160 **126** 205 **128**
294 **136** 318
Abigail (King) **125** 287
Abigail (Perry) **115** 193
Abigail (Sandford)
 114 91
Abigail Frost **76** lxxxix
Abigail P. **87** 233 241
Abijah **99** 198
Abraham **65** 351 **83** 267
Achsah **83** 267 **84** 50
Adam **61** 233 **78** 410
Addie **143** 23
Adelaide **89** 180
Adeline **79** 31
Adeline M. **81** 282
Agatha Strother **102** 163
Aggephe **54** 49
Albert **82** 22
Albert H. **114** 307
Albert N. **70** 154
Alberta Hildegarde **77**
 237 **78** 202
Alex S. **82** 442
Alexander **104** 102 **108**
 188 **118** 45 49 56 **125**
 196 258
Alexander H. **88** 339
Alexander J. **116** 124
Alfred **91** 251
Alfred George **85** 326
Alfred S. **91** 35
Alice **66** 356 **87** 173 **90** 333
 101 12 15
Alice (Edwards) **101** 15
Alice (Homeyard) **101** 23
Alice Prowde **101** 11
Allen **72** 182
Alma Eloise **90** 136
Almira **74** 304 **82** 22
 123 93
Almira Cynthia **63** 184
Almira E. **120** 222
Almira S. **121** 177
Alonzo **65** 13 14 17 18
 101 75 **110** 17 **120** 304
 144 60 **148** 331
Althea **74** 298
Amanda F. **73** 36
Amelia **117** 163
Amelie **62** 85
Ammon **73** 166
Amos **79** 35 **89** 180 **96** 79
 115 120 **125** 293 **128**
 300
Amy **55** 49 **91** 189 248
 250 251 **105** 108
Amy (Clarke) **91** 250
Amy (Hopkins) **105** 109
Anabel **82** 430 441
Andreiss **109** 100
Andrew **54** 408 409 **60** 28

LEWIS *cont'd*
82 284 292 **84** 381 **101** 6-
 9 12-17 23 86 **111** 230
 112 304
Angeline M. **120** 136 **122**
 72 233
Ann **55** 294 **65** 73 **73** 218
 76 136 **82** 46 216 **99** 25
 109 97 **142** 377
Ann (Burrows) **116** 285
Ann (Gaines) **132** 163
Ann (Welch) **100** 299
Ann Jenckes (Vose) **120** 7
Ann Jenks **120** 11
Anna **51** 286 **53** 207 **63** 84
 66 164 165 **67** 315 **76**
 139 **79** 77 **82** 292 293 **91**
 251 **92** 64 **99** 46 **102** 223
 107 108 201 **108** 189
 109 35 96 97 **111** 308
 116 285
Anna (Barlow) **132** 42
Anna (Hamilton) **118** 61
Anna (Huntley) **101** 143
Anna (Lothrop) **97** 277
Anna Burrows **116** 285
Anna Gilpin **81** 338
Anna Newton **94** 138
Anna Phillips **98** 343
Anne **51** 133 **55** lxv **66** 270
 101 7 15 **102** 165 **107**
 108
Anne (Sotherne) **101** 10
Anne Adelia **118** 61
Anner **99** 254 **103** 69
Annette **96** 160
Annie (Reynolds) **127** 35
Annie Burr (Auchincloss)
 97 383
Annie D. **127** 35
Annie E. **77** 179
Annie Olive (Pearson)
 96 333
Ansel **75** 172
Antipas **105** 86 88
Apphia **83** 266 395
Arabella **69** 207
Arch. S. **76** 46
Archebus **82** 322
Archibald **76** 137
Ariel M. **85** 409
Arnold Angell **82** 499
Arozona (Rich) **84** 48
Asa **55** 178 **85** 409
Asa Packard **94** 44
Asenath **87** 228 234
Augustus **73** 213 **128** 217
Augustus Marion **82**
 427 430 441 442
Aurelia **108** 265
Azubah **127** 178 179
B. F. **91** 328
Barachiah **55** 262 **91** 189
Barachias **57** 259
Barnabas **116** 40
Barrent **106** 300
Bartlett **109** 35
Barzillai **51** 40
Basha C. **108** 265
Bathsheba **86** 395 **129** 34
Bathsheba (Swift) **109** 35

LEWIS *cont'd*
Beason **97** 82
Benajah **73** 320 321 **127**
 106 107
Benjamin **53** 314 **73** 320
 80 427 **82** 46 288 292 **83**
 267 395 **84** 50 **96** 79 **98**
 106 **103** 280 **105** 87 195
 309-311 **106** 102 182-
 184 **107** 108 198 201 270
 271 274 289 292 **108** 54
 122 192 **127** 106 **128**
 191 294
Benjamin Bryan **82** 430
 442
Benjamin F. **83** 18
Benjamin Franklin **85**
 219 **126** 191
Benjamin Gorham
 108 259
Benjamin M. **117** 212
Benoni **66** 356
Bertha **91** 247 **93** 350
 106 310
Bertha Estelle **82** 22
Bethany **120** 251
Bethiah **58** 259 **106** 270
Bethiah (Smith) **122** 49
Betsey **55** 421 **60** 306 **68**
 317 **76** 265 **83** 34 **108**
 208 262 **114** 307 **117**
 212 **127** 178 179 **128**
 187 191
Betsey (Stayson) **125** 217
Betsey A. (Lucas) **120** 217
Betsey G. **78** 306
Betty **87** 256 **95** 74 **105** 309
 107 271 **108** 190
Beula **118** 61
Beulah **55** 421
Billie Redding **141** 253
Blanch (Corbet) **101** 14
Blaney **108** 264
Borden **100** 264
Burriah **128** 217
Byron Ray **82** 237 252
C. F. **124** 206
C. G. **91** 328
Calvin **82** 21 **89** 42 **124** 63
Calvin Smith **57** 375
Calvin Winfield **51** 228
 57 xxxiii **61** xxxiv **64**
 xxxi
Camila (Phillips) **98** 343
Candace **57** 137
Candis **115** 44
Capitola Alberta
 (Hannum) **91** 45
Carlisle **123** 100
Carll Andrews **91** 250
Caroline **57** 286 **60** 306
 114 191
Caroline Antoinette
 76 lvii
Caroline E. **93** 350 **118** 191
Caroline Louisa **92** 351
Caroline S. **141** 148
Caroline Wesley **82** 22
Carolyn Trowbridge
 (Brown) **86** 93
Carrie Lincoln **74** 304

LEWIS *cont'd*
Carrie Lincoln (Stover)
  86 197
Catherine **55** 399 **65** 132
  250 **85** 167 **107** 299 **110**
  142
Catherine (Fry) **88** 131
Catherine Cubin **94** 44
Catherine Cubin
  (Cannell) **94** 44
Catherine E. (Jackson)
  88 335
Catherine Fry (Knowles)
  88 131
Catherine Prowde **101** 10
Celia **81** 311 **82** 18
Celia (Chase) **88** 26
Charity **146** 374
Charles **63** 257 **64** 19 **70**
  153 **73** 321 **84** 382 **91** 45
  97 131 222 **101** 143 **109**
  35 234 **111** 305 **127** 106
  107 **136** 270
Charles E. **69** 187 **70** 155
Charles H. **125** 238
Charles Hildreth **61** 217
Charles Preston (Mrs.)
  105 128
Charles Sheldon **85** 296
Charles W. (Mrs.) **101** 179
  102 239
Charles Winslow (Mrs.)
  99 148
Charlotte **73** 166 **103** 280
Charlotte S. **81** 338
  125 290
Chester Evert (Mrs.)
  109 130
Chloe **61** 233
Christian **111** 57
Christopher **108** 208 263
Christopher Clarke
  91 250 251
Christopher D. **125** 176
Christopher E. **125** 176
Churchill Gorham
  82 430 442
Clara **114** 184
Clarissa **70** 154 155 **76** 142
  107 108
Clark **107** 108
Clementine **57** 286
Clemmie May **82** 22
Content (Langworthy)
  91 250
Cora **86** 300 **97** 139
Cora P. **117** 213
Cordelia A. (Rathbun)
  100 89
Cornelia **111** 305
Cornelia G. **114** 315
Cornelius **118** 211
Curtis **114** 315
Cynthia **61** 233 **114** 7 **119**
  320 **126** 207
Cynthia (Sanford)
  128 212
Cynthia E. S. (Parker)
  114 7
Cynthia Sanford **128** 212
Cyrus Oliver **118** 61

LEWIS *cont'd*
Daily **115** 114
Daniel **63** 49 111 **69** 282
  73 153 **76** lxxxix **86**
  395 **87** 398 **91** 249-251
  371 **92** 33 64 **101** 13-15
  23 **104** 242 **121** 216 **122**
  22 **123** 37 **128** 301 **129**
  39 60 **136** 270 332
Daniel B. **81** 282
Daniel Clark **91** 142 251
  96 79 80 88 166
Daniel Clark (Mrs.)
  83 126 232
Daniel Davis **132** 242
Daniel Frank **84** 295
Daniel R. **106** 79
Daniel Wells **114** 315
Daniolt **101** 14
David **57** 190 **58** 259 **63**
  263 **66** 232 233 **74** 179
  180 **76** 149 **78** 307 **85**
  167 **88** 334 **98** 343 **99**
  249 **106** 102 182 **114** 7
  115 193 **116** 285 **121**
  142 **123** 80 93 **128** 224
  140 162
David H. **72** 204
Davis Draper **96** 80
Debby **57** 262
Deborah **85** 369 **86** 396
  95 360 **101** 12 13 **105** 86
  106 49 **129** 34 35
Deborah (Herd) **90** 253
Deborah (Luff)
  (Pleasanton) **106** 45
Deliverance **55** 49
Desire **63** 182
Desire (Parker) **113** 20
Desire Bacon **85** 219
  126 191
Dexter Wadleigh **79** 34
Dianah **115** 223
Diantha **88** 292
Diconson **66** 112
Dimon **54** 445 **116** 141
Dinah (Rich) **83** 266
Dio **55** xciv **69** lxix
Dora Bellows **99** 146
Dorcas **57** 157 **61** 42 **100**
  302 **126** 145
Dorothy **52** 309 **54** 420
  101 82 **111** 230 **114** 130
Dorothy (Bragdon)
  116 131
Drusilla **95** 16
Dyantha (Croel) **108** 262
E. E. **56** 323
Ebenezer **54** 274 **61** 42 **68**
  321 **77** 80 **83** 418 **97** 277
  99 198 **106** 212 270 **115**
  308 **116** 297 **143** 343
Eber **100** 270 **101** 141
Edgar **108** 259
Edith **82** 376
Edith Chase **86** 197
Edmund **59** 302 **73** xxxiii
  76 lvii **101** 23 77 **106**
  143 **108** 94 **143** 124
Edna E. (Jennings)
  121 180

LEWIS *cont'd*
Edward **51** 133 134 **58**
  282 362 363 **59** 65 **101**
  14 15 **106** 183 **108** 208
  109 39 **114** 315
Edward H. **79** 16
Edwin Ashley **82** 430 441
  442
Edwin Coffin **85** 221
Edwin James **57** lxix
Edwin P. **81** 282
Edwin R. **91** 251
Edwin S. **69** 187
Edwin Whitney **76** lviii
Eldad **61** 285 **141** 49
Eleanor **52** 273 **70** 37 **101**
  16 86 **127** 35
Eleanor (Eynes) **101** 11
Eleanor (Green) **96** 79
Eleanor (Johnson) **129** 34
Eleanor (Waring) **101** 11
Eleanor (Webber) **115** 308
Eleanor Parke **81** 198
Eleazer **76** 137-140 142
  143 147 172 **77** 80 **80** 18
  96 79
Elias **128** 223 301
Elihu **76** 131 136
Elijah **60** 338 **102** 235 **125**
  100 **135** 43
Elijah P. **78** 304
Elisha **79** 166 **126** 60
Elisha I. **81** 290
Eliza **60** 239 **72** 257 **73** 213
  78 237 **82** 289 292 **88**
  278 **91** 250 **92** 63 **108**
  183 **125** 105
Eliza (Allen) **119** 67
Eliza (Hull) **111** 304 305
Eliza (Kinsbury) **88** 334
Eliza A. **79** 152
Eliza Allen **89** 361
Eliza C. (Carter) **101** 213
Eliza P. **77** 235
Elizabeth **51** 133 134 286
  52 78 **54** 274 421 **58** 52
  60 239 **62** 257 **63** 267
  65 165 180 **66** 19 125
  164 165 **77** 203 316 **81**
  429 445 **82** 499 **83** 266
  88 279 **91** 250 **94** 157
  97 7 **100** 264 298 **101** 12
  16 19 21-23 86 **105** 87
  106 182 **108** 259 **109** 35
  110 315 **111** 19 **114** 5
  115 114 217 **116** 136
  121 44 45 **123** 74 **127**
  179 **143** 343 **145** 234
Elizabeth (Borden)
  100 264
Elizabeth (Clapp) **114** 315
Elizabeth (Ellis) **119** 173
Elizabeth (Foster) **92** 170
Elizabeth (Gallison)
  118 283
Elizabeth (Gifford) **129** 39
Elizabeth (Huntley)
  100 264
Elizabeth (Manser)
  125 293

LEWIS *cont'd*
Elizabeth (Marshall) **101**
16 91
Elizabeth (Merrill) **108**
189 **132** 269
Elizabeth (Merriman)
106 212
Elizabeth (Penfield)
109 35
Elizabeth (Shepherd)
87 111
Elizabeth (Vickery)
(Dixon) **143** 343
Elizabeth (Welch) **115** 135
Elizabeth (Whiton)
135 43
Elizabeth Foster **92** 170
Elizabeth Greenough **62**
213 **71** lix lxvi 99 100
92 351 **95** 351
Elizabeth H. **70** 155
Elizabeth Heywood
101 21
Elizabeth M. **73** 270
Elizabeth McKie **114** 315
Elizabeth Munroe (Chace)
117 213
Elizabeth Prowde **101** 10
Ella Beach **90** 209
Ella May **79** 201 **82** 124
251 **87** 304 **125** 124 **148**
221
Ella May (Swint) **83** 246
Ellen **74** 298 **89** 382 **101** 8
Ellen J. (Dow) **86** 300
Ellen L. **88** 140
Ellen Stearns **79** 34
Ellis **82** 284 292
Elmanson **73** 321 **127** 107
Elnathan **105** 87 89 202
106 101 102 182 **108**
208 **109** 43
Elvira (Mann) **96** 79
Ely **100** 264
Elzada **73** 321 **127** 107
Emeline **70** 5 **71** 100
91 251
Emeline (Wells) **91** 251
Emily **83** 194
Emily Eugenia **82** 430
441 442
Emily Harriet **82** 421
Emily Huntington **71** lii
Emily Johonnot **58** lx
Emma Margaret **77** 267
Enoch **74** 304 **81** 338 **97**
268 **125** 238 **128** 129
Enoch B. **88** 132
Ephraim **86** 131
Eresmen Fell **73** 275
Ernest Grant **96** 390
Ernest Grant (Mrs.) **84**
341 **85** 195 **96** 149 166
390
Esther **60** 68 **69** 161 **75** 200
89 385 **116** 285 **124** 61
148 327
Ethel Borden **99** 333
Ethelinda (Huntley)
101 202
Etta A. **91** 190

LEWIS *cont'd*
Etta M. **117** 221
Eunice **63** 265 267 **67** 224
76 147 **128** 186 **143** 343
Eunice G. **111** 305
Eunice M. **108** 260
Eva (Parker) **121** 142
Evan **107** 319
Evelina **111** 241
Everett E. **57** 234
Everett Edward **58** xlv
Experience **54** 274 **105** 87
Experience (Bassett)
125 150
Ezekiel **60** 239 **84** 260
104 242 **106** 212
Ezra **67** 54
Fannie **114** 315
Fannie B. **83** 434 435
Fanny **60** 28 **93** 257
102 289
Fanny (Gray) **114** 315
Fanny Bowers **93** 350
Fanny C. **91** 250
Fear **118** 283
Flavel **55** 286
Flavia A. **82** 380
Flora **82** 430 441 442
128 95
Florence M. **82** 430 441
Florence Sherman (Davis)
96 80
Florentius **51** 286
Frances **73** 166 **77** 230 **85**
437 **89** 131 **93** 257
Frances Amelia **63** 386
65 95
Frances Amelia
(Smallage) **85** 296
Frances Cordelia **70** 155
Frances Jane **82** 427 430
441 442
Frances M. **70** 155
Frances Maria **76** lvii
Francis **51** 133 **66** 80 81
100 188 **113** 25 127 **115**
225
Francis B. **113** 25
Francis Beecher **113** 127
Francis Bucker **113** 127
Frank **116** 124
Frank Grant **75** 81 316
76 xxii **88** 306 **108** 273
Frank H. Erwin **109** 234
Frank Percival **82** 430
441 442
Frank W. **56** xxxii
Franklin Henshaw
73 xxxiii
Frederic **52** 433 446 **108**
210 258-260 263 **109** 44
114 315 **123** 204
Frederic (Mrs.) **108** 260
G. B. **76** 53 54
G. Frank **117** 221
Gardner **69** 187 274
Genevieve Neva **85** 296
Genvieve Neva **85** 296
Geo. **128** 312
George **51** 207 **55** 309 **57**
371 **58** 260 **60** 28 **65** 95

LEWIS *cont'd*
152 **66** 356 **71** 100 **77** 45
78 443 **80** 55 **82** 72 376
83 266 **84** 48 295 **86** 395
90 328 **91** 202 **96** 79 **99**
25 **102** 180 **109** 35 **113**
20 **116** 124 **128** 298 **129**
34 39 **143** 343
George (Mrs.) **84** 342
85 195
George Amasa **76** lvii
George Arthur **76** lviii
George B. **101** 124
George Cressy **118** 61
George Edward **63** 111
67 96
George F. **84** 299
George Harlan **65** xxxiv
73 xix **76** xxx lvii
George Howard **85** 326
George Howard (Mrs.)
75 xxiii **85** 187 201 326
George R. **101** 202
George W. **65** 135
George Washington
93 350
George Willis **118** 61
Georgia **75** 38
Georgia Ellen **104** 145
Georgina **120** 228
Gershom **52** 78
Gilbert Newton **136** 321
Grace **51** 207
Green **128** 300
Griffin **55** 49
H. S. **126** 233
Hannah **55** 49 262 399 **57**
261 **58** 363 **60** 239 306
61 96 **63** 49 293 **64** 373
65 353 **67** 132 **75** 193
77 xcix **78** 443 **80** 26 **83**
266 **86** 338 395 **90** 328
91 19 189 250 251 **97**
183 **100** 264 **101** 141
102 261 **106** 155 182
107 108 289 292 **108** 54
188 192 **109** 35 78 **111**
112 **113** 25 114 135 **116**
129 179 **121** 272 **122** 49
124 18 **127** 179 **128** 59
139 36 37 46 **142** 64 **143**
343
Hannah (Baker) **148** 327
Hannah (Chipman) **84** 53
Hannah (Donnell) **113**
25 127
Hannah (Hopkins)
102 58
Hannah (Junkins)
90 231 249
Hannah (Lincoln)
121 211
Hannah (Pierce) **128** 186
187 190 191
Hannah (Sage) (Wilcox)
106 211
Hannah (Tibbetts) **100** 35
Hannah A. (Trow) **124** 63
Hannah B. **127** 177
Hannah Newell **75** 200

LEWIS *cont'd*
Harold Mann (Mrs.) **84** 234 **85** 195
Harriet **66** 108 **71** lii **80** 55 **82** 421 **83** 24 25 **108** 76
Harriet (Cox) **140** 54
Harriet A. **117** 212
Harriet Amanda **147** 182
Harriet Ann (Bancroft) **96** 333
Harriet Ann Townsend **78** 443
Harriet Augusta **126** 142
Harriet E. **81** 478
Harriet E. (Russell) **88** 341
Harriet M. (Penniman) **88** 282
Harriet Matilda **79** 16
Harriet Southworth **63** 386 387 **65** 93 95
Harry Lincoln **76** lviii
Harry R. (Mrs.) **100** 112
Harvey A. **58** 259
Hattie Bancroft **96** 333
Hattie M. **104** 102
Hattie Mabel **81** 43
Helen Virginia (Worrell) **96** 79
Helen Worrell **96** 80
Henry **51** 286 **73** 104 **90** 233 254 **92** 358 **93** 61 64 115 121 124 **94** 41 **107** 319 **114** 315 **117** 201
Henry A. **101** 202
Henry F. **123** 203
Henry Martyn **63** 387 **65** 93
Henry R. **126** 112
Henry S. **90** 327
Henry Wells **114** 315
Herbert Radnor (Mrs.) **86** 93
Herman Enoch **74** 304
Herman Enoch (Mrs.) **86** 197
Hester Heywood **101** 21
Hezekiah **82** 380 **85** 167 **128** 221
Horace Holden **125** 150
Howard **81** 43
Howard Clinton **82** 22
Howard F. **117** 213
Howell **109** 234
Hubbard R. **101** 202
Hugh **73** 151
Huldah **107** 274
Huldah (Mitchell) **132** 269
Humphrey **55** 438
Ichabod **75** 194
Ida **78** 108 **94** 139 **118** 68
Ida Eleanor **85** 221
Irena (Norman) **121** 303 **122** 148
Irene **108** 259
Irene (Fitgerald) **120** 304
Isaac **66** 108 **76** 143 **91** 189 **123** 190 **132** 42 **136** 270
Isaac B. **76** 264 265
Isaac M. **78** 399
Isaac Newton **55** xxix **63** 389 391 **64** xxix **65** 18

LEWIS *cont'd*
84 180 **90** 124 **91** 189 297 **92** 149
Isabel **101** 14
Isabel (Millard) **101** 14
Isabella **51** 133 **89** 381
Isabella R. **117** 212
Isaiah **78** 443 **80** 22 **86** 396 398 399 **90** 400 **113** 194 **119** 67 **121** 71 **140** 54
Israel **128** 301 **143** 343
Israel Ashley **114** 315
Ivory **90** 329 **91** 20 **120** 217
J. J. **57** 16
J. Morrell **111** 305
J. P. **54** 363
J. W. **52** 193
Jabez **63** 267 **73** 320 321 **76** 172 **78** 25 **88** 334 **105** 86 88 **108** 259 261 **109** 41 43 44 **127** 106 107
Jacob **101** 273 **118** 283 **129** 60
Jael (Rooker) **127** 57
James **54** 393 **55** 19 **59** 194 **60** 39 **63** 182 **68** 315 317 320 **70** 218 297 **73** 320 321 **78** 443 **79** 77 440 **80** 260 **82** 208 499 **87** 263 **88** 26 **91** 190 **92** 170 **95** 60 **96** 79 **99** 209 332 **104** 242 **108** 260 307 **117** 311 **127** 106 107 **128** 59 186 187 190 191 294 **129** 34 **136** 30 **138** 25 **143** 343 **147** 343
James A. **66** 34
James B. **103** 280 **121** 180
James D. **120** 249 251
James F. **119** 77
James Franklin **99** 332
James Hawkes **75** 200
James M. **75** 207
James N. **84** 53
James R. **121** 180
James S. **136** 251
Jane **51** 133 **58** 282 362 363 **59** 65 **67** 285 **76** 90 **100** 264 **101** 16 86 **125** 301
Jane (Snelling) **105** 55
Jane M. **75** 172
Jane Pelletreau **114** 315
Jane Withington **75** 207
Jared **62** 85
Jason **82** 116 **87** 234 242 **94** 386
Jeannette (Wells) **114** 315
Jedediah **70** 154 155
Jedediah S. **70** 155
Jemima **115** 279
Jemima (Huntley) **100** 270
Jenny (Young) **83** 267
Jenny Frances **76** xxii **99** 134 152 332 333
Jenny Francis **75** 316
Jeremiah **111** 19 **112** 214 **115** 224 **119** 61 **120** 136 **142** 377

LEWIS *cont'd*
Jerusha (Rich) **84** 47
Jesey **128** 303
Jessymin Thurman **91** 210
Joan **101** 22 **123** 249
Joan Prowle **101** 10
Joanna **112** 304 **115** 224 **123** 198 233
Joanna (Booth) **119** 198
Joanna (Chase) (Franklin) **87** 262
Joanna E. (Bradeen) **91** 35
Job **57** 280 **60** 239 **97** 108 109
Joel **75** 200
Joh **121** 107
Johanna **115** 140
John **51** 131-134 140 252 286 **52** 78 309 **54** 97 **58** 128 **59** 384 **60** 28 306 **62** 92 **63** 142 189 263 **64** 19 **65** 26 **66** 125 229 354 356 **67** 26 **75** 220 **76** lvii lxxxix 174 **78** 74 443 **79** 45 77 **80** 351 **82** 46 47 208 210 214 216 282 293 312 317 320 322 413 **83** 266 401 **86** 397 **90** 155 **91** 189 230 **97** 271 **98** 300 **100** 264 299 **101** 7 8 11 13 23 77 244 **102** 52 58 266 275 **103** 18 89 **105** 86 283 **108** 213 **110** 168 317 **113** 120 290 **116** 285 **118** 61 **119** 173 320 **120** 7 **121** 109 211 213 273 280 **125** 175 217 **126** 233 **127** 57 **128** 220 295 **129** 57 **131** 128 **140** 68 **144** 321 329 **148** 334
John (Mrs.) **97** 271
John A. **88** 341
John Addison Cobb **109** 234
John B. **55** 179 **67** 224 **90** 55 **91** 121 **96** 333
John B. (Mrs.) **114** 191
John Bevens **96** 333
John C. **105** 108 109
John Churchill **82** 430 442
John Cobb **109** 234
John Grant **96** 390
John L. **75** 38
John Saunders **98** 264
John Thomas **77** 183
Jon **109** 38 229 234
Jona. **128** 294
Jonah **55** 49
Jonas **57** 259 **98** 104 105 **143** 363
Jonathan **59** 93 **76** lvii **96** 79 **119** 320 **120** 79
Joseph **52** 145 **55** 421 **56** 25 **63** 25 190 191 265 **66** 270 273 356 **79** 46 **84** 47 **90** 231 237 238 249 253 330 333 400 **91** 21 23 **95** 393 **97** 326 **100** 35 264 **101** 12 **105** 225 **107** 236 **108** 208 **109** 44 **115** 226

LEWIS *cont'd*
116 136 124 26 136 28
139 49 143 123 124 342
343 148 43
Joseph E. 86 300
Joseph P. 91 142
Joseph Saunders 53 460
Joseph W. 77 179 92 351
94 52
Joseph Warren 92 358
Josephine 85 195
Josephine (Billings)
94 52
Josephine G. 94 52
Joshia Flint 118 61
Joshua 55 399 57 261 262
371 375 64 19 101 14
Josiah 107 313 111 112
117 225
Judah 80 427 87 234 238
Judith 52 433 101 19 21 23
120 107
Julia (French) 123 75
Julia (Murphy) 125 176
Julia A. 91 29 113
Julia Ann 75 200 78 399
92 351
Julia S. (Sayward) 91 230
Juliann 123 93
Justus 72 36
Katharine 75 xxiii 82 46
Katharine (Bell) 85 106
Katharine (Fitz Randolph)
98 228
Katharine B. 64 131
Katharine Bell 85 187 327
Keziah 52 446 108 264
111 115
Keziah (Chamberlain)
88 337
Laban 75 200
Lathby 105 283
Lathley 91 198
Lathy 87 14
Laura 70 155 105 128
114 315
Lavator B. 61 201
Lavenia 111 305
Lawrence 81 198 93 305
Leicester C. 105 319
Lela (Hutton) 93 350
Leland 101 202
Lemuel 98 300
Lena 75 81
Lendall 108 213
Leonard 104 102 106 300
Lester A. 111 305
Levi 55 286 100 188
Lina Nichols 77 187
Lincoln 98 228 111 112
Lois (Gifford) 130 138
Lois (Tibbetts) 100 35
Lorry 70 155
Lot 127 178
Lothrop 70 37 90 400
Lothrop Howland
108 259
Louisa 84 51
Louisa S. (Blaisdell)
123 75
Louise 100 200

LEWIS *cont'd*
Lucia 106 212
Lucinda 127 178 179
Lucinda (Silvester) 86 131
Lucinia Ann 73 275
Lucretia 78 25 106 212
Lucretia (Crowell) 109 39
Lucy 52 78 55 399 80 18
83 267 84 50 104 102
118 242 143 343
Lucy Anner 108 259
Lucy Jane (Rich) 84 299
Lucy Marion 105 3
Luther 126 207
Lydia 58 259 63 49 68 320
74 202 75 200 80 22 83
83 84 99 102 266 271
273-275 278 106 182
115 122 125 182 127
178 179
Lydia (Allen) 119 61 64
Lydia (Chase) 87 263
Lydia F. 116 124
Lydia M. 121 71 73
Lyman 108 196 114 314
315
Lyman Samuel 123 93
M. 63 184
M. B. 76 53
M. Louise 73 xix 74 xxvi
M. S. 127 106
Mabel (Hoyt) 120 79
Mabel A. 77 156 78 203
Magdalen 101 86
Malachi 106 211
Malcolm (Mrs.) 92 81
Malin Wilson (Mrs.)
108 134
Marcia F. 114 7
Margaret 63 190 76 xli
82 216 83 404 84 131
90 89 110 101 12 13 21
22 86 104 102 114 315
131 128 134 224
Margaret (Ashley)
114 315
Margaret (Lathly) 83 404
Margaret (Tate) 125 196
Margaret (Webster)
90 328
Margaret Ann 125 196
Maria 65 250 125 175
Maria (Crossman) 135 76
Maria A. 116 124
Maria Clarissa 89 186
111 148
Maria Newman 62 lvii
Maria Richards 54 lxi
Marian Gove 105 128
Marie 66 164 165 355
Marietta (Combs) 112 240
Marjorie (Ireland) 101 11
Mark 78 308
Mark C. 114 262 264
Marsh 128 301
Martha 66 164 165 73 320
321 79 305 408 82 499
91 250 105 86 89 114 11
123 216 127 106 142
381
Martha (Benson) 90 327

LEWIS *cont'd*
Martha (Hopkins) 102 52
Martha (Prosser) 91 250
Martha (Smith) 98 264
Martha (Westcott) 127
106 107
Martha Ellen (Radcliffe)
96 80
Martha Heywood 101 21
Martha J. 104 102
Martha Sophronia 118 61
Martin 123 93
Marvin H. 76 161
Mary 51 133 134 52 78 53
314 54 393 394 55 421
57 lxix 190 261 60 68
306 61 63 62 92 63 187
191 248 65 250 66 270
273 69 374 70 243 73
143 75 148 77 37 39 183
229 78 299 443 79 194
80 22 427 82 46 282 286
293 376 413 83 266 84
29 295 332 85 102 243
86 395 87 111 234 240
88 27 90 229 250 92 291
93 283 96 90 99 198 209
100 238 239 264 101 11-
16 20 22 75-77 86 102
290 105 87 106 101 218
107 270 271 274 108 54
265 302 109 32 229 111
19 114 47 115 223 116
285 119 198 121 282
122 143 125 214 126
256 127 178 179 128 20
59 302 134 151 143 102
Mary (Atkins) 126 204
Mary (Bray) 108 264
Mary (Burrill) 102 266
Mary (Chamberlain)
88 339
Mary (Cole) 132 42
Mary (Davis) 109 68
Mary (Dyer) 132 242
Mary (Ellis) 122 262
Mary (Gardner) 101 14
Mary (Harding) 101 22
Mary (Herring) 101 16
Mary (Hopkins) 102 52
Mary (Hopkins) (Snow)
127 179
Mary (Jones) 143 124
Mary (Junkins) 115 65
Mary (Lewis) 101 86
Mary (Liddons) 125 175
Mary (Lloyd) 101 11
Mary (Lumbard) 96 79
Mary (Lunt) 126 145
Mary (Nichols) 127 179
Mary (Perry) 116 40
Mary (Strong) 136 332
Mary (Turrell) 136 270
Mary (Whitehead) 101 21
Mary A. 69 32
Mary A. (Hopkins)
123 203
Mary Alice 123 80
Mary Ann 69 172 78 71 79
51 156 101 31 102 223
118 61 140 144 144 321

LEWIS *cont'd*
329
Mary Ann (Grant) **97** 228
Mary Ann (Holmes)
  88 334
Mary Anne **82** 499
Mary Anner **108** 259
Mary Augusta **93** 350
Mary B. **78** 179 **90** 389
  108 260
Mary C. B. (Bangs)
  123 204
Mary D. **82** 430 441
Mary Draper **93** 64
Mary E. **65** 135
Mary Eliza **81** 311 **82** 18
Mary Elizabeth **117** 201
  118 61
Mary Elizabeth
  (Goodwin) **96** 166 390
Mary Freeman
  (Heueston) **88** 335
Mary Fry **91** 183
Mary Gelston **114** 315
Mary Haworth (Ellis)
  121 240
Mary Hawthorne **109** 131
Mary Hinckley (Sheldon)
  136 321
Mary Jane **106** 143
Mary Jane (Sanborn) **90**
  333 **91** 23
Mary Louise **81** 363 **82**
  234 244 499 500
Mary Prowde **101** 10
Mary W. **84** 295
Mary Winslow **92** 351
Matthew **116** 7
Maudlin **64** 260
Maxon **70** 243
Maxson **128** 300
May A. **82** 430 441
Mehitable **57** 90 **114** 11
Mehitable (Hallet)
  108 263
Mehitable (Pepper)
  123 119
Mehitable (Phinney)
  126 191
Mehitable (Richards) **90**
  330 **91** 21
Mehran **82** 22
Melissa **101** 202 **104** 102
Mercy **82** 216 **142** 125
Mercy (Atkins) **126** 204
Mercy Ann **132** 242
Mercy Maria (Rich)
  (Hopkins) **84** 295
Meribah (Walker)
  117 225
Meriweather **51** 500 501
  65 204 **136** 87
Merritt Bradford **96** 79
Micah **123** 75
Michael **101** 6 13-15
Mildred **109** 234
Mindwell **57** 209 **106** 212
Minerva **73** 320
Minnie O. **65** 135
Miriam **92** 53 **116** 302
Miriam (Rich) **84** 59

LEWIS *cont'd*
Molly **57** 209 **58** 260 **63** 49
  95 393 **102** 69 **107** 201
  145 45
Molly (Baker) **95** 393
Molly (Seavy) **108** 122
Molly LeBaron **96** 391
Morgan **59** 287 **76** lxxxix
  91 230 **101** 23 **111** 19
  112 214 **115** 65
Moses **80** 23 **100** 264
  123 119
Myra **102** 290
Myra Philinda **89** 19 235
Myrtle Irene (Mosher)
  88 169 **106** 116 130 142
Nabba **57** 262
Nabby **63** 255 **67** 54
  140 34
Nabby K. **108** 264
Nabby Turner **60** 337
Nancy **53** 460 **55** 421 **73**
  320 **100** 188 **127** 106
  107
Nancy (Young) **83** 267
Nancy Jane **124** 63
  136 270
Nancy Jane (Quint)
  91 121
Naomi **70** 92 **105** 86 202
  108 260
Nathan **63** 255 **70** 92 **76**
  140 **79** 77 **86** 395 **91** 251
  106 184 **126** 233 **129** 39
  227 **145** 45
Nathan B. **134** 209
Nathan Kenyon **91** 251
Nathaniel **57** 209 **72** 36
  75 190 **76** lxxxix **79** 43
  83 266 **97** 326 **101** 11
  13 **106** 270 **111** 19 258
  304 305 **112** 216 219
  114 48 **115** 44 114 144
  128 220 **132** 163
Nathaniel E. **89** 382
Nathaniel L. **111** 305
Nathaniel T. **136** 270
Nehemiah **54** 274 **101** 15
Nellie M. (Kimball)
  125 161
Nelson **82** 173 **108** 210
Newton **123** 93
Nicolas Seavy **107** 271
Norman **123** 93
Obadiah **70** 155 **128** 59
Olive **90** 240 315 **96** 333
  116 131 297
Olive (Fitzgerald) **119** 67
Olive J. (Brown) **91** 122
Olive P. (Cole) **90** 329
  91 20
Oliver **128** 221
Oliver F. **123** 75
Oliver P. **125** 287
Olpardo **109** 100
Orrin **82** 376
Ozial **115** 293
Ozias **52** 78
Palemon **73** 321 **127** 107
Patience **110** 308
Patience (Look) **96** 79

LEWIS *cont'd*
Patience (Woodward)
  90 237
Patty **125** 102
Patty (Walker) **117** 144
Paul **63** 265 **130** 138
Peggy **90** 89
Peleg **70** 155 **127** 5
  128 217
Perry E. (Mrs.) **84** 234
  85 195
Peter **54** 409 **74** 298 **76**
  lxxxix **94** 334 **100** 188
  108 189 **112** 286 287
  115 65 **116** 140 **132** 269
Phebe **52** 446 **66** 229 **85**
  409 **93** 308 350 **106** 102
  182 **108** 208 **112** 320
Phebe (Adams) **108** 188
Phebe (Gorham) **108** 263
Phebe Experience **113** 299
Phebe Gorham **108** 258
Philena **55** 49
Philip **58** 391 **85** 121 **98** 60
  105 55 **106** 299 **108** 183
  258 **113** 299
Philip Bullard (Mrs.)
  103 74
Philo **76** 149
Phineas **111** 305
Polly **55** 421 **58** 260 **82** 46
  89 312 **95** 393 **107** 271
  274 **108** 123 **111** 240
  116 285 **120** 7 **127** 178
  179
Polly (Baker) **108** 261
Polly (Perry) **116** 40
Prentis **108** 259
Priscilla **70** 37 **78** 408 **79**
  332 **83** 266-268 **105** 309
Priscilla (Rich) (Rich) **83**
  267 395 **84** 50
Priscilla N. **78** 422
Prudence **66** 103
Prudy A. **116** 260
R. A. **84** 59
Rachel **65** 352 **81** 141 **99** 25
  116 221 **123** 93
Rebecca **53** 55 **55** 178 **58**
  362 **75** 200 **80** 23 **84** 133
  108 259 **141** 12
Rebecca (Bourne) **120** 248
Rebecca (Tibbetts) **98** 300
Rebecca A. **65** 135
Rebecca Chalkley **98** 264
Rebecca Crofts **58** 310
Richard **51** 133 134 **62**
  265 328 **64** 19 255 **65** 44
  76 46 155 **85** 394 **101** 7
  11 12 15 **127** 7 **146** 348
Richmond **76** 155
Robert **51** 134 **57** 280 **59**
  173 **64** 255 **66** 164 165
  68 323 **78** 237 **101** 14 16
  109 234 **127** 175
Robert Barnard **100** 50
Robert Benjamin **88** 335
Robert Colt **114** 315
Robie W. **92** 333
Rodman **76** 50
Rogers **82** 22

LEWIS *cont'd*
Rose A. **79** 34
Roseter J. **79** 35
Rosetta **69** 187
Rosina (Hodgkinson)
  89 182
Roxa **55** 421
Roxena **115** 293
Roxse **69** 187 274
Ruhama **105** 251
Russell **91** 230 **108** 263
Ruth **61** 285 **72** 219 **82** 116
  105 87 **106** 183
Ruth (Bussell) **125** 100
Ruth (Rich) **84** 47
Ruth (Taylor) **109** 38
Ruth (Wilkinson) **94** 386
Ruth B. (Sisson) **125** 238
Ruth Ellen **82** 115 116
Ruth Parmelee **93** 368
S. **84** 47
Sabin **73** 320 321 **127** 106
  107
Sabina **65** 351 352
Sallie B. **79** 25
Sally **58** 259 **70** 155 **78** 74
  90 233 254 **108** 91 **109**
  220 **115** 36 **116** 285 **120**
  39 **125** 109 149 **127** 178
  179
Sally (Allen) **119** 61
Sally (Beal) **116** 305
  117 141
Sally (Clifford) **83** 418
Sally (Lewis) **90** 233 254
Sally (Merrill) **108** 192
Sally Ann **109** 313
Samuel **52** 78 **60** 337 **62**
  357 **63** 143 **65** 238 **66**
  301 356 **82** 376 **87** 111
  91 266 328 **95** 16 **96** 247
  97 228 **100** 264 **101** 13-
  16 217 **105** 205 **106** 212
  107 201 271 274 289
  112 219 276 **113** 194
  114 314 315 **115** 56 57
  116 131 137 **117** 144
  118 211 **119** 61 64 **121**
  71 **124** 210 **127** 179 **132**
  269 **143** 343
Samuel Clapp **114** 315
Samuel E. **121** 303 **122** 148
Samuel Edward **100** 112
Samuel Edwards (Mrs.)
  106 125
Samuel M. **101** 217
  102 223
Samuel P. **51** 16
Samuel Shaw **73** xxxiii
Sarah **51** 134 139 140 252
  52 372 **54** 394 **58** 379
  59 342 **60** 239 338 **62** 92
  63 43 174 265 **65** 351 **66**
  108 164 165 354 356 **70**
  78 92 **72** 258 **73** 166 213
  320 321 **74** 249 **75** 194
  220 **76** 138 **78** 443 79
  385 **80** 153 **81** 79 **82** 46
  207 216 288 293 299 312
  83 266 466 482 **86** 96
  395 **87** 234 241 **91** 230

LEWIS *cont'd*
  93 375 **96** 79 **97** 277 **98**
  353 **99** 198 **100** 35 264
  101 12 14 **104** 215 **105**
  89 309-311 **106** 102 155
  183 184 **107** 108 200 274
  108 122 123 263 **111** 19
  112 258 **114** 227 314 315
  116 134 **120** 249 **121**
  276 **122** 200 **123** 136
  141 251 **124** 63 **125** 160
  126 204 **127** 106 107
  128 175 **129** 255 258
  133 43 **134** 278 **136** 332
  143 138
Sarah (Arey) **129** 39
Sarah (Bassett) **139** 299
Sarah (Blackleach) **148** 43
Sarah (Bliven) **130** 157
Sarah (Butler) **127** 195
Sarah (Dexter) **100** 35
  107 236
Sarah (Dutton) **101** 14
Sarah (Fettiplace) **123** 251
Sarah (Goff) **127** 106
Sarah (Gray) **111** 19
  114 48
Sarah (Howard) **91** 266
Sarah (Hutchins) **108** 189
Sarah (Jenkins) **96** 79
Sarah (Kenyon) **91** 251
Sarah (Kimball) **96** 247
Sarah (Knowles) **88** 132
Sarah (Lane) **143** 343
Sarah (Lewis) **96** 79
Sarah (Marsh) **143** 343
Sarah (Morgan) **91** 230
Sarah (Parker) **113** 120
Sarah (Stephens) **101** 14
Sarah (Stockbridge)
  135 43
Sarah (Thompson)
  112 219
Sarah (Tibbetts) **98** 300
Sarah (Tripe) **112** 214
  115 65
Sarah (Wakefield) **97** 222
Sarah (Wyman) **87** 234
  242
Sarah Ann **93** 121 **110** 52
  115 38
Sarah Ann (Northrup)
  91 250 **92** 64
Sarah B. **66** 112 **88** 339
Sarah Borden Durfee **66**
  lii **73** xxix xxxiii xxxiv
  73 xxxiii
Sarah Caroline **82** 421
  83 181 183
Sarah Content **91** 251
Sarah Dexter (Hasey)
  107 236
Sarah E. **78** 422
Sarah Elizabeth **66** 232
  233
Sarah Gorham **108** 260
Sarah Jane **142** 377
Sarah Kimball **75** 172
  99 187
Sarah Matilda **82** 427 429
  430 441 442

LEWIS *cont'd*
Sarah Tate **125** 196
Sarah Wilkinson **94** 386
Seena (Hancock) **113** 299
Seraphine (Handy)
  126 112
Seth **79** 169
Seth Ames (Mrs.) **78** 330
  79 192 201 **87** 188 **88**
  185 **89** 147 **90** 151 **91**
  157 92 161 **93** 153 94
  154 **95** 161 **96** 175 **97**
  173 **98** 142 162 **99** 164
  100 47 126 152 184 277
  101 140 **102** 139 **103**
  136 **104** 159 **125** 124
Seth Clark **96** 79
Shubael **127** 177-179
Shubael Barton **85** 326
Shubael D. **88** 337
Sibylla **66** 270 273
Silas **75** 193
Silas Huntington **71** lii
Simeon **108** 261 **109** 43
Simon **116** 138
Simpson H. **88** 335
Solomon **108** 213 **119** 67
Sophia **81** 290 **93** 61 **94** 41
  117 229 **123** 93
Sophronia (Bacon) **118** 61
Stephen **56** 38 **69** 187 **73**
  166 **100** 35 **129** 60
Stephen (Mrs.) **106** 45
Sturges **70** 37
Submit **55** 400 **57** 371
Sukey **91** 198
Sukey (Ruggles) **84** 260
Susa **106** 102
Susan **60** 28 **101** 13 14
Susan (Bailey) **87** 226 234
Susan (Nye) **113** 249
Susan (Sears) **108** 263
Susan B. **125** 244
Susan G. **78** 302
Susan Henry **83** 108
Susanna **55** 262 **59** 287
  63 238 **70** 155 **72** 258
  320 **82** 46 320 **91** 230 **92**
  74 **101** 12 21 **106** 102
  121 275 **125** 217
Susanna (Cook) **90** 231
Susanna (Ireland) **101** 12
Susanna (Tolman)
  (Fracker) **124** 26
Susanna H. **94** 45
Susanna Hickling **78** 443
  82 13
Susanna Wallis (Curtis)
  126 207
T. **139** 257
T. G. **78** 296
T. H. **53** 384
Tamsin **58** 239
Temperance **53** 207
  107 224
Terrissa **55** 179
Thankful **96** 79 **105** 86 87
  106 101 102 182 212
  108 208
Thankful (Hallet) **108** 261
Thankful (Lewis) **96** 79

LEWIS *cont'd*
Thankful Hallet **108** 259
Theda **119** 143
Theda A. **121** 71
Thede **55** 421
Theodore **90** 231 251
Theodore G. **55** xxxii
Theodosia **119** 67
Theodosia (Lewis) **119** 67
Theresa (Miller) **90** 55
Thomas **54** 341 393 421
 55 437 **58** 52 142 310 **60**
 68 347 **62** 92 **63** 187 **66**
 355 **67** 72 **69** 32 **71** 123
 73 270 **78** 318 **82** 155
 293 299 421 **83** 318 **84**
 29 **93** 228 **97** 326 **99** 79
 198 209 **100** 238 **101** 3 6-
 8 12-20 22 81 85 91 304
 102 117 172 173 176 223
 106 270 **107** 292 **111**
 112 241 **114** 7 **117** 34
 119 198 **120** 248 **123**
 192 **125** 29 39 **126** 204
 127 195 **128** 212 **129** 34
 136 270 **138** 25 **139** 49
 299 **140** 162 329 **141**
 101 **143** 204 **148** 327
Thomas Ashley **114** 315
Thomas Gorham **82** 430
 442
Thomas H. **54** 445
Thomas S. **83** 24 25
Thomas W. **101** 213
 117 212
Timothy **57** 138 **87** 262
 97 269 **105** 86 **116** 136
 138 29
Timothy A. **70** 155
Tristram S. **91** 122
Ursula (Trappes) **101** 9
Vintin **128** 59
Violet **79** 38
Wait **80** 260
Waitstill **130** 157
Walter Herrold **93** 115
Walter W. **107** 319
Warren **108** 262
Warren Billings **93** 350
Warren G. **127** 35
Warren L. **111** 305
Welcome **91** 251
Whitman **92** 63
William **51** 286 **52** 143
 54 393 394 420 **59** 342
 62 247 **63** 174 234 **64**
 108 113 159 **65** 73 370
 66 37 **69** 172 **76** lvii **77**
 37 203 **80** 26 **81** 311 **82**
 18 317 **83** 83 282 **87** 226
 234 **88** 131 **91** 189 202
 328 **93** 384 387 **100** 35
 238 264 **106** 79 310 **108**
 189 **111** 324 **115** 135
 308 **116** 305 **117** 141
 119 67 **121** 240 **125** 41
 128 223 **136** 270 **145**
 352
William Bliss **91** 251
William Draper **93** 124
William F. **93** 257

LEWIS *cont'd*
William Guilford **82** 430
 441 442
William J. **119** 194
William L. **88** 282
William M. **91** 251
William P. **126** 145
William Penn **75** lxxx
William Reed **54** xxxviii
William Russel **108** 259
William S. **108** 259
William Whitney **93** 257
Wilmarth S. (Mrs.) **97** 383
Wilson F. **117** 213
Winda J. **92** 168
Winslow **52** 104 **54** lxi
 71 lix lxvii 64 100 102
 75 67 **77** 227 **78** 443 **79**
 52 194 **80** 22 **86** 398 **94**
 157 159 **99** 11 14 16 21
 140 34
Woodrow Lyles (Mrs.)
 108 134
Zadock **106** 79
Zebulon **115** 293
Zenas Winslow **108** 260
Zilpah **125** 219
Zintha (Merritt) **96** 79
Zipporah **141** 8
LEWISGER John **65** 236
LEWISHALL J. **108** 203
LEWISSON
Louis **85** 429
Sarah MacCalmont
 85 430
Walter Updike **84** 180
 85 108 206 429
LEWKNOR Joan **112** 308
John **96** 21 **112** 308
Nicholas **96** 21
Sibill **96** 21
Sibyl **96** 21 22
Sibylla **96** 21
Thomas **96** 21 22 **112** 309
LE WOLFE —— **54** 106
LEWORTHY Ruth **97** 139
LEWSON
Martha **51** 422
Thomas **51** 422
LEWTHWAITE
John **65** 25
LEWTON Effie Mildred
 105 128
Lewyn *see* Lewin
LEXINGTON
Alice de **103** 200
John de **103** 200
LEY ____ (Hoffelbauer)
 148 183
Johan Gorg **148** 183
LEYBOURNE Leyborne
Eleanor de **96** 116
Jane **71** 175
Nicholas de **96** 116 118
Robert de **96** 116
Sarah de **96** 116
William **71** 175
LEYDET Bruno **85** 196
LEYE Richard **147** 17
LEYER Margery **58** 404
LEYNERK Edmund **60** 340

LEYONARD
Edmund **60** 240
LEYOUGE
Elizabeth **136** 186
LEYSON Thomas **81** 488
LEZARE Francois **70** 183
LEZER Mary A. **64** 181
L'FABEURE
Rachel **64** 215
L'HOMMEDIEU
La Hommedieu
Le Hommedieu
Ann Amelia **100** 187
Arthur William **107** 79
Benjamin **53** 413 **54** 59
 82 355 **100** 187 **118** 213
 289
Charity **53** 169
Cornelia **58** 37
Elizabeth **118** 289
Ezra **53** 169 170 **54** 59
 118 289
Lucy Cable **100** 187
Martha **54** 59 **118** 213
Martha (Bourne) **118** 213
Mary (Conklin) **118** 289
Mary Catherine **54** 59 60
 82 355
Patience **53** 413 **54** 59
 82 355
Sally **81** 330
Susanna **53** 81 413
Sylvester **53** 81
William **58** 37
Libbey *see* Libby
Libbie *see* Libby
LIBBINS —— **143** 29
LIBBY Libbey Libbie
 —— **92** 347 **147** 282
 — Capt. **83** 194
 — Maj. **103** 191
 — Mr. **82** 218
 — Mrs. **83** 193 **93** 324
 — Widow **82** 46 95 **97**
 373 **103** 195 196
Aaron **103** 196
Abba C. **91** 119
Abba Chase **99** 202
Abbie L. **98** 196
Abial **103** 195 266
Abigail **63** 171 **65** 114 339
 68 93 **70** 319 **74** 213 215
 216 224 226 227 246 249
 252 257 **78** 427 **82** 214
 325 326 328 329 331 503
 84 324 **87** 126 **103** 260
 267 **142** 205
Abigail (Farrington)
 84 324
Abigail (Libbey) **84** 324
Abigail Johnson **99** 202
Abner **63** 178 **87** 124 **88**
 345-349 354 355 **99** 197
 199-201 203 **103** 259
Abraham **81** 445 **90** 169
Agnes **74** 259 **77** 188 **78**
 427 **83** 154 **103** 265
Ai **142** 205
Albert **103** 268
Alice **63** 175 **74** 214 218
 228 248 261

LIBBY *cont'd*

Allen **77** 188
Allison **103** 192 193
Alma W. **121** 142
Almira **65** 340
Alvan **92** 333
Amelia Ann **69** 35
Amos **87** 125 **103** 190 195
  197 255 257 261 **121** 142
Ancil **103** 262
Andrew **97** 142 **102** 307
  103 193 254 258 260 263
  266
Andrews **98** 311
Angie (Davis) **98** 196 197
Angie E. **147** 270
Ann **74** 248 266 **82** 205
  209 215 330 **89** 357
Ann (Seavey) **84** 445
Ann Maria **103** 263
Anna **55** 372 **63** 170 **65** 115
  74 214 226 227 229 255
  82 80 95 329 **83** 13 **87**
  124 **88** 346 347 349 354
  355 **97** 141 267 **103** 193
  115 225 **142** 205
Anna (Lazell) **88** 361
Anna Small **87** 124
  88 348 355
Anne **99** 197 199-201
  121 142
Annie J. (Billings) **98** 107
Annie Laurie **95** 39
Anson O. **95** 39
Ansyl **103** 268
Anthony **82** 362 **84** 324
  445 **103** 192 258
Apphia **88** 355
Arsenath **103** 263
Arthur **82** 362 **84** 445
  125 92
Asa E. **85** 441
Azariah **55** 254
Bathsheba **64** 123
Benjamin **74** 212 215 216
  219 220 226-230 248 252
  253 **76** 47 **78** 427 **81** 429
  82 77-80 83-85 92-94 96
  98 205 325 326 **83** 153
  87 122 **88** 346 356 **95**
  185 **97** 374 **103** 255
Benjamin Carll **88** 356
Bertha May (Sanborn)
  95 188
Bethshua **74** 43
Betsey **65** 115 335 340 **74**
  255 **76** 30 **87** 123 **103**
  196
Betsey (Crosby) **84** 445
Betsey Pettingill **88** 354
  99 200
Betty **65** 354 **74** 219 220
  227 229 230 **97** 374
Bradford **103** 267
C. F. **54** xxxv **56** xxix **57**
  xxx **59** xxxix **60** xxxii
  61 xxx **62** xxxiii
C. T. **124** 100
Calob / Calop **103** 263
  267 268
Caroline **99** 202 **103** 269

LIBBY *cont'd*

Caroline (Twaits) **113** 314
Caroline M. **79** 276
Catherine **103** 263
Catherine (Skillin)
  103 263
Caziah **103** 195
Celia Louia **99** 203
Charles **74** 185 222 246 250
  78 427 **82** 84 217 312
  314 318 321 325 326 328
  329 331 503 **91** 328 **98**
  56 **103** 192 **113** 314
Charles Edward **113** 314
Charles Frank **113** 314
Charles Freeman **59** lvi
  82 362 **84** 445
Charles Milton **103** 269
Charles O. **89** 357
Charles Perley **90** 169
Charles Perley (Mrs.) **76**
  xxi 78 **89** 81 135 **90** 169
Charles T. **103** 98 **147** 270
Charles Thornton **63** 383
  64 376 **65** xxxiv 86 293
  294 **66** xlix 89 189 **69**
  35 36 **70** 185 **71** 91 194
  72 xx **75** 42 **76** 315 316
  79 222 286 379 **80** 6 119
  265 **81** 139 240 367 **82**
  185 **83** 257 **85** 78 **87** 305
  359 **90** 130 209 **98** 11 **99**
  218 **101** 121 **102** 307
  103 77 122 188 270 **104**
  177 **116** 97 176 **120** 242
  243 **121** 229 **124** 288
  303 **131** 248 251 252
  133 94 **141** 114 314 **142**
  111 **143** 38 148 **144** 29
  141 **147** 315 **148** 36 134
Charlie S. **98** 196
Charlotte **65** 115 **103** 197
Charlotte (Tibbetts)
  100 37
Charlotte Neal **88** 355
  99 201
Clara A. **92** 333
Clarissa **83** 340 **103** 259
Clarissa (Noble) **95** 185
Clement **99** 55
Clymena **121** 142
Cornelia M. **103** 267
Cyrus **103** 254 257 259
  268 270 **121** 142
Daniel **51** 45 **55** 311 **59**
  286 **74** 213 215 216 219
  224 226 227 229 250 **79**
  276 **82** 77 85 88 205 212
  214 218 314 318 321 322
  325 **83** 153 183 185 **85**
  447 **87** 124 **88** 346 **98** 55
  99 202 **103** 191 254 260
  261 266 267
David **54** 408 409 **65** 115
  340 **74** 261 **87** 122 **88**
  346 **97** 369 **99** 202 203
  103 257 **127** 224
Dearborn **95** 187
Deborah (Smith) **84** 445
Deborah Bartlett **82** 46
Deliverance **82** 413

LIBBY *cont'd*

Demas **103** 260 264 265
  270
Dolly **97** 367 **98** 56 **99** 200
Dolly (Belknap) **88** 334
Dominicus **103** 195 196
  268 270
Dorcas **74** 261 **79** 276 **82**
  319 **88** 347 **103** 196 261
Dorothea **92** 145
Dorothy **65** 115 **88** 348
  97 374 **103** 191 195 258
  260
Drusilla **103** 254
E. **103** 261
Ebenezer **74** 250 **82** 314
  103 188 194 197 255 260
  264
Edgar **82** 77 **83** 154
Edward **65** 115 340 **97** 374
  103 260 263 264 270
Edward Lewis **69** 35
Edward Watson **69** 35
Edwin **103** 269
Elbridge **103** 258 261
Eleanor **71** 133 **74** 223
  247 261 **88** 356 **97** 374
Eli **103** 264
Eli (Mrs.) **103** 266 269
Eliakim **103** 264
Elias **78** 427 **87** 126 **88** 346
Elisha **82** 85 325
Eliza **97** 369 **98** 56 **99** 201-
  203 **103** 254 261 269
Eliza (Hall) **88** 196
Eliza A. **80** 309
Eliza Jane **103** 262
Eliza Lawrence (Vaughan)
  93 324
Elizabeth **55** 311 314 315
  63 168 171 172 **65** 115
  354 **69** 35 **71** 132 216
  217 **74** 212 214 216 219
  220 226-229 248 250 257
  258 **80** 309 **81** 429 430
  445 **82** 318 330 **83** 9 11
  94 32 95 271 **99** 198
  102 80 **103** 194 195
Elizabeth (Lakeman)
  126 67
Elizabeth (Shorey) **83** 9
Elizabeth A. **68** 154
Elizabeth Goodridge
  (Parlin) **84** 324
Elizabeth Jennie Sarah
  (Taylor) **89** 135 **90** 169
Ellen **78** 363
Ellen Waring **89** 357
Elliott **91** 328
Elmira **65** 115 **103** 264
Elsie L. **94** 374
Elvira S. **98** 196
Ely **103** 270
Emerly **103** 258
Emma Hayes (Dame)
  113 314
Enoch **103** 259
Enos **103** 256
Ephraim **55** 250-252 255
  80 129 **99** 55
Ernestine **96** 78

LIBBY *cont'd*
Ervin **103** 195
Esther **102** 307 **103** 270
Eunice **68** 99 **74** 229 260
  87 122 123 **88** 348 **99**
  197 **103** 191
Eva **68** 154
Experience **74** 228 246
Ezra **97** 300
Ezra B. **68** 154
Fannie S. **92** 110
Fanny **74** 264 **103** 189
Fanny Ward **99** 201
Ferdinand **88** 356
Foxwell **103** 259
Frances A. **69** 36
Frank R. **83** 431 434
Franklin **99** 203
Frederic H. **103** 264
Frederick James **55** xxxv
  231 **81** 238 **82** 246 361
  362 **84** 445
Frederick M. **77** xxviii 78
Freeman **103** 257 269
Freeman Henry **55** 353
George **91** 328 **97** 273
  103 197 255 257 258 266
George Dexter (Mrs.)
  91 142
George P. **103** 266
George Porter **95** 39
George W. **103** 264-266
Gideon **88** 346 **97** 267
Gilman C. **98** 311
Grace **78** 359
H. L. **91** 96
Hannah **55** 314 **59** 286 **65**
  352 **74** 251 255 **82** 217
  321 **83** 10 **87** 121 **100** 42
  103 194 195 254 257 262
  268 **111** 118
Hannah (Tibbetts) **98** 294
  99 53
Hannah E. (Hancock)
  90 169
Hannah F. **89** 357
Hannah F. (Neal) **83** 183
  185
Hannah J. **92** 333
Hannah T. **84** 29
Hanson **74** 216 255 **82** 46
Harriet **88** 347 **99** 199
  103 193 266 268
Harriet L. **148** 175
Harrison **88** 356
Harry **78** 359 **95** 188
Harvey **65** 115 340 **99** 202
Hattie **103** 268
Hattie S. **95** 378
Helen L. (Noble) **113** 314
Helen Marjorie **83** 433
  434
Helena **65** 114
Henrietta B. **82** 362
Henrietta D. **98** 252
Henry **81** 429 430 **99** 202
  103 191 269
Herbert Leslie **87** 174
Hezekiah **103** 189
Horatio K. **68** 154
Horatio Smith **69** 36

LIBBY *cont'd*
Horris **103** 257
I. Harding **99** 202
Ichabod **63** 177 **74** 219 259
  82 329 **103** 193 254 257
Ira **74** 264 **76** 30
Isaac **65** 352 **66** 148 150
  67 276 **82** 362 **84** 324
  445 **98** 294 **99** 53 **125** 92
Isabella (Shapleigh)
  95 268
Isaiah **103** 257
Ivory **103** 260
J. **98** 55
Jacob **103** 196 **125** 102
Jacob George Lewis
  69 35
Jacob S. **65** 115
Jacob Small **99** 199
James **51** 45 **65** 339 353
  354 **74** 219 223 255 262
  81 429 **82** 46 288 293
  329 362 **83** 145 **84** 445
  87 124 **88** 348 **92** 258
  347 **93** 324 **95** 375 **96**
  337 **97** 374 **98** 196 197
  99 197 **100** 37 **103** 191
  192 257 266 **109** 183
  125 95 **142** 203
James Albert **98** 196 197
James Irish **99** 201
James W. **98** 107
Jane **66** 148 **88** 347 **92** 324
  97 267 99 198 **113** 145
Jefferson W. **103** 268
Jemima **97** 143 267
Jemima (Littlefield)
  (Shapleigh) **95** 267
Jemima (Smith) **98** 55
Jeremiah **74** 222 **82** 79
  314 325 **94** 354
Jerusha **97** 375
Jesse **87** 121 **88** 347
  105 290
Jesse M. **98** 196
Jethro **84** 324
Joanna **98** 64
John **51** 45 **74** 220 222 251
  258 **78** 427 **81** 429 **82** 46
  216 285 293 321 328 362
  83 34 **84** 324 445 **87** 121
  88 345-347 349 **91** 328
  97 144 367 **99** 197 199
  202 **102** 307 **103** 189
  192 255 258 261 263 268
John A. **103** 267
John Adams **87** 126
John Bartlett **82** 46
John Franklin **103** 269
John Fuller **61** 217
John Mills **68** 93
John S. **103** 268
Johnson **74** 223 **103** 259
  263 265
Jonathan **93** 397 **100** 63
  103 191 192
Jordan **103** 267 270
Joseph **55** 314 316 **59** 284
  64 123 **65** 114 **74** 220
  81 430 445 **82** 77 205
  207 209 215 319 325 329

LIBBY *cont'd*
330 **83** 9 12 **88** 346 347
  99 197 199 **103** 190 192
  195 197 257 264 **138** 108
  147 270
Josephine Rachel **88** 196
Joshua **74** 222 **81** 429 430
  82 46 **97** 374 **102** 307
  103 190 193 194 196 254-
  256 258-261 **145** 45
Josiah **103** 192 196 255
  258-260 265 267 **142** 199
Josiah W. **88** 196
Joslin S. **97** 369
Jotham **142** 207
Judith **97** 367
Julia Augusta **82** 362
Julia Augusta (Tinker)
  84 445
Julian **103** 258
Juliann (Rogers) **147** 270
Katharine **95** 187
Keziah **74** 227 **88** 347
Kittie P. **98** 196
Levi **84** 324
Lizzie H. **98** 196
Lois **74** 219 229 250 260
  99 202
Looranzo **103** 261
Lottie **103** 268
Louis **103** 268
Louisa **103** 255 269
Louisa Abby **98** 196
Love **81** 445
Lovina **128** 268
Lucy **97** 373 377 **98** 56
  103 258
Lucy (Grant) **147** 270
Lucy Hannah **103** 270
Lucy T. **97** 224
Luke **82** 46 **103** 261 262
  265
Lute Blanche (Morrell)
  91 142
Luther **103** 197 257 259 260
Lydia **55** 316 **63** 171 **74**
  227 247 258 260 **76** 32
  82 87 **83** 12 **97** 369 **98**
  56 **103** 197 256 259 262
  263 266
Lydia (Bean) **98** 56
Lydia (Shorey) **83** 12
Lydia A. **91** 121
Mabel A. **83** 299 300
Margaret **74** 229 **82** 285
  293 **88** 356 **103** 263
Margaret E. **81** 385
Maria **99** 201
Mariam **97** 369 **103** 256
Marietta **92** 113
Mark **74** 219 223 247 248
  263 **103** 192 255 258 260
  262
Martha **55** 250 252 311 **69**
  36 **74** 255 **82** 88 322 **88**
  346 348 355 **97** 267 271
  99 197 201 203 **142** 204
Martha (Hanscom) **95** 267
Martha (Parker) **121** 142
Martha Ellen **99** 203
Mary **55** 314 315 **58** 295

LIBBY *cont'd*
59 190 **65** 352 353 **66**
148 150 **74** 224 228 251
78 427 **81** 445 **82** 78 205
211 312 321 **83** 9 10 **87**
124 **88** 90 346 **97** 145
271 **99** 198 **103** 194 255
257 260-262 264 265 267
142 199
Mary (Batson) **126** 208
Mary (Chandler) **98** 196
Mary (Cleves) **96** 145
Mary (Mosier) **109** 183
Mary (Tibbetts) **98** 294
Mary A. **107** 317
Mary Alice **121** 142
Mary B. **98** 194
Mary B. C. **83** 300 302
Mary C. **68** 203
Mary Chandler **98** 196
Mary Crosby **84** 445
Mary E. **80** 310
Mary Elizabeth **78** 427
99 202
Mary Ingerson **87** 125
Mary Jane (Bradeen)
90 335
Mary L. **92** 333
Mary L. (Lougee) **118** 94
Marynn **98** 56
Matthew **55** 250 253
102 307
Matthias **102** 307 **103** 192
195
Mehitable **55** 316 **78** 427
82 321 **83** 12
Mehitable (Low) **96** 337
Menta Belle **68** 154
Mercy **59** 284 **99** 248
103 255
Meribah **55** 314 **83** 9
Meribah (Lord) **83** 9
Merrit **103** 264
Meserve **99** 197-200
Milton **103** 269 270
Miriam **65** 114 **74** 213
228 253 **82** 205 **103** 197
Molly **63** 177 **74** 230 258-
260
Molly (Lazell) **88** 361
Moses **103** 189 195 259 269
Moses Gilman **84** 324
Moses M. **98** 196
Nancy **98** 196 311 **103** 261
263
Nancy Yeaton **99** 203
Naomi **103** 192
Nathan **55** 254 **74** 252 **95**
267 **97** 143 267 **103** 189
190 192 195 197 254 260
Nathaniel **65** 114 **74** 212
213 219 220 223 228 229
247 **82** 205 207 210 214
216 318 321 **88** 355 **99**
199 **103** 189 191 192 197
255 257 **124** 291 **134**
153
Nathaniel (Mrs.) **103** 257
Nathaniel Smith **92** 347
Nehemiah **103** 193 197 258
Nicholas **103** 191

LIBBY *cont'd*
Octavius B. **84** 29
Olive **59** 38 **63** 168 **71** 133
74 223 247 257 263 **76**
35 **95** 186 **115** 227 **142**
205
Olive Ann **79** 277
Olive B. **92** 333
Oliver **103** 256
Ollie May **98** 197
Osgood **103** 256 257 261
267 268 270
P. **99** 202
Pamela **88** 356
Parmenio **99** 201-203
Patience **82** 329 **88** 346
Patty **87** 123
Paul **55** 314 **80** 309 **82** 92
83 9 **98** 294 **99** 53
Peggy **88** 346
Permenia **88** 346
Peter **80** 27 **88** 361
Phebe **65** 355 **88** 347 **103**
196 262 263 268
Phebe (Tibbetts) **99** 55
Philander **118** 94
Philemon **88** 348 355
99 197
Phineas **103** 189 190 267
269 **142** 199 **145** 164
Polly **59** 286 **74** 253
Polly (Ayer) **97** 374
Priscilla **88** 346 347
99 197 199
Rachel P. **98** 311
Rebecca **81** 430 **103** 267
112 149
Rebecca J. **68** 154
Reuben **55** 250 252 254
66 150 **82** 293 300 318
97 271 **103** 197 255 267
142 386
Reuben (Mrs.) **97** 271
Reuben A. **59** 286
Rhoda D. **95** 271
Rhoda Davis **96** 35
Rhoda Webster (Noble)
95 39
Richard **88** 347 **103** 256
257 **145** 167
Robert **65** 115 340 **97** 369
98 56 **99** 198 **103** 256
258
Robert (Mrs.) **103** 256 258
Robert Elmar **99** 202
Robert J. **147** 270
Rosanna Jane **148** 175
Rosco **103** 266
Rufus **87** 121 **88** 355 **103**
194 196 197 254 258 264
Ruth **74** 252 **145** 353
Sally **59** 35 **65** 340 **74** 262
80 129 **87** 123 **97** 372
377 **98** 55 56 **99** 197 **103**
189 258 261 266 270 **142**
199 **145** 164
Sally (Tomson) **125** 102
Samuel **51** 45 **55** 250 252
255 **58** 295 **65** 115 **74**
216 218 255 **81** 430 **96**
145 **97** 300 367 **99** 113

LIBBY *cont'd*
114 **103** 188 189 195 256
262 268
Samuel Hubbard **100** 37
Samuel Marr **103** 193
Sara L. (Holmes) **83** 431
434
Sara Morrill **84** 174 324
Sarah **55** 312 **59** 190 **65** 115
353 **67** 276 **74** 214 222
224 229 245 249-252 254
256 260 **76** 34 **78** 427 **81**
430 **82** 46 77-80 85 92
207 211 213 288 293 300
331 510 **84** 215 **88** 346
97 265 **98** 197 **99** 197-
200 **103** 265 267 **142**
204
Sarah (Davis) **103** 267
Sarah (Drake) **84** 324 445
Sarah (Goss) **84** 324
Sarah (Waldron) **98** 294
99 53
Sarah Ann **74** 266 **79** 277
118 241 **121** 142
Sarah Jane **97** 359
Sarah Morrill **68** xxxiv **84**
174 324 **85** 204
Seth **97** 271 **103** 190 257
262 263
Sewall **103** 254 258
Shirley **103** 261 270
Shuah **87** 122 **88** 346
Sidney **65** 114
Silas **103** 190 259
Simeon **142** 205
Simeon F. **148** 175
Simon **55** 254 **89** 357 **95**
268 **97** 267 271 272 274
300 **98** 196 197 **103** 189
190 194 196 197 268
Sofey **97** 265
Solomon **95** 267 **97** 267
300 **142** 199 **145** 164
Statira **65** 115 340
Stephen **65** 115 340 **74**
218 228 248 251 **79** 277
82 205 210 **88** 346 **90**
335 **97** 377 **99** 202 **103**
189 193 195 259 265 269
142 205
Stephen M. **99** 202
Stephen Ruthven **99** 202
Stilman **103** 267
Storer **102** 307 **103** 195 267
268 270
Sumner J. **103** 267
Susan **68** 93 **91** 122 **103**
262 266
Susanna **74** 258 **82** 205
Susie **74** 229
Tappan **103** 261 262 268
Thankful **64** 123 **74** 226
Theodore **103** 192 197
255 265 268
Thomas **65** 115 **97** 367 **103**
190 194 196 197 256 258
262-264 270 **128** 94
Thomas I. **83** 146
Tobias **67** 276 **68** 93
Tristram **88** 334

LIBBY cont'd
Una **90** 169
Veramus **103** 268
Viola **92** 231
Walter **121** 142
Walter B. **69** 35
William **55** 311 **65** 115
335 340 **69** 36 **82** 87 **88**
355 **97** 367 374 **98** 56
103 195 257-259 262 265
267 **142** 199
William G. **69** 35
William Henry **103** 264
Woodbury **103** 268 269
Z. **98** 55
Zebulon **74** 249 **82** 214
97 377 **98** 55 **103** 267
268
Zenus **103** 260
LIBERTY
Francis **63** 90
Phebe **63** 90
LICENER James **64** 155
Loisa **64** 155
LICERWORYTT
Joan **71** 170
Thomas **71** 170
LICHTENSTEIN
Elizabeth **69** 113 114
Richard C. **94** 212 **114** 265
LICHTY Daniel **89** 232
Esther **89** 232
Margaret (Kelso) **89** 232
LICKEY —— **137** 311
LICKLEY
Marguerite Ellen
97 220
LICKLY Phebe **57** 247
LICORISH Lykyris
Alice **71** 317
James **71** 317
John **59** 174
LIDCOMBE
— Col. **96** 362
Samuel **67** 366 **96** 362
LIDDELL Liddel
Alice **132** 47
Anne **132** 49
John **99** 206 **132** 49
Joris **100** 95
Mark Harvey **84** 173
85 196
Mary Stanley Field **95** 399
Sarah **104** 281
Thomas **104** 279 281
Vinton **96** 231
LIDDER
Killian de **70** 262
LIDDLE Adam **78** 358
Betsey **78** 358 **116** 114
George **65** 244
J. L. **116** 114
Leonard **70** 261
Mary **63** 195 **78** 358
LIDDONS Mary **125** 175
LIDDY
G. Gordon **145** 200
Hugh **66** 307
LIDE Jane **136** 101
Thomas **103** 182 **136** 101
LIDFORD James **59** 219

LIDFORD cont'd
Matthew **59** 219
LIDGETT Desire (Joseph)
90 54
Elizabeth **65** 293
John **90** 54
Peter **65** 293
LIDLES G. B. **91** 328
LIDMAN Emma **81** 495
LIDNESCEY
Nathaniel **65** 43
LIDRA William **63** 199
LIDSTON Frances **144** 35
LIDSTONE Mary **101** 52
Roger **85** 424
Thomas **101** 52
LIDVETTER —— **53** 451
Lidyard see Ledyard
LIEBE Olga **80** 243
LIEBMANN Adolf **73** 316
74 xxiv **84** 111 184 193
85 218
Joseph **85** 218
Kathryn J. **84** 111 184
85 218
LIEBOWITZ Daniel (Mrs.)
108 134
LIECHTENSTEIN
Elizabeth (Princess of)
77 94
LIEDIUS —— **51** 335
LIEM James **93** 77
LIEN Abel E. **88** 208
Bernard (Mrs.) **100** 112
101 179 **105** 125 **107**
240 **112** 164 **120** 232
LIENOW ____ (Piemont)
140 236
Henry **140** 236
LIENS Jacob **93** 76
LIESE Sylva **76** 274
LIETNER Mary S. **88** 284
LIETZ W. Filler **52** 275
Lievsay see Livesey
LIEZEAR —— **130** 314
LIFFERMAN
C. F. **75** 247
Catherine Lois **75** 247
LIFFORD
Joseph **82** 280
Louise **82** 280
Mary **82** 280
LIFORD Ann **121** 11
Ruth **121** 15
LIGALLIS Sarah **118** 282
LIGGETT Ligett
Elizabeth J. (Galbraith)
96 395
Hiram Shaw **96** 395
Jenny Cowan **68** 124
John **52** 312
John Albert **68** 124
John Edmund **96** 395
Laura Colman **67** lv
Laura Kate (Colman) **96**
395 **97** 161
Mary Boyd **68** 124
LIGGINS Thomas **63** 240
LIGHT — Capt. **118** 35
Abigail (Leeman) **83** 418
Adelia **111** 128

LIGHT cont'd
Alonzo **111** 128
Andrew **83** 418
Anga S. **111** 128
Betsey **72** 273
Dana **111** 123
Dana F. **111** 128
Diodana **101** 234
Dorothy (Pike) (Andrews)
121 164
Elizabeth **72** 273 **88** 190
Ella Louisa **111** 128
Elsie **63** 378 **64** 375
Esther **111** 128
George **63** 378 **64** 375
Hannah **83** 21 25 **118** 32
38
Hannah (Lord) **118** 38
Hannah W. **72** 273
Helen **111** 128
Henry **111** 125 128
Isaac **101** 234
Iva D. **111** 128
Jane E. (Cutler) **111** 125
128
Jane L. **111** 128
Jemima **103** 306
John **55** 66-68 **66** 245 249
118 35 38 **121** 164 **134**
233
Joseph **111** 128
L. Augusta **111** 128
Livia A. **111** 128
Louisa A. (Beardsley)
111 123 128
Lovina **111** 129
Mary **63** 378 **64** 375
101 234
Maydalene V. **125** 53
Oscar D. **111** 128
R. Smith **111** 128
Rebecca **63** 378 **64** 374
Richard S. **111** 128
Robert **72** 243 273 **83** 419
Thomas **66** 246
William **125** 36
LIGHTBODY
Agnes **112** 293
Anna **69** 208
Elizabeth **112** 293
Gabriel **112** 293
LIGHTFOOT Lightfoote
Lyghtfoote
Cuthbert **109** 315
Hannah **96** 83
Hannah M. **117** 111
Mary **67** 253
Michael **147** 30
Rachel **117** 111
Robert **57** 280 **58** 68
70 316
Samuel **62** 321 **117** 111
120 236
Sarah **64** 24
Thomas **52** 132 **54** 196
William **59** 219
LIGHTHALL
W. D. Schuyler **62**
xxxvii
LIGHTLE
Margaret **122** 147

LIGHTLE *cont'd*
Sarah W. **120** 218
LIGHTLY
Elizabeth (Post) **84** 171
Joseph **84** 171
LIGHTNER
Elizabeth K. **94** 59
LIGHTON John **97** 269
LIGHTSENT
Ellen **84** 429
LIGHTWOOD
Thomas **56** 87
LIGON
Mary Alice **85** 195
Richard **140** 108 109
Thomas **84** 465 **108** 32
William D. **92** 97 **107** 79
112 75
LIKELY William **85** 25
LIKIBIE —— **83** 194
— Mr. **83** 194
LILGRAVE —— **57** 316
LILJEVALCH Mary
(Delano) **109** 286
Olof **109** 286
Lilley *see* Lilly
LILLIBRIDGE
—— **62** 283 290
Abby **63** 45 50 **127** 88
Abby (Hoxsie) **127** 88
Abby Frances **63** 50
Abigail **63** 45
Addie **63** 46
Aletta Aycrigg **101** 69
Alice **63** 44 45 **69** 274 **72** 75
Allen Ellis **63** 51
Amanda J. **63** 48
Amanda Lydia **63** 46
Amos **63** 45 46 48 49
70 243
Amos A. **63** 45
Amy **63** 44 46 48 49
Andrew **63** 48
Ann **63** 44 45
Anna **63** 46 48
Anna G. **63** 50
Anna Maria **63** 47
Anne **63** 49
Annis **63** 49
Augusta **63** 49
B. D. **69** 274
Benjamin **63** 43-50
69 274 276
Benjamin Dwight **63** 46
Betsey **63** 44 48 49 **70** 243
Buel **63** 44 47
Burnham **63** 49 **70** 243 244
Byron J. **63** 49
Carmi **63** 44
Caroline **63** 45
Caroline G. **63** 46 **69** 274
Catherine **63** 43
Champlain **63** 44
Charity **63** 49
Charles **63** 47 49
Charles Slocum **63** 50
Charles W. **63** 45
Charlotte **63** 45 48
Chester **63** 45
Chloe **63** 50
Chloe Maria **63** 50

LILLIBRIDGE *cont'd*
Christopher **63** 44 46
Clarissa **63** 45 47 48
Clark **63** 46 48 49 **70** 243
92 185
Clark R. **63** 51
Clifford Burnham **63** 49
Clymena **63** 48
Corinne **63** 49
Cynthia **63** 50
Dan C. **63** 49
Daniel **63** 44 46 49
Daniel O. **63** 49
David **63** 44-50 **70** 243
144 120
David R. **63** 49
Deborah **63** 44 46 47 49
69 274
Desire Slocum **63** 50
Dolly **63** 50
Dora **63** 51
Dorcas **63** 43 45 47
Edward **63** 43-45 **127** 139
Edward H. **63** 45
Edward T. **63** 44
Eleanor **80** 178
Elias **63** 44
Elisha **63** 44
Eliza **63** 45 48 49
Eliza Ann **63** 50
Elizabeth **63** 43 47
Elizabeth E. **63** 49
Ella **63** 50
Elmira Vandora **63** 47
Emeret S. **63** 48
Emily **63** 49
Emma Violet **63** 47
Erastus **63** 44 47
Esther **63** 43 49
Eunice **63** 46 **144** 110 120
122
F. Janette **63** 45
Frank **63** 49
Frank M. **63** 48
Freeman Cady **63** 49
Gardner **63** 44-47
Gardner B. **63** 46
Gardner Clark **63** 47
Gardner R. **63** 45
George **63** 44 49 50
George Washington
63 51
Gideon **63** 44 **128** 125
Green **63** 46
Hampton **63** 44-46 **69** 274
Hampton B. **125** 36
Hampton R. **63** 46 **69** 274
Hannah **63** 44-47 49
Harlan Page **63** 48
Harriet **63** 46 47 50 **72** 147
92 185
Harrison **63** 48
Hattie E. **63** 45
Henry **63** 46 49 50
Henry C. **63** 47
Henry Gilbert **63** 46
Henry R. **63** 50
Henry Reynolds **63** 50
Herbert M. **63** 49
Horace **63** 45 47
Horatio **63** 46 **69** 274

LILLIBRIDGE *cont'd*
Horatio Francis **63** 46
Hoxie **63** 45
Ida Mercy **63** 50
Ira **63** 48
Ira C. **63** 48
Jacob **63** 44 47
James **63** 44 48
James B. **63** 47
James D. **63** 50
James H. **63** 46
James Willett **63** 51
Jane **63** 48 50
Jane E. **63** 49
Jane Smith **63** 47
Jenney **63** 49
Jenny F. **63** 45
Jeremiah **63** 49
Jerome Bonaparte **63** 47
Jerusha **63** 46
Jesse **63** 43 **127** 139
Jesse Potter **63** 49
Jesse R. **63** 49
Jireh **63** 44
Johanna E. **63** 50
John **63** 43-45 47 49 **125**
31 33 41
John David **63** 50
John H. **63** 45
John Oliver Hampton
Baxter **63** 45
John Tyler **63** 46
John Work **63** 46
Jonathan **63** 44-46 49 50
128 297
Jonathan Reynolds **63** 50
Joseph **63** 44 47
Joseph Thomas
Wilkinson **63** 47
Joseph W. **63** 46
Joshua **63** 44
Josiah **63** 44 **128** 297
Julia **63** 49
Kate **63** 46
Laura **63** 46 48
Lauraette **63** 48
Lester **63** 44
Lewis **63** 50
Lodica A. **70** 243
Lodice **63** 49
Lodowick **63** 44
Lowell **72** 75
Lucinda **69** 275
Lucy **63** 46 49
Luella **63** 47
Lydia **63** 45 46 49 50
69 274
Lydia A. **63** 46
Lydia Ann **63** 50
Lydia Cynthia **63** 51
Lydia Lewis **63** 49
Lydia Mary **63** 50
Lyman **63** 46 **69** 274 275
Lyman R. **63** 50
M. E. **69** 274
Mahala **63** 47
Marcia **63** 48
Marcy **63** 43
Margaret **63** 43
Maria **63** 45 48 49
Maria Stone **70** 243

LILLIBRIDGE *cont'd*
Marion **63** 49
Martha **63** 46
Mary **63** 43-47 49 50 **69** 274 **127** 86
Mary (Hobson) **147** 42
Mary (Woodmansee) **147** 42
Mary Ann **63** 46 49 50
Mary Anna **63** 50
Mary B. **63** 49
Mary C. **63** 49
Mary D. **63** 51
Mary Jane **63** 46 **69** 276
Mary Josephine **63** 49
Mary R. **63** 50
Mary S. **63** 48
Mary W. **69** 274
Mary Work **63** 46
Matilda **63** 50
Matilda Caroline **63** 45
Meda **63** 47
Mercy **63** 48
Meriam **63** 48
Merrill S. **63** 49
Minerva **63** 48
Miriam **63** 45 **70** 243
Morton Mowry **63** 49
Muroel **63** 47
Nancy **63** 44 **72** 73
Nancy M. **63** 47
Nathan **63** 44
Nathan Andrew **63** 50
Nathan B. **70** 243
Nathan Bates **63** 50
Nathan Burnham **63** 49
Nellie E. **63** 49
Octavius C. **63** 48
Olive **63** 47
Oliver Martin **63** 45
Paris **63** 44
Patience **63** 43-45
Phebe **63** 44-46 49 50
Phebe Esther **63** 50
Polly **63** 47 49 **70** 243 244
Rachel **63** 44 47
Reynolds **63** 46 49 50
Robert **63** 43-45 **125** 31 **127** 9
Roger Sherman **63** 49
Rouse **63** 44
Rowena **63** 48
Rowena Sophia **63** 48
Ruth **63** 44 45
Ruth Lucinda **63** 50
Sally **63** 45 47
Sarah **63** 43-47 50 **127** 31 87
Sarah A. **63** 51
Sarah Adelaide **63** 49
Sarah Ann (Champlin) **130** 70
Sarah Artless **63** 49
Sarah M. **63** 45
Sarah Maria **63** 49
Seth E. **63** 49
Sheffield **63** 44
Silas **63** 50
Silas Barber **63** 50
Simon **63** 44 46
Sophia **63** 48

LILLIBRIDGE *cont'd*
Sophronia **63** 48
Stephen Lee **63** 47
Susan **63** 49
Susan A. **63** 51
Susan Ann **63** 51
Thankful **63** 44 45 47
Thomas **63** 43-50 204 **72** 75 **92** 185 **125** 28 **147** 42
Thomas Baxter **63** 45
Thomas J. **63** 47
Thurston B. **63** 46
Wallace M. **69** 274
Wanton **63** 45 46 **130** 70
Warren **63** 44 46 47 49
Willard **63** 47
Willard M. **63** 43
Willard Merrick **63** 48
Willard Stephens **63** 47
Willett R. **63** 50
Willett Reynolds **63** 51
William **63** 44 45 47
William Clark **63** 50
William Smith **63** 50
William W. **63** 45
William Wells **63** 45
Willie M. **69** 275
Zipporah **63** 47
Zipporah Maria **63** 47
Lillie *see* Lilly
LILLINGSTONE
Lillingston
Ann Agnes **117** 114
Charles **117** 114
George **59** 219
John **59** 219
Mary **63** 164
Thomas **63** 164
LILLINGTON
Alexander **124** 102
John **124** 102
Joseph **124** 102
Sarah **124** 102
Sarah (James) **124** 102
Thomas James **124** 102
LILLIS
Maria Palmer **64** 151
Miriam **82** 282 293
Patrick **82** 282 293
LILLY Lilley Lillie
—— **63** 52 **145** 48
Abigail **54** 286
Abigail (Wright) **148** 145
Abigail C. **78** 417
Amanda **132** 305
Amy **79** 121
Apollos **132** 304
Arethusa **90** 53
Benjamin **105** 280 **132** 305
Charles Wesley **132** 305
Converse **66** 106 107
Daniel **78** 314 **133** 308 **140** 162
Deborah **53** 445
Delia Ann **86** 18
Dorcas (Seymour) **132** 304
Dorothy **132** 305
E. **78** 314
Edward **68** 203 **128** 63
Edward W. **132** 305

LILLY *cont'd*
Eli **101** 79
Elisha **87** 269
Eliza S. **51** 369
Elizabeth (Vose) **91** 185
Emma **98** 353
Enoch **75** 305
Ezra T. **129** 395
George **53** 445 **60** 186
George C. **132** 305
George Leavens **63** 314 **64** 94 379
Hannah **84** 411 **109** 309 **126** 156 **132** 304
Hannah Hinton **66** 105 106 111
Henry A. **96** 137
Huldah **126** 306
Ichabod **53** 234
J. W. **63** 101
James **64** 320
James W. **132** 305
Jerusha **120** 50 **132** 304
John **51** 94 **99** 26 119 **129** 271 **132** 304 **140** 162
John Sweetsen **133** 308
Jonathan **84** 411
Joseph **65** 30 **132** 304 **140** 162
Julius W. **60** 186
Justin **123** 10
Lavinia **134** 225
Levi L. **78** 397
Lewis C. **132** 305
Lorenzo Dow **132** 305
Lucia **85** 297
Lucy **132** 305
Luke **81** 74
Lydia C. **66** 110
Margaret **136** 19
Margery **84** 273 275
Mary **53** 445 **148** 147
Mary (Brewster) **88** 367
Mary (Emes) **128** 63
Mary (Howlett) (Emms) **128** 63 64
Mary Etta **93** 137
Mehitable **59** 374 **66** 108
Nabby **77** 231
Nabby (Cogswell) **133** 307
Nancy **78** 410
Nancy (Bancroft) **96** 137
Nimrod A. **132** 305
Nora J. **132** 305
Patrick **72** 177
Phebe **53** 234
Rachel **90** 105 **99** 26 119 **100** 63 **137** 29 **148** 147
Reuben **53** 445 **93** 397
Rufus **132** 305
Rupert Ballou **97** 150 **98** 143
Ruth **126** 208
Sally **66** 107 110
Sally (Andrews) **133** 306
Samuel **55** 141 **112** 174 **128** 63 **148** 145-147
Sarah **53** 445 **66** 103 106 **78** 181 **90** 105 **98** 81
Sarah (Gilpin) **132** 305

LILLY *cont'd*
Sarah (Knight) **87** 269
Scott Barrett (Mrs.)
  103 119
Silas **53** 445
Stephen **86** 435
Susan (McIntosh) **123** 10
Theodore **84** 262
Theophilus **57** 280 **92** 55
Thomas **84** 260 **99** 26 119
Thomas (Mrs.) **86** 344
William **64** 106 **80** 409
LILLYWHITE Eleanor
Vilate **109** 128
Horesa **99** 147
LIMBARD
James **117** 126
Marguerite Victoria
  (Taylor) (McQuary)
  117 126
LIMBOCKER Charles
Cogswell **98** 147
LIMBURG
Anna B. **85** 167
Casper **85** 167
Frederick F. **85** 167
Gertrude **85** 167
LIMEBAUGH
Mary Elizabeth **78** 48
Limeburner *see*
Lymburner
LIMESI Alice (Harcourt) de
  97 342
John de **97** 342
Robert de **96** 39
LIMFORD
Elizabeth **65** 34
LIMING
Elizabeth **77** 183
Millville D. **109** 157
William **77** 183
LIMMY Charles **63** 53
LIMOGES
Gyomar de **124** 306
LIMPUS
Lowell M. **107** 246
LIMUR Andre M. A.
  (Countess de) **92** 403
LINA George **143** 258
LINACRE Ann **65** 50
Thomas **97** 346
Thomas De **96** 312
LINAH
Michael **110** 322
Thomas **110** 322
LINARD Conrad **51** 41
LINCAL Eugenia **87** 110
LINCH — Rev. **119** 202
Charles **76** 50
Christopher **100** 28
Daniel **65** 28
Deborah **100** 28
Katharine **129** 42
Leonora M. **121** 179
Maybelle M. **121** 181
Nicholas **65** 32
Sibyl **89** 74
LINCOLN Lenekin
Lennakin Lincon
Linnekin
— Bp. of **54** 104

LINCOLN *cont'd*
— Capt. **119** 205
— Countess of **53** 70
— Earl of **52** 354 **53** 71
  54 192 **61** 280 **65** 87
— Gen. **61** 11 **85** 123 130
  131 **95** 66 **119** 289
— Judge **70** 138
— Lieut. **62** 19
— Maj. Gen. **84** 384 386
— Mr. **51** 24
— Mrs. **95** 50
— Professor **54** 248
____ (Lewis) **121** 215
____ (Revere) **140** 163
A. H. **62** 187
Abby **59** 27
Abel **76** lxxiv
Abiathar **57** 189 **124** 198
  200
Abigail **58** 83 **59** 27 311
  312 389 **60** 62 63 **114**
  103 271 **121** 193 280
  124 201
Abigail (Haynes) **114** 103
Abigail (Nichols) **124**
  199 200
Abigail (Paine) **123** 119
Abigail Bigelow **76**
  lxxxviii
Abigail Reed (Walker)
  145 298
Abijah **60** 371 **125** 211
Abisha **55** 41
Abner **132** 163
Abraham **51** 71 **52** 381
  53 256 **54** xlix lvi lxvi
  lxx cxliv 248 375 461 **55**
  l lxxvii 366 **56** lvii lxix
  57 232 245 **58** c ci 106
  115 210 **59** lx lxi 348 **60**
  105 **61** lii 113 377 **62** 12
  217 **63** 388 **64** 201 **65** 97
  101 205 **66** lxiii lxv
  lxxiii **67** lviii **69** xxv
  lxx lxxi 87 95 **70** lvii 5
  71 xlviii 197 **72** liv **74**
  165 **75** lxxx 160 **76** xliv
  lxxvii 81 163-169 **77**
  xvii xxiv 243 244 247 **78**
  80 90 249 437 **80** 140
  163 305 **81** 3 120 243
  244 247 330 478 **82** 15
  355 **84** 389-391 395-400
  97 66 **99** 87 **103** 36 84
  149 **105** 83 **108** 75 **109**
  78 **113** 45 233 **114** 79
  158 318 **115** 238 **117**
  315 **143** 128 132 133 166
  144 56 **145** 314
Abraham (Mrs.) **84** 390
Abraham Orne **91** 86
  145 300
Adeline **60** 293 **145** 300
Adeline (Lincoln) **145** 300
Adeline E. (Bancroft)
  103 65
Agnes Wyman **56** 214
  66 lii **76** xxxi lxxxviii
Albert Lamb **59** xliv
Alexander **104** 324 **106**

LINCOLN *cont'd*
158 **145** 309
Alfred Varnum **75** ix
  xxiii **76** xxix lxxiv **93**
  182
Algernon Sidney **76**
  lxxxviii
Alice Thayer **76** lxxiv
Alma **80** 46
Almira **53** 461 **56** 46
  68 255
Amanda **134** 85
Amasa **76** lxxxviii
Ambrose **55** 41
Amelia (Howard) **145** 299
Amos **54** xcvi **140** 163 **145**
  297-300
Ann **121** 276
Ann (Wilkinson) **125** 106
Anna **71** 202 **114** 103
Anna Matilda **78** 421
Anna T. **88** 340
Annis (Lane) **131** 128
Apollis Riley **81** 384
Apollos **124** 201 **132** 163
Arba N. **124** 198 201
Arthur **78** 408
Asa **141** 346
B. **54** 99 **93** 263
Bathsheba **122** 86
Bela **77** 283 **84** 364 **85** 124
  131
Bella **116** 111
Ben **121** 271
Benia **121** 214
Benjamin **51** 176 373 **52**
  426 **53** 147 **58** lxvii **59**
  154 **60** 181 **61** 131 **65**
  367 **70** 98 **74** 284-292
  81 30 **84** 268 383 **86** 342
  88 222 **92** 118 119 **94**
  297 **95** 55 **113** 318 **119**
  22 124 **121** 16 119 121
  124 191 195 282 **124** 199
  201 **129** 333 130 275
  137 315 **140** 52 298 **141**
  14 15
Bersheba **84** 389 392
Bessie **62** lxxvi **85** 197
Bethiah **58** 175 **121** 125
Betsey **56** 258 **60** 95 **77** 317
  126 198 210 **134** 241
Betsey R. **123** 124
Beza **55** xx xlii lxi lxiii
Bradford **53** 461
Bridget **51** 290
Caleb **121** 16 17 214 270
  285 **132** 163
Caroline **95** 50
Caroline Augusta **53** 461
Caroline Howard **77** lxx
  91 85 86
Caroline J. **101** 34
Carrie Lizzie **82** 170
Castine (Hartwell)
  125 292
Catherine **53** 461 **63** 14
Catherine (Blankinship)
  134 241
Catherine Russel **125** 284
Celia **93** 192

LINCOLN cont'd
Charles 55 lxii 70 327 80
46 134 85
Charles Augustus
145 300
Charles H. 115 168
Charles Henry 58 107 61
319 65 386 108 134 116
144
Charles L. 55 xxxii
Charles Plimpton 56
xxxii 65 xxxiii xxxvi
366 69 xxx 89 262 283
90 141
Charles S. 78 91
Charles Sprague 89 263
Charlotte S. 69 334
Chloe 117 305
Chloe (Blackwell) 117 306
Christopher 65 367 369-
371 78 404 79 41 89 263
Clara Emma 75 270
Constance 125 83 84
Constant 102 143 134 292
Cornelius 144 225
Daniel 55 lxii 58 261 71
202 254 78 403 443 88
260 89 263 114 103 120
234 121 16 103 104 106
108 116 120 124 126 201
203 271 274 124 198-201
140 163 142 357 143 50
Daniel W. 84 340
Daniel Waldo 85 196 87
307 310 313 107 151
David 121 280
David 61 22 113 131 114
103 121 122 282 123 65
124 201
Dawson 123 118
Dawson W. 123 123
Dean 120 234
Debby 145 298
Deborah 58 173 175 59
311 86 87 88 260 93 380
94 290 100 162 121 18
195 201 215 274 129 170
260 134 298 140 163
Deborah (Burr) 119 13
Deborah (Hersey) 121 271
134 138
Deborah (Hobart) 88 260
121 118
Deborah (Revere) 145
297 298 300 309
Deborah H. 145 298
Desire 60 293
Diadamia (Briggs)
126 270
Dinah 116 36
Doane 123 118
Dorothy 57 367 87 313
314
Drolly 70 327
Drusilla 53 461
Dwight 69 334
E. Joshua 107 158
Ebenezer 121 281 124 200
Edith 53 461
Edward 79 39 83 375
95 49 51

LINCOLN cont'd
Edward (Earl of) 53 66
Edward Baker 81 243
Edward Winslow 89 266
Elias 124 201
Elijah 91 328 114 103
Elisha 119 13 121 279 123
9 129 258
Eliza 67 350 79 152
Eliza Jane (Revere)
140 163
Eliza Langdon
(Frothingham)
145 298
Elizabeth 51 79 173 52 426
53 461 58 173 60 30 61
174 290 70 324 71 202
78 69 178 82 170 86 342
87 148 113 131 138 121
111 201 209 274 125 87
88 90 126 205 129 166
366 369 135 300 143
132 133 145 300
Elizabeth (Fearing)
123 65
Elizabeth (Hall) 140 150
Elizabeth (Haukes)
121 110
Elizabeth (Jacobs) 135 300
Elizabeth (Jones) 113 131
Elizabeth (Lincoln)
121 201
Elizabeth (Revere) 145
297 298
Elizabeth Howe 106 159
Elizabeth Maria 145 300
Elizabeth Otis 68 23
Elizabeth Seekins 98 96
Elizabeth Tomlinson
70 327
Elizabeth Wilder 73 xlv
80 443
Elkanah 76 lxxxviii
Ella 122 112
Ellen B. 62 lxxvi
Emeline 54 xcvii 76 lxxiv
Emily Caroline 54 xcvii
Emma 126 141
Emma Cushman 125 284
Emma Jane 77 182
Emma S. 122 112
Enoch 51 144 425 427 59
238 87 307-309 140 163
145 298 300
Enos 76 lxxxviii
Ephraim 55 lxii 121 109
110 120
Ernest Avery 95 146
Eugenia 87 110
Eunice 101 145
Everett D. 120 234 235
Experience 61 22 114 102
Experience (Lanphere)
135 300
Experience (Willis) 114
102 271
Ezekiel 78 419 125 284
130 313
Ezra 63 14 125 292
F. W. 140 150 145 301
Fanny 129 151 376

LINCOLN cont'd
Florence 76 lxxiv 136 326
Florence Agnes 84 342
85 196
Frances Revere 145 300
Francis Henry 56 xxxiv
57 xxxi 62 xxxv 66 lx
lxxvii lxxviii 95
Francis Henry (Mrs.)
121 4
Francis / Frank
145 297 298
Franklin 81 290
Frederic 125 107
Frederic W. 51 102 56 l 61
104 140 163 145 301
310
Frederic Walker 53 253
54 xcv 229 65 xxv 145
297-299
Gamaliel 53 461 59 29
George 60 326 64 101 65
11 69 334 73 20 77 84
117 190 124 199 142
107 145 157 300 148
323
George Chandler 87 313
George Gilbert 53 461
George Russell 125 284
Gerusha 124 200
Gideon 130 313
Gilbert 60 151
Gilbert de Gant (Earl of)
96 103
Grace 129 168 258 268
Grace (Stockbridge)
(Thaxter) 134 138
Grace Sprague 76 lxxiv
93 182
Hananiah 84 391 397
85 465
Hannah 53 230 55 lxv 57
399 58 87 169 171 173
175 59 137 60 95 61 22
62 130 71 202 78 443
83 479 85 131 94 195
295 121 109 211 124
199 200 125 83 126 124
129 166 134 296
Hannah (Atkins) 127 43
Hannah (Baker) 123 123
Hannah (Eveleth) 114 102
Hannah (Haynes)(Eveleth)
135 31 32
Hannah (Hopkins)
102 52
Hannah (Knapp) 124 199
Hannah (Leonard) 124
198 200
Hannah (Luce) 98 367
Hannah (Pudney) (Gloyd)
119 13
Hannah (Salter) 143 133
Hannah (Smith) 136 165
Hannah (Stone) 114 103
Hannah (Woodward)
123 202
Hannah H. (Knowles)
123 201
Hannah Sprague (Wales)
145 300

LINCOLN *cont'd*
Harriet **96** 30 **125** 290
Harriet Abbot **54** xcvii
Hawkes **77** 84
Helen Frances **125** 284
Helen M. F. **120** 147
Hepzibah (Bouvee)
125 107
Hezekiah **58** 173 **121** 209
125 106
Hinckley **123** 203
Huldah **60** 177 179
Ichabod **53** 461 **123** 120
Ida Hannah **76** lxxiv
Ida Mabel **76** lxxiv
Ira **80** 46
Ira W. **91** 328
Isaac **53** 349 **58** 83 171 **59**
311 312 314 389 **60** 62
63 **61** 22 **68** 164 **69** 172
74 103 **84** 39 391 **90** 400
114 42 102 103 271 **121**
278 **123** 202 **129** 156
166 168 **135** 31 32 **143**
132 133
Israel **58** 175 **119** 13
121 215
J. Gardner **83** 130
J. J. **91** 328
J. Thayer (Mrs.) **92** 162
93 153
Jacob **60** 63 **71** 202 **82** 384
107 320 **121** 193 207
124 200 **129** 366 **135**
300 **143** 132 133
Jael (Garrett) **143** 133
James **121** 209 **123** 120 201
141 346
James M. **90** 109
James Minor **52** 96 **53** 459
54 xxxviii **59** xliv 118
61 xxxiv **64** 65 328 **65**
383 **66** xxxviii xlviii lii
124 201
James Otis **68** 23 **92** 119
Jane **90** 394
Jared **88** 284
Jedediah **62** lxxvi **78** 404
87 307 **121** 279 **140** 163
145 297 300 309
Jedidiah **58** 175
Jemima (Bowen) **134** 85
Jeremiah **121** 209
Jerusha **78** 355 **119** 188
Jesse **123** 202
Jessie Harlan **81** 247
John **53** 461 **58** 161 **64** 189
69 283 **71** 202 **81** 243
97 328 329 **102** 52 **111**
311 **121** 121 **124** 198
199 **125** 90 **126** 270 **145**
166
John Randolph **145** 309
Jonah **62** 183 **124** 199 201
125 81 83 **135** 300
Jonathan **55** lxii **76**
lxxxviii **121** 214 **125** 200
134 241
Jonathan Thayer (Mrs.)
92 146
Joseph **86** 45 **118** 282 **119**

LINCOLN *cont'd*
11 13 119 **121** 13 210
211 284 **123** 117 119
Joseph F. **81** 290
Josephine Rose **87** 313
Joshua **58** 84 169 **59** 137
140 309 311 387 389 **60**
177 179 181 **65** 368 **88**
260 **89** 263 **95** 52 56 **98**
96 **121** 17 118 123 125
195 200 205 215 275 279-
281 **135** 130
Joshua Revere **145** 300
Joshua W. **123** 123
Josiah **60** 43 **84** 392 **120**
234 **121** 285
Jotham **103** 65
Katy **124** 201
Kenneth C. (Mrs.) **85** 105
Keziah **53** 349 **119** 13
126 68
L. **134** 53
Laura **69** 334
Laura Ashley **69** 334
Laura E. **69** 334
Lazarus **129** 151
Leah **101** 31 **121** 284
Leantes **123** 121 124
Levi **51** 425-427 **52** 193 226
60 293 326 **69** 302 **70**
306 **75** 86 **85** 121 **87** 308
309 **96** 278 **140** 163 **144**
266
Lewis **140** 163 **145** 297 299
Lillah D. (Rogers)
123 203
Lois **55** 41
Lois Rebecca **81** 384
Loring **57** 367
Louis **54** xcvi **145** 297 299
Louis Revere **54** xcvii
Louise Sears (Cobb)
92 146
Lucia **81** 290
Lucia Josephine **81** 290
Lucia Woodruff **93** 288
Lucinda **113** 152
Lucy **62** 130 **68** 164 **70** 327
72 254 **133** 42
Lucy Lane **88** 286
Lucy Page **70** 327
Luke **56** 258 **76** lxxiv
121 282
Luther **88** 16 **108** 166
Lydia **52** 397 **53** 461 **67**
380 **84** 322 **109** 310 **121**
3 278 279 285 290 **122**
258 259 **123** 267 **124**
199 **135** 299 300
Lydia (Bates) **145** 300
Lydia (Hobart) **121** 276
Lydia (Pratt) **88** 16
Lydia L. **105** 224
Lydia Pratt **88** 16
Lyman **82** 170
Lyman Washington
82 170
Mabel Mumford **78** 207
Marcia Scott **74** 103
Marcy **135** 300
Margaret **53** 428 **58** 175

LINCOLN *cont'd*
121 200 213 280 281
134 137 138
Margaret (Caldwell)
129 365
Margaret (Langer)
130 178
Margaret (Lincoln)
121 280
Margaret (Stodder)
119 13
Maria **82** 170
Maria (Freeman) **123** 120
Maria Revere **145** 300
Marian **89** 266
Mark **76** lxxiv
Marshall **84** 362
Martha **51** 427 **52** 226 **58**
261 **71** 254 **87** 307 **113**
45 **121** 120 280 **129** 257
130 313
Martha (Fearing) **123** 65
Martha (Lyford) **143** 131
Martha (Perkins) **130** 313
Martha Ann **89** 263
Martha Eugenia **80** 46
Martin **51** 292
Mary **53** 428 461 **54** xcvi
55 xxxii lxii **57** 189 **58**
173 **59** 155 389 **73** 236
81 243 247 **84** 97 392 **87**
314 90 394 **92** 118 119
93 263 **99** 192 **113** 233
121 15 20 113 114 196
213 270 276 280 282 284
124 199 201 **125** 287
133 192 193 **135** 131
300 **140** 163 **145** 300
Mary (Austin) **125** 83
Mary (Brattles) **126** 213
Mary (Chubbuck)
121 114
Mary (Hobart) (Chapin)
143 131-133
Mary (Holbrook) **129** 366
143 133
Mary (Lafferty) **126** 270
Mary (Lewis) **121** 282
Mary (Revere) **145** 296
300
Mary (Robeson) **143** 133
Mary (Shores) **124** 200 201
Mary A. **103** 81
Mary Ann **53** 461
Mary B. (Freeman) **123**
121 124
Mary Eliot **125** 284
Mary Fleet (Eliot) **125** 284
Mary Hathorne (Knight)
145 298
Mary Knight **54** 229
Mary Molly (Brattles)
126 213
Mary Otis **70** lii
Mary Vinal **145** 300
Mary Waldo **107** 151
Mehitable **62** lxxvi **66**
lxxvii **102** 240 **118** 135
132 161
Mehitable (Foster) **90** 89
Mercy **51** 176 **53** 231 461

LINCOLN cont'd
58 84 59 137 140 309
311 387 389 102 100
114 176 123 203
Mercy (Chipman)
123 123
Mercy (Faunce) (Carver)
88 222
Mercy (Rich) (Russell)
84 39
Mercy (Russel) 123 202
Merrick 79 6 87 313
Merriel P. 90 105
Mical 62 135
Minor Sprague 53 461
Miriam 69 172
Mirriam (Tirrell) 130 313
Mollie 60 43
Molly 102 143
Mordecai 59 155 76 164
81 243 113 45 121 105
107 129 365 142 276
143 128 131-133
Moses 58 261 121 272
N. 91 328
Nancy 60 326 79 51 84 392
Nancy (Hanks) 84 396 397
Nathan 53 230 123 65
Nathaniel 53 461 71 202
125 87 127 43 135 300
136 41
Nehemiah 119 13 121 272
Nicholas 124 199
Noah 54 xcvii
Obadiah 58 261 121 203
129 366
Olive 71 202
Paul 75 270
Paul Revere 145 298
Peggy 129 365
Peleg 70 324
Perez 79 15 124 201
Peter 114 103 121 120 121
125
Phebe 60 371 123 122 198
126 270
Phebe (Gould) (Godfrey)
127 43
Phebe (Littlefield) 93 344
Phebe (Walker) 123 117
Phebe J. 84 85
Polly 145 298
Prudence 53 461 119 11
121 283
Prudence (Ford) 119 13
121 210
Rachel 51 425 59 140 154
275 73 171 88 260 102
56 106 230 115 135 121
273
Rachel (Doane) 123 118
Rachel (Fearing) 145 298
300
Rachel (Holmes) 102 56
Rachel (Macomber) 88 16
Rachel (Tirrell) 119 13
Ralph 59 27
Ralph S. 84 85
Rebecca 71 202 254 99 61
111 311 143 133

LINCOLN cont'd
Rebecca (Manchester)
102 21
Rebecca (Walker) 111 311
Rebecca Hill (Butler)
145 298
Rebecca M. 79 37
Rebecca Trevett (Bartol)
145 298
Rhoda 141 346
Robert Todd 73 316 74
xxiv 76 163 168 77 xvii
81 109 120 230 243-247
Rolliston Woodbury
(Mrs.) 87 201
Roxana Taft 75 270
Roxey Gorham 95 51
Rufus 53 461 59 118 64
65 328 372 65 260 125
201 142 36
Ruth 60 338 96 375 99 327
106 306 121 114 215
123 117 202 129 156
166 130 178
Ruth (Bate) 121 214
Ruth (Beal) 129 156 166
168
Ruth (Cox) (Delano)
136 41
Ruth (Wade) (Curtis)
129 366
Ruth (Ward) 123 118
Ruth Howard (Bates)
88 284
Saba 120 5
Sally 55 94 64 xlvii 88 330
124 200 145 298
Samuel 51 173 53 461 55
lxii 58 175 62 lxxvi 65
383 68 110 71 202 254
76 lxxiv 164 77 241 80
108 81 243 87 307 312
97 328 113 45 121 10 23
103 112 113 116 123 126
194 271 275 277 122 154
124 198 125 87 134 138
135 299 300 143 131
Sarah 52 372 53 461 59 373
389 71 254 77 84 84 397
94 195 295 113 45 121
15 18 22 23 108 116 123
126 196 271 275 282 124
199 125 293 143 132
133 253 145 297
Sarah (Bush) 84 399 400
Sarah (Cummings)
143 133
Sarah (Fering) 121 119
Sarah (Haynes) 114 103
Sarah (Jones) 113 45 143
128 131-133
Sarah (Lewis) 129 258
Sarah (Nicols) 121 271
Sarah (Royce) 135 299 300
Sarah D. (Dill) 123 121
Sarah D. (Gill) 123 124
Sarah Louisa 82 271 409
Sarah Louise 77 83 84
Sarah R. 89 118
Sarah Rebecca 81 384
Serena Lambert 145 300

LINCOLN cont'd
Seth 102 21 124 199
Sherman 117 306
Silas 98 367
Solomon 52 99 53 431 55
lxv 163 57 399 58 87 169
171 173 59 311 61 290
62 xlix lxxvi 101 65 11
66 lxxvii 99 8 121 211
142 107 143 132 145
300
Stephen 52 397 398 84 352
120 234 121 15 22 108
110 111 114 117 125 193
200 279 135 130
Sumner 79 152
Susan 53 461 59 29
132 163
Susann 121 197
Susanna 51 292 52 372
55 lxii 58 261 59 29 62
lxxvi 71 254 75 206 82
384 88 260 121 13 19
104 118 273 281 124 199
200
Susanna (Beal) 145 309
Susanna (Marble) 143 133
Tamson 123 121
Thankful 91 87
Theophilus 53 69
Theophilus Fiennes
alias Clinton (Earl of)
75 236
Thomas 52 23 372 53 428
461 54 89 57 333 58 175
59 89 154 275 65 383 69
283 76 lxxxviii 77 84
81 243 84 389-400 87
307 97 328 329 102 56
119 13 120 234 121 10
13 16 103 108 109 112
114 116 197 211 212 215
276 279 283 286 124 198
125 81-83 127 43 130
178 131 128 135 300
139 130 134 143 132
Thomas Fiennes alias
Clinton (Earl of)
86 262
Timothy 123 121
Varnum 60 lviii 76 lxxiv
Vilatia 60 151
Waldo 52 213 397 399 53
254 54 v xxii 55 v 232
56 xvi xviii xix xxx 113
203 57 xxxi 108 229 60
325 61 v vi xiii 62 v vi
63 v vi 64 vi xiv 65 v
vi xiv 66 v vi 67 v viii
68 vi ix 110 300 69 vi x
70 viii 94 183 71 viii 72
viii 73 viii 121 122 74
viii 75 viii 76 viii 77
viii 241 78 220 79 216
338 80 197 219 221 222
81 233 235 236 243 82
222 249 83 219 84 180
87 297 307 311 88 163
173 402 96 278 114 103
119 109 143 131 144
168 225 145 298-300 309

LINCOLN *cont'd*
Walter Hayes **87** 148
Warren **55** lxii **123** 121
124
Welcome **62** lxxvi
107 320
Willard **66** 21
William **51** 427 **58** 377
60 62 **62** lxxvi **83** 375
90 89 **94** 43 **126** 270
William (Mrs.) **94** 43
William de Roumare
(Earl of) **96** 104
William Ensign **84** 352
William Henry **145** 300
William Otis **145** 300
William S. **51** 79 **64** 330
William Simpson **98** 96
William Wallace **81** 243
Zilpha **68** 164 **124** 201
Zilpha (Lincoln) **124** 201
LIND *see also* Lynde
Arthur Carlton (Mrs.)
105 128
George **63** 238
Ingebrough **115** 180
Jenny **82** 12
Jonas **115** 180
Nathaniel **125** 33
Sylvia Marion **117** 200
LINDALL
— Mrss **127** 17
Abigail **67** 206 370 **95** 78
99 254
Azeiah **127** 222
Caleb **124** 173
Elizabeth **86** 221
Fenia **127** 306
James **56** 69 **67** 203 **94** 241
131 107
Mary **67** 203
Mary (Henchman)
102 278
Mary (Verin) **131** 104 107
108
Nathaniel **99** 79 **129** 64
Timothy **67** 369 **102** 278
104 181 **124** 173 **131**
104 107 108
LINDBACK
Christian **88** 169
LINDBERG
Marcia Wiswall **144**
271 **148** 331 335 339 340
LINDBERGH Charles
Augustus **90** 6
LINDBÖRG
Earl Emanuel **108** 68
LINDE Simon **110** 219
LINDEBOHM
Anders Pehr **111** 100
Susanna **111** 100
Lindell *see* Lindall
LINDEMAN Paul Richard
(Mrs.) **100** 340 **101**
124 338
LINDEN Abby **125** 244
James **95** 132
LINDENBERGER Edith
Atherton (Vaughan)
91 142

LINDENBERGER *cont'd*
Ruth **94** 96
Ruth Winifred (Eason)
106 77
William James (Mrs.) **91**
142 **101** 338
LINDENFIELD
Nicholas **134** 171
William John **134** 171
LINDER Abby **64** lxvi
August P. **128** 98
Caroline Bodelson **128** 98
Ethie Bigelow **68** xxxv
George **64** lxvi
John P. **128** 98
L. **128** 98
Mary A. (Farnham)
128 98
Mary F. **55** lxi
Matilda (Smallwood) **64**
lxvi **125** 302
LINDERGREEN
H. F. **95** 91
LINDHOLM
Ernest G. **122** 289
LINDLE Marie **123** 88
LINDLEY Lindly
____ (Freeman) (Ford)
97 84
Allen Ledyard **84** 110 185
97 78 83 84 160
Arthur **67** 71
Daniel **97** 84
Daniel Allen **97** 83 84
Demas **97** 84
Elizabeth **100** 304 **115** 62
Elizabeth Ann **97** 84
Ellen **128** 147
Ellen (Dayton) **128** 147
148
Experience (Ide) **96** 269
Francis **97** 83 **128** 147
Hannah **53** 234 **128** 147
Hannah (Dickey) **97** 84
Jacob **97** 84
Joanna (Prudden) **97** 84
John **67** 68 70 71 **97** 83 84
119 116 **128** 147
Levi **53** 234 **56** 74
Louisa A. **123** 98
Lucy Virginia (Allen)
97 84
Mabel **78** 112
Mabel Elizabeth **80** 195
208
Margaret **67** 68 70
Mary **89** 57 **128** 147
Mary Grace (Field) **97** 83
84
Sarah **53** 234 **125** 236
128 147
Sarah (Plum) **97** 84
Sarah Elizabeth
(Ellsworth) **97** 84
Thomas **96** 269
Timothy **53** 234
William **61** 348
LINDON
Augustin **112** 123
Henry **81** 124 127 130 133
134

LINDON *cont'd*
John **81** 127
LINDQUIST
Eliza **125** 293
LINDSAY —— **58** 223 **59**
225 **60** 213 **61** 314 **95**
405 **143** 366
Abigail **74** 210
Abigail (Perry) **125** 103
Achsah **89** 321
Agnes **94** 395
Alice **114** 232
Alice de **96** 94
Amos D. **125** 220
Andrew R. **100** 86
Annie **86** 401
Archibald Lionel **107** 46
C. S. (Mrs.) **89** 259
Charles **68** 328
Clarissa **86** 401 **87** 8
Clarissa S. **125** 238
Cora B. **68** 328
Crawford Easterbrooks
62 113
David **94** 395-397 **107** 48
229 **114** 183 184 **120**
311
David K. **120** 312
Deborah **86** 401
Edmond **120** 311
Edwin **106** 231
Eliza **86** 401
Eliza (Coombs) **86** 401
Elizabeth **100** 86 **146** 327
Elizabeth (Mason) **100** 86
Ephraim **86** 401 **97** 394
395
Ethan **86** 401
Eulogia **109** 291
Frank H. **120** 312
George **61** 135 **120** 311
George F. **94** 395
Grace **95** 352
Hannah **86** 401
Hannah (Dyer) **86** 401
Hannah (Lazell) **89** 115
Hannah (Munroe) **100** 86
Hannah Rowe **79** 325
120 82
Harriet F. **97** 66
Harriet Isabella **75** xlvii
Helen **94** 395
Helen (Lady) **79** 58-60 64
Henry **120** 311
Hierome **94** 395 **107** 48
Hugh **125** 103
Isadora **100** 86
James **100** 86 **120** 311
James (Lord of the Byres)
79 58 59 64
James M. **100** 86
Jane **107** 228
Jeannette **100** 86
Jesse **120** 311
John **62** 301 **75** 53 **79** 325
86 401 **112** 27 306
John D. **72** 322
John F. **100** 86
John Summerfield **59** 229
John T. **59** 221
John William **72** 80

LINDSAY *cont'd*
Joseph **61** 351 **106** 205
  112 105 306
Joseph (Mrs.) **79** 103 202
Julia Hill **106** 123
Julia Willsie **79** 202
Julia Willsie (Wingate)
  91 148
Louisa **68** 328
Louise Elizabeth **94** 138
Lucy **86** 401
Mabel Mildred **107** 131
Margaret A. **100** 86
Margaret Isabella **94** 386
  395 397
Martha **112** 27 **114** 182
Mary **86** 401 **112** 27 306
Mary (Arey) **86** 401
Mary (Muchemore)
  112 306
Mary O. **100** 86
Matilda **120** 311
Matthew **87** 206 **112** 306
Moses Crosby **86** 401
Nabby **86** 401
Olive (Harmon) **112** 105
Olive M. (Stanton) **92** 62
Oliver N. **100** 86
Polly **86** 401
Polly (Ryder) **86** 401
Ranulf de **96** 319 **97** 249
Robert **117** 52
Sally **86** 401
Sally (Ryder) **86** 401
Samuel **75** 53 **112** 26 105
  306
Sarah (Blodget) **88** 277
Sarah (Fowle) **95** 352
Susan **117** 169
Thomas **112** 306 **120** 311
Timothy **89** 115
Uctreda de **96** 319
Walter de **96** 112 314
Walter Manville **61** 322
William **106** 282 **112** 306
  120 311
William de **96** 94 106
Zula L. **100** 86
Lindscott *see* Linscott
LINDSELL Anne **71** 243
John **71** 243
LINDSEY Lynsey
  —— **128** 311 **136** 34
— Mr. **54** 148
A. J. **78** 321
Abigail **115** 217
Adelia **135** 76
Alfred **105** 206
Alfred O. **91** 328
Allan V. **78** 321
Alpha **78** 321
Amos **135** 76
Andrew **91** 79 **136** 39
Anna **135** 76
Anne **136** 35
Athelbert **105** 205
B. **64** 288
Benjamin **73** 116 **124** 178
Buck **78** 321
Catherine **147** 75
Charles **92** 333

LINDSEY *cont'd*
Christopher **111** 55
Content **56** 73 **95** 83
David **135** 76
Edward Delano **78** 285
Edwin Parker **95** 271
Eleanor **73** 270 **135** 76
Eleazer **56** 73
Eliza J. **110** 206 210
Elizabeth **56** 73 **73** 270 **115**
  62 **146** 327 **147** 75
Elizabeth (Gifford)
  135 142
Elizabeth (Monro) **128**
  311 **133** 192
Ephraim **136** 34 35 37
Esther **81** 430
Ethelbert **136** 37
Frederic Cushman **95** 271
Gammy **136** 38
George **73** 224 **135** 142
George W. **91** 387
Grace **95** 352
Hallie **78** 321
Hannah **135** 142
Harriet **66** 111
Harriet E. **97** 66
Harriett F. **97** 66
Helen **92** 333
Israel **66** 111
James **105** 205
Jane **81** 258 259
Janet **56** 185
Jno **123** 192
John **56** 21 **64** 99 216 336
  73 270 273 **78** 321 **88**
  277 **105** 206 **116** 172
  128 311 **133** 192 **135** 76
  136 24 **147** 75
John H. **78** 321
John Taylor **78** 321
John W. **92** 334 **110** 202
John William **91** 67
Jonathan W. **110** 51
Joseph **76** 251 **78** 321 **91**
  78 **113** 26 28 **116** 129
Joseph (Mrs.) **91** 59 78 148
Julian Ira **92** 96
Kesiah (Josselyn) **133** 192
Lester **78** 321
Lewis **78** 321
Lucien Nelson (Mrs.) **83**
  123 232
Lydia **81** 430
Martha L. (Woodbury)
  91 387
Mary **76** 256 **81** 388 **111** 55
Mary (Miller) **88** 340
Mary (Muchemore)
  115 136
Mary Ann **76** 256
Matilda **73** 262
Matthew **76** 196 250-252
  256 **92** 334 **115** 136
Monro **128** 311
N. Allen **55** 360
Nancy **76** 197 250-252 256
  78 401
Nancy (Quin) **125** 220
Nancy G. **92** 334
Noble **73** 268

LINDSEY *cont'd*
Olive **116** 221
Olive (Harmon) **113** 26
  116 129
Priscilla S. **92** 334
Rachel **73** 228
Rosella **92** 334
Samuel **73** 116 263 **76** 252
  92 334 **113** 26 **133** 192
Samuel P. **92** 62
Samuel R. **95** 271
Sarah **83** 59 **92** 334
Sarah E. **92** 334
Semantha E. **92** 334
Sukey (Inman) **84** 360
Susanna **73** 276 **135** 76
Susie **92** 334
Thomas **64** 261 **73** 150 **78**
  321 **88** 340 **92** 334 **111**
  55 **115** 211 **127** 227
Thomas Bond **64** 101
Thorne **95** 352
Waltha **73** 116
William **76** 250
Woodbridge **135** 142
Zeluma **135** 76
LINDSKOG Anna
  Charlotte (Swanson)
  90 108
Carl Daniel **90** 108
LINDSLEY
  —— **62** 87 90 **95** 405
  — Rev. Mr. **80** 60
Abby Foster (Gibbs)
  106 81
Albert **118** 79
Alice **62** 380
Annie Halstead **83** 481
  106 81
Benjamin **106** 82
Daniel **119** 182
David **114** 182
Dorcas (Harrison) **106** 82
Ebenezer **62** 147 **106** 82
Eleazer **106** 160 **119** 193
Elis **62** 292
Elizabeth **98** 99 **100** 201
  291 **119** 112
Elizabeth Jane **81** 221
Esther **62** 147
Frances Alphia
  (Shapleigh) **95** 271
Francis **106** 82 **119** 113
Hannah **114** 182 **119** 80
Isaac **62** 147
Jane **83** 490
John **62** 147 **63** 394 **106** 82
  119 113 193
Joseph **119** 179
Joseph Camp **106** 81 82
Lydia **62** 147
Mary **62** 147
Mary (Miller) **106** 160
Mary (Morris) **106** 82
Mary Henderson **62** 189
Matthew **60** 331
Mercy **62** 147
Michael **114** 182
Nancy **106** 160
Nancy L. **100** 257
Phebe (Baldwin) **106** 82

LINDSLEY cont'd
Phillis **62** 379
Sarah (Camp) **106** 82
Susanna (Cullpepper)
  106 82
Sylvanus **80** 434
Thomas **114** 182
LINDY — Mrs. **62** 290
LINDZY Lindzey
— Capt. **85** 22
Betsey **108** 205
Clarissa **108** 205
Greenough **108** 205
Jane **108** 205
Jonathan **108** 205 206
Joseph **108** 166
Maria **108** 205
Olive (Harmon) **113** 28
Phebe **108** 205
Sally **108** 205
Line see Lines
LINEHAN John C. **53** 135
  147 **57** 127
Katharine **106** 69
Margaret May **106** 69
Patrick **106** 69
LINEINGE Thomas **83** 327
LINEKIN
Benjamin **136** 76
Mary **136** 76
LINELL Arthur Ellsworth
  60 186
David **60** 332
Hannah **60** 332
Robert **60** 186
LINELY John **64** 239
LINES Line
— Widow **76** 133
Abigail **55** 369 **56** 297
Alice **59** 69
Amarilla **104** 46
Anna **59** 68 69
Ashael **77** 81
Ashbel **77** 81
Belisle **104** 46
Benjamin **59** 68 69
Calvin **82** 352
Christopher **101** 22
Clara Belle **82** 353
David Harpin **136** 320
Dorcas **59** 71
Dorothy **109** 221
Ebenezer **82** 352
Eber **82** 352
Edwin Stevens **82** 353
Elizabeth **117** 157 **119** 237
Elizabeth Maronette
  Pease **65** 134
Ellie Munger **82** 353
Esther **54** 26
Ferdinand **104** 46
Frances Amelia **82** 483
Francis **114** 182
H. Wales **74** xxiv 77 **77**
  241 **82** 234 244 352 353
Harriet **82** 352
Harriet Louisa **82** 353
Henry **60** 101 **65** 134
  136 320
Henry Washington
  82 353

LINES cont'd
Henry Willis **82** 352
Ida Wilmot **125** 3 **136** 320
Joanna **104** 46
John **82** 352
John J. **84** 137
John L. **84** 137
Joseph **55** 369 **56** 297
Julia **104** 46
Julia Anne (Morse)
  136 320
Julius **109** 269 270
Laura M. **109** 170 269
Louisa **104** 46
Lydia **67** 230 **84** 214
Marlow **67** 49
Martha **51** 242
Mary **59** 71 168
Mary Anne (Wilmot)
  136 320
Mary E. **104** 46
Maxine **120** 317 320
Maxine Phelps **120** 235
Pamelia **104** 46
Patty **67** 129
Ralph **59** 69 **60** 101 **82** 352
Ransom **101** 234
Rufus **104** 46
Ruth **108** 291
Samuel **59** 71 **82** 352
Sarah **59** 70
Sarah (Kelsey) **109** 269 270
Sarah Congdon **82** 353
Sarah Lavinia **82** 353
Susan Amanda **134** 91
Thomas **90** 274 **145** 354
Titus **67** 49
William **104** 46 **114** 182
  143 261
LINEY Mary Ann **110** 227
LINFERD
Elizabeth **89** 233
LINFIELD
Ansel **128** 284
Dorothy (Willis) **114** 43
Elizabeth Porter **113** 297
Hannah **78** 244
Hiram **128** 284
Ira **128** 284
Joel **128** 284
Jonathan **113** 297 **128** 284
Lucy Swan **128** 284
Mary **75** 211
Mary S. **128** 284
Nathaniel **114** 43
Samuel **126** 118
Sarah **60** 41
William **60** 41
LINFORD
James Henry **101** 335
LING Linge
Abraham **114** 193
Alice **55** 412
Ann **68** 324
Benjamin **81** 127 132
  131 129
George Washington
  110 52
Jane Maria **110** 52
Joanna **81** 127 **131** 129
John **112** 255

LING cont'd
Matthew **63** 19
Nicholas **98** 116
William **51** 254 **63** 284
LINGARD —— **68** 361
Ann **65** 166
Ruth **65** 50
Linge see Ling
LINGEN Simon **68** 182
LINGENFELTER
David **108** 80
Eliza Jane **108** 80
George **108** 80
George W. **108** 80
Isaac **108** 80
John **108** 80
John F. **108** 80
Keith **108** 80 **124** 72
Keith Edwin **105** 128
Lydia **108** 80
Mary A. **108** 80
Mary E. **108** 80
Peter **108** 80
Thomas **108** 80
William **108** 80
LINGLE
Elizabeth **110** 116
LINGLEY James **123** 107
LINGNER
Elizabeth **85** 314
George **85** 314 **86** 321
John **85** 314
Martha G. **86** 321
Peter **85** 314
LINGWOOD W. **51** 254
William **51** 496 **56** 275
LINIARE Annas **65** 170
LINING Charles **54** 197
LINK Lyncke
Arthur S. **101** 258
Edward **110** 239
Elizabeth **67** 35
Eugene Perry **96** 210
Freda A. **70** 155
Helmus **110** 239
Muriel F. **110** 53
Muriel Florence **102** 124
Susan Snow **102** 289
Thomas Betts **110** 239
William **67** 35
LINKER Eduard **112** 247
LINKFIELD
Benjamin **63** 293
Edward **63** 292 295
Hannah **63** 292
Susan **109** 232
LINKHORN
— Widow **63** 81
LINKHORNEW Sarah
  (Remick) **123** 117
LINKLETTER
Alexander **78** 267
George Onderdonk
  108 31
Keziah **78** 267
LINLEY Linlee Linly
Albert E. **117** 288
Alonzo **117** 286
Elizabeth **117** 288
James **112** 48
Josua **127** 228

LINLEY cont'd
  Libbie A. **51** 52
  Luke **65** 129
  Mary E. **117** 286
  Maud D. **117** 286
  May H. E. **117** 286
  Mildred H. **117** 286
  Miriam T. **117** 288
  Samuel **117** 288
  Solomon **112** 47
  Susanna **117** 286
  Thomas **66** 35
  Walter J. **51** 52
LINN
  Catherine **128** 269
  Edith Willis **70** 369
  Elizabeth **85** 78
  George **96** 209
  Henry **85** 78
  Isaac **58** 142
  James R. **91** 328
  John **128** 172
  Joseph **113** 268
  Joseph (Mrs.) **82** 257
  Mary **54** 275
  Mary A. (Campbell)
    128 172
  Mary Ann **81** 334
  Mary Carnes **88** 290
  Mary D. **113** 295
  Sarah **85** 78 **128** 172
  Susan Elizabeth **81** 334
  Warren Byron **96** 209
  William **65** 56 **81** 334
    85 348
Linnal see Linnell
LINNE George **98** 70
  Karl Von **54** 392
LINNEHAN
  Mary **100** 298
Linnekin see Lincoln
LINNELL Linnal Linnel
    Lynnell
    —— **59** 331 **95** 44 **102** 290
  A. F. **102** 286
  Abby Sophronia **77** 183
  Abigail **80** 121 **105** 63
  Abigail (Smith) **102** 290
  Abner **87** 327
  Abner F. **102** 282
  Absalom **102** 283
  Amelia A. **99** 257
  Arthur Ellsworth **59**
    xlvii 331
  Arthur Percival **83** 143
  Benjamin **110** 311
  Bethiah **85** 104 **102** 49
  Charlotte E. **102** 281
  David **130** 7
  Dean G. **102** 287 289
  Dean S. **102** 286 290
  Dean Smith **77** 183
  Desire **103** 172
  Eben H. (Mrs.) **102** 289
  Edmund **102** 286
  Edward **83** 143
  Edward S. **83** 143
  Elisha **83** 482 **107** 39
  Elizabeth **83** 146 **103** 173
  Elizabeth Ann **83** 482
  Elkanah **123** 119

LINNELL cont'd
  Emogene (Eldredge)
    102 286
  Esther (Chase) **87** 327
  Eunice (Moser) **87** 234 235
  Eva May (Snow) **99** 257
  Experience **81** 97
  Frank W. (Mrs.) **120** 80
  George Worth **83** 143
  Gould **102** 289
  Gould (Mrs.) **102** 289
  Hannah **123** 124
  Hannah C. **83** 143
  Hannah C. (Walker)
    123 119
  Harriet (Webster) **83** 482
  Helen E. **102** 281
  Heman **80** 11 **107** 289
    123 119
  Herbert Montague (Mrs.)
    85 196
  Imogene **102** 286
  Jamie **102** 282
  John **102** 287 290 **130** 7
  John Wesley (Mrs.) **84** 98
  Jonathan **102** 285 **105** 101
    130 7
  Joseph **80** 19 **118** 75
  Julia Maria **123** 201
  Julia W. **102** 282
  Lucinda (Belt) (Wells)
    110 311
  Marrietta **102** 290
  Mary Belle **102** 124 **118**
    75 216
  Mehitable **102** 289 **107** 39
  Mercy (Mayo) **105** 101
  Mercy P. **123** 200
  Olive **132** 92
  Oliver **102** 287
  Pamelia Ann (Snow)
    102 290
  Pamelia Ann Snow
    102 290
  Penninah **69** 284
  Pininna **67** 260 261
  Priscilla **125** 19
  Ray Lorenzo (Mrs.)
    84 111 190
  Richard **63** 164
  Robert **51** 50 **59** 331 **67**
    261 **69** 284
  Ruth **105** 101
  Samuel **87** 234 235
  Sarah **79** 386 **80** 11
  Sarah (Walker) **123** 119
  Silumeth **102** 284
  Solomon **102** 285 290
  Susan **102** 286
  Thankful **80** 24
  Thankful (Hopkins)
    102 52
  Thomas **102** 52 288
  Zerviah **80** 19
LINNET Heman **109** 44
  Jabez **109** 42
  Robert **112** 191
Linnex see Lennox
LINNEY F. A. **70** 289
LINNIN
  Andrew **100** 301

LINNIN cont'd
  Mary (Shurtleaf) **100** 301
LINNON William **65** 244
LINNVILE
  Margaret **128** 268
LINS. Winiford **64** 155
LINSA James **55** 68
Linsay see Linsey
Linscit see Linscott
LINSCOMB —— **62** 283
  Maude **97** 121
LINSCOTT Lindscott
    Linscit Linscot Linscut
    Linscutt
  Abigail **110** 290 **114** 131
  Abigail (Knowlton)
    86 134
  Albert L. **73** 96
  Almira **73** 234
  Anna **90** 251
  Annie **123** 153
  Benjamin **115** 309
  Beriah **110** 94
  Betsey **73** 92
  Betsey Ann **73** 96
  Catherine **120** 65
  Charles **73** 92
  Clorinda **73** 96
  Daniel **63** 378 **64** 375 **82**
    496 **97** 268 **115** 141
  Daniel J. **73** 234
  David **66** 365
  Dorcas **65** 115 **74** 105
  Elijah **73** 92 **84** 426
  Eliza J. **76** 25
  Elizabeth **84** 423
  Elizabeth (Peake) **114** 292
  Ephraim **73** 87
  Esther **73** 89 **82** 293 302
  Eunice **84** 426 **90** 328
  Eva **92** 113
  Frank D. **73** 234
  Hannah **73** 87 92 167 **84**
    423 **112** 103 **115** 212
    116 132 **117** 221 **119**
    224
  Hannah (Bragdon)
    110 290
  Hepzibah **97** 145
  Hepzibah (Came) **114** 50
  Hepzibah (Kingsbury)
    112 103 **114** 291
  Hiram **73** 87
  Ichabod **76** 103 **82** 293 302
    119 21
  James **73** 96
  Jane **73** 87
  Jeremiah **84** 423 **97** 270
    115 60 **116** 129
  Jerusha **63** 378 **64** 375
  John **66** 363 **73** 87 92 **110**
    94 290 **111** 95 **132** 326
  John E. **73** 184
  John G. **73** 96
  Jonathan **73** 87 **95** 52
  Jos. **66** 366
  Joseph **73** 87 **76** 103 179
    110 290 **114** 134 292
  Joshua **63** 377 **64** 374 **66**
    363 **80** 29 **86** 134 **110**
    290 **112** 103 **114** 291

LINSCOTT *cont'd*
Josiah **114** 50 **115** 306
  132 326
Lois **74** 264
Love **110** 94
Lucinda **73** 92
Lucy **63** 170 **73** 92 **115** 221
Lucy (Beedle) **115** 305
Lucy (Clapp) **84** 426
Lydia **63** 378 **64** 374 **73**
  95 96 **111** 95 **114** 49 **115**
  136
Mabel **115** 219
Mahala (Slater)
  (Hoisington) **141** 45
Martha **84** 423
Martin **73** 96
Mary **63** 377 **64** 374 **65** 115
  66 365 **73** 87 **74** 104
  110 290 **114** 44 **115** 218
  116 296
Mary (Kingsbury)
  115 217
Mary E. **119** 69
Mary J. **73** 96
Mary Jane **86** 135
Mellon **73** 96
Mercy **76** 179 **116** 139
Meribah **114** 154
Merribe **115** 223
Molly **110** 290
Moses **97** 18
Nabby **73** 87
Nancy **63** 379 **73** 89
  112 241
Nancy (Nowell) **117** 224
Noah **141** 45
Olive **95** 361 **112** 103
  115 222
Patience **73** 181 **115** 216
  120 219
Phebe **110** 94 **115** 64
Phebe (Stevens) **97** 18
Polly **84** 423
Polly (Linscot) **84** 423
Ralph Joseph **103** 119
Rhoda **65** 313
Sally **63** 377 **64** 374 **66**
  363 366 **87** 125
Samuel **55** 374 **63** 170 **74**
  105 264 **83** 15 **110** 290
  115 217 305 **116** 130
  297 **117** 140 224
Samuel H. **121** 147
  122 147
Sarah **63** 378 **64** 375 **76** 103
  179 **80** 29 **84** 427 **110** 94
  115 138 308 **116** 142
Sarah (Favour) **114** 134
Sarah (Kingsbury)
  132 326
Sarah E. **73** 87
Shuah **115** 58
Stephen **116** 134
Susanna **55** 374 **73** 96 173
  83 15 **116** 225
Susanna (Lord) **83** 15
Susanna (McIntire)
  115 217
Tabathy **110** 94
Tabitha **110** 94 **112** 103

LINSCOTT *cont'd*
Theodore **65** 115 **115** 226
Urania (Kingsbury) **121**
  147 **122** 147
William **73** 95 96 **112** 103
  115 217 **116** 134 **125** 33
Zoa **73** 92
LINSDELL Martha
  (Dolbeare) **112** 175
Thomas **112** 175
LINSET Samuel **71** 219
LINSEY Lensey Linsay
— Capt. **84** 270
____ (Tilden) **140** 253
Alexander **82** 293 299
Anne **77** 308
Barbury **65** 44
Catherine **93** 95
Catherine (Denny) **93** 95
Charles **84** 40
Dorcas **71** 127
Dorothy **71** 219
Elizabeth **71** 129 **73** 151
Johanna **82** 293 299
John **71** 127 **77** 308 **84** 360
  93 95 **140** 299
John Inman **140** 141 253
Joseph **129** 382
Martha (Hill) **112** 26
Rebecca **77** 308 310
Richard **77** 308 310
Rose **140** 141
Sarah **99** 280 **118** 245
Saunder **51** 410
Thomas **51** 159
William **99** 280 **129** 382
LINSFIELD
David **60** 42
Hannah **60** 42
LINSFORD
Elizabeth **71** 91 92
John **71** 91 92
Margaret **59** 90
Thomas **71** 92
LINSLEY Linzley
— **56** 264 **57** 134 **71** 49
Abigail **54** 177 **70** 85 **123**
  89 **124** 186 187
Alfred **59** 218
Ammi **60** 392
Amy **70** 80
Charles **71** 55 117
Charles J. **71** 55
Curtis **75** 191
Dan Evelyn **111** 295
Daniel **54** 177
Delight Urania **111** 295
Elizabeth **60** 385 **70** 80
Elizabeth Maltby **111** 295
Ellen **123** 88 89
Emily **111** 295
Esther **111** 295
Francis **123** 89
Hannah **70** 80 85 **123** 88
  89 **124** 186 187
Harriet **70** 85
Israel **70** 80 85
James **111** 295 **136** 326
James Harvey **111** 295
  136 326
Jeremiah **111** 295

LINSLEY *cont'd*
Joanna **123** 89
Joel H. **52** 294
John **58** 180 **60** 385 **70** 56
  70 80 **123** 88 89 **124** 186
John Stephen **111** 295
Jonathan **123** 89
Joseph **123** 89
Josiah **123** 89
Lydia **70** 82 **71** 8
Marie **123** 88
Mary **57** 134 **58** 180 **61** 392
  70 70 **123** 88 89
Mercy **70** 80 83
Olive **70** 77 **111** 295
Phelin **61** 392
Polly **59** 217
Rachel **53** 311
Reuben **70** 80
Richard **70** 82
Sabra **75** 191
Samuel **71** 8
Sarah **123** 88 89
Sarah (Maltby) **111** 295
  136 326
Sarah (Page) **123** 89
Sarah (Pond) **123** 88
Sarah Melvina **111** 295
Sophia Brainerd (Lyon)
  136 326
Sophia Emilia Lyon
  136 326
Timothy **70** 77
Tryphena **70** 80
LINST Robert **57** 388
LINSTER
Alfred P. **76** 177
Anna M. **76** 177
Mary **76** 177
LINSTON Simeon **54** 441
LINT Peter **73** 104
LINTHICUM
Thomas **87** 97
LINTHORN
— Widow **127** 12
LINTON — **95** 405
Adelin **104** 79
Ann **78** 282 **83** 20
Anne **73** 222
Blanche **78** 165
Elizabeth (Breese) **113** 279
Fanny **124** 258
Frances **124** 258
Frank **124** 258
George **65** 120
Hannah (Sikes) (Sawyer)
  135 78
John **63** 30
Joseph **59** 301
M. Albert **98** 351
Margaret (Roberts)
  98 351
Martha **73** 152
Ralph **104** 79
Richard **56** 241 243 **58** 200
Robert **135** 78
Samuel **113** 279
Sarah **126** 145
William **64** 113
William C. **118** 248

LINTOT
Bernard **76** 140
Sarah **76** 140
LINTOUN
John (Lord) **79** 65
LINUS Peter **97** 274
LINZEE Linzey Linzie
Ann **53** 20
Christopher **103** 149
Dorothy Evelyn **103** 149
Edward **53** 20 21
Hannah **127** 164
Hannah Rowe **120** 82
J. W. **52** 278 **123** 171
James (Mrs.) **103** 227
John **53** 21 **55** 422 **103** 148
John Inman **103** 149
John W. **60** 278 **102** 234
   103 114
John William **68** xxxii
   111 **98** 145 **103** 111 148
   149 **104** 148 **145** 239
   240 310 **148** 65
Martha (Atkins) **84** 40
Robert **53** 20
Robert Bernerd **103** 149
Rose **56** 46
Sarah **53** 20
Sarah Inman **55** 422
Susanna **53** 20 21
Theodora Marylyn
   103 149
Thomas C. **52** 380
Thomas Edward **103** 149
William **102** 246
Linzley *see* Linsley
LIONBERGER
Esther **67** 350
I. H. **84** 353
Joseph **67** 350
Mahala Elizabeth **67** 350
Minerva Phillips (Davis)
   117 51
Reuben **117** 50 51
Lipcombe *see* Lipscomb
LIPDRY Jacob **63** 24
LIPE Peter **91** 328
LIPHOT John **64** 340
LIPMAN
Hyman L. **97** 290
Samuel **82** 326
LIPPENWELL
Emily M. **103** 46
Esther **79** 397
Isabel **79** 397
Michael **79** 397
Lippet *see* Lippitt
Lippett *see* Lippitt
LIPPINCOTT Lippincot
   —— **59** 236 **60** 214 **62** 104
   145 371 **147** 39
Abia Swift **74** 241 **90** 361
Abigail Maria (Howe)
   98 350
Amelia **70** 325
Anne **106** 311
Arthur Horton **75** xxiii 64
   95 137 **96** 163 **98** 350
Bertram **142** 18 **145** 367
Charles **133** 233
Charles Albanis **133** 233

LIPPINCOTT *cont'd*
Constance **56** 215
Edward **98** 350
Edward Philip **98** 350
Eliza **70** 325
Elizabeth **70** 325
Elizabeth (Wills) **111** 278
Emily (Hannum) **90** 344
Emma **84** 49
Emogene (Bryant)
   133 233
Eunice **70** 325
Freedom **111** 278
Hannah (Shaddock)
   128 254
Helen Stillman **70** 325
Henrietta (Porter) **98** 350
Horace Mather **66** xlix
   191
J. B. **51** 240 **52** 285 **53** 132
   142 **55** 126 237 **56** 215
   218 412 418 **57** xxx 128
   230 **59** xxxix 334 **60**
   xxxii 214 **62** 388 **67** 384
James **111** 272
James Edward **70** 325
Jane J. **70** 325
Joanna **70** 325
Job **111** 286
John **70** 325 335 **128** 254
John Leander **70** 325
Josephine Sarah **70** 55
Mary **70** 325 **103** 226
Mary (Talbot) **98** 350
Mary Ann (Cassidy)
   98 350
Mary Bertha **94** 138
Rachel S. (Hawn) **133** 233
Remembrance **54** 213
Restore **125** 232 **128** 254
Richard **98** 350 **128** 254
Samuel **90** 344
Sarah **70** 325 335
Sarah (Huett) **128** 254
Sarah B. **70** 335
Susan **77** 54
LIPPITT Lippet Lippett
   Lippit
   —— **57** 343
— Col. **57** 157 162
Abraham **129** 270
Albert E. **93** 216
Alfred Joseph George
   145 371
Ann (Green) **87** 363
Ann Fillice **144** 165
Anne **144** 165
Anne Phillis (Whipple)
   144 165
Bembo **129** 273
Catherine **96** 296
Cezer **129** 270
Charles Warren **61** 404 **62**
   xxxvii **71** xxi 88
Charles Warren (Mrs.) **78**
   108 205
Christopher **65** 149 **89**
   362 **102** 235 **128** 51
Eliza Young **80** 147
Elizabeth **70** 209
Freelove **137** 74

LIPPITT *cont'd*
George Warren **145** 371
Henry **76** lxxii
Henry F. **69** 210 **115** 76
   145 371
Jeremiah **147** 373
John **87** 363 **89** 362 **129**
   275 **133** 235 **136** 216
Joseph **129** 275
Loaden **128** 52
Lucy Hayes **69** 210
Margaret Barbara **78** 205
Maria Low **92** 82
Martha **87** 363
Mary **87** 363
Mary (Knowles) **87** 363
Matilda Floriana (Von
   Miller zu Aichholz)
   145 371
Moses **87** 363 **89** 362 **128**
   52 **129** 270 275 **144** 165
Nathaniel **93** 216
Peleg Wilbur **89** 362
Rebecca **87** 363 **115** 42
   133 235
Rebecca (Lippitt) **87** 363
Sarah **83** 217 **84** 186
Sarah Waldo **78** 205 **89**
   362 **90** 79 140
Warren **92** 82
LIPSCOMB Lipcombe
   Lipscom
   —— **57** 406
G. **118** 262
George **66** 343 **110** 250
   119 314 **142** 151 229
   233
James **65** 119
John **64** 342
LIPSEY
Hesakiah H. **134** 252
Lavina **96** 300
LIPSON Joseph **93** 137
Samuel C. **92** 146
LIPTON —— **95** 405
LIRE William **143** 260
LISBURN — Lord **53** 323
LISBY Ann **73** 217
Eleanor **73** 263
LISCO
— Capt. **101** 246
Elizabeth **100** 27 **101** 270
Mary **101** 247
Matthew **100** 27 **101** 270
LISCOMB Liscom
   Liscome Liscum
   Lyscom Lyscomb
Charles S. **68** 109
Charles Sutton **83** 122 232
Deborah A. **79** 139
Desire **75** 79 198 **85** 365
   366 **93** 265 **108** 116
Desire (Silvester) **85** 366
Ebenezer **140** 299
Eliza A. **135** 159
Elizabeth **53** 429 **85** 370
   112 316 **120** 6
Elizabeth (Addoms)
   112 316
Grace **108** 115
Hannah **113** 33 40

LISCOMB cont'd
Hannah (Fay) **137** 145
Hannah (Whitney)
137 145
Hannah T. **125** 183
Jane Adelaide **107** 308
Jno **123** 192
John **97** 326
Leah **107** 75 76
Levi **90** 53
Lucy **90** 315
Mary (Smith) **112** 316
Mary O. (Akerman) **90** 53
Miriam **60** 359
Nehemiah **108** 116
Phebe **61** 343
Philip **60** 359 **75** 79 198
85 366 **108** 115 116
Sally **59** 290
Samuel **129** 381 **137** 145
Samuel B. **113** 33
Samuel S. **147** 260
Sarah **61** 343 **67** 375
108 116
Sophia **79** 139
Thomas **67** 375 **112** 316
Thomas D. **79** 139
LISH George **90** 89 **100** 30
John **63** 347
Mary / Polly (Hendley)
90 89
Sarah **100** 30
LISHMAN John **65** 118
LISHUT Sarah **111** 268
LISK Andrew **116** 7
Huldah **126** 93
Sally **91** 197
William **116** 7
LISLE Lysle
—— **53** 263
— Viscount **59** 180
Alice **53** 298
Alice (Beconsawe)
110 218
Alice (Rogers) **113** 323
Alicia (Lady) **53** 188 292-
294 299
Ann **53** 293
Bridget **53** 188 292 298
300 378 **107** 43 **110** 218
123 184 **131** 168
David **85** 6
Edmund **54** 283
Fanny **85** 7
George **54** 283
Humfrey **116** 175
James **109** 149 **113** 323
John **53** 293 **110** 218
123 184
John (Lord) **53** 188 292
298
Julian **116** 169
Mary Barry **109** 149
Peter **114** 316
Robert **116** 175
Thomas **116** 169 175
William **54** 283 **109** 20 26
LISLEY
Bartholomew **112** 310
Elizabeth (Bohun) **112** 310
John **112** 310

LISLEY cont'd
Maud **112** 310
LISNEY Richard **54** 192
LISPENARD —— **59** 113
Abigail **104** 308
Anthony Leonard
104 308
Anthony / Antoine
104 308
Leonard **104** 308
Marie **104** 308
Sarah **104** 308
LISPER Henry **65** 26
LISSANT
Elizabeth **138** 14
Philip **81** 322
LISSEN Mary **97** 182
LISSINTON Thomas **76** 67
Lisswell see Liswell
LIST
Adrienne F. **88** 344
Anthony **83** 76
Elizabeth **83** 76
Mary Reigh **101** 165
LISTER — Mr. **98** 204
Andrew **125** 26
Avelyn **53** 23
Benjamin H. **93** 218
Bryan **51** 413
George **60** 25
Harriet **133** 56
James **60** 25
Jane **116** 244
Jeremy **98** 203 204
John **88** 387
Joseph **51** 413 **136** 257
Mary (Taylor) (Jowett)
94 102 104
Rosamond **52** 83
Ruth Weston (Alden)
96 185
William **94** 102-104
LISTON —— **140** 68
Alice **71** 237
John **103** 295
Marcia **79** 202
William **71** 237
LISURE Hannah **115** 34
LISWELL
Ann **100** 28 303
James **100** 33 **140** 163
Joannah **100** 28 30 32 33
133 136
John **91** 206 **94** 95 **99** 118
100 28 30 32 33 65 133
136 139
Mary **99** 118 **100** 136 242
Thomas **100** 133
William **99** 118 **100** 32
LITAN Pierre **77** 108
LITCH Josiah **123** 122
LITCHFIELD
— Mr. **57** 229
— Rev. Mr. **82** 416 417
Abigail **129** 168 373
Abigail (Buck) **129** 169
Alfred **61** 176 292
Allen **90** 57 110
Amos **60** 339 **61** 291 **129**
164 167 168 254 257 361
365 367-370 372 376 **135**

LITCHFIELD cont'd
44
Ann (Murray) **125** 219
Anna **61** 381
Anna (Gordon) **129** 164
Asenath **60** 339 **61** 174
Asenath (Stockbridge)
135 44
Atwood **60** 40
August C. **117** 291
Azotus **129** 165 378
Bathsheba **129** 157 167
168 269 370
Bathsheba (Clark) **129** 168
Bathsheba (Litchfield)
129 157 167 168
Benjamin **84** 213 **90** 90
103 173
C. D. **85** 316
Carrie Maville **82** 172
Charles Manfred **113** 309
Charlotte **129** 377
Daniel **129** 152-157 160-
164 171 250-254 256 260
261 265 267 361-365 371
372 374-378
Deborah **129** 169 **134** 143
145
Delight (Beale) **129** 168
Dependence **53** 465
Desire (White) **129** 167
Dolly **61** 175
Edith Florence **113** 309
Edwin **77** 148
Eleazer **129** 167
Elisha **129** 162 168 171
267 377
Eliza **82** 171
Elizabeth **65** 216 **129** 151
164 **144** 31
Elizabeth (Litchfield)
129 164
Elizabeth P. **92** 113
Ellen **82** 171
Elwood Brownell **82** 172
Emily **77** 148
Enoch **82** 171
Ensign **129** 377
Ephraim **129** 167 250 251
371
Esther Cole **61** 292
Everett Haven **82** 172
Everett Starr **88** 169
Experience **53** 465 **129** 168
Fanny (Lincoln) (Kilby)
129 151 376
Festus **135** 44
Florence (Brinton)
113 309
Foster **147** 65
Francis **129** 153 157-159
161 163 166 251 253 256
361 362 364 374-376 378
Fred J. **147** 65 67
George William Henry
82 171
Gracy **61** 288
H. W. **63** 111
Hannah **53** 465 **57** 183 **129**
168 268 269 362
Hannah (Pratt) **129** 165

LITCHFIELD *cont'd*
Hannah (Willcutt)
  129 170
Harriet Tisdale **82** 172
Henry Kimball **61** 381
Isaac **129** 252 269
Israel **60** xxix **61** 207 292
  129 150-171 250-269
  361-378 **135** 43 44
J. M. **85** 316
Jacob **129** 168 368-371
James **55** 277 **129** 151 153-
  155 163-165 170 251 253
  260 261 361-364 371 372
  377 378
James A. **57** 333
Joab **129** 170 364
Joan **64** 52
Joanna (Woodward)
  125 220
John **65** 26 **129** 371 372
John Ripley **82** 171
Joseph **63** 168 170 297
  65 216
Josephine **85** 315 316
Josiah **53** 465 **57** 183 184
  129 151 166 168 170 250
  251 255 361 362 364 360
  377 378 **135** 41 43 **142**
  123
Judith **53** 465
Julia **61** 289
Julia F. **83** 421 434
Julia Winter (Weeks)
  113 309
Katharine Pennington
  113 309
Lawrence **52** 85 **53** 459
  465 **56** 99 **57** 229 **58** 99
  59 421 **60** 186 **129** 151
  152 165 260 373
Lilly **129** 167
Lot **61** 175 291 **129** 152-
  158 160 161 163 164 167
  250 251 253 256 361 363-
  365 372 374 376-378
Lothrop **129** 153 166 376
Lucy **60** 339
Lucy Elizabeth (Smith)
  147 65
Lucy Hyland **82** 171
Lydia **137** 154
Lydia (Cowing) **129** 269
Lydia K. **61** 177
Mabel **142** 298
Mary **61** 58 176 **64** 189
  129 269
Mary E. **77** 148
Mary Frances (Higgins)
  82 171
Mary Frances Bell **82** 172
Mary Jane **82** 172
Matilda Packard **84** 213
  103 173
Melvina **147** 67
Melvina (Weston) **147**
  65 67
Mercy **90** 110 **129** 168 170
Mildred Bancroft **85** 196
Nancy (McClellan) **84** 213
  90 90 **103** 173

LITCHFIELD *cont'd*
Nellie Norton **82** 171
Nicholas **53** 465 **55** 277
  57 184 **129** 151 162-164
  166-168 369 371 **135** 44
Noah **129** 170 **142** 298
Patty **60** 338
Paul Weeks **85** 188 **113**
  232 309
Penelope **129** 154 167
  251 363
Penelope (Litchfield)
  129 154 167 251
Penelope (Stockbridge)
  135 44
Phineas Francis **82** 172
Priscilla **129** 169 362
Priscilla (Vinal) **129** 165
  169 268 362
Rachel **61** 175 **129** 164
Rachel (Clapp) **129** 165
Rachel (Litchfield)
  129 164
Raymond Weston **147** 66
Remembrance **53** 465
Rhoda **70** 353
Rhoda (Perry) **129** 166
Rhoda (Studley) **129** 168
Rowland **125** 219
Rufus **61** 57 58 175 288 289
Ruth **55** 277 **92** 94 **129** 251
  147 66 67
Ruth (Cole) **129** 168
Ruth (Tilden) **129** 260
Samuel **53** 455 **129** 164
  165 169 268 362
Sarah **53** 465 **57** 183 **129** 69
  250 252 253 369 378 **135**
  43
Sarah (Baker) **142** 123
Sarah (Cass) **129** 151 **135**
  43 44
Sarah (Jackson) **90** 57
Sarah (Litchfield) **129** 369
Sarah (Studley) **129** 164
  135 44
Sarah (Whitcomb)
  129 164
Sarah (Willcutt) **129** 170
Sibea **135** 43
Simeon **60** 339
Susanna **60** 339 **129** 154
  167
Susanna (Morey) **129** 168
  135 43
Thomas Tilden **90** 110
Ward **90** 109
Wilford Jacob **52** 85 **53**
  252 **54** xxxvi **55** xxix
  56 xxx 99 107 **57** xxxi
  226 229 398 **58** xliii 82
  99 168 260 387 **59** 74
  134 308 387 421 **60**
  xxxiv 61 82 85 86 175
  186-189 271 335 **61** vii
  xxxiii 56 172 207 288 372
  62 vii xxviii xxxv 383
  63 vii xxii 391 **64** vii
  xxix **65** vii xxi xxxiii **66**
  xxxvii xlviii 83
William **125** 220

LITCHFIELD *cont'd*
Zoa **55** 225
LITCHMAN
George **140** 163
LITCHMORE
Elizabeth **100** 303
LITERAL
Charles W. **128** 264
Elen (Knox) **128** 177
Emma (Mays) **128** 264
John **128** 264
John H. **128** 177
Lettes E. (Knox) **128** 264
Sarah **128** 177
LITHGOW Lithcow
  Lithgoe
— Col. **146** 335
— Mr. **64** 322
Alfred J. S.J. **66** 111
Andrew **65** 245 **118** 43 46
  50 56
Ann (Gardiner) **97** 113
Arthur **97** 113
Charles **97** 113
Charlotte **97** 113
Elizabeth **65** 245
Hetty Green (Langdon)
  97 291
J. **145** 159
James **97** 113
Jane **65** 245 **97** 113
Jane Caroline **65** 38
Margaret **147** 73
Martha **74** 100
Martha (Bridges) **97** 113
Martha C. **66** 111
Mary **74** 101 **97** 113
Mary (Warler) **100** 242
Matthew **100** 242
Nancy **97** 113
Phebe Langdon **97** 291
Robert **65** 245 **74** 100 101
  97 103 113
Robert Alexander
  Douglas **64** 299
Sarah **67** 312 **97** 103 112
  113
Sarah (Noble) **97** 103 113
Susanna **97** 113
William **52** 471-473 **63** 267
  67 312 **97** 103 112 113
  291 292 **98** 300 **147** 73
  75 76 185
LITHMAN
Catherine **64** 323
Litilbury *see* Littlebery
Litlebury *see* Littlebery
Litlehale *see* Littlehale
Litlepage *see* Littlepage
LITLER Thomas **72** 56
LITMAN
Ray Frank **111** 324
Simon **111** 324
LITSTER Henry **94** 7
LITTANY
Margaret E. **69** 141
Littlefield *see* Littlefield
Littlefield *see* Littlefield
LITTELL —— **54** 382
Eliza. **136** 243
Emlen T. **83** 434

LITTELL cont'd
Helen A. (Howell)
  83 432 434
Jim **117** 319
Joseph **117** 319
Mary (Ludlam) **98** 332
Mary Catherine (Wilson)
  105 218
Mercy **117** 80
Sarah Jane (Fitz
  Randolph) **98** 332
Thomas **117** 80
LITTERLY
Catherine **88** 119
LITTIG
Elizabeth **84** 453
M. D. **99** 257
Peter **99** 257
LITTILE
Rachel W. **78** 402
LITTLE Lytle
—— **51** 17 28 87 **62** 21
  70 xxxiii **92** 357 **93** 63
  65 116 117 121 **98** 127
  111 217 **119** 32 **120** 133
  123 52 **136** 211 **140** 163
  145 51
— Col. **85** 18
— Mme **97** 4 8
— Mr. **71** 53 **75** 114
  91 140
— Mrs. **120** 133
— Widow **70** 24
Abigail **51** 462 **52** 81 233
  94 64 165 **129** 251 252
Abijah **70** 217
Abijah Brooks **57** 69
Abner **51** 462
Abraham **112** 302
Adelaide **70** 209
Alexander **74** 32 **106** 108
Alice **128** 202
Almena **68** 156
Althea **58** 197
Alvin **58** 403
Amelia **58** 402
Amos **94** 64 **97** 355
Andrew **60** 160 **81** 368
Anjalene **116** 26 27
Ann **55** 72 73 77 **63** 140
  106 82 **110** 141
Ann (Warren) **120** 197
Ann Huntress **97** 4
Anna **70** 163
Anna (Warren) **143** 122
Anne **59** 213
Annie **128** 95
Anthony **91** 328
Archibald (Mrs.) **89** 303
Archibald Stinson **116** 26
Arthur **53** 136
Arthur D. **62** xxxi **97** 5
Arthur Dehon **62** xxxvii
Asahel **58** 401
B. K. (Mrs.) **120** 159
Barnabas **52** 81 **118** 129
  129 159 169 256
Barzillai **58** 196-198 401
  60 78
Beatrice **78** 85
Benjamin **62** 20

LITTLE cont'd
Bertram Kimball (Mrs.)
  95 152 **100** 117 **104** 151
  108 129 **113** 304
Bethiah **53** 428 **55** 73 162
  134 138
Betsey (Hammond)
  83 493
Betty **60** 78 **69** 118 119
Bond **64** 123
Calvin **84** 43
Caroline **74** 32
Caroline Amelia **77** 182
Caroline Gore **124** 149
Catherine **76** 268
Catherine Stinson **116** 26
Charles **55** 162 **87** 339
Charles Lowell **93** 65
Charles Walter **81** 368
Charlotte **116** 26 27
Charlotte Barton **116** 26
Christopher **75** 241
  114 241
Clara L. **87** 93 **94** 93 98
  208 **101** 329
Clarissa **119** 32
Clarissa (Bourne) **119** 32
Consider **60** 371
Constant **52** 55 **53** 429
Constant (Fobes) **136** 333
Daniel **83** 435 **84** 21 29
  113 318
Daniel C. **87** 207
David **52** 56 81 **55** 376 **61**
  192 **66** 132 **83** 17 **84** 43
  87 207 **118** 128 129 **129**
  169 251 256 263 266 **130**
  213 **135** 16
David Elsworth **61** 192
David S. **84** 43
Denial **58** 197
Donald Goodridge (Mrs.)
  86 447
Dorothy **63** lxii **83** 210
  211
Dorothy (Perkins) **83** 211
Doty **105** 210
Earl J. **130** 55
Ebenezer **76** 268
Edmund **134** 215
Edna **66** 131 135 **79** 89
Edna (Hale) **139** 52 55
Edward **72** 37
Edward Porter **57** 227 334
  60 85
Eliphalet **74** 63
Eliza **59** 289 **60** 160
Eliza (Rich) **84** 125
Eliza R. **125** 175
Elizabeth **51** 401 **52** 56 81
  57 200-202 **69** 15 121
  70 xliii 24 **76** 10 215 **81**
  190 **82** 478 **92** 352 **94** 39
  97 4 5 **99** 208 **100** 25
  105 63 **106** 108 317 **113**
  223 **118** 128 129 **129**
  169 **139** 51 53
Elizabeth (Norton) **98** 93
  94
Elizabeth (Searle) (Poor)
  139 55

LITTLE cont'd
Elizabeth (Twombly) **83**
  435 **84** 21
Elizabeth (Woodbridge)
  101 148
Elizabeth H. **94** 160
Elizabeth Henry **92** 352
Elizabeth Powers
  (Knight) (Little) **94** 64
Elizabeth Taylor **139** 52
Ellen **124** 149
Ellen C. **103** 47
Emily **84** 43 **116** 26
Emlen T. **83** 432 434
Emma **116** 26 27
Emma J. **84** 125
Ephraim **52** 81 **55** 73 **57**
  18 **60** 205 **98** 93 94 **99**
  79 **101** 148 **142** 170
Esther Hope (Low)
  90 293
Ethel **108** 135
Eunice (Gaines) **85** 53
Ezekiel **66** 131-133
Faith **74** 114
Fobes **104** 242 **136** 333
Fobes Francis **127** 115
Frances **74** 32
Frances (Boyd) **140** 163
Frances Amelia **100** 230
Francis **100** 239 **147** 47 48
Francis Kinzer (Mrs.)
  90 293
Francis Nichols **93** 121
Frederick S. **121** 178 179
Freelove (Brooks) (Rich)
  83 409
Gay **124** 149
George **52** 68 **55** 73 **66** 135
  78 414 **79** 89 **88** 303 **91**
  328 **101** 59 104 69 **110**
  141 **139** 52-55
George Brown **93** 117
George T. **52** 486 **54** 243
  111 10 180 181 **114** 258
  266 268
George Thomas **64** 96
  69 lvii **104** 69 **122** 292
  131 250 **146** 336
George W. **88** 339 **97** 19
  125 183
Gladys Margaret
  (Vosburgh) **86** 447
H. M. **76** 46
Hannah **53** 39 **54** 84 **55** 73
  65 331 **66** 133 **69** 104
  92 325 **106** 108 **133** 289
  134 140 **144** 199
Hannah (Chase) (Craw)
  87 339
Hannah (Leigh) **94** 64 165
Hannah (Moody) **94** 64
  97 355
Hannah (Noyes) **133** 43
Hannah Morril **90** 54
Hariett M. **116** 26
Harriet **94** 64
Harriet F. **113** 161
Harriet M. **116** 27
Harriet S. **94** 161
Harriet Sophia **93** 63

LITTLE *cont'd*
Harriett **94** 64
Helen **59** xciv
Helen Lee **92** 108 **95** 213
Henry **105** 63 **113** 223
119 21
Henry F. W. **64** 134
Henry G. **92** 98
Henry N. **93** 116
Homer Parson **106** 125
Hortentia C. **78** 406
Howard James **96** 160
Hugh Ruthven **105** 218
Huldah **72** 37
I. Runnel **124** 149
Isaac **53** 428 **55** 73 162 **86**
6 7 **98** 332 **100** 25 **127**
253 **136** 79 **52** 273
Jacob **98** 231 **100** 25
James **65** 121 **85** 313 315
90 396 397 **116** 26 27
119
James B. **84** 43 **91** 328
James L. **84** 207
James Lovell **145** 311
James R. **116** 27
James S. **84** 43
Jane **60** 160 **97** 355 **127** 253
Jean **57** 202
Jedida **51** 197
Jemima **122** 101
Jenny **57** 69 202 **64** 123
70 307
Joan **84** 77
John **52** 55 **53** 39 **57** 202
60 28 160 371 **64** 319 **70**
305 **77** 318 **81** 368 **84** 43
75 125 226 **93** 258 **108**
253 **112** 174 **118** 128
120 200 **128** 293 **132**
194 **133** 43 **136** 333
John Barton **116** 26
John Dozier (Mrs.) **86** 436
John J. **55** xxxii
John Mason **59** xciv
John Moody **94** 64
John R. **116** 27
John T. **91** 328 **132** 194
Jonathan **79** 165
Joseph **57** 202 **90** 43 49
112 302 **134** 215 **140** 68
Joseph Barton **116** 26
Joseph Taylor **139** 56
Josiah Stover **88** 155
Judith **97** 4
Judith (Bailey) **97** 4
Julia Agusta (Cook)
145 311
Juliana Submit **91** 107
Kate (Dunlap) **86** 436
Katharine P. **109** 130
Keziah **115** 14
Lemuel **51** 197 199 **90**
396 397 **136** 39
Leola **100** 195
Leonard **70** 261 **75** 241
110 320
Lerinda (Bourne) **119** 32
Levi **125** 101
Lida **124** 149
Louisa **84** 43

LITTLE *cont'd*
Louisa L. (Lord) **97** 19
Lucinda **115** 14
Lucinda (Bourne) **119** 32
Lucy **66** 133 **90** 396 **113**
156 **126** 67
Lucy B. **126** 22
Lydia **66** 131 **89** 48 **90** 396
105 63
Lydia (Barker) **136** 79
Lydia (Coffin) **106** 144
110 141 **121** 168
Lydia (Little) **105** 63
Lydia (Young) **90** 396
Lydia Young **90** 396
Mabel **70** 84 **118** 128 129
Marcy **120** 197
Margaret **57** 202 **60** 160
65 85 **66** 132
Margaretta Artemisia
94 198
Maria (Seymour)
Salsbury) **132** 194
Marion (Borden) **84** 226
Martha **69** 17 214 **115** 172
52 273
Mary **51** 197 199 **52** 81 **55**
73 376 **71** 57 **75** 241 83
17 **87** 338 **88** 302 303 **90**
392 **94** 65 **97** 5 **100** 195
114 186 **115** 141 **120**
197 **122** 101 **125** 180
182 241 243 **127** 9 **134**
297 **135** 40 75 **139** 56
Mary (Briggs) **90** 43
Mary (Hovey) **83** 17
Mary (Kimball) **139** 55
Mary (Lapham) **136** 79
Mary (Lovering) **125** 101
Mary (Otis) **136** 79
Mary (Vose) **95** 213
Mary (Woodmansee) **147**
47 48
Mary Ann **82** 487 **94** 64
Mary E. **116** 26
Mary E. (Gilman) **121** 179
Mary Emeline **83** 492 493
Mary Jane **84** 43
Mary Jane (Fitz
Randolph) (Reynolds)
98 231
Mary Jane W. **94** 161
Mary R. **145** 310
Mary Robbins (Revere)
145 311
Mary Simmons **83** 231
Mary T. **53** 43
Mary W. (Chadwick)
103 47
Maryella R. **87** 98
Maud **81** 42
Mercy **52** 81 **55** 73 **124** 118
129 170 **135** 36
Michael **88** 155 248 **94** 64
165
Mildred Prince **108** 133
Milly **72** 37
Moses **53** 368 **64** 64 **65** 80
111 114 **66** 133 **106** 144
107 161 **110** 141 **121**
168 **135** 100 102 **142** 31

LITTLE *cont'd*
36
Myron H. **84** 43
Nancy **125** 106 **127** 239
Nancy B. **84** 43
Nathaniel **52** 81 **53** 36 **74**
63 114 **104** 242 **110** 141
115 141 **118** 129 **136** 79
Nicholas **67** 347 **92** 352
357 **93** 63 65 116 117
121 **94** 39 161
Nina Fletcher **91** 140 **92**
152 **94** 146 **97** 164 **98**
153 **99** 154 **104** 151 **106**
131 **107** 130 222 **110**
221
Nina Jarvie (Fletcher)
113 304
Noah **133** 43
Octavia E. **74** 88
Olive (Littlefield) **133** 43
Oliver John Clark **116** 26
Omar **126** 245
Orrie Delle **86** 371
Otis **59** 193 194 **83** 211
104 242 **105** 210 **118**
128
Patience **55** 73 **70** 163
143 122
Paul **100** 230 **109** 54
Penelope **90** 396
Phebe W. **109** 109
Philip F. **115** 172
Polly **118** 14
Priscilla **120** 200
Priscilla (Ellis) **120** 200
Rachel **51** 401 402 **66** 133
101 148 **131** 235
Rebecca **57** 200 **60** 371 **69**
119 216 296
Rebecca (Dodge)
(Caldwell) **97** 5
Rebecca (Rich) **84** 43
Rebecca C. **116** 26 27
Rhoda J. **75** 211
Richard **54** 341 **63** 235
110 141
Richard H. **84** 43
Robert **60** 28 **62** 352 **63** 78
78 417 **128** 95
Robert C. (Mrs.) **109** 130
Roger **84** 73
Rufus **85** 53
Russell **55** 35 **56** 356
Ruth **55** 73 **64** 123 **75** lxxxi
96 382 **109** 155 **113** 21
136 333
Ruth (Rich) **84** 43
Sally **88** 155 248 302
106 108
Sally (Williams) **128** 80
Sallyann Barton **116** 26 27
Samuel **52** 273 **55** 73 **61**
217 **65** 286 **66** 132 **82**
320 **91** 328 **96** 354 **104**
229 **125** 94 **127** 163 **129**
272 **140** 68
Samuel A. **100** 195
Samuel H. **91** 107
Sarah **53** 39 429 **55** 73 162
163 167 **60** 72 **76** 10 **83**

LITTLE *cont'd*
481 **92** 372 **93** 349 **97** 4
100 230 239 **106** 144
110 50 **121** 169
Sarah (Baker) **136** 333
Sarah (Brown) **125** 183
Sarah (Dole) **105** 63
Sarah (Jackson) **94** 65
97 4 5
Sarah (Moody) **106** 144
Sarah (Redington)
(Emerson) **109** 54
Sarah (Ryley) **90** 49
Sarah (Wicom)(Hale)
139 55
Sarah A. **115** 172
Sarah B. **64** 205
Sarah Jackson **94** 65
Sarah Jane (Fitz
Randolph) **98** 332
Sarah McKensie **100** 239
Sarah W. **123** 150
Simon Addis **116** 26
Stephen **65** 286 **87** 98 **94**
65 **97** 4 5
Submit (White) **91** 107
Sukey **57** 202
Susan **106** 68
Susan D. **126** 245
Susan D. (Munroe)
126 246
Susan G. (Bearse) **88** 339
Sussan **106** 68
Sylvester **92** 108 **95** 213
Taylor **139** 56
Thomas **51** 197 **55** 72 73
57 202 **63** 140 353 **64**
123 **69** 9-14 **70** 163 **74**
240 241 **85** 260 **94** 10 **99**
208 **100** 25 **120** 32 197
122 252 **126** 225 **127** 24
143 122
Toby **93** 204
Tom **70** 219
Tristram **53** 39 **57** 280 **76**
10 **105** 63 **110** 141
Violet **77** 190
W. J. **91** 328
Wallace **69** 12 127 215 218
297 303 306 **70** 10-14 16
18 20 139 141 143 212
216-220 295 299 300 305
306 **76** 268
Wallis **57** 69 202
Warren **58** 401
Warren L. **114** 241
William **57** 200-202 **58** 197
401-403 **59** 213 413-15
119 120 122 127 212 215-
220-22 138 307 **83** 409
493 **84** 43 **87** 398 **103** 47
113 161 **125** 183 **134**
217 **140** 29 163 **147** 84
William B. **94** 161
William Baldwin **92** 357
William Bernard **78** 85
William C. **70** xxxiii
William J. **84** 43
William M. **84** 43
William Meeker **77** 190
William R. **98** 332

LITTLEBERY Litilbury
Litlebery
John **84** 230
William **93** 224 **94** 75 76
LITTLEDALE
Willoughby A. **57** 226
62 385
LITTLEFAIR
Ann **115** 26 110
Horatio **115** 110
John **115** 26
Joseph **115** 26 110
LITTLEFIELD Littlefield
Littelfield Littlifield
—— **105** 263
— Mrs. **117** 168
A. **91** 328
A. A. **94** 29
Aaron **57** 146 **65** 115 **76**
103 105 110 247 **82** 366
91 230 **96** 146 **113** 123
Aaron J. **93** 333
Aaron Stevens **107** 198
Abbie **93** 244
Abbie A. **92** 334
Abbie E. **93** 108
Abbie F. **93** 329
Abbie M. **92** 334
Abbie S. **93** 247
Abigail **59** 363 **63** 169 **65**
115 **67** 348 **75** 44 46 47
105-108 111 112 114-122
313-315 **76** 103 108-111
179 181 183 184 187 192
195 254 255 259 **92** 334
93 103 108 114 242 243
335 **94** 33 35 **96** 147 337
341 **113** 123 **115** 219
228 **119** 68 **123** 74
Abigail (Littlefield)
96 147
Abigail (Smith) **95** 86
Abigail A. **120** 138
Abigail Ann **94** 29 37
Abigail Haumer **82** 366
Abigail J. **94** 29
Abigail M. **94** 35
Abigail Russell
(Whitman) **84** 222
Abner **76** 107 **91** 328 **94** 33
95 200 **107** 275 **108** 60
191
Abraham **65** 115 **75** 111
76 104 107 109-111 185
196 250 **87** 206 **108** 121
115 211 227
Achsa **136** 270
Acut **113** 123
Ada R. **92** 334
Ada V. **92** 334
Adaline (Chaney) **83** 19
Adeline **83** 19
Agnes **63** 271 **67** 345-347
76 109 111 112 184 188
190 251 252 256 262 **79**
15 **92** 334
Agnes E. **93** 112
Alanson **93** 242 243
Albert **79** 270 **92** 334
Albert H. **94** 35
Albert J. **92** 334

LITTLEFIELD *cont'd*
Albra W. **93** 247
Alcult **116** 133
Alden L. (Mrs.) **120** 3
Alden Llewellyn **84** 223
105 69 125
Alfred **93** 242 243
Alfred H. **55** 190
Alice **75** 113 **108** 123
Alice P. **120** 305 306
Alice W. **93** 247
Almeda P. **93** 108
Almedia (Welch) **120** 138
139
Almira **76** 256 **93** 112 238
Almira N. **93** 244
Almon A. **92** 334
Alonzo F. **94** 35 36 373
Alpheus **76** 109 250 251
255 **81** 384 **93** 113 239
116 133 **117** 230 **118**
154 155
Alpheus F. **94** 373
Alta G. **94** 29
Alvah W. **94** 33
Amanda F. **93** 242
Amaziah J. **93** 335
Amos **64** 181 66 155 157
76 104 **87** 206 **93** 332
115 310
Amos Augustus **105** 65
114 154
Andrew **91** 328
Andrew J. **92** 334 337
93 54 56
Andrew Jackson **93** 242
Angeline **92** 334
Angie M. **92** 334
Ann **67** 345-347 **83** 88 88
388 **93** 242 244 248
Ann (Davidson) **96** 335
Ann (Ricker) **98** 205
Ann (Shapleigh) **95** 274
Ann E. **93** 243
Ann J. **93** 250
Ann M. **93** 332
Ann Ricker **98** 205
Anna **51** 369 **59** 363 **65** 115
75 44 117 319 **76** 110-
114 181 185 186 188 189
249 253 260 **82** 194 **93**
355 **98** 205 **110** 174
Anna Brooks **124** 208
Anna L. **92** 334
Anne **67** 343-348 **76** 108
185 **88** 388 **94** 29
Anne Hinxe **52** 263
Annie **123** 232
Annie (Littlefield)
123 232
Annie E. **93** 108
Annie L. **92** 334 **98** 258
Annie M. **93** 108 109
Annie S. **93** 335 **120** 304
Annis **67** 345-347 **105** 262
Annis (Austin) **105** 261
Anson B. **92** 334 336
Anthony **67** 345 347 348
75 113 **76** 191 **84** 222
402 **86** 71 73-75 179 **105**
262 **112** 320 **120** 315

LITTLEFIELD *cont'd*
Arabell L. **89** 275
Arletta V. (Redmond) **84** 223
Armine W. **92** 334
Arthur M. **92** 334
Arthur W. **93** 246
Asa **75** 114 **76** 106 **93** 103 **94** 33 **105** 281 **118** 170
Asahel **76** 106 108 **118** 170
Ashel **113** 123
Augusta **93** 244
Augustus **76** 250 **92** 334
Augustus A. **114** 153
Augustus M. **93** 111
Augustus T. **92** 334 335 337 **121** 309
Austin S. **93** 111
Bancroft **96** 335
Barbara **96** 335
Bathsheba **75** 115 311 **76** 103 104 179
Beatrice B. **102** 319
Belinda B. (Clark) **117** 164
Benaiah **65** 115 **76** 251 **93** 108
Benjamin **75** 107 311 312 **76** 104 107 110 114 179 181 188 195 249 250 252 253 255 256 261 **79** 48 **87** 206 **92** 334 335 337 **93** 108 109 **107** 198-200 270 273 275 **108** 57 59 189 **115** 60 309
Benjamin H. **93** 108
Benjamin W. **119** 61
Bertha B **92** 334
Bethiah **52** 216
Bethiah (Waldo) **84** 222 **136** 313
Bethulah **116** 133
Betsey **65** 115 **66** 315 **76** 185 189 249-251 256 **92** 334 338 **93** 107 108 238 246 248 **96** 338 339 **97** 232 **117** 141 142 **131** 233
Betsey (Chaney) **119** 62
Betsey (Davis) **97** 21
Betsey (Shapleigh) **95** 274
Betsey L. **114** 154
Betsey Mitchel **96** 245
Betsey S. (Rice) **114** 154
Betty **75** 119 **76** 183 255 **95** 88
C. C. **93** 329
C. J. **89** 275
Caleb **67** 24 26 248 **74** 84 **82** 159 **86** 71-77 179 180 330 **104** 12 **105** 177 234 255 261-263 271 **136** 211
Calvin **76** 250 **93** 248 **119** 62
Calvin C. **93** 248
Caroline A. (Morse) **114** 154
Caroline A. (Parsons) **119** 287
Caroline Amelia (Morse) **105** 65
Caroline H. **91** 230 **93** 247

LITTLEFIELD *cont'd*
Caroline Morse **114** 154
Carolyn Maria **105** 65
Carrie C. **92** 334 336 337
Carrie J. **94** 35 36
Carrie Maria **114** 154
Cate **86** 75
Catherine **67** 27 **86** 76 330 **105** 167 263 **136** 270
Catherine (Sands) **86** 75
Charity **67** 348 **75** 117 **76** 184 **86** 75
Charity G. **97** 18 238
Charles **76** 109 **92** 334 336 **93** 109 **94** 116
Charles B. **92** 334
Charles C. M. **92** 334 336
Charles Clement **68** xxx xxxiv
Charles E. **93** 338
Charles F. **92** 334 336 337 **93** 327
Charles H. **56** 203 **92** 334-338
Charles Harrison **56** xvi xxx **57** xxxl **74** xxviii **79** 196 **80** 204 **81** 216 363 **82** 216 266 267
Charles L. **92** 335
Charles M. **94** 35 36
Charles Oscar **93** 242
Charles P. **94** 35
Charles S. **92** 239 334 335
Charles W. **95** 378
Charlie A. **92** 335
Charlotte **65** 115 **81** 384 **90** 206 **93** 113 329 **114** 154 **123** 72 149 **124** 208
Charlotte (Bowden) **118** 154 155
Charlotte B. **114** 154 **118** 318
Charlotte M. **92** 335 336
Chessie **92** 335
Christopher **92** 334 335 337 338
Christopher C. **119** 288
Christopher Columbus **93** 329
Clara **93** 242
Clara E. **92** 335
Clara F. **92** 335
Clarina **94** 29
Clarinda **117** 164
Clarissa **94** 35
Clement **76** 108 251 252 256 262 **92** 334-336
Cora B. **92** 335
Cynthia **86** 77 **92** 335
Cynthia J. **92** 335
Cyrus K. **92** 335 337
Daniel **66** 158 **67** 348 **75** 43 44 108 112 113 311 **76** 108 110 113 114 183 184 186 187 248 249 251 253 259 **84** 222 **85** 448 **86** 75 **87** 206 207 **92** 335 **93** 242-244 246 329 **94** 35 **99** 327 **105** 252 282 **115** 212 **119** 288
David **63** 169 **64** 11 **67** 348

LITTLEFIELD *cont'd*
75 45-47 105 106 108 111 112 116 117 119 **76** 103 250 257 **91** 328 **93** 248 **96** 146 245 **97** 16 **98** 205 **115** 227
David Blair **96** 335
David G. **93** 111 112
Deborah **59** 364 **66** 78 **67** 348 **71** 129 **75** 113 121 **76** 104 106 107 112 181 182 185 187 256 258 **93** 329 **117** 142
Deborah (Perkins) **115** 138
Deliverance **86** 76
Dependence **67** 348 **70** 291 **75** 46 106 **76** 103 106 107 109 179 180 182 190 194 258 **87** 206 **92** 334 335 337 **93** 335
Dorcas **65** 115 66 262 **75** 118 311 312 **76** 104 106-111 179 181 184 185 188 259 **92** 334 335 **93** 329 333 335 **95** 267
Dorcas (Black) **115** 60
Dorcas (Boston) **119** 61
Dorothy **59** 174 **67** 348 **74** 252 **75** 117 120 313 **76** 253 **92** 337 **93** 248
Dorothy (Chatman) **108** 121
Dorothy A. **92** 335
Dorothy Maria **94** 35
Dummer **76** 248
E. J. **93** 327
Eastman **93** 335
Eben **108** 60
Ebenezer **65** 263 **66** 78 263 312 **75** 105 311 **76** 104 105 107 110 179 182 253-255 261 **87** 207 **91** 230 **93** 108 109 **116** 128 139 **118** 318
Edgar H. **94** 29
Edith **93** 327
Edmond W. **93** 242
Edmund **52** 216 **59** 90 91 153 363 364 **67** 24 66 343 345-348 **70** 291 **71** 133 **74** 84 **75** 113 **76** 111 **82** 366 **84** 222 **86** 71-73 77 **88** 388 **105** 262 263 **108** 121 **136** 313
Edmund D. **92** 335
Edna **76** 107 109 111 182 183 185 187 259 **87** 225 234
Edward **67** 343 345-347 **76** 103 104 248 **90** 325 **107** 155
Edward H. **92** 335
Edward L. **93** 242
Edward S. **85** 422
Edwin **93** 244
Edwin M. **92** 335 341
Elbridge **93** 242 243
Elcey **94** 116
Eleanor **75** 45 119 **76** 179
Eleazer **93** 111 112

LITTLEFIELD *cont'd*
Eleazer C. **93** 111
Eli P. **93** 327
Eliab **67** 348 **75** 106 115
  311 **76** 103-107 110 179
  181 184 **82** 366
Elias **70** 291 **76** 107 **133** 41
Elijah **66** 157 **75** 106 108 **76**
  103 107 **93** 340 **105** 211
  107 195 197
Elisha **64** 181 **75** 106 107
  111 114 **76** 103 104 106
  108 110 112 114 181 184
  187 247 249 250 258 260
  93 327 **94** 34-36 **96** 339
  97 21 **133** 42
Elisha L. **94** 28
Eliza **80** 127 **93** 248 **94** 35
Eliza (Ingersoll) **122** 294
Eliza A. **90** 303 **97** 232
Eliza Ann (Brann) **133** 123
Eliza Jane **92** 335
Eliza U. **93** 250
Elizabeth **57** 393 **59** 90
  153 363 364 **64** 11 **67** 24
  345-348 **75** 44 47 105
  106 108 115-117 313-315
  76 105-108 179 180 184-
  187 190 191 193 196 247
  259 261 **92** 335 **93** 107
  328 329 **96** 247 **110** 57
  113 123 **116** 135 **127** 12
  136 270
Elizabeth (Beal) **114** 130
Elizabeth (Brinley) **86** 76
  330 **105** 263
Elizabeth (Mott) **84** 222
  86 72 **105** 262
Elizabeth C. **103** 236
Elizabeth H. **92** 335 337
Elizabeth J. **93** 107
Elizabeth M. **92** 335
  93 243
Elizabeth R. (Dore)
  103 236
Elizabeth S. (Turner)
  117 164
Elizabeth U. (Parsons)
  117 140
Ella F. **93** 333
Ella Kimball **82** 367
Ella M. **92** 335
Ellen **93** 243
Ellen C. **93** 111
Ellen F. **93** 333
Elmer **98** 10
Elmira **93** 111
Elmus **94** 29
Eloisa **76** 190
Elsey **94** 116
Elsie S. (Perkins) **90** 387
Elva **93** 243
Elveretta **93** 138
Elvira **83** 183 185
Emeline **56** 384
Emeline E. **94** 28 29
Emily **93** 244
Emily A. **92** 335
Emily Elizabeth **79** 270
Emily W. **128** 281
Emma **92** 335 **117** 167

LITTLEFIELD *cont'd*
Emma E. **93** 108
Emma G. **92** 335
Emma Jane (Noble)
  95 377
Emma L. **92** 335
Emma Warren (Bancroft)
  96 334
Emme **92** 338
Enoch **76** 109 112
Ephraim **57** 393 **66** 157
  75 54 **76** 189 **92** 335 337
  115 220 225 **116** 143
Esther **63** 270 **75** 44 122
  76 103 106 107 109-111
  179 180 182 184 **113** 123
  116 137 **136** 313
Esther (Banks) **113** 123
  115 135
Esther J. **94** 28
Etta **123** 232
Eunice **75** 122 315 **76** 179
  93 108
Eunice (Mitchell) **98** 205
Eunice (Winn) **117** 225
Eunice M. **93** 108
Everett **93** 328 331 338
Experience Pray **118** 170
Fanna **94** 118
Fannie **94** 118
Fannie (Larrabee) **95** 378
Fannie A. (Barker) **95** 376
Fanny **76** 189
Florence **93** 243
Florence A. **92** 335
Florence A. M. **93** 108
Florence E. **92** 335
Florence L. **83** 425 434
Florence Lord **92** 335
Florence P. **92** 335
Frances **67** 345-347 **75** 53
  108 117 **76** 193
Frances Georgiana
  82 367
Frances Jane (Blair)
  96 334
Frances Judith **92** 113
Frances Kingsbury
  96 335
Francis **67** 343-348 **70** 291
  75 44 53 55 108 116 118
  76 103 110 111 **82** 366
  95 360 **98** 205 225 **105**
  262 **109** 220 **141** 329
Frank **92** 337 **93** 335 **124**
  240 **136** 270
Frank E. **94** 29
Frank R. **95** 375
Frank W. **95** 379
Frankie A. **94** 35
Franklin E. **121** 70
Franklin M. **121** 69 70
Freddie **94** 28
Frederick **76** 114 **92** 335-
  338 **93** 57 337
Frederick Billings **98** 10
Frederick James **98** 10
Frost **76** 249
Georgana M. **92** 336
George **76** 106 110 111 114
  82 366 **93** 248 332 **119**

LITTLEFIELD *cont'd*
  225 **136** 270
George A. **92** 335 **93** 329
  94 371 373 **95** 379
George A. (Mrs.) **69** lxvi
George Abner **96** 334
George Emery **51** 226 504
  52 88 392 484 **53** 258 **54**
  358 **55** xix 107 **56** 104
  212 **57** xxxi 125 **58** xliii
  212 327 **62** 110 **63** 108
  391 **66** vii 97 **67** vii **68**
  vi **69** vi **70** xxviii lviii
  291-293 **71** 102 105 **93**
  328 **94** 175 176 212 **104**
  91 92 **105** 83
George F. **93** 244
George H. **91** 230 **92** 334-
  336 **93** 333
George Martin **82** 367
George P. **93** 250
George S. **65** 19
George Sherman **51** 369
George Thomas **51** 368
George W. **93** 103 108 109
  123 232
Georgia Anna **133** 123
Georgiana (Weeks)
  123 152
Gertrude Elizabeth
  70 294
Gideon R. **92** 335 **93** 246
Gideon Richardson
  76 107 250
Grace **67** 346
H. E. **93** 112
Hannah **60** 191 **63** 169
  270 271 **66** 265 **67** 348
  75 46 113 115 118 122
  314 **76** 102 110 180 182-
  186 188 189 248 254 259
  260 **86** 76 **89** 275 **91** 230
  92 334 336 **93** 108 329
  340 **94** 33 **102** 239 **105**
  263 **107** 275 **108** 57 59
  60 **112** 304 **115** 141 **117**
  143 144 **118** 241 **119**
  228 288 **121** 73 146 **136**
  270
Hannah (Coes) **133** 42
Hannah (Littlefield)
  118 241
Hannah (Stone) **95** 200
  108 191
Hannah (Straw) **90** 325
Hannah (Swett) **116** 128
Hannah (Thompson)
  108 191
Hannah (Webber)
  119 285
Hannah A. **122** 71 232
Hannah E. **93** 331 **94** 36
Hannah E. (York) **92** 336
Hannah G. **92** 336
Hannah H. **81** 384
Hannah J. **120** 307 309
Hannah Maria **77** 51
Hannah O. **92** 336
Hannah S. **91** 230
Hannah W. **93** 103
Harriet **76** 188 **92** 336

LITTLEFIELD *cont'd*
116 293
Harriet Abby **82** 367
Harris N. **93** 247
Harry **92** 335
Hartley B. **93** 108
Hattie **92** 336
Hattie A. **94** 35 36
Hattie A. (Junkins)
122 229
Hattie F. **92** 336
Hattie N. **92** 336
Haven D. **93** 242 243
Helen T. **93** 250
Henrietta (Kimball)
97 235
Henry **76** 249 **86** 75 **94** 29
30
Henry O. **93** 327
Henry Willis **96** 335
Hephzibah **75** 44 53 55 116
119 **76** 105-107 110 180
181 184 **115** 65
Hiram **76** 251 **88** 335 **93**
238 239 **118** 320 **119**
288 **120** 64
Hiram H. **93** 247
Horace **96** 245 **97** 225 232
Horace P. **92** 336
Horatia A. **76** 241
Hosea **117** 171
Howard **92** 336
Huldah **63** 270 **75** 46 121
122 **76** 182 188 193 **92**
336 **93** 243 247 **95** 377
Huldah (Gifford) **134** 238
Huldah (Jacobs) **118** 154
Huldah A. **91** 230 **92** 336
Huldah E. **93** 243
Huldah M. **93** 242 243
Ida E. **93** 243
Ina M. **93** 111
Isaac **57** 393 **63** 270 **67** 348
75 46 108 119-121 **76**
103 104 107 109 111 113
183 187 189 257 259 **80**
127 **95** 195 267 **96** 244
122 294
Isaac Avery **96** 244
Isabella **75** 116 **76** 180
195 253 **86** 338 **92** 334-
336 **95** 267
Isabella (Gunnison)
120 64
Isaiah **76** 114 **93** 108 109
Israel **76** 248 **93** 108 **96** 245
97 235 **117** 225
Ithamar **75** 105 112 113
123 314 315 **76** 104 107
109 111 179 182 183 185
187 259
Ivory **92** 335-337 **96** 335
116 305
Ivory W. **87** 7
J. **93** 114 **94** 29 30
J. B. **94** 29
J. E. **94** 29
J. Q. **91** 328
Jabez **75** 106
Jacob **70** 291 **75** 110 **76** 110
111 184 186 188 248 260

LITTLEFIELD *cont'd*
87 206 **95** 86 **116** 221
124 208 **133** 41
Jacob Fisher **96** 244
Jacob H. **93** 327
James **60** 191 **65** 115 **67**
343-348 **75** 46 54 55 106
109-111 113 115-118 **76**
108 109 113 114 187 248
249 253 254 260 **90** 87
93 247 353 **95** 267 **96**
147 334 **105** 282 **112**
217 **114** 317 **118** 320
125 33 **136** 270
James Bancroft **96** 334
James Dorance **96** 244
James Eaton **76** 113
James L. **114** 154
James M. **92** 336
James Mitchel **96** 245
James S. **93** 114
James Warren **96** 335
Jane **67** 347 **75** 108 119-121
76 180 187 191 195 254
92 334-337 **95** 267 **96**
339 **97** 271 **107** 63 305
119 279
Jane (Hill) **95** 360 **98** 225
Jean **63** 270
Jeannett **123** 152
Jemima **75** 115 119 **95** 267
Jennie **94** 373
Jennie M. **93** 248
Jenny (Chatman) **108** 121
Jeremiah **66** 157 **75** 45 51
107 109 111 112 114 117-
120 122 311 315 **76** 103
104 106-112 114 181-185
187 188 195 257-259 **116**
296 **119** 288
Jeremiah S. **92** 334 336 337
93 53
Jeremy **75** 313
Jerusha **76** 185
Joan **67** 345-347
Joanna **67** 348 **75** 44 115
117 144 **132** 122
Joanna (Garlen) **95** 88
Job **67** 348
Joel **65** 115 **76** 112 **95** 88
John **66** 262 **67** 26 27 343-
348 **75** 44 49 51 53 54
105-107 111 113 114 121
312 313 **76** 103-106 108
111 113 181 189 248 249
82 366 **83** 88 **85** 347 **86**
73-76 330 **90** 240 315 **92**
336 **93** 247 335 397 **94**
28 29 **100** 63 **104** 11 **105**
167 256 263 270 **108** 59
110 57 **114** 294 **115** 221
133 42 **136** 270
John E. **94** 373
John F. **94** 33
John J. **92** 334 336 337
John Moulton **76** 252
John P. **119** 287
John Royal **76** 109
John S. **92** 335-337 **93** 247
329 **94** 33
John Storer **76** 106 256

LITTLEFIELD *cont'd*
262
John Stover **76** 250
John W. **94** 28
John Walley **96** 335
Johnson **65** 115 **76** 103
248 250 253-255 **87** 207
93 108 109 **119** 63
Jonathan **67** 348 **75** 43-47
55 113 122 314 **76** 102
105-108 110 180 186 193
250 259 **92** 335-337 **93**
246 **95** 274 **103** 236 **114**
228 **118** 320 **136** 270
Joseph **63** 170 270 271 **67**
348 **75** 47 105 107 108
113 115 311 312 **76** 104-
106 108 110-114 180 183-
186 188 189 249 251 254
258 260 261 **87** 206 207
92 335-338 **93** 114 243
250 **94** 29 34-36 **95** 274
98 205 **105** 211 **108** 190
115 304 **116** 128 **117**
140 **119** 64 66 **133** 42
Joseph A. **93** 328 329 **123**
150 234
Joseph B. **93** 112 **94** 30
Joseph C. **93** 112 329
Joseph Edwin **93** 243
Joseph F. **93** 335
Joseph H. **92** 334 336 337
94 36
Joseph L. **94** 28
Joseph M. **93** 242 243
Joseph N. **93** 114
Joseph S. **93** 246
Josephine **92** 336
Josephine (Sampson)
(McCausland)
114 317
Josephine H. (Herrick)
98 10
Joshua **75** 109 **76** 112 113
251 **87** 206 **92** 334 336
337 **93** 242 243 245-247
94 28-30
Joshua A. **93** 334
Joshua C. **94** 34 36
Joshua D. **94** 28
Joshua O. **93** 243
Joshua S. **85** 423
Joshua Thornton **76** 105
Josiah **67** 348 **75** 43-46 49
113 **76** 106 107 109-111
251 260 **82** 366 **87** 207
92 335-337 **93** 246 **110**
174 **114** 130 **117** 141
Josiah G. **119** 287
Josias **76** 250 254 255 **87**
206 **121** 144
Jotham **65** 115 **75** 113 312
76 110 113 184 186-188
192 249 254 **108** 120
119 285 288
Jotham B. **93** 108 109
Judith **136** 79
Judson **95** 274
Julia A. **70** lvii **93** 335
Julia A. (Witham) **123** 150
Julia Ann **93** 335 **94** 33

LITTLEFIELD *cont'd*
Julia F. **93** 243 244
Kate F. (Goodwin) **92** 336
Katharine **96** 335
Katharine Frances **96** 334
Katrina (Porter) **98** 10
Keziah **75** 117 **93** 344
Keziah (Ames) **84** 222
L. A. **61** 105 **98** 258
Laura A. **92** 336
Laura R. **93** 111 112
Laura R. M. **93** 112
Lavinia **76** 253 **93** 244
Leander **93** 244
Leander N. **93** 329
Lebbeus **93** 248
Leslie **92** 336
Lester **92** 336
Leta G. **92** 336
Lettie J. **93** 335
Levi **75** 112 **76** 107 111
  113 114 196 248 259 **87**
  207 **90** 387 **93** 108 109
  119 282
Levi W. **93** 108
Levina **76** 255
Levisa **76** 254
Lewis **94** 28
Lewis L. **92** 336 337
Lida **92** 336
Lillian (Pierce) **98** 10
Lillian R. **93** 108
Lincoln C. **92** 232 335 336
Lizzie E. (Steuart) **123** 234
Lizzie O. **93** 103
Lois **75** 119 **76** 188 **111** 117
Lorenzo D. **93** 111 112
Louie M. **92** 336
Louisa F. **90** 107
Louisa H. **92** 336
Lovey I. **93** 112
Lovina **93** 244
Lovina L. **93** 244
Lucinda **51** 368 **93** 108
Lucinda P. **93** 250
Lucretia **63** 269 **76** 253
Lucy **93** 109 **95** 374 **96** 245
  107 270 **108** 122 192
Lucy S. (Perkins) **75** 315
  76 113 114 183 248 253
  260 **90** 387 **93** 108 109
  95 374 **119** 282
Lura Mabel **94** 373
Lydia **59** 363 **60** 191 **63**
  270 271 **66** 264 **67** 24
  348 **75** 45 54 55 105 106
  108-111 113 115-119 312
  315 **76** 104-107 109 180
  183-189 192 195 196 248
  249 251 253 255 257 258
  86 72-74 183 **92** 334-338
  93 243 **94** 28 **95** 267 **98**
  205 **105** 234 254 255 262
  271 **115** 307 **116** 296
Lydia (Joy) **116** 305
Lydia (Merrill) **132** 269
Lydia (Mott) **86** 72 **105**
  177 262
Lydia (Roberts) **96** 147
Lydia A. **94** 373 **98** 258
Lydia J. **93** 242 244

LITTLEFIELD *cont'd*
Lydia Olive **93** 243
Lydia Patten **93** 243
Lydia W. **95** 376 378
Lydia Winn **98** 205
Lyman **91** 230
Lyman F. **123** 234
M. **94** 29 30
M. Ella **92** 336
M. Isabel **92** 336
M. J. **93** 329
Mabel **75** 44 **76** 192
Mabel B. (Ramsdell)
  93 109
Malissa O. (Young)
  121 309
Malvina Louisa **100** 164
Marcy **96** 337 **104** 12 **105**
  263 271
Marcy (Mott) **105** 177 263
Margaret **75** 112 113 123
  314 315 **76** 104 179 183
  190 **82** 460 **85** 422 **86** 75
  77
Margaret (Mitchell) **86** 74
  105 263
Margaret La Martine
  (Cole) **96** 335
Margaret Penniman
  134 329
Maria **119** 288
Maria C. **114** 154
Mariah (Hutchins)
  116 296
Marie **67** 345
Marietta **93** 327
Martha **55** 310 **75** 45 **76**
  104 105 107 180 188 251
  252 255 **86** 77 **92** 336 **93**
  52 **94** 29 30
Martha (Frazer) **86** 77
Martha (Jellison) **118** 320
Martha (Lord) **124** 70
Martha A. **94** 35 36
Martha E. **92** 336
Martin U. **83** 19
Martin V. B. **94** 116
Mary **53** 249 **55** xcv **59**
  91 155 246 363 **60** 42
  295 **65** 115 **67** 343 346
  348 **70** 291 **75** 45 47 105
  111 113 115 117 121-123
  76 108 109 113 114 180
  187 193 194 251-256 259
  82 194 **86** 72 75 77 179
  180 **89** 58 **91** 230 **92** 335
  336 **93** 109 112 242 243
  245 247 327 335 **94** 28
  33 36 373 **95** 360 **96** 245
  336 **97** 20 **98** 205 225
  101 70 **102** 239 **107** 199
  200 270 **108** 227 **109**
  220 **115** 211 **122** 160
  125 301 **127** 239
Mary (Clarke) **85** 422
Mary (Dickens) **86** 76 179
  104 12 **105** 263
Mary (Frost) **108** 120
Mary (Goodwin) **133** 41
Mary (Jaques) **114** 294
Mary (Murphy) **108** 189

LITTLEFIELD *cont'd*
Mary (Page) **84** 222
  105 261
Mary (Smith) **96** 339
Mary (Sprague) **86** 75
Mary (Winn) **117** 141
  119 63
Mary A. **92** 337 **93** 109 243
  94 36 **95** 378 **98** 258
  117 170
Mary A. (Boston) **123** 150
Mary A. (Goodale)
  123 234
Mary A. (Heagan) **117** 164
Mary A. (Toolin) **95** 379
Mary Ann **76** 256 **92** 337
  94 30 **118** 318
Mary Ann (Adams)
  88 335
Mary Ann (Vinal) **87** 7
  109 7
Mary B. **93** 333
Mary E. **89** 351 **92** 337
  93 109
Mary Eliza **119** 227
Mary Ellen (Noble)
  95 375
Mary F. **84** 295 **93** 109
Mary F. (Smith) **119** 288
Mary H. **92** 337
Mary H. (Allen) **121** 144
Mary Hill **98** 205
Mary J. **93** 112
Mary Jane (Kimball)
  97 225 232
Mary Jane (Wakefield)
  118 320
Mary Jaquish **76** 180
Mary L. **94** 29
Mary L. (Brown) **91** 230
Mary Russell (Walley)
  96 335
Mary S. **92** 337
Mary Wheaton (Ellis)
  84 223
Matilda **85** 422
Matthias **76** 250 **93** 239
May A. **92** 337
Maybelle Gifford
  (Kingsbury) **96** 334
Mehitable **75** 55 107 108
  113 116 119 120 311 **76**
  104 105 110-112 114 179
  180 182-184 186-188 195
  196 249 252 255 256 260
  261 **92** 337 **93** 247 **95**
  195 **96** 244 **108** 120 **117**
  164
Mehitable (Black) **90** 390
  114 51
Mehitable (Littlefield)
  95 195
Melissa **91** 230
Melissa A. **92** 337
Melissa O. **92** 334 335 337
Melville **93** 243
Mercy **67** 26 348 **74** 83 **75**
  121 **76** 181 183 **86** 74 77
  180 184 **94** 36 **105** 234
Mercy (Chase) **87** 140
Mercy (Mott) **86** 73 330

LITTLEFIELD *cont'd*
Mercy E. **93** 248
Mercy G. **94** 36
Merebah Wardwell
98 205
Meribah **67** 348 **75** 46 117
76 184
Mina E. **123** 74
Minard **93** 247
Minnie **82** 182
Miranda H. **119** 145
Miriam **75** 315 **76** 184 189
115 221
Miriam J. (Bowden)
119 288
Miriam Phillips **96** 335
Molly **76** 187 **108** 57
Molly (Farnham) **116** 221
Moses **60** 42 **67** 348 **75** 46
105 115 **76** 110 113 185
260 **82** 366 **87** 207 **92**
337 **93** 108 109 243 335
96 244 **105** 282 **107** 200
108 59 **119** 227 **124** 70
Moses F. **93** 108 109
Myron B. **92** 337
Myrtle Bell (Rose) **95** 379
N. G. **97** 232
N. W. **59** 335
Nabby **76** 189 **108** 57
Nahum **76** 249 **94** 118
Nancy **76** 189 256 262 **83**
88 **86** 76 330 **92** 336 337
93 238 239 246 **104** 58
105 263 **116** 184 185
295 301 304 305 **119** 201
Nancy (Currier) **97** 235
Nancy (Wilson) **116** 300
301
Nancy L. **92** 337
Nancy S. (Moulton)
123 150
Nancy S. (Norton)
119 287
Nancy T. **124** 208
Nancy U. **94** 29
Naomi **75** 122
Narcissa (Weare) **118** 318
Narcissus **66** 263
Nathan **67** 348 **75** 45 105
106 108 112 115-117 119
76 105 107 183 184 187
259 **77** 51 **98** 205
Nathan W. **52** 379 **105** 69
Nathan Whitman **75**
xxiii 76 **84** 194 222 223
232 **105** 125
Nathaniel **59** 363 **60** 296
75 105 315 **76** 103 105
111 114 180 183 249-251
261 **82** 460 **86** 72-75 179
92 334 335 **93** 329 **94** 33
96 339 **97** 271 **105** 234
263 **114** 294
Nathaniel G. **96** 342 **97**
231 234 236-238
Nathaniel L. **93** 344
Nathaniel S. **93** 114
Nathaniel Stevens **76** 105
Nehemiah **60** 295 **75** 46
108 109 114 120-123 314

LITTLEFIELD *cont'd*
76 106 114 183 188 193
259 **112** 304
Nelle (Moulton) **116** 128
Nellie **92** 337 **94** 30
Nellie F. **92** 337
Nellie M. **93** 334
Nicholas **67** 343-345 347
356 **76** 106 **87** 207 **88**
388 **92** 334 336 337 **116**
133
Noah **66** 158 **76** 103 **87** 207
93 247
Noah M. **65** 115
Noah Moulton **75** 108
76 104 105 107 180 196
93 397 **100** 63
O. **91** 328
O. B. **93** 112 **94** 29
Obadiah **75** 106 312 **76** 111
257 **95** 374
Olcut **76** 108
Olive **75** 118 **76** 188 189 **90**
230 **92** 337 **108** 57 60
116 294 **133** 42
Olive (Durrell) **108** 190
133 42
Olive (Rhoads) **90** 332
91 26
Olive (Seavey) **117** 230
118 155
Olive (Winn) **118** 320
Olive A. **92** 334-337 **93** 243
Olive G. **93** 246
Olive Gifford **96** 335
Olive J. **94** 29
Olive Luella **94** 36
Olive M. **94** 35 36
Olive S. **93** 112
Olive V. **92** 337
Oliver **93** 108 109 **118** 241
123 150
Oliver B. **93** 112 **94** 29 37
Oliviah **92** 337
Olle **76** 179
Ora M. **93** 335
Oren **92** 337
Orin H. **93** 108 109
Orrin **97** 235
Otis **93** 243
Owen B. **93** 111 112
Pamela **76** 255
Patience **67** 348 **75** 121
76 106 114 183 188 259
Patience (Dickens) **86** 75
179
Paulina (Talpey) **119** 288
120 64
Paulina E. (Beal) **121** 69 70
Pauline **93** 239
Peggy **86** 75
Pelatiah **57** 146 **75** 44 107
108 113 116 119 120 312
76 104 195 251 252 255-
257 **87** 206 207 **90** 390
94 115 **114** 51
Penelope **86** 77
Persis **75** 120 **76** 184 186
82 293 295 **95** 274 **113**
123 **115** 307
Peter **55** 58 **63** 270 **66** 265

LITTLEFIELD *cont'd*
67 346 **75** 44 105 106
108 112 115-117 119-121
76 103 108 110 111 184
189 192 248 255 259 **105**
213 **113** 123 **115** 135
116 300 301
Peter Augustine **105** 262
Phebe **63** 270 **64** 181 **67** 27
75 115 314 **76** 103 104
106 108 110 112 181 184
186 187 258 **83** 88 **86** 76
330 **92** 337 **93** 344 **96**
146 147 **105** 263 **116**
140 **118** 243
Phebe (Littlefield) **96** 146
Phebe (Ray) **86** 75 330
105 167 263
Phebe (Whitacre) **136** 270
Phebe A. (Brewer) **122** 232
Phebe Ann **92** 337 **136** 270
Phebe K. **119** 68 **123** 72
Philadelphia **76** 254
Phineas **76** 111
Polly **63** 170 **90** 229 250
96 245 247 **113** 123
Polly (Mitchel) **96** 146
Polly (Perkins) **115** 304
Priscilla **63** 270 **75** 45 120
76 182 184 **93** 247
R. P. **93** 245
Ralph **92** 337 338
Ralph H. **87** 347
Rebecca **63** 270 **67** 347 348
75 117 119 **76** 183 184
186 188 **92** 337 **94** 36
112 217 **113** 123 **115** 64
223 **116** 223
Reuben **54** 98 **76** 113 **87**
206 **95** 86 **132** 269
Rhoda **57** 393 **75** 315
Richard **67** 343 346 **76**
111 113 188 251 260 **91**
230 **94** 372
Richard Bancroft **96** 335
Richard Yeaton **118** 170
Robert **67** 344 **95** 377
133 123
Roger **75** 108 **76** 105 108
113 180 185 186 258 **87**
206 **98** 205
Rosamon **97** 16 237
Rosewell **120** 64
Rosie (LaBonte) **92** 337
Roswell **123** 152
Ruby **124** 240
Ruby Steere **82** 367
Rufus **76** 113 **91** 328
Rufus (Mrs.) **117** 172
Rufus Ames **84** 222
Ruth **67** 348 **75** 202 **76** 181
91 229 **92** 337 **115** 225
Ruth B. **92** 337
S. A. **93** 114
S. Abbie Winn **93** 247
S. B. **117** 172
S. L. **98** 258
Sabrina **76** 255 **91** 230
Sadie **92** 337
Sally **60** 297 **64** 181 **65** 115
76 251 **87** 125 **92** 337

LITTLEFIELD *cont'd*
  108 191 **116** 221 **117**
  222 **132** 242
Sally (Garland) **90** 240 315
Samuel **67** 348 **70** 291 **75**
  44 46 53 105 106 108 111-
  113 115-117 121 122 313-
  315 **76** 102 103 106 107
  109 112 180 181 257 **86**
  73-75 77 **92** 334-337 **93**
  49 **96** 245 **105** 234 262
  271 282 623 **107** 197
  108 57 **118** 154 **119** 225
  132 119
Samuel A. **93** 108 109 **120**
  138 139
Samuel B. **92** 334-338
  93 57
Samuel Black **76** 104 107
  87 206
Samuel C. **93** 248
Samuel H. **94** 35 36
Samuel L. **98** 258
Samuel N. **94** 373
Samuel S. **92** 335-337
  93 58
Sarah **59** 363 **63** 169 **64** 180
  65 115 **66** 263 312 **67**
  348 **70** 291 **75** 46 51 53
  54 105-109 111 112 116
  117 119 121 122 311 **76**
  103 104 107 110 112 113
  179 181-188 191 192 248-
  250 253-255 258 **85** 147
  86 75 77 **92** 334 337 **93**
  109 239 327 332 **94** 373
  95 195 **97** 230 233 **105**
  228 252 **107** 195 **108**
  188 **109** 312 **115** 303
  119 69 **133** 42
Sarah (Crane) **84** 222
Sarah (Gardiner)
  (Sheffield) **86** 75 **104** 11
  105 256 263 270
Sarah (Hill) **133** 41
Sarah (Mott) **86** 75
Sarah (Smith) **95** 86
Sarah (Weare) **115** 310
Sarah A. **93** 327 335
Sarah Belle **93** 243
Sarah E. **87** 347 **92** 335 337
  93 248 **120** 64
Sarah Goodwin **76** 256
Sarah J. **92** 337
Sarah Jane **136** 112
Sarah M. **92** 335-337
Sarah W. **119** 65
Sarah W. (Fitzgerald)
  123 74
Seth **66** 157 **75** 311 **76** 110
  113 114 248 253 261 **84**
  222 **87** 207
Shadrach **93** 242-244
Sheldon **92** 336 337
Sheldron **93** 107
Shuah **60** 295 **75** 123 314
Sibyl (Wilcox) **86** 74
Sidney A. **92** 337
Sidney E. **92** 336 338
  93 112
Sidney H. **92** 338

LITTLEFIELD *cont'd*
Silas M. **94** 36
Silva **93** 112
Simeon **113** 50
Simon **76** 114 **93** 247
  108 60
Simon B. **117** 164
Simon Ray **83** 88 **86** 76
  330 **105** 263
Solomon **66** 157 **76** 109
  112 187 188 251 260 **83**
  88 **86** 75 **92** 232 334-338
  93 333 **105** 263 **117** 224
  226 **122** 103 **127** 16
Sophia **93** 248 **123** 71
Sophia (Fluent) **96** 342
Sophia (Perkins) **119** 225
Sophia Ann **93** 114
Sophia Ann (Swett) **119**
  64 66
Sophia C. **92** 338
Spencer **114** 154
Stephen **66** 78 158 **75** 53
  108 109 **76** 102 104 106
  107 112 113 181 182 185
  187 258 **87** 207 **90** 87
  105 282 **115** 138 **117**
  164
Stimpson **93** 329
Stimson **76** 104 254 256
Storer **76** 251 **93** 246
Stover **76** 111
Susan **92** 335 338 **94** 29 30
  119 224 226 **124** 208
Susan (Clark) **97** 16
Susan Abigail **101** 325
Susan B. **93** 108 109
Susan B. (Shapleigh)
  95 274
Susan E. **93** 329
Susan F. **93** 109
Susan M. **94** 36
Susanna **56** 31 **60** 296 **65**
  115 **66** 262 **75** 114 115
  312-315 **76** 102-107 111
  113 114 180 181 187 248
  254 256 258 259 **92** 338
  119 68
Susanna (Jaques) **114** 294
Susanna (Maxwell)
  98 205
Susanna (Raymond)
  96 339
Susanna Maxwell **98** 205
Susie M. **93** 112
Suthern M. **92** 338
Swett O. **93** 103
Sylvester **93** 333
Tabitha **60** 295 **67** 348 **75**
  44 47 51 108 109 114 120-
  123 314 **76** 193 253 261
  86 74 **119** 146 **123** 232
Tabitha (Perkins) **115** 309
Tabitha Staples **76** 105
Temperance **76** 107 109
  111 113 183 187 189 259
Thaddeus **93** 335
Thatcher Elbert (Mrs.)
  83 217 **84** 190
Theodore **66** 264 **75** 114
  76 111-113 251 **91** 230

LITTLEFIELD *cont'd*
  113 123 **116** 221 **123** 74
Theodosia **76** 183 185 188
  93 333 **120** 216
Theodosia (Hutchins)
  117 224 226
Theodosia (Norton)
  119 225
Theodosia E. (Clark)
  92 336 338
Thomas **51** 368 **67** 346 348
  90 332 **91** 26
Thomas B. **93** 107 247
Timothy **76** 102 113 189
  248 250 **89** 384 **115** 223
Tristram **92** 338
W. H. **93** 327
Wait R. **86** 77 179
Wallace F. **92** 338
Walter **76** 114 **92** 334-336
  338
Walter Herbert **93** 109
Warren **122** 232
Wesley **92** 334
Wesley C. **92** 336 338
  93 112
William **63** 270 **65** 149
  67 27 344 345 347 **75**
  109 **76** 109 111 112 182-
  184 188 190 **86** 76 330
  92 336 338 **102** 235 **105**
  263 **107** 155 **115** 139
William B. **122** 229
William Bartlet **76** 113
William G. **92** 334 338
  93 103
William H. **117** 164
Willie E. **93** 109
Willie H. **93** 109
Willis B. **92** 338 **93** 110-112
Winfield C. **93** 109
Woodbury **92** 338
Zebadiah **76** 113
LITTLEFORD Esther
  Deidamia **111** 244
Frank W. **116** 315 **117** 157
John **73** 225 229
Mary **73** 149
Thomas **73** 222
LITTLEGROOME
Anne **51** 403
Joan **51** 403
John **51** 403
Margaret **51** 403
Mary **51** 403
LITTLEHALE Litlehale
  —— **56** 335
Abraham **134** 175
Betsey **91** 261
Elizabeth **137** 336
Eugenia **86** 308
Ezria **91** 260 261 266
Hannah (Jaquith) **137** 336
Harriet **51** 248
James **137** 336
Katerine **91** 260
Lydia R. (Richardson)
  91 266
Martha (Bean) **86** 308
Mary (Stearns) **134** 175
Rebecca (B___) **91** 267

LITTLEHALE cont'd
Sibyl **91** 265
Thomas S. **86** 308
LITTLEJOHN
David **60** 105
Lavinia Polk **78** 161
Margaret **78** 161
Mary Rebecca **78** 161
Thomas **78** 161
Tilly **58** 130 131
W. S.J. **124** 35
William Whitson **78** 161
LITTLEPAGE Litlepage
Daniel **65** 64
Elias **65** 64
Elizabeth **65** 64
Elizabeth Southerland
112 151
George **65** 64
Joan **52** 131 **65** 64
John **65** 64
Samuel **65** 64
Sarah **65** 64
LITTLEPROWE
John **143** 298
LITTLETON Lytelton
Aaron **147** 276
Almoda (Rogers) **147** 276
Antoinette **81** 205
Barbara **122** 176 177
Edgar **81** 205
Edward **64** 85 **122** 176 177
Elmeda **147** 276
Frank Campbell **81** 205
Frank Campbell (Mrs.)
78 110 205
Grace **104** 314
Henrietta Olive **78** 205
80 218 **81** 205
James **94** 275 338
James R **75** lxxvii
James R. (Mrs.) **75** lxxvii
Lavinia **86** 441
Mary King **75** lxxvii
Nathaniel **112** 246
Sophia C. **104** 70
Thomas **98** 115 **103** 285
Timothy **64** 85
Trowbridge **81** 205
William **64** 85 87
William E. **104** 314
LITTLEWOOD
Benjamin **64** 106
Joseph **138** 93
Sophia Appleton (Foss)
105 227
Littlifield see Littlefield
LITTON Grace **67** 364
Judith **91** 70
Mary **67** 364
Nathaniel **67** 364
Rowland **91** 70
William **67** 364
LITTRELL
Ada Octavia **78** 169
Beth Lenore **117** 206
Emma (Mays) **128** 264
Sarah **128** 177
LITWIN Leo **106** 62 121
LITZENBERG
Lenna May **99** 146

LITZMANN
Fredricka **106** 70
LIVEEN John **133** 112
LIVELY Mary **128** 266
Warren Powell **94** 139
LIVER Catherine **88** 341
LIVERMAN
Hannah **125** 223
O. S. **91** 328
LIVERMORE Levermore
——— **53** 434 **56** 95 **57** 119
69 121 213 295 **96** 286
112 204 **114** 202
— Capt. **54** 74 75
— Mr. **67** 133 **69** 13 123
A. G. **79** 38
Abiel Abbot **64** 233
Abigail **71** 268 **113** 156
127 293
Abigail A. (Jarvis)
125 222
Abijah **77** 313
Adeline Maria **127** 291
Amos **77** 289 **127** 291
Amos Henry **127** 291
Ann **79** 424 438
Anna **54** xlviii **57** 119 **69**
310 **77** 274 **110** 225 **127**
288
Anna (Howard) **118** 140
Annie **69** 314
Anson Gould **96** 286
Arthur L. **78** 447
Arthur Leslie **79** 202
Benjamin **77** 313
Beulah **71** 150 268 **141** 51
Caroline Matilda **75** 257
Catherine **57** 202
Charles Frederick **61** 217
Charles Herbert **144** 60
Clara Perkins **96** 212
Daniel **51** 509 **57** 202 **69**
221 223 300 **70** 15 **71**
268 346 **77** 272 274 **83**
377 **92** 271 **114** 201 202
132 273 **144** 220 221
147 181
Daniel Austin **96** 286
Daniel Gould **96** 286
David **57** 202 **70** 141 216
306 **118** 140
Dorothy Thelma (Perry)
101 318
Edmund **86** 239
Edward **83** 376
Edward St. Loe **104** 69
140 248
Eliza **127** 291
Elizabeth **54** 346 **71** 268 **77**
236 **81** 445
Elizabeth (Tilton) **114** 202
Elizabeth Cunningham
67 110
Emma Gertrude **61** lxiii
Ephraim **114** 202 **144** 224
Esther **58** 167 **71** 150 268
Eva **100** 200
Ezra **121** 93
Fannie Garner (Iselin)
86 337
George **53** 255 **57** 119 **67**

LIVERMORE cont'd
110 **69** 314
George W. **92** 275
Giles **54** 346
Grace **77** 273
Grace Sanderson **127** 291
Hannah **77** 273 **107** 307
108 27 **109** 154 **114** 201
127 291 **141** 224
Hannah (Cutting)
114 202
Hannah (Sanderson)
127 291
Harriet **57** 119 **96** 290
Henry **54** 345 346
Hepzibah **77** 289 **136** 333
Hepzibah (Coolidge)
127 291
Homer Fiske **66** 100
97 358
Huldah **71** 268
Ira Warner (Mrs.) **101** 124
Isaac **69** 109
James **54** 345 **59** 245
104 302
Jason **62** 374 **117** 138
Jesse **121** 94
Joanna **52** 77
John **51** 448 **54** 346 **55** 114
57 119 202 **69** 299 **77**
273 **82** 27 **107** 307 **109**
153 154
Jonas **57** 202 **70** 18 138
139 146 211 213 214 218
219 296 297 300 **71** 150
268
Jonathan **118** 313
Joseph **144** 218
Julia **96** 288
Julia Almira **96** 286
Julia Putnam (Bancroft)
96 286
Lois (Mixer) **127** 291
Lot **121** 93
Louisa **96** 327
Lucinda **57** 202 **70** 141
Lucy **57** 202 **127** 291
Lucy H. **57** 202
Lydia **54** 345 346 **77** 320
123 126
Lydian Loring **118** 140
Maria **118** 140
Martha **51** 448 **99** 334
Mary **54** 345 346 **62** 374
71 268 346 **77** 274 **81**
327 445 **82** 288 293 **87**
295 **106** 268 **117** 138
Mary Anna Dana **127** 291
Mary Hoyland **109** 130
Mary I. **88** 337
Mary Jane **104** 69
Matthew **51** 468 **54** 387
81 445 **82** 27 **90** 400
106 268
Mehitable Jane **89** 368
Nabby **83** 214
Nathaniel **57** 202 **70** 140
141 219 220 303
Nellie Bezin (Brown) **66**
100 **97** 358

LIVERMORE cont'd
Nellie M. (Sawyer)
  121 307
Oliver 57 202 69 11 216
  218 223 77 276 282 284
  83 378
Peter 54 346
Philip 92 65 66
Philip Walton (Mrs.)
  86 337
Polly 57 202 70 18
Polly (Glover) 88 287
Rebecca 59 245 121 92
S. M. 91 328
Sally 57 202
Sally (Loring) 118 140
Sally Knowles (Hopkins)
  104 302
Samuel 52 77 54 xlviii
  74 75 346 57 119 77 274
  104 69 129 371 144 222
Sarah 53 348 63 289 69 109
  95 279 110 228
Sarah (Poland) 96 286
Sarah Amelia 57 361
Sarah Crese (Stackpole)
  140 248
Sarah Jane 96 286
Solomon K. 125 222
Solon Augustus 96 286
Stephen 54 346
Susan (Platts) 126 64
Susanna 71 346 88 331
  133 70
Tabitha 55 114 98 84
  127 292
Thomas 54 345 57 119 88
  287 112 212 127 291
Thomas L. 65 205
Thomas Leonard 64 135
Walter 57 202
William 79 424 438
  118 140
William R. 90 364
William Roscoe 67 110
Willie W. 121 307
LIVESEY Leivsay Levesey
  Lievsay Livsey
Celia Anna 77 181
Ellen B. 117 209
Gilbert 64 261 340 65 172
James 117 209
Jane 65 172
Jonathan 64 159 164 254
  339 345
Rachel 69 376
Richard 69 376
Squire 77 181
William 56 21 82 187
LIVING John 65 165
LIVINGSTON
  Levengston Leving-
  stone Livingstone
—— 59 113 106 321
Abigail 83 167
Abraham Henry 52 79
Abram 86 245 106 64
Angelica 104 310 311
Anne 76 12
Anne Temple 52 79
Ardelia 113 158

LIVINGSTON cont'd
Brockholst 65 149
Catherine 86 245 106 64
Charles Frank 59 xliv
  61 xxxiii
Chloe 62 329
Clarissa Hazeltine 81 404
Cornelia 81 175
Cortlandt 66 34
Daniel 55 280
Deborah 78 306
Edward 81 404
Edward Philip 110 128
Edwin Brockholst 125 64
Eliza 76 12
Eliza (Owen) 91 242
Elizabeth 121 319
Elizabeth (Stevens)
  110 128
Emelia 133 308
Emeline Cornell
  (Hopkins) 104 221
Engeltie 51 340
Felicia Hemans 89 180
Frances Clarissa 81 404
Frank Alexander 85 196
Gertrude 92 184
Gertrude Laura 75 xl
Gilbert 81 175
Helen 105 218
Henry 76 34
Henry Braithwait 92 344
Henry W. 65 55
Herman 104 221
Irving G. 83 433 434
James 81 175 121 319
  125 279
James Benedict 81 403
Jane 95 168
Jane Augusta 83 56
Joann (Williston) 126 142
Joanna 55 280 281
John 73 218
John (Mrs.) 111 101
John Ashe 76 12
John H. 85 348
John J. 125 73
John Leslie (Mrs.) 106 125
John R. 125 64
Juliet Birckhead 81 402
Juliet Turner 81 403
Livingston 81 402 404
Lucy 65 383
M. A. 91 242
Mabel 81 404
Mae E. (Lane) 83 433 434
Margaret 51 342
Margaret (Beekman)
  125 64
Margaret (Sheafe) 125 64
Maria 81 402
Mary 121 184
Mary Catherine (Tully)
  105 218
Mary Celia 81 402 404
Mary S. 51 342
Maryia 53 118
Namee 125 73
Peter 118 313
Peter R. 51 342
Philip 51 87 81 403

LIVINGSTON cont'd
116 111
Philip Henry 81 402
Philip L. 81 402 403
Rebecca 51 462
Rebecca J. 52 79
Robert 52 476 73 104 81
  175 83 202 86 264 104
  311 125 64 133 113
Robert Clermont 110 128
Robert James 55 362
Robert Le Roy 73 266
Robert R. 59 121 60 111
  125 64
Robert T. 51 342
Ruth 99 47
Sarah 76 34
Sarah K. 81 404
Seth 83 167
Solomon M. 126 142
Stanley (Mrs.) 101 170
  102 121
Walter 65 53 149
Walter H. 52 79
William 55 125 105 218
LIVIUS Peter 116 111
Livsey see Livesey
LIZARRA A. De 117 96
LJUNGSTEDT Ljungstadt
  Hannah Milnor
  (Robinson) 97 163
Milnor 123 216
Milnor (Mrs.) 79 223
Llaw see Law
LLEWELLYN Lewellen
  Llewellen Llewellin
— Capt. 115 9
Emme 148 109
Jorwerth Ap 119 98
Mildred 118 78
Nathalie Walker 147 383
Robert 93 300
Llewis see Lewis
LLOYD Loyd
—— 59 327 113 66
— Dr. 56 51 85 123
— Lieut. 58 68
— Miss 84 260
— Mr. 51 473
—— (Breck) 140 44
Aaron 76 10
Abigail 105 275
Abigail Hannah 105 275
Andrew 55 332 76 116
Ann 53 82 101 276
Anna 60 359
Anna (Long) 89 111
Anna Belle (Jameson)
  89 111
Anne 141 95 96
Anne (Stratton) 135 294
  297
Annie (Spackman) 95 328
Bathsheba 89 111
Benjamin 110 24 104
  114 191
Benjamin R. 110 104
Byfield 85 125
Caroline Augusta 76 10
Catherine 76 21 101 53
Charles 52 31 32

LLOYD *cont'd*
Charles S. **125** 178
Charlotte A. (Emerson)
  91 225
Clement **108** 295 296
Clinton Homer **89** 111
Cornelia **110** 104
Dale C. **128** 312
Dale C. (Mrs.) **121** 79 **124**
  78 79
David **51** 117 **54** 189 **85**
  242 **101** 11 12 **102** 238
  108 295 296 **128** 172
Dean David (Mrs.)
  107 133
Dennis **89** 111
Dennis Lafayette **89** 111
Dixie Marie **107** 133
Edward **52** 31 32 **70** 262
  101 85 **107** 254 **110** 166
  114 191
Eleanor B. **81** 357
Eli J. **83** 423 434
Eliza Ann **110** 104
Elizabeth **53** 83 302 **78** 407
  107 254 **130** 216
Elizabeth Ann **105** 275
Elizabeth R. **122** 15
Emma Louise **87** 209
Eunice Floyd (Pearson)
  94 167
Frances **53** 82 **89** 111
Frances (Churchill)
  110 24
Frances (Lazell) **89** 111
Frances Lusk **77** 158
George **53** 82 83 **108** 283
Grant Ulysses **89** 111
Griffin **51** 391
Hannah (Griffin) **107** 254
Hannah P. (Weeks)
  125 178
Harold Evans (Mrs.)
  107 133
Hazel Pearl **96** 160
Henry **65** 165 **77** 158 **89**
  111 **140** 172
Henry Demerset **102** 167
Horatio Gates **89** 61
Horatio Gates (Mrs.) **75**
  xxv 65 **89** 61 81 135
Howard Williams
  54 410 411
Ira F. **117** 291
James **55** 141 **61** 199 **78**
  266 403 **95** 307 308 **99**
  83 267 **113** 318 **127** 115
  137 37 **140** 44 163 324
Jane **52** 83 **54** 347 **85** 424
Jessie Louise (Bross)
  102 167
John **53** 82 83 272 **54** 341
  60 359 **64** 160 163 256
  345 **78** 300 **110** 170 **128**
  217 **135** 294 297
John A. **128** 172
John Adams **89** 111
John Edward **116** 279
Joseph **105** 275
Judith **68** 29
Katharine **126** 80

LLOYD *cont'd*
Lettie (Long) **128** 172
Lewis **104** 316 **112** 61
Lewis C. **116** 171 **142** 235
Lola (Maverick) **102** 167
Louisa (Leahy) **126** 80
Lovina / Lovinia **89** 111
Lucius **128** 175
Lucy **62** 249
Lydia A. **77** 151
Lydia T. **113** 66
Margaret **64** 337
Margaret (Sands) **89** 111
Maria **126** 80
Maria Christie **76** 10
Martha **64** 253 **65** 174
Martin **58** xcviii
Mary **57** 139 **75** xxv **101**
  11 **110** 168 **112** 226 **114**
  191
Mary Ann **125** 178
Mary E. **98** 287
Mary E. (Brady) **128** 172
Mary Helen (Wingate)
  89 135
Mary Jane **89** 111
Mary M. **76** 276
Maud (Betteker) **83** 423
  434
Morgan **52** 32
Nathaniel B. **78** 309
Nathaniel Byfield **85** 126
Nora **78** 174
Polly **126** 80
R. Louis **102** 238
Rachel **107** 70
Richard W. **84** 172
Richard Wingate **85** 188
  89 61
Robert **102** 238
Robert T. **108** 283
Sally **114** 181
Samuel **54** 43 **79** 164 **85** 7
Sarah **85** 424 **113** 220
Stacy B. (Mrs.) **81** 357
Susan **58** xcviii
Thomas **52** 31 32 **57** 139
  64 115 160 338 **65** 33 **79**
  164 **101** 85 88 **106** 166
  266 **107** 70
Ulysses Grant **89** 111
William **105** 275 **125** 178
William Bross **102** 167
William R. **110** 104
Llucas *see* Lucas
LLYNE
Wenlion ap Jevan
  51 211
LOAN Adam **67** 30 31
Adam C. **67** 31
Melvin **67** 31
Mercy **67** 31
Robert Harcourt **67** 31
LOATHER
Benjamin **73** 136
LOBB Lobbe
— Mrs. **51** 352
Abigail (Hurd) **132** 89
Richard **51** 352 **54** 340
Roger **132** 89
LOBDAN Nicholas **84** 152

LOBDELL Lobdel
—— **121** 13
Abigail **76** 89 90 **143** 340
  348
Agnes **78** 313
Anne **143** 348
Benjamin **121** 123 **142** 394
Caleb **70** 202
Charity **70** 202
Cromwell **142** 358
Darius **76** 136
Ebenezer **52** 365 **120** 275
Elizabeth **86** 219 **93** 194
  113 135 **121** 113 **126** 93
  133 192 **142** 394 **143**
  348
Elizabeth (Perkins)
  143 348
Elizabeth (Price)
  (Townsend) **143** 348
Emily (Hoisington)
  141 47
Esther **76** 96
Eunice **76** 136
Hannah **121** 110 113 209
  142 394
Hannah (Leavit) **121** 109
Hannah (Leverett)
  142 394
Isaac **121** 107 112 **143** 334
  339 340 347 348
Jared Charles **119** 248
John **113** 49 **121** 109 117
  141 47 **142** 276 277 394
  143 134 347
Joseph **113** 49 **140** 163
  143 138 334 347 348
Judith / Judah (Collier)
  142 358
Julia Harrison **142** 277
Leighton **86** 120
Leighton (Mrs.) **87** 172
Lydia **120** 275 **143** 348
Lydia (Shaw) **120** 275
Lyman **87** 303
Martha (Ward) **143** 334
  340 347
Martha Anne **104** 142
Mary **75** 178 **142** 277
  143 348
Mary (Bosworth) **142**
  276 277
May Agnes **105** 225
Mercy **52** 356 **142** 394
Nancy (Hoisington)
  141 47
Nathaniel **142** 277 394
Nicholas **121** 115 **140** 163
  142 277 394 **143** 347
  348
P. B. **117** 160
Persis **75** 178
Rebecca **85** 3 **143** 138 333
  334 348
Ruth (Adams) **86** 120
  87 172
Samuel **121** 112 **143** 348
Sarah **53** 445 462 **140** 163
  142 277 394 **143** 129
Sarah (Bryant) **143** 348
Simon **75** 178 **87** 303

LOBDELL *cont'd*
142 277
LOBEL
Louye de 115 255 256
Mary de 115 256 355 356
Mathieu de 115 255
Matthias 115 256
Matthias de 115 255 256
LOBENSTINE
H. G. 54 ci
LOBINEAU —— 119 234
LOBINGIER
Kate 67 xxxv
LOBLEY Hannah (Hughs)
101 34
Isaac 101 34
LOCHARD
W. G. (Mrs.) 124 319
LOCHARY
John 87 191 192
Mary Adelaide 87 178
191 203
Patrick 87 191
LOCK Alice 98 364
Betsey 97 371
Sarah (Whitmore) 86 350
Susan (Tileston) 126 206
LOCKARD
Audrey Lucia 123 15
LOCKARY Margaret Ann
(FitzRandolph)
98 128
LOCKE —— 53 385 56 181
58 131 132 135 62 153
64 86 83 307 92 285 316
322 118 21 129 86 188
315 140 259
— Elder 96 200
— Mr. 56 386 73 73
83 307
— Mrs. 119 137
— Widow 58 33
Abby Cummings
110 309
Abel 108 251
Abigail 55 223 59 152 66
153 68 330 75 127 90
360 111 160 141 226
Abigail (Heywood)
148 239
Abigail (Merriam)
141 226
Abigail (Poulter) 141
225 226
Abigail Tibbetts
(Shannon) 99 246
Abner 56 291
Abram 83 307
Ada Rytherwood (Gayer)
106 70
Alice 65 352 98 364
105 264
Alma 87 79
Almira H. 83 181 183
Alphia 95 271
Ann 93 299
Anna Wellington 84 452
Anne 58 138 135 292 296
Anne (Maurice) 88 144
Apphia 88 286
Arthur 67 183

LOCKE *cont'd*
Arthur Horton 61 404
62 xxxvii 67 88 138 71
95
Asa 55 59 425 56 380
Belle F. 61 346
Benjamin 75 lxxx 81 30
108 248 126 206 131
317
Betsey 65 219 76 39 81 30
97 69 371
Bezaleel 70 12 13 19-22
144 145 212-214
Blake 90 48
Caleb 71 221
Calvin 55 115 99 246
Caroline C. (Garland)
122 73
Catherine A. 84 29
Catherine R. 56 389
Charity (Marden) 92 211
Charles 70 204 81 107 219
90 200 360 91 146
Charles S. 92 338
Christophine Gayer
106 70
Daniel 56 257 88 144 91
200 116 275
Darius 78 309
David 66 153 70 296 82 46
92 321
David Ross 90 360
Deborah 65 351 73 3
Deborah (Butterfield)
84 452
Deliverance 65 352
Delmont 87 79
Don 129 188
Dorothea Renee 90 360
Dorothy 66 145
Dorothy (Blake) 105 264
Ebenezer 55 59 57 353 363
82 472 113 30 37
Edna May (Oakes) 90 360
Edwin R. 83 181 183
Eleanor 97 371
Elijah 105 301 302
Elisha 103 43
Eliza 56 389 67 139
Eliza (Roberts) 97 235
Eliza G. 67 143
Elizabeth 58 131 62 152 65
351 67 80 68 260 75 196
209 90 274 360 126 209
Elizabeth (Berry) 105 264
Elizabeth (Page) 92 274
Elizabeth (Plympton)
90 360
Elizabeth (Winship) 84
452 141 221
Elizabeth Frances 113 302
Elizabeth S. 127 89 90
Ellen E. 84 29
Ellen M. 98 311
Elvin W. 98 311
Enoch B. 76 28
Ephraim 95 193
Esther 93 299
Eunice 98 311
Fanny 55 51 56 389
Fortunatus 70 152

LOCKE *cont'd*
Frances Ellen 82 473
Francis 58 131 65 352 75
196 209 77 139 78 419
84 452 92 274 141 221
Franklin Day 73 317 74
xxiv 82 122 245 472
Frederick Clarence (Mrs.)
82 382 83 232
Genny 67 142
George Turell 84 452
George Washington
84 452
Georgianna 122 73
Hannah 56 29 389 65 351
78 401 82 46 96 247
125 95
Hannah B. 92 338
Hannah F. 98 311
Hannah W. 97 18
Harriet 78 68
Hayes (Don) 129 86
Helen Lavinia 84 452
Helen May 84 29
Henry H. 84 29
Hepsey 125 41
Hester (Ross) 90 360
Hiram C. 84 29
Hosea P. 91 328
Howard J. 83 432 434
Increase 123 287
Irena 117 282
Irene 78 91
Isaac S. 91 328
J. 59 180
Jacob 73 73 93 299 135 129
James 58 131 62 152 65
351 352 354 82 46 472
473 107 261 137 108
James H. 91 327
James L. 56 292
Jane 129 77
Jane Whitney (Levet)
90 48
Jemima 58 131
Jeremiah 125 95
Jesse 98 311
Jesse F. 97 221
Jethro 76 29 125 95
Joanna 141 226
John 55 51 56 29 379 389
62 315 65 71 66 244 71
95 73 75 82 472 86 435
90 360 98 311 105 264
118 63 124 99 125 95
129 86 188 315 131 183
317 135 260-262 292
143 115 148 62
John D. 122 73
John F. 68 207
John G. 55 115 100 2 111
159 160
John Goodwin 58 209
79 223 97 163 141 225
John L. 145 177
Jonathan 51 42 58 135 66
151 153 82 46 105 264
107 227 116 11 128 125
Joseph 62 306 65 351 70
138 139 73 74 105 263
264 119 289 125 95 140

LOCKE *cont'd*
259 **141** 225
Joshua **77** 239 **92** 211
Joshua R. **127** 90
Josiah **78** 415 **86** 44 **92** 285
Laura **56** 389
Lavina (French) **103** 43
Lavinia (Smith) **84** 452
Leander N. **79** 52
Lois M. **83** 300
Lottie H. **92** 338
Louisa (Harrington)
131 317
Louise H. (Johnson)
83 432 434
Lucinda Howard **82** 472
Lucretia **80** 440 **111** 149
Lucy **58** 135 **68** 251 **81** 30
Lucy (Wood) **141** 226
Luther **56** 290 **117** 282
Lydia **93** 299
Lydia K. **87** 344
Mabel (Dunham) **88** 169
Marcy (Honeywell)
105 264
Margaret **78** 314 **118** 296
129 77
Margaret (Adams) **84** 452
Maria **88** 285
Marshall **78** 315
Marshall H. **78** 414
Martha **75** 209 **82** 46
Martha Hannah (Bodine)
90 360
Martha Learned **84** 452
Mary **65** 353 **66** 151 **68**
xxxiv 251 **75** 19 **77** 50
78 73 306 402 **81** 150 **83**
74 **94** 223 **97** 15 **98** 311
100 240 **121** 160 **129**
365 **135** 129 **141** 225
226
Mary (Clarke) **84** 452
90 360
Mary (Reed) **90** 360
Mary A. **77** 190 **99** 246
Mary Ame **75** lxxx
Mary Anne **89** 100
Mary E. **92** 338
Mary Elizabeth **85** 94
Mary Jane **56** 389
Mary Learned **66** lii **84**
452 **85** 107 204
Mary P. **76** 33
Mary White (Learned)
84 452
Matilda **125** 290
Mehitable **65** 353
Mehitable (Higgins)
135 129
Mehitable D. **97** 21
Mehitable G. (Hill) **97** 221
Mercy **65** 354
Nancy **80** 330 **82** 46
Nancy S. **55** 62
Nancy W. **79** 44
Nathan **78** 177
Nathan B. **91** 328
Nathaniel **58** 31 **67** 80 **71**
95 **105** 264
Nathaniel Reed **90** 360

LOCKE *cont'd*
Nicholas **77** 76
Olive (Gates) **121** 48
Oliver **84** 452
Olivia S. **84** 29
Olivia S. (Hall) **83** 181 183
Olivia Shores **83** 173
Oren **55** 59
Otis Russell **106** 70
Patience **107** 227
Peggy **97** 371
Persis (Matthews) **86** 44
Peter **135** 294 297
Phebe **57** 363 **141** 226
Phebe (Chapman) **94** 22
Phebe M. **55** 51
Philena Hephzibah
77 182
Philip **121** 48
Polly **56** 290 291 **119** 137
Polly Wiley **56** 292
Rebecca **91** 366 **128** 45
Reuben **56** 290-292 **94** 22
117 282
Richard **145** 350
Richard Foss (Mrs.) **103**
119 160 **119** 148
Robert **64** 138 **68** 180
Robert Winter (Mrs.)
85 233
Robinson (Mrs.) **88** 169
Ruhamah **107** 261
Ruth **78** 304
Ruth (Faxon) **90** 360
Sally **56** 257 **62** 152 **65** 312
76 28
Salome **65** 351 355
Samuel **58** 32 33 36 **63** 191
68 251 **78** 303 **80** 440
82 472 **84** 261 264 371
452 **91** 328 **92** 316 **97**
371 **111** 149 160 **116**
111 **137** 109 111
Samuel B. **92** 321
Sarah **54** cxxxiii **65** 352
354 **66** 151 153 336 **67**
142 **75** 196 **82** 473 **125**
42 **137** 73 **141** 226
Sarah (Cutler) **107** 261
Sarah (Foss) **85** 193
Sarah (Whitmore) **84** 452
86 350 **141** 221 226
Sarah A. **70** 204
Sarah C. **88** 338
Sarah J. **67** 141
Sarah L. **98** 311
Sarah P. **67** 141
Simeon P. **87** 344
Simon **95** 190 200 **96** 146
116 275 276
Stacy H. **92** 338
Sukey **76** 29
Susan (Tileson) **126** 206
Susanna **54** 92 **57** 353
Susanna (Cole) **129** 77
Thomas **79** 51
Thomas D. **97** 235
Timothy **59** 222 **105** 264
114 180 **128** 129
Tryphena **70** 152
Varney **76** 39

LOCKE *cont'd*
Vera Nash **92** 146
Waity (Sheldon) **127** 90
Warren Andrew **71** lv
William **55** 115 **57** 351
58 131 **65** 312 **82** 472
84 452 **85** 455 **86** 349
350 **90** 360 **125** 95 **129**
77 **141** 221 226
Lockeman *see* Lockman
LOCKER Amany **73** 264
Ann **73** 263
Barbara **73** 271
David **73** 218
George **74** 117
Isaac **73** 219
Ora Butler **117** 237
Philip **73** 145
Richard H. **73** 277
Sarah **73** 274
LOCKERT Frances **66** 196
LOCKHART
— Capt. **104** 178
Abigail (Ryder) **137** 216
Abigail (Trask) **137** 215-
217
Aletha (Swift) **93** 137
Burton W. **53** 257
Elizabeth **134** 334
Fanny **77** 100
George **106** 292
Henry (Mrs.) **93** 137
J. Bicknell **117** 237
J. Bicknell (Mrs.) **117** 237
Jacob **120** 16
James **63** 202 **111** 205
116 7
John **137** 215-217
Mary (Fogal) **134** 334
Mary Eliza **120** 16
Miriam **99** 298
Oliver C. (Mrs.) **113** 81
Robert **134** 334
LOCKHEAD Alexander
Clarke **144** 317
Clara Jane (Wilson)
144 317
James **144** 317
Jeanette **144** 317
LOCKINGEN
Henry **117** 294
Reba G. **117** 294
LOCKINGTON
Mary **53** 86
William **61** 92
LOCKLEAR
James A. **78** 322
Mary Elizabeth **78** 322
LOCKLIN —— **75** 302
Isaac **115** 79 **116** 76
LOCKLYN Helen **79** 349
LOCKMAN Lockeman
Ann **122** 188
Harriet **122** 188
Maria **122** 188
LOCKRIDGE
Andrew M. **122** 125
Christine Hance **78** 176
Dulcena **122** 125
Elizabeth **122** 124 125
Elizabeth Hill **78** 176

LOCKRIDGE *cont'd*
Hazel Boykin **78** 176
Kenneth **137** 52
Kenneth A. **125** 265
Louisa **122** 125
Luther Polk **78** 176
Margaret **122** 125
Permelia **122** 125
Rachel **122** 125
Robert **122** 125
Robert Darden **78** 176
Ross F. **95** 306
Sarah **130** 276
Virginia **122** 125
LOCKSON Henry **63** 160
LOCKSONNE
Christian **148** 9
LOCKWARD Harriet
Louise (Johnson)
145 309
William **145** 309
LOCKWEER
Samuel **64** 323
LOCKWOOD Lockwoed
—— **52** 390 394 397 **54**
66 155 **58** 405 **60** 140 **62**
97 **72** 315 **112** 177
— Mr. **55** 287 **60** 205
— Widow **86** 41
Abby **78** 345
Abigail **57** 325 **112** 79
Abigail M. **106** 108
Abraham **93** 376 **112** 79
118 79 **129** 271
Adam **129** 271
Adelaide Elizabeth **68** 282
Agnes **52** 42
Amos **93** 376 **112** 79 **117**
9 15 **129** 271
Ann **66** 323
Ann (Perry) **115** 289
Ann Maria **62** 97
Anna **112** 79 **136** 130
Anna (Blanchard) **112** 79
Anne **141** 37
Anne Louisa **82** 484
Arna S. **62** 98
Asa **145** 149
Asenath **112** 79
Ashael **112** 79
Augustin **106** 108
Barbara **106** 148
Beal Burr **109** 261
Benoni **93** 376
Bethiah (Field) **112** 79
Betsey **72** 315 **127** 249
C. L. (Mrs.) **101** 318
Candace **76** 274
Caroline **62** 98
Cathalina Lansing **62** 97
Catherine **72** 315
Charles **62** 97
Charles C. **62** 98
Charles E. **86** 154
Charles Henry **112** 227
Charles M. **116** 258
Charlotte **62** 97
Charlotte (Fayerweather)
145 149
Christopher **114** 180
Clark **106** 108

LOCKWOOD *cont'd*
Closson **62** 97
Closson Lyman (Mrs.)
103 119
Daniel **57** 325 **108** 294
112 79
David **62** 97 **72** 315
Dianah (Harris) **90** 94
Dinah **90** 94
E. Dunbar **62** 97 **144** 240
145 149
Ebenezer **114** 180 **145** 149
Edmund **99** 238 **108** 292
294
Edward **66** 323
Elijah **112** 79
Eliza **62** 97
Eliza Ann **62** 97
Elizabeth **59** 207 **62** 97 **85**
167 **141** 37
Elizabeth Bogart **136** 322
Elizabeth Olive **112** 227
Elizabeth R. **62** 97
Ellen Maria (Rich) **84** 122
Elsa **112** 79
Elzina **112** 79
Emily **62** 97
Emily E. **80** 152
Emma Habicht **86** 197
98 78 89 151
Enoch **112** 79
Ephraim **72** 315 **98** 78
Esther **72** 315
Esther (Field) **112** 79
Ethelannah (Westcott)
106 148
Eunice **106** 108
Eunice (Smith) **109** 265
Ezekiel **112** 79
Ezra **61** 90 **124** 64
Francis **66** 323
Genevieve **106** 124
George **66** 323
Gershom **93** 376
Grace S. **76** 217
Hamilton Davidson **82**
484 **93** 376
Hannah **72** 315 **109** 192
261 **112** 79 **144** 240
Hannah (Whitlock) **98** 78
Henry **62** 97
Henry R. **84** 122
Henry Roswell **62** 97
Hezekiah **72** 315
Hortence **115** 37
Hos. **144** 41
Huldah (Barton) **107** 298
Isaac **52** 370 **59** 205 207
72 315 **127** 249 **144** 45
Isabel **66** 323
Ithamar **62** 97
J. **91** 328
Jacob **112** 79 **118** 79
James **53** 212 **72** 210 **98** 78
115 289 **116** 97 **141** 260
142 340
James P. **76** 274
James R. **62** 97
Jerusha **62** 97
Joan **52** 42
Job **98** 78

LOCKWOOD *cont'd*
John **66** 323 **91** 71 **107** 298
108 291 **109** 265 **112** 79
128 52 **141** 36 37 **143**
260
John David **62** 98
John H. **71** 96
Jonathan **62** 97
Joseph **61** 191 **72** 315 **106**
148 **114** 180 **128** 53 **144**
41
L. Pardee **78** 345
Laetitia **109** 259
Largin **112** 79
Laura **61** 273 **62** 97
Lewis **72** 315 **112** 79
Lewis C. **85** 315
Lois (Hicks) **106** 148
Lucy **80** 47
Lucy Cordelia (Quintard)
109 261
Lucy Jane **62** 97
Lucy Sophia (Ballou)
106 148
Luthana **112** 79
Luther **112** 79
Lydia (Smith) **98** 78
Lyman **62** 97 **112** 79
Lynda (Field) **112** 79
Lynn J. **110** 240
Margaret S. **123** 199
Margery **66** 323
Maria **109** 265
Maria (Dunbar) **98** 78
Marie **66** 323
Martha H. (Harriman)
116 258
Mary **54** lvii **60** 249 **62** 97
66 323 **70** 104 **100** 166
141 37
Mary (Godfrey) **145** 149
Mary (Street) **141** 259 260
Mary Ann **62** 97 **84** 418
Mary Elizabeth (Nugent)
112 227
Mary J. **76** 274
Mary Jane (Booth) **89** 41
Mary N. **85** 167
May Davidson **78** 204 **82**
484 **93** 376 **94** 80 144
Mercy **53** 212 **72** 210
Mercy (St. John) **98** 78
Meriba **61** 90 191 389
62 375
Minerva **106** 108
Nancy **75** li **85** 290
115 121
Nathan **112** 79
Newton Leavenworth
102 124
Noah **97** 294
Parateen **112** 79
Phebe **54** 212 **80** 171
Polly **62** 97 **100** 166
Priscilla S. **85** 167
Prudence **131** 238
Rachel (St. John) **98** 78
Reuben Benson **109** 261
Rhoda **59** 395
Rhodes Greene **93** 376
Richard **51** 140 **66** 323

LOCKWOOD cont'd
  68 179
  Robe 112 79
  Robert 62 97 66 323 72
    315 93 376 98 78 144
    240 145 149
  Rollin C. 106 108
  Roswell 62 97
  Ruth 62 97 72 315
  Sally 72 315 125 215
    145 247
  Sally Jane 145 148
  Samuel 52 410 412 413
    62 97 98 78 106 108
    144 242
  Samuel S. 85 167
  Sarah 52 79 62 97 72 216
    85 167 108 291 129 271
    141 37
  Sarah (Betts) 98 78
  Sarah (White) 112 78 79
  Sarah Ann 80 161
  Sarah Jerusha 62 97
  Sarah Sophia 62 97
  Stanley C. 62 97
  Stephen 90 94
  Susan 62 97 141 37
  Susan (Ferris) 109 261
  Susan (Strutt) 141 36
  Susanna 51 140 93 376
    136 165 141 260 145
    154
  Susanna (Norman) 98 78
  Thalia 62 97
  Theodosia 97 189
  Thomas 66 323 141 37
  Thomas St. John 98 78
  Timothy 61 90 191 389
    62 375 114 180
  Tuswell 112 79
  Virginia 86 154
  Virginia (Preston) 86 154
  W. D. 80 47
  William 69 370 85 167
    91 206 112 78 79 141 37
LOCKWYK Alice 145 10
  John 145 10
LOCKY Jane 75 58
  John 75 58
LOCKYER Lokyer
  Mary Ann 69 202
  William 52 66
LOCOTT John 143 321
  Mary 143 321
  Thomas 143 321
LODEN William 53 15 77
  112 78 57
LODENWICK John M.
  (Mrs.) 123 99
LODER Andrew 84 275
  Ann Elizabeth 86 224
  Gilbert 61 278 79 417
    88 388
  James 84 275
  John 80 406
  Robert 63 162 105 10
  William 61 278 65 298
LODEWYCK Anne 83 118
  Hercules 83 118
LODGE —— 63 277 66 179
  74 xxiv 78 102 321

LODGE cont'd
  Abigail H. 55 xci
  Anna Cabot Mills (Davis)
    79 233 234 243 136 321
  Anna Sophia 79 229 231
  Augusta L. 99 71
  Constance 85 189 102 308
    103 77 123
  Constance Davis 79 233
    243
  Edmund 52 382
  Elizabeth 66 179 79 228
    96 401
  Francis 79 53 228
  George Cabot 79 243
    136 321
  Giles 79 228 231 102 308
  Giles (Mrs.) 130 314
  Giles Henry 79 231
  Helena 79 243
  Henry Cabot 51 100 52
    483 57 342 60 219 62
    392 74 xxviii 77 xvii
    248 302 79 211 227 228
    230-237 240 242 243 80
    200 82 484 87 166 91
    311 96 85 97 212 99 92
    259 102 308 136 321
  Henry Cabot (Mrs.)
    136 325
  J. 64 286
  James 117 16
  John 71 235 236
  John Davis 79 243
  John E. 78 305
  John Ellerton 79 228 229
    231 232 243 102 308
  Mary 79 228
  Mary C. 79 243
  Mary Felecia 99 71
  Mary G. 74 xxiv
  Matilda Elizabeth
    Frelinghuysen
    (Davis) 79 243 136 321
  Matthew 65 123 77 314
    79 228
  Robert 95 255 96 401
  William 99 71
  William (Mrs.) 99 68 71
    150
  William Jacob 96 401
LODGYER John 67 345
LODI Charles 109 189
  Julia (Leake) 109 189
LODNES Geoffrey de 103
  155 156
LODON J. M. 91 328
LODWICK Frank 93 278
LODY William 127 163
LOEB Fanny 77 xlviii
  Solomon 77 xlvii xlviii
    85 344
  Theresa 77 xlviii 85 344
LOEBKE Henry 105 49
  Marcella (Hamilton)
    105 49
LOECHEL
  Charles F. 91 50
  Emily May (Hannum)
    91 50

LOEFFLER
  Charles 110 322
LOESCH Helen Louise
  Sweet 124 313
LOESCHER
  Burt G. 124 243
  Conrad 58 321
  George 58 321
  Sebastion 58 321
LOEW Florence Bellows
  (Baker) 86 5
  William Goadby (Mrs.)
    86 5
LOFFEHAM John 76 284
LOFGREEN
  Gladys Juline 98 146
LOFKIN Isaac 55 67
  S. 91 328
LOFLIN Mary 73 144
LOFSTROM
  Karl 103 252
LOFT
  Caroline Augusta
    134 335
LOFTHOUSE
  Alice 126 24
LOFTMAN
  Benjamin 64 114
LOFTS Norah 121 234
LOFTUS —— 57 98
  Florence Frances
    (De Graf) 95 316
  Harry H. 95 316
  John 61 68
LOFTY Mary 51 463
  William 51 463
LOGAN Loggan
  —— 54 113 233 56 210
    122 270 273
  Adam 72 273
  Agnes L. (Hurin) 136 243
  Alexander 107 235
  Allen 112 93
  Angeline 85 217
  Ann 72 273 112 88 89 97
  Ann Elizabeth (Shapleigh)
    96 34
  Anne 112 90
  Anne (Montgomery)
    112 89 96 97
  Annie Raeburn 68 xxxiv
  Benjamin 112 87-93 96 97
  Betsey 112 97
  Betsey (Briggs) 112 88
  David 112 88-90 97 120 14
  Deborah Norris 54 121
  Elizabeth 112 88 97
    123 160
  Eva 79 143
  Frances A. 54 121
  Freelove 69 62
  Frisby Briscoe 107 234
  George 54 121 123 61 351
  Hannah 61 272
  Harold Edward (Mrs.)
    119 149
  Hugh 91 202 112 88 93
    117 33
  Hugh Adair 96 34
  Isabel 112 88
  James 62 313 63 311 343

LOGAN *cont'd*
  64 xxxi 201 295 **65**
  xxxiv **66** xlix **91** 328
  117 79 279
  Jane **112** 88 97
  Janet **51** 493
  Jean **112** 88
  Jenny **112** 97
  John **51** 198 **65** 117 **91** 264
    107 234 235 **112** 88 90-
    92 97 **117** 33 **125** 115
  John A. **55** 52 **69** 62
  Lloyd **73** 228
  Lucy **107** 234 235
  Margaret **112** 88
  Margaret (Bishop) **112** 97
  Mary **112** 88 97
  Mary (Cox) **91** 264
  Mary P. (Clark) **89** 380
  Mary Susan **107** 235
  Meda **89** 131
  Melinda **107** 234 235
  Nathaniel **112** 88
  Polly **112** 97
  Robert **71** 58 **112** 97
  Samuel **112** 88 93
  Sarah **112** 88 **120** 14 **125**
    115 119 197
  Sarah C. **136** 243
  Sarah Cadwalader **78** 92
  Sonora **107** 235
  Walter **55** 390
  Walter Seth **61** 109
  William **51** 493 **60** 25 **79**
    40 **98** 106 **111** 202 **112**
    88 92 97 **136** 243
  William P. **89** 380
LOGAY Hannah **127** 304
LOGE Samuel **112** 17
LOGEE
  Abraham **146** 348
  Hannah **146** 348
  Hopestill **146** 348
  John **114** 180
  Moses **114** 180
  Philip **146** 348
  William G. **114** 180
LOGES Margaret **82** 56
  Simon de **79** 228
Loggan *see* Logan
LOGGINS Annie **67** 256
  Elizabeth **51** 298
  Gilbert **67** 256
  Richard **51** 298
  Susanna **51** 298
  Sylvester **67** 256
  Thomas **67** 251
  Vernon **106** 77
LOGHEAD — Mr. **55** 390
LOGIE Comfort (Chase)
  87 247
  James **92** 283
  Philip **87** 247
LOGIN Hannah **59** 247
  John **59** 247
LOGLEY Margeria **94** 17
LOGUE
  Edward J. **115** 229
LOGUN Hannah **106** 196
  John **106** 196
  Thomas **106** 197

LOHMANN August W.
  81 107 219 **103** 77 125
  Carl A. **94** 305 **105** 157
LOHNES
  Barry J. **147** 265 267
  Harold George (Mrs.)
    101 124
LOISEAU Jean **143** 8
  Margaret (Mouton) **143** 8
LOISELLE
  Mathilda **95** 378
LOJIER Eva **58** 321
  John **58** 321
LÓK Michael **52** 481
LOKE William **55** 99
LOKER —— **57** 337 **58** 101
  143 220
  — Capt. **65** 361
  — Mrs. **53** 34 **65** 360
  Ann **63** 280 **143** 329 331
  Anne **143** 330 331
  Artemas **53** 34
  Benjamin **63** 241
  Bridget **55** 226 **63** 280 281
    143 329 330
  Daniel **64** 136
  David C. (Mrs.) **111** 327
  Elizabeth **52** 73 **63** 280 **143**
    329-331 **147** 381
  Ephraim **65** 365
  Faith **111** 186
  Hannah **63** 280 **114** 24 **143**
    330 331
  Hannah (Brewer) **143** 330
  Henry **55** 226 **60** 357 **63**
    280 281 **64** 136 **65** 357
    68 271 272 **91** 213 **114**
    24 **143** 328-331 **147** 381
  Hugh **64** 136
  Isaac **56** 265
  Joan **64** 136
  John **55** 226 **60** 357 **63**
    280 281 **64** 136 **143** 327
    329 330 **147** 381
  Lucy **64** 136
  Margaret Lugene
    (Cotton) **113** 68
  Mary **55** 267 **63** 280 **64** 136
    107 151 **108** 243 **143**
    330
  Mary (Draper) **143** 330
  Mehitable **56** 265
  Robert **64** 136
  Sarah **55** 392
  Stephen **144** 224
  William **53** 34 **64** 136
    113 68 **143** 329
LOKERSON Abraham L.
  90 390 391
  David H. **90** 391
  H. **90** 390
  Harriet (Rogers) **90** 391
  William Augustus **90** 391
Lokyer *see* Lockyer
LOLE Peter **100** 336
L'OLINOIS — Mr. **83** 84
Lolley *see* Lolly
Lollie *see* Lolly
LOLLIER
  R. R. (Mrs.) **116** 83
LOLLIS Ann **117** 213

LOLLO Marie **147** 73 174
LOLLY Lolley Lollie
  Charles William **119** 286
  Edward **51** 122
  Janet **72** 61
  John H. **84** 29
  Lucy Ann (Welch)
    119 286
  Mary **65** 37
  Olive (Austin) **117** 227
  Richard **72** 61
  Samuel **117** 227
LOMAN
  Christopher **111** 6
  Edmund **111** 6
  Jerome **111** 6
  Marie **111** 6
  Patience **111** 6
  Sarah **126** 68
  Thomas **111** 6
  William **111** 6
LOMAS Samuel **142** 54
  Sarah (Smith) **142** 54
LOMASK Milton **119** 154
LOMAX D. A.N. **112** 274
  113 88
  Elizabeth **52** 249 **144** 345
  Ellis **80** 87 88
  James **80** 87 88
  John **52** 249 **80** 91
  Lawrence **52** 249
  Peter **80** 88
  Richard **80** 89
  Roger **142** 261
  Susanna **89** 202
  Thomas **93** 300
LOMB Carl Ferdinand
  99 177
  Konrad **99** 177
LOMBARD Lambard
  Lambarde Lumbard
  —— **129** 86
  — Mr. **80** 18
  Aaron **84** 55
  Abigail **79** 441 **84** 129
    103 74 **105** 63
  Abner **70** 201
  Alice **99** 65
  Alice May (Clark) **92** 146
  Ammi C. **88** 337
  Anna **59** 170
  Annie (Noble) **95** 186
  Asenath **116** 198
  Atkins **125** 102
  Barnabas **140** 326 **147** 75
  Bathshua **79** 442
  Benjamin **55** 77 **123** 205
  Bernard **79** 441 442 **147**
    154 161
  Bethiah **79** 442
  Betsey **80** 18 **99** 197
  Betsey H. (Rich) **84** 49
  Betty **123** 117
  Caleb **67** 370 **83** 271 **115**
    279 **145** 53
  Calvin **87** 122
  Carrie **96** 331
  Chester **70** 201
  Daniel **86** 396 **104** 218
  David **72** 143
  Delight **70** 201

LOMBARD *cont'd*
Desire **115** 279
Desire (Perry) **115** 279
Edith **75** xxiii 75 **98** 84 88
    149
Edith E. **83** 427 434
Edward **115** 279
Edward E. **97** 292
Edwina **148** 174
Eliane / Eliony **87** 64 **89**
    262 **95** 355 **97** 188
Elijah **136** 77
Elioney **95** 355
Eliza (Wharf) **144** 348 354
Eliza Ellen **118** 131
Elizabeth **79** 441 442 **84** 53
    99 60
Elizabeth (Binney) **98** 84
Elizabeth (Lombard)
    84 53
Elizabeth (Pike) **111** 29
Ella J. (Bailey) **96** 331
Elsie Boyd **83** 230 247
Emory **145** 53
Ephraim **80** 12 **83** 268 272
    86 338 **93** 251 **94** 161
    140 150
Eunice **97** 184
Evalina **148** 174
Everett F. **108** 134
F. **112** 311
Fane **104** 35 **116** 17
Fanny **70** 201
Franklin **70** 201
Fred **95** 186
Freelove (Springer)
    135 338
George **72** 232 236 **82** 312
George Francis Fabyan
    86 338
George Simpson (Mrs.)
    92 146
Grace **72** 232 236 **82** 312
Hannah **79** 137 442 **83** 399
    84 43 45 **86** 396 **88** 66
    104 298 **145** 53
Hannah (Coan) **98** 84
Hannah (Lewis) **86** 338
Hannah (Wing) **86** 338
Harriet (Rich) **84** 53
Harriett H. (Jones) **88** 337
Hepzibah **79** 441
Hiram **70** 201
Hitte **88** 66
Huldah (Rider) **83** 268 272
    88 169
Isabel (Fabyan) **86** 338
    88 169
Israel **84** 53 **98** 84
Jabez **79** 440-443
Jacob Hall **86** 338
James **83** 398 **135** 338
James D. **96** 331
Jane **55** 77 **83** 398 **148** 172
Janet (Scott) **144** 348 354
Jedediah **98** 84 **125** 10
Jedidiah **86** 338
Jemima **84** 122
Jemima (Atkins) **98** 84
Jemima (Lewis) **115** 279
Jennie (Bradley) **96** 331
Jesse **59** 170

LOMBARD *cont'd*
Joanna (Vickery) **86** 338
Joel **70** 353
John **79** 441 **84** 49 **140** 326
John L. **51** 506
Jonathan **118** 205
Joseph **88** 66 **125** 37 **144**
    348 354
Joshua **105** 63 **147** 154 161
Joyce **98** 84
Julia **70** 201 **79** 153
Lena J. (Rich) **84** 123
Lewis **84** 53 **123** 201
Lucina **70** 201
Lucinda C. (Collins)
    123 201
Luther **148** 174
Luther H. **148** 174
Lydia **83** 404
Margaret **147** 154 161
Martha **79** 442
Mary **72** 143 **79** 441 442
    83 270 **86** 395 396 **88** 66
    96 79 **110** 121 **123** 264
    145 53 **148** 174
Mary (Arey) **86** 396
Mary (Cushman) **136** 77
Mary (Gaines) **132** 163
Mary (Newcome) **98** 84
Mary (Swift) **86** 338
Mary (Wing) **98** 84
Mary Ann **96** 185
Mary Elizabeth **93** 251
Mary Elizabeth (Hall) **86**
    338 **93** 251 **94** 161 **140**
    150
Matilda **113** 295
Matthew **79** 441
May **92** 230
Mehitable **79** 441 **80** 12
    106 160 **126** 67
Mehitable (Knowles)
    86 338
Mercy **83** 487 **123** 65
Nancy **125** 214 **126** 65
Nancy (Penn) **125** 102
Nathan **55** 69
Nathaniel **79** 441 **87** 302
Nathaniel Knowles
    86 338
Olive **84** 49
Oliver C. **83** 273
Orville Dewey **82** 13
Pamelia **70** 201
Patience **79** 442
Paul **83** 271 **99** 197
Peggy **125** 101
Percival Hall **68** xxxvi
    74 xxviii **76** 77 **77** 79 **78**
    109 110 211 **79** 104 112
    194 209 **81** 236 **86** 184
    338 **87** 177
Percival Hall (Mrs.)
    88 169
Percy **129** 86
Persis **129** 86
Phebe Ann **97** 292
Polly **84** 38 55 **123** 117
Rachel **87** 122 **105** 63
Rebecca **79** 442 **80** 12
    83 404

LOMBARD *cont'd*
Richard **55** 300
Richard P. **83** 406 **103** 27
Rosamond **86** 338
Rufus **129** 86
Ruth (Carlson) **96** 331
Sabra (Covell) **83** 273
Sally **84** 55 **104** 217
Sally (Rich) **83** 406 **103** 27
Salome **84** 37 **87** 123
Samuel **88** 66
Sarah **70** 201 **78** 445 **79**
    441-443 **80** 18 **83** 398
    103 28
Sarah (Hopkins) **104** 218
Sarah Brown (Rich) **84** 55
Simon **80** 18
Solomon **80** 12 **90** 400
Sophia **70** 201
Susan **84** 119
Susan (Stickney) **98** 84
Susanna **125** 10
Susanna (Snow) (Collins)
    84 35
T. A. **97** 292
Thankful **83** 271 **88** 66
    92 81
Thankful (Rich) **83** 271
Thomas **79** 442 **83** 404 **84**
    129 **86** 338 396 **88** 66 **98**
    84 **147** 154 161
Timothy **84** 35 **105** 282
W. C. (Mrs.) **112** 240
Wentworth **148** 172
William **84** 53 **91** 328
    110 199 293 **132** 163
William A. **84** 123
William E. **97** 292
Wintworth **87** 123
LOMBARDO
Daniel **141** 362
H. **117** 168
LOME Bennett **73** 275
LOMES Richard **63** 345
Lomis *see* Loomis
LOMUST Lydia
    (Hutchings) **126** 68
LOND Matthew **98** 117
LONDENOYS
—— **56** 41 319 320
Katharine **56** 40
Mary **56** 40
Richard **56** 40
Robert **56** 40
LONDERVILLE
Armaline **81** 148
Fabien **81** 148
Mary **81** 148
LONDON Charles
    Marion Henry **112** 320
Edward **147** 317 318
H. S. **108** 69 70
H. Stafford **95** 303 **145** 100
H. Stanford **111** 68 **118**
    171 172
Hawkins **58** 335
Hoyt H. **112** 320
Hugh Stanford **113** 310
Jane (Sparrow) **147** 318
Joan (Sparrow) **147** 317
John **83** 313 **125** 38

LONDON *cont'd*
L. S. **52** 96
Mabelle **83** 232
Robert (Bishop of) **96** 46
Robert de **122** 266
Sally **86** 38
Stanford **113** 310
LONDRY Joseph **81** 272
Katharine **81** 272
LONDY John **73** 104
LONE
Anthony **84** 307 312
Elizabeth **64** 317 **84** 307 310-312
John **86** 420
Margaret **84** 307
Robert **84** 307 310
LONEGAM John **79** 50
LONERGAN Henry **78** 70
LONES Lellie Capitola (Southwick) **93** 137 **97** 161 182
William Franklin **97** 183
William Franklin (Mrs.) **93** 137 **96** 150 **97** 161 162
LONG Longe
—— **59** 106 337 **67** 38 284 **92** 245 **100** 188
— Capt. **101** 50 **124** 96
— Col. **56** 29
— Mrs. **54** 389
— Widow **96** 321
A. S. **91** 328
Abby **78** 325
Abiel **104** 39
Abigail **81** 445 **82** 46 **100** 254 **104** 39 **105** 80
Abraham **128** 292
Abram Heath **102** 77
Adeline (Leigh) **94** 164
Aden F. **65** 135
Albert F. **65** 135
Alden B. **100** 255
Alexander **67** 38 42 **104** 40
Alice **104** 36
Allin **107** 305
Almira D. **100** 254
Amelia Juliana **130** 315
Ann **58** 92 **70** 367 **104** 38
Ann E. **74** 265
Ann Maria **83** 25 28
Anna **53** 463 **54** 82 **83** 161 **89** 111 **100** 254
Anne **51** 114 **53** 95 **57** 416 **67** 42 **77** 251 **100** 220 328 **104** 37 38 **143** 76
Anne (Costable) **104** 39
Annie **67** 353
Anthony **80** 361 **124** 100
Archibald **94** 164-166
Armistead Rosser **95** 98
Arnold H. **83** 161
Arthur I. (Mrs.) **85** 440
Asahel **83** 161
Aurelia Jane (Handy) **126** 112
Azubah **72** 75
Benjamin **53** 143 145 **104** 39
Berenice Clement **98** 146

LONG *cont'd*
106 61 130
Bertha C. **65** 135
Bessie **77** 251
Betsey **70** 356 **100** 254
Brian Bancroft **95** 283
Bridget **62** 302
Bryant Alden **100** 255
Caleb **91** 312 **100** 254
Caleb A. **118** 132
Caleb C. **100** 254
Calista Cralle **95** 98
Carleton M. **100** 255
Caroline Ellen **89** 325
Caroline Mae (Comey) **83** 426 434
Carrie **92** 361
Catharina Kern **120** 315
Catherine **90** 90
Catherine (Burke) **95** 283
Charles **51** 114
Charles Henry **94** 165
Charles W. **91** 328
Christiana **121** 137
Christiana (Coffin) **122** 262
Clark **63** 48
Clement Ross (Mrs.) **98** 147 **100** 47 116
Conrad **91** 328
Cynthia **65** 370
David **61** 263 **71** 202
Deborah **54** 421 **104** 38 **122** 262
Deidamia (Perry) **122** 206
Denis **95** 283
Diana **90** 276
Diana (Snow) **102** 288
Dorothy M. **100** 255
Dudley **53** 82
Ebenezer **91** 312 **100** 254
Edward **56** 312 **60** 291
Edye **78** 144
Eleanor **100** 254 **104** 40
Eleanor (Jackson) **104** 39
Eli L. **65** 135
Eliza **62** 368
Eliza (Rogers) **125** 214
Eliza (Sterry) **94** 165
Eliza Jane B. **90** 105
Eliza L. **100** 255
Elizabeth **57** 416 **65** 34 **68** 178 **78** 175 **80** 353 **94** 378 **100** 220 254 328 **104** 37 38 40 **131** 129
Elizabeth Ann **90** 105
Elizabeth C. **126** 144
Evart H. **65** 135
Fannie **91** 230
Fannie Elizabeth **81** 223
Frances **77** 251
Frances Kittredge **95** 283
Frances Marsh (Bancroft) **95** 283
Francis **104** 38
Fred **109** 288
Gabriel **77** 251
George **63** 19 **69** 360 **82** 46 **94** 379 **124** 227 **143** 202
George A. **100** 255
George E. **65** 135

LONG *cont'd*
George Washington **77** 251
Gertrude E. **100** 255
Giles **53** 95 **100** 220 328 **104** 37 38
Hallock Porter **80** 225 449 **82** 122 237 **91** 312 **100** 255 328 337 **102** 82 254 **103** 154 **104** 36 **116** 310 **120** 147
Hannah **63** 381-383 **64** 189 **71** 202 **104** 38 39 **113** 297 **133** 251 **140** 209
Hannah W. (Lyman) **83** 183 184 **84** 29
Harry Vinton **56** xxxiv
Helen Cole **108** 222
Henry **51** 114 **54** 326 **63** 143 **104** 40 **120** 315
Henry C. De **53** 456
Henry L. **83** 161
Henry S. **91** 230
Herodias **85** 428 **91** 289 **105** 258 **106** 309
Ida Clarissa **61** 274
Ida Merriam **70** 203
Ira **100** 254
Isaac G. **127** 158
Isabella **101** 165
Isabella (Slappey) **102** 77
Isarance **127** 159
Ivorine **117** 131
Ivory A. **100** 255
J. C. **89** 98
Jacob **100** 328 **104** 37
James **61** 134 **87** 5 **100** 328 **102** 313 **104** 37 **110** 82
James Hall **108** 134
James Henry **78** 325
James R. **74** 305
James S. **65** 135
Jane **51** 114 115 162 **56** 91 **69** 169 **104** 38
Jane (Smalley) **102** 51
Jane (Totten) **126** 67
Jasper **100** 220 328 **104** 37
Jasper S. **120** 315
Jean (Northrup) **95** 283
Jennie A. **136** 311
Jerusha **54** 178
Joan **56** 312 **78** 150
Joanna **104** 38
Joel **125** 214
John **51** 162 **56** 91 312 **57** 416 **60** 291 **61** 279 **63** 163 **64** 115 **67** 37 38 42 **69** 298 **70** 247 **73** 224 **78** 150 **81** 489 491 **82** 59 **90** 82 **91** 328 **98** 208 **100** 328 **102** 51 **104** 37-40 **105** 80 **110** 82 **113** 297 **124** 95 102 **128** 172 **144** 10
John Davis **52** 483 **54** lxxviii cxxvii **57** xxxiii xlviii 122 **58** lxxxv **59** ci 336 **60** 90 104 **62** lxxvii **63** 111 216 **64** 71 **65** liii **67** 189 **68** xiv xx xlviii **99** 92 **100** 171 **101** 325

LONG *cont'd*
111 165
John Edwin (Mrs.)
104 144
John H. **100** 255
John Joseph **77** 251
John L. **74** 265
John Nicholas **98** 289
Jonathan **53** 448 **56** 91 **72**
75 **100** 254 **104** 39
Jonathan Dean **91** 312 313
Joseph **52** 182 **61** 29 280
70 312 **83** 161 **85** 42 **92**
245 **94** 378 379 **100** 220
254 328 **104** 37 39 40
Joseph A. C. **97** 238
Joseph M. **100** 255 337
Joseph Mansfield **91** 312
313 **100** 255
Joseph Philip **92** 245
Joshua **57** 416 **104** 38
Katharine (Kellar)
94 165 166
Katharine E. **100** 255
Kety **90** 90
Lemuel **54** 82 **83** 161
Lemuel McKinney **77** 251
Lettie **128** 172
Levi **102** 288
Levi C. **102** 281
Lois Bancroft **95** 283
Londace **81** 445
Louisa **76** 17
Lovina **74** 305
Lucretia de **122** 244
Lula **102** 77
Lunsford **77** 251
Luther E. **65** 135
Lydia **51** 55 **94** 379 **97** 272
107 305
Lydia (Coffin) **121** 137
Lydia Bangs (Snow) **102**
281 290
Lydia Nash **92** 208
Mabel **105** 128 **108** 218
109 134
Mae **117** 167
Margaret **51** 114 115 **81**
445 **111** 165
Margaret Wooley **91** 142
Margaretta **81** 201
Mariah **100** 254
Marie **104** 38
Martha **57** 416 **65** 135 **77**
251 **104** 39 **125** 205
Martha (Viemont) **94** 165
Mary **51** 56 **53** 211 **57** 416
70 312 **77** 251 **78** 325
81 445 **82** 46 291 293
413 **85** 377 **97** 357 **100**
220 254 328 **104** 11 37-
39 **111** 179 **115** 56 320
128 292
Mary (Giles) **126** 204
Mary (Marshall) **128** 292
Mary Ann **79** 36 **107** 308
108 260
Mary Ann (Snider)
94 165
Mary Elizabeth **74** 305
Mary H. **90** 276

LONG *cont'd*
Mary J. (Crawford)
128 172
Mary Rebecca A. **77** 216
251
Mary Russel **94** 379
May **104** 142
Mercy **100** 165
Michael **57** 416 **85** 455 **86**
348 349 **104** 38 40 **143**
259
Miles **104** 40
Minnie A. **100** 255
Minnie R. H. **98** 97
Moses **55** 66 **92** 309
N. **91** 328
Nabby (Scott) **126** 66
Nabby A. (Taylor) **109** 39
Nathan **114** 316
Nathaniel **68** 178 **104** 40
Nicholas **77** 251 **79** 418
430 **104** 40 74
Oliver **83** 161
Orman R. **83** 426 434
Ovilla **74** 305
Patience **51** 161 **83** 161
Pearl (Stonecipher)
117 131
Peter **115** 39 **122** 262
Peter G. **126** 143
Phebe **120** 118
Phebe Staples **100** 254
Philip **104** 39
Pierce **58** 235 **65** 77 80 82
109 112 257 264 339 **80**
116 **81** 445 **82** 46 291
293 413 **100** 41 **104** 40
136 137
Polly **124** 278
Rebecca **56** 91 **57** 416 **61**
263 **104** 38 39 **121** 265
124 96
Rebecca (Boardman)
92 309
Rebecca Edwards **77** 251
253
Remembrance (Pierce)
127 159
Reuben D. **117** 131
Reuben S. **100** 254
Richard **51** 114 115 **58** 92
67 35 **77** 251 **78** 150 **91**
312 **100** 254 328 **104** 36-
40
Robert **54** 345 **56** 91 **57**
415 416 **62** 67 **63** 25 **94**
165 **100** 242 254 328
104 36-40 **115** 320 **124**
95 **131** 9 19 129 **135** 234
148 137 138
Robert J. **126** 94
Roger **104** 39
Roxa **83** 161
Ruel **100** 254
Ruth **97** 355 **100** 254 **104**
38 **124** 96
Sally **94** 166 **97** 272
Sally (Howard) **126** 143
Sally Maria **71** 202
Samuel **51** 55 **64** 22 **67** 38
42 **73** 144 **83** 307 **104** 39

LONG *cont'd*
121 137
Samuel P. **83** 183 184
Sarah **51** 114 **57** 416 **61** 29
355 **72** 5 **100** 254 **104** 38-
40 **108** 119 **121** 122 **125**
216 **131** 125 **132** 86 **143**
45
Sarah (Cahoon) **122** 206
Sarah (Haviland) **109** 288
Sarah (Strangman)
100 242
Shubael **104** 39
Sophia **63** 48
Sophia Lillibridge **83** 161
Stephen **52** 182 **81** 445
100 254
Susanna **51** 493 **67** 286
100 254 **104** 39 40 **122**
206 **125** 255
T. W. **92** 208
Theodore K. **98** 289
Thomas **51** 114 115 **72** 5
80 357 **96** 122 **100** 328
104 37-39 **109** 39
Valentine **100** 188
Violet **76** 17
W. H. **59** 142
W. S. **57** 335 336
Waldo **91** 328
Warren **91** 328
William **56** 404 **62** 202
63 381 383 **65** 370 **73**
140 **74** 130 **80** 357 **81**
445 **91** 312 328 **94** 379
100 149 220 254 328
103 185 **104** 37 39 40
106 23 **122** 206 **138** 7
William A. **100** 255
William F. **126** 112
William G. **86** 465
William H. **65** 135 **76** 17
91 328
William J. **126** 204
William Joseph **95** 283
Zachariah **125** 58
Zachary **57** 416 **104** 38
Zelotes **63** 48 **83** 161
LONGA Abigail **118** 97
William **118** 97
LONGACRE Ethel **91** 48
LONGBON J. W. **80** 163
LONGBOTTOM Long-
bothome
Abel **70** 226
Anna **78** 26
Anne **129** 315
Daniel **78** 26 **121** 74
129 315
Elijah **129** 315
Elizabeth **129** 315
James **70** 225
Judith **129** 315
Lydia **129** 315
Mary **70** 225 **78** 26
Mary (Caswell) **129** 315
Thomas **72** 57
Weltha **70** 226
LONGDEN Charles
Scudamore **97** 99
Elizabeth **61** 393

LONGDEN *cont'd*
Henry Errington **97** 99
Henry Isham **81** 136 138
94 252 **97** 99-102 **103**
41
Isham **94** 200 252 260 266
269 338 **97** 101 102 **98**
32 39
Lavinia (Johnson) **97** 99
Lavinia Mary **97** 99
Louisa (Isham) **97** 99
Roger **97** 99
Thomas Hayter **97** 99
LONGDENE
Thomas **54** 336
Longe *see* Long
LONGEE James **115** 34
LONGEL Sarah Abby
(Bragdon) **120** 223 304
William A. **120** 223 304
LONGELY
Jane G. **147** 269
LONGESPEE Longspee
Longespeye
Longuepee
Alfred **131** 90
Ela (Fitzpatrick) **140** 221
Elsa de **116** 279 280
Emeline de **116** 279 280
Matilda de **75** 62
Stephen de **116** 279
William **119** 98 100 101
140 221
William de **116** 279
LONGEST Daniel **65** 29
LONGFELLOW Langfellow
Abigail **101** 59
Abigail (Tompson)
88 200 295
Alexander Wadsworth
64 xxxiii **65** xxi **78** 287
88 200 203 398 **89** 136
Alice **88** 296
Alice Mary **106** 154
Alice Pearl **86** 197
Amelia H. **83** 434 **84** 21
Anna **101** 59
Anne (Sewall) **88** 295
Annie **106** 154
Annie Allegra **85** 199 **88**
203 295 **89** 136
Charles Appleton
106 154
David **101** 59
David P. **63** 272
Edith **86** 235 **88** 296
106 154
Elizabeth **85** 325
Elizabeth (Porter) **88** 398
Elizabeth Clapp (Porter)
88 200
Elizabeth O. **135** 79
Elizabeth P. **88** 398
Ernest Wadsworth
106 154
Fanny E. **106** 154
Frances Elizabeth
(Appleton) **86** 235 **88**
295 **106** 154 **136** 321
Green **140** 21
Hannah **63** 272

LONGFELLOW *cont'd*
Henry Wadsworth **52**
93 303 **54** 439 **56** 181 **57**
347 **59** 237 **60** x 108 235
62 106 209 **63** 385 **64** lx
296 **66** lxxiv **68** lvii
283 340 363 **70** 292 **71**
68 **74** 115 **75** 166 **86** 235
88 200 295 **98** 3 **103** 242
106 154 **116** 8 **124** 136
128 67 **136** 90 321
Jacob **63** 272 **125** 91 92
Jane **63** 272
Jonathan **101** 59 **125** 91
92 94
Joseph **112** 241
Joseph W. **91** 286
Lucia Wadsworth **67** xlix
Lucinda C. (Hanscom)
91 386
Marcia **93** 366
Marian **68** 383
Mark **63** 272
Martha (Hull) (Crow)
112 241
Mary (Davis) **125** 60
Mary (Fowler) **112** 241
Mary (Green) **125** 91
Mary King **88** 200
Nathan **101** 59 **125** 91
140 21
Patience (Young) **88** 200
295
Rebecca **63** 272
Richard King **88** 200
Samuel **71** 68
Samuel (Mrs.) **109** 58
Sophia (Storer) **109** 58
Stephen **51** 149 **54** 31 **88**
200 295 **110** 317 **114**
293
Tabitha (Bragdon) **88**
200 295 **114** 293
Taphenas **63** 272 **101** 59
Taphenas (Huntley)
101 59
Tracy (Merida) **112** 241
William **55** 197 **86** 355
88 200 295 **101** 59 **125**
60
Zilpah (Wadsworth) **88**
200 295
LONGFORD —— **141** 99
Elizabeth **110** 263 **135** 135
Margery **111** 268
Philippe **83** 318
Ralph **110** 263
William **111** 68
Longglay *see* Longley
Longly
LONGHEAD John **60** 161
Robert **60** 161
Thomas **60** 161
LONGHORNE
Elizabeth **93** 46
Mary (Crosby) **113** 70
119 248
Richard **113** 70 **119** 244
248
LONGHURST Willard
Leslie (Mrs.) **99** 148

LONGINO
Helen Maxwell **112** 75
Lovick P. (Mrs.) **112** 75
Sam W. (Mrs.) **119** 240
LONGLAND —— **53** 68
Charles **53** 116-118
Francis **124** 116 117
Joan **94** 268
William **94** 268
LONGLE Joan **67** 162
LONGLEY Longglay
—— **57** 337
— Dea. **70** 301
____ (Eaton) **140** 138
Abel **57** 202 203 **70** 15 17
138 213 306 307
Abigail **76** 32
Abigail (Sawtell) **87** 234
238
Alice **57** 203 **69** 120 **71** 95
Amy **57** 202
An. E. (Tonkinson)
128 262
Anna **61** 70
Anna B. **57** 202
Anna True (Peabody)
95 295
Artemus **57** 203 **70** 11
298 305 306
Asa **57** 204 **69** 299 **70** 17
212 303 **97** 395
Benjamin **97** 395 **125** 222
Betsey **57** 203 **70** 303
Bridget **57** 202 203
Calvin **70** 17
Charles **57** 203
Charles Hiram **82** 125 237
Clementine **103** 235
Cynthia **61** 358
Deborah **54** 52 **79** 397
Deliverance **64** 194
Desire **57** 203
Dissama **99** 39
Edmond **119** 258
Edmund **57** 203 **61** 358
69 12 14 15 119 120 126
127 211 213-215 217 218
220 221 300 302 306 307
70 138 142 **87** 234 238
95 294 **119** 258 **125** 107
132 107
Edmund (Mrs.) **69** 222
Edmund Waters **95** 294
96 87 160 166
Edward **119** 258
Edward M. **57** 203
Eleanor **118** 309
Elijah **64** 194 195
Elizabeth **90** 105 **99** 300
100 29
Elizabeth (Patterson)
95 294
Elizabeth Peabody **95** 295
Esther **57** 203
Eunice **89** 17
Ezekiel **69** 298 **70** 140
George **100** 29
Hannah **57** 203 **61** 70
Horace **57** 203
Huldah **123** 52
Isaac **106** 238

LONGLEY *cont'd*
Israel **61** 169 **70** 11 17 20
  140 307
Ivory **57** 203 **70** 137 140
  142 144 145 212 215 219
  299
James **67** xxxiv **71** xxxiv
  lii **118** 309 **140** 138
James F. **128** 262
James R. **118** 309
Jane **69** 127
Jane G. **147** 267
Jane P. **57** 203
Joanna **61** 70 71
John **61** 169 **64** 37 194 **65**
  297 **69** 298 300 303 **70** 9
  12 15 140 **79** 397 **95** 294
  100 29
John B. **128** 262
Jonas **57** 202 203 **69** 10 13-
  16 120 126 214 221 **70**
  139
Joseph **57** 203 **69** 13 15 16
  118 123 125 213 218-221
  223 304 **70** 13 16 17 295
  302 **95** 294
Joshua **57** 202 203 **69** 13-15
  17 119 121 212 218-222
  295 303 306 **70** 17 21-23
  214 300
Josiah P. **64** 155
Julia **71** liii
Keziah (Gates) (Fairbanks)
  121 48
Lavina **70** 144
Lizzie **118** 309
Louinah **57** 203
Lucy **70** 20
Lucy Bartlett **57** 68
Luther **57** 68 203 **70** 217
Lydia **56** 246 **57** 203 **70**
  299 **126** 14 132 **145** 36
Mary **57** 68 203 204 **69** 11
  118 120 125 **87** 234 238
  125 24 **126** 138
Mary (Learned) **125** 107
Mary (Pratt) **95** 294
Mary Ann Manning
  (Reed) **95** 294
Mary Josephine **82** 407
Molly **57** 203
Nehemiah **69** 120 **87** 234
  239
Nicholas **64** 350
Olive **57** 203 **69** 125 127
  213
Pamela **57** 203
Phineas **69** 296 307 **70** 9 16
  139
Phineas A. **57** 203
Polly (Smith) **87** 234 239
R. B. **140** 68
Rebecca **57** 204
Rebecca Ann **64** 155
Rhoda **70** 144
Richard **95** 294
Robert **77** 295 **136** 269
Robert Dalton **106** 238
Roxanna **70** 303
Roxanna W. **57** 203
Roxey **57** 204

LONGLEY *cont'd*
Rufus **70** 216
Sally **57** 204 **61** 169 **71** lii
Sally (Sawtell) (Tarbell)
  126 138
Samuel **57** 204 **70** 303
Sarah **57** 204 **61** 169 **64** 37
  69 299 **87** 234 240 **136**
  269
Sarah (Gill__h) **121** 118
Sarah (Prescott) **95** 294
Sarah Ann (Chiles)
  128 262
Sisley **85** 455
Stedman **79** 51
Stephen **70** 24 137 138
  140 142 143 145 210 215-
  220 295-297 299-305 307
Susan **70** 305
Susan (Adams) **125** 222
Susanna **69** 217
T. **123** 285
Thomas **75** 305 **119** 259
Timothy **76** 32
William **57** 204 **61** 70 **64**
  194 **68** 195 **69** 12 16 119
  121 127 218 223 224 298
  299 **70** 11 12 138 **71** 95
  85 30 33 **95** 294 **106** 238
  108 95 **123** 167 **125** 26
Zachariah **97** 395
LONGLINE Alice **104** 260
LONGMAN Ann **67** 362
F. G. **82** 258
Rufus Adolphus **66** xlix
  191
Thomas **67** 362
LONGMIRE
— Dr. **55** 341
LONGMORE
Luella B. **83** 430 434
Mary A. Smyth **130** 50
LONGREY Rachel **132** 96
LONGSHORE
Alfred **86** 462
Louisa (Sylvester) **86** 462
Peter **86** 462
Rhody (Bodwell)
  (Sylvester) **86** 461 462
Robert **117** 276
Longspee *see* Longespee
LONGSTAFF Longstaffe
Eleanor **145** 254
W. Hylton Dyer **90** 60
LONGSTONE
— Mistress **148** 111
Hester **148** 117
Thomas **148** 117
LONGSTREET
— Gen. **56** 329
Abby Buchanan **81** 290
C. S. **81** 290
LONGSTRETH Mary Ann
  81 369 **96** 83 **111** 322
LONGSWORTH
Mary Esther **93** 136
Longuepee *see* Longespee
LONGUEVILLE
Osbern de **105** 294
Walter Gyffarde (Count
  of) **75** 59 60

LONGUST Reuben **64** 315
LONGWELL
Henry **110** 170
Thomas **110** 169
LONGWOOD
Matthew **124** 72
William **65** 117
LONGWORTH Alice Lee
  63 106 **76** 217
Bethiah **53** 327
Catherine **106** 65
Deborah **53** 327
Israel **77** xlvi
John **95** 257 258
Nicholas **61** 215 **76** 217
  106 65
Peter **105** 97
Roger **105** 97
Susan **76** 217
Thomas **53** 327
LONGY Georges **94** 390
LONGYEAR
Abby Beecher **85** 338
Barbara **85** 239
Clyde Stanley **109** 226
Edmund J. **85** 239 **97** 98
  106 78
Edmund Joseph **81** 219
  237 **86** 352 **109** 121 133
  226
Helen McGaw **85** 338
Isaac **109** 226
Jacob **85** 239 **97** 98 **109** 226
Johannes **109** 226
John Munro **85** 337 338
John Munro (Mrs.) **76**
  xxi **85** 337 345 **86** 203
John Wesley **85** 337
Margaret **109** 226
Mary Beecher **75** 316
  85 338
Mary Hawley **76** xxi
Petrus **109** 226
Philip Owen **109** 226
Richard Patten **109** 226
Robert D. **106** 78
Robert Davis **109** 226
Robert Dudley **85** 338
Sarah Mathews **94** 138
LONNIS Eleanor Jane
  (Davis) **117** 56
Henry **117** 55 56
Jane **117** 55
LONNON John **93** 384
Olive **128** 277
William **128** 277
LONSDALE
— Earl of **67** 318
Lionel (Mrs.) **85** 340
Margaret **116** 239
LONT
Charles Henry **99** 48
Ethel Lassell **99** 48
George D. **104** 46
Mary Emeline (Van Allen)
  99 48 **104** 46
LONUS John **54** 45
LONWELL
Arthur **114** 65
John P. **114** 65
Leslie **114** 65

LOOFBURROW —— **143** 78
LOOFT Will **145** 111
LOOK Aaron **59** 383
  Bethiah **75** 47 48
  Catherine **64** 80
  Cheney **52** 369
  Damaris **93** 188
  Daniel **59** 259
  Elijah **66** 80 81
  Elizabeth **60** 143
  George **59** 201 259 380 381
  Hannah **76** 257
  Jean **60** 143
  Job **59** 263
  Johan **142** 156
  Johan (Montague) **142** 154-156
  John **75** 47 48 **142** 154 156
  Jonathan **65** 353 **145** 358
  Joseph **66** 80
  Lois **59** 259
  Lot **59** 262
  Lydia L. **80** 127
  Mary **75** 48 **87** 62
  Nancy **59** 259
  Nathan **66** 80
  Patience **96** 79
  Persis **59** 259 380 381
  Peter **66** 80
  Prince **59** 196 200 261-263
  Rebecca **122** 190
  Robert **66** 80
  Roger **142** 156
  Samuel **59** 259 **66** 80 81
  Sarah **59** 196 200 261-263 **65** 353 **104** 56
  Seth **66** 80 **118** 205
  Susanna **59** 262
  Thomas **60** 143 **66** 80 81
  William **63** 162
LOOKABAUGH
  Adam **68** 255
  Adam Frederick **68** 255
  Clementine D. **68** 255
  Elizabeth **68** 255
LOOKER Cylinda (Hanks) **86** 16
  Elizabeth **57** 301
  Henry **57** 301
  John **57** 223 **86** 16
  Mary **57** 223
  Sarah **57** 223
LOOKHOUSE
  Eliza **88** 284
LOOKIN Sally **61** 238
LOOME Mary (Canney) (Tibbetts) **98** 62
LOOMER Addie Eugenia **106** 307 **107** 135
  Augustus Hart **113** 323
  Caroline **120** 17
  Charles J. **86** 170
  Charles N. **86** 170
  Electa **113** 323
  Elijah **120** 17
  Elizabeth **120** 257 **126** 86 178
  Elizabeth (Sanford) **104** 76
  Elizabeth (Wheland) **120** 16

LOOMER *cont'd*
  Elizabeth Jane (Bennett) **120** 15
  Eunice **62** 293
  Eunice B. **86** 170
  Hannah (Chapman) **104** 76
  Henrietta (Fitch) **113** 323
  Henry **120** 15
  Jemima **80** 139
  John **120** 16
  John G. **113** 323
  John N. **86** 170
  Jonathan **104** 76
  Levi **87** 135 **99** 298
  Lois **99** 298
  Lois (Chase) **87** 135
  Lucy Ann (Coats) **113** 323
  Mahala A. **113** 323
  Mary (Sanford) **104** 76
  Nathan **104** 76
  Nellie A. (Woodworth) **86** 170
  Otis **108** 250
  Philip **101** 78
  Rebecca **99** 298
  Rebecca E. **120** 17
  Sara Alice (Newcomb) **120** 15
  Stephen **104** 76 **115** 69
  Thomas **120** 15
LOOMER-SHEPARD
  Addie E. **101** 78
LOOMIS Lomis Loomas Loomes Lummis
  — Widow **71** 302
  Aaron **61** 310 **136** 329
  Abel **71** 86 87 153 154 156 157 277 299 300
  Abial **72** 37
  Abiel **52** 309 **83** 99
  Abigail **52** 184 308-310 412 414 415 418 419 **53** 448 **54** 81 **56** 165 **59** 65 **69** 334 **71** 84 282 **72** 33 42 75 166 204 **83** 99 340 **89** 246 **116** 67 **147** 57
  Abigail (Clark) **147** 57
  Abigail (Gillett) (Birge) **100** 277
  Abigail S. **69** 334
  Abijah **71** 83 158 276 **72** 32 34 168 171
  Abner **52** 184 **54** 81 **55** 34 39 **58** 195 **83** 99
  Addah (Harder) **133** 25
  Affa **63** 337
  Agnes **92** 188
  Alfred **72** 105 **89** 246
  Alfred Lee (Mrs.) **83** 487
  Alice **55** 37 **56** 353
  Alice Marie (Garlock) **84** 188
  Almira **61** 310
  Almon **72** 204
  Alvin **58** 403
  Amasa **52** 311 **54** 83 **55** 37 283 **58** 402 **59** 412 **60** 262 **79** 151 161 **101** 204
  Amos **57** 213 **60** 402 **74** 63 **80** 186 **89** 254 **145** 332

LOOMIS *cont'd*
  Amy (Browning) **91** 250
  Andrew **52** 408 **54** 81 258 **55** 35 **56** 163 165 350 **71** 163 **72** 36 **83** 99
  Andrew H. **82** 376
  Ann **52** 183 **64** 262 **71** 155 297
  Ann (Lyman) **123** 115
  Anna **54** 83 85 254 **55** 37 **56** 350 **60** 202 **61** 310 **72** 33 42 **83** 99 **125** 75
  Anna (Watson) (Allen) **123** 279
  Anna M. **61** 310
  Anne **64** 262 **71** 87 277 296 **101** 48
  Annie M. **82** 379
  Anstrus G. **89** 246
  Aretas **61** 340
  Ariel **72** 75 **74** 63
  Arphanso **142** 190
  Asenath **81** 454
  Austin **55** 38 **56** 355
  Axa **55** 39
  Becce Bechee **71** 274
  Benjamin **52** 181 412 **54** 253 **56** 350 352 **72** 174 **78** 92
  Beriah **52** 180 410 412
  Betsey **55** 37 **60** 201 **61** 398 **83** 99 359
  Beulah **54** 81 258 **56** 352 **83** 99
  Britzal **61** 398
  Burdett **65** xxxiv
  Caleb **123** 137
  Caroline Adele **104** 308
  Catherine P. **82** 380
  Celestin R. **61** 398
  Charity **104** 124
  Charles **52** 181-184 310 311 410 420 **54** 256-259 **55** 35-37 **56** 164 165 347 348 352 356 **61** 398 **83** 99
  Charles Bacon **72** 297
  Charlotte **61** 398
  Charlotte (Bliss) **93** 190
  Charlotte M. **72** 104
  Chauncy **61** 35
  Chauncy Chester (Mrs.) **97** 92
  Chester **55** 282 **56** 350 **92** 188
  Chester Clark **104** 308
  Chloe **52** 310 **55** 34 **61** 398 **72** 184
  Christiana **52** 184
  Clara **55** 36 **61** 398
  Clarence F. **82** 380
  Clarissa **55** 34 **58** 403 **72** 89 101
  Cleora Adelaide Josephine Bonaparte **72** 296
  Clyrana **66** 38
  Cynthia **72** 105
  Dan **72** 75
  Daniel **52** 382 **58** 195 **61** 398 **71** 154 **81** 454

LOOMIS *cont'd*
David **54** 258 **72** 38 168
  136 329
Deborah (Egleston)
  136 329
Desdemonia **83** 99
Desire **120** 160
Diademia **52** 415 **71** 81
  271 281 **72** 44
Dolphorus **54** 256 **56** 163
Dorcas **61** 398 **71** 156 281
  136 329
Dorsey **72** 101
Ebenezer **54** 255 **72** 36 **98**
  302 **126** 86
Edify **61** 398 **147** 68
Edward **96** 381
Edward Eugene **73** 316
  74 xxiv **92** 148 188 199
Eleanor **52** 310 417
Electa **59** 97 **60** 200
  136 274
Electa (Chase) **87** 257
Electa Spafford **66** lxiv
Eliakim **71** 75 87 154 155
  298 **72** 36 169
Elias **65** 93 **80** 189 **89** 246
  147 57
Elias G. **80** 189 **89** 246
Elihu **79** 402
Elijah **52** 182 58 194-197
  402 403 **59** 214 415 **60**
  79 202 262 **71** 83 157
  276 282 **72** 33 34 42 168
  177 **80** 189 **83** 359 **89**
  246 **101** 206
Elijah G. **89** 246
Elijah Griswold **80** 189
Eliphalet **71** 78 155 157-
  160 278 297 300 301 306
Elisha S. **60** 186 402 **61**
  310 398 **86** 352 **90** 385
  92 203 303 **112** 110 **142**
  288 **145** 329 330 332
Elisha Scott **58** xlv **65** 93
  69 xxxii 192
Eliza **111** 128 188
Eliza H. **79** 80
Elizabeth **52** 182 184 308
  309 412 **54** 82 **56** 166
  352 **58** 194 **60** 80 **63** 340
  64 262 **71** 83 156 278 **72**
  74 317 **78** 92 **83** 47 99
  87 198 **108** 190 **109** 309
  123 259 **136** 324
Elizabeth (Fowler)
  123 115
Elizabeth Hawley
  (McLanahan) **97** 92
Elizabeth Mason **61** 340
Elizabeth W. **74** 63
Ellen A. **89** 246
Ellen Holman
  (Farnsworth) **83** 487
Elmira **55** 282 287
Elven **71** 275
Emeline **55** 285
Emeline S. **69** 334
Emily **72** 102
Enos **63** 337 340
Epaphras **72** 204

LOOMIS *cont'd*
Erastus **72** 89
Esther **64** 262 **72** 75 **98** 302
  103 219
Esther (Colt) **145** 330 332
Esther (Eades) **136** 274
Esther A. **64** 251
Eunice **55** 35 **56** 354 355
  63 340 **71** 86 277 282
  299 **72** 33 173 289 **80**
  160 **83** 99 **123** 50 **126**
  172 178 179
Eunice Aurelia **72** 92
Ezekiel **58** 196 **59** 213
Ezial **60** 205
Ezra **52** 183 415 417 **54**
  253-256 **56** 163 **58** 196
  197 **60** 205 **71** 153 296
  123 47
Ezra S. **123** 49
Fanny **75** 259 **79** 151
Fanny (Ford) **133** 25
Farnsworth (Mrs.) **112**
  318 **113** 73
Flora **72** 105
Francis **133** 25
Frank L. **83** 99
Fred **61** 398
Freddie **83** 99
Freedom **71** 44 115
Freeman **58** 206
George **54** 85 **55** 36 **56** 350
  71 277 **72** 43 92 **83** 99
George A. **115** 131
George T. **83** 99 100
Gideon **72** 37
Glenn **91** 246
Grace **71** 154 278 280 **72**
  41 170 **136** 329
Guy **89** 246
H. (Hanchet) **123** 260
H. L. **128** 263
Hannah **52** 181 **54** 253 **56**
  166 307 308 349 352 **57**
  213 **58** 196 **59** 214 60 75
  61 310 **64** 250 **71** 277
  72 179 **83** 99 **92** 203 303
  98 302 **145** 330 332
Hannah (Hunt) **123** 115
Harriet **55** 282 284
Harvey **55** 36 286
Helen Mary **90** 339
Heman **71** 276
Henry **72** 288
Hester **71** 278
Hester (Gillett) **100** 277
Hezekiah **58** 194 401 403
  59 97 416 **60** 79 202 263
  61 143 **71** 157 **83** 365
Horatio **63** 214 **72** 297
Horton **71** 51
Hubbel **68** 334
Huldah **71** 158 281 **72** 32
  126 172
Huldah (Jones) **126** 172
  179
Ichabod **72** 37
Irvin W. **133** 25
Isaac **69** 334 **72** 35 **90** 385
  92 203 **106** 108
Isabel **64** 262 **102** 143

LOOMIS *cont'd*
Isaiah **98** 302
Israel **71** 159 300 **81** 454 **91**
  197 **98** 302 **115** 16 17
  126 86 **145** 332
Jabez **52** 183 311 **56** 163
  353 **83** 99 100
Jacob **52** 311 **71** 81 155
  271 272 274 281 **72** 31
  33 34 44 89 172 179 **83**
  99 100 **86** 161 **89** 258 **91**
  250
James **52** 420 **53** 447 **56**
  165 **79** 80 **83** 99 100
James Angel **79** 80
Jeannette S. **82** 376
Jedediah **71** 278 **72** 37
Jeffrey **112** 116
Jemima **83** 100 **86** 161
Jennet **60** 79 **123** 47
Jennie K. **82** 380
Jerijah **52** 184 308-310 408
  418 **53** 447 **54** 81 83 **55**
  34-37 **56** 163 165 166
  348 349 353 **83** 99 100
  86 161
Jerusha **52** 410 **54** 81 **55** 34
  60 200 201 **68** 334 **71** 77
  79 160 279 **72** 40 179
  118 176
Jesse **71** 277
Jessie Black **110** 149
Joab **71** 308 **72** 31 34 45
  94 95 **90** 162
Joel **52** 183 417 **56** 162
  163 352 **71** 278
John **54** 259 **55** 321 323 328
  329 **57** 384 **58** 403 **59**
  413 **64** 262 **65** 149 **66** 38
  71 75 77 300 302 **72** 34
  80 89 189 **81** 454 **83** 365
  89 246 **92** 188 **98** 302
  100 274 277 **101** 47 48
  115 16 **123** 115 116
John G. **66** 49
John S. **70** 155
John W. **69** 334
Jonathan **64** 250 **136** 325
Joseph **51** 496 **52** 181 417
  53 315 **55** 23-25 28 30
  56 275 **58** 194 402 403
  59 413 415 **60** 74 79 200
  262 **64** xxxi **65** 93 **80**
  186 **81** 454 **83** 365 **89**
  254 **90** 385 **92** 188 203
  303 **100** 277 **104** 308
  108 152 **112** 110 **113**
  229 **142** 288 **145** 329-
  331 **147** 57
Josephine Marion **72** 297
Josiah **58** 384 **72** 36
Julia A. (Card) **133** 25
Julia Anna **72** 89
Julia S. **83** 99
Julianis **55** 287
Justie **60** 78
Justin **148** 283
Keziah **71** 164
L. **72** 42
Lata **58** 403
Laura **55** 38 39

LOOMIS *cont'd*
Laura C. **82** 376
Lauren **82** 376 380
Lawrin **59** 98
Lebbeus **70** 155
Leicester **59** 96 **72** 102
Levi **52** 308 **54** 84 258 259
 55 36-39 283-287 **56** 347
 349 353 354 **58** 194 **83**
 99
Levy **91** 197
Lewis H. **85** 409
Libbeus **65** 149
Lidea (Colt) **147** 384
Lizze **71** 160
Loice **120** 257
Lois **53** 447 **58** 196 402 **60**
 79 200 262 **71** 18 **83** 365
 85 56
Lois (Gaines) (Simons)
 85 56
Lora **105** 66
Love **142** 287 **143** 153
Lowell **72** 168
Lucia **96** 76
Lucinda **60** 202 **136** 312
Lucretia D. **80** 189 **89** 246
Lucretia R. **89** 258
Lucy **54** 256 **70** 155 **71** 279
 74 63 **78** 92 **103** 219
Luke **58** 195 **59** 96-98
 60 80 203
Luna **55** 38
Lyana **58** 196
Lydia **52** 410 412 420 **54**
 81 82 258 **55** 282 284 **56**
 356 **59** 416 **60** 79 **61** 310
 72 40 177 **74** 63 **83** 365
 86 382 **91** 198 **136** 320
 330
Lydia (Marsh) **136** 329
Mabel **52** 410 **54** 84 259
Mahlon **69** 187 192
Marcy **98** 302
Marcy (Colman) **91** 197
Margaret **113** 298 **125** 75
 136 325
Maria **79** 151 **83** 99
Martha **52** 308 309 311
 410 419 **54** 81 84 258 **56**
 166 **60** 402 **65** 371 **83** 99
 90 338
Martha (Osborn) **123** 115
Mary **52** 180 183 311 419
 53 315 **54** 82 83 254 **55**
 23-25 28 30 35 321 323
 326 **56** 166 353 **57** 384
 58 194 **60** 79 402 **61** 143
 71 80 154 280 282 **72** 42
 74 87 170 171 204 **75** 39
 80 189 **83** 100 **89** 246
 98 302 **145** 327 332
Mary (Canney) (Tibbetts)
 98 62
Mary (Chauncey) **90** 385
Mary (Dart) **101** 106
Mary (Huntley) **101** 206
Mary (Jerome) **90** 339
Mary (Sherwood) **90** 385
 92 303
Mary (White) **90** 385

LOOMIS *cont'd*
 103 147
Mary Ann **72** 297 **83** 100
Mary Clarke **72** 100
Mary Elizabeth **86** 200
Mary J. **85** 409
Mary Lucretia **86** 382
Matthew **52** 181 182 184
 308 309 311 408 410 420
 54 84 253-255 259 **55**
 282 **56** 162 166 349 350
 354 **83** 99 100 **88** 321 **90**
 385 **92** 203 **145** 332
Mattie **66** 49
Medad **54** 84
Mercy **108** 45 **115** 16 17
Merrill **136** 274
Mindwell **65** 371 **83** 100
Molly **54** 257 **71** 271 272
 304 **72** 99
Moses **56** 162
Nabby **72** 100
Nancy **58** 402 **72** 104
 89 246
Naomi **54** 84
Nathaniel **52** 180 310 311
 409 **53** 448 **55** 35 **60** 402
 90 162 **98** 62 **123** 279
Nehemiah **123** 263
Norman **83** 100
Olive **58** 197 **71** 115
Olivia **61** 398
Olivia Langdon **92** 189
Owen **64** 262
Patience **60** 74
Patty **54** 85 **55** 36 **106** 108
Phebe **113** 154 **125** 180 239
Phebe (Vinton) **91** 246
Philura **98** 302
Phineas **71** 87
Polly **70** 152
Porter **65** 149
Priscilla **54** 83 **58** 194
 60 79 204
Prudence **52** 308 **54** 84
Rachel **52** 181 182 184 415
 417 420 **53** 449 **58** 194
 197 **60** 79 199 205 262
 71 83 273 **80** 189 **83** 100
 88 321 322 **89** 246
Rachel (Wryte) **88** 321
Ralph **71** 273
Rebecca **71** 154 278 281
 304 **72** 99 104 **98** 302
Reuben **71** 84 87 154 155
 157-159 278 282 296 304
 72 41 101 169
Reuben Harrison **72** 95
Rhoda **108** 46
Richard **64** 262
Riley **89** 365
Robert N. **85** 315
Roger **52** 182-184 308 309
 311 **56** 165 **58** 194-196
 60 73 75 204 **79** 158 **83**
 99 100
Rosel **71** 276
Roswell **60** 80 **87** 257
Roxana Marie **89** 365
 90 74
Roxanna **57** 293

LOOMIS *cont'd*
Roxy W. **82** 380
Royal T. **72** 75
Ruamah **54** 253
Russell **55** 282 **58** 402 **59**
 97 **71** 277 **83** 100
Russell T. **83** 99 100
Ruth **52** 408 418 **54** 81 85
 56 354 **58** 196 **60** 80 **62**
 85 **72** 75 288 289 **83** 105
 145 328 331
Sabra **58** 384
Sally **54** 84 **61** 345 **64** 251
 72 101 **83** 100 **114** 184
Sally M. **83** 100
Salmon **55** 37 **56** 355 **60**
 201 **83** 99 100 365
Sam **123** 259
Samuel **52** 410 415 **55** 36
 56 164 165 **58** 402 **60** 79
 71 77 79 160 277 279 **72**
 38 40 174 **123** 47 260
Sarah **52** 181-184 310 409
 410 418 420 **53** 448 **54**
 81 83 **55** 34 35 **56** 349
 353 **60** 78 80 **61** 310 **71**
 155 **72** 167 **80** 189 **83**
 100 **89** 246 **113** 298 **115**
 43 **145** 332
Sarah (Higley) **136** 325
Sarah (White) **123** 115
 116 279
Sarah A. **52** 382 **72** 75
Sarah Ann **72** 95
Sarah C. **71** 115
Seba **54** 259
Selina M. **89** 258
Seth **71** 278 **72** 35
Sibyl **60** 78 **71** 278 **72** 37
 98 302
Silas **52** 182 **55** 283 **58** 196
 83 359
Silas Lathrop **90** 339
Simeon **72** 36
Simeon L. **79** 151
Simon **74** 63 **86** 382
 92 188
Solomon **52** 183 **53** 449
 58 194-197 **59** 213 416
 60 79 204 262 402 **72** 75
 204 205 **101** 106
Starling **83** 161
Stephen **71** 80 84 87 154
 156-158 163 164 271-273
 275 276 278 280 304 309
 72 33 41 167 **90** 385 **92**
 203 **136** 329 **145** 332
Sterling **73** 40
Susa **83** 161
Susan **73** 40
Susanna **71** 157 **72** 95 **83**
 100 **86** 161
Sylvester **71** 276 **72** 168
Tabitha **60** 402 **61** 310
 71 278
Tabitha (Kingsley) **90** 162
Thankful **136** 333
Thankful (Weller)
 123 263
Thedean **71** 157
Theodosia **71** 78 278 281

LOOMIS *cont'd*
Thomas **52** 180-183 409
  414 415 419 420 **53** 449
  55 35-39 282 **56** 163 165
  354 355 **64** 251 **72** 74 **81**
  454 **83** 99 100 **123** 115
  116 **145** 329 **147** 57
Timothy **71** 276 **72** 43 92
  102
Timothy Dwight **72** 92
Tirzah **55** 284 287 **56** 349
Trumbull C. **133** 25
Tryphena **58** 196 197 **59**
  213 **60** 199 **106** 63
Vielatte (Metcalf) **91** 197
Virginia Langdon **92** 189
Walter W. **71** 47
Warren W. **73** 40 **83** 161
Wealthian **71** 159 **72** 102
Wealthian Ann **72** 92
Welthy **125** 104
William **61** 398 **64** 25 **65**
  371 **72** 101
Zachariah **98** 302 **125** 75
  126 172
Zedekiah **72** 38
Zerviah **54** 83
Zilpah (Hannum) **90** 162
Zuba **72** 36
LOON Patience **84** 96
LOONEY
Robert F. **144** 114
Samuel **111** 208
LOOP Loope
Andrew **79** 417
R. Maria **76** 273
LOOS Louis (Count Of)
  96 42 48
LOOSELY Loosley
Agnes **83** 314
Mary **84** 338
Richard **84** 338
LOPAUS Lopeaus Lopus
Hannah **73** 285
Hannah A. **85** 378
Henry **110** 198
Katie P. **85** 381
Mary A. **78** 397
Melinda R. **85** 372 373
Nancy **73** 285
LOPER Daniel **126** 53
Elizabeth **55** 89
Elizabeth (Trepania)
  91 193
Henry David **81** 57
John **91** 193
Keziah **55** 89
Margaret Baird **88** 79
Mary **91** 193
Ruth **58** 359
Sarah B. **81** 57
Stephen A. **81** 57
William **55** 89
LOPETEGUI
Juana Maria **109** 286
LOPEZ
—— **54** 313 **62** 287
— Mr. **62** 356
— Mrs. **62** 354
Aaron **54** 312 **94** 401
  136 190

LOPEZ *cont'd*
Chloe Ann **78** 353
Dorothy Isabel **83** 425 434
Francis **78** 353
Hannah **126** 141
Jacob **88** 141
Joseph **89** 52 **92** 128
Mary (Harmon) **92** 128
Molly (Knowles) **88** 141
Moses **54** 312 **62** 361
Samuel **88** 141
LOPHAM Mary **67** 175
LOPS Ambrose **65** 26
LORA
Anna Maria (Zeller)
  96 396
John **96** 396
Mary **96** 396
LORAINE
Dorothy M. **97** 210
LORANT Stefan **114** 159
LORD
— Capt. **101** 149 209
— Dr. **118** 109
— Mr. **62** 273 **83** 307
  85 38
— Mrs. **121** 299 **122** 70
— Rev. Mr. **126** 236
— Widow **71** 140 **74** 127
____ (Hussey) **98** 217
____ (Stillman) **140** 327
Aaron **82** 79 206-208 213
  217 314 319 324 327 328
  97 19
Abby L. **108** 187
Abel **78** 368
Abiel **82** 316
Abigail **53** 403 **54** 450 **55**
  373 375 376 **59** 248 **60**
  80 **63** 168 173 178 **74**
  224 259 262 **77** 199 **79**
  387 **80** 434 **81** 59 **82** 77
  78 216 314 327 332 **83**
  14 17 155 **87** 116 **90** 331
  92 55 **102** 303 **107** 305
  108 123 **118** 31 32
Abigail (Goodwin) **83** 17
Abigail Adell **110** 305
Abigail Batrigo **104** 294
Abigail C. **73** 40
Abigail D. **126** 141
Abigail F. **119** 224
Abigail Partridge **128** 80
Abigail T. **109** 15
Abigail W. **109** 15
Abner **51** 96 **65** 220
  78 368 382
Abra **55** 376 **83** 18
Abraham **55** 310 **74** 126
  190 212 213 215 217 219
  82 74 78-80 85 87 88 90
  91 93 210 212-217 312-
  314 316 319 320 322 324
  325 333 500 503 504 507
  83 153 **108** 123 **133** 45
  144 142 **148** 169
Abram **148** 169
Adah **97** 20
Adam **55** 316 **82** 314 **83** 12
  133 218
Addie **135** 18

LORD *cont'd*
Agnes **96** 342 **116** 277
Agrippa **88** 24
Alexander **140** 163
Alice **51** 297
Alice Nancy **110** 305
Alice Tullis **86** 198
Almira **124** 150
Amanda **80** 424
Ambraic **82** 507
Amelia **64** 309
Amelia Bulkeley **90** 275
Ammi Ruhamah **55** 374
  82 314 **83** 15
Amos P. **110** 212
Amy **55** 311 373 **63** 171
  82 85 212 509 **83** 14
Amy (Lassell) **88** 362
  108 122
Andrew **77** 203 **104** 193
Andrew E. **92** 338
Andrew S. **78** 368
Angier W. **110** 305
Ann **73** xxxvi **74** 265
  82 79 324
Anna **55** 315 **74** 226 230
  260 **77** 203 **78** 368 **81** 47
  82 215 327 328 **83** 52
  115 216
Anna (Perkins) **116** 302
Anne **55** 310 **66** 159 **74** 45
  92 95
Anne (Anderson) **91** 108
Anne (Tibbetts) **100** 38
Annie Augusta **97** 300
Annie L. **110** 298
Apphia **74** 264
Arthur **51** 297 **61** xix 91
  62 xxxvii **77** xxiii 78 79
  94 286
Arthur L. **110** 298
Arthur W. **89** 290
Asa **82** 507 **108** 54 **133** 40
  135 19
Augusta **110** 298
Augustus **82** 506 **83** 24
  25 34 307
Augustus J. **78** 368
Azubah **78** 367
B. C. **128** 268
Barnabas **78** 387
Benjamin **55** 374 **59** 413
  65 254 342 **74** 214 220
  224 226 230 251 254 255
  265 **77** 203 **78** 368 **82**
  206 207 209 211 214 314
  316 320 325 **83** 15 **88**
  362 **90** 327 **92** 95 **93** 352
  96 339 **97** 17 **99** 209
  100 38 **107** 274 **108** 122
  111 131 **113** 223 **115**
  213 266 **134** 231 **147** 62
Benjamin Meeds **133** 216
  217
Bertha **76** lxxxvi
Betsey **65** 115 **69** 282 **74**
  255 256 259 261 263 **81**
  59 **87** 85 122 **88** 331 **90**
  247 252 **92** 320 **96** 147
  104 294 **108** 191 **133** 40
Betsey (Campbell) **126** 65

LORD *cont'd*
Betsey Watts **67** 104
Betty **74** 255 **82** 325 **107**
   272 **108** 189 **118** 33
Bridget **74** 226 256 **82**
   207 213 312
Butler **76** 271
C. C. **124** 69 70
C. W. **106** 49 50 **128** 97
Caleb **74** 125 255 **82** 503-
   506
Calvin **64** xxxiv
Caroline **65** 254 313
   101 205
Caroline A. **94** 114
Caroline Matilda (Dam)
   (Dorwin) **111** 50
Catherine **77** 204 207 **82**
   318 **83** 148 **99** 209
Catherine (Junkins)
   115 214
Catherine T. **83** 183 184
Chance **82** 213
Charity **107** 196-200 270
   272
Charles **51** 297 **55** 312 **82**
   86 314 317 321 323 421
   507 509 **83** 34 **113** 223
   134 197
Charles Asaph **113** 222
   223
Charles Austin **96** 78
Charles C. **60** xxxvi
   64 230
Charles E. **107** 129 **110** 304
   113 222
Charles Edward **62** xl
   67 v vi viii xiii xxx 190
   68 v vi x xli **69** v vi ix
   xli **70** xii xxvi **72** 77 158
Charles Edwin **109** 15
Charles Haven **82** 421
   83 34
Charles M. **110** 241 298
Charlotte **74** 194
Charlotte A. (Haven) **83**
   24 25 178 183
Christine **96** 179
Christine (Billings)
   96 179
Christopher **77** 203
   78 368
Clarence J. **110** 298
Clarissa (Junkins) **117**
   144 222
Clement **107** 272 **108** 192
   133 45
Clement Augustus
   133 45
Clifford **118** 72 78
Concurrence **52** 325
Cora E. **110** 299
Cyrus E. **110** 304
Dana Boardman **97** 300
Daniel **56** 90 351 **59** lxiv
   96 413 **60** 198 **65** 115 **74**
   192 218 **78** 387 **80** 424
   82 91 212 314 322 328
   500 **90** 53 **97** 271 273
   108 122 **115** 214 **116** 39
   131 **136** 331

LORD *cont'd*
Daniel (Mrs.) **97** 271 273
Darling **90** 247 **147** 70
David **78** 387 **82** 91 330-
   332 500-502 504 **83** 148
   90 254 **97** 265 270 **107**
   196 272 **133** 40 **134** 225
David Durrell **133** 218
Deborah **52** 480 **78** 370
   110 212
Delia **89** 24
Dorcas **63** 168 171 **74** 182
   230 248 256-258 **82** 207
   312 331 505 **100** 38
Dorcas (Welch) **115** 213
Dorcas Kenney
   (Goodwin) **95** 327
Dorothea **79** 322 323
Dorothy **53** 248 **59** 46
   107 109
Earl Theodore (Mrs.)
   86 231
Eben **109** 112
Eben D. **109** 204
Ebenezer **60** 198 **66** 147 **74**
   186 212 213 215-217 226
   228 229 250 261 **82** 79
   84 211 216 217 312 315
   319 322 324 **100** 148
   109 204 **110** 26 **125** 103
Edith A. **110** 298
Edmond **82** 502
Edmund **55** 374 **83** 15
Edmund B. **88** 287
Edna Waldron
   (Shapleigh) **95** 327
Edward Locke **111** 323
Edward Oliver **64** 134
   97 300
Eleanor A. **92** 338
Eleanor Cordelia
   76 lxxxvi
Eleanor Louisa **52** 394
Eleanor Wellman **92** 338
Eleazer **85** 430 **113** 223
Elias **65** 254 334 337 **74** 256
Elijah **74** 218
Eliphalet **83** 12
Elisha **55** 314 **63** 168 **65**
   149 **71** 277 310 **72** 89 99
   166 168 172 **74** 214 217
   219-221 226 228 229 252
   257 **79** 387 **82** 207 210
   331 **83** 10
Elisha Bidwell **72** 89
Eliza **111** 227
Eliza Abba **110** 299
Elizabeth **52** 480 **55** 313
   372 **57** 88 **59** 248 **61** 117
   65 254 335 337 **66** 218
   220-222 225 295 305 **71**
   310 **74** 213 215 217 224
   253 260 266 **77** 203 204
   78 368 387 **79** 384 387
   82 207 212 293 297 314
   322 326 327 329 331 421
   500 503 504 511 **83** 13
   155 **89** 133 **92** 338 93
   352 **97** 273 366 **99** 27
   107 64 200 **108** 37 121
   109 204 **115** 213 266

LORD *cont'd*
   133 322
Elizabeth (Billings)
   (Tisdale) **93** 352
Elizabeth (Charles)
   111 317
Elizabeth (Clark) **100** 240
Elizabeth (Dunham)
   109 112
Elizabeth (Haggens)
   83 13
Elizabeth (Lougee) **118** 32
Elizabeth (Remick)
   124 69
Elizabeth (Welsh) **88** 287
Elizabeth E. **92** 338
Elizabeth L. **110** 105
Elizabeth P. (Jackson)
   90 50
Elizabeth Susan **82** 421
   83 34
Elizabeth Wellington
   102 319
Ellen Agnes **52** 328 329
Ellen Augusta **68** xxxiv
Elmir T. **110** 298
Elsie **62** lvi
Emanuel **111** 50
Emily **92** 338
Emily Harrington (Esty)
   86 231
Emily Jane (Knight)
   133 218
Emma Augusta **97** 300
Emma Lucretia
   (Woodman) **95** 314
Enoch **74** 259 **77** 203 204
   82 331
Epaphras **80** 434
Ephraim **82** 504 **133** 154
   155
Erastus Abel **78** 367
Ernestine **96** 78
Ernestine (Libby) **96** 78
Erskine D. **121** 236
Erskine Daniel (Mrs.)
   106 125
Esther **55** 312 **69** 132 **74**
   179 195 196 262 **77** 200
   203 204 **82** 322 328 329
   331 332 510 **118** 38
Esther M. **95** 394
Ethan **62** lxxii
Eugene Clifton **110** 298
Eugene Howe **91** 108
Eugenia E. **92** 341
Eunice **55** 376 **74** 247 249
   254 260 264 **82** 209 321
   330 **83** 18 **90** 234 236
   132 269
Eunice (Emons) **95** 199
Eva M. **110** 298
Eva Mabelle **110** 298
Everett L. **110** 298
Experience **52** 420 **60** 204
   63 176 **74** 259 261
Fannie M. (Decker)
   128 268
Fanny B. **69** 282
Fanny Farnham **110** 298
Fidelia **92** 38

LORD *cont'd*
Esther M. **95** 394
Ethan **62** lxxii
Eugene Clifton **110** 298
Eugene Howe **91** 108
Eugenia E. **92** 341
Eunice **55** 376 **74** 247 249
254 260 264 **82** 209 321
330 **83** 18 **90** 234 236
132 269
Eunice (Emons) **95** 199
Eva M. **110** 298
Eva Mabelle **110** 298
Everett L. **110** 298
Experience **52** 420 **60** 204
63 176 **74** 259 261
Fannie M. (Decker)
128 268
Fanny B. **69** 282
Fanny Farnham **110** 298
Fidelia **92** 38
Florence E. **110** 298
Frances **93** 66
Frances (Jones) **93** 61
Frances Ann **93** 66
Frances Blunt **96** 27
Frances Caroline (Ward)
135 74
Frances H. **60** 23
Frances Jane **77** 204
Frances Jones **93** 61 **94** 43
Frances Veazie **69** liii
Francis **135** 18
Frank **95** 37
Fredd **106** 47
Frederick **79** 387
Frederick Augustus
74 211 266
Friend Drake **133** 218
Frost **89** 290 293
George **65** 169 **74** 194 **78**
420 **80** 434 **82** 500
George A. **92** 107 **94** 114
George Boardman **97** 300
George H. **51** 13
George L. **124** 70 **126** 155
George Pease **95** 314
George S. **90** 325 **91** 16
138 322
George Stone **133** 218
Gershom **82** 322 **97** 366
Gertrude Mary **110** 298
Grace **115** 146
Grace Davison **136** 331
Grace Low **110** 298
Granville W. **92** 338
Griswold **69** 379
Grizzel **74** 249
H. C. **128** 268
Hannah **53** 340 **55** 374 **60**
196 198 **63** 176 **65** 115
254 342 **69** 89 **74** 226
251 253 255 256 261 **78**
370 **82** 95 206 500 501
504 505 **83** 14 **90** 233 **96**
200 **107** 272 **118** 32 33
38 **137** 259
Hannah (Blaisdell) **135** 18
Hannah (Durrell) **133** 218
Hannah (Emmons)
95 191

LORD *cont'd*
Hannah (Kilgore)
134 173
Hannah (Light) **118** 32
Hannah (Perkins)
108 189
Hannah (Shackley) **132**
122 269 **133** 41
Hannah (Waterhouse)
104 193
Hannah (Wiswal) **108** 121
Hannah H. **76** 28
Hannah W. **90** 326
Harold M. **82** 257
Harold S. **110** 298
Harriet **77** 204 **78** 368
Harriet Bliss **109** 224
Harriet E. **78** 367
Harriet H. (Hill) **133** 218
Harriet P. **109** 204
Haven E. **92** 338
Haynes **79** 154
Helena **79** 387
Henry **51** 297 **60** 267 **82**
421 **83** 34 **105** 280
Henry A. **122** 149
Henry Augustus **82** 421
Henry C. **95** 327
Henry Dutch **51** 93 96 **52**
96 99 **93** 66 **135** 74
Henry E. **88** 284
Henry Gardner (Mrs.)
84 341 **85** 196
Hepsabeth **96** 344
Hepzibah **77** 203 204
Hervey A. **113** 128 **122** 149
Hester **69** 371
Hezekiah **120** 263
Horace **91** 35
Hosea **97** 372 **98** 57
Huldah **63** 270 **77** 203 **90**
234 **96** 145
Humphrey **55** 374 **74**
213 220 222 230 246 247
250 261 264 **82** 316 332
507 **83** 15 149 **116** 132
Ichabod **55** 372 374 **58** 194
65 254 335 339 **74** 214
255 **82** 319 327 **83** 13 15
Irene A. **88** 24
Isaac **51** 297 **74** 181 194
82 215 320 **119** 281 283
Isaac Morrill **133** 218
Isaac Walker **135** 74
Isaiah **104** 294 **110** 210 212
Ivory **82** 507
Ivory S. **110** 298
J. H. **52** 85
Jabez **55** 313 **77** 181 **82** 91
323 326 328 330 511
Jack **106** 47
Jacob **55** 316 **74** 222 249
263 264 **82** 217 **83** 12
James **53** 338 **55** 376 **57** 88
65 255 **72** 179 **74** 217
248 256 265 266 **76** 46
79 387 **82** 79 92 97 206
208 209 215 217 314 318
320 322 325 **83** 17 153
87 122 **96** 341 **100** 38
110 106 **133** 218

LORD *cont'd*
James Cooper **136** 331
James Freeman **133** 218
James H. **91** 385 **110** 105
106
James K. **69** 282
James Laidley **71** 277
James Monroe **128** 97
James Nicholas **82** 504
James Ralph **110** 298
James T. **109** 15 **110** 298
Jane **56** 351 **63** 178 **74** 214
259 **85** 53 54 **107** 196
197 272 274 **108** 54 **133**
40
Jane (Ayer) **98** 57
Jane (Smith) **133** 40
Jane (Stone) **133** 45
Jane Alma **110** 212
Jane Kirby **85** 54
Jane Stone **133** 45
Jedediah **82** 293 297 321
124 69
Jemima **65** 255 **123** 41 44
Jemima (Davis) **96** 339
Jenny **74** 229 **82** 313 **87**
105 **108** 124
Jenny (Stone) **108** 123
Jeremiah **97** 267
Jeremiah **55** 314 373 **66**
218 220 221 305 **74** 220
249 262 266 **82** 90 323
329-332 501 502 504 507
83 9 13 **91** 206 **100** 38
104 59 294 **105** 212 **115**
226 **117** 143 144
Jeremiah E. **92** 338
Jeremy **66** 222 225 295 **67**
232 233 237 238
Jerusha **80** 434 **82** 257
114 12
Jerusha (Gates) **120** 263
Jerusha (Webster) **114** 12
Joab **55** 374 **83** 15
Joanna **90** 52
Joel **82** 501 **114** 12
John **51** 107 297 **52** 308 417
420 **53** 208 448 **55** 315
373 **56** 21 **59** 248 **65** 243
66 168 295 **69** 89 **74** 130
196 217 260 305 **78** 370
82 46 76 79 83-85 88 92
94 207 208 213 215-217
292 293 312 313 317 321
323 327 329 332 413 500
505 506 **83** 11 13 148
151-153 307 **85** 54 **87**
122 **90** 231 248 **95** 37 **97**
21 **100** 30 239 **104** 61
294 **105** 211 **107** 196-
200 270 272 **108** 284
109 15 **110** 180 **117** 144
222 **118** 31 32 **124** 69
John (Mrs.) **82** 413 **83** 153
John H. **65** 342
John Haynes **79** 387
John Hurd **60** 185
John Knight **133** 218
John M. **77** 203 **83** 173
John McClary **82** 421
John Mills **59** xliv

LORD *cont'd*
  108 121 123 191 **134**
  173 **135** 16 **139** 107 **142**
  54
Joseph E. P. **54** xxxviii
Joseph Nathan **79** 323
Josephine **77** 204
Josephine Caroline
  73 lvii
Joshua **82** 88 **110** 180
  114 294
Josiah **104** 294
Jotham **82** 501
Judith **55** 311 **60** 293 **82**
  76 509 **99** 27
Judith (Conley) **124** 70
  128 37
Julia A. (Sinclair) **91** 385
Julia Ann **77** 204
Julia F. **110** 212
Julia Frances **74** 305
Katharine **51** 297
Katurah **76** 33
Kenneth **98** 147 **99** 338
  100 338 **111** 61 **113** 222
  223 **148** 18
Keziah **74** 250 **82** 87 212
  320
Laura Ann **89** 290
Laura Ann (Cutting) **89**
  290 293
Laura F. **72** 75
Lavina **93** 114
Lawrence **96** 179
Levi **118** 131
Lizzie (McCay) **128** 268
Lizzie O. (Mott) **97** 300
Lois **65** 254 335 339 **113** 81
Loise **55** 372 **83** 13
Loise (Shackley) **83** 13
Louisa **74** 305 **93** 340 **104**
  294 **108** 286 **109** 14 15
Louisa (Bowden) **108** 284
Louisa L. **95** 330 **97** 19
Louise **92** 208
Love **74** 214 224 226 230
  246 262 **82** 320 **110** 180
Lovey **90** 229 248
Lucille Otis **115** 146
Lucinda **60** 200
Lucy **55** 376 **69** 162 282
  74 186 **77** 204 **82** 211
  212 314 326 502 **83** 17
  381 **88** 283 **96** 201 **133**
  216
Lucy (Emery) **83** 17
Lucy (Mitchell) **108** 123
  135 16
Lucy M. (Goodwin)
  122 230
Lucy Maria **83** 194
Lucy Treadwell **60** 198
Luella Leverne **95** 327
Luke **65** 115
Lydia **51** 361 **53** 403 **54**
  450 **55** 374 **63** 171 **69**
  282 **74** 181 189 194 248
  251 255 257 260 **82** 84
  206 209 316 **83** 15 149
  135 16

LORD *cont'd*
Lydia (Buckland) (Brown)
  148 18
Lydia (Daniels) **97** 15
Lydia (Gilpatrick) **97** 17
Lydia (Hezletine) **90** 230
  251
Lydia (Leavit) **83** 15
Lydia (Meserve) **133** 218
Lydia (Perry) **116** 39
Lyman **97** 15
Lyman S. **110** 298
Lynde **136** 318
Margaret **55** 310 374 **66**
  222 **74** 126 182 190 248
  251 266 **82** 76 77 79 85
  87 88 91 321 332 501 **83**
  15 **104** 294 **108** 280 **110**
  299 **115** 227 **125** 287
  137 19
Margaret L. **110** 106
Margaretta Hunter
  (Brown) **136** 331
Margery **55** 313 315 **66**
  261 **82** 206 510 **83** 11
Maria **78** 70
Mariah L. (Davis) **91** 35
Marion Bird (Hannum)
  91 108
Mark **82** 321 **97** 270
Martha **55** 310 311 314 316
  73 315 **74** 186 213 215-
  217 226 228 229 251 264
  266 **79** 55 **82** 75 76 78
  80 85 209 217 323-325
  83 10 13 **90** 52 **92** 78 **99**
  244 **124** 70 **138** 321
Martha (Bragdon)
  110 180
Martha (Emery) **100** 148
Martha (Everett) **144** 142
Martha Hyde **76** lix
Martin **52** 325
Marvin **77** 204
Mary **51** 297 **55** 313-316
  373-375 **56** 90 **60** 364
  63 168 **65** 254 **69** 132
  371 379 **73** 206 **74** 128
  183 215-217 224 226 228
  248-250 257 266 **76** 26
  107 184 259 **77** 204 **79**
  387 **82** 79 80 83-85 87 89
  90 92 95 206 208 214 217
  288 293 318 321 324 327-
  329 331 332 501 504 510
  511 **83** 10-12 14-16 **84**
  126 456 **89** 24 **90** 192
  234 **92** 329 **107** 274 **108**
  54 55 **110** 180 **111** 97
  114 125 **115** 94 136 **116**
  277 **118** 33 **122** 69 **124**
  70 **133** 40 216
Mary (Butler) **97** 234
Mary (Davis) **83** 15
Mary (Davis)
  (Waterhouse) **116** 277
Mary (Dixon) **95** 335
Mary (Dunham) **133** 154
Mary (Frost) **100** 38
Mary (Gerrish) **83** 14
Mary (Hight) **83** 11

LORD *cont'd*
Mary (Huntriss) **83** 12
Mary (Lord) **133** 40
Mary (Lyman) **136** 318
Mary (March) **133** 216
Mary (Norton) **116** 298
Mary (Preston) **137** 259
Mary (Smith) **123** 258
Mary (Struble) **128** 97
Mary (Tupper) **99** 297
Mary (Washborne)
  108 122
Mary (Waterhouse)
  97 228 233
Mary (Welch) **90** 327
Mary (Wise) **133** 216
Mary (Wright) **133** 218
Mary A. **85** 167 **97** 300 301
Mary A. (Marshall)
  122 149
Mary Abby **97** 301
Mary Abby Stevens
  97 300
Mary Adeline (Polk)
  110 297 306
Mary Ann **90** 333
Mary Ann (Marshall)
  113 128
Mary B. **69** 96
Mary Chesebrough
  81 176
Mary D. (Smith) **97** 236
Mary Durrell **133** 40
Mary E. (Allen) **91** 35
Mary Edith **92** 338
Mary Elizabeth **77** 181
  82 421 **83** 173 183 184
  133 45
Mary F. **95** 335
Mary Jane **137** 77
Mary Ladd **82** 508
Mary P. **93** 300
Mary Pease **69** 320 333
Mary R. **94** 59
Mary S. **73** 41
Mary Sheldon **136** 318
Mary Stinson (Pillsbury)
  112 151
Mary W. G. (Stevens)
  97 299
Mary Y. **77** 204
Matthew **77** 204
Mattie H. **74** 211
Mehitable **55** 373 **83** 13
  148 151 152
Mehitable (Perkins) **83** 13
Mehitable (York) **90** 231
  248
Mehitable Smith **71** li
Mercy **63** 176 **66** 138
  74 254 258
Meribah **55** 314 373 **63** 168
  82 90 207 330 **83** 9 13
Micajah **65** 254 342
Minerva **98** 231
Minnie E. **110** 298
Miriam **55** 280 **71** 202
  111 317 **132** 122
Miriam (Thorn) **97** 21
Molly **55** 374 **66** 221 225
  74 251 252 **76** 111 186

LORD *cont'd*
  82 210 83 15 155 107
    270 272
Molly (Durrill) 108 123
Molly (Frost) 83 15
Morris E. 110 304
Moses 55 315 82 79 80
    207 208 210 216 315 323
    326 83 156
Myra 147 80
Myra B. 87 401
Myra B. (Horn) 97 300
Myra Belle 64 232
Myra E. (Barrett) 91 385
Nabby 74 198 261 76 186
Nancy 55 372 69 320 74
    194 82 272 83 13 109 15
    110 105 116 304 118 93
Nancy A. 110 106
Nancy B. 110 112
Nancy D. 82 421 83 34
Nathan 55 312 313 65 254
    342 71 202 74 179 180
    182 195 196 215 254 256
    82 74 76-79 84-88 93
    204 206 211 257 313 316
    317 319 322 324-329 331
    332 500 501 503 506 509-
    511 83 13 17 148 149
    111 20 110 223 115 214
    124 69 70 128 37 132
    122 140 68 144 142
Nathan Augustus 82 508
Nathaniel 55 372 376 62
    lvi 74 192 215 81 59 268
    82 76 207 213 216 83
    154 91 328 108 189
Nathaniel J. 51 367
Nehemiah 82 288 293
Newton 109 15 110 299
Nicholas 55 312 74 224
    253 260 82 87 313 321
    325 327 510 145 349
Noah 74 250 75 253 82 315
    95 335
Noah Emery 95 327
Olive 55 312 313 316 373
    374 63 176 65 254 342
    74 214 220 222 230 246
    247 250 255 263 305 82
    46 292 293 321 322 325
    329 506 509 510 83 12-
    14 87 173 91 232 95 326
    103 161 104 294 109
    255 115 223
Olive (Hodsden) 83 14
Olive (Knight) 83 12 90
    325 91 16 133 218 138
    322
Olive Eliza 95 326
Olive Mary 110 298 306
Oliver 55 376 73 40 41
    83 17
Oliver H. 97 299 300
Olivia Anderson 100 110
Oravilla C. 94 37
Orlando Marcellus
    56 xxxiv
Oswald Bates 112 151
Owen Martin 102 124
Patience 55 311 374 62 123

LORD *cont'd*
  65 254 74 230 251 82 76
    84 86 97 206 207 315 316
    329 83 15 111 23 114 47
Patience (Nason) 92 95
Patience (Paul) 83 15
Patty 55 373 83 13
Patty (Marshall) 83 13
Paul 74 255 82 212 91 35
Paulina 65 260
Paulina K. 97 21 238
Pearl W. 110 298
Peggy 55 374 63 176 74
    262 83 15 124 69
Persia (Ramsdell) 117
    222 223
Peter 78 367 368 82 210
    101 304
Phebe 82 312 330 331 500-
    502 504 85 152 107 270
Phebe (Crary) 136 331
Phebe (Walker) 108 189
Phebe Ann P. (Bragdon)
    117 222
Phebe Griffin 77 204 208
Philip 110 205
Philo 110 241
Philomela 55 374 83 15
Philomela (Emery) 83 15
Philura H. 123 92
Polieme 74 261
Polly 55 376 60 198 63 176
    74 258 262 265 83 17 90
    232 252 96 146 98 297
Polly (Chadbourn) 83 17
Polly (Fairfield) 108 191
Priscilla 74 253 96 144 339
    98 231
Prudence 55 313 76 271
    82 323 330 332 333 501
    502 511 118 240 242
R. 82 218
Rachel 68 287 69 132 376
    79 387 80 434
Ralph 106 47
Ralph W. 92 332 338
Rebecca 53 208 67 43
Rebecca (Dennis) 133 322
Rebecca Jane 113 302
Renold 77 204
Reuben 78 368 385
Richard 51 297 55 106 373
    56 90 61 117 163 63 168
    65 125 254 76 107 111
    184 186 259 77 203 204
    79 387 82 79 84 85 87
    89-91 97 208 316 326 83
    14 104 294 105 211 108
    37 123 258 148 24-26
Robert 51 58 56 181 335
    68 174 287 69 132 371
    372 93 32 34 38 89 93
    125 26 135 74 142 51 52
Robert W. 135 74
Robert Waterston 63 113
Roger 55 316 82 313 83 12
Rosamond 55 xxxii
Royce E. (Mrs.) 114 297
Rufus 104 294
Rufus S. 76 lix
Russel H. 110 304

LORD *cont'd*
Russell D. 72 75
Ruth 52 308 417 420 55
    312 316 56 411 60 204
    65 254 335 74 214 224
    256 82 321 325 327 510
    83 12 90 328 96 147 248
    99 247
Ruth (Beal) 83 12
Ruth (Perkins) 110 212
Ruth (Richardson)
    125 103
Ruth G. (Hooper) 97 19
Sabra Julia 62 lxxii
Sally 55 375 74 63 254
    257 262 265 82 369 83
    16 90 231 248 107 272
    108 189 192 148 169
Sally (Demerit) 90 254
Sally (Noble) 95 37
Sally (Snowman) 117
    143 144
Sally (York) 90 247
Samuel 55 310 56 156 67
    43 69 132 372 74 181-
    183 186 188 194 196 215-
    217 224 226 255 262 78
    312 82 75 76 78 79 81 84
    85 89 92 95 97 206 207
    212 214-217 312 314 318
    321 325 333 421 422 505
    83 34 153 307 87 207 90
    230 251 92 239 338 95
    86 190 104 193 124 70
    126 254 140 163 327
    143 37 145 163
Samuel O. 80 434
Samuel Philips 80 434
Samuel S. 116 298 122 230
Samuel Smith 95 314
Sarah 51 297 54 450 55 310
    312-314 374 60 53 198
    295 61 201 65 115 254
    342 66 147 69 89 73 306
    74 217-221 224 226 228
    229 249 250 253 254 262
    266 75 89 78 183 368
    370 385 79 154 82 74 79
    80 84 92 97 206 209 215
    216 314 323 328 330-332
    504 509 511 83 9 10 15
    154 84 422 92 109 93
    340 95 199 201 324 97
    234 235 99 209 107 198
    108 188 109 15 110 180
    115 58
Sarah (Abbot) 90 247
Sarah (Clevs) 95 86
Sarah (Drew) 95 190
Sarah (Durrell) 108 192
    133 45
Sarah (Gill) 88 284
Sarah (Hambleton) 83 9
Sarah (Hill) 96 341
Sarah (Hubbard) 83 15
Sarah (Kirk) 100 239
Sarah (Quimby) 88 24
Sarah (Shackley) 83 10
Sarah (Spelman) 133 218
Sarah (York) 90 231
Sarah Ann 73 xxxvi

LORD *cont'd*
111 227
Sarah Auuusta **110** 298
Sarah Boyd (Stevens)
133 218
Sarah Frances **86** 119
Sarah Jane **97** 235
Sarah Kimball **133** 45
Sarah M. (Frizzell) **94** 59
Sarah Mehitable **82** 422
83 34
Sarah Pierson **85** 430
Sarah W. **78** 368
Seth **101** 57
Seth B. **91** 385
Sewell B. **109** 15 **110** 298
Shebe **82** 332
Shuah **55** 372 **83** 13
Sibyl **125** 43
Sidney **91** 201
Sila **98** 231
Simeon **63** 176 **65** 11 256
334 338 **74** 258 **82** 319
323 **93** 397 **97** 268 **100**
63
Simeon Locke **133** 218
Simon **74** 251 **82** 77 79 216
319 504 **90** 260
Solomon **52** 308 **71** 202
82 93
Solomon E. **123** 313
Sophia **56** 308 **65** 254 **82**
507 508 **83** 150 153 **96**
337
Sophia Elizabeth **94** 291
Stephen **60** 364 **76** 107
82 93 **95** 191 **133** 322
Stillman **92** 335 338
Susan **65** 254 **102** 67
108 169
Susan (DeForest) **136** 331
Susan Durrell **133** 45
Susan H. **65** 342
Susan Hayes **82** 508
91 232
Susan M. (Marshall)
90 53
Susanna **55** 310 374 375
56 156 318 **72** 99 **76** 184
82 217 500 506 **83** 15 17
148 **116** 130 **144** 142
Susanna (Dearing)
108 188
Susanna (Hezelton)
90 250
Susanna (Morse) **135** 74
Sylvanus **77** 203
Sylvester **91** 108
T. **77** 84
T. N. **64** 132
Temple **93** 114 **113** 302
117 222
Thankful **62** lxxii
Theodosia **72** 166 **74** 264
Theophilus **52** 480
78 370 371
Thomas **53** 248 403 **54** 450
55 313 **69** 89 **70** xlix **74**
127 220 221 **76** 111 **77**
200 204 **82** 83 314 318
321 326 328 329 331 332

LORD *cont'd*
510 **83** 154 **86** 270 **93** 61
66 **94** 43 **95** 199 **97** 228
233 234 **99** 27 338 **100**
240 269 338 **107** 109 272
274 **108** 54 55 123 **110**
180 **111** 317 **113** 223
116 277 **118** 38 **133** 40
216 217
Thomas Knowlton
64 309
Thomas N. **99** 297
Tirzah **74** 228 260 **100** 148
Tobias **67** 190 **82** 85 207
211 217 313 **87** 206 **107**
196 **108** 188 189 **133** 40
41 44 216
Tobias (Mrs.) **83** 155
Tozier **63** 171 172 175 **82**
88 **100** 38 **103** 161
Violet **55** 373 **63** 172 **83** 14
Virginia Justine **92** 338
Waitstill **133** 155
Wallace Dow **110** 106
Walter **82** 81 82
Walter A. **89** 290
Walter H. **85** 167
Walter T. **85** 167
Warren **90** 50
Wentworth **65** 254 **74** 215
William **51** 297 361 **53** 403
54 450 **59** 46 63 176 270
65 115 149 **66** 159 **74**
216 248 256 259 266 **76**
28 **77** 203 **78** 368 **79** 387
80 427 434 **82** 80 92 209
216 502 **87** 116 206 **90**
231 247 **93** 8 **110** 105
113 223 **116** 302 **117**
222 223 **118** 32 **124** 70
137 259
William A. **97** 236
William B. **90** 33
William C. **80** 434
William Crofford
76 lxxxvi
William E. **92** 338
William G. **69** xxxii 96
109 158
William H. **94** 59
William Reuben (Mrs.)
109 130
William S. **109** 15
William Wentworth
74 216
Willis **52** 329
Wilmot **110** 212
LORDINGE
George **57** 316 317
LORE —— **61** 100
Auley **66** 366
Charles B. **59** lxi **66** 367
Eldad **66** 366 367
Jane **66** 366
LOREE
Elizabeth **53** 232
Leonor Fresnel **89** 132
LORENZ Annette (Lewis)
96 160
Lewis (Mrs.) **96** 160

LORESEN
Abiel Paige **132** 38
Cornelius **132** 38
LORETZ
Catherine A **95** 164
LOREY Emanuel **142** 120
LORIMER Grace **96** 385
Thomas **83** 322
LORIN Carolina **128** 172
LORING Loringe
— Capt. **77** 63 65 98 100
84 371 372
— Commodore **84** 163
— Maj. **85** 21
— Mr. **98** 166
____ (Bradford) **140** 43
____ (Lovell) **140** 164
____ (Perkins) **140** 235
Abigail **79** 390 **113** 169
143 137
Abigail (Wood) **118** 140
Abigail W. **118** 140
Abner **81** 313 **113** 138
Alathea **115** 235
Alathea (Hall) **115** 235
Alden **89** 67
Aletha (Alden) **129** 170
Alethea (Drinkwater)
83 342
Alice (Honor) **143** 135
Alida (Mattson) **97** 124
Almira **116** 256
Angelica **75** 36
Ann **80** 329 **85** 120 **92** 131
259 **100** 33 134
Ann (Greely) **85** 3
Ann (Sharp) **88** 342
Ann Sophia **81** 313
Anna **92** 352 355 358 **93** 66
94 42 **108** 207 **143** 139
Anna (Alden) **84** 323
Anna (True) **127** 68 70
Anna (Vickery) **143** 46
139 343 346
Anna A. **79** 52
Anna Pierce (Brace) **85** 3
Anna Powell **72** xx
Arthur Greene **51** 239 243
52 52 101 **53** 385 388 **54**
xxxvi 387 **55** xxix 116
443 **56** xxx **57** xxxi 223
335 350 **58** xliii 48 101
125 322 **59** vii xli 104
144 216 418 **60** vii xxvi
xxxiv **61** vii xxxiii 94
151 **62** vii xxxv 58 150
308 **63** vii 96 **64** vii xii
78 **65** vii xxxiii 83 187
66 vii xlviii **67** vii xxx
68 vii xxx **69** vii xxx 90
70 vii **71** vii **72** vii **73**
vii **74** vii **75** vii **82** 382
83 230 **84** 195 232 323
Asa **88** 150 248
Augustin L. **118** 141
Augustus Peabody **73**
317 **74** xxiv **85** 5 **88**
397 **92** 294 392 393 **93**
139 **94** 139 **106** 62 130
144 145 **107** 131

LORING cont'd
Augustus Peabody (Mrs.)
   99 154 **100** 117
Barbary **100** 236
Barbary (Murphy)
   100 303
Becky **139** 97
Benjamin **58** 175 **78** 41
   84 323 **121** 17 125 279
   140 163 164 **142** 124
   125 **143** 46 47 135-137
   139 255 343 345 346 **144**
   266
Betsey **118** 139 140 **126** 220
   139 97
Betsey (Chase) **88** 114
Betsey (Condry) **126** 65
Betsey White (Faxon)
   84 323
Bezaleel **88** 153
Braddock **92** 117 **94** 41
   140 163 327
C. G. **93** 66 **94** 42
C. W. **93** 256
Caleb **55** 163 390 422 **78** 41
   80 329 **85** 3 **92** 122-125
   131 248 253 259 393 **93**
   326 **94** 156 297 **113** 45
   47 **125** 223 **140** 162 163
   247 **142** 125 **143** 49 127
   130 136-138
Caleb Gould **74** 309 **78** 41
Caleb L. **94** 42
Caleb P. **140** 163
Caleb William **52** 381 **85**
   3 **92** 352 392
Calop G. **103** 269
Carl **73** 41
Caroline **94** 157
Caroline M. **90** 384
   140 164
Catherine Peabody
   93 256
Charles **99** 128 **120** 86
Charles G. **52** 381 **92** 352
   355 358 **94** 160 **140** 163
Charles Greely **85** 3 **92**
   123 **93** 66
Charles Greely (Mrs.)
   96 395
Charles Harding **61** 217
Charles P. **65** xxxiv
Charlotte **74** liii **85** 196
Charlotte (Buck) **108** 264
Charlotte (Hay) **126** 141
Chloe (Draper) **118** 140
Clarissa **75** 214
Clayton **91** 193
Cordelia **96** 190
Cordelia O. **118** 141
Cornelia **79** 49 **108** 210
Cornelia (Amory)
   (Goodard) **120** 86
Daniel **57** 367 **65** 149 **84**
   323 **90** 400 **118** 139-141
   143 138
David **127** 68 **143** 136 139
   346
David C. **125** 42
David Haws **108** 207
David Webster **74** 309

LORING cont'd
78 41
Deborah **58** 26 27 175 **78**
   180 **86** 100 **94** 41 **104**
   314 **118** 141 **121** 124
   136 122 **143** 46 49 136
Deborah (Cushing) **84**
   323 **143** 136
Delia **91** 193
Desire **114** 3
Dexter H. **118** 141
Dolly **118** 139-141
Dorothy (Pitman) **88** 337
Ebenezer **90** 384
Edward **93** 316
Edward G. **53** 156 157
Edward I. **143** 133
Edward Payson **124** 72
Edward Wells **108** 260
Eleanor J. **88** 333
Elisha **108** 264
Eliza (Ayres) **118** 141
Eliza A. **75** 214
Eliza G. (Browning)
   90 49
Eliza P. (Orcutt) **125** 220
Elizabeth **55** 305 **62** 199 **78**
   415 **92** 15 **93** 256 **94** 160
   106 145 **113** 138 **118**
   275 276 **121** 192 **126**
   220 **134** 297 **140** 163
   143 49 139
Elizabeth (Baker) **142** 125
   143 138
Elizabeth (Bourne)
   118 276
Elizabeth (Collier) **143**
   131 139 361 365
Elizabeth (Cushing)
   113 138
Elizabeth (Goold) **143** 46
Elizabeth (Hayden)
   126 220
Elizabeth (Howe) **139** 97
Elizabeth (Lloyd) **130** 216
Elizabeth (Otis) (Allyne)
   143 136
Elizabeth (Prince) **129** 36
   38 **143** 135 249 250
Elizabeth (Tupper) **99** 128
Elizabeth A. **109** 39
Elizabeth Ann **90** 105
Elizabeth Anner **108** 209
Elizabeth B. (Bronsdon)
   126 68
Elizabeth Smith
   (Peabody) **85** 3 4
Ellen (Gardner) **106** 144
Ellen Gardner **106** 145
Elsa Eldredge **94** 299
Elsey (Hamden) **118** 140
Emily **73** 41
Emma **83** 332 342
Emma J. **75** 214
Emma Teresa **74** 309
   78 41
Ernest **136** 158
Ernest Johnson **56** xxxv
   57 xxxv
Esther **75** 214
Esther Coffin **108** 260

LORING cont'd
Eunice **92** 17 **113** 259
   122 59
Experience **143** 49 139 140
Experience (Collier) **142**
   358 **143** 140 365
Ezekiel **113** 260
Frances **93** 316
Francis C. **78** 189 **140** 235
Francis Caleb **52** 381 **92**
   131 248 **93** 375
Francis G. **140** 163
Francis M. **90** 384
Frank Edward **78** 41
George B. **53** 53
George Bryant **75** 214
George F. **60** 187
George H. **88** 342
George Henry **108** 210
Gertrude **93** 375
Gilbert Lyon **91** 193
Hannah **67** 211 **84** 163 **88**
   150 248 **90** 384 **118** 139
   140 **121** 117 280 **134**
   297 **141** 221 385 **143**
   135 136 139 140
Hannah (Jackson)
   130 216
Hannah (Jacob) **84** 323
   143 135 136 138
Hannah (Leavitt) **121** 213
   143 138
Hannah (Vickery) **127** 68
   143 346
Hannah B. **90** 384 **126** 208
Harold Angellotti **74** 309
   78 41
Harriet **74** 309 **78** 41
Harriet B. (Lee) **125** 291
Harriet Boott **53** 157
Harrison **62** 213
Helen (Swope) **91** 193
Helen Curtis **92** 125
   93 326
Henry **75** 214 **125** 65 **126**
   141 **140** 164
Henry W. **90** 49
Hiram **108** 208
Innocent **94** 299
Isaac **88** 114 **121** 11 14 17
   119 **143** 135 138
Isabel **110** 186
Isannah Elizabeth **92** 259
   94 156
Israel **56** 36 **61** 124 **65** 358
   75 37 **84** 272 **87** 398 **92**
   13-15 17 19 21 **93** 195
   140 43 163 **143** 133 134
   137
Jacob **143** 138
James **118** 141 **136** 37 **143**
   131 139
James G. **125** 287
James L. **75** 36
James S. **99** 8
James Speare **72** 80 **143**
   133 135 334 **145** 223
James T. **78** 181 **140** 34
Jane **78** 41 **92** 110 227 **121**
   115 **129** 36 38 **140** 163
   143 49 140

LORING cont'd
Jane (Baker) **142** 125 **143**
138 140 365
Jane (Collier) **142** 358
143 47 49 140 365
Jane (Goold) **143** 48 49
Jane (Lathrop) **140** 162
Jane (Newton) **84** 323
130 216 **143** 134 250
Jane A. **118** 141
Jane B. **90** 384
Jane Gray **106** 145
Jane Lathrop **92** 355
94 160
Jane T. **94** 42
Jean **143** 47
Jean (Goold) **143** 49
Jennie **86** 369
Jenny (Hunt) **85** 128
Jessie May (Lyon) **91** 193
Joanna **79** 182
Job **90** 51 **121** 124
John **53** 429 430 **62** 199
78 313 **85** 3 128 **99** 79
100 33 134 236 303 **108**
207-210 259 260 **109** 42
43 **113** 45 47 **118** 139
141 **121** 107 108 **139** 97
140 163 **142** 116 117
122-125 276 351 358 359
143 127 133-135 137-
140 334 345 361 365 **145**
168
John A. **79** 90
John Arthur **56** xxxii **60**
187 **72** 80 **143** 133
John B. **143** 135
John Coffin **108** 260
John F. **140** 163
John G. **125** 289
Jonathan **107** 313 **121** 194
125 220 **130** 43 **140** 164
143 49 140
Jonathan Hurd **75** 214
Jonathan T. **126** 119
Joseph **59** 374 **63** 76 **93** 39
100 63 **112** 267 **118** 139
140 **121** 111 213 214 277
125 223 **127** 68 70 **139**
97 **140** 31 164 **141** 221
222 225 226 **143** 138
144 102
Joseph B. **90** 384
Joseph Gray **123** 159
Joshua **84** 256 260 377 **88**
335 337 **94** 299 **112** 269
121 273 **125** 220 **130**
216 276 **136** 283 **140** 43
163 **143** 135
Josiah **91** 328 **121** 118 122
192 285 **129** 36 38 **143**
135 249 250
Jotham **130** 276
Judah **84** 323
Judith **126** 204
Judy Williams (Elwell)
125 223
Julian **85** 386
Julian (Cowes) **85** 386 387
Katharine (Page) **96** 395
Katharine Peabody **72** 80

LORING cont'd
85 5 **100** 107 **143** 133
Keziah **61** 22 **139** 97
Larus **145** 168
Leah **121** 273
Leah (Buckland) **143** 138
Lemuel **113** 131
Levi **99** 201 **113** 169 **115**
235 **122** 59
Lindsley **86** 197 **104** 314
Lindsley (Mrs.) **74** liii
Louisa Putnam **85** 5
Love (Rand) **125** 223
Luce **143** 49
Lucinda Alden **51** 103
89 67
Lucious Augustin
118 140
Lucious Pitts **118** 140
Lucy **53** 431 **57** 367 **92** 376
108 168
Lucy (Parker) **113** 260
Lydia **88** 150 153 **100** 33
107 262 **113** 260 **118**
139 **120** 281 **125** 290
141 142
Lydia (Fiske) **141** 221
Lydia (Gray) **143** 136
Lydia (Landell) **143** 140
Mabel Velma **78** 41
Mabethe C. **118** 141
Marcy **143** 49 140
Margaret **77** 231 **126** 119
140 163
Margaret (Beaupel)
110 186
Margaret (Smith) **88** 335
Maria C. **88** 337
Maria L. (Bradford)
123 159
Marjorie Angellotti **78** 41
Martha (Melton) **143** 131
Martha (Rand) **125** 289
Mary **59** 373 **78** 406 **88** 214
92 14 17 **110** 31 **113** 47
118 139-141 **121** 121
125 292 126 208 **140**
163 164 **143** 43 47 48
127 136 138 139
Mary (Bacor) **121** 107
Mary (Baker) **113** 47 **143**
127 135 137 138
Mary (Breck) **113** 169
Mary (Curtis) **130** 216
Mary (Dillaway) **125** 287
Mary (Freeman) **84** 323
Mary (Hartshorn)
126 206
Mary (Hawke) **121** 125
143 47 135 139
Mary (Hayman) **143** 138
Mary (Thayer) **84** 323
Mary Ann **55** 422 **92** 122
Mary Margaret **104** 314
Mary Richmond **88** 150
Mason **75** 36
Matilda (Pitts) **118** 140
Matthew **70** 263 **90** 384
125 104 106 **140** 164
142 358 **143** 49 136 140
May Bowditch **106** 145

LORING cont'd
Melinda **75** 36
Mercy **90** 384
Mercy (Bates) **125** 106
Meribah (Ellis) **122** 59
Mira (Ellis) **122** 59
Nancy **59** 374 **90** 384
Nancy (Floyd) **90** 384
Nancy (True) **127** 68 70
Nathan **61** 22
Nathaniel **112** 178 **126** 220
143 138
Nathaniel Thomas **118**
139-141
Nathaniel W. **79** 182
Nehemiah **55** 305 **121** 269
Nele **110** 186 188
Nicholas **62** 277 **104** 242
143 133
Olive **86** 294
Otis **113** 18
Pearl Dow **109** 182 183
Peleg **118** 141
Perez **140** 163
Polly **92** 117 **132** 277
Polly (Selsbry) **140** 163
Polycarpus **113** 169
Prescott **74** 309 **78** 41
Priscilla **53** 429 **118** 141
Priscilla (Mann) **143** 138
Rachel **53** 394 **143** 138 140
Rachel (Bradford) **140** 163
Rachel (Wheatley)
(Buckland) **85** 3 **143**
135 137 138
Rebecca **106** 306 **113** 137
138 **118** 141 **125** 290
143 139
Rebecca (Lobdell) **85** 3
143 138
Richard **118** 140
Rollin S. **118** 141
Rosamond (Bowditch)
106 145
Rose **106** 145
Russell **90** 42
Ruth **53** 429 **78** 207 **94** 297
118 141 **125** 218
Ruth (Sturtevant) **118** 141
Sally **118** 139 140
Sally (Johnson) **125** 220
Sally Lewis **108** 207
Samuel **78** 41 **79** 45 **121**
122 195 **142** 358 **143** 47-
49
Samuel G. **118** 141
Sarah **53** 394 **54** 317 **90** 384
93 195 319 **113** 138 **118**
141 **121** 116 277 **125**
105 223 290 **140** 164
143 49 138 139
Sarah (Blake) **90** 384
125 104
Sarah (Bradford) **85** 3
Sarah (Lewis) **143** 138
Sarah (Watson) **118** 139
140
Sarah (Young) **143** 138
Sarah Ann (Huff) **90** 51
Sarah Elizabeth **118** 141
Sarah Francis **80** 329 **92**

LORING *cont'd*
253 **94** 156
Sarah Stewart **75** 214
Sarah T. **88** 332
Simeon **118** 140
Simeon W. **118** 141
Solomon **83** 342
Sophia **108** 246
Sophia B. **75** 37
Sophia Stetson **81** 313
Submit **121** 277
Susan Mary **92** 358
Susan Mason **71** 287
Susan Mason (Lawrence)
85 5
Susan Sophia **74** 309
78 41
Susanna (Breck) **143** 138
Susanna (Butler) **143** 138
Susanna (Cocks) **143** 138
Sylvia **118** 141
T. **85** 23
Theodore **118** 139 140
Thomas **60** 187 **72** 11 **78**
41 **84** 323 **85** 3 **92** 392
106 144 **113** 260 **115**
265 **118** 139 140 **121** 18
107 112 113 124 270 **124**
72 **130** 216 **139** 129 **142**
110 115 116 279 280 351
354 359 **143** 133-140 250
254 343 346 **144** 266
Thomas B. **126** 206
Thomas Coffin **108** 259
Thomas Robson **92** 21
Thomas W. **118** 141
William **125** 291 **128** 9
129 163 170 **140** 163
William Caleb **77** lxxxiii
78 311 **84** 181 **85** 3 106
204 **92** 392 **106** 144 145
William Deane **108** 209
William Henry **75** 214
William Joseph **92** 124
William P. **90** 384
William Stowell **74** 309
78 41
Zubah **118** 141
LORINI
Domenico Bragioni
90 224
Raffaele **90** 223
Raffaele (Mrs.) **90** 223 224
99 266
LORK Ann **55** 413
Lorkin *see* Larkin
Lorkyn *see* Larkin
LORMAN
Esther May **114** 180
Mary **114** 180
LORMEIASSE
Isabeau **98** 370
LORNE Charles **83** 173
John **83** 307
LORNEL Hannah **58** 19
61 307
LORRAINE C. E. **117** 78
LORRANE Mary **116** 119
LORREY
Emma C. **69** 204
Mary Ann **72** 303

LORRIMORE
George **62** 248
LORRY Martha **126** 205
LORT —— **52** 135 **53** 15
LORTE Lawrence **80** 88
Lorthrop *see* Lothrop
LORY Mable Geraldine
133 269
LOS SALDIVIA
Catalina de **109** 290
LOS SANTOS
Isabel de **107** 224
LOSARES Andrew **78** 301
LOSAW David **116** 206
LOSE Elizabeth **108** 24
LOSEE Elizabeth **105** 62
LOSELER P. **143** 222
LOSEY Jane **112** 227
John **112** 227
John P. **98** 49
Sarah (Wood) **98** 49 79
LOSHBROOK
Phebe **76** 264
LOSIER
Hannah **110** 116
Philip **55** 329
LOSSING
Benjamin **130** 208 209
Benson J. **59** 121
John **130** 208
Miriam (Dorland)
130 208
LOSSLYN Eliza (Huntley)
101 206
LOT Ferdinand **105** 292
LOTH Anne Marie **97** 68
LOTHER Elizabeth **66** 73
LOTHERON
Deborah **73** 224
LOTHIAN Hannah **85** 381
LOTHROP Lorthrop
—— **51** 301 **56** 221 **59** 332
95 45 330 **112** 194 **119**
264 296 **120** 99 209
— Capt. **101** 44 **125** 27
— Col. **122** 51
— Dr. **65** 368 370 **92** 128
130
— Miss **79** 299
— Mr. **55** 149 **57** 228 229
65 366 **67** 46 **95** 43 44
47 48
— Mrs. **79** 298 **112** 191
— Rev. Dr. **92** 344
— Widow **81** 360
Abigail **72** 75 **86** 447 **97**
276 **102** 301 **112** 261
263 **127** 254
Agnes **126** 141
Agnes (Patterson)
125 289
Albert **85** 314
Alden **69** lx
Aletha **76** 266
Alice (Bacon) **90** 356
Alice (Chubbuck) **134** 174
Alice Putnam **82** 497
Alice Putnam (Bacon)
136 312
Alvin M. **72** xlviii
Amanda **86** 382

LOTHROP *cont'd*
Amy **94** 137 **100** 2
Amy Peabody **77** 300
90 356
Anna **97** 277
Anne **51** 297 **84** 438
Anne Avery (Parker)
113 257
Anne M. **74** xxiv
Anne Maria (Hooper)
77 300 **85** 106 **90** 355
136 312
Annie **56** 184 **71** 119 **72** 75
Ansel **93** 253
Anselm **93** 123 **94** 163
Asenath (Spear) **120** 50
Aurelia **72** 74 75
Azariah **84** 85
Azariel **65** 147
Barnabas **86** 455 456 **87** 50
112 193 **119** 170 **124** 55
143 340
Bartholomew **54** 92 93
Bathsheba **86** 456 **87** 277
102 48 51
Bathshua **86** 456 457
87 277
Benjamin **52** 423 **71** 202
86 382 **96** 390 **99** 289
100 2 **101** 99 **102** 75
112 261 **113** 174
Benjamin H. **71** 202
Benjamin Harvey **80** 42
Bethiah **65** 319 **125** 133
127 254 **133** 234
Betsey **71** 202 **80** 42 **86** 382
Betsey (Crane) **125** 288
Caroline **89** 258
Carrie A. **89** 351
Charity **120** 266
Charity (Perkins) **120** 266
Charles **125** 290
Charles Lowell **93** 123
Clayton H. **86** 386
Clorinda **72** 205
Cornelia Penfield **81** 239
84 466 **101** 76
Cornelia W. **62** lx
Cynthia (Cutler) **90** 104
D. F. **91** 200
Daniel T. **88** 333
David **72** 205 **74** 62
David W. **124** 37
Davis **125** 251
Deborah **67** 373 **75** lxxxi
96 382 **112** 263
Deborah (Perkins) **112**
262 263
Dixwell **71** 36
Don F. **72** 74
Dorothy **54** 93
Dudley **86** 382
E. M. **79** 156
Ebenezer **80** 187 **89** 258
107 224
Edmund **104** 69
Edward **125** 288
Eleanor (Abbott) **136** 312
Eliel Gilbert **92** 40
Elijah **65** 148 **85** 152 **97** 275
Elisha H. **84** 85

LOTHROP *cont'd*
Eliza Alden **69** lx
Eliza Ann **74** 168
Eliza Davis **107** 223
Eliza Lee **58** lxxvi
Elizabeth **51** 297 298 **55**
168 **58** 77 **66** 198 **78** 316
79 159 297 **81** 271 **84**
438 **86** 382 **93** 253 **94**
163 286 **100** 2 302 **120**
87
Elizabeth (Matthews)
109 39
Elizabeth Handy
(Freeman) **125** 251
Elizabeth Moore **93** 123
Elizabeth R. (Whelden)
123 123
Elizabeth W. **72** 204
Ella R. **113** 295
Ellen **132** 37
Elvira **72** 205
Emily J. **71** 15
Eunice **71** 36
Everett B. **84** 85
Experience (Gorham) **112**
196 **113** 166
Ezra **120** 266
Fanny (Baxter) **125** 290
Francis Anna **81** 201
Francis Bacon **136** 312
Frank **104** 69
Frederick **73** 7
Freeman H. **60** 113
George **71** 15 202
George A. **72** 74
George H. **85** 314
George Van Ness **104** 68
69
Grant **72** 75
Gurdon **86** 382
Hannah **66** 357 **72** 74 204
205 **94** 198 **101** 99 **102**
74 75 **112** 261 263 **113**
120 **123** 65
Hannah (Crocker)
112 261
Hannah (Hathaway)
127 254
Hannah C. **72** 204
Harriet **93** 253
Harriet A. **72** 74
Helen A. **104** 149
Helen Ames **78** 206
104 67
Helen Harriet **92** 292
Henry Monroe **92** 292
Henry Monroe (Mrs.)
82 125 **83** 232 **92** 136
291
Henry St. Clair **80** 67
Hillie **78** 410
Hope **72** 74 75 **100** 2
Horace C. **86** 21
Howard **104** 69
Huldah **86** 382 386
Ichabod **72** 74 75
Isaac **57** 280 **99** 79 **104** 69
119 254
Isaiah F. **91** 328
J. **79** 300

LOTHROP *cont'd*
Jacob **104** 206
James **74** 62 **79** 161 **91** 328
107 225
James O. **72** 75
Jane **51** 297 **54** 92 **62** 185
84 438
Jane A. **85** 314
Jane Charlotte **92** 40
Jason **90** 104
Jay **81** 496
Jerusha (Kirkland)
136 312
Jerusha Ann **76** 269
Jesse **86** 379 382
Joanna (Prince) **143** 251
John **51** 49 50 298 **52** 81
423 **54** 93 222 **55** 300 **56**
184 **60** 112 168 **62** 185
66 lxxiii 357 **67** 46 261
69 lx 284 358 **72** 75 205
78 8 **79** 320 **84** 254 268
437-439 **86** 382 455-457
87 277 **90** 155 156 **91** 67
372 **95** 42 45 46 48 **96**
325 **97** 47 275 **100** 2 **101**
99 **107** 225 **113** 65 **120**
87 **124** 60 **127** 254 **128**
18 **133** 95 **134** 174 **143**
251 **147** 110
John C. **72** 204
John H. **79** 166
John Hosmer **100** 2
136 312
John Pierce **81** 201
Jonah **87** 25
Jonathan **72** 75
Joseph **53** 449 **72** 75 **79**
159 **100** 2 **107** 225 **112**
261 263 **119** 270 **128**
248 249
Joshua **126** 117
Judith **101** 169
Julia **89** 31
Julia A. **120** 307
Julia H. **84** 85
Justin **72** 75
Laura Jane (Shapleigh)
95 330
Lawrence **54** 93 **84** 437
113 65
Lebbeus **71** 202
Lois **86** 382
Loring **62** lx **63** xlv
Louisa J. Adams **84** 85
Louise **92** 110
Lucretia Jeanette **113** 304
Lucretia S. **104** 163
Lucy **54** 92 **71** 53 **72** 205
Lydia **79** 156 **86** 382
Lydia (Daniels) **128** 18
Lydia A. **88** 343
Lydia Rathbun **89** 258
Mamie C. (Knight)
99 246
Margaret **125** 288
Margaretta **81** 201
Margery De **112** 318
Maria **72** 75 **88** 287 **89** 258
Marietta **72** 74
Mark **54** 92 93 **69** lx

LOTHROP *cont'd*
Martha **52** 423 **73** 7 **81** 496
94 190 **96** 390 **101** 99
102 75 **126** 117
Martha Stockton **65**
xxxvii **69** xlii lx
Martin **54** 93
Mary **51** 297 298 **54** 93 **60**
168 **66** 179 **72** 75 **84** 438
102 75 **125** 236 **127** 94
136 57
Mary (Buckminster)
90 355
Mary (Joyce) (Gorham)
(Parker) **112** 196
Mary A. **78** 181
Mary Ann **72** 204 **81** 199
Mary B. **100** 2
Mary Buckminster **90** 356
136 312
Mary H. **84** 417
Mary K. **72** 75
Mary Lyman
(Buckminster) **136** 312
Mary Thaxter **85** 194
Mehala **71** 36
Mehitable **51** 197 **75** 249
113 166 118 288
Mehitable Hinckley **66**
lxxiii **95** 289
Melatiah **76** 266
Mercy **72** 75
Milton **99** 246
Mitchell Lee **125** 262
Nancy **85** 152
Nathaniel **72** 75 **118** 313
119 254 127 254
Nelson **74** 168 **91** 327
Phebe **80** 187 **89** 258
Polly **72** 75
Prudence **72** 75
Rachel **71** 36 **72** 75 **74** 62
Rebecca **72** 75 **112** 261-263
Rebecca (Parker) **112** 259
261 **125** 254
Rebecca (Tupper) **99** 289
Rhoda **86** 382
Richard **54** 93
Robert **84** 437 **113** 65
Robert Penfield **92** 292
Roswell **71** 202
Rowland **72** 204 205
Ruth **54** 222 **93** 123
Ruth Jane **93** 123
Ruth P. **72** 75
S. Pearl **71** 53
Sallie B. Comer **100** 79
Sally **74** 168 **125** 290
Sally H. **86** 382
Salmon **113** 304
Samuel **54** 93 **69** lx **88** 260
104 69 **112** 261 **120** 118
Samuel Kirkland **90** 355
100 2 **136** 312
Sarah **54** lxviii **59** 197 69
358 **71** 202
Sarah Jane **93** 123
Seth **69** lx **80** 187 **89** 258
Seth E. **89** 258
Sibyl **71** 202 **80** 45
Sibyl (Backus) **113** 174

LOTHROP *cont'd*
Simon **55** 69 **74** 53 62
Simon de **112** 318
Solomon **72** 75
Sophia **72** 75
Sophia C. (Albray) **84** 85
Sophronia **87** 25
Stephen **71** 52
Stillman **60** 40
Susanna **91** 182
Sylvanus **69** lx
T. J. **99** 311
Talitha Huntington **84** 85
Temperance **89** 184 **112** 263 **113** 23
Thankful (Sanders) **124** 60 **127** 254
Thatcher **85** 51
Thomas **51** 197 297 **54** 93 **58** xli **66** 43 179 357 **69** 358 **71** 202 **84** 437-439 **107** 225 **112** 196 197 261 262 **113** 65 166 **130** 17
Thomas Charles **113** 259
Thomas de **112** 318
Thomas J. **52** 421 **53** 143 147 **57** 420 **148** 260 261
Thomas Jackson **58** xlv **62** 314
Thomas W. **91** 328
Thornton Kirkland **73** 317 **74** v vi xi xxiv 160 163 **75** v vi xi xxi **76** v vi x xx 169 **77** v viii xvi xvii xxvii 300 **78** 192 201 217 220 **79** 187 201 213 216 **80** 196 205 219 222 **81** 208 217 233 236 **82** 221 234 249 250 **83** 219 244 246 **84** 175 203-205 **85** 177 212 214 **86** 186 187 214 **87** 188 **90** 355 356 **100** l 2 44 114 **136** 312
Thornton Kirkland (Mrs.) **73** 317 **74** xxiv **85** 202 **90** 355
Tisdale **125** 289
Veranes **66** 23
Vesta A. **126** 117
Walter de **112** 318
Warren (Mrs.) **92** 196
Washington **120** 50
William **51** 298 **54** 92 93 **72** 74 75 204 **84** 438 439
William Anselm **93** 123
William Gilbert **92** 292
William Henry **92** 292
William Sturgis Hooper **82** 497 **90** 356 **136** 312
Zebadiah **86** 382
Zebulon **72** 75 **86** 382
LOTLAND
Solomon **104** 118
LOTT James **114** 80
Maria **108** 199
Sarah Marie **78** 296
LOTTE Charles Eugene **75** xxiii 75 **110** 135

LOTTESHAM
Oliver **84** 281
LOTTINVILLE
Armand J. **97** 397
LOTTISHAM Frances **66** xxiii **67** 76
Oliver **67** 76
LOTZ Edward Harrington (Mrs.) **103** 119
LOUCKS Ann **134** 152
Laura **97** 219
Myrtle **97** 219
Vern **97** 219
LOUD Lowd
—— **53** 396 **82** 47 **130** 72
— Mrs. **83** 194 307
Abby **74** 28
Abigail **65** 213 **68** 159 **81** 430 445 **117** 255
Abigail (Dam) **111** 46
Abigail (Keith) **125** 221
Adalaide S. **84** 29
Allen **76** 50
Andrew J. **90** 107
Ann Elizabeth **83** 183 184
Annie Frances **71** lviii
Asphia **82** 46
Augustus Sherburne **82** 46
Benjamin **81** 445 **82** 27 46 47 **97** 372 **142** 198
Benjamin Sherburne **82** 46
Bethea **82** 286 293
Betsey **59** 40 **82** 46
Caesar **82** 27
Caleb **53** 265 267
Callista S. (Whitney) **90** 107
Caroline A. (Goodwin) **88** 339
Charity **122** 52
Charles E. **59** xcv
Clifford A. **83** 425 434
Daniel **82** 46 47
David **82** 46 47 282 293 422 **122** 52
Debby **97** 372
Deborah **97** 372 **142** 198
Eben **66** 37
Edward **82** 46 47 283 293 **83** 34
Edward B. **68** 159
Edward Brown **82** 46
Eleanor **82** 283 293
Eliphalet **89** 16
Elizabeth **58** 296 **81** 445 **82** 47 282 283 293 302 **126** 144
Elmira B. **77** 177
Emily Keith **71** lix
Ephraim **97** 372 **130** 72 **147** 277
Essau **125** 43
Etta L. (Clough) **83** 425 434
Eugene Francis **63** 214
Francis **53** 265 267 **54** 406 **61** 42 **71** lviii **113** 139 **143** 253
George **82** 46

LOUD *cont'd*
George D. **68** xxxii **130** 72
George Tucker **82** 46
Harriet **126** 144
Helen Frances **71** lix
Henry **84** 29
Henry M. **53** 265
Honor (Prince) **113** 139 **143** 253
Honor Prince **53** 265
Honour **54** 406
Hunking **82** 47
Ida **89** 40
Jacob **71** lviii
James **82** 46
Jane **81** 445
John **76** 34 **81** 445 446 **82** 47 **125** 93 **130** 72
John Henry **83** 173
John Hermann **71** lix
John J. **54** 113 **58** 90
John Jacob **55** xxix 240 **56** xxx **59** xli 104 **60** xxxiv **61** xxxiii **63** 298 **65** xxxiii **71** xxxiv lviii
John White **71** lviii
Jonathan **81** 446
Joseph **58** 296 **68** 159 **81** 430
Joshua **97** 372 **142** 198
Julia Ann (Perry) **130** 72
Leonard Holmes **82** 422
Louise Flora **79** 18
Lucy **81** 446 **82** 46
Margaret (Smith) **89** 16
Margaret Mead **82** 47
Maria **122** 52
Mark **81** 430 **82** 46 47 293 302 **83** 34
Martha Alice **71** lix
Mary **68** 159 **81** 430 **82** 46 284 293 **83** 25 26 **97** 372 **113** 139 **126** 68
Mary Elizabeth **83** 173 **84** 29
Mehitable **82** 46 47
Mercy **54** 406
Moses **97** 372
Nancy **82** 46 **147** 277
Nathaniel **82** 46 **83** 25 26 **97** 372
Nathaniel Jones **82** 46
Olive **82** 46 **83** 34
Oliver Blanchard **71** lix
Olly **82** 293 300
Polly **82** 47
Ralph White **71** lix
Roger Perkins **71** lix
Rufus Woodbury **117** 240
Ruth **82** 293 294
Sally **97** 372
Samuel **82** 47 **117** 240
Samuel P. **75** 203
Sarah **53** 254 **76** 34 **81** 430 446 **83** 34
Sarah A. **147** 277
Sarah Humphrey **71** lviii
Solomon **65** 213 **81** 446 **82** 47 **111** 46 **125** 221
Susan (Perry) **130** 72
Susanna Bird **75** 203

LOUD *cont'd*
Thomas **81** 445 446 **82** 283 284 293
Thomas Dalling **82** 47
Thomas J. **88** 339
Watson **53** 265 **54** xxxviii
William **81** 430 **82** 27 46 47 293 300 **125** 93
LOUDACE Mary **100** 224
LOUDEN Jacob **111** 19
Mary **111** 19
LOUDON Loudoun
— Earl of **53** 366 **94** 226
— Lord **123** 15
Ann **59** 399
Joanna **88** 283
John **112** 291 **133** 233
John Campbell (Earl of) **63** 188 189
Lovina (Leigh) **133** 233
Richard **59** 399
Robena A. **121** 182
LOUDUIN
Margaret **67** 252
LOUER Mary B. Williams Kinney **127** 71
LOUGEE Louge Lougie Lowgie
—— **92** 316 **143** 99
____ (Emerson) **118** 190
____ (Packard) **118** 91
Abbie G. **118** 189
Abby L. **118** 92
Abigail **115** 73
Abigail (Hall) **115** 73 **118** 187
Abigail G. **118** 189
Abigail J. **118** 189
Abraham Folsom **118** 99 **124** 68
Adelaide **118** 97
Adeline D. M. **118** 186 187
Albion K. P. **118** 192
Alcy **118** 98
Alfred C. **118** 196
Alonzo Pitt **118** 190
Alpheus F. **118** 101
Amos D. **118** 94
Amy A. (Pierce) **118** 190
Ann **118** 32 94 98 191 291
Ann (Delano) **118** 195
Ann B. **118** 192
Ann Elizabeth **118** 293 294
Anna **118** 32 38 94 191 192
Anna (Parsons) **118** 37
Anne **118** 31 32
Anne (Gilman) **118** 31
Anne E. **118** 291
Anne Elizabeth **118** 293
Anne W. **118** 196
Annice **118** 37
Apphia **118** 93 94
Apphia (Swazey) **118** 92
Arabella **118** 195
Asa B. **118** 193
Augusta C. **118** 98
Augusta Cornelia **118** 191
Augustus Leavitt **118** 191
Barry H. **118** 195
Benjamin **118** 34 96 98 99

LOUGEE *cont'd*
124 68
Benjamin L. **118** 191
Betsey **115** 75 **118** 34 37 91 92 100 101 190 194 196
Betsey (Fletcher) **118** 193
Betsey (Marsh) **118** 91 92
Betsey Scribner **118** 186 187
Bettie (Bryan) **118** 191
Betty **115** 154 **118** 35 38 100 193 196
C. H. **118** 94
Caroline **118** 97 191
Caroline E. (Lewis) **118** 191
Caroline E. (Spring) **118** 190
Caroline Elizabeth **124** 68
Caroline Emily **118** 292 924
Catherine **118** 100
Catherine C. **118** 195
Charles **118** 37 91 93
Charles A. **118** 196
Charles E. **118** 94 196
Charles F. **118** 196
Charles H. **118** 91
Charles T. **118** 196
Charlotte **118** 97 190
Charlotte Burrows **118** 100
Chauncey Vester **124** 68
Clarinda M. **118** 91
Clarinda S. **118** 192
Cordelia **118** 98
Cynthia **118** 100 196
Daniel **118** 94
Daniel Felch **118** 101
Daniel Gilman **118** 191
David **118** 194 196
Dearborn **118** 94
Dolly **118** 35 100 196
Dudley **118** 91 92 95
E. F. **118** 94
Edman **118** 38
Edmond **118** 38
Edmund **116** 76 **118** 32 38 39 97 100 190 193
Edson Melvin **118** 190
Edward **118** 39
Eleanor C. **118** 190
Elisha **118** 93 94
Eliza B. **76** 31 **118** 196
Elizabeth **118** 32 34 35 91 94 96 97 99 101 193 196 **124** 68
Elizabeth (Lougee) **118** 99
Elizabeth (Mitchell) **118** 96
Elizabeth (Morgan) (Hewitt) **118** 193
Elizabeth (Scribner) **118** 34
Elizabeth M. **118** 94
Ella M. **118** 196
Ellen **104** 177
Ellen (Wheeler) **118** 94
Elmira B. (Richardson) **118** 192

LOUGEE *cont'd*
Elsie **118** 33 95 98
Emerson **118** 34
Emily **118** 291
Emily Caroline **118** 293
Emma E. **118** 91
Emmaline **124** 68
Enoch **115** 75
Enoch B. **118** 188
Enoch Bunker **118** 189 **119** 314
Eunice W. (Hibbard) **124** 68
F. Marion **115** 154 **118** 30 34 37 99 100 185 188 191 195 295
Fanny **118** 99
Frances Caroline **118** 101
Franklin W. **118** 195
Frederick W. **118** 96 97
George **118** 91 97
George Eldad **118** 191
George Gilman **118** 191
George I. **118** 190
George M. **118** 91
George Washington **118** 100
Georgia Augusta **118** 94
Gilman **118** 32 34 36 37 192
Grace **85** 398 399
Greenleaf T. **77** 148 **118** 196
Hannah **76** 29 **118** 38 39 95 100 196
Hannah (Blanchard) **118** 193
Hannah (Dolloff) **118** 194
Hannah (Elkins) **118** 90
Hannah (Lord) **118** 38
Hannah (Perkins) **118** 187
Hannah (Sanborn) **118** 93
Hannah (Watson) **118** 37
Hannah A. **118** 94
Hannah Nutter **118** 190
Hannah T. (Bickford) **118** 190
Harriet **118** 97
Harriet Biron **118** 100
Hazen **118** 91
Helen **118** 94
Henrietta (Wheeler) **118** 94
Henry **118** 33 98
Henry Clement **118** 100
Henry W. **118** 195
Hugh Bartis **118** 192
I. **118** 189
Irene **118** 195
Isaac **118** 91
Isaac William **118** 94
J. **118** 189
J. S. **118** 94
Jacob Moody **118** 91
James **118** 39 195
James Edwin **118** 293 294
James H. **118** 101
James William **118** 195
Jane **118** 189 291
Jane (Perkins) **118** 189

LOUGEE *cont'd*
Jane Catherine **118** 292-294
Jemima (Bridgeman) **118** 96
Jennie **118** 94
Jennie A. (Morse) **118** 190
Jerusha (Tibbetts) **118** 37
Jesse **118** 33 91 95 96
Joanna **118** 32 33 192
Joanna (Kimball) **118** 94
Joanna (Smith) **118** 192
Joel Bunker Hawkins **118** 100
John **85** 398 399 **115** 75 154 **116** 76 **118** 30-33 35-37 39 89-94 96-101 184-192 194-196 291 **119** 314 **124** 68
John A. **76** 29 **118** 186 187 190
John F. **118** 91 94
John Fogg **118** 94
John G. **118** 37
John H. **118** 98
John M. **118** 193
Jonathan **118** 33 35 37-39 96 97 99 190 191 193
Jonathan Folsom **118** 36 93 190-192 291
Jonathan Lord **118** 38 39 193
Joseph **92** 316 **115** 75 154 **118** 32 34 35 38 91-95 98-101 190 192 194 196
Joseph Bunker **118** 189 190
Joseph L. **118** 99
Joseph Leavitt **118** 33 92 192 291
Joseph Merrill **118** 190
Joseph S. **118** 94
Josephine (Adams) **118** 191
Josiah **118** 100 196
Judith **118** 98
Judith (Jackson) (Chattle) (Beal) **118** 33
Judith (Perkins) **118** 91
Julia **118** 192 **124** 68
Julia A. **118** 91 92
Julia A. (Rose) **118** 94
Julia Augusta **118** 101
Julius **118** 99 **124** 68
Kate **118** 195
Laura **118** 91
Leavitt **118** 91
Levi **118** 38 99 **124** 68
Lewis **118** 191
Lewis E. **118** 195
Lewis T. **118** 98
Luis **118** 96
Lucretia (Evans) **118** 189
Lucy **118** 91 95
Lucy (Wells) **118** 195
Lucy Ann **118** 195
Lydia **76** 32 **115** 75 154 **116** 76 **118** 34 35 37 38 98 100 101 185 191 196
Lydia (Folsom) **118** 35
Lydia (Lamson) **118** 34

LOUGEE *cont'd*
Lydia (Swain) **118** 97
Lydia C. (Felch) **118** 101
Lydia Lamson **118** 186
Lyman **118** 100
M. G. **118** 94
Mae Belle **118** 190
Manthano **118** 101
Maria **118** 291 292
Maria Augusta **118** 293 294
Maria Augusta (Frank) **118** 195
Maria Bloomfield **118** 100
Mariah **118** 292
Mariah Franks **118** 294
Marianna **118** 91
Mary **118** 90 94 95 99 100 186 192 196 **124** 68
Mary (Buzzell) **118** 192
Mary (Marsh) **118** 90
Mary (Ross) **118** 91
Mary (Smith) **118** 94
Mary (Thurston) **118** 192
Mary (Tibbetts) **118** 100
Mary A. **77** 148 **118** 196
Mary A. (Young) **118** 91
Mary Ann **76** 41 **118** 190 **119** 314
Mary Ann (Sargent) **118** 91
Mary E. (Jennison) **118** 94
Mary G. **118** 37
Mary J. (Goulding) **118** 190
Mary Jane **124** 68
Mary L. **118** 94
Mary W. **118** 37
Mehitable **84** 447 **118** 36 97
Mercy **118** 99
Mercy Elizabeth (Clough) **118** 193
Merrill **118** 91
Miriam **118** 93
Miriam (Fogg) **118** 92
Molly **116** 76 **118** 33 38 185 186
Molly (Avery) **118** 184
Molly (Leavitt) **118** 33
Moses **118** 32 35 36 99 191 192 291
Nancy **69** 255 **118** 39 40 91 186 187 191 194 196
Nancy (Hodsdon) **118** 94
Nancy (Lord) **118** 93
Nancy (Thompson) **118** 190
Nancy (Turner) **118** 100
Nathaniel **116** 76 **118** 38 39 93 184 192-195
Nehemiah **118** 33 90
Newell R. **118** 91
Nicholas **115** 73 154 **118** 35 187 188
Nicholas Gilman **115** 73 **118** 188
Nicholas N. **118** 190
Noah **118** 30 36 187 191 195 291 292 294 295
Olive **90** 334 **118** 91

LOUGEE *cont'd*
Oliver B. **118** 191
Orinda (Morrill) **118** 192
Parker Morgan **118** 193
Peggy (Cate) **118** 39
Phebe **118** 196
Phebe (Carter) **118** 195
Philander **118** 97
Pitt **115** 75 154 **118** 35 100 185 188 189
Polly **115** 75 **118** 37 91 92 94 95 101 186
Polly (Edgerly) **118** 37
Polly (Lougee) **118** 91 95
Polly (Rollins) **118** 91 95
Rebecca **118** 185
Rebecca (Bunker) **118** 188
Rebecca (Collins) **118** 192
Rebecca (Edgerly) **118** 91
Richard **147** 154 160 161
Richard J. **118** 93
Ruth **118** 99
Ruth (Folsom) **118** 98 **124** 68
Ruth Emily (Heath) **118** 190
Ruth M. (Tibbetts) (Crillis) **118** 195
Sally **115** 75 **118** 92 93 94 95 98
Sally Felch **118** 101
Sally Hodgdon **118** 186
Samuel **115** 75 **118** 37 94 98 188 190
Sanford Page **118** 91
Sarah **90** 327 **118** 32-34 98
Sarah (Brown) **118** 97
Sarah (Mason) **118** 98
Sarah (Rand) **118** 37
Sarah A. (Leavitt) **118** 191
Sarah Ann **115** 73 **118** 188
Sarah B. **118** 190
Sarah Bunker **119** 314
Sarah E. (Foss) **118** 196
Sarah L. **118** 195
Sarah Noble **118** 189
Semira J. (Brown) **118** 191
Seth **118** 94
Shuah **118** 32 33
Simeon **115** 75 154 **118** 35 37 100 101 185
Stephen N. **118** 190
Susan **88** 336 **118** 34 98 190 196 **124** 68
Susan (Hull) **118** 33
Susan (Wheeler) **118** 91
Susan Avery **118** 195
Susan B. **118** 192 195
Susane **118** 33
Susanna **116** 76 **118** 37 99 192 193 195 **124** 68
Susanna (Avery) **118** 194
Susanna (Mudgett) **118** 36
Sylvester **124** 68
Taylor **118** 37
Thomas **118** 98
Virginia H. **118** 101
W. S. **118** 94
Weston G. **118** 191
William **118** 33 38 39 97 98

LOUGEE *cont'd*
William A. **118** 195
William B. **118** 191
William Bruce **118** 190
William Edwin **118** 94
William H. **118** 195
William James **118** 191
William Mitchell **118** 96
William Pitt **118** 35 185
　188
William S. **118** 94
William Wallace **124** 68
LOUGH Gladys **82** 437
Harriet (Millis) **111** 128
　189
Robert **111** 128
LOUGHBOROUGH
Grace Van Arsdale
　(Burt) **98** 78
Robert Henry Rose (Mrs.)
　98 78
Ross **84** 234
Thomas Rossington
　85 196
LOUGHERY
Bernard **116** 154
LOUGHRAN
Brizb'r **61** 348
Robert **61** 348
LOUGHREY
Mary Ellan **99** 177
LOUGHRIDGE
Eliza **60** 242
James **60** 242
Jane **60** 242
Mary **69** 32
Mg. **60** 242
Paul **95** 209
William **60** 242
LOUGHTON
William **147** 17
Lougie *see* Lougee
LOUIS IV King of
　France **62** 388 **141** 103
LOUIS NAPOLEON Prince
　60 225
LOUIS PHILIPPE King of
　France **54** lxxviii **55**
　362 **60** 225 **88** 99
LOUIS THE FAT
　of France **140** 222
LOUIS XI King of
　France **59** 236
LOUIS XIII King of
　France **71** 103
LOUIS XIV King of
　France **52** 477 **60** 260
　142 126
LOUIS XV King of
　France **52** 281
LOUIS XVI King of
　France **53** 225 **71** 103
　130 27 **143** 238
LOUIS
　—— **83** 34
Hannah (Hopkins) **102** 58
John **143** 262
LOUISE Princess
　(Marchioness of
　Lorne) **69** lxii
LOUISON Didama **123** 110

LOUK Elizabeth **102** 70
LOULASE
Lawrence **76** 235
LOUNDE
Alexander **116** 174
LOUNDERS Jane **73** 294
Tabitha **73** 294
LOUNSBURY
　Lounsberry
　Lounsbery
　—— **62** 206 309
Abigail **108** 291 293
　127 246
Amelia **75** 192
Ann **108** 290
Ann Teal (Richardson)
　95 287
Betsey (Devers) **126** 207
Clarence **102** 124 **119** 148
Crownage Frederic
　76 170
Delia Annor (Scofield)
　109 264
Edward Haskell **61** 217
Elizabeth **107** 293 **108**
　289 290
Elizabeth (Pennoyer)
　108 289
Enos **108** 294 295
Epenetus **108** 292-295
Esther **78** 264
George **108** 294
George E. **54** 355
George Frederic **76** 170
Gideon **108** 293-295
Hannah **108** 293
Harriet (Post) **147** 53
Henry **108** 290-295
Jairus **76** 170
James H. **95** 287
Jane Ann **114** 237
Jemima **108** 291
John **108** 290 291 296
Jonathan **108** 291
Joshua **108** 291 293
Josiah **66** 331 **108** 291
Lucy **73** 16
Margaret **127** 320
Martha **66** 331
Mary **88** 190 **106** 171 **108**
　290 291 293
Matilda **109** 264
Mercy **108** 293 294
Michael **108** 290-292
Monmouth **108** 291 293
　295
Nathan **108** 293-295
　109 264
Nathaniel **108** 293-295
Nehemiah **108** 291
Phineas **108** 294
Rachel **108** 293 294 296
Rebecca Bird **95** 287
Richard **60** 187 **106** 171
　108 288-291 **119** 315
Sarah **108** 291
Stephen B. **147** 53
Thomas **108** 290 291
William **108** 290
William W. **126** 207

LOUPE
Christiana Marie **71** 67
LOURAINE Dorothy M. **92**
　210 **93** 98 **95** 402
LOURE Thomas **51** 117
　54 189
LOURIE —— **143** 366
LOURIER
Susanna **113** 276
LOURNEDALE
Katharine **116** 244
LOUSHONG
Antoine **105** 277
LOUTHE Elizabeth
　(Blennerhasset) **98** 277
Lionel **98** 277
Margaret **110** 126
LOUTHER
Juliana **115** 231
William **115** 231
LOUTHROP Hawise de
　(Nevil) **112** 318
Margery **112** 318
LOUTITT Mary **81** 457
LOUVAIN
Alice (Hastings) (Cornhill)
　96 42
Godfrey (Count of) **96** 42
　48 **101** 294
Lovaine **96** 42
LOVAT — Lord **123** 6
Lovatt *see* Lovett
LOVE —— **140** 252
Abigail **116** 210 **141** 350
Abraham **116** 210
Agnes **75** 220 **114** 72 73
Albert Haller **112** 49
Andrew **92** 296
Andrew H. **128** 93
Ann **116** 208
Anna **116** 208
Anne **137** 294
Archibald B. **116** 210
Arthur **111** 194
Benjamin **109** 295
Bennet **76** 201
Catherine **96** 230
Charlotte Cutler **112** 49
Comfort **141** 350
Deborah **76** 201
Donald M. **98** 98
Dorcas **116** 131
E. Paul (Mrs.) **93** 196
Earle E. **91** 41
Ebenezer **82** 27
Edna **117** 128
Eleanor **64** 11
Elizabeth Murray **112** 49
Emeline **80** 164
Eusebius **66** 59
Flora A. (Wood) **128** 93
Florence Speakman
　144 329
George Maltby **112** 49
Gladys Davenport
　(Hannum) **91** 41
H. D. **113** 12
Harlow Swaine **112** 49
Helen Douglas **85** 196
James **82** 205 **85** 349
　96 230

LOVE *cont'd*
James A. **91** 328
James W. **114** 191
Jane **80** 164
Jannet **140** 252
Jeannie **112** 49
John **64** 11 **84** 66 318 **116**
208 **129** 65 **137** 294
John Lord **112** 49
Joseph **62** 170
Josiah **141** 349
Julia **112** 49
Katharine **55** 209 **66** 59
Lawrence **75** 227
Lelia **112** 49
Linda **96** 228
Lyda **141** 352
Malinda J. **96** 230
Margaret **65** 132 **73** 142
110 312 **111** 153 **114** 72-
74 **134** 335 **137** 362
Margery **137** 303
Maria **112** 49
Maria (Maltby) **112** 49
Marie **112** 49
Martha **129** 63
Martha Church (Maltby)
112 49
Martha Maltby **112** 49
Mary **62** 303 **80** 58 **116** 206
Maryett **116** 210
Nath **82** 80
Nathaniel **73** 222 **83** 154
Olive **66** 134
Phila **116** 208
R. T. **60** 91 97 207
Richard **110** 312 **111** 153
114 47 72 73 **147** 134
135
Robert **129** 66
Robert A. **105** 77 **109** 158
Robert M. **114** 191
Rose **62** 170
Sally Keyes **84** 318 **85** 425
Samuel **111** 194 **116** 206
143 260
Sarah **82** 80 205 **83** 154
Susan **115** 131
Susan Ann **80** 58
Thomas **76** 201 **80** 164
147 132
Thomas C. **112** 49
Wilhemina Rogers
(Royall) **109** 295
William **65** 26 **69** 343 **86**
425 **116** 208 **129** 66 **147**
131 132
William DeLoss **54** 231
69 xxxii 97 **104** 92 **120**
157 **148** 13
LOVECRAFT
Joseph **133** 181
LOVEDAY Anne **103** 106
Anne (Brandon) **103** 106
John **74** 137
Margaret **74** 137
William **74** 69
LOVEE Ann B. (Shaw)
125 236
James **125** 236
Susan **125** 238

LOVEGREEN
Rebecca **76** 17
LOVEGROVE Betsey **70**
121 **115** 133
Elizabeth **115** 36
Love **115** 43
Wellington **115** 37
LOVEJOY —— **92** 272
278 280 282 322 **122** 91
— Capt. **77** 46
— Mr. **92** 278
Abby F. (Junkins) **120** 309
121 71
Abial **89** 391
Abigail **87** 234 238
Abigail (Ambrose)
92 318
Abigail Read **53** 41 **61** 381
Abijah **132** 104
Abiud **107** 108
Alethea A. **129** 189
Alexander **73** 137 218
Alice Vernon **82** 170
Almira Marion (Gore)
89 390
Althea C. **129** 189
Althea D. **129** 189
Alvan D. **90** 116
Ann **73** 150
Anne **59** lxxix **112** 23
Arethusa **61** 242
Azubah **92** 316
Betsey **70** 151 **136** 312
Betsey (Pattee) **147** 78
C. E. **97** 55
Caroline (Hall) **91** 386
Catherine **64** 310
Chandler **92** 272 275 314
316
Chloe **61** 237
Christopher **93** 286
Clarence E. **147** 78
Clarence Earle **85** 196
D. R. **60** 187
D. Ross **55** 348
Daisy (Dean) **144** 120
Daniel **111** 116 **147** 78
E. M. **116** 99
Ebenezer **82** 344 **89** 260 **92**
275 278 280 282 316 **122**
91
Edward Everett **89** 390
Edwin A. **90** 115
Elbridge **91** 386
Eleanor **73** 147
Elijah **127** 100
Elijah P. **58** lxxix
Elijah Parish **147** 78
Eliza Gray **89** 390
Elizabeth **147** 78
Elizabeth (Francis) **88** 333
Elizabeth (Pattee) **111** 116
147 78
Elizabeth Miles (Dean)
144 120
Esther B. **88** 276
Evelina **88** 338
Evelyn Mary Wood **66**
xlix 193 **100** 131 **116** 77
Ezra **136** 138
Frances James **89** 390

LOVEJOY *cont'd*
Francis **94** 318 **147** 78
Frederick Bates **84** 110
185 **89** 260 **90** 79 140
Frederick Bates (Mrs.)
90 137
Frederick Horr **89** 261
George **115** 119 **126** 144
George Freeman **59** 40
George Henry **90** 109
George N. **73** 218
George Trundy **89** 390
Gertrude Russell **122** 91
Hannah (Chandler)
92 274
Hellen Augusta **89** 390
Henry **88** 333 **92** 269 274
Henry L. **92** 314
Hepzibah (Farley)
136 138
Howard **108** 211
Ida Gertrude **89** 390
Isaac **61** 384
James A. **82** 170
Jeremiah **89** 260
John **56** 21 **60** 187 **89** 260
92 270 316 318 **145** 353
147 78
Jonathan **53** 41 **61** 237
Joseph **67** xxxiv
Joseph Cammett **147** 78
Joshua **112** 23 **122** 91
Josias **73** 150
Judith Clark **59** 40
Julia A. (Gordon) **90** 115
Katharine Pease (Horr)
90 137
Kimball A. **90** 57
Lettice **73** 219
Lid. **70** 312
Lizzie **96** 333
Louise **88** 170
Love **115** 43
Loyal **89** 390 **103** 313
Lura J. (Hayes) **83** 431 434
Lydia **61** 383
Lyman **90** 354
Mabel Woodbridge
(Hannum) **90** 354
Mahala **87** 234 238
Maria **78** 357
Martha **93** 291
Martha Trundy **89** 390
103 313 314
Mary **61** 237 **62** 31 **84** 328
89 285 **91** 389 **111** 138
Mary (Bancroft) **94** 318
147 78
Mary (Fitz) **126** 144
Mary Amelia **89** 390
Mary Ann (Lakin) **90** 104
Mary Augusta **89** 390
Mary Elizabeth **82** 170
Mary T. (Stevens) **89** 390
Mary Weeks **59** 40
Matilda Jones (Domett)
122 87 91
Mattie T. **89** 391
Mehitable **55** xciii
Michael **73** 149 264
Minnie Domett **122** 91

LOVEJOY *cont'd*
Miriam **93** 286
Miriam (Virgin) **92** 275
Molly **91** 266
Moses **90** 104
Naomi **97** 54 **125** 59
Nathaniel **125** 23
Nealey **92** 270
Obadiah **93** 397 **100** 63
Olive **53** 41 **61** 237
Olive (Blaisdell) **114** 293
Olive (Trafton) **112** 23
Owen **147** 78
Patience **61** 237
Peter **92** 322
Phebe **59** 251 **82** 344
    85 341
Phebe (Russell) **122** 91
Polly **61** 239 **107** 108
Prudence **80** 167
Rebecca **73** 230
Rowland **89** 260
Sadie Luella **86** 364
Samuel **59** 40 **73** 217 **112**
    23 **145** 353
Samuel Sylvester **59** 40
Sarah **61** 236 237 **97** 85
Sarah A. (White) **90** 57
Sarah Ann (McClure)
    134 89
Sarah C. (Porter) **134** 89
Sibyl Pattee **147** 78
Sophia **61** 384
Sophia (Amsden) **90** 116
Stephen **112** 23 **114** 293
Susan **64** 310
Susan (Virgin) **92** 278
Susan B. (Wheeler)
    126 293
Susanna **61** 240 **107** 108
Theodore **112** 23
Thomas Cotton Noyes
    59 40
Thomas H. **120** 309 **121** 71
Warren K. **134** 89
Warren Scott **144** 120
William **92** 324
William Bates **89** 260
William H. **62** 31
William Russell **89** 260
Willis A. **83** 431 434
Winslow Meston **89** 261
Xerxes **92** 324
LOVEKIN Lovekyn
Abigail **113** 295
Alice **92** 385
Arthur C. (Mrs.) **100** 316
Christian **92** 385
David **145** 350
Jacob **61** 42
Mehitable **61** 237
Michael **92** 387
Nicholas **92** 384 385
Stephen **92** 385
William **92** 385
Lovel *see* Lovell
LOVELACE Loveless
    Lovelesse
—— **133** 38
— Col. **52** 204 205
Ambrose **54** 215

LOVELACE *cont'd*
Ann **73** 277
Anne **106** 167
Arial **129** 47 49
Ariel C. **129** 49
Ashby Lawrence **97** 82
Basil **73** 227
Charles **51** 280
Daniel D. **82** 257 **84** 240
    85 241 **86** 241 **129** 47
Delilah **129** 47
Dora (Ashby) **84** 190 **93**
    142 **97** 82
Elisha **73** 150
Eliza (Hyde) **129** 49
Eliza J. **129** 49
Elizabeth **129** 49
Elizabeth Sarah **73** 276
Ellen **80** 347 366
Frances (Cole) **97** 82
Francis **64** 80 **65** 305 **96**
    237 **106** 167
George **132** 244
Griffin Morton **97** 82
Henderson **73** 270
Ignatius **73** 226
Isaac **73** 218
James **120** 17
Johanna **73** 222
John **73** 230 **97** 82 **129** 49
John H. **129** 49
Lawrence **51** 280
Luke **73** 227
Lydia H. **129** 49
Mary **141** 143
Mary Ann **73** 231
Mary LaClaire **97** 82
Meredith (Sherman)
    133 38
Milicent Ann **73** 143
Orcelia **129** 49
Samuel Henry **97** 82
Samuel Henry (Mrs.) **84**
    105 **92** 295 **93** 142 **97** 82
Susan **98** 121
Susanna Rebecca **120** 17
Unie **73** 217
Uretta M. **129** 47
William **97** 207
LOVELAND Aaron **71** 46
Abigail **86** 53
Abigail Moulton **69** 329
Abner **61** 390
Amos **61** 389
Anna **60** 380 **61** 89 388
Asa **61** 84 392
Asa J. **86** 170
Ashbel **59** 71
Avanell **100** 198
Avis **141** 47
Benjamin F. **84** 49
Betsey **61** 195 **62** 90 193
    86 162 317
Betsey (Derbon) **87** 229
    234
Betsey (Rich) **84** 49
Betty **61** 85
Caroline **70** 84
Cate **61** 190
Catherine H. **86** 317
Caty Eliza **86** 321

LOVELAND *cont'd*
Charity **60** 382 **61** 392
Charles **62** 270
Chester **61** 194 **62** 193 **85**
    164 167
Christopher Vansant **60**
    377 **62** 86
Clara Jane **92** 364
Clarissa **54** 254
Clinton S. **85** 167
Clitheroe Mason (Parker)
    96 296
Comfort **106** 213
D. **104** 96
Daniel **61** 89 389 **62** 299
    104 96
David **59** 21 **60** 378 379
    61 387 390 **62** 296
Deborah **61** 194 195 389
    392 **62** 376
Dinah (Andrews) **85** 46
Dorothy **62** 272
Drusilla **62** 270
Edith (Pardue) **100** 198
Electa **85** 167
Eli **59** 21 **85** 167
Elijah **60** 376 377 379 **61**
    194 **62** 193 296 **86** 162
Elisha **60** 377 **61** 86 387
    62 194 376 **63** 71 **86** 321
Elizabeth **60** 140 381 **61**
    191 192 194 195 390 **62**
    192 292 376 **63** 71 **85** 63
    167
Elizabeth (Gaines) **85** 46
Elizabeth A. **68** 154
Elizabeth Ann **75** 191 192
Elizur **60** 377 378 380 381
    61 85 87 90 **62** 86 378
    86 161
Elizur M. **86** 170
Elsie A. **62** 294 **86** 170
Emily **61** 387 **62** 293
    86 170
Epaphroditus **62** 270
Erastus **60** 377
Esther **60** 381 **61** 191 195
    62 193 298 **70** 84 **86** 162
Eunice **61** 194 **62** 270 **85**
    51 63 **116** 117
Experience **60** 140 **85** 63
    145 40
Ezekiel **62** 270
Fidelia **116** 117
Frances **61** 387
Francis **60** 377 **61** 194 195
    293 295 297 298 390 **62**
    193 **63** 68 71 **86** 170
Frank O. **51** 510
Frankie **104** 96
George **77** 153
George W. **86** 170
Gilbert **62** 293
Hannah **60** 376 381 **61**
    194 293 390 392 **62** 193
    86 170
Harriet **60** 334 **62** 84
    64 209
Harvey **61** 295
Honor **61** 85 **85** 167
Idris **74** 314

LOVELAND *cont'd*
Ira C. **86** 170
Ira Chester **61** 298
Irena R. **85** 167
Isaac **61** 389
James **61** 293 **86** 170 **87**
229 234 **145** 359
James Monroe **85** 409
Jared **61** 195
Jemima **61** 389
Jessie **85** 409
Joab **85** 63
Joel **61** 88 **62** 86 193 **85** 63
86 162 **100** 198
John **60** 140 334 **61** 191 192
194 195 390 **62** 192 376
70 84 **85** 63 167 **145** 321-
324 327 333
John F. **86** 317
Jonathan **54** 254 **56** 162
60 379
Joseph **78** 261 **84** 49
Joshua **61** 295 392 **86** 318
Judah **61** 389
Keturah **61** 87 392
Keziah **85** 63
Laura A. **86** 318
Lavinia C. **86** 170
Lazarus **85** 409
Leonard **85** 167
Levi **60** 141 381 **61** 85 87
88 90 191 194 195 **62** 90
193 298 380 **86** 162
Lewis **77** 80
Lois **61** 87 90 390 **78** 261
86 162
Lorry **62** 84
Lot **60** 377 378 **62** 86 87
193 194
Lovina C. **86** 170
Lovisa **62** 84 268
Lucia **62** 85
Lucinda **104** 96
Lucretia **85** 409
Lucy **60** 377 **61** 388 **62** 83
379 **85** 63
Luther **61** 195 **62** 85
Lydia **70** 203
Lydia Jane **85** 409
Mabel **60** 377 378 **61** 389
Malachi **62** 271
Marah **62** 84
Martha **59** 71
Mary **60** 140 382 **61** 86 88
90 190 192 194 195 392
62 193 **85** 63 **145** 322
Mary Ann / Anne **60** 378
62 86
Mary Jane **77** 153 **107** 154
Mary Lowana (Munroe)
100 198
Matilda **100** 198
Mehitable **60** 378 **61** 387
Mercy **86** 170
Merrenda E. **86** 321
Milly **60** 378
Molly **61** 84 195 **86** 162
Moses Bascom **62** 271
Nancy **85** 167
Nancy M. **86** 317
Nathan **61** 194 195 389 **62**

LOVELAND *cont'd*
90 376
Norman **61** 192 **62** 192
85 63
Oliver **85** 409
Onner **85** 167
Orlanza **86** 321
Otis **62** 270
Pelatiah **60** 382 **61** 84 86 88
90 190 192 194 195 **62**
193 291 298 **86** 162
Penelope **61** 390
Philander Cook **61** 387
Philatha **61** 194
Polly **61** 88 194 **62** 193
84 49
Prince Albert **100** 198
Prudence **56** 352 **62** 378
Rachel **86** 318
Rebecca **61** 388 **62** 270
Remembrance **104** 96
Reuben **61** 90 **86** 317
Robert **60** 377 **85** 42 46
142 331
Roger **62** 270
Ruth **61** 89 389 **62** 299
86 161
S. A. **104** 96
Sally **62** 83
Samuel G. **116** 117
Sarah **60** 379 **61** 90
Solomon **85** 63
Sterling Nye (Mrs.)
96 296
Sylvester **61** 195
Sylvester G. **86** 170
Thomas **60** 140 **62** 268 **85**
42 63 **145** 322 330
Tirzah **63** 71 **86** 321
Titus **62** 270-272
Truman **75** 192 **76** 174
Vesta Gilbert **61** 297
Vier **61** 192
Watson **86** 318
William **60** 378
Ziba **61** 194 **62** 193
Loveless *see* Lovelace
LOVELL Lovel
— Capt. **57** 396
— Col. **104** 131
— Gen. **59** 147
— Mr. **51** 127
— Mrs. **109** 44
____ (Bethune) **140** 164
____ (Gorham) **140** 164
Abia **106** 160
Abigail **52** 273 **54** 292 **56**
254 **57** 326 **58** 371 **64**
372 **127** 110
Abigail L. **89** 242
Abner W. **109** 38
Adeline **82** 500
Albert (Mrs.) **79** 193
Albert A. **65** 19 **66** 240
Alexander **58** 345 **110** 227
125 104 **138** 115
Alexandrew **127** 311
Alpheus **56** 250
Amy C. **120** 41
Andrew **70** 259 **124** 53
Ann **55** 147 **67** 114 **138** 123

LOVELL *cont'd*
Anna **58** 371
Anne **74** 136
Anne (Bethune) **125** 64
Asa **58** 371
Augusta A. **84** 54
Beliza **56** 250
Benjamin **52** 14 **100** 188
144 266
Betsey **68** 312
Betsey Prince **121** 140
Betty **58** 371
Bulah **106** 160
Caroline **56** 254
Charlotte (Norcross)
125 216
Christopher **56** 258
64 372
Clarissa **64** 372
Clarissa (Downes)
125 221
Clarissa D. **64** 372
Cyrus **78** 67
Dabby **140** 164
Daniel **52** 273 **92** 25
Daniel G. **126** 145
Darius **138** 123
David **90** 400
Deborah **63** 91 **110** 227
Desire **51** 35
Dorcas (Lewis) **126** 145
Dorothy May **106** 125
Ebenezer **57** 109 **100** 63
120 41
Edmund **77** 118 **84** 285
Edward **77** 118 **109** 146
Edward Francis **109** 146
Eleanor **106** 160 **119** 7 9
104 190 **137** 34
Eli **106** 160
Elijah **54** 292 **56** 254 384
Eliza **64** 372
Eliza M. **64** 372
Elizabeth **57** 185 **58** 345 **69**
358 **70** 259 **74** 136 **119** 9
Elizabeth (St. Clair)
139 283
Ellen **119** 9
Ellen F. (Fuller) **103** 48
Ellis **133** 215
Ernest L. (Mrs.) **119** 77
Esther **68** 314
Eunice **57** 392 **58** 371
121 140
Eva G. **95** 97
Fanny (Swain) **125** 215
Francis Lord **94** 323
Franklin Corey **55** 63
Franklyn Hallett **82** 500
Franklyn Hallett (Mrs.)
73 319 **74** xxvi
Frederick Solon **55** 63
Frederick W. **95** 97
Frink **56** 249
George **81** 312 **82** 500
George Hyrum (Mrs.)
109 130
Hannah **53** 394 **54** 293 **56**
249 250 256 386 **58** 371
105 85 **108** 244 **113** 21

LOVELL *cont'd*
Hannah (Williston)
  125 104
Hannah Ellen **68** xxxiv
Hannah Lucilla **81** 312
Harriet **55** 61 63
Harriet Lovell **55** 63
Harriet Martha **66** 127
Helen **125** 65
Helen (Sheaffe) **125** 64 65
  140 164
Helen Estella **88** 169 **104**
  67 68 149 162
Helena (Norcross) **125**
  107 108
Henry **81** 312 **111** 266 267
  121 232
Herbert **90** 157
Hope **58** 371
Horace **56** 249 259
Huldah **109** 69
Isabel **82** 234 500
James **52** 14 273 **56** 48 **70**
  259 **79** 441 **84** 269 **118**
  313 **119** 10 11 104 105
  125 64 65 **130** 176 **132**
  138 **140** 164 323 **142**
  146
James G. **88** 330
James S. **140** 164
James Smith **125** 64 65
Jane **51** 35 **70** 259 **112** 197
  120 248 249 **123** 129
Jane Balcome **104** 102
Jemima (Landers) **124** 53
Jerusha **106** 160
John **51** 35 **52** 14 **54** 201
  202 290 293-296 **55** 147
  429 **56** 249 250 388 391
  392 **65** 97 **66** 127 **67** 114
  70 259 **79** 367 **80** 98 201
  81 5 **97** 320 **99** 79 109
  108 174 **115** 186 **117** 15
  119 21 **124** 220
John D. **64** 372
John King **54** 290
John Prince **121** 140
Jonathan **57** 287 **124** 53
Joseph **51** 35 **52** 14 **56** 35
  57 185 285 **60** 39 43 **61**
  42 **68** 311 312 314
Joshua **113** 253 **124** 220
Julia A. (Perry) **103** 46
Loisa J. **120** 41
Louise **73** 319 **74** xxix
Louise (Bearse) **113** 253
Louise Lewis **76** 158
Lucy **62** 187
Lydia **57** 53 **58** 371
  123 320
Lydia (Gifford) **133** 215
Lydia D. **73** xxx
Lydia Isham (Scudder)
  113 253
M. **120** 41
M. Louise **73** xix 321 **74**
  xxvi **127** 106
Mahlon **104** 102
Malinda **120** 41
Margaret **103** 105 106
  111 266 **121** 232 **138**

LOVELL *cont'd*
  116
Margaret (Brandon)
  103 106
Margaret Livingston
  125 65
Mariah **123** 159
Marmaduke **81** 180
Marsha Melinda **120** 41
Martha **54** 201 202 290
  293 295 **55** 63 429 **56**
  249 250 257 388 **66** 127
  114 9 **124** 53 **126** 104
Mary **52** 14 **58** 230 **62** 372
  79 441 **86** 370 **125** 214
  133 46 **135** 20
Mary (Middleton) **125** 64
Mary Ann **81** 312
Mary Laura **109** 146
Mary Louise **81** 363 **82**
  234 244 499 500
Mary Middleton **125** 65
Mary V. (Dillaway)
  88 330
Maud **108** 174
Mehitable **57** 287 **79** 441
  106 160
Mehitable (Lombard)
  106 160
Mellindia (Ford) **120** 41
Mercy (Ellis) **121** 139
Michael **56** 390 **62** 381
Michael L. **103** 48
Nathan **58** 371
Nathan Prince **121** 140
Nathaniel **127** 311
Olive **106** 305 306
Olive (Crocker) **109** 38
Olive Gould **61** lvii
Oliver **54** 293 **56** 249 250
  391 392 **64** 372 **125** 221
Oliver Sturgis **64** 372
Ovid **55** 59 61 63 **66** 127
Patty **56** 384
Phebe **56** 258 **70** 259
Philadelphia **56** 259
Phineas **92** 25
Polly **54** 290 **56** 253 256
  384
Polly Ellis **121** 140
Rachel **86** 294
Ralph **111** 266 267 **121** 232
Randal **56** 254
Rebecca **55** 146 **121** 140
Rhoda **78** 406 **88** 279
Richard L. **100** 188
Robert **70** 259 **84** 238 **104**
  162 **117** 75 **119** 7 9 10
  103 **124** 220
Rosemary **119** 77
Russell **125** 108
Russell A. **132** 185 **141**
  251 254 361
Ruth **78** 404
Sabra **54** 293
Sabre **58** 371
Sally **56** 256
Sally (Sheafe) **125** 64
Sally Ann **147** 180
Samuel **68** 82 **78** 304 **106**
  306 **125** 215

LOVELL *cont'd*
Sarah **52** 273 **53** 394 **54**
  cxxxi **56** 35 **64** 372 **83** 4
  108 91 **124** 220
Sarah (Isham) **124** 220
Simeon **121** 139 140
Solomon **119** 190 **147** 74
Splan **58** 230
Stephen **56** 21
Susanna **60** 43 **86** 348
  118 277
Sylvia Pond **57** 285
Tabby **58** 371
Thomas **55** 336 **74** 136 322
  95 97 **103** 105-107 **125**
  216
Velina **113** 253
Vryling **54** 293
William **60** 399 **62** 253
  70 259 **79** 441 **106** 160
  139 283
William Horace **104** 68
  162
William M. **103** 46
William R. **104** 162
LOVELLEY
Mitchell **74** 318
Victor Haman **74** 318
LOVELOCK
Sarah (Rice) **88** 277
William **88** 277
LOVELY
Carrie **111** 138
Ida **83** 423 434
John **111** 138
Ruppert L. **114** 5
Sabra Melvina **111** 140
Susan (White) **111** 138
Sylvester I. **100** 76
LOVEMAN
— Mrs. **122** 307
Rachel **62** 269
Thomas **62** 265 268 269
LOVEMOND Lewis **77** 80
LOVEN John **51** 448
Phebe **51** 448
LOVER James **65** 117
John L. **91** 328
LOVERAN Anne **51** 309
John **51** 309
LOVEREL Daniel **62** 39
Esther **62** 39
Hannah **62** 41
John **62** 47
Lois **62** 47
Mary **62** 47
LOVERIDGE
— Mr. **148** 13
Archibald **100** 141
Edward **116** 7
Lucretia **100** 141
Rebecca **100** 141
LOVERIN
Dorothy **53** 163
Ebenezer **53** 163
Emma **53** 163
Jonathan **98** 265
Sarah A. **98** 265
Sarah Alvina **98** 265
LOVERING —— **130** 314
Aaron **88** 158 **89** 275

LOVERING *cont'd*
Abigail **62** 95 96 **133** 280
Alice **62** 95 96
Alice (Craft) **102** 3
Ann **56** 184 **71** 99 **75** 128
Anna **136** 269
Benjamin **62** 40
Charles Taylor **67** xxxiv
  70 xxviii xxxviii **90** 137
Clara **81** 255
Clifton **97** 134
Daniel **88** 158 **89** 275
  102 3
David **88** 158
Ebenezer **58** 233 **62** 37
Eliza **88** 158
Eliza R. **75** 128
Elizabeth **62** 95 96 **78** 291
  399 **114** 200
Ellen **76** 15
Elmer **97** 134
Esther **52** 276 **62** 38
George **88** 158
Hannah **61** 334 **62** 38
Hannah (Bowland)
  140 164
Harry Franklin (Mrs.)
  81 222 **82** 228 229
Henry Morton **51** 230
  60 xxxvi
Ira J. **97** 134
Jacob T. **88** 158
Jane **62** 95
Jerusha **114** 196
Jesse **58** 372 **102** 3
John **52** 276 **56** 184 **61** 336
  62 36 46 **65** 90 **140** 164
  145 315
John Parker **75** 128
Jonas **61** 22
Joseph **62** 95 96 **64** lx **70**
  xxxviii **71** 99 **75** 128 **97**
  57 **140** 164 328 **145** 315
Joseph Foster **75** 128
Joseph Swain **70** xxxviii
  81 192
Julia Esther **70** xli
Leah **130** 314
Lewis H. **51** 247
Lovilla Frances **76** lxvi
  95 361
Lucy **81** 255
Luke **58** 372
Lydia **58** 233
Mahalia **56** lxii
Margaret **62** 95 **75** 202
  126 65
Margaret (Gutch) **102** 3
Marian Shaw **70** xxxviii
Martha Y. (Bancroft)
  97 134
Martin **70** 97 **114** 204 280
Mary **58** 35 **62** 37 **70**
  xxxviii **81** 192 **84** 205
  351 **86** 214 350 **87** 188
  89 147 **90** 151 **92** 161
  125 101 **147** 20 152 251
Mary (Leland) **102** 3
Mary Ann **75** 128
Mary Campbell **62** xxxix
  102 4 **109** 289 **143** 99

LOVERING *cont'd*
  100
Mehitable **61** 357
Moses **61** 357
Nabby **88** 158
Nancy **52** 156 **71** 99
Nancy (Phillips) **97** 57
Olive **58** 372
Orissa Lavers **80** 106
  81 222
Phebe **88** 158 **89** 275
Philip **61** 199
Polly (Phillips) (Fox)
  97 57
Rebecca **100** 300 **145** 302
  315
Rebecca (Ellis) **145** 315
Richard Sears **70** xxxviii
Robert **62** 95 96 **102** 3
S. H. **91** 328
Sally **61** 23 **88** 158 **89** 275
  125 100
Samuel **62** 36 95 96 **81** 255
  102 3
Sarah **92** 124 **140** 164
Sarah Cook **75** 128
Sarah Eatat **92** 124
Sarah Foster **75** 128
Susan **68** 93
Susan Henry **75** 128
Teresa Beatrice **81** 192
Thomas **56** 184 **77** 307
Washington **61** 23
William **56** 184 **62** 42 95
  65 90 **70** xxxviii **92** 124
  97 57 **102** 3 **134** 228
  140 164 **145** 315
Winifred **141** 20
LOVETOT
John de **102** 192
LOVETT Lovall Lovet
  —— **71** 245 **119** 129 299
—Capt. **77** 63 64 107
—Mr. **65** 365
Abigail **54** 223 **57** 55
Ann **111** 64
Anna Ekin **72** xlv
Anna Eliza **92** 127
Anne **71** 245
Antoinette **80** 215
Augusta **126** 207
Benjamin **88** 281
Bethiah (Standly) **144** 54
Betsey **71** 50
Betty **142** 75
Beulah **98** 338
Caroline **72** xlv
Charles Henry **89** 132
Charles Walley **92** 127
Daniel **54** 222 223 **92** 24
  136 314 322 327
David **71** 50 **119** 20
Dolly **73** 306
Eleanor G. (Bridge)
  83 178 183
Eliz. **103** 73
Elizabeth **74** 136 137 **88**
  276 **92** 127 **93** 325 **94**
  377
Elizabeth (Matthews)
  142 36

LOVETT *cont'd*
Emma (Ray) **88** 361
Evaline Eudora **85** 197
Frank **98** 279
George Sidney **72** xlv
Hannah **67** 323
Henry **59** 102 **108** 83
Henry Almon **92** 146
Isaac **71** 122
Israel **54** 45 **88** 361
James **69** 361 **76** 47
  129 387
Jane E. **86** 323
Jeremiah **97** 269
Joan **75** 133 **76** 121
Joanna **54** 222
Joanna (Blott) **136** 314
  322 327
Joanna B. **67** xlvi
Joanna Batchelder **89** 371
John **66** 120 122 124 **102**
  193 **129** 385 **140** 68
John W. **88** 279
Jonathan **104** 75 76
  117 146
Joseph **97** 269 **99** 79
Joseph (Mrs.) **97** 269
Joseph M. **83** 178 183
Josephine Elizabeth
  136 317
Josephus **86** 323
Liflit **129** 385
Louisa Kilham **77** lxxxvi
Marcy **80** 240
Margaret **76** 122
Martha **136** 314 322
Martha R. (Francis)
  88 279
Mary **67** 77 **80** 180 **82** 47
  111 I **136** 327
Mary (Penn) **88** 281
Minerva **71** 122
Phineas **92** 24 **98** 338
Richard **76** 121
Robert **145** 105
Robert W. **116** 72 **119** 238
Robert Williamson (Mrs.)
  85 196
Ruth **88** 361
Samuel **70** 264 **78** 387
  113 211
Sarah **59** 61
Sidney **112** 321
Thomas **74** 322 **75** 133 **98**
  288 **144** 54
William **58** 202 **77** 231
  92 127 **93** 325 **94** 377
LOVEWELL
Abigail L. **89** 242
Anna **55** 186-188 **63** 288
Benjamin **132** 323
Betty **85** 361
Bridget **93** 237
C. H. **60** 187
Ebenezer **93** 397
Eleanor **85** 229
Elizabeth **63** 288
Enoch **94** 244
Esther **51** 222 **91** 262
  124 227
Esther (Hassell) **93** 237

LOVEWELL cont'd
Hannah **63** 288 290 **89** 315
Hepzibah **89** 315
James **85** 25
John **51** 101 143 **52** 394
54 77 80 **55** 186-188 **58**
411 **59** 84 85 144 145 **60**
187 **61** 106 **63** 288-296
64 35 37 98 **85** 257 **89**
315 **93** 376 **107** 99 **124**
227
Joseph **144** 222
Lucy **91** 263 **93** 234
Marguerite E. H. **84** 238
351
Mary Ann **95** 329
Molly **91** 263 **132** 323
Nehemiah **91** 257 259
107 100
Noah **91** 254
Nora **93** 347
Robert **84** 238 **91** 259
Sarah **91** 263 264 **124** 227
Zaccheus **51** 222 **93** 234
237 **124** 227
Zach **91** 254
Zacheus **91** 257
LOVEY
Alson H. **101** 210
Benjamin F. **101** 210
Charles C. **101** 210
Freelove **114** 12
Harriet M. **101** 210
Lorinda (Huntley)
101 210
Sary **95** 189
William P. **101** 210
LOVEYNE Margaret **138**
318 319 **139** 283 284
Nicholas **138** 318
LOVIE Ann B. (Shaw)
125 236
Susan **125** 238
LOVIS
Adeline S. **90** 49
Alice **141** 143
Catherine (Crofts)
125 218
Else **141** 143
Gridley **125** 218
Mary **125** 215 **141** 140
Ruth **141** 140 142
Ruth (Mansfield) **141** 140
Sally **125** 216
Sophia **125** 216
Sophie **137** 361
Thomas **141** 140
William **79** 40
LOVISE Ada **134** 67
LOVKIN Abigail (Parker)
105 160
LOVSGRAN
Betsey J. **70** 316
Low see Lowe
LOW Abigail **84** 447 **86** 122
Abigail (Choate) **90** 292
Abigail (Smith) **96** 145
Agnes (Meyeer) **88** 188
Alice Adeline **94** 140
Ann Curtis **90** 293

LOW cont'd
Anne Davison (Bedell)
90 292
Anthony **147** 337
Azubah **147** 185
Elizabeth (Stone) **105** 80
Emily Crosby **95** 342
Esther Hope **90** 293
Hannah (Haskell) **90** 292
Isit **97** 226
Jeanie (Isham) **97** 122
Joan Rebecca (Chapman)
87 174
Lois Robbins (Curtis)
90 293
Margaret (Tod) **90** 292
Martha **88** 398
Martha (Boreman) **90** 292
Mary **147** 185
Mary (Lamb) **90** 292
Mary (Langdon) **90** 184
Mary (Porter) **90** 292
Mary Elizabeth **90** 184
Rebecca B. **94** 380
Rosamond Curtis **90** 293
Sarah (Andrews) (Cole)
86 68
Susanna **90** 292 **118** 169
Susanna (Low) **90** 292
Virginia Marie **97** 122
Lowall see Lowell
LOWARDEN Jane **81** 34
LOWBER Hannah (Luff)
(Freeman) (Robinson)
106 45
Isaac **106** 47
Mary **106** 47
Mary (Bowers) **106** 47
Matthew **106** 45
Michael **106** 47
LOWCOCK Harry **63** 35
Lowd see Loud
LOWDEN Lowdin Lowdon
—— **136** 41
Abigail **59** 244
Andrew **59** 244
Antho: **98** 215
Benjamin **59** 244
Elizabeth **51** 465 **59** 244
94 61
Experience **111** 70
Florence **98** 145
Frank Orren **54** 105 **84**
110 185 **91** 183 **97** 287
98 145 149
George **102** 30
Hannah **59** 244
James **59** 244 **106** 95
John **54** 105 **59** 243 244
134 72
Joseph **59** 243 244 **107** 98
Joshua **54** 105
Lydia **82** 18
Lydia C. **127** 62
Martha Jane **110** 144
Mary **57** 356 **59** 243 244
60 52
Mary (Cole) **131** 129
Mary Ann **119** 280
Nahum **136** 41
Priscilla **104** 227

LOWDEN cont'd
Rachel **73** 143
Richard **59** 243 244 **106** 91
131 129 **136** 41
Ruth (Josselyn) **134** 72
Sarah **59** 243
LOWDER
D. (Mrs.) **105** 210
Hannah **78** 67
Henry **125** 104
James **53** 22
John **53** 72
Jonathan **84** 260 **90** 87
Mary Ann **119** 285
Orpha **117** 124
Polly (Searls) **125** 104
Ruth **93** 155 **118** 290
Ruth (Bussey) **93** l 154 155
S. **93** 155
Samuel **93** 154 155
William **90** 87 **140** 165
LOWDERMILK
Polly **78** 40
LOWDHAM
Jane **98** 274 275
Jane (Kelvedon) **98** 275
John **98** 274
Lowdin see Lowden
Lowdon see Lowden
LOWE Low
—— **76** 249 **82** 413 **83** 35
93 123 **104** 57
— Capt. **96** 357 **97** 143
— Goodman **81** 131
— Goodwife **81** 131
— Gov. **124** 134
— Mr. **65** 166 **73** 77 **92** 14
Aaron **86** 68
Abba C. (Libby) **91** 119
Abia **93** 114
Abiel Abbot **136** 321
Abigail **63** 167 **74** 224 **75**
106 107 116 118 119 **76**
110 179 182 193 **78** 317
79 36 **84** 447 **86** 122 **92**
17 **102** 146 **116** 304 **136**
323
Abigail (Choate) **136** 321
Abigail (Gould) **95** 88
Abigail (Smith) **96** 248
Abigail (Varney) **136** 323
Abigail Hale **90** 171
Abigail M. **97** 227
Abraham **76** 248
Abraham Annis **76** 248
Abram **93** 243
Ada Clarissa **78** 50
Adeline **88** 334
Adeline (Ford) **101** 227
Alce **96** 144 336
Alexander **95** 399
Alfred M. **97** 122
Alice Adeline **94** 140
Almira S. **91** 121 **97** 230
Almon **91** 119
Alpheus **91** 17 **96** 341
Ambrose **121** 272 282
143 50
Andrew **81** 128 131 **100**
197 **121** 82 83
Ann **64** 262 **70** 121 **73** 217

LOWE *cont'd*
220 **82** 27 **100** 303 **115**
132
Ann Curtis **90** 293
Anna **52** 200 **78** 399 **95** 191
100 91
Anna (Moriarty) **101** 227
Anne **61** 129
Anne (Parkhill) **136** 323
Annie L. **75** 261
Annis **52** 67
Anthony **61** 129 **62** 181
63 129 **97** 326 **129** 276
Arthur Houghton
136 323
Arthur Moore **102** 139
Arthur Moore (Mrs.)
100 112 **103** 136 **104**
160
Asa **75** 312 **76** 111-114 248
249 253 260
Augustus G. **83** 34
Barbara **73** 267
Barbara (Wells) **129** 79
Barsheba **73** 147
Barton **73** 141
Basil **73** 146 **114** 193
Benaiah **75** 114
Benjamin **76** 13 **100** 298
105 279 **143** 18
Benjamin Franklin
134 334
Benjamin R. C. **79** 337
Benjamin Robbins
Curtis **90** 293
Berger **98** 336
Betsey **65** 255 **96** 147
116 137
Betsey (Farrington)
88 275
Betsey (Kingsley) **88** 282
Betsey (Smith) **90** 230 251
Betsey B. **97** 226
Bezaleel **65** 255
Blanche Beal **117** 76
Caleb **86** 311 **136** 323
Caroline **116** 223 298 300
Cassie **76** 13
Catherine **64** 122 128
79 54
Charity **100** 91
Charles **64** 138 **80** 202 **82**
47 **83** 34 173 **89** 263 **103**
268 **105** 276
Charles F. **73** 220
Christina **76** 13
Claflin (Mrs.) **93** 280
Clarissa **65** 255
D. Grenville **90** 114
Daniel **76** 103 113 **90** 333
91 23 24 **96** 339 **100** 91
103 269 **105** 282 **113**
138
Daniel W. **61** xxxiii
Darling **90** 333
David **75** 48 112 113 121
122 312 313 **76** 102 103
110 111 194 **78** 313 **90**
184 292 **92** 351 **94** 380
136 311 321 323
David W. **55** xxix xxxv

LOWE *cont'd*
122 313
Deborah **64** 123 **73** 268
Delia (Ebbets) **134** 334
Dennis **73** 146 **114** 193
Dorcas **56** 318 **74** 224
116 131
Ebenezer **75** 110
Edith Frances **82** 122 235
Edith G. **123** 235
Edmund Augustus
75 260
Edward **70** 216 **75** 261 **78**
402 **96** 357 **113** 125 263
116 222 224 **119** 288
320 **120** 64
Edward F. **113** 125
Eleanor **75** 122
Eleanor (Berrey) **100** 298
Elias **73** 146
Elijah **76** 187 **90** 326
105 282
Elisha **82** 47
Eliza **78** 185 **82** 47
Eliza-Jane (McCulla)
90 114
Elizabeth **61** 129 **62** 181 68
225 **73** 150 **75** 45 110
120 **80** 394 **81** 446 **82** 47
83 22 25 31 **89** 188 **101**
223 **105** 80 **112** 40 **116**
129 265 **121** 23 **135** 105
Elizabeth (Crosby) **92** 323
Elizabeth (Eveleth)
(Haradin) **135** 27
Elizabeth (Folsom)
(Noble) **95** 29
Elizabeth (Hyde) **126** 28
Elizabeth (Stodder)
121 71
Elizabeth Abbot **92** 312
Elizabeth Ann **90** 109
92 351
Elizabeth Emma **109** 66
Elizabeth P. **83** 25
Elizabeth Stevens **82** 422
Ellen **65** 170
Ellen Almira (Dow)
136 321
Elmira S. **97** 226
Emily Crosby **93** 122 **95**
342 **102** 145
Enoch Louis **67** 192
Ephraim **74** 216 224
75 50 120
Esther **73** 142 **75** 116
116 221
Esther Hope **90** 293
Eunice **58** 258 **76** 111 112
186 187 189 248 253 260
78 419
Fannie **93** 243 **107** 211
Florence Withington
75 261
Frances **64** 138
Frances Catherine (Titus)
114 175
Francis **81** 329 **93** 122 **94**
158 **109** 160
Frank **134** 334
Frank B. **114** 175

LOWE *cont'd*
Franklin **82** 47
George **64** 166 **73** 219 **82**
47 **83** 35 **92** 17 19 21-23
101 227 **117** 16
George Ann **82** 422
George D. **52** 386
George M. **93** 243
George W. **88** 283
George Washington
92 127
Grace Gardner **61** 243
Hannah **59** 283 **65** 255 **75**
121 **76** 106 182 184 186
259 **81** 124 **90** 246 **92**
124 **100** 197
Hannah (Buzzell) **90** 333
91 23 24
Hannah (Fitz Randolph)
98 336
Hannah (Gardner)
133 321
Hannah (Haskell) **136** 321
Hannah (Lincoln)
121 109
Hannah W. (Lakeman)
88 283
Hannah W. (Lord) **90** 326
Harriet **86** 122 **90** 46
Harriet Gertrude **75** 261
Helen M. (Hopkins)
104 124
Henrietta **53** 464 **90** 293
Henrietta Margaret
109 66
Henry **52** 67 **133** 182
Henry Mazyck Clarkson
(Mrs.) **88** 188
Henry Somes **108** 250
Hiram **76** 249 **93** 114 247
Horace **97** 227
Horace (Mrs.) **123** 117
Horace P. (Mrs.) **126** 81
Horace Wales **75** 261
Hudson **61** 101
Hugh **80** 388
Isabel **61** 129
Isabella C. **87** 383
Isabella Crawford
125 291
Isit **97** 226 227
Izetta / Iset (Gooch) **96**
146 **133** 43
Jacob **73** 67-70 72 **76** 114
James **65** 49 **68** 227 **73**
140 151 **76** 111 **104** 124
James Adrian **101** 227
James Jeremiah **115** 135
James Rector Magruder
73 230
Jane **83** 25 26 **133** 182
134 334
Jean **125** 301 302
Jedediah **75** 112 **76** 106
182 184 186 259
Jemima **78** 67
Jen. **58** 60
Jesse **104** 324
Joab **76** 112
Joanna (Partridge) **98** 219
Job **75** 46 52 110-114 120

LOWE *cont'd*
122 **76** 102 111 112 186
189 191 192 194 248 253
260
John **51** 45 **52** 67 **55** 413
56 335 **61** 42 129 269
336 337 **62** 46 181 243
63 22 25 **64** 128 342 **65**
45 149 261 **66** 35 **67** 355
73 75 142 144 **74** 224 **75**
107 112 119 120 122 **76**
110 179 194 **82** 422 **83**
24 25 35 **84** 465 **87** 206
207 **88** 282 **92** 123-127
129 131 246 **94** 265 276
95 191 199 **96** 143 145
248 **97** 227 **98** 219 **104**
230 **107** 84 **116** 222 268
121 21 105 108 109 204
129 79 275 276 **144** 266
John Adams **67** 385
68 385
John Allan (Mrs.) **87** 174
John Brown **92** 22
John F. **92** 315
John Gardner **62** 113
John Gorham **93** 123
John H. **73** 149
John Holden **129** 79
John J. **101** 227
John M. **123** 235
John W. **73** 263
Jonathan **79** 14 193 **81** 446
82 27 **105** 55 **108** 183
140 164
Jonathan Loring **92** 131
Joseph **63** 15 27 **73** 74 **82**
47 292 293 **83** 25 26 35
91 328 **92** 312 315 **95** 29
113 125 **116** 141 301
302 **119** 66 **136** 323
Joseph G. **97** 227
Judah **65** 255
Keziah **73** 149
Kitty **73** 264
Lavinia **97** 19 226
Lawrence **52** 124
Lawrence Janson **59** 419
Leithy **73** 151
Lester Dony (Mrs.)
104 144
Levi **105** 276
Lillian Annie **75** 261
Lois Curtis **90** 293
Louisa **93** 123
Louisa (Dairy) **86** 311
Louisa Adeline
(Messenger) **136** 323
Lucy **74** 255 **79** 12
Lydia **75** 53 **76** 194 **82** 47
83 25 26 **116** 142
Lydia (Cook) **126** 179
Lydia (Gooch) **96** 147
Lydia (Rhodes) **90** 335
91 25
Lydia (Vickery) **143** 50
Mamie E. **93** 243
Margaret **92** 129 **118** 260
126 28
Margery **59** 326
Maria **82** 47 **83** 25 27

LOWE *cont'd*
Maria Frances **82** 422
Marie **55** 413
Martha **88** 398 **96** 144 340
Mary **61** 382 **62** 303 **73** 136
74 216 224 **75** 45 46 48-
50 52 53 120 **76** 111-114
248 253 260 **81** 124 **83**
35 **93** 243 **116** 138 **125**
99 **136** 311
Mary (Lamb) **136** 311
321 323
Mary (Porter) **136** 321
Mary (Sawyer) **136** 323
Mary (Springer) **86** 122
Mary (Towne) **133** 43
Mary (Whittemore)
107 186
Mary (Wise) **136** 323
Mary A. **130** 157
Mary Ann **83** 21 25
102 240
Mary B. **97** 227
Mary Cassandra **86** 311
Mary D. **93** 243
Mary D. (Towns) **97** 221
Mary Elizabeth **90** 184
Mary Ellen **77** 186
Mary Emma **75** 261
Mary Foote **89** 263
Mary G. **97** 235
Mary H. **88** 275 278
Mary Haden **92** 124
Mary M. (Clark) **125** 53
Mary Wells **129** 79
Mary Wilkerson **104** 324
Mehitable **74** 250 **93** 247
96 337
Mercy **75** 122 **91** 229
Mercy (Norcross) **125** 215
Mercy B. **97** 227
Miriam **75** 122 313
Miriam (Lockhart) **99** 298
Moses **90** 229 248
Nancy **76** 253 **91** 29 **92** 21
Nancy (Moore) **119** 66
Nancy Adaline **86** 368
Nathan **105** 208
Nathaniel **53** 338 **63** 167
78 185 **95** 88 **96** 146 **97**
226 **133** 43 **139** 49
Nicholas **133** 182
Obadiah **52** 200 **53** 72 **68**
225 227 **74** 216
Olive **75** 120 **109** 256
116 221
Orin Messinger **59** xli
Pamelia Delaverne
64 128
Parley **91** 328
Patience **116** 294
Peter **62** 61 **125** 53
Peter Cornelius **112** 315
Phebe **75** 119
Phebe (Rhodes) **90** 333
Philip **104** 324
Phillipe (Snelling) **105** 55
Phineas **65** 255
Polly **65** 255 **76** 253 **82** 47
Polly (Smith) **96** 339
Priscilla **73** 224 **76** 186

LOWE *cont'd*
Rachel **73** 141 149 232 **82**
291 293 **113** 263 **116**
225
Rachel Parkhill **94** 137
136 323
Rebecca **73** 137 **96** 389
Rebecca B. **92** 351 **94** 380
Reynes **112** 40 **118** 260 261
Richard **82** 47 413 422 **83**
35 **85** 390 393
Robert **88** 275
Robert Henry **109** 66
Roger **53** 97
Rosamond Curtis **90** 293
Rosetta **108** 135
Russell Cutle **96** 160
Ruth **121** 215 **125** 105
Ruth (Andruce) **121** 272
Ruth (Joye) **121** 204
S. **82** 422
Sabra Jane **97** 227
Sally **75** 261 **95** 199
Sally A. **93** 243
Sally H. **97** 227
Samuel **61** 129 **62** 181 **64**
162 **75** 111 **78** 71 **90** 230
251 335 **91** 25 **92** 127
106 43 44 **121** 210 **125**
215
Sarah **52** 67 **61** 382 **62** 61
64 315 **65** 255 **73** 141
74 252 **75** 111-114 118
120-122 312 313 **76** 102
103 **79** 193 **81** 446 **82**
291 293 **83** 24 25 **92** 14
23 **98** 219 **127** 8 **129** 276
134 146 **135** 123 126
Sarah (Davis) **135** 123
Sarah (Herrick) **95** 199
Sarah (Pitts) **90** 229 248
Sarah (Tupper) **99** 61
Sarah A. **84** 29
Sarah Ann **83** 173 **90** 326
129 79
Sarah Elizabeth **76** l
Seth **64** 382 **79** 337 **90** 292
99 61 **117** 302 **136** 321
Simon **107** 186
Sophia V. **122** 71
Stephen **78** 301 **92** 19
129 270 275
Sukey **116** 137
Sukey (Perkins) **116** 301
302
Susan **81** 329
Susan (Fernald) **123** 235
Susan E. **119** 277 278
Susan Elizabeth **75** 260
Susan Ella **75** 261
Susan Gilchrist **81** 329
Susan J. **113** 125
Susan J. (Raynes) **113** 125
120 64
Susan Jane (Raynes)
119 288
Susan M. **91** 385
Susan P. **93** 243
Susanna **75** 112 119 120
122 **90** 292 **92** 131 **118**
169 **136** 311 321-323

LOWE *cont'd*
Susanna Cane **92** 126
Susanna Hayden **92** 246
Symonds **135** 123
T. H. **53** 453
Tabitha **75** 49 **76** 187 **121**
  103 104 108
Taylor **73** 75
Temperence (Getchell)
  91 17 **96** 341
Thomas **52** 67 **56** 314 **63**
  17 **74** 252 **77** 318 **90** 292
  92 125 **96** 147 **97** 221
  226 **100** 141 **105** 276
  119 320 **133** 43 **140** 164
Thomas Dean **92** 126
Thomas Gerrish **82** 47
Thomas T. **119** 320
Timothy **76** 102
Vincent **133** 182
Virginia Marie **97** 122
Walter **52** 67 **93** 243
Walter Grant **101** 124
William **52** 126 **58** 60 **61**
  243 **73** 143 262 **75** 45
  106 107 116 118 119 **76**
  192 **79** 341 **80** 397 **81**
  446 **92** 323 **119** 320
William C. **126** 178
William Gilman **73** 235
  74 xxiv **89** 170 190 **90**
  292 293 **91** 57 145
William Henry **90** 292
William Lewis (Mrs.)
  108 134
Winfield Eldridge **90** 137
Winifred **73** 217
LOWELL Lowall Lowle
— Capt. **134** 271
— Dr. **92** 346 354 **93** 322
— Judge **54** 315
  Mr. **65** 368 371 **69** 221
  78 187 **142** 135
— Rev. Dr. **94** 297
____ (Amory) **140** 32
____ (Bradbury) **91** 262
A. O. (Mrs.) **117** 79
Abbott Lawrence **63** 207
  64 92 **73** 235 **74** xxi 166
  78 80 81 **80** 136 **81** 13
  88 214 397 **89** 215 **97**
  148 211 214 **98** 148 **136**
  90 321
Abigail **54** 315 316 319
  61 51 **64** 9 **72** 273 **96**
  325 **141** 250
Abigail (Coney) **110** 313
Abigail (Lowell) **141** 250
Abner **78** 110 **90** 87
  105 283
Abram **53** 376
Adeline L. **141** 143 144
Albert **95** 186 **145** 139
Alice **84** 51 52 131
Amanda H. **117** 164
Amy **97** 213 **105** 82
Ann **84** 377
Anna **54** 315 **93** 121 122
  254
Anna (Cabot) **93** 120
Anna (Hassell) **85** 257

LOWELL *cont'd*
Anna Cabot **93** 115 120
Anna Cabot Jackson
  93 120
Anna M. (Jordan) **83** 207
Anna Parker (Lowell)
  97 213 **136** 321
Anne **94** 64 **137** 362
Annie (Harris) **117** 167
Arabine **110** 235
Augusta **103** 266
Augustus **89** 215 **97** 211
Benjamin **97** 286 **105** 283
  141 244 **147** 259
Betsey **80** 27
C. **82** 416
Catherine Elizabeth
  (Peabody) **84** 327
Charles **51** 445 **53** 42 135
  216 376 **54** 315 **58** 203
  64 296 **91** 341 **92** 132
  245 247 251 259 349 352
  93 315 **94** 378 **136** 225
  140 155
Charles R. **93** 120-122 254
Charles Russell **60** 220
  226 **92** 245 **93** 121
Charlotte C. **97** 235
Clara Augusta **92** 109
Colford **54** 316 319
Cynthia **147** 259
D. O. S. **98** 184
Daniel **58** 43 **83** 207
Daniel Ozro Smith **59**
  xlvi **74** 161 **81** 483 **82**
  381 **83** 206 236
David **64** 9 **141** 244 250
Delmar R. **53** 373 381 454
  54 xxxvi 315 317 319
  110 313 **141** 143 244
  148 134
Diana **64** 212
Eben **97** 140 396
Ebenezer **54** 315-319 **93**
  397 **96** 325 326 **100** 63
  110 313 314
Ebenezer B. **72** 273
Edward **137** 362
Edward Jackson **58** 326
  93 257 **136** 321
Eliphalet **105** 211
Eliza **54** 315 319 **88** 127
Eliza Maria **82** 485
Eliza Warren **92** 109
Elizabeth **52** 428 **53** 376 **54**
  315-319 **57** 179 **63** 300
  85 257 **94** 106 **96** 325
  110 313 314 **142** 304
  145 162 **148** 133
Elizabeth (Goodale)
  148 134
Elizabeth (Mayo) **104** 183
Elizabeth (Silvester)
  85 257
Elizabeth Cabot **70** lv
Elizabeth Shapleigh
  96 35
Ella **89** 60
Ella Bancroft **70** lv **77** lix
Emma E. **92** 338

LOWELL *cont'd*
Emma Woodman
  (Jordan) **83** 207
Enoch **92** 109 **104** 183
Frances **117** 128
Frances (Colby) **83** 207
Frances H. **74** 103
Francis C. **52** 389 **63** 390
  93 64 115 120 122 257
  315 **94** 44
Francis Cabot **77** 300 **78**
  287 **93** 64 374 **94** 45 **97**
  92 211
George **72** 273
George A. **121** 179
George Gardner **93** 115
  136 321
George H. **117** 167
George O. **121** 180
Georgia A. (Barton)
  121 180
Georgianna (Amory)
  120 85
Georgina **93** 63 115 122
Georgina Amory **93** 63
Georgina M. **94** 43
Gideon **83** 207 **86** 460
Grace (McFadden) **134** 66
Gran **103** 298
Guy **117** 161 **136** 321
H. B. **92** 259 349
H. B. L. **92** 259
H. B. S. **92** 352
Hannah **52** 428 **55** 264 **61**
  307 **63** 300 **68** 260 **91**
  258 **93** 315 **97** 352 **147**
  259
Harriet **92** 251 **93** 122
Harriet B. **92** 245 247
Harriet Brackett **94** 40
Harriet I. **72** 273
Harriet M. **97** 140 396
Harriet Whiting **66** lxiii
Helen Augusta
  (Shapleigh) **96** 35
Henry **86** 36
Holford **54** 316
Jacob **58** 237 **103** 298
  134 66
James **58** 42 43 **145** 163
James Arnold **52** 381
James Burnett **85** 188
  102 62 71 121 127
James Jackson **93** 254
James R. **93** 257
James Russell **53** 136 376
  58 13 115 **70** 292 **74** 103
  76 166 **81** 10 **91** 341 **92**
  352 **93** 253 255 **96** 35
  102 121 **115** 66 **139** 3
Jennie (Abar) **145** 137
Joan **53** 376
Joanna **53** 376 **67** 105
John **51** 45 **52** 381 428 **53**
  155 376 **54** 315-319 **57**
  86 178-180 **62** 253 63
  214 300 **66** 111 **67** 209
  74 206 **77** 90 **81** 7 **85**
  257 261 **90** 400 **91** 311
  93 63 115 **94** 43 106 **96**
  325 **97** 213 **110** 313 **114**

LOWELL *cont'd*
259 **116** 111 224 **118**
313 **120** 82 85 **136** 361
140 32 165 324 **141** 244
148 134
John (Mrs.) **85** 196
John A. **94** 37
John Amory **52** 381 **70** lv
89 60 **91** 311 **140** 324
Joseph **52** 428 **57** 178 **63**
300 **85** 257 **91** 262 **96**
325 **105** 212
Joseph Dam **92** 109
Joseph Q. **80** 235
Joshua **78** 111
Josiah **64** 9 **105** 210
Jotham Grant **134** 66
Julia A. (Chase) **94** 37
Kate **94** 54
Ladora L. **80** 235
Lavina **147** 259
Levi **141** 250
Louisa **147** 259
Louise H. **95** 250
Lucy (Foster) **83** 207
Lucy Ann **90** 108
Lucy B. **52** 381
Lucy Buckminster **52** 381
Lydia **74** 94 **103** 193
142 304
Lydia (Messer) **91** 263
Mabel **93** 255 **102** 71
Margaret (Paro) **145** 139
Maria **93** 253 255 257
Maria (Burnell) (Noble)
95 186
Martha **52** 428 **145** 137
Martin Luther **96** 98
Mary **52** 428 **54** 315-319 **58**
124 **63** 300 **77** 300 **93** 64
115 120 374 **97** 91 92
110 314 **118** 80
Mary (Blaisdell) **86** 460
Mary (Blood) **141** 244 250
Mary (Chandler) **83** 207
Mary (Reed) **110** 313 314
Mary A. **92** 338
Mary Amanda (Smith)
83 207
Mary Chandler **94** 118
245 **95** 205 206 **142** 245
Mary Ellen (Parker)
136 321
Mary L. **93** 122 257 **94** 44
Mary Lowell (Gardner)
97 92
Mary Shapleigh **96** 35
Mary Somes (Merrill)
134 66
Mary Traill Spence
92 251
Mary Walker **83** 207
Mary Wolcott (Goodrich)
136 321
Matilda **103** 304
Matilda (Goodrich)
103 235
Melinda **66** 111
Melvin Nelson **92** 109
Melvina M. **145** 139
Metilla **80** 235

LOWELL *cont'd*
Michael **54** 315 316 319
61 51 **110** 313 314
Miriam (Knowlton)
83 207
Miriam (Swett) **83** 207
Molly **91** 258 **105** 61
Moses **83** 207 **91** 258
Muriel Emma **83** 207
Nancy (Bowen) **97** 140
396
Naomi **54** 315
Naomi (Sylvester)
136 361
Nathaniel **105** 283
Nehemiah **58** 42 43
Olive Jane **110** 224
Oliver **58** 43
Olivia F. (Gunnison)
121 179
Pascal **145** 137
Patience **57** 178 **63** 300
85 257
Paul **142** 304 **145** 162
Percival **53** 376 **54** 315
317 318 **63** 300 **67** 105
77 lx **78** 287 **82** 153 **83**
207 **95** 263 **97** 213 214
136 361 **141** 244
Peter **63** 300
Phebe **57** 179 **63** 300
85 257
Priscilla **147** 259
Ralph (Mrs.) **84** 342
85 196
Rebecca (Amory) **120** 82
Rebecca Russell **84** 327 **92**
247 **93** 290 **94** 43 **98** 270
Reuben **91** 328
Reynold **95** 263
Rhoda (Farnham) **141** 143
Richard **53** 376 **83** 207
139 140
Robert Traill Spence
92 349
Ruth **91** 257 **109** 149 **136**
361 **141** 244 249 250
Ruth (Bruce) **141** 250
Ruth (Woodman) **97** 286
Samuel **78** 111 **80** 27
92 109
Sarah **51** 461 **54** 315-319
61 47 **91** 263 **110** 313
314
Sarah Ethel **98** 352
Sarah W. **101** 32
Stephen **60** 44 **91** 257 258
263
Susan **52** 381
Susanna **64** 9 **86** 348
Thomas **85** 32 **104** 118
Walter **93** 257
William **53** 376 **60** 44
103 235 304
William Keith Spence
92 259
Zaccheus **57** 180 **85** 257
Zerebiah P. **90** 107
Ziba Wright **141** 143
LOWEN Nicholas **63** 163
LOWER —— **61** 36

LOWER *cont'd*
Ellen Florence **82** 278
John **82** 278
Joyce **84** 190
Katrine **82** 278
Mark Anthony **65** 88 **99** 8
Mark Antony **74** 16
LOWEREE —— **101** 179
LOWERRE Sarah Burling
(Helme) **102** 239
LOWERSON
Mary **65** 123
Richard **63** 138
LOWERY
Barbara **68** 150
Caroline Ford **60** 88
Carrie L. **119** 110
Catherine **68** 150
Edna Hopkins **82** 105
Edwin Eugene **68** 150
Ellen **68** 150
Ellen S. (Ford) **137** 51
George **68** 150
Ida **68** 150
John **91** 328
Kate **68** 150
Marie Caroline **68** 150
Mary **68** 150
Melinda **68** 150
Rachel **99** 40
Stewart S. (Mrs.) **82** 105
Thomas **68** 150
William **68** 150
William Pierson **68** 150
Woodbury **67** 96
LOWES Richard **103** 11
LOWEY James **61** 348
Jane **61** 348
John **61** 137
Mary **61** 348
Robert **61** 348
T. K. **112** 276
William **61** 136 348
Lowgie *see* Lougee
LOWLAND John **108** 189
Olive **108** 189
Olive (Wildes) **108** 189
Lowle *see* Lowell
LOWMAN
A. Marshall **95** 399
John **51** 80
Moses **60** 36
Seymour **95** 399
LOWN Clarence **87** 87
Eliza **83** 471
Mary Alvinette (Coleman)
87 87
LOWNDES Lownds Lownes
—— **53** 134 **117** 14
— Mr. **53** 418
Anne **75** xl
Arthur **107** 245
Charles **107** 267
E. R. **83** 428 434
Edith H. (Farmer) **83** 428
434
Elizabeth **73** 268
George **117** 58
Gertrude Laura **75** xl
Jane **117** 58
John **117** 4 9 12 15

LOWNDES *cont'd*
Mary L. **125** 238
Rawlins **75** xl
Rebecca **73** 140
Richard **104** 163
LOWNEY Sarah **80** 27
William **80** 27
LOWRIE Harriet **86** 195
LOWRY Lowrey Lowrie
—— **54** 117 **58** 207 **112** 19
— Mr. **76** 132
Adelia Lafayette **92** 291
Betsey **71** 355
Betty **77** 267 **99** 44
Caroline **77** 291 **78** 163
Caroline Ford **58** xlviii
Cleo E. **78** 175
Clyde E. **78** 175
Curtis **71** 355
Daniel **76** 132
David **112** 19
Dorcas **112** 19
Dorcas (Montgomery)
112 19
Emily Isabel **72** 165
Estelle Gale **78** 175
F. N. (Mrs.) **84** 172
Frances **69** 324
Fred E. (Mrs.) **116** 233
Frederick Eugene (Mrs.)
115 231
Frederick Nichols (Mrs.)
85 196 **118** 159
Harriet **86** 195
Helen (Bullitt) **99** 44
Isaac **111** 89
Israel Hugh **85** 329
James **78** 69 **99** 44 **112** 19
117 15 **145** 295
Janet **71** lvi
John **59** 219 **73** 229 231
106 108 **112** 17 19
John M. **112** 19
Kate Celina Adele **111** 52
Laura **78** 175
Lois Akin **116** 233
Louisa M. **106** 108
Mamie Dorcas **78** 175
Martha L. **106** 108
Mary **65** 123 **99** 76
Mary Ann Clark **72** 165
Michael **111** 52
Nehemiah **71** 355
Ophelia Jane **78** 175
Philip **77** 291
Rachel **99** 40
Robert **72** 165 **112** 302
Robert E. **112** 19
Rosina (Billings) **98** 7
Ruth Cleveland **97** 118
Sallie **117** 319
Sarah Ellen **97** 118
Sophie Wager **77** 291
Susan Elizabeth **85** 329
Thomas **76** 132
Virginia Polk **78** 175
William **69** 324 **112** 19
William (Mrs.) **99** 183
William S. **78** 175
William Stephen **97** 118

LOWSLEY Lowsleye
Barzillai **117** 200
Richard **83** 320
LOWTH Anne **98** 118
LOWTHER Lowthe
Lowthier
Ada **79** 204
Ada May **81** 220 **95** 292
296 **96** 164
Alexander **95** 293
Anthony **54** 325 335 **56**
204 **96** 101
Aquilla (Reese) **95** 293
Beatrice de **96** 312
Charles Centennial
95 293
Elizabeth **56** 204
Elizabeth Ann (Boyce)
95 292
Granville **95** 292 293
Hannah (Leeson) **95** 293
Hazel **85** 192
Hugh de **96** 119
Jesse **95** 293
John **98** 117
John de **96** 121
John Frank **95** 293
Joseph **62** 81
Joshua **139** 42 43
Lola Edith **95** 293
Mabel Elizabeth **95** 293
Margaret **54** 325 334 335
56 204
Margaret (Morrison)
95 293
Martha **95** 292
Mary **63** 140
Nathaniel **139** 42
Robert **56** 204 **95** 293
101 244
Sarah (Ireland) **95** 293
Sudna (Hughes) **95** 293
Thomas de **96** 312
William **95** 292 293
LOWTON Ralph **82** 189
LOWTRIDGE
Archibald **102** 29
Lucretia **102** 29
Rebecca **102** 29
LOXHAM Henry **63** 159
LOXLEY —— **54** 117
Loyd *see* Lloyd
LOYE Loy De Loy
Bethiah **57** 180
Elizabeth de **92** 229 230
John **57** 180
Percival Elliot **121** 156
William **121** 156
William E. **57** xliv
LOYER
Electa A. **76** 272
George **76** 272
LOZIER —— **53** 232
Eliza (Wallace) **114** 60
Hannah **53** 232
John L. **123** 74
Margaret (Griggs) **123** 74
Mary (Averill) **123** 74
Nettie M. (Norton) **123** 74
LOZUM Charles **62** 329
LUBEC Emma **68** lxxi

LUBTAN Abigail **55** 200
LUBY William A. **68** 306
LUC Maria I. **65** 231
Peter **65** 231
LUCAN —— **56** 341 343
LUCAR Mark **122** 107
LUCAS alias HILL
Katharine **52** 253
LUCAS Leucas Llucas
Luckis Lucus
—— **57** 423 **60** 70 **67** 274
95 320 **132** 163
— Mr. **82** 452 **85** 120
— Mrs. **101** 270
— Widow **67** 38
—— (Henderson) **113** 323
Abigail **132** 163
Adam **73** 262
Agnes **73** 254
Alden **60** 70
Alfred **85** 167
Alice **82** 444 450
Alice L. **85** 315
Alice R. **83** 299 300
Alma Jerusha **59** 212
Almeda Minerva **59** 212
Amanda M. **77** 151
Andrew **73** 254
Ann **73** 271
Anne **71** 213 334
Annie **93** 55
Annie (Moore) **121** 147
122 146 **123** 232
Arthur **147** 166
Asa Milo **59** 212
Auguste **107** 268
Augustus **80** 174
Aurelia Lerinna **59** 212
B. Washington **123** 232
Barnabas **125** 277
Bathsheba **80** 174
Baza **77** 266
Benjamin **55** 390 **111** 271
113 324 **116** 304 305
119 287 **123** 232
Benjamin W. **120** 66
Benoni **88** 223 **121** 40
Bethiah **148** 143 147
Betsey **60** 70
Betsey (Clough) **118** 242
122 73
Betsey Ann **120** 217
Betsey Ann (Clough)
118 240
Bryan **52** 253
Calvin **127** 97
Catherine (McCoy)
113 324
Charles E. **85** 315
Charlotte A. (Andrews)
116 259
Christian **71** 329 334
Critchett **132** 163
Cyrenius Edwin **59** 212
60 76
Daniel **73** 254 **132** 163 164
David Sherman **85** 167
Deborah **60** 70 **127** 65
Dorcas **119** 64 65
Dorothy **61** 391

LUCAS *cont'd*
Dorothy M. (Main)
  118 241
Edith Brittain **80** 244
Edward **110** 171 **111** 271
Eldora C. **110** 223
Eldora Catherine **110** 223
Electa **62** 268
Elisha **144** 318
Eliza **144** 156 158 159 345
Eliza (Briggs) **86** 300
Eliza Ann **119** 284 286
Eliza Y. **114** 192
Elizabeth **51** 465 **60** 166 **71**
  329 334 **82** 446 450 **91**
  271 **102** 31 **111** 271 **132**
  163 **144** 156 223
Elizabeth (Scott) **111** 271
Ella Maud **65** xlviii
Emily F. (Underwood)
  120 305 307
Emma J. **86** 147
Emma Jane **86** 300
Esther **111** 271
Esther (Heulings) **111** 271
Frances **71** 329 334
Frances McIver **109** 145
  112 224
Frederick **117** 49
Geofry **91** 328
George **58** 64 **99** 285 **144**
  156 157
George E. **122** 73
Griselda (McCollister)
  113 324
Halsey B. **116** 259
Hannah **77** 320 **111** 271
Harriet Cynthia **112** 145
Hart Newell **59** 212
Henderson **114** 192
Henry **51** 465 **102** 31
  144 223
Henry S. **102** 78
Hepsibeth (Boston)
  116 301
Hewill **62** 331
Hugh **113** 323
Israel **61** 391 **85** 409
James **73** 104 254 **104** 118
James A. **77** 151
James Jonathan **109** 145
Jane **58** 391 **77** 266 **80** 174
  82 444 452
Jean **80** 257
Jenet **116** 172
Jerusha **60** 267 **62** 83
Joan **65** 328 **79** 250 **80** 257
  82 444 450
Joanna **52** 364
John **52** 253 **53** 302 **54** 240
  59 212 **60** 76 267 **61** 392
  62 83 **64** 214 **65** 149 169
  185 186 **73** 139 148 **94**
  332 **95** 58 **110** 166 **111**
  271 **113** 55-57 **114** 192
  140 165 323 **144** 156
John Bunyan Wesley
  86 300
John Y. **93** 294 **118** 241
  120 305 307
Joseph **55** 78 **115** 281

LUCAS *cont'd*
Josiah G. **122** 73
Josiah Gilman **118** 240
  242
Lavina **77** 153
Lilla M. **98** 258
Lucy **72** 285 **79** 219
Lucy Jane (Robes) **120** 66
  123 232
Lydia **85** 167 **132** 163
Lydia Wells **59** 212
Mabel **85** 409
Margaret **73** 254 **77** 181
  81 446 **111** 271 **114** 192
  116 167 172
Margaret (Portyngton)
  116 167
Margaret J. **83** 434 **84** 23
Margaret N. **114** 192
Martha **73** 254
Martha O. (Fisher)
  123 232
Martin Luther **110** 223
Mary **58** 391 **71** 243 329
  334 **73** 254 **82** 444 452
  90 51 **132** 163 **144** 26
  156 158 159
Mary (Shurtleff) **110** 223
Mary Ann **85** 315 **137** 75
Mary Jane **120** 65
Mary T. **77** 146
Matthew **144** 222
Mollie J. **77** 266
Molly **54** 274 **132** 163
  144 159
Nancy **72** 301 **88** 281
Nellie M. **95** 33
Nicholas **82** 444 450
Olive (Preble) **116** 304 305
Oliver **91** 271 **98** 258
  131 112
Patience **55** 78 **115** 281
Perceval **65** xxxiv
Persis (Shaw) **115** 281
Philander Hodge **59** 212
Polly **144** 158 223
R. S. **77** 266
Rebecca **67** 274 **111** 271
Rebecca (Fenimore)
  111 271
Rebecca (Verin) **131** 112
Repentance **88** 223
Richard **52** 253 **62** 268 **71**
  22 23
Robert **71** 329 334 **82** 443
  111 271 280 281 285
  116 167 172
Robert M. **77** 181
Robert T. **65** xlviii
Rosalinda **62** 268
Roxanna S. **98** 258
Rufus **62** 268
Russell Henry **106** 158
Ruth **61** 392
Ruth (Godfrey) **127** 97
Rutha **113** 324
Samuel **55** 78 **85** 63
Samuel M. **121** 147 **122**
  146 **123** 232
Sarah **65** 185 186 **82** 444
  450 **88** 223 **125** 219

LUCAS *cont'd*
Sarah (Hancock) **111** 271
Sarah Y. **119** 286
Sereno Goodale **59** 212
Seth **111** 271
Silas Emmett **115** 237
Stephen **90** 268 371
Susan **70** 248 **90** 268 371
  103 46
Susanna **61** 392 **71** 329
  334 **99** 285
Susie F. (Connor) **122** 73
Thomas **71** 243 329 334
  78 71 307 **94** 332 **114**
  192 **144** 156 **147** 28 **148**
  147
Viola L. **123** 232
W. **91** 328
William **55** 78 **65** 172 **73**
  254 **78** 304 **94** 332 **111**
  271 **125** 35
William A. **114** 192
William Henderson
  113 324
LUCASTE
Elizabeth Anne **131** 93
  96 97
LUCE Luse - *see also*
De Luce
—— **62** 133
— Mr. **62** 135
— Mrs. **70** 315
Abby Bradford **88** 290
Abiah **59** 198 **98** 367
Abiah (Hough) **98** 366 367
Abigail **59** 380-382 **98** 366
  129 340
Abigail (Wilson) **126** 64
Abigail Lena **88** 376
Abishai **66** 81
Abraham **52** 233 **66** 80
  88 8
Adelia (Light) **111** 128
Adeline **126** 65 199
Albert R. **72** 114
Albon **72** 114
Alexander **81** 430 446
Alice de **96** 93
Almira (Luciver) **89** 106
Alsberry **59** 262 **145** 352
Amabel de **96** 93
Anna **72** 114
Anna (Utley) (Parsons)
  88 376
Anna Maria **88** 375
Annie Budlong **95** 343
Anthony de **96** 119
Archless **145** 364
Arvin **79** 76
Aurelia **72** 114
Barzillai **59** 302
Belinda **86** 401
Benjamin **59** 258 260 305
  66 81 81 430 446 **129**
  340
Bethuel **66** 80
Betsey **98** 367
Betsey N. (Roe) **98** 367
C. E. **89** 383
Caroline Elizabeth **68** 214
Carrie Louisa **68** 214

LUCE *cont'd*
Cathcart **79** 76
Catherine (Dann) **98** 367
Charles C. **79** 76
Charles Walter **88** 376
Christopher **59** 204 207
  208 406
Clare Boothe (Brokaw)
  136 321
Cyrus S. **85** 456
Damaris **59** 260
Daniel **59** 380-382 **98** 367
  145 363 364
David **59** 202 384 **88** 375
  100 188
David Wing **68** 214
Deborah **81** 430 **86** 401
Deborah (Arey) **86** 401
Delorne Gilkey **85** 456
Diana **79** 76
Ebenezer **59** 202 384
  98 367
Edmund **69** 243 382 **79** 76
Eleazer **98** 367
Eleazer H. **98** 367
Elgiva **85** 456
Elgiva Bird **85** 456
Elijah **100** 188 **123** 268
Elisha **89** 383 384 **122** 201
  145 352
Elizabeth **69** 382 **126** 215
Elizabeth (Lazell) **88** 264
Elizabeth Middleton
  (Root) **136** 321
Ellis **145** 359
Elsie Jane **88** 376
Emma Elizabeth **96** 129
Enoch **66** 80
Esther **81** 430
Experience **56** 79 99
Ezekiel **66** 80 81
Fanny **72** 114
Francis de **79** 55
George **59** 408
Georgia Ellen **85** 456
Georgiana (Barton)
  85 456
Grace (Baker) **142** 125
Hannah **59** 258 261 307
  66 51 **81** 446 **98** 366 367
Hannah (Bushnell) **98** 367
Hannah (Butler) **98** 367
Hannah (Morton)
  117 302
Hannah (Moulton)
  132 324
Harriet **95** 343
Harriet (Luce) **95** 343
Harriet (Patrick) **116** 310
Harriet B. **88** 285
Harvey **98** 367
Henry **56** 99 **60** 187 **66** 80
  136 90
Henry Robinson **136**
  321 327
Henry Winters **136** 321
Hepsibah **59** 260
Hezekiah **66** 80
Hiram **69** 243 382 **78** 139
Hosea **132** 324
Huldah (Squires) **98** 367

LUCE *cont'd*
Isaac **66** 80 **79** 134
Israel **59** 199 **72** 114 **89** 384
  142 125
Jabez **59** 259
James F. **64** 79
James Madison **132** 324
Jane **51** 162 **56** 79 91
  72 114
Jason **59** 203 204 299 402
  410
Jedidah (Claghorn)
  69 382
Jedidiah **98** 367
Jemima **59** 307 **98** 367
Jeremiah **89** 115
Jeremiah S. **72** 114
Joanna **56** 75
John **59** 307 **66** 80 81
  81 430 446
John A. **98** 367
John Ayres **98** 367
Jonathan **66** 80 81 **69** 382
  72 114
Joseph **66** 81 **69** 382 **72**
  114 **81** 430
Joshua **72** 114
Josiah **72** 114
Julin **86** 401 **133** 324
Juliet C. **72** 114
Juliet E. **72** 74
Juliet G. **72** 114
Juliette Elizabeth (Howe)
  88 375
Lizzie Lazell **88** 376
Louisa (Lazell) **89** 115
Louisa Jane (Hawks)
  88 376
Love **59** 406
Lovey **96** 61
Lucy **81** 430
Lydia **52** 232 **69** 382
Lyman **116** 310
Malatiah **66** 80
Margaret **100** 298
Maria P. **126** 65
Marion **97** 187
Mark **72** 114
Martin **98** 367
Mary **59** 40 **64** 13 **81** 430
  86 401
Mary (Handy) **126** 106
Mary (Prentice) **88** 264
Mary A. **79** 76
Mary E. **72** 114
Mary Ellen (Morse)
  85 456
Mary Evelyn **88** 376
Matthew **62** 135 **66** 81 **69**
  100 **78** 97
May **79** 134
Mayo **56** 75
Mercy **72** 114 **77** 233
  120 264
Minnie **84** 191
Nancy **80** 155 **89** 36 **99** 127
Nancy Adelia (Corson)
  88 376
Nathan **66** 80 **88** 264
  145 352
Nathaniel **88** 264 **89** 383

LUCE *cont'd*
Nathaniel K. **98** 367
Obed **66** 81 **100** 188
Peter **55** 306 **57** 280 **63** 187
  66 81
Phebe (Tibbetts) **99** 328
Polly (Handy) **126** 106
Priscilla **72** 114
Prudence **59** 258 **64** 80
Rachel (Bouton) **98** 367
Ralph **69** 20
Rebecca (Ayres) **98** 367
Rebecca B. **100** 188
Reliance **59** 259
Rhoda **72** 114
Richard **59** 260
Richard de **96** 93 94
Robert **67** xxxiv **69** 18 20
  22 25 **88** 375 **145** 364
Robert Edwin **88** 375
Rowland **145** 363
Ruth **59** 408 410
Sally **59** 258 **69** 243 382
  96 80
Samuel Wing **126** 106
Sarah **59** 207 262 410 **78**
  139 **79** 76 **83** 418 508 **88**
  375 **132** 324
Sarah (Allen) **83** 508
Sarah (Blackwell) **117** 302
Sarah (Chase) **88** 8
Sarah (Lazell) **88** 375
Sarah (Sargent) **132** 324
Sarah Ann **88** 376
Seth **66** 81 **117** 302
Sheldon R. (Mrs.) **113** 240
Shubael **59** 261
Simeon **98** 366 367
Solomon **145** 358
Sophronia S. **133** 285
Stedman **98** 367
Stephen **111** 128
Susanna **81** 430 **98** 367
  101 179
Susanna (Kingsley)
  98 367
Sylvanus **66** 80
Sylvia **126** 198
Thankful **79** 76
Thomas **66** 80 81 **69** 243
  382 **79** 76 **95** 343 **98** 366
  367
Thomas de **96** 93 312
Thomas Martin **88** 376
Uriah **86** 401
Warren **59** 258
William **66** 81 **125** 31 34
  132 324
William Warren **88** 376
Zachariah **66** 80
Zephaniah **59** 263 **66** 82
LUCELLES
Agnes de **79** 363
Beatrice de **79** 361 363
Hugh de **79** 361 363
Isabel de **79** 361
Muriel de **79** 361
Richard de **79** 361 363
William de **79** 361
LUCENA
Mary Dolores **68** 24

Lucey *see* Lucy
LUCIA Fred **74** 318
  Sarah **74** 318
LUCIVER Almira **89** 106
Luck *see* Lucke
LUCKAM Jane **100** 240
  Judith **100** 301
LUCKCOAT
  Joshua **70** 262
LUCKE Luck
  Ambrose **54** 92
  Anne **53** 71
  Edward **64** 325
  Elizabeth **53** 71
  Fred Winston **104** 144
  John **92** 56
  Samuel **53** 71
  Sarah **66** 87
  Thomas **66** 87
LUCKERST Ellen **66** 63
LUCKETT James **91** 328
LUCKIN John **78** 68
LUCKINGE
  Thomas **59** 173
Luckis *see* Lucas
LUCKLAND
  Ann Maria **73** 278
LUCKMAN James **65** 34
LUCKNOW
  Edward **138** 88
LUCKNUM
  Judith **122** 84
LUCKSY Judith **122** 84
LUCKUM Judith **100** 301
LUCKY Carrie **138** 214
Lucus *see* Lucas
LUCY Lucey
  Abijah **105** 205
  Bethuel **105** 205 206
  Elizabeth **124** 307
  Geoffrey de **105** 38 41
  Gloria Joan **105** 126
  Isham **124** 297
  John **73** 72
  Malatiah **105** 205
  Mary **76** 22
  Richard de **105** 38 40 41
  Roese de **105** 40
  Sarah **71** 340 **93** 373
  Sarah F. **76** 35
LUDAM James **71** 321
LUDDEN Luden
  Ann **60** 42 **85** 154
  Anna **60** 42 **110** 235
  Anna M. **110** 235
  Augustus **110** 235
  Benjamin **60** 41 **85** 154
    104 266
  Bertrand **110** 235
  Bethiah **110** 235
  Bethrac **110** 234
  Betsey **113** 137
  Bettee (Jones) **113** 138
  Charles M. **56** xxii 89
  Clarence E. **110** 235
  Content **110** 234-236
  Cornelia **110** 234 235
  Daniel **110** 235 236
  Deborah **60** 42
  Dorothy **60** 42
  E. A. **110** 235

LUDDEN *cont'd*
  Edith M. **110** 236
  Edwin A. **110** 235
  Edwin A. M. **110** 234
  Edwin Alonzo **110** 235
  Elizabeth **60** 41 **110** 234-
    236
  Esther **60** 41
  Esther (Capen) **85** 154
    104 266
  Etta **84** 120
  Eunice **52** 438 **104** 266
  Frank **110** 235
  Frank Verne **110** 235
  Frederick **103** 227
  Hannah **65** 378 **110** 235
  Hezekiah **60** 42
  Hiram **110** 235
  Jacob **110** 234 235
  Jacob C. **103** 226
  Jeannette **103** 227
  Joanna **60** 41 **79** 182
  John Brown **110** 234 235
  John Emerson **110** 234
    235
  Joseph **60** 41 **110** 234-236
  Levi **110** 234-236
  Lewis / Louis Vanburen
    110 234 235
  Louisa **110** 234 235
  Lucy E. **110** 235
  Lydia **110** 234 235
  Mary **60** 43
  Mehitable **60** 42
  Milford **103** 227
  Nathaniel **60** 42
  Sally **126** 39
  Samuel **113** 138
  Sarah **110** 234-236
  Sewell **110** 234 235
  Sewell R. **110** 235
  Sidney **110** 234 235
  Sophia (Hannum) **90** 256
  Sylvanus **90** 256
  Vinton **110** 235
  Wallace **125** 267
  Warren V. **110** 236
  William **110** 235
  William Augustus **110**
    234 235
  William H. **103** 227
  William Henry **80** 102
    206 **103** 226 **104** 65 148
LUDDINGTON
  Luddinton Ludenton
  Ludington
  —— **58** 72 76
  Aaron **58** 77 78
  Abby **65** 134
  Abigail **58** 76-78 81 **79** 384
  Abraham **58** 79
  Amos **58** 81
  Amy **58** 81
  Ann L. **88** 343
  Anna **58** 76 78 81 82
  Anne **58** 77 81 82 **79** 384
  Appeline **58** 81
  Asa **58** 81
  Asenath **58** 81
  Betsey **77** 158
  Catherine **58** 79

LUDDINGTON *cont'd*
  Charles Henry **62** xxxvii
    106
  Christian **58** 72
  Collins **58** 77
  Daniel **58** 77 78 81
  David **58** 76 77
  Desire **58** 79
  Dinah **58** 77
  Dorcas **58** 76 82
  Dorothy **54** 324 **58** 76 81
  Elam **58** 82
  Eleanor **56** 285 **58** 75 76
    78 79
  Eliphalet **58** 75 76 81 82
  Elisha **58** 78
  Elizabeth **58** 76 79-81
  Ellen **54** 324 **58** 73
  Ethel Saltus **80** 450
  Eunice **58** 76 78
  Eunice (Jones) **83** 343
  Ezra **58** 77
  Fanny **59** 67
  Hannah **58** 74 76 77 80 81
    81 129
  Helen **58** 73
  Henry **58** 74-78 **62** 106
    79 384 **81** 128 129 **103**
    308 **104** 53
  Hopestill **58** 76
  Horace **60** 187
  Hulda **58** 81
  Isaac **58** 81 **83** 343
  James **58** 76 79
  Jane **58** 81
  Jared **58** 81
  Jesse **58** 81
  John **58** 73-77 79-81
  Joseph **58** 79
  Jude **58** 75 80 81
  Lavinia Elizabeth **62** 106
  Lemuel **58** 76
  Lucinda **58** 81
  Lucy **58** 78 **76** 134
  Lydia **58** 77 78 **79** 384
    83 342
  Mabel **54** 324 **58** 77 79 82
  Martha **55** 184 **56** 285 **58**
    74 75 81 **81** 131
  Mary **55** 183 184 **58** 74 76-
    79 81 **79** 384
  Mary Ann **88** 336
  Matthew **58** 74 79 82
  Mehitable **58** 81
  Mercy **54** 324 **55** 183 **58** 74-
    76 79 81 82
  Moses **58** 77 78 **76** 134
  Naomi **58** 79 81
  Nathaniel **58** 77 78 81
  Olive **58** 81
  Phebe **58** 77
  Rebecca **58** 74 76 77 **79** 384
  Ruth **58** 79 **79** 384
  Samuel **58** 77 79 **79** 384
  Sarah **58** 74-78 81 **79** 384
  Sibyl **58** 81
  Solomon **58** 77
  Stephen **79** 384
  Submit **58** 77 **79** 384
  Susanna **58** 77
  Thomas **58** 73 74 77 78

LUDDINGTON *cont'd*
Timothy **54** 324 **58** 79
Titus **58** 77
William **54** 324 **55** 183 184
56 285 **58** 72-82 **60** 101
187 **79** 384 **81** 128 129
LUDDLETON Ruth **59** 65
Timothy **59** 65
Luden *see* Ludden
LUDENDORFF August
Wilhelm
Theodor **111** 99
Erich Friedrich Wilhelm
111 99-101 103
Ludenton *see* Luddington
Ludewig *see* Ludwig
LUDGATE John **107** 101
LUDGATER Jo. **71** 32
Ludington *see*
Luddington
LUDKIN Ludkins
Gorge **121** 20
Lydia **121** 10
Samuel **121** 14
William **63** 382 **144** 255
LUDLAM Ludlum
Abigail **97** 335
Abraham **132** 243
Anthony **54** 430 **123** 85
Catherine / Catrina
(Ackerman) **132** 243
Clarence **56** 316
Clemence **53** 413
Edmunde **56** 316
Elizabeth **71** 288
Frances **53** 413
Francis **56** 316
Grace **56** 316
Hannah **56** 197 **124** 189
Helen Rosella **108** 133
John **56** 197 **132** 243
Mary **98** 332
Patience **123** 85
Patience (Barnes) **123** 85
Thomas **56** 316
William **53** 413 **56** 316 317
94 342
Ludlaw *see* Ludlow
LUDLEY Eleanor **65** 129
LUDLOW Ludlaw Ludloe
Ludloue Ludlowe
— Mr. **53** 25
Agnes **136** 242
Anne **110** 271
Anne E. **56** 46
Augustus **71** 43
Augustus C. **66** 33
Benjamin **51** 255
Catherine **51** 389
Catherine (Cooper)
136 242
Christopher **86** 270
106 164
Daniel H. **101** 124 **147** 211
Edmund **51** 255 389
Edward **53** 292
Elizabeth (Barton) **107** 55
Ephraim **107** 55
Gabriel **106** 164 **123** 247
141 102
George **51** 255 **86** 270

LUDLOW *cont'd*
147 152 161
Henry **51** 255 **55** 206
Jemima **119** 197 198
137 38
John **51** 343 389 **123** 247
136 242
Jonathan **51** 255 **110** 271
147 152 161
Joseph **110** 271
Katharine **51** 396
Margaret **51** 389
Martha **51** 255
Mary **51** 255 **53** 232 **79** 152
110 186 271
Mary (Coggan) **110** 186
147 152 161
Roger **51** 66 496 **57** 197
86 270 **87** 273 **99** 229
110 186 270-272 **111**
247 **117** 82 **118** 168 **123**
241 247 **141** 101 102
142 113 **145** 378 **147**
151 152 160 161
Rowe **66** 33
Sarah **57** 197 **79** 330 **110**
271 **123** 247 **141** 102
Stephen **53** 232 **117** 46
Thomas **74** 277 **110** 186
270 271 **123** 247
William **64** 158
William H. **123** 175
Ludlum *see* Ludlam
LUDMAN VON
HADUSFALVA Gabor
125 163
LUDOVICI —— **96** 11
Leopold **106** 8
LUDWELL
Philip **57** 110
Thomas **57** 110 **124** 102
LUDWIG Agnes **100** 330
Albert **91** 393
Ellen (Abbott) **91** 393
Hermann E. **99** 9
Newell W. **91** 393
Robert **91** 393
William W. **91** 393
LUE ___ (Greenough)
92 28
Barzillai **92** 28
LUEDEMAN Judith
Miner Hine **143** 362
147 62 63 **148** 270
LUEDER Areline Byron
(Mrs.) **84** 190
Mary E. **84** 107
LUEN Mehitable **56** 127
LUES William **51** 469
129 276
LUEWKS Matthew **144** 222
LUEY
John William **83** 203
Mary Frances **83** 203
Mary Jane **88** 342
Mary Jane (Wiggin)
83 203
LUFCY Herman (Mrs.) **82**
123 237
Lola **82** 237

LUFF Luffe
—— **136** 335
___ (Cogan) **110** 195
Bridget **136** 102
Caleb **106** 46
Deborah **106** 45
Edward **110** 195 262
Eliza (Bignal) **125** 219
Hannah **106** 45
Hugh **106** 42-45
Joan **136** 101
John **136** 86 102
Mary **106** 45
Nathaniel **106** 44-46 49
116 230 231
Nicholas **110** 195 262
Sarah **106** 45
Sarah (Hunn) **106** 42 45 46
116 230
Thomas **110** 195 262
William **54** 182 **125** 219
LUFFENHAM
William **61** 68
LUFFIELD
— Prior of **142** 235
LUFFLEYN Edward **76** 279
LUFKIN Lufkyn
—— **93** 226
— Mrs **83** 35 **117** 170
Abby S. **74** 307
Abigail **113** 295 **121** 156
Abigail (Parker) **105** 160
Alice **93** 75
Anna **113** 51 146 **133** 234
135 160
Anne **134** 93
Arabella Maria
(Partridge) **94** 23
Bartholomew **93** 173 228
Benjamin **105** 160 207
120 222
Bridget **122** 29
Charles **74** 307
Cora **95** 33
Cora A. **74** 307
Daniel **111** 112
David **111** 112
David B **74** 307
Dorcas **75** 154
Dorothy **60** 42
Ebenezer **133** 234
Eddie **74** 307
Edith Louise (Hall) **87** 174
Edwin B. **64** 129
Elmira B. **77** 177
Elmira Evelyn **83** 122 233
Florence **131** 89
George **77** 177
Gilbert **94** 152
Grace Edna **98** 81
Hannah **59** 340 **111** 112
Harry McCurdy (Mrs.)
87 174
Henry **105** 207
Isaac **60** 42
Jacob **75** 154
James **111** 112
John **93** 77 **111** 112
Jonathan Eaton **94** 23
Julian **94** 235
Keziah (Drew) **98** 81

LUFKIN cont'd
Lois **89** 69
Mabel **74** 307
Mary **84** 190
Mary E. **131** 89
Merriam **118** 169
Nancy M. **110** 210
Nehemiah **76** 41
Olive **75** 264
Prince C. **140** 266
Rachel **63** 14
Richard F. **113** 233 **117** 150
Sally **76** 41
Sarah **111** 112
Stephen **93** 75 77 **94** 233
   234 **111** 112
Susan **145** 166
Susan L. (Wilson)
   140 266
Thomas **76** 281 **83** 75
   105 160
Uriah Davis **98** 81
LUFMAN Jane **66** 255
Roger **66** 255
LUGER Elizabeth
   (Crowninshield)
   105 234
Elizabeth (Groundsel)
   105 234
Hannah **105** 234
Samuel **105** 234
LUGG Andrew **93** 384
Humfry **111** 171
Jane **52** 17 22
Jane (Deighton) **141** 100
John **52** 22
Mary **96** 366
LUGHTON
Bartholomew de
   102 45
LUIMA Joseph **62** 289
LUIS Hannah **106** 155
LUISIGNAN
Alice de **120** 259
LUIST
Elizabeth **52** 221
Rebecca (Jenner) (Lynde)
   143 38
LUITWEILER
Clarence S. **97** 208
Marion Bassett **84** 239
LUKE Abiel **100** 140
Alice **98** 36
George **90** 345
John **104** 109-111 **126** 175
Margaret **90** 345
Margaret (Lumberdey)
   (Jackson) **144** 32
Mary **85** 231
Oliver **65** 285
Ottoson (Mrs.) **99** 148
Rebecca (Power) **90** 345
Richard **144** 32
Sally (Cook) **126** 175
Samuel **98** 36
Sarah **78** 137
William **66** 244
William H. (Mrs.) **105** 128
LUKENS Lukyn Lukyns
Ann **117** 68
Charles **92** 387

LUKENS cont'd
E. F. (Mrs.) **121** 160
Elizabeth **71** 32 250
Godfrey **141** 129
Isabelle Pennock **92** 387
John **55** 115
Katharine (Dowsett) **141**
   128 129
Mary (Wilbore) **113** 99
Rebecca **92** 387
Robert **71** 32 250
Sarah **55** 115
William **112** 253 **113** 99
LUKER
Charles **143** 259
R. G. **118** 75
LUKERS John **143** 261
William **143** 257
LUKINICH Emeric **96** 141
LUKYE
Elizabeth **55** 97
Hugh **55** 97
John **55** 97
Lukyn see Lukens
Lukyns see Lukens
LULETT Lewis **106** 31
LULEY Charles Volney
   113 229
Georgia Ann **113** 229
LULL Abner **92** 311
Amanda **142** 377
Amy **116** 310
Belinda **59** 375
Clare Louise **104** 144
Clarissa (Slate) **110** 31
   111 135
Elizabeth **60** 52 **98** 77
Emma Elvira **104** 46
H. H. **104** 46
Harriet (Patrick) **116** 310
Hattie **102** 152
Jesse **104** 196
Joanna **94** 48 **122** 240
Joseph **104** 58
L. B. **116** 310
Levi R. **102** 152
Lucia E. **104** 197
Lucien **116** 310
Lucina **116** 310
Lucina (Francisco)
   116 310
Lucius D. **102** 152
Lyman **116** 310
Morris **104** 197
Newton **51** 240
Phebe **82** 23
Susan (Thomas) **104** 197
Sylvanie **102** 152
Lum see Lumm
LUMACKS
Elizabeth **62** 35
John **62** 35
LUMAN Frances **116** 185
Lumas see Lummas
Lumb see Lumm
Lumbard see Lombard
Lumbart see Lumbert
LUMBER Eliony **97** 188
   130 208
Elisha **145** 358
Joseph **145** 359

Lumberd see Lumbert
LUMBERDEY
Margaret **144** 31 32
LUMBERT see also
   Lombard
—— **61** 375
Abigail **112** 200
Abishai **59** 264 379 384
Abishai Hayden **100** 188
Bathsheba **59** 258
Belinda **59** 259
Benjamin **114** 82
Bethiah **130** 130
Betsey **58** 369 **59** 25
Caleb **119** 267
Chloe **120** 247
Deborah **59** 202 260
Deliverance **126** 237
Elisha **112** 200
Elisibeth (Vickre) **143** 342
Elizabeth **59** 25 **69** 382
   112 200
Elizabeth (Derby) **112** 257
Francis **59** 378
Gideon **112** 200
Hannah **126** 68
Hannah (Parker) **112** 196
Hayden **59** 202 260
Hezekiah **114** 10
Jonathan **59** 259 **112** 200
Joshua **112** 197
Joyce **98** 84 **114** 82
Laura **59** 260
Lemuel **112** 200
Lewis **112** 265
Love **59** 259
Mary **59** 257 **83** 270 **112**
   257-259 265 **130** 44
Mary (Parker) **112** 200
Mehitable **106** 160
Mercy **123** 65
Moses **59** 202
Parker **112** 197 198
Parnell **59** 258 262-264
   379-381
Patience (Bourne) (Allen)
   118 205
Peter **145** 353
Polly **114** 10
Prudence **59** 202 258
Rebecca **112** 265
Samuel **112** 200
Sarah **106** 243 **112** 197 198
Sarah (Gibbs) **123** 205
Sarah (Parker) **112** 197
   265
Thomas **59** 202 258 262-
   264 379-381 **106** 243
   112 196 257 **114** 82 **143**
   342
William **59** 260
LUMBY —— **68** 361
LUMCREE Hannah **55** 49
Mary **55** 50
Polly **55** 49 50
LUMET Gloria Morgan
   (Vanderbilt)
   (Stokowski) **136** 321
   322 330
Sidney **136** 90 321 330
LUMLEY —— Lord **93** 34

LUMLEY *cont'd*
 Diana **63** 137
 Elizabeth **132** 45
 Jane (Lady) **81** 178
 John **63** 29 137 **93** 5
 John (Lord) **81** 178
 Mary **111** 8
 Mary (Cogan) **111** 8
 Ruth **63** 137
 Thomas **63** 137 **121** 187
   189 **124** 307
 William **111** 8
LUMLIE Mary **141** 37
LUMM Lum Lumb
 Adam **76** 135 144 145 149
   150 153 **109** 264
 Agnes **93** 205
 Amy **75** 185
 Bennett Davis **109** 264
 Betsey (Curtis) **109** 264
 Betsey (Day) **106** 144
 Billy **76** 146
 Charles **122** 299
 Clarissa A. **68** 93
 Daniel Bircham **76** 172
 David **75** 191 **76** 145 146
 Edward H. **71** 287 **82** 130
 Edward Harris **65** xxxvi
   90 **90** 126 **106** 62 130
   143 144
 Georgianna Baird
   (Torrey) **106** 143
 Grace **76** 151
 Hannah **76** 145 **106** 144
 Harvey Mandred **106**
   143 144
 Henry **76** 147 **78** 260
 Isaac **76** 149
 Israel **106** 144
 James **76** 149
 Jemima **53** 230
 John **65** 90 **76** 141 **106** 144
 Jonathan **76** 135 145-147
   149 151 153
 Joseph **76** 135
 Katharine Heath
   (Woodruff) **106** 143
 Martha (Clark) **106** 144
 Martha (Day) **106** 144
 Mary Elizabeth (Quintard)
   109 264
 Mary Jane **122** 299
 Matthew **53** 230
 Merritt Bruen **106** 144
 Nancy **76** 153
 Nicholas **94** 220
 Obedience **78** 260
 Phebe Jane Smith (Bruen)
   106 143
 Polly **75** 191
 Reuben **76** 135 145 146 149
   151 152 171-173
 Richard **106** 144
 Samuel **106** 144
 Samuel Day **106** 144
 Sarah **76** 144 145
 Sheldon **76** 149
 William **76** 171
LUMMAS Lumas
 Lummus - - *see also*

LUMMAS *cont'd*
 Loomis
 Charles A. **60** 187
 Edward **60** 187 **76** lvii
 Elizabeth **61** 333 336
 Henry T. **60** 187
 Jonathan **61** 226
 Margaret **61** 226
 Margaret (Redington)
   109 114
 Welthy **125** 104
 Lummis *see* Loomis
LUMPEY Ambrose **65** 22
LUMPKIN Ann **51** 47
 Hannah **136** 81
 Richard **53** 345 **63** 285
 Sarah **53** 345 **63** 285
 Tamesin **51** 47 **52** 81
 Thomasine **95** 46
 William **51** 47 **52** 81 **95** 46
LUMSBURY
 Hannah Maria **145** 309
LUMSDEN James **63** 143
 Lun *see* Lunn
LUNCEFORD
 Alvin Mell **111** 78
LUNCHER Thomas **71** 30
LUND
 —— **64** 42 **91** 257
 — Mr. **64** 343
 Anthon H. **65** 203
 Betty **91** 259
 C. **91** 328
 Dora **107** 133
 Elizabeth **94** 190
 Elizabeth B. **90** 51
 Fanny **107** 153
 Fred Bates **60** xxxvi
 Hannah **91** 264
 Joanna **64** 207
 John **94** 20
 Jonathan **91** 264 265
 Joseph Wheelock **59** xliv
 Levi **91** 257
 Lucy **106** 307
 Margaret **63** 288
 Mary **85** 198
 Mary (Hardy) **94** 190
 Olive **91** 265
 Olive (Sargent) **91** 264
 Priscilla (Cumings)
   91 265
 Rebecca **64** 207 **66** lxiii
   88 342 **94** 20 21
 Rhoda **91** 265
 Sarah **64** 42 207 **94** 21
 Stephen **94** 190
 Thomas **55** 188 **63** 288 **91**
   257 259 **142** 275
 William **55** 188 **64** 207
   94 21
LUNDAIIL Harry White
   (Mrs.) **120** 147
LUNDAY Robert **59** 193
LUNDELL
 Charles Gustavus
   62 394
LUNDERS
 Mary **100** 193 913
LUNDES
 Caroline **133** 267

LUNDGARD
 Anton Martin **113** 223
 Mabel **113** 223
LUNDIN
 Thomas de **122** 272
LUNDQUIST
 Bessie **99** 146
LUNDVALL
 Ida M. **128** 170
LUNDWALL —— **147** 229
 N. B. **147** 227 228
LUNDY
 Anna Harriet **102** 229
 Benjamin **52** 396 398
 George R. **116** 64
 J. Eugene **116** 64
 James **116** 64
 Jane A. **116** 61
 John **61** 348
 Mary **116** 58 67
 Raymond **116** 64
 Rhoda Elizabeth **107** 135
 Richard **101** 79
 Sarah **56** 128
LUNEA Elizabeth **100** 25
LUNEY
 Elizabeth (Oakes)
   100 296
 John **100** 296
LUNG William Le **102** 45
   195
LUNGER
 Charlotte **102** 73
LUNGREN Cary **128** 263
LUNHAM
 Gertrude **117** 203
LUNHERD K. **91** 328
LUNN Lun
 Amos L. **128** 177
 Charity (Chase) **88** 124
 Irene Theresa (Howley)
   86 366
 Isabella **98** 358
 Joseph William **86** 366
 Josephine V. (McAfee)
   128 177
 Joshua **86** 304
 Katharine H. (Stone)
   86 366
 Leonora **86** 304
 Marcia E. (Blake) **86** 304
 Margaret **98** 358
 Nicholas **94** 220
 Phebe (Chase) **88** 124
 Rachel **81** 154 **86** 304
 Susan Phebe (Cole)
   86 366
 Thomas **60** 367 **88** 124
 Vadis Lucinda **86** 366
 Verle Nelson **86** 366
 William **86** 366 **88** 124
   98 358
LUNNEN
 William **111** 217-219
LUNNINGHAM
 Alex. **62** 320
LUNNY Patrick **60** 162
LUNQUIST
 Charles William **80**
   332 **81** 219 **87** 70 177 **95**
   75 76

LUNQUIST *cont'd*
Lillian Marie **95** 76
Louisa Christine
(Anderson) **95** 76
Robert **95** 76
Robert Peter **95** 76
William **95** 76
LUNT —— **59** 236 **70** 300
83 194 **87** 329 **119** 63
145 45 47 313
Abel **101** 336 **118** 75 **141**
94 97
Abigail **51** 464 **53** 123 167
113 123 **114** 182
Abigail B. **104** 60
Abraham **105** 162 **112** 100
143 3 4 18 19
Albert **97** 222
Albert C. **83** 300
Alice (Cottle) **94** 62
Alice E. **98** 197
Allen P. **83** 173
Amy **82** 422
Ann **105** 162 **147** 363
Ann G. **83** 25
Ann S. (Jones) **83** 182-
184 188
Anna **51** 461
Anne Pearson **89** 368
109 233
Augustus **130** 155
Benjamin **94** 62 **104** 59
105 212 **114** 182
Benjamin J. **104** 60
Betsey **113** 124
Catherine **143** 19
Catherine Chase **143** 19
Charles **94** 62
Charles C. **98** 197
Charles Henry **82** 422
Charles P. **120** 67 69
Clementine M. **98** 197
Cutting **137** 254
Daniel **53** 37 38 **65** 108 255
91 206 387 **94** 95 **100** 65
112 100 **115** 217 **125** 62
Deborah (Jaques) **137** 254
Dorcas **113** 123 **116** 132
Edward **64** 262
Edward H. **91** 394
Eleanor **114** 182
Eliza J. **104** 60
Elizabeth **65** 43 **81** 145 **88**
335 **94** 223 **104** 59 291
113 265 **114** 182 **117**
142 **119** 60 62 63 **133** 42
Elizabeth (McIntire) **105**
161 **113** 123
Elizabeth Simes **82** 422
Ellen **82** 422
Ellen Hobart (Hedge)
145 312
Elsie (Merchant) **130** 155
Elvira **143** 19
Emeline A. **91** 275
Esther **104** 59 **108** 285
Esther (Robertshaw /
Robichaux) **143** 4
18 19
Esther P. **104** 60
Eunice **63** 169 **115** 305

LUNT *cont'd*
Eunice (Cambridge)
88 329
Eva J. (Nutter) **83** 300
Ezekiel **53** 167
Ezra **64** 64 **65** 78 114 149
93 397 **100** 63 **114** 182
George **66** 301 **84** 441
Hannah **53** 37 **65** 255 **73**
199 **83** 194
Hannah (Smith) **119** 69
Hannah Rebecca **143** 19
Hannah S. **83** 173
Hannah Simes **82** 422
Harriet (Weare) **117** 142
144
Harriet S. **120** 67 68
Henry **53** 167 **62** 124 **63**
101 **64** 198 **78** 224 **99**
113 **105** 162 **110** 288
115 225 **116** 221
Henry S. **98** 197
Horace **113** 265
Isaac S. **114** 182
James B. **104** 60
James Boothby **104** 291
James J. **104** 60
James R. **91** 328
Jane **98** 197 **105** 4 **110** 288
Jane G. **119** 225 228
Jane Sewall (Durrell)
134 225
Jason Landen **134** 225
Jeremiah Libbey **82** 422
Joanna **65** 381 **100** 302
Joanna (Bale) **110** 289
114 47
Job **66** 301 **104** 60 **114** 182
John **94** 107 **113** 124
John P. **104** 60
John R. **85** 381
Johnson **110** 289 **114** 47
Joseph **53** 38 **55** 196 **65**
381 **104** 59 **107** 313
Joseph M. **85** 375
Joseph P. **104** 59 60 133
114 182
Joshua **98** 197 **105** 277
112 100 **114** 182
Josiah **53** 123
Kate G. **91** 394
Katie P. (Lopaus) **85** 381
Lewis J. **98** 197
Lillian Verteen **83** 434
Lorana **143** 19
Louisa **114** 304
Louisa (Ring) **114** 303
Lucretia Watson **145** 312
Lydia **135** 17
Lydia (Dodge) **105** 161
162
Lydia Josephine **105** 161
Lydia S. **97** 229
M. Parry **83** 183 184
M. Parry (Mrs.) **83** 194
Marcia **94** 62
Marcia (Leigh) **94** 62
Maria L. **85** 380
Maria S. (Chase) **120** 67 69
Mark J. **98** 197
Martha **53** 38

LUNT *cont'd*
Martin Parry **83** 173
Mary **78** 224 **82** 422 **83** 307
91 78 **98** 77 **102** 142
125 62 **126** 145 **148** 134
Mary (Chase) **87** 329
Mary (Peabody) **94** 63
Mary Chase (Sargent)
94 62
Mary I. **104** 59
Mary Simes **82** 422
Mary W. **119** 277 280
Micajah **68** 19 **105** 207
113 124 **116** 294 **117**
142 144
Miriam (Moulton)
112 100
Molly **113** 124
Moses D. **88** 329
Nancy E. **85** 381
Narcissa **113** 265
Narcissa (Lyman) **113** 265
116 221
Nathan **137** 254
Nellie **91** 393
Olive **74** 306
Olive (Hooper) **105** 161
Otis L. **104** 60
Patience (Bryant) **137** 254
Paulina (Avery) **116** 221
Phebe (Tilton) **141** 97
Polly **98** 197
Rachel M. (Reed) **85** 375
Rebecca **104** 60 133
Rebecca Gertrude **103** 74
Rufus **113** 124 **134** 225
Ruth (Smith) **134** 225
Ruth (Wood) (Jewett)
94 107
Ruthy **116** 221
Samuel **51** 464 **66** 301 **82**
422 **84** 29 **91** 393 105
162 **112** 100 **113** 123
265 **116** 132 221 **117**
142
Samuel Johnson **91** 394
Samuel L. **119** 69
Samuel Lyman **82** 422
113 265
Sarah **53** 37 **78** 224 **82** 422
96 400
Sarah B. **83** 173
Silas **67** 239
Silas N. **98** 197
Skipper **112** 100 **116** 221
Sophia **68** 19
Sophia (Hill) **97** 222
Stephen **105** 161 162
Susan (Dawes) **130** 155
Susan Boyd (Coffin)
94 63
Susanna **113** 124
Theodore H. **68** 19
Thomas **82** 422 **83** 194
Thomas S. **145** 312
W. Washington **89** 351
William **94** 62 **105** 162 277
112 100 **113** 123 **114**
182 **128** 125
William Durant **143** 19
William E. **98** 197

LUNT cont'd
William Edward **82** 422
William P. **59** 87
William Parry **83** 173
William Parsons **62**
xxxvii **89** 368 **145** 312
William Pike **114** 182
William W. **88** 92
William Wallace **54** xli
68 xiv **114** 230
Williams Parsons
61 xxxiv
Willie **91** 393
Woodbridge **94** 62
LUNTLEY
Alice **148** 117
Averye **148** 117
LUPELL Susie **73** 141
LUPSON Elizabeth **70** 59
61 132
LUPTAINE
Richard **146** 270
LUPTON
—— **56** 287 **59** 174
Abigail **66** 167
Christopher **66** 167
Hannah **56** 281 **71** 5
Thomas **56** 281 **71** 5
81 129
LUPUS Hugh **141** 94
LUQUES Luquis
Abigail (White) **96** 342
Andrew **96** 148 337
Anthony **96** 148 342
Betsey (White) **96** 337
Hannah **96** 148 340
Herbert L. **93** 401
LURAAS Gunhild
(Kittlesdatter) **86** 221
Gunhild Nelson **86** 221
John Nelson **86** 221
LURFETE Joan **144** 33 34
LURKEN Helen **65** 184
LURKER Thomas **64** 352
LURNEY Moses **88** 317
Ruth (Carver) **88** 317
LURRON John **51** 282
LURTON
Deborah (Rich) **84** 48
Freeman **84** 48
Patty **84** 47
LURVEY Lurvy
Abigail **73** 283 288 289 291
Alice (Middleton) **146** 323
Cyrus **85** 373
Ebenezer **86** 63 **146** 323
Eleazer **137** 141
Eliezer **146** 323
Elizabeth (Pattee) **146** 323
Enoch **73** 283 290
Hannah **71** 47 116 **73** 281
Hannah D. **85** 372 373
Hannah Boynton **73** 289
Isaac **73** 283 288 290
Jacob **73** 281 283
James **53** 147
Levi **85** 373
Lydia (Marshall) **85** 372
Mary (Cole) **86** 63
Mary Ann **85** 372 373

LURVEY cont'd
Mary Ann (Lurvey)
85 372
Peter **86** 63 **146** 323
Polly **122** 165
Rebecca **73** 286
Rhoda **73** 283
Samuel **73** 283 289 290
Susanna **73** 282
LUSARDER
George E. **91** 199
LUSBY Eleanor **73** 142
Henry **63** 25
John **73** 135
Robert **63** 25
Susan **73** 266
Thomas **62** 251
LUSCH Ida **83** 424 434
LUSCOMB Luscom
Luscombe
Catherine (Goddard)
88 333
Hannah C. **104** 165
Humphrey **102** 185
106 19
John **61** 137
John G. **88** 333
Lucinda **125** 237
Robert **87** 327
Salome (Chase) **87** 327
Shadrach **71** 124 127
William **62** 249 **71** 124
Luse see Luce
LUSENDY — Miss **96** 341
LUSH —— **101** 207
Charles W. **113** 315
Delia B. (Huntley) **101** 207
George **84** 357 **140** 165
John **66** 254
Katharine **100** 302
Lyntje (Fonda) **109** 189
Maria **109** 189
Mary **84** 357
Richard **109** 189
Sarah **79** 271
LUSHA Sally **56** 258
LUSHER
— Maj. **96** 372 373
— Mrs. **95** 252
Ann **54** 215
Eleazer **55** 194 **62** 68 224
225 **71** 99 **79** 339 **86** 434
87 275 **88** 267 **94** 216
349 **95** 252 390 **96** 283
372-374 **97** 345
Elia. **141** 181
Eliazer **121** 192
Elizabeth **86** 434 **88** 267
John **65** 129
Lydia **88** 293
Mary **62** 69 **95** 252 255 **96**
372 374-376
Mary (Bunker) (Gwin)
95 252 **96** 283 372 376
Nicholas **96** 374
LUSHINGTON
Abigail **76** 57 70
Edward **76** 57 70
Jane **76** 57 70
John **76** 57 70
Thomas **76** 57 70

LUSIGNAN Hugh de **109**
178 **110** 43
LUSK Alice Kessler
105 145
Alzina **76** 268 269
Bridget **122** 29
Christina **111** 305
Christina (Phillips)
111 305
Daniel **76** 268
Daniel H. **76** 269
Edward Park (Mrs.)
102 124
Eliza **76** 269
Eliza Jennings **77** 157
Elizabeth **82** 118
Eunice **54** 106
James **51** 360 **80** 60 **112** 18
Jane **51** 360 **54** 106 **57** 113
John **51** 360 **54** 106 **57** 113
111 209 **112** 17
Joseph **111** 192
Levi **59** 21
Love **79** 299
Margaret **135** 250
Margaret Olive **135** 250
Matilda (Myer) **105** 145
Pamela **76** 268
Robert **112** 18
Sally **111** 192
Sarah **76** 268 **82** 118
Sarah Maria **68** lxviii
Sylvester **79** 299 **82** 118
William **111** 209 **112** 18
William Thompson
105 145
LUSLEFORD
Mary **73** 139
LUSON Anne **53** 462
John **53** 462
LUSTESHULL
— de **53** 263
LUTER
Clorinda A. **85** 292
LUTEY
Mary Jane **88** 82
Sarah (Phillips) **88** 82
Thomas **88** 82
LUTH Anna **102** 166
Lawson C. **102** 166
Mary Elizabeth (Ambrose)
102 166
LUTHARDT —— **56** 15
LUTHE
Dorothea **68** 150
John C. H. **68** 150
Marie Caroline **68** 150
LUTHER Leuther
—— **54** 43 **63** 58 **139** 34
35 39 46 47
— Mr. **63** 54 **80** 56
— Mrs. **63** 57 **80** 56
Abiah **125** 270 **128** 59 **138**
27-29
Abial **138** 31
Abiel **138** 24 26
Abner **129** 380
Adam Albert **83** 435 **84** 23
Adelaide Grafton **77** 185
Alaph (Chase) **88** 23
Albert W. **125** 238

LUTHER *cont'd*
Alfred **70** 29
Alice (Bressey) **112** 31
Amos **71** 342
Anu **125** 74
Ann Elizabeth **123** 179
Anna (Easterbrooks)
88 22
Anne **88** 30
Anthony **80** 352
Asahel N. **122** 288
Barnabas **129** 276
Barton **88** 107
Benjamin **88** 22 **125** 271
Bertha K. **101** 177
Bethany (Chase) **88** 22
Betsey **70** 29 30 **87** 339
120 11
Charles Fisher **65** 204
Charles P. **123** 179
Clair Franklin **87** 205 208
88 165
Claire F. **54** xxxviii
Constant **127** 224
Curtis **76** 272
Curtis Pierce **124** 68
Dar **110** 52
David **88** 22
Deborah (Briggs) **126** 216
Delana **87** 338
Dorothy **84** 306
E. **122** 288
E. P. **123** 179
Ebenezer **70** 25 **129** 379
Edith B. (Pierce) **83** 435
438
Edward **97** 322 **144** 199
200
Eleanor (Gansey) **88** 30
Eleazer **87** 320 339
Elias P. **123** 179
Elisha **144** 199
Eliza **70** 30
Eliza (Burdick) **125** 238
Elizabeth **60** 69 **70** 30
84 306
Elizabeth (Mason)
144 199
Elizabeth Reynolds
113 227
Ellery Spencer **70** 29
Ellis **144** 199 **147** 60
Esick **87** 128
Eunice W. (Hibbard)
(Lougee) **124** 68
Ezra **127** 148
Frances **84** 306
Frankie C. **123** 179
Frederick **70** 29 30
129 379
Freelove **54** 80
Giles **120** 11
Hannah **144** 198 199
Hannah (Earnshaw)
126 23
Hannah (Hale) (Carr)
(Wilson) **102** 205 206
Harriet **76** 272
Harvey **122** 288 **125** 238
Harvey S. **122** 290
Henry **84** 306

LUTHER *cont'd*
Hepsibah **88** 107
Herbert A. **83** 435 438
Hezekiah **63** 228 328 **70** 30
97 326 **139** 41 **144** 199
Himan **122** 288
Huldah **60** 69
Irene **84** 300
Irene B. **66** lxxxii
Isabell **123** 179
Jabez **80** 175 **123** 179
James **70** 30 **80** 175
87 138 252
Jared **80** 56
Jeremiah **87** 338 **139** 44
Joan **84** 306
Joanna **70** 30
Jobish **129** 277
John **70** 30 **79** 335 **87** 208
93 207 **101** 177 **102** 155
103 158 **104** 169 **105**
156 **112** 31
John P. **70** 30
Jonas **90** 52
Jonathan **87** 135
Joshua **70** 30
Jotham **138** 24
Julia (Lougee) **124** 68
Keziah **88** 22 29
L. Mabel (Williams) **83**
435 **84** 23
Leslie L. **93** 207 **101** 177
102 155 **103** 158 **104**
169 **105** 156 **119** 75 **144**
199 **147** 60
Levi **70** 30 **78** 375
Linas A. **78** 367
Louisa **66** 243
Lucy **119** 320
Lucy E. **122** 288
Lydia **80** 175 **87** 137 249
Maria (Colby) **90** 52
Maria B. (Tibbets) **88** 283
Marianna **77** 185
Martha (Slade) **87** 138
Martin **53** 245 **70** 29 **86** 16
104 46 **127** 307 **129** 276
134 184 **138** 171 **145**
200
Mary **79** 257 **83** 465 **92** 223
129 379
Mary (Brown) **88** 107
Mary (Chase) **87** 262 320
Mary (Howland) **138** 45
Mary Ann **81** 60 270
Mary Emily **77** 181 182
Mary Jane **123** 179
Mary Jane (Lougee)
124 68
Mary Martha **122** 288
Matthew **88** 30
Mercy (Cole) (Chase)
87 252
Nathan **60** 69 **63** 58 **127** 7
Nathan Beckett **119** 320
Nathaniel **70** 30 **139** 43 45
Oliver **127** 224
Pamelia **70** 29 30
Patience **87** 338 **88** 15 22
Patience (Chase) **87** 128
Paul **58** 142

LUTHER *cont'd*
Phebe **87** 260 **88** 107
122 288
Philanda **80** 175
Philip **88** 23
Polly **96** 92 **119** 320
Preserved **70** 30
Rachel **70** 29
Rhobe **138** 45
Richard **58** 142
Richmond G. **122** 160
Rilly **119** 320
Ruth **70** 30 **135** 140
Sally **79** 335 **119** 320
120 11
Sally E. **120** 11
Sally P. **123** 179
Sally P. Russell **123** 179
Samuel **53** 321 **57** 33 **70** 30
83 465 **97** 322 324 325
102 206 **129** 276 **138** 45
139 22 25 43 46 49
Samuel P. **70** 30
Sarah **78** 375 **83** 466 **90** 191
104 46 **126** 215 **139** 41
Sarah (Butterworth)
144 199
Sarah (Callender) **144** 199
Sarah (Chase) **87** 135
Sarah (Hanks) **86** 16
Sarah (Merrils) **147** 60
Sarah V. **78** 367
Sarah Willard **92** 308
Seth **127** 227 **143** 225 227
Sibyl (Post) **147** 60
Slade **88** 283
Squire **128** 59
Stephen **87** 262
Susan S. **70** 30
Susan Slocum **77** 185
Susanna **70** 30
Sylvester **62** 359
Thomas **87** 338 **127** 306
Thomas S. **125** 43
Wheaton **126** 23
William **70** 29 30 **100** 188
129 379
William Henry **77** 182
Z. **70** 30
LUTHERS John B. **91** 328
LUTHY Florence Corinne
(Batchelder) (Conolly)
95 338
Godfrey (Mrs.) **95** 338
LUTIUS George **73** 271
LUTLEY Adam **110** 248
Margaret **110** 247
LUTMAN Edward **52** 122
Jane **54** 95
Johan **142** 156
Katheren (Montague)
(Golding) **142** 154 156
Roger **142** 154 156
LUTON
Adelaide **78** 325
Maggie McCorkle **78** 325
William **78** 325
Lutterell *see* Luttrell
LUTTON John **63** 141
LUTTRELL Lutterell Luttrel
—— **141** 99

LUTTRELL cont'd
Agnes (de Sutton)
 145 268
Andrew **145** 267 268
Elizabeth **135** 288
Geoffrey **145** 267 268
Hawise **145** 267
Hawise (Le Despenser)
 145 267 268
Joan (Talboys) **145** 267
 268
Laura Elizabeth **104** 171
LUTWYTCHE
Edward **101** 54
Maria **98** 342
Thankful **101** 54
LUTZ Augusta **68** 328
Cora B. (Forman) **86** 361
Elizabeth **114** 186
John S. **128** 269
Josephine **86** 200
Roger A. **102** 157
Samuel G. **86** 361
Sydney **89** 240
Vera Forman **86** 361
LUX John **85** 386
Margaret (Mason)
 100 241
Mary **85** 386
Richard **100** 241
LUXFORD Elizabeth
 (Albone) **131** 129
James **93** 42 **131** 129
Margaret **90** 72
LUXON
Andrew H. **89** 237
Anthony **73** 147
Blanche (Lazell) **89** 237
Jay **89** 237
May **89** 237
Ruth (Smith) **89** 237
LUYSTER
Isaphene Moore
 55 lxx
LUZMORE James **97** 104
LUZZATO Giovanni Wel-
 ding **90** 209
LYALL Irene M. **103** 119
LYBARGER
Donald Fisher **115** 76
 117 155 **118** 74
Henrietta Harmon
 118 165
LYBIA
Abraham **82** 293 299
Mary **82** 293 299
LYBRAND Elizabeth **76** 79
 105 220
LYBYER Albert H. **76** 162
 77 162
LYCAN
Gilbert L. **113** 242
LYCEL
Catherine **58** 372
John **58** 372
Mary **58** 372
LYDAT Henry **60** 283
Lyddiard see Ledyard
LYDDS Sarah **111** 177
LYDE
—— **122** 85 **130** 231

LYDE cont'd
— Capt. **84** 379
— Mrs. **52** 111
____ (Foster) **140** 142
Andrew Belcher **69** 112
Ann **122** 84
Ann (Domett) **122** 85
Betsey (Oliver) **84** 361
Byfield **57** 280 **69** 111 112
 84 256 372 **90** 400
Catherine **84** 171
Catherine (Gooch) **84** 171
Dale C. (Mrs.) **122** 320
Deborah **69** 112 **140** 165
Edward **57** 275 **61** 394 **69**
 112 116 **84** 171 361 **89**
 47
Elizabeth **69** 112 116
Elizabeth R. **122** 15
George **69** 112 **122** 85
 145 32
Grace **69** 112
Hannah (Foster) **85** 126
John **140** 165
Katharine **61** 394 **69** 112
Louisa **84** 372
Mary **67** 111 **69** 112
Mary (Wheelwright)
 89 47
Mary L. **145** 32
Nathaniel B. **140** 142 165
Nathaniel Byfield **130** 231
Sarah **69** 111 112 **84** 256
Sarah (Belcher) **84** 256
Sarah Louisa **69** 112 116
Susanna (Callender)
 145 32
Lydeard see Ledyard
LYDEGRAF Vera E.
 (Baldwin) von **120** 154
LYDENBERG
H. M. **112** 210
LYDGATE
Elizabeth **53** 131
Peter **53** 131
Lydiard see Ledyard
LYDIAT Mary **78** 417
LYDIG
Catherine (Suydam)
 86 447
Florence **86** 447
Philip Mesier **86** 447
LYDING James **78** 397
LYDSON Eunice **97** 144
LYDSTON
Alice M. **127** 132
Daniel **55** 249 252
John **54** 409 **65** 294
John M. **127** 131
Mary **65** 294
Robey **55** 250
Sarah **55** 253
Tillie O. (Tobey) **127** 131
Walter Clarence **127** 132
Waymouth **55** 249 252
LYE Anne **51** 186
Elizabeth **83** 480
John **52** 46
Joseph **102** 276
William **64** 218

LYEBBORNE
Edward **104** 276
LYENDS Susan **88** 342
LYETH Mary **112** 147
LYFE Richard **146** 270
LYFORD Alonzo **68** 329
Annie May **68** 329
Arthur Elgar **68** 329
Bessie Holmes **84** 295
Charlotte **68** 329
Columbia D. **140** 265
David **73** 309 **74** 48 189
 114 180
E. L. **112** 235
Epaphras K. **88** 330
Fannie Bradley **67** xxxiv
Fifield **114** 180
Francis **57** 120 **58** lxxxi
 lxxxii **94** 355
George Nathaniel **68** 329
Grace **68** 329
Guy Alonzo **68** 329
Harriet M. **88** 342
Harrison **114** 180
Harry B. **91** 51
Harvey **114** 180
James O. **147** 112
James Otis **68** 386 **81** 138
 93 374 **98** 361 362 365
 118 40 97 100
John **53** 162 **57** 120 **76** 317
 98 164 **114** 180 **142** 110-
 112
Jonathan **114** 180
Josephine Goyette **91** 51
Malvina Fitzalan **58** lxxxi
 91 292
Martha **143** 131
Mary **91** 369
Maud Alice **68** 329
Miriam **53** 162
Mordecai **98** 164 **142** 110
 111
Nathaniel **68** 329
Ned Everett **68** 329
Obadiah **98** 164 **142** 110
 111
Peter **114** 180
Ralph Earl **68** 329
Ruth **142** 110
Sarah **73** 309 **74** 48 **98** 164
 142 110 111
Sarah R. (Fletcher) **88** 330
Sidney **114** 180
Susan **68** 329
Thomas **114** 180
William **66** 344
William Luther **68** 329
Lyghtfoote see Lightfoot
LYGON Anne de
 (Beauchamp) **97** 343
Ciccly **54** 192
Elizabeth **97** 343
Elizabeth (Berkeley)
 97 343
Henry **97** 343
Isabel **97** 343
Margaret (Greville)
 97 343
Richard **97** 343
William **54** 192

LYILYN John **60** 284
LYINGWOOD
 William **112** 115
LYKE Delila (Barton)
 107 ?99
 George W. **107** 299
Lykyris *see* Licorish
LYLBOURNE
 Henry **71** 108
 Margaret **71** 108
LYLE Carrie **144** 118
 Daniel **100** 338 **111** 209
 112 19
 Elizabeth **111** 210
 Jane **111** 209-211
 John **111** 210
 Lois Marjorie **104** 146
 Matilda (Wheeler) **85** 290
 Matthew **118** 326
 Oscar K. **111** 201 **112** 21
 Samuel **85** 290 **111** 209-
 211
 Sarah **108** 71 73 **112** 148
 Sarah (McClung) **111** 211
 Sarah Delina **74** xxxvii
 xlvii
 Seth Snow **74** xlvii
 Sophia **74** xlvii
 T. R. **98** 289
 William Thomas **63** 205
LYLES
 Eleanor West **73** 229
 Eliza **73** 264
 Elizabeth **73** 220
 Emily **73** 267
 Margery **73** 231
 Martha **73** 218
 Mary **73** 222
 Priscilla **73** 137
 Richard **73** 146
 Sarah Magruder **73** 270
 Sidney **73** 271
 Thomas **73** 137 151
 Zachariah **73** 271
LYLIAT John **70** 62
LYLY William **71** 326
LYMAN ____ **54** 134 **55**
 154 **57** 209 **76** 172 **80**
 168 **84** 85 **118** 11 116-
 120 124 126 220 222 224
 226-235 297-301 303-308
 119 44 45 47 48 51 54-56
 59 129 132-134 138 206-
 209 212 214-220 222 223
 289-293 295-298 300-302
 304-306 **120** 57-61 63
 123-135 203-209 211 213
 214 293-298-100 297-300
 302-304 307 309 **123** 27
 130 72 **140** 43 297
 — Col. **94** 227 **111** 291
 120 295
 — Gen. **94** 226 227
 — Mrs. **83** 194 **118** 124
 223 224 231 234 301 305
 119 130 206 212 220 290
 291 302 **120** 61 125 209
 211 297 300 **121** 96 99
 300 **122** 65 69 227
 — Rev. Mr. **75** 123 313
 82 504 505

LYMAN *cont'd*
 ____ (Bracket) **140** 43
 ____ (Otis) **140** 232
 ____ (Robins) **140** 241
 ____ (Williams) **140** 263
 A. A. **96** 167
 Aaron **54** 273 **61** 288
 Abby B. **82** 380
 Abby Frances **82** 422
 83 25 28
 Abigail **60** 385 **63** 169 **75**
 190 **81** 397 **98** 302 **112**
 305 **113** 124
 Abigail (Lewis) **136** 318
 Abigail (Moseley)
 136 331
 Abigail (Moulton) **112**
 305 **115** 136
 Abigail F. **113** 263
 Achsah (Colburn)
 (Bancroft) **96** 127
 Achsah (Parsons) **136** 333
 Albert J. **55** 354
 Alvah **78** 239
 Alvan **74** 63
 Amanda **82** 380
 Amanda M. **74** 63
 Ann **123** 115
 Anna **57** 269 **118** 126
 Anna Jean **82** 110
 Anna Maria **80** 167
 Anna Mason (Grant)
 97 53
 Anna Whitney **63** 258
 Anne **54** lxxxiii **70** liv
 109 224
 Anne (Phelps) **136** 333
 Anne (Pratt) **83** 201
 Anne Jean **77** 297
 Anne Jean (Robbins)
 136 327
 Annie **97** 53
 Annie Jean **76** l
 Anson **84** 85
 Anson M. **64** 105 379
 Anson Marshall **58** 198
 59 xxvi
 Arna S. **62** 98
 Arthur **70** lv **77** lx **98** 86
 Arthur Theodore **67**
 xxxiv **70** xxvii liv lv **77**
 ix xc **89** 60
 Arthur Theodore (Mrs.)
 75 lxxxi
 Asa **66** 103 **74** 63
 Augusta **112** 305 **116** 295
 Azariah **54** li
 Benjamin **57** 209 **62** lxxiii
 129 368 **136** 318 328
 142 346 348 349
 Benjamin Smith **71** 291
 92 209
 Bessie Huntington
 85 196
 Bethiah **70** 198 **74** 63
 119 290
 Bethiah (Clark) **136** 330
 Betsey **113** 27
 Betsey (Whiting) **134** 173
 Billy **119** 220 291 302
 Caleb **57** 388 **58** 68 **118**

LYMAN *cont'd*
 26 113 230 234 **119** 43
 50 **123** 21 **136** 325 **144**
 226
 Caroline (Atwood)
 132 75
 Catherine **54** 177
 Catherine Robbins **75**
 lxxix **82** 110 **107** 227 228
 136 327
 Charles **97** 53 **113** 263
 123 27
 Charles Frederic (Mrs.)
 87 65 **96** 188
 Charles Frederick **97** 53
 Charles Parker **83** 215
 Charlie F. **82** 380
 Charlotte Kimball **55** 230
 Chester **59** 97 **60** 151
 Clarissa **85** 338
 Clarissa Lawrence **78** 239
 Cora **79** 97 **82** 493 **83** 337
 Daniel **56** 284 **65** 149 **77**
 325 **82** 380 **125** 178 182
 244 **126** 22
 David **80** 168 **136** 326
 David Belden **88** 208
 Delight (Wilson) **136** 325
 Dolly **119** 293 295
 Dorcas **53** 449
 Dorcas (Chadbourn)
 96 341
 Dosia **112** 305
 Dwight **89** 314
 Ebenezer **57** 209 **136** 310
 325 **142** 335 346
 Edna G. **82** 380
 Edna Maria **103** 312
 136 333
 Edward Hutchinson
 Robbins **76** l
 Edwin G. **84** 85
 Effie (Witham) **86** 366
 Eleanor **55** 154 **57** 213 **80**
 168 **101** 288
 Eleanor Grant **97** 53
 Eleanor Lee **81** 469
 Elias **57** 269 **93** 182 **103**
 312 **136** 333
 Elihu **103** 64 **104** 195
 Elihu Oliver **54** xlvii li
 Elijah **57** 213 **96** 127
 119 135
 Eliphalet **58** 403
 Eliza **80** 167
 Eliza B. **125** 182
 Elizabeth **57** 209 210 213
 61 310 **79** 153 **91** 80 **97**
 53 **112** 24 **116** 130 **123**
 261 **136** 330
 Elizabeth (Cowles)
 136 320
 Elizabeth (Richardson)
 139 147
 Elizabeth (Seward)
 136 325
 Elizabeth (Wright) **88** 199
 Elizabeth R. **122** 297
 Ella **70** lv **77** lx **85** 189 **89**
 60 80 135
 Ella Bancroft **70** lv **77** lix

LYMAN *cont'd*
Ellen Flinn **80** 168
Ellen Goodale **88** 208
Emily **64** 207
Emily A. **54** li
Emma **89** 314
Erastus **60** 397 **140** 43
Esther **57** 213 **122** 226
  136 310
Eunice **57** 269 **85** 409
Eunice (Graves) **95** 370
  103 64
Eunice A. **77** 325
Experience **57** 209
Experience (Pomeroy)
  136 310 325
Falvia Elizabeth **85** 334
Fanna **56** 354
Fanny **119** 292 305 **120** 58
  62 126 131 133 209 212
  213 300 303 **121** 57-59
  63 68 95 98 100 297 **122**
  64 117 221 226 304
Francis **113** 263
Francis F. **78** 315
Frederick **82** 380
Gad **57** 212 **118** 135
  123 306
Gaius **79** 156 **144** 104
Gen. **147** 52
George **138** 211
George Chilcott **64** 125
George D. **69** 259
George H. **79** 233
George Hinckley **81** 469
George Sheafe **113** 263
George Theodore **62** 394
George W. **54** lxxxiii
  140 232
George Williams **70** liv
  83 201 **89** 60
Georgianna **64** 125
Gideon **57** 213 **118** 113
Grace **142** 346-348
Hannah **57** 209 211 **62**
  lxxiii **64** 125 **69** 259 **84**
  458 **98** 82 301 302 **112**
  305 **116** 128 **119** 292
  306 **120** 61 63 128 131
  134 213 297 300 302 **129**
  368 **136** 319 325 330
Hannah (Birchard) **98** 302
Hannah (Huntington)
  136 330
Hannah (Sewall) **113** 197
Hannah Cogswell (Fiske)
  136 333
Hannah Pickering
  113 263
Hannah S. **79** 156
Hannah W. **83** 183 184
Harriet **77** 44 **85** 88 89
  125 173 178
Harrison Franklin (Mrs.)
  84 172 **85** 190
Harry S. **69** 259
Hattie M. **82** 380
Henry **93** 182
Henry Bull **126** 22
Henry M. **82** 380
Hepzibah **57** 211 **74** 57

LYMAN *cont'd*
101 237 239 240 **136**
  314
Hepzibah (Ford) **136** 310
  313 314 320 325 328-330
Herbert **70** lv **77** lx
Hope **53** 313
Hope (Hawley) **136** 310
  326
Innia **56** 348
Irene **109** 80
Isaac **63** 169 297 **71** 188
  89 60 **93** 391 **97** 269
  109 80 **112** 24 304 305
  113 25 27 263 **114** 45 46
  293-295 **115** 58-62 64 65
  135-142 211 214 215 222
  225 227 228 303-310 **116**
  127-135 137 139 140 142
  301 **118** 26 **127** 115 **132**
  75 **134** 102
Isabella Ogden Reed
  (Macomber) **96** 188
  97 53
Israel **118** 118
Jacob **54** 258 **55** 36 37 **56**
  165 348 350 353 **83** 100
James **58** 196-198 401 403
  59 97-99 213 **60** 204 205
  83 365
James D. **82** 380
Jane **103** 87
Jerusha **58** 196 401 **59** 213
  60 205 **74** 63 **82** 380 **83**
  365
Jesse **134** 173
Jesse P. (Mrs.) **77** 321
Jesse Philyer (Mrs.)
  78 205
Joanna **83** 97 100
Joanna S. **74** 63
Job **112** 305 **113** 124 197
  265 **115** 136
Joel **103** 312 **109** 80
  136 333
John **54** li **57** 212 **80** 399
  89 60 **90** 161 **93** 182 **98**
  301 302 **103** 312 **111**
  298 **123** 310 311 **136**
  310 326 330 331 **137** 315
John P. **83** 173 184 185 307
  84 29
John Pickering **82** 422
  83 173 **113** 263
John R. **80** 167
John Reed **85** 188
John Wanton **125** 244
Jonathan **60** 385 **62** 277 **74**
  63 **121** 297 **122** 117 303
  136 320 330
Joseph **61** 310 **77** 297 **82**
  110 **107** 227 228 **119** 83
  122 121 **136** 318 327
  330 **140** 241
Joseph A. **132** 75
Joshua **90** 161
Josiah **60** 371 **137** 26
Josiah Dwight **63** 258
Judson G. **82** 380
Judson M. **82** 380
Julia **70** lv **74** 157 **75** xxiii

LYMAN *cont'd*
77 xxxv lix lx **82** 380
Julia A. **84** 85
Julia L. Roberts **85** 315
Junia **55** 36
Justin **79** 169
Laura Gertrude **69** 259
Lena (Roberts) **86** 366
Lottie A. **82** 380
Lottie C. **86** 170
Lovinia **112** 305
Lucia **83** 365
Lucius **83** 365
Lucretia **96** 161
Lucretia (Pickering)
  113 263
Lucretia A. **84** 29
Lucretia Ann **82** 422
  113 263
Lucy **52** 224 **112** 24 **115**
  226 **119** 306
Lucy Ellen (Pope) **83** 215
Lura **83** 365
Lydia **74** 63 **92** 170
Lydia (Loomis) **136** 320
  330
Lydia (Wright) **142** 346
Lydia Williams **90** 179
M. S. **82** 376
Mabel **53** 398 **70** lv **77** lx
Margaret Perkins
  75 lxxxi
Mark Perkins (Mrs.)
  101 124
Martha **88** 199 **90** 340
  130 72 **136** 328
Martha (Hannum) **90** 161
Martha (Richards)
  123 306
Mary **51** 241 **55** 37 **57** 213
  74 63 **79** 97 405 **81** 3 9
  83 100 173 **85** 409 **112**
  24 **115** 310 **136** 312 318
  330
Mary (Bassett) **136** 328
Mary (Sargent) **116** 303
  305
Mary (Sheldon) **136** 318
  327
Mary (Wanton) **125** 178
  182 244 **126** 22
Mary Ainsworth **83** 215
Mary Grace **78** 205
Mary R. **82** 376
Mary R. (Peabody)
  83 184 185
Medad **136** 328
Melvin **86** 366
Mindwell **57** 213 **80** 398
  399 **112** 305 **116** 135
  136 331
Mindwell (Sheldon) **136**
  330 331 333
Morison **91** 328
Moses **61** 286 **89** 60 **93** 182
  97 271 **103** 312 **112** 305
  113 25 26 **116** 303 305
  136 333
N. **79** 302
N. Parker **83** 307
Nabby **59** 171 **115** 304

LYMAN *cont'd*
Nancy **141** 48
Naomi **95** 370 **103** 64
Narcissa **112** 305 **113** 197
 265 **116** 221 **119** 60
Nathan Parker **113** 263
Norman **85** 409
Norman R. **82** 380
Normand **79** 153
Olive **112** 24 **115** 218
 118 135
Patty **119** 43
Payson Williston **67** 193
 68 xxxii
Phebe **84** 208 **105** 219
 136 330
Philate **83** 100
Phineas **53** 366 **57** 213 **70**
 109 **94** 226 229 **118** 111
 120 231 232 **119** 44 304
 120 205
Phyllis **87** 374
Polly **59** 99
Rachel **52** 326 **60** 267
 118 118
Ransom **92** 170
Rebecca **54** 273
Rebecca (Swift) **134** 173
Rebecca (Wheeler)
 134 173
Rebecca B. **79** 158
Rhoda (Gifford)
 (Clements) (Smith)
 138 211
Rhoda E. **82** 380
Richard **54** li **57** 210 211
 61 310 **70** liv **74** 57 **77**
 lx **85** 89 **89** 60 **93** 182
 101 239 240 **103** 312
 136 310 313 314 320 325
 328-330 **142** 336 346
Richard Warren **97** 53
Robert Hunt **85** 89 187
 93 82 139 182
Robert Hunt (Mrs.) **85** 89
Ronald Theodore **70** lv
 77 lx
Ruamah **54** 82
Ruth **56** 351 **61** 286 **109** 80
 112 24
Ruth (Holton) **136** 310
Ruth (Plummer) **112** 24
 114 294
S. Justin **82** 376
Sally **76** 172 **136** 326
Sally Outram **108** 105
Salome (Maltby) **111** 298
Samuel **54** 82 **56** 165 **58**
 196 **59** 415 **60** 73 199 **83**
 365 **85** 89 **93** 182 **109** 80
 132 75
Samuel Tucker **93** 182
Sarah **54** li 178 **60** 151 199
 61 286 310 **74** 63 **83** 365
 84 85 **86** 170 **92** 188
 102 230 **107** 157 **109** 80
 136 310 313 325 328-330
 137 115
Sarah (Comstock)
 136 326
Sarah (Harris) **99** 303

LYMAN *cont'd*
Sarah (Narman) **90** 161
Sarah (Swan) **89** 314
Sarah Cordelia (Hannum)
 90 343
Sarah Elizabeth **76** l
Sarah Joiner **88** 208
Sarah Pratt **54** lxxxiii **83**
 201 **86** 340
Seth **95** 370 **103** 64
Sophia **60** 151 **95** 360
 98 226
Stephen **93** 182
Susan Bulfinch **77** 297
Susan Elizabeth **93** 183
Susan Lowell **70** lv
Susan P. **83** 182 184
Susan P. (Warren) **97** 53
Susan Pickering **82** 422
 113 263
Susanna **61** 288
Sylvester **88** 199
Thankful **57** 209 212
Thankful (Pomeroy)
 129 368 **136** 318 328
Theda **112** 305 **116** 226
Theodah **74** 63
Theodora **83** 173
Theodore **51** 79 **59** xciv
 60 225 **61** 214 **62** lxiii
 71 291 **75** 66 **79** 97 309
 81 9 **82** 4 **86** 141 **89** 60
 95 85 **112** 24 **122** 297
 140 146 263
Theodore Benedict (Bp. of
 N.C.) **64** 297
Theodosia **112** 24 **115** 215
 116 298 300
Thomas **52** 326 **54** 178 **123**
 259 **136** 310 **142** 347
Thomas J. **134** 173
Timothy **112** 24 **119** 50
 123 17 **140** 165
Welthy **83** 365
William **58** 401 **60** 265
 64 125 **66** 159 **74** 63 **85**
 315 **86** 170 **90** 343 **91**
 200 **97** 269 **112** 305 **113**
 197 **116** 224
William H; **84** 85
Willis Lester **86** 366
Zadoc **54** li **123** 19-21 28
 29
LYMARK Thomas **53** 93
LYMBOTE
William **100** 293
LYMBURNER Limeburner
Alice (Tapley) **104** 132
Augusta M. **109** 203
Cunningham **105** 212
David **104** 61
Eleanor M. **105** 116
Elizabeth **108** 279
Elsie **108** 279
Esther **108** 284
Eugene B. **110** 296
Eva (Harlow) **98** 109
Everett L. **110** 296
Grace **97** 350 **111** 243
Grace (Smith) (Kane)
 98 109

LYMBURNER *cont'd*
Hannah E. (Means)
 110 22
Hattie May **110** 296
Hollister **110** 296
Horatio A. **110** 296
Isashrene (Condon)
 104 182
James **105** 116
James Condon **105** 116
Jane **104** 133
John **104** 132 182 **105** 116
 284
Joseph **105** 116 **110** 296
Juliann **109** 111
Katharine **105** 116
Kathrine (Condon)
 104 182
Katie C. **110** 296
Margaret **104** 134
Mary **105** 116 **109** 205 206
Mary (Walker) **110** 23 25
Maurice Llewellyn
 110 296
Oscar P. **110** 296
Paul **98** 109
Phebe **109** 203
Phebe Emma **109** 203
Robert **109** 206 **110** 23 25
Roscoe M. **110** 296
Rufus P. **109** 206
Samuel **105** 116
Samuel M. **105** 116
Scott R. **98** 109 **110** 296
Scott R. (Mrs.) **98** 109
Susan **107** 306 **108** 280
Sylvester **110** 296
Sylvester P. **109** 203
Thomas **105** 116 **110** 22
William **109** 199 203
LYME Fran **126** 256
Mary (Tinker) (Huntley)
 101 144
LYMER Paul **66** 36
LYMES Polly **125** 103
LYMYTORY
Peter **84** 81 82
LYNCH Lynche
A. C. **109** 269
Abigail (Priestly) **125** 104
Addie **74** 302
Alice Clare **89** 305 401
Amelia **73** 148
Ann (Spearman) (Russell)
 137 284
Anne **137** 302
Annie **75** xxvi 65 **80** 103
 218
Annie Maria **77** 187
Belle **82** 431
Caroline **88** 281
Catherine **90** 110
Charles **60** xvii
Clay F. (Mrs.) **113** 241
Clemence **137** 302
Cynthia **62** lxxv
Dorothy **137** 302
E. L. (Mrs.) **125** 301
Eleanor Head **113** 241
Eliza **118** 244
Elizabeth **68** 126 **137** 303

LYNCH *cont'd*
304
Elizabeth (Baker) (Court-
hope) **137** 301 302
Elizabeth Royce **81** 356
Ellen **116** 210
Ellen (O'Dowd) **116** 187
Ellen Agnes **72** 302
Ellen Maria **82** 19
Ellen V. (Siebert) **110** 54
Emily Knox **68** 126
Frances Priscilla **62** lxxv
Gabriel **90** 165
George **80** 63
Gertrude Bradford
(Powers) **110** 54
Gervase **137** 302
Hagar **90** 41
Harriet Louise (Husted)
86 197 **98** 82
Harry Pinkney **68** 126
Hector Pierre **68** 126
Helen Bradford **110** 54
J. **66** 259
James **63** 18 **73** 266 273
90 37
James Henry **82** 19
Jane **73** 227
Jeremiah **72** 302
Jerome Morley **98** 82
Jerome Morley (Mrs.)
86 197 **98** 82 89 152
Joan (Courthope) **137** 301-
303
John **62** 301 **64** 25 113
116 210 **137** 302
John L. **73** 274
John S. **73** 141
Julia **82** 19 274 **101** 216
Kateryn **137** 302
Louis Ward **109** 153
Louise Adele **79** 150
M. B. **126** 25
Marcus **62** 129
Margaret **72** 302 **125** 222
137 302
Maria (Lloyd) **126** 80
Martha **130** 72
Martin **90** 110
Mary **127** 78 **137** 302
Mary Ann **101** 215
Mary N. **99** 51
Matilda **92** 227
Maybelle M. **121** 181
Nora **82** 274
Parker **62** lxxv
Patrick **60** 243 **81** 356
Peter **117** 4 5 9 12 15
Polly (Lloyd) **126** 80
R. Le B. **63** 318
Robert **54** 289 **137** 284 302
Rose **137** 302
Royal F. **110** 54
Sarah **109** 269 **145** 28
Simon **71** 172 **137** 301-304
Stephen H. **81** 357
Susan Ann **81** 356
Thomas **109** 96 **116** 187
137 302
Walter **73** 273
William **84** 74 **118** 51

LYNCH *cont'd*
137 284 301-303
William H. **110** 54
William R. **109** 269
William Vance **125** 104
LYNCH-ROBINSON
Adrian **103** 320
Christopher **103** 320
LYNCHAKIN
Denis **60** 163
Lynche *see* Lynch
Lyncke *see* Link
LYNCKER Erhard **112** 247
LYNDE Lynd - *see also*
Lind
—— **53** 266 **72** 184
— Mr. **124** 101 **144** 14
Aaron **56** 290
Abel **78** 264
Adoniram **56** 290
Alonzo Vinton **56** 293
Amanda **57** 137
Amos Porter **66** 317
Arma **78** 264
Barnard **55** 144
Bathsheba **66** 330
Benjamin **54** lxiv **57** 137
280 **63** 362 **90** 400 **95** 27
107 185 **130** 202 **139**
292 293
Benjamin Franklin
81 273
Betsey **56** 290
Cecilia de la **94** 14
Charlotte **70** 85
Daniel **56** 293
David **56** 65 **59** 144
Deborah **66** 331
Dorothy **54** 212 **56** 153
155 **136** 314
Dorothy (Stanton) **136**
314 **143** 39
Edward **61** 350
Elihu **56** 66
Eliza Jennette **66** 198
Elizabeth **51** 299 300 **60**
167 168 **70** 69 **81** 127
132 89
Emma **78** 352
Enoch **56** 291
Esther **51** 305 **70** 34
Eunice **126** 122
H. Wales **81** 207
Hannah **51** 133 **56** 65 66
289-291 **79** 70 **143** 38 39
Henry **70** 69 **81** 127
Hepzibah **56** 65 66 289-291
Hopestill **70** 69
Jabez **56** 65 66 289-291 **66**
317 **92** 50 52
Jacob **54** 211 **55** 143 144
Jacob Perkins **66** 317
James **95** 27
James Edgar (Mrs.)
78 352
James Lawrence (Mrs.)
99 148
Jane **51** 285
John **66** 317 331 **70** 69
John Hart **70** 85
Johnson **59** 144

LYNDE *cont'd*
Jonathan **54** 211 **147** 179
Joseph **51** 299 **56** 153 **60**
168 **66** 317 **67** 210 **85**
455 **90** 400 **92** 50 56 57
136 314 **143** 36 37
Joshua **126** 122
Larkin F. **88** 340
Lizzie **55** 32
Lora **56** 291
Lydia **53** 212 **54** 211 212
72 210 **78** 314 **83** 472
Margaret **67** 210
Margaret (Jordan) **131**
129 **143** 36
Margaret (Martin) **143** 39
Maria **81** 273
Martha **81** 273
Mary **51** 302 **53** 326 **55**
143 144 293 **63** 362 **66**
199 300 317 **74** liii **78**
299 318 **81** 133 **130** 202
207
Mary (Lemmon) **136** 314
Mary Eliza **136** 328
Mehitable **56** 290
Nancy **66** 317
Nathan **92** 51 53 57
Nathaniel **53** 326 **79** 70
Nicholas **56** 153 155 **136**
314 **143** 39
Otis **56** 289
Phebe **56** 65 **66** 317
Polly **56** 290
Prudence **56** 293
Rachel **77** 233
Ralph **66** 330 **81** 135
Rebecca **59** 144 **60** 167
143 37
Rebecca (Jenner) **143** 38
Rebecca (Trerise) **143** 36
37
Ruth **92** 54
Sally **56** 66 289 **66** 109
Samuel **51** 64 65 **57** 275 **61**
394 **66** 200 **145** 236
Sarah **55** 306 **56** 153 **67** 210
74 253 **85** 455 **127** 221
Sarah (Belcher) **125** 63
Sarah E. (Cobb) **88** 340
Simon **51** 132 133 **57** 275
61 40 **63** 382 **99** 233
102 180 **106** 17 259
Stephen **56** 65 66 289-291
Sukey **56** 66
Susanna **81** 190
Thomas **51** 299 300 302
54 211 212 **55** 143 306
85 455 **92** 50 **131** 9 13
19 129 **143** 36 37 39
Vesta (Gibson) **125** 292
Walter de la **94** 14
William **66** 317 **92** 179
104 242 **125** 292
Lyndehurst *see* Lyndhurst
LYNDENBURGER
Dorcas **63** 157
LYNDES
Benjamin **69** 374
Eliza J. **69** 199
Grace **69** 374

LYNDES *cont'd*
Jairus F. **69** 199
LYNDESELL
Alice **68** 192 193
Edward **68** 191-193
Joan **68** 193
Mary **146** 268
Peter **68** 193
LYNDFORD John **75** 227
LYNDHURST Lyndehurst
— Lord **57** 343 **99** 9
Georgiana (Lady) **56** 222
John Singleton Copley
(Baron) **56** 222 **68** lv
Sarah (Lady) **56** 222
LYNDON —— **62** 353
Abigail **136** 332
Josiah **147** 347
Josias **56** 296 **69** 350 **70** 30
96 15 **104** 73 **143** 231
Mary **125** 244
LYNDSELL Mary **132** 22
Lyne *see* Lynn
LYNES Elizabeth **141** 125
126
Ignatus **111** 192
Joan **141** 124-126
Robert **141** 125 126
LYNFIELD Mary **126** 142
LYNFORD
Dorothy **56** 405
Martha **102** 96
Lyng *see* Ling
LYNGFIELD
Gilbert **52** 244
Sarah **52** 243
LYNN Lyne Lynne
— Capt. **55** 381
Agnes **61** 287 **123** 249 250
Agnes (Fettiplace)
123 249
Andrew **67** 384
Ann **73** 220
Catherine **119** 78
Clemens **94** 327
Colarton **73** 220
Cyrus **73** 254
David **73** 254
Eleanor (Venable)
123 249
Eliza B. **67** 384
Eliza Belle **68** xxxii
Elizabeth **51** 211 **71** 5 6
George **71** 19 **73** 254
Henry **59** 215 **71** 6
James **64** 111 **73** 254
John **71** 5 **73** 254 **111** 201
123 249 250
John F. **114** 186
Joseph **73** 254
Louisa Maria **103** 70
Margaret **123** 249
Martha **60** 78
Mary Ashercraft **67** 384
Michael **114** 186
Nancy **73** 245
Nathaniel **73** 254
Polly **66** 110 **73** 254
Rebecca **73** 254
Richard **123** 250
Robert **66** 110 **114** 186

LYNN *cont'd*
Roger **123** 250
Sally **73** 254
Sarah **59** 215
Sarah (Fairman) **113** 268
Simeon **60** 78
Susan **71** 19
Susanna **100** 302
Thomas **63** 144 **139** 315
William **51** 211 **112** 256
LYNNAN Mary **80** 25
Lynnell *see* Linnell
LYNNET Polly (Webber)
108 264
Prentiss **108** 264
Lynsey *see* Lindsey
LYNSFORD
Margaret **59** 362
LYON Lyons
—— **54** cxviii **56** 96 305
58 206 317 **61** 317 **62**
387 **68** 377 **91** 191 **112**
296 **117** 18 **118** 125 **119**
302 **120** 134 206 207
— Lord **96** 207
— Miss **57** 423
— Mr. **55** 146 **79** 404
— Mrs. **127** 138
— Rev. Dr. **66** 67
___ (Oakes) **128** 160
A. B. **58** 206 **60** 213
Aaron **70** 146 212 215 296
298 **72** 305
Abbie F. (Gifford)
138 215
Abel **91** 191 193
Abel S. **91** 192
Abiel **55** 318 **67** 375
Abigail **52** 57 **56** 31 **58** 405
59 393 **60** 359 **64** 210
67 374 **68** 175 377 **69** 46
231 377 378 **72** 305 **97**
42 255 **99** 254 **133** 233
136 76 **137** 35
Abigail (Brothwell) **145**
73 75
Abigail (Ogden) **134** 255
334
Abigail (Polly) **97** 42
146 278
Absolom **100** 133
Adah **141** 195
Adaline (Woodruff)
122 239
Adelia Collier (Watkins)
91 192
Albert Brown **61** xxxiv
63 303 **64** xxxi
Albert S. **91** 192 193
Albert Williams **69** xxxvi
70 ix x
Alice **84** 125
Alice A. **91** 377
Almira M. **116** 259
Almon H. **87** 234 240
Alvin **72** 305 **101** 256
Amanda **72** 305
Ambrose **70** 261
Amelia **58** 405 **91** 192
Amelia Eunice **72** 305
Ameriah **116** 7

LYON *cont'd*
Amy **91** 377 **121** 67 69
125 176 **126** 22
Andrew **72** 312
Ann **71** 52 **78** 11 **88** 141
Ann Elizabeth **91** 192
Anna **70** 227
Anne **68** 377 **69** 231
111 292
Annice Jeannette **68** 257
Anson **145** 73 **146** 384
Arthur E. **100** 255
Asahel **59** civ **107** 240
120 318 319 **122** 239
Asahel Dimock **107** 240
120 318 **122** 239
Augustus **133** 119
Azubah **66** 40
Barna **73** 254
Barzillai **55** 264 **57** 410 411
Baxter **133** 119
Benjamin **60** 39 **63** 264
68 173 220 221 223 226
228 230 233 238 313 314
321 **69** 370 371 **91** 191
377 **115** 38 **133** 119
Benjamin R. **73** 254
Bethiah **91** 263 **107** 156
Betsey **72** 308 **73** 254
145 75
Betsey (Wilkins) **133** 119
Beulah **91** 191 192
Caleb **58** 405 **98** 329
133 119
Caroline M. (Smith)
91 377
Caroline Margaret
55 lxxii
Catherine **132** 326
Catherine (Hamilton)
112 296
Catherine Cecilia **72** 305
Charles **86** 53 **117** 15
125 42
Charles Treat **72** 305
Charlotte **91** 191 192
Chester **70** 155
Clarence Cady **69** xxxii
Clarence Edwin **85** 196
Clarissa **64** 124
Clement **112** 296
Cornelia Peck **73** 131
Damaris Williams
66 lxvii
Dana **93** 214
Daniel **60** 187 **61** 379 **64**
253 **68** 173 **69** 370 **80**
434 **89** 378 **91** 191-193
377 **145** 75
David **56** 74 **60** 359 **72** 305
120 14 **145** 73
David A. **72** 305
David W. **60** 346
Deborah **55** 262
Deliverance **51** 167
Diana **61** 42
Dorothy **112** 295
Dorothy (Montgomerie)
112 295
Dorothy J. **100** 255
Dow **58** 206

LYON *cont'd*
Dupont Bayard (Mrs.)
  83 370 **84** 190
Ebenezer **51** 167 **56** 31 148
  57 28 **97** 27 42 254 255
Ebenezer Vorse **68** 315
Edward **61** 236
Edward James **93** 278
Edward S. **125** 182
Edwin Daniel **91** 377
Effie Estella **68** 257
Eleanor **64** 210 **68** 292 **69**
  366 **70** 35 **100** 133
Eleanor (Adkins) **122** 240
Eleanor (Bradley) **145** 73
  146 384
Eleanor (Nichols) **145** 73
  146 384
Eleazer **84** 465
Elhanan **55** 141 **60** 359
  78 11
Eliah **145** 75
Elijah **86** 13 **128** 277 **145** 75
Eliphalet **68** 292 **69** 46
  366 373 **70** 35 41
Elisha **55** 397 399 **57** 373
  376-378
Elisha Hiram **57** 377
Eliza **58** 406 **69** 30 **122** 240
  125 180 241
Eliza S. **126** 20
Eliza W. **58** 405
Elizabeth **53** 229 **55** lxxiii
  58 405 **63** 90 264 **66** 40
  67 373 **68** 290 377 **69**
  134 376 **90** 283 **91** 77
  193 **93** 355 **96** 270 **103**
  175 **111** 292 **125** 183
  291 **132** 297 **136** 361
Elizabeth (Bannister)
  91 192
Elizabeth (Barnes)
  125 260
Elizabeth (Bugbee)
  133 119
Elizabeth (FitzRandolph)
  91 191
Elizabeth (Maltby)
  111 292
Elizabeth A. **125** 182
Elizabeth B. **87** 386
  112 150
Elizabeth Bannister
  91 192
Elizabeth Bowers **87** 380
Elizabeth FitzRandolph
  91 191
Elkanah **115** 188
Elkanan **56** 74
Ellen Frances **57** 380
Elvira (Landers) **124** 278
  279
Emily **86** 53
Enoch **64** 121 122
Ephraim **53** 229 **63** 85 **68**
  287 377 **69** 46
Esther **56** 146 **63** 88 **69** 133
  70 39 **72** 305 **93** 213
Eunice **58** 405 **68** 176 287
  320 **69** 46 **70** 36 **91** 191
  131 297 **145** 73

Eunice (Haynes) **140** 305
  307
Experience **67** 372
Ezra Perry **77** 180 184
Fear **59** civ
Florence **102** 124
Frances Matilda **73** 131
Frank A. **91** 377
Frederick Denison
  72 305
Freegrace **54** 213
George **60** 135 213 **63** 303
  69 xxxv **107** 240 **115** 230
  120 17 318 **122** 240
George Armstrong (Mrs.)
  90 187
George H. **68** 161
George P. **74** 97
George W. **122** 239
George W. A. **58** 206 **60**
  213 **63** 303
Georgette Ernestine
  74 97
Gershom **69** 370
Gilbert **134** 255 334
Gilbert D. **91** 377
Gilbert FitzRandolph
  91 191-193
Gilbert Miner **72** 305
Grace **70** 41
Grace (Webb) **145** 73 75
Griswould **68** 377
Grizell (Brothwell) **145** 75
Grizzel **69** 377
H. W. **55** lxxiii
Hamilton **91** 377
Hannah **51** 223 **55** 391 **57**
  378 **60** 135 359 **66** 40 **68**
  377 **70** 34 **87** 190 **89** 189
  93 216 **102** 105 **107** 35
  69 **108** 226 **115** 118 **119**
  222
Hannah (Kimberly)
  102 105
Hannah M. **91** 377
Harriet **70** 160 **75** xxvi
  79 122 **91** 192
Harriet Newell (Pearson)
  133 119
Harvey **101** 216 **103** 175
Henry **55** xlii lxxii lxxiii
  60 40 **68** 317 **87** 380
  115 230 **125** 242 **132** 95
Herbert Kent (Mrs.)
  115 146
Hester **68** 377
Hezekiah **59** 393 **69** 46
  70 34
Hiram D. **138** 215
Hugh **112** 296
Huldah E. **77** 146
Humphrey **65** 149 **80** 434
Ida A. **78** 166
Ida M. **68** 161
Isaac **58** 405 **107** 240 **120**
  318 **122** 239 240
Isaiah **60** 187
Israel Whitney **57** 379
J. B. **57** 343 **60** 407
Jabez **69** 134 **111** 146

LYON *cont'd*
Jacob **60** 187 **93** 397 **100** 63
James **51** 19 324 **60** 346
  64 318 **68** 173 175 287
  377 **69** 46 377 378 **71** 52
  88 118 **103** 175 269 **114**
  232
James B. **52** 89 **55** 127 **56**
  329 **57** 237
James Hazelton **92** 131
Jane **56** 193 **73** 131 **75** 198
  100 316
Jane (Both) **91** 192
Jane (Kniffin) **134** 255 334
Jason **78** 419
Jedediah **66** lxviii
Jelina (Foot) **120** 17
Jemima **58** 259 **68** 377
Jennet **91** 192
Jerre **72** 308 **73** 254
Jesse **69** 231 **107** 240 **114**
  277 **120** 318 319 **122**
  239 240
Jessie May **91** 192 193
Joanna **58** 241 **116** 157
  122 228
Job **58** 405 406
Joe **145** 75
Joel **91** 191-193
John **53** 302 **56** 193 **60**
  348 349 **61** 133 **62** 21
  126 289 301 **64** 210 256
  323 **65** 54 149 **68** 173
  257 290 377 **69** 134 374
  376 **72** 114 **86** 389 390
  88 285 **91** 191 **97** 42 **98**
  324 **100** 133 **102** 105
  107 240 **112** 295 296
  114 232 **120** 318 **122**
  240 **125** 260 **127** 307
  133 119 **141** 200 **145** 73
  146 278
John D. **73** 131
John E. **125** 245
John F. **62** 121
John Fisher **58** 372
John Howard **73** 131
  111 292
John P. **120** 14
Jonathan **67** 373 **93** 215
Jose **145** 75
Joseph **59** 393 395 **65** 237
  68 171 **69** 46 231 379 **73**
  131 **125** 173 177 182 242
  245 **127** 139 **145** 75
Joseph Lorenzo (Mrs.)
  99 148
Joshua Brown **57** 376 380
Josiah **56** 145 146 148 **70**
  36 **81** 53 98 105
Judah **133** 119
Judith **128** 277
Julia (Todd) **91** 192
Julia L. **91** 192
Julius **66** 40
June **87** 173
Katharine Wallen **91** 235
  238 **97** 388
Keziah **99** 29
Laurinda (Ketchum)
  133 119

LYON *cont'd*
Lemuel **55** lxxii **57** 373
 379 380 **68** 226 321 **94**
 228 **115** 194
Lois **54** 49 **59** 393 395 **68**
 177 **69** 46 231 379 **86** 53
 92 195 **111** 146
Lois (Bennett) **145** 75
Lorene Jones **119** 156
Lorenzo **73** 254
Louisa **57** 373
Louisa Rathbun **86** 389
Lucinda **69** 366
Lucinda (Holcomb)
 122 240
Lucy **62** 121 125 **93** 217
Lucy Mehitable **57** 380
Luella R. **58** 206
Luke **73** 254
Luna (Baldwin) **91** 192
Luther **58** 372 **62** 121 123
 83 380
Lydia **62** 121 127 **114** 182
Lydia (Perry) **115** 194
Lyman **66** 40
Marcelia E. **116** 259
Marcia **127** 238
Marcus **133** 119
Marcy (Underwood)
 125 182
Margaret **51** 223 **68** 377
Margaret (Thomas)
 120 14
Maria (Flood) **88** 285
Marie **55** 413
Marie Louise **74** 97
Marjorie Randolph
 (Van Wickle) **90** 187
Martha **91** 263 **125** 218
 133 119
Martha (Morris) **146** 278
Martha Dana **96** 76
Martin Armstrong
 91 293
Mary **52** 201 **55** 264 **56** 32
 59 civ **61** 114 **62** 328 **64**
 371 **67** 375 **68** 228 257
 292 **69** 40 133 231 378
 70 34 **72** 114 211 305
 308 312 **73** 254 **76** 266
 77 188 **78** 11 **80** 64 141
 434 **91** 191 192 **93** 321
 99 43 **111** 292 **125** 239
 128 277
Mary (Turner) **83** 380
Mary (Wilson) **91** 192
Mary A. **116** 259
Mary Amanda **72** 305
Mary Ann **57** 377 **77** 184
 78 322 **91** 192
Mary Ann (Carlisle)
 101 215
Mary Ann (Chase) **88** 118
Mary Ann (Wyckoff)
 91 192
Mary Belle Elizabeth
 92 145
Mary Clap **68** 321
Mary Eliza **68** 257
Mary Elizabeth **58** 405
Mary P. **91** 377

LYON *cont'd*
Mary Ward **78** 108
Mary Wilson **91** 192
Matthew **55** 125 **60** 213
 79 160
Matthias **91** 191 193
Mehitable **81** 469
Melinda **61** 300
Mercy **81** 53
Meriah **136** 119
Michael **69** 370
Miriam **57** 410 **61** 236
Molly **61** 344
Moses **93** 214 216
Moses H. **60** 346
N. M. **125** 177
Nancy **73** 254 **80** 184
 111 292
Nancy Clarissa **68** 257
Nancy Fisher **64** 122
Nathan **63** 90 **131** 297
 136 141
Nathan H. **73** 254
Nathaniel **56** 269 **57** 411
 69 371 **111** 292 **112** 48
 145 73
Nehemiah **51** 189 **65** 374
 66 21 **145** 75
Nehemiah May **133** 119
Nelson John **91** 377
Nettie **78** 322
Newton Thomas **91** 377
Noah Frank Bray **68** 257
Obadiah **125** 207
Olive **92** 131 133 **93** 317
Olive (Gardner) **101** 216
Oliver **58** 405 **64** 122
 65 305
Otto Jamieson (Mrs.)
 101 124
Parley **66** 38
Patience **63** 90 **64** 122
Patty **66** 40 **68** 318
Pauline Henrietta **93** 278
Peggy **87** 124
Pelatiah **67** 374
Persis E. **140** 305 307 308
Peter **60** 213 **63** 303 **68**
 230 291 **69** 40 231 378
 78 11 **103** 150 **112** 48
Phebe **66** 38 **81** 273
Phebe (Mumford) **125**
 173 177 242 245
Phebe (Seaver) **122** 240
Phebe V. **125** 242
Philena **66** 40
Philena (Hanks) **86** 13
Polly **55** 399 **61** 379 **63** 85
 68 316 **91** 377 **97** 42
 127 66 **145** 75
Polly (Esten) **89** 378
 91 377
Polly (Farley) **136** 141
Polly (Strickland) **89** 378
 91 377
Priscilla **145** 73
Priscilla (Wakeman)
 (Wilson) **146** 384
Prudence Barger **72** 305
Rachel **55** 395 **70** 119
 115 134

LYON *cont'd*
Ransom **69** 373
Rebecca **60** 359 **68** 288 **69**
 40 **93** 97
Rebecca F. **68** 95
Rebecca Lizzie **103** 175
Reuben **101** 215
Rhoda **69** 377 **70** 35 **91** 191
 192
Richard **51** 223
Robert **76** 53
Robert M. **60** 346
Rosalette I. **91** 377
Rowland **69** 366 **70** 41
Royal Corbin **133** 119
Ruth **70** 35 **78** 299
Ruth (Newcomb) **120** 14
Sally **55** 397 **68** 313 **70** 155
Sally (Durrell) **133** 119
Sally Brown **57** 373
Samuel **51** 167 223 **66**
 lxviii **67** 375 **68** 173 233
 264 286 318 377 **69** 40
 46 231 374 **92** 131 133
 93 317 **94** 377 **140** 307
 145 73
Samuel B. **60** 387
Samuel Belcher **61** 42 **68**
 315 317 318 320
Samuel C. **66** 40
Sarah **51** 166 167 **60** 346 **62**
 121 124 **63** 131 **67** 374
 375 **68** 174 **69** 40 46 133
 370 377 **71** 263 **88** 319
 89 378 **91** 191 377 **98**
 172 **101** 256 **109** 263
 111 292 **115** 43
Sarah (Titus) **89** 377
 91 377
Sarah (Tolman) **87** 234
 240
Sarah Ann **64** 122
Sarah Ann (Vaughn)
 133 119
Sarah Booth **112** 48
Sarah Brown **57** 379
Sarah Caroline (Lazell)
 89 310
Sarah E. **63** 272
Sarah Maria **133** 119
Sarah Thorpe **91** 172
Sarah Young **77** 180
Seth **68** 292 **69** 46 133 375
 70 34 39 **128** 277
Seth Augustus **72** 305
Sidney **58** 206
Simeon **91** 191
Sophia **80** 434
Sophia Brainerd **136** 326
Sophie **91** 293
Sophronia **72** 114 **91** 192
Stephen **145** 73 75
Susan **91** 192
Susan L. **81** 406
Susanna **51** 223 **67** 375
 68 377 **86** 390
Susanna Glover **68** 314
Tamer **141** 193 200
Thankful **55** lxxii **68** 238
 377 **126** 142
Theophilus **56** 74

LYON *cont'd*
Thomas **60** 187 **63** 303 **68**
  223 313 315 316 318 321
  69 134 **134** 255 334
Thomas A. **81** 53 **89** 310
Thomas W. **64** 122
Vinal **66** lxvii lxviii
Vivian Elsie **80** 208 337
W. J. **78** 322
W. P. (Mrs.) **119** 156
Waitstill **75** 147
Wakeman S. **69** 366
Walter **69** 133 **77** 146
William **60** 213 **62** 251
  63 303 **64** 214 **66** lxviii
  76 265 **85** 276 283 **89**
  377 **91** 377 **108** 258 **111**
  292 **127** 17 **133** 119 **145**
  73 **146** 278 384
William B. **60** 346 **91** 377
William H. **53** 136
William Henry (Mrs.)
  85 196
William Howard **73** 131
William Huntington
  133 119
William P. **63** 272
Zerviah **67** 375
LYSARDE
  — Goodman **148** 111
Lyscom *see* Liscomb
Lyscomb *see* Liscomb
LYSETH
  Amy Coburn **97** 163
LYSINGE Sisley **141** 124
Lysle *see* Lisle
LYSON —— **54** 68 **59** 291
  296
LYSONS Daniel **110** 19
LYSSON Mary **66** 291
LYSTER
  Armstrong **145** 370
  Frederick Edward
    145 370
  Graciana **145** 370
  John **117** 115
  Laurence **114** 58
  Richard **90** 62
  Susan Alice **117** 115
  William Narcissus
    145 370
LYSTON
  Thomas de **109** 22
  William de **109** 22
LYTCOTT
  Christopher **101** 22
LYTE
  Agnes (Ash) **96** 186
  Agnes (Blomvill) **96** 186
  Anna Maria (Oliver)
    96 186
  Constance (Baskerville)
    96 186
  Dorothea (Kellway) **138** 9
  Edith (Horsey) **96** 186
  Edmund **96** 186
  Elizabeth (Cooper) **96** 186
  Elizabeth (Mohun) **96** 186
  Emily Jeanette (Craigie)
    96 186
  Frances (Fownes) **96** 186

LYTE *cont'd*
  Frances (Tiptoft) **96** 186
  Frances (Worth) **96** 186
  Gertrude **138** 9
  Henry **96** 186
  Henry C. Maxwell **141** 99
    145 4 267
  Henry Francis **96** 186
    138 10
  Henry Maxwell **103** 21
  Hugo **138** 10
  Isabel (de Draycot) **96** 186
  Joan (Fitz James) **96** 186
  Joan (Ilberd) **96** 186
  John **77** 113 **96** 186
  Katharine **138** 8-10
  Margaret (Goathurst)
    96 186
  Margaret Maxwell **96** 186
  Margery (Blaunfield)
    96 186
  Margery (Blomvill)
    96 186
  Margery (Drew) **96** 186
  Margery (Hippesley)
    96 186
  Mary (Down) **96** 186
  Peter Le **96** 186
  Robert Le **96** 186
  Thomas **96** 186 **138** 9
  Thomasia (Carent) **96** 186
  William **138** 9
  William Le **96** 186
Lytelton *see* Littleton
LYTH John **55** 340 341
LYTHAM James **62** 253
LYTHERLANDE
  Thomas **51** 258
Lytle *see* Little
LYTLEHARE —— **65** 316
  Agnes **65** 316
  Anne **65** 316
  Katharine **65** 287 316
LYTLINGTON
  Nicholas **119** 99
LYTTLEBYE
  Joan **142** 263
LYTTON —— **52** 320
  Thomas **104** 30
LYVER John **66** 37
LYVERSEDGE
  Jennett **109** 7
  John **109** 7
Lyveryche *see* Leverich

MAAN Johnson **73** 279
MAAR
  Charles **68** xxxii 111
MAAS
  Isidor I. **72** 295
  Katharine Lucile **72** 295
  Martin **72** 295
MABBDE Robert **111** 263
MABBETT Sarah **81** 103
MABBS —— **51** 219
  Elizabeth (Stone) **100** 301
  Jonathan **100** 141 301
    102 31
  Sarah **100** 300

MABEE Mabie Maby
  —— **54** 456
  Anna E. (Barton) **107** 211
  Clara (Aulls) **114** 65
  H. P. **127** 74
  Hamilton Wright **64** 296
  John Eber (Mrs.) **102** 124
    106 160
  Rachel A. (Williams)
    127 71
  William A. **114** 65
MABEL Dorothy **128** 190
MABEN
  Benjamin S. **123** 232
  Betsey **92** 170
  Betsey (Gregroy) **92** 170
  Catherine **92** 170
  Catherine (Wyckoff)
    92 170
  Catherine A. **92** 170
  Eliza I. **92** 170
  George S. **92** 170
  Gregory **92** 170
  Hannah **92** 170
  Hugh **92** 170
  Hugh M. **92** 171
  John **92** 171
  Libbie **92** 171
  Louisa **92** 171
  Mary E. **92** 166
  Sally **92** 169
  Sally (Pearce) **92** 171
  William **92** 170 171
MABER Henry **61** 278
    79 432
  Martha **79** 432
  Mary **72** 232
MABES Sarah **100** 300
Mabie *see* Mabee
MABILLON —— **107** 286
MABLE
  Hamilton W. **58** 326
MABLETUFT
  Samuel **62** 325
MABRY Delia **82** 434
MABURY —— **145** 47
  Bella **94** 381
  Hiram **94** 381
  Josephine (Hardman)
    94 381
  Paul Rodman **80** 334 **81**
    219 **94** 79 142 381
  Richard **94** 381
Maby *see* Mabee
MacDUFF
  Donald **122** 272
MACA Thomas **148** 20
Macadams *see* McAdam
MACAFEE M'Afee McAfee
  — Capt. **92** 310
  Achsah **56** 252
  Agnes **61** 351
  Catherine H. **109** 221
  Daniel **59** 193
  Ida A. **68** 210
  Ira **56** 252
  James **55** 430 **56** 250-252
    60 103
  Jane **56** 250 **115** 240
  Jeanett **115** 240
  Josephine V. **128** 177

MACAFEE *cont'd*
Mabel **84** 185
Mary **56** 251 **92** 310
Reid Dana **94** 139
MACALLAN
Barbara **147** 129
MacAllister *see* McAallister
MACAR Rethaan (Baron)
106 13
Macarta *see* McCarthy
MacArthur *see* McArthur
Macarthy *see* McCarthy
Macartney *see* McCartney
Macarty *see* McCarthy
MACARY Leonce **92** 402
MACAULAY McCauley
—— **101** 197
— Dr. **54** 120
Catherine **60** xvi
Eliza Ann (Drury)
109 231
Genevieve F. (Garvan)
(Brady) **93** 140 **98** 349
Hannah More **83** 344
Isabella **119** 319
J. B. **58** lxv
James **101** 201
Kate McGill **58** lxv
Leora Arvesta **109** 231
Ruth **142** 178
Selina (Mills) **83** 344
T. B. **56** 204
Thomas B. **53** 96 **57** 15 240
William J. B. (Mrs.) **93** 125
140
Zachary **83** 344
MACAY
____ (Leach) **105** 150
MacBean *see* McBean
MacBeane *see* McBean
MACBETH John Gordon
(Mrs.) **98** 147
Lucia Shaw (Holliday)
89 132
MACBRAYNE
Agnes R. **86** 297
MACBRIAR Ruth Patience
(Flather) **94** 86
Wallace Noble (Mrs.)
94 86
MACBRIDGE
Sarah **82** 291 293
MACBRINE
Edith Grierson **74** xxi
83 222 369 383 **84** 105
176 190 205 **85** 213 214
86 213 214 **91** 141
Lucy **97** 123
Ruth **83** 222
Ruth Wilmot **89** 146 **90**
137 150 **91** 141 157 **92**
161 **93** 152 **94** 154 **95**
161 **96** 174 **97** 172 **98**
161 162 **99** 163 164 **100**
125 126 **101** 139 140
102 138 139
MACBRYDE
David Caldwell **89** 97
Maccae *see* McKay
MacCafery *see* McCaffrey
MacCafrey *see* McCaffrey

MacCALMONT
Sarah **85** 430
MACCAMAN Maccamey
Esther (Reed) **125** 105
Francis L. **125** 105
MACCANE —— **125** 105
Daniel **57** 57
Mary **57** 57
William **81** 368
MACCARTER Alice R.
(Snow) **102** 286
Everett **102** 286
MacCarty *see* McCarthy
MacCasland *see*
McAusland
MACCASTLE
Mary **73** 153
MacCausland *see*
McAusland
MacCay *see* McKay
MACCHONE Hannah **85**
90 **88** 251 255
MACCLAMROCH James
Gwaltney Westwarren
107 133
MacClary *see* McCleary
MacClewain *see* McElwain
MacClintock *see*
McClintock
MACCLOY —— **104** 204
MacClung *see* McClung
MacCOLGIN
Catherine **73** 227
MacCollister *see* McAllister
Maccomb *see* McComb
MACCONE Mary **83** 377
MACCOVEY
James Stuart **66** lxv
Julia **66** lxv
Mary Stuart **66** lxv
MacCoy *see* McCoy
MacCray *see* McRae
MACCU Martha **62** 84
MacCulloch *see*
McCullough
MacCurdy *see* McCurdy
MACCUS —— **62** 163
MacDaniel *see* McDaniel
MacDaniels *see* McDaniel
MacDermott *see*
McDermott
MacDonald *see* McDonald
MacDonell *see* McDonnel
MacDonnel *see* McDonnel
MacDonnell *see* McDonnel
MacDonough *see*
McDonough
MacDougal *see* McDougall
MacDougall *see*
McDougall
MacDowal *see* McDowell
MacDowell *see* McDowell
MACE *see also* Macy
— Mrs. **83** 35
Abigail **66** 147 221 305
87 126
Abraham **66** 304
Agnes **66** 142 144
Andrew **58** 137 139 **66**
142 143 150 153 209 302
67 59-61 134 135

MACE *cont'd*
Benjamin O. **88** 285
Betsey **59** 286 **92** 310
Betty **66** 155 **82** 293 295
Charles **105** 102
Daniel **79** 40 **88** 331
90 113
Deborah **66** 142 143 150
153 209
Elizabeth **51** 462 463 **66**
146 148 219 220 222 223
305
Elizabeth F. (Johnson)
90 113
Eveline T. (Howland)
88 285
Gibbons **66** 142 146 148
150 153 155 211 **67** 145
146 232 233
Hannah **64** 155 **66** 142
150 219 221 301 **67** 244
247 355
Henry **67** 247 **90** 105 113
Hepzibah **90** 113 **125** 292
Ithamar **66** 221 302 **67** 356
James **51** 399 **66** 153 221
Joanna **66** 142 150
John **66** 146 219 220 222
223 302 303 **82** 47 **113**
55
Jonathan **108** 85
Jos. **66** 302 303
Joseph **66** 142 150 152
154 211 223 **67** 59 60
132 133 135-137 142 144-
146 **82** 27 **86** 148
Josiah **66** 211 225
Judith **66** 142 148 150 153
155 211
Levi **66** 219 221 302 **82** 27
Lois **61** 379
Martha (Whittemore)
108 85
Mary **66** 142 144-146 150
152 154 209 211 303 **67**
139 **82** 47 413 **123** 125
Mary (Morrow) **88** 331
Mary A. O. (Hopkins)
105 102
Mary C. **100** 188
Mary E. **88** 341
Nancy **93** 103
Nancy (Durrell) **134** 154
Olive A. **93** 103
Priscilla **55** 407
Rachel **66** 302
Rebecca **66** 146
Reuben **66** 304 **93** 103
134 154
Rheney **61** 384
Robert **66** 303 **67** 137
Ruth **84** 135
Samuel **66** 153 **83** 506
Sarah **63** 177 **66** 142 144
225 306 **67** 354 355 **82**
342 **83** 35
Sarah (Morer) **90** 105
Sarah N. **99** 58
Thankful D. (Smith)
105 102
Thomas **66** 146 154 225

MACE *cont'd*
 67 137 244 245 247 355
 98 104 105
 Wayne (Mrs.) **106** 125
 William **51** 463 **78** 55
  82 342
MACEL — Mr. **71** 140
MACELFRESH Mackelfresh
 Anna **63** 273
 Caroline **83** 65
MacElvine *see* McElvine
MACEVERS
 Elizabeth **110** 134
MacEvoy *see* McEvoy
MacEwen *see* McEwen
Macey *see* Macy
MacFaden *see* McFadden
MacFarland *see* McFarland
MacFarlane *see* McFarland
MacFee *see* McFee
MacGeachey *see* McGeachey
MacGill *see* McGill
MacGowan *see* McGowan
MacGregor *see* McGregor
MACGUNNIGLE Bruce
 Campbell **143** 78 250
  147 285 286 **148** 150
MACHAN
 George **112** 159
 Susan (Mountford)
  112 159
 Susan (Parish) **112** 159
MACHANT
 — Widow **127** 13
Machard *see* McHard
MACHEATH
 Malcolm **122** 272
MACHELL Machel
 —— **64** 86
 Alason **61** 199
 Jane (Woodroofe)
  135 158
 John **135** 158
 Mary **135** 158
 May **135** 158
 Micah **76** 61
MACHEN
 Minnie Buckner
  136 316
 Thomas **85** 112
MacHerd *see* McHard
MACHETT Machet
 —— **106** 254
 Elizabeth (Perkins)
  140 165
 John **140** 165
 Mary **140** 165
MACHIR Lewis W. (Mrs.)
  118 248
 Violette Somerville **118**
  167 248 **120** 314
 William F. (Mrs.) **118** 248
  120 314
MACHLIN Mary **63** 22 214
MACHOLD
 Doris Ward **95** 35
 Jenny (Ward) **95** 35
MACHOME David **53** 268
MACHYN Thomas **70** 55
Macie *see* Macy
MacIntier *see* McIntire

MacIntire *see* McIntire
MacIntosh *see* McIntosh
MacIntyre *see* McIntire
MACK
 —— **56** 324 **58** 101
 Aaron **120** 189
 Abby **81** 53
 Abby Jane **81** 53
 Abigail **101** 208 **120** 189
 Abigail (Peterson)
  120 189
 Abigail Newton **127** 118
 Abihu **80** 424
 Adeline Louisa **126** 144
 Alexander **98** 209
 Alice Ritchart **86** 199
 Almira **111** 128
 Alvin Ebenezer **134** 155
 Anabel Stevens **85** 189
  113 232 303
 Anna **81** 53
 Anne **81** 53
 Asenath **61** 34
 Augusta (Tupper) **99** 297
 Azubah **100** 269 **101** 151
 Belinda **127** 118
 Bezaleel **121** 256
 Calvin C. **81** 53
 Caroline Stevenson
  (Saltonstall) **93** 198
 Catherine Eleanor
  127 118
 Charles Samuel **117** 156
 Charles Standish **117** 156
 Charlotte Matilda **128** 33
 Cleave Benjamin **100** 188
 Daniel **55** 185 **146** 364
 David **70** 100 **85** 325
  120 189
 Deborah **52** 480 **100** 269
  127 118 203 **128** 32 113
 Desire **80** 121 **126** 160
 Desire (Cahoon) **126** 160
 Dorothy **81** 53
 Ebenezer **100** 269 **134** 155
 Edward **127** 118
 Edward G. **81** 53
 Elijah **79** 78
 Elijah B. **101** 234
 Elijah S. **81** 53
 Elisha **78** 385 **100** 269 **120**
  189 **127** 204
 Eliza **56** 388 **128** 114
 Elizabeth **126** 160
 Elizabeth (Ewens) **105** 159
 Ellen B. **77** xlix
 Ellice **95** 363
 Eloisa **127** 118
 Emily **101** 235
 Emma (Hall) **111** 127 128
 Emma Frances (Durrell)
  134 155
 Emma J. **72** 205
 Enoch **78** 385 **101** 234
 Ephraim Dean **128** 33
 Eunice (Fish) **120** 28
 Frank P. **72** 205
 George Mitchell **128** 33
 George William **54** 150
 Gurdon **61** 34
 Hannah **100** 269 **121** 226

MACK *cont'd*
 Hannah (Huntley)
  100 269
 Harold A. (Mrs.) **93** 198
 Harriet **101** 235
 Harriet B. **81** 53
 Harry W. **109** 318
 Hazel Ladd **72** 205
 Helen Whaley **57** xxxiii
 Henry **97** 218
 Hepzibah **100** 269 **128** 32
 Hezekiah **81** 53 54
 Horace **54** 150
 Isabel **51** 493
 J. W. **56** 214
 Jason **116** 221 **127** 118
 Jerusha **101** 205
 John **51** 493 **55** 348 **58** 101
  78 368 **79** 72 **81** 53 57
  95 363 **100** 269 **111** 127
  120 28 189
 John Dean **128** 33
 John J. **111** 128
 Jonas **128** 32
 Jonathan **61** 33
 Josiah **78** 385 **101** 231 234
  235 **120** 189
 Julia Whiton **54** 150
 Julian Ellis **117** 156
 Julian Standish **117** 156
 Laura (Test) **117** 156
 Laura White **54** 150
 Lauriston B. / L. **81** 53
 Leucina **127** 118
 Livermore **81** 35
 Lizzie E. **54** cxxxix
 Lois **101** 231 **120** 189
 Loue **78** 368
 Lucy **54** 150 **81** 53
 Lucy (Hill) (Smith)
  121 256
 Lydia **78** 385 **79** 78 **101**
  202 **120** 189
 Lydia (Dean) **128** 32 33
 Lydia (Gilbert) **146** 362
 Lydia M. **79** 78
 Margaret Ann (Ryder)
  113 303
 Martha **51** 493 **120** 189
 Martha Desiah **128** 33
 Martin **130** 235
 Mary **81** 35 **90** 49 **120** 189
  128 113
 Mary (Bancroft) **97** 218
 Mary (Burbank) (Parker)
  127 204
 Mary (Ellis) **120** 189
 Mary (Talcott) **120** 189
 Mary J. **111** 122 129
 Mary M. **90** 106
 Matilda **128** 33
 Mehitable **78** 368
 Mercy **66** 315
 Mercy (Tinney) **116** 221
 Mindwell **120** 189
 Moses **120** 189
 Patience **52** 276
 Patrick Doran **127** 118
 Paul Collins **127** 118
 Phebe **100** 269 **101** 143
  200 207

MACK *cont'd*
Phebe (Miller) **100** 270
Philip Frank (Finnegan)
130 235
Rachel **81** 53
Ralph **146** 362
Robert **105** 159
Robert F. **90** 116
Ruth **79** 78
Samuel **80** 121 **100** 269
126 160 **127** 118 203
128 32 114
Samuel S. **111** 128
Sarah **60** 398 **84** 220
120 189
Sarah (Bagley) **100** 269
Sarah (Blossom) (Howes)
120 189
Sarah (Richards) **120** 189
Sarah E. (Barnes) **90** 116
Solomon **100** 269 **126** 160
128 32 33
Sophia **80** 121 **128** 114
Sophia (Knowles)
127 118
Sophia (Larabee) **120** 189
Sophronia (Harding)
134 155
Stephen **55** 345 **81** 46 **99**
297 **100** 269 **101** 151
126 160 **127** 118
Taphena **78** 385
Thomas **63** 352
W. R. **84** 466
Wallace **79** 225
Warren **120** 189
Wealthy **81** 57
William **79** 72 78 **126** 160
127 203 **128** 113
William Atwood Dean
128 33
William Orlando **109** 71
William Stuart **113** 303
Winifred Maud **95** 363
Zerviah **127** 118
Zopher **79** 72 **100** 270
101 62 207
MACK-RHEDERY
John **82** 84 **83** 155
Katharine **82** 84
Mackall *see* McCall
MACKAMAN
Etta V. **116** 126
MACKANON Will **65** 149
MACKARTY
Daniel **55** 330
MacKay *see* McKay
MACKAY-SMITH
Alexander **64** 296
MacKaye *see* McKay
Mackclaflin *see*
McLaughlin
Mackdaniel *see* McDaniel
MACKDOLON
James **143** 257
Mackdonald *see* McDonald
Mackdonnel *see* McDonnel
MacKECHNIE
Horace K. **115** 156
Prudence S. **115** 156
MACKEE Mild'e **62** 85

MACKELAND
William **143** 262
Mackelfresh *see* Macelfresh
MACKEN
Elizabeth **88** 255
Elizabeth (Poingdestre)
88 255
Jean **88** 255
MACKENALL
Mary **58** 143
MacKENNETH
Beatrix **108** 174
Bethoc **108** 174
Malcolm **108** 174
Mackenny *see* McKenney
Mackentire *see* McIntire
Mackentosh *see* McIntosh
Mackenzie *see* McKenzie
Macker *see* Maker
Mackerel *see* Mackrell
Mackerell *see* Mackrell
MACKERNES
John **54** 193
MACKERWETHE
Mackerwithy
Mackiwithe
Bethiah (Lewis) **106** 270
Hannah **106** 270 271
James **106** 270
Mary **106** 270
Sarah **106** 270
MACKET Asahel **51** 292
Lydia **51** 292
MACKEY Mackie
Aeneus **58** 68
Andrew **123** 276 **127** 256
Anna **78** 412
Annie Maria **68** 383
Charles **92** 27
Daniel **81** 159 **108** 224
Dorothy **81** 159
Elizabeth **92** 22 **105** 75
125 109
Elizabeth Ann **108** 224
Eva S. (Seymour) **133** 31
Evelyn **133** 31
Fanny **92** 25 118
Fletcher **92** 171
Hamden Jordan **108** 224
Henry **79** 35 **92** 28
Jane E. (Kilpatrick) **92** 171
John **55** 202 **125** 35
142 333
John Lewis **68** 383
Joseph **92** 27
Lewis **98** 345
Lydia **98** 53
Mabel L. **97** 210
Martha **81** 495
Mary **81** 159 **113** 307
142 333
Mary (Thorpe) **142** 333
Mary-Frances L. **143** 266
Mungo **65** 368
Ophelia (Pugh) **98** 345
Peter **119** 180
Robert **125** 30
Ruth **92** 20 22 25-28
Sally **62** 84 **78** 306
Samuel **92** 26
Sarah Ann (Hill) **108** 224

MACKEY *cont'd*
Sarah Bell **132** 241
Susanna **127** 8
Thomas **113** 63
W. II. **133** 31
Wilcomb L. **92** 171
William **80** 277 **92** 20
Mackfarland *see* McFarland
Mackfield *see* Maxfield
MACKFUN McFun
Agnes **133** 305
Patience **71** 44
Robert **141** 205
Mackhard *see* McHard
Mackie *see* Mackey
MACKIM Julia **132** 327
Mackinnon *see* McKinnon
MACKINSON
Emma F. **127** 59
Isabella Arethusa Louisa
(Harris) **89** 310
William Henry **89** 310
Mackinteir *see* McIntire
Mackintir *see* McIntire
Mackintire *see* McIntire
Mackintosh *see* McIntosh
Mackiwithe *see*
Mackerwethe
Mackkenny *see* McKenney
Macklaflen *see* McLaughlin
MACKLAIN
Eliza **125** 218
Macklelland *see* McClellan
Macklewain *see* McElwain
MACKLIN
George T. **106** 46 50
John **63** 22 214 **143** 258
Mary **97** 104 106
R. **80** 66
Mackloflen *see*
McLaughlin
MACKLON
Eunice **113** 32
John **113** 32
Macklothlan *see*
McLaughlin
Mackmallin *see*
McMillan
Mackmarnis *see*
McManus
Mackneel *see* McNeil
MACKNESS
Samuel **73** 137
MACKNEY Sarah **88** 329
MacKnight *see* McKnight
MACKOLDS
John **127** 228
Mackphail *see* McPhail
Mackranney *see* McCranny
MACKRELL Mackerel
Mackerell Mackrille
Benjamin **64** 89
Edward **64** 324
Edwin **96** 390
George **84** 433
James **64** 324
John **84** 433
Margaret Grandage
96 390
Michael **52** 45 **54** 343
55 340

MACKRELL *cont'd*
Nellie (Grandage) **96** 390
Robert **84** 433
Thomas **84** 433
William **84** 433
MACKRISS Phebe **140** 22
Macksfield *see* Maxfield
Mackson *see* Maxon
Mackswell *see* Maxwell
Macksy *see* Maxey
Mackvarlow *see*
Magvarlow
MACKWORTH Agnes **57**
406 **108** 176
Arthur **101** 17 20 84 85 **104**
177 **107** 48
Elizabeth **101** 84 85
Humphrey **57** 406 409
108 176
Jane **104** 177 178
Jane (Andrews) **104** 177
178
John **108** 176
Mary (Barker) **101** 85
Richard **108** 176
Sarah **108** 179
Thomas **108** 176
MacLachlan *see* McLachlan
MacLatlen *see* McLaughlin
Maclain *see* McLean
Maclane *see* McLean
MACLAREN
Alice Austin **97** 83
Donald **97** 83
Elizabeth Stockton
(Green) **97** 83
Ian **54** 101
MacLaughlan *see*
McLaughlin
MacLaughland *see*
McLaughlin
MACLAURIN Elfriede
(Carter) **110** 147
William Rupert **110** 147
MACLAY
Edgar Stanton **64** 71
John **61** lxiv
Minnie **61** lxiv
MACLEA Florence **81** 110
222 **82** 228 251 **83** 246
Maclean *see* McLean
MACLEISH
Andrew **136** 322
Archibald **136** 90 322 329
Elias Brewster **136** 322
Julia (Whittlesey) **136** 322
Martha (Hillard) **136** 322
Moses **136** 322
Patty (Brewster) **136** 322
Maclellan *see* McClellan
MACLENNA
Deborah **64** 310
William **64** 310
Macleod *see* McLeod
Macloon *see* McLoon
MACLOTH Amy **115** 121
Maclure *see* McClure
MacLYSAGHT
Edward **148** 333 335
MacMahon *see* McMahon

MacMANIMON
Emma L. **105** 150
MACMARR
— Mrs. **101** 270
MacMaster *see* McMaster
MacMEACHAN
Macmechan
Archibald **56** xxxii
Archibald M. **55** 354
MacMICHEL
Mary **117** 43 121
MacMILLAN *see also*
McMillan
—— **62** 163
Carrie (Dauchy) **111** 302
305
Edward P. **115** 239
Harold **136** 87
Josephine **77** 190
Margaret **91** 375
Margaret Burnham **98** 98
Peter G. **77** 190
Ruth **115** 298
Somerled **115** 239
Susan Polk **77** 216
William J. **115** 293
MacMONNIES
Frederick **78** 229
MacMORRIS John A.
(Mrs.) **99** 148
Mary MacDougall **119** 77
MacMULLEN
John **107** 13
MacMUNN Katharine
Seward **102** 124
120 149
MacMurphy *see* McMurphy
MacMURROUGH
Dermot **145** 268
MACNEE Ellen Frances
(Breck) **83** 489
Forrest Frew (Mrs.)
83 489
MacNeel *see* McNeil
MacNEES Mary **114** 291
MacNeil *see* McNeil
MacNeill *see* McNeil
MACNEMAR Jane **59** 64
MACNERE John **129** 275
Robert **129** 270
MacNichol *see* McNichol
MacNicoll *see* McNichol
MacNUTT Francis
Augustus **105** 186
MACOCK Macoke
Lettice **83** 128
Thomas **57** 250 **83** 128
MACOLESTOR Nancy
(Smith) **125** 109
MACOLLY John **96** 324
MACOMB
— Capt. **54** 165
Duncan **107** 98
Edward **107** 98
Elizabeth **65** 149
Mary (Hoare) **107** 98
Ruth (Whittemore)
107 98
William **65** 149

MACOMBER Macumber
Maycomber
Maycumber McOmber
McCumber
—— **54** cvii **57** 338 **61**
314 **148** 284
— Lieut. **54** 72
— Mr. **95** 134
— Mrs. **51** 376 **62** 284
Abiel **77** 81 **132** 217
Abigail (Brown) **88** 281
Abigail (Gifford) **137** 150
Abigail (Hoxie) **94** 51
Abner **148** 269
Ada Frances (Sears) **94** 51
Alexander C. **94** 145
Almira **66** 84
Ann (Jepson) **126** 209
Anne Johnson **109** 68
B. Frank **117** 218
Benjamin **73** 297 **105** 213
117 22 **118** 311
Bernice May (Yeobett)
94 51
Betsey (Sawdy) **148** 283
284
Botsey Maria (Billings)
94 51
Bryant **125** 37
Caleb **72** 17 21 26 27
137 150
Charilla **68** 95
Charles **132** 216
Charles Thurston **94** 51
Christiana **117** 23
Clara Elizabeth **78** 205
Clara Elizabeth (Robison)
87 65 179 **96** 188 **97** 53
Comfort **135** 140
Constant **135** 147
Cora B. **74** 295
Deborah **88** 108 **131** 294
132 297
Deborah A. (Keith) **88** 342
Dianna H. **118** 311
Donald **100** 109
Donald (Mrs.) **99** 148
Dorothea Elizabeth
(Taber) **94** 51
Ebenezer **65** 149 **102** 235
Edgar Thurston **94** 51
Edith **53** 461 **131** 295
Edith G. **125** 181 182
Edward **117** 23
Elijah **80** 100 **131** 295
Eliza **68** 95 **134** 313
Elizabeth **74** 295 **80** 100
102 15 **117** 294 **131** 294
Elizabeth (Cornell) **131**
216 **135** 307
Elizabeth (Crandall)
102 15
Elizabeth (Gifford)
135 318
Elizabeth (Rogers) **P132**
297
Ellen M. **52** 210
Elliot Harvey **94** 51
Elsie May (Westgate)
94 51
Emory D. **117** 221

MACOMBER *cont'd*
Ephraim **127** 12 217
  134 313
Esther **72** 26 27 **129** 21 22
Eunice **138** 216
Ezra B. **117** 294
Florence Billings **94** 51
Frank Gair **87** 65 **88** 169
  96 149 166 187 **97** 53
Frank Gair (Mrs.) **77** 156
  78 205 **87** 65 72 179
Frederick **74** 295
Frederick Clarence **94** 51
Frederick H. **74** 295
George Ellison **109** 68
Gideon **87** 261 **102** 10
Grace Ethel **83** 435 **84** 22
H. N. **97** 231
Hannah **51** 176 **134** 313
Harmon **134** 337
Harold Sears **94** 51
Henry E. **74** 295
Henry Eaton **61** xxxvi
Hope **138** 206
Ichabod **87** 65 **88** 281
  96 187
Isaac **116** 123 **118** 311
Isabella Ogden Reed **87**
  65 **96** 188 **97** 53
Jacob **126** 116
James **126** 209
James P. **88** 342
Jeremiah **129** 21
Joanna **53** 429
Job **105** 214
John **51** 454 **53** 436 **57** 334
  60 187 **61** 314 401 **62**
  234 345 **63** 327 331 386
  80 100 **97** 328 329 **111**
  245 **125** 83 **143** 77
John H. **66** 84
Jonathan **128** 217
Joseph **68** 95 **145** 355
Joshua **90** 191
Joshua Mason **51** 376 384
Julia **74** 295
Julia Ann (Julse) **83** 331
Lemuel **124** 61
Lila May **94** 51
Lillis **135** 307
Lois Rogers **94** 51
Lucy **124** 120 **134** 297
Lucy (Philbrick) **124** 61
Lurana **127** 299
Lydia **53** 436
Lydia E. (Wright) **134** 337
Maria **110** 111
Marianna B. **81** 258
Marie **110** 107
Mary **71** 9 **91** 329 **105** 216
  118 311 **131** 139
Mary Antoinette **83** 331
Mary Elizabeth (Brewer)
  87 65 **96** 187 188
Mary F. **79** 33 **94** 51
Mary J. **116** 123
Matthew **102** 10 **105** 75
Mercy **137** 150
Merit **83** 331
Nathaniel **132** 213 **148** 154
Nehemiah **78** 304

MACOMBER *cont'd*
Olive **127** 299
Patience **135** 52
Peace (Gifford) **132** 216
  217
Perry **81** 259 **88** 108 **131**
  216 294 295
Perry R. **81** 258
Peter **148** 269
Phebe (Brightman)
  132 217
Philip **132** 215
Phyllis **74** 295
Rachel **72** 26 **81** 259 **88** 16
  131 295
Rachel (Gifford) **88** 108
  131 294
Russell Frederick **94** 51
Ruth **108** 67 68 **117** 22
Ruth (White) **96** 187
Sally **88** 27
Samuel **98** 244 **113** 35 40
Sarah **53** 429 **73** 297 **87** 321
  90 191 **102** 143 **125** 82
  130 232 **131** 215 216
Sarah (Cooper) **129** 21
Sarah (Gifford) **131** 295
  135 309
Sarah (Howard) **96** 187
Sarah (Johnson) **109** 68
Sarah (Manchester) **87**
  261 **102** 10
Simeon **94** 51 **135** 318
Sophia **135** 147
Susan C. **117** 22
Susanna **87** 261
Sylvanus B. **118** 131
Tabitha **131** 214
Thomas **53** 429 **96** 187 **119**
  186 **133** 191 **145** 355
Thurston **92** 377 **94** 51
Timothy **132** 297
Ursula **90** 191 **125** 201
Ursula (Mathew) **125** 82
Vivienna G. **116** 123
Wesson **105** 216
William **60** 187 **61** 314 401
  63 228 386 **90** 191 **96**
  187 **97** 312 **102** 15 **125**
  82 202 **129** 342 **131** 295
  148 269
William Henry **94** 51
Zebedee **131** 216 295
  135 307
MACON —— **51** 324
Althea Jane **111** 323 **120** 78
Elizabeth **53** 87
Gideon **111** 323
Jane **120** 78
Nathaniel **55** 353 **59** 118
MACONDA
Charlotte **89** 249
MACOONE Macoon
Abigail **115** 301
Deborah **77** 35
Hannah **77** 34 35
James **127** 307
John **77** 35
MACOY Sarah **90** 50
MacPhedris *see* McPhedris

MacPherson *see*
  McPherson
MacQuarrie *see* McQuerry
MacQueen *see* McQueen
MacQUESTON
James **83** 255
Leona B. **83** 255
Robert **83** 255
William **83** 255
MACQUET Peter **62** 245
MacQUINERY
Alexander **54** 410
MACQUIRE John **70** 264
Peter **65** 239
MACRAE Donald **89** 254
Donald O. (Mrs.) **96** 86
Jessie Ann (Kennedy)
  89 254
Pauline Le Roy (French)
  (Wagstaff) **96** 86
MACRATE
Margaret **68** 237
Thomas **68** 237
MACRAY William Dunn
  52 94 **142** 362
MACREADY Agnes **89** 66
Agnes (Houston) **89** 66
Dorothy Louise **94** 84
Dorothy Madison (Stone)
  94 84
John **89** 66
Louise May **78** 205
Louise May (Kemp) **94** 84
Mary Augusta Kemp
  94 84
Robert Ashton (Mrs.) **77**
  322 **78** 205 **83** 229
MACRINAN
Meldred **107** 157
MacSPANER
Miriam **116** 231
MacSPARRAN McSparren
  —— **144** 293
Hannah (Gardiner)
  105 257
James **62** 210 **71** 61 **105**
  257 **124** 164 165 **131**
  192 **136** 106 173 **144**
  228 301
MacTaggart *see* McTaggart
MACTAKET Jane **100** 27
John **100** 135
Margaret **100** 27 28 31 135
Peter **100** 27 28 31 135
MacTAVISH Alexander
  113 84 86 87
Duncan C. **114** 150
MACULLAR
Addison **70** xxxvi
Macumber *see* Macomber
MACUNE
Elizabeth **58** 372
John **58** 372
William **58** 372
MACURDA Donald
Bradford **91** 142
MacVarlo *see* Magvarlow
MacVEAGH Charles (Mrs.)
  78 109 205
Fanni Davenport **78** 205
MACWELL William **65** 245

MACWHA
George W. **74** xiv
MacWILLIAM
Donald **122** 266
Donald Ban **122** 272
Guthred **122** 266
MacWITHEY
Ephraim **120** 264
MACY Macey Macie - *see also* Mace
—— **54** 112 **61** 207 **141** 363
Alan Dent **75** xliv
Alexander **100** 188
Alice **67** 187
Almira **100** 188
Anna **100** 188
Anna Kathryn **75** xliv
Augustus J. **100** 188
Barzillai **100** 56 152
Caleb **87** 260 **100** 56
Caroline **76** xxxiv
Cecile Rusch / Rushe **76** xxxiv **86** 194
Charles **100** 188
Charles Henry **100** 188
Cornelia Walker **76** xxxiv
Daniel **100** 188
Deborah **62** 235 **63** 127
Edward **100** 161
Elbert B. **107** 79
Eliza **69** 176
Eliza (Gifford) **134** 241
Eliza Leggett **76** xxxiv
Elizabeth **62** 234 **113** 252
Elizabeth (Gardiner) **113** 252
Eunice **51** 164 **134** 314
Eunice Gardner **100** 188
Frederick **100** 188
George **62** 234 235 **63** 127 **97** 327 328 343 **134** 241
Gorham **100** 188
Hannah **117** 309 **141** 59
Harriet **100** 188
Harry **109** 130 **144** 273
Helena Wright **75** xliv
Isaiah **100** 49
James **56** 25
Jane **75** xliii
Jedidah **100** 188
Joanna E. **78** 179
Job **100** 188 **113** 252
John **72** 232 **76** xxxiv **100** 188
John R. **56** 25 **100** 188
John Wendell **100** 188
Jonathan **76** xxxiv
Joseph **115** 320
Josiah **75** xliii **76** xxxiv **100** 188
Josiah (Mrs.) **94** 62
Josiah Henry **75** xliii
Judith **100** 152
Judith (Folger) **87** 260
Juliet **76** xxxiv
Louisa M. **77** 176
Lydia **75** xliii **88** 8
Lydia (Coleman) **134** 241
Lydia Hussey **75** xliii

MACY *cont'd*
Malcolm Dunbar **75** xliv
Margaret B. **100** 188
Maria **116** 216 **117** 136
Marion **75** xliv
Marion Marjorie **75** xliv
Mary **82** 351 **100** 188 **115** 320
Nathaniel **100** 188
Nelson **67** 187
Obed **100** 188
Orrin **63** 90
Paul **100** 188
Paul Bunker **100** 188
Peleg **100** 188
Peter **100** 188
Phebe (Barnard) **88** 8
Philip (Mrs.) **125** 177
Polly **63** 90
Rebecca **62** 235 **97** 343 **100** 281
Robert **100** 158
Ruth **87** 260 **98** 135
Sally **100** 188
Samuel **97** 329
Sarah **62** 234 235
Sarah Ridgway **76** xxxiv
Shubael **100** 188 281
Solomon **134** 241
Stephen **100** 188
Susan **72** 232
Susanna **62** 235 **63** 127 128 **100** 188
Susanna (Street) **97** 343
Sylvanus Jenkins **75** xxxvii xciii **76** xxxiv **83** 216
Thomas **76** xxxiv **82** 351
Thomas W. **100** 188
William A. **60** 84
William Alec **75** xliv
William Austin **58** xlvlii **59** xli **60** 87 185 186 277 280 **75** xxxvi xliii xliv
William Charles **75** xliv
William F. **116** 11
William Henry **76** xxxiv
William W. **100** 188
Zaccheus **100** 188
MADAI —— **58** 223
MADARA Ruth **129** 188
MADDEN Maddin
— Mr. **85** 19
Abram **69** 31
Adeline **69** 31
Alex **112** 282
Amy **69** 324
Ann **66** 79
Anne (Woods) **112** 106
Anthony **112** 282
Bessie **91** 248
Charity **85** 371
Charity (Silvester) **85** 371
Dan **112** 282
E. **76** 50
Edward **125** 107
Elizabeth **112** 282 **137** 36
Ella **69** 31
Emily H. **69** 31
Florence **74** 294
Frederick **59** lviii

MADDEN *cont'd*
George **112** 106 **114** 293
Georgeanna A. **69** 31
Harriet **69** 31
Hester **69** 31
Hugh **61** 133 134
J. A. **66** 79
James **69** 31 **97** 221
James Alexander Woods **112** 106 **115** 217 224
James Joseph **69** 31
Jane **69** 324
Jean (Reed) **125** 107
John **57** 204 **65** 120 **69** 214 **70** 261 **85** 371 **91** 329
Laura A. **59** 420 **60** 280
Margaret **93** 275
Maria **74** 89
Mary **69** 31 **125** 290
Mary (Lowber) **106** 47
Mary Eliza **69** 31
Michael Lester **96** 160
Noah **69** 31
Robert Marshall **69** 31
Sally **86** 296
Sarah **69** 31
Sarah K. **98** 288
Thomas H. **69** 31
Thomas J. (Mrs.) **106** 47
Thursy (Andrews) **97** 221
Maddin *see* Madden
Maddison *see* Madison
MADDOCK Maddack Maddick Maddocke Maddocks Maddox
—— **52** 259
— Mrs. **101** 274 **117** 167
—— (Andros) **90** 234
Abigail **75** 120 **90** 233 235
Abigail (Hooper) **90** 333 **91** 27
Agnes **80** 389 390
Aney (Robarts) **95** 191
Anne (Reade) **112** 120
Anthony **80** 389 390 393
Asa Dyer **56** 91
Benjamin **110** 111 212
Benjamin W. **110** 212
Betsey **90** 333 **91** 27 **96** 339 **97** 19
Caleb **55** 311 **75** 109 111 118 120 **82** 89-92 205 **86** 138 139
Daniel **70** 265
Daniel A. **91** 35
Dorothy **64** 137
E. B. **64** 130
Elizabeth **55** 311 **75** 109 111 118 120 **82** 89 205 **113** 302 **124** 41 **148** 119
Emily J. (Gowen) **91** 35
Esther **96** 145 341
Esther (Roberts) **90** 251 **96** 145
Eunice (Andrews) **90** 236 **138** 321
Eunice C. **97** 20 236
Florietta **109** 12 **110** 212
Frances **73** 223
George Tapley **110** 212
Hannah **56** 318

MADDOCK *cont'd*
Harriet R. **91** 204
Henry **65** 255 **75** 50 105
106 115 **77** 273 **90** 328
96 147 343
Jacob **90** 234 236 251 **96**
145 **138** 321
James **56** 318 **65** 44 **95** 191
97 237
Jane Prynn **118** 81
Jesse **97** 222
John **53** 346 **64** 155 **75** 50
105 114 **82** 89 **90** 250
104 184 **107** 64 **110** 166
Jonathan **56** 83
Joseph **76** 108 **90** 333 **91**
27 **105** 206
Joshua **71** 219 **82** 91
Judith **56** 318
Katharine **64** 339
Lydia **82** 87 **90** 235 **95** 195
96 336
Lydia (Clark) **90** 328
96 343
Martha Ann **95** 329
Mary **55** 313 **56** 141 **75** 105
106 115 **76** 194 **77** 273
82 511
Mary (Courtney) **104** 184
107 64
Mary (Green) **97** 222
Mary J. **64** 155
Miriam **96** 340
N. **91** 329
Nabby **96** 248
Nathan **73** 141
Notley **73** 228
Olive **109** 12
Olive (Varnum) **110** 111
212
Palsgrave **75** 106 **76** 108
109
Patience (Waterhouse)
96 147
Polly (Lewis) **108** 123
Rebecca **53** 346
Rebecca (Barker) **90** 250
Richard **75** 111 **82** 92
110 166
Robert **80** 389 390
Ruth **75** 115 118
Sally **96** 340
Samuel **75** 109 **82** 205
Sarah **75** 114
Sarah Ann **73** 228
Sarah Jane **97** 229 233
Thomas **76** 108 **84** 75 225
108 123 **112** 120
Thursey (Andrews)
97 237
W. H. (Mrs.) **90** 98 **96** 402
William **64** 137 345
William H. (Mrs.) **108** 129
MADDY James **105** 77
Olive **105** 77
William **105** 77
Maddyson *see* Madison
MADEIRA
Albert P. (Mrs.) **72** xiv
MADEN Joanna M. **78** 397

MADEY
Maria Antoinette
64 17
MADGWICK
Edward **113** 220
Jane (Kittier) **113** 220
MADIGAN
— Mrs. **95** 50 52
Catherine **66** 306
John **95** 51 53 54
Matthew **95** 51
Walter **66** 306
MADIOL —— **134** 89 90
MADISON Maddison
Maddyson
—— **76** 304 **143** 202
— Canon **98** 17
— Capt. **125** 31
— Col. **85** 9
— Lieut. Col. **84** 376
— Mr. **55** 274 276
— Rev. Canon **59** 222
A. R. **58** 286 **98** 12 **141** 96
106 **145** 100
Alice **128** 267
Almond Z. **76** 263
Alphonsine C. **64** 124
Ambrose **110** 65
Amy **51** 124
Ann **79** 172
David **125** 41
Deborah **51** 123 **76** 263
Dolly **99** 139
Dorothy **51** 121-124
Elaine (Baldwin) **95** 147
Eliza Ann **109** 309
Elizabeth **51** 122-124 **77**
245 316 **96** 367
Ellen **51** 124
Fanny **110** 65
Frances **51** 123
Frances (Taylor) **110** 65
George W. **64** 124
Hiram **106** 160
James **51** 19 21 22 153 156
426 **54** 123 **60** lvi **64**
195 **65** 83 **66** 156 **75** 86
77 215 245 **89** 161 162
95 210 **101** 190 **105** 42
111 319 **136** 67 87
John **51** 123 124 **90** 37 38
111 201
John (Mrs.) **85** 196
John Ripley **107** 155
Lionel **96** 367
Maria Church **107** 155
Marie (Westerbrook)
128 267
Mark **51** 124
Mary **51** 124
Mira (Bissell) **106** 160
Pauline **95** 316
Peter **128** 267
Polly **114** 181
Rebecca **90** 43
Richard **51** 123 124
Thomas **51** 121 123 124
111 210
Violanthe **126** 212
William **51** 123 124
109 309

MADLING Sarah **94** 275
MADOC 52 28 **69** 65
Madocks *see* Maddock
MADORE Sophia **111** 139
Madox *see* Maddock
MADRYN Hugh **111** 317
Mary **111** 317
MADSEN John B. (Mrs.)
84 172
Pauline **95** 316
Ruth C. **109** 130
MAELLER
Catherine Louisa
77 181
M'Afee *see* Macafee
MAFFET George West **60**
355 **62** xxxvii 104 206
64 xxxi 92 **69** 287
Maggie **128** 92
MAGAM — Mrs. **121** 94
MAGAN Frances **112** 301
MAGARIAN Oscar K. (Mrs.)
120 234
MAGDALYN
Mary **101** 324
MAGEE —— **140** 140
— Mrs. **127** 141
Amanday **105** 274
Andrew **109** 13 **110** 216
Ann **104** 78
Anthony **112** 287
Augusta Smith **67** 15 187
Bernard **140** 150
C. **109** 14
Carolyn Sturgis **84** 295
Celia **109** 14
Cevilla **109** 14
Charles **67** 187
Charlotte **109** 14
Cornelius **108** 280 284
109 13 14
Cornelius J. **110** 212
Daniel **108** 280 **109** 13 14
Eleanor **100** 300 **125** 142
Eleanor May **96** 57
Eliza **88** 279
Elizabeth **110** 108 111
112 297
Elizabeth Richmond
84 295
Eva (Higgins) **84** 295
Everline **109** 14
F. **109** 14
Harriet **109** 13
Harriet (Colson) **108** 280
284
Harriet F. **109** 14
Harriet Maria **109** 14
Henry **112** 297
Horace A. **84** 295
James **67** 15 187
Jane **112** 297
John **109** 13 **112** 297
Joshua **53** 447
Lillian S. **110** 216
Lydia Maria **100** 248
Manford Seymour
110 212
Margaret **67** 187 **112** 297
Margaret J. **89** 242
Mary **110** 216 **112** 297

MAGEE *cont'd*
Mary C. **109** 14
Mary Frances **109** 14
Mary Jane **91** 398
Nellie **125** 142
Sally **105** 274
Seth **105** 274
Susan **108** 284
Susan (Hall) **140** 150
Susanna **109** 13
Thomas **112** 297
William **112** 297
MAGELIS Robert **143** 204
MAGELLAN Fernando **53** 253 **54** xxvii
MAGER Noah **128** 19
Phebe **128** 19
MAGET — Sergt. **54** 441
MAGEVNEY Elizabeth Berchmans **145** 195
Elizabeth Rose (O'Driscoll) **145** 195
John Maxwell **90** 298
MAGGART Maynard E. (Mrs.) **121** 159 **124** 78 159 239 319
MAGGETT Eliza **90** 111
Elizabeth **100** 26 **101** 270
Hepzibah **100** 26 **101** 270
Webster **100** 26 **101** 270
MAGGONE
James **121** 119
John **121** 114 115 117 118
MAGGS Ann **67** 365
George **67** 365
MAGGUIRE
Elizabeth **64** 220
MAGHILL Mary **84** 209
MAGIE A. H. **104** 299
E. Flora **104** 299
MAGILL
Myrtle Bernadine **109** 131
Samuel **60** 26
William **60** 349
MAGINNIS Maginnes Maginniz Maginniz
Alexander **80** 194 **89** 249
Arthur Whittlesey **89** 249
Daniel **114** 187
Donald Ambrose (Mrs.) **94** 183
E. L. **80** 194
Edward **80** 194 **89** 249
Edwin **80** 194
Eliza (Larkin) **89** 249
Eliza Tully (Whittlesey) **89** 249
Elizabeth **73** 146 **114** 187
Elizabeth A. (Lamb) **88** 334
Etha Mabel **82** 125 237
Jennette Morgan (Whittlesey) **89** 249
John **82** 294 295
John S. **88** 334
John T. **89** 249
Margaret **80** 194 **89** 249 **114** 187
Martha Scribner **85** 191
Mary **82** 294 295

MAGINNIS *cont'd*
Ruth (Hobson) **94** 183
Sarah **114** 187
Susan **114** 187
W. H. **89** 249
MAGISTER
Baldwin **110** 292
Henry **110** 292
Thomas **110** 292
MAGLEBY
John Bert (Mrs.) **108** 135
MAGMISON
Brita Lena **128** 264
C. **128** 264
MAGNA Edith (Scott) **75** 316 **76** xxii **80** 230 **90** 78 **91** 140 **94** 155 **95** 162 **115** 67
Russell William **75** 316 **76** xxii **90** 78 **91** 140 **95** 162 **115** 67
MAGNAUS John **86** 421
MAGNER
Catherine **78** 420
John **140** 166
Mary **79** 46
Mary Euphrosina **103** 148
MAGNESS Alfred Parsons (Mrs.) **84** 106 190
MAGNEY — Mrs. **82** 413
MAGNIER Peter **65** 230
MAGNIES John **54** 196
MAGNONI
Elizabeth M. **90** 106
MAGNUS Annette Barbara (Kollberg) **111** 101
MAGNUSSON
Albert **107** 192
Hakan **111** 100
MAGOFFIN —— **60** 104
MAGOGRAY
Catherine **114** 186
MAGOUN Magoon
—— **56** 241
Abigail **59** 77 135 138 140
Abner **59** 370 **136** 39
Adelia Adelaide **113** 231
Alexander **58** 92 **100** 254 **104** 40
Alfred **69** 270
Ann **58** 92
Ann (French) (Long) (Mudgett) **100** 254 **104** 40
Benjamin **69** 270 **100** 229 **147** 258
Betsey **70** 349
Charles N. **69** 271
Charles V. **70** 334
Clara M. **69** 168
Cornelius Briggs **59** 370
Cynthia **136** 39
Daniel **69** 270 **70** 334
David **58** 86
David Crooker **89** 178
Dolly **147** 258
Eliab **57** 181
Elias **58** 86 88 **89** 178 **133** 292
Elisha **89** 178

MAGOUN *cont'd*
Elizabeth **69** 270 **147** 258
Elizabeth W. **69** 271
Franklin **69** 270
George H. **69** 270
Hannah **57** 180 398 **58** 86 171 **59** 140 **134** 73
Hannah (Perry) **116** 195
Hannah Crooker (Webb) **89** 178
Harriet Hatch **89** 179
Harrison **70** 272
Henry **118** 323
Henry Albert **89** 178 191 **90** 135 138
Henry S. **75** x xxiii
Isaac **69** 168 **86** 129 **119** 14 113 114
James **58** 89 **119** 14 106 113 119
Jerusha **70** 354
John **57** 180 181 324 398 **58** 86 171 176 **59** 77 135 138 140 **69** 284 **85** 259 **89** 178 **119** 14 113 **147** 257
John Wallace **89** 178
John Warren **89** 179 **90** 135
Jonathan **147** 257
Joseph **147** 258
Joshua **70** 349
Joshua M. **70** 354
Josiah **69** 270
Judith **67** 271
Katharine Hawthorne **89** 179
Louisa (Cutting) **114** 202
Lucia **136** 39
Lucy **70** 354
Lusanna **59** 77
Lydia **147** 258
Lydia (Neal) **89** 178
Margaret (Silvester) **86** 129
Maria **59** 370
Martha **70** 334
Martha Bradshaw **123** 67
Mary **58** 86 **69** 270 **90** 46
Mary W. **69** 270
Mehitable A. **92** 310
Moses **60** 44 **147** 258
Nancy **61** 174
Neal W. **114** 202
Olive Clarissa **82** 398
Phebe **69** 270 **70** 334
Phebe H. **69** 271
Polly **147** 258
Priscilla **53** 430 **89** 179
Rebecca **67** 279 **119** 14
Recompense **89** 178
Ruth **59** 370 **133** 292
Ruth (Crooker) **89** 178
Ruth (Dedham) **133** 292
Ruth Neal **89** 179
Sabra (Burnham) **100** 229
Sarah **58** 89 **70** 349 **119** 14 106 119 **147** 258
Sarah (Ford) **119** 14 113 119
Seth **70** 352

MAGOUN *cont'd*
  Stephen **67** 272
  Susan B. **100** 229
  Susanna **70** 352
  Thomas **53** 430 **58** 89 **119**
    14 106
  Woodman **69** 271
MAGOWNAN
  — Mr. **52** 171 332 463
Magquier *see* Mequier
MAGRA Thomas **70** 263
MAGRANE
  Adeline Gertrude
    87 385
  Anna Bertha **87** 385
  Bridget (Byrne) **87** 385
  Charles Edward **87** 385
  Mary (Gernon) **87** 385
  Mary Cecilia **87** 385
  Mary Woods (Thornton)
    87 385
  Michael **87** 385
  Patrick **87** 385
  Patrick Byrne **80** 195 206
    87 384 **88** 87 173
  Thomas Frederick **87** 385
MAGRATH Abigail
    (Myrick) **102** 200
  Hannah (Hopkins)
    102 200
  Patrick **60** 24
  Thomas **102** 200
MAGRAW Clara Adeline
    (Clark) **83** 297 300
  M. Henry **83** 297 300
MAGRAY Eliza **108** 301
  Frederick **108** 211
  John **108** 211 301 **116** 43
  Susanna **116** 43
  Tamasine (Kinney)
    108 211
MAGREGORY
  Margaret **106** 29
MAGRUDER A. F. **51** 32
  Alexander **73** 151
  Alexander F. **53** 156
  Alexander Richardson
    53 156
  Alexander Wilson **73** 146
  Anna **73** 152
  Barbara **73** 149
  Caleb Clarke **64** 94 **65** 304
    67 xxxi 192 **68** 304 **69**
    xxxii **70** 287 **73** 160 **84**
    239
  Cassandra **73** 140
  Clarissa Harlowe **73** 262
  Dennis **73** 137 261 272 276
  Edward **73** 142 227 268
  Egbert Watson **69** 97
  Eleanor **73** 138
  Elizabeth **53** 375 **73** 148
  Elizabeth Ann **73** 231
  Elizabeth Hawkins
    73 153
  Emma C. **73** 270
  Enoch **73** 140
  Francis **73** 147
  Harriet **73** 146 223
  Harsell **73** 229
  Henrietta **73** 228

MAGRUDER *cont'd*
  Isaac **73** 229 **84** 239
  Isabella Richardson
    53 156
  James **73** 149
  James A. **73** 218
  James M. **145** 28
  James Trueman **73** 231
  Jane **73** 149
  Jane B. **73** 275
  Jane Contee **73** 227
  John **70** 287
  John Bowie **73** 152
  John Read **73** 218 266 275
  Kenneth Dann **80** 335 **81**
    222 **90** 209
  Kitty **73** 224
  Margaret S. **73** 264
  Martha **73** 265
  Mary **73** 149 218
  Mary Bowie **73** 149
  Nathan **70** 287 **73** 151
  Nathaniel **73** 160
  Polly B. **73** 266
  Priscilla **73** 148
  Rebecca **73** 150
  Rebecca D. **73** 277
  Samuel **73** 153 230
  Sarah **73** 145 149
  Sarah Ann **73** 139
  Thomas **73** 226 231
  William **73** 220
  William Richardson
    53 156
Maguarlow *see* Magvarlow
MAGUINNIS Dan **89** 305
MAGUIRE
  Alma Lettice **86** 155
  Bethiah (Brown) **86** 155
  Bridget **62** 80
  Charles **94** 167
  Daniel **63** 350
  Dorothy Eleanor (Berry)
    94 167
  Eldon Sylvester **86** 155
  Eliza Ann (Ellis) **122** 260
  Ella Frances (White)
    86 155
  Ezekiel **86** 155
  Francis **62** 80
  Frank Hain (Mrs.) **86** 197
  Harriet Estella **86** 155
  Jeremiah D. **78** 89
  John **86** 155
  Paulina (Cole) **86** 155
  Ruth May **78** 88
  Thomas **60** 348
  Thomas Henry **62** xi
MAGVARLOW
  MacVarlo Maguarlow
  Hannah **121** 203
  Margaret **119** 13 **121** 124
    276
  Mary **121** 202 270 274
  Patience **121** 121 122
  Patience (Russell) **121** 120
  Purdy **121** 120 124 191
    194 200 207
  Rachel **121** 269
  Sarah **121** 210 270
  Solomon **121** 278

MAHAFFY Nancy **114** 187
MAHAM Etta S. (Hurd)
    121 179
  Henry **105** 318
  Stephen **121** 179
MAHAN —— **56** 106
  Alfred T. **54** 360
  Eliza I. **102** 287
  Harriet (Hanscome)
    126 206
  Jane **136** 308
  John **126** 206
  Mary **105** 146
  Nancy **136** 126
  Phebe **121** 250
  Sarah Elizabeth **101** 252
  Walter C. **102** 283
MAHANER
  Cornelius **70** 262
MAHANNAH
  Bradley **127** 239
MAHANY Betsey (Trewog)
    125 100
  Dennis **65** 234
  Peter **125** 100
  Rebecca **125** 289
MAHAPPY
  Helen Maria **65** 134
  James **65** 134
MAHAR Maher
  Alice Farrington **94** 187
  Alwilda Ann **103** 280
  Anna **102** 220 **103** 100
  Araletta **103** 280
  Asenath Ann **103** 101
  Avery Rich **103** 280
  Chester Earnest **103** 100
  Cyrus Edwin **101** 314
  Edith Emeritta **101** 314
  Edmund **103** 277
  Edward W. B. **103** 280
  Edward Wilson **103** 280
  Edwin A. **103** 277
  Elizabeth **103** 277
  Elizabeth T. **103** 280
  Elizabeth T. (Blackwood)
    101 32
  Emeline **103** 100
  Ernest **101** 32
  Francis **103** 100
  Hannah **76** 148 **101** 314
  Hannah C. **101** 36
  Harry B. **103** 277
  Isaac Putnam **103** 280
  James **72** 170
  Jane **103** 100
  Jane (Antone) **101** 31
  John **103** 280
  John B. **101** 32 **103** 280
  Joseph W. **103** 280
  Josephus **103** 277
  Josephus F. **103** 100
  Josiah Washington
    103 280
  Jotham L. **103** 100
  Jotham S. **101** 314
  Jotham Sewell **102** 220
  Lizzie S. **101** 36
  Lucretia N. (Damon)
    101 36
  Martin F. **144** 323

MAHAR *cont'd*
Mary **69** 38
Mary Ann **102** 221
Mary Anna **101** 34
Mary Jane **103** 100
Monica **69** 38
Munroe **103** 101
Myron Willis **101** 314
Nancy **101** 217 **103** 100
Orin Lucius **103** 100
Otis L. B. **101** 33 **103** 101
Patrick **69** 38
Robert L. B. **101** 36 **102** 220 **103** 280
Samantha **101** 217 **103** 100
Sarah **103** 100
Sarah Elizabeth **103** 280
Smantha (Daily) **101** 36
Susan **103** 101
Susan (Clark) **101** 33 **103** 101
William **102** 220 221
William A. **103** 277
William R. **101** 31 36 **103** 100
MAHARD Edwin Pratt (Mrs.) **96** 160
Marguerite (Shattuck) **96** 160
MAHARNEY
Edelburgodis **73** 148
MAHAWNY Hannah **77** 28
Jemima **77** 28
MAHE Anne Brigette **103** 148 149
MAHEGAN
Mary Theresa **109** 218
Maher *see* Mahar
Mahew *see* Mayhew
Mahieu *see* Mayhew
MAHIN Frank W. **69** 384
MAHINNICK
Eliza **90** 58
MAHIR Mary **61** 349
Thomas **61** 349
MAHLON
Ann (Ladd) **133** 155
Joseph **133** 155
Susanna **133** 155
MAHN Ella Syrene (Holbrook) **65** xxxvii **74** xxviii
Frederick Louis **74** xxviii
MAHON Edward **64** 320
Elizabeth **117** 288
Ellen **117** 288
Eugene **117** 218
John **143** 258
Mary **136** 271
Richard **117** 288
Timothy **117** 16
MAHONA Israel **66** 262
MAHONE Dorothy (Jones) **100** 240
Thomas **100** 240
MAHONEY Mahony
Anne **61** 138
Annie **139** 215
Annie Filomina **92** 359
C. Ray **101** 124
Catherine **99** 120 **109** 228

MAHONEY *cont'd*
Catherine (Johnson) **100** 242
Cornelius **99** 120 **100** 242
Daniel **139** 214
Daniel Sullivan **91** 88
Edward **73** 147
Elizabeth **124** 296
Elizabeth (Hilton) **124** 296 298
Evie S. **124** 230
Frances Josephine **139** 214 215
Francis S. **137** 219
Frederick Louis **139** 214 215
Gertrude **139** 215
Hannora Gately (Fallon) **91** 88
Henry Joseph **139** 215
Henry Patrick **139** 215
Humphrey Charles **139** 212 214
James **128** 170
Jasper **65** 21
Jesse **124** 298
Joanna L. (Kennedy) **139** 212 214
John **73** 145 **77** 188 **91** 329 **105** 287 **123** 175
Jos **64** 320
Josephine Frances **139** 215
Julie (Burke) **89** 132
Margaret **61** 138 **77** 188
Mary **78** 69 **139** 214
Mary (Noonan) **128** 170
Mary E. **139** 214
Mary Elizabeth (Farley) **139** 215
Mary M. **128** 170
Mary Sargent **91** 87
Matthew **99** 120
Patrick **105** 289
Polly **124** 298
Rose (Weare) **116** 132
Silas **116** 132
Thomas **115** 213
William Henry **139** 214
MAHOONE Dorman **71** 10 **95** 134
MAHOS — Mr. **61** 394
MAHURA
Charles E. **117** 221
MAHURIN McHuron
—— **136** 26 118 128
Aaron O. **136** 131
Abigail **136** 121 127 246 252
Abigail (Dickerman) **136** 119 120
Abigail (Mattison) **136** 247
Abigail (White) **136** 247
Achsa **136** 27 124 125
Agnes (Ludlow) **136** 242
Agnes L. **136** 243
Alanson **136** 247 248
Albert **136** 247
Alexander M. B. **136** 132
Alfred **136** 245 246

MAHURIN *cont'd*
Alice **136** 243
Allen **136** 251
Allen E. **136** 246
Almira D. **136** 126
Alson **136** 250
Althea **136** 247
Alvarado F. **136** 252
Alvin **136** 247
Alvira **136** 250
Amanda **136** 242 247 248
Amanda K. **136** 131
Amasa **136** 120 121 249 250
Andrew J. **136** 126
Ann **136** 248
Ann Maria (Druggs) **136** 248
Anna **136** 115 117 126 130 250
Anna (Haskins) **136** 250
Anne **136** 115 116
Annette **136** 132
Armina **136** 249 250
Asa **136** 252
Asaph L. **136** 249 250
Ashley **136** 246
Athalia **136** 131
Augustus B. **136** 126
Bathsheba **136** 19 22 25
Bathsheba (Joyce) **136** 21
Bathshua **53** 436 **136** 27
Belinda **136** 126
Belle M. **136** 244
Benjamin **136** 19 20 26 27 121-124 229 248 250 252
Benjamin Abbott **136** 131
Bethiah **136** 124 131 248
Bethiah (Churchill) **136** 252
Bethiah (Pratt) **136** 25 117 118
Bethiah (St. John) **136** 130
Bethiah A. **136** 131
Betsey **136** 243 250
Betsey (Hutchins) **136** 249
Betty **53** 436 **136** 22 28 118
Beulah (Howe) **136** 30
Caleb **136** 126
Caleb R. **136** 126
Calvin **136** 246
Candace **136** 127
Caroline (Sherell) **136** 248
Caroline P. **136** 126
Caroline W. (Cone) **136** 244
Catherine **136** 29 126
Catherine (Hogaboom) **136** 246
Catherine (Robinson) **136** 248
Catherine C. **136** 242
Charles **136** 244
Charles J. **136** 132
Charlotte (Marshall) **136** 246 247
Chloe **136** 120 121 250
Chloe (Sabin) **136** 121
Clara **136** 244
Clarissa **136** 246 247 251
Cora **136** 246
Cynthia **136** 126

MAHURIN *cont'd*
Cynthia A. (Halsey) **136** 243
Cynthia J. **136** 132
Daniel **136** 249 250
Daniel Hazeltine **136** 247
David **136** 24 26 115-117 244-247 250 252
David L. **136** 247 248
Deborah **136** 122 123
Delia **136** 250
Ebenezer **53** 436 **136** 17-22 27 28 125-128 130 131 242
Edilda G. **136** 244
Edmond M. **136** 131
Edward A. **136** 132
Edway **136** 246
Eleazer **136** 250
Eli **136** 29 131
Eli H. **136** 131
Elias **136** 129
Elijah **136** 131
Eliza **136** 246 247
Eliza (Littell) **136** 243
Eliza Jane **136** 130
Eliza L. **136** 243
Elizabeth **136** 20 21 29 126 127 243 248
Elizabeth (Tryon) **136** 250
Elizabeth A. **136** 126
Ella M. **136** 243
Ellen **136** 244
Ellen A. **136** 250
Ellen E. **136** 252
Elvira **136** 250
Elvira C. **136** 247
Emily **136** 246
Emily (Curtis) **136** 244
Emily (Senteny) **136** 132
Emma J. **136** 132
Enos **136** 29 131 132
Ephraim **136** 23 30 243
Ephraim H. **136** 30 243 244
Esther A. **136** 131
Ettamine **136** 132
Ettie **136** 244
Eunice **136** 249
Eunice (Galpin) **136** 249
Experience **136** 130
Florilla **136** 247
Frances **136** 244
Francis H. **136** 131
Frank E. **136** 244
Frank W. **136** 243
Frederick **136** 127
George **136** 126 247 248
George A. **136** 131
George H. **136** 247
Grace (Hersey) **136** 251
Hannah **134** 86 **136** 17 20 21 29 117-119 130 243
Hannah (Kilburn) **136** 125
Hannah (Snow) **136** 26 121
Hannah F. **136** 132
Hara **136** 132
Harriet **136** 132 248
Harrison **136** 126

MAHURIN *cont'd*
Harvey **136** 247
Harvey H. **136** 131
Hazen **136** 132
Henry **136** 244
Henry H. **136** 246
Hezekiah **136** 27 117 119-121 249 250
Hiram **136** 247
Hollis **136** 246
Horace A. **136** 246
Horace K. **136** 246
Hugh **115** 156 **136** 17-21 23 24 26-28 30 115 117-119 121-123 125 126 128 130 131 242-246 248-250
Ida L. **136** 132
Isaac **136** 27 123 124 126 244 250
Isabel **136** 132
James **136** 123 251
James Adams **136** 251
James Allen **136** 124 250-252
James F. **136** 130
James H. **136** 243
James Kemper **136** 243
James M. **136** 244
James W. **136** 132
Jane **136** 29
Jennie N. **136** 132
Jennie R. **136** 126
Jeremiah **136** 131 132
Jeremiah T. **136** 132
John **136** 117 120 121 123 126 128-130 247 250
John A. **136** 132
John Adams **136** 244
John L. **136** 126
John Ludlow **136** 242
John W. **136** 132
Jonas **136** 126
Jonathan **136** 19 22 23 26 27 30 117 122 243 245 246
Josiah **136** 17 25 26 117 118 248 252
Julia **136** 244 250
Julius A. **136** 244
Katharine (Harding) **136** 131
Katie **136** 244
Laura L. **136** 247
Lavica **136** 246
Leslie T. **115** 156
Levi **136** 246
Levina **136** 126
Lewis F. **136** 132
Linus **136** 247
Louisa **136** 126 131
Louisa (Shedd) **136** 246
Lucia (Snow) **136** 115 116
Lucinda **136** 247
Lucretia **136** 28 132 249 250
Lucretia (Martin) **136** 131
Lucy **136** 27 118-121 248
Lucy (Galloway) **136** 129 130
Lucy A. **136** 246
Luellen A. **136** 131

MAHURIN *cont'd*
Lunceford **136** 130
Lydia **136** 120 121
Lydia (Johnson) **136** 243
Lydia (Marsh) **136** 29
Lydia (Pratt) **136** 26 27
Lyman **136** 247
Madeline (Stephenson) **136** 132
Marcus **136** 248
Margaret E. **136** 126
Margaret W. **136** 132
Maria **136** 120 129 242
Maria (King) **136** 132
Maria E. **136** 248
Martha **136** 25 117
Martha (Conant) **136** 117 118
Martha B. **136** 132
Martha J. **136** 130
Martin **136** 130
Mary **53** 436 **60** 402 **136** 22 24 27 29 126 128 130 132 244 250 251
Mary (Allen) **136** 123 124
Mary (Bailey) **136** 244
Mary (Campbell) **136** 18 19
Mary (Doran) **136** 250
Mary (Edson)(Packard) **136** 23
Mary (Hazen) **136** 28
Mary (McClain) **136** 130
Mary (Ritter) **136** 126
Mary (Snell) **136** 23 24 119
Mary (Wetherel) **136** 121 252
Mary A. **136** 130 247
Mary C. **136** 132
Mary E. **136** 130 131 244
Mary F. **136** 132 243
Mary J. **136** 247
Mary Jane (Lane) **136** 132
Mary L. (Foster) **136** 243
Mary M. **136** 132
Maryette **136** 248
Matilda (Freeman) **136** 126
Matilda (Ross) **136** 130
Matilda L. **136** 126
Medad **136** 250
Mehitable (Williams) **136** 26 27 124
Melvin **136** 248
Melvina S. **136** 247
Melzar **136** 250
Milo **136** 244
Nabby **136** 120
Nabby M **136** 120
Nahum **136** 248
Nancy **136** 128 129 248
Nancy (Mahan) **136** 126
Nancy (Pierce) **136** 248
Nancy A. **136** 132
Nancy Ann (Wiles) **136** 132
Nancy M. **136** 131
Oscar F. **136** 250
Othniel **136** 18 22 28 29 125 127-130
Othniel J. **136** 131

MAHURIN *cont'd*
Otho **136** 22
Patience **136** 126 128
Patience (Pierce) **136** 248
Patsy **136** 126
Paulina D. **136** 247
Persis **136** 244
Phebe **136** 28 29 118 119 126-129 131
Phebe L. **136** 131
Polly **136** 247
Preston A. **136** 248
Priddy **136** 127
Priscilla **136** 28 122 123 129
Prudence M. **136** 132
Rachel **136** 126 132 250
Rebecca **136** 244
Rebecca (Bundy) **136** 243
Rebecca N. **136** 130
Reliance **136** 26
Reuben **136** 121 132
Reuben S. **136** 246
Reuel **136** 121 250
Rhoda **136** 248
Robert **136** 126
Rosa **136** 248
Royal Stearns **136** 247
Rufus E. C. **136** 132
Ruth **136** 116 117 211 247 248
Ruth (Dunbar) **136** 115 116
Ruth (Kingman) **136** 122
Ruth A. **136** 247
Sally **136** 118 120 121
Samuel **136** 28 126-129
Samuel B. **136** 132
Samuel Francis **136** 132
Samuel W. **136** 126
Sarah **136** 27 117 118 126-130 245 246
Sarah (Bassett) **136** 115 116
Sarah (Meek) (Green) **136** 127
Sarah (Proctor) **136** 129
Sarah A. **136** 126 243
Sarah D. **136** 131
Sarah H. **136** 242
Sarah J. **136** 131
Sarissa (Miner) **136** 247
Servey A. **136** 246
Seth **53** 436 **136** 22 28 29 116 117 126 130-132 242 246-248
Seth J. **136** 131
Seth T. **136** 131
Silas **136** 27 29 126-130 132 242 247
Silas E. **136** 132 243
Silas Gray **136** 243
Silas Marshall **136** 248
Stephen **53** 436 **115** 156 **136** 17 22 27 125-128
Susan **136** 244
Susan M. **136** 248
Susan T. **136** 242
Susanna **136** 117 127 243 249

MAHURIN *cont'd*
Susanna (Hamblin) **136** 244
Sylvester L. **136** 248
Sylvia **136** 27 124 252
Thankful **136** 116
Thankful (Howes) **136** 244
Thomas **136** 129
Thomas E. **136** 126
Thomas S. **136** 132
William **136** 126 132 243 244 247 250
William C. **136** 244
William Cooper **136** 243
William H. **136** 126 127 132 248
William M. B. **136** 131
William N. **136** 132
William W. **136** 132
Willis B. **136** 131
Winfield F. **136** 252
Zerviah (Spaulding) **136** 246
MAHURN
Charles E. **117** 221
MAIDSTONE Maidston
John **110** 276 **138** 101
Robert **63** 281
MAIF
Dallas V. **103** 236
Hugh **76** 289 **103** 183
Hugo **103** 182
James Herbert **103** 120
MAIER Christian Jacob (Mrs.) **106** 125
Mailard *see* Maillard
MAILER Norman **136** 88
MAILEY
Maude Ellen **71** xxiv
MAILLARD Mailard
Agnes **51** 184 **52** 47
James **110** 317
Lawrence **51** 184 **52** 47
Rowland **110** 317
MAILLER
Ida Malvina **90** 209
MAILLONS
Amant **145** 130
Domitille (Denno) **145** 130
Josette (Demerse) **145** 130
MAILMAN Catherine (McKinlay) **125** 261
Henry **125** 261
MAIN Maine Mayne
—— **56** 96 **63** 50 **84** 129 **99** 114 **101** 94 **143** 362
— Mrs. **74** 191
A. H. **111** 129
Abel **77** 39 **143** 363
Abigail **115** 139 **143** 363
Abram **70** 243
Adaline L. **111** 129
Agnes **73** 131 **118** 253
Albert **111** 127 129
Albert N. **83** 161
Alice **81** 430
Alice Appleton **97** 387
Alice Josephine **83** 161
Almira (Emery) **117** 142

MAIN *cont'd*
144
Alva **111** 129
Amanda **80** 309
Amos **68** 382 **74** 191 **99** 79 **109** 300 **111** 96 **114** 51
Amos W. **80** 309
Andrew **70** 243 **80** 309 **142** 167
Andrew Jackson **89** 115
Angie M. **111** 128
Anna **73** 213
Anne **118** 258
Asenath (Teal) **117** 141 142
Barbara **113** 92
Belinda (Sessions) **110** 119
Benajah **143** 362 363
Betsey **63** 169 **68** 334 **70** 243 **80** 308
Betsey E. **70** 243
Betty **111** 230 **115** 307
Betty (Trafton) **115** 303
Carl J. (Mrs.) **109** 130
Catherine **83** 69
Cecelia **79** 99
Charles **84** 30 **111** 124
Charles A. **111** 129
Charles E. **83** 183 184
Charles Reed **97** 387
Charles Thomas **84** 233 **85** 188 **97** 287 387 **98** 149
Chester **69** 334
Christian **55** 310
Clarence A. **96** 294 **97** 154
Collins **83** 161
Cordelia Green (Reed) **97** 387
Cornelia **83** 161
Daniel H. **83** 161
Daniel L. **70** 243
David **80** 307 309
Deborah **69** 334
Deborah (Phillips) **97** 387
Dolly **63** 50 **143** 363
Dolly (Woodward) **143** 362
Dorcas **81** 430
Dorothy **82** 291 293 **93** 294 **109** 300 **111** 230 **114** 50
Dorothy (Lewis) **111** 230
Dorothy M. **118** 241
Dudley C. **70** 243
E. **91** 329
E. G. **56** 324 **57** 112 **60** 187
Edith E. **111** 124
Edith E. (Burdick) **111** 129
Edward **63** 49 **83** 161 **111** 127 129 **112** 300
Edwina A. **70** 243
Eleanor A. **123** 151
Elias **63** 169 **115** 303
Elithia Cornelia (Carver) **88** 322
Eliza A. **111** 124 129
Elizabeth **57** 112 157 **80** 309 **82** 293 300 **111** 96 129

MAIN *cont'd*
Elizabeth (White) **111** 96
Elizabeth F. (Appleton) **97** 387
Ellen R. (Higgins) **111** 127 129
Elvira (Meeker) **111** 124
Emily **79** 99
Esther **80** 307 309
Eugene M. **111** 129
Ezekiel **60** 187 **65** 302 **143** 362
Ezekiel S. **73** 213
Fear **70** 243
Fear (Holmes) **142** 167
Flora (Sumners) **111** 124
Floyd H. **111** 129
Frank D. **111** 129
Franklin B. **83** 161
George H. **111** 129
Georgie V. **83** 300
Grace M. **83** 429 435
Hannah **81** 430
Hannah E. (Wilson) **121** 310 **122** 313
Harriet Delilah (Colegrove) **101** 94
Harrison **111** 129
Hattie D. **111** 129
Hattie M. **83** 161
Helen Augusta **89** 115
Henry **78** 213 **79** 99
Herbert **79** 99
Howard E. **111** 129
Isaac **65** 378 **70** 314
Isobel **113** 91 92
J. Estelle **111** 129
Jacob **80** 309
James **73** 131
Jane **111** 127 **126** 207
Jane Ann W. (Laighton) **83** 183 184
Jeanette **137** 283
Jeremiah **143** 362
Jerusha **70** 243
Jerusha A. **70** 243
Jesse **143** 363
John **56** 324 **69** 282 **79** 412 **80** 352 **84** 76 **109** 300 301 **111** 230 **114** 130 **115** 138 **117** 141 142 **118** 258 **120** 139 **123** 151 **143** 363
John Henry **79** 99
John L. **72** 205
Jonas **57** 155
Joseph **109** 300 **111** 97 **114** 126 **115** 44
Josephine Lillibridge **83** 161
Joshua **57** 112 155 **68** 334 **70** 243
Josiah **80** 309 **109** 300 **110** 97 **111** 96 230 **117** 142 144
Jozinah D. (Johnson) **111** 127 129
Justus B. **101** 94
Katie **83** 430 435
Loren S. **83** 161
Lucretia **111** 123

MAIN *cont'd*
Lucy **111** 97 230 **115** 137
Lucy (Farnam) **115** 138
Lucy M. **70** 243
Lydia **117** 223
Lydia A. **119** 286
Madison **111** 129
Maria E. **83** 161
Marie **118** 258
Marietta **110** 119
Martha **77** 39 **79** 99
Mary **68** 334 **80** 309 **102** 228 **111** 96 230
Mary (Pendleton) **143** 362
Mary (Randall) (Miner) **143** 362 363
Mary (Shepherd) **118** 258
Mary Josephine **63** 49
Mary Margaret (Carlton) **89** 115
Mercy **63** 169 **109** 300 **110** 97 **111** 97 **114** 126 **115** 216 303
Meribah **80** 309
Meribah Ann **80** 307
Molly **143** 363
Nathan S. **83** 161 **88** 322
Nathaniel **68** 265 **70** 315
Nellie **104** 102
Nellie E. **84** 30
Nicholas **56** 324
Noah **70** 315
Olive E. **128** 175
Parker **68** 334
Patience **57** 155 156 **81** 430
Perry J. **70** 243
Peter **83** 69
Phebe **143** 363
Phebe H. **70** 243
Philander Jervis **69** 334
Polly **70** 244 **109** 313
Rachel **57** 112 155 **109** 301
Ray Leon **104** 102
Reuben **68** 334 **70** 243
Rhoda J. (Grover) **120** 139 **123** 151
Robert **55** 98 **118** 258
Rosa A. **111** 129
Rosie E. **111** 129
Samuel **116** 132 **143** 363
Sarah **72** 205 **143** 363
Sarah (Fleming) **128** 175
Sarah M. (Jenkins) **83** 161
Sesian **55** 98
Simeon **65** 302 **143** 362
Sophronia **119** 284 285
Stephen **65** 378 **73** 213
Susan **69** 282 **122** 298
Susan A. **80** 310
Susan E. **83** 161
Susan L. **83** 161
Susan R. **80** 310
Susanna (McIntire) **111** 97 **114** 126
Theodore **97** 387
Theresa **83** 69
Thomas **51** 45 **81** 430 **97** 387 **104** 102 **118** 258 **143** 362
Van Rensselaer **73** 213
W. R. **128** 175

MAIN *cont'd*
Wallace **121** 310 **122** 313
William **73** 131 **80** 309 310 **113** 92 **118** 253 258
William Comstock **110** 119
William H. **80** 309
Williams **55** 310
Willie E. **80** 309
Zeruah **83** 161
MAINS Blanche (Rich) **84** 129
Elvira **90** 343
Sarah **71** 132
MAINTENON Francoise d'Aubigny de (Marchioness) **52** 476
MAINWARING
Manwaring
Manwaringe
Manwarren
Manwarring
Manwearing
— Dr. **52** 111
— Mr. **144** 299
Ann **144** 297 299 300
Anne (Gregson) **128** 107
Benjamin **79** 72
Betsey S. **77** 204
C. E. **112** 67 125
Charles F. **77** 204
Charles W. **105** 198 **144** 49 **147** 119
Charles William **59** xliv **60** xxxvi 113 **72** 222 **100** 274 332 **116** 97 **118** 272 **119** 91 **120** 95 **122** 37 39 41 42 **123** 231 278 279 301 **142** 123 329 333 334 337 339 344 **143** 304 306 308-310 312 314 317 321 322 324 **145** 319 **148** 17 218 228
Curtis **79** 72
Esse **79** 111
Frances **120** 248
G. A. **60** 187
Hannah (Raymond) **86** 327 **144** 297
Harriet A. **77** 204
Isaac **79** 79
Jerusha **79** 79
John **73** 156 **77** 204 205 **112** 28 **128** 107
John J. **77** 204
Joseph George Ross **86** 197
Josiah **79** 72
Judith **86** 327 **105** 166 **144** 300
Julia Ann **79** 72
Keturah **79** 79
Latham **79** 72
Love **79** 111 **144** 237
Lydia **79** 72 **126** 256 **128** 21
Mary **53** 375 **112** 28 **141** 102
Nancy **133** 56
Norman **116** 290
Oliver **79** 110 111 **82** 153

MAINWARING *cont'd*
  86 327 **104** 189 **105** 166
  141 96 104 105 **144** 297
  Peter **141** 105
  Pierpoint H. **79** 72
  Prudence **79** 111 **104** 193
  Ral. **141** 29
  Ranalphus **60** 187
  Roger **53** 375
  Sabra **79** 72
  Sally **79** 72
  Sarah **77** 204 205
  Syvilian **79** 72
  Thomas **79** 79 **126** 256 **128**
  21 **141** 105
  Zerviah (Gifford) **133** 36
Maior *see* Major
Mair *see* Mayer
Maire *see* Mayer
MAIRS Eliizabeth (Gaston)
  111 313
  Elizabeth Atwater **93** 138
  111 310 312
  Ethel D. (Morrell) **83** 435
  436
  Frances Bradford (Tyller)
  111 312
  George **111** 313 **137** 362
  James **137** 362
  John **111** 313 **137** 362
  John Gaston **111** 312
  Margaret **137** 362
  Margaret (Whiteside)
  111 313
  Ralph **83** 435 436
  Sarah (McFadden)
  111 313
  Thomas **137** 362
MAISONFORT
  Boisdescourt
  Alexandre (Marquis
  du) **77** 97
Maister *see* Masters
Maisters *see* Masters
MAISY Francis **55** 438
MAITHAM Richard **92** 396
MAITLAND
  — Col. **84** 256
  Anne **61** 265 270
  Emily (Rising) **85** 296
  F. W. **119** 100 101
  Frederic W. **147** 8
  James **73** 226
  Jennet Lenox **104** 235
  John Robert **85** 296
  Mary Ann **61** 265 270
  Rebecca Seton **101** 250
  Thomas **61** 265 270
MAJERSON
  Sarah Ann **64** 212
MAJOR Maior
  — **52** 267 **99** 113
  146 367
  Abigail **111** 67
  Anna Rosabell (Hopkins)
  105 109
  Anthony **112** 138
  Aurelius **105** 109
  Catherine **115** 61
  Eleanor **100** 300
  Elizabeth **100** 241

MAJOR *cont'd*
  Francis **100** 287
  Henry **98** 35
  James **62** 243
  James Edward **112** 138
  John **75** 227
  Martha Lenora (Glass)
  112 138
  Nettie Leitch **118** 166
  Peggy **93** 202
  Priscilla **88** 362
  Rebecca **64** 122
  Robert **51** 351
  Tirsa **125** 106
MAJORY
  Benjamin **105** 76
  John **55** 68
  Joseph **100** 242
  Rachel (Howard) **100** 242
Mak *see* Mack
Makar *see* Maker
MAKAROFF
  — Admiral **62** 55
  Marie Josephine
  (Hartford) **94** 137
MAKE Richard **138** 29
MAKECHNIE
  Flora W. Mabel
  124 228
  Josie A. M. **124** 228
  Sarah A. H. (Moore)
  124 228
MAKEMIE
  Francis **117** 106
MAKEMSON
  Eliza Jane **107** 228
  Jane **107** 228
  Jane Lindsey **107** 228 229
  Thomas **107** 228 229
MAKENY Daniel **64** 29
MAKEPEACE Makepiece
  — **53** 301 **55** 229 **56** 99
  — Capt. **136** 245
  — Widow **63** 327
  ____ (Hughes) **140** 36
  Abel **93** 392 **94** 257
  Abel (Mrs.) **94** 257
  Abigail **57** 75 **90** 72
  Anna (Hodges) **126** 116
  Betsey **54** lxxxi
  Calista **126** 116
  Elizabeth **61** 55 56 **76** 198
  Esther **53** 378
  F. B. **83** 223
  George **140** 166
  Hannah **51** 291 **93** 191
  Hester **53** 378
  Isaac **126** 116
  Jane **94** 257
  Jonathan **125** 208
  Lawrence **94** 257 **98** 30
  Mary **129** 86
  Mary (Chase) **87** 51
  Mary (Washington) **93**
  393 **94** 257
  Russell **120** 145
  Sarah **87** 51
  Sukey **140** 161
  Thomas **53** 378 **61** 55 56
  76 198 **80** 282 **85** 249
  87 51 **120** 145

MAKEPEACE *cont'd*
  Wait A. While **54** 213
  147 68
  William **57** 75 **63** 81 **106**
  22 23 **140** 36
MAKER Macker Makar
  Alice **104** 292
  Arabella G. **89** 242
  Clarissa Emeline **77** 188
  Cora Ada (Lazell) **89** 117
  David **104** 292
  Edwin **89** 117
  Elizabeth **124** 239
  Eunice (Elwell) **89** 117
  Hepzibah **104** 59
  James **60** 187 **65** 27 **89** 117
  John **87** 327 **102** 49
  Lucy Ann **113** 66
  Mary **80** 125
  Mary (Hopkins) **102** 49
  Oliver **104** 292
  Robert **104** 292
  Rosilla Sophronia **89** 117
  Seth **113** 66
  Solomon **59** 353
  Tabitha **125** 275
  Thankful **87** 327 **104** 292
  William **105** 209
MAKERNES Agnes **71**
  325 326 332-333 **75** 139
  Agnes (Sare) **89** 154
  Alice **71** 325 326 330 334
  Anne **71** 328 330-332 334
  335
  Annis **71** 325 333
  Barbara **71** 328 329 336
  74 283
  Bridget **71** 331 336
  Dorothy **71** 331 336
  Edith **71** 331 334
  Edmund **71** 325 328 330-
  336
  Edward **71** 329 331 336
  Eleanor **75** 58 139
  Elizabeth **71** 325 326 328-
  336 **74** 283
  Ellen **71** 175 324-326 330
  332 333 335 336 **75** 139
  89 154
  Frances **71** 332 335
  George **71** 326-328 330-
  332 334 336 **89** 152-154
  Hannah **71** 331 332 334
  Henry **71** 327-329 331 332
  334-336
  Humphrey **71** 327 329-332
  334
  Jacob **71** 330 334
  Jane **71** 328 329 331 332
  335 336
  Joan **71** 326 327 329 331-
  336 **89** 151 154
  Joel **71** 331 332 335
  John **71** 324 325 328-336
  89 154
  Joseph **71** 331 333 336
  Katharine **71** 328 331 332
  335 336
  Margaret **71** 327 330 332
  333 335
  Margareta **71** 331

MAKERNES *cont'd*
Margery **71** 326 330 332 334-336
Marie (Goodfellow) **89** 154
Mary **71** 326 328 330-332 334-336
Peter **71** 327-331 334
Priscilla **71** 331 334 336
Rebecca **71** 331 336
Richard **71** 325-336 **74** 283 **89** 152 153
Samuel **71** 329 336
Susan **71** 331 332 336
Susanna **71** 327 328 332 335
Theophilus **71** 331 334
Thomas **71** 325-336 **74** 283 **89** 151 153 154
William **71** 175 324-336 **75** 139 **89** 154
MAKIN Alice **66** 326
Daniel **66** 325 326
Elizabeth **66** 326
Grace **51** 309 310 313 **66** 324 **86** 223
James **66** 325
Joan **51** 309 313
Martha **66** 325 326
Mary **66** 326
Robert **66** 325 326
Samuel **66** 325
Sarah **94** 89
Thomas **51** 313 **66** 326
Tobias **51** 310 313 **66** 324
MAKING Elias **64** 115
MAKINSON
— Mr. **82** 187
Amy (Briggs) **127** 59
John **127** 59
MAKLEBUST
Mercy **118** 79
MAKUNE
Elizabeth **99** 27
Lydia **99** 26 27
William **99** 26 27
MAKUSET
Mordecai **59** 153
Sarah **59** 153
MAKYES
Albert C. **109** 103
Edwin L. **109** 103
Emma L. (Moseley) **109** 103
MALABERGE
Madeline **106** 230
MALALLEY
William **55** 251
MALAPOGNE
Jeanne **143** 236
Magdeleine **143** 234-236 366 **145** 292
MALARNEE
Sarah Ann **95** 288
MALAVERY
Deliverance **106** 148
MALBANC Hugh **112** 27
William **112** 27
MALBISSE
Richard **102** 296

MALBONE Malbon
Malborn
—— **54** 323
— Capt. **84** 252
— Col. **67** 12 **96** 12 13
Ann **60** 18
Catherine **96** 14
Catherine (Scott) **96** 193
Ceaser **127** 138
Charles **100** 330
Daniel **107** 319 **108** 157
Deborah **85** 220
Edward G. **125** 30 44
Evan **60** 18 **125** 240
Francis **67** 211 **127** 16 139
Godfrey **96** 12 14 193 **104** 11 **105** 238 267 **108** 297 **110** 317
John **65** 149 **80** 254 **125** 44 **127** 17
Katharine **67** 211 **96** 12
Katharine (Scott) **96** 12
Mary E. (Isaacs) **125** 240
Polly **127** 14
Ralph **125** 240
Richard **128** 66 70 71
Solomon **60** 18
Thomas **116** 111
Winfield S. **107** 319 **108** 157
MALBURGH John **100** 20
MALCASTER
William **54** 215
MALCHAM
Maylam William **100** 42
Meribah (Tibbetts) **100** 42
MALCOLM II King of Scotland **79** 371 **136** 102
MALCOLM Malcom
Malcomb
—— **62** 388
— Mr. **52** 312
Abbot of Aberbrothock **56** 190
Allan **119** 20
Andrew **108** 42
Ann **84** 265 **102** 29
Anne **100** 28 30 32 33 133
Carolina **100** 33 **101** 273
Daniel **84** 260 265 **100** 28 30 32 33 133 139 **101** 273 **102** 29
David **124** 79
Edith **108** 305
Elizabeth **103** 25
Elizabeth (Killeran) **90** 90
Ernest E. **72** xx
Granville **51** 72
Hannah **51** 72 **90** 91
Howard **51** 72 **88** 337
J. P. **60** 32
James **90** 91 **125** 32
James Fudge **100** 133
John **51** 72 **92** 91 **119** 21
John James **51** 72
John Karl **105** 156
Lucy **90** 91
Mary **100** 228
Michael **105** 55 **108** 184

MALCOLM *cont'd*
119 20
Rebecca (Snelling) **105** 55 **108** 184
Ruth **102** 123
Ruth Ann (Dyer) **88** 337
Sarah **101** 273 **128** 171 **140** 166
Sarah Fudge **100** 28
Susanna **100** 30 303
Thomas **125** 37
William **90** 90-92 **119** 21
MALCOVENANT
Geoffrey **116** 170
MALDAN
John Lewis **65** 231
MALDEN
Henry C. **54** 289
John **56** 275 **80** 403
Margaret **80** 405
MALDONADO
Antonia **68** 24
MALDRED —— **79** 371 372
MALE John **125** 220
Lavias (Jones) **125** 220
MALESTON Mary **71** 297
Malet *see* Mallett
MALEY Maude **81** 221
MALING
Richard **105** 79
Sarah Jane Urann **118** 170
Thomas H. **118** 170
MALINS Malyns
Christopher **70** 340
MALISSEN
Peter **51** 343
Sophie **51** 343
MALKEM John **111** 212
Mikel **146** 326
Sarah **146** 326
MALKMES Henry **85** 315
MALL — Mr. **54** 43
Hans Wendel **109** 77
Jesse M. **109** 77
Mary **92** 53
Roger **126** 8
MALLABAR Ann **52** 267
Mark **104** 281
Nicholas **52** 267
Robert **104** 280 281
MALLABY Elizabeth Bleeker **111** 53
Sarah Elizabeth (Popham) **111** 53
Theodore **111** 53
Thomas **85** 458
MALLACKE Mallack
Marie **141** 26
Richard **61** 280
Roger **67** 364
William **141** 26
MALLALEY —— **70** 264
MALLALIEU
Eliza Frances **66** lxxix
Ellen Bromfield **66** lxxx
Francis **66** lxxix
John **66** lxxix
Lydia **66** lxxix
Willard Emerson **66** lxxx
Willard Francis **60** xxxiv **64** xxix **66** lix lxxviii

MALLALIEU *cont'd*
lxxix
MALLAPAR Matilda M.
(Eaton) **145** 157
MALLARD Anna **63** 156
Betsey **59** 287
Cyrus Stevens **95** 16
Frances D. (Porter) **83** 300
301
George **126** 145
Harriet **95** 15
Henry **128** 128
Henry Martyn **95** 16
James **127** 176
John **59** 287 **66** 20
John D. **83** 300 301
John W. P. **100** 188
Lazarus **95** 16
Mary **66** 20 23
Rebecca **95** 15
Robert **104** 281
Sarah A. **69** 142
Susan (Ridley) **126** 145
Thomas **66** 20 **95** 15
Mallary *see* Mallory
MALLBY
Katharine **51** 119
MALLENDER
Elizabeth L. **69** 263
John **69** 263
Mary **69** 263
Thomas **69** 263
Mallery *see* Mallory
MALLET-PREVOST
Paul Henri **85** 240
Severo **85** 240
MALLETT Malet Mallet
Mallette
— Col. **62** 382
— Mr. **63** 231
Ann **91** 353
Anna **78** 410
Beatrice **100** 306
Catherine (Brown)
125 223
Collet **97** 284 285
Eliza **116** 179
Hannah **78** 405
Isaac **91** 353 **125** 105
John **60** 291 **98** 296 **119** 21
Lawrence Edward
105 128
Lawrene Edward **114** 77
Martha (Wilson) **98** 296
Mary **60** 400 **64** 30 31
96 388
Mary (Rogers) **125** 105
Mary (Wood) (Wilcox)
103 275 277
Nancy **125** 105
Nathaniel **60** 290
Peter S. **147** 182
Phebe **98** 296 **115** 117
Philip **70** 37
Richard **74** 231 232 267
Robert **96** 104 **102** 292-295
105 293 294
Roger **90** 268
Sally **78** 310
Samuel **60** 290
Sarah **70** 37

MALLETT *cont'd*
Sarah E. **71** 12
Solomon **115** 117
Susanna **125** 106
Thomas **60** 400 **63** 331 **64**
30 31 **103** 275 277
William **100** 306 **105** 294
125 223
MALLEY
Dorothy Swan **109** 135
Elizabeth **82** 267
Helen Blackstone **82** 267
John Keep **82** 267
Josiah Keep **82** 267
Julia Eleanor **89** 59
Thomas **89** 59 **119** 20
MALLIBROKE
William **54** 333
MALLIE Mary **132** 77
MALLINCKRODT
Edward **92** 145
Ethel **85** 100
Florence (Kelsey) **85** 100
Louis **85** 100
MALLINSON
— Mrs. **83** 445
Alice (Pearson) **94** 110 112
Ellen **94** 107 110 111
Helen **94** 107
Joseph **122** 252
Judith **94** 111 112
Marie **94** 110
Martha **94** 110-112
Mary **68** 58 **93** 44 **94** 102
105 107 110-112 **148** 133
Rebecca **94** 110 112
Richard **94** 105 107-112
Sarah **94** 108 110-112
Sarah (Waterhouse) **94**
105 110 112
Thomas **94** 107-109 111
112
MALLIOTT
Alice **141** 119
Richard **141** 119
William **141** 119
MALLIS
Katharine **110** 254
MALLISON
Betsey **70** 227
Elisha **70** 227
Polly **91** 246
MALLIT Andrew **55** 68
MALLMAN Mallmann
Alfred William **82** 479
Jacob E. **79** 176 **80** 82
Rosamond Fay **82** 478
479
MALLO George **112** 89
Michael **112** 89
MALLOCH Anna **103** 52
Daniel **103** 52
Peter **103** 52
MALLOCK Grace **62** 48
Jane **101** 31
Richard **62** 48
Samuel **144** 335
Sylphine Mary
(Holberton) **144** 335
MALLON
Betsey **147** 176

MALLON *cont'd*
Charlotte (Bird) **126** 142
Daniel **126** 142
Dorcas **84** 5
Guy **70** 287
Jerusha (Hyde) **90** 57
Michael **66** 307
MALLOON Anna (Harris)
115 320
MALLOR
Rachel **111** 123 129
MALLORY Mallary
Mallery Malorie
Malory Meelery
Mellory
—— **61** 317 **69** 160
Aaron **54** 320 321
Abigail **54** 321-325 **68** 278
102 111
Ada **68** 278
Alice (de Driby) **142** 232
Alza Amelia **133** 265
Amos **54** 325 **133** 265
Amy **54** 324 **71** 12
Anketil **142** 232
Anna **68** 298
Anne **103** 106
Anne (Bruyn) **103** 106
Asa **54** 324 **58** 82
Azariah **68** 278
Benjamin **54** 321-325 **58**
75 76 82 **78** 47
Benjamin Irvin **78** 47
Brown **65** 136
Burr **65** 136
Caleb **54** 321 323 **56** 281
68 285 **117** 16
Calestra (Plumer) **133** 265
Calvin **54** 323
Caroline **65** 136
Catherine (Dorrah)
133 265
Charity **67** 52 229
Charles Payson **51** 236
Culver **72** 101
Curtis **133** 263 265 269
Daniel **54** 320 321 323 324
68 278 **78** 263
David **54** 323 324 **58** 82
69 47
Deborah **54** 323 **68** 298
69 47
Dorothy **54** 324 **58** 76 82
Dwight Harcourt **94** 49
Ebenezer **54** 321 **68** 298
Edmund **68** 278
Eliakim **53** 249 **54** 323
Elisha **53** 249
Elizabeth **54** 321 322 325
56 280 **68** 275 **102** 103
148 135
Elizabeth (Kimberly)
102 103
Elsie Jane (Luce) **88** 376
Emeline **65** 136
Estelle Dora (Margetts)
97 158
Esther **54** 323 334
Eunice **54** 321 323-325 **68**
287 **69** 47 **107** 71
Ezra **54** 325

MALLORY *cont'd*
Flora Maude **87** 17
Fred **122** 290
Freelove Amy **68** 278
Garrick Bolter **133** 266
Gertrude **94** 49
Gideon **65** 136
Hannah **54** 322-324
    68 173 286
Hannah (Minor) **133** 265
Herbert **72** 17 111
Horace Curtis **133** 265
Ira **71** 15
Isaac **54** 324 **58** 79 82
James **54** 323
Jane Fidelia **133** 266
Jared **54** 324 **58** 82
Jasper Benjamin **88** 376
Jean (Putnam) **94** 49
Jerusha D. **68** 334
John **54** 320-324 **56** 280
    62 364 **68** 298 **102** 103
    105 315 **142** 231
John Clinton **69** 160
John L. **71** 13
Jonathan **68** 298
Joseph **54** 321 322 324 325
    58 82 **69** 160
Joseph Minor **133** 262 265
Jubal Williston **133** 266
Judith **54** 321
Juliet **133** 265
Katharine **52** 260
Laura **69** 32
Leah **72** 16
Lecie Amelia **78** 47
Levi **54** 324
Lois **54** 324 **68** 278 **78** 263
Lorana **54** 324 **58** 82
Louella Kate (Billings)
    94 49
Lydia **68** 298
Lydia Maria (Emmons)
    133 265
Mabel **54** 324 **58** 79 82
    68 278
Margery **142** 232
Mary **54** 320 321 323 324
    58 75 82 **67** 126 **68** 278
    286 **78** 47 263 **145** 20
Mary (Pugh) **133** 266
Mary E. **133** 265
Mary G. **133** 265
Mary V. **69** 160
Mehitable **54** 322
Mercy **54** 323 324 **58** 82
Merriam **56** 281
Miriam **54** 323 **62** 364
Nancy **133** 263
Nancy (Bolter) **133** 262
    265 269
Nathan **122** 217
Nathaniel **116** 204
Noah Woodruff **54** 324
    325
Obedience **54** 322
Olive **65** 136
Omar **94** 49
Parthena **133** 265
Parthena (Smith) (Bolter)
    133 262 269 270

MALLORY *cont'd*
Peter **53** 249 **54** 320-325
    68 298 **76** 123 **81** 126
    140 184
Philip **107** 49
Philippa (Chetwynd)
    142 231
Polly **133** 270
Rachel **116** 204
Rachel (Perry) **116** 204
Rebecca **54** 320-323 **59** 67
    168 **68** 278
Rene **68** 278
Rhoda **72** 101
Rhode **69** 47
Richard **58** lxxxvii
Roger **107** 49
Rudena **143** 75
Rudena K. **146** 390
S. S. **68** 334
Sally **71** 13
Sally (Cheney) **125** 218
Samantha **59** 160
Samuel **54** 321-323
Sarah **54** 323 324 **65** 136 **68**
    172 286 298
Silence **54** 322
Simeon **54** 324
Stephen **54** 321 **144** 43
Susan **71** 15 **76** 123 **90** 177
Thankful **54** 322 324 325
Thomas **54** 321 323 324
    68 275 **95** 361 **102** 103
    315 **107** 49 **133** 262 269
Thomas Ebb **78** 47
Thomas Lyles **78** 47
Walter Langdon **106** 237
Warren James (Mrs.)
    97 158
Willard J. **69** 160
William **54** 321 **61** 287
    68 173 287 298 **69** 47
    374
Williston **133** 265
Zaccheus **54** 321
Zipporah **54** 321
MALLOY
— Capt. **101** 219
Eloiza (Shipley) **105** 222
Helen Franklin **74** 307
Joseph Drum **74** 307
Luke **93** 299
Margaret Louisa **105** 222
    223
Mary **101** 225
Paul **105** 223
MALLUS
Amelia P. **80** 26
John **140** 166
Mary **59** 313
Sarah Hart **59** 313
William **59** 313
MALLYN —— **94** 272
MALM Andrew **62** 248
MALMAINS Agnes
    (Montague) **140**
    222 223
Alice **140** 224
Beatrice **140** 223 224 228
    287 **69** 47 **107** 71

MALMAINS *cont'd*
Eleanor (DeVitre)
    (Parnell) (Tillieres)
    (Fitzpatrick) **140** 221
Joan (Tillieres) **140** 221
    222
Nicholas **140** 220 223 224
    228
Pernell **140** 220 224
Petronilla **140** 220
Thomas **140** 221 222
MALMQUIST
Carl G. **83** 422 435
Edith (Barrack) **83** 422 435
MALONA Daniel **66** 35
Martha A. **101** 35
MALONE Maloon
Abigail **51** 465 **65** 354
    114 180
Abigail (Tibbetts) **100** 39
Ann **65** 355 **71** 221
Anna **59** 284
Benjamin **105** 113
Betty **74** 22
Caroline A. **74** 294
Catherine **73** 135
Daniel **90** 57
Dumas **144** 168 233
Ebenezer **59** 289
Edmund **78** 69
Fanny **79** 127
Hannah **65** 351
Hannah (Yetten) **125** 105
Jane Isabel **117** 198
John **65** 35
Joseph **59** 288 **100** 39
    130 55
Kate **59** 283
Katharine **59** 288
Lane **59** 284
Mark **63** 134 **65** 354
Martha **88** 362
Mary **65** 353 **90** 114
Mary Ann **128** 177
Mollie **109** 70
Polly **59** 285
Samuel **59** 283 **65** 353
Sarah **59** 284 **89** 114
    142 266
Sophia **59** 289 **73** 131
Susanna **59** 283
William **125** 105
MALONEY Malony
    Meloney Melony
    Moloney Molony
— Capt. **71** 64
Ann **73** 219
Anna **82** 437
Betsey **127** 304
Charles **100** 25
Dorothy Brintnall (Fitch)
    (Thurman) **96** 298
Eleanor **99** 205
Francis **77** 153 **93** 138
Francis Xavier **118** 146
Hannah **65** 354 **82** 290
    294 295
Harry James (Mrs.)
    96 298
James **82** 290 294 **108** 275
John **77** 228 **99** 205

MALONEY *cont'd*
John James (Mrs.) **82** 237
John M. **117** 156
John Tarr **100** 25
Leah W. **82** 237
Leah W. B. **81** 363
Love **78** 187
Ludowick **140** 166
Margaret **99** 205
Mary **77** 153
Mary Ann **125** 292
Mary Ann (Wheaton)
  (McClain) **108** 275
Nona **81** 196
Pierce Vincent **82** 293 300
Rachel **82** 293 300
Rebecca Fling **100** 25
Ross (Mrs.) **88** 83
Sarah **78** 179
Walter **65** 354
Maloon *see* Malone
Malorie *see* Mallory
Malorye *see* Mallory
MALOY Patrick **139** 214
MALPAS Philip **71** 239
  109 31
Philippa **71** 239
MALQUIST Vaughn
  Edward (Mrs.) **99** 148
MALSCH Olive **107** 135
MALTBY Maltbie
  Maltboy Maltbye
  ——— **60** 93 **121** 57 63 98
  — Capt. **84** 366
  — Mr. **77** 13
  ___ (Culver) **112** 50
Abial Holmes **112** 48
Abigail **62** 147 **111** 292
  295 296 **112** 45 50
Abigail (Holmes) **111** 295
Abigail (Munger) **112** 45
Abigail (Wilford) **111** 295
Abigail (Williams) **112** 49
Adin **111** 298
Albert Sylvester **112** 53
Alice **111** 299
Almira **80** 145
Alva **111** 298
Ammi **112** 45
Amoret Submit **112** 48
Ann **99** 280 **101** 162
  110 171
Anna **111** 298
Anne **110** 171 172 **112** 44
  50
Anne (Peto) (Jenks)
  110 165
Anthony **110** 171
Augustus Williams
  112 50
Aurelia **112** 49
Beligur **112** 50
Benjamin **53** 314 **111** 294
  298 **112** 45 46 49 **136**
  326
Birdsey L. **111** 291
Catherine **111** 297
Catherine (Lee) **111** 297
Chandler **111** 296 297
Charles David **112** 53
Chester **112** 52

MALTBY *cont'd*
Clarissa (Pardee) **112** 48
Daniel **60** 210 **70** 73 **111**
  293 294 296 **112** 44 45
Daniel Munson **112** 44
David **59** 255 **60** 210 **101**
  106 **108** 294 **111** 295
  296 **112** 53
De Grasse **112** 46
Deborah **111** 298
Deborah (Jones) **111** 292
Deborah (Scovall)
  111 298
Dorothy **111** 291 **112** 44
Dorothy L. **60** 93
Dorothy Lord **60** 187 210
Ebenezer Davenport
  112 53
Edin **111** 298
Elbridge **112** 46
Elihu **111** 294
Elija **112** 50
Eliza **80** 145
Eliza Rebecca **112** 46
Elizabeth **53** 314 **56** 264 **62**
  147 **71** 6 **110** 171 **111**
  292 293 295-297 299 **112**
  46 48 **146** 360 **147** 63
Elizabeth (Allen) **112** 52
Elizabeth (Fowler) **111**
  294 **136** 326
Elizabeth (Gifford)
  132 300
Elizabeth (Pratt) **111** 293
Elizabeth White **112** 49
Elon **112** 45
Epaphras Chapman
  111 147
Ephraim **111** 298
Erastus **111** 297 **112** 46
Esther **59** 255 **60** 210 **62** 49
  70 74 **111** 292 294
Eunice **112** 50
Fannie **104** 96
Frederick **111** 298
George **112** 48
George W. **111** 299
Grace **111** 297
Grove **111** 297
Hannah **58** 281 **111** 293
  294 296 297 **112** 45
Hannah (Hoadley)
  111 147
Harriet Amelia **111** 147
Harriet Grace **112** 48
Henry **112** 50
Huldah **111** 298
Ira **111** 298
Isaac **111** 295 298 **112** 49 52
  132 300
Isaac Fowler **112** 49
Isaac Taintor **112** 48
Jacob **80** 145 **112** 45 52
James **56** 264 **111** 295 **112**
  48 50-52
James Rufus **112** 53
Jane **59** 65
Jane (Smith) **111** 292
Jane Betsey (Dixon)
  112 48
Jehiel Merriman **112** 44

MALTBY *cont'd*
Jerusha **112** 46
Jerusha (Rose) **112** 45
Jesse **111** 299 **112** 45
John **58** 281 **59** 65 **60** 187
  81 128 **110** 165 171 **111**
  291-293 296-298 **112** 50
  53
John Davenport **111** 296
John Robert **112** 53
Jonas **127** 246
Jonathan **108** 294 295
  111 293 295-299 **112** 46-
  48 50-52 **127** 246
Joseph **111** 293 296-298
Josiah **111** 299
Julia **112** 45
Julia Ann **112** 49 50
Julius **112** 46
Lois **112** 45
Lucinda **112** 49
Lucinda (Murray) **112** 49
  132 300
Lucius **112** 48
Lucretia **53** 315 **111** 294
  112 46
Lucy **112** 52
Lydia **111** 294 297 299
Lydia (Bartholomew)
  111 298
Lydia (Ritter) **111** 297
  147 63
Margaret **68** 66 **111** 296
Margaret (Munson)
  112 44
Maria **112** 49
Martha **111** 293 299
Martha Church **112** 49
Martha Humphreys
  71 95
Mary **53** 316 **60** 210 **70** 73
  111 293 294 297 **127**
  246
Mary (Fowler) **111** 295
Mary (Harrison) **111** 293
Mary Catherine **112** 53
Mehitable **111** 291 292
Mehitable (Clarke)
  111 291
Molly Rose **112** 46
Morris **112** 50
Nancy (Davenport)
  112 53
Nathaniel **111** 292
Nathaniel Harrison
  112 45
Noah **111** 293 298
Oliver Ellsworth **112** 48
Patience **112** 46
Patty B. **111** 299
Percy **111** 298
Polly **111** 298
Polly (Foote) **112** 51
Rebecca **111** 295 **112** 46
Rebecca (Foote) **111** 295
Rebecca (Taintor) **112** 46
Rhoda J. **123** 95 305
Rosanna (Coe) **112** 50
Sabra **111** 294 **112** 46
Sally **111** 298 **112** 44
Salome **111** 298

MALTBY *cont'd*
 Samuel **53** 316 **62** 147 **99**
  280 **101** 162 **111** 295
  112 46 48 50-52
 Sarah **101** 106 **108** 295
  111 292-295 **112** 50 53
  136 326
 Sarah (Coe) **112** 50
 Sarah (Davenport)
  111 292
 Sarah (Harrington)
  111 294
 Sarah (Holly) **111** 295
 Sarah Booth (Lyon)
  112 48
 Sarah Matilda **112** 46
 Seth Murray **112** 49
 Simeon **112** 45
 Sophia **111** 298
 Stephen **111** 295 **112** 49 50
 Stephen Elutherous
  112 50
 Stephen Lee **111** 297
 Subbmitta (Gibbs)
  111 297
 Submit (Taintor) **112** 47
 Susanna (Hutchnings)
  111 296
 Symon **110** 171
 Thaddeus **111** 294 295
  112 46 47
 Thankful **111** 294
 Thomas **145** 101
 Timothy **112** 50
 Wealthy W. (Chittenden)
  112 46
 William **58** 357 **60** 93 187
  62 147 **71** 6 **111** 291-
  293 296-298 **112** 50-52
  147 63
 William Davenport
  112 53
 Zaccheus **111** 294 **112** 45
  46 **132** 300
MALTEN
 Dorothy **80** 175
 Michael **80** 175
MALTER
 Katharine **109** 20
 Thomas **109** 20
MALTHOUS Malthouse
 Malthus
  —— **76** 305
 John **141** 106 107 **142** 157
 Margaret **141** 106 107
  142 156-158 160
 Margaret (Bullock)
  141 107
MALTIS
 Katharine **110** 254
MALTMAN
 Bessie Hannah **97** 295
 Candace S. (Fisher)
  97 294
 Ellen **76** 267
 Fisher James **97** 295
 Jennie B. **96** 292
 John **97** 294
MALTON John de **114** 221
MALUM John **62** 357
MALYERD Guy **116** 170

Malyns *see* Malins
MALZOR Milton **94** 276
MAMANASH
 Hannah **85** 58
MAMBRUT —— Lady **66** 18
 Sarah **66** 18
MAMINOT Hugh **139** 228
Man *see* Mann
MANACK —— Mr. **54** 166
MANAGAN Jane **65** 27
MANAHAN
 Ellen J. **67** 351
 Ellen Montgomery
  75 xc xci
 Esther **88** 78
 Hugh **90** 388
 Jane **90** 388
 Jean **90** 388
 John **67** 351
 Winnie **67** 351
Manally *see* McNally
MANARD
 Mary Jane **90** 104
MANATT
 J. Irving **57** 232
MANAY Benjamin **82** 47
 Frank Addison **82** 253
 Mary **82** 47
MANBY William **58** 70
 145 101
MANCELL Robert **81** 491
MANCER Mary E. **147** 276
MANCHESTER
 Mancester Mancrester
  —— Mr. **62** 290 **63** 54
  —— (Turner) **102** 21
 A. C. **108** 315 316
 Abby **116** 123 **118** 65
 Abby (Whitaker) **102** 21
 Abby Knight **102** 18
 Abel G. **117** 210
 Abigail **73** 288 **101** 330
  102 10 13-15 25-27
 Abigail (Brown) **102** 14
 Abigail (Knight) **102** 18
 Abigail (Redding) **102** 26
 Abigail (Richmond)
  102 10
 Abigail (Thompson)
  102 27
 Abraham **101** 330 **102** 12
  14 22 26 **116** 219 **117**
  284 **118** 309
 Abraham E. **116** 219
 Adaline **70** 121 **115** 132
 Adam **102** 21
 Adeliza **102** 26
 Albert **102** 26
 Alcy Ann **102** 18
 Alden Coe **101** 254 308
  331 **102** 10 124 **113** 78
  118 309 **148** 153 268
 Alex **101** 313
 Alexander **118** 150
 Alexander Sampson
  102 19
 Alfred **52** 153 387 **79** 345
  102 20
 Alice **102** 11 14 18 **117** 211
  118 309
 Alice (Burden) **102** 12

MANCHESTER *cont'd*
 Alice (Taber) **102** 25
 Alice D. **117** 284
 Alice Wheaton **73** xix **90**
  131 **118** 69
 Alix **101** 313
 Almira **102** 26 **117** 284
 Almy **117** 217 **144** 362
 Almy (Gray) **102** 24
 Amelia (Smith) **102** 18
 Amy **101** 310
 Amy Ann **117** 220
 Andrew **102** 26
 Andrew H. **117** 217
 Ann **87** 270 **101** 175 329
  102 19 24 **105** 75 **127** 8
  148 153
 Ann (Slocum) **102** 19
 Ann F. (Bush) **102** 22
 Ann Hovey (Bartlett)
  102 25
 Ann M. **118** 311
 Ann Maria **102** 21
 Anna **101** 175 313 330
  102 13 15 24 26 27 **118**
  309
 Anna (Cook) **102** 26
 Anna (Sowle) **102** 25
 Anna (Williston) **101**
  175 311 329
 Anna A. **117** 217
 Anna B. **118** 66 **137** 155
 Anna M. (Young)
  (Corsin) **102** 22
 Anne **101** 312 **102** 19
 Anne (Bunker) **102** 27
 Annie B. **117** 210 211
 Ansy L. **122** 289
 Archer **101** 175 311 329 330
  102 12 22 **104** 168 **131**
  54
 Armenia **81** 391
 Armida **138** 220
 Arnold **102** 17
 Arthur **101** 175 311 329
  102 12
 Asa **102** 20
 Avis **102** 20
 Baize / Bayes **101** 312 **102**
  13 **128** 49
 Barbara **102** 17 **118** 148
 Benjamin **102** 10 20 27 **118**
  150 **120** 5 **127** 150
 Benjamin F. **102** 22
 Beriah C. **116** 219
 Bersheba **101** 312
 Bertha E. **117** 210
 Betsey **110** 236 **118** 310
 Betsey (Potter) **102** 17
 Betsey C. **117** 209
 Bridget **102** 25
 Caleb **102** 28
 Calvin **116** 123
 Caroline (Pettey) **102** 25
 Caroline F. **117** 284
 Caroline L. **117** 209
 Catherine **118** 311
 Catherine L. **102** 17
 Catherine W. (Chase)
  88 27
 Charles **102** 20 22 26 **116**

MANCHESTER *cont'd*
213 219 **117** 27 294
Charles (Mrs.) **118** 152
Charles Sowle **137** 156
Charlotte (Durfee) **101**
330 **102** 22
Christopher **102** 12 **105**
215 **118** 65 310 **127** 150
137 151
Christopher H. **116** 50
Cinderella **102** 24
Clarence F. **122** 289
Clarissa **102** 22 26
Clarissa Anna (Coe)
102 24
Clark S. **118** 308 **137** 156
Clarke **102** 26
Comfort **73** 283 288 **102**
27 314 315
Comfort (Bunker) **102** 15
Comfort T. **118** 151
Content **105** 75 **148** 153
Cordelia **118** 308
Cordelia (Gifford)
137 156
Cornelia **134** 90
Cornelius **102** 25 **118** 149
Cory **102** 25
Cynthia **102** 18 **118** 309
Cynthia (Phillips) **102** 24
Cynthia (Sawyer) **102** 26
Cyrus **102** 17
Damaris **101** 310
Daniel **102** 12 17
Daniel W. **108** 315
David **101** 312 **117** 137
David Greene **79** 345
102 20
Deborah **101** 309 **102** 25
103 216 **105** 214 **118** 65
310 **127** 150 **148** 281
Deborah (Briggs) **101**
175 330 **102** 21
Deborah (Brownell)
102 12
Deborah (Cook) **102** 14
Deborah (Pearce) **102** 12
Delia W. **117** 284
Delilah (Briggs) **102** 22
Diana **126** 34
Dorcas **101** 330 **102** 13
Dorcas (Gifford) **101** 330
102 13 **129** 342
Drucilla **137** 155
Ebenezer **102** 27
Eber **101** 313
Edith **102** 21
Edward **101** 175 309 311-
313 329 330 **102** 10 12
15 16 21 314 **118** 310
127 216 **129** 342 **131** 54
Edward B. **117** 211
Electa A. **102** 23
Eli **102** 25
Elias **101** 313 **102** 16 27 28
Eliphal **102** 24 **137** 152
153 158
Eliphal (Cory) **102** 25
Eliza **102** 20 **118** 310
Eliza S. **116** 215
Elizabeth **73** 281 **77** 194 **87**

MANCHESTER *cont'd*
396 **101** 175 308-313 330
102 10-13 17 20-22 24
314 315 **104** 9 167 **105**
268 **117** 217 **122** 102
126 20 **131** 54
Elizabeth (Anthony)
102 16
Elizabeth (Bailey) **101** 311
Elizabeth (Barnes) **85** 374
Elizabeth (Britton) **102** 25
Elizabeth (Cruff) **102** 18
Elizabeth (Dolley) **102** 27
Elizabeth (Gifford) **101**
175 330 **102** 12 **131** 54
Elizabeth (Gray) **102** 24
Elizabeth (Harding)
120 5
Elizabeth (Jennings)
101 312 **102** 15
Elizabeth (Kelley) **102** 26
Elizabeth (LeValley)
102 17
Elizabeth (Macomber)
102 15
Elizabeth (Norton)
101 312
Elizabeth (Sawyer) **101**
175 330 **102** 22 **104** 167
Elizabeth (Sheldon) **102**
13 **110** 236
Elizabeth (Simmons)
102 24
Elizabeth (Wodell)
101 310
Ellen B. **117** 286
Ellery **102** 25 **116** 123
Elnathan **102** 20
Elsie **102** 18
Emily **118** 309
Enoch **102** 26
Ephraim **102** 27 **113** 78
Ephraim C. **102** 22 **118**
310 311
Esthel / Esther (Church)
101 175 330 **102** 21
Esther **102** 22 27 **118** 310
Eunice **102** 19 27 **105** 215
Eunice (Davenport)
102 19
Eunice (Hopkins) **102** 18
Eveline **102** 22
Ezekiel **102** 26
Fannie **116** 213
Fannie D. **117** 27
Fanny **116** 219
Fizeweed (Snell) **101** 175
330 **102** 12
Florinda **102** 18
Fobes **102** 22 **117** 139
Forbes W. **116** 219
Frances **116** 50
Frances (Pearce) **102** 26
Frances Amelia **117** 217
Frances Pitman **118** 309
Frank D. **116** 219
Frederic **102** 26
Frederick A. **117** 213
Freeborn **102** 19
Freelove **102** 10 13 15-17
Freelove (Gorton) **102** 10

MANCHESTER *cont'd*
Gardner F. **118** 150
George **101** 308-312 330
102 10 11 13 16 17 19 25
314 **105** 75 **116** 219 **118**
65 310 **148** 153
George C. **117** 213
George Cook **102** 19
George S. **118** 310
George W. **116** 215
117 217
George Washington
102 24
Gershom **101** 310 313
102 15 27
Gideon **101** 311 **102** 10
11 17 23 **117** 220 **128** 52
Gideon F. **117** 294
Gilbert **102** 14 24 **116** 123
127 217 **137** 152
Giles **102** 12 20 21 **122**
105 214 **125** 244
Godfrey **102** 14 24 **117** 217
127 217
Grace **102** 315 **122** 289
Grace (Farrar / Farrow)
102 14
Greene **102** 24
Hannah **79** 281 291 **79** 345
101 310 312 313 330
102 12 13 15-17 19 20 26
28 314 315 **116** 123 **117**
215 **118** 309 **122** 105
137 160
Hannah (Almy) **102** 24
Hannah (Bailey) **102** 26
Hannah (Carr) **102** 16
Hannah (Cranston)
102 20
Hannah (Cundall) **102** 11
Hannah (Ingols) **102** 25
Hannah (Potter) **102** 16
Hannah (Seabra) **102** 16
Hannah (Taber) **102** 23
Hannah (Wilcox) **102** 19
Harriet **102** 22
Harriet (Warner) **102** 17
Harriet Dana **102** 19
Harriet E. (McAlister)
102 22
Harriet K. (Fiske) **102** 18
Harriet O. **117** 217
Henrietta **102** 19
Henry **102** 17 18 **117** 210
211
Henry Alden **102** 22
Henry D. **101** 308
Hepsibah Dana
(Sampson) **102** 18
Herman W. **116** 219
Hiram Sowle **137** 156
Hope (Miller) **102** 25
Hope (Taber) **102** 22
Horace H. **117** 27
Huldah **102** 27
Humphrey **102** 25
Ichabod **101** 330 **102** 13 23
Ira **102** 16
Isaac **55** 83 **79** 345 **101**
311 313 330 **102** 11 12
14 19 20 22 25 27 **105**

MANCHESTER *cont'd*
213 214 216 **117** 292
118 148 309 **122** 102
105 **127** 143 150 **148**
281
Isaac D. **117** 284
Isabella **117** 220
Israel **102** 11 18
Israel G. **102** 18
Jabez **101** 175 330 **102** 12
117 284
Jabez B. **117** 284
Jacob **101** 175 330 **102** 12
22 25 27 **104** 167 168
Jael (Kent) **102** 17
James **102** 17 19 24 26
117 220 284 **118** 309
James Hardy **102** 22
James Harvey **102** 22
James L. **109** 270
Jane **102** 27 **118** 308
Jane (Cook) **102** 11
Jane (Gifford) **137** 156
Jane (Morse) **102** 22
Jay L. **109** 270
Jean **102** 19
Jeremiah **102** 18 21 **118** 65
131 54
Job 63 329 **101** 175 308
310 311 329 330 **102** 10
12 16 18 21 314 315 **118**
309 **128** 52 **129** 61 **131**
54
John 62 350 **73** 288 **79** 345
100 189 **101** 308-313
330 **102** 10-15 17 19-25
27 28 314 **108** 316 **110**
236 **113** 77 78 **117** 19
209 **118** 64 **122** 102 105
218 **127** 149 221 302 312
128 52 **135** 140 **137** 153
157 **148** 280
John A. **117** 213
John B. **125** 179
John E. **85** 379 **117** 286
John M. **122** 218
John S. **117** 284
Jonathan Gilbert Hadlock
73 288 **102** 27
Joseph **79** 345 **87** 77 **101**
175 311 312 330 **102** 10-
13 18 20 22-24 **110** 236
121 55 **122** 105 **127** 312
129 67 **134** 206
Joseph T. **118** 150
Judith **101** 330 **102** 13 23
131 54
Judith S. **117** 284
Julia A. (Sheldon) **102** 22
Julia Ann (Havens)
102 18
Katharine Hunter **102** 20
Lauretta **118** 150
Lavina (Briggs) **102** 12
Leander Cornelius **56**
xxxii **58** xliv **59** xliv **60**
xxxvi **61** xxxiv
Lemuel **105** 214 **118** 148
Levi **117** 219 220
Levi T. **117** 220
Lewis L. **122** 288

MANCHESTER *cont'd*
Lewis P. **122** 288
Linda **102** 27
Lois **101** 330 **102** 13 23
Loring **102** 25 **118** 151
Lottie **117** 294
Louisa M. **117** 27
Lucinda **102** 24
Lucinda (Mayo) **85** 379
Lucretia **117** 213
Lucy **102** 16 25
Lucy (Hopkins) **102** 24
Lucy (Nason) **102** 11
Lucy (Wilmot) **102** 26
Luman **113** 78
Lydia **101** 312 **102** 10-12 15
19 21 22 24 28 **113** 77 78
117 19 22 **122** 102 105
127 148 305
Lydia (Austin) **102** 27
Lydia (Chichester) **102** 28
Lydia (Crooker) **102** 22
Lydia (Dagin) **102** 20
Lydia (Earl) **137** 156
Lydia (Gifford) **131** 54
135 140
Lydia (Griswold) **113** 77
Lydia (Manchester) **101**
312 **102** 15
Lydia (Seabury) **102** 25
Lydia (Sheldon) **102** 11
Lydia B. **116** 219
Lydia Briggs **116** 125
Lydia M. **122** 288
Lydia S. **116** 219
Mabel Edith **100** 111
Mabel May **117** 284
Madeline H. **102** 19
Manton **101** 312
Marabee **101** 311
Marbrey **102** 21
Marcy **102** 17
Marettee **102** 25
Margaret **69** 189 **101** 309
310 **102** 10 **105** 75 **148**
153
Margaret (Depuy) **102** 22
Margaret (Lake) **102** 16
Margaret (McGowen)
102 20
Margaret (Wood) **101** 308
Maria **102** 21
Maria (Bishop) **102** 25
Maria E. **117** 210
Maria L. **102** 22
Mariah (Tompkins)
102 23
Marietta (Smith) **102** 25
Martha **101** 313 **102** 23
Martha (Allen) **102** 27
Martha (Taber) **102** 23
Martha Jane (McClane)
102 20
Mary **73** 281 286 288 **77**
194 **88** 26 **101** 308-313
330 **102** 10-13 15-17 19
23 24 27 28 314 **105** 75
115 173 **116** 123 **117** 22
213 292 294 **118** 64 148
122 102 **125** 178 **127**
149 **137** 180 **148** 153

MANCHESTER *cont'd*
Mary (Arnold) **102** 18
Mary (Bailey) **102** 15
Mary (Brownell) **101** 311
Mary (Browning) **101** 308
329 **102** 314
Mary (Cook) **101** 309
102 314 **103** 216
Mary (Farron) **101** 313
Mary (Hadlock) **102** 27
Mary (Hannaford) **102** 27
Mary (Irish) **101** 330
102 13
Mary (Jenckes) **102** 24
Mary (Manchester)
102 314
Mary (Nason) **102** 27
Mary (Pottle) **102** 16
Mary (Ricker) **102** 26
Mary (Roberts) **102** 13
Mary (Slocum) **102** 13
Mary (Smith) **101** 309
Mary (Whitman) **102** 17
Mary A. **117** 27 287
Mary A. (Bradish) **102** 25
Mary Ann **53** 461 **102** 17
20 27 **122** 295
Mary C. **117** 213
Mary E. **117** 294
Mary Eliza **117** 213
Mary J. **117** 217
Mary Jane **117** 284
Matthew **65** 149 **101** 311
102 10-12 16 **118** 65 310
128 52
May **88** 26
Mehitable **122** 295
Mehitable (Albro) **102** 19
Mehitable (Coggeshall)
102 20
Mehitable (Eddy) **102** 14
Mercy **102** 10 16 19
Mercy (Burlingame)
101 311
Mercy (Coggeshall)
102 19
Mercy (Durfee) **102** 24
137 152
Mercy (Remington)
102 18
Meribah **102** 27
Minerva (King) **102** 22
Miriam **131** 214
Moses **85** 374
Nabby **102** 18 27
Nabby (Knight) **102** 18
Nahum **102** 27
Nancy **102** 11 25 **118** 310
137 157
Nathaniel **101** 309 312
102 13 24 **127** 307 **129**
380
Nehemiah K. **102** 18
Niles **102** 16
Ober **101** 313
Olive **113** 78
Oliver **117** 22
Orpha (Slocum) **102** 24
Otis **102** 25
Owen C. **116** 219
Pamelia **122** 218

MANCHESTER *cont'd*
Pardon **102** 11 **105** 217
 110 236 **118** 66
Patience **102** 28
Patience (Boyce) **102** 28
Peace **102** 22
Peleg **102** 11 19 **116** 50 123
 118 64 **127** 217
Peter **102** 20 28 **117** 294
Phebe **73** 285 **87** 326 **101**
 330 **102** 10-14 17 19 20
 24 26 28 **116** 219 **117**
 284 **118** 65 310 **131** 54
Phebe (Fenner) **102** 16
Phebe (Gray) **101** 312
Phebe (Hill) **102** 17
Phebe (Manchester)
 102 12
Phebe (Randall) **102** 24
Phebe (Stedman) **101** 330
 102 23 **108** 316
Phebe (Truman) **102** 22
Phebe A. **117** 284
Phebe Amanda **77** 183
Phebe C. **118** 309
Phebe Hannah
 (Doddridge) **102** 20
Phebe Hannah (Taylor)
 102 20
Phillp **101** 312 **102** 11 14
 18 25 **105** 214 216 **118**
 65 310 **127** 148
Polly **102** 23 24
Priscilla **56** 398 **101** 312
 330 **102** 13 14 **119** 266
Priscilla (Taber) **101** 330
 102 22
Rachel **102** 26
Rachel G. **117** 286
Rebecca **101** 308 310 311
 102 21 **105** 214 **127** 216
Rebecca (Bartlett) **102** 21
Rebecca (Batty) **102** 20
Rebecca (Cook) **102** 14
Rebecca (Stafford) **102** 18
Rhoda **120** 10 **131** 54
 137 157
Rhoda (Sanford) (Diman)
 120 5 10
Rhoda M. **116** 219
Rhody **102** 14
Richmond **118** 309
Rita C. **101** 308 **102** 10
Robert **102** 25
Roby **131** 297
Roland **117** 220
Ruth **101** 175 310 311 329
 102 19 20 25 26 213 **106**
 223 **118** 149 **125** 181
 135 140
Ruth (Kilborn) **102** 27
Ruth (Remington) **102** 18
Ruth (Sisson) **102** 19
Ruth B. **118** 309
S. **76** 52
Saba (Lincoln) (Peck)
 120 5
Sally **124** 160
Sally (Fish) **102** 19
Sally (Ralph) **102** 18
Sally (Wells) **102** 22

MANCHESTER *cont'd*
Samuel **102** 12 20 22 24
 116 123 122 105 295
Samuel G. **117** 217
Samuel S. **117** 211
Sarah **79** 345 **87** 261 **88** 13
 101 309 311 **102** 10 11
 14 16-20 23 25 28 **105** 75
 118 150 319 **148** 153
Sarah (Brown) **102** 21
 125 244 245 **126** 22
Sarah (Cornell) **102** 11
Sarah (Durfee) **102** 23
Sarah (Earl) **101** 312 313
Sarah (Seabury) **102** 21
Sarah (Smith) **102** 26
Sarah (Spink) **102** 17
Sarah (Stone) **102** 16
Sarah (Wood) **102** 12
Sarah A. (Scaritt) **102** 25
Sarah B. **116** 219
Sarah B. (Baker) **102** 20
 125 179
Sarah Brightman **102** 22
 120 4
Sarah Church (Bailey)
 102 24
Sarah L. **117** 27
Seabury **118** 309 **120** 5 10
 129 381
Seafair (Mayberry) **102** 14
Sena (Shaw) **113** 78
Shadrach **101** 330 **102** 13
 24
Sibyl D. **102** 22
Silas H. **125** 244
Simeon **101** 331 **102** 13 22
 117 19 27
Simon **102** 21
Sophia **116** 123
Stephen **73** 288 **101** 308
 310 311 313 **102** 14-16
 18 19 27 28 314 **127** 216
 134 90 **137** 160
Susan **102** 17 22
Susan (Harris) **102** 17
Susan A. **117** 210 217
Susan F. **117** 220
Susanna **101** 175 310 330
 102 12 17 19 21 25 **104**
 168
Susanna (Eldridge)
 102 23
Susanna (Hinkenbotham)
 102 16
Tabitha (Fenner) **102** 18
Thaddeus **102** 14
Thankful **101** 331 **102** 13
 27
Thankful (Stevens)
 102 25
Theodore J. **117** 213 217
Thomas **73** 281 288 290
 291 **101** 175 254 308-312
 329 330 **102** 10-17 19 26
 27 314 **105** 75 **118** 309
 311 **122** 102 105 **125**
 245 **127** 146 216 **129** 61
 64 342 **136** 216
Thomas F. **118** 311
Thomas I. **125** 244

MANCHESTER *cont'd*
Thomas J. **126** 22
Thomas Jefferson **102** 21
Thomas W. **116** 215
Timothy **101** 312
Ursula **117** 19
Victoria **116** 123
Wanton **102** 24 **115** 173
 117 217 **118** 150
Wealthy **102** 24
Willard **102** 25
William **61** 345 **77** 194
 88 27 **101** 175 308-310
 312 313 330 331 **102** 10-
 13 15-19 21-23 26-28 314
 315 **103** 216 **104** 9 **105**
 214 268 **122** 105 **127**
 148 **129** 61 **137** 153
William C. **102** 17
William Cook **102** 25 26
William K. **102** 18
William L. **118** 151
William Leonard (Mrs.)
 85 196
William Manton **102** 14
William W. **116** 219
Zebedee **101** 175 312 330
 102 12 21 314 315 **105**
 214 **131** 54
Zilpha **102** 18 21 **113** 77 78
Zilpha (Woodman) **101**
 175 330 **102** 21
MANDELL Mandall
 Mandel - *see also*
 Mendall
Abigail **56** 79 **58** 55
Abijah **57** 411
Anna **57** 410
Anna I. (Clark) **89** 296
Anna J. **89** 297
Caroline Foster **93** 256
Eliza (Jones) **125** 289
Francis **57** 413
Henry **132** 76
Henry Russell **62** 113
Luthera **56** 79
M. J. **93** 256
Marian **96** 160
Marie Louise **93** 256
Mason **56** 79
Mercy **57** 414
Moses **56** 79 **61** 324 **89** 296
 297
Noah **57** 410-414 **58** 55
Sidney **125** 289
Sophia Williams
 (Trumbull) **132** 76
Susan **115** 285
MANDERS Basil **73** 140
 Thomas **65** 118
MANDERSON
 Charles F. **68** 25
MANDEVILLE Mandevile
 —— **55** 229
 — Miss **63** 23
Arnulf de **97** 243
Bernard **131** 175 176
Eliza **118** 143
Geoffrey de **82** 146 **95** 395
 96 37 **97** 241 **106** 276
 121 233

MANDEVILLE *cont'd*
John **121** 231
Roger de **122** 267 272
William de **79** 376
139 228
MANDIGO Julie **69** 261
Phebe **69** 261
MANDIN James **91** 329
MANDLEY Daniel **51** 159
MANDYE William **51** 349
MANEN James **82** 27
Thomas **82** 27
MANENT Julia **119** 279
122 310
MANES Polly **87** 122
MANESS
George Raymond
104 144
MANESTY Francis **51** 254
MANEY Morris **64** 320
W. **91** 329
MANFORD Mae **81** 343
MANGAM
William D. **95** 399
MANGAN John Joseph
60 320 **61** xxxiv
MANGANO Antonio (Mrs.)
85 196
MANGER Moses **73** 269
MANGIER Green **66** 37
MANGOLD Anna **92** 208
MANGRUM
Charles William **78** 42
Hiram L. **106** 70
Jane **78** 42
Martha **106** 70
Nancy (Tunnell) **106** 70
Rhoda Jeannette **78** 42
MANGUM
Annie Laura **93** 137
Eleanor **73** 146
George Addison **108** 135
Henry **73** 222
James **73** 263
John **73** 146
Josias G. **73** 230
Levi **73** 262
Lucinda **113** 231
Margaret **73** 273
Mary **73** 151
Rachel **73** 265
Sarah **73** 270
Willie P. **55** 353
Zachariah **73** 273
MANGUS J. **91** 329
MANIERRE Julie Edson
103 318 **120** 147
Louis **103** 318
MANIFORD
Henry **61** 279
John **68** 178
MANILUS ——— **58** 221
James **60** 164
MANIM — Mrs. **103** 302
MANIMON
James W. **74** 318
Jemima **74** 318
William **74** 318
Maning *see* Manning
MANIS Cuff **55** 68
MANISTIE John **53** 20

MANK Augusta (Webster)
100 58
Edith Webster **84** 340 **85**
190 196 **87** 207 **97** 394
100 44 58 115
Elizabeth **100** 58
Georgianna (Wells)
100 58
Helen G. **100** 58
Herbert Gardner **100** 58
Isaac **100** 58
Jacob Gardner **100** 58
Mary (Havener) **100** 58
Mary Elizabeth (Gross)
100 58
Paul **100** 58
Peter **100** 58
Valentine **100** 58
MANLEY Manly
——— **67** 245
— Capt. **53** 430 **70** 187
71 164 **85** 27 28 118 119
122
— Commodore **85** 130
145 56
— Mr. **71** 76
Abigail **116** 281 282
Abigail (Hinsdale)
116 282
Adin **133** 233
Allen **116** 281 282
Allin **71** 163
Almira **116** 282
Amasa **58** 255
Ann Elizabeth **77** 224
Anna (Briggs) **126** 36
Anna (Perkins) **120** 257
Annis **56** 187
Anthony **94** 257
Asa **72** 35
Atalina **101** 256
Betsey **58** 255 **125** 293
Betty (Phillips) **133** 322
Calvin **72** 37
Caroline **101** 256
Cecily (Pargiter) **98** 36
Charles **83** 342 **91** 329
Chatman **77** 224
Clarissa **77** 224
Cordelia Maria
(Ingerson) **109** 233
Daniel **72** 38 **74** lxviii
Daniel W. **85** 381
David **72** 38
Ebenezer **71** 77 80 162-
164 166 272 280 306 **116**
282 283 **122** 281
Edward **94** 257 **98** 36
Eleazer **111** 131
Eliza **101** 256
Eliza Jane **77** 224
Elizabeth **73** 146
Elizabeth M. (Argent)
111 137
Elizur Newell **109** 233
Emily C. **69** 168
Emma (Loring) **83** 342
Eunice **58** 255
Flavel **72** 37
Frances J. **84** 30
Friswith **78** 411

MANLEY *cont'd*
George **71** 78 157 278 **72**
30 35 37 38
Hannah **58** 255 **60** 341 **100**
139 142 **101** 277
Hannah V. **76** 277
Harmon H. **116** 282 283
Henry **68** xxxiv **74**
xxxviii lxviii lxix **75** 82
Henry S. **120** 155
Hiram **76** 50
Horace **87** 321
Horace S. **116** 282 283
Howard **133** 233
Howard Tisdale **74** lxix
Ira **56** 187
Iza Annette **74** lxviii
J. M. **105** 15
James **58** 255
James H. **116** 282 283
Jane Sybilline **74** lviii
Jesse **58** 255
Joan **98** 36
John **58** 255 **71** 289 **72** 38
73 147 **100** 139 142 **101**
277 **130** 170 **131** 45 **137**
122
Laura **110** 65
Laura Weston **77** 224
Laurence Bradford
74 lxix
Lavina **111** 137
Lawrence **98** 36
Lorin **101** 256
Luke **58** 255
Lydia **58** 255
Marcia (Chase) **87** 320
Marcie (Gillet) **116** 282
Margaret **71** 279
Margaret P. (Rich) **85** 381
Marilla **116** 282
Martha C. **84** 302
Martha Hinsdale **116**
281 282
Martin **72** 38
Mary **71** 78 158 278 279
304 **76** 277 **116** 282
Mary (Wadleigh) **92** 310
Mary Esther **109** 233
Mercy **58** 255 **71** 77 80
280 282
Miriam (Dewing)
133 233
Molly **71** 85 309
N. V. **69** 168
Nathaniel **58** 255
Obed **133** 322
Olive **120** 257
Paley **116** 282
Pamela **72** 99 169
Pearlley **72** 38
Permena **71** 272
Phebe (Calkins) **116** 282
Polly **58** 255 **71** 162 **93** 182
116 282 283
Rebecca **119** 12
Reuben **75** 151
Russell **71** 164 **72** 169
116 282
Ruth **71** 78 278 **72** 37
Sally **58** 255 **60** 371

MANLEY *cont'd*
Salmon **74** xlviii
Samuel **125** 35
Sarah **111** 131
Seth **58** 142 **133** 322
Shubael **72** 30
Susan Elizabeth **74** lxix
Sylvester **60** 371 **120** 257
Thankful **75** 151
Thomas **59** 21 **73** 145
   74 lxviii
Verneria (Webster)
   116 282
William **55** 141 **58** 255
   63 82 83 130 131 **65** 32
   71 78 84 85 157 158 166
   278 300 304 309 **72** 37
   38 170 171 **73** 150 **74**
   lxviii 82 **92** 310 311 **98**
   171 172 **116** 282
William Burton **77** 224
William H. **111** 137
   116 283
William Lewis **116** 282
   283
MANLOVE George **106** 42
MANLUFMORE
Mary **63** 344
Manly *see* Manley
MANN Man
  — Capt. **65** 360
  — Dea. **65** 365
  — Lieut. **65** 249
  — Mr. **56** 384 **57** 329
   69 102
  — Mrs. **56** 384
  — Widow **63** 229 **65** 365
A. C. **143** 18
Aaron **104** 118
Abby (Martin) **125** 180
Abiathar **52** 409 **54** 359
Abigail **55** 264 **61** 395 **62**
   283 384 **64** 104 **99** 115
   125 235 **134** 144 **142**
   141
Abigail (Belknap) **125** 235
Abigail (Gill) **134** 144
Abigail E. **76** 9
Abijah **57** 145
Albert W. **63** 212
Alexander **63** 14
Alfred Allen **92** 378
Alice **59** 87 157 158 284 290
   64 103 **124** 250 253
Alice (Fessenden) **99** 115
Alice (Whitney) **126** 126
Alicia Augusta **139** 218
Alrick H. **126** 102
Amar **133** 155
Amherst **142** 142
Amy (Brayton) **126** 220
Andrew **148** 47 58
Ann **54** 177 **58** 312 **59** 65
   127 54
Anna **55** 263 **80** 330 **81** 306
   142 142
Anne **60** 338 **65** 354
   144 200
Anne (Berry) **132** 326
Anne (Post) **146** 360
Annis **124** 253

MANN *cont'd*
Ariel **138** 117
Asa **133** 155 **146** 348
Asal **93** 348
Augusta S. **85** 380
Avery **124** 253
Azubah **127** 178 179
Azubah (Nichols) **127** 179
B. Pickman **51** 305 511
Bathsheba **121** 225 226
Bela **60** 338
Benjamin **52** 310 408 409
   411 412 414 418 420 **54**
   81 258 **56** 348 **57** 143 **58**
   380 **61** 373 **92** 266 **110**
   150 **134** 144
Benjamin Percy **84** 234
   85 196
Beriah **92** 265 **130** 208
Bethiah **63** 141
Betsey **63** 156 **81** 67 **94** 286
   116 119
Betsey (Burrows) **116** 119
Betsey G. (Eddy) **88** 337
Bette **54** 81
Bezaleel **92** 266
Calvin **116** 114
Caroline 40 **92** 40
Caroline E. **88** 339
Caroline Elizabeth **56** lxv
Carrie Wildes **64** 105
Catherine **93** 367
Catherine (Vernon)
   125 237
Catherine Cleek **113** 321
Charles **54** 201 **56** 253
   79 151
Charles A. **79** 269
Charles E. **51** 101
Charles Edward **54** xxxvi
   55 xxxv **65** xxxiii 103
   188 303 304 384 **66**
   xlviii 82 **67** viii xxi 87
   303 **68** vi xxx **69** vi **70**
   vi **71** vi **72** vi **73** vi 78
   160 **74** vi **75** vi **78** 216
   80 329-331 **82** 372
Charles Henry **148** 178
Charles Hooper Trask
   51 243
Charles W. **51** 376
Charlotte **92** 378 **103** 144
Charlotte Billings **92** 378
   115 78
Christopher **124** 250 253
Clarissa **54** 259
Conklin **97** 344 **109** 130
   115 192 **145** 338
Cylinda **88** 284
Cynthia **55** 399 **57** 382
Cyrus **113** 34
Daniel **56** 92 **62** 283 **87**
   123 **105** 279 **133** 155
   136 346 **146** 348
Daniel Fisher **86** 229
David **57** 288 **99** 115 116
   105 279 **127** 204 **130**
   210 **141** 187 193 197 200
   332 333 335 340 342 345-
   347 349 350 353 534 **142**
   58 60 61 63 66 81 130

MANN *cont'd*
   142 **143** 11 12
David Whitcher **87** 288
Deborah **60** 63 **125** 234
   235 **136** 134
Deborah (Dyer) **123** 320
   139 307
Dorothea Lawrence **80**
   331 **103** 119
Dorothy **102** 122
Ebenezer **56** 144 **57** 153 **92**
   265 **132** 326 **142** 80
Ebenezer C. **88** 337
Ebenezer Corey **57** 374
Edith Luella **76** 9
Edmund **84** 152
Edward **54** 96 **64** 139 **101**
   101 136 346
Edward I. **125** 180
Edward J. **125** 237
Eleanor **125** 220
Electa T. **115** 199
Elijah **57** 410-412 **58** 55 56
   58
Elisha **57** 396 **98** 104 **141**
   337 342 343
Elisha Burrows **116** 119
Eliza (Tupper) **99** 305
Eliza Jane **86** 229 **136** 236
Elizabeth **54** 96 258 **60** 42
   71 **63** 264 65 285 **79** 151
   92 266 **97** 116 **107** 226
   116 114 **125** 216 235
   136 79 **148** 47
Elizabeth (Dyer) **123** 320
Elizabeth (McLeod)
   127 204
Elizabeth (Southworth)
   87 287
Elizabeth Adelia **76** 9
Elizabeth Helen **90** 106
Elizabeth Jenkins Clapp
   (Holton) **87** 288
Elly **53** 34
Elvira **96** 79
Emma **88** 285
Ensign **64** 103 104 **121** 247
   126 126
Ephraim **61** 42 **68** 225
   226 229
Ernest Withington **76** 9
Esther **55** 225 **66** 90 **80** 330
   81 188 **92** 266 **119** 240
   133 155 **142** 131
Esther (Ware) **130** 208
Esther Eliza **67** lvi
Eunice 105 **52** 414 **53** 442
   57 188 379 **92** 105 **99**
   115
F. W. **54** 127
Fanny **125** 293
Fisher **57** 145 **133** 155
Floyd **110** 148
Frances (Hopkins) **95** 287
Franklin **136** 346
Frederick **146** 360
George **56** 383 **64** 21
George Henry **67** lvi
George Hewins **67** lvi
George Sumner **51** 229
   52 377 **54** xxii xxiv 220

MANN *cont'd*
221 **55** xiii xxix 107 220
57 109 **58** lii **59** xli **60**
vii 207 **61** vii xix xxv
xxxiii **62** vii xxv 198
215 389 **63** vii **64** xvii
xliii lxx 103-105 183 184
279 **65** xvii 83 97 **92**
265 **93** 74 **142** 142 **144**
200
Georgianna Holton
87 288
Gertrude Edith **83** 217
84 190
Gertrude Whitney **64** 105
65 xxxiv **91** 141
Gideon **63** 156
Grace **85** 197
Hannah **55** 397 **56** 38 **58**
162 **66** 90 **80** 330 **83** 48
86 295 **88** 284 **92** 265
120 5 8 10 **126** 126 **133**
155
Hannah (Carter) **120** 5 10
Hannah (Moody) **87** 287
Hannah (Whitcher)
87 287
Harriet **92** 378
Harvey **62** 283
Helen **116** 119
Helen R. **109** 158
Henry **84** 72
Henry N. **83** 435 **84** 20
Henry Sanford (Mrs.)
75 xxvi 76
Hepzibah **107** 36
Herman **62** 283 **92** 378
136 346
Hezekiah **61** 395 **104** 242
115 293
Hollis **57** 379
Horace **51** 306 **53** 33 34
54 lxxxii **56** 176 **61** 315
64 105 **93** 348 **110** 47
279
Horatio L. **85** 409
Howard **82** 490
Howard Walter **77** 237
78 205
Ichabod **61** 395
Isabel **124** 253
Isabella Belcher
(Shapleigh) **95** 271
Israel **128** 58
Jabez **53** 34
Jacob **87** 327 **99** 115 116
141 353 **142** 75 76
James **55** 263 **56** 148 **57**
255 257 **59** 284 **65** 21
356 **73** 196 **80** 330 **98**
106 **117** 319 **142** 69 75
144 200 **148** 178
James Austin **87** 287
James Otis **80** 329 330
James Whitcher **87** 288
Janet **73** 228
Jedediah **56** 383
Jemima **58** 20 **80** 330
Jemima (Farrington)
130 210
Jeremiah **54** 201 **141** 335

MANN *cont'd*
353 **143** 14
Jerusha **57** 288
Jho. **141** 197
Joanna **126** 220
Joel **125** 237
Joel Richards **57** 373
Johab **129** 383
John **56** lxv **57** 257 **58** 20
58 **59** 87 157 158 **63** 351
67 169 **80** 330 **86** 121
87 287 **102** 185 **104** 118
124 253 **125** 235 **127** 54
212 **145** 115 116 **146**
348
John C. **90** 42
John Rogers **136** 79
Jonathan **92** 266
Joseph **55** 436 **56** 275 **59**
193 **60** 70 **76** 9 **93** 124
94 156 160 **99** 115 **104**
24 **125** 235 **136** 78
Josiah **57** 183 **60** 63-65 **92**
265 **93** 74
Judith **53** 163
Julie Edson (Manierre)
101 124 **103** 318 **104** 78
140 **105** 124
Katie **56** lxv
Keziah **53** 34
Lawrence Bacon **80** 331
Leonard **61** 395 **88** 330
Lester W. **76** 9
Levi **140** 248
Lilian **109** 129
Lishua **125** 235
Lizzie Cass **67** lvi
Llewellyn M. **95** 271
Lois **87** 64
Lois E. **109** 80
Lois Elizabeth **100** 112
Lois F. **148** 178
Lorena **104** 213
Louisa **77** 187
Lucinda **136** 270
Lucius **76** 9
Lucy **55** 399
Lurana (Mayhew) **99** 115
116
Luther **116** 119
Lydia **56** 92 **62** 283
Lydia (Porter) **104** 118
Lydia A. **64** 105
Lydia Sophia **69** lxvii
Mabel Maria **87** 288
Maley **115** 293
Margaret **63** 93 **78** 302
Margaret (Peters) **87** 287
104 118
Margaret (Stone) **95** 180
Margaret (Tufts) **83** 394
Maria Jane **93** 348
Maria Sophia **125** 290
Martha **57** 401 **58** 390 **59**
157 **94** 156
Martha H. (Rich) **88** 330
Mary **51** 45 **52** 412 **55** 260
56 141 **57** 150 **59** 158
289 **60** 42 63 64 70 **63**
151 **67** lvi **68** 226 **75**
254 **80** 330 **90** 48 **93** 348

MANN *cont'd*
95 287 **104** 24 **108** 185
116 120 **133** 155
Mary (Barker) **125** 103
Mary (Blake) **99** 115
Mary (Budge) **101** 101
Mary (Collis) **86** 229
Mary (Howe) **87** 287
Mary (McCleland) **126** 80
Mary (Root) **87** 287
Mary (Webster) **142** 268
Mary Ann **57** 396 **111** 52
Mary E. **79** 269
Mary Ella **67** lvi
Mary Esther **90** 44
Mary Milnor **80** 331
Mary Nash **75** xxvi
Mary Sanderson **64** 105
Matthew **64** 192 **87** 287
Maude **124** 250 253
Mehitable **56** 36
Mercy **56** 373 **60** 70 **92** 265
133 155 157
Mercy (Finney) **104** 24
Mercy (Fisher) **133** 155
Michael **116** 84 **130** 213
Milly **62** 283
Minna S. (Steffens) **83**
435 **84** 20
Molly (Whiting) **142** 142
Morris T. **101** 80
Morris Townsend
101 124
Moses **55** 266 **57** 373 374
Moses Whitcher **64**
xxxiii 192 283 **87** 287
296 **88** 175
Nabby **65** 366
Nancy **57** 373 **99** 115 **116**
114 **127** 212 **141** 355
Nancy (Oldman) **132** 243
Nathan **51** 306 307 **53** 163
57 412
Nathaniel **55** 260 **56** 38
141 144 **57** 145 146 149
150 153 **80** 427 **87** 287
93 74 **106** 19 **125** 235
146 348
Nicholas **57** 218
Noah **120** 5 10
Noah C. **116** 114
O. **105** 210
Obadiah **133** 155
Olive **55** 394 **75** 153
Olive (Ware) **143** 14 16
Patience (Adams) **133** 155
Patty **62** 283
Pelatiah **80** 330 **117** 319
130 210 **141** 191 **142**
142
Peleg **83** 394
Peter **65** 165
Phebe **56** 148 **57** 255
Phebe (Parkhurst)
104 118
Phebe L. **93** 348
Philip **54** 177 **59** 65
Pliny **93** 273
Polly **99** 115
Polly (Whiting) **142** 142
Priscilla **62** 383 **143** 138

MANN *cont'd*
144 198 200 201
Priscilla (Grice) 144 200
Provided 115 293
Rachel 52 310 408 412 414
418 420 80 427 109 194
Ralph 57 188 125 103
Ralph H. 111 155 114 149
Rebacca 119 93
Rebecca 55 266 397 57 410
91 239 119 93
Rhoda 67 lvi 83 485 100
250 103 224 128 175
Richard 64 103 184 87 287
92 265 100 292 141 330
331 340 352 142 142
Robert 55 394 98 106 107
179 112 250
Robert Colgate Vernon
(Mrs.) 95 180
Robert Neville 113 321
Royal 146 348
Ruby Grace 87 288
Sabin 130 213
Sage 90 47
Sally 99 115
Sally (Ingraham) 104 118
Sally (Melvin) 104 118
Samuel 51 306 307 57 146
61 305 80 330 87 207
92 265 117 16 127 204
130 208 132 324 133
155 141 143 142 142
Samuel Chandler 136 346
Samuel Vernon 125 180
Sarah 54 96 61 345 62 283
68 225 127 204 134 144
136 79 346 141 355
Sarah (Luce) 132 324
Sarah (Rigets?) 136 78
Sarah (Silvester) 86 121
Sarah (Tibbetts) (Osgood)
99 115
Sarah A. (Bowdoin)
85 409
Sarah Lydia 76 9
Sarah Marshall 80 329 330
Seabury 52 418
Seth 58 389 60 42 123 320
Sherod 60 40
Shuah M. 132 243
Solomon 104 118
Sophia 126 122
Statira 99 324
Stephen 105 277
Sukey 141 355
Susan 79 54 82 490 83 485
Susan Alzea 64 105
Susan Josephine 82 490
Susan Prudence 89 61
Susanna 57 411 60 65
80 183
Sylvia 116 114
Sylvia L. (Hedge) 90 42
Tamzin (Chase) 87 327
Theodore 62 283 141 201
Theodosia 52 411
Thomas 51 306 307 57 183
62 231 64 103 66 90 84
308 97 319 326 99 94 99
108 109 115 121 111

MANN *cont'd*
139 49 143 14 146 348
Thomas C. 117 232
Timothy M. 99 305
Vashti 133 155
Verona D. 79 137
Walter A. 76 9
Walter Scott (Mrs.)
105 128
Will 142 268
William 51 306 307 58 162
64 103 104 80 329 84 72
92 378 95 287 116 119
124 253 141 192 142
142
William Brayton (Mrs.)
120 147
William Frost 108 318
William Haynes 92 378
William Leake 108 318
William Marion 125 262
William R. 57 397
William Rufus 67 xliii lvi
William S. 77 187
William T. 78 407 91 329
William Willard 55 399
57 382
Yelverton 125 235
Zerviah 56 253
Zipporah 55 393 92 265
Zoa 125 180
MANNEN Mary 77 157
MANNERING —— 69 380
Elizabeth 66 142 304
John 66 170
Mary 141 105
Richard 141 105
Thomas 66 304
MANNERS
— Baron 136 335
Anne (St. Leger) 148 140
George 148 140
Hannah 61 203 311
John 80 385
Katharine 148 140
MANNERY
Hannah 59 319
Solomon 59 319
MANNET George 95 30
Hannah A. (Moulton)
95 30
MANNEY Manny Many
Daniel 58 204
Dorothy Jones 116 82
Frank Addison 58 204
83 233
Hugh 58 204
Jean 116 82
Robert 58 204
Wallace T. (Mrs.) 116 82
MANNING Maning
Mannin Manninge
Mannings Mannyng
Mannynge
—— 80 360
— Capt. 55 45
— Mr. 60 289
— Rev. Mr. 62 276
Aaron B. 101 210
Abby 78 97
Abby F. 78 98

MANNING *cont'd*
Abby Hone 85 196
Abial / Abiel (Wight) 92
194 106 147
Abiel C. 59 xcviii
Abigail 69 156 87 255
93 296
Abigail (Alden) 100 183
137 79
Abigail (Maverick)
96 234
Abigail (Watson) 93 296
Adah A. 130 53
Agnes 51 389-391 395-
399 404
Alice 51 397
Alice Lee 103 74
Alice S. 83 25 26
Alice Sherburn 82 47
Andrew 72 114 115
Andrew H. L. 86 382
Ann 69 156 75 251 76 228
90 110 148 142
Ann (Parker) 96 234
148 142
Anna 51 389 56 207 71 203
Anna Cora 79 142
Anna Jane 99 184
Anne 51 389 391-396 401-
404 66 55 94 334 142
257 146 378
Anne (Jackson) 124 6
Anne (Willoughby)
94 334
Anne M. 69 256
Annie F. 78 98
Annis 73 254
Anstice 56 326 78 97
Anstice (Calley) 111 317
Asahel 69 144
Asenath 68 335
Asenath (Beaman)
100 183
Barbara 51 402
Bartholomew 51 389 398
Benjamin 65 54
Benjamin F. 59 xcviii
Betsey 55 373 63 172 83 14
88 330
Betsey (Tower) 100 183
Bridget 51 389 394
Caleb 140 68
Calvin 63 370
Caroline 72 114
Caroline Lord 88 186
Catherine 51 389 108 217
Catherine (Clarkson)
84 102
Catherine (Innes) 143 335
Charles 51 389 92 106
106 147 148
Charlotte Barrett 78 98
Charlotte C. 93 296
Christiana 97 278
Christiana (Laing) 84 102
Cicely 51 394 403 142 262
Clarissa Louisa 68 199
Cook 71 202
Cora May 69 144
Cornelia Hull 82 499
Daniel 55 347 78 178

MANNING *cont'd*
90 357
David **120** 113 **124** 6
  144 153
Dennis **143** 335
Dinah **143** 335
Doris Way **81** 364 **82** 237
Dorothy **51** 389 390 394
  396 406 **106** 147
Durand S. **68** 335
Earl G. **77** 162
Ebenezer **125** 23
Edith O. **81** 259
Edmond **121** 118
Edmund **51** 394 406
Edward **51** 389 390 392
  397 399-404 406 **63** 34
  70 59 **94** 259 334 **98** 39
  140 327 **143** 142 143
  147 148
Edward A. (Mrs.) **82** 499
Edward S. **83** 25 27 35
Edward Sherburn **82** 47
Edwin B. **81** 259
Eleanor **51** 394 402
Eleazer **98** 302
Elizabeth **51** 389-391 393-
  399 402 406 **53** 462 **56**
  207 **72** 115 **78** 97 **82** 47
  90 42 **93** 324 **97** 278
  106 147 **113** 73 **125** 214
  293 **143** 143 147 148
Elizabeth (Ellis) **120** 113
  122 256
Elizabeth (Fitz Randolph)
  84 102 **97** 280
Elizabeth (Stearns)
  106 147
Elizabeth Bennet **82** 47
Elizabeth L. **79** 45
Elizabeth Lucy **106** 141
Ellen **51** 401
Ellen Gordon (Whittier)
  89 386
Emma **51** 390
Ephraim **73** 254 **97** 280
Ephraim Brackett **93** 296
Esther **57** 111
Eunice **118** 170
Eylmer **51** 389
F. C. **54** lxi
Fortune Mildred **51** 389
  404 405
Frances **90** 385 386
Francis **51** 389 397
Francis Cogswell **78** 97
Francis Henry **77** xxxvii
  78 97 98
Frederick **71** 202 203
Frederick Johnson (Mrs.)
  84 248
George **51** 389-391 394 399
  401 405 406 **60** 39 **61** 42
  64 8 **68** 320 **75** 251 **92**
  106 **93** 163 164
George L. **68** 335
George Washington
  100 183
Gertrude (Devol) **111** 317
Gurdon **72** 114 115
Hannah **59** 411 **61** 394 **78**

MANNING *cont'd*
307 **90** 167 **93** 163 **97**
264 **100** 183 **107** 219
  135 79 **137** 79
Hannah (Gorham)
  143 335
Harriet Avis **106** 147 148
Harry **51** 390 391 393-396
Helen Herron (Taft)
  84 248
Henrietta Hamblin (Pratt)
  92 195
Henry **51** 389 397 399 400
  402 404-406 418 419 **88**
  186 **92** 106 **143** 143 147
  148
Henry L. **79** 142
Hepzibah (Andrews) **84**
  102 **97** 278
Hugh **51** 389 390 393 395
  397 400 403-405
Ignatius **73** 269
Isaac **84** 102 **107** 257
J. **54** lxi
Jacob **51** 389 398 **59** xcvii
  84 102 **90** 110 **92** 194
  195
Jacob Warren **55** 353 **56**
  xxx **59** xxvi lvi xcvii
  xcviii **92** 194 915
James **51** 383 385-397 **65**
  149 **84** 102 **94** 275 **97**
  278 **145** 249
James M. **128** 96
Jane **51** 394
Jane M. **69** 144
Jannet **88** 351
Jared **71** 202
Jean **56** 405
Jeffrey **84** 102 **97** 278
Jeremiah **97** 336
Jeremy **51** 396 397 400
  402 403
Jessie A. **98** 178
Jessie Ruth **107** 134
Joan **51** 389 394 399
  94 324 334
Joanna **51** 389 **107** 257
Joanna (Whittemore)
  (Bodge) (Webber) **106**
  234 **107** 257
Jocosa **51** 389
Joel **100** 183
John **51** 389 390 393-397
  399-406 **53** 303 **57** 110
  111 **60** 289 **61** 237 **69**
  156 **71** 202 282 **73** 254
  74 63 **78** 97 **82** 321 **84**
  102 **86** 383 **96** 234 **100**
  183 **106** 147 **111** 317
  140 107 **143** 31 147
John Henry **63** 394
John W. **68** 335
Joie **70** 358
Jonas **61** 237
Jonathan **83** 167
Joseph **78** 97 309 **88** 351
  91 93 **99** 79 **106** 148
  114 104 **116** 111
Joseph C. **120** 20
Josiah **71** 202

MANNING *cont'd*
Julia **78** 324
Julia Ann (Edgar) **84** 103
Julian **51** 390
Juliana **51** 389 403
Junias **71** 202
Katharine **51** 391 394-396
  400 405 406
Lathrop **68** 335
Laura Brown **79** 203 **84**
  102 109 196
Lazarus **56** 405
Leila O. **81** 259
Leonard **51** 389 405
Lorenzo **92** 106
Lucinda **113** 33 40
Lucretia **70** 155
Lucy **51** 394 395 **78** 97
Lucy (Andrews) **92** 195
Lucy E. **68** 335
Lydia **61** 237 **63** 370 **71**
  282 **72** 206 **74** 257 260
  78 97 410 **79** 38 **100** 183
  113 33 40
Lydia Brooks (Chandler)
  59 xcviii **92** 194 195
Lydia Brown **107** 150 151
Mansur **70** 155
Margaret **51** 389 391 394
  396 400 **77** 129 **78** 98 **79**
  449 **84** 407 **92** 106 **97**
  278 **122** 258
Margaret (Eager) **107** 257
Margery **51** 389
Maria **51** 389 **101** 210
Martha **51** 389 **83** 167
  126 141
Martha (Beard) **92** 194
Martin **51** 393 395 396
  399 402 405
Mary **51** 390 395 403 **55**
  290 312 347 **56** 207 **59**
  xcvii **61** 378 **63** 34 171
  64 37 **69** 144 156 **71** 202
  74 63 250 257 **82** 47 318
  510 **83** 167 301 **96** 234
  97 339 **106** 141 **125** 106
  216 **143** 143 147 **144**
  164
Mary (Brigham) **88** 186
Mary (Cutting) **114** 104
Mary (Fletcher) **92** 195
Mary (Giddings) **111** 317
Mary (Hamby) **145** 121
Mary (Robinson) **143**
  142 143 145 147
Mary (Shed) **92** 194
Mary (White) **106** 148
Mary Ann S. **83** 22 25 27
Mary E. **141** 258
Mary Jane **69** 206
Mary Pierce **82** 47
Matilda **63** 367
Matilda (Morgan) **89** 28
Matthew **91** 395 397 400
  406
Matthew H. **70** 155
Maybelle **107** 130
Mildred **51** 419
Mildred Fortune **51** 396
  418

MANNING *cont'd*
Minerva **68** 335
Miriam **51** 389 **92** 106
Miriam (Lord) **111** 317
Myles **51** 389 405
Nancy **88** 351 **89** 28 **93** 380
  94 290 **100** 162
Nanna Wier **90** 361
Nathaniel **63** 367 **89** 28
  97 278
Nathaniel L. **90** 110
Nellie Cora **89** 386
Nicholas **51** 389 397 398
  402 **53** 86 **65** 189 **110** 27
  148 25
Owen **63** 99
Pascal R. **70** 155
Patrick **55** 312 **63** 171 **74**
  257 **82** 214 318 321 323
  510 **83** 153
Peggy **88** 351
Percivall **51** 389
Peter **51** 389 390 394 396-
  398 404 406
Phebe **51** 389 394 399 404
  406 407 **59** 307 411 **78**
  303 **106** 308 **107** 49
Phebe Jane **68** 335
Philena Small (Brown)
  84 102
Philip **51** 395
Phineas **100** 183 **135** 79
  137 79
Polly **70** 268 **88** 351
Prudence **139** 96
Prudence (Fitz Randolph)
  97 278
Purcell **71** 69
Rachel **51** 45 397 404
Rachel (Ford) (Fitz
  Randolph) **97** 336
Rebecca **51** 56 **56** 207
  57 110 111
Rebecca Dodge
  (Burnham) **111** 317
Richard **51** 389-394 396-
  399 401-406 **52** 125 **56**
  326 **69** 53 **78** 97 **93** 80
  111 317 **148** 142
Richard Clarke **92** 146
  111 316 317 **112** 72
Rizpah (Thatcher)
  (Brown) **100** 183
Robert **51** 389 392 394
  395 399 403 405 **65** 129
  111 317
Rockwell **70** 155
Ruth **72** 114 115
S. **62** 122
Sally **71** 203 **74** 263
  100 183
Sally Rogers
  (Chamberlain) **92** 203
Sampson **51** 394 399
Samuel **51** 392 **59** xcvii **64**
  37 38 **74** 257 **82** 323 **84**
  102 103 **92** 194 **106** 147
  113 33 38 **136** 57 **145**
  121
Sarah **51** 403 **54** 419 **57** 111
  61 237 **64** 38 **65** 312 **69**

MANNING *cont'd*
  53 **70** 155 **82** 293 298 **89**
  385 **100** 300 **104** 287
  128 292 **134** 91 **143** 147
Sarah (Butterfield)
  92 194 195
Sarah (Spaulding)
  106 147
Sarah (Walbridge)
  100 183
Sarah Ann **71** 69 **82** 47
Sarah C. **141** 53
Sarah Elizabeth (Yeaton)
  (Gould) **111** 316
Sarah R. **92** 203
Sarah Wiswell **75** 251
Serepta A. **62** 122
Simon **51** 389 395 403
  405 406
Solomon **59** xcvii **92** 195
Statira **71** 69 **82** 47
Stephen **51** 389 403
Susan **70** 155
Susan B. **90** 394
Susan May (Avis) **106** 147
Susanna **51** 306 391 402
  403 **88** 351 **106** 147
Thomas **51** 389 390 393-
  397 399 401-406 **53** 31
  61 378 **65** 248 **69** liv
  354 **71** 69 **78** 97 **82** 47
  293 298 **101** 7 **111** 317
  125 220 **143** 147
Thomas Augustus **82** 47
Thomas Daniel **55** 347
Thomasin **51** 389 405
Timothy **83** 167
Toby **51** 399
Trimelius **71** 202
Tryphena **86** 383
Ursula **51** 393 395 396 405
Venus (Sylvester) **125** 220
Wade Hampton (Mrs.)
  107 134
Warren H. **59** xcviii
  79 193
Warren Harold **92** 195
Warren Henry **90** 137 **92**
  194 195 199 **93** 142
Wayland **65** xxxiv
Wealthy **120** 20
William **51** 389-391 393-
  395 399 403 405 406 **55**
  353 390 **56** 326 **59** xcvii
  102 411 **60** 298 **64** 217
  65 54 **77** 162 **78** 72 89
  82 47 **88** 351 **92** 194
  101 13 **106** 147 148 234
  107 257 **108** 152 **113** 73
  143 335
William B. **93** 296
William Barker **92** 203
William F. **101** 210
William H. **56** 326 **57** 111
  223 **61** 304 **63** 318 381
  64 xxxi 194 **88** 351 **93**
  167 **124** 6 **144** 164 **148**
  142
William Henry **57** xxxiii
  60 xxxvi **89** 386

MANNING *cont'd*
William S. **59** xcviii
William Thomas **81** 341
William W. **73** 226
Willie P. **68** 335
Zelinda (Huntley)
  101 210
Zeruiah (Fitzrandolph)
  84 102
MANNINGHAM
Henry **108** 31
Mary **108** 31
Mannings *see* Manning
MANNION Mary Isabelle
  (Bulch) **133** 229
MANNISON
William **70** 21
MANNOCKE
Bridget **63** 278
MANNOO Marie (Mahieu)
  (DeLannoy) **143**
  198 199
Robert **143** 198
Symone (Pachette)
  143 198
Manny *see* Manney
Mannyard *see* Maynard
Mannyng *see* Manning
Mannynge *see* Manning
MANON
— Rev. Mr. **124** 279
MANOR Metcalf **138** 116
MANOXON Anne **105** 271
MANRICK
Thomas J. **91** 329
MANRO Daniel **61** 33
MANROW
Jakemiah **148** 282
MANSBACH Kenneth
  Leonard (Mrs.)
  107 134
MANSBRIDGE
—— **105** 189
Albert **103** 42
MANSDOTTER
Katarina **111** 100
MANSELL Donald E. **108**
  160 **114** 71 78 **115** 237
  117 156
E. P. **114** 78
Edwin **108** 160
Frank **108** 160
Ira **108** 160
Isaac **105** 289
Jane **63** 93
John **51** 279 **63** 93 **105**
  278 289 **114** 71
Joseph **105** 276
Robert **54** 412
Sarah Ann (Rollins)
  108 160
Mansell *see* Manson
Manser *see* Mansur
MANSFIELD Mansfeild
— Col. **95** 57 **135** 102
  145 159
— Lord **125** 154
____ (Avery) **140** 35
A. **123** 97
Aaron **59** 340
Abigail **81** 128

MANSFIELD *cont'd*
Abigail A. **127** 67
Abigail Ann **76** 173
Abigail Grace **76** 149
Abijah **76** 150
Achilles **76** 131
Achsah **124** 10
Aiken L. **125** 294
Alice Cushing **92** 136 **93** 142 **94** 82 83
Allen Bancroft **96** 336
Alpheus **124** 8
Amos **124** 8
Andrew **85** 30 **108** 95 **112** 242 **123** 167 **142** 361
Ann **108** 246
Anna **76** 130 136 138-144 **98** 81 **121** 274 **124** 10
Anna Maria **63** 47
Anne **61** 41
Arthur **95** 254
Asenath **124** 10
Augusta McKim (Davies) **84** 208
Bethiah **55** 292 **83** 342 **85** 447 **103** 144 **112** 242
Betsey **59** 340 **76** 145 **77** 228 **78** 419
Betsey J. **84** 346
Betsey P. (Jenkins) **84** 346
C. W. **91** 329
Calvin **111** 298
Celia A. **69** 164
Charles Ennis **92** 126
Charles F. **56** xxxii
Chastina Elizabeth **84** 346
Clarissa **59** 340
Colloredo (Countess) **86** 336
Comfort **66** 308
Damaris **51** 347
Daniel **51** 301 **71** 358 **84** 346 **102** 272 275 **107** 183
David Lufkin **58** 379 382 384 **59** 340 **61** xxx
David Murray (Earl of) **67** 103
Deborah (Dayton) **83** 331
Dorcas **124** 18
Drucilla E. (Boynton) **123** 97
Ebenezer **66** 308 309
Eleonora (Iselin) **86** 336
Elijah **71** 359
Elisha H. **60** 18
Eliza Ann **92** 128
Elizabeth **51** 301 **55** 438 **59** 221 **61** 41 **63** 238 **66** 308 **76** 136 **85** 391 393 **90** 105 **111** 18 **121** 193 **124** 10 **135** 105
Elizabeth (Montgomery) **112** 294
Elizabeth (Needham) **94** 82
Elizabeth (Nourse) **94** 82
Elizabeth (Spring) **124** 10
Elizabeth (Walton) (Conant) **142** 361

MANSFIELD *cont'd*
Elizabeth (Whittemore) **108** 83
Elizabeth (Williams) **94** 82
Elizabeth Hyde **60** 194
Elma **96** 336
Emily Dwight **78** 204 **83** 217 331 **84** 196
Epes **55** 395
Esther **66** 204
Eunice **76** 172 173 **97** 65
Ezra **59** 340
Florence Stone (Bancroft) **96** 336
Francis **112** 294
Gideon M. **77** xxxiv
Giles **83** 331
Gillian **66** 308 **81** 128
Gillian (Drake) **131** 121
Glover **83** 331 **133** 308
Grace **76** 144
Hannah **51** 462 **56** 285 **58** 164 **59** 340 **66** 308 **69** 57 **79** 39 **81** 128 **127** 164
Hannah (Parker) **125** 294
Hannah Elizabeth **75** 207
Harriet (Stanley) **83** 331
Haysom R. **83** 129
Helen **51** 221 225 **52** 84
Helen Amelia (Cushing) **94** 82
Helen J. (Hubberley) **96** 336
Henrietta **76** 138
Henry S. **138** 126
Horace **66** 308
Isaac **57** 49 50 **76** 152 **92** 120 **110** 317 **125** 23 **129** 363 **140** 35
Isaac (Mrs.) **93** 317
James **113** 88
James S. **147** 20
Jane (Goodridge) **94** 82
Japhet **59** 168 **66** 308
Jared **64** 362 **76** 143
Jeremiah **121** 279
Jesse J. **59** 340
Joanna (Burrage) **102** 275
Joel **71** 358
John **55** 438 **61** 41 **65** 24 65 66 **66** 308 **75** 91 **95** 112 **99** 77 **102** 243 **106** 262 **113** 93 **121** 106 115 117 121 212 214 274 **123** 258 **125** 101 **128** 284 **147** 19
John F. **54** 151
John William **83** 331
Jonathan **76** 130 140 141 **83** 331 **94** 82
Jonathan N. **75** 257
Joseph **51** 462 **54** 24 **59** 168 **66** 308 309 **70** 75 **76** 138 **81** 122 128 131 **92** 126 128 **94** 82 **100** 254 **141** 17
Josiah **91** 265 **124** 10
Kiersted **76** 131 **77** 81
King William **62** xxxvii
Lois **75** 310 **124** 18

MANSFIELD *cont'd*
Louis **76** 131
Lucie C. **83** 435 **84** 18
Lucretia **76** 142
Lucy **84** 137
Lucy (Avery) **93** 317
Lucy (Corey) **84** 346
Lucy H. **60** 18 **75** 257
Lucy Tryphena **84** 346
Lydia **75** 91 **78** 408 **96** 188
Lydia D. **60** 18
Lyman **84** 137 **100** 189
Margaret **101** 225 **102** 272 273 **104** 289
Margaret (Crownin-shield) (Murphy) **104** 290
Maria Adaline **54** 151
Martha **56** 280 **66** 172 308
Martha (Stocker) **94** 82
Martin **117** 52
Mary **54** 24 421 **59** 70 168 **63** 73 **65** 63 66 **66** 308 309 **75** 186 **76** 131 **81** 128 **84** 30 **94** 313 **100** 239 **114** 294 **121** 119-121 **124** 8
Mary (Aikins) **83** 331
Mary (Badlam) **141** 137
Mary (Brington) **94** 312
Mary (Clapp) **129** 363
Mary (Dorchester) **126** 78
Mary (Gilbert) **91** 265
Mary (Jackson) **124** 8
Mary (Morris) **147** 19 20
Mary (Newhall) **94** 82
Mary Ann **70** 75
Mary Ann (Avery) **92** 120
Mary Antoinette (Macumber) **83** 331
Mary B. **141** 147
Mary Badlam **141** 17
Mary Jane **84** 346
Mary Louisa **76** 143
Matthew **94** 82
May Stansbury **61** 204
Mercy **59** 168 **62** 364 **66** 198 308 **81** 128
Mercy (Glover) **83** 331
Moses **59** 70 **62** 219 **66** 198 **76** 131 132 **78** 188 **81** 121-123 125 126 128-130 133-135 **83** 331
Nancy **84** 346 **88** 279 **128** 278
Nancy Elvira **84** 346
Nathan **76** 131 138 143 145 147 152 153 **83** 331
Patience (Badlam) **141** 16 17 147
Paul **51** 347
Polly (Atkins) **133** 306
Polly (Maltby) **111** 298
R. **143** 304
Rachel **59** 70 **78** 396
Rebecca **59** 340
Rhoda (Orton) **124** 8
Richard **54** 23 **62** 113 **66** 308 309 **76** 130 131 135-144 148-150 153 171 **81** 128 **83** 331 **92** 187 **108**

MANSFIELD *cont'd*
  83 **120** 244
Richard S. **75** 207
Richstead **77** 81
Robert **66** 173 **76** 235 **94**
  82 **122** 315
Ruth **51** 347 **141** 140
Ruth (Cheever) **129** 363
Sally **60** 18 **76** 147 **78** 262
  141 17
Sally (Pritchett) **125** 101
Samuel **59** 168 **63** 257 **66**
  309 **78** 317 **94** 312 **112**
  152
Sarah **55** 395 **59** 72 **66** 13
  75 91 **76** 130 137 172
  112 152 **121** 116 216
  122 90 **126** 78
Sarah (Alling) **83** 331
Sarah (Waters) **141** 17
Sarah F. **90** 109
Sarah M. (Hunt) **84** 347
Shubael **141** 17
Sibyl (White) **124** 8 10
Silence **66** 308 309
Sophia **76** 153
Stanley Allen **96** 336
Stephen **76** 139
Susanna **62** 219 **76** 138
  103 139
Susanna Badlam **141** 17
Theophilus **124** 8 10
  144 215
Thomas **102** 275 **121** 117
Wallace H. **69** 164
Walter D. **61** 204
Walter Damon **60** 185 277
William **56** 84 **70** 115 **76**
  138 172 173 **84** 346 **101**
  225 **104** 290 **141** 17 **145**
  126
William H. (Mrs.) **105**
  267 269 271 272
William Murray **52** 293
Young Farrar **124** 18
MANSHIPPE Manship
 — Rev. Mr. **90** 388
Joan **64** 53
William **64** 53 54
Mansir *see* Mansur
MANSON Mansen Mansson
Abigail (Rich) **84** 58
Abigail Fearing **58** civ
Ada **110** 304
Ada E. **110** 304
Alexander **118** 56 **125**
  195 259
Alfred Small **54** xxxvi xli
  58 lv civ cv
Annah **87** 125 **99** 200
Arrie M. **123** 153
B. S. **122** 147
Barbara **65** 246
Bertha **83** 435 **84** 20
Caleb **125** 182
Charles A. **92** 360
David R. **122** 149
Dennis **119** 288
Eaton **58** civ
Eben **79** 33
Edith **75** 251

MANSON *cont'd*
Eliza (Whitham) **125** 290
Eliza Emerson (Vance)
  83 479
Elizabeth **65** 246
Elizabeth Emerson **82**
  252 **83** 233 370 479 **84**
  196
Elizabeth H. **83** 435 **84** 21
Ellen **79** 33 **125** 195
Ellen Doane **79** 33
Emma **73** 190
Estelle **73** 191
Frederic Hurlbut **75** 251
Frederic Irving **75** 251
Frederic W. **75** 251
George **87** 126 **118** 56
  125 195
Grace E. **83** 435 **84** 21
Hannah **68** lxiv
Hans **115** 4
Hiram N. **92** 338
Hugh O. **110** 304
Ida J. (Hart) **83** 298 300
James **84** 58
Jane **59** 40 **66** 51 **87** 124
  100 335 **125** 195
Jane (Waters) **125** 195 259
Jane D. (Drummond)
  100 335
John **58** civ **83** 479 **87** 123
  125 195 290
Joseph H. **123** 153
Joseph W. **120** 137 139
  123 72 153
Josephine **75** 251
Joshua B. **125** 182
Kate Withington **75** 251
Lillian Josephine **75** 251
Louisa **100** 335
Louisa Catharina **99** 200
Louisa J. **100** 335
Louise M. **81** 252
Lucy **51** 178
Lucy Jane (Blaisdell)
  119 288
Mabel **75** 251
Mabel E. (Mugridge)
  123 153
Margaret **65** 246
Maria **88** 336
Martha A. **83** 435 **84** 22
Martha O. **73** 190 191 195
Mary **81** 446 **82** 293
Mary (Bliss) **125** 182
Mary (Turner) **83** 479
Mary Ann **75** 251
Mary Eliza **58** cv
Mary J. **92** 338
Mary J. (Moore) **122** 149
Mary L. **125** 217
Mary Turner **83** 480
Nehemiah **83** 479
Nettie **76** 100
Nicholas **79** 35
Nicholas W. **97** 20 238
Noah **82** 293
Parker **83** 25 28
Richard **58** civ
Robert **73** 190 191 195
Sally (Clark) **97** 20 238

MANSON *cont'd*
Samuel **51** 46 **58** civ **81**
  446 **87** 122
Sarah **59** 57
Sarah Ellen **75** 251
Sophia **125** 288
Susan D. **100** 335
Susan P. **83** 25 28
Sylvester **83** 398 300
Theodore **97** 269
Thomas **65** 246
Thomas Lincoln **83** 479
W. G. **94** 30
Waite H. (McIntire) **120**
  137 139 **123** 72 153
Waldo Searsmont **58** cv
William **58** civ **76** 100 **85**
  447 **99** 200 **125** 36
William Rufus **100** 335
Mansor *see* Mansur
MANSPERGER Martin
  Matheny **93** 305
Mansson *see* Manson
MANSTER Lydia **100** 296
MANSUR Manser
  Mansir Mansor
  Mansure
 — **109** 44
Abby **60** 196
Charles H. **56** 100
Daniel **116** 231
Ebenezer **78** 189
Elijah **92** 323
Eliza Cunningham
  60 196
Eliza Jane **94** 93
Elizabeth **56** 100 **125** 293
Esther C. **94** 93
Eunice **61** 357
Ezra **60** 196
Frank A. **85** 63
Frank L. **117** 235
George **94** 93
George Bradley **60** 196
George H. **94** 93
Hannah (Benson) **126** 204
Helen Maria **60** 196
Horace **60** 196
Isabella **60** 196
James **61** 357 **145** 352
James Munroe **60** 196
Jefferson **94** 93
John **109** 44
John H. **56** 100
Lucy A. **88** 332
Lucy Ann **92** 323
Martha **92** 49 50
Martha (Collins) **126** 207
Mary **61** 357 **107** 252
Mary (Smith) **94** 93
Mary A. **78** 399
Mary Hay **60** 196
Matthew **91** 329
Nancy **60** 196 **94** 92
Nancy R. **94** 93
Olive **78** 346
Robert **56** 100 **126** 204
Ruthy **78** 422
Samuel **126** 207
Samuel Crombie **60** 196
Sarah **60** 196

MANSUR cont'd
Sukey (Stodder) **125** 287
Susan **60** 196
Susanna **60** 196
Thomas **92** 50 **94** 237
Valeria **116** 231
William **60** 196 **70** 59 **77**
81 **125** 287
William Earl **60** 196
William H. M. **78** 300
MANTEL
Robert de **62** 165
MANTELL
Dorothy **103** 17
Margaret (Wood) **103** 17
Walter **103** 17
MANTER
Belcher **123** 272
Benjamin **100** 189 **123** 229
Charlotte **70** 350
Deborah **100** 53
Elizabeth **59** 384
Eunice **59** 307
George **100** 53 189
James **66** 80
Jerauld A. **118** 77 158
Jeremiah **59** 384
John **66** 80
Jonathan **66** 80
Love **59** 259
Lucinda **100** 189
Mary **123** 229
Mary (Whiton) **123** 229
Mary Pease **88** 290
Matthew **66** 80 81
Reuben **100** 189
Sally **59** 380
Samuel **59** 201 379 380
66 80
Seth **100** 189
Whiten **66** 80 81
Whitton **123** 229
MANTET
D'Ailleboust de **52** 476
477
MANTEYER
—— **110** 42 43
Georges de **103** 153 **107**
276 **110** 41 **111** 265-267
114 295 296
MANTHORN Abiel
(Kinney) **127** 125
George **127** 125
James **127** 125
Sally **127** 125
William **127** 125
MANTIER Mary (Barton)
107 293
MANTLE Betty **115** 44
Henry **115** 123
John **115** 120
Martha **115** 119
Mary **115** 43
Mary Ann **115** 39
MANTLO Mariah **78** 47
MANTON — Dr. **53** 297
— Mr. **51** 273
Amos **55** 68
D. **145** 159
Daniel **67** 300
Edward **71** 95

MANTON cont'd
Henry **116** 219
Jane **74** lxiv
Kate **74** lxiv
Mary A. **88** 140
Shadrach **88** 140
William S. **74** lxiv
MANTONOMI **98** 20
MANTONYA Charlotte
Cyrena (Falley)
108 201
MANTOOTH Edwin James
81 107 219
MANTOR James **57** 410
75 305 **103** 299
John Lewis **57** 411
Robert **57** 410 411
MANTRAVERS
Alice **75** 62
MANTUE
Benjamin **145** 360
Henry **145** 357
MANUEL
Anthony **92** 272
Martin **123** 202
Rebecca F. (Mayo)
123 202
MANVEL Allen **123** 234
Annah (Fellows) **123** 234
Florence **123** 234
MANVILLE
Addison **136** 311
Charles **80** 272
Charles Brayton **136** 311
Clara Louise (Johnson)
89 132
Estelle Romaine **103** 69
136 311
Frederick (Mrs.) **89** 132
Henrietta Estelle
(Romaine) **94** 139 **103**
69 **136** 311
Hiram Edward **103** 69
136 311
Hiram Edward (Mrs.)
94 139 **102** 113 129 **103**
69
James **76** 147 150 152
Jennie A. (Long) **136** 311
John **75** 193
Mary Ann **80** 272
Murray **76** 147
Nicholas **104** 316
Ruth **75** 193
Salome (Calkins) **136** 311
Stewart Roebling
104 316
Vanbon **76** 152
Manwaring see
Mainwaring
Manwaringe see
Mainwaring
Manwarren see
Mainwaring
Manwarring see
Mainwaring
Manwearing see
Mainwaring
Many see Manney
MANYOR Patrick **62** 252

MANZER
Lola Adah **81** 221
Lydia Permelia **89** 317
MANZIARLY
Mima de **82** 363
MAPEN John **104** 70
Mary Lucinda **104** 70
Pamelia (Bradford)
104 70
MAPES — Mr. **83** 74
Desire (Chase) (Jolly)
87 336
Gladys Merwin
(Blakeslee) **90** 69
Idiel **87** 336
Milton Crawford (Mrs.)
90 69
Persis Ann **115** 128
Richard John **119** 319
Sarah **55** 379
MAPLE
Benjamin **105** 71
Katrine **82** 278
Margaret Ann **111** 326
Phebe **83** 435 **84** 21
T. Grant **105** 71
MAPLEDDE Jane **91** 14
MAPLEHEAD
Mary **127** 185
MAPLERDEN John **92** 72
MAPLES Debora **141** 46
Eunice **81** 360
J. **90** 33
William **71** 233
MAPLESDEN Maplisden
Anne **51** 257 **112** 34
Edward **51** 257-261 264
89 282 **92** 398
Elizabeth **53** 302
Felix **112** 35
Francis **92** 370
George **51** 257-261 **53** 302
Henry **51** 258 259
Jervis **51** 257 259
John **51** 259 260 266 **112** 35
Katharine **51** 257-259
Lydia **51** 258 259
Mary **51** 257 260 **89** 282
92 398
Peter **51** 259-261 264
Richard **51** 259 260 264
Robert **51** 259 268
Thomas **84** 73
Thomasine **51** 258 259
MAPLESON —— **116** 291
MAPLETT Mayplet
— Mr. **70** 117
Ann **51** 200
Anne **70** 116 118
Edward **51** 200
Elizabeth **70** 116-118
Ellen **51** 200 **70** 115-118
282
Henry **51** 200
John **51** 200 299 **70** 115-
118 282 **82** 341 **103** 214
105 259 260
Margaret **51** 200 **70** 115
118
Mary **51** 199 200 **70** 115-
118 282 **82** 186 341 **103**

MAPLETT *cont'd*
  214 **105** 259
  Sarah **70** 117 118
  Thomas **51** 200 **70** 115
    117 118 282
Maplisden *see* Maplesden
MAPP Joseph **58** 202
MAPPLESHALL
  Gilbert de **102** 299
MAPS Charles **90** 392
  Cornelia C. **90** 392
  Elizabeth **90** 392
  Hannah **90** 392
  Hannah (Throckmorton)
    90 392
  Hannah W. **90** 392
  Julia Ann (Hooper)
    90 392
  Lewis T. **90** 392
  Mary **90** 392
  Mary Ann (Tucker)
    90 392
  Michael **90** 392
  Sibyl **90** 392
  Unice H. (Ferguson)
    90 392
  William R. **90** 392
MAQUET
  Anthony **65** 231
  Peter Robert **65** 231
MAR Alexander Erskine
  (Earl of) **74** 16
  Isabella Erskine
    (Countess of) **74** 16
  Jane (Bradley) **100** 239
  Robert Erskine (Earl of)
    74 16
MARA
  Avice de **140** 226
  Francis **63** 28
MARABEL
  Adelaide **78** 49
  Mary (Knower)
    (Whittemore) **106** 33
MARABLE John **106** 33 37
MARAHAL Thomas **66** 37
MARAKEL Jane **89** 95
MARAN Rebecca **73** 146
MARANBILLA
  Gifford B. **135** 129
  Mary (Rundlett) **135** 129
MARANVILLE *see*
  also De Moranville
  E. C. **123** 98
  Louisa A. (Lindley)
    123 98
  Mary A. (Petty) **122** 288
  Stephen **122** 288
MARASPIN Alice G.
  (Higgins) **114** 5
  Anne Howland **114** 5
  Davis Goodwin **88** 210
    91 203 **92** 92 93-5 68
  Dorothy Blanche (Howe)
    114 5
  Dorothy Lothrop **114** 5
  Francis Lothrop **114** 3
  Mary Eliza (Davis) **114** 3
  Maud Isabel (Goodwin)
    114 3
  Paul **91** 198 202 **114** 3

MARASPIN *cont'd*
  Sally Davis **114** 5
MARBADCHER Elizabeth
  Catherine **68** 123
  John **68** 123
  Maria Catherine **68** 123
MARBLE Marbell
  — Mr. **148** 113
  Aaron **75** lxxxiii
  Abby De Woolf **88** 244
  Abigail **57** 417 **58** 84 **59**
    138 139 309
  Abigail (Leland) **124** 17
  Adeline F. **88** 244
  Allura **88** 243
  Almira **79** 303
  Alpheus **143** 161
  Alvin **96** 285
  Amanda **76** xlvi
  Angeline B. **88** 244
  Ann **87** 256 **142** 293
    143 161
  Anna Theresa **75** lxxxiii
  Arethusa L. **88** 244
  Benjamin **87** 249 **88** 148
    237 **95** 65 **97** 130
  Benjamin David **88** 241
  Charles **87** 249 **130** 158
  Cornelia J. **120** 319
  Cyrus **69** 304 307
  Danforth **79** 303 307
  Daniel **62** 185 **78** 111
    88 147 244
  Daniel C. **89** 275
  David **58** 84 **59** 138 139
    309 **88** 147 241
  Delaney True **88** 241
  Delia Henrietta
    (Parmenter) **95** 238
  Dorcas **88** 241
  Eben **88** 244
  Ebenezer **56** 319 **76** 268 **85**
    86 **88** 147 237
  Edith May **103** 121
  Eleazer **85** 86 **105** 320 **107**
    240 320
  Elias **133** 297
  Eliza **76** xlvi
  Eliza Tainter (Bancroft)
    96 285
  Elizabeth **87** 256 **118** 170
  Elizabeth (Emerson)
    85 87
  Elizabeth Dana **85** 87
  Emaline **127** 78
  Emily **76** 263 **79** 303
    81 283
  Emily Greene **75** lxxxiii
  Enoch **75** lxxxiii **143** 161
  Ephraim **59** 309
  Ezra **124** 17
  Fanna **76** 268
  Fanny **114** 179
  Fred E. **74** xviii
  Fred Elmer **73** 154
  Frederick **79** 302 303
  Freegrace **75** lxxxiii
    143 161
  Freeland **76** xlvi **88** 48 243
    245
  George P. **88** 241 **98** 259

MARBLE *cont'd*
  Guilford Lionel **85** 87
  Hannah **56** 319 **75** 208 253
    86 44 **113** 300 **132** 324
  Hannah (Carey) **85** 86
  Hannah Davis **88** 241
  Harriet B. **88** 244
  Helen Chace **75** lxxxiii
  Henrietta **88** 244
  Henry **91** 206 **94** 95 **100** 65
  Jacob **66** 22
  Jacob O. **88** 244
  James **91** 107 **118** 170
  James E. **109** 189
  Jane **126** 66
  Jerome **55** lxiv **73** lx **75**
    lxxxiii **83** 375
  Joel **65** 149
  John **62** 185 **90** 273 **104**
    206 **118** 170 **139** 257
  John E. **107** 240 320
  John E. (Mrs.) **105** 320
  John Emerson **71** xxiv
    74 xxviii **85** 87 **90** 130
    117 148
  John Miner Carey **60**
    xxxviii **61** xxxiii xxxvi
    62 xxxv 105 **67** xliii **85**
    86
  John Putnam **75** lxxxiii
  Jonathan **62** 185 **126** 22
  Joseph **139** 257
  Joseph Russel **73** xix **75**
    xxxiv lxxxii lxxxiii
  Joyce (Sears) **108** 181
  Julia Wolcott **79** 303
  Laura **79** 303
  Lawson Mellon **88** 243
  Lena Olive **73** lx
  Leslie **95** 238
  Louisa **88** 148
  Lovisa **88** 237
  Lucinda **88** 148 237
  Lucretia (Leake) **109** 189
  Luther **59** 139
  Lydia **62** 185
  Lydia B. **88** 244
  M. M. **101** 338
  Margaret (Harwood)
    126 22
  Maria **79** 303
  Mariah (Gifford) **133** 297
  Martha (Goss) **95** 65
    97 130
  Mary **61** 96 252 **101** 64
    133 42
  Mary (Richards)
    (Thomson) **85** 86
  Mary Ann **125** 181
  Mary Elizabeth (Coleman)
    85 87
  Mary Skinner **79** 303
  Mehitable (Putnam)
    143 161
  Miner Carey **60** xxxiv
  Miriam T. **88** 244
  Moses **76** 268
  Nathaniel **62** 185
  Oliver **88** 148 237 241
    98 259
  Patience **95** 65 **97** 130

MARBLE *cont'd*
103 64
Persis **108** 164
Persis Ann **88** 241
Phebe **75** lxxxiii
Priscilla **88** 244 **125** 220
Rachel **62** 185
Rebecca **62** 185 **76** 139 **88**
241 **98** 259
Rebecca D. **88** 241
Rebecca H. T. **88** 244
Robert **60** 356
Rosannah **114** 179
Russel **75** lxxxiii
Ruth **57** 417 **87** 249
Ruth (Chase) **87** 249
Ruth Banister (Hannum)
91 107
Ruth Putnam **75** lxxxiii
Sally **76** 268 **88** 148 237
241
Sally (Bullard) **105** 320
107 320
Samuel **57** 417 **62** 185 **73**
70 72 **75** lxxxiii **87** 249
143 161
Samuel F. **88** 148 237
Sarah **84** 429 **88** 147 237
Sarah (Bullard) **105** 320
Sarah Almy **75** lxxxiii
Sarah E. **88** 241
Stephen **87** 249 256
Stephen M. **88** 243
Susan **73** lx
Susanna **76** 139 **88** 241
143 133
Warren **118** 170
William **79** 302 303 307
118 170
William Allen **65** 205
William Carey **85** 87
William D. **88** 241
MARBLEY Jemima **91** 106
MARBOIS — Mr. **55** 276
MARBURNY
James **112** 303
MARBURY Marburie
Agnes **138** 319
Anne **51** 119 **56** 409 **60** 168
67 200 **71** 103 **72** 136
79 94 170 249 **80** 140
176 **85** 323 **86** 262 **88**
401 **90** 312 **96** 9 **98** 15-
17 **103** 211 **106** 230 **118**
275 **122** 246 **125** 180
136 87 155 175 189 211
212 215 217 290 **138** 317
141 96 101 **145** 3 15 99
258 265
Bridget **60** 168 **66** 87
Bridget (Dryden) **85** 323
96 8
Caroline **73** 265
Catherine **60** 168-174 318
74 134 **86** 262 **104** 7
127 214 **136** 211 212
217 **141** 101 107
Francis **51** 255 **60** 168 171
66 87 **68** 79 **71** 103 **85**
323 **96** 8 **98** 16 17
Henrietta Beans **73** 232

MARBURY *cont'd*
Jane Contee **73** 279
John **73** 272 **109** 282
Katharine **51** 255 **66** 87
88 401 **92** 202 **96** 8 9 **98**
11 16 17 19 **119** 141 **123**
180 **138** 317 **145** 3 15 21
Leonard **110** 9
William **73** 227 **138** 319
MARBUT C. F. **57** 237
MARBYLL
John Miner Carey **66**
xlviii
Roger **66** 353
MARCELLUS
Henry **130** 53
John E. **130** 53
MARCEY —— **92** 348 351
353 **93** 60
Christian **94** 41
MARCH —— **86** 247
— Capt. **100** 225
— Dr. **52** 272
— Mr. **77** 30
— Mrs. **83** 194 307
— Widow **70** 129 **103** 194
Abigail **52** 479 **53** 122-125
82 502
Abigail Robinson **52** 479
Agnes **70** 131
Alce **86** 79 248 250
Alice **86** 78 248-250
Amias / Amyas **86** 78-80
249-251
Ann **53** 125 **82** 47
Ann (Bickne) **131** 129
Anna **53** 123
Avis K. **137** 31
Benjamin **53** 122 124 **54**
409 **64** 226
Bette **53** 124
Caroline **75** 88
Catherine **63** 115
Catherine (Monroe) **58** lx
63 115 **75** xlvi **84** 96 **86**
231
Charles **82** 422 **125** 238
Christopher **142** 256
Clement **52** 478 479 **53**
124 125 **73** 67 **82** 422
104 319 **144** 266
Daniel **53** 122 123 **55** 17
63 314
David **63** 115 **84** 96 **86** 231
Dorcas **53** 121
Dorcas (Bowman)
(Blackleach) **148** 30-
32 35
Dorcas Bowman **53** 268
Dorothy **53** 124
Earl **80** 165
Ebenezer **53** 124
Edmund **53** 122 124 **82**
332 **91** 93 **106** 268
Eleanor **52** 479 **53** 125
Elizabeth **52** 430 **53** 122-
125 **54** 341 **55** 71 **82** 47
289 293 **86** 78 83 248-
251 **91** 188 **106** 75 **112**
138 **142** 256
Elizabeth (Voysey) **86** 83

MARCH *cont'd*
Elizabeth Shannon **71** lx
Ellen Gates **52** 479 481
53 121 125 265 **54**
xxxviii **104** 319
Emily Susanna **86** 231
Emma **84** 30
Enoch **53** 124
Esther **107** 270 **108** 189
Eulalia **86** 218 **93** 194
Eunice **53** 123 **55** 314 **74**
265 **83** 10 **108** 121
Eunice (Hill) **83** 10
Flora **55** 375 **83** 16
Fortune **55** 373 375 **63** 172
83 14 16
Frances (At Fenne)
142 256
Francis **55** 71 **82** 422
George **53** 121 122 124
125 268 **55** 314 **73** 73 **83**
10 **86** 78 83 217 248 249
106 71
Grace **86** 216 248
Hannah **53** 122-125 **59** 372
107 270
Henry **53** 121 122 **58** 45 59
372 **75** 88
Hugh **53** 121-124 268 **84**
238 **96** 77 **148** 30 31 35
Isott **86** 83
Israel **53** 121 123 124
Jacob **53** 123 **107** 201
James **53** 121 122 124 268
71 327 **82** 47 48 291 293
413 **103** 196
Jane **53** 121 122 124 **86** 78
248 249 251 **88** 348
Jemima **53** 122
Jesse **107** 269
Joan **86** 78 248 249 251
Joan (Martyn) **86** 249
Johanna **82** 47
John **52** 430 **53** 121-124
268 **58** 42 44 45 **67** 207
70 263 **82** 47 **83** 24 25
86 83 216 247 **93** 397
100 63 **106** 266 268 **107**
269 **108** 189 **131** 129
John P. **125** 238
Jos **64** 226
Joseph **51** 461 **52** 479
53 122-124
Joseph W. **82** 422
Josephine A. **83** 300 302
Joshua **53** 122 123
Judith **53** 38 121-123 268
Leonard **83** 183 184
Leslie G. **80** 165
Lora **80** 165
Louise H. **83** 300
Louise Harriet **83** 173
Lucy M. **83** 184 186
Lydia **51** 461
Lydia (Seavey) **108** 189
Lynn **80** 165
Margaret **52** 478
Margery **82** 47 291 293
Maria **58** 124
Maria L. **83** 182 184
Marie **86** 79 250 251

MARCH *cont'd*
Martha **53** 123-125
Martha I. **80** 165
Martha P. **83** 24 25
Martha R. (Laighton) **83**
    183 184
Mary **52** 479 **53** 121-125 **55**
    314 **58** 42 **65** 353 **82** 332
    501 502 **83** 10 **86** 82 248
    250 251 **104** 319 **106**
    267 268 **108** 191 **121**
    174
Mary (Angier) **106** 268
Mary (Folsom) **106** 71
Mary (Goodwin) **83** 10
Mary (Whittemore)
    106 268
Mary Frances **75** 88
Mary L. (Lowndes)
    125 238
Mary Wainwright **82** 422
Mehitable **83** 122 **82** 48
Mercy **53** 124
Merrill **53** 123
Merry **53** 124
Miriam **82** 48
Molly **53** 124 **82** 48 **107**
    270 274
Morris **58** 44
Nanne **53** 124
Nathaniel **53** 122-124
    82 48
Nehemiah **57** 265
Nichola **86** 216
Nicholas **86** 83
Nizaula **54** cxiv
Oliver **83** 194
Paul **53** 123 **61** 367 **107** 201
    269 270 273
Pelatiah **53** 124 **55** 314 **82**
    332 501 502 **83** 10 148
    154
Peter **86** 216 247
Philip **53** 123
Polly **59** 372
Prudence **86** 249
Rebecca **131** 129
Rhoda **53** 123 **107** 201
    269 270 273 **108** 192
Richard **86** 78 216 219
    247-249
Robert **59** 372 **86** 216 247
    105 96
Roy **80** 165
Ruth **107** 270 **108** 188
Sabrini **100** 76
Samuel **53** 122-124
    103 191
Sarah **53** 121 122 124 125
    268 **54** cxiv **80** 227 **82**
    332 **86** 249 **106** 71 **107**
    270
Sarah M. **83** 298 300
Sarah Martha **83** 173
Sibyl (Taylor) **86** 83
Stephen **52** 479 **53** 121
    123 125 **88** 388
Susan **108** 192
Susan Sparhawk **82** 422
Susanna **53** 124 **82** 286
    293 **83** 23 25 **84** 409 **121**

MARCH *cont'd*
173
Tabitha **53** 122 **111** 107
Theophilus **85** 455
Thomas **53** 123 125 **86** 78
    79 216 250 251 **106** 268
Trueman **53** 122 123
Ulalia **72** 142 **86** 77 78 83
    217 218 220 247 249 250
    89 68 **98** 78
Violet **55** 373 **63** 172 **83** 14
Violet (Lord) **83** 14
Will **86** 216
William **53** 124 **86** 77-79
    216 217 247-251 **142** 257
William King Atkinson
    82 422
MARCHAND
Alfred **131** 87 90
C. A. **56** 112 **61** 318
Caroline-Elizabeth
    (LeBlanc) **131** 94 95 97
Elysee **131** 87
Felix **131** 87 94 95 97
Louise **131** 96
Philip **131** 87
Richard N. **114** 5
Sally Davis (Maraspin)
    114 5
Sidney A. **107** 319 **120** 78
MARCHANT *see also*
    Merchant
— Goodman **142** 52
— Mr. **64** 176
— Widow **142** 53
Abigail **87** 9
Abigail (Butler) **87** 12
Abigail (Raynes) **87** 9
    115 141
Abisha **53** 105
Abishai **59** 207 298 301
    306 411
Ann **52** 359
Ann Catherine **109** 259
Anna **59** 409 **109** 43 **114** 12
Anthony **115** 141
Apphia (Parker) **113** 183
Azubah **106** 101
Betty **106** 101
Bial **108** 207 262
Cornelius **52** 230 369 370
    53 106 **59** 204 302 409
Crowell **108** 207
Deborah **125** 14
Edgar **59** 302
Edward **145** 349
Eleanor **60** 378 **144** 338
Elihu **59** 301 304
Elizabeth **59** 306 410 411
Elmira **86** 401
Ensign **108** 205
Ephraim **59** 206 297 404
Eunice (Chase) **88** 10
Freeman Augustus
    120 16
Gamaliel **53** 107 108
    59 304 410
George **59** 302 304
Hannah **59** 204 **86** 344
Harriet Beetle **74** lxx
Heman **113** 183

MARCHANT *cont'd*
Henry **53** 107 **59** 406-408
    82 197 **118** 313 **128** 126
Hepzibah **59** 410 411
Hepzibah (Jones) **113** 178
Hepzibah (Pease) **87** 12
Hepzibah Y. **141** 148
Huxford **52** 232 **59** 203
Jabez **106** 101
James **108** 207
Jane **59** 298 306 410
Jean **52** 371
Jesse **117** 16
John **52** 231 **53** 102 105 108
    59 303 306 402 410 411
    71 17 **86** 394 **113** 235
    127 239
Josiah **52** 359
Juliana **105** 270
Love **113** 178
Lydia **52** 371 **59** 207 406
    407 409 410
Margaret **81** 489 491
    122 193
Marjory **86** 401
Martha **52** 233 **128** 260
Martha (Dalrymple)
    120 16
Mary **87** 9 **12 99** 298
Mary Ann (Arey) **87** 12
Matilda **59** 306
May W. **52** 446
Mercy **108** 207
Mercy Hallett **108** 207
Miriam **53** 106 108
Molly **106** 101
Naomi **59** 307 411
Oscar **115** 130
Polly **59** 206
R. **111** 253
Rebecca **100** 190
Remember /
    Remembrance **106** 101
Ruben **106** 184 **107** 37
Sarah **59** 402 **71** 17 **86** 394
    141 4
Seth **52** 230 **59** 409 410
    122 193
Silas **52** 230 369 **113** 178
Stephen **117** 9
Susanna **53** 105 **59** 207
    411
Sylvanus **106** 101
Thankful **53** 108 **59** 307
    410 **108** 205 **113** 183
    128 210
William **81** 489 **88** 10
    142 51 52
MARCHAUNTE
Robert **51** 354
Marche *see* March
Marchent *see* Marchant
MARCHIE Martha **65** 44
MARCHIONE
Dale Parsons **148** 237
Marcie *see* Marcy
MARCOM Justina **111** 62
MARCOTTE
Ida A. (Ray) **98** 197
Thomas P. **98** 197

MARCOVIUS
—— **56** 341 343
MARCRAFT
Sarah **81** 305
MARCREASE Amanda
  (Cutting) **89** 293
Harvey **89** 293
MARCUS Moses **56** 23
MARCY —— **51** 51 **58** 99
  92 343 351 353 357
— Col. **51** 188
— Mrs. **51** 188
Abigail (Sargent) **141** 52
Abraham **111** 128
Angeline **68** 335
Anna Laura (Plummer)
  87 174
Anne **72** 141
Bessie Scott (Smith) **83**
  435 **84** 19
Betsey (Parks) **125** 108
Catherine T. (Lord)
  83 183 184
Charles D'W. **54** 114
Charles Dustin **58** 239
  78 6
Christian **94** 41
Christian Morris **92** 343
Clara Kendall **58** 239 **78** 6
Constance (Buckminster)
  94 89 **113** 228
Daniel **68** 43 **83** 183 184
Dorothy (Newell) **109** 191
Dwight **126** 254
Edward **126** 159
Edward D. **68** 335
Edward Wilson **89** 230
Edwin **73** 116
Elias **98** 339
Elijah **51** 188
Eliza (Mott) **109** 191
Eva Luella **111** 128
Fanny G. **68** 335
Fanny W. **68** 335
Frances N. (Shackford)
  83 307
Francis **125** 108
George D. **84** 30
George Daniel **83** 435
  84 19
George N. **68** 335
Hannah **70** 241
Hannah S. **70** 241
Harriet M. (Benham)
  111 123
Harriet M. (Walby)
  111 128
Harry **83** 307
John **58** 272 **72** 141
John J. **91** 201
Lavina **54** 287 288
Lemuel **93** 215
Louisa M. **68** 335
Lucy Sumner **70** 241
Lydia Ann **73** 116
Martha **81** 33
Martha K. **68** 335
Martha R. **70** 241
Marvin **92** 343 348 351
  353 357 **93** 60 **94** 41 380
Marvin Richards **92** 348

MARCY cont'd
Mary **64** 72 **110** 113
Mary A. **73** 116
Mary B. **68** 335
Mary Chastina (Lazell)
  89 230
Mary Dell **111** 128
Mary Kendall **58** 239 **78** 6
Matthew K. **68** 335
Mayer **98** 339
Moses **52** 98 **64** 72 **124** 169
N. A. **111** 123
Nancy M. **116** 260
Newman S. **68** 335
Newton A. **111** 128
Olive **51** 51 **141** 52
Oliver **52** 100
Otis Field **93** 60
Phebe **68** 335
Priscilla **54** 287 **69** 334
  93 215
Prudence **64** 72
Ralph Wales (Mrs.)
  109 130
Reuben **70** 241
Rhoda (James) **126** 254
Rosa **111** 128
Samuel **68** 335 **85** 17
  109 191
Sarah **69** 334 **72** 141 **83** 343
  106 215
Sarah A. **68** 335
Sarah Ann (Wilbur)
  111 128
Sarah E. **125** 183
Thompson (Mrs.) **94** 89
Timothy **68** 335
William Lake **113** 228
William Learned **57** 229
  109 191
William Rutherford
  (Mrs.) **87** 174
William W. **68** 335
William Winchester
  92 357
Winthrop **141** 52
Zebadiah **68** 335
Zebediah **54** 287 **69** 334
MARCYES
Hannah **73** 283 284
Lambert **73** 284
MARDEN
— Goodman **66** 353
— Mr. **82** 285 293
— Mrs. **83** 194
— Widow **83** 35
Abigail **58** 337 **82** 285 293
Agnes (Booreman) **84** 79
Agnes (Borden) **84** 227
Alfred **83** 183 184
Alice **59** 191 **74** 43
Ann (Borden) **84** 227
Anna **59** 290
Annie **84** 30
Bathshua **74** 43
Benjamin **66** 145 **92** 211
  105 299
Betsey **59** 287
Betsey E. **105** 299
Blanche **69** 142
Caroline **126** 145

MARDEN cont'd
Carrie Eliza **77** 181
Charity **81** 430 **92** 211
Charles H. **69** 142
Clara I. **83** 434 435
Daniel Nicher **100** 189
Deborah C. **100** 189
Ebenezer **65** 354
Eleanora J. **117** 165
Eliza **59** 284
Eliza (Denton) **90** 44
Eliza E. **67** 351
Elizabeth **74** 43 49 182 **82**
  48 290 293 300 **90** 109
Ella F. **69** 315
Else **105** 299
Elsie **59** 191
Emery **117** 164
Esther **65** 354
Eunice F. **98** 206
G. A. **58** 215
George Augustus **61** 218
Hannah **59** 40 **61** 243
  81 430
Harriet **105** 299
Harriet E. **105** 299
Harriet Seavey **107** 309
Harris **105** 299
Henry **69** 315
Horace Lockhart **83** 307
James **58** 337 **59** 284 **81**
  446 **82** 27 48 290 293
  125 92 94
James Libbey **74** 43
Joan **66** 56
John **58** 337 **73** 199 **74** 43
  81 446 **82** 48 **84** 79 227
  105 299 **123** 155
John B. **100** 189
John C. **90** 44
Jonathan **105** 114
Joseph **74** 193 **81** 446
Josiah **67** 351
Lucy S. **105** 299
Lucy W. **105** 299
Lydia **74** 43
Maria (Perkins) **90** 47
Mary **74** 43 **82** 48 293 301
Mary Ann (Langdon)
  83 183 184
Mary C. **88** 332
Mehitable **67** 351 **86** 150
  153 **105** 299
Mehitable Hardy **82** 48
Mehitable S. **105** 299
Moses **68** 131
Nancy **82** 48 **120** 221
Nathan **105** 299
Nellie Beck **86** 196
Newell **105** 299
Nicholas **85** 135
Noah **81** 446
Oliver M. **98** 206
Pauline **69** 142
Phedora A. **117** 166
Philip Sanford **63** xxxiii
  72 251
Rachel **59** 286 **105** 299
Rachel (Dowrst) **92** 211
Rebecca **66** 145
Rhoda **117** 227

MARDEN *cont'd*
 Richard **82** 48
 Robert **66** 55
 Salome **82** 27
 Samuel **67** 351 **82** 48
 Sarah **92** 211
 Stephen **81** 430
 Susan M. **105** 299
 Thomas L. **59** 286
 Timothy **82** 293 300
 Uceba (Hillman) **117** 164
 William **65** 323 324 **66** 354
  81 446 **82** 48 **90** 47
 William C. **67** 352
 William P. **105** 299
MARDOCK
 Viola **128** 269
MARE Ann **54** 346
 Elizabeth **147** 13
 Hannah **63** 131
 Henry **86** 457 **87** 275 276
MAREAN Mareen Marene
 Betsey (Blood) **89** 228
 Catherine **97** 236
 Catherine Brewer **113** 295
 Emma Endicott **76** 76
 Emma Frances **76** xxii
 Esther **78** 186
 Ezekiel **79** 164 **80** 72
 John **61** 92 96 **78** 25
 Joseph Mason (Mrs.)
  76 xxii
 Katharine **57** 411
 Laura Etta **89** 113
 Margaret **71** 343
 Rebecca **61** 92
 Samuel **61** 92
 William **57** 411 **140** 68
MAREAU Alonzo **91** 52
 Frederick Alonzo **91** 52
 Jessie Roe (Robinson)
  91 52
Mareen *see* Marean
Marene *see* Marean
MARENELL
 Andrew **102** 184
MARESCALLO
 Andrew **116** 171
MARESQUELLES
 — Col. de **62** 108
 Lewis de **61** 43
MARET
 Richard **110** 168
 William **64** 54
MARETT ____ (Knapp)
  140 160 166
 Elizabeth **55** 420 **140** 166
 Elizabeth Esther **55** 420
  140 166
 Ellen **55** 421
 Martha **55** 421
 Philip **55** 420 421 **140** 160
  166
MAREY Sarah **77** 291
MARGARET John **55** 97
 Laura **96** 159
 Sampson **140** 174
MARGERRY Margeri
 Alice **64** 353
 Jonathan **142** 33
 Luke **142** 33

MARGERRY *cont'd*
 Sarah **142** 33
MARGESON
 R. S. **104** 234
MARGETTS
 Estella Dora **97** 158
 William **93** 6
MARGIN John **62** 362
MARGOLIS
 Max L. **81** 370
MARGOT
 L. Stanley (Mrs.) **115**
  79
MARGOTTE
 Jean Marie **110** 133
 Therese F. (Lemaire)
  110 133
MARGRAGE
 Serena **74** 296
MARGRATE
 George **120** 319
 Mary **120** 319
 Susanna **120** 319
MARH Rhoda **108** 192
MARHSFIELD
 Rachel **85** 48
MARIA HENRIETTA
 Queen of the Belgians
  88 102
MARIA —— **144** 226
 Patience **87** 259
MARIAM Elizabeth **68** 218
  106 45
 John **105** 284 **106** 45
 Mary (Luff) **106** 45
 Thankful **68** 219
 William **68** 218 219
MARICA William **73** 136
MARICHON
 James **91** 329
MARICK Stephen **63** 82
  128 327
MARICLE
 Cora Letts **61** 205
MARIE Countess of
 Flanders **88** 99 102
MARIE-JOSE Crown
 Princess of Italy
  88 104
MARIENVILLE
 Robert de **87** 245
 Sarah (Chase) **87** 245
Marifield *see* Merrifield
MARIGER Vivian Kane
 (Mrs.) **108** 135
MARIGNY Abbe **56** 116
MARIL Lo. **64** 239
MARILLEY
 Richard **63** 343
MARILLIAS
 Don Juan de **54** 269
MARIN M. **77** 103
 Prudence (Butler) **88** 283
 Thomas **88** 283
MARINE
 Louisa **112** 141
 William Pierrepont
  82 122 237
MARINER Marriner
 Merriner
 Abigail **82** 293 302

MARINER *cont'd*
 Catherine **80** 25
 Ellice **82** 292 293
 Georgiana **92** 338
 James **69** 363 **92** 338 339
 Jonathan **105** 286
 Mary **92** 339
 Mary Lou (Craver)
  143 168
 Nailer **105** 286
 Philip **105** 286
 Ruth **63** 382
 Sally **96** 248
 Sarah **63** 269
 Stephen **80** 25
MARINES
 Philippe **143** 198
MARINO Alexander **66** 34
MARION
 —— **53** 134 **54** 370
 — Mrs. **51** 282
 Addison Gardner **75** 267
 Anna **75** 151
 Carrie **114** 62
 Catherine **114** 191 **125** 73
 Eliza Jane **75** 267
 Elizabeth **75** lxxix 151
  86 449
 Ellen **144** 239
 Esther **75** 151
 Francis **53** 455 **65** 230 **90**
  183 **114** 191 **130** 185
  137 312
 Gabriella M. **114** 191
 H. Riddell **110** 149
 Isaac **75** 151
 J. C. **112** 316
 Jessie A. (Black) **110** 149
 Jno. **139** 313 **144** 17
 John **51** 171 **96** 325 **106** 19
  114 250 251 **139** 299
  302 **142** 267
 John Ernest **51** 95 99
 Jonathan **139** 312
 Jos. **63** 278
 Joseph **57** 277 280 **84** 152
  157 **112** 180 **125** 73 **144**
  239
 Judeth **105** 76
 Louisa C. **114** 191
 Lydia **75** 151
 Margery (Webster)
  (Godfrey) **142** 267
 Mary **75** 151
 Mary G. **88** 332
 Mary V. **114** 191
 Nathan Kellogg **75** 267
 Nathaniel **75** 151
 Otis H. **61** 109
 Phebe Rose (Addoms)
  112 316
 Prudence **114** 250 251
 Rebecca **75** 151
 Ruth Ann **75** 267
 Sarah **75** 151
 Thankful **75** 150 151
 William **60** 39 **75** 150 151
MARIPINE
 Amme **102** 29
 Anthony Valentine
  102 29

MARIPINE *cont'd*
 Elizabeth **100** 304
 Joseph **102** 29
MARIS
 Emilie **77** xxviii
 Margaret **98** 126
 Mary **80** 319 322
 Rachel **51** 74
MARISCIS Christiana de
 116 279
 Robert de **116** 279
MARISH Lydia **97** 272
MARJARY
 Jonathan **103** 195
MARJORAM
 Sarah (Lilly) **90** 105
 William Waterson **90** 105
MARJORIBANKS-
 EGERTON P. M.
 113 87
Mark *see* Marks
MARKALL Cicely **54** 161
Markam *see* Markham
MARKAME
 Augustine **72** 55
MARKANT
 John **63** 281 282
 Robert **63** 282
 Thomas **63** 281 282
MARKBY
 John **60** 309 **68** 68
MARKEE Gates **121** 140
MARKELL
 William Bruce **68**
 xxxiv
MARKEN Ruby C. **66** 49
MARKETMAN
 Mary **65** 320
 Phillis **65** 320
 Richard **84** 72
 Roger **84** 72
 Steven **65** 320
 Thomas **65** 320
MARKEY
 Sarah Jane **84** 101
MARKHAM
 —— **89** 74 **117** 279
 — Admiral **62** 55
 Abigail **124** 13
 Abigail (Chadwick)
 124 13
 Abijah **124** 13
 Alice **111** 68
 Artemas **115** 36
 Asher **124** 224
 Charlotte A. Turner
 85 168
 Clements **87** 32
 Daniel **60** 187 **86** 349 350
 124 13
 Denison Gorham **85** 168
 Dolly (Joslin) **124** 13
 E. A. **54** xxxviii **55** xxxii
 56 xxxii **60** 187
 Elijah **124** 13
 Elizabeth **55** 340 341 **57** 80
 127 7
 Elizabeth (Whitmore)
 86 349
 Erastus **124** 13
 Ernest A. **57** xxxiii **58** xlv

MARKHAM *cont'd*
 61 xxxiv **62** xxxvii **64**
 xxxi **67** xxxi **68** xxxii **69**
 xxxii
 Esther **117** 79
 Eunice **113** 40
 Francis **63** 164
 George **54** 335 **65** 129
 George Dickson **83** 336
 Guy **57** 80
 Hannah **115** 125
 Henry **115** 37
 Hubbard **62** 362
 Isaac **71** 45
 James **60** 398
 Jane **60** 398
 Jeanette Sumner **83** 495
 Jehial **115** 124
 Jemima **89** 380
 Jerusha **124** 13
 Joan **63** 164
 John **55** 340 341 **111** 68
 Joseph **115** 123
 Justina **111** 62
 Justus **124** 13
 Lucy (Landers) **124** 224
 Phila **89** 206
 Robert **94** 264
 Sarah Marie **78** 296
 Stephen **124** 13
 Submit (House) **124** 13
 W. M. **91** 329
 Wiley **91** 329
 William **52** 368 **54** 334 335
 63 237 **115** 124
MARKLAND
 Edward **90** 299
 Oliver **63** 160
MARKLE
 Alvan (Mrs.) **93** 98
 Caspar **87** 389
 Christian **87** 389 390
 Elizabeth (Grimm) **87** 389
 Emily Alexander
 (Robison) **87** 389
 107 113
 Gaspard **88** 82
 George **87** 389
 George Bushar **87** 389 390
 107 113
 Gladys Jones **93** 98
 Ida **75** xxii **115** 229
 Jemima (Weurtz) **87** 389
 John **75** xxiii 64 **87** 389
 390 **88** 86 172
 Leah **88** 82
 Magdalena (Coehorn)
 87 389
 Mary (Rathermel) **88** 82
 Mary Christina (Hill)
 87 389
 Mary Estelle (Robinson)
 87 390
 Peter **87** 389
 Sophia Maria (Beaudoin)
 87 389
MARKLEY Edith (Denno)
 145 138
 Elizabeth **64** 161
 Franklyn **145** 138
 Gladys **145** 138

MARKLEY *cont'd*
 Leslie **145** 138
MARKMAN Edith **99** 330
MARKOE —— **98** 371
 Frances E. (Caldwell) **97**
 158 **98** 77
 Harry **98** 77
 Harry (Mrs.) **97** 158 288
 98 77 151
 Maria **105** 219
 Peter **140** 68
 Stephen **98** 77
MARKQUICK Hercules
 Richard (Mrs.) **117** 153
 118 163 **119** 153 **120**
 153
MARKRES Clair **89** 290
 Gertie Ione **89** 290
 H. A. **89** 290
 Rachel A. (Cutting)
 89 290
 Ruby S. **89** 290
MARKS —— **76** 172
 — Mr. **62** 285 **72** 176
 Abigail **76** 147 **79** 17
 Abraham **76** 134
 Agnes **68** 58
 Albion F. **109** 109
 Alice **51** 276-278 **65** 133
 Asa **113** 35
 Asa (Mrs.) **113** 35
 B. H. **98** 358
 Benjamin **106** 219
 Betsey **108** 285 **113** 41
 Betty **76** 144
 Caroline Ellen (Hurlbut)
 87 191
 Catherine **82** 16
 Catherine Emeline **86** 197
 87 72 178 191
 Charlene **104** 144
 Cornwell **61** 391
 Daniel **82** 16
 Deborah **63** 354
 Eben **110** 110
 Eben (Mrs.) **109** 109
 Ebenezer **107** 64 **110** 110
 Edmund **51** 276 277 280
 Edward **51** 279
 Elijah Samuel **90** 168
 Eliza Ann **76** 142
 Eliza C. **125** 237
 Eliza J. **69** 199
 Elizabeth **51** 214 **63** 354
 106 312
 Ellen **91** 329
 Emily **91** 329
 Galen **109** 14 15
 Galen O. **108** 284 **109** 109
 George **65** 133 **68** 58
 George B. **69** 203
 George Beckwick **76** 151
 Gregory **86** 177 **105** 264
 Hannah **56** 288 **58** 181 **76**
 144 **109** 109
 Hannah (Day) **110** 110
 Hannah (Gott) **108** 284
 Harriet **90** 168
 Harriet (Sandusky)
 90 168
 Henry **87** 191

MARKS *cont'd*
Hepzibah **104** 59
Ida A. **69** 203
Irena **107** 64
Irene **110** 25
Irving **95** 98
Isaac **63** 354
J. **91** 329
James **56** 288 **110** 105
James E. **110** 105
Jane **87** 127
Jeannette **141** 314
John **62** 332 **76** 138 150
   91 329 **98** 7 **105** 212
   111 208
John Nicol **91** 220
John Shenur **115** 16
Jonas **55** 69
Joseph **52** 243 **76** 148
Josiah **115** 16
Julia **98** 358
Julia A. **69** 203
Kenneth L. **100** 259
Lillian Jeanette **82** 16
Lydia **107** 64
Mabel Eleanor (Ayer)
   97 158
Malvina **110** 110
Margaret (Henman)
   126 64
Maria (Gramley) (Baer)
   87 191
Maria J. **110** 24
Martha (Billings) **98** 7
Mary **55** 187 **63** 354 **98** 108
   107 63 **114** 186
Mary (Galley) **114** 186
Mary (Hayden) **110** 105
Mary A. **65** 133
Mary Ann Catherine
   98 358
Mary F. **109** 109
Matilda **107** 64 **108** 284
Mercy (Dickens) **86** 177
   105 264
Michael **76** 147
Miles **51** 276 277 **52** 248
Mona C. **125** 238
Mordecai **76** 134
Nancy **104** 132
Nathan **75** 92
Nehemiah **76** 142 144 151
Orson **91** 329
Phebe **78** 235
Phebe (Haskell) **109** 12
   109
Philip **63** 141 **82** 16
Polly **107** 64
Prudence **51** 276
Rachel **110** 105
Rebecca **107** 64
Richard **115** 16
Robert **63** 282 **105** 10
Samuel **51** 276 277 **91** 329
Sarah **61** 391 **63** 354
Sarah Elizabeth **110** 105
Sheldon **76** 139 148
Stephen **105** 212 **108** 285
   109 109 **110** 105
Stephen (Mrs.) **109** 109
Susan **107** 64 **108** 280

MARKS *cont'd*
Susan H. **110** 21
Susan J. **109** 109
Susanna **75** 92
Tente **115** 16
Theodore **94** 266
Thomas **63** 354 **107** 64
Upton **91** 329
Victor **110** 105
Wanton **107** 64
Warren **109** 12 109
William **51** 276 277 **66**
   245 252 **76** 139 148 **129**
   56
William Henry **87** 191
William J. **91** 329
William Percy (Mrs.)
   97 158
Zachariah **76** 138 150
MARKSTED
Edward **95** 259
MARKUS
Gunner **100** 303
Mary (Duckous) **100** 303
Oscar A. (Mrs.) **107** 134
Theresa **103** 241
MARKWELL
F. C. **147** 340
MARLAND
Abby Billings **75**
   lxxvii
George Abbott **75** lxxvii
Helen **75** lxxvii
Mary King **75** lxxvii
Salome Jane **71** xxiii **74**
   xxviii **75** xxxiv lxxvi
   lxxvii
Sarah **75** lxxvi
Thomas **64** 165 166
William **75** lxxvi lxxvii
William (Mrs.) **74** xxviii
   86 133 143
William Sykes **75** lxxvi
MARLATT Helen Stuart
   Mackay-Smith **116** 82
MARLBOROUGH
— Duke of **53** 261 322
Sarah **85** 164
MARLEBURG James (Earl
   of) **52** 127
MARLEN Willm. **147** 13
MARLER Peter **111** 169
Ralph **82** 188
Robert **82** 188 **116** 169
Tamsin (Cogan) **111** 169
MARLERE Isabel **93** 75
William **93** 75
MARLETT Gideon **57** 12
Jane **57** 12
Sally M. **57** 12
MARLIN Aeltye **66** 18
Aeltje **66** 18
Anna **66** 18
Hendrick **66** 18
Jean (Manahan) (Patten)
   90 388
Orr (Mrs.) **99** 48
William **90** 388
MARLOUT Sophia **78** 401
MARLOW
Abraham **73** 137

MARLOW *cont'd*
Amelia **73** 137 138
Ann Middleton **73** 231
Butler D. **73** 221
Buttler **73** 142
Charles **76** 272
Edward **73** 263
Eliza **73** 272
Emeline **76** 272
Esther **91** 300 303
George Francis **100** 259
   102 157 **108** 159
Isaac **51** 291
John **73** 153
John L. (Mrs.) **119** 5
John S. **73** 275
Julia **105** 82
Maria C. **73** 265
Martha **73** 271
Samuel **73** 271
Sarah **73** 137
Susanna **51** 291
Thankful **85** 44
Thomas D. **73** 148
William **73** 147 230
MARMADUKE
— Gen. **62** 52 53
John Sappington **77** 223
MARMAN
Betsey **114** 181
Dama **114** 181
John **114** 181
Lucinda **114** 181
Mark **114** 181
Rebecca **114** 181
MARMIAR Jenny
   (Montgomery)
   125 101
Peter **125** 101
MARMION Le Marmion
   Marmyon
   —— **141** 103 104 **144** 268
   269
Elizabeth **111** 198
Lora (St. Quintin) **111** 198
Mabel **99** 273 274
Maud **120** 173
Osbert **98** 111
Philip **98** 112
Robert **99** 273 **120** 173
William **105** 36 **139** 229
MARNEY
John **110** 124 125
Robert **109** 22
William **109** 23
MARON Alfred Conrad
   81 107 219 **88** 89 174 **90**
   356
Anna (Miller) **90** 356
Conrad **90** 356
Dewa (Davis) **90** 357
Don Edward **90** 357
MARONE Nicholas **78** 311
MARONEY Loise **106** 226
MAROWE Elisha **53** 173
Katharine **98** 115
Thomas **98** 115
William **98** 115
MARPLE Jane **128** 96
Marie **64** 86
Mary (McGren) **128** 96

MARPLE cont'd
Samuel **128** 96
MARPLEHEAD
Mary **93** 206
MARPOLE Nancy **63** 271
MARQUAND Christian
Sedgwick **94** 98
John Phillips **136** 90 322
328
Joseph **136** 322 328
Laura Margaret **85** 199
Margaret (Fuller) **136** 322
Margaret Searle (Curzon)
136 322
Peter **140** 172-174 178
Philip **136** 322
Sarah Winslow (Tyng)
136 322
MARQUARD Mary **51** 462
MARQUESS
Effie Lee **95** 145
MARQUESSEE
— Maj. **76** 146
Lewis **76** 146
MARQUETTE Jacques **51**
386 **64** 95 **68** lxxiii
Jacques C. de **99** 138
Jacques D. de **100** 106
MARQUIS
Albert Nelson **79** 224
MARR see also Mar
—— **71** 124
Abigail **99** 198
Adaline **85** 447
Adelaine **112** 241
Andrew **63** 103 **148** 59
Anne **131** 74
Benjamin **65** 255
Betsey **65** 255
Caroline **80** 27
Caroline Jean **83** 435 436
Catherine **87** 125
Charles A. **80** 152
Cyprius **82** 331
Cyrus **148** 172
Dennis **99** 199 **103** 193 197
Dennis (Mrs.) **103** 197
Dianna **148** 169 173
Dolly **99** 199
Ellen Arabella **148** 169 173
Else **82** 293 297
Esther Mary **80** 152
Eunice **83** 15
George **63** 103
Hannah **87** 123
Helen E. **83** 300
Ichabod **55** 373 **63** 173
83 14
Isaiah **80** 25 **127** 158
James **64** 319 **65** 255
99 198
James Eldred **128** 133
Jane (Bradley) **100** 239
Jane (Shirley) **130** 158
John **83** 15 **99** 205 **148**
169 173
John Amos **112** 241
John E. **76** 242
Joseph **112** 241
Joshua **65** 255 **73** 136
Joshua Libby **99** 198

MARR cont'd
Kingsmill **71** xlvii
Laura **71** xlvii
Lawrence **76** 242 318
Lydia **65** 255 **99** 198
Lydia Hill **99** 198
Marcy **82** 331
Mark **99** 198 199
Mary **83** 11
Mehitable **55** 373 **83** 14
Mercy **63** 173 **80** 25 **83** 14
Mercy (Oliver) **127** 158
Molly **55** 373 **63** 173 **83** 14
Molly (Nason) **83** 14
Parker **103** 258
Polly **99** 198
Rufus **65** 255 **99** 198
103 190
Ruth **80** 28
Salome **65** 255
Sarah **82** 331 **83** 13 **99** 205
Sylva **99** 202
Thomas **55** 373 **76** 242 **83**
14 **99** 205
Walter **71** 124
William **63** 173 **83** 449
130 158
William Parker **99** 198
William Price **76** 242 318
MARRABLE
Robert **140** 167
MARRAGE — Widow **84** 306
MARRANCE
Robert **84** 77
MARRANT Robert **67** 166
MARRARO
Howard R. **107** 19
MARREL Peter **104** 22
MARRETT Marret
—— **59** 85
— Capt. **57** 111
— Rev. Mr. **59** 147 150
Abigail **112** 69 70
Abigail (Richardson)
112 70
Alexander **63** 279
Amos **83** 378
Anne **63** 279
Basil Joseph **65** 230
Hepsibah **128** 44
John **52** 144 **65** 375 **74** 203
79 40 **112** 70 **121** 247
Margaret **63** 279
Martha **74** 203 **77** 319
Mary Elizabeth **60** lxxv
Mary W. **124** 150
Peter **65** 230
Thomas **121** 247
MARRIAN Elizabeth **68** 72
111 238
Isaac **56** 275
John **56** 275 **68** 72 **111** 238
MARRIBLE —— **102** 321
MARRICK
Frances Fiske **107** 151
John **107** 95
Ruth **107** 242
MARRIL Nathen **127** 222
MARRIN John Francis **56**
xxxii
Marriner see Mariner

MARRIOTT Marriot
Marryat Marryot
Marryott Maryatt
Maryote Merriot
—— **52** 100
Abigail **53** 462
Abraham **111** 281 **113** 210
Adda **83** 69
Allina **83** 68
Anna **83** 69 **113** 210
Benjamin **113** 210 211
Charles **83** 68 69
Charlotte (Geyer) **140** 144
Cora **83** 68
Earl **83** 69
Edward **83** 68
Edward L. **83** 68
Elijah **83** 68
Elizabeth **83** 68
Elsie **83** 69
Emily Bayley **108** 151
Felix **127** 79
Frederick **52** 388
George **83** 68
Georgie **83** 69
Grace **83** 68
Henry **65** 323 **127** 79 142
Hubert **83** 68
Isaac **113** 205 210 270 271
Isaac Franklin **83** 68
James **65** 87
John **93** 393 **111** 271
Joseph **113** 210 211 271
140 144
Joseph S. **83** 68
Joyce **113** 205 210 270 271
Joyce (Ollive) **113** 210
Laura **83** 68
Louisa **83** 68
Malinda **83** 68
Mary **111** 286
Mary (Fenimore) **111** 281
Mary (Mullen) **111** 281
Middleton **65** 21
Nicholas **54** 277
Oliver **83** 69
Oscar **109** 160
Phelix **127** 12
Polly **88** 119
Powers **58** 68 **84** 256
Richard **113** 210
Samuel **62** 285 **109** 160
113 210 **127** 79
Samul **111** 56
Sarah **113** 210
Sarah Ellen **83** 69
Susanna **113** 205 210 271
Susanna (Field) **113** 205
210 211
Thomas **65** 71 **113** 210
W. Smith **35** 209
Walter Scott **83** 69
Will Clark **83** 69
William **94** 339 **141** 116
MARRIS Elizabeth **67** 67
MARRISON
Mary **113** 312
MARROTT William **120** 77
MARROW
— Capt. **56** 372
Anne **63** 172

MARROW *cont'd*
David **145** 360
Ebenezer **66** 271 **114** 298
Edmund **63** 172
John H. **51** 194
Katharine **98** 115
Lucy Frances **51** 194
Lydia **63** 171
Sally **84** 374
Samuel **65** 163
MARRS Mars
Alice **100** 239
Anna **123** 308
Benjamin **116** 226
Eunice **55** 374
Jane **115** 221
John **55** 374 **100** 239
Katharine **74** 253
Kingsmill (Mrs.) **79** 95
Mary **55** 315 373 **83** 11
Mehitable (Huntress)
 83 14
Mercy **83** 14
Robert **100** 239
Sarah **55** 316 **83** 13
Unice (Abbot) **83** 15
MARRY Barnat **65** 121
Dolly **99** 198
Robert **54** 214
Marryat *see* Marriott
Marryatt *see* Marriott
Marryott *see* Marriott
Mars *see* Marrs
MARSCRAFT
Daniel **55** 66
MARSDEN —— **54** 230
— Mr. **65** 44
Christopher **65** 44
Dorothy **83** 452
George **116** 233
John **64** 253 **65** 168 169
Kenneth L. **116** 233
Levi **83** 194
Mary C. **68** 203
R. G. **70** 337 340
Samuel **68** 203
William **83** 451 452
MARSELUS
Sarah **90** 378
MARSER John **109** 38
Mercy (Marston) **109** 38
Thomas **72** 53 55
MARSEREUX
Estienne **66** 18
Marie **66** 18
MARSH — Capt. **118** 15
 18 235
— Col. **74** 285
— Miss **79** 304
— Mr. **57** 228 **62** 362 **71**
 135 **73** 72 194 **79** 301 **80**
 64
— Mrs. **51** 189 **79** 301
 302 308 408 409 **80** 60
 83 194 **121** 94 **127** 14
— Mrs. William **130** 72
— Widow **71** 134 **91** 256
Abby **79** 303 408 **80** 58
Abigail **57** 286 **79** 401 **90**
 289 **91** 258 **98** 337 **118**
 92 **121** 126

MARSH *cont'd*
Abigail (Clapp) **92** 146
Abigail (Merrill) **91** 263
Abram **72** 205
Adam **56** lxv
Ade **77** 177
Adoniram Judson **69** 32
Alexander **59** 155-157 364
 365 **60** 128-131 **61** 40
 129 130 **64** 255 **86** 455-
 457 **87** 277 **92** 263
Alice **61** 130 **71** 319 **81** 57
 112 34 **138** 40
Alice (Nicholson) **139** 235
Amariah **65** 39
Amaryllis (Squires)
 130 72
Amasa **115** 320
Amos **118** 91 92
Amy (Taylor) **133** 229
Andrew **52** 105
Ann **61** 285 **79** 401 404
 406 409 **80** 58 60 **117**
 275 **125** 245
Anna **69** 32 **86** 26 **110** 140
 142 72
Anne **56** 255 **79** 150 303 **80**
 66 **140** 179
Anne (Brown) **98** 51
Anne (Webster) **102** 230
Ansel C. **82** 376
Anstiss **62** 188
Arah **110** 150
Arthur M. **113** 240
Atwood **126** 181
Avis K. **137** 31
Barachias Washburn
 86 366
Bathsheba **86** 455 456
 87 277
Bathsheba (Lathrop) (Bale)
 86 455-457
Becca **118** 221 224 232 234
 299 305
Becky **118** 27
Benjamin **56** lxv 255 **125**
 172 174
Benjamin F. **90** 54
Benjamin Wilson **114** 157
Bertha (Ellis) **89** 132
Bertha S. **89** 305
Bessie A. **80** 202 **88** 91
Bethiah **87** 390
Betsey **54** 290 **56** 255 **57** li
 101 204 **118** 91 92 **121**
 69
Betsey (Huntley) **101** 205
Betsey (Lougee) **118** 91 92
Betsey Ann **80** 46
Betty **72** 283 **120** 208
Bower **90** 402 **143** 363
C. C. **77** 161
Caleb **74** 107 **140** 167
Calvin **123** 27 28 30
Carlos E. **75** 41
Carlotta **94** 136 **95** 144
Carmi Lathrop **65** 161
Caroline Amelia **81** 196
Caroline E. (Mann)
 88 339
Caroline Elizabeth **56** lxv

MARSH *cont'd*
Catherine **79** 152 **125** 172
 126 110
Catherine (Castoff)
 125 174
Catherine Lucy **89** 187
Celia F. **75** 206 **77** 146
Charitable **71** 38
Charles **55** 295 296 **61** 285
 69 32 **70** 230 **75** 206 **90**
 282
Charles B. **132** 295
Charles D. **61** 277
Charles Edwards **80** 46
Charles Grant **80** 62 66
Charles P. **62** 188
Charles Thomas **102** 143
Charles Thomas (Mrs.)
 96 160 **102** 62 129 142
 143
Charles Webster **85** 224
Charles William Strong
 80 46
Christobel **60** 350
Christopher **98** 51
Christopher Bridge
 121 247
Clarissa **118** 92
Clark **57** 410
Clement **64** 15
Constance **145** 111 113
Constance (Hamby) **145**
 110-113
Cora Ellen (Vandemark)
 96 160 **102** 142
Cyrus **70** 221 226
Daniel **54** 290 **55** 389 **99**
 304 **102** 230 **110** 150
 118 108 **121** 297 **123** 16
 19-21 24 27 28 30 **128**
 284
Daniel L. **99** 211 **100** 108
 102 119 **114** 70
David **79** 303 **81** 189
 121 280
David W. **65** 150
Deborah **88** 358 **106** 230
 136 328
Deborah (Buell) **136** 313
 328
Donald Buckham **102** 230
Dorcas **110** 278
Dorothea **56** lxv
Dorothy (Mason) **102** 230
Douglass **87** 247
Dudley **145** 351
Duty **121** 93
Eben **125** 36
Ebenezer **70** 76 **91** 259 267
 101 155 160 **118** 124
 218 304 306 **119** 52 212-
 214 219 **120** 60 209 295
 123 16 17 **136** 313 328
Ebenezer Grant **80** 62 70
Edmund **81** 57 **145** 113
Edward **68** 49 **96** 160
Edward P. **125** 172
Elam (Mrs.) **92** 146
Elam Smith **83** 490
Eleanor **55** 336 **81** 57
Elias **97** 335

MARSH *cont'd*
Elijah **133** 229
Elisha **82** 376 **105** 108
  107 313
Eliza **69** 32 **125** 294
Elizabeth **55** 71 **56** lxv **64**
  343 **65** 351 **70** 225 **72**
  317 **79** 301 **81** 189 261
  82 236 **93** 279 **94** 195
  101 155 158-160 **108** 64
  121 21 269 **126** 142 **142**
  270 **143** 361 **145** 111
  113
Elizabeth (Burbank) **102** 3
Elizabeth (Gillett) **101** 160
Elizabeth (Harding)
  90 46
Elizabeth (Lincoln)
  121 209
Elizabeth (Pitkin) **136**
  313 328
Elizabeth (Webster)
  125 175
Elizabeth W. **126** 23
Elizabeth Wales **81** 222
  237
Ella B. **69** 32
Ellen **114** 182
Ellen Story **86** 366
Ely T. **101** 205
Emily **69** 32
Emma **102** 158
Emma Frances **59** lxix
Enoch **109** 56
Enos **101** 159
Ephraim **121** 105 209 212
Esek **95** 237
Esther **56** 259 **81** 39 **111**
  225 **112** 242 243
Esther A. **82** 376
Ezekiel **56** lxv
Fannie Irene **80** 46
Fanny **95** 282
Fanny D. **61** 277
Fennimore C. **75** x xxiii
Florence Christine
  (Boynton) **94** 195
Frances **79** 404 **80** 66
Frances A. **82** 376
Frances Ann **79** 409 **80** 62
Frances Fowler **80** 62
Frances T. **79** 153
Francis **75** 34 40
Francis G. **75** 41
Freeman L. **75** 41
Frieda Lawrence **81** 196
George **94** 195 **121** 20
  126 141 **145** 111 113
George W. **81** 265 **138** 122
Gould **127** 140
Grace **56** 275
Gyles **105** 96
Hannah **51** 188 **70** 76 **75**
  206 **83** 261 **91** 259 262
  263 **92** 99 **101** 288 **121**
  107 **126** 37 **136** 325 329
  330
Hannah (Cutler) **121** 105
Hannah (Lincoln) **94** 195
Hannah C. (Harris) **90** 54

MARSH *cont'd*
Hannah Withington
  75 206
Harriet **85** 224 **118** 92
Harriet (Adlington)
  126 141
Harriet (Gifford) **132** 295
Harriet Cranston **80** 46
Harriet Eliza **85** 224
Harriet G. **125** 175
Harriet Moore **77** xl
Hattie **82** 268
Helen (Percival) **106** 142
Helen Willard **102** 230
Henry **56** lxv **60** 291 **79**
  302 **82** 376 **86** 258 **113**
  273 **139** 235
Henry W. **85** 188
Henry Wheelwright
  98 87 149
Hepzibah **136** 310
Hepzibah (Ford) **136** 329
Herbert J. **118** 92
Hiram **81** 273 **114** 182
Horatio W. **75** 206
Howard **106** 142
Huldah **56** 255
Ira **101** 204
Irene Graffin Lee **113** 239
Irene Lee (Graffin)
  113 240
Israel **69** 32
J. (Mrs.) **79** 406 409
Jacob **91** 255 **101** 204
  110 150
James **56** 394 **71** 328 **87**
  247 **97** 340 **102** 230
Jared **110** 150
Jason **77** xl
Jehieha Lord **60** 44
Jemima **61** 130
Jerusha **54** 290 **56** 255 **61**
  130 **70** 76
Job **121** 61 **123** 19 **129** 207
  136 321
John **51** 188 **56** lxv 256 275
  59 157 363-365 **61** 129
  130 **63** 69 **65** 351 **72** 317
  75 227 **79** 150 153 303
  404 405 **80** 62 63 66 70
  81 57 265 **82** 48 293 298
  83 35 **88** 285 **90** 87 **91**
  256 257 259 262 **94** 195
  97 340 **99** 79 **102** 230
  105 108 277 **114** 313
  121 103 115 247 270
  125 175 **134** 53 **136** 310
  313 325 328-330 **138** 125
  142 270 **143** 18 **145** 334
John B. **118** 92
John C. **98** 51
John Edward **81** 196
John L. **83** 110
John L. (Mrs.) **83** 110
John Lee **113** 240
John M. **62** 188
John Tallmadge **79** 406
  80 62
Jonathan **71** 203 **72** 29 317
  87 398 **90** 393 **91** 258
  109 165 **111** 225 **114**

MARSH *cont'd*
  312 313 **121** 272-274
  127 14
Joseph **51** 224 **56** 255 **63**
  91 **72** 283 **76** 139 **82** 48
  265 **87** 398 **97** 335 **99** 79
  102 230 **118** 91 92 306
  119 53 121 138 **121** 287
  140 175 176
Joseph DuBois **80** 46
Joseph M. **66** 112 **113** 255
  256 **140** 167
Joseph Walker **102** 230
Julia Ann **59** lxix
Julia Louise LeBrun
  83 110
Julia M. (Barrett) **90** 282
Katharine **97** 340 **145** 113
Keziah **87** 247 **125** 292
Laura (Wheelock) **102** 230
Laura A. **75** 41
Laura Louisa **80** 62
Lawrence **71** 319
Leonora **69** 32
Leslie W. **95** 314
Levi **110** 150
Levi B. **82** 376
Levi H. **140** 167
Lewis **123** 31
Lois **104** 162 **135** 337
Lomira (Kennon) **86** 366
Lora Elizabeth **80** 46
Lot **94** 195
Louisa **76** 139
Louisa Adelaide (Taft)
  94 195
Louisa L. **75** 206
Lucia (Wheelock) **102** 230
Lucina **72** 316 317
Lucinda **81** 273
Lucius Bolles **56** xiv xli
  lxiii **57** 337 **88** 339
Lucy **57** 411 **64** 209 **70** 76
  138 125
Lucy Dolph **80** 46
Lucy Frances **77** xl
Lucy M. **75** 206
Lydia **51** 224 **79** 303 401
  409 **91** 256 **110** 150 **136**
  29 329
Lydia (French) **94** 195
Lydia (Jewet) **91** 262
Lydia (Kingsley) **110** 150
Lydia (Tupper) (Fuller)
  99 304
M. **81** 265
M. L. **128** 91 94-96 172-
  175 264 266 268
Mabel **118** 307 **123** 19
Mabel Minott **90** 282
Madeline Adel (Crosby)
  95 314
Mae **92** 339
Marcius **130** 72
Margaret **61** 277 **74** 107
Margaret Helen **106** 142
Margaret J. **69** 32
Margaret Marsh (Aymar)
  97 340
Maria **75** 206
Maria L. **82** 376

MARSH *cont'd*
Marietta **92** 339
Marshall Stuart (Mrs.)
82 125 **83** 233
Martha **97** 335 **136** 321
Martha (Fitz Randolph)
97 335
Martha (Severance)
91 262
Martha Ethel **90** 137
Martha Eugenia **80** 46
Martha S. **82** 376
Mary **60** 128 129 **61** 129
66 176 **69** 32 **71** 115 **75**
41 **79** 150 298 303 **86**
234 **93** 282 **114** 182 **117**
274 **118** 90 92 **121** 107
109 213 **136** 313 **145**
113 334
Mary (Allison) **145** 334
Mary (Buckham) **102** 230
Mary (Burr) **88** 358 **94** 195
Mary (Coates) **111** 225
Mary (Cross) **91** 265
Mary (Demarest) **102** 158
Mary (Fitz Randolph)
98 51
Mary (Shotwell) **97** 340
Mary A. **69** 32
Mary Ann **73** 194 **104** 162
Mary Bradford **63** 275
Mary Brimmer **80** 62
Mary C. **125** 172 174
Mary C. (Williams)
125 178
Mary Frances **85** 224
Mary H. **72** 205
Mary Lizzie **83** 490
Mary T. (Hollenbeck)
83 490
Matilda **109** 165
Mehitable **109** 165 **141** 153
Mehitable (Duston)
109 165
Mehitable (Porter) **129**
206 207 **136** 321
Melista (Cook) **126** 181
Mercy **59** 153 155 **102** 267
123 24
Mercy (Bill) **102** 230
Miles **82** 376
Miles W. **82** 376
Miriam **72** 317
Miriam Webster (Gilbert)
(Hopkins) **114** 313
Molly **91** 257 258 **118** 303
307 **119** 43 47-49 51 55-
57 130
Moses **54** 290 **56** 249 250
255 259 **61** 130 **91** 260
110 140 **118** 14 306
Nabby **56** 256
Nancy **79** 299 **81** 343
Nancy Falls (Davis)
89 187
Nathan **145** 356
Nathaniel **60** 350 **70** 315
71 38 **72** 317
Nehemiah **118** 90 92
Nettie Harrison **90** 382
Nicholas **54** 63

MARSH *cont'd*
Noah **69** 32
O. C. **55** 366
Olive **62** 29 **92** 61 **118** 92
Oliver **123** 28
Onesiphorus **91** 255 256
262 **121** 105 125 **139**
131
Page **62** 247
Parsons **123** 21
Patty **56** 255 **118** 306
123 24
Perez **113** 318 **136** 321
Perlina S. **75** 34 40
Phebe **56** 250 258 **59** 157
81 57 **118** 16 27 115 118
119 126 217 **119** 133
120 62
Phebe (Porter) **123** 126
Phebe M. **125** 179 **126** 23
Phebe Parsons **123** 21
Philena **147** 178
Philip Gridley **95** 317
Philippa **139** 235
Philippa (Raynsford)
139 235
Phineas **97** 340
Pierces **122** 122
Polly **56** 249
Priscilla **70** 176 225
Rachel **59** 156 **79** 246
Ralph **117** 274
Randolph **97** 340
Rebecca **52** 112 **56** lxv
118 24 228 234 **121** 300
123 126
Reuben **51** 190 **115** 320
Reuben P. **75** 41
Rhoda **72** 205
Richard **70** 264 **76** 58
105 96
Robert **105** 96
Robert Wesley (Mrs.)
81 222
Roscious C. **92** 339
Roscoe **138** 122
Roswell **100** 189
Roxana Bruce **93** 367
Ruth **82** 376
Ruth (Chase) **87** 247
S. **79** 301
Sadie Louise (Bugbee)
95 317
Sally **56** 255 **87** 122 **118**
306 **119** 57 **138** 37
Samuel **56** 249 **57** 410 411
59 67 **61** 130 **79** 405 **91**
255 256 258-260 263 **97**
340 **98** 42 **102** 234 **114**
182 **118** 230 233 234 300
119 138 210 **120** 62 **123**
20 126 **145** 334
Samuel (Mrs.) **119** 133
Samuel Edward **59** lxix
Samuel H. **137** 219
Samuel I. **125** 172
Samuel J. **125** 178
Sarah **59** 91 363-365 **61** 129
63 91 **69** 32 **71** 203 **72**
317 318 **73** 8 **77** 192 **82**
293 298 **86** 458 **91** 258

MARSH *cont'd*
92 100 **97** 340 **98** 45
100 9 **113** 272 **116** 257
121 22 114 122 208 **143**
343
Sarah (Beal) **94** 195 **121** 21
Sarah (Crosby) **110** 140
Sarah (Farnham) **125** 293
Sarah (Fitz Randolph)
97 340
Sarah (Kimball) **90** 393
Sarah (Lincoln) **94** 195
121 196
Sarah (Lyman) **102** 230
136 310 313 325 328-330
Sarah (Williams) **136** 321
Sarah Adelaide **94** 195
Sarah Curtis **56** lxiii
Sarah R. **66** 112
Sarah Rice (Parker)
113 256
Sheila Maurine **109** 130
Simeon **90** 207
Solomon **101** 159
Sophia (Allen) **135** 73
Sophronia (Alden)
133 229
Sophronia (Keith)
116 259
Squires **130** 72
Stella Grace **95** 316
Stephen **118** 92 **121** 274
Submit **91** 256
Sukey **142** 72
Susa **110** 150
Susan **105** 108 **138** 37
Susan Amelia **80** 155
Susanna **56** lxv **70** 221
226 230 313 **75** 206 **97**
340
Susanna (Chase) **91** 267
Susanna (Skelton)
142 270
Susanna Lincoln **75** 206
Sylvester **81** 57
Theodore Taft **89** 132 **94**
126 145 195
Theodosia **114** 313
Theodosia (Kellogg)
114 313
Thomas **56** lxv **60** 26 **75**
206 **77** 192 **88** 358 **91**
258 259 265 **94** 195 **104**
242 **121** 21 24 108 119
196 199 **145** 110 111 113
Thomas Charles **69** 32
Thomas Clapp **90** 46
Thomas DeWitt **133** 229
Thomas Hartshorne
56 lxiii
Thomas Jefferson **89** 187
Timothy **123** 17 18
Trace **80** 155
Tracy H. **114** 78
Tryphosa Colton **113** 167
Tryphosa Colton (Parker)
113 255 256
W. E. **125** 178
Warren **75** 206
Warren Leslie **102** 234
103 120

MARSH *cont'd*
Willard C. **116** 259
William **56** 21 **70** 176 221
  313 **76** 62 **79** 303 **89** 335
  338 **113** 273 **125** 293
  145 110 113
William Parmelee **95** 145
  102 218 230 **103** 123
William R. (Mrs.) **114** 78
William Russell **102** 158
Wilson **61** 130
Woodward **81** 265
Zebulon **111** 225
Zipporah (Fitz Randolph)
  98 42
MARSHALL VON
BIERBERSTEIN
Wilhelm (Baron)
  133 272
MARSHALL Marshal
  Marshel Mershel
  —— **52** 257 **54** 341 **61** 207
  76 151 **82** 48 413 **89** 385
  91 267 **100** 32 189 **120**
  130 **140** 38 167 **143** 114
  145 52 163
— Capt. **83** 194 307 **84** 251
  102 181 **142** 145
— Col. **53** 462 **55** 390
  84 252
— Dr. **57** 115 239 **71** 118
— Mrs. **63** 343 **83** 307
  84 152
— Widow **105** 207
  148 236
A. **72** 172
A. R. **98** 234
Aaron **105** 238
Abiel **66** 111
Abigail **53** 248 **62** 179 **78**
  125 179 **82** 48 **85** 373 **91**
  256 262 **108** 65
Abigail (Banks) **136** 76
Abigail (Barney) **147** 334
Abigail (Phelps) **108** 65
Abigail (Pollard) **91** 266
Abigail Parker **91** 258 267
Abraham **55** 341
Ada Elizabeth **79** 18
Adelia **116** 210
Agnes **61** 68 **103** 11
Albert G. **69** 165
Albertus McLaren **96** 29
Alexander **71** 81 154 165
  72 30 39 169
Alice **59** 293 294 296
Alice Frances **69** 35
Alice Maud **113** 300
Alice Ruth (Hall) **84** 94
Alice Sarah (Whittlesey)
  113 300
Allen **115** 91
Almina (Lawrence)
  124 228
Almira **126** 207
Almira T. **117** 163
Amaretta A. **69** 165
Amelia **116** 210
Amos **52** 412 **55** 285
Andrew **74** 184 **82** 48
Andrew (Mrs.) **87** 384

MARSHALL *cont'd*
Ann **71** 332 **81** 446 **82** 413
  422 **83** 173 **126** 22
Ann (Doane) **110** 266
Ann (Marshall) **126** 22
Ann (Simkins) **125** 182
Ann C. **83** 307
Ann Catherine **82** 422
Ann L. **82** 422
Ann M. **84** 30
Ann Mary **83** 173
Ann Mary (Bennett)
  83 178 184
Anna **54** 254 **69** 35 **72** 211
  82 292 293
Anna (Cathcart) **121** 132
Anna Maria Susanna
  62 383
Anne **52** 250 **55** 341 **59** 293
  295 **71** 335 **110** 266 270
  271
Anne (Gifford) **135** 56
Annie Bartram **85** 95
Annie E. **69** 35
Annie E. (Eastman)
  121 309
Anson S. **73** xxxix
Anthony **60** 187 **67** 174
  98 105
Antipas Percival **81** 155
Asahel **99** 133
Augusta **84** 132 **93** 180
  96 50
Aurilla **116** 210
Aurilla M. (Nelson)
  116 210
Austin **116** 64
B. D. (Mrs.) **117** 236
Barbara **67** 179
Belle **123** 179
Benjamin **52** 250 **57** 135
  61 354 **69** 35 **73** 135 **90**
  90 **91** 262 **95** 239 **103** 46
  105 209 **125** 182 **126** 22
  127 11 227 304 **142** 20
Benjamin Clarke **82** 48
Benjamin De Forest
  68 lxii
Benjamin Soper **100** 30
Bertha **65** lxii
Betsey **55** 283 **82** 48
  103 316
Betsey (Cleaves) **125** 214
Betsey W. **81** 155
Betty **90** 228 **91** 257
Bridget **55** 375 **73** 315 **82**
  502 **83** 16
Caleb **96** 50
Caroline E. (Hadley)
  85 291
Carrie Maud **72** 303
Catherine **99** 285 **101** 91
Catherine Larison **85** 113
Catherine Russell **68** lxii
Charles **117** 276
Charles R. (Mrs.) **98** 183
Charlotte **89** 293 **136** 246
  247
Chester **98** 110
Christopher **65** 150 255
  93 397 **100** 63 **140** 38

MARSHALL *cont'd*
167
Clarissa (Fletcher) **90** 43
Clark **116** 210
Comfort **82** 48 293 302
Damaris **52** 418 420 **54**
  254 **56** 162
Daniel **82** 48 **91** 256 258
  259 262 **105** 238
Daniel F. **123** 124
Daniel Tompkins
  103 316
David **63** 21 **85** 156 **91** 257
  100 189 **108** 65
David W. **90** 43
Davis **101** 201
Deborah **52** 414 **59** 271
  73 196 **82** 27 293 298
Deborah (Reed) **91** 262
Deborah Shackford **82** 48
Deliverance **59** 363 **86** 458
Denzil Price (Mrs.) **117** 73
Derexia **74** 174
Dimis **103** 316
Dinah **56** 61
Dolly **119** 211 300 304
  120 59 129
Dolphus **85** 291
Donald **98** 110
Dorcas **82** 48
Dorcas Y. (Swain)
  126 205
Dorothy **82** 48
Dorothy (Morriss)
  (Everett) **144** 19
Dotty **119** 214
Drury M. **69** 35
Ebenezer **115** 284 **124** 160
Edith Cushing **110** 281
Edmund **53** 238 **63** 335
Edward **59** 295 **98** 24
Edward C. **111** 154
Edward Chauncey **64** 63
Edward Parker **81** 258
Edward S. **83** 300
Edward Simpson **113** 128
Elaine **98** 110
Eleanor **58** 234 **81** 446 **82**
  48 290 291 293
Eleanor Jarrett **96** 29
Electa **116** 210
Elijah **124** 228
Eliza **55** 284
Eliza Ann **120** 14
Eliza Henshaw
  (Comerbach) **84** 93
Eliza M. **84** 30
Eliza Morrill **82** 422
Elizabeth **57** 20 **59** 170
  291-297 **63** 335 **68** 318
  74 lxix **78** 46 **81** 5 446
  82 155 284 293 **83** 25 26
  35 347 **100** 30 237 304
  101 3 16 81 87 90 91
  102 117 **109** 4 **124** 228
  125 257 **135** 78 **147** 334
  335
Elizabeth (Franks)
  125 289
Elizabeth (Potter) (Hilton)
  124 294

MARSHALL *cont'd*
Elizabeth (Winn) **124** 228
Elizabeth Augusta
  63 xxxiv
Elizabeth F. G. **78** 420
Elizabeth Fendall **73** 149
Ella (Fitz Randolph)
  98 234
Ellen **110** 266
Emily **140** 232
Emily F. **69** 35
Emma A. (Ferguson)
  83 20
Ephraim **105** 207
Erminie Northcutt
  117 236
Ernest Clifton **59** xlvii
Estelle E. **116** 64
Estelle Miriam (Hooper)
  98 110
Esther **82** 286 293 **96** 189
  124 160
Eunice **52** 181 414-416 **53**
  449 **55** 286 **56** 200 **60** 78
  204 298 **83** 161 **113** 129
  127 186
Eunice (Grant) **113** 128
  123 149
Eunice (Rhodes) **113** 129
Ezra **80** 52
Fanny **131** 157
Fanny G. **123** 179
Farnsworth **71** 359
Farwell **91** 262
Florence **69** 35 **105** 63
Florence Goodwin **83**
  435 **84** 22
Francis **105** 208 **141** 298
Francis Bacon **113** 128
Frank (Mrs.) **85** 196
Frank White **72** 303
G. W. **118** 172
George **51** 469 **81** 446 **82**
  48 286 290 293 **84** 93
  124 228 **141** 108 **144** 19
George A. **121** 309
George Albert **113** 128
George E. **51** 240
George Sidney **105** 238
George W. **53** 43 **54** 455
  461 **56** 210 **57** 239 **59** 48
  321
George William **58** xliii
  187 **60** xlvi lxxix **63**
  100 **84** 93 **98** 13
Georgie V. (Main) **83** 300
Gilbert **109** 192
Greenleaf **121** 132
H. B. **123** 233
Hamlet **72** 55
Hannah **55** 340 341 **84** 210
  85 380 **91** 255 259 267
  147 259
Hannah (Lockwood)
  109 192
Hannah (Swift) **115** 91
Hannah H. (Knowles)
  123 124
Hannah M. **109** 192
Harold **65** lxii
Harriet **78** 310 **94** 308

MARSHALL *cont'd*
Harriet (Bangs) **125** 217
Harriet N. (Frink) **121** 179
Harriett **94** 308
Harvey J. **124** 62
Helen **81** 155
Helen P. **83** 435 **84** 21
Henry **91** 261 262 266
  109 309 **115** 56
Henry G. **101** 201
Henry Norton Foster
  113 300
Henry S. **135** 56
Herbert I. **116** 210
Hester **57** 135
Holman Thompson
  72 303
Holmes **103** 316
Hopley **82** 293 302
Horace **83** 20
Humanus **62** 383
Humphrey **55** 341 **80** 52
  117 119
Ichabod **52** 412 413 415-
  417 **54** 254 256 **56** 162
  163 349 352 **57** 145 **83**
  161 **124** 15 **136** 246
Ida M. **123** 151
Ida Maria (Moulton)
  123 72
Ida May **113** 128
Ida Reed **81** 258
Imogene (Cofran)
  121 179
Isaac **55** 341 **63** 100 **78** 125
  79 42 **84** 93
Isaac Hill **72** 303
Isaac Newton **84** 60
Isabel **76** 226
Isabella **56** xlii
Israel **63** 138
Israel Z. **135** 56
J. **51** 170
J. Furber **122** 315 **125** 295
J. M. **64** 130
Jacob **103** 316
James **53** 303 **55** 141 341
  59 293-296 417 **63** 40
  343 **79** 43 **81** 446 **91** 329
  104 79 **125** 34 **140** 106
James Woodbury **137** 218
Jane **59** 293 294 296 **99** 285
Jane Ann **92** 89
Jane E. **90** 388
Jane Elizabeth **72** 303
Jane Libbey (Moore)
  90 50
Jeremiah **103** 315 316
Jessie (Ames) **87** 384
Jessie Ames **72** 81
Joan **59** 295-297 **71** 237
  101 88 **143** 118
Joan (Benyon) **101** 87
Joanna **56** 61 **71** 84 155
  280 308
Johannah **92** 339
John **51** 23 24 171 395 **52**
  181 414 415 420 **53** 238
  372 449 **54** 367 **55** 141
  282-284 341 353 **56** 353
  378 **57** 20 280 388 **58** 27

MARSHALL *cont'd*
  154 **59** 89 153 271 272
  274 293-296 361 363 364
  60 133 406 **64** 159 254
  256 264 365 **65** 47 **66**
  173 175 **67** 385 **68** 318
  70 246 **73** 315 **74** 189
  80 434 **81** 446 **82** 27 48
  292 293 413 416 **83** 161
  347 **84** 164 254 **86** 458
  90 50 66 **91** 255-257 262
  92 287 **94** 110 308 **99**
  207 **101** 86 87 **103** 11 14
  316 **105** 281 **113** 128
  204 **116** 293 **121** 229
  123 149 **124** 294 **125**
  217 **126** 141 **127** 9 **136**
  76 **143** 44 **144** 46 **148** 65
John J. **98** 333
John K. **62** xxxvii
John Knox **61** 322
John Murray **68** lxii
John Patten **85** 346 **86** 191
John Rutgers **62** 383
John Woodbury **79** 18
Jonathan **59** 170
Jonathan Lyman **76** 151
Joseph **52** 249 **57** 145 **58**
  23 **61** 42 **66** 132 **68** 321
  75 124 **76** 46 **82** 48 **109**
  44 **112** 302 **121** 179 **124**
  63 160 **125** 214
Joseph B. **108** 236
Joshua **58** 142 **81** 155
Joshua P. **80** 52
Josiah **59** 361 **72** 37 **91** 93
  100 189 **121** 289
Josias **73** 222
Judith **101** 87 90 91
Julotta **61** 42
Julia **69** 35
Julia Etta **113** 128
Julia Mathilde **101** 201
Julietta **83** 300 **121** 307
Justine **121** 179
Katey **82** 48
Katharine **101** 90 **108** 306
Katharine (Mitton) **101**
  89 90
Langdon **101** 201
Laura **84** 106
Laura Alexander **84** 190
Laura D. **116** 210
Leonard **124** 228
Leonora **63** 347
Levi Winfield **66** 1
Lewis **103** 316
Lizzie B. **122** 300
Lorinda **103** 316
Lucena C. **124** 228
Lucy **58** 372 **81** 446 **82**
  293 299 **119** 135-138 208
  209 211 214 215 291 **120**
  125 129 130 132 207 **121**
  62 **122** 308
Lucy (Woodbury) **137**
  218 219
Lucy C. **99** 133
Lucy Grace **103** 316
Lydia **55** 285 **71** 81 165
  72 43 90 171 **80** 417 **81**

MARSHALL *cont'd*
446 **85** 372 373 **103** 316
125 290 **140** 68
Lydia (Stearns) **124** 15
136 246
Lydia G. (White) **124** 62
Lydia L. **99** 133
M. C. **54** xxxviii
Mabel **107** 121
Mae Kendall **91** 38
Margaret **75** 124 **76** 226
81 446 **82** 294 **100** 32
Margaret A. G. **81** 383
Margaret H. **83** 23 25
Margaret Rowland
(Clapp) **56** xxxiv **68**
xlii lxii
Margaret T. **68** 100
Margery Le **71** 238
Maria **72** 103 **81** 155
Maria (Fitz Randolph)
98 333
Marian **117** 203
Marilyn Jane **98** 110
Mark **82** 48
Martha **55** 314 **58** 299 **63**
335 **65** 198 **73** 315 **74**
189 **81** 446 **82** 27 284
287 291 294 502 **83** 10
Martha (Lord) **83** 10
Mary **51** 55 **52** 249 **54** 367
55 341 **59** 153 271 272
274 361 363 364 **61** 72
62 71 **64** 248 **66** 173 175
72 30 **73** 148 273 **74** 254
75 32 124 319 **78** 286
318 **79** 42 357 **80** 52 **81**
446 **98** 24 **101** 87 90 91
116 211 **122** 132 **125**
258 **128** 292
Mary (Cotton) **110** 266
Mary (Elder) **96** 29
Mary (Sheffield) **86** 458
Mary (Wilton) **143** 118
119
Mary (Woodward)
124 228
Mary A. **122** 149
Mary A. Dalton (Huckins)
69 35
Mary Ann **88** 335 **113** 128
124 228
Mary Ann (Talpey)
123 149
Mary E. **109** 192
Mary Elizabeth (Varney)
84 60
Mary J. (Wilson) **90** 108
Mary Janverin **82** 48
Mary Marshall **80** 52
Mary Moore **83** 307
Mary S. **77** 314 **88** 332
Mary S. (Goodwin) **122**
72 233
Mason **99** 133
Maud **108** 252
May E. **123** 179
Mehitable **67** 285
Mehitable (Gordans)
98 54
Mercy **72** 99

MARSHALL *cont'd*
Moses **61** 42 **119** 317
Nahum **55** 314 **63** 169
171-173 **73** 315 **74** 189
254 **82** 502 **83** 10 **116**
111
Nancy **82** 48 **114** 179
127 12
Nancy (Blasdell) **114** 179
Nancy (Dame) (Seaver)
89 385
Nancy C. **66** 111
Nancy Lewis **82** 422 **83** 35
Naomi **85** 156
Nathan **52** 417 **55** 284-286
56 349 350 **83** 161 **91**
261 **124** 228
Nathaniel **81** 446 **82** 48
83 194 **106** 302 **128** 292
Nathaniel G. **109** 297 **110**
178 **111** 254 **112** 106
215 306 **113** 27 28 127
129 193 195 197 **114** 45
115 227 **116** 89 299 302
117 140 142 143 222 225
230 **118** 154 320 **119** 63
64 69 143-146 225 226
228 285 **120** 68 306 **121**
304 **122** 71-73 145 231-
234 310 311 **123** 71-74
149 151
Nathaniel Grant **113** 128
Nathaniel S. **111** 230
Nelson **137** 161
Nicholas **59** 295 **76** 225
226 **110** 266 **143** 118
Noah **71** 78 278 **72** 37
Obadiah **58** 299 **81** 446
Obed **100** 189
Olive **55** 284 **71** 283
77 xliv
Olive Jane **77** 183
Oliver **71** 165 **72** 170
Oriana F. **77** 179
Orin **137** 161
Otis **124** 228
Patty **55** 373 **83** 13
Pearle Kathleen **109** 309
Perez **74** lxix
Peter **147** 334 335
Peter Benjamin **69** 36
Peter Morse **69** 35
Phebe **116** 201 **121** 132
126 156
Phebe (Ellis) **120** 279
122 132
Phebe (Godfrey) (Wolf)
128 292
Phebe (Hoar) **142** 20
Phebe (Young) **90** 90
Philena **80** 52
Philip **54** 96 **76** 226
Philomela (Hesselton)
147 259
Philotheta **103** 317
Phineas **54** 256
Polly **123** 45 **128** 284
147 259
Polly (Cowles) **123** 45
Rachel **127** 69
Rachel (Greele) **91** 262

MARSHALL *cont'd*
Rachel Robinson **91** 257
Ralph **101** 86 **148** 21
Rebecca **68** 318 **80** 434
103 316
Rebecca Ann **91** 41
Rebecca M. (Haney)
126 141
Reuben **72** 30 **100** 189
Rhoda (Audley) **148** 65
Richard **51** 181 **59** 293-296
71 106 **73** 142 269 **101**
86-88 90 91 **132** 45
Richard B. **62** 383
Robert **59** 295 296 **73** 275
79 50 **110** 267
Robert Le **71** 238
Roger **59** 295 **101** 87-90
109 23
Ruhama **122** 244
Russel **76** 151
Ruth **54** 367 **57** 20 **60** 243
71 278 **72** 39 90 102 **82**
107
Ruth (Kempton) **148**
342-344
Ruth (Rawlins) **85** 256
S. **117** 47
Sabra **71** 81 280
Sally **55** 375 **76** 151 **83** 17
91 268 **114** 173
Sambo **81** 446
Samuel **55** 341 **56** 200 **57**
20 **58** 234 **60** 243 **69** 305
70 10 **71** 81 84 154 155
165 272 280 308 **72** 29
168 169 174 **73** 265 **75**
218 219 **76** 151 **77** xliv
81 446 **82** 27 48 **83** 35
84 164 271 **85** 256 **91** 93
261 267 **94** 274 **98** 54 **99**
205 207 **116** 111 **123**
319 **124** 13 **125** 289 **143**
118 119 342 **148** 344
Samuel Bradley **113** 128
123 72
Samuel H. **83** 184 **84** 30
Samuel Henry **82** 422 **83**
173 178
Sarah **52** 413 417 420 **54** 84
55 284 **56** 249 253 **57**
354 **58** 23 **60** 243 **62** 383
69 31 **71** 347 **73** 231 **80**
208 **83** 161 **86** 185 213
88 80 282 **89** 123 **100**
237 **106** 65 **121** 222 **138**
211 **141** 20
Sarah (Abbott) **103** 46
Sarah (Gifford) **135** 56
Sarah (Macoy) **90** 50
Sarah (Walker) **108** 188
Sarah A. **116** 210
Sarah A. (Barrell) **116** 210
Sarah D. **114** 60
Sarah Knapp **109** 192
Sarah Knapp (Quintard)
109 192
Sheffield **59** 364
Sibyl **95** 239
Solomon **105** 208
Solomon D. **90** 108

MARSHALL *cont'd*
Solomon David **90** 50
Sophia **113** 128 **122** 314
Sophia Baker (Bragdon)
　113 128 129 **119** 225
　228 **123** 72 151
Stephen **58** 237
Susan **59** 293-295 **81** 383
　89 320
Susan Elizabeth **74** lxix
Susan Gibson **77** 287
Susan J. (Baker) **124** 63
Susan M. **90** 53
Susanna **92** 77 **119** 257
　125 72
Susanna (Rule) **94** 308
Sussa **55** 283
Thankful **82** 48 413 **91** 263
Thomas **56** 163 **57** 20 **59**
　295 296 **61** 72 **63** 141
　283 **65** liv 384 **70** 246
　71 237 **73** 315 **76** 225
　242 **77** 230 **78** 418 **80**
　331 434 **84** 167 251 **93**
　397 **98** 24 **100** 63 **101** 50
　86 87 90 91 **103** 11 316
　105 209 **108** 65 188 **110**
　266 **116** 208 211 **120**
　279 **122** 132 139 315
　124 160 **136** 233 **140**
　167 **143** 44 119 **144** 234
　148 232
Thomas Parker **77** 183
Thomas Worth **93** 210
　94 303 306 **103** 247
Tom A. **128** 174
Vera Lee (Kearl) **119** 316
Vernon (Mrs.) **117** 239
Walker **126** 205
Wallace **78** 113
Walter **100** 237
Walter Leonard **102** 124
Warren W. **123** 179
Wealthy (Huntley)
　101 201
William **58** 372 **59** 295 296
　62 321 **64** 188 189 **65**
　150 **68** 321 **73** 265 **75** 32
　320 **79** 357 **80** 417 434
　81 383 **82** 48 294 **84** 93
　93 382 388 **94** 110 **96**
　310 311 **98** 103 105 **99**
　209 285 **101** 86 87 **102**
　297 **108** 252 **112** 116
　292 **119** 21 **120** 14 **147** 3
William Forbes **147** 107
William G. **84** 30 **122** 72
　233
William Graham **83** 173
William H. **81** 155 **109** 192
Wiltse **116** 210 211
Wyzeman W. **124** 228
Zachariah **105** 209
Zachariah L. **100** 76
Zerubbabel **100** 30
Zerviah **72** 30
MARSHAM
Elizabeth **54** 95
Henry **54** 95 **141** 115
Jane **54** 95
Joan **54** 95

MARSHAM *cont'd*
Robert **54** 338
Thomas **54** 95
William **54** 95
MARSHAM-TOWNSEND
Robert **64** xxxii
Marshel *see* Marshall
MARSHEY
Adeline **75** 18
Michael **75** 18
Sloma **75** 18
MARSHFIELD Marshfeild
— Mr. **80** 136
Abilene **87** 303 **123** 260
Catherine (Chapin)
　148 225
Elizabeth **114** 313
Elizabeth (Legg) **85** 48
Hannah **123** 261
Hester **87** 303 **123** 261
Jonas **87** 303
Joseph (Lenord) **123** 260
Josiah **65** 382
Josias **87** 303
Katharine **87** 303
Margaret **123** 262 **148** 224
Rachel **65** 382 **85** 48
Sam **123** 259 260
Samuel **65** 382 **85** 48 **87**
　303 **148** 224 225
Sarah **88** 188 **123** 259 **136**
　318 324
Thomas **87** 270 272 273
MARSHIA Samuel **74** 318
MARSHMAN
James **73** 138
Mary **66** 255
MARSIN
Edward B. **140** 266
Mary E. (Simpson)
　140 266
MARSLAND
Ethel 43 **92** 43
Joan **83** 453
Judith Ames **107** 134
MARSLY Richard **111** 89
MARSON Marsson
— Mme de **105** 188
Abner **99** 206
Ann **99** 279
Benjamin **99** 280
Elizabeth **99** 121 206 208
　279 280 282 283 **100** 138
　298
Elizabeth Harris **100** 138
Lydia (Sawyer) **125** 107
Mary (Bennett) **100** 299
Nancy **66** 110
Polly **66** 110
Samuel **99** 121 206 208
　279 280 282 283
Sarah **99** 283
Sibyl **99** 208
Stephen **99** 121 **100** 138
　299 **125** 107
Thomas **110** 82
William **110** 82
Marstan *see* Marston
Marstass *see* Masters

MARSTELLER
John Andrew
　Thompson **93** 400
Marsters *see* Masters
MARSTON Marstan
　Marstin Marsting
　Marstins
— Capt. **58** 30
— Ensign **58** 31 33
— Mrs. **83** 35 307
Abiah **60** 51
Abiel **58** 35
Abigail **51** 61 461 **59** 37
　113 302
Abigail (Dearborn)
　90 359
Abigail (Nudd) **142** 263-
　265
Abigail (Verin) **131** 107
Abraham **95** 91
Adeline Swift **113** 307
Alice **69** 343 **131** 107
Alice Emma **73** xxxviii
Almerin (Mrs.) **76** xxii 78
　86 194
Almira **95** 92
Amelia (Rollins) **111** 139
Andrew J. **95** 92
Ann **76** 259 **102** 304
Ann (Treadway) (Ellis)
　90 360
Anna **78** 70
Anna (Moulton) **90** 359
Anna (Philbrick) **116** 271
Anna Maria **53** 156
Anne **76** 108 111
Annie A. (Lord) **97** 300
Asa **104** 119
Augusta H. **83** 181 184
Benjamin **57** 280 **58** 34
　64 97 117 **66** 155 **81** 329
　91 93 **95** 92 **113** 252 318
　131 107
Benning **83** 24 25
Betsey **59** 286 **109** 38
Beverly Lorraine **94** 28
Caleb **58** 33 **76** 108 **90** 359
Catherine **67** 139
Charles E. **97** 300
Clarence James **100** 204
Daniel **58** 31 **84** 328
　138 113
Daniel S. **134** 294
David **73** 71 **91** 370 **109** 39
　140 167
David K. **95** 92
Deborah **95** 91 92
Dinah **51** 61
Edgar Jean **71** xxiii **90** 129
　360
Edgar Lewis **73** 318 **74**
　xxiv **90** 80 139 359
Edward Everett **95** 92
Elbridge G. **95** 189
Elijah **73** 199 200
Elisha **116** 271
Eliza **64** 117
Eliza (Nason) **99** 56
Elizabeth **51** 461 **64** 117 **67**
　xxxiv **83** 24 25 **95** 91 92
　116 271

MARSTON cont'd
Elizabeth (Brown) **90** 359
Elizabeth (Davis) **104** 119
Elizabeth (Poor) **106** 232
Elizabeth Howland
  90 127
Elizabeth Weston (Swift)
  113 307
Ella Matilda (Baldwin)
  115 230
Ella N. **83** 432 435
Ella Virginia (Graham)
  112 224
Ellen J. **67** 351
Ellen M. **77** 149
Elmira **69** 327
Emeline E. **67** 351
Enoch Quimby **52** 286
  289 **55** xxxii 121
Ephraim **51** 61 **58** 29 30
  35 138
Ernest **111** 139
Ernestine (Munroe)
  (Hugaboom) **100** 204
Esther Ann **102** 304
Eunice **96** 390
Eunice (Blish) **113** 252
Everett Edward **95** 92
Fanny **95** 92
Frances Ann **73** 200
Frederic **83** 179 184
Frederick William
  112 224
George **113** 307
George H. **55** xxxii
  57 xxxiii
George Milton **100** 204
Gilman **54** lxxix **72** lv
Hannah **55** 344 **56** 199 **58**
  33 **90** 358 359 **95** 92 **97**
  182 **100** 133 302 **104**
  119 **134** 149
Hannah (Drake) **138** 107
  108 113
Hannah (Knowles) **95** 92
Hannah (Marston) **90** 359
Hannah (Post) **104** 118
  119
Harold E. **94** 28
Haven **68** 157
Huldah **138** 112
Hunter Sylvester **90** 360
Ida **69** 327
Ida Lovell **90** 95
Irene Louisa **100** 204
Isaac **90** 359 **110** 287
Isabella Tracy **92** 247
Israel **58** 18 **76** 111
J. **59** 184
Jacob **58** 137 **104** 118 119
  106 232
James **51** 61 **58** 19 136
  100 133
James Graham **102** 124
  112 222 224
James Henry **112** 224
Jennie **90** 360
Jennie C. (Hunter) **90** 360
Jere **58** 19
Jeremiah **58** 30 32 36 137
  67 351 **90** 359 **95** 91

MARSTON cont'd
111 289 **138** 112
John **58** 92 **69** 342 343 345
  360 **90** 359 **99** 56 **104**
  119 **109** 43 **112** 224 **113**
  274 **114** 233 **124** 299
  300 **131** 107 **140** 167
John B. **56** lxiii
John F. **69** 327
John M. **77** 149
Jonathan **53** 156 **58** 32 34
  140 **133** 287
Joseph M. **91** 386
Julia **138** 322
Katharine **58** 17
Katharine Von Webber
  89 266
Lavinia Dearborn **91** 370
Leafy B. (Slack) **94** 28
Lemuel **82** 284 294
Leota **115** 230
Louise **56** lxiii
Lucy A. **114** 233
Lydia **58** 233 **65** 351
Mabel **95** 189
Mahala J. **68** 157
Manasseh **55** 327 **140** 167
Margaret **82** 284 294
Margaret (Moulton)
  (Goose) **147** 135 137
  142 145
Martha **106** 232
Martha Abigail (Noble)
  95 189
Mary **51** 63 463 **66** 155 **67**
  138 **88** 290 **95** 92 **109** 39
  110 287 **126** 209
Mary (Brown) **114** 233
Mary (Chayton) **112** 224
Mary (Estow) **90** 359
  142 260
Mary (Hilton) **124** 300
Mary (Hutchings)
  126 204
Mary (Robinson) **84** 328
Mary (Stockbridge)
  134 294
Mary (Tasker) **95** 92
Mary A. **105** 301
Mary Ann **83** 150 153
Mary Ann (Vail) **111** 289
Mary Hunter **109** 221
Mary J. (Forbes) **91** 386
Matthias **126** 204
Maud **92** 101 **95** 189
Maude Benson **100** 335
Maude Longfellow
  76 xxii
Mercy **109** 38
Nabby (Hallett) **109** 39
Nancy **58** 16
Nathan **125** 94
Nathaniel **140** 68
Obadiah **58** 34 137
Patience **81** 329 **102** 145
Patience (Rogers) **131** 107
Paul Smith **76** 108 111
Phebe **58** 18
Polly **58** 19
Polly (Stockbridge)
  134 294

MARSTON cont'd
Rebecca (Page) **141** 120
Reuben **58** 29 30
Richard **61** 322 **110** 168
Robert **69** 342 343 **142**
  263-265
Robey / Robie **138** 107
  108 113
Sally **95** 92 **125** 218
Samuel **51** 63 **58** 31
Samuel H. **84** 59
Sarah **51** 63 **53** 156 **58** 33
  77 41
Sarah (Clough) **138** 113
Sarah (Roby) **112** 224
Sarah Robinson **84** 328
Simon **58** 29 31 **69** 343 344
  147 135 142
Sophia **113** 252
Susan H. (Carpenter)
  90 359
Susanna **58** 92 138 **68** 260
Sylvester W. **90** 359
Tabitha (Dearborn)
  138 112
Tabitha (Page) **90** 359
Theresa M. (Cotton)
  83 179 184
Thomas **51** 58 59 63 **58**
  233 **90** 359 **95** 91 92 **125**
  94 **142** 260
Thomas E. **95** 92
Tryphena **68** 157 **92** 247
William **51** 58 60 61 **53**
  156 **55** 344 **68** 260 **69**
  342 **90** 359 **92** 247 **100**
  204 **141** 120
Willie **100** 335
Wyatt **69** 327
Zechariah **77** 41
Zerviah **133** 308 309
MARSTOP
Abigail **137** 144
Martain see Martin
MARTEL
Aubrey **102** 296
Bertha **109** 178
Charles **109** 176-178
  110 38
Geoffrey **79** 373
Karl **101** 110 112 **107** 281-
  283 285 **109** 179 **114**
  297
Landreda **107** 285
Landrée **107** 283
Mary Emma **142** 297
N. N. (of Laon) **109** 173
William **102** 294 296 299
Marten see Martin
MARTENE Edmond **116** 22
MARTER Peter **148** 112
MARTHER
Richard **121** 123
William **72** 169
MARTHIS C. H. **76** 53
MARTIAL —— **57** 42
Joseph **68** 319
MARTIEN — Mrs. **51** 44
MARTIN alias TWIG Joan
  (Holyoke) **147** 18
Margery (Eaton) **147** 18

MARTIN alias *cont'd*
William **147** 18
MARTIN alias WIGNALD
John **51** 129
MARTIN Martain Marten
Martyn
— Capt. **54** 75 **84** 268
 85 121
— Dr. **51** 128
— Lieut. **83** 194
— Mr. **51** 347 **56** 407 **57**
 114 **59** 354 **81** 430
— Mrs. **62** 24 382 **79** 20
 85 121 **103** 302
— Rev. Mr. **77** 21 23 24
 26 27
— Widow **71** 134 **138** 25
 26 28
___ (Bowen) **104** 119
___ (Hawkes) **137** 74
___ (Welch) **136** 81
Aaron **67** 271 272
Abbie **115** 294 **125** 180
Abby **125** 180
Abigail **55** 312 **82** 510 **87**
 341 **98** 268 364 365 368
 99 173 **100** 74 **108** 121
 114 234 **122** 101 **125**
 291 **126** 21 **136** 314 **143**
 231 **148** 182
Abigail (Butler) **119** 188
Abigail (Norton) **148**
 181 182
Abigail Currier **89** 364
Abigail Staniels **73** xxxix
Abijah **105** 247
Abraham **58** 159 **65** 378
 98 167 **99** 235 **148** 182
Abro **143** 231
Absalom **64** 361 366 **65**
 51 54 229 231
Adam **93** 397 **100** 63
Agnes **95** 320 **110** 293
 142 351
Agnes (Chamber) **95** 324
Albert Clark **111** 135
Albert J. **128** 267
Albert M. **116** 64
Albert Pray **107** 134
Albro **122** 101
Alexander **61** 268 **83** 265
 100 189
Alfred Henry **82** 422
Alice **54** 28 29 **75** lxvii **91**
 67 **96** 135 **110** 292 **116**
 242 244 **125** 291
Alice (Master) **110** 292
Alice (Mattson) **128** 267
Alice (Penrose) **116** 242
Alice Virginia **92** 109
Almira **132** 77
Alonzo **95** 187
Althea **79** 29
Alton **115** 294 **116** 64
Amanda M. **77** 151
Amarilla (Ingalls)
 115 294
Amasa **119** 188
Ambrose **85** 249
Amias **61** 280
Amy **116** 120

MARTIN *cont'd*
Amy (Hall) **115** 294
Anderson **74** 63 64
Andrew **64** 254 **86** 290
 104 119
Ann **100** 237
Ann Eliza (Holman)
 111 135
Ann Eliza (McMannis)
 90 177
Ann Maria **126** 65
Anna **55** 50 **67** 376 **97** 332
 111 133 **115** 293
Anna (Chase) **88** 10
Anna (Goodwin) **108** 320
Anna D. (Whitmore) **83**
 184 188
Anna E. (Norton) **116** 64
Anna Statia **73** 262
Anne **60** 162 **77** 251 **112**
 158 159 **116** 242 244
Anne (Slate) **111** 133
Anne E. (Walls) **98** 346
Annie Louise **133** 322
Annis **63** 79 **142** 351
Anselm **115** 294 **116** 120
Armin **111** 135
Armina (Slate) **110** 31
 111 135
Arnold **83** 100
Asa **52** 434
Atlanta Elizabeth **111** 65
Atwood **76** 177
Augusta **54** 29
Azariah B. **78** 31
Azubah **73** 254
Barbara **122** 101 105
Barbara (Phillips) **143**
 231 232
Bartholmew **143** 232
Bathsheba **125** 179 **127** 218
Belinda **91** 384
Benigna Dunlap **77** 145
Benjamin **104** 119 **105**
 154 155 **126** 132 **127**
 228 **138** 29 30
Benjamin Franklin
 115 24
Bethiah **57** 65 **74** 119 **86**
 334 **143** 232
Betsey **57** 114 **79** 151 **103**
 235 **108** 320 **125** 103
Betsey (Chase) **89** 25
Betsey (Martin) **103** 235
Betsey (Ward) **112** 325
Betsey (Wolcott) **111** 133
Bette **104** 119
Betty **82** 283 294 **104** 22
Betty (Brown) **95** 86
Blanche Mae **94** 23
Bradley **85** 347
Bradley Anthony **78** 47
Bridget **110** 171
Brotherton **116** 7
Bryan **87** 125
C. Griffin (Mrs.) **86** 197
C. R. **93** 402
Caleb **58** 237
Carlos Slate **111** 136
Caroline **68** 165
Caroline (Pike) **134** 89

MARTIN *cont'd*
Caroline Hunley **104** 146
Caroline M. **67** xix
Catherine **73** 141 **78** 72
 100 200 **125** 287 **142**
 386
Catherine Augusta C.
 (Bull) **126** 144
Catherine S. **81** 53
Charles **60** 25 **71** 45 **75** 322
 79 337 **80** 339 **81** 241
 88 47 **102** 153 **110** 31
 111 135 **144** 323 **146**
 363
Charles C. **116** 64
Charles Frederick **82** 422
Charles H. **98** 259
Charles Henry **69** lxii
Charles L. **116** 64
Charles Lawburgh (Mrs.)
 109 130
Charles Newell **111** 136
Charles O. **88** 47
Charles William Parker
 72 xx
Charles Yeamans **54** 28
 29
Charlie D. **115** 294
Charlotte **76** lxx **125** 290
Chester E. (Mrs.) **118** 248
Chloe **73** 265
Christian **66** 257 **86** 79 80
Christiana **115** 294
Christiana (Maynard)
 116 64
Christine E. **92** 171
Christopher **67** 382 **104**
 119 **105** 154 **123** 320
Christopher Leroy **116** 64
Clarence **115** 294 **116** 64
Clarence Reynolds **95** 96
Clarinda **138** 117
Clarissa **89** 275
Clarissa (Grover) **123** 151
Clark Van Buren **116** 64
Claude Nichols (Mrs.)
 84 111 190
Clement **51** 129
Clinton E. (Mrs.) **116** 236
Clora Amanda **97** 132
Colleen Tower **106** 80
Cornelia **111** 135
Cynthia **78** 164
Cynthia Sophia (Buskirk)
 91 47
Cyrene Victoria 109
 92 109
D. K. **122** 240
D. P. **115** 300
Dabney A. **65** 93
Damaris **74** 64
Dan **66** 34
Daniel **53** 358 **62** 129 **65**
 378 **66** 35 **80** 245 **104**
 120 **111** 135 **115** 293
 118 75 **125** 189
Daniel B. **119** 189
Darius A. **92** 109
Darwin D. **74** 156
Darwin Denice **75** xxiii
 90 117 177 **91** 141 144

MARTIN *cont'd*
Darwin Reidpath **90** 178
  91 141
David **65** 255 **71** 214 **81** 53
  92 309 **97** 332 **113** 11
  115 226 227 **117** 137
  118 46 **127** 303
David Kendall **116** 64
  118 247 248 **147** 241
  253
David P. **115** 293
Deborah **91** 290 **125** 223
Degory **55** 99 104 105
Delia R. **116** 64
Dinah **67** 271 272
Dinah (Bailey) **104** 119
Dolly **92** 309 **103** 301
Dorcas P. **64** 124
Dorothy **71** 245 **82** 48 **87**
  199 299 **120** 47 **121** 31
  146 278
Dorothy (Brown) **125** 301
Dorothy (Smith) **90** 177
Dorothy Reidpath **90** 178
Duane **115** 294
Duressa **111** 135
Eben G. **89** 275
Ebenezer **57** 114 **69** 334
  111 135 **119** 188
Edilda **115** 301
Edith **55** 104 105
Edmund **136** 131
Edward **51** 129 **54** 31 **59**
  295 **62** 382 **76** 40 **86** 423
  87 253 261 **89** 25 **98** 368
  99 120 **106** 162 **115** 24
  318 **125** 92 **138** 24-27 29
Edward Byam **54** 31
Eleanor **61** 138 **74** 118 **76**
  126 **77** 185
Eleanor P. **111** 141
Eleanor Pope **71** xxiii
  90 129
Eleazer **79** 245
Eli **76** 177 **111** 135
Eliezer **138** 26 28 29
Elijah **108** 320
Eliphalet **110** 31 **111** 135
Elisha H. **73** 41
Eliza **62** 79 **65** 255 **81** 430
  120 10
Eliza (Coal) **128** 267
Eliza J. **67** 272
Elizabeth **51** 118 **52** 432 **53**
  104 108 **54** 28-31 **56** 318
  411 **57** 114 **58** 227 **61**
  339 **74** 64 **77** 223 **79** 39
  81 61 **82** 48 **85** 425 **86**
  362 **87** 262 **91** 188 **92**
  171 **93** 291 **96** 145 343
  98 368 369 **100** 27 241
  105 316 **107** 209 **110**
  171 **111** 65 **115** 294 **119**
  188 **120** 5 **122** 101 102
  105 **125** 101 106 **130** 39
  133 321 **137** 280 334
  143 231 **145** 133 **147** 18
Elizabeth (Borden) **130**
  38 39
Elizabeth (Chase) **87** 253

MARTIN *cont'd*
Elizabeth (Fitz Randolph)
  (Leper) **98** 335 336
Elizabeth (Ford) **119** 188
Elizabeth (Gay) **130** 38 39
Elizabeth (Lougee) **118** 91
Elizabeth (Lund) **94** 190
Elizabeth (Salter) **127** 28
  142 351
Elizabeth (Sax) **92** 171
Elizabeth (Welman)
  90 177
Elizabeth Dewolf **120** 5
Elizabeth Humphrey **86**
  231 **97** 96
Elizabeth Jane **105** 128
Elizabeth Phebe (Noble)
  95 187
Elizabeth R. (Mason)
  90 46
Elizabeth W. **83** 25 29
Ella Dora (Leek) **89** 21
Elmer E. **123** 151
Emily **54** 31 **72** 301 **142** 75
Emily E. **116** 64
Emma **81** 53 **115** 299
Enoch **88** 279
Enos **73** 254
Ephraim **65** 51 **86** 231 **97**
  96 **98** 328 **104** 119 **105**
  154 155 **138** 25 26 28-30
Erastus **54** 31 **76** 177
Esther **63** 43 **81** 61 **104** 264
  115 27
Esther (Hughes) **103** 236
Esther (Kimball) **92** 318
Etha Lee **78** 47
Ethel Almira **86** 194
Etta Gertrude (Young)
  (Witherspoon) **99** 33
Eunice **87** 82 **115** 294 **119**
  188 **136** 316
Eunice (Chase) **88** 120
Eva M. **68** 333
Evangeline **92** 109
F. Jennie **74** 152
Fannie B. (Lewis) **83** 434
  435
Flora **145** 132 138
Flora E. **103** 146
Florence **104** 13
Florence B. **116** 64
Florence Giffin **121** 235
Forrest **83** 23 25
Frances **54** 27-29 **98** 340
Frances (Fitz Randolph)
  98 336
Francis **63** 23 79 **147** 18
Frank **118** 91
Frank H. **114** 81
Fred **116** 64
Fred Eastman **104** 163
Frederick **92** 171
Freelove M. **85** 380
Freeman S. **99** 33
George **54** 27 **61** 351 **67** 38
  72 17 **75** 41 241 **80** 201
  95 96 **111** 133 135 **112**
  292 **115** 27 **119** 121 **122**
  101 **125** 301 **127** 17 **143**
  231 232 **148** 75

MARTIN *cont'd*
George A. **66** lii
George C. **57** 341 **58** xlv
George Castor **66** 1 **67** 92
  69 xxxii 93 **70** 191
George Harris (Mrs.) **83**
  233 247
George W. **54** 457 **68** 333
  78 164
George Wiley **128** 269
Georgeanna A. **69** 31
Georgianna **89** 185
Gideon **119** 121
Glenn H. (Mrs.) **105** 239
Grace **63** 79 **86** 66 **98** 242
H. B. **54** xxxviii 119
H. M. **78** 367
Hannah **51** 114 118 **54** 31
  56 208 252 **68** 274 **74**
  118 **85** 386 **98** 364 **124**
  288 **125** 108 **127** 131
  131 236 **148** 75
Hannah (Chase) **87** 137
Hannah (Gemmes)
  83 383
Hannah B. **61** 384
Hannah H. **76** 177
Harriet **83** 474 **96** 135
Harriet (Foster) **98** 362
Harriet Susan **81** 222
Heale **86** 79
Helen **92** 109
Helen (Lady) **68** lv
Helen M. **99** 148
Helen R. (Hite) **110** 64
Henrietta **82** 422
Henrietta Maria **83** 25 29
Henry **51** 116 117 433 **54**
  27 28 31 **55** 223 **73** lv
  79 417 **86** 79 249-251
  87 63 **92** 285 318 **97** 91
  114 235 **122** 310
Henry A. (Mrs.) **99** 148
Henry Byam **54** 28
Henry E. **95** 16
Henry H. **75** lxvii
Henry William **54** 28
Herbert A. **116** 64
Hester **85** 292 **135** 336
Hezekiah **81** 53 **138** 29 30
Hiram **69** lxii **75** xxiii
  90 177
Holbrook **105** 210
Horace Johnson **103** 120
  104 137 158 **105** 142
  106 139 **107** 126 **108**
  238
Hugh **80** 379 **114** 187
Hulda (Freeman) **97** 332
Huldah **103** 314
Hutson **65** 93
Ida A. **103** 48
Ida F. (Warren) **116** 64
Ira **104** 119 **105** 154
Ira Wright **92** 146
Isaac **56** 183 **65** 27 **70** 265
  87 82 **123** 151 **133** 321
Isabell **94** 233
Isabella **94** 233
Isabelle (Reidpath) **90** 178
Isobel (Bancroft) **95** 70

MARTIN *cont'd*
Isobel (Gordon) **95** 324
J. **128** 267
J. D. **78** 367 **115** 294
Jacob **65** 54 **105** 154 **108** 4
James **56** 411 **62** 24 **63** 43
    68 liv **87** 137 **88** 204 **90**
    87 **92** 397 **95** 86 **99** 120
    103 300 **111** 65 133 **122**
    101 105 **125** 42 116 **134**
    89 **137** 74 **143** 231 232
James Foster (Mrs.) **80**
    332 **81** 222
James Henry **77** 145
James L. **84** 110 185
James P. **126** 144
James Sullivan **114** 301
Jane **51** 118 **59** 297 **65** 247
    83 23 25 **113** 53 **115** 27
    117 314
Jane (Durke / Durgee)
    125 302
Jane (Forren) **83** 23
Jane Margaret **116** 64
Jane Vernette **85** 188 **103**
    77 123
Jeannette (White) **111** 65
Jemima **51** 320
Jennie **113** 307
Jerusha (Durge) **119** 188
Jerusha (Linkon) **119** 188
Joan **63** 34 **67** 382 **86** 219
    249 **93** 384 **106** 207 **139**
    41 **147** 18
Joan (Adam) **92** 397
Joan (Upham) **127** 28
Joanna **71** 214 **127** 28
    143 291
Joanna (Fassett) **111** 135
Joanna (Rines) **95** 192 200
Joanna Leland (Baker)
    86 231 **97** 96
Job **115** 293 **116** 64
John **51** 129 255 **59** 293
    60 27 184 347 **61** 131 **62**
    350 **63** 79 83 131 **65** 56
    68 165 **70** 262 **73** 254
    76 281 **78** 402 **80** 379
    82 294 **83** 374 **85** 121
    86 80 251 **88** 10 **89** 328
    90 177 **91** 62 93 329 **92**
    48 109 **93** 384 **94** 264 **95**
    320 321 **96** 255 **97** 256
    277 319 326 **98** 172 336
    361 368 **99** 94 97 98 108
    100 241 **102** 288 **103**
    235 301 **104** 119 **110**
    293 **112** 285-287 **114**
    234 **117** 160 **119** 21 189
    120 161 **123** 192 **125**
    302 **131** 129 **134** 191
    138 25 27-31 **139** 33-36
    41 49 **140** 167 **141** 230
    142 303 **144** 323
John A. **77** 145
John B. **79** 29
John Foster **117** 160
John H. **116** 64
John Harding **77** 185
John P. **63** 377 **64** 76
John W. **92** 289

MARTIN *cont'd*
Jonah **136** 81
Jonathan **53** 41 **56** 318 **81**
    61 **104** 119 120 **105** 154
    155 **143** 232
Jos **64** 107
Joseph **63** 348 **65** 33 **66** 33
    81 430 **105** 247 **112** 325
    114 234 301 **115** 61 294
    116 114 **119** 122 188
    189 **122** 101 105 **126**
    217 247 **127** 139 146 302
    140 167 **143** 231 232
    147 330-333 341
Joseph Francis **72** 301
Joseph H. **86** 191
Joseph N. **83** 184 188
Joseph P. **87** 226 **105** 279
    114 298 300
Josephine Bacon **91** 210
    114 159 160
Josephine Frances **92** 109
Joshua **61** 280 **73** 254
    147 84
Josiah **54** 27 31 **129** 144
Josie E. **116** 66
Jotham **65** 255
Judith **86** 298
Kate (Knight) **98** 197
Katharine **71** 241
Keziah **53** 358 **82** 294
Knowles **81** 430
L. P. **115** 294
Late **86** 82
Laura **81** 53 **128** 93
Laura A. **80** 163
Lavinia **93** 283
Leah **142** 386
Lee A. W. (Mrs.) **117** 320
Lemuel **70** 261 **122** 101
    127 15 **143** 231
Levi **103** 236 **105** 280 **115**
    293 294 **116** 64
Levi P. **116** 64
Lewis **62** 329 **116** 258
    145 133
Libbie C. (Edwards)
    116 64
Lois **116** 69
Lora (Higley) **116** 64
Lora Blanche **91** 142
Loraine **105** 154
Loranora **104** 119
Lottie E. **105** 150
Lottie Edna **72** 301
Louisa
    (Van Valkenburgh)
    92 171
Louisa Sampson **71** lx
Luce **86** 79 80 216 250
Lucia A. **75** 41
Lucile **108** 135
Lucinda **117** 160
Lucretia **136** 131
Lucretia (Dexter) **135** 158
Lucy **70** 197 **86** 82 249 251
    108 4 **114** 301
Lucy (Clewley) **114** 300
Lucy A. **133** 322
Lucy R. **78** 367
Lydia **53** 41 **54** 27 30 **67**

MARTIN *cont'd*
    271 **97** 277 **98** 259 **115**
    293 **142** 303
Lydia (Chase) **87** 254
Lydia (Clark) **116** 64
Lydia (Gates) **121** 223
Lydia (Stearns) **105** 155
Lydia Ann **89** 25
Lydia M. **73** 41
M. Johnson **115** 294
Mabel (Hubbard) **108** 197
Malinda (Crofut) **97** 132
Margaret **51** 117 **84** 215
    143 39
Margaret (Barnough)
    116 258
Margaret (Brown) **98** 338
Margaret (Langill) **125**
    116 120
Margaret (Richardson)
    90 177
Margaret Teresa **83** 423
    435
Margery **147** 243 244
Marguerite **143** 5
Maria **96** 288 **114** 188
Maria (Dempsey) **114** 188
Marie **82** 235 252
Marjorie **92** 147
Marren **68** 56
Marshall (Mrs.) **102** 77
Marshall P. **104** 126
Martha **78** 319 **79** 39 **98**
    311 **115** 79 **121** 260 **137**
    74 **138** 30 **143** 150
Martha (Clark) **111** 135
Martha (Goodwin)
    116 64
Martha J. (Brown) **116** 64
Mary **51** 269 **52** 404 **53** 465
    54 28 29 **57** 65 114 **60**
    347 **63** 318 377 **64** 76 **66**
    363 **69** 92 **79** 245 **82** 48
    86 301 **89** 392-394 **92**
    397 **94** 166 **95** 337 **97** 91
    98 368 **100** 27 **103** 235
    108 83 **111** 152 **115** 30
    117 62 **118** 64 119 189
    122 101 **125** 103 106
    216 **126** 217 **136** 316
    143 231 **144** 323 **145**
    133 **148** 182
Mary (Bullis) **135** 337
Mary (Chase) **87** 261
Mary (Coggeshall) **147**
    330 332 333
Mary (Favour) **111** 243
Mary (Headley) **94** 166
Mary (Lincoln) **135** 300
Mary (McCarter) **90** 89
Mary (Pinder) **148** 181
Mary (Simon) **147** 21
Mary (Thompson) **95** 190
Mary A. **92** 109
Mary A. (Ellis) **114** 81
Mary Ann **70** 325 **73** lv **87**
    62 63
Mary Ann (Trescott)
    87 63
Mary Ann Bishop **92** 109
Mary Anne **98** 351

MARTIN *cont'd*
Mary Coleman **77** lxiii 295
Mary Douglas **78** 47
Mary E. **115** 294 **116** 61
Mary Eliza **117** 160
Mary Elizabeth **54** 28 **82** 422 **83** 173
Mary Hunt **125** 216
Mary J. **135** 336
Mary Jane **89** 225
Mary Olive **120** 307
Mary Pearl **90** 136
Mary Susan **111** 145
Mason **88** 120 **116** 64
Matilda **63** 89
Maxwell **116** 64
Mehitable **79** 245 **105** 79
Mehitable (Wiggins) **103** 236
Melatiah **53** 358 **58** 52 **138** 31
Melinda A. **76** 177
Mercy (Billington) **90** 177
Michael **51** 117 118 **98** 368 **139** 305 **140** 44 **147** 21
Mildred **73** 153
Miles **89** 239
Minnie Belle **62** xl **69** xliii lxii
Miriam (Wakefield) **58** 124 **95** 86 190
Miriam B. **89** 275
Moses **58** 124 **129** 272
Moses B. **137** 41
Myrtie (Holmes) **89** 239
Nancy **77** 145 **78** 397 **81** 113 **93** 161 **98** 311 **133** 282
Nancy (Carter) **124** 298
Naomi **104** 119
Narcissa **78** 164
Nathan **53** 358 **56** 252 **111** 135 **114** 301
Nathaniel **54** 31 **58** 68 **98** 368 **99** 172 **104** 119 120 **105** 205 **108** 320
Nathaniel Ford **119** 188
Nellie **137** 51
Nellie A. **80** 245
Nettie **145** 132 138
Nicholas **110** 198
Noah **67** xix **68** 42 **70** 5
Nola Estelle (Leffingwell) **108** 225
Noler **82** 48
O. W. **115** 300
Obadiah **124** 298
Octavia H. **98** 311
Olive **108** 320
Olive (Wheeler) **123** 50
Olive Eliza **105** 109
Olivia **64** 123
Olledine A. **115** 294
Ora A. **99** 75
Orr (Mrs.) **98** 346
Otis **115** 293 **138** 117
Otis J. **116** 64
Otis William **116** 64
Parker **103** 301
Patience **91** 68 **104** 120

MARTIN *cont'd*
Patrick **112** 18 **135** 337
Penelope **54** 29-31
Penelope Ann **54** 31 **69** lviii lix
Percy **83** 478 **95** 187
Percy Alvin **109** 284
Peter **53** 108 **64** 316 **70** 265 **86** 80 251 **135** 337
Phebe **53** 41 **90** 47 **115** 293
Phebe (Bisby) (Bressey) **112** 43
Philip **66** 363 **69** 31 **70** 263 **104** 120 **127** 306
Phillis **82** 294 301
Polly **58** 385 **87** 378 **108** 83
Priscilla **51** 116 117
Prudence **73** 254 **98** 368
Rachel **54** 28 29 **62** 15 **66** 58 **70** 348 **89** 282 375 **92** 300 397 398 **93** 297 **115** 294
Rachel (Barnes) **100** 241
Rachel C. **81** 53
Randolph **98** 336
Rebecca **53** 358 **57** 307 **58** 52 **127** 218 **131** 129
Rebecca (Higgins) **97** 277
Rebecca (Lawton) **125** 243
Remembrance Chamberlain **94** 23
Reuben **69** lxii **94** 21 **104** 120
Rhoby **100** 67
Rhoda **54** 31
Rhoda (Flint) **88** 279
Rhoda (Nichols) **104** 163
Richard **51** 118 **56** 369 **58** 227 **62** 301 **63** 34 79 **67** 351 **69** 360 361 **71** 172 241 **73** 138 **74** 70 280 **81** 61 **86** 79 80 82 251 252 421 **90** 89 **91** 188 **93** 384 386 387 **94** 254 264 **96** 255 **97** 319 **98** 362 368 **99** 96 **100** 27 **110** 292-294 **114** 234 235 **127** 28 **130** 38 **142** 351 **147** 21
Richard A. **57** 229 337 **58** xlv **60** 84 187
Richard Allen **65** 302
Richard Byam **54** 28
Robert **57** 65 218 **64** 19 225 **65** 244 67 248 382 **70** 265 **74** 119 **79** 171 **86** 421 422 **88** 47 **90** 177 **96** 255 105 113 **112** 286 **116** 242 244 **127** 28 **142** 386 **147** 243 244
Robert Everard **108** 225
Robert H. **133** 322
Robert Harper **115** 24
Roger **57** 316
Rosanna **142** 386
Rose **68** 333
Roxanna (Patch) **123** 151
Ruby **104** 119
Ruth **125** 240
Ruth (Silvester) **86** 290
Ruth E. **79** 143
Ruthie Elizabeth **77** 186

MARTIN *cont'd*
Sabrina (Slate) **110** 31 **111** 135
Sallie Maria **113** 226
Sally **52** 25 **65** 255 **76** 40 **88** 25 **108** 320 **125** 215 **140** 130
Sally (Barker) **105** 154 155
Sally Ann **98** 338
Sam **112** 276 288
Samuel **54** 27 28 30 31 **57** 229 **60** 187 **63** 89 **69** lix lxii **81** 53 **85** 49 **95** 192 200 **97** 132 **104** 120 **105** 205 **112** 43 **148** 181 182
Samuel Billings **117** 160
Samuel George Thomas **54** 29
Samuel M. **113** 39
Sarah **51** 118 **52** 233 **54** 27 31 222 **58** 297 **59** 411 66 129 **69** 31 **81** 430 **82** 294 296 **86** 67 **90** 228 308 **98** 52 338 361 368 **99** 105 **104** 18 120 267 **105** 154 247 **111** 116 133 **119** 199 **120** 50 **125** 214 **126** 131 132 **129** 379 **143** 232 **148** 181 182
Sarah (Armstrong) **89** 185
Sarah (Clark) **111** 133
Sarah (Cluff) **95** 193 200
Sarah (Durkee) **111** 133
Sarah (Gaines) **85** 49
Sarah (Harris) **105** 247
Sarah (Parker) **119** 189
Sarah (Quimby) **104** 119 120
Sarah (White) **98** 368
Sarah (Willmarth) **90** 177
Sarah A. **83** 296 300
Sarah A. (Crawford) **89** 225
Sarah A. (Hayes) **94** 23
Sarah Ann **82** 422 **83** 182 184 **98** 338
Sarah L. **73** 41 **94** 291
Sarah N. (Hopkins) **104** 126
Sarah R. (Ford) **137** 51
Sarah S. **69** lxii
Sarah T. **83** 25 29 35
Sargent **57** 114
Scipio **82** 294 301
Serena H. **115** 294
Seth **98** 311 **138** 25 26 28-30
Sibyl **76** 127
Sibyl F. **114** 81
Silence **76** 177
Silv. **98** 244
Silveneas **127** 306
Simeon **65** 141 **76** 155 **127** 14
Simon **76** 122 127
Smith **73** 277
Solomon **115** 24 **148** 181
Sophia **60** xxxvi **123** 13
Sophia (Smith) **121** 225 226

MARTIN *cont'd*
Sophia S. **56** 324
Sophronia **137** 76
Stephen **115** 294
Stephen S. **120** 138 139
Stilman **142** 386
Stoddard **123** 50
Susan **54** 112 **56** 252 **57** 34
  115 24 **121** 230 **126** 64
Susan Lambert **118** 248
Susan M. (Winn) **120**
  138 139
Susan T. **79** 110
Susanna **54** 419 **68** 165
  69 112 334 **70** 66 **78** 308
  81 101 430 **82** 48 294 **98**
  368 **99** 204 **104** 120 **114**
  301 **115** 142 **121** 230
  125 103 **126** 247 **133** 72
  136 131 **147** 329-333
  338 347-349 **148** 66
Susanna (Dantrey)
  100 241
Susanna (Davis) **115** 61
Susanna (Holyoke) **98**
  368 **147** 21
Susanna (Ives) **123** 320
Susanna (North) **115** 27
  144 358
Susanna P. **114** 301
Sylvanus **97** 41 **138** 30
Tabitha **124** 305
Temperance (Fitz
  Randolph) **97** 277
Thankful **108** 320
Thankful (Rich) **83** 265
Theodore **51** 42 **68** xliii
  liv lv
Theodosia **69** 334
Thomas **51** 117 **60** 283 **62**
  15 **63** 226 **65** 93 116 255
  68 274 **74** 118 **76** 122
  127 **79** 311 **81** 92 **83** 383
  434 435 **86** 79 251 **90** 46
  93 385 387 **94** 233 **95** 70
  320 324 **97** 277 **100** 237
  101 244 **103** 238 **105**
  211 **112** 158 159 **114**
  234 235 **116** 7 **120** 48
  121 223 **122** 101 **131**
  129 **143** 231
Thomas Byam **54** 28
Thomas D. **91** 329
Thomas Goldthwait
  114 301
Timothy **53** 358 **138** 26
  28 29
Tom **80** 323
Urania L. **78** 31
Ursula **67** 253
Ursula (Utley) **119** 188
Vincent **135** 336
Vine **104** 120
W. S. **118** 248
Washington N. **98** 259
Wealthy J. **91** 384
Wilbert Wallace **70** 197
William **51** 117 **54** 27-31
  241 **57** 307 **59** 294 **60**
  347 **63** 234 318 **64** 107
  66 34 **67** 382 **69** lix lxii

MARTIN *cont'd*
71 49 54 **73** 142 **76** 55
77 251 **82** 422 **83** 25 29
  35 **87** 254 **89** 185 **92** 386
93 75 **94** 166 **95** 86 190
  193 200 **98** 311 338 **99**
  51 204 317 **100** 241 **103**
  235 236 **111** 133 243
  114 234 301 **115** 293
  116 64 **117** 53 **118** 40
  121 230 **125** 243 **127**
  227 **128** 59 **138** 26 28 30
  143 232 **147** 18
William B. **71** 45 **92** 171
William Bates **51** 116 117
William Byam **54** 28
William C. **95** 16
William Charles **116** 64
William Clarke **54** 30 31
William Fanshawe **54** 27
  28
William Gamble **117** 155
William H. **116** 64
William Henry **89** 225
William L. **125** 243
William Lewis **82** 422
William M. **116** 64
William R. **84** 30
William Roy (Mrs.)
  108 135
William Scott **115** 24
William Thomas **54** 27
  29 30
Willis E. **68** 333
Wilmot **95** 228 **114** 234
Zadoc **69** lxii
Zalmon **111** 133
Zephaniah **73** 220
Zilpah **79** 246
MARTIN-HOLLOWAY
Celia Sabina **97** 382
George **97** 382
MARTINDALE
  Martindel Martindell
— Capt. **85** 27 28
— Col. **136** 247
Anna **62** 266
Bethiah **62** 269
David **62** 269
Diana **62** 267
Dolly **62** 268
Electa **62** 269
Elias **62** 266
Godsgift **111** 57 **147** 333
Henry C. **92** 42
Isaac **51** 298 **63** 331 **83** 85
  86 **105** 265 **147** 331 333
John **120** 315
Joseph C. **66** 190 191
Lemuel **62** 266-269
Lillie **98** 147
Margaret **82** 175
Mary **62** 268 **111** 57
Minta Belle **96** 128
Nanny **63** 54
Olive **62** 268
Pelatiah **62** 267
Pliny **62** 270
Rachel **116** 187
Sihon **129** 382
Theodore **62** 270

MARTINDALE *cont'd*
Timothy Dwight **62** 270
Tubal **62** 268
Uriah **62** 269 270
William **103** 239
MARTINEAU
Daisy **95** 378
John **63** 45
Joseph **117** 138
Mary **63** 45
Matthew **63** 45
P. E. **65** 160
Peter **63** 45
Sarah **63** 45
William **63** 45
MARTINESO
Huldah **71** 35
John **71** 35
MARTINEZ Carmel Grace
  St. Jeanne **85** 196
  Rosa Molina **109** 288
MARTINFIELD
Edward **114** 234
MARTINGALE
Hawser **95** 29
MARTINIE
  Ernest Frederick Julius
  89 304
MARTINOU
  François **52** 34
MARTINS C. **62** 312
Mary Susan **111** 145
MARTIR Peter **51** 264
MARTIS Sarah **90** 104
MARTLIN Susanna **65** 351
MARTOCCIA
  Lionel Joseph (Mrs.)
  103 120 **106** 240
MARTON
  Lawrence Bruce
  103 120
  Richard de **120** 172
  Walter de **120** 172
MARTY Samuel Clinton
  103 120 **116** 73
Martyn *see* Martin
MARTZ John **100** 90
  Margaret (Voltz) **100** 90
  Sophia **100** 90
MARUMBERG
Abiel **77** 81
MARUS Mary **98** 53
MARVEL Marvell Marvle
—— **138** 121
Abbie **81** 222
Asenath **95** 117
Benjamin **87** 256
Betsey **87** 256 **88** 23
David **59** 312 314
Edward I. **117** 136
Frances (Stall) **125** 245
Hannah **59** 312 **73** 65
  132 324
Huldah **87** 256
John **73** 69 70
John Francis (Mrs.)
  80 334 **81** 222
Jonathan **59** 312
Marianna **93** 376
Mark **95** 117
Martha M. **93** 274

MARVEL *cont'd*
Mary Brayton **117** 136
Mehitable **59** 312
Nathaniel **59** 312
Rhoda **59** 314
Robert **76** 237
Sam **73** 71
Samuel **73** 70
Sarah Ann **113** 305
Susanna **82** 384
Thomas S. **125** 245
Marverick *see* Maverick
MARVILL Harry Edward
(Mrs.) **99** 148
MARVIN Marvyn
Aaron **76** 53 **115** 16 108
Abby **77** 205
Abigail **51** 330-334 **92** 300
Abigail Mary **115** 114
Abijah Perkins **65** 12 19
141 8
Abraham **69** 211 **115** 16
108
Alice **51** 330 334 **59** 109
92 385
Alpheus **61** 77
Amanda **78** 251
Anna **53** 128
Anna (Lee) **116** 288
Anne Maria **68** 118
Asahel **78** 367
Asahel Mather **78** 367
Azubah **78** 371
Benjamin **77** 205 **116** 40
Catherine **68** 115 **78** 371
Charles Benjamin **77** 205
Charlotte **70** 207 **111** 311
Chloe Bradley **58** 93
Comfort **96** 384
Curtis Warner **115** 108
Dan **78** 251
Daniel **78** 251
Deborah S. **78** 371
Diademy **101** 207
Edward **59** 116 **68** 115
91 184
Edward Lee **77** 205
Edwin E. **65** 154
Elihu **68** 115
Elihu H. **72** 205
Elisha **68** 115 **78** 371
Elisha Thomas **78** 367
Eliza Crane **87** 388
Elizabeth **51** 331 **59** 116 **68**
115 **69** 58 211 **71** 111 **72**
209 216 **77** 205 **78** 371
79 72 **83** 311 **96** 384
139 235
Elizabeth Chloe **58** 93
Elizabeth Clara **57** 138
58 93
Elizabeth Eliot **68** 118
Emma S. **77** 200
Esther **116** 40
Eunice **116** 286-288
Fanny Spaits **78** 113
Florence **68** 118
Florence Ruth **68** 118
Florence Ruth (Dennis)
91 185
G. F. **116** 40

MARVIN *cont'd*
George **115** 108
George F. **116** 288
George Franklin **59** 116
68 117
George Ritchie **57** xxi
xxviii **60** xxxviii **68** xxx
xxxiv 118 **69** vi xxx **70**
viii **71** vii 88 **72** vii **73**
vii 78 **74** vii **75** vii 76
76 vii **77** vii **82** 235 253
83 256 **84** 206 **85** 109
112 214 215 466 **86** 215
91 129 184 **92** 149 **144**
29
Grace W. **68** 118
Hannah **51** 331 **53** 128 213
71 111 **72** 209 **75**
lxxviii 177 181
Harlow **148** 273
Harlow (Mrs.) **148** 273
Harriet G. **125** 173
Henry **115** 108
Hephzibah **78** 251
Huldah **78** 251
Israel **100** 63
James **78** 251 **115** 17
Jane **61** 77 **115** 108
Jarvis Edson **115** 21
Jerusha (Peck) **137** 39
Joan **79** 72
John **57** 138 **58** 93 **77** 200
205 211 **113** 39 **115** 114
144 31
John C. **115** 112
John Clinton **115** 16
John Milton **115** 114
John Reginald **58** xlv
68 118
Joseph **61** 77 **78** 371 **79** 72
Julia Ann Coleman
(Coggeshall) **68** 115
Julia Rogers **68** 118
Laurana **77** 205
Lewis Rockwell **115** 108
Lois **72** 36
Lucius M. **77** 205
Lydia **121** 255
Martha **68** 115 **77** 205
Marty **51** 331
Mary **52** 448 **53** 209 210
213 214 **59** 109 116 **62**
304 **63** 100 **68** 118 **72**
210 **75** 188 **78** 130 376
79 78 **84** 220 **89** 150 **92**
300 **101** 142 **115** 16
Mary (Ritchie) **91** 184
Mary Ann Frances
115 112
Matthew **51** 330-334 **52**
447 448 **53** 209 214 360
54 238 241 **59** 116 **68**
177 **71** 111 **72** 209 **77**
205 **79** 78 **92** 300 **96** 384
105 5 116 40 288
Mehitable **78** 251 **116** 40
Mehitable (Marvin)
116 40
Melissa **115** 16
Merze **67** xxxi 94

MARVIN *cont'd*
Mignonette de la Force
80 209
Miles **70** 227
Miranda **115** 17
Moses **78** 251
Nancy **115** 112
Nathan **53** 128 **141** 259
Phebe **77** 205 **78** 371
Polly **70** 227 **115** 17 21
114 313
Rachel **51** 333
Rebecca **51** 331 333
Reinold / Reynold **53**
302 360 **54** 238 240 241
384 **58** 300 **59** 116 **61** 77
62 304 **68** 115 117 **77**
205 **78** 251 376 **89** 150
91 184 **100** 263 **101** 145
106 147 **116** 40 288
Richard **63** 100 **127** 228
Rising **130** 72
Robert **63** 100 **92** 385
137 39
Samuel **51** 333 **77** 205
137 39
Samuel E. **78** 102
Samuel M. **113** 39
Samuel Manning **113** 31
Sarah **51** 331 **54** 384 **61** 77
62 172 **68** 115 **72** 313
77 211 **78** 371 376 **83**
311 **92** 300 **96** 383 384
110 142 **115** 16 108
Sarah A. **78** 251
Selden **78** 371
Seth P. **78** 371
Sophie **95** 173
Susan R. **83** 311
Susanna **58** 181
Sylvester S. **76** 159
T. E.O. (Mrs.) **83** 307
Temperance **79** 72
Theophilus Rogers **51**
330 364 **52** 99 **54** 232
451 **55** 228 **56** 325 **57**
119 120 **58** 209 **59** 116
60 112 **61** 98 99 206 212
401 **68** 115 118 **91** 184
185
Thomas **58** 181 **72** 36
Thomas O. **71** xxiii
Timothy **78** 371
Ulysses **58** 93
Ulysses L. **58** 92 93
Uretta Clinch **115** 16
William **61** 77 **78** 251 369
79 72 **115** 16
William Bent **83** 311
William E. **83** 311
William Theophilus
Rogers **51** 330 **52** 446
53 214 360 **54** xx xxxvi
238 241 **55** xxix xxxv-
vii xvii xxxi 109 121 211
58 xvi xliii 93 219 **59** vi
xviii xli 109 116 **60**
xxxiv **65** 207 **67** xxx **68**
xliii 115-118 304 **91** 184
116 288 **P68** lxxix
Zachariah **77** 205 **116** 288

MARVIN cont'd
Zilpah **78** 251
Marvle see Marvel
Marvyn see Marvin
MARWICK George (Mrs.)
76 xxxiv
Lawrence **115** 319
Sarah Ridgway **76** xxxiv
Susanna **100** 29
MARWOOD Anne **104** 279
Harry **74** 69
Henry **104** 279
MARX
Alexander **81** 370
Brothers **145** 200
Edmund (Mrs.) **117** 78
Karl **70** xliii
MARY Princess of
England **57** 44
MARY Queen of England
51 488 **53** 293 **56** 191
276 376 **57** 43 173 **59** 53
60 31 32 **61** 235 **62** 139
164 200 **136** 287 **143**
291
MARY Queen of Scotland
55 212 **66** xx
MARY —— **109** 171
MARYASH Sarah **147** 259
Maryatt see Marriott
MARYHEW
Charles M. **116** 124
Clarissa **116** 123 124
Matthew **116** 123 124
Maryon see Marion
Maryote see Marriott
MARZOLF
William A. **94** 211
MASAOKA Naoichi **69** 289
Masarene see Mascarene
MASARY Betsey **88** 280
MASCARENE Masarene
Mascaren Maserean
— Lieut. Gov. **97** 109 112
— Mr. **144** 159
Jean Paul **71** 102 **106** 261
John **65** 279 **110** 317 **140**
167 **144** 223
Margaret **65** 279 **108** 186
140 167
Paul **52** 186 **67** 213 **84** 151
116 5 9 12
MASCAW
Beatrice **104** 102
Felix **104** 102
Frank **104** 102
Frederick **104** 102
Maschcal see Maskell
MASCHER
Virginia **102** 226
MASCHEREL Alexander
96 46 47 **101** 292 293
Alice **101** 292 293
Cecily **96** 46
Edith **96** 46 47 **101** 292
Emengarde **96** 42
Ralf **96** 47
Robert **96** 47
Walter **96** 42 46 47 **101** 292-
294
William **96** 47

Mascoll see Maskell
MASCROFT
Daniel **99** 314
Harriet **94** 59
Harriet D. **63** 1
John **99** 314
Samuel **99** 314
MASCY Hamon **139** 287
Isabel **139** 287
Isabella (Beauchamp)
139 287
Mary (Beauchamp)
139 287
MASE Adam **106** 320
Anna Belle **77** xcv
Jane Elizabeth **77** xcv
Maximilla (Fisher)
106 320
Willard Horace **77** xcv
MASEFIELD
John **117** 155
Maserean see Mascarene
Maserve see Meserve
Maservey see Meserve
MASH
Ann (Bird) **88** 285
John **143** 261 262
Jonathan **127** 222
Mary (Mitchel) **125** 219
Peter **125** 219
MASHAM Abigail (Lady)
56 379
Damaris (Lady) **64** 86
Elizabeth (Barrington) **91**
70 **113** 189
Francis **64** 86
Francis Cudworth **64** 86
Samuel **64** 222
William **52** 90 **56** 379 **91**
69 70 **98** 67 **113** 189 **138**
88
Winifred (Lady) **56** 379
MASK
Elizabeth (Butman)
86 66
MASKELL Mascol
Mashcal Maskal
Abigail **148** 233
Bethiah (Parsons) **148**
230-233
Constant **148** 234
Elizabeth **148** 232 234
Henry **62** 322
James **84** 404
John **148** 234
Margaret **93** 75
Mary **148** 233 234
Patience (Barton) **84** 404
Thomas **81** 497 **148** 230-
233
MASKERS
Henry A. **85** 409
Mary **85** 409
Samuel **85** 409
MASON Masson Massone
—— **140** 167 **146** 377
— Capt. **53** 45 **59** 315 **61**
323 **89** 174 176 177 **96**
369 **98** 62 **121** 11 **133**
107
— Dea. **71** 141 142

MASON cont'd
— Dr. **132** 87 **138** 116
— Lieut. **96** 369
— Miss **83** 35
— Mr. **58** 29 **62** 363 **73**
199 **80** 323
— Mrs. **51** 190 **58** 31 59
65 365 **83** 307 **127** 139
— Rev. Mr. **79** 309
— Widow **97** 337 **99** 96
____ (Harndine) **148** 146
____ (Peck) **121** 11
____ (Powell) **140** 237
A. A. **104** 96
A. K. **100** 207
Aaron **54** 44 46 **58** 133 **64**
310 **105** 299 **108** 26 **127**
224
Abbott **95** 210
Abby A. **83** 179 184
Abby Francis **63** 50
Abel B. **104** 96
Abigail **55** 62 426 427 **56**
79 **57** 53 **58** 133 **59** 37
325 **66** 19 **69** xlviii **72**
194 **74** 40 **87** 320 **116**
160 163 **125** 82 **135** 126
Abigail (Conn) **87** 88
Abigail (Dodge) **104** 126
Abigail (Gregory)
112 147
Abigail Belcher **145** 69
Abigail Brown **83** 173
Abigail M. **55** 62 427
Abigail Sawyer **56** 396
Abner **62** 372 **86** 311
125 217
Abraham **63** 29
Ada **82** 76
Ada Estelle **102** 303
Adam **135** 76
Addie Hodge **68** lxxviii
Addison **84** 56
Agnes **54** 345 **56** 311 312
Albert **108** 60
Albert Clark **61** 310 **62** xl
65 195 302 **67** xxxiv
Alexander **129** 379
Alfred Bishop **51** 373
Alice **56** 312
Alveda J. **117** 165
Alverdo Hayward **52** 97
55 xxix 122 132 **56** 328
57 xxxi **60** 187 **74** 147
Amanda **82** 453 **141** 48
Amasa K. **100** 207
Amory N. **113** 197 **119** 145
Amos Lawrence **64** xxxi
Amy **84** 56
Andrew J. **123** 98
Andrew J. (Mrs.) **123** 98
Angeline **111** 80
Ann **53** 462 **54** 345 **94** 328
99 280 **106** 198 **126** 208
145 69
Ann (Fayerweather) **144** 4
235 **145** 68 69
Ann A. **70** 26
Ann Marcy (Gifford)
133 212
Anna **74** 209 260

MASON *cont'd*
Anna Powell **97** 53
Anna W. **87** 340 341 **88** 16
Anne **56** 308-312 **57** 318
 71 203 **72** 194
Anne (Chase) **87** 252
Anne (Peck) **89** 328
Anne (Sanford) (Noyes)
 103 275 **111** 58
Anne Janette **66** 19
Anne Rebecca **96** 400
Archie Church **111** 61
Arthur **102** 181 188 **105**
 196 **144** 13
Asa **65** 366 **87** 231 234
 125 85
Asahel **114** 192
Aurora P. **82** 453
Barachias **58** 345 **110** 317
 112 147 **148** 146
Barbara **56** 309
Barker **84** 56
Barnet **87** 261
Benjamin **58** 140 **62** 361
 73 70 74 **74** 36 83 35 **84**
 426 **88** 19 **95** 190 196 **96**
 14 **98** 65 96 **107** 275 **108**
 58-60
Benjamin Franklin
 108 58
Betsey **56** 396 **59** 289 **87**
 231 234 **108** 60 283 **123**
 47 48 303 **133** 281
Betsey Jane **68** lxxviii
 108 60
Betty (Stone) **95** 190
Broadstreet **105** 282
 114 179
Calista **104** 96
Carol Y. **101** 172
Caroline Atherton
 (Briggs) **126** 120
Caroline Augusta
 101 321
Caroline H. **86** 383
Carrie **77** 181 **123** 224
Catherine **68** 258 **87** 232
 234 **98** 65 **135** 77
Catherine (Dunbar)
 84 426
Catherine (Hartshorn)
 112 147
Caty **134** 54
Ceaser **127** 138
Celia A. **71** 42
Charles **63** 50 **64** lx **123**
 100 **126** 120
Charles (Mrs.) **123** 98
Charles Francis **78** 256
 79 225 **83** 379
Charles Frank **74** xxviii
 84 180 **90** 123 **96** 154
 101 116 172 **102** 127
Charles Gilbert **133** 72
 136 361 362
Charles O. **89** 241 **108** 283
Charlotte **64** 17
Charlotte (Lazell) **88** 368
Chloe **73** 151 **80** 182
Christopher **54** 345 **70** 31
 87 252 **110** 168

MASON *cont'd*
Clara (Decker) **125** 73
Clarence B. **83** 298 300
Clementina (Crocker)
 101 32
Cyrenus **111** 80
Dale R. (Mrs.) **84** 213
Daniel **55** 427 **56** 396 **58**
 56 **64** 195 **65** 374-376
 73 67 **74** 64 **81** 176 **83**
 42 **98** 327 **101** 172 **103**
 44 166 **116** 116 **121** 205
 126 143
Daniel B. **91** 384
Daniel Wilbur **77** 187
David **57** 280 **60** 149 **64**
 xliv xlvi **84** 159 **86** 383
 91 345 **93** 397 **97** 45 46
 118 **100** 63 **116** 116 **133**
 261 **137** 256 **140** 255
David Robinson **88** 105
David W. **125** 73
Deborah **84** 154
Delia N. **82** 453
Deliverance **87** 256
Desire P. **63** 338
Diademia **104** 58
Doras (Staples) **108** 190
Dorinda **110** 22
Dorothy **56** 309 311 312
 64 195 **66** 24 **102** 230
Dwight **147** 263 265
E. W. **113** 73
Ebenezer **59** lxxxii **62** 381
 65 12 **72** 115 194 **112**
 147 **142** 390
Edgar **84** 56
Edmund **100** 242 **137** 310
 312 **143** 113
Edna Warren **91** 208
 145 68
Edward **61** 93 **70** 26 **73**
 65 70 71 73 **104** 186 **129**
 379 **133** 212
Edward Beecher **54** 242
Edward C. **84** 190
Eleanor (Long) **104** 40
Eleanor (Longe) **100** 254
Elias **75** 208
Elijah **123** 46-48
Eliphalet **53** 398 **123** 47
 133 72 **136** 362
Eliphalet Fales **101** 172
Elisha **125** 36 **138** 29-31
Eliz **91** 346
Eliza **53** 398 **125** 109
 133 72
Eliza A. **58** 345
Eliza J. (Leeman) **91** 384
Eliza L. (Grindle) **109** 12
Elizabeth **51** 300 **52** 432 **54**
 270 **56** 309 396 **57** 395
 60 228 **66** 191 **69** 38 **70**
 31 **71** 224 **74** 50 183 **77**
 290 **91** 396 **93** 366 **98** 65
 217 **100** 86 **107** 275 **108**
 58-60 **110** 144 **112** 175
 116 163 **125** 292 **126**
 255 **128** 19 **132** 90 **133**
 72 103 **135** 76 **142** 279
 280 **144** 199 **145** 69

MASON *cont'd*
Elizabeth (Brooks)
 87 227 234
Elizabeth (Chase) **88** 22
Elizabeth (Gilbert?)
 136 361
Elizabeth (Hammond)
 101 172
Elizabeth (Knowles)
 88 128
Elizabeth (Sewall) **145** 69
Elizabeth (Spring) **145** 68
Elizabeth (Tibbetts) **98** 65
Elizabeth (Ward) **141** 121
Elizabeth Boyd
 (Worcester) **84** 213
Elizabeth L. **53** 398
Elizabeth R. **90** 46
Elizabeth Rogers **98** 86
 103 222
Elizabeth Street **141** 258
Elizabeth Venable **87** 400
Ellen **110** 171
Ellen Barker **117** 292
Elsa (Whitin) **89** 31 **94** 290
Emily Amanda **77** 187
Emily C. **69** 35
Emma **69** 207
Emma (Gifford) **87** 231
 234
Emma Hoven **79** 135
Emme **75** 220 **79** 108
Enoch **66** 191
Ephraim **59** 289
Estelle Hart (Kimball)
 112 146
Esther **54** 189 **56** 396 **59**
 145 **74** 36 50 185 **77** 281
 92 77
Esther A. **74** 147
Eunice **63** 182 **74** 64
Evelyn E. **83** 429 435
Evelyn L. (King) **91** 393
Experience **56** 396 **62** 371
 120 268
Experience (Newcomb)
 101 172
Ezekiel **88** 279
Fanny (Peabody) **95** 147
 103 73 77 125
Frances **55** 338
Frances Eldredge **81** 176
Francis **63** 243 **65** 352 **68**
 73 **116** 163
Francis Eliphalet **101** 172
Frank **87** 88
Frank Asa **95** 373
Frank Hamilton
 59 lxxxiii
Fred A. **100** 207
Fred H. **82** 453
Frederick **81** 176
Frederick Clark (Mrs.) **82**
 382 **83** 233
Freelove **58** 345
Freeman C. **108** 276
G. **56** 150
Gardner **129** 277
George **55** 276 **56** 309 **63**
 283 **64** 266 **78** 161 **84** 56
 94 275 **109** 62 **113** 62 63

MASON *cont'd*
117 258 125 73 135 76
George C. 96 27 103 159
125 171
George Carrington 100
80 106 238 117 247
George Champlin 69 352
96 13 15 118 156
George E. 91 393
George L. 71 42
George R. 59 289
Gertrude 104 96
Gertrude Cogswell
103 145
Gilman 73 189
H. O. 104 96
Hannah 52 217 57 53 59
289 69 331 72 316 80
175 89 58 239 94 223 97
45 102 226 106 201 108
283 109 253 110 26 107
111 65 120 116 122 258
125 109 127 307 128 41
135 250 136 319 320
141 58 144 225 145 69
Hannah (Child) 101 172
Hannah (Clark) 112 147
Hannah (Millar) 108 121
Hannah (Symmes) 97 45
Hannah (Turner) 88 335
Hannah C. 59 190
Hannah L. 105 299
Hannah Stone 108 60
Harold F. (Mrs.) 83 487
Harriet 104 96 126
Harriet (Bennett) 86 311
Harriet Brown 80 256
Harris 87 328
Harrison Denning
64 xxxi
Harry E. 71 42
Helen 86 194 100 44 115
Helen Augusta (Palmer)
112 146
Helen Evelyn 95 373
Helen Hart 112 146
Helen Ripley (Baker)
101 172
Henry 56 309 311 312 81
176 112 146 135 77
Henry L. 100 80
Henry Lowell 65 xxxvi
90 126 112 72 146
Hepzibah 58 51
Hester 54 189 78 256-258
86 349 101 172 113 73
Hester (Welles) 113 73
Hezekiah 53 462 71 203
Hiram 65 376 66 19 20 25
Hobart 81 176
Holding 129 277
Howard 66 liii
Hubbard 128 217
Hugh 54 86 87 189 56 396
66 187 78 256-258 79
225 85 112 86 352 91
208 96 369 99 332 101
172 106 65 113 73 145
68 69
Ida Bell 128 91
Ida Menage 77 187

MASON *cont'd*
Ira 91 329 132 240
Irena (Chase) 87 261
Isaac 74 36 130 184 87 341
97 319 138 117
Isabel 56 311 123 114 116
278
Isabel Hopewell Hayden
96 296
Israel 123 278
J. Bradford 77 181
J. F. 103 239
J. O. 94 93
Jacob 66 24 25 121 115
James 59 37 80 175 92 320
104 96 108 283 118 46
129 379 138 30 142 280
286
James A. 127 59
James Bryant 93 138
James H. (Mrs.) 85 196
111 61
James J. 104 96
James Murray 63 258
James Witherell 55 69
Jane 52 271 65 29
Jane (Sutton) 105 299
Jane A. 70 155
Jane E. 86 383
Jane Frances 70 155
Jane Sutton 105 299
Jason Rogers 70 203
Jehiel W. 103 44
Jemima 113 78
Jeremiah 60 228 61 241
96 225 111 132
Jeremiah Vinton (Mrs.)
109 130
Jerusha (Owen) 126 79
Jerusha T. 104 96
Jesse 63 101
Joan 56 312 66 261
Joanna (Sewall) 113 197
119 145
Joanna M. 87 88
Joanna R. 59 290
John 51 75 52 217 262 318
320 53 22 48 52 54 45
189 55 324 333 56 231
308-312 396 57 318 58
59 294 59 141-143 283
61 360 64 160 195 216
65 299 70 4 339 71 124
171 249 72 83 194 316
74 36 40 185 269 76 224
239 315-317 78 256 258
79 135 167 80 176 81
138 176 82 155 86 351
87 229 234 271 88 22 89
177 328 90 274 91 202
94 186 95 221 222 228
96 369 378 381 393 97
345 98 58 101 172 103
275 104 186 188 105
280 106 262 107 226
262 110 168 111 58 116
7 117 82 118 46 56 123
278 125 32 151 293 126
211 305 129 277 132 90
133 104 134 287 135 76
218 138 29 31 140 68

MASON *cont'd*
141 121 142 390
John (Ensign) 145 68
John A. 93 215
John Alford 126 225
145 69
John Andrew 98 147
John Brackett 113 307
John Brackett (Mrs.) 109
130 113 232 306
John C. 108 283
John G. H. 74 64
John Knight 113 307
John L. 61 301
John Lane 107 318
John Lufton 61 359
John Raines 117 255
John S. 69 207
John Stone 108 58
John T. 58 156
John Tufton 59 57
Johnson 58 345 112 147
Jonas 87 227 234 107 262
Jonathan 55 337 69 89 82
76 83 154 84 152 375
379 85 124 99 8 107 226
129 383 139 6 140 167
233 236 237 244 247 324
325 145 68
Jonathan Tufton 135 125
Joseph 51 58 59 54 86 87
189 56 328 59 lvi lxxxii
lxxxiii 145 288 67 116
71 226 265 72 194 73 18
74 260 77 276 281 78
256 258 80 144 85 455
89 88 97 319 107 226
108 121 117 258 126
159 129 379 132 264
Joseph (Mrs.) 114 183
Joseph Parker 59 lxxxiii
87 311
Joseph Warren 108 59
Josiah 79 47
Jotham 108 190
Joycelynn 118 167
Judith 56 309 59 285 68 75
106 231
Judith (Smith) 121 125
Julia 107 226
Julia A. 138 287
Julia Ann (Terry) 126
143 208
Julia F. 71 203
Julia L. 97 134
Julian S. 94 401 104 170
Julie E. 100 207
Juliet 94 185 186
Junia Killen (Russell)
83 487
Katharine 51 75 52 247
58 393 68 69 71
Katharine Elizabeth
(Baird) 133 72 136 361
Kathryn Harrod 105 238
Keturah 126 36
Keziah 104 80 110 4
Lafayette N. 82 453
Larkin D. 96 227
Laura 102 167
Laura E. 115 202

MASON *cont'd*
Leila Venable **114** 70
Lemuel **55** 338 **59** 289
　66 19
Lemuel B. **106** 153
Leonard (Mrs.) **115** 317
Lewis **66** 19
Lillian Irene **123** 225
Lizzie **90** 349
Louis B. **86** 351
Louisa (Hunnewell)
　125 293
Louise (Conn) (Smith)
　87 88
Love **58** 345
Love (Whitney) (Battle)
　112 147
Lowell **100** 80 **112** 146 147
Lucinda **72** 15 **86** 311
Lucy **89** 386 **108** 283 285
　142 390
Lucy (Fales) **101** 172
Lucy E. **93** 215
Luke **125** 287
Luke M. **82** 453
Lydia **72** 316 **78** 404 **79** 39
　99 114
Lydia (Loring) **107** 262
Lydia (Perry) **126** 120
Lydia J. **89** 351
Lyman **59** lxxii
M. A. **82** 453
M. Phillips **111** 79 165
Mabel Dorcas **113** 307
Mabel Dorcas (Barnes)
　113 306
Malinda **117** 24
Mandruk **129** 379
Marcia L. (Smith) **103** 44
Margaret **74** 52 **100** 241
　109 236
Margaret (Partridge)
　112 147
Margery **57** 50 51
Marie **55** 337
Marmaduke **64** 318
Martha **58** 140 **145** 69
Martha (Cowen) **87** 229
　234
Martha (McMullen)
　135 77
Martin **62** 371
Mary **51** 280 **53** 406 **54** 170
　55 230 **57** lxvi **58** 378
　59 37 145 289 **61** 93 241
　62 303 **63** 14 **64** 344 **65**
　352 **66** 105 **72** 194 195
　74 36 146 147 **77** 281 **78**
　258 **83** 25 29 **86** 383 **87**
　341 **103** 166 **105** 299
　108 59 156 311 **116** 160
　161 163 **121** 202 **126** 38
　211 268 305 **134** 87 **137**
　280 **139** 30 46
Mary (Arnold) **112** 147
Mary (Day) **137** 256
Mary (Fales) **101** 172
Mary (Miller) **135** 76
Mary (Nichols) **125** 287
Mary (Veaton) **105** 299
Mary A. (Colburn) **103** 44

MASON *cont'd*
Mary Ann **90** 168 **91** 291
　135 77
Mary E. **105** 299
Mary Eliza **77** 153 **86** 352
Mary Eliza (Merrick)
　113 307
Mary Ellen **108** 277
Mary F. **85** 196 **111** 61
　123 225
Mary Fales (Sisson)
　101 172
Mary Frances (Bigelow)
　101 172
Mary Huntress **83** 173
Mary Murdock **51** 373
Mary Nettie **113** 307
Mary S. **73** 291
Mary T. **73** 286
Mary Yeaton **105** 299
Matilda **64** 310 **79** 135
Matthew **56** 310 **76** 155
Mehitable **73** 17 18 **90** 183
　123 49
Mehitable (Andrews)
　125 217
Mercy **58** 59 **82** 453 **108**
　283 **126** 305 **135** 18 **142**
　390
Mercy Ann **85** 331
Mercy Jane **73** 286
Meriam **84** 375 379
Michael **54** 345
Mildred **102** 123
Millard **104** 96
Minerva **135** 48
Minerva Slater (Briggs)
　127 59
Minnie **80** 140
Miriam **112** 318 **140** 244
Miriam Clarke **93** 196
Molly **51** 465
Mortimer B. **55** 21
Moses **135** 76
Nancy **59** 288
Nancy (Adams) **88** 279
Nancy (Chase) **88** 105
Nancy Maria **88** 340
Naomi Dorinda **108** 283
Nathan **138** 29
Nathaniel **58** 29 31 **100**
　254 **104** 40 **114** 179 **116**
　8 162 **138** 30
Nehemiah **81** 176
Nellie Bosworth **70** 203
Nelson **88** 335
Nicholas **53** 406 **54** 270
　62 303 **73** 65 **76** 240
Noah **73** 69 **74** 146 149 150
　93 215 **97** 38 319 **98** 323
　328 329 **99** 97 105 **127**
　225 **139** 41
O. H. **52** 79 80
Olive **57** 77 **74** 35 36
Oliver **134** 54
Orion T. **67** 386 **68** xxxii
Orman B. **104** 96
Orray Tillinghast **80** 256
Otis Tufton **63** 113
Owen **67** 300
P. H. **53** 129

MASON *cont'd*
Pamelia W. **100** 207
Patience **63** 181 **74** 36 40
Patrick **118** 46 56
Pauline (Goddard) **94** 186
Pelatiah **58** 51
Peleg **86** 383
Peleg Sanford **74** 64 **111**
　56 **116** 7
Peletiah **108** 280 285
Peletiah W. **109** 12
Pella Hull **66** l
Peter **82** 453 **98** 65 **123** 279
　147 37
Phebe **87** 378 **88** 7 **122** 214
Phebe (Gilbert) **137** 360
Phebe Ann **80** 144
Philadelphus **66** 19 20 25
Philip **97** 330 **125** 211
Polly **73** 283 **137** 256 **140**
　22 255
Polly (Miller) **135** 76
Polly Cary **100** 259
　103 159
Prudence **59** 283 **64** 151
Prudence (Balston)
　132 90
Puella Follett **51** 94
R. Osgood **107** 17
Rachel **56** 312 **75** 208
　105 55
Rachel R. **59** 290
Ralph **72** 194
Rebecca **64** 17 **72** 177 **81**
　462 **112** 139 **116** 163
　126 211 **144** 4 **145** 68
Rebecca (Perley) **96** 400
Rebecca (Williams)
　145 68
Reginald **68** 355 369
Relief (Smith) **94** 93
Reuben **128** 59
Rhoda **57** 162
Rhoda (Crocker) **126** 204
Rhoda (Green) **128** 94
Richard **63** 36 **65** 28 **68**
　353 **84** 307 **109** 211
Rishworth **88** 368
Robert **51** 60 **56** 309 310
　57 53 **59** lxxxii 333 **60**
　399 **64** 324 **79** 425 431
　82 188 **83** 262 **95** 222
　223 225-228 **112** 147
　148 146
Robert Means **60** 228 229
Robert Tufton **58** 393 **95**
　221 223 224 228 231
Rosanna (Rich) **84** 56
Rose **65** 34 **80** 175 176
Rose (Norcross) **100** 242
Roy Wallace **85** 196
Rufus **64** 151
Ruhamah S. **118** 188
Ruth **61** 391 **75** 208
S. H. **82** 453
S. Howard **82** 453
S. R. **89** 31
Sadey **148** 146
Sadie A. **123** 225
Sally **58** 345 **83** 108
　117 143

MASON *cont'd*
Sally Talbot **61** 301
Sampson **52** 97 99 **55** 300
  56 328 **58** 51 **60** 187 **67**
  300 **78** 66 **97** 319 326 **99**
  98 108 **139** 30 49
Samuel **54** 198 **55** 425-428
  56 259 260 389 394 396
  58 378 **59** 285 325 **70** 25
  31 **72** 15 194 **96** 269 **97**
  34 114 116 319 **121** 124
  126 204 **133** 113 **142**
  390
Sarah **51** 189 **52** 217 **61** 344
  62 219 **70** 31 **73** 140 144
  74 147 **82** 74 **91** 236 **97**
  337 **108** 283 **118** 98 **123**
  99 **135** 76 101 **142** 280
Sarah (Bates) **125** 73
Sarah (Bourne) **88** 19
Sarah (Chase) **87** 328
Sarah (Clarkson) **97** 337
Sarah (Rife / Riffe) **135** 76
Sarah A. (Sayles) **89** 241
Sarah Ann **76** 36
Sarah Catherine **89** 198
Sarah Frances **77** 185
Sarah Harrison (Cargill)
  117 255
Sarah I. **96** 330
Sarah J. (Fogg) **83** 298 300
Sarah Jane (Huntley)
  132 240
Sarah Rebecca **59** lxxxiii
Seth Clark **96** 400
Sibyl **84** 424
Silas **70** 155
Silence **85** 230
Simeon **64** 17
Sophia **59** lxxxii
Sophronia **59** 290 **104** 125
Sophronia H. **89** 351
Sounde **103** 11
Stephen **56** 20 **68** lxxviii
Stephen O. **82** 453
Stephens **91** 345
Stevens Thompson **51**
  23 158 324
Submit **107** 261
Submit (Whittemore)
  107 262
Sukey **70** 150
Susan **56** 309 **59** 290
Susan A. **97** 134
Susan Lawrence **130** 204
  207
Susan Powell **82** 492
Susanna **60** 149 **63** 336
  81 132 **86** 383 **87** 234
  237 **123** 46 47 **134** 54
  135 76
Sydney Russell (Mrs.)
  94 290
Sylvester Shemway **66** 1
  191
Sylvia **63** 101
Sylvia M. **63** 202
T. Beria **125** 85
Tabitha **58** 56 **63** 93
Tabitha (Jenkins) **103** 166
Thaddeus **77** 236 **99** 79

MASON *cont'd*
  106 198 **126** 120 **144** 4
  232 235 **145** 68 69
Thamar **68** 65 68
Thankful **66** 19
Theodore West **64** 195
  65 xxxiv
Theodosia **93** 283
Theresa (Southworth)
  108 245
Thomas **56** 309 312 **57** 50
  51 **59** lxxxii **63** 90 **68**
  64 65 68 **70** 263 **71** 28
  72 194 **73** 148 **80** 398
  81 181 **102** 172 **108** 245
  112 147 178 184 **128** 52
Tilla **145** 350
Tilly **61** 353
Timothy **62** 372 **73** 286
  290 **80** 182 **127** 227
Tryphena J. **82** 130
Valentine **126** 268
Victor W. **117** 285
Vida Calista **104** 96
Vinton (Mrs.) **105** 128
Virlinda **73** 138
Walter **116** 160-163 165
Walter Dwight **82** 453
Ward **73** 67 69
Ward B. **76** 36
Wealthy **86** 383
Wheaton **87** 98
Willaby **105** 210
Willard **96** 330
William **52** 432 **56** 309 311
  63 113 **64** 160 **67** 116
  70 263 **73** 272 **86** 352
  88 128 **91** 329 **101** 172
  105 209 210 **116** 162
  165 **117** 24 **118** 46 **123**
  30-35 94 **135** 76
William F. **128** 94
William L. **51** 94 **56** xxxii
  59 xliv 329 **148** 146
William McGeorge **80**
  335 **81** 219
William P. **101** 32
William Phillips **64** xxxi
William Powell **99** 8
  103 73
Willis Brower (Mrs.)
  106 79 125
Zipporah **72** 115
Zoa **125** 241
MASSAME John **147** 167
MASSARE Francis **60** 309
MASSASOIT Sachem **53**
  317-322 382 **54** 261 262
  58 326 **89** 281 **90** 156
  94 346-348 **95** 134 **143**
  301 **144** 211-214
MASSAU ____ de
  (Baroness) **104** 175
MASSCHOP
Agnes **106** 10
Claes **106** 10
Frans **106** 10
Gerhardt **106** 10
Grietie (Hendricks)
  106 10
Johan **106** 10

MASSCHOP *cont'd*
Johann Wilhelm **106** 10
MASSE Angelique
  (Legris-dit-Lepine)
  143 13
Antoine **143** 13
Jean-Baptiste **143** 13
Luce **143** 13
Marie-Angelique Louise
  143 13
Marie-Louise Esther
  (Robichaux) **143** 13
Pierre Antoine **143** 13
Richard **87** 208 **127** 170
Massee *see* Massey
MASSEN Mary **127** 228
MASSENBURG Lucy
  (Cargill) **117** 251
Nicholas **117** 251 254
MASSERBACK
Felix **65** 243
MASSETT Thomas **91** 329
MASSEY
  Massee Massia Massie
  Massy Massye
  ——— **84** 166 **112** 213
— Mrs. **93** 274
Aileen (Fairey) **93** 274
Aileen Isobel **93** 274
Benigna **77** 268
Benjamin **78** 111
Betty **77** 264
Cecilia **106** 66
Charles Harper **78** 171
Charles Polk **77** 264
Clara Heverin (Clark)
  106 45
Cynthia Benigna **77** 264
Dave (Mrs.) **93** 273 274
Edmund **66** 58
Edward **112** 34 35
Edward R. (Mrs.) **96** 186
Eliza **77** 264
Elizabeth **66** 58
Emily **77** 264
Frances **52** 123 125
Frances Ewell **105** 126
Geoffrey **112** 34
George **75** 235 **83** 35
  111 245
George Valentine **104**
  321 322 **105** 77 **106** 38
  48-50 **107** 127
Hannah **83** 173 194
Isobel (Wendt) **93** 274
Jane **112** 33
Jeffrey **53** 50 **112** 34 35
Joel Vincent **77** 264
John **72** 284 **84** 166
  125 109
John H. **77** 264
Lorena **98** 147
Lucy **72** 284
Margaret **112** 30
Margaret (Bressey)
  (Forset) (Amice)
  112 29
Margaret Benigna **77** 264
  78 174
Margaret Maxwell (Lyte)
  96 186

MASSEY *cont'd*
Mary **112** 33
Mary Ann **77** 264 **78** 174
Nathaniel **53** 67 **54** 361
Ollie **77** 270
Orpha **78** 171
Ruby **95** 187
Sarah B. **77** 147
Susan **77** 255
Susanna (Mock) **125** 109
Thomas **112** 34
Thomas Drury **93** 274
William **52** 123 125 **97** 297
    112 29 30 34
William S. **77** 264 **78** 174
Massia *see* Massey
Massie *see* Massey
MASSINGBERD
William **103** 11
MASSINGBERG
Thomas **68** 73
Massinger *see* Messinger
MASSLIN Robert **63** 344
Masson *see* Mason
Massone *see* Mason
MASSUERRE
Peter **125** 93
MASSURE
Adeline **81** 153 263
Catherine Sophia **86** 301
Chloe (Jackson) **86** 70
Hannah **81** 263
Hannah (Blake) **86** 70 301
James **81** 153 154 263
    86 70 301
John **81** 153 263 **86** 70
Lois **86** 71 207 307
Sophia **81** 154 **86** 305
Massy *see* Massey
Massye *see* Massey
MAST
Catherine **135** 250
Christian Z. **66** 287
    67 xxxi
Helen Murray **103** 116
Jacob **66** 287
MASTELLER
Cloris Augusta **89** 115
William Thomas **89** 115
Masten *see* Maston
MASTENS Rachel **125** 104
Master *see* Masters
MASTERIION
Marmeduke **100** 33
MASTERMAN
Ellen **64** 262
MASTERS Maister
    Maisters Mastass
    Marsters Master
    —— **92** 398
— Capt. **76** 132
Abigail **56** 345 **61** 334 **62**
    37 **137** 144 218
Abraham **56** 345 **62** 40
    91 71 **99** 281 **120** 17
Addie Jane **100** 86
Agnes **71** 175 176 **74** 281
    75 137 139 **110** 292 294
Alice **85** 297 **110** 292
Andrew **130** 279 280 **137**
    218 219

MASTERS *cont'd*
Angeline **120** 17
Ann **56** 345 **61** 334 **62** 42
    43 46
Anna Woodbury **137** 234
Anne **110** 292 **129** 75 77
Arthur Allen **77** 174
Caroline D. C. **66** 112
Catherine **125** 218
Charles **135** 252
Clark **85** 297
Daniel **76** 132
David **136** 270 **137** 282
Dennis **51** 261
Dorcas **73** 136
Edmund **110** 292
Edward **51** 272 **54** 92 **90**
    45 **95** 255 **110** 294
Eleanor Augusta **135** 252
Eliza Jane (Aiken) **135** 252
Elizabeth **71** 172 173 175
    74 279-281 **75** 177 **76**
    132 **90** 44 **91** 71 **92** 398
    110 292-294
Elizabeth (Brown)
    125 216
Elizabeth (Smith) **135** 252
Elizabeth (Tomson)
    110 293
Ellen (Beckwith) **120** 16
Ezekiel **73** 150 231
Fred **91** 329
Fred Nation (Mrs.)
    101 124
George **68** 183 184 **89** 282
    91 286 **92** 368 **110** 293
    123 250 **129** 77
George Streynsham **110**
    292 293
Giles **107** 44
Grace **54** 91 92
Hannah **51** 463 **58** 338
    62 38
Hannah (Woodbury)
    137 218
Henry **66** 112
Isaac **120** 13
J. H. **91** 329
J. T. **91** 329
James **55** 146 **64** 147 **71**
    172 173 176 **74** 279-281
    75 177 **110** 294 295 **120**
    16 **125** 219
Jane **89** 282 **91** 71 **95** 173
Joan **110** 293
Joan (Ensyng) **110** 293
Joan (Sawtell) **128** 154
John **54** 92 **55** 146 **71** 171-
    173 175 176 **73** 136 **74**
    279 280 **75** 137 **76** 132
    89 282 **91** 68 286 **92** 140
    398 **95** 173 **110** 292-294
    120 17 **137** 218 233
John M. **137** 220 223
John Marshall **61** 218
    137 219
Joseph Edward **135** 252
Josiah **76** 173
Josiah Samuel **76** 173
Katharine **64** 189 **92** 398

MASTERS *cont'd*
Katharine (Gilbarte)
    110 294
Katharine Louise **77** 174
Keziah (Felch) **137** 234
Lavinia Jane (Beckwith)
    120 17
Lewis **85** 297
Lucy (Woodbury)
    (Marshall) **137** 218 219
Lucy Jane **80** 331 **137** 219
    223
Lucy Maria **137** 218 234
Lydia **55** 74 **62** 40 **64** 147
    91 71 **95** 173
Magdalen **54** 92 **129** 75
Malinda **136** 270
Margaret **54** 91 92 **136** 270
    272
Margaret / Martha (Hoyt)
    125 219
Martha E. (Newcomb)
    120 13
Martin **57** 100
Mary **73** 217 **100** 86 **110**
    293 294 **125** 221
Mary (Redman) **90** 45
Mary A. **88** 344
Mary Ann **90** 114
Mary C. (Dow) **88** 331
Mary Delphine **85** 297
Mildred **66** 65
Nathan **73** 218
Nathaniel **56** 345 **91** 71
    137 218
Olive **54** 91 92
Peter **71** 172 173 176 **74**
    279-281 **89** 282 **91** 286
    92 368 398 **93** 298 **110**
    292-294
Phebe **85** 297
Philip **58** 338 **99** 207 209
    281
Rachel **58** 338 **99** 207 209
    281
Rachel (Bigg) (Starr) **89**
    282 **92** 368 398
Ralph **81** 488
Rebecca **55** 146 **62** 42
    95 346
Richard **110** 292 293
Robert **125** 216 **128** 154
Ross **100** 86
Ruth **56** 345 **62** 39 43
S. **91** 329
Sally **125** 109
Samuel **56** 345 **62** 43
    76 132
Sarah **79** 51 **91** 71
Sarah (Snelling) **108** 183
Sophrona (Goltry) **85** 297
Streynsham **110** 293 294
Susan **110** 295
Susanna **121** 50
Susanna (Leach) **137** 218
Thomas **71** 172 173 176
    74 280 281 **99** 207 **108**
    183 **110** 292-294
Tryphena **88** 130
W. **137** 219

MASTERS *cont'd*
Wilhelmina (Rigel) **136**
270 **137** 282
William **88** 331 **89** 282
91 286 **92** 368 **103** 18
110 292-294 **119** 21 **140**
167
William F. **73** 278
Woodbury **137** 218 219
233 234
MASTERSON
Alfred **133** 268
Clara Ellen (Rutherford)
133 268
Elizabeth (Cogswell)
144 24
Hannah **125** 218
James **64** 221
James R. **108** 237
John **143** 206
Lillian (Fleener) **133** 268
Margery **51** 263
Mary (Goodall) **144** 24 25
Nathaniel **144** 24
Richard **119** 161 162 **143**
203 206 **144** 24 25
Sarah **144** 24-27 **148** 323
Thomas **112** 29
MASTICK —— **65** 359
Sarah **55** 393
Mastin *see* Maston
MASTINES Theresa **77** 58
Mastins *see* Maston
MASTON Masten Mastin
Mastins Mastons
—— **101** 269
Eleanor **65** 355
Hannah **65** 352
J. H. **91** 329
Joan **142** 159
Joseph **65** 352
Mary (Clewley) **114** 298
Mary (Moulton) **141** 235-
237
Nathan **65** 355
Nathaniel **114** 298
Peter **141** 327
Simon **141** 325
Thomas **92** 54
William **67** 78
Mastons *see* Maston
MASURY
Ellen **52** 150 372
Joseph **102** 235 **147** 43
Margaret **83** 480
Mary **52** 372
Mary (Woodmansee)
147 43
Samuel **147** 37 43
Sarah **147** 43
Stephen **52** 150 372
Susanna **55** 111
MATAR Francois **125** 98
Matcalf *see* Metcalf
MATCHETT Matchet
Bridget **88** 273
Charles Frederic **92** 243
Elizabeth Perkins **92** 249
George **92** 246
Horatio **79** 47
James **52** 247

MATCHETT *cont'd*
Joanna Louisa **92** 348
John **100** 140
Mary **100** 140
Mary Hacey **100** 140
Theodore **92** 255
W. P. **94** 42
W. P. (Mrs.) **94** 42
William **92** 243 246 249
255 348
MATCHIN Matchyn
Christiann (Leich) **109** 67
Edmond **142** 266
James Hiatt **109** 67
Joan (Webster) **142** 266
Mary Hurley **109** 67
MATEE Charles **63** 143
MATEER
Gladys (Keay) **96** 83
John Gaston (Mrs.) **96** 83
May **80** 43
MATENSOIR
John **55** 432
MATH Daniel **107** 103
Mathar *see* Mather
Mathasson *see* Matheson
Mathenson *see* Matheson
MATHER Mathar
—— **129** 395
Capt. **118** 21 27
— Dr. **53** 297 **123** 164 168
— Mr. **53** 25 **55** 145 149
56 51 **59** 106 **84** 153 **85**
249 **95** 103 105 106
— Mrs. **118** 115 304 **119**
47 **120** 133 **122** 120
— Rev. Dr. **84** 367
Abigail **52** 424 **136** 320
Abraham **53** 22
Albert Increase **107** 305
Alberta **98** 345
Alexander **98** 117
Alice **77** lxxi **78** 387
Allyn **72** 181 **81** 84
Allyn M. **80** 54 60
Amanda P. **72** 274 **115** 260
Amasa Stone **86** 246
Ann (Lake) (Cotton)
86 244
Anna **77** 203 **81** 265
Anne **52** 275 **77** 205
Anne (Porter) **98** 94
Asa Ferdinand **112** 141
Atherton **61** 140 **73** 116
112 141 **120** 178 179
186
Augustus **81** 265
Augustus C. **88** 337
Azariah **53** 210 **87** 398
Benjamin **53** 22 **116** 7
Betsey **78** 238
Burton C. **81** 290
Caroline **77** 200 205
Catherine **68** 115
Catherine (Atherton)
106 64
Catherine (Holt) **86** 243
106 64 **140** 13
Catherine (Livingston)
86 245 **106** 64
Catherine (Wise) **86** 245

MATHER *cont'd*
106 64
Charles **66** 191 **79** 161
397 402 **100** 174 **112**
141
Charles C. **100** 174
Charles J. **143** 66
Charles L. **98** 358
Clara **78** 239
Clinton **81** 290
Constance **86** 246
Cotton **51** 252 **52** 36 281
53 37 42 255 290 291
347 **54** 41 67 **55** lxxvi
lxxxvii 19 20 236 297 **56**
110 216 221 343 **57** 411
58 298 377 **59** 117 **60** 36
37 301 **61** 39 51 128 198
281 282 **62** 141 **63** 383
65 189 253 **66** 266 268
340-342 **67** 82 109 114
208 **69** 102 105 106 **71**
lxvii 102 **72** liii 155 223
76 li 170 201 307 308 **78**
17 430 **84** 8 **86** 244-246
89 149 151 **91** 167 **94**
220 **95** 44 103 104 106
107 **96** 249 98 94 99 216
101 187 **102** 263 265
277 **103** 37 39 41 **104** 82
84 87 92 286 **106** 41 194
107 93 **108** 114 112 41
44 176 **115** 12 **117** 242
118 86 251 **121** 3 **123**
162 **124** 164 **128** 66 145
130 110-112 264 **131**
163 176 179 182 184 185
132 102 107 108 **133**
102 133 **134** 182-184 186-
188 190 191 **136** 9 113
150 255 256 **140** 6 7 **142**
122 147 **144** 159 199 200
203 **145** 203
Dan W. **77** 206
Daniel **105** 99
Deborah **77** 205 206
Deborah (Champion)
106 64
Deborah (Ely) **86** 245
106 64
Dewar **112** 141
Diana **81** 290
Edgar Cotton **101** 124
Edgar R. **98** 345
Edmund **98** 117
Eleazer **55** lxxvi **77** 205
78 387 **81** 265 **86** 244
112 152 **116** 7
Eli **81** 290
Elias **77** 205
Eliezer **52** 367
Elihu **71** 276
Elisha **62** 17 **72** 100
Eliza **63** 344
Elizabeth **63** 172 **69** 102 **72**
35 **77** lxxi 206 **81** 84
Elizabeth (Atherton)
(Weeks) **86** 244
Elizabeth Lucy (Gwinn)
86 245 **106** 64
Eloisa **98** 358

MATHER *cont'd*
Elvira (Warren) **112** 141
Esther **61** 77 **72** 100
Esther (Wareham) **86** 244
    112 152
Eunice **55** lxxvi **77** 205
    206 **79** 72
Eunice M. **79** 72
Ezekiel **95** 104 106
Ezra **77** 205 206 **84** 137
F. G. **107** 90
Flora A. **81** 290
Flora Amelia (Stone)
    86 246
Frances White **79** 25
Francis Amanda **115** 260
Frank J. **69** 194
Frederick **77** 205 206
Frederick W. **78** 238
George **77** 206
George D. **81** 290
George W. **82** 453
George William **112** 141
Georgia **77** 206
Georgiana Pomeroy
    (Woolson) **86** 243 245
Hannah **52** 367 368 **72** 184
    83 59 **117** 68 **124** 170
    171
Hannah (Hutchinson)
    124 170 181
Hannah A. (Blodgett)
    110 23 104
Hannah M. (Barnes)
    88 337
Harriet Almira **96** 133
Hattie **98** 345
Helen Talcott **60** 306
Henry **77** 205
Hepzibah **77** 206 **78** 251
Herbert **78** 239
Horace E. **52** 366 **104** 92
Increase **51** 84 362 **52** 275
    367 424 **53** 291 **54** 41
    194 234 235 241 **55** 40
    236 380 **61** 129 **69** 102
    105 111 **71** lxvii **76** 170
    78 430 **79** 223 **86** 244-
    246 **91** 167 **95** 44 101-
    104 106 108 **101** 194 196
    103 37-42 **107** 305 **109**
    201 **112** 9-12 **128** 145
    129 352 **132** 33 **133** 127
    132 134 189 **136** 5 12 13
    149 150 **137** 268 **139**
    305 **140** 13 **142** 147 **144**
    196 203 212 **148** 20
Irene **107** 305
Irene (Blodgett) **109** 201
Isaac **53** 22
Isabella (Hoffman) **112**
    141 142
Jacob **53** 22
James **53** 22 **77** 200 205
    101 202 **126** 255
Jane **70** 225
Jane Ann (Barratt)
    112 141
Jane M. **73** 16
Jarius **143** 66
Jehoiada **77** 205 206

MATHER *cont'd*
Jeremiah **53** 22
Jerusha **77** 205 206
Joan (Riddlesdale)
    143 217
Joanna **77** 205
John **53** 22 210 **56** 386 387
    58 118 328 **61** 77 **77** 205
    206 **78** 251 **116** 7
John R. **110** 23 104
Joseph **53** 22 **66** 191 **75**
    150 **77** 205 206 **86** 244
    115 25 **116** 7
Joseph Harvey **96** 133
Katharine **52** 366-368
    75 149 150
Katharine Livingston
    86 245 246 **106** 64
Keziah **112** 75
L. Arabella **81** 290
Lester **81** 290
Lizzie Palmer (Merrill)
    106 64
Lodice **97** 117
Lois **61** 140 **77** 206 **115** 25
Lois (Fairbank) **112** 141
Lois (Griswold) **86** 245
    106 64
Louisa (Marine) **112** 141
Louisa C. **77** 200
Lucretia Helm **78** 346
Lucy **77** 206 213
Luther P. **77** 206
Mabel Lay **104** 145 **112**
    73 141
Margaret **54** 348 349
Maria **69** 102
Marie **104** 84
Mary **53** 22 **61** 140 **73** 116
    76 220 **98** 345 **106** 231
Mary (Cotton) **86** 244
Mary (Lamb) **112** 141
Mary A. **77** 206
Mary K. **100** 174
Mary W. (Benchley)
    (Getman) **143** 65 66
Medusy **71** 276
Mehitable **77** 206 **81** 265
Mercy **77** 205 206
Minerva **98** 345
Nabby **98** 358
Nancy **79** 307
Nancy (Starr) **126** 255
Nathan **53** 22
Nathaniel **52** 367 368 **57**
    64 **61** 281 **72** 35 **77** 205
    83 59 **86** 244 **89** 149 **94**
    176 **96** 281
Norman R. **77** 206
O. M. **84** 398
Obadiah **53** 22
Oliver M. **114** 307
Orlando **77** 206
Otis M. **76** 81
Peggy (Gerrish) **84** 377
Persis Electa (Wright)
    96 133
Phebe **77** 206 207 **84** 137
    98 356
Philip Richard **86** 246 452
Rebecca **53** 210 **63** 337

MATHER *cont'd*
Reuben **97** 294
Rhoda (Huntley) **101** 202
Richard **52** 366 **53** 22 190
    54 43 44 348 **55** lxxvi
    lxxxvii 299 **57** 64 **58** 328
    60 lxxii **61** 56 127 140
    65 63-13 15 16 **143** 217
Richard Henry **77** lxxi
    78 346
Robert **53** 22
Robert Seymour **104** 144
Rufus Graves **100** 180
Ruth (Kelsey) **112** 141
Sally **114** 307
Sam **77** 206
Samuel **52** 366-368 **57** 64
    72 181 **75** xxiii 64 77
    203 206 207 **78** 387 **79**
    44 **84** 377 **86** 109 202
    243-246 452 **87** 166 **91**
    93 352 **94** 176 **95** 100 **97**
    43 **106** 64 **124** 170-172
    144 208
Samuel B. **78** 387
Samuel Livingston **86**
    243 245 246 **106** 64
Sarah **56** 387 **61** 56 **67** 373
    75 150 **77** 206 **93** 179
    129 395 **134** 87
Sarah (Cotton) **86** 244
Sarah (Huntley) **100** 268
Sarah (Story) (Cotton)
    106 64
Sarah Anne **78** 387
Silence **63** 337
Simon **77** 206
Stephen **56** 387
Stephen Douglass **79** 25
Sylvester **77** 206
T. **77** 206
Thankful **81** 84
Thomas **54** 348 349 **67** 373
    84 153 165 **86** 243 98
    358 **106** 64 **108** 196
Thrusden **64** 253
Timothy **52** 367 **77** 205
    206 **86** 244 245 **100** 267
    268 **101** 56 58 62 **106** 64
    112 141 **144** 121
Ursula **81** 290
Warham **72** 35
William **60** 306 **63** 172 337
    77 206 98 345
William B. **77** 206
William Cotton **72** 274
William G. **74** xxiv
William Gwinn **73** 318
    86 245 246 **105** 232 **106**
    64 128
William L. **72** 274 **98** 345
    115 260
Zelinda **115** 25
Zilpah **72** 223
MATHERS
Alberta **98** 345
Charlotte (Fitz Randolph)
    98 345
Elizabeth **122** 320
Hattie **98** 345
James **128** 19

MATHERS *cont'd*
Mary **98** 345
Minerva **98** 345
Nancy (Starr) **128** 19
Polly **56** 255
Rebecca (Fitz Randolph)
  98 345
MATHERSHAW
Joseph **64** 315
MATHERY Mary **132** 305
MATHES Mathis Mathies
—— **83** 194
— Mr. **82** 298
Abraham **61** 360
Ada **117** 119
Alice **59** 317
Alice (Andrews) **99** 167
Ann **67** 276
Anna **66** 48 **82** 294 298
Arthelia Jane **83** 217 **84**
  190 **99** 138 167 **100** 116
Baldwine **55** 143
Benjamin **61** 360
Caroline (Durrell)
  134 149
Cassie **117** 119
David **66** 47
Dorothy **73** 192
Eliza Caroline **134** 149
Elizabeth **54** 395 **55** 113 **82**
  294 297
Emma **99** 167
Francis **132** 264
Gideon **66** 47 48 **67** 276
J. M. **83** 194
Jane (Corson) **99** 167
Jennings Gaskill **99** 167
Jesse **66** 47
Job **66** 47
John **59** 317 **66** 47 **99** 167
John Shields **96** 305
Joseph **54** 395 **55** 143
Judith **66** 47
Julia Ann (Carver) **96** 305
Lois **66** 47
Lydia **64** 186 **67** 276
Marcy (Cranmer) **99** 167
Marguerite **99** 148
Martha **73** 74
Mary E. (Rutherford)
  117 119
Mary F. **84** 30
Mercy (Shreeve) **99** 167
Micajah **99** 167
Molly **73** 70
Peter **82** 294 298
Reuben **66** 47
Robert **74** 270
Ruth **82** 293 294
Sally **86** 300
Sally (Laskey) **134** 149
Samuel **82** 293 294
  134 149
Samuel J. **134** 149
Sarah Jane **67** 98
Solomon **64** 185
St. Helena (Hand) **99** 167
Stanley M. **82** 123 237
Susan E. **73** 193
Thomas **117** 119
Timothy **54** 395

MATHES *cont'd*
Valentine **61** 360 366 368-
  371 **73** 201
MATHESON Mathasson
  Mathenson Mathison
Abner **101** 204
Alexander **63** 351
Anna Emily **100** 245
Catherine (Campbell)
  93 190
Catherine (Maltby)
  111 297
Catherine W. **93** 190
Charles **63** 88
Donald **93** 190
Flora **93** 190
Flora (Matheson) **93** 190
Harriet May (Torrey)
  100 244
Hugh Merritt **100** 245
Israel **111** 297
John **91** 329
John Alexander **81** 107
  219 **93** 83 141 190
Josephine Mary (Merry)
  93 190
Lucretia **101** 204
Lucretia (Huntley)
  101 205
Malcolm **100** 245
Rebecca **63** 88
Samuel Hallett **77** 182
Sarah Frances **77** 182
Thomas **128** 50
William John **100** 245
William John (Mrs.) **86**
  194 **100** 232 244 245
  101 128
Matheus *see* Matthews
Mathew *see* Matthews
Mathewe *see* Matthews
Mathews *see* Matthews
MATHEWS-RICHARDSON
Elizabeth **60** 81
Mathewson *see*
  Matthewson
MATHEY
Alexandre **88** 400
Frederic **64** 115
MATHIAS
Abraham **67** 247
Clara L. **95** 314
Frederica G. **97** 53
John J. **91** 193
MATHIE Caroline
  Hamilton (Briggs) **89**
  132 **113** 302
Cornelia Zoa **113** 302
Eleanor **85** 397
Elizabeth **74** 258
Francis S. **113** 302
Karl **113** 302
Karl (Mrs.) **89** 132 **103** 116
  113 147 302
Karl Theodore **113** 302
Katharine (Discher)
  113 302
Katharine Elizabeth
  113 302
William **74** 258
Mathies *see* Mathes

MATHIEU Remi **114** 263
Mathis *see* Mathes
Mathison *see* Matheson
Mathues *see* Matthews
MATILE
Anna Grace **112** 317
MATLACK Asa **103** 248
MATLAT Anna **85** 144
MATLOCK
Edgar Lee **87** 174
MATLY Martin **66** 36
Maton *see* Mattoon
Matoon *see* Mattoon
MATOSIUS —— **62** 168
MATOTT
Jessie Mary **102** 124
MATRAU Ruth **109** 73
MATRESS
Ezekiel **88** 284
Sarah (Landerson) **88** 284
MATROP Thomas **52** 234
MATROSS
____ (Chase) **87** 141
MATRY Peter **65** 230
MATSON Matsone Mattson
— Dea. **71** 134
Abigail **77** 206
Albertina **85** 410
Alice **128** 267
Alida **97** 124
Ann **89** 47
Ann B. **85** 410
Anna **81** 51
Archelaus H. **85** 409
Asa **71** 80 161
Azra **85** 410
Carl **97** 124
Catherine **77** 206
Charles Randolph (Mrs.)
  94 139
Charles W. **85** 410
Charlotte Chapman
  85 410
Christian **77** 136
Clara L. **83** 217
Clara Lois **84** 190
Clement **85** 410
David **71** 154
Delorane P. **85** 410
Desire **71** 164
Dinah **77** 206
Eastman J. **85** 410
Edward **71** 280 **72** 37
Eli **81** 51
Eliza **104** 122
Elizabeth **71** 87 280 303
  101 48
Elizabeth (Gillett) **101** 48
Elizabeth (Maltby)
  111 293
Elizabeth Pelton **86** 170
Ella **83** 249 **84** 190
Ella Cornelia **60** lix
Emily M. Castle **85** 410
Eunice **78** 375
Ezra **85** 410
Flora Pluma **105** 220
Frank H. **85** 410
Freeborn **101** 94
George **62** 83
Harriet F. **85** 410

MATSON *cont'd*
Helen **85** 291
Isabella **66** 111
Israel **77** 207
Joanna **77** 206
John **52** 35 **71** 81 87 154
164 165 299 302 303 **72**
38 **95** 132
Joseph **59** 21
Keziah **72** 38
Laura **86** 49
Lois **77** 206
Lucretia **71** 161
Luther **85** 410 **86** 170
Lydia **85** 410
Margaret A. **71** 35
Mary **71** 279 **85** 410
Mary E. **85** 410
Matilda (Sjernberg)
97 124
Minnie A. (Bradley)
94 139
Moses **71** 165 303
Nathan **77** 206
Nathaniel **56** 96 **77** 206
207
Penelope **62** 83
Phebe **77** 207
Philo **86** 170
Polly **77** 207
Rachel **85** 410
Ralph **77** 136
Rebecca **62** 83
Rosabelle **85** 410
Ruth **61** 392 **85** 410 **101** 94
Sarah **71** 299 **85** 410
Thomas **55** 141 **56** 96 **58**
205 **85** 410 **89** 47 **95** 132
Wallace H. **85** 410
Washburn N. **85** 410
William **78** 375 **81** 51
MATSUNGA
Alicia **123** 160
MATT Dorothy **128** 73
MATTEINI Giuseppe
Carlo **78** 248
Harriette Henchman
78 248
MATTER
Catherine **114** 186
MATTESON Matterson
Abel **104** 46 **129** 61
Allen **129** 270
Alvira **72** 146
Andrew **102** 159 **116** 259
Benjamin **129** 67
Caleb **113** 53
Carrie Alice **74** 308
Catherine **76** 273
Clara L. **102** 159 **104** 323
Clarinda **98** 358
Climena **98** 358
Daniel **76** 264 **129** 67
David **127** 34 35 **129** 58
60 270 **134** 205
Deliverance **72** 25
Dorcas (Waite) **127** 34 35
Ebenezer **127** 147
Edmond **129** 60
Edwin A. **111** 127 129
Elijah **127** 93

MATTESON *cont'd*
Elizabeth **72** 17
Emily F. **117** 208
Emily Louisa **61** 274
Erastus P. **74** 308
Ezekiel **129** 60
Fannie A. (Harrington)
111 127 129
Freelove **104** 46
Hannah **64** lii **76** 264
Henry **82** 467 **87** 266
129 57
Henry A. **117** 208
Hiram **72** 146
Huldah **114** 307
Isabel **109** 270
Jane C. (Rathbone)
116 259
Job **72** 25 **116** 64 **129** 60 67
John **109** 270 **129** 58 61
Jonathan **129** 60 61 67
Joseph **129** 59 67
Joshua **98** 368
Josiah **114** 307 **127** 93
Josias **129** 58
Lewis Spafard (Mrs.)
103 120
Lois **127** 35
Lucy (Spink) **127** 34
Lurania **114** 307
Lydia **72** 17 25
Lydia (Himes) **102** 159
Marcy (Manchester)
102 17
Maria (James) **127** 34
Mary **89** 205
Mary (James) **127** 34
Moses **129** 66
Nathan **129** 59
Nathan W. **98** 358
Nathaniel **56** 126
Nicholas **129** 271
Obadiah **129** 61
Oliver **102** 17
Peleg **127** 34
Polly (James) **127** 34
Price **72** 146
Richard **129** 58
Rufus **127** 34 **129** 60
Russelle **127** 34
Sally **98** 358
Samuel **129** 61
Sarah **113** 53
Silas **129** 61
Solomon **129** 270
Susan **99** 301
Thomas **127** 34 **129** 60 65
67 270
Uriah **129** 60
William **129** 61 274
MATTHEWS Matheus
Matthew Mathewe
Mathews Mathues
—— **54** 456 **55** 40 **57** 338
58 101 **66** 87 **68** 138 **92**
230 **105** 325 **106** 32 **109**
44 **111** 251
— Mr. **79** 408 **89** 88
93 301
— Mrs. **61** 134
— Rev. Mr. **58** 73

MATTHEWS *cont'd*
— Widow **56** 293
____ (Gray) **108** 262
____ (Putnam) **86** 44
____ (Thompson) **123** 308
A. **57** 343
A. G. **148** 243
A. W. **86** 46
Aaron **86** 44
Abbie Frances (Knowles)
86 96
Abbie Knowles **86** 109
Abel **65** 150
Abigail **66** 224 **78** 413 **86**
32 45 **88** 192 **105** 203
309 311 **106** 101 **116**
142 **126** 96
Abigail (Averell) **111** 258
114 129
Abigail (Willis) **86** 32 44
Abner **66** 332 **92** 339
Abraham **66** 217 **67** 247
109 44
Adelaide **92** 230
Adeline **92** 339
Albert **54** 359 461 **55** xxix
xxxv 239 344 440 **56** xxx
111 216 417 418 **57** v
vii xviii xxxi xxxvi 221
234 239 243 **58** xliii 11
59 v vii xxvi xxvii xli
lxxxv xcvii 121 122 177
214 337 **60** vii xxxiv
xcii 30 108 109 217 222
407 **61** vii xxxiii **62**
xxxv 110 **63** vi 111 213
64 286 298 381 **65**
xxxiii 279 284 304 **66**
xlviii 95 **67** xxx 303 **68**
xxx 112 **69** 290 **71** 97 **72**
248 **73** 82 74 162 **82** 261
264 **84** 181 **90** 124 **94**
176 **96** 154 **100** 232 249
101 128 **103** 32 **142** 118
Albertine **59** xcvii
82 259 261
Albertine (Bunker)
100 249
Alexander **91** 329
Alfred **86** 45
Alfred Russell **108** 260
Alice **53** 10 **108** 260
Alice (Hallet) **108** 264
Alice R. **94** 52
Alice Southworth **59**
xcvii **82** 261
Almira **57** 291
Amanda **108** 207 **109** 42
Amos **71** 50 115 118 **117**
170 172
Angeline **95** 115
Ann **73** 254 **100** 136
133 235
Ann (Butler) (Penfield)
109 229
Anna **56** 64 **81** 430
Anna Angenora **44** 211
Anna Bangs **108** 260
Anne **54** 97 **64** 347 **73** 254
Anne Chace **62** xxxvii
Anner **108** 206

MATTHEWS *cont'd*
Annie **71** 119
Ansel **108** 108 264
Anthony **112** 287
Arthur **100** 189 **133** 124
Asa **109** 43
Asa Eldridge **107** 289
Asahel **62** 85 **86** 43
Atkins **105** 203 **107** 289
  290 **108** 108 **109** 43
Augustus **71** 117 119 120
Avis **125** 109
B. L. **86** 46
Barbara Jean **148** 83
Barnabas **105** 89 **106** 183-
  185 **107** 37 38 289 **108**
  206 262
Basha C. (Lewis) **108** 265
Benjamin **67** 122 **82** 260
  100 249 **103** 72 **105** 203
  108 207-210 262 **109** 41-
  43
Benjamin (Mrs.) **108** 260
Bethiah **105** 203 **108** 206
  260 261
Bethiah Gorham **108** 208
Bethiah S. **109** 38
Betsey **51** 52 **86** 45 **107** 289
Betsey (Bryant) **137** 327
Betsey (Leavens) **86** 32
  45 46
Betsey (Rider) **108** 262
Betsey Leavens **86** 45
Betsey M. **123** 52
Bickford C. **114** 180
Brander **59** xcvi **65** 97
C. H. **91** 329
Caleb **56** 137 **60** 159 **66**
  328 **76** 132 **129** 273
Caroline **59** xcvii **82** 261
  92 339 **108** 260
Caroline A. **92** 339
Carrie L. **121** 306
Catherine **99** 205 **101** 54
  163 276 **108** 108 **142** 36
Catherine Van Cortlandt
  62 389
Charles **53** 186 300 **86** 45
  91 106 **105** 287 **108** 205
  110 217
Charles G. **104** 64
Charles Henry **51** 52
Charlotte **108** 207 264
  125 215
Charlotte A. (Stover)
  120 220 222
Clara **84** 216
Clara C. **52** 446 **109** 39
Cleo **104** 141
Clifton **81** 363 **82** 237
Constant Southworth
  59 xcvii **82** 261
Cornelia (Whiting)
  104 64
Cyrus **108** 209 210
Daisy B. **124** 258
Daniel **86** 32 43-45 **114** 180
  138 26
David **66** 22 **107** 37 **108**
  109 264

MATTHEWS *cont'd*
Debby Eliza (Harris)
  145 154
Deborah **66** 294
Deborah (Donnell) **118**
  241 242
Dennis **57** 291
Desire **106** 183-185 **107** 37
Desire (Gifford) **130** 45
Dorcas **82** 260 **105** 203 311
Dorcas (Howes) **100** 249
  103 72
Dorman **95** 134
E. L. **92** 339
E. R. Norris **62** xxxvii
Ebenezer **100** 35 **105** 311
  106 182 **108** 205 207-
  209 **109** 44
Ebenezer Bryant **56** 293
Edith Dillon **86** 45
Edmond **108** 209 **109** 41
Edmund **51** 352 353
Edward **54** 192 **59** xcvi
  66 218 **86** 43 45 **108** 206
  207 **109** 44
Elcina **91** 106
Electa **57** 291
Eli **56** 64 **71** 54 **86** 44
Eli J. **71** 119
Elijah **113** 26 **115** 140 222
Elisha **62** 23 **86** 43 44 **105**
  85 **106** 184
Eliza **61** 136 **82** 285 294
  92 339
Eliza (Crowel) **108** 262
Eliza (Harris) **145** 154
Eliza (Hedge) **109** 38
Elizabeth **53** 22 23 **59**
  xcvii **66** 146 154 217-220
  222 224 294 328 **67** 49
  73 254 **82** 261 **86** 44 **99**
  282 101 163 **105** 203
  108 205 207 208 **109** 39
  122 320 **142** 36
Elizabeth (Crowell)
  125 236
Elizabeth (Hannum)
  90 350
Elizabeth J. **121** 308
  122 152
Elizabeth Rider **107** 289
Elizabeth Selby **77** 226
Ella **108** 259
Ellen Bacon **82** 264
Ellen Bacon (Sargent)
  103 72
Ellen M. (Freeman) **120**
  220 222
Ellen Nathalie **82** 264
  101 124 **103** 72 73 77
  125
Elmira Augusta (Arey)
  87 105
Elvira **94** 389
Elvira (Eldridge) **108** 264
Emeline (Hallet) **108** 264
Emma J. (Bridges) **92** 339
Enoch **107** 288 **108** 109
  109 42
Esther **79** 43
Eunice **86** 43 44 **107** 37

MATTHEWS *cont'd*
  126 220
Eunice (Morse) **86** 43
Eunice (Payne) **137** 327
Eunice B. **73** 179
Ezekiel **108** 109 110 206
  119 315
Fanny **125** 292
Fanny (Matthews)
  125 292
Frances **52** 446
Frances (Bray) **109** 38
Frances (Kress) **114** 63
Frances Halarub **88** 107
Francis **82** 285 294 **85** 82
Francis Joseph **73** 179
Francis Weeks **73** 179
Frank (Mrs.) **108** 260
Franklin **108** 260 **109** 39
Frederick **107** 291
Freeman **108** 109
G. F. **58** 185 288
George **68** 85 **85** 279 280
  285 **86** 97 **108** 109 260
  264 **109** 43 **125** 218 292
  143 257 **145** 154 155
George Allen **118** 131
George Clifford **86** 97
George Clifford (Mrs.)
  86 96 197 204
George E. **54** 121
George F. **128** 281
George L. **90** 350
George Prince **108** 260
George W. **61** 109 **119** 315
  121 71 73
George Williams **84** 172
  85 196
Gertrude M. (Barnes)
  126 293
Grace **86** 44
Grace (Ferguson) **96** 397
Gretchen Elizabeth **86** 97
  87 174
Hannah **52** 445 **56** 137 **57**
  290 **82** 260 **86** 44 **88** 313
  103 260 **105** 89 203 310
  106 101 **108** 209 265
  109 44 **142** 36
Hannah (Bray) **108** 265
Hannah (Matthews)
  108 265
Hannah (Ryder) **100** 249
  103 72
Hannah (Snow) **86** 44
Hannah Hodges **114** 11
Hannah Hodges (Parker)
  114 11
Hannah T. (Matthews)
  108 263
Hannah Thacher **108** 205
Harriet Adele **51** 52
Harriet Louise **60** xxxviii
  62 xxxv **66** xlviii
Hawes Hallet **108** 110
Helen Louise **51** 52
Heman **108** 209 **109** 44
Henrietta **60** 159
Henry **62** 22 **86** 43 45 **107**
  290 **108** 109 262 **109** 44
  128 219

MATTHEWS *cont'd*
Hepzibah (Beal) **113** 26
Hepzibah (Bryer) **115** 140
Hopey **62** 85
Howes H. **108** 265
Huldah (Putnam) **86** 32 44
Increase **86** 32 33 37 43-46 466
Irene Buel **82** 181
Isaac **82** 260 **86** 343 **100** 249 **103** 72 **105** 88 89 309-312 **106** 102 182 183 **107** 107 **108** 108 206 207 265 **109** 42 44 **123** 311
Isaiah P. **109** 39
J. **58** 185 288
J. A. **52** 487
J. F. **92** 339
J. Frank **92** 339
J. M. (Mrs.) **123** 310
James **51** 52 **57** 291 **59** xcvi **67** 119 120 122 218 **73** 254 **82** 259 260 **100** 249 **103** 72 **106** 102 **108** 205-208 263 **109** 39 42 **123** 312 **131** 129
Jane **125** 18
Jedidah (Kenney) (Wilson) (Baker) **108** 216
Jo. **123** 312
Joan Cutting **96** 397
Joanna **113** 27
Joel **58** 372 **86** 43 **108** 208
John **53** 22 189 300 378 **56** 313 **62** 324 **63** 28 173 280 **64** 344 **65** 32 51 59 150 **66** 22 **76** 132 133 **78** 423 **80** 9 316 **86** 32 37 43-45 **91** 329 **92** 339 **93** 51 **96** 397 **98** 119 **99** 205 282 283 **100** 136 **101** 54 163 276 **103** 254 255 **105** 202 203 **108** 77 **110** 217 **111** 258 **113** 27 **114** 129 **116** 11 **118** 241 242 **119** 21 **123** 260 308 **125** 43 **133** 235 **141** 117 **142** 36 **143** 330 **144** 37 **148** 62
John (Mrs.) **89** 132 **96** 396 **97** 78 162
John Alexander **108** 236
John F. **120** 305 **121** 71
John Gillette **73** 319 **74** xxx
John Henry **96** 397
John Mabry **74** 241
John R. **73** 213
John T. **76** 276
Jonas **56** 64 **71** 122
Jonathan **66** 219 **107** 37
Jorge **108** 109
Joseph **66** 220 **92** 60 **99** 205 283 **101** 54 **105** 203 280 **107** 289 **108** 208 210 258 **109** 40 **117** 223 224 **123** 311 **137** 327
Joseph R. **103** 268

MATTHEWS *cont'd*
Joseph W. **117** 164
Joshua **105** 310 311 **106** 102 182 183 185 **108** 205 206 259
Joshua Atkins **108** 260
Josiah **105** 203
Julia Ann **77** 265
Julia E. **51** 52
Julius **83** 428 436
Katharine **99** 282 283
Katie (Schermerhorn) **89** 132 **96** 396 **97** 162
Keziah **107** 38
L. B. **76** 277
Lawrence **52** 256 258 **77** 226
Leander **91** 329
Leroy **92** 230
Libbie (Hannum) **90** 350
Lila E. **106** 125
Lizzie J. (Brewster) **121** 71 73
Lois **56** 66 **66** 332 **71** 120 122
Lois Kimball **65** 199
Louis **86** 43 45
Louisa **77** 226
Louiza (Field) **128** 281
Lovina **90** 76
Lucille **92** 230
Lucina **71** 50
Lucretia **72** 284
Lucy **58** 372 **66** 22 **86** 45 **107** 288
Lucy Tyler **104** 68
Lucy Wyman **56** 66
Luther **86** 44
Luthera **141** 52
Lydia **57** 290-292 **66** 217 **86** 43 **107** 95 **108** 108-110 **109** 44 **111** 258
Lydia (Bickford) **91** 106
Lydia (Hussey) **84** 423
Lydia Baker **108** 209
Lyman **64** 235
M. **128** 171
M. C. **118** 131
Mabel **92** 339
Madelon **78** 205
Marcy **105** 310-312
Margaret **53** 150 **60** 61 **68** 193 **88** 3
Margaret (Dillon) **86** 45
Margaret (Hunt) **86** 43
Margery **53** 186 189 300 378 **56** 313 **78** 423
Margery (Hoar) **110** 217
Maria **108** 260
Maria (Parsons) **125** 218
Marmaduke **54** 236 **87** 46 **90** 270 **142** 118 119 **143** 123
Martha **99** 327
Martha F. (Hawes) **117** 164
Martin Irwin **67** xxxiv
Mary **52** 445 **58** 393 394 **61** 134 **63** 173 344 **65** 353 **66** 149 153 **73** 254 **79** 397 **81** 430 **86** 43 45

MATTHEWS *cont'd*
92 339 **100** 146 **104** 27 **105** 18 87 203 310 **108** 207 260 **117** 167 **126** 96 **133** 235
Mary (Crowfoote) **123** 260
Mary (Hedge) **108** 263
Mary (Johnson) **86** 43
Mary (Varrell) **120** 305 **121** 71
Mary A. **90** 357
Mary Ann **103** 255 **108** 207
Mary E. **90** 42
Mary Elizabeth (Kellog) **86** 97
Mary J. **58** lxxix
Mary Jane **66** 53
Mary L. **83** 371
Mary Louisa **84** 190
Mary N. **88** 343
Mary V. **87** 89
Matilda **117** 41
Mehitable **66** 224
Melissa **86** 45 46
Mercy **87** 226 234 **105** 309-312 **106** 102 182 **107** 288 **108** 206 209 260
Mercy (Hopkins) **105** 101
Mercy M. **120** 308
Merriman **109** 229
Milly Thacher **108** 206
Minnie Lee **93** 274
Miriam Jane **73** 179
Molly **66** 222 **73** 70
Moses D. **120** 220 222
Nancy **114** 182
Nancy (Slocum) (Swan) (Meloy) **120** 5
Nathan **59** xli lv xcvi xcvii 231 **64** xxix **71** v vi x **72** v vi **73** v vi **74** vi xi **75** vi **76** v x 78 240 241 **77** v xv **78** 192 217 **79** 112 187 196 213 **80** 196 204 219 **81** 208 216 233 **82** 223 246 252 253 259-264 385 **100** 249 **103** 72 73 **108** 207 260
Nathan F. **68** 130
Nathaniel **105** 203 **106** 182 **108** 206 259 263 **109** 42
Nellie **117** 172
Nellie E. (Drew) **83** 428 436
Nicholas **95** 244
Obadiah **115** 293
Olive **107** 289 **108** 206 208
Oliver **108** 206 260 264
Oliver Ellsworth **57** 291
Oliver Russell **108** 260
Orimal **62** 133
Orphia **81** 387 **82** 178
Pamelia **71** 122
Patia **108** 263
Patia Baker **108** 209
Patience **107** 289 **108** 261 **115** 293
Patty **66** 22

MATTHEWS *cont'd*
Patty Russel **108** 205 206
109 42
Paul **58** 372
Paulina **108** 210
Peggy **142** 36
Persis **86** 44
Peter **58** 393 **64** 19 160 **65**
353 **66** 152 213 **81** 430
82 413
Phebe **57** 290 **82** 260 **105**
203 312 **107** 289 **108**
207 260 264 **125** 18
Phebe (Howes) **100** 249
103 72
Phebe (Matthews) **108**
264 **125** 18
Philip **93** 382 386 387
Phineas **86** 44
Polly **66** 22 **107** 291 **108**
108 109 206
Prince **105** 309 **107** 291
108 108 109 206 207
109 42 44
Rebecca **86** 343 **87** 105
105 310 311 **106** 102
182 183 185 **107** 107 289
108 108 206 207 209 264
Rebecca (Crowell) **86** 343
Rebecca C. **109** 38
Rebecca Howes **108** 207
Reuben **105** 203 **106** 184
108 208 209 **109** 38 42
Rhoda **81** 387
Richard **63** 25 **80** 363 **108**
206 **109** 44
Robert **51** 451 452 **64** 162
73 200 **79** 314 **108** 22
Roger **81** 122 **144** 37
Roger A. **92** 339
Ruby (Parker) (Wyman)
133 124
Ruth **58** 167 **86** 43 **107** 38
108 208 261 **109** 42 **133**
213
Ruth M. **104** 126
Sabra **107** 288 **108** 206
207 261
Sabra Temperance
108 206
Sally **56** 65 **66** 186 **108**
109 205-208 262 265 **109**
39 **119** 147 **142** 36
Sally (Donnell) **117** 223
224
Sally (Hallett) **100** 249
Sally H. (Taylor) **109** 39
Salmon Hows **57** 290
Samuel **57** 290-292 **66**
142 149 152-154 211 213
215 217-220 222 224 294
302 **67** 119 **86** 43 44 **103**
194 254 259 **105** 87 280
311 **108** 206 207 **125**
234 236
Samuel Wooster **87** 105
Sarah **59** xcvi **66** 142 149
152-154 211 213 215 217
301 **67** 120 **71** 120 125
80 9 **82** 260 **84** 325 **86**
32 44 45 **106** 184 **107**

MATTHEWS *cont'd*
289 290 **108** 77 108 206
109 39 220 **118** 260 **124**
218 **133** 235
Sarah (Cary) **106** 24
Sarah (Garfield) **86** 43
Sarah (Hallett) **100** 249
103 72
Sarah (Hedges) **131** 129
Sarah (Matthews) **109** 39
Sarah (Tibbetts) **100** 35
Sarah (Woodbridge)
86 44
Sarah Almira **51** 52
Sarah Bryant **56** 293
Sarah Hallet **59** xcvii
Sarah Hallett [Sister
Paula] **82** 261
Serena **108** 208 **109** 42 43
Sibell (Giffard) **95** 244
Silas **71** 122 **86** 44
Solomon **86** 43 **106** 183
Stanley **69** 210
Stephen **132** 141
Sukey **66** 22 **142** 36
Sullivan Amory **82** 264
Susan **86** 45 46
Susan (Thatcher) **108** 264
Susan A. **94** 373
Susanna **60** 159 **64** 154
83 208 **85** 302 **86** 37 44
107 37
Susanna Baker **108** 258
Sylvanus **106** 185 **108** 207
109 38
Temperance **114** 10
Thankful **86** 44 **105** 310
107 289
Thomas **57** 290 291 **61** 136
63 345 **64** 345 **76** 133
100 136 **105** 101 **107**
289 **108** 264 **109** 43 **125**
18 **130** 45 **132** 141 **140**
68
Thomas Clark **91** 142
Timothy **56** 63-66 **71** 48 50
115 119 120 122
Tobias (Archbp. of York)
64 88
Toby **52** 348 **67** 70
Toby (Archbp. of York)
67 70
Ursula **52** 257-259 **125** 82
Vance E. **230 92** 230
Walter **113** 27 **116** 134
117 169
Watkins **108** 208
William **51** 222 351 **52** 445
63 214 **65** 34 66 211 **75**
229 **84** 423 **91** 329 **92**
230 **100** 180 189 **104**
172 **105** 203 286 311
106 101 **107** 250 **108**
216 260 **113** 27 **118** 260
William A. **109** 42 43
William Atkins **107** 289
William D. **73** 213
William G. **108** 220 222
William Henry Howells
51 52
William L. **91** 329

MATTHEWS *cont'd*
William Peter **62** 301
Willie G. **92** 339
MATTHEWSON Mathewson
Allen Hunt **82** 467
Almira **108** 160
Amy **63** 157
Amy Ann **77** 178
Andrew P. **90** 57
Ann **63** 157
Anna **115** 37
Augustus **88** 15
Azubah **89** 231
Barbara (Lockwood)
106 148
Benoni **108** 160
Bethiah **88** 7
Brockholt **63** 157
Catherine **142** 112
Catherine (Hathaway)
134 200
Celia Ann **69** 200
Cora Agnes (Clark)
106 148
Daniel **128** 58 **138** 115
Darius **82** 467
Dearborn **72** 115
Deliverance (Malavery)
106 148
Dolly **121** 179
Edward Payson **82** 467
Edward Payson (Mrs.)
73 105
Elizabeth **106** 148
Elizabeth (Clemence)
106 148
Elizabeth (Mathewson)
106 148
Ellen **77** 183
Emma Annette **80** 248
Flora S. **65** xxxiv
Forrest Earle **89** 231
George **63** 157
George Bowen **82** 467
George Edwin **77** 178
Hannah **80** 78 **82** 467
Hannah (Field) **106** 148
Helen **82** 467
Helen L. **121** 178
Helen Washburn **82** 467
Henry **82** 467
Henry Lewis **104** 144
Henry Smith **64** xxxiii
69 xxx **73** 105 **82** 123
247 467
Hope **82** 467
Imogene **78** 203
Ira **80** 248
Isabel **80** 78 84
James **67** 300 **80** 78 **97** 207
106 148 **116** 230
James William **106** 148
Jeffery **65** 61
Jeremiah **127** 310
John **106** 148 **127** 304 **128**
58 59 **146** 348
Joseph **82** 467
Joshua **128** 59
Judith (Peirce) **128** 313
Judith S. (Pierce) **90** 57
Linn N. **107** 129

MATTHEWSON *cont'd*
Louie Clark **99** 148 **106**
  62 130 148 **107** 129
Louis C. **97** 207
Lydia **115** 37 43
Marcy (Herendeen)
  142 141
Maria W. **72** 115
Marian Chandler **73** 105
  82 467
Mary **69** 200 **82** 467 **87** 253
  103 218 **115** 35
Mertie Carleton (Lazell)
  89 231
Nancy **138** 124
Nelson A. **106** 148
Noah **128** 313
Perigrene **128** 58 **138** 120
Phebe Ann (Chase) **88** 15
Philip **115** 41
Priscilla H. **80** 248
Rhoda **133** 308 310
Richard **129** 55
Rollin **63** 157
Sarah **142** 141
Sarah (Randall?) **108** 160
Susanna **63** 157
Thomas **128** 50
Vela **88** 25
William **69** 200
Winchester **142** 141
MATTHIES Anna Louise
  (Putnam) (Wooster)
  91 290
Bernard Harrison **91** 290
Eva **91** 290
George E. **74** xxiv 77 **91**
  144 176 290
Katharine **80** 105 206
  91 390
Martin **91** 290
Matticks *see* Mattocks
MATTINGLY
Eleanor Rutha **73** 267
Joan **67** 251
Joseph **73** 145
Martha **67** 256 **73** 262
William **67** 251 257
MATTIS
Sophie Levering **71** lv
MATTISON Abigail **65**
  344 345 **136** 247
Agnes E. **69** 30
Albert **115** 293
Alice **65** 344
Allen **80** 166
Almond Zina **75** 78
Ama **75** 78
Anna **80** 50
C. W. (Mrs.) **122** 240
Caroline Sophronia
  80 166
Charles Hamilton **80** 166
Daniel H. **69** 30
Daniel J. **80** 166
David **80** 50
David Maydole **73** 82
David Ovendo **80** 50
Ebenezer **73** 213 **80** 166
Edwin **69** 30
Francis **65** 344

MATTISON *cont'd*
Gertrude **80** 166
Harry Allen **80** 166
Helen **80** 50 **85** 291
Henry **73** 304 **75** 78
Ira **75** 78
James A. **73** 213
Jane **75** 78
Joanna J. **73** 213
John **65** 344
Lois **75** 78
Lucy **80** 166
Lucy A. **69** 30
Mary (Hawkins) **100** 295
Myra D. **80** 166
Oliver **100** 295
Parmer **65** 345
Patience **73** 213
Phebe **80** 166
Roxana **73** 213 **80** 166
Samuel **65** 344
Susanna **75** 78
Thankful **73** 304
Thomas **65** 344
William **65** 345
MATTOCKS Matticks
  Mattock Mattocke
  Mattoks Mattox
  Mattucks
— Widow **105** 277
Agnes **51** 348
Ann **75** 146 149 **97** 56
Anney (Robarts) **95** 190
Betty (Littlefield) **95** 88
Bridget **100** 300
Elizabeth **97** 56 **132** 40
Grace **81** 133
Helen Ruth **109** 128
Henry **95** 88
Hepzibah **95** 86
James **95** 131 190 **96** 273
Joanna (Cane) **95** 88 190
John **107** 64
Martha **132** 165
Palgravs **95** 88
Pelatiah **95** 190
Richard **81** 133
Samuel **97** 56 **122** 79
  143 43
MATTOON Maton Matoon
— **56** 214
— Col. **120** 63
— Gen. **121** 65 297
— Maj. **119** 217 223
Abel **73** 104 **121** 184
Amanda Louise **121** 183
  184
Anne **57** 268
Ebenezer **140** 296 300
Emily **78** 357
Haile **80** 176
Ida E. **93** 347
Isaac **78** 357
Isabella F. **77** 176
Jane **124** 289
Jane (Hilton) **124** 289 290
John L. **77** 176
Lydia **102** 158 **117** 80
Martha **78** 357
Mary **121** 60 63 64 68 97
  99 303

MATTOON *cont'd*
Mary (Livingston)
  121 184
Mary Emily **78** 357
Mary Livingston **122** 240
Oliver **78** 357
Phebe **121** 184
Philip **69** 286
Polly **120** 201
Richard **124** 290 292
Roxana **92** 100
Schuyler **121** 184
Sylvia Ann (Sherman)
  121 184
William **80** 176
Winford Lecky **69** 286
  70 xix
Mattox *see* Mattocks
Mattson *see* Matson
Mattucks *see* Mattocks
MATTYSEN Jan **96** 94
Mattys **96** 94
MATURIN Maturine
Elizabeth **51** 439
Gabriel **84** 256 382
MATZ
Caroline Rebecca
  95 164
Catherine A. (Loretz)
  95 164
Johan Michael **95** 164
MAUBUIT Georges Marie
  de (Mrs.) **88** 168
MAUCALLY Mary **60** 348
MAUD Maude Mawde
  Mawdes
Aner **94** 101
Daniel **96** 368 **99** 230
Esther (Hawks) **125** 103
Isaac **145** 112
Mary **60** 153
Sarah **78** 399
William **125** 103
MAUDANT —— **74** 28
MAUDINE
Hepzibah **134** 252
MAUDLIN —— **111** 312
Maudsley *see* Mawdsley
MAUDUIT
Beatrice **76** 300
Georges Marie de (Mrs.)
  89 262
Isabel de **97** 342
Priscilla Alden (Griffin)
  89 262
Robert **76** 300
William de **97** 342
MAUEAU William **140** 45
MAUG Augustin P. **107**
  19 251
MAUGANS Fay E. **120** 234
MAUGER Mary **148** 62
MAUGHAM
Isabel **104** 280
MAUGHER
Edward **60** 243
MAULE Maul Maull Mawle
—— **56** 212
Ann (Garrigues) **98** 44
Cornelia **95** 335
Edward **94** 275 **117** 111

MAULE *cont'd*
Edward W. **99** 50
Ethelbert Rounds **95** 335
Florine (Shapleigh)
95 335
Hannah (Penrose)
117 111
Harry **80** 375
Israel **98** 44
John **64** 353 **79** 41
Margaret **143** 328
Mary (Fitz Randolph)
98 44
Sarah Jane **94** 51
Shapleigh **95** 335
Thomas **90** 306 **102** 189
191
William **60** 253 **98** 44
99 50
MAULEY
Christina de **106** 287
Edmund de **116** 167
Elizabeth **73** 144
Maud **116** 174
Maud de **116** 174
Maull *see* Maule
MAULMER Ann **143** 236
MAULMON
Anne **143** 234-236
MAULSBY John **61** 207
Mary **61** 207
MAUNCEFELD
Richard **94** 339
MAUND
Anna Martin **79** 332
Bryan Martin **79** 332
George Tasker **79** 332
Harriet Lucy **79** 332
Henry Lee **79** 332
John James **79** 332
Julia Carter **79** 332
Newton **79** 332
Robert Carter **79** 332
MAUNDRE Joan **63** 39
Richard **63** 39
MAUNDY Richard **69** 362
MAUNEY
Walter de **109** 21
Maunsell *see* Munsell
MAUNSER William **70** 59
MAUREN —— **52** 97
MAUREPAS
— Count de **116** 9
MAURER Grace **98** 147
MAURICE Bishop of
London
56 375
MAURICE Elector of
Saxony **88** 100
MAURICE Prince **143** 105
MAURICE Anne **88** 144
Annie (Fitzgerald)
106 142
Anthony **106** 42
Benjamin Wistar **106** 46
Frederick **88** 202 **106** 142
Frederick Barton **89** 130
106 116 127 142
Frederick Michael
Percival **106** 142
Helen **106** 142

MAURICE *cont'd*
Joan Violet **106** 142
John Frederick **106** 142
John R. (Mrs.) **106** 311
Lewis **106** 173
Margaret Esther **106** 142
Margaret Helen (Marsh)
106 142
Mary **106** 82
Phillis Marjorie **106** 142
Theodore William **73** 275
MAURIEAU —— **56** 342
MAURY Alice **88** 170
Hannah **102** 206
James **52** 460
Jane Lewis **102** 168
Jesse Lewis **102** 168
John **80** 238
Kate F. **80** 238
Lillian Hope Woods
80 238
Lucy Jane (Price) **102** 168
Richard L. **56** 416
MAUTRAVERS
Alice **142** 241
Joan (Foliot) (Percy)
142 241
John **142** 241
MAUVES Honorée
Jeanne Georgine
98 338
MAVERICK
— Mr. **96** 236
____ (Reavis) **97** 63
____ (Stetson) **86** 349
Aaron **69** 146 147 156 **78**
448 **96** 233 360
Aaron Howell **97** 59
Abigail **58** 242 **69** 154
156 157 **78** 448 **96** 234
239 359 364 365 **143** 349
147 152 161
Ada (Bradley) **102** 165
Ada (Robards) **102** 167
Agatha **102** 165 168
Albert **102** 165 168
Alexander **69** 148 152
Alice **69** 148 152
Amias **67** 366 **69** 158 **96**
235 361 362
Amias (Cole) (Thompson)
96 235
Andrew **97** 57-59
Angelica **97** 59 63
Ann **97** 57 58 60
Ann (Anderson) **97** 59
Ann (Harris) **89** 281
Ann (Reynolds) **97** 58
Ann / Nancy **97** 57
Anna **69** 154
Anna (Harris) **96** 239
131 129
Anna (Luth) **102** 166
Anne **96** 240
Anne (Johnson) **96** 240
Anne (Maverick) **96** 240
Anne Caroline **97** 63
Antipas **69** 157 **78** 448 **85**
77 **95** 264 **96** 234 **147**
152 161
Audrey **69** 148 152

MAVERICK *cont'd*
Augusta **102** 165
Augusta Lewis **102** 167
Augustus **97** 59 **102** 168
Bella **67** 366 **96** 362 363
Benjamin **97** 63
Bersheba **96** 365
Caroline **97** 59
Catherine **69** 154 **97** 58
Catherine (Coyer) **97** 61
62
Catherine (Skipper)
96 239 240
Cicely **69** 146-149 152
Cornelia **97** 58
Daniel **69** 148 149 153
Dorothy **69** 148 149 152
159 **78** 449 **96** 235 **97** 60
Edward **69** 146-149 152
153
Elias **67** 367 **68** 202 **69**
148-151 153-155 157 **78**
448 **85** 455 **86** 349 **89**
281 **96** 233 236 239 240
363 364 **97** 57 59 61 62
131 129 **147** 152 161
148 7
Elizabeth **67** 366 **68** 203 **69**
146-149 152-156 **96** 239
240 359 360 362 364 **97**
56 58-60 **102** 165
Elizabeth (Anderson) **97**
63 **102** 163
Elizabeth (Baxter) **102** 168
Elizabeth (Hanniford)
97 59
Elizabeth (Mattucks) **97**
56 **132** 40
Elizabeth Given **102** 166
Ellen **102** 168
Ellen (Grover) **97** 59
Emily **97** 58
Emily Virginia **102** 166
Emily Virginia (Chilton)
102 167
Esther **96** 365 **132** 39
Eunice **62** 384 385 **69** 155
156 **96** 359 360
Eunice (Latham)
(Bowman) **102** 168
Eunice (Roberts) **96** 358
Fannie **97** 63
Frankie Cordelia (Cure)
102 166
Genevieve (Bunker)
97 59
George (Mrs.) **100** 78
George Madison **102**
165 166 169
George Madison (Mrs.)
102 163
George Vance **102** 167
Georgia **102** 166
Glenn (Scanling)
(Worthington)
102 167
Gloria Margaretta
(Nichols) **97** 56
Gloriana **97** 56
Grace **97** 59

MAVERICK *cont'd*
Grace Madeline (Fox) **102** 167
Hannah **69** 159 **96** 238
Hazel (Davis) **102** 169
Henry **69** 146-149 153
Hester **96** 364 366
Isaac Jacob **97** 63
Isabella **96** 363
James **69** 155 **96** 240 364 365
James Slayden **102** 169
Jane **67** 366 **69** 147 159 **78** 448 449 **96** 234 363
Jane (Andrews) **96** 234 **97** 60
Jane Lewis (Maury) **102** 168
Jean Nelson (Evans) **102** 168
Jemima **69** 155 **96** 366 **97** 57
Jemimah (Smith) **96** 365
Jenny Byrd (Rousseau) **102** 167
Jessie **102** 168
Joan **67** 367 **69** 148 149 153 **96** 363
Joan (Battin) **107** 62
John **51** 434 **52** 344 **55** 11 57 388 **67** 366 **68** 202 **69** 146-150 152-154 157-159 382 **76** lxxvi **78** 448 449 **79** 321 **96** 232-236 238-240 358 362 366 **97** 56 57 59-63 152 **100** 218 **114** 237 **115** 248 251-253 **122** 282 283 **131** 32 **132** 40 **142** 113 **143** 349 **147** 151 152 161 **148** 8
John Frost **102** 166
John Hayes **102** 165
Joseph **58** 242 **97** 63
Jotham **84** 377 **96** 366 **97** 56 57 59
Judith **69** 148 153
Julia Augusta **97** 59
Katharine **67** 366 **69** 157 **96** 234 362 **97** 60 **98** 93 **107** 62
Katharine (Coyer) **97** 60 62
Laura (Blocker) **102** 167
Laura Wise **102** 168
Laurabel (Grice) **102** 168
Lavinia **97** 58
Lewis **102** 166 167
Lewis A. **102** 165
Lewis Adams **102** 167
Lewis Antonio **102** 165
Lillian (Williams) **102** 168
Lilly **102** 166
Lola **102** 167
Lola Ruth (Newell) (Edenborough) **102** 169
Lucy Madison **102** 167
Lydia **97** 63
Lydia (Turpin) **97** 63
Lydia Ann **97** 64
Manton **74** xxx **97** 59

MAVERICK *cont'd*
Margaret **69** 155 **96** 363 **97** 25
Margaret (Sherwood) **96** 363
Maria **97** 59
Maria Ann **97** 58
Marie **69** 148 149 153
Martha **69** 155 156 **96** 360 364 365 **97** 57 61
Martha (Bradford) **96** 364
Mary **58** 242 **64** lv **67** 366 367 **68** 202 **69** 147 149 153 155 156 159 **78** 448 **84** 377 **96** 233 235 238 240 359 360 362 365 **97** 57 **98** 93 **102** 98 164 169 **115** 248 **122** 282 **147** 152 161
Mary (Gallop) **98** 93
Mary (Griffin) **97** 58
Mary (Gye) **96** 232 **97** 62 **115** 248-252 **122** 282 **131** 32 **141** 97 **148** 8
Mary (Howell) **97** 59
Mary (Palgrave) **102** 98
Mary (Walker) **96** 365
Mary (Williams) **97** 56
Mary Agatha **102** 166
Mary Ann (Adams) **102** 163
Mary Ann (Van Vorhees) (Ruggles) **97** 59
Mary Brown **102** 165
Mary Elizabeth **97** 64
Mary Elizabeth (Vance) **102** 166
Mary Esther **97** 63
Mary H. (Dean) **97** 59
Mary Rowena **102** 166
Mary V. **96** 232
Mary Vance **100** 77
Matilda (Brown) **97** 58
Maury **102** 169
Mehitable **97** 57
Mehitable (Banks) **97** 56
Moses **54** 278 357 416 **62** 384 385 **67** 366 **68** 202 203 **69** 147 155-157 159 **78** 448 93 163 **96** 233 234 238 358-360 362 366 **97** 61 **100** 81 **143** 349 **147** 152 161
Nancy **97** 57
Nathaniel **67** 365-367 **68** 179 **69** 146-148 150 151 153 157-159 **78** 449 **85** 70 73 **96** 235 238 360-363 **97** 60-62 **98** 93 **107** 62 **140** 111
Noadiah **69** 148 149 153
Octavia **97** 58
Paul **69** 155 **96** 241 365 366 **97** 56
Penelope **97** 59
Peter **69** 146 148-155 157 382 **96** 232 236 239 240 364 366 **97** 58 61 62
Peter Rushton **97** 58
Philip **102** 168
Pirie (Davidson) **102** 167

MAVERICK *cont'd*
Radford **69** 146-154 156 **96** 233 **115** 248 252 **122** 282 283
Raphael **97** 59
Rebecca **69** 147 148 153 155 156 159 **96** 238 241 359 **97** 58 59
Rebecca (Reynolds) **97** 58 59
Rebecca (Wheelwright) **96** 238 239
Remember **54** 357 **62** 384 **69** 155 156 **96** 360
Remember (Allerton) **96** 358 **143** 349
Rena **102** 166
Reuben **102** 168
Robert **69** 146 148 150-153 157 **96** 232 **122** 283
Robert Anderson **97** 64
Robert Van Wyck **102** 168
Ruth **69** 155 **96** 240
S. **59** 184
Sally (Frost) **102** 166
Samuel **61** 163 **65** 298 **67** 366 **68** 16 **69** 146 149-151 153-159 **76** 316 **78** 448 449 **84** 263 264 **85** 70 73 185 **87** 272 274 **89** 280 **90** 270 **96** 232 233 235-239 279 358 360-364 **97** 57 59-63 **98** 93 **99** 237 **102** 98 163-166 **115** 252 **134** 287 289 **140** 107 **143** 29 30 32 **148** 7 9
Samuel Augustus **78** 449 **97** 63 **102** 163 164 166 **103** 112
Sarah **62** 384 **69** 148 149 153 155 156 **96** 240 360 365 **97** 57 58 60 **113** 320 **137** 184
Sarah (Frost) **102** 166
Sarah (Rushton) **97** 58
Sarah (Smith) **96** 363 **97** 61 62
Sarah Frost **102** 166
Silence **96** 365
Skipper **97** 60
Stella (Cook) (Cutrer) **102** 168
Terrell Louise (Dobbs) **102** 169
Wilemotte **69** 148 152
William **69** 148 149 152 382
William Benjamin Nicoll **97** 56
William Chilton **102** 167
William H. **102** 165 167
William Henry **97** 58
William Mann **97** 58
MAVIS Betsey **77** 186
Lydia **74** 256
William **74** 256
William Henry **77** 186
Mawde *see* Maud
Mawdes *see* Maud

MAWDLIN Joan **144** 259
MAWDSLEY Maudsley
  Ebenezer **52** 199
  Sarah **52** 436
  Thomas **52** 199
MAWE —— **52** 257
  — Dr. **52** 258
  John **52** 259
  Martha **52** 258
MAWER Agnes **74** 52
  Joan **74** 52
  Katharine **74** 52 53
  Margaret **74** 52
  Thomas **74** 51-53
MAWHA
  James (Mrs.) **100** 112
MAWHINNEY
  William Thomas **99**
    148 **103** 161 **105** 158
    106 160 **114** 239
Mawle see Maule
MAWNEY Mawny
  —— **136** 191
  Amy **127** 228
  Pardon **129** 56
MAWRER A. **144** 335
MAWSON Harry P. **65** 97
MAWSUP Sachem **103** 215
MAX Margaret (Penrose)
  (Pim) **117** 57
  Simon **117** 57
Maxcey see Maxey
Maxcy see Maxey
Maxell see Maxwell
Maxen see Maxson
MAXEY Macksey Maxcey
  Maxcy Maxy
  —— **105** 170
  A. **91** 329
  Abigail **61** 332 **62** 37
    141 200
  Alexander **61** 334 **62** 38
    41 43 44 **102** 154
  Almira R. **83** 142
  Benjamin **62** 44
  Benoni **61** 335 **62** 35 42 44
  Betsey **83** 142
  D. **61** 336
  David **62** 47
  Ebenezer **62** 42 44
  Elizabeth **62** 35 39
  Elizabeth B. **83** 147
  Esther **62** 41 **70** 119
    102 154
  Hannah **141** 351
  Henry **141** 351
  Isaiah **51** 165
  John Crosby **83** 142
  Jonathan **116** 134 **141** 351
  Joseph **62** 40
  Josiah **62** 43
  Leonard **83** 142 145
  Levi **141** 351
  Mary **51** 164 **56** 345 **61**
    331 334 **62** 39
  Milton **141** 351
  N. R. **91** 329
  Ruth **51** 165
  Sabary **141** 351
  Sarah **56** 346 **61** 336 **62** 34
    47

MAXEY cont'd
  William **62** 34
MAXFIELD Macksfield
  Mackfield Maxfeld
  —— **70** 264 **118** 233
  Abby F. **120** 6
  Abby Finney (Fales)
    120 10
  Albert **64** 129
  Almy S. **59** 27
  Amos **68** 234 **88** 239
  Ann **68** 236
  Ann (Lady) **86** 222
  Ann Elizabeth **77** 183
  Benjamin **117** 211 **118** 150
  Betsey **142** 38 **145** 166
  Betsey C. **77** 186
  Charles A. **69** 309
  Charles P. **94** 299
  Clement **54** 90 **65** 63
  Cyrus E. **69** 309
  Daniel **129** 381
  Daniel W. **141** 145
  David **120** 9 10 **127** 221
  David C. **124** 61
  Deborah (Southwick)
    125 288
  Dinah **135** 141
  Dorcas **87** 245
  Ebenezer **53** 73 **68** 234
    236 237
  Eda V. **121** 179
  Edmund **59** 22
  Elizabeth **51** 460 **68** 234
    131 134 **135** 45
  Elliot **142** 38
  Elsa Eldredge (Loring)
    94 299
  Eugenia M. **121** 179
  Fanny **126** 233
  Freeman R. **118** 150
  George **60** 56 **68** 218 **99** 26
    125 288
  Gilbert **100** 300
  Hannah **68** 229 **94** 381
    120 5 9
  Hannah (Adams) **100** 300
  Henry **59** 27
  Henry E. **121** 179
  Herbert N. **69** 309
  James **71** 133 **90** 38 **91** 329
    94 381
  Jesse S. **69** 309
  Joanna **88** 239
  Joe **68** 237
  John **68** 216 231 234 **87** 245
  Joseph **69** 309 **70** 334
    116 262
  Joseph Estes **70** 328
  Josiah **57** 186 **70** 334
  Judith **86** 3 **135** 142
  Kate L. (Carr) **121** 179
  Lady Ann **86** 222
  Lillian May **72** xxi
  Louisa R. **69** 309
  Lovey **75** 252
  Lucy **68** 238
  Lydia **68** 216 234 **99** 26
  Lydia C. **70** 328
  Margery **52** 428
  Mary **54** 169 **57** 186 **118**

MAXFIELD cont'd
    150 **127** 57 **134** 66
  Mary A. **69** 309
  Mary Ann **69** 174 **70** 328
    334
  Mary Cook **88** 239
  Mary E. **124** 62
  Mary P. **121** 178
  Mehitable (Harrison)
    87 245
  Melvina (Stanstead)
    121 178
  Mercy (Prindle)
    (Whittemore) **108** 84
  Merebah **120** 9 10
  Mildred Elizabeth
    104 144
  Moses **101** 55
  Nancy **57** 186 **70** 334
  Nancy Elizabeth **70** 328
  Nathaniel **60** 56
  Obadiah **55** 66
  Orville Eldred **108** 135
  Patrick **94** 299
  Polly **147** 257
  Rachel **59** 22
  Rebecca **57** 162
  Reuben **145** 166
  Robert **142** 38 **145** 166
  Rufus **69** 174 **70** 328
  Russell **121** 178
  Ruth **51** 463 **53** 278 **68** 232
  Samuel **65** 63 **68** 229 231
    232 234 236 238 **77** 149
    123 193
  Sarah **51** 464
  Sarah E. S. **77** 149
  Sibyl D. **69** 309
  Susan **142** 38
  Susanna **68** 236
  Tabitha **142** 38 **145** 166
  Thankful (Cutts) **124** 61
  Warren **57** 162
  William **57** 186 **99** 26
    104 120 **108** 84
MAXHAM Maxam Maxum
  Addie Mary **82** 268
  Belvia **66** 19
  Benjamin **88** 334
  Chandler **114** 272
  Cordelia **96** 60
  David **66** 19
  Edmund **96** 60
  Edna M. **121** 182
  Edwin Burns **82** 268
  Eva Lillian **82** 268
  Harriet Isabel **82** 268
  Hattie Belle **82** 268
  James **66** 19
  John **96** 60
  Kate Williamson **82** 268
  Kingman **96** 60
  Lucinda **112** 324
  Lyman **82** 268
  Marietta **96** 60
  Minerva (Shurtleff)
    88 334
  Myra Hammond **82** 268
  Sally **66** 19
  Samuel **75** 306 **96** 60 61 63
  Winslow **82** 268

MAXIM Briant **128** 207
Lucy (Willis) **114** 272
Mary **115** 185
Samuel **105** 71
Silas Packard **64** 132
Thankful **128** 207
MAXIMILIAN Archduke
of Austria **88** 102
Emperor of Mexico
76 xliv
MAXSON Mackson
Maxen Maxon
—— **136** 189
Abby (Barker) **125** 245
Abigail **80** 166
Amos **77** 207 **128** 302
Asa **128** 220
Barrodel (Ross) **107** 160
Benjamin **128** 303
Bethiah **105** 64
Caleb **105** 64 **118** 59
127 138
Catherine **127** 86
Clara G. **104** 46
Clarke **128** 301
Cordelia A. **104** 46
Daniel **107** 160
David **128** 222
Elisha **128** 303
Eliza S. **126** 21
Elizabeth **77** 207 **87** 354
105 64
George **128** 299
Hannah **110** 160 **116** 84
Harriet E. **80** 234
Horace **78** 87
Isaac **122** 105
James M. **125** 245
Jared **80** 234
Jesse **128** 302
Jesse L. **107** 160
Joel **107** 160
John **63** 198 **87** 355 **107**
160 **118** 60 **127** 15 **128**
300
John S. **125** 245
Jonathan **63** 56 **126** 22
127 142
Joseph **87** 355 **105** 64 **128**
224 302
Levi **104** 46
Lovina **78** 87
Lucelia Harriet **80** 234
Lucretia **107** 160
Lucy (Minor) **136** 329
Lydia **86** 442
Lydia (Ketchum) **107** 160
Maria E. **51** 380
Martha **128** 220 299
Martin L. **70** 210
Mary **87** 140 **105** 64
Mary E. **80** 45
Mary Starr **78** 87
May **80** 45
Nancy (Potter) **126** 22
Nellie L. **104** 46
Olive Marie **107** 133
Paul **128** 222
Peleg **128** 299
Phineas **128** 299
Richard **136** 216

MAXSON *cont'd*
Ruth **85** 221
S. R. **80** 45
Sally (Bills) **107** 160
Samuel **95** 16 **128** 302
Sarah Catherine **78** 87
Stephen **128** 303
Susanna **136** 329
Sylvenus **128** 302
Wallace G. **105** 124 **106**
122 **107** 129 **108** 130
Wealthea Ann **70** 210
William **126** 22 **128** 302
136 329
Zackyers **128** 303
MAXSTED Robert **67** 173
Maxum *see* Maxham
MAXWELL Mackswell
Maxell Maxwel
—— **52** 398 **56** 326 **62**
xxxviii **76** 249 251 253
261 **92** 339 **101** 161 **140**
68
— Lady **89** 43
— Mrs. **100** 138
Aaron **76** 109 114 **93** 239
Abbie S. **93** 239
Abigail **75** 9 50 112-114
123 313 **76** 104 105 179-
181 186 **93** 239 240 335
100 138 140
Adam **129** 53
Albert B. **93** 239 240
Alexander **75** 113 **76** 108
109 111 112 188 189 196
250 252 253 260 **87** 206
93 239 240 **114** 44 **141**
328
Alfred E. **89** 357
Alice L. **93** 239
Alpheus **76** 251
Amanda Caroline **93** 239
Andrew **114** 187
Ann **52** 396 **98** 197 **118** 50
55 56
Anna **76** 104-106 109 183
186 252 258 **77** 264 **93**
239 **145** 162
Anne **96** 186
Annie Lou **112** 75
Arthur **148** 179
Audley **95** 16
Barak **62** 154 **75** 106 **76**
104-106 109 113 114 183
186 252 258 **93** 239 240
Benjamin **76** 105 **81** 430
Bernard Love **94** 139
Betsey **62** 154
Betsey Ames **93** 239 240
C. J. **98** 370
Catherine **76** 255 **93** 248
Cedora E. **148** 176
Charles **92** 339 **93** 335 **98**
259 **141** 17 147
Charles Edward **95** 16
Charles H. **148** 179
Charles J. **104** 78
Charles Thomas **127** 62
Charlotte (Stover) **117**
226 227
Clara F. D. **148** 179

MAXWELL *cont'd*
Clarisy W. **93** 239
Clement **76** 251 **117** 226
227
Conillia A. **148** 179
Cornelia **77** 264
Daniel **75** 112 114 **76** 111
247 **96** 344 **114** 187
Daniel F. **93** 239 240
Daniel W. **92** 339
David **65** 244 **75** 54 112-
114 123 313 **76** 104 105
112 179-181 193 252 256
262 **93** 239 240 **117** 16
Deborah **76** 253
Dorcas **76** 186 253
Dorothy **93** 239 **102** 154
Dwight **148** 176
Ebenezer **64** 12 **76** 249
Edward **126** 209
Edwin W. **93** 239
Eleanor **76** 180 255 **93** 239
107 211
Eleanor (Hunn) **106** 46
Eliza **63** 1 **93** 239 **108** 161
114 187
Eliza (Jackson) **127** 62
Elizabeth **76** 189 252 **78**
178 **108** 136 **148** 179
Elizabeth Agnes **93** 239
Elizabeth B. **141** 147
Elizabeth J. **93** 239
Elizabeth J. (Jones) **95** 16
Ella L. **93** 239
Ellen **148** 170
Elma Blanche **108** 136
Elmer **117** 43
Elwin S. **89** 357
Emarentha **64** 155
Emily Jane **92** 339
Emma **83** 426 436
Emma F. **89** 357
Emma J. **92** 339
Emma J. (Welch) **120** 140
Ernest **117** 43
Esther **74** 64
Eunice **76** 197 249-251
Eunice G. **93** 335
Frances **118** 50
Francis **118** 51 56
George **66** 32 **93** 248 **120**
221 222
George A. **148** 179
George L. **92** 339
George W. **92** 339 **93** 51
Georgianna **148** 176
Gershom **75** 50 52 54 106
109 115-117 **76** 104 109
182 186 193 247-252 259
87 207 **96** 344 **97** 237
102 154
Gilbert **100** 140
Golder **148** 176
Hamilton **112** 201 203
204 209 265-270 272-274
Hannah **64** 12 **75** 123 **76**
248 250 252 253 255 256
261 **83** 146 **93** 248 **98**
197 **100** 139 140 **128**
262
Hannah (Adams) **108** 189

MAXWELL *cont'd*
Hannah O. **93** 239
Hannah Persis **93** 248
Harriet **88** 392 **93** 248
Hattie O. **93** 248
Helen A. **93** 239
Helena Philae Olive
   Virginia **89** 43
Henry D. **52** 396
Herbert D. **93** 239
Hubert W. **148** 179
Hugh **63** 75 **65** 150 263
   77 239 **93** 304 **100** 66
   136 60
Ida **64** xxxiii
Isabel **93** 239
Isabella **76** 183 **115** 309
J. W. **148** 172
James **66** 306 **76** 105 248
   250 251 253 255 256 261
   87 206 **99** 27 **101** 51
   103 234 **106** 46 **114** 187
   129 276 **148** 176
James Audley **95** 16
James Giboney **77** 264
James Gilford **117** 43
James Henry **93** 239
James Mordecai **99** 324
James Nathan **117** 43
Jane **82** 399 **93** 239 **112** 272
   148 179
Jane J. **91** 196
Jenny **76** 256
Jeremy **76** 109
Joanna (Westcott) **88** 14
John **52** 396 **65** 131 **74** 64
   75 52 112 122 123 311
   76 103 107 180-182 193
   250 **81** 430 **87** 206 **88**
   123 **89** 43 **93** 335 **100**
   138 140 **103** 270 **111**
   202 **114** 187 **122** 72 **127**
   62 **148** 31
John B. **93** 248
John Brock **76** 252
John Guy **77** 264
John Jackson **90** 183
John S. **93** 248
John Shapleigh **76** 106
   252 255 256 **87** 206
John Wesley **148** 176
Jonathan **76** 106 **87** 207 **92**
   339 **93** 248
Joseph **76** 104 249 255 261
   87 207 **93** 239 240
Joshua **76** 109 **90** 328
   93 239 240
Kate **77** 264
Laura (Ewell) **126** 209
Level **129** 380
Lilian M. (Beckwith) **92**
   207 **100** 178
Lilly **75** 303 **89** 266
Lincoln L. **93** 239
Llewellyn **148** 176
Loruhamah **75** 311
Louise **78** 203
Lovina **98** 259
Lucy **75** 122 **76** 252 **116**
   297 **123** 149
Lucy L. **148** 179

MAXWELL *cont'd*
Lydia **63** 270 **73** 126 **76**
   182 **99** 25 27 **101** 51 161
   148 172
Lydia (Warren) **93** 239
Lydia A. **93** 248
Lydia A. (Perkins) **122**
   72 310
Lydia Elizabeth **99** 133
Lydia T. **138** 208
Lydia Warren **93** 239
Margaret **63** 74 **77** 47
   87 294
Mariah T. **83** 147
Mariam **95** 194
Martha **75** 117 **76** 181 255
   93 239
Martha C. **93** 240
Martha M. **98** 197
Mary **54** 169 **64** 12 **75** 106
   109 115-117 123 210 **76**
   113 114 182 192 252 256
   262 **81** 430 **87** 294 **93**
   239 240 248 **95** 16 **117**
   224 226 **123** 280 **148**
   176
Mary A. **92** 339
Mary Ann **93** 240
Mary Ann (Baker) **90** 183
Mary Ann Elizabeth
   (Welch) **120** 221 222
Mary Badlam (Mansfield)
   141 17 147
Mary E. **93** 248 **148** 179
Mary Eliza (Rutherford)
   117 43
Mary J. **93** 240
Mary J. (Briggs) **127** 62
Mary Jane (Swett) **119** 228
   229 276
Mary Pierson **76** 255
Matthew **61** 348 **100** 138
Melinda (Chase) **88** 123
Miriam **75** 115 116
Miriam (Drown) **96** 344
   97 237
Moses **76** 108 **93** 239 240
   119 228 229 276
Myron Ames **93** 240
Myrtle **117** 43
Nancy **60** 27
Nancy (Tower) **102** 154
Nellie **102** 124
Olive **76** 253 **83** 300 **93** 248
Oliver S. **92** 335 339 **93**
   248 **120** 140 **122** 72 310
Pauline **77** 264
Pearl (Bradford) **117** 43
Pearl Louise **102** 124
Persis **76** 253
Peter **64** 25
Phebe **75** 112 122 123 311
   76 103 107 180-182 **117**
   226
Phebe (Stevens) **96** 344
Philadelphia **76** 108 109
   111 112 188 189 196 252
   253 260 **93** 240
Priscilla **85** 193 **114** 187
Ralph W. **92** 339 **93** 248
Rebecca **148** 176

MAXWELL *cont'd*
Rebecca F. **76** 50
Richard **148** 170 172
Richard E. **99** 133
Robert **60** 27 **64** 220
Robert C. **121** 316
Rosewel **76** 251
Ruth **98** 197 **145** 162
Ruth (Lord) **90** 328
Ruth W. **97** 223 231
S. M. **95** 16
Sally **93** 240
Sally (Tibbetts) (Brackett)
   99 324
Samuel **64** 155 **74** 64 **76**
   103 249 **88** 285 **114** 187
Samuel Raymond
   71 xxi 88
Samuel S. **93** 240
Sarah **75** 313 **76** 109 182
   186 188 247 248 252 259
   82 294 299 **93** 239 **96**
   145 **116** 222
Sarah (Pennewell) **114** 44
Sarah A. **93** 240
Sarah E. **99** 133
Sarah L. **148** 179
Scott **148** 179
Sedora **148** 176
Seth **76** 248
Solomon **74** 64
Sophia Helen **90** 183
Squire **88** 14 **138** 31
Stephen **76** 102 247
Sukey **93** 240
Susan **93** 240
Susan Huston **86** 330
Susan W. (Heard) **88** 285
Susanna **75** 117 **76** 179
   183 249 256 **93** 240 248
   98 205
Sylvester **75** 305
Tabitha **76** 256 **93** 240
   119 69
Tamma **98** 259
Thomas **112** 75
Thomas Jefferson
   121 316
Wilbray J. **93** 240
Will J. **107** 248
William **62** 161 **63** 76 **82**
   294 299 **84** 378 **92** 339
   93 249 **95** 16 **98** 197 **99**
   25 27 **101** 51 161 **108**
   189 **112** 270 **140** 68 **145**
   162 **148** 172 176 179
William M. **76** 50
William N. **93** 240
Willie O. **92** 339
Wilt **54** 148
Winfield Scott **148** 176
Zerviah **76** 180
Zuruah **147** 115
MAXWELL-BOYD
David **73** 131
Margaret **73** 131
MAXWELL-LYTE
Agnes **96** 186
Arthur **96** 186
Edith **96** 186
H. C. **147** 5

MAXWELL-LYTE *cont'd*
Henry **97** 240
Henry Churchill **78** 331
  79 201 **81** 314 **82** 67 **96**
  149 162 185
John **96** 186
John Walker **96** 185 186
Margaret **96** 186
Walter **96** 186
Maxy *see* Maxey
MAY —— **51** 139 260 272
  414 418 **52** 124 132 **58**
  114 309 **59** 338 **61** 43
  315 **101** 260 **140** 44 167
  168
— Capt. **101** 102
— Mr. **58** 199
— Mrs. **62** 132 **80** 56
— Widow **84** 361
____ (Cravath) **140** 168
Aaron **77** 293 **85** 462 **140**
  167 168
Abby Keith (Worcester)
  84 213
Abby V. **89** 195
Abigail **67** 375 **78** 419 **83**
  380 **85** 462 **99** 334 **110**
  131 **136** 308 310
Abigail (Fellows) **140** 168
Abigail (Gore) **109** 66
Abigail (Stansfull)
  146 275
Abigail (Varney) **89** 194
Abigail (Williams) **109** 66
  136 308 310
Alexander **54** 341
Alice **65** xxxv **80** 412
Almira **82** 169 173
Amasa **111** 305
Ann **83** 380 **89** 223 **117** 298
Ann Elizabeth **86** 104
Ann G. **78** 301
Ann M. (Allen) **111** 299
  305
Anna (Carver) **118** 106
  107
Anna (Wilber) **111** 305
  308
Anna M. (Rose) **111** 305
Anna Maria (May) **99** 256
Anne **55** 161 **111** 56
Anne (Pimm) **90** 349
Arthur **51** 414
Bathsheba **117** 297
Bathsheba (Blackwell)
  117 298
Benjamin **136** 311
Bessie Tuttle **104** 144
Bethiah **67** 373
Caroline Simpkins
  58 113 115
Catherine **106** 148 **140** 55
Catherine (Mears)
  105 242
Cecily **65** 330
Charles **64** 225 **68** 282
Charlotte **55** 419 **85** 462
Clara **78** 399 **85** 197
Clarissa **85** 462
Close Hutton Davies
  136 326

MAY *cont'd*
D. **101** 235
Daniel **78** 240
David **82** 169 **128** 278
Deliverance **98** 327
  133 293
Dollie Leota **117** 128 129
Dolly (Sewell) **140** 168
Dorothy **73** 116 **141** 94
  108
Dorothy (Sewall) **136** 308
Dorothy Wells (Hannum)
  90 348
E. **111** 192
Earnastus **62** 134
Ebenezer **61** xlvii **82** 198
  85 462 **109** 66 **110** 131
  140 168
Edith Sibyl **136** 333
Edward **63** 353 **77** 236
  148 327
Edwin Hyland **90** 348
Eleanor Swan **61** xlviii
Eleazer **67** 375 **73** 116
Elijah **128** 129
Eliza R. **111** 305
Elizabeth **69** 92 **72** 176 **77**
  293 **85** 462 **92** 181 **120**
  54 **141** 8
Elizabeth (Child) **99** 256
Elizabeth (Tupper) **111** 30
Elizabeth Caroline
  105 201
Ella Sena/Seva (Guild)
  104 68 162
Elna Jean **118** 248
Enoch **140** 167 328
Ephraim **55** 419 **84** 358
  360 **85** 462 **140** 167 168
Ephraim (Mrs.) **84** 360
Erastus **111** 299 305
Esther (Palfrey) **125** 108
Esther (Tupper) **99** 290
  291 **111** 30
Ethyle **94** 140
Eunice **85** 462
Ezekiel **61** 96
Ezra **92** 100
Francis **64** 219
Frederick **65** 150 **85** 462
  136 310 333 **140** 167
Frederick Goddard **95**
  147 **108** 218 **109** 66 134
Frederick Warren
  Goddard **61** xlv xlvii-
  xlix **82** 198 **109** 66
George **97** 326 **106** 90
  140 167
George C. **83** 173
George H. **83** 184 186
George Henry **74** 237 **75**
  xxiii **99** 256 **100** 44 114
  101 121
George Henry (Mrs.)
  101 121
George W. **111** 305
George Washington
  128 278
Gideon **55** 311 **74** 212 213
  82 95 211 324
Hannah **54** 394 395 **78** 240

MAY *cont'd*
  124 78 **125** 109
Hannah (King) **148** 316
  327
Hannah Colby
  (Goodwin) **139** 145
Hannah O. **65** 312 **89** 194
Hannah Owen **89** 192
Harmon **111** 305
Helen Estella (Lovell)
  (Skidmore) **88** 169 **104**
  68 162
Henry A. **54** xxxix **55**
  xxxii **56** xxxii **57** xxxiii
  58 xlv 104 206
Henry K. **140** 167
Henry Knox **65** 150
Henry W. **91** 199
Herbert A. **133** 303
Herman Eugene **111** 192
Hester **51** 414
Hezekiah **61** 96 **62** 295
Hugh **100** 224
Ida Cordelia **111** 192
Ira **128** 278
Irena **111** 305
Isaac **116** 256 **128** 278
James **54** 393 **69** 91 92 **89**
  192 92 181 **140** 168
James R. **53** 453 **83** 300
  84 30
James Rundlett **83** 173
Jane Rundlett **84** 30
Jessie **100** 246
Joan **67** 267
Joanna **85** 430
John **51** 414 **54** xcvi 392-
  395 **55** 161 **58** 113 **61**
  xlvii 43 **64** 320 368 369
  65 59 60 62 141-143 145
  146 149 150 221-225 227
  228 369 **67** 35 **68** 99 **78**
  13 316 422 **80** 410 412
  82 198 **85** 462 **99** 256
  291 **104** 63 120 **108** 112
  109 66 **116** 156 **117** 75
  298 303 **120** 114 115
  125 108 222 **136** 310
  140 167 168 173
John Birchard (Mrs.)
  84 213
John Cravath **85** 462
John Frederick **136** 333
John Howard **104** 68 162
John J. **57** 196 **59** xcviii
John Jacob **57** 414
John Joseph **51** 228 **53** 452
  54 xix xcvii cxxiv **55**
  vii xxv xxix **56** vii 413
  57 xxxi 329 414 **58** xlix
  liv cxiv 90 111-115 198
  199
John Shepard **104** 68 162
John Shepard (Mrs.) **88**
  169 **104** 67 68 149 162
John W. **88** 340 342
John W. M. **65** 150
Jonathan **79** 91 **121** 270
  276 **128** 278
Joseph **55** 389 **65** 150 **98**
  359 **136** 308 **140** 167

MAY *cont'd*
168
Joshua **111** 305 **115** 18 22
Julia Matilda **136** 310
Julia Matilda (Slocum)
  136 310 333
Katharine **67** 45 **70** 249
L. **62** 131
Lena **78** 206
Leota **117** 129
Lettice **115** 25 109
Lois **55** 419 **85** 462
Louisa **140** 55
Louisa C. **84** 30
Louisa C. (Rundlett)
  83 184 186
Louise **98** 359 **140** 145
Lucretia **140** 33
Lucretia Emeline **115** 109
Lucy **111** 192 305 **115** 18 22
Lucy (Goddard) **99** 256
Luke **115** 109
Lynde Elliott **90** 349
Margaret **67** 45 **68** 99 **70**
  249 255 **80** 402 412
Margery (Knopp)
  147 319
Maria **76** 53 **77** 293
Maria Frazee **109** 66
Mariah **105** 201
Marjorie Merriweather
  (Post) (Close) (Hutton)
  (Davies) **133** 302
  136 323
Martha **140** 168
Martha (Howell) **136** 308
Martha Ann **83** 380
Martha Ann (Turner)
  83 380
Martha Ann Turner
  83 380
Martha Louise **77** xxviii
Martha Rand **61** xlviii
  82 198
Martha Rand (Morse)
  109 66
Martin **67** 45 **70** 249 255
Mary **55** 311 **58** 112 **61**
  xlvii **68** 99 282 **74** 213
  249 **77** 220 **78** 204 **79** 98
  82 95 198 294 298 **90** 47
  96 76 **104** 120 **105** 227
  125 293 **140** 168
Mary (Goddard) **109** 66
Mary (Hunt) **125** 222
Mary (Morison) **83** 300
Mary (Williams) **136** 311
Mary Ann **70** 191 **128** 278
Mary Jackson **81** 109 231
  82 198
Mary Perrin **105** 151
Mehitable **105** 24 **141** 343
Mills **104** 120
Moses **85** 462 **140** 168
Nancy **83** 380 **140** 167 168
Nancy (Beeks) **101** 260
Nehemiah **110** 32
Orra **90** 52
Penuel **115** 22
Perrin **140** 44 168 260
Phebe **105** 201 **108** 88

MAY *cont'd*
Polly **125** 216
Polly (Mills) **104** 120
Polly (Upham) **116** 256
Prudence **78** 13
Prudence (Bridge) **99** 256
  109 66
R. H. **91** 329
Ralph **79** 157 **81** 241
  83 295
Rebecca **54** 393 **77** 254
Richard **80** 410 412
Richard Arnold **109** 66
Robert **66** 37 **76** 53
Robert E. **89** 351
Robert Morse **109** 66
Robond **75** 293
Roxanna (Butler) **90** 52
Ruth (Witter) **99** 256
S. N. **111** 192
S. P. **114** 12 **121** 267
Sally **82** 169 **124** 64
  140 167
Salome Morton **102** 302
Samuel **52** 193 **58** 111-113
  59 xli xlvii **60** xxxiv **61**
  xlvii **63** 210 **78** 183 **82**
  198 **85** 462 **94** 157 **109**
  66 **128** 58 **136** 308 310
  140 33 55 **115** 167 169
  141 8 **142** 187 292 **146**
  275
Samuel (Mrs.) **79** 402
  92 257
Samuel Edward **84** 352
Samuel J. **61** 176
Samuel P. **52** 321 **141** 139
Samuel Pearce **68** xxxii
  124 24 26
Sarah **54** 392-395 **79** 98
  85 462 **100** 42 **104** 120
  121 278 **126** 66 **136** 334
  140 168
Sarah (Brewer) (Bruce)
  99 256 **109** 66 **128** 278
Sarah (Langle) **121** 270
Sarah (Paine) **99** 256
Sarah (Russell) **94** 157
Sarah Maria (Mills)
  136 333
Sarah Russell **96** 189
Sargent W. **65** 150
Seth **99** 291
Silas **139** 145
Simond **71** 21
Sophia **115** 25
Sophia L. (House) **88** 340
Susan **51** 414
Susan N. (Gray) **88** 342
Susanna **80** 412 **110** 131
  136 311 324
Thomas **51** 414 **54** 392 **57**
  316 **67** 175 **68** 263 **73**
  271 **74** 274 **83** 380 **99**
  256 **101** 248 **104** 120
  106 34 **110** 123 **140** 167
  168 **147** 379
Virginia Sargent (Poor)
  99 256
Walter **111** 305 308
Wilbur J. **89** 351

MAY *cont'd*
William **57** 315 **65** 32 **67**
  169 **99** 256 **104** 120 **105**
  201 **111** 192 **138** 36 **140**
  168 **147** 379
William Hyatt (Mrs.) **77**
  xxviii 77
William P. **89** 194 195
William Rufus **65** 150
Zabiah **85** 462
Zabiah (Cravath) **85** 462
MAYALL Robert **87** 126
MAYBANK Andrew **95** 16
  Martha **95** 16
MAYBEE
Abraham **115** 127
Charity **115** 21
David **115** 21
Elizabeth **63** 271
Mary **115** 128
Simon **115** 125
Solomon **115** 21
MAYBERRY Maybry
  Maybury
  —— **145** 53 54
Amelia M. **125** 238
Elizabeth **107** 317
Harriet B. **125** 237
Lucy **142** 300
Molly **117** 80
Nancy **142** 300
Rebecca **142** 300
Richard **65** 255 259 342
  91 272
Sarah **128** 285
Seafair **102** 14
William **102** 15 **106** 267
  142 300
MAYBORN
Donald Ward **83** 351
Frank Willis **83** 351
Leroy Henry **83** 351
Lura (Burns) **83** 351
Nellie Cole (Welton) **81**
  222 **83** 217 351 **84** 196
Theodore Welton **83** 351
Ward Carleton **83** 351
Ward Carleton (Mrs.)
  81 108 222
Maybry *see* Mayberry
Maybury *see* Mayberry
MAYCOCK John **77** 76
Maycomber *see* Macomber
Maycumber *see* Macomber
MAYDEWEL
Richard **79** 367
Maydstone *see* Maidstone
Maye *see* May
MAYER Mair Maire Mayre
  —— **87** 335 **140** 30
Alfred Goldsborough
  65 34 303 **70** 288
Alfred Marshall **70** 288
Anne **63** 360 **68** 325
Annis (Chase) **87** 335
Benjamin **71** 126
Charles **66** 108 **123** 233
Durand Churchill **82** 346
Elizabeth **66** 108 109 **71**
  126 **82** 345
George **66** 103 109 **80** 237

MAYER *cont'd*
  82 346
  Georgia Margaret **80** 237
  Hannah (Merriam)
    126 145
  Harriet Hyatt **66** 191
  Jasper Joseph **100** 112
  Jeremiah **141** 30
  John George **117** 16
  Judith **71** 126 127
  Lena E. **123** 232
  Love **71** 126
  Malinda (Mayer) **123** 233
  Mary **71** 126 **148** 340
  Nancy **66** 110
  Olga **97** 119
  Peter **62** 252
  Polly **66** 109 110
  Rachel **105** 55 **108** 185
  Rachel (Vaughan) **108** 185
  Rebecca **71** 126 **132** 121
  Rhoda **66** 109
  Richard **65** 33
  Robert **56** 86
  Rose **80** 237
  Ruth **71** 126
  Sarah **71** 126
  Stephen **66** 110
  Thomas **63** 358 **126** 145
  Walter **71** 126
  Walter Scott **104** 144
  William **56** 86 **66** 110
    108 185
MAYERES
  Josiah **64** 257 259
MAYERS
  Barbara **109** 146
  Elizabeth **56** 77
Mayes *see* Mays
MAYETTE
  Francis A. **81** 393
  Lizzie Nellie **81** 393
MAYFIELD
  Edward **140** 330
  Merle Carter **107** 132
Maygatt *see* Mygatt
MAYHAM
  Clarissa A. **107** 150
  Louisa **97** 132
MAYHEN
  Elizabeth **51** 198
  Zaccheus **51** 198
MAYHEW Mahew Mahieu
  ―― **58** 406 **60** 214 **61** 100
    62 xxxviii **91** 170 **140**
    238 **145** 44
  ― Capt. **77** 110
  ― Col. **91** 170
  ― Dea. **59** 203 206
  ― Dr. **91** 171
  ― Gov. **86** 394
  ― Mr. **66** 363
  ― Mrs. **59** 198
  ― Rev. **91** 171
  ____ (Cooper) **128** 173
  Abbie D. **122** 194
  Abiah **59** 199 **83** 508
  Abigail **59** 195 261 262 409
    83 508 509 **99** 116 **118**
    205

MAYHEW *cont'd*
  Abigail (Parkhurst)
    123 240
  Abigail (Tibbetts) **99** 115
  Abigail D. **122** 195
  Abishai **59** 198
  Abner **59** 259 381-384
  Addie D. **122** 194
  Adelaide A. **73** 178
  Adelaide S. **73** 178
  Adeline Mahala **89** 18
  Alice **73** 135
  Allen **59** 197 258 264 378
    111 290
  Amanda Lucretia (Avery)
    89 18
  Andrew **105** 279 **109** 160
  Ann **73** 218 **83** 508
  Anna **59** 198 411 **127** 52
  Anna (Newcomb)
    106 308
  Anson Kendrick **89** 18
  Antonette **143** 198
  Arad **105** 289 **109** 160
  Arletta **73** 178
  Armenia **89** 17
  Armenia (Lazell) **89** 18
  Benjamin **59** 261-263 378-
    381 **70** 263 **111** 290
  Bethiah **59** 196 199
  Betsey **59** 198 259 260 379-
    382 **60** 70
  Brian **73** 137
  Catherine (Sippell)
    86 362
  Charles **59** 406
  Charles B. **73** 178
  Charlotte **110** 321 **122** 78
  Charlotte Jane (Hillman)
    101 253
  Clara **59** 198
  Clarissa **59** 258 260
  David **59** 202 380-384 **86**
    362 **122** 194
  David Porter **69** 210
  David S. **128** 173
  Davis **59** 384
  Deborah **52** 233 **59** 197
    258 262-264 378-380
    127 213
  Dinah **83** 508
  Drusilla **59** 301 307
  Ebenezer **73** 178
  Edward D. **73** 178
  Elbridge Gary **99** 116
  Eleanor **59** 196
  Eleanor S. **73** 144
  Elijah **56** 318 **59** 198 **99** 116
  Elisha **99** 115 116 **109** 160
  Elizabeth **52** 371 **59** 195 **73**
    277 **84** 272 **92** 12 **93** 260
    102 122 **104** 314 **106**
    308 **113** 303
  Elizabeth (Allen) **83** 508
    118 205
  Elizabeth (Clarke)
    118 205
  Elizabeth (Nugent)
    86 307
  Emma **128** 173
  Emma Vincent **92** 145

MAYHEW *cont'd*
  101 249 253 **102** 128
  Ephraim **59** 197 201 259
    261-264 381 383 **104** 314
    122 194
  Ethelinda **59** 382
  Eunice **56** 318 **59** 197 258
    259 264 378 380-383 **60**
    245 **93** 91 **118** 205
  Experience **60** 159 245 **91**
    93 **118** 205
  Fanny Jane (Cooper)
    89 18
  Fear **59** 195
  Frances **73** 137
  Francis **59** 199 261 262
  Francoise **143** 199
  Frederick **59** 260 382
  Freeborn **89** 18
  Freeborn Lazell **89** 18
  George **59** 260 374 **75** 308
    89 18
  George Washington
    89 18
  Hannah **55** 112 **59** 200
    262 264 **88** 289 **106** 71
  Hannah (Skiff) **89** 18
  Hannah Curtis
    (Huntington) **99** 16
  Hannah Elizabeth **89** 18
  Harriet **59** 201
  Harrison P. **59** 260
  Hebron **59** 197 258 262-
    264 378-380
  Henry **73** 226
  Hester **117** 189 **127** 94
    129 235 **143** 169 195-
    199 205
  Hilliard **59** 202 **105** 214
  Isabel **63** 164
  Jacques **143** 199
  James **59** 304 **73** 149
    109 160
  Jane **52** 203 **55** 112 **59** 198
    257 305 308 **99** 116 **143**
    198
  Jane (Gallyon) (Payne) **99**
    60 **101** 253 **106** 308
  Jane (Nickerson) **122** 194
  Jane N. **122** 195
  Jeanne **143** 196 198 199
  Jedidah **59** 198 261-264 380
    382 411
  Jenny **60** 182
  Jeremiah **59** 195 198 199
    258 260
  Jerusha **59** 196 199
  Jethro **59** 201
  John **52** 206 **57** 218 **59**
    195 198 262 264 378 **64**
    80 **73** 220 86 307 **95** 106
    103 32 **118** 323
  John Wesley **101** 253
  Jonathan **59** 196 199-201
    258 263 264 378 **61**
    xxxiv **73** 144 **84** 250 251
    272 **91** 340 351 **92** 12 14
    16 **93** 259 **110** 317 **118**
    205 **129** 100 **130** 33
  Jonathan (Mrs.) **84** 251
  Joseph **56** 20 **59** 258 380

MAYHEW *cont'd*
382-384 405 406 **99** 79
   111 290
Josias **59** 200
Juliana **122** 195
Katharine Burke **85** 199
Laura Jane **86** 361 362
Laurana **99** 115
Letitia **73** 231
Lewis **86** 307
Lois **59** 197 200 **99** 128
Lucia (Huntington)
   99 116
Lucina Augusta (Bishop)
   89 18
Lucy **59** 198 203 205 207
   258 382-384 **73** 178
Lucy Ann **89** 18
Lurana **99** 115 116
Lydia **52** 233 **59** 262 263
   378 381 389 **60** 338
Lydia (Farnsworth)
   99 116
M. Juliana **122** 195
Maltiah **59** 198 382 384
Margaret **59** 306 308
   109 64
Marie **143** 198 199
Mark **59** 202 **111** 290
Martha **55** 112 **59** 384 **99**
   60 **113** 108 109 **114** 7 8
   135 **115** 182 **122** 194
   123 63 **128** 252
Martha (Parkhurst)
   106 308
Martha B. **59** 260
Mary **57** 218 **59** 200 207
   259 261-263 306 **73** 135
   147 **79** 297 **87** 5 **109** 160
   111 290 **118** 323 **127** 52
Mary (Allen) **83** 508
Mary (McFadden) **99** 115
Mary (Skiffe) **106** 308
Mary Ann **73** 275
Mary C. **111** 290
Mary J. **122** 195
Mary Maria Middleton
   89 18
Matilda **59** 258
Matthew **52** 203 205 206
   53 105 **59** 195 196 201
   205 207 260 262-264 304
   307 401 411 **72** 202 **83**
   508 **106** 308
Mehitable **59** 195 199 **104**
   314 **109** 160
Mercy **59** 195
Mercy (Skiffe) **123** 129
Micajah **106** 308
Moses Adams **101** 253
Nancy **53** 375 **59** 196 260
   406 **99** 116 **112** 241
Nathan **59** 195 198-200 261
   104 242 **118** 205
Nathaniel **59** 260 264 378
   379 **60** 182 **99** 115 **109**
   160
Nathaniel A. **111** 290
Nathaniel B. **73** 178
Oliver **59** 198 199

MAYHEW *cont'd*
Ollie May (Montgomery)
   86 307
Pamelia **59** 261 **63** 377 **64**
   17 76 **66** 363
Parnell **59** 196-198 201
   258 260-264 378
Parnell (Adams) **101** 253
Patty **59** 201 380 381 383
   384
Peggy **59** 195 199 258 260
Persis **59** 260
Phebe **52** 368 **53** 105 **59**
   198 263 264 307 378-384
   411 **109** 160
Phebe (Manning) **106** 308
Polly **59** 258 259 264 378
   379 382
Priscilla **86** 14
Prudence **59** 196 257 259
   379-383 **83** 509 510
Prudence (Allen) **83** 509
   510
Rebecca **59** 196-198 207
   258 260 262-264 308 **101**
   253 **111** 290
Rebecca (Allen) **111** 290
Rebecca (Pope) **101** 253
Remember **60** 245
Remember (Bourne)
   118 205
Royal **99** 116
Ruhamah **59** 197 258
Ruth **59** 195 202 261 **118**
   323 **147** 271
Ruth (Davis) **118** 323
Sally **59** 260 **66** 364 **99** 116
Samuel **59** 197 200
Sarah **59** 207 307 **63** 377 **64**
   157 **83** 508 **87** 12 **92** 16
   113 109 **133** 153
Sarah (Ripley) **106** 308
Sarah (Skiffe) **101** 253
Sarah (Smith) **99** 116
Sarah Welles **69** 210
Seth **59** 195 196 198 200
   259 379-382 **123** 129
Simon **59** 197 199 200
Sophia **111** 290
Sukey **59** 381
Susan **59** 260 383 **111** 290
Susan Brimmer **75** xlv
Susan Ware **64** 17
Susanna **59** 257 259 262
   381 **73** 223 **93** 188
Susanna (Perry) **116** 31
Susanna (Wade) **101** 253
Thaddeus **116** 31
Thankful **59** 197
Thomas **52** 177 179 203
   206 **53** 130 54 180 **55**
   112 448 **58** 406 **59** 197
   306 308 403 **60** 159 160
   64 80 **65** 296 **66** 180 **72**
   202 **73** 140 **79** 297 **83**
   373 **84** 238 **86** 267 353
   393 **98** 84 **99** 60 **101** 253
   281 **106** 71 308 **111** 290
   114 124 **127** 52 **137** 342
   144 254
Thomas N. **122** 195

MAYHEW *cont'd*
Thomas W. **59** 201 259 382
   384 **132** 216 **138** 207
Thomas Wade **59** 263 383
   101 253
Timothy **59** 195 261
   73 148
Tristram **59** 201 401 **122**
   194 195
Verlinda **73** 263
W. Nelson **64** 187
Wade **59** 261 262 382
William **59** 198 205 207
   260 263 264 305 308 378-
   384 **73** 218 220 **77** 235
   105 276 **125** 23
William B. **59** 202 259
   379-384 **83** 509 510
William Manning **59** 206
Wilmot **59** 196 197
Zaccheus **52** 371 **59** 207
   261 308 **63** 377 **64** 17
   157 **101** 253 **113** 109
Zach. **66** 364
Zachariah **59** 195 198 201
   83 508 **118** 205 **145** 352
Zelinda **59** 260 382
Zephaniah **59** 201 264
   379-382
MAYHOW Eleanor **63** 34
   John **63** 34
MAYKYN Richard **108** 254
MAYLAM Maylem
   George **66** 58
   John **91** 93
   Mary **66** 58
   Meribah (Tibbetts) **100** 42
MAYLIN —— **107** 316
MAYNARD Mannyard
   Maynerd
   — Mrs. **71** 26
   ___ (Taverner) **139** 233
   Abigail **52** 338
   Abner **84** 86
   Abraham **54** 343
   Adam **82** 407
   Adelbert **116** 64
   Adin H. **74** 319
   Alice J. **74** 318
   Allen Tinker **85** 410
   Amby **115** 294 **116** 64
   Amelia **73** 255
   Amos **89** 300
   Amy **75** 12
   Amy D. **75** 27
   Andrew **85** 410
   Ann **115** 294 **116** 78
   Anna **116** 114
   Anna Louisa **89** 14
      145 307
   Anna W. **75** 17
   Antipas **79** 31
   Artemas **77** 27 28 32
   Arthur H. **74** 318 **75** 24
   Arthur S. **110** 320
   Ashley J. **74** 318 319
   Autenia H. **75** 13
   Banister **77** 26
   Barnabas **52** 425
   Benjamin **114** 40 41 43
   Betsey **61** 346 **74** 318 319

MAYNARD *cont'd*
75 12 77 186
Betsey (Clapp) 114 43
Betsey (Thayer) 125 289
Betsey Ann 81 60
Betsey M. 74 319
Bezaleel 77 24-29
Burroughs 116 114
Burton H. 74 317 319
C. 75 12
Calvin 74 319 75 12
Caroline E. 52 339
Caroline Ellen (Long)
  89 325
Charles A. 145 307
Charles F. 52 339
Charles Tracy 74 318 319
Charlotte A. 52 339
Charlotte Augusta
  (Nelson) 105 62
Charlotte M. 52 339
Christiana 116 64
Chrystia 73 255
Clarissa W. 74 311
Clarissa Williams 85 410
Cora D. 76 276
Corneli 103 260
Cornelia L. 75 14 23
Daniel 52 338 339 58 316
  78 184
Daniel Wallace 52 339
David 63 222 225
Deborah 54 343
Deborah (Coates) 111 109
Deliverance 56 168
Deliverance (Leland)
  124 16
Della 56 168
Dolly 108 239 110 159
  114 43
Dolly (Maynard) 114 43
Dorothy 75 197
E. A. 121 92
Editha (Stebbins) (Day)
  147 384
Edna Long 89 325
Edward 75 13 89 325
  116 64
Edward Flint 52 339
Edwin 132 295
Elihu 114 104
Elijah 116 114
Elisha 77 19-21 116 114
Eliza 52 339 114 181
Eliza (Field) 114 181
Eliza K. 75 13
Elizabeth 61 23 71 3 73
  151 254 255 77 19 24 93
  94 115 80
Elizabeth (Gray) 103 236
Elizabeth Agnes 82 470
Elizabeth K. 89 384
Ella M. 74 318 319
Ellen 52 339
Elsie Sophia (Walden)
  104 308
Emily 75 24 115 294
Emily (Gates) 116 64
Emma 116 65
Emma F. (Spring) 116 65
Ephraim 74 318 319 75 12

MAYNARD *cont'd*
114 38 43 109
Esther 61 23 114 32 33
Esther (Gifford) 132 295
Esther (Rice) 114 33
Eunice 114 109
Fannie A. (Cotton) 116 64
Fanny Therese Walling
  52 339
Fanny W. 57 xlvii
Flora Ardelia 75 13
Fordyce 108 215
Frances 69 115 116 182
Frances (Huff) 116 182
Frances Maria Russell
  (Curow) 52 339
Francis 77 27
Frank Burton 75 12 13
Frank William 75 12
Fred Augustus 105 62
Fred W. 53 151
Gardner 77 20 115 204 294
Gaylard H. 75 13
George 52 128 53 259
George B. 74 319
George Willie 74 319
Gideon 61 23
Grace 74 319 116 65
Grace Mildred (Dean)
  144 120
Hannah 52 337 338 54 343
  58 316 61 311 77 317
  92 369 94 171 172 95
  254 124 16
Hannah Ann 116 114
Hannah O. 75 12
Harold G. 116 64
Harriet 74 153 75 12 21
  85 410
Harriet N. 52 338
Harrison S. 75 12 13 27
Hartwell 82 470
Heber 82 407
Helen Nelson 105 62
Henry 71 25 73 254
Henry N. 52 339
Hepzibah 52 338
Horace 116 114
Horace H. 75 12
Huldah 114 43
Ireney 63 89
Isaac 61 23 126
Isabel 74 317 75 23
Isabel A. 74 319
Israel 56 168 114 43
James 75 13 81 60 270
  126 255 128 18
Jane 73 254
Jesse Knowles 74 171 75
  13 14
Joan 54 343
John 52 337 53 151 359
  54 343 60 357 61 23 311
  62 220 223 227 228 337
  63 60 61 66 121 125 221
  222 64 73 68 264 75 13
  76 lxiii 85 455 93 94 94
  67 170-172 103 194 113
  57 114 33 116 65 120
  163 124 16 136 314 147
  21

MAYNARD *cont'd*
John B. 81 270
John H. 53 151
John W. 53 151
Jonathan 65 258 262 100
  66 143 17
Joseph 63 225 103 236 303
  114 43
Josiah 52 338
Judson W. 116 65
Julia S. 75 13
Julian A. 54 151
L. P. 89 383
Laura (Staplin) 98 288
Laura A. 116 118
Lee 116 65
Lemuel 98 359
Lena M. 74 319
Lenora (Beecher) 116 65
Leslie 116 65
Levi G. 116 65
Levi P. 91 329
Lewis A. 52 338
Lizzie Alita 82 407
Lizzie M. 74 171 311
Lodisa 85 410
Lois 52 337 338 61 23
Lois L. 85 410
Lorette H. 74 171
Louisa 77 25
Luana S. 75 13
Lucinda 103 298
Lucy 58 316 73 254 75 13
  14 77 27-29
Lydia 74 319 78 252
  94 171 172
Lydia S. 74 318 319
Lyman 57 144 381 98 288
M. Elizabeth 75 13
Malvina 74 174
Margaret 82 407
Margaret Emma 116 65
Maria 75 12
Maria Cornelia Durant
  74 liii 136 314
Maria J. 74 319
Marian 114 181
Marian (Ellis) 114 181
Martha 52 338 75 13
Martha Isadore 75 12 13
Mary 51 270 52 337 338
  425 53 359 54 343 61
  311 64 73 77 lxxiv 93
  93 94 172 95 256 114 43
  115 293 136 303 304
Mary (Axtell) 94 172
Mary (Balcom) 114 38 109
Mary (Beebe) 126 255
  128 18
Mary (Durant) 136 314
Mary (Gates) 120 163
Mary (Martin) 103 235
Mary (Starr) 93 94 94 170
  171 95 253 256
Mary Elizabeth 75 13
Mary J. 75 12
Mary Lewis 85 410
Mary Louise 116 114
Mary Noyes 114 43
Micah 52 338
Miriam 77 32

MAYNARD *cont'd*
Miriam (Willard) **114** 43
Moses **52** 337 338 **57** 307
  60 363 **61** 23 **76** lxiii
  108 239 **114** 40 42 43
Myron B. **75** 13
Nancy **73** 254 **95** 346
Nancy E. **79** 31
Nathan **136** 299
Nathaniel **52** 338 **61** 261
  137 317
Ophelia P. **74** 314
Orin **79** 78
Orlando **75** 13
Orlando S. **74** 319
Orra S. **75** 13
Orrilla **74** 174
Patty P. **75** 13
Phebe **74** 172 **75** 13 24
  116 64
Philip **83** 356
Polly **57** 284 **73** 254
Pruella **74** 319
Raymond Williamson
  82 407
Rebecca **57** 395 **61** 126
Reuben **61** 23
Rhoda **73** 254 **75** 27
Richard **54** 343
Robert **76** 225 **124** 117
Roxana **74** 177
Russell **84** 86
Ruth **51** 347 **77** 24 **114** 43
Sally **61** 23 **132** 295
Sally (Brigham) **114** 104
Sally (Willis) **114** 104
Salome **76** lxiii
Samuel **52** 338 **75** 12 **76**
  lxiii **111** 109 **114** 43 **125**
  289
Sarah **61** 23 **73** 254 **75** 13
  84 86 **98** 359 **108** 239
  114 43 **145** 158
Sarah (Blanchard) (Keyes)
  120 163
Sarah (Hall) **145** 307
Sarah (Maynard) **108** 239
  114 43
Sarah A. **52** 339 **75** 13
Sarah A. (Waller) **116** 65
Sarah D. **81** 270
Selden **78** 252
Sibyla **61** 23 **114** 40 43
Sibyla (Willis) **114** 42
Silence **114** 40 43
Silence (Willis) **114** 43
Simon **74** 319 **75** 13 24
  103 235 303
Sophia **72** 146 **81** 60 270
Sophia Eliza **73** 255
Sophia Maria **81** 60
Stephen **60** 236 238 **74** 150
  75 13 **121** 219
Stillman **75** 12
Susan **82** 470
Susan M. **52** 339
Susanna **63** 89 **114** 71 81
Susanna (Gifford)
  132 295
Sybilla (Willis) **108** 239
  114 43

MAYNARD *cont'd*
Tabitha **57** 307 **114** 43
Thaddeus **73** 254 255
Theodore Frelhuysen
  104 308
Thomas **77** 28 **112** 112
  113 58
Vashti M. **74** 311
Verna Eureta **104** 308
Warren **61** 23
Willard **114** 43
William **53** 151 **54** 343
  65 122 **73** 254 **77** lxxiv
  93 304 **100** 66 **112** 190
  116 65 **132** 295 **144** 120
William Davis **75** 13
William Stewart **73** 255
William T. **75** 13
Willis **114** 43
Zachariah **61** 23 **76** lxiii
  113 77 **141** 248
Zachary **52** 337
Zebediah **61** 23
Zelinda **52** 338
Zurry **116** 117
Mayne *see* Main
Maynerd *see* Maynard
MAYNERS — Capt. **59** 354
MAYNES Eliza **92** 36
  James M. **92** 361
  Robert **92** 361
Maynord *see* Maynard
MAYO ——— **72** 152 **103**
  172 **104** 218 **109** 205
  — Capt. **55** 421
  — Lieut. **85** 118
  — Mr. **95** 45 47-49 102
  — Mrs. **95** 105
  A---od **105** 289
  Abigail **53** 436 **81** 401 403
  104 61 **108** 278 **123** 119
  122
Abigail (Gates)
  (Sparhawk) **120** 164
Abigail (Gould) **124** 239
Abigail K. **116** 257
  123 199
Abijah **116** 257 **123** 122 199
Adelia **84** 123
Alfred **84** 35
Alice **83** 143 **102** 47 288
  123 200
Alice K. **123** 122
Allen **124** 239
Alvina Artemis **106** 114
Ama **83** 142
Amanda **105** 274 **108** 284
  109 14
Amariah **102** 281
Amaziah **84** 35
Ambrose **108** 278 **109** 205
Amory Dwight **61** 322
Amos **87** 317
Amy (Davis) **101** 325
Amy Richardson **85** 194
Angerina **109** 205
Ann **67** 365 **73** 151
Ann R. **83** 143
Anna (Davis) **101** 325
Anna Doane **61** 345
Anne **80** 9

MAYO *cont'd*
Anne Bakeman **106** 114
Annie **75** 255
Apphia Freeman **92** 118
Arza **104** 284
Asa **125** 8
Avis **108** 278
Avis M. **110** 107
Barbara **79** 293
Barbara (Knowles)
  126 238
Barnabas **123** 121
Barnabas K. **123** 198
Bathsheba (Smith)
  123 121
Benajah **87** 336
Benjamin **78** 320
Benson **62** 382
Bertha (Newcomb)
  102 290
Bethiah **80** 8 20 23 **123** 118
Bethiah (Knowles)
  123 117
Bethiah C. **123** 122 200
Bethiah Collins **80** 270
Betsey **77** 230 **104** 132
  106 114 **123** 118 124
Betsey (Atwood) **123** 119
Betsey C. **123** 124
Betty **84** 322 **123** 119 120
Betty (Knowles) **123** 117
Betty (Lumbard) **123** 117
C. G. **79** 191
C. H. **88** 390
C. Johnson **132** 165
Caleb Bateman **106** 114
Caroline **69** xlvi
Catherine **125** 216
Charles C. **91** 394
Charles E. **52** 392 **54** 169
Charles Herbert **54** 115
Charlie **102** 283
Chester Garst **87** 174
  120 315
Clara D. **109** 205
Clarenton **102** 289
Crosby **83** 143
D. R. **86** 197
Daniel **59** 218
Daniel T. **83** 141
Deborah **108** 278
Deborah (Chase) **87** 336
Deborah (Rich) **83** 401
Debrane **108** 278
Delilah **102** 284
Desire **80** 7
Dianry B. (Smith) **123** 204
Dora Malana **102** 288
Dorcas (Chase) **87** 317
Dorothy **80** 270
Dorothy (Collins)
  123 117
E. Jean **120** 155
Ebenezer **53** 436 **105** 289
Edmond Gardner
  128 150
Edmund **58** 372 **128** 150
Edward **67** 365
Edward E. **83** 142
Edward P. **75** 255
Edward Richards **101** 325

MAYO *cont'd*
Elisha **69** xlvi **80** 20 **83**
 142 145 **105** 288 289
 126 236 **130** 14
Elisha Y. **123** 204
Eliza **100** 189 **123** 118
 126 141
Elizabeth **51** 204 206 **67**
 365 **79** 293 **80** 12 21 24
 83 273 **95** 41 48 **104** 183
 106 229 **107** 63 **117** 299
 123 80 **143** 341
Elizabeth (Davis) **101** 325
Elizabeth (Farley) **101** 325
Elizabeth (Ring) **102** 47
Elizabeth F. **94** 53
Elizabeth Fisk **128** 150
Elizabeth Mary **106** 114
Ella F. (Freeman) **102** 290
Elna Jean (May) **118** 248
Emma **75** 255 **83** 142 143
Emma F. **122** 311
Enoch **105** 290
Enoch M. **83** 141 142 144
Ephraim **108** 278
Esther **123** 204
Esther A. **83** 299 300
Eunice **80** 12 **83** 143 **94**
 193 **123** 117 **125** 11
Eunice (Higgins) **111** 156
Ezekiel **128** 150
Ezra **85** 369
F. B. **76** 9
Florence V. **93** 109
Francis **108** 285
Francis Evans **106** 114
Freeman **102** 288
Freeman (Mrs.) **102** 287
Freeman D. **123** 121
George **62** 321
George W. **83** 142
Gertrude **91** 142
Gertrude Ellen **104** 144
Gideon **79** 386
Guy (Mrs.) **118** 248
 120 155
Hannah **79** 293 **80** 20 **81**
 329 **84** 35 **86** 398 **95** 41
 45 **102** 52 145 **108** 118
 111 134 **113** 126 **121**
 209 **123** 119 **124** 239
 126 96 239 **146** 277
Hannah (Bassett) (Covell)
 125 8
Hannah (Cahoon)
 124 239
Hannah (Ford) **102** 281
Hannah (Freeman) **102**
 54 55 **121** 208
Hannah (Graves) **101** 325
 146 277 278
Hannah (Knowles)
 123 117
Hannah (Prence) **95** 48
Hannah (Prince) **102** 49
Hannah (Rich) **84** 35 52
Hannah (Rycroft) **95** 48
Hannah D. **123** 199
Harriet **80** 124 **82** 367
Harriet (Snow) **123** 124
Harriet T. **75** 255

MAYO *cont'd*
Helen Isadore (Merrill)
 101 325
Henry **80** 8 23 270 **103** 42
 123 117 **132** 239
Henry Lenord **106** 114
Hitty **123** 118
Hope (Rich) **83** 272 400
Howes **105** 289
Isaac **73** 284 **83** 142 143 145
 105 205 **124** 239
Isaiah **83** 143
Israel **70** 365 366 **79** 293
J. C. **91** 329
J. George **132** 165
Jacob **124** 239
Jacob W. (Mrs.) **102** 287
James **79** 379 **80** 6 12 22 24
 86 96 **105** 289 290 **123**
 118
James Crawford **106** 114
Jane **83** 272 **102** 286
Jemima (Gifford) **133** 56
Jennie Carolyn (Palmer)
 98 184
Joanna **123** 119
Joel R. **83** 143
John **51** 206 **55** 265 **56** 74
 62 315 **65** 63 207 **71** 192
 73 274 **78** 450 **79** 379
 80 201 **81** 213 329 **82**
 227 **83** 272 **84** 35 **95** 39-
 49 100 207 **98** 104 105
 101 325 **102** 47 52 54 55
 145 **103** 32-42 **106** 229
 108 278 **118** 248 **119**
 160 **120** 155 315 **121**
 208 212 277 **123** 117
 131 173 146 277 278
John (Mrs.) **103** 40
John H. **112** 322
John L. **109** 205
Johnnie **102** 284
Jonathan **102** 288 **111** 156
Joseph **55** 272 **61** 344 **75**
 255 **83** 401 **102** 288 **104**
 61 **105** 210 **106** 114 **120**
 164
Joseph C. **80** 124 **123** 124
Joseph Knowles **80** 20
Joseph S. **75** 255
Josephine C. **98** 151
Josiah **80** 9 **123** 119 120
Josiah S. **85** 380 **140** 266
Joyce **103** 41
Judah **79** 293 **113** 126
 127 42
Judith **109** 205 **110** 111
Judith A. **109** 205
Judith M. **110** 110
Lawrence **101** 325
Lawrence Shaw **75** 322
 90 306 **99** 145 **101** 325
 102 61 128 **103** 237 246
 247 **110** 271 **111** 13 **116**
 153 154 **144** 11 232 233
Leonard **75** 255
Lewis **83** 147 **93** 109
Livonia A. **85** 372 373
Lizzie E. **75** 255
Loui **102** 281

MAYO *cont'd*
Louisa Rogers **102** 289
Lovey **80** 22 271
Lucina **85** 379
Lucinda **83** 141 142 **85** 379
Lucinda W. **83** 142
Lucy **58** lxxx **112** 226 **123**
 118 119 **128** 238 311
Lucy Richard **92** 390
Lucy Richards **92** 390
Luther M. **83** 142
Lydia **60** 179 **79** 293 **123**
 118 202 **127** 46
Lydia (Cole) **123** 199
Lydia (Doane) **123** 118
Lydia (Knowles) **123** 121
 198 201
Lydia (Mayo) **123** 118
Mae **78** 320
Marcellan Cram **104** 284
Marcia B. **102** 290
Marcy **121** 272
Margery **54** 87
Maria **124** 239
Martha **80** 22 24 **83** 272
 400 **102** 283 **143** 341
Martha (Rich) **83** 272 400
Martha A. (Hopkins)
 102 283
Martha B. (Snow) **123** 124
Martha Miller **101** 252
Mary **56** 36 **60** 179 **73** 283
 79 293 **83** 272 **86** 343
 396 **87** 13 **95** 108 **102** 55
 103 93 **121** 282 **124** 239
Mary (Hamilton) **127** 42
Mary Ann (Watkins)
 128 150
Mary C. **109** 205
Mary Elizabeth **76** 9
Mary Ellen **84** 123
Matilda **123** 120
Matthew **76** 50
Mehitable **104** 58 **128** 292
 146 278
Meletiah (Rich) **83** 403
Melinda F. (Collins)
 123 204
Melissa B. **102** 281
Mercy **79** 293 **80** 20 **83** 142
 102 54 **105** 101 **123** 117
 120 **126** 238
Minnie **78** 320
Molly **60** 179
Moses **51** 204
Myra **88** 212
Nabby **125** 288
Nancy **75** 255 **108** 278
Nancy F. (Smith) **132** 239
Nancy J. **109** 205
Nancy Pierce (Reed)
 101 325
Nancy R. (Allen) **85** 380
 140 266
Naomi **123** 121 198
Nathaniel **60** 179 **70** 366
 79 293 **80** 279 **95** 41 45
 48 103 **102** 49 **105** 289
 290
Nathaniel E. **125** 37
Nehemiah Doane **83** 272

MAYO *cont'd*
403
Nettie **117** 127
Noah **83** 272 400 **84** 35
Obed **100** 189
Olive **80** 270
Olive C. (Doane) **102** 286
Oliver **123** 202
Ovey P. **102** 290
Patience **119** 160 **135** 73
Patty **123** 119
Patty (Doane) **123** 119
Patty K. **123** 199
Paul **79** 386
Phebe **72** 151
Phebe (Gould) **123** 123
201
Phebe K. (Cobb) **116** 257
123 122 199
Priscilla **126** 169
Priscilla (Hopkins)
103 172
Rachel **75** 255 **79** 293
Rachel (Hopkins) **102** 56
Randall **124** 239
Rebecca **79** 293 **80** 21 24
94 388 **102** 101 **121** 279
122 144 **123** 120 **126**
239
Rebecca (Knowles) **123**
118 202
Rebecca A. **83** 143
Rebecca F. **123** 202
Reliance **105** 104
Reuben **104** 61 **105** 210
108 278 **124** 239
Reuben M. **109** 205
Richard **70** 365 366 **79** 293
103 40
Robert **62** 247 **123** 199
Roline **69** xlvi
Roxanna **102** 288
Ruth **79** 293 386 **123** 118
Ruth (Cole) **123** 120
Ruth (Hopkins) **102** 49
Ruth A. **123** 202
S. Emery **102** 286
Sabra (Rich) **83** 400
Sally **73** 284 290 **105** 227
274 **110** 308 **123** 119
Sally (Will) **109** 183
Samuel **70** 365 **80** 21 22 24
83 272 **84** 35 **95** 41 46-
48 102 104 108 **102** 49
52 **103** 41 **121** 214 **123**
117 118
Sarah **51** 208 **55** 265 **59** 217
218 **67** 365 **79** 379 386
80 12 **83** 145 **108** 285
127 42 48 99
Sarah (Elkins) **86** 96
Sarah (Hopkins) **104** 218
Sarah J. **69** 275
Sarah Jane **108** 286
Sarah Young **106** 114
Sears **109** 183
Seth **104** 132 **105** 274
133 56
Seth Washington **106** 114
Simeon **92** 118 119 **123**
119 **140** 168

MAYO *cont'd*
Solomon **102** 285
Solomon H. **123** 123 201
Sophronia **128** 150
Susan **102** 287 **123** 200
Susanna **84** 35 **123** 119
Sylvanus **62** 382
Tabitha **51** 206 **123** 118
Tamsen **95** 41 47 108
103 41
Tamzen Doane **102** 289
Thankful **79** 296 **83** 273
123 117 118
Thankful (Smith) **123** 204
Theodore **128** 150
Theophilus **64** 284 **79** 293
102 56
Thomas **61** 43 **64** 284 **70**
365 **79** 293 **80** 7 20 **83**
272 273 400 **101** 325
123 204 **125** 37 **126** 238
130 15
Thomasine (Lumpkin)
95 46
Timothy **84** 35 **123** 117
118 201
Uriah **80** 20 **84** 35 **123** 117
Uriah R. **84** 52
Wallace **102** 283
Walter **102** 290
Warren D. **123** 204
Wesley H. **93** 109
William **102** 47 286
William F. **102** 281
William Holbrook
128 150
William Withington
75 255
Zilla **123** 119
MAYO-SMITH
Amabel **92** 390
Lucie **92** 390
Mabel Percy (Ford) **92**
390 **93** 140
Richmond **92** 390
Richmond (Mrs.) **86** 193
92 390 **93** 82 140 140
MAYOR
Alfred G. (Mrs.) **93** 138
Amy **89** 242
Harriet (Hyatt) **93** 138
Joan (Riddlesdale)
143 215
John **63** 142 **148** 62
Launcelott **143** 215
Rose **89** 267
William **64** 55
MAYOU Josephine C. **80**
208 **97** 288 385
Leon **97** 385
Samantha Matilda
(Haughey) **97** 385
Mayplet *see* Maplett
MAYRAND
George **111** 51
Jenny Mary (Dame)
111 51
Mayre *see* Mayer
MAYS Mayes Mayse
Catherine Elizabeth
(Gardner) **93** 291

MAYS *cont'd*
Emma **128** 264
Ida (Whitlock) **128** 177
Joseph **128** 177
Margaret **93** 374
Mercy **88** 304
Richard **94** 345
Thomas **51** 254
William Mayer (Mrs.)
93 291
MAYSANT Robert **51** 253
Mayse *see* Mays
Maysten *see* Mayston
MAYSTER John **59** 173
Margaret **59** 173
MAYSTON Maysten
John **92** 385 386 **93** 75
MAYWORTH
Sophia **82** 179
MAZARIN ———— **123** 102
MAZEEN Ezekiel **80** 72
MAZERGUE Aimee **71** 14
MAZURE Michael **65** 230
MAZUZEN
Elizabeth **72** 221
MAZYCK Isaac **62** 108
K. **102** 279
MAZZINI
Giuseppe **77** liii
MAZZONE
Mary Caroline **82** 267
MCAAIN Hughston
Maynard **122** 95
John **125** 258
Margaret **125** 258
MCAAY
William B. **114** 185
MCACHRAN John **99** 44
Julia Ann **99** 44
Rosanna (Halut) **99** 44
MCADAM MacAdam
Macadam McAdams
Abigail (Hardey) **91** 267
Archbald **114** 150
David **107** 10
Edward Pope **91** 142 **105**
119 314 **106** 129
Eugene Perrott **105** 314
George **127** 268 269
Gloriana Margaretta
(Nicoll) **136** 322
Greta **148** 130
Hannah **127** 268
Hannah (Slocombe)
127 268
Henry Kenneth (Mrs.)
112 88
John Loudon **136** 322 328
Mary Elizabeth (Pope)
105 314
Nancy **127** 268
Raymond **148** 130
Samuel **104** 201
MCADOO
Eleanor Randolph
81 119
Eleanor Randolph
(Wilson) **136** 322
William **57** 341
William Gibbs **81** 119
98 79 **136** 322

McAfee *see* Macafee
McAFOOSE
  Georgianna **92** 221
McALARNEY
  William M **55** xxx
McALEER Alonzo
  William (Mrs.) **96** 160
  Catherine **64** 293
  George **58** 215 **64** 293
   65 xxiv
  Helen Etheridge (Jewett)
   96 160
  Hugh **64** 293
  Lawrence **64** 293
McALEXANDER
  Alexander **65** 6 84
McALISE D. M. **89** 392
McAlister *see* McAllister
McAleer *see* McAleer
McALLISTER
  MacAllister
  MacCollister
  McAlister McAllester
  McAllister McAlloster
  —— **106** 80
  Aaron **74** 318
  Agnes **69** 328
  Alexander **73** 94 **147** 265
   267
  Angus **123** 154
  Archibald **73** 94 167 **89** 34
   117 253
  Arthur Walker **77** 226
  Benjamin Franklin
   106 80
  Bessie (Hannum) **90** 345
  Betsey **73** 94
  Cavanagh Jacobs **125** 72
  Chester W. (Mrs.) **115** 157
   116 154 **121** 76
  D. M. **68** 384
  Duncan M. **69** xxxii
  Eliza Melville **54** lxi
  Ethel Beatrice **100** 111
  Fanny **93** 243
  Frances **54** lxi
  Frances Wardale **71** 1
  Frank **73** 94
  Garland **106** 80
  George C. **113** 323
  George I. **79** 225
  Georgia **67** 283
  Hall (Mrs.) **85** 196
  Harriet **74** 318
  Harriet E. **102** 22
  Hiram **73** 94
  James B. **77** 153
  James S. **90** 345
  Jane B. **67** 283
  Jesse **74** 318
  Johanna **124** 67 68
  Johanna (Holland) **124** 67
  John **54** lxi **62** 30 **71** 1
   98 106
  John Allister **54** xlvii lxi
   lxii
  Lucy (Faulkener) **106** 80
  Lydia **74** 318
  Margaret **91** 263
  Margaret (Cavanagh)
   (Jacobs) **125** 72

McALLISTER *cont'd*
  Maria **106** 80
  Mary **73** 94 **74** 318 **79** 131
   124 67 **145** 132 **147** 265
   267]
  Mary (Beedle) **124** 67
  Mary (Blair) **124** 67
  Mary Eliza **77** 226
  Matilda Willis **67** 321
  May **51** 492
  Nabby (Wright) **106** 80
  Ned **125** 303
  Patsy (Willliams) **125** 303
  Randall **124** 67
  Rebecca W. **77** 153
  Richard B. **67** 283
  Robert **61** 239
  Robert Vincent **103** 119
  Rosanna **73** 94
  Ruth **73** 94
  Ruth A. **73** 94
  Ruth Brown **115** 157 **116**
   154 **121** 76
  Sally **106** 80
  Samuel **124** 67
  Sarah **61** 239 **73** 94
  Thomas **124** 67 68 **125** 109
  Ward **62** 314
  William **60** 25 **93** 397
   100 63
McALPIN McAlpine
  —— **58** 207
  Adelaide (Rose) **89** 56
  Albert Harford **103** 176
  Bede Eliza **75** 96
  Caroline W. **103** 176
  Caroline W. (Clark)
   101 36
  Charles Percival **103** 176
  Christian **127** 52
  Claudia Thomas **103** 122
  Corabelle **103** 175
  David Hunter **77** xci
   89 56
  David Hunter (Mrs.) **77**
   323 **78** 205 **89** 56 137
   137 190 190
  Donald **117** 16
  Elaine Rockefeller **89** 56
  Emma **77** xci **78** 205
  Emma (Rockefeller)
   89 56 137
  Francis Green **127** 52
  Geraldine Rockefeller
   89 56
  Harvey Foster **103** 176
  James **101** 36 **103** 176
  James R. **101** 315
  Jane **127** 52
  John **101** 315 **103** 175 **117**
   16 **127** 52
  Kenneth **79** 359
  Mariona Waterhouse
   Caswell (Angell)
   103 219
  Mary F. **101** 33
  Peter **127** 52
  Rebecca **127** 52
  Rebecca (Barss) **127** 52
  Samuel C. **101** 315
  Selden Kilby **103** 176

McALPIN *cont'd*
  Susan **101** 315 **103** 175
  William **84** 379 **127** 52
  William Rockefeller
   89 56
  William Rockefeller
   (Mrs.) **103** 219
McALVINE McAlvin
  —— **56** 387
  Ebenezer **56** 258
  Elizabeth **56** 258
McAnally *see* McNally
McANANEY
  Peter **112** 315
  Vincent X. **112** 315
McANDREW
  Alexander **65** 245
  Caroline (Robar) **125** 261
  Shirley **80** 110
  William **125** 261
McAnnally *see* McNally
McANTUN —— **53** 152
McAnulty *see* McNulty
McARTHUR MacArthur
  McArthour McArthur
  McAurther McCarther
  —— **53** 152 **92** 11 13
  — Mr. **92** 11-13
  Alex. **128** 267
  Annie **82** 176
  Archibald **113** 13
  Arthur **97** 343 **99** 201 202
  Aurelia (Belcher) **97** 343
  Catherine **87** 122 **99** 201
  Catherine (Barton)
   107 301
  Charles Stuart **99** 202
  Daniel **52** 408 **91** 352
  Douglas **97** 342-344 **98**
   203 **109** 176 **115** 87 90
   192 **119** 148 **136** 87
  Eleanor **87** 121
  Elizabeth **89** 385
  Eunice **115** 43
  Helen **115** 287 **119** 28
  Isabella **92** 12
  James **99** 198 **112** 206
  Jane **109** 183
  Jennet **77** 184
  Jerusha **109** 182
  John **52** 408 **91** 352-354
   99 198 **114** 187 **145** 255
  Joseph **112** 203
  Lydia **91** 352-354
  Malcolm **99** 202
  Margaret **114** 187
  Mary **91** 354 **99** 198 **100**
   303 **125** 106
  Mary C. **92** 228
  Mary Pinkney (Hardy)
   97 343
  Moroni (Mrs.) **104** 144
  Neal **52** 312
  Pamelia **99** 198
  Peggy **87** 122
  Rebecca **114** 187
  Sarah **99** 201 202 **114** 187
  Selim Walker **93** 137 **116**
   71 **118** 248
  Selim Walker (Mrs.)
   118 248

McARTHUR *cont'd*
Selina Walker **147** 242
Virginia Shackelford
(Bostick) **93** 138
William **107** 301 **114** 187
William Miltimore
99 201
McATEER
Isabella **73** 131
John **73** 131
McAuley *see* McCauley
M'Cauley *see* McCauley
McAurther *see* McArthur
McAUSLAND
MacCasland
MacCausland
McAuslan
McCauseland
Abigail **115** 222
Amelia Bovey (Robinson)
100 251
Barnaby **100** 252
Gloria **102** 117
Gloria Natalie **93** 138 **96**
205 **99** 76
Grace Amelia **100** 252
Grace Ellen (Barnaby)
100 251
John **100** 251
William Alexander **78**
447 **79** 202 **82** 250 429
83 126 243 246 **84** 112
174 203 205 **85** 214 **86**
109 110 214 463 466 **87**
188 **88** 185 **89** 146 **93** 84
94 81 **100** 232 251 **101**
129 **115** 159
William Alexander (Mrs.)
100 252
McAUTUN John **52** 419
McAVA Ellen **109** 289
McAVERY Hugh **60** 160
Jane **60** 160
McAVITY Elizabeth
Frances (Dixon)
145 154
John **145** 154
McAWARD
Ferrol **60** 163
McAWSEY
David **73** 104
McBEAN Macbean
Macbeane
Donald **113** 4 84 87
Frank Nelson **93** 348
John **123** 154
Ruth Adele **93** 348
William **107** 18
William M. **66** 194
McBEATH Randolph
Price (Mrs.) **105** 128
McBEE John Harbour
(Mrs.) **99** 148
Louise **110** 281
May Wilson **145** 32
McBERNEY
Alice **62** 79
William **62** 79
McBETH Anna **83** 69
Joseph **83** 69
McBONE Thomas **65** 125

McBRAYER
Campie **77** 218
Samuel **77** 218
McBRIDE
Adam **112** 283
Alice Leonard (Crosby)
95 314
Allen **76** 276
Ann **92** 172 **112** 283
Ann (Montgomery)
112 283
Catherine **60** 241
Charles **128** 263
Edna D. (Kirlin) **128** 266
Eliza Jane **92** 174
Elizabeth **82** 113
Elizabeth (Pilson) **128** 263
Elizabeth A. **76** 275
Ellen **93** 370
Emma **139** 198
Fanny **139** 198
Glenna **105** 127
Hannah E. (Williams)
128 266
Hattie **139** 198
Henry Thomas **128** 263
Hugh **60** 27
James **54** cxxxvii **60** 241
61 351
Jane **58** 372
Jas. C. **128** 266
Jennie **104** 197
John **58** 372 **111** 210 **112**
282 283
John A. **76** 275
John F. **128** 266
John McLaren **64** xxxi
Lavinia **139** 198
Margaret **139** 198
Margaret (Hews) **120** 15
Martha **65** 237
Martha (Steepleton)
128 263
Martha F. **83** 435 **84** 17
Mary **126** 234 **128** 173
Robert **114** 187
Samuel **60** 242 **139** 198
Sarah **61** 351 **67** 81 **69** 266
Sarah E. **76** 276
Sarah Whitfield **104** 165
Thomas **120** 15
Virginia **117** 77
W. **60** 27
William **58** 372 **60** 28
61 351
William Arthur **95** 314
McBRIEN Joseph (Mrs.)
85 196
McBRIER Fannie **93** 365
McBRINE
Edith Grierson **84** 179
204 205
McBROOM Linda
(Eggleston) **147** 156
McBryde *see* McBride
McBURNEY Annie
(Beattie) **87** 59
Christian **144** 231
Elizabeth **87** 59
Elizabeth (Irwin) **133** 233
John **133** 233

McBURNEY *cont'd*
Mary Ruth **106** 309
William Henry **87** 59
McCAA Agnes **142** 192
379-381
John **142** 379
Mary **142** 379
McCABE McCabb
McCabes
Arthur **114** 188
Benjamin Chidlaw **89** 179
Bridget (Kelley) **89** 179
Charles **89** 179
Charles Cardwell **61** 217
Clara J. **113** 79 **122** 60 61
132 294 295
Clara Joan **104** 144
D. M. **130** 234
Electa Ann (Hannum)
91 45
George Henry **89** 179
Hannah **86** 382
Hannah (Riley) **115** 293
Hannah (Smith) **86** 382
Harry **89** 179
James **89** 179
Jane (Barlow) **89** 179
Janette **91** 45
Jennie Carter (Chidlaw)
89 179
John **66** 35 **91** 45 **114** 188
Julius P. Bolivar **66** 96
Margaret Fleming (Ward)
96 390
Mary **97** 190
Mary (Dyar) **128** 313
Mary Ann **80** 169
Mary Elizabeth **91** 39
Mary Jane (Graham)
89 179
Nancy (Owen) **91** 39
Obadiah **114** 188
Robert Emmet (Mrs.)
96 390
Thomas J. (Mrs.) **119** 320
W. Gordon **74** 160
William **91** 39 **115** 293
William John **81** 107 219
89 81 135 179
Winfield S. **91** 45
McCAFFERTY
Bridget **66** 32
James **60** 161
William **66** 36
McCAFFREY
—— **133** 278
Fanny **83** 417
John H. **107** 267
Matthew **107** 267
Sally **114** 231
McCAHAN
Rena Shull **96** 98
McCAIN
— Rev. **104** 172
Alma **78** 174
David **124** 61
Frank **82** 405
Grover Gerow **82** 405
James Edward **82** 405
John **115** 120
Melvin Henry **82** 405

McCAIN *cont'd*
Minnie **82** 405
Peter Kenneth (Mrs.)
104 144
Polly (Bickford) **124** 61
Verona Elvira **82** 405
William **78** 174
McCalester *see* McAllister
McCALL Mackall McCaul
—— **54** 456 **95** 372 **97** 133
— General **51** 202
— Mr. **61** 298
— Rev. Mr. **64** 288
Albert **98** 336
Archippus **124** 78 **127** 283
136 167 328
Benajah **124** 78 **136** 167
137 79
Betsey **136** 328
Charles **70** 205
Cicero B. **116** 65
Clare M. **124** 78
David **116** 65
Debbe **91** 197
Deborah (Marsh) **136** 328
Dolly **61** 296
Dorothy **61** 296 392
62 377
Ebenezer **124** 78 **136** 167
Elijah **136** 167
Elisha **61** 294 296 298 392
62 377
Eliza **98** 336
Emily **70** 205
Estella F. (Brown) **116** 65
Ettie **80** 208
Ettie Tidwell **85** 465
Eunice Bates **85** 326
Fannie **70** 205
George **70** 205
George G. **73** 229
Hannah **127** 281-283
Hannah (Clark) **127** 283
Hannah (Green) **136** 166
Hardy Bertram **120** 173
Hobart **136** 328
Howard Henry (Mrs.)
80 102 208 208 **96** 306
James **123** 155 **124** 78 **136**
166 167
John **70** 205 **73** 149 **124** 78
136 167 **137** 79
John Cooper **137** 79
Joseph **124** 78 **127** 282 283
136 167
Levis **123** 320
Lois **137** 79
Louis **127** 282
Lucy (Bancroft) **95** 372
Lucy (Strong) **136** 328
Margaret **89** 378
Margaret J. **73** 269
Mark **64** 361
Mary **73** 151
Mary (Williams) **137** 79
Matilda Seymour **133** 155
Maud (Day) **116** 65
Mercy (Lee) **137** 79
Meta **84** 348
Olive **86** 21 **136** 167 **137** 79
Polly **127** 282

McCALL *cont'd*
Rachel **136** 167
Rachel (Turner) **136** 166
Rebecca **73** 221 **136** 167
Rebecca Covington
73 268
Robert **70** 205
Samuel Walker **71** 187
72 xvii
Sarah **61** 294 **98** 336
Susan **70** 205
Thomas **116** 65
Walter **70** 205
Warner Sherman **81** 111
222
William **64** 221 **112** 302
William Harry (Mrs.)
95 147
McCALLEN
Jane **100** 297
Patrick **60** 27
McCALLEY McCally
Elizabeth **74** 249
Eunice (Royce) **101** 201
McCalloster *see* McAllister
McCALLSON
Phyllis **107** 133
McCALLUM
Angus J. **99** 38
Angus J. (Mrs.) **99** 37 38
Duncan **114** 150
Edward Davison **99** 148
James Dow **94** 401
Lorena **77** 265
Margie **89** 242
Susanna Menzies (Fitz
Randolph) **99** 38
McCally *see* McCalley
McCALMON
Jane **118** 330
McCAMANT
Wallace **76** 82
McCAMBLY
Patrick **145** 253
McCAMEY McCamy
Bernice Berrien **78** 176
Thomas Stokely **78** 176
Tilleman Calvin **84** 106
190
McCAMLEY
Bridget **145** 253
McCAMMON
Claire **109** 129
McCAMPBELL Mary
Marguerite **106** 125
McCamy *see* McCamey
McCANCE
Alexander **94** 211
Andrew **66** xlix **67** xxx
xxxiv **76** vi **77** vi **78** 218
79 104 209 214 **80** 104
105 214 220 **81** 208 233
234 **82** 249 **83** 244 **84**
175 **87** 73 186 **88** 89 182
90 127 **94** 80 144 211
Catherine May **94** 211
Elizabeth **61** 137
Hugh **61** 137
Jane **61** 137
John **94** 211
Margaret **94** 211

McCANCE *cont'd*
Margaret (McRoberts)
94 211
Margaret Hester **94** 211
Mary Craig (Shaw)
94 211
Robert **91** 328
Robert Thomson **94** 211
Samuel **61** 137
McCANDLESS
McCandlish
McCanless
Anne **107** 233 234
Deborah **107** 233 234
Deborah (Wheeler)
107 234
Elizabeth **67** xxxi
James **89** 95
Malinda Thomas **101** 122
Robert **107** 234
Sallie Benbridge **89** 95
Sarah **89** 95
Sarah Truxton
(Benbridge) **89** 95
William **112** 17
McCANEL
James **82** 316
McCanless *see*
McCandless
McCANLY Abial **76** 46
McCANN McCanne
— Mrs. **71** 50
Althea A. **89** 357
Ann (McKeon) **90** 115
Betsey **89** 357
Bobbey **89** 357
Caroline (Chellis) **128** 79
Charles Edward Francis
93 365
Charles Edward Francis
(Mrs.) **84** 233 **85** 188 **92**
294 **93** 140 365 365
Constance Woolworth
93 365
David **88** 158 241 **89** 357
Eliza **88** 158
Eliza R. **118** 326
Ella E. (Webster) **89** 351
Ella E. Webster **89** 351
Felix **60** 241
Frank Edgar **89** 357
Frankie **89** 357
Frasier Winfield **93** 365
Frederick (Mrs.) **100** 112
Hannah **60** 241 **88** 158
Hannah H. **89** 357
Hannah S. **89** 357
Hattie **89** 357
Helena Maude
(Woolworth) **93**
140 365
Helena Woolworth
93 365
Isaac **88** 241 **89** 357
James **60** 160 **89** 357
91 328
James W. **89** 357
Kate **117** 42
Kenneth S. **109** 77 156 238
Louise H. **100** 163
Lucy Snell **89** 357

McCANN *cont'd*
Mary **60** 241 **88** 241 **89** 357 **100** 163
Mary E. **89** 357
Mary Frances **117** 122
Mercilla **89** 357
Michael **60** 241
Mildred Olive Bates **118** 326
Molly **88** 158
Nelly **60** 241
Patrick **60** 241 **62** 81
Peggy **88** 158
Peter **60** 241
Polly **88** 158
R. B. **106** 78
Sally **88** 158 241
Samuel **88** 241
Sarah Elizabeth (Gilman) **109** 77
Sophronia S. **89** 357
Susan **60** 241 **88** 241
Thomas N. **109** 238
Thomas Nash **109** 77
W. A. **89** 357
Wesley D. **118** 326
William **89** 357 **90** 115
William H. **88** 158
William R. **118** 326
William Ray **112** 162
William W. **89** 351
Willie **89** 357
McCANNA
Barny **61** 267
Barry **60** 162
McCANNON —— **83** 35
Emma Ann **125** 53
Matilda (Crawford) **125** 53
Silas W. **125** 53
McCARAN
Edwin **62** 169
James **62** 169
McCARLEY
Felix **78** 310
Jeremiah **78** 300
McCARNEY
Michael **61** 43
McCarrel *see* McCarroll
McCARREN Patrick Henry **64** 102
McCARROLL McCarrel McCarrill
Abigail **63** 178 **74** 215 228 260 **82** 509
Abraham **74** 218
Ann **114** 187
Jacob **114** 187
James **74** 215 218 228 229 **82** 509
John **114** 187
Molly **74** 229
Patrick **61** 351
Polly **74** 261
Rachel **63** 178 **74** 229 260
William **112** 281
McCARRON
Fanny **60** 160
James **60** 160
Jane **60** 160
John **60** 160

McCartee *see* McCarthy
McCARTER
—— (Hills) **122** 66
Anna **107** 112
Elizabeth (McLellan) **90** 90
Eunice **115** 45
Hannah **90** 91
James **71** 49 **90** 90
Jane **90** 90
John **51** 462 **107** 112 **111** 219
Mary **90** 89
Mary (Sherer) **111** 219
McCARTHY Macarta Macarthy Macarty Maccarty McCartee McCartey McCarthey McCarty
—— **51** 37 **69** 29 **112** 301 **140** 247
— Dr. **57** 69
— Mr. **59** 354
— Rev. Mr. **77** 26
—— (Smith) **140** 247
Alice **109** 64
Ann **73** 217 **100** 243
Arthur **99** 202
C. **101** 273
Caler **99** 281
Callaugham **99** 284
Catherine **74** 307 **114** 183
Charles **78** 58 **99** 281 **100** 143 234 236 **101** 222 **102** 29
Charles Cunningham **85** 350
Charles Piercy **100** 143 **102** 29
Charlotte **67** lvii
Clarissa **73** 139
Daniel **62** 71 **73** 227 **92** 52 53
Daniel Edward **139** 217
David **78** 355
Denis **85** 439
Denis Aloysius **75** 157 **76** xx **77** xv **78** 198 **85** 439 **86** 107 200
Dennis **73** 152
Dermond **63** lxiii
Dervengal **95** 205
Divie Bethune **56** xiv xl xlii
Duncan **99** 202
Edward **85** 350
Elam S. **109** 39
Eliza Jane **75** 205
Elizabeth **67** 214 **70** 34 **83** 86-88 **95** 172 **119** 182
Elizabeth (Williams) **105** 265
Emilie Putnam **107** 134
Esther **101** 174
Florence **83** 415 **101** 175 **106** 245
Francis **72** 286
Guy A. **96** 330
Hannah **99** 281 284
Helen **74** 91
Helen (Walsh) **139** 217

McCARTHY *cont'd*
James **61** 265 350 **85** 350 **88** 389
Jennie F. **107** 86
Jerry **74** 91
Joan **63** lxiii
John **85** 350 **116** 150
John Collins **85** 350
John Henry **88** 389
Joseph Capewell **85** 350
Justin **67** xlii lvii
Justin Huntley **67** lvii
Katharine **68** 125 **100** 296
L. P. **139** 218
Louis **73** 318 **74** xxiv **88** 86 171 389 **89** 130
Louis Blalock **88** 389 **89** 130 **117** 71
Luke **100** 303
Margaret **110** 80
Mariah **83** 223
Marion Theodosia **88** 389
Martha **72** 286
Mary **83** 223 **100** 143 234 236 **102** 29
Mary A. **74** 91
Mary Elizabeth **94** 138
Mary Louise (Connelly) **139** 217
Matilda M. S. **73** 270
Matthew James **139** 217
Michael **102** 28
Michael Francis **67** lvii
Peter **56** xlii
Polly **83** 223
Richard Justin **90** 402
Robert **56** xlii **75** 205
Rufina Morris **85** 440
Samuel **60** 241
Sarah **73** 227 **99** 202 **116** 150
Susan Ann **85** 350
Susan Story **78** 355
Thaddeus **67** 214 **100** 221 **107** 191 313 **148** 333
Thomas **62** 321 **70** 262 **83** 87
Thomas James Caines **85** 350
Timothy **83** 86 **105** 178 265
Vivian **96** 330
William **83** 223 **85** 350
McCARTNEY Macartney MacCartney
Elizabeth Mearns **124** 194
Laura Keyser (Fracker) **124** 194
McCarty *see* McCarthy
McCaul *see* McCall
McCaulay *see* Macaulay
McCauley *see* Macaulay
McCausland *see* McAusland
McCawley *see* Macaulay
McCay *see* McKay
McChord *see* McHard
McCLAIN McCleane - *see also* McLean
Martha Jane **102** 20

McCLAIN cont'd
Mary **136** 130
Mary Ann (Wheaton)
  108 275
Moses **114** 187
Peter **88** 394 **103** 68
Sarah (English) (Frambes)
  103 68
Sarah Wilkinson
  (Elsberry) **103** 68
Wiliam **114** 187
William Page **88** 394
  103 68
McCLANAHAN
M'Clanachan
David **67** 370
Elizabeth **67** 370
Hannah **112** 92
Jennie P. **128** 262
Nathaniel **67** 370
W. S. **128** 95-97 171 174
  176 177 262 263 269
McCLANATHAN
Abby Ann **111** 312
Harriet Rose (Brown)
  111 312
Warren **111** 312
McClane see McClain
McCLANEN
Brice **91** 32
Dorothy (Hill) **91** 32
McCLANNAN
Juley **125** 216
Margaret **85** 349
William **52** 312
McCLARANCE
Anne **77** 182
Peter **77** 182
McCLARE
Archa'd **113** 92
McClaren see McLaren
McCLARET
Juley **125** 216
McCLARKEY
James **76** 50
McClarn see McClaren
McCLARTY McLarty
Alexander **77** 217
Charles Bingley **77** 217
David **116** 65
Edith Wiggins **106** 125
George **116** 65
George Washington
  77 217
Hannah **77** 217
Harvey Ezekiel **77** 217
James **77** 263
John **116** 65 119
John C. **77** 217
Katie **77** 263
Lillian P. **116** 67
Maria W. (Barker) **116** 65
Martha **77** 217
Martha Jane **77** 217
Mary **77** 217 **116** 65 119
Mary Amanda **77** 217
Myra E. **116** 65
Nancy **116** 119
Nancy (Lamont) **116** 65
Polly **77** 262
Ruby **116** 65

McCLARTY cont'd
Samuel Marion **77** 217
Samuel Wilson **77** 217
Sarah Ellen **77** 263
Sophia Caroline **77** 217
William James **116** 65
McCLARY McCleary
M'Clary
Ann F. **92** 312
Elizabeth (Dearborn)
  92 315
James H. **92** 312 315
McCLASH M'Clash
Margaret **127** 7
McCLAY A. **107** 174
Isabella A. Howe **86** 170
James S. **86** 170
Samuel **79** 50
McCLEA Andrew **78** 189
McClean see McLean
McClearn see McLaren
McCLEARY MacClary
McClary
Andrew **130** 245
Charles R. **77** 176
Edward **61** 135
Elizabeth **100** 304
Elizabeth M. **77** 176
Frances **80** 236
Frances B. **81** 148
Frank P. **117** 280
Horace P. **65** xxxiv
Isaac **79** 54
Jesse K. **117** 280
Jonathan **117** 280
Mahaly **117** 280
Margaret **80** 236
Martha **66** 94
Mary **78** 70
Moses **80** 236
Sally B. **78** 413
Samuel **77** 315
Samuel F. **110** 134
Samuel Foster **56** 220
Thomas **55** 81 **76** 318
William W. **117** 280
McCLEAVE
Hannah **128** 292
Joseph **128** 292
Mary **70** 83
Robert **128** 292
Sally (Godfrey) **128** 291
McCLEES Ann **84** 448
Ann Augusta **95** 399
Peter **84** 448
McCleland see McClellan
McCLELHILL
Joseph **111** 202
McCLELLAN M'Lellan
Macklelland
  McCleland McLellan
— Col. **63** 371 **101** 146 148
— Widow **103** 266
__ (Bradford) **110** 56
A. **145** 167
Abigail **90** 52 **97** 83
Alexander **94** 245 **145** 166
Alfred **74** 106
Anna (Arbuckle) **111** 93
Anna Isadora **55** lxiv
Arthur D. **95** 359

McCLELLAN cont'd
Arthur Daggett **55** xliii
  lxiv
Aubrey Lester **121** 76
Bertha (Lee) **96** 332
Betsey **90** 90 **127** 294
Betty **65** 313
Beulah **95** 359
Bryce **75** 51 52 54 56
Caree **75** 107
Charlotte **99** 148
Chloe **145** 56
Daniel **73** 255
David **91** 328 **111** 93
  127 294
Deborah **113** 243 324
Diana **113** 243 324
Diana (Jordan ?) **113** 243
  324
E. J. **79** 123
Edward **137** 183
Elina Meneta Leslie
  85 192
Elizabeth **75** 107 **127** 294
Elizabeth **58** 59 **90** 90
Elizabeth (Robinson)
  90 89
Elizabeth Holman **72** 304
Elizabeth Sophia
  (Brinton) **136** 322
Esther Anne **109** 296
Eunice **135** 317
Eunice (Eldredge)
  136 322
Florence **55** lxv
Florence (Armsby)
  95 359
Frances Decker **68** 145
Frank A. **75** lxxxiii
George **75** 56 **93** 257
  136 322
George B. **54** lxx lxxix
  cxlv **55** 52 **59** lxxxv
George Brinton **64** 69
  78 100 **79** 340 **136** 322
Grace M. **105** 52
Hannah **58** 57
Harriet E. **98** 82
Harriet Maria (Walton)
  93 120
Harry R. **96** 332
Helen **103** 266
Helen Livingston **85** 114
Hugh **73** 255 **75** 107
Hugh Davis **64** 131
Isaac **113** 243 324
James **53** 229 **73** 255 **90** 90
  91 91 **97** 366 **98** 55 **106**
  99 **136** 322
Jane **71** 226 **75** 51 52 56
  91 91
Jane D. **94** 245
Jane Elizabeth **110** 243 244
Jean **73** 255
Jeanette **71** xl
Jemima **113** 243 324
John **55** lxiv **73** 255 **75** 51
  78 142 **111** 93
John H. B. **93** 257
John H. B. (Mrs.) **93** 120
John Jay **109** 59

McCLELLAN *cont'd*
Joseph **113** 243 324
Josephine Maria (Sands)
  137 183
Kate Lucy (Pierce) **88** 383
Lizzy **93** 257
Lucia F. (Snow) **88** 342
Lydia (Redington) **109** 59
Margaret **65** 138 **71** xl **72**
  304 **73** 255 **74** 106
Margaret A. **102** 124
Margaret (Johnson)
  94 245
Margaret Smiley **72** 304
Maria **93** 257
Martha **78** 142
Mary **65** 138 **125** 288 **126**
  80 **137** 280
Mary (Finney) **114** 161
Mary (Montgomery)
  112 293
Mary A. **55** lxiv
Mary Ann **101** 323
Melinda **72** 304
Michael **71** xl **73** 255
Moses **58** 57 59
Nancy **84** 213 **90** 90 **95** 153
  103 173
Nancy V. **99** 153 **100** 117
Nathaniel **97** 366
Oliver Eldridge **93** 257
Peggy **58** 59
Phebe **113** 243 324
Polly (Rivers) **90** 90
Prince **145** 56
Quindley Sleight **101** 124
Rebecca **98** 55
Rebecca W. **90** 92
Robert **72** 304 **73** 255 **88**
  342 **112** 285 293
Robert Lawson **73** 255
Robert Smiley **72** 304
Ruth **113** 243 324
Sally **114** 182
Samuel **65** 138 **73** 255 **75**
  54 **91** 328 **104** 206
Sarah **53** 229 **73** 255 **123** 10
Sarah (Preble) **116** 130
Sarah Jane Boynton **98** 55
Simon **90** 89
Stanley Raymond **95** 147
William **75** 56 **78** 110 **91**
  328 **97** 366 **113** 243 324
  114 161 **116** 130 **119** 21
William Albert **91** 142
William Brownlow
  121 76
William Henry **58** 59
William Smith **67** 194
McCLEMENT
Arthur **85** 427
Catherine **77** 144
John Hall **75** ix xxiii **85**
  427 **86** 107 200
John Wesley **85** 427
Lena **85** 427
Lena (Morgan) **85** 427
Mary Ann (Hall) **85** 427
Morgan Hall **85** 427
McCLENACHAN
Charles T. **107** 13

McCLENACHAN *cont'd*
Robert **84** 382
McCLENAN
Ebenezer **97** 377
Elizabeth **58** 123
James **97** 377
McCLENCH M'Clench
  McClinch
Frances **77** 56
George B. **140** 265
John **77** 317 **79** 44 **140** 165
Joseph **79** 36
Katharine Amanda
  77 xxviii
Martha G. (Rose) **140** 265
Mary **77** 56
Mary A. **76** 53
Nancy (Robertson)
  133 309
Sally **147** 267 269
Samuel **133** 308
William Wallace (Mrs.)
  77 xxviii 78 78
McCLENDEN
Amy **93** 274
McCLENING
— Capt. **70** 235
McClentick *see*
  McClintock
McClerren *see* McLaren
McClinch *see* McClench
McCLINE James **65** 6 84
McCLINTOCK
  MacClintock
  McClentick McClintic
  McClintoch
—— **60** 96 **130** 313
— Mrs. **83** 194
— Rev. Dr. **83** 35
— Widow **83** 35
Alexander **71** lv lvi
Ann **71** 65 66
Caroline **69** lxi **71** 65 66
  82 422
Caroline Augusta **71** lv
Catherine **71** lv
Catherine M. **83** 21 25
Catherine Montgomery
  82 422
Charles **83** 194
Charles Henry **82** 422
Chester Lewis (Mrs.)
  85 196
Eliza Ann **82** 422 **83** 194
Eliza D. (Fernald) **83** 23 25
Elizabeth **82** 422
Elizabeth Knight **90** 357
Ellen **82** 422
Emily **71** 65 66
Emory **55** 352 **59** 291 **60**
  xxxviii **65** xxi **71** xxxiv
  lv
Esther **102** 226
Frances **82** 422
Frances M. **83** 307
Francis Babcock **83** 173
George Warwick **90** 357
George Warwick (Mrs.)
  83 122 233 233 **89** 82
  137 137 **90** 357
Isabella **71** lvi

McCLINTOCK *cont'd*
James **71** lvi
Jenet **71** lvi
John **71** lv lvi **81** 36 **82**
  422 **83** 194 **106** 108 **123**
  80
John Norris **59** xlvii
Lydia **102** 301
Margaret **71** lvi
Martha **71** lvi
Martha Jane **66** 112
Mary A. (Mathews)
  90 357
Mary Ann **81** 36
Mary Ethel (Knight) **89**
  137 **90** 357
Rachel **85** 426
Rebecca Hestor **112** 141
Samuel **69** lxi **73** 280 **82**
  422 **83** 23 25 173 **116**
  111 **140** 39
Sarah (King) **123** 80
  130 313
Thomas **112** 141 **123** 80
  130 313
William **71** lvi
William II. **90** 357
McCLISH
Margaret **127** 7
Robert **73** 146
McCLISTER
Jane **78** 316
McClod *see* McCloud
McCLONEY
Ichabod **145** 352
McCLOSKEY McClosky
Eliza **134** 332
Elizabeth **134** 332
George **134** 332
James **134** 332
John **66** 32 **134** 332
Joseph **134** 332
Mary (Gilman) **134** 332
Matilda (McConechy)
  134 332
Robert **134** 332
Rosanna (Mitchell)
  134 332
Rose **66** 32
Sarah (McCartney)
  134 332
William **134** 332
McCLOTHLAND
M'Clothland
Katharine **70** 264
Thomas **70** 264
McCLOTHLIN
Sarah **133** 73
McCLOUD McClod - *see*
  also McLeod
—— **84** 129
Abigail **108** 57 58
Abigail (Seavy) **108** 124
Alexander **108** 57
Angus **61** 31 **112** 207 **116**
  96 100
Anne **116** 97 100
Anson **116** 96
Betty **108** 58
Charles **63** 22
Curtis **66** 112

McCLOUD *cont'd*
Daniel **108** 58 **116** 96-100
231
Eli **116** 98 99
Elizabeth **116** 96 97
Ellen **90** 110
Fanny (Chase) **87** 322
Forest **116** 99
Harvey **116** 99
Herman **87** 322
John **62** 244 **90** 110 **108**
57 58 124
Louis **108** 57
Mary **116** 97-99
Mary (Cleveland) **116** 98
Matthew **90** 110
Michael **116** 97 98
Norman **116** 99 100
Oliver **108** 57
Robert R. **116** 12 13
Roderick **64** 325
Ruby (Wright) **116** 99
Rufus Bailey **116** 99
Sally **108** 58
Samuel (Mrs.) **116** 147
Sarah **116** 97 98 231
Sarah G. **66** 112
Sophia **108** 57 192
Thankful (Rich) **84** 129
Wallace **116** 314
McCLOUGHRY
James **83** 57 61
McCLOUTH
John **76** 157
Sarah **76** 157
McCLUNG MacClung
Alexander Keith (Mrs.)
93 138
Aurelia **83** 206
Charles **83** 206
Charles Henry **86** 230
Charles J. **83** 206
Eliza Ann (Mills) **83** 206
Ellen **83** 206
Florence E. (Juhling)
93 138
Franklin Henry **83** 206
Henry **111** 209
Mary Imboden **86** 230
Matthew **83** 206
Quantrille Day **95** 147
Robert Gardner **71** xxiii
74 xxviii **82** 381 **83** 206
236
Sarah **111** 211
McCLURE McCluer
M'Clure Maclure
Mclure
—— **70** 299 **93** 117 124
— Rev. Mr. **95** 92
Agnes (Wallace) **108** 80
Alexander **111** 208 209
Alice Pauline (Moor)
94 60
Andrew **101** 339
Annie **84** 297
Archibald **94** 400 **98** 290
Arnold **84** 36
Benjamin **108** 80
Betsey **79** 151
Charles Walter **103** 119

McCLURE *cont'd*
Chester **136** 250
Chloe (Mehurin) **136** 250
Clarence Alfred **95** 318
Cyrus **93** 117 121 124 256
94 156
Cyrus Benjamin **93** 256
D. **80** 65
David **54** 113 **57** 271 **62**
lxxiii **79** 151 158 301 **80**
65 **82** 504 **98** 106 **117** 82
89 **145** 351
Deborah **64** 43
Dorothy **104** 146
Dorothy Gertrude **95** 318
Elizabeth **80** 65
Elizabeth (Gill) **84** 36
Elizabeth Davison **93** 124
Emeline **98** 80
Florence Elsie **95** 318
Hannah **57** 271
Hugh **111** 207
Ida May (Jessell) **95** 318
Irene **103** 309
James **52** 10 **64** 43 **80** 65
94 400 **101** 339 **106** 153
108 80 **112** 92 **134** 173
145 350
James Alexander **70** 191
Jane **70** 264 **108** 80
Jane (Ahll) **108** 80
John **70** 264 **108** 80 **111**
203 **125** 103
John Robert **86** 99
Jonathan **145** 351
Joseph **108** 80
Joseph Hall **93** 121
Lindley **94** 60
Lois **61** 383
Mabel Frances **95** 318
Margaret **101** 339
Mariam **115** 123
Martha Rogers **52** 10
Mary **80** 65 **85** 226 **108** 80
111 209
Mary (Clayton) **101** 339
Mary Ann **78** 70
Mary Belle **86** 99
Matilda **114** 190
Mattie Byrne **86** 99
Mercy (Miles) **134** 173
Mildred Geraldine **95** 318
Moses **111** 208
Nancy **93** 121 256 **94** 156
101 339
Nancy Jane **93** 117
Octavia **126** 22
Peter **95** 318
Rachel **108** 80
Raymond Edwin **95** 318
Russell **80** 65
Sally **133** 308 309
Sally (Queenyard)
125 103
Salome **115** 119
Samantha **134** 173
Samuel **92** 280 **145** 350
Sarah **82** 428
Sarah Ann **134** 89
Susan Elizabeth (Winfrey)
86 99 109 199

McCLURE *cont'd*
Thomas **74** 94 95 **101** 339
Walter Burtell **95** 318
William **95** 318 **101** 339
110 130
McCLURG —— **55** 274
— Dr. **56** 55 56
Gilbert **76** 320
McCLUSKEY McLuskey
Rachel **107** 209
McCLUSTER
Jane **58** 145
McCOBB McCobbs
—— **145** 173
— Col. **98** 300
Abby **74** 28
Abigail **74** 20
Albert **74** 20
Alexander **83** 375
Andrew **73** 184
Beatrice **90** 89 **93** 95
Betsey **74** 20
Dana **74** 20
David **83** 375 415
Elizabeth **73** 184
Elizabeth (McFarland)
83 415
Irene **74** 28
James **83** 375 **93** 95
Lydia **74** 20
Maria **74** 23
Mary **53** 395 **93** 95
Nancy **74** 20
Ruth **74** 20
Samuel **74** 20 28 **89** 34 **93**
95 **119** 22 **133** 263 **147**
74-76 80
Thomas **79** 55
McCOCKELL
Archibald **60** 240
McCOLEY Laurel
Catherine (Perry)
116 33
Susanna **116** 303 305
McCOLGAN Eleanor
Dunn **104** 146
McCOLL
Duncan **118** 51
Madeline **109** 307
Ora John **109** 307
McCOLLA
Susanna **116** 303
McCOLLESTER
Alexander **70** 262
Archibald **105** 288
Sullivan Holman **70** 369
McCOLLEY
Benjamin **63** 235
Caroline **89** 310
Eliza A. **59** lxi
Eliza Caroline (Lassell)
(Stuart) **89** 310 311
H. W. (Mrs.) **114** 229
James **62** 79 **124** 244
Jean (Stark) **124** 244
John **89** 310
Michael **93** 300
Nathaniel **145** 348
McCOLLISTER
Amos **83** 275
Betty **83** 275

McCOLLISTER *cont'd*
Elmer Ellsworth **94** 139
Ethel Morrill **76** 158
Griselda **113** 324
Hannah **104** 196
James **83** 275
Jennie (McBride) **104** 197
Lemuel **83** 275
Mary **83** 275
Patience **83** 275
Reuben **104** 197
Thurman Paul **85** 196
McCOLLOCK
John **112** 291
Margaret **108** 124
McCOLLOM McCullom
    McCollum McCullum
    —— **126** 156
Alvah **112** 58
Andrew **115** 112
Anna **115** 108
Archibald **59** 258 378-383
Chester **115** 108
Daniel **115** 108
David **51** 493
Duncan **55** 179
E. **59** 212
Eben **115** 108
Electa R. **83** 365
Electa Rosannah **59** 212
Erastus **59** 210-212 **60** 76
    266 **83** 365 **84** 85 86
Erastus Selden **59** 210
Hannah **55** 179 **59** 201
Harriet B. **84** 86
Henry Field **59** 212
Horatio Nelson **115** 108
Israel **115** 108
James **128** 170
Jane (Gregory) **112** 58
Janet **136** 326
John **112** 303 **114** 187
John D. **128** 170
John Hildreth **61** xxxiv
    104 **62** xxxv xl
Lydia **83** 365
Lydia C. **84** 86
Margaret **51** 493
Marie **110** 145
Mary Maria **59** 211
Patty **59** 258 380-383
Polly **59** 378 379
Polly Noyes **115** 108
Sarah **115** 112
Sarah M. **114** 187
Sarah Sophia **115** 112
Susan **114** 187
McCollough *see*
    McCullough
McCollum *see* McCollom
McCOLM Sarah S.
    (Grover) **128** 170
McCOMAS
Louis Emery **62** 113
McCOMB Maccomb
    McCombe
Alexander **65** 56 149
Ann **108** 80
Eleanor **108** 80
George **108** 80
Hugh **62** 301 **108** 79 80

McCOMB *cont'd*
Jane (Burch) **108** 79 80
Jean **108** 80
John **108** 80
Joseph **108** 80
Martha **108** 80 **113** 31
Mary **108** 80
Matilda **108** 80
Parker (Mrs.) **117** 71
Susan **55** 229
Thomas **108** 80
Virgil Juriene **84** 105 190
McComber *see* Macomber
McCOMISA
John S. **91** 328
McCONAGHY
    McConaha
    McConaughy
David **60** 163 **116** 311
Hannah E. **116** 65
John **98** 106
Robert **116** 311
Samuel **116** 311
Thomas **60** 348
William **116** 65 311
Zavier **116** 65
McCONE Edward **69** 214
McCONECHY
Matilda **134** 332
McCONIHE Hugh **61** 379
    129 50
Isaac **51** 493
John **51** 469 470 493
Nancy **61** 379
Sarah **51** 493
McCONNELL McConell
    McConnel
Alexander **68** 29 **111** 214
Burt **81** 41
Caroline Augusta **88** 192
Catherine **125** 260
Clara (Beymer) **124** 191
Clyde **81** 41
Cyrus **86** 446
David Ross **118** 76
Eliza **70** 334
Elizabeth **70** 326 334 **87** 65
Elizabeth Ellen
    (Robinson) **136** 317
Emma **81** 41
Experience (Mills) **115**
    315 **125** 257
F. M. (Mrs.) **112** 323
F. Wright (Mrs.) **113** 161
    114 240 **117** 157
Flora Theresa **81** 41
George E. **118** 73
George Edward **118** 76
Glen **81** 41
H. **76** 50
Helen **124** 191
Helen Sarah **74** 318
Henry C. **136** 317
Henry Lloyd **68** 29
Hugh **107** 170
Ida **81** 41
James Blakeley **95** 16
Jane **74** 318
Jane Sinclair **74** 318
John **74** 318 **91** 263 **112**
    281 **133** 235

McCONNELL *cont'd*
Judith **68** 29
Kitty **62** 170
Leigh **81** 41
Lola **68** lxxv
Louella A. **74** 318
Louisa **116** 115
Lucenia Maria **81** 41
Margaret (McAlloster)
    91 263
Margaret Wallace Brown
    113 161 **117** 157
Maria L. **90** 112
Martha **103** 161
Mary **108** 151
Mary Ann **74** 318
Mary Ann (Crowell)
    108 212
Mary Elizabeth **68** 29
Mary Robinson **136** 317
Minnie **81** 41
Nina Lillian **83** 435 438
Ora May **81** 41
Patrick **62** 170
Peter **115** 315 **125** 257
R. C. **95** 16
Rebecca **121** 159
Rebecca (Emligh) **86** 446
Robert **74** 318 **81** 41
    90 112
Robert Hall **82** 125 237
Samuel **147** 260
Sarah **95** 16
Sarah Ann **74** 318
Sarah Helen **86** 446
Washington J. **68** lxxv
William **70** 334 **81** 41
    108 212
William Oliver **124** 191
Wilson Hall **84** 173
    85 196
McCONWAY
John **61** 267
Mary **61** 267
McCOO M'Coo
David **70** 265
McCOOK
— Gen. **55** 117
Frances Agnes **78** 332
    79 201
Henry Christopher **64** 71
Nannie (Davis) **92** 74
Thomas E. **92** 74
McCOOL Ann **81** 249
Carolyn Jean **99** 46
Charles **99** 46
Frances Ann **81** 249
Frances Ellen **81** 249
James **60** 241
John **60** 241
Mary **60** 241
Mary Jane (Rutzell) **99** 46
Mary Louise **81** 248 249
Robert **81** 249
Samuel **119** 22
McCOON
Abigail **80** 180
Anne **80** 180
John **80** 180
McCORD
Alvin Carr **90** 70

McCORD *cont'd*
Alvin Carr (Mrs.) **82** 125
237 **90** 70 81 142
David Thompson
Watson **117** 231 **120**
150 151 233 310 **121** 75
151 **122** 208 **123** 220
Emily Davis **82** 237
Emily Davis (Rowe)
90 70 142
J. B. **80** 242
Joseph **111** 202
Maria L. (Barton) **107** 207
Maria L. (Underhill)
107 207
Marjorie Carr **90** 70
Mary Jane (Campbell)
90 70
Minnie Dee **80** 242
R. L. **128** 263 267 269
Robert **82** 381 **83** 233
Roy Spencer (Mrs.)
109 130
William Berry **90** 70
Zelma **106** 125
McCORDICK Abigail
(Hickey) **86** 307
Abigail Jane **86** 307
William **86** 307
McCORKLE McCorkall
McCorkell
Archibald **62** 78 **105** 110
Elizabeth S. **119** 316
James **111** 202 205
Nettie Eliza (Hopkins)
105 110
William C. (Mrs.) **119** 316
McCORMICK-
GOODHART
Leander **89** 209
McCORMICK
McCormach
McCormack
—— **136** 90
Adeline M. **74** 296
Andrew T. **73** 221
Anna (Mullens) **97** 50
Annie **75** 255
Annie E. **80** 144
Aurelia Baird **98** 147
Brooks **81** 378
Catherine **116** 186
Catherine (Cody) **108** 271
Charles **67** 19
Charles Deering **81** 378
Chauncey **81** 378
Chauncey (Mrs.) **90** 186
98 145 182 **119** 148
Comfort **133** 281
Cyrus Hall **51** 378 **64** 201
86 113 **87** 60 **90** 306
136 322
Daniel **122** 264
Dennis **100** 141
Donald **90** 180
Dorothy Hale (Dudley)
127 127
Edith **75** xxiii **111** 139
Edith (Rockefeller) **87** 59
60 70 176
Edna Haynes **112** 320

McCORMICK *cont'd*
Edward **68** 152
Eleanor **63** 175 **108** 124
117 159
Eliza **68** 152
Elizabeth **63** 269 **83** 468
97 50
Elizabeth (Carruth) **106**
111 113 114
Elizabeth Day **100** 117
112 238
Elizabeth Heming **78** 125
Ella **71** 72
Elsie **76** 169 **83** 222 **84** 179
85 178 **86** 214 **87** 174
188 **88** 185 **89** 124 125
145 146 **90** 150 151 **91**
141 156-158 **92** 101 160-
162 **93** 151-153 **94** 153
154 **95** 160 161 **96** 173
175 **97** 171 172 **98** 139
160-162-164 **100** 102
105 125 126 **101** 139 140
102 62 138 139 **103** 135
136 **104** 158 159 **105**
123 142 143 **106** 120 140
107 128 146 147 **108**
128 148 149 **109** 124 143
144 **110** 138 139 **111**
143 **112** 71 136 223 242
315 **113** 62 150 234 294
114 71 143 229 310 **115**
69 147-149 230 314 **116**
74 146 147 228 307 **117**
74 148 152 153 232 312
118 70 162 163 246 324
119 72 152 153 236 312
120 56 152 153 233 310
121 75 152 **122** 208 **123**
221 277
Emily Charlotte **67** 19
Genevieve (Cater)
134 171
George **108** 271
George Chalmers **67** 384
68 xxxii
Grisella **120** 156
Harold Fowler **87** 60
106 111
Harold Fowler (Mrs.) **75**
ix xxiii
James **93** 319 **145** 49
James M. **97** 50
John **118** 243
John Gilchrist **54** 458
John Rockefeller **87** 60
John Steele **118** 327
John W. **92** 38
Leander James **51** 379 381
106 111
Lydia A. **80** 144
Mamie **126** 154
Margaret Rachel **72** 310
Margaret Rose **68** 152
Marion **81** 378
Marion (Deering) **90** 186
98 182
Mary L. **100** 211
Mathilde **87** 60
Minnie **82** 405
Muriel **87** 60

McCORMICK *cont'd*
Nancy Maria (Fowler)
136 322
Nettie (Fowler) **87** 60
Olivia Cox **94** 400
Phebe A. **80** 144
Raymond Louis **134** 171
Robert **52** 486 **89** 209
Robert Hall **59** 421 **60**
xxxvi **79** 104 202 **112**
238
Roger **90** 186 **91** 140
Roger Simon **81** 378
Ruby **96** 160
Ruth A. **80** 144
Sarah Bessie **92** 38
Thomas **78** 125 **106** 111
W. S. **128** 93
William C. **80** 144
William H. **80** 144
William Lee **112** 320
McCORNACK
David C. **120** 157
McCORNSTINE
Rachel M. **79** 37
McCORRIE McCory
Andrew **87** 136
Anna (Chase) **87** 136
Mary Ann **127** 238 239
McCOSH
James **76** lxxxiii
McCOSKRY
James **64** 377
McCOTTER A. **106** 108
Ann **116** 206
Charles T. **64** 304
Dennis **116** 206
Fred W. **116** 65
George F. **116** 65
Grace (Maynord) **116** 65
Hugh **106** 108
Judson W. **116** 65
Lydia **106** 108
Nelson **106** 108
Sarah (Baker) **116** 65
Smith **116** 206
Thomas **116** 206
William **116** 65
Workman **116** 65
McCOULL Jennie
Frances **79** 142
John William **79** 142
McCOUN —— **60** 104
McCOURTIE
John **68** 304
William Herbert Lee **68**
304 **69** xxxii **71** 94
McCOWN Francis **112** 17
McCOY M'Coy MacCoy
McCoye
—— **74** 93
Abigail **67** 372
Amelia Bridgett **95** 168
Amy **117** 294
Catherine **113** 324 **114** 187
Celenda A. **68** 334
Charles **117** 294
Charlotte **64** lx
Clara **84** 126
Daniel **125** 214
Daniel Allen **97** 198

McCOY *cont'd*
Edna E. **118** 106 107
Edward **67** 372
Eliza **126** 204
Elizabeth **81** 36 **97** 198
Elizabeth (Furber)
  125 214
Elizabeth J. **69** 322
Emeline **114** 187
Francis **100** 297
Frank R. **117** 294
George H. **83** 435 **84** 18
George Madison **107** 134
Gilbert **115** 45
Harry Bacon **110** 319
Henry Bacon **114** 155
Ida M. (Reynolds) **83** 435
  84 18
Isaac **68** 334
Isaac H. **68** 334
Isabella **105** 302
James **97** 207 **111** 206
  112 209
Jane **104** 263
Janet **68** 156
Jean Emeline **103** 119
Jeannette (Snowden) **83**
  435 **84** 20
John **60** 163 **69** 322 **81** 392
  84 126 **100** 299 **101** 274
  112 209
John Ernest (Mrs.)
  104 144
Joseph **69** 322
Kitty **113** 324
Mabel Lee **105** 319
Margaret **74** 93 **91** 187
Mary **64** lx **67** 373 **72** 292
  101 274 **115** 40
Mary (Lord) **84** 126
Mary (Mills) **100** 297
Mary E. **101** 215
Mary Helen **69** 322
Matilda **118** 238
Merrill Hoerner (Mrs.)
  87 174
Nehemiah **67** 373
Nettie Day (Foskett)
  87 174
Patience (Colten) **100** 299
Phebe **81** 392 **107** 63
Phebe (Gray) **104** 62
Phebe Catherine **81** 392
Priscilla **73** 141
Rachel **94** 27
Rebecca **126** 205
Rosanna **108** 305
Sally (Briggs) **126** 212
Samuel **64** lx
Samuel Duff **93** 305
Sarah **128** 175 268
Susanna **67** 372
Thomas **114** 187
Thomas H. **83** 435 **84** 20
Walter **126** 212
William **104** 62 **112** 209
  114 187 **128** 223
William F. **117** 292
William J. **117** 292

McCRACKEN
McCrackan
McCrackin McCraken
—— **54** 249 **140** 296
Archibald **116** 26
Asa **58** 372
Betsey **58** 372
Charlotte (Little) **116** 27
Charlotte Barton **116** 26
Dorothy **83** 161
Electa Johnston **70** xxxvii
Francis (Mrs.) **124** 78
George E. **104** 221 317 **106**
  168 290 **107** 49 111 202
  292 **108** 128 155 **110**
  185 258 **111** 5 74 84 168
  245 **112** 65 119 154 235
  317 **113** 197 267 **116** 26
  82 237 239 **117** 57 106
  195 **121** 234 **122** 36 **124**
  66 **125** 5 6 **147** 242 243
  245-248 251 254 **148** 324
Henry Noble **112** 163
Hopkins **79** 302 405
James **83** 161
Jane **103** 139
Jennie **77** 184
John **79** 166 **80** 58 **81** 51
  148 32
John Wesley **116** 26
Joseph **57** 116
Joseph Hill (Mrs.) **109** 130
Judith (Skidmore) **148** 32
Leroy **116** 27
Mary **80** 58
Nancy **79** 166 302
Samuel **58** 372
Sarah **80** 58 **81** 51
William **79** 403 **80** 58 61
McCRADY —— **53** 134
Edward **52** 88
George **77** 230
Grace Bell (Billings) **94** 49
John Cranson **94** 49
Louisa De Berniere **91** 76
Louisa Rebecca (Lane)
  91 76
McCraken *see* McCracken
McCRANNEY
Mackranney
McCraney
Benjamin **61** 397
Deborah (Gifford)
  135 317
John **135** 317
Mary **61** 308 397
Rachel **61** 397
Ruth **61** 397
Timothy **61** 397
William **61** 308 397
McCRARY Benjamin
  William (Mrs.) **108** 134
John **101** 207
Logan **85** 97
Mahala (Ayres) **85** 97
Mary **85** 97
Sally (Huntley) **101** 207
Susanna Marian **59** 416
McCRATE
Ann S. **72** 274
John D. **72** 274

McCRATE *cont'd*
Sarah **72** 274
Sukey (Dennis) **84** 424
Susan S. **72** 274
Susanna **72** 274
Thomas **72** 274 **84** 424
McCRAY McCrae McCrea
—— **57** 93
— Dr. **55** 287 **56** 350
Alice **113** 82
Annie **128** 262
Aubine **101** 126
Catherine **128** 203
Edwin **55** 285
Eleazer **55** 285 287 **56** 351
  59 99 **60** 199 **62** 296
Eunice **56** 351 **59** 99
  60 199
Farguire **73** 140
Fred Wilton **95** 147
George **61** 349
Grant **113** 82
Isaac **57** 93
James **60** 161
John **59** 98 414 **60** 161 204
  66 31 **83** 365 **128** 263
Lucy **66** 109
Margaret (Simpkins)
  113 82
Mary **111** 139
Philander **113** 82
Polly **59** 98
Robert **60** 162
Robinson **113** 82
Roxanna **57** 93
Sally **55** 285
Sarah **57** 93
William **55** 287
McCREADY McCreedy
Alexander **91** 328
Anna **94** 49
Anthony **94** 49
Belva **96** 160
Dorothy Louise **94** 84
James Plunkett **82** 267
Jessie Edith **82** 267
Katharine **94** 49
Louise May **82** 219
Mary Augusta Kemp
  94 84
Rachel (Buell) **94** 49
Robert **94** 84
Robert Ashton **94** 84
Robert Ashton (Mrs.) **82**
  219 **94** 79 84 141
Susan **82** 267
McCREARY McCreerey
McCreery
Alexander **124** 78
Donald Chalmers (Mrs.)
  95 147
Eunice (Armstrong)
  124 78
Gilbert B. **128** 177
John **116** 76
Julia A. (Calkins) **128** 177
Julia Blanche **113** 225
Laura **124** 78
Madelon **78** 205
Marjorie **116** 76
Martha **128** 177

McCREARY cont'd
Robert Samuel (Mrs.)
  78 108 205
William **112** 17 **128** 177
McCREE William **117** 16
McCREEDY
Belva **96** 160
McCreerey *see* McCreary
McCreery *see* McCreary
McCREKY
Samuel **64** 256
McCRILLIS McCreles
  McCrellis McCrellos
  McCrielles McCrullis
—— **54** 460
Amanda **67** 274
Anna **82** 330
Benjamin **67** 274
Carrie **100** 212
Daniel **63** 178 **74** 259
  82 330
Eleanor **73** 255 256
Elizabeth **81** 150 252
George W. **52** 148 385
Gertie May **100** 212
Hannah **73** 255 **74** 264
  147 258
John K. **147** 258
Herbert O. **65** 192
Hiram **67** 274
James **73** 256
Jane **73** 255
John **63** 177 **65** 192 **73** 255
  74 259 **90** 53 **95** 332
John P. **73** 256
Lavina (Shapleigh)
  95 332
Lydia **63** 177 **74** 259
Mary **73** 255 **74** 251 **123** 73
Mary Sophia **82** 353
Nancy A. **67** 274
Nelson **100** 212
Polly **63** 178 **74** 259
Rebecca **73** 255
Robert **73** 256
Sally B. **124** 61
Sarah **73** 255
Sarah (Palmer) **132** 244
Sophia S. (Bacon) **90** 53
Thomas **60** 348
Tonie **100** 212
William **65** 192 **73** 255 256
  132 244
William H. **121** 178 179
McCROGGE Margaret
  (Webster) **100** 302
William **100** 302
McCromb *see* McCrum
McCRONE
Rebecca **80** 169
Sally P. **80** 169
William **80** 169
McCRORY McRorie
  Mcrory
Alice **111** 129
Calvin **111** 129
Emily **111** 129
G. W. **113** 324
James **114** 193
James T. **128** 96 174 175
  262

McCRORY cont'd
Peter **111** 129
Warren **111** 129
McCROSKEY —— **56** 210
Ann (Montgomery)
  112 19
Betty M. **103** 318
James Harrison (Mrs.)
  104 144
John **103** 318 **112** 17
McCROY Robert **66** 307
McCrullis *see* McCrillis
McCRUM McCromb
Elizabeth **100** 235 239
Ephraim Banks **120** 76
George **100** 239
James **62** 79
Joseph **100** 235
Katharine **100** 235
Mary **107** 115
Sarah **62** 79 **100** 239
McCRUMMIN
Donald **117** 16
McCUE John **62** 171
John N. **67** 384
John Nolley **68** xxxii
McCUEN Charles
  Nicholas **76** 95
Delbert **148** 275
Elizabeth Putnam **76** 95
McCUGE Mary **78** 302
McCULLEN
Ann **125** 214
Martha **76** 93
Sarah Coe **71** lxvii
McCULLISTER
Deliverance (Rich)
  83 275
Mary (Flood) **83** 275
McCULLOCH
  McCullock
  MacCulluch
  McCollough
  McCulloh - *see also*
  McCullough
—— **52** 151
Adam **134** 276
Alexander **97** 264
Alice Rebecca **81** 218 **110**
  308 **111** 60
Alice Rebecca (Wilson)
  110 308
Ann **128** 238 311
Ann Greenough (Brown)
  97 264
Barbara **65** 245
Ben **64** 67
Emeline **100** 248 **102** 65
George **110** 308
Henry **141** 15
Hugh **53** 153 **63** 239 **134**
  276 281 **135** 16
Isabella **109** 221
Isabelle **114** 186
James **73** 256
John **110** 308
John Lewis **110** 308
Lucy **73** 256
Margaret **81** 194
Maria (Weaver) **110** 308
Mary **62** 253

McCULLOCH cont'd
Otis **73** 256
Robert **110** 80 **117** 16
Sally **73** 256
Sarah **73** 256 **77** 215
Sophia **73** 256
Temperance **73** 256
Thomas **125** 116
William **65** 245
McCullom *see* McCollom
McCULLOUGH *see also*
  McCulloch
—— **101** 108 **135** 251
— Mrs. **60** 164
Abiel **107** 275 **108** 57
Abiel (Perkins) **108** 188
Adam **107** 195 197-201
  269 273 **108** 57 **132** 269
Agnes **122** 5 15
Alexander **60** 164 **107** 199
Andrew **60** 164
Anna (Gager) **101** 108
Catherine **90** 109
Clare **103** 69
Eliza Jane **90** 114
Elizabeth **75** lviii **107** 198
  108 189
Emeline **100** 248 **102** 65
Frank (Mrs.) **83** 122 233
Frisby Henderson **99** 41
George **60** 164
Hall Park **69** xxxv **76** xx
  90 128
Hers **60** 27
Hugh **72** liv **107** 197 275
  108 57 188
Isabel **107** 269
Isabella **108** 190 **132** 269
Jean **60** 164
John **61** 349 **90** 109
Kate **69** 168
Kendrick **100** 112
Louisa **107** 194 195 197-
  201 269 273 **108** 57
Louisa (Brown) **132** 269
Margaret **107** 195
Patrick **61** 136
Roderic **107** 201
Sally **61** 137
Thomas **108** 57
William **90** 109
McCULLY
George **64** 301
Mary **126** 218
Pamelia **110** 141
McCUNE Allen **117** 52
Amy Edna (Ramey)
  101 335
Anna **117** 52
Betsey **117** 52
Catherine Elizabeth (Fitz-
  Randolph) **98** 234
Eliza **117** 52
Elizabeth **72** 305
Elizabeth Claridge **79** 225
Emma **117** 52
Esther **72** 305
James **117** 52
Jane **101** 335
Joseph King **115** 159
Lewis O. (Mrs.) **101** 335

McCUNE *cont'd*
    Martin **117** 52
    Matthew **117** 52
    Nelson **117** 52
    Polly **117** 52
    Robert **72** 305 **101** 335
    S. **98** 234
    Samuel **117** 52
    Susan **117** 52
McCUNN John **65** 117
    Matthew **63** 141
McCURDY Maccurdy
    —— **55** 365
    Abiel **73** 166
    Alexander **77** 204 **80** 110
        123 15
    Alexander Lynde **80** 110
    Alice **103** 121
    Ann **73** xxxvi
    Anna **60** 213
    Anne **77** 204
    Archibald **123** 204
    Betsey **104** 96
    Calvin **73** 166
    Charles **104** 96
    Charles J. **77** 204
    Charles Johnson **55** 364
        73 xxxvi
    Elizabeth **56** 255 **77** 212
    Eveline Griggs **113** 231
    Evelyn **55** 364 **73** xxix
        xxxvi
    George S. **104** 96
    Gertrude Griffin **80** 110
    Gertrude Mercer **77** xcix
    Hannah **79** 45
    Hannah Keen (Yard)
        105 48
    Hannah M. (Doane)
        123 204
    Horace Winslow **119** 75
    Ira **104** 96
    Isaac **73** 166
    Isabel **78** 204
    J. L. **104** 96
    James **73** 166 **90** 87
        125 259
    James Winslow **119** 75
    Jesse **104** 96
    John **60** 213 **73** xxxvi 166
        77 204 212 **137** 361
    John E. **73** 181
    Jonathan **104** 96
    Josephine **77** 204
    Josephine Lord **80** 110
    Julia A. Hill **104** 96
    Luther **73** 166 181
    Lynde **77** 204
    Margaret **125** 115
    Mary **62** 31 **73** 166 **77** 204
    Mary E. **104** 96
    Matilda **104** 96
    Nancy (Archibald)
        125 199
    Neil Barclay **119** 75
    Ophelia **73** 181
    P. M. **104** 96
    Pamela **73** 184
    Patrick **73** xxxvi
    Pliny Merrick **104** 96
    Richard **73** xxxvi **77** 204

McCURDY *cont'd*
        137 361
    Robert K. **105** 48
    Rosanna **73** 166
    Samuel **56** 255 **105** 209
    Sarah **125** 199
    Sarah (Harris) **137** 361
    Sarah (Watts) **137** 361
    Sarah Ann **73** xxxvi
        77 204
    Ursula **77** 204
    William **65** 150 **73** 166
McCURLEY
    Hugh **78** 309
McCURRY McCurrie
    Andrew **127** 146
    Mahala **122** 296 299
    William Earle (Mrs.)
        108 134
McCusick *see* McKusick
McCUTCHEON McCutchen
    Elizabeth **112** 18
    Franklin **89** 318
    Hugh **118** 42 43 46 47
        125 258
    James **81** 151
    Jane (Hemloe) **125** 258
    Mary Abbie (Stone)
        89 318
    Mary B. **98** 73
    Mary Barr **88** 393
    Nancy **81** 151
    Nora **89** 318
    Robert **111** 208
    Thomas **112** 303
    William **111** 208
McDADE James **66** 31
    Owen **60** 162
McDALE Anna **115** 129
    John **60** 243
McDanald *see* McDonald
McDANIEL MacDaniel
        MacDaniels
        Mackdaniel McDaniels
        —— **55** 271 **72** 175 **99** 280
        101 246 **102** 34 **103** 196
        136 39
    — Capt. **101** 246
    Abigail **68** 222
    Albert A. **68** 99
    Alexander **64** 226
    Allen **73** 278
    Ann **100** 25 143 238 302
    Archibald **73** 224
    Betty **69** 245
    Catherine **68** 229 **73** 266
    Catherine (Bowldin)
        100 299
    Cephas **73** 222
    Charles **68** 99
    Daniel **55** 141 **91** 68
    Dorothy **99** 117
    Eleanor Jeannette **73** 230
    Eliphalet **147** 186
    Elizabeth **73** 226 271 **99**
        206 282 285 **100** 140 143
        101 55 276
    Elizabeth (Burrell)
        100 301
    Foster **68** 93
    Freelove **57** 66

McDANIEL *cont'd*
    Henry **118** 43 51 53
    Hugh **57** 389 **58** 64 68 **84**
        150 264 265 **100** 25 138
        102 29 37
    Isaac **99** 206 285 **100** 140
        143 301 **101** 55
    J. **91** 123
    Jacob **91** 28 **97** 231 **99** 285
    James **55** 177 **70** 202 **111**
        39 **115** 224 **118** 43 51 52
        54 56
    Jane (Sewall) **147** 76 186
    Janephen **73** 139
    John **68** 222 226 229 231 **75**
        311 **88** 280 **98** 103 106
        100 238 299 **102** 32 **118**
        53 56 **136** 39 **137** 8
    Joseph **68** 231
    Laura **82** 436
    Lavinia **119** 143
    Leney **73** 231
    Lucina **115** 122
    Martin N. **73** 264
    Mary **73** 224 **99** 282
        100 238
    Mary (Sutton) **91** 68
    Mary (Wood) **100** 299
    Mary Elizabeth **68** 99
    Nancy **70** 202 **84** 205
    Paul **97** 368
    Pelatiah **75** 311
    Peter **59** 193
    Phebe **69** 245
    Richard **98** 103 105
    Ruth **55** 177
    Sally **70** 202
    Sally E. (Simpson) **88** 280
    Sarah **68** 99 **73** 152 262
        107 188
    Sarah Ann **70** 202
    Sarah H. **68** 93
    Stephen **84** 466
    Sukey **118** 154 240 242
    Susan **117** 229
    Susanna **75** 311 **119** 67
    Thomas **118** 43 51
    Timothy **58** 68 **99** 206
        280 282 285 **100** 140
        101 55 276 **103** 190
    Una Ione **98** 146
    William **73** 138 **118** 43 46-
        49 51
McDanold *see* McDonald
McDarmee *see* McDermott
McDAVIE Peter **61** 42
McDAVITT Caroline
        (Hanson) **87** 67
    Clarence G. (Mrs.) **82** 350
    Edith **82** 350
    Mildred **117** 125
    Mina Percelia **87** 67
    William H. **87** 67
McDERMOTT
        MacDermott
        McDarmeed
        McDermaid
        McDermond
        McDermont
        McDiarmid
    Andrew **126** 142

McDERMOTT *cont'd*
Carrie R. **91** 385
Donald Kenneth (Mrs.)
  96 383
Edward **61** 270
Elizabeth K. (Ames)
  126 142
Frank Paine **59** xlvii
Jane **86** 306
Janet Campbell **85** 222
John **61** 265
John Francis **103** 320
Margaret **125** 259
Marjorie Ruth
  Dallhousie (Armitage)
  96 383
Mary **89** 32 **93** 218
Mary (Faithen) **125** 290
Mary Ellen **92** 223
May Ann **77** 56
Ronald **118** 43 47 52
  125 259
William **92** 223 **125** 290
McDEVITT
Mary **97** 123
William **97** 123
McDiarmid *see* McDermott
McDIVITT
B. Olive **120** 157
James **62** 81
Ruth K. **120** 157
Ruth Wright **120** 157
Thomas B. (Mrs.) **120** 157
McDOLE Anna **70** 124
Elizabeth Forestine
  94 139
Frances B. (Bowers)
  103 47
James **103** 47
Matthew **61** 138
Rosannah **121** 319
T. **61** 138
William **121** 319
McDONALD M'Donald
  MacDonald McDanald
  McDanold
—— **60** xxiv **98** 8 **100** 85
  122 269 **124** 78 **147** 226
A. B. **123** 110
A. R. **128** 177
Aaron Burt **80** 47
Abigail **128** 277 278
Abner **142** 35
Adelaide **80** 47
Adolphus Cranston
  80 46
Agnes (McNutt) **128** 29
Albion H. **83** 435 **84** 20
Alex **111** 212
Alexander **52** 312 **61** 268
  62 301 **73** 104 **108** 318
  111 202 **113** 92 94 **116**
  288 **118** 49 56
Alexander Niel **125** 194
Alfred **83** 428 435
Allan Lane **96** 32
Ambia Harris **89** 264
  101 119
Angus **62** 301 **73** xxxv
  118 43 48 51 52 **125** 257
  259

McDONALD *cont'd*
Anna **76** 22
Anna (Stinson) **83** 435
  84 20
Anne **125** 116 121
Anne Alexander **99** 250
Annie **83** 435 437
Archibald **84** 103
Arlene (Emmons) **96** 32
Arthur D. **91** 328
Belle Godman **80** 47
Benjamin **87** 242
Bertha (Evans) **83** 428 435
Bessie **83** 232
Betsey **87** 108 **111** 44 117
  125 195
Betty **112** 214
Burns **116** 288
Catherine **93** 190 **102** 303
  125 121 197 **128** 177
Catherine (Fitz-
  Randolph) **98** 232
Catherine (McGillivray)
  125 258
Cecilia Frances **76** 22
Charles **80** 47
Charlotte (Carver) **87** 7
  88 328 **109** 7
Christina **82** 272
Clara (Cooke) **84** 104
Clarissa Evelina **85** 292
Clarissa Saville (Rising)
  85 292
Daniel **112** 214
David **74** 318 **111** 44 **118**
  43 52 57 **123** 110
David Archibald **125** 195
David Ashley **109** 130
Deborah (Bulyea) **123** 107
Delea **133** 72
Delos G. **120** 81
Donald **100** 236 **145** 255
Dorcas **87** 124 **142** 35
Dorothy (Best) **96** 32
Dorothy Sloan (Allen)
  94 139
Drusilla **127** 51 **128** 29
Drusilla (Drew) **127** 51
Duncan **63** 25 **73** 104
  125 256
Duncan Cameron **80** 36
Effie **81** 252
Eleanor **125** 197 259
Eleanor (Bancroft) **96** 329
Eliza (Durrell) **133** 219
Eliza A. (Berry) **88** 341
Elizabeth **74** 264 **111** 44
  125 199 258 **127** 51 **133**
  72
Elizabeth (Elliot) **125** 195
Elizabeth (McDonald)
  125 199
Elizabeth Blandy
  (Shapleigh) **96** 32
Elizabeth Elliot
  (Archibald) **125** 194
  196-198 258
Elizabeth H. (Miller)
  84 103
Elizabeth Wood **128** 277
Elspeth **84** 294 **127** 51

McDONALD *cont'd*
Emaline **116** 288
Emma **85** 292
Ethel I. **83** 431 435
Ethel Janet **104** 144
Experience **116** 288
Experience (Ford) (Snow)
  116 288
F. B. **65** 118
Fanny (Snead) **96** 32
Flora **64** 97 **84** 104 **86** 194
Florence Isabelle (Julliard)
  92 188
Frances **81** 260
Francis **88** 341
George W. **91** 328
Gladys **121** 156
Gladys Emma **107** 132
Grace Ann (Baker) **96** 32
Grace E. **110** 101
Hannah **103** 46
Harriet (Snell) **98** 197
Harriet Alice **85** 292
Harry Peake **96** 32
Harry T. (Mrs.) **118** 73 80
  121 156
Henrietta **75** 268
Horatio **118** 52
Hugh **88** 339 **115** 315 **118**
  41 43 44 47 49 52-54 56-
  58 **125** 194 195 258
Humphrey **127** 51 **128** 29
Isaac **111** 44
Isaac Archibald **125** 199
Isabel **100** 236
Isabella **127** 51
Isabella (McKay) **116** 288
James **52** 312 **73** 104 **77**
  239 **84** 103 **87** 7 **88** 328
  111 39 44 **112** 214 **118**
  52 **125** 259 **127** 51
James Allan **75** xxv 65
  84 103 104 107 195
James Garfield (Mrs.)
  104 144
James H. **118** 43 52
James Hugh **125** 199
James Ranald **125** 197
James S. **73** 104
Jane **111** 44 118 **125** 194
  257
Janett **102** 313
Jeanette C. **115** 206
Jemima (Belyea) **123** 110
Jennie **116** 61
Jenny **125** 116
Jessie Louise **79** 17
Joan **115** 211 212
Joan (Young) **112** 214
Joanna (Rounds) **115** 65
John **64** 107 **69** 263 **76** 22
  80 46 **81** 252 **85** 292 **87**
  122 **99** 200 **111** 206 **115**
  65 **118** 49 50 52 **125** 258
  259 **128** 179 **142** 35 **145**
  45
John Adolphus **80** 46
John Angus **125** 196
John Carlisle (Mrs.)
  94 139
Joseph **98** 192 197 252

McDONALD *cont'd*
Kate **69** 263 **133** 72
Kenneth **118** 50 52 59
Kenneth A. **96** 329
L. D. **133** 219
Lauchlan **90** 87
Laura E. (Harris) **115** 293
Laura Field **74** 318
Laurence Emmons **96** 32
Lelia Ramsey **111** 201
  210 211
Lemuel **127** 51
Lewis **71** 45
Lillian **80** 46
Lillian (Billings) **98** 8
Lora Elizabeth **80** 47
Loraine Dow **108** 132
Lucinda (Angell) **147** 226
Lucy **80** 47
Lucy A. **80** 46
Luzetta **80** 47
Lydia **99** 200 **102** 240
  123 110
M. J. Harden **116** 117
Manuel N. **115** 293
Margaret **81** 252 **125** 197
  198 258
Margaret (McLean)
  125 195
Maria (Carter) **88** 339
Marie Thayer **80** 36
Marion **116** 288
Mark Lindsay (Mrs.)
  92 188
Martha **125** 198
Martha (Fisher) **125** 116
  119
Martha (Tye) **85** 292
Martha Ann **125** 197
Martha J. **89** 205
Martha Laura **85** 292
Mary **99** 200 **100** 236 **111**
  50 **125** 119 256 **127** 51
  130 314
Mary Alastair **96** 32
Mary Ellie **116** 288
Mary Elmore (Coumans)
  116 288
Mary J. **79** 145
Mary Maria **85** 218
Mary N. **121** 310 **122** 230
Mary Philomel **80** 47
Mary Roxanna **85** 292
Mary S. **100** 337
Matthew Archibald
  125 199
Maud Isabel **75** xxvi
Maud Mabel **75** 65
Michael **64** 220 **112** 214
Michael Todd **128** 278
Moriah **116** 288
Nancy **128** 266
Nancy (Palmer) **136** 271
Nancy Agnes **98** 331
Naomi Gae **92** 364
Niel **125** 195 258
Pamilla (Chase) (Smith)
  87 242
Paul **105** 282
Pelatiah **142** 34
Perry **127** 160

McDONALD *cont'd*
Peter **62** 301
Phebe Ann **80** 46
Philip **62** 252
Philomela **80** 46
Polly **111** 44
Samuel **111** 206
Sarah **101** 324 **111** 44 **115**
  293 **125** 198
Sarah E. **116** 58
Sibyl **111** 44
Soirle **117** 16
Solomon **88** 304
Sophronia J. (Bull)
  115 293
Susan **133** 72 **142** 35
Susan M. **125** 291
Terence **62** 243
Theophilus **98** 232
Thomas **75** 268
Udolpho Snead **96** 32
Waldron Shapleigh **96** 32
William **62** 93 **85** 292
  111 44 **113** 288 **115** 293
  125 197
William G. **115** 293
William Thompson
  125 197
William Wallace **116** 288
McDONNELL
  MacDonell
  MacDonnel
  MacDonnell McDonel
  McDonnal McDonnel
  Meckdonol
— Mr. **62** 355
— Mrs. **71** 50
Andrew **77** 316
Daniel **143** 260
Frederick Cook **108** 134
Hope (Pierce) **116** 256
James **143** 257
John **64** 342 **75** 110 111 113
  121 **76** 257 **112** 203 **116**
  256
Joseph **75** 113
Margaret **116** 187
Mary **75** 121
Michael **148** 112
Mildred A. **121** 77
Nanita Callier **84** 218
Patrick **60** 163
Robert **75** 111
Robert Walker **84** 218
Susanna **75** 110 111 113
  121
Tabitha (Williams) **84** 218
Theresa **82** 405
William **91** 328
McDONOUGH
  McDonogh
  McDonogher
—— **55** 53 **61** 270 **110** 52
  140 233
Beatrice (Tripp) **83** 435
  84 21
Catherine **60** 160
Charles **86** 363 **139** 207
Charles J. **83** 435 **84** 21
Dorcas **79** 276
Gladys May **86** 363

McDONOUGH *cont'd*
Hugh **60** 160
James **60** 160 **61** 270
John Patrick **107** 134
  120 147
Julia Ann **100** 289
Lloyd Charles **86** 363
Lucy Ann **79** 163
Mabel (Cole) **86** 363
Morris James **73** 151
Patrick **61** 269
Richard **60** 160
Rodney **54** 372 **55** xxix
  xxxv **56** xxx 100 **63** 388
  64 xxxi
Thomas **54** 372 **56** 100 **60**
  112 160 **63** 388 **78** 73 **79**
  163 **104** 80 **140** 233
McDouell *see* McDowell
McDOUGAL
  MacDougall
  McDougald
  McDougall McDugel
— Gen. **141** 14
— Mrs. **113** 10
Alan Nicholson **90** 347
Alex **125** 257
Alexander **73** 143 **102** 222
Augusta Ann **133** 322
Carrie E. (Day) **111** 130
Catherine **134** 54
D. S. (Mr.) **125** 180
Daniel **73** 256 **102** 222
  110 160
Donald **107** 251 **109** 238
Duncan **110** 160 **126** 21
Elizabeth **73** 256 **102** 222
Eva (Sommer) **110** 160
George **91** 328
George S. **90** 347
Gilbert Donald (Mrs.)
  104 144
Grissell **112** 294
James **128** 97
James B. **68** 95
Jane **63** 271 **68** 95 **102** 222
John **73** 256 **111** 138 **112**
  294 **126** 21
Katharine **68** 121 **111** 138
Margaret **105** 108
Margaret A. (Jewell)
  128 97
Mary **54** lxxii **73** 256
  102 222
Mary Elizabeth **99** 148
Mary Elizabeth (Hannum)
  90 347
Moses **128** 97
Nancy **85** 449 **125** 122 247
  257
Nancy (Weaver) **110** 160
Patrick **113** 4 10 13
Peter **113** 11
Rachel **102** 222
Richard (Mrs.) **119** 159
Robert **90** 347 **109** 238
Sally (Smith) **125** 180
  126 21
Sarah **86** 312
Sarah (Palick) **128** 97
T. F. **92** 338

McDowall *see* McDowell
McDOWE Aldus **87** 220
McDOWELL MacDowal
    MacDowell McDouell
    McDowall McDowle
    —— **53** 457 **60** 104
  — Lieut. **111** 213
  Agatha Ann **89** 91
  Alexander **54** 166 **116** 111
    136 54
  Angus **87** 138
  Ann **73** 225
  Anna Margaret **90** 187
  Charles **112** 92
  Edna **99** 332
  Edward Alexander **62** 213
    136 322 331
  Elizabeth **73** 152 **94** 42
    100 133
  Elizabeth (Mann) **125** 216
  Elizabeth A. **115** 201
  Erasmus **77** 143
  Evelina Louisa **77** 143
  Grace (Greenlee)
    (Bowman) **112** 92
  Hiram **120** 319 **132** 326
  Hugh **112** 302
  James **112** 17
  John **79** 54 **125** 216
  Margaret **83** 482
  Marian Griswold
    (Nevins) **136** 322 331
  Mary **90** 366
  Mary Elizabeth **112** 92
  Mercy (Chase) **87** 138
  Nora B. **92** 338
  Rebecca **114** 188
  Rebecca (Wilson) **114** 188
  Richard **116** 65
  Rosannah **121** 319
  Sally **132** 326
  Samuel **73** 261 **112** 17
  Sarah **120** 319
  Sarah Jane **120** 319
    132 326
  William **73** 149 **100** 133
    116 63 65 **121** 319
  Zebulon **90** 366
McDOWLAND
  Jerusha **75** 178
  Thomas **75** 178
McDowle *see* McDowell
McDUFFEE McDuffie
  —— **53** 134 **57** 337
  Abigail **69** 258 **80** 309
    123 69
  Abigail (Young) **123** 69
  Alice Longworth **86** 306
  Andrew J. **80** 309
  Betty (Knock) **123** 69
  C. W. L. **86** 306
  Catherine (Doremus)
    125 53
  Daniel **83** 150 152 **123** 69
  David **123** 69
  Frank P. **69** 258
  Franklin **63** lxi **64** 232
    67 275 348 **80** 309 **123**
    69
  George **123** 69
  Hannah **65** 219 **94** 392

McDUFFEE *cont'd*
  Hannah Edna Isabelle
    69 258
  Harriet **68** 382
  Huldah (Tibbetts) **100** 38
  Ida (Covert) **125** 53
  Isaac **123** 69
  James **69** 258
  Joanna **65** 310
  John **65** 219 310 **80** 309
    88 330 **94** 392 **123** 69
    125 53
  John Randolph **68** 382
  Julia Ann **68** 382
  Luther **123** 69
  Lydia **123** 69
  Mary **79** 129 **80** 309
  Mary Ann (Varnum)
    88 330
  Mary Frances
    (Lautenschlager)
    125 53
  Mortimer **125** 53
  Nancy **123** 69
  Polly **123** 69
  Sally **123** 69
  Samuel **100** 38
  Tommy **123** 69
McDugel *see* McDougal
McDUGG
  Margaret **104** 120
McDUGGART M'Duggart
  —— **70** 265
McEACHERN McEachren
  Angus **118** 243
  Archibald **118** 243
  Finlay **56** xlii
  Hugh **118** 243
  Margaret **82** 279
McEAUGHIN
  Ann **99** 119 121
  David **99** 119 121
  Sarah **99** 119
McELDERRY
  Horatio C. **73** 271
  Mary **73** 225
  Patrick **73** 150
McELERY Sally (Chenay)
    125 218
McELHANEY McElhany
  James O. **91** 328
  John **125** 130
McELHINNEY
  George W. **101** 33
  Mary L. (Annas) **101** 33
McElleroy *see* McElroy
McEllroy *see* McElroy
McELRATH McElreath
  Elsie Anne (Alden)
    136 330
  John Edgar **136** 330
  Katharine **136** 330
  Walter **97** 98
McELROY McElleroy
  McEllroy McIlroy
  Mckleroy
  —— **124** 78
  Alice **112** 283
  Anne **74** 47
  Catherine **125** 221
  Charles **122** 167 **126** 142

McELROY *cont'd*
  Clarriet **80** 237
  Elbridge G. **60** 40
  Elizabeth **61** 42
  Elizabeth Jane (Church)
    122 161 167
  Ella March **80** 237
  James **61** 42 **85** 450
  John **74** 183 **77** 230 **80** 237
    112 283
  Lyda **122** 167
  Martha **74** 183
  Mary C. **125** 294
  Peter **61** 42
  Robert **125** 218 **140** 165
  Roxie Elizabeth **122** 167
  Sarah (Drew) **126** 142
  William H. **55** 125
McELVAIN Mary **55** 64
McELVINE Macelvine
  Helen **94** 393
McELWAIN
  Macclewain
  Macklewain
  Anna (Spear) **113** 224
  Betsey **75** 35
  Daniel **75** 35
  David **57** 293 294
  Edgar Marshall (Mrs.)
    105 128
  Frances **113** 224
  George **57** 292
  Hannah (Melvin) **113** 224
  Ida Eloise **68** xxxiv **72**
    xxxi liii
  James **72** liii **113** 224
  James Franklin **63** xxxiii
    93 138 **113** 60 224
  Joanna (Farley) (Burge)
    136 144
  John **91** 348 **136** 144
  John Allen **72** liii **113** 224
  Laura **57** 292
  Maria **57** 292
  Martha Jane **57** 292
  Martha Philura **57** 292
  Mary **54** 222 **113** 224
  Mary Barton (Pratt)
    113 224
  Mary W. (Wilder) **113** 224
  Melinda **57** 292
  Nancy **57** 293 294
  Obediah **57** 292
  Rufus Payn **57** 294
  Sally Dickson **57** 292
  Sarah **91** 350
  Susan **72** liii
  Susan (Gilbert) **113** 224
  Timothy **57** 292 **72** liii
    113 224
  William **72** liii **113** 224
  William Howe **63** xliii li
  Zilpah **57** 242
McELWEE
  Pinckney G. **112** 237
McELWELL
  Margaret **85** 297
McELWIN
  William Howe **62** xl
McENERY Lillian Irene
    (Mason) **123** 225

McENLTOFFES
  Catherine **136** 271
McENNIS Edward **65** 30
McEntash *see* McIntosh
McENTEE Anne **86** 105
McEowen *see* McEwen
McERNY
  Margaret **99** 280
  Mary **99** 280
  Sylvester **99** 280
McEVER Charles **73** 136
McEVERS —— **59** 113
  Elizabeth **92** 184
McEVOY MacEvoy
  Barbara Frances **85** 115
  Helena Ray (Palmer)
    85 117
  James **85** 115
  Theresa (Meredith)
    85 115
McEWEN MacEwen
  McEowen McEwan
  Adelaide Nina **68** 157
  Alexander **112** 22
  Alfred (Mrs.) **74** xxiv 155
    98 137 149
  Alfred Francis **99** 165
  Alfred Francis (Mrs.)
    99 165
  Alfred Robinson **99** 165
  Andrew B. W. **116** 156
    118 295 **119** 315 **141** 92
    105 **143** 141
  Anna Laura **99** 165
  Caroline **146** 363
  Charles **114** 187
  Charles F. **116** 154
  Eleanor Frances **99** 165
  Frank W. **68** 157
  Harry **73** 131
  Isabella **86** 375
  J. W. **128** 174
  James **105** 105
  Janet **86** 375
  John Auguste **99** 165
  John B. **91** 328
  Joseph **68** 157
  Margaret **68** 157
  Margaret (Houston)
    112 22
  Margaret (Robinson)
    99 165
  Margaret R. **74** xxiv
  Mary **98** 46
  Mercy **146** 363
  Muriel **89** 133
  Rebecca (Goodrich)
    (Hopkins) 105 **105** 105
  Thomas **114** 187
McFADDEN MacFaden
  McFadean McFaden
  McFadin McFading
  —— **91** 348
  Abner **63** 378 **64** 375
  Andrew **74** 99 **80** 25
    122 78
  Anna **84** 424
  Betsey **80** 27
  Daniel **57** 242 **135** 121 122
    146 335 **147** 74
  Edward **65** 27

McFADDEN *cont'd*
  Elizabeth **80** 25 **82** 179
  Emiline **115** 170
  Fay (Mrs.) **81** 222
  Grace **59** 376 **134** 66
  Grace Gertrude **81** 108
    222
  Henretta (Lancaster)
    91 386
  James **109** 160 **115** 170
    119 21
  John **55** 390 **80** 27 **91** 345
    119 21 **146** 335
  Letis **146** 335
  Margaret **57** 242 **80** 25
    146 335
  Martha **80** 25 **91** 345 348
  Mary **57** 242 **63** 378 **64** 375
    80 27 **82** 179 **91** 345 **99**
    115 **109** 160
  Mary (Daniels) **122** 78
  Norman T. **115** 170
  Patience (Pattee) **146** 335
  Polly **84** 424
  Rachel **146** 335
  Robert **91** 386 **146** 335
  Robert J. **115** 170
  Samuel **80** 25
  Sarah **111** 313
  Susanna **80** 27 28
  Thomas **103** 299 **112** 209
  William **140** 165
McFAE Angus **115** 134
McFALL McFaul
  —— **99** 281
  Daniel **99** 205 207 209
    101 55 **111** 213
  James **111** 213
  Mary **99** 205 207 209 **101**
    55 163
McFARLAND
  MacFarland
  MacFarlane
  Mackfarland
  McFarlain McFarlan
  McFarlane McFarlin
  McFarling
  —— **60** 104 **70** 89 **92** 271
  — Capt. **70** 89 **98** 220
  — Mr. **125** 30
  — Mrs. **83** 415
  — Rev. Mr. **92** 130 **94** 377
  A. **91** 329
  Abigail **114** 182
  Adalaide S. **91** 385
  Albert **130** 304
  Alexander **95** 208 **130** 304
    137 282
  Alice Lilla (Emery) **86** 364
  Allen Smith **137** 282
  Andrew **119** 22
  Anna **69** 264
  Annie A. **60** 319
  Annie M. **116** 214
  Asa **60** 319 **92** 271 272 313
  Azubah **136** 141
  Benjamin **136** 141 142
  Betsey **137** 282
  Betty **57** 366
  Caroline **68** 334 **86** 145
    150 **137** 282

McFARLAND *cont'd*
  Caroline E. **68** 334
  Catherine **77** 153 **114** 182
  Charles **89** 40
  Charlotte **74** 31
  Clarissa **92** 271
  Clessie **86** 364
  Cynthia **137** 282
  Dan **145** 173
  Daniel **61** 273 **62** 307 **69**
    84 **86** 145 **134** 277
  Daniel Young **65** xxxiv
    93
  Duncan **118** 42 52 **130** 304
    131 237
  Eleanor **71** 218
  Elijah **145** 173
  Eliza **69** 84 **80** 167 **114** 182
  Elizabeth **82** 173 **83** 415
    101 165 **136** 141
  Elizabeth Lydia (Potter)
    86 150
  Elvira (Wheeler) **86** 364
  Emily **68** 334
  Emily Rockwood **102** 3
  Emily Victoria **111** 138
  Ephraim **105** 284 **119** 22
  Eunice **114** 182
  Eunice Ann **114** 182
  Eva Josephine **113** 324
  Fanny F. **114** 182
  G. **91** 329
  George E. **68** 334
  George Sidney **64** xxxi
    65 xxxvi
  Gracey (Smith?) **137** 282
  Hannah **58** 89
  Helen Augusta (Griffith)
    102 4
  Henry **60** 319 **61** xxxiv
    114 182
  Hepzibah (Ward) **102** 3
  Horace D. **134** 277
  Irma **113** 299
  J. Horace **85** 184
  James **57** 366 **58** 175 **61**
    135 **65** 93 **68** 334 **117**
    103
  James C. **114** 182
  James D. **68** 334
  Jane **55** 147 **65** 93 **113** 223
    114 320
  Jane (Bushfield) **126** 306
  Jared D. **86** 364
  Jennie May **72** 311
  John **53** 142 **55** 147 **58** 87
    89 **72** 311 **78** 111 **116** 52
    119 20 22 **140** 165 **148**
    172
  John Gardner **117** 292
  Joyce **111** 270
  Judith (Carver) **89** 40
  Julia **111** 139 **114** 182
  Laura Etta **130** 304
  Lindley James (Mrs.)
    107 134
  Lorinda Adelaide
    (Webber) **85** 334
  Lucy **61** 273 **70** 177 **71** lx
  Lydia (Toothacre) **137** 77
  Margaret **65** 93 **89** 58

McFARLAND *cont'd*
  91 38
  Marshall **85** 334
  Martha **58** 87 89 **61** 273
    69 121
  Mary **53** 249 **68** 334 **81** 27
    89 323 **108** 239 **110** 159
    114 240 **137** 77
  Mary Ann **88** 277
  Mary E. **128** 94
  Mary Elizabeth **145** 68
  Maynard **99** 33
  Mercy Williams **126** 144
  Moses **93** 397 **100** 63 **114**
    182 **146** 332 **147** 181
  Muriel L. **102** 281
  Nancy **72** 311 **115** 174
  Nancy (Dwight) **92** 272
  Nanna **51** 494
  Naomi **51** 494
  Nathan **65** 57 58
  Nelson **86** 150
  Osgood **114** 182
  Patty **136** 141
  Patty Crawford (Bell)
    86 145
  Pauline **85** 196
  Pauline Carolyn **99** 33
  Polly **136** 141
  Rachel **58** 175
  Reuben **86** 150 **130** 304
    137 282
  Robert **120** 319 **125** 221
    126 306
  Ruby **126** 220
  Sally **56** 47 **137** 77
  Sally (Plumely) **125** 221
  Sarah **58** 175 **70** 163
  Serena Amanda (Durrell)
    (Kelley) **134** 277
  Silas **136** 142
  Sophia (Sargent) **134** 277
  Stanton Maynard **99** 33
  Susan **114** 182
  Susan (Pearson) **109** 166
  Susan Adelia **100** 111
  Thedessa Becket
    (Witherspoon) **99** 33
  Thomas **65** 93 94 **102** 3
  Ursula Nancy **85** 334
  Vera **78** 203
  Virginia **69** 264
  Walter **61** 248 **120** 319
  William **69** 264 **70** 163
    105 287 **136** 141 142
    137 77
  William S. **76** lviii
McFARRIN
  Thomas **111** 213
McFASSEN Charlotte
    (Butterfield) **87** 234
McFASSON
  Daniel **64** 318
McFATE Sarah **99** 76
McFaul *see* McFall
McFAULIN
  Joyce **111** 270
McFAUN
  Charlotte **95** 314
McFEE Macfee
  Angus **70** 121

McFEE *cont'd*
  James **88** 91
  Leon Worrick **95** 147
  Martha **56** 27
  Mary **88** 91
  William **56** 27
McFerlin *see* McFarland
McFEY Benjamin **73** 268
McFUN Mackfun
  Agnes **133** 305
McGAFFEE Betsey
    (Hubbard) **88** 96
  Mabel **88** 170
  Neil **88** 96
  Sally **88** 96
McGAFFERTY
  Patrick **60** 162
McGAFFEY
  Andrew **59** 284
  Hannah **59** 284
  Jane **59** 283
  Laura **126** 81 171
  Molly **59** 284
  Neil **60** 187
McGAHAN
  Henrietta **98** 232
  Phebe Ann **127** 136
McGAHEY Henry **75** 36
  Melinda **75** 36
McGALVEY
  Andrew **114** 187
  Isabella **114** 187
  Margaret **114** 187
McGAN
  Adelbert **116** 65
  Bernice Adelbert **116** 65
  Edith May **116** 65
  Eleanor **60** 241
  Elizabeth **60** 241
  Emeline **116** 66
  Emeline R. (Bump)
    116 66
  Gilman T. **116** 66
  John **60** 240 241
  John P. **115** 293
  Marilla **116** 66
  Mason **116** 65 66
  Polly (Powell) **116** 65
  Sarah **60** 241
  Thomas **116** 65 119
  William J. **116** 66
McGARRAUGH Mary
    (Maverick) **102** 169
  Robert Oscar **102** 169
  Robert Smith **102** 169
  Sarah (Kinkead) **102** 169
McGARRY
  Peter **61** 268
McGARTY
  John E. **116** 66
McGARVAS
  William **91** 329
McGARVEY Albert
    Gayton **86** 370
  Frances Alida (Cole)
    86 370
  Henry **86** 370
  Mary (Postlethwaite)
    86 370
  Mary Eleanor **86** 370
  Ruth Cole **86** 370

McGARVEY *cont'd*
  William A. **145** 99
McGATHERN
  Robert **119** 20
McGAUGHEY
  Eliza Adeline **78** 37
  Felix Polk **78** 37
McGAVIN James Edgar
    (Mrs.) **108** 134
McGAW
  Alexander **90** 250
  Alice (Rhoads) **90** 250
  Anna R. **82** 110
  Isabella **61** 243
  Jacob **81** 398
  Marcy **95** 190
McGAWLY
  Patrick **62** 169
McGEACHEN Jeanie /
    Jennie **98** 283
McGEACHEY MacGeachey
  Elizabeth Jean **85** 190
McGEE McGehee
    McGhee McGhie
  Amanda **91** 190
  Andrew **62** 79
  Ann **73** 256 **114** 277
  Anna **73** 256
  Annie **117** 121
  Anstis **73** 256
  Archibald **114** 188
  Benjamin **117** 38
  Calvin **73** 256
  Chester **73** 256
  Clara **94** 375
  Clarissa **73** 256
  Daniel **63** 352
  David **73** 256
  Eleanor (Barrett) **100** 301
  Eliphal **80** 448
  Eliza **68** 152 **79** 353
  Eliza Ann **80** 448
  Elizabeth **81** 106
  George **80** 448
  Hannah **61** 135
  Hazel **117** 121
  Hes **117** 121
  Jacob **105** 148
  Jane R. **73** 256
  Jean **73** 256
  Jenny **73** 256
  John **65** 170 **100** 301
    114 188
  Jonas **73** 256
  Jonathan **73** 256
  Joseph **73** 256 **114** 188
  Joseph B. **73** 256
  Joseph W. **73** 256
  Juliana **79** 353 **80** 448
  June (Whitton) **125** 222
  L. H. (Mrs.) **102** 71
  Levi **73** 256
  Levin **114** 188
  Lucy Kate **113** 244 **115** 77
  Luther **73** 256
  Maggie **117** 121
  Martha **73** 256
  Mary **61** 135 **73** 256
  Mary Ann (Rutherford)
    (Carver) **117** 38 121
  Montford **77** 215

McGEE *cont'd*
　Neal **105** 210
　Patrick **106** 259
　Rachel **73** 256
　Robert **73** 256
　Rolla **117** 121
　Sally Polk **77** 215
　Sam **91** 346
　Samuel **79** 353
　Samuel Perkins **80** 448
　Sarah **73** 256 **79** 353 **80** 448
　　105 148
　Sarah Maria **80** 448
　Terrence **125** 222
　Thomas **73** 256 **78** 188 **114**
　　188 **115** 69
　Thomas (Mrs.) **109** 130
　Thomas R. **73** 256
　William **114** 188
　William Bolton **73** 256
McGEHEE Eleanor
　(DeJarnette) **105** 148
　Sarah **105** 148
McGeoch *see* McGooch
McGEORGE ―― **121**
　96-98 100 297 298 300
　301 303 **122** 63 74 117
―― Mrs. **122** 67
　Ruth A. **101** 213
McGERAGH
　Patrick **60** 161
McGhee *see* McGee
McGhie *see* McGee
McGIFFIN M'Giffin
　Jane **122** 19
　O'Shemas **89** 380
　Sarah (Clark) **89** 380
McGILCHRIST
　Daniel **65** 20
McGILL Macgill
―― Capt. **112** 291
―― Mr. **93** 256
　Alexander T. **76** lxxxiv
　Andrew **64** 108
　Ann **73** 150
　David **79** 65
　Edward Hicks **73** lxii
　Eleanor **73** 143
　Elizabeth **73** 136 **79** 65
　Hannah **142** 304
　Helen **73** lxii
　James **82** 47 293 296
　　112 302
　John **62** 332 **73** 147 **111**
　　244 **122** 256
　Joseph **100** 188
　Lydia (Ellis) **100** 188
　　122 256
　Martha **142** 304
　Mary Clare (Spence)
　　93 256
　Mary Gorden **73** 268
　Mary Margaret **103** 117
　Peter **142** 304
　Robert **73** 150
　Roberta Brooke **93** 256
　Sarah **82** 47 284 293 294
　　296
　William **142** 304
McGILLIS
　Randolph **107** 155

McGILLIVRAY
　McGilvarey McGilvery
　McGilvry
　Alexander **125** 216
　Anne **125** 116 121
　Catherine **125** 258
　Elizabeth (Hayden)
　　126 65
　John **62** 301 **123** 7
　Lachlan **62** 301
　Mary **61** 166
　Nancy (Rupell) **125** 216
McGINLEY
　Edward **118** 53-56
　Gertrude **80** 206
　Holden (Mrs.) **79** 325
　　80 206
　W. A. **123** 151
McGINN Mary **60** 161
　Nancy (Chase) **87** 331
　Theresa **86** 370
　Thomas **60** 161
McGINNESS ___ (Oakes)
　　128 160
McGINNIS
　Adele **136** 319
　Annie Mary **80** 140
　Ella Card **109** 270
　Francis Kamp (Mrs.)
　　95 147
　John **87** 251 **139** 203
　Lorenda **68** 150
　Louisa (Chase) **87** 251
　Mary Frances **68** 150
　Percy A. **109** 270
　William **68** 150
　William C. **117** 238
　Zachariah T. **68** 150
McGINTA Elia **76** 276
　Nettie **76** 276
McGINTY
　Eveleen **95** 251
McGIVERN
　Susan **116** 186
McGLANCHY Catherine
　(Connelly) **88** 339
　John **88** 339
McGLATHRY McGlathery
　Jane **89** 340
　Jane Mary **135** 39
　Margaret **89** 340
　William **105** 281
McGlauflin *see*
　McLaughlin
McGlaughlan *see*
　McLaughlin
McGLENEN
　Edward Webster **52**
　　389 402 **54** xxxviii **56**
　　xxx xxxiv **57** 221 414 **58**
　　xxx xliii **59** xli **64** xxix
McGLENHY
　Mary **61** 268
　Owen **61** 268
McGLINCHEY
　Esther **122** 194
McGLOGHIN
　Gitte **76** 270
　J. **76** 270
McGLOTHNEY
　James **145** 350

McGLOTTEN
　George **119** 20
McGLOWN John **119** 21
McGlucas *see* McLucas
McGLYNN Ann
　Filomina
　　(Mahoney) 359
　James Devitt (Mrs.) **108**
　　134 **111** 153
　John Joseph **92** 359
　Katharine Regina **92** 359
McGOGGIE
　Mary Ann **78** 359
McGOMERY
　Mary **61** 267
　Thomas **61** 268
McGonagal *see*
　cGonegal
McGONE Edward **91** 329
McGONEGAL McGonagal
　Elizabeth **87** 331
　Emma **117** 213
　James **60** 27 163
　William **117** 213
McGOOCH McGeoch
　McGouch
　Alexander **55** 376 **74** 198
　　252 **82** 505 507 **83** 17
　　148
　George **82** 505
　Henry **82** 507
　James **74** 198 262 **82** 505
　Jane **55** 375 **83** 16
　Jane (Plaisted) **83** 16
　John **65** 257 **74** 198 **82** 505
　Lydia **74** 262
　Martha **55** 376 **83** 17
　Martha (Palmer) **83** 17
　Mary **55** 376 **82** 507 **83** 17
　Olive **74** 198 252 **83** 148
　Robert **55** 375 **74** 198 **82**
　　505 **83** 16
　Rosanna Key **55** 376 **82**
　　505 **83** 17
McGOODIN
　Margarette **61** 345
McGORLEY
　Hannah **82** 174
　Jessie Eliza **82** 174
　John **82** 174
　Peter Francis **82** 174
McGouch *see* McGooch
McGOUGAT
　John **78** 317
McGOUN
　Rebecca **117** 253
McGOVERN
　George L. **116** 79
　Maria B. **123** 97
　Mary **139** 215
McGOW Jane **131** 86
　John **131** 86
　Margaret **131** 86
McGOWAN M'Gowen
　MacGowan McGowen
　McGowin McGown
―― **60** 104
―― Mr. **52** 61
　A. **91** 329
　Ann **139** 212
　Barbara **110** 224

McGOWAN *cont'd*
Daniel **55** 186 **60** 26
Edward **61** 135
Eliza (Manchester) **102** 20
Francis **61** 268
Grace **61** 135
Isabella **73** 131
J. W. **118** 62
James **127** 53
James Doliver **127** 53
John **102** 20 **115** 45
Margaret **102** 20 **127** 120
Margaret (Chalmers)
  118 62
Margaret Bell **73** 131
Margaret Nancy **118** 62
Mark **61** 268
Mary **116** 187
Mary (Chisolm) **127** 53
Michael **127** 53
Owen **60** 26
Patrick F. **67** 97
Peter **60** 26
Philip **61** 135
Rebecca **117** 253
Robert **54** 46
Susanna **127** 53
Thomas **61** 268
William **61** 351 **79** 52
McGRADY
Anne **145** 134 135
Edward **91** 76
Leon L. (Mrs.) **102** 226
Louisa de Berniere **91** 76
McGRAFFEE
Gertrude **76** 263
McGRAI Eleanor
  (Johnson) **100** 301
Moses **100** 301
McGRAL Jane **55** 266
John **55** 266
McGRATH ——— **118** 44
Abigail **83** 359 **97** 228 233
Alfred J. **124** 32
Angelona H. **60** 296
Barnard **83** 359
Charlotte (Broughton)
  125 100
Dora Steele **60** 296
Hannah **60** 296
Henry **60** 296
J. Howard **139** 194
James Franklin **97** 158
Mary **96** 382 383
Matthew **118** 47
Michael **139** 204
Patrick **139** 204
Richard **125** 100
Sarah Katharine
  (Granger) **124** 32
McGRAW ——— **70** 87
— Mr. **83** 307
— Mrs. **83** 307
A. H. **60** 82
Eleanor **108** 309
Elizabeth Jane **146** 387
Grace Ingersoll (Butler)
  83 330
Harrison Beecher **64** xxxi
Letitia **115** 171

McGRAW *cont'd*
Sarah Edma (Simpson)
  136 318
Thomas **136** 318
McGRAY
Almira D. **108** 304
Asa **108** 304
Catherine **91** 384
Eliza Ann (Doane)
  108 304
Leland R. **123** 80
Miriam (Webber) **123** 80
Persis (Turner) **134** 144
Sabiah **111** 139
Sophia **134** 126
Susanna (Turner) **134** 144
William **123** 80 **134** 144
McGREEVY
Catherine **81** 258
McGREGOR
  MacGregor
  McGregger
  McGreggor McGriger
  McGrigor
  ——— **58** 323 **93** 351
  — Capt. **51** 452
Abigail **61** 384
Ada Ruth (Cole) **86** 308
Alexander **112** 207 **117**
  245 **123** 319
Alexander (Mrs.) **99** 148
Alexander Buchanan
  82 20
Alexander M. **126** 24
Annis **51** 466
Betsey **70** 226
Carrie Mabel **82** 21
Charles **64** 135
Charles F. **86** 308
Daniel **117** 245
David **61** 384 **80** 444 **106**
  153 **117** 245
Eleanor **106** 242
Elizabeth **53** 375 **117** 245
Emma Jane **82** 20
Helen **76** 169 **95** 147
Helen May **82** 180
James **80** 444 **114** 314 **117**
  242 243 245 248 **123** 319
  125 116 256
Jane **117** 245
Jane (Verity) **123** 319
Janet **68** 152
Jeannie **99** 255
John **64** 79 **70** 226 **82** 20
  117 245 **118** 52 56 **129**
  64
John Chambers **82** 21
Lizzie Catherine **82** 21
Malcolm Murry **82** 20
Margaret **117** 245 **123** 319
Marion (Cargill) **117** 245
Mary **77** 183 **80** 444 **82** 20
  89 215 **91** 381 **117** 245
Mary (Drummond)
  123 319
Mary (Gray) **126** 24
Nancy **114** 314
Philura Jane **82** 180
Rebecca Ann (Fitz-
  Randolph) **98** 129

McGREGOR *cont'd*
Robert **117** 245
Robert G. **98** 129
Rumsey Miller **106** 69
Ruth Abbie (Hill) **106** 69
Ruth Miranda **82** 20
Susan **82** 180
Thomas **119** 21
Tracy William **106** 64
Violet **77** 190
William **82** 180 **103** 119
William Wallace **82** 180
McGREGORY
David **65** 114
Emma **87** 87
Lydia **90** 315
Thomas J. **90** 38
McGREN Mary **128** 96
McGRENAN
John **60** 162
McGREW
Alexander **128** 173
Archibald B. (Mrs.) **81** 325
Cynthia **128** 173
Martha **118** 247
Nancy (Beamer) **128** 173
Ogda **102** 122
Phyllis **81** 325
Washington **128** 173
McGriger *see* McGregor
McGrigor *see* McGregor
McGRILLIS
Dorcas **100** 38
Fred **92** 362
McGROARTY William
  Buckner **94** 402
McGROWN
Charles **91** 329
McGUIGAN
James **115** 51
John **115** 51
John I. (Mrs.) **121** 257
Margaret **115** 51
Mary **115** 51
Mary Jane **115** 51
Michael **115** 51
McGUIN
James D. **129** 50
McGUINESS
John P. **81** 381
Margaret **81** 381 **106** 108
Mary **81** 381
Patrick **106** 108
Richard **106** 108
McGUINEY
John **111** 208
McGUIRE
Abner **88** 114
Alice **91** 387
Amanda Pauline **77** 263
Belle **102** 124
Catherine **87** 385 **139** 204
Catherine Prigmore
  117 237
Charles Polk **77** 263
Charles Polk (Mrs.)
  105 128
Edmund J. **73** 242 **75** 161
Edna Mae **77** 263
Edward **82** 130
Edward J. **71** 97 **76** 160

McGUIRE *cont'd*
77 242
Elisha Whipple 72 xx 90
130 92 305
Fanny 77 263
Henry 74 18
James 62 81
Jane 105 62
Joel Seaborn 77 263
John 63 158 122 260
Lena 77 263
Lucy Eveline (Chase)
88 114
Lydia (Hamilton) 122 144
Maggie Evelyn 77 263
Margaret 74 18 23
Mary 81 383
Mary Jane 77 263
Minnie 77 263
Nancy 74 18
Patrick 74 23 117 237
Prudence 105 215
Robert 103 161
Sarah Chambers 63 158
Thomas 74 18 122 144
William David 77 263
McGUYER McGuyre
Henry 84 425
Peggy (Hanley) 84 425
Prince (Mrs.) 111 326
Ruth C. 147 89
McHAFIE John 112 291
McHARD MacHard
MacHerd Mackhard
McChord McHarde
McHeard
—— 119 304
Alexander 81 24
Anne 62 271
Elizabeth 62 271
Hannah 62 272
J. H. 97 98
James 124 246 144 331
146 325
John 62 271
Lucinda 62 271
Mary 144 331
Matthew 71 10 144 21 44
331
Sarah 71 10 98 78
Sarah (Fayerweather)
144 21 331
Temperance 62 271
Trueman 62 271
William 62 271 272 93 301
McHATTON
Neil 114 150
McHEAN Maria 63 353
Stewart 63 353
McHELEN
Elizabeth 114 185
Elizabeth (Burns) 114 185
McHENCH
John 113 161
McHENRY Catherine
(Mahurin) 136 29
Henry 60 348
James 95 210
John 105 287
Van 136 29

McHERG
Judith 54 201
Patrick 54 201
McHINCH
Marie 90 381
McHOLLOND
Mary J. 91 386
McHUGH
Bridget 116 119
Bryan 115 293
Emma 115 299
John 116 119
Joseph Daniel (Mrs.) 84
190 120 149
Marie Tylee 83 217 102
153 105 72 107 320
Mary 116 69
Patrick 116 119
William 115 293
McHURIN
Hugh 104 168
McHURON
Clarissa 136 247
Mary 136 252
Polly 136 247
Ruth 136 247
McIAN Elizabeth 54 451
106 228
Robert 54 451
Sarah 54 451
McIEHERRY
Thomas 60 347
McILHENNY
McIlhaney McIlhany
Henry P. 96 167
Hugh M. 103 99
Lily 118 169
Mary 78 33
McILREEVY
James 69 321
Jane 69 321
Winifred 69 321
McIlroy *see* McElroy
McILVAINE McIlvain
McIlvane
Abigail 56 251
Angeline 81 36
Benjamin Franklin 81 37
Caroline Frances 68 122
Daniel 81 36
Ebenezer 56 251 252
Edward S. 106 226
Emily G. 99 47
Frances McClelland
68 122
Hannah 62 28 81 36
Harriet P. 81 36
Henry Clay 68 122
Hiram B. 81 36
John 56 252
John Lamont 68 122
Josephine 68 122
Margaret Shippen
106 226
Robert 111 271
Sabrina S. 81 37
McILWAIN McIlwaine
Andrew 57 303
H. R. 115 13 117 251
Hasadiah 57 303
Mary Ann 99 296

McILWRATH
Isabel 60 402
Samuel 60 402
McINDOE —— 56 114
McINNERNEY
Thomas Henry 88 169
McINNESS McInnes
McInnis
Addie 82 174
Bessie 108 132
Donald 125 258
Edward Thomas 82 174
Elizabeth 82 174
Emily Rebecca 82 174
Jennie 82 174
Jessie Eliza 82 174
Lizzie Maria 82 174
Margaret (McBain)
125 258
Maria 82 174
Thomas 82 174
Thomas Hall 82 174
McINTIRE M'Intire
MacIntier MacIntire
Mackentire Mackintier
Mackintir Mackintire
McIntyre
—— 57 338 61 104 65 360
110 62 113 26
— Mr. 85 121
— Mrs. 83 307
Abbie C. (Emerson) 121
306 122 149
Abigail 57 258 104 132
115 64 116 297 118 240
241
Abigail (McIntire) 118
240 241
Abigail (Webber) 114 129
Abraham 114 204
Addie E. (Bird) 99 31
Adelbert C. 96 331
Agnes 90 90
Albert 110 211 212 119 286
120 223 225
Albert Augustus 110 211
Alex 61 135
Alexander 55 374 58 341
63 176 66 313 314 74
186 83 14 111 22 112 24
113 26 28 124 264 114
49 116 136 225 294-299
302 303 305 117 140-143
224-230 118 155 240-
242 317-321 119 60-69
143 145-147 224-229 275-
288 120 64 65
Alexsander 110 62
Alice (Willis) 114 204
Alice Mabel 74 305
Allyn Brewster 103 119
Almira (Bancroft) 96 331
Amelia Augustine 51 104
Amelia Bigelow 75 lxxi
Amiliah 111 41
Amos 120 67 69
Andrew 118 321
Andrew J. 117 292 120 140
123 151
Andrew Jackson 120 215
Angelie C. 110 212

McINTIRE *cont'd*
Angus **105** 285
Ann **92** 205 **95** 115 **98** 99
  120 308 **140** 306
Anna **89** 180
Annette **95** 373
Annie E. **121** 71 72
Arthur F. (Mrs.) **124** 240
  125 228
Asa **85** 315 **93** 293 294
  117 226 **123** 74
Augustus **110** 212
Barbara Camilla **113** 91
Benjamin **57** 249 **70** 315
Benjamin E. **75** lxxi
Benjamin Franklin
  113 26
Benjamin Mesura Giron
  82 47
Betsey **103** 297
Caroline **69** 205
Caroline (Brooks) **93**
  293 294 **117** 226 **123** 74
Caroline B. **120** 309
Catherine **83** 25 28
Charles **116** 294
Charles Ezra **110** 212
Charles J. **51** 104 **52** 400
  61 xxxiv 104
Christiana **114** 184
Clara S. Littlefield (Came)
  91 223
Clarence **99** 31
Clarisa (Nichols) **119** 276
Cynthia (Silvester) **86** 90
Daniel **91** 329 **97** 269 **110**
  287 **114** 133 **115** 216
  116 223
Daniel B. **123** 74
David **88** 285
Deborah **120** 12
Deborah (Russell) **120**
  12 13
Deborah (Silvester) **86** 90
Dolle **115** 306
Dorcas **115** 222 **118** 321
  120 306
Dorcas (Hutchings)
  92 205
Dorcas (McIntire) **118** 321
Dorothy **82** 293 297 **111**
  23 **112** 24 **114** 291
Duncan M. **123** 160
Ebenezer **51** 104 **110** 287
  114 131 **115** 212 **117**
  221
Edgar **113** 26 264 **118** 240
  241
Edgar A. **113** 125 129 193
  119 225 275 282 **120** 65-
  70 135-140 216
Edgar Augustus **113** 26
  193 **119** 282
Edith W. **117** 292
Edward **97** 216
Edward Warren **74** 307
Edwin **99** 31
Eleanor (Junkins)
  119 145
Eliza Ann **75** xci
Eliza H. (Murrey) **120** 216

McINTIRE *cont'd*
Elizabeth **55** 393 **56** 37 147
  57 188 255 **74** 305 **88**
  339 **90** 91 **92** 205 **105**
  161 162 **113** 123 **121** 70
Elizabeth (Lunt) **119** 60
Elizabeth Frazier **113** 267
Elizabeth Jane **75** lxx
Elizabeth L. **120** 224
Elizabeth Lunt **68** 19
Elizabeth M. (Cousins)
  110 106
Elva F. **99** 31
Emily B. (Rix) **90** 105
Ernest Eugene **74** 305
Esther (Nowell) **115** 135
Evalina **113** 26 264
  119 224
Evaline **118** 320
Fanny (Peabody) **116** 255
Flora **117** 315
Flora Alma **99** 149
Florence **96** 331
Florence A. **123** 151
Frances (Fogg) **97** 216
Frances Ann
  (Witherspoon) **99** 31
Frank **74** 305
Frank Palmer **60** xxxviii
  75 xxxv lxx lxxi
Franklin **113** 264
Fred E. **69** 286
Fred H. **85** 315
Fred W. **103** 300
Freelove (Phillips) **120** 5
George **61** 138 **91** 91 **92**
  205 **116** 255 **119** 276
George E. **110** 212
George O. **120** 137
Grace (Stratton) **97** 216
Hannah **55** 260 266 **56** 33
  144 145 267 **57** 106 149
  153 252 **61** 242 **110** 287
  112 104 **114** 51 **116** 132
  118 241 **119** 61 **127** 126
Hannah (Linscit) **115** 212
Hannah (Shaw) **120** 307
  308
Hannah (Smith) **122** 49
  126 167
Hannah S. (Glynn)
  121 147
Hannah S. (Welch)
  120 137
Harriet **92** 362 **117** 224
  120 67 69
Harriet Elizabeth (Moody)
  120 140 215 **123** 151
Harriet F. **57** 225
Harriet S. (Lunt) **120** 67
  68
Harry **117** 23
Harry B. **96** 331
Harvey Howard **74** 307
Hattie L. (Blaisdell) **123** 74
Helen G. **121** 71 73
Henry **114** 184
Hugh **104** 118
Ida May **74** 305
Ingleson **74** 305 307
  110 106

McINTIRE *cont'd*
Ingleson Roy **74** 305
Isabel **74** 307 **110** 211 212
Isola Eliza **97** 216
Jacob **61** 379 **92** 205
James **82** 47 293 295 **91**
  329 **106** 108 **115** 308
  120 5
James H. **120** 307 308
James Thornton **113** 193
  119 282
Jane **90** 90 **91** 91 **111** 23
  115 219
Jane (Procter) **133** 309
Jedidiah **115** 222 **116** 136
Jemima **55** 261 **57** 102
Jerah **114** 204
Jeremiah **80** 128 **97** 146
  270 **116** 133 **119** 60 **121**
  306 **122** 149
Jeremiah L. **121** 147
Jerry **114** 204
John **56** 146 **57** 27 253 **74**
  266 **75** lxx **78** 407 **90** 92
  91 91 **92** 205 **97** 266 **99**
  31 **104** 118 **105** 162 281
  106 193 **107** 187 **110**
  287 **111** 97 **112** 104 **113**
  123 **114** 129 115 135
  306 **116** 296 **119** 145
  122 49 **126** 167 168 **127**
  126
John E. **99** 31
John M. **124** 31
John R. **121** 71 73
John W. **91** 91 **118** 321
Jonathan **133** 308
Joseph **55** 261 **56** 144 145
  147 148 267 270 **57** 27
  102 153 253 255 256 **61**
  96 **79** 40 **86** 90 **97** 272
  110 287 **113** 91 **115** 136
  116 224 **119** 21 285 **120**
  13
Josephine Curran **85** 315
Joshua **116** 138
Julia **138** 124
Keziah **63** 169 **110** 62 **111**
  93 **114** 129 115 304
Lena M. **74** 305
Leonard **115** 128 **120** 215
  216
Lewis **91** 91
Livingston **113** 26 264
  267 **120** 65
Lizzie **120** 306
Lizzie Noble **74** 305
Lois **57** 249 **82** 293 295
Louisa **74** 305 **119** 283 285
Love (Grover) **119** 284
  285
Lucy **66** 275 **106** 108 **115**
  212 **117** 228
Lucy (Kingsbury)
  115 136
Lucy E. **85** 315
Lydia **55** 259 265 266 **56**
  34 141 **57** 27 106 150 **74**
  266 **80** 128 114 204 **116**
  130 **126** 278 **136** 222
Lydia (Briggs) **126** 278

McINTIRE *cont'd*
Lydia A. (Main) **119** 286
Lydia L. (Winn) **120** 215
Maney **111** 116
Margaret **92** 205 **111** 129
130 **126** 167 **127** 126
Margaret Antoinette
(Brecht) **109** 149
Margaret Frazier **113** 267
Margaret Frazier (Nelson)
113 267 **120** 65
Maria (Curtis) **118** 321
119 62
Martha **108** 221
Martin V. B. **121** 308
Mary **56** 148 **57** 256 **63** 171
74 257 **83** 261 **85** 315
88 339 **97** 267 272 **106**
225 **110** 62 **111** 23 **116**
304 305 **117** 228
Mary (Barron) **88** 285
Mary (Junkins) **113** 26
264 **116** 136
Mary (Tibbetts) (Beath)
100 145
Mary (Weare) **111** 22
114 49
Mary A. **113** 193 **119** 282
Mary A. (Thompson)
113 193 **119** 225 282
Mary Ann (Enslin)
126 204
Mary Avery (Freeman)
84 299
Mary E. **99** 43
Mary Ella **110** 212
Mary Frances **84** 299
Mary G. (Cooper) **118** 317
Mary H. (Blaisdell)
121 308
Mary H. (Junkins) **120**
215 216
Mary Susan **113** 193
119 282
Matilda **119** 63 285 **120** 70
123 150 233
Mehitable (Whittemore)
106 193
Mehitable Peters **74** 307
Mercy **115** 226 **116** 133 140
221 **118** 321
Mercy (McIntire) **118** 321
Micum **95** 209 **110** 62
111 93 **115** 215 **116** 133
Mildred Harriman **87** 17
Milton Donald (Mrs.)
98 147
Minnie **85** 315
Molly **116** 136
Moses **56** 148 270 **57** 256
Nabby **97** 269
Nabby (Junkins) **117** 221
Nancy **76** 273 **116** 136
119 68 **125** 291
Nathaniel **126** 204
Nellie F. **74** 307
Oliver H. **120** 67 68
Palmer **75** lxx
Patty **78** 328
Patty (Heral) **116** 138
Perley **86** 90

McINTIRE *cont'd*
Phebe **95** 114 **97** 216
Phenis **97** 145
Phenis (Mrs.) **97** 145
Philip **92** 304 **97** 208 **100**
145 **120** 13
Philip Willis **63** 307
Phineas **97** 395 **115** 215
118 321 **119** 62
Rachel **78** 309
Rebecca **61** 379 **92** 205
Rebecca (Sturges) **92** 205
Rebecca M. **91** 91
Rhoda **117** 139 **119** 226
228
Rhoda (Allen) **115** 215
Rhoda (McIntire) **119** 228
Rhoda (Moulton) **115** 213
Rhoda L. **119** 227
Robert **75** lxx **91** 91
Robert H. **92** 304
Robert Harry **95** 209 **97**
208 **120** 13
Roger Doane **108** 134
Rose L. **69** 145
Rufus **118** 317 **128** 58
Ruth **82** 283 293
Ruth A. **118** 145 146
S. **145** 133
Salla **57** 257
Sally **55** 374 **63** 176 **83** 14
97 85
Sally (Cotton) **83** 14
Sally (Thompson)
118 243
Samuel **55** 260 266 **56**
141 143 145-148 267 **57**
27 106 149 150 152 252
253 255 257 258 **82** 293
297 **88** 337 **92** 348 **95**
114 153 **97** 146 216 272
108 140 **110** 287 **114**
227 **115** 140
Sarah **56** 31 145 **57** 253 **58**
341 **61** 96 **63** 169 **94** 286
115 214 303 **119** 229
277
Sarah (Came) **114** 227
Sarah E. **120** 309 **121** 70
Sarah E. (Trafton) **120**
223 225
Silas **83** 25 28
Simeon **128** 58
Solomon **63** 76
Sophia Jane **119** 66
Susan **118** 316 317 **119** 62
281
Susan (Holt) **148** 267
Susan H. (Kidder) **88** 337
Susanna **110** 287 **111** 97
114 126 **115** 138 217
116 142 **119** 61
Susanna (Blaisdell)
115 306
Susanna (Simpson)
115 216
Susanna (Young) **110** 287
Sylvester **119** 228 283
120 65 66 136 138 139
216 305

McINTIRE *cont'd*
Tabitha (Chandler)
104 118
Thankful **55** 259 **57** 27
Theodore **57** 225 **71** 225
115 213 **134** 222
Theodore B. **84** 299
Thomas **61** 268 **90** 105
119 200
Timothy **56** 147 **57** 255
116 130 139 222 226
118 243
Tobias **116** 129
Waite **123** 72 153
Waity H. **120** 137 139
Walter **85** 315
Washington **103** 297 300
William **75** lxx **82** 283 293
105 213 **108** 221 **116**
224 **119** 66 145 **120** 215
McINTOSH MacIntosh
Mackentosh
Mackintosh McEntash
McIntoch
—— **52** 270 398 **53** 316
123 11 12 14 160
—Capt. **84** 171
—Col. **59** 147 148 281 **97**
29 30 33 41 115 252 253
101 102
— Mme. **97** 25
Aaron Smith **57** 378
Abbie Jennie (Dutton)
123 12
Abbie Louise **123** 13
Abi (Clark) **90** 376
Abigail **56** 33 **57** 105 204
70 299 **78** 241 **122** 228
Aemas **123** 160
Alexander **124** 78
Alexander Day **109** 127
Alvira (Morse) **123** 13
Amanda **102** 166
Andrew **60** 40 **63** 47
123 160
Angus **106** 154 **112** 203
204 212
Ann (Foster) **126** 256
128 19
Appleton Isaac **123** 13
Archibald **123** 8
Austin **63** 48
Bathsheba **57** 105 257
Bertha **123** 13
Carlton Wintrock **123** 12
Catherine **57** 105 371
87 122
Charles **57** 380 **124** 79
Charles A. **68** 212
Charles Fleming **68**
xxxiii **69** xxx 96 **76** 321
79 106 **88** 160 **89** 134
91 77
Charles Newell **123** 13
Charlotte **57** 373
Christianna (French)
122 228
Clark **63** 48
Curtis **57** 371 380
Cynthia (Collins) **90** 91
Cynthia I. **87** 20

McINTOSH *cont'd*
David **126** 256
Davis **128** 19
Don Wilbur **123** 12
Donald **123** 14
Dorcas **63** 48
Ebenezer **56** 39 **57** 371-
  373 375 **97** 56
Ebenezer W. **57** 380 382
Ebenezer Whiting **57** 372
Edward **123** 12
Edward Earl **123** 12
Edward Martin **123** 13
Eleanor E. **123** 13
Elisha **122** 228
Eliza **125** 260
Eliza (Dutton) **123** 12
Eliza Ann **77** 149
Eliza S. (Sargent) **123** 12
Elizabeth **51** 255 256 **55**
  266 297 298 **56** 33 **57**
  105 371 **63** 48 **97** 56 **122**
  228 **123** 8
Elizabeth (Lion) **91** 77
Elizabeth (Maverick)
  97 56
Elizabeth (Moore) **91** 77
Elizabeth Dewing **57** 378
Elizabeth Mason (Walker)
  91 77
Ellen **57** 380
Ellen Jane **123** 11
Emeline (Preston) **123** 14
Ephraim Dewing **57** 379
Esmeralda **124** 79
Ethan **63** 48
Eva **106** 154
Eva (Chilson) **123** 12
Finlay **123** 14
Fitz **124** 79
Francis **57** 375
Frederic **57** 380
Frederick William **123** 13
George **91** 77 **124** 79
George Herman **123** 13
Gideon **55** 394 **57** 105
Gisey **123** 10
Hannah **57** 105 372 382
  63 47
Hannah (Davis) **123** 239
Hannah (May) **124** 78
Hannah (Prince) **123** 11
  13 14
Hannah Maria **124** 79
Harriet E. **124** 240
Hattie Belle **123** 13
Helen Annie **80** 208
Helen L. (Tallman) **123** 11
Helen Marr (Haven)
  123 13
Helen Worthington
  78 205
Henry **51** 255 **90** 91
  127 163
Henry S. **69** li
Herbert Miller **123** 11
Hervey **124** 79
Hezekiah **63** 48
Ida Anosima (Bailey)
  123 13
Isaac **123** 10 11 13 14

McINTOSH *cont'd*
Isaac Appleton **123** 11
Isaac R. **91** 329
Isabella **123** 9 10
Isabella Donaldson
  (Thornburn) **91** 77
J. **91** 329
Jael **67** 24 25
James **51** 145 **103** 171 **106**
  154 **122** 144 **123** 9 160
James B. **118** 54
James McKay **95** 14 16
James Miller **123** 10 11
James N. **124** 78 79
Jane **89** 33 **122** 144
Jane (Patterson) **123** 10 11
Jemima **56** 39
Jennie Grace **87** 114
Jennie Rebecca (Dyke)
  123 13
Jennie S. (Smith)
  (Wilkinson) **123** 13
Jeremiah **122** 228
Joanna (Lyon) **122** 228
John **55** 266 **65** 245 **77** 313
  91 329 **99** 312 **112** 203
  118 41 44 52 54 56-12 14
  15 160 373 **125** 260 **142**
  299
John Elphenstone **91** 77
John Wyatt **123** 11 12
Jonathan Haskell **124** 79
Joseph **104** 80 **122** 228
Josephine **57** 380
Julia Emily (Burbank)
  123 12
Juliette Eliza **123** 12
Kate H. **70** 95
Lachlan **51** 255
Lawrence E. **123** 13
Leander James **124** 79
Leland **107** 253
Lisle Dwight **123** 12
Lois (Batchellor) **123** 13
Lucetta **123** 11
Lucetta Elizabeth (Hatch)
  123 11
Lucia Isabel **123** 14
Lucinda **123** 11
Lucinda (Woodworth)
  (Dutton) **123** 12
Lucy **55** 395 **57** 259 **61** 346
  63 48
Lucy Fisk **57** 105
Lula **123** 13
Lura **63** 48
Lydia **122** 228
Lyman Durkee **123** 11 14
March **67** 286
Margaret **122** 144
Maria **57** 379 **63** 48
Maria (Haskell) **124** 79
Marilda **63** 48
Martha **123** 8 9 16
Martha (Henry) **123** 7 10
Martha Bascom (Tucker)
  123 12
Martha Jane **123** 10 11 13
Martha Smith **57** 378
Mary **51** 255 **55** 265 **106**
  156 **122** 228 **123** 10

McINTOSH *cont'd*
Mary (Appleton) **106** 154
Mary (Merrifield) **122** 228
Mary (Saunders) **91** 77
Mary A. **123** 13
Mary H. **123** 10
Mary Jane **123** 13
Maude Eva **123** 12
Mehitable **55** 394 398
  57 105
Mercy **67** 24 26
Michael **57** 373
Miles **118** 41 44
Montgomery E. **51** 245
Nancy **57** 105 **114** 320
  122 228
Naomi **63** 48
Nathan **57** 373
Nicholas **65** 233
Olive **63** 48 **122** 144
Olive (Hopkins) (Graub)
  103 171 **122** 144
Orange **123** 11
Orange S. **123** 12
Paschal Paoli **90** 376 **97** 56
Patrick **123** 160
Penelope **67** 25
Persis L. (Wheeler) **123** 13
Peter **91** 77 214 **140** 165
  329
Phebe **61** 380
Phebe (Wyatt) **123** 10 12
Phebe Jane **123** 11
Philena **63** 48
Polly **120** 239
Priscilla **57** 105 371
Priscilla Broad **57** 380
Priscilla Jane **120** 142
Raymond Drew **123** 12
Rebecca (Holt) **123** 14
Rebecca (Metcalf) **122** 228
Rebecca Hannah **123** 14
Rebecca Holt (Preston)
  123 14
Reuben Mussey **123** 11 13
Robert **63** 48 **122** 144
Robert James **106** 154
Roland Burbank **123** 12
Ronald **106** 154
Royal **56** 33 **57** 105 371 372
  378
Sally **142** 299
Samuel **57** 105 371 378-380
  61 380 **122** 228 **123** 10-
  12
Sarah **67** 25 **123** 11
Sarah (Briggs) **107** 253
Sarah (Griggs) **122** 228
Sarah J. **124** 79
Shaw **51** 255
Solomon Prince **123** 11
  13
Stephen **122** 228
Suel **142** 299
Suky Gurney **57** 105
Susan **123** 10
Susan Maria **57** 379
Susan Pratt **57** 380
Susanna **122** 228
Susanna (Blake) **122** 228
Sylvester **57** 380

McINTOSH *cont'd*
Tamasin Ashcroft
(Dutton) **123** 12
Theron William **123** 13
Thomas **122** 228
W. H. **120** 44 **122** 160
Walter **123** 195
Walter C. **127** 137
Walter H. **121** 149 **122**
144 228 **123** 6 126 145
160 **124** 79
Walter Harrison **123** 12
Wendell (Mrs.) **80** 208
120 148
Wendell P. (Mrs.) **79** 324
Wilbur Fisk **123** 12
William **55** 265 397 **57**
105 204 257 259 **67** 24
25 **70** 212 214 220 297
299 304 305 **82** 456 **89**
214 **99** 312 **105** 169 **116**
157 **122** 228 **123** 8-11 13
15 160
William Appleton **123** 13
William Henry **57** 378
William Washington
57 380
McIntyer *see* McIntire
McIntyre *see* McIntire
McISAAC
Murdoch **114** 150
McIVER
Augus **114** 150
Carrie **109** 145
Helen H. **78** 113 225
80 225
Judith **60** 161
Mary **60** 161
Shane **60** 161
William W. (Mrs.) **109**
292 **113** 66
McIVOR Nancy **77** 266
McJEFFERDS
Samuel **87** 206
McKAIN
Annabelle **90** 347
Thomas **90** 347
McKALL
Lucy **146** 360 361
McKÁMEY McKamy
—— **56** 210 **60** 104
McKAN James **66** 35
McKANE Lavina **87** 23
Nancy **87** 23
Robert **87** 23
Thankful **60** 345
McKANER Ann **100** 241
McKARTE
Margaret **113** 279
McKAY M'Kaye Maccae
Maccay Mackay
Mackaye McCay
—— **60** 100 **80** 370 **92**
251 349 **140** 36 156 165
166
— Dr. **66** 48
— Maj. Gen. **84** 258
—— (Hussey) **140** 156 166
Abigail (Mixer) **124** 38
Aeneas **110** 100
Agnes **93** 204

McKAY *cont'd*
Alex J. **92** 205
Alexander **61** 268 **73** 136
92 338 **104** 203 **118** 55
140 165
Ann **129** 49
Archibald **52** 312
Barbara **73** 146 **96** 334
Benjamin **82** 47 **88** 378
Betsey **92** 129 **124** 80
Caroline **92** 251
Catherine **68** 328
Catherine S. **73** 264
Charles **111** 80 **129** 49
Charlotte Elizabeth
(Hoag) **90** 170
Clarence Hungerford
84 333
Clarissa (Hoar) **134** 117
Claude (Mrs.) **105** 150
Crafts **140** 165
Daniel **91** 206 **94** 95
100 65
Donald **54** 240 **76** 241
125 43
Donald Dana **100** 112
Donald Sage **63** 113
81 485
Eliza **93** 218
Elizabeth **54** 244 **68** 255 **96**
384 **110** 100
Elizabeth (Mears) **96** 384
Ellen **61** 138 **84** 333
134 117
Emerette L. (Harris)
92 205
Eppert Rudolf **93** 138
Frances **92** 243
Francis **62** 301
G. L. **124** 103
George L. **107** 8
Gordon **76** lxvii
Hannah **104** 203
Helen **81** 485
Helen Esther (Baker)
90 170
Hugh **54** 238 **73** 151
145 375
Hunter **84** 238
Hunter Branson **84** 105
190
Isabella **116** 288
Jack **112** 266
James **104** 203
Jane **82** 47 **111** 80
Janet **104** 203
Job **92** 23
John **54** 244 **59** 393 **62**
250 301 **63** 352 **92** 243
251 349 **94** 378 **104** 203
120 15 17 **140** 165 **145**
375
John Alexander **63** 134
John Robert **96** 384
John Singleton **74** 206
John William **84** 333
Joseph W. **105** 156
Katharine **84** 333
Katharine Alexander
(Duer) **84** 333 342
85 205

McKAY *cont'd*
Lexia **92** 129
Lillian D. **105** 156
Lizzie **128** 268
Lucy Ann **66** 48
Lydia **98** 53
M. **93** 263
Margaret **54** 244
Margaret Susan (Hobbie)
100 111
Marie Louise (Hunger-
ford) (Bryant) **84** 333
Mary **54** 244 **59** 393 **66**
lxxxv **110** 100
Mary (Hodgkins) (Nason)
88 378 379
Mary (Long) **85** 377
Mary E. **92** 338
Mary Eliza (Videto)
120 15
Mehitable **82** 47
Mehitable Wilson **74** 206
Michael **61** 269
Mungo **88** 204 **92** 18-20 22
23 25-28 118 **93** 318 **140**
156 165
Murdoc **92** 129
Nancy **61** 268
Neil **145** 375
Patrick **61** 268
Percy **81** 208 **82** 229
Phebe **134** 117
Reuben **124** 38
Robert **62** 81 **84** 238
131 253
Robert Gordon (Mrs.)
90 75
Rufus **85** 377
Ruth **92** 19 20 22 23 25-28
93 263 321
Ruth Augusta (Sanford)
120 17
Ruthey **88** 204 **92** 18
Sally **92** 19 **140** 165
Samuel **62** 301 **110** 100
Sander **145** 375
Sarah **88** 205 **106** 126
134 117
Stephen **62** 301
Thomas **61** 138 **134** 117
Virginia Sturges
(Osborn) **90** 75
William **84** 379 **91** 201
104 203 **140** 36 156 165
166 252 **145** 375
William Eshorne **84** 180
90 81 141 169 170
William Osborne **94** 139
Woodbury Eshorne
90 170
McKEAN —— **54** 246 247
55 272
Agnes **101** 277 **140** 34 166
Andrew Jackson **117** 101
Annis **117** 246
Barnabas **117** 100-102
Barnabas Henry **117** 101
Barnabus H. **140** 305 306
Caroline **117** 102
David **98** 364 **117** 246
Elizabeth **89** 20 **117** 101

McKEAN *cont'd*
245 **140** 166
Elizabeth Perkins **76** 214
Emily **140** 305
Emily (Smith) **140** 305 306
Hannah **78** 310
Hannah (Eveleth) **135** 31
Harry **117** 101
Henry Pratt **76** 214
Honor **117** 100
Hosea **117** 101
Hugh **103** 163
James **60** 196 **98** 364 **115**
56 **117** 100 242 243 245
246
Jane Amelia (Cardinal)
117 101
Janet **117** 245 246
John **61** 28 **117** 245 246
135 31 105 106
Joseph **83** 148 **140** 166
Joseph W. **140** 166
Keturah **117** 100
Laughton **117** 100
Lorie Amanda **82** 272
Lucy Ann (Bullock)
117 101
Lucy Jane **103** 163
Mabel **117** 100
Mabel (Hall) **117** 100
Margaret **117** 246
Margaret Williams
(Sargent) **90** 369
Marian **76** 214
Martha **117** 246
Mary **57** 265 **60** 195 **75** 253
98 364 **99** 173 **117** 100
101 245 246
Nancy **61** 28
Patrick **57** 141 **117** 100
Pierce Urban **117** 101
Polly **117** 101
Prudence (Brownson)
117 100
Quincy Adams Shaw
(Mrs.) **90** 369
Rachel **57** 141
Rachel (Bradley) **117** 100
Samuel **117** 246
Sarah Ann **117** 101 102
Susan **117** 102
Susan (Townsend)
117 101
Thomas **51** 89 **117** 245
Walter Ernest **101** 124
William **101** 277 **117** 245
246 **140** 34 166
McKECHNIE McKenchnie
Agnes Finlayson **117** 199
Alexander **92** 302
Alice Burt **103** 119
Elizabeth **92** 302
Hannah **92** 302
Jane **92** 302
John **92** 301 302 **107** 153
147 80
Joseph **92** 302
Lydia **92** 302 **111** 117
Mary **92** 302
Mary (North) **146** 327
147 80

McKECHNIE *cont'd*
Mary Pattee **92** 302
Rebecca **92** 302
Sarah **92** 301 302
Thomas **92** 302
William **92** 302
William Tileston **71** xxiii
McKEE
—— **51** 452 **123** 96
— Mrs. **60** 163
— Rev. **113** 81
Aaron **106** 315
Alex **60** 161
Alexander **58** 195
Andrew **60** 163
Andrew J. **78** 354
Anna **62** 298
Anna Margaret
(McDowell) **90** 187
Bessie **71** xxiii **74** xxviii
Bessie (Pardee)
(Van Wickle) **90** 187
91 146
Bessie Pardee **90** 129
Bettey **94** 384
Bille **54** 254
Caroline **85** 315
Chester **55** 283 **62** 292
Dudley **55** 284
Eleazer **58** 195
Electa **121** 160
Eli **62** 294
Eliza J. **86** 165
Elizabeth **62** 298 **83** 68
107 112
Ellen B. **95** 402
Elliott Bates **112** 151
Fanny **60** 161
Florence Margaret **70** xix
Florence McCutcheon
85 465
Hannah (Langdon) **123**
96 309
Harriet C. **86** 165
James H. **85** 315 **123** 309
John **62** 298 **111** 202
112 290
Joseph **54** 254 **58** 195
Julia Ann **113** 153
Katharine Stevens
(Pillsbury) **112** 151
Leander **90** 187
Lucretia **62** 292
Margaret **62** 297
Martha (Henry) **106** 315
Mary **78** 313
Michael **78** 185
Nancy **60** 163 **128** 266
Nathaniel **55** 283 284 **56**
347 348 356 **58** 195
Patrick **60** 163
Robert **58** 195 **62** 298
S. W. (Mrs.) **79** 193
Salmon **55** 283
Samuel **56** 347
Sarah **56** 356 **58** 195 **94** 165
147 232
Susan Emily **78** 354
William **61** 266 **62** 362
92 42 **112** 17
William Leander **90** 187

McKEE *cont'd*
William Leander (Mrs.)
74 xxviii 159 **90** 117 187
91 146
McKEEL Mary **83** 67
McKEEN —— **52** 390
Abner **105** 284
Adam **125** 115 260
Agnes **106** 69
Alexander **84** 424 **125** 197
Ann **85** 448
Annis (Cargill) **117** 245
Betsey (Hammon) **84** 424
Catherine (Kirk) **125** 257
Charlotte Jane **125** 196
Daniel **108** 4
David **118** 44 45 52 55 57
125 114 115 256
David Kergill **118** 55
David Taylor **125** 117
Dorothy Carol **106** 69
Edward **125** 197
Eliza **125** 260
Elizabeth **108** 4 **117** 245
125 256
Elizabeth (Dinsmore)
117 246
Elizabeth (Harris) **125**
115 118
Elizabeth (Taylor) **125** 120
256
Elizabeth Hull **106** 69
Ephraim **105** 284
Isaac **125** 260
James **108** 4 **125** 96
Jane **85** 448
Janet **117** 245 246
Janet (Cochran) **108** 4
117 245
Janet (Graham) **106** 68
Jean **117** 246
Jenny (Taylor) **125** 115
117
John **106** 68 69 **118** 41-43
46 58 **125** 115 257
John Duncan **125** 117
John Kergill **118** 41 44-
53 55 57 58 **125** 117 196
256
John L. **118** 55
John Leroy **106** 69
John W. **118** 51 53 55 56 58
Joseph **74** 103
Julia Hull (Stoughton)
106 68
Lucy (Martin) (Nesmith)
108 4
Lucy H. **85** 448
Lyman Arthur **106** 68
Margaret **125** 115 116
Margaret (Glencross)
125 258
Martha **117** 246
Martha (Cargill) **117** 246
Martha (Dunn) **106** 68
Martha (Kergill) **125** 115
116
Mary **100** 74 **117** 245 246
Mary (Gregg) **106** 68
Nancy **74** 103
Philena **80** 445

McKEEN *cont'd*
Polly (Brigham) **106** 68
Rachel **125** 115 260
Rachel (Archibald) **125** 115 257
Rachel (Johnson) **125** 115
Rosannah **125** 117 119 256
Sabrina (Atwater) **125** 122 196 256
Samuel **105** 284 **106** 68 69 **118** 42 44 45 52 53 55 58 **125** 115 197 256
Sarah (Logan) **125** 115 119 197
Sarah Ann (Brown) **106** 68
Sarah Elizabeth **125** 196
Sarah Susanna **125** 197
Shirley Irene (York) **106** 69
Shirley York **106** 69
Silas **64** 235 **68** 250 **118** 96
Thomas Alvarus **125** 196
Walter Earl **106** 69
Walter Ernest **106** 61 68 69 130
William **85** 448 **118** 50 **125** 257
William Logan **125** 197
McKEEVER
Alexander **62** 171
John **118** 56
Nancy **61** 267
McKEIGHAN
Alexander H. **80** 43
Amy Ruhama **80** 43
Sarah **80** 43
William Arthur **80** 43
McKEISZY
John **73** 218
McKELLA
Howard **81** 385
Mary **81** 385
Selinda **81** 385
McKELLOR
Angus **114** 150
McKELLUP
Daniel **115** 117
John **115** 117
Mary **115** 117
McKELPIN
Isaac **79** 52
McKELSEY
Blake **100** 260
McKELVEY McKelvy
—— **67** 231
— Mrs. **61** 137
Ann **77** 262
Bridget **77** 179
Charles Pinckney **77** 262
Charles W. (Mrs.) **75** lxii
Dothea Anna **67** 231
Edward **61** 137
Ezekiel A. **77** 262
Flora **77** 262
Frances **77** 262
George **77** 262
Hannah Elizabeth **77** 262
Harold B. (Mrs.) **109** 232
Ira **77** 262
Isaac **77** 262

McKELVEY *cont'd*
James Peter **139** 220
Jane **77** 262
John **77** 179 262
Lude **77** 262
Lulu **77** 262
Nancy (Ryon) **139** 220
Robert (Mrs.) **86** 197
Sarah **77** 262
Savilla **77** 262
Sydney Maleia (Lawford) **139** 220
William Sheldon **139** 220
William Thomas **77** 262
McKenchnie *see* McKechnie
McKENCY
Judith **80** 26
McKENDLEY Betsey **65** 312 **89** 385
McKENDRICK
Norman Shaw **88** 169 **92** 402
McKENDRY Benjamin **55** 398 **57** 105
Elizabeth **55** 398 **57** 105 **134** 226
Ellen **93** 265
John **86** 460
Mary **87** 379 **93** 156
Mary (Tolman) **86** 460
William **93** 265 304 **100** 66
Winnifred **97** 219
McKenestry *see* McKinstry
McKENNA
Arthur **134** 90
Catherine Alice **96** 204
Charles **87** 121
Elizabeth **87** 121
Elizabeth (Haines) **124** 160
Ellsworth **134** 90
Isoline Orne **79** 202
James **134** 90
John **124** 160
John Sebastopol **134** 90
Kate **134** 90
Margaret **139** 202
Nugent **134** 90
Roger **139** 202
Susanna **87** 121
Theresa **134** 90
William Jay (Mrs.) **78** 330 **79** 202
McKENNAN
William **65** 54
McKENNE Ann **90** 328
Elizabeth (Cohoon) **128** 113
Gardner **128** 113
John **128** 113
Rebecca **128** 113
McKENNEN
Thomas **60** 161
McKENNEY Mackenny Mackkenny
Abigail **82** 330
Abram **148** 171 176
Ann **90** 328 **91** 19
Ann F. **90** 52
Benjamin **116** 180 184
Bert L. **100** 208

McKENNEY *cont'd*
Betty **99** 198
Catherine **55** 313 **82** 511
Charles **81** 250 **103** 194
Clara Ella **148** 175
Clarissa **80** 28
Cynthia **116** 184
Daniel **80** 28 **82** 205 **87** 123
David **82** 208 330
Eda **116** 184
Ede **116** 180
Edith **116** 180 184
Edith (Huff) **116** 184
Elias **87** 125
Elisha **72** 274
Ethel Delight **81** 363 **82** 237
G. W. **98** 197
George W. **148** 175
Hannah **111** 116 **148** 171 176
Hannah R. **80** 28
Henry **112** 288 **145** 364
Henry H. **91** 20
Horatio **116** 184
Humphrey **87** 126 **99** 198
Ira T. **100** 207
James **87** 122 **111** 116
Jane R. **72** 274
Jeremiah **82** 277
John **61** 135 **112** 90 **139** 215
Joshua **87** 122 123
Katharine **82** 205
Lester **105** 128
Lewis **98** 314
Lucy A. **100** 207
Lucy Ann **80** 28
Lydia (Gould) **97** 223
Mahali **103** 196
Margaret **111** 138
Maria D. **98** 197
Martha **82** 330
Mary **80** 27 **82** 205 **87** 124 **99** 198 **148** 175
Mary B. **103** 236
Mary Jane **111** 138
Mary Sophronia **81** 250
Matthew **80** 28
Miriam **142** 35
Moses **103** 190 191
Nancy **80** 28
Olive (Emery) **91** 20
Phebe **116** 184
Polly **87** 124
Salome **103** 258
Samuel **97** 223
Sarah **80** 27 **127** 78
Sarah Frances **82** 277
Sarah H. (Pulsifer) **98** 314
Sarah Jane **82** 277
Sophronia **72** 274
Stillman **116** 184
Susan **65** 80 **148** 176
Sylvia H. **100** 207
Thomas **105** 287
Thomas B. **100** 207
Timothy **111** 116
Walter Davis **78** 205
William **78** 412 **81** 368

McKENNEY *cont'd*
 100 63 **142** 35
McKENNON
 Willena **83** 430 435
McKENSTRE —— **120** 60
McKENZIE M'Kenzie
 Mackenzie Mackinzie
 McKensey McKensie
 McKensy McKenzey
 McKinzey
 —— **84** 123
 — Capt. **59** 406
 — Maj. **137** 313
 — Mr. **54** 291 **56** 253
 — Prof. **133** 39
 Adeline **59** 410
 Agnes **135** 248
 Alexander **51** 100 **52** 300
  55 230 **57** 130 **63** 308
  69 99 **77** xliii **86** 28
  100 2 **113** 87 **118** 41 44
  45 48 50 55 56 **125** 116
 Alexander Wedderburn
  113 87
 Alfred **68** 134
 Andrew **91** 353
 Angus **112** 207
 Ann **138** 288
 Ann Elizabeth **125** 197
 Anna **51** 361
 Anne **118** 329 **125** 263
 Barbara **118** 329
 Bessie Amelia **85** 191
 Catherine **118** 329
 Christian (Jordan)
  125 259
 Christiana (Gordon)
  125 197 198
 Christy **118** 329
 Colin **112** 201 203 212 213
  113 3 84-87
 Daniel **59** 410 **118** 329
 Deborah **73** 144
 Donald **118** 47 48
 Dougal **51** 361
 Duncan (Mrs.) **98** 147
 Elizabeth **113** 87 **118** 329
 Frederick **85** 241 **113** 8
 G. N. **112** 311
 George **62** 330 **64** 318
  107 191 **113** 93
 George N. **79** 337
 George Norbury **62** 390
  116 237
 Grenville C. **113** 64
 Hannah **118** 329
 Hector **118** 45
 Isabella **118** 55 **125** 197
 James **73** 140 **118** 309 310
  329 **125** 180 238
 James (Mrs.) **85** 196
 James A. **116** 284 **118** 309
  125 240
 Jane **118** 55 329 **125** 197
 Jennet **125** 197
 Jessie **118** 329
 Joanna F. (Hoxsie) **125**
  180 238 240
 John **62** 301 **64** 317 **73** 261
  80 127 **118** 45 329 **125**
  197 259

McKENZIE *cont'd*
 Joseph Philander **118** 310
 Kenneth **105** 276 **118** 45
  55 58 **125** 197 **126** 225
 Lois **54** 291 **56** 253
 Malcolm **118** 329
 Margaret **125** 197
 Margaret Brodie **87** 57
 Mary **59** 410 **107** 191 **118**
  329 **125** 263
 Mary Ann **68** 134
 Mary Graves **104** 309
 Mary S. **118** 309 310
 Nancy **125** 220
 Neil Campbell **104** 309
 Olive **83** 167
 Peter **56** 189 **62** 325
  118 329
 Phebe **59** 406
 Phebe Mayhew **59** 410
 Polly **66** 100
 Robert **118** 45 55
 Robert Gordon **125** 198
 Roderick **70** 17-20 138
  139 141 142 144-146 211
  303 **112** 210 274 **113** 92
 Rodrick **66** 100
 Sarah **91** 353 **118** 309
 Sarah Jane **118** 309
 Sarah Jane (Christ)
  104 309
 Stephen **142** 293
 Susan M. (Moares) **126** 67
 Susanna **80** 127
 Thomas **62** 252 **63** 240 **118**
  55 57
 William **117** 16
 William Douglas **71** 98
 Zachariah **73** 150
McKEON
 Alexander **62** 171
 Ann **62** 171 **90** 115
 William **62** 171
McKEOUGH
 Jane **131** 86 89
 John **127** 180
 Ruth (Godfrey) **127** 180
McKEOWN
 Agnes **85** 167
 Alexander **60** 349
 David Armstrong **85** 167
 Jane E. **85** 168
 John **85** 168
 Josephine **89** 360
 Robert **85** 167
McKERNELLY
 Patrick **65** 235
McKERNS
 Elizabeth **100** 300
McKERRAL
 Andrew **114** 150 151
McKEVER
 Dorothy **80** 167
 William **80** 167
McKEVY Philip **61** 348
McKEY Elizabeth Ann
  108 224
 James **60** 240 **144** 44
 Margaret Ann
  (McTetridge) **120** 16
 Patrick **61** 136

McKEY *cont'd*
 Robert **120** 16
McKIBBEN McKibbon
 Edna **80** 152
 Emma Eudora **80** 152
 Esther May **80** 152
 Etta May **90** 137
 Frank Pape **117** 216
 Hugh Byard **80** 152
 James **106** 235
 Jefferson **88** 93
 Mary Olevia (Betts) **88** 93
 Maud **80** 152
 Ralza Grant **80** 152
McKIE
 Thomas **118** 55 56
McKILLIPS
 David **104** 120
 Electa Mehitable
  (Wheelock) **142** 193
 George W. **86** 149
 Harriet Capron
  (Whipple) (Smith)
  86 149
 Hattie B. **142** 193
 John **142** 193
 Patrick **51** 469 470
 Resign (Davis) **104** 120
McKIM McKimm
 —— **55** lxxiii
 Abigail **120** 6
 Annie M. **75** xxv
 Annie Moore (Clymer)
  (Brooke) **83** 123
  214 236
 Augusta E. **111** 66
 Augusta Elizabeth **84** 208
 Catherine (Harrison)
  83 215
 Elizabeth **120** 6
 Haslett **77** 296
 James **99** 248
 John **83** 215
 John Windsor **62** 394
 Mabelle **61** xx
 Mary (Tibbetts) **99** 248
 Randolph Harrison
  83 214
 Randolph Harrison
  (Mrs.) **75** x xxv
 Rogé **77** 296
 Sally **77** 296
 William Duncan **77** 296
McKIMMY G. **91** 329
McKinistry *see* McKinstry
McKINLEY McKinlay
 — Maj. **81** 355
 Alexander **61** 135
 Anna Maria **67** 280
 Catherine **125** 261
 Chittannah (Rankin)
  135 251
 Clara Gibson **81** 106
 Duncan **99** 119 121 205
  208 **100** 241
 Edward **67** 280
 Eleanor **93** 377
 Eleanor (Metcalf) **126** 306
 Elizabeth **67** 280 **125** 260
 James **61** 267 **67** 280
  99 205

McKINLEY cont'd
Joan **99** 119
John **99** 121 **126** 306
Mary **99** 119 121 205 208
114 189
Mary (Frost) **100** 241
Samuel **61** 267
Vesta Lenore **85** 195
William **52** 285 288 **53**
201 206 373 377 **55** 231
58 154 **60** 111 **63** 388
66 lxxxiii **68** xiv xlviii
26 **69** lvii **72** xlix lv **73**
lxi **75** lxxxvii **77** 243
247 **79** 236 **105** 241 **136**
67
McKINNEY McHinney
McKinnie
Alexander **60** 74 76 **73** 41
83 36 365
Alice **108** 309
Ann **51** 339
Archibald **117** 36
Betsey **55** 80 **83** 366
Burt **84** 86
Candace **59** 101
Chester **60** 201
Chloe **59** 210 **60** 200
Daniel **51** 339 **60** 74 **117**
34 35 40 133 **119** 21
David **59** 98 208
Dorcas **117** 133
Ebenezer **117** 34
Elizabeth **83** 365
Elizabeth (Borton)
108 275
Ellen Depuy **77** 226
Elsje **108** 309
Erastus **59** 100 101 208-211
60 75 76 200 264 **83** 366
Eunice **59** 210 **60** 76
83 366
Fanny **59** 209
George **96** 35 **119** 21
Harrison **117** 35 133
Henry **77** 265
Hiram **117** 133
Jane **76** 88 **77** 226 **117** 36
John **77** 251 **108** 104 **115**
312 **125** 41
Jonas **76** 88
Jula **59** 98 208
Julia **84** 86
Justus **60** 200
King **117** 133
Lauricy **117** 133
Lois **96** 35
Lora **59** 210 **60** 75 **83** 366
Lorenzo **59** 211
Lydia **60** 200 **83** 366
Margaret **51** 339
Marie Adeliza (Falley)
108 104
Mary **77** 251
Mary B. **103** 236
Mercy (Blackley) **117** 34
Miles **117** 133
Mordecai **117** 132
Myrinda **60** 200
Ophelia Amanda **77** 265
Owen **59** 210

McKINNEY cont'd
Phila **60** 200
Philena (Barber) **126** 296
R. Kay **120** 155
Rachel **83** 366
Ralph **59** 208
Rosanna **59** 209
Roxey **83** 366
Sallie (Wheeler) **115** 312
Samuel **108** 275
Sarah A. **92** 225
Seldin **60** 200
Sophia **60** 201
Starling **59** 100
Susanna **117** 34
Susanna (Rutherford)
117 34
Thomas **77** 226
Vianna **117** 133
Walter D. **77** 323
Warren **59** 98 101 208-210
60 76 204 266 **83** 366
William **93** 397
McKINNON MacKinnon
Calvin **77** 262
Elizabeth **77** 262
Helen **62** 301
John **108** 211 215
Letitia (Piggot) **108** 215
Mary **77** 178 **82** 278
Olive Jane (Kinney)
108 211
Rhoda (Kenney) **108** 215
Robert Collins **108** 215
Samuel **62** 301
McKINSEY Mary Beale
118 163 **119** 314
McKINSTRY M'Kinstry
McKinistry
McKenstrey
McKinstrey
—— **52** 480 **61** 315
145 167
— Dr. **92** 310
— Mrs. **80** 67
Addis Emmet **88** 169
Adeline Margaret **80** 43
Caroline **113** 165
Charles **80** 43
Chloe (Elmer) **120** 43
Erwine **80** 43
James **91** 329
James T. **74** lx
John **111** 290 **113** 165
Keziah (Batcheller)
113 165
Lee **91** 329
Louisa **59** 260
Lucy **120** 43
Mary Allura **80** 43
Moses **59** 260
Roger Augustus **120** 43
William **92** 310
McKinzey see McKenzie
McKIRAHAN
M. F. **128** 92 96
McKISSICK
Hannah **90** 332
Lydia B. **90** 335
McKlean see McLean
McKLEM Robert **140** 298

McKleroy see McElroy
McKLISH Ann **125** 244
McKnab see McNab
McKnally see McNally
McKneely see McNeely
McKNIGHT Macknight
Alice **112** 154
Althea **77** 267
Betty **56** 255 **61** 269
Calvin **61** 287
Charles **145** 245
Daniel **111** 212
Dodge **81** 67 68 70
Eliza **61** 269
Esther **101** 205
George W. **89** 317
Helen (Lazell) **89** 317
Hu **61** 269
James **61** 269 **111** 212
John **61** 269
Margaret **61** 269
Martha B. **59** lxx
Mary **87** 284 **95** 359
Moses W. **98** 314
Nellie A. **98** 314
Sumner Thomas **80** 106
206 **118** 68
Susan Maria **85** 329
Wealthy **61** 287
McKOIN Thomas **62** 243
McKOWN
Ann Maria **74** 96
Caroline Elizabeth
136 270
Ellen / Helen (Henderson)
136 270
John **84** 271
John Alexander **136** 270
Josephine **89** 360
Rebecca **117** 253
Robert **60** 346
Sarah **89** 268
Sarah (Harwood) **111** 305
William George **136** 270
McKoy see McCoy
McKune see McCune
McKUSICK
Evalina Jane **89** 388
Jeremiah **147** 264 266
Nancy **83** 147
Victor A. **115** 80 **120** 160
121 320
McKvicker see McVicar
McLACHLAN MacLachlan
Juliana **89** 188
Margaret Mary **67** 19
McLACHLIN
Ann **106** 108
Daniel **125** 31
William **106** 108
McLain see McClain &
McLean
McLallan see McClellan
McLANAHAN Elizabeth
Hawley **97** 92 **98** 351
Ella Amsbry (Spendley)
97 162 **98** 351
Helen Spendley **97** 92
98 351
John King **97** 92 **98** 351
John King (Mrs.) **83** 249

McLANAHAN *cont'd*
84 190 **97** 79 92 162 **98**
351
Mary Anne (Martin)
98 351
McLANATHAN
Oreanna **66** 54
Richard B. K. **110** 221
McLANE *see also* McLean
Alberta **65** 135
Angus Wilton **97** 208
Arthur **114** 190
Benjamin **75** 152
Charles Bancroft **97** 71
Clarissa **90** 108
Daniel **75** 152
Deliverance **75** 152
Edward **140** 166
Elizabeth **97** 71 **114** 190
Elizabeth (Bancroft) **97** 71
Enoch **114** 190
Georgiana **91** 56
Hannah E. **88** 331
Jane **126** 127
John **140** 57 166
John Roy **97** 71
Maclean W. **114** 5 71 134
Mary **75** 152
Mary Ann (Payton)
136 362
Nancy (Amory) **140** 57
Rebecca **132** 241
Rebecca W. **77** 147
Rebecca Willie **98** 263
310 311
Robert **114** 190
McLANIN Dinah **115** 225
McLANLIN
— Col. **120** 48
McLAREN McClaren
McClearn McLarn
Abner West **127** 50
Bethiah **127** 50
Elizabeth **127** 50 126
Elizabeth (Crichton)
89 231
Hannah **92** 318
Harold Johnston **86** 197
Hugh **127** 50
Isabella **89** 230 **127** 50
117 126
James **92** 318 322 **108** 119
127 50 117 126
Jane **108** 303
Jerusha (Hamilton)
108 118
John **73** 150 **89** 231
128 130
Lydia **92** 318
Mary **76** lxxi **127** 50
128 31
Matthew **123** 14 **127** 50
Nancy **128** 30
Robert **127** 50 **128** 31
Sarah **127** 50 **128** 30 31
Sarah (West) **127** 50
Sarah Lucinda **84** 114
Thomas **127** 50
McLarty *see* McClarty
M'Clary *see* McClary
M'Clash *see* McClash

McLATCHEY Caroline
Sophia **89** 197
Charles Henry **89** 197
Charlotte Ann **89** 197
Ellen Amelia **89** 197
James Harris **89** 197
John Thomas **89** 197
Mary Eliza **89** 197
Olivia Arabella **89** 197
Otis Samuel **89** 197
Rebecca Jane **89** 197
Sarah Alice **89** 197
Sophia **89** 197
Sophia (Calkins) **89** 197
Susan Isabella **89** 197
Thomas **89** 197
McLAUGHAN
Priscilla **73** 232
McLAUGHLIN
Mackclaflin
Macklaflen
Mackloflen
Macklothlan
MacLaughlan
McGlauflin
McGlaughan
—— **61** 338 **66** 32 **106** 254
— Capt. **123** 9
Abbie E. **101** 217
Abby Eliza **103** 176
Abigail **62** 34 **102** 220
Abigail S. **102** 220
Adela **101** 217 **103** 176
Albert **101** 215
Albert J. **102** 220
Albion K. P. **102** 220
Alice **103** 178 277 278
Alice Maria **103** 278
Almira **51** 194
Almira S. **102** 220
Alvah Rufus (Mrs.)
108 134
Alvin **103** 278
Alvira **102** 220
Amanda **128** 94
Amy Hamilton Gray
(Williams) **109** 228
Andrew Cunningham
66 95
Annie **137** 183
Archie **137** 183
Benjamin **87** 234 235
Benjamin F. **101** 36
103 176
Benjamin Franklin **70**
198 **102** 220
Bertha **102** 223
Bertha V. **89** 302
Betsey A. **124** 61
Caroline (Bartlett) **124** 62
Charles **70** 364 **109** 228
Charles (Mrs.) **94** 136
120 148
Charles Jasper (Mrs.)
93 185
Clara (Starkey) **128** 264
Clifford L. **89** 302
Daniel **62** 34 **78** 436
103 299
David **91** 329
Della **103** 119

McLAUGHLIN *cont'd*
Dugald Campbell
105 315
Edward **91** 329
Eliza **103** 176
Eliza (Clark) **101** 36
Eliza Jane (Ackerman)
137 183
Elizabeth **100** 298 **137** 183
Elizabeth (Kerr) **85** 349
Elizabeth Rena **81** 460
Ella L. **121** 179
Ellen M. **102** 223
Elsie **103** 278
Elsie Jane **95** 378
Emeline **101** 215 **103** 278
Emeline (Furge) **111** 137
Emily G. (Gunnison)
124 63
Emma **113** 316
Emma J. (Hardy) **121** 179
Emma Victoria **105** 315
Ernest Thurston **103** 176
Esther **103** 278 **137** 183
Eva E. **121** 182
Ezra **101** 35 36 **102** 220
103 176
Francis H. **121** 179
Frank Benjamin **103** 176
Fred (Mrs) **103** 119
Fred Lewis **103** 176
Frederic **111** 137
Frederick Chase (Mrs.)
100 112
G. C. **109** 270
George **109** 228
George H. **128** 264
George W. **70** 327
Gertrude **103** 277
Hannah **70** 353 **101** 34 **102**
220 **128** 175
Hannah Eliza **102** 220
Harriet **70** 198
Harriet L. **103** 280
Harry Lewis **103** 178
Helen **102** 220
Herbert A. **89** 302
Hitty **102** 220
Isaac **102** 220
Isaiah **137** 183
James **61** 239 **70** 327 **85**
349 **101** 33 **102** 220 **103**
280 **108** 130 **137** 183
Jas. **128** 94
Jesse Benton **102** 223
Joanna **61** 331 **78** 436
Joanna (Warner) **93** 280
John **101** 33 **102** 220 223
124 62 **137** 183
John Charles Fremont
102 223
John S. **102** 220
John W. **70** 327
Joseph **137** 183
Joseph A. **89** 302
Josephine A. **102** 223
Joshua **62** 42
Josiah **101** 34 **102** 220
103 277
Julia E. **87** 21
Laura **102** 220

McLAUGHLIN *cont'd*
Lavinia **103** 280
Lewis **102** 220 **103** 278
Lillian Rich **83** 232 **109**
    216 228
Lorimer **101** 214 215 **103**
    178 278
Lovilla **103** 280
Lucy (Stearns) (Keys)
    93 185
Lydia (Wilder) **105** 315
Lydia Curtis **70** 364
Margaret **101** 215
Margaret E. (Griffin)
    101 34 **103** 277
Maria **137** 183
Martha **103** 280
Martha A. (Greenlaw)
    101 33
Mary **63** 179 334 **101** 33
    109 228
Mary (Wendall) **109** 228
Mary A. **95** 378
Mary A. (McLaughlin)
    95 378
Mary Ann **77** 187
Mary C. W. **70** 327
Mary E. **103** 280
Mary Elizabeth **70** 327
Mary Ellen **103** 277
Mary M. **101** 33 **102** 220
Mary W. **86** 331
Mason **70** 353
Melissa Ann **103** 176
Melissa Ann (Sprague)
    101 35 36
Nancy **89** 298 **102** 220
Nellie Augusta **78** 206
Nellie L. **102** 223
Nelly **66** 32
Oliver Wendall **109** 228
Owen **66** 32
Parker **81** 460
Paulina S. (Damon) **101**
    214 215
Pauline **68** 158
Pauline S. **103** 178
Polly **102** 220
Rachel **111** 139
Rachel W. **102** 220
Rebecca **61** 239
Rena **81** 222
Robert **58** 98 **61** 111 331
    63 334 **78** 436 **93** 280
Robert A. **89** 298
Roberto **103** 280
Ruth **100** 300
Ruth (Niles) **87** 234 235
Ruth Ann **106** 126
Sally **102** 220
Samuel T. **102** 220
Sarah **78** 436 **101** 34
Sarah (Young) **137** 183
Sarah B. **102** 220
Sarah Lillias **103** 277
Susan S. (Morgan) **101** 33
Susanna **103** 280
Terrance **77** 187
Thomas **89** 298 **101** 33 **103**
    278 **137** 183
Thomas J. **102** 220

McLAUGHLIN *cont'd*
William **61** 269 **101** 31 218
    102 220 **135** 149
William C. **95** 378
William Henry **103** 278
William S. **101** 33 **102** 220
    103 280
William Vance **102** 220
Willis G. **102** 220
McLAUGHTON
Ira **124** 63
McLAUREN
Maria Blakely **78** 35
McLAURIN
Alexander **107** 170
McLAUTHLIN
—— **102** 321
Elizabeth Pease (Vincent)
    102 67
Elizabeth Rena **102** 67 68
Hannah Howard (Reed)
    102 67
Jane **75** 129
Jane (West) **102** 67
John **102** 67
Joseph **102** 67
Margaret (Miller) **102** 67
Martin **102** 67
Martin Parris **102** 67
Rena **102** 61 128
McLEAN Maclane
    Maclean McKlean
    McLain - *see also*
    McClain & McLane
—— **76** 144 **91** 349
    112 273
— Capt. **133** 308
— Hutchins **133** 308
— Lieut. **112** 269
— Pres. **58** 412
Abigail **61** 87 89 90 193
    294 296 389 **62** 90 193
    379 **63** 71 **72** 106 **86** 318
Abijah **98** 45
Addie **69** 334
Alexander **56** 164 **58** 196
    197 401 402 **59** 95 98
    208 209 416 **60** 73 74 76
    78 201 205 265 **83** 359
    366 **109** 160
Alice **89** 58
Allan **79** 284 **83** 106 366
    128 179
Allan Alexander (Mrs.)
    106 125 **117** 148
Allen **58** 401 **59** 413 **60** 201
    205 264 **69** 246 **71** 274
    72 167
Amelia (Blair) **120** 17
Amelia L. **86** 318
Amzi Chapin **109** 160
Ann (Fraser) **127** 279
Ann (Lake) **98** 332
Ann Elizabeth (Fitz-
    Randolph) **98** 332
Anna **85** 409 **86** 53
Anne (Amory) **120** 82
Annie A. **91** 386
Annie Elliston **98** 82
Archibald **72** 30 **83** 359
    113 88 89 92

McLEAN *cont'd*
Barbara **79** 284
Benjamin **130** 281
Betsey **83** 359
Betsey Goodwin **71** 276
    72 42
Betty **60** 74 **83** 166
Catherine **81** 251 **126** 292
Catherine A. **96** 287
Charles **59** 209 **71** 162 **84**
    86 **89** 105 **92** 171
Charles Batchelor
    62 xxxvii
Charlotte A. L. **86** 53
Christina **79** 284
Clara Stanley **58** 412
Clarence T. **69** 334
Clarissa **60** 266
Cornelius **98** 332
Crosby Chamberlain
    85 196
Cyrus **61** 90
Daniel **69** 246 **104** 102
    118 45 **125** 115
Dennis **83** 166
Duncan **104** 118
E. L. **91** 329
Edith Alice **104** 145
Edward **59** 211 **69** 223
    224 294 70 24 **89** 58 **127**
    280 **128** 28
Edward Lee (Mrs.) **98** 279
Egbert F. **86** 318
Eleanor **125** 198
Eleanor Weir **85** 315
Eliza **69** 32 **125** 218
Eliza Augusta **86** 53
Elizabeth **60** 201 **127** 280
    128 28
Elizabeth (McKeen)
    125 256
Elizabeth M. **96** 287
Elizabeth Mearns
    (Macartney) **124** 194
Ellen **53** 234
Ellen S. **84** 86
Emily Smith **82** 20
Emma L. **84** 86
Emma R. **84** 86
Ethel Louise **89** 58
Eugene F. **84** 86
Finlay **118** 54
Flavel **61** 194 **86** 318
Francis **59** 100 101 208
    209 211 212 **60** 74 201
    204 265 266 **84** 86 **137**
    309
Frederick **127** 280 **128** 28
George **127** 279
George Elbridge **82** 20
Georgiana **91** 56
Hannah **58** 196 **60** 80 **79**
    386 **125** 222
Harry **72** 46 101 175 176
Hector **71** 63 **72** 29 **86** 318
    112 266
Helen **89** 58
Henry **72** 106 **79** 53
Hugh **118** 45 **125** 115 198
Ida Gertrude (Billings)
    94 49 50

McLEAN *cont'd*
Inez Mabel (Tyler) **89** 105
Isabella **127** 280 **128** 28
Isable (King) **126** 292
Ivon **115** 35
J. P. **53** 383 **113** 12 **118**
    175 177
Jabez **83** 106
James **61** 87 89 90 193 194
    294 296 389 **62** 90 193
    292 379 **63** 71 **69** 32 **71**
    275 **72** 184 **86** 318 **89** 58
    118 45 **125** 115 256 **127**
    280 **128** 28
James (Mrs.) **84** 341 **85**
    188 **89** 58 134 190
James L. **86** 318
Janet Ann **145** 255
Joanna **60** 76 78 **83** 366
John **56** 186 **69** 322 **71**
    273 275 276 303 **72** 32
    34 41 171 178 **91** 349 **96**
    137 **110** 232 **116** 100
    118 45 46 **120** 82 **125**
    115 **127** 279 **141** 104
    145 106
John Hall **59** 208 **84** 86
John Patterson **59** xliv
    70 191
John S. **96** 287
Kenneth **127** 279
L. Cordelia **84** 86
L. Louisa **84** 86
Lauchlan **71** 80 162 164
    280 **72** 29 30 33 **122** 269
Lester **62** 90
Lora **59** 100
Louis **106** 47
Louise Elizabeth **104** 143
Lovisa **62** 84
Lucy **71** 80 280 **72** 33
Lydia Maria Slater **84** 86
M. W. **123** 211
Maclean W. **93** 399 **112**
    190 257 **113** 15 104 166
    249 **115** 86 181 268 **116**
    27 100 103 149 191 313
    117 180 295 **118** 83 197
    275 323 **119** 26 161 162
    260 **120** 26 97 187 272
    121 37 127 224 260 **122**
    51 131 196 254 **123** 54
    129 183 266 **124** 69 70
    146 **125** 141 **126** 103
    127 18 108 193 250 **141**
    57 206
Maclean Warren **85** 196
Margaret **56** 186 **72** 101
    109 191 **125** 195 **127**
    279 280 **128** 28
Margaret (McDonald)
    125 258
Margaret (McFarland)
    89 58
Margaret (Wallace)
    96 137
Margaret Alberta Barton
    106 168 298 299 **107**
    111 115 293
Margaret Ann **125** 198
Maria **84** 86

McLEAN *cont'd*
Mariann **71** 164
Martha (McDonald)
    125 198
Mary **58** 197 402 **59** 98
    101 208 413 416 **69** 246
    322 **83** 106 366 **98** 45
    332 **125** 118 256 **126**
    292
Mary Jane Reid **69** 322
Mary T. Palmer **84** 86
Maryetta **92** 171
Maude Millicent **82** 20
Mercy **115** 121
N. Emeline **86** 56
Nancy **51** 50
Neal **71** 303
Newton G. **85** 315
Niel **79** 386
Norman **125** 32
Norman Campbell
    133 86
Norris Windon **124** 194
Obed P. **86** 53
Octa Strong **84** 86
Ogden **61** 296 **86** 318
Oscar **85** 409
Otis **59** 100 **84** 86
Pamela **98** 45
Pamelia **86** 318
Patty **83** 166
Peter **106** 165
Phebe **86** 53
Rachel Ann **118** 79
Rebecca Willie **98** 263 311
Rhodrick **71** 274
Robert **86** 438 **91** 329 **111**
    140 **117** 207 258
Robert Caldwell **86** 438
Robert Cutler **133** 86
Robert Elbridge **82** 20
Rockland **71** 275
Rosanna **59** 95 **60** 73
    83 366
Roxey **59** 212 **60** 74 **84** 86
Ruby **89** 105
Ruby C. **115** 122
Ruth **102** 122
Sabra Melvina (Lovely)
    111 140
Sabrina **125** 198
Sally **72** 34
Samuel **76** 476
Sarah **59** 212 **60** 201 **72** 41
    176 **95** 190 **107** 56
Sarah (Throckmorton)
    89 58 134
Sarah B. **84** 86
Sarah Wells **86** 438
Silas **85** 409 **86** 53
Silas O. **86** 53
Sophia **92** 115
Stafford (Mrs.) **92** 184
Susan H. **72** 106
Susanna **60** 78 **72** 46 101
Timothy **118** 45 46 **125**
    115 256
Vine **61** 193 294 **62** 193
W. T. **84** 86
Walter **89** 105
Warden **86** 438

McLEAN *cont'd*
Warren McLean **84** 234
Wealthy A. **86** 318
William **71** 275 **84** 86 **91**
    328 **127** 279
William L. (Mrs.) **145** 234
William Lippard **81** 107
    219 **86** 203 236 438
McLEARN
Elizabeth **108** 304
James **88** 128 **108** 304
Jane **88** 128 **108** 303
Julia Ann (Bishop) **120** 17
Richard Judson **120** 17
McLEARY
Deborah **77** 136
Samuel **77** 136
McLEISH
John **142** 293
Rhoda (Bassett) **142** 293
McLELLAN McLallan
    McLellen McLellon
M'Clenachan *see*
    McClenachan
McLENATHAN Caroline
    (McFarland) **137** 282
M'Clench *see* McClench
McLENDON
Betty Randolph
    104 144
Posey Augustus **103** 318
McLENICHON
William **97** 106
McLENNAN
Duncan D. **97** 219
J. S. **119** 248 250
Mary **97** 219
Sarah Catherine **97** 219
McLEOD Macleod
    McLoad McLoud - *see*
    also McCloud
—— **57** 286 **79** 19
— Mr. **95** 236
— Mrs. **70** 19
— Widow **70** 298
Alexander **52** 312 **140** 166
Alexander Byron
    65 xxxvii
Anson **52** 391
Aylse **127** 202
Cameron **68** lxxv
Catherine **77** 262 **140** 166
Charles **77** 262
Christie Ellen **96** 136
Colin Campbell (Mrs.)
    85 196
Cornelia Jane **77** 262
Daniel **80** 130
David **69** 213 220 222 224
    296 298 303 305 306
Donald **127** 204
Dora Ellen (Bancroft)
    96 136
Eldon **68** lxxv
Eleanor **125** 121
Elizabeth **77** 262 **80** 130
    127 204 **145** 135
Elizabeth (Lee) **126** 282
Ellen Elizabeth **77** 226
Elsie May **96** 136
Ernest John **96** 136

McLEOD *cont'd*
Evelyn **68** lxxv
George **127** 202
George Henry **77** 226
Harrison Lowell **96** 136
Helen **68** lxxv
James **77** 262 **99** 128 **127** 202 **128** 118
Jedida **128** 118
John **51** 297 **52** 312 **127** 202 276
Katharine **92** 228
Lola **68** lxxv
Lowell **96** 136
Malcolm **61** 406
Margaret **126** 282
Mary **80** 130
Mary (Murray) **99** 128 **127** 202
Mary E. **78** 205
Mary V. **79** 19
Michael Sanders **77** 262
Norman **51** 449 **112** 201 **113** 94
Norman (Mrs.) **77** 237 **78** 205
Philena **57** 286
Rebecca **127** 276
Rebecca (Darss) **127** 276
Robert R. **59** 92 93 234
Robert Randall **59** xliv
Sally **82** 397
Samuel (Mrs.) **109** 130 **115** 149 **117** 153 **118** 163 **119** 153 **120** 153
Sarah **77** xliii **91** 54
Sarah (Giddings) **116** 96
Wallace G. **111** 75
William **68** lxxv **77** 262 **117** 4 13 16
William Alexander **68** xliii lxxiv

McLEON
Alexander **54** 259
Francis **54** 259
John **81** 290
Rhoda **81** 290

McLESTER
Daniel **78** 304
Eleanor **137** 256
John **101** 52

McLINDEN
John **117** 4 16

McLINZEY
Murray **64** 110

McLISH
Margaret **73** 144
McLoad *see* McLeod

McLOON Macloon
Ebenezer **66** 107
Ebenezer C. **90** 105
Eliza Ellen **54** cxxvii
Rachel (Lilly) **90** 105
M'Clothland *see* McClothland
McLoud *see* McLeod

McLOUGHLIN
Alexander **61** 269
John **61** 269
Mary **61** 269
Patrick **61** 347

McLOUGHLIN *cont'd*
R. **61** 347
Sarah **97** 84

McLOUTH Lucy **90** 69

McLUCAS McClucas
McGlucas
Abraham **90** 327 **91** 19 116
Benjamin **115** 308 **116** 301
Dorcas (Young) **115** 308
Hannah **71** 221 **110** 289
Hannah (Young) **116** 297
Isaiah **91** 116
Jane **91** 116
Jane (Nason) **90** 327 **91** 19
John **71** 218 **110** 289 **114** 46 292
Joshua **110** 289
Lucy **71** 225 **79** 219 **93** 354
Mary **71** 217 **110** 289
Mary (Cole) **110** 289 **114** 46
Oliver **116** 297
Peggy **90** 235
Phebe **95** 185
Sally **90** 326 **91** 17
Sarah **71** 220 **91** 116 **100** 36 **110** 289
M'Clure *see* McClure

McMACKIN
Martha **71** lvi
Matilda **89** 30

McMAHAN
Elizabeth D. **80** 27
Frances Sarah **112** 140
Isabella **112** 89
Joel **112** 140
John **80** 27 **112** 89
Lucy **80** 27
Mary (Austin) **112** 140
Samuel **91** 387

McMAHON Macmahon
Alice Isabel (Russell) **97** 119
Alice Jeanette (Roach) **97** 119
Alice Myrtle **97** 119
Amy Josephine **97** 119
Andrew M. **97** 119
Anna Holland **72** 274
Benjamin **101** 216
Betty Jean **97** 119
Bonnie Eva **97** 119
Charles Cushing **83** 295
Charlotte Eloise (Alvord) **90** 172
Dobson W. 68 281
Dorothy Esther **97** 119
Edward Thomas (Mrs.) **90** 172
Elizabeth Donnell **72** 274
Ethel Louise (Williams) **83** 435 **84** 23
Fanny Blanche **97** 119
Frances Sarah **112** 140
Frances W. (Spindler) **97** 119
George Warren **97** 119
Harold Kenneth **97** 119
Howard Spindler **97** 119
Ida Cushing **83** 295
Irma H. (Drost) **97** 119

McMAHON *cont'd*
James **77** 269 **81** 201 202 **86** 364
James H. **61** 109
Jane **52** 339
John **83** 299 300
Josie (Israel) **83** 299 300
Kate (Israel) **83** 299 300
Laura R. **81** 202
Lydia **82** 47 **117** 168
Margaret **82** 465
Margaret Helen **86** 364
Martin T. **58** lxiii
Mary Ann **81** 202
Mary Ann (Radcliff) **137** 77
Maud Cyrene (Johnston) **97** 119
Mercy **82** 47
Michael **111** 115
Nathaniel **105** 277 320
Nellie (Gilbert) **86** 364
Roger **81** 201 **137** 77
Russell Andrew **97** 119
Sarah **81** 201 202
Sarah Jane **79** 210 **81** 201 202
Terrence **72** 274
Thalia **68** 281
Thalia Maria **68** 281
Thomas **117** 171
Thomas (Mrs.) **117** 168
William **83** 299 300
William Howard **97** 119
William John **83** 435 **84** 23

McMAIN Mary **147** 115
McMan *see* McMann

McMANAN
James **97** 375
Martha **97** 375
Rebecca **97** 375

McMANIGAL
Helen Foster **92** 43
William **92** 43

McMANN McMan
Elizabeth **92** 389
James **105** 210
John **51** 465
Margaret **51** 465

McMANNERS
Catherine **142** 303
Elizabeth **142** 303
John **142** 303

McMANUS
MacManus
McMannes
McManness
McMannis
Amanda **57** xlix
Ann Eliza **90** 177
Anne **128** 177
Barnard **118** 64
Bryan **61** 268
Catherine (McDonald) **128** 177
Hannah **67** 375
Kenney **90** 177
Lucyann **109** 184
Martha (Foster) **90** 177

McMANUS *cont'd*
　Mary **85** 315 **118** 64
　　128 177
　Patrick **74** 99 **139** 196
　Robert **57** xlix
　Susanna **118** 64
　Thomas **128** 177 **139** 196
McMARNASS
　Hannah **100** 300
McMARNE
　Elmira **80** 26
McMARR
　Francis **112** 286
　Mary **100** 27
　William **100** 27
McMARSTON
　Isabel **111** 92
　John **111** 92
McMARTIN
　Anginette **69** 324
　Ettie **69** 324
　Peter **69** 324
McMASTER MacMaster
　McMasters
　Algernon **88** 8
　Anna **96** 128
　Anne **72** xxxvi
　Byron **71** 50
　Caroline **86** 101
　Caroline T. (Bancroft)
　　96 128
　Daniel **83** 145 146
　Dimmis (Skeel) **136** 360
　Elizabeth (Brown) **91** 264
　Elizabeth (Chase) **88** 8
　Elizabeth (Wattrous)
　　86 445
　Eloisa M. **148** 172
　Gertrude (Stevenson)
　　86 445
　Guy H. **114** 67
　Hannah **136** 360
　James **72** xxxvii **86** 444
　　445 **117** 4 16
　Jennie **64** 123
　John **86** 445 **108** 194
　John Bach **52** 382 **54** 456
　　57 xxxi 232 **61** 106 **84**
　　180 **86** 444 **87** 70 175
　Julia Anna Matilda (Bach)
　　86 44 445
　Marget **91** 262
　Mary **71** 50
　Miriam (Weaver) **108** 194
　Philip Duryee **86** 445
　Rachel **105** 219
　Samuel **91** 264
　Sarah **64** 123
　Theodore James **86** 445
　William **64** 123
　William J. **96** 128
　Young **136** 360
McMEAL
　Archibald **51** 464
　Mary **51** 464
McMEEKIN
　Alexander **60** 27
McMEIKAN
　Grace **104** 231
　John **104** 231

McMEIKAN *cont'd*
　Mary L. (Wetmore)
　　104 231
McMELLAN
　Samuel **62** 81
McMICHAEL —— **54** 456
　Catherine (Fitz-
　　Randolph) **98** 231
　E. **98** 231 232 **99** 51
　Grace Evelyn **84** 192
　Jane (Rankin) **135** 251
　Margaret (Rankin)
　　135 251
　Maria **126** 296
　Martha **98** 231
　Mary **98** 231
　Robert **98** 231
　Thomas **98** 231
　William H. **111** 80
McMILLAN McMillin
　—— **111** 185
　Alastair **106** 191
　Ananias **119** 79
　Angeline E. **125** 53
　Anna (White) **106** 80
　Anne **104** 232
　Anne (Russell) **104** 231
　Archibald **125** 217
　Bertha Lee **102** 124
　Carrie (Dauchy) **111** 302
　　305
　Catherine **67** 281 **116** 289
　Claud Nelson **111** 164
　Daniel **119** 79
　David **119** 79
　Dorothy (Fouts) **104** 232
　Elizabeth **80** 49 **119** 79
　Elizabeth (Colby)
　　(Walker) **125** 112
　Elizabeth (Murray)
　　104 231
　Ellise **119** 79
　Elsie **104** 232
　Fannie J. **116** 66
　Grace (McMeikan)
　　104 231
　Hannah **106** 191
　Harriet **89** 233
　Helen Russell **104** 231
　Hugh **95** 305 **117** 11
　James **119** 79
　James McMeikan **104** 231
　James Thayer **100** 108
　　104 231 232 237 **105**
　　131
　Joel **91** 329
　John **68** 158 **73** 103 104
　　107 159 **114** 150 **116**
　　149 **119** 79 **125** 112
　Joshua **106** 191
　Kate Louise **60** 276
　Laura A. **68** 158
　Lydia E. **68** 158
　Margaret **91** 375
　Marie Louise **104** 231
　Marie Louise (Thayer)
　　104 231
　Mary **69** 32 **119** 79
　Mary (Whittemore) **108**
　　167 **125** 216
　Richard Frederick **91** 142

McMILLAN *cont'd*
　Robert **119** 79
　Robert Dudley **95** 305
　Ruth **115** 298
　Sally **125** 219
　Sarah **119** 79
　Sarah (Cogan) **111** 185
　Sarah (White) **106** 80
　Virginia (Cutting)
　　104 231
　William **104** 231 **108** 167
　　119 79 **125** 216
　William Charles **104** 231
　　232
McMILLIAN
　Anna **78** 74
　Joseph **127** 147
　Mary **137** 339
　Timothy **79** 44
McMillin *see* McMillan
McMillion *see* McMillian
McMINN
　Margaret **87** 23
　Mary A. **115** 208
McMITCHELL
　Rebecca **51** 362
McMORDY
　Anthony **61** 266
McMORRINE
　Robert **88** 366
McMORRIS Macmorris
McMORROW
　James **61** 268
　John **61** 269
　Michael **69** 127
McMULLEN M'Mullen
　McMullan McMullin
　Agnes **97** 163
　Alexander **61** 353
　Andrew **61** 353
　Ann Bradford **110** 56
　Anna (Bradt) **110** 72
　Annette **110** 72
　Archibald **56** 147 **57** 255
　　105 205
　Barbara **61** 353
　Betsey **61** 352
　Charlotte **128** 94
　Christina **95** 168
　Daniel Joseph **91** 53
　Dennis **106** 253
　Eli Glover **147** 226
　Esther **61** 353
　Fanny **61** 352
　Frederic Bogart **68** 385
　　74 322
　Helen (Apted) **110** 56
　Henry **110** 72
　Herbert Garber **86** 197
　Hugh **117** 16 17
　James **61** 266
　Jane **61** 352 **133** 156
　John **61** 351 352
　John B. **110** 56
　Jonathan **61** 352
　Josephine **97** 163
　Latham (Mrs.) **96** 189
　Lucile Devereux **74** 297
　Lucy **73** 285
　Mae Pearl (Hannum)
　　91 53

McMULLEN *cont'd*
Margaret **61** 351
Marietta **108** 135
Martha **135** 77
Mary **61** 352
Mary Jeanne **110** 56
Molly (Thomas) **96** 189
Nora **92** 10
Orland **74** 297
Patrick **60** 161 **97** 163
Phebe Ann (Angell)
147 226
Robert **121** 238
Samuel **61** 351
T. **91** 329
Thomas **61** 353
William **61** 352
McMUNN
Martha Ann **82** 22
McMURDY John **61** 265
McMURPHY
M'Murphy
MacMurphy
Annis **51** 466
Betsey **74** 18
George **54** 293
James **92** 273
Jane **54** 293
Jesse **113** 82
Jesse G. **79** 225
John **101** 260 **113** 82
140 17
Margaret **74** 18
Nancy **54** 293 **84** 125
William **51** 466
McMURRAN Joseph P.
(Mrs.) **113** 308
McMURRAY —— **92** 36
Alexander **111** 74
Cooksen **108** 79
Eliza **116** 66
Elizabeth **123** 319
Ella J. (Hughes) **116** 66
Emma Lincoln **78** 326
James **116** 66
John **81** 347
Mary **81** 347
Maura Maud **81** 347
Olive **116** 66
Rebecca **111** 73
Susanna (Cline) **108** 79
William **116** 66
McMURTRIE McMurtry
Abraham **106** 304
Amelia (Barton) **106** 304
Catherine (Ryerson)
88 290
Doris Irene **82** 347
Douglas C. **91** 97 **104** 92
93
Edward Painter **82** 347
Edward Painter (Mrs.)
82 347
George Gibson **82** 347
Gerald **111** 164 **112** 162
118 166
Mary Elizabeth **75** xxiv
88 86 171 290
Mary Gould **85** 194
R. Gerald **94** 305 **113** 161
114 157 **115** 156 **116**

McMURTRIE *cont'd*
155 **117** 155 **119** 155
120 155 **121** 156
Robert Roscoe (Mrs.)
106 125
Sarah **128** 266
William **88** 290
McMUTTEN
John **58** 372
Mary **58** 372
Polly **58** 372
McNAB McKnab
Allan **88** 169
Harriet B. **83** 25 28
James **83** 25 28 **118** 42 43
46 48 50-52 54-57 59
John **118** 43 47
McNAIL
Stanley D. **112** 75
William B. **112** 75
McNAIR
Andrew **84** 354
Boyd **92** 400
Daniel **90** 209
David D. **69** 287
James Birtley **78** 113 **85**
240 **110** 319 **115** 76
John **130** 155
Mary Wilson **69** 287
McNAIRY Abigail Esther
(Bush) **98** 350
Amos **98** 350
Amos Bush **98** 350
Amos Bush (Mrs.) **75**
xxiii 64 **94** 278 **95** 144
148 **98** 350
Elizabeth **98** 350
Gladys **95** 144 **98** 350
Mary **75** xxiii
Mary (Pack) **98** 350
McNALL
George M. **128** 268
Joseph **93** 397 **100** 63
Lucinda R. (Middaugh)
128 268
Minerva (Hesser) **128** 268
Otis O. **128** 268
McNALLY McKnally
McAnally McAnnally
McKnally McNalliu
Harriet **87** 389
James **61** 352
Luke **70** 261
McTagues **112** 282
Michael **60** 187 **62** 329
Ridgway **99** 148
McNAMARA McNamar
Anna **100** 203
Anne **101** 260
Anne (Smyth) **100** 203
Charles E. **104** 102
Daniel George **54** 229
64 329
Dennis **100** 203
Dorothy A. (Kimball)
110 223
F. N. **141** 98
J. B. **57** 342 **65** 154
Mary **104** 102
Michael Henry **64** 329
Myrtie Martha **144** 117

McNAMARA *cont'd*
Nancy **100** 296
Nancy Ann (Bannister)
101 260
Thomas **104** 102
William T. (Mrs.) **110** 223
McNAMEE
Ann Eliza **115** 26
James **115** 25 26 112
James Lawrence **115** 25
John Lawrence **115** 27 112
Lawrence **115** 27 110 112
Maria **115** 27 110 112
Nancy **115** 25 26 112
Patrick **62** 80
Richard **115** 112
Theodore **115** 110
William James **115** 110
McNANTZ
Charles **73** 226
McNANY
Elizabeth **75** 13
James **75** 13
Mary Elizabeth **75** 13
McNARY
George **81** 418
Hephzibah Melissa
109 38
Jerusha **81** 418
Joseph Rea **69** xxxii 191
192
Julia A. **81** 418
Katharine **100** 117
Minnie **82** 236
Morris **109** 38
Sarah **123** 74
Sarah (Doan) **109** 38
Sarah Parmelee **109** 38
McNAST
Dorothy **143** 159
McNAUGHT
Nancy M. **77** 53
McNAUGHTON
Duncan **59** 286 288
Eleanor **59** 288
Jane **59** 286
Margaret **81** 222
McNAY
Bertha S. Farrow
122 125
McNEADER
William **63** 16
McNEAL —— **123** 100
Adam **58** 68
Archable **99** 193
Betsey **89** 205 **112** 140
Daisy **123** 225
Elizabeth **91** 343
Henrietta **134** 337
Jane **81** 146
Olivia **123** 51 308
Patty **56** 257
William **60** 298
McNEALY Mary
(McClure) **108** 80
McNEAR Agnes **74** 93
Alexander **74** 21
Almira **74** 21
Anne **74** 93
Baker **74** 21
Betsey **74** 21

McNEAR *cont'd*
Catherine **74** 21
Christopher **74** 21
David **74** 21
Eleanor **74** 93
Elizabeth **72** 274 **74** 21 93 95
Emeline **74** 21
Frederick William **82** 105
George W. **72** 274 **74** 21
Georgina **82** 105
Hannah **74** 93
Hiram H. **74** 21
James **72** 274 **74** 21 93 94 **130** 311
Jane **74** 21 93
Jane (Erskine) **130** 311
John **57** 38 **72** 274 **74** 21 93-95 **119** 21 **130** 311
John Augustus **74** 21
Joseph **74** 93
Josephine Greenleaf **74** 21
Lydia **74** 21
Lydia (Erskine) **130** 311
Margaret **74** 93 96
Mary **74** 21 93 95
Mary (Shirley) **130** 311
Mary Ann **74** 21
Mary Eliza **74** 21
Mary Elizabeth **74** 21
Phebe **57** 38
Rebecca **72** 274 **74** 21 94
Robert **72** 274 **74** 21
Ruth **74** 21
Samuel **121** 219
Sarah **74** 21 93 95
Sarah T. **72** 274
Susan **74** 21
Susanna **121** 218
Susanna (Gates) **121** 219
Thomas **74** 21 93
Thomas H. **74** 21
William **74** 21
Wilson **74** 21
McNEARIN
John **70** 119
McNEEL Emma Safrona (Flowers) **102** 168
James Shelby **102** 168
Jessie (Maverick) **102** 168
McNEELY
Isabelle **108** 272
Lorenzo Dow **108** 272
Louise Benn **144** 118
Mary (Culbertson) **108** 272
McNEICE Mary **83** 345
McNEIL M'Neil
Mackneel McNeile
McNiel McNeill
— Capt. **70** 188 **80** 277 **85** 125 **92** 53
— Major **54** 29
— Mr. **84** 152
— Mrs. **120** 301 **121** 60 66
— Widow **84** 152
Adam **76** 132
Albert Thomas **77** 143
Alexander **78** 49
Alfred **77** 320 **109** 76

McNEIL *cont'd*
Alva **109** 72
Anna Elizabeth **78** 49
Anne **77** 143 **112** 292 295
Anne (Montgomery) **112** 295
Annie Charlotte **117** 200
Annie Polk **76** 21 **78** 49
Archibald **84** 168 360 **92** 118 **112** 292 295 **140** 166 **143** 320
Bethiah **77** 40
Betsey **112** 140
Cath **112** 292
Catherine (Watts) **92** 132
Charles **51** 469 470 **75** 190
Clarissa **77** 143
Daniel **62** 301 **92** 117 **110** 128 **118** 42 43 53
Donald Southworth **120** 239
Edmund **117** 200
Elizabeth **91** 343
Elizabeth Walker **77** 143
Ernest Webb (Mrs.) **87** 174
Evelina Louisa **77** 143
Ezekiel Polk **77** 143
Fanny **109** 72
Franky Matilda (Vannoy) **109** 76
George **109** 72
Hannah **126** 142
Harold Franklin (Mrs.) **85** 196
Hector **77** 160 **91** 343 **112** 292 295
Henrietta **134** 337
Henry **91** 265 **148** 282
Hester **112** 292
Hopestill **127** 303
Jack **78** 49
James **109** 72 75
Jane **112** 295
Jane Frances **77** 143
John **73** 14 **77** 40 **78** 316 **109** 72 **112** 292 **117** 15 16
John Charles **78** 49 50
Julia **78** 49
Katharine **92** 53
Katharine Elnora **78** 50
Lottie S. (Palmer) **123** 100
Lycurgus **77** 143
Lyndon **112** 293 295
Mamie Frances **78** 50
Margaret **62** 301 **97** 219
Maria **134** 336 337
Martha Ann **78** 49
Mary **76** 132 **92** 53 **112** 292
Mary (Ranger) **91** 265
Mary Ann **77** 235
Mary Eliza **77** 143
Mary Jane **77** 143
Nancy **84** 360 **127** 222
Neil **91** 343 **112** 292 295
Olivia **123** 51 308
Peter **62** 301
Polly **73** 14 **109** 72
Priscilla **77** 143
Prudence **77** 143

McNEIL *cont'd*
Prudence Tate **77** 143 **78** 171 326
Rachel (Eller) **109** 72
Rebecca **109** 75
Robert **55** 418 **140** 68 166
Roger **112** 292 293 295
Samuel **60** 349
Samuel L. **77** 143
Sarah **55** 418 **112** 292
Susanna **67** 351
Thankful **75** 190
Thelma Pauline (Whitney) **87** 174
Theresa **78** 49
Thomas **77** 141 143
Tymoxena **78** 49
Virginia **78** 49
William **73** 196 **78** 310 **140** 166
William H. **79** 52
William Wallace **77** 143
Willie Polk **78** 50
McNEILLIE Alice Winifred (Raymond) **85** 427
McNEIR John **66** 36
McNELAUS
Alexander **91** 347
Isobell **91** 347
Mary **91** 347
McNELLEY McNellie
Arthur **111** 112
Betsey **111** 112 117
George G. (Mrs.) **85** 427
Isabella **111** 113
Jefferson Huston **111** 113
John **111** 112
Lucy **111** 112
Michael **111** 112 113
Nancy **111** 112 116
Susanna **111** 112 113
William **111** 112
McNEMALL
Ann **100** 300
McNETT
George **116** 313
Margaret **106** 307
McNETTEN
Douglas **124** 34
James **124** 34
Lucinda **124** 34
Mary **124** 34
McNEW Mary **73** 136
Thomas **73** 229
McNEY William **119** 21
McNIAH John **70** 263
McNICHOL MacNichol
MacNicoll McNichols
Archibald **85** 222
Archibald Ford **85** 222
Daniel **55** 402
Delia Helen (Burrall) **85** 222
Edward Ford **85** 222
Elizabeth **78** 206 **85** 222
Ethel Laurice (Laxson) **86** 363
Eunice **55** 402
Frances A. **69** 263
George Pope **74** 237 **75**

McNICHOL *cont'd*
  xxiii **85** 106 202 222
  Hugh Lyle **86** 363
  Isaac **114** 190
  James **69** 263
  Janet Campbell
    (MacDermott) **85** 222
  John **85** 222
  Laura Blaine (Ford)
    85 222
  Laura Ford **85** 222
McNiel *see* McNeill
McNiell *see* McNeill
McNISH
  Illa Maude **117** 44
McNITT David **75** 307
  James **75** 305
  Lucinda **52** 341
  Patty **75** 302
  Sally **75** 305
  Samuel **52** 341
  V. V. **105** 318
McNOSSEN
  Andrew **61** 270
McNUBENS
  B. A. **91** 329
McNULTY McAnulty
  — Father **56** 24 25
  A. **118** 64
  Agnes **75** 241 **85** 98 99
  Amy Sophronia (Kibby)
    90 277
  Ann Arabella (Rhea)
    85 99
  B. **118** 64
  Eloise **124** 34
  George Washington
    85 99
  Helen **125** 54
  Jane **88** 31
  John **118** 64
  Marvin **110** 229
  Mary Ann Valley **124** 263
  Mary Jeanette **110** 229
  Mary Jeannette
    (Brinkerhoff) **110** 229
  Prudence **91** 44
  Rosanna **134** 335
  Sarah Adeline **84** 188 **90**
    277 295 **91** 147
  William Michael **90** 277
McNUTT — Col. **116** 6
  Agnes **128** 29
  Alexander **117** 8
  Caroline Georgie
    71 xlvii
  Elizabeth **54** 174
  James **112** 18
  Jane E. **128** 116
  John **128** 116
  John Johnson **71** xlvii
  Margaret **71** xlvii
  Martin **128** 29
  Mary **128** 116
  Rebecca **128** 29
  Robert **112** 90
  Sarah **70** 87 **84** 320
McOmber *see* Macomber
M'Coo *see* McCoo
McOWEN Arabella
    (Briscoe) **98** 349

McOWEN *cont'd*
  Francis Anthony **98** 349
  Frederick **75** xxiii 65 **93**
    82 139 **98** 349
  Louise R. **98** 349
M'Coy *see* McCoy
McPARLIN
  William **73** 271
McPARTLAN
  Hugh **62** 80
  Mary **62** 80
McPEAK Neal **60** 241
McPHAIL Mackphail
    McPhaill
  Alexander **120** 13
  John **125** 216
  Margaret Louisa **120** 13
  Ruth **122** 300
  Sarah **90** 44
  Sarah (Longe) **125** 216
  Thomas **62** 93
McPharlan *see* McFarland
McPhearson *see*
    McPherson
McPHEDRIS Macphedris
  John **83** 155
McPHEE
  Daniel **65** 126
  Julia **82** 174
McPheeters *see* McPhetres
McPHERAN
  Fanny **128** 176
McPHERN Annie
    (Gorham) **128** 265
  John **128** 265
  Mary Jane **128** 265
McPHERON
  Harry (Mrs.) **98** 369
McPHERREN
  Mary Jane **128** 265
McPHERRIN
  John Munson
    80 102 208
McPHERSON
  M'Pherson
  MacPherson
  McPhearson
  — Brig. Gen. **80** 161
  A. H. **72** 205
  Adam **112** 238
  Allan **127** 277 **128** 32
  Andrew **127** 277 **128** 32
  Angus **69** 31
  Asa **83** 141-143 145
  Benjamin D. **83** 143
  Caroline A. **72** 205
  Catherine **127** 277
  Charles **137** 306
  Charlotte (Butterfield)
    87 228 234
  Clarence **72** 205
  Cynthia **83** 141-143
  Daniel **67** lii **101** 327
    127 277
  Donald **62** 301
  Dougal **112** 209
  Eben **128** 32
  Edmund **81** 257
  Elizabeth **60** 346 **78** 410
  Elizabeth Weir **101** 335
  Emily **69** 31

McPHERSON *cont'd*
  Emily H. **69** 31
  Evan **127** 277 **128** 32
  H. S. (Mrs.) **79** 192
  Hannah **127** 277 **128** 32
  Henrietta **73** 271
  Hugh **58** 60
  Isabella **81** 257
  James **127** 277
  James Eben **104** 144
  John **83** 142 **104** 78
    127 277
  John Dunivan **128** 32
  John Q. A. **60** 346
  John Sydney Smith **58** 60
  Joseph **59** 36
  Julia Ann **67** lii
  Kate **83** 385
  Lewin D. (Mrs.) **94** 97
    101 335
  Lewin Dwinell **94** 97
    101 327 335 **106** 158
    112 161
  Lizzie **128** 263
  M. M. **72** 205
  Margaret **82** 279
  Martha W. **88** 278
  Mary **119** 194 **128** 32
  Mary Ann **83** 141
  Mary Brown **77** 189
  Mary E. **81** 257
  Mary Jane **90** 346
  Neil **82** 279
  Nettie **83** 385
  Patrick **110** 131
  Paul **87** 228 234
  Reuben **107** 212
  Sally **59** 36
  Sally (Steward) **128** 32
  Sarah **82** 279
  Sarah (Barton) **107** 212
  Susan **125** 223
  William **63** 142
  William H. **69** 31
McPHETRES
  McPheeters McPheters
  —— **56** 210
  ____ (Scott) **111** 211
  Archibald **74** 104 **105** 276
    278
  Charles **105** 277
  Eliza **74** 104
  John **105** 277 **119** 21
  Rebecca (Averill) **85** 349
  William **85** 349 **105** 278
McPHETTRAGE
  John **147** 185
  Sarah (Sewall) **147** 185
McPHORD
  Elizabeth **52** 432
McPHUSAN
  Richard W. **73** 276
McPIKE
  Eugene Fairfield **56** 96
    58 206 **59** xliv **60** 86 89
    183 185 187 190 212 213
    279 **61** 206 **62** xxxvii
    63 101 111 **64** xxxi 91
    65 xxxiv 92 299 **66** xlix
    287 **67** xxxi 93 384 **68**
    xxxii

McPIKE *cont'd*
James **60** 187
McQUAID
Bernard **132** 256
Jane **62** 30
Jennie **128** 263
Mary Jane **103** 46
Paul **139** 200
McQUAIN
D. C. **91** 329
Joseph **91** 329
McQuaren *see* McQuarren
McQUARLER
Missoni **77** 218
Thomas **77** 218
McQUARREN McQuaren
Daniel **101** 35
Sarah Ann (Fisher) **101** 35
McQUARRY
McQuarrie Mcquary
Allan **118** 57 58
Angus **118** 57
Anne **125** 116 121
Donald **118** 57
Frank **117** 126
Hector **125** 116
Margaret **84** 120
Marguerite Victoria
(Taylor) **117** 126
Neil **125** 116
McQUEEN
Alice **134** 334
Alice (Strathearn) **134** 334
David **118** 46 57
Donald Hugh **99** 148
Dorothy **100** 296
Dorothy (Southack)
100 295
Elizabeth (Hamilton)
134 334
Jane **66** 307
Mary **84** 104
Peter **134** 334
Timothy **100** 295
William **66** 307
McQUERRY
Abraham **82** 278
Mary **82** 278
Maud Hannah **82** 278
McQUESTEN McQueston
David **59** 112
Elizabeth (Cotton) **94** 190
Elizabeth (Lund) (Martin)
94 190
Esther (Harwell) **94** 190
George **94** 190
Harriet **94** 299
Helen Barnet **103** 118
Herbert Eugene (Mrs.)
95 379 394 **96** 160 174
206 **97** 172 **98** 161 **99**
163
Joseph **94** 190
Lenora White **87** 396 **88**
46 146 231 **89** 269 343
98 188 251 310 **99** 57
131
Margaret (Arbuckle)
94 190
Maria Tyler **84** 185 **94**
190 278 **95** 149

McQUESTEN *cont'd*
Relief Judith **93** 311
Simon **94** 190 **117** 159
William **94** 190
McQUEW Thomas **115** 37
McQUILLAN
Andrew **61** 351
Mark **62** 170
Sarah **133** 218
McQUILLIS
Andrew **145** 363
McQUIN Ann **62** 171
Baxter J. **102** 223
Bernard J. **102** 223
Byron M. **102** 223
James **102** 223
John **62** 171
Mary E. **102** 223
McQUIRK Adam **102** 28
Margaret **102** 28
McQUISTION
McQuistian
McQuistin McQuiston
David **91** 257
Leona Bean **92** 305 **117**
159 **141** 95
Margaret (Nahor) **91** 263
Robert **60** 163
Sarah **91** 262
William **91** 257 263
McQUOID John **60** 160
McRAE Maccray McRay
Alexander **52** 312
Anna **60** 79
Annie **128** 263
Beatrice **94** 139
Calvin **60** 80
Eleanor **58** 196
Eleazar **58** 197 **60** 264
Elizabeth **60** 80 **145** 156
Flora **94** 54
Jane **58** 195 **60** 80
John **58** 194-197 **59** 213
60 204 **90** 55
Julia Ann **79** 31
Levina (Buttry) **90** 55
Margaret **60** 78
Rebecca **58** 195
Richard **79** 31
Sarah **58** 196
Thomas **61** 145
M'Cray *see* McRae
McREA Annie **128** 263
Flora **94** 54
McREADY Susan **97** 94
McREDDING
Edward **78** 311
McREE
Deborah **77** 136
Dinah **77** 136
Harriet **77** 136
James **77** 136
Margaret **77** 136
Mary **77** 136
Rachel **77** 136
Robert **77** 136
Susan **77** 136
Thomas **77** 136
William **77** 136
McReedy *see* McCready

McREILLIPS
May **83** 233
McREYNOLDS Evan
Shelby Polk **77** 269
Hadley **117** 42
Hallie (Hickman) **117** 42
Isaac B. **77** 269
John Alsup **103** 119
Kathleen **117** 42
Laura S. **77** 269
Mary Elizabeth **77** 269
McROBERT
Charles **89** 233
Gertrude May (Lazell)
89 233
Ilma **89** 233
Mary (Walker) **89** 233
Melvin **89** 233
Myrne **89** 233
William Smith **73** xix
McROBERTS
Andrew **94** 211
James **122** 219
Jane (Ritchie) **94** 211
Lusetta A. **122** 219
Margaret **94** 211
Prudence **122** 219
Rosella **122** 219
McRorie *see* McCrory
McRory *see* McCrory
McROSTIE
Elizabeth **105** 127
McSHANE
Susan **81** 383
McSHAY
Mary Jane **101** 215
McSHEA
Edward **103** 176
Ellen **103** 176
Fred **103** 176
George Bernard **103** 176
Lucy **103** 176
Rosanna **103** 176
McSHERRY M'Sherry
Hugh **73** 151
Richard **64** 67
McSPADDEN —— **61** 100
McSparran *see*
MacSparran
McSTERLING
—— **124** 243
McSURGAN
Mary **60** 162
Thomas **60** 162
McSWEENEY
McSweeny McSweney
Edward F. **78** 114 **82** 386
Hannah (Colby) **83** 416
John **89** 132 **145** 72
Mary **63** lxiii
Owen **63** lxiii
Peter **83** 416
McTAGGART MacTaggart
Sophia **100** 112
McTAGGET
— Mrs. **101** 272
Jane **101** 271
Margaret **101** 271 272
Peter **101** 271 272
McTEER Carroll K. (Mrs.)
99 148

McTEER *cont'd*
    Frances (Davis) **114** 22
        96 193 268 **116** 260 **117**
        44 **119** 235 **123** 280
    Mildred F. **99** 148
    Wilson (Mrs.) **105** 128
McTETRIDGE
    John **120** 16
    Margaret Ann **120** 16
McTHERSON
    A. L. **128** 97
    Catherine A. (Leaman)
        128 97
    L. **128** 91
    Leander **128** 93 97
    Lizzie (Guthrie) **128** 97
McTIGUE Marguerite
    Jamison **115** 317
M'Cullough *see*
    McCullough
McURANEY
    Owen **61** 137
McURICH
    Archbald **114** 150
McVAIL Thomas **65** 119
McVEY Isabella Mary **89**
        392 394
    John **66** 35 **89** 392
McVICAR Mckvicker
    McVickar McVicker
    McVickor
    —— **53** 464
    Andrew **114** 150
    Archibald **127** 119
    Barnabas **65** 121
    Claude Allen (Mrs.)
        87 377
    Collin **127** 119
    Donald **114** 150
    Dorothy Allaben
        (Holmes) **87** 377
    Duncan **114** 150
    Edward **63** 304 **64** xxxi
    Elizabeth (Cahoon)
        (Smith) **122** 49 **127** 119
    John **63** 304 **122** 49
        127 119
    Malcolm **79** 321
    Mary **127** 119
    Nancy **127** 119
    Thomas **73** 315
McVITTY Albert Elliott
    (Mrs.) **94** 139
    Ruth (Dwight) **94** 139
McVOY
    Hannah Townley
        100 76
McWAIN
    Abraham **123** 179
    Ada **86** 371
    Amanda M. **78** 30
    Amy **69** 324
    Harmon **78** 30
    Mark **69** 324
    Rebecca **57** 368
    Viletta **69** 324
McWATERS
    Elizabeth **112** 182
    Hannah **97** 182
McWETHY
    George **133** 235

McWETHY *cont'd*
    Harriet (Barnes) **133** 235
McWHIRH
    Alexander **88** 283
    Matilda (Mitchell) **88** 283
McWHIRTERS
    Elise Farrel **103** 147
    Rachel **100** 32
    William **100** 32
McWHORTEN
    Elizabeth **126** 93
McWHORTER
    Agnes **116** 66
    Hance **133** 235
    Hobart Amory (Mrs.)
        96 160
    James **116** 66
    John **127** 144
    Keziah **128** 265
    Marjorie Abigail
        (Westgate) **96** 160
    Mary Ann (Graham)
        116 66
    Robert G. **116** 66
McWILLIAMS
    M'Williams
    McWilliam
    Duncan **105** 169 171
    Eva B. **68** 331
    James **73** 131
    Joseph **68** 331
    Margaret **73** 131
    Thomas **140** 68
McWILLIAMSON
    Duncan **82** 456 **105** 169
    Dunkety **105** 171
McWINNE Daisy **81** 43
    Myron **81** 43
McWITHEY McWithee
    Abigail **55** 260
    Eliza **76** 268
    Mary **76** 268
McWOOD
    Maria Jane **100** 312
M'Donald *see* McDonald
M'Duggart *see* McDuggart
Meach *see* Meech
MEACHAM Meachem Mea-
    chum
    Abner **60** 307
    Agnes **72** 175
    Alice **53** 29
    Angelina **98** 354
    Ann Smith **93** 194 195
    Anna C. **73** 41
    Anna E. **73** 41
    Anna May **101** 124
    Archibald **70** 122 **115** 130
    Asa **86** 339 **98** 359
    Ashbel **118** 20
    Ava Ardelia **89** 231
    Barnabas **72** 293 **83** 51
    Benjamin **60** 306 307
    Caroline (Bottom) **123** 52
    Caroline M. **73** 41
    Catherine **72** 70
    Celia W. **106** 80
    Charles **73** 41
    Chloe **98** 359
    David **115** 35 37

MEACHAM *cont'd*
    Deborah (Browning)
        (Perkins) **86** 339
    Ebenezer **62** 42
    Elijah **73** 41
    Eliza (Hoyt) **123** 92 307
    Elizabeth **60** 307 **61** 333
        335 **62** 41 **113** 30 37
    Else Matilda (Lazell)
        89 231
    Emily Clark **73** 41
    Emily F. **98** 359
    Emma P. **123** 98
    Enoch **73** 41
    Enoch G. **73** 41
    Enos **73** 41
    Ephraim **89** 231
    Esther **55** 47 48 **113** 37
        119 122
    Eunice **73** 41
    Florence Lazell **89** 231
    Frankie Matilda **89** 231
        232
    Freelove **114** 12
    George Washington **84**
        219 **86** 339
    Hannah **62** 44 **98** 359
        134 173
    Hershell Lyon (Mrs.)
        100 112
    Hiram **93** 195
    Ichabod **86** 339
    Idah **80** 209 **86** 237
    Isaac **60** 399 **66** 286 **86** 339
        87 358 **108** 309
    J. **123** 52 92 306 307
    James **61** 334 **62** 40 41 43
        46 **71** 56 **113** 30 37 **123**
        303
    James H. **98** 354
    Jehial **61** 31
    Jeremiah **86** 339 **98** 359
        113 29 37
    Jesse **73** 41 **109** 317
    Joel **60** 396 **61** 34
    John **81** 122 **115** 37
    Jonathan **113** 30 37 39
    Joseph **72** 70 **87** 398 **115**
        33 124 **122** 41
    Josephine **104** 144
    Larned Everett **98** 147
    Laura Idah **86** 339 **87** 178
    Levi **73** 41
    Lewis **123** 92 303 307
    Lorena **98** 359
    Love **115** 37
    Lovey **114** 12
    Lovisa **60** 307 **119** 122
    Lucy **113** 30
    Lucy Ann **84** 219
    Lusalla **73** 41
    Lydia **57** 293 **61** 31 **91** 295
    Maranda **98** 359
    Margaret **72** 293 **83** 51
        134 173
    Martin **61** 32
    Mary **62** 46 **72** 293 **108** 309
        123 303
    Mary (Case) **122** 41
    Mary (Gifford) **123** 92
    Mary (Stedman) **84** 219

MEACHAM *cont'd*
Mary A. **98** 354
Mehitable **60** 307
Nathan Truman **86** 339
Peggy **73** 41
Persis **60** 396
Phebe Amelia (Craiger)
  86 339
Philip **57** 293
Phineas **61** 32
Pleadase Maria **57** 293
Priscilla **61** 31
Rachel **73** 41
Rebecca **113** 29 30
Robert **62** 40
Ruth **134** 337
Saloma (Gorham) **93** 195
Sarah **56** 72 200 **95** 83
Sarah (Truman) **86** 339
Sarah J. **73** 41
Tamerson **81** 96
Thankful **113** 30
Titus **72** 172 174 175
Wilber L. **73** 41
William G. **73** 41
MEACOM George **63** 113
Nancy H. **124** 149
MEAD Meade Meads
  Meed Meeds
—— **70** 22 218 **92** 58
— Bp. **61** 211
— Capt. **85** 25
— Dr. **71** 119
— Gen. **57** 60
— Mr. **56** 250 **92** 58
— Squire **135** 73
Abby **76** lxxxvii
Abigail **58** 295 **59** 282 **64**
  122 **75** 184 **77** 231 **81**
  458 **106** 263 **124** 34 35
Abigail (Eveleth) **124** 12
  135 32
Abigail (Whittemore)
  106 262
Abigail Jane **80** 152
Abigail R. **59** 282
Abraham **54** 209 **144** 46
Ada Lawrence **99** 252
Adaline Kinnicut **103** 1
  314
Agnes **139** 234 235
Albert Philo **90** 345
Alfred **76** 265
Alice **53** 431 **66** 363-366
Andrew **75** 322
Ann **66** 354 356 **76** 265
  81 446
Ann Eliza **90** 345
Anna **62** 72 158 **66** 354 356
  124 208
Anne **63** 363 **66** 353-355
  84 338 **139** 234 235
Artemas **69** 248
Asa **62** 159 **79** 168
Asenath **115** 80
Benjamin **55** 311 **75** 184
  81 446 **82** 80 **90** 345
Betsey **64** 151 **124** 208
Bridget **106** 108
Catherine **77** 316

MEAD *cont'd*
Cecilia Marie (Neuhalfen)
  90 345
Charles Henry **103** 143
Charles Henry (Mrs.) **89**
  132 **103** 79 126 143
Charles Stanley **103** 143
  104 144
Charlotte **57** 1 **76** lxxxvii
  135 73
Clara Hapgood **103** 143
Clara Learned (Hapgood)
  89 132 **103** 143
Clarissa **126** 164
Cora E. **124** 208
Cyrus **135** 73
D. M. **75** 13
Daniel **58** 78
Daniel M. **66** 289
Daniel W. **76** 265
David **64** 151
Dinah **83** 300 302 **121** 49
Donald Gaylord (Mrs.)
  101 124
E. **123** 306
Edward **103** 143 **139** 234
  235
Edward D. **53** 136
Edward Sherwood
  136 322
Edwin D. **61** 319
Edwin Doak **56** 332 407
  57 xxii **63** xix 96
Eliza **58** 406 **76** 265
Eliza W. **58** 405
Elizabeth **52** 184 **55** 293 **66**
  353-355 **76** 266 **81** 430
  82 80 284 294 **83** 325-
  327 **88** 294 **103** 314 **110**
  116 **135** 75 **139** 234
Elizabeth (Glover)
  83 181 184
Ella E. **124** 208
Ella Josephine (Kirby)
  90 345
Elsie **58** 405
Emily (Fogg) **136** 322
Emma Augusta **85** 101
Enoch **123** 45
Esther **105** 150
Esther Crafts **76** lxxv
  lxxvi
Ethan **83** 384
Eva Carey **100** 111
Florence Ina **90** 345
Frances **97** 68
Francis **52** 250 **69** 248
Frederick Sumner **99** 252
Frederick Sumner (Mrs.)
  93 138 **99** 69 152 252
Frederick Verner **90** 345
George **66** 354 **77** 218
George Gordon **136** 322
  334
George M. **83** 181 184
Gertrude **71** xlix
Giles **76** 265
Girard **61** 233
Grace Carson **99** 149
Grace Hartley (Jenkins)
  88 394

MEAD *cont'd*
Hannah **52** 40 **58** 295 405
  62 305 306 **67** 284 **69**
  331 **81** 430 **82** 286 294
  83 297 300 **108** 291 **124**
  208 **135** 73
Harriet Sarah **53** 431
Harry Benjamin **90** 345
Hasaniah **62** 306
Hattie E. (Goodwin)
  83 430 436
Henry Hibbard **81** 353
Henry S. **71** xlix
Hepzibah **125** 292
Holliday S. (Mrs.) **85** 229
Isaac **53** 431 **59** 369
Israel **59** 106 **61** 42 **62** 306
  124 12
J. M. **75** 13
Jabez **124** 12 **135** 33
Jacob **101** 151
James **65** 24 381 **66** 353-
  356 **81** 430 **114** 190
Jane **76** 266 **139** 235
Jasper Huntley **101** 151
Jemima **109** 192
Jeremiah **112** 238
Jeremie **143** 143
Joan **66** 353 355 **139** 234
Joanna **120** 20
Job **58** 405 **83** 430 436
  84 30
John **51** 462 **52** 184 250
  54 192 **58** 295 **61** 23 **62**
  77 **63** 351 64 319 **66** 353-
  356 **67** 284 **70** 264 **78**
  422 **83** 325 326 **84** 30
  135 32 **139** 234 **144** 46
John Abner **65** 300
John Lyman **67** 284
John Samuel **90** 345
Jonathan **58** 405 **63** 290
Joseph **55** lxii 293 **63** 75
  64 114 **71** 11 **75** 30 **76**
  lxxxvii **81** 430 458 **82** 48
  101 107 **106** 234
Judith **55** 311 **82** 80 205
Julia Corinthia **61** 233
Katharine (Rand) **93** 138
  99 252
Laura **62** 97 **81** 458
Le Roy **135** 73
Lewis **140** 122
Lois **62** 78
Lucy **80** 437 **144** 46
Lydia **53** 215
Marcus **135** 73
Margaret **81** 446 **136** 322
Margaret Ellen (Hannum)
  90 345
Margaretta (Sergeant)
  136 322
Maria **100** 260
Marie **66** 354
Martha **133** 302
Mary **52** 184 250 **53** 448
  54 192 **59** 369 **62** 306
  64 lvii **66** 354 356 **69**
  248 **76** 227 231 **80** 208
  81 430 446 **97** 388 400
  109 92 **115** 262 **121** 160

MEAD *cont'd*
Mary (Freeman) **133** 155
Mary Ann **82** 479
Mary E. **123** 92
Mary Eliza **76** lxxxvii
Mary Elizabeth (Hartwell)
    85 101
Mary Webster **81** 353
Mary Wilhelmina
    (Vogelsang) **90** 345
Matthew **52** 250
May **100** 260
Minnie Maria Dix
    76 lxxvi
Nabby **62** 150
Nancy Ambler **135** 73
Nancy Fisher **64** 122
Nathaniel **52** 250 **124** 208
Nehemiah **107** 54
Nicholas **83** 325 326
Oliver **69** 245 246 **124** 208
Oliver Warren **85** 101
Oscar J. **119** 160
Pamela **76** 265
Patience **66** 355 **75** 147
Phebe (Huntley) **101** 151
Philena **138** 120
Philip **114** 190
Polly **125** 103
Polly (White) **110** 116
Priscilla **63** 290
R. W. **53** 135
Rachel **107** 208
Rebecca **52** 250
Relief **123** 52
Repentance **66** 354 355
Reuben **135** 73
Richard **52** 250 **65** 293 **66**
    354 **83** 325 326 **139** 234
    235
Richard Fitzgerald **82** 48
Richard W. **52** 90
Richard Worsam **64** 296
Robert **52** 250 **66** 353-355
    76 266
Ruth **55** 293 **71** 11 **75** 30
    82 294 299
Sadie J. **75** 13
Sally **78** 188 402 **115** 313
    124 204
Samuel **52** 250 **67** 364
    106 262 263 **124** 208
Samuel H. **64** 122
Samuel O. **76** lxxvi
Sanford **133** 155
Sarah **51** 462 **58** 78 **63** 76
    66 354-356 **115** 313 **127**
    291
Sarah (Barton) **107** 54
Sarah (Gager) **101** 107
Sarah (Husted) **140** 122
Sarah Ann **81** 353
Sarah Barton **107** 54
Sarah C. **67** 284
Simion **144** 47
Solomon **83** 251
Spencer P. **148** 41
Spencer Percival **56** xxxii
    60 275 **63** 304 **64** xxxi
    66 289 **67** xxxi **68** xxxii
    144 19 **145** 146

MEAD *cont'd*
Spencer R. **55** 348
Stephen **55** 293 **59** 282
    64 122 **65** 248 **66** 353-
    356 **75** 30 **110** 116 **120**
    20
Sumner Rust **99** 252
Susanna **81** 327 446
Susanna (Chadwick)
    124 12
Susanna (Whitney)
    124 12
Theodore **73** 270
Theodosia **83** 251
Thirza **90** 174
Thomas **62** 305 306 **66**
    354-356 **76** lxxxvii 227
    231 **81** 430 446 **82** 284
    294 **83** 326 **106** 108 **121**
    160 **139** 234 235
Tryphena **58** 204
Warren Judson **109** 130
William **52** 250 **53** 132
    65 234 **66** 353-355 **73**
    221 **81** 446 **83** 325-327
    100 178 **103** 99 **117** 247
William H. **100** 189
Winter (Mrs.) **88** 394
Zadok **58** 204
MEADER Meder Meeder
    Meeders
Abigail **73** 44 **114** 181
Abigail (Ewer) **114** 181
Abigail Moulton **69** 329
Alexander **100** 189
Alonzo E. **93** 113
Alvin A. **59** xliv
Benjamin **100** 189
Betsey **57** 114
Betsey (Edgerly) **132** 277
Carrie W. **121** 145
Charles **72** 257
Charles Albert **82** 256
Content **69** 172
Daniel **97** 230 **98** 224
Daniel Downs **114** 154
Deborah **100** 189 **113** 252
Deborah (Knight) **102** 74
Doritha (Straw) **97** 230
Edward Kirby **97** 208
Eleanor (Hall) **98** 224
Elijah **65** 219 **73** 46 **94** 392
Eliza **68** 245
Elizabeth **57** 114 **72** 272 **73**
    46 **98** 224
Elizabeth (Chase) **87** 248
Elizabeth (Hanscomb)
    108 189
Elizabeth (Norton)
    120 118
Elizabeth Ann **69** 320
Ellen Jane (Whidden)
    114 154
Francis **53** 107
George **82** 294 297
    100 189
Georgie Elizabeth **69** 329
Hannah **51** 162 **65** 219 **75**
    8 **120** 117
Hannah (Dame) **94** 392
Hannah D. **76** 37

MEADER *cont'd*
Hannah Hussey **69** 172
Hanson **70** 333 **73** 49
Hepzibah **130** 287
Isaac **133** 120
Jacob Q. **88** 340
James **69** 172
Jane **69** 172 **70** 333
Jeremiah **87** 248
Jesse **76** 37
Joanna **82** 294 297 **98** 299
Job Winslow **69** 172
John **51** 162 **72** 272 **98** 216
    132 277
John Joseph **72** 272
Jonathan **69** 172 **76** 31
    120 118
Joseph **72** 257 **73** 44 50 51
Joseph Hanson **72** 257
Joshua **72** 269 **73** 44
Judith **68** 243 **69** 174
Katie E. **121** 306
Lydia **69** 172
Maria **76** 32
Mary **69** 172 **72** 257 263
    269 **73** 51 **76** xl 31 **132**
    240
Mary Ann (Grant) **97** 230
Mary F. (Hunt) **88** 340
Mary G. **88** 342
Mehitable **72** 257 **73** 50 51
Mercy **72** 257 **73** 50
Mercy C. **123** 310
Mercy M. **123** 310
Micajah **68** 243 244 **70** 333
    134 238
Molly (Downs) **95** 190
Nathaniel **73** 46 **98** 224
Nicholas **132** 277
Olive Black (Parker)
    113 252
Patience **68** 244 **70** 322
Paul **102** 74
Peace **73** 46
Phebe **68** 245 **72** 269 **73**
    44 50 **89** 90
Phebe H. **73** 49
Rachel **68** 243 **134** 238
Rachel Paddock **100** 189
Rebecca **68** 244
Robert **100** 189 **121** 76
Rose (Quimby) **132** 277
Samuel **69** 329 **95** 190
    100 189
Samuel B. **113** 252
Sarah **68** 243 244 **70** 333 **73**
    49 **98** 136 216 **134** 238
Sarah (Follett) **98** 216
Sarah (Tibbetts) **99** 328
Stephen **73** 49 **132** 277
Susan L. **73** 49
Thomas **108** 189 **113** 252
Tobias **73** 49
Valentine **68** 245 **72** 257
    73 49 50
MEADES
    William **53** 237 238
MEADOR William Frank
    (Mrs.) **107** 134
Meadow *see* Meadows

MEADOWCROFT
Ann **80** 89
Margaret **80** 91
MEADOWS Meadow
Meadowes Meddowes
Medowe
—— **54** 188 **64** 139
135 281
Alma **81** 221
Ayner Oree **106** 126
Elizabeth **65** 187
Fanny Louisa Steed
120 55
Hannah **65** 187
John **91** 329
Mary **103** 143 **107** 152
Philip **65** 187
Sara **82** 436
Thomas **63** 278
Meads *see* Mead
MEAGHER Sally **66** 109
William **66** 109
MEAHL
Elizabeth **87** 387
Henry **87** 387
Mary Edith (Knight) **87**
387 **88** 87 176
Walter V. **87** 387
William Kirk **87** 387
Meaker *see* Meeker
MEAKINS Meakin
Meakyn Meekin
Abigail **122** 41
Bennett **114** 190
Elizabeth **65** 166
Hannah **68** 196 **104** 235
122 41 **136** 325
John **56** 86 **62** 356 **122** 41
Joseph **72** 288 **122** 41
Joseph S. **114** 190
Margaret **82** 467
Mary **122** 41 **148** 219
Rebecca **122** 41
Samuel **62** 326 **122** 41
Sarah **68** 196 **104** 235
122 41
Thomas **68** 196 **104** 235
MEAL Elizabeth **88** 66
John **88** 66
MEALEY Martin **64** 320
MEALLY Fred **91** 329
John **91** 329
Thomas **91** 329
MEANE
Katharine **144** 134
MEANS —— **58** 323
Agnes **78** 205 **109** 221
Agnes Barr **111** 311
Alice **74** 104
Alice (Finney) **114** 161
Alice (Phinney) **114** 161
Amy **88** 394 **103** 68
Ann Haseltine **74** 304
Anne Middleton **72** xx 79
79 212 **80** 444 445
Augustus G. **102** 308
Caroline W. (Sherman)
91 275
Carroll Alton **125** 6
Carroll Gates Alton
102 124

MEANS *cont'd*
Catherine **61** 379 **80** 444
142 205
Catherine Atherton
89 220
Charles J. **60** 31
Charlotte **54** 11
Charlotte Abigail **74** lxiv
Constance **79** 243
David M'Grigors/Mac-
Gregor **61** 379 **80** 444
Dorcas **142** 201 **145** 163
Eleanor **142** 205
Elizabeth **61** 242
Elnora **74** 305
Emily Sperry **95** 77
Frederick Howard **54** xli
58 xliii **69** xxx **74**
xxxvii lxiv
Freeman **91** 275
Gardiner Coit **74** lxv
George **54** 98 **78** 71
Hannah **133** 217
Hannah E. **110** 22
Helen Chandler **74** lxv
Helen Coit **68** 304
Henry **87** 217 218
Hugh **114** 193
Huldah Rosalind **95** 77
Isaac **74** lxiv
James **74** lxix **145** 44
James (Mrs.) **77** 156
78 205
James H. **60** 31 **80** 445
James Howard **54** 11
74 lxiv
Jeannie B. **72** xlv
John **95** 76 **124** 72 **140** 168
John Alfred **95** 76
Margaret **142** 201 **145** 163
Margaret (Chase) **87** 329
Margaret Keady **95** 77
Mark Boardman **74** 304
Martha **80** 444
Martha Ann (Keady)
95 76
Mary **61** 241 **74** 305 **80** 444
Mary (McGregor) **89** 215
Nancy **61** 381 **89** 215
Nathan **95** 76
Nathan Amzi **95** 76
Paul Howard **74** lxv
Polly **140** 168
Rebecca (Chase) **87** 330
Robert **72** 47 79 **80** 444
89 215 **121** 243
Rosalind Ladd (Sperry)
95 77
Ruth **116** 186
Samuel **142** 205
Sophie **103** 225
Susan **95** 252
Thomas **74** lxiv 305 **80**
444 **87** 329 330 **114** 161
119 20 **142** 201 204 **145**
163
Walter K. **60** xxxvi
William Alfred **70** xix
90 129 **95** 75-77 150
William Gordon **79** 243
80 444 445

MEANS *cont'd*
Winthop Johnson **74** lxv
MEANTINOMO 97 345
MEANTYS — Mr. **63** 159
Edmund **63** 159
John **63** 159
Thomas **63** 159
MEANY
James Russell **98** 147
MEARA
Adelaide **83** 337
Alice May (Sykes) **83** 237
248 337
Alice Sykes **73** xix
Eugenia Eliza (Norton)
83 337
Frank Sherman **83** 337
Sherman Timothy **83** 337
MEARD Agnes **83** 326
MEARE John **52** 235
Margaret **52** 235
Roger **56** 86
MEARNS
David Chambers
124 194
Mary Beard (Fracker)
124 194
Mary Hume (Richardson)
124 194
Mildred Sellars (Haines)
124 194
William Andrews
124 194
MEARS Meere Meeres
—— **52** 231
—— (Durell) **140** 62
Abigail **130** 214
Abigail Kendall (Holden)
105 242
Ann Brown **75** 205
Catherine **105** 242
Catherine Marshall
78 248
Catherine Marshall
(Raymond) **125** 107
Charles Edwin **68** 21
Daniel **90** 105
Dowkes **83** 168
Edwin A. **68** 21
Elijah **78** 248 **125** 107
Eliza **59** 282
Elizabeth **58** 91 **78** 415 **96**
384 **138** 229
Garrison **59** 307
George Washington
75 205
Granville **140** 62
Harriet Henchman **67** li
78 248 **82** 361
Harriet P. **126** 64
Henry **51** 261
James **61** 199 **105** 195 197
Jane **59** 307 **78** 403
John **52** 125 **56** 74 **58** 142
67 370 **68** 179 **75** 205
130 214
Laura Ann **68** 21
Lemuel Robinson **75** 205
Lucy **75** 20-25
Lucy Withington **75** 205
Lydia **62** 26

MEARS *cont'd*
Marie **112** 158
Mary **58** 91 **68** 179
Mehitable **105** 242
Neal Francis **76** 241 **77**
xxviii **101** 78 **109** 275
Robert **51** 261 **83** 168
105 195
Rollin **68** 21
Samuel **58** 92
Samuel May **105** 242
Sarah **66** 334 **68** 21 **75** 205
Sarah E. **77** 150
Sarah Elizabeth **75** 205
Sarah Robinson **75** 205
Solomon **125** 32
Stephen **66** 334
Susan **81** 385
Susan (Norris) **90** 105
Susanna **59** 307
William **84** 436
William Savage **68** 21
MEASE William **119** 247
MEASEL Martha **78** 73
MEASURE Measurer
Alice **56** 182
Alice (Smith) (Tinker)
100 263
William **56** 182 **100** 262
263
MEAULX Joan (Blenner-
hasset) **98** 277
John **98** 277
MEBOON
Jonathan **52** 429
Mehitable **52** 429
MECAMENY
William **77** 231
MECARTA
Priscilla (Cash) **109** 39
MECARTY James **141** 198
MECCENS —— **118** 221
MECHAN Sally **61** 346
MECHANT Fanny **125** 291
MECHER
James **82** 294 301
Mary **82** 294 301
MECHLIN A. H. **64** 63
MECKSTROTH
Anna Lydia **74** xxv
110 63
MECLALOR
William **143** 258
MECLARE
Richard **143** 260
MECLURA Eunice
(Kimbal) **87** 233 234
James **87** 233 234
MECOM Mecum
Benjamin **104** 88
Jane **106** 78
Lucy L. **138** 218
Susanna **56** 318
MECON —— Mrs. **62** 354
MECONNACK
John **143** 257
Thomas **143** 260
MECORKINGAL
Peter **51** 160
MECORY Mary Ann
(Sawdy) **148** 285

MECOUEN James **143** 260
MECRESS
Joseph **125** 91 92
Mary **125** 91 92
Mary (Green)
(Longfellow) **125** 91
MECUE William **143** 260
Mecum *see* Mecom
MECYRE
Benjamin **143** 260
MEDAHY
Elizabeth **126** 207
MEDAR Edward **80** 26
Francis **145** 352
Sarah **80** 26
MEDART Harriet
Elizabeth **78** 45
John **78** 45
MEDARY
Henry Martyn **85** 184
MEDBURY Medberry
Medbery
—— **97** 36 325
— Mr. **71** 135
Amanda **82** 181
Benjamin **62** 351 **146** 348
Benjamin Franklin **96** 76
Charles **92** 39
Deliverance **80** 179
Dorothy **80** 179
Ephraim **71** 141 143
Frank **63** 166
Hannah **62** 351
Henry **63** 166
Isaac **92** 39 **127** 310
John **62** 346 350 351 **71** 141
97 317
Joseph **96** 76
Mabel **99** 147
Mary Hope **67** xxxiv
Mary Hope (Bigbee)
96 164
Mary Hope (Bugbee) **96**
76 87 164
Nancy (Irons) **96** 76
Nathaniel **62** 351 **63** 165
80 179 **91** 89 **97** 36 **133**
72 **146** 348
Nicholas **64** lxv
Polly (Hall) 39 **92** 39
Remember **90** 94 **91** 89
Ruth **70** 231
Sarah **62** 346 351 **92** 39
Sarah (Campe) **97** 36
Sarah (Humphrey) **133** 72
Sarah Frances 39 **92** 39
Susan **76** xlv
Thomas **62** 351 **63** 164
Medcalf *see* Metcalf
MEDCAP — Mrs. **69** 227
Medcolf *see* Metcalf
MEDD T. H. **114** 20
MEDDIX
David E. **126** 207
Lydia H. (Jones) **126** 207
Meddley *see* Medley
Meddowes *see* Meadows
MEDECINE John **65** 46
MEDEENOR
Abigail **100** 242
Meder *see* Meader

MEDES Lydia **58** 404
Medeway *see* Medway
MEDFORD Grace **111** 84
MEDGET Jos **64** 218
Medgley *see* Midgley
MEDHOITT
Richard **139** 311
MEDHURST Francis
Henry **103** 120
MEDILMOR
William **98** 116
MEDLEY Meddley
Henry **98** 70
Isabell **94** 8
Jane **106** 230
John **64** 344 **66** 36
Mary **73** 222
William **54** 217 **63** 287
Zella Loretta **68** 331
MEDLICOTT Medlycott
Andrew **101** 9
Elizabeth Prowde (Lewis)
101 10
Joseph **101** 9
Judith **101** 9
Martha **101** 9 10
Stephen **101** 9
Thomas **101** 9
William **101** 9 10
MEDLOCK
Annie E. **125** 54
Carrie (Robinson) **125**
54 545
Ella W. (Spear) **125** 54
Fred **125** 54
Mayme B. **125** 54
William R. **125** 54
Medlycott *see* Medlicott
Medowe *see* Meadows
MEDUANA
Walter de **75** 62
MEDWAY Medeway
Elizabeth **64** 23
Henry **79** 417
Lydia **64** 23
Robert **64** 23
Susannna **64** 23
MEDYCOTE
William **85** 76
MEE Joyce **56** 86
Thomas **110** 267
William **65** 236 **69** 363
MEECH Meach
Amy **81** 359 361
Charles **60** 352
Charles B. **121** 152
Charles K. **121** 152
Cynthia **60** 352
Daniel **81** 361 **93** 193
David **121** 152
David B. **120** 10 **121** 153
Desire **55** 177
DeWitt C. **120** 18
Elisha **55** 177
Eliza **120** 20 **121** 152
Eliza Ann **121** 152
Elizabeth **120** 20
Ephraim **80** 427 428
Eunice **80** 427
Fannie Gertrude **89** 254
Frances A. **121** 152

MEECH *cont'd*
Frances Rosita **120** 20
Hannah **120** 264 265
  121 152
Hannah (Yeomans)
  93 193
Harriet Ann **121** 152
Henry **120** 20
Henry B. **120** 18
Hezekiah **80** 427
Hugh **121** 152
John **64** 217 **93** 193
Joseph **121** 152
Lucretia **120** 20 **121** 152
  153
Lucy **63** 95 **81** 177
Lucy Ann **80** 427
Nathan **120** 20 **121** 152 153
Noyes Billings **93** 193
Polly **60** 352
Rosina **121** 152
Sally **121** 152
Sarah **55** 178
Sarah W. **75** 272
Sophia **80** 427 428
Sophia H. **80** 428
Stephen **81** 177 **93** 193
Susan (Spicer) **93** 193
Susan Billings **67** xxxi
  68 xxxiv **71** xviii **77** 325
  81 156 **90** 128 **93** 83 141
  193 **145** 143
Susan S. **60** 276
Susan Spicer **52** 272 278
  145 143
Susanna **120** 20
Thomas **93** 193
Timothy **136** 120
Meed *see* Mead
Meeder *see* Meader
Meeders *see* Meader
Meeds *see* Mead
MEEHAN
Catherine **68** 253
Florence G. (Munroe)
  100 195
George L. **100** 195
James **60** 24
MEEK Meekes Meeks
Adeline **82** 432
Carleton L. **109** 239
  117 237
Charity (Vickery) **110** 278
Cula **82** 432
Daniel **53** 285 **94** 164
Edward Colton **86** 197
Elizabeth **53** 285
Eva **128** 93
Frederick M. **113** 59 **114**
  139 **115** 68
Jane **110** 105
Jonathan **53** 285
Julia Ann **118** 170
Mary (Phillips) **110** 278
Mary Ann **73** 277
N. D. **91** 329
Reuben (Mrs.) **99** 148
Salina (Dolph) **94** 164
Sally (Shumaker) **94** 164
Sanford Basil **94** 164
Sarah **136** 127

MEEK *cont'd*
Susan **73** 274 **81** 354
  95 342
Thomas **110** 278 **128** 71
Western **73** 227
William **73** 265
MEEKER Meaker
—— **56** 214 **61** 317
  127 239
Aaron **60** 396
Abigail **69** 131 374 379
  70 35
Ahaz **111** 124 129
Alice **111** 123 129
Anna **52** 324
Anne **69** 39 **122** 290
Benjamin **60** 396 **70** 35
  121 318
Benjamin Shear **134** 89
Betsey **111** 129
Betsey Gould (Jones)
  134 89
Caleb **70** 35
Caroline Melinda (Hurd)
  108 67
Charles H. **101** 235
Daniel **69** 135 **122** 286 290
Daniel G. **111** 129
David **60** 396 **68** 173 **69**
  131 135 378 379
Eleanor **60** 396 **122** 218
Elizabeth **69** 39 **86** 338 **94**
  359 **101** 235 **108** 67
Elizabeth (Begg) **111** 123
  129
Elizabeth (Bryce) **111** 124
  129
Elvira **111** 124 129
Esther **133** 302 **146** 367
Frank A. **111** 129
G. D. **111** 129
George **111** 123 129
Hannah **60** 396 397 **68** 176
  69 135 **70** 33 34
Hannah (Street) **141** 259
Harriet **111** 129
Harriet M. **69** 167
Henry **111** 129
Jared **122** 290
Jemima **106** 143
John **57** 289 **68** 173 **69** 39
John M. **86** 339
Joseph **52** 324 **141** 259
Josiah **60** 396 397
Levi **60** 396
Lyman **111** 129
Mabel **69** 39
Mary **52** 324 **55** 257 **68**
  173 302 **69** 131 135 **70**
  35 39 **75** 178
Mary (Beardsley) **111**
  123 129
Mary (Darling) **141** 259
Mary (Taylor) **121** 318
Moses Taylor **121** 318
N. Arvestus **111** 129
Nancy S. **111** 129
Orrin **101** 235
Phebe **133** 307 308
Phebe (Price) **86** 339
Philo **111** 123 129

MEEKER *cont'd*
Rhode **70** 35
Rufus **60** 396
Ruth **70** 35
Samuel **52** 324 **60** 396
Sarah **58** 318 **69** 39 131
  81 126
Sarah Ann **121** 318
Seth **69** 379
Stephen **69** 39 **70** 35
Susan **101** 235
Theodosia **57** 289
W. D. **69** 167
William **70** 69 **81** 126
William Henry **108** 67
MEEKHAM
Samuel **64** 217
Meekin *see* Meakins
MEEKS Meekes
MEEKSOY
Jeremiah **127** 304
MEELER Ruth **75** 12
Meelery *see* Mallory
MEELES Rebeca **91** 266
MEEM
Faith (Bemis) **90** 284
John G. (Mrs.) **90** 284
MEENE Mary **53** 126
Meere *see* Mears
Meeres *see* Mears
Meers *see* Mears
MEERT
Sarah A. **109** 218
Sarah Atwood **78** 436
MEETKERKEN Adolf von
  143 201-203
MEETUP Bethiah (Beers)
  123 184
Daniel **123** 183 184
MEGAN Martha **61** 240
MEGEE
Cornelius **105** 201
Daniel **105** 201
Mary **117** 288
Susan **105** 201
Thomas **117** 288
William E. **117** 288
Meges *see* Meigs
MEGGE William **67** 169
MEGGETT Gertrude Eliza-
  beth **70** 294
J. M. **70** 294
MEGHILL Mary **84** 429
MEGILL Mary **133** 232
MEGINNIS Leila **89** 389
MEGIS
Elizabeth (Martin)
  85 425
MEGOOK
Alexandorg **97** 142
MEGOON
Abigail **116** 263
Nathaniel **116** 195
Thomas **116** 263 266
MEGOW
Nettie Adell **107** 135
MEGOY
Alexander **95** 199
Elles (Roads) **95** 199
MEGQUIER Abigail **88**
  239 **98** 197

MEGQUIER *cont'd*
Amy Adelaide Smith
  98 197
Benjamin Clark **88** 239
Betsey A. **98** 197
Betsey C. **98** 197 252
Betsey C. (Perkins) **98** 197
Edmund C. **98** 197
Edwin W. **98** 197
Emeline **88** 239
Emma G. (Brown) **98** 197
Frank P. **98** 197
Hope **98** 197
Louisa **98** 197
Louisa H. **98** 197
Louisa M. **98** 197
Mary Abigail **88** 239
Mary J. **98** 197
Moses M. **98** 197
Olive W. **98** 197
Polly **98** 197
Rilla K. **98** 197
Sally (Merrill) **98** 197
Samuel **88** 239 **98** 197
Samuel Augustus **88** 239
Silas A. **98** 197
Thomas I. **98** 197 252
Thomas Lewis **88** 239
William **98** 197
MEGRATH
Martha Cordelia
  103 225
MEGREGORY
Lydia **91** 15
MEGREW
Alden Frick **97** 389
Annie Louisa (Goudy)
  97 389
George **97** 389
George (Mrs.) **85** 196 **88**
  186 **89** 147 **90** 152 **97**
  389 **98** 87 151
Jane Shelley **97** 389
Megs *see* Meigs
MEHALF Daniel **143** 261
MEHAN Elizabeth (Rinhart)
  125 287
Samuel **125** 287
MEHAND Agnes Theresa
  123 234
Ann **123** 234
Patrick **123** 234
MEHANES
Patsy **114** 188
Patsy (Milleway) **114** 188
MEHEGAN
Mary Theresa **95** 291
MEHOES
George W. **91** 329
MEHRINGER Ernest H.
  (Mrs.) **109** 130
MEHURIN Mehuren
  Mehuron
Armina **136** 249 250
Bethiah **136** 124 252
Clarissa **136** 251
Grace (Hersey) **136** 251
Hezekiah **51** 159
Priscilla **126** 205
Ruth **136** 117
Sophia **125** 220

MEHURIN *cont'd*
Susanna **136** 117 249
MEIER Babette **104** 71
Laura **69** 257
MEIGS Megs Meges
  Meiggs Miegs
—— **53** 379 **59** 421 **61** 100
— Col. **102** 216 **112** 47
Abigail **61** 30
Abner **105** 287
Amelia **100** 189
Ann **67** 365
Anne **57** 138
Anson **108** 154
Anson H. **81** 57
Arabelle A. **65** 134
Artimesia **55** 33
Asenath **52** 326
Bertha **84** 319
Caleb **125** 35
Caroline (Lazell) **89** 25
Concurrence **55** 112
  86 226
Daniel **55** 33 **59** 47 **89** 25
Dorothy (Leavitt) **108** 154
Ebenezer **58** 142 **113** 112
Edgar **89** 23
Eliza **80** 68
Eliza A. **65** 134
Elizabeth **58** 282 **59** 66 67
  103 226
Elizabeth (Hamlin)
  84 318
Elizabeth (Wallace) **86** 95
Elizabeth Blair (Hubbard)
  87 386
Elizabeth Martin **85** 425
Esther **65** 9
Ezekiel **52** 326
Felix **123** 47
Gardner C. **91** 329
George **67** 365
George A. **76** 48
Hannah **56** 161 **59** 64
Hannah (Willard) **84** 318
Hannah E. (Kimberly)
  102 111
Henry Benjamin
  57 xxxiii
Irene **56** 161 **60** 334
Isaac **102** 111
James R. **65** 134
Jane Boyd **85** 425
Janna **57** 138 **84** 318
Jarusha **123** 47
Jehiel **55** 32 **56** 156 **138** 171
Joanna **55** 32
Joe Vincent **59** 421 **60**
  xxxvi **61** xxxiv 100 **62**
  113
Joe Vincent (Mrs.) **86** 95
John **52** 466 469 **55** 255
  56 156 358 **57** 135 **59**
  386 **65** 150 **66** 199 **75**
  xxxvii xciii **81** 131 132
  84 318 319 **85** 425 **89** 23
John F. (Mrs.) **87** 386
Jonathan **125** 33
Joseph **100** 189 **105** 159
Josiah **55** 32
Keziah **111** 115

MEIGS *cont'd*
Lois C. **81** 57
Lovisa **138** 171
Lucia (Lazell) **89** 29
Lucretia **138** 171
Lucretia (Tuller) **89** 23
Lucy **55** 32 **56** 156 **138** 171
Lydia **52** 466 **58** 359
  66 199
Mabel **53** 58
Margaret Trimble **85** 425
Martha **105** 159
Mary **55** 32 **56** 358 **84** 222
  85 306 **129** 18
Mary (Lazell) **89** 23
Maude **84** 319
May Clendenin **85** 425
Millicent **59** 47
Mindwell **52** 469 **54** 271
Nathan **81** 57
Nathaniel **57** 138
Olive **53** 312
Orton Love **84** 319
Phineas **58** 282 **59** 67
Rachel **56** 300
Rebecca **58** 301 302 **59** 65
Return **84** 318
Return Jonathan **55** 32
  65 59 **79** 162 391 **84** 318
  319 **85** 425 **86** 107 200
Rosa **105** 127
Ruth **57** 138
Sally (Keyes) **84** 318
  85 425
Sally (Orton) **84** 319
Sally Keyes (Love) **84** 318
Samuel **54** 271 **61** 30
Sarah **56** 156 106 214
Sarah (Wilcoxson) **84** 318
Sibyl **57** 138
Statira **56** 161
Thankful **55** 255
Thomasine (Fry) **84** 318
Timothy **53** 58 **56** 161 **57**
  138 **59** 66 **138** 175
Titus Benjamin **89** 29
Vincent **84** 318 319 **85** 425
William **57** 316
Zerviah Townsend
  108 154
MEIKLE
Harriet Amelia **79** 202
MEIN
Elizabeth **125** 178
Isabella **90** 45
John **130** 25
MEINDERS Maria **107** 49
MEINERTH
Charles **83** 173
Charles Anton **83** 173
John Haven **83** 173
Josephine Louise **83** 173
MEINILL Nicholas de **120**
  171 174
MEINS Isaac **84** 378
Jane **71** 220
John **71** 218 **84** 260 261
Margaret **71** 133
Mary **71** 216
Sophie **103** 225
Thomas **71** 218

Meinzies *see* Menzies
MEIR Babette **104** 72
  Benedict Menko **104** 72
  Isaac Benedict **104** 72
  Regina (Weil) **104** 72
  Rosa (Dreifus) **104** 72
MEISNIL
  Robert de **106** 280
MEISSNER Sophie
  Radford de **82** 514
MEISTER
  Carl Theodore **148** 180
  Carlena Louise **148** 180
  Edward Victor **148** 180
  Frederick William
    148 180
  Gustave Alban **148** 180
  Harriet **148** 179
  Louis G. A. **148** 180
  Louis Herman **148** 180
  Rudolf Bernhardt **148** 180
Meixter *see* Mixter
MEJER Percy G. **89** 188
MEKE Thomas **83** 443
MEKEEL Caleb **80** 59
  Charles Haviland **67** xxxi
MEKER Elvira **111** 124
Mekin *see* Meakins
MEKYLBURGH
  Agnes (Bartram) **91** 8
  Robert **91** 8
MELANS John **83** 377
MELANSON Anne
    (Robichaux) **143** 9 10
  Charles **143** 5
  Jean **143** 9
  Jean-Baptiste **143** 10
  Marguerite **143** 9
  Marie (Dugas) **143** 5
  Marie-Anne **143** 5
  Roselle **131** 94 97
MELATZ John **86** 383
MELBONE — Mr. **52** 319
MELBOURNE Melborn
  Abigail **93** 216
  William **139** 229
MELCHER Mellcher
  — Mrs. **83** 194
  Aaron **74** 107
  Abbie N. (Vennard)
    83 300 303
  Abby U. **84** 30
  Abigail **82** 48 **95** 54
  Benjamin **51** 465
  C. J. (Mrs.) **83** 307
  Caroline J. **83** 183 184
  Caroline Jones **83** 174
  Catherine **80** 144 **83** 35
    194
  Catherine H. **83** 25 28
  Charles Cheever **83** 174
  Comfort **82** 48
  D. **83** 307
  Daniel **68** 40
  Deborah **82** 48
  Dolly **82** 48
  Dorcas **82** 48
  Dorothy **82** 422
  E. Adelaide **81** 352 **82** 374
  Edith March **83** 295 422
    436

MELCHER *cont'd*
  Edward Harding **82** 374
  Eliza **82** 294 298
  Eliza Cecelia **83** 25 28
  Elizabeth **71** 216 218 **74**
    107 **81** 430 **82** 48
  Elizabeth P. **145** 37
  Ellen Louise **83** 174 **84** 30
  Ellen Stevens **60** xxxvi
  Esther **81** 430 446 **82** 48
    413 **88** 285 **133** 281
  Frances **82** 422 **84** 30
  Frank H. **83** 296 300
  George **82** 48 **83** 174 194
    307 **125** 292
  George A. **83** 300
  George Augustus **83** 174
  Gershom **83** 307
  Gershom F. **83** 300 303
  Hannah **81** 446
  Hannah B. (Beckett)
    83 296 300
  Harriet Ellen **82** 374
  James **81** 446 **82** 48 49 413
    83 35
  John **74** 104 **81** 430 446 447
    82 48 49 294 300 413 **83**
    35
  John Stevens **76** lxxxii
  John Vicar **82** 48
  Jonathan **81** 446
  Josiah **74** 104
  Justin **80** 144
  Katharine **82** 49 294 298
  Levi **96** 275
  Lois **74** 107
  Louise H. **84** 30
  Louise H. (March) **83** 300
  Lydia **83** 194
  Lydia Furnald **82** 49
  Margaret **74** 104
  Marguerite Fellows
    95 306
  Mark **82** 49
  Martha **82** 422 **83** 25 29
  Mary **51** 465 **81** 430 446
    82 49 294 300 413
  Mary G. **95** 56
  Nancy **83** 26 27 **91** 275
  Nathaniel **51** 45 **81** 430
    440 446 447 **82** 48 49
    294 298
  Olive **81** 446 **82** 49 284
    294 422 **83** 23 26 307
  Olive (Goodwin) **125** 292
  Paul **81** 446
  Rebecca B. **63** 379 **64** 375
  Rhoda T. (Cole) **140** 132
  Robert **82** 49
  Samuel **74** 107 **82** 49
  Sarah **71** 130 217 **82** 294
    298 422
  Sarah Ann **82** 422 **83** 35
  Stephen **82** 49
  Thomas **82** 49
  Titus **82** 48
  Tobias **81** 447 **82** 49
  William **82** 49 **140** 132
  Woodbury **82** 49
MELDEAR
  Molly (Downs) **90** 228

MELDEAR *cont'd*
  Samuel **90** 228
MELDRUM Meldram
  Meldrem Meldrom
  — Mr. **81** 431
  Betty **76** 186
  Esther **66** 146 302 **76** 187
    90 235
  Hannah **76** 180
  James **64** 224
  John **65** 255 **76** 186 187 260
    81 431
  Mary **66** 142 303 **76** 180
    182 196 **81** 431
  Mary Ann **77** 187
  Samuel **87** 206
  Sarah **76** 186 187 260
  Thomas **65** 255 **66** 302 **76**
    180 182 **81** 431
  William **81** 431
MELENDIA Sarah **85** 343
MELENDY Mellendy
  — Miss **61** 380
  Annie M. (Hannum)
    90 354
  Clara **61** 382
  Clarissa **53** 41 **61** 384
  Elizabeth **61** 236
  Emery Arnold **90** 354
  Flora Azubah **113** 155
  Josiah **61** 381
  Lucy **61** 381
  Lucy W. **78** 422
  Lucy W. (Edes) **125** 287
  Martha **134** 254
  Mary **53** 41
  Patience **61** 381
  Rebecca **61** 382
  Richard **53** 41
  Thomas W. **61** 382
  William **125** 287
MELES Edmund **84** 77
MELGAREJO Luisa
    Enriqueta (Trumbull)
    109 291
  Ramón Corbalán **109** 291
MELGRAVE
  —— **89** 329 339
MELHINCH Jennie M.
    (Bonesteel) **104** 102
MELICK Harry C. W. **106**
    168 172 173 175 178 **107**
    121
MELIUS
  Wheeler B. **108** 16
MELL
  Alexander **66** 135
  Henry **72** 56
  Thomas **72** 56
  William **72** 56
MELLANDER
  Grace Dyer **145** 22
Mellcher *see* Melcher
MELLE
  William At **70** 245
MELLEFONT
  Harriet H. **116** 210
MELLEGAN — Mr. **64** 24
MELLEMY Ione **85** 290

MELLEN Mellens Mellin
  Melling Mellins
  —— **56** 387 **145** 173
  — Rev. Mr. **77** 20 22-24
    92 130 131
  Abigail **92** 272 **125** 155
    127 186
  Abner **104** 216 **127** 186
  Addie **66** 242
  Ailsa **92** 3 10
  Andrew **92** 3 6 7 **105** 219
  Andrew William **87** 297
    88 167 **92** 3 5 90 147
  Ann **96** 365
  Anne **127** 186
  Archibald **92** 3 **105** 219
  Betsey **116** 138
  Carol Frances **84** 187
  Charles **125** 215
  Charles S. **83** 335
  Charlotte **92** 284
  David **96** 365
  Deborah **104** 216
  Dorcas **82** 294 297 **111** 258
  Edward **66** 242
  Elizabeth **55** 374 **63** 176 **83**
    14 **86** 349 **88** 80 **111** 258
    127 186
  Elizabeth (Fiske) **127** 186
  Elizabeth (Hovey) **83** 14
  Elvira **76** 270
  Esther **111** 258
  Esther (Towne) **96** 365
  Experience (Briggs)
    126 220
  George S. **85** 162 168
  George W. **66** 242
  Grenville **72** 84
  Harriet (Homer) **127** 80
  Harriette **56** 46
  Helen M. **88** 205
  Henry **55** 374 **63** 176 **83** 14
    100 151 **134** 150
  Isabella **111** 258 **115** 226
  James **86** 349 **93** 397
    127 186
  James Ross **105** 219
  Joanna **119** 115
  John **55** 147 **63** 353 **73** 85
    78 303 **86** 349 **92** 272
    284 **95** 60 **96** 365 **110**
    317 **126** 225 **127** 79
  Jonathan **111** 258 **114** 290
    115 211
  Josephine **81** 200
  Joshua **127** 186
  Judson **76** 270
  Lucy **96** 365
  Margaret **55** lxxxiv
    105 219
  Martha Wentworth
    100 151
  Martha Wentworth
    (Frost) **100** 151
  Mary **86** 349 **87** 88 **93** 211
    212 **96** 365 **106** 36 **110**
    70 **113** 305
  Mary (Creighton) **127** 79
  Mary (Maverick) **96** 365
  Matthew Taylor **105** 219
  Nabby (Randall) **125** 215

MELLEN *cont'd*
  Pamela **73** 84
  Paul **92** 10 **136** 322
  Philip Edwin (Mrs.)
    84 109 190
  Polly **92** 319
  Rachel Larimer **105** 219
  Rachel Lowe (Lambert)
    136 322 323
  Rebecca **92** 272
  Richard **92** 6 7 **106** 36
    116 111 **124** 96
  Richard Beatty **92** 5 8 9
  Samuel Fairbank
    69 xxxii
  Simon **96** 365 **124** 96
    127 186
  Sophia Ann **88** 205
  Thomas **86** 349 **92** 3 4
    105 219 **125** 31 **126** 220
  W. F. **91** 329
  Washington **66** 242
  William **86** 349 **127** 79
  William H. **119** 158
  William Larimer **84** 111
    185 **92** 6 **104** 239 **105**
    131 219
  William P. **91** 329
  Zurvilla G. **66** 242
Mellendy *see* Melendy
Mellens *see* Mellen
MELLENS
  Elizabeth **88** 80
MELLENT
  — Earl of **53** 219
  Robert (Earl of) **76** 297
MELLER Samuel **61** 34
  William **125** 43
MELLERS George **63** 27
  Gustavus **91** 329
  Henry I. **91** 329
  James **63** 134 **91** 329
MELLERSHE
  —— **51** 353 **56** 404
MELLET Elizabeth Phillips
    133 309
  John **133** 308
MELLICK
  Andrew D. **93** 204
  Elizabeth Dunn (Ayers)
    93 204
  Kate La Rue **83** 339
MELLIES Woodrow
    Wilson (Mrs.) **99** 148
Mellin *see* Mellen
Melling *see* Mellen
MELLINGER
  Asa Wright **104** 308
  Edith Marion (Ford)
    104 308
MELLINGS Robert **52** 244
Mellins *see* Mellen
MELLISH Mellis Mellishe
  Betsey **68** 238 312
  Elizabeth **110** 259 268 269
    111 55
  Esther **68** 229
  Eunice **68** 237 314
  Hannah **68** 231 313
  Henry **68** 225
  John **68** 223 313 314 316

MELLISH *cont'd*
    318 320 321
  John Thomas **63** xxxiii
  Lydia **68** 320 **111** 55
  Molly **68** 233
  Nancy **68** 318
  Philip **52** 137 138
  Phineas **68** 316
  Polly **68** 321
  Robert **110** 260 268 269
  Samuel **68** 221-223 225 227
    229 231 233 235 237 238
    312 **91** 206 **94** 95 **100** 65
  Sarah **68** 222
  Stephen **68** 235
  Thomas **62** 301 **127** 306
  William **68** 227
MELLMAN
  Elizabeth **125** 260
MELLON Abigail
    (Sanderson) **127** 186
  Ailsa **92** 3 10
  Elizabeth **127** 186
  Elizabeth (Armour) **92** 3
    105 219
  Margaret **105** 219
  Mary Hill (Taylor)
    105 219
  Nora (McMullen) **92** 10
  Rachel Hughey (Larimer)
    105 219
  Rachel Larimer **105** 219
  Rebecca (Wauchob) **92** 3
    105 219
  Sarah Jane (Negley) **92** 3
    4 **105** 219
MELLOR Mellur
  — Mr. **84** 152
  Elizabeth **82** 175
  Joseph Samuel **82** 175
  Mary Eliza **82** 175
  Samuel **82** 175
MELLOSWY
  Elizabeth **51** 269
MELLOWALIE
  Elizabeth **51** 265
  John **51** 265
MELLOWS Mellowe
  Mellowes
  —— **54** cv
  Abraham **51** 256 257 **53** 24
    76 79 198 **131** 10 12 19
    129
  Edward **76** 198 **131** 130
  Elisha **76** 199
  Elizabeth **61** 55 56 **76** 198
    199 **87** 282 **135** 301
  Hannah **76** 198
  Hannah (Smith) **131** 130
  John **76** 198 199
  Joseph **76** 199
  Lawrence **57** 317
  Martha **51** 256 **53** 24 **61**
    55 56 **76** 198 199
  Martha (Bulkeley) **131** 129
    141 100
  Mary **61** 55
  May **76** 198 199
  Oliver **61** 55 **76** 198 199
  Samuel **61** 55 **76** 198
  Sarah **76** 199

MELLS Mary **92** 262
Richard **92** 396
Mellur *see* Mellor
MELLUS — Dr. **76** 70
Deborah H. **88** 276
E. Lindon (Mrs.) **76** 318
Eliza Ann **88** 333
Jerusha **52** 453
John **52** 453
Mary **74** 94
May Gardner **69** xxxv
72 xvi
MELLWIN
Elizabeth **99** 281
Hony Frankling **99** 281
MELLYS Elizabeth **110**
259 269
MELMAN Margaret **105** 33
MELNICK Melnik
Louis Daniel **117** 319
119 201 **121** 55 318 **122**
315 **123** 69 **125** 149 **127**
133
Michael A. **124** 64
MELONA Keziah **82** 294
Patrick **82** 294
Melone *see* Malone
Meloney *see* Maloney
Melony *see* Maloney
MELOON — Mr. **83** 194
Charles C. (Mrs.) **87** 288
Eliza **82** 294
Eliza Davis **86** 101
John **82** 294
Joseph **56** 27 **83** 26 29
Josiah **106** 153
Louisa A. (Yeaton)
83 300 303
Mabel Maria (Mann)
87 288
Sarah **83** 26 29
Sarah H. **84** 30
William T. **83** 300 303
MELOTT Augustin **86** 349
MELOY Edward **53** 409
120 5 9
Eunice **120** 5
Mary **53** 409
Nancy (Slocum) (Swan)
120 5
Walter Orval (Mrs.)
100 112
William **120** 48
MELRETH William **109** 26
MELS Alice **107** 214
Phillippe **107** 214
MELSON William **64** 315
MELTON Melten
Agnes **59** 397
Bathsheba (Jones) **113** 46
Cora B. **79** 19
Edward **72** 53
John **67** 70-73 **72** 53 **111**
196 **114** 223-226
Joseph **113** 45-47 49
Lola **117** 131
Margery **111** 199 **114** 226
Mariora **111** 196 199
Philip **72** 53
William **72** 52 53
Meluen *see* Melvin

MELUNE Samuel **119** 21
Melven *see* Melvin
MELVHER John Stevens
76 lxxxii
MELVILLE Melvil Melvill
—— **60** 102
— Adm. **62** 55
— Mr. **63** 342
Abby **125** 183
Allan **117** 249 **140** 168
Andrew **125** 238 239
Betsey **55** 407
David **79** 292 **93** 91 **127** 16
Emma Augusta **69** lv
George H. **125** 182
Hannah (Barnes) **125** 238
Henrietta E. **125** 183
Henry **122** 178
Herman **117** 249
J. **56** 192
James **63** 141 **125** 239
Jean (Cargill) **117** 249
John **88** 336
Jonas M. **55** 407
Lucina D. (Langley)
125 240
Lydia **125** 242
Malcolm L. **120** 156 315
Malvina A. **88** 336
Margaret **56** 192
Maria (Gansevoort)
117 249
Mary Ann Augusta
(Hobert) **125** 293
Mary F. (Knox) **88** 336
Mary Jane **69** lv
Nancy W. **79** 43
Priscilla (Scollay) **117** 249
140 168 244
Rosanna (Bosemdesed)
125 239
Sarah **84** 348
Susan (Huddleston) **125**
182 241
Thomas **54** xcvi **117** 249
253 **125** 293 **126** 225
127 16 **140** 168 244 322
Thomas D. **125** 240
Thomas H. **125** 240
William **69** lv
William L. **125** 182 241
MELVIN Meluen Melven
—— **130** 155
Abigail **54** 53 **63** 324
111 114
Abraham / Abram T. **88**
302 303
Almon **76** 267
Andrew **66** 307
Andrew A. **56** 323
Anna **93** 189
Anna Little **61** 355
Benjamin **83** 166 **107** 180
Bridget **57** 203
Charles **92** 317
David **54** 53 **62** 33 **63** 293
Eleazer **54** 52 **62** 33 **63** 293
Ellen C. (Little) **103** 47
Ephraim **62** 33
George **83** 166
Hannah **63** 73 293 **113** 224

MELVIN *cont'd*
Harriet Little (Poor)
88 302 303
Helen Fisher (Seaverns)
102 310
J. M. **122** 209
Jacob **62** 33
James **56** 323
James Crombie **65** xxxv
Jeneve Mulle **103** 120
107 126 **113** 149 **116**
148 **117** 153 **118** 163
119 153 **120** 153
Joanna **83** 166
John **60** 102 **62** 33 **63** 293
145 365
Joseph C. **65** 199
Joshua **54** 52
Josiah **103** 47
Lucy M. **90** 56
Margaret **63** 293
Marietta **88** 303
Mary **54** 52 **63** 74 293 **92**
313 **130** 155
Mehitable **107** 180
Nathan **62** 33
Nathaniel **63** 324
Prudence **54** 51 **108** 162
Rebecca **71** 359
Reuben **83** 166 **91** 268
Robert **54** 45 46 **62** 33
108 26
Robert W. (Mrs.) **102** 310
Sally **104** 118
Sally (Marshal) **91** 268
Samuel **54** 53 **65** 199
Susanna **101** 69
MELYEN Abigail **147** 47
MELZAR Harold Eber **87**
174 **88** 88
MELZARD Thomas **91** 200
MELZER Harriet Russell
103 164
MEMORY John **59** 106
MENAGER
Claudius Romaine
65 230
MENAND
Catherine S. **143** 73
MENARD Rene **51** 386
MENCER William **77** 81
MENDALL Mandell
Mendell
Abby (Dickerman)
126 207
Amos **123** 60
Caleb **123** 60
Daniel **123** 60
Hannah (Wood) **123** 61
Isaac **99** 177
Joanna **87** 84 **121** 129 **123**
60 **127** 25 108 112 **130**
137
Joanna (Standlake) **123**
60 **127** 25
John **87** 84 **99** 177 **118** 285
119 171 173 **121** 129
123 60 **127** 25 **130** 137
Lydia **123** 61
Mary **98** 259
Mary (Briggs) **125** 206

MENDALL *cont'd*
  Mary (Ellis) **120** 121 **121**
    129 **123** 61
  Mary A. **98** 259
  Moses **118** 277
  Patience **121** 129 **123** 60
    130 137
  Paul **125** 206
  Phebe **116** 107 **122** 259
    138 209
  Polly (Soule) **124** 153
  Prudence **123** 60
  Prudence (Gibbs) **118** 285
    121 129 **123** 60 **130** 137
  Remember (Dillingham)
    123 61
  Ruth **117** 306 **119** 173
    122 56
  Samuel **118** 285 **123** 60
    125 185 186
  Sarah **118** 285
  Sarah (Bourne) **118** 285
    123 60
  Seth **120** 121 **121** 129 262
    123 61 **128** 230
  Susanna **118** 277
  Susanna (Church) **123** 60
  Susanna (Sprague)
    123 60
  Sylvanus **98** 259 **118** 199
    123 60 **124** 153
  Synthia **126** 196
  Thankful Bates (Handy)
    126 198
  William A. **126** 207
Mendam *see* Mendum
Mendell *see* Mendall
MENDENHALL Mendinghall
  Anna **98** 342
  Catherine (Barton)
    107 212
  Elizabeth **92** 387
  Judith **100** 189
  Mary **105** 313
  Samuel Brooks **113** 161
  Thomas **107** 212
MENDHAM
  John de **103** 292
Mendinghall *see*
  Mendenhall
MENDITH Alfred **91** 329
MENDOZA Garcia
  Hurtado de **68** 206
MENDUM Mendam
  — Mr. **81** 447
  — Mrs. **81** 447 **83** 194
  Adeline **54** cxxiii
  Alice **55** 280 **81** 447
    82 294 295
  Anna **63** 174 **65** 255
  Charles **64** 342
  Charles H. **83** 296 300
    84 30
  David **61** 256 **81** 447
  Eleanor **58** 234
  Elizabeth **81** 447 **82** 287
    294
  Elvira P. **84** 30
  Elvira P. (Barnabee)
    83 296 300
  Hannah **63** 170

MENDUM *cont'd*
  John **54** cxxiii **61** 256 **81**
    447 **83** 194
  John F. **83** 35
  Jonathan **55** 280 **61** 255
    256 **83** 194
  Joshua **61** 256 **82** 287 294
  Margery **61** 256 **63** 174
  Mary **58** 296 **81** 447
  Maud B. **83** 436 **84** 19
  Nathaniel **58** 234 **61** 256
  Olive (Moore) **118** 241
  Oliver P. **83** 307
  Patience **61** 255 256 **82** 287
    294
  Robert **61** 256
  Samuel **61** 256
  Sarah **61** 255 **67** 364
  William **61** 256 **63** 174
    65 255 **118** 241
  Willis Barnabee **54** xlviii
    cxxiii
MENEELY
  Andrew **86** 21 22
  Philena (Hanks) **86** 22
MENEFEE Menefie
  Ferdinand Northrup
    108 135
  George **53** 302
  John **128** 177
MENEUST Marie A. F.
    (Fagard) **110** 133
MENG Charles Henry
    70 xlii
  Katharine **70** xlii
  Malvina **70** xlii
MENGEL Charles Chris-
    topher **108** 64
  Emily Mason (Tryon)
    108 64
  Faith **95** 35
  Jane Potter **108** 64
  Sara (Slater) **95** 35
MENGOUS Ann / Anna
    Aspasia **89** 30
MENIAC Levi **105** 33
  Louisa (Hopkins) **105** 33
MENING Joseph **127** 224
MENINGER
  Christian **143** 258
  Michael **143** 258
MENL Daniel **100** 96
MENNABB Robert **143** 259
MENNARD
  George **63** 243
  Robert **63** 243
MENNESSIERS
  Francis **65** 231
MENNIS John **73** 262
MENOIRE Catherine
    Eléonore **110** 131
MENSEENE John **65** 294
MENSING Adeline Lorette
    79 125
  Lewis **79** 125
MENTELLE Augustus
    Waldemard **65** 231
Menter *see* Mentor
MENTIETH Walter (Earl of)
    96 296

MENTOR Menter
  John **60** 24 **78** 375
  Thomas **143** 257
MENTPACE
  Nicholas **67** 176
MENTYS Peter **53** 23
MENYS Agnes **71** 172
    110 294
MENZ James T. (Mrs.)
    111 150
  Jane Taylor (Gallup)
    111 150
MENZIES Meinzie
    Meinsies Minzee
    Minzie Minzies
  — Maj. **85** 123
  Abigail **140** 168
  Alexander **77** 239
  Elsie Louise **103** 122
  James **112** 174 **125** 101
  John **117** 14 16
  Margaret (Geyer) **125** 101
  Mary **125** 289
  Phebe (Price) **99** 37
  Robert **113** 4 12 13
  Sally **78** 307
  Sarah **78** 190
  Susan Byles **99** 37
  Thomas **77** 239 **99** 37
  William **99** 207 **101** 56
    140 168 326
MEOLL Janet **65** 85
MEPHAM John **61** 25
MEPHUM George **84** 81
MEQUIER
  Edmund C. **89** 360
  Sally **89** 360
MERATRAZ Hannah
    (Carlton) **125** 293
  Joseph **125** 293
MERAY James **143** 260
Merburbie *see* Marbury
MERCANT
  Christopher **86** 432
MERCAT A. **143** 239
MERCER Mercier
    Mercur Mersher
  — Dr. **52** 169
  — Lieut. **113** 91
  — Mr. **79** 299
  Alberta **145** 255
  Alexander **73** 131
  Alice **68** 188 **102** 166
  Amy **68** 188
  Andrew **66** 36 **68** 187 188
  Ann **68** 187
  Anna **68** 187
  Anna Cofer **87** 174
  Anne **68** 188
  Annis **68** 187
  Bartholomew **68** 187 188
  Catherine **68** 188
  Catherine Singleton
    86 223
  Christian **68** 187-189
  Constance **68** 188
  Desiré Cardinal **76** 1
  Eleanor **68** 187 188
  Elizabeth **68** 187 188
  Emma F. **68** 332
  Frederick W. **77** 186

MERCER cont'd
Freesan **57** 94
George **52** 333 **65** 28
  68 187 188
Georgia Anderson **74** 1
Grace **117** 103
Harriet **68** 332
Henry **68** 187 188
Hester **95** 337 **106** 223
Hugh **52** 63 **105** 128
Hugh Weedon **74** 1
Isabel **68** 187
Jacquine **76** lxxxiii **91** 76
James **117** 103
James Watt **105** 53
James Watts **99** 50
Jane Delzell **86** 223
Jean **60** 187
Joan **68** 187 188
John **55** 273 **65** 48 150 **68**
  187 188 **77** 234 **117** 103
John D. **65** 55
Joseph A. **77** 229
Julian **68** 188
Lavinia (Fayerweather)
  145 255
Lizzie Bennett **77** 186
Lydia **107** 28
Margaret **68** 187 188
  73 131
Marietta Elizabeth
  Honore (Denis) 53
  105 53
Marion I. **117** 292
Mary **68** 188 **74** 1 **114** 186
Michael **68** 187
Nicholas **59** 294 295
  68 187
Polly (Watts) **114** 187
Rebecca **98** 130
Richard **87** 208
Robert **68** 187 188
Rose **68** 187 188
Sarah **68** 187
Sarah Davis 53 **105** 53
Sarah Davis (Albert)
  105 53
Sarah E. (Watson) **128** 93
Susan **68** 187
Thomas **68** 187 188 **112**
  246 **145** 255
Thomasine **68** 187 188
Timothy **67** 39 **68** 187 188
Ulysses **105** 53
Wilbur F. **68** 332
William **57** 94 **68** 187 **82**
  335 **91** 349 **128** 93
William Ralph **102** 124
MERCEY George **63** 348
MERCHANT see also
  Marchant
Abigail **53** 154 **87** 9
Abigail (Hutchinson)
  140 28
Ann **125** 105
Ann (Tufts) **110** 47
Anna **109** 43
Anthony **87** 6 9 **105** 207
  208
Benjamin **100** 189
Bethiah **105** 202

MERCHANT cont'd
Charles **85** 292
Claribel **85** 292
Clarissa **72** 291
Cornelius **87** 12
Daniel Basset **105** 89
Edwin **85** 292
Elizabeth **105** 89
Elsie **130** 155
Ensign **105** 89
Frances D. **85** 292
George **87** 12
George Ripley **87** 12
Hallet **75** 194
Hannah **78** 67
Helen Burnham **66**
  xxxvi 82
Hezekiah **105** 89
Isaac **131** 87
Ivo **80** 379
Jabez **105** 86
James **105** 89
Joanna **53** 204 **105** 86
Joanna Phebe **105** 222
John **85** 124 **92** 118 **94** 297
  105 270 **110** 47
Josiah **105** 89 306
Julia Celestia (Rising)
  85 292
Julia M. **85** 292
Juliana **105** 270
Katharine **66** 65
M. A. Caroline **131** 94
Margaret Jackson
  (Hansone) **113** 235
Marshall A. **92** 171
Martha **105** 86
Mary **87** 9 12
Mary Etta **79** 129
Matthew **80** 379
Nancy **92** 118
Oscar **70** 122
Philip A. **131** 87 97
Rachel **75** 194
Rebecca **100** 190
Robert **58** 70
Roxanna **100** 148
Samuel **53** 204 **105** 86 89
  202
Sarah **53** 154 **75** 188 194
Sarah Parr **100** 189
Sylvanus **105** 86
Thomas **75** 228
William **53** 154 **60** 178
Mercier see Mercer
Mercur see Mercer
MERCY — Miss **62** 289
Ann **79** 259
Hephzibah **79** 49
Hinckley **84** 120
John **62** 125 **104** 195
Naomi **123** 121 198
Nathan **123** 124
Natta (Schemerer) **98** 339
Sarah (Fitz Randolph)
  98 339
William **85** 10
MERDEN Samuel **83** 74
MERE John de **80** 381
Sarah **65** 171
Thomas **65** 168

MEREAN
____ (Brewer) **140** 45
MERECK Lewis **100** 299
Ruth (Wheeler) **100** 299
MEREDITH Meredeth
  Meridithe
— Mr. **54** 268
____ (Amory) **140** 32
Ann **97** 123
Benjamin **91** 329
Charles **52** 127
David **110** 170
Elizabeth **93** 384
Eve **110** 170
Frances Maria (Amory)
  120 83
George **107** 307
Gertrude Euphemia
  55 349
J. Owen (Mrs.) **103** 120
Joanna **65** 168 173
Jonathan **91** 329
Kate **85** 199
Kathryne Marie **86** 196
R. R. **53** 271
Robert **52** 127
Robert R. **54** 462
Samuel **120** 83 **140** 32
Theresa **85** 115
Thomas **84** 307
William Henry **59** 337
  60 xxxvi
MEREEN
Betsey Parsons **88** 12
John **104** 218
John Dunning **98** 147
Rebecca **104** 218
Merefield see Merrifield
MEREKIN Frances **51** 124
MERELY
Agnes de **94** 207
Roger de **94** 207
MERENSHAWE
Robert **63** 36
MERESEAU
Joshua **106** 30
Mary (Craven/Cursen)
  106 30
Rachel **106** 30
MERFLET
Stephen de **114** 218
MERGOTTEN
Henry C. **91** 329
Meriam see Merriam
MERIAN Agnes **67** 163
MERIC Blanche Brooke
  (Oliver) **97** 382
Victor de **97** 382
Merick see Merrick
MERIDA Tracy **112** 241
MERIDEN
Abigail **65** 64
John **65** 64
MERIDON
Elizabeth **70** 115
MERIEL — Father **51** 226
Merifield see Merrifield
MERIHEW Merrihew
Albert J. **100** 90
Charles Dyar **100** 90
Elizabeth **111** 56

MERIHEW *cont'd*
Gustina (Nhare) **100** 90
Josiah **148** 288
Martha Jerusha (Monroe)
100 90
Samuel **128** 250
Sarah (Kirby) **128** 250
Stephen **81** 296
MERIJWAY Sabina **82** 85
83 155
Merill *see* Merrill
Meriman *see* Merriman
MERING
Margaret **142** 243
William **142** 243
MERINO
Francisco **100** 287
MERINY Samuel **127** 223
MERION
Beulah **128** 278
David **128** 278
Elijah **128** 278
Elijah Grover **128** 278
Hannah **128** 278
Mary **128** 278
Mille / Milly **128** 278
Nathaniel **128** 278
Pelatiah **128** 278
Thankful **128** 285
William **128** 278 285
Merit *see* Merritt
MERIT Mary (Mullen)
111 281
MERITHEW Merrithew
Andrew J. **91** 329
E. Northup **116** 65
Elizabeth (Manchester)
102 24
Emma E. (Northup)
116 65
Fanny **115** 294 **116** 65
Ira **87** 9 **115** 294 **116** 65
Jane (Arey) **87** 9
Jay **116** 65
Lovinia **109** 254
Lucy **114** 300
Martha Jerusha (Munroe)
100 90
Parisandra **87** 8
Philip **102** 24
Roger **105** 206
Sam **128** 51
Samuel **115** 294
Sarah **116** 69
Sarah L. **109** 109
William **105** 205
MERITON Henry **57** 196
Meritt *see* Merritt
Meriweather *see*
Merriweather
Meriwether *see*
Merriweather
MERKE Merk
Alulf de **79** 362 363
Ralph de **71** 238
MERKLE
Enoch von **114** 13
Jerusha (Parker) von
114 13
MERKLEY Elida Ann
(Wilson) **84** 210

MERKLEY *cont'd*
George W. **84** 210
Mary Emma Swan **84** 210
Rose Anna **108** 136
MERKS Robert **57** 97
MERKYNGFELD
Thomas **118** 177
MERLAY —— **136** 102
Agnes de **79** 362 363 369
372
Alice de **79** 362 372 373
377 378
Anseri de **79** 369
Emma de **79** 369
Gosfrid de **79** 369 370
Isabel de **79** 372
Joanna de **79** 373
Juliana de **79** 370 371 373
97 251
Mary de **79** 372
Menialde de **79** 369
Morello de **79** 369 370
Osbert de **79** 370
Ralph de **79** 369-372
Ranulf de **97** 251 **118** 181
Robert de **79** 369
Rodolph de **79** 369
Roger de **79** 362-364 369
370 372 373 377 378 **115**
47
Walter de **79** 373
William de **79** 363 369
370 372 373
MERLE-RAOUL Merlay
Foulques de (Lord)
79 369
MERLE-SMITH
Wilton (Mrs.) **86** 197
MERLIN Asa **91** 329
E. H. **91** 329
Nancy **88** 304
MERLINO Bennit **110** 133
MERLOTT
Elizabeth **52** 123 125
MERMOD
Augustus S. **85** 228
Augustus S. (Mrs.) **75**
xxiii **85** 227 235 **86** 201
Hezediah (Hastings)
91 385
Justine **85** 228
Mary E. **75** xxiii 64
Mary Elmina (Jewell) **85**
227 **87** 168
Nehemiah **91** 385
Mero *see* Merrow
MERON M. H. **58** 103
MERONEY Polly **78** 416
Merow *see* Merrow
Merrall *see* Merrill
Merrel *see* Merrill
Merrell *see* Merrill
MERRER — Col. **53** 418
Merret *see* Merritt
Merrett *see* Merritt
MERREY Joshua **145** 362
MERRIAM Meriam
Miriam Mirriam
— Capt. **83** 35
— Dea. **62** 158
— Mr. **52** 322

MERRIAM *cont'd*
— Rev. Mr. **62** 295 **88** 91
Aaron **77** 81 **141** 227
Aaron Brooks **99** 332
Abel **69** 245 246
Abigail **57** 362 **67** 124
121 85 **141** 226
Abigail (Norcross) **99** 168
108 220
Abigail (Wheeler) **99** 332
Abraham **93** 320 **125** 107
219
Adeline **90** 48
Adeline Sabra (Taylor)
109 257
Adolphus **113** 165 166
Albert **66** 25
Alfred B. **106** 121
Alfred B. (Mrs.) **106** 121
Alfred Brooks **70** xix **90**
129 **99** 68 152 332
Ann **89** 58
Anna **63** 74
Annie (Chapman)
113 166
Asa **113** 38 39 **125** 44
Asaph **77** 81
Augusta Maria **125** 44
Benjamin **66** 269 **77** 81
113 33 40 41 **141** 225
226
Bethiah **111** 46
Betsey **61** 380
Betsey (Eaton) **125** 109
Burrage **62** 276
C. Hart **63** 393
Caroline **61** lxiii **81** 192
Caroline (McKinstry)
113 165
Caroline (Ware) **92** 196
Caroline Louisa **61** xiii
92 196
Caroline McKinstry
113 166
Catherine (Jennings)
88 281
Charles **52** 150 **61** xliv lxii
lxiii **81** 192 **92** 196
Charles Edwin **84** 334
Charles H. **79** 43
Charles Pierce **55** xxxii
115 **61** 100
Charlotte **59** xcvi **126** 67
Clement **125** 30
Constance Elizabeth
113 166
Cora **105** 68 132
Cora Alice **108** 220
Cynthia **114** 279
Cyrus Lincoln **103** 120
Deborah **113** 31 39
Delia **87** 201
Diana (Hudson) **114** 279
Dorothy **81** 192
Dorothy (Brooks) **99** 332
Ebenezer **57** 143 **66** 269
141 226 **148** 341
Edith **53** 216
Edmond **77** 81
Elbridge **62** 78 161
Elisa (Miller) **125** 107

MERRIAM *cont'd*
Elisha **78** 418
Eliza **78** 305
Eliza (Edes) **126** 65
Eliza Ann (Rowell) **90** 49
Elizabeth **55** lxxxi **63** 172
  66 269 **67** 124 **74** 214
  218 220 221 228 246 258
  95 13 **120** 167 **126** 129
  141 226
Elizabeth (Locke) **141** 226
Elizabeth (Townsend)
  120 167
Elsie (Gilson) **115** 155
Emily Davenport **113** 166
Emily Roberta **106** 124
Ephraim **77** 81 **126** 145
Ermina **113** 231
Esther (Gleason) **141** 226
Ethelred (Berry) **148** 338
  340
F. **63** 375
Florence S. (Sahler)
  99 332
Frank **55** xxxiv **61** xxxiii
  lxiii **72** 250 **79** 211 **81**
  192
Franklin Asbury **84** 240
Frederic Jones **99** 168
Galen **90** 45
George **52** 150 **145** 305
George Washington
  109 257
Ginger (Porter) **141** 227
Grace Page (Andrews)
  99 168
Greenlief Augustus
  99 168
Hannah **53** 228 **61** 153 244
  62 76 **124** 12 **126** 145
Hannah (Gregory) **99** 168
Hannah (Jones) **99** 168
  108 220
Hannah (Perley) **99** 168
  108 220
Hannah (Picket) **125** 218
Hannah B. (Nichols)
  127 179
Hannah Matilda
  (Wentworth) **99** 332
Harold A. **115** 155
Harriet **113** 31 35 39
Harriet Brooks **84** 100
Helen **61** lxiii
Helen Bradford **61** lxiii
Helen I. **99** 168
Helen Louise (Burleigh)
  99 168
Henrietta C. **147** 366
Henry Augustus **99** 168
Henry J. **79** 26
Henry Jonathan **96** 97
Hephzibah **75** 258
Herbert **61** lxiii
Ignatious **92** 51
Jacob **125** 218
Jacob A. **90** 38
James **95** 67 **103** 64
James S. **61** xxxiv
James Sheldon **61** 100
Jane (Dwelly) **145** 305

MERRIAM *cont'd*
Jerusha (Berry) **148** 338
  341
Jesse **79** 37 **113** 31 39
John **61** lxiii **63** 75 **65** 374
  74 220 261 **81** 192 **94**
  321 **99** 168 332 **108** 220
  112 67 **113** 166 **114** 279
  141 226
John M. **85** 464
John McKinstry **71** viii
  xxiii **72** viii **73** viii **74**
  viii xviii 159 **75** xviii
  76 169 **87** 188 **88** 184
  89 146 **90** 130 150 **91**
  157 **92** 160 **93** 152 **94**
  129 136 152 153 **95** 159
  160 **96** 173 174 **97** 150
  151 172 **98** 161 **99** 163
  223 **100** 125 **101** 139
  102 138 238 **113** 147
  165 166
Jonas **56** 38 **62** 72 73 **63**
  190 **69** 245 **85** 128 **116**
  111 **125** 109 **141** 226
Jonathan **91** 329 **96** 97
Joseph **55** 214 **61** lxiii **66**
  269 **77** 81 **81** 30 192 **99**
  168 332 **108** 220 **113**
  166
Joseph Chapman **113** 166
Joseph S. **102** 106
Joshua L. **113** 38
Josiah **61** lxiii **81** 192
  113 166
Josiah W. **90** 49
Lillian A. **86** 367
Lucy **62** 76 160 **81** 192
  113 32 40
Lucy (Wheeler) **99** 332
Luther **66** 25 **147** 366
Lydia **63** 75 **81** 192 **91** 293
  113 38
M. **125** 39
Mary **55** 213 214 **56** lxxii
  57 385 **59** 146 **60** 43 **63**
  74 **66** 269 **75** 30 **79** 102
  81 192 **108** 82 **109** 307
  110 3 **113** 33 38 40 **125**
  44 290 **141** 226
Mary (Bancroft) **94** 321
Mary (Brooks) **99** 332
Mary (Cooper) **99** 168
  108 220
Mary (Dam) **111** 46
Mary (Hersey) **126** 145
Mary (Poulter) **141** 225
  226
Mary (Sheafe) **131** 130
  137 291
Mary (Stone) **99** 332
Mary (Wheeler) **141** 226
Mary Lovering **81** 192
Matthew **63** 168 171 172
  176 297 **74** 184 213 218
  220 221 228 246 249 **82**
  504 **107** 237 **118** 313
Matthew Henry **52** 291
  55 22
Matthew Thacher **74** 221
Mehitable **63** 190 **74** 258

MERRIAM *cont'd*
Miranda W. **79** 53
Nancy **62** 72
Nathan **99** 332
Nathaniel **68** 217 **74** 218
  258 **75** 30 **77** 81
Nelson **84** 334
Oliver **113** 318
Pamela **113** 38
Patience **74** 261 **121** 53
Paul Adams **113** 166
Persis **66** 25 **74** 246
Phebe **67** 52 230 **81** 30
Phebe (Locke) **141** 226
Philip Russell **81** 30
Polly **113** 34 36 41
Ralph **96** 97
Rebecca **55** 290 **63** 74
Robert **55** 213 214 **131** 130
  137 291 **143** 36
Rufus **113** 34
Ruth **51** 222 **86** 153 **113**
  137 **137** 238 242
Ruth Davis **81** 30
Sabra Anne (Allen)
  108 220
Sally **78** 407 **93** 320
Sally (Henderson)
  125 219
Samuel **62** 73 158 **77** 81 **88**
  281 **99** 332 **120** 167
Sarah **63** 76 **66** 269 **67** 123
  70 75 **74** 228 **81** 192 **87**
  56 **147** 366
Sarah (Chardon) **85** 128
Sarah (Goldston) **99** 168
  108 220
Sarah (Jones) **99** 168
  108 220
Sarah (Wheeler) **99** 168
  108 220
Sarah B. **147** 366
Sibyl Priscilla **79** 26
Sidney Augustus **82** 122
  237 251 **83** 125 246 **84**
  205 240 **85** 214 **87** 73
  186 188 **99** 138 168 **100**
  116
Silas **113** 11
Silence S. (Baxter) **90** 45
Sophia **57** 392
Susanna **92** 51
Susanna (Kimberly)
  102 106
Tabitha (Stone) **126** 129
Teresa Beatrice **81** 192
Teresa Lovering **81** 192
Theophilus **66** 269
  106 194
Thomas **61** 199 **62** 72 158
  126 129
Waldo **61** lxiii
William **51** 222 **61** lxiii
  62 70 **66** 25 **68** 217 **77**
  81 **81** 192 **99** 332 **108**
  220 **113** 32 40 166 **148**
  340
William Rush **57** xxxiii
MERRICK *see also* Myrick
—— **148** 117
Abigail **60** 140 386 **67**

MERRICK *cont'd*
118 295 **85** 63 **147** 259
Abigail (Hopkins) **102** 48
Alice **81** 42 **136** 321
Almira (Chase) **97** 137
Ann **77** 239
Anna **68** 335
Anna James **68** 336
Anne **67** 117-119 216
Artemas B. **77** 181
Barbara Lambert **141**
206 213 **145** 380
Benjamin **79** 40
Betsey A. **86** 53
Caleb **60** 76 **67** 118
Caroline E. **77** 257
Catherine (Edwards)
126 85
Charlotte **68** 335
Chloe **60** 386 **67** 119
Clara **95** 317
Clarissa **97** 137
Constant **67** 119
David **121** 247
Deborah **67** 115 117 217
78 304
Deborah (Snow) **102** 48
Delilah **81** 42
Delos S. **97** 137
Desire **132** 324
Dighton (Bird) **120** 280
Electa **122** 124
Eliza **147** 259
Elizabeth **67** 120 **77** 207
108 212 **138** 19 22
Elizabeth (Twining)
126 85
Elizabeth A. **68** 336
Ellis (Bango) **102** 111 112
Esther Burnham **68** 335
Eunice **67** 119 216 **68** 199
86 334 **133** 308 309
Evelina **68** 335
Frances (Clark) **132** 324
Frances Fiske **87** 307 310
107 151
Francis Taliaferro **87** 310
Frederick L. **54** 225
Gad **70** 78
George **67** 115 **86** 53
George Alonzo **91** 80
George Alonzo (Mrs.)
91 60 79 148
George B. **97** 140
George Dana Boardman
91 80
George E. **86** 53
George W. **97** 137 **147** 259
Gideon N. **68** 336
Hannah **52** 82 **57** 213 **67**
119 **68** 335 **113** 268
Hannah (Hopkins)
102 55
Harriet L. **83** 26 29
Harvey **68** 335
Hopestill **128** 197 201
Irene **68** 335
Isaac **119** 266 **120** 280 281
122 131
Jacob **116** 226
James **60** 140 **85** 63 **117** 75

MERRICK *cont'd*
144 216
Jeremiah **116** 115
Joanna **68** 335 **69** 83
John **67** 115 117 216 295 **68**
335 **132** 324 **136** 135
John Alonzo **97** 137
John M. **83** 26 29
Joseph **54** 288 **67** 116-120
68 335 336 **77** 207 **91**
260 329 **101** 43 **126** 85
147 259
Josiah **67** 119
Julia **77** 181
Justina Hall **94** 385
Laban **147** 259
Levi Conn **81** 42
Lodicea **54** 288
Lodicea Dunton **68** 336
Maria **84** 330
Mark **83** 359
Mary **67** 116 **81** 42 **86** 125
91 260 **102** 111 112 **114**
187 **119** 27 **121** 49 **126**
84 172
Mary Buckminster (Fiske)
87 312
Mary Eliza **113** 307
Mary P. **83** 366
Mehitable **119** 264 266
120 281
Mehitable (Ellis) **119** 266
120 99 281 284 286 **122**
131
Mehitable Pearl **68** 336
Mercy **120** 280 281 **122** 131
Miner **60** 386
Moses **67** 117
Nancy (Star) **125** 292 294
Nancy Hollister **86** 53
Naomi **63** 48
Noah **121** 247
Olive H. **72** 115
Paris M. **81** 42
Polly **87** 121
Polly N. **68** 336
Rawson C. **78** 334
Rebecca Jenisin **61** 265
Rufus **147** 259
Ruth **58** 120 **107** 242
S. V. **81** 332
Sally **64** 125 **86** 125 **117**
222 **147** 259
Samuel **72** 115 **91** 206 **93**
397 **125** 292
Samuel D. **68** 335
Samuel Rush **117** 99
Sarah **51** 206 **68** 335 **77** 146
81 475 **87** 203 **119** 160
147 259
Sarah (Congdon) **94** 385
Sarah (Hitchcock) **123** 263
Sarah (Hopkins) **102** 259
Sibyl **70** 78
Silas **147** 259
Silvey (Daggett) **102** 260
Sophia **77** 176
Sophronia **63** 48
Stephen **64** 29 30 33 **67**
118 119 **68** 199
Thomas **65** 30 236 **67** 116

MERRICK *cont'd*
68 335 336 **69** 83
Thornton Alexander
61 265
Tilly **126** 119 **144** 266
Timothy **68** 336 **94** 385
Vina **81** 42
Wayne William **108** 135
Willard **63** 48
Willard F. **81** 42
William **55** 333 **60** 283
63 277 **79** 290 291 **83**
366 **94** 241 **130** 15
Zerviah (Payn) **97** 137
MERRICLE
John **107** 297
Permelia (Barton) **107** 297
MERRIELL — Mr. **54** 91
MERRIET Phill **101** 247
MERRIFIELD Merefield
Merifield Merryfield
Abigail **55** 259
Abraham **123** 282
Adelaide G. **54** xciv
Alice S. **93** 331
Ann J. **93** 334
Arthur W. **93** 331
Asaph **58** 372
Benjamin **56** 74
Betsey Bird **68** 311
Betsey Jane **103** 44
Charles **78** 400
Charlotte **136** 273
D. Jane **120** 306
David **93** 331
Dorcas **93** 331
Elizabeth **55** 315 **83** 10
Elizabeth (Hearl) **83** 10
Esther **87** 124
Eunice **58** 372 **76** 90
Eunice (Watkins) **136** 273
Fannie P. (Dodge)
121 178
George **55** 259
Grace **58** 372
Hammond **93** 331
Hannah **58** 242 372
Harriette **74** xxvii **82** 123
221 229 230 249 258 **83**
244 **84** 204 **85** 177 **86**
228 **106** 62 129 **141** 294
306
Harvey P. **121** 178
Hepzibah **93** 331
Hosea **90** 330 **91** 22 33
Increase **141** 195
Isaiah **91** 329
Joanna (Sedgley) **115** 309
John **63** 143 **75** 109 **76**
185 260 **115** 309 **127**
159 **136** 273
John H. **61** 218
John P. **93** 334
Joseph **58** 242
Julia **102** 306
Leroy S. **93** 331
Lois H. **99** 306
Louisa B. (Hobbs) **91** 33
Lydia **55** 374 **83** 15
136 273
Lydia (Abbott) **83** 15

MERRIFIELD *cont'd*
Lydia A. **93** 331
Lyman **136** 273
Maria (Allen) **125** 222
Maria Caroline (Brigham)
  86 228
Mary **61** 43 **66** 303 **75** 120
  76 192 **122** 228
Mary Jane (Hobbs) **90**
  330 **91** 22
Mercy **58** 372
Nathaniel **55** 374 **83** 15
Oliver **136** 273
Ozem **136** 273
Philena Electa **136** 273
Pleiades **136** 273 **147** 70
Prudence Piper (Larg.)
  88 283
Robert **56** 74 **64** 218
Ryal Justus **136** 273
Salathiel B. **93** 331 **94** 371
Samuel **68** 311 318
Sarah **76** 185 260
Silas **136** 273
Simeon **55** 315 **75** 109
  110 112 114 120 **83** 10
  115 308 **125** 222 **127**
  159
Simon **87** 125
Sophia **136** 273
Submit **99** 306
Susan **93** 331
Sylvinia **92** 339
Thankful **75** 109 110 112
  114 120 **76** 247
Thomas **75** 114 **136** 273
Thomas Chandler
  136 273
Valouruas Smith **88** 283
William **75** 112
William Trowbridge
  86 228
Merrihew *see* Merihew
MERRILL Merrel Merrell
  Merrills Merrils
  Mirrill
—— **95** 273
— Mr. **55** 296 **56** 105 **70**
  143 **83** 417-419 **91** 253
  92 324
— Rev. Mr. **71** 48 **91** 253
— Widow **73** 70
____ (Durant) **91** 264
A. M. **82** 376
Aaron **82** 454
Abbie M. (Osgood) **87** 94
Abel **53** 38 **73** 12 **91** 255
  260 261 265 268 **92** 285
  107 194 199-201 270 272
  108 55 58 121 **134** 225
Abigail **52** 429 **69** 28 **81**
  282 **83** 417 **86** 227 **91**
  263 **114** 303 **120** 159
  121 259 **127** 239 **145**
  171
Abigail (Livermore)
  113 156
Abigail Marsh **91** 260
Abijah **124** 8 13 15
Abraham **60** 56 **81** 255
  101 159

MERRILL *cont'd*
Adams **94** 125
Adams H. **74** 108 **94** 125
  250
Addie M. **87** 80 **147** 273
Addie Maria (Osgood)
  96 228
Adelaide Keith **89** 97
Adolphus **94** 125
Agnes (Carr) **108** 191
  132 269
Alanson **81** 282
Albee Weeks **94** 23
Albert Mem **94** 23
Albert Remembrance
  94 23
Albert S. **76** 86 87 99 **87** 83
Alexander P. **110** 153
Alfred E. **82** 453 454
Alice **78** 294 **89** 200
  113 185
Alice (Gosnold) **105** 7
Alice Marion (Johnson)
  94 23
Allard S. **83** 299 300
Allie G. **98** 197
Almira Ann **68** 332
Almira J. (Dixon) **119** 283
Alousia J. (Dixon) **119** 283
Amanda **77** 150
Amanda H. **76** 86 87
Amy **106** 210
Ann **109** 150 **113** 156
Ann (Walker) **113** 230
Ann M. **82** 454
Anna **51** 464 **52** 432 **53** 164
  280-282 411 **58** 46 **82**
  453 454 **88** 157 **92** 273
  95 325 **136** 144
Anna (Redington)
  109 166
Anna Riggs **84** 60
Anna S. **98** 197
Anne **52** 434 **53** 163 282
  283 **71** 83 274 307 **95** 54
Annie **98** 207
Annie M. **83** 427 436
Annis **82** 454
Ansel **112** 240
Ariel Bell **82** 454
Asa **72** xxxv 100 290 **73** 72
  91 261
Asa Baldwin **72** 289
Asenath **81** 290 408 **83** 141
  108 60 **110** 152 153
Asenath (Merrill) **110** 153
Asenath Hart (Goodwin)
  124 13
Asher **82** 453 454 **107** 210
  147 57
Augusta Meriwether
  109 130
Aurelia **76** 86 96 99 **82** 453
Barbara (Ridgely) **84** 60
Barbara M. **73** 233
Belle J. **82** 454
Benjamin **51** 462 **52** 432
  53 164 166 282 **62** 120
  121 123 174 **63** 377 **64**
  75 **73** 65 68 **91** 257 259
  107 270 275 **108** 60 192

MERRILL *cont'd*
  132 269 **134** 66
Benjamin Franklin
  135 18
Benjamin W. **91** 329
Betsey **56** 29 **73** 233 **88** 244
  92 315 **96** 144 338 **99**
  173 **135** 251 **137** 73
Betsey (Annis) **98** 365 **99**
  173 **100** 74
Betsey (Knight) **90** 229
  249
Betsey Nason **88** 244
Betty **91** 259
Betty (Bancroft) **95** 113
Betty Bradstreet **91** 254
  259 265
Beulah Etonia (Lufkin)
  94 23
Blackstone **95** 54
Blanche Mea (Martin)
  94 23
Bradbury E. **91** 330
C. A. **82** 453
C. H. Sayre (Mrs.) **77** 322
Caleb **124** 13
Caleb Barton **124** 7
Camaralzaman **82** 453
Candace **82** 379
Caroline **65** 337 **82** 453
Caroline A. **82** 379 454
Caroline Augusta **83** 26
  28
Caroline Augusta
  (Tibbetts) **100** 151
Carrie **96** 29 **133** 157
Catherine F. **82** 454
Catherine J. **82** 454
Catherine L. (Manchester)
  102 17
Catherine R. **61** 234
Charity **73** 67 **148** 168
Charity N. **110** 153
Charles **68** 329 **96** 228
Charles (Mrs.) **97** 158
Charles Edward **84** 233
  85 188 **111** 61 **113** 155
Charles H. **148** 168
Charles Henry (Mrs.) **83**
  126 233
Charles Hudson Sayre **79**
  92 **82** 466
Charles Hudson Sayre
  (Mrs.) **78** 205
Charles Morton **113** 155
  156
Charles S. **105** 299
Charlotte **65** 337 **88** 149
Charlotte A. **121** 179
Charlotte Howe **122** 187
Charlotte M. **82** 453
Chester Wright **122** 187
Christiana Cram **134** 66
Clara Augusta **122** 187
Clara Fossett **122** 187
Clarence N. **82** 454
Clarinda **82** 453
Clarissa **68** 332 **72** 90 100
  88 158
Clarissa (Flint) **113** 230
Clifford H. **82** 454

MERRILL *cont'd*
Clore **81** 408
Cora May **82** 376
Cora Parker (Dame)
94 393
Cornelia **89** 235
Cornelius **76** 151
Curtis **74** 211
Cynthia (Silvester) **86** 121
Cyprian **71** 83 274 307
Cyrus Strong **75** 160
D. W.C. **118** 192
Dan C. **82** 453
Daniel **61** 241 **65** 78 81
112 114 255-257 259 261
334 337 338 **69** 37 **72**
xxxv **73** 10 **81** 255 281
282 408 **86** 337 **91** 255-
259 263 **93** 397 **98** 6 **100**
63 **107** 196-198 **108** 58
189 **121** 226 **122** 26 27
132 269 271
Daniel Clarke **94** 23
David **59** 286 **68** 332
104 121
Davis **83** 141
Deborah **52** 433 **68** 329
Deborah (Allen) **83** 509
510
Deborah A. **83** 511
Delight (Sawyer) **107** 210
Diadama **81** 282 408
Dina **136** 90 323
Dorcas (Richardson) **94**
22 24
Doris **113** 155
Dorothea Ellen (Barbour)
94 23
Dorothy **53** 164 160 275
91 256 265 **107** 198
Dudley **53** 168 **58** 46
Duth **91** 256
Ebenezer Redfield **87** 285
Edgerton **72** xxxv
Edmund **95** 113
Ednah (Griffin) **126** 69
Edward **51** 72
Edward A. **81** 418 **82** 454
Edward Henry **75** 160
Edwin **81** 282 **108** 55
Edwin A. **75** 39
Edwin R. **82** 453
Edwin Seymour **122** 186
187
Edwin W. **98** 198
Eldad **72** 318
Eleanor **78** 205 **79** 92
82 466
Eleanor (Robinson)
147 369
Eleazer **71** 280 **72** 37
Eli **72** 90
Eliakim **101** 158
Elias **126** 275
Elias W. **148** 168
Elijah **82** 453
Eliphalet **52** 427 434 **53**
166-168 276-280 282 **73**
68 **142** 397
Eliza **82** 454 **126** 273
Eliza A. **82** 453

MERRILL *cont'd*
Eliza J. **76** 86
Eliza Jane **77** 177
Eliza M. **81** 282
Eliza Olmsted **82** 453
Eliza P. **82** 453
Eliza Watson (Newbury)
86 337
Elizabeth **51** 74 **52** 428 **53**
404 **68** liii **72** 35 290 **81**
408 **83** 141 146 **107** 196
210 **108** 189 **122** 35 **132**
269 **137** 73
Elizabeth (Clarke)
104 121
Elizabeth (Rickard) **108**
190 **132** 269
Elizabeth (Tippetts)
98 221
Elizabeth (Weare) **119** 227
Elizabeth (Wyatt) **136** 146
Elizabeth Brown **63** xxxiv
113 60 230
Elizabeth F. **96** 203
Elizabeth Sophia **76** lvi
Elizabeth U. (Fletcher)
90 47
Ella Agnes **76** 86 87 99
Ella Marion (Griswold)
94 23
Ellen Eliza **81** 408
Ellen Sophia **89** 200
Elvira M. **86** 365
Emeline **67** 282 **82** 454
123 226
Emily **62** 294
Emily L. **82** 454
Emma D. (Knight)
83 299 300
Emma Francis **94** 24
Emma J. **75** 39
Emma Marie Lareau
(DeLangis) **135** 18
Enoch **58** 20 **66** 360 **73** 66
84 425 **95** 113 **125** 92
Enos **53** 278 282
Estelle Minerva (Hatch)
86 337
Esther **53** 404 **62** 125
106 228
Etta **69** 37
Etta (Dearborn) **94** 23
Etta Gordon **89** 200
Eudora **73** 233
Eunice **107** 197 **108** 189
114 180
Eunice (Johnson) **100** 74
Eva **83** 342
Eva G. (Rundlett) **105** 299
Evan **109** 166
Ezekiel **53** 163 280 **86** 121
91 260
Ezra **134** 66
F. F. (Mrs.) **100** 112
Fanny **95** 110 **133** 154
Fanny (Bancroft) **95** 110
Fayette **82** 454
Fenwick D. **110** 153
Ferrand Fossett **122** 187
Floyd Walter **94** 23
Ford **73** 68-70 77

MERRILL *cont'd*
Frances **82** 377
Frances (Whitcomb)
94 24
Frances F. **82** 379
Frances M. **76** 41
Francis **82** 454
Frank **67** 282
Frank Abner (Mrs.)
110 146
Frank Allen **94** 23
Frank Herman **94** 393
Franklin **82** 453 **95** 53
142 35
Fred **118** 192
Frederick James
Hamilton **54** xxxvi 127
72 xxxi xxxv
Frederick W. **54** 364
George **67** 282 **68** 155 **81**
408 **128** 98
George A. **77** 322
George Arthur **78** 205
George B. **96** 228
George Edmands **62** 394
George N. **133** 24
George P. **110** 153
George W. **58** 209 **94** 24
George Willard **148** 168
Georgia Drew **88** 47
Gertrude Bradley **78** 206
Gideon **107** 195 198
Giles **86** 337 **110** 153
118 313
Giles W. **110** 153
Grace **123** 226
Grace E. **100** 315 **102** 126
Granville L. **98** 197
Hamilton **72** xxxv
Hamilton Wilcox **54** 127
72 xxxv
Hannah **51** 462 **52** 429 430
53 166 168 283 404 **54**
353 **57** 87 **58** 122 **61** 241
62 121 **64** 155 67 182
73 76 **78** 105 **82** 454 **86**
232 **88** 149 248 **89** 357
91 255 **94** 23 **100** 167
101 339 **104** 39 **108** 190
124 13 **132** 269 **134** 66
Hannah (Chadwick)
124 13
Hannah (Howk) **124** 13
Hannah Elizabeth
(Blanchard) **83** 342
Hannah L. **81** 251
Hannah Moody (White)
97 356
Harriet **82** 454 **89** 319
Harriet (Hand) **122** 186
Harriet (Woods) **94** 24
Harriet Bradbury **68** 329
Harriet D. (Barnes) **88** 339
Harriet Davis **102** 230
Harriet Hurd Hand
122 185
Harriet K. **82** 378 454
Harriet L. **98** 198
Harriet Ursula (Brown)
113 230
Harry **96** 228

MERRILL *cont'd*
Harvey F. **91** 330
Helen **80** 146
Helen E. **82** 453
Helen Isadore **101** 325
Helen Russell Brown
  122 185
Hellen (Ingram) **113** 155
Hellena W. **110** 107
Henry **81** 408 **82** 454
  91 259
Henry A. **99** 202 **110** 153
Henry Adams **94** 125
Henry C. **82** 454
Henry M. **82** 376 453
Hephzibah **73** 10
Hephzibah L. **81** 275 282
Hollis **96** 228
Horace **81** 251
Horace Wells **81** 408
Horatio **72** 50
Howard **80** 146
Howard W. **122** 78
Huldah (Ellis) **121** 226
Humphrey **108** 124 190
  132 269 270
Ida **148** 168
Ida Jane **135** 18
Ira **82** 454 **94** 22 24
Ira Allen **94** 23
Irene **51** 248 **70** 77
Isaac **81** 408 **91** 260-262
  266 **113** 210 **119** 227
Isabel **82** 454
Isabella (McCullough)
  108 190 **132** 269
Israel **72** xxxv
Israel S. **97** 356
J. D. **96** 222
J. Frankie **89** 357
J. Henry **82** 454
J. T. **95** 52
J. W. **55** 353
Jabez **73** 233 **88** 244
  126 275
Jabez H. **73** 233 **98** 198
Jabez Henry **88** 244
Jacob **65** 337 **71** 279 **107**
  200 **108** 123 **116** 177
  178 183 **127** 320 **136**
  146
Jacob L. **88** 339
James **53** 165-168 276 **73**
  18 65 70 **82** 454 **84** 60
  86 441 **98** 365 **99** 173
  100 74 **132** 269 **145** 350
  353
James Flint **113** 230
James Hooper **88** 149
James Ingram **113** 155
James O. **105** 299
James Russell **147** 273
James S. **125** 36
Jane **63** 376 **64** 76 155 **66**
  360 **68** 329 **95** 55 **108**
  191 **134** 225
Jane L. **82** 454
Jane M. (Hillman)
  147 273
Jared **72** xxxv
Jasper Haskell **88** 244

MERRILL *cont'd*
Jemima **108** 122
Jennet **113** 163
Jennie **83** 299 300
Jennie Luella **94** 24
Jenny **108** 58
Jeremiah **53** 168 **88** 158
  98 365 **99** 173 **100** 74
Jerusha **73** 18
Jerusha Caroline (Dean)
  134 66
Jerusha Jane (Tuttle)
  (Gore) (Fuller) **125** 301
Jess **73** 65
Jesse **88** 149 248 **104** 121
Joan (Kinney) **113** 230
Joanna **52** 430 432 **53** 278
Joanna (Davis) **116** 262
  263
Joel **89** 357
John **51** 74 **53** 164 280 404
  54 129 **65** 239 **72** xxxv
  73 10 12 **84** 424 **88** 149
  91 255 261 **92** 273 **94**
  393 **98** 221 365 **100** 74
  107 195 272 **108** 190
  109 164 **113** 230 **121**
  161 **122** 35 **124** 13 **132**
  269 **134** 215 **142** 35 **147**
  273
John B. **110** 153
John L. **77** 237
John Lee **106** 125 **115** 67
John Lee (Mrs.) **96** 395
John Lenord **78** 205
John Leverett **64** 228
  72 152
John Lund Woods **94** 24
John Pearl **87** 80
John T. **88** 248
John Tappin **88** 149
Jonas **65** 337
Jonathan **62** 120 **81** 408
Joseph **52** 428 432 **53** 165
  166 280-283 411 **64** 155
  331 **73** 7 64 65 69 **76** 86
  82 454 **87** 94 **89** 275
  115 27 **121** 313 **125** 92
  132 270
Joseph Durrell **134** 66
Joseph Edward **62** xxxvii
Joseph F. **92** 305 **93** 400
Joseph K. **110** 153
Joshua **55** 353 **91** 256
  94 22 24
Josiah **73** 63
Josiah E. **110** 105
Josiah G. **110** 105
Joyce Blanche **94** 23
Judith **53** 275 **62** 122 **107**
  196 197 199 **132** 270
Judith (Durrell) **132** 269
  270
Judson **68** 303
Julia **82** 454 **94** 125
  100 194
Julia A. **57** 361
Julia A. (Moore) **87** 80
Julia Ann **82** 454
Kate **96** 127

MERRILL *cont'd*
Katharine Langdon (Hill)
  96 395
Keith **84** 341 **85** 188 **114** 68
Keziah **73** 7
L. J. **82** 376
Laura Ann **98** 361 364 365
  99 173
Lavisa **88** 157
Lemore (Gale) **97** 158
Lemuel **62** 126
Leonard E. **89** 200
Leonard W. **89** 200
Levi **53** 167 277 **58** 122 **66**
  279 **105** 289
Levina **54** 199
Levinia **56** 253
Lewis Albee **94** 23
Lillie D. **82** 454
Lizzie Palmer **106** 64
Lois **71** 280 281
Loren W. **81** 408
Loretta (Dearborn) **94** 23
Louisa **72** xxxv **83** 146
  88 157
Louise **81** 281
Louise Edgerton **72** xxxv
Lucius H. **82** 453
Lucy **63** 379 **65** 337 **76** 271
  88 157 **124** 15
Lucy (Cushing) **86** 337
Lucy (Tobie) **86** 441
Lucy A. **97** 182
Lucy Ann **102** 303
Lucy Ann (Worthley)
  94 23
Lucy E. **76** 271
Lucy L. **81** 282
Lucy Maria (Draper)
  (Page) **94** 24
Lucy Tobie **86** 441
Luella **94** 22
Lydia **52** 432 **53** 162 280
  62 120 124 125 **79** 89 **81**
  35 281 282 **83** 417 **91**
  261 **107** 272 **127** 239
  132 269
Lydia (Haynes) **113** 230
Lydia (Redington)
  109 164
Lydia E. B. **77** 184
Lydia Mitchell (Durrell)
  135 18
M. A. **82** 454
Mabel **73** 12
Marcia Wheelock **135** 18
Margaret **87** 292 **143** 320
Margaret Ann (Combs)
  112 240
Margery **145** 51
Maria **68** 95 **74** 108
Maria Eliza **87** 285
Marian I. **82** 454
Marietta **82** 436
Marion F. **83** 432 436
Marriner Wood **92** 305
  93 400
Marshall **82** 454
Martha **52** 434 **53** 123 **88**
  195 **94** 24 **112** 223
Martha Bernett **98** 148

MERRILL *cont'd*
Martha C. **68** 155
Martha Smith **136** 309
Martin **82** 378 454
Martin S. **91** 107
Mary **52** 427 428 433 **53**
    165-168 276-280 **58** 123
    62 258 **63** 378 **64** 375
    65 337 **68** 153 **71** 279
    81 255 **82** 294 298 454
    91 255 **95** 113 **107** 199
    108 189 **112** 223 **114**
    184 **132** 269 270 **136**
    146
Mary (Chamberlin)
    91 268
Mary (Clough) **86** 337
Mary (Emery) **98** 365
Mary (Hale) **91** 263
Mary (Hutchins) **132** 269
Mary (Rich) **83** 410
Mary (Wilson) **147** 273
Mary Ann **123** 239
Mary Augusta **122** 187
Mary B. **90** 44
Mary Bartol **112** 312
Mary E. **89** 200 **103** 49
    134 67 **147** 369
Mary Elizabeth **87** 61
Mary Ella **76** 99
Mary Ellen (Clarke) **94** 23
Mary L. **82** 454
Mary Louise **106** 150
Mary N. **82** 376
Mary North **82** 453
Mary O. **105** 299
Mary Sedgwick **124** 13
Mary Somes **134** 66
Mattie H. **74** 211
Maude Alice (Fenton)
    94 23 24
Mead **113** 156
Medad W. **81** 408
Mehitable **107** 199-201
    270 272 **108** 55 58
Mehitable (Burbank)
    108 121 **134** 225
Mehitable Daw **82** 269
Meletiah **51** 464
Melvin Clarence **92** 305
Mercy (Flecher) **91** 267
Mercy (Mason) **135** 18
Mercy (Sedgwick) **124** 13
Mercy C. **82** 453
Merlin **81** 275 282
Merro Joseph **76** 86 96 99
Milburn **73** 278
Mildred Florence **94** 393
Mildred L. **82** 376
Miles **81** 408
Minnie Francis **94** 23
Miriam **53** 165
Miriam (Putnam) **86** 337
Molly **53** 277 282 **91** 258
    267 **99** 173 **107** 198 **126**
    275
Molly (Stevens) **134** 66
Monroe **88** 334
Mortimer D. **82** 453
Moses **52** 433 **71** 154 155
    281 **72** 35-37 39 **86** 337

MERRILL *cont'd*
    91 256 **122** 279 **145** 51
Myron **80** 146
Myron W. **81** 282
Nabby **58** 20
Nancy **64** 155 **68** 95 **87** 18
    94 25
Natalie **91** 254
Nathan **53** 166 167 **77** 150
    90 229 249 **125** 291 **127**
    63 **142** 35 **145** 171
Nathaniel **53** 168 275 277
    278 411 **54** 129 222 **61**
    139 **62** 121 123 258 **72**
    xxxv **73** 10 12 **82** 294
    298 **85** 448 **86** 337 **88**
    304 **91** 253-262 265 **94**
    394 **98** 365 100 74 **104**
    121 242 **105** 224 **107** 99
    113 230 **114** 238 **125** 23
    132 269 **145** 351 **147**
    258
Nathaniel E. **119** 281
Nathaniel William **83** 26
    28 **100** 151
Nellie **89** 391
Nellie (Colby) **94** 393
Nellie Mary **81** 255
Nelson **103** 265
Noah **106** 228
Noel **125** 301
Norman **82** 454
Obed **91** 330 **107** 195-197
    199 **132** 269 270
Octavia (Wilson) **113** 155
Olin Lee **68** 330
Olive **81** 408 **91** 230 256
    262 266 **108** 120 **122** 26
Olive (Lund) **91** 265
Olive (Merrill) **91** 266
Olive (Record) **122** 27
Oliver **91** 260
Orlando **126** 273
Oscar S. **76** 86 87
P. **73** 74
Parker **53** 279 411 **77** 184
Parthena Robinson
    (Hannum) **91** 107
Patience **63** 377 **64** 76
Paul **96** 29
Persis **94** 125
Persis H. **74** 108
Persis Poor (Greenliaf)
    94 125
Peter **64** 116 **78** 110 111
Phebe **62** 174 **103** 260
    107 275 **108** 60 **113** 230
Phebe (Merrill) **113** 230
Phebe (Robinson)
    108 192
Philip **73** 223 277
Phineas **142** 397
Platt **68** 95
Plumey **81** 408
Polly **86** 120 **90** 245
    136 146
Polly (Blake) **122** 279
Polly (Haskell) **122** 279
Praxo **69** 262
Priscilla **53** 38 **69** 331 **82**
    368 **88** 158

MERRILL *cont'd*
Priscilla (Huff) **108** 124
    132 269 270
Priscilla (Sweetser)
    127 320
R. A. **91** 330
Rachel **72** 36 **73** 9 **134** 66
Rachel Fidelia **72** 289
Ransom **81** 35
Rebecca **62** 258 **125** 294
Rebecca (Blodget) **91** 262
Rebecca (Foster) **125** 291
Rebecca Durrell **134** 66
Rebecca W. **69** 37
Reuben **83** 342
Reukal **91** 257
Rhoda **55** 353 **71** 155 **76** 87
    94 123
Rhoda (True) **126** 275
Richard **52** 430 **53** 278
    116 262 263
Richard (Mrs.) **114** 232
Richard Lewis **94** 23
Riley **113** 156
Riley Mead **113** 156
Rockwood G. **68** 332
Rosina **87** 126
Ruby **72** 205
Russel **76** 173
Ruth **52** 427 **72** 39 **84** 328
    91 257 267 **94** 122 123
    108 121 192
Ruth (Win) **91** 265
S. M. **55** 353
S. P. **52** 85
Sally **83** 417 **92** 321 **98** 197
    99 173 **108** 192 **114** 179
Sally (Chadwick) **124** 7
Sally (Jackson) **124** 7
Sally (Woods) **94** 22
Salome **88** 157
Samuel **51** 233 **52** 85 **53**
    168 **56** xxx **58** xliii **59**
    xliii **60** xxxiv **63** 379 **66**
    xlviii 291 **67** xxx 85 **68**
    xxx **74** x **79** 196 **80** 204
    81 113 216 282 **82** 231
    84 179 **85** 176 **86** 184
    337 **87** 168 171 177 **88**
    157 **91** 256 257 260 262
    263 330 **95** 110 **99** 173
    107 197 **108** 191 **124** 7
    132 269 **142** 35
Samuel Eastman **113** 230
Samuel H. **64** 129
Samuel Haseltine **94** 24
Samuel S. **95** 110
Sarah **51** 464 **53** 163 276
    281 **59** 286 **61** lvi **62**
    120 123 124 **63** 377 **64**
    76 **65** 337 **66** 362 **67** 277
    68 155 **71** 154 **72** 318
    76 86 **81** 147 408 **83** 107
    87 194 **91** 260 263 266
    99 324 **107** 196-198 **108**
    58 121 **116** 177 178 183
    124 8 **136** 271 272 **142**
    35 **147** 60
Sarah (Barton) **124** 8 15
    125 8 15
Sarah (Briggs) **126** 275

MERRILL *cont'd*
Sarah (Bucknam) **110** 153
Sarah (Chadwick) **124** 7
Sarah (Huff) **108** 123
  116 177
Sarah (Jackson) **124** 7
Sarah (Jaquith) **88** 334
Sarah (Roling) **84** 425
Sarah (Towne) **108** 189
Sarah (True) **86** 337
Sarah (Wagg) **126** 273
Sarah (Wilson) **134** 66
Sarah (Woods) **94** 22 24
Sarah A. **82** 453
Sarah Ann **88** 244 **148** 168
Sarah E. **67** 282 **74** 108
Sarah Emily **76** 86 96
Sarah Kitredge (Somes)
  134 66
Sarah L. **57** 361
Sarah S. **81** 408
Selah **63** 214
Sereno T. **51** 495
Seward **103** 265 266
Sibyl (Mason) **84** 424
Simeon **68** 95
Spencer **129** 273
Stephen **83** 417 **107** 195
  200 **108** 58 **134** 66 67
Susan **56** 28 **63** 376 **64** 76
  66 362 **132** 269
Susan (McIntire) **119** 281
Susan A. **88** 281
Susan B. (Lougee)
  118 192
Susan Bliss **94** 24
Susan M. **83** 183 184
Susan Stout **107** 213
Susanna **53** 280 **54** 222
  61 139 308 **73** 10 **84** 446
  91 261 264 **94** 394 **113**
  230 **127** 320 **129** 18
Susanna (Fitz Randolph)
  97 278
Susanna (Hamlet) **91** 263
T. J. (Mrs.) **95** 52
Tabitha **91** 261 265
Temperance French
  134 66
Thankful **73** 12
Thede **83** 52
Theodore **91** 258 267
  107 198
Thomas **53** 168 404 **54** 353
  57 87 **58** 123 **63** 376 **64**
  76 **66** 360 **83** 509 510 **91**
  258 **105** 7 289 **134** 215
  145 51 351
Thomas A. **71** 56
Timothy **122** 187
Timothy Robinson
  122 187
True **68** 155
True Chipman **88** 149
Uel **125** 32
Valeria **69** 262
Viola V. **68** 155
W. P. **123** 73 74
W. S. **96** 224
Wainwright **86** 338
Waitstill **71** 281

MERRILL *cont'd*
Walter L. **82** 454
Walter McIntosh **110** 220
Wiggins **94** 125
Willard G. **81** 408
William **53** 166 **57** xxxiii
  58 209 **69** 275 **81** 408
  83 52 410 **87** 124 **90** 47
  91 264 **99** 58 **107** 201
  122 35
William B. **102** 17
William C. **119** 283
William E. **119** 283
William Franklin **135** 18
William G. **124** 13 **147** 369
William Henry **62** 113
  94 23
William Louis **66** 91
Winifred **72** xxxv **115** 174
Winifred Mabel **86** 198
Winthrop **53** 276
Zacharias **51** 72
Zebulon **82** 453
Zilpha Jane **88** 244
MERRIMAN Merryman
Aaron **77** 81
Abigail **55** 369 **74** 106
  121 85
Addison **57** 292 295 357
Andrews Taggart **57** 295
Ann **101** 102
Asaph **77** 81
Benjamin **77** 81
Betsey **57** 292
Caleb **55** 372 **70** 92
Clark Spencer **57** 296
Cynthia **57** 292
Daniel **57** 292 295 296 357
Daniel Watson **57** 296
David **66** 111
Edmond **77** 81
Eliezer **70** 92
Eliza Seaman **80** 147
Eliza Young **80** 147
Elizabeth **53** 21 **66** 309 **74**
  105 **106** 212
Elizabeth Julia **57** 360
Enoch **70** 92
Ephraim **77** 81
George **53** 21
Hannah **60** 166
Harriet **125** 160
Henry **57** 292 359 360
Henry P. **80** 110
Henry Payne **57** 359
Hiram **57** 292
Israel **108** 314
Jehiel **60** 166 **121** 84
Jemima **66** 309 310
Joan **91** 11 12 14 285
Joan (Peck) **89** 338 339
John **53** 21 **66** 309 310 **91**
  330 **136** 362
John Adams **57** 357
John Churchill **57** 295
Joseph **77** 81 **136** 362
Levi **70** 92
Louisa **66** 111
M. **69** 287
Mansfield **67** 304 **68** xxxii
Margy **59** 66

MERRIMAN *cont'd*
Martha **57** 292 295 296 357
Martha (Bowen) **136** 362
Mary **56** 140 **117** 32-34
  136 362
Mehitable **103** 27
Moses **121** 84
Nathan **125** 35
Nathaniel **53** 21 **55** 369
  372 **67** 304 **68** 304 **69**
  287 **77** 81 **81** 125 **89** 175
Norman Mansfield
  66 309
Oliver Addison **57** 357
Phebe **112** 44
Polly **70** 92
Prudence **57** 295 357
Rebecca **136** 362
Robert **91** 285
Roger B. **79** 6
Rosa E. **128** 92
Rosa F. **128** 92
Roxana **129** 396
Ruth **55** 372 **86** 152 153
Sally **57** 292
Samuel **77** 81 **92** 100
Sarah **60** 166 **65** 7 **108** 314
  114 206
Sarah B. **57** 359
Seymour Wheelock
  57 357
Sidney **128** 92
Sidney Augustus **86** 214
Susan Webb (Cushman)
  84 334
Susanna **56** 285
Thankful **136** 320
Theoph **59** 66
Thomas **117** 32 133
Timothy **74** 105
William **77** 81
William Edward **57** 295
William L. **80** 147
Merriner *see* Mariner
Merriott *see* Marriott
MERRIPIN Amme **100** 31
  33 134 137 **101** 272 274
  275
Amme (Riont) **100** 299
Amy **100** 138
Andrew Cooper **100** 134
  101 274
Ann **100** 138
Anne **100** 141
Anthony **100** 141
Elizabeth **100** 31 33 304
  101 272
Joseph **100** 31 33 134 137
  138 141 299 **101** 272 274
  275
MERRIS Merriss
  — Mrs. **63** 57 58
Anne **70** 155
John Acie (Mrs.) **102** 124
William **70** 155 **128** 298
Merrit *see* Merritt
Merrithew *see* Merithew
MERRITT Merit Merritt
  Merret Merrett Merrit -
  see also De Merritt
  — Mr. **57** 228 **125** 29

MERRITT *cont'd*

Abigail **57** 399 **58** 262 **81** 390 **115** 185 **129** 164
Abigail (Woodworth) **133** 101
Abraham **99** 281 **111** 281 **140** 123
Adeline Bach **91** 56
Agatha **58** 262
Alan Douglas **82** 357
Alexander Henry (Mrs.) **85** 196
Alice **55** 422
Amanda **140** 123
Amos **78** 74
Amy **58** 262
Ann **55** 225 **64** 324
Ann Eliza (Hollister) **111** 312
Anna **61** 242 **72** 296
Anna M. (Doubleday) **120** 255
Anna T. **96** 34
Anstis **140** 123
Antoinette Polk **78** 169
Arthur Henry **85** 346 **86** 191
Benjamin **55** 225 **59** 134 **60** 210 273 **61** 242 **82** 356
Benjamin Dean (Mrs.) **103** 120
Berry **60** 210
Bert Howell **72** 296
Betsey (Dodge) **126** 256 **128** 21
Catherine **55** 225
Catherine (Weaver) **100** 240
Celia (Munroe) (Youtsey) **100** 86
Charles **55** 225 **60** 271
Charles Edward **111** 312
Charles Edward (Mrs.) **93** 138 **102** 320 **111** 310 312 313
Charlotte May **72** 296
Chloe (Haines) **89** 260
Christina **55** 225
Clara Louise (Ketcham) **96** 81
Consider **60** 273 **129** 253 266
Cynthia **140** 124
Cynthia (Howland) **140** 118 119 123
Daniel **87** 134 **89** 260 **101** 276 **112** 102 103
Daniel Hasbrouck **89** 259 260
David **60** 176
David Schuyler **144** 116
Deborah **113** 287 **129** 265
Deborah (Litchfield) **129** 169 **134** 145
Desire **55** 225
Diantha **55** 225
Douglas **55** 225 **60** xxxvi 210 **65** xxxv 95 **66** 1 93 **68** xxxii 111 **69** xxxii 94 384 **71** 192 **73** 81 **74**

MERRITT *cont'd*

xxiv 156 **81** 363 **82** 244 356 357
Ebenezer **55** 225
Edward **60** 210 **81** 447
Edward Alford **75** ix xxiii **89** 259 **90** 79 138
Electa Elizabeth **111** 313
Elijah **55** 225
Elisha **55** 225 **129** 253
Elizabeth **55** 225 **69** 167 **73** 226 **99** 284 **115** 185 **119** 239
Elizabeth (Hyland) **133** 100 101
Elizabeth (Tower) (Whiton) **129** 169
Elizabeth (Underhill) **89** 259
Elizabeth (Wyborne) **133** 100
Elizabeth Atwater (Mairs) **93** 138 **111** 312
Elizabeth Cleveland **82** 357
Elizabeth Lee (Dame) (Miles) **89** 260
Eloisa S. **123** 52
Emilie Catherine **111** 313
Emily Maria **106** 224
Esther **140** 124
Ethel Claire (Dean) **144** 116
Ethel Douglas **82** 357
Eugene Turhan **72** 296
Eunice **112** 103
Ezekiel **55** 225
Frances Ann **111** 313
Frances Fern **102** 124 **105** 125
Francis **81** 431 447
Frank **105** 319
Franklin Williams **72** 296
Fred Holman **72** 296
George **55** 225 **60** 210 **82** 356 **89** 259 **91** 207
Gilbert **55** 225
Glorianna (Purdy) **89** 259
Hannah **57** 390 **59** 137 **60** 176 210 **63** 272 **66** 333 **81** 413 **108** 239 **110** 159 **114** 240 **115** 185 **137** 29
Hannah Skinner (Fitz-Randolph) **98** 126 127
Harriet Louise (Alford) **89** 259
Henry **57** 402 **59** 76 **60** 188 210 **68** 111 **71** 192 **79** 279 **133** 100 101 **134** 145
Hepzibah **72** 295
Huldah Jane **72** 295
Hulett Clinton **78** 169 **81** 108 219
Ichabod **59** 76 77 134 137 **140** 123
Isaac **55** 225 **60** 210 **68** 111 336 **71** 192 **140** 124
Izetta M. **83** 26 27
J. R. **55** xxxii
Jacob **96** 34

MERRITT *cont'd*

James **60** 210 **81** 413 447
James D. **98** 127
Jane **123** 52
Jane (Rich) **83** 400
Jane Huntington **89** 260
Janette (Wilson) **89** 260
Jennie Sophia **72** 296
Jerome **55** 422 **90** 50
Jesse **83** 400
Jesse F. **78** 338
Joanna **55** 225
Joce **60** 273
John **55** 225 **57** 389 **60** 210 **68** 111 **91** 330 **111** 271 **112** 103 **133** 100 101 190 **134** 145 **140** 168
John Carlton **111** 312 313
Jonathan **55** 225 **58** 82 **59** 138 **115** 185 **129** 169 260 **134** 145
Joseph **55** 225 **59** 76 **60** 273 **81** 364 **82** 237 356 **100** 86 **140** 123
Julia **82** 356
Katharine **114** 123 **126** 280
Katrina **55** 225
Keziah **55** 225
Leonard Vincent Atkins **96** 81
Levi **106** 224
Lewis Howell **72** 295
Lovering **60** 210
Lucy **55** 225
Lusanna **59** 76
Mahala **140** 124
Margaret **55** 225 **57** 402 **59** 76
Margery **60** 210
Martha **55** 225 **99** 208 209 284
Martha (Smith) **100** 242
Mary **55** 225 **58** 262 **59** 77 134 137 **63** 47 272 **67** 209 **81** 431 **84** 121 **99** 208 **129** 266
Mary (Adams) **125** 218
Mary (Mullen) **111** 281
Mary (Fowler) **89** 260
Mary (Gowell) **112** 102
Mary (Perry) **115** 185 278
Mary (Stodder) **129** 167
Mary L. **140** 124
Matilda **72** 296
Matilda (Huntington) **89** 260
Maud R. **72** 296
Mehitable **55** 225 **58** 82 **59** 138 **115** 185
Meyer **60** 210
Michael **55** 225
Mildred Mae **106** 125
Minnie Antoinette **72** 296
Minta Clifton **79** 279
Moses **55** 225
Naheba **140** 124
Naomi **52** 439
Napoleon B. **72** 295
Nathaniel **55** 225 **60** 210
Nehemiah **55** 225 **75** 10 **82** 356 **129** 259 260

MERRITT *cont'd*
Nellie L. **72** 296
Nicholas **55** 225 **60** 210
  68 111 **71** 192
Noah **60** 271 **61** 96 **83** 26
  27 **134** 145
Obadiah **129** 159 169
  134 145
Paul **55** 225
Pearl Ketcham **96** 81
Percival **77** 242 **81** 370
Phebe **55** 225 **113** 301
  140 123
Pheleck **60** 210
Philip **55** 225 **60** 210 **68**
  111 **71** 192 **99** 208 209
  281 284 **100** 242 **145**
  293
Polly **55** 225 **60** 273
Power **100** 240
Priscilla **129** 369
Priscilla (Holbrook)
  129 253
Prissa **60** 273
Rachel **55** 225 **127** 296
  134 141
Rebecca **55** 225
Richard **55** 225 **60** 210
  140 123 **145** 355
Roger **55** 225
Roxa **60** 273
Ruth **86** 287 289
Sally **61** 175 242
Sally (Tibbetts) **99** 54
Sally Hilliard **78** 169
Salora (Bacon) **106** 224
Samuel **60** 210 **68** 111 **71**
  192 **89** 259 260 **92** 55
  107 253 **128** 299
Samuel Suel **99** 298
Sarah **55** 225 **61** 96 **81** 431
  88 331 **129** 253 **140** 123
Sarah (Tibbetts) **99** 54
Sarah (Tupper) **99** 298
Sarah (Wade) **129** 260
Sarah (Wing) **140** 123
Sarah Elizabeth **72** 296
Sarah J. (Jenks) **90** 50
Sarah James Bradford
  95 93
Sarah Jane (Bradford)
  95 93
Sebe **55** 225
Seth **129** 155-157 160-163
  167 253 259
Sibyl **55** 225
Simeon **59** 138
Susan **107** 306
Susanna **73** 275 **123** 52
  145 294
Susanna (Gannett)
  129 167
Thomas **55** 225 **57** 399 **58**
  262 **60** 210 **68** 111 **71**
  192 **81** 390 **82** 356 **89**
  259 **133** 101
Thomas Albert **72** 296
Timothy **56** 21
Uriah **57** 390
William **55** 225 300 **60** 210
  63 47 **68** 111 **71** 192

MERRITT *cont'd*
  112 103 **120** 255 **126**
  256 **128** 21
Ziba **125** 218
Zintha **96** 79
Zoa **55** 225
MERRITZ
Rosalind **129** 52
MERRIWAY
Sabina **83** 155
MERRIWEATHER
Meriweather
Meriwether
Merryweather
Colyer **53** 132
Edward **67** 178
Ella Letitia **118** 166 **133**
  302 **136** 326
Nelson Heath **119** 75
Richard **67** 178
Thomas **59** 219
MERRIX Ann **108** 230
Elizabeth **108** 230
Mary **108** 230
William **108** 230
MERROW Mero Merow
—— **102** 321
— Mr. **83** 415
Abigail **74** 247 **83** 415
Abra **69** 282
Almon H. **120** 304 307
  123 150
Ann **100** 300
Anna **74** 36
Betsey (Hardy) **125** 218
Charles **74** 223
Charles E. A. **81** 460
Daniel **81** 460 **100** 240
  118 80
Deborah **74** 129 **100** 35
Dorcas **74** 41
Dorothy **95** 65
Eleanor (Turner) **100** 240
Elizabeth **58** 52 **74** 247
  83 415
Elizabeth (Merrow)
  83 415
Elizabeth L. (Webber)
  120 304
Elizabeth Rena **81** 460
Elizabeth Rena
  (McLauthlin) **102** 67
Everett B. **85** 354
Fanny (Upton) **90** 108
Hannah **74** 36 223
Hartford **133** 122
Henry **58** 52 **81** 460 **98** 278
  109 157
Isaac **74** 37 223
James **69** 282 **74** 36 223
Jane **58** 52 **81** 460
Jane (Trask) **83** 417
Jefferson **99** 56
John **140** 168
Jonathan **74** 36 192 **83** 417
Joseph **97** 365
Josephine E. **81** 460
Josiah **53** 73
Lillian C. **84** 456
Lizzie L. (Webber)
  120 307

MERROW *cont'd*
Lucy M. **79** 156
Lydia **74** 247
Lyford Ambrose **74** xxx
  80 106 217 **81** 460 **102**
  68
Lyford Ambrose (Mrs.)
  80 106 **81** 222 **102** 61 67
  68 128
Margaret **142** 301
Maria Elizabeth **81** 460
Mary **63** 378
Mary A. (Leonard) **90** 56
Mary Ann (Nason) **99** 56
Mehitable **97** 365
Miriam **58** 52
Nancy **74** 247
Olive **74** 247
Oscar Earl **97** 158 **98** 278
  102 120 **109** 157
Parker McLauthlin **81**
  460 **102** 68 **103** 120
Phebe **74** 36 37
Rena **81** 222
Robert **81** 460
Sally **74** 37 **83** 417 **97** 365
Samuel **83** 417
Seth **125** 218
Susanna **74** 247
Thomas **74** 36
Timothy **83** 415
Uriah **90** 56 108
William **142** 301
Zenobia (Wells) **133** 122
MERRY Merrey
—— **63** 383 **75** 249
— Mrs. **79** 304
___ (Rust) **140** 243
Abigail **59** 259
Agnes B. **63** 272
Agnis **127** 265
Alice **127** 261 265
Alicia **128** 106
Ann **127** 167 261
Anna **60** 395
Asa **145** 357
Bathsheba **59** 410
Benaiah **66** 81
Benjamin **66** 81
Bethiah **148** 234
Bethiah (Morgan) **148** 235
Bethiah (Williams)
  148 235
Betsey **125** 218
Betsey (Callender)
  144 320
Charles **79** 304
Charles Hamilton **93** 190
Christopher **79** 311
Cornelius **60** 392-396
  100 340 **148** 234 235
Daniel **61** 202 **78** 186
  140 168
David **66** 81 82 **145** 357
Elizabeth **58** 52 **68** 371
Elizabeth (Ellice) **87** 230
  235
Elizabeth Viall **82** 373
Hannah **63** 176
Henry **58** 52 **127** 172 173
  261 265

MERRY *cont'd*
Irwin L. **148** 235
Isaac **63** 176
Isabella G. **148** 235
James E. **101** 32
Jane **58** 52
John **127** 169 265 **128** 106
  144 319 320
Jonathan **140** 168 243
Joseph **66** 81 **68** 82 371
  79 311
Josephine Mary **93** 190
Lathrop **59** 259
Lucy **61** 202
Margaret **79** 311
Marie **127** 265
Mary **59** 306 411
Mary Elizabeth **82** 495
Matthew **66** 81 82
Miriam **58** 52
Myra **100** 111
Norman **60** 394
Polly **97** 187
Rachel **148** 235
Ralph **127** 304
Robert **79** 311
Rosanna (Carlisle) **101** 32
Sally L. **77** 313
Samuel **87** 230 235 **100**
  189 **127** 311
Sarah **78** 71
Sarah Rossella (Rock)
  93 190
Simon **127** 265
Susan **75** 249
Susanna **60** 394-396
T. T. **63** 272
Thomas Henry **133** 153
Trueman **60** 396
Walter **63** 383
William H. **79** 304
MERRYALL
Arthur **51** 406
Merryfield *see* Merrifield
Merryman *see* Merriman
Merryweather *see*
  Merriweather
MERSCER John **51** 348
MERSEAR Ariadne B.
  (Chase) **88** 125
Charles **88** 125
MERSELIS —— **57** 236
MERSEREAU Joshua **65** 55
  112 208 213 270 **113** 5 8
  86 **137** 309-312
Sarah Elizabeth **71** lxi
MERSERVE
Nathaniel **147** 81
MERSEY
Edward W. **115** 268
Ella A. **115** 268
MERSHAN Edwin **77** 152
  Mary Frances **77** 152
MERSHE
Elizabeth **60** 286
Isabel **60** 285
Mershel *see* Marshall
Mersher *see* Mercer
MERSHON Ann **97** 279
  Grace Lucile Olmstead
    100 338

MERSHON *cont'd*
Henry **97** 279
Joab **134** 226
Katharine **105** 126
Luella (Billings) **98** 54
Luella (FitzRandolph)
  98 54
Oliver Francis **100** 338
Rebecca **97** 279 **134** 226
Sarah (Dilworth) **134** 226
MERSON Abraham **78** 371
MERSSEY William **62** 243
MERSTON Betty **58** 124
Constance De **79** 365
MERTON Richard **64** 160
MERVEILHAUD
Magdeleine
  143 234 237
Pierre **143** 234
Simon **143** 234 237
Suzanne (Rivoire)
  143 234
MERVELL William **52** 67
MERVIENNE
Patrick **143** 262
MERVILLE
Loren **111** 129
Lovina (Light) **111** 129
Nathan **111** 129
MERVINE William M. **70**
  190 **75** 241
MERWICK
Giles **93** 383 387
MERWIN Merwon Murwin
A. A.C. **108** 101
Abigail **69** 238
Abijah **68** 294 **69** 370 **70** 37
Andrew **52** 41
Ann **59** 68
Arthur F. **81** 39
Celestia P. **81** 39
Charles L. **114** 78
Damaris **70** 36 42
Daniel **52** 326 **59** 68
  68 171
David **68** 291 **69** 238
Davis **96** 28
Davis Underwood **96** 29
Dorothy **69** 240
Edward Payson (Mrs.)
  102 121
Elizabeth **59** 68 **96** 31 **118**
  296 **138** 42
Emma Jane **90** 180
Eunice **59** 394 **68** 292 **69**
  237 **70** 34
Florence B. **114** 318
Hannah **59** 68 171 **68** 291
  69 238
Hull **69** 370
Israel **93** 397
John **68** 171 **69** 240 **70** 36
  37
Joseph **102** 109
Josephine Cronkhite
  (Underwood) **96** 28
Josephine Underwood
  96 28
Justina **57** 265 **59** 171
Lyman **69** 238
Martha **102** 109

MERWIN *cont'd*
Mary **53** 410 **70** 34 35 37 38
  103 88
Miles **53** 410 **59** 68 **88** 304
  114 318 **118** 296 **138** 42
Mordecai **69** 240
Nathan **69** 237
Rebecca **52** 326
Rhue **69** 370
Ruth **53** 57 **68** 294 **70** 34 37
Samuel **59** 171 394 **68** 292
  69 237 **70** 34 **138** 43
Samuel Edwin **61** 322
Sarah **70** 37
Tamar **52** 41
Thalia A. **90** 68
Thomas **68** 171 **69** 235 **70**
  40 **138** 43
MESCHIN Maud **121** 233
Ranulf le **96** 102
William **121** 233
William le **96** 315
MESERVE Maserve
  Maservey Meservey
  Meservie Meservy
  Messervey Messervie
  Messervy Miserve
  —— **62** 316
— Mr. **66** 362
Abigail **66** 107 110 **88** 350
  89 84 **98** 62 **99** 198 **108**
  123 **125** 216 **132** 274
  275
Abigail Frances **68** 93
Alden **73** 171
Andrew **87** 344
Andrew E. **67** 82
Andrew Jackson **113** 300
Benjamin **99** 198 199
Betty **56** 318 **134** 146
Caroline **73** 171 178
Charity **70** 319
Clement **58** 249 **68** 93
  132 274 275
Damaris **73** 185
Daniel **103** 190 192 270
  132 274 275
Daniel (Mrs.) **103** 192
David **66** 104 110
Dora E. (Hackett) **113** 314
Edward George **67** xxxiv
Eleazer **103** 270
Elethere **66** 110
Elisha **103** 193
Eliza J. **87** 344
Elizabeth **66** 107 **88** 350 **99**
  198-200 **101** 325
Elizabeth (Foster) **135** 132
Elizabeth Pray (Ricker)
  113 300
Elsie **73** 171 175
Elzira **73** 184
Emily **73** 175
Emily J. **87** 344
Eunice **66** 109
Eunice (Willey) **124** 61
Frank L. **113** 314
George **98** 198 **99** 196
  198 199
George P. **69** xxxii
H. N. **85** 375

MESERVE *cont'd*
Hannah **99** 198 199 **124** 61
Henry H. **73** 178
Isaac **91** 330 **99** 198
James D. **125** 113
Jane **73** 171
Jane Y. **73** 185
Jemima **99** 198 199
John **58** 237 **73** 171 **82** 33
  88 350 **96** 247 **99** 199
Jonathan **89** 84
Jonathan S. **73** 175
Joseph **88** 350 **89** 84
  99 198 199
Lizzie Frank **113** 300
Lydia **88** 350 **99** 199 **105**
  228 **133** 218
Maria Lunt **112** 144
Mark M. **88** 350
Martha **98** 198
Martha (Nock) **96** 247
Mary **67** 314 **68** 93 **73** 185
  88 350 **99** 196 198 199
  144 219
Mary C. **84** 30
Mary H. (Brooks) **120**
  217 218
Mehitable **63** 271
Miles **73** 171 185
Nancy **73** 171 178 **87** 344
Nathaniel **55** 67 80 **63** 294
  65 353 **73** 171 175 **92**
  102 103 **124** 41 **130** 103
  142 203 **146** 330-332
Oliver **87** 344
Orin **103** 269
Parnel / Pernal Foster
  88 350 **99** 198
Paul **87** 344
Paul T. **87** 344
Polly **88** 350 **99** 198 199
R. U. **101** 34
Rachel **73** 175
Rebecca **73** 178 184
Reuben **66** 110
Robert McKenny **99** 199
Rufus **88** 350 **99** 198
Ruth **73** 171
Sally **73** 171 **99** 123
Samuel **73** 171 **88** 350 **99**
  198-200 **124** 61 **132** 275
Samuel S. **88** 350
Sarah **65** 353 **142** 203
Sarah (Demerritt) **132** 275
Sarah (Pendergast)
  132 275
Sarah Venner **87** 343
Solomon **88** 350
Stephen **99** 198
Susan **99** 123
Susanna **99** 196
Tabitha **88** 350 **99** 198
Tamson **98** 216
Theresa R. (Herriman)
  (Colby) **125** 113
Thomas **73** 178 **135** 132
Thomas J. **120** 217 218
Timothy **99** 200
William **73** 171 **99** 198
Winthrop Smith **68** 305
  69 97 **132** 115

MESHAKA Marguerite
  Ricker **99** 57
MESQUEY William **91** 330
MESSENBERG
George **64** 112
Messenger *see* Messinger
MESSER Messers Messor
  —— **70** 16 **91** 259
Abby Frances **81** 381
Abigail **146** 334
Abigail Francis **110** 308
Alice **70** 11
Ann Elizabeth **94** 27
Asa **56** 12
Asenath (Baker) **88** 282
Augusta L. (Perley)
  103 47
Carroll L. **83** 424 436
Charlotte A. (Merrill)
  121 179
Daniel **88** 331
Edwin F. **103** 47
Eliza (Cutts) **121** 182
Eliza W. (York) **121** 177
Elizabeth **64** 117 **69** 297
  305
Ella M. (Allen) **103** 48
Emerson J. **121** 178
Emma J. **92** 108
Ernest L. **87** 208
Frances Abigail **81** 381
  382
Francis P. **103** 47
Grace B. (Burrell) **83** 424
Hannah **83** 144 **86** 149
Harriet Record **66** lii
Harvey H. **121** 180
Hellen L. (Everett)
  121 178
Jacob **103** 47
John E. **121** 178 182
John M. **103** 47
Jonathan **69** 304 **70** 308
Joseph H. **103** 47
Judith S. (Whittier) **103** 47
Laura A. (Putney) **103** 47
Lenora M. (Ganbern)
  121 178
Louisa C. (Whittaker)
  121 180
Lucy (Lord) **88** 283
Lucy Ann **67** 350
Lydia **91** 263
Lydia (Sanderson) **128** 45
M. **91** 330
Martha (Dam) **100** 227
Mary **125** 53
Mary C. (Johnson) **103** 47
Mehitable **86** 362
Milton **121** 177
Moses **121** 178
Nathaniel **124** 62
Nathaniel P. **121** 179
Nellie S. **103** 127
Nellie Stearns **108** 140
Nelson Augustus **81** 381
  382
Olive Martha **81** 381
Oliver **100** 227
Phebe **64** 117

MESSER *cont'd*
Reginald Augustus
  81 382
Richard **87** 208
Rose E. **121** 179
Rosie E. **121** 179
Sarah **91** 263 **117** 80 **122** 80
Sarah (Merritt) **88** 331
Sarah Melvina **81** 382
Sarah S. **88** 333
Stephen **91** 259
Stillman **88** 282
Sylvia (Booth) **124** 62
Sylvia J. (Laney) **121** 178
Thomas **117** 80
Wealthy C. (Williams)
  103 47
Willard **88** 283
William H. **103** 48
Messervey *see* Meserve
Messervie *see* Meserve
Messervy *see* Meserve
MESSICK —— **78** 234
Jane (Hunt) **86** 462
John **86** 462
Margaret Ann **78** 234
Sarah Matilda **86** 462
MESSIER Emily **74** 312
Emily E. **74** 312
Ida **74** 312
Joseph **74** 312
MESSING Edward **101** 244
MESSINGER Massinger
  Messenger
  —— **64** 55 **93** 258
— Mr. **64** 181 182
A. W.B. **101** 326 327
Abigail **52** 420 **60** 204
  115 131 **135** 301 302
Almon **81** 413
Amanda Fitzalen **77** 185
Andrew **64** 286 **135** 301
Anoxie **64** 286
Austin **134** 173 **136** 167
Betsey **132** 106
Bronson **111** 129 **136** 167
Calvin **58** 55
Caroline (Hopkins)
  104 54
Catherine **83** 44
Charles **104** 54
Charles W. **79** 41
Chloe **64** 286
Chloe (Jackson) **87** 283
Clarissa **64** 286
Cyrus **64** 287 **134** 173
  136 167
Daniel **64** 286 287 **136**
  167 312
David Sewell **86** 232
Dora **64** 286
Dorcas **64** 286 **110** 142
Dorcas (Bronson) **136** 167
Ebenezer **87** 282 **91** 342
  344 **93** 258 **130** 213 **135**
  301 **142** 83
Edgar **64** 286
Edward **135** 301
Edward F. **108** 128
Edward Foster **94** 139

MESSINGER *cont'd*
Edward Foster (Mrs.) **95** 147
Eldridge **81** 282
Elias **58** 55
Eliza **64** 286
Elizabeth **135** 301 302
Elizabeth (Mellows) **87** 282 **135** 301
Ella Marion (Cobb) **94** 59
Elvira **64** 286
Emily **52** 228
Emory F. **81** 413
Esther (Cheevers) **135** 302
Eveline **64** 287
Fidelia B. **82** 376
George D. **64** 287
George W. **92** 266
George Washington **99** 14
Giles A. **82** 376
Hannah **64** 286
Hannah Ellis (Hartshorn) **87** 289
Harriet **92** 203
Harriet (Sawyer) **86** 232
Harriet Josephine **61** lxi
Henry **60** 188 **87** 282 **91** 93 **102** 185 **135** 301 302
Herbert Stanley **94** 59
Hiram King **61** lxi
Horace H. **81** 277
Hubert N. **81** 282
James **92** 203 **121** 247
Jemima (Everett) **130** 213 **135** 302
Jennie I. **81** 277
Jerusha **135** 302
Jho. **141** 196
John **55** 289 **92** 24 **135** 302 **142** 130
John E. **81** 413
John S. **71** 288
Jonathan **87** 283
Josephine Louise **87** 289
Katharine **72** 38
Laura J. **81** 413
Laury **64** 287
Leady **64** 286
Levina (Blake) **89** 285
Lizzie E. **82** 376
Lois Ann **64** 286
Louisa **81** 413
Louisa Adeline **136** 323
Lucinda (Hiscock) **136** 167
Luther **58** 55
Lydia (Royce) **136** 312
M. E. **81** 413
Martha **55** 289 **138** 217
Martha A. **81** 277
Martin **64** 286
Mary **58** 55 **68** 282 **73** 227 **78** 291 **89** 367 **92** 24 **135** 301 302
Mary A. **61** lxi
Mary Ann **73** 195
Mary Ann (Dunbar) **87** 282 283 **104** 312 **111** 65
Mary Fidelia **87** 176 203 282 **93** 364 **104** 312 **111**

MESSINGER *cont'd*
65
Mary P. **111** 129
Maryette **81** 280
Molly **135** 302
Nancy **58** 55
Nathan **52** 420 **60** 204
Nathan Harvey **119** 80
Nathaniel **52** 413
Olive **58** 55 **66** 91
Olive (Ware) **135** 302
Oliver **52** 413
P. **59** 183
Peter **64** 286
Polly **135** 302
Priscilla **134** 332
Rebecca **91** 342 344 **93** 258 **135** 301
Rebecca (Sweetser) **87** 283 **130** 213 **135** 301
Rebecca Orswell **77** 185
Return **118** 329 **119** 80
Rhoda **81** 413
Richard **64** 336
Roderick **64** 286
Rosewell **113** 25 123 **116** 135 221-223
Ruth **71** 288 **135** 301 302
Rutherford S. **81** 413
S. E. **81** 413
Sadie M. **81** 413
Samantha (McClure) **134** 173
Samuel **64** 286 **89** 285 **116** 136
Sarah **81** 413
Sarah A. **71** 288
Sherman **81** 413
Stephen **64** 286
Sukey **58** 57
Susan **97** 66
Susanna **136** 312
Susanna Sawyer **86** 232
Sweetser **135** 301 **141** 346 **142** 57
Thomas **54** 334 **58** 55-57 **87** 282 **91** 342 **135** 301 302 **142** 83
Timothy **58** 56
Ursula **135** 301 302
Virgil Jackson **87** 282 283 **104** 312 **111** 65
Wigglesworth **87** 283 **130** 213 **135** 301 **136** 167 **141** 330
William Harrison **87** 289
Winthrop **60** 188
MESSMORE
Jessie **88** 95
MESSNER Margaret
Rhoda (Henry) **105** 313
V. E. (Mrs.) **105** 313
Messor *see* Messer
MESSUERRE
Francis **81** 447
James **81** 447
Peter **81** 447
Sarah **81** 447
MESTON Isabel **89** 260
Margaret Scott **89** 260

MESTON *cont'd*
Peter **89** 260
MESUARD Eri **91** 242
Lucy (Hill) **91** 242
MESUM
Juliana **71** 311 323
MESURIER H. G. **83** 256
METACOM Sachem **132** 14 **144** 211
METCALF Matcalf
Medcalf Medcolf
Metcalfe Metcalk
Mydcallf
— Lieut. **57** 23
— Maj. **114** 302
— Mr. **57** 229
— Mrs. **73** 74
Abel **141** 339
Abiel **72** 205
Abiel (Adams) **148** 42
Abigail **56** 395 **60** 370 **98** 302 **126** 212 **136** 328
Abijah **126** 212 **141** 346
Abner **141** 339
Achsah **63** 94
Adam **86** 253 254
Albert **67** xlii lxix
Alexander **111** 263 264
Alfred **56** 21
Alice **122** 285
Almira **142** 76
Almira (Landers) **124** 280
Alvah **142** 76
Amelia **72** 205
Amy **78** 64 **80** 312 313
Amy Abigail **83** 230
Andrew **115** 118
Ann **122** 285
Anna **60** 370 **74** 64 **98** 302
Anna (Fisher) **142** 131
Anna Sophia **72** 103
Anne **59** 373 **78** 64
Anne (Chickering) (Paine) **143** 302
Arthur Hobart **59** xcix
Augustine **86** 253 255
Barnabas **141** 332
Benjamin **91** 330 **141** 346
Bethuel **142** 76
Betsey **91** 197 **122** 285
Brian **111** 198
Brian (Mrs.) **111** 198
Bryce **93** 210 **144** 322 **145** 31
C. A. **91** 330
Caleb **59** xcviii
Caleb Hardy **138** 137
Candace **138** 137
Caroline **59** xcviii **97** 49 **120** 95
Carrie Ethlyn (Wilson) **100** 94
Catherine **99** 334
Charles Everett **139** 214
Charlotte Anne **81** 393
Clara **57** 285
Clare L. **74** xxiv
Clare L. (Burt) **113** 59
Clarissa **74** 64
Clifton A. **66** 52
Cyrus **138** 137

METCALF *cont'd*
Daniel **60** 370 **74** 64
  81 393
David **60** 370 **74** 64 **98** 302
  103 299 **138** 136 137
  141 346 **142** 131 **147**
  260 **148** 177
David (Mrs.) **147** 260
Deborah **58** 372 **141** 190
Deborah (Revere) **145**
  293 294
Dennis **86** 252
Diantha **81** 393
Dionis **86** 254
Ebenezer **62** 381 **74** 64 **98**
  302 **129** 384 **141** 339
  142 82 **147** 257
Edmond **86** 253
Edward **72** 103 **86** 252
Eleanor **117** 250 **126** 306
Eleazer **59** xcviii **142** 79
  130
Elia (--)nder **141** 339
Elias **142** 76
Eliphalet **60** 149 **98** 302
Eliza **115** 118
Eliza G. **105** 148
Elizabeth **57** 223 **59**
  xcviii xcix **60** 370 **74** 64
  77 130 **78** 64 **79** 449 **86**
  256 **94** 215 **108** 64 308
  141 346
Elizabeth Mason (Paine)
  98 86 **103** 222
Elizabeth Vincent **82** 472
Ellyn (Benson) **86** 253
Elvira **138** 137
Erastus **138** 137
Esther **55** 260 **61** 141
Esther Henrietta (Pierce)
  105 148
Eunice Dench
  (Houghton) **105** 148
Frances Hale **54** cxxi 139
Frank Hamilton (Mrs.)
  75 155 **76** xxii
G. S. **91** 330
Geoffrey **86** 254 255
George **74** 64 **91** 330
George Cook **74** 64
George Pierce **105** 148
Gertrude Margaret (Kane)
  139 214
Grace **106** 270
H. **91** 330
Hannah **59** 220 **60** 370 **63**
  188 **74** 64 **98** 302 **121**
  217 **130** 212 **138** 137
  141 197
Hannah (Kenrick)
  105 148
Hannah Elizabeth (Bruce)
  97 126
Helen **122** 285
Helen Adelia (Rowe)
  105 148
Helen Pierce **105** 148
Henry **86** 252
Henry B. **55** 189
Henry Brewer **59** xii
  xxvi lvi xcviii xcix

METCALF *cont'd*
Henry Harrison **65** 198
Hepzibah (Mann) **107** 36
Houghton Pierce **105** 148
Irving W. **56** xxxii
Isaac **56** 100 **125** 41
  142 131
Isaac Stevens **56** 100
J. G. **112** 213
Jabez **74** 64
James **86** 253 **90** 89 **141**
  202 339 342
James A. **100** 94
James Sparks **148** 177
Jane **78** 64 65 **96** 261 264
Jeffery **86** 254 255
Jerusha (Bliss) (Shaw)
  104 24
Jesse **105** 148
Joan **86** 252
Joan (Cooke) **86** 253
Job **98** 302
Joel **105** 148 **127** 226
John **57** 41 **62** 371 **63** 93
  187 **76** 79 **78** 64 80 312
  86 252 253 256 **104** 24
  106 270 **118** 43 46 52 56
  57 **122** 285 **124** 280 **145**
  293 348
John Brockway (Mrs.)
  82 472
John G. **113** 84 86
John George **65** 14
John Morris **115** 118
John Thomas **74** 64
Jonathan **60** 370 **63** 187
  191 263 **74** 113 **98** 302
  105 148 **119** 82 **130** 212
  141 15
Joseph **58** 372 **63** 263 **74**
  64 **87** 398 **112** 264 **128**
  257
Jubal **126** 234
Julia **79** 403 407
Julia (Buckminster)
  89 120
Katharine **78** 64
Katharine (Herrick)
  105 148
Leonard **78** 63 64 **80** 312
  313 **86** 252 253 256
Lizzie Nellie **81** 393
Lois **57** 392 **115** 118
  141 339
Louisa **114** 72
Lucian **138** 137
Lucretia Ann (Bingham)
  92 323
Lucy **81** 393 **95** 238
Lucy (Gay) **105** 148
Lydia **56** 32 270 **98** 302
Mabel Armine **76** xxii
Malinda **89** 120
Margaret **142** 130 131 141
Margaret (Smith) **86** 253
Maria **74** 64 **78** 64
Marie **80** 313
Marion **56** 100
Marquis **142** 62
Martha **78** 64 **83** 493 **94**
  217 **142** 130 131

METCALF *cont'd*
Mary **56** 39 **57** 53 **58** 240
  59 xcviii **60** 149 **63** 91
  93 **74** 64 **78** 64 65 **86**
  253 **89** 120 **99** 312 **107**
  35 179 **114** 162 **137** 109
  142 130 131 **147** 260
Mary (Cazneau) **142** 82
  128 130 139-141
Mary (Fairbanks) **105** 148
Mary (Fisher) **145** 293
Mary (Gay) **106** 227
Mary (Whittemore)
  107 36
Mary Caroline **67** xlix
Mary Elizabeth **78** 47
Matilda **111** 263 264
Matilda J. **66** 52
Matthew **60** lvi **72** 57 58
  78 64 **80** 312 313 **86** 254
Mehitable **57** 23 **58** 167
  59 153 373 **60** 370 **63** 93
Melatiah **126** 34 **141** 346
  142 141
Melatiah (Fisher) **142** 130
Meletiah **57** 396 **126** 34
Melissa **138** 137
Michael **56** 100 **57** 223 **58**
  208 **59** xcviii 373 **60**
  188 **62** 381 **63** 187 **65**
  362 **67** xlix **78** 63-65 **80**
  312 313 **82** 225 **85** 181
  86 190 252-256 **94** 215
  96 264 **98** 84 **105** 148
  106 259 **107** 36 **127** 226
  138 80 **141** 339 **142** 130
Nathan **65** 360
Nathaniel **105** 148 **106** 227
Nicholas **78** 64 **80** 312 313
  86 256
Nynian **78** 64 **80** 312
Obededom **141** 339
Olive **57** 153 **63** lx
Olivia **98** 84
Patty **79** 41
Paul **89** 120 **93** 384
Peletiah **59** xcviii **107** 36
Pleasance **86** 254
Polly **138** 137
Polly (Whittemore)
  107 36
Ralph **92** 323
Rebecca **59** 373 **65** 38 **78**
  64 **122** 228
Reginald **86** 252
Reuben G. **67** xlix
Richard **78** 64 **80** 313 **86**
  252 253 255
Robert **86** 253
Rosa (Jones) **139** 214
Ruth **63** 263 **84** 186 **115** 67
Ruth (Whiting) **105** 148
Sabra **141** 339
Samuel **57** 153 **58** 345 **99**
  312 **122** 285 **141** 339
Samuel L. **68** 306
Sarah **58** 372 **78** 64 65 **80**
  313 **81** 38 **106** 227 **130**
  212 **142** 130 131 139
Sarah (Elwyn) **94** 215
  105 148

METCALF cont'd
Sarah Ann **67** xlix
Sarah T. **96** 288
Sarah W. **148** 177
Seth **95** 120 **116** 80
Sibyl **74** 64
Silva **141** 346
Simon **86** 252
Sophia **122** 285
Stephen Card **148** 177
Stephen Olney **75** xxiii
155 **105** 68 131 148
Susan **86** 254
Susanna **78** 65 **142** 130
131 140 141
Sylvester **86** 254
Tabitha **58** 372
Tamer **141** 192
Tewil **141** 346
Theodore **80** 68
Theron **79** 403 **80** 69
Thirza (Danforth) **123** 319
Thomas **56** 269 **59** xcviii
153 **78** 64 **86** 255 **104**
121 **143** 302 **145** 293
Thomas Newell (Mrs.)
98 86 **103** 222
Timothy **63** 188 **142** 128
130 131
Victor Howard **63** 312
Vielatte **91** 197
Walter C. **57** 330 **66** 342
71 174 319 **74** 136 **102**
254 **104** 36 **105** 21 **111**
154 **141** 95 96 **145** 99
100 **148** 253
Welthy **115** 118
William **60** 370 **63** 146
65 26 **66** 37 **98** 302 **99**
79 **111** 264 **123** 319 **139**
214
William Henry **81** 393
Winship Whitten **148** 177
Zachie **76** 116
METELLI
Fratelli **107** 251
METER see also Von Meter
Thomas **144** 31
METERRE
Richard **143** 260
METFORTH John **93** 28
METHAM
Agnes **114** 225 226
Elizabeth **111** 200
John **116** 167
John de **116** 167
Richard de **116** 172
Sibyl **116** 167
Thomas **116** 166
Thomas de **116** 167 170
METHERST James **67** 38
METLAR
Elizabeth **96** 387
METLIN
Robert **82** 283 294
Sarah **82** 283 294
METLINE Carrie **81** 41
Daniel **81** 41
METLOCK Annie **78** 319
METRE Jacob von **84** 392
METTE Nicholas **76** 55

METTEE
Andrew H. **84** 354
METTENSIS
Albertus **104** 210
METTERNICH-WINNEBURG
Clemens Wenzel
Nepomuk Lothar von
(Prince) **77** 94
METTLACH Frank Robert
(Mrs.) **107** 134
METTLER
Alice Lorraine **97** 119
Amanda M. (Rea) **112** 325
Amy Josephine
(McMahon) **97** 119
Andrew **97** 119
Dolly May **97** 119
Don (Mrs.) **112** 325 **114** 82
Frances Amy **97** 119
George Howard **97** 119
John A. **97** 119 **112** 325
John McMahon **97** 119
Russell William **97** 119
Wilhelmina (Kropinske)
97 119
METTON
Elizabeth **53** 86
Michael **53** 86
METYARD —— **79** 427
Elizabeth **84** 434
Martin **84** 434
Robert **84** 434
METZ Ann **78** 422
Anna **126** 308
Benjamin F. **97** 380
Edith **135** 338
Jacob **86** 352
Mary L. **97** 380
Matilda **109** 226
W. Ray **101** 337
METZGER
Mary J. **139** 216
Nellie Louise **103** 138
MEULAN Robert
Beaumont (Count of)
95 123
Waleran Beaumont
(Count of) **95** 123
96 317
Marie de **79** 373
MEUNIER
Jean-Baptiste **131** 90
Jeanne **88** 194
MEURANT
Gloria M. **116** 96
MEURER
Gerhart Wiemar
125 73
Henry **125** 74
Peter J. **125** 74
MEURIG Roger ap **119** 97
MEUSHETT
Andrew **77** 232
MEVERS
Frank C. **148** 187
MEW James **61** 279
Richard **129** 32
MEWCE Mews Mewse
— Mr. **127** 17
— Mrs. **60** 207 **98** 41

MEWCE cont'd
Elizabeth (Washington)
98 30 41
Francis **98** 30 41
Hannah **84** 374
Lucy **98** 30
Peter **86** 353
Samuel **77** 122
Thomas **84** 374
MEWERS
Eliza E. **67** 351
Luke **67** 351
MEWHORTER Emma
Celia **71** xxxviii
Mews see Mewce
Mewse see Mewce
MEXON Ann **73** 147
MEYER Adolf **59** 419
Agnes **88** 188
Albert Cook **115** 66
Alfred Reuben **88** 188
Anna **112** 139
August Robert **88** 188
August Robert (Mrs.)
86 346 **88** 187
Carl **80** 105 206 **120** 149
Catalyntje **94** 60
Charles Fisher **105** 68 131
Earl Schenck **115** 238
Edward L. **117** 293
Eliza G. (Lovejoy) **89** 390
391
Emma J. **75** 157
Emma Jane (Hixon) **87**
177 **88** 187
Emmetje (Van Dyke)
94 61
Frances **98** 9
Frank M. **97** 85
Frederick **117** 16
George Forest (Mrs.)
108 135
George Steven (Mrs.)
108 135
George Von Lengerke
66 193 **67** 305 **74** lvii
Gertrude Vanatta **105** 126
Harold L. (Mrs.) **117** 158
Heinrich Peter **88** 188
Helen (Hornblower)
95 350
Henry Hixon **88** 188
Howard (Mrs.) **120** 80
Isidore S. **115** 319
Jacob **98** 223
James Newton (Mrs.)
98 147
Jeremiah **117** 16
John G. **117** 55 56
John H. **74** xxiv
Julius **112** 139
Margaret A. **108** 201
Margaretha (Krafts)
88 188
Maria (Palmer) **112** 139
Martinus Jansen **94** 60
Mary H. **108** 135
Mary K. **145** 271
Matilda **105** 145
Micah **59** lxxxi

MEYER *cont'd*
Miriam Badlam (Pearce)
105 129
Myer **109** 77
Nicholas de **55** 378
Ortha Loomis (Wright)
109 128
Philip **88** 188
Ruth **88** 188
Sarah Willets (Leavitt)
84 98
William **105** 112
William Kulp (Mrs.)
108 135
MEYERS Bethiah Hayward
(Clifton) **90** 53
Burtha **95** 360
Charles G. (Mrs.) **84** 98
Eliza **107** 112
Ellen (Canon) **84** 217
Emma Jane **84** 217
Gardiner Howland **84** 98
Harriet **125** 280
John **84** 217
Joseph H. **107** 72
Margaret A. **108** 201
Marie Anne (Rouse)
91 81
Martha Pamelia **91** 80 81
143 126
MEYSER
Fanny (Gale) **124** 17
George A. **124** 17
MEZANAH
Ann (Pike) **91** 381
John **91** 381
MEZCRELIS
— Widow **82** 331
Daniel **82** 331
MEZELACA
— Mr. **54** 347
MEZZARA
Joseph **77** lxxvi
M'FISHER Jane Buck
(Morgan) **96** 33
M'Giffin *see* McGiffin
M'Gowen *see* McGowen
MIADEN Mary **125** 216
MIALS Elizabeth **67** 372
MIANTONOMI **54** 265 **89**
176 177 281 **94** 347 **96**
272 **98** 18 20
MIARS Amanda **91** 386
MIBROSS Jane **65** 246
MICAH Sampson **78** 111
MICHAEL Micall Mycaell
Mycall
John **60** 347 **94** 7
Maud Allen (Weeks)
87 77
Peter **111** 197
Mary **85** 146
Rebecca **60** 93 **119** 111
133 257
Thomas **56** 315
Watson **91** 330
MICHAELIUS
Jonas **143** 196
MICHAELS —— **56** 210
Mary **117** 163
Mindwell **134** 67

MICHAELSON
Michelsen Michelson
Barbara **86** 31
Bastian **106** 175
Clarina Shumway
(Hanks) **86** 31
Herman **86** 31
Jan **52** 475
Joan **86** 31
John **56** 378
Reyer **106** 173 175 177
178 291 292
Richard **106** 175 176
Roger **106** 178 292
MICHAU Joseph **65** 230
MICHAUD John **139** 193
MICHEAL
— Mrs. **71** 119 121
John **71** 119
MICHEL Katharine
(Sedgley) **90** 336
Lewis **129** 42
Mary **148** 258
Mary L. (Sands) **97** 20
MICHELBORNE
Michelburne
Edward **52** 122
Elizabeth **52** 122
George **52** 121
John **52** 121 122 **70** 127
William **52** 121
MICHELENA Y SALIAS
Carmen **103** 310
MICHELINI Mildred
Lewis (Swett) **96** 333
Romero Mark **96** 33
MICHELL —— **142** 365
— Widow **147** 169
Ezabell **142** 162
Joan **143** 116
Marie **100** 273
Michelsen *see* Michaelson
Michelson *see* Michaelson
MICHENER Michiner
Able **148** 150
Adelaide Richards
81 109 222
John G. **91** 330
Mary **98** 349
MICHIE — Mr. **91** 303
M. E. Ann (Carter) **91** 303
MICHIEL Watson **91** 330
MICHIELS Mary **128** 168
MICHIELSDR
Lijsbeth **128** 162
Michiner *see* Michener
MICK George **117** 80
Isaac **117** 80
Peter **117** 80
Peter Kidd **117** 80
Sarah **96** 53
MICKEL Mickell
— Capt. **85** 460
Cordelia **129** 49
Edmund **112** 58
Elizabeth **129** 49
Ephraim Christian **64** 214
Isaac **129** 49
MICKELS Betsey **111** 115
MICKELWRIGHT
Humfrey **147** 166

MICKLE Elizabeth (Morris)
125 223
Thomas **125** 223
MICKLEFIELD
Ann **58** 312
Edward **58** 312
Hannah (Hitchins)
125 105
John **58** 312
Mary **58** 312
Richard **79** 84
Sarah **77** 228
Thomas **58** 312
William **125** 105
MICKLEHEUNEY
John **125** 130
Sarah (Handy) **125** 130
MICKLETHWAITE
Anne **67** 76
Joseph **67** 76
MICKLEY
Minnie F. **66** lii
MICKMAN John **107** 37
Mary (Whittemore)
107 37
MICKUM Mary (Wheeler)
127 54
Samuel **127** 54
MICO Micoe
—— **51** 417 **52** 125 140
53 23
John **61** 199 **69** 360 **131**
175 178
Joseph **53** 324 **54** 196
MICOMTIER
Jane (Grant) **114** 44
Micom **114** 44
MICTON
George **110** 168
Richard **110** 168
Rowland **110** 168
Midaugh *see* Middaugh
MIDCLAIRE
Mary **64** 340
MIDDAUGH Midaugh
Middagh
Alice (Kerns) **124** 298
Florence Marie **124** 298
Harriet Alice (McDonald)
85 292
Ira Otis **124** 298
Julia **92** 171
Lucinda R. **128** 268
Mary Alice (Kerns)
124 298
Thomas **128** 268
Willard **85** 292
MIDDENDORF
Henry Stump **110** 156
J. William **117** 156
MIDDLEBOROUGH
James **70** 264
MIDDLEBROOK
— Mrs. **70** 43
Abiah **145** 243
Anne **69** 131 **70** 40
Burr **69** 373
Deborah **69** 130
Dorothy **69** 131
Eleanor **69** 130 **70** 34 35
Elizabeth **69** 373 378

MIDDLEBROOK *cont'd*
Ephraim **69** 373
Eunice **69** 130 131 **70** 37
Grace **62** 203
Hubble **69** 368
Huldah **69** 368
James **69** 373
Jane **68** 289 **69** 376
Jerusha **68** 293 **69** 368
Jonathan **68** 171 175
  69 128 368
Joseph **51** 331 **64** 92 **68**
  170 171 176 289 **69** 130
  131 376 **70** 39
L. F. **113** 13
Louis F. **101** 147 211 **144**
  236 **145** 70 **146** 368
Louis Frank **64** xxxi 92
Mary **51** 331 **68** 293 **69** 240
Michael **62** 203
Morris **69** 239
Odel **69** 240
Oliver **68** 293 **69** 128 239
  240
Rebecca **69** 128
Rhode **69** 130 **70** 35
Robert **69** 373
Salome **69** 128 **70** 36
Samuel Wheeler **69** 240
Sarah **68** 176 **69** 130 131
  376
Sarah A. **145** 244
Submit **69** 130 131
Sylvanus **68** 293 **69** 128
  368
MIDDLEBURGER
Margaret A. **109** 223
MIDDLECOTT
  Middlecot Middlecote
Richard **87** 153 **139** 299
Sarah (Winslow) (Paine)
  87 153
Thomas **53** 45
MIDDLEMORE
—— **59** 333 **147** 29
— Mr. **57** 322
Caroline **57** 286
Catherine **53** 357
Frances **57** 286
Grace **57** 321
John **53** 357
Mary **57** 319
Moses **57** 286
Samuel **57** 320
Thomas **53** 357 **56** 213
  57 xxxiii 319-321 **60**
  xxxvi
Uriah D. **57** 286
MIDDLESWART
Teunis **136** 54
Middlesworth Von *see*
  Von Middlesworth
MIDDLETON Midleton
  Midlton Myddelton
  Mydelton
— Mrs. **104** 173 175 **105**
  184 **106** 235
A. **116** 119
Alan de **96** 105
Alexander **52** 13
Alice **90** 60 62 65 197 **93**

MIDDLETON *cont'd*
177 **146** 323
Andrew **51** 287
Ann **52** 13 **73** 142 **129** 45
Ann (McNemall) **100** 300
Anna **116** 119 **129** 45
Anne **67** 252 **104** 275
Arthur **51** 410 **52** 14
Arthur E. **106** 278
Bernard de **96** 105
Cemantha (Butterfield)
  128 97
Charles **100** 300
Charles (Earl of) **52** 13
Chloe Ann **73** 274
Clawson R. **115** 122
David **73** 276
Diana **52** 13
Edmund **110** 171
Edward **51** 410 **104** 280
Edy **60** 284
Eliza (Garrett) **88** 331
Elizabeth **90** 109
Elizabeth F. **69** 262
Else **78** 316
Elspeth **52** 13
Faith **67** 201
George **52** 13 **70** 229 **79** 56
  104 280
Griffin **110** 170
H. **59** 181
Harriet **82** 179
Helen **52** 13
Helen I. **116** 119
Henry **107** 191 **125** 263
  130 166
Henry O. **73** 269
James **69** 262 **88** 331
  119 18
Jane (Skelton)
  (Blennerhasset) **98**
  272 274
Jane (Strickland) **114** 53
Jeanne **88** 254
Joan **98** 274
Joan (Jenks) **110** 164
John **60** 25 **93** 177 **98** 33 35-
  37 39 272 274 **100** 235
  239 **110** 164 169-171
  113 70 267
John (Earl of) **52** 13
John T. **128** 96
Joseph **68** 206
Joshua **110** 169 170
Katharine **54** 216 **63** 286
  100 274
L. **116** 119
Lucy **78** 310
Mabel (Ogel) **104** 274
Margaret Simons **108** 78
Mary **52** 14 **100** 235 239
  125 64
Mary E. **69** 262
Matthew **67** 201 **93** 19
Peter **90** 62 65 **93** 177
Phebe **98** 44
Prudence **52** 13
Richard **51** 410 **63** 83 **88**
  252 254 **110** 169 170
  142 365
Robert **52** 13 **64** 258 **93** 17

MIDDLETON *cont'd*
  104 274 **110** 170 171
  112 185
Sally **70** 229
Samanth D. (Butterfield)
  128 97
Sarah **73** 272
Sarah (Minnick) **128** 96
Stephen **51** 410
Theodore **73** 151
Thomas **51** 404 **68** 181 **90**
  64 65 **104** 274 **114** 53
  135 224 229 231 **139**
  229
Thomas de **96** 105
William **51** 410 **64** 216 259
  65 239 **93** 177 **116** 119
  129 45
MIDEL Gilbert **79** 173
MIDGLEY Medgley
  Midgeley Midgely
Bertha **96** 288
Bertha Ann **96** 288
Carrie Amanda (Bancroft)
  96 288
Florence Elizabeth
  (Millett) **96** 288
Florence Ida (Sullivan)
  96 288
Fred **96** 288
Frederick **96** 288
Harold Austin **96** 288
John **94** 107 **113** 199
Leonard **96** 288
Lilla May (Noble) **96** 288
Lorey Frederick **96** 288
Mary J. **77** 189
Mildred **96** 288
Mildred Pomeroy **96** 288
R. I. **53** 450
Ruth Amanda **96** 288
Samuel **65** 45
Sarah Ann (Clegg) **96** 288
Susan **113** 199
William Bancroft **96** 288
MIDHURST
Sarah Sophia **62** 97
MIDJAAS Mildred
  Bilderback **117** 159
MIDKEFF Ann **126** 144
MIDLAND John **84** 281
MIDLEDICHE
John **80** 315
MIDLING Mary A. **105** 34
MIDLINGTON
— Mr. **71** 135
Midlton *see* Middleton
MIDWOOD
Charles N. **63** liii
Miegs *see* Meigs
MIELS Abigail **126** 67
MIELZINER Ella McKenna
  (Friend) **89** 132 305
Leo (Mrs.) **89** 132
MIER Elizabeth **73** 137
MIERN Nathan **91** 330
William **91** 330
Miers *see* Myers
MIETH Audrey Lucia
  (Lockard) **123** 15
MIETT Susan **89** 241

MIFFIN Philip **93** 9 11
MIFFLIN —— **53** 460
Elizabeth (Bagnell) **131** 45
Elizabeth Crowninshield
76 217
Eugenia **89** 369
George H. **51** 87 **110** 279
Jane Appleton (Phillips)
110 279
John **131** 45
Sophia **106** 309
Thomas **55** 54 **131** 45
Walker **106** 47
MIGEOT Gaspard **114** 265
MIGHILL Mighel
Mighell Mighells
Mighil
—— **61** 374
Abigail **65** 255
Benjamin **58** 28 **67** 373
Daniel **67** 373
Elizabeth **53** 203 377
65 255
Elizabeth (Ferman)
123 263
Ezekiel **53** 203 377
Hannah **107** 33
Joanna **52** 226
John **107** 33 **123** 263
Margaret **130** 280
Mary **89** 67
Moses **65** 255
Nathaniel **60** 307 **123** 265
131 156 **133** 72
Samuel **87** 398
Sarah **52** 82 **58** 28 204
67 373
Sarah (Bliss) **123** 265 **127**
178 **133** 72
Susanna **67** 373
Thomas **107** 33 **121** 214
274 **131** 156 **133** 188
MIGNEL Joseph **78** 180
MIGNERON Jean-Baptiste
128 182
Magdeleine (LeBlanc)
128 182
Marie-Magdeleine
(Bomer dit LaPlante)
128 182
MIGNET —— **60** 225
MIGOY
Alexander **96** 337
Sarah (Jones) **96** 337
MIHALES Betsey **111** 44
112 115
David **111** 44
George **111** 44
James **111** 44 116
John **111** 44 112
Lucretia **111** 112 115
Mindwell **111** 44
Moses **111** 44
Polley **111** 112
Rachel **111** 44
Rebecca **111** 44 115
Samuel **111** 112
Susanna **111** 44 112 115
William **111** 112
MIHELL Henry **52** 238
Joan **52** 238

MIHELL *cont'd*
Robert **52** 238
Thomas **52** 238
MIKEL —— **91** 387
MIKEN Abigail **125** 289
MIKESELL
Sarah Jane **147** 226
MIKYLBURGH
Agnes **89** 338
Agnes (Bartram) **89** 336
338
Robert **89** 336 338
MILAN W. D. **91** 330
MILBANK
A. G. (Mrs.) **75** xli
Albert Goodsell **88** 169
89 130 **104** 65 69 70 148
Albert Jouvneay **104** 69
Elizabeth (Hall) **104** 70
Georgiana (Goodsell)
104 69 70
Marjorie **75** xli
Marjorie Elizabeth
(Robbins) **104** 70
Mary (Watkinson) **104** 70
Nichols **79** 103 202
Robbins **104** 70
Robert **104** 70
Samuel **104** 70
Samuel Robbins **104** 70
Sophia C. (Littleton)
104 70
MILBERRY Milburey
Milbury
Benjamin **110** 62 **115** 142
Betty **111** 257
Dorcas **111** 257 **116** 129
Dorcas (Came) **111** 257
Eliphalet **110** 62
Elizabeth **71** 225 **110** 62
112 105 **115** 62
Elizabeth (Kingsbury)
110 62
Eunice **111** 92 **115** 211
George **111** 257
Gustavus **111** 257
Hannah **110** 62 **111** 92 **112**
214 **115** 63
Henry **148** 36
John **109** 300 **110** 62 **111**
92 **112** 220 **114** 49 **147**
252 253
Joseph **109** 300 **111** 257
114 130
Jotham **111** 257
Lucy **113** 128 **115** 224
Lucy (Higgins) **111** 257
Lydia **111** 257 **113** 128
115 223
Mary **110** 62 **111** 92 254
114 134 **117** 226 227
148 33 36 37
Mary (Harris) **115** 142
Mercy **115** 61 **116** 134
Mercy (Webber) **114** 130
Miriam **111** 92 **112** 220
115 64
Nathaniel **111** 92 **115** 59
Olive **71** 225 **111** 257
Richard **109** 300 **110** 98
111 92 257 **115** 218

MILBERRY *cont'd*
Samuel **109** 300 **110** 62
111 254 257 **112** 105
214 **113** 128 **114** 190
115 211
Sarah **109** 300 **110** 98 **111**
92 **115** 140 218
Sarah (Simpson) **115** 59
Susanna **111** 92 **115** 64
213
Susanna (Sayword) **111**
92 **114** 49
Theodore **111** 257
Timothy **111** 257
William **109** 297 **111** 257
MILBOURNE Milborn
Milborne
—— **70** 264
— Rev. Mr. **71** 124
Andrew **64** 317
Blanche **122** 176
Christopher **64** 317
Eleanor **122** 176
Elizabeth **65** 246
Gawen **104** 275
Joan **74** 69 136
John **74** 136
Mary **64** 260 **132** 39
Nathaniel **114** 84
Peter **114** 86
Polly **83** 144
Sally **77** 48
Sibyl **122** 176
Simon **122** 176-178
Thomas **77** 48
Ulysses Sumner **82** 383
83 227
Milburey *see* Milberry
MILBURNE
Agnes **147** 23
Lucy **104** 275
Milbury *see* Milberry
MILBY
Elizabeth **135** 252
Priscilla **135** 252
MILCH John **51** 461
Sarah **51** 461
MILCOME
Eleanor **144** 33 34
MILD James **60** 349
MILDMAY
Alicia **56** 378
Amy **56** 378
Anne **53** 289 **71** 249
Dorothy **71** 249
Elizabeth **71** 249
Henry **53** 289 **56** 378 379
110 218 **114** 84 85
Jane **71** 249
John **71** 249
Robert **71** 249
Thomas **56** 375 378
Walter **56** 377 **103** 19
148 127
William **71** 249 **107** 47
MILDRAM
A. Clifford **92** 339
A. Hurbert **92** 339
A. Olevia **92** 339
Abigail **94** 37
Abigail E. **94** 37

MILDRAM *cont'd*
Charles A. **94** 37
Charles J. **92** 339
Clara F. **94** 37
Clement **94** 37
Clement L. **92** 339
Frank Benton **94** 37 38
Georgia A. **92** 339
Gertrude M. **92** 339
J. Sidney **94** 37
Joseph H. **92** 339
Laura R. **94** 37 38
Mary A. **94** 37
Mary G. **94** 37
Olive **94** 37
S. Jane **92** 339
Samuel **94** 37 38
Samuel A. **94** 38
Sarah Eliza **94** 38
Sylvia **92** 339
Willey G. S. **94** 37 38
MILDRED Jean **117** 126
MILDREN Mary **114** 76
Richard **114** 76
MILDWINTER
John **62** 301
MILEHAM Christopher J.
(Mrs.) **82** 349
Helen W. **82** 349
John **63** 362
Matthew **63** 362
MILENER John **64** 256
MILES Myles
—— **99** 240 **130** 70 **139**
23 46
— Capt. **77** 110
— Goodman **81** 121
— Mr. **70** 298 **98** 168
144 154
Aaron O. **86** 303
Abbie B. **57** xlix
Abigail **59** 68 69 **65** 137 **66**
197 **81** 126 **88** 279 **104**
89 **127** 191
Abigail M. **76** 35
Abraham **87** 345
Ada (Lovise) **134** 67
Agnes (James) **138** 40
Alfred Harry **85** 244
Alfred Hart (Mrs.) **89** 189
Alice **138** 40
Alice (Marsh) **138** 40
Alice Gertrude **87** 345
Anna **62** 180
Anne **58** 372 **138** 40
Archibald **136** 319
Arey Newton **87** 23
Arlina **61** 273
Asa **58** 372
Augusta **87** 345
Benjamin **51** 252 **65** 24 140
110 307
Benoni **76** 141
Bethiah **75** 94 177 178
76 134
Betsey **130** 70
Betty **74** 257
Calista M. **65** 10
Caraline **92** 126
Catherine **81** 470 **106** 15
16 **111** 13

MILES *cont'd*
Charles **55** 354 **85** 10
Charlotte **76** 147
Chary **76** 149
Clarke **65** 10
Cynthia **76** 152
Cyrus M. **119** 320
Daisy (Von Braun)
(Savell) **89** 367
Daniel **85** 63 168 **127** 191
David **76** 142 145
Edith G. Russell **78** 205
Edward Brown **92** 244
Edward C. **62** lxxviii
Eleanor **73** 135
Elisha **115** 116
Eliza **87** 345 **88** 340 **92** 125
Eliza H. **87** 345
Eliza H. (Walker) **87** 345
Elizabeth **51** 139 251 252
53 242 **54** 173 **58** 55 **66**
209 **67** 128 **78** 419 **81**
125 **91** 79 **92** 125 126
244 **94** 376 **96** 74 **110**
307 **138** 40
Elizabeth (Adams) **130** 71
Elizabeth (Arey) **87** 23
Elizabeth Gilmer (Tyler)
89 189
Elizabeth Lee (Dame)
89 260
Ella Celeste **136** 310
Erastus **136** 319
Eunice **85** 63
Eva **65** 10
Fannie M. **87** 345
Flora Annie **106** 124
Frances **63** 195
Frances Damon (Swift)
91 142
Francis **65** 22 **134** 67
Frank C. **65** 10
Frederick **73** 141 144
George **92** 125 126 132 244
94 376
George H. **87** 345
George M. **65** 10
Hannah **54** 173 **59** 68 **66**
209 **75** 178 309 **76** 143
93 363 **118** 194
Hannah Adams (Dean)
88 336
Harold M. **65** 10
Harriet **134** 67
Harry **138** 40
Hazen Tichenor **87** 345
Henry **73** 143
Henry A. **65** 10
Henry M. **65** 10
Herbert James **75** lx
Horace **119** 320
Isaac **113** 34 35 41 **119** 320
Jacob **119** 320
Jafferye **138** 40
James **67** 128 **69** 54 **71** 48
56 **97** 320 **119** 320
James Benjamin **86** 303
Jane **78** 303
Jesse **111** 116
Joel **119** 320
Joel E. **119** 320

MILES *cont'd*
John **53** 196 300 **55** 122
60 171 **61** 118 159 164
65 222 302 306 **66** 197
70 95 **73** 139 **75** lx 178
77 81 **81** 125 **86** 425 **87**
23 **88** 336 **93** 384 **97** 103
320 325 326 **99** 94 99
229 **105** 5 **110** 181 **119**
320 **127** 120 **138** 40 **139**
21-23 41 46 49 **148** 36
John (Mrs.) **139** 24
Jonas Keyes **75** lx
Jonas Maynard **75** lx
Jonas Michael **64** xxxiv
65 192 303 305 306 **66**
xlviii **70** 95 **75** xxxiv lx
Jonathan **75** 177 178 **76**
141 142 144 152 **99** 79
Joseph **51** 139 251 252
91 330
Josephine Helen **87** 345
Joshua **65** 150
Judith **87** 345 **113** 313
Julia Ann **90** 46
Katharine **81** 128 **108** 173
131 11 26 **138** 39-41
139 46
Keziah **114** 101
Keziah (Smith) **114** 101
Laban **87** 345
Laura **85** 293
Lettice (Green) **142** 261
Lewis **88** 336
Lizzie B. **75** lx
Louisa **90** 45
Lowell Milton **75** lx
Lucinda **75** 178
Lucretia **76** 150
Lucy **75** 178
Lucy S. **65** 137
Lydia **87** 345 **119** 320
Lydia (Adams) **130** 71
Lydia (Melville) **125** 242
Lydia Ann **87** 345
Malina **115** 116
Manoah Smith **65** 137
Mara **76** 149
Margaret **54** 214 **92** 132
Marilla **113** 34
Marion E. **65** 10
Martha **81** 128 **86** 230
113 41 **127** 120 **138** 40
Mary **53** 196 300 316 **54**
173 **57** 367 **63** 195 **67**
126 321 **69** 332 **73** 147
149 227 **75** 178 **80** 343
81 125 **125** 216 **126** 218
136 316 319
Mary (Brayton) **88** 278
Mary (Treese) **136** 319
Mary Abbie **87** 345
Mary Ann **81** 251
Mary Elizabeth **65** 10
144 119
Matilda **125** 289
Mehitable **75** 178
Mercy **134** 173
Molly **73** 73
Nancy **87** 345
Nathaniel **97** 320

MILES *cont'd*
Nellie M. **65** 10
Nelson A. **51** 38 **55** 126
  56 329 **57** 238 **105** 82
Nelson Appleton **91** 100
Olive **71** 48
Parnell (Reve) **138** 40
Patience **133** 73
Paulina **115** 116
Phebe **75** 177
Phineas **88** 278
Polly **142** 381
Priscilla **73** 136
Rebecca **70** 78
Rebecca Bragdon **75** lx
Relief **58** 55
Reuben **58** 372 **87** 345
Richard **54** 24 173 352 **57**
  298 **66** 209 **75** 177 **80**
  107 **81** 121 122 124-130
  132-134 **90** 202 **128** 70
Richard Kirby (Mrs.)
  91 142
Robert **127** 120 **138** 40
Robert Cunningham
  (Mrs.) **77** 323 **78** 205
Ruth Maria **87** 345
Sada Alida (Cole) **86** 303
Sally **84** 209
Samuel **55** 380 **59** 68 **62**
  136 **67** 297 **75** lx 177 **81**
  125 126 128 129 **97** 103
  320 **121** 83 **144** 164
Sarah **55** 369 **61** 118 **62** 136
  73 219 **76** 142
Sarah (Boudle) **86** 303
Sarah (Fiske) **136** 319
Sarah (King) **88** 336
Sarah B. **76** 34
Sheldon **76** 151
Stephen **59** 68 **63** 195
  81 126
Susan **119** 320
Susanna **78** 418 **93** 384
  127 191
Thankful (Freeman)
  127 120
Theophilus **59** 68 **75** 177
  178 **76** 142 143 145 147
  149-151 **81** 126
Thomas **59** 69 **63** 345 **75**
  lx **125** 242 **131** 156 **138**
  40 **142** 362
Thomas R. **125** 242
Tichenor **87** 345
Timothy **81** 251
Walter Herndon **89** 260
Watson **91** 330
Will **119** 320
William **63** 344 **92** 132
  127 120 **138** 40
Winona **76** 98
Zerviah **75** 177 178
MILEY
Mary Louise **96** 295
MILFORD Ann **72** 157
Humphrey **69** 288 **77** 82
  92 401 **95** 306
Mary **64** 9
Thomas **59** 294
MILHAM Simon **71** 368

MILHAM *cont'd*
Willis Isbister **71** 368
MILHOUS Dorothy Z.
  120 157 236
Hannah **120** 157
Phebe **120** 157
Rachel **120** 236
MILICK
Elizabeth **126** 219
Hannah **126** 219
Miliken *see* Milliken
Milikin *see* Milliken
MILIS
John **93** 174 222
Robert **93** 174 222
MILK
Abigail **87** 332 335
Cynthia **134** 334 **136** 167
David **135** 145
Dorcas **72** 84
Isabel **130** 154 **135** 145
James **72** 84
Job **87** 333 **135** 145
John **78** 311 **91** 96 **132** 39
Lemuel **135** 145 312
Mary **135** 145 **136** 167
Mary (Scolley) **132** 39
Patience **125** 230
Phebe **135** 145
Rebecca **135** 146
Rebecca (Lawton) **135** 145
Sarah **87** 333
Susanna **77** 313
MILKIGAN
Willard **128** 173
MILKS Henry Joseph (Mrs.)
  82 253 **83** 233
Mill *see* Mills
MILLAIS —— **54** xcvii
Millakin *see* Milliken
Millar *see* Miller & Millard
MILLARD *see also* Miller
____ (Hall) **87** 358
Abigail **127** 276
Ann (Aldrich) **113** 228
Anne **127** 209
Betsey (Snow) **116** 288
Corinthia **110** 230
Dorcas (Tucker) **127** 202
Elizabeth (Saben) **113** 228
Experience (White)
  113 228
Frances Virginia (Child)
  113 228
Hannah (Crowell)
  127 211
Hannah (Thayer) **113** 228
Isabel **101** 14
Joan (Cogan) **111** 247
  123 34
Louisa (Hitchcock)
  113 228
Nancy (Barney) **96** 92
Olive Lydia **86** 98
Phebe **111** 80
Ruth **126** 165 **127** 207
Sally (Williams) **113** 228
MILLBROOK
Minnie Dubbs **116** 83
Mille De *see* De Mille

MILLEDGE Milledge
—— **56** 326
Betsey **100** 236
Elizabeth **78** 398 **100** 233
  102 30
John **100** 233 236 **102** 30
Stephen **117** 9 12 16
Susanna **100** 233 236
  102 30
MILLEDOLLAR
— Rev. Mr. **79** 299
MILLEMAN
Freelove **70** 111
MILLEN
— Lt. Col. **136** 249
— Mr. **125** 36
David **88** 285
Gurder **125** 38
Joseph **60** 188
Maria (Locke) **88** 285
Melinda **86** 145
MILLENS Hannah **64** 118
MILLEQUET
William **77** 317
MILLER Millar Millard
  Millerd Myller
—— **51** 492 **52** 437 **54** 67
  55 351 **56** 106 214 320
  342 **58** 321 386 405 **60**
  398 **62** 216 **69** 58 **81** 447
  83 35 **86** 54 **88** 123 **92**
  312 **101** 247 **108** 54 **109**
  40 **117** 319 **118** 150 297
  119 132 **127** 16 **139** 33-
  37 39 42 47 **143** 366
— Capt. **124** 278
— Col. **54** 150 **122** 88
  142 130
— Dr. **71** 49
— Maj. Gen. **94** 185
— Miss **83** 35
— Mr. **57** 229 **62** 19 **66**
  132 **70** 171 314 **76** 131
— Mrs. **65** 359 **71** 47 117
  122 88 **127** 14
— Rev. Dr. **62** 277
— Widow **71** 50 **73** 69
____ (Hall) **87** 358
____ (Kincaid) **113** 243
A. **91** 330
A. Lee (Mrs.) **98** 265
A. M. **101** 235
Abbie Green **96** 400
Abby F. **77** 181
Abel **81** 386
Abiathar **136** 313 316
Abigail **56** 38 **58** 383 386
  59 248 **61** 179 **70** 26 **74**
  37 127 251 **78** 412 **85**
  431 **87** 254 **100** 240 **106**
  215 **126** 165 **127** 276
  138 119 **140** 21
Abijah **61** 390 **85** 410
Abiram **106** 108
Abner **100** 173 **136** 326
Abraham **55** 205 206 **135**
  250 **136** 304 **142** 355
Ada **113** 243
Ada Perkins **94** 138
Adah Leona **103** 118
Adalaide **92** 171

MILLER *cont'd*
Addie A. **92** 171
Addison Charles **84** 212
Adelia A. **86** 53
Agnes **146** 267
Albert **117** 43
Albert Henry **78** 328
Albert S. **89** 246
Albert Sherman **86** 156
Alburtus **128** 269
Alexander **55** 271 **62** 76
  322 **81** 431 **90** 109 **107**
  33 **112** 286
Alexander C. **90** 342
Alice **56** 312 **85** 168 **97** 74
  134 283
Alice Chapman **95** 337
Alice Gordon (Coffin)
  83 425 436
Alice Maude **103** 146
Alice W. **86** 53
Allen **65** 40 42
Allis Hardenberg **94** 82
Almira **94** 121 **108** 261
  115 25
Alpha **80** 68
Alpheus **108** 58
Alvin **58** 403 **86** 53
Ama **100** 270 **101** 201
Amanda **72** 98
Amasa **79** 72 **91** 330
Amma **100** 270 **101** 201
Amy **107** 200
Ananias **54** 301
Andrew **55** 34 36 **58** 195
  81 102 **87** 378 **95** 336
  97 208 **107** 116 195 197-
  200 270 271 **108** 58 **133**
  153
Andrew II. **122** 130
Andrew J. **89** 116
Angerona Erickson
  82 237
Angerona Erickson
  (Powell) **84** 112 197 211
Ann **72** 291 **73** 228 **77** 151
  81 431 447 **111** 74 206
  140 21
Ann (Bolt) **140** 18 21
Ann (Buell) **85** 56
Ann (Reist) **87** 378
Ann L. **78** 185
Anna **56** 199 258 **57** 140 **65**
  256 334 **72** 46 89 105 **73**
  255 **79** 156 **82** 292 294
  85 168 **90** 356 **107** 155
  198-200 270 271 **108** 56
  58 **118** 190 191 **121** 317
  125 111 112
Anna (Ames) **88** 332
Anna (Starr) **90** 172
Anna De Peyster (Douw)
  88 188
Anna Eliza **80** 157
Anna Eva **117** 318
Anna Maria **97** 380
Anna Pancoast **81** 102
Anna Ridgway **75** xxiii
  79 201 210 **81** 102 **85**
  216
Anna W. Welles **85** 315

MILLER *cont'd*
Anne **70** 31 **90** 356 **101** 43
  107 201 273 **127** 202
  207 209 276
Anne (Burbank) **108** 121
Anne (Chandler) **85** 141
Anne (Crowell) **126** 165
Anne B. **104** 58
Annetta **110** 130
Annie **69** 168 **125** 111
Annie C. **64** 283
Annie Elizabeth **86** 113
Annis **55** 406
Archibald **64** 314
Arthur **54** 218
Asa **58** 81 **107** 200
Asa H. **86** 53
Asenath **58** 81
Ashby Dunbar **115** 24
Augustus **68** 336
Barbara **108** 82
Barbary **70** 31
Barnard **129** 277
Bathsheba **133** 71
Bathsheba (Bowker)
  136 304
Batney **65** 42
Baylies (Mrs.) **113** 226
Beatrice (Baylies) **113** 226
Belva (McCreedy) **96** 160
Ben Robertson **117** 237
  121 236
Benedicta (Lawton) **111**
  248 **123** 261
Benjamin **56** 58 **60** 43 **69**
  91 322 **70** 31 **72** 144 **85**
  63 168 **88** 15 **94** 121 **97**
  319 **106** 182 **107** 198
  273 **136** 304 **148** 266
Benjamin Kuntz **95** 336
Benjamin L. **78** 401
Benjamin W. **57** 80
Bernard **60** 157
Bert **70** 203
Bertha **101** 123
Bethena **101** 202
Bethuel **100** 270 **101** 202
Betsey **58** 403 **72** 178 **79** 72
  92 171 **116** 288 **130** 71
  132 243 **147** 257
Betsey (Brown) **140** 20
Betsey (Swan) **94** 121
Betty **60** 79 **66** 147 211 **94**
  121 **136** 304
Beulah **126** 53
Blanche **116** 65
Bridget (Clark) **94** 357
Brister **129** 380
Bruno William (Mrs.)
  95 147
Burnet **54** 210 **55** 85 203-
  205
C. **116** 115
C. J. **57** 342
C. R. **55** 321
Calvin **58** 195
Cameron **78** 37
Candora P. **70** 206
Carlos Arthur **92** 364
Caroline (Todd) **94** 202
Caroline Augusta **107** 71

MILLER *cont'd*
Caroline Elizabeth
  (Kuntz) **95** 336
Caroline Lavinia **83** 298
  300
Caroline M. **78** 305
Caroline T. **94** 202
Caroline Tucker (Chace)
  90 172
Carrie Borden (Johnson)
  87 379
Carrita St. Clair **87** 379
Catherine **73** 275 **86** 321
  90 57 112 **107** 155 **108**
  235 **115** 25 **125** 221 **127**
  267
Catherine (Byers) **95** 336
Catherine (Fitz Randolph)
  97 338
Catherine (Nash) **126** 143
Catherine (White) **125** 109
Catherine Cecelia **72** 305
Catherine D. **69** 341
Catherine Doane (Riggs)
  103 313
Catherine S. **90** 54
Caty **99** 199
Cecil Hale **112** 225
Charity **70** 33
Charles **56** 252 **60** 22 **66**
  152 154 211 301 303 **67**
  133 134 136 146 147 232-
  234 **70** 360 **71** 134 **83**
  375 **84** 258 **119** 278 **122**
  86 **134** 132 **138** 30 **140**
  168 169 239
Charles Adams **100** 112
Charles Duncan **104** 308
Charles Edwin **83** 425 436
Charles H. **100** 189
Charles J. **66** lxxxiii
Charles Kingsbury
  71 311
Charles O. **92** 171
Charles Robert (Mrs.)
  99 148
Charles W. **101** 235 **111** 74
Charles William **111** 74
Charlotte **55** 205 **111** 190
Charlotte Chapel **81** 188
Chloe **88** 364
Christian **81** 431 447
  87 378
Christiana **73** 131
Christine (Stabley) **87** 378
Christopher Columbus
  94 81
Clara **82** 237
Clara Gardner **93** 96
Clarabelle (Fitz
  Randolph) **98** 341
Clarissa **108** 60
Clarissa Amanda **113** 230
Clarke C. **106** 317 318
Comfort **62** 133 **114** 188
Comfort (Clark) **114** 188
Conrad **107** 116
Corinthia **110** 230
Cynthia **95** 377 **115** 25
Cynthia Jervis (Brayton)
  84 212

MILLER *cont'd*
Cyrena A. **80** 39
Cyrus **65** 256
Daisy **76** 90
Dan **123** 48
Dan (Mrs.) **123** 48
Daniel **55** 203 205 **107** 201
   108 58 **113** 228 **129** 386
   136 304 **138** 30
Daniel G. **79** 87
Daniel Jackson **78** 328
Daniel Leeds **81** 102
Darby **78** 190
Darius **99** 251
Darius (Mrs.) **81** 107 219
   93 127 **94** 142 **99** 251
David **54** 45 **55** 85 205 **61**
   135 **62** 83 **70** 123 233 **77**
   151 **78** 399 **86** 53 54 **87**
   378 **100** 135 **105** 285
   110 34 **111** 320 **115** 130
   117 212 **127** 267 **131**
   238 **140** 21 22 **141** 205
   206 209
David (Mrs.) **117** 212
David A. **98** 128
David C. **140** 122
David M. **96** 92
David P. **73** 255
David S. **134** 59
David W. **86** 54
Deborah **55** 204 **73** 308
   74 37 **81** 34 **107** 198 275
   108 58 189 **123** 263
Deborah (Millar) **108** 189
Deborah (Templar)
   (Chamberlain) **142** 355
Deborah A. **70** 205
Deborah Crowell
   (Richardson) **106** 62 72
Delmar James (Mrs.) **77**
   xxviii 154
Desire **101** 43
Dolly **94** 120
Dolly Goodhill **75** 272
Dorcas **71** 222 **74** 214 230
   255 **81** 431 **82** 413 **85**
   410
Doris **103** 121
Doris M. (Sheldon)
   98 265
Dorothy **140** 21
Dorothy (Root) (Chapin)
   111 248
Dorothy Ruth (Durkee)
   112 225
E. Irene **122** 74
E. K. **101** 235
Ebenezer **53** 378 **63** 192 **73**
   255 **81** 102 **84** 161 265
   87 303 **90** 172 **91** 93
   136 304 **137** 22 **138** 25
   140 22 172-175 **141** 49
Ebenezer Templeton
   113 243
Edgar Gail **87** 379
Edith **108** 82
Edith H. **98** 280
Edmund **94** 121
Edmund Howe **61** 109

MILLER *cont'd*
Edmund Thornton
   102 166
Edward **65** 221 **72** 104
   106 200 **140** 168
Edward D. **86** 53
Edward Franklin **113** 228
Edward Gore (Mrs.)
   90 137
Edwin **86** 53 54
Edwin Child **108** 82
Edwin Child (Mrs.) **108**
   62 81 82 139 **109** 124
Edwin P. **61** xxxiv **86** 54
Effie **79** 147
Elbert H. T. **66** 1 **105** 238
Eleanor **94** 121
Eleanor (Pope) **131** 130
Eleanor E. **92** 190
Eleazer **54** 209 **55** 201 202
   204 205 **90** 48
Eli **55** 34 **60** 200 **83** 359
Eliakim **74** 37
Elias **141** 205 206
Elihu **51** 165
Elijah **86** 54 **136** 304
Eliot **59** 97
Eliphaz **81** 391
Elisa **125** 107
Elisha **53** 314 **55** 205 **79**
   71 72 **88** 188 **90** 172 **101**
   202 **106** 182-184 **111**
   148
Eliza **75** lxx **77** 151 **81** 447
   86 54 **110** 130
Eliza (Hollis) **102** 166
Eliza (Hyde) **83** 199
Eliza Ann **73** 201 **74** 33
   107 72
Eliza T. **86** 54
Elizabeth **54** 210 430 **55**
   85 88 205 207 **60** 20-30
   143 **61** 135 **65** 373 **66**
   142 152 154 211 229 335
   68 167 **70** 31 **71** 62 **76**
   131 **79** 71 **80** 41 189 **82**
   49 169 **85** 64 **89** 246 **100**
   302 **103** 308 **104** 249
   107 116 198 199 270 273
   108 190 **110** 130 **125**
   292 **132** 21 **136** 304 **140**
   169 **141** 49 50 **142** 384
   146 261-263 267
Elizabeth (Barton)
   107 203
Elizabeth (Bull) **106** 211
Elizabeth (Cary) **84** 258
Elizabeth (Chase) **87** 328
Elizabeth (Cordner)
   96 400
Elizabeth (Dorby) **142** 278
Elizabeth (Haggelton)
   83 415
Elizabeth (Hamock)
   84 265
Elizabeth (Hill) **127** 32
Elizabeth (Huntley)
   101 144
Elizabeth (Jellison)
   119 278
Elizabeth (Lazell) **88** 262

MILLER *cont'd*
Elizabeth (Lewis) **88** 279
Elizabeth (Parsons)
   136 326
Elizabeth (Rollins) **140** 21
Elizabeth (Wetzell) **87** 378
Elizabeth B. (Jones)
   89 246
Elizabeth B. Jones **89** 246
Elizabeth Cambell
   109 235
Elizabeth H. **84** 103
Elizabeth Lee **104** 143
   117 207
Elizabeth Mary **88** 134
   104 250
Elizabeth Pearl **103** 121
Elizabeth Trumbull
   136 323
Elizer **85** 64
Elkanah **106** 72
Ella Jane **81** 385
Ella S. **83** 199
Ellen S. (Shapleigh)
   95 328
Elmer **123** 222
Elona **94** 120
Elvira **110** 257
Emily **72** 104 **114** 282
Emily (Brown) **89** 319
Emily E. **92** 171
Emily Virginia
   (Maverick) **102** 166
Emma **61** 346 **102** 123
Ephraim **71** 117 **72** 92
   105 286 **113** 228
Erasmus Darwin **87** 212
Erwin **92** 171
Estella **133** 29
Esther **61** 389 **80** 39 **81** 391
   100 270 **107** 198 270
   108 162 191
Esther Ann **79** 130
Ethel **95** 145
Ethel D. (Elliot) **83** 428 436
Ethel Irene (Smith)
   (Haynes) **86** 156
Ethelyn **100** 111
Etta (Fuller) **92** 171
Etta Lucille **102** 125
Eunice **79** 247 **100** 270
   101 202 **107** 198 **108**
   188 **126** 165 **137** 22
Eva **69** 322 **85** 216
Eva M. (Pike) **143** 164
Eveline **80** 434
Eveline L. **85** 315
Evelyn **116** 143
Evelyn Spencer
   (Witherbee) **104** 308
Experience **123** 262
Experience (Hawes)
   (Sproat) **141** 203-205
Ezra **77** 207 **79** 79 **83** 415
F. D. **128** 269
F. W. **83** 307
Faith **124** 118 119
Fanny **58** 386
Fanny M. (Welch) **85** 376
Fay (Mrs.) **85** 196
Ferdinand G. **86** 54

MILLER *cont'd*
Festus **115** 127
Flora **125** 107
Flora (Hull) **87** 378
Flora Payne (Whitney)
   (Tower) **85** 103
Florence **88** 297
Florence (Farrington)
   (Young) **88** 188
Florence (Sawdy) **148**
   275 276
Florence Andyman **74** x
   75 xxvi
Florence Valentine
   83 126
Forrest F. (Mrs.) **111** 148
Frances **55** 321 **123** 251
Frances (Fettiplace)
   123 251
Frances (Neble) **86** 95
Frances A. **78** 320
Frances Helen **103** 80 114
   107 238 **110** 267 **112**
   151 **118** 146 **136** 326
   141 20 **142** 326 **143** 99
   325 **146** 274 **147** 152
   241 251 252 **148** 45 65
   226
Frances Virginia **86** 448
Frances Virginia (Child)
   86 448
Francis **62** 101 **78** 407
   100 300 **126** 207 **141**
   203-206 209 211 212
Frank **60** 188 **133** 29
Frank A. **117** 43
Frank Augustus **80** 334
   81 219 **94** 81 82 142
Frank B. **60** 188 **90** 89
   91 90
Frank E. **92** 171
Frank H. **51** 386
Frank Seward (Mrs.) **81**
   237 **82** 237
Frank W. **83** 184 188
Franklin A. **78** 37
Fred **116** 65
Frederick **72** 205 **86** 321
Freeman C. **148** 276
G. MacCulloch (Mrs.)
   85 103
Genevieve **100** 339
George **66** 33 **72** 90 **78** 313
   79 72 **80** 370 371 **83** 199
   86 23 321 **87** 328 **101**
   227 **115** 25 **134** 283 284
   286 **139** 218 **143** 164
George A. **61** 207 **79** 72
   95 328
George B. **85** 410 413
   101 235
George Douglas **51** 334
   337 338 344 **53** 118 119
   84 179 **88** 188 203 309
   89 134
George Graigg **108** 56
George Howard **104** 144
George J. **100** 173 **117** 234
George Manville **61** 274
George Norton **73** 317 **74**
   xxiv **90** 139 172 199

MILLER *cont'd*
George Oscar **107** 155
George P. **89** 311
George Peckham **81** 110
   219 **95** 74 149 336
George R. **92** 205
George R. (Mrs.) **106** 47
   50
George Robert **60** 157
George W. **100** 330
   125 289
George Washington
   94 120
Georgia **142** 285
Georgia M. (Blair) **98** 198
Georgiana Parker **68** 145
   87 211 212
Georgiana Peet (Mrs.)
   122 281
Georgie **92** 171 **101** 227
Gertrude **55** 345 **86** 54
Gertrude (Hussey) **84** 300
Gertrude Ann **139** 218
Gertrude L. (Sherrel)
   85 315
Gideon **73** 104
Giles **61** 279 **136** 326
Glen H. (Mrs.) **86** 95
Glenn Eugene (Mrs.)
   87 174
Grace **80** 238
Grace Lillian (Clarke)
   95 294 **96** 160 208 **97**
   207 **98** 209
Grace Pratt **95** 145 **105** 125
Griffey Garten **113** 79
Gurdon W. **98** 286
H. **116** 115
Halsey Doan **88** 135
Ham **83** 307
Hannah **51** 33 34 192 195
   225 **53** 378 **55** 204 205
   56 58 256 **59** 244 **60** 22
   61 34 **63** 175 **65** 332 373
   66 112 301 **67** 374 **71**
   226 **81** 102 **85** 56 **86** 54
   89 246 249 370 **92** 268
   99 129 **101** 43 **106** 184
   199 **107** 116 155 197
   108 121 124 189 192
   109 59 **112** 197 **125** 107
   126 165 **131** 123 **135**
   250
Hannah (Burt) **141** 49
Hannah (Nickels) **109** 59
Hannah (Parker) **112**
   196 197
Hannah (Rider) **92** 171
Hannah (Smith) **131** 238
Hannah (Taylor) **86** 54
Hannah H. **73** 193
Hannah Maria **89** 107
Hannah Rider **92** 171
Harriet **78** 295 **85** 162
Harriet (FitzRandolph)
   98 128
Harriet (Rogers) **147** 276
Harriet J. (Stebbens)
   126 142
Harriet L. **77** 146

MILLER *cont'd*
Harriet Lovisa (Hanks)
   86 23
Harriet Maria **57** 285
Harriet Sophia **108** 301
Harris **70** 326
Hector **72** 104
Helen **85** 195 **87** 113
Helen Day **79** 86 87 **93** 197
Helen J. (Gates) **116** 65
Helen LeRoy **90** 172
Helen Ludlow (Bingham)
   94 139
Helen Mar **104** 145
Henrietta (Howard)
   89 311
Henrietta (Roberts)
   101 227
Henrietta Zahm
   (Killough) **72** 298
Henry **55** 390 **57** 47 **69** 362
   72 183 **79** 267 **92** 171
   97 269 **98** 341 **102** 166
   107 203 **115** 25 **123** 251
Henry A. **102** 75
Henry C. **116** 65
Henry F. **77** 56 **85** 376
Henry F. (Mrs.) **83** 489
Henry Franklin **86** 448
   108 82 **113** 228
Henry G. **86** 54
Henry Hollis **117** 237
Hepze **77** 207
Hepzibah **115** 119
Herbert **123** 222
Hezekiah **73** 274 **78** 403
   138 29 31
Hezekiah Reed **61** 42
Hiram **101** 235
Hiram Allen **66** lii
Hollis Henry **117** 237
Hope **102** 25
Horace **89** 244 246
Howard Cullen **84** 212
Howard Cullen (Mrs.)
   81 363 **82** 237
Huldah **54** 83 **58** 195 **60**
   266 **104** 322
Huntting **54** 430
Ichabod **65** 373 **72** 35
Ida Louise (Farr) **54** vii
   461 **55** vii xxi xxix **56**
   vii **59** vii 330 **60** vii **61**
   v vii xiii **62** v vii xxxv
   63 v **64** xiv xv **65** xxxiii
   67 viii **68** liii 109 **70** v
   vi x **71** v vi **72** vi xi 76
   73 vi **74** vi 78 **75** vi 242
   76 vi **77** vi x xii xiii xv
   78 218 **79** 214 **80** 220
   81 234 **83** 370 **84** 181
   89 169 **90** 124 **93** 131
   96 154 **99** 183 **108** 81
Inloe L. **78** 174
Inman Lyon **131** 73
   133 153
Ira **106** 108
Irene **85** 216
Isaac **58** 386 **107** 155 **109**
   235 **116** 43 **125** 216
Isaac Wheler **109** 235

MILLER *cont'd*
Isabel **98** 356 359 **101** 14
  106 72
Isabel (Rankin) **135** 251
Isabelle (Peckham) **95** 336
Isabelle Demorest
  (Hardenberg) **94** 82
Isabelle Pauline Louise
  85 196
Israel **105** 286
Israel P. **53** 453 **83** 300 301
  84 30
Ithamar **125** 218
Iva C. **116** 65
J. C. **61** 315 **65** 197
J. R. **92** 339
Jabez **54** 441
Jacob **55** 261 **56** 144 **58** 383
  72 291 **90** 209 **94** 204
  107 71 72 **124** 34
James **55** 390 **58** 386 **59**
  lxxxiv 244 248 **60** 188 **61**
  239 **65** 237 **70** 31 **74** 297
  84 30 **85** 10 **101** 274
  104 121 **105** 285 **106** 91
  197 **107** 198-200 270 273
  275 **108** 58 189 **114** 184
  115 25 **119** 21 **123** 10 11
  127 5 7 14 **129** 379 **135**
  250 **136** 304 **140** 20
James Blaine (Mrs.) **95**
  294 **96** 160
James D. **57** 285
James F. **142** 293
James Harvey **94** 202
James M. **76** 275
James Mann **103** 313
James P. **85** 315 **89** 249
James Peyser **83** 307
James Raglan **86** 197
James Raglan (Mrs.)
  103 120
Jane **63** 346 **65** 166 **73** 132
  74 104 **77** 269 **78** 190
  345 **79** 122 **81** 386 **84**
  267 **85** 138 **107** 198 **108**
  295 **109** 112 **140** 21
Jane (Galbraith) **95** 336
Jane Briar **73** 131
Jane E. **101** 235
Jane Edgar **98** 128
Jane Moody **69** 269 **97** 202
Janet (McCollum)
  136 326
Janetta (Ford) **92** 171
Jannett Snow **116** 288
Jason **58** 195 **59** 412
  60 205
Jean **51** 491 **71** xl **73** 255
  80 371 **125** 196
Jedediah **61** 233 **109** 119
Jemima (Huntley)
  100 270
Jeremiah **54** 208 209 301
  433 **55** 85 204-206 **58** 20
  73 131 132 **88** 262 **98**
  246 **107** 198 200 201 270
  271 **108** 23 57
Jeremy **55** 207
Jerusha **55** 85 261 **65** 373
  81 391

MILLER *cont'd*
Jesse **136** 312
Jessie **146** 390 391
Jewel **78** 320
Jo. **99** 96
Joan **111** 245 246 **123** 260
Joan (Cogan) **111** 247
Joanna **71** xlv **111** 248
Joanna (Whittemore)
  106 200
Joanne **123** 34
Joe Haynes **90** 137
John **51** 25 33 34 192 195
  224 225 **52** 274 **54** 183
  207 308 428 **55** 203 **56**
  256 **57** 161 **58** 68 102
  194 **59** 218 **60** 143 188
  400 **61** 397 **62** 274 275
  63 238 348 382 **64** 252
  65 40 42 164 169 255
  332 **66** 35 301 335 **67**
  171 **69** 343 **71** 220 224-
  27 29 30 **140** 20 169 **141**
  204-206 **142** 264 **143**
  260 **144** 33 **147** 257
John Alexander (Mrs.)
  83 233 **104** 144
John B. **131** 90
John Barnes **74** xxv 155
  87 378 **88** 86 171
John Bolt **140** 18-20
John Borden **87** 379
John E. **113** 243
John Edgar **87** 378
John F. **77** 146 **87** 231 235
John Francis **115** 21
John Franklin **109** 226
John H. **83** 300 302
John Henry **92** 344
John Leland **57** 239
John Leslie **115** 320
John O. **89** 291
John P. **92** 171
John T. **125** 44
John William **96** 400
Johnnie **92** 171
Jonathan **85** 64 **90** 172 **99**
  195 **115** 45 **140** 21 22
Joseph **60** 188 **62** 23 **65**
  129 **68** 238 **71** 130 **77**
  142 207 **81** 102 431 **85**
  410 **86** 401 **91** 206 **94** 95
  357 **96** 306 **100** 65 **101**
  43 144 **105** 284 107 198
  199 **127** 211 **132** 21 **138**
  25 27-30 **140** 68 **141** 201
  143 324
Joseph John **110** 130
Joseph Kingsbury **108** 59
Joseph Lyon **67** xxxi 190
Joseph Nelson **63** 392
Joseph R. **91** 330
Josephine **70** 360
Josephus **113** 243
Joshua **51** 34
Joshua Newton **116** 288
Josiah **51** 33 34 224 **54** 209
  55 204 205 **138** 24 25 27-
  30
Judith **51** 224
Julia **72** 90 105 **73** 7

MILLER *cont'd*
Julia A. **82** 455
Julia Ann (Chase) **88** 123
Julia Belle (Rutherford)
  117 43
Julia Ella **109** 128
Julia Margaret (Ver
  Plank) **84** 94
Justin **80** 189 **89** 246
Justin L. **89** 246
Justus **115** 294
K. D. Mrs. **112** 75
Kate E. **83** 174 **84** 30
Kate E. (Weeks) **83** 184
  188
Katharine **87** 303 **100** 301
  108 185 **136** 316
Katharine (Wheeler)
  100 304
Katharine Allen **107** 132
Katharine Chace **90** 172
Katharine Marie
  (Tallman) **92** 394
Katharine V. **74** 297
Kathleen **84** 212
Kennard W. **84** 30
Kenneth D. (Mrs.) **110** 78
Kenneth Duane **110** 78
  112 75
Keziah **89** 291
Kibbie **124** 257
L. **60** 161
L. M. Gildersleeve **86** 54
Laura **61** 233 **101** 235 **105**
  238 **109** 119
Laura (Wales)
  (Redington) **109** 119
Laura Appleton
  (Chapman) **95** 337
Laura Delphina **89** 311
Laura E. **86** 54
Laura Isabelle **95** 337
Laura Isobel **97** 75
Lavinia **72** 104
Lazarus **61** 308 397 **111**
  248 **123** 261
Leah **92** 171
Leavitt **83** 359
Leman **111** 116
Lemuel **65** 256 333 **93** 397
  100 63 270 **101** 202 **107**
  198-201 270 271 273 **108**
  56 58 121
Lena **102** 75
Lena (Van Deusen)
  102 75
Lenore **117** 43
Leonard **65** 24 **68** 238 **93**
  397 **100** 63
Leslie W. **63** 309 388
Leverett **58** 403 **59** 96 99
  60 79 203
Leveretta (Talcott) **86** 54
Levi **98** 359 **101** 235
Levi M. **98** 359
Levina **61** 384
Levitt **58** 915
Lewis **55** 203 **61** 42 **88** 73
  141 208
Lizzie **127** 238
Lois **77** 207

MILLER *cont'd*
Loraine (Jackson) **88** 188
Loudon **58** 195 403 **59** 413 **60** 203
Louisa **78** 345 **126** 142
Louisa (Boardwell) **70** 203
Louisa (Clarke) **87** 212
Louisa M. **86** 54
Louisa Malzena (Lazell) (Gibbs) **89** 116
Louise **74** xlvii
Love **107** 275 **108** 57 58 60
Lovy **108** 59
Lucinda **136** 312
Lucinda (Loomis) **136** 312
Lucretia **54** 301 **55** 204 **58** 383 **107** 155
Lucy **56** 259 **61** 390 **72** 220 **77** xliv **78** 68 **115** 126 **125** 220 **136** 304
Lucy (Husted) **140** 122
Lucy (McKinistry) (Ford) **120** 43
Lucy (Stanley) **104** 249
Lucy (Wadsworth) **141** 208
Lucy Hannah **72** 90
Lucy Narcissa **78** 320
Lucy S. **86** 53
Lucy Stanley (Knowles) **88** 135
Luella **92** 171
Lydia **51** 33 34 192 195 **52** 274 **57** 390 **58** 403 **60** 79 157 203 266 **63** 175 **83** 359 **88** 262 **90** 342 353 **93** 280 **106** 89 **108** 124 **128** 285 **138** 131 **148** 50
Lydia (Coombs) **141** 204
Lydia (Pierce) **107** 71 72
Lydia (Porter) **148** 49
Lydia A. **85** 441
Lydia Pierce **107** 71
Lydia S. **106** 108
Lyndes **78** 371
Lynn Smith (Mrs.) **85** 196 239
M. **101** 43
M. A. **101** 258
M. L. **128** 177
Mabel **55** 36 **86** 54
Madeleine (Tinkham) **103** 116 **119** 148
Mae Lawrence **98** 362
Maggie **77** 269
Maggie Oliver **78** 52 329
Malloy Myron **123** 221 **124** 265 **125** 212
Malvina (Wilson) (Perry) **89** 265
Mamie Elizabeth **77** xxviii
Marcella **96** 159
Marcus Peter **61** 218
Margaret **51** 33 34 224 **61** 138 **64** lxv **68** 257 **70** 205 **71** xl **72** 308 **73** 245 255 **74** 104 106 **77** lxx **78** 35 345 **92** 170 **94** 357

MILLER *cont'd*
98 148 **102** 67 **107** 198-200 270 273 **118** 197 **124** 34 **143** 49 **146** 267
Margaret (Arey) **87** 23
Margaret (Carnegie) **100** 317
Margaret (Dennis) (Lamberton) **90** 172
Margaret (Hildreth) **126** 207
Margaret A. **97** 392
Margaret Adele (Breck) **83** 489
Margaret C. **128** 266
Margaret Crandall **66** 83
Margery **51** 33
Maria **92** 176
Maria (Ham) **88** 282
Maria (Runnells) **91** 41
Maria Catherine **85** 410
Maria Louise **91** 41
Marie Walcott **85** 239
Marion Isabella **96** 158
Marion Louise (Clark) **94** 82
Marjorie Dean **103** 69
Marsena V. **79** 72
Martha **61** 135 397 **66** 11 73 255 **77** 207 **81** 431 **82** 169 **83** 359 **85** 64 **92** 78 **108** 192 **122** 85 **123** 261
Martha (Terrell) **102** 165
Martha A. **68** 336
Martha LeRoy (Glover) **90** 172
Martin **84** 351
Martin T. **104** 121
Mary **51** 34 224 302 443 **52** 134 457 **53** 210 54 209 301 433 **55** 86 204 205 207 271 **58** 20 **60** 43 **61** lix 308 397 **64** 128 **65** 256 372 373 **68** 167 255 **69** 323 **70** 31 203 **71** 130 258 **72** 47 91 105 144 **73** 200 255 **74** 37 297 **76** 12 **77** 141 207 319 **78** 328 421 **79** 157 **81** 431 **85** 64 168 410 **86** 401 **88** 188 340 **89** 54 311 **98** 302 **99** 298 **100** 173 **101** 43 **106** 89 160 182-184 **107** 195 197-201 270 271 **108** 57 58 123 189 **109** 40 235 **110** 53 **111** 57 **114** 187 **115** 116 123 126 294 **116** 65 **123** 251 265 **131** 126 **135** 76 **136** 304 **140** 22 **147** 257
Mary (Allen) **140** 21
Mary (Beckwith) **100** 270
Mary (Burbank) **111** 248 **123** 261
Mary (Bushnell) **106** 213
Mary (Crofters) **100** 300
Mary (Fyers) **109** 235 **125** 216
Mary (Jackson) **144** 33
Mary (Luce) **86** 401

MILLER *cont'd*
Mary (Morgan) **120** 13 **133** 270
Mary (Morgan) (Williston) **133** 270
Mary (Rankin) **135** 251
Mary (Roberts) **117** 165
Mary (Zahm) **72** 298
Mary A. (Clark) **94** 81
Mary A. (Sweetser) **83** 300 302
Mary A. E. **54** xi
Mary Alice Edwards **78** 203 **88** 161 **91** 131 **94** 89 **96** 154 **113** 59 228
Mary Ann **77** 56 **79** 122 **80** 434 **88** 343 **95** 293 **110** 130 **127** 211 267
Mary Ann (Douglas) **88** 188
Mary Ann (Perry) **116** 43
Mary Delia **112** 139
Mary E. **69** 322 **115** 294
Mary Elizabeth **61** 274
Mary Hannah **66** lxxxiii
Mary Jane **66** lxxxiii **82** 480
Mary Josephine (Nelligan) **139** 218
Mary Kent (Davey) **96** 400
Mary L. **106** 74
Mary Lane **80** 110
Mary Louise (Paull) **109** 226
Mary M. **109** 235
Mary Margaret **115** 118
Mary Maud **99** 146
Mary Mayo **51** 34
Mary Meretor **109** 235 236
Mary Tibbetts **94** 120
Mary Valinda (Alexander) **88** 73
Matthew **55** 59 205 431 **56** 252 256 **61** 384 **85** 168 **95** 336 **104** 121 **143** 319
Maude (Delano) **133** 29
May **109** 157
McKendry **147** 276
Mehitable **51** 33 34 **56** 199 **70** 31 **88** 15 **123** 262 **136** 314 **140** 21
Mehitable (Stanyan) **140** 18-20
Mehitable (West) **127** 267
Mehitable S. **140** 21
Mercy **51** 192 195 **54** 207 **56** 252 256 **57** 80 **134** 336
Merecetplone **107** 116
Meribeth Vernette **100** 90
Michael **70** 205 **78** 320 **87** 378
Michael M. **73** 255
Milbery Walker **108** 60
Milo H. **88** 305 **91** 208
Milton **78** 113
Mina **88** 73
Minerva **73** 255 **84** 56
Minnie **81** 37

MILLER *cont'd*
Minnie C. **90** 402
Minnie Cecilia **76** 101
Miriam B. **141** 9
Miriam Badlam (Pearce)
  (Myers) **141** 6
Miriam Walley **97** 52
Molly **99** 199 **107** 195 199
  200 **140** 21
Molly (Strout) **140** 20
Morris Barnes **87** 379
Moses **65** 373 **79** 72 **126**
  142 **138** 30
Muriel Jarvis **78** 35
N. **91** 330
N. F. **72** 97
Nabby **78** 188 **108** 261
Nancy **62** 83 **72** 305 **73** 255
  84 424 **86** 54 **96** 92 **125**
  107
Nancy (Powers) **86** 156
Nancy (Yancy) **100** 257
Nancy Brown **128** 266
Nancy H. **72** 106
Nancy Lamb **58** xlv
Nanny **66** 146 154
Nath. **99** 96
Nathan **60** 72 **65** 150 **70** 31
  129 271 277 **138** 31 **147**
  350
Nathan F. **72** 106
Nathaniel **54** 441 **61** 397
  87 212 **120** 43 **129** 273
  138 24-26 30
Nehemiah **138** 25-27
Nelle Dean (Young)
  90 137
Nellie **78** 175
Nellie E. (Harris) **92** 205
Nellie Grace **68** lxxviii
Nelson **65** 40 42
Nettie E. (Moak) **128** 269
Nicholas **65** 119
Nicodemus **100** 269 270
  101 201 202
Nini Cecilia (Hull) **87** 174
Noah **56** 129 **61** 397 **85** 56
  105 286 287 **127** 307
  309 **138** 30
Obadiah **61** 397 **111** 245
  246 248 **123** 261
Olive **98** 359 **108** 191
  115 125
Olive E. (Brayton) **115** 294
Olive Lydia **86** 98
Oliver **116** 288 **126** 165
Olivia **81** 495 **107** 155
Orlando D. **127** 62
Orni **61** 34
Ozni **61** 32
P. **75** 28
Pamela **94** 121
Pathama **100** 270
Patience **51** 165 **65** 42 **70**
  31 **85** 64 **104** 216 **126**
  119 **142** 336 **143** 313
Patience (Bacon) **90** 172
Patty (Poor) **140** 21
Paul **142** 278
Paulina **60** 45
Peggy **73** 255 **107** 198

MILLER *cont'd*
Peleg **55** 205
Permelia (Symonds)
  131 73 **133** 153
Perry **124** 137 **127** 32
  136 254
Peter **78** 67 **80** 39 **88** 279
  113 228 **114** 184 **129**
  386
Peter H. **92** 171
Phebe **54** 209 428 **55** 204
  205 **63** 372 **79** 72 **100**
  189 270 **111** 80 **132** 75
  136 316
Phebe (Huntley) **100** 269
  270 **101** 201
Phebe (Mackriss) **140** 22
Phebe Rogers **94** 120
Philadelphia (Borden)
  87 379
Philip **73** 273 **143** 15
Philip (Mrs.) **98** 145
Philip W. **91** 330
Philma **64** 252
Philomela **80** 46
Phineas **107** 155 **136** 304
Phineas Gleason **75** 209
Polly **56** 258 **62** 136 **65** 42
  94 204 **97** 268 **110** 34
  135 76
Polly (Mason) **140** 22
Polly (Needham) **110** 34
Priscilla **51** 192 195 **95** 343
  99 195 **140** 21
Priscilla (Thompson)
  140 20
Proctor **108** 82
Prudence **85** 63
R. B. **106** 303
R. V.G. **84** 300
Rachel **69** 141 **79** 267 **81**
  102 **83** 144 **97** 385 **107**
  112 **115** 212 **116** 204
  148 265-267
Rachel (Acres) **125** 218
Rachel (Rollins) **140** 22
Rachel Ledfield **126** 209
Ralph **87** 23
Rathbun **137** 148
Rebecca **51** 33 34 **56** 59
  60 132 **65** 42 **80** 176 **97**
  9 **111** 148 210 **114** 188
  117 276-278 **123** 240
  262 **147** 350
Rebecca (Leanord)
  123 260
Rebecca (Parkhurst)
  90 48
Rebecca Novaline **78** 37
Rebecca Paull **109** 226
Rebecca Peck **60** 157
Rena Alberta **83** 422 436
Reuben **89** 54 **133** 270
Rhoda **59** 98 **129** 170
Richard **62** 243 330 **63** 351
  73 131 132 **79** 72 113 **80**
  434 **94** 259 324 344 **111**
  197 **131** 130
Richard Esselstyn **73** 132
Richard G. **102** 165
Riley W. **101** 235

MILLER *cont'd*
Robert **56** 368 **58** 236 **60**
  157 **61** 267 279 **66** 152
  303 **70** 31 33 **71** xl **72**
  305 **73** 255 **77** 207 **78**
  404 **93** 385 **94** 120 121
  174 **97** 319 326 338 **99**
  96 **105** 284 290 **113** 228
  122 251 252 **123** 251
  125 111 **126** 165 **127**
  202 207 209 276 **128** 266
  137 148 **138** 24-27 29
  139 25-27 36-40 46 **140**
  17-21 169 **142** 19 **147**
  257
Robert B. **60** 187 188 355
  63 303
Robert Dexter **63** 214
Robert H. **140** 21
Robert Lake (Mrs.) **94** 91
Robert Loren (Mrs.)
  103 120
Rosalvo Delmonmort
  92 318
Rosannah **88** 333
Roswell **73** 245
Roswell (Mrs.) **100** 317
Rowena A. **92** 172
Roxana **64** 252 **94** 120
  100 330
Roxana H. **91** 387
Rozina **79** 247
Russell **85** 410
Russell E. **135** 149-151
Ruth **54** 209 **55** 204 **70** 31
  230 **73** 191 **80** 176 **83**
  145 **94** 102 121 122 **105**
  307 **107** 155 126 165
  127 207 **136** 304 **138** 31
Ruth (Beamon) **123** 261
Ruth (Carr) **94** 120 121
Ruth (Fish) **87** 231 235
Ruth (Phillips) **111** 148
Ruth Elizabeth (Headley)
  111 74
Ruth G. **92** 172
Ruth K. (Raynes) **83** 300
  301
Ruth Matrau **109** 74
S. **101** 43 **124** 100 103
Sabara **72** 35
Sally **59** lxxxiv **60** 201 **65**
  362 **73** 255 **81** 345 **85** 91
  293 **94** 120 121 **98** 286
  108 57 192 **125** 220
Sally (James) **127** 32
Sally (Lyman) **136** 326
Sally (Mitchel) **94** 120
Sam **123** 261
Sampson **63** 33 **72** 188
Samuel **51** 491 **54** 209 301
  55 85 **56** 74 199 **58** 403
  59 212 **60** 132 201 361
  398 **61** 34 **62** 347 348 **63**
  84 **64** 28 **65** 373 **70** 26
  31 **72** 274 **80** 176 **87** 23
  303 **88** 134 188 282 **96**
  262 268 **97** 319 **98** 323
  99 105 **101** 43 **104** 249
  105 286 **107** 155 **118**
  313 **125** 109 **129** 273

MILLER *cont'd*
277 **140** 172 **141** 10 **147**
257
Samuel A. **92** 190
Samuel Carroll **72** 298
Samuel Hulda **58** 195
Samuel R. **140** 169 232
145 299
Samuel Ridgway **66** 335
Samuel S. **99** 257
Samuel Snow **116** 288
Samuel Thompson (Mrs.)
96 160
Sandy **122** 93
Sarah **52** 199 **53** 314 **61** 43
65 40 42 **66** 45 **70** 31
326 **72** 198 **74** 37 **75** 209
76 191 193 **77** 207 **78**
404 **81** 102 **84** 409 **85** 64
86 440 **87** 123 303 339
341 **88** 11 15 **90** 342 **94**
97 121 **107** 271 **108** 122
123 **111** 74 75 **115** 21 24
111 **117** 167 **123** 259
261 **133** 283 **136** 304
140 21 **141** 105
Sarah (Allen) **90** 172
Sarah (Baker) **89** 54
Sarah (Bruce) **136** 302 304
Sarah (Fowler) **90** 172
Sarah (Gifford) **134** 132
Sarah (James) **127** 32
Sarah (King) **125** 289
Sarah (Marshfield) **88** 188
Sarah A. **79** 170
Sarah Amelia (Barnes)
87 378
Sarah Ann (Allen) **90** 172
Sarah C. **76** 275
Sarah F. **128** 268
Sarah Green **72** 291
Sarah Jane **61** 182
Sarah L. **100** 330
Shadrach **66** 11
Sidney **83** 428 436
Sidney Trowbridge
136 323
Silas **77** 207
Silas Warren (Mrs.)
106 125
Simeon **56** 144 **82** 292 294
Simeon Danforth **94** 120
121
Solomon **66** 38 **72** 98 **88**
188 **98** 324 **101** 43
Sophia **106** 108
Sophia Lulu **78** 174
Spencer **79** 113 **83** 370 **84**
190 465 **96** 306 **97** 155
135 135 **146** 267
Squire **129** 273
Starr **72** 97
Statira P. **140** 21
Stella **60** 45
Stephen **71** 142 **140** 173
174
Stocks **78** 35
Submit **57** 393 **136** 304
Susan **100** 256 257 **141** 48
Susan E. **83** 174 184 185
Susan F. (Hall) **128** 269

MILLER *cont'd*
Susan Ridgway **81** 103
Susanna **51** 33 **58** 195 **60**
78 **61** 239 **65** 256 **77**
lviii **85** 56 64 **108** 189
119 261 **123** 10 **125** 101
136 304 **140** 22
Susanna C. **81** 219
Susanna C. (Brown)
99 251
Susey **107** 200
Sylvanus **54** 301
Syntha **108** 57
Tabitha (Hopkins) **136**
312 316
Tama **125** 216
Temperance **54** 308 **55**
205 **73** 196 **79** 72
Thankful **51** 33 34 224 **59**
217 218 **97** 277
Theda **89** 249
Theodore **117** 207 **128** 268
Theresa **78** 328 **90** 55
Thereza **110** 130
Thomas **55** 204 **61** 135 179
63 346 **66** 229 **68** 167
69 269 **71** 344 345 **73** 7
255 **74** 37 **78** 320 **80** 189
83 326 **85** 83 **87** 303 **88**
188 **89** 246 **94** 262 **98**
302 **112** 287 **115** 123
116 13 **123** 259 260 **126**
165 **127** 227 **132** 21 **136**
304 **146** 267 **147** 257
Thomas C. **74** 33
Thomas Matthew **126** 165
127 202
Thomas Woodnut (Mrs.)
92 394
Timothy **55** 88 204 205
107 126 146 221 **108**
148 **109** 142 144 **110**
137 140 **111** 144 **112**
134 136 137 223 315 **113**
61 149 151 234 294 **114**
71 142 228 310 **115** 68
145
Tobias Ham **73** 193 200
Uriah **55** 87 204
Valentine **78** 371
Vespasian **58** 386
Victor Arthur **83** 122 233
118 159
Virginia Estelle **92** 364
W. H. **80** 157
Wade Hampton (Mrs.)
108 135
Walter **59** 96
Walter Herbert **94** 89
113 228
Warwick Price **65** xxxv
Washington **73** 255
Wilbur F. **91** 41
Wilhelmina **100** 113
Willard I. **80** 111
William **51** 491 **53** 210
54 218 441 **60** 45 **61** 269
389 **63** 342 **64** 115 **73**
139 187 201 202 255 **78**
393 **80** 375 **83** 35 375 **84**

MILLER *cont'd*
358 374 **85** 64 162 168
86 54 **90** 172 **91** 330 **98**
128 **100** 256 257 **107**
201 270 271 **109** 59 283
111 245 **113** 243 **114**
187 **117** 165 277 278
126 143 **127** 32 **128** 285
129 385 **141** 6 **145** 349
William Abeel **70** 203
William Alexander **76**
241 **77** xxviii
William Augustus **87** 23
William Chauncey
115 111
William D. **144** 301
William Davis **96** 351
109 237
William Douglas **82** 125
237
William Edward (Mrs.)
105 129
William Ellery **77** 181
William Fowler **72** 40 41
44 87 88 92 98 99 166
176 **90** 172
William Frank **68** lxxviii
William H. **116** 115
William James **78** 37
William R. **79** 55 **89** 265
William Starr **72** 89
William T. **129** 277
William Taylor **81** 188
William W. **80** 39
Willima **64** 115
Willis Alanson (Mrs.)
86 197 **87** 208 **90** 135
Willis Harry **99** 257
Zenas **126** 165
Zerviah **55** 205 **57** 161
136 304
Zerviah (Mowly) **133** 153
Zilpah **51** 192 195
Millerd *see* Millard
Milles *see* Mills
MILLETT Millet
—— **61** 161 **95** 133
— Capt. **98** 220
A. Wesley **120** 313 **123**
154 155
Abigail **73** 312 **87** 346 **88**
54 64
Abigail (Coit) (Eveleth)
134 307
Ada F. **98** 195
Alice I. (Campbell)
83 424 436
Alma **120** 313 **123** 155
Anna **88** 54 71 **108** 60
145 46
Annie P. G. (Fuller)
83 180 184
Archie Lane (Mrs.) **99** 148
Benjamin **88** 71
Bethiah **95** 133
Betsey **147** 362-364
Charles **88** 71
Charles C. **83** 180 184
Clarissa **88** 238
D. Caldwell **54** 373
Dana **83** 298 300

MILLETT cont'd
David **88** 54 71
Deborah **53** 339
Dorcas **88** 71
Dorcas Dinsmore **88** 238
Ebenezer **58** 372
Elisha **88** 64
Eliza **108** 192 **116** 179
Elizabeth **147** 362 364
Ellen Ursula **85** 439
Ellice (Averill) **109** 183
Emma Francette **88** 9
Eunice **56** 319 **88** 54
Fidelia **88** 71
Florence Elizabeth **96** 288
George Bown **52** 150
George Francis **95** 147
  101 122 **114** 318
Hannah (Powers) **129** 316
  136 79
Hannah (Prince) **147** 362
Hiram **87** 334
Jabez **88** 71
Jean Francois **55** lxx lxxi
John **88** 54 **107** 275 **108**
  56 58-60 191 **145** 46
Joseph **129** 316 **136** 79
Josiah **88** 64
Kate **58** 372
Leaffee **58** 372
Lewis **101** 102
Louis **125** 217
Love **74** 183
Lydia **58** 372 **88** 71 **108**
  59 60 **145** 46
Lydia (Hutchins) **108** 191
Marah **59** 215
Maria **108** 58 **145** 46
Mary **53** 30 **58** 372 404 **89**
  117 **108** 56 58 **145** 46
Mary (Eveleth) **134** 302
  307
Mary Ann **129** 316 **136** 79
Mary Jane **125** 221
Mary Sergeant **108** 191
Mary W. **83** 184
Mehitable **53** 30 **64** 14
Morice Baker **108** 59
Morris **145** 46
Moses **88** 54
Nathaniel **58** 372
Pauline (Chase) **87** 334
Powers **129** 316
Pratt **129** 316
Ralph L. **83** 424 436
Ruth **127** 320
Sally H. **116** 126
Samuel **88** 71 238 **91** 330
  109 183
Sarah **88** 54 64 71
Sarah (Bodge) **101** 102
  125 217
Sarah E. (Brown) **83** 424
  436
Simeon **88** 71
Solomon **88** 71
Stephen Caldwell **73** 318
  74 xxv **82** 380 **83** 230
  105 124 **124** 231 **133** 85
  145 367
Susanna **82** 294

MILLETT cont'd
Thomas **51** 468 **53** 30 **56**
  319 **67** 180 **88** 54 **98** 66
  224 **107** 45 **114** 318 **134**
  302 307 **147** 362
Thomas Wheeler **58** 372
Thyass **88** 64
Wealth **101** 125
William **88** 54
William F. **83** 424 436
William Howard (Mrs.)
  102 124
MILLETTE Myllette
Richard **72** 55
MILLEVASHE —— **56** 111
MILLEWAY
Isaac **114** 188
John W. **114** 188
Nancy **114** 188
Patsy **114** 188
Rachel **114** 188
Susan **114** 188
MILLEY John **60** 242
MILLICAN
Esther **61** 378
Margaret **61** 236
Mary Ann **97** 18
Percy **111** 158
Robert **61** 236
Millidge see Milledge
MILLIGAN
Elise **78** 203 **96** 57
Elizabeth **98** 359
George **98** 359
George Baldwin **96** 57
George M. **62** 157
James **83** 345
Julia **74** 49
Margaret Anne Wylie
  83 345
Mary (Trumbull) **83** 345
Mary Ellen **62** 157
Robert **98** 359
Samuel **53** 460
Sophia Gough (Carroll)
  96 57
MILLIKEN Miliken
  Milikin Millakin
  Millikan Millikin
  —— **57** 127 **62** 103 **104** 57
  145 167
Abigail **73** 286 **145** 47
Abigail (Norton) **90** 281
Abigail Smith **104** 184
Abner **105** 287
Abraham **103** 260 **105** 264
Achsah **145** 47
Alexander **57** 296
Ann (Baldwin) **108** 68
Anne Bennett **88** 390
Archibald **105** 264 265
Arthur **90** 282 **91** 141
Arthur Norris **84** 105 107
  185 186 **90** 281 294 **91**
  141 145
Asa **110** 24 104
Ashbeline **106** 219
Barbara (McKay) **96** 334
Benjamin **105** 208 265
  115 60
Benjamin Carll **96** 334

MILLIKEN cont'd
Bessie Della (Thomas)
  (Cahoon) **97** 158
Betsey **105** 264
Caroline (Chase) **87** 330
Catherine (Harmon)
  136 270
Charles **142** 198
Charles Alfred (Mrs.)
  97 158
Charlotte Jellison
  (Tincker) **77** xii **90** 281
Clarissa **104** 183
D. **89** 301
Daniel **104** 133 182
  106 219
Daniel L. **65** 105
David **104** 132 133
Dominicus **89** 301 **108**
  311 **104** 133 183
Dorothy **104** 184
E. C. (Mrs.) **99** 183
Ebenezer Coolbroth
  90 281
Edward **90** 281 **105** 265
  134 92
Eliza **67** 186 **142** 198
Elizabeth **91** 396 **105** 265
Elizabeth (Alger) **90** 281
  105 265
Elizabeth (Harman)
  90 281
Elizabeth G. (Town)
  103 45
Flora A. **91** 385
Frances A. **103** 45
Frances L. **122** 71 232
George **104** 184
George L. **89** 301
Gerrish Hill **89** 132
Hannah **142** 198
Hannah (Rathbone)
  105 264
Helen Josephine **82** 9
Helen L. **79** 16
Hester Lee **101** 235
Hugh **105** 265
Isaac **97** 369
Isabel **57** 296
J. Hopkinson **142** 198
James **85** 120 **105** 265
  142 198
Jesse L. **108** 68
Joel **145** 47
John **90** 281 **91** 396 **105**
  265 **108** 68 **136** 270 **142**
  198
John (Mrs.) **83** 477
Joseph **90** 281
Josiah **142** 198
Julia **107** 155
Louisa Wylie **87** 59
Lucinda **104** 184
Lucretia **101** 235
Lucretia (Davis) **105** 264
Lucy **145** 47
Mabel Minott (Marsh)
  90 282
Margaret Ann (Smith)
  108 68 **110** 24 104
Maria **106** 143

MILLIKEN *cont'd*
Martha **55** 424
Martha (Orr) **87** 59
Martha Ann **96** 334
Mary **73** 233 **91** 396 **97** 369
125 103 **126** 272
Mary (Wyatt) **108** 68
Mary Ann **97** 18 369
Mary Belcher (Tarbox)
90 281
Mary Elizabeth (Simonds)
83 477
Mattie **134** 92
Nancy **104** 183
Nathaniel **59** 284
Phebe **73** 282 **100** 146
Rebecca **62** 261 **101** 235
106 219 **108** 311 **115**
225
Rebecca (Smith) **104** 132
133 182
Robert **57** 296 **62** 261
87 330
Royal B. **103** 45
Sally **57** 296 **73** 284 **104**
133 **145** 47
Samuel **73** 284 **105** 265
108 68
Sarah **59** 284 **68** 100 **71** 225
89 301 **99** 301 **136** 270
142 198
Sarah (Burnett) **91** 396
Sarah (Flood) **134** 92
Sarah (Hartzell) **108** 68
Sarah Amanda **57** 296
Sewel **103** 261
Silva Lucina **57** 295
Simeon **73** 282
Sophia **67** 276
Susan **126** 142
Susanna **73** 282 283 291
William **87** 59 **88** 304
101 235 **105** 264 **108** 68
132 162 **136** 270
MILLIMAN
Aaron **67** 286
Anne **67** 286
MILLIN — Mrs. **62** 24
Isabella S. **81** 248
John **81** 248
Sarah **81** 248
MILLINER —— **140** 31
Francis **63** 24
James **92** 47
MILLINGS
Ella Veronica **99** 148
MILLINGTON Millinton
Agnes **113** 70 **120** 24 25
Agnes (Sotheron) **113** 70
120 24 25
Alice **120** 24 25
Ann (Lady) **93** 376
Barbara **120** 24 25
Charles Fremont **100** 291
Christopher **120** 25
Clara Ellen **78** 320
Clarinda **122** 112
David **73** 104
Dorothy **120** 25
Eleanor **101** 17
Elizabeth **113** 70 **120** 25

MILLINGTON *cont'd*
Ella **100** 291
Ellen **120** 25
Esther M. **122** 112
Franklin **100** 291
Harold W. **78** 320
Henry **119** 159 **136** 167
Isabel **120** 25
James B. **100** 291
Jennet **113** 70 **120** 25
Jennett **120** 24 25
John **58** 398 **99** 118 **101** 52
119 247 **120** 25 **136** 167
Margaret **120** 25
Martha **52** 409
Mary **52** 409 410 **99** 118
100 242 **101** 52
Mary Ann (Howland)
100 291
Mary Eveline **100** 291
Matthew **119** 246 **120** 25
Nathaniel **63** 238
Phillippa (Sotheron)
120 25
Richard **120** 25
Robert **119** 247 **120** 23-25
Samuel **52** 409 410
Samuel C. **100** 291
Sarah (Smith) **136** 167
Solomon **122** 112
Thomas **120** 24 25
Wilfred **120** 25
William **120** 24 25
William Cullen Bryant
100 291 **147** 70
MILLIOR John **115** 19
MILLIQUET —— **140** 169
MILLIS Anne (Davis) **111**
125 129
Elva I. **111** 122 129
Everett **111** 129
Frank A. (Meeker)
111 129
Harriet **111** 128 129
Hart W. **111** 125 129
Samuel **106** 298
William L. **111** 129
Millner *see* Milner
MILLORD
Mabel **56** 353 354
MILLS Mill Milles
—— **52** 112 **54** 232 **57** 337
61 207 **65** 360 **67** 336
98 94 **118** 118 **130** 235
— Capt. **70** 42 **108** 25
— Mr. **63** 342
— Mrs. **71** 121 **119** 137
— Widow **65** 361 **70** 300
—— (Coleman) **140** 52
A. R. **100** 214
Abbie A. **89** 351
Abbie D. (Holt) **83** 20
Abiah **81** 283
Abial **71** 275
Abigail **55** 259 **57** 24 **68** 93
70 34 **71** 81 281 **78** 419
99 29 **107** 118 **110** 175
111 21 **114** 48
Abigail (Treat) **110** 142
Abigail Frances **68** 93
Abigail H. **68** 93 **69** 320

MILLS *cont'd*
Abijah **57** 26
Abraham A. **142** 185
Ada L. **110** 302
Adaline W. **79** 219
Adam Lee **83** 206
Addie J. **89** 351
Addison N. **81** 282
Addison O. **81** 282
Adia **56** 39
Agnes (Smith) **98** 350
Albert D. **110** 304
Albert R. **109** 198 **110** 304
Alberta C. **93** 355
Alce **101** 244
Alice D. **110** 302
Alice Eliza **62** 367
Alice F. **109** 198
Aligood **82** 49
Allen **71** 54 122 **123** 52
Alligood **81** 447
Alma W. **93** 339
Amanda **72** 47 49 97 106
133 122
Amanda J. **128** 91
Amasa **81** 282 408
Ammi **72** 49 104 180
Amos **56** 36 **85** 10 **107** 118
Andrew **71** 121 **93** 203
123 46 47
Andrew R. **123** 311
Ann **55** 266 **59** 219 **63** 45
81 260 **91** 381
Ann Eliza **81** 275
Ann M. (Hutchins) **89** 351
Anna **55** 398 **56** 38 **123** 47
53 304
Anna (Chase) **88** 29
Anna Doris **111** 148
Anna Kellogg **110** 141
142
Anna Maria **133** 232
Anne **55** 265 **57** 145 261 **61**
399 **63** 166 **68** 192 197
71 86 **112** 303 **123** 50
Annette W. **72** 50
Anson G. **81** 283 408
Antoinette **72** 106
Archibald **104** 121
Archibald L. **81** 283
Arnon **81** 283
Arthur **61** 218
Asa **57** 259
Asa C. **125** 302
Asenath **57** 259 **81** 290
Asphia **125** 302
Austin **87** 10
Azro Downs **93** 355
Bathsheba (Allen) **83** 508
118 204 205
Beebee **69** 49 233
Bellewynn Elnora **103** 164
Belvider E. **81** 382
Benaiah **62** 120
Benjamin **55** 262 266 392
56 36 38 145 268 **57** 22
261 262 **81** 408 **105** 205
206 **118** 133 **136** 321
Benjamin T. **81** 283
Bethiah **56** 37
Betsey **71** 276 **72** 33 **79** 219

MILLS *cont'd*
81 283 390 93 354 123
90 304
Betsey (Goodwin) 93 354
Betsey Ann 129 48
Beulah 56 142 265 57 150
Bildad 71 164
Boardman 133 122
Borden Hicks 66 1 93
Bracket 125 302
Bruce 75 38
Calcie A. 81 281
Calvin Rawson 86 334
Calvin Rawson (Mrs.)
77 xxviii 86 109 204 334
Caroline 57 378 81 289
125 302 142 184
Caroline Adelaide 62 367
Caroline H. 79 306
142 185
Caroline H. (Jenks) 142
183-185
Catherine 68 93 106 73 9
255 83 55 98 350 137
282
Catherine (Hickson)
91 29 34
Catherine (Lewis) 110 142
Catherine Haven 57 380
Celia 56 39
Charles 61 353 62 367 64
339 90 319 91 26 31 330
Charles Blunt 93 354
Charles Ferdinand 99 148
Charles H. 129 45
Charles Lewis 110 142
Charles P. 79 219
Charlotte 81 277 282
Charlotte (Arey) 87 8
Charlotte Eugenie
(Colby) 125 113
Christina 63 378 64 375
Christopher S. 77 149
Clara 100 214
Clarissa 65 346 66 98
104 56
Clarissa A. 68 93
Clark 78 450
Climena 81 416
D. O. 70 xlv
Daniel 57 22 60 188 61
389 71 75 85 86 79 219
88 30 125 302
Darius 87 8
David 55 259 265 56 142
147 267 57 145 146 148
149 151 255 260 371 373
98 350 107 117 119 198
133 218 145 359
Davis Kendrick 125 113
Day 69 328
Debby 56 148 57 256
Deborah 55 262 267 79
220 99 172
Deborah Selden (Wilson)
97 379
Dexter 104 56
Dexter Townsend 57 380
Diademia 71 157
Dorcas (Messinger)
110 142

MILLS *cont'd*
Dorothea 141 140
Dorothy 68 288 109 198
Dorothy (Farnham)
109 12
Dorothy (Fitz Randolph)
(Fell) 99 47
Dorothy (Webster)
97 379
Drusilla 71 277
Drusilla Emery (Durrell)
133 122
Durston 125 302
E. Merle (Mrs.) 123 33
Ebenezer 57 260 68 171
69 372
Edmund 68 106
Edmund Foster 71 277
Edson W. 100 91
Edward 63 232 79 220 81
290 447 84 77 87 320
115 120
Edward Augustus 57 380
Edward C. 60 188 114 189
Edward E. 109 198
110 302
Edwin W. 100 91
Effie 129 48
Eleanor (Arey) 87 9
Eleanor (Lawrence) 96 85
Eli 69 233 71 82 157 273
275 281 72 31 33
Eligood 53 249 71 224 225
79 219 220 93 354
Elihu 71 160 283 72 46 47
97 101 102 172 176 178
184
Elijah 71 78 87 154 155
157-159 161 162 164 302
303 72 166 104 56
Elijah H. 79 166
Elijah Hunt 136 321 325
Elisha 55 262 397 56 147
148 57 29 255-260 71
275 85 10 110 142 118
228
Elisha Treat 110 142
Eliza 78 398 129 46 48
Eliza (Harmon) 90 338
Eliza A. 86 306
Eliza Ann 83 206
Elizabeth 55 262 264 265
267 393-396 398 56 32
33 147 268 57 24 146
255 257 261 59 270 63
47 73 9 74 249 78 308
81 260 408 86 222 100
299 112 227 114 189
119 180 125 257
Elizabeth (Snow) 133 218
Elizabeth Ann 57 377
75 190
Elizabeth B. 83 509 510
Elizabeth Greene 81 222
Elizabeth Marsh 133 218
Elizabeth Shown 141 111
Elizur L. 81 283
Ella 53 143 56 416
57 xxxiii
Ellen F. 89 351
Ellen Ryerson 81 480

MILLS *cont'd*
Elligood 90 249
Ellis 82 49
Elmer W. 93 339
Elvira (Davis) 111 148
Emeline 81 287
Emily 89 238
Emily (Corbin) 86 334
Emily E. 81 290
Emily Jane 90 338
Emily S. 109 198
Emma T. 81 283
Enoch 55 395 56 147
Ephraim 57 259 81 283
408 98 105 125 101
Esther 55 392 56 142 57
28 151 63 238 68 93
Ethel Louise 83 436 84 21
Eunice 56 36 145 57 252
Eunice (Sibley) 124 20 22
Eunice Louisa 92 321
Eunice M. 79 219
Experience 115 315 125
247 257
Ezekiel 72 39
Ezra 55 395 56 39 57 149
261
Ezra Hayden 72 97
Fannie 82 433
Farwell 133 122
Flora 104 308
Frances Adelaide 62 367
Francis Joseph 62 367
Frank 71 122
Frank B. 83 20
Frederick 72 29
Frederick M. 81 290
Freeman 87 10
Fuller 56 34
G. J. 82 433
Gardner 81 283 408
George 57 260 377 60 188
66 93 72 31 49 50 97 98
106 76 268 81 289 290
89 238 92 321 126 144
George C. 76 268
George H. 56 417
George Morey 57 379
George Pilsbury 92 310
George V. 109 12 198
110 206
George Woodford
81 290
Georgena E. 85 87
Gideon 72 29 73 9 81 408
Grace 55 261
Grace Evelyn 86 197 334
88 186 89 147 90 152
96 158
Gustavus 87 10
H. 72 172
Hadassah 56 38 147 57 255
Hannah 55 259 262 392
395 56 269 57 149 256
259 59 88 269-274 361
362 61 131 69 233 71 78
87 280 72 35 46 166 171
79 218 220 81 260 408
447 83 52 141 193 202
Hannah (Browne) 131 31
Hannah (Chase) 88 30

MILLS *cont'd*
Hannah A. **69** 28
Hannah Clementine
93 355
Hannah Newman (Sleigh)
97 379
Harriet **57** 378 **81** 287
123 50
Harriette Blake **136** 321
325
Harry Willard **104** 144
Harvey **81** 283
Helen Whittington
77 292
Henrietta **90** 329 **91** 20
93 354 **115** 315 **125** 260
Henry **62** 80 **88** 119 **90** 72
92 47 **121** 236
Henry James **59** xlvii
Hepzibah **60** 43
Herbert Lee (Mrs.) **84** 234
85 196
Hester **73** 219
Hezekiah **55** 393
Hiram **57** 380
Hiram Roberts **72** 98
Honour **53** 302
Horace A. **110** 302
Horace S. **93** 339
Huldah **72** 101 172
Ida May **75** 18 **129** 48
Ida Olive **69** 328
Ida S. (Monroe) **100** 91
Ira **57** 371 **71** 52 **123** 311
312
Irene L. **81** 283
Isaac **71** 85 **81** 290
Isaiah **59** 405
Israel **56** 266
Jacob **56** 37
James **56** 141 **57** 22 146
150 **69** 296 297 305 307
308 **70** 15 146 **77** civ **79**
219 220 **90** 237 238 319
92 282 **110** 317 **112** 303
115 315 **118** 56 58 **125**
257 302 **128** 247 249
129 34 46 **145** 349
James E. **79** 219
James H. **129** 45 48
James K. **140** 52
James Layng (Mrs.)
82 478
James M. **89** 351
James William **129** 48
Jane **63** 376 **64** 76 **66** 360
90 319 335 **91** 24 **123**
125
Jane (Johnson) **115** 315
125 247 257
Jane (Robbins) **126** 144
Jane M. **81** 282
Jared **81** 290 **118** 134
Jeannette **107** 134
Jedediah **71** 85 277 **79** 168
110 142
Jemima **55** 259 393 **56** 39
142 **57** 151 259 261 **60**
43
Jenny **57** 259
Jeremiah **76** 38

MILLS *cont'd*
Jeremie **101** 244
Jerome B. **93** 354
Jerusha **68** 293 **69** 233 **70**
35 42 **71** 75
Jesse **57** 261 **71** 163
148 282
Joanna **81** 290
Joanna (Case) (Russell)
118 134
Joanna (Porter) **110** 142
Job Smith **64** 102
Joel **81** 290
John **55** 259 264 281 **56** 141
143 145-147 270 **57** 22
23 144-146 148-150 152
252 253 255 378 **59** 83
88 156 269-274 361 362
60 188 **61** 131 399 **64**
260 339 345 **65** 323 324
358 **68** 293 **69** 190 233
282 307 372 **70** 35 141
73 141 255 **74** xxv 155
192 **78** 334 **79** 219 220
81 447 **83** 508 **90** 253
91 206 216 330 **94** 95 **97**
208 287 378 379 **98** 104
105 149 **99** 29 99 **100** 65
241 **101** 244 **103** 161
161 165 **104** 56 **105** 225
111 148 **115** 315 **118** 46
204 **123** 25 27 30 31 **125**
257 302 **128** 170 247 249
250 **139** 235 **140** 169
142 34
John B. **81** 283
John Boardman **111** 41
133 122
John Kendrick **125** 113
John P. **68** 93
Jonas **56** 37 148 **57** 27
87 9 18
Jonathan **56** 32 **57** 146 **59**
88 90 269 361 362 **60** 43
63 300 **70** 120 **79** 220
81 447 **91** 93 **115** 134
147 258
Joseph **56** 31 267 **57** 24 27
148 259 260 377 378 **62**
367 **69** 233 **72** 35 **79** 219
220 **86** 334 **87** 123 **93**
216 **111** 41 **131** 31 **133**
122 **142** 185
Joseph E. **110** 302
Joseph Freeman **62** 367
Joseph Hunting **57** 377
Joseph Larkin **69** 28
Joseph W. **89** 351
Josephine **69** 28
Josiah **55** 394 **57** 259 263
Josue **88** 256
Judith **55** 259 **57** 146
71 158
Julia **79** 306 **88** 334
128 122
Julia B. **81** 283
Julia Frances **87** 10
Julia L. **123** 226
Julia M. **78** 318
Kate **82** 433
Kate M. (Hunt) **123** 225

MILLS *cont'd*
Katie (Haddick) **128** 170
Katie R. **105** 317
Kendall Andrews (Mrs.)
106 125
Keziah **55** 394 **56** 35 147
57 146 255 **71** 81 163
280
L. May **129** 45
Laura **99** 303
Laura A. (Paul) **129** 45
Laura C. **81** 408
Lauren C. **81** 283
Lawrence **123** 304
Lemuel **55** 392 **56** 143 **57**
152 373 379 **81** 408
Levi **56** 35
Lewis Hunt (Mrs.) **96** 85
Linda **71** 165
Lois **66** 364 **71** 80 162 280
Lois Huckins **68** 93
Loretta (Monroe) **100** 91
Lorette Matilda **57** 381
Louisa Woolworth
88 191
Lucia Ann **123** 309
Lucina **71** 155
Lucinda **100** 226
Lucretia **81** 290
Lucy **57** 262 **79** 219 220
81 408 **90** 234 254 319
91 113 126
Lucy (Weatherbee)
125 113
Lucy Amelia **81** 283
Lucy Bolton **110** 302
Lucy G. **79** 219
Lucy L. **81** 282
Lucy M. **109** 198
Lucy Morey **57** 379
Luke **55** 295 **57** 147 **79**
218-220 **81** 260 447 **93**
353
Lydia **55** 265 **56** 31 34 36
37 143 **57** 152 **71** 118 **79**
219 **90** 252
Lydia C. **93** 354
Lydia Jane (Chase) **88** 119
Margaret **57** 145 **73** 255
100 296 **114** 189 **116**
169
Margery (Sumner)
89 238
Maria **108** 65
Maria A. (Kellogg)
110 142
Marianna B. **82** 478
Mark **79** 220
Mark Laighton **93** 354
Marten **64** 225
Martha **55** 264 397 **56** 36
57 377 **69** 189 190 **71**
155 156 278 281 297 307
79 219 **87** 6 **101** 284
136 316
Martha (Ridlon) **90** 253
Martha R. **79** 219
Mary **53** 232 **54** 367 **55**
260 264 393 **56** 38 145
372 **57** 145 252 377 **59**
88 90 91 153 155 269 273

MILLS *cont'd*
363 364 **61** 199 **63** 190
65 44 167 **66** 14 **70** 42
120 **71** 60 81 280 303 **72**
98 **74** 251 **78** 334 410 **79**
153 219 220 **81** 283 408
447 **82** 292 294 **90** 319
331 **91** 23 **95** 272 **100**
297 **106** 303 **109** 305
111 21 240 **115** 134 **125**
302 **128** 247-249 **129** 33
34
Mary (Bell) **100** 241
Mary (Bull) **111** 240
Mary (Forest) **110** 142
Mary (Hunt) **136** 321
Mary (Kennedy) **115** 315
125 247 257
Mary (Ware) **107** 35
Mary Ann **71** 122 **87** 10
Mary B. **109** 198
Mary C. (Finney) **90** 72
Mary E. **81** 279
Mary F. **81** 408
Mary Folger **121** 236
Mary Holbrook **90** 72
Mary J. **72** 106
Mary Loula **75** 38
Mary R. **72** 50
Mary S. **81** 283
Matilda N. (Holtzman)
83 206
Maud **129** 45
Mehitable **71** 283
Melissa **68** 93
Mercy (Hopkins) **104** 56
Minette G. **89** 131
Miriam **72** 102 176
109 111
Molly **62** 120 123 **71** 272
79 219
Moses **56** 146 **57** 147 253
Myra C. **54** 407
Nabby **61** 239 **71** 83 159
275 308
Nabby Griswold **71** 166
72 99
Nancy **68** 93 **87** 9 **137** 282
Nancy L. (Wasson)
110 206
Nancy M. **63** 47
Nancy Yates **117** 291
Naomi **69** 49 **123** 46 47
Nathan **57** 27
Nathaniel **56** 36 141 **57**
22 150 258 262 **59** 91
155 363 364 **85** 26 **92**
310 313
Nehemiah **55** 264 **56** 36
142 143 145 147 148 265
268 269 **57** 144-147 149
152 153 252 255 259
Nellie **87** 9
Nellie Emma **93** 354
Nicholas **59** 219
Norman **81** 290
Obed **133** 122
Ogden **99** 47
Ogden Livingston **99** 47
Olive **69** 328
Olive Lucena **86** 23

MILLS *cont'd*
Oliver **55** 263 **56** 34 37 **57**
145 **71** 162 302 **107** 35
133 122
Oscar Coles **62** 367
P. L. **79** 306
Pareni **78** 334
Patience **55** 265 **56** 36 269
57 149 **81** 282
Patience (Carle) **90** 237
238
Patience (Geary) **90** 237
Patty **72** 40
Paul **56** 39 **57** 259 **121** 236
240
Pelatiah **71** 76 80 154-157
159 160 162-164 271 273
280 297 301 309 **72** 29
39 40 **83** 52
Percy A. **110** 304
Persis (Chase) **87** 320
Peter **71** 75 76 299 **73** 9
110 142 **130** 235 **148**
354
Phebe **62** 367
Philip **55** 266 **57** 260
Philo Lewis **71** 277
Phineas **57** 259
Phinelopa **72** 35
Pieter Wouters **110** 142
Polly **104** 120 **123** 48
Polly (Woodward)
90 229 250
Polly M. **81** 283
R. **123** 47 304
Rachel **61** 380 **125** 302
133 122
Rachel J. **79** 219
Ralph **80** 291 **89** 351
123 304
Rebecca **72** 104 **73** 9 **79**
219 **104** 301
Rebecca (Gridley) **125** 101
Rhoda **55** 393 **56** 148
62 120
Rhoda (Putney) **92** 313
Richard **57** 144 **63** 353 **81**
260 **82** 49 **116** 32 169
125 302
Richard Stokes Jones
62 367
Robert **60** 346 **64** 22 **68**
288 **69** 372 **116** 84
Roger **71** 81 154 164 166
272 273 275-277 280 281
303 **72** 31 33
Rosanna **81** 408
Rufus **57** 373 379-381 **72**
33 **136** 236
Rufus Haven **57** 379
Ruth **61** 389 **69** 296 **83** 52
Ruth (Livingston) **99** 47
S. H. **79** 153
S. V. **82** 433
Sabra **71** 154 280
Sally **55** 397 **57** 261 **65** 361
72 31 **79** 219 **90** 319 **91**
31 **111** 41 **133** 122 **137**
282
Sally (Knight) **91** 26 31
Sally (Simpson) **90** 249

MILLS *cont'd*
Samuel **56** 148 **57** 259 **65**
192 **71** 81 163 165 280
72 39 **73** 9 **79** 169 **88** 29
89 351 **137** 132
Samuel C. **125** 302
Samuel I. **72** 106
Samuel J. **72** 50 **79** 300
Sarah **51** 464 **55** 262 266
392 394 **56** 30 36 38 148
57 30 259 373 **59** 269
274 **61** 399 64 339 **70** 34
71 54 82 85 164 271 281
303 **73** 9 **74** 251 **76** 38
81 283 **84** 322 **104** 121
105 225 **122** 79 **128** 247
249 **133** 122 123 **142**
185
Sarah (Bowman) **97** 378
Sarah (Hadley) **93** 203
Sarah (Pettibone) **105** 225
Sarah (Whittemore)
107 35
Sarah (Wolfin) **128** 170
Sarah A. **81** 284 **129** 45 48
Sarah A. (Woodcock)
129 48
Sarah Apame **74** 58
Sarah E. **77** 149
Sarah Elizabeth **57** 379
Sarah H. **68** 93
Sarah Hunt **136** 325
Sarah J. **77** 152
Sarah Jane **112** 313
Sarah Maria **136** 333
Sarah Reed **103** 296
Schuyler **71** 122
Selina **83** 344
Shora **63** 167
Sibyl **56** 37
Simeon **81** 283
Simon **111** 240 **120** 77
Simon Huckins **68** 93
Solomon **57** 27
Solon **90** 338
Sophia **69** 282 **123** 93
Sophia (Arey) **87** 18
Stella Emeline (Johnson)
77 xxviii 77 **86** 334
Stephen **79** 219
Stephen Palmer **57** 379
Susan **63** 378 **64** 375 **68** 93
Susan D. **90** 319
Susan Jane **76** 37
Susan Lincoln **82** 382
83 233
Susan W. **109** 198
Susanna **55** 263 **56** 34 **59**
156 **71** 76 86 159 276
279 281 **81** 290 **105** 242
Susanna (Beeman)
137 282
Sylvia **123** 304 **133** 122
Syrena **90** 332 **93** 354
Thomas **51** 351 **52** 49 **53**
143 146 302 **55** 262 **57**
195 259 **62** 325 **63** 346
65 34 **69** 189 **71** 124
104 56 **114** 189 **128** 170
Thomas G. (Mrs.) **85** 242
Thomas J. **63** 47

MILLS cont'd
Timothy **57** 149
W. Robert **144** 345 351
Walter **89** 351
Walter B. **75** 38
Walter S. **89** 351
Walter Truman **62** 367
Westchester **62** 367
Wilber **129** 48
William **53** 302 **55** 259 393
56 36 76 78 141 142 147
148 269 270 **57** 22 146-
151 **61** 380 **65** 262 264
71 118 **73** 255 **78** 309
403 **79** 219 220 **90** 229
250 319 **91** 29 34 **94** 95
97 378 379 **100** 65 **101**
244 **107** 35 **111** 21 **115**
120 **123** 225 **124** 20 22
137 282
William E. **81** 290
William Eligood **80** 102
208
William F. **79** 219 **123** 226
William Howe **59** xlvii
William Ritchie **57** 380
William Stowell **54** 229
55 xxxii 122 **56** xxxii 60
198 344 418 **63** 98 **65**
xxxv
Xenephon Elihu **103** 164
Zechariah **57** 22-24 26-30
145 **73** 149 266 **77** 231
Zenas **71** 55 **123** 48
Zillah **68** 93
MILLSAPP Mary **117** 118
MILLSPAUGH —— **69** 321
Abner **95** 116
Adam **77** xciv
Anna Belle **77** xcv
Anna Eva **77** xciv
Caroline **69** 321
Deborah Barron **77** xciv
Dorothy **77** xciv
Edward Judson **74** 157
75 xxiii **77** xxvii xxxv
xciv xcv
Francis C. **111** 241 **114** 78
Francis Corwin **77** xxvii
xcv
Isaac Little **77** xciv
Jane **77** xciv
Mary B. **95** 116
Matthias **77** xciv **111** 241
Nicholas **111** 241
Philip **111** 241
Pieter **77** xciv
Samuel **77** xciv
Susanna **77** xciv
MILLUM
Avice de **96** 106
William de **96** 107
Millwarde see Milward
MILMAN —— **60** 225
MILMERE George
Parsons (Mrs.) **93** 292
MILMINS
Alexander **115** 26
Hannah **115** 26
Lucinda **115** 26

MILNE Milnes Milns
A. D. **125** 172
Alice **128** 109 110
Alice (Gregson) **128** 106
Ann (Tennant) **125** 172
Caroline Jean (Marr) **83**
435 436
Catherine **136** 78
Celia Adelaide **82** 101
Dorothy (Woodward)
128 109
Fanny **136** 78
George G. (Mrs.) **82** 101
Helen Durthie **57** 327
J. M. **121** 235
James Norman **83** 435 436
John **90** 194-196 264 266
127 261
Mary **126** 143
Peter **62** 322
Richard **128** 109 **136** 78
Susan (Wilcox) **136** 78
Susan Jane **136** 78
William **77** 230 **125** 172
128 106
MILNER Millner Milnor
— Rev. Mr. **79** 300
Abigail (Barton) **107** 293
Alice **83** 446 **84** 14 16
Ann **83** 445
Ann Frances **99** 250
Ann Frye Hewes
(Hunneman) **94** 47
Anna **125** 240
Anne **84** 13 16
Edward T. **78** 416
Elizabeth **52** 129 **63** 244
George W. **88** 337
James **88** 95
John **101** 83 84
John T. **114** 318
Jonathan **63** 244
Joseph **78** 74
Joseph F. **88** 343
Joseph F. (Mrs.) **94** 47
Lucy L. (Sprague) **88** 343
Margaret **82** 445 **138** 129
Mary **94** 264
Nathaniel **114** 249
Ralph **83** 446 **84** 14 16
Richard **94** 259
Robert **77** lii
Susan Sarah (Vanbuskirk)
88 337
Thomas **56** 315 **97** 297
109 9
W. C. **116** 8 11 13
William **103** 185
MILNER-GIBSON
Jasper **77** lii
Susanna Arethusa **77** li
Thomas **77** li lii
MILNER-GIBSON-
CULLUM George
Gery **67** 67 **73** xix **76**
xxviii xc **77** li-liii **86**
324 **97** 205 **104** 107
Milnes see Milne
Milnor see Milner
Milns see Milne
MILOM John **61** 48 **94** 69

MILOM cont'd
70
MILROY
Margaret **85** 298
Margaret (Rising) **85** 298
MILSOIN John **84** 437
MILSON — Mrs. **51** 134
Joseph **115** 254
Josias **115** 254
Martha **115** 254
Mary **70** 347 348
MILSTEED John **63** 144
MILTIMORE
— Mr. **73** 70
Caleb Wiggin **73** 70
MILTON Mylton
—— **65** 83
— Mr. **67** 156
Alice W. **110** 158
Amelia **81** 102
Anna Ridgway **75** xxiii
79 201 210 **81** 102 103
Anne **101** 10
Anthony **138** 219
Bathsheba **113** 46 **143** 131
Bathsheba (Jones) **143**
130 131
Benjamin **64** 85 87 **70** 262
265
Betsey **125** 214
Christian **67** 156
Christopher **57** 218
Dorcas **104** 177
Elijah **143** 260
Elizabeth **56** 91
George **65** 234
George Arthur **81** 242
82 100
George Arthur (Mrs.)
77 022 **78** 205 **81** 242
George Bruce **82** 100
H. Harvey **123** 126
J. Elet **90** 207
Jael (Hobart) **143** 131
John **53** 118 131 **56** 227
59 183 **60** 133 **61** xlix
63 242 **64** xlvi 87 **67** 72
80 408 **101** 10 **110** 253
133 127 **138** 161
John C. **98** 311
Joseph **113** 46 **143** 127
130 131 345
Lucy Kidder **82** 100
Lulu M. **86** 297
Lydia **143** 131
Margaret (Hore) **141** 24
Martha **143** 131
Mary **60** 133 **102** 278
Mary Bond (Bancroft)
96 290
Myldred **92** 296
Priscilla **123** 125
Priscilla (Trussell)
123 126
Rebecca **64** 87
Robert **60** 188 **142** 353 **143**
122 131 333
Ruth (Gifford) **138** 219
Sally **78** 189
Sarah **85** 121 **97** 229
143 131

MILTON *cont'd*
Sarah (Chamberlain)
  142 353 **143** 131
Sarah E. **98** 311
Sumner **78** 205 **81** 110
  231 242 **82** 100
Theodora **60** 133
Thomas **59** 400 **65** 234
  141 24
William C. **96** 290
William Frederick **81** 102
William Frederick (Mrs.)
  75 xxiii 65 **85** 216
William Hammat **81** 102
MILWARD Millwarde
  Milwarde
— Mr. **53** 26
Alice **101** 14
Ann **80** 259
Clement **110** 19
Isabel **101** 14
James **80** 259
Jeffery **101** 272
John **95** 321 322
Thomas **52** 342 **54** 218 **56**
  316 **112** 34 37
William **112** 34 37
MILWOOD — Mr. **53** 237
MIMMY
Abraham **73** 311
Ann **73** 311
James **74** 180
Jane **73** 311 **74** 38 180 188
  191
John **73** 311
Mary **73** 311
Molly **74** 180
Phebe **73** 311
Sarah **74** 188 191
MIMS Georgia **77** 266
MINARD
Abigail **56** 256
Alline **127** 268
Anna (Waterhouse)
  104 195
Charles E. **91** 104
Christopher **116** 7
Clara Derby **81** 258
Clement **121** 10
Cynthia **89** 250
Darius **116** 7
David **127** 268
Deborah **63** 84
Didama **104** 194
Dimmis **80** 189 **89** 246
Eldred **128** 115
Elijah **126** 162 **127** 268
Elizabeth **91** 104 **127** 268
Ephraim **121** 14
Fear **127** 268
Henry O. **91** 104
Isaac **118** 243 **125** 228
Jane **127** 268
Jesse **104** 195
Joseph **121** 17
Levi **126** 162 **127** 268
  128 115
Lucy **127** 268
Lucy (Taylor) **91** 104
Lydia **89** 244 246

MINARD *cont'd*
Martha (Freeman)
  128 115
Mary **127** 268
Mary (Stephens) **126** 162
Nancy **89** 246
Nathan **80** 189 **89** 246
Peter S. **63** 84
Rebecca **127** 268 **128** 115
Rebecca (Kempton)
  127 268
Richard Kempton
  128 115
Sarah **128** 114
Sarah I. **80** 189
Sarah Isham **89** 246
Susanna **128** 114
Thomas **116** 7 **121** 12
Wealthy **132** 76
Wheeler **128** 114
William **56** 256
MINCE Albert **85** 315
Emma **85** 315
John **85** 315
Mark **85** 315 **86** 321
Martha **86** 321
Martha Loveland **85** 315
Mary **85** 315
Sarah E. **86** 321
Willie L. **85** 315
MINCHER Isaac **91** 385
Phebe (Jones) **91** 385
MINCHIN
Edward **130** 314
Elizabeth (Wentworth)
  130 314
Emma Eliza **80** 141
John **130** 314
Nancy (Thayer) **130** 314
MINCK Ella **83** 423 436
MINCKLER
Mattie Jane **82** 272
MINDELEFF
Jessie Louise **70** xxxvii
Victor **70** xxxvii
MINDWELL
Eldora **82** 237
MINE Mary Margaret
  (Carlton) **89** 115
MINEHAN
Henry **126** 204
Mary J. (Edes) **126** 204
MINER Minor
—— **51** 321 **55** 50 **57** 420
  72 100
— Miss **76** 270
— Mr. **56** 221 385
— Mrs. **56** 78
Abigail **72** 102 **78** 368
  83 342
Abigail E. **68** 258
Ada (Barber) **126** 296
Adelaide Arvilla **82** 108
  109
Alice Emma (Trainer)
  84 457
Alice Maude **95** 147 **100**
  109 **112** 71 143
Allan Gerard (Mrs.)
  109 130
Alonzo A. **52** 298 **62** 218

MINER *cont'd*
  135 150
Alonzo Ames **58** 333
Alonzo Gilbert **72** 309 310
Alvin John **75** 13
Amanda **95** 366
Amy **78** 368 **79** 72 73 **80**
  194 **81** 360
Anderson **54** 82 **55** 34 35
  56 165 356 **58** 402 **59**
  413 **83** 100
Andrew C. **89** 256
Andrew Cole **86** 304
Angeline D. **84** 86
Anna **72** 306 **81** 360
Anna Mary **72** 310
Augustus P. **134** 334
Austin **72** 306 309
Benjamin **81** 170
Benjamin C. **123** 224
Bertha **89** 319
Bethiah **81** 173
Betsey **72** 308 **80** 424
  83 359
Betsey Mehitable **84** 86
Calvin **55** 34
Caroline **78** 373
Carroll Alonzo Lyons
  72 310
Catherine **80** 143
Cedora A. **68** 258
Champlin **123** 224
Champlin (Mrs.) **123** 224
Charles **81** 265 **86** 304 365
  142 169 **143** 362
Charles Elbert **72** 309
Charles Frees **72** 311
Charles Henry **72** 310
Charles Oram **86** 304
Charlotte (Dunphey) **86**
  304 365
Charlotte Hoskins
  107 134
Chloe **114** 181
Chloe (Field) **114** 181
Christopher **60** 397 **62**
  173 174 **79** 72 73 **127**
  199 200 **128** 20 **142** 175
  143 362
Christopher A. **80** 193
  89 251
Clara Augusta **54** cvii
Clarence **83** 64
Clarence Horatio Gilbert
  72 310 311
Clarence J. **83** 64
Clement **78** 368 **79** 72 **84**
  457 **108** 95 **138** 184
Clement S. **84** 457
Coral Henry **72** 311
D. Y. **80** 193
Daisy Gertrude **72** 311
Daniel **78** 368
Daniel S. **78** 373 **81** 265
David **78** 368 **81** 173
Delia A. **76** 270
Dudley T. **83** 359 **84** 86
E. B. **128** 173
Edgar Samuel **72** 309 311
Edith **138** 184
Edna W. **103** 120

MINER *cont'd*
Edward B. **128** 93
Edward Burnham **77** 207
Edward S. **69** 202
Elbert **72** 308
Elbert Spencer **72** 311
Electa **57** 91 **68** 258
Elias **77** 207
Eliphal **104** 194
Elisha **79** 72 73 **101** 212
Eliza (Green) **91** 291
Eliza (Stark) **89** 256
Eliza Ann (Bancroft)
    95 366
Elizabeth **52** 39 **78** 85 **89**
    72 251 **93** 254 **115** 123
    138 184 **142** 169
Elizabeth Call (Herring)
    94 47
Elizabeth Shepard **72** 308
Ella Grace **72** 311
Ellen M. **89** 256
Ellen Matilda **72** 309
Ellen P. **68** 258
Ellen R. **84** 86
Elnathan **72** 288
Emeline S. **80** 193
Emeline S. (Ransom)
    89 254
Emily B. **81** 287
Emily G. **68** 258
Emily Holman **72** 309
Emma Frances (Palmer)
    112 143
Emma J. **75** 13
Emma W. **101** 216
Ephraim **78** 85 **118** 265
    143 362
Erwin Avery **72** 311
Esther **77** 207 **78** 385 **79** 72
Ethan A. **68** 258
Ethan N. **68** 257
Etta Alice **72** 310
Etta Martha **80** 143
Eugene M. (Mrs.) **112** 74
Eunice **80** 193 **89** 251
    128 20
Eunice (Holmes) **142** 168
    169
F. Alfred **84** 86
Fairy H. **111** 79
Fannie Gertrude (Meech)
    89 254
Frances (Burcham)
    (Willey) **108** 95
Frances Jane **69** 202
Frances Maria **72** 309
Franklin **138** 218
Freelove **89** 256
George **80** 193 **89** 251
George A. **51** 232
George Bancroft **95** 366
George Clement **93** 254
George Edward **72** 309
George H. **84** 86
George Hiram **80** 143
George Leland **101** 178
George W. **93** 254
George W. (Mrs.) **94** 47
Gertrude E. **116** 60
Gideon **136** 249

MINER *cont'd*
Gilbert Prentice **72** 309
Gilbert Smith **72** 306 308
Grace **78** 85 **81** 168 **87** 62
Grace (Palmer) **131** 130
Griswold **80** 424
Handel Pond **72** 311
Hannah **56** 154 **72** 306 **73**
    255 **78** 85 **83** 359 **126**
    255 **128** 18 **133** 265 **142**
    168
Hannah (Ward) **126** 156
Hannah (Wheeler)
    136 329
Harlow **82** 179
Harriet Pond **72** 310
Harry W. **84** 86
Hattie Luella **72** 310
Hattie R. **89** 254
Hazen H. **68** 258
Helen **104** 231
Helen A. **123** 223
Helen H. **68** 258
Helen Maria **82** 109
Henry **138** 182
Henry Austin **72** 309 310
Henry C. **66** 34
Hepzibah (Belding)
    84 157
Hiram **57** 286
Huldah S. **68** 257
Isaac **65** 302 **143** 362
Isaac Williams **91** 291
Isaiah **55** 38
Israel **138** 184
Iva May **72** 311
Jabes **128** 18
James **126** 255 **143** 362
James Fontaine **105** 129
James H. **76** 267
Jane (McDermont) **86** 306
Jane H. **81** 286
Jane Maria **91** 291
Jared **78** 373
Jared L. **100** 189
Jean Elizabeth **85** 196
Jennie May **72** 311
Jennie Pond **72** 311
Jerre Lorenzo **72** 309
Jerusha **58** 402 **59** 413
    83 100
Jesse **83** 359
Joan **138** 183 184
Joanna **62** 174
Joel **60** 396-398 **61** 35
    77 207
John **52** 39 **68** 235 **75** 13
    115 33 **128** 18 **138** 183
    184
John C. **116** 65
John M. **78** 368
John Prannell (Mrs.)
    86 197
John S. **77** 207
John Tyler **82** 109
Jonathan **101** 57
Joseph **60** 144 370 **62** 174
    74 108 **77** 207 **79** 72 **81**
    168
Joseph Eastman **112** 143
Joshua **57** 290

MINER *cont'd*
Julia Josephine **69** 202
Kate Pleasants **67** 194
Katharine **72** 288 304 306
L. W. **75** 13
Laura **104** 56
Laura (Titus) **89** 379
Laura A. **78** 373
Laura Florence (Fitz
    Randolph) **98** 341
Laura M. **75** 14
Laura W. **51** 232
Leo **75** 14
Leonard **83** 64
Leroy Matthew Simpson
    72 311
Leroy Matthew Simpson
    (Mrs.) **103** 120
Lilla E. **68** 258
Lillian **86** 306 364
Lillian Eugenia Sophia
    72 310
Lillian Lounsberry **83**
    130 **100** 332 **101** 106
Loraina **86** 130
Loren F. **68** 258
Lorinda **76** 267
Louisa G. **86** 383
Loyal Frank (Mrs.)
    106 125
Lucian W. **68** 258
Lucinda **86** 365
Lucius **81** 265
Lucius B. **81** 265
Lucretia **78** 385
Lucretia W. **89** 254
Lucy **136** 329
Lucy (Stebbins) **126** 255
    128 18
Lucy H. **72** 309
Lucy R. **116** 68
Lucy Sevign **75** 13
Lurmtha **75** 13
Lydia **79** 73 **101** 57
Lydia (Dominy) **84** 457
Lydia (Miner) **101** 57
Lydia Ann **68** 258
M. Grace **112** 144
Manasseh **72** 288
Margaret **68** 258
Maria **83** 359 **95** 366
Maria C. **76** 267
Maria Catherine **72** 309
Maria R. **84** 86
Marietta **69** 202
Martha **54** 82 **56** 356 **58**
    402 **72** 305 **83** 100
Martha (Clapp) **84** 457
Martha Asby **72** 311
Martha Esther **68** 258
Martha G. **80** 193 **89** 251
Mary **54** 291 **56** 253 **60** 144
    62 173 174 **72** 305 307
    79 73 **81** 170 265 **99** 251
    101 212 **138** 184
Mary (Lay) **127** 198
Mary (Randall) **142** 175
    143 362 363
Mary Eliza **72** 311
Mary F. **68** 258
Mary H. **77** 207

MINER *cont'd*
Mary Jane **72** 309 **116** 57
Mary P. **84** 86
Mary Pomeroy **72** 310
Mary Richards **72** 308
Mary S. **112** 74
Matthew **80** 194
Mattie A. **83** 64
Mehitable **84** 86
Mercy **60** 144
Mina **72** 311
Nabby **80** 194
Nancy **72** 307 **73** 255 **79** 23
Nancy Melissa **72** 309
Naomi **79** 73
Nathan **72** 288 304
Nathan L. **68** 258
Nathaniel **54** 291 **56** 253
68 235 **80** 193 **89** 254
Nathaniel Emmons
89 254
Nathaniel S. **80** 193
Nellie Caroline **93** 380
O. **73** 255
Olin **83** 64
Olive **72** 308
Olive E. **72** 309
Oliver **116** 65
Orpha Ada **82** 179
P. A. **84** 86
Parkhurst Ward **98** 341
Patty **57** 290
Persis **57** 286
Peter **86** 306
Phebe **77** 207 **125** 102
Phebe (Cole) **86** 304
Philippa (Simons)
138 184
Prudence **60** 370 **74** 108
Rebecca **78** 368 385
Rebecca S. **78** 368
Relief **72** 309
Richardson **72** 288 304
Robert **116** 231
Rossy Elizabeth Amanda
72 310
Roswel **70** 151
Rufus **57** 290 **68** 258
Ruth **79** 73 **101** 212
S. H.C. **54** cvii
Sally **72** 288 304
Sam **104** 94
Samuel **55** 35 **56** 165 **72**
288 **77** 207 **83** 100
Samuel Elbert **72** 308 309
Samuel H. **73** 255
Samuel Haven **72** 309 311
Samuel Holman **72** 305
306
Sarah **72** 288 304-306 **77**
207 **81** 360 **82** 179 **127**
200
Sarah A. **86** 170
Sarah Elizabeth **72** 308
Sarah M. **68** 258 **78** 373
Sarissa **136** 247
Sebra **60** 397
Seth **79** 73
Shelumiel **80** 424
Shirley Gardner **72** 311
Sibyl Amanda **72** 310

MINER *cont'd*
Sidney Roby **56** xxxii 109
Simeon **136** 329 **142** 174
Sophronia Augusta
72 308
Stephen **55** 141 **79** 73
Susanna (Gifford)
138 218
Temperance **60** 397 398
Thankful **67** 130
Theoda **83** 112
Thomas **54** 41 **69** lx **72**
288 **77** 207 **78** 85 **81** 198
360 **82** 153 **89** 256 **100**
263 **131** 130 **138** 182-
185 **143** 362
Thomas R. **72** 308
Turner **81** 265
Unice **128** 20
Walter W. **75** 14
William **69** 202 **78** 385 386
79 73 **86** 170 **95** 366
138 183 184
William Avery **72** 310 311
William Harvey **73** 236
74 xxv
William Henry **84** 457
85 106 202
William Woodward
82 179
Willis Haven **72** 310
Ziba **70** 151
MINES Caroline (Rich)
84 129
John Flavel **107** 17
MINESORA Caroline E.
(Stephenson) **91** 385
William J. **91** 385
MINETT
Henry **115** 53 54
Mary **115** 53 54
Mary Jane **115** 53
MINGAY John **64** 219
Mary **51** 266
MINGE Ming
— Mr. **51** 40 41
John Henry **101** 125
Robert **104** 323
MINGINS Charles Robert
(Mrs.) **101** 125
MINGLES Abigail (Booker)
125 292
Asa **125** 292
MINGO **148** 188
Eli **53** 165
Esther **51** 163
Phebe **128** 29
Prince **128** 29
Violet **53** 165
William **51** 163
MINGUN
Anthony Henry
65 230
MINICUS
Arlina **111** 130 188
Catherine A. **111** 130
Matthias **111** 130
MINK Eliza **88** 335
L. **63** 95
Lucinda **90** 113
Mabel Gertrude **78** 205

MINK *cont'd*
Mary **133** 22
Mary (Feller / Fellows)
133 22
Oliver Willard (Mrs.) **77**
237 **78** 205 **89** 148 **90**
152 **91** 59
Peter **133** 22
Philip **133** 22
MINKEMA
Kenneth P. **148** 6
MINKLEROY
Benjamin **51** 461
Mehitable **51** 461
MINKS
Artie Francis **80** 151
Bert **80** 151
Elmer Albert **80** 151
Floyd Atwood **80** 151
Guy Marion **80** 151
Milton Harold **80** 151
Phebe Jane (Huff) **116** 181
Raymond Dow **80** 151
MINMA John **112** 295
MINNE Judith **128** 164
MINNERBY
Jane **114** 187
MINNICK
Anthony **91** 55
Eliza (Rogers) **91** 55
James Stanley **107** 149
Julia **91** 55
Ruth (Stephens) **107** 149
Sarah **128** 96
MINNS Minis Miniss
Minnis Mins
Constant Freeman **69** 99
Elizabeth **73** 265
Frances Ann **69** 99
George **85** 196
Grace Winchester **78** 131
James **63** 237
John **143** 258
Mary **90** 189
Nancy **125** 108
Polly **140** 169
Samuel **60** 349
Sarah **140** 169
Susanna **55** 420
Thomas **55** 420 **58** xvii
xx 12 **61** 397 **62** xxxv
lxxxiii **63** xxi lxxii **64** vi
xx xxix **65** vi xxii **67**
viii **68** xliii lxxix **69** 99-
101 **99** 189 **140** 169
William **78** 304 **112** 283
140 169
MINNY Thomas **93** 385
Minor *see* Miner
MINORD
Elizabeth **88** 283
MINOT Minott
—— **91** 263
— Mr. **63** 190 **93** 235
____ (Davis) **140** 169
____ (Dawes) **140** 59
____ (Fosdick) **140** 58
Abigail **52** 450 **68** 232
Albert Thomas **81** 353
Anna Lodge **79** 243
102 308

MINOT *cont'd*
Betsey **52** 470
Charles Sedgwick **93** 370
Charles Sedgwick (Mrs.)
  85 190 **93** 276 369 **94**
  142
Charles Vincent (Mrs.)
  99 148
Christopher **52** 470 **91** 93
Constance **79** 243
Elizabeth **52** 469 472 **55**
  147 **68** 219 **92** 55 **93** 235
  140 68
Elizabeth (Bartlett)
  108 311
Ellen Sears **81** 99
Eunice **68** 313
Francis **55** 148 423 **84** 382
  91 208 **95** 392
Francis (Mrs.) **98** 227
George **52** 98 450 469-473
  54 cxi **57** 280 388 **60** 39
  68 221 311 313 315 318
  320 **93** 275 **116** 111 **131**
  189 **137** 333 **140** 59
George R. **51** 476 477 **54**
  446 **140** 169 323 324
George Richards **91** 208
Grafton Winthrop **79** 243
Hannah **55** 147 **68** 230 **93**
  235 **140** 162 169
Harriet Gaut **67** xxxiv
Helen Louise **81** 353
Henry Whitney (Mrs.)
  81 99
James **52** 470 473 **57** 388
  62 33 **93** 235 **100** 221
  106 225 **109** 222 **136** 52
James Clark **140** 323
James Jackson **89** 97
  91 208
Jerusha **55** 400 **111** 106
John **52** 470 **53** 73 **55** 391
  57 280 **58** 158 **61** 358
  63 83 **68** 219 221 225
  228 230 232 311 315 **93**
  81 175 224 **94** 75 **105**
  276 **134** 145
John Clair **114** 264 265
John Marston **125** 23
John S. **56** 171 **87** 241
Jonas Clark **80** 277
Jonathan **66** 127
Joseph Grafton **52** 98 473
  59 xlviii **62** 198 **68** xxx
  70 vi **71** vi **72** vi **73** vi
  74 vi **75** vi **76** vi
Julia **55** 423 **95** 392 393
Katharine (Sedgwick)
  93 370
Lavina **88** 83
Love **86** 116
Lucy **108** 280
Lucy (Fosdick) **93** 369
Lydia **54** cxi
Martha **58** 404 **68** 225 320
  93 235 **106** 225
Martha (Lane) **93** 235
Martin Timothy **140** 169
Mary **80** 228 **84** 257
  140 323

MINOT *cont'd*
Mary (Kittredge) **98** 227
Mary (Speakman)
  140 169
Mary Augusta **108** 311
Mehitable **100** 221
Nathaniel **60** 40
Olive **112** 129
Otis **108** 311
Rebecca **53** 196
Rebecca (Blanchard) **91**
  263 **93** 235
Rebecca (Wheeler)
  106 225
Robert Sedgwick (Mrs.)
  85 196
Sally **84** 272
Samuel **55** 147 **77** 319
  126 10 **140** 58 68 162
  169
Sarah **52** 473 **56** 171 **58** 92
  93 235
Sarah Elizabeth **81** 353
Sarah Parkman **55** 423
Sarah Parkman (Blake)
  95 392
Sophia **68** 318
Stephen **51** 64 65 **52** 469
  470 473 **57** 280 389 **58**
  92 **67** 257 **84** 257 **99** 79
  116 111 **140** 169
Susanna (Sawtell)
  (Gilson) **126** 10
Thomas **52** 98
Timothy **91** 93 **113** 318
Timothy Martin **140** 169
Truecross **54** 213 **67** 257
Will **94** 234
William **54** lxix **66** 34-37
  91 208 **93** 80 81 370 **94**
  234 **140** 169
William Amory Gardner
  79 243 **102** 308 **114** 255
MINOTTO
James (Mrs.) **91** 296
MINPHEY Samuel **65** 30
Mins *see* Minns
MINSEE Grace (Russell)
  84 366
John **84** 366
MINSES Mary **126** 145
MINSHALL
Jeffrey **118** 248
Sarah **75** 140 141 **131** 208
William **75** 140 141
MINSHEW Thomas **72** 133
MINSHULL Ann **84** 450
Edward **84** 424
MINSON Lucretia (Sears)
  84 214
MINTER Desire **143** 209
  212 **147** 280
Elizabeth (Teal) **128** 269
Joseph **128** 269
Mary **128** 269
Sarah (Willet) **143** 209
William **143** 209
MINTHORN M. **97** 58
Maud Aileen **86** 197
Polly F. **119** 197
M'Intire *see* McIntire

MINTON Myntton
Alvan James **96** 288
Bertha Ann (Midgley)
  (Towne) **96** 288
Henry **143** 144
Marion Grace **86** 197
Telfair M. **108** 10
MINTURN Hannah **80** 81
Jonas **80** 81
Penelope **80** 81
William **127** 12
MINTY
Frank E. **69** 165
Minnie E. **69** 165
Minzee *see* Menzies
Minzie *see* Menzies
Minzies *see* Menzies
MIOT John **62** 301
MIRABEAU — M. **59** 334
MIRACH Sally **117** 222
MIRANDA Elizabeth
  (Andrews) **125** 289
Margaret **88** 285
Stephen **125** 289
MIRCH Julian **68** 57 58
Mires *see* Myers
MIRFIN Mirfyn
Edith **83** 456
Elizabeth **67** 68
John **83** 457
Robert **67** 68 69
William **83** 441 457
Miriam *see* Merriam
Mirick *see* Myrick
Mirik *see* Myrick
MIRMAN
Abraham Zalman
  99 330
Alexander **99** 330
Edith **99** 330
Edith (Markman) **99** 330
Elizabeth **99** 330
Ida **99** 330
Jacob **80** 333 **81** 219 **99** 68
  151 330
Joseph **99** 330
Raphiel **99** 330
Mirriam *see* Merriam
Mirrick *see* Merrick
Mirrill *see* Merrill
MIRTEN Sarah **90** 246
MISER Adam **118** 80
George **118** 80 **132** 76
Henry **118** 80
Johann Jorg **118** 73
John **118** 80
John George **118** 73
Joseph **118** 80 **132** 76
Rebecca **118** 80
Samuel **118** 80
Sophia (Beidler) **132** 76
Susan **132** 76
Wealthy **147** 68
Wealthy (Minard) **132** 76
Miserve *see* Meserve
Miservey *see* Meserve
MISES Dorothy **82** 422
MISGATT Henry **91** 201
MISH Fred J. (Mrs.)
  118 248
Mary Vernon **93** 96

MISH *cont'd*
  118 248
Misharve *see* Meserve
MISKELLY
  Kitty **60** 349
  Owen **60** 349
MISNER Peter **54** 423
MISON John **54** 278
MISPLEE
  Elizabeth **56** 209
  Thomas **56** 209 **68** 239
MISSELHORN Henry
  Gerhard (Mrs.) **85** 196
MISSEN Thomas **101** 50
MISSENDEN
  Elizabeth de **75** 132
MISSILLOWAY
  Daniel **90** 213
MISSIMER
  Hannah **124** 240
MISSROON Effie
  Verplanck **65** 38
  Frank Dupont **65** 38
  Gertrude **65** 38
  Hermann Hoffman **65** 38
  John Downes **65** 38
  John S. **65** 38
  Julia Emily **65** 38
  Julia Maria **65** 38
  Martha Louise **65** 38
  Mary Alice **65** 38
MISUE Susanna **105** 148
Mitchall *see* Mitchell
MITCHAM
  Christopher **65** 240
MITCHELL Mitchall
    Mitchel Mithcel
    Mithcell Mittchell
    Mychell
  —— **53** 137 297 **56** 114
    59 223 242 **68** 281 **76**
    254 261 **96** 228 **98** 207
    100 190 **120** 23 **121** 121
    136 211
  — Capt. **77** 63 105 **101** 271
  — Col. **91** 272 **136** 252
  — Judge **79** 308 407
  — Mr. **56** 367 **83** 379
    95 103
  — Mrs. **54** 267 423 425
    80 57
  —— (Watson) **120** 23
  —— (Wylies) **83** 415
  A. **80** 186 **89** 254
  A. C. **91** 330
  Aaron **56** 25
  Abiel **89** 38
  Abigail **58** 38 **63** 173 **82**
    461 **85** 164 168 **86** 22 **93**
    291 **99** 128 **107** 272 **109**
    166 **112** 232 **126** 84 **127**
    123
  Abigail (Dickens) **86** 178
  Abigail (Tupper) **99** 128
    123 131
  Abner **69** 304 **70** 10 299
    88 348 **99** 199 202
  Abner Woodell **89** 310
  Abraham **66** 154 **134** 293
    294
  Abram **66** 106

MITCHELL *cont'd*
  Adam **100** 142 **118** 249
  Addie May (Norris)
    89 115
  Adelbert **109** 270
  Agnes **73** 132 **82** 56 58 62
    91 263
  Agnes Mary **112** 313
  Albert **100** 189
  Albert Eliphalet **65** xxxvi
  Albertina **92** 228
  Albion Lewis **99** 202
  Alexander **73** 275 **111** 116
  Alexander F. **51** 246
  Alexander Fergurson
    73 289
  Alexius **73** 219
  Alfred **79** 168 **80** 61 186
    89 254 255 **114** 188
  Alfred G. **90** 32
  Alice **127** 94
  Alice (Bradford) **127** 94
  Alice Eunice **108** 135 **110**
    135 **113** 222
  Almeda P. **148** 174
  Almina **114** 184
  Alonzo **80** 309
  Althea **71** 15 **89** 199 200
  Amanda **80** 424 **109** 270
  Amasa **81** 265 **96** 200 201
  Amelia **73** 142
  Amy (Cumpton) **100** 297
  Andrew **56** 208 **77** 153
    86 104 **118** 43 46 47 56
    125 152
  Andrew B. **89** 351
  Andrew C. **88** 247
  Angeline **80** 424
  Ann **61** 54 **73** 148 **80** 78
    131 130 **148** 170 174
  Ann Eliza **75** 36
  Ann Hodge **105** 156
  Ann Loisa **99** 202
  Ann Maria **96** 201
  Ann S. **89** 351
  Anna **72** 287 **87** 123 **92** 104
    100 142 **109** 183 270
    122 106 **126** 84
  Anne **51** 391 **62** 260 **87** 246
  Anne (Peck) **105** 179
  Anne Maria **96** 201
  Annie **96** 71 **128** 115
  Annie Marie (Knowlton)
    110 225
  Anson **133** 270
  Arabella **90** 299
  Arabella M. **123** 153 154
  Ariana **100** 189
  Arnold **101** 94
  Asa **89** 15
  Asahel **85** 104
  Augustus **84** 37
  Bancroft **97** 69
  Barzillai B. **85** 422
  Benjamin **54** 351 **76** 170
    78 426 **82** 458-460 462
    91 272 **93** 283 **94** 360
    108 55 **111** 306 **114** 129
  Bera **109** 270
  Bertha Jane **81** 40
  Bethiah **80** 424

MITCHELL *cont'd*
  Bethiah (Lazell) **89** 15
  Betsey **71** 120 **83** 416
    133 283
  Billy **136** 323
  Boyce Spurgeon **103** 120
  Bradley **64** 117
  C. W. **114** 8
  Calvery **138** 118
  Caroline (Stoddard)
    136 323
  Caroline A. (Kimball)
    119 285
  Caroline Augusta
    (Hannum) **91** 46
  Caroline Elois **75** lviii
  Caroline Laura
    (Langdon) **85** 104
  Carter **79** 331
  Catherine **79** 308 **86** 181
    91 46 **99** 203 **106** 108
  Charity (Breese) **113** 279
  Charles **94** 165 **100** 189
    109 270 **114** 184
  Charles E. **90** 32
  Charles Edwin **84** 339 **85**
    188 **89** 115 **110** 220 225
  Charles Elliott **67** xxxi
  Charles Langdon **54**
    xxxvi **60** xxxiv **84** 180
    85 104 107 206
  Charles Lucius **112** 148
  Charles R. **148** 170 174
  Charlotte A. J. **75** 260
  Charlotte Frances **70** lviii
    76 lv
  Charlotte Jones **89** 116
  Chauncey Leeds **85** 104
  Christiana Drummond
    77 299
  Christopher **54** 351 **78**
    426 **81** 193 **93** 283 **148**
    187
  Clara **109** 270
  Clara (Beach) **88** 290
  Clarence Blair **81** 240
  Clarence Van Schaick
    (Mrs.) **89** 269
  Clarissa **109** 151
  Clement Adams **99** 202
  Constance **114** 215
  Constant **52** 55 **107** 308
    112 146 **136** 86 100 308
  Content A. **75** 36
  Cora B. **83** 436 438
  Craig Knowlton **110** 226
  Cynthia (Parkhurst)
    113 222
  D. F. **75** 15
  Daniel **70** 265 **93** 283 **107**
    201 270-272 274 **108** 55
    56 **122** 295 **128** 58
  David **61** 376 **65** 250 **69**
    136 **85** 104 100 189 **105**
    112 114 **116** 111 **125**
    179 **145** 366
  David Allen **113** 222
  Debby **114** 188
  Deborah **54** 351 **78** 426
    83 418 **88** 241 **126** 98

MITCHELL *cont'd*
Deborah (Andrews)
  109 151
Delilah **105** 147
Derius **128** 58
Desire **82** 463 **135** 141
Dianthe (Shaw) **90** 50
Dicy (Collins) **117** 40
Dolly **58** 39
Donald Grant **54** 401 **63**
  214 **80** 65
Donald Grant (Mrs.) **84**
  173 **85** 196
Donella **61** 383
Dorcas M. **90** 57
Dorothy **81** 491 **82** 62 461
Dorothy (Dickens) **86** 178
Dorothy (Hart) **111** 167
Dummer **96** 200-202 **107**
  275 **108** 55 122 **111** 227
Ebenezer **95** 195
Edith M. **147** 275
Edward **65** 307 **73** 267
  268 273 **78** 25 **80** 78 **107**
  177 **127** 94
Edward C. **55** 72 **59** 107
  108
Edward H. **75** 36
Edward Henry **93** 283
Eleanor **54** 351 **73** 223
  264 266
Eleanor Varnum **83** 174
Eleazer **85** 168
Electy **123** 31
Elijah **62** 266-268
Elisha **89** 15 **90** 50 **98** 268
  114 184 **128** 59
Eliza **61** 345 383 **73** 277
  79 358 **96** 200 202 **133**
  270
Eliza Ann **87** 375 **100** 245
Eliza Caroline **85** 104
Eliza Katharine **89** 193
Eliza Leeds (Silliman)
  85 104
Elizabeth **53** 375 **54** 351 **59**
  107 **60** 12 **61** 71 **62** 266
  63 lx 173-175 **73** 145 **75**
  lviii **78** 25 **80** 69 **81** 123
  128 **82** 462 463 **83** 428
  436 **85** 321 **89** 95 **90** 56
  298 **91** 186 **92** 47 **95** 358
  98 84 **105** 255 **106** 69
  107 179 **111** 116 **115** 62
  118 96 **121** 257 **122** 106
  211 213 **127** 94 95 **131**
  130
Elizabeth (Anthony)
  125 179
Elizabeth (Cole) **134** 293
Elizabeth (Curtiss) **85** 104
Elizabeth (Lamb) **121** 258
Elizabeth (Rend) **110** 226
Elizabeth (Simm) **86** 104
Elizabeth (Tenney)
  121 245
Elizabeth Adams **99** 203
Elizabeth Jane **90** 299
Elizabeth L. **92** 339
Elizabeth Trumbull
  (Miller) **136** 323

MITCHELL *cont'd*
Elkanah **99** 128 **123** 131
  127 123
Ella Grant (Wilson)
  144 315
Ellen Ann **90** 298 299
Ellen Douglas **81** 357
Emily Morton **76** lv
Emma (Newbury) **85** 375
Emma E. **75** 36
Emma Virginia **90** 299
Enoch F. **92** 339
Enoch L. **115** 319
Ephraim **108** 55 **128** 135
Erasmus **51** 395
Esther **68** 294 **69** 136 **70** 37
  75 182 **108** 192 **127** 94
Ethel (Kinney) **91** 46
Eunice **62** 267 **76** 254 **82**
  106 **98** 205 **121** 257
Experience **52** 216 **55** 439
  63 lx **65** 307 **74** liii **78**
  426 **81** 204 **82** 127 **94**
  241 **95** 358 **105** 179 **106**
  69 **107** 308 **114** 215 **127**
  94 95 **128** 58 **136** 77 100
  308 **143** 169
Ezekiel **128** 58
Fanny W. Pratt **100** 329
Flora **89** 351
Floyd **91** 46
Forest R. **83** 425 436
Frances **73** 144
Frances Lewis **93** 277 283
  94 143
Frances Merritt (Smith)
  97 69
Frances Tasker **79** 331
Francis **73** 147 **106** 108
Francis Ignatius **73** 264
Francis N. **99** 8
Francis W. **80** 424
Frederick M. (Mrs.)
  85 105
G. B. **91** 330
Gelston **126** 84
George **66** 35 **75** lviii **78**
  371 **81** 491 **82** 458 459
  462 463 **83** 87 **100** 189
  103 197 266 **105** 156
  178 266 **109** 270 274
  128 115 171 **145** 272
George Edwin **110** 225
  226
George Gorham **100** 189
  190
George W. **91** 330 **100** 329
George Washington
  127 62
Gertrude (Bancroft) **97** 69
Giles **75** 281
Godfrey **75** 281
Grace **75** lviii **96** 201
Grace (Huff) **96** 200
Grace (Smith) **96** 201
Grace M. **147** 277
Grace Webster **74** lv
H. E. **61** xliii
Hallett **135** 141
Hannah **63** lx **73** 228 **77**
  320 **79** 167 **80** 53 **81** 128

MITCHELL *cont'd*
  82 284 294 **88** 81 241 **99**
  128 **100** 336 **103** 188
  194 **108** 55 **125** 294 **126**
  98 **127** 94 95 123
Hannah (Anson) **125** 294
Hannah (Mayo) **113** 126
  126 96
Hannah (Sayward)
  123 153
Hannah (Tomson) **89** 15
Hannah B. **85** 373
Hannah Hart **90** 299
Hannah Hill (Belcher)
  110 226
Harold Nash **105** 145
Harold Nash (Mrs.) **88**
  169 **104** 238 **105** 132
  145 146
Harriet **79** 331 **80** 57 **88**
  356 **89** 11 **92** 45 **99** 201
Harriet (Rich) **84** 37
Harry E. **118** 249
Harvey **108** 78
Hattie **128** 262
Helen **109** 270
Henrietta **73** 271
Henry **64** 102 121 **81** 92 **82**
  284 294 **87** 375 **99** 133
  100 189 **111** 89
Henry H. **61** 233
Hepzibah **87** 246 **100** 189
  122 106
Horten **66** 303
Hugh **73** 132
Huldah **81** 265 **132** 269
Ida **122** 289
Ida Mount **112** 317
Irving Byron **144** 315
Isaac **85** 447 **87** 123 **88**
  345 347-355 357 **99** 199-
  202 **100** 190 **120** 215
  122 106 213
Isaac L. **99** 203
Isaac Lee **88** 355 **99** 200
Isabell (Roberts) **97** 235
Isabella (Bragdon) **114** 48
J. **96** 201
J. C. **91** 330
J. H. **76** 52
Jack **70** 304
Jack K. **96** 275
Jacob **59** 107 **70** 296 **91** 46
  127 94 203
James **57** 154 **60** 28 **63**
  170 175 **71** 120 **73** 274
  75 lviii **76** 46 249 **78** 188
  303 **81** 40 **87** 246 **90** 285
  99 128 **100** 189 **107** 196
  108 55 **111** 116 **112** 18
  114 191 **116** 65 **122** 106
  211 **125** 179 **126** 64 **127**
  144 228
James C. **88** 247 **89** 351
James Evans **112** 313
James Henry **74** lv
James L. **83** 174
James Lynde **83** 174
James Madison **89** 116
James W. **125** 244
Jane **60** 152 **64** 121 **68** lxxi

MITCHELL *cont'd*
74 lxiv 78 426 81 204 82
127 104 201 111 246
112 22 118 249
Jane (Cooke) 105 179
106 69 127 94 95 136 77
Jane (Kennedy) 116 65
Jane (Smith) 147 277
Jane (Walton) 91 33
Jeanette 145 272
Jefferson Button 88 290
Jemima 81 193 119 199
Jennie Irene (Olds) 93 283
Jeremiah 82 461 85 422
111 116
Jerusha 63 156
Jethro 100 189 112 148
122 106 212
Jethro F. 122 213 295
Jianet (Jordan) (Berni)
97 69
Joanna 54 351 66 149 78
426 105 222 111 227
122 213 125 180 127 64
134 254
John 51 467 469 52 118 263
54 351 55 101 420 56 63
186 59 215 63 18 65 34
69 136 70 37 72 287 73
140 149 152 273 74 100
75 lviii 120 122 260 76
46 192 249 254 79 55 81
87 488 489 491 82 58-60
62 127 458 460 461 463
83 313 85 104 347 89
223 92 60 93 77 94 334
96 200-202 100 143 239
273 103 258 270 104
201 202 105 180 106
199 107 179 197 108
124 111 205 227 246
114 128 115 63 120 64
122 106 212 213 125 99
102 294 127 94 128 58
129 134 225 136 27 77
138 116 140 169 145
272 273 146 328 147
175
John Charles 90 299
John J. 75 lviii
John Kearsley 80 105 206
104 239 105 131
John Michael 66 1
John R. 100 189 144 315
John W. 91 46
John Watson 120 18
Jonathan 53 245 370 54
267 422-425 58 320 64
131 82 461 86 178 179
183 95 207 386 110 236
129 359 136 148
Joseph 54 410 56 124 63
175 66 149 151 154 303
73 267 78 426 79 358
80 53 82 127 458-464
83 87 86 178 179 183 88
241 93 283 105 164 106
108 108 55 111 116 114
48 116 128 117 141 142
121 257 122 106 295
126 84 98 127 94 142

MITCHELL *cont'd*
144 206 148 169
Joseph B. 85 375
Joseph F. 97 235
Joseph Whitman 89 351
Joshua 63 14 90 336 91 25
Josiah 83 35
Jotham 87 206
Juda (Crosley) 125 102
Judith 52 235 263 73 287
78 67 85 374 101 276
107 275 108 55
Judith (Dorman) 108 122
Julia 79 331 114 191
Julia (Young) 120 215
Julia Clark 54 cii
Justus 85 104
Karl Maurice 105 129
114 69
Kate L. 125 286
Katharine (Sedgley)
91 25
L. G. 142 231
L. M. 80 186 89 254
Laura 81 204
Laura A. 121 310 122 230
Lavina (Clarke) 85 422
Lavinia Hathaway 74 lv
Lawrence C. (Mrs.)
111 167
Lemuel 119 286
Lena 91 53
Leola A. 147 275
Lewis 79 164 407 88 352
99 200
Lewis (Mrs.) 107 134
Lewis W. 92 228
Libbie 69 166
Lilla 90 285
Lois 82 460
Lorenzo Dow 110 226
Louisa 99 149
Lovinia D. B. 88 241
Lucinda 80 419 109 270
Lucinda Elizabeth 75 lvii
lviii
Lucretia 59 377 80 186
89 255
Lucretia W. 80 186 89 255
Lucy 63 173 75 122 82 274
107 270 108 123 191
135 16
Lucy (Newbury) 85 374
Lucy Ann 73 154
Lyal 70 306
Lydia 62 261 268 75 120
122 79 273 90 298 299
94 173 95 386 96 200
108 55 126 84
Lydia (Sewall) 111 227
114 128
Lydia P. (Parker) 114 8
Lydia S. 80 309
M. Nellie 92 339
Malinda E. 121 181
Margaret 65 307 68 95
73 275 82 458-464 86
74 87 375 105 179 254
255 263 116 285 120 23
Margaret (Mitchell)
87 375

MITCHELL *cont'd*
Margaret (Rathbone)
105 179
Margaret (Williams)
(Stocking) 136 86 100
Margaret Bartlett
(Tenney) 85 104
Margery 63 170 175
Marguerite L. (Chesley)
83 425 436
Maria 65 307
Marie 100 273 120 23
Mark 63 16 113 222
Mark Lincoln 83 348
Martha 56 186 208 61 70
88 241 348 352 355-357
97 389 99 199-202 136
323 146 374
Martha (Sherman) 85 104
Martha (Wylie) 83 415
Martha D. 75 35
Martha M. 75 36
Martha R. 125 292
Martin Van Buren
147 277
Mary 54 351 56 128 62 189
63 270 66 142 149 151
154 69 328 71 120 72
287 73 148 149 217 75 7
14 15 82 294 300 461
463 83 87 86 104 91 262
263 380 96 200-202 100
143 189 239 303 106 313
107 196-199 272 273
109 270 274 111 246
112 92 113 223 114 184
117 163 185 122 106
125 219 126 84 127 94
145 272 148 169
Mary (Bonney) 89 223
127 94
Mary (Callender) 144 206
Mary (Dickens) 86 183
Mary (Fairfield) 96 200
201
Mary (George) 105 164
Mary (Hayward) 127 94
Mary (Lathrop) 127 94
Mary (Lazell) 89 310
Mary (McKean)
(Westover) 117 101
Mary (Prior) 127 94
Mary (Smith) 96 200 201
108 124
Mary (Starbuck) 112 148
144 206
Mary (Stuart) 89 310
Mary (Suter) 112 148
Mary (Wales) 125 244
126 21
Mary A. 118 244
Mary Abbie (Cross)
89 351
Mary Alden 64 122
Mary Ann 57 xxxv 114
65 188
Mary B. 94 165
Mary Cornelia 99 202
Mary Elizabeth 69 328
78 48 81 386

MITCHELL *cont'd*
Mary Elliott (Atkinson)
  97 69
Mary Frances **70** lviii
Mary J. **89** 254 **120** 67
Mary J. (Obear) **85** 377
Mary Jane **120** 66
Mary Jane (Moulton)
  119 286
Mary L. **93** 201
Mary M. **90** 347
Mary P. **80** 186
Mary R. (Dickins) **144** 315
Mary Ruth **90** 298 299
Massy Ann **73** 222
Matilda **88** 283
Matthew **54** 235 **85** 104
  131 130
Matthew Freeman **78** 52
Maude Elizabeth **88** 290
May J. **120** 67
Medad **99** 128
Mehitable **78** 426 **82** 460
  461 **111** 306 **118** 96
Mehitable (Bragdon)
  114 129
Mehitable (Pool) **118** 96
Melzah / Melzer **99** 133
Mercy **63** 174 **74** 100
Mercy (Dunlng) **115** 63
Mercy Damon (Briggs)
  127 62
Meroby H. **83** 146
Middleton **73** 153
Miles **75** 35
Minerva **82** 276
Minnie J. **128** 171
Minnie Murphy **78** 48
Minot **85** 104
Miriam **54** 351 **115** 139
Molly **82** 287 294 **107** 198
  199
Mordecai **82** 463
Mordica Miles **73** 138
Nabby (Lazell) **89** 11
Nahum **52** 362 **53** 431 **65**
  189 **72** 201 **74** lv **89** 11
  93 161 **94** 242 **99** 8 **102**
  86 **114** 22 **115** 84 **116**
  310 **124** 54 152 **134** 49
  141 297 **145** 43
Nancy **58** 19 **64** 117 **89** 36
  99 202
Nancy (Tuker) **125** 99
Nancy A. (Montgomery)
  128 171
Naomi (Dickens) **86** 179
Natalie Laura **93** 138
Nathan **99** 128
Nathaniel **82** 463 **97** 20
  108 55 **114** 188
Nehemiah **117** 279
Nicholas **100** 297
Norman **109** 270 **116** 65
Obed **133** 137
Olive (Root) **85** 104
Oliver F. **91** 33
Olivia Ann **79** 331
Olzira **83** 24 26
Ormsby MacKnight
  81 330

MITCHELL *cont'd*
Otis **85** 349
Paul **100** 51 161 189
Pauline **109** 270
Perley **112** 320
Pernal (Jenney) **117** 185
Peter **96** 228 **117** 101 **122**
  213 **125** 244 **126** 21
Peter G. W. **125** 244
Peternell **106** 92 **107** 179
Phebe **56** 63 **99** 133 **100**
  189 **127** 133 **136** 77
Phebe (Coffin) **100** 189
Phebe (Lewis) **112** 320
Philemon Libby **88** 357
  99 201
Philena **61** 81
Philip **58** 19
Philip Whitman **89** 351
Polly **56** 63 **63** 175 271 **73**
  267 **83** 416 **96** 146 **100**
  239 **114** 180 **119** 60
Polly (McKean)
  (Westover) **117** 101
Polly (Perce) **111** 116
Polly (Simmons) **111** 116
Priscilla **73** 223 **79** 331
Rachel **73** 262 **89** 193 194
Rachel Elisa (Cooper)
  120 18
Ray Wesley **91** 46
Rebecca **77** 320 **79** 159
  170 308 **80** 66 **81** 193 **82**
  463 **90** 298 299 **119** 111
  124 225 **126** 84 **128** 285
Rebecca (Cook) **126** 84
Rebecca (Sawyer) **90** 299
Rebecca (Ulmer) **89** 116
Rebecca Sawyer **90** 299
Rector **73** 232
Reuben **90** 298 **123** 153
Rhoda **54** 450 **57** 154 **73**
  286 **122** 211
Rhoda (Gray) **134** 294
Rhoda Ann **81** 357
Rhoda Freeman **73** 289
Rhoda Susan **125** 292
Richard **54** 351 410 **64** 216
  70 lviii **76** lv **100** 189
  107 196-199 273 **110**
  285 **112** 148 **122** 104
  106 213 **126** 21 **127** 144
  307 **144** 206
Richard Tasker **79** 331
Rita Rend **110** 226
Robert **51** 395 **54** 450 **79**
  331 **83** 415 **85** 378 **105**
  284 **110** 288 **118** 249
  120 23 159
Robert Bladen **79** 331
Robert Logan **78** 48
Robert Stewart **112** 148
Roger **54** 410 **63** 173
  111 228
Rosanna **134** 332
Rosella Putnam (Frisbie)
  113 222
Rotheus **93** 397 **100** 63
Royal **70** 306
Rue Burcham **113** 222
Russell **61** 384

MITCHELL *cont'd*
Ruth **76** 170 **90** 298 **126** 84
Ruth (Charlton) **85** 105
Ruth (Winslow) **135** 141
S. Weir **96** 275
Saba **128** 285
Sally **61** 376 384 **94** 120
  108 190 **116** 139
Sally (Gerrish) **117** 141
  142
Sally (Pineo) **85** 349
Sally Coles Stevenson
  (Colston) **83** 348
Samuel **54** 351 445 **63** 18
  70 170 **73** 218 270 **82**
  463 **87** 206 **91** 330 **100**
  189 190 **113** 279 **118** 49
  50 **126** 84 **128** 224 **145**
  355
Samuel Augustus **81** 357
Samuel Finley **78** 48
Samuel H. **88** 241
Sarah **51** 57 **52** 235 **54** 351
  56 186 **59** 215 61 351
  63 14 **73** 153 270 271
  275 **75** 260 **78** 426 **80** 53
  82 127 284 294 460 461
  463 **83** 377 **84** 121 **89** 39
  95 394 **96** 200 375 **106**
  313 **107** 201 270-272 274
  108 55 56 **109** 151 **110**
  285 288 **111** 228 **114**
  129 **120** 159 **122** 211
  127 94 **131** 315 **134** 100
  294 **136** 77 **148** 187
Sarah (Andrews) **93** 283
Sarah (Littlefield) **95** 195
Sarah (Mahurin) **136** 27
Sarah (McKee) **94** 165
Sarah (Sellers) **115** 62
Sarah Ann **86** 313
Sarah E. **77** 148
Sarah H. **94** 201 202
Sarah Harris **89** 15 **94** 201
Sarah Jane **77** 153
Sarah Jane (Mills) **112** 313
Sarah L. **97** 234 235
Sarah Loring **113** 297
Sarah M. **90** 114
Sarah March **99** 202
Sarah Tabitha **78** 51 52
Selden **126** 84
Serene **103** 300
Seth **69** 328 **78** 426 **100** 189
  109 151
Silas Weir **65** 195
Simeon **75** 182
Sina **61** 383
Solomon **78** 426 **111** 305
Sophia **79** 331 **108** 55
Sophia Peters **73** 132
Spencer **73** 231 267
Stella Josephine **61** 233
Stephen **79** 308 **80** 424
  108 56
Stephen M. **79** 158
Stephen Mix **66** 23 **80** 61
  65 69
Stewart **84** 232 **85** 196 350
  104 318 **109** 62 125 **112**
  72

MITCHELL cont'd
Sumner **96** 201
Susan **73** 278
Susan (Hancock) **125** 103
Susan (Wood)
 (Butterfield) **131** 130
Susan Ann **134** 134
Susan Hyde (Burleigh)
 96 228
Susanna **52** 74 **53** 163 **54**
 351 **55** 420 **63** 173 **73**
 142 **89** 12 **105** 164
Susanna (Pope) **127** 94
Sylva **62** 266
Tabitha **63** 173
Temple **82** 294 300
Thalia McMahon **68** 281
Theadora **73** 135
Theodore **114** 188
Theodore M. **75** 36
Thomas **51** 161 **52** 263 **59**
 107 **60** 399 **61** 70 **62** 246
 64 129 333 **65** 307 **73**
 136 140 144 229 278 **75**
 281 **81** 128 **82** 457-464
 86 73 74 178 **96** 272 274
 97 312 **100** 140 **105** 175
 179 180 254 255 263 **111**
 246 **119** 285 **122** 83 **124**
 225 **127** 94 95 **128** 135
 285 **131** 130 **136** 86 100
 211
Thomas G. **112** 148
Thomas I. **91** 330
Thomas Lee **73** 153
Thomas Mayo **113** 126
Thomas W. **89** 299
Top: **112** 284
Truman **109** 270
Virginia (Baker) **105** 145
Virginia B. **88** 169 **104** 238
Virginia Baker **105** 146
W. K. (Mrs.) **118** 236
Walter **79** 304 403 **91** 53
Warren **80** 424
Webster C. **75** 36
William **51** 391 395 **52** 263
 56 186 **60** 242 **62** 248
 264 268 **63** 173 271 **65**
 117 **73** 154 **75** 6 **85** 375
 90 298 299 **97** 69 **105**
 282 **111** 246 **112** 287
 113 126 **114** 184 **115** 62
 227 **117** 40 185 **118** 43
 46 47 96 **121** 245 **122**
 295 **125** 103 **126** 96 98
 133 270 **145** 351
William De Witt **97** 69
William J. **114** 188
William James **83** 174
William Lawton **62** 113
William Lendrum
 136 323
William Sawyer **90** 299
Willie Lewis **93** 283
Willie M. **109** 270
Wilmot Brookings
 107 159
Zebulon D. **88** 241
Zephaniah **73** 265 272
 80 424

MITCHELSON
Edward **74** 243
Ruth **74** 243 **90** 290
Susanna **72** 319
MITCHEM
Granville **82** 180
Malinda Melissa **82** 180
Rebecca **82** 180
Sylvanus **82** 180
Timothy Simeon **82** 180
William Frederick **82** 180
MITCHINER
William Arthur
 101 125
MITCHINSON
William **64** 23
MITFORD —— **54** 192
Baron Redesdall **56** 327
Constance (Ogle) **104** 273
Eleanor **132** 47
Jasper **132** 46
Jessica **148** 292
John **104** 273
Margaret **132** 46
Margery **104** 273
Robert **104** 273 **132** 47
MITFORD-BARBERTON
I. **89** 305
Mithcel see Mitchell
Mithcell see Mitchell
MITNER Robert **64** 106
MITSON John **64** 320
Mittchell see Mitchell
MITTELSTADT Dorothea
 (Wells) **114** 81
John David Peter **114** 81
O. L. (Mrs.) **114** 81
MITTELSTAEDT-
 KUBASECK Carla
 148 183
MITTEN
Elizabeth **89** 309
Marah (Kidd) **89** 311
Samuel **89** 311
Sarah Jane **89** 311
MITTIMORE
— Rev. Mr. **82** 416
MITTING
Ebenezer **61** 240
Sally **61** 240
MITTLEBERGER
Francis **87** 335
Lucy (Chase) **87** 335
MITTLEBURG
— Miss **101** 166
MITTON De Mitton
 Mytton
Ann (Skrymsher) **101** 89
Constance (Beaumont)
 101 89
Dorcas **104** 177
Edward **101** 89-91
John **101** 89
Katharine **101** 87 89 90
Margaret (de Pesale)
 101 89
Michael **101** 17 **104** 177
Richard **71** 326 **101** 89
 110 170
Roger **59** 219
Thomas **101** 89 **110** 170

MITZOR Mahalia **128** 175
MIVILLE Ernest **116** 246
MIX —— **72** 98
— Mr. **56** 137 **72** 95 96
— Rev. **143** 308 318 320
 324
Abigail **59** 69
Ann **70** 108 **132** 243
Artemisia **61** 272 274
Aurella **132** 243
Benjamin **132** 243
Caleb **57** 135 **66** 201
Caroline **69** 161
Caroline Bessie Belle
 85 191
Charles F. **95** 331
Clifton H. **72** xx
Dan **132** 243
Daniel **61** 395
Deborah **61** 311
Dorcas **132** 243
Dorothy **70** 108 **127** 239
Elihu **69** 161
Elisha **61** 274 **132** 243
Elizabeth **59** 68 69 **81** 126
Elo **132** 243
Ephraim **132** 243
Esther **59** 69 **68** 276 **71** 6
Ethan **132** 243
Eunice (Aylsworth)
 101 174
Freelove **132** 243
Hannah **60** 166 **61** 118 **70**
 108 **78** 433 **85** 337
Henry **132** 243
Hester **81** 126 127
Irene **93** 134
Irene Howe **92** 147
James **72** 98 **81** 127
John **59** 68 66 201 **68** 276
 71 6 **81** 126 **132** 243
Joseph **59** 69 **61** 118 **71** 8
Lucinda **132** 243
Lucy **70** 93
Lydia **61** 395
Mary **57** 135 **58** 304
 115 294
Mary L. (Shapleigh)
 95 331
Mercy **59** 69
Minnie **70** 85
Moses **132** 243
Myrtle M. **117** 129
Noble **101** 174
Polly **61** 274
Rachel **61** 284
Rebecca **59** 68 66 201
Rufus **127** 239
Sarah **58** 304 **65** 64 **66** 201
 71 8
Sibyl **72** 220
Stephen **59** 69 **75** 178
Temperance **112** 58
Theophilus **132** 243
Thomas **59** 68 **61** 311 395
 70 108 **127** 239
Timothy **58** 304
William **65** 64
Zerviah **75** 178
MIXAN —— **98** 20
MIXER Abagail **124** 38

MIXER cont'd
Abigail **66** 178 179 **124** 38
Abigail (Fobes) **102** 159
Adam **66** 178
Almira **70** xxxvii
Amy **63** 277 **66** 179
Ann **102** 159
Anna **65** 380 **66** 178 179
Anne **77** 289
Betty **115** 37
Charles Galloupe (Mrs.)
  77 322
Charles T. **92** 322
Daniel **79** 48
Dorothy **63** 277 **65** 380
  66 178 179
Edmund **66** 179
Electa Johnston **70** xxxvii
Elizabeth **66** 178 179
Esther A. (Durgin) **89** 351
Eunice **77** 315
Frances **63** 277 **66** 178 179
Francis **66** 178
George **63** 277 **65** 380 **66**
  178 179 **124** 37
Horace **70** xxxvii
Horace F. **89** 351
Isaac **63** 277 **65** 74 380 **66**
  178 179 187 **77** 272
Jane **63** 277 **65** 380 **66** 178
  179
Joel **77** 314
John **63** 277 **66** 178 179
  78 70
Joseph **77** 289 **109** 306
Josiah **127** 291
Judith **56** 35
Julia F. (Durgin) **89** 351
Julius **102** 159
Laura **102** 159 **105** 65
Lois **78** 183 **127** 291
Louis **102** 159
Lura Lucille **69** 203
Lydia **63** 277 **66** 179 **77**
  228 **115** 34 **116** 80
Mary **63** 277 **66** 178 179
  77 272 273 289 **109** 306
Mary C. **124** 36
Moses **115** 36
Nellie **89** 351
Nellie (Mountfort) **89** 351
Phineas **102** 159
Rebecca **53** 357 **66** 179
Robert **66** 178
Rupert A. **89** 351
Ruth (Doten) **124** 37
Samuel J. (Mrs.) **77** 324
Sarah **63** 277 **65** 380 **66** 178
  179 **77** 272 273 **83** 478
  93 185
Sarah (Mead) **127** 291
Susan **66** 178 179
Thomas **63** 277
William **66** 179
William R. **89** 351
MIXSON
John Leslie **125** 262
MIXTER Meixter
—— **62** 22 135
— Col. **62** 21 133
Anne (Dudley) **99** 252

MIXTER cont'd
Charles Galloupe **81** 348
Charles Galloupe (Mrs.)
  78 205
Daniel **131** 317
David Mason **97** 53
Deborah (Brown) **131** 317
Dorothy (Fay) **97** 53
Elizabeth **61** 341
Elizabeth Elliot **97** 53
Esther **116** 316
George **81** 348
George Gilbert **60** 307
Helen Worthington
  78 205
Henry Fay **97** 53
Jacob **97** 137
James **62** 24
Lucy **62** 20
Madeleine Curtis
  61 xxxiv
Maria Annunciate **60** 308
Mary **81** 348 **87** 282
Samuel **62** 20 **81** 348
  99 252
Samuel J. **58** cx
Samuel Jason **59** xliv **81**
  347 348 **97** 53
Wilhelmina (Galloupe)
  58 cx **80** 217 **81** 347 348
  97 53
William **62** 135 **81** 348
William Jason **81** 348 **84**
  340 **85** 197 **97** 53 391
MIXTURE
Joseph **77** 235
Sarah Ann (Payn) **97** 137
MIZE
Harlan Edgar (Mrs.)
  107 229
MIZENER Cora **109** 73
MIZER Lloyd E. **121** 156
M'KAYE see also McKay
Jane **111** 80
Mary (Adams) **111** 80
M'Kenzie see McKenzie
M'Lane see McLean
M'Lellan see McClellan
M'Mullen see McMullen
M'Murphy see McMurphy
M'Neil see McNeil
MOAK
Elizabeth Winnie
  128 269
Henry **128** 269
Nettie E. **128** 269
MOAL Johannah (Hore)
  100 240
Samuel **100** 240
MOANAM **144** 213 214
MOANE John **100** 287
MOARES Susan M. **126** 67
MOARN Elizabeth
  (Lindley) **100** 304
William **100** 304
MOARY John **129** 58
MOAT William J. **84** 30
MOBBERLY
Elizabeth **73** 222
Hezekiah **73** 221
Mary **73** 154

MOBBEY John **78** 393
MOBBS John **67** 136
  82 286 294
Jonathan **99** 284
Lucy **80** 434
Lydia (Gaines) **85** 52
Polly **80** 434
Richard **99** 284
Samuel **80** 434 **85** 52
Sarah **99** 284
Tabitha **66** 146 **82** 286 294
MOBLEY Ann **73** 277
Beney **73** 268
James **73** 266
Jonathan **73** 217
MOCECUP **63** 328 329
MOCK Adam **110** 175
Allen **140** 169
Andrew J. **140** 169
James **110** 175
Mercy **115** 62 **131** 235
Sarah **110** 175
Sarah (Rankin) **110** 175
Susanna **125** 109
William **140** 169 328
  143 260
MOCKBEE Mockeboy
Alexander **73** 262 266
Ann **73** 138
Basil **73** 138
Breck **73** 149
Darkey **73** 152
Eleanor **73** 144
Hickerson **73** 277
John **73** 134
Linna **73** 226
Mary **73** 228
Matilda **73** 268
Nelly **73** 276
Philip **73** 264
Rachel **73** 136
Rebecca **73** 222
Sarah **73** 228 232
Virlinda **73** 217
William **73** 138 139
MOCKLAR Anna
Katharina **138** 229
Catherine **138** 229
Jacob **138** 229
John Philip **138** 229
Margarette Christina
  138 229
Philip **138** 229
MOCKRIDGE
Hannah **76** 263
Lavinia I. **96** 167
William **76** 263
MODENA
— Duke of **77** 259
MODERN
Ada Johnson **105** 318
Modey see Moody
MODION Patrick **76** 46
MODLEY Rebecca
  (Marchant) **100** 190
Thomas **100** 190
MODRICKER George R.
  (Mrs.) **118** 329 330
MODSLY Thomas **59** 106
Modye see Moody

MODYFORD
Thomas **109** 96
MOE Beryl (Packard)
104 132
John Gregor (Mrs.) **104**
127 144
Mercy **107** 298
Pluma (Barton) **107** 298
Silas **107** 298
MOELLERS
Margaret **85** 70
Vincent **85** 70
MOENS W. J.C. **59** 52
MOERY Caroline **109** 111
MOES E. W. **106** 7
MOESER Jessie **113** 308
MOFFATT Mofet Moffat
Moffet Moffett Moffit
Moffitt Muffet Muffit
Muffitt
—— **60** 355 **117** 14
143 366
— Dr. **63** 53
Abbot Low **81** 111 222
117 315
Abigail **129** 316
Alexander W. (Mrs.)
111 83
Altania (Wilson) **102** 304
Alton Reid **82** 433
Amanda Malvina **77** 183
Angelina **138** 121
Anna Robson
(McCartney) **112** 4
Antoinette S. (Jones)
88 334
Aquila **113** 53
Benjamin **63** 361
Burnham **64** 293
Catherine **58** 233
Charles C. **70** 155
Charles Denny **72** xxxvii
Charles Todd **72** xxxviii
Cornelia (Dopp) **90** 378
Cynthia Whitney **89** 324
David **113** 53
David George **75** xvii
Dorothy Lake (Gregory)
102 65
Earle Mortimer
72 xxxviii
Edith Hill **101** 332
Edith L. (Hill) **101** 332
Edward Stewart **112** 4
Eleanor Stewart **112** 4
Eleazer **70** 155
Eliza **68** 155
Elizabeth **58** 233 **66** 130
131 **76** 110 184 260 **129**
316
Elizabeth H. **75** xvii
Ella Bowman **72** xxxviii
Emily D. **70** 155
Emily Hayman **72** xxxvii
Enoch **54** 74
Eunice (Young) **126** 233
129 316
Eva L. **107** 238 318 **108** 55
157 **109** 157
Eva Louise **72** xx **102** 304
103 77 124

MOFFATT *cont'd*
Frances **57** 286 **126** 233
129 316
Frances Pamela
72 xxxviii
Frances Smith **72** xxxviii
Freda A. **70** 155
George W. **70** 155
Godfrey **77** 183
Grace Emily **72** xxxviii
Hannah **64** 23 **113** 53
Hannah (Battin) **114** 293
Helen **83** 344
Huldah **79** 335
Irene Louise **82** 433
James **117** 9 16
Jeannette Todd
72 xxxviii
Jeremiah **69** xxxv
Jesse **80** 85
Jessie **70** 155
Johanna **76** 184
John **58** 233 **64** 293 294
76 110 184 260 **82** 49 **84**
265 **85** 131 **129** 316
John C. **109** 192
John Fletcher **70** xix **72**
xxx xxxvii xxxviii
John Tufton **89** 198
Jonathan **102** 304
Joseph **72** xxxvii **102** 304
105 289
Joseph L. **88** 334
Julia Ann **129** 316
Lieze S. **119** 238
Lois Amanda **120** 155
Macajah **128** 58
Malinda Frances **133** 268
Mary **64** 23
Mary Elizabeth **110** 225
Mary Jane **115** 121
Mary Tufton **89** 198
Melvin **102** 304 **107** 238
Millie H. **98** 283
Nancy (Treadway)
102 304
Nancy Jane (Stice) **133** 268
Nancy Maria **107** 238
Nannie Marie (Britton)
102 304
Phebe **70** 155
Rachel Maria
(Brinkerhoff) **129** 316
Reuben Burnham **59**
xliv 113 **65** xxxv **67** 302
68 xxxii **75** 90
Rhody **80** 85
Robert **70** 263
Robert H. **101** 332
Robert Tucker **82** 123 237
Ross **83** 513
Ross E. (Mrs.) **102** 65
Salome **56** 77
Sam **90** 378
Samuel **66** 33 **114** 293
118 313
Samuel Cutt **89** 198
Sarah **114** 80
Sarah (White) **102** 304
Sarah B. (Decamp) **111** 83

MOFFATT *cont'd*
Sarah Catherine (Mason)
89 198
Sarah Knapp (Marshall)
(Freeland) **109** 192
Tamar **107** 36
Thomas Spencer **102** 304
W. A. **98** 181
William **56** 77 **60** 188 **64**
23 **70** 155 **72** xxxvii
102 304 **126** 233 **129**
316
William A. **70** 155
William Fountain
133 268
William G. **78** 181
William H. **70** 155
Willie A. **70** 155
MOFFEWE
Abigail **82** 288 294
Moffit *see* Moffatt
Moffitt *see* Moffatt
Mog *see* Mogg
MOGER Jehiel **137** 78
Jemima **137** 78
Noah **126** 256
Phebe **126** 256
MOGG Mog
Dorothy **77** 76 115-117
84 273
John Valentine **83** 311
Richard **77** 115-117
Valentine **83** 311
William **77** 76 115-117
84 273
MOGGIN Peggy **133** 263
MOGGS Petter **143** 262
MOGRAGE Mogredge
Mogridge Morgrage
Benjamin **82** 211 213 324
Burridge **110** 286
John **80** 352 **110** 286
Lorana **91** 230
Lydia **52** 75
Mary **110** 286 **114** 133
Mary (Whitten) **110** 286
Peter **105** 211
Sarah **110** 286
Simeon **105** 288
Thomas **54** 409
William **91** 230 **110** 286
MOHAN
Emily Elizabeth **76** 21
MOHAT
Elizabeth **132** 245
Elizabeth A. **132** 245
Francis **132** 245
Mary **132** 245
MOHEGAN Rudy **148** 294
MOHLER Hannah **99** 45
Rebecca **76** lxxviii
Sarah **86** 333 **114** 186
Sarah (Galley) **114** 186
MOHO Jereniah **114** 182
MOHR
John George **65** 243
Michael A. **129** 87
Wilson (Caroline) **129** 87
MOHRBACH
Mary W. **107** 170
Sadie **107** 170

MOHRING Ellen **128** 176
MOHUN - De Mohun
—— **141** 96 99 **145** 267
Alice **103** 21 23 24 **139**
283 286 287
Alice (Briwere) **103** 23
Alice (Tiptoft) **103** 21
Baldwin **103** 22
Deborah **103** 161
Eleanor **103** 22
Elizabeth **96** 186 **103** 23
Elizabeth (Fitz Rogers)
103 22
Hervey **103** 22
John **103** 21-23
John (Lord) **103** 21 24
Juliana **103** 23
Laurence **103** 22
Margaret **80** 365
Mariot **103** 23
Mary **103** 22
Maximilian **103** 21 22
Patrick **103** 22
Payn **103** 22
Reginald **139** 286
Reynold **103** 21 23 24
Richard **103** 21-23
Robert **80** 365 **103** 21 22
Thomas **103** 22-24
William **103** 23 24
Mohurin see Mahurin
MOIES Edward **60** 40
John **61** 43 **140** 328
MOIGNE Thomas **116** 172
MOIR
Alexander **66** 367
Alexander James (Mrs.)
85 190 **106** 117 **107** 136
Alexander L. **66** 367 **68**
xxxii 111
Andrew **63** 27
James **63** 27 **66** 367
Jane **62** 247
Robert **66** 367
Ruth **100** 139
MOISE — Widow **84** 77
Abraham **116** 313
Frederic Stith (Mrs.)
105 129
Harold **116** 313
John **128** 165
Marie **128** 165
Sarah **116** 313
MOISER
Lancelot **113** 191
MOLAN James **63** 240
73 139
MOLAND
Daniel **100** 296
Margaret (Mills) **100** 296
William **64** 107
MOLAS
J. Sala **109** 174 175
Molay see De Molay
MOLDEN Henry **127** 12
Moldoon see Muldoon
MOLDS Samuel **72** 236
MOLDSON
Isabell **83** 463
Thomas **83** 449 463
MOLE James **91** 330

MOLE cont'd
William **98** 36
Molenaux see Molineaux
MOLENS Return **139** 300
MOLER —— **57** 121
MOLES
Mary **97** 55 **101** 50
MOLESWORTH
— Capt. **84** 258
Bysse **125** 64
Eliza **125** 64
Elizabeth **51** 132
Hender **109** 96
Ponsonby **125** 64
Susanna (Sheafe) **84** 258
125 64
MOLEYNS Thomas **81** 314
MOLHUYSEN
P. C. **143** 295
MOLIERE — M. **60** 407
MOLINA
Alfred Diaz de **98** 145
Olegario **60** 320
Molinaux see Molineaux
MOLINE
John **82** 79 **83** 154
MOLINEAUX Molenaux
Molinaux Molineux
Mollineaux Mollineux
Mollinex Molyneaux
Molyneux
Agnes **75** 287
Cicely **71** 241
Diana **65** 44
Elizabeth **72** 157 158
77 229
Ellen Zada (Rice) **92** 146
Fanny **61** 235
Gideon **75** 11
James **72** 157
Jane **125** 100
John **65** 173 **71** 241 **75** 287
Margery **82** 187
Myrtle Anita **92** 145
Nellie Zada Rice **66** 93
Richard **58** 70 **80** 91
Robert **82** 187
Robert Anthony (Mrs.)
92 146
Roland B. **82** 475
William **84** 368 379 380
85 124 **90** 87 **113** 71
131 272
Molines see Mullins
Molineux see Molineaux
MOLINIER Marie **114** 260
MOLINS Laurent **143** 4
MOLL Justus Reiniger **86**
197 **120** 76
MOLLEN J. M. **91** 330
MOLLENES
Thomas **67** 264
MOLLER
Elizabeth F. **83** 483
MOLLESON
Sarah **97** 278
William **73** 140
MOLLET Mollett
Elizabeth **63** 345
John **92** 118 120 121 **94** 297
John S. **77** 232

MOLLET cont'd
Perrine **88** 253
Polly **92** 120
Richard Call **92** 118
Thomas **86** 255
MOLLEY — Mrs. **63** 350
MOLLINEUM Anna **83** 35
Mollineux see Molineaux
Mollinex see Molineaux
MOLLING William **64** 227
MOLLINGIN
John **55** 141
MOLLON
Erasmus T. **78** 301
MOLLOY
Benjamin **74** 125
Keiran **117** 108
Mary **104** 289 **117** 108
Mary (Crowninshield)
104 289
William **104** 289
MOLLY Thomas **139** 207
Moloney see Maloney
Molony see Maloney
MOLOON Oliver **91** 330
MOLOTTS Martin **76** 131
MOLSHE Francis **94** 265
MOLSON
Eliza Josephine **78** 247
Herbert S. S. **78** 247
MOLT Robert Nelson
(Mrs.) **101** 327 **102** 121
Rudolph Friedrich
Wilhelm **80** 333 **81** 219
114 70
Molten see Moulton
MOLTER
Philip Ludwig **88** 98
Ruth **91** 198
MOLTHROF
Benjamin **76** 172
Benjamin Anson **76** 172
Betty **76** 172
MOLTKE Carl (Count) **68**
lxxviii
Carl Adam Nathaniel **68**
lxxviii
Cornelia Van Rensselaer
(Countess) **68** lxxviii
Molton see Moulton
Molyneaux see Molineaux
Molyneux see Molineaux
MOLYNS John **102** 193
John de **102** 193
William de **102** 193
MOMENT John J. **66** 193
Momford see Mumford
MOMMSEN
— Mr. **82** 470
MOMY Lydia **82** 294 297
MON William **80** 381
MONAHAN Monaghan
—— **112** 302
Annie Abigail **82** 399
Elizabeth (Fitzsimmons)
86 305
Frank **92** 97 **102** 157
107 19
Mary Janette **86** 305
Michael **82** 399

MONAHAN *cont'd*
Mildred Priscilla **82** 399
Rose Ann **85** 377 378
Sarah (Montgomery)
112 302
Thomas **86** 305
MONAHON
Clifford P. **106** 238
MONCEAUX Monceux
Simon **94** 323
William **118** 177
Monck *see* Monk
Monckton *see* Monkton
MONCRIEFF Moncreaf
Moncreft Moncreiffe
Moncrief Muncrief
Abigail (True) **127** 69
Alexander Bain **98** 342
Catherine **125** 220
Hannah **125** 106
Ian **107** 157 **108** 70 **145**
369
James **113** 13
Jane **140** 169
John **127** 69
Lucy **125** 104
M. Hartley **98** 342
Mary Bonson (Simter)
98 342
Sally **78** 70
Wallis **77** 234
MONCURE Cornelia P.
(Ensign) **103** 117
MONDAL Oliver **62** 19
Monday *see* Munday
MONDIE
Elizabeth (Capen)
84 336
MONDINDALE
William **63** 25
MONDING Alice **65** 171
Mondy *see* Mundy
Mone *see* Moon
MONELL Claudius L. **107**
10 163
James **101** 79
MONESON
Dorothy **113** 191
MONET —— **62** 101
Aley (Slagle) **90** 278
Ann (Hilliary) **90** 278
Catherine (Braucher)
90 278
Claude **81** 67 68
Elizabeth (Kent) **90** 278
Elizabeth (Osborne)
90 278
Orra E. **62** 101
MONEY Mony
— Mr. **71** 134
Ann **65** 234
Catherine **68** 76 77 **74** 51
Edward **111** 91
Jane **66** 162
Joan **66** 162
Joan (Cogan) **111** 91
John **68** 74 77 **74** 51
Joseph **128** 297
Samuel **128** 296
Thomas **66** 162
W. **53** 42

MONFORD
Amanda **89** 311
Emma (Richardson)
89 311
Hendrick **100** 96
Henry **100** 98
Hiram **89** 311
John **89** 311
Martha Thirza (Lazell)
89 311
Mary (Ingersoll) **89** 311
MONFORT
Sarah E. Y. **94** 202
MONGEHAM
Richard **76** 56
MONGER
Elizabeth **76** 226
Ferdinand **85** 168
Harriet (Stana) **126** 170
John **147** 237
Luke **126** 170
May **147** 237
MONGO John **129** 380
Mongomery *see*
Montgomery
MONICHAN
Bridget **77** 181
MONIERIE
Elizabeth Ann **92** 82
MONINGTON
William **96** 181
MONIOY John **68** 49
MONIS
Judah **65** 83 **91** 93
MONK Monck Monke
Monnck Mounck
Munck Munk
—— **56** 204 **61** 38 **126** 156
— Gen. **61** 281 **89** 149
— Mr. **52** 469 470
— Mrs. **124** 225
Abigail **75** 152
Agnes **66** 347 348 **93** 76
Amy **67** 253
Ann Wadsworth **128** 278
Anna **58** 256 **69** 318 **75** 152
Anne **66** 349
Benjamin **75** 151 **128** 278
Caroline (Townsend)
78 442
Charles F. **100** 214
Chloe **128** 285
Christian **54** 213
Christopher **75** 152 **84**
263 373 **144** 198
Clara E. **100** 214
Clement **72** 56
Dorothy (Boson) **109** 208
Ebenezer **128** 278
Edward **70** 129 131
Elias **75** 152 **77** 283
109 208
Elijah **75** 152 **124** 226
128 278
Elijah Wadsworth
128 278
Eliphalet **75** 152 **128** 278
285
Elizabeth **56** 31 **70** 129 131
71 106 **78** 188 **128** 278
Enoch **75** 152

MONK *cont'd*
Frances **115** 253
Freelove **51** 496 **54** 213
77 283
George **55** 400 **57** 388 **75**
249 **85** 77 **101** 163 **115**
253 **121** 189 **128** 278
George (Duke of
Albemarle) **66** 291
Grace M. **69** 318
Hannah **66** 316 **75** 152
Henry **85** 137 138 **132** 19
Hope **54** 213 **77** 283
Isaac Morton **128** 278
Isabel **85** 77
James **58** 68
Janet **64** 338
Jerusha Catherine **128** 278
Joanna **145** 55
John **66** 345 **71** 28 **83** 315
126 209 **128** 278 285
Joseph **64** 338 339 341
Lemuel **124** 226
Leon A. **69** 318
Lester Hawthorne **78** 442
Lillian Hoag **75** 82
Lydia **75** 249 **128** 285
Margaret **65** 180
Margaret (Chandler) **85**
138 **132** 19
Maria **109** 286
Marion **93** 137
Mary **75** 152 **128** 285
Mary (Summers) **126** 209
Meredith **128** 278
Nancy **75** 249
Nicholas **54** 242
Phebe **132** 94
Rachel **75** 152
Richard **65** 180 **85** 77
93 76 79
Ruth **75** 151
Sally **92** 256 **93** 322
Samuel **128** 278 285
Sarah **55** 400 **75** 152
128 285
Sarah (Raymond) **116** 256
Silence **75** 152
Simon **66** 349
Submit **128** 278
Susanna **75** 152 **128** 285
Thomas **66** 345 349 **78** 151
Wendal **128** 278
William **64** 23 **66** 345 **67**
253 **92** 51 **128** 278 **145**
361 **148** 32
Monkhouse *see* Munkhouse
MONKS
Caroline S. **116** 76
David **55** 83
George Gardner **98** 270
George Howard **98** 270
George Howard (Mrs.)
94 139 **98** 250 270 **99**
152
John Peabody **98** 270
123 67
Joseph **60** 27
Marion **93** 137
Olga **98** 270

MONKS *cont'd*
Olga Eliza (Gardner) **94**
139 **98** 270
Robert **60** 27
Stillman **116** 256
Thomas **60** 27
William **116** 76
MONKTON Monckton
— Brig. Gen. **84** 149
— Gen. **56** 192
Elizabeth **67** 69
John **67** 69 72
Robert **64** 97 **67** 72
116 172
MONMOUTH — Duke of
53 292-294 299
— Earl of **60** 317
Eleanor (Needham)
105 183
Henrietta Maria
(Wentworth) **105** 183
Mary Louise (O'Brien)
84 348
Monnck *see* Monk
MONNET Elizabeth
(Williams) **90** 278
Jullen C. (Mrs.) **82** 128
MONNETTE
Abraham **90** 278
Carrie Lucile (Janeway)
90 279
Ella Elizabeth (Crim)
90 279
Helen Hull **90** 279
Helen Marie (Kull) **90** 279
Isaac **90** 278
Jeremiah Crabb **90** 278
Mervin Jeremiah **90** 278
Olive Adelaide (Hull)
90 278
Orra Eugene **63** xxxiii 98
65 89 **66** 84 **68** 302 **70**
97 98 **74** xxviii **82** 513
86 354 **87** 210 305 **88**
402 **90** 126 201 278 **91**
146 **97** 331 332 **113** 276
277 **119** 13 114 116 179
William **90** 278
MONNYNGHAM
Charles **52** 249
William **52** 249
MONOT Stephen **65** 231
MONRAL Job **91** 330
MONROE Monro - *see also*
Munroe
— Capt. **77** 47
— Col. **70** 13
— Dr. **54** 187
— Mr. **73** 51
— Mrs. **62** 355 **63** 57
129 381
A. **62** 147
Abby A. **71** 35
Abel **90** 43
Abigail **63** 55 **67** 117 121
216 **78** 235 **100** 6 7 88
129 381
Abigail (Read) **100** 6 7
Abigail T. **62** 77
Achsah **70** 201
Addie (Johnson) **100** 197

MONROE *cont'd*
Addie Blanche **100** 94
Adelbert Alfonso **100** 90
Adele Orville **75** 255
Adoniram Judson **100**
86 93
Albert Deloss **100** 194
Albert Nelson **112** 320
Alexander **73** 234
Alfaretta **100** 93
Allen **88** 15
Allie (Hopkins) **100** 203
Almeda **100** 13
Almeda Ellen **100** 91
Alonzo **100** 10 87-89 194
Alonzo DeCarto **100** 87
Alonzo Wilson **100** 196
Alpha **100** 199
Alta **100** 196 204
Altia Fitch **70** 201
Alvin **100** 87
Alzina **100** 90
Amanda **100** 87
Amelia Frances
(Hannum) (Smith)
91 45
Ammitty **100** 8
Amos **69** 371
Andrew Jackson **100** 88
Angeline (Moss) **100** 90
Angeline Estella **100** 196
Ann Sarah **68** 145
Anna **69** 371 **70** 201
100 204
Anna (Kendall) **83** 477
Anna (Lowe) **100** 91
Anna (McNamara)
100 203
Anne **100** 92
Anne (Monroe) **100** 92
Annie Mary **100** 88
Annis **100** 9
Annis Sophronia **100** 88
Aravilla **100** 198
Archibald **129** 381
Aristarchus **100** 13 198
199
Arthur **100** 204
Artie Rozell **100** 203
Artus Judson **100** 94 199
Asa A. **70** 201
August Willick **100** 196
202
Augusta Olivia **70** 206
Averell **100** 205
Barbara **100** 197
Beatrice **100** 200
Bedent B. **69** 30
Ben **112** 97
Benjamin **100** 4 **136** 38
Benjamin Barney **100** 11
88
Bennet **136** 34
Bennie Cleo **100** 203
Bernice **100** 195
Bertha **130** 156
Bessie (Stocks) **100** 203
Betsey **140** 131 132
Betsey Ann **107** 150
Betsey Ann (Crandall)
100 193

MONROE *cont'd*
Betsey M. **100** 193
Betty **68** 309 **121** 49
Beulah (Davenport)
100 196
Billie **100** 203
Blanche Laverne **100** 200
Bridget **63** 75
Burton Lewis **100** 201
Byron A. **100** 88
Caleb Bradley **68** 315
Carl **100** 201
Carlton Albert **100** 194
Caroline French **76** 15
Caroline Sanford **78** 205
Carrie E. (Bland) **100** 199
Catherine **63** 115 **84** 96
86 231
Catherine (Britton)
100 197
Celia **100** 86
Charity **100** 85
Charles **62** 330 **81** 34 **100** 9
92 93 **129** 383
Charles B. **100** 91 197
Charles Bertram **100** 197
Charles Bland **100** 200
Charles Conrad **100** 195
Charles Dever **100** 198
Charles Edward **91** 366
Charles Fremont **100** 93
199
Charles Seymour **100** 195
Charlotte **61** 340
Charlotte Ann **100** 199
Chauncey **70** 201
Chester Irving **100** 203
Chrysanthis **100** 14
Claire Stocks **100** 203
Clara **100** 196
Clara (Slater) **100** 205
Clara (Wheeler) **100** 196
Clara A. (Hubbard)
100 196
Clara Cordelia **100** 195
Clarence **100** 205
Clarence Ona **100** 203
Clarissa **100** 11 12
Claud Lee **100** 203
Clifford **100** 201
Cora **100** 196
Cora (Bennett) **100** 205
Cora Livingston **75** 255
Cordelia A. (Rathbun)
(Lewis) **100** 89
Cordelia Celestia **100** 90
Cornell **71** 35
Cynthia (Montgomery)
112 97
Cynthia Lee **100** 204
Cyrenius C. **100** 14
Cyrus **77** 148 **100** 92 197
136 38
Cyrus Moore **100** 204
Dan **100** 8 9 12
Daniel **62** 147 **100** 4
Daniel Wilson **100** 201
David **69** 372 373 **70** 201
265 **78** 186 235 **85** 159
100 4-6
David Bates **75** 255

MONROE *cont'd*
Day Moore **100** 204
Deborah **62** 147 **98** 354
  100 4 6 7 10
Deborah (Hogabone)
  100 193
Deborah (Sexton) **100** 12
Deborah C. (Johnson)
  90 43
Delia **100** 87
Della **100** 93
Diana **100** 14 91
Donald **100** 2 3
Donald Rouse **100** 197
Dora Louise **136** 327
Dorah E. **100** 193
Dorcas **84** 100
Dorothy **100** 196
Dorothy C. **100** 195
Dorothy Jean **100** 197
Duncan **65** 246
Dyar **100** 8 9 13 89
E. Cornell **71** 35
E. L. **100** 8
Earl **100** 205
Earlie Wilbert **100** 203
Ebadena **100** 94
Ebaline **100** 87
Ebenezer **59** 396 **81** 34
  85 10
Edgar **100** 203
Edith **95** 147 **123** 190
Edmund **100** 63
Edward **129** 381
Edward J. **100** 202
Edward N. **100** 108
Edwin Wallace **75** 255
Elbert Lorenzo **100** 202
Eleanor **100** 4-6 13
Elery A. **100** 105
Elijah **100** 9
Eliza **100** 14 87 **107** 5
Elizabeth **68** 221 232 **70**
  329 **71** 8 **73** 267 **78** 183
  88 279 **100** 4-6 11 **128**
  311
Elizabeth (McNairy)
  98 350
Elizabeth (Peck) **100** 9
Elizabeth C. (Leake)
  109 189
Ella **69** 30
Ella Dell **100** 8 88
Ellen Aramintha **100** 194
Elmer **100** 197
Elmer Omega **100** 202
Elmon LaVerne **100** 197
  203
Elnora **100** 197
Elora B. **100** 198
Elsie **100** 10
Elvira C. **77** 180
Elwin James **100** 204
Emeline **70** 201
Emeline C. **116** 259
Emeline E. **78** 397
Emily **100** 12 91
Emily (Morgan) **100** 89
Emily Marina **100** 193
Emizetta **100** 94
Emma **77** 188

MONROE *cont'd*
Emma (Hyle) **100** 196
Emma Frances **68** xxxv
  71 xviii **90** 128 **91** 297
  366
Emma J. **75** 255
Encie **100** 197
Enoch **91** 366
Ephraim **126** 120
Eri **91** 45
Ernest **100** 200
Ernestine **100** 199 204
Eugene **100** 195
Eugene Bronson **100** 90
Eugenia (Potter) **100** 90
Eunice **71** 35
Evadena **100** 94
Evaline **100** 87
Ezra Barrows **75** 255
Ezra J. **100** 202
F. T. **107** 79
Factor **112** 47
Fannie B. **83** 429 436
Fannie Lee **100** 202
Fern (Johnson) **100** 204
Fidelia **100** 13
Floda May **100** 194
Flora Louisa (Dilts)
  100 94
Florence G. **100** 195
Florence Lydia **85** 197
Florence Olive **100** 199
Floyd Lavern **100** 203
Frances **75** 255 **100** 199
Frances H. **100** 90
Frances Medora **89** 232
Francis Lerotus **100** 194
  201
Frank D. **100** 94
Frederick **70** 80 83
Frederick Augustus
  100 198
Frederick David **100** 92
  198 200
Genevieve **100** 201
George **90** 344 **91** 366
  100 3 4 92
George B. **77** 147 **100** 91
George Edwards **75** 255
George Frederick
  100 201
George Lester **100** 197
George O. **100** 92 198
George Verlin **100** 202
George W. **112** 97
Georgetta **100** 94
Gerald Elmon **100** 203
Geraldine L. **100** 195
Gertrude (Smith) **100** 195
Gertrude E. **100** 203
Gladys **100** 193 194
Gladys Marian **100** 195
Grace **100** 201
Grace Eva **81** 389
Grace Ludeena **100** 201
Hannah **89** 264 **100** 4 9
  11 13 86 91
Hannah (Josselyn) **136** 34
Hannah (Low) **100** 197
Hannah (Munroe) **100**
  11 13

MONROE *cont'd*
Hannah (Smith) **100** 87
Hannah Augusta
  (Boyden) **86** 145
Harriet **100** 87 89 194
Harriet Arvilla **81** 35
Harriet D. **78** 185
Harriet Elizabeth **100** 12
Harriet Stone **136** 323 327
Harry Britton **100** 197
Harry Lytle **100** 195
Harry Orlando **100** 200
Havilla **100** 14 198 199
Havilla V. **100** 88 193
Hazel Helen (Henry)
  100 195
Helen **100** 195
Helen Magoon **100** 229
Helen Whiting **83** 247
  248 **84** 110 190 206 **85**
  215
Helena D. (Trainor)
  100 203
Henry **66** 36 **70** 329 **136** 33
  34 40 323
Henry Lewis **100** 90
Henry Smith **76** 320
  81 113
Henry Stanton **136** 323
Hester A. (Huston) **100** 93
Hezekiah **73** 278 **129** 381
Hile Ann (Fisher) **100** 199
Hiram Leonard **100** 91
  197
Howard Wright **100** 93
Hubert **100** 201
Hugh **100** 3
Huldah (Fox) **100** 89
Hurley Anne (Monroe)
  100 198 200
Ida **100** 201
Ida C. **75** 255
Ida Mae **100** 200
Ida S. **100** 91
Idabelle (Helfrich)
  100 199
Irene Hile **100** 203
Irma Jane **100** 201
Irving Wilbert **100** 196
  202
Isaac **77** 30 **100** 7-10 13 85
  90 93 129
Isaac Everett **100** 195
Isabel Louise **100** 200
Isadora **100** 94
Israel Daniel **100** 92 198
  199
Ivers **81** 34
Jacob **77** 30 **89** 232
James **51** 23-25 153 156 157
  323 **54** 456 **57** 238 **58**
  198 **59** xxvi 235 **61** 214
  65 83 220 **66** 315 **67** 326
  72 76 **78** 71 **91** 204 **100**
  87 88 **105** 189 **112** 269
James Austin **100** 197
James Donald **100** 197
James Madison **100** 90
  196
James Morris **68** 317
James P. **59** 232

MONROE *cont'd*
James Phinney **100** 2 4
James Sexton **100** 8 13
Jane **68** 231 **81** 34 **100** 86
Jasper **100** 87
Jeanette **100** 88
Jedediah **85** 10
Jennie **100** 88
Jennie Ophelia **100** 94
Jerusha **100** 205
Jerusha (Tyler) **100** 198
Jesse **70** 201
Jesse Franklin **100** 93
John **62** 288 355 **68** 236 309
    313 315 **71** 35 **81** 34 **100**
    3-5 236 **115** 123 **130** 156
John Bland **100** 200
John Edward **71** 35
John Hamilton **100** 93
John Quincy Adams **100**
    90 196
John Wiswell **68** 312
Jonas **62** 77
Jonathan **59** 282 **86** 145
Joseph **65** 348 **100** 4 6 8 9
    11 13 91
Joseph Alonzo **100** 89 194
Joseph E. **100** 193
Joseph M. **100** 195
Joseph Marcus **100** 90
Josephine **100** 205
Josephine (Burson)
    100 199
Josephine (Cardwell)
    100 203
Josiah **63** 75 **65** 220 **68**
    217 219 221 222 **70** 201
    100 2 5 6 **142** 387
Julia Ann **75** 255
Julia Augusta **86** 145
Juliana Appleton **75** 255
Juliette (Rogers) **100** 201
Karl R. **100** 195
Katharine **100** 197
Katharine (Sullivan)
    100 203
Keith **100** 205
Kenneth **100** 205
Keziah **54** 51 **100** 87
Kitty **100** 205
L. F. **100** 10
Laura Ann **100** 85
Laura Ann (Schrock)
    100 198
Laurena **100** 205
Lee **100** 2 85 193 198 204
Lee Sawyer **100** 204
Lemuel **68** 217 229
Lemuel Franklin **100** 10
    85
Lena **100** 90
Lena Blanche (Smith)
    100 94
Lenore Moore **100** 203
Leona **100** 200 201
Leonard **100** 7-10 87
Leonore Moore **100** 204
Lerotus **100** 88 89 193
Lerotus Jeremian **100** 201
Leslie **100** 201
Lewrania **71** 35

MONROE *cont'd*
Lila **100** 201
Lilla Day (Moore) **100** 204
Lillian May **97** 69 **100** 201
Llewellyn **100** 205
Lloyd Raymond **100** 196
Lorene **100** 203
Loretta **100** 91 93
Loring **81** 34
Louis Gonzaga **100** 203
Louisa **100** 88
Louisa Jane **100** 88
Louise **100** 195
Lovina **100** 92
Lucia (Anderson) **89** 232
Lucia S. **81** 34
Lucretia **100** 89
Lucy **68** 236 **78** 420 **81** 34
    100 8 9 85
Lucy A. **75** 255
Lucy M. **81** 34
Luella (Hemingway)
    100 195
Lulea **70** 83 85
Lurilla **100** 89
Lydia **68** 233 **75** 35 **81** 34
Lydia (Cutting) **100** 89
Lydia A. (Killips) **100** 194
Lydia Evans **68** 235
Lydia Ophelia **100** 93
Maggie (Williams)
    100 202
Margaret **100** 197 **136** 33
Margaret (Brown) **100** 85
Margaret A. **71** 35
Margaret R. **77** 178
Maria **100** 87 88 91
Mariah (Newton) **100** 89
    90
Marie Harriet **100** 203
Marion **100** 87
Marjorie Jean **100** 203
Marrianne **100** 86
Martha **81** 382 **87** 289
    100 4 9 **107** 155 **129** 380
Martha (Bixby) **107** 155
Martha (Mitchell) **136** 323
Martha A. **81** 34
Martha Ann (Brown)
    100 93
Martha Augusta **81** 389
Martha Jerusha **100** 90
Mary **65** 348 **68** 321 **69** 30
    372 **87** 129 **100** 3-6 92
    128 45 **136** 41
Mary (Ely) **100** 90
Mary (Smith) **100** 199
Mary (Sullivan) **100** 201
Mary (Vorys) **100** 93
Mary Agnes (Smith)
    100 203
Mary Ann **100** 91 203
Mary Ann (Chase) **88** 15
Mary Ann (Dewey)
    100 197
Mary Ann (Larkin)
    100 90
Mary Belle **100** 93
Mary E. **100** 90
Mary Ellen **100** 201
Mary Farwell **81** 34

MONROE *cont'd*
Mary Lowana **100** 92 198
Mary Viola **100** 88
Massie Belle **100** 202
Mather Withington
    75 255
Maurice **100** 195
May **70** 208
Mercy **136** 34
Mercy (Atherton) **126** 120
Mildred **100** 201
Mildred M. **100** 195
Minerva **71** 35 **100** 14 85
Miranda **86** 437
Myron Frederick **100** 201
Myrtle Olive **100** 93
N. W. **61** 340
Nabby **68** 311 **78** 398
Nahum Parker **68** 145
Nancy **71** 35 **100** 85
Nancy C. **78** 180
Nancy J. **81** 34
Nancy Whitney **81** 34
Napolean W. **100** 88
Nath. **129** 381
Nathan **128** 135 **129** 380
Nathaniel **129** 382
Nellie **100** 196 201
Nellie Estelle **100** 202
Nelson **100** 90
Nina Belle **100** 92 200
Nina Mable **100** 202
Olive **115** 218
Ophia **100** 93
Ora Belle **100** 197
Ora Leone (Gray) **100** 194
Orlando **100** 92 193 198
    200
Orsamus **100** 85
Orsamus Leonard **100**
    14 91
Oscar **100** 87
Oscar Edward **75** 255
Oscar Hatfield **77** 188
Pauline **100** 203
Perlina **100** 194
Peter Lafayette **100** 194
    201
Phebe (Button) **100** 204
Philena A. **71** 34
Philetus **100** 13 90
Phylurah **100** 88
Polly Mariah **100** 90
Polly Mariah (Newton)
    100 89 90 195
Porter **100** 204
Prudence **75** 206
Publius Virgil **100** 194
Publius Virgilius Bogue
    100 12 89
Quincy Mitchell **100** 202
R. A. **122** 311
R. Maynard **77** 323
Rachel **91** 45 **100** 87
Rachel Bates **75** 255
Raymond **100** 205
Rebecca **70** 80 83 **100** 195
    126 120
Rebecca (Clerk) **68** 309
Rebecca (Foster)
    (Prentice) **100** 11

MONROE *cont'd*
Rebecca (Locke) **128** 45
Rebecca (Thompson)
100 195
Rhoda **59** 282
Richard **100** 200
Richard Edward **100** 202
Richard Johnson
Madison **100** 88 94
Richard Leeds **68** 318 320
Richard S. **122** 80
Robert **77** 239 **85** 10 **100**
3 201
Robert Augustus **100** 201
Robert Maynard **78** 205
Roger Edward **100** 202
Rowena **100** 199
Royal **75** 255
Rufus **100** 196
Ruie Gladys **100** 202
Russell **100** 195
Ruth **100** 205
Ruth (Niles) **85** 159
Ruth (Woodin) **100** 197
Ruth E. **100** 195
S. D. **70** 206
Salaman Harrison **100**
88 193
Sally **100** 11 12
Sally (Barney) **100** 11
Sally (Davidson) **100** 87
Sally B. **100** 89
Samantha **100** 88 89 194
Samuel **67** 116 117 121
68 229 231 235 309 312
71 35 **100** 6 7 9 10 85 87
88 92 205
Samuel L. **100** 87
Sanford **88** 15
Sarah **59** 282 396 **69** 371
373 **71** 35 **100** 4-6 10 88
90 236 **136** 266
Sarah (Fassett) **100** 8
Sarah (Sayles) **100** 92
Sarah A. **100** 92
Sarah Ann **71** 35
Sarah B. **77** 147
Sarah E. **77** 148
Sarah Elizabeth **100** 195
Sarah Elsie **100** 94
Sarah Jane **100** 88 198
Sarah L. **54** cvi
Sarah Louise **62** 189
Sarah Tapley **77** 293
Sarah Thompson **75** 255
Sidney Spencer **100** 198
205
Silas **100** 86
Simeon **129** 381
Smith **100** 87
Sophia **88** 278 **100** 87
Spencer **100** 87 93 198
Stanley Marvin **100** 203
Stella **100** 198
Sue (Humphrey) **100** 202
Sukey **68** 311 316
Susan (Wagner) **100** 93
Susan A. J. **78** 401
Susanna **70** 201 **78** 410
100 85 **137** 251
Susie Bradley **68** 309

MONROE *cont'd*
Suzanne (Perry) **130** 156
Sylvia (Thomas) **136** 323
Thankful **68** 219
Thomas **123** 192 **129** 380
Thomas Evans **68** 236
Thomas Francis **100** 201
Thomas Samuel **100** 198
204
Timothy **85** 11
Tommie **100** 202
Vergie Cordelia **100** 202
Victor Garfield **100** 195
Vivian F. **100** 198
Walter Hubbard **100** 197
Warren Walter **100** 196
Wayne Leroy **100** 196
Wilfred Harold **68** xiv
Will S. **100** 5
Willard Barr **100** 89
Willard Taylor **100** 199
Willard Ursino **100** 93
William **67** 116 **68** 232
233 235 236 309 311 316
318 320 **70** 201 **75** 255
77 239 **91** 45 366 **100** 2-
8 10 11 13 85 86 88 193
204 **123** 192 **128** 45 **129**
381
William Alfred **100** 93
William Bennett **65** xix
William Bennett (Mrs.)
77 322 **78** 205
William C. **71** 35
William Christy **100** 200
William Edward **100** 201
William H. **77** 180 **81** 389
William Henry Harrison
100 90 195
William Locke **75** 255
William M. **100** 89
William Morris **68** 317
William R. **104** 144
William Wheaton **100**
12 88
Willie Roy **100** 197 203
MONS Anna **120** 20
R. **120** 20
MONSALL
Claude G. **105** 238
Elizabeth **105** 226
Joel **105** 157
Ruth **105** 228
MONSEIGNAT
— Mr. **52** 476
MONSEL Enos **80** 54
MONSISE
Cornelius **111** 109
Elizabeth (Coates)
111 109
MONSON —— **58** 110
— Lord **98** 12 13
— Mr. **82** 413
Abigail **75** 50 51 56
Catherine Amelia **82** 108
Edwin Beach **82** 108
George **113** 313
Hannah Jane **100** 310
John **54** 409 **75** 49
Jonathan **93** 273
Joseph **75** 49

MONSON *cont'd*
Lucy Ann **108** 68
Mary **75** 47 53
Mary Burton **81** 369
Mary Gertrude **82** 108
Myron Andrews **65** 195
Richard **65** 195 **82** 283 294
Robert **65** 195 302 **75** 47-
49 51 53 56
Samuel **54** 445 **81** 125
129 447
Sarah **75** 48 **81** 414 415
Stephen **75** 56
Susanna **82** 283 294
Theophilus **145** 241
Thomas **81** 121 122 124-
127 129-131
Wait **81** 415
MONTAGUE Montagu
— Adm. **84** 270 376
— Bp. **104** 33
— Capt. **77** 97 102
— Gov. **84** 255
— Mrs. **119** 128 207 209
218 **120** 210 **121** 61 66
67 **122** 308
Abbie T. **53** 251 **54** 228
55 xxxii
Abigail **60** 302 **64** 126
106 217 218 **118** 115
217 **123** 18 22 24 **142**
161
Abigail (Camp) **106** 217
Abigail (Downing) **142**
149 161
Agnes **140** 222 223 **142**
152 154-156
Albert **75** 14
Alice **104** 315 **108** 178
142 153
Amanda **75** 14
Ann **142** 161
Ann Maria **52** 151
Anna **123** 21
Anne **106** 217 **142** 159 160
Anne (Belden) **106** 218
Annie S. **52** 151
Arthur E. **77** 57
Azubah **104** 123
Benjamin **97** 58
Cassie **77** 57
Charles (Lord) **58** 411
Charles H. **52** 151
Cicily **142** 161
Daniel **123** 29
Dudley **123** 27
Edward **98** 33 34
Edwin **123** 30
Eleanor **142** 149
Elijah **123** 25-28
Elizabeth **118** 26 **142** 154
159 161
Elizabeth (Harrington)
98 34
Elizabeth (Montfort)
110 186
Elizabeth G. **77** 57
Ellen **142** 161
Ellen (Allen) **141** 107 **142**
159-162 164
G. W. **79** 349

MONTAGUE *cont'd*
George **142** 151 158 159
George W. **142** 149
George William **141** 107
   142 161
Gertrude **106** 124
Gertrude Alice **118** 159
Griffin **56** 378 **84** 402
Hannah **88** 303 **118** 111
   123 20
Harry **75** 14
Helen **142** 149
Helen (Allen) **141** 107
   142 159-162 164
Henry **98** 34 **142** 160 161
Henry (Lord) **96** 183
Henry Pole (Lord) **96** 182
Holland **93** 273
Irene **94** 390
Isabel **140** 222
Jedediah **120** 302 **123** 18
   20 22 24 26 27 30
Jediah **123** 21
Joan **142** 152-156
Joan (Maston?) **142** 159
Joanna (Rackley) **142** 156
John **55** 343 **84** 270 **106**
   218 **118** 227 231 232
   119 48 135 294 **170** 210
   212 **122** 120 **123** 23 **142**
   152 153 161
John (Earl of Sandwich)
   129 138
John (Mrs.) **119** 135 139
Julia B. **85** 168
Katharine **142** 153 154 156
Katharine (Spencer)
   98 34
Lawrence **142** 154-156
Lucy **59** 36
Margaret **56** 378 **142** 155
   160 161
Margaret (Catton) **142**
   152 153 160
Margaret (Malthous)
   (Grove) **142** 156-
   158 160
Martha **106** 218
Mary **110** 186 **142** 161
Mary Elizabeth **52** 151
Moses **90** 162
Nathaniel **59** 30 **118** 222
   119 210 **123** 29
Natt **118** 221
Persis **79** 348
Peter **98** 203 **107** 191 **118**
   221 **141** 106 107 **142**
   149-151 159 162 164 **144**
   124
Polly **120** 298
Rhoda **119** 218 307 **120**
   206 295 **122** 64 68 119
   222 303 305
Richard **60** 302 **79** 160
   106 217 **117** 79 **138** 83
   84 103 **141** 106 107 **142**
   149-151 156 161 **144** 124
Robert **142** 152-156 158-
   161
Ruth **59** 36
Samuel Leland **52** 151

MONTAGUE *cont'd*
Sarah **117** 79 **119** 212 290
   120 134 **121** 64 **142** 159
   161
Sarah (Maverick) **97** 58
Sarah Goodrich **123** 23
Seth **120** 301
Steven **123** 23-27 29
Susan (Norris) **142** 159
William **51** 472 **52** 147 148
   58 68 **67** 250 317 **80** 68
   110 186 **123** 29 **140** 169
   222 **142** 150 152-164
William H. **99** 5 8 11 **116**
   87 **140** 169 **145** 205 208
William Henry **52** 147
   68 xlvi **74** xiii **75** 66 **89**
   167 169 **99** 6 23
William L. **142** 149
William Lewis **63** 113
Zebina **81** 396
MONTAINIE
Abraham de la **59** 420
MONTAMBAULT
Joseph **143** 8
Marie (Landry)
   (Robichaux) **143** 8
MONTANARI
Marie C. **91** 366
MONTANYE
Jane **118** 106
John **118** 106
MONTARGIS
Sarah de **117** 132
MONTCALM —— **56** 383
— Gen. **84** 148 149
   146 332
— Marquis de **57** 128 **60**
   1 **135** 41
Louis Joseph (Marquis
   de) **63** 190 **130** 186
Moses **100** 280
Nabby **100** 280
Nancy **108** 263
Sally **100** 280
MONTCHAL Charles de
   Barentin de (Vicomte)
   105 188
MONTCHANIN Anne
   Alexandrine de **95** 84
MONTCHENSEY
Montchensy
Montechensy
Mountchensy
Muntchensy
Hubert de **96** 102
Thomas de **103** 290
Walter **73** 28
Warin de **102** 298
Warine de **75** 62
William **139** 284
MONTDIDIER — Count
   136 102 **141** 98
MONTEATH Monteith
Caroline (Lowe) **116** 298
   300
Jay Waldo **96** 128
Mary Bancroft (Strudley)
   96 128
Walter N. **116** 298 300
Montejoye *see* Mountjoy

MONTEN Boston **77** 232
MONTENEY
Lewis **110** 124
MONTFICHET
Richard de **105** 39 40
Montfort De *see* Mountfort
Montfort *see* Mountfort
MONTGOMERY
Mongomery
Montgomerie
Mountgomery
Muretgomery
—— **112** 94 95 293 294
— Capt. **84** 167
— Gen. **54** 56 **85** 27 118
   123 299 **137** 315
— Mr. **65** 370 **66** 363
— Mrs. **95** 50
— of Cubley **141** 99
____ (Dawson) **112** 298
A. C. **112** 20
Abigail **125** 216
Abigail (Cope) **112** 298
Adam **91** 348 **112** 293 295
   297 302 303
Adam John **112** 297
Agnes **79** 124 **112** 282
   288 301
Agnes (Cox) **112** 301
Agnes (Hugart) **112** 20
Agnes (Lane) **112** 288
Agnes Mary (Olsen)
   96 286
Alex **102** 313
Alexander **112** 15 18 19
   90 92 96 280-282 284
   285 288-290 296 299-301
   303
Alexander T. **76** 266
Alexandretta **112** 296
Alice **112** 283 301 303
Alice (McIlroy) **112** 283
Alicia **112** 284
Andrew **112** 288 290 295
   297 298
Andrew Jackson **85** 97
Angel (Archdale) **112** 298
Ann **84** 118 **112** 15 19 96
   283
Ann (Hull) **112** 292
Ann M. **142** 28
Anna **112** 282 292 295
Anna C. (Anderson)
   112 97
Anna Maria **112** 292 300
Anne **112** 89 90 95-97 280
   282 288 290 291 294-296
   298 300-302
Anne (Burke) **112** 282
Anne (Cairnes) **112** 304
Anne (Deey) **112** 304
Anne (Faulkner) **112** 295
Anne (MacNeill) **112** 295
Archibald **112** 280 281 303
Archibald Armar **112**
   298 299
Archibald MacNeill **112**
   293 295
Armantha **76** 270
Barbara **112** 299
Benjamin **112** 96

MONTGOMERY *cont'd*
Bernard Law **112** 278
Bertha Isabella **96** 286
Betsey **99** 50 **112** 90 95 98
Blanche Comfort
  (Bancroft) **96** 286
C. C. **112** 94
Caroline **71** 122
Caroline (Poland)
  100 146
Catherine **73** 139 **76** 266
  112 294-296 298-301
Catherine (Auchinlech)
  112 288
Catherine (Dillon)
  112 294
Catherine (Dunbar) **112**
  298 299
Catherine (Jones) **112** 294
Catherine (Montfort)
  112 299
Catherine (Moore)
  112 301
Catherine (Willoughby)
  112 289 300
Catherine (Younger)
  112 288
Cato **88** 282
Charles **91** 330 **112** 294
  295
Charles F. **111** 310
Charlotte Ruby **76** 97
Chetwynd **112** 284
Christian **112** 282
Christopher **84** 382
  91 348
Clarence W. **133** 35
Clayton **112** 98
Clayton C. **112** 92
Clemence **112** 303
Colville **112** 295
Cynthia **112** 97
D. B. **112** 14 88
David **112** 287 290 291 303
  117 246
Davida Virginia **85** 340
Deborah **84** 366 **91** 348
Dixie **112** 292
Dorcas **112** 15 19 288 289
  293 300
Doresh **112** 297
Dorothea **112** 289
Dorothy **112** 295 303
E. L. **91** 330
Earle Saunders **96** 286
Edith C. (McCauley)
  96 286
Edmond **112** 294
Edmondson **112** 292
Edward **76** 97
Edward Soule **76** 97
Effie Stephenson
  (Winlock) **112** 97
Eleanor **112** 295
Eleanor (Anderson)
  125 223
Eleanor (Barnewell)
  112 294
Eleanor (Burke) **112** 289
Eliza **76** 36 **90** 298 **112** 93
  295 301

MONTGOMERY *cont'd*
Eliza (Pennefeather)
  112 301
Eliza J. **112** 98 99
Elizabeth **67** 349 **72** 305 **91**
  345 **103** 118 **112** 95 97
  98 281 282 288 289 292-
  294 296 297 299-302 **117**
  246 **120** 239
Elizabeth (Armar) **112** 298
Elizabeth (Batten) **112** 292
Elizabeth (Brabazon)
  112 293
Elizabeth (Connor)
  112 299
Elizabeth (Edmonstowne)
  112 294
Elizabeth (Montgomery)
  112 297 299
Elizabeth (Piercy) **112** 301
Elizabeth Jane **112** 91 99
Ellinor (Moore) **112** 289
Esther (Houston) **112** 15
  18 20
Esther H. **112** 22
Eveline (Whitley) **112** 94
Flora **112** 92
Florence **112** 91 95
Frances (Howth) **112** 294
Frances (St. Lawrence)
  112 293
Francis (Magan) **112** 301
Grissell (MacDougall)
  112 294
Hannah **112** 91 282
Hannah (Clements)
  112 284
Hugh **101** 260
Isabel (Pibells) **112** 280
Isabella (Campbell)
  112 294
Isabelle (Stewart) **112** 281
Jane **112** 92-95 98 282 293
  301 302
Jane (Macneil) **112** 295
Jane (Patterson) **112** 94
Jane (Phillips) **112** 296
Jane (Reasoner) **110** 65
Jane (Ward) **112** 96
Janet (Montgomery)
  112 293
Jean **112** 89
Jean (Alexander) **112** 293
  294
Jean (Cargill) **117** 246
Jenet **112** 292
Jenny **112** 92
Jenny (Ward) **112** 96
John **112** 21 22 90-96 278
  280-297 299-304 **115** 57
  125 223 **140** 169
John C. **112** 20
John F. **88** 305
John Francis **51** 230
John J. **112** 93
John Love **85** 340
John S. **76** 44
John W. **133** 35
Jonathan H. **113** 313
Jordan **112** 98
Joseph **112** 92 280 282

MONTGOMERY *cont'd*
  283 288 293 303
Josias **112** 281
Juda (Morrison) **112** 92
Judith **112** 300
Judith (Montgomery)
  112 300
Julia **126** 217 218
Juliet **112** 20
Katharine **52** 434 **112** 288
  299
Katharine (Stewart)
  112 294
Knox **112** 98
L. J. **133** 302
Leanna **80** 48
Leila (Young) (Post)
  133 302
Leslie **112** 299
Logan **112** 98
Louisa **112** 296 303
Louise **112** 282
Lovisa **88** 375
Lovisa (Lazell) **88** 375
Luanne Lillian **91** 203
  113 313
Lucinda **112** 283
Lucy **90** 49 **112** 304
Lucy (Saunders) **88** 282
Lula **76** 97
Lydia **76** 264 **88** 305
  90 92 315
Mabel E. **94** 382
Manettie Arabella (Cole)
  86 152 307
Margaret **73** 95 **112** 18 91
  92 280-283 288 293 294
  297-299 301 303 **125** 217
  141 100
Margaret (Campbell)
  112 289
Margaret (Cole) **112** 294
Margaret (Edmonson)
  112 91 95
Margaret (Fitzwilliam)
  112 294
Margaret (Greenlee) **112**
  92 96
Margaret (Johnstone)
  112 300
Margaret (Leslie) **112** 288
Margaret (Weir) **112** 17
  18 20
Margaret Ann **73** 277
Margaret Leslie **112** 284
Maria **112** 98 289 300
Maria Dolores (Plink)
  112 298
Marion **112** 303
Marjorie Selina **76** 97
Marshall Hugh **102** 124
Martha **107** 64 **111** 210
  112 98 99 282 283 290
  294 303
Martha (Crawford)
  112 20
Martha (Crockett) **85** 97
Martha H. (Orn) **90** 92
Martha J. **68** 258
Martha P. **112** 91
Mary **112** 91 96 97 279-

MONTGOMERY cont'd
284 288 289 292 293 295
296 299-303 **117** 246
120 239 **126** 145 218
318
Mary (Archibald) **112** 298
Mary (Crane) **112** 289
Mary (Dalway) **112** 290
Mary (Dawson) **112** 298
Mary (McCrary) **85** 97
Mary (Moore) **112** 294
Mary (St. Lawrence) **112**
293 294
Mary Angelica **112** 294
Mary Ann **112** 302
Mary Anne (Boyd)
112 300
Mary C. (Ellis) **112** 98
Mary Catherine **74** 304
Mary E. **76** 42
Mary Millicent **112** 298
Mary Robt (Cumins)
112 302
Mary W. **112** 92
Mary W. (Montgomery)
112 92
Mary Wright Ellis **112**
93 98 99
Matilda Virginia
(Campbell) **85** 340
Matthew **112** 280 282 284
288-290
May **60** 28
Mervyn **112** 298
Michael **112** 292
Mildred Comfort **96** 286
Molly **112** 15 19 **120** 239
Morton L. **116** 253 **117** 60
Moses **76** 35
N. **125** 39
N. E. **91** 330
Nancy **53** 460 **84** 216 **112**
92 94 96
Nancy (Babcock) **96** 286
Nancy (Brown) **112** 296
Nancy (Roberts) **85** 97
Nancy A. **128** 171
Nancy Agnes (Crockett)
112 20
Nathaniel **52** 343 **112** 290
300
Nicholas **112** 298 299
Nicola **112** 288 299
Nina Elizabeth **86** 307
Noble **88** 375
Ollie May **86** 307
Oscar Fred **86** 307
Patience **112** 289
Patrick **112** 290 293
Peggy **112** 20
Philips **112** 296
Polly **112** 20 92 96 97
Polly (Lee) **112** 92
Polly (Smith) **112** 96
Priscilla (Wallace) **112** 97
Rachel (Givens) **112** 93 96
Rebecca **60** 28 **73** xxxiv
112 283 284 288 299 302
Rebecca (Aikin) **112** 295
Rebecca (Montgomery)
112 299

MONTGOMERY cont'd
Richard **69** 369 **112** 245
278 282 296 298 301 **129**
326 **130** 185 186 217
131 48 **132** 136 **147** 82
Robert **54** 46 **74** 304 **81**
431 **85** 97 **91** 345 349
112 15 19 20 89-91 95
278 280-285 288-293 295-
301 303 **119** 20 153
Robert Alexander **112** 303
Robert H. **106** 157 **107** 79
109 126 238
Robert Humphrey **78** 109
205 **108** 127 147 148
109 122 142 **110** 137
138 **111** 141 142 144 201
112 14 70 87 134 135
137 222 276 314 **113** 61
147-149 151 233 234 293
114 70 140 142 144-147
227 228 306 307 **117** 73
74 148 149 151 153 **118**
163 **120** 153
Roger **63** 306 **112** 283
Rose **112** 282
Rose Ann **112** 302
Royal Cole **86** 307
Ruth Leona **86** 307
Sally **65** 370 **112** 20
Salsbury Wilhemina
(Tipping) **112** 304
Samuel **60** 28 **64** 366 **110**
65 **112** 20 91 280 282-
284 289 291 293 295 296
303
Sarah **54** cl **81** 431 **84** 320
110 65 **112** 18 281 282
289 293 295 296 298 300
302 303 **128** 160
Sarah (Campbell) **112**
280 281
Sarah (Colville) **112** 20
Sarah (Davis) **112** 98
Sarah (Hardy) **112** 295
Sarah (Heries) **112** 293
Sarah Adelaide **63** 49
Sarah Ann **76** 35 36
Sarah E. **113** 313
Sidney **112** 298-300
Sidney (Gamble) **112** 299
Smith **112** 92 96
Sonata **112** 98
Sophia **112** 98 282
Sophie (Tipping) **112** 300
Sophie P. **112** 94
Stella **81** 222
Stella (Scarborough)
85 340
Stewart **106** 109
Susan **76** 37 **88** 280
112 283
Susan (Lucas) **103** 46
Susan (Steyning) **112** 293
Susan M. (Dennison)
96 286
Susanna **52** 41 **112** 280
293
Sydney (Gamble) **112** 299
Thomas **85** 97 **92** 285 **110**
125 **112** 89-96 98 278

MONTGOMERY cont'd
280 281 284 285 287-290
292 294-296 300-304
120 239
Thomas B. **112** 94 99
Thomas Harrison
112 276
Thomas L. **80** 338
Thomas Lynch **71** 96
Thomas McBurney
112 281
Tom **112** 96
Troilus **112** 293
U. **112** 297
W. G. **54** 125
Walter Crockett **85** 97
Webster Clay **85** 340
Webster Clay (Mrs.) **81**
111 222 **85** 340 346 **86**
204
Will **112** 304
William **54** 123 **60** 28 **76**
97 **79** 123 **88** 375 **89** 103
103 46 **112** 87 89-99 276
279-284 289-295 299 301-
303 **119** 20
William Bancroft **96** 286
William G. **112** 15
William L **112** 93
William P. **112** 93
Willis Edgar **79** 186 **80**
208 **85** 97 107 205
Winslow Lewis **74** 207
Woodson C. **112** 93 98
Zibella **112** 287
MONTGOMERY-MOORE
Acheson **112** 301
Alexander James **112** 300
Anne **112** 301
James **112** 300
Nathaniel **112** 301
Robert **112** 300
MONTIER Peter **114** 250
MONTMORENCI
Mathieu de **119** 97 100
MONTO Mary **126** 67
MONTOEU
Joseph **125** 108
Mary (Sterling) **125** 108
MONTRE Conrad **85** 338
Louisa (Blinn) **85** 338
Sophia Eliza **85** 338
MONTRESOR
John **65** 203
MONTROSE
David A. **111** 305
James Grahame
(Marquis of) **52** 13
Joseph J. **111** 300 305
Myrtle A. (Baulch)
111 300
MONTROSS —— **54** 456
MONTS DU GUAFT
Pierre Sieur de **68**
lxxv
MONTSOREL
Isabel **145** 4 5
James **145** 4
MONVILLE
Nigel de **100** 305
Mony see Money

MONYASH
William de **80** 381
MONZINGER
Sarah D. **69** 265
MOO Peter **61** 360
Mooar *see* Moore
Mooars *see* Mooers
MOOBAT Joseph **65** 234
MOOBERRY
Alva Wilson **90** 345
Ethel Leona (Bishop)
90 345
Lintner **90** 345
Lucretia (Hale) **90** 345
MOOD Fulmer **83** 374 507
92 401 **104** 30 **105** 18
James M. **108** 215
Peter **95** 208
Rosanna **63** 379
Sarah **63** 379
Sarah Ann (Harding)
108 215
MOODY Modey Modye
Moody Mowdye
Mowdye
— Mr. **53** 454 **56** 26 110
71 54 118 **76** 141
____ (Impson) **105** 240
A. **66** 362
Aaron **88** 206 207
Abby A. (Talpey) **119**
283 285
Abigail **55** 310 **63** 378 **64**
374 **66** 277 **73** 102 **84**
426 **103** 258
Abigail (Hopkins)
103 169
Abigail Peaslee **91** 186
Abraham **56** 213
Adelia (Van Zile) **131** 156
Adelphia **85** 95 **89** 181
Adonijah **72** 318
Agnes **80** 319 320 323
Albert **73** 185 **92** 226
Alfred L. **123** 151
Alice **66** liii **80** 320 **82**
124 247 490 **100** 254
Alice Fairfield **100** 107
Alma C. **148** 175
Alma F. **148** 175
Almira **64** 154
Almira (Kingsbury) **116**
304 305
Alvin **103** 264
Amanda **56** 171 **66** 47
Ambrose **80** 318 325
Amos **63** 378 **64** 374 **91**
265 **118** 313
Amos Ralph (Mrs.)
117 150
Ann **56** 182 **58** lxxxvi **80**
318 319 325
Anna **51** 442 **72** 318 **103**
191 **108** 54
Anna (Jacobs) **89** 150
Anne **80** 314-316 318-320
322 323 325 326 **87** 38
Anne M. **69** 256
Anson **72** 318
Asaph **107** 201
Augustus B. **98** 259

MOODY *cont'd*
B. Maria **72** 50
Barbara **131** 100
Barberry Ann **119** 229 276
Beatrice Robbins (Porter)
83 436 438
Benjamin **85** 95 **91** 266
103 256 258 259 261
104 284
Betsey **58** 17 **63** 378 **64**
117 374 **66** 362 **87** 124
103 268 **135** 339
Betsey (Chase) (Ayer)
(Whitney) **88** 9
Betsey (Holton) **136** 323
Betsey (Rolf) **103** 235
Betsey (Uran) **135** 339
Betsey S. **81** 418
Bridget (Davis) **95** 87
Caroline **73** 185 **93** 332
Caroline P. **93** 109
Carrie P. **93** 109
Catherine **81** 418 **104** 284
Catherine (Ho___) **84** 425
Catherine B. **57** 291
Charles **56** 171 **107** 272
108 55 **117** 223 224
Charles Benjamin **83** 436
438
Charles H. **93** 109
Charles S. **148** 178
Chester **57** 290-292
Chester E. **93** 332
Chrissa (Kinsley) **88** 206
Chrissa K. **88** 206
Chrissa K. (Kinsley)
88 207
Christian **80** 316 319 323
326
Christopher C. **117** 165
Clara A. **93** 332 339
Clara J. **93** 332
Clement **55** 66 **90** 228 245
Cordelia **57** 290
Cotton **57** 357 358
Cutting **133** 156
Cyrena **64** 117
Cyrus **72** 50
Daniel **58** 32 **64** 117 155
82 490 **92** 339 340 **98**
259 **107** 197 **111** 232
114 127 **135** 339 **145**
348 **147** 272
Daniel W. **92** 339
Darius **64** 117 **135** 339
David **55** 442 **56** 42 **92** 226
David F. **56** xxxii
Deborah **55** 377 378
93 317
Dorcas **118** 241
Dorothy **56** 309 **58** 122
Dorothy Rose **113** 126
116 130
Dudley **88** 9
Dwight L. **82** 116
Dwight Lyman **76** lvi
136 153 323
E. E. **72** 98
Eben E. **93** 332
Ebenezer **72** 318 **80** 327 **93**
332 **111** 232 **116** 141

MOODY *cont'd*
143 226 **133** 155 156 233
Edith I. **92** 339
Editha **80** 327
Edmond **53** 464
Edmund **56** 213 **80** 314-
316 319-321 323 325
Edmund E. **72** 50
Edward **80** 325
Edward C. **83** 300 **121** 307
Edward F. **98** 198
Edward Fairfield **82** 490
Edward Lyman **57** 358
Edwin **103** 270 **136** 323
Elbridge **103** 260
Elbridge G. **103** 262 265
Eleazer **80** 317 **106** 34
Eli **88** 206 207
Elias **103** 190 **105** 240
148 170
Eliezer **112** 173
Elijah **63** 378 **64** 374 **93** 332
Elisha **147** 260
Elisha William Budd
95 169
Eliza **51** 65 **56** 171 **64** 117
89 66 **123** 234 **148** 178
Eliza (Dixey) **120** 219
Eliza (Powers) **147** 128
Eliza H. **72** 50
Elizabeth **56** 70 **60** 360 **63**
377 **64** 76 **65** 256 334 **66**
142 335 **73** 101 181 **79**
44 **80** 316-320 324 325
88 206 207 **90** 227 244
99 200 **103** 188 254 **108**
122 **113** 126 308 **116**
317 **118** 98
Elizabeth (Go___) **91** 266
Elizabeth (Jacques) **133**
156 233
Elizabeth (Moore) **113**
126 **115** 58
Ellen **57** 358
Ellen E. (Ellis) **117** 165
Elmira **66** 263
Elvira **93** 332
Emeline **57** 292
Emerson **72** 49 98
Emily **103** 260
Emily (Boston) **119** 277
Emily (Rich) **84** 298
Emma C. **121** 306 **122** 149
Emma R. **98** 259
Emmy **103** 268
Enoch **78** 110
Epaphras **72** 318
Ephraim **145** 364
Ermina **72** 50
Esther **87** 125
Esther (Davice) **91** 268
Eunice **90** 107
Eunice Balch **89** 63
Eunice Stratton **93** 187
Evitts **125** 37
Ezekiel **84** 424
Ezra **56** 172 **62** 261 **90** 342
113 32
Fairbanks **56** 385
Fannie P. **123** 74
Filpah **56** 171

MOODY *cont'd*
Florence **103** 266
Frances **80** 318 319 324
Francis **56** 213
Frank **108** 268
Frederick **108** 268
Friend **91** 268
G. W. **91** 330
George **56** xxx 213 **65**
  256 334 **66** 261 263 **80**
  314-320 322-326 **99** 198-
  200 **116** 304 305 **119** 61
George W. **82** 490 **108** 268
Grace **80** 315 316 323
Granville **119** 240
H. **66** 362
Hannah **52** 221 **56** 42 169
  171 **63** 377 **64** 76 **67** 211
  212 **80** 318 327 **87** 287
  392 **88** 206 207 **94** 64 **95**
  86 87 **97** 355 **108** 56 **110**
  288 **113** 126 **114** 294
  119 287 **121** 174
Hannah (Sewell) **109** 301
Hannah (True) **121** 174
Hannah (Warner) **88** 206
Hannah Irene **56** 171
Harriet **99** 202
Harriet (Baker) **117** 221
  222
Harriet E. **120** 140 **123** 151
Harriet Elizabeth **120** 215
Henry **53** 302 **55** 377 **66**
  277 **80** 318 325 **97** 355
  107 46
Henry P. **91** 200 203
Henry Pike **97** 355
Hepzibah **56** 171
Herbert A. **75** 241 **101** 258
Honor **113** 301
Howard A. **92** 339
Huldah **147** 272
Humphrey E. **69** 256
I. P. **119** 285
Ida M. (Marshall) **123** 151
Isaiah **93** 187
Isaiah P. **119** 283 **120** 219
Iva **92** 226
J. H. **54** 236
J. P. **119** 285
Jacob **107** 63
James **64** 117 **100** 76 **127**
  139 **135** 339
James Cotton **57** 357
James W. **56** xxxii
Jane **63** 377 378 **64** 374 **66**
  277 366 **89** 361 **95** 169
Jane (Chamberlain) **85** 95
Jane Little **83** 472
Jane Little (Brown) **97** 355
Jenne **115** 306
John **54** 148 **56** 41 42 182
  213 **58** lxxxvi 17 **61** 25
  62 327 **63** 202 355 **64**
  116 117 260 **66** 245 277
  362 366 **80** 313-316 318
  319 321 323 325-327 **84**
  336 426 **85** 30 **88** 206
  207 **99** 79 **103** 191 194
  197 257 260 262 264 **108**
  32 **110** 288 **115** 225 **116**

MOODY *cont'd*
  317 **133** 156 233 **135**
  339 **147** 129
Joseph **66** 262 **87** 206 **90**
  390 **91** 93 **95** 86 87 **103**
  264 **109** 301 **110** 62 288
  113 126 **114** 46 50 51
  125-127 129 132 291-295
  115 58 59 309 **117** 221
  222 **118** 189 **123** 234
  145 364
Joseph A. **120** 216
Joseph F. **148** 178
Joseph H. **93** 332 **120** 140
  123 74 151
Joseph Howard **120** 215
Joshua **60** 384 **61** 281 **63**
  378 **64** 374 **66** 35 141
  142 **70** 267 **87** 398 **89**
  150 **91** 93 **95** 224 228 **96**
  379 **97** 346 **121** 166 **134**
  146 **145** 47
Jotham **56** 171
Judith **80** 319 323 **88** 195
Julia M. **148** 175
Julietta (Marshall) **83** 300
  121 307
Julyann **103** 262
Katharine V. **69** 256
L. B. **127** 26
Laura Ann **90** 342
Lawrence Elliott **104** 144
Levi **84** 425
Levi W. **121** 240
Lewis **87** 92
Lizzie J. **93** 332
Lois **87** 123 **90** 228 246
Lois E. (Seymour) **133** 26
Lorenzo **93** 332
Louis **103** 264
Louisa **103** 266
Love **115** 306
Lucina **72** 318
Lucinda Delphia **57** 290
Lucy **57** 357 358 **63** 379
  72 318 **74** 102 **109** 301
  110 288 **113** 126 **115**
  227 **116** 138 296 **123**
  153
Lucy (White) **110** 288
  114 46
Lucy P. **56** 171
Lydia **80** 319 324 **131** 171
  133 155 233
Lydia (Bartlett) **133** 155
  233
Lydia (Preble) **115** 309
Mager **103** 256 257 259
Malvina **100** 193
Margaret **56** 42 **63** 377
  64 374 **66** 277 366 **80**
  315-317 319 320 323-326
  90 337 **119** 145
Margaret (Umberhind)
  84 426
Margaret E. **92** 339
Margery **80** 319 323
Maria (Barrell) **115** 309
Marian **82** 490
Marinus A. **131** 156
Martha **55** 197 **60** 383 **61**

MOODY *cont'd*
  281 **62** 261 **90** 337 339
Martha (Collins) **89** 150
Martin **81** 418
Mary **53** 38 **55** 197 **56** 41
  42 172 **58** lxxxvi **64** 155
  66 245 301 **72** 49 315 **75**
  105 **79** 51 303 **80** 315
  316 318-320 323 325-327
  84 220 **95** 86 87 **97** 355
  99 199 **103** 194 **107** 73
  197 198 200 201 270-272
  108 54-56 192 238 306
  109 301 **111** 228 **113** 32
  114 290 **115** 226 **135**
  339 **136** 315
Mary (Jones) **87** 92
Mary (Pearce) **111** 232
  114 127
Mary (Smith) **107** 63
Mary A. **120** 68 **123** 234
Mary D. **95** 330
Mary Elizabeth **103** 262
Mary Elizabeth (Davis)
  120 64 65
Mary Fitch **56** 42
Mary J. **123** 234
Mary L. **119** 284 285
Mary Louisa (Falley)
  108 268
Mary P. **121** 71
Mary S. **72** 50 106 **120** 304
Mary Sophia **56** 171
Matilda S. (Putnam)
  119 61
Mehitable **64** 117 **135** 339
Mehitable (Scribner) **90**
  228 245
Mercy **113** 40
Mildred **103** 120
Miriam **63** 169
Miriam (Emery) **133** 156
  233
Miriam (Sewall) **115** 228
Molly (French) **133** 156
  233
Moses **64** 117 **87** 123 **103**
  257 259 **133** 156 233
  135 339
Nancy **56** 171 **57** 290-292
  63 377 **64** 76 116 117 **66**
  277 362 **73** 93 **135** 339
Nancy (Uran) **135** 339
Nancy E. **121** 178
Narcissa **103** 256
Nathan **103** 235 297
Nathaniel **78** 111 **140** 170
Nathaniel Green **60** 360
  75 105
Nettie M. **93** 109
Nora **78** 428
Olive **63** 377 **64** 76 **66** 362
Oliver B. **93** 332 339
Orrin **103** 265
Paron **76** 45 46
Pearce **103** 254
Peggy **119** 145
Persis A. **98** 259
Phebe **64** 117
Phebe Jane **95** 335
Phila (Alexander) **93** 187

MOODY *cont'd*
Polly **64** 117 **115** 226
Polly (Benner) **84** 424
R. **66** 366
Rachel **100** 76
Rachel (Hodgkins)
  134 146
Ray (Mrs.) **108** 135
Rebecca **63** 378 **64** 374 **65**
  256 334 **99** 198-200 **133**
  324 **145** 47
Rebecca A. **148** 178
Rebecca Ruth (Wilkinson)
  108 268
Rhoda **92** 339 340
Richard **53** 302 **55** 377 **58**
  122 **80** 314 315 319-324
Robert **66** 261 **80** 315 320
  323 **93** 317
Robert E. **86** 192 **101** 337
  114 141
Robert Earle **92** 295
  93 132
Robert F. **131** 248
Robert Rose **113** 126
  115 308
Roswell **90** 337
Roxalina **72** 318
Rufus **103** 195
Rufus A. **120** 64 65
Ruth (Currier) **135** 339
Sally **63** 378 **64** 116 117
  374 **73** 90 **83** 231 **104**
  284 **107** 272 **135** 339
Sally (Bragdon) **117** 223
  224
Samuel **54** 403 **55** 196
  343 391 **56** 209 **63** 169
  392 **64** 117 **69** 349 350
  75 56 57 105 303 **76** 257
  80 314 316-319 324 325
  327 **82** 73 82 **91** 93 **97**
  269 **100** 76 **106** 144 **107**
  161 200 **109** 301 **110**
  288 **113** 126 318 **114** 46
  48-51 125-132 228 290
  291 **115** 228 309 **121**
  174 **127** 115 **133** 156
  233 **134** 102 **135** 339
  145 361
Sarah **51** 303 462 **53** 122 **56**
  35 171 318 **61** 25 **72** 317
  318 **80** 314 316 318 319
  324-327 **82** 498 **90** 227
  245 **92** 326 **106** 144 **113**
  126 **121** 166 169 **133**
  233 **143** 77
Sarah (Knight) **106** 144
Sarah A. **121** 309 **122** 230
Sarah A. (Boston) **120** 216
Sarah Ann **147** 272
Sarah E. **86** 344
Sarah Rachel (Harding)
  95 169
Seth E. **63** 202
Sewall **103** 255 **148** 175
Sidney S. **93** 109
Silas **63** 175 **107** 197 198
  200 201 270-272 **108** 54-
  56 **121** 247
Silas S. **72** 50

MOODY *cont'd*
Solomon **56** 169 171
Sophia **107** 271
Susan **80** 320 **82** 490
  135 339
Susan Jane (Preble) **120**
  140 215 **123** 74 151 234
Susanna **56** 209
Susanna (Landers) **121**
  240 **124** 282 283
Sylvanus **72** 50
Tabitha (Cocks) **134** 146
Thaddeus **63** 379 **66** 277
Thankful **141** 259
Thomas **56** 213 **80** 318
  320-322 325 **107** 194
  110 288 **116** 131 139
Thomasine **80** 315 316 319
  323
W. P. **70** 289
Wealthea **70** 267
William **53** 464 **55** 310
  56 42 86 318 **57** 358 **63**
  202 **66** 277 **71** 118 **75**
  241 **78** 110 111 **80** 319
  87 206 **95** 330 **100** 190
  105 287 **107** 198 **111**
  232 **116** 82 137 **119** 277
  134 146 **140** 206 **143** 77
  148 178
William E. **91** 330
William Falley **108** 267
  268
William H. **58** 103 327
  93 332
William Henry **64** 201
  78 287
Zerviah **72** 318

MOOERS Mooars Moores
——— **97** 400 **145** 45
Abigail (Farwell) **89** 65
Abigail (Hazen) **109** 167
Abigail Hubbard
  (Farwell) **103** 146
Adelia **136** 167
Alida **136** 167
Betsey **61** 169 **109** 205
  138 209
Cynthia **136** 167
Cynthia (Milk) **136** 167
Cynthia Merial (Lazell)
  (Lazell) **89** 103 106
Daniel **143** 259
David **61** 169
Delphina (Reynolds)
  140 265
Dorcas (Pitts) **89** 103
Elizabeth **61** 169 **97** 335
Elizabeth (Gilson) **89** 65
  103 146
Esther **54** 199 200 290
  136 167
Experience (Fitz
  Randolph) **97** 332
Fairbanks **54** 199 200 290
Francis **129** 382
Grace **98** 48
Hannah (Sawtell) **126** 135
Henry **136** 167
Henry C. **136** 167
Joanna **109** 182

MOOERS *cont'd*
John **126** 135
Jonathan **61** 74
Joseph **61** 74
Joseph Benjamin **59**
  xlviii **62** 198
Josiah **140** 265
Levi Van Renceleer
  126 209
Luch **127** 130
Lucinda **54** 200 290
Lucy **127** 130
Lucy (Stone) **103** 146
Margaret (Crage) **97** 332
Maria Buckminster
  89 65 137
Mary **59** lxxxi **121** 132
  136 167
Mary (Colburn) **126** 209
Mary Buckminster (Jones)
  89 65 **103** 146
Mary E. (Doyle) **88** 297
Mercy (Briggs) **123** 118
Millie Chandler
  (Hathaway) **88** 297
  89 136
Nancy **109** 167
Priscilla (Poor) **89** 65
Samuel **54** 199 **136** 167
Sarah **121** 132
Sarah (Ward) **89** 65
Sibyl **61** 74
Virginia (Fisher) **103** 66
  146

MOOGENS Relphe **143** 259
MOOK Leonard Courtney
  (Mrs.) **107** 134
Mary E. **142** 186
MOON Mone Moone
  Moons Moones
  ——— (Barton) **107** 52
Alice **79** 433 **80** 343 353
  356 365 **81** 91 92 317
  318
Amy **65** 289
Angeline **127** 159
Ann **81** 94 316 **82** 67
  107 52
Anna Jane **98** 342
Anna Mary **93** 400
Anne **66** 349 **81** 94 316 317
  107 52
Anthony **65** 289 **76** 278
  81 91 92 318
Beth **120** 79
Catherine **81** 317
Charles **98** 342
Churchill **81** 317 **82** 67
Deanes **81** 186
Deborah **117** 96
Deborah (Peabody)
  117 96
Deborah Hoxie **103** 161
Delos Rensselaer **127** 159
Dennis **55** 334 **93** 385 387
Dionisia **81** 93 317
Ebenezer **117** 97 **128** 296
Edith **80** 357 **81** 91 182
  183 186 317
Eleanor **73** 299 **81** 317
  82 67

MOON *cont'd*
Eleanor (Wiles) **93** 377
Elizabeth **69** 92 **81** 316 317
  82 67
Elizabeth (Manchester)
  101 312
Francis **73** 137 **81** 317
  82 67
George **81** 91 317 318
  82 67
Gilbert **81** 93 184
Hope **101** 312
J. W. **91** 241
J. W. (Mrs.) **91** 241
Jacob **107** 52
James **61** 266 **63** 146 **126**
  156 **129** 60
Jennie **90** 351
Joan **80** 356 357 **81** 91 92
  315 317 318 **82** 66 68
John **63** 146 **73** 104 **81** 91-
  94 179 317 318 **82** 67 **83**
  319 **111** 119
John de **81** 314
Jonathan **115** 294
Julia E. **115** 303 **116** 70
Lydia **73** 301 302
Margaret **80** 356 365 **81** 91
  92 94 182 184 315 320
  82 67 **93** 176
Maria **126** 156
Marie **126** 156
Martha **81** 91 92 318
Mary **73** 301 **81** 92 315-317
Mary Cadwalader
  (Eastburn) **98** 342
Maximilian **81** 92-94 179
  182 183 185 316 317 **82**
  66 67
Meliora **81** 93 94 316
Mercy **116** 212
Morgan **80** 356 366 **81**
  91-93 180 182 185 186
  317 318
Myra **90** 351
Norah (Goldsmith)
  (Craig) **104** 311
Phineas **93** 377
Rebecca **69** 92 **117** 96
Richard **80** 355 356 **81** 91
  92 180 182-185 314 318
  82 66-69
Robert **64** 344 **73** 299 **79**
  433 **80** 355-357 365 **81**
  91-94 178-186 314-320
  82 67 68 **93** 176
Robert C. **52** 85 **53** 458
  459 **54** xvii xxxix **63**
  304 **64** xxxi
Ruthy (Brown) **126** 68
Sabrina (Wright) **126** 156
Sally **115** 294
Seth **126** 156
Tamzine **82** 67
Thomasine **81** 317
Waitey **117** 196
Walter **79** 418 **80** 356 357
  81 91 93 179-186 315
  317 **82** 68 **101** 312
William **63** 243
William de **81** 314

MOON *cont'd*
Zenas **83** 145
Zilpha **124** 45
MOONEY Moony
——— **67** 182 **136** 191
Anna **59** 285
Annie **99** 249
Caroline **92** 313
Clarinda **92** 324
Daniel **65** 311
Elizabeth **82** 17 **85** 234
  95 53
Ellen **82** 17
Hannah **134** 152
Henry Clay **85** 234
Hercules **82** 291 294
  125 96
Hester **65** 311
James **60** 26
James E. **120** 316 **144** 322
Judith P. **69** 137
Lucy G. (Holbrook)
  85 234
Marion **83** 436 **84** 18
Mary **82** 291 294
Michael **62** 129
Nicholas **79** 51
Russell E. **119** 317
Samuel **92** 278 312 313 317
Sylvester **126** 145
Thomas **82** 17
MOONS
Charles **121** 152
Ella **121** 152
Frances O. **121** 152
MOONSOM
William **116** 10
Moony *see* Mooney
Moor *see* Moore
MOORCOCK
  Moorecock Morecock
Amy (Burnham) **145** 338
Audria (Cook) **123** 228
Audrian **123** 228
Bennett **84** 322 **123** 228
  229
Henry **123** 228
Mary **123** 228
Nicholas **123** 228 **145** 338
MOORE Mooar Moor More
——— **51** 126 52 286 289
  53 374 380 415 **55** 351
  57 97 337 **58** 101 321 **59**
  lxxix 80 116 **60** 102 **61**
  207 **63** 45 **67** 276 340 **68**
  357 **70** 305 **71** 124 **73** 68
  75 134 **77** 138 **79** 400
  89 40 **91** 172 342 344
  347 349 350 **92** 63 279
  340 **93** 355 **97** 65 340 **99**
  98 **105** 116 **110** 104 **111**
  280 **112** 105 200 **117**
  124 **119** xiii **136** 32 **145**
  171 **148** 309
—— Bp. **80** 54 **115** 14
—— Capt. **65** 115 **73** 67 **78**
  268 **85** 23 **91** 161 171
  172 **125** 27
—— Col. **66** 116 **77** 137 138
  97 64 **119** 137
—— Dr. **66** 264 312 **67** 70

MOORE *cont'd*
—— Maj. **70** 213
—— Miss **83** 307
—— Mr. **54** 28 **55** 299 **80**
  361 **82** 452 **84** 359 **142**
  367
—— Mrs. **62** 290 353 354
  73 73
—— Prof. **59** 20
—— Rev. **90** 388
—— Widow **73** 68 **77** 25
  83 416 **93** 228
A. **58** 61 62
A. B. **91** 378
A. Frances **52** 75
Aaron **57** 362 369 **104** 124
Aaron Pitts **89** 103 106
Abbie **99** 280
Abby **52** 74
Abby Frances **52** 75
Abel **57** 307 309 368 369
  70 14 15 146 219 **139**
  257
Abiah **59** lxxix **79** 5
Abigail **51** 490 491 **52** 73
  74 **53** 175 325 **54** 222
  387 **55** 378 **57** 302 304-
  309 362-364 366 368-370
  58 177 178 **60** 364 **61** 23
  65 xlvi **70** 345 **71** 222
  281 **77** 25 303 315 **78** 31
  79 400 **82** 206 **91** 347
  349 **98** 56 **105** 57 **109**
  303 **110** 98 **116** 45 300
  140 170
Abigail (Field) **113** 280
Abigail (Peck) **105** 58
Abigail (Stevens) **119** 64
Abigail Ann **61** 23
Abigail Harding **57** 287
Abigail L. **117** 280
Abijah **52** 73 **57** 304 307
  309 364 368 **58** 372 **62**
  304 **71** 281
Abner **57** 308
Abraham **51** 494 **55** 80
  57 303 362 **59** lxxviii
  lxxix **69** 296 **89** 65 **97**
  395 **103** 146 **137** 107
  140 62 **145** 357
Absalom Jackson **78** 43
Acheson **112** 289 300
Achsah **75** 216 263
Ada **81** 254 262 **113** 302
Ada Waterman (Small)
  65 xxxv **66** lii **71** xviii
  90 127 **109** 151
Ada Williamson **82** 266
Adaline **61** 23
Adam **91** 378
Addie (Pulsifer) **98** 311
Addison True **105** 299
Adelaide **65** xlvi
Adelia FitzAlan **86** 341
Adeline **90** 115
Adonijah **57** 368
Agnes **51** 490 **55** 271 **57**
  204 368 **67** 40 42 **71** 312
  73 213 **80** 364 369 **85** 47
  95 263
Alba **76** 74

MOORE *cont'd*
Albert **94** 201 **114** 307
Albert Wilder **94** 28
Alberta Louise (Peters)
90 137
Alex P. **125** 181
Alexander **71** 175 **74** 275
75 138 **76** 50 **111** 209
127 203 **128** 33 **141** 140
141
Alexander Pope **52** 74
Alexander Thompson
82 112
Alfred **53** 465 **121** 190
Alfred Fitler **78** 281
Alfred Fitler (Mrs.) **75** 316
76 xxi
Alfred Thomas **87** 148
Alice **51** 492 493 **55** 378
57 363 365 **58** 312 **78**
294 **88** 32 **105** 19 **106**
315 **129** 51 **139** 231
Alice Leigh **113** 297
Alice Medora **72** xx
Alice Medora (Rogers)
83 112 123 237
Alice Pauline **94** 60
Allen **51** 492
Allen L. **117** 156
Alma Ruth **80** 245
Almira Chauncey **82** 49
Alonzo P. **83** 19
Alta E. **69** 169
Alvena (Riley) **119** 284
Alvin **78** 230 **94** 201
Alvira **59** lxxv
Alwilda **117** 165
Alydia B. **107** 154
Amanda **57** 390
Amanda (Davis) **131** 155
Amanda H. **69** 142
Ambrose **63** 42
Amelia **52** 74 **63** 174
Amos **52** 74 **57** 303 **83** 43
Amy **72** 205 **112** 215 **133**
233 **136** 333
Andrew **51** 494 **63** 161
65 173 174 **71** 298 **105**
113
Angeline **114** 285
Ann **51** 490 494 **52** 73 **53**
175 413 **54** 223 **58** 177
61 23 **67** 334 **73** 219 **78**
182 **79** 165 **82** 86 **93** 89
96 291 **98** 349 **100** 303
114 44
Ann (Moore) **96** 291
Ann (Van Wyck) **97** 64
Ann Elizabeth (Bedell)
103 236
Ann Louisa Whette
90 108
Anna **53** 325 **57** 362-365
367-369 **58** 372 **59** 286
71 261 **72** 47 97 **80** 97
84 440 **104** 121 **111** 41
114 **114** 270 **121** 252
122 29
Anna (Bostwick) **92** 389
Anna (Fitz Randolph)
98 50

MOORE *cont'd*
Anna (Gates) **121** 253
137 361
Anna (Moor) **104** 121
Anna (Smith) **105** 195
Anna Buckham **68** xxxiv
71 xxxiv xliv
Anna F. **72** 104
Anne **55** 311 **57** 301 **58** 177
372 **59** lxxix **67** 340 **82**
90 **90** 66 197 **109** 167
110 98 **114** 134 **118** 257
122 30 32 35 **135** 159
136 332
Anne (Sayre) **119** 182
Annie **98** 334 **123** 232
Annie M. **121** 147 **122** 146
Antiphus Holland **52** 74
Aphrodoza **78** 276
Appachia **55** 80
Arannah **72** 35
Archelaus **78** 294
Archibald **112** 300 **137** 361
Artemas **57** 368 **79** 53
137 361
Artenatus **57** 368
Arthur Scudder **96** 333
Arthur Wendell **65** xlvi
96 160 **103** 66 109 146
104 149
Arthur Wendell (Mrs.) **77**
156 **78** 205 **99** 69 153
103 66
Asa **57** 305 365 366 **69** 246
101 200 **117** 265 **145**
355
Asa W. **103** 235
Asahel **57** 306 **58** 178
Ashbell **57** 307 369 **65** 357
144 219
Augusta **91** 394
Augusta L. **117** 280
Augustus **57** 307 367 368
Augustus Edwin **113**
301 302
Aurelia M. **68** 336
Azariah **105** 58
Azubah **57** 305 306 365 367
Barsheba **57** 368
Bathsheba **52** 73 **57** 362
363 **105** 58
Beatrix **51** 489-491
Belle **89** 302
Benjamin **52** 72 73 **53** 175
325 413 **55** 80 **57** 300-
302 306-345 346-370 **58**
176 177 **59** lxxix **65**
xlvi **73** 69 72 **83** 167 **85**
47 **89** 65 **94** 125 **97** 395
98 104 105 **100** 190 **103**
146 **105** 57 109 167 **111**
280 **112** 367 **115** 25
Benjamin F. **95** 368
Benjamin Franklin **52** 74
Benjamin W. **69** 175
Benoni **57** 302 306 **61** 304
Bernice **73** 213
Bess Louisa (Acree)
100 252
Bessie M. (Shropshire)
117 197

MOORE *cont'd*
Bethiah (Cole) **112** 215
Bethuel **103** 252 **111** 280
285
Betsey **55** 80 81 **57** 365
368 369 **59** 280 **75** 307
77 230 **86** 24 **91** 250
104 59 61 132 **109** 205
116 115 119 183 **125**
102
Betsey (Ruth) **84** 95
Betsey Plume **72** 97
Betty **57** 309 362 365 366
61 207 **112** 105 **113** 128
115 218 **136** 35
Beulah **57** 306 368 **58** 372
Bezaleel **57** 306 367
Blanche **92** 400
Bloomfield Haines **103**
249 253
Bloomfield Haines (Mrs.)
103 249 253
Boaz **57** 367 **135** 34
Bridget **122** 30
Bridget (Lufkin) **122** 29
Burt Wallace (Mrs.) **80**
106 **81** 222
C. W. **57** xxxiii
Caleb **57** 309 **105** 57 60
Calvin **57** 309
Calvin Cooper **119** 75
Calvin G. **88** 334
Candace (Bailey) **92** 171
Carl W. **89** 311
Caroline **83** 21 26 **92** 124
94 39
Caroline (Blunt) **83** 21
Caroline F. (Somes)
85 380
Caroline Matilda **126** 24
Caroline T. **148** 21 35
Carrie A. **110** 106
Carrie Estelle **89** 104
Carrie Evelyn **80** 225 **83**
256 **84** 240 **85** 240 **86**
241 **87** 209 **88** 209 **89**
209
Catherine **57** 309 366 367
73 213 **112** 301 **114** 164-
168 **122** 29 30 **124** 85
Catherine (Moore)
114 164
Catherine (More) **124** 85
Catherine L. (Fonda)
118 291
Celia **78** 281
Celina A. **118** 131
Celinda (Heath) **104** 116
121
Celinda Jane **104** 121
Charles **51** 494 **94** 14 **100**
200 **104** 121 **116** 211
120 65 304 306 **123** 74
140 170 327
Charles Alvah **124** 228
Charles B. **53** 414 **59** 116
91 330 **94** 212
Charles C. **90** 352
Charles Church **65** 94
Charles E. **52** 75
Charles Henry **92** 112

MOORE *cont'd*
  Charles Huntington
    94 23
  Charles T. **77** 235
  Charles V. **91** 330
  Charles W. **51** 91 **72** 205
  Charles Warren **92** 63
  Charles Whitlock **88** 284
  Charles William **83** 295
    92 63
  Charlotte **61** 24
  Charlotte (Tolman)
    88 284
  Charlotte A. **117** 280
  Charlotte Lavern
    (Bradley) **92** 63
  Chauncey **82** 49
  Chester **72** 47 182
  Chester N. **72** 104
  Chloe **72** 39
  Christeen M. **90** 52
  Christina M. **69** 138
  Christopher **112** 286
  Clara **78** 295 **92** 389
  Clara Lillian **89** 311
  Clara M. **92** 163
  Clara Sophia (Jessup) **103**
    249 253
  Clarence Bloomfield
    103 249
  Clarissa (Harlow) **128** 113
  Clarissa Amy **70** 92
  Clarissa Washburn
    75 192
  Clark **68** 336
  Clark B. **68** 336
  Clark L. **92** 171 172
  Climena (Bradley) **84** 118
  Collins **52** 73 **57** 304 362
    364 **64** 35
  Comfort **57** 302 305
  Cornelia **75** 23
  Cornelia L. **75** 14
  Cornet **73** 68
  Crayton M. **75** 14
  Cummin **57** 366
  Curtis **57** 370 **58** 178
    61 23 24
  Cynthia **52** 74
  Cynthia (Milk) **134** 334
  Dallas (Mrs.) **121** 319
  Damaris **71** 277 279
  Daniel **51** 492 498 **52** 73 74
    55 81 **57** 202 301 304
    305 365 366 **59** 59 **61** 23
    91 378 **94** 200 201 **99**
    302 **104** 121 134 **105** 57
    116 212 **109** 205 **110** 24
    104 105 114 **119** 182
    137 334 **143** 261 **145**
    362
  Daniel C. **61** 23
  David **51** 492 **52** 73 **55** 81
    57 308 362 363 370 **61**
    218 **72** 35 **74** 125 182
    184 185 187 192 **77** 295
    81 171 **82** 500 **83** 167
    91 161 **104** 59 61 132
    105 211 **109** 205 **110** 94
    111 204 **112** 17 215 **114**
    43 200 **115** 307 **126** 250

MOORE *cont'd*
    132 323 **137** 322 **145**
    352
  David Fellows **51** 381 **52**
    286 **54** xxxix **55** xxxii
    57 xxxiii **60** xxxvi **61**
    xxxv **65** 94 **70** 96
  David M. **87** 125
  Deborah **53** 171 **55** 80 81
    57 306 364 **73** 213 **110**
    94
  Deborah (Butterfield)
    125 72
  Deborah (Smith) **94** 200
  Della **95** 169
  Dennis **103** 236
  Desire **57** 362 **97** 335
  Dinah **57** 303 307 308 367
    368
  Dolly **112** 215
  Dolly L. **92** 176
  Don Lorenzo **52** 74
  Donald H. (Mrs.) **97** 158
  Donald Kimball (Mrs.)
    80 103 208 337 **89** 379
    90 380 **91** 194 377
  Donald R. **128** 183
  Dorcas **72** 205 **88** 294 **103**
    314 **110** 98 **112** 107 **114**
    132 **115** 307 **116** 89
  Dorcas (Hilton) **110** 98
  Dorcas (Moore) **115** 307
  Dorcas (Raynes) **115** 64
  Doris **100** 112
  Doris Jean (Rutherford)
    (Wright) (Hart)
    117 124
  Dorothy **52** 73 **57** 302
    305-308 363 364 366 367
    81 127 **84** 414 **109** 205
    110 94 **148** 253
  Dorothy (Learned) **84** 414
  Dorothy (Shouldham)
    148 253
  Dorothy May **92** 63
  Dorothy Parsons **113** 302
  Dwight **74** xxx **78** 215
    294 295
  Eben **72** 176
  Eben S. **103** 235
  Ebenezer **54** 387 408 410
    57 364 **70** 345 **71** 224
    83 419 **99** 323 **108** 21
    145 355
  Edith **78** 294 **89** 104
  Edith (Garrison) **92** 63
  Edith (Henry) **91** 247
  Edith Austin **79** 113
    106 77
  Edward **54** 387 **55** 378 **57**
    302 307 364 368 369 **65**
    256 **71** 281 **97** 268 **99**
    206 **101** 55 **112** 302 **113**
    302 **114** 29 **122** 29-33 35
    127 176 **128** 111
  Edward C. **63** 390
  Edward Caldwell **87** 174
  Edward Caldwell (Mrs.)
    84 341 **85** 197
  Edward Livingston
    65 94

MOORE *cont'd*
  Edward Parsons **113** 302
  Edward Procter **113** 302
  Edward Small **109** 151
  Edward Vance **89** 311
  Edwin **119** 284
  Edwin King **58** xlv
  Edwin Roberts **95** 147
  Eleanor **51** 492 493 **52** 73
    57 304 363 **71** 223 **110**
    94 98 **112** 153 289 300
    122 176 177 **124** 182
    183 **135** 159
  Eleanor (Milbourne)
    122 176
  Eleanor Freudenburg
    69 210
  Eleanora **114** 164
  Electa (Tupper) **99** 302
  Eliab **57** 306 366
  Eliakim **127** 67
  Elias **57** 306 366 370 **89** 310
  Elias Crane **79** 73
  Elijah **52** 73 **57** 304 307
    363 364 369 **84** 414 **92**
    171
  Elijah D. **83** 184
  Eliphal **67** 130
  Eliphalet **57** 305 **58** 178
    85 368
  Elisha **72** 39 90 **79** 73
  Eliza **52** 74 **73** 268 **81** 371
    82 294 **109** 205
  Eliza (Durell) **140** 62
  Eliza (Smith) **103** 235
  Eliza A. **117** 280
  Eliza J. **139** 294
  Eliza Jane (Fitzjarald)
    120 224 304
  Elizabeth **51** 490 492 493
    52 72-74 469 **54** 152 387
    55 80 **57** 94 300-302 304-
    306 308 309 362-368 **58**
    176 177 **59** 418 **60** 286
    62 136 **70** 63 228 340 **71**
    279 380 **72** 37 214 **73**
    145 256 **75** 134 **77** 235
    78 294 **79** 79 **81** 30 150
    380 447 **82** 294 301 **83**
    112 292 **91** 77 344 378
    94 121 **97** 335 **99** 329
    103 238 104 124 172
    105 57 58 **110** 94 **111**
    280 **113** 126 302 **114**
    167 115 58 **116** 115 **120**
    255 **121** 48 132 **122** 30
    33-35 **124** 160 **128** 33
    142 200
  Elizabeth (Bryant) **137** 322
    334
  Elizabeth (Burton) **122** 29
  Elizabeth (Dunwell)
    125 237
  Elizabeth (Fitz Randolph)
    97 336
  Elizabeth (Loker) **143** 330
  Elizabeth (Maddox)
    113 302
  Elizabeth (Martin) **120** 5
  Elizabeth (Sackett) **105** 58

MOORE *cont'd*
Elizabeth (Varney)
100 301
Elizabeth (Whale) **114** 155
Elizabeth A. **90** 115
Elizabeth Catherine
(Lazell) **89** 310
Elizabeth Estelle (Wilson)
92 115
Elizabeth Fox **110** 79
Elizabeth Rice **57** 302
Elizabeth Stickney
102 306
Elizabeth Thayer **78** 294
Elizabeth Vaughan **52** 75
Elizabeth W. **124** 228
Ella **89** 104 **90** 136
Ella Carlton **103** 249 250
Ellen **114** 163 **124** 85
Ellen (Moriarty) **89** 226
Elmira **52** 74 **87** 21
Elvira M. **69** 169
Emeline **114** 196
Emery N. **88** 339
Emily **79** 73 **90** 358
Emily Ann **94** 24
Emily Ida (Crandall)
100 200
Emily Louisa (Kellogg)
76 xxi **78** 214 280 281 **79**
73 81 **80** 231 **81** 62 **82**
54 **83** 8 **84** 69 **85** 29 **86**
59 **87** 39 **88** 6 **89** 9 **90**
103 **91** 6 **92** 29 **93** 47 **94**
19 **95** 89 **96** 58 **97** 147
98 90 **99** 70 **100** 127
101 278 **102** 197 **103** 20
240 **104** 212 **105** 248
106 181 **108** 313 **109**
107 **110** 184 **111** 59 **113**
130 **114** 114
Emily M. **75** 14 **77** 207
Emily Maria **74** 314
Emma **80** 245 **87** 21
Emma Emily **111** 240
Emma Palmer **68** xxxv
Enoch **122** 29 30 32-35
Enoch N. **85** 375
Ephraim **57** 306-309 365
366 **61** 23 **89** 104 **100**
204
Erastus A. **98** 314
Esther **53** 171 **55** 80 81 **57**
308 367 369 **78** 230 **81**
345 **101** 200 202 **109**
205
Esther (Ryerson) **86** 341
Esther M. **72** 104
Ethan **57** 368
Ethan Allen **121** 319
Ethel Louise **96** 333
Ethel Lyman **78** 205
Ethel Prescott **65** lxvi
Ethel Sivley **101** 259
Ethelbert Allen **105** 238
Eugene **116** 65 **144** 317
Eunice **53** 175 **55** 197 **57**
304 305 309 365 366 368-
370 **58** 178 372 **61** 23 24
91 378 **97** 340 **114** 99
194 **119** 183 199 **124** 77

MOORE *cont'd*
134 56
Eunice (Farnsworth)
(Weston) **134** 65 66
Eunice (Fitz Randolph)
97 340
Eunice (Ford) **119** 182
Eunice (Haynes) **126** 256
Eunice (Hines) **126** 256
Eunice (Needham)
110 119
Eunice (Owen) **85** 47
Eunice (Willis) **114** 196
Euphemia **51** 490
Eva **116** 67
Eva Carleton **57** xxxiii
Evelyn Hortense **96** 178
Ezekiel **78** 294 **92** 389
Ezra **77** 27
F. B. **91** 201 330
F. C. **77** 303
Fairbank **57** 303 308
58 382
Fanny **57** 365 **72** 102
110 33
Fanny (Lazell) **89** 311
Felice **122** 30
Fidelia Leverett **82** 112
Fidelia Wellman
(Leverett) **81** 217
82 112
Flagg **57** 369
Flavilla R. (Trask) **85** 376
Flora Alice **102** 232
Flora J. **134** 331
Florence L. **104** 140
106 122
Florence Wylie (Wilcox)
102 125
Floyd Warren **94** 139
Frances **53** 175 **55** 68 **76**
117 **82** 275
Frances L. **90** 48
Frances May **78** 161
Frances Wharton **84** 187
Francis **55** 378 **58** 178 **65**
267 **67** 130 **76** 73 74 **80**
97 **93** 89 **99** 280 **101** 161
122 28-30 34-36 **124** 182
Francis J. (Mrs.) **76** xxxiii
117 72
Francis Joseph **65** xlvi
Francis Marion **82** 266
Frank **59** lv xcvi **110** 106
113 90
Frank Barrett (Mrs.)
97 158
Frank H. **88** 297 **127** 282
Frank Remick **60** xxxviii
Frank S. **86** 369
Franklin S. **92** 171
Fred **91** 330
Frederick Porter **83** 112
113
Fuslam **106** 208
G. J. **118** 292
Gardner **57** 309
Garnett Taylor (Mrs.)
100 112
George **51** 492 **52** 456 **58**
207 208 **59** lvi lxxviii-

MOORE *cont'd*
lxxx **63** 27 **69** 362 **73** 85
153 **75** 234 **77** 207 215
250 **85** 455 **90** 66 198 **91**
330 **112** 295 **115** 64 **116**
139 **117** 107
George A. **95** 401
George B. **85** 376
George D. **73** 220
George Ellis **82** 267
George Gordon (Mrs.)
81 345
George H. **92** 64 **123** 75
George J. **92** 64 **118** 292
George James **118** 291
George Morse (Mrs.) **96**
160 **97** 157
George W. **91** 330
George Washington
127 282
George William **80** 245
Georgiana (Atherton)
85 379
Georgie E. **75** 14
Gerry **117** 265
Gershom **105** 58
Gertie M. **75** 14
Gideon **57** 368 369
Gladys Viola (Elwell)
94 28
Goffe **55** 80
Golden **136** 46-48 55
141 220
Grace **52** 73 **57** 304 365
58 177 **98** 48 **109** 205
Grace Guernsey **82** 266
Grace Hyacinth **103** 149
Grace M. (Brayton) **116** 65
Grace Owens **107** 80
Grace Van Dyke **110** 239
Gratia **57** 362
Gregg **100** 200
Grove **132** 144
H. J. **74** 314 **75** 14
Hallie **78** 321
Hannah **51** 493 **52** 73 74
53 175 **54** 223 **55** 81 200
57 302 303 305 306 309
362-367 370 **58** 178 **59**
lxxix **61** 242 250 **68** 168
69 323 **70** 345 **72** 36 **78**
294 **79** 79 **85** 381 **88** 32
89 110 **90** 383 **103** 68
104 124 **110** 94 98 **111**
280 **114** 103 290 **116**
136 141 **119** 182 **121**
223 **125** 92 94 **127** 140
Hannah (Carney) **104** 124
Hannah (Eayre) **111** 280
Hannah (Gillett) **101** 49
Hannah (Harris) **114** 295
Hannah (Hayes) **123** 75
Hannah (Hill) **125** 92 94
Hannah (James) **126** 249
Hannah (Jordan) **110** 97
Hannah (Stover) **85** 304
114 292
Hannah (Studley) **96** 185
111 241
Hannah A. **116** 211
Hannah C. **114** 307

MOORE *cont'd*
Hannah G. (Rutherford)
    117 119
Hannah Gleason **57** 302
Hannah J. **75** 247
Hannah Maria **120** 64
Hariet **126** 170
Harold Nies **92** 389
Harriet **71** 286 **72** 102 **78**
    294 **96** 291 **119** 202 203
    126 170 **132** 323
Harriet (Gibbs) **125** 173
Harriet Amelia **72** 299
Harriet E. D. **91** 330
Harriet L. **72** 126
Harriet N. **120** 137
Harriet Newell **52** 456
Harriet W. **90** 206
Harry **71** 55 **100** 200
Harry Denton **80** 103 205
    92 199 389 **93** 139
Harry Gove **92** 389
Harry Oliver **99** 148
Harry W. **105** 299
Hartshorne **97** 340
Harvey **73** 64
Hasadiah **57** 302 303
Hattie **96** 135
Hazard L. **53** 171
Helen **82** 56 **84** 188 **89** 112
Helen A. **83** 19 **114** 307
Helen A. (Burleigh) **83** 19
Helen Blackstone **82** 267
Helen Catherine **96** 333
Helen L. (Beal) **120** 304
    306 **123** 74 235
Helen M. (Stanley) **85** 377
Helen Marie **71** 72
Helen Rhodes (Bancroft)
    96 333
Helen Rosannah **72** 97
Henry **51** 494 **52** 126 **57**
    304 **61** 24 **71** 79 158 279
    72 35 **83** 35 **90** 45 110
    92 63 **100** 287 **123** 251
    125 104 **134** 334
Henry Clarke **92** 63
Henry D. **120** 69
Henry Porter **69** 169
Hepzibah **57** 309 370
Herbert **145** 362
Herbert W. **71** 72
Hercules **111** 319
Hester W. **125** 54
Hezekiah **57** 302 306 307
    366 369 370 **144** 219
Hiram **70** 345 **78** 31
Hiram D. **77** 303
Hobart **109** 151
Holland **75** 14
Horace Leon **89** 311
Horatio **73** 230
Howard **78** 294
Howard P. **72** 248 **124** 242
Howard Parker **103** 237
Hoyt Augustus **90** 137
    113 232 301
Hugh **51** 489 492-494 **55**
    80 **57** 204 **84** 152 368
    376 **112** 302 **124** 228
Hugh (Mrs.) **70** 17

MOORE *cont'd*
Huldah **69** 175
Humphrey **57** 367 **61** 242
Ida **98** 314
Ida Florence **78** 177
Ida L. **116** 61
Increase **57** 305
Irene (Huntley) (Ryan)
    101 143
Isaac **52** 73 74 **53** 87 **57** 303-
    305 362 363 365 366 **61**
    23 24 **66** 240 **87** 21 **90**
    110 **94** 24 **96** 185 **106**
    228 **111** 241 **137** 322
    334
Isaac Elijah **96** 185
Isaac Perry **52** 74
Isabel **51** 492 **55** 81 **72** 60
Isabella **72** 274 **74** 146
Isabella Graham (Boyd)
    125 244
Isham **77** 260
Israel **57** 304 305 309 365
    114 99 **131** 120
Israel Gordell **57** 287
J. B. **55** 188 **93** 274 **124** 303
J. C. **116** 211
J. K. (Mrs.) **83** 124 233
J. Staunton **59** xliv 119
J. W. **52** 98
Jabez **91** 378
Jacob **52** 72 73 **57** 300 301
    303-306 309 362-366 **58**
    176 177 **98** 55 **105** 58
    143 330
Jacob B. **59** xcvi **92** 312
    99 9
Jacob Bailey **64** 228 **92** 312
    102 86
Jael **83** 205
James **51** 488 489 491-494
    53 175 **55** 80 81 **57** 301
    302 305 365 **58** 177 178
    60 242 346 **61** 137 **63** 26
    69 163 **71** 124 217 **72**
    205 **73** 220 256 **77** 25
    250 268 **82** 91 **83** 416
    420 **84** 153 **85** 304 **92**
    171 **97** 332 **99** 206 **100**
    243 304 **101** 55 **104** 121
    105 282 **111** 210 **114**
    292 **116** 115 **117** 265
    125 237 **127** 239 **135**
    159
James (Mrs.) **83** 418
James F. **103** 29 30
James Fullerton **127** 203
James H. **69** 142 **76** 50
James Perazim Gilboa
    53 175
James W. **55** 230 **59** xliv
    116
Jane **51** 491 492 494 **53** 175
    57 366 **61** 24 **63** 174 **67**
    353 **68** 332 **71** 55 **91** 378
    94 201 **104** 266 **111** 255
    122 30 **124** 182 183 **127**
    203
Jane (Andrews) **90** 68
Jane (Doremus) **97** 386

MOORE *cont'd*
Jane (Foliott) (Clifton)
    124 183
Jane (Montgomery)
    112 20
Jane G. **82** 128
Jane Libbey **90** 50
Jane R. **95** 246
Janet **51** 490 492-494 **82** 91
    110 141 **127** 203 **128** 33
Jasper **104** 116 121 **114**
    163 164 167 **124** 85
Jean **51** 490
Jeannette **94** 28
Jeduthun **57** 307 366 367
Jefferson **117** 261 265 268
Jeffrey **80** 364 369
Jehoida **51** 490
Jennet **55** 81
Jennie M. **52** 75
Jenny **55** 81
Jenny E. **63** 273
Jeptha **57** 368 **58** 372
Jeremiah **55** 378 **83** 418
Jeremy **55** 378
Jerusha **53** 175 **57** 363
Jerusha (Beal) **117** 144 224
Jesse **57** 366 367 **61** 24
Jesse Ozias **70** 92
Jessie Fremont **82** 267
Joab **51** 490
Joan **80** 385
Joan (Champney) **136** 47
Joanna **82** 49 **108** 21 **109**
    182 **113** 302 **115** 62
Joanna (Deering) **108** 21
Joanna C. **83** 26 27
Joanna H. **88** 382 **118** 154
    242
Joel **57** 369 **117** 225
Joel Roscoe **67** 386
John **51** 144 488-490 492-
    494 **52** 68 72-74 98 337
    53 49 **54** 222 223 387 **55**
    80 81 351 **57** 204 300-
    309 347 362-370 **58** 176-
    178 316 323 **59** 78 116
    136 326 **60** 27 242 283
    364 **61** xxxiv 207 **62**
    329 388 **63** 24 75 142
    174 293 295 **64** 158 198
    325 **65** 30 233 234 **66**
    259 260 **68** 168 **69** 175
    219 **70** 63 340 **71** 218 **72**
    248 274 73 76 132 143
    213 256 **75** 238 **77** 75
    239 **78** 294 313 **79** 73 **81**
    380 431 **82** 49 **83** 21 26
    319 **84** 95 118 **86** 72 341
    349 **88** 32 269 **91** 330
    378 **92** 171 397 **93** 385
    387 **94** 171 **96** 185 **97**
    335 **98** 55 **100** 139 274
    277 **101** 47 **102** 35 **104**
    121 **105** 57 58 195 212
    106 20 153 **109** 205 298
    303 **110** 97 119 289 **111**
    41 117 173 280 **112** 105
    113 128 270 **114** 155
    182 **115** 223 251 **116**
    115 **117** 144 224 **121**

MOORE *cont'd*
223 253 260 **122** 176 178
123 193 **126** 249 250
256 **127** 203 229 **128** 20
36 113 269 **134** 65 **137**
361 **141** 25 **142** 107 **145**
354
John B. **61** 233 **125** 54
John Bartlett **73** 213
John C. **73** 264 **101** 120
John Calvin **83** 112
John Clark (Mrs.) **90** 137
152 **91** 158
John D. **75** 14 23
John F. **103** 147
John Farwell **64** 331
65 xlvi
John Farwell (Mrs.) **77**
238 **78** 205
John Fredrick **110** 104
John H. **77** 207 **104** 121
John Henry **82** 422
John Hubbard **57** 367
John Leverett **75** xxiii 64
81 109 217 230 **82** 112
John M. **91** 330
John Polk **78** 169
John White **78** 169
Jonadab **54** 387 **57** 362
Jonas **57** 308 365
Jonathan **52** 73 **53** 329 **54**
223 **55** 251 253 **57** 204
301-303 305 306 309 362
363 365 368 369 **58** 178
372 **83** 412 **100** 190 **118**
131 **120** 255 261 **121**
132 247 **125** 59
Jonathan H. **78** 411
Joseph **51** 449 492 **52** 72 73
55 80 81 **57** 300-303 306
309 366-368 **58** 131 176
63 74 **64** 9 231 320 **70**
345 **71** 224 **73** 224 **78**
281 414 **89** 65 **91** 350 **93**
355 **94** 60 170 171 200
95 253 256 **96** 380 **97**
369 377 **98** 55 56 **103**
146 299 **105** 57-60 **113**
77 196 **116** 128 **121** 106
135 22 **137** 93
Joseph Benjamin **65** xlv
xlvi **89** 65 **103** 146
Joseph Clifford **63** 314
Joseph H. **119** 229
Josephine **92** 63 **97** 386
109 263
Josephine Harriet **103** 49
Joshua **52** 74 **53** 175 **57**
303 308 **63** 169 175 **79**
73 79 **111** 280 **115** 139
303 304 **119** 83 **123** 187
126 256 **128** 20 **131** 155
145 354
Joshua S. **85** 380
Josiah **57** 305 309 365 368
68 lxxviii **73** 135 **79** 49
105 290 **110** 94 **112** 105
120 224 304
Jotham **94** 125 **113** 128
Judah **57** 306 **58** 178
Judith **57** 301 304 308 **122**

MOORE *cont'd*
29 30
Judith G. **81** 151
Julia **89** 226 **125** 54
Julia (Lee) **126** 182
Julia A. **87** 80
Julia A. (Wadleigh)
123 75
Julia Frances (Carlton)
110 106 210
Julia King **127** 282
Julia Mary **61** 233
Julia S. **85** 380
Julie L. **52** 75
Juliette (Wilson) **144** 317
Kateryn **90** 66
Katharine **51** 494 **52** 74
77 268 **90** 198 **92** 389
114 165-167 274 **122** 36
Katharine (Nies) **92** 389
Kathryn Van Tassel **92** 63
Keturah **111** 280
Keturah (Van Hoesen)
92 389
Keziah **57** 306 307 366 369
114 28
Keziah (Goodnow)
114 29
Keziah (Willis) **114** 29
L. A. **116** 211
L. H. **116** 211
LaRue **117** 119
Laura **71** 52
Laura Cunard **71** 72
Laura M. **59** xcvi
Lavina **116** 300 301
Lavinia **113** 196 **116** 301
Lavinia D. **120** 139 140
Lavinia Gordon **81** 324
Lawrence L. **98** 50
Leila Carter (Curtis)
99 148
Lemuel **79** 79 **85** 373
Lenstanday **57** 368
Leonard **109** 205 **110** 210
Leonard Irish **110** 106
Letitia **51** 490
Letitia (Carver) **89** 40
Letty **73** 266
Levi **57** 309 363 **73** 213 228
77 19 24-27 **117** 265
Levinia D. **120** 140
Lewis **57** 369 **61** 24
117 265
Lewis C. **110** 106
Libbie (Maben) **92** 171
Lilla Day **100** 204
Lillian Augusta Stuart
103 249
Lillian Sophia (Keller)
97 158
Linda A. **117** 166
Lindsley A. **92** 171
Linus **97** 386
Lizzie **83** 100
Lizzie M. **75** 23
Lizzie O. **118** 131
Loammi **119** 198
Lois **51** 490 **57** 309 368
Lois M. (Locke) **83** 300
Lora (Parsons) **113** 302

MOORE *cont'd*
Lorenzo **94** 201
Lorin **73** 256
Lorinda (Needham)
110 114
Louis Trenchard **69** 210
Louisa **78** 399 **92** 171 172
Louisa (Beal) **123** 235
Louisa (Sanford) **92** 171
Louisa Pettitot St. Leger
(Atkins) **117** 107
Louisa Sanford **92** 171
Louisa Sophia (Hixon)
114 196
Louise Alice **82** 275
Louise Virginia **105** 126
Love **57** 367
Lucia W. **52** 75
Lucinda **57** 368 **58** 178 **84**
209 **110** 117 **113** 229
Lucinda (Trask) **85** 375
Lucinda (Wells) **96** 291
Lucretia **57** 307 **79** 73
Lucy **57** 307 309 363 365-
367 369 **73** 229 **111** 41
114 270 **126** 205
Lucy Ann (Chase) **88** 13
Lucy E. (Barrett) **127** 282
Lucy H. **52** 74
Luke **57** 307 369
Luther **53** 329 **57** 365 369
Lydia **51** 494 **52** 72 73 **57**
300-303 305 306 370 **58**
177 **63** 330 **72** 100 299
94 171 201 **96** 75 **108** 22
112 226 **116** 208 298
300 **122** 53 **136** 47-49 53
57
Lydia (Daggett) **103** 235
Lydia (Milberry) **113** 128
Lydia A. (Faulkner)
114 196
Lydia Fullerton **127** 203
Lydia J. **52** 74
Lydia Jane **113** 197 **119**
283 284 **123** 75
Lydia R. (Goodwin) **117**
140 141
Lyman **117** 265
M. F. **113** 91
M. J. (Mrs.) **114** 261
M. T. **73** 213
Mabel **89** 104
Mae Emily **92** 63
Marcia M. (Church) **94** 28
Marcus **52** 74
Marcy **57** 364
Margaret **51** 492-494 **55**
80 81 **57** 308 **59** 81 **60**
360 **62** 252 **65** 233 **69**
163 **81** 222 **82** 487 **84** 80
91 342 **105** 116 **109** 12
116 115 **122** 35 176 **125**
102 **140** 170
Margaret (Crage) **97** 332
Margaret (Lymburner)
104 134
Margaret Crawford
78 294
Margaret Ellen **68** lxxviii
Margaret H. **83** 174 182

MOORE *cont'd*
184
Margaret Ham **82** 422
Margaret Jenny (Forrest)
145 174
Margaret Phillips **78** 169
Margaret R. **77** 268
Margery **63** 175 **95** 358
98 84
Maria **52** 73 **57** 301 303
85 426 **114** 164
Maria Adeline **82** 266
Maria Buckminster **65**
xlvi **78** 203 **89** 65 81 137
Maria Cynthia **113** 295
Maria Naomi **77** 223
Marie **57** 301 **58** 177 **74**
275 **75** 138 **90** 66 198
Marion (Wright) **84** 206
85 215
Marjorie Standish
(Devlin) **76** xxxiii **84**
181 **90** 124 **96** 154
Mark **82** 49
Marrietta **115** 121
Martha **51** 492 493 **53** 175
55 81 222 **57** 303 305
363-366 368 **58** 382 **61**
24 **69** 262 73 213 **78** 43
83 43 **99** 280 **103** 145
105 58 **109** 303 **110** 98
111 285 112 105 **115**
219 222 **116** 119 **128** 36
113
Martha (Cobb) **127** 203
Martha (Houghton)
89 104
Martha (Hovey) **88** 334
Martha (Philbrook)
112 105
Martha (Rider) **126** 208
Martha (Walford) **109** 303
Martha (White) (Cooke)
142 367 368
Martha A. **82** 375
Martha Eliza **128** 181
Martha Elizabeth **127** 203
Martha M. **125** 183
Martha N. **125** 183
Martin **57** 369 **61** 23 24
117 265 **144** 317
Marvin **57** 364
Mary **51** 489-494 **52** 72-74
126 337 **53** 329 **54** 387
55 80 81 378 401 423 **57**
300-307 362-367 **58** 178
316 **59** 78 326 **61** 24 **62**
304 **63** 174 **65** 165 **67**
375 **68** 336 **71** 175 177
203 **72** 293 **73** 70 219
270 286 **77** 250 **78** 294
79 86 100 **82** 291 294
422 444 452 **84** 4 300
374 376 **85** 333 **87** 390
90 68 **91** 296 **92** 171 **95**
273 375 **97** 302 **99** 206
323 **101** 55 272 **104** 59
61 **105** 57 58 **107** 69 **108**
88 199 268 **109** 151 303
110 94 98 **111** 280 **112**
132 215 294 **113** 30 37

MOORE *cont'd*
114 44 130 134 175 **115**
221 **117** 37 221 222 **118**
317 **121** 132 **122** 29 30
123 149 **126** 79 **127** 203
128 36 113 **136** 38 333
145 262
Mary (Allen) **111** 280
Mary (Ayres) **119** 183
Mary (Barber) (James)
126 250
Mary (Blaisdell) **119** 229
Mary (Bolton) **110** 104
Mary (Brown) **94** 24
131 120
Mary (Cole) **115** 139
Mary (Collins) **89** 150
Mary (Crow) (Allen)
125 236
Mary (Dougherty)
100 304
Mary (Easton) **125** 181
Mary (Elwell) **110** 94
Mary (Faulkner) **92** 171
Mary (Fiske) (Brame)
88 269
Mary (Gates) **121** 54
Mary (Gregson) **127** 176
128 111
Mary (Hamlen) **92** 389
Mary (Harris) **105** 58
Mary (Johnson) **106** 30
Mary (Pattey) **100** 243
Mary (Silvester) **85** 368
Mary (Titus) **114** 175
Mary (Whitcomb)
111 173
Mary (Woodman) **110**
97 98
Mary A. **84** 95
Mary Ann **51** 494 **72** 88 **78**
351 **82** 487
Mary Ann (Herrington)
119 63 66
Mary Ann (Lombard)
96 185
Mary Anna **82** 487
Mary B. (Clouston)
88 339
Mary Curtis (Clarke)
92 63
Mary D. (Langley)
105 299
Mary E. **52** 75 **61** 24 **114** 64
Mary E. (Schurr) **111** 73
Mary Elizabeth **76** 5
78 169
Mary Ellen **110** 106
Mary Faulkner **92** 171
Mary Fitch **69** 195
Mary Gould (Barnard)
92 389
Mary H. (Platt) **125** 54
Mary J. **111** 73 **122** 149
Mary Jane **91** 378
Mary Jerusha (Clarke)
92 63
Mary Lucretia **78** 43
Mary M. **52** 75
Mary Richardson **96** 185
292 **97** 160

MOORE *cont'd*
Mary Stone **82** 237
Mary Susanna **124** 77
Mary Virginia (Burdick)
92 64
Matilda **115** 121
Matthew **64** 22 **82** 444 452
Matthias **78** 294
Matthias Jones **78** 294
Mattie E. **77** 266
Maud **74** 307
Maurice **52** 469 471
Mehitable **52** 73 **57** 304
306 **58** 177 **123** 202
Mercy **57** 306 367 **67** 76
Mercy (Easton) **126** 249
Mercy A. **123** 204
Meriam **71** 223
Merrick **61** 24 **90** 32
Micah **53** 175 325 **57** 307
Mildred Bishop **88** 168
Millard Fillmore **80** 334
81 219 **110** 64 69
Milton **117** 280
Miner B. **92** 171
Minerva **72** 47 **123** 92
Minnie Marilla **100** 254
Miriam **63** 45 **109** 205
110 94 **114** 292
Mitte **73** 73
Molly **51** 492 494 **57** 365
77 26
Moody **123** 75
Mordicai **73** 261 **111** 41
Moses **111** 208
Murray Stuart (Mrs.) **84**
109 190
Myrtie A. **75** 14
Nabby **63** 175 **97** 377
98 55
Nancy **51** 492 **55** 80 81 **58**
16 **61** 24 **68** 336 **90** 110
94 125 **95** 345 **98** 56
105 76 **109** 167 **114** 180
116 222 **117** 222 224
119 66 **124** 28 **125** 103
134 222 **137** 361 **145** 36
Nancy (Bolton) **110** 24
Nancy (Covell) **114** 180
Nancy (Little) **127** 239
Nancy C. (Gilley) **85** 373
Nancy Campbell **82** 112
Nancy Clark **82** 112
Nancy Foster **77** 44
Nancy P. W. **78** 300
Nanna **51** 494
Naomi **51** 494 **55** 378
Nathan **57** 307 363 364
368 369 **68** 168 **69** 175
83 35 **111** 73 **126** 182
Nathan C. **111** 73
Nathan W. **52** 75
Nathaniel **52** 73 **55** 81 **57**
301 302 304 305 **58** 177
78 294 **83** 419 **105** 58
112 300
Nathaniel Ford **109** 151
Nathaniel M. **78** 410
Nehemiah **57** 364
Nellie **92** 171
Nelson **91** 378

MOORE *cont'd*
Nettie Iola **69** 142
Newell **58** 372
Nicholas **122** 29 32 34 35
Norma **142** 4
Obadiah **57** 302 366 370
  90 87
Okey **91** 247
Olive **55** 80 81 **57** 362 370
  58 178 **61** 24 **118** 241
  120 219 220 **122** 73 **123**
  151 233
Oliver **57** 303 309 362 **113**
  197 **117** 140 141 **119** 63
  66
Olivia V. (Morse) **92** 171
Orinda **71** xli
Orphia Williamson
  82 267
Orrin **70** 92
Orson B. **101** 329
Oscar S. **116** 115
Otis **117** 265
Pamela **126** 254
Parnel **57** 307 308
Patience **51** 494 **55** 253
  111 231 **114** 48
Patience (Gates) **121** 260
Patience (Sellers) **115** 60
Patrick **54** 424 **89** 226
Patty **92** 171
Paul **57** 305 306 308 367
  109 151 **115** 66 **139** 96
  240
Peace **125** 179 243
Pearl Blanche (Kilpatric)
  83 433 436
Peggy **55** 80 **139** 253
Pelatiah **71** 226 **142** 200
Penelope **63** 169
Penelope (Philbrook)
  115 304
Perazim Gilboa **53** 175
Persis **57** 307 365 367-369
  117 265
Persis (Gates) **121** 223
Peter **51** 490 **57** 302 305
  307 365 368 **73** 64 69 70
  73
Peter S. **85** 377
Phebe **52** 74 **57** 363 **66** 240
  70 359 **71** 298 **103** 144
  111 73 **119** 183
Phebe (Sayles) **111** 73
Phebe Adell **100** 254
Phebe Adell (Leigh)
  100 254
Phebe P. **67** 309
Phebey (Cannada) **83** 416
Philip **122** 29 32 34
  132 324
Phineas **57** 204 307 309
  367 368 **58** 372 **65** 12
Pliny **58** 372
Polly **52** 74 **57** 370 **61** 23
  24 **70** 345 **97** 375 **108** 88
  113 227 **131** 155
Polly (Ayres) **119** 183
Polly (Collier) **132** 323
Polly (Smith) **94** 200 201
Portius **52** 74

MOORE *cont'd*
Prince G. **134** 132
Priscilla **55** 80 102 **59**
  lxxix **73** 141
Priscilla (Arey) **87** 21
Prudence **57** 302 309
Prudence W. **116** 115
Rachel **57** 368 **83** 41
  116 208
Rachel (Ballinger)
  111 280
Rachel (Billings) **83** 417
Rachel (Brown) **135** 22
Rachel (Chase) (Billings)
  122 239
Rachel (Haines) **103** 248
Rachel (Homer) **140** 154
Rachel (Roberts) **92** 400
Rachel A. **100** 204
Rachel Arvilla (Beckwith)
  109 151
Rachel C. **116** 312
Ralph **78** 273
Raphael Mingo **82** 266
Raymond L. **92** 340
Readuck **124** 77
Reasin **91** 378
Rebecca **52** 74 **55** 81 **57**
  307 309 362 365 366 368
  369 **58** 131 **69** 92 **79** 400
  126 17
Rebecca (Fenimore)
  111 280
Rebecca (Hodsdon)
  99 323
Rebecca D. (Hurd)
  123 202
Rebecca Jane (Lord)
  113 302
Relief **57** 309 368 **58** 131
  372
Reny (Huntley) (Ryan)
  101 143
Reuben **55** 68 81 **57** 305
  366 369 370 **58** 178 **61**
  23 24 **77** 24 25
Reuben Barton **58** 62
Reuben P. **92** 112
Reynold Marvin **57** 364
  62 304
Rhoda (Pettigrew) **87** 148
Rhoda Cotton (Coombs)
  96 160 **97** 157
Rhoda E. **92** 172
Richard **52** 73 **57** 301 303
  304 362-364 **58** 177 **61**
  318 **62** 304 **63** 330 **67** 37
  38 42 **68** 182 **71** 124 **74**
  235 **89** 150 **94** 6 95 262
  263 **107** 313 **113** 30 37
  114 163 164 167 **121** 27
  122 168 **124** 85 111 182
  183 **135** 61 152 **141** 97
  108 **144** 169 **147** 25
Richard A. **120** 15
Richard Allan **119** 75
Richard Channing **79** 407
Robert **51** 489 490 492 493
  54 387 **55** 80 **62** 360 **64**
  25 112 **67** 37 38 42 70 76
  72 205 **77** 49 **78** 72 80

MOORE *cont'd*
  385 **93** 17 20 28 **95** 262
  263 358 **98** 311 **100** 190
  104 121 **112** 286 **113**
  279 280 **126** 249 **147** 41
Robert Allan **119** 75
Robert Eldridge **104** 121
Robert Leverett Goodale
  101 125
Robert R. **119** 64
Roger **52** 473 **69** 346 **77**
  250 **106** 30 **131** 130
Rosa (Briggs) **127** 67
Rosa B. **123** 74
Rowena A. (Miller)
  92 172
Roxa **114** 196
Roxanna **83** 199
Roy **117** 197
Ruby May **92** 146
Rufus **57** 364 368
Rufus King **89** 103
Russell **82** 487
Russell Franklin **118** 75
Russell Wellman **71** xliv
Russell Wellman (Mrs.)
  69 lxxvi
Ruth **52** 74 **53** 87 **55** 271
  57 302 306 307 363 364
  366-369 **59** 251 **65** 294
  71 281 **72** 217 **93** 93 355
  95 256 **100** 139 **105** 57
  106 228
Ruth (James) (Harris)
  105 57
Ruth (Lovis) **141** 140 142
Ruth (Stanley) **106** 228
Ruth (Starr) **93** 355 **94**
  170 171 **95** 253 256 **96**
  380 **121** 106
Ruth Miller **119** 75
S. B. **116** 211
Sabina Chloe **126** 182
Sallie Moye (Billings)
  93 274
Sally **55** 80 **57** 365 **58** 372
  64 118 **74** 180 **78** 93 **81**
  171 **83** 35 **97** 221 369
  377 **98** 56 **103** 235 236
  109 205 **112** 156 **113**
  128 **114** 181 **125** 103
  106 108
Sally (Baker) **83** 418
Sally (Cook) **125** 104
Sally Ann **136** 143
Salome **57** 362
Samantha **55** 80
Samson **51** 492
Samueila **122** 32
Samuel **51** 44 461 488-491
  494 **52** 73 74 **55** 79-81
  250 378 **57** 214 215 301
  302 305 306 308 363-365
  58 177 **60** 349 **63** 175
  295 **64** 115 189 **69** 362
  78 294 **82** 266 **86** 124
  89 112 **92** 171 172 **97**
  332 336 **100** 190 276
  104 121 **105** 58 287 **107**
  93 **108** 285 **109** 303 **110**
  98 **111** 255 **112** 107 **113**

MOORE *cont'd*
207 279 280 **114** 164-168
115 60 306 **119** 183 199
122 28-31 33 35 36 168
124 85 **125** 72 92 94 **134**
229 233 **145** 356
Samuel C. **57** 364
Samuel French **103** 248
Samuel P. **69** 169
Samuel W. **131** 155
Sanders **71** 279
Sapphira **57** 306
Sarah **51** 493 **52** 73 74 **53**
414 **54** 387 **57** 284 302
304 305 307 309 362-366
368 369 **58** 319 **59** lxxix
63 174 **67** 336 342 **72**
205 **73** 136 228 231 **75**
14 **77** 49 215 **78** 294 **79**
53 79 **80** 155 **82** 266 **98**
126 **100** 298 **103** 146
104 121 **105** 57 **109** 201
303 **110** 177 289 **111**
241 255 280 **114** 196
119 183 **121** 132 223
122 28-33 36 **123** 233
125 173 175 176 **127**
191 229 **133** 249 250
134 91 **144** 317 **148** 37
Sarah (Daniels) **125** 223
Sarah (Gates) **120** 261
Sarah (Halsey) **105** 57
Sarah (Mulliken) **83** 184
Sarah (Pryor) **92** 389
Sarah (Rich) **83** 412
Sarah (Stokes) **111** 280
Sarah (Webber) **121** 319
Sarah A. (Towle) **105** 299
Sarah A. H. **124** 228
Sarah Adelia **72** 302
Sarah Amelia (Hathaway)
96 185
Sarah Ann **61** 384 **83** 214
85 375 92 320 **120** 15
Sarah C. **92** 168
Sarah E. **87** 148 **93** 136
Sarah E. (Grant) **120** 65
Sarah Isham **77** 260
Sarah L. (Winn) **124** 228
Sarah M. **63** 45
Sarah Rosaltha **64** 211
Saraphina **124** 204
Seth **72** 37
Seth A. **92** 115
Sharpless **92** 400
Sibyl **57** 204 364 367
Sibylla **52** 73 **57** 304
58 177
Silas **57** 305 306 366 367
97 369 **98** 56 **114** 196
Silence **57** 362
Simon **53** 175 176 **72** 36
Solomon **86** 102
Solomon E. **81** 290
Sophia **57** 191 303 **68**
lxxviii **78** 404 **117** 227
132 324
Sophia (Hodges) **94** 23
Sophrona **100** 287
Sophrona (Barlow)
100 287

MOORE *cont'd*
Sophronia **73** 77
Stanley L. **100** 253 254
116 152
Stanley Leigh **100** 112
Statira **82** 49 **83** 26 27
Stephen **55** 81 **57** 309 **66**
62 **119** 182
Sumner **125** 42
Susan **59** lxxix **61** 23 24
78 302 **90** 57 **94** 201
125 243
Susan (Kuhn) **90** 45
Susan Cutter **79** 285
Susan Jane **72** 97
Susan S. (Seely) **86** 102
Susan Seely **86** 101 102
Susan W. (Tucker)
113 301
Susanna **51** 461 493 **52**
73 74 **55** 314 **57** 204 304
305 308 309 363 365 366
370 **60** 193 **73** 256 **79** 55
82 206 **83** 9 **91** 172 **115**
60 **135** 17
Susanna (Allen) **116** 128
Susanna (Frost) **117** 225
Susanna (Jackson) **97** 6
Susanna (Woodward)
114 99
Susie **74** 197 **87** 21
Sydney (Wingfield)
112 300
T. J. **117** 119
Tabitha **57** 307 369 **109**
298 303
Tamar **57** 306 307 368 **64** 9
77 32 **83** 167
Tamzine **71** 203
Thaddeus **57** 365 366 370
Thankful **57** 305 309
Thelma 229 **92** 228 229
Thelma (Carver) **97** 158
Theodosius **92** 389 **127** 66
Theodotus **96** 185
Thomas **51** 490 492 494
52 73 74 246 **53** 171 329
414 **55** 80 334 **57** 94 302
362 363 368 369 **58** 388
60 283 **63** 41 362 **64** 163
65 370 **66** 352 **72** 42 87
88 90 174 **73** 67 68 70 72
77 239 **79** 44 **82** 86 90
89 336 **91** 378 **92** 124
389 **93** 383 385 387 **96**
185 **97** 6 **101** 49 **104** 80
107 **107** 214 **110** 94 **111**
231 255 **112** 286 **114**
182 227 **115** 57 **116** 119
117 16 **122** 28-30 32-36
126 225 **136** 32 35 **140**
170 **144** 234 **148** 252
253
Thomas Alexander **52** 75
Thomas H. **137** 361
Thomas Paine **52** 74 75
Thomas Ransom (Mrs.)
102 124
Tilley **57** 309 367
Timothy **57** 370 **59** lxxix
Tirzah **70** 92

MOORE *cont'd*
Treat **123** 118 202
Triphena **52** 74 **54** 354
Trythena V. **117** 280
Ulysses G. **92** 172
Unice (Minor) **128** 20
Unity **57** 308
Uriah **57** 302 307-309 362
366 370 **58** 178 **61** 24 **79**
41 **114** 195 196
Uriah B. **57** 390
Uriel **61** 24
Ursula **73** 213 **81** 413
Victoria Josephine **77** 303
78 31 **87** 99
Virginia **78** 205
Virginia Dunham
103 223
Vivian Elsie **80** 208 337
W. De Witt **83** 433 436
W. F. **55** xxxii
Walter **100** 200
Walter A. **52** 75
Walter Burritt **61** 406
Walter Henry **82** 275
Walter Lindley **93** 98
106 157
Wareham **79** 167
Warren **71** 52 **94** 28
114 196
Warren Harold **94** 28
Warren James **92** 63
Washington **73** 256
Welcome **52** 74
Whitney McKendree
143 267
Willamin **122** 29-33
Willard **57** 367
Willard B. **105** 299
William **51** 489 490 492-
494 **52** 72 73 **55** 80 81
311 **57** 300-302 306-308
362 364-370 **58** 61 176
319 388 **59** 81 **60** 360 **61**
23 **62** 288 **64** 164 **65** 294
69 175 245 **71** 177 203
277 286 **72** 100 205 299
73 20 67 104 138 232 **74**
180 **78** 187 276 294 **79**
79 **82** 86 90 206 500 **83**
417 420 **84** 80 **88** 13 **91**
206 342 344 347 349 350
378 **94** 95 95 246 **96** 333
100 65 190 301 **101** 143
104 121 172 **105** 209
282 **109** 205 **110** 94 98
111 209 282 **112** 18 20
105 **113** 125 126 128
114 182 270 295 **116**
119 208 **119** 22 **121** 54
319 **122** 239 **125** 23 93
96 173 223 232 233 **135**
159 **143** 259 **146** 270
147 350
William A. **82** 128 **125** 33
William C. **85** 379 **96** 291
William Coffin **100** 190
William Cutter **125** 244
William E. **77** 223
William E. B. **83** 100
William Francis **88** 297

MOORE *cont'd*
William Francis (Mrs.)
  86 197 **88** 297 300 **89**
  136
William Henry **89** 209
  93 305 **105** 60 **109** 151
  114 307 **125** 173 244
William Henry (Mrs.)
  84 173 **85** 189 **109** 121
  151
William I. **83** 300 **84** 30
William J. **116** 115
William John **112** 281
  116 115
William McLannin
  92 389
William S. **72** 274
William Sutcliff **127** 203
William Van **90** 68
William W. **72** 205
William Wells **78** 351
Willie T. **75** 14
Willis L. **55** 125
Winifred **117** 319
Winifred B. **130** 73
Winnie May (Woods)
  94 28
Wyatt **71** 133 **113** 302
Zadok **73** 137 142
Zebulon **59** 21
Zenus **94** 125
Zephaniah Swift **58** 178
  79 161
Zephina Jackson **78** 43
Zeresh **57** 308
Zerviah **57** 303 306 364
  79 399
Zibiah **57** 306 366
Zillah Imogene **92** 63
Zilpah **57** 309 368
Zulima **72** 42
Moorecocke *see* Moorcock
Moorecroft *see* Morecroft
MOOREGALWAY
  William **112** 287
Moorehead *see* Moorhead
Moorehouse *see*
  Morehouse
Moores *see* Mooers
MOOREY Nicholas **63** 132
MOORFIELD
  ____ (Eaton) **140** 138
  James **140** 138
MOORHEAD Morehead
  Moorehead
  — Mr. **66** 114
  — Rev. Mr. **63** 51
  Betty Jane **78** 325
  Caroline Ticknor
    (Hunnewell) (Scott)
    108 242
  Elizabeth **88** 286
  Horace R. **108** 242
  Jemima **56** 319
  John **60** 349 **74** 101 **84**
    370 382 **107** 236
  John Motley **75** 241
  Joseph M. **52** 102
  Ora Bell **78** 325
  Robert Young **78** 325
  Samuel **56** 319

MOORHEAD *cont'd*
  Sarah **84** 382
  Susan **88** 330
  W. K. **59** 424
  Warren King **83** 249 371
    84 182 192
Moorhouse *see* Morehouse
MOORIB Thomas **71** 316
MOORING
  Andrew **65** 238
  James **64** 218
  Thomas **63** 242
Mooris *see* Morris
Moors *see* Mooers
Moorton *see* Morton
MOORY Eliza (Charles)
    126 145
  Sylvester **126** 145
  Warren **126** 254
MOOTE
  Anne (Knop) **108** 256
  Thomas **108** 256
MOOTHAM Mooteham
  Katharine **141** 237
  Thomas **96** 369
MOOTREY Annabel **97** 338
MOPHETTE
  Josia **143** 258
MOQUET Francis **57** 280
MORAN Alfred **131** 83
  Ann **134** 335
  Anne **125** 98
  Catherine **134** 335 **136** 270
  Catherine (Sinnott)
    134 335
  Charles **143** 159
  E. **75** 24
  Edmund **143** 160
  Edward C. **85** 463 **120** 235
  Edward Carleton **83** 384
    91 207 **97** 97 **98** 147
  Edward Carleton (Mrs.)
    84 105 190
  Elizabeth (Reed) **136** 271
  Elizabeth Marie **125** 99
  Elizabeth Mary **88** 77
  Ellen (Mullen) **136** 270
  Friend **104** 121
  G. **91** 330
  Harold B. **123** 79 159
  Helen Louise (Anderson)
    119 149
  Henry **125** 99
  J. Bell **104** 170
  James **134** 335
  Janet **79** 285
  Jesse **73** 273
  Joseph **134** 335 **136** 270
  Lucy **61** 288
  Maria Jane **143** 159
  Mary **73** 195 **134** 335
  Mary Ann (Shumway)
    143 159
  Patrick **58** 73 **90** 165
    134 335
  Richard **134** 335 **136** 270
  Rosanna **134** 335
  Rosanna (McAnulty)
    134 335
  Roseanna **136** 271
  Rupert **108** 221

MORAN *cont'd*
  Sarah **73** 228 **136** 271 331
  Theodore Thomas **88** 77
  William **136** 270
MORANDAY Morandy
  Bristow **78** 302
  Flora **79** 55
MORANDO
  Louis (Mrs.) **109** 130
MORANDUS
  C. H. **82** 454
  Daisie C. V. **82** 454
  Henry C. **82** 454
  Juliette **82** 454
  V. **82** 454
  Willie **82** 454
MORANG
  Charlotte M. **101** 31
MORANT
  Francis **98** 122
  Philip **56** 107 **71** 235 **73** 28
    74 134-136 **141** 95 **148**
    242
MORANVILLE *see also*
  De Moranville
  Sarah (Chase) **87** 321
MORARS
  Elizabeth **66** 68 75
MORAS Catherine
    (Higgins) **90** 114
  Emanuel **90** 105 106 114
  John **68** 309
  Louisa (Babington)
    90 106
  Polly **68** 309
  Sally A. (Steel) **90** 105
MORAWETZ Adelheid M.
    (Arens) **83** 421 436
  Albert R. **83** 421 436
MORBEY Jane **138** 22
MORBILL — Count **98** 86
MORBURY Anthony **52** 125
MORCOUX
  Celina **113** 299
MORDAN — Mr. **91** 166
MORDAUNT
  Alice **98** 29 30 41
  Edward A. B. **59** 227 **60**
    xxxvi 408 **65** xxxv 202
  John **123** 255
  L'Estrange **98** 30
  Margaret **123** 255
  Robert **98** 30
MORDECAI
  Jacob **125** 35
  Julius **91** 330
MORDEN Anne **75** 121
  James **64** 257 **75** 121
  Jane **75** 121
  John **127** 215
  Marion **108** 111
MORDOCKE Morduck
  Joseph **54** 216 **63** 286
MORDOUGH
  Abigail **95** 345
MORDRUM Henry **115** 57
Morduck *see* Mordocke
More *see* Moore
MOREAU Caroline (Friese)
    84 448

MOREAU *cont'd*
Charles Combault **58**
xlix **60** xxxix **61** xxxvii
62 xl **63** xxxiv **64** xxxiv
65 xxxvii **66** liii **67**
xxxv **68** xxxvi **69** xxxvi
70 xx **71** xxiv **72** xxi **83**
123 235 **84** 448
Charles L. **84** 448
Clotilde (Lecour) **84** 448
D. H. **95** 399
Francoise **143** 8
Jeanne **91** 76
John Bostwick **84** 448
Joseph **84** 448
Morecock *see* Moorcock
MORECROFT Moorecroft
Brian **68** 364
Edmund **53** 302
Hector **68** 364
William **68** 364
MOREDICK John **73** 104
Morehead *see* Moorhead
MOREHOUSE
Moorehouse
Moorhouse Morhous
——— **51** 95 239 380 **60** 93
61 317 **69** 43 **123** 296
125 230
— Mr. **90** 35
Abigail **69** 43
B-Ann **115** 320 **116** 317
117 319
Benjamin **112** 58 **115** 122
Betsey **112** 58
Betsey (Brothwell) **145** 74
Betsey Ann **112** 58 59
C. F. **64** 331
Caroline **132** 243
Daniel **69** 43
David **73** 104
Edwin **86** 312
Emily (Higby) **98** 75
Eunice **60** 80 **145** 74
Frances Milton I. **71** 98
George Allen **112** 58
Gould **112** 58
Hannah **69** 377
Isaac **58** lxx **145** 74
Isabell Rainey **86** 312
James **55** 341
Jeannette **68** 121
Jerusha **69** 43
Joanna **54** 271
John **51** 110 **98** 7
John Hoffnagh **98** 75
John Ransom **98** 75
Jonathan **68** 287 **69** 131
371 **144** 40
Julia Eliza **95** 297 **96** 162
98 75
Laurana Kimberley
52 373
Louise M. **80** 161
Lucinda Euphemia
132 243
Lucy (Warren) **98** 75
Luther **132** 243
Margaret **68** 121
Marshall **113** 239
Martha **69** 376

MOREHOUSE *cont'd*
Mary **69** 376 **102** 65 **112** 58
Mary Elizabeth **58** lxx
Matilda Helen **132** 243
Mercy **69** 43
Othniel **69** 377
Peter **70** 37
Phebe **70** 37 **116** 114
Rebecca **60** 91 **69** 371
Robert Owens **68** 121
Robert Thomas **68** 121
Rosanna (Hoffnagh)
98 75
Samuel **69** 43 **70** 41
Sarah **69** 371 **109** 192
Sarah Elizabeth
(Johnston) **86** 312
Sibyl **108** 67
Stephen **63** 353
Susanna **69** 377
Sylvanus **68** 290
Thaddeus **69** 43 376
Thomas **51** 332 **60** 80 **98**
75 **134** 174 **144** 46
MOREIRA Luis **92** 97
MOREL
Elisa S. **114** 191
John **146** 323
Margaret S. **114** 191
Sarah (Dustin) **146** 323
MORELAND Morland
Ann **73** 270
Bertha M. **69** 168
David **87** 208
Elias **73** 223
Harriet (Jackson) **140** 157
Harry **69** 168
Hetty **73** 273
John **140** 157
Mary Ann **73** 271
Matilda **73** 272
Nancy **90** 106
Philip **73** 140
Rachel **73** 272
Robert **140** 157
Samuel **73** 228
Sarah **73** 277
Theresa **73** 268
Thomas **109** 315
Thomas B. **73** 225
MORELAYE
John **145** 106
Morelin *see* Morelyne
MORELL — Mr. **51** 72
MORELLI Domenico **74** xl
Morely *see* Morley
MORELYNE Morelin
Anna **66** 58
Gervais **65** 291
Jarvis **66** 58
Margaret **65** 291
Richard **65** 175 177
MORENI Louis **119** 100
MORENO Anna Maria
(Valle) **141** 149
Manuel Argumosa
141 149
Maria-de-las-Nieves
141 149
Mariano **141** 149
Morepeth *see* Morpeth

MORER Sarah **90** 105
MORERAN William **65** 235
Mores *see* Morris
Moreson *see* Morrison
Moreton *see* Morton
MOREWELL
Agnes de **109** 18
Gilbert de **109** 18
MOREY — Mrs. **127** 141
A. C. **125** 239
Abia (Swift) **123** 273
Abigail (Daniels) **114** 171
Alfred **120** 47
Ann **107** 207
Anna **57** 390
Augusta **128** 135
B. F. **128** 267
Barak **107** 57
Barbara **90** 55
Benjamin **104** 10 11 **118**
199 **120** 27 188 **123** 273
Bethiah **105** 257
Betsey **64** 117
Caroline **109** 111
Caroline C. **126** 64
Caroline Coventry
142 73
Catherine **87** 81
Catherine (Ginnedo)
87 81
Christopher **128** 224
134 202
Constance (Bressey)
112 43
David **140** 170
Deborah **106** 239 **112** 77
125 228
E. **100** 80
Edmund **129** 168
Edward **60** 249
Elias **105** 207
Elisha **121** 264
Elizabeth **64** 117 **100** 242
Elizabeth (Swift) **118** 199
Elizabeth (Titus) **114** 177
Emily (Braman) **87** 81
Ephraim **114** 171
Eunice **111** 134
Ezekiel **105** 206 207 **109**
204 **125** 228
Florence Broughton
90 135
Frank **69** 333
George **61** 313 **98** 243
123 192
George M. **128** 176 265
268
Gideon **128** 59
Hannah **74** 259 **110** 177
118 199 **120** 119
Hannah (Bourne) **118** 199
Hannah (Howard)
109 204
Harris **144** 100
Henry **104** 121
Isaac **74** 259
Israel **62** 311 **82** 49 **104** 121
128 58
J. S. **118** 311
Jacob **64** 117
James **105** 188

MOREY cont'd
Jane Bell **103** 120 **107** 131
  109 315 **111** 49 51
Jeremiah **128** 296
Jerusha **60** 370
Jerusha C. **123** 268
John **57** 392 **60** 370 **64** 117
  89 275 **105** 287 **112** 43
  128 130 135 295 296
Jonathan **55** 72 **64** 117 **108**
  152 **118** 199 **119** 171
  120 26 32 34 103 201
  121 39 **123** 61 62 **127** 20
  23 108
Juverd **114** 177
Linsford **104** 263
Lucretia **125** 293
Lucy (James) **126** 254
Lydia **58** 19 **104** 263 265
  125 220
Lydia (Ellis) **122** 56
Lydia J. **53** 249 **54** 106
Maria **118** 199
Martha T. **89** 275
Mary **55** 72 **57** 389 392 **98**
  68 **100** 138 104 263 **108**
  152 **118** 199 **120** 194
  121 227
Mary (Bartlett) (Foster)
  108 152 **118** 199
Mary L. (Barton) **107** 57
Mary L. (Sutherland)
  107 57
Nathan **58** 19 **144** 266
Nathaniel N. **105** 234
Palmer **57** 390
Patience **78** 401 **125** 228
Penny Clement **62** 301
Reliance **118** 199
Robert **128** 296 298
Roger **99** 239
Rosanna **114** 171
Ruth **87** 81
Ruth (Browning) **87** 81
Rutson **105** 188
Sally **64** 117
Salome L. **118** 311
Samuel **69** 333 **104** 121
Sarah **69** 333 **85** 359 **87** 81
  95 79 **104** 134 **127** 60
Sarah (Dewey) **104** 263
Sarah (Ewell) **129** 168
Susan **103** 88
Susanna **98** 86 **129** 168
  135 43
Sylvanus **123** 268 **128** 58
Thankful **118** 199 276
  125 248
Thankful (Swift) **118** 199
Thomas **100** 190
Walter **99** 242
William Pitt **104** 121
MORFEW —— **76** 282
Alice **76** 280 294
Ann **76** 291
John **76** 280 294
MORFIT Henry **114** 187
MORFOLK D. **91** 330
MORFOLT Thomas **68** 73
MORFORD Annette Della
  (Allen) **128** 268

MORFORD cont'd
Benjamin **106** 297
Catherine **94** 85
Charles **106** 297
Esther M. (Hazem)
  128 268
Harriet **98** 78
John **106** 297
John Jasper **128** 268
John T. **128** 268
Lewis **106** 297
Mary **106** 297
Mary (Denton) **106** 297
Mary (Hambleton)
  106 297
Noah **106** 297
Sarah **106** 297
Stephen **106** 297
Susanna **106** 297
Susanna (Barton) **106** 297
Theodosia **106** 297
Zebulon **106** 297
MORGAN Morgain
  Moreghen Morgin
  —— **51** 406 **53** 233 **54** 215
  57 lii **59** 416 **60** 100 **62**
  xxviii **70** 223 **71** 135 **74**
  154 **83** 35 **84** 118 **95** 366
  105 107 **112** 30 **124** 200
  143 202
—— Capt. **117** 32
—— Lady **54** 215
—— Rev. **100** 257
—— Widow **71** 137
A. R. **128** 174 176 177 264
  265 268 269
Abby (Barber) **89** 249
Abigail **63** 367 **65** 353 **68**
  31 336 **86** 64 **101** 218
  128 197 198
Abigail (Blashfield)
  137 25
Abigail (Gardner)
  123 259
Abigail (Herrick) **86** 64
Abigail (Phelps)
  (Parsons) **148** 225
Abigail (Wood) **103** 141
Abigail Talcott **82** 479
Abner **144** 266
Abraham **66** 285 **78** 386
  126 256 **128** 20
Achsha **109** 165
Adeline **76** 53
Alabama **78** 321
Albert **89** 249
Alden Kendrick **84** 110
  185 **103** 108 123 141
Alfred Waterman **88** 76
  173
Alice **63** 367 **70** 176 177
  221-223 **84** 461
Allen **114** 187
Alvie **80** 191
Amanda **78** 386
Amanda Maria (Alden)
  103 141
Amasa **70** 316
Amos **109** 165
Amy **60** 352 **125** 109
  136 308

MORGAN cont'd
Andrea **53** 315 **136** 312
Andrew **62** 373 **117** 45 47
  48
Ann **68** 217 **89** 207
Ann Frances **111** 311
Anna **63** 370 **70** 222 **81** 51
  94 389
Anna (Doran) **116** 187
Anna (Pierce) **131** 237
Anna (Shapleigh) **96** 32
Anna S. **96** 33
Anne **79** 417 **81** 361
  128 107
Anne (Redman) **107** 305
  108 279
Anne Cameron (Dold)
  136 324
Annie **63** 367
Annis **81** 51
Arthur M. **103** 47
Asenath **57** 326
Ashby **91** 265
Asher **63** 367
Augusta E. **101** 34
Augusta Ellen **103** 57
Augustus **131** 237
Avery **65** 137 **78** 100
  89 246 254
Azubah **57** 295
B. L. **91** 330
B. S. **103** 57
Barbara (Spofford) **94** 139
Benjamin **55** 177 **91** 206
  94 95 **100** 65 **104** 121
Benjamin D. **72** 115
Bessie **122** 16
Bessie Hamilton **81** 341
Bethiah **63** 366 **148** 235
Betsey **101** 218 **114** 281
Betsey (Millar) **132** 243
Betsey (Sanborn) **118** 193
Betsey H. **109** 116
Betsey W. **101** 218
Bridget **136** 316 329
Caleb **107** 121
Calvin Cogswell **136** 324
Calvin R. **103** 52
Caroline **78** 322
Caroline Knox **61** liv
Caroline L. **137** 362
Carrie Lydia **79** 280
Cate **73** 12
Catherine (Copp) (Avery)
  88 76 **136** 331
Catherine A. **136** 331
Cecil (Mrs.) **99** 148
Charles **60** 352 **65** 32 **72** 38
  73 12 **84** 428 86 383 **96**
  32 **109** 260 **143** 201 202
Charles A. **89** 207
Charles Almeron **57** 295
Charles Augustus **97** 193
Charles E. **91** 330
Charles L. **55** xx lxiii
Charles Lincoln **73** xx
Charles Torrance **112** 234
Charles West **100** 190
Charlton Hunt **136** 324
Christopher **79** 417
Clarence Merton **86** 197

MORGAN *cont'd*
Climena **57** 295 359
Consider **70** 222
Cynthia **63** 367 **83** 100
Cyprian **70** 222
Cyrene (Redman) **109** 200
D. M. (Mrs.) **123** 310
Daniel **53** 444 **58** 221 **60** 248 **64** 65 **81** 202 **109** 165 **120** 263 **136** 329
David **55** lxii **68** 179 **81** 361 **100** 295 **123** 259
Deborah **55** 177 **56** 93 **60** 146 **85** 229 **136** 273
Deborah (Blake) **136** 273
Denison **144** 111
Desire **60** 248 **86** 383 **136** 329
Diantha **109** 165
Dolly **53** 233
Dorothy **53** 287 443 **81** 358 361 **85** 192 **94** 332 **136** 308 310 311 320 322
Dorothy (Avery) **136** 323
Dorothy (Parke) **136** 99
Drusilla **64** 117
Dudley **100** 190
E. Delmar **59** lxii
Ebenezer **103** 141
Edgar L. **117** 76
Edith Denison **87** 294
Edmund S. **112** 163 **121** 238
Edmund Sears **124** 137 144
Edward **81** 341 **121** 26 29
Edwin **57** 359
Edwin Denison **60** lxiii **77** ix xxvii **79** 81 **80** 231 **81** 62 **82** 54 **83** 8 **84** 69 **85** 29 **86** 4 59 **87** 39 **88** 6 76 77 87 173 **89** 9 90 103 **91** 6 **92** 29 **93** 47 **94** 19 **95** 89 **96** 58 **97** 147 **98** 90 **99** 70 **100** 127 **101** 278 **102** 196 **103** 20 240 **104** 212 **105** 248 **106** 181 **108** 313 **109** 107 **110** 184 **111** 59 **113** 130 **114** 114
Edwin Vernon **81** 189
Eleanor **53** 12
Eleanor Birk **103** 57
Elijah **79** 73
Eliphalet **79** 73
Elisha **60** 352 **63** 367 370 **70** 223 **81** 473 **89** 246 **138** 33 38
Eliza **81** 51
Eliza Caroline **98** 264
Eliza L. **76** 34
Elizabeth **53** 441 444 **60** 165 248 **65** 237 354 **77** 318 **81** 341 **91** 288 289 **97** 336 **100** 236 **103** 141 **105** 4 **109** 165 **112** 29 30 **118** 193 **120** 262 **121** 26 29 **122** 175 **136** 271 317 323
Elizabeth (Bliss) **97** 341 **101** 167 **123** 258

MORGAN *cont'd*
Elizabeth (Bressey) **112** 30
Elizabeth (Brewster) **136** 308
Elizabeth (Dixey) **103** 141
Elizabeth (Forsyth) **136** 322
Elizabeth (Gates) **120** 263 **136** 329
Elizabeth (Jones) **136** 308 312 331
Elizabeth (Neal) **100** 295
Elizabeth (Parsons) **142** 246 249
Elizabeth A. **89** 250
Elizabeth Gertrude **52** 465
Elizabeth K. **72** 115
Elizabeth Mary (Moran) **88** 77
Elizabeth Sarah (Archer) **88** 76 77
Elizabeth Wilbourn **103** 141
Ellen A. (Loomis) **89** 246
Ellen Key (Howard) **136** 324
Emily **100** 89
Emily (Atwood) **123** 308
Emily (Reeves) **109** 260
Emma **75** 28
Emma (Herrick) (Cole) **86** 66
Enoch **114** 187
Erastus **60** 352
Ernest Hall **64** xxxi
Ernest Ray (Mrs.) **96** 160
Esther B. **136** 266
Eunice **60** 351 352 **63** 367 **124** 188
Eustis Parker **92** 109
Evan **68** 180
Eveline A. (Rutherford) **123** 307
Experience (Smith) **97** 341 **136** 318
Ezra **136** 145
Fanny B. **105** 129
Flaake **87** 302
Fordyce **123** 308 **132** 243
Frances (Irby) **136** 316
Frances A. **52** 464 465
Frances B. **107** 305
Frances Goodridge **61** liv
Frances Louisa (Tracy) **97** 341 **101** 166 167 **136** 323
Frances Tracy **97** 341
Francis **54** 351 **59** 215 **71** 90 **75** 160 **94** 332 **142** 246 249
Francis B. **108** 279 **109** 200
Francis Elizabeth **109** 260
Francis M. K. **80** 191 **89** 250
Francis Perkins **131** 237
Frank B. **109** 320
Frank Herbert **79** 280
Franklin **57** 359
Gad **65** 379

MORGAN *cont'd*
George **64** 274 281 356 **73** 12 **81** 51 **100** 236 **123** 307 **130** 236 **136** 316 **144** 111
George D. **72** 115
George Earnest **97** 215
George P. **97** 215
George Walker **103** 141
Georgiana **65** 137
Georgiana C. **72** 115
Gertrude **54** lix
Gertrude A. **75** 40
Gideon **136** 316 324
Gifford (Mrs.) **105** 129
Gilbert **80** 192 **89** 252
Gloria **136** 322
Grace **54** 417
Grace (Smith) **136** 322
Grace Beulah **104** 144
Grace Price **96** 33
Griffith **111** 275
Hannah **51** 116 463 **61** 130 231 **62** 373 **65** 354 355 **66** 15 **77** 207 **86** 360 **89** 247 **91** 263 **100** 302 **103** 52 **104** 162 **109** 165 **123** 261 **133** 270 **136** 311 313 319 320 322 325 **137** 23
Hannah (Bird) **97** 341 **101** 167
Hannah (Chapin) **133** 269
Hannah (Dagget) **101** 218
Hannah (Grele) **91** 265
Hannah (Haynes) (Redington) **109** 119 165
Hannah (Lincoln) **124** 200
Hannah Almira **103** 52
Hannah Colby (Hoyt) **100** 255
Harriet **86** 442 **103** 57
Harriet (Steele) **136** 324
Harriet (Stoddard) **89** 250
Harriet A. **103** 57
Harvey **85** 291 **86** 383
Hattie P. **91** 385
Henrietta (Hunt) **136** 324
Henrietta Judd **85** 168
Henry **79** 407 **80** 191 **89** 250 **121** 29
Henry C. **65** 137
Henry E. **90** 33
Henry Sturgis **84** 233 **85** 188 **97** 341
Hiram **78** 31
Hopestill (Merrick) **128** 197 201
Horace **73** 257
Howard McKay **103** 57
Hugh **60** 24
Inez Scott **89** 43
Irving Bancroft **97** 217
Isaac **70** 221-223 **87** 302 **101** 218 **114** 187 **123** 259
Isaac C. **103** 52
Israel **86** 66 **136** 308
Italy N. **74** 316

MORGAN *cont'd*
J. P. **105** 82
J. Pierpont **55** xci **86** 119
  87 166 **99** 259 **104** 310
Jabez **73** 257 **75** 304
Jacob Gray **51** 463
James **53** 238 239 **55** 177
  59 266 267 **60** 352 **63**
  367 **68** 112 **78** 114 **88** 76
  105 76 **114** 187 **117** 277
  128 201 **133** 107 **136** 86
  101 309 313 316 317 322
  323 327 329 331
James Ethington (Mrs.)
  81 363 **82** 237
James H. **65** 137 **103** 57
James P. **122** 217
James Sanford **64** 95
James W. **89** 43
Jane **53** 12 238 239 **65** 48
  74 xli **114** 187
Jane Buck **96** 33
Jane E. **89** 250
Jane Norton **65** li **75** lxv
  97 341
Jane Norton (Grew)
  97 341
Jasper **88** 76 77 **136** 331
Jedediah **136** 324
Jennie Emily **85** 193
Jenny Lind (Beaman)
  97 193
Jerusha **63** 367 **65** 137 **78**
  100 **90** 261 **136** 309 327
Jessie June (Jack) **93** 138
Jo. **79** 156 **80** 69
Joanna **53** 444 **136** 273
Joel **109** 165
John **53** 12 315 441 **54** 215
  271 **55** 179 311 **56** 93
  297 **60** 165 351 352 **64**
  117 163 255 345 **65** 150
  66 113 **67** 262 **73** 137
  77 229 **78** 221 374 **80** 58
  383 **85** 26 **88** 76 148 **93**
  383-385 387 **103** 141
  114 281 **117** 65 **123** 265
  129 21 **133** 269 270 **136**
  273 308 311 312 316 322
  324 329 331 **137** 25
John Alden **103** 141
John Avery **86** 443
John Bickford **100** 255
John Edward (Mrs.)
  93 138
John G. **115** 157
John H. **85** 168
John McGlauflin **103** 52
John Pierpont **65** li **70** 52
  73 316 **74** xxv **75** lxv
  77 xvii **82** 493 **97** 287
  341 **98** 149 **101** 166 167
  104 311 **115** 4 **136** 90
  323
John S. **103** 57
John T. **76** 34
John Williams (Mrs.) **86**
  197 **98** 78
Jonath **123** 260
Jonathan **61** 246 **66** 113
  123 124 **119** 90

MORGAN *cont'd*
Jos. **70** 265
Joseph **51** 116 **53** 287 441
  54 417 **59** 189 **60** 402
  70 51 54 **80** 192 **81** 358
  87 157 **89** 249 252 **97**
  341 **101** 167 **104** 311
  109 120 **136** 99 318 323
Joshua **60** 146 **61** 231 **109**
  117 119 120 165
Josiah **78** 386
Judith **53** 12 **88** 148
Julia **80** 233
Julia (Rich) **84** 118
Julia E. **79** 154
Julia Eliza **81** 51
Julian **53** 12
Juliet (Pierpont) **97** 341
  101 167 **104** 311 **136**
  318 323
Juliet Pierpont **104** 310
  311
Julius **57** 295
Junius Spencer **70** 51 **84**
  108 185 **97** 341 **101** 167
  104 311 **115** 67 **136** 318
  323
Justus R. **85** 168
Katharine **86** 240
Katharine Avery **88** 77
Kendrick Ebenezer
  103 141
Kendrick Pierpont
  103 141
L. N. **68** 209
Laura **86** 24
Laura (Ford) **89** 43
Lavina Gardner **103** 52
Lavinia **72** 144 **80** 62
  103 57
Lena **85** 427
Lewis **65** 23
Lewis Henry **136** 324
Littleton T. **125** 289
Lois **61** 375
Loisa **63** 367
Lot **70** 221
Louisa Pierpont **86** 194
  101 24 129 166
Louise (Johnson) **96** 33
Lovina (Rising) **85** 291
Lovinia A. **103** 57
Lowell Goodridge **61** liv
Lucretia (Brown) **111** 311
Lucy **63** 366 **70** 51 54 95
  79 73 156 305 **94** 285 **95**
  366 **122** 276
Lucy Ann **127** 58
Lucy Ann (Brightman)
  127 58
Lucy Celia **81** 473
Luke **88** 148
Luodovic **77** 113
Luther **136** 324
Lydia **60** 352 **61** 246 **71**
  137 **73** 12 **75** 89 **80** 192
  89 246 252 **101** 218 **123**
  260 **129** 87
Lydia (Leach) **126** 256
  128 20
Lydia (Smith) **88** 76

MORGAN *cont'd*
  136 331
Lydia L. **103** 57
Lydia Smith **78** 99 100
  112 3
Mabel **73** 12
Mabel (James) **96** 160
Mabel Ann **97** 215
Madeline Gertrude
  96 289
Mahala **59** 189
Marcella L. **96** 33
Margaret **51** 318 320 **71**
  367 **114** 187 **136** 99
Margaret (Avery) **136**
  309 323 327
Margaret (Hopkins)
  105 107
Margaret (Norman)
  103 141
Margaret Lovina **103** 52
Margarette **103** 52
Margery **52** 428 **53** 12 **56**
  298 **136** 322
Margery (Hill) **136** 101
Maria **60** 325
Mariette **103** 57
Marion Haviland (Burt)
  98 78
Marjorie Burr (Shepard)
  96 161
Marshall **92** 146 400
  98 280
Marshall Shapleigh **96** 33
Martha **61** 103 **62** 373 **63**
  367 **70** 177 222 **84** 215
  94 385 **136** 311 312 322
  324 328
Martha Lena **97** 193
Martha M. **137** 28
Mary **52** 56 134 **53** 12 **54**
  215 271 **55** 311 **70** 222
  72 115 **74** 305 **77** 113
  78 125 137 **79** 156 **80**
  191 192 **81** 100 **89** 247
  250 252 **97** 81 **103** 57
  107 51 **120** 13 **133** 269
  270 **136** 323 331 **147** 30
Mary (Averill) **136** 316
Mary (Avery) **88** 76 **136**
  308 331
Mary (Basford) **101** 218
Mary (Clarke) **123** 259
Mary (Schreiner) **130** 236
Mary (Stebbins) **97** 341
  101 167
Mary (Vine) **136** 309 313
  317 323 327 331
Mary A. **80** 57 **103** 57
  126 254
Mary Agnes **83** 260
Mary Ann **63** 21 **79** 155
  299 307 407
Mary Brewer (Penniman)
  88 77
Mary Brown **65** 137
Mary Calista **55** lxxxv
Mary E. **65** 137 **85** 168
Mary Eleanor **70** lviii
Mary H. **91** 313 **100** 255
Mary J. **65** 137

MORGAN *cont'd*
Mary Jane (Nash) **131** 237
Mary Livonia **100** 164
Mary Lyman **136** 318
Mary McLean **72** 115
Mathe **88** 148
Matilda **63** 367 **89** 28
Matilda C. **65** 137
May Jane **89** 207
Mehitable **71** 14 **109** 165
Melinda (Ball) **136** 145
Melvin M. **103** 57
Mercy **87** 302
Mercy (Cooley) **123** 265
Mercy (Rich) **83** 273
Micajah **64** 117
Miles **53** 238 239 **58** lxxii
    70 54 **76** 170 **97** 341
    101 167 **104** 311 **123**
    258 259
Milo M. **122** 217
Miriam **55** 179
Molly **88** 148
Musidora **136** 316
N. H. **105** 246
Nabby **88** 148
Nancy **60** 352 **125** 179
    135 251
Nancy (Dunn) **125** 289
Nancy J. (Sewall) **103** 47
Nancy Ward **56** 171
Nathan **63** 366 **80** 192
    89 252
Nathan Denison **65** 137
Nathaniel **97** 341 **101** 167
Nellie (Bancroft) **97** 217
Olive **58** 93 **61** 272 **109** 116
Olive (Coit) **138** 33
Oliver **114** 187
Oliver W. **98** 288
Orlando S. **56** 171
Orville **80** 191 **89** 250
Ozias **76** 53
Parker **118** 193 **136** 271
Patience (Cogswell) **136**
    316 324
Paul **52** 428
Paul Beagary **95** 147
Paulina (Bancroft) **95** 366
Pauline **103** 311
Peggy **72** 115
Pelatiah **68** 336 **148** 225
Perlina **122** 217
Permelia Hewins **90** 68
Peter **89** 207 **116** 187
Phalla **73** 12
Phebe **60** 352 **64** 117
Phebe Ann (Lang) **105** 74
Philendia **83** 100
Philip **128** 201
Philip Maynard (Mrs.)
    96 161
Polly **60** 352 **81** 473 **137** 26
Portia May (Bordwell)
    101 123
Prudence **123** 264 **136** 323
Prudence (Avery) **136** 323
Rachel **78** 31 **148** 235
Rachel (Deming) **136**
    311 316 322 324 329
Rachel (Kibbe) **136** 316

MORGAN *cont'd*
Rachel (Merry) **148** 235
Ralph **66** 306 **68** 217
Randal **96** 32 33
Raphael **55** 364
Rebecca **61** 375
Rebecca (Corning)
    103 141
Reuben Dodge **111** 311
Richard **77** 207 **83** 273
    102 32 **110** 197 **117** 156
Richard F. **97** 217
Richard Rhys **128** 201
Richard Rose **128** 197 201
Richard S. (Mrs.) **130** 232
Robbinson P. **103** 57
Robert **61** 103 **73** 138 **77**
    149 **103** 141 **121** 29 **137**
    23
Robert Crary **60** 352
Roger **131** 130
Roswell **89** 249
Rozal **70** 222
Ruth **53** 286 441 **56** 319
    70 109
Ruth (Shapley) **136** 324
Sally **60** 352 **70** 51 54 **90** 90
Sally (Bond) **114** 281
Sally (Spencer) **97** 341
    136 318
Sally F. **75** lxiii
Samuel **53** 444 **54** 276 **60**
    352 **63** 366 367 **65** 354
    73 257 **80** 191 **88** 148
    89 247 250 **103** 141 **120**
    154 **132** 264 **136** 316
    322 **142** 41
Samuel (Mrs.) **106** 126
Samuel Davidson **75** lxii
Samuel Tate **73** 318 **74**
    xxv **75** xxxiii lxii lxiii
Sanford **60** 352
Sara Ann **90** 172
Sarah **54** 351 **55** 177 **59** 215
    61 246 67 362 **70** 106
    78 386 **79** 154 **84** 426
    88 148 **90** 90 **91** 230 255
    265 **92** 107 **95** 204 **100**
    236 **103** 239 **125** 172
    138 33 34 38
Sarah (Basford) **101** 217
Sarah (Bond) **137** 25
Sarah (Cobb) **136** 324
Sarah (Cooley) **123** 260
Sarah (Herrick) **103** 141
Sarah (Leeds) **136** 324
Sarah (Pierpont) **103** 141
Sarah (Spencer) **104** 311
Sarah (Taylor) **103** 141
Sarah (Whittridge)
    103 141
Sarah Ann **90** 172
Sarah Cordelia **98** 288
Sarah E. (Bancroft) **97** 215
Sarah Elizabeth **103** 57
Sarah Helen **97** 215
Sarah L. **89** 379
Sarah Osgood **77** 149
Sarah R. **88** 332
Seth **86** 383

MORGAN *cont'd*
Shepard Ashman (Mrs.)
    94 139
Shubael **83** 100
Sibyl **63** 367
Sidney **89** 250
Sidney C. **103** 57
Silence **87** 194
Simeon **88** 148
Solomon **70** 223
Sophia **57** 295
Sophia M. **74** 316
Stella **82** 237
Stephen H. **74** 316
Stokeley **70** lviii
Susan **86** 383 **101** 35 **103**
    57 174
Susan Amelia (Pendleton)
    86 443
Susan Everett (Emerson)
    112 233 234
Susan S. **101** 33
Susan Viana **101** 35
    103 57
Susanna **60** 402 **126** 68
Susanna (Bray) **125** 109
Susanna (Westcott)
    103 141
Sylvanus **105** 73 187
Sylvia **60** 352
Talithia Adaline **75** lxii
Taylor Wescott **103** 141
Temperance **86** 383
Temperance (Avery) **88**
    76 **136** 308 331
Theda **72** 38 **73** 12
Theodore Moran **88** 77
Theophilus **75** 90 **80** 191
    89 250 **129** 20 21
Theophilus B. **101** 217 218
Theophilus Bachelor
    103 57
Thisbe **60** 352
Thomas **64** 220 **65** 125 236
    67 362 **98** 35 40 **103** 52
    132 243 **136** 324 **148**
    235
Thomas Archer **88** 77
Thomas Hunt **136** 324
Thomas J. Swan **103** 174
Timothy **80** 191 **89** 250
Tracy **97** 400
Tryphenia **73** 257
W. Y. **54** 457
Walker **104** 144
Wallace **52** 465
Washington **103** 57
Watson **132** 243
Webster Dunbar **103** 57
Wheeler **72** 115
William **62** 242 **63** 26 367
    67 365 **71** 14 **73** 12 **80**
    192 **81** 51 176 **88** 76 **89**
    252 **105** 283 **116** 316
    117 156 **127** 15 58 **128**
    201 **136** 308 309 323 327
    331
William Avery **88** 76
William F. **138** 284
William G. **65** 137
William Henry **103** 52

MORGAN *cont'd*
William James **115** 168
William Manning **82** 254
 83 233 **145** 128
William P. **52** 464 465
Williams Fellowes **86** 197
Zachariah **86** 64
Zerviah **86** 383
MORGANDOLLAR
Elizabeth (Strobel)
 109 294
Frances **109** 294
John **109** 294
MORGENSON
Annie M. **72** 205
Charlie **72** 205
Mary **72** 205
Peter **72** 205
Morgrage *see* Mograge
MORGRET
Catherine **107** 213
Morhous *see* Morehouse
MORIAN
Mary Jane **78** 352
MORIARTY Moriaty
— Mr. **95** 302 303 **96** 93
— Mrs. **107** 315
Abigail **101** 225
Abigail (Moseley) **101**
 224 **104** 289 **107** 314
Anna **101** 227
Bridget **101** 222
Caroline Andrews
 101 227
Daniel **101** 220 222
David **101** 220
Deborah **101** 222 223
Deborah (Bowditch) **101**
 222 **107** 314
Deborah Althea **101** 226
Elizabeth **86** 170
Elizabeth Lowell **54** 316
 317
Elizabeth Lowell
 (Hancock) **101** 227
Elizabeth Lowell
 Hancock **101** 228
Elizabeth Moseley (Webb)
 101 225
Ellen **89** 226 **101** 219 221
 222
Ellen Maria **101** 226
George Andrews **77** vii
 xv xx 71 110 160 190 238
 305 325 **78** 54 144 192
 196 217 219 272 391 **79**
 82 170 187 191 213 215
 311 336 358 410 **80** 86
 136 196 200 219 221 313
 337 338 343 **81** 91 157
 178 208 211 233 235 314
 486 **82** 55 123 124 136
 146 185 220 221 225 248
 250 251 257 303 333 443
 456 514 **83** 70 84 129
 218 226 244-246 251 278
 391 **84** 70 174 181 203
 205 206 225 229 236 273
 433 437 **85** 69 79 133
 176 177 181 183 212 214
 215 347 396 417 **86** 71

MORIARTY *cont'd*
174 185 188 190 191 212
214 215 238 252 256 266
324 406 **87** 40 74 97 141
162 169 186 188 189 217
264 352 367 **88** 142 161
165 183-185 265 383 386
89 122 123 127 144 146
147 151 154 166 **90** 119
124-126 215 292 328 **101**
37 97 110 115 117 118
138-140 219 227-229 242
290 **102** 3 40 42 45 75 76
81 87 113 115 117 118
120 137-139 187 189 192
277 279 292 312 313 **103**
21 102 110 112-114 134-
136 152 153 156 182 198
208 271 283 287 317 **104**
3 14 15 40 76 107-109
113 114 137 138 158-160
176 227 244 285 304 317
105 25 36 75 81 95 122
123 142-144 153 154 162
167 187 234 237 249 292
106 52 76 119 120 139-
141 237 **107** 40 109 126-
128 147 148 264 **108** 62
127-129 148 149 **109** 124
142-144 **110** 138 139
111 31 55 57 74 142-144
158 195 200 261 265 **112**
61 66 136 137 158 168
113 63 65 69 72 74 150
151 184 189 235 236 319
114 51 57 83 84 89 143
144 150 152 217 229 232
295 **115** 46 48 49 105-
107 148 150 209 246 **116**
13 21 23 79 147 152 153
170 173 308 **117** 94 152
153 233 234 271 **118** 162
163 180 **119** 4 8 70 71
101 102 152 153 174 175
120 152 153 170 **122**
241 245 248 291 **123** 3
45 180 181 **141** 92 94 98
101 **144** 169 **145** 198
147 188 191 315 381
148 45 335
Georgie (Miller) **101** 227
Harriet Carpenter **93** 88
 101 225
Henry Augustus **101** 220
Honnora **101** 222
James **122** 92
Jemima Crocker (Paul)
 101 226
John **101** 219-227 **104** 289
 107 314 315
John H. **107** 16
John Hancock **54** 316 317
 101 228
John Moseley **74** 245
 101 219 224-227 **104**
 181
Joseph **54** 316 317 **101**
 221 225 227 228
Joseph Moseley **101** 228
Judith **101** 222

MORIARTY *cont'd*
Judith (Fitzgerald)
 101 220
Lilias Sanford Sheffield
 101 229 **123** 5
Lottie E. **86** 170
Louise (Dittmore) (Alfau)
 101 229 **123** 5
Margaret **101** 221 222
 122 92
Martha Ann **101** 225
Mary **74** 86 **101** 220 222
Mary (Trant) **101** 220
Mary Anne (Sheffield)
 101 228 **104** 14 **123** 3
Mary B. (Adams) **101** 228
Mary Bowditch **101** 225
Nancy **101** 222
Nancy Page (Andrews)
 101 226 **104** 181
Nelly **101** 222
Olga (Gillming) **101** 229
 123 5
Peggy **101** 221 222
Philip **86** 170
Rosamond Augusta
 101 226
Sylvester **101** 220
Thomas **101** 220-223 226
 107 314
Thomas Fitz Owen
 101 226
William **101** 220
William Andrews
 101 227
MORIEN John **62** 248
MORIEUX Thomas **121** 186
MORIEY Francis **87** 123
MORILLO
Eleanor **66** 40
Stephen **66** 40
MORIN —— **136** 200
Asa **127** 119
Auguste **131** 83
Daniel **127** 119
Desiah **117** 172
Desiah (Lampher)
 117 164
Eliza A. (Kneeland)
 117 164
Elizabeth **127** 119
Elizabeth (Viconte)
 109 185
Fidele **131** 83
Jean **109** 185 **131** 83
John **109** 185 **117** 164 **127**
 55 119
Lucy **117** 164
Marie **131** 96
Marie Anne (Quintard)
 109 185
Marselles **117** 164
Samuel **109** 185
Stephen **127** 55 119
Susan Maria (Osborne)
 95 313
Susanna **127** 55 56 119
Susanna (Patterson)
 127 119
Thomas **127** 119 120
William **117** 251 **127** 119

MORINE Eliza **92** 340
Elizabeth (Foster) **127** 55
Elmira **120** 16
Richard **92** 340
MORING Alexander **68**
112 **69** 286
Lucy (Cargill)
(Massenburg) **117** 251
MORION Mary **115** 120
Morison *see* Morrison
Moriss *see* Morris
MORISSEY
— Capt. **104** 304
MORIZE Andre **83** 248 **84**
182 **91** 131 **92** 142
Morland *see* Moreland
Morlay *see* Morley
MORLEY Morelaye Morely
— Mrs. **92** 369
Aaron **60** 380 **61** 387
65 372
Abel **65** 371-373
Abigail **65** 372
Abner **65** 373
Adam **110** 198
Ann **110** 260
Anna **61** 296 **85** 410
Anne **63** 69 **65** 374
Asahel **65** 373
Betsey **62** 269
Betty **61** 391 **62** 269
Catherine **131** 130
Catherine S. **85** 410
Cave **148** 119 120
Charles **61** 387
Charles H. **85** 315
Christiana **61** 192 390
65 372
Clarissa **61** 296
Constance **91** 289 **93** 93
95 254-257
Constance (Starr) **92** 369
94 240 **95** 254 256 260
Daniel **65** 372
David **65** 373 **77** 207
Deliverance **61** 389
Derrick **65** 373
Dimmick **131** 73 **133** 153
Dorcas **65** 373
Dorothy **67** 175
E. W. **65** 373
Ebenezer **65** 371 372
Edwin **85** 168
Elijah **65** 372
Elizabeth **64** 72 **65** 371 372
67 68 74 **78** 92 **110** 196
197 260 263
Elizabeth (Cogan) **110**
196-198
Elizabeth (Pratt) **94** 328
Enos **61** 85 387 **63** 70 72
65 372 **85** 168
Esther **65** 373
Eunice **60** 379 **65** 373
80 66
Eveline **63** 184
Experience **85** 410 **145** 40
Experience (Loveland)
145 40
Ezekiel **61** 389 **65** 372
Francis **110** 196 198 263

MORLEY *cont'd*
Gabriel **110** 196 198 263
George **61** 296 **62** 291 **63**
69 **65** 372
Gideon **65** 372 373
Hannah **65** 373
Harriet M. **85** 315
Hattie L. **85** 315
Henry **55** xcv
Herbert Small **65** 371
66 lii
Huldah **65** 373
Isaac **65** 372 373 **85** 410
Israel **65** 373
James **67** 72
Jasper **76** 266
Jerusha **61** 389 **65** 372 373
John **62** 265 269 **63** 183
64 72 **65** 371-373 **67** 68
74 **84** 167 359 **90** 272 **91**
289 **92** 368-371 **93** 93
94 240 351 **95** 134 254
256 260 **96** 369 **133** 153
John (Mrs.) **90** 272
Joseph **85** 410
Katharine **110** 260
Kilborn **65** 373
Laura **85** 410
Lionel **55** 433
Lucy **65** 373
Mabel **85** 410
Margaret (Green) **142** 261
Martha **65** 371 372
Martha (Wright) **85** 44
Martin **61** 387
Mary **61** 392 **65** 371 374
84 359
Matilda **62** 269
Mercy **65** 371 372
Mindwell **65** 371 373
86 162
Miriam **65** 373
Moses **60** 378 **65** 372
Nancy **61** 142 296 **65** 374
Obadiah **65** 373
Orrin **86** 170
Penelope **64** 72
Perlinia **76** 266
Prudence **65** 372 **94** 328
Ralph **131** 130
Robert **78** 74 **148** 119
Roderick **65** 374
Ruth **65** 372 373
Ruth (Weston) **131** 73
133 153
Sabeah **65** 373
Samuel **65** 372
Sarah **61** 296 **62** 84 **65** 372
373
Sarah (Green) **133** 153
Sarah G. **77** 207
Sibyl **65** 373
Susanna **65** 372
Thankful **65** 371 373 **85** 44
Theodosia **65** 373
Tho **123** 261
Thomas **64** 72 **65** 173 371-
373 **85** 44 **86** 162 **110**
197 198 260 263 **142** 261
331
Timothy **60** 378-380 398

MORLEY *cont'd*
61 85 **62** 84 196 **65** 372
Valentine **94** 328
Walter **65** 373
William **61** 387 **65** 173 371-
373 **85** 309 314 315 410
145 40
William Cave **148** 120
Willim Wickham **61** 192
MORMSON
— Mr. **145** 110
MORNINGSTAR Edna
Emily (Lazell) **89**
238 239
Freeman **89** 239
Lucille Victoria **89** 239
Wilma May **89** 239
MORONEY
Frances Trumbull **69**
lxxii
Percy Stuart **69** lxxii
MOROT Aimé **77** lxxvi
MOROTH Samuel **68** 227
Morow *see* Morrow
MORPETH Morepeth
Morpath
Peter de **79** 370
Roger de Merely (Baron
of) **94** 207
Thomas **61** 329 **94** 253 262
96 194
MORPHEW —— **73** 20 21
Morphey *see* Murphy
Morphy *see* Murphy
MORRAH Dermot **108** 70
Morrall *see* Morrill
MORRANTE
William **98** 123
MORRATT John **143** 304
Rachel (Blinn) **143** 304
MORRE —— **64** 211
— Col. **119** 131
Bathsheba **64** 35
Cambridge **64** 46
Morrel *see* Morrill
Morrell *see* Morrill
MORRELLY Anne **84** 304
MORREN Richard **74** 271
MORRER John **58** 17
Sukey **58** 17
MORRES
Margaret **146** 275
MORRIAM Aluna **96** 203
MORRICE
William **146** 275
MORRICK —— **121** 23
John **121** 20
MORRILL Morrall
Morrel Morrell Morril
—— **53** 266 **58** 100 **59** 337
60 107 **66** 280 **76** 14 **92**
311 **98** 198 **140** 170
— Mr. **54** 183-188 395
75 114
— Mrs. **83** 194
— Rev. Mr. **62** 65
—— (Glover) **140** 170
Aaron **56** 205 **73** 127 **87** 94
119 227 229 276
Aaron H. **94** 250
Aaron Hall **94** 124

MORRILL *cont'd*
Abby C. (Osgood) **87** 94
Abel **52** 430 **53** 165 279
Abigail **52** 431 **53** 166
   279 282 **59** 188 284 **62**
   152 **73** 125 **87** 123 **123**
   12
Abigail B. **81** 151
Abigail C. (Osgood)
   87 94
Abner **53** 165-168 276
Abraham **52** 431 **56** 205
   58 100 **70** 96 **72** 257 269
   73 125 **75** 7-9 **81** 151 **85**
   465 **109** 312 **136** 271
Adam **53** 166
Adonijah **51** 462
Affia **58** 122
Alexander H. **72** 272
Amos **88** 331 **91** 206 **94** 95
   100 65
Andrew Jackson **127** 137
Ann Elizabeth **94** 124
Ann Maria **76** 256 **94** 249
Anna **53** 163 278 279 **55**
   315 **58** 124 **63** 177 **72**
   255 265 269 **75** 8 **78** 411
   83 156 **90** 247
Anna T. **98** 193
Annath **83** 140
Anne **75** 10
Annie **96** 331
Archales L. **72** 272
Arkil **97** 248 249 **103** 284
Asa **68** 243 **69** 173 **72** 255
Augustus **81** 152 **127** 137
Barnes **53** 167
Benjamin **53** 164 283 **58**
   100 **63** 251 **105** 213
Benjamin J. **88** 337
Benjamin Winslow
   72 255
Benning **83** 35
Bersheba **52** 433
Betsey **93** 365
Betsey L. **90** 332 **97** 18
Betsey S. **91** 23
Betty **52** 435 **53** 276 282
   58 125
Blanche **81** 128
Cadwallader **62** 153
Camilla **81** 152
Caroline (Cousens)
   89 351
Catherine **69** 155 **96** 240
Charles **81** 151 **127** 137
Charles C. **103** 47
Charles G. **89** 351
Charles Henry **94** 249
Charles J. **78** 446
Cincinnatus **92** 323
Clara Ellen (Dam)
   100 229
Climena A. **69** 255
Comfort **72** 255 257
   73 44 46
Cordelia Chadwick
   115 159
Cornelia Dean **54** 371
Cynthia **68** 243 **69** 173
Cyrus Peverly **81** 151

MORRILL *cont'd*
D. T. **136** 143
Daniel **89** 357 **145** 354
Daniel J. **72** 272
David **52** 431 **53** 163 **64**
   208 **72** 255 258 272 **73**
   44 48 **75** 7 8 10 **81** 150
   91 199 **127** 137
Davis **83** 140
Delia **75** 14
Dorcas Ellen (Gordon)
   89 199
Dorcas Hall **94** 124
Dorothy **53** 168 278 **66**
   321 **78** 69
Ebenezer **53** 283
Eleanor **74** 248 266
Eleanor Cordelia
   76 lxxxvi
Electa **57** 284
Eliakim **57** 372 **65** 364
Elijah **91** 330 **105** 284
Eliza **72** 257
Eliza Ann **94** 250
Eliza Davis **89** 351
Eliza S. **83** 23 26
Eliza S. (Frost) **83** 23
Elizabeth **52** 431 **53** 164
   165 277 278 280 **55**
   xlviii **64** 11 **72** 255 261
   269 **73** 46 48 **75** 10 **78**
   294 **88** 334 **92** 340
Elizabeth (Harper) **92** 73
Elizabeth (Severance)
   126 234
Elizabeth J. **134** 234
Elizabeth N. **92** 340
Ellen M. **94** 249
Elsie L. **97** 68
Emeline H. **81** 151
Emeline L. (Partridge)
   98 198
Emily **69** 318
Enoch **74** 260
Ephraim **53** 166 **72** 267
   73 47 **75** 9 **120** 269
Ephraim L. **72** 267
Esther **53** 314 **73** 48
Ethel D. **83** 435 436
Eugene A. **98** 198
Eugene F. **92** 340
Eunice **58** 17
Ezekiel **53** 165-167 275
   278-280 **62** 124 **78** 294
Ferdinand Gordon **62**
   213 **109** 312
Florence E. (Graves)
   121 180
Francis Maria **94** 124
Francis Wellington
   Brown **94** 250
Frank E. **92** 340
Fred L. **81** 151
Frederick Charles **94** 124
Frederick Hall **94** 124
George **83** 194 **124** 22
   127 137
George A. **98** 198
George F. **69** 318
George Henry **63** 314
George I. **84** 47

MORRILL *cont'd*
George Peverly **81** 151
George W. **103** 47
George Washington
   94 124
Giles **58** 340
Green **126** 234
Guly Elma Maria **72** 255
Hannah **51** 462 **52** 430 **53**
   165-167 276 277 279 **54**
   31 **58** 47 **63** 178 **67** 182
   68 168 243 **71** 212 216
   224 **72** 254 255 269 **73**
   44 48 **74** 248 259 260 **76**
   253 **86** 451 **92** 340
Hannah Elizabeth **94** 124
Hannah Rogers **72** 267
Harriet Richardson
   94 249
Helen Maria **94** 250
Henry **58** 41 124 **76** 19
   81 128
Herbert Percy **99** 57
Hibbert **53** 278
Hiram Baker **120** 318
Hiram Kelley **61** xxxv
Hope **72** 255 **74** 264
Horace Edwin **58** xlv 100
Horatio S. **72** 272
Huldah F. (Gordon)
   89 199
Humphrey **75** 10
Isaac **53** 40 165 **62** 152 **63**
   178 **70** 96 **74** 250 259 **81**
   151 **85** 465 **107** 313 **109**
   312 **136** 271
Isabella **76** 254
Israel **126** 234
J. **91** 330
J. Willard **94** 250
Jabez **58** 47
Jacob **56** 205 **72** 255 **85** 465
   90 331 **98** 198 **124** 61
James **53** 276 **75** 14 **85** 125
   111 183 **139** 295 **140**
   170
James A. **72** 272
James B. **92** 340
James William **111** 139
Jane **74** 260 **97** 265
Jedediah **72** 255 269 **73** 48
   75 7 9 **94** 249 **126** 275
Jemima **53** 167
Jennet **113** 163
Jeremiah **53** 168
Joanna **53** 166 278 **74** 250
Joel **97** 144 268
Joel (Mrs.) **97** 144
John **52** 432 **53** 314 **54** 31
   408 409 **58** 18 **68** 142
   260 **71** 212 **72** 254 255
   75 7 **76** 158 **81** 151 **82**
   79 **90** 390 **91** 200 **107**
   238 **109** 312 **125** 94 **136**
   271
John A. **95** 299
John Barstow **98** 147
   114 309
John Calvin **81** 151
John D. **106** 320 **108** 319
   320 **109** 78 80 126 **110**

MORRILL *cont'd*
158 160 321 **111** 246
112 76 80 239 241 **117**
157 160 **118** 244 245
120 318 320 **121** 74 **122**
78-80
John Dorrance **105** 129
115 314 **135** 285
John E. L. **72** 272
Jonathan **53** 279 **72** 255
Joseph **53** 165 166 276 282
59 290 **71** 224 **89** 351
357 **100** 229 **134** 90
Joseph G. **69** 255
Josiah **73** 125 **75** 7 8
Judith **58** 18 340
Julia A. **98** 198
Keziah **72** 254
Lair Davis **92** 73
Laura Jane **76** 14
Leonard W. **89** 199
Levi **53** 278 **69** 177 **75** 10
81 447 **111** 239
Levina **72** 255
Lewis **81** 152
Lewis W. **81** 151
Lincoln L. **92** 340
Linwood L. **89** 351
Louise **81** 152
Lovilla **127** 137
Lovilla (Walton) **127** 137
Lucia Janet **73** lvii
Lucinda **64** 208
Lucinda (Stoning)
139 293
Lucy **86** 194
Lucy Amanda **92** 73
Lurana **64** 208
Lute Blanche **91** 142
Lydia **52** 433 **53** 165-168
276 **69** 177 **72** 255 266
269 **75** 10 **82** 413 **111** 69
132 219
Lydia (Briggs) **126** 275
Lydia (Yeaton) **90** 335
Lydia A. **98** 198
Malvina P. (Farley)
136 143
Marcellus **92** 323
Margaret **54** lx **59** 188
Margaret Elizabeth
81 151
Maria (Pico) **88** 337
Martha **53** 165-168 275-277
Mary **51** 462 **52** 432 **53**
165 276 278 281-283 **67**
271 **68** 260 **72** 255 267
73 47 **76** 35 254 **82** 295
301 **90** 390 **99** 205 **127**
137 **133** 284
Mary (Adams) **126** 234
Mary (Cofran) **124** 61
Mary (Currier) **111** 239
Mary (Shinn) (Crosby)
(Fenimore) **111** 269
Mary A. **80** 140 **127** 137
Mary Angelina **75** liv
Mary Ann **81** 151 152
Mary Ann (Coolidge)
88 331
Mary Ardilla **89** 351

MORRILL *cont'd*
Mary Augusta **94** 250
Mary D. (Adams) **103** 47
Mary E. **72** 267
Mary J. **69** 255
Mary Jane (Pelkey)
111 139
Mary Nelson **99** 57
Mary W. (Millett) **83** 184
Mattie A. **103** 47
Mattie A. (Morrill) **103** 47
May **53** 165
Mehitable **73** 45
Mercy **73** 44 **92** 340 **94** 124
Mercy (Hall) **94** 124
Mercy Jane **94** 124
Merriam **72** 254
Micah **53** 280
Micajah **52** 433 **53** 277
279 280 282 **81** 151 **145**
351
Milo Sanborn **81** 151
Miriam **52** 429 **53** 165 **58**
100 124 **59** 38 **81** 150
Molly **53** 279 282 **58** 123
Moses **52** 429 **71** 212 216
76 251 **85** 465 **92** 340
107 313 **109** 312
Nahum **72** 269 **73** 48 **75** 8
9 **76** 248 250-254 256
261 **87** 206 **92** 340 **109**
312
Nancy **53** 276 **81** 151
Nathan **72** 267 **118** 37
Nathaniel **53** 277 278 280
58 41 **66** 141 302 303 **67**
61 **81** 447 **82** 49 **89** 351
356 **91** 93 **125** 91
Nathaniel E. **119** 281
Nellie B. **76** 19
Nicholas **54** 409 **61** 202
Olive **59** 290
Orinda **118** 192
Orlando **91** 200
Patience A. (Rich) **84** 47
Paul **53** 165-168 275-277 **81**
151 **127** 137
Paul E. **89** 199
Paulina (Grant) **119** 227
229 276
Peace **72** 254 **73** 46 **74** 256
Peaslee **72** 255 **74** 256 **87**
225 226 230 239 **94** 124
145 364
Pelatiah **72** 255
Peter **68** 243 **72** 255 **73** 44
75 7 8 **94** 124
Peter Chadbourne **94** 124
Peter J. **90** 335
Peter Winslow **72** 255
Phebe **105** 104
Philip **53** 280
Prudence **115** 37
Rachel **53** 279 **55** 314 **59**
286 **68** 260 **74** 250 **78** 94
83 10 **92** 292
Rachel (Warren) **83** 10
Rebecca **73** 45
Reuben **81** 150 **115** 159
Reuben C. **87** 227
Rhoda **111** 239

MORRILL *cont'd*
Richard **115** 124
Richard B. **119** 227 229
Robert Codman **99** 57
Robert G. **121** 180-182
Robie **116** 111
Rosetta E. (Angell) **99** 292
Rowena **62** 122 127
Ruth **53** 263 277 279 **72**
254 255 267
S. **92** 322
Sadie (Strout) **89** 351
Sally **98** 221
Sally (Ambrose) **111** 239
Samuel **52** 433 **53** 163-
168 276 282 **57** 284 372
62 153 **67** 271 **69** xxxv
76 248 250 **90** 128 **92**
340 **96** 182 **102** 88 **109**
312 **110** 63 **125** 23
Samuel J. **83** 23 26
Samuel Jordan **71** 212
Sarah **51** 463 465 **52** 429
431 **53** 164-168 276 278-
280 **72** 255 257 258 266
269 **73** 44 48 **75** 8 **76**
248 250-254 256 261 **77**
235 **81** 151 **82** 49 **90** 170
92 340 **97** 144 **111** 147
120 319 **125** 91
Sarah (Blaisdell) **120** 318
Sarah Ames **67** 271 **69** 331
Sarah Anne **69** 331
Sarah Catherine **81** 152
Sarah E. **72** 272
Sarah M. (Guptill) **90** 331
Sarah Sanborn **81** 150
Sarah Thurston **94** 249
Sarah Worthen **76** 19
Simeon **53** 167 168 276
278-280
Simon **106** 153
Smith L. **69** 255
Sophronia J. **89** 357
Soviah **73** 47
Stephen **72** 255 **83** 184
98 198 **99** 205
Susan **56** 205 **62** 153
Susan (McIntire) **119** 281
Susan Ann (Roberts)
119 227 229
Susan L. **73** 45
Susanna **52** 428 432 **53**
163 279 280 **58** 47 63
251 **72** 255 258 263 267
272 **73** 45 46 **75** 8
Susanna (Gates) **120** 269
Thaddeus **72** 272 **75** 9
P75 6
Thaddeus C. **72** 272
Thankful **111** 117
Thankful H. (Tobie)
89 351
Theodate **55** xciii **72** 255
Theodore **83** 35
Theophilus **52** 429 **53** 278
Thomas **59** 188 **72** 255 **83**
140 **87** 122 **91** 330 **92**
324 **125** 73 **126** 234 **136**
271
Timothy **53** 280 282

MORRILL *cont'd*
Timothy H. **72** 274
Vienna G. **72** 272
Walter Goodale **94** 250
Walton **127** 137
Weston **107** 134
Wiggins **105** 284
William **53** 165 276 **55** 314
  74 248 **76** 47 **83** 10 **103**
  298 **105** 285 **111** 183
  269 272 **134** 234 **140**
  170 **145** 354
William Chadbourne
  94 249
William Creighton
  103 298
William L. **92** 340
William Pepperill **72** 255
William S. **81** 152
Winthrop **72** 258 267 **73**
  45 46 **75** 7
Zerviah **72** 267
MORRILL Mooris Moriss
  Morriss
—— **52** 394 **54** xvii 459
  460 **57** 121 **59** 113 **62**
  290 **68** 275 **69** 51 53 **86**
  351 **92** 320 362 **100** 190
  119 234 **120** 207 **122**
  303 304 307 **128** 312
— Capt. **62** 290 353
— Ensign **96** 369
— Lieut. **53** 45
— Mr. **55** 274 276 **57** 222
  79 298 **148** 152
— Mrs. **52** 112 **83** 194
  85 120
— Sgt. **96** 369
Aaron **71** 8 17
Aaron K. **71** 13
Abby E. **73** 39
Abigail **60** 50 **71** 6 7 9 11
  12 18 **136** 309
Abraham **84** 277
Adam **95** 6 7
Adeline **71** 19
Adonijah **53** 311 **71** 6 9
  97 36
Agnes **53** 459 **66** 253
  119 126
Aimee **71** 14
Al **145** 377
Alanson **71** 13 18
Alethea **71** 12 15
Alexander **67** 290
Alexander Gardner
  100 190
Alexander Pollard
  100 190
Alfred **71** 13
Alice Gertrude (Howe)
  362
Almira **71** 15
Almira Miller (Nickerson)
  84 453
Amanda **90** 374
Amelia **71** 13 19 **136** 29
Amelia Lucretia **71** 19
Amos **62** 137 **71** 5 7 8 10-
  14 **144** 332
Amy **71** 12 18

MORRIS *cont'd*
Amy (Silvester) **86** 124
Andrew **71** 8 17
Angeline **71** 13
Ann **53** 459 **67** 288 371 **71**
  4 6 7 12 **73** 150 **128** 34
Ann (Lattimer) **145** 321
Ann Elizabeth (Kittow)
  87 281
Ann Elizabeth (Lazell)
  89 14
Ann Elizabeth (Revere)
  145 307
Ann Jane (Johnston)
  128 264
Ann Louise **71** 15
Anna **53** 311 460 **71** 6 10
  13 14 19 **88** 81 **112** 50
  121 152 153
Anne **65** 161 **71** 6 **91** 356
  102 43
Anne (Holyoke) **147** 19
  32
Annie **81** 357
Anthony **52** 85 **53** 458-460
  63 304
Anthony John **85** 440
Anthony Paschall **53** 460
Armour **86** 192 **103** 115
  140
Arthur **65** 29
Arthur B. **107** 13
Arvil **71** 13
Arza C. **71** 12
Asa **71** 8 10 12
Asher **71** 13
Augusta (Goodell) **126** 35
Augusta (Shaw) **104** 96
Barnabas **125** 37
Bela D. **71** 19
Benjamin **71** 7 9 **73** 143
  77 264 **143** 260
Bennett Franklin **71** 15
Bertha May **108** 133
Bethel **71** 13
Bethiah **78** 243
Bethiah (Peake) **84** 454
Betsey **62** 137 **71** 9 13 15 19
Betsey (McDonald)
  125 195
Betsey (Wallace) **92** 317
Betty **62** 382
Bevans (Mrs.) **114** 188 189
Cadwalader **53** 459
Caroline **71** 12 13 **84** 133
Caroline M. **81** 357
Caroline Margaret
  101 319
Caspar Wistar **53** 460
Catharina A. **71** 12
Catherine **83** 26 29 **112**
  56 58 **125** 195
Catherine Cox **115** 14
Catherine E. **71** 15
Catherine Julia (Ford)
  142 195
Catherine W. **53** 460
Charity **66** 22 **71** 15
Charles **51** 104 **52** 400 **67**
  287-290 **71** 13 64 **78** 305
  87 281 **100** 190 **103** 194

MORRIS *cont'd*
257 **107** 250 **109** 171
  111 130 **116** 7 **117** 7
  144 18 19
Charles Gould **71** 14
Charles H. **109** 270
Charles Newton **71** 18
Charles Valentine **115** 18
Charlotte (Gennens)
  125 102
Chauncey **71** 13
Chezia **76** 170
Chloe **71** 9
Christopher **65** 233
Clara **71** 13
Clara Elizabeth **76** lxxix
Clarania **71** 16
Clarissa **71** 13
Clarissa D. **71** 15
Cornelia **71** 12 15
Cortland **71** 13
Curtis **71** 12
Cynthia **71** 19
Cynthia J. **71** 12
Daniel **71** 7-12 **144** 20 21
  331 332
Davenport Alger **142** 195
David **71** 16-19 **73** 257 **76**
  152 170 **110** 171
David Albert (Mrs.)
  94 139
Davis Harrington **75** 239
Deborah **52** 418 **133** 232
Desire **71** 6
Diodama H. **111** 130
Dorcas **72** 15 **77** 157 158
Dorman **71** 10
Dorothy **67** 288 **71** 7 **144**
  18 19
Dorothy (Martin) (Howe)
  146 278
Ebenezer **71** 9 11 **146** 278
Edith **108** 132
Edmund **71** 8 13
Edward **53** 384 **76** lxxix
  79 101 **84** 453 454 **99**
  311 **128** 176 **146** 261
  262 275-278
Edward J. **97** 332
Edward Livington **71** 18
Edwin **71** 14
Effingham Buckley
  81 357
Effingham Buckley (Mrs.)
  74 ix xxv
Eleanor **63** lix **71** 10
Eleanor B. **81** 357
Eleazer **61** 118 **71** 5-8 10
  81 129
Elgy **104** 96
Eli **71** 13
Eli A. **71** 14
Eli F. **71** 12
Eli Gould **71** 12 14
Eli James **71** 14
Elijah **71** 13 **92** 317
Elisa G. **90** 46
Elisha **71** 17 **145** 75
Eliza **71** 14 15 **100** 190
  118 46
Eliza (Richards) **126** 205

MORRIS *cont'd*
Elizabeth **51** 218 **53** 459
460 **59** 361 **62** 137 **63**
142 238-14 16 19 **76** 25
78 291 **81** 129 **85** 98 **89**
58 **99** 311 **100** 237 239
297 **108** 64 152 **109** 111
114 58 **115** 24 **119** 126
125 101 223 **144** 331
146 261 262 275-278
147 19 20
Elizabeth (Bowen)
146 278
Elizabeth (Brown) **84** 454
Elizabeth (Burritt) **144** 332
Elizabeth (McDonald)
125 258
Elizabeth A. **71** 15
Elizabeth Ann **78** 34 **115**
24 **128** 34
Elizabeth Ann (Adams)
114 188 189
Elizabeth Constance
76 25
Ella **81** 403
Ellen Ann **71** 14
Ellen Douglas **74** xxv **80**
102 215 **81** 357
Elliott **71** 19
Elsie **60** 78
Emeline **71** 18
Emily Eugenia **71** 14
Emily J. **71** 15
Emily M. **71** 12
Emma **104** 102 103
128 264
Emma J. **87** 281
Emma O. (Nelson) **104**
102 103
Ephraim **71** 5 7 9 11 13 **76**
lxxix **84** 453 454 **146** 277
Esther **59** 168 **67** 288 **68**
276 **71** 6-8 10 **102** 109
144 19
Esther (Woodworth)
86 351
Ethel Mounteney **92** 146
Eugenia Laura **71** 14
Eugenia Laura (Tuttle)
84 332
Eunice **63** 195 **68** 275 **71**
11 12 14 15 17-19 **76** 152
88 374 **96** 64 **144** 332
Eunice A. **111** 139
Eunice Atwater **71** 14
Experience Taft (Perry)
116 202
Ezra **71** 13
Fanny **77** lxxxvi
Fanny Jennet **71** 18
Finly **64** 163
Flora V. (Ball) **111** 300 305
Florence Bellinger
Skottowe **94** 310
Florence Eddowes **95** 152
Fordham **51** 386
Foster **71** 9
Frances Anne Henrietta
(Penrose)
(Thorneycroft) **117** 114
Frances L. **71** 15

MORRIS *cont'd*
Frances Martha
(Morrison) **94** 139
Francis **52** 236 351 **67** 290
102 43
Francis Pratt **71** 18
Frank **78** 40
Freddie S. **104** 103
Frederick **71** 13
Frederick K. (Mrs.) **91** 177
92 142 **93** 125 132 **94**
145
Gainor **117** 67
Garry **71** 12 18
George **63** 41 **64** 314 **68**
275 325 **69** 53 **71** 13 16-
19 **76** 235 **96** 305 **101** 4
George C. **104** 102
George Calvert **63** 303
George Franklin **71** 15
George M. **71** 15
George Seymour **71** 15
George W. **128** 264
Gouverneur **64** 179 **65** 97
119 192
Grace **79** 101 **146** 278
Grace (Bett) **84** 453
146 277
Granville W. **71** 13
Grissie **76** lxxix **84** 453
Guy **118** 46
H. **91** 330
H. A. **91** 330
H. C. **128** 176
H. O. **128** 176
Hannah **53** 459 **56** 281 **71**
5-9 11 13 18 **85** 98 **104**
96 **106** 46 **119** 182
Hannah (Chaffee) **84** 454
Hannah (Ford) **119** 182
Hannah (Mayo) **146** 277
Hannah (Rodney) **106** 46
Hannah A. **121** 152
Harriet **71** 14 15 **91** 330
Harriet E. (Brown) **109**
171 270
Harriet Helen **71** 18
Harry Joseph (Mrs.) **118**
77 **119** 78 158 **120** 158
121 158 315
Harvey **71** 12 15
Harvey (Mrs.) **84** 111 190
Hattie **77** 263
Helen Harrison **71** 14
84 332
Henrietta **122** 12
Henry **51** 354 **59** 220 **60** 50
63 27 **71** 15 **94** 338
Henry Calvin (Mrs.)
104 144
Henry Newton **71** 14
Herbert **71** 15
Hester **71** 7 11 18 **131** 130
Hezekiah **67** 289
Hilles **96** 399
Hobart Hotchkiss **71** 15
Homer **104** 102 103
Homer M. **104** 102 103
Hugh **64** 337
Ida **75** xxiii **89** 87

MORRIS *cont'd*
Ida Nesbitt (Tucker) **76**
lxxx **103** 140
Imogen **71** 15
Isaac **71** 9 **76** lxxix **84** 454
146 277
Isaac Amos **71** 14
Isabel **71** 10
Israel **93** 296
Israel B. **71** 11
Israel W. **81** 357
Israel Wistar **53** 460
J. L. **104** 103
Jachin **71** 11 13
Jacob **71** 7 **83** 24 26 29 **91**
330 **100** 190 **115** 14 17
18 26
James **53** 459 **65** 29 150
67 288 **71** 5-7 9 11 12
77 263 **87** 400 **91** 330
103 255 256 **104** 242
105 205 **117** 80 **118** 46
124 187 **126** 205 **144**
332
James Allen **71** 15
James Eliot **115** 17
James M. **110** 130
James Ranstop **67** 290
James Tarrant **90** 352
James Thomas **137** 39
Jane **72** 295 **115** 122
Jane (Bordman) **88** 331
Jane Eliza **102** 302
Jane Elizabeth **71** 14
77 261
Janet **73** 257
Jared **71** 17
Jason **71** 19
Jean **68** 275 **71** 16
Jemima **71** 7 10
Jerusha **67** 130 **71** 13 14
Joan **66** 253 **93** 8 **146** 275
276
Joanna (O'Neill) **85** 440
Joel **91** 330
John **51** 218 219 **53** 433
55 24 **59** 315 **60** 24 291
62 159 382 **64** 226 337
338 **66** 22 **67** 288 289
371 **68** 275 310 **69** 149
70 69 **71** 5 6 9 12 13 15-
18 **73** 226 **76** 25 **81** 128
129 486 **97** 278 **100** 239
101 271 **110** 199 **117** 80
119 126 125 102 **128**
264 **145** 6 307 **147** 19
John Anthony Grant
108 36
John E. **52** 398 **61** 213 **62**
98 **128** 176
John H. (Mrs.) **99** 167
John Moses **65** 154
John N. **71** 15
John P. **100** 190
John Plumb **71** 18 19
John Spry **67** 290
John Stevens **71** 13
Jonathan **104** 96 **126** 35
Jonathan B. **100** 190
Jonathan Flynt **53** 384
Jonathan Ford **119** 182

MORRIS *cont'd*
Joseph **53** 459 **59** 168 **68**
275 **69** 53 **70** 70 **71** 5-9
16 17 **76** lxxix **81** 129
101 4 6 52 81 82 85 86
115 169 **116** 17 **119** 182
196 **125** 220
Joseph Lucius **71** 16
Joseph N. **71** 13
Joseph Riggs **71** 13
Joseph Saunders **53** 460
Judah **104** 90
Judith **64** 355 **83** 75 292
136 100
Judson **67** 130 **71** 12 14
144 332
Julia **71** 19
Julia Ann **71** 19
Julia Louisa **71** 18
Julia S. **71** 18
Juliet Birckhead **81** 402
Julius **71** 18
Kate Eugenia **75** viii **76**
viii **77** viii **78** 220 **79**
216 **80** 222 **81** 236 **84**
112 195 453
Katharine **71** 14 **76** 116
94 282 383
Katharine (Grinnell)
90 70
Katharine J. (Ford)
142 194
Katy **71** 14
Keturah **71** 9
Keziah **52** 418 **71** 17 19
92 48
Kitty **77** 263
Laura **71** 12
Lawrence Johnson **88** 401
Leonard A. **71** 15
Levi **71** 10 12
Levi C. **71** 12
Lewis **86** 264 **115** 169
126 121
Lewis G. **125** 216
Lewis Lee **115** 24
Lewis S. **68** 25
Lois **71** 9 10 18
Lois (Bennett) (Lyon)
145 75
Louisa **71** 19 **103** 195
Lovel **104** 96
Lovice **71** 8
Lucretia **71** 13
Lucy **68** 25 **71** 13 18
145 307
Lucy Ann **71** 13
Lucy Thom **68** 25
Luke **53** 459
Luke Wistar **53** 460
Luzon B. **78** 101 **84** 332
Luzon Burritt **71** 14
Lydia **71** 8 9 11 14
Lyman **71** 19
M. C. **104** 103
Mabel **71** 7-9 11
Mabel Madeline **105** 221
Major **71** 11 13
Malga M. **71** 15
Marcus **71** 15 18
Margaret **53** 459 **55** 29 66

MORRIS *cont'd*
lxv **67** 372 **68** 275 **69** 51
53 **71** 7 8 16 **111** 56 **146**
278 **147** 54
Margaret Smith (Even)
119 182 **137** 36
Maria **71** 12 19 **118** 46
Maria H. **71** 15
Marietta **71** 15
Marshall Eliot **71** 15
Martha **71** 12 **111** 83
146 278
Martha B. **71** 15
Martha Jane **71** 14
Martin **63** 142
Martin F. **51** 81
Mary **51** 421 **53** 459 460
54 201 **56** 253 **58** 147
61 166 **65** 43 48 **67** 14
288-290 372 **71** 6-10 12-
15 18 19 **75** 241 **83** 23
26 **85** 99 228 **93** 296 **99**
207 **100** 239 **106** 82 **111**
287 **115** 14 17 18 26 **120**
6 11 **121** 319 **122** 160
123 239 **144** 331 **146**
277 **147** 20
Mary (Conway) **126** 67
Mary (Fitz Randolph)
97 278
Mary (Ford) **119** 126
Mary (Harrison) **93** 296
Mary (Philipse) **94** 310
Mary (Ruggles)
(Pierpont) **146** 277
Mary (Shumway) **125** 216
Mary (Skinner) **126** 35
Mary Ann **71** 12
Mary Cox **115** 26
Mary Dent **73** 149
Mary Elizabeth **71** 15
120 238
Mary Etta **71** 16 19
Mary Jane **71** 18
Mary Maria **71** 14
Mary Norman **73** 151
Mary O. **71** 12
Mary Seymour **71** 14
Mary Tama **88** 71
Matilda **128** 176
Matthew Mackhard/
McHard **71** 11 12
144 332
Maurice Morgan **117** 114
Mehitable **71** 9 12 14 15
123 202
Mehitable (Judson)
144 332
Mehitable (Mayo) **146** 278
Melinda **71** 17
Melvin Ebenezer (Mrs.)
99 148
Mercy **61** 118 **66** 285 **69** 53
71 7 16
Merritt Noyes **71** 14
Miles **66** 37 **71** 14
Minnie **77** 264
Molly **71** 14
Monroe C. **111** 130
Morris **101** 31
Myron Newton **71** 18

MORRIS *cont'd*
Myrtle M. **96** 305
Nancy **71** 12 15
Nancy (Thompson)
126 66
Naomi **57** 400
Nathan Ruel **71** 13
Nellie **77** 264 **114** 188
Nellie Maria (Thompson)
72 xx **90** 130
Nelson **71** 13
Newton **71** 14
Newton John **63** 195
71 16 18
Nicholas **130** 313
Nola **77** 264
Olive **71** 13
Oliver **63** 189
Oliver B. **99** 9
Pamela **76** lxxix
Pamela (Converse) **84**
454 **146** 277
Patty **126** 35
Pauline **77** 264
Peleg **71** 18
Phebe **71** 7 8
Phebe (Barnes) **124** 187
Philip **71** 6
Philo **71** 13
Polly **68** 314 **71** 10 13 15 18
100 190 **117** 80 **121** 319
122 160 **123** 239 **128**
312
Polly (Knapp) **123** 239
Polly (Knoles) **109** 183
Polly Ann **71** 16
Polly H. **71** 12
Powhatan Randolph
(Mrs.) **86** 197
Priscilla **54** 287
Priscilla (Ford) **119** 126
Priscilla Pratt
(Woodward) **106** 311
Prudence **71** 10
Prudence (Summers)
(Curtis) **144** 331
Rachel **71** 8 11 **78** 40
Rachel Helen **89** 232
Ralph **54** 161 **69** 18
Ray **71** 14
Ray (Mrs.) **90** 70
Ray Sells **87** 264
Rebecca **52** 200 **71** 6 11 13
17
Rebecca (Russell) **125** 220
Redmond **109** 183
112 292
Rhody **103** 195
Rice **131** 130
Richard **60** 188 **62** 382 **68**
275 **69** 53 **71** 16 **82** 341
88 71 **100** 237 **105** 115
109 111 **121** 152 153
125 195 258 **136** 66
Richard B. **87** 210 **94** 210
107 16 **108** 237 **109** 89-
91 **115** 168
Richard H. **119** 126
Ritta Ann **71** 19
Robert **51** 89 373 **53** 417
55 24 27 **61** 143 **64** 340

MORRIS *cont'd*
  65 44 **66** 22 **88** 331 **96**
  258 **97** 179 **103** 213 **111**
  287 **112** 178 **121** 319
  128 312 **130** 172 173
  175 **145** 321
  Robert Clark **87** 400
  Robert Tuttle **71** 14
  Roger **61** 134 **94** 310
  107 202
  Rosa 111 **92** 111
  Rosalie **63** 303
  Roswell **71** 12
  Ruphine Antonia **85** 440
  Ruth **71** 9 11 15 **147** 54
  Rutisha **94** 166
  S. **91** 330
  S. B. **80** 68
  Sal **129** 167
  Sally **71** 10-13 15 **126** 276
  Samuel **53** 459 **67** 290 **71** 7
  11 13 16 **80** 68 **100** 302
  304 **146** 278 348
  Samuel B. **71** 13 **80** 68
  Samuel Buckley **53** 460
  Samuel M. **71** 15
  Samuel Wells **53** 460
  Sarah **51** 421 **53** 460 **66** 203
  67 288 290 371 375 **71** 6-
  11 16 17 19 **72** 15 **93**
  205 **99** 207 **115** 24 **125**
  107 287 **144** 331
  Sarah (Bell) **137** 40
  Sarah (Davis) **146** 278
  Sarah (Fayerweather)
  (McHard) **144** 20 21 331
  Sarah (Fiscus) **128** 176
  Sarah (Gilbert) **144** 331
  Sarah (Hunt) **114** 147
  Sarah (James) **101** 31
  Sarah A. **90** 352
  Sarah Ann **71** 13 14
  Sarah Catherine (Bone)
  105 221
  Sarah E. **71** 12 **77** 263
  Sarah E. (Ramsey) **128** 176
  Sarah Jane **71** 13
  Sarah M. **71** 15
  Sarah Sabrina **78** 435
  Seymour **61** 177 314 **72**
  209 312 **73** 6 160 **76** xxx
  lxxix lxxx **86** 187 189
  192 **87** 170 **88** 87 163 **90**
  133 **93** 305 **99** 261 **103**
  140
  Seymour (Mrs.) **75** x xxiii
  86 192 **87** 171 **88** 87
  103 78 115 123 140
  Seymour Tucker **76** lxxx
  103 140
  Shadrach **71** 11 13
  Sheldon **71** 14 15 19
  Shubael **71** 17
  Sibyl **68** 275 **71** 16
  Sibyl (Chancelor) **100** 304
  Sibylla **118** 46 48
  Sibylla Eliza **118** 43 56
  Solomon **71** 17
  Sophronia **71** 15
  Staats Smith **89** 14
  145 307

MORRIS *cont'd*
  Stephen **65** 24 **71** 7
  119 182
  Stephen G. **71** 13
  Susan **51** 421 **71** 13 15 19
  Susan (Waggoner)
  128 176
  Susanna **68** 275 **71** 16
  130 301
  Susanna (Florance)
  130 313
  Susanna (Wickham)
  100 302
  Susanna Jackson
  (Weston) **84** 454
  Sylvan Herbert **105** 221
  Sylvester **54** 241 **84** 454
  T. A. **91** 200
  Temperance (Bushnell)
  (Post) **146** 371
  Thalia J. **71** 15
  Thankful **68** 319
  Thomas **52** 200 **53** 460 **64**
  163 **66** 285 **68** 275 **69** 53
  71 5 6 8 10 16 17 **72** 15
  73 257 **76** lxxix 235 **77**
  76 **81** 128 129 **83** 35 **84**
  453 **93** 8 99 235 **100** 237
  114 147 **144** 331 **146**
  275 **147** 19 20
  Thomas D. W. **104** 103
  Thomas Gardner **100** 239
  Thomas W. **73** 278
  Thomas Willing **53** 460
  Timothy **71** 6 9 **104** 96
  Tryphene **115** 127
  Tyler Seymour **54** xxxvi
  458 460 **55** xxx 124 128
  132 **57** xxxi 121 **59** xlii
  60 xxxiv **61** xxxiii **62**
  xxxv **64** xxix **66** xlviii
  67 xxx **146** 277
  Uriah **54** 201 **56** 253
  61 166
  Victorina **115** 169
  Violet **83** 24 26
  Warder **53** 460
  Weyant (Mrs.) **105** 159
  160
  Whit **105** 78
  William **54** 347 **61** 43 **62**
  382 **64** 363 **65** 27 43 256
  66 xvi 248 259 **67** 289
  290 **68** 310 314 316 319
  69 153 **70** xliii **71** 7 13
  17-19 **86** 394 **91** 330 356
  93 8 34 385 **96** 233 **99**
  207 **100** 190 **115** 252
  253 **116** 202 **128** 34
  William Augustus **71** 19
  115 14
  William B. **111** 300 305
  William D. **71** 13
  William F. **71** 15
  William Henry **81** 403
  121 153
  William M. **65** 150
  William Scudder **85** 98
  William W. **64** 361 366
  Winthrop **71** 12
  Woodbury **63** 54

MORRIS *cont'd*
  Woolaston **63** 344
  Zada **71** 8
  Zebiah Christy (Gregg)
  85 98
MORRISETTE
  Charles A. **81** 238
  82 237
MORRISEY Delia Agnes
  (Powers) **120** 239
  Michael **120** 239
MORRISHE
  Agnes **110** 199
MORRISON Moreson
  Morison Morrisson
  —— **121** 301 **143** 202
  — Capt. **108** 25 **117** 167
  — Maj. **113** 10
  — Mr. **61** 58 **71** 51
  — Mrs. **127** 16
  — Prof. **96** 370
  — Rev. Mr. **71** 359
  Aaron **72** 284
  Abby Arianna **110** 26
  Abigail **71** 54 **73** 286 **75**
  115 121 **76** 194 **95** 31
  Abigail B. **76** 41 **101** 217
  Abigail B. (White) **101** 215
  Abraham **76** 248 **85** 374
  Abram **75** 311
  Alexander **52** 312 **71** lxvii
  79 43 **92** 129 **115** 39
  133 247
  Alfred J. **64** xxxi
  Alice **51** 285
  Andrew **60** 165 **62** 49
  136 362
  Ann **54** 275 **73** 257 **126** 66
  Ann Maria **93** 355
  Anna **73** 257 **134** 281
  Annah **56** 256
  Armida **115** 204
  Augusta E. **83** 180 184
  Benjamin **66** 37 **75** 312
  76 112 113 248 255 260
  87 206 **108** 122
  Benjamin F. **52** 283
  Betsey **56** 259
  Betty **63** 172
  Bradbury **63** 172 **76** 105
  Brenda Vance de Vere
  97 190 **98** 147
  Cameron (Mrs.) **89** 132
  Caroline A. **110** 26
  Carrie **83** 307
  Catherine **114** 186 **125** 31
  Catherine (Garvey /
  Garvin) **114** 186
  Catherine (McDonald)
  102 303
  Charity **75** 314 **76** 103 258
  Charles E. **68** 336
  Charles F. **68** 336
  Charles H. **110** 26
  Charles K. **126** 243 244
  Charles R. **56** 44
  Charles W. **84** 30
  Comfort **94** 31
  D. **91** 330
  Daniel **55** 375 **75** 48 49 51
  52 54 106 107 112 114

MORRISON *cont'd*
115 118 121 312 313 **76**
103 193 **83** 16
Daniel B. **97** 190 **115** 294
Daniel Moor **61** 241
David **51** 494 **73** 257 **75**
51 112 **76** 107 259
David J. **101** 215 **103** 176
Dependence **76** 249
Doll **92** 129
Dorcas M. **68** 154
Dorothy Steuart **76** 260
Ebenezer **75** 107 **134** 280
Eda **72** 284
Edgar **68** 336
Edward **68** 336 **76** 103 **77**
239 **146** 268 276 277
Eleanor **75** 52 106 107 115
118 315 **76** 182
Eleanor Addison **136** 324
Elijah **76** 112
Elisha **76** 109
Eliza **92** 340
Eliza (Moody) **123** 234
Elizabeth **51** 494 **72** 62 **73**
257 **74** 145 **75** 311 315
76 104 105 107 182 185
195 **84** 330 **108** 65 **146**
276
Elizabeth (Cargill)
117 245
Elizabeth (Fayerweather)
145 254
Elizabeth (Penrose)
117 62
Elizabeth (Rice) **106** 160
Elizabeth Hawkins
(Williams) **136** 324
Elizabeth Shaw (Greene)
136 324
Elizabeth W. **84** 30
Emily Hurd **51** 232
Emma **144** 349 355
Esther **76** 249 253 261
Ethel Louise (Ream)
96 129
Eunice **76** 253
Evelyn **109** 70
F. **59** 182
Florence Inez **96** 129
Frances Martha **94** 139
Francis **112** 247
Francis Johnson **76** 104
Frederick William **109** 70
George **91** 330 **145** 254
George A. **80** 246 **116** 79
George Abbot **106** 158
109 130 158
George Austin **66** 1 **67**
xxxi **68** xxxii **71** xxiii
xxxvi lxvii lxviii **74** 72
133 **75** 274 **85** 418 **91**
249 **92** 61 **105** 254
George W. **68** 154
Grace (Bett) **146** 277
Granville Price **83** 513
Hannah **75** 49 **76** 180
Hannah Caroline **61** 273
Hannah I. (Hollis) **88** 339
Harriet E. **110** 26
Harriet M. **59** xliv **68** 336

MORRISON *cont'd*
Hattie A. **79** 23
Hazel Cleo **109** 128
Henry Lawton **84** 320
Hepzibah Eames **82** 176
Hiram **93** 203
Horace **83** 183 184 **106** 153
107 129 **108** 130
Horace Eugene **68** 154
Horace H. **68** 154
Howard Schofield **92** 146
Hugh **73** 257 **112** 283
Hugh A. **54** 375
Hugh Alexander **61** 319
63 313
Huldah **75** 315 **76** 103
107 180 182 184 185 258
I. R. **91** 330
Ida M. **68** 154
Isaac **146** 276 277
Isabella **66** 110 **144** 349
355
J. D. **91** 330
J. H. **90** 98
J. R. **91** 330
Jack **96** 129
James **51** 491 **71** 45 **84** 320
109 199 **110** 26 **117** 62
144 349 355
James Addison **79** 29
James Britton **110** 141
James H. **76** 41
James Work **61** 273
Jane **51** 494 **61** 241 **98** 53
Janet **51** 491 492
Janet Diane **96** 129
Jennie Belle **109** 130 **110**
63 141
Jeremiah **76** 248
Joel **71** 51
Johannah (Hadley) **93** 203
John **51** 491 **52** 311 **65** 127
70 88 202 **71** lxvii **73**
257 **75** 107 114 **76** 108
109 260 **77** 231 **91** 330
94 31 **110** 141 **114** 192
118 6 145 298 **119** 54
208 **120** 52 **123** 32 **125**
31 40 96 **127** 319 **134**
281 **144** 201
John A. **89** 402
John H. **64** xxxi 198
John Hopkins **51** 232
John M. **93** 355
John Mitchell (Mrs.) **98**
147 **108** 287 291 295
Jonathan **56** 252 256 **73**
257 **84** 459
Jorn **87** 207
Joseph **73** 257 **75** 311 315
76 104 105 107 114 182
185 195 **105** 288
Josephine M. (Lapham)
110 141
Josiah **76** 249 253 261
87 125
Juda **112** 92
Julia N. **110** 26
Keziah **76** 114
L. **146** 331
Larry **60** 200

MORRISON *cont'd*
Leila (Howard) **97** 190
Lenny **92** 340
Leonard Allison **51** 93
96 379 381 384 **52** 248
390 **53** 382 **64** 233 **70** 86
117 245 **124** 248 303
125 162 **145** 239 **147** 78
Leslie McGregor **85** 191
Lilly **76** 113
Louisa **68** 336
Louville **92** 340 **93** 48
Lucie Anne **71** lxvii
Lucinda **73** 257
Lucy **73** 257 **76** 112 248
110 26
Lucy (Littlefield) **108** 122
Lulu B. **123** 234
Luvill **123** 234
Lydia **60** 192 **75** 54 314
76 194
Lydia A. **115** 294
Lydia M. **83** 183 184
M. D. **85** 106 **102** 303
Mabel **102** 303
Magdalen Sophrona **71**
lxviii
Mahala Chase **133** 121
Malcum **73** 132
Margaret **51** 491 **56** 186
92 46 **95** 293 **102** 302
Margaret (Morrison)
102 302
Martha **73** 257 **88** 280
Martha C. **119** 145
Mary **51** 491 **56** 185 **61** 349
69 258 **75** 112 114 121
312 313 **76** 103 184 247
82 216 294 296 **83** 300
91 203 **100** 248 **126** 244
128 172 **146** 276 277
Mary A. **69** 258 **103** 44
Mary Ann **51** 232 **78** 235
Mary E. **84** 30
Mary Elizabeth (Lord)
83 183 184
Mary G. **72** 253
Mary Jane **90** 109
Mary Kent **73** 132
Mary Watrous **70** xix **84**
173 320 **85** 204
Maurice **92** 46
Meribah **76** 185
Miranda **70** 202
Miriam **67** 280
Morris **65** 236
Moses **51** 491 **76** 103
Murdock Daniel **85** 186
102 302 **103** 77 122
Myrta **79** 29
Nancy **76** 253 **125** 107
141 146
Nancy Pamela (Castle)
84 320
Nancy T. **115** 294
Nathan **76** 107
Nathan J. **54** xxxix
Nathan Littlefield **75** 106
314 **76** 103 258
Nathaniel **51** 232 **106** 158
Nathaniel P. **58** 20

MORRISON *cont'd*
Nehemiah **69** 258
Neil **102** 302
Newton **92** 340
Nicholas Gowen **76** 114
Noah **76** 107
Noah Farnham **59** xliv
  61 xxxv
Olive **76** 107 259
Olley (Shackley) **134** 280
Pamelia (McCully)
  110 141
Parker **91** 330
Patty **60** 200
Peter **144** 201
Peter J. **88** 339
Priscilla **76** 248
Priscilla (Callender)
  144 201
Prudence **146** 276
Prudence (Heath) **146**
  268 277
Rachel **51** 492
Rebecca **73** 257
Rebecca A. **126** 243
Rebecca Adams (Munroe)
  126 244
Richard **112** 247
Richard Snow (Mrs.)
  107 134
Robert **51** 492 **101** 260 **106**
  160 **112** 247 **113** 82 **115**
  294 **117** 245 **145** 359
Robert Brown **136** 324
Robert J. **114** 192
Romelia J. **68** 336
Rosamond **134** 280 281
Royal **76** 107
Ruth **73** 69
Ruthena **84** 459
S. E. **87** 170 **103** 41
Sally **55** 375 **56** 252 **76** 255
  83 16 **94** 31 **120** 52 **136**
  362
Sally (Nason) **83** 16
Salome (Gott) **85** 374
Samuel **61** 349 **70** 236 **73**
  257 **75** 106 315 **76** 103
  107 180 182 184 185 248
  258 **82** 294 296 **88** 304
  89 305 **146** 328
Samuel Eliot **76** 241 **77**
  xxiii 162 **82** 253 **83** 230
  84 466 **85** 241 350 **87**
  397 **90** 81 132 306 **91** 60
  137 **94** 18 176 210 **95**
  101 108 **96** 369 **97** 205
  104 91 92 **106** 20 319
  108 78 **109** 239 **111** 78
  115 168 **117** 238 **119** 77
  124 112 122 137 146 286
  136 90 324 **143** 110 **144**
  24 **148** 336
Sara Virginia Ecker
  (Watts) **89** 132
Sarah **60** 165 **62** 49 **68** 154
  71 51 359 **75** 315 **76** 108
  109 185 260
Sarah (McNutt) **84** 320
Sarah (Montgomery)
  84 320

MORRISON *cont'd*
Sarah A. **114** 192
Sarah E. **68** 336
Sarah Eunice **82** 176
Sarah J. **68** 336
Sarah Jane **81** 366
Sarah Luetta **68** 154
Sarah P. **110** 26
Solomon **73** 257
Susan **56** 44 **58** 20
Susanna **75** 121 **76** 253
  78 411
Tabitha **75** 118
Thomas **51** 491 **56** 186 **63**
  350 **72** 62 **74** 146 **91** 330
  145 108
Tirzah Adaline (Johnson)
  84 459
Uriah **76** 113 **124** 302
Ursula Jean **80** 246
Viola Fay **80** 246
W. E. (Mrs.) **106** 121
Will **101** 247
William **64** 22 **76** 114 248
  261 **84** 320 **91** 330
William E. **84** 30
William Eric (Mrs.)
  81 106
William F. **125** 44
William Robert (Mrs.)
  86 197
William Wallace **82** 176
Zerviah **73** 257
Morriss *see* Morris
Morrisson *see* Morrison
MORRON —— **57** 338
MORROW Morrough
— Capt. **63** 249
Alexander **105** 316
Andrew **61** 348
Anna (Bailey) (Wells)
  108 80
Benton **88** 93
C. M. **91** 330
Dorothy **87** 287
Ebenezer **75** 33 **107** 105
  252 **111** 157 158
Edna Young **109** 130
Francelia Sarah **89** 320
Frank C. **109** 240
Frank Chapman **87** 174
Hannah **109** 189
Hannah (Conklin)
  109 189
Harriet **115** 39
Hugh **61** 344
Jane **61** 348 **88** 288 **125**
  116 121
Jean **125** 116 121
Jennie B. **72** xxx lix
Jennie Brown **68** lxv
John **73** 132 **80** 34 **89** 320
  98 106
John B. **68** lxv **72** lix
Lewis **88** 241
Margaret (Gardner)
  105 316
Margaret B. **68** lxv **72** lix
Mary **88** 331 **105** 316
Mary (Hopkins) **103** 87
Mary (Hunewell) **126** 68

MORROW *cont'd*
Mary E. L. (Alexander)
  88 334
Nancy **79** 42
Nancy C. **61** 96
Nicholas **65** 239
Rispah **88** 241
Sarah B. **80** 34
Sarah Jane **92** 291
Susan (Betts) **88** 93
Susan (Marshall) **89** 320
Susan J. **115** 38
Timothy **145** 360
W. B. **78** 328
William **108** 80
William H. **88** 334
MORSE Mors
—— **62** 290 **112** 187
  148 315
— Col. **119** 130
— Dea. **71** 49
— Dr. **92** 131
— Mr. **57** 229 **83** 278 284
  85 120
— Mrs. **62** 17 **65** 360 **83**
  83 **94** 43 **121** 95
— Rev. Mr. **62** 277 **82** 315
— Widow **65** 363 **83** 72
  79
—— (Bradford) **103** 47
—— (Torrey) **140** 253
Aaron **92** 24 **106** 242
  125 109
Abbie F. **98** 198
Abbie Lillian **106** 310
Abel **81** 29 **84** 446
Abigail **53** 164 **58** 344 **59**
  287 **60** 165 384 **61** 132
  66 48 126 **67** 127 **69** 275
  72 284 **75** 14 **83** 75 76
  285 290 292 **114** 30 **115**
  51 **118** 263 **119** 313 **121**
  169 **125** 276 **126** 278
  136 301 **145** 171
Abigail (Coney) **90** 71
Abigail (Gibbs) **123** 270
Abigail (Gleason) **114** 30
Abigail (Gregory) **143** 15
Abigail (Ingalls) **84** 446
Abigail (Merrill) **145** 171
Abigail (O'Brien) **99** 192
Abigail E. **74** 172
Abigail Thomas **53** 146
Abijah **65** 361
Abner **52** 286 484 **53** 165
  55 317 56 20 **57** 55 254
  58 305 323 **60** 102 **69**
  288 **76** lxxxv **77** 277 **83**
  280 287 292 **85** 185 **91**
  174 **92** 24 25 **99** 16 **107**
  253 **109** 153 **119** 111
  125 150 **126** 157 **140**
  318 **142** 328 **146** 315
Adaline **103** 300
Adam **56** 34 **58** 345 **64** liv
Adelia Almira **75** 14
Afton **82** 200
Agnes **57** 142 **83** 71 82 83
  280-283 285 **95** 372 **120**
  5
Alathrair **95** 202

MORSE *cont'd*
Albert B. **85** 410
Alexander R. **96** 81
Alice **83** 71 75 79 83 281
  286 **104** 112
Alice (Chubbuck)
  (Lothrop) **134** 174
Alice (McGuire) **91** 387
Alice Sarah **89** 203
Alice Walker **61** xxxvi
  90 125 **106** 309 **107** 67
  138
Almira **103** 44
Almira Bernice (Phinney)
  106 241 242
Almond **57** 204 **97** 129
Alpha **131** 199
Alpheus **58** 372 **77** 22
  136 335
Alsbn (Dowsett) **141** 128
  129
Alsimony Lavina **64** 252
Alvira **123** 13
Amanda **133** 284
Amasa **69** 275 **72** 147 **75**
  14 **95** 202
Ambrose **125** 36
Amherst **77** 26 33
Amity **54** 213 **64** 370
  93 342
Ammi C. **100** 190
Amos **56** 34 **57** 106 **58** 258
  75 93 **91** 267 **106** 310
  133 284
Amy **69** 161 **83** 81 **137** 242
Andrew **92** 172 **145** 359
Angeline **100** 90
Ann **75** 93 185 **83** 73 78
  79 81-83 284 286 290
  294 **91** 309
Ann (Cox) **110** 202 203
Ann (Jasper) **83** 284 286
  289
Ann (Morse) **83** 294
Ann (Porter) **83** 282
Ann Brooks **75** 93
Ann Louisa **77** 179
Anna **58** 345 **59** 283 **69** 35
  76 177 **92** 82 **93** 291
Anna (Cook) **125** 106
Anna Bathsheba (Fisher)
  90 71
Anna Hooker **104** 143
Anna Kast **93** 200
Anna Maria (Fitz
  Randolph) **99** 39
Anna Smith **78** 344
Annah (White) **106** 310
Annas **100** 79
Annas (Chickering) **83**
  290 **90** 71 **100** 79 **106**
  310
Anne **51** 400 **57** 254 **83** 79
  80 82-84 281 282 **94** 334
Anne (Edwards) **83** 294
Anne (Hedge) **83** 282
Anne (Johnson) **91** 267
Anne (Kirkham) **83** 281
Anne R. **95** 202
Annes **83** 72 284 288 294
  91 308

MORSE *cont'd*
Annie Louisa **89** 203
Annis **77** 27 33
Anson Ely **58** 410 **64** 382
  65 xxxv
Anthony **58** 323 345 **60**
  102 188 **61** lvi **65** 195
  67 158 **81** 387 **82** 481
  83 71 72 279 287 **84** 446
  88 195 **90** 214 **105** 4
  109 162 **110** 202 203
  119 160 313 **121** 164
  313
Apame **75** 183
Arnold **55** 396 400
Arthur **76** 48
Arthur Moore (Mrs.)
  78 103
Arthur T. **103** 47
Arthur W. **92** 208
Asa **58** 20 372 **65** 40 **77** 283
  78 401 **125** 108
Asa Porter **51** 93 **52** 96
  61 xliv lvi lvii
Asabell **83** 83
Asahel **83** 72 287
Asarelah **64** 80 **125** 23
Avis **123** 298
Azubah **77** 33
Azubah (Tupper) **99** 286
B. **139** 257
Barbara **83** 77
Barnett **147** 360
Barton (Mrs.) **116** 81 312
Bathsheba **83** 291
Bathshua **83** 291
Benajah **77** 81
Beniah **56** 35
Benjamin **55** 262 **56** 147
  58 238 **59** 283 **61** lvi **62**
  370 **65** 195 **66** 126 **83** 76
  80 285 **84** 446 **91** 267 **92**
  269 313 **98** 105 **105** 4
  119 160 **131** 198 **140**
  170 **145** 171
Benoni **98** 105 **106** 109
  141 191
Bentley Watrous (Mrs.)
  83 123 233
Bertha (Lewis) **106** 310
Bethiah **58** 256 259 **83** 290
  291
Betsey **59** 286 **65** 364
Betsey (Jepson) **125** 108
Betsey B. **69** 341
Beulah **58** 303 364 **59** 66
  102 110
Beulah (Kimberly)
  102 111
Brian **83** 79
Bridget **83** 82 84 281
C. C. **56** 218 329 **57** xxx
  423 **58** 105
C. F. **57** 118
Cabot Jackson **91** 312
Caleb **51** 465 **59** 283 287
  103 300
Caleb K. **92** 313
Calvin **90** 71
Camille W. **99** 47
Carissa **113** 155

MORSE *cont'd*
Caro **74** 91
Caroline **78** 407 **81** 313
Caroline (Mann) 40 **92** 40
Caroline A. **77** 149
  114 154
Caroline Amelia **105** 65
Carrie E. **98** 253
Carrie L. **96** 70 **100** 163
Catherine **66** 49 **80** 332
  96 392 **120** 268
Caty **93** 68 **97** 349
Charity Thompson
  84 140
Charles **66** 48 49 **69** 114 **83**
  77 80 **135** 74
Charles A. **66** 49 **117** 317
Charles A. (Mrs.) **110** 145
Charles Anthony **75**
  xxiii 64 **82** 122 234 245
  481 **88** 195 **112** 226
Charles Edward **89** 203
Charles F. **52** 484 **53** 143
  74 166
Charles F. D. **98** 198
Charles H. **54** 233 425
  70 155
Charles Leland **66** 49
Charles M. **66** 49
Charles P. **109** 270
Charles Parker **92** 39 40
Charles T. **84** 140
Charles W. **86** 345
Charles Ward **97** 219
Charlie **98** 198
Charlotte **126** 145
Charlotte A. (Averill) **83**
  177 184
Charlotte Eliza **73** xli
Charlotte Gertrude **91**
  312 **93** 138
Chester **60** 102
Chloe **65** 41
Christopher **51** 173
Clara Rebecca (Boit)
  84 447
Clarissa A. **61** 376
Clarissa C. **77** 225
Clark R. **69** 275
Constance **88** 196
Cynthia **89** 27
Cynthia G. (Smith) **88** 286
Cyprien **67** 373
Daniel **53** 462 **56** 74 **58**
  345 61 lvi **64** liv **89**
  195 **75** 14 **78** 124 **83** 70
  71 74 76-78 283-285 287-
  291 293 **91** 308 309 **98**
  355 **105** 159 **106** 242
  134 92 215
David **57** 392 **58** 361 **77**
  292 **110** 216 **132** 281
  284 287
David B. **91** 330
David J. **99** 39
David Lewis **58** 258
Deborah **55** 259 **57** 57
  72 78
Deliverance (Ellis)
  106 310
Della Martha **72** xx

MORSE *cont'd*
Dennison **95** 202
Dinah **51** 303 **76** 177
  83 293
Dinah (Knight) **83** 293
Dolly **123** 24
Dorcas **57** 51 **83** 76 291
Dorcas Louisa **61** lvii
Dorothea **109** 79
Dorothy **51** 400 **83** 70 75
  284 292 293 **94** 334
Dorothy (Burnap) **83** 284
Dorothy (Pike) **121** 168
Dorothy Hattie Chipman
  83 230
Ebenezer **77** 17-19 23 24 33
  81 431 **83** 375 **91** 310
  107 313 **141** 189
Eddy **140** 170
Edith (Sherman) **96** 161
  112 225 226
Edna **68** 158
Edward **76** 138 283 **83** 71
  72 74 75 83 278 279 286
  287 **104** 112 **125** 253
  126 61 258 **139** 309
Edward A. **90** 37
Edward Leland **66** 49
Edward S. **71** 96
Edward Warren **66** 49
Edwin **74** 29
Eleanor **112** 226 **137** 339
Eleanor (McGregor)
  106 242
Eleazer **125** 106
Electa **79** 124
Eliakim **58** 344 346 **62** 371
  77 22 25 33 **91** 310 **140**
  29 170
Elijah **56** 44 74 **57** 106 **61**
  xlviii **65** 39 **83** 375 **98**
  105 **105** 76 **107** 106 **109**
  66 **142** 61
Elisha **56** 35 **65** 362 **76** 177
Eliza **59** 288 **84** 441 **109** 69
  125 222
Elizabeth **51** 400 401 **53**
  122 **57** 57 98 142 **58** 255
  258 345 346 **60** 41 246
  76 266 **77** 30 **78** 124 **82**
  225 **83** 70-73 75 79 81-
  83 279 282-288 290-294
  85 156 **87** 282 **88** 383-
  385 **89** 102 154 **91** 307-
  309 **93** 61 64 344 **94** 259
  334 **102** 179 **106** 242
  117 290 **125** 291 **127**
  305
Elizabeth (Barbour)
  106 242
Elizabeth (Brown) **103** 45
Elizabeth (Daniel) **83** 290
Elizabeth (Eaton) **139** 56
Elizabeth (Haines)
  126 157
Elizabeth (Jasper) **83** 186
  284 286 288 **90** 70 71 **91**
  307 308 310 **106** 310
Elizabeth (Moore) **83** 292
Elizabeth (Morse) **83** 294
Elizabeth (Sawtell) **126** 7

MORSE *cont'd*
Elizabeth (Smith) **113** 158
Elizabeth (Stewart)
  136 335
Elizabeth (Underwood)
  126 157
Elizabeth (Weeks)
  87 235 241
Elizabeth (Wood) **91** 310
Elizabeth A. **143** 15
Elizabeth E. **118** 147
Elizabeth Emma (Lowe)
  109 66
Elizabeth Frances **89** 203
Elizabeth Gardner **86** 197
Elizabeth K. **66** 49
Elizabeth W. **143** 15
Ellen **91** 190 394
Elmer W. **121** 181
Elvira **114** 241
Emeline T. **77** 175
Emily **98** 356
Emily Adele **79** 23
Emily F. **88** 333
Emma J. **69** 137
Emma S. **93** 218
Enoch **78** 110 111 **124** 149
  132 189
Enoch R. **61** 406
Ephraim **60** 102 **66** 20 **78**
  239 **83** 290 **125** 277
Ephraim W. **143** 59
Esther **55** 262 **56** 269 **69**
  161 **71** 255 256 **72** 219
  83 293 **110** 202 203
Esther (Pierce) **83** 293
Esther (Tilden) **142** 70
Ethel **82** 196
Eunice **57** 22 58 106 **58** 258
  64 liv **86** 43 **87** 235 **95**
  202 **108** 168 **142** 68
Eunice Elizabeth **114** 241
Everett **84** 172 **85** 188 **88**
  172 195 196 202
Everett (Mrs.) **82** 196
Ezekiel **57** 287 **59** 289
Ezra **58** 258 259 **83** 290 **90**
  71 **106** 310 **110** 216 217
  219
Ezra Dwight **58** 258
Fanny **103** 62
Fanny (Torrey) **140** 253
Fanny Pope (Hovey)
  91 312
Florence A. **74** 309
Francene E. **73** xli
Frances **61** 382 **83** 82 83
  294
Frances Amelia **136** 335
Frances Hicks (Torrey) **76**
  210 **91** 310 **140** 170
Frances Rollins **76** 210
Francis **63** 282 **83** 73 77
  82 84 282
Frank A. **69** 137
Frederick H. **117** 290
Friend Moody **119** 160
Genevieve **84** 447
George **57** 142 **67** 224 **69**
  275 **83** 82 83 **93** 115 **136**
  248

MORSE *cont'd*
George A. **74** 309
George Anson **58** 345
George F. **76** 266
George W. **56** 99 **75** 14
  118 131
George Washington **56**
  xxx **84** 446
Gertrude Elizabeth
  84 447
Gertrude Leslie **90** 385
  386
Gervase **83** 77
Gilead **78** 397 **106** 310
Glenn Tilley **69** xxxv **77**
  viii 323 324 **78** 198 220
  79 104 105 112 216 324
  80 104 196 202 222 **81**
  111 214 236 **82** 124 221
  229 251 **83** 246 **84** 206
  86 185 213 **87** 187 **88**
  183 **89** 123 **90** 129 **93**
  144 **105** 3 5 68 132 **106**
  120
Grace **83** 82 83 **86** 231
Grace (Parker) **84** 446
Grisle **83** 79
Guilford **99** 39
H **91** 330
H. Amanda **77** 178
H. Raymond **118** 170
Handley Chipman **99** 301
Hannah **53** 124 **58** 238
  282 300-304 360 361 372
  59 65 288 289 **60** 22 **76**
  148 **77** 283 **83** 79 285
  291 293 **84** 140 **89** 102
  96 81 **107** 307 **117** 215
  135 74
Hannah (Badcock)
  107 307
Hannah (Frost) **123** 13
Hannah (Hall) **136** 320
Hannah (Hoare) **106** 310
Hannah (Phillips) **83** 291
  91 310
Hannah D. **90** 377
Hannah M. **92** 170
Hannah M. (Salter) **83** 184
  186
Hannah Parker **96** 81
Happy **78** 110 111
Harold Wilbur **74** 309
Harriet A. (Phippeny)
  84 140
Harriet Clara **84** 447
Harriet Jackson **76** 209
Harvey **58** 258
Hattie E. **66** 49
Helen **100** 227
Helen Mariah **79** 128
Helen Shaw **78** 103
Henry **69** 275 **80** 353 **83** 78
  278 279 **100** 230
Henry Adams **112** 226
Henry Adams (Mrs.) **96**
  161 **112** 133 225 226
Henry Boit **84** 447
Henry D. **61** lxiii
Henry Lee **76** 210
Henry O. **83** 184 186

MORSE *cont'd*
Hepzibah **53** 346 **65** 41
  84 209
Herbert Richardson
  99 148
Hester **73** 181 **110** 202 203
Hiram **114** 241
Hiram J. **69** 275
Homes **91** 174
Horace F. **83** 184 186
Horatio Gilead **106** 309
  310
Hosea B. **98** 198
Howard J. **83** 290
Huldah **93** 219
Humphrey **85** 156
Ida **74** 309
Ida Estelle **74** 309
Ira Herbert (Mrs.) **89** 132
Irena **95** 202
Irene **106** 310 **128** 278
Irene (Briggs) **126** 211
Irene (Morse) **106** 310
Irene (Needham) **110** 37
Irene G. **117** 290
Irving G. **69** 137
Isaac **57** 142 **60** 41 **61** 382
  65 358 **83** 293 **105** 4
  113 158
Isaac Smith **76** 171
Isabel **83** 85 **94** 330
Isabel A. **66** liii
Isabel Curtis (Barnes)
  93 194
Isabel Elizabeth **77** 183
Isaiah **142** 64
Israel **65** 357 **99** 286
J. C. **91** 330
J. Howard **58** 323 **60** 102
  75 185 **76** lxxxv **83** 280
  100 79
J. R. **143** 15
J. W. **98** 198
J. W. (Mrs.) **103** 238
Jabez **57** 106
Jacob **53** 165 **60** 56
James **58** 345 346 **71** 53
  83 71 74 75 77 79 80 284-
  286 288 291 **86** 293 **89**
  27 32 203 **95** 201 202
  100 190
James King **93** 305
James R. **77** 232
James Reed **82** 481
James Winthrop **98** 198
Jane **55** 400 **57** 58 **66** 208
  209 **83** 79 83 **84** 332 **90**
  187 **102** 22 **105** 168
Jedelal (Norton) **135** 159
Jedediah **53** 42 430 **57** 288
  58 259 **64** 198 **66** 299
  67 137 239 244-246 248
  354 355 **68** 139 **79** 164
  93 305 **105** 189 **135** 202
  139 6 11 **141** 335
Jedidiah **146** 384
Jemima **67** 372 **78** 66 **95**
  202 **130** 214
Jennie A. **118** 190
Jeremiah **56** 74 **83** 73 79
  285 288 291-293 **85** 455

MORSE *cont'd*
  98 105 **123** 13
Jeremy **54** 86 **83** 71 73 75
  79 82 278 281
Jerry L. **92** 172
Jerusha **67** 373
Jerusha (Tupper) **99** 301
Jessie Frances Lizzie
  76 210
Jessie Gwendolen **85** 197
Jethaniel **61** 42
Joan **51** 400 406 **83** 71 79
  281 **94** 334
Joan (Manning) **94** 324
Joanna **63** lxvii **97** 96
  110 216 219
Joanna (Hoar) **90** 71
  110 217
Joanna (Kimball) **88** 195
Joel **65** 41 **67** 127 **136** 320
John **51** 189 303 304 400
  401 406 **52** 45 **53** 346 **57**
  96 99 **58** 300 303 304
  323 345 360 361 **60** 102
  165 188 **62** 58 **65** 270 **66**
  198 208 **69** 137 **72** 281
  284 **74** 212 217 224 225
  227 248 249 **75** 185 **76**
  195 210 **77** 20 30 31 33
  80 109 **81** 123 124 130
  83 70-83 278 280-290
  292 293 375 **88** 286 **90**
  71 **91** 308-310 **94** 333
  334 **96** 376 **100** 79 **102**
  179 184 185 **105** 7 **106**
  310 **107** 307 **110** 216
  115 51 **116** 111 **118** 263
  264 **121** 82 **124** 280 **127**
  185 **134** 215 **135** 159
  140 1 253 **141** 128 129
  142 81 **143** 12 14-16
John Howard **119** 313
John Martin **92** 24 25
John Robichaux **143** 15
John S. **69** 341
John T. **60** 215 **79** 235
John Torrey **61** 109 **74**
  165 **90** 137 **91** 298 307
  310 312 **92** 140 150
Jonah **83** 375
Jonas **58** 372
Jonathan **57** 58 **69** 275 **83**
  291 293 **92** 277 **99** 298
  118 264 **139** 308
Jonathan Church **92** 24
Joseph **55** 262 **56** 382 **57**
  25 **58** 142 256 323 345
  372 **59** 323 **60** xxiii 102
  166 188 384 **62** 357 **64**
  324 **65** 359 362 **69** 161
  70 345 **71** 256 **76** 148
  151 152 171 **77** 17 22-24
  29 33 225 283 292 **78**
  111 344 **81** 122 124 127
  129 134 213 **83** 70-77 80-
  82 278 280 282 284-294
  84 137 **88** 383 **91** 307-
  310 **92** 277 **93** 397 **95**
  132 201 202 **100** 63 **108**
  167 **119** 160 **126** 7 **128**
  278 281 **137** 339 **142**

MORSE *cont'd*
  300 **148** 146
Joseph Chipman **106**
  241 242
Joseph Fred **83** 125 233
Joseph P. **84** 30
Joseph Samuel **77** 225
Joseph W. **95** 202
Joseph Wheat **95** 201
Josephus **83** 375
Joshua **58** 345 **62** 369 **77**
  17 23 33 **82** 481 **88** 195
  91 310 **128** 278 **134** 174
  148 146
Josiah **62** 381 **90** 214
Jotham **57** 143 **143** 15
Judith **52** 432 **53** 123 **60**
  249 **83** 74 79 80 **136** 322
Judith (Moody) **88** 195
Judith (Starr) **96** 376
Julia **58** 258
Julia Anne **136** 320
Julian **83** 72
Julian (Forth) **83** 287
Juliana Perkins **72** lii
Julie (Burke) (Mahoney)
  89 132
Juliet M. **79** 450
Justus **100** 340
Kate Olive **85** 192
Katharine **83** 71 82 83 281
Keziah **70** 345 **71** 17
Keziah (Bullen) **87** 292
  95 81
Kitty **57** 106
Lancelot **83** 71 282 285
Laura E. (Goodin)
  121 181
Laurance Preston (Mrs.)
  102 124
Lavinia (Chipman)
  106 242
Lavinia (Fitz Randolph)
  99 39
Lawrence **80** 353
Leander Samuel **79** 128
Lelia Dyer **98** 148
Lemuel Foster **61** 218
Lena **85** 195
Lenna Margaret **97** 219
Lenora Augusta **74** 309
Leonard **88** 281
Leopold **99** 92
Leprelette **58** 258
Levi **145** 171
Lewis **93** 344
Linda Marion **137** 3
Lionel **57** 98 **75** 280 **105** 11
Lizzie Belle **74** 309
Llewellyn J. **96** 70
Lois **54** 49 **58** 300 302 304
  59 64 **108** 167
Loisa **81** 274
Lora (Neff) **98** 356
Louise **78** 52
Louise Jane **66** 49
Lovell **126** 278
Lovicia (Brewster) **89** 27
  32
Lucinda **57** 204 **97** 129
Lucinda (Pond) **140** 170

MORSE *cont'd*
Lucinda (Wait) **90** 71
Lucretia **55** 261
Lucy **58** 300 344 372 **59** 64
290 **68** 144 **70** 231 **76**
148 **93** 341 **119** 276 **135**
74
Lucy (Ayres) **135** 74
Lucy Ann **66** 49
Lucy Cabot (Jackson) **91**
307 310
Lucy F. **99** 298
Lucy M. **84** 30
Lucy Smith **86** 352
Luther **55** 398 **58** 258 **70**
124 **95** 202
Lydia **51** 465 **53** 462 **56** 34
57 106 **60** 166 **63** 91 **64**
liv **83** 73 82 83 282 284
291 **85** 328 **86** 397 **92** 24
98 355 **100** 190 **108** 83
84 **119** 160 **129** 65
Lydia (Church) **106** 242
Lydia (Fisher) **83** 290
106 242
Lydia T. (Blaney) **88** 281
M. **91** 330
Mabel (Riley) **100** 340
Mabel Edna **69** 137
Mahala **117** 215
Major **91** 174
Manly **114** 241
Margaret **51** 173 **61** lvi
83 71-75 78-82 84 281-
284
Margaret (Beckwith)
99 298
Margaret (King) **83** 283
287 **90** 70 **91** 308
Margaret (White) **126** 258
Margaret Catherine **66** 49
Margaret J. (Wight)
98 198
Margerie **83** 283
Margerie (Wood) **83** 282
Margery **83** 78 79 82 83
283
Margery (Boggas) **83** 283
91 308
Margery (Symsone) **83**
280 285 287
Maria **58** 345 346
Maria L. (Russell) **83** 184
186
Marian **82** 481
Marie **83** 80 82
Marietta **100** 340
Marion Adelaide **90** 136
96 158
Marry (Eddy) **91** 310
Martha **57** 142 **83** 77 78
108 185
Martha (Bartholomew)
136 320
Martha (Merrill) **88** 195
Martha Ann (Walker)
106 309
Martha Houghton **82** 481
Martha Rand **61** lxviii
82 198 **109** 66
Martha Rebecca **89** 203

MORSE *cont'd*
Martin **102** 111
Mary **51** 304 400 401 **52**
438 **53** 394 **55** 262 398
56 38 **57** 56 **58** 258 318
61 lxviii **63** 91 **64** 253
69 275 **71** 352 **77** 17 21
28 33 277 283 **78** 317 **81**
29 121 431 **83** 70 72 73
76-84 282 285 287-289
291 293 294 **84** 137 **90**
214 **91** 309 **94** 334 **100**
230 **105** 159 **109** 168
114 241 **117** 215 **127**
189 **136** 167 **141** 189
Mary (Adams) **88** 195
Mary (Barnard) **109** 162
Mary (Goodnuff) **134** 174
Mary (Guild) **90** 71
Mary (Hills) **100** 230
Mary (Jackson) **109** 66
Mary (Penniman) (Paige)
91 310
Mary (Stewart) **126** 66
Mary A. (Zimmerman)
84 137
Mary Ann **72** 147
Mary Ann Butrick
(Winchester) **78** 239
Mary B. **60** 276 **68** xxxii
77 182 **93** 73 **94** 56
Mary Bennett **60** 82
Mary Caroline **66** 49
Mary Dewese (Frazee)
109 66
Mary Elizabeth **82** 481
91 295
Mary Elizabeth (Wells)
88 195 **112** 226
Mary Ellen **85** 456
Mary Elvira (Randall)
84 446
Mary Ethel **84** 447
Mary Frances **74** 29
Mary Holmes **58** 258
Mary J. **69** 275
Mary Jane (Herrick)
135 159
Mary Lee **76** 210
Mary Lewis **69** 275
Mary Louisa **61** lvii
Mary Louise (Cushing)
96 70
Mary Marcy **69** 275
Mary T. **97** 129
Matilda **58** 258
Matthew **51** 400 **94** 334
Mattie **66** 49
Mehitable **55** 394 **56** 382
57 57 **59** 286 **74** 227
107 151 **130** 213
Melatiah **134** 174
Mercy **75** 185 **81** 129
Mercy (Walker) **106** 242
Merriam **61** lvi
Michael **83** 78
Mima **95** 202
Mindwell **135** 159
Minerva **81** 274
Minor **114** 175
Miriam **66** 49

MORSE *cont'd*
Miriam P. **75** 14
Molly **58** 17 372
Molly (Adams) **88** 195
Molly (Merrill) **91** 267
Moody **64** 122 **146** 329
Moses **58** 17 **59** 288 **65** 195
75 93 **77** 277
Moses Leland **66** 49
Nancy **59** 283 **92** 375
135 74
Nancy S. **59** 287
Naomi **84** 418
Nathan **69** 275 **76** lxxi
86 383
Nathan G. **69** 275
Nathan L. **59** 287
Nathaniel **55** lxxix **57** 22
24 **77** 277 **83** 71 72 74
76-79 83 283 285 287
288 290 291 **92** 24 **105**
159 **110** 216
Nehemiah **76** 151 **84** 140
Newbury **123** 270
Newbury LeB. **112** 321
Nicholas **75** 183 **83** 278
84 140
Noah **114** 30
Noel **88** 196
Obadiah **51** 45 **65** 363 364
83 291 **92** 60 **106** 242
114 176 **119** 160
Olive **58** lxxxii 346 **62** 370
66 275
Olive (Goodell) **90** 70 71
Olive R. **103** 64
Oliver **65** 359 **83** 375
139 56
Olivia V. **92** 171
Orville Curtis **84** 140
Ozias **135** 74
Parker **104** 242
Patty **69** 137 **113** 158
Patty (Robichaux) **143** 12
15 16
Paul **119** 155
Payne **90** 38
Peggy **57** 395
Persis **77** 17 19 21 33 **122**
303 306 **123** 24
Persis (Bush) **91** 310
Peter **57** 142 **84** 446
110 216
Phebe **98** 355 **104** 125
Philip **83** 71 74 79 83 283
285 288 **98** 119 **105** 4
Philip Reed **82** 234 481
Phillius **90** 71
Polly **57** 106 **58** 20 **59** 287
289 **81** 387
Pruda **65** 361
Prudence **51** 173 **61** 383
85 355
R. W. (Mrs.) **68** xxi
Rachel **58** 256 **65** 41 **76** 138
80 353 **83** 83 286 290
128 278 285 **141** 189
Rebecca **57** 287 **77** 24 **83**
76 **86** 383 **97** 262
Rhoda **76** 141
Rhoda (Mehurin) **136** 248

MORSE *cont'd*
 Richard **68** 355 369 370
  83 71-74 77-83 278 279
  281-283 285 287 **125** 216
 Richard C. **114** 189
 Richard Page **84** 447
 Robert **65** 27 **82** 481 **83**
  71-77 79 80 82 83 278
  280-283 286 287 **88** 195
  91 357 **99** 39
 Robert M. **81** 337
 Roger **52** 45
 Rosalind **84** 447
 Roxa (Ellis) **128** 281
 Rufus **100** 90
 Rufus Osgood **74** 309
 Russell **135** 159
 Ruth **53** 56 **57** 392 **58** 303
  60 22 **61** lvi **69** 341 **83**
  81 290 **89** 109 **92** 172
  142 61
 Ruth (Sawyer) **84** 446
 Ruth A. **126** 278
 Ruth S. **57** 392 **83** 509 510
 Ruthe **128** 278
 S. F.B. **55** 22
 Sadie May **93** 144
 Salathiel **58** 372
 Sally **55** 396 **59** 287 **77** 225
  89 32 **128** 278
 Sally (Johnson) **125** 109
 Sally (Sawyer) **133** 284
 Sally Monk **58** 259
 Samuel **53** 122 **57** 25 206
  58 162 323 345 346 **60**
  102 188 **62** 370 381 **64**
  liv **65** 195 360 **69** 288 **77**
  17 **82** 225 **83** 70-78 81
  280 284-294 375 **84** 137
  140 **88** 383 384 **90** 70 71
  91 307-310 **92** 24 **96**
  376 **98** 198 **100** 79 **105**
  75 **106** 242 310 **110** 216
  113 50 **125** 29 **141** 341
 Samuel A. **99** 192
 Samuel Adams **128** 278
 Samuel Butterfield **66** 49
 Samuel Finlay Breese **51**
  378 **55** 366 **77** 164 **119**
  183 **136** 324 **139** 11
 Samuel Finlay Brown
  84 447
 Samuel J. **98** 198
 Samuel T. B. **114** 189
 Samuel Torrey **76** 209
 Sanford A. **84** 464 465
 Sanford Alexander
  90 137
 Sarah **51** 173 250 302 **53**
  165 **55** 153 261 **56** 35 37
  57 284 **58** 16 238 **59** 283
  60 166 **61** lvi **64** 75 157
  74 213 217 224 225 227
  76 177 **77** 277 **81** 387
  431 447 **83** 71 76-79 83
  84 283-285 287 288 291-
  293 **85** 97 **89** 41 211 **91**
  309 **92** 379 **96** 84 **118**
  131 **128** 180 181 **141**
  354
 Sarah (Brown) **84** 446

MORSE *cont'd*
 Sarah (Draper) **112** 178
 Sarah (Ellis) **108** 167
 Sarah (Enuch) **125** 216
 Sarah (Peaslee) **109** 162
 Sarah (Pike) **121** 164
 Sarah (Starr) **96** 376
 Sarah A. **69** 275
 Sarah Abigail **57** 284
 Sarah Ann **69** 114
 Sarah Elizabeth **66** 49
  93 194
 Sarah Elizabeth
  (Griswold) **136** 324
 Sarah G. **100** 329
 Sarah Ingalls **97** 358
 Sarah J. **84** 140
 Sarah Jane **118** 131
 Sarah L. **75** 14 **117** 290
 Sarah M. **69** 137
 Sarah Minerva **75** 93
 Sarah R. (Townsend)
  126 68
 Seraphina (Titus) **114** 176
 Seth **53** 56 **55** 153 **58** 282
  300 360 **60** 22 **76** 177 **87**
  292 **95** 201 **110** 216
 Shepard **117** 215
 Sherman **112** 226
 Sidney (Mrs.) **79** 450
  83 71
 Sidney E. **93** 215 **114** 189
 Silas **95** 201 202
 Silas Hibbert **136** 335
 Silas Livingston **95** 147
 Silvester **91** 330
 Simeon **83** 375
 Sion **54** 213
 Solomon B. **100** 190
 Sophia **57** 392 **77** 23
 Sophia O. **87** 376
 Sophronia N. **57** 392
 Spachett **83** 77
 Stearns **120** 316
 Stephen **65** 41 **76** 152 **84**
  446 **91** 174 **93** 61 64 115
  98 355 **100** 190 340 **134**
  215
 Stoughton **128** 278
 Street Hall **136** 320
 Susan **55** lxxix **83** 76 78 80
 Susan Alice (Ensign)
  106 241
 Susan Amelia (Fitz
  Randolph) **99** 39
 Susan Read **73** lviii
 Susan Toy **106** 241
 Susanna **55** 314 **58** 258
  59 284 **71** 256 **74** 225
  135 74
 Susanna (Guild) **106** 310
 Susanna (Holbrook)
  106 242
 Sylva **83** 79
 Sylvanus **57** 284
 Sylvia J. **98** 193
 Sylvina (Silvester) **86** 293
 Thankful **57** 24 **78** 437
 Thankful (Titus) **114** 175
 Theoda Mears **115** 158

MORSE *cont'd*
 Theodory (Crane)
  136 335
 Thomas **64** 343 **83** 70 71
  76-84 278 280-290 292
  294 **90** 70 **91** 308 309
  139 232 **144** 113
 Thomas M. **103** 45
 Thomas Perry **105** 3 4
 Thomas Tilley **105** 4
 Timothy **57** 57 392 **58** 372
  60 246 **65** 40 **98** 356
  121 164 168 **125** 281
  134 215
 Tryphenia **108** 82
 Unity **54** 213
 Uriah **59** 301 **62** 370
 Velma Maria **61** lvii
 Virginia **112** 226
 Virginia Fisher **116** 81
  312
 Waitstill **57** 287 393
 Waldron Lewis (Mrs.)
  99 148 **100** 109
 Warren **66** 49
 Wells **112** 226
 Willard Samuel **57** xxxv
  59 329 **64** xxix **90** 70 81
  141
 Willard Vaughan **90** 72
 William **55** 261 **58** 323
  345 364 **60** 102 188 **61**
  lvi **63** 37 **64** 252 **65** 195
  359 363 **68** 239 **75** 185
  76 138 139 141 **77** 29 **78**
  189 **83** 71 72 77-80 82
  278 281 286 287 **94** 333
  100 190 **106** 242 **110** 37
  114 316 **140** 206
 William A. **52** 289
 William Frederick **93** 194
 William H. **89** 59 **91** 387
  116 65
 William Inglis **79** 105 450
  80 206 **91** 402 **92** 210
  98 97 370 **99** 338 **106**
  241 242 **107** 67 127 137
  148 315
 William James **89** 203
 William L. **83** 177 184
 William M. **100** 190
 William Parker **92** 40
 William R. **118** 147
 Wilson **73** xli
 Winnifred (McKendry)
  97 219
 Zachariah **91** 174
 Zebulon **87** 235 241
 Zilpah **69** 275
 Zipporah **56** 30
MORSELANDER
 Cornelius **100** 190
 Deborah **127** 195
 Hepzibah **100** 190
 Mary Barnard **100** 190
 Zebulon **100** 190
MORSELL
 Benjamin Ked **73** 271
 Caroline **73** 275
 Jane F. **111** 289
 John **73** 266 272

MORSELL *cont'd*
Kidd **73** 230
Richard J. **73** 271
MORSEMAN I. **108** 197
Margaret (Hubbard)
108 197
MORSES Eben **81** 447
Mary **81** 447
MORSHAM
Richard **55** 97
MORSLY — Mr. **54** 336
MORSMAN Betsey
Dunham (Chase)
88 127
William H. **88** 127
Morss *see* Morse
MORTAIN Robert **140** 229
MORTARY John **68** 51
MORTENSEN
Effie **94** 139
Lars **86** 94
MORTEYN —— **136** 102
Joan **138** 319
MORTH
Anthonette **143** 198
MORTIFIELD
Ione **114** 234
Ione (Parris) **114** 234
MORTIMER Mortimore
—— **122** 178
— Mrs. **100** 138
Agnes **60** 291
Alianore **116** 16
Ann Elizabeth (Quintard)
109 261
Anne **94** 111 **148** 140
Constantine **99** 271
Dorothy **60** 93 284-287 291
64 185 **88** 79
Edmond **117** 99
Edmund **104** 270 **108** 176
116 16 17
Edward **125** 257
Eleanor (Cornwall)
116 15
Eleanor (Holand) **148** 140
Eleanor West **116** 15
Eliza Harriet **81** 249
Elizabeth **108** 176 177
115 169 **116** 15 16 **132**
244
Elizabeth Percy (Lady)
66 192
Ellen **84** 337
Francis **60** 291 **81** 249
George **81** 466 **109** 261
George Harding (Mrs.)
107 134
Guillaume **99** 274
Hannah **84** 365
Henry **116** 14 17
Hue **99** 272
Hugh **99** 272 273 **116** 15
17 **121** 233
Ida C. (Tourtellot) **96** 96
Isolt **104** 270 **116** 13 16 17
James **84** 365 **115** 250 251
Jane **115** 250-252
Jennie **51** 54
Joan **60** 291 **99** 273 **116** 16
John **60** 291 **71** 311 **94** 110

MORTIMER *cont'd*
103 106 **115** 120 **116** 14
15 **142** 119 **148** 32
Juliane **116** 14
Katharine **104** 270 **122** 268
Llewelyn **116** 16 **117** 99
Luce (Waffren) **116** 13
Margaret **60** 291 **64** 185
103 106
Margaret (de Fiennes)
116 16
Maria **60** 291
Martha (Blinn) **143** 321
Mary (Briggs) **84** 296
Mary Adelaide **84** 296
Maud **116** 16 **121** 233
Maud (De Herle) **116** 15
Nicholas **52** 76
Owain **117** 99
Peter **84** 365
Philip **80** 16 **143** 321
Ralph **116** 17
Richard **116** 14
Robert **99** 272 273 **116** 174
Roger **116** 13-17 **117** 99
100 **121** 233 **148** 140
Samuel **84** 296
Sarah **80** 102 217 **81** 465
466
Sarah W. **71** 88
Sibyl **116** 174
Susan **81** 249
Susan Harriet **81** 249
Thomas **100** 20
Veda J. **107** 134
William **60** 282 285 291
64 185 **71** 233 **99** 271
108 203
MORTIMORE alias
TANNER Eleanor
52 76
Henry **52** 76
Matthew **52** 76
William **52** 76
MORTLOCK Margaret **63**
359 **68** 326
MORTMAYNE
Anne **98** 123
MORTON Moorton
Moreton Mourton
—— **147** 216
— Capt. **98** 106 **116** 197
— Mr. **83** 451
— Mrs. **118** 125
-- Sec. **62** 142
Abbie **91** 41
Abigail **75** 148 **126** 96 281
128 285 **145** 335
Abigail S. **85** 168
Abigail Talcott **85** 168
Abraham **145** 335 **147**
213 216
Adele Allen (Waterman)
95 116
Albert N. **106** 80 **107** 238
Albert Nowell **100** 112
Alice **75** lxviii **111** 68
Alice (Miller) **134** 283
Alice (Newcomb) **99** 67
Alpha **123** 149
Alvira **71** 120

MORTON *cont'd*
Amasa **120** 33 **128** 278
Amity **128** 278
Andrew **65** 369 **83** 375
114 181
Andrews **88** 331
Ann **55** 164 **60** 67
Ann (Cooper) **148** 326 343
Anna **142** 209
Anna Livingston
75 lxviii
Anna Livingston Reade
81 175
Anna May **132** 165 **133** 74
Anne **71** 175 **75** 138 **94** 140
Annie C. **58** cxi
Anthony **83** 455 **84** 8
111 68
Arabel **82** 498
Armina (Leavitt) **119** 288
Asenath **98** 198
Barbara **55** 434
Bathsheba **71** 47 121 122
Benjamin **55** 165 **60** 68
114 121 **116** 190 **145**
334
Bertha C. **83** 424 136
Bessie **137** 362
Betsey **68** 166 **71** 46 **142**
33 207 **145** 53
Boston **61** 42
Brayton **104** 313
Bryant **55** 368 **68** 166 **74**
249 **142** 209
C. **90** 33
Caleb **71** 55
Carnelius B. **91** 330
Caroline **57** 285
Caroline Edwards (Smith)
96 80
Caroline Elizabeth **71** 45
Catherine de **79** 365
Charles **67** 208 **76** 243 **95**
98 **106** 199 **137** 362
Charles A. **98** 101
Charles Augustus **95** 116
Charles Silas (Bigelow)
119 155
Charles T. **85** 168
Charles W. A. **78** 317
Charlotte (Goodridge)
88 292
Charlotte (Hodges)
89 183
Charlotte Frances **70** lviii
76 lv
Chauncey **102** 155 **114** 207
Clara **90** 356
Clarence H. **98** 198
Comfort (Deming)
(Beckley) **145** 334
338 339
Consider **102** 100
Constance de **79** 365
Cornelia (Sibley) **125** 215
Cornelia Joy **95** 339
Cornelius **57** 285 **83** 375
Cynthia **71** 45
Dana **66** 14
Daniel **64** xxxi **71** 120 122
102 100 **145** 335

MORTON *cont'd*
Daniel O. **71** 55
Daniel Oliver **75** lxvii
  136 324
David **117** 304 **118** 299
  123 160 **142** 208 **145**
  335
Deborah **71** 45 121
  123 160
Deborah (Blackwell)
  117 304
Donald Wadsworth
  100 112
Dorothy **61** 393 **145** 335
E. F. **98** 198
Eben **55** 368
Ebenezer **60** 68 **71** 121 **83**
  375 **87** 122 **145** 335
Edith Livingston
  75 lxviii
Edmund **55** 146 **61** 42 43
  142 33 **145** 53
Edmund de **74** 232 **75** 131
  79 365 **94** 206
Edward **71** 120
Eleanor (Blood) **96** 80
Eleanor (Lyman)
  (Pomeroy) **101** 288
Eleazer **71** 47 57 **120** 31
  141 205
Electa (Belden) **90** 189
  95 353
Eliakim **99** 192
Elijah **126** 99 **145** 335
Elisha **55** 368 390 **71** 46 47
  98 198 **145** 335
Eliza **71** 52 53
Eliza J. **98** 253
Eliza W. (Gould) **97** 229
  234
Elizabeth **55** 146 **59** 57 **61**
  393 **63** 183 **71** 49 **74** 233
  277 **75** 126 **99** 63 **116**
  315 **120** 30 33 114 283
  123 274 **125** 185 186
  141 59 **142** 275 278 **143**
  40 **145** 335
Elizabeth (Clarke) **120** 33
Elizabeth (Easton)
  137 362
Elizabeth (Holmes) **99** 67
Elizabeth (Newcomb)
  99 192
Elizabeth (Whitman)
  136 324
Elizabeth (Worthington)
  145 334
Elizabeth A. **136** 236 241
Elizabeth de **79** 365 367
Elkanah **99** 67 **119** 261
Elsey **142** 209
Emily (Cannedy) **104** 313
Emmet **137** 362
Ephraim **55** 77 164 168
  60 67 68 332 **71** 47 57
  85 360 **96** 80 **114** 121
  116 189 **119** 170 **120**
  278 **128** 244 **148** 326
  343
Esther **142** 209
Esther (Bardwell) **102** 100

Eunice **128** 278 **145** 335
Eunice (Gray) **101** 174
Eustace de **94** 206
Experience (Ellis) **120** 33
Frances Wood **89** 182 183
Frank **112** 319
Freddie E. **112** 319
Frederick **71** 51 **96** 80
Frederick D. **98** 198
George **55** 78 162 **58**
  lxxxii **63** 304 **71** 47 57
  119 **75** lxvii **79** 320 **89**
  304 **96** 80 **99** 67 **111** 68
  114 116 117 124 **116**
  188 189 **118** 71 78 **119**
  266 **122** 281 **123** 229
  135 253 **136** 271 **148**
  343
George C. **58** lxxxiii
George W. **72** 115
Georgia (Howland)
  112 319
Gervaise **74** 273 **75** 138
Guy **115** 233
Hannah **55** 78 164 165 **60**
  67 68 **66** 262 **71** 278 **84**
  272 **101** 287 **117** 302
  125 207 290 **142** 34 376
  143 250 **145** 53 **148** 326
Hannah (Chambers)
  94 58
Hannah (Faunce) **114** 121
  116 189
Hannah (Finney) **148** 326
Hannah (Gibbs) **123** 267
Hannah (Gillett) **101** 288
Hannah (Gore) **99** 67
Hannah (Morse) **96** 81
Hannah Lucretia **147** 232
  233
Harriet A. C. **98** 198
Harriet Electa **90** 189
  95 353 357
Harriet M. **112** 319
Helen **75** lxviii
Hepzibah **71** 115 121
  127 293
Hugh **104** 313 **127** 159
Huldah **126** 115
Huldah (Briggs) (Brown)
  126 115
Ichabod **71** 45 47 57 121
  122 **120** 30 **123** 160
Isaac **63** 14 **83** 375 **112** 319
  115 219 **128** 285 **142** 34
  145 53 364
Jabez **59** 93 **99** 63
Jacob **65** 150
James **59** 93 **61** 393 **71** 47
  50 **75** 229 **83** 375 **119** 21
  126 96 **127** 278 **136** 241
  142 207
James Ferdinand **94** 139
  96 80 81 149 166
James Madison **59** ci
  104 313
James Madison (Mrs.)
  84 341 **85** 190 **104** 313
  105 68 132
Jane **71** 53 **98** 193 198 **125**

MORTON *cont'd*
  106 **145** 103
Jane (Haskell) **98** 198
Janet **136** 66
Jemima **99** 63
Jeremiah **58** lxxxii
Jerusha **58** 255
Jesse Whitman **103** 120
Joan **74** 233
Joan de **79** 365 368 369 378
Joanna **70** 349 **143** 250 251
Joanna (Kempton) **116**
  189 **119** 266 **148** 342
  343
Job **99** 63
John **51** 211 **60** 68 **61** 393
  66 262 **71** 45 49 52 54
  57 **74** 232 233 **83** 375 **87**
  330 **93** 385 **94** 339 **95** 49
  102 47 **114** 207 **120** 30
  31 283 **127** 159 **128** 200
  142 278 **145** 332 334
John D. **81** 30
John de **75** 131 **79** 158
  364 366-369 378
John Dwight **54** xli **58** lv
  lxxxii lxxxiii **82** 498
John N. **102** 155
Jonathan **145** 335
Joseph **60** 68 **83** 146 **96** 80
  122 258 **140** 170 **145**
  334
Joseph P. **145** 358
Joseph T. **98** 198
Joshua **83** 375 **122** 141
  140 170
Josiah **87** 123 **120** 30 33
  114 201
Julia **71** 52
Juliana (Carpenter) **111**
  78 **114** 117 **116** 188
Katharine **68** 75
Lemuel **86** 8 **99** 67 **120** 35
  123 267
Lemuel (Gibbs) **123** 267
Lena **75** lxviii
Leonard **71** 49
Lettice **142** 278
Levi P. **55** 78
Levi Parsons **75** xxxiv
  lxvii lxviii **78** 90 **81** 175
  135 253 **136** 90 324
Lewis **75** lxviii
Lillie **95** 116 **98** 101
Lindley Calhoun **84** 108
  185
Louisa **91** 41 **128** 278
Louise **145** 255
Love **68** 166 **74** 249
Lovisa **71** 120
Lucetta (Chase) **87** 330
Lucretia **75** lxvii **120** 302
  121 57 69
Lucretia (Parsons)
  136 324
Lucy **59** 93 **60** 339 **74** 233
  127 278 **145** 335
Lucy (Gorham) **126** 283
Lucy de **75** 131 **79** 359
  365 378
Lucy Young **75** lxviii

MORTON *cont'd*
Lydia **94** 58 **127** 293
  145 335
Lydia (Cooper) **142** 278
  143 250
Malin **66** 61
Manasseh **117** 192 **125** 185
Marcus **55** 164 **59** 335 **89**
  183 **109** 233
Marcus (Mrs.) **93** 138
Marcy **119** 266
Margaret **75** 229
Maria **71** 50
Maria E. **58** lxxxiii
Maria Eldredge (Welch)
  93 138
Maria Elizabeth **82** 498
Maria Louisa **91** 40
Mark **65** 242
Martha **99** 63 **142** 34 **145**
  53 335
Martha (Brewster) **89** 119
Martha (Doty) **120** 35
Martha (Newcomb) **99** 67
Martha (Tupper) **99** 63
Mary **51** 163 **52** 418 **55** 168
  60 332 **63** 14 **71** 120 **75**
  lxviii **88** 190 **99** 67 **111**
  68 **113** 46 47 **114** 86 **117**
  192 **126** 96 281 283 **142**
  207 278 **143** 127 131
  144 5 318 **145** 332-335
  337 **147** 384
Mary (Burnham) **145** 327
  332
Mary (Carey) **99** 63
Mary (Ellis) **120** 35
Mary (Faunce) **114** 121
Mary (Marsh) **145** 334
Mary (Ring) **102** 47
Mary (Taber) **125** 185
Mary (Waite) **135** 253
Mary Ann **142** 207
Mary Evelyn **77** 254
Mary Jane **72** 115
Mary Lavalette Gilliam
  119 155
Matthew **64** 165 166 259
Mehitable (Graves)
  145 334
Melinda **59** 93 **98** 198
Mercy **71** 121 **81** 356 **105**
  149 **119** 264 266 **127**
  255
Mercy (Clark) **102** 100
Mercy (Ellis) (Dotey)
  (Barnes) (Wilson) **119**
  266 **120** 98 99 103
Mere **61** 280
Minerva (Philbrick) **147**
  267 269
Mitty **80** 64
Molly **71** 44 49
Moses **145** 335
Myrtle Ellis **79** 203
N. **67** 96
Nabby **127** 278
Nancy **63** 377 **64** 374 **71** 47
Nancy Jarrette Bowers
  (Brayton) **104** 313
Nathaniel **53** 317 **55** 70

MORTON *cont'd*
71 129 **57** 62 **68** 339 340
  358 **70** 349 **71** 47 57 **81**
  76 356 **82** 185 **86** 8 **87**
  49 **95** 43 **98** 170 317 318
  99 63 **105** 149 **114** 121
  117 188 **120** 30 31 35
  197 **122** 281 **128** 278
  285 **142** 276 278 **143**
  250 **144** 318 **147** 261
  263
Nellie **108** 118
Nicholas **52** 144
Noah **145** 335
Norman **90** 116
Olive **58** lxxxii
Olive (Paul) **126** 209
Olive Martha **89** 119
Oliver **101** 287 288 **145** 335
Oren F. **111** 201 **112** 14 88
Oscar Elisha **70** xix
Patience **55** 78 162 **85** 94
  108 118 **114** 116-119
  116 188 189 **122** 144
  123 229
Patience (Purrington)
  99 63
Paul **59** 339 **60** 110 **88** 292
  142 33
Pauline **88** 292
Pearl Ketcham (Merritt)
  96 81
Perez **54** 99 **55** 164 **65** 150
  85 21 124 **126** 225 **140**
  170 183 324 **145** 305
Phebe **136** 271 **147** 214
Phebe (Langford)
  147 213
Phebe Ann **147** 213-218
  232 233
Phineas **126** 115
Polly **142** 209
Polly (Snow) **123** 160
Priscilla **98** 198
R. R. **91** 330
Ralph H. **89** 304
Randall **142** 207
Rebecca **60** 68 **71** 55 **99**
  63 67 192 **117** 188 **120**
  30 31
Rebecca (Clark) (Ellis)
  91 296 **99** 63 **103** 141
  117 188 **120** 31
Rebecca (Needham)
  136 241
Rebecca (Tupper) **99** 67
  119 261
Rebecca (Verg) **126** 100
Reliance **60** 68
Remember **89** 56
Reuben **51** 163 **113** 231
Richard **58** lxxxii **60** 356
  135 253 **136** 271 **142**
  209 **145** 317 322 327 332
  333 335
Richard L. **97** 394
Richard Tower **90** 189
  95 353
Robert **87** 146 **112** 285
  143 251
Robert de **94** 206

MORTON *cont'd*
Robert Stone **96** 81
Roger de **94** 206
Roland **99** 67
Rosette **109** 270
Ruth **55** 168 **57** 34 **99** 63
  114 122 **120** 33 **145** 333
  334
Ruth (Edwards) **145** 322
  327 330 333 334
Ruth (Huston) **100** 242
Ruth Davis **81** 30
Sabra Nye (Ellis) **122** 258
Salmon **125** 215
Salome **102** 302
Samuel **52** 418 **60** 356 **99**
  67 **116** 316 **145** 335
Samuel Gillett **101** 288
Sarah **55** 165-168 **99** 67
  101 288 **104** 313 **111**
  177 **113** 231 **120** 33 **128**
  200 285 **145** 334 335
Sarah (Belding) **145** 335
Sarah (Kellogg) **145** 335
Sarah (Otis) (Ellis)
  120 197
Sarah (Smith) **145** 335
Sarah (Whitman) **96** 80
Sarah C. **71** 115
Sarah Copeland **136** 311
Sarah H. **70** 350
Sarah J. (Kidder) **90** 116
Sarah M. (Hoyt) **113** 231
Sarah Wentworth **86** 241
Seth **58** 255 **61** 43 **71** 115
  121 **75** 148 **123** 160 **124**
  226 **127** 293 **128** 278
  285 **145** 335
Silas **75** 125 126 **93** 304
  100 66 **118** 132
Simeon **120** 33 **145** 335
Sophia **94** 58 **128** 285
Stephen **101** 288 **145** 364
Susan **122** 141
Susan Hall **78** 233
Susan Nason (York) **95**
  116 **98** 101
Susan Tillinghast **109** 233
Susanna **55** 146 168 **61**
  393 **73** 271
Susanna (Freeman)
  126 283
Susanna H. (Field) **88** 331
Sylvanus **59** 93 **126** 96
Taber **100** 53
Thankful **145** 334
Thomas **55** 168 368 **59**
  178 179 183-186 **90** 155
  96 271 **98** 100 **100** 223
  101 174 **120** 33 35 **124**
  285 **134** 282-290 **142** 33
  112 **145** 53 333 334 338
  339 **146** 348
Thomas de **79** 365
Timothy **119** 266 **120** 103
Westley **128** 285
William **55** 167 168 **61** 268
  64 200 **68** 75 **71** 51-53
  166 **83** 375 **89** 119 **94** 58
  96 356 **97** 104 **100** 242
  104 187 **120** 33 **123** 274

MORTON *cont'd*
  126 209 **145** 167 326
    327 332 333
  William C. **116** 316
  William E. **98** 198
  William H. **119** 288
  William Jasper **116** 316
  William L. **109** 270
  William Seymour **71** 52
  William Thomas Green
    136 236 324
  Zacheus **140** 170
  Zechariah **97** 229 234
  Zephaniah **145** 358
MORTS Henry **60** 39
MORUM Adonijah **83** 57
MORVEN
  John **51** 183 **52** 47
  Margery **52** 47
MORVILLE
  Ada de **96** 93
  Alice de **96** 310
  Elena de **108** 174
  Hugh de **97** 243 244
  John de **96** 113 114
  Margaret de **95** 396
    103 201
  Richard **108** 174
  Robert de **96** 310 **115** 47
  William de **96** 45
MORVOIS
  Berthe de **97** 342
MORWAY
  Beatrice S. **75** 14
  Homer S. **75** 14
  Jennie I. **75** 14
  Rhoda A. **75** 14
MORY Mary (Johnson)
    106 23
  Susanna **98** 86
MORYFIELD
  Stephen **97** 270
MOSART Mary **88** 338
MOSBY
  Charles W. **114** 192
  Clarissa **114** 192
  John **114** 192
  Nathaniel M **91** 330
  Robert **114** 192
  Susanna **114** 192
MOSCRIP Virginia **121** 77
    142 194
MOSCROP Joseph **52** 311
MOSE Anne **61** 117
  John **61** 117
MOSELEY —— **100** 233
  — Capt. **62** 357 **99** 108 109
    105 314
  — Miss **79** 300
  ____ (Hancock) **100** 96
  Abby **85** 168
  Abigail **60** 140 **91** 374 375
    101 224 **104** 289 **107**
    314 **109** 104 106 **136**
    331
  Abigail (Chapin) **109** 105
  Abner **60** 140 **85** 64 168
    91 375 **136** 330
  Achsah C. **114** 182
  Alice (Poore) **93** 87
  Alice Lydia **109** 103 105

MOSELEY *cont'd*
  106
  Angeline **109** 105
  Angeline (Head) **109** 103
    106
  Anna **109** 104-106
  Anna (Abbot) **109** 105
  Anna Maria Susanna
    62 383
  Anne **100** 224
  Anne (Hargrave) **100** 96
  Ardelle **99** 147
  Arthur **100** 96 98 99
  Augusta (Chapman)
    93 86
  Ben: Perley Poore **93** 87
    107 70
  Benjamin **61** 392 **85** 168
    91 375 **109** 103 105
  Bethiah **81** 162
  Caroline **70** 198 **93** 220
  Caroline Augusta **78** 293
  Catherine **78** 413
  Charles Henry **102** 301
  Charles Talcott **109** 103
  Charles W. **109** 103 106
  Charles Whiting **109** 104
  Charles William **54** 383
    57 xxxi **68** xxx **72** vi **73**
    vi **74** vi **75** xiv xxxv xci
    xcii
  Charlotte **68** 315
  Charlotte A. **75** xci
  Charlotte Augusta
    (Chapman) **54** 380 382
    383 **107** 70
  Charlotte Chapman **93**
    87 **107** 70
  Cicely **78** 292
  Consider **109** 103 105 106
  Constant **115** 36
  Cynthia **57** 289
  Daniel **109** 103-106 **115** 37
  Daniel T. **109** 105
  Daniel Talcott **109** 104
  David **57** 289 **64** 250 **74**
    243 **78** 422 **108** 96 **145**
    315
  David C. **145** 295 296
  David Colson **145** 295
  Deborah **78** 292
  Dolly **114** 182
  Ebenezer **54** 377-379 **68**
    220 310 312 315 **75** 145
    119 188
  Edward Augustus **54** 383
    68 112
  Edward S. **137** 47
  Edward Strong **54** 377-
    383 **55** xlii xcvi **56** 332
    75 xci xcii **93** 86 87 **107**
    70
  Elisha **75** 199
  Eliza **81** 46
  Eliza Eaton **109** 105
  Eliza S. **85** 168
  Elizabeth **62** 249 **68** 221 **75**
    145 199 **78** 410 **81** 46 **85**
    64 **91** 375 **97** 91 **101** 225
    104 289 **109** 99 105 **119**
    189

MOSELEY *cont'd*
  Elizabeth (Colson)
    145 295
  Elizabeth (Crownin-
    shield) **101** 224 **104** 289
    107 314
  Elizabeth (Lyman)
    136 330
  Elizabeth (Moseley)
    109 105
  Elizabeth (Revere)
    145 295
  Elizabeth M. **109** 103
  Elizabeth M. (Pierce)
    145 296
  Elizabeth Winston
    108 157
  Elizur **109** 104
  Ella M. **109** 103
  Ellen (Worthington)
    109 103
  Emily **85** 64 168
  Emma L. **109** 103
  Esther **68** 226 **75** 199
    109 104
  Eunice **85** 64 168
  Fanny **62** 383
  Flavel **75** 199 **140** 235
  Frances **145** 296
  Frederick Strong **54** 383
    68 xxxii **75** xcii **80** 335
    81 222 **93** 83 86 87 143
    107 40
  Frederick Strong (Mrs.)
    94 139 **107** 67 69 138
  George **85** 168 **117** 16
  George Cabell **108** 157
  Hannah **93** 87 **108** 307
  Hannah (Basset) **110** 129
  Hannah (Dewey) **109** 105
  Hannah Odin (Dorr)
    (Carpenter) **93** 87
  Harold A. **86** 383
  Harriet **57** 289 **107** 70
  Harriet S. (Hopkins)
    105 107
  Helen Annie **80** 208
    120 148
  Helen Campbell **107** 70
  Helen Carpenter **93** 87
  Helen Dalton (Carpenter)
    107 69
  Helen Graham **78** 293
  Henry **57** 289 **85** 168
  Hopeful **85** 168
  Hopy **91** 375
  Hopy (Robbins) **91** 375
  Increase **62** 383 **78** 292
  Isaac **60** 140 **85** 64 168
  Isaac Newton **85** 168
  Israel **109** 103 105
  James Otis **57** 295
  James S. **109** 103
  James Sackett **109** 104
  Jane **104** 106
  Jane (Curtis) **109** 103
  Jane A. **109** 105
  Jane Ann **109** 104
  Jane B. **75** 199
  Jennie Glover **70** xix **74**
    xxviii 160 **79** 104 **90** 129

MOSELEY *cont'd*
99 68 151 **102** 301
Jerusha **85** 64 168
John **54** 377 **64** 250 **72** 143
  78 292 293 **85** 64 168 **91**
  375 **93** 87 **108** 99 **109** 99
  118 313
John B. **85** 162 168
John Graham **54** xxxvii
  55 xxx **56** xxx **57** xxxi
  58 xliii **59** xlii **60** xxxiv
  61 xxxiii **62** xxxv **64**
  xxix **78** 215 292 293
John Thomas **78** 328
Johnnie Ina **104** 144
Jonathan **68** 231
Joseph **60** 140 **73** 213 **85**
  63 64 168 **91** 374 375
  100 99 **101** 224 **104** 289
  107 314 **108** 307
Josey **145** 296
Josiah **109** 104
Julia M. **75** xcii
Katharine **73** xxxii
Lucretia **60** 140 **85** 64
Lucy **79** 151 **109** 104-106
Lucy Annette **109** 103 104
Lucy Augusta **109** 103
  105 106
Lydia **109** 103-106
Lydia (Noble) **109** 105
Maria **78** 292 293
Maria L. (Gibbs) **109** 105
Marie **69** 250
Martha **54** 378
Martha Alger **55** xxxv
Mary **57** 289 **74** 243 **78** 292
  85 168 **90** 290 **109** 103
  105 **115** 42 **136** 330
Mary (Gookin) **100** 96
Mary Alice **54** 383
Mary Ann **54** 379 **70** xxxv
  75 199
Mary Augusta **78** 293
Mary Benton **85** 168
Mary E. **109** 103
Mary Eliza **57** 295
Mary Elizabeth **109** 104
  106
Mary J. **62** 190
Mary Louisa (Glover)
  102 301
Mary Matilda **78** 293
Mary Preston **75** 153 199
Maryanne **109** 104
Mattie **78** 328
Melatiah **58** 28
Miriam **72** 143
Molly Preston **68** 316
Nathaniel **60** 41
Nicholas (Mrs.) **84** 332
Noah **120** 42
Ogden B. **85** 168
Oliver **81** 46
Ora **57** 295
P. **91** 330
P. W. **86** 383
Patience **62** 383 **78** 292
Peabody **115** 32 40
Phebe **115** 36
Phineas Holden **68** 310

MOSELEY *cont'd*
Pliny **109** 103-106
Polly **61** 392
Rachel **57** 212 269
Rachel (Tolman) **126** 64
Rebecca **57** 289 **115** 35
Rhoda **85** 168 **109** 103 105
Richard **69** 250
Robert **85** 168 **91** 375
Robert B. **100** 99
Robert Warner **78** 47 329
Robert Warren **78** 329
Rowland **82** 334
Ruth **60** 140 **85** 64 **109**
  103 105
S. M. **86** 383
Sally **68** 319
Samuel **53** 192 **54** 377
  378 383 **64** 8 **68** 229 **70**
  173 174 **72** 194 199 **81**
  162 **99** 79 102 103 **105**
  256 **110** 129 **118** 266
Samuel S. **120** 48
Sarah **60** 41 **75** 34 153 199
  201 260 **78** 292 **85** 64
  119 189
Sarah (Ford) **119** 189
Sarah Day **85** 168
Seneca **85** 64
Sibyl **80** 56 **109** 104 105
Sophia **109** 104-106
Sophia (Pomery) **109** 105
Sophia A. **85** 168
Stacey **73** 221
Susanna **100** 94-96 98 99
  292
Susanna (Burnet)
  (Blackmore) **100** 96
Talcott **109** 104 106
Theodore **57** 289
Thomas **53** 72 **54** 377 **61**
  46 **68** 220 221 224 226
  229 231 316 319 **75** 153
  199 **78** 292 **81** 46 51 **94**
  6 **119** 189
Thomas Mather **75** 199
Tryphena **109** 104
Unite **54** 213 **145** 295
Verda Ray **78** 47
Virginia **78** 47
W. H. **53** 249
William **60** 140 **62** 383
  79 162 307 **82** 154 **85** 64
  168 **100** 94-99 292 **109**
  105
William Basset **110** 129
William D. **100** 99
William Gibbs **109** 105
William Graham **78** 292
  293
William O. **61** 176
William Oxnard **75** xcii
William Q. **85** 64
William T. **109** 103 106
William Tudor **109** 104
  106
William W. **105** 107
Wylie Amanda **78** 170
MOSELL
Margaret **135** 288
Mosely *see* Moseley

MOSENTHAL
Hermann **107** 251
MOSER Elizabeth
  Colclough **77** 217
Eunice **87** 234
Frederick **85** 315
Jason C. **77** 217
Sally **69** 381
Sophia Wrisley **85** 315
MOSES — Dea. **82** 413
— Mrs. **83** 194
___ (Hill) **125** 178
Aaron **58** 227 234 392 **61**
  83 **72** 319 **81** 414 431
  447 **82** 49 **114** 241
Aaron (Mrs.) **83** 194
Aaron Seymour **72** 319
  81 414
Abel **61** 33 34
Abigail **81** 431 447
Abner **61** 32
Abraham **81** 408
Alice Freeman **79** 285
Amasa Cassius **83** 477
Amos **65** 360
Amy **61** 32 **71** 85
Andrew **76** 140
Andrew J. **79** 285
Ann C. **126** 22
Anna **59** lxxxiv **81** 414 415
Anna C. **81** 414
Anna Melissa **76** 18
Annie **83** 297 300
Asenath **72** 319
Ashbel **61** 31 **81** 408
Augusta Marsh **83** 296
  300
B. **72** 174
Benjamin F. **83** 184
Benoni **72** 37 **83** 477
Bertha **80** 167
Betsey **58** 234 **113** 158
  142 299
Betsey (Campbell) **83** 477
Bildad **112** 127
Candace **81** 408
Catherine **81** 414 **82** 49
  114 184
Cathryne Lottridge
  (Teasdale) **106** 70
Charlotte **83** 26 29
Chauncey **81** 414
Clarissa **81** 414
Daniel **81** 148 414 415 431
  82 49 **142** 299 387
Darius **72** 319 **81** 414
Deborah (Thrall) **83** 477
  112 127 **122** 39
Delia H. (Wells) **83** 300
  303
Delia Lottridge **106** 70
Delilah **81** 414
Dorcas **71** 155
Dorothy **81** 447 **82** 49
  282 295
Edward Walter **83** 477
  84 107 184
Eleanor **82** 292 295
Elias **81** 408
Elisha **71** 79
Eliza D. **83** 181 184

MOSES *cont'd*
Elizabeth **58** 234 **71** 84 301
  81 414 431 447 **82** 49
  295 300 **110** 203 **112**
  127 **128** 165 **145** 172
Elizabeth (Law) (Reade)
  112 69 126 127 129 130
Ella F. **84** 30
Ellen E. **81** 408
Elnathan **72** 37 **83** 477
Esther **61** 31
Eunice **54** lxviii
Faithe **81** 414
Fannie **80** 167
Frances Ann (Buswell)
  133 124
Frank **118** 238
Franklin C. **81** 283
Franklin Wheeler **118** 239
Frederick **81** 414
Gaylord **81** 414
George **81** 431 **82** 27
  124 218
George F. **68** 207
Gertrude (Tucker) **83** 477
Hannah **81** 431 **82** 49
Hannah (Humphrey)
  112 127
Hannah J. (Mugridge)
  83 184
Harriet Almira **118** 239
Harriet E. (Wheeler)
  118 238
Harry **81** 414 **118** 238
Harry Field **118** 239
Hattie **118** 238
Hattie M. **125** 176
Henry **118** 238
Hiram **83** 477
Huldah **72** 104
J. G. **125** 178
J. M. **59** 117 **67** 239
J. W. **83** 194
Jabez C. **123** 121
James **58** 234 **81** 431 447
  82 49 **103** 270
James M. **81** 414
James O. **81** 283
Jan **128** 163 164 166 167
Jane Amelia **84** 102
Jay B. **144** 273
John **58** 227 234 **67** 273
  72 35 319 **81** 431 447 **82**
  27 49 **83** 477 **112** 127
  122 37 39 **128** 165 **148**
  231
John G. **125** 176
John Gilman **84** 30
John H. **83** 300 303
John R. **86** 170
John S. H. **103** 267
Jonas **76** 140
Joseph **65** 366 **78** 315 **81**
  431 447 **82** 292 295 **92**
  313 314
Josiah **81** 431 **142** 298
  145 172
Katharine **81** 447
Katie Frank **133** 124
Keziah **71** 154
Levi **83** 194

MOSES *cont'd*
Lijsbeth **128** 163 164 167
Lincoln Ellsworth **74** xxv
  78 **83** 477 **84** 107 184
  193
Linda **86** 170
Lois C. (Cotton) **113** 298
Louise Bobo **84** 189
Love **81** 447
Lucy **72** 301
Lydia **61** 34 **71** 80 156 163
  79 245 **81** 414 **82** 49
Lydia (Ramsdale) **83** 477
Lyon **63** 345
Mabel **83** 436 438
Margaret **81** 143 431
  83 477
Margery **83** 35
Mark **58** 234 **65** 119 **81** 431
Martha **71** 302 **81** 431 447
  82 49 288 295
Martha Ann **83** 179 184
Martha Simpson **82** 49
Martin **61** 31 **69** 202 **71**
  80 87 163 302
Martin Levi **72** 319 **81** 414
Mary **51** 460 **58** 228 392
  73 192 **81** 143 414 431
  82 49 **84** 30 **89** 51 **100**
  241 **116** 176
Mary (Brown) **83** 477
Mary (Sargent) **112** 220
Mary A. **103** 49
Mary Ann **83** 178 184
Mary Aurelia **69** 202
Mary M. **67** 273
May (Delauny) **118** 238
Maybel **83** 436 438
Mehitable **142** 299
Mehitable (Dill) **123** 121
Merab **81** 290
Mercy **81** 408
Miles **81** 414
Molly **82** 49
Nadab **82** 49
Nancy **67** 273
Naomi A. (Tyler) **83** 477
Nathaniel **81** 431 **103** 257
Nehemiah **83** 307
Norman **81** 414
Norman W. **72** 104
Oliver Thomas **133** 124
Peletiah **81** 431
Phebe **82** 49
Phebe (Woodruff) **83** 477
Rachel **72** 319
Rhoda **72** 35 319 **81** 414
Roxey **81** 414
Ruby **81** 414
Rufus **83** 477
Rufus J. **81** 408
Russell A. **86** 318
Ruth **54** 354 **58** 227 **61** 83
  81 431
Sadie (Delauney) **118** 238
Samuel **79** 245 **81** 143
  431 447 **82** 49
Sarah **71** 279 297 300 **72**
  29 319 **81** 414 431 447
  114 241
Sarah (Alderman) **122** 39

MOSES *cont'd*
Sarah (Tuller) **83** 477
Sarah Ham **81** 148 149
  82 49
Sarah Jane **88** 331
Sarah L. **76** 272
Seymour A. **81** 414
Seymour Aaron **72** 319
Silas **103** 257 267
Solon **81** 408
Sophrona (Hurd) **123** 198
Stephen S. **123** 198
Susan **79** 285 **81** 283
Susanna **72** 319 **81** 414
Thaddeus **81** 290
Theodore **81** 431
Thomas **81** 143 **122** 39
Thomas (Mrs.) **83** 194
Thomas Lanier **106** 70
Timothy **71** 75 84-87 154-
  156 297 300-302 309 310
  72 29 166 319
William **81** 148 **82** 49 413
  112 69 126 127 129 **142**
  299
Winfred **80** 167
Zebina **58** 228 **62** xxxvii
  308
Zeruiah **71** 86 279
MOSEZOON Moseszoon
  Jan **128** 163 169
MOSGROVE
Catherine **86** 170 318
Isabella **86** 170
Mary K. **86** 318
Thomas **86** 170 318
MOSHER Moshier
  Mosier Mozier
Abby G. (Babb) **126** 68
Abel **114** 182
Abiel **91** 379 380
Abigail **87** 395 **105** 216
Abigail (Tripp) **87** 395
Abijah **114** 182
Abner **110** 52
Abner D. **130** 53
Albert Booth **82** 404
Alice Edna (Dean) **106** 142
Alida M. (Graham)
  116 206
Allen **91** 379 380
Allie F. **130** 53
Amanda **115** 294
Amy **91** 380
Andrew **117** 218
Anna (Nims) **129** 397
Anna Lewis **110** 52
Annie E. **117** 218
Anson A. **113** 53 64
Arabella **88** 129
Asa **131** 134
Asa T. **117** 218
Bardine J. **130** 48
Barnabas **131** 134
Benjamin **87** 395 **125** 184
Benona **135** 77
Bethiah **131** 134
Bethiah (Walker) **131** 134
Betsey **59** 25
Bruce **135** 146
Caleb **87** 395

MOSHER cont'd
Campbell **106** 303
Caril **106** 303
Catherine **98** 129
Catherine (Tosh) **113** 244
Charles **114** 182
Charles Albert **82** 404
Charles Bradford **110** 52
Charles D. E. **118** 65
Charlotte Mary **91** 379
Cora **116** 60
Cora Estella **82** 404
Daniel **87** 395 **106** 143
  108 67 **114** 182
Daniel A. **117** 284
Deborah **72** 306 **91** 379
  131 139
Diana **134** 314
Ed. **130** 47
Edward **87** 395
Electa W. **109** 183
Elias **115** 294
Elihu **148** 288
Elizabeth **87** 395 **91** 380
  113 53 **124** 240 **135** 77
Elizabeth (Briggs) **91** 380
Elizabeth (Green) **113** 244
Elizabeth (Jackson)
  106 143
Elizabeth M. **145** 177
Elmer H. **118** 65
Emma B. **117** 218
Eugene Henry **106** 142
Eunice **87** 234 235 **98** 288
Experience (Kirby)
  128 250
Freelove (Weaks) **87** 235
  240
G. Abbott **117** 218
G. Aloutsous **117** 218
Gardnor **129** 387
George **91** 379 **130** 47
George H. **130** 46
Gideon **117** 218 220 **129**
  58 **131** 134
Grace **116** 66
Hannah **91** 379
Hannah (Dunning)
  118 143
Hannah L. **117** 220
Harold Otto **83** 436 437
Harriet **91** 246 **134** 127
Henry **106** 143 **135** 77
Henry C. **98** 288
Hepzibah **59** 29
Hiram **118** 143
Hope **87** 395
Hugh **126** 156 **128** 250
  136 216
Ichabod **128** 295
Ina **117** 212
Israel **87** 395 **129** 344
  135 77
J. **91** 330
James **113** 244 **128** 297
James D. **116** 65
Jane Maria (Ling) **110** 52
Jehu **88** 130
Jesse **129** 344
Jethro **112** 156
Job **91** 379 380

MOSHER cont'd
John **87** 258 **91** 380 **104**
  222 **106** 143 **114** 182
  127 93 **128** 250 **134** 311
John A. **96** 50
John Pinkham (Mrs.) **84**
  234 **85** 197
John Wardwell **110** 52
Jonathan **91** 379 **129** 387
  132 214
Joseph **59** 25 28 **91** 379 380
  129 337 **148** 154
Josephine D. **118** 65
Josher **135** 142
Josiah **131** 134
Katie **130** 46 47
Leah **130** 53
Lemuel **102** 217 **131** 134
  135 45 142
Lena Aldrich **130** 53
Leonard Jarvis **110** 52
Levi **135** 77
Levina (Westover) **135** 77
Levina S. **115** 177
Lora Anna **82** 404
Loren Augustus **82** 404
Luther **129** 387
Lydia **87** 395 **107** 297
  118 148
M. Etta **117** 218
Mamie E. **130** 53
Margaret **91** 379
Martha **87** 395
Martha (Knowles) **88** 130
Martha Ovitt **130** 53
Mary **59** 28 **91** 379 380
  102 217 **109** 183
Mary (Carr) **102** 217
Mary (Niedham) **125** 105
Mary Ann **115** 294
Mary Jane (Lewis)
  106 143
Mary Lucretia **82** 404
Mary Margaret (O'Brien)
  83 436 437
Maxen **87** 395
Mehitable **59** 28
Mercy **108** 67
Meribah **91** 379
Michael **115** 177
Minnie J. (Corlew) **130** 48
Myrtle Irene **88** 169 **106**
  116 130 142
Nan **110** 52
Nancy G. **88** 105
Nathaniel **59** 29 **132** 214
Nellie **117** 212
Nicholas **88** 129 **129** 337
  135 77
Norman **116** 65
Obediah **127** 216
Oliva Loisa **81** 274
Patience **117** 284
Paul **127** 216
Pauline **91** 379 **103** 239
Peace (Gifford) **135** 146
Peter **135** 77
Phebe **107** 57 **116** 219
Phebe (Hart) **131** 134
Philip **87** 394 395 **118** 64
  65

MOSHER cont'd
Philip M. **118** 65
Rachel **96** 50
Rebecca **87** 336 **88** 130
  108 117 **128** 250
Rebecca (Chase) **87** 258
Rebecca (Horndell)
  128 250
Reuben **134** 314
Rhoda **113** 244
Rhoda Ann **118** 64
Ruth **59** 29 **87** 335 **102** 159
  109 183
Ruth (Gifford) **131** 134
Ruth (Huested) **106** 303
Ruth (Talbot) **110** 52
Sabra **88** 130
Sally (Hathaway) **112** 156
Samuel **127** 93
Sanford A. **87** 97 400
Sarah **82** 265 **87** 395 **123**
  239 **131** 134
Sarah (Burges) **87** 395
Sarah (Gifford) **134** 314
Sarah (Mosher) **131** 134
Sarah Dean **110** 52
Selinda **99** 302
Seth **127** 26
Silar **88** 130
Sophia Ann **118** 64 65
Stephen **81** 274 **107** 297
Susan Jarvis (Bradford)
  110 52
Susanna (Sherman)
  127 26
Susanna (Wilbore)
  107 297
Tibitts **115** 294
Vesta (Lee) **116** 65
Warren B. **117** 220
Warren E. **117** 220
Wilbur **130** 47
William **87** 235 240 **88** 130
  116 206 **125** 105
William Henry **110** 52 53
William Henry Bradley
  110 52
Zilpha **58** 370
MOSIE Aaron **62** 284
Mosier see Mosher
MOSLEY Adam **65** 169
Anne **66** 284
Anthony **66** 284
Dolly (Root) **114** 182
Edward **66** 284
Elizabeth **66** 284
Elizabeth M. **109** 103
Ellen **66** 284
Francis **66** 284
Helen Dalton (Carpenter)
  94 139
Laura Beaumont (Hadley)
  84 332
Lydia **114** 182
Marianna **125** 113
Nicholas **66** 284
Oswald **66** 284
Richard **66** 284
Robert **103** 104
Rowland **66** 284
Samuel **67** 202

MOSLOVA Tatiana **96** 386
MOSMAN Mossman
  Alexander Hyde **82** 499
  Anna **86** 344
  Caroline Bemis **82** 499
  Cornelia Hull **82** 499
  Eliza **90** 55
  Elizabeth **56** 39 **114** 38
  Elizabeth (Balcom) **114**
    38 41
  Ellen (Harvey) **106** 311
  Frances A. **82** 513
  Francis **108** 240 **110** 159
    114 240
  George **82** 499
  George H. **84** 137
  Helen Hyde **82** 499
  James **61** 24 **82** 499 513
    111 321 **114** 38 41
  Lucy Theodora **82** 499
  Marguerite **106** 311
  Mary **61** 18 24
  Mary Helena **84** 137
  Matthias **114** 40 41 201
  Melzar Hunt **106** 311
  Moses **61** 18 24 **114** 195
  Nathan **82** 499
  Olive **114** 269
  Rhena (Conner) **108** 240
  Sarah **61** 24 **114** 40 110
  Sarah (Haynes) **114** 41
  Sarah O. **84** 137
  Sibyl **114** 197
  Silas **82** 499
  Timothy **82** 499 **93** 397
    99 311 **100** 63
  Walter Bemis **79** 103 203
    82 248 253 499
MOSMER Abel **105** 210
MOSOLOVA
  Tatiana **96** 386
MOSS Mosse
  —— **133** 322
  Abigail **62** 219
  Alexander **59** 219
  Angeline **100** 90
  Anna **133** 302
  Camille W. **99** 47
  Donald Ernest **101** 70
  Eleanor **147** 25
  Elizabeth **59** 219 **87** 282
  Ellen **91** 190
  Ernest Goodman **101** 70
  Ethel Doris **101** 70
  Evelyn **101** 70
  Evelyn Lawrence **101** 70
  Fra: **100** 293
  Harry William **101** 125
  Jane **84** 332 **90** 187 **105** 168
  Jennie Edith Somerville
    (Donnelly) **101** 70
  John **93** 97 **101** 70 **125** 34
    131 130
  Joseph **59** 420 **62** 219
    144 41
  Josephine (Sanford)
    101 70
  Lucy A. **101** 131
  Lydia **59** 420
  Martha **108** 185
  Mary **100** 241

MOSS cont'd
  Philip **127** 7
  Rebecca (Lyons) **93** 97
  Reuben **144** 102
  Robert (Mrs.) **100** 340
  Samuel **144** 41
  Samuel Lyons **101** 70
  Sanford Alexander **93** 97
    101 25 70 71 130
  Sarah **89** 211 **96** 84 **131** 25
  Stephen **55** 391
  Unity **141** 5
MOSSER Esther **87** 377
MOSSETT John **80** 310
MOSSEY
  Marion Bernice
    100 109
Mossman *see* Mosman
MOSSO Carlos Emilio
  Porter **109** 290
  Emilia **109** 290
MOSSOCKE
  Henrie **105** 96
MOSSON William **64** 158
MOSSWELL Anne **57** 100
  John **57** 100
MOST Thomas **65** 44
MOSTON William **116** 172
MOTARD Richard **66** 56
MOTE Anne **67** 69
  Dorothy **67** 69
  Emmanuel **67** 68 70 71 79
  Mary **67** 68 69 71
  Sibyl **82** 57
  Thomas **82** 57
MOTHAM
  Elizabeth **51** 109
  James **51** 109
  Jeremy **51** 109
  Peter **51** 109
  Thomas **51** 109
MOTHERS J. L.D. **91** 330
MOTLEY ____ (Lathrop)
  140 162
  Ann **140** 170
  Anna **85** 144
  Anne **97** 53
  Catherine M. E. **77** 56
  Charlotte Elizabeth **79** 7
  Edward **64** lvi **97** 52
    140 162
  Edward Preble **63** 113
  Eleanor (Warren) **97** 52
    53
  Elizabeth Cabot **136** 318
  Ellen **64** lvi
  Ellen (Rodman) **97** 52
  John Lothrop **51** 363 **54**
    438 **55** 93 **59** 235 **136** 90
    318 324 **140** 162
  Joseph **96** 56
  Margaret (Fay) **97** 52
  Maria Davis **79** 7
  Mary **77** 56
  Mary Elizabeth
    (Benjamin) **136** 318 324
  Phyllis **97** 53
  Rebecca Rodman **64** lvi
    97 52
  Richard **77** 316 **140** 170
  Sarah **96** 56

MOTLEY cont'd
  Thomas **97** 52 **140** 162
  Thomas Lawrence **79** 7
  William W. **77** 56
MOTON Margery **142** 229
  232 238
  Margery (Malory)
    142 232
  Robert **142** 232
MOTRAL Thomas **65** 127
MOTT Motte
  —— **55** 229 **62** 283
    136 211
  ____ (Shooter) **105** 176
  Abbott (Mrs.) **78** 240
  Abel **91** 243
  Abiah **83** 5
  Abigail **55** 178 **67** 26 287
    101 80 **106** 105 **112** 155
    156 **113** 273 **118** 315
  Abigail (Field) **113** 287
  Abraham Rathbone
    67 186
  Adam **56** 100 **60** 318 **68**
    179 **69** 52 **71** 85 **101** 80
    104 304 305 **105** 92 **112**
    156 **123** 109 **145** 348
    148 158
  Adrian **51** 496 **55** 24 27
    56 274
  Agnes **69** 341
  Albert **92** 42
  Alice **98** 117 **132** 214
  Alma **62** 272
  Ann **119** 194
  Anna **67** 24
  Anna (Beckwith) **111** 305
  Anne (Knopp) **147** 317
    318
  Anstis (Merritt) **140** 123
  Apphia (Hathaway)
    148 158
  Asher **117** 111
  Atwood **129** 267 268
  Bathsheba **67** 25 **86** 182
    183
  Benjamin **88** 20 **122** 102
  Cassandra **56** 124
  Catherine **67** 186
  Charity **67** 186
  Charles **106** 296 **107** 51
  Charles Bouton **109** 191
  Clarissa (Quintard)
    109 190
  Daniel **67** 186
  De Witt **92** 42
  Deborah **67** 25 **129** 267
  Desire **129** 167
  Diedama **112** 57 58
  Dolly **86** 23
  Dorothy **51** 496 **55** 24 **99**
    74 **148** 258
  Ebenezer **67** 24 26 **105** 177
    111 287 **129** 267
  Edward **65** 7 **67** 24-26 **78**
    445 **86** 72 **101** 152 **105**
    176 177 180 **106** 104 105
  Edwin C. **66** 232
  Eliza **109** 190 191
  Elizabeth **51** 252 **56** 127 **59**
    153 **67** 24 26 **70** 155 **74**

MOTT *cont'd*
134 **79** 258 **84** 222 **86** 72
94 48 **105** 262 **109** 190
147 379 **148** 149
Elizabeth (Dunn) **105** 254
Ella Ann **88** 198
Ellis L. **56** 415
Elvira (Penrose) **117** 111
Emily Abigail (Hoyt)
109 191
Esther **98** 348
Experience **67** 24 25
Ezra R. **67** 186
Fanny **69** 202
Florence B. **83** 428 436
Frank L. **107** 249
Frank Luther **104** 92
145 225
G. F. **69** 202
Gershom **69** 93 **70** 155
101 80
Grace **67** 26
Hannah **67** 25 26 **122** 101
102
Hannah R. **67** 186
Harriet (Bouton) **109** 191
Harriet E. **109** 191
Henry **147** 116
Hepzibah **67** 25
Hepzibah (Winsley) **105**
172 177
Hopper Striker **74** 96
107 16
Ida **92** 42
Irene T. (Barbour) **110** 70
Jacob **56** 127 **63** 81 **66** 228
229 **68** 275 **79** 258 **85**
457 458 **97** 311 **103** 231-
233 **122** 102 **127** 145
128 247 248 **129** 224
Jacob S. **85** 458
James **59** lxxvii **62** 354
63 57 **66** 287 **67** 23 **106**
177 **140** 123
James S. **66** 232
Jeremiah **68** 275 285
69 51-53
Jesse **66** 229
Joan **83** 119
John **67** 24-26 **68** 179 **83** 86
86 72 73 180 **105** 175-
177 252 263 **147** 379
148 258
John A. N. **85** 458
John Langdon **109** 191
John R. **76** lvi
John Thomas **67** xxxi
Jordan **110** 70
Jordan L. (Mrs.) **77** 322
78 205
Joseph **51** 56 **62** 272 **101**
93 94 96 **128** 304 **144**
203
Josiah **111** 305
Julia Ann **144** 312 316 317
Katharine Jerome **78** 205
Keturah **66** 229
L. **111** 305
Lent **71** 279
Leslie Cornell **123** 225
Lizzie O. **97** 300

MOTT *cont'd*
Lodowick **67** 186 **104** 12
105 252
Louise **109** 191
Lucretia **59** lxxvii
Lucretia Dodge **67** 186
Lucretia Dodge (Ball)
67 186
Lucy A. **83** 99
Lydia **67** 24 25 **83** 87 **86** 72
105 177 262
Marcy **105** 177 263
Marcy (Tosh) **105** 177
Margaret **67** 25 **68** 275 285
69 51-53 **101** 243 **111**
57
Margaret Ann **85** 457 458
Maria **59** lxxvii
Marietta **109** 191
Mark **51** 496 **56** 274 378 **89**
77 78
Martha **62** 272 **111** 287
Martyn **64** 54
Mary **64** 85 **66** 232 **67** 24-
26 381 **71** 279 **79** 267 **80**
176 **85** 457 458 **122** 100
102
Mary (Anderson) **85** 458
Mary Ann **72** 297
Mary Brockway **85** 148
Mary Catherine **67** 186
Mary Elmira **85** 458
Mary Weaver **122** 102
May H. **74** 96
Mercy **62** 272 **67** 25 26 **69**
93 **86** 73 330 **105** 252
Mercy (Goold) **125** 104
Mercy (Tosh) **86** 73
Miriam **67** 25
Naomi **62** 272
Nathan **67** 186 **86** 183
Nathaniel **67** 23-26 186 381
69 341 **82** 463 **83** 92 **86**
72 182 **105** 172 175-177
252 262 **129** 259 **144**
298
Owen **62** 272
Parnel **148** 149
Patience **67** 26
Penelope **67** 26 **106** 104
Penelope (Niles) (Tosh)
105 177 **106** 104
Pernel **148** 158 287
Phebe (Tuttle) **109** 190
Phebe C. **67** 186
Phebe D. **67** 186
Rachel (Rider) **112** 156
Rebecca **51** 56 **55** 179
99 31
Rebecca (Phelps) **105** 252
Rest (Perry) **128** 247
Reuben **94** 48 **109** 190
Rhoda **85** 95
Richard **70** 329 **92** 42
113 287
Robert **51** 252 496 **64** 85
Samuel **55** 177-180 **67** 24-
26 **105** 177 254
Samuel M. **120** 49
Sarah **67** 25 186 **82** 463 **106**
243 **111** 287 **134** 337

MOTT *cont'd*
Sarah (Belyea) **123** 109
Sarah (Chase) **88** 20
Sarah (Merritt) **140** 123
Sarah (Tosh) **86** 182
105 177
Sibyl **105** 254
Simon Littlefield **107** 72
Sophia **101** 93 94
Sophia Wright **101** 96
Sophronia **62** 272
Stephen **109** 190 **125** 104
128 304 **145** 146
Susan **126** 65
Susan L. **111** 305
Susanna (Sheffield)
104 12
Thomas **101** 243 244 **122**
102 **140** 123 **147** 317
318
Valentine **107** 11 **145** 314
Wait (Dickens) **86** 180
Walter R. **67** 186
Waty R. **67** 186
William **51** 252 **64** 85 **68**
179 181 **83** 375 **113** 55
140 123
William H. **66** 34
MOTTERN Hugh H. **117**
237 **118** 247
William **117** 237
MOTTEROZ —— **58** 103
MOTTERSHED
Mottersheade
Adam **64** 256
Elizabeth **69** 357
Humphrey **69** 357
Roger **64** 256
MOTTEY Sarah **96** 56
MOTTRAM
Elizabeth **92** 201
John **92** 201
Lois **92** 201
Mary **92** 201
Othniel **92** 201
Primrose **92** 201
Thomas **92** 201
Moubray *see* Mowbray
MOUCOVIUS —— **56** 341
MOUDAY
Briget (Davis) **95** 86
Hannah **95** 86
Mary **95** 86
MOUDY Barbara **131** 100
MOUET DE MORAS
Elizabeth (Jutras)
128 182
Pierre **128** 182
MOULD Moulde Moulder
Christian **61** 198 199
106 213
Edward **61** 198
Esther **106** 213
Jane **74** 278 **106** 213
Mary **67** 201 **74** 278 **89** 29
98 368
Nichols **61** 198 199
Prudence W. **96** 203
MOULDING Hannah
(Murphy) **85** 374
James **85** 374

MOULE Thomas **72** 185
MOULSON
— Mr. **52** 111 112
Anne **52** 120
Anne (Lady) **74** 5
Joan **52** 113
Nathaniel **52** 113
Rebecca **52** 112 120
Thomas **52** 120 137
MOULTE Moult
Francis **52** 142 **53** 302
William **53** 302
Moulten *see* Moulton
MOULTHROP
Moulthrop Moultrop
Moultrup
Abigail **57** 135
David **67** 126
Elizabeth **81** 129
Enoch **67** 51
Eunice **67** 226
Hannah **59** 70 **66** 197 **70**
80 85 **81** 129
Hepzibah **67** 126
Jane **81** 129
John **57** 135 **81** 129
Lydia **59** 67
Margaret **85** 297
Mary **58** 80 **67** 51 **81** 129
86 198
Mary Agnes **84** 320
Matthew **58** 72 74 **66** 197
73 241 **75** 322 **81** 123
125-131
Samuel **59** 70 71
Sarah **59** 70 71 **71** 6
Sheldon **67** 226
MOULTON Molten
Molton Moulten
Moultin Multon
—— **54** 230 **55** lxxxiv
57 261 **58** 32 **61** 338 **92**
273 275 **103** 300 **112**
219 **118** 27 **141** 321 322
— Capt. **62** 355 359 **97** 271
— Col. **55** 68 **120** 275
— Mr. **62** 289
— Mrs. **83** 194 307
— Msgr **141** 315
— Widow **58** 35
____ (Littlefield) **141** 329
____ (Spolding) **141** 327
Aaron **56** 34 **77** 292
Aaron M. **68** 157
Abel **55** 312 **82** 510 **110**
288 **114** 293 **115** 136
116 133 295
Abigail **55** 197 **59** 290 **62**
39 **80** 424 **83** 148 **96** 336
365 **109** 300 **110** 61 282
111 229 **112** 305 **113**
155 **115** 136 214 **116**
132 **118** 154 155 240 242
119 160 188 **123** 74 **141**
320 321 326 329 **144** 260
147 143
Abigail (Bryant) **124** 160
Abigail (Goode) **98** 81
Abigail (Harmon)
113 127
Abigail (Hill) **91** 18

MOULTON *cont'd*
Abigail (Littlefield)
119 68
Abigail (Page) **138** 112
Abigail (Stackpole)
119 65
Abigail (Webster)
141 323
Abigail (Young) **116** 132
Abigail Ruck **112** 216
Able **109** 300
Abra (Wentworth) **134**
152 153
Adaline S. **119** 67
Adam **59** 290
Ade **66** 159
Agnes **141** 315 316 **147**
131 138 141
Alan de **96** 93 94
Albert **51** 52 **56** 77 **122** 71
231
Albert Gallatin **107** 227
Albert Sweetser **94** 139 **98**
81 88 152
Albion Wesley **123** 73
Alden **81** 150
Alexander **118** 320
Alice **83** 118 **111** 232 **131**
130 **141** 314 315
Alice (Anderson) **144** 259
Alice (Chadbourne)
(Donnell) **141** 329
Alice M. **68** 157
Allen C. **123** 75
Almeda G. (Perkins)
119 62
Alvah **78** 89
Amasa **110** 34 117
Angelia (Snow) **119** 229
Ann **51** 62 **121** 73 145 **125**
221 **141** 328 **144** 262
Ann Watts **95** 30
Anna **56** 34 **59** 284 287 **61**
310 **68** 160 **71** 203 **77**
292 **90** 359 **147** 138 143
Anna (Mansfield) **98** 81
Anna M. (Jelleson)
123 150
Anne **141** 313 320 322 328
147 143
Anne (Bradbury) **113** 127
Anne (Green) **107** 227
142 260 263 **144** 261
262
Anne (Taylor) **141** 319 320
144 248 257 **147** 138
142
Annette **69** 319
Annie (Smith) **97** 262
Annie M (Ferbish)
123 149
Annis **93** 373
Aphia (Boston) **119** 63
Arthur J. **78** 447
Arthur Julian **79** 203
Asa **123** 235
Asa L. **120** 309 **121** 70
Augustus F. **77** 161
Augustus Freedom
68 xxxii
Benjamin **58** 29 138 140 **62**

MOULTON *cont'd*
44 **63** 48 84 **115** 309 **116**
220 **119** 62 143 145 **125**
97 **141** 321 323 **144** 257
147 138 143
Bethiah (Swaine) **141** 323
Bethulah **64** 181
Bethulah (Sayward)
115 307
Betsey **54** 402 **59** 285 289
63 170 **115** 305 **116** 140
141
Betsey (Mace) **92** 310
Betsey P. **59** 290
Betty **82** 293 295
Brewse / Brice (Warner)
141 326 327 **144** 260
Bridget **141** 313 326 328
144 260 262
Caleb **62** 43
Calvin **59** 290 **71** 203
Caroline **69** 139 **89** 261
Caroline E. **69** 145
Caroline S. **123** 123 200
Caroline S. (Rankin)
92 340
Catherine **110** 33 **119** 63
141 315
Catherine (Hudson)
98 81
Catherine (Keyes) **104** 122
Catherine H. **113** 193 194
Catherine Jane **118** 240
Cecilia **141** 315
Cecilia (Haughton)
144 259
Cecyle **141** 315
Celinda **71** 203
Charles **65** 256 **97** 367
113 266 **120** 140 **122** 71
231 **123** 72
Charles A. **81** 396
Charles D. **97** 19
Charles F. **124** 160
Charles J. B. **64** 152
Charles Wells **55** 231
Charlotte **113** 265 266
120 216
Charlotte Elizabeth **88** 75
Charlotte Hiller **52** 455
Cheney **110** 34
Chloe **54** 84 **55** 284 285
56 355 **83** 100
Christian de **96** 94
Christopher **68** 160
Cordelia F. (Jellerson)
121 71 73 **123** 235
Cutler **110** 34
Cyrene **97** 377
Daniel **58** 340 **61** 240 **62**
40 **81** 431 **82** 49 **86** 460
97 376 **98** 57 **107** 227
110 61 289 **111** 254 255
112 215 307 **113** 194
114 45 132 **115** 137 214
217 222 **116** 90 132 136
142 **134** 107 **141** 329
Daniel J. **92** 318
Daniel W. **121** 71 73
123 235
David **58** 31 136 **63** 46 **77**

MOULTON *cont'd*
153 **97** 370 376 **98** 57
107 227 **116** 298 300
304 305 **119** 278 **123** 73
Deborah **55** 344 **68** 260
97 375 **98** 81 **115** 226
116 303
Deborah (Hilton) **97** 375
Dolly **58** 35 **59** 289
Dorcas **68** 93 **95** 268 **110**
61 **111** 255 **114** 290 291
116 225 295
Dorcas (Lucas) **119** 64 65
Dorothy **59** 288 **81** 431
91 78 **115** 139 **138** 112
141 314 **145** 318-322
327 331-333 341
Ebenezer **61** 310 **63** 46 **110**
29 32 33 **113** 127 194
114 126 **115** 215 219
118 242 318
Edith Lorraine **72** xx
Edmund **113** 266 **141** 315
147 138 142
Edward **58** 31 32 **81** 262
147 143
Edward Brown **97** 262
Edward Everett **142** 377
Edward L. **120** 68 **123** 151
Edward Lee **142** 376
Eleanor **82** 288 295
Eleanor (Bane) **110** 288
Eleazer **141** 322
Electa **110** 114 **142** 376
Eliezer **147** 143
Eliza **118** 242
Eliza (Blaisdell) **123** 152
Eliza (Grover) **119** 281 282
Elizabeth **58** 339 **61** 330
332 **62** 35 43 **66** 151 **69**
53 **81** 396 **82** 285 295 **96**
269 **110** 31 **111** 231 **114**
130 **119** 282 284 **141**
322 325-327 **144** 260
147 143
Elizabeth (Cole) **115** 137
Elizabeth (Fosket)
114 202
Elizabeth (Giggs) **141** 322
Elizabeth (Godfrey)
144 260
Elizabeth (Harmon)
114 126
Elizabeth (Perkins)
111 92
Elizabeth (Rush) **141** 322
Elizabeth (Towns) **123** 73
Elizabeth Abigail (Tyler)
107 227
Elizabeth H. (Roberts)
121 70
Elizabeth J. **77** 153
Elizabeth May **69** 145
Elizabeth Medora **68** 157
Ella Perley **82** 277
Ellen J. (Woodward)
123 73 74
Ellen Louise (Chandler)
63 113
Elmer L. **123** 235
Elvira **110** 34

MOULTON *cont'd*
Emma E. (Abbott) **123** 73
Emma Elizabeth Parker
81 396
Emma F. (Danielson)
123 74
Ephraim **58** 139 **97** 369
Esther **63** 84 **68** 336 **115**
212 **141** 320 321 **147**
143
Esther S. **68** 336
Eunice **59** 288 **110** 30
Eva V. (Ferbish) **123** 235
Eveline (Jellerson)
117 223
Everet E. **142** 377
Ezekiel **58** 139 **98** 81
Fanny D. (Kingsbury)
119 69
Florence Dell **68** 151
Frances **65** 256 **91** 32
Frances Parsons **98** 55
Francis Severn **84** 109 190
Frank Pierce **107** 227
Fred M. **68** 151
Frederick E. **80** 424
Freedom **103** 265
G. Frank **123** 74
Geneva May **82** 277
George **99** 202 **112** 216
113 194 **116** 142 224
303 **117** 222 **119** 63 229
120 218 **123** 73
George A. **123** 100
George D. **119** 286
George Edwin **62** 113
George Henry **92** 340
George L. **119** 279 280
George Lyman **123** 73
George M. **55** 347
Georgia (Hutchins)
123 235
Gilman **85** 334
Grace **141** 318 319 **144**
247 252 258 **147** 137 138
142
Grace Edna (Lufkin)
98 81
Grizel (Norridy) **144** 253
H. R. **110** 191
Hannah **51** 63 463 464 **52**
433 **56** 77 **58** 32 340 **62**
41 **63** 169 **84** 410 **86** 460
96 247 **97** 376 **99** 201
245 **110** 61 **111** 229 233
254 **112** 138 307 **113**
127 **114** 132 **115** 215
227 306 **116** 293 294
119 226 228 **123** 153
132 324 **141** 321 323
327 329 **147** 143
Hannah (Gowen) **116**
298 300
Hannah (Groves) **110** 28
Hannah (Noble) **95** 29
Hannah (Preble) **111** 254
114 132
Hannah (Sayward) **111**
229 **114** 130
Hannah (Wall) **141** 323

MOULTON *cont'd*
Hannah (Woodis?)
141 329
Hannah A. **95** 30
Hannah Harmon **94** 65
Harley S. **92** 340
Harriet F. **93** 107
Hattie Gray **62** xxxix
Helen F. **92** 340
Helen Winifred (Shute)
74 xxvii **85** 334
Henry **51** 52 **58** 32 **82** 293
295 **92** 284 310 **95** 219
112 25 **114** 125 **119** 283
123 74 **125** 243 **127** 12
141 313 315 325-328
144 260 262 **147** 135
Henry A. **68** 151
Henry H. **68** 157
Henry K. **80** 424
Henry L. **123** 151
Henry W. **141** 313
Hepzibah **76** 196
Hester **141** 320 321
144 257
Hiram **113** 265
Hiram H. **119** 62
Horace A. **123** 101
Howard **55** 284
Hubert **141** 315
Hugh de **96** 106
Huldah **67** 270
Ida Maria **123** 72
Ida O. **92** 340
Irene **113** 265 **119** 147
Isaac **125** 23
Isabell **141** 315 317 **144**
246 256 **147** 141
J. K. (Mrs.) **84** 30
J. Sidney **57** 236
Jacob **58** 34 35 138 **59** 283
288 **97** 262 **124** 160
James **59** 191 **61** 330 338
62 39 **69** 53 **71** 203 **92**
275 318 **117** 142 **127**
306 **136** 240 **141** 314
325-327 **144** 245 253 254
260 263 **147** 129
James C. **126** 25
James W. **90** 109
James William **82** 277
Jane **61** 332 334 **69** 53 **131**
131 **141** 313 328 **144**
262
Jane (Godfrey) **135** 19
Jane Berry **135** 19
Jedidiah **135** 19
Jemima **111** 255
Jennie M. **121** 308
Jennie Silver **72** xlvii
Jeremiah **55** 68 69 314 **67**
111 **74** 101 **77** 68 70 **83**
10 **97** 16 **109** 299 303
110 61 173 **111** 92 229
233 **112** 100 216 305
114 50 125-133 291-295
115 60-63 136 **116** 224
117 141 **119** 65 **134** 106
141 328 329
Jerusha **97** 375 **113** 127
116 142

MOULTON *cont'd*
Jerusha (Libbey) **97** 375
Joan **96** 94 **141** 322 **147**
   131 143
Joan (Green) **141** 323 324
   142 260 261 **144** 251
   252 256 259 **147** 141 142
Joanna **99** 284 **115** 219 **144**
   248 249
Joanna (Tilden) **88** 378
   112 216 **115** 139
Job **111** 231
Joel **111** 229
John **51** 52 63 466 **57** 261
   58 34 137 **59** 288 **61** 334
   62 38 41 43 44 **64** 212
   65 360 **66** 188 **69** 342-
   344 **71** 203 **81** 431 **97**
   262 376 **99** 203 247 284
   107 227 **110** 30 33 288
   111 231 **115** 216 **116**
   221 **117** 229 **125** 97 **141**
   313-323 325-328 **142**
   260-264 376 **144** 246-
   263 **147** 129-132 134-
   143 145
John Bound **114** 202 203
John Grant **61** xxxvi
John J. **68** 336
John M. **123** 73
John S. **95** 329
John Shackford **97** 262
John Tilden **52** 455
John Todd **98** 81
John Watts **95** 29 30
John Wesley **86** 146
Johnson **54** 132 **64** 129
   133 **94** 62 **97** 261 **115**
   224
Jonathan **54** 98 **58** 31 32
   35 139 140 **59** 289 **61**
   310 334 **62** 40 41 45 **66**
   151 **69** 360 **74** 124 **92**
   273 **112** 216 **119** 280
   285 **123** 149 **126** 116
   144 266
Jonathan B. **123** 150
Joseph **55** 197 311 **58** 29
   138 **59** 191 **65** 142 150
   256 **68** 336 **74** 187 **86**
   146 **98** 81 **105** 162 **109**
   299 300 **110** 173 282
   111 92 96 231 232 **112**
   100 **114** 44 129 **115** 139
   116 135 **141** 313 320-
   323 328 329 **144** 257
   147 136-138 143 145
Joseph E. **119** 281 282
   123 152
Joseph Parsons **97** 368
Joseph R. **59** 288
Josiah **51** 463 **55** 285 **58**
   30 32 139 140 **62** 40 **116**
   221 **118** 320
Jotham **61** 11 **65** 80 **76** 196
   88 378 **111** 229 **112** 216
   115 139 **116** 137 140
   117 223
Joy Wade **143** 72 **144** 245
   147 129 130 134 135 138
   139 141 **148** 296

MOULTON *cont'd*
Judith **55** 312 **82** 510 **102**
   67 **116** 225 **119** 224 **123**
   75
Judith A. **121** 144 145
Julana **51** 52
Julia **123** 151
Julia Ann (Trafton) **119**
   143 145
Julian (Straw) **97** 16
Justin A. **119** 69
Kate **51** 52 **59** 283
Kattrin (Chestney)
   141 322
Katy **116** 135
Keziah **71** 203
Lambert de **96** 93 94
Laura **64** 152
Leon **123** 150
Leonice Marston
   Sampson **52** 401
Linus **63** 46
Lizzie A. (Sewall) **123** 75
Lizzie H. (Roberts) **120**
   309 **123** 235
Lois **112** 225
Loraine (Jellison) **118** 320
Louise M. **68** 151
Lucia **58** 33
Lucretia **63** 46
Lucretia Ann **68** 160
Lucy **62** 44 **63** 169 **66** 151
   81 431 **108** 87 **110** 61
   117 **111** 229 **112** 100
   114 292 **115** 225 **119**
   144
Lucy (Harris) **115** 227
Lucy (Perkins) **117** 141
Lucy (Smith) **141** 323
Lucy Sewell **61** 110
Lydia **59** 283 287 288 290
   65 256 **66** 188 **92** 106
   97 375 376 **111** 92 255
   112 307 **114** 294 **115**
   214 **116** 128 129 **119**
   277 278 **120** 66 67 **123**
   151
Lydia (Berry) **97** 262
Lydia (Pease) **97** 376
Lydia (Taylor) **107** 227
   141 328
Lydia Ann (Dearborn)
   85 334
Lydia Miller **59** 287
Marcia **114** 204
Marcia Ella (Atwood)
   107 227
Margaret **51** 61 **69** 343
   82 291 295 **141** 315-319
   144 246 247 250 252 256-
   258 **147** 131 135-137 141
   142 145
Margaret (Page) **109** 162
   163 **141** 120 322 323
Margaret (Wattes)
   147 141
Margaret de **96** 106
Maria **51** 52 63 48 **119** 69
   123 232
Maria (Bradbury) **118** 320
Maria (Fernald) **120** 68

MOULTON *cont'd*
Maria Amanda **78** 89
Mariah **105** 300
Marie (Smith) **141** 326
Marietta **55** 284
Marion Elizabeth **102** 122
   107 222 227 **108** 139
Mark **97** 376
Martha **81** 431 447 **115** 59
   118 321 **119** 276 278
   123 232 **141** 320 321
   328 **144** 257 260 **147**
   138 143
Martha (Hanson) **117**
   144 224
Martha (Shaw) **114** 125
Martha A. **120** 224 306
Martha Ann **123** 149
Martha Jane (Shapleigh)
   95 329
Mary **51** 54 63 466 **55** 56
   196 197 311 314 **59** 290
   61 11 330 **62** 38 **63** 46
   68 94 **78** 89 **83** 10 **85**
   302 **90** 390 **97** 376 **99**
   284 **107** 227 **109** 162
   299 302 303 **110** 28 33
   111 96 229 **112** 25 **113**
   265 **114** 51 176 **115** 58
   216 **116** 138 302 303
   117 228 **118** 240 242
   119 64 **141** 313 321-329
   142 259 263 264 **144**
   252 253 255 259 260 262
   147 129 135 136 138 142
   143
Mary (Batcheldor) **97** 376
Mary (Beedle) **119** 63
Mary (Henshaw) **126** 20
Mary (Jacobs) **117** 229
Mary (Lord) **83** 10
Mary (McIntire) **116** 304
   305
Mary (Pulman) **114** 44
Mary (Smith) **141** 324
   142 264 **144** 249 252
   259 260
Mary (Smythe) **147** 142
Mary (Stevens) **119** 65 66
Mary (Toothacer) **111** 231
Mary (Weeks) **116** 303
Mary (Wickham) **126** 67
Mary (Young) **119** 285
   141 329
Mary A. **123** 152
Mary A. (Benchley) **142**
   376 377
Mary Amanda **81** 150
Mary Ann **59** 290 **119** 146
Mary E. (Spencer) **121** 309
   122 313
Mary Eliza (Avery) **119**
   279 280 **123** 73
Mary Etta (Abbott) **121**
   308 **122** 153
Mary F. **92** 237
Mary J. **68** 204 **76** 43 **119**
   278 **123** 73
Mary Jane **119** 286
Mary L. **110** 34
Maryann **98** 57

MOULTON *cont'd*
Matilda **141** 315
Matilda (Pike) **86** 146
Matthew **119** 64 65
May A. **123** 152
Mehitable **59** 283 **68** 100
  71 203 **97** 369 375 **110**
  30 33
Mehitable (Needham)
  110 33
Mehitable (Salter)
  (Tibbets) **99** 247
Melissa **68** 93 **73** 195
Mercy **59** 283 **113** 127
  116 134
Mercy (Hammond)
  119 228
Mercy (Young) **119** 280
  123 149
Merean **141** 313 326
Meribah **118** 318 **123** 235
Meribah (Thompson)
  115 64
Meribah L. **121** 307
  122 150
Meribah T. **118** 318
Merrick **110** 34
Michael **125** 243
Milan C. **123** 149
Mina Grace **69** 137
Miriam **83** 468 **112** 100
  141 314 322 325 327
  144 260 **147** 143
Miriam (Mitchell) **115** 139
Miriam (Weld) **110** 33
Miriam S. **92** 340
Molly **110** 28
Molly (Boyce) **90** 227 244
Moses **59** 286 288 290 **97**
  262 **104** 122
Nabby **97** 375
Nabby (Bryant) **124** 160
Nancy **59** 289 **71** 203 **97**
  370 **98** 57 **104** 128 **113**
  127 194 **116** 142
Nancy (Green) **110** 34
Nancy (Hains) **115** 308
Nancy (Noble) **95** 29 30
Nancy F. (Young)
  119 286
Nancy M. **120** 67 69
  122 286
Nancy S. **113** 194 **120** 136
  123 150
Naomi **61** 240
Naomi (Plaisted) **120** 218
Nathan **58** 139 140 **97** 375
Nathan Smith **59** 283 286
Nathaniel **62** 46 **113** 127
  115 137 **116** 221
Needham **110** 33 34 117
Nelle **116** 128
Nellie B. **71** xxxviii
Newel **91** 18
Noah **107** 227 **114** 126
  116 142 295 **117** 144
  224
Olive **97** 374 **99** 294 **119**
  288 **120** 64 **123** 75
Olive (Lowe) **116** 221
Olive E. **121** 307 **122** 151

MOULTON *cont'd*
Olive M. **101** 64
Olive S. **92** 340
Olivia **89** 289
Oraville A. (Norton)
  123 150
Orlando M. **68** 204
Orrill **110** 34
Patience (Locke) **107** 227
Patty **59** 287
Paulina **118** 321
Peggy **59** 286
Pelatiah **119** 68 147
Peter **58** 32
Phebe (Green) **110** 117
Phebe (Needham) **110** 34
  117
Phebe (Philbrick) **107** 227
Philip **108** 300
Polina **118** 321
Polly **59** 286 289 290 **63** 46
  77 146 **82** 49 **97** 370
  112 241 **114** 202 **116**
  129
Polly (Quimby) **118** 242
  318
Polly J. S. **68** 336
Porter **110** 34
Rachel **126** 24 **141** 314 327
Rachel Ann **119** 67
Rebecca **58** 34 **59** 288 **110**
  37 **141** 320 321 324 **144**
  257-259 **147** 133 136 138
  142 143
Rebecca E. **108** 300
Redmond **68** 93
Relief (Todd) **98** 81
Reuben **82** 291 295
Rhoda **115** 213 **119** 287
  120 64 236
Rhoda (Plaisted) **117** 142
Robert **51** 60 **58** 31 140
  61 310 **69** 343-345 **74**
  69 **86** 460 **98** 81 **110** 28
  31 **112** 225 **131** 130 141
  314 316-328 **142** 259 264
  144 245-263 **145** 319
  147 129-143
Robert C. **116** 222
Robert Lufkin **98** 81
Roger **141** 315
Roswell **71** 203
Roy Elmer (Mrs.) **84** 106
  190
Royal **71** 203
Rufus **112** 216
Ruth **51** 61 **141** 313 314
  322 323 325-328 **144** 260
  262 **147** 143
Ruth (Bound) **110** 30
Ruth (Quimby) **119** 62
Ruth Sargent **86** 465 **87**
  95 **88** 93 **89** 295
Ruth Stevens **95** 187
Sally **55** 284 **59** 191 290
  65 256 **97** 366-368 372
  374 375 377 **98** 57 **116**
  128
Sally (Knapp) **107** 227
Sally (Myrick) **117** 222
Sally (Tripp) **97** 19

MOULTON *cont'd*
Sally M. **59** 288
Samuel **52** 433 **54** 84 **55**
  284 **56** 209 355 **58** 139
  62 41 44 **64** 31 **65** 256
  66 22 68 260 **81** 431 **83**
  100 **97** 374 **113** 265 266
  114 129 **115** 139 216
  307 308 **116** 141 **141**
  326 327 **144** 245 252 253
  260 261 **145** 319 322 324
  327 332 333
Samuel A. **121** 309 **122** 313
Samuel Perkins **59** 287
Sara **147** 136 143
Sarah **53** 348 **59** 189 284 **61**
  330-332 336 **62** 34 37 41
  43 45 **63** 294 **66** 47 **67**
  353 **68** 157 **69** 53 **81** 150
  92 244 365 **93** 319 **109**
  163 **110** 288 **115** 227
  141 320 321 323 **144**
  257 **147** 178
Sarah (Cutler) **126** 25
Sarah (Cutter) **125** 243
Sarah (Donnell) **115** 136
Sarah (Lilley) **98** 81
Sarah (Nowell) **115** 137
Sarah (Smith) **97** 262
Sarah A. **119** 287
Sarah Frances (Sweetser)
  98 81
Sarah H. **80** 424
Sarah J. **92** 340
Sarah Maxwell **100** 313
Sarah Olive (Goodwin)
  123 151
Seba (Munger) **110** 33
Silas **134** 215
Simeon **65** 256 **97** 366-
  368 372 374-377 **98** 55
Simon **58** 136 **59** 287
Sobriety (Hilton) **95** 219
  141 328
Sophia **113** 265 **117** 140
  142-144
Sophronia **51** 52
Sophronia W. (Emmons)
  122 71 231
Stephen **58** 137 **97** 374 375
  98 326 **113** 265 **141** 315
Susan **126** 204 **147** 143
Susan (Emms) **141** 322
Susan (Hill) **122** 71 231
Susan H. (Card) **119** 147
Susan M. **119** 283 **123** 74
Susanna **115** 140 227
  141 322
Sylvester **119** 228
Syrena **65** 256
Temperance **59** 191
Temperance (Cotton)
  86 146
Theodore **111** 229 255
  115 222 **119** 65 66
Theodosia **113** 265 **119** 61
Theodosia J. (Langton)
  120 140 **123** 72
Thomas **59** 288 **64** 132 **69**
  342 **83** 118 **105** 285 **106**
  32 282 **109** 302 **110** 61

MOULTON *cont'd*
  111 229 **115** 64 65 **116**
  135 **125** 97 **131** 14 131
  141 313-315 317-319
  323-328 **142** 260 261
  144 245-254 256 259-
  263 **145** 333 **147** 129
  131 133-138 140-142
  Thomas de **96** 93
  Thomas M. **141** 313
  Thomasine **141** 317 318
  142 260 262 **144** 247
  248 256 257 **147** 136-139
  141 142
  Timothy Pike **59** 284
  97 262
  Turner **110** 34
  W. L.G. **92** 340
  Walter L. **123** 235
  Warren Joseph **85** 334
  Warren Joseph (Mrs.)
  73 319 **74** xxvii **85** 334
  346 **86** 203
  Wesley F. **69** 145
  Wilbur **51** 52
  Wilhelmina M. **73** 141
  William **51** 59 61 63 **55**
  197 **58** 31 33 137 **62** 34
  38 41 43 44 46 **63** 169
  65 150 **66** 180 **69** 53 342
  71 203 **90** 227 244 **94**
  262 **97** 366 **109** 162 **111**
  255 **113** 127 **115** 219
  227 **116** 136 **126** 20 **138**
  112 **141** 120 313-315 321-
  324 **142** 259 260 **144**
  248 252 259 262 **145** 173
  147 142
  William C. **71** 1
  William D. **92** 340 **93** 51
  116 141
  William F. **92** 340
  William G. **119** 224 **123** 75
  William Pitt **134** 152
  Willis G. **121** 308 **122** 153
  Worthington **58** 31
  Worthy **58** 140
  Zachariah **84** 378
  Zelotes **110** 34
MOULTON-BARRETT
  Edward R. **141**
  314 **144** 251
Moultrhop *see* Moulthrop
MOULTRIE —— **53** 134
  — Gen. **58** 156
  William **53** 455 **58** 411
Moultrop *see* Moulthrop
Moultrup *see* Moulthrop
MOUNCE
  Alexander **136** 79
  David **136** 79
  Jeremiah **136** 79
  John **136** 79
  Mary A. (Walker) **136** 79
  Maudyea **104** 142
  Nancy **136** 79
  Sally **136** 79
  Samuel **136** 79
  William **136** 79
Mounck *see* Monk

MOUNDFORTH
  John **75** 287
MOUNDYN
  Thomas **79** 425
MOUNIGLE
  Patrick **60** 241
MOUNT Mownt
  Dorothy **67** 35
  John **67** 166 **143** 259
  Leslie C. **109** 307
  Madeline (McColl)
  109 307
  Sarah **98** 178
  Stephen **70** 248
  William Sidney **99** 82
MOUNTAGNE
  Francis **60** 286
MOUNTAIR
  Dorothy **63** 355
  Francis **63** 355
Mountchesny *see*
  Montchensey
MOUNTENEY
  John **109** 27
  Margaret **109** 27
  Margaret (Tyrrel) **109** 31
  Robert **109** 27 31
  William **109** 27 31
MOUNTEYNE
  John **110** 188 189
MOUNTFLORENCE
  James Cole **110** 134
MOUNTFORT
  De Montfort Montfort
  Mountford
  —— **54** 446 **82** 413
  — Dr. **85** 13
  Albert **89** 351
  Anne **112** 159 **121** 29
  Benjamin **107** 106
  Betrade de **99** 35
  C. **89** 351
  Caroline T. **89** 351
  Catherine **112** 299
  Caty **125** 220
  Dorothy **112** 158
  Dorothy (Curteys)
  112 158
  Eben **125** 106
  Ebenezer **87** 298
  Edmund **89** 351
  Elizabeth **110** 186
  Eunice (Whittemore)
  107 106
  Francis **124** 149
  Hannah **125** 106
  Henry **96** 321 **97** 195 **102**
  185 **112** 158 159 299
  Isabel (Chipley) **112** 159
  John **77** 239 **91** 93
  Jonathan **57** 389
  Joseph **77** 239 **97** 57
  Lovicy M. **89** 351
  Marie **112** 158
  Mary **89** 351 **112** 159 **133**
  308 310 **135** 93
  Nellie **89** 351
  Peggy (Bass) **125** 106
  Piers **110** 186
  Polly **85** 13
  Sarah (Gyles) **97** 57

MOUNTFORT *cont'd*
  Simon **106** 286 **121** 29
  Susan **112** 159
  Thomas **112** 158 159
  Timothy **82** 413
  William de **116** 92
Mountgomery *see*
  Montgomery
MOUNTJOY Montejoye
  Munjoy Muntjoy
  — Lady **113** 220 221
  — Lord **55** 223 **82** 309
  Daniel **56** 239 **135** 251
  Edmund **55** 437 438
  Ephraim **69** 295
  Gardiner Luke (Viscount)
  85 324
  George **59** 274 **82** 69 70
  136 186
  Grace **100** 242
  Joan **82** 70
  Joanna **59** 274
  Katharine **55** 438
  Louise de (Baroness)
  107 42
  Martha **100** 241
  Mary **59** 274 **66** 177 **72** 199
  100 242
  Mary Philips **135** 251
  Ned **69** 295
  Philip **82** 69
  Rebecca **56** 239
  Walter Blount (Baron)
  72 136
  William Blount (Baron)
  72 136
MOUNTRATH
  — Countess of **52** 127
MOUNTS
  Elizabeth Polk **78** 173
  Jonathan Clark **78** 173
  Olga (Polk) **78** 173
MOURRAILLE
  Jeannette Louise **79** 323
MOURSUND
  John S. **120** xxx
MOURT
  —— **55** 129 **145** 215
  G. **142** 109
Mourton *see* Morton
MOUSALL Mousal Mousel
  —— **55** 116
  Alice **125** 58 **131** 131
  Ann **106** 196
  Anna **106** 196
  Anna (Fowle) **107** 258
  Dorothy (Hett) **143** 50
  Elizabeth **61** 94 **99** 77
  Eunice **58** 49 50
  Hannah **106** 196
  Joanna **58** 49 **106** 198 199
  Joanna (Thompson)
  131 131
  John **57** 351 **58** 48-53 127
  61 94 **85** 455 **106** 95 196
  199 **131** 19 131 **143** 50
  Mary **61** 94 **99** 77 **107** 258
  Ralph **61** 94 **94** 66 **99** 77
  106 196 199 **107** 258
  108 27 **123** 230 **125** 58
  131 19 131

MOUSALL *cont'd*
Ruth **99** 77 **123** 230 **125**
57 58
Sarah **58** 48 52 53
Thomas **61** 94 **106** 34 196
MOUSER
Grant E. **77** 246
Henry **144** 131 132
Robert **144** 132
Sabina (Aldous) (Smith)
144 131 132
William **144** 131 132
MOUT Jan **128** 164
MOUTON Jacques **143** 8
Margaret **143** 8
Marguerite **143** 10
Marguerite (Caissie)
143 8
MOVER Hannah **79** 321
MOVEY Hannah **110** 107
MOVIUS
Alice Lee (West) **84** 341
85 197
MOW
Eliza Ruth **81** 380
Ellis **81** 127 129
Ezra **81** 380
James Leroy **81** 380
Sarah Leonard **81** 380
Sarah Rogers **81** 380
MOWAT Mowatt
— Capt. **85** 26
Elisha **65** 150
Elizabeth **65** 40
Harvey **65** 217
Henry **51** 143 **52** 221 **65** 97
66 xxiii
James **101** 22
John **65** 150
Ralph **65** 40
William Augustus **65** 201
MOWBRAY
De Mowbray
Moubray
—— **53** 257 **60** 218
141 100
— Barons of **123** 243
Alexander **120** 173 174
Alice **120** 172
Anne **96** 368
Eleanor **120** 173 174
Elena **120** 172 174
Elizabeth **120** 170 173 174
Helena **120** 171
Hilda **120** 171 174
Isabel **120** 172
Jane **104** 271
John **104** 270 **111** 263 **114**
225 **120** 170 172-174
Margaret **120** 172 173
Maud **97** 249 **120** 171
Neel **120** 174
Philip **106** 285 **120** 174
Richard **120** 171 174
Robert **97** 249 **102** 292 **106**
283 **120** 174
Roger **79** 374 376 **103** 198
201 **120** 174
Thomas **120** 172 174
Walter **120** 170 171 174
William **107** 155 **120** 170-

MOWBRAY *cont'd*
174
Mowdy *see* Moody
Mowdye *see* Moody
MOWER
Albion P. **64** 155
Alice **88** 32
Ann **64** 155
Charles **64** 156
Daniel **142** 286
Earl A. **59** 116
Ebenezer **61** 262
Ebenezer L. **125** 35
Eleta **64** 155
Elias A. **133** 123
Ellen **90** 136
Emarentha **64** 155
Ephraim **51** 380 **52** 285
57 388 **58** 68
Hannah **52** 73 **57** 363
Harriet Hammond
(Robinson) **142** 369
Isabella (Wing) **90** 352
Joanna **54** 224
Job **142** 9
John **52** 73 **57** 363
Jonathan **63** 375
Lydia **122** 53
Mary **107** 69
Mary Olive (Kimball)
(Durrell) **133** 123
Milicent **64** 155
Nahum W. **59** 116
Oliver **142** 369
Olivet **63** 375
Parthena (Hannum)
90 352
Peter S. **64** 155 156
Richard **54** 224 **59** 116
Samuel **51** 383 **54** 224
Sarah **61** 262
Sarah D. **64** 155 156
Thomas **59** 116
MOWERS Sarah Ann (Coy)
100 200
MOWLING Ann **86** 433
MOWLSON
Ann (Lady) **54** 217
MOWNDER
Thomas **120** 21
Mownt *see* Mount
MOWRY Moorey Mowrey
—— **136** 200
— Mrs. **138** 125
Abigail **52** 209 212
Ahaz **122** 213
Albert **52** 209 **138** 122
Alfred **91** 330
Alpha (Chase) **87** 264
Amanda M. **77** 180
Amasa **52** 209 **84** 445
138 126
Ann (Brownell) **113** 102
Anna **52** 209 **97** 71
Anna (Hamilton) **84** 445
Arlon **52** 207 209 210 212
397 399 400 **58** xlviii
84 445 **85** 107 204
Arnold **138** 121
Arnold W. **138** 121
Atwell **52** 209

MOWRY *cont'd*
Augustus **96** 306 **138** 126
Barney **52** 209 210 **84** 445
Benjamin **52** 207 211
67 286
Bethiah **52** 207 211 **105** 257
Blanche Swett **72** xlvi
Burrill **87** 340
Caleb **52** 209 **84** 445
138 115
Caroline Eliza **72** xlvi
Caroline F. **77** 181
Catherine **87** 80-82
Catherine (Ginnedo) **87**
80 81
Charles Bowen **52** 209
Daisy B. **52** 210
Daniel **72** xlv **138** 121
146 348
David **52** 209 **130** 137
Deborah **52** 209 **106** 239
138 117
Deborah (Wing) **84** 445
Dorcas **52** 209
Duane **67** xxxi 95
Duty **52** 209
Elebette **87** 81
Eliakim **52** 209
Elisha **52** 208 **146** 348
Elizabeth **52** 207 208 211
Elizabeth (Clark) **114** 283
Elizabeth (Gifford)
130 137
Emma L. **52** 210
Emma Lillian **84** 446
Emor H. **77** 180
Erwin A. **52** 209
Esek **79** 335
Eugene C. **52** 210
Eugene Clayton **84** 446
Eunice **87** 81
Experience **52** 208 **80** 174
Ezekiel **106** 239
Foster **138** 122
Gideon **52** 208 **72** xlv
Hannah **52** 207 208 211
72 xlv **101** 309 **102** 206
110 107
Harriet **52** 210
Harriet (Whitman) **84** 446
Harriet W. **52** 210
Harvey **80** 309
Hassard **87** 81
Henry **52** 208 **84** 445
146 348
Isabel (Chase) **87** 339
Israel **70** 151
James **129** 384
Jeremiah **52** 208 **138** 122
125 **146** 348
Jerusha **74** 64 114
Jesse **52** 209
Joanna **87** 81 **123** 253
Joanna (Inman) **84** 445
123 253
John **52** 207 208 212 **55** 448
64 92 **72** xlvi **74** 64 **114**
81 283 **146** 348
Jonathan **52** 207-209 211
72 xlv **84** 445 **138** 115

MOWRY *cont'd*
117
Joseph **52** 207 208 **72** xlv
  87 81 **113** 102 **146** 348
Joshua **87** 81
Lavina **122** 213
Lewis **87** 81 **106** 72
Lilian T. **116** 82
Lois Adeline **138** 288
Lucy **70** 151
Lucy Ann **138** 122
Lucy Malvina **77** 188
Lucy W. **79** 335
Lydia **122** 55
Marcy **52** 208
Martha **52** 208 209
Mary **52** 207 208 211 **63**
  154 **67** 286 **106** 24
Mary (Bull) **84** 445
Mary (Johnson) **84** 445
  106 23 30 **113** 102 **146**
  261 274
Mary (Wilbore) **113** 102
Mary Agnes **77** lxxv
Mehitable **52** 207 **58** 51 52
Mendol **69** 334
Meribah **80** 309
Nancy **52** 209 **84** 445
Napolean B. **91** 330
Nathaniel **52** 207 208 210
  212 **55** 448 **64** 92 **72** xlv
  xlvi **84** 445 446 **116** 82
  123 253 **146** 348
Oliver **146** 348
Orrin P. **52** 209
Osborne **122** 213
Patience **52** 208
Peleg **52** 209
Phebe **52** 208
Phebe (Chase) **87** 340
Phebe (Tillinghast)
  (Hazard) **114** 81
Phila **52** 209 **84** 445
Philip **52** 208 **116** 82
Phylura **80** 309
Polly **63** 49 **70** 243
Rebecca **52** 209
Richard **52** 212 **64** 92 **72**
  xlv xlvi **87** 339
Richard Dennis **77** 188
Robert **52** 209 **87** 81
Robert C. **87** 81
Roger **52** 207 208 210-212
  55 448 **58** 52 **84** 445 446
  106 30 **113** 102 **136** 216
  146 274
Rufina **138** 126
Russell **138** 115
Ruth **72** xlvi **87** 81
  138 124
Sally Ann **138** 120
Sarah **52** 208 **87** 81 **125** 206
  127 239
Sidney M. **69** 334
Silas **122** 213 **138** 119
Stafford **52** 209
Stephen **52** 208 **87** 264
  146 348
Susanna **52** 212
Sylvanus **122** 56
Thomas **52** 207 211 212

MOWRY *cont'd*
106 24
Urania **52** 208 209
Urania (Paine) **84** 445
Uriah **52** 208 209 **84** 445
  138 120 **146** 348
Walter G. **77** lxxv
Walter H. **72** xlvi
Walter Sylvester **91** 394
Wanton **52** 208 **146** 348
Wilfrid L. **52** 210
William **91** 330 **138** 121
William A. **51** 376 384 **52**
  207 210 399 400 **55** 448
  58 212 325 **60** 217
William Augustus **56**
  xxx **58** xliii **59** xli **63**
  xxxiii 106 **64** xxix 92 202
  67 96 **72** xxix xlv xlvi
Zerviah **133** 153
MOWT Robert **129** 60
MOXAM Thomas **54** 337
MOXCEY
Desiah **83** 184 188
MOXHAM Joseph **93** 385
MOXLEY Jonas **54** 327
  55 332
Joshua **73** 268
MOXON — Mr. **55** 160
George **133** 164-166
  140 10
Grace **61** 385
Union **87** 302
MOYA
Salvadore de **101** 121
Moye *see* Moyse
Moyes *see* Moyse
MOYLAN John **131** 45
Stephen **131** 45
MOYLE
Edith Luella **76** 9
John **74** 74 **76** 9 **94** 265
Judith **100** 98 293
Lovedy **79** 111
Lucia **74** 74
Margaret **74** 74
Richard **71** 233 **74** 74
Walter **74** 74
MOYNAHAN
Patrick A. **80** 226
MOYNES John **113** 56
MOYSE Moye Moyes
  Moys Moysse
  —— **55** 432
Agnes **128** 165
Hannah **90** 3
Jan **128** 162
John **65** 179-183 **66** 56 68
  92 385 **93** 76 79 **128** 165
Joseph **90** 3
Lettice **65** 183
Margaret **75** 281 288 289
Mary **90** 3 **143** 292
Rebecca Jane **93** 274
Richard **128** 165
Robert **65** 180 182 **66** 68
Samuel **128** 165
Simon **65** 182
Thomas **128** 165
William **95** 257

MOZART
Charles A. **123** 232
George F. **123** 150
George W. **88** 339
Julia M. (Goodwin)
  123 150
Maria B. (Hawes) **88** 339
Mary **88** 338
Mercy (Holman) **123** 150
  232
Sadie (Shutts) **123** 232
William F. **123** 150 232
MOZEY Benjamin **58** 52
Mozier *see* Mosher
M'Pherson *see* McPherson
M'Sherry *see* McSherry
MTOHKSIN
Jehoiakim **54** 162 164
MUCARY William **115** 59
MUCCRANNY
William **123** 261
MUCHMORE
Muchemore
Mutchemore
Mutchermore
—— **83** 35
— Dea. **64** 11
— Widow **82** 423 **83** 35
Abigail **64** 7 **66** 142 145
  301 302 **67** 242 **115** 59
  211 **121** 176
Anne **64** 7 **66** 142 145 155
  211 214 304 **67** 242
Arthur **82** 50
Barnard **67** 243
Benjamin **66** 209 225 295
  297 298 **67** 239 242 **81**
  142 **82** 50
Bernard **66** 148 217 **127** 15
Betsey **113** 128 **116** 222
Betty (Moore) **113** 128
Daniel **59** 35
Deborah **66** 294 **67** 244
Eliza Ann **82** 50
Elizabeth **66** 144 146 154
  67 242 **82** 49 295 297
Elizabeth Kinsman
  81 142
Henry **66** 215 296 299 301
  67 242
Henry Carter **66** 224
  67 244
Jacob **66** 217 218 **67** 242
  113 128 **115** 218
James **66** 216 **82** 295 297
Jane **82** 49
Jeffrey **66** 147 212 296 299
  67 237 239-241 **115** 224
Joanna **66** 143 146 154
  209 211 213 214 216 217
  67 242
John **51** 462 **64** 7 **66** 142
  143 145 155 211 214 220
  221 301 302 **67** 59-62
  132 134-136 143-145 242
  243 **81** 142 **112** 306 **115**
  220 **121** 176
John Kinsman **82** 49
John Kinsman Peverley
  82 423
John Tucke **66** 296 299

MUCHMORE *cont'd*
Joseph **55** 374 **64** 7 **66**
    143 146 224 294 295 297
    298 **67** 234-244 **83** 15
Josiah Ladd **113** 128
Katharine **51** 462
Lemuel **66** 213
Love **66** 147 296 299
Martha **59** 35
Mary **66** 143 146 211 224
    294 295 297 298 **67** 242
    244 **112** 306 **114** 129
    115 136
Molly **55** 374 **66** 294 295
    67 244 **83** 15 **113** 128
Molly (Spencer) **83** 15
Nathaniel **67** 242 **81** 447
Patty **113** 128
Rachel **64** 7 **66** 146 150
    67 243
Rebecca **66** 214 295
    82 289 295
Richard **64** 7 **66** 302
    67 242 243
Ruth **66** 143 145 212 213
    215 217 218 220 221 304
Samuel **66** 143 145 155
    212 213 215 217 218 220
    221 296 305 **67** 143 146
    232 234 **119** 198
Sarah **64** 7 **66** 142 143 145
    147 148 150 153 213 225
    67 242 243 **81** 142 **82**
    295 298 **110** 289 **114** 47
Tamzine **66** 225 295 297
    298 306
Trueworthy **113** 128
Tryphena **66** 296 299 306
William **64** 7 **66** 142 148
    150 153 154 209 211 213
    214 216 298 302 303 **67**
    59 61 62 132 134 135 137
    143 145-147 232 234-240
    242 243 **81** 142 **82** 49 50
    423
MUCK Hannah **125** 214
MUDD Ann **73** 141
Benjamin N. **73** 269
Elizabeth **73** 151 221 263
Harriet **73** 277
Hezekiah **73** 137
James **103** 81
John **96** 357 **101** 52
Joseph **73** 148
Mary **73** 152
Mary Ann **73** 274
Mary Tabitha **73** 152
Michael **73** 274
Nettie **117** 315
Richard D. **103** 81 160
    106 77 **117** 315
Richard Dyer **103** 120
Samuel **58** 137
Samuel A. **117** 315
Sarah **73** 267
Thomas **103** 160
MUDDIFORD
William **64** 341
MUDGE Abigail **53** 403
    54 450 **58** lxxix
Abigail J. **68** 258

MUDGE *cont'd*
Adeline **68** 258
Alfred **51** 93 95 377 **52**
    285 483 **54** 366 **56** 103
    104 **57** 118 238 **58** 108
Anna **61** 230
Beatris **53** 432
Caroline (Woodbury)
    105 313
Caroline Matilda **80** 441
    442
Charles **115** 18
Cranston Richard **80** 158
Daniel Lee **80** 442
Daniel W. **68** 258
Deborah **115** 18
Delia **115** 18
Dorothy **85** 457 458
Ebenezer **53** 403 **54** 450
Edmund Webster **81**
    108 219 **105** 232 313
    106 128
Edna May **80** 158
Edward A. **83** 181 184
Elizabeth **53** 432 **76** 220
    222
Elizabeth (Burrill) **105** 313
Enoch **105** 278 279
Enoch Redington **52** 279
Eunice **63** 367
George McClelland
    80 158
Hannah (Ingalls) **105** 313
Harriet **77** 147
Henry Seymour **84** 351
Hiram **115** 18
Ichabod **63** 367
Isaac B. **83** 194
Jane **115** 40
Jarvis **84** 351 **148** 11
John **61** 230 **105** 313 314
    106 193
Joseph **55** 394
Josephine **80** 158
Leonard Seeley **105** 313
Lois **55** 394
Lora Elizabeth **80** 158
Louisa J. **84** 30
Lucy **115** 40
Lydia **105** 313
Margaret A. **84** 30
Margaret A. (Hall)
    83 181 184
Marie Louise **72** xx
Martha **55** 40 **115** 40
Mary **105** 314 **106** 33 **115**
    18 **123** 263
Mary (Albright) **105** 313
Mary (Waite) **105** 313
Mary I. **68** 258
Mary Louise **105** 313
May Emma (Foster)
    (Sheppard) **105** 313
Nathan **105** 313
Nathan A. **88** 32
Olive **68** 258
Osceola Warren **68** 258
Pamelia Boardman
    (Chase) **88** 32
Pauline Gordon (Seeley)
    105 313

MUDGE *cont'd*
Presby **68** 258
Rachel **63** 255
Ruth **106** 193
Ruth (Burditt) **105** 314
Sabre **115** 40
Samuel **63** 255
Sarah (Chauncey) **119** 302
Sarah (Kimberly) **102** 110
Simon **105** 313
Solomon **102** 110
Thomas **53** 432 **80** 442 **105**
    314 **134** 29
Thomas Henry **105** 313
William **51** 495 **53** 127
MUDGETT Mudget Mugett
    ——— **60** 107
Abigail **67** 271 279
    147 362
Abraham R. **117** 163
Abram **117** 171
Abram (Mrs.) **117** 168
Ann **58** 92
Ann (French) (Long)
    100 254 **104** 40
Anna **68** 100
Benjamin **67** 270 271 **68** 96
    160 **69** 331
Betsey (Farnham) **94** 391
Betsey (Varnum) **113** 313
Bruce D. **115** 318
Calvin Huckins **68** 97
Camilaus **94** 392
Caroline **68** 100
Clara **68** 97 **81** 255
Cyrus P. **94** 391
David **59** 290
Dorothy **91** 31
Eleanor S. **67** 271
Elisha **94** 391 **113** 313
Eliza M. **117** 163
Elizabeth **59** 283 **101** 331
Emeline **94** 391
Eunice **68** 97
Frank **117** 170
Fred S. **94** 392
Frederick J. **80** 310
George Leland **94** 392
George Washington **94**
    391 392
Gratia **91** 393
Hannah **51** 466 **67** 183 271
    68 96 153 **69** 331
Hannah Huckins **68** 97
Hattie Bell **94** 392
Herman W. **81** 255
Ira **94** 391
J. W. **117** 168
James H. **67** 271
Jennie **89** 300 **99** 29
Jeremiah **105** 280
Jesse **68** 159
John **67** 271 **68** 100
    105 279
John C. **67** 271
John Huckins **67** 271
John Hull **69** 331
John Philander **68** 97
Joseph **67** 271 279 **68** 97
    69 331 **117** 171
Judith B. **117** 164

MUDGETT cont'd
Julia **68** 97
L. H. **91** 330
Laura Lettice **68** 97
Louisa **94** 391
Lucinda **94** 391 **113** 313
Luther **117** 169 170
Lydia **67** 270 271
Martha Ann **68** 160
Mary **67** 270 **68** 159 **69** 331
 94 391 **125** 96
Mary A. (Peaslee) **94** 392
Mary Ann **67** 271
Mary J. **68** 97
Mary Mooney Smith
 68 97
Maude Gertrude **94** 392
Mehitable **67** 279 **68** 97
Mildred D. **111** 317
 115 318
Moses **51** 466
Nancy **67** 271
Nancy B. **67** 271
Nancy H. **67** 271
Nancy S. **67** 270
Nathaniel **105** 282
Nehemiah **117** 168
Nellie R. **94** 392
Nellie Ruth **94** 392
Nicholas **125** 96
Orinda Mehitable **68** 97
R. F. **91** 330
Ruby Jane (Bassick)
 117 163
Ruth **51** 466 **68** 159
Sally **59** 290
Samuel **94** 391 **105** 289
Sarah **67** 271
Sarah Ann Baker **68** 97
Simeon **118** 37
Stephen **94** 391
Susan **67** 270
Susan A. **80** 310
Susanna **118** 36
Temperance **71** 261
Thomas **51** 466 **58** 92 **100**
 254 **104** 40 **111** 317 **115**
 318
William **68** 97
William Chase **86** 198
William S. **68** 100
MUDGIN Margaret **112** 69
MUDIE
Lydia H. **92** 340
Mitchell **92** 340
MUELLER
Ernest **68** 123
Hugo **111** 54
Ralph Scott **88** 169
Sarah Frances **68** 123
MUENSTER
Joseph **78** 323
Josephine **78** 323
Minnie Pearl **78** 323
MUERS —— **120** 123
Muffet see Moffat
MUFFIN
Jonas **111** 276 277
Mary **111** 276
Mary (Burroughs)
 111 277

Muffit see Moffat
Muffitt see Moffat
MUFREY Bryan **95** 134
MUGATT Arys (Byington)
 127 239
Mugett see Mudgett
MUGFORD —— **52** 361
— Capt. **85** 122
George **77** 131
John **142** 36
Mary **77** 131 **142** 36
Sarah **137** 329
W. E. **58** 190
MUGGE Mugg Muggs
— Mr. **51** 265
— Mrs. **65** 361
Richard **137** 301
MUGGOTT — Mr. **84** 153
Muggredg see Mugridge
Muggs see Mugge
MUGGY Mary **54** 189
MUGOON
Hannah **134** 72 73
MUGRIDGE Muggredg
— Miss **83** 35
Abigail (Moore) **116** 300
Annie (Linscott) **123** 153
Eliza Ann **77** 146
Elizabeth (Peabody)
 90 106
George **116** 300 **120** 21
Hannah **63** 174
Hannah J. **83** 184
J. H. **123** 152 232
John **54** 445 **63** 174
John H. **123** 151
Mabel E. **123** 153
Nancy (Marden) **120** 221
Rebecca **63** 173
Samuel **123** 153
Temperance **63** 174
Thomas **63** 173
William **54** 445 **77** 146
William P. **90** 106
MUHLECK
John A. **83** 429 436
Sarah (Geller) **83** 429 436
MUHLEMAN
Beulah McLeyne
 111 151
Elizabeth (Cunningham)
 111 151
Harriet Fracker (Pettes)
 122 91
Maurice L. **122** 91
Samuel **111** 151
Viva Gertrud (Ewing)
 111 151
MUHLENBERG Muhlenburg
F. **51** 25
Henry Melchoir **66** 287
William Augustus
 72 xxxvii
MUHLENBEY
Mary Ann C. **93** 291
MUIKIS Jonathan **58** 142
MUIR Adam **122** 268
Alexander **63** 214
Anna **111** 66
Betsey (Haynes) **92** 388
Catherine (Victor) **98** 54

MUIR cont'd
Elizabeth **110** 308
Isabella (Brown) **110** 308
Jasper **110** 308
Mungo **110** 308
Ophelia **98** 147
Robert **98** 54
Robert Edmenston
 92 388
Sarah Catherine **92** 388
William **110** 308
MUIRHEAD
Elizabeth Yates **91** 105
Margaret McNab
 (Connor) **91** 105
William Row **91** 105
MUIRSON —— **55** 449
MULBERRY Ann **58** 144
Benjamin **58** 144 **84** 253
MULCASTER
Eleanor **54** 215
John de **98** 272
Peter **52** 112
Richard **52** 112
William **54** 215
MULDA Henry **79** 267
Rachel **79** 267
MULDER Cornelis
 Stephense **86** 464
MULDOON Moldoon
 Muldown
Aleen **92** 190
Frank M. (Mrs.) **113** 296
James **60** 160
Margaret **91** 54 **93** 300
Mary Ann **77** 182
Mary Elizabeth **79** 282
MULENOX William **58** 68
MULFORD —— **56** 214
— Capt. **55** 279
— Mr. **51** 419
Abiah **55** 88 201
Abigail **55** 84 294
Abraham **55** 88 204
Amy **54** 433 **55** 88 202 203
 109 5
Andrew A. **137** 41
Anna **54** 307 **55** 203
Anne **83** 263
Barnabas **55** 204 **75** 309
Benjamin **55** 207
Bettee **62** 147
Catterina **55** 201
Charles L. **54** 200
Christopher **54** 433
 55 202
Daniel **55** 204 205
David **54** 206 301 433 **55**
 84 204 205
Deborah **55** 201 204
Dorcas **51** 47 48
Ebenezer **54** 433
Edward **54** 433 **55** 202 203
Eleazer **63** 47
Elias **54** 62 206 **55** 201 203
Elisha **55** 84 85 204
Elizabeth **265 54** 301 304
 55 203 **63** 47 **79** 293 **83**
 265 **124** 184
Esther **54** 206 433 **55** 202
 206

MULFORD *cont'd*
Ezekiel **55** 88 201 204 206
  106 160
Frances **51** 419
Freezneed **55** 207
Hannah **52** 81 **55** 201 204
  206 207 **58** 127 **79** 292
  80 279
Isaac **55** 202
James Hervey **55** 424
Jane **55** 201
Jeremiah **55** 84 88 201 204
Jerusha **55** 206
Joanna **55** 84 202 205
Job **55** 204
Joel **62** 147
John **54** 88 206 307 **55** 200
  201 206-208 **105** 59 **107**
  115 **108** 310
Jonathan **54** 301 **55** 203
Josiah **55** 201 206
Juliana **54** 301
Lemuel **55** 88 204
Lewis **55** 201
Mary **51** 47 **54** 62 206 301
  433 **55** 84 201 203 206-
  208
Mary Moore **55** 424
Matthew **54** 206 301 304
  55 201 202 205
Mehitable **75** 309
Mercy **54** 433 **55** 202
Nancy (Lindsley) **106** 160
Nathan **54** 307 433 **55** 203
Patience **79** 292 **80** 279
Phebe **54** 301 307 **55** 84
  85 201 203 204
R. A. **91** 330
Rachel **55** 201 205 207
Robert L. **54** 206
Samuel **54** 62 204 206 304
  55 201-203 205-207 **108**
  310
Sarah **54** 304 433 **55** 202
  207
Sarah (Barton) **107** 115
Susan **76** 319 **92** 400
  108 310
Susan (Kitchell) **92** 400
Thomas **51** 47 48 **52** 81
  54 433 **55** 85 201 204
  207 **79** 292 **83** 263 265
Timothy **54** 433 **55** 201-
  203 **108** 310
William **55** 201 205 207
  124 184
Zeruiah **54** 62
MULGRAVE Constantine
  (Baron) **60** 61
Timothy **52** 132
MULGREW
Anne (Grey) **109** 64
John **109** 64
Mary Anne **109** 64
MULHALEN
John **112** 280
MULHAUSER
Bertha D. **96** 29
Fred P. **96** 29
Virginia Ruth **96** 29
MULHERON John **62** 81

MULHOLLAND Mulhollan
Ann **61** 350
Elizabeth **108** 197
Jane **61** 182
Mary (Bell) **108** 101 197
Owen **106** 109
Muliken *see* Mulliken
Mulin *see* Mullins
MULKEARN Lois **104** 79
MULKEY Mary **72** 282
MULKINS Lusa **65** 344
MULKOW E. **64** 366
MULKS Nancy **100** 326
Mullagin *see* Mulligan
MULLAHY John **61** 349
MULLAN Arthur **59** 138
James **59** 238
Mary **59** 138
Patrick **61** 136
MULLANDER
Elizabeth **51** 421 422
Lydia **51** 421
Margaret **51** 421
Martha **51** 421
Rose **51** 421
Thomas **51** 421 422
MULLANE George **68**
  xxxii **71** 63
MULLE —— **117** xii
Mullen *see* Mullins
MULLENDER
Thomas **65** 236
MULLENERS
William **53** 11
Mullens *see* Mullins
MULLER
—— **66** xxvi **117** xii
Amelia **119** 178
Anna Maria **97** 380
Casper Otto **119** 176
Charles **77** 181
Christina **102** 70
Christine K. **85** 315
Elizabeth A. (Teaure)
  119 176
F. **59** lxii
Gertrude **77** 181
Gertrude Fanny Adeline
  (Erbsloh) **96** 389
Henry J. **115** 150
Jacob **77** 239
John **85** 168
Julius **56** 15
Margaret K. **85** 168
Melusina **83** 332 **119** 176
Olga Helen Clara
  (Erbsloh) **96** 389
Robert Otto (Mrs.) **96** 389
Samuel **85** 315
MULLERY
Charles Waldorf
  112 247
Helen Marie **112** 247
John **112** 247
MULLET Mullett
Abraham **62** 19 20
Adeline **58** 62
Agnes **143** 112
Daniel **58** 61
Dulcina **58** 61
Ephraim **78** 69

MULLET *cont'd*
George **62** 20
Henry **62** 20
J. **58** 61 62
John **58** 61 62
Lucetta **58** 62
Lucina **58** 61
Lydia **58** 61
Lyman **58** 62
Mary Simon **88** 277
Mercy **125** 294
Rebecca **58** 61
Sally **79** 49
MULLEY Mary M. **70** 124
  115 129
Mullicken *see* Mulliken
MULLIGAN — Mr. **81** 42
Alice **81** 42
Annabel **91** 110 **111** 152
Annabella (Garrard) **91**
  110 **111** 152
Frederick W. **66** 228
James **91** 110 **95** 53
  111 152
John **66** 37
Nabby **100** 304
MULLIKEN Muliken
  Mullicken Mullikin
Ann **73** 265
Asa W. **127** 320 **128** 312
Barak **73** 278
Benjamin **73** 229 **125** 183
Betsey (Clifton) **125** 183
Eleanor **73** 275
Eliza **77** 290
Francis **73** 271
Henrietta **73** 263
Henrietta B. **73** 274
James **73** 140 220 267
John **128** 47
John B. **73** 267
John R. **59** 288
Joseph **73** 222 **128** 47
Lucy **73** 149
Lydia (Sanderson) **128** 47
Lydia (Stone) **128** 46 47
Martha **73** 264
Martha Hall **73** 223
Mary **73** 225 232 267 **128**
  46 47
Nathaniel **128** 46 47
Polly **59** 288
Rebecca A. **79** 38
Rechel (Campbell) **127**
  320 **128** 312
Richard **73** 146 **77** 290
Robert **146** 320
Samuel **128** 47
Sarah **83** 184 **121** 173
Sarah Ann **73** 276
Thomas **73** 224
Walter **73** 225
William **73** 139
Mullin *see* Mullins
MULLINER
Richard **75** 284
Robert **75** 288
Thomas **75** 282

MULLINS Mulin Mullen
  Mullens Mullin
  Mullines Mullings
  Mullyn Mullyns
  —— **103** 55 170 **117** 14 15
  — Mr. **83** 307
  Abigail **63** 174
  Alice **51** 428 **99** 269 **110** 44
    118 82 **124** 140
  Ann **51** 428 **111** 279 286
  Ann (Fenimore) **111** 281
  Anna **97** 50
  Anna (Sutton) **112** 313
  Anne **111** 281
  Barbary (Tullock) **127** 211
  Bridget (Butler) **86** 360
  Charles Emerson **86** 360
  Charles Ward **86** 360
  Charlotte **101** 36
  Dora (Stanley) **86** 360
  Elizabeth **71** 352 **103** 55
    111 281 286
  Ellen **136** 270
  Frederick L. **120** 235
  Hannah **59** 93 **111** 281 **127**
    209 211
  Hannah D. **79** 41
  Hannah D. (Robinson)
    125 217
  Hannah Smith **101** 69
  Harriet Ann **103** 55
  Helen Alzinella (Cole)
    86 360
  Isaac **51** 428 **144** 13
  Iuer **112** 286
  James **63** 174 **78** 397 **103**
    55 **105** 113
  Jane **123** 110
  Joanna **51** 428
  Joe **117** 124
  John **59** 93 **60** 24 **111** 281
    286 **116** 119 **127** 209
    211
  Joseph **111** 279 281 286
    112 313
  Joseph Norman **86** 360
  Lavina (Hopkins)
    103 170
  Margaret **56** 183
  Marion Day **105** 129
  Martha Ann **112** 313
  Marvin **116** 119
  Mary **110** 243 244 **111** 281
    116 119
  Myra Eleanor (Tuck)
    86 360
  Priscilla **51** 95 428 429 **53**
    206 **54** ciii **56** xlv **58**
    lxxv 217 **59** 221 **60** 144
    65 103 **67** li **73** xxxiv
    78 424 **85** 330 **87** 97 98
    182 316 **99** 269 **101** 334
    102 83 308 **103** 83 148
    154 **105** 221 **106** 82 **110**
    44 **115** 263 **118** 82 **119**
    124 **120** 282 **124** 111
    126 154 **128** 202 **144** 55
  Rebecca **59** 93 **111** 281
    127 209
  Returne **76** 219
  Richard **73** 23

MULLINS *cont'd*
  Robert **82** 59
  Sally Tracy **127** 211
  Samuel **66** 36 **111** 281 286
  Sarah **51** 428 **52** 436
  Sarah LaMent **92** 172
  Thomas **73** 264 **117** 16
  William **51** 428 429 **52** 436
    61 318 **65** 103 **69** lx **70**
    337 **75** lvii **86** 238 360
    91 330 **99** 269 **100** 318
    101 170 **110** 44 **118** 82
    124 111 140 **144** 55
  William F. **84** 30
MULLISON
  Ann (Carver) **118** 107
  Reuben **118** 107
MULLOY Muloy
  Abigail **99** 201
  Anne **99** 197 203
  Catherine **99** 199
  Dennis **87** 122 **99** 197 199
    203
  Edward **87** 126 **99** 201
  Hugh **93** 397 **100** 63
  Jane **85** 447
  Jenny **99** 199
  Mary **99** 199
  Sally **65** 256
  Thomas **87** 125
  William **99** 201
MULLOYNE — Mr. **53** 23
MULLUNLY
  Margdin **64** 114
MULLY
  Elizabeth **75** 288
  Robert **75** 286-288
  Mullyn *see* Mullins
  Mullyns *see* Mullins
MULOCK
  Charles **67** 227
  Maria Louise Forbes
    67 227
  Muloy *see* Mulloy
MULSHOE Mulshow Mulso
  —— **71** 325
  — Mrs. **71** 328
  Robert **71** 327 328 **89** 152
    153
  Thomas **89** 152 153
    139 229
  William **89** 152 153
MULTER
  Sarah Jane **76** 271
  Multon *see* Moulton
MULVANEY
  Patrick **84** 168
MULVIHILL
  M. J. **85** 466
MUM Henry V. **73** 152
MUMATOGUE Abigail
  (Wampatock) **122** 21
  Jeremiah **122** 21
MUMBRUE A. **123** 79
MUMBY Estar **145** 111
MUMFORD Momford
  Munford
  —— **62** 359 **88** 95 **125** 242
    130 279 **144** 293
  — Capt. **77** 67 102 104

MUMFORD *cont'd*
  Abby Christophers **80**
    186 **89** 255
  Abigail **53** 115 **69** 380 **98**
    182 **144** 300
  Abigail (Cheesborough)
    144 300
  Abigail (Cory) **125** 179
  Ada **81** 106
  Andrew **71** 85
  Angelina S. (Jenkins)
    88 95
  Anna **69** 380
  Ann / Anna (Wilson)
    (Ray) **144** 299-302
  Ashbel Woodward
    86 383
  Augustus **69** 380 **102** 235
    144 300
  Augustus Grey **55** 186
  B. Goddard **126** 24
  Benjamin **62** 354 **125** 175
    126 24 **127** 140
  Benjamin A. **125** 176
  Benjamin B. **125** 176
  C. A. (Barker) **125** 176
  C. D. **125** 176
  Caleb **80** 186 **89** 255
  Caroline **55** 186
  Charles Frederick **55** 186
  Charles H. **125** 176
  Clara Gibson **81** 106
  Clarissa **86** 380 383
  Cuff **127** 11
  Deborah **63** 44
  Edmund **53** 115
  Edward **91** 93
  Elihu Hubbard Smith
    88 95
  Elisha **63** 54
  Eliza **127** 15
  Eliza C. **81** 105
  Eliza H. **138** 283
  Eliza Rebach **55** 186
  Elizab **146** 264
  Elizabeth **67** 285 **136** 331
    146 268 269
  Francis **127** 11
  Gardner William **128** 126
  George **125** 23 **142** 4
  George A. **125** 242
  George Elihu **76** 218
  George Huntington
    88 95
  George Saltonstall
    76 218
  Gertrude **81** 105 106
  Gideon **69** 380 **129** 54
    144 300
  Hannah **55** 227 **60** 210 **67**
    286 **112** 184
  Hannah (Latham) **144** 300
  Hannah (Remington)
    125 176
  Harriet **55** 186
  Helen Francis **88** 95
  Helen S. **78** 204
  Helen S. (Ford) **86** 235
  Henrietta Saltonstall **85**
    432 433 **88** 95 **95** 167
  Henry **71** 281

MUMFORD *cont'd*
Henry Huntington **88** 95
Hepzibah (Snelling)
  108 184
Isabella Lee **76** 218
Isabella Mason (Lee)
  76 218
James **125** 179 **126** 21
James Gregory **86** 235
  144 300
James H. **86** 380 383
  126 21
Jane **65** 380 **126** 24
Jireh **63** 44 **88** 41
Jo **63** 53
Johane **85** 137
John **65** 150 **71** 301 **80** 186
  85 82 **89** 255 **98** 118
  108 184 **109** 313 **118**
  269
John B. **126** 24
John P. **125** 238
John R. **125** 176
Joseph **88** 41 **96** 348
Julia Ann **55** 184
Julia Emma **76** 218
Julian Vaill **55** 186
Lucretia **80** 186 **89** 255
Lucretia Christophers
  90 185
Marcy (Goddard) **126** 24
Martha **82** 413
Martha Ann **86** 380
Martha T. **125** 173
Mary **67** 286 294 **71** 85 280
  111 55 **125** 100 179 241-
  243
Mary (Tillinghast) **126** 24
Mary Abigail **55** 186
Mary B. (Prie) **125** 243
Mary E. (Ginkins) **125** 175
Mary L. (Wilson) **125**
  238 242
Mary M. **125** 239 243
Mary Pierce **88** 95 96
Mary S. **88** 95
Mary Sheldon (Smith)
  85 433 **88** 94
Mercy **86** 383
Mercy (Helme) **138** 283
Mercy (Reynolds)
  109 313
Nancy **72** 42 89
Naomi **62** 284
Nathaniel **66** 29 **86** 383
  128 125 **138** 283 **144**
  300 302 304
Patty **79** 45
Paul **69** 380 **144** 300
  147 351
Peace **148** 154
Peleg **67** 286
Peter **55** 186 **127** 140
Phebe **125** 173 177 242 245
Polly **63** 84
Ray **69** 380
Ruth **129** 55
Samuel **128** 135 **147** 335
Samuel S. **125** 243
Sarah **69** 380 **71** 281 **88** 41
  127 87 **144** 300

MUMFORD *cont'd*
Sevilla (Dean) **126** 21
Simon **69** 380
Simon Ray **144** 300
Stephen **111** 55 129 55
Susanna **57** 155 **127** 140
T. **88** 95
Thomas **85** 433 **88** 94 95
  125 179 **136** 177 216
  144 294 296 300
Thomas C. **126** 24
Thomas G. **125** 238 242
Thomas J. **74** xxv 155
Thomas Jefferson **79** 210
  81 105
Thomas Lillibridge
  81 105
William **62** 286 287 **69** 380
  86 383 **144** 299-301
William A. **125** 243
William Woolsey **88** 95
MUMLER
Frederick **78** 302
William H. **74** lxiii
MUMMERY
Mary E. **121** 179
MUMMERYES
Richard **76** 57
MUMTER Henry **58** 202
  Julian **58** 202
MUNCERRY
James A. **121** 178
Mehala (Worthington)
  121 178
Munck *see* Monk
Muncrief *see* Moncrieff
Muncy *see* Munsey
MUND
W. C. (Mrs.) **81** 204
MUNDAY Monday
  Mundy Mundye
  —— **60** 107
Ann **53** 20 **77** xciv
Anne **55** 215 219
Anne May (Seymour)
  96 161
Burt C. **125** 54
Claude (Tunison) **125** 54
Crowell **77** xciv
Deborah Barron **77** xciv
Elizabeth **100** 302
Ezekiel Wilson **58** cix
  59 xlviii
Ezra F. **62** xxxvii 104
Francis **55** 219
John **62** 355 **66** 34
John James (Mrs.) **96** 161
Jonathan **129** 382
Mahlon **99** 41
Martha **88** 284
Mary **74** 13
Mary Jane (Fitz
  Randolph) **99** 41
Matthew **54** 343
Nathaniel **74** 13
Nicholas **62** 104
Richard **65** 125 **141** 98
Samuel **62** 104
Sarah **72** 216
Sarah Ann **89** 183 **142** 377
Thomas **53** 20

MUNDAY *cont'd*
William **61** 342
MUNDELEIN
George **132** 256
MUNDELL
Alexander **73** 279
Elizabeth **60** 241
Ephraim **58** 204
Isabella **60** 241
Jane **60** 241
John **60** 241
Margaret **60** 241
Mary **60** 241
Samuel **60** 241
Sibyl **58** 204
Susanna **73** 275
Thomas **73** 218
William John **60** 241
MUNDEN Elizabeth **58** 296
  64 13
Richard **54** 333
MUNDERSOL
Vincent **84** 152
MUNDINE
Marietta **59** 257
William **59** 257
MUNDON
Daniel **112** 174
John **62** 357
MUNDONE
Angeline **105** 308
MUNDREY
Moris **143** 260
MUNDROW John **61** 366
MUNDS —— **62** 300
Ida **85** 296
Israel **62** 301
Mundson *see* Munson
Mundy *see* Munday
Mundye *see* Munday
Mune *see* Munn
Munford *see* Mumford
MUNGE Mynge
John **67** 35
Mary **67** 35
MUNGEON
Addie W. **103** 48
MUNGER —— **110** 33
— Mr. **71** 51
— Mrs. **71** 45
Abigail **54** 47 49 **112** 45
Abner **54** 50
Ada (Barber) (Miner)
  126 296
Aggephe **54** 49
Albert **54** 50
Alice Marjorie **91** 143
Alonzo **145** 138 139
Amasa **110** 33
Ann **53** 55
Anna **53** 58 **54** 48 **123** 46
Anne **54** 48 49
Anthony **110** 36
Asa **110** 30
Asahel **141** 47 48
Aurelia (Barker) **110** 30
Azubah **54** 48 275
Bela **54** 48 **71** 45
Benjamin **54** 49
Billy **54** 50
Caleb **54** 47 48

MUNGER *cont'd*
Caroline **79** 156
Catherine (Moulton)
110 33
Charles **84** 348
Charlotte **58** lxiv
Chauncey **54** 49 **55** 258
Chloe **54** 49 50
Clarissa (Quackenbush)
110 30
Claude G. **145** 138
Clorinda **54** 48
Daniel **54** 49
Deborah **54** 48
Delancy **110** 36
Deliverance **54** 47
Dinah **54** 48
Dorothy **54** 50 **61** 26 **110**
30 **111** 135
Dorothy (Evarts) **110** 30
Dudley **54** 49 **71** 51
Ebenezer **53** 55 **54** 47-49
56 264
Eber **54** 48
Edward **54** 49
Elam **110** 33
Eleanor **58** lxiv
Elias **54** 48
Elihu L. **54** 49
Elijah **110** 30
Elijah Hinds **56** 374
Elisha **71** 50
Eliza **54** 48 **67** 55
Elizabeth **54** 48 49
Elizabeth (Dudley) **112** 45
Elizur **54** 49
Elnathan **54** 50
Emegene (Wilkenson)
145 138 139
Emeline **54** 50
Emma E. **80** 149
Esther **55** 33
Esther D. **56** 374
Esther Maud (Denno)
145 139
Eunice **110** 36
Eunice (Andrews) **110** 33
Eunice (Needham) **110**
33 36
Everette H. **145** 139
George **57** 139
George C. **84** 140
George Goundry **58** xi
xxxi lvi lxiii
Georgine Dows **58** lxiv
Hannah **54** 48-50 **58** lxiii
Hannah (Corbin) **110** 33
Hannah (Fiske) **110** 30
Hepzibah (Wolcott)
115 103
Hester **54** 49
Hiram **71** 119
Huldah **54** 48 **58** 359
71 119
Increase **54** 50
Irene **54** 50 **110** 36
James **54** 48 50 **55** 33 257
Jane **54** 48 **71** 52
Jehiel **54** 48
Jemima **110** 29
Jeremiah B. **69** 384

MUNGER *cont'd*
Jeremiah Bly **55** xxxv
64 89
Jerusha **54** 49
Jesse **54** 48 **67** 55
Jesse Wescott **80** 149
Joel **54** 49 **58** 359
John **54** 47-49 **61** 26 **110** 36
Jonathan **54** 47 49 **59** 64
Joseph **54** 47 50 **58** lxiii
110 29 30
Josiah **53** 58 **54** 47-49
Julia **54** 49
Levi **54** 50
Levi Henry **145** 139
Linus **54** 49
Lois **54** 49 **58** 302 **59** 64
Lorinda (Chapin) **110** 30
Lorrain **54** 49 **55** 257
Louisa **82** 353
Louise S. (Denno)
145 138
Lovina (Bishop) **110** 29
Lucy **54** 48 **117** 100
Lydia **54** 48
Lyman **54** 48
Lynthia **80** 149
Mabel **54** 49 **56** 360
Marie **58** lxiv
Mary **54** 47-50 **58** 359 **61**
26 **123** 307
Miles **54** 48 49
Miriam **54** 50
Myrtle A. **145** 139
Naomi **110** 30
Naomi (Needham) **110** 29
Nathan **110** 29 30
Nathaniel **54** 48 **123** 311
Nicholas **54** 46-50 **64** 89
Olive **54** 48
Parnel **57** 139
Perley **58** lxiii **110** 30
Philip **54** 50 **56** 24
Rachel **54** 47 50
Rebecca **54** 48 49 **59** 65
61 29 **110** 32 256
Reuben **54** 48 49 **71** 45
110 30 **112** 45 **123** 46
Sally **55** 258 **71** 51 **110** 36
Samantha **110** 36
Samuel **54** 47 49 50 **61** 26
110 29 30 32
Sara S. (Denno) **145** 138
Sarah **54** 46-50 **56** 264
81 113
Sarah Congdon **82** 353
Sarah Elizabeth (Knapp)
(Hoisington) **141**
47 48
Seba **110** 33
Sibyl **54** 50
Sibyl (Parsons) **110** 36
Simeon **54** 49 **110** 36
Submit **55** 33
Subrint **54** 50
Susanna **54** 48-50 **55** 257
110 36
Susanna (Fuller) **110** 30
Timothy **54** 49 50 **55** 257
56 360 **59** 65 **61** 29
Titus **54** 49

MUNGER *cont'd*
W. **91** 374
Wait **54** 48
Washington **82** 353 **91**
374 **110** 33 115 120
Wyllys **54** 49 **55** 33
Zerviah **58** lxiii
MUNGEY John **68** 49
Munnings *see* Munnings
Munion *see* Munnion -
Munjoy *see* Mountjoy
Munk *see* Monk
MUNKHOUSE Monkhouse
Anna Sophia Savage **67**
318 319
Arthur Savage Thornton
67 318
Bird Thornton Savage
67 318
Dorothy **67** 318
Eliza Mary Thornton **67**
318 319
Faith **51** 473 **67** 319
Faith (Savage) **144** 349
Fidelia **51** 473 **67** 318
Fidelia (Savage) **144** 349
Fidelia Savage Thornton
67 318 319
Jane **65** 127
Jane Eleanor Bird **67** 318
319
Lucy Savage Sturgis **67**
318 319
Mary **67** 318
Richard **51** 473 **67** 318 319
144 349
Richard Savage Thornton
67 318 319
MUNN Mun Mune Munne
—— **76** 149 **104** 22
128 312
— Capt. **110** 36
— Mrs. **81** 273
Abigail **89** 303 **123** 259-
261
Abigail (Burt) **148** 224
Abigail (Burtt) (Ball)
86 219
Abigail (Munn) **89** 303
Abigail (Parsons) **123** 260
148 223-225
Ann (Maverick) **97** 58
Benjamin **86** 219 **89** 174
175 **101** 158 **147** 123
148 223 224
Betsey **62** 271
Calvin **62** 271
Calvin Lorin **62** 271
Caroline **62** 366
Charles **62** 271 **79** 167
Christiana **73** 132
Clarissa **89** 303
Clarissa (Munn) **89** 303
David **105** 160
Elijah **89** 206
Eliza **89** 206
Emeline Weld **98** 79
Emma **89** 303
Esther **147** 259
Eunice **89** 303
Eunice (Munn) **89** 303

MUNN *cont'd*
Fanny **62** 271
Hannah **105** 160
Harrison **128** 312
James **104** 122 **105** 160
Jane **89** 303
Jane (Munn) **89** 303
Jessey **89** 303
John **62** 271 **64** 107 **73** 132
  89 303 **104** 22 122 **105**
  160 **123** 260 **144** 221
  148 223 224
Joseph **89** 303
Josiah **105** 160
Levi **62** 267
Lucy **93** 194
Mahala **128** 312
Margaret **105** 160
Mary **104** 220 **105** 160
Nancy **62** 271 **73** 132
Orson Desaix **61** 218
Patrick **97** 58
Phebe **89** 303
Polly **75** 302
Ralph **147** 259
Ransom **147** 259
Rebecca **76** 14
Reuben **62** 266
Sally **89** 303 **125** 294
  128 312
Samuel **62** 264 266 267
Simeon **62** 266
Thankful **62** 265
Thomas **51** 279 **108** 156
Thomas W. **89** 303
Thomas Williams **89** 303
Vincent **65** 177
William B. **104** 220
William Garfield **86** 198
MUNNINGS Munings
  Munning Munninges
  — Mr. **52** 248
Abigail **57** 331
Alice (Wilchine) **141** 243
Anne **57** 331
Catherine **147** 320
Edmond **121** 118
Edmund **62** 168
Elizabeth **57** 331 **73** 239
George **57** 331 **60** 357
  89 174
Gilbert **57** 331
Heed **147** 68
Henry **73** 239
Humphrey **57** 331 **73** 239
John **78** 62 **141** 243
Margaret **56** 183 **141** 236
  237 241
Returne **121** 116 121
Sarah **121** 201
Sarah (Hobart) **121** 116
Take Heed **54** 213
Thomas **57** 331 **73** 239
  141 236
William **59** 103
MUNNION Munion - *see*
  also Lamunyon
Edward **123** 318
Eliza Ann **91** 38
Mary **123** 318
Sarah (Proctor) **123** 318

MUNNON Dorcas **97** 293
MUNNS Iona M. (Curtis)
  83 427 436
John **85** 390
William H. **83** 427 436
Munnter *see* Munter
MUNOWES
Robert **103** 185
MUNROE Munro - *see*
  also Monroe
—— **55** 116 275 357 **56**
  106 **92** 354 **93** 120 **100** 9
  89 202 **120** 211 **121** 302
____ (Daniels) **100** 85
____ (Frazier) **100** 194
____ (Lunt) **145** 313
A. Bradford **117** 288
Abbie (Gorham) **110** 149
Abbie M. **110** 214
Abel **126** 240-245
Abel B. **126** 244-246
Abigail **79** 355 **100** 6 **126**
  240 241 **131** 31 33
Abigail (Richardson)
  100 129
Abigail West **79** 355
Adelaide B. **100** 12
Adelia M **109** 270
Alexander **53** 246
Alfred **56** 217
Alice **127** 166
Almeda Ellen **100** 91
Alpha **100** 199
Alta **100** 204
Amanda **100** 87
Ann **98** 354
Anna **100** 204 **127** 159
  135 305 **146** 340
Anna A. **98** 354
Annis **100** 9
Archibald **126** 23
Arletta A. **110** 214
Armarentia (Fales) **120** 5
Averell **100** 205
Barney **110** 214
Belle (Howard) **100** 92
Belle (Wright) **100** 93
Belvidera **93** 120 **94** 158
Benjamin **114** 109 **121** 52
  217 **124** 177 **127** 164-
  166 **133** 192 **145** 313
Bennett James **120** 6
Bethany (Barron) **126**
  240 242
Betsey **136** 165
Betsey (Briggs) **126** 213
Betsey Ann **107** 150
Betty **121** 49
Beulah **126** 240 241
Beulah (Potter) **126** 240-
  242
Catherine A. (O'Hearn)
  100 12
Celia **100** 86
Charity **100** 85
Charles **117** 213 **124** 177
Charles G. **79** 38
Charlotte A. **126** 246
Clara **100** 196
Clara Jane (Austin)
  100 197

MUNROE *cont'd*
Clarence **110** 214
Comfort **127** 166
Cora **100** 196
D. Eldridge **117** 315
Dan **114** 307
Daniel **114** 184 **117** 16
Daniel N. **110** 149
David **79** 355 **92** 256 354
  94 40 **126** 240 241
David W. **79** 41
Deborah **98** 354 **100** 7 10
  126 245
Deborah (How) **100** 4
Deborah C. (Johnson ?)
  126 245
Deliverance **55** 407
Della **100** 93
Dorothy **82** 282 295 413
  100 196
Edith **114** 229
Edmond **56** 74
Edmund **93** 397
Edmund D. **74** 91
Edward **120** 8
Eleanor **100** 13
Eliza **100** 14 **107** 5
Eliza (Brown) **126** 240 243
Elizabeth **88** 279 **92** 354 **94**
  40 **100** 6 **127** 166 **133**
  192
Elizabeth (Briggs)
  126 213
Elizabeth (Johnson) **100** 3
Elizabeth (Peck) **100** 9
Ella (Pearson) **100** 197
Ellen Aramintha **100** 194
Elsie **100** 10
Elvira A. **126** 244
Emeline C. **116** 259
Emily **100** 12 91
Emily A. **109** 270
Emma (Hicks) **100** 198
Emma F. **92** 139 **93** 129
Emma Frances **92** 149
Emma N. **110** 214
Ernest V. **126** 244
Ernestine **100** 204
Esther **114** 307
Esther (Plumb) **100** 13
Fannie B. **83** 429
Fannie Lee **100** 202
Fidelia **100** 13
Florence G. **100** 195
Frances **100** 199
Francis A. **126** 246
Francis James **126** 243
Frank Adair (Mrs.) **98** 350
Frederick K. **74** 91
George **79** 267 **110** 214
  113 90 **127** 5
George C. **109** 189
Gertrude E. **100** 203
Gladys (Eldred) **100** 201
Grace (Clark) **100** 93
Grace Ludeena **100** 201
H. P. **58** 153
Hannah **79** 321 **89** 264 **100**
  10 11 86 **120** 8 **127** 165
  166

MUNROE *cont'd*

Hannah (Rosbotham) **127** 165
Hannah A. **110** 53
Harriet **85** 337 **126** 244
Harriet Elizabeth **100** 12
Harriet Jane **74** 91
Harriet T. (Hadley) **126** 243
Hattie **110** 214
Helen (Christy) **100** 200
Hurley Anne **100** 198
Irene Hile **100** 203
Irma (Rouse) **100** 197
Isabella Baltimore **126** 243
Iva May (Dean) **100** 202
Jame **127** 304
James **58** 110 **109** 14 **114** 162 241 **116** 84 **117** 221 **126** 242-244
James Henry **92** 248
James L. **109** 270 **126** 246
James Phinney **55** xxxii 230
Jane **100** 86
Jannet **126** 272
Jefferson **110** 214
Jennet **126** 273
Jennie (Eccleston) **100** 200
Jennie (Robinson) **100** 93
Jennie (White) **100** 201
Jessie (Lamoreux) **100** 197
Joanna Ida **126** 244
Joel **117** 213
John **79** 321 **82** 282 295 **102** 32 **108** 247 **116** 111 **126** 240 242 243 245 246 **127** 140 165 166 **133** 192 **140** 240 **145** 24
Joseph **79** 355 **127** 166 **146** 340 341
Josiah **55** 401 407 **98** 354 **126** 23
Jotham **126** 242 243
Jotham Bradley **126** 243 244
Jotham Edward **126** 243 244
Julia (Merrill) **100** 194
Kitty **100** 205
Laurena **100** 205
Lavinia (Gates) **121** 217
Lenzey **127** 305
Leola (Lytle) **100** 195
Leona **100** 200
Lillie (Reines) **100** 202
Lilly Ann **110** 214
Lizzie E. **74** 91
Lois **64** lv
Lois (Smith) **100** 9
Lorette **100** 93
Louisa Jane **100** 88
Louise **100** 195
Lovina **100** 92
Lucinda (Hinckley) **100** 14
Lucretia **92** 256 **145** 313
Lucretia (Gates) **121** 217

MUNROE *cont'd*

Lucy **100** 9 85 **126** 243
Lucy (Silvester) **126** 209
Lucy Ann **100** 12
Lundy (Brooks) **100** 203
Lydia **133** 72
Lydia (Nickerson) **126** 244
Lydia Ellen **94** 55
Lydia Ophelia **100** 93
Mabel L. **94** 27
Madalena A. **126** 245
Madeline **114** 162 241 **116** 84
Madeline Augusta (Ferrar) (Sanchez) **126** 245
Marcella (Sabin) **100** 13
Maria **100** 88 91
Marrett **55** 407
Martha **87** 289 **100** 9
Martha (George) **100** 3
Martha Jerusha **100** 90
Martin A. **126** 245 246
Mary **53** 246 **64** 375 **79** 355 **98** 354 **100** 6 **108** 214 **124** 177 **126** 241 244-246 **127** 166 **133** 232
Mary (Ball) **100** 3
Mary (Carter) **126** 23
Mary (Gladding) **120** 5
Mary (Josselyn) **133** 192
Mary (Miller) **110** 53
Mary (Sawyer) **100** 204
Mary (Swan) **144** 309
Mary (Vallet) **100** 6
Mary (Wadley) **126** 245
Mary (Wardwell) **120** 5
Mary (Wormwell) **127** 165
Mary A. **126** 244
Mary Ann **109** 109
Mary Ann (Hamilton) **100** 14
Mary Belle **100** 93
Mary Bethania **126** 244
Mary Ellen **100** 201
Mary H. **109** 270
Mary Helen (Dame) **91** 204
Mary K. (Lane) **126** l 244
Mary L. (Hannum) **90** 344
Mary Lowana **100** 198
Mary R. **126** 244
Massie Belle **100** 202
Mehitable Converse **92** 256
Melville E. **74** 91
Mercy **124** 177
Millie (Church) (Newton) **100** 198
Minerva **100** 14 85
Minnie (Doty) **100** 202
Miranda **86** 437
Nancy **114** 181
Nathan **127** 165 166 **133** 72
Nathaniel **110** 53 **117** 16 **120** 10 **127** 163 164
Nellie **100** 196 201
Nellie Estelle **100** 202
Nina Belle **100** 200

MUNROE *cont'd*

Nina Mable **100** 202
Olive (Slater) **100** 198
Ora Belle **100** 197
Peter G. **126** 23
Phebe Ann (Clarke) **120** 6
Phebe Ann (Cole) **120** 6
Philip **126** 213 240-242
Rachel **79** 267
Rebecca **108** 247 **126** 240-243 246
Rebecca (Ross) **100** 195
Rebecca (Sadler) **126** 241
Rebecca (Wellington) **108** 247
Rebecca Adams **126** 244
Richard S. **118** 73 **121** 76 **126** 240
Robert **114** 162 241 **116** 84 **126** 245
Robert William **114** 162 241
Rosalthe **109** 270
Rosbotham **127** 166
Rosbothom **98** 245
Ruth (Savage) **100** 205
S. B. **92** 248
Sabrina **109** 270
Sally **100** 12
Sally B. **100** 89
Samuel **109** 270 **120** 5 6 **127** 93
Samuel T. **126** 243 244
Sarah **55** 230 **79** 56 **100** 6 88 **120** 8 **133** 192
Sarah (Burns) **126** 64
Sarah (Fassett) **100** 8
Sarah (Ryan) **125** 293
Sarah (Throop) **126** 23
Sarah Catherine **126** 244
Sarah Elizabeth **100** 195
Sarah Jane **126** 246
Sarah L. (Fish) **120** 6
Sarah Throop (Child) **126** 23
Shubael **124** 177
Sibyl (Tyler) **100** 92
Solomon **126** 209
Solomon Dockendorf **74** 91
Sophia **88** 278
Sophia B. **126** 246
Stephen **127** 166
Stephen Cranston **79** 355
Susan **92** 252 **110** 214
Susan Barney **92** 246 **93** 319
Susan Barney (Grinnell) **92** 246
Susan D. **126** 246
Susan Sophia **92** 252
Susanna **55** 401 407 **79** 321 **100** 85
Theodore J. **126** 244
Thomas **127** 165 166 305
Timothy **121** 217
Viola (Hall) **100** 204
Vivian F. **100** 198
W. H. **118** 290
Walter G. **109** 270
Washington **125** 293

MUNROE *cont'd*
Wilfred H. **119** 41 109
  124 176
Wilfred Harold **64** xix
William **55** 230 **92** 248 252
  93 319 **98** 354 **109** 270
  114 229 **118** 73 **121** 76
  124 176 177 **126** 240
  242 243 245 **127** 163 164
  144 218
William Augustus **92** 248
William Bennett **64** 283
William C. **93** 120 **94** 158
William H. **126** 240
William Henry **126** 243
William W. **126** 244
William Wallace **126** 243
  244
Wilson S. **74** 91
MUNROSS
Hephzibah **71** 281
Timothy **71** 281
MUNS
Elizabeth **80** 364
Jerome **80** 406-408
John **80** 364 406 408
Richard **80** 407
Robert **61** 268
MUNSELL Maunsel
  Maunsell Munsel
  Munsill
— Mr. **57** 239
Anna **52** 411 **116** 39
Azubah **101** 143 144
Azubah (Huntley)
  101 144
Betsey **78** 379 **101** 144
Charity **71** 281
Charlotte **80** 64
Chloe (Squire) **114** 182
Daniel **52** 411 **118** 105
  145 368
Dorothy **61** 229
Dorothy (Redington)
  109 114
Elisha **61** 229 **109** 114
Elizabeth **90** 62
Esther **101** 202
Esther (Miller) **100** 270
Eunice **52** 411 420 **118** 105
Eunice (Downer) (Carver)
  118 105
Evelina **80** 64
G. **55** 38
Gurdon **55** 37 38 283
  88 321
Hannah **71** 280
James **100** 270 **101** 202
Joel **52** 88 280 **54** xxxv 118
  55 xxviii 129 130 **56**
  xxix 215 **58** 99 **59** xxxix
  65 xxviii **66** xxxiv **75**
  67 **89** 168 **99** 92 **103** 98
  145 232 233
John **59** 353 **78** 379 **90** 62
  101 144 205 **145** 368
Joseph **101** 144 **145** 368
Lois **52** 224
Lucina **55** 283
Lucy **55** 37
Luman **101** 144

MUNSELL *cont'd*
Lydia **78** 379 **100** 271
Lydia (Huntley) **101** 205
Mary **100** 270 271
Mehitable **101** 144
Olive **56** 354
Olive (Carver) **88** 321
Phebe **63** 336
Richard **145** 368
Sherman **101** 200
Solomon **73** 104
Thomas **100** 271 **142** 235
Timothy **80** 64
Ursula (Huntley) **101** 200
William **94** 13
Zaccheus **71** 280
MUNSEY Muncy
— **59** 331
Andrew **81** 483 **104** 219
Andrew Chauncey **74** 161
  81 483 **104** 219
Betsey (Sawyer) **104** 219
David **61** 96 **81** 483
Emma **91** 274
Emma Jane **81** 484
Francis **60** 314 316 **106** 169
  112 75 **118** 53 56
Frank Andrew **73** 318
  74 xxv 161 **80** 106 216
  81 483 484
Hannah **60** 314 316
Henry **95** 382
John **60** 314 **61** 96 **81** 483
Margaret **61** 96
Mary **59** 221 **61** 96
Mary Jane Merritt **74** 161
  81 483
Mary Jane Merritt
  (Hopkins) **104** 219
Nathaniel **105** 284
Olive (Davis) **95** 382
Samuel **60** 314
Solomon **96** 222 223
Timothy **59** 221 **61** 96 **81**
  483 **104** 219
William **60** 188 316 **61** 96
  201 202 **81** 483
Munsill *see* Munsell
MUNSON Mundson
— **54** 388 **56** 286 **58** 110
  60 111
— Dr. **79** 307
— Rev. Mr. **124** 276
Abigail **59** 359 **66** 332
  115 38
Abigail (Preble) **119** 68
Aeneas **79** 164
Albert **108** 68
Albert M. **92** 172
Alfred S. **79** 152
Almira **75** lxxviii
Althana **111** 306
Amy Treadwell **85** 89
Asa **76** 53 **118** 106
Asahel **97** 392
Augustus **75** 95
Betsey Norcross **79** 166
C. D. **127** 72
Caleb **58** 180
Caroline **75** 310
Catherine **88** 394

MUNSON *cont'd*
Celia H. **111** 130
Charles **111** 306
Charles D. **127** 70 73
Comfort **104** 71
Daniel **85** 89
David **54** 26 **111** 306
Delilah A. **124** 34
Don Alonzo **111** 306
Dorcas **54** 26
Dunham Ockerman **78**
  331 **79** 203
Ebenezer **66** 332
Edward A. **79** 21
Eliza J. **101** 34
Elizabeth **57** 331 332 **58**
  180 **66** 310 **67** 55 **111**
  306 **115** 43 119
Elizabeth (Andrus) **85** 89
Emma **85** 349 **111** 306
Ephraim **123** 311
Esther **56** 138 286 **59** 69
Esther J. **127** 72 73
Esther J. (Williams)
  127 70
Eunice **52** 78 **75** 97
  136 313
Ezra **69** 164
Garry **77** 44 **85** 88 89
George **111** 130
George Thomas **111** 306
Hannah **57** 134 **59** 70 72
  62 203 **69** 57 **75** 194
Hannah (Booth) **85** 89
Hannah Lyman **93** 183
Harriet **77** 44
Harriet (Johnson) **92** 172
Harriet (Lyman) **85** 88 89
Harriet A. **79** 21
Harriet Johnson **92** 172
Harvey **84** 214
Henry **91** 330
Hester Ann **101** 33
Huldah **87** 376
Irene **70** 82
Isaac **75** 310 **111** 306
Jared **111** 306
Jennie Belle **89** 30
Jerusha (Fowler) **85** 89
Jesse **115** 44
Joanna **66** 310
Joel **71** 7 **79** 166
John **56** 280 **57** 331 332
  66 310 **67** 50 **71** 9 **141**
  36
Jonathan **75** 97 **85** 349
  112 48
Joseph **75** 193 **121** 85
Joshua **119** 68
Julia Ann **111** 306
Julia M. **111** 130
Lavinia Lucy **69** 164
Levi **112** 47
Lorana **111** 306
Loretta **93** 88 **101** 225 226
Loveland **105** 73
Lucinda **75** 193
Lucretia **71** 13
Lucy (Riley) **106** 212
Lucy Ann **108** 68
Luisa **115** 20

MUNSON *cont'd*
Lydia **109** 188
Mabel **77** 92
Magnis **145** 349
Mansfield **108** 68 **115** 20
Margaret **75** 178 **112** 44
Margery **57** 331
Margery (Hitchcock)
  121 85
Martha **57** 134 **66** 310 311
  67 49
Martha (Bradley) **85** 89
Mary **54** 388 **59** 72 **66** 310
  67 49 **115** 43
Mary (Pineo) **85** 349
Mary (Wilcox) **85** 89
Mary A. **79** 152 307
Mary Ann **124** 34
Mary Elizabeth **84** 214
Mary Jane (Orr) **89** 30
May **71** 7
Mehitable **71** 9
Merriam **56** 138
Milton Delos **89** 30
Mindwell **131** 316
Moses **112** 44
Myron A. **51** 380 383
  75 97
Myron Andrews **66** 1 310
  85 89
Nicholas **124** 34
Obadiah **59** 70 72 **85** 89
  108 68
Obedience **67** 49
Phebe (Merriman) **112** 44
Phebe (Robinson)
  111 130
Polly **75** 95 310 **115** 308
Rachel (Tyler) **85** 89
Rebecca **53** 88
Richard **57** 331 **61** 309 310
Robert **61** 309 310 **85** 89
Ruth **67** 50
Samuel **56** 134 **57** 134 **66**
  310 311 **67** 49 **85** 89 **108**
  68 **112** 51 **115** 140
Samuel L. **74** 157
Samuel Lyman **75** xxiii
  77 44 **85** 88 89 106 187
  202 **93** 139 182 183
Sarah **56** 283 **67** 50 **71** 9
  85 349
Seneca L. **71** 13
Serena Ann (King)
  97 392
Serena Narcissa **97** 392
Stephen **68** 173 **85** 89
  106 212 **115** 37 **119** 195
Submit **115** 20
Susan **57** 331
Susan B. **101** 215
Susan Babcock **77** 44
Susan Babcock (Hopkins)
  85 89
Tamar **67** 49
Thankful **116** 203
Theophilus **56** 280 **59** 69
Thomas **51** 98 **56** 283 **57**
  134 331 332 **66** 310 **78**
  158 **85** 88 89 **89** 175 **108**
  68 **121** 82

MUNSON *cont'd*
Titus **112** 47
Waitstill **56** 286
Walter **59** 72 **108** 68
William **69** 54
MUNSTEAD Ascar **76** 46
Muntchesny *see*
  Montchensey
MUNTER Munnter
Alice **139** 324
Ann (Rawlings) **139** 324
Elizabeth **139** 322-324
Elizabeth (Johnson)
  139 323
Henry **139** 322
Jane **139** 323 324
John **139** 322
Katharine **139** 323 324
Margery **139** 322
Nicholas **139** 324
Phineas **139** 322-324
Sarah (Baker) **139** 322
Susan **67** 172 **68** 142 **75**
  225 **86** 334 **87** 211 **131**
  127 **139** 322 324
Thomas **139** 324
Muntjoy *see* Mountjoy
MUNTLE William **115** 42
MUNTON William **65** 131
MUNUE Francis **66** 58
Katharine **66** 58
Munyan *see* Munion
Munyon *see* Munion
MUNZIG
George Chickering
  62 314
MURAN James **73** 138
MURAT —— **145** 201
MURCH Abigail **71** 220
Benjamin **105** 290
Charlotte **142** 299
Colman W. **91** 199
Daniel **142** 299
Deborah **71** 217 **111** 94
  114 47
Deborah (Emery) **120** 79
Dorcas **142** 299
Elizabeth **90** 52
Emily **88** 287 **92** 131
Ephraim **105** 290
George W. **83** 421 436
Hannah **71** 219 220 224
Hannah (Kent) **114** 49
Hattie L. (Allen) **83** 418
  421 436
Joanna **111** 24
John **71** 217 221 **111** 24
  114 49
M. B. **66** 1
Mary **90** 50
Matthias **92** 129 131
  142 299
Oliver **83** 412
Phebe **90** 56
Philena **88** 338
Polly **142** 299
Priscilla **90** 47
Rosanna (Newcomb)
  (Rich) (Chase) **83** 412
Samuel **71** 220 **88** 336
  120 79

MURCH *cont'd*
Sarah **71** 222 **92** 131
  126 144
Sarah L. (Sawyer) **88** 336
Tabitha **71** 220 **111** 24
Tabitha (Young) **111** 24
  114 48
Thomas Perkins **92** 129
Walter **71** 130 218 220
  111 94 **114** 47
William **71** 222 **105** 290
  111 24 **114** 48
MURCHIE Murchy
Ruth Elizabeth **101** 125
  119 149
William **117** 16
MURCHISON
Alma **82** 438
Daisy **78** 328
Iza Polk **78** 328
John **52** 312 **78** 328
John Le Gory **78** 328
John Smith **78** 328
Josephine Augusta
  78 328
K. M. **81** 204
Kate **81** 204
Katharine **109** 221
Laura **77** 265
Luola **81** 204
Martha **78** 328
William Polk **78** 328
MURCOTT Edward **140** 181
MURDAC Alice **75** 63 **76**
  295 298-300
Beatrice **75** 63 **76** 300
Eva **76** 295 298-300
Geoffrey **96** 318
Joan **76** 301
Maud **76** 301
Ralph **76** 295 298-300
  102 296
MURDAGE Laura **65** 8
MURDICK
Betsey **123** 92 302
Henry Francis **123** 302
Josiah Wallace **123** 302
Martha Elizabeth **123** 302
Mary **123** 229
Mary Eliza **123** 302
Nathaniel Turner **123** 302
Samuel **123** 302
Samuel H. **123** 92
Murdo *see* Murdough
MURDOCK Murdoch
—— **55** 53 **87** 262 **95** 103
— Miss **69** 69
— Mrs. **64** 288
— Prof. **62** 172 177 238
  239
Abigail **71** 148
Abraham **62** 239
Adaline Sarah **88** 373 374
Addison **73** 232
Agnes **78** 206
Alexander **118** 56
Amos **85** 339
Anna **62** 238 239 **71** 203
Anna Cleveland **143** 160
Anne (Dillingham)
  85 340

MURDOCK *cont'd*
Ariel **85** 339
Bartlett **122** 134
Beamish **67** 290 **116** 12
Benjamin **52** 276
Bethiah **71** 149
Betsey C. **90** 114
Calvin **93** 345
Carrie **69** 207
Charles **89** 242 **145** 173
Charlotte **145** 173
Clarissa Jane **137** 181 182
Dan **71** 203
Deborah **122** 134
Deborah (Perkins)
   122 134
Edmund **145** 173
Edward **143** 160
Edward Hamilton
   143 160
Eliphalet **71** 203
Elizabeth **71** 148 **84** 99
Enoch **62** 238
Esther **71** 148
Eunice **71** 203 **85** 339
Eunice (Dix) **137** 181
Eunice (Murdock) **85** 339
Frances **62** 239
Frances E. **77** 15
George **70** 311 **80** 225
   94 298
George L. **93** 345
Grace A. (Wheeler)
   126 293
H. K. **69** 207
Hannah **51** 320 **62** 239 **71**
   148 151 267 346 **84** 99
Hannah (Stedman)
   85 339
Harold **63** xxxiii **65** 384
   79 325 **80** 202
Hephzibah **77** 207
Irvine **85** 339
Jacob W. **78** 73
James **62** 239 **73** 132 **122**
   134 **145** 172
Jane **64** 210 **134** 334
Jerusha **98** 181 **121** 65
Jesse **122** 135
John **52** 56 **55** 77 **57** 280
   62 171 239 **63** 355 **71**
   149 267 **73** 104 **77** 207
   85 339 **120** 12
John Andrew **72** 115
John Nelson **85** 339
Joseph B. **80** 225
Joseph Ballard **72** xx **78**
   112 **85** 339 345 **86** 204
Joshua **71** 148 **87** 262
Lois **68** 205
Loretta (Wardwell)
   89 242
Louise M. Hamilton
   143 160
Lucia K. **70** 345
Lucinda (Chase) **87** 262
Lucy **71** 203
Lucy Ann **72** 115
Lydia **62** 239
M. D. **128** 175
Mariamne Craik **73** 265

MURDOCK *cont'd*
Martha **71** 267
Martha Ann (Ballard)
   85 339
Martha Elizabeth
   (Benchley) **143** 159 160
Mary **52** 276 **61** 306 **62** 238
   65 371 **74** 64 **93** 345 **94**
   298 **104** 268 **121** 179
Mary (Paine) **104** 268
Mary A. **94** 298
Mary Florence **101** 167
Mary Taft **95** 175
Peter **80** 225 **86** 181
Phebe **55** 77 **114** 252
   123 132
Philina (Walker) **143** 160
Rebecca **73** 218 **93** 346
Rebecca B. **93** 345
Rebecca W. **77** 153
Robert **71** 148 151 152 267
   78 112 **80** 225 **85** 339
Ruth **52** 56
Ruth (Chase) **87** 262
Samuel **61** 306 **63** 355 **68**
   205 **71** 148 203 **79** 54
Samuel R. **72** 115
Sarah **71** 149 267
Sarah (Himes) **85** 339
Sarah (Read) **85** 339
Sibyl (Flint) **85** 339
Sophia **90** 370
Stephen **137** 181
Submit **71** 203
Susanna (Ellis) **122** 135
Thankful **71** 148
Thomas **63** 355 **93** 360
Thomas J. **70** 345
Tressa Isabelle **101** 123
William **80** 225 **104** 268
William A. **77** 151
William G. **65** 302 **66** 1
William Henry **145** 173
MURDOUGH Murdo
Edgar A. **121** 182
Hannah A. **90** 57
James **117** 282
John **80** 225 **117** 282
Josie A. (Pollard) **121** 182
Mary A. **117** 282
MURDY Sara **101** 120
   102 120
Muretgomery *see*
   Montgomery
MURFEILD
Christopher **65** 288
MURFIN Anne **89** 180
MURFORD
Marie **112** 158
Marie (Leake) **112** 159
William **112** 158 159
MURFREE — Col. **145** 31
MURFYN
Frances **51** 211
Thomas **51** 211
MURHOFF Sarah Jane
Clark **94** 52
MURIOLO
Geoffrey de **102** 296
MURIOUS
Alexander de **103** 156

MURIOUS *cont'd*
Alvered de **103** 156
Geoffrey de **103** 156
Gua de **103** 156
Roger de **103** 156
MURKLAND Mary **97** 130
Mary A. **125** 113
MURLIN
Lemuel Herbert **74**
   160 161
MURMEEL
Mary Lathrop **81** 392
MURÓ
Margarita de **86** 195
MUROE
Abigail **131** 31 33
MUROUGH
Deliverance **54** 47
Richard **54** 47
MURPHY Morphey
   Morphy Murphee
   Murphey
   —— **62** 362 **76** 13 **124** 78
   — Capt. **101** 219
Abigail **116** 119
Ada S. **84** 30
Agnes **73** 102 103
Alice **107** 272 274 **108** 54-
   57 59
Alice (Littlefield) **108** 123
Alice B. (Murrey) **128** 93
Amos **108** 54
Ann **51** 461 **88** 389 **125** 302
Ann Elizabeth **78** 47
Anna **78** 190
Anne **86** 360
Annie M. **87** 376
Arthur **61** 267
B. **64** 223
B. J. (Mrs.) **125** 75
Barbary **100** 303
Bartholomew **92** 228
Benjamin **96** 245
Bertha Louise (Bradford)
   110 55
Bertram (Mrs.) **103** 227
Betsey **96** 245
Betsey (Waymouth) **95**
   196 **96** 143
Blossom **82** 269
Bridget **139** 211 213 215
Caroline **96** 133
Cassie **76** 13
Catherine **73** 102 **84** 378
   142 77
Charity **74** 264
Charity (Heard) **96** 337
Charles **64** 325 **100** 190
Charles Stuart (Mrs.)
   91 142
Charles T. **127** 80
Charlotte **73** 285
Claire Warren **82** 269
Clara **116** 119
Cora **101** 217
Cora Anna **78** 47 329
Daniel **64** 345
Darwin D. **127** 80
David **73** 98 **111** 139
Dennis **100** 329
Ebenezer **62** 353 **102** 23

MURPHY *cont'd*
Edward **127** 10
Eliza **73** 98 **77** 54 **97** 16
Elizabeth **73** 102 267 **74**
  308 **77** 52 **78** 40 **95** 16
  100 136 **108** 192 **117**
  289 **139** 215
Elizabeth (Brinton)
  100 300
Elizabeth (Downing)
  108 120
Elizabeth B. **91** 3
Elizabeth Miller **96** 245
Ellen (Beaumont) **126** 234
Elmira **73** 98
Emily **96** 245 **97** 224 232
Emma **101** 215
Florence N. **117** 293
Francis **61** 135
Francis P. **139** 194
Franklin **55** 126
Gardiner **73** 98
George **95** 199 **96** 144
  100 190
George A. **110** 55
George Charles Henry
  100 190
George W. **85** 378
Georgiana Augusta
  110 55
Hannah **85** 374 **86** 301 **96**
  340 **108** 121 123 189
  142 77
Hannah (Giles) **96** 344
Hannah (Lazell) **88** 262
Hannah M. **85** 372 373
Hannah S. (Reed) **85** 375
Harrison **108** 191
Henry **91** 331
Henry C. **119** 161
Hugh **60** 27
Isabel H. **85** 375
Isaiah **142** 77
James **51** 461 **60** 24 161
  61 351 **63** 31 **72** 310
  117 293 **142** 28
James L. **127** 80
Jane **109** 295
Jane (Seavy) **108** 192
Jane Elizabeth (Patton)
  97 384
Jemima **83** 51
Jennie E. **130** 54
Jeremiah **64** 315 **77** 229
  142 77
Jerry S. **100** 328 329
John **53** 436 **57** 237 238
  58 xli **60** 348 349 **68** 20
  73 102 103 **85** 375 **96**
  340 **97** 14 229 233 **104**
  290 **108** 59 120
John B. **127** 80
John Bradford **110** 55
John E. **108** 301
John H. **101** 34 **115** 294
John J. **80** 226
John James **90** 299
John L. **59** 120
Joseph **114** 188
Joseph P. **142** 28

MURPHY *cont'd*
Josephine (Bridges)
  85 373
Joshua **71** 224 **85** 372 **107**
  272 274 **108** 54 55 57 59
  123
Josiah Fitch **100** 190
Julia **125** 176 **126** 233
Katharine **100** 236 **102** 32
Keziah **73** 315 **96** 146
Lily M. D. **114** 19
Lois (Manchester) **102** 23
Loreetta **96** 245
Louisa A. (Abbott) **85** 378
Luke **117** 16
Lukey **142** 201
Lydia (Tibbets) **96** 340
M. W. **101** 214
Mabel Henrietta (Fellows)
  91 142
Margaret **104** 160 289
  111 290 **117** 118 126
  125 175 260 **139** 212
  213 215 **142** 77
Margaret (Crownin-
  shield) **104** 290
Margaret (Nowlan)
  92 228
Margaret Bradford
  110 55
Margaret H. (Dawes)
  85 372
Margaretta Alice **81** 339
Maria **73** 102
Martha A. **127** 80
Martha Ann (Kinney)
  108 301
Martha B. (Hanson)
  97 229 233
Martin **60** 220 **142** 77
Mary **53** 436 **60** 361 **61** 351
  73 102 **77** 182 **85** 375
  89 111 **93** 350 **100** 234
  329 **108** 189 191 **117** 40
  125 179 **139** 211 212
  142 77 201
Mary (March) **108** 191
Mary (McCray) **111** 139
Mary (Nason) **97** 14
Mary A. **127** 80
Mary Agnes **55** lxxxiv
Mary E. **100** 329
Mary E. (Adams) **100** 329
Mary E. (Shubael) **100** 328
Mary Eliza **77** 153
Mary H. **116** 184
Mary L. **97** 235
Mary May **72** 310
Mary Ruth (Mitchell)
  90 299
Mattie **82** 269
Mellen **73** 98
Michael **65** 240
Mildred **107** 318
Moses **108** 55
Murdock **95** 16 18
Murray Griffin **104** 145
Nancy (Colby) **83** 416
Nicholas **100** 136 233 236
  300 303 **101** 276 **102** 32
Olivia **68** 20

MURPHY *cont'd*
Owen **61** 135 **78** 411
Patrick **73** 315 **74** 125 127
  194 **95** 196 **96** 143 245
  344
Patrick Waymouth
  96 245
Peter **83** 416
Peter Henry **97** 384
Pierce **108** 123 192 **142** 200
Polly **93** 350 **125** 242
Rebecca (Walker) **95** 199
Rebecca (Worthen)
  96 144
Reuben **85** 373
Reynold **62** 355
Rhoda E. **85** 374
Richard **52** 42 **64** 261 **114**
  188 **139** 211 212
Robert **111** 290
Robert Hanley **78** 47
Ruth **84** 378 **100** 233 236
  102 32
Ruth (Adams) **100** 303
Sally **96** 146 **97** 17
Samuel **74** 264 **96** 245 337
  107 272
Sarah **61** 267 **73** 103 **86** 122
  96 245 **100** 136 **108** 191
  111 290 **142** 201
Sarah (Adams) **108** 123
Sarah (Moran) **136** 271
Sarah B. (Ferris) **101** 34
Sarah Florence **117** 128
Statira **73** 98 **114** 146
Stephen **96** 245
Sukey **73** 98
Susan **108** 57
T. F. **90** 9
Terence **61** 269
Thomas **60** 161 361 **63** 26
  73 315 **77** 318 **84** 30 **93**
  299 **95** 86 **96** 245 **119** 21
  128 93
Timothy **95** 401
Timothy C. **144** 113
Virginia Eleanore **110** 55
Walter James (Mrs.) **102**
  124 **120** 149
Walter Patten **88** 169 **89**
  130 **97** 148 161 384 385
William **100** 190 234 **107**
  272 **114** 188 **116** 119
William D. **108** 12
William J. **77** 153
William Walton **126** 234
William Warren **82** 269
MURRAUGUN **145** 341
MURRAY Murrey Murry
  Mury
  —— **56** 333 **69** 168 **97** 127
  112 266 **117** 15 17 **123**
  308
— Col. **119** 134 206 292
  296 **120** 205
— Maj. **119** 43
— Mr. **73** 71 **76** 142
— Mrs. **104** 67 **121** 63
— Rev. Mr. **74** 182
A. **53** 247
Abigail **55** 257 **99** 128

MURRAY cont'd
116 288 126 98 281 127
125
Abigail Wiggin 86 235
106 309
Abner 55 256
Abraham 124 160
Ada F. 89 351
Addie (Hurd) 97 127
Adelia 56 171
Agnes (Gray) 111 139
Albert N. 72 xx 90 130
Albert Nickerson
77 xxvii
Alexander 83 297 300 98
198 117 9 11 16 118 45
46
Alfred R. A. 114 190
Alice 74 228
Alice B. 128 93
Alice Isadora (Purinton)
108 309
Alice R. 132 306
Alta (Munroe) 100 204
Amasa 55 256
Ann 55 255 256 56 112 62
170 125 219
Anna 54 271 55 255 256 57
135 76 145 97 48
Anna Bronson 78 133 134
Anna Morris 113 225
Anthony 86 122
Asahel 55 256 257 126 170
Augusta 107 235
Augustus 55 257
B. M. 89 351
Barbara (Bennet) 110 143
Barbara Bennet 54 xcviii
Benjamin 75 197 100 146
Benjamin D. 101 34
Beriah 55 256 257
Betsey 62 170 73 71 90 249
Betsey (Hopkins) 102 261
Beulah 55 257
Beulah Maria 55 258
Calvin 55 258
Calvin Nelson 55 258
Catherine 55 257
Catherine (Bourne) 89 57
Catherine Wilhelmina
83 112
Charles 99 128 126 98
127 202 203
Chauncey D. 55 258
Chester P. 125 54
Christianna Wilhelmina
83 112
Clarissa A. 89 246
Cornelia E. (Eastman)
125 54
Cornelia Groot 108 309
Curtiss 55 257
Cynthia Ann 123 128
Daniel 55 255-257 126 225
David 56 190 65 244 69
385 127 125
David W. 86 16
Deborah (Brindley)
84 262
Della 117 206
Diademia 55 258

MURRAY cont'd
Dickinson 55 258
Dorcas 55 256 57 91
Dorothy 54 xcviii 110 143
112 266
Dorothy (Emerson)
91 230
Dorothy Bruce 54 1
Ebenezer 123 128
Eber 55 257 258
Edward 102 28
Edward Morris 113 225
Edy 123 128
Eleanor 96 127
Eleanor Vinton (Clark)
113 224
Electra 107 235
Elijah 84 137
Elisha 53 247
Eliza Bradlee Winchester
78 134
Eliza H. 120 216
Elizabeth 53 247 55 257 86
65 104 231 106 23 230
112 212 266 272-274 296
113 5 10 114 190 124
160 140 241 145 309
Elizabeth (Cheesman)
89 57
Elizabeth (Tibbetts) 99 55
Elizabeth (White) 112 49
Elizabeth S. (Gowen)
97 234
Ellen F. 82 279
Elmira 89 13
Elspeth Mona 68 121
Emeline B. (Hurlbut)
89 246
Emily 55 258
Erva Jane 107 235
Esther 55 256 123 128
Ethel Gwynna 76 xxi 89
57 82 135
Etta D. (Keeler) 125 54
Eunice 53 247 74 256
Eunice Gould 97 382
Ezra 55 256
Ezra Burbank 127 125
Florence (Boardman) 83
297 300
Florence Ione 71 xxiii
Frances L. (Porter)
123 128
Frank 58 xiv
George 100 204
George Henry 108 309
George M. 123 128
George Monticellane
123 128
George Mudd 107 235
Georgia S. 147 63
Georgiana 78 205 100 204
Georgiana (Groot)
108 309
Gertrude 96 179
Gilbert 80 191 89 246
Gilbert E. 83 112
H. H. (Mrs.) 77 322
Ham W. 97 234
Hannah 53 247 63 176 65
353 74 258

MURRAY cont'd
Hannah (McGlauflin)
101 34
Hannah (Silvester)
(Newell) 86 122
Hannah (Tibbetts)
100 146
Hannah Ann 84 137
Hannah Haskell 126 68
Harriet A. (Thompson)
123 128
Harriet S. 73 194
Hart 55 257
Harvey 55 258
Henrietta M. 107 235
Henriette 131 97 207
Henry Alexander 95 147
Henry Franklin 97 382
Henry Franklin (Mrs.) 96
161 97 149 382 98 151
Henry Hotchkiss 108 309
Henry Hotchkiss (Mrs.)
78 205 108 125 140 309
Hester 52 468 55 255
Hope 53 55 55 255
127 202
Hope (Freeman) 99 128
Horace 55 257
Hugh 61 268 68 121 78
407 114 190 130 158
Huldah 55 257 99 303
123 128
Isaac H. 100 144
Isabella 53 247 86 16
Isabelle 81 381
J. 123 127 144 207
Jacquith 94 291
James 51 42 53 247 54
xcviii 56 332 60 162 62
93 301 63 44 176 191 67
9 74 218 259 265 89 16
110 143 111 139 112
266 272-274 114 190
117 16 129 57 137 315
James A. 115 314 116 156
James Augustus Henry
67 62
James B. 78 133
James E. 117 236
James M. 114 190
Jane 90 44
Jane (Shirley) (Marr)
130 158
Jane Melville (Hunt)
107 235
Jean 108 221
Jehiel 55 255 256 57 114
Jeremiah 91 331
Jesse 54 272 55 256-258
Joanna 126 98 281 127 53
125 202 203
Joanna (Tupper) 99 128
123 131 126 98
John 53 247 55 255-258
61 43 62 301 64 188 65
220 68 144 72 105 73
151 74 189 215-218 224
225 72 228 246 250 77 239
82 384 84 262 377 382
87 298 89 57 91 203 97
113 99 128 100 190 105

MURRAY *cont'd*
10 **107** 45 **109** 245 **115**
222 **123** 128 **125** 42 54
218 263 **126** 98 **127** 53
129 104 **130** 187 **135**
150 **137** 10
John E. **89** 203
John Frank **123** 128
John Kneeling **76** 143
John L. **100** 204 205
107 235
John R. **107** 235
Jonathan **51** 491 **52** 468 **53**
55 **55** 255-258 **57** 91 116
135 **60** 188 **76** 158
Joseph **53** 247 **54** 196 **76**
143 145 **106** 28
Joseph King **89** 57
Judith Sargent **85** 353
Julia M. **107** 235
Julius **55** 257
June **107** 235
Kate R. **124** 148
Katharine **68** 121
Kendall G. **94** 30
Laura C. (George)
123 128
Laura Dell **123** 128
Laurena Alta **100** 205
Lawrence George
100 204
Leo **107** 235
Leroy Samuel **100** 205
Lilly (Campbell) **137** 315
Lindley **89** 57
Lois **55** 257
Lorrain **54** 49 **55** 257
61 29
Louisa **55** 50
Louise Welles **60** 188
Lucinda **112** 49 **132** 300
Lucy **55** 256 257 **127** 125
Lucy (Ford) **99** 128
127 125
Lucy (Hanks) **86** 16
Lurana (Tibbetts) **100** 146
Lydia **55** 256 257 **57** 92
72 105 **74** 260
Mabel **55** 256 257 **56** 263
Margaret **51** 491 **73** 139
74 251 **87** 26 **88** 330
116 187 **122** 270 **127**
125
Margaret (Killgore)
134 173
Margaret Francis **107** 235
Maria **78** 133 **94** 160
Marjorie Louise **100** 205
Martha **53** 247 **74** 260 265
86 16 **145** 140
Mary **53** 247 **55** 111 256
257 **63** 239 **73** 92 **74** 224
257 **82** 403 **90** 228 244
92 146 **96** 158 **99** 128
100 108 138 **115** 220
126 66 98 **127** 202
Mary (George) **123** 128
Mary (Lindley) **89** 57
Mary (Talbot) **100** 144
Mary A. **107** 235
Mary Ann **55** 257

MURRAY *cont'd*
Mary B. **123** 128 **130** 53
Mary E. **94** 30
Mary Eunice M. Bell
123 128
Mary G. **123** 128
Mary Grace **87** 173
Mary Vinton **113** 225
Matthew **100** 138
Maude M. **107** 235
Maude Venita **123** 128
Menerva Jane **116** 316
Mindwell **55** 257
Molly **90** 246 **109** 147
N. **64** 223
Nabby **63** 176 **74** 259
Nancy (Smith) **125** 218
Nancy Morris **113** 225
Nathan **55** 256 **63** 171 **74**
217 258
Nehemiah **102** 261
127 125
Nellie Hamlin **107** 135
Nicholas **114** 190
Nicholas Russell **106** 77
Noah **60** 188
Olive **63** 171 **74** 258
Onslow **125** 31
Parthena **53** 247 **67** 126
Patience **53** 247
Patrick **61** 136 **119** 21
Patrick Henry **72** 309
Peleg **62** 289 **127** 202
Peres Ford **127** 202
Peter Warren **55** 256
Phebe **93** 214 **96** 179
Phebe (Campbell) **96** 179
Phebe (Manchester)
102 28
Phedora **69** 168
Philemon **53** 247
Philip **96** 179
Philo **55** 257
Pierce **55** 257
Polly **55** 257 **58** 18 **126** 170
Polly (Murry) **126** 170
Rachel **54** 272 **55** 257 258
Rainey (Tibbetts) **100** 146
Rebecca **55** 257 **61** 29
Reuben **55** 256 **74** 218
Richard **117** 75
Richard Koska **107** 235
Robert **89** 57 **95** 52
Rosa B. (Dunn) **98** 198
Rosamond Willing
113 225
Rose E. (Sweeney)
107 235
Rose L. E. **107** 235
Rosella Elizabeth **72** 309
Roxana (Beals) **89** 16
Ruby **53** 247
Ruth **55** 256 **58** 359 **75** 197
Ruth Mabel (Gould) **96**
161 **97** 382
Sabra **55** 257
Sally **55** 258 **82** 50 **142** 209
Sally Ann **55** 257
Samuel **55** 256 **73** 75 **74**
215 251 260 **82** 50 **105**
282 **134** 173 **144** 266

MURRAY *cont'd*
Samuel Plumb **55** 257
Sarah **51** 466 **55** 256 257 **61**
136 **74** 212 215-218 224
225 228 246 **90** 44
Sarah (Ford) **99** 128
127 53
Sarah Ann (Becket) **108** 83
Sarah G. (Hastings)
89 203
Selah **54** 50 271 **55** 255-257
57 92
Seth **75** 320 **92** 100 **95** 365
112 49
Seymour **55** 257
Stephen **55** 257
Susan **55** 257
Susan (Seymour) **123** 308
Susan (Tibbetts) **100** 144
Susanna **54** 50 **55** 257 **74**
214 246 250 **90** 229 248
Susanna (Lithgow)
97 113
Sylvia **55** 256
T. C. **123** 128
T. Morris (Mrs.) **113** 147
Tamar **55** 256
Terence **60** 24
Thankful **55** 255-257
Thomas **74** 216 256 257
77 239 **89** 246 **91** 230
99 128 **100** 146 **108** 83
123 128 **126** 98 **127** 53
134 198
Thomas Cornelius
123 128
Thomas Hamilton **53**
135 147 **54** 363 **55** xxxii
451 **56** xxxii **57** 123 329
330 343 **58** 323 **60** 219
61 319 **62** xxxvii 392
394 **65** 151 155 **139** 209
Thomas Harrison **52** 379
Thomas Morris **113** 225
Thomas Morris (Mrs.)
85 188 **113** 224
Timothy **61** 366 **81** 447
107 235
Vilatte **136** 331
Virginia Frances **102** 124
106 123
W. B. **60** 188
W. F. **89** 351
Walter **65** 248
Warren **55** 257
Washington **78** 134
William **54** 1 **55** 258 **65**
353 **74** 215 **76** 46 **99** 55
128 **117** 16 **123** 131 **125**
154 295 **126** 98 **127** 53
125 202 203 **130** 182
William B. **57** 116 **76** 158
William Breed **102** 124
William F. **89** 352
William F. (Mrs.) **119** 240
William H. **123** 128
William Hubbard
55 257 258
Zilpah **127** 202
Zubah **55** 258

MURRELL Murrel
  Murrelle Murrells
  Cordelia **116** 205
  Elmira N. **116** 206
  George **112** 93
  George W. **116** 206
  Henry H. **116** 206
  Hiram **116** 206
  Joseph Harlan (Mrs.)
    91 142
  Levi **111** 285
  Rhoda **116** 206
  Sarah **116** 206
  Sarah Ann **116** 206
  Sophronia **116** 206
  Stephen **116** 206
  William **111** 272 **113** 186
    116 206
MURRELLE Marietta
  (Gregg) **91** 142
MURREN
  Abigail **69** 377
  Abijah **69** 131
  Daniel **68** 175 289 **69** 131
  David **69** 379
  Hannah **69** 379
  John **69** 373
  Mary **68** 175 289 **69** 129
    131
  Meeker **69** 131
  Peter **69** 131
  Ruth **69** 131
  Samuel **68** 175 **69** 129
  Sarah **69** 131
  Thomas **69** 373
Murrey see Murray
MURROW Murrough
  Edward R. **136** 90
  Edward Roscoe **136** 324
  Janet Huntington
    (Brewster) **136** 324
  John **64** 342
Murry see Murray
MURTAGH
  Catherine **92** 115
MURTHE Michael **61** 270
MURTIS John **63** 144
MURTON John **100** 73
  Robert **87** 146
Murwin see Merwin
Mury see Murray
MUSARD Isabel **75** 62
MUSCOTE
  Francis **63** 165 166
MUSCOTT
  Elizabeth **74** 283
  Foulk **74** 283
  Susanna **94** 276
MUSE Eliza **114** 191
  Elizabeth **75** 99
  Hannah (Pribble) **104** 122
  Marianne **109** 130 **114** 321
  Richard **117** 33
MUSGRAVE - De Musgrave
  —— **54** 226 **55** 446 **57** 409
  — Major **53** 178
  Anna **114** 187
  Avice **94** 206
  Barthow: **117** 16
  Christopher **110** 201
  Cuthbert **132** 46

MUSGRAVE cont'd
  Francis **62** 324
  Grace **71** 243
  James **114** 187
  John **114** 187
  Mary (Cogan) **110** 201
  Richard **94** 206
  Thomas **94** 206 **96** 113
  William **54** 451 **114** 187
MUSGROVE
  Richard Watson **64**
    228 **65** 94 **67** 183 350
    351 **68** 98 258 332 **69** 38
MUSHAWAY Mushway
  Frances **82** 27
  John **83** 35
  Lois **82** 27 293 295
  Mary **83** 35
  Peter **81** 447 **82** 27
  Sarah **81** 447
MUSICA Philip **145** 378
MUSICK Ben (Mrs.) **116**
  312 **120** 154
  G. C. **119** 155
  Velma Cottle **116** 312
    120 154
MUSKETT Musket
  —— **57** 331
  Andrew **65** lxvi
  Anne **65** lxvi
  Catherine Charlotte
    (Dalgairns) **58** 411 **65**
    lxvii
  Elizabeth **65** lxvi
  Henry **91** 356 357
  J. J. **108** 175 **111** 154
  Joan **65** 69
  John **65** lxvi
  Joseph **65** lxvi
  Joseph James **51** 234 424
    52 250 **53** 114 268 269
    54 xxxvii **55** 234 239 **56**
    xxx 413 414 **57** xxxi 98
    99 219 **58** xliii 411 **59**
    xlii 337 **60** xxxiv **61**
    xxxiii **62** xxxv **65** xxxiii
    xliv lxvi lxvii **105** 22
    123 171
  Margaret (Ralegh) **145** 20
  Mary **65** lxvi
  Richard **145** 20
  William **65** lxvi 69
MUSKOLL
  Thomasine **75** 228
MUSON Cyrus **85** 349
MUSPRATT Musprat
  Ambrose **51** 187
  James Sheridan **84** 334
  Thomas **51** 187
Musse see Muzzey
MUSSELMAN
  Amos **78** 104
  Elizabeth Hetty **93** 190
MUSSELWHITE
  John **66** 254
MUSSENDON
  Elizabeth de **74** 231
  Thomas de **74** 231
MUSSER Sarah **103** 226
MUSSETT John **143** 295
Mussey see Muzzey

MUSSILOWAY
  Daniel **104** 39
  Mary (Long) (Griffin)
    104 39
MUSSON —— **71** 312 324
  Matilda Margaret **89** 59
Mussy see Muzzey
MUSTARD Musterd
  — Mrs. **67** 177
  Catherine **109** 307
  D. French **128** 266
  Margaret **74** 102
  Thomas **53** 22
MUSTEL Alan **96** 110
  Richard **115** 47
  Robert **115** 47
  William **96** 110
MUSTELUS
  Adam **142** 240
MUSTERS Elizabeth **120**
  173 174
  Henry **120** 173 174
  John **120** 173
  Robert **120** 173
MUSTIN —— **107** 316
MUSTO Christian **69** 92
MUSTON Anne **102** 248
  251 **103** 10
  Anne (Whetehill)
    (Selling) **102** 248
  Elizabeth **102** 249 **103** 5 18
  Joan **116** 169
  Mary **52** 350
  Thomas **102** 252 **116** 169
  William **102** 248 250-252
    103 5 10 11 18 **116** 169
MUTCH Herman **92** 226
Mutchemore see
  Muchmore
Mutchermore see
  Muchmore
MUTH
  Johan Peter **95** 208
MUTTAR
  Elizabeth **56** 270
MUTTENRIDGE Maria
  Amarilla **132** 307
MUTTERY James **63** 19
MUX Daniel **128** 218
  John **128** 218
  William **128** 218
Muxam see Muxham
MUXFELD
  Louise Berta **105** 129
MUXHAM Muxam
  Muxom Muxsom
  Muxum
  Abigail **120** 115
  Abigail (Ellis) **120** 116
  Abigail (Faunce) **114** 214
  Caleb **123** 132
  David **123** 132 272 276
    132 294
  Dinah **123** 272 276
  Edmund **114** 214 **115** 92
    93 **119** 274 **120** 116
  Edward **115** 92 **120** 120
  Elizabeth **121** 139 **123** 132
  Elizabeth (Gibbs) **123**
    131 272
  Eura **123** 132 272

MUXHAM *cont'd*
Ezra **120** 122 **121** 139
Hannah **132** 294
Hannah (Bumpas) **115** 93
Hannah (Perry) **120** 116
　123 131
Jesse **123** 276
Joseph **58** 142
Lemuel **114** 214
Lucy **123** 272 276
Nathan **123** 132
Phil S. **123** 68
Priscilla **116** 41
Rebecca (Besse) **123** 272
　276 **132** 294
Rebecca (Faunce) **114** 214
Samuel **115** 92 93 **120**
　116 120 **121** 139 **123**
　131 132 272
Tabor **123** 275
Zachariah **115** 93
MUYDERMAN
Aleyda **106** 11
MUZZEROLE
Richard **115** 146
MUZZEY Musse Mussey
　Mussy Muzey Muzzy
　—— **60** 107 **70** 22 **75** 253
　91 261 **92** 260
— Mr. **71** 116
— Mrs. **56** 248 389
Abigail **75** 210
Abraham **60** 94
Amos **107** 28
Anna **55** 61
Benjamin **55** 391 **58** 52
　75 210 **85** 455 **144** 266
Betsie Culver **91** 261
Bridget **60** 94
C. F. **82** 508
Charles **61** 219
Clarindon F. **67** 359
Cora Jane **81** 251
Ebenezer **78** 177
Edward **55** 279
Elizabeth H. **95** 372
Ellis S. (Stacey) **125** 220
Esther (Green) **107** 28
Hannah **61** 379
Hannah (Pribble) **104** 122
Hester **55** 279 **71** 114
Isaac **85** 10
James **78** 400 **98** 134 **108**
　223 **125** 220 **132** 120
Joanna Crumbie
　(Fletcher) **108** 223
John **60** 94 **61** 241 **82** 211
　108 223 **132** 42
John C. **81** 251
Jonas Bridge **92** 260
Joseph **55** 59 61 62 **56** 248
　388
Josephine Emma **81** 251
Judith **97** 182
Julius **99** 133
L. **91** 331 **109** 270
Letitia Howard **60** liv
Lizzie T. **99** 133
Lucy **81** 34 **108** 89 **137** 31
Lydia **60** 94
Mary **75** 210 **123** 11

MUZZEY *cont'd*
　137 333
Mary Ella **108** 223
Moses **104** 122
Nellie M. **71** 118
Orilla S. **109** 270
Patience **61** 24
Polly **56** 255
Rebecca **118** 140
Rebecca (Ingham) **132** 42
Robert **60** 94 **93** 397 **100**
　63 **148** 120
Ruth **75** 253
Sally **61** 307 379
Sarah **77** 287 **118** 140
Susan (Hayes) (Doe)
　82 508
Susanna **61** 241
T. **145** 167
Thaddeus **92** 260
Theo. **55** 391
Thomas **60** liv 94
William Hadley **81** 251
Zadock **121** 92
Mvnge *see* Munge
M'Williams *see*
　McWilliams
Mycaell *see* Michael
Mycall *see* Michael
Mychell *see* Mitchell
MYCOCK
Edwin S. **98** 362
Frederick C. **98** 362
Marjorie E. (Foster)
　98 362
Mydcallf *see* Metcalf
Myddelton *see* Middleton
Mydelton *see* Middleton
MYERS Miers Mires Myer
— Mr. **62** 362
＿＿ (Hays) **140** 152
Abe **83** 64
Abigail (Mrs.) **132** 42
Adelia **90** 376
Adelia (Allen) **90** 376
Adolph **91** 330
Albert Cook **52** 478 479
　481 **57** xxxiii 127 **60** 85
　64 376 **90** 117 **91** 140
　99 68 143 **106** 319 **111**
　325 **116** 238 248 252
Albert Marcellus **92** 45
Alfred Reuben (Mrs.)
　95 350
Amanda **91** 386
Angie **85** 290
Ann **65** 348 349
Ann Maria **82** 477
Anna **60** 345 **83** 65
Anna Barbara **82** 347
Annie E. **82** 101
Annie Elizabeth **82** 347
August Robert (Mrs.)
　76 xxi **87** 177
Barbara **83** 65
Ben **91** 347
Burtha **95** 360
Calista (Snow) **90** 113
Caroline **83** 65
Carrie Louise **92** 45
Catherine **88** 340 **133** 323

MYERS *cont'd*
Charles **91** 330
Charles A. **83** 65
Charles Fisher **85** 188
Christian Charles (Mrs.)
　106 125
Christopher **55** lxxx
Clell **83** 65
Daniel **87** 259 **134** 175
David **83** 64-66 **90** 344
David C. **90** 376
Doris Irene **82** 347
Dorothy (Munroe)
　100 196
E. H. **100** 196
Earl Schenck **114** 318
Electa **71** 52
Elizabeth **65** 349
Elizabeth (Simonds)
　134 175
Ella M. **82** 404
Ellen **77** 182 **83** 65
Ellen Isabella (Wheeler)
　107 72
Ellen Rowley **76** 24
　93 369
Elton H. **85** 169
Emeline **69** 80
Emily **109** 187
Emma E. **83** 65
Emma Jane **76** xxi
Ernest **100** 196
Esther **65** 45 **89** 288
Esther (Rising) **85** 290
Flora **83** 65
Francaline **85** 290
Frank A. **106** 317
Frank H. W. **125** 105
Frederick **90** 113
G. W. **64** 295
Gardiner Howland
　82 234
George **90** 338
George Hewitt (Mrs.)
　89 366
Gideon **65** 349
H. Frederick **82** 347
Harmon **85** 315
Harriet **125** 280
Henry **66** 36 **77** 182 **82** 477
　133 323
Hezekiah **65** 349
Hiram **102** 289
Howard (Mrs.) **119** 320
Howard C. **59** 420 **60** 183
Isaac **83** 63 65
Jacob **62** 356 **127** 304
　137 161
Jacob L. **77** 151
James **69** 80 **73** 132
James N. (Mrs.) **103** 239
James T. **83** 65
Jeannette **82** 477
Jeremiah **71** 52
John **85** 290 **90** 53 **125** 257
　133 323
John Francis **65** xxxv
John H. **73** 317
John Henry **81** 230 237
　82 347
John Melchior **91** 81

MYERS *cont'd*
Joseph **85** 315 **89** 390
Joshua **91** 330
Lottie **83** 65
Louisa Rebecca (Bacot)
  91 76
Louise S. (Chase) **89** 366
Lucy (Chase) **87** 259
M. A. **128** 266 267
Marcia **77** 57 **85** 90
Marcia A. **92** 88
Marcia Ann **111** 146
Margaret **81** 273 **129** 42
Margaret (Johnson)
  125 257
Margaretta **55** lxxx
Margaretta LeCompt
  125 53
Mariette **81** 395
Marrible Eva **102** 124
Martha **83** 65 66
Martha Ann **146** 386
Martha Elizabeth **71** 56
Martha Pamelia **90** 209 **91**
  80 81
Mary **65** 349 **73** 132 **90** 344
  91 343 349
Mary Davis (Dean)
  144 117
Mary Ellen **76** 20
Mary Frances **77** 151
Mary Magdalene
  (Kemmerer) **110** 224
Marya **147** 329 **148** 66
Matilda **105** 145
Minerva **83** 64
Miriam Badlam (Pearce)
  141 6
Nancy (Gardner) **125** 105
Nathan **52** 433
Nicholas **65** 349
Nichols **129** 59
Norma **100** 196
Oliver **65** 348 349
Oscar **85** 290
Peter Lymaster **110** 224
Philip **133** 323
Reuben **60** 345
Robert **91** 349
Rosa W. **82** 347
Sadie **95** 187
Sally (Hays) **140** 152
Sally Ann **133** 323
Samuel **76** 20 **140** 152
Samuel P. **100** 76
Sarah **76** 20 **90** 113 **129** 170
Sarah (Green) **126** 306
Sarah (Pinkham) **98** 223
Stephen **133** 323
Steven W. **142** 4
Susan **99** 45 **133** 323
Sylvester **126** 306
Tarsy Salome **110** 224
Theodore B. **52** 479
Theodorus Bailey **64** 65
Thomas E. (Mrs.) **91** 76
Veda **90** 338
Wayne **100** 196
William **66** 37 **71** 56
  90 109 113
William H. **78** 186

MYGATT Maygatt Myggot
Christian (Fairchild)
  124 66
Comfort Starr **119** 91
Dorothy **73** 13
Eli **119** 90
Elisha **72** 177
Elizabeth **106** 109 **119** 90
  91
Elizabeth (Starr) **118** 271
  119 85 86 91 **125** 45
Ezra **106** 109
F. E. **96** 294
Frederick T. **124** 66
Hannah **124** 66
Hannah S. **106** 109
Jacob **52** 182 **85** 33 37
  119 91
John **145** 328
Jonathan **52** 182
Joseph **106** 109 **118** 271
  119 85 86 90 91 **124** 66
Joseph E. **106** 109
Mary **72** 319 **73** 6
Nelson H. **127** 239
Rachel **60** 306
Sabreay **92** 20
Sarah **96** 392 **107** 57
Thomas **124** 66
Zebulon **60** 306
MYHRE Hazel (Wallace)
  96 161
Peter Young (Mrs.)
  96 161
MYLAM Constance **58** 309
MYLDENALE
  William **93** 80 81
MYLER Dorothy Carol
  (McKeen) **106** 69
James Lovell **106** 69
Kittie Eva (Young)
  110 54
William **110** 54
Myles *see* Miles
MYLIN
  Abraham **106** 312
Amos Herr **106** 312
Anna (Herr) **106** 312
Barbara **106** 312
Barbara (Bear) **106** 312
Barbara (Kendig) **106** 312
Barbara Kendig **100** 112
  106 312 **107** 67 138
Caroline Emily
  (Hepburn) (Powell)
  106 312
Elizabeth (Herr) **106** 312
John **119** 245
Martin **106** 312
Myller *see* Miller
Myllette *see* Millette
MYLNER alias BROWNE
  Mary (Twigden)
  94 259
MYLNER Alyson
  (Bradford) **84** 16
Mylton *see* Milton
MYNDERSE
  Wilhelmus **64** xxxi
MYNG
  Anthony de **60** 361

MYNG *cont'd*
Elizabeth de **60** 361
MYNK John **95** 259
MYNORS — Capt. **57** 93
MYNSKIPP
  Alexander **83** 451
Myntton *see* Minton
MYOTT M. E. **122** 218
Oliver **122** 218
MYRAM Jane **89** 11
MYRAND —— **52** 53
MYREHOLT Mary Velora
  (Hannum) **91** 55
Wilbur William **91** 55
MYRFYN John **83** 441
Thomas **83** 441 457
MYRICK *see also* Merrick
— Mrs. **109** 42
Abigail **51** 207 **71** 351
  102 200
Abigail (Hopkins) **102** 48
Alona B. **109** 108
Alonzo K. **109** 108
Andrew **51** 162 **100** 190
Ann C. **126** 294
Anne **88** 197
Annie S. (Hoyt) **102** 260
Augusta Ann **113** 152
Avis **100** 190
Barbara **126** 239
Barna **57** 413
Barnabas **57** 411-413 **102**
  111 259
Barney **102** 259
Beman Parker **113** 152
Benjamin **57** 161 **87** 132
  101 101
Betsey **135** 341
Betsey (Rich) **84** 123
Caleb **58** 372
Charles B. **100** 190
Charles C. **100** 190
Constant **102** 259
Cynthia (Kincaid) **102** 260
Cynthia (Kneeland)
  102 260
Daniel **61** 346 **139** 242 244
Deborah **51** 162 207 **52** 82
  57 161 **100** 160 **102** 48
Deborah (Snow) **102** 48
  55
Dorcus **102** 287
Dorothy **58** 372
E. **109** 256
Eben **109** 108 200 **110** 21
  23 210
Ebenezer **110** 111 206
Edward Coffin **100** 190
Electa **122** 124
Elisha **57** 367
Eliza **61** 344
Eliza (Knowles) **123** 118
Eliza Jane **102** 260
Elizabeth **59** 245 **61** 345 **80**
  11 **104** 161 **108** 212 **123**
  261
Elizabeth (Harding)
  126 239
Elliot **102** 260
Elliot T. **102** 260
Ephraim **58** 372

MYRICK *cont'd*
Esther **56** 396 **80** 122 **88** 32
Eunice **58** 372
Eunice Augusta (Gott)
   91 80
Fear **126** 239
George Alonzo (Mrs.)
   85 196
George D. **109** 108
Grace Fidelia (James)
   (Gillette) **91** 79 148
Hannah **52** 82 **80** 122 **88**
   32 **95** 54 **102** 55 **113** 268
   123 259 **127** 179 180
Hannah (Chase) **87** 132
Hannah (Dumbleton)
   123 262
Hannah (Hopkins)
   102 55
Hannah (Paine) **103** 92
Harding **113** 34 41
   123 119
Harriet Anola **109** 108
Huldah **102** 55
Isaac **51** 162 **61** 345 **80** 11
   100 156 160 186 190
   111 116 **144** 219
Jabez **51** 207 **102** 48
James **58** 372 **100** 190 **123**
   263 319
Jane (Tucker) **102** 260
Jedida **51** 162
Jesse **61** 343 346 **80** 11
   123 118
Jethro **51** 207 **102** 48
Job **100** 191
Johanna **145** 365
John **59** 245 **84** 123 **123**
   203 261 265 **125** 42 102
John C. **100** 190
John E. **109** 108
Jonathan **100** 190
Joseph **61** 344 **80** 21 **101**
   43 **102** 260 **126** 239
Joshua **51** 207 **57** 412 **79**
   293 **102** 48 **126** 239
Joshua T. **102** 260
Josiah **95** 50 **123** 200
Julia **109** 131
Julia Ann **102** 260
Katharine **57** 413
Katy **57** 413
Levi **102** 260
Lizzie R. **104** 219
Louisa **109** 108
Lucinda **71** 3
Lucretia R. (Green)
   113 152
Lucy **61** 344
Lydia **79** 293 **126** 239
   128 119
Lydia (Godfrey) **126** 239
Lydia (Hopkins) **103** 92
Margaret **123** 319
Martha **111** 117
Martha (Bodge) **101** 101
Mary **57** 161 **58** 372 **66** 99
   80 21 **97** 357 **101** 43
   102 49 **126** 239
Mary (Day) **123** 261
Mary (Smith) **102** 259

MYRICK *cont'd*
Mary Eliza **113** 307
Maryann **140** 266
Mercy **80** 11
Mercy (Lincoln) **123** 203
Mercy A. **123** 200
Myrtle **103** 119
Nabby (Philbrook)
   111 116
Nathan **102** 260
Nathaniel **102** 100 259 260
Oliver **51** 207 **102** 48
Osborn **103** 92
Paul **105** 205
Persis **57** 367
Persis Moore **58** 372
Peter Coffin **100** 190
Phebe **59** 27 **102** 55
   123 199
Polly **58** 372 **102** 260
   111 115
Polly (Cobb) **123** 120
Prince **102** 259
Priscilla **100** 190
Rebecca **59** 245 **102** 48 49
   113 34 41
Rebecca (Higgins)
   123 119
Ruth **126** 238
Ruth (Godfrey) (Gould)
   126 239
Ruth (Smith) **123** 118
Sally **61** 344 **100** 156 190
   102 260 **117** 222 **123**
   118
Samuel **58** 372 **61** 344 **94**
   95 **100** 63 165 **102** 48
   115 33 **123** 118
Sarah **59** 324 **89** 47 **93** 281
   123 258 **124** 288
Sarah (Cooly) **123** 263
Sarah (Hopkins) **102** 259
Sarah (Parson) **123** 265
Sarah Sylvester **59** 377
Seth **51** 207
Seth G. **100** 190
Silvey (Daggett) (Myrick)
   102 260
Simeon **51** 207 **102** 48
   143 18
Snow **51** 207 **102** 48
Stephen **51** 207 **52** 82
   102 48 55
Susan **61** 344
Susan (Mayo) **123** 200
Susanna **102** 260
Susanna (Gardner)
   125 102
Susanna (Lawrence)
   102 259
Thankful **71** 148 **105** 103
Thomas **51** 207 **52** 82 **102**
   48 55 **123** 259 262 **126**
   239
Tilla/Tilly **58** 372 **123** 263
Timothy **100** 158 159
W. W. (Mrs.) **110** 322
Wayne **110** 322
William **51** 207 **57** 411
   102 48 49 **103** 92 **111**
   116 **123** 120 **126** 239

MYRICK *cont'd*
Zenas **57** 413
MYRIES — Miss **65** 246
MYRTLE Katie **114** 64
   Minnie **83** 231
   Philip **114** 64
   Rebecca (Walters) **114** 64
MYTCH Barbara **63** 35
MYTROOD Hannah **60** 347
Mytton *see* Mitton

NABBS —— **52** 45 124 132
   139 **53** 302 **54** 92 93
   Edward **76** 79
NABE
   Elizabeth **81** 418
   William **81** 418
NACKEY
   Margaret **82** 292 295
NADEAN William **125** 142
Naef *see* Neff
NAEGLE Adelaide (Savage)
   97 158
   Lawrence Heber (Mrs.)
   101 125
   Robert Wilford (Mrs.)
   97 158
NAEVE Milo M. **144** 227
NAGE John **65** 126
NAGEL Nagle
   Anne **75** xxv
   Anne (Shepley) **106** 70
   Anne Dorothea **106** 70
   Charles **89** 322 **106** 70
   Charles (Mrs.) **75** xxv 65
   106 61 70 128
   Edith **106** 70
   Edward J. **88** 93
   Herman **106** 70
   Jan **59** 419
   Mary Edney (Wyman)
   88 93
   Mary Ella (Lazell) **89** 322
   Mary Shipley **106** 70
   Tanneka **96** 386
NAHOR
   Margaret **91** 263
   Mary **91** 259
NAILE John **62** 328
Nailor *see* Naylor
NAINBY William **64** 112
NAIRNE David **76** 60
NAISBY John Russell (Mrs.)
   109 130
NAKIN —— **55** 159
NALDER
   Minnie Watt **99** 146
NALLE
   John (Mrs.) **108** 131
   Leslie **87** 174
NALLERAN
   George **61** 349
   Jane **61** 349
NALLIS William **98** 102
NALON William **127** 302
NAMATH Joe **145** 200
NANCE
   George W. **126** 144
   Ruth (Dean) **126** 144
   T. F. **91** 331

NANCREDE
P. I.G. de **140** 230
Nancy *see* Nance
NANFAN John **112** 249
NANGLE Peter **60** 240
William **64** 321
NANIN Aimone (Mrs.)
103 149
NANNING
Andrew **92** 126
Andrew (Mrs.) **93** 262
Mary (Carnes) **93** 262
Mary Barber **92** 126
NANSCAWEN
Mary (Davis) **127** 198
William **127** 198
NANSEGLOS Nansicles
Alice **74** 279
Elizabeth **74** 279
Lucy **74** 279
Mary **71** 175 **74** 279 **75** 136
Richard **74** 279
Robert **74** 279
Thomas **74** 279
William **71** 175 **74** 279
75 136
NANSEN ―― **62** lv lvi
Nansicles *see* Nanseglos
NANUMETT **127** 20
NAPEY George **81** 418
Mary E. **81** 418
NAPHEY D. A. **82** 454
Frank Allen **82** 454
S. L. **82** 454
NAPIER Nappier
A. S. **103** 156
Eva L. **122** 79
Jos **64** 224
Theophilus **94** 275
NAPOLEON I of France
51 100 441 509 **54** cxlv
61 101 **67** 306 **136** 311
NAPOLEON III
of France **77** liii **88** 102
NAPOLITAN Marjorie
Louise **112** 153
NAPPER Alice **72** 186
John **72** 186
Mary **55** 337
Thomas **55** 337
Nappier *see* Napier
NAPPING
Theodocia **100** 239
NAPTON ―― **141** 98
Robert **142** 228
NARAMORE Narramore
Abigail **126** 120
Caroline **106** 109
John **71** 355
Justin **106** 109
Lois **71** 355
M. L. **75** 14
Mary A. **71** 355
Nelson C. **71** 355
W. M. **75** 14
Zaidee **75** 14
NARBEY Catherine
(Martin) **125** 287
John **125** 87
NARBOTH John **100** 190

NARDEN Nardin
―― **112** 145
Charles S. **84** 304
Mary Ann (Rich) **84** 304
NARMAN Sarah **90** 161
NARMORE
Abiel **126** 142
Tamson (Snow) **126** 142
NARR
John Peter **88** 335
Margaret Amelia
(Howard) **88** 335
NARRACOT David **86** 84
Joan (Beard) **86** 84
Joan (Chapin) **83** 354
Narramore *see* Naramore
NASBY
Petroleum V. **90** 360
NASCOMOS **55** 157
NASE Mary T. **79** 122
NASH Nashe
―― **54** 108 **56** 327 **60**
188 338 **118** 22 116 233
119 106 289
― Lieut. **120** 131
― Mr. **53** 450 **57** 228
― Mrs. **62** 273 **119** 46 52
―― (Atkins) **140** 33
Aaron **58** 196
Aaron P. **79** 276
Abel **60** 182
Abigail **54** 404 405 **56** 281
61 398 **80** 127
Abigail (Haynes) **135** 76
Abigail Thomas **127** 65
Abner **64** 202
Abner Porter **133** 47
Abraham **54** 405 406
Alexander **118** 166
Alice **54** 448 **60** 130
Almena **133** 46
Alvan **57** 360
Amasa **132** 324
Ann **54** 406 **60** 41 **64** 202
71 281 **88** 150
Ann Eliza **89** 94
Anna **54** 406 **71** 161
138 210
Anna Maria **89** 262
Anne **71** 79 279
Anne (White) **119** 111
Ansel **60** 267 **72** 47 104
Arabella Tressie
Elizabeth **109** 128
Arthur Irving **54** xli
Atherton **119** 191
Bartholomew **88** 285
Bathsheba **54** 406
Benjamin **54** 404 406
116 20
Betsey **63** 379 **119** 190
135 77
Betsey (Fayerweather)
145 146
Bridget **63** 19
C. A.W. (Mrs.) **123** 96
Caleb **54** 406
Caroline **135** 77
Carrie **123** 99
Catherine **126** 143 **135** 77

NASH *cont'd*
Catherine Van Bergen
(Curtis) **89** 94
Charity **54** 404
Charles **119** 190
Charles A. **76** 50
Charles Dennis **123** 302
Charles E. **52** 379
Charlotte **82** 274
Chauncey Cushing **74**
237 **75** xxiii **96** 151 173
97 171 **98** 160 **99** 139
141 **100** 46
Christian **85** 397
Christiana **88** 341
Christopher **73** 142 **124**
312 **125** 73
Church **58** 372 **59** 391
63 379
Clarissa **77** 176 **125** 292
Cotton **123** 29
Cyrus **119** 184 185 187 255
120 46 **126** 257
D. W. (Mrs.) **123** 99 223
Daniel **54** 406 **62** 264 272
68 222 223 **115** 14 21
118 **145** 146
David **58** 174 **127** 14
135 77
David P. **123** 91 310 311
David R. **78** 306
Debby **60** 338 **61** 175
Debby Cushing **60** 273
Deborah **59** 388 **61** 173
70 99 **78** 412 **99** 170
119 111 191 **135** 43
Deborah (Merritt)
129 265
Delight **129** 265
Diana **123** 288
Dora **69** 262
Dorastus Wright **123** 302
Dorcas **54** 406 **60** 199
Dorothy **59** 154
Dyer **54** 405
E. T. **57** 360
Ebenezer **54** 405 **60** 76
Edith **123** 49
Edward **76** 57
Edward Fessenden
70 102
Edward Phelps **123** 303
Electa **136** 269
Elijah **123** 26 30 31
Elisha **58** 264 **105** 209
Eliza **58** 372 **61** 59 176
126 64
Elizabeth **54** 404 **58** 174 **61**
48 49 52 54 56 **69** 262
70 76 99 100 **81** 129 324
82 384 **94** 327 **111** 295
118 81 **119** 190 **123** 27
303 308
Elizabeth (Nash) **123** 308
Elizabeth (Porter) **148** 52
53
Elizabeth Flint **108** 4
Elizabeth Gould **123** 104
Elizabeth Todd **56** 327
57 xxxiii **60** xxxviii 188
Ellen **88** 191

NASH *cont'd*
Ellen V. (Smith) **123** 309
Enos **118** 24 117 219 **119**
  295 299 **120** 300 **123** 18
Ephraim **54** 404 405
Erastus **122** 225 **123** 23
  25-28 31
Esther **52** 76 **88** 283
Eunice **72** 47 **119** 190 **123**
  30 **126** 261 **136** 40
Eunice (Ford) **119** 190
Eunice (Jenkins) **126** 208
Eunice (Pomeroy)
  119 214
Experience **54** 404
Fidelia **91** 80
Flora **79** 51
Florence **135** 77
Fordyce T. (Mrs.) **123** 99
Fordyce Theron **123** 99
  302
Fordyce W. **123** 99
Frances **81** 368
Frances (Selick) **123** 308
Francis **54** 404-406 **58** 372
  59 90 154 362 **85** 147 **89**
  94
Francis Philip **57** xxxv
Frank (Mrs.) **123** 226
Frank T. **123** 99
Freeman Knowles **80** 127
Garrett Van Bergen **89** 94
George Kilbon **59** 335
Georgiana **145** 146
Gilbert **53** 392 395 **60** 108
  65 19 189 **67** 382 **73** 164
Gregory **131** 131
H. Hewitson **113** 42
Hannah **54** 404 406 **56** 281
  57 399 **58** 174 260 264
  388 **61** 118 **70** 99 **74** 91
  81 129 **126** 267 **129** 267
  136 37
Harriet **123** 52 303
Harriet Maria **81** 237
  82 237
Helpa **123** 47 308
Henry **63** 343
Henry William **123** 303
Herbert A. **91** 105
Hope **94** 280
Hopestill (Bradford)
  110 48
Huldah **143** 320
Hutchinson J. **69** 262
Isaac **54** 405 **59** 154 **86** 72
Isaiah **54** 405 **80** 127
  122 292
Israel **61** 288
J. **71** 52
Jacob **54** 405 **88** 150 **119**
  105 **122** 53 **133** 47 257
James **54** 404-406 **55** 221
  58 174 **60** 42 130 **64** 223
  321 **68** 222 **70** 99 **119**
  117 119 **133** 47 **134** 50
James Ford **119** 190
James Hervey **58** 372
James Jewett **123** 302
James N. **54** 405
James S. **77** 52

NASH *cont'd*
Jane Frances **123** 101 305
Jared **62** 269
Jemme **71** 165
Jerusha **58** 372 373 **76** 85
  105 150
Jesse **135** 77
Jessie Elizabeth **91** 105
Joanna **88** 150 **126** 267
Job **133** 47 **135** 76
Joel **58** 196 197 **60** 205
John **52** 273 **54** 404 405
  55 343 **56** 281 **58** 174
  60 251 273 274 **61** 56 57
  59 118 173 288 **62** 270
  64 202 **69** 113 **70** 99 100
  71 157-159 300 **77** 52
  81 121-124 126-129 133-
  135 **88** 150 **109** 316 **123**
  20 22-24 26 29 **124** 17
  134 50 **143** 320
John Frederick **90** 137
  115 21
John King **61** 56 176
John Stephen **126** 234
Jonathan **57** 289 292 293
  88 150 **90** 228 **115** 14
  123 96 302 **128** 219
Jonathan Wilcox **123** 304
Joseph **54** 405 **57** 399 **58**
  174 260 264 388 **62** 266
  270 **68** 180 **70** 99 **71** 79
  159-163 165 279 300 303
  80 127 **81** 129 **110** 48
  119 190 **123** 308 **125**
  222 **129** 265 **133** 47
Joseph R. **123** 99
Joseph R. (Mrs.) **123** 99
Joseph Rush **123** 302
Josephine S. **67** lxi
Joshua **59** 330 **91** 331 **140**
  33 **148** 53
Josiah **115** 116 **118** 118
  122 123 224 230 **120** 204
Judah **95** 66
Judith **58** 372
Julia **135** 77
Keziah **54** 405
Laurana **89** 39
Lemuel **88** 150
Llewellyn **69** 262
Lorana **89** 39
Lorena Elizabeth **86** 196
Lorenzo Samuel **135** 77
Louis **76** 50
Loyal **123** 52 303
Lucy **60** 339 **78** 419
  118 228
Lucy (Cushing) **119** 191
Lucy A. **79** 275
Lucy M. (Leonard) **88** 285
Lucy Turner **70** 99
Luther **58** 372
Lydia **54** 406 **59** 314 391
  60 182 **82** 19
Lyman Junius **89** 94
Margaret **54** 404 405 **60** 42
  61 43 **123** 47
Margaret (Merrill)
  143 320
Maria **123** 52

NASH *cont'd*
Mariah Matilda **123** 303
Martha **52** 273 **62** 266 **88**
  150 **96** 270 **123** 25 26
Martha Caroline **69** xxxv
Mary **52** 196 197 436 **53**
  450 **54** 404 405 **59** 154
  155 171 **60** 130 **61** 130
  64 154 **71** 157 **78** 178
  309 **81** 129 **88** 124 **89**
  904 **93** 91 **112** 173 **115**
  25 116 **119** 118 119 184
  121 83 **131** 131
Mary (Foster) **112** 173
Mary (Ingersoll) **122** 292
Mary (McBride) **126** 234
Mary (Munger) **123** 307
Mary (Murry) **126** 66
Mary (Purchase) (Niles)
  85 147
Mary (Sprague) **119** 190
Mary Ann **77** 52 **145** 146
Mary Elizabeth **123** 305
Mary Elvira **89** 318
Mary Gyles **59** 330
Mary Jane **131** 237
Mary P. **123** 302
Mary Peninah **123** 91
Mary S. **123** 96
Mary T. **87** 223 233 235
Matilda (Lock) **125** 290
Matthew **120** 199
Mehitable **88** 206 **91** 240
Melvin S. **67** lxi
Mercy **54** 406 **58** 260
Molly **54** 405
Molly (Emery) **90** 228
Moses **60** 41 **66** 364 **71** 84
  158 300 **101** 158 159
  119 111 **120** 54
Nabby **88** 151
Naby (Gale) **124** 17
Nancy **88** 150 **123** 50
Nancy (Nottage) **125** 222
Nancy (Remele) **89** 94
Nancy Eliza **89** 94
Nathan **128** 124
Nathaniel **119** 190 **125** 290
Nathaniel Cushing **58**
  xv-vii xiv xvii xliv **61**
  vii xii xiv xlii 57 **62** vii
  63 vii **64** vii xx **65** vii
  66 vii **70** xxviii lviii 99-
  102
Nellie Munro **70** 102
Newman Curtis **89** 94
Noah **70** 100
Noah P. **123** 309
Noah Preserved **123** 302
Olive **115** 15 21 24 108
  116 117
Olive S. **79** 53
Oliver **54** 405 **58** 373 **59**
  391 **88** 286
Oran **119** 191
Peter Micajah **145** 146
Phebe **120** 54
Phelps **123** 303 308
Phineas **60** 199
Pliny **62** 270
Polly **80** 128 **88** 150

NASH *cont'd*
Rachel **54** 406 **88** 150
  134 92
Ray **117** 233
Rebecca **54** 406 **60** 251 **68**
  223 **71** 162 **78** 404 **127**
  224 **135** 77
Rebecca (Tirrell) **116** 20
  120 54 **121** 244
Relief **60** 337
Remembrance **62** 270
Reuben **54** 405
Richard **118** 166
Rivera **71** 163
Robert **61** 48
Robert L. (Mrs.) **92** 146
Roger **75** 227
Ruth **54** 405 **69** 113
  119 184
Sally **77** 52
Sally M. **89** 94
Samuel **52** 76 229 **54** 404
  405 **55** 343 **56** 205 **58**
  197 372 373 **59** 90 155
  362 **60** 182 **65** 126 **89**
  174 **94** 241 242 **118** 123
  123 303 307 **143** 320
Samuel P. **123** 93 305
Sarah **54** 406 **60** 42 **61** 18
  66 327 **72** 283 317 **80**
  127 **81** 129 **83** 298 300
  88 150 291 **119** 119 183
  129 370 **136** 315 332
Sarah (Damon) **119** 190
Sarah (Keen) **127** 65
Sarah Seymour **83** 56
Silence Webb
  (Humphrey) **133** 47
Simeon **58** 174 **59** 314
  388 391 **60** 182 **62** 269
Solomon **54** 406 **58** 373
Sophia Ladd **132** 324
Sophie **122** 53
Sophronia K. **72** 47
Susan **135** 77
Susan A. (Edwards)
  88 286
Susan Elizabeth **123** 304
Susanna **54** 404 405 **60** 78
  62 272 **79** 275 **80** 127
  128 **88** 150
Sylvanus **62** 273
Sylvester **64** 190 **115** 14
Thomas **54** 404 **59** 193 **60**
  182 **64** 20 **81** 129 **127** 65
  134 335 **136** 40 **143** 209
  320
Timothy **52** 196 197 **62**
  270 **63** 299 **81** 129 324
  101 155 **112** 173 **133** 47
  143 320 **145** 379
Treadway **122** 178 **124** 182
Treadway Russell **65** 163
Tryphena **62** 273
Uriah **117** 53
Wallace **123** 302
Will J. (Mrs.) **123** 224
William **54** 405 **58** 372
  65 22 28 **71** 52 **88** 150
  89 94 **123** 91 302 311
  131 131 **135** 77

NASH *cont'd*
William Francis **89** 94
William Humphrey
  63 214
William Phelps **123** 96
  302
William Phelps (Mrs.)
  123 96 222
William R. **89** 94
Zacheriah **60** 271
Zaidee (Skidmore)
  145 146
Nasmith *see* Nesmith
NASON Nasson Nayson
  Neason
—— **53** 250 **54** 230 **56** liv
  67 276 **88** 380 **129** 396
  130 235 **131** 244
— Miss **83** 35
— Mr. **79** 299
— Mrs. **83** 35
— Widow **82** 314
A. H. **95** 301
Aaron **82** 332 **99** 56 198
Abbie J. (Taylor) **93** 112
Abiah **97** 142
Abigail **55** 313 314 373 376
  63 168 **73** 125 **82** 84 90
  212 213 317 510 **83** 9 14
  17 **88** 349 350 355 **90**
  245 **95** 189 191 **99** 197-
  200 **107** 198 273 **108** 57
  189 **133** 45 217
Abigail (Currier) **108** 123
Abigail (Curtis) **108** 120
  133 45
Abigail (Lord) **83** 14
Abigail (Wodlin) **83** 9
Abraham **82** 503
Agabial **95** 189
Albury **83** 150
Alice **61** 256 **82** 294 295
Alice L. **93** 112
Almira **97** 273
Amos **55** 373 **82** 319 331
  83 13
Amy **82** 320
Ann **82** 91 216
Anna **55** 316 **82** 78 **83** 11
  12
Arlbury **82** 509 **83** 152
Arthur C. (Mrs.) **75** xcii
Avoline (Chadbourn)
  91 31
Barsheba **88** 151
Bartholomew **82** 327 **83**
  149 **140** 230 329
Bathsheba **57** 186
Benjamin **55** 310 376 **66**
  188 **71** 214 217 218 **82**
  76-78 80 83-86 88 89 91
  92 95 205 501 **83** 17 19
  154 **87** 121 **99** 200 201
  108 57 123 **134** 153
Benjamin E. **87** 126
Benjamin Small **88** 350
  99 198 199
Betsey **55** 373 **63** 172 **83**
  14 149 151
Betsey (Lord) **108** 191
Betsey (Manning) **83** 14

NASON *cont'd*
Betty **74** 254 **82** 214 319
  107 198
Bridget **55** 316 **82** 77 90
  204 332 333 503 **83** 13
Caleb **63** 177 **74** 254
  82 329
Charity **109** 147
Charles **118** 195
Charles A. **83** 184
Charles William **92** 230
Clara **86** 301
Claresy (Davis) **97** 16
Comfort (Manchester)
  102 27
Daniel **55** 373 **63** 168 **82**
  209 332 **83** 14 19 **93** 103
  108 190
Daniel G. **119** 60
David **82** 328 **90** 335 **91** 25
Deborah **53** 164
Dolly **70** 283
Dolly (Getchell) **99** 56
Dorcas **82** 330 503 **88** 64
  90 231 251
Dorcas (Hoit) **91** 32
Durrell **133** 217
Ebenezer **91** 32 **102** 27
  107 317
Edith **91** 390
Edmund **108** 57
Edward **65** 256 335 336
  71 214 **82** 89 212 **87** 121
  124 **88** 349 350 **99** 197-
  200 **108** 121
Edward C. **84** 106
Elias **51** 497 **52** 88 **59** 330
  64 229 335 **65** 41 **92** 204
  99 13 14 16 **112** 274 **146**
  383
Elijah **141** 55
Elisha **82** 92 312 **116** 132
  135
Eliza **90** 336 **99** 56
Eliza A. **97** 230 233
Eliza Jane (Whitten)
  91 28 120
Elizabeth **55** 310 314 **74**
  249 252 **82** 76 317 326
  83 9 **94** 249 **96** 200 **99**
  198 201
Elizabeth (Lake) **91** 390
Elizabeth (Street) **148** 294
Elizabeth (Wells) **94** 249
Elizabeth Chickering
  75 lxxi
Elizabeth H. **96** 202
Elizabeth S. (Wentworth)
  99 56
Elizabeth T. **98** 198
Elizabeth T. (Battles)
  98 189 198
Elizabeth W. (Huff)
  96 200
Eloisa **55** 375 **83** 16
Elwell **83** 20
Emma Huntington **51**
  364 **63** 210 **64** xxxi 197
  144 60
Enoch **87** 121 **133** 217
Essie Lydia **92** 230

NASON *cont'd*

Esther **55** 375 **63** 171 **65**
336 **83** 16 **114** 182
Eugene Hilston **92** 230
Eunice **55** 313 375 **58** 258
82 208 329 511 **83** 16
Eunice (Goodwin) **83** 16
Eveline / Evertine
(Chadbourn) **91** 26
97 222
Ezra Davis **99** 198
Fanna **82** 331
Francis L. **113** 313
Francis M. **71** 119
Frank **68** 282
Frank Leon (Mrs.) **78** 205
85 184 **87** 187 **88** 183
185 **89** 53 145 147 210
90 120 150 **91** 157 **92**
161 **93** 84 152 **94** 81 154
95 161 **96** 88 174 **97** 172
98 162 **99** 164 **100** 126
101 139 **102** 138 **103**
135 **104** 67 159 **105** 143
110 137 138 **111** 78 142
112 70 135 222 314 **113**
61 148 **141** 203
Fred A. **93** 112
Freeman **91** 28 120
Gee Hodgkins **88** 380
112 219
George **82** 76 **83** 154
George W. **65** 205
Ham **55** 316 **82** 322 **83** 12
Hannah **55** 315 373 **65**
256 336 **82** 332 503 **83**
10 13 **91** 27 34 114 **96**
340 **99** 56 198 **111** 117
126 142 **134** 153
Hannah (Gubtail) **90** 335
91 25
Hannah (Hodsden) **83** 10
Hannah (Nason) **83** 13
Hannah P. **83** 153
Hannah Plummer **83** 150
Harriet **88** 380
Harriet Matilda **88** 378
Hepzibah **81** 431
Hepzibah (Roberts) **97** 16
Horace **91** 26 **97** 222
Horris **91** 31
Irena **99** 56
Isaac **88** 64 **99** 56
Isabel Emery **96** 200
Isabella **78** 205 **80** 222
81 236
Isabelle **82** 250 251 381
Isabelle (Cushman) **78**
109 **83** 227 247 370 **84**
182 206 **85** 215 **86** 109
215 **87** 163 **90** 119 **98** 98
101 24 119
Jacob **78** 421 **82** 214 291
295 503 **107** 198 **108** 30
Jacob Morrell **88** 355
James **82** 214 503 **87** 121
123 **88** 355 **93** 112 **95**
193 200 **97** 17 221 231
237 274 **99** 133
Jane **82** 83 **83** 25 **90** 327
91 19 114

NASON *cont'd*

Jane (Hoyt) **111** 138
Jemima **71** 214 225 **87** 124
115 240
Jeremiah **75** 110 **76** 190
Joanna **82** 332 **88** 380
Joanna (Tilden)
(Moulton) **88** 378
Joel **90** 228 246
John **55** 314 **70** 283 **74** 252
76 264 **82** 77 88 90 96
208 212 214 216 319 332
500 504 **83** 9 **90** 248 326
91 17 114 **97** 16 144 146
99 197 198 **105** 287 **107**
198 **108** 57
Jonathan **54** 408 **65** 256 **82**
79 **83** 154 **87** 122 **97** 144
135 22
Joseph **82** 92 93 214 216
318 503 **95** 193 **99** 56
198 108 191 **125** 177
Joshua **55** 302 **74** 224 254
82 86 212 314 315 510
107 198 273 **108** 120
123 189 **133** 41 45 216
Josiah **82** 316 **98** 189 198
115 213
Katharine **84** 56
Katharine (Dame) **113** 313
Keziah **55** 315 **82** 320 328
331 501 502 **83** 10 **128**
232 233
Keziah (Ricker) **95** 193
200
L. Howard **93** 112
Leonard **138** 125
Lois **82** 332
Louisa **71** 119
Love **55** 316 **82** 216 321
504 **83** 13
Lucia W. **83** 19
Lucy **74** 249 **88** 355 **96** 73
102 11
Lucy (Durrell) **133** 217
Lucy Ann (Lougee)
118 195
Lydia **82** 88 **87** 125 **95**
191 194 **99** 197 198
Lydia (Towne) **108** 190
Lydia (Waterhouse) **97** 17
Lydia H. (Wells) **83** 19
93 103
Marcy (Boyce) **90** 246
Margaret **55** 312 **82** 90 510
Mark Fisk **82** 509
Martha **55** 316 375 **66** 188
74 253 **82** 77 205 **83** 12
16 **93** 333 **99** 197
Martha (Emery) **83** 12
Martha (Varney) **83** 16
Mary **55** 310 314 315 **65**
256 **74** 252 **81** 425 431
82 76-78 80 83-86 88 89
204 205 212 217 289 295
315 319 328 331 **83** 10
11 **88** 377 379 380 **91** 26
31 114 **95** 87 **97** 14 145
99 198 200 201 **102** 27
108 57 **133** 217 **135** 18
19

NASON *cont'd*

Mary (Bean) **99** 56
Mary (Dearing) **108** 122
Mary (Durrell) **133** 45
Mary (Fletcher) **88** 377
Mary (Hodgkins)
88 378 379
Mary (Millar) **107** 195
108 189
Mary (Shores) **88** 378 379
112 219
Mary A. **83** 179
Mary A. (Nason) **83** 184
Mary Ann **99** 56
Mary E. **99** 133
Mary F. (Ramsdell)
119 60
Mary J. **126** 24
Mary Jane **97** 146
Mary S. **99** 133
Matilda **55** 376 **83** 17
Mehepsabah (Tibbetts)
99 56
Mehitable **98** 57
Melissa (Boyle) **83** 20
Mercy **55** 373 **81** 431 **82**
50 328 330 **83** 14 **107**
200 **127** 192
Mercy (Boyce) **90** 228
Mercy (Hammond)
129 396
Meribah **55** 312 **82** 319 328
329 510
Merson **92** 230
Michael **82** 502
Miller **97** 146
Milly **99** 199
Mina **87** 122
Molly **55** 316 373 **63** 173
82 214 503 **83** 13 14 **87**
125 **88** 151 **99** 197-199
Molly (Jillison) **83** 13
Moses **55** 314 **65** 256 **74**
249 **82** 98 204 319 329
331 332 502 **83** 9 **94** 249
99 197 **108** 122
Myer **92** 230
Myrtress Isabel **92** 230
Nabby **82** 323
Nahum **145** 362
Nancy **78** 298 **114** 183
Nancy Elizabeth **94** 249
Nancy Hyde **141** 55
Narcissa (Stone) **133** 217
Nathan **74** 259 **82** 325 502
506 **88** 151 **97** 145 267
Nathaniel **55** 312 373 375
56 74 **63** 172 **82** 204 294
295 319 322 327-329 333
503 510 **83** 14 16 35 **88**
151 **91** 206 **94** 95 **98** 105
100 65
Nehemiah **96** 342
Nellie L. **98** 253
Nellie M. B. **113** 313
Nicholas Edgecombe
99 200
Noah **82** 76 216 312 317
320
Olive **55** 314 373 **63** 168 **74**
254 **82** 320 329 331 332

NASON *cont'd*
502 **83** 9 14 **91** 114 **116**
133
Olive (Bagley) **90** 248
Olive (Davis) **83** 9 **96** 342
Oliver **96** 200 202
Olivia S. (Hubbard) **55**
376 **83** 17 19
Olly **99** 199
Patience **55** 310 314 **82** 216
83 9 **92** 95 **104** 74
Patty **87** 123
Pelatiah **55** 375 **83** 16
Peter **88** 380 **112** 219
Phebe **76** 264 **87** 124 **88**
350 **99** 199
Phebe A. **125** 174
Philadelphia **82** 79
Phineas **97** 16
Polly **63** 177 **74** 259
87 122 126
Polly (Gray) **95** 193
Prudence **55** 314 **82** 216
332 500 **83** 9
Prudence (Nason) **83** 9
Rachel **82** 318
Rebecca **88** 151
Richard **57** 186 **58** 249 **80**
281 **82** 204 205 319 322
323 331 332 **136** 360
141 121
Richard Tweedie **92** 230
Robert **55** 375 **83** 16 **99**
197 198 200 **129** 396
Robert Edgcomb **71** 214
Robert W. **85** 436
Rufus **99** 56
Ruth **82** 291 295
Ruth (Earl) **125** 177
Ruth (Hyde) **141** 55
Sabra **97** 224
Sally **55** 375 **83** 16 **91** 114
97 273 **130** 235
Sally (Joy) **116** 132
Sally (McLucas) **90** 326
91 17
Sally (Plaisted) **83** 16
Sally (Wyer) **125** 221
Salome **88** 355
Samuel **82** 90 91 93 95 98
209 214 216 314 318 321
327 328 330 **88** 64 377-
380 **99** 198-200 **112** 219
115 219
Samuel Baker **82** 504
Sarah **51** 61 **55** 312 313
316 372 375 **65** 256 335
71 225 **74** 224 **75** 110
76 257 **81** 431 **82** 90 91
95 204 209 214 316 319
323 327 332 333 510 511
83 12 13 17 **87** 121 **88**
64 355 **93** 68 69 **97** 272
108 57 121 **116** 138 **130**
235
Sarah (Baker) **136** 360
Sarah (Chick) **135** 22
Sarah (Dyar) **108** 123
Sarah (Merril) **108** 121
Sarah (Wilkinson) **83** 17
Shirley Isabell **92** 230

NASON *cont'd*
Shuah (Colcord) **141** 121
Shubal **115** 212
Simon **87** 124 **88** 64
Sophia **88** 380
Stephen **55** 316 **82** 318
83 13 **111** 138
Steve **134** 93
Susan **93** 91
Susanna **70** 283 **82** 332
88 380 **91** 114 **99** 197
198 200 **108** 57 **112** 219
Thaddeus **133** 217
Thomas **98** 105
Uriah **57** 186 **75** 110 **76**
257 **82** 216 **88** 151
Ursula **99** 56
W. H. **96** 200
Willard **70** 283
William **55** 314 315 375
70 263 **81** 431 **82** 78 93
217 317 320 323 326 328
330-332 501-503 **83** 9 10
17 **88** 151 349 377-380
91 114 390 **99** 197 **112**
219 **125** 221
William Bracey **133** 45
William H. **96** 202
William Henry **92** 230
NASSAU
Josephine K. **114** 186
Nasson *see* Nason
NATERLOW Jos **65** 116
NATHAN Abigail (Lucas)
132 163
Joseph **110** 129
Matthew **112** 322
Ruth **126** 140
Samuel **132** 163
NATHANIEL
Harriet Ella **70** 203
William **70** 203
NATICK Sarah **91** 391
NATIONS
Abigail **100** 234
John **100** 141 234 237 301
102 30
Lewis **101** 276
Mary **100** 237
Mary Mitchel **102** 30
Rebecca **100** 234 237
102 30
Rebecca (Whitteker)
100 301
NATTERSTROM
Sukey **79** 39
NAUDAIN Andrew **90** 84
141 310
Lydia **90** 84 93 **141** 310 311
NAUFFTS
Alexander **125** 261
Anne (Ridman) **125** 257
Jacob **125** 257
Margaret (Murphy)
125 260
Martha (Rogers) **125** 261
NAUGHTON
Patrick **139** 207
Sophia (Hatcher) **120** 15
Stephen A. **120** 15

NAUGHTY
Margaret **54** 178
NAUHAWTON **142** 110
NAUNTON — Mrs. **58** 311
105 8
Elizabeth (Wingfield)
105 12
Margery **109** 19
Robert **105** 17
Thomas **109** 19
Ursula **105** 8 12 15 16 20
21
William **105** 12
NAUSIM
Edmund **100** 239
John **100** 239
Margaret **100** 239
NAUTEPUM
Peter **120** 26
NAUTROPP Abel **69** 40
Abigail **69** 40
Ama **68** 288 **69** 40
Anna **68** 288
Caleb **69** 40
Elizabeth **69** 40
Johanna **68** 175 **69** 40 374
Lois **69** 40
Mary **69** 40 376
Nehemiah **69** 40
Rhoda **69** 40 375
William **68** 174 **69** 40
NAVARRE
— Queen of **148** 117
Robert **119** 250
NAVARRO
Carlos Besa **109** 287
Cristina **109** 285
Jose Antonio **109** 285
Rosario **109** 285
Teresa (Foster) **109** 287
Theodora **81** 325
NAVE
Jane Mahalia **94** 140
NAVESTOCK
Ellis de **100** 22
NAVINA Naoma **132** 191
NAW James **100** 235
Jane **100** 235
Martha **100** 235
NAWTE
Elizabeth **67** 76
William **67** 76
NAY *see also* Nye
Abigail (Webster)
142 268
Ann (Gyles) **100** 303
Anna **59** 287
Anthony **59** 287
Bessie Celia **86** 151
Hannah J. **124** 207
Harriet **126** 80
Jerusha **126** 80
John **58** 29 33 138 139
142 268
Nicholas **100** 303
Ormsby Henry **86** 151
Sarah Jane (Horn) **86** 151
NAYLE
Charles F. **114** 191
Henry M. **114** 191
Jane **114** 191

NAYLE *cont'd*
John **84** 282
Mary **114** 191
Philip A. **114** 191
Richard **111** 85
Susan **114** 191
NAYLOR Nailor Nayler
Abraham **117** 111
Ann **65** 35 **73** 143 144 149
  108 212
Baston **73** 136
Benjamin **73** 146 218 223
  262
Christopher **54** 92
Deborah **74** 34
Edmond **93** 19
Elizabeth **64** 344 **65** 35 43
  73 269
Elizabeth (Hamby)
  145 106
Frantz (Mrs.) **98** 147
George **73** 146 228
Henry (Mrs.) **85** 425
Isaac Jones **73** 228
James **73** 222 227 **74** 34
  143 33
John **57** 316 **109** 6
Joshua **73** 139 225
Judson **73** 269
Lydia **74** 34
Margaret **73** 138 **109** 6 7
Martha **73** 143 **74** 34
  103 143
Mary **73** 223 **74** 34 **95** 288
Mary (Penrose) **117** 110
Mary Jane **117** 111
Nicholas **73** 143 **109** 9
Philip **51** 220
R. Veldon **106** 126
Rachel **117** 111
Richard **90** 194 265
Susanna **73** 217
Thomas **73** 267 **101** 161
William **101** 10 **145** 106
Nayson *see* Nason
NAZITER Jane **71** 126
John **71** 125
Michael **71** 124 125 127
William **71** 124
NAZRO Arthur Francis
  76 246
Arthur P. **76** 246
Arthur Phillips (Mrs.)
  75 65 **77** 156 **78** 206
Elizabeth **100** 296
Eveline Blunt **76** 246
Henry **93** 372
Isaac **102** 31
Mary **59** 325 **60** 254
Mary Elizabeth **93** 372
Mary Evert **78** 206
Matthew **59** 325 **140** 230
  327
Stephen **60** 254
Thomas W. **76** 246
NEAD
Daniel Wunderlich **69**
  xxxii
NEAFLE —— **57** 236
NEAGLE Neagles
Joan **92** 53

NEAGLE *cont'd*
John **102** 112
Lydia (Kimberly) **102** 112
Mary **92** 52
Mary Jane **91** 386
Richard **60** 104
NEAGOOSE — Mr. **71** 26
NEALAND Edward **148** 336
NEALE Neal Neall Neele -
  see also Neil
—— **53** 360 **54** 101 109
  238 **59** 141 **61** 97 **65** 135
  72 56 **74** 217 227 **83** 35
  194 **108** 80 **111** 327 **116**
  248
— Mr. **71** 251
— Mrs. **55** 141 **76** 223
  83 194
— Rev. Dr. **90** 115
— Rev. Mr. **145** 33
A. G. **91** 331
Abby L. (Tarlton) **83** 185
  187
Abigail **55** 375 **57** 399 **58**
  176 264 **59** 275 **61** 131
  65 352 **73** 66 **83** 21 26
  87 122 **123** 263
Abigail (Haines) **125** 62
Abijah **60** 41
Abraham **117** 58
Adeline **83** 174
Agnes **52** 261
Alanso S. **82** 454
Albert B. **97** 67
Albert Barnes **85** 197
Albert G. **90** 83
Alexander **81** 490 **86** 147
Alice **59** 310 313 391
  125 62
Andrew **54** 408 **55** 315
  74 263 **82** 50 **83** 11 **116**
  142
Andrew J. **73** 204
Andrus **82** 327
Ann **55** 392 **59** 310 **108** 104
Ann Eliza **79** 44
Ann S. (Trefethen) **90** 83
Anna **59** 191 **60** 181
  136 313
Anne **51** 121 122 **74** 263
Anne (Bland) (Culverwell)
  148 116-120
Asa M. **72** 257
Barker **124** 148
Benjamin **59** 89 275 361
  393
Betsey **72** 269 **73** 44 **79** 37
  97 142
Bridget **72** 62 63
Cara Gertrude **83** 174
Caroline **72** 274 **78** 322
  83 232
Catherine **58** 385 **72** 267
  82 454
Charles Abbot **90** 83
Charles E. **90** 83
Charlotte **124** 147-149
Clarence Robert (Mrs.)
  108 135
Clarinda **73** 191
Comfort **72** 255 257 **73** 44

NEALE *cont'd*
Cora Lee **112** 77
D. M. **91** 331
Daniel **91** 93 387 **94** 98
  102 155
Daniel W. **88** 335
Daniel Wunderlich
  68 385
David G. **97** 268
Deborah **56** 93
Dominicus **95** 199
Dorothy **83** 177 185
E. D. **100** 78 **105** 188
Edith **82** 290 295
Edmund **74** 264 **115** 217
  116 269 270 294 **117** 48
Edward **76** 132 133
  127 174
Edward A. **92** 340
Edwin **72** 274
Elbridge **72** 274
Elbright **54** 336
Eleanor **73** 230 **90** 3
Eleanor (Cole) **86** 147
Elijah **72** 255 257 259 **73** 44
Eliza **109** 183
Eliza Jane (Amazeen) **83**
  177 185
Elizabeth **52** 261 **54** 336 **55**
  315 **59** 154 156 274 **65**
  351 **71** 32 249 **72** 256
  257 259 **73** 44 126 127
  75 5 6 8 11 **83** 10 **89** 260
  90 167 **99** 74 **100** 295
  125 287
Elizabeth (Haley) **90** 274
Elizabeth (Hubbard)
  83 10
Elizabeth (Locke) **90** 274
Elizabeth Bancroft **97** 67
Elizabeth Duffield
  108 187
Elizabeth Martigini
  Whittredge **85** 322
Elsie **59** 313
Emily M. (Swain) **90** 83
Emma E. **92** 400 **116** 99
Emma J. **115** 32
Enos **116** 187
Enos H. **72** 257
Ethelbright **54** 336
Eugene B. **69** 256
Eugenia **82** 454
Fielder **73** 268
Frances **52** 261 **148** 120
Frances J. **84** 30
Francis **52** 261 **71** 249
  104 177
Frank K. **94** 32
Fred **73** 189
Gay **87** 173
George **59** 309 **72** 259 **75** 9
  80 280-282 284-287 290-
  295 299 446 **82** 58
George Alfred **78** 322
Gideon **75** 9
Grace **86** 78 248
Grace (Marche) **86** 248
Hannah **52** 436 **55** 315 **59**
  274 275 **63** 169 **74** 228
  257 **83** 11 **87** 288 **95** 192

NEALE *cont'd*
116 133
Hannah (Hooper) **83** 11
Hannah (Pray) **113** 48
143 128
Hannah (Smith) **90** 274
Hannah F. **83** 183 185
Hannah Fields **83** 174
Hannah W. **72** 257
Harriet Charlotte **76** 212
Helen **82** 56
Henrietta **73** 220
Henry **58** 385 **59** 156-158
99 231 **105** 199 **112** 112
113 48 58 **143** 128
Henry R. **90** 37
Hiram **72** 257 259 **75** 12
Honora **52** 261
Humphrey **97** 67
Ichabod **59** 136
Ida Belle **68** 152
Ida M. **92** 340
Isaac **72** 257
James **54** 446 **68** 152 168
72 256 257 259 **73** 44 **75**
10 **82** 50 423 **83** 194 **97**
270 **101** 29
James William **85** 197
Jane **59** 135
Jane (Andrews) **104** 177
Jane (Came) **115** 217
Janet **68** 152
Jennie Sinclair **83** 433 437
Jeremiah **74** 117
Jeremiah H. **73** 198
Jerry **73** 73
Jerusha **59** 363
Joan **82** 55 57 62
Joanna **59** 154 158 **91** 348
Job **58** 176 **59** 390 392 **60**
64 178 179 181
John **51** 119-121 147 **53**
107 108 **55** 254 315 **57**
403 **58** 83 **59** 77 78 134-
137 309 390 **60** 176 **65**
351 **68** 152 **71** 32 249 **72**
56-58 60 61 84 257 **74**
144 145 218 220 **76** 236
79 173 **82** 50 55 57 **83**
10 **86** 41 **87** 227 230 237
88 252 **105** 113 **111** 107
112 17 **116** 294 **124** 148
143 20 259 **145** 359
John R. **59** 334
John W. **83** 185 187
Johnson **74** 218 220 228-
230 **82** 327
Jonathan **59** 361 **91** 93
Joseph **57** 399 403 **58** 176
264 **59** 89 274 275 310
313 362 389 391 **60** 64
74 117 **90** 274 **99** 257
105 199 **115** 156 **118**
107
Joshua **65** 352 **125** 62
Julius **114** 317
Katharine **72** 60
Katharine V. **69** 256
Letitia (Platts) **116** 187
Letitia G. **116** 188
Lillian **95** 250

NEALE *cont'd*
Lois **53** 108 **59** 298 306 409
Lois Smithers **145** 31
Louisa **72** 257
Lucy **73** 192 194
Lucy (Sampson) **114** 317
Lucy A. (Fernald) **90** 83
Lucy G. **97** 143 266
Lucy M. **90** 83
Lydia **59** 89 274 275 361
363 **60** 41 **63** 168 **68** 168
72 257 259 **73** 44 **89** 178
113 48 **129** 165 **135** 43
143 128
Lydia Louisa **72** 257
Lydia N. **72** 257
Malcome E. **114** 65
Margaret **65** 351 **82** 295
298
Margaret C. **90** 83
Margaret E. **83** 434 436
Margery **51** 120 121 **72**
58 60 62 **74** 142 144 145
Maria **78** 31 **83** 308
Marie **148** 120
Martha **59** 137 **96** 347
Mary **52** 261 **55** 313 **57** 403
58 83 **59** 78 89 134 136
274 306 362 409 **60** 176
71 249 **73** 194 **74** 203
75 264 **82** 50 423 511 **83**
11 21 26 **90** 324 **109** 68
115 151 **116** 139 **117** 62
Mary (Downs) **95** 199
Mary D. **83** 308
Mary Elizabeth **68** xxxv
74 xxvii **90** 274 **91** 57
145
Mary Emily H. (Newhall)
88 335
Mary Frances **83** 436
84 19
Mary Janet **68** 152
Mary N. **72** 257
Mary T. **83** 179 185
Mary Thomas **83** 422 437
Minnie Grace **68** 152
Molly **95** 192
Nancy **74** 306 **114** 179
128 160
Nancy A. (Stone) **90** 83
Nathan **72** 257
Olive **74** 252
Olive S. (Getchell) **94** 32
Parmenia **124** 148
Patience **74** 229 230 261
263 **95** 198
Peace **63** 175
Peggy **82** 50
Persis M. **124** 37
Peter M. **72** 257
Phebe **76** 132 **82** 283 295
Philemon C. (Mrs.)
107 134
Philip J. **72** 257
Rachel **59** 154 157 **74** 308
78 40 **93** 73 **98** 185 **143**
337
Rachel H. (Eldridge)
91 387
Rebecca **59** 389 391

NEALE *cont'd*
111 116
Rebecca (Penrose)
(Forbes) **117** 58
Rebecca P. **116** 188
Rhoda **120** 241
Richard **82** 50 **97** 142
Robert **82** 50 283 290 295
423 **83** 174 177 185 194
Rollin H. **90** 113 **124** 192
Ruby Adell **105** 126
Rufus **74** 264
Sally **116** 269 270 **117** 47
48 **124** 16
Sally (Davis) **117** 47 48
Samuel **65** 351 **73** 67 204
82 50 **83** 35 **90** 274
Sarah **53** 62 **59** 390 392 **60**
178 335 **65** 120 **74** 214
218 220 227-230 255 264
82 327 **83** 35 **116** 220
124 148 **125** 220
Sarah (Coates) **111** 107
Sarah (Davis) **116** 270
Sarah Ann **73** 194
Sarah Ann (Jewett) **90** 51
Sarah Elizabeth **114** 317
Sarah Elizabeth (Smith)
90 274
Sarah Jane **89** 227
Serena **58** 385
Shuah **55** 372 **83** 13
Shuah (Lord) **83** 13
Smith **90** 274
Solomon **55** 375 **97** 269
Stephen **97** 267 300
Sukey **74** 264
Susanna **73** 273
Susanna R. **90** 45
Sylvester W. **90** 83
Theadora **73** 135
Theodore Augustus
85 322
Thomas **52** 230 261 **53** 108
55 390 **59** 306 409 **62**
328 331 **73** 137 **80** 280
281 286 **82** 56 57 **83** 174
182 185 299 300 **91** 348
148 118 120
Thomas S. **90** 51
Thomasine **104** 33
Titus **76** 133
Vivian Ellen **108** 135
Walter **51** 45 **52** 261 262
53 355 **54** 240 **65** 299
71 90 **90** 274 **148** 120
William **51** 121 122 **52** 261
53 355 **55** 372 **58** 385
72 62 **73** 194 224 **78** 31
80 408 **82** 55 58 **91** 348
104 33 **105** 113 **148** 116
118-120
William A. **92** 320
William F. **107** 134
William H. **68** 152
Nealey *see* Nealley
Neall *see* Neale
NEALLEY Nealey
Abby (Pray) **94** 189
Abby Josephine **94** 189
Anna G. **83** 20

NEALLEY *cont'd*
Benjamin F. **65** 217
Benjamin Mason **94** 189
Ella **83** 437 438
Fannie **65** 217
Hannah E. (Grant) **121**
303 **122** 312
John B. **82** 508
Mary Elizabeth **82** 508
Robert **121** 303 **122** 312
Susan Emerson **65** 217
NEALOR William **94** 277
NEANDER —— **61** 12
NEANE Margaret **112** 120
NEARE Near
Albert A. **122** 195
I. W. **114** 68
M. Juliana (Mayhew)
122 195
NEARGRASS Edward **67**
111 **80** 257 **96** 15
Mary **67** 111 **80** 253 257
96 15
Rebecca **67** 111 **69** 92
96 15
Susanna **67** 111 **96** 15 193
NEARING Nearin
A. H. **72** 184
Ahasel **72** 42 87 90 99
Albert G. **72** 47 96 105
Ann E. **112** 58
Asa **112** 58
Asabel **72** 89 97
Asabel Henry **72** 89
Asahel H. **72** 47 103
Betsey **114** 307
Charlotte **112** 58
Cynthia L. **112** 58
Cyrenus **112** 58
Electa **112** 58
Elizabeth **53** 247
Emily A. **112** 59
Emily Graham **72** 97
George **112** 58
H. L. **112** 58
Harry **72** 181
Harvey **112** 58
Hector **72** 184
Hector Latimer **72** 97
Heman Loomis **72** 90
Henrietta **112** 58
Henrietta M. **112** 59
Henry **112** 58 59
Henry Thrall **72** 97
Hezekiah **72** 181
J. S. **112** 58
John Henry **53** 247
John M. **115** 134
Joseph **112** 58
Julia **72** 46 96
Leander B. **112** 59
Lewis A. **112** 58
Lois **112** 58
Louise N. **112** 58
Margaret **112** 58
Maria **72** 89
Mary Ann **72** 47 48 97 103
112 58
Mary E. **112** 55 58
Matilda **112** 58
Melissa **72** 87

NEARING *cont'd*
Minerva **112** 58
Molly **72** 42 99
Myra **112** 58
Nancy A. **72** 105
Philo **112** 58
Polly **112** 58
Polly Van **72** 89
Russell **112** 59
Samuel **112** 58
Sylvester **112** 58
Thankful **112** 58
Thankful M. **112** 58 59
Truman **114** 307
Neason *see* Nason
NEAT Neate
Eleanor **63** xlvii **109** 64
Elizabeth **108** 185
Elizabeth (Clark) **125** 102
140 230
Hannah **77** 231
Hulda **100** 197
John **78** 312 **125** 102 **140**
230 328
NEATHERD John **76** 288
NEAU John **86** 317 318
Lydia **86** 317 318
Mary M. **86** 317
NEAVE John **64** 214
Mary **63** 357 **64** 61
Pierson Mitchell **109** 66
Richard **63** 357 **64** 61
NEAVENS Anna **72** 145
NEAVERS Joshua **56** 74
NEAVORD
Edmund **101** 244
Sewsan **101** 244
William **101** 244
NEBEKER Ida **101** 124
Lewis Hebert (Mrs.)
102 124
Myrtilla **105** 127
NEBEL Edith A. (Hales)
103 119
NEBLE
Beverly Ruth **86** 95
Christine (Larsen) **86** 94
Eyvind M. **86** 95
Frances **86** 95
Karen (Paulsen) **86** 94
Martin **86** 94
Olivea (Hansen) **86** 95
Sophus Frederik **81** 107
219 **86** 94 95 109 203
NEBLETT
Eliza D. **107** 80
NECHANICKY
Anna K. **80** 161
NECHETT —— **96** 192
NECKER Amons **143** 262
NECKLAS Fortune **78** 178
Necol *see* Nichol
NED Neds
Bathsheba (Lloyd) **89** 111
Simon **70** 262
Nedam *see* Needham
Nedham *see* Needham
Neds *see* Ned

NEEDHAM
Nedam Nedham
Needom Niedham
— Lady **52** 251
— Mrs. **105** 184
___ (Pease) **110** 34
Abbie **110** 122
Abbie (Pratt) **110** 118
Abigail **101** 64 **110** 27 30
34 256
Abigail (Perry) **110** 32 35
Abigail (Walbridge)
110 371
Abigail (Wales) **110** 120
Abigail G. **110** 120
Abner **110** 30 34 35 116
117 258
Achsah (Thayer) **110** 119
Achsah L. **110** 119
Addie **110** 258
Adelbert **110** 117
Adelbert Jordan **110** 117
Alanson Andrews
110 117
Alfred **110** 113 257
Alfred Allen **110** 114
Alfred C. **110** 121 122
Alice **110** 257
Alice (Thompson)
110 121
Alvin **110** 37 256
Amanda (Cooley)
110 115
Amanda Jane (Holton)
110 37
Amelia **110** 120
Amelia G. **80** 47
Amy **110** 116
Andrew A. **110** 114 256
Ann **143** 50
Ann (Potter) **110** 27
Ann E. **110** 115
Anna **82** 181 **110** 27 32 35
116
Anna (Thayer) **110** 37
Anna Hosick **110** 121
Annah **110** 32 120
Anne **76** 309-311
Annis **110** 37
Annis E. **110** 257
Anthony **55** 328 **60** 188
110 27-29 31 32 34 36 37
114 256
Anthony Matthias **110** 37
Anthony Storrs **110** 37
Arabel **110** 117
Asa **110** 115
Asa H. **110** 115
Azariah C. **110** 120
Azubah **110** 34 118 258
Bashaba **110** 258
Bathsheba (Ferry) **110** 116
Belle E. **110** 115 258
Benjamin **110** 31 119
136 56
Benjamin A. **110** 256
Benjamin Agard **110** 117
Benjamin Cooley **110** 119
Betsey **108** 319 **110** 37 116
Byrdee M. **110** 36 37

NEEDHAM *cont'd*
Campbell Gertrude
  (Nickson) **110** 122
Candace **110** 37
Carlos D. **110** 257
Caroline **110** 121
Caroline (Cook) **110** 120
Caroline (Woodward)
  110 121
Caroline Amelia **110** 119
Caroline D. **110** 120
Catherine (Walbridge)
  110 114
Catherine (Warner)
  110 36
Chandler **110** 115 257
Charles **110** 35 120
Charles G. **110** 257
Charles Osgood **110** 122
Charles Stillman **110** 122
Charlie **110** 37
Charlotte (Bowers)
  110 119
Charlotte A. **110** 257
Charlotte Adele **110** 117
Charlotte Alaxa
  (Phetteplace) **110** 117
Chester **110** 115
Chloe **110** 120
Chloo (Strong) **110** 32 120
Chloe M. **110** 114
Clarra **110** 35
Content **72** 184
Corlistis **110** 258
Cornelia (White) **110** 119
Cynthia (Baxter) **110** 117
Danford **110** 35 118 121
  257
Daniel **55** 322 **58** 305 **95**
  280 **103** 82 **110** 30 31 34
  35 116 117 257
Daniel D. **110** 36
Darius Munger **110** 34
  117
David **110** 31 32 113 256
David A. **110** 114 257
David B. **110** 257
David Besse **110** 114
Deborah (Fuller) **110** 34
Deidamia **110** 256
Deidamia (Walbridge)
  110 114
Della C. **110** 119 258
Desire **110** 30
Dinah (Foster) (Amos)
  110 121
Dolly **110** 115
Dora A. **110** 121
Dorothy **51** 390 **76** 308-
  311 **110** 27 30
Dorothy (Munger) **110**
  30 **111** 135
Ebenezer Brigham **110** 37
Edgar **93** 199
Edmond **148** 340
Edmund **52** 320 **58** 305
Edward **97** 216 **104** 174
Edward W. **110** 257
Eleanor **104** 173 **105** 183
  184 **106** 235
Elisha **110** 32 35 120

NEEDHAM *cont'd*
Eliza **110** 257
Elizabeth **52** 251 256 **76**
  308 309 **94** 82 **110** 27 28
  116 257 **141** 332 **143**
  341 342
Elizabeth (Gardner) **110**
  32 34
Elizabeth (Mead) **110** 116
Elizabeth (Moulton)
  110 31
Elizabeth (Wilder)
  110 115
Ella A. **110** 118
Ella Viantha (Hiddleson)
  110 37
Ellen A. **110** 257
Ellen E. **110** 258
Emeline **69** 35
Emma **110** 122
Emma (Souder) **110** 37
Emmerette P. **110** 37
Enoch Gardner **110** 120
Ernest T. **110** 257
Esther (Wales) **110** 120
Esther Burnet **110** 120
Eugene **110** 258
Eunice **110** 32 36 119 120
Eunice (Fiske) **110** 114
Eunice (Fuller) **110** 32
Eunice (Moulton) **110** 30
Eunice M. **110** 115 257
Eva **110** 119
Ezekiel **57** 141 **58** 305 **66**
  125 **141** 332
Fayette O. **110** 118 257
Frances **76** 309 311
Francis **52** 251
Francis A. **110** 121
Francis M. **110** 115 257
Frank **110** 258
Frank A. **110** 122
Frank M. **110** 257
Fred J. **110** 114
Frederic **110** 35
Gabrielle **110** 37
George **110** 27
George A. **110** 114 115
George E. **110** 257
George H. **110** 36 257
Georgiana **110** 37
Gertrude **110** 122
Gertrude (Sears) **110** 121
Hannah **110** 28 29 34 118
  256
Hannah (Agard) **110** 117
Hannah (Berry) (Hood)
  148 335 338 340
Hannah (Gibbs) (Nichols)
  110 117
Hannah (Heaton) **110** 35
Harriet **57** 392 **110** 116 257
Harry **110** 116
Heaton **110** 35
Helen E. (Chapman)
  110 115
Helen G. **110** 257
Helen M. **110** 114
Helen P. **110** 115
Henry **110** 119

NEEDHAM *cont'd*
Henry Chapman **110**
  115 117
Henry H. **110** 257
Henry M. **110** 257
Henry Miles **110** 115
Hester Ann (Hiatt)
  110 121
Horace **110** 120
Horatio **110** 118
Horatio G. **110** 119 258
Howard Chamberlain
  110 117
Huldah **110** 34 116
Humphrey **110** 28 30 256
  111 135
Ida L. **110** 257
Irene **110** 37
Isaac **110** 27
Isabel **110** 117 258
J. A. **110** 258
James **110** 122
James Francis **110** 121
James H. **110** 35 256
Jane **51** 390 **76** 309 **104** 173
  105 184 **106** 235 **110**
  258
Jane Ann **110** 37
Jane Elizabeth **110** 120
Jared Gardner **110** 119
Jasper **56** 71 **110** 28 30 31
  34 117 256
Jeremiah **110** 28 30 32 34
  35 116 119 120
Joan **58** 305
John **51** 390 **57** 143 **58** 305
  76 310 **80** 387 **82** 181
  110 27 34 122 **114** 182
John A. **110** 114
John S. **110** 257
John Sample **110** 37
John Varnum **82** 181
Jonathan **110** 34 114 115
  257
Joseph **110** 30
Josephine (Turner)
  110 117
Josephine M. **110** 119
Julia **110** 120
Julia (Tiffany) **110** 117
Julia F. (Warren) **110** 114
Julia Jane **110** 118
Laura **110** 37
Lauretta (Howe) **110** 115
Laurette H. **110** 257
Levi **71** 49
Lewis **110** 120
Lodisa (Pratt) **110** 115
Lodisa F. **110** 257
Lois (Huntley) **110** 119
Lois A. **110** 119
Loretta **110** 258
Lorinda **110** 114
Louisa **110** 120 121
Lovina **110** 37 **137** 27
Lovina (Nelson) **110** 34
  117
Lovisa **110** 117
Lucretia O. **110** 119
Lucy **63** 76 **110** 33 36 118
  257 **137** 74

NEEDHAM *cont'd*
Lucy (Green) **110** 117
Lucy D. **110** 117 121
Luke **110** 113
Luke B. **110** 114
Lurancy **110** 120
Lydia (Blodgett) **110** 32
Lydia A. **110** 114 257
Lyman **110** 115 117 257
Lyman H. **110** 119
Lyman W. **110** 37
Lysander **80** 47
Mabel **110** 120
Marcena **110** 120
Margaret **76** 310 **97** 216
Margaret J. (Coye) **110** 118
Margaret J. Coy **110** 257
Margery **76** 309
Maria A. **110** 258
Marsena **110** 120
Marsena Wales **110** 120
Marsilvia **110** 114 256 257
Martha **110** 35
Martin **110** 120
Mary **55** 322 **58** 305 **62** 62 **63** 54 **76** 309 **90** 284 **93** 199 **110** 27 28 31 32 34 36 118 120 121 257 258 **111** 135 **125** 105
Mary (Cook) **110** 31
Mary (Foster) **110** 120
Mary (Fuller) **110** 36
Mary (Moulton) **110** 28
Mary (Swinerton) **110** 27
Mary Ann (Town) **110** 120
Mary C. **110** 257
Mary E. **110** 118
Mary Elizabeth **110** 37
Mary Elizabeth (Gordon) (Wells) **110** 121
Mary Helena **110** 121
Mary Jane (Davidson) **110** 115
Mary M. **110** 36 114 118 256 258
Mary M. (Worthington) **110** 117
Matilda **110** 115
Maud **76** 309
Mehitable **110** 33
Mehitable (Moulton) **110** 30
Melinda **110** 35 116 117 258
Melissa Clarissa **110** 37
Milton W. **110** 257
Miner **110** 258
Miner G. **110** 118
Miriam **110** 116
Molly **110** 28
Monroe **110** 118
Nancy (Belcher) **110** 114
Nancy A. **110** 256
Nancy E. (Janes) **110** 121
Naomi **110** 29 34
Nehemiah **110** 30 32 34
Nellie **110** 119
Nettie E. **110** 119 258
Ninna N. **110** 121

NEEDHAM *cont'd*
Noah L. **110** 119
Norman G. **110** 120
Olive (White) **114** 204
Olive A. **110** 114
Olive M. **110** 257
Olive M. (White) **110** 114
Oliver **110** 114
Orenda **110** 120
Orinda (Nelson) **110** 114
Orril **110** 37 257
Orrin **110** 36 37 256
Orrin O. **114** 204
Otis **110** 114 257 **114** 204
Pearl Emmerette **110** 37
Persis **110** 114 257
Phebe **110** 31 34 117 256
Phebe Green **110** 117
Polly **110** 120
Polly (Miller) **110** 34
Polly Marcy **110** 113
Priscilla **58** 305
Provided **110** 27
R. Jane **76** 269
Rachel **84** 414 **110** 27 30
Ralph Burnham **103** 120
Rebecca **107** 183 **110** 27 28 35 256 **136** 241
Rebecca (Jaquith) **136** 56
Rebecca (Munger) **110** 32
Rebecca M. **110** 114
Robert **52** 251 **76** 308 309 **110** 34 115 258 **112** 292
Robert W. **110** 116 258
Roswell **110** 115 257 258
Ruth **58** 305 **110** 28-30 34 120
Ruth (Cooley) **110** 28 116 119
Ruth (Sibley) **110** 27
S. J.C. **58** 305
Sabra **57** 392
Sally **110** 114-116 257
Sally (Colburn) **110** 115
Sally (Gates) **110** 32 33
Salome **110** 114
Samuel **110** 32 34 **141** 356
Samuel Strong **110** 120
Sarah **65** 170 **66** 125 **97** 216 **110** 30 34 36 115 116 119 257 258
Sarah (Gage) **110** 120
Sarah Jane **82** 181
Sarah Jane (Olds) **110** 37
Sarah Jane Clarkson **59** xlviii **60** 188
Sarah P. **110** 114
Sidney F. **110** 116 258
Silas Thayer **110** 119
Sophia **69** xlix **82** 114 **110** 36 256
Sophia (Pratt) **110** 37
Sophia (Willis) **114** 204
Sophia Caroline **55** 321
Sophia W. **110** 119
Stephen **110** 31 33 35 36 121 256
Stephen Mead **110** 116
Stillman **110** 121
Susan **110** 257
Susan (Deming) **110** 119

NEEDHAM *cont'd*
Susanna **110** 34 36
Sylvester **110** 37
Thankful (Corley) **110** 35
Theodore P. **110** 258
Thomas **52** 251 **76** 309-311 **110** 27 28
Timothy S. **137** 42
Truman **110** 116
Tryphena **110** 120
Varnum **78** 317
W. B. **110** 258
W. E. **110** 122 258
W. Eugene **110** 257
W. W. **110** 257
Wales **110** 114
Wales Foster **110** 114
Walter **55** 321
Walter H. **110** 257
Ward S. **110** 121
Warren **110** 115 257
Watson **110** 257
Willard M. **110** 37
William **51** 390 **57** 392 **110** 114 120 **128** 300
William A. **110** 114 256
William L. **110** 257
William Loring **110** 121
William M. **110** 257
William Merritt **110** 117
William Minot **110** 117
Wilma Icle **110** 122
Wyles **110** 117
Zalmon **110** 120
NEEDS James **63** 18
Neef *see* Neff
Neele *see* Neale
NEELES — Mr. **141** 151
NEELY Neeley
—— **64** xlix **103** 161
Adela Clarissa **77** 144
Bertha Amanda **77** 263
Charles Lea **77** 144
Charles Rufus **77** 144
Christopher **68** 242
Clemmie **77** 263
Elizabeth **77** 144
Fanny **77** 144
Haiden **77** 263
Jack **78** 328
James **77** 140
James Jackson **77** 144
John **117** 76 79
Louisa **77** 144
Margaret **111** 208
Margaret Viana **77** 263
Mary **77** 263
Mary Catherine **77** 144
Myrtle **77** 263
Nicholas Jackson **77** 263
Rufus Polk **77** 144
Sarah **77** 144
Sophia **77** 140
Thomas **77** 144
William **77** 144
NEFF Naef
Abiah **128** 271
Amos E. (Mrs.) **107** 134
Bertha P. **107** 134
Caroline **85** 315
Catherine (Wolf) **128** 97

NEFF *cont'd*
Christian **128** 97
Cornelia **83** 359
Cynthia Amelia **128** 271
Ebenezer **58** 373
Ebenezer Augustine
    58 373
Ebenezer C. **123** 13
Edward **128** 271
Edwin **128** 271
Eleanor E. (McIntosh)
    123 13
Eliza **128** 271
Elizabeth Clifford **54**
    xxxix 127 **59** 106
Emma **85** 315
Esther **128** 271
Esther (Webb) **128** 271
Florinda (Porter)
    (Holmes) **128** 271
Francis Joseph Nicolas
    110 130
Frederick **83** 359
Frederick W. **85** 315
George **128** 263
George H. **117** 59
Hannah M. **77** 177
John H. **128** 263
John J. **85** 315
John W. **112** 58
Jonathan **83** 359
Joseph **98** 356 **128** 271
    135 261
Joseph Henry **128** 271
Lewis **113** 236
Lewis E. **124** 140 141 **128**
    161 162 **135** 152
Lewis Edwin **100** 112
    115 159
Lora **98** 356
Louisa Barkley **85** 315
Lucy **120** 48
Lucy (Ford) **120** 48
Manvers B. **72** 205
Maria Antoinette
    (Pinkerton) **128** 263
Mary **83** 359 **128** 271
Mary (Coburn) **120** 48
Mary E. (Kas) **128** 263
Miriam **98** 356
Nancy **112** 58 **128** 271
Polly **112** 54 58
Polly (Bennett) **112** 58
Roxana **72** 205
Roxana S. (Kibby)
    116 258
Rudolph **54** 128
Silas **112** 58
Tilla Hughes **107** 318
Voral **73** 41
W. **128** 97
Warner **128** 97
Warren **128** 97
Waterman **114** 161
William **115** 237 **120** 48
    128 271
William L. **77** 177
Zebulon **72** 205 **116** 258
NEGERS —— **101** 247
NEGLES
Elizabeth **78** 414

NEGLEY Anna B.
    (Winebiddle) **92** 4
Jacob **92** 4
Peter **89** 228
Priscilla (Lazell) (Brooks)
    89 228
Sarah Jane **92** 3 4 **105** 219
NEGRE George **143** 261
NEGUS — Capt. **64** 33
Abigail **89** 380 381
Abigail (Pease) **89** 380
Alice **135** 277
Amanda (Jewett) **133** 233
Bena **127** 149
Benjamin **105** 192 **106** 26
    127 148 **146** 274
Carrie M. **117** 208
Darius **133** 233
Desire **70** 81
Edgar C. **117** 211
Elizabeth **106** 26 **135** 277
Ellen A. **117** 24
Esther Bertha **117** 214
George **117** 24
Grace **146** 274
Grove **133** 233
Hannah **52** 17 22 **135** 314
Hannah M. **117** 215
Isaac **52** 17 22 **97** 328 **127**
    148 **131** 218
Israel **133** 233
Jabesh **64** 188
Jabez **106** 26
James Fred **117** 214
James I. **117** 214
Jane **52** 17 22
Jane (Deighton) (Lugg)
    141 100
Job **127** 148
John **70** 81 **127** 148
John Jared **133** 233
Jonas **89** 380 381
Jonath **102** 182
Jonathan **52** 17 22 **139** 302
    142 110 **146** 274
Lavinia (Gifford) **131** 218
Lillian C. **117** 211
Lora M. **117** 208
Maria **52** 22
Mary L. **117** 214
Nathaniel **127** 139
Phebe **75** 302 **117** 24
Richmond **117** 208
Samuel **117** 24 **133** 233
Susanna **89** 380 831
Thomas **63** 350 **86** 351 **94**
    268 **117** 218 **127** 149
Thomas H. **117** 215
William **105** 192
William A. **117** 215
William H. **117** 24
NEHUS Hannah **51** 455
Isaac **51** 455
Jonathan **51** 171 172
Joseph **51** 413
William **51** 109
NEIGHBORS
Ann Elizabeth **77** 262
R. S. (Mrs.) **114** 158
William **77** 262

NEIGHBOUR
Elizabeth **66** 302
Francis **66** 153 302
Mary **66** 153 302
Sarah **66** 153
NEIKERK Floyd Edwin
    104 78 145 **118** 68
NEIL Neile Neill - *see also*
    Neale
—— **56** 402
— Col. **77** 141
— Mr. **64** 215
Adeliza **127** 276
Alice **127** 275
Anna Maria **77** 291
Carrie E. (Bancroft) **97** 67
Charlotte **127** 276
Daniel **60** 220
Edward Duffield **70** 337
Elizabeth **64** 189
Filius **60** 188
Henry **127** 275
Henry Moore **64** xxxi 200
    70 287
Jennie Sinclair **83** 433 437
John **127** 275
John Godfrey **77** 291
Julia Evans **70** 287
M. Carrie (Jackson)
    83 299 300
Mary (Parke) **127** 275
Mary L. (Hanscom)
    83 182 185
Mary Thomas **83** 422 437
Rebecca **54** 273
Rebecca Park **127** 275
Richard **64** 58 **140** 5 6
Sarah Jane **89** 227
NEILD John **64** 165
Neill *see* Neil
NEILSON Neylsonn
—— **59** 225 **143** 366
Abigail **83** 311
Agnes **79** 171
Alexander Sliddell **83** 311
Arstanus Humboldt
    Socrates (Mrs.) **105** 129
Augusta Jay (Balch)
    83 488
Charles Homer **108** 222
Cornelia **87** 66
Edith Howard **108** 222
Elizabeth **60** 240
Elizabeth Ann **83** 311
Elizabeth Coolidge
    83 311
Francis **78** 88
Helen Louise **78** 88
Howard Stout **108** 222
Howard Stout (Mrs.) **81**
    363 **82** 237 **108** 63 139
    222
J. L. Hubert **64** 95
James **60** 160 240 **95** 98
Jane **60** 240
Jane Ballouci **108** 222
Jane Wallace **82** 237
John **60** 240 241
Joseph **60** 240
Kate **108** 69

NEILSON *cont'd*
Katharine Amelia Brown
  65 lv
Katharine Bishop **108** 222
Margaret **60** 240
Marian Redfield **108** 222
Mary **60** 160 **94** 386
Mary Elizabeth **97** 157
Robert **60** 349
Robert Hude (Mrs.)
  83 487
Samuel **60** 349
Sarah E. (Russell) **83** 487
Simon **60** 160
Thomas **60** 349
Wallace Platt **108** 222
William Allan **81** 9
NEILY Anne Elizabeth
  (Fitz Randolph) **98** 333
Catherine (Durland)
  98 334
Kinsman **98** 334
Mary Charlotte (Fitz
  Randolph) **98** 334
Owen **98** 333
NEITHAMER
Clara **85** 298
NEIVE John **52** 107
Nekerson *see* Nickerson
NELAH John **83** 379
NELE Dorcas **146** 272
Nelis *see* Nellis
NELL Casper **124** 313
Christian **124** 313
Louis Maximilian **133** 85
Peter Christian **124** 313
NELLE Margaret **67** 41
William **67** 41
Nelles *see* Nellis
Nelley *see* Nelly
NELLIGAN
Mary Josephine
  139 218
Michael **76** 53
NELLIS Nelis Nelles
Cornelia Eliza **76** 275
Eliza H. (Jenks) **90** 108
Esther Elizabeth **76** 275
George H. **142** 192
Jacob **76** 275
James **116** 258
Jonas **76** 275
Mabel **144** 119
Mary (Vaslette) **116** 258
Nancy **76** 275
Patrick **60** 240
Saunders K. G. **90** 108
Nellson *see* Nelson
NELLUM James **54** 192
Martha **54** 192
NELLY Nelley
Joanna **76** 185
Olive **76** 185
Sarah **56** 194
Thomas **76** 185
NELMS Eliza **77** 216
Matilda **109** 310
Ruth Earle **101** 124
Thomas **109** 310
NELONDE John **139** 286

NELSON Nellson Nelsen
—— **55** 350 **57** 230 **63** 334
  73 257 **81** 448 **82** 50 **92**
  42 **95** 24 **101** 221
— Capt. **60** 324
— Chief Justice **62** 72
— Col. **56** 150
— Gen. **61** 95
— Judge **143** 12
— Lord **54** 98
— Mr. **52** 163
— Mrs. **83** 35
____ (Deckers) **83** 417
A. J. **128** 170
A. W. **122** 109
Aaron **90** 256 **137** 22
Abigail **68** 249 **89** 295 **97**
  370 372 376 **103** 57
Abigail (Brewster) **89** 295
Abigail (Briggs) **125** 270
Abigail (Tebbetts)
  90 228 246
Active **104** 103 **147** 69
Ada **77** 145
Adam R. **110** 75 76
Agnes **81** 447
Albert Gallatin **110** 228
Albert R. **73** 257
Albertina (Anderson)
  106 223
Alexander **77** 145 **106** 223
Alfred T. **76** 22
Alice Josephine **76** 22
Andrew **55** 389 **92** 27
  100 300
Andrew J. **75** 272 **128** 92
Angeline **58** lxvii
Ann **73** 93 **81** 431 447 **82**
  50 **89** 295 **114** 186
Ann (Merrow) **100** 300
Ann Marshall **82** 50
Ann Mary **76** 275 **82** 50
Ann-Louisa T. **90** 54
Anna **105** 92 105 **110** 76
Anna (Warren) **113** 136
Anna Belle **80** 43
Anna C. (Weingarth)
  110 228
Anna Elizabeth **110** 75
Anna Louise **80** 43
Anna M. **116** 69
Anne **116** 135 **126** 217
Anne (Lambert) **148** 134
Anthony **117** 77
Archibald **110** 117
Argenia **104** 103
Arline M. (Cann) **83** 424
  437
Arthur (Mrs.) **129** 86
Aurilla M. **116** 210
Austin **66** 185
Austin M. **73** 257
Azubah (Needham)
  110 34
Bathsheba **56** 28
Benigna Ellen **77** 145
Benjamin **115** 142
Bernice **62** 124
Betsey **112** 318 **116** 211
  126 218
Betsey (Shaw) **111** 117

NELSON *cont'd*
Betsey (Simpson) **88** 286
Betsey J. **62** 125
Carl Matthew (Mrs.)
  104 145
Catherine (O'Flaharty)
  125 218
Catherine (Parkhurst)
  113 136
Catherine Hubbard
  67 329
Cephas **71** 48
Charles **77** 145 **116** 66
  147 85
Charles Colfax **110** 75
Charles E. **116** 66 115
Charlie **110** 76
Charlotte **116** 115
Charlotte Augusta **105** 62
Christian **66** 35
Christian Edgar **113** 155
Christopher **104** 103
Clara Bell **110** 75
Clara J. **83** 300 302
D. **83** 35
Daniel **74** 158 **82** 50 **89**
  295 **98** 230
Daniel B. **116** 211
Daniel Crocker **103** 57
David **110** 228
David V. **104** 233
Deborah Isabel **95** 166
Dexter C. **101** 214
Docia Melvina **104** 233
Dolly **82** 50
Dora **110** 76
Dora Gertrude **86** 199
Dora Hannah **110** 75
Dorothy **82** 50 295 296
  113 301 **148** 131 133
Dorothy (Stapleton) **128**
  82 **148** 130-133 135-137
  139 140
E. **78** 300
Ed **110** 76
Eddy Preston **110** 75
Edith Warren **75** 270
Edmond H. **104** 233
Edward **103** 57 **110** 228
Eleanor **88** 286
Eliza **52** 339
Elizabeth **55** 167 168 **58**
  297 **68** 202 **73** 142 **75**
  251 **101** 36 54 **104** 103
  110 75 **117** **112** 297
  122 124 **125** 287 **126**
  217 **135** 127 **141** 6
Elizabeth (Briggs)
  126 218
Elizabeth (Campbell)
  112 297
Elizabeth (Lowell) **94** 106
  148 133
Elizabeth (Warren)
  112 318
Elizabeth J. **62** 122
Elizabeth W. (Crocker)
  79 153
Elmer Lafayette **109** 231
Elmer Lafayette (Mrs.)
  104 145 **108** 235 **109**

NELSON *cont'd*
217 231
Emma O. **104** 102 103
Emma S. **104** 47
Ephraim **111** 97
Erasmus D. **99** 133
Estelle Caroline **80** 161
Esther **125** 40
Eugenia **77** 145
Eva **97** 128
Fannie S. **116** 211
Fanny **86** 17
Fanny (Cole) **126** 208
Flora Eliza (Sheldon)
    110 228
Frances **67** 68 74
Frances A. **51** 193
Fred Langley (Mrs.)
    108 135
Gene W. **110** 228
George **64** 57 **65** 79 **68** 352
    363-365 **69** 33 **101** 31
    103 57
George Samuel **103** 57
George W. **80** 111
Gilbert **68** 364
Glade Ian **141** 92 101 105
    109
Gordon Bruce **110** 76
Hamilton **104** 46 47
Hannah **58** 125 **82** 294 295
    110 76 **113** 144 **126** 217
Hannah (Sheffield)
    113 144
Harriet **122** 109
Harriet Elizabeth (Betts)
    110 229
Harrison Allen **109** 231
Hattie **77** 145
Helen Josephine
    (Chipman) **98** 184
Helen M. **116** 115
Helen Maria **106** 65
Helen Mary (Stetson)
    94 65
Henry **94** 95 **100** 65 **113**
    136 **114** 182 **125** 218
    144 7
Henry Nutter **82** 50
Herbert W. **122** 109
Hezekiah **110** 34
Hial F. **121** 180
Hilma Leontina **85** 187
    106 221 223 **107** 136
Horace D. **116** 115
Horatio **51** 376 **68** 179
    88 315
Howard Ross **107** 134
    110 221 228
Hugh **77** 145
I. M. (Mrs.) **98** 265
Ida **128** 92
Ida L. (Farr) **121** 180
Isaac **82** 50 295 296 **126** 218
J. W. **70** 192
Jacob **76** 275 **83** 417 **90** 228
    246 **97** 376
James **56** 28 **58** 297 **60** 243
    62 301 **64** 324 **81** 447
    448 **110** 75
James Augustus **98** 184

NELSON *cont'd*
James C. **109** 231
James M. **91** 123
James Newton (Mrs.)
    99 148
James Y. **91** 331
Jamin E. **94** 65
Jane **60** 69 **81** 448 **111** 115
    114 119
Jemima **142** 249
Jemima (Brown) **110** 229
Jennet J. **104** 103
Jennett **99** 133
Jenny **56** 42
Joan (Dummer) **148** 133
    134 140
John **51** 69 **52** 166 **53** 461
    55 73 **56** 149 152 **63** 129
    65 79 **67** 68 74 **78** 186
    79 54 **80** 43 **82** 50 **83** 35
    85 427 **88** 286 **89** 295
    91 331 **98** 200 **101** 54
    106 177 **107** 111 **110** 45
    75 **111** 117 **112** 292 297
    113 267 **141** 6 102 **148**
    20
John H. **66** 288
John Home **110** 75
John J. **80** 43
John S. **80** 161
John V. **125** 221
Joseph **74** 143 **148** 81 431 **82**
    50 **89** 295 **111** 117
Joseph B. **90** 33
Joseph H. **116** 211
Josephine M. **76** 22
Josiah **106** 264 **113** 136
Julia **85** 427
Katharine **148** 131-133
Laura E. **99** 148
Laura Ida **122** 109
Lazzie (Johnson) **128** 92
Leader **81** 431 **82** 50 **89**
    295 **92** 105 106
Ledu **97** 372
Lewis J. **121** 180
Lillian Julia **74** 296
Lo Ruhamah **56** 169 172
Lois Leverett **85** 88
Loretta M. (Coates)
    101 214
Loretta R. **104** 233
Loretta Rowley **97** 158
Louisa (Tukesbury)
    125 221
Louisa M. **75** 272
Lovica Jane (Carbine)
    100 111
Lovina **110** 34 117
Lucy (Hannum) **90** 256
Lucy (Moulton) **110** 117
Luther **116** 115
Lydia **52** 56 **55** 73 **66** 47 **82**
    50 **89** 295 **120** 35
M. B. **116** 115
Mabel Christine **98** 184
Mansel Hyrum **92** 146
    104 233
Mansel Hyrum (Mrs.)
    104 237 **105** 132
Marcus **114** 182

NELSON *cont'd*
Margaret **59** 57 **69** lxvii
    32 **74** 158 **81** 431 448 **92**
    106 107 **110** 115 **112**
    297 **141** 102 **143** 139
Margaret (Henderson)
    112 297
Margaret F. **120** 65
Margaret Frazier **113** 267
Maria (Harvey) **106** 75
    141 107
Maria B. **116** 115
Maria C. **128** 264
Mark **82** 294 295
Martha **51** 174 **52** 84 **130**
    138 140
Martha (Ford) **114** 119
Martha Eunice Ensign
    116 232
Martin Van Buren
    115 294
Mary **58** 296 **64** 211 **79** 272
    81 448 **82** 50 **83** 25 26
    89 295 **95** 86 **113** 223
    115 294 **148** 131 133
Mary (Hanchett) **110** 229
Mary (Harmon) **110** 229
Mary (Lunt) **148** 134
Mary (Southwell) **110** 229
Mary A. **116** 211
Mary Ann **99** 133
Mary Caroline **104** 233
Mary E. **116** 66
Mary Esther **106** 235
Mary L. **88** 333
Mary Martha **103** 57
Matthew **51** 45 **58** 296 **59**
    329 **60** 96 **81** 447 448
Maurice **91** 51
Mehitable **53** 461 **101** 167
Mercy **121** 177 **148** 133 134
Merriel **51** 416
Mildred Eva **113** 155
Miles Grant **110** 75
Millicent **77** 228
Mira A. **121** 179
Moses **110** 228
Murry **67** 329
Myron E. **73** 257
Nancy **67** 353 **83** 24 26
    147 116
Nancy (Beverstock)
    126 145
Nannie A. **110** 76
Nannie Amanda **110** 75
Nathaniel **62** 381 **83** 416
Nathaniel Marshall **82** 50
Nehemiah **113** 144
Nelson (Mrs.) **147** 370
Nicholas **75** 272
O. N. **54** 362
Obed **73** 257
Olaf N. **55** xxxii
Olive **82** 50 **136** 327
Oliver **126** 145
Oril **99** 168
Orinda **110** 114
Orpheus T. **73** 257
Paggey **89** 295
Pamelia **60** lxxiv
Parley **64** lxvi

NELSON *cont'd*
Pascal **91** 93
Patience **112** 318
Paul **116** 211
Paul E. (Mrs.) **116** 232
Pegei **95** 88
Peggy **111** 116
Peggy (Deckers) **83** 416
Percy **110** 45
Perry G. **104** 103
Phebe H. **99** 133
Philip **54** 260 **58** 125 **94**
    106 **128** 82 **140** 206-208
    148 130 131 133 134
Philippa (Andrews) (Felt)
    (Platts) **148** 134
Polly **74** 158 **75** 272 **97** 376
Price (Mrs.) **106** 126
Rachel **74** 101
Ralph J. **83** 424 437
Rebecca (Fitz Randolph)
    98 230
Richard **125** 42
Richard H. **55** 126
Richard Leader **82** 50
    89 295
Robert Rutherford (Mrs.)
    102 124
Ruth **113** 144
Ruth (Stainbrook) **91** 51
Ruth J. **126** 205
S. **116** 115
Sally **111** 118
Sally Hall **92** 27
Salome W. **69** lxvii
Samuel **103** 57 **148** 133
    134
Samuel Nichols **55** 168
    112 318
Sarah **61** 95 **63** 334 **66** 185
    74 158 **77** 145 **93** 85
    104 47 **110** 75 228 **115**
    215 **132** 218
Sarah (Bond) **137** 27
Sarah (Carver) **88** 316
Sarah (Grover) **115** 142
Sarah (Jewett) **94** 106
    148 133
Sarah A. (Nelson) **110** 75
Sarah A. Lyon **104** 46
Sarah Ann **110** 75
Sarah E. (Farr) **121** 180
Sarah Maria **115** 294
Sarah Sprague **103** 57
Seth **113** 143
Silence (Cheney) **113** 143
Sophia **77** 145
Stephen **104** 103
Stephen R. **79** 153
Susan **69** lxvi **104** 103
    122 109
Susan C. (Smith) **91** 123
Susanna **111** 117
Swain **81** 431
Temperance **65** 79
Temple **51** 69 **52** 166
Thomas **52** 58 **56** 54 55
    64 lxvi **69** 147 **74** 321 **94**
    106 **106** 264 **110** 228
    126 217 **128** 82 **136** 87
    148 130-136 139 140

NELSON *cont'd*
Tirzah Jane **110** 75
Verena **133** 230
Vivian M. (Sheldon)
    98 265
W. R. **76** 315
W. Ripley **120** 158
Wallace S. **94** 402
Wheeler **122** 109
William **51** 74 77 87 100
    52 91 101 102 281 285
    287 290 **53** 127 128 369
    370 **54** lxi 112 113 124
    126 366 **55** 130 236 237
    56 xxxi **58** xliii 214 **59**
    xlii 57 225 233 234 329
    60 xxxiv 82 108 184 188
    61 315 **62** xxxv **64** xxix
    24 200 284 299 **65**
    xxxiii **66** xlviii 97 185
    67 xxx 95 193 **68** 202 **69**
    xlii lxvi lxvii **71** 194 **77**
    145 **79** 446 **82** 50 **88** 316
    106 19 75 **111** 117 **112**
    297 **114** 119 **115** 294
    137 27
William (Earl of) **53** 21
William (Mrs.) **105** 189
William Henry **124** 65 66
William Miller (Mrs.)
    108 135
NELTHORPE
Richard **53** 292 294
NELY John J. **96** 224
NEMOURS
— Duke of **88** 99
NENNE John **65** 323
Robert **65** 323
William **65** 322
NENNEY
Catherine **63** 204
NEPAUPUCK **145** 319
NEPE Richard **86** 417
NEPOS
Cornelius **56** 341 343
NEPTUNE Sabatis **143** 17
NERBOTH John **100** 188
NERTHAM John **59** 194
NESBITT Nesbete Nesbett
    Nesbit Nisbet Nisbeth
    Nisbett Nisbit
— **57** 121 **91** 344
— Col. **85** 7 9
— Lieut. Col. **84** 380
Agnes Carolyne **107** 132
Alexander **86** 265 **112**
    284 300
Allen **101** 33
Andrew **112** 301
Annie **104** 217
Bell **128** 92
Charles **74** 260
Charles Francis **87** 98
Clarence Clarke (Mrs.)
    101 125
Edward **53** 96
Eleanor **109** 208
Elizabeth (Harris)
    (Wheeler) **143** 306 **148**
    40 41
Ellen **77** 266

NESBITT *cont'd*
Hannah **72** 17
Henry **112** 301
Hetty (Ellis) **125** 290
Hugh **87** 190 **148** 41
Hugh O'Keefe **87** 190
James **55** 141 **90** 209
John **59** 194 **63** 241 **65** 242
    87 190
John Pratt **95** 165
Jos'a **112** 296
Judith **74** 260
Marco **125** 290
Margaret Sophia
    (Hannum) **91** 54
Martha **53** 96 **95** 166
Martha Ann **76** lxxx **82**
    479 **103** 140
Mary **87** 190
Mongo **69** 362
Nicola (Montgomery)
    112 299
Rachel (Conant) **101** 33
Robert **61** 348 **72** 17 23
    110-112 **87** 190 **112** 299
Robert G. **91** 54
Robert Taylor **87** 190 191
Sarah **129** 188
William **67** 112 **91** 344
William Duncan **81** 108
    219 **87** 72 177 190
NESHAM Ralph **54** 45
NESMITH Nasmith
— **136** 268
Abigail **117** 256
Agnes (Gilmore) **117** 256
Alexander **51** 469
Alfred **117** 256
Anne **108** 4
Annis **56** 187
Benjamin **56** 251 **105** 284
    113 243 **116** 272 274
    117 256
Benjamin I. **54** xxxix
David **56** 251
Eleazer **73** 221
Elizabeth **56** 186 187
    117 256
Fisher Hildreth **100** 112
    102 115 137 **103** 134
    104 141 158 **105** 120
    108 3 4 61 138 **109** 124
Hannah **116** 274
Henrietta Hudson
    Curger **90** 8
Hugh **56** 251
James **105** 284 **108** 4 **113**
    82 **117** 245 256
Jeanette **117** 259
John **64** 116 **108** 4
Judith **116** 273
Judith (Pettingill) **116** 274
Leonora S. Pendleton
    58 xlv
Mary **137** 76
Mary Baldwin **108** 4
Mary Jane **117** 256
Robert **77** 130
Sallie **117** 256
Sally (Cargill) **117** 256
Susanna **117** 256

NESMITH cont'd
Thomas **56** 187 **108** 3 4 **117** 256
Thomas Llewellyn **90** 8
NESPER —— **143** 369
NESS see also Von Ness
Orabella of **112** 63
NESSE John **56** 312
Robert **56** 312
NESSON Mary **95** 87
NESTON Mollie **90** 351
NETCHER
Amanda Maria **59** 28
Elizabeth **125** 176
George F. **59** 28
Helen Eliza **59** 28
NETHAWAY
Ebenezer **66** 227
Hannah **66** 227
Thomas **66** 227
William **66** 227
NETHERCLIFT
F. G. **59** lviii lix
Thomas **125** 29
NETHERCOOL Christian **105** 195 **148** 22 26 27
NETHERCOTE Nethercoate
Anthony **52** 260
H. O. **97** 100
NETHERSOLE
— Mr. **84** 30
Joan **80** 349 366
John **80** 349 366
NETHERSON
Elizabeth **82** 289 295
Lawrence **82** 289 295
NETHERTON
Hester **105** 314
NETHERWOOD
Joseph **63** 355
Netleton see Nettleton
NETLEY Michael **148** 64
NETTAR John **84** 73
NETTELS
Curtis P. **97** 394
NETTER Julian **66** 59
NETTERVILLE OF DOWTH John (Viscount) **74** 139
Nicholas (Viscount) **74** 139
NETTERVILLE
Eleanor **74** 139
Elizabeth **74** 139
Mary Ann **73** 8
NETTLEFORD
Edward **54** 95
NETTLES Cora W. (Chadbourne) **104** 198
John **61** 68
Richard **101** 91
Stephen **104** 198
NETTLESHIP
Elizabeth **55** 438
Katharine **55** 438
Roger **55** 339 340 438
NETTLETON
— Mr. **57** 229
Aaron **124** 61
Abigail **104** 70 **147** 40
Agnes **76** 138

NETTLETON cont'd
Anne **54** 275
Annie T. **95** 251
Damaris **52** 325
Dina (Healy) **147** 40
Elizabeth **71** 12 **147** 40
Enos **76** 172
Enos Gunn **76** 140
Eunice **71** 14
Ezra **52** 325
Fannie **84** 222
Fanny Elizabeth **87** 390
Freelove **76** 146
George **71** 14
Hannah **53** 210 **57** 90 **72** 210
Isabel **70** 136 **78** 259
James **54** 275
Jennie Maria **92** 112
Jeremiah D. **87** 390
Jerusha **61** 30
John **140** 230 **147** 37 40
Jonah **77** 80
Joseph **53** 210 **72** 210 **76** 138
Josiah **76** 140 145-147 149 **77** 80 **147** 40
Lucy **147** 40
Martha **135** 75 **147** 40
Martha (Hull / Hall) **147** 40
Mary **59** 45 **70** 136 **147** 40
Mary (Brooks) **147** 40
Mary Ann **75** 192 **76** 149
Nancy **76** 172
Rebecca (Lovering) **100** 300
Ruth **52** 57
Samuel **70** 136 **147** 40
Sarah **61** 27 **76** 147 **147** 40
Sarah (Carter) **147** 40
Sarah (Davis) **147** 40
Sarah (Rutley) **147** 40
Sarah (Woodmansee) **147** 37 40
Thankful **147** 37 40
Thomas **78** 301 **100** 300 **145** 315
NETTON William **58** 396
NEUBECKER
Ottfried **93** 394
NEUFVILLE
Leonard de **65** 142
NEUHALFEN
Cecilia Marie **90** 345
Peter **90** 345
NEUHAUSER —— **143** 78
Neuil see Neville
NEULEY Thomas **75** 220
NEUMANN
Charles E. **89** 304
NEUNER
John J. W. (Mrs.) **101** 125
NEUSCHELER
Frederick C. **85** 315
John A. **85** 315
Katharina Decker **85** 315
NEUSOM William **116** 176

NEUSTADT
Adele Gertrude **77** xlviii **85** 345
Agnes **77** xlviii
Sigmund **77** xlviii **85** 345
NEUWANGER
Mary **74** 211
NEVARD Henry **93** 77
NEVE
Agnes **86** 418 420
Edna **77** xlvii
Elizabeth **86** 420
Jaffrey **86** 418
Jeffrey **86** 432
John **100** 19
Reginald **77** xlvii
NEVELLS Emma Prudence **110** 303
NEVELS Sarah **60** 380 **62** 297
Neven see Nevins
Nevens see Nevins
NEVERS Abigail (Bixby) (Sawtell) **126** 130
Ann **123** 111
Hannah (Morgan) **133** 270
Jerusha (Weare) **119** 70
John **78** 313
Joshua **126** 130
Polly **133** 308 310
Rapha H. **119** 70
Susan C. **78** 409
NEVES Agnes **69** 250 251 **79** 82-84
Ann / Anne **69** 252 **79** 83
Joan **69** 18 19
Richard **69** 252
Sarah **100** 241
Nevett see Nevitt
NEVEU Cecile (Denno) **145** 130
Octave **145** 130
NEVIELS —— **62** 86
NEVILLE De Neville Neuil Nevel Nevell Nevil Nevill
—— **51** 260 355 **52** 254 **53** 301 **58** 191 286 **112** 39
— Mr. **56** 378
Agnes **106** 280
Alesia (Lady) **100** 23
Alexander **111** 264 **118** 178 179
Alice **71** 32 246 **104** 271 272 **108** 178
Amy **52** 260
Andrew **61** 248
Anne **139** 238
Bridget **100** 135
Cecily **104** 270 **148** 140
David **100** 135
Edmund **96** 121
Edward **98** 70 115 **105** 7 **108** 178 **117** 115 201
Eleanor **108** 177
Elizabeth **52** 260 **96** 107
Ellen **122** 175
Ferdinand **57** 240
Floria **79** 363

NEVILLE cont'd
Geoffrey **106** 186
George **99** 280
Gervase **111** 250
Hawise **112** 318
Henry **71** 30
Hugh **79** 363
Isabel **106** 186 **115** 48 50
Isabel Montserrat **117** 201
Jane **96** 183 **118** 180 259
Joan (Beaufort) **148** 140
John **52** 255 260 **54** 191 192
  67 267 269 **100** 135 **105**
  21 **106** 188 **114** 55 **116**
  15 174
Jolland **76** 301
Katharine **93** 5 35 **98** 70
  105 21 **108** 178 **118** 179
Katharine (Eure) **111** 264
Lawrence **71** 69
Louisa **71** 69
Luke **79** 49
Mable Frances (Penrose)
  117 115
Margaret **75** 62 **100** 22 23
  114 55 56 **116** 15
Marie **124** 256
Mary **54** 191 **99** 280
Mary B. **61** 248
Maud **76** 301
Philip **62** 323
Ralph **104** 270 271 **106** 188
  108 178 **118** 178-180
  148 140
Ranolph **106** 188
Rebecca **52** 255
Rhoda Frances **117** 115
Richard **108** 178 **122** 175
  139 238
Robert **106** 188 **115** 231
  118 178
Roger **112** 318
Ruth **61** 248
Thomas **52** 255 260 **54** 195
  61 248 **71** 240 **73** 20 **94**
  75-78 **99** 280 **118** 178
  122 175 **124** 256
William **118** 179 181
NEVINS Neven Nevens
  Nevin
—— **53** 203
— Widow **71** 136 341
Adelia **76** 25
Allen **106** 320
Anna **88** 69
Archibald **117** 62
Asa **125** 107
Asher **71** 341
Aurelia **98** 354
Betty **71** 341
Christian **73** 7
Cornelia Leonard
  (Perkins) **136** 322
Daniel **107** 56
David **71** 340 341 **113** 223
David Henry **136** 322
Delos **98** 354
Edward P. **65** xlvi
Elias M. **98** 311
Elizabeth **88** 68
Elmina E. **98** 354

NEVINS cont'd
Fanny **51** 466
Frank E. **94** 92
Grace (Penrose) **117** 62
Hannah **88** 69
Hannah M. **128** 96
Harry **74** 295
Helen Louise (Andrews)
  94 92
Hepzibah **51** 466
James M. **74** 295
John **51** 466 **73** 7 144 **88** 68
  98 311 **111** 306 **136** 336
Joseph **64** 313 **126** 137
Josephine McCloskey
  75 xlix
Julia **65** xlvi
Julia Ellen **65** xlvi
Lucy **64** 313
Lucy (Sawtell) **126** 137
Mabel Annie **74** 295
Mabel Marguerite **74** 295
Marian Griswold **136**
  322 331
Mary **51** 466 **64** 313 **74** 295
  88 68 **91** 294
Mary (Hazelton) **136** 336
Mary Lathrop **113** 223
Minerva (Tucker) **125** 107
Polly **61** 241
Rachel **117** 64
Rachel (Pim) **117** 64
Rebecca **61** 238
Rosamond C. **98** 311
Sarah **59** 40 **88** 69
Sarah A. **128** 174
Tamesin **88** 280
Thomas **112** 290 295
  117 64
NEVINSON Sarah **53** 348
NEVITT Nevett Nevit
Ann **73** 143 153
Charles **73** 138
George Paine **92** 146
James **73** 134
John **132** 326
Lavina **73** 225
Martha **55** 433
Mary **73** 224
Richard **73** 148
Sarah Ann (Rovine)
  132 326
Susan **63** 165
Thomas **73** 223 **132** 326
William **73** 230
William Miles **73** 136
NEVIUS
Cornelius **113** 289
David **129** 43
Jane (Ten Eyck) **113** 289
NEW — Mrs. **85** 120
John **121** 248 **137** 92
Martin **63** 143
Newall see Newell
NEWARK Newarke
Alan De **116** 174
Bridget **54** 192
Elizabeth **94** 14 **111** 261
John **54** 192 **148** 252
Roger **111** 261 264
Susan **148** 251-253

NEWARK cont'd
Thomas **111** 261 264
William **83** 315
NEWAY James **98** 116
NEWBEGIN
Cyrena **97** 367
Dennis **97** 367
Elisa **90** 51
Ethelyn Rose **80** 249
Harvey **97** 367
Isabella **83** 491
James **100** 190
Lydia **97** 367
Phebe **100** 190
Robert **80** 249
Sarah **97** 367
Newberry see Newbury
NEWBERT Edith Zeluma
  Vinal (Arey) **87** 108
G. A. **87** 108
Jessie (Keating) **96** 160
  100 44 116
Philip **73** 185
Newbery see Newbury
NEWBIT Jacob **125** 32
NEWBOLD
Anna P. **75** lxx
Arthur Emlen **73** 235 **74**
  xxv **75** xxxiii lxx
Caroline **54** xci **81** 476
Dorothy **75** lxx
Fitz-Eugene **75** lxx
Harriet **75** lxx
John **81** 476 **86** 352
John S. **75** lxx
Joseph Whitaker (Mrs.)
  80 195 208
Mary Elizabeth **77** 302
Mary Ruth **80** 208
Michael **60** 355 **65** 90 **111**
  272 **119** 155
Robert C. **110** 80
Sarah **136** 95 334
Sarah Lawrence **75**
  lxxxviii **77** 302
Thomas **75** lxxxviii **77**
  302 **119** 155
Thomas Haines **77** 302
Thomas Jefferson (Mrs.)
  85 197
William Romaine **60** 355
NEWBON
Henry **66** 352 353
NEWBONE
Ann (Cogan) **110** 192
Margaret (Cogan)
  110 192
Robert **110** 191 192
NEWBOROUGH
Jane **64** 86
Matthew **100** 222
Walter **64** 86
NEWBRE Cora **92** 147
NEWBROUGH George F.
  (Mrs.) **122** 124
NEWBURGH Alice de **97**
  342 **98** 203
Roger de **97** 342 **116** 94
Waleran de **97** 342 **98** 203
Walter **61** 278

NEWBURN
James **73** 152
Thomas de **103** 290
NEWBURY Newberry
Newbery Noebury
Nubery
——— **53** 142 145
— Capt. **85** 36 **148** 235 236
— Lieut. **71** 309
— Widow **105** 206
A. E. **89** 254
A. W. **79** 401
Abel P. **143** 61
Abigail **71** 281 304
Amasa **113** 298 **136** 325
Ann **79** 254
Ann Mercy **79** 254
Anna (Ford) **113** 298
Anne **71** 166 **74** 134
Aurelia **71** 162
Barnes **98** 145
Benjamin **55** 200 **71** 280
304 306 **79** 253 **113** 298
Benjamin H. **85** 381
Bolivar **69** 202 **147** 69
Cathren (Crowley) **85** 381
Chauncey **72** 93
Clarinda **53** 142 **70** 54
Daniel **144** 348 354
Dolly **72** 100
Doris **69** 163
Dorothy **67** 167
Elihu **113** 298
Eliza **72** 183
Eliza Arora **72** 92
Eliza Watson **86** 337
Elizabeth **71** 305 **113** 268
Emma **85** 375
Frances Jane **69** 202
Frederick **72** 30 43 87 92
93 100 172 183
George **72** 87 **79** 401
Grace (Watson) **86** 337
H. W. **137** 77
Hannah (Kelly) **144** 348
354
Harriet **72** 105
Helen (Handy) **126** 109
Helen Hall **91** 84 **100** 108
113 59 298
Helen Parmelee (Handy)
113 298
Henry **72** 88
Henry Oliver **137** 77
Huldah **72** 93
James **62** 354 **71** 272 275
304 **72** 101 181 **116** 223
119 21
Jane **128** 73
Jerusha (Stoughton)
113 298
John **52** 68 **64** 323 **81** 431
106 83 **115** 223
John S. **126** 109
John Stoughton **91** 84
113 298
John Strong **69** 384
Joseph **113** 298
Josiah **71** 306
Leonard **86** 337
Lucy **85** 374

NEWBURY *cont'd*
Mary **54** 399 **72** 43 100 172
81 431 **101** 285 **128** 22
Mary (Allyn) **113** 298
Mary A. **72** 105
Mary Ann **71** 164 309 **72**
47 88
Mary Jane (Perkins)
119 65
Narcissus **55** 50
Nathaniel **70** 340
Nicholas **51** 465
Polly **71** 274
Rachel **72** 49 **141** 342
Rebecca **60** 383 **95** 166
128 73
Rhoda (Phelps) **113** 298
Richard **63** 160
Robert **51** 435
Roger **71** 305
Ruth (Warner) **113** 298
136 325
Sally **72** 101
Samuel **79** 161
Sarah **71** 164 280 309 **81**
431 **109** 224 **136** 224
315 324
Sarah (Loomis) **113** 298
Susan **134** 299-301
Susan Aurelia **72** 92
Susanna **81** 431
Thomas **53** 145 **60** 383 **69**
384 **71** 80 162 164 166
272 274 275 304 309 **72**
30 170 **73** 104 **99** 232
109 224 **113** 298 **128** 73
Truman Handy (Mrs.)
84 233 **85** 188 **97** 287
98 145 149
Tryphena **51** 465
Walter **74** 134 **79** 254 **92**
202 **100** 219
Walter Loomis **136** 325
William **81** 431 **119** 65
William E. **89** 254
NEWBY Agnes **52** 107
95 320
Anna R. **122** 128
Anna Robinson **122** 127
Blakely **122** 126
Caroline Cecilia **122** 127
Caroline Whyte **122** 126
127
Cecilia **122** 126 127
Cecilia Walker (Pearce)
122 126-128
Duncan Thompson
122 128
Frank Olmstead **122** 127
128
George Clinton **122** 126-
128
George Larkin **122** 126-
128
Hannah A. **122** 127
Hannah A. (Stuart)
122 126
Jesse **122** 126 127
John **52** 107
Johnston Blakely **122** 128
Joseph **117** 77

NEWBY *cont'd*
Julia West **122** 126 127
Kate Cannon **122** 127 128
Kate Clinton **122** 126 127
Keziah **122** 126 127
Keziah (Tatom)
(Goodwin) **122** 126
Larkin **122** 125-128
M. **122** 128
Maggie Vance **122** 126
127
Margaret **52** 107 **122** 126-
128
Margaret (Tyson) **122** 126
Mary Cecilia **122** 126 127
Mary Pearce **122** 126 128
Mayme **95** 335
Mollie (Spence) **122** 126
Oliver Walker **122** 127
128
Richard **52** 107
William **52** 107 **117** 77
William Clinton (Mrs.)
122 125
William Raiford **122** 126-
128
NEWCASTLE ——— **59** 418
— Duke of **54** 27 **132** 33
John Lock **97** 146
Louisa **73** 213
Peter **73** 213
Thomas Pelham Holles
(Duke of) **77** 102
NEWCE Mary **52** 126
NEWCOMB Newcom
Newcombe Newcome
Newcomen Nucom
——— **51** 48 **55** 230 **67** 123
108 217 **109** 44 202
— Mrs. **62** 135
Abigail **52** 181 183 184
58 262 **59** 155 157 **60** 41
85 231 **103** 54 **104** 76
119 126 **125** 37
Abigail (English) **99** 192
299
Abigail (Sanford) **104** 76
Abigail T. **90** 54
Abitha (Post) **146** 359
Abner **67** 215
Abraham **99** 192
Adeline **68** 336
Alfred **108** 265
Alice **99** 65 67
Alice (Gascoigne) **113** 68
Alice (Potter) **104** 76
Alice Loring **75** xxvi
77 viii
Alice Vernon **82** 170
Almira **72** 115
Almira (Knowles)
123 198
Almira (Rich) **84** 55
Alphonso **83** 67
Alvira N. (Damon)
101 213
Amelia J. **68** 336
Andrew **53** 130 **58** 169 262
67 92 **78** 113 **81** 196 **88**
10 **113** 153 **121** 319 **122**
160

NEWCOMB *cont'd*
Angeline A. **104** 96
Ann **59** 363 **124** 34
Ann (Dickie) **99** 192
Ann (Townsend) **124** 34 35
Ann Bracket **125** 222
Anna **53** 130 **56** 78 **72** 115 **88** 384 **106** 308
Anna (Bayes) **121** 319 **122** 160
Anna (Hughes) **104** 297
Anna Turner **72** 115
Annie Sarah **81** 196
Asa **123** 122 198
Aurelia (Lewis) **108** 265
B. M. **67** 92
Bathsheba **123** 59
Bathsheba (Bourne) **118** 207 212
Bell Cora **82** 407
Benjamin **104** 76
Bertha **102** 290
Bertha M. **69** 263
Bethiah **56** 202 **59** 156
Bethiah (Young) **113** 153
Bethuel **89** 290
Bethuel Merritt **68** xxxv **72** xvi **78** 113 **79** 211 **80** 113 **81** 196 338
Betty **60** 43
Betty (Rich) **84** 48
Boylston **78** 178
Bryant **77** lxxviii **112** 153 **125** 216
Bryant Barter **77** lxxviii
Caroline (Gibbs) **123** 269
Caroline (Loomer) **120** 17
Caroline Baxter **77** lxxviii
Caroline E. **104** 96
Caroline W. **68** 336 337
Carrie Edda **112** 153
Catherine **89** 293
Charles **51** 122 127 130
Charles Silas **82** 407
Cordial **67** 215 **72** 115
Cyrenius **123** 319
Danforth P. **90** 108 112
Daniel **52** 181 **93** 318 **103** 266 **126** 225
David **100** 173
Deborah **74** 64 **78** 302 **99** 65
Deborah Charlotte **81** 196
Delight **125** 223
Dellon **83** 142
Desire **118** 212
Diana **89** 203
Dwight **68** 336
Earlbert **81** 197
Ebenezer **52** 182 **59** 272 **83** 399
Eddy **99** 192 299 **104** 76
Edgar J. **68** 336
Edith **84** 120 133
Edmund **59** 273 **78** 411
Edward **104** 76
Edwin G. **104** 103
Eleazer **52** 181
Eliakim Tupper **99** 192

NEWCOMB *cont'd*
Elias **113** 68 69
Elisha **83** 270 402 **142** 77
Eliza **102** 221 **103** 262
Eliza A. **101** 35
Eliza Ann **101** 31
Elizabeth **52** 438 **59** 88 89 270 272 361 363 **60** 149 **78** 309 **99** 192 299 **102** 261 **118** 212 **125** 220
Elizabeth (Cook) **102** 49 **113** 153 **143** 335
Elizabeth (Harding) **102** 261
Ellen Frances **83** 488
Emily **69** 263
Emma **60** 149
Erastus C. **109** 202
Esther **104** 216
Eunice **102** 261
Eunice (Bullard) **102** 261
Experience **56** 396 **85** 155 **101** 172
Ferdinand **103** 54
Francis **62** 94 **70** 182 **77** lxxviii
Frank B. **72** 115
Frederick W. **68** 336
G. W. **84** 133
George **69** 263 **104** 96 103 **124** 34 35
George B. **72** 98 107
George F. **55** 347
Grace **67** 220 **84** 38
Grace (Ricks) **121** 319
Hannah **59** 90 155 **67** 215 **83** 67 **118** 202 207 212 **135** 340
Hannah (Lewis) **102** 261
Hannah (Witherly) **102** 261
Hannah S. **123** 200
Harding **102** 261
Harriet **78** 308 **104** 96
Harriet (Swain) **125** 216
Hart **90** 260
Henry **102** 221 **123** 121 198
Hepzibah **102** 221
Herman Danforth **90** 137
Hezekiah **74** 64 **84** 133 **105** 289 **120** 17
Hiram **72** 115
Hope **67** 221 **74** 64
Horatio Cooley **93** 378
Isaac **59** 157 361 **77** lxxviii
Isaac Gilford **120** 15
Israel **89** 290
J. K. **104** 96
J. M. **58** 104
Jabez **67** 123
James **57** 282 **77** lxxviii **83** 141 142 **99** 192 **104** 96 **125** 220 **126** 142
James Lemuel Atkinson **113** 153
Jane **113** 118
Jane Bicknell **104** 96
Jane E. **83** 100
Jedediah **81** 196
Jemima **52** 183 **84** 133

NEWCOMB *cont'd*
104 297
Jeremiah **86** 399
Jerusha **74** 64
Jesse **103** 261 262 265 266 **104** 297
Jesse Smith **102** 261
Jessie Elvira (Bath) **88** 169
Joan **51** 122 127
Joanna **99** 65 **103** 239
John **59** 88-90 155-157 270 272 361 **77** lxxviii **87** 24 **99** 65 **104** 76 **113** 68 69 **120** 15 **123** 269 **145** 245
John B. **51** 223 **84** 131 **133** 72
John Bearse **78** 113 **144** 101
John C. **79** 45
John Jay **78** 286
John Lawson **120** 13
John Loring **103** 54
John M. **68** 336
Jonathan **59** 89 159 **99** 65 **105** 290 **133** 72
Joseph **67** 123 215 218 220 221 **68** 336 **102** 221 **103** 265 **125** 9
Joseph Warren **61** 306
Joshua **58** 169 **102** 261
Judith **86** 460
Judith (Woodworth) **123** 319
Laura **72** 115
Laura A. **89** 293
Laura Ann **89** 290
Leila Frances **78** 286
Lemuel **86** 399 **113** 153 **123** 269
Leonard **67** 215 **83** 147
Levi **88** 340
Loren **72** 115
Loring **125** 294
Louisa **84** 133 **108** 265
Louisa M. (Barton) **90** 108
Luanna (Greeno) **120** 13
Lucindia (Wiley) **123** 122 198
Lucy **84** 56
Lucy Jane **103** 54
Luther **66** 21 23
Lydia **52** 184 **103** 27 54 **113** 77 78
Lydia (Brown) **103** 27 **113** 153
Lydia (Huntington) **99** 192
Lydia (Manchester) **113** 77
M. **104** 96
Mabel Caroline **93** 378
Mahew **120** 14
Mamie **102** 288
Marcus C. **142** 77
Marcy **104** 76
Margaret **102** 221
Margaret (Bowles) **120** 15
Margaret E. (Sheffield) **120** 14
Margery **51** 122

NEWCOMB *cont'd*
Maria **89** 203
Maria E. **104** 96
Maria T. **68** 336 **72** 115
Marietta Wallace **109** 202
Martha **99** 67 **104** 96
Martha (Rich) (Cobb)
   83 402
Martha E. **120** 13
Martha Goodwin (Snow)
   113 153
Martyn Le **113** 68
Mary **51** 48 **53** 108 **59** 362
   61 306 **68** 336 337 **72**
   115 **77** 317 **78** 286 **98** 84
   99 192 **102** 261 **105** 165
   113 146 **118** 212 **127** 46
   143 129 335
Mary (Chase) (Post)
   146 361
Mary (Eldredge) **125** 8 9
   126 238
Mary (Rich) **83** 402
Mary (Tupper) **99** 192
Mary (West) **104** 76
Mary (Wood) **99** 192
Mary Ann **90** 112
Mary DeWolf **113** 300
Mary Elizabeth **77** xxxvi
   lxxviii
Mary Ella Wallace
   109 202
Mary J. **83** 100
Mary J. (Rich) **84** 133
Mary R. **90** 112
Mary Warren **61** 306
Matilda (Jarvice) **126** 142
Matilda Ann **104** 103
Matthew **56** 273 **113** 68 69
Maude Corabell **82** 407
Mehitable (Atwood)
   113 153
Mercy **58** 169 262 **83** 142
   145 **118** 202 212
Mercy (Brown) **113** 153
Mercy (Smith) **118** 212
Minnie Herman **103** 54
Nabby (Clough) **125** 220
Nabby (Wild) **125** 215
Nancy **105** 105 **125** 218
Nathaniel Leprelate
   77 188
Obadiah **52** 181-184 420
   99 192 **146** 359 361
Oliver **78** 415 **79** 39 **84** 55
   125 215
Orline V. **68** 336
Peter **59** 87 156-159 270
   363 **105** 290 **118** 212
Phebe **104** 76 **125** 15 **126**
   207 **142** 77 **144** 101
Phebe (Thayer) **83** 270
Polly **102** 261 **142** 208
Polly L. (Rich) **84** 55
Priscilla **123** 119 **133** 322
Rachel **52** 449 **59** 87 88
   155 156 158 **68** 336 **77**
   lxxviii **79** 51 **93** 71 154
   125 275
Rachel (Briggs) **125** 275
Ralph **83** 100

NEWCOMB *cont'd*
Ralph Pitcher **81** 197
Rebecca **102** 221 **142** 77
Rebecca (Merril) **125** 294
Rebecca (Morton) **99** 192
Reuben **105** 290 **113** 153
   125 37
Rhoda **57** 282 **67** 218
   68 336
Rial **67** 123
Richard **59** 363 **142** 77
Richard E. **61** 306 **104** 199
Robert **101** 31 **102** 221 **103**
   54 **120** 17
Robert H. **101** 213
Robert T. (Mrs.) **124** 239
Romulus **103** 54
Rosanna **83** 412
Roxana **80** 310 311
Royal **68** 336 337
Rubee **99** 65
Rufina S. **103** 54
Rufus **127** 68
Ruth **59** 361 **97** 184 **98** 186
   104 76 **120** 14
Sally **103** 265
Sally (Atwood) **102** 261
Samuel **59** 88 153 271-273
   361-363 **60** 149
Samuel Lewis **103** 54
Samuel P. **72** 115
Sara Alice **120** 15
Sarah **59** 88 153 158 271-
   273 361 362 **78** 419 **113**
   153 **115** 193 **118** 212
   123 319
Sarah (Chase) **88** 10
Sarah (Fayerweather)
   145 245
Sarah (Hatch) **102** 261
Sarah (Hopkins) **102** 261
Sarah (Kinner) **123** 319
Sarah (Loring) **125** 223
Sarah (Smith) **123** 319
Sarah A. **77** 188
Sarah A. (Ball) **88** 340
Sarah Alvord **61** 306
Sarah Ellis (Rich) **84** 131
Sarah M. **103** 269
Sarah Margaret
   (Anderson) **113** 153
Sarah Wells **61** 306
Shubael W. **68** 337
Silas **74** 64 65 **81** 196
   105 205
Simeon **113** 153 **142** 77
Simon **74** 64 65 **83** 402
   86 399 **102** 261 **103** 27
   109 202 **113** 153 **120** 13
Sophia (Hannum) **90** 260
Stephen **113** 68 69
Submit **74** 65 **88** 11 12 **108**
   239 **109** 308
Sumner **103** 54
Susan **89** 290 293
Susanna **59** 87 156 158
   159 270
Tamsey Ardellice
   (Davison) **120** 17
Thankful **83** 39 399

NEWCOMB *cont'd*
Thankful (Freeman)
   83 399
Theophilus **84** 48
Thomas **61** 229 **77** lxxviii
   81 196 **83** 46 **84** 55 **100**
   322 **102** 49 **111** 131 **112**
   153 **113** 68 69 153 **118**
   212 **123** 319 **125** 223
   274 **140** 230 **143** 335
Thomas (Mrs.) **102** 287
Thomas S. **80** 266
W. A. **123** 150
Waity (Sanford) **104** 76
Walter **67** 221 **68** 336 337
Waterman **103** 54
William **63** 235 **69** 263
   73 139 **81** 196 **91** 93
   102 221 **104** 96 **118** 207
   211 212 **125** 275 **142**
   208
William A. **103** 54
William C. **68** 336 **72** 115
William H. **120** 14
William Wood **113** 59 153
Willis Edwin (Mrs.)
   88 169
Willis Wood **80** 332
   81 219
Zemiah **103** 54
Zilpha **99** 65
NEWCOMER Anne **78** 88
Anne (Connelly) **88** 74
Hortense **78** 88 **88** 74
Olive Gall **107** 318
Theodore Philip **78** 88
   88 74
NEWCOURT Richard **51**
   200 **71** 235
NEWDIGATE   **53** 266
Amanda **119** 204
Anne **51** 132
Catherine **119** 204
Charles **119** 204
Elizabeth **51** 133 **74** 69 136
   119 204 **130** 196 206
Emma **119** 204
George Washington
   119 204
Hannah **51** 133
Hannah Jane **119** 204
Herman **119** 204
Isabella **51** 132-134
James **119** 204
James Henry Harrison
   119 204
John **52** 64 **56** 183 **74** 69
   136 **119** 203 204
Lisebeth **119** 204
Lucinda **119** 203 204
Margaret **119** 204
Mary **119** 204
Mary Ann **119** 204
Nancy **119** 204
Nathaniel **51** 131-133 **52**
   64 **68** 304
Sarah **51** 133 **130** 196 206
Sarah Bell **119** 204
Susan **119** 204
Thomas **119** 204
William **119** 204

NEWE Giles **54** 343
NEWELL Newall Newel
—— **53** 379 **54** 230 **56** 326
62 24 **71** 25 **72** 317 **86**
56 **92** 253 260 **100** 190
112 22 **121** 60 **136** 33
— Capt. **65** 113 **84** 374
— Col. **65** 110 **122** 62
— Dea. **56** 141
— Dr. **62** 131
— Mr. **57** 150 375 **62** 22
66 40
— Mrs. **62** 20 **65** 363 **69**
11 124 126 **121** 69 **126**
113
— Rev. Mr. **72** 32
____ (Grubb) **140** 149 230
____ (Scott) **140** 155
Aaron **58** 373
Abbie Anna **68** xxxiv **85**
356 **88** 89 176 193
Abby Frances **97** 96
Abel **71** 300
Abigail **55** 394 397 **57**
103 205 **103** 160 **115** 79
Abigail (Allen) **88** 193
Abigail (Nightingale)
88 281
Abigail Newton **58** 373
Abigail S. **67** 351
Abigail Weeks (Burleigh)
88 193
Abijah **145** 361
Abraham **51** 173 **57** 103
76 lix **81** 368 **83** 488 **88**
193 **94** 286 **98** 369 **104**
314
Adeline **57** 377
Alice Blake **94** 286
Almond **75** 256
Amanda **71** 355 **116** 126
Amelia Brown **90** 259
Amy **138** 116
Amy (Carpenter) **90** 137
93 142
Andrew **51** 161 **55** 147 223
57 280 **76** 204 **78** 308
140 230
Ann **57** 380 **59** 366 367
Ann Cartwright **93** 253
Anna **55** 445
Anne **55** 392 **143** 342
Annie B. **81** 368
Ardell **89** 313
Artemas **55** 397 **57** 261 380
382
Augustus Carpenter
93 186
Augustus T. **83** 488
Barbara **116** 126
Baxter H. **126** 38
Bertha Stafford **80** 449
Betsey **55** 396 **57** 371
75 256
Betsey (Mann) **94** 286
Betty **66** 213
Beulah **55** 263 **57** 144
Birdsey **71** 355
Caleb **138** 115 118
Calvin **55** 398
Caroline **77** 146

NEWELL *cont'd*
Caroline (Lazell) **89** 313
Caroline Webster (Swett)
94 286
Catherine Howe **66** 40
Cephas **139** 93
Charles **57** 380 **58** 346 **78**
398 **101** 256
Charles Artemus **58** 346
Charles Henry **77** 183
Charles Howe **66** 40
Charles Stark **92** 260
Charlotte **116** 126
Charlotte (Peabody)
86 299
Charlotte M. **75** 206
Chester **86** 307
Chloe **77** 228
Clarissa M. **116** 258
Cynthia **73** 116
Daniel **58** 373 **73** 116 **88**
281 **100** 190 **113** 32 40
134 56 **145** 362
Daniel Edwin **77** 258
Deborah **54** 421
Delia (Coombs) **148** 171
Dinah **72** 223
Dorcas **55** 398
Dorcas Evans **112** 22
Dorothy **109** 191
E. F. **79** 56 **101** 214-216
Eben **86** 122
Ebenezer **54** civ **55** 263
56 31 **57** 29 144 146 153
252 254 257-259 261 **60**
255 **65** 363 **76** 157 80
449 **88** 193 **107** 240 **118**
288
Ebenezer F. **101** 31
Eleazer **56** 146 269 **57** 254
Elijah **55** 398 **91** 40
Elisha **58** 373 **104** 122
129 385
Eliza **94** 379
Elizabeth **55** 146 147 262
263 266 399 **56** 31 **57** 28
103 153 260 355 **59** 249
366 367 **61** 260 **76** 201
204 **79** 44 **84** 374 **89** 61
116 127 **136** 308 **142**
137
Elizabeth (Bullard) **88** 193
Elizabeth (Curtis) **88** 193
94 286
Elizabeth (Hawley)
136 318
Elizabeth Collvil **112** 22
Elizabeth Emma
(Spilman) **94** 286
Elizabeth Lothrop
(Rogers) **94** 286
Ellen Frances **83** 488
Emily **90** 104 **116** 126
Emily J. **79** 41
Enoch **114** 278
Ephraim **55** 110
Esther **56** 33 142 **57** 151
Esther Montgomery
112 22
Eunice **51** 161 **107** 240
126 206

NEWELL *cont'd*
Experience **56** 31 **114** 29
30
Frances **86** 310
Frances F. **86** 299
Frances Read **113** 239
Francis **76** lix
Francis William **92** 260
Fred Dexter **86** 307
Frederick Haynes
65 xxxv
Gad **95** 61
Gamaliel **125** 32
Garry T. **79** 154
George **54** 421 **58** 346
114 9
George Curtis **57** 378 379
Gertrude Bradley **78** 206
Gordon **119** 75 **126** 113
Grace **51** 173
Grace K. **82** 273
H. M. **100** 77
Hannah **51** 177 **55** 396 **56**
30 32 39 269 **57** 106 144
147 260 261 **58** 346 **59**
367 **72** 219 **75** 200 **104**
314
Hannah (Fisher) **88** 193
Hannah (Fletcher) **94** 286
Hannah (Silvester) **86** 122
Hannah (Whitney) **94** 286
Harriet **88** 331 **90** 45 47
102 282
Harriet (Perry) **116** 202
Harriet Adwood **100** 147
Harriet E. **81** 45
Harriet Emily **94** 166
Harriet G. **125** 172
Harriet G. (Peckham)
125 175
Hart **56** 159
Helen S. **79** 11
Henry **71** 25
Henry Oscar **89** 313
Hiram **116** 126 127
Huldah **62** 135
Isaac **55** 260 **57** 103 213
88 193 **94** 286 **104** 314
114 29 30
Isaac F. **71** 355
Isabel Spencer **77** 183
J. **113** 33
Jabez **57** 374
Jacob **57** 103 **114** 30
James **57** 380 **64** 79 **72** 223
117 33 **140** 230
James Montgomery **94**
128 139 286 **95** 150
James Webster **94** 286
Jane **112** 22 **114** 187
134 222
Jane (Kinkead) **112** 22
Jane (Montgomery)
112 21
Jane (Nichols) **83** 488
Jasen **125** 269
Jason **129** 385
Jason W. **54** 457
Jean **112** 21 22
Jemima Hathaway **90** 56
Jerusha **72** 223

NEWELL *cont'd*
Jesse **94** 382 **105** 217
Jessie McIver **77** 258
John **55** 223 **57** 205 **70** 12
  16-18 139 302 **77** 235 **86**
  162 **89** 313 **93** 186 **101**
  49 **112** 267 **124** 297 **127**
  69 **136** 308 **140** 68 230
  145 366
John Edmund **93** 186
John Edmund (Mrs.) **90**
  137 **93** 125 142 186
John G. **93** 253 **94** 163
John H. **125** 172 175
John Montgomery
  112 22
John P. **125** 172 175
John S. **88** 332
Jonah **86** 87
Jonas **62** 18
Jonathan **51** 294-296 **52**
  37 38 **55** 397 399 **56** 141
  57 150 261 372 375 376
  378 379 389 **76** 204 **112**
  242 **126** 225
Jonathan Kingsbury
  57 375
Joseph **55** 146 **57** 377 379
  59 366 367 370 **85** 359
  88 193 **93** 217 **122** 86-
  88 **136** 33 **138** 118 **140**
  149 230
Joseph Allen **57** 377
Joseph Black **112** 22
Joseph Keith **64** 329
Joshua **56** 33 **57** 262
Josiah **56** 31-33 269 270
  57 22 28 30 107 144 146-
  148 260-262 **65** 361 **88**
  193 **94** 286
Joyce **114** 30
Julia **57** 261
Juliana Magdalena
  (Snyder) **105** 217
Juliana Magdelena
  (Snyder) **94** 382
Julius **57** 379
Laura **75** 101
Leonard **57** 376
Loftus **62** 16
Lois **57** 258
Lola Ruth (Stribling)
  102 169
Lot **71** 355
Louise (Smith) **94** 166
Lucena **126** 38
Lucinda **57** 380
Lucius **57** 377 **85** 356
  88 193
Lucretia **125** 222
Lucretia (Silvester) **86** 87
Lucy **55** 397 **57** 372 374
  73 116
Luke **90** 45
Lydia **55** 259 263 **57** 144
  153 374 **86** 162
Lyman **75** 256
M. H. **55** 110
Marah **52** 54
Margaret **56** 91 **59** 367
  66 213

NEWELL *cont'd*
Margaret E. **112** 22
Maria (Hannum) **91** 40
Maria A. **77** 150
Marshall **57** 379
Martha **55** 397 **57** 260 **62**
  57 **131** 315 **140** 154
Martha Jane (Skinner)
  94 286
Mary **55** 223 260 **56** 33 **57**
  22 103 106 148 260 389
  58 346 373 **59** 367 **60**
  146 372 **72** 283 **75** 256
  82 79 **88** 281 **89** 106 **95**
  353 **100** 77 **101** 256 **109**
  227 **116** 126 127 **122** 28
  125 215 **136** 34 310 **140**
  230
Mary (Amory) **120** 81
  140 230
Mary (Hart) **136** 308 310
  319
Mary (Walker) **89** 313
Mary Ann **58** 346 **79** 154
Mary Cabot **124** 29
Mary Catherine **76** lix
  94 382 **105** 217
Mary G. (Marian) **88** 332
Mary Morcy **57** 379
Matthew **64** 254
Mehitable **55** 392 **57** 254
  72 223
Melissa **80** 146
Melissa (Shepard) **106** 74
Milbury **148** 171
Millicent **112** 242
Mindwell **56** 159
Minnie Belle **84** 109 190
Mira **125** 32
Montgomery **57** 262
  140 155
Moses **57** 153 **134** 215
Munson **106** 74
Myra M. (Deith) **86** 307
Nabby **55** 398 **58** 373
Nancy **59** 367 **72** 317 **86**
  306 **107** 240
Nancy (Owens) **112** 22
Nancy Kendall (Prentiss)
  126 113
Nathan **55** 392 **56** 144 **57**
  152 371 374
Nathan S. **86** 299
Nathaniel **57** 103 150 **77**
  232 **99** 79
Noble W. **71** 355
Olive **55** 395 **57** 257
  140 230
Oliver Stebbins **102** 169
Oscar Alonzo **77** 187
Pascal J. **116** 127
Patience (Jenks) **91** 267
Patty **71** 343 **116** 126
Peggy (Beatie) **112** 22
Phebe **62** 16
Philip **116** 127
Philip W. **116** 126
Philip Wilder **116** 202
Polly **57** 374 **59** 367 **71** 355
  116 126 127 **142** 73
Priscilla **55** 398

NEWELL *cont'd*
Prudence **127** 69 **133** 308
  309
Rachel **55** 266 398 **57** 148
  213
Rachel (Briggs) **126** 38
Rachel (Silvester) **85** 359
Rachel Flagg **75** 256
Rebecca **52** 216 **54** ciii **55**
  259 264 396 397 **57** 147
  259 382 **73** 257 **85** 330
  116 126 127
Reuben **55** 397 **56** 39
  57 262
Rhoda **76** 157
Richard **64** 165 **82** 443
  125 41
Robert **82** 79 **127** 227
Rosanna (Nichols) **86** 307
Roxana (Whiting) **90** 45
Roxana P. **88** 330
Rufus **58** 373
Russell S. **116** 126
Ruth **55** 260 **57** 103 **126** 64
  89 323 **125** 104
Sally **56** 39 **57** 262 **78** 304
  89 323 **125** 104
Sally (Tisdale) **88** 193
Samuel **53** 87 **57** 103 **60**
  372 **72** 94 **73** 257 **92** 253
  260 **94** 379 **99** 307 308
  112 21 22 **136** 308 310
  319
Samuel A. **112** 22
Samuel B. **112** 22
Samuel Henry **92** 253
Sarah **53** 87 **55** 262 **56** 31
  33 270 **57** 30 **58** 373 **59**
  367 **61** 396 **86** 162 **111**
  282 **118** 135 **130** 211
  136 319
Sarah (Mackintire) **94** 286
Sarah (Norton) **136** 319
Sarah Adelia **77** 187
Sarah Newell **59** 367
Sarah Thornton **59** 367
Sarah Tisdale **57** 377
Silas **132** 192
Simon **72** 223
Solomon **71** 343
Solomon Newton **58** 373
Sophronia **107** 240
Stanford **61** 322
Stella **89** 313
Stephen **57** 103 **124** 278
Stephen A. **67** 351
Susan H. **93** 253 **94** 163
Susan L. (Sprague)
  101 31
Susanna **52** 212 **58** 373
  59 367 368 370 **112** 22
Susee **57** 252
Tabitha **114** 298
Thankful **116** 126
Theodore **57** 146
Theron **57** 380
Thomas **55** 146 **59** 249
  366 367 **60** 188 **72** 223
  76 204 **80** 449 **85** 124
  455 **87** 273 **91** 267 **94**
  166 **99** 308 **125** 32 35
  141 353 **142** 56

NEWELL *cont'd*
Timothy **53** 179 **55** 259
56 142 144 146 269 **57**
144 146-148 150-152 254
59 367 **120** 81 **140** 230
147 174
Titus **134** 56
Tryphosa **116** 126 127
Walter **57** 377
Willard **57** 380
William **57** 380 **73** 116
112 21 22
William Allen (Mrs.) **77**
156 **78** 206
William Palmer **57** 262
William S. **71** 355
William Stark **98** 369
William T. **112** 22
William Wells **61** 218
Winfield W. **71** 355
Winifred (Parker) **114** 9
Ziba **142** 73
NEWENDEN Joan **84** 81
William **84** 81
NEWENT
Elizabeth **101** 65
NEWFOILLE
Benjamin **114** 191
William **114** 191
NEWGAR
Abigail **55** 308
Peter **55** 308
NEWGATE John **52** 42 43
89 47 **96** 367 **97** 393
Philip **52** 42-44
Newgent *see* Nugent
NEWHALL *see also* Newell
—— **60** 320 **137** 99
Abby Rogers **93** 199
Abigail **68** 165
Abijah **68** 165 381 **69** 177
Albert **126** 141
Alfred (Mrs.) **79** 12
Alice M. **92** 340
Allen **59** 144 **74** lx **97** 50
102 275
Almond **70** 278 327 **75** 256
Amos **68** 168 247 **70** 278
327
Anna **78** 186
Annie E. Durgin **92** 340
Asa **61** 167
Aymeline **125** 106
Beaumont **120** 76
Benjamin **59** cvi
Benjamin S. **92** 340
Bethiah **112** 152
Celeste **97** 50
Charles Henry **65** 201
Charles Lyman **55** xxx
xxxv 115 116 **60** xxxiv
102 **66** xlviii **69** xxx **71**
xviii **74** xxxviii lx lxi
118 182 184
Charles W. **111** 110
Cheever **62** lxxxviii
63 lxxvii
Cynthia **69** 177
Daniel **69** 178 **74** lx **78** 416
116 80
Dorcas **136** 165

NEWHALL *cont'd*
Edward **78** 408 **92** 58
Effie **69** 180
Elijah **95** 56
Elisha **94** 321
Eliza **78** 72
Eliza Ann (Coates)
111 110
Elizabeth **68** 168 247 **70**
278 327 **83** 471 **90** 76
131 233
Elizabeth (Bancroft)
94 222
Elizabeth (Hills) **126** 141
Ellen Augusta **103** 229
Esther (Adams) **125** 289
Eunice **111** 108
Everett E. **92** 340
Ezra **93** 304 **95** 57 **100** 66
Florence Dana **74** lxi
Frances Ann **83** 340 341
Francis **98** 147
George Harrison **97** 66
Gertrude **82** 237
Gustavus **122** 278 279
Hannah **52** 73 **57** 363 **68**
168 **70** 327
Hannah B. **92** 340
Harriet **91** 237
Harriet E. (Lindsey) **97** 66
Henry **69** 178
Henry Whiting (Mrs.)
84 106 190
Henry Willard **83** 108
Howard Mudge **63** 214
65 201
J. R. **118** 216
James **125** 289
James R. **144** 60
James Robinson **65** 13
14 17 18 **123** 161
Jane (Breed) **94** 321
Jane Y. **68** 247
Jemima **57** 56
Joel **78** 70
John **74** lx **85** 31 33 **121**
221 **140** 230 **148** 337
John Breed (Mrs.) **82** 122
237 **103** 115
John Davis **70** 278 327
John J. **91** 331
John M. **68** lxxii
Jonathan **68** 168 **111** 108
Joseph **55** 53 **61** 171 **78** 71
88 331 **94** 321 **102** 190
112 152
Josephine Emily
Augusta **74** lxi
Kizia (Lincoln) **126** 68
Laura C. **92** 340
Leroy **74** 28
Louisa **78** 309
Lucy **68** 381 **69** 177
Lucy Mansfield **68** lxxii
Luther **92** 52
Lydia **126** 142
Lydia (Blake) **122** 279
Martha **104** 116
Martha Jane **95** 54
Martha Jane (Robinson)
95 54 56

NEWHALL *cont'd*
Mary **54** 107 **72** 161 **75** 256
78 85 **88** 199 **89** 72 **92**
60 **94** 82 **95** 56 **101** 70
108 86 **111** 108
Mary (Cheever) **95** 56
Mary (Hancock) **88** 331
Mary Emily H. **88** 335
Mary H. **97** 66
Moses **111** 108
Nathan **92** 48
Nathan Hussey **70** 327
Otis **74** lx
Ozias **70** 327
Patience **79** 56
Phebe **66** 317
Porter **74** 28
Rebecca **79** 37 **88** 27
137 238
Reuben **74** lx **111** 187
Richard **55** 68
Ruth **83** 116 **94** 321
Ruth (Bancroft) **94** 321
S. W. **118** 131 **122** 278
Sally **108** 186 **125** 217
Samuel **70** 327
Samuel C. **68** 247
Sarah **61** 167 **74** 201 **77** 231
232 **85** 435 **97** 308 **106** 4
108 83
Sarah Anne (Howe) **97** 50
Sarah Catherine **111** 152
Sarah Dana **74** lx
Sarah Frances **74** 28
Sarah Jane Hopkins
95 54
Susan **111** 187 **126** 273
Susan Augusta **83** 108
Susan Henry **83** 108
Thomas **52** 73 **54** 107 **65**
12 **74** lx **78** 85 **85** 31 **94**
222
Thomas B. **56** lxxiii
Thomas Bancroft **52** 486
William **78** 314 **95** 56
William W. **92** 340
NEWHAM
Dorothy **62** 58
John **106** 207
Richard **62** 58
NEWHARD Anne K.
(Wallace) **110** 223
Chapin S. (Mrs.) **110** 223
NEWHAVEN
— Lord **113** 91 92
NEWHOUSE
— Mr. **142** 366
Amy **122** 91
Edward **126** 243
Henrietta **126** 243
Isabella Baltimore
(Munroe) **126** 243
Otto H. **126** 243
Sophia **72** 107
William **73** 146
NEWICK Ethel Sargent
(Jewett) **83** 432 437
Ira Aaron **83** 432 437
NEWKIRK
Annie **107** 121
Flora Douglas **86** 198

NEWKIRK *cont'd*
Thomas J. **71** 288
NEWLAND Newlands
—— **89** 382
Abigail **54** 397 **141** 196
Abigail (Grover) **125** 274
Amos **125** 273
Annie **126** 276
Annie (Briggs) **126** 276
Anthony **62** 180
Elizabeth **92** 120 **125** 202
Esther **125** 273 274
Esther (Finney) (Briggs) **125** 273 274
Francis Griffith **58** xlv
Henry **63** 17 **77** 269
Huldah **123** 126
Israel **55** 171
Jabez **52** 365 **123** 59
James **76** 63
Jeremy **63** 227
Jo. **76** 61
John **63** 241 **125** 85 200 **128** 247
Joseph **89** 382
Josiah **54** 397 **125** 274
Katharine **63** 227
Keziah **126** 116
Mary **76** 63 **88** 398 399 **89** 59
Mary P. (Handy) **126** 111
Peabody **126** 111
Rebecca (Cushman) **123** 59
Rose (Allen) (Holway) **128** 247
Sarah **52** 365
Thomas **65** 24
William **92** 120 **97** 330 **117** 182 **128** 247
NEWLANDS Rose (Fitz Randolph) **97** 330
NEWLIN
Algie I. **120** 156
Alonzo **80** 168
Anna **80** 168
Earl Mortimer (Mrs.) **87** 64
Harvey **120** 156
Jacob **68** 249
John **68** 249 **120** 156
Mary Pyle **120** 156
Nicholas **86** 351
Rena Robinson (Cranston) **80** 168
Ruth **68** 249
Sarah W. **68** 249
NEWLING Annie (McDonald) **83** 435 437
Charles H. **83** 435 437
Daniel **144** 348 354
Sarah (Crane) **144** 348 354
NEWLON
Lulu Maria **92** 147
NEWMAN Newmans
Newnam Numan
—— **51** 411 413 **63** 285 **81** 121 **92** 246 **99** 234 235 **121** 115
— Dea. **62** 348 **96** 268 **97** 258 **98** 236

NEWMAN *cont'd*
— Dr. **58** 35
— Lord **140** 327
— Miss **79** 298
— Mr. **52** 172 **53** 299 **55** 180 **62** 141 **66** 117 **96** 261
—— (Stillman) **140** 230
Abigail **55** 197 198 **57** 179 **114** 321 **127** 79
Abigail (Perrin) **96** 263
Abraham Chandler **120** 313
Albert Harding **59** xliv **65** xxxv
Alexander **100** 238
Alice **61** 385
Ames B. **85** 376
Amos **85** 376
Andrew **66** 36 **103** 267 **111** 295
Ann **62** 37 **92** 246 **132** 21 22
Anna Brewster **94** 40
Anne **100** 239
Antipas **67** 298 **121** 192
Augustus **127** 7 **140** 230 234
Barnaby **85** 389 392
Basheba (Chickering) **97** 257
Bathsheba **97** 35
Benjamin Lincoln **140** 230
Bertha D. **86** 318
C. F. **65** 23
Caroline **94** 39
Caroline Savage **67** 323
Cate **111** 295
Catherine **73** 225 **125** 42
Charles R. **69** 201
Charlotte M. **79** 53
Chloe (Gill) **96** 263
Christian **68** 64 67
Christopher **51** 352
Clara (Reed) **86** 198
Daniel **51** 465 **100** 299 **101** 106
David **96** 263 **97** 38 39 319 **98** 326
Deborah **93** 323 **100** 240 **140** 56
Deborah (Cushing) **140** 56 230
Dora **66** 242
Dorinda G. **73** 286
Dorman **144** 213
Dorothy Stover **82** 50
Edmund **94** 263
Edward **59** 418 **63** 20 **94** 339
Eleanor **70** 129 133
Eliza **55** 197
Eliza Ann **73** 286
Eliza H. **126** 65
Eliza S. **77** 150
Eliza Sophia (Shaw) **88** 190
Elizabeth **61** 125 334 385 **63** 285 **65** 320 **67** 298 **72** 186 **78** 38 **131** 123

NEWMAN *cont'd*
Elizabeth (Ellis) **120** 118
Ellen **85** 374 **99** 47
Emma **123** 232
Enoch S. **73** 286
Eva J. **95** 247
Ezekiel **115** 23
Francis **81** 121 122 129 133 134
Frank W. **86** 318
George **135** 103 **140** 230
George E. **88** 190
George Nathan **76** xxii 76
Gustavus **90** 48
H. **93** 323
Hannah **67** 368 **83** 293 **101** 106
Hannah (Jagger) **101** 106
Hannah (Kendrick) **96** 263
Hannah (Locke) **141** 226
Hannah (Morse) **83** 293
Hannah S. **77** 233
Harriet **81** 392
Harry Wright **88** 98 **118** 247
Henry **51** 354 **58** 68 **85** 124 **92** 246 **93** 323 **94** 39 40 **97** 320 **140** 56 230 231
Hopestill **97** 300
Horatio **73** 268
James **73** 274
James Franklin **78** 38
James H. **125** 41
Jane **53** 122
Jennie **75** 213
Jennie (Smith) **98** 81
Jeremiah **101** 106
Joan **66** 244 **67** 45 46 **70** 249 254
Joanna **53** 189 291 300
John **51** 196 **52** 230 369 **53** 122 **54** 92 **55** 390 **60** 159 **62** 35 **66** 37 **68** 64 67 **73** 268 **75** 213 **80** 317 **81** 392 **82** 443 **86** 425 **96** 263 **100** 236 **107** 313 **110** 202 **114** 321 **121** 248 **125** 26 **127** 15 **142** 52 **143** 295
John Henry **70** xli **71** 235
John L. **85** 373
Jonathan **73** 285 290
Joseph **100** 236
Josephine **78** 38
Julia B. **71** xxiii **88** 89 176
Julia Betsey **88** 190
Katharine **125** 44
Lucy **81** 392
Lucy (Coburn) **125** 106
Lydia **96** 263
Malina S. (Newman) **85** 379
Maltbie **111** 295
Margaret **79** 40 **93** 323 **115** 254 255 **140** 56
Margaret (Fletcher) **140** 56 231
Margaret Anna **75** 213
Marinda **101** 250
Mark **140** 235

NEWMAN *cont'd*
Martha **65** 237
Martha (Lynch) **130** 72
Martin **78** 38
Mary **51** 196 465 466 **69**
144 **73** 228 **93** 323 379
97 257 **108** 150 293 **115**
23 **125** 181 **126** 141
Mary (Carberry) **90** 48
Mary (Cooks) **125** 220
Mary Ada **69** 201
Mary B. **117** 73
Mary Jane **78** 38 323
Mary L. **126** 208
Maud **87** 174
Nancy **78** 406
Nancy (Turner) **125** 105
Nancy S. **85** 374
Nathaniel **88** 190 **108** 293
Nathaniel G. (Mrs.)
108 220
Nicholas **70** 129 133
Nicholas Clinton (Mrs.)
86 198
Noah **53** 189 201 291 300
96 261 **98** 325 330 **99** 94
95 97 99 102 104 **121**
201 **128** 305 **138** 31
Patience **84** 98 **97** 300
Peter **59** 418 **88** 190
R. **140** 248
Rachel (Salmon) **100** 299
Ralph **111** 295
Rebecca **100** 235 238 **101**
106 **111** 295
Richard **51** 112 **54** 335 **59**
418 **65** 320 322 **81** 489
Robert **56** 83 **60** 192 **63**
36 39 **67** 45 **70** 249 254
78 69 186 **81** 132 135 **85**
373 **96** 278 **100** 235 238
125 106 **140** 327
Robert H. **115** 32
Roger **139** 235
Rufus **111** 295
Ruth **61** 331 **62** 36 **114** 125
Sally **111** 295 **126** 142
Sally (Phillips) **140** 235
Samuel **62** 183 332 **63** 79
83 131 132 **93** 304 **95** 77
97 257 300 316-319 **98**
166 171 244 **99** 96 98
228 236 **100** 66 **125** 220
139 24 **140** 10 230
Samuel Stillman **140** 230
Sarah **53** 433 **73** 285 **78** 418
96 263 **97** 356 **100** 236
107 118 **110** 204
Sarah (Maltbie) **111** 295
Sarah (Smith) **110** 202
Sarah Ann **92** 63
Sarah J. **77** 150
Scudder **130** 72
Sibyl **62** 38 **67** 298
Stephen **101** 106 **111** 295
Susan **92** 246
Susan D. **94** 44 **140** 230
Symon **143** 114
Thomas **57** 179 **64** 315 **70**
125 **83** 293 **88** 190 **101**
106 **141** 226

NEWMAN *cont'd*
Thomas C. **120** 118
Thomas M. **85** 379
Timothy H. **125** 105
Viola E. (Spear) **85** 376
Voldo **103** 120
William **51** 351 **52** 49 **61**
385 **65** 242 **85** 124 **88**
190 **111** 295 **115** 23 **125**
44 **140** 230 **148** 60
William John **67** 323
William L. **79** 56
NEWMARCH Newmarsh
— Capt. **77** 63 69 98
— Mr. **54** 408
— Rev. Mr. **75** 57
Ann **74** 120
Clarinda R. F. **60** 294
Elizabeth (Lowden) **94** 61
George **74** 120
Jno. **54** 409
John **53** 124 **67** 61 **81** 141
133 232
Joseph **70** 186 **74** 120 **99**
79 **105** 112 114 **130** 86
Laura R. **60** 294
Martha **76** 7
Martha (Gould) **133** 232
Mary **51** 460 **94** 61
Sarah **63** 173 **112** 153
Susanna **58** 338 **74** 120
Thomas **60** 294 **94** 61
Newnam *see* Newman
NEWNING James **129** 381
NEWORK Esther **100** 315
101 175
Sarah **101** 175
NEWPORT Newporte
— Mr. **71** 137
Audrey **51** 121-123
Blount Mountjoy (Earl of)
74 139
Dorothy **51** 123
Emanuel **81** 322
Florence **81** 322
Frances **81** 322
Francis **51** 123
James **65** 238
John **51** 123
Richard **65** 69
Robert **51** 123
Sarah **57** 32 **109** 223
William **51** 121 123
Newsame *see* Newsome
Newsames *see* Newsome
NEWSE Hannah (Rickard)
100 302
Thomas **100** 302
NEWSOME Newsame
Newsames Newsom
Newsum
A. R. **116** 234
Agnes Mary **105** 227
Eleanor **147** 34
Experience (Titus) **98** 171
Isabel **96** 254 **98** 171
John **147** 34
Laura Elizabeth **78** 47
Lenord **98** 171
Leonard **64** 28 **96** 255
98 171

NEWSOME *cont'd*
Mary **84** 452 **97** 39 **98** 171
Mercy **98** 171
Nancy **78** 33
Nathaniel **78** 33
Robert **124** 255
Susan **78** 33
William **93** 17
NEWSON
Charlotte (Chase)
87 262
Daniel **87** 262 **138** 92
Jane (Fiske) **87** 44 372
John **92** 182
Mark **63** 347
Mary **110** 129
Robert **63** 143
Samuel **144** 127
Thomas **87** 44 372
NEWSTEAD
Robert **65** 29
NEWSTEP Sarah **77** 220
NEWSTUBBES
John **94** 236
Newsum *see* Newsome
NEWTEL —— **62** 356
NEWTH Marion Alice **83**
437 **84** 20
Samuel **65** 27
NEWTHEWETT
Robert **83** 452
NEWTON —— **52** 316 **55**
248 **56** 106 114 197 **57**
338 **86** 423 **89** 255 **118**
125 **119** 55 132 209 289
120 302 **121** 68 **122** 222
— Col. **111** 293
— Mr. **52** 127 **59** 181 **62**
355 **67** 214 **85** 445 **93**
361
— Mrs. **62** 20 **71** 48 **85**
444 **94** 11 13 **119** 127
137 218 294 298 305 **120**
129-131 204 210 214 295
296 299 **121** 60 66 95
122 64 116 117 223 226
227 305 **123** 17
A. G. **78** 312
Aaron **58** 374 **77** 18 20
103 239
Abbie (Needham) **110** 122
Abiah **81** 280 283
Abigail **62** 264 267 **64** 370
66 220 75 182 **85** 444
124 177 182 **127** 207
Abigail (Perkins) **127** 207
Abigail (Phelps) **124** 60
Abner **73** 257
Abraham **83** 300 302
88 341
Adam **60** 202
Adeline **66** 243
Adeline (Hanks) **86** 26
Adelle P. **108** 135
Agnes **111** 197 200
Alice **51** 360 **52** 84 **76** 122
108 76
Alice (Thorpe) **111** 195
196
Alvan **88** 277
Alyson **111** 197

NEWTON *cont'd*
Amos **89** 383 **114** 29
Ann **68** 103 **100** 25
Anna Coleman **58** 316
Anna Parmalee **69** 201
Anne **69** 160 201
Anne (Loker) **143** 330
Annie **125** 303
Annie A. (Staples)
  83 300 302
Artemas **124** 60
Arthur **100** 299
Asa **80** 190 **89** 255
Asahel **115** 294 **137** 257
Asenath **108** 76
Asintha **80** 331
Avis **76** 136
Azariah **113** 136
Azubah **57** 287
Basswell **55** 332 338
Bellows **60** 76
Benjamin **114** 171 **125** 182
Benjamin B. **65** 138
Benoni **71** 114
Bertha **116** 207
Bethiah **137** 257
Betsey **56** 168 **115** 16
  120 63
Betty **77** 27 **118** 305 **119**
  48 59 127 133-136 140
Brian **55** 332 338 339
Bridget **143** 331
Burwell **62** 270
C. G. **84** 455
Caleb **79** 12
Caroline **79** 12
Caroline Jacques **138** 210
Catherine **56** 197 **95** 315
Charles **89** 312 **114** 29
Charles Hamilton **89** 238
Charlotte **127** 207
Charlotte Ann **127** 207
  128 37
Chester **111** 53
Chester V. **52** 338
Christian **68** 102 103
Christopher **76** 136
Clair A. Hemenway
  101 336
Clarissa **97** 91
Clarissa D. **67** 139 144
Claude William (Mrs.)
  104 145
Comfort **63** 195
Cyrus **62** 268 **91** 192
  121 92
Daniel **58** 316 **63** 226 **111**
  287 **115** 19
Daniel Butler **126** 91
Daniel Edmund **91** 192
Deborah **55** 179
Deborah C. (Cook)
  88 341
Delight (Chapman)
  137 257
Dexter **56** 256
Dirius **91** 192
Dorothy Elizabeth **111** 53
Duane H. **73** 213
Ebenezer **100** 246
Ebenezer S. **77** 177

NEWTON *cont'd*
Edmund **55** 338 **94** 11
  111 197 200
Edward **77** 25 27 **94** 179
Edward Augustus
  68 102 103
Edward C. **66** 243
Elbert **86** 449
Elbridge Ward (Mrs.)
  84 190 232
Eleanor **73** 225 **93** 22
  119 208
Elijah **77** 24
Elisha **58** 373
Eliza **55** 449
Eliza (Lewis) **88** 278
Eliza A. **80** 47
Eliza Taft **77** xxvii 77 **100**
  232 246 **101** 128
Elizabeth **55** 339 **58** 373 **60**
  72 316 **62** 265 **63** 195 **68**
  102 **86** 195 **94** 6 7 9 10
  12 16 18 **98** 93 **99** 285
  100 138 **110** 227 **111**
  197 **113** 35 41 **115** 16 19
  121 223 **125** 243 **143**
  331
Elizabeth (Davenport)
  125 173 182
Elizabeth (Hinton) **94** 6
  16
Elizabeth (Lazell) **89** 238
Elizabeth Anne **58** 316
Elizabeth Scott **65** 138
Ellen **52** 339 **93** 22 23 40 46
  94 3-5 7-10 12 13 15-18
  99 100 106 **97** 388 **98**
  200 **107** 111 111 195
  199 260 265 **112** 157
  113 71 **114** 74 75 226
  116 166 **124** 312 **141**
  101
Elmira **73** 213
Elvin **68** 45 131-133 137
  138 140 141
Elviria Lavinia **113** 230
Emily Charlotte **66** lxxxv
Emma **91** 192
Enoch **69** 160 201
Ephraim **127** 187
Ephraim H. **110** 32
Ephraim Holland **63** 388
Esther **63** 195 **77** 32 **119**
  48 50 52 53 55 58 59 127
  130 133-136
Eunice **58** 255 **63** 195
  71 18
Ezekiel **75** 182
Ezra **55** 179 **105** 285
Fannie C. **73** 213
Fanny **125** 287
Fergus **62** 250
Frances **55** 338 **94** 7-10 12
  18 **118** 120 **120** 302 **123**
  18
Francis **94** 6-8 10 12-14 16
  17 **111** 197 **123** 20 21
  124 117 **125** 29
Francis Albert **77** 148
Francis L. **86** 26
Gabriel **94** 12 17

NEWTON *cont'd*
George **55** 332 338 **66** 37
  80 47 **96** 63 **138** 15
George H. **115** 294
George W. L. **88** 341
Gershom **136** 303
Gertrude **80** 395
Gideon **122** 62 **143** 18
Gilbert **56** 87 197
Gilbert Stuart **68** 103
H. W. **119** 160 320
Hannah **53** 246 **54** 222 **68**
  102 103 **69** 201 **77** 32 **88**
  284 **102** 309
Hannah (Loker) **143** 330
Hannah M. **78** 315
Hannah P. **73** 193
Harmony **60** 201
Harold Wilson **120** 232
Harriet Augusta **67** 144
Harriet N. **52** 338
Harriet P. (Bump) **92** 172
Harriet W. **65** 138
Harry B. **111** 53
Harry Heustis **61** xxxvii
Hattie F. (Preble) **83** 437
  438
Heirome **94** 7
Helen **94** 9 15 **122** 78
Helen Vanderveer **83** 491
Henry **67** 112 **68** 103 **69**
  201 **93** 217 **94** 11 12 17
  127 207 **137** 51
Hezekiah **88** 278
Hibbert **57** 277 280
  68 101-103
Hierome **94** 8 9 11
Hiram Camp **72** 87
Hollis B. **91** 192
Howard Dunlap (Mrs.)
  85 188 **103** 77 123 **106**
  123
Hubert A. **51** 233
Huldah **61** 260 **63** 388
I. R. **125** 173
Ida **68** 45
Isaac **57** 114 **62** 265 266 268
  269 **67** 246 **68** 34-37 **72**
  43 87 **73** 213 **75** 320 **94**
  16 **115** 19
Isaac B. **84** 54
Isaac Elvin **67** 144
Isaac K. **67** 144 **68** 142
Isaac Lafayette **60** 72
Isabel **55** 338
Isabella **82** 237
Israel **80** 190 **89** 255
Ithamar **115** 16
J. B. **79** 300
J. R. **110** 122
J. T. **60** 316 **63** 195
Jacob **60** 124
James **55** 339 **66** 294 **100**
  246 **116** 7
James B. **100** 246
James E. **130** 46
James Hale **100** 246
Jane **78** 41 **84** 323 **85** 3 **92**
  392 **94** 11 12 14 **111** 197
  130 216 **143** 134 250
Jane (Rich) **84** 54

NEWTON *cont'd*
Jane Eliza **55** 449
Jennett **55** 339
Jenny **55** 339
Jerome **94** 7 11 13-15
  111 197
Jerusha (Bruce) **136** 303
Jerusha (Child) **88** 277
Jesse **62** 269
Joan **94** 12 17
Job **78** 124
John **54** 360 **60** 316 **62**
  265 268-270 **63** 61 66
  121 195 224 **64** 226 254-
  11 13-15 17 **99** 285 **107**
  215 **111** 195-200 260 261
  265 **113** 69 **114** 226 227
  122 68 **124** 177 178 **125**
  279 **127** 8 **138** 102 **143**
  331 **147** 158
John Breckenbrough
  87 295
John C. **67** 139 **73** 193 206
John H. **90** 37
John Marshall **67** 192
John W. **65** 138
Jonah **58** 373
Jonathan **136** 303
Joseph **63** 220 226 **100** 246
  113 213 275
Joseph C. **68** 38
Joseph M. **67** 139
Joshua **127** 207 **128** 37
Josiah **53** 246 **67** 117
Jotham **127** 187
Julia H. **77** 177
Julius **62** 122
Katharine **56** 87
Katharine Lucile **72** 295
Lancelot **93** 24 40 **94** 7-10
  12 13 15 17 18 **111** 198-
  200
Laura **115** 291
Laura Maria **80** 190 **89** 255
Laurena **99** 303
Lavina **56** 36
Lemuel **77** 24
Leverett Thompson
  (Mrs.) **82** 219 237
Liberty **80** 331
Lillian **115** 294
Lois **80** 190 **89** 255
Louisa **80** 190 **89** 255
Louler **83** 200
Lucinda **60** 202
Lucinda Ellen **64** 252
Lucy **58** 316 **103** 239
  118 120
Lucy E. 437 **83** 437
Lydia **51** 293 **60** 72 124
  67 117 **80** 190 **89** 255
  108 76
Lydia (Rich) **84** 39
Margaret **62** 271 **73** 265
  94 7 11-13 **111** 197
Margaret (Clayton)
  143 331
Margaret (Grimston) **94**
  7 13 **111** 260 265
Margaret (Thorpe) **111**
  195 198 200

NEWTON *cont'd*
Margery **94** 12 18
Maria **65** 138 **100** 89 90
  116 303
Marie (**94** 8 9 12 14 15 17
Marie (Skipsey) **94** 9 14
  15
Mark **67** 139 144 246
Mark C. **68** 36 37
Martha **60** 316 **63** 195 **64**
  258 **100** 240 **103** 239
  122 187 **126** 25
Martha (Gibbs) **100** 299
Martin **66** lxxxv **88** 334
Mary **53** 228 **58** 47 **59** 68
  61 129 **62** lxxv 265 **63**
  195 **64** lvi **65** 122 **67**
  138 139 144 **68** 103 **69**
  161 **71** 352 **74** 173 **78** 21
  86 454 **91** 192 **94** 9 10
  12 **99** 285 **119** 160 320
Mary (Field) **113** 213
Mary (Lee) **93** 24 40 **94** 17
Mary A. **73** 213
Mary Agnes **77** 184
Mary Amelia (Fassett)
  104 124
Mary Ann (Dam) **111** 53
Mary C. **67** 139 144
Mary J. **68** 45 **103** 48
Mary Jane **77** 148
Mary Mann Page **87** 295
Marye **94** 12
Matilda (Gates) **121** 217
Matthew **65** 127 **69** 384
  119 160 320
Maude (Prawokr ?) **94** 12
Michael **94** 12 17
Miles **63** 195
Millie (Church) **100** 198
Miranda **61** 250
Miriam **108** 76 **136** 304
Moses **57** 114 **63** 220 226
  100 246 **136** 300
Nahum **66** 243 **127** 187
Nancy **67** 246 **81** 394
  136 327
Nancy A. **68** 46
Nancy Ann **67** 144
Nanny **66** 222
Naomi **63** 195 **77** 26
Nathan **61** 250 **63** 195
Nettie **102** 287
Norman Thomas King
  101 125
Obed **62** 270
Olive **86** 455
Olive (Maxwell) **83** 300
Orlando L. **92** 172
Ovid **64** 252
Parateen (Lockwood)
  112 79
Patience **125** 279
Patty **55** 179
Peggy **73** 140
Persis **57** 114 **62** 270 **103**
  68 **137** 257
Phebe **67** 246 **127** 299
Philena **78** 236
Philip **60** 244
Phillips **68** 103

NEWTON *cont'd*
Philo Slocum **58** 316
Phineas **78** 21
Polly **56** 256 **115** 16
Polly Mariah **100** 89 195
Polly Melinda (Turner)
  89 312
Priestly **62** 270
Prudence **127** 187
R. **54** 26
Rachel **60** 316 **73** 218
Rebecca **57** 385 **60** 244
Rebecca A. (Bump) **92** 172
Rejoice **62** 269
Reuben **58** 255
Rhoda **91** 193
Rhoda (Lyon) **91** 192
Richard **60** 72 188 357 **62**
  220 223 226-228 337 342
  63 61 66 121 124 125
  218 225 **66** 218 **69** 384
  76 122 **80** 387 **94** 12
  100 246 **110** 267 **111**
  197 **114** 37 **141** 339 **143**
  330 331
Robert **81** 487 **94** 7-9 11
  13 15 **143** 331
Roger **60** 316 **61** 129 **62**
  lxxv 263-272 **63** 195 **69**
  384 **94** 62
Ruby A. **83** 200
Russell D. **52** 456
Ruth E. (Winter) **92** 172
Ruth G. (Miller) **92** 172
S. E.C. **72** 295
Sabra (Titus) **114** 171
Sally **67** 137
Sally Williams **68** 103
Samuel **62** lxxv 269-271
  73 104 **111** 281 **127** 187
Sarah **62** 456 **56** 38 **58** 373
  59 66 **60** 134 **61** 129 **62**
  269 **63** 195 **66** 143 145
  147 216 218 220 222 224
  294 305 **67** 117 138 246
  73 257 261 **77** 19 24 **106**
  71 **127** 187 **129** 395
Sarah (Field) **88** 341
Sarah (Jones) **113** 136
Sarah E. **68** 46
Sarah Elizabeth **67** 144
Sarah Jane (Searles)
  88 334
Sebra **62** 268
Selim **147** 261 263
Seraph Huldah **63** 388
  71 1
Sewall **112** 79
Shadrach **73** 104
Sherman Chauncey
  69 201
Sherman T. **83** 437 438
Sibyl **60** 316 **68** 275 **71** 16
Silas **77** 184 **121** 217
Silence **136** 304
Simeon **95** 237
Simon **63** 57 74 **125** 173
  182 **127** 8
Solomon **77** 32
Stephen **94** 11
Submit **78** 124

NEWTON cont'd
Susan **66** lxxxv
Susan C. **121** 179
Susan E. **79** 119
Susanna **59** 168 369 **60**
316 **62** lxxv 267 268 **63**
195 **73** 257 **94** 62
Susanna (Cook) **126** 91
Tabitha **114** 37 **127** 186
Tabitha (Sanderson)
127 187
Thankful **71** 52
Thankful (Willis) **114** 29
Thomas **51** 240 **55** 339 **61**
394 **68** 101-103 **69** 384
80 385 395 **94** 3 6 8 11-
14 16-18 **98** 105 **111** 197
200
Thomas H. (Mrs.) **108** 135
Thomas Wodehouse
Legh (Baron) **77** 253
Timothy **61** 250
Tryphene **119** 223 298
Tryphenia Adeline **80** 331
Vivian **91** 192
W. M. **82** 228 **110** 267
W. N. **122** 61
Walter **52** 338
Willard A. **83** 300
William **55** 002 008 009
58 47 **68** 103 **94** 4 12 13
16 17 **100** 25 **101** 161
104 124 **111** 195-197
200
William C. **68** 37-44 134
135 137 141
William H. **115** 294
William Monroe **78** 331
79 203 **124** 16 **141** 151
William T. **51** 77
William Ward **84** 39
Woodman W. **83** 200
Zachariah **53** 228
NEWTONIUS
Esther **55** 438
Ney see Nye
Neye see Nye
Neylson see Neilson
NEYRUNYT
John **102** 193
NIAH Huldah **62** 370
NIBLO Niblow
Cuba Mary **94** 25
Esther **129** 52
Margaret **129** 51
NIBLOCK Maria **81** 99
Niblow see Niblo
NICARY
Jonathan **105** 279
Niccolls see Nichols
Niccols see Nichols
Nice see Von Nice
Nichelson see Nicholson
NICHIPOR
W. (Mrs.) **130** 314
Nichol see Nichols
NICHOLAS V Pope **66** x
NICHOLAS Nickolas
Nickulas Nicolas
—— **63** 327 **69** 15 **74** 74
Abbie M. **86** 366

NICHOLAS cont'd
Abigail **111** 55
Ann **100** 32
Edward Mithoff (Mrs.)
97 186
Elizabeth **92** 47
Elizabeth D. (Clark)
106 149
Esther Stevenson **113** 295
George **54** 343 **55** 276
Hannah **71** 48
I. **58** lxxxviii
Jack **55** 276
James **62** 159 **92** 46 **120** 12
John **85** 10 **93** 382 386 387
100 32
John S. **106** 149
Joseph **145** 361
Lucy **91** 364
Mary **100** 32
Mary Carrington (Cram)
(Greene) (Thurston)
97 186
Nicholas Harris **58** 288 **99**
272 **145** 16
Plassce **78** 420
R. C. **55** 383 384
Rebecca **87** 235 237
Rice **60** 188
Richard **64** 114
Robert Carter (Mrs.)
86 198
Roberta Wood (Johnson)
86 198
Samuel **93** 382 384 385 387
Sarah **60** 192
Thomas **110** 170
Wealthy W. **76** 272
William **76** 56
Wilson **55** 276
NICHOLS Necol Niccolls
Niccols Nichol Nicholl
Nicholls Nickalls
Nickel Nickels
Nickolds Nocholl
—— **51** 348 **52** 134 260
270 **56** 108 **57** 191 **58**
102 201-203 210 317 **59**
225 **60** 103 107 147 212
61 374 401 **62** 360 **65**
189 **66** 233 **73** 299 **74**
119 **75** 28 **76** 174 **82** 413
91 346 **92** 256 259 313
317 351 355 **97** 217 **100**
191 233 237 238 **103** 11
104 47 **109** 207 **118** 261
122 287 **137** 240 **147** 59
— Capt. **61** 305
— Col. **54** 183 184 **59** 275
277 **94** 20 **139** 102
— Gen. **52** 34 204 205
Mr. **63** 22 **70** 16 233
71 48 116 118 139 140
— Mrs. **58** 60 **62** 28 **63** 57
71 48 **82** 413
— Rev. Dr. **83** 194
— Widow **63** 162 **66** 364
—— (Low) **112** 40
Aaron **58** 203 **61** 236
Abah **88** 335
Abbie E. **109** 16

NICHOLS cont'd
Abbie M. **110** 215
Abby **104** 163
Abby J. **85** 416
Abel **128** 143
Abiah (Chase) **87** 337
Abiel **88** 117
Abigail **68** 169 244 **69** 81
104 **71** 254 **73** 299 **75**
185 **104** 294 **109** 12 16
121 270 **124** 199 200
129 269 **137** 329-331
141 336
Abigail (Barton) **107** 299
Abigail (Beal) **129** 269
Abigail (Ford) **120** 50
Abigail (Gale) **127** 179
Abigail (Kendall) **137** 251
Abner **72** 263
Abraham **105** 280 **139** 312
Ada Sophia
(FitzRandolph) **99** 39
Adam **91** 387 **93** 171
140 231
Adelaide **78** 32
Adna **90** 112
Agnes **76** 136 **114** 234
Agnes Eliza **93** 188
Aholiab **103** 299
Alanson **61** xlvi
Albert **86** 366
Albert C. **76** 52
Albert P. **78** 184
Alden **77** 320
Alexander **91** 346 **92** 313
317 **119** 21 **125** 101 **129**
53
Alfred **65** 379 **71** 54
Alice Elizabeth **89** 13
Allen Chase **141** 336
Allora (Chase) **88** 117
Almira **60** 150
Almira A. **81** 36
Althea **66** 233
Ambrose **52** 133 **133** 231
Amelia **69** 366
Amos **71** 55 **103** 160
Amy **54** 219 **69** 114
109 270
Andrew **100** 241 **104** 80
128 128 143
Ann **66** 233 **69** 331 **72** 219
74 116 119 **109** 206 207
113 77
Ann (Barnard) **98** 135
Ann (Devereux) (Boasum)
109 207
Ann (Eno) **123** 309
Ann (Humphrey) **89** 13
Ann Elmira **68** 248 **69** 311
72 263
Ann F. **93** 112
Ann Maria **89** 13
Ann Maria (McAuley)
98 93
Anna **58** 373 **63** 57 **72** 261
81 123 **108** 92 **121** 320
133 73
Anna (Williams) **98** 337
Annah **133** 72
Anne **58** 373 **66** 342

NICHOLS *cont'd*
Anne (Sanders) **109** 168
Annie **138** 287
Annie May **69** 312
Annie R. **80** 38
Annis **78** 284
Anthony **52** 255
Arthur Howard **58** xlv
  63 151 199 211 **59** xi
  xxiv xxxiv xlii xlviii
  214 **65** xxxiii 275 **66**
  194 **67** xxx **70** 147 **78**
  215 284 285
Arvard Bradley **110** 215
Asa **61** lxiii **62** 266 **75** 306
  78 32
Aseneth **88** 283
Asher **127** 178 179
Augusta A. (Holmes)
  (Porter) **85** 169
Augustine **66** 341 342
Augustus Barton **92** 343
Avery L. **108** 284
Azubah **127** 179
Bathsheba **57** 183
Benjamin **54** 402 **61** xlvi
  379 **62** 355 **63** 53 **71** 130
  75 182 **80** 38 **97** 22 56
  127 **109** 212 **114** 127
  125 218 **127** 6 7
Benjamin Floyd **70** 193
Benjamin Ropes **76** lx
Benjamin Thomas
  110 215
Bethiah **58** 262 **129** 251 377
Betsey **56** 259 **59** 258 **61**
  239 **63** 184 **78** 411 **114**
  303
Betsey (Gardner) **127** 179
Betsey (Pettee) **125** 218
Betsey Ann **92** 375
Betty **58** 203 373
Brett Selpho **81** 111 222
Bromfield Bradford
  148 66
C. **126** 170
C. A. **61** 102
Caleb **59** 314 **65** 344 **68**
  169 246 **69** 75 179 180
  72 263 **127** 307 **135** 44
Calvin **71** 115
Caroline **95** 51
Caroline (McColley)
  89 310
Caroline E. **113** 295
Carrie **71** 116
Catherine **79** 155 **137** 251
  325
Catherine (Clifford)
  114 300
Catherine (Cushing)
  129 168
Catherine (Miller) **90** 112
Catherine M. (Egan)
  90 112
Catherine T. Wendell
  144 210
Celia **121** 280
Cephas **71** 135
Charity **71** 254 **99** 205
  121 108

NICHOLS *cont'd*
Charity S. **84** 140
Charles **61** xlvi **68** 245
  69 305 **72** 263 **75** 14 **79**
  308 **95** 51 **100** 191 **107**
  299 **113** 158 **147** 60
Charles (Mrs.) **95** 51
Charles A. **93** 217
Charles B. **75** 14 28 **109** 16
  110 215
Charles C. **93** 352
Charles D. **78** 317
Charles E. **84** 140
Charles H. **94** 114 **96** 54
Charles Henry **69** 180
Charles J. **99** 82 **101** 259
Charles Lemuel **59** cii
Charles Moses **113** 158
Charles R. **84** 140
Charles W. **75** 14
Charlotte **74** 154 **75** 14 28
Charlotte A. **75** 14 28
Charlotte E. **74** 154
Chirdsey **80** 434
Christian **67** 156
Christopher **55** 412
Clarissa **103** 144 239 **119**
  276 **135** 44
Clarissa B. **89** 42
Clarissa H. (Gilman)
  88 285
Clark **101** 94
Comfort **61** 379
Comfort Hoag **72** 261
Cornelius **125** 237
Cushing **92** 256 259 315
  355 **93** 326 **94** 379
Cynthia **60** 336 **61** 173
Cyprian **81** 83 84 **105** 246
  148 34
Cyrus **101** 329 **110** 117
Cyrus H. **91** 42
D. **139** 257
Daisy **96** 161
Damaris **96** 377
Daniel **129** 269
Daniel B. **125** 293
Daniel Furber **98** 125
David **57** 282 **61** lxiii **62**
  23 129 **68** 293 **69** 78 180
  368 **70** 36 230 **71** 54 116
  72 264 **74** 42 189 196
  197 **75** 141 304 **76** lxxiv
  86 224 **87** 137 **92** 54 **98**
  333 **104** 80 **105** 279 **109**
  270 **114** 300 **127** 87 **128**
  301 **129** 66
David H. **69** 308
Deborah **70** 40
Deborah (Hobart) **110** 79
Deborah Currier **134** 66
Deborah S. **57** 67
Desire **106** 182 **125** 240
Dimmick **104** 80
Dorcas **63** 88 177 **68** 169
  245 **69** 81 177 **71** 254 **72**
  262 263 **73** 47 49 **126**
  141
Dorothea Folsom
  (Gilman) **86** 224
Dorothy **135** 288

NICHOLS *cont'd*
Dorothy M. **78** 203
E. P. **88** 325
Ebenezer **55** 52 **57** 355 **61**
  203 **62** 61 **68** 292 **69** 365
  366 **70** 34 **79** 321 **80** 424
  90 112 **94** 320 **108** 26
  125 33 **137** 240 251 325
  330
Edgar Guernsey **109** 160
Edward **52** 260 **73** 139
  75 220
Edward E. **98** 93
Edward F. **141** 148
Edward L. **141** 148
Edward M. **52** 484
Edwin **95** 50
Eleanor **89** 15 **120** 10 **124**
  242 **145** 73 **146** 384
Eleanor (Robertson)
  127 179
Elijah **104** 80
Eliza **114** 321
Eliza (Hannum) **91** 42
Eliza Ann **69** 331 **82** 203
  109 129
Eliza P. **125** 243
Eliza Woodhull **86** 103
Elizabeth **55** 345 412 **58**
  133 173 261 **59** 314 **62**
  266 **64** 41 152 340 **65**
  349 **68** 192 197 251 **69**
  164 **71** 47 248 254 **72**
  263 **73** 49 **75** 141 **78** 184
  86 318 **89** 13 **94** 320 **99**
  119 205 **100** 26 214 240
  104 163 **116** 66 **121** 16
  119 **125** 223 251 **129**
  164 170 **135** 40 **143** 231
Elizabeth (Bates) **88** 193
Elizabeth (Boyd) **128** 171
Elizabeth (Gowen)
  125 293
Elizabeth (Hazelton)
  136 336
Elizabeth (Lincoln)
  129 369
Elizabeth (Pitman)
  125 180
Elizabeth (Snowman)
  110 105 107
Elizabeth (Trask) **126** 66
Elizabeth Ely (Randolph)
  98 125
Elizabeth Fisher **78** 285
Elizabeth Huntington
  62 190
Elizabeth Keith **67** xxxiv
  76 lxxv **86** 110 205 224
Ella B. **68** 159
Ellen **97** 192
Ellen J. (Carver) **89** 42
Ellis **61** 380 **122** 80
Elmira A. **69** 311
Elnathan **75** 190
Eloise A. **76** 90
Emily Baker **112** 312
Emma **68** 246 **91** 108
Emma Eliza (Bancroft)
  97 128
Emma Gertrude **61** lxiii

NICHOLS *cont'd*
Emma H. (Young) **89** 13
Emmaline **90** 42
Ephraim **58** 373 **64** 152
　70 38 40 **71** 254 **121** 21
　197 204 208 209 212 280
Erasmus **89** 76
Esther **68** 245 **75** 191
　76 220
Esther (Smith) **133** 231
Esther Rice **108** 83
Esther T. **55** 199 **141** 148
Ethan Harry **86** 366
Ethel Daveneille **108** 135
Ethelbert Belknap **98** 337
Etta M. (Noble) **94** 352
Etta Maria (Noble) **95** 36
Eunice **61** 238 **68** 169 **69**
　75 78 179 365 **70** 35 200
　230 **74** 196 **91** 343 348
　127 59 **128** 143 **146** 384
Eunice (Nichols) **128** 143
Eunice H. **69** 180
Evelina **89** 40
Experience **58** 262
Ezra **119** 75 **136** 336
F. **91** 331
Fanny **55** 180 **81** 153 **90** 43
Fanny (FitzRandolph)
　98 337
Fanny (Leavitt) **86** 150
　367
Fanny F. R. **99** 51
Ferdinando **52** 93
Florence **93** 217
Frances **74** 32
Frances Elizabeth (James)
　127 89
Frances Oriana **55** 199
Frances Sabrina **61** xlvi
Francis **66** 34 **87** 231 235
　91 331
Francis Alanson **61** xlv-
　vii
Frank **75** 14
Frank Billings **107** 226
Frank Cheever **106** 126
　115 67
Frank I. **110** 215
Frankie **108** 135
Gabriel **52** 254
Genevra **97** 128
George **61** 322 384 **62** 360
　63 57 58 **72** 261 263 **76**
　131 133 **104** 80 **109** 160
　125 251 **128** 134 **129** 55
　137 48
George (Mrs.) **97** 341
　101 125
George B. **66** lxix
George Henry **76** lxxiv
　86 224 225 **89** 343
George Leslie **62** xxviii
　xxxvii
George Little **92** 198
George Louis **89** 13
George Roseman **107** 226
George Roseman (Mrs.)
　87 62 172 **107** 125 225
　226 **108** 138
George S. **90** 38 **93** 112

NICHOLS *cont'd*
George W. **68** 251 **83** 185
　187
George Washington
　104 163 **110** 79
George Wolcott **89** 232
Georgiana **82** 353
Gilman Nevins **82** 353
Gloria Margaretta **97** 56
Gold **69** 366
Grace **70** 40
Grace Bancroft **97** 128
Grace C. (Staniford)
　97 128
Grace Gardner **61** 243
Grizel **58** 59
Guy Carlton **79** 321
H. M. **81** 36
H. S. **57** xxxiii
Hannah **52** 82 **58** 58 204
　59 389 **61** 238 261 **63**
　271 **66** 233 **68** 245 247
　248 293 **69** 78 81 311
　368 **70** 36 **71** 254 **72** 263
　264 274 **73** 47 **74** 42 196
　197 256 **78** 284 **79** 40 96
　80 424 **81** 104 **84** 365
　86 89 **88** 325 **109** 59
　118 81 **121** 18 **124** 12
　127 178 179 **129** 169
　136 145
Hannah (Caldwell)
　88 325
Hannah (Cushing)
　129 169
Hannah (Gaskill) **86** 224
　120 159
Hannah (Gibbs) **110** 117
Hannah (Myrick) **127** 179
Hannah (Tompkins)
　125 288
Hannah (Whittemore)
　106 94
Hannah B. **127** 178 179
Hannah Broughton
　127 180
Hannah Elizabeth **69** 311
　72 263
Hannah P. **68** 247 248
　69 78
Hannah Pierce **127** 59
Harriet **79** 302 **101** 94
Harriet (Lazell) **89** 13
Harriet Elizabeth **70** xlix
Harriet Maria **69** 311
Harry Frederick **54** xli
　61 xlv lxiii
Hay **78** 184
Hazel **91** 51
Helen J. **77** 175
Helon **123** 309
Henrietta **78** 311
Henrietta Fivilla **92** 146
Henrietta Maria **77** 297
Henry **71** 45 **78** 386 **89** 310
　129 61
Henry Clay **61** lxiii
Henry Joseph **103** 120
Henry S. **114** 180
Henry Wilber **91** 51
Herbert **62** 283 **63** 57

NICHOLS *cont'd*
　102 207
Herbert W. **95** 36
Hester **52** 133
Hezekiah **104** 163
Horace **71** 47 53
Horace H. **80** 424
Horatio **100** 191
Huldah **58** 203 **86** 447
　108 279
Huldah (Kimberly)
　102 109
Huldah (Snow) **104** 132
　133
Humphrey **72** 248
　104 163
Ichabod **51** 143 **74** 42 **76**
　lxxiv **82** 413 **86** 224 **101**
　224 **124** 148
Inez Scott **89** 43
Irene **72** xlix
Isaac **54** 352 **76** 134-136
　141 142 144 **84** 140 **89**
　13 **93** 397 **100** 63 **101**
　225 **108** 222 **128** 134
　140 174
Isabel Perkins **61** xlvi
Isabella **68** 144 **146** 361
Isabella C. **115** 320
Isabella Johnson **92** 344
Isaiah **97** 128
Israel **57** 320 **59** 314 389 **71**
　254 256 **91** 93 **104** 47
　105 210 **121** 23 204 209
　213 272 273 **129** 163 170
J. B. **53** 143
J. G. **58** 288 **60** 82 85 183
　184 187 188 190 **104** 271
　123 295
J. G. (Mrs.) **119** 202
Jabez **52** 82 **58** 204 **127**
　178 179
Jack **123** 107
Jacob **127** 178 180 **139** 312
James **54** 46 **61** xlvi 239
　62 74 **63** 246 **64** 111 **69**
　104 **70** 170 171 **75** 254
　78 410 **79** 192 321 **81**
　104 146 **88** 325 **90** 87 **91**
　343 346 348 **99** 82 **103**
　300 **105** 277 279 280
　106 94 **125** 96 **128** 171
　132 41 164 **137** 330 **143**
　257 **144** 343
James D. **119** 198
James O. **91** 388
James Robinson **70** xlix
Jane **72** 274 **75** 182 **83** 488
　104 133 294 **109** 16 **110**
　111
Jane (Jameson) **86** 224
Jane Maria **84** 460
Jane Norton (Morgan)
　97 341
Jazaniah **58** 173 262 **121**
　287 **129** 169
Jazeniah **121** 278
Jeanette P. **92** 207
Jeannette **146** 390 391
Jeannette Paddock **91** 97
Jeremiah **109** 212

NICHOLS *cont'd*
Jerome **92** 344 350 **93** 325
Jerusha **57** 363 **133** 73
Jesse **63** 87 **76** 146 **77** 175
Jesse Clyde **146** 390 391
Jessie (Miller) **146** 390 391
Jo. **79** 308
Joan **93** 171
Joanna **64** 189
Joel M. **85** 169
John **55** 199 **56** 214 **57** 363
  58 56 203 **59** 193 **60** 18
  181 **61** lxiii 391 **62** 323
  63 57 58 87 165 234 246
  64 165 **65** 189 **66** 27 342
  68 169 174 244 **69** 81
  177 **71** 117 248 **72** 263
  73 152 262 **74** 154 196
  75 14 28 **76** 133 177 **80**
  357-360 **85** 410 **90** 38
  92 55 179 259 343 **93**
  324 385 387 **94** 318 380
  96 375 **98** 337 **104** 132
  133 163 294 **107** 31 105
  309 **109** 16 212 **113** 64
  115 320 **117** 15 **118** 313
  119 21 **123** 180 **127** 178-
  180 **128** 51 125 143 **129**
  56 67 **137** 249 **139** 303
  311 312 **142** 228 229 242
  243 **143** 43 **145** 355
John Benjamin **94** 208
John Edward **69** 312
John Gorham **89** 13
John Gough **102** 6 253
  103 18
John H. **114** 180
John Homan **109** 229
John K. **85** 416
John L. **145** 25
John Perkins **78** 284
John S. **87** 337
John T. **66** 27
Jonas **58** 373 **69** 17 **94** 316
Jonathan **58** 60 203 373
  61 xlvi **62** 355 **63** 87 **81**
  153 **86** 367 **129** 67 **143**
  221 222 225 227 231 **147**
  332 341
Jonathan Clifford **89** 43
Jonathan Clifford (Mrs.)
  89 43
Jonathan Lyman **76** 142
Joseph **56** 35 **66** 11 **67** 156
  69 331 **71** 135 140 **73**
  303 **76** 131 **79** 301 **88**
  193 **98** 135 **106** 182 **109**
  212 **118** 245 **124** 228
  128 217 **129** 59 60
Joseph B. **69** 311 **72** 263
  127 89
Joseph Dean **88** 22
Joseph Evans **88** 359
Joseph Stickney **134** 69
Joseph T. **127** 89
Joseph Taylor **138** 287
Josephine G. **122** 19
  146 362
Josephine Genung **57**
  112 116 **60** 89 **63** 305 **64**
  xxxi **71** 191 **73** 241 **145**

NICHOLS *cont'd*
  40
Joshua **52** 73 **137** 360
Joshua B. **89** 42
Joshua Meader **72** 261
Josiah **71** 48
Josias **94** 66
Judith **52** 260 **56** 35 **62** 153
  109 16
Judith (Bulyea) **123** 107
Judith (Darby) **108** 279
Judith (Durrell) **134** 69
Julia Ann **121** 180
Julia E. **93** 186
Julianna **104** 80
Katharine **52** 246 **93** 211
Katrina **92** 198
Katy **140** 49
Kendall **57** 282 **111** 56
Kitta Louisa **71** 117
L. N. **57** 116 **60** 82 85 183
  184 187 188 190
L. N. (Mrs.) **113** 276
Laura **78** 31
Lela **101** 125
Lemuel **102** 109
Lena Bancroft **97** 128
Leon Nelson **61** xxxv 99
  73 160 **113** 276
Levi **58** 373 **69** 368 **86** 126
Lewis **104** 47
Lila **102** 239 240 **103** 81
Livona Ellen **86** 367
Lloyd (Mrs.) **92** 194
Lois **60** 147 **121** 51
Lorna **81** 496
Louisa **66** 11 **82** 353
Louisa (West) (Post)
  147 60
Louisa Jane **69** 78 178
Louisa Jane (Hobby) **68**
  248 **69** 312
Love **100** 191 292
Lucena (Corbett) **88** 359
  124 228
Lucinda **52** 457 **63** 87 **82**
  353 **127** 179
Lucinda Allen **92** 351
Lucretia **104** 80
Lucy **58** 60 147 203 **63** 87
  67 376 **75** 186 **104** 294
  106 109
Lucy Ann **89** 232
Lucy Augusta (Waste)
  113 158
Lucy M. **93** 274 **94** 52
Lucy Orne **76** lix lx **119** 5
Luke **71** 35
Luther Western **125** 288
Luthera B. **75** 28
Lydia **58** 136 203 373 **61**
  239 **68** 168 169 245 **69**
  77 78 182 **76** 133 **87** 92
  340 **88** 107 **95** 280 **127**
  179
Lydia (Kent) **135** 44
Lydia (Ropes) **86** 224
Lydia (Wade) **127** 180
Lydia R. **127** 87
Lyman **61** 218 **101** 225
M. **94** 320

NICHOLS *cont'd*
M. T. **92** 343
Mabel **75** 98
Mae **90** 136
Magaret **104** 294
Malachi **112** 59 **127** 178
  179
Marcy **137** 25
Margaret **65** 45 **68** 169
  70 xlix **79** 37 96 **93** 91
  104 133 294 **143** 292
Margaret (Billings)
  87 172
Margaret (Romley)
  86 366
Margaret Atherton
  89 343
Margaret B. **68** 246 **125**
  237 240
Margaret Homer **78** 285
Margaret Nelson **81** 146
Maria **79** 155 **89** 232
  93 363
Maria S. **69** 180
Maria Theresa **92** 259
  93 324
Marian Clarke **78** 285
Marietta (Hazard) **127** 89
  138 287
Marion J. **64** 119
Marion Josephine **95** 36
Marjorie Louise **106** 124
Martha **57** 414 **58** 57 78
  264 **91** 79 **112** 59 **129**
  369 **136** 273
Martha (Merwin) (Tolles)
  102 109
Martha Ann (Moriarty)
  101 225
Martha Winifred
  Whitney (Smith)
  112 313
Martin Lazell **89** 13
Marvin Curtis (Mrs.)
  108 175
Mary **52** 254 260 **53** 32 **54**
  352 402 **56** 73 **57** 141
  182 **58** 203 373 **59** cii
  68 169 **69** 81 104 181 **71**
  130 254 256 **72** 264 271
  274 283 **73** 303 **74** 42 **75**
  254 **76** lx **79** 39 289 321
  80 438 **92** 344 350 **93**
  325 **94** 221 224 **98** 333
  104 163 **107** 220 **108** 93
  162 222 **109** 160 168
  111 291 **114** 312 **115**
  140 **121** 103 206 275
  122 100 **125** 287 **127**
  179 **129** 58 **130** 88 89
  148 42
Mary (Bancroft) **94** 314
Mary (Bugbee) **127** 179
Mary (Burdett) **98** 125
Mary (Felt) **106** 94
Mary (Woodbridge)
  114 127
Mary Ann **65** 10 **78** 284 79
  320 321 **127** 87 89
Mary Ann Cushing
  92 256

NICHOLS *cont'd*
Mary Bates **88** 192 193
Mary C. **68** 247 **69** 311 **72** 263 **96** 53
Mary Chickering **74** 161
Mary Elizabeth **71** lxiii
Mary Elizabeth (Badlam) **141** 148
Mary G. (Aldrich) **91** 387
Mary H. (Low) **88** 275
Mary Jane **109** 16
Mary Jane (Leach) **108** 279
Mary Jean **95** 144
Mary Jewett **71** lxiii
Mary Josephine **61** 99
Mary Josephine Genung **61** xxxv
Mary M. **109** 16
Mary Runey **92** 350
Mary Virginia **78** 166
Matilda **63** 372
Matthew **125** 237
Matthias **61** 279 **96** 235 **106** 167 169 170
Maude (Yunks) **113** 158
Mehitable **78** 284
Mehitable (Bancroft) **94** 318
Mercy **92** 53
Meribah **104** 47
Merriam **122** 244
Merriam (Stafford) **122** 244
Miller **146** 390 391
Miriam **58** 373 **70** 38 **75** 254
Moses **58** 157 **69** 177 **78** 294 **93** 274 **97** 128 **100** 26 **106** 109 **147** 85
Myron Leslie (Mrs.) **108** 135
Nabby **61** 175
Nancy **63** 87 **113** 73 **122** 244
Nancy (Stafford) **122** 243
Nancy Dearborn (Blake) **134** 66 69
Nat **121** 208
Nath **121** 103 209 216 269
Nathan **63** 257 **129** 58
Nathan Round **78** 337 **80** 113
Nathaniel **56** 259 **58** 173 261 **71** 254 **114** 189 **121** 271 **122** 287 **129** 156 168 258 369
Nathaniel Gilman **134** 66 69
Nehemiah **114** 189
Nellie **85** 192
Nicholas **71** lxiii **86** 318
Noah **61** 174 **65** 10 **88** 275
Octavia **72** 274
Olive **79** 321 **93** 274
Olive (Staples) **83** 185 187
Olive W. **68** 247
Olive Wing **69** 78
Ozias **91** 51 108
Parna **75** 304 **127** 179
Parthena Baker (Chase) **88** 22

NICHOLS *cont'd*
Patience **57** 320 **71** 254 **121** 112 216 **141** 211
Paul Allen **92** 259
Paul Louis **89** 13
Paulina (Ireland) **91** 388
Paulina Rebecca **91** 104
Penelope **60** 339
Peregrine **103** 160 **144** 131
Perkins **58** 157 **79** 302
Perthena (Faught) **87** 231 235
Peter **145** 73 **146** 384
Phebe **69** 81 311 **72** 263 **74** 196 **79** 31 **80** 434 **143** 251
Phebe (Caswell) **125** 237
Phebe (Chase) **87** 137
Phebe (Stimpson) **137** 251
Phebe J. **109** 16
Phebe W. (Barton) **107** 115
Philip **63** 88
Phineas **88** 285 **109** 168
Pierre **51** 40
Pliny **109** 160
Polly **58** 203 **61** 242 **78** 67 **93** 326 **101** 94 **109** 168 **127** 179 **137** 337
Polly (Law) **127** 179
Preston Foster **109** 130
Price **76** 131
Prudence B. **78** 386
Rachel **54** cxxxiii
Rachel (Petell) **100** 241
Rachel (Smith) **119** 198
Rachel B. **69** 78 308
Rachel O. **93** 112
Rebe **57** 141
Rebecca **55** 303 **57** 180 282 **58** 59 173 262 **61** 310 **62** 101 **63** 87 **68** 168 **69** 78 **71** 253 254 256 **72** 263 **73** 47 **78** 284 **79** 398 **88** 334 **91** 104 **94** 218 **97** 308 **121** 16 115 283 **139** 312
Rebecca (Hobart) **121** 287
Rebecca (Raynsford) **139** 311
Rebecca H. **75** 28
Reliance **58** 373 **59** 259
Reuben **92** 379
Rhoda **79** 321 **104** 163
Rhoda (Carpenter) **96** 377
Rhoda (Millard) **129** 170
Richard **52** 34 254 **54** 196 **61** xlvi lxiii 163 164 **69** 158 **76** 131 133 **78** 284 **79** 321 **80** 88 **96** 237 **106** 169 170 **109** 211 **129** 54 63 64
Richard H. **68** 159
Richard Johnson **61** xxxvii
Richard Maurice **96** 161
Robert **57** 414 **58** 57-60 **71** 312 **72** 284 **95** 289 **109** 206-208 **114** 80 161

NICHOLS *cont'd*
Roger **58** 262 **63** 16 **112** 40
Rosalia (Bancroft) **97** 217
Rosanna **86** 307
Rose Standish **78** 285 **103** 120
Roxanna B. **85** 219
Ruhama **117** 159
Ruth **51** 167 **52** 73 **57** 363 **58** 18 **61** 391 **69** 177 **71** 263 **85** 410 **121** 271 **139** 312
Ruth (Sargent) **96** 54
Ruthanna H. **69** 308
S. **96** 197
Sabra **122** 287
Sally **53** 165 **58** 60 **61** 381 **63** 87 **78** 32 **125** 173 **127** 179 **133** 307 309 **136** 138
Samson **120** 50
Samuel **55** 89 **58** 56 57 173 373 **63** 177 **68** 169 245 **69** 311 **72** 262 263 271 **73** 47 49 **74** 196 **78** 31 406 **79** 289 **82** 413 **91** 348 **92** 53 **93** 382 383 385 **94** 314 **96** 377 **98** 125 **104** 133 294 **105** 212 280 **108** 279 **109** 15 16 **114** 189 **121** 280 **127** 10 **133** 307 309 **137** 249 329 **141** 246
Samuel B. **69** 311
Samuel O. **69** 177
Sarah **52** 82 128 **56** 125 **58** 204 **61** 236 384 **67** 307 **68** 244 292 **69** 81 177 181 365 **70** 34 40 200 **71** 254 **72** 217 257 264 266 271 **74** 196 **75** 186 **76** 134 135 173 174 **77** 142 **78** 264 **89** 263 **96** 196 **98** 333 **109** 16 **121** 105 271 272 **125** 215 **126** 68 **133** 73 **136** 40 **141** 222 **148** 42
Sarah (Bates) **108** 284
Sarah (Bliss) (Mighell) **127** 178 **133** 72
Sarah (Brown) **127** 179
Sarah (Bryant) **137** 325
Sarah (Chamberlain) **140** 50
Sarah (Dodge) **98** 333
Sarah (Glazier) **137** 360
Sarah (Lincoln) **121** 271
Sarah (Page) **91** 51
Sarah (Preston) **89** 232
Sarah Ann **65** 10 **76** lxxiv
Sarah Ann (Atherton) **86** 224 225
Sarah Ann (Bancroft) **96** 54
Sarah Anna **82** 21
Sarah Frances **77** 182
Sarah Hazzard **80** 38
Sarah Louise **69** 312
Sarah O. **73** 98
Sarah Swain **100** 191

NICHOLS *cont'd*
Sarah Vose
(Cunningham) **89** 13
Sebiah (Bates) **129** 156 168
Shubael M. **66** 233
Sidney Homer **78** 285
Silas **55** 180 **80** 434
Silence **58** 262
Simeon **78** 264
Sophia **61** 380
Sophia (Carter) **97** 128
Stephen **68** 168 169 245
247 248 **69** 77 78 178
311 312 **72** 263 **73** 47 **74**
196 **96** 54 **122** 243 **145**
355
Stephen Pope **74** 42
Suretonhie **65** 325
Susan **61** 382 **62** 153
94 114
Susanna **57** 183 **61** 203
73 230 **74** 102 **76** 177
78 284 **79** 321 **94** 320
121 276 **126** 99
Susanna (Damon)
137 325
Susanna (Monroe)
137 251
Susanna (Rust) **125** 101
Susanna E. **100** 210
Symond **109** 212
Tabitha **63** 246 **72** 284 **92**
276 **107** 309
Tabitha (Floyd) **132** 41
Tamar **76** 131 **78** 264
Thaddeus **58** 373 **140** 50
Thankful **66** 11 **81** 83
121 282
Theophilus **75** 186
144 332
Thomas **55** cxi 303 **57**
180 182 183 320 **58** 173
60 181 **62** 101 264 **63** 19
66 342 **69** 15 17 121 **71**
253 254 256 **72** 264 **74**
42 196 197 **76** lxxiv **78**
284 337 **86** 224 **94** 314
99 119 **104** 163 294 **108**
279 **109** 16 **121** 16 111
192 197 208 210 212 213
282 285 **122** 80 244 **128**
135 **129** 53 57 **132** 164
137 243 249 250 **147**
331 332
Thomas Baker **112** 313
Thomas Butman **69** 78
308
Thomas P. **55** 124 **57** 337
62 108
Thomas Pitman **125** 180
Thomas Russell **62** 190
Thomas T. **146** 390
Timothy **61** 261 **78** 284
Timothy Russell **76** 144
Urana (Bradley) **146** 384
Vadis Lucinda (Lunn)
86 366
Walter **125** 243 **127** 10
131 131
Walter Bancroft **97** 128
Walter Garfield **84** 107

NICHOLS *cont'd*
190
Warren B. **63** 372
Washington **52** 457
Willard Atherton **62** xl
66 xlviii 94 **76** xxxi
lxxiv lxxv **86** 225
William **52** 82 254 **54** 53
56 73 251 **57** 388 **58** 204
373 **60** 150 **61** lxiii **66**
24 **72** 274 275 **73** 135 **79**
96 97 **80** 38 **81** 496 **84**
365 **99** 39 119 205 **100**
26 191 210 **104** 163 **106**
182 **109** 211 **110** 105
107 **127** 178 179 **128**
171 **129** 60 63 **133** 72 73
137 251 **140** 231 327
146 264
William (Mrs.) **109** 59
William George **92** 146
101 119 **104** 135 149
163
William H. **69** 312
William Maurice **110** 215
William N. **109** 16
William S. **125** 180 243
William T. **66** 233 **107** 115
William W. **55** 199
William Wight **104** 163
Zilpah **79** 35
NICHOLSON Nicholson
Nicholsen
—— **59** 113 **61** 392 **65** 262
84 10 100 191
— Capt. **58** 68
— Mr. **52** 117 249
A. W. **77** 268
Abel **81** 102
Albert J. **104** 198
Alice **139** 235
Amaziah J. **80** 150
Ambrose **85** 64 **143** 58
Angus **106** 109
Anna **106** 109
Anna Browning **77** 268
Anne **83** 118
Anne Rosemary **117** 205
Arthur **52** 118
Benoni **100** 191
Betsey **133** 72
Christopher **52** 118 **91** 67
Clara Etta **76** 20
Deliverance **91** 67
Edmond **85** 64
Edward **94** 173
Eleanor **64** 138
Elijah **100** 191
Elizabeth **90** 347 **104** 176
132 40 **133** 247
Elizabeth (Atkins) (Davis)
121 242 243
Elizabeth (Faulkner)
132 39
Elizabeth Mary (Rand)
86 105
Frances **73** 149
Francis **64** 138 139 **112** 248
142 127
Fred Cranston **80** 150
George **62** 301 **64** 225 **67**

NICHOLSON *cont'd*
267 269
George Blount **83** 344
Hannah **60** 181 **70** 286 **81**
102 **84** 449
Hannah (Brown) **100** 243
Hannah (Redknap) **91** 67
Hannah (Spencer)
137 183
Hannah (Wood) **111** 276
Harold Joseph (Mrs.)
86 105
Helen (Moffat) **83** 344
Henry **58** 295 **60** 54 **104**
198 **137** 183
Isaac Lea **61** 109
Isaiah **100** 191
James **60** 181 **65** 220 **89** 87
110 128
Jane **89** 87 88 **113** 96
Jared **85** 64
Jeremiah **73** 226
Joan **83** 452
Joan (Bradford) **84** 10
John **60** 181 **64** 261 **65** 85
94 173 265 **100** 243 **104**
280 **107** 115 **114** 190
141 354 **142** 66
John P. **56** xxxii **57** xxxiii
59 335 **60** xxxvi
John Page **66** 1 **67** xxxii
Joseph **63** 199 **111** 276
112 251 **113** 96
Laura **57** 361
Lydia **59** 105
Mabel **61** 391
Malcom **77** 321
Margaret **52** 118 **85** 64
Martha Adaline
(Chadbourne) **104** 198
Martha F. Sayles **100** 318
102 121
Mary **59** 105 **79** 56 **82** 192
339 **94** 173 **95** 253 261
129 254
Mary A. **117** 293
Mary Ella **80** 150
Mary Helen **83** 344
Mehitable **92** 265
Meredith **108** 158
N. D. **66** 33
Nathaniel **133** 136
Otho **64** 138 139
Paul **82** 339
Paul Coe **101** 170
Paul Coe (Mrs.) **101** 116
122 170 **102** 121 127
Phebe **89** 87
Polly **85** 64
Rebecca **100** 73 **111** 273
114 10
Rebecca Lloyd **78** 224
Robert **64** 138 139 **89** 87
109 206 208 **112** 251
113 96 **121** 243
Ruth **126** 50
Samuel **59** 105 **65** 81 369
78 418 **111** 273 274 **120**
106
Sarah **58** 295 **111** 273

NICHOLSON *cont'd*
Sarah (Burroughs)
    111 273
Simon **62** 321
Susan **93** 23 **104** 190 198
    112 251 **113** 96
Thomas **89** 87 **112** 251
    114 95
W. Sayles **101** 170
William **59** 175 **64** 138 139
    78 224 **83** 452 **90** 270
    114 90 **132** 39 46
Wright **78** 450
NICK
Grace **54** 413 417
Mary **54** 413 417
Richard **54** 417
William **54** 413 414 417
    94 353
Nickalls *see* Nichols
Nickason *see* Nickerson
Nickel *see* Nichols
Nickels *see* Nichols
NICKERSON   Nekerson
    Nickason Nikerson
—— **59** 105 **79** 386 **86** 400
    92 226 **95** 48 **109** 43
    122 204 **143** 341
— Goodman **79** 440
— Mrs. **110** 236
____ (Crowel) **108** 263
Aaron **105** 281
Abba Lillian **102** 286
Abby B. **123** 202
Abby Miner **71** lxx
Abigail **59** 196 200
Abigail (Gould) **123** 201
Abner **125** 8
Abraham L. **117** 220
Absalom **94** 388 **108** 119
    212
Achsah **127** 51 205
Achsah (Crowell) **127** 50
Adam **125** 16
Adelaide Trego (Daniels)
    94 387 388
Adeline T. (Beck) **83** 21 26
Alexander C. **117** 208
Alice **79** 386
Allen **52** 446 **109** 38
Almira (Chase) **84** 454
Almira Miller **84** 453 454
Alville B. **102** 288
Alvin B. **117** 286
Amanda E. **117** 215
Amos **85** 91
Amos R. **123** 52
Ann **62** 382 **126** 110
Ann (Bishop) **106** 229
Ann (Busby) **94** 387
Anna **105** 101 **127** 100 268
Anna (Godfrey) **127** 100
Anna (Nickerson) **125** 14
Anne **79** 441 **127** 51
Annie **52** 10
Ansell **84** 361 365 **122** 203
Arthur **111** 139
Asa **102** 284 **125** 8 19
Asa G. **123** 203
Asa S. **123** 203
Asa W. **109** 39

NICKERSON *cont'd*
Azubah **79** 391 **123** 117
Bassett **125** 8
Bathsheba **87** 322 **126** 287
    127 259
Ben H. **102** 289
Benjamin **124** 41
Bennie **102** 290
Bethiah **87** 319 **123** 117
    126 164
Betsey (Bassett) **125** 16
Caleb **126** 237
Catherine (Handy) **126** 63
Catherine (Stuart) **113** 15
Charlotte **97** 68 **108** 308
Christian **125** 8 10 **133** 42
Clarissa **127** 96
Clarissa (Gage) **108** 261
Cora **77** lxxii
Daniel **105** 278 **108** 211
    127 268
David **127** 42
David Nye **127** 96
Davis **108** 217
Dean **102** 283 **126** 63
Deborah **61** 191 **101** 80
    108 206 **126** 237
Deborah (Chase) **87** 316
    324
Deborah (Ryder) (Rogers)
    127 259
Deliverance **62** 203
Deliverance (Lumbert ?)
    126 237
Desire **108** 211 213 263
Diana **92** 226 **117** 215
Dora Malana (Mayo)
    102 288
Dorcas **127** 268
Dorcas (Bassett) **125** 8 10
Dorcas A. **108** 216
Ebenezer **64** 295 **65**
    xlviii xlix **86** 405 **105**
    309 **106** 229 **126** 94 **127**
    267
Edith (Child) **97** 68
Edward **125** 41
Edward H. **108** 214
Eldad **127** 54 272
Eleanora J. (Marden)
    117 165
Eleazer **105** 281
Eliphalet **105** 278
Elisha **125** 12 17
Eliza M. **52** 9
Elizaann **123** 199
Elizabeth **55** 424 **79** 441
    442 **108** 117 **126** 237
    127 40 54
Elizabeth (Arey) **86** 405
Elizabeth (Chase) **88** 123
Elizabeth (Doane) **123** 199
Elizabeth (Ellis) **121** 41
Elizabeth (Mayo) **106** 229
Elkanah **126** 96
Ella Sophia **93** 364
Emerline S. **123** 203
Enos **121** 41
Ensign **94** 388 **108** 214
    126 44
Epiphany **127** 271 **147** 68

NICKERSON *cont'd*
Esther **127** 96
Esther (Ellis) **122** 200
Ethel F. **117** 215
Etta **102** 285
Eudoxa **65** xlviii
Eudoxa (White) **106** 229
Eunice **108** 217 **127** 259
Eunice (Hopkins)
    103 169
Eunice Howard **89** 114
Experience **113** 15 114 **124**
    52 216
Experience (Chase)
    87 337
Fanny (Baxter) **108** 265
Francis **96** 286
Francis C. **108** 214
Frank **109** 130
Fred N. **117** 208
Frederick **77** lxxii **83** 21
    26
Frederick William
    77 lxxii
G. Franklin **117** 215
George **108** 216 **127** 96
George F. **117** 215
Georgianna Prentiss
    (Langmaid) **134** 225
Georgie V. **117** 216
Glenn Inman (Mrs.)
    105 129
Grace Livermore (Tobey)
    106 228
Hagar **142** 304
Hannah **79** 391 **102** 199
    122 205 **125** 106 **127** 42
    272
Hannah (Dexter) **126** 287
Hannah (Taylor) **108** 264
Hannah J. (Piper) **124** 41
Hannah Jane **81** 251
Hannah Russell **105** 111
Harriet **62** 156
Harriet B. **123** 201
Helen **94** 387 388
Helen Davis **67** 282
Heman **108** 304
Henry **79** 102 **97** 68
    102 199
Henry B. **102** 283
Henry C. **102** 288
Herman **101** 218 **141** 92
    103 109
Hester **79** 442
Hiram **108** 265 **125** 244
Hitta **59** 160
Hoffman **86** 198
Huldah (Bassett) **125** 10
Isaac **109** 42 **125** 8
Isabel **92** 116
Isaiah **105** 279 **125** 16
    127 47
Israel **108** 214
James **84** 50 **107** 290 **108**
    213 **117** 167 **127** 101
    259 271 272
James Henry **71** lxx
Jane **59** 202 261 379 **108**
    118 **122** 194 195 **127**
    267

NICKERSON *cont'd*
Jane M. **117** 215
Jarvis **92** 116
Jedidah **123** 118
Jennie (Giberson)
  111 139
Jeremiah **93** 267 **127** 50
  51 122 **132** 88
Jerusha **80** 119
Jesse **67** 282 **80** 19
Joanna **125** 19
Joanna (Mayo) **123** 119
Jobel **123** 120
John **79** 441 442 **80** 119
  107 290 **125** 8 10 **127** 50
  51 205 **133** 42 **142** 304
John Franklin **134** 225
John J. **134** 225
Jon. H. **117** 168
Jonathan **85** 91 **103** 170
  105 289 **108** 263 **127** 42
Joseph **88** 123 **106** 185
  108 216 **133** 42
Joshua **105** 111 **108** 216
  122 200 **126** 237 **127**
  100 259
Joshua W. **123** 121 124
Josiah **55** 424 **78** 178 **93**
  123 **125** 19
Katharine **126** 237
Kermit Spearing **98** 147
Keziah (Godfrey) **127**
  101 259
Keziah (Smith) **123** 119
L. T. **76** 50
Laura A. **102** 284
Laura A. (Gould) **123** 203
Lendal **103** 169
Leonard **103** 169
Levi **108** 216 262 **122** 144
Lizzie E. **134** 279
Loisa **52** 446
Loisa (Gorham) **109** 38
Lombard **125** 15
Lot **61** 191
Louisa **108** 217
Louisa R. **65** xlix
Lovina **125** 17
Lucretia **78** 313
Lucy **91** 42
Lucy (Simmons) **127** 272
Lucy Blanchard **77** lxxii
Lucy Stanley (Bancroft)
  96 286
Luke **142** 304
Lumbert **127** 258 259
Lusania H. **123** 204
Lydia **59** 261 262 **60** 154
  125 17 **126** 244
Lydia (Godfrey) **127** 47
Lydia A. **103** 171
Lydia Sturges (Handy)
  126 111
M. P. **143** 19
March **127** 96
Marinda **125** 21
Martha **108** 216
Martha (Ellis) **121** 41
Martha Tillinghast **106**
  22 229 **107** 134

NICKERSON *cont'd*
Martha Tillinghast
  (Westcott) **106** 228
Mary **51** 204 **55** 424 **67** 282
  75 126 **79** 441 442 **84**
  131 **99** 61 **105** 309 **108**
  214 216 304 305 **126** 237
  287 **127** 54 **134** 175
Mary (Atwood) **108** 217
Mary (Godfrey) **126** 237
Mary (Snow) **106** 229
Mary A. **103** 170
Mary Almona **71** lxx
Mary C. **85** 197
Mary Eldridge (Chase)
  87 319
Mary M. **117** 215
Matilda **108** 119 212
Matilda Pinkham
  (Crosby) **94** 388
May (Smith) **106** 229
Mehitable **125** 21 **126** 94
  164
Mehitable (Burgess)
  102 199
Mehitable (Crowell)
  94 388
Mehitable (Phillips)
  133 42
Mercy **108** 118 **126** 237
  127 40 **128** 291
Mercy (Godfrey) **126** 237
  127 96
Mercy (Walker) **105** 111
  123 121 124
Mercy (Williams) **94** 388
Miller Wheldon **84** 454
Miranda **105** 110
Molly **127** 169
Moses **108** 119 213 **126**
  237 **127** 96
Moses Godfrey **108** 213
Myra (White) **108** 262
Nabby **138** 219
Nancy (Kenney) **108** 217
Nathan **108** 265 **118** 329
Nathan B. **123** 203
Nathan E. **117** 165
Nathan H. **125** 17
Nathaniel **59** 261 262 **70**
  365 **79** 390 391 **80** 21
  109 38 **113** 15 113 **117**
  167-169
Nehemiah **108** 117 216
Nellie (Cummings)
  102 289
Nicholas **65** xlix **79** 439
  441 442 **106** 229
Norman Dunning
  105 129
Olga **98** 362
Osborn **51** 225
Patience **79** 441 442
Patience (Cahoon)
  125 244
Paul **105** 278
Peggy **59** 260
Phebe **86** 401 402 **116** 194
  122 205
Phebe (Avery) **86** 402
Phebe (Hopkins) **102** 260

NICKERSON *cont'd*
Phebe (Horton) **123** 203
Philip Tillinghast **95** 39
  100 207 **96** 161 **103** 32
  106 222 228 **107** 137
Phineas **125** 8
Polly **93** 267 **108** 206
  125 19
Polly (Chase) **87** 318
Priscilla **108** 119 217
  126 287
Priscilla P. (Hopkins)
  103 170 **123** 204
R. **117** 169
Rachel **127** 98 271
Rachel (Dexter) **126** 287
Rebecca **59** 260 **79** 390 391
  80 21 **103** 29 **114** 10
  122 49 **125** 12 **126** 96
  168 **127** 50 51 96 122
Rebecca (Atkins) **126** 237
  127 96
Rebecca (Bassett) **125** 19
Rebecca (Covel) **123** 120
Rebecca (Homer) **109** 38
Rebecca (Hurd) **132** 88
Rebecca (Jones) **126** 237
Rebecca (Mayo) **94** 388
Rebecca (Robinson)
  125 12
Rebecca (Rogers) **125** 14
Rebecca C. (Gould)
  123 203
Rebecca Dyer (Watkins)
  134 225
Reliance (Chase) **87** 321
Reuben **59** 160 **86** 396
  102 286 **105** 281 **123**
  119 198 199 203
Rhoda **80** 18 **122** 203
Richard **108** 119 213 264
  109 43 **126** 237
Robert **103** 29 **126** 237
Rogers **86** 402
Roland Crosby **94** 387
  388
Rose Brooks **55** 240
Roxana **65** lxvi **127** 44
Ruth **86** 396 **125** 19
Ruth (Arey) **86** 396
Ruth (Hinckley) **127** 47
Ruth (Lincoln) **123** 202
Ruth (Rich) **84** 50
Ruth A. (Nickerson)
  109 39
Sabina **102** 285
Sabrina (Sears) (Crowell)
  122 257
Safford S. **125** 244
Sally (Paine) **123** 120
Salome **127** 51 122 205
Samuel **59** 260 261 379
  108 216 261 **115** 79 **120**
  107-109 **122** 194 **123**
  119 202 **125** 14 **126** 111
  244
Samuel Mayo **94** 388
Sarah **61** 191 **79** 442 **102**
  199 **108** 119 210 216
  120 109 **127** 42 96 **143**

NICKERSON *cont'd*
340 341
Sarah (Bassett) **106** 229
  125 15
Sarah (Covell) **127** 259
Sarah (Doane) **123** 203
Sarah (Godfrey) **127** 42
Sarah (Hamilton) **122** 144
Sarah (Vickery) **143** 341
Sarah Godfrey **108** 214
Sarah Goodenow **133** 42
Sarah Jane **117** 216
Sereno Dwight **51** 91 **54**
  xxxvii **55** xxix **56** xxxi
  57 xxxi 344 **58** xliii 109
  59 xlii **60** xxxiv 220 323
  408 **61** 107 215 319 405
  62 211 313 393 **64** 295
  65 xlv xlviii xlix
Seth **51** 204 **65** xlix **85** 91
  102 260 **105** 309 **106**
  229
Shabour / Sheber **122** 200
Silas **125** 14
Simeon **108** 216
Simeon H. **117** 168
Sophia **93** 123 **108** 214
Sophia Bangs **93** 123
Stephen **60** 365
Stillman **108** 304
Susan (Spear) **126** 208
Susan Jane **108** 302
Susanna (Bassett) **125** 14
Sylvanus **117** 215
Sylvia **93** 364
Tabitha **108** 118 **126** 44
  127 100
Tabitha (Eldredge)
  (Ryder) **126** 45
Tabitha (Howes) **127** 100
Tamsin (Gray) **125** 16
Temperance (Sherman)
  108 265
Thankful **86** 400 **87** 11
  121 43
Thankful (Arey) (Wixon)
  86 400
Thankful (Bassett) **125** 17
Thankful (Chase) **87** 323
Thankful (Eldredge)
  122 200
Thomas **59** 260 **85** 91 **93**
  364 **105** 278 **108** 216
  118 57 **120** 105 **127** 47
Thomas P. **123** 201
Thomas White **106** 228
Thomasine **80** 19
Timothy E. **68** 141
Tully **86** 402
Uriah **123** 120 204
Vernon R. **123** 117 154 198
Vinson **125** 10 19 **133** 42
Warren **105** 278
Warren Sears **79** 323
  80 208
William **51** 171 **52** 10 **61**
  191 **63** 101 **64** 96 **65**
  xlix **66** 191 368 **79** 439
  441 442 **85** 91 **94** 387
  388 **101** 80 **106** 229 **108**
  119 213 214 **117** 167

NICKERSON *cont'd*
  121 41 **122** 74 **125** 8
  126 235 237 **127** 42 259
  133 42
William E. **96** 157 **99** 261
  143 338
William Emery **54** xli **63**
  101 **78** 450 **79** 336 **82**
  381 **83** 230 **84** 181 **85** 91
  92 106 203 **96** 155
William Gifford (Mrs.)
  93 379
William J. **62** 156
William S. **117** 215
Winslow **108** 217
Winsor **102** 289
Zehiva **102** 287
Zenes **108** 216
Zoath **126** 237 **127** 96
Zurvia **108** 214
NICKLE
  Edgar Burr (Mrs.)
  102 124
Nickles *see* Nichols
NICKLIN John Bailey
  Calvert **104** 135
  145 150 165
  Joseph **104** 165
Nickolas *see* Nicholas
Nickolds *see* Nichols
Nickson *see* Nixon
Nickulas *see* Nicholas
Nicol *see* Nicoll
Nicolas *see* Nicholas
NICOLET John **70** 288
NICOLL Nicol - *see also*
  Nichols
  Anne Willett (Floyd)
  136 328
  Benjamin **56** 298 **136** 331
  Charity **56** 298
  Charlotte Anne **136** 328
  331
  Eliza Woodhull **86** 103
  Elsie **136** 331
  Gloriana Margaretta
  136 322
  Grace Davison (Lord)
  136 331
  James **137** 313
  Janet **137** 313
  Joanna (D'Honneur)
  136 322 328
  Mary Townsend **136** 328
  331
  Samuel Benjamin **136** 328
  Sarah Brown (Payne)
  136 328
  Solomon Townsend
  136 328 331
  William **55** 200 **136** 322
  328
Nicola *see* Nichols
Nicson *see* Nixon
NICUM John **107** 245
NIEBUHR
  Mary Alden **101** 64
  Mary Marland **56** xxxii
NIECE Jane **131** 75
NIEDERER Zetta **115** 317

NIEDERLANDER
  June **95** 335
NIEDERLITZ Elizabeth
  Louise **92** 65
Niedham *see* Needham
NIEHAUS Eliza **93** 278
  John David (Mrs.) **93** 278
NIELSON Nielsen
  Clarence Floyd (Mrs.)
  109 130
  Donald M. **143** 239 **145**
  291 **148** 212
  Irene A. (Allen) **129** 85
  Johannah **138** 210
NIELY
  Elizabeth **60** 163
  Sarah **128** 96
NIERLING Bertram Victor
  (Mrs.) **84** 340 **85** 197
NIES John **92** 389
  Katharine **92** 389
NIESS Hannah **126** 206
NIETERT Anna Eliza **79**
  203 **80** 334 **81** 231 **82**
  112
  Caroline Wilhelmina
  Dorothea **82** 112
  Gertrude Eleanor **82** 112
  Henry John **82** 112
  Henry John (Mrs.) **78** 332
  79 203
  John Henry Gotlieb
  82 112
  Roscoe Henry **82** 112
NIETO Rafael **110** 319
NIEWANGER
  John **65** 221
NIFONG Frank Gosney
  (Mrs.) **99** 148
NIGEL — Dea. **76** 298
NIGERS Silvia **135** 318
Nigh *see* Nye
NIGHTINGALE
  Nightengale
  Nightgale Nightingal
  —— **65** 220
  Abiah (Ellis) **121** 262
  Abigail **60** 245 **88** 281
  Abigail (Belcher) **109** 4
  Ann **108** 223
  Augusta Wahrendorf
  (Harrison) **109** 3
  Benjamin **59** 269
  Bertha (Deering) **109** 4
  Bethiah **59** 87 156 158 159
  269
  Boylston **79** 50
  Crawford **82** 119 **109** 4
  Daniel **59** 159 **135** 251
  David **118** 244
  Ebenezer **59** 158 **141** 331
  Elizabeth (Thompson)
  109 4
  Ella (Trowbridge) **109** 3-5
  Experience **79** 52
  George Corlis **60** v xiv
  xxxiv **61** v xiii xxxiii
  xxxvi **62** v xv **63** v xv
  96 **64** v xiii xxix **65** v
  xiii xxi **66** 281
  Hannah (Paine) **109** 4

NIGHTINGALE *cont'd*
143 43
John **59** 156 274 **141** 16
John T. **109** 123
John Trowbridge **103**
  120 **105** 120 142 **106**
  139 **107** 146 **108** 127
  109 3 4 61 134
Joseph **59** 157 **65** 141 **109**
  4 **127** 225 **143** 43
Lionel Brydges **133** 271
Mary **60** 41 **93** 269
Mary (Goold) **143** 43
Mary (Williams) **109** 4
Mary Hoyt **82** 119
Mary Williams **82** 119
Mirian S. **54** 134
Nancy (Morgan) **135** 251
Nancy V. **126** 216
Nina **109** 3
Rebecca **59** 271 272 274
  108 163
Samuel **59** 156 **60** 245
  109 4 5 **121** 262 **127** 303
  305
Samuel Crawford **109** 3 5
Samuel Crawford (Mrs.)
  84 342 **85** 197
Susanna (Crawford)
  109 4 5
Thomas **61** 133
William **59** 87 88 156-159
  269 271 272 274 **109** 4
  143 43
NIGNIE Dolly **72** 104
Nikerson *see* Nickerson
NILBERT Al **128** 98
NILES Nile Nills Nyle
—— **57** 141 **106** 103 **119**
  131 140 203 218 **136** 211
  140 179
— Mrs. **80** 34
— Rev. Mr. **62** 277
A. H. **68** 337
Aaron T. **81** 266
Abbott Howe (Mrs.)
  122 188
Abigail **85** 146 148 149 151
Abigail (Avery) **85** 154
Abigail (Hazard) **85** 151
Abigail (White) **85** 153
Abigail E. **76** 9
Albert H. **68** 337
Alice **68** 337
Alice (Reed) **85** 158
Alice (Scripture) **85** 158
Alice M. **85** 156
Almira **85** 152
Amanda **85** 158
Ambrose **78** 372 373 **81**
  266 **85** 146 148 **106** 105
Ambrose E. **78** 373
Amos A. **80** 191 **89** 250
Amos Avery **85** 154
Ann **85** 150
Ann (Codington) **85** 149
Ann (Ludden) **85** 154
Ann-Jane (Erskine) **90** 54
Anna **60** 42 **81** 266 **89** 250
  138 279 280
Anna (Avery) **85** 154

NILES *cont'd*
Anna (Dickinson) **85** 150
Anna (Thayer) (Wild)
  85 150
Anna (Woodman) **85** 152
Anna Hester (Cross)
  (Seymour) **97** 158
Anna Lillian **85** 156
Anne **85** 149 152
Anne (Coddington) **106**
  155 **145** 264
Anne (Cornish) **85** 148
Anne Lothrop **54** lxviii
Anthony **132** 191
Archibald **128** 20
Arria **109** 312
Asa **85** 157
Asa H. **85** 157
Asenath M. **81** 266
Augusta E. **85** 156
Austin Herbert **68** 337
Barnabas **85** 148
Bathsheba **85** 151
Bathsheba (Palmer)
  85 151
Benjamin **59** 88 90 154
  272 361 363 364 **73** 233
  78 372 **85** 145-148 152
  154 **105** 175 176
Benjamin Cone **78** 373
Bertha (Olmsted) **85** 158
Bethiah **85** 147 151
Betsey **71** 355 **85** 151
  87 235 237
Bridget (Avery) **85** 154
Caleb **73** 104
Catherine **85** 148 149 151
  154 **90** 367
Charity **54** 274 **85** 151
Charles **85** 158
Charles William **85** 156
Charlotte **88** 56
Charlotte Polly **85** 159
Christiana (Griswold)
  85 156
Clarissa **72** 307 **75** 216 **79**
  23 **85** 153
Clarissa Orton **72** 307
Cyrus **85** 158
Dan **85** 152
Daniel **73** 234 **85** 151 155
  158
Daniel Swift **85** 158 **88** 56
David **59** 361 **85** 146 151
Deborah **85** 147 149 155
Delia (Woodruff) **85** 158
Dorcas **83** 224 **85** 155
Dorcas (Beckwith) **85** 148
Dorothy **85** 155
Dorothy (Ingraham)
  85 152
Dorothy (Reynolds)
  85 155
Ebenezer **59** 367 **67** 286 **85**
  146 147 151 155 157
Edla Maud **91** 142 207
Edward Samuel **54** xli
Elbert Sanford **72** 307
Elijah **85** 155 156
Eliphalet **85** 148
Elisha **59** 216 **60** 42 **85**

NILES *cont'd*
150 154 **107** 313 **126** 92
Eliza **78** 313
Elizabeth **65** 349 **85** 149
  151-153 156 157 **125** 107
  288 **127** 90
Elizabeth (Adams)
  (Whiting) **85** 149
Elizabeth (Cottrell)
  85 151
Elizabeth (Hunt) **85** 157
Elizabeth (Morse) **85** 156
Elizabeth (Niles) **85** 157
Elizabeth (Randall)
  85 155
Elizabeth (Thacher)
  85 149 150
Elizabeth (Vinton)
  85 151 157
Elizabeth (Watson)
  85 153
Ellen Maria **72** 307
Elvira **85** 158
Emeline (Pomeroy)
  101 34
Emily (Grover) **119** 203
Emma A. **72** 307
Ephraim **85** 155 **123** 159
Esther (Hazard) **85** 150
Experience **85** 155
Experience (Newcomb)
  85 155
Francelia Mary **72** 307
Frances (Cotton / Collon)
  123 159
Freedom **72** 306
Freedom Hale **72** 307
Freelove **85** 155
George **129** 59
Giles **85** 150
H. L. **68** 337
Hannah **59** 273 **60** 43 **72**
  306 **85** 145-151 154 **88**
  42 43
Hannah (Ames) **85** 145
Hannah (Niles) **85** 149 151
Hannah (Secomb) **85** 146
Hannah (Sekin) **85** 146
Hannah (Thayer) **85** 151
Hannah Cornelia **72** 307
Harriet **85** 152
Harvey **85** 152 153
Henrietta W. **85** 169
Henry **85** 151
Herbert **75** 14
Hiram **85** 154
Horace Samuel **72** 307
Humphrey **85** 156
Increase **54** 404 **85** 145
  147 151 **106** 23
Isaac **67** 123 **68** 337 **85**
  145 152 155 158
Isabel **94** 288
James **67** 123 215 216 **68**
  337 **72** 307 **73** 233 **85**
  155 157 158 **101** 34 **128**
  218
Jane **85** 149 158 **88** 56
Jane (Pratt) **85** 156
Jane (Reed) **85** 145
Jason **85** 158

NILES *cont'd*
Jeremiah **85** 150 153 **93**
  397 **100** 63 **128** 124 **129**
  59 **148** 171
Jeremiah A. **148** 175
Jesse **85** 151 **90** 54
John **54** 404 405 **59** 193
  68 223 337 **85** 145-149
  151 155 158 **91** 207 **92**
  186 263 **105** 175 176
  106 105 **136** 333 **143**
  116
John A. **80** 191 **89** 250
John Avery **85** 154
John Milton **85** 156
Jonas **85** 154
Jonathan **68** 220 222 223
  228 **80** 34 **85** 151 155
  101 235 **129** 59
Jonathan Sands **86** 22
Joseph **54** 274 **59** 88 90 272
  85 145 146 148 151 152
  156 **129** 61
Joseph R. **148** 172
Joseph S. **80** 191 **89** 250
Joseph Stanton **85** 154
Joshua **136** 333
Joshua H. **68** 337
Joshua Holt **67** 216 **85** 158
Judith **85** 155 158
Julia Ann **78** 373
Justin **85** 152
Katharine **85** 146 150 151
Keziah **85** 155
Keziah (Howard) **136** 333
Laura **85** 153
Lester Eugene (Mrs.)
  97 158
Lizzie C. **75** 14
Lois **78** 372 373
Lois (Brockway) **85** 148
Louisa **72** 307
Lucius H. **85** 169
Lucy **85** 151 152 155
Lucy (Sill) **85** 152
Lucy Tucker **72** 306
Lydia **85** 151 152 154 157
  158
Lydia (Clay) **128** 20
Lydia (Seacum) **85** 146
Margaret **54** 404 405 **85**
  149 151 155 **132** 191
Maria **57** 141
Maria (Hanks) **86** 22
Marietta J. **85** 158
Martha **85** 150 **129** 61
Martha (Coombs) **126** 68
Mary **52** 450 **54** 404 **59** 89
  90 154 272 273 364 **60**
  43 131 **67** 286 **68** 337 **75**
  14 **78** 372 **85** 146-155
  92 262
Mary (Billings) (Belcher)
  85 147
Mary (Clark) **85** 147 149
Mary (Dodge) **85** 153
Mary (Hannah) **85** 150
  152 **144** 295
Mary (Jenkins) **85** 157
Mary (Micall) **85** 146
Mary (Niles) **85** 150

NILES *cont'd*
Mary (Northrup) **85** 154
Mary (Purchase) **85** 147
Mary (Sawin) **85** 157
Mary (Wiswall) **85** 150
Mary (Woodward) **85** 157
Mary Brockway (Mott)
  85 148
Mary Dodge **85** 153
Mary E. **89** 250
Mary F. **80** 191
Mary Frances **136** 333
Mary J. (Knowles) **85** 156
Mary Jane **72** 307
Mary Jane (Thayer)
  136 333
Mary N. **132** 243
Mehitable **85** 153 157
Melissa **85** 152
Mercy **73** 233 **85** 155
Mercy (Sacan / Secomb)
  85 147
Millie **85** 148
Milton **85** 152
Minerva **76** 268 269
Mingo **128** 128
Miranda **85** 152
Miriam **85** 152
Miriam D. (Hill) **85** 156
Miriam Jane **85** 156
Miriam Josephine **85** 156
Molly **67** 215 **85** 158
Moses **85** 152 156
Nahum **85** 156
Nancy **85** 154 **95** 355 **97**
  188 **148** 172
Nancy (Lothrop) **85** 152
Nancy Lavinia **72** 306
Naomi **85** 147
Naomi (Marshall) **85** 156
Naomi Griswold **85** 156
Nathan **67** 286 **85** 148 150
  151 154 155 158 159 **88**
  56
Nathaniel **60** 43 **82** 459
  85 145-154 **98** 25 **104**
  122 **105** 173 175 176
  106 105 **125** 23 **144** 295
  145 264
Northrup **85** 154
Olive Ann **72** 307
Olive H. **76** 269
Oliver **85** 151
Oliver Perry **72** 307
Palmer **85** 152
Pamela **85** 156 157
Patience **85** 146
Paul **85** 150 151
Paul Frederick **85** 154
Pearl **75** 14
Peggy **78** 302
Penelope **85** 151 **106** 104
  105
Peter **60** 39 **61** 43 **85** 146
  151 155
Phebe **85** 151 152 154 158
Polly **85** 152 **88** 56
Priscilla **80** 34
Rachel **85** 155
Rachel Ann **81** 266
Rebecca **59** 86 **73** 234

NILES *cont'd*
  85 146 158
Rebecca (Bryant) **85** 158
Rhoda **85** 152
Rhoda (Phelps) **85** 152
Richard **85** 156
Robert **85** 150 154
Russell **85** 152
Ruth **59** 154 361 363 364
  85 147 155 159 **87** 234
  235 **88** 56
Ruth (Scant) **85** 146
Sabra (Avery) **85** 154
Sally **85** 157-159 **88** 56
Salmon **85** 148 158
Salmon T. **75** 14
Samuel **52** 222 **54** 404-406
  58 95 **59** 89 90 273 **60**
  41 66 131 **65** 190 **67** 214
  72 306 **78** 419 **79** 47 **82**
  456 **83** 84 **85** 145-154
  156 159 **86** 72 326 **88** 56
  92 262 263 **93** 264 **101**
  174 **104** 242 **105** 165
  173-176 182 **106** 105 155
  128 218 **140** 177 178
  143 78 **145** 264
Samuel Burke **85** 159
Sands **85** 151 153 154
Sanford H. **68** 337 **85** 158
Sarah **54** lxviii **59** 90 273
  67 286 **68** 222 307 **72** 307
  73 108 **75** 261 **85** 147
  149-155 **95** 175 **98** 25
  101 332 **126** 155
Sarah (Burrows) **85** 154
Sarah (Cook) **85** 157
Sarah (French) **85** 155
Sarah (Frink) **85** 151
Sarah (Littlefield) **85** 147
Sarah (Niles) **85** 149 150
  152
Sarah (Robinson) (Howe)
  85 156
Sarah (Sands) **85** 146 **98**
  25 **105** 173 176 **144** 295
  145 264
Serena **126** 207
Shirley **85** 156
Sibyl (Hughes) **85** 158
Silas **61** 43 **65** 370 **73** 108
  85 150 155
Silas N. **85** 154
Sill **85** 152
Sophia **85** 158
Sophia S. **61** 346
Stephen **85** 151 156
Stephen Brainard **72** 307
  79 23
Susan (Cole) **85** 156
Susanna **68** 220 **85** 148
  150 151
Sylvanus **85** 151
Sylvia **88** 332
Tabitha **85** 146 150 151 154
Thomas **85** 148 152 156
Thomas Northrup **85** 154
Thomas Phelps **85** 152
William **73** 104 **78** 373
  85 149 152 153 **136** 40
William Ambrose **81** 266

NILES cont'd
William B. **78** 373
William Francis **85** 156
William Jenkins **85** 157
109 312
William P. **80** 191 **89** 250
William Pitt **78** 373
William Woodruff
85 158
Winslow Bryant **85** 158
Zerviah **85** 154
Nilson *see* Nelson
NIMMO
Anna Belle Koenig
108 77
Nimms *see* Nims
NIMOCKS
Calista **73** 15
Frances Augusta **101** 66
NIMROD Sachem **148** 294
NIMROD Alice E. (Mitchell)
110 135
Daniel Albert **113** 222
Jesse **58** 142
Juanita Jane **113** 222
Merle Robert **113** 222
Merle Robert (Mrs.) **108**
135 239 240 **110** 135
113 222
Norris Patrick **113** 222
Suzanne **113** 222
NIMS Nimms
—— **53** 232
— Mr. **62** 267
Abigail **62** 266 **72** 80 **75**
304 **126** 133 211
Abigail (Briggs) **126** 211
277
Albert Gilman **81** 350
Albert Hull **62** 272
Alfred **129** 50 397
Alpheus **126** 277
Anna **75** 307 **129** 397
Bethiah (Banks) **104** 56
Betsey **129** 50 396
Betsey (Holden) **129** 396
Betsey (Rice) **136** 141
Charles **62** 272
David **79** 400 **126** 211
Dorothy Louise **106** 126
Eleanor **81** 350
Electa **75** 307 **136** 141
Electa (Hopkins) **104** 56
Eliakim **126** 211
Elizabeth **136** 317
Elizabeth Maria **79** 203
80 103 217 **81** 350
Esther **62** 272
Eunice (Call) **129** 50 397
George **116** 187
Godfrey **70** 287 **129** 397
Hannah **62** 267 272
Harriet Augusta **81** 350
Hull **62** 272
Israel **104** 56
Jemima **79** 400
John **62** 272 **75** 308 **129**
397 **136** 141
Justus **104** 56
Lizetta C. M. **129** 50
Lucius **62** 272 **71** xli

NIMS cont'd
Lucy **75** 308 **129** 51
Margaret **129** 397
Mary **62** 272 **71** xli
Mary (M'Gowen) **116** 187
Mary Ann (Reynolds)
129 50 397
Mary J. **129** 50
Mary Sophia (Arey)
(Reynolds) **87** 25
Norman Granville **81** 350
Norman Granville (Mrs.)
78 330 **79** 203
Ormand F. **67** 98
Patty **75** 306
Polly **75** 307
Reuben **62** 266 267
Ruel **129** 50 396
Sally S. **129** 50
Sarah **62** 267 272
Silas **75** 303 **129** 50 397
Susan C. **71** xli
Thankful **75** 307
Thomas **62** 264 272
W. Newton **93** 272
Walter T. **68** 111
NIMUS Edwin **102** 112
Eunice (Kimberly)
102 112
NINDE
Edward Summerville
108 268
Frederick Ward **108** 268
George Falley **108** 268
Henry S. **85** 114
James **85** 114
Mary Louise **108** 268
William **108** 268
William Frederick
108 268
William Zavier **108** 268
Ninecraft *see* Ninigret
NINEZERGH
Orm de **96** 311
NINIAN Nancy **73** 146
NINIGRET Ninecraft
Ninicraft
—— **136** 178
Charles **77** 34 37
Sachem of the Niantics
87 353 **89** 177 **144** 231
145 78
Thomas **57** 156 **137** 342
NIOSS
Francis G. **106** 207
Nisbet *see* Nesbitt
Nisbeth *see* Nesbitt
Nisbett *see* Nesbitt
Nisbit *see* Nesbitt
NISH Henry **51** 188
NISLET Patrick **65** 85
NISMES
Peter de **137** 306
NISSEN
Dorothea **68** 333
Henry **68** 333
Lena **68** 333
Maude **86** 363
NISSENBAUM Stephen
144 142 360 **148** 145

NITCHER Elizabeth
(Manchester) **126** 20
Mary **126** 20
William **126** 20
NITES Abraham **145** 361
NITSCHKE —— **51** 94
NITSER Jeptha **122** 79
NIUS Richard **99** 204
Sarah **99** 204
NIVEN
C. E. (Mrs.) **96** 208
NIVER Mildred **113** 294
NIX Nixe
Edith Augusta Rooch
115 151
John **67** 330
NIXON Nickson Nixen
—— **75** 267 **145** 160
— Capt. **145** 56
— Col. **65** 338 **85** 18
— Mr. **82** 443
— Mrs. **63** 54
Aaron **75** 205 215 **114** 181
Abraham **85** 323
Amanda C. **81** 328
Ann **83** 470
Anna Parker Bulley
75 205
Armine **75** xlv
Beatrice **107** 133
Benjamin **114** 181
Campbell Gertrude
110 122
Christiana **85** 323
Delia M. **75** 267
Eliza Jane **75** 205 214 215
Elizabeth **75** 205 **104** 319
320 **114** 40
Elizabeth (Haynes) **114** 41
Elizabeth Tucker **75** 205
215
Ensign R. **108** 260
Eunice Tucker **75** 205
Frances Wilhelmina
85 324
George F. **104** 319
George W. **104** 319
Hamilton **91** 331
Hananh Hart (Mitchell)
90 299
Hannah **104** 319 320
Henry **85** 324
Hepzibah **57** 370
Horace F. **104** 319
Huldah **108** 260
James **126** 234
Jane S. **76** 48
Jeremiah **104** 319 320
John **60** 256 363 **61** 265
67 315 **75** 205 **78** 267
93 398 **100** 63 **107** 180
110 167 **114** 33 40 41 43
103 107 134 181 197 200
121 220 **130** 275 **147** 75
175 178 181
John Warren **75** 205
Joseph K. **90** 299
Lucy Withington **75** 205
Marcy **105** 264
Mary **68** 257 **126** 133
Mary Henry **124** 91 191

NIXON cont'd
  Nelphia **127** 229
  Norton **104** 319 320
  Polly **57** 370
  Raymond G. **104** 319
  Reuben **104** 319
  Rhoda **104** 320
  Richard **65** 233 **115** 247
  Richard M. **108** 77 **136** 66
    67
  Ruth **104** 320
  Samuel **59** 194
  Sarah Ann **75** 205
  Thankful **114** 41
  Thomas **65** 79 114 220 257
    83 376 **142** 38
NOAD C. A. **52** 96
  Henry Edward **52** 96
NOAH Andrew Hale **80**
    105 207 **88** 87 172 **98**
    348
  Elmus H. **98** 348
  Esther (Mott) **98** 348
  Isabella **98** 348
  Robert H. **98** 348
NOAILLES ⸻ **145** 201
  — Count de **54** 285
  Louis Marie (Viscount de)
    112 246
Noakes see Knox
Noaks see Knox
NOANTICO Job **128** 246
NOAR William **115** 57
NOBBES Simunde **86** 422
Nobel see Noble
Nobels see Noble
Noblat see Noblit
NOBLE Nobel Nobels
    Noblee Nobles
  ⸻ **59** 349 **81** 448 **83** 36
    194 **95** 30 375 381 **97**
    103 **103** 197 **115** 19 **145**
    164
  — Col. **97** 108 110-112
  — Ens. **97** 105
  — Lieut. **97** 106
  — Lieut. Col. **97** 107 109
  — Mr. **51** 462 **64** 144
  — Mrs. **51** 356 **123** 16
  — Rev. Mr. **62** 275
  ⸻ (Howard) **97** 114
  ⸻ (Keniston) **94** 357
  Abbie **95** 188
  Abbie (Ela) (Sanborn)
    95 248
  Abbie (Sanborn) **95** 185
  Abbie Josephine **95** 36
  Abigail **63** 183 336 **67** 31
    32 **74** 42 **94** 360 361 363
    95 31 36 **112** 152 **115** 21-
    23 25 26 108 109
  Abigail (Hodgdon)
    94 358
  Abigail (Whidden)
    94 359-361
  Abigaill (Sackcut)
    123 261
  Ada Bertha (Jewell) **95** 187
  Addie **95** 38
  Addie May **95** 378 379
  Adeline **95** 187

NOBLE cont'd
  Adoniram **85** 411
  Adrian Arthur **95** 187
  Agnes **95** 186
  Aileen (Omallley) **95** 251
  Alansen **77** 41
  Albert Porter **95** 39
  Albertina M. (Bernier)
    95 378
  Alfred I. (Mrs.) **94** 352
  Alfred Ira **95** 39
  Alice A. **95** 377
  Alice E. **81** 39
  Alice M. **95** 377
  Allen **82** 433
  Allen B. **82** 433
  Allwin Franck (Leidy)
    95 250
  Alma (Rickard) **95** 188
  Almira **94** 362 **95** 38 383
  Almira (Farrington)
    95 38
  Alonzo **124** 279
  Alpheus A. **95** 375-377
  Althea Louise **95** 376
  Alwina Elizabeth **95** 250
  Amanda (Bennett) **95** 188
  Amanda S. **81** 291
  Amaziah **95** 375
  Amosy **95** 188
  Ann **81** 448 **94** 352 359 **95**
    30 38 246
  Ann C. (Anderson)
    95 376
  Ann Elizabeth **95** 37
  Ann Maria **97** 114
  Ann Victoria **95** 251
  Anna **63** 205 335 **94** 363
    104 163 **115** 24 26 108
  Anna (Leeman) **95** 188
  Anna Florence **95** 379
  Annie **95** 186
  Annie Belle **95** 376
  Annie E. **95** 377
  Annie L. **95** 186
  Annie R. **95** 378
  Anthony **142** 208
  Ari (Barker) **95** 187
  Arthur **63** 267 **66** lxxvi
    67 289 312 **76** 170 **78**
    306 **96** 350 355 357 **97**
    31-33 103-106 108 109
    112-114 **100** 300 **111** 66
    117 249
  Arthur Chadbourne
    95 37
  Arthur H. **117** 154 **122** 81
  Arthur Meritt **95** 187
  Augustus **91** 199
  Aurelia **113** 304
  Aurelia (Landers) **124** 279
  Averilla M. **128** 98
  Barbara Elizabeth
    (Warner) **95** 251
  Beatrice Elizabeth
    (Robinson) **95** 376
  Belinda **95** 32
  Benjamin **94** 359 361 **95** 31
    38
  Benjamin Hartt **67** 32
  Bethiah **67** 220

NOBLE cont'd
  Betsey **95** 30
  Betty **74** 42 **94** 358 **95** 382
  Betty (Nutting) **95** 382
  Bion Elbridge Gerry
    95 248
  Bloomy (Chase) **95** 38
  Brown **128** 171
  Caroline **95** 35 **115** 21
  Caroline Howe (Young)
    95 37
  Caroline Young **95** 37
  Carrie Dane **95** 379
  Carrie Leola **95** 189
  Carrie M. **95** 376
  Cassandria **115** 108
  Catherine **95** 185 **110** 241
  Catherine (Clark) **95** 36
  Catherine (Dougherty)
    95 185
  Catherine Frances (Bligh)
    95 251
  Charles **68** 337 **95** 38 185
    187 247
  Charles Burroughs
    95 246
  Charles C. **95** 383
  Charles Curtis **115** 24
  Charles Howard **95** 377
  Charles Loring Jackson
    95 252
  Charles Richard **95** 186
  Charlotte **67** 119 220 **73** 14
    95 31 **97** 114
  Charlotte (Emery) **95** 39
  Charlotte Elsie **95** 37
  Chester **95** 185-187
  Christian **67** 116-119 217
    219 220
  Christopher **81** 139 401
    432 **94** 352-354 356 361
    362 **95** 28 31 184 185
    245 250 252 374 **96** 89
    202
  Christopher Herman
    95 185
  Christopher Marlan
    95 188
  Clara **95** 187 247
  Clara (Noble) **95** 187 247
  Clara Jane **95** 39
  Clara Luella (Toothaker)
    95 247
  Clarence A. **95** 376
  Clarissa **85** 291 **95** 185
  Clark **85** 292
  Clayton Jewell **95** 376
  Clement **95** 375 376 378
  Clifford **95** 188
  Comfort **94** 357
  Constantine **67** 220
  Content **95** 39
  Cora E. **95** 376
  Cordelia D. **69** 319
  Curtis **115** 24 26 108
  Cynthia **95** 383
  Cynthia (Goodrich)
    95 185
  Cyrenus **115** 23 24 27 109
    110
  Cyrus Freeman **95** 187

NOBLE *cont'd*
247
Damon Granderson
115 17
Dana L. **95** 378
Daniel Cram **95** 247
David **53** 398 **54** 163 **63**
336 **93** 398 **100** 63
David F. **128** 98
David Fred **95** 379
Delia **95** 188
Delia (Ryan) **95** 247
Delia Sprague (Bowen)
95 250
Delmore P. **95** 376
Diana **76** 264
Dolly **82** 50
Dorcas V. **68** 337
Doris Adelaide **95** 39
Dorothy **95** 30 38 375 380
381
Dorothy (Thayer) **90** 370
Dorothy Ann **95** 30
Drusilla Bonneau **77** 297
125 106
Ebenezer **63** 183
Edith (Dearborn) **95** 186
Edith (Phillips) **95** 379
Edith Elnora **95** 248
Edna **77** 269
Edna (Hennen) **95** 188
Edna Lois (Wood) **86** 223
Edward **95** 188 **97** 114
Edwin Eleazar **95** 187
Elbridge Gerry **95** 32
185 186 247
Eleanor Gray **95** 251
Eleanor Neale (Gerrie)
95 250
Eleazer **67** 31 32 **95** 32 185
Eleazer P. **95** 186
Electa **67** 220 **68** 337 **71**
122 **95** 39
Electa A. **68** 337
Elias Meritt **95** 186
Elijah **65** 344
Eliza **83** 150 152 **95** 39
Eliza (Kellogg) **95** 188
Eliza G. **81** 97
Elizabeth **63** 179 180 340
82 317 **94** 356 357 **95** 28
30 37 38 186 380 383
120 186 **123** 263 **126** 78
Elizabeth (Crockford)
95 380 381
Elizabeth (Folsom) **95** 29
Elizabeth (Meeker) **94** 359
Elizabeth (Nutter) **94** 356
Elizabeth (Rolf) **95** 38
Elizabeth (Rowe) **94** 362
Elizabeth A. **72** 115
Elizabeth Cate **82** 50 **95**
30 380 381
Elizabeth E. **95** 376 377
Elizabeth J. (Denney)
95 246
Elizabeth Johnson **95** 37
Elizabeth M. (Hodgdon)
95 188
Elizabeth P. **95** 247
Elizabeth Phebe **95** 187

NOBLE *cont'd*
Elizabeth S. **83** 22 26
Elizabeth Sarah (Green)
95 378
Elizabeth Stoodly **95** 29
Ella Annie (Boole) **95** 39
Ella Ostelena **95** 246
Ellen **95** 185
Ellen (Jones) **123** 235
Ellen (T___) **95** 376
Ellen Iva **95** 379
Ellen M. **95** 186
Ellen Miller **95** 247
Elnathan **115** 16 22 23 109
Elsie Jane (McLaughlin)
95 378
Emelie **95** 250
Emeline (Sanborn)
(Burnell) **95** 185
Emma **95** 185 **109** 267 270
Emma D. (Lee) **95** 185
Emma Irene **95** 378
Emma J. (Trotter) **95** 37
Emma Jane **95** 35 377
Emma Webber **95** 37
Ephraim **63** 335
Esther **95** 32 **99** 295
Etta M. **94** 352
Etta Maria **95** 36
Eugene Frank **95** 376
Eunice **51** 165 **59** 343
128 291
Eunice (Turner) **99** 295
Eusebia Sawyer **81** 97
Evaline **115** 21
Ezekiel **99** 295
Fannie **82** 433
Fannie A. (Barker)
(Littlefield) **95** 376
Fannie Sanborn **95** 189
Fannie W. (Baker)
123 235
Fanny **94** 363 **95** 31 32 39
97 114
Fanny (Boardman)
103 89
Fanny S. **94** 35 352
Flora (Cousins) (Chase)
95 376
Flora Belle (Judkins)
95 39
Floyd Clarke (Mrs.)
90 370
Forrestine Shirley **95** 376
Frances **94** 359-361
Frances (Teale) **95** 247
Frances Eleanor **95** 39
Frances I. (Gowell) **95** 376
Francis **67** 289 312 **78** 415
96 355 **97** 103 111 112
114
Francis A. **95** 376
Francis Lister Hawks **94**
352 **95** 250
Frank Alpheus **95** 378
Frank Charlton **75** 157
76 xxii **79** 211 **81** 97
Frank Elbridge **95** 185
Frank Stillman **95** 379
Frank Treby **94** 352 355
356 **95** 30 37

NOBLE *cont'd*
Franklin H. **95** 35
Fred **95** 187
Frederick A. **55** 247
Frederick Alphonzo
95 246
Frederick C. **68** 337
Frederick E. **95** 378
Frederick Leslie **95** 379
Frederick Perry **95** 247
Fremont Chase **95** 378
Genevieve **95** 247 383
George **63** 35 **84** 30 **95** 31
184 185 250 **97** 106 114
114 251 **140** 49 **143** 141
George C. **95** 383
George Davis **95** 36
George E. **95** 376
George H. **95** 376
George Hayes **115** 24
George Henry **95** 36 187
188
George W. **95** 382
George Washington
95 247
George Washington
Copp **70** 100 **76** lxxvii
77 lxxiii lxxxiii lxxxvi
92 392 **93** 311 **94** 389
95 246 249 308 **99** 268
George Watson **115** 22
Georgianna **95** 185
Georgianna E. **95** 375
Gerrie **95** 250
Gertrude (Clement)
95 186
Gideon **67** 115-121 123 216
217 219 220 **68** 337 **85**
61 64
Gilbert Le **94** 352
Goodman **121** 320 **122**
160 **125** 150 **128** 312
Gorham **94** 359
Grace (Whiting) **95** 376
Grace Lillian **95** 187
Grace M. **95** 39
Grace May **95** 378
Gracie A. **95** 377
Hannah **57** 208 209 **64** lxii
73 281 **74** 42 **94** 357 358
362 363 **95** 29 37 191
101 217 218 **102** 224
115 17 22-25 27 109 110
123 136
Hannah (Dewey) **123** 262
Hannah (Simes) **95** 28
Hannah (Stebbins)
123 265
Hannah J. **95** 376 377
Harriet **68** 337 **115** 16
Harriet (Pike) **95** 35
Harriet Ann **110** 72
Harriet Eliza **78** 361
Harriet H. **78** 181
Harris **95** 38 39
Harvey Daniel **86** 223
Hazel Elsie **95** 378
Helen **95** 187
Helen L. **113** 314
Henrietta Maria **72** 294
Henry Carrington **115** 26

NOBLE *cont'd*
Henry H. **107** 90
Henry Harmon **66** 1
Henry Lane **115** 18
Herman **95** 185
Herman S. **115** 110
Hezekiah **70** 122 **115** 128
Hiram **95** 383
Hiram Benjamin **72** 294
Horace **78** 361 **95** 376 378
Horace M. **95** 383
Horace Mann **95** 247
Horatio **67** 220
Howard **95** 186
Hugh Le **94** 352
Huldah **68** 337
Huldah (Dalton) **95** 30
  381
Huldah (Hill) **85** 292
Hurriold **145** 253
Ida (Perkins) **95** 188
Ida Belle **95** 186
Ida L. **95** 37
Ida Leona **95** 378 379
Ira **109** 149
Ira Burnell **95** 187
Irene **95** 377
Irene Grace **95** 376
Irma **95** 378
Irvin **95** 377
Isaac **94** 362
Isabel Helen **64** lxii
  95 249
Isabel S. (Richardson)
  95 378
Isabella **95** 379 380
Isabella (Crockford)
  95 380
Isabelle **95** 376
Isetta **82** 50 367 **95** 30 380
  381
J. **57** 343
J. H. **95** 383
Jacqueline Hawks **95** 251
James **67** 312 313 **68** 337
  81 174 **82** 27 **84** 360 **95**
  31 185 246 383 **97** 45
  103 112-114 **106** 150
  109 149
James Byron **95** 247
James C. **95** 30 381
James Hammond **109** 149
James R. **68** 337 **72** 115
Jane **81** 139 **95** 38 383 **97**
  114 **125** 216 **140** 49
Jane (Cram) **95** 246
Jane (Spencer) **95** 186
Jane (Vaughan) **97** 103
Jane Loring **95** 251
Jane R. (Moore) **95** 246
Jay Laurence **95** 247
Jemima **95** 382
Jennie **77** 265
Jenny (Leonard) **95** 188
Jeremiah **83** 194 **95** 30 36
  38 246 383
Jeremiah Constantine
  95 246
Jesse **130** 132 135
Jessie **102** 124
Joan **85** 135 **95** 39

NOBLE *cont'd*
Joanna **67** 119 220 **95** 31
  102 224 **115** 16 22-24
Joanna (Rowe) **95** 31
John **51** 165 **52** 101 **54** 359
  56 xxxi 109 110 **58** 12
  214 215 **59** xlii 228 **60**
  xxxiv 90 222 **63** 179 **64**
  xliv lxii **69** lxxv **71** li
  73 312 **74** xlv 42 **81** 97
  448 **82** 50 292 295 423
  83 36 **84** 381 **85** 135 **94**
  352 355 356 358 359 361
  362 **95** 29-31 36-38 188
  246 248 249 251 252 379
  380 382 383 388 **97** 114
  110 11 **112** 283 **123** 261
  128 291 **142** 274 **148** 25
John Cyrenus **115** 110
John Frederick **125** 219
John Hancock **94** 357
John Harmon **95** 30 381
John Hawks **95** 250 251
John Jay **95** 188
John Le **94** 352
John M. **123** 235
John Matthew **95** 189
John Oren **95** 38
John S. **95** 383
John Sumner **95** 247
John W. **95** 383
Joseph **73** 312 **81** 448 **94**
  358-361 **95** 29 31 36 37
  185 375 383
Joseph A. **95** 375
Joseph B. **95** 383
Joseph E. **95** 378
Joseph T. **73** 229 **95** 375
Josephine **95** 188
Josephine Hawks **95** 250
Julia **67** 123 **82** 433 **95** 375
Julia Agnes **95** 247
Julia Frances **94** 359
Junior **71** 47
Karen H. **84** 30
Kate Tyler **95** 247
Katharine (Libby) **95** 187
Katharine Nash **95** 249
Katharine Williams
  64 lxii
Katharine Williams
  (Sheldon) **95** 249
Kathleen **95** 247
Kathleen Louise **86** 223
Kenneth Eugene **95** 376
Keziah **94** 355 357
Keziah (Booth) **125** 219
Keziah (Emery) (Briggs)
  95 375
Ladanta **95** 188
Lafayette M. **123** 235
Laura (Hawks) **95** 249
Laura E. **123** 223
Laura H. **95** 246
Laura Hawks **95** 250
Lay **115** 18
Lazarus **64** lxii **81** 139 431
  94 353-356 359-361 **119**
  21
Leader **81** 448 **94** 358

NOBLE *cont'd*
Leila Moss (Crandon)
  95 247
Leonora Dougherty
  116 313
Leroy Cyrus **95** 187 247
Lew Maurice **95** 247
Lewis H. **95** 187
Lewis Leonard **115** 107
Lida C. **95** 37
Lilla May **96** 288
Lloyd Delmont **95** 376
Loren **103** 89
Louisa **115** 24
Louisa (Rowley) **92** 164
Love (Clark) **94** 359
Lovisa **71** 53 56
Lucetta Frances **95** 36
Lucia Mah-Mak-Soo
  72 294
Lucinda **120** 297 304
Lucy **54** 444 **85** 64 411 **95**
  376 **108** 45
Lucy (Littlefield) **95** 374
Lucy Ann (Spinney)
  95 246
Lucy Augusta (Perry)
  95 246
Lucy Ladd **82** 423 **95** 30
  381
Luke **123** 265
Lulu (Gorman) **95** 187
Lulu L. **95** 188
Lurana **71** 56
Lydia **72** 317 **73** 312 **74**
  42 184 187 **81** 431 432
  94 356 358 **95** 32 186
  379 383 **96** 89 **109** 104
  105
Lydia (Berry) **94** 357
  131 77
Lydia (Jackson) **94** 356
Lydia A. **95** 375
Lydia W. (Littlefield) **95**
  376 378
Lyman W. **81** 291
Mabel L. **95** 377
Marcia Cordelia **81** 344
Margaret **73** 312 **81** 432
  94 358
Margaret (Kennison)
  94 357
Margaret (Miller) **94** 357
Maria (Burnell) **95** 186
Marian Allen **95** 247
Marian Caroline **78** 134
Marietta Josephine
  (Edmand) **95** 247
Mark **64** lxii **67** 121 220
  68 43 **94** 357 **95** 28 29
  36 37 245 246 250 251
  134 254
Mark Edwin **95** 37
Marshall Roy **95** 378
Martha **71** 47 **81** 139 432
  94 353 354 356 361-363
  95 31 185
Martha (Blackledge)
  95 375
Martha (Peverly) **94** 353
Martha (Rowe) **94** 361

NOBLE *cont'd*
95 31
Martha Abigail **95** 189
Martha Ann **95** 376-378
Martha Foote **71** 122
Martin **115** 18 21 23 25 26
108
Mary **56** 288 **63** 335 **65** 354
69 319 **71** 44 **74** 265 **81**
432 448 **82** 292 294 295
413 433 **94** 355-357 359
361 363 **95** 28 29 31 37
38 186 188 246 247 375
380 381 **96** 337 **97** 114
101 281 282 **115** 22 **130**
135
Mary (Barnes) **94** 355
Mary (Conlon) **106** 150
Mary (Glass) **94** 358
Mary (Goffe) **97** 114
100 300
Mary (Leavitt) **95** 30 380
381
Mary (Macklin) **97** 104
106
Mary (Sias) **94** 362
Mary (Staples) **94** 356
Mary (Wallace) **94** 357
Mary A. (Littlefield)
95 378
Mary Abigail **54** cxxxiv
14
Mary Adelaide **95** 36
Mary Ann **95** 186 **102** 224
106 150 **115** 24 **135** 77
137 183
Mary Carr (Copp) **64** lxii
95 246
Mary Dow **95** 188
Mary E. **72** 115 **95** 35
Mary E. (Day) **95** 376
Mary E. T. **95** 30 381
Mary Ellen **95** 375
Mary Emily (Potter)
95 250
Mary F. **83** 26 28
Mary Folsom **83** 481
95 29
Mary Frances **95** 247 378
Mary Furnald **82** 423 **83**
36 **95** 30 381
Mary Gorham (Hedge)
94 359
Mary Hunking **82** 50 **95**
30 380 381
Mary Jane **72** 299
Mary Jane (Dow) **95** 35
Mary Jane (Thompson)
95 376 377
Mary L. **100** 198
Mary N. **88** 337
Mary Nichols **94** 359
Mary Perry **95** 247
Mary Shannon (Davis)
95 38
Mary Weston **115** 27
Matthew **67** 120 220 **77**
xxxix **123** 262
Mehitable **95** 32 **96** 202
Mehitable (Thompson)
95 376

NOBLE *cont'd*
Melissa (Ross) (Kimball)
95 377
Mildred Evelyn **95** 187
Mildred Irene **95** 377
Mildred K. (Edwards)
95 383
Millard Victor **95** 186
Millie **95** 383
Milton Bird **116** 313
Minnie (Wilkinson)
95 379
Minot **95** 187
Mira **77** xxxix
Miriam **63** 183
Moses **63** 335 **64** lxii **94**
354-357 **95** 28 30 37 38
246
Nancy **83** 150 152 **95** 29
30 32 37 **96** 202
Nancy Ann (Gannett)
(Gerald) **95** 36
Nancy M. (Simpson)
95 375
Naomi **72** 220 **131** 291
Nathan **52** 401 **69** 319
101 281
Nathan Bundy **109** 149
150
Nellie Caroline (Keene)
95 39
Nelly **95** 185
Newell Perkins **95** 247
Nina O'Malley **95** 251
Obadiah **77** xxxix
Olive **81** 174 448 **94** 355
359 **95** 382
Olive (Cram) **95** 32 247
Olive (Libby) **95** 186
Oliver **54** 444
Olivia Folsom **95** 29
Olivia Jane **95** 187
Opal **95** 188
Ora **95** 186 187
Orren R. H. **95** 376
Orvillia **95** 383
Osephine **95** 188
Pamela **73** 283 **83** 36
108 46
Pamelia **82** 423 **95** 381
Pamelia (Sellars) **95** 30
381
Patience **53** 398
Patience (Drew) **95** 32
Patty **123** 47
Paul **67** 220 **95** 188 251
Percy **95** 187 188
Perley **95** 185
Perlina **95** 39
Peter **77** xxxix
Phebe **68** 337 **73** 283
94 355
Phebe (Gifford) **130** 132
135
Phebe (McLucas) **95** 185
Philip **103** 79 114
Philip Schaff **95** 247
Polly **56** 291 **74** 42 **94** 358
95 31 193 **123** 47
Pomeroy **115** 17
Priscilla **73** 282

NOBLE *cont'd*
Queenie **95** 187
Rachel **63** 183 **67** 312 **69**
266 **84** 381 **94** 355 357
97 114 **117** 186 **140** 234
Rachel (Burnell) **95** 32 185
Rachel (Savage) **97** 103
Ralph **95** 187
Randolph **77** 269
Rebecca **94** 357 **123** 22
Rebecca (Richards) **95** 251
Rebecca Everingham
(Wadley) **132** 221
Rena Catherine **95** 251
Reuben **63** 336 **73** 281
94 357
Rhoda **67** 220 **95** 31 39
109 270
Rhoda Webster **95** 39
Richard **73** 221 **81** 432 **94**
355 358
Robert **60** 25 **67** 289 **94**
352 **95** 29 30 36-38 **102**
224
Robert Austin **95** 251
Robert Bligh **95** 251
Robert P. **102** 224
Robert Valentine **95** 246
251
Rocksey **68** 337
Rodney **95** 379
Roger **71** 47 122 **94** 352
123 47
Roger Elliott **95** 379
Roger Le **94** 352
Rosa M. **94** 352
Rosa Mary **95** 248
Rose (Hatch) **95** 378
Rose (Labarge)
(Bombard) **95** 379
Rose Ann **95** 39
Royce Jennings **95** 187
Ruby (Massy) **95** 187
Rufus G. **95** 376
Ruth **59** 343 **95** 186 247
108 200 **109** 62 133
Ruth Amelia **79** 201
109 149
Ruth May **95** 376
Ruth Stevens (Moulton)
95 187
Sabina **71** 53
Sadie (Myers) **95** 187
Sadie B. **95** 185
Sally **68** 337 **73** 281 **77** 41
82 50 **83** 150 153 **94** 352
95 30 32 37 380-383 **115**
107 110 **128** 291
Sally (Austin) **95** 37
Sally (Sanborn) **95** 35
Sally (Spencer) **95** 184 185
Sally Jennette **115** 110
Samuel **71** 44 53 56 **81** 97
94 355 **95** 188
Samuel H. **95** 375
Samuel Sanford **95** 39
Sanford **95** 31
Sarah **52** 428 **63** 182 336 **64**
lxii **67** 116 219 312 **74** 42
81 448 **83** 150 152 **89**
112 **94** 355 358 363 **95**

NOBLE *cont'd*
31 247 375 **97** 103 113
130 135
Sarah (Chadbourne) **94**
358 **95** 36
Sarah (Doe) **94** 361
Sarah (Green) **89** 112
Sarah (Jones) **94** 355
Sarah (Partridge) **94** 355
Sarah (Pratt) **128** 98
Sarah (Richardson)
(Sanborn) **95** 185
Sarah (Rumrell) **95** 30 381
Sarah (Tyler) **121** 320
122 160 **123** 240 **125**
150 **128** 312
Sarah Abbie (Huff) **95** 377
Sarah Austin **95** 38 246
Sarah E. T. **95** 30 381
Sarah Elizabeth **95** 379
Sarah Jane (Harrigan)
(Jillson) **95** 377
Sarepta **68** 337 **95** 39
Seth **99** 115
Sias **95** 35
Sias Eugene **95** 36
Solomon **67** 117 220 **68**
337 **77** xxxix
Sophia **68** 337
Sophia (Dow) **95** 187 247
Stephen **54** 323 **59** 343
73 312 **81** 448 **94** 352
354 355 358 359 **95** 374
375 379
Stephen Atwood **95** 376
Stephen N. **132** 221
Susan **94** 362
Susan (Means) **95** 252
Susan Loring (Jackson)
95 251
Susanna **73** 282 **82** 50
95 383
Sylvanus **115** 107 110
Sylviditia (Grey) **95** 187
Tamar **95** 31
Tamar (Chase) **95** 31
Tamsen H. (Small) **95** 35
Thankful **95** 39
Thankful (Canon) **95** 38
Theodora **132** 323
Theodore T. **95** 376
Thomas **52** 428 **57** 209 **73**
312 **74** 42 124 **77** xxxix
81 432 448 **84** 30 **94** 356-
358 362 363 **95** 32 36 **97**
113 **101** 82 **120** 186 **131**
77 **134** 254 **142** 68
Thomas Bostwick **115** 23
Thomas Chadbourne
95 37
Thomas Freeman **95** 379
Thomas Le **94** 352
Thomas Nelson **95** 376
Thomas R. **51** 377
Velora E. (Jones) **87** 92
Victoria **95** 246
Walter **95** 186 376
Walter E. **95** 39
Walter Galbraith **95** 247
Washington **56** 292
Webber **89** 112 **94** 362

NOBLE *cont'd*
Wilbur W. **72** 50
Wilder Stiles **95** 376
Willard **95** 187
William **82** 50 **94** 352
115 22
William C. **95** 37
William F. (Mrs.) **94** 352
William Frank **95** 39
William Frederick **95** 36
William Henry Harrison
95 375
William J. **95** 383
William James **95** 247
William Le **94** 352
William M. **63** 309
95 378 379
William Mark **64** xxxi
William Rufus **95** 375
William Shove **95** 376
William T. **95** 37
Wilson **78** 134
Zella **95** 186
NOBLIT Noblat Noblett
Noblitt
Anthony **88** 268
Esther (Fiske) **88** 268
John Hyndman **61** 207 **62**
xxxvii
Joseph **67** 394
Loren Scott **111** 323
Minnie Walls **111** 323
Robert **64** 255
William **61** 207 208
NOBSER — Mr. **51** 190
Nocholls *see* Nichols
NOCK Nocke - *see also*
Knox
Abigail **83** 15
Abigail (Thomas) **98** 220
Elizabeth (Emery) **98** 61
Esther (Philbrook) (Beard)
98 61
Margaret **97** 371
Olive **83** 15
Patience **98** 220
Rebecca **98** 61 132
Rebecca (Tibbetts) **98** 60
61
Sarah **83** 12
Sarah (Adams) **98** 62
Sarah (Gould) **95** 190
Nocks *see* Knox
NODD Richard **111** 89
NODDIN Charles Alvin
103 101
Emily A. **103** 101
Ernest James **103** 179
Esther Frances **103** 101
Harriet R. **101** 35
Harriet Roxanna **103** 101
Irma Roxanna **103** 179
James **101** 35 **103** 101
James William **103** 101
179
Jane Esther **103** 179
Jane H. **103** 179
Michael **63** 244
Olive A. **101** 34
Olive Aurilla **103** 101
Oscar Varnam **103** 179

NODDIN *cont'd*
Roxanna **103** 101
NODDS Robert **85** 275
NODELL Agnes **124** 256
NODINE
Julia A. **129** 396
Polly **127** 159 **134** 254
NODOWAHUT **55** 157
NODSOM John **83** 447
NOE Pierre **98** 48
Sara Ann **98** 48
Noebury *see* Newbury
NOEL Noell
Ann Isobel **117** 207
Jennie **107** 135
Martin **140** 101
Paul **107** 313
Thomas **56** 310
NOERS Hugh de **95** 123
NOES Joseph **100** 63
NOETHER Carl Frank
(Mrs.) **102** 124
NOFTSGER
Mary (Clark) **116** 232
NOGÁROLA
— Countess **67** 101
Noise *see* Noyes
NOISEAU
Francois **143** 13
NOKE Joan **66** 56
NOKER
Charles **126** 205
Joanna (Chambers)
126 205
NOKES Anne **105** 150
NOLAN Noland Nolen
Nolin
Anne **139** 204
Catherine (Fallon) **90** 182
Charles **133** 263
Henry **133** 263
Hitty **61** 238
James **91** 331 **126** 209
139 204
Johanna **139** 205
Kate **124** 228
Lola Edith Iva (Hannum)
91 54
M. K. **91** 54
Marie **143** 12
Martin **125** 107
Mary **73** 228 **133** 263
Mary (Bouvy) **125** 107
Mary Ann (Garman)
126 209
Patrick **90** 182
Philip **56** 332
Samuel **61** 145
Sarah Ann **90** 105
Susanna **139** 204
Thomas **55** 390 **73** 221
NOLBROW William **64** 22
NOLE Nancy **117** 226
Nolen *see* Nolan
NOLENS Betsey **114** 179
NOLES *see also* Knowles
Joanna **81** 432
Samuel **81** 432
Stephen **81** 432
NOLETH
____ (Fiske) **87** 368

NOLETREE Allin **55** 141
Nolin *see* Nolan
NOLL William **64** 217
NOLONIER — Mr. **64** 322
NOLOTH John **86** 408 415
    417 **92** 178 179 183
    Nicholas **86** 408 **92** 178-
    180
    Robert **92** 180
NOLROYNDE
    Gilbert **80** 405
NOLTDEMAS
    Hendrik **106** 8
NOLTE
    Catherine **113** 323
NOLTEN
    Eveline S. **101** 213
NOLTING
    Alice Ann **93** 278
    Carl Frederick Philip
    93 278
    Charles Adolph **75** xxiii
    64 **93** 83 139 278 279
    Edwin Garfield **93** 278
    Florence Matilda **93** 278
    John Frederick **93** 278
    Lillie Ann **93** 278
    Mildred Ida **93** 278
    Myrtle Helen **93** 278
    Wesley Lewis **93** 278
Nolton *see* Knowlton
NOMUCH Jonas **125** 126
NOMYS John **80** 360
NONESUCH Belle **79** 76
    John **79** 76
NONEY Louise **125** 36
NONIS George **65** 242
NONN
    Elizabeth **93** 300
    Thomas **93** 300
NONS Thomas **143** 202
NOODES —— **54** 334
NOOK Judith **72** 258
Noon *see* Noone
NOONAN Noonnan
    Annie **81** 302
    Cristiana **85** 377
    Mary **128** 170
    Nancy I. **85** 376
    Thomas **63** 76
NOONE Noon
    —— **62** 129
    Alfred **65** 13 **142** 288
    Betsey **58** 17 **61** 307
    Michael **115** 294
    Sally **115** 294
    Thomas **115** 294
NOONEY James **60** 78
    Ruby **81** 354
    Sarah **60** 78
NOONING Elizabeth
    (Harding)
    (Manchester) **120** 5
    Jane (Brown) **100** 242
    Thomas **100** 242
    Timothy **120** 5
Noonnan *see* Noonan
NOORDSTRAUT Jacob
    Jansen von **80** 438
NOOSTRANT
    George **113** 285

NOOSTRANT *cont'd*
    Hannah **113** 285
NORBURY
    Elizabeth Susan **80** 335
    81 222
    Joseph **120** 253
    Lydia (Doubleday)
    120 253
NORCLIFF Norcliffe
    C. B. **59** 52 **93** 23
Norcot *see* Northcott
Norcott *see* Northcott
NORCROSS
    —— **55** 1 **56** 106
    —— (Homer) **140** 154
    Abigail **79** 93 **99** 168
    108 220
    Abigail (Tibbetts) **99** 328
    Abigail C. **88** 330
    Adline (Florida) **103** 45
    Alice N. **68** 254
    Almira **68** 254
    Anna **123** 172
    Betsey (Fay) **136** 314
    Betsey (Masary) **88** 280
    Charlotte **125** 216
    Christiana (Nash) **88** 341
    Cornelius Hinckley
    68 254
    Daniel **78** 401 **79** 93
    104 130
    David **104** 122 **125** 40
    Eliza **77** 314
    Eliza I. **88** 286
    Elizabeth **77** 232 287 **79** 93
    Emily **136** 314
    Emily Cutter (Ingols)
    88 341
    Fanny **78** 24
    Frank W. **107** 247
    George **127** 182
    George S. **103** 45
    Grace **71** 349
    Grenville Howland **55**
    424 **58** xliii **61** xxxiii
    257 353 **65** xx **66**
    xxxvii **68** xxi **70** xv **71**
    xlvii **72** xvi **74** 6 **77** xxv
    78 333 **79** 94 95 196 **80**
    204 **81** 216 **82** 231 **84**
    179 **89** 170 **90** 123 **91**
    177 187 **92** 149 **100** 171
    Hannah **52** 456 **79** 93
    127 182
    Hannah (Sanderson)
    127 182
    Helena **125** 107 108
    Henry **88** 280
    Isaac **88** 341
    James **100** 145
    James E. **85** 242
    Jane A. **140** 265
    Jemima **77** 287 **108** 31
    Jeremiah **67** 78 **79** 93 **91**
    187 **104** 122 **118** 266
    127 182
    Joel **79** 156 **136** 314
    John **111** 283 **127** 182
    Joseph **127** 182
    Josiah **77** 233 287
    Laura **71** xlvii

NORCROSS *cont'd*
    Louisa **78** 335
    Lucy **78** 417 **104** 267
    111 288
    Lucy Ann **67** xxxiv **71**
    xxxiv xlvi xlvii **79** 93 94
    Lucy Ann (Lane) **91** 187
    Lydia **124** 15
    Mary **78** 24 **79** 93 **100** 241
    111 236
    Mary (Brooks) **127** 182
    Mary (Gilbert) **111** 236
    Mary Cunningham **71**
    xlvi **79** 94
    Mary Lavinia **111** 152
    May **100** 241
    Mercy **125** 215
    Moses **78** 24
    Nancy **125** 101 **147** 213
    Nancy (Tibbetts) **100** 145
    Nathaniel **78** 24 **83** 377
    378 **86** 238 **92** 20 **111**
    236
    Nehemiah **140** 231
    Noah **144** 223
    O. H.B. **91** 331
    Otis **71** xlvi xlvii **78** 215
    79 93-95 **91** 187 **140**
    154
    Peter **79** 93 **127** 182
    Philip **53** 215 **71** 349
    Rachel **111** 281 283
    Rebecca **78** 410
    Richard **79** 93 **98** 165 **118**
    263 266 **123** 183 184
    127 182
    Rose **100** 242 **127** 182
    Ruth **127** 182
    Sarah **53** 215 **71** 349 **77** 21
    79 156
    Sarah P. **88** 330
    Susanna **86** 238 239 **98** 83
    Susanna (Shattuck) **86**
    238 **118** 264
    Susanna Ruggles **79** 95
    Thankful **53** 215
    Uriah **92** 20 **140** 231
    William **77** 21 **109** 77
    111 279 **127** 182
    William Rowland **88** 341
Norcut *see* Northcott
Norcutt *see* Northcott
NORD
    Herman Joel (Mrs.)
    109 130
NORDASH John **69** 357
NORDEN *see also* Von
    Norden
    —— **56** 276
    Eleanor Johnson (Hale)
    83 476
    Ernest (Mrs.) **83** 476
    Hannah **112** 179
    John **52** 117
    Margaret **52** 110 117
    Maria **86** 309
    Mary **52** 110
    Nathaniel **60** 238 239
    112 179
    Samuel **95** 135
NORDGREN N. **128** 264

NORDIKE Elizabeth
(Fenimore) **111** 271
Isaac **111** 271 287
NORDLIE Eugene **93** 248
NORDQUIST
Anna **128** 172
Christina **128** 172
Johanna Mathilda
128 172
John M. **128** 172
NORDSTROM Norstrom
Clarissa **66** 112
Erick H. **66** 112
Mabel **79** 134
NORE Frances **147** 173
NORFOLK — Duke of **53**
115 **57** 97 193 **123** 243
Agnes **100** 15
Bernard Edward
Howard (Duke of)
79 152
Edward (Duke of) **95** 24
John **100** 15
Margaret **52** 124 125
Mary **52** 124 125
Richard **52** 124 125
Roger (Earl of) **95** 242
Sarah **52** 124 125
Thomas (Duke of) **57** 194
Thomas (Earl of) **57** 193
Thomas Howard (Duke
of) **57** 194
NORFORTH —— **52** 245
NORGARD Stuart Neil
(Mrs.) **105** 129
NORGATE Edward **52** 235
236 **118** 172
Henry **52** 236
John **52** 236
Nicholas **52** 236
Noriss see Norris
NORKOT John **148** 111
NORLAND
Jonas J. **98** 232
Margaret (Fitz Randolph)
98 232
NORLEIGH
John **115** 249
NORLIE
Olaf Morgan **113** 241
NORMAN —— **70** 264 **79**
323 **140** 322
— Capt. von **54** 187
Abbie Kinsley **108** 150
Abby **55** lviii
Abby Durfee **55** lviii
Agnes **68** 62 **69** 358 359
Alexander **83** 24 26
Ann **66** 72 **68** 62
Anna **116** 298 300
Annie **112** 75
Arabella **122** 148
B. W.T. **148** 256
Beatrice Elizabeth **79** 285
Benjamin **62** 384 385 **96**
360 361 **117** 225 226
Betsey (Grover) **115** 306
Bradford **55** lviii
Caleb **73** 152
Cecil Ray **78** 323
De Lafayette **78** 323

NORMAN cont'd
Deborah (Plaisted) **117**
223 224
Delilah P. **84** 86
Ebenezer **117** 227
Edith **55** lviii
Edward **80** 406
Eleanor **52** 478
Eliza Ann **119** 144
Elizabeth **53** 21 **68** 62 **69**
321 359 **78** 323 **95** 18 **96**
361 **123** 73
Elizabeth Ann **120** 215 216
Ella **78** 323
Emily **120** 138
Eunice **96** 350 360
Frances **69** 321
Frances D. **84** 86
Frances Hanstep **73** 144
George H. **55** xx xliii lviii
108 150
Guy **55** lviii
Hannah **115** 213 **123** 152
Hannah (Beal) **117** 225 226
Hannah (Welch) **117** 227
Hannah Jane **120** 140
Hugh **68** 62
Hugh K. **55** lviii
Irena **121** 303 **122** 148
Isabella **121** 305
J. **90** 280
James **112** 40
Jeremiah **117** 223 224
123 73
Joan **147** 14
Joel **83** 359 **84** 86
Joel E. **84** 86
John **52** 257 **53** 21 **55** 54
98 332 341 **59** 229 **62**
384 385 **63** 351 **64** 20 **69**
156 358 359 **96** 360 **104**
122 **140** 28
John W. **69** 321
Joseph **90** 355
Joseph P. **83** 359
Keziah **102** 68
Lionel **63** xxxiii
Lucy **117** 222
Mabel **55** lviii
Margaret **103** 141 **105** 15
Margaret (Gosnold)
105 15
Margery **65** 85
Martha Lavinia **79** 132
Mary **52** 257 **62** 384 **64** 164
68 62 **93** 384 387 **95** 169
96 360 **104** 113
Mary (Coes) **96** 361
Mary (Collins) **90** 355
Mary (Welch) **116** 303
Mary J. **123** 73
Maxwell **55** lviii
Mercy P. **83** 24 26 36
Moses **96** 360 361 **110** 47
127 8
Nettie Adella **74** xxx
Nettie Hall **74** 77
Philippa **68** 62
Phillis **68** 62
Priscilla (Bradford)
110 47

NORMAN cont'd
Priscilla B. **125** 172 175 177
Rachel (Peckham) **125** 173
Reginald **55** lviii
Richard **55** 332 **69** 358 359
Richard C. **125** 173
Richard Henry **125** 173
Robert **52** 257 **56** 85 **69**
321 **80** 408
Ross Cumnor **78** 323
Sadie **78** 323
Sarah **62** 384 385 **69** 156 **83**
359 **84** 86 **96** 360 361
Sarah (Maverick) **96** 360
Senath **119** 283
Susanna **98** 78
Thomas **55** 333 **94** 270 **115**
306 **116** 303
Thomas P. **125** 173
Traber (Mrs.) **74** xxx
Walter **148** 62
William **65** 75 85 **68** 62
95 16 **112** 40 **113** 290
140 28
Zachary **105** 15
Normandie De see
De Normandie
NORMANSELL
Thomas **147** 14
NORMANTON
— Earl of **53** 293 294
NORMANVILLE
Hugh de **106** 280
Thomas de **114** 219
NORMIDGE
James **61** 349
Mary **61** 349
NORRACOTT
James **83** 354
Johan **83** 354 356
John **83** 354 356
NORRIDY Grizel **144** 253
NORRINGTON
Elizabeth **53** 19
Joan **53** 19
Sarah **53** 20
Vincent **53** 20
NORRIS Noriss
—— **92** 280 284 **102** 74
129 395
— Capt. **54** 31
— Mr. **65** 369
— Mrss **127** 12
Abbie **92** 203
Abby C. **74** li
Abigail **55** 206 207 **99** 64
102 159
Addie May **89** 115
Albert Lane **72** xx **74**
xxxviii lxi lxii
Albert Perley **74** lxii **84**
172 **85** 197 **104** 238 **105**
61 132
Alice **64** 123
Alice Waterman
(Greenough) **83** 490
Allen A. **70** 95
Amelia Caroline **90** 297
Andrew **73** 227
Ann **59** 288 **65** 233
Anna (Hilton) **124** 302

NORRIS *cont'd*
Annah (Hanks) **86** 7
Annis **70** 60 136
Benjamin **73** 72 73 75 **125**
   254 **127** 256 **129** 395
   136 336
Benjamin Franklin **136**
   90 325
Bertha **102** 287
Bertha L. **75** 15
Bethuel **136** 29
Betsey (Spencer) **129** 395
C. **104** 47
C. Maud **105** 61
Carl B. **74** li
Caroline Amelia **89** 93
   90 297
Caroline F. **74** li
Caroline Matilda **59** lxix
Catherine **83** 26 27
Charles **102** 159 **112** 283
Charles Henry **57** xlii **58**
   xi xxxi **59** lxviii lxix
Charles M. **68** 44
Charles S. **59** lxix
Charles Sewall **73** xx **74**
   xxxviii li
Charles Sheppard **93** 119
Charles Sumner **71** xxiii
   83 490 **84** 107 196
Charlotte Wright **93** 119
Christian **82** 50
Clara Elizabeth **74** lxii
Clara Elizabeth (Perley)
   105 61
Clara Maud **74** lxii
Cyrenus A. **64** 123
D. W. **96** 401
Daniel Wells **98** 145
   112 73
David Holden **83** 490
Dolly **59** lxviii
Dorothy **110** 253 255
Dorothy (Combe) **138** 13
Ebenezer **136** 22
Edna May **92** 363
Edward **51** 39 41 **59** lxviii
   74 li **102** 159
Edward John **96** 35
Effie Louise (Shapleigh)
   96 35
Elbridge **95** 55
Eleanor **105** 61
Eliza **81** 432 **102** 159
Eliza Bourne **120** 6
Elizabeth **82** 50 **93** 119 **94**
   157 **96** 35 **120** 7 **125** 254
   133 285
Elizabeth (Whittemore)
   106 272
Elizabeth D. **63** 182
Elizabeth Sewall **93** 119
Ellen **110** 253 255
Ellen (Hearne) **110** 250
   253
Emeline **102** 159
Emerson Shapleigh
   96 35
Emma Frances **59** lxix
   74 li
Ensign **102** 159

NORRIS *cont'd*
Ethel **68** xxxv **73** xvii **83**
   490 **90** 128
Frank **80** 43 **136** 90 325
Frank (Mrs.) **81** 222
Frank J. **75** 15
George **70** 60 61 136 **90** 50
   103 228 **110** 253 255
George Everett **74** li
George Henry **68** 160
George Sullivan **89** 114
George W. **83** 490
George Walter **93** 119
George Washington
   89 114
Gertrude Glorvina
   (Doggett) **136** 325
Gould **147** 258
Grace **55** 101
Grace (Wyeth) **105** 61
Grace May **74** lxii
Greenleaf Dudley **93** 119
Greenleaf Rufus **74** lxi **78**
   416 **105** 61
Guy Holden **83** 490
Hannah **82** 376 **102** 159
   120 6 **136** 22
Hannah (Bevens) **136** 22
   27
Hannah (Colby) **129** 395
Hannah (Donne) **132** 38
Hannah (Kelley) **83** 490
Harriet **105** 186
Harriet B. (Luce) **88** 285
Harriet W. **108** 265
Harry **55** 207
Helen M. **59** lxix
Henrietta **108** 80
Henry **70** 61 136 **82** 187
   102 159 **103** 8 **118** 262
   142 243
Henry McCoy **60** 318
Howard **118** 152
Hugh **65** 238
Ida A. **97** 295
Isaac **147** 258
J. A. **76** 98
J. Anna **108** 135
Jacob **83** 490 **114** 190
   136 336
James **74** lxi **82** 187 **83** 490
   105 61 **106** 153 **110** 233
   111 274 **138** 113 **142** 36
   144 348 354 **147** 258
Jane **83** 26
Jemima (Benson) **99** 64
Jeremiah **59** lxviii **73** 66
   68 **120** 7
Jesse **125** 291
Joan (de Vere) **141** 107
Joanna **99** 64 **123** 209
John **55** 101 **60** 27 **79** 312
   80 43 **82** 376 **83** 490 **86**
   7 **88** 285 **99** 64 **120** 6 7
   124 78 **125** 108 **129** 383
   136 22 **144** 31 **146** 265
John C. **114** 190
John W. **105** 61 **116** 236
Jonathan **60** 318 **82** 50
   145 356
Joseph **70** 61 136 **73** 64 65

NORRIS *cont'd*
   68-70 **111** 275 276
Joseph Warren **89** 114
Julia **102** 159
Katharine **96** 35
Keziah **136** 22
Lewis **58** 17
Lizzie Amanda **89** 114
Lowell **74** lxi **105** 61
Lowell Ames **85** 184
Lucinda **74** lxi
Lucinda (Lane) **105** 61
Lucy **59** 409 **88** 370
Lucy (Hazelton) **136** 336
Lucy (Lazell) **89** 114
Lucy Adelia **89** 114
Lucy Mary **70** lvii
Lula May **76** 98
Lydia **69** 377 **82** 50
   138 113
Lydia (Rundlett) **83** 490
M. **104** 47
Margaret **70** 61 136
   141 107
Margaret (Heath) **146** 265
Margery **68** 107
Margery (Doggett) **99** 64
Marion Chase **75** 15
Marjoria Estella **100** 109
   103 79 126 228
Martha **106** 272
Martha Ann **68** 160
Mary **59** 289 **60** 402 **66**
   lxix **69** 155 **72** 12 **78** 426
   89 93 **96** 358 **99** 269
   105 61 **108** 231 264 **110**
   253 255 **124** 133 **134** 92
   136 22 **138** 113
Mary (Brown) **83** 490
Mary (Mahurin) **136** 22 27
Mary (Tupper) **99** 64
Mary (Whiting) **90** 297
Mary (Woodin) **125** 254
Mary D. **99** 47
Mary E. **90** 115
Mary Ida **68** 160
Mary Lizzie (Marsh)
   83 490
Mary Shaw **59** 404
Mary Whiting **90** 297
Mercy **65** 376
Mira (Holden) **83** 490
Molly (Lowell) **105** 61
Mordecai **90** 110
Moses **74** lxi **83** 490
   105 61
Nabby **147** 258
Nancie W. **118** 131
Nancy **68** 249 **95** 32 **97** 183
Nancy (Hilton) **124** 302
Nancy Maria (Cookson)
   89 114
Nathaniel **65** 375 376
   136 336
Nellie Maria **80** 43
   81 110 222
Nicholas **74** lxi **83** 490 **105**
   61 **136** 22
Oliver **99** 64 **129** 344
Patience **120** 7
Patty **133** 307 309

NORRIS *cont'd*
Peter **60** 402 **136** 22 27
Phebe (Mahurin) **136** 29
Phillis (Jones) **125** 108
Polly **58** 17 **147** 258
Priscilla **83** 490 **90** 55
Ralph Thomas (Mrs.) **83** 124 233
Rebecca **57** 334 **111** 275 276 **120** 7
Rebecca (Hazelton) **136** 336
Rebecca Ann **76** 269
Rebecca B. **108** 265
Rhoda **147** 258
Richard **99** 47 **109** 10 **110** 250 253-255
Richard Greenough **83** 490
Robert **83** 313 **89** 93 **103** 228 **133** 271
Robert A. **90** 297
Robert Lane **105** 61
Robert P. **105** 61
Rosetta M. **127** 62
Rufus Granville **89** 115
Ruth **72** 115 **82** 50
Ruth (Folsom) **83** 490 **105** 61
Ruth (Mosier) **102** 159
Ruth Blake **83** 490
Ruth Blake (Norris) **83** 490
Sally **147** 258
Sally (Beaverstock) **125** 291
Sally (Robinson) **105** 61
Sally (Stokley) **125** 288
Samuel **57** 334 **59** 288 403 409 **63** 362 **72** 115 **82** 50
Samuel Martin **72** 115
Sarah **54** 31 **59** 288 **65** 352 **79** 54 **105** 224 **114** 187 **129** 395
Sarah (Coxe) **83** 490 **105** 61
Sarah (Dobson) **99** 47
Sarah (Hazelton) **136** 336
Sarah (Knight) **102** 74
Sarah (Maloon) **89** 114
Sarah Ann (Frost) **90** 50
Sarah Louisa **89** 114
Shepard H. **93** 119 **94** 157
Silas Ensign **103** 228
Simeon **74** lxi **105** 61
Sophia Jane **89** 114
Susan **90** 105 **142** 159
Susan M. **80** 43
Susanna **53** 459
Sylvia **108** 262
Tamesin **60** 318
Tennie **123** 240
Thomas **66** 307 **90** 110 **102** 274 **106** 272 **111** 275 **120** 7 **125** 288 **132** 38
Tristram Wesley **89** 114
True L. **84** 331
Walter **104** 93 **136** 22
Walter E. **121** 175
Walter Greene **89** 115

NORRIS *cont'd*
Walter Henry **96** 35
William **102** 159 **124** 78 302 **127** 140 **138** 13 **141** 107
William Bond **53** 459
William S. **59** lxix
Willie **104** 47
Willie R. **86** 54
Ziba **136** 22
NORSEN Henry Norman (Mrs.) **108** 135
Irene Ward **113** 161
NORSTER Margerette (George) **91** 385
William **91** 385
Norstrom *see* Nordstrom
NORSWORTHY Deborah (Wheelwright) **126** 209
Thomas **126** 209
NORTH —— **51** 127 **52** 146 **130** 235
— Miss **73** 36
Abi **52** 150 **109** 65
Alexander **120** 311
Alexander Lovell **58** 373
Anna (Whipple) **107** 57
Arthur **51** 127
Asher **72** 220
Asinthe **80** 331
Betsey **72** 220
Caleb **130** 235
Catherine **55** 345 **59** 221
Charles J. **51** 240 243
Charles Jackson **68** xxx **69** xxxi **78** 216 **80** 331 332
Charlotte **127** 69
Daniel **56** 161 **58** 373 **100** 297
Darius Robinson **89** 372
David **52** 474 **73** 7
Dexter **73** 159 **76** 242 **142** 333
Dora **80** 332
Dudley **53** 82
Eliza S. **109** 65
Elizabeth **109** 65
Elizabeth (Gilbert) **105** 11
Elizabeth (Gosnold) **105** 11
Esther **136** 311
Esther (Stanley) **136** 311
Frances **148** 58
Francis **62** 92
Frederick **130** 182
George **66** 34
Hannah **53** 87 **71** 121 **72** 219
Hannah Flagg **96** 78
Hannah Root **52** 474
Harriet (Corbet) **120** 17
Harris **120** 16
Henry **105** 11
Isaac **52** 474 **72** 220
James **72** 220 221 **109** 65
James D. **91** 394
Jane **84** 331
Jedediah **52** 474
John **51** 118 **52** 474 **58** 373 **61** 134 **62** 301 **72** 211

NORTH *cont'd*
219 220 **73** 159 **76** 242 **83** 316 **92** 302 **111** 117 **132** 142 **136** 311 **142** 333 **148** 58
Joseph **74** 190 **106** 232 **111** 117 **125** 39 **147** 74
Katharine **53** 82
Lavenia (Wood) (Seacord) **120** 16
Lemuel **52** 474
Lydia **72** 220 **111** 240
Lydia Muncil **89** 371 372
Madeline **51** 127
Martha **72** 220
Martha (Jewett) **91** 394
Martha Elizabeth **106** 232
Martha Jewett **91** 394
Mary **58** 373 **72** 211 **92** 302 **108** 309 **146** 327 **147** 80
Mary (Cocks) **100** 297
Mary (Fuller) **148** 266
Mary (Price) (Petersfield) **148** 18
Matilda (Osgood) **87** 94
Mercy **58** 373 **72** 221
Nancy (Conig) **125** 290
Orpha **136** 328
Ralph H. **69** 288
Rebecca **52** 474
Rhoda **72** 221
Richard **108** 309
Roger **105** 11
Roxana **56** 161
S. D. **93** 179
Sally **73** 7 **79** 114
Samuel **53** 87
Sarah **65** 121 **72** 220 221 **121** 274 **134** 333
Selah **59** 21 **107** 57
Seth J. **109** 65
Simeon **69** 288
Simon Newton Dexter **64** 100 **69** 288
Solomon **148** 266
Stephen **62** 92 **125** 290
Susan **54** 112
Susanna **72** 220 **93** 308 **106** 215 **115** 27 **128** 4 **144** 358 **146** 317 320
Thomas **51** 118 **52** 474 **72** 219 220 **81** 126
Ursula **108** 309
William **65** 260 **91** 206 **93** 17 **116** 242 **121** 59
NORTHAM Northom
Abigail **57** 211
Ann **57** 211 **126** 25
Ann Burdick **125** 178
C. H. **126** 23
Caroline **51** 169
Elijah **83** 54
Elizabeth **57** 211
Experience **57** 211 **90** 383
Ferdinand **51** 169
Hannah **57** 211
Hannah (Houghton) **88** 278
J. Lewis **125** 242
John **57** 211 **127** 140
Joseph **51** 169

NORTHAM *cont'd*
Katharine **57** 211
Lois **83** 53 54
Lurana **57** 211 213
Mary **51** 169 **125** 242
Mary (Langley) **125** 242
   126 23
May N. **125** 176
Ruhama **57** 211
S. T. **126** 23
Sally M. **83** 100
Samuel **55** 343
Sarah **57** 211
Stephen **55** 343
Stephen T. **51** 169 **88** 278
William Langley **51** 169
NORTHAMPTON
William Compton
   (Earl of) **66** 343
Northand *see* Northend
NORTHBRIDGE
Cassie **80** 232
NORTHCOTT Norcot
   Norcott Norcut
   Norcutt Northcote
   Northcutt
Ann **75** 221
Edmund **115** 252
Elizabeth **125** 276 **126** 67
Elizabeth (Bonney) **89** 223
Ephraim **89** 222 223
Eva Ann **82** 235
Isaac **111** 7
John **51** 135 **111** 6 **115**
   248 249 **122** 136 **142**
   366
Katharine **52** 185
Lydia **107** 151
Mary **125** 220
Nancy **125** 220
Olive **123** 269
Patience **79** 293
Philip **142** 366
Richard **111** 6
Ruth **79** 293
William **69** 151 **79** 293
NORTHCRAFT
Lucy Ann **89** 310
NORTHCROSS
Andrew Taylor **77** 224
Clarissa Sarah **77** 224
Henry **138** 213
James M. **77** 224
Phebe Jane (Gifford)
   138 213
Northcutt *see* Northcott
NORTHEAST
Peter **143** 213
NORTHEND Northand
   Northen
Caleb **55** 67
Christopher **66** 352
Edna **80** 96 **93** 186
Elizabeth **53** 203 377
   66 352
Ezekiel **53** 203 377 **66** 352
   80 96 **131** 166 169
Jeremiah **66** 352
John **60** 152
Margaret **60** 152
Mary **63** 371

NORTHEND *cont'd*
Ralph **66** 352
Richard **61** 67
Robert **66** 352
Sarah **80** 96 **83** 476
Thomas **93** 81
William Dummer **69** 3
NORTHEY Northie Northy
Abraham **104** 122
Adelia **134** 92
Ann **73** 143 151 222
Anna **59** 313 **133** 289
David **104** 122
Deborah **59** 313 **133** 289
Ebenezer **59** 313 **133** 289
Eleanor **60** 272
Eliphalet **59** 76 **60** 181 182
   133 288 289
James **58** 84 **59** 76 313 **60**
   176 273 **133** 287-289
   134 234
Jane **73** 271
Jesse **59** 313 **133** 289
John **54** 421 **133** 289
   143 338
Joseph **54** 421
Marcy **60** 181
Mary **58** 84 **59** 76 313 **60**
   176 **73** 137 266 **133** 289
Mary (Sanderson)
   133 289
Mary (Stockbridge) **133**
   287 288 **134** 234
Mehitable **58** 83 **59** 313
   133 289
Nathaniel **73** 228
Robert **60** 272 274
Sally **60** 274
Sarah **59** 313 **75** lxxvi **76**
   281 **133** 289
Sarah (Elwell) **133** 289
William **65** 240
NORTHGATE
Eser **57** 411
Peter **57** 411
Northie *see* Northey
NORTHINGTON
Alice (Smith) **91** 108
Hector **91** 108
Mary Emeline **91** 108
Sada Victoria **78** 46
Samuel **78** 46
Sarah Willis **78** 46
NORTHLAND
Richard **119** 99
NORTHLY John **61** 241
Sally **61** 241
NORTHMORE —— **59** 418
Northom *see* Northam
Northon *see* Norton
NORTHRIDGE Nortridge
—— **52** 112
NORTHRUP Northrop
   Northup Northupp
—— **55** 245 **75** 181
— Mrs. **62** 290
A. J. **56** 220
Abigail **69** 58 **115** 295
Ada **92** 34 44
Ada (Fayerweather)
   145 256

NORTHRUP *cont'd*
Adda A. **115** 295
Addie **116** 66
Alexander H. **73** 116
Almira **92** 34
Amanda **76** 86 **107** 302
Amelia M. **109** 173 268
Amelia Maria **92** 36 38
Amigh **92** 42
Amos **53** 247 **76** 86
Amy Lewis **92** 36
Andrew **52** 41 **71** 12
Andrew Jackson **76** 87
Ann **94** 92 **129** 40 **137** 74
Ann Maria **97** 383 **105** 314
Anna **91** 250 **92** 35 **102** 69
   112 146
Anna (Wells) **92** 35
Anna E. **115** 295
Anna Maria **105** 314
Annie Valeria **92** 42
Annis **115** 123
Augusta Eudora **92** 41 42
Barbara Reed **92** 46
Barzillai **124** 9
Benjamin **66** 28 29 **102** 217
   128 296
Benjamin Wooster **76** 86
Bessie **92** 44
Betsey **115** 295
Betsey A. **76** 87
Betty **92** 34
Caroline Elizabeth **92** 40
Carr **91** 251 **92** 32-34
   115 294
Catharina A. **71** 12
Catherine **92** 34 35
Catherine Barnes **92** 40 44
Charles **92** 42 **136** 267
Charles Edwin **144** 317
Charles G. **100** 173
Charles Henry **92** 43
Charles M. **116** 66
Charles Roy **92** 44
Charles S. **116** 66
Charlotte (Worden)
   145 251
Chloe **92** 34 **125** 280
Chloe (Baldwin) **125** 280
Chloe E. **116** 62
Christopher **91** 251 **92**
   33 35 **100** 173 **109** 270
Christopher Carr **92** 35
   37 40
Clara **115** 295
Clara B. **122** 299
Clara Minerva **52** 41
Clarina **52** 41
Clarissa **115** 295
Clarissa Comb **76** 91
Clarissa S. **76** 87
Clark C. **109** 271
Clark Carr **92** 39
Clark N. **115** 294
Clark Sutherland **92** 32
   38 45
Clarke **52** 41 **88** 37 **92** 33-
   35
Clayton **115** 295
D. F. **75** 15
Daniel Lewis **92** 41

NORTHRUP *cont'd*
Daniel Wier **92** 42
David **122** 299 **128** 134
144 317
De Witt Clinton **92** 42
Della E. **116** 66
Dorcas **88** 43
Dorcas T. (Kingsley)
144 317
Dwight **92** 41 42
Edgar **92** 36
Edmund Dwight **92** 42
Edward Barber **92** 44
Edwin **145** 256
Eliza (Pollack) **92** 36
Elizaann (Nekerson)
123 199
Elizabeth **79** 262 **92** 34 35
109 270
Elizabeth (Barnes) **92** 44
Elizabeth (Sutherland)
107 57
Elizabeth Barnes **92** 44
Elizabeth Bliss **92** 34
Elizabeth F. B. **75** 14 15
Ella **92** 34 **115** 292
Ellen Ann **92** 43
Elmina M. **115** 295
Elvira P. **115** 295
Emeline **76** 86 **92** 31 65
Emeline (Sutherland) **109**
270 273
Emma **92** 34 **115** 295
Emma E. **116** 65
Emma Frances (Wilson)
144 317
Emma J. **115** 295
Enos **102** 69
Ephraim **92** 34 35 **115** 295
Etta J. **115** 295
Eunice **76** 86 87 97 **83** 252
Eveline M. **115** 290
Fanny E. **115** 294
Frances **128** 135
Frances E. **116** 66
Fred D. **116** 66
Frederick **92** 44
Freelove **67** 286
G. S. **100** 2 5 6
Gardner **115** 294 295
Gardner Hall **92** 35 38 39
44
Gardner Harold **92** 45
Gardner Herrick **92** 35
41 45
George **92** 33 **102** 108
115 295
George Ernest **92** 44
George Foster **92** 38 40 44
George Thomas **145** 256
Gideon **79** 346 **128** 135
Grace **116** 66
Grace Marian **92** 45
Hannah **78** 264 **92** 33 34
145 251 256
Hannah (Sutherland)
107 57
Hannah Elizabeth (Fayer-
weather) **145** 256
Harmon **76** 86
Harriet **78** 223 **115** 297

NORTHRUP *cont'd*
Harriet (Sutherland)
107 57
Harriet D. **115** 295
Harriet S. **115** 295
Helen **92** 34 39 **109** 171
270
Helen Frances **92** 46
Henry **66** 27 **79** 263 **128**
129 134
Henry Bliss **92** 35 36 42
Hiram **92** 44
Hopestill **52** 317
Hosea B. **54** 458
Immanuel **92** 33-35
128 131
Isaac **76** 86 **131** 219
Isaac H. **109** 270
Isaac Hall **92** 35 38
Isaac Herbert **92** 39
James **97** 383 **105** 314 **128**
134 **129** 60
James C. **92** 34 **116** 66
James M. **115** 295
Jane **68** 258 **74** 316 **97** 76
Jane Elliot **76** 86 87 99
Jay **92** 34
Jennie Mary **92** 44
Job **125** 280
Joel **78** 264 **84** 140
Joh. **128** 134
John **92** 33
John Carr **92** 34 **115** 295
John H. **115** 295
John Henry **92** 42
John Holmes **92** 33-36
John S. **115** 295
John Spafard **92** 35 39
John Wesley **107** 302
Jonathan **75** 15 **102** 108
Jonathan (Mrs.) **75** 15
Joseph **52** 317 **60** 331 **92**
34 **128** 134 **129** 60
Josiah **144** 47
Julia A. **115** 295
Julia Electa **92** 42
Laodomia **52** 41
Laura E. **115** 295
Lebeous **128** 134
Lena Kate **92** 44
Leroy **115** 295
Lewis **107** 57
Louisa **61** 35 **92** 42
Louise **92** 34
Lucretia **92** 39 **109** 270
Lucretia Carter **92** 39
Lucretia Maria **92** 39
Lucy **92** 34 44 **97** 186
115 294
Luther G. **123** 199
Lydia **92** 36
Lydia Ann **92** 42
Lyman **92** 36
Margery **124** 9 **128** 135
Margery (Rockwood)
124 9
Maria (Gates) **109** 267 270
Maria Louise **92** 44
Marian Gardner **92** 45
Mariette **92** 37
Martha Jane **115** 295

NORTHRUP *cont'd*
Mary **53** 247 **67** 286 **71** 38
73 116 **83** 91 **85** 104 154
92 34 36 42 **100** 173 **115**
295
Mary (Darling) **136** 267
Mary (Kimberly) **102** 108
Mary (Knowles) **88** 37
Mary A. **115** 295
Mary Ann **52** 41 **92** 38
109 272
Mary E. **73** 116 **115** 295
116 58
Mary E. (Barton) **107** 302
Mary Eliza **76** 87
Matie **115** 295
Mercy **52** 41 **66** 28 **85** 228
102 69
Millia E. **115** 295
Minnie J. **115** 295
Nabby **79** 54
Nancy **85** 222 **92** 33
Nathan **83** 252
Nicholas **66** 26 **67** 286 **92**
33 35 **128** 134
Nicholas Augustus
92 41 42
Nicholas Carr **66** 27 **79**
346 **91** 250 **92** 33 35 36
39 41 42 46 64 **109** 270
Nicholas Clark **92** 39
Nicholas Gardner **92** 34
Olive Emelyn **92** 45
Penelope **92** 38 **109** 270
Penelope Hall **92** 36
Phebe (Beecher) **121** 251
Polly **52** 41 **109** 262
115 295
Rebecca **76** 86
Reynolds **92** 34 35
Robert **128** 131
Rowse **128** 134
Ruth **84** 140
Ruth Louise **92** 45
Samuel **66** 26 **79** 262 **121**
251 **128** 128 135
Sarah **52** 41 **70** 177 **72** 115
79 346 **80** 260 **91** 251
92 33 34 **107** 302 **109**
270
Sarah (Barton) **107** 302
Sarah (Clarke) **91** 251
92 33
Sarah Ann **91** 250 **92** 33 36
64 **107** 302
Sarah C. (Denison)
109 270
Sarah Clarke **92** 35
Sarah Eddy **109** 270
Sarah F. **115** 295
Sarah Frances (Medbury)
92 39
Sarah Harris **76** 86
Sarah T. **116** 63
Selina **76** 87
Stephen **66** 28 **68** 384
128 130 134
Stukely **66** 27 **128** 130
Susan **102** 217
Susan (Smith) **97** 383
105 314

NORTHRUP cont'd
Susan S. (Carr) **102** 217
Susanna **75** 181
Taylor **92** 42
Theron W. **107** 302
Thomas L. **115** 295
Thurston **66** 28
Tibbets **115** 295
Tildena Eudora **92** 42
Tucker **127** 14
Waite Smith **52** 41
Waity **92** 34
William **92** 34 35 **107** 57
    109 270 **115** 294 **128**
    134 **138** 285
William B. **116** 66
William H. **109** 267 270
    271 273 **116** 66
William Hall **92** 35 36 39
William Henry **92** 39 44
Willie J. **115** 295
Willis **76** 86
Wolcott **52** 41
Zadoc **145** 251
Zebulon **128** 134
Zorah **76** 86
NORTHUMBERLAND
— Earl of **52** 136 **136**
    102
Aldred (Earl of) **79** 371
Eadulf (Earl of) **79** 371
Gospatric (Earl of) **79** 371
    96 101
Osulf II (Earl of) **79** 371
Percy (Earl of) **55** 16
Percy Hugh (Duke and
    Earl of) **79** 325
Uchtred (Earl of) **79** 371
    372
Northup see Northrup
Northupp see Northrup
NORTHWAY —— **63** 230
Susanna **115** 262
Northy see Northey
NORTON Northon
    —— **51** 431 **52** 230 **53** 89
    379 **56** 344 **58** 284 **61** 99
    100 **65** 179 **66** 81 82 **90**
    60 **91** 170 **93** 23 **95** 43
    102 313 **104** 62 **116** 206
    118 304 **119** 45 127 132
    213 219 296 306 **121** 22
    68 113 207 **122** 65 **140**
    156 **141** 108 **143** 202
    145 250
— Capt. **119** 222 **120** 127
    133 205 206 304 **122** 66
    222 223
— Col. **52** 444 **59** 404
    141 14
— Mr. **52** 230 **53** 237 **57**
    322-324 **60** 202 **62** 18
    66 314 **79** 304 **91** 161
    95 103
— Mrs. **59** 265 **120** 133
    300 302 **121** 64 98 299
    122 116 117 122 308
— Rev. **111** 14
____ (Boardman) **132** 245
____ (Eliot) **140** 139
____ (Mills) **98** 94

NORTON cont'd
Aaron **54** 271 273-275 **59**
    306 400 **115** 295 **118**
    170
Abby P. (Porter) **121** 309
Abel **54** 275 **56** 157
Abiel Abbot **79** 159
Abigail **54** 270 271 273
    275 276 404 **59** 410 **64**
    249 **90** 281 **104** 60 **108**
    286 **109** 109 **115** 295
    148 181 182
Abigail (Green) **126** 66
Abigail (Orcutt) **86** 116
Abigail Jane **78** 361
Abijah **54** 274
Abisha **59** 306
Abner **52** 232 **66** 80
    145 357
Abraham **54** 271 **59** 205
Achsah **54** 273
Ada **54** 275 **58** 359 362
    116 133 134
Adaline **115** 292
Addie Perkins **74** 302
Addie S. **115** 295
Addison G. **120** 221 222
    123 72 149
Adeline Mary **74** 303
Albert B. **54** 451
Albion P. **121** 307
Alexander **54** 275 **60** 247
    61 285
Alexzena A. **121** 145
Alfred **80** 127
Alice Elvira **89** 316
Alice M. **123** 232
Alice W. **123** 232
Almira E. **121** 309
Alonzo **115** 295
Alvah R. **116** 207
Alvinia (Hillman)
    147 272
Ama **59** 298
Amanda (Miars) **91** 386
Amanda O. **121** 144 145
Amos **54** 275
Amy **59** 411
Andrew **54** 271 275 **58** 301
Andrews **81** 8 **93** 60 **129**
    362 **140** 139 143
Andrews (Mrs.) **92** 122
    93 320
Ann **51** 221 361 **54** 273 275
Ann Amelia **79** 154
Ann Frances **51** 197 **59**
    401 404 409
Anna **52** 233 **53** 91 **54**
    270-275 **55** 256 **58** 363
    59 62 **78** 303 **101** 88
    116 67 **117** 29 **121** 61
    122 117
Anna (Belknap) **129** 362
Anna E. **116** 64
Anna F. **123** 149
Anne **51** 309 **53** 87 88 91
    54 269 274 275 **59** 66 **98**
    94 **117** 29
Anne (Porter) **98** 94
Anne Bradstreet **52** 272
Anne Porter **98** 94

NORTON cont'd
Annie **77** 178 **93** 51
Annie E. (Treat) **83** 300
    302
Annis **59** 304
Ansel **145** 358
Arah **54** 272 **55** 258 **59** 65
Arden Lathrop **90** 97
Ariel **124** 7
Arixiene P. **105** 100
Arthur **91** 274
Arthur Blaisdell **92** 340
    341
Asahel **54** 271
Asenath **53** 91
Ashbel **54** 272 **59** 95
Asher **59** 61
Augusta **79** 153
Augusta A. **74** 303
Augustus Nathaniel
    82 507
Avis **53** 104
Azubah **54** 48 272 275
    56 161
Barna Cousins **53** 104
Bartlett **59** 204
Bayes / Baze **51** 198 **52** 232
    53 102 **59** 299 305 306
    404 411
Belinda **109** 36
Benjamin **52** 327 **53** 104
    315 **54** 48 272 275 **57** 91
    58 359 **59** 406 **61** 399
    68 82 **112** 47 **145** 358
Benjamin B. **91** 331
Benjamin H. **79** 153
Benjamin R. **85** 372
Beriah **51** 197 **53** 102 107
    54 271 **59** 300 401 402
    409
Bethiah **54** 272 **59** 66
Betsey **59** 202 **98** 94 **115**
    295 **116** 142
Beverly June
    (Underwood) **106** 228
Birdseye **54** 274
Bonus **85** 388
Bradbury **82** 507
Byron Thomas (Mrs.) **102**
    124 **103** 234
Cadelia F. (Jelleson)
    123 150
Caroline (Haley) **119** 67
    120 68
Carrie **132** 245
Cassandia **73** 150
Catherine **81** 8 **93** 60 **116**
    206 **119** 147
Catherine (Eliot) **92** 122
    93 320
Catherine Jane **93** 60
Chadbourn **82** 507
Charity **54** 272 274 275
    59 65
Charity Maria **82** 354
Charles **53** 88 **54** 276 **59**
    400 **76** 265 **79** 408 **81**
    250 **88** 349 **112** 49
Charles A. **92** 227 **116** 66
Charles Adams **110** 106
Charles E. **55** 376 **82** 507

NORTON *cont'd*
508 **83** 18 150 152
Charles E. (Mrs.) **83** 153
Charles Eliot **52** 483 **61**
214 **63** 110 113 **69** 293
294 **81** 8 **129** 362
Charles G. **86** 54
Charles M. **91** 331 **94** 373
Charles Oliver (Mrs.)
68 114
Charlotte A. **116** 117
120 137
Chauncey H. **101** 235
Chloe **58** 363 **98** 94
Chloe (Butler) **98** 94
106 213
Christianna N. (Shaw)
83 300 302
Clara (Brewster) **120** 223
225
Clarissa **54** 272 **66** 112
70 111
Clarissa (Adams) **123** 151
Clarissa (Sheldon) **124** 7
Clement Bassett **59** 200
Clyde **81** 250
Constantia **82** 507
Content **120** 118
Cordelia **120** 42
Cornelius **66** 81 **145** 358
Cotton **123** 152
Cyrus **58** 361
D. N. **83** 308
Daniel **54** 272 273 **57** 137
58 281 302 362 363 **59**
61 65 203 **66** 263 **76** 16
115 296 **116** 225 **119** 64
66 **122** 240 **123** 134
Daniel Russell **120** 118
Daniel W. **116** 66
Darius **90** 91
David **52** 232 **54** 81 178
271 274 275 **55** 308 **58**
301 302 361-363 **59** 61
64 299 300 **104** 57 62
108 280 285 **109** 15 109
122 192 **125** 40 **135** 159
Davis **108** 285
Deborah **51** 197 **52** 233
467 **54** 273 **74** 302 **82** 9
Deborah (Mayhew)
127 213
Delphine Elizabeth
(Rising) **85** 297
Dennis **54** 269 **59** 298
Desire **59** 306 410 **83** 508
106 71
Diadema **54** 272 **55** 258
59 65
Diana **59** 61 **122** 192
Diantha **54** 275
Dinah **54** 274 **59** 305
122 192
Dolly **59** 308 **82** 507
83 149 151
Dorcas **53** 87 **57** 273 **59**
304 404 **82** 507
Doris Vincent **124** 42
Dorothy **53** 87 **63** 172 **74**
258 **93** 23 **106** 228
E. B. **122** 111

NORTON *cont'd*
Eben **61** 29 30
Ebenezer **51** 197 **52** 231
233 **53** 87 **54** 270 273
274 **127** 213 **142** 60 **145**
352 358
Eber **54** 272 275 **58** 301
59 63
Ede (Clark) **126** 90
Edey **53** 91
Edith (White) **84** 185
Edith White **83** 216
Edmund **59** 304
Edna Celia **61** 274
Edward **67** 41 **76** 57 **93**
385 **112** 49 **116** 206 **122**
189 190
Edward E. **69** xxxii
Edward H. **121** 71 72
Edward Russell **90** 137
Edwin **82** 507 **98** 94
Elah **54** 275
Eleanor **93** 24
Eleanor (Knight) **131** 131
Eliakim **51** 192 **52** 370 **66**
80-82 **145** 353
Elias **53** 88 91
Elihu **54** 273
Elijah **54** 272 **57** 273 **58** 94
91 90 **105** 214 **115** 21 23
24 27 **120** 87 88 **145** 352
Elisha **54** 273 **93** 398 **100**
63 **128** 211
Eliza **54** 275 **61** 28 **66** 263
95 31 **98** 93 **108** 285
117 226 227
Eliza (Wilson) **117** 223
224
Eliza J. **116** 207
Elizabeth **51** 303 361 **52**
326 327 **53** 87 91 102
242-244 315 380 **54** 177
270-276 402 451 **57** 91
270 271 **58** 281 302 **59**
64 65 196 199 307 409
411 **61** 398 **67** 208 **71** 8
131 **72** 217 218 **74** 75 **79**
156 **81** 250 **82** 507 **85**
300 **91** 11 12 **98** 93 94
101 312 **104** 62 **108** 285
111 24 **116** 207 **120** 118
121 284 **134** 138
Elizabeth (Bennett) **137** 35
Elizabeth (Bradish)
125 289
Elizabeth (Galpin) **144** 49
Elizabeth (Gregson)
128 111
Elizabeth (McIan) **106** 228
Elizabeth (Sikes) **107** 111
Elizabeth (Thaxter) **134** 73
Elizabeth Ann **108** 306
120 216
Elizabeth Anna **108** 307
Elizabeth B. **137** 362
Elizabeth Gaskell **94** 139
Elizabeth H. **79** 408
Ellen **53** 87 **67** 41 **82** 171
Ellen Cogswell Wright
90 97

NORTON *cont'd*
Ellen Maria (Leavitt)
91 274
Elmira **104** 60
Elnathan **54** 275 **60** 399
Elon **54** 272 **58** 362
Elvira J. (Hillman)
147 272
Emeline (Frisbie) **83** 349
Emeline A. **76** 265
Emily **98** 94
Emily Ann **119** 225 229
276
Emma Louise **109** 308
Emme (Shepardson)
109 12
Enoch **52** 230 231 **59** 411
Enoch B. **116** 66
Ephraim **54** 275 **145** 352
Esther **54** 273 274
Esther (Merrill) **106** 228
Eugenia Eliza **83** 337
Eunice **53** 91 **54** 273 **61**
398 **63** 174 **84** 458 **115**
45
Eunice (Shepardson)
109 12 109
Eunice Averill **110** 106
Eunice Ophelia **78** 327
Eva Geneen **101** 125
Evelyn Polk **78** 327
Experience **54** 274 275
F. B. **91** 331
Faith **93** 24
Felix **54** 272 **59** 61 62 **70** 81
Florence Mary **81** 250
Florilla **62** 126
Florinda J. **113** 54
Frances **72** 61 **74** 145 **79**
408 **82** 507 **92** 340 **93** 23
Frances (Ramsdell) **123**
73 149
Frances Cogswell Wright
90 97
Francis **66** 80 81 **67** 208
76 317 **91** 11 12 71 72
93 23 24 **94** 66 **108** 33
131 19 131 **143** 28 34
Frank Porter **90** 97
Fred D. **116** 66
Fred Dunham **110** 106
Fred Lewis **66** lii **90** 127
92 92 151 **93** 183
Frederic Horace Grant
109 308
Frederick **53** 107
Frederick H. **95** 153
Frederick Rowland
78 327
Freegrace **54** 222 **71** 124
126 **148** 181 182
Gail Herbert **122** 195
Galen O. **104** 60
George **59** 302 **64** 92 **66**
263 **76** 46 **85** 297 **91** 11
12 **101** 46 285 **104** 60
108 285 **109** 245 246
111 24 **117** 223 224 **119**
61 **123** 263 **148** 181 182
George D. **109** 12 109
George L. **110** 106

NORTON *cont'd*

George W. **83** 300 302 **118** 321
Georgia **92** 340
Gertrude **86** 54
Gideon **53** 88 **77** 228
Giles **59** 62
Grace **51** 221 **52** 323 **54** 269
H. **116** 205
Hannah **52** 432 **53** 87 108 243 311 410 **54** 270-275 **58** 340 363 **59** 63 66 258 307 308 406 410 411 **63** 174 **66** 263 **67** 128 **70** 81 **74** 302 **76** 187 **78** 71 **79** 352 **82** 288 295 **88** 349 **105** 62 **107** 111 **116** 206 **122** 240 **126** 79 107 **147** 272
Hannah (Bolter) **133** 257
Hannah (Carver) **87** 6 **88** 328
Hannah (Staples) **116** 304
Hannah (Stover) **119** 68 69
Hannah (Younglove) **123** 263
Hannah E. (Goodwin) **121** 307
Hanson **147** 272-274
Harriet **59** 307 **98** 94 **104** 60 **121** 147
Harriet A. **86** 54
Harriet Cleveland **122** 190
Harriet Lincoln **86** 115 116
Harry H. **123** 151
Helen **93** 23
Helen Hinckley **74** 302
Helen M. **74** 302
Heman **79** 154
Henry **52** 231 **59** 409 **70** 203 **85** 300 **112** 49 **128** 111 **145** 352
Henry Barker **83** 349
Henry Bruce **78** 41
Henry Lot **106** 227 228
Henry Sidney **62** 50 **106** 228
Henry T. **88** 16
Hepzibah **51** 198 **52** 232 **59** 406 410 411 **91** 379
Herbert L. **122** 195
Hervy **59** 63
Hilyard **59** 302
Hooker **54** 272 **57** 138
Hope **59** 299 306
Howard **91** 274
Huldah **54** 271 275 **59** 304 307 308 **60** 247 **61** 285 **73** 15
Huldah Lavinia **72** 300
Humphrey **54** 60 **106** 27
I. **91** 331
Ida E. **123** 152
Imogene **84** 124
Ira **120** 40
Irvin (Mrs.) **77** 321 **78** 206
Isaac **52** 231 370 **53** 87 106

NORTON *cont'd*

130 **54** 273 451 **58** 363 **59** 205 307 410 411 **66** 22 **72** 218 **115** 295 **144** 49
Isabella (Parsons) **119** 64
Isabella F. **75** xxi **83** 217 349 **84** 193
Isabella M. **121** 39 309
Isaiah **54** 271
Ishi **54** 271 **57** 91
J. Albert **121** 308 **122** 152
J. B. **92** 341
Jabez **53** 104 **54** 274 **61** 399 **109** 36 **115** 298 **145** 363
Jacob **53** 91 **59** 199 **76** 248
James **53** 103 **54** 271 **59** 201 202 **62** 251 **100** 191
James A. **115** 295
James E. **116** 206
James Edward **90** 97
James Hatch **74** 302
James Safford **54** xxxix **67** xxxii
Jane **54** 356 **59** 410 **62** 122 **84** 214 **90** 181 **104** 60 **114** 180
Jane (Andrews) **129** 362
Jane (Reeve) (Reynolds) **131** 131
Jane B. (Berry) **88** 336
Jane L. **109** 111
Jarvis **62** 129
Jean **52** 233
Jedediah **54** 273 **80** 16 **135** 159
Jedidah **54** 272 **59** 204 207
Jefferson **84** 30
Jeffrey **106** 228
Jemima **59** 308 409
Jenks **141** 356 **142** 56-58 60
Jennie W. **123** 72
Jeremiah **53** 302
Jeremiah B. **92** 340 341 **94** 373 **119** 284
Jeremiah N. **120** 224
Jeremiah S. **74** 302
Jerusha **52** 233 **59** 306 409 **108** 285 **109** 12 109
Jerusha (Ford) **120** 40
Jerusha (Ware) **143** 14 16
Jesse **58** 94 **88** 328
Jesse Rowland **78** 327
Jethro **53** 102 **59** 299 407 410
Joan **91** 10-12
Joanna **54** 271
Job **53** 88 **54** 275 **59** 307 **98** 94
Joel **54** 273 275 **58** 359 **59** 61 **66** 79 **116** 304 305
John **51** 198 221 361 **52** 369 **53** 55 87 88 90 91 243 311 **54** 177 269-273 275 451 **55** 33 57 409 **58** 25 **59** 265 304 343 **61** 39 **62** 323 **63** 19 174 **64** 92 **70** 260 261 263 264 **72** 61 214 217 218 **73** 104 **74** 145 **75** 239 294 **82** 171 **83** 406 **90** 195 265 **92**

NORTON *cont'd*

184 **93** 23 **95** 40 44 100 102 103 206 207 **98** 94 **103** 11 **105** 287 **106** 228 259 266 **111** 130 **112** 42 217 **113** 54 **116** 223 294 **117** 29 **119** 147 **121** 114 202 204 288 **123** 260 **125** 289 **126** 90 **129** 362 **134** 73 **135** 87 **136** 148 **147** 272 **148** 133
John A. **115** 295 **141** 245
John B. **92** 34 **100** 260 **115** 296
John Buck **91** 142
John C. **111** 130
John F. **114** 207
John Finn **52** 272
John Foote **64** 229 332
John Homans **91** 274
John Neal **122** 190
John T. **79** 156 **80** 61
John Treadwell **79** 152
Jonathan **54** 275 410 **74** 302 **116** 206
Joseph **51** 198 **52** 369 467 **53** 130 **54** 270 271 273 451 **59** 205 298 305 406 410 **63** 265 **73** 104 **86** 395 **101** 312 **108** 285 **145** 352
Joshua **54** 451 **74** 302
Josiah **54** 273 **66** 37 **71** 131 **76** 187 **120** 223 225 **123** 151 **125** 36
Josiah N. **120** 224 **123** 232
Jotham P. **123** 153
Judah **52** 232 **59** 303
Judith **54** 269 **115** 28
Judith A. **148** 80
Julia **60** 333 **72** 275 **112** 49
Julia (Adams) **106** 228
Julia (Porter) **98** 94
Julia Ann (Maltby) **112** 49
Julia Frances (Ramsdell) **120** 221 222
Julian **98** 94
Julietta A. **58** 94
Juliette A. (Stover) **121** 71 72
Katharine **52** 262
Katharine Marie **52** 272
Katie J. (Vedder) **122** 195
Keziah **54** 271 **56** 262
L. G. **61** 399
L. M. **54** 269 270 274
Laforest **147** 272
Laurael **147** 272
Laurain **54** 275
Laurana Kimberley **52** 373
Lavina **59** 380
Lavinia (McDaniel) **119** 143
Lawrence Harper **74** 77 **75** xxvi **84** 173 **85** 190 **115** 228
Leah **54** 272
Lemuel **104** 61
Levi **54** 274 **145** 358
Lewis **54** 276

NORTON *cont'd*
Lewis Mills **52** 291 390
Lewis Rufus **63** 114
93 183
Lilla E. (Bowden) **123** 151
Lillian Adelaide **66** lii 92
81 238 **82** 237
Lois **54** 272 275
Lorenzo **122** 190
Lot **52** 232 **53** 103 **59** 303
304 **106** 228
Lottie Elouise **68** xxx
xxxv
Louisa **59** 259 **145** 313
Louisa P. (Talpey) **121**
308 **122** 152
Love **52** 368 **53** 106 **59**
198 262-264 378 379
Lucia **109** 129
Lucia Marie **100** 111
Lucinda **59** 63 **112** 49
122 192
Lucretia **54** 275
Lucy **53** 55 88 **54** 274 275
56 157 **58** 284 **59** 257
109 108 **113** 54 **122** 190
Lucy (Cleveland) **122** 189
Lucy (Hotchkiss) **58** 284
Lucy (Johnson) **111** 130
Lucy (Rathbone) **100** 9
Lucy (Wass) **128** 211
Lucy A. **109** 108
Lucy Alvina **104** 233
Lucy Ann (Bakeman)
109 12
Lucy Beardsley **115** 27
Lucy Cleveland **122** 190
Lucy Jane **109** 108
Lucy Martha (Todd)
106 228
Lucy Matilda **62** 50
Lucy Winthrop **52** 272
Luke **55** 435
Luther Calvin **74** 302
Luzernia **122** 111
Lydia **54** 271 273 274 **57** 91
59 197 304 308 402 **60**
247 **66** 263 **71** 126 **72**
275 **82** 329 507 **83** 149
86 395 **93** 323 **100** 191
119 229 **123** 262
Lydia (Boyce) **88** 16
Lydia (Fowler) **115** 28
Lydia Esther **92** 188
Lydia Maria **55** 376 **83** 17
149 151
Lyman **54** 276 **115** 296
Mabel **54** 272 **61** 29
Mabel Florence (Jeffrey)
106 228
Malinda **116** 206
Manely **104** 62
Marana **54** 274
Marella **53** 88
Margaret **54** 274 **82** 171
85 300 **90** 60 **93** 19 23
24 36 37
Margaret (Hellyar) **93** 23
Margaret W. **77** 150
108 285
Margery **63** 170 173 175

NORTON *cont'd*
Margit Ann **115** 295
Maria **76** 265 **82** 507 **116**
302 303
Maria (Shepardson)
110 106
Maria Julia (Elliot) **89** 316
Mariam **90** 387
Mariam N. **123** 152
Marian Pease **111** 311
Marion Vedder **122** 195
Marjorie (Coler) **106** 228
Martha **54** 272-275 **59** 305
410 411 **61** 399 **115** 295
126 127 128
Martha A. (Adams) **121**
308 **122** 152
Martha W. (Brewer)
96 161
Mary **51** 197 198 221 **52**
370 **53** 87 88 130 402 **54**
134 269-275 **55** 33 58
362 363 **59** 62 207 208
304 306 307 343 401 409-
411 **60** 22 **63** 174 **67** 208
72 223 75 239 **78** 206
79 408 **82** 507 **83** 340
86 54 **90** 91 **91** 11 12 **98**
80 **100** 312 **104** 38 61
112 217 **116** 206 298
119 118 147 **121** 281
125 244 **128** 211 **137** 35
145 352 **148** 182
Mary (Bayes) **86** 395
101 312
Mary (Daggett) **106** 71
Mary (Hickok) **106** 228
Mary (Houghton)
(Phillips) **131** 131
Mary (Junkins) **119** 61
Mary (Lawrence) **125** 222
Mary (Mason) **121** 202
Mary (Porter) **119** 118
Mary (Williams) **122** 189
Mary A. **55** 376 **83** 18
Mary A. (Averill) **120** 307
Mary Ann **82** 507
Mary Ann (Cogswell)
82 508 **83** 18
Mary C. **74** 203 **92** 172
Mary E. **92** 340 **93** 334 **94**
373 **116** 67 **120** 221 **121**
306
Mary E. (Goodale) **92** 341
119 284
Mary E. (Norton) **121** 306
Mary Ella **94** 373
Mary H. **79** 152
Mary Hart **110** 106
Mary J. **83** 20
Mary J. (Shackford) **83** 19
Mary L. **120** 136
Matthew **51** 198 **52** 370
59 300 306 307 406 **106**
71
Maxwell Z. **61** 274
Mayhew **59** 258 **66** 81 82
Medad **54** 276
Mehitable **53** 278 **54** 273
59 400 409 **104** 57 61
127 213

NORTON *cont'd*
Mercy **53** 106 **54** 272 **59**
410 411 **101** 285
Mercy (Barber) **148** 181
Mercy (Barber) (Gillett)
101 46
Mercy Rust **74** 230
Merit Milton **115** 23
Merriell **74** 230
Miles **54** 273 274
Mindwell **54** 271 276
Minerva (Smedley) **98** 94
Minton **143** 262
Miranda **61** 285
Miriam **53** 163 411 **54** 275
59 207 **79** 258
Miriam (Winn) **119** 144
Miriam L. (Chase) **121** 71
123 234
Molly **54** 274 **59** 407
Montgomery **59** 63
Moody **104** 62 **108** 285
Moses **54** 275
Nancy (Gay) **90** 91
Nancy S. **119** 287 **121** 303
Naomi **54** 271
Nathan **54** 271 **73** 71
123 121
Nathaniel **54** 274 **64** 222
72 275 **73** 104 **74** 213
230 **82** 329 **88** 349 **126**
217
Nathaniel Reed **86** 198
Nettie M. **123** 74
Nicholas **53** 103 **59** 301
410 411 **61** 399 **64** 92 **66**
92
Noadiah **54** 275 **59** 47 61
60 333
Noah **54** 271 274 275 **59**
203 **104** 57 **105** 210 **108**
285
Obed **52** 232 **53** 105 **59** 409
Olive **54** 274 276 **114** 230
116 305
Olive J. **120** 69
Olive Jane (Hutchins)
118 321
Oliver **54** 275 **59** 307 **66**
265 **118** 240 242 **119** 68
69
Oliver E. **52** 272
Oliver J. **94** 116
Olivia S. **115** 296
Oraville A. **123** 150
Oren A. **121** 306
Orlando **89** 316
Orrin **123** 150
Ozias **53** 410 **54** 276 **58** 361
Parnel **54** 272 **59** 63
Patience **59** 207 299 306
Patty **54** 274
Peggy **59** 298
Peleg **59** 404
Percy Hawes **122** 195
Perkins **88** 336
Peter **53** 107 **59** 299 304
305 308 **66** 80 **100** 191
145 351 352
Phebe **54** 272-275 **59** 65
72 282 **76** 16 **142** 58

NORTON *cont'd*
Philemon **54** 271
Philip **54** 348
Philippa **74** 274 **75** 137
Phineas **54** 273 **59** 207 306
  86 116 **104** 60 62 133
Pluma E. **116** 66
Plummer D. **83** 302 **84** 30
Polly **53** 102 **58** 302 **59**
  201 258 260 262-264 378
  104 61 **115** 23 24 27 **126**
  217 **142** 57
Polly B. **59** 260
Prince **53** 106 **59** 300 304
Prudence **54** 273
Rachel **54** 272 274 275 **55**
  258 **58** 300 **63** 185 **67**
  131 **139** 237
Rachel (Starr) **91** 287
Ralph **104** 145 **106** 222
  227 228 **107** 137
Ralph Tolles **90** 97
Ransom **59** 197 257
Rebecca **53** 88 **54** 271 273
  59 195 200 304 **88** 349
Rebecca P. **74** 302 **104** 61
Reuben **54** 272 **58** 363
  111 117
Rhoda **54** 273 275 **61** 285
Richard **52** 262 **53** 87 **59**
  407 **72** 275 **74** 274 **75**
  137 **91** 10-12 **101** 88 269
Richard (Mrs.) **115** 146
Robert **53** 103 **62** 321 **73**
  263 **86** 417 418 **89** 339
  91 10-12 14 **119** 143
Roger **53** 88
Rowland **115** 28
Rufus **58** 302 362 **59** 63
  121 309
Ruth **53** 87 88 130 **54** 271
  273 275 **59** 63 65 201
  208 410 **60** 304 **71** 112
  72 217 **73** 6 **92** 341 **136**
  308
Ruth (Moore) **106** 228
S. **116** 205
Sabrina **54** 273
Sally **108** 285 **133** 306 309
Sally (Freeman) **117** 227
Sally (Matthews) **119** 147
Sally (Pease) **111** 311
Sally (Pelton) **109** 36
Sally Ann (Van Valken-
  burgh) **92** 172
Sally W. (Bragdon)
  120 138
Sam (Mrs.) **120** 209
Samuel **53** 87 104 **54** 270
  271 273 274 **55** 308 **57**
  265 270 **58** 300 357 **59**
  196 199 200 202 207 302
  382 383 401 409 **61** 77
  398 **63** 173 174 **66** 310
  70 264 **83** 53 105 205
  116 294 **119** 118 144
  129 362
Samuel M. **119** 67 **120** 68
Samuel W. **94** 116 **120** 138
Sarah **53** 87 88 **54** 222 271-
  275 **57** 137 328 **58** 302

NORTON *cont'd*
  357 362 363 **59** 47 61 67
  205 299 308 410 **61** 391
  72 218 **73** 135 **76** 187
  248 **88** 326 **102** 70 **115**
  221 **119** 67 **136** 319 **142**
  248
Sarah (Martin) **148** 181
Sarah (Sherbourne)
  123 232
Sarah (Stockbridge)
  (Silvester) **85** 362 **86** 92
  134 73
Sarah (Street) **141** 259 260
Sarah (Walden) **125** 242
Sarah A. **115** 295
Sarah Adams **55** 375 **82**
  507 **83** 17
Sarah Agnes **74** 302
Sarah Ann (Moody)
  147 272
Sarah Foster **74** 302
Sarah H. **123** 153
Sarah M. (Sherborn)
  120 224
Sarah W. **94** 116
Seba (Elder) **132** 188
Selah **98** 94 **106** 213
Seth **62** 277 **93** 183 **104** 60
  109 12 108 199 **116** 111
Shubael **54** 169 **59** 262-
  264 299 302 305 378 379
  400 **104** 61
Sibyl **54** 272 274 **57** 138
  80 16
Sidney Jeffrey **106** 228
Silas **61** 28
Simeon **54** 271 **58** 362 363
  59 62 63 **60** 22
Simon **111** 311
Solomon **116** 206
Solon F. **74** 302
Sophia **119** 287
Sophia (Wilson) **116** 304
  305
Sophia M. **86** 54
Sophronia **104** 62 **116** 206
Sophronia L. **108** 285
Stanley **54** 272
Stebbins **59** 63
Stella **76** 16
Stephen **54** 275 276 **59** 206
  86 54 **145** 353
Submit **54** 178 271 **58**
  361-363 **59** 61 64 65 **96**
  384
Sullivan Sedgwick
  115 24
Susan **84** 172 **85** 197 **100**
  191 **122** 189 190
Susan P. (Weare) **118**
  240 242
Susan Stover **74** 302
Susanna **51** 192 **54** 81 **59**
  197 257 **63** 265 **66** 265
  98 94 **122** 190
Susanna (Olmsted) **98** 94
Suza **54** 271 **58** 362
Sylvania Helen **147** 272
Sylvanus **53** 105 **54** 273
  59 206

NORTON *cont'd*
Sylvester **59** 197
Sylvia **54** 275
T. B. **91** 331
Tappen **53** 411
Temperance **60** lii
  63 170 175
Thankful **53** 88 **54** 271
  56 91 **59** 307 **66** 309 310
Theodosia **119** 225
Thomas **51** 221 399 **52**
  262 323 **53** 87 208 **54**
  269-276 451 **58** 300 340
  59 259 380 400 411 **62**
  147 **74** 75 **78** 402 **91** 11
  12 93 **93** 13 19 23 24 35-
  37 41 **100** 191 **106** 228
  107 47 111 **108** 285 **117**
  227 **125** 30 **147** 173
Thomas Fred **62** 251
Thomas Herbert **76** 159
Thomas Martin **59** 303
  122 189 190
Timothy **52** 231 369 **53**
  105 **54** 272 **59** 64 204
  207 411
Timothy Cutlon **82** 507
Tristram **59** 204 260 410
  145 357
Tristram Warren **122** 190
Truman **115** 295
Tryal **54** 271 **57** 265
Uriah **105** 205
Viona (Branscom) **85** 372
Walter **54** 356 **74** 302 **90**
  181 **91** 10-13 **93** 360 361
  107 47 **131** 131
Walter Whittlesey
  64 xxxi 92
Wilber F. **121** 308 **122** 152
Wilbur Harrington (Mrs.)
  101 125
William **51** 221 **52** 231 373
  53 106 **54** 269 271 275
  55 308 415 **59** 200 203
  205 258 262-264 301 304
  307 308 378 400 411 **67**
  269 **83** 36 **85** 362 **86** 54
  92 **91** 10-12 331 **98** 94
  100 9 **104** 187 **115** 308
  116 304 **121** 11 **125** 222
  134 73 **137** 35 **139** 129
  145 163
William A. **77** 150 **120** 307
  123 74
William Anderson (Mrs.)
  96 161
William D. **116** 66
William H. **83** 20 **121** 71
  123 234
William O. **92** 188
William S. **125** 242
William Shepard **52** 272
William Upton **122** 240
William Wallis **147** 272
Winefred F. **123** 234
Winslow **91** 386
Winthrop **79** 352
Winthrop B. **63** 172 **82**
  507 **83** 149 151

NORTON *cont'd*
  Winthrop Benjamin
    74 258
  Zachariah **53** 106 **145** 352
  Zadock **59** 406
  Zebul **58** 363
  Zebulon **54** 271
  Zerviah **54** 272
  Ziba **58** 362
  Zina **59** 62
  Zipporah **54** 273
Nortridge *see* Northridge
NORTRUGS
  Agnes **67** 249
NORTWYCK
  Blandine von **135** 74
NORWARD Bathsheba
    (Greenleaf) **125** 103
  John **125** 103
NORWELL Norwel
  Helen Hunter **88** 170
  Patience **74** 263
NORWICH
  Elizabeth **64** 54
  Henry **141** 116
  Joan **64** 53
  Margaret (Warde) **141**
    115 116
  Richard **64** 54
  William (Bishop of) **96** 38
NORWOOD —— **55** 215
    62 387 **70** 264 **95** 265
    102 74
  —— (Sheafe) **137** 292
  Abby Maria **94** 295
  Abigail **94** 42 **101** 32
    110 132
  Abigail (Brooks) **124** 319
  Abigail (Eames) **145** 38
  Abigail Harding **144** 328
    145 37 38
  Adeline A. **51** 79
  Agnes **78** 151
  Alice **52** 424 **73** 287 **111**
    254 **142** 249
  Alice (Donnell) **109** 300
  Aljava C. (Carver) **85** 380
  Almeda **120** 67 69
  Almeda (Parsons) **93** 295
    119 225 226
  Ann Mary (Parsons)
    119 143
  Anna **117** 319
  Anne **114** 155
  Annie J. **123** 232
  Atheldirst **79** 246
  Awderie **101** 244
  Betsey **62** 155
  Caleb **109** 300
  Candace **117** 319
  Charles **93** 295 **119** 225
    226
  David **61** 167
  Diana **73** 284 291
  Ebenezer **145** 38
  Eliza (Pierce) **123** 232
  Eliza Alves **92** 190
  Elizabeth **61** 167 **73** 239 **75**
    140 **109** 300
  Elizabeth (Coldam) **125**
    24 27

NORWOOD *cont'd*
  Elizabeth Russell **145** 38
  Ellen L. (Scofield) **93** 295
  Emery H. **85** 377
  Emily J. **85** 378
  Francis **51** 79 **117** 319
    123 80 **125** 24 27
  Francis R. **93** 295
  George **75** 140
  George Macy **89** 14
    145 38
  Gustavus **111** 254 **114** 134
  Helen E. **120** 304 305
    123 153
  Henry D. **93** 295 **119** 143
  Ida F. **97** 217
  Israel M. **85** 373
  Jemima **93** 295
  Jemima (Donnell) **93** 295
  Jerusha **124** 319
  Job **101** 244
  John **101** 244
  John E. **93** 295
  John Edward **93** 295
  John Greene **145** 38
  Jonathan **126** 225
  Joshua **137** 141
  Joshua D. **91** 331
  Julia (Lazell) **89** 14 **145** 38
  Lemuel S. **85** 374
  Louisa **62** 155
  Lucy E. **93** 295 **121** 309
  Lulu M. **131** 93 94
  Margaret **73** 143
  Marietta **64** 211
  Martha A. (Reed) **85** 377
  Mary **51** 79
  Mary (Milberry) **111** 254
  Mary J. **93** 295
  Mary Jane **93** 295 **119** 61
    62
  Mary Russell (Callender)
    89 14 **140** 48 **145** 34 38
  Matilda **117** 319
  Melissa (Otis) **85** 377
  Micajah **117** 319
  Mildrid A. (Gott) **85** 374
  Moses **124** 319
  Nancy (Rhoades) **116** 255
  Nathaniel **93** 295 **116** 139
  Richard **78** 151 **101** 244
  Robie M. **85** 380
  Ruth **73** 281 290
  Samuel **89** 14 **93** 295 **111**
    254 **115** 142 **140** 48 49
    145 34 38
  Samuel Smith **145** 38
  Sarah **82** 285 295 **111** 254
    117 319
  Sarah (Knight) **102** 74
  Sarah J. (Ellis) **85** 379
  Setira J. M. (Richardson)
    85 373
  Stephen **73** 282
  Thomas **125** 27
  William **62** 155 **70** 264
    116 255
  William A. **85** 379
  William D. **93** 295 **123** 232
  William G. **85** 377
  Zaccheus **97** 44

NORWOOD *cont'd*
  Zecheiell **69** 254
NOSSITER Rebecca Mayer
    132 121
NOSTRAND *see also*
    Van Ostrand
  Cornelia **110** 131
  Cornelius **110** 131
  John **110** 131
NOSTRAS Jann **71** 126
  Michael **71** 126
Notage *see* Nottage
NOTBEAM —— **141** 97
NOTCHELL Notchel
  — Mr. **92** 11
  Johanna Sophia **92** 11
  Nicholas **127** 139
NOTCLIFFE
  William **110** 274
NOTEWARE
  Frederick **107** 298
  Hannah **76** 177
  Harriet (Barton) **107** 298
  Nelson **76** 177
Notingham *see*
    Nottingham
NOTLEY
  Elizabeth **73** 267
  Peter **62** 323
NOTMAN Arthur Lane
    (Mrs.) **84** 447
  Rosalind (Morse) **84** 447
  Winifred **98** 147
NOTON Notton
  Cyrus **65** 364
  Hitty **61** 238
  J. **121** 93
  Rice **61** 334
NOTT Nots
  —— **91** 285
  — Mr. **60** 263
  — Rev. Dr. **86** 378
  Abernethy **80** 45
  Abigail **86** 383
  Abigail (Gibbs) (Dix)
    143 308 317
  Agnes A. **133** 230
  Ann (Parmalee) **106** 149
  Ann Augusta **133** 230
  Anne **61** 178 **142** 334 336
    340 **143** 313
  Chloe (Spencer) **133** 230
  Chloe Lucinda **133** 230
  Deborah **70** 241 **86** 383
  Diodate **86** 383
  Edmund **51** 259
  Eliphalet **77** lxvii
  Frances (Hopkins)
    104 220
  George W. **104** 220
  Gershom **104** 191 **105** 325
    108 37 **111** 221
  Guy Spencer **133** 230
  Hannah **57** 92 **61** 177 178
  Harriet (Child) **133** 230
  Harriet L. **133** 230
  Harriet Newell **86** 383
  Irene Ward **80** 45
  John **61** 178 **89** 175 **106**
    149 **142** 336 340 **143**
    313

NOTT *cont'd*
Joseph P. **133** 230
L. P. **106** 305
Laura **80** 45
Louisa F. **133** 230
Lucretia **86** 383
Mehitable **61** 392 **111** 221
Olive **91** 283
Patience (Miller) **142** 336
143 313
Peninah **106** 149
Phebe Marie **133** 230
Richard **91** 15 283
Roxana **86** 383
Samuel **86** 383 388
Sarah (Waterhouse)
104 191
Sarah M. **86** 383
Simeon **133** 230
Simeon M. **133** 230
Sophronia **133** 230
Stephen **70** 241 **86** 383
Stephen T. **86** 383
Thaddeus **133** 230
Thankful **143** 307 313 315
William **55** 101 **143** 317
NOTTAGE Notage Nuttage
—— **101** 247
— Mr. **65** 368
Abigail **78** 315
Catherine **55** 148
Elizabeth **140** 231
Elizabeth (Chandler)
125 214
Emma Janett (Cheney) **83**
233 **87** 172 **98** 178 179
George L. **125** 292
Henry Bailey **63** 114
Joseph **78** 407
Josiah **78** 412 **140** 231
Josias **100** 242
Louis Millard **98** 179
Louis Millard (Mrs.) **98**
138 178 179 **99** 145 150
Mabel Eloise **92** 364
Marion Mildred **98** 179
99 145
Mary **78** 178
Nancy **125** 222
Nathaniel **125** 214 **140**
231 326
Olle **77** 228
Sally **77** 235 **79** 44
Sally (Savels) **140** 231
Sally S. (Stevens) **125** 292
Sarah **55** 148 **65** 219
100 295
Sarah (Ranger) **100** 242
NOTTINGHAM Notingham
——— (Gurdon) **94** 369
Gervase de **80** 379
Ralph de **96** 109 112
Richard **70** 338 **74** 271
Notton *see* Noton
NOTYERE Robert **109** 23
NOUGHTOP
Electa T. **70** 93
NOUGUIER
Anthony **144** 19
Jane **144** 19

NOUGUIER *cont'd*
Sarah (Sherwood)
(Wheeler) (Fayer-
weather) **144** 20 334
NOULDING Ama **61** 90
Betsey **61** 193
Dudley **61** 195
Elizabeth **60** 381 **61** 85 86
90 193 195 **62** 87 88
Fanny **61** 193
Honor **61** 90
Lorana **62** 87
Lorania **61** 85
Mary **60** 381
Noah **61** 103
Samuel **60** 381 **61** 85 86
90 193 195 **62** 87 88
NOURSE Nurse
—— **58** 204
— Dr. **51** 130
— Mr. **53** 367
— Mrs. **56** 389
Abigail **62** 60 **64** 152
Addie Mable **133** 235
Anne **76** 211
Annie Endicott **83** 217
84 190
Annie Thorndike **69** 294
Annie Thorndike (Rand)
95 362 363
Annis **55** 61
Asa **119** 39 313
Benjamin **61** 167 **64** 152
73 116 **92** 388 **125** 105
126 7 **133** 73 235
Benjamin F. **76** 50 53
Benjamin Read **58** 56
Billy **62** 54
Byron Heywood
70 xxxvii
Chauncy **117** 264
Clara Ann **92** 388
Crucy **117** 265
Cynthia **119** 313
Cynthia (Bourne) **119** 39
313
Daniel **55** 59 **58** 56
David **55** 61 63 **56** 259
Ebenezer **62** 37 **85** 321
Elizabeth **56** 410 **59** 221 **61**
156 **79** 154 **94** 82 83 **117**
271 **120** 12 **144** 170
Elizabeth (Sawtell)
(Morse) **126** 7
Elsie Thorndike **85** 322
Emma F. (Watkins)
133 235
Eunice **58** 204
Florence **102** 145
Francis **56** 410 **58** 217 **59**
41 **61** 71 332 338 **84** 404
85 321 **128** 160
Francis Walkup **117** 265
Frederick Russell **85** 321
322
Gertrude Maria **70** xxxvii
Grata **55** 65
H. S. **111** 158
Helen Lucy **89** 132
Henry F. **143** 330
Henry S. **54** 149 **57** li **58**

NOURSE *cont'd*
130 **61** 341 **78** 423 **93**
260 **120** 162 163 167
147 112
Henry Stedman **53** 92
186 289 374 378 **57** 422
58 xlv 217 218 **59** 229 **64**
332 **65** 11 12 17 282 **69**
189 **141** 22
James **58** 56 **59** 221
Jane P. **114** 146 147
Jerusha Bruce **117** 264
John **70** 69 **118** 131 **140** 30
John Frederick **69** 294
85 321 322 **95** 363
John K. **79** 154
Jonathan **58** 54 56 57
62 60
Joseph **65** 220
Joshua **133** 73
Julius Augustus **117** 265
Lizzie A. **58** 218
Lucius **117** 265
Lucy **55** 61 63 **56** 259
114 274
Lydia **55** 61 **56** 258
Marcia B. **141** 249
Marcia Baldwin **63** 208
Maria Treat **70** xxxvii
Martha **58** 57 **117** 240 271-
273
Mary **58** 218 **61** 71 **133** 73
Mary (Fedrick) **125** 105
Mercy **64** 152
Nathan **78** 181
Patty **56** 257 **58** 217
Peter **55** 59 61 65 **56** 257
Philip **55** 61 62
Rebecca **56** 410 **58** 217 **59**
41 **61** 71 156 **70** 66 68
81 456 **117** 319 **128** 160
Rebecca (Nurse) **128** 160
Rebecca (Towne) **84** 404
144 170
Reuben **117** 264 265
Rufus **85** 322
Ruth **61** 167
Sally **110** 160
Samuel **55** 59 **58** 204 **70** 69
85 321
Sarah **57** 309 **76** 50 53
Sarah (Tarbell) **128** 160
Stedman **58** 217
Stephen **85** 322
Tameson **114** 171 174
Thankful **57** 192
Thomas W. **117** 264
Vashti H. **140** 132
William **58** 54
NOUS Thomas **143** 202
NOVAK
R. L. (Mrs.) **117** 318
NOVEY Novy
Marguerite Felice **109** 130
Mary **83** 16
Mary (Lord) **83** 16
Temple **83** 16
NOWELL Nowel Nowill
—— **83** 194 **96** 381 **99** 230
106 15 32 **121** 105
— Mrs. **85** 120

NOWELL *cont'd*
Abigail **97** 142
Abraham **109** 303 **111** 232 **114** 129
Alexander **137** 77
Alfred Increase **57** lxvii
Alice P. **57** lxvii
Amy **82** 290 295
Ann Allen **83** 174 194
Ann Isobel **117** 207
Anna **119** 64
Anna (Preble) **117** 143
Anstross **148** 178
Anthony **83** 194
Anthony F. **83** 174 194
Bethiah **116** 136
Bethiah (Leavett) **115** 306
Betsey **59** 107 **65** 257 **74** 260 264
Betsey A. **120** 69
Betsey Ann **95** 273
Bradford L. **121** 307 **122** 150
Celeste Amanda **120** 223
Charles **57** lxvii **102** 94
Daniel **116** 135 **117** 222 **118** 154 155 **142** 387
Daniel Weare **115** 216
Delia **148** 177
Delia Frances **148** 177
Ebenezer **74** 259 **97** 265 **109** 303 **112** 23 218 **113** 126 **114** 132 **116** 128
Edward G. **57** lxvii
Effie Alexander **57** lxvii
Eleanor **117** 228 229
Eleanor (Junkins) **115** 216
Eliza **65** 257 **102** 70
Elizabeth **51** 398 399 **65** 257 **112** 306 **115** 140 **148** 127
Elizabeth (Eavans) **100** 297
Elizabeth (Leavitt) **115** 60
Emily A. **57** lxvii
Esther **89** 382 **109** 303 **111** 233 **114** 227 **115** 135
Eunice **59** 107
Eunice (Kingsbury) **118** 154 155
Eunice E. **120** 309
Fanny **142** 387
Frances Catherine **83** 174 194
Frances F. **84** 31
Frank **83** 174
Frank Leland **118** 166
Frederick W. **84** 31
George **57** xlii lxvi lxvii **71** 92 **77** 314 **140** 231 327
Georgiana Mason **57** lxvii
Grace G. **57** lxvii
Grant William **57** lxvii
Hannah **112** 23 218 **113** 129 **115** 65 **116** 225 294 **118** 317 **119** 146
Hannah (Came) **111** 233

NOWELL *cont'd*
113 129
Harriet A. **120** 139 215 **123** 152 153
Harriet Augusta **92** 77
Harriet P. (Hill) **83** 299 300
Henrietta M. L. **57** lxvii
Herbert W. **83** 299 300
Humility **115** 214
Humility (Preble) **111** 232 **114** 129
Increase **53** 60 61 **65** 269 **67** 200 **68** 179 195 372 **89** 173 **97** 307 **99** 229 **100** 218 **106** 15 16 **123** 34 **124** 90 **129** 353 **131** 10-12 19 131 **137** 77 **138** 41 **148** 127
Isabella G. **57** lxvii
James **61** 358 **73** 223 **97** 265 270 **112** 305 **115** 306 **116** 139 299 302
James H. **123** 234
Jane **97** 267
Jane (Towne) **108** 191
Jane Pepperell (Frost) **112** 306
Jeremiah **116** 300 301 **148** 178
Joanna **116** 225
Joanna R. **57** lxvii
Joel **119** 67 283 284
John **51** 398 **52** 228 **78** 309 **84** 153 **90** 230 **109** 302 **111** 20 **112** 306 **114** 49 **115** 60 213 **116** 135 296 **120** 219 **148** 127 171
Jonathan **65** 79 112 254 256 261-264 334 335 339 **112** 23 **115** 141
Joseph **51** 462 **100** 235 238 **111** 21 **112** 305 **115** 308 **117** 143
Jotham **112** 305 **117** 229 230
Jotham M. **93** 294 **119** 65 66
Katharine **51** 398 **82** 289 295
Laura **57** lxvii
Laura M. (Leavitt) **121** 307 **122** 150
Lavina **65** 257
Lizzie (Langley) **83** 299 300
Locadias **95** 378
Louisa **117** 222
Lucy **115** 215
Lydia **57** lxvii **65** 257 **115** 219 **116** 133 221 306
Lydia (Junkins) **111** 94 **114** 50
Margaret **142** 387
Margery G. **116** 142
Mark **59** 107 **65** 257 **92** 77
Martha **51** 464 **57** lxvii **68** 301 **115** 225 **119** 62
Mary **51** 462 **52** 228 **57** lxvi lxvii **61** 358 **65** 353 **92** 106 **95** 269 **97** 145

NOWELL *cont'd*
265 **100** 235 238 **104** 38 **109** 302 **111** 94 97 98 **112** 23 107 **113** 126 **114** 46 **115** 58 60 64 **116** 226 296 **117** 140 228 230 **119** 224 **123** 74 **142** 387
Mary (Carr) **137** 77
Mary (Hoppin) **137** 77
Mary (Nutting) **111** 98
Mary (Preble) **114** 50
Mary (Thompson) **112** 305
Mary (Usher) **86** 349
Mary (York) **137** 77
Mary A. (Moody) **120** 68 **123** 234
Mary B. **126** 66
Mary Eliza Roberts **118** 166
Mary Frances **95** 249
Mary G. **116** 136
Mary Waldo **84** 99
Mehitable **124** 90
Mercy **112** 305 **115** 136 **119** 67
Mercy (Nowell) **119** 67
Mercy (Teal) **119** 65 66
Mercy A. **119** 288
Michael **106** 26
Milbury **148** 177
Molly **61** 358
Moses **82** 289 295
Nancy **59** 107 **117** 224
Nathaniel **95** 273 **111** 232 **116** 222
Olive **111** 233 **113** 129
Olive (Littlefield) **90** 230
Oliver **59** 107 **97** 144
Parnell (Gray) (Parker) **106** 16 **131** 11 131 **138** 41
Patience **74** 259 **111** 233 **115** 136 219
Patience (Hamilton) **112** 23
Patience (Kingsbury) **116** 225
Paul **82** 290 295 **109** 303 **111** 98
Peter **57** lxvi lxvii **59** 107 **109** 302 **110** 95 283 **111** 94 97 **112** 107 305 **113** 129 **114** 50 **115** 63 214 **116** 225
Polly **140** 156 157
Polly (Bennett) **117** 222
Rachel **74** 259
Rachel (Linkorn) **115** 135
Rebecca **117** 229 **120** 219
Rebecca (Nowell) **120** 219
Reuben **91** 331
Rhoda (Allen) **95** 273
Robert **56** 86
Rosanna **120** 221 222
Rose **82** 434
Sally **65** 257 **116** 300 301 **140** 251
Sally (Junkins) **116** 299 302
Sally (Nowell) **116** 300

NOWELL *cont'd*
301
Samuel **56** 242 **59** 107 **86**
  349 350 **99** 103 **100** 235
  238 **111** 232 **116** 139
Samuel G. **78** 302
Samuel Johnson **83** 174
Samuel York **137** 77
Sarah **57** lxvii **68** 301 **73**
  218 **78** 67 **100** 299 **109**
  302 **110** 95 283 **111** 20
  115 137 **119** 65 **125** 301
Sarah (Gray) **115** 63
Sarah (Weare) **109** 302
Sarah A. **120** 139 **123** 232
Sarah Elizabeth (Junkins)
  119 283 284
Shadrach **57** lxvi lxvii
  97 266 **115** 215
Silas **51** 464 **59** 107 **74** 191
  109 303 **111** 233 **113**
  129 **114** 133 **115** 135
  120 68 **123** 234 **125** 41
Simon **108** 191
Susan **118** 318
Susanna **115** 212
Tabitha **55** 312 **74** 261 **82**
  509 **111** 20 **114** 290 **115**
  63
Tabitha (Came) **111** 20
  114 49
Theodore **97** 268 **112** 305
  116 133
Theodosia (Smith) **117**
  229 230
Thomas **57** 208 **101** 246
  111 20 21 **115** 140
W. H. **91** 331
Will **100** 297
William **68** 301
William G. **83** 299 300
William Gray **83** 174
William Harrison
  148 178
Winslow Warren **83** 174
Zachariah **93** 398 **100** 63
  137 77 **142** 387
NOWERS
Edward H. (Mrs.)
  75 316
Nowill *see* Nowell
NOWLAN Daniel **66** 306
Eliza **94** 247
James **94** 247
Jathniel S. **94** 247
John **94** 247 **118** 50
Katharine **94** 247
Maldreth **94** 247
Margaret **61** 134 **92** 228
NOWLAND Elizabeth **60**
  379 380 382 **62** 86 88
James **63** 17
Joshua **60** 380
Lorana **60** 382
Samuel **60** 379 380 382
  62 86 88
NOWLIN
Ama Lana **118** 165
Mary **101** 257
Mary Bacon **101** 257

NOXON Noxen
Anna (Ruggles) **84** 442
Annis B. **127** 249
John **73** 104
Laura Ann **84** 442 **112** 150
Richard **65** 117
Robert **84** 442
NOYES Noise   Noyce
—— **53** 35 36 41 **57** 336
  420 **58** 101 338 **59** xxx
  61 258 **79** 18 **92** 272 276
  347 **120** 205 **147** 282
— Dr. **54** 184
— Mr. **51** 359 **57** 242 378
  71 51
— Widow **84** 152
Aaron **73** 168
Abby **74** 30
Abby Sill **77** 207
Abby Smith **55** 199
Abel **114** 270 **115** 25 109
Abial **73** 168
Abiel **73** 96 167
Abigail **53** 36 37 348 **55**
  197 198 **60** lxii **75** 89
  80 115 **99** 298
Abigail (Hayden) **114** 270
Abigail Read **53** 41
Abigail Reed (Lovejoy)
  61 381
Abram **73** 169
Addie **133** 47
Alan **92** 178 179
Albert **133** 47
Allen **74** 30
Allen Samuel **53** 40
Almira **53** 40 **72** 84
Almirce C. (Follansbee)
  114 270
Alonzo B. **76** 50
Amelia **53** 39
Amos **54** 315
Amos Jewett **55** 198
Andrew **114** 270
Ann **55** 197 **73** 169 **80** 176
  177 **98** 189
Anna **53** 163 **69** 107 112 **77**
  207 318 **119** 287
Anna Emery **70** 365
Anna Margaret Deering
  102 142
Anne **53** 35 36
Anne (Sanford) **103** 275
  111 58
Anne Lathrop **54** lxviii
Anne Rebecca (Mason)
  96 400
Annie **55** 197 198
Arthur L. **119** 64
Asa **61** 24 **88** 148
Atherton (Mrs.) **85** 197
Audrey Pearson **94** 168
Austin **88** 376
B. Lake **52** 481 **60** 186
Bathsheba **55** 196 197
Bela **88** 148
Belcher **69** 107 **99** 79 **108**
  30 **112** 178 **119** 20 **121**
  248
Belinda **73** 168
Benjamin **52** 429 **73** 96 169

NOYES *cont'd*
  88 61 **103** 67 **140** 132
Benjamin Lake **55** xxxv
  66 xlviii **82** 128 129 **84**
  181 **90** 124 **93** 131 **96**
  154 **100** 47 117 **103** 67
Benning **92** 276
Bethiah **55** 198
Betsey **53** 41 42 104 216
  55 199 **73** 169 **92** 357
  94 47 **108** 164
Betty **55** 198
Bridget **81** 165 **109** 223
Caroline **75** 261 **115** 240
Catherine **77** 204 207
Catherine B. **77** 207
Catherine L. **77** 207
Chandler **73** 97
Charles **56** 30 **66** 37
Charles Lloyd **100** 108
Charles Lothrop **79** 114
Charles P. **60** 238 401
Charles P. (Mrs.) **74** 241
Charles Phelps **62**
  xxxvii 104 **143** 252
Charles Reinold (Mrs.)
  90 70
Charles Townsend
  77 207
Charles William
  61 xxxvii
Charlotte (Crooker)
  87 91
Charlotte Newman
  55 198
Clarissa **53** 41 **77** 207 208
  126 156
Clarissa Dutton **77** 207
Constance **52** 404
Cornelia B. **57** 288
Cutting **53** 36 37 **55** 196-
  199 **102** 142 **133** 47
Cynthia **55** 198
Cyrus **73** 169 **115** 43
Daniel **52** 338 **53** 37 38 **54**
  lxviii **58** 19 **59** 354 **61** 24
  73 97 **89** 275 **98** 364
  114 33 **118** 313 **121** 169
Daniel R. **77** 204 207
David **55** 197
David J. **103** 67
Denison **101** 304
Dolly **58** 19
Dorcas **53** 39 40
Dorothy **77** 208 **80** 177
  95 338
Dorothy Prince **59** 39
Dorothy Quincy
  (Crinnell) **90** 70
Ebenezer **118** 313
Edith Pearson (Leigh)
  94 168
Edmund **92** 179 **113** 318
Edward **54** cxxxii **91** 331
Edward Deering **72** xx
  84 86 **74** xxviii **90** 130
  102 114 142 **103** 123
Edward F. **84** 291
Edward Griffin **77** 207
Edward Roland **93** 348
Edwin M. **129** 85

NOYES *cont'd*
Edwin M. (Mrs.) **118** 170
  129 85
Elana **83** 468 469
Eleanor **75** xxiii **93** 82
  139 364
Eli **73** 97
Elijah **98** 364
Elijah Withington **75** 262
Eliphalet **85** 39 **91** 331
  96 400
Eliza **55** 197-199 **73** 168
  126 120
Eliza Ann **55** 199
Eliza Frothingham
  75 262
Elizabeth **52** 432 434 **53**
  37-39 **54** lxix **55** xlviii
  196 197 199 **57** 1 **59** 39
  61 24 **81** 165 171 **88** 148
  114 96
Elizabeth (Eaton) **114** 270
Elizabeth (High) **86** 339
Elizabeth (Poole) **96** 400
Elizabeth (Sanford)
  103 275
Elizabeth (Wright) **145** 37
Elizabeth Adams **92** 357
Ella (Pike) **94** 168
Ellen E. **55** 199
Emily (Chandler) **123** 239
Emily C. **74** xxvi **89** 170
  190
Emily Caroline **108** 34
Emily Cushing **93** 370
  94 79 141
Emily F. **102** 234
Emily H. **62** 104
Emily Leavitt **96** 97
  104 246
Emma Florence (Leigh)
  94 167
Enoch **53** 39 **55** 198 199
  77 204 207 208 **92** 277
  114 278 **134** 215
Ephraim **53** 35 36 **73** 169
Ernest Henry **82** 390
Esther (Melcher) **88** 285
Esther Ann **55** 199
Esther M. **55** 199
Eugene **103** 120
Eunice **55** 197 **73** 169 **77**
  208 **81** 165
Fanny **73** 97
Florence A. **94** 167
Florence A. (Noyes)
  94 167
Florence Ethel **95** 146 **96**
  400 **97** 78 162
Frances Mary Edwena
  54 lxxxii
Frances Oriana **55** 199
Francis **123** 193
Francis Clark **59** 40
Frank Alton **96** 400
Fred **74** 30
Fred L. **98** 206
Fred Leigh **94** 168
Fred Sewell **94** 168
G. Howard **103** 67
Genice Arlene **103** 67

NOYES *cont'd*
George **59** 40 **93** 370
  145 350
George B. **103** 67
George Clement **93** 364
  365
George Freeman **72** 86
  102 142
George Newman **55** 199
  79 99
Gerald Snow **94** 168
Gibbs Eddy **55** 199
Gladys Douglas (Jewett)
  94 168
Grace **75** xxvi **79** 216 **80**
  222 **81** 164 165 236
Grace (White) **86** 109
H. E. **51** 228 **114** 270
H. Wallace **55** 196
Hannah **52** 433 438 **53** 36-
  39 41 **59** 40 **68** 97 **73** 97
  167 **77** 207-209 **86** 84
  93 195 **133** 43
Hannah (Dow) **133** 47
Hannah (Freethy) **119** 64
Hannah Graham **55** 198
Harriet **82** 279 **86** 298
Harriet Hayes **74** lxix
Harriet Livermore **86** 297
Harriet N. **55** 199
Harriette Eliza **54** xli 235
  55 xxx **57** 336 **58** xliii
  105 **59** xlii 116 **64** 230
  84 181 **88** 173 **115** 28
  145 37
Harrison **91** 331
Hattie **131** 77
Helen Gilman **78** 203
Helen Maria **75** 262
Helen Wescott **104** 145
  105 125
Henry **53** 39 **115** 25
Henry Craft **55** 199
Henry E. **59** 116 **145** 37
Henry Erastus **54** xli
  59 xlii
Henry Justin **94** 167
Henry T. **91** 331
Hepzibah **55** 197
Hester **55** 199
Hezekiah **73** 97
Hiram **73** 168
Horace Pearson **75** 262
Horatio S. **103** 44
Ichabod **119** 256
Ida Helen **79** 99
Ilsley **72** 86
Isaiah **73** 97
Israel **59** 39
J. B. (Mrs.) **91** 207
Jacob **53** 42 **55** 196 **93** 365
  102 142 **127** 62
James **52** 481 **53** 35-37 41
  267 **57** 336 **59** 116 306
  60 188 **61** 43 381 **62** 213
  70 xxxiv **76** xxxix **77**
  208 **80** 176 **81** 165 171
  198 **88** 148 **93** 370 **103**
  275 **111** 58 **114** 270 **118**
  263 271 272 **120** 95 176
  131 164 **133** 114 **143**

NOYES *cont'd*
  362 **145** 37
James Atkins **52** 404 **53**
  35 214 265 269 374 381
  426 **54** xxxvii 127 **55**
  196 **84** 179 **90** 123 **96**
  154 **100** 46 116 246 247
  108 34
James Beaumont **94** 139
  103 310 **104** 65 149
James Sullivan **53** 42 267
  92 347 **100** 246 247
Jane **51** 466 **53** 38 39 108
  55 197 198 **60** 42 **77** 208
Jane (Gowell) **96** 400
Jane (Richardson) **98** 364
Jane Elizabeth **77** 208
Jane P. **114** 147
Jane Todd **55** 199
Jerusha **125** 66
Jesse D. **77** 52
Joanna (Record) **96** 400
John **53** 36-41 121 267 **54**
  lxviii **55** 196-199 **59** 40
  143 **73** 168 **74** 30 **77** 52
  207 208 **81** 171 **88** 143
  148 **92** 179-181 **93** 370
  96 400 **100** 246 **103** 310
  104 242 **107** 102 114
  103 255 257 264 **118** 183
  119 107 **125** 95 **126** 225
  136 309 **137** 258
John Bradford **131** 75
John Buttrick **63** 214
John E. **88** 285
John H. (Mrs.) **85** 99
Johnson **77** 176
Jonathan **52** 432 **73** 169 **93**
  365 **94** 314 **119** 256
Joseph **55** 196 197 **61** 187
  188 **62** 273 **65** 296 **73** 96
  75 89 **77** 208 **80** 93 94
  81 171 **93** 398 **102** 142
  114 33 **116** 84 **125** 100
  128 222 **134** 216
Joseph C. **102** 142
Josephine H. **100** 231
Joshua **53** 282 **103** 67
  118 313
Josiah **55** 197 **102** 142
Judith **53** 38 39 122 **68** 261
  75 262 **98** 184
Judith (Gaines) **85** 39
Judith (Knight) **121** 169
Judith (Pike) **121** 168
Julia Gilman **78** 202
Katharine Dodge **75** 262
Leonard **53** 41 **125** 218
Letitia H. **73** 287
Levi Prelight **96** 400
Lewis E. **127** 62
Lizzie C. **119** 309
Loammi **53** 41
Lois **73** 96 169
Lorana **88** 61
Louisa (Willis) **114** 278
Louisa M. **77** 176
Louisa Stanton **76** xxxix
Lucinda **55** 199
Lucy **53** 41
Lucy A. **59** lxxxvii

NOYES *cont'd*
Lucy A. (Briggs) **127** 62
Lucy Maria **79** 18
Luther **53** 37
Lydia **53** 39-41 **73** 97
 94 314
Lydia (Bancroft) **94** 314
Lyman A. **61** 218
M. **70** 23
Margaret **73** 168
Margery **73** 169
Marian **72** 86
Marie (Batchler) **94** 168
Marinda **88** 61
Martha **53** 38 **55** 197 **73** 97
 74 264 **77** 208 **116** 294
Martha (Caldwell)
 125 218
Martha R. **55** 199
Mary **52** 338 430 433 **53**
 35-39 41 121 **55** 196-198
 56 365 **59** 40 **61** 187 188
 65 295 296 **66** 275 **73**
 169 **74** 30 102 **77** 202
 208 **80** 93 94 115 **81** 171
 90 302
Mary (Cutting) **96** 400
Mary (Gallup) **136** 309
Mary (Matthews) **100** 146
Mary (Poore) **96** 400
Mary Ann **77** 208
Mary Ann (Willis)
 114 270
Mary Augusta (Chandler)
 103 44
Mary Ball **53** 42
Mary Coffin **53** 36
Mary E. **55** 199 **77** 52
Mary Evelyn (Luce)
 88 376
Mary H. B. (Cole) **140** 132
Mary J. **86** 312
Mary Kannaday **88** 148
Mary W. **55** 198
Matthew **77** 202
Mehitable **55** 198 **119** 256
Mehitable (Ford) **119** 256
Mehitable (Wright)
 131 75
Mehitable Hunt **70** 364
Mercy M. **55** 199
Mille **53** 39
Millicent (Orcutt) **119** 256
Milton **73** 169 **74** 30
Moses **53** 38-41 216 267
 280 **55** 197 198 **73** 97 **77**
 202 208 **78** 111 **92** 272
 100 246 269 271 **114**
 270
Nancy **58** 19 **59** 40 **73** 167
 169 180 **88** 60 **114** 146
Nancy Worth **58** 20
Natalie Priscilla **103** 67
Nathan **52** 67 **53** 35 **54**
 lxviii **75** 261
Nathaniel **52** 431 **53** 38
 267 280-282 **55** 197-199
 62 275 **73** 169 **88** 327
 108 30 **121** 248 **140** 231
Nathaniel Dodge **75** 262
Nathaniel H. **59** 290

NOYES *cont'd*
Nathaniel Newman **55**
 198 **83** 469
Nehemiah **55** 197-199
Nicholas **52** 481 **53** 35-41
 267 **54** lxviii **55** 196-
 199 **57** 336 **59** 116 **63**
 361 **80** 115 **83** 259 **88** 60
 61 63 **93** 364 **96** 400 **100**
 246 **102** 142 **103** 67 310
 113 157 **114** 270 **121**
 168 **129** 360 **131** 191
 133 47 **144** 358 **145** 37
Olive **127** 62
Oliver **57** 275 **61** 24 **67** 108
 69 107 **131** 178 181 182
Parker **52** 431 **53** 281 282
Paul **53** 39 41 282 **73** 168
Peleg **81** 165 171
Penelope Barker **52** 404
 84 105 190 **100** 247
Peter **52** 481 **57** xlix 1 **59**
 116 **60** 59 357 **61** 24 **72**
 84 **88** 60 **114** 96 270 **137**
 252 253 **145** 37
Pheaney **78** 414
Phebe **53** 39-41 216 **81** 165
 88 61 **90** 348
Phebe Griffin **73** xxxvi
 77 204 207 208
Polly **55** 198 **81** 165
Polly (Richardson)
 98 364
Priscilla **53** 38 **77** 52
Prudence **81** 165 171
Rachel **53** 36 37 **73** 168 **88**
 60 **89** 275 **115** 45
Rebecca **51** 466 **52** 82 **53**
 37 **54** lxviii **74** 30 **81**
 165
Rebecca (Harding)
 102 239
Richard **53** 35 **77** 208
Richard S. **133** 47
Robert **53** 35 **66** 27 **103** 15
Robert H. **99** 201
Rose (Smith) **83** 437 **84** 20
Roswell Leigh **94** 167
Rufus King (Mrs.) **74** 238
 75 xxvi **83** 514 **90** 210
 402
Ruth **55** 198 **74** 30 **77** 208
Ruth (Read) **114** 33
S. C. **54** cxv
Sabin **140** 132
Sally **59** 290 **77** 207 208
 83 382 **114** 184 **135** 248
 140 129-131
Sally (Carver) **88** 327
Sally (Lovering) **125** 100
Sally Brown **55** 199
Samuel **52** 82 **53** 38 41 42
 216 267 **54** lxviii **55**
 xlviii 196 **60** 18 42 **61** 43
 66 230 **68** 317 **88** 148
 92 256 347 357 **94** 47
 379 **100** 246 **102** 239
 103 310 **119** 107 256
 128 278 **133** 47
Samuel Adams **92** 256
Samuel Bradley **55** xli

NOYES *cont'd*
 xlviii xlix **103** 310
Sanford **128** 222
Sarah **52** 338 429 431 **53**
 35-37 41 104 108 280-
 282 **54** lxviii **55** 197 **59**
 143 306 **61** 24 **69** 107 **73**
 97 169 **75** 261 **77** 208 **83**
 259 **88** 148 **95** 338 **97** 4
 261 **103** 151 **114** 37 240
 270 **130** 211 **134** 216
 137 252 258
Sarah (Hand) **140** 132
Sarah (Hearsey) **96** 400
Sarah (Lunt) **96** 400
Sarah Ann **55** 198 199
Sarah Ann (Carver)
 83 469
Sarah B. (Callender)
 145 37
Sarah E. **125** 287
Sarah Griswold **77** 208
Sarah Jane **77** 189
Sarah Luella **102** 310
Sarah M. **76** 41
Sarah Putnam **113** 301
Sarah Worcester **79** 99
Sewell Henry **94** 168
Sibyl **90** 209 **98** 11 **99** 218
 116 176 **120** 242 243
 124 100 303 **131** 251
 252 **133** 93 **136** 309 **141**
 114 314 **142** 111 **143** 38
 148 **144** 29 141 **147** 315
 148 36 134
Sibyl (Whiting) **136** 309
Sibyl I. **121** 229
Silas **53** 39-41 **75** 262
Silence **77** 13
Simon **53** 39
Sophia **115** 25 109
Sophia Hatch **115** 109
Statina **111** 110
Stephen **53** 39 **92** 277
 134 215
Stephen L. **77** 208
Stillman **55** 198 199
Susanna **53** 39 40 **73** 96 97
 86 85 **137** 258
Sylvanus **93** 365
Thomas **53** 36 37 122 **54**
 cxxxii **55** 258 360 **56** 30
 60 357 **63** 124 126 220
 65 295 296 **74** 102 **81**
 165 171 **90** 302 **103** 275
 127 5 **128** 222 **134** 215
 136 226 228 **145** 37
Thomas Branch **59** 40
Timothy **53** 36 37 **58** 19
 93 365 **103** 67 **134** 215
Wadleigh **93** 398 **100** 63
Wadsworth **72** 86
Walter Foss **55** 199
Walter R. **114** 270
Weller Hayward (Mrs.)
 95 147
Wiley Davis **94** 167
William **52** 438 **53** 35-41
 267 **55** 196-199 **57** 336
 60 18 **77** 207-209 **88**
 148 **92** 178 179 **93** 364

NOYES *cont'd*
370 **96** 400 **125** 246 **133**
47 **134** 215 **136** 309
William Curtis **93** 370
William H. **76** 41 **83** 437
84 20
Winchester **79** 18
Zebulon **55** 197 391
Zibia (Pratt) **96** 400
Nubery *see* Newbury
NUBEY John **59** 64
Prudence **59** 64
NUCCIO Joseph **99** 33
Vernetta Caro (Fletcher)
99 33
NUCHTEN Emma H.
(Genest) **83** 429 437
Nuckolls *see* Nichols
Nuckols *see* Nichols
Nucom *see* Newcomb
NUDD Nud Nudde
—— **144** 263
Abigail **55** 344 **99** 54 **142**
263-265
Abigail (Reade) **142** 264
Agnes **142** 264
Almira **83** 22 26
Amy (Kempte) **142** 265
Benjamin **51** 163
Elizabeth **141** 327 **142** 264
144 257
Frances **142** 265
Hannah **87** 229 235 **92** 315
142 266
Isabell **142** 264
Jacobe **142** 264
James **69** 344 **142** 264 266
Jane **90** 289
Joan **112** 138 **142** 257 258
265
John **141** 327 **142** 263-266
Joseph **142** 264
Judith **87** 229 235
Margaret **142** 265
Mary **51** 463 **142** 266
Mary (Moulton) **141** 325-
327 **142** 263 264 **144**
260
Nicholas **69** 343-345
Robert **69** 343-345 **141**
325 327 **142** 261 264
144 256
Roger **90** 289 **142** 257 264
265
Samuel **142** 266 **145** 349
Sarah **68** 72 **96** 85 **142** 266
Sarah (Dearborn) **142** 265
Sarah (Maloon) **142** 266
Thomas **58** 34 **68** 72 **69**
342 343 361 **125** 93 **141**
322 327 **142** 257 263-266
Thomas T. **79** 42
Walter **69** 344 345
Will **141** 327
William **69** 343 344 **141**
327 **142** 259 263-265
NUENS Elizabeth **65** 66
NUGENT Newgent Nugen
—— **97** 55
Amos **114** 184
Anna Marios **142** 139

NUGENT *cont'd*
Anthony **70** 262
Elisa **114** 184
Elizabeth **86** 307
Ellen **66** 284
Harry **114** 184
John **114** 184
Margaret **66** 284
Mary **118** 64
Mary Elizabeth **112** 227
Michael **64** 315
Nell Marion **115** 13 **117**
132 **123** 257 **124** 25 **141**
39
Richard **55** 67 69 **63** 21
Russel **114** 184
Ruth (Blunt) **97** 55
Walter **66** 284
William **86** 198
NUGGASSET
Wiaro **143** 17
NUILLE
Emmelina de **105** 293
Gilbert de **105** 293
NUIR Alexander **62** 244
63 214
NUKIN Widow **76** 280
NULIN Richard **147** 173
NULL
Ruth Neal (Magoun)
89 179
NULRYNE James **125** 32
NULTNY Jonathan **108** 42
NUMACKES
Nunquid **118** 86
Numan *see* Newman
NUMMUMPAUM **54** 262
Nun *see* Nunn
NUNAN
Dorothy A. **92** 341
Laura Jane (Stevens)
(Eaton) **134** 279
William H. **134** 279
NUNCRIEF Sarah **79** 41
NUNE Thomas **57** 315
NUNEMAKER
Catherine **92** 391
NUNIE
Cornelius **100** 140
Elizabeth **100** 140
Timothy **100** 140
NUNN Nun Nunns
Abraham **63** 160 **141** 240
Agnes **141** 233
Agnes (Devereux)
141 241
Agnes (Osborne) **141**
239 240
Agnes (Samson) **141** 241
Alice **141** 239 240
Alice (Nunn) **141** 240
Anne **141** 239-241
Annis (Osborne) **141** 240
Beatrice **141** 241
Elizabeth **141** 237-239 242
George **67** 38 **141** 239-241
Isabel **141** 237 **144** 357
James **141** 239-241
Jane **141** 240
Joan **141** 237 241
John **141** 233 239-241

NUNN *cont'd*
Katharine **141** 240
Margaret **141** 233
Margery **141** 241
Martha **141** 240
Matthew **141** 240
Randall **63** 160
Robert **141** 239-241
Susan **141** 242
Ursula **141** 241
William **141** 34 237 241
242 **144** 357
Winifred **141** 240
NUNNELEY
Mamie Dorcas **78** 175
Samuel **78** 175
Nunns *see* Nunn
Nurse *see* Nourse
NURSED Hannah **140** 177
NUSBAUM Fred B. (Mrs.)
113 323
NUSON —— **63** 131
NUTBROWNE
Mary **74** 275
NUTCHEN
Fred R. **83** 429 437
NUTE Abigail **63** 178 **74**
260 **83** 22 26
Albert James **83** 430 437
Ann **100** 225
Anna **82** 295 299
Anna P. **113** 314
Annie P. **91** 204
Charlotte A. **77** 150
Eliza J. **76** 43
Everline (Parsons) **93** 294
Francis **93** 294 **119** 66
Grace Lee **106** 78
Hannah Lock (Hayes)
113 314
Henry W. **93** 294
Isaac **74** 191 255
Isaac F. **77** 150
Isetta (Keen) **90** 42
James **90** 42 **92** 101 **99** 75
103 312
Jeremy O. **68** 44
Jonathan **63** 178 **74** 260
Josiah **103** 312
Jotham **92** 102 **103** 312
L. S. **118** 94
Leah **82** 286 295 **92** 102
Levi M. **80** 309
Louisa (Brooks) **93** 294
119 66
Louisa B. **119** 225
Lucy A. **62** 122
Martha **92** 101 **97** 145 **98**
66 **100** 225
Mary **92** 102
Mary (Hayes) 102 **92** 102
Mary Elizabeth **103** 312
Orsamus **103** 312
Pamela **59** 189
Patience **83** 154
Percy E. **92** 102
Perle Ethelyn (Goodsoe)
83 430 437
Phebe Ann **113** 314
Polly **80** 309
Russell Freeman **113** 314

NUTE *cont'd*
Samuel **100** 225 **103** 312
Sarah **68** 94 **74** 255 **103** 312
Sarah T. **80** 309
Tristram **59** 189
Nuting *see* Nutting
NUTMAN Nuttman
Carrie D. **104** 309
Margery (Nunn) **141** 241
Sarah **98** 337
William **141** 241
NUTSON
Lawrence **100** 139
NUTT — Mr. **63** 159
Abigail **91** 38 **111** 153
Abigail Prentice **73** lvi
Abraham **60** 356
Ada Sophia **73** lvii
Adam **98** 53
Alpha M. **90** 394
Anne **59** 280 **127** 284
Arthur **73** lvii
Belinda **84** 59
Charles **57** xxxv 227 **58**
    xliii **60** 188 **61** 98 **62**
    xxxv **64** xxix **66** xlviii
    70 191 **72** 81 **73** xxviii
    lvi lvii **114** 195
Charles Stanley **73** lvii
Dorothy May **73** lvii
Elizabeth **127** 284
Elizabeth (Jackman)
    141 56
Elizabeth (Steuart) **76** 190
Hannah **127** 284
Hannah / Anna (Fitz
    Randolph) **98** 53
Harold **73** lvii
Hiram S. **76** 273
Isabel Ella **73** lvii
James **64** 259 **127** 284
Joanna **76** 273
Joe **74** 71
John **84** 59 **124** 242
John Budd (Mrs.) **92** 389
Joseph **98** 53
Laura **84** 59
Lucia Janet **73** lvii
Martha **127** 284
Mary **127** 284
Mary (Walker) **91** 38
Michael **141** 56
Miles **66** 270 **141** 56
Pamela **98** 53
Portus R. **76** 273
Richard **80** 359
Ruhannah **127** 283 284
Ruth **73** lvii
Samuel **101** 217
Sarah **57** 352 **70** 87 **77** 231
    141 56
Sibyl **66** 270
Walter Ernest **100** 112
William **57** 227 **60** 188 **73**
    lvi **91** 38 **98** 53 **111** 153
    140 17
Nuttage *see* Nottage
NUTTALL Nuttell
Anne **71** 28
Charles **71** 27 28
Cora Lillian Jane **96** 160

NUTTALL *cont'd*
Elizabeth **71** 28
James **71** 27 28
John **71** 28
Joseph **62** 322
Julia Riddiough **94** 282
    96 301
Kate B. **117** 293
Margaret **71** 247
Mary **68** 18 **71** 27 28
    100 236
Mary Wallace **68** 18
Olivia F. **117** 293
Peter Austin **94** 282
Susanne **71** 28
Thomas **65** 69-71 **71** 27 28
    80 88
W. L. F. **148** 246
William **100** 236 **117** 293
William B. **68** 18
NUTTAU Charles **80** 90
Geoffrey **80** 90
Nuttell *see* Nuttall
NUTTER —— **58** 249 **73**
    206 **77** 135 **82** 413 **103**
    299
Abigail **65** 215 **73** 191
    196 200 201 **83** 351 **109**
    151 **111** 46
Adaline B. **73** 198
Adeline **72** 275
Agnes Marian **79** 218
Alfred Hoyt **81** 149
Alice M. **90** 362
Alice Maria **79** 218
Ann **52** 82 **59** 284 **81** 148
    82 50
Anna **65** 313 **81** 148 149
Anna (Manchester)
    102 26
Anna Maria **66** lxviii
Anne **94** 111
Anthony **65** 215 **82** 295
    297 **91** 365 **95** 225-228
    111 47
Antoinette **73** 190 199 204
Antoinette Susetta
    Fredericka Alberta **73**
    192 **81** 149
Ariadna **73** 195
Armaline **81** 148
Belinda N. **101** 35
Betsey **59** 286 **73** 192 **76** 29
    97 142
Betty **65** 215
Betty (Dam) **111** 47
Bridget **81** 148
Charles **73** 199 202 204
Charles Amos **73** 194
Charles Edward **73** 199
Charles Latham **66** lxviii
Charles W. **73** 190 192 204
Charles Wesley **81** 148
    149
Charlotte E. **73** 193
Christopher **73** 197
    77 135
Clarinda L. **73** 194
Deborah **73** 197
Ebenezer **79** 217
Edward **79** 218 **82** 50

NUTTER *cont'd*
Edward Hopkins **79** 218
Eliza **65** 311 **73** 194
Eliza Ann **73** 193 **81** 148
Eliza B. **73** 202
Eliza D. **81** 148
Elizabeth **65** 354 **67** 279 **73**
    194 203 205 **79** 218 **81**
    149 **91** 32 **94** 356
Elizabeth Ann **73** 193
Ella **69** 36
Ellen **81** 148
Ellis **94** 111
Emily **73** 195
Emily Augusta **81** 148
Enoch P. **85** 445
Esther **65** 214 **91** 380
Esther (Dame) **91** 390
Ethel Olmstead **69** 36
Eunice **74** 261
Eva J. **83** 300
Everett **120** 216
Francis **103** 298
Francis Douglas **79** 218
Frank **93** 340
George **82** 50
George Peverly **81** 148
George R. **82** 261 262 385
George Read **84** 106 190
    91 178 365 **92** 150
George S. **85** 445
Grafton **59** 286
Hannah **73** 194 **80** 310 **82**
    50 **94** 356
Hannah (Decker) **91** 390
Harriet **81** 149
Harriet Atwood **81** 148
Harriet Emily **81** 148 149
Harriet Louisa **79** 217 218
Hatevil **52** 82 **58** 249 252
    65 215 **91** 365 390 **95**
    226 **109** 151 **111** 47
Henry **58** 249 250 **82** 50
Ichabod **91** 365
Ida A. **73** 190
Isaac **66** lxviii
Isaac Newton **66** lix lxviii
Izetta Shaw **85** 445
J. **97** 265
J. H. **113** 312
Jacob **97** 142 270
Jacob S. **90** 111
James **65** 214 **73** 192 198
    81 149
James T. **85** 445
James W. **73** 193
James William **81** 148
Jenney E. (Armstrong)
    120 216
John **58** 249 252 **64** 344
    65 215 **67** 43 **80** 310 **85**
    445 **111** 47
John Darius **81** 148
John L. **85** 445
Joseph **73** 198 205 **81** 148
    97 145
Joseph Henry **79** 218
Joseph Matthius **81** 148
Joseph S. **73** 197 **87** 93
Joseph Simes **64** lvii
    73 200

NUTTER *cont'd*
Joshua **73** 201
Joshua M. **73** 189 193 202
   203 206 **87** 93
Josiah W. **110** 23
Jotham **85** 445
Judith (Roberts) **110** 23
Juliette **73** 204
Lavinia **73** 193
Loammy **82** 295 297
Lucy Ann **73** 192 **87** 93
Lydia **97** 265
Lydia B. **73** 193
Lydia Walker **82** 50
Margaret **76** 30
Margaret Orr **66** lxviii
Maria Latham **66** lxviii
Mark **73** 191 194 201 202
Martha **82** 295 296
Martha Ann **73** 192
Martha Jane **81** 148 149
Mary **59** 284 287 **79** 217
   82 50 423 **89** 61 **97** 272
   100 147 **132** 275
Mary Abigail **81** 148
Mary Ann **73** 193
Mary Augusta **79** 217 218
Mary C. **81** 306
Mary Chapman **79** 218
Mary Esther **85** 445
Mary Jane **69** 36
Mary R. **73** 193 **87** 93
Mary Ryder **64** lvii
   95 357
Matilda **85** 376
Matthias **58** 253 **81** 148
   149 448 **82** 295 296
Mehitable **67** 43
Melissa **73** 195
Miriam **76** 28
Nathan **79** 217 218
Ned **82** 50
Peter **71** 349
Phebe P. **73** 205
Phebe P. (Hoit) **87** 93
Phebe Pickering **64** lvii
Phebe Simes **73** 202
Phillis **73** 197
Rebecca **97** 270
Richard **91** 365 **145** 356
Richard W. **66** lxviii
Rufus O. **81** 149
Ruth **88** 369
Ruth B. **91** 28
Ruth H. **91** 34
Sally **59** 290 **63** 176 **74** 259
   85 445 **116** 197 297
Sally (Hurd) **85** 445
Samuel **74** 261 **76** 28
   102 26
Samuel H. M. **73** 198
Samuel Hoyt **81** 148
Sarah **65** 351 354 **73** 189
   193 203 **82** 284 295 **96**
   247
Sarah E. **79** 218
Sarah J. **73** 193
Sarah O. **73** 194
Simes **73** 198
Sophia Ann **85** 445
Susan **81** 255 256

NUTTER *cont'd*
Thomas Franklin **91** 365
Volatine **82** 413
W. B. **117** 122
William **65** 311 **73** 192 285
   79 218 **88** 369
William Burligh **97** 273
William Henry **73** 194
   195 203
Winfred N. **81** 148
Winthrop H. F. **73** 194
Wyndham Hunt (Mrs.)
   103 120
NUTTING Nuting Nuttin
—— **69** 299
— Capt. **95** 64
— Mrs. **69** 213
Abel **63** 269
Abiah **75** 15
Abiah (Varnum) **136** 166
Abigail **56** 44 **61** 276 277
   63 291 **64** 35
Abijah **70** 300 **97** 395
Alice Gertrude **92** 112
Annie Jennie **118** 131
Annis **56** 45
Axie **75** 15
Betty **95** 382
C. H. **92** 101
Catherine **136** 61
Catherine (Smith) **89** 45
   92 112
Catherine Eliza **72** xxxiv
Charles H. **71** lxiii
Charles Herbert **92** 112
Clifford Porter **92** 112
David **52** 79 **63** 323 **64** 37
David Hubbard **65** xxxvi
   67 95 **71** xxxiv lxii
   lxiii
Deborah **95** 347
Elizabeth **63** 325 **86** 239 **90**
   90 **92** 266 **93** 167 **98** 84
Elizabeth (Gardner) **90** 91
Elizabeth B. (Gray)
   103 235
Elizabeth J. (Penniman)
   88 286
Ephraim **63** 380 381
   64 42 146
Ernest W. **75** 15
Esther **89** 45 **93** 170
Ezekiel **61** 276
Frank G. **74** 172 316 **75** 15
Frederick **88** 286
Frederick W. **71** lxiii
George **75** 15 **90** 262
George F. **75** 15
George Hale **64** xxxi **65**
   xxxvi **67** xxx 95 **71** lxiii
   90 126 **112** 133
Grace Anna **92** 112
Hannah **64** 37 **92** 266
   126 145
James **126** 14
Jane **56** 405
Jane A. **128** 233
Jennie M. **75** 15
John **59** 417 418 **60** 355
   61 396 **63** 304 319 380
   381 **64** 34 **65** 187 **66** 369

NUTTING *cont'd*
71 lxii lxiii **87** 398 **89** 45
   92 112 266 **95** 347 **103**
   235 **104** 122 **139** 147
   148
John David (Mrs.) **82** 380
   83 233
John Keep **63** 304
Jonah **97** 395
Jonas **86** 87
Jonathan **59** 242 244 247
   71 lxiii **90** 89 **92** 266
   111 98 **142** 127
Joseph **55** 263 **64** 107
Josiah **136** 166
Judith **90** 262
Julia Seraphine **77** 185
Lorna **63** 269
Lucretia **89** 45
Lucy (Silvester) **86** 87
Luther **88** 332
Lydia **63** 325 380 381 **93**
   232 **126** 14 **132** 76 **144**
   219
Lydia (Longley) **126** 14
Mabel **89** 324
Margaret (Trask) **126** 66
Martha **138** 322
Mary **56** 79 **61** 396 **63** 319
   380 381 **64** 34 146 **100** 4
   111 98
Mary (Butler) **90** 89
Mary Adeline **90** 45
Mary Barrett **71** lxii
Mary Elizabeth **71** lxiii
Mercy M. (Meader)
   123 310
Nancy **112** 223
Nancy Amelia **90** 262
Nellie E. **75** 101
Nellie Edna **74** 316
Nellie H. **71** lxiii
Olive **55** 263 **57** 257
   144 219
Pamelia Williams
   89 291 292
Patience **126** 129
Polly **64** 42
Porter **92** 112
Rachel **63** 323 **125** 216
Relief **64** 208
Rena L. **93** 344
Rhoda **64** 310
Ruth **64** 37
Samantha **81** 272
Samuel **83** 378 **126** 225
   144 219
Samuel W. **123** 310
Sarah **53** 346 347 **59** 418 **65**
   187 **95** 347 **139** 155
Sarah (Eggleston) **95** 347
Sarah E. (Richardson)
   88 332
Silas **90** 91 **95** 382
Simeon **56** 45
Stephen **81** 272
Stephen (Mrs.) **123** 97
Susan J. **84** 41
Tamar **52** 79
Thankful **74** 316
Wallace **78** 331 **79** 194

NUTTING *cont'd*
  100 163
  Walter M. **89** 45 **92** 266
  Walter Merriman **86** 198
  Wells Porter **92** 112
  William **61** 171 **67** 95 **71**
    lxii lxiii
  William Henry **92** 112
Nuttman *see* Nutman
NUTTONG John **64** 261
NUTWELL
  Catherine **73** 144
  Elias **73** 140
  Martha **73** 139
Nuys *see* Van Nuys
NYBORG
  Mildred Johanna
    91 142
NYCE Mary **96** 75
Nycholl *see* Nichols
NYCUM Homer C. **119** 238
NYE Ney Neye Nigh - *see*
  also Nay
  —— **60** 141 **62** 17 **93** 263
    96 51 **100** 191
  — Capt. **67** 18
  — Col. **123** 300
  — Mr. **51** 263 **86** 34
  — Mrs. **62** 20
  Aaron **130** 136
  Abby F. (Clark) **133** 54
  Abigail **72** 205 **118** 209
    278 **127** 29
  Abigail (Batchelder)
    128 205
  Abigail (Gifford) **123** 218
    130 132 **133** 134
  Achsah **57** 413
  Achsah Bourne **120** 251
  Alexander Gibbs **120** 251
  Alfred Atwood **76** 90
  Alice **57** 412
  Almira **60** 202
  Almira (Phillips) **115** 285
  Almira Colton **83** 366
  Amy **60** 146 **72** 205
  Anna H. **72** 205
  Anne Swift **81** 381
  Annevery **72** 205
  Annie E. **67** 18
  Apollos **115** 285
  Aretonius **115** 285
  Ariel G. **91** 331
  Asa **113** 115
  Asenath **72** 205 206
  Aurelia **68** 106
  Austin **72** 205
  Barlow **68** 106
  Barnabas **121** 225
  Bartlett **81** 469 **121** 37 38
  Bathsheba **57** 412 **115** 190
  Benjamin **56** 75 **57** 410 413
    60 188 **67** 115-123 216
    68 337 **76** 90 91 **81** 469
    99 59 **115** 285 **119** 262
    120 97 101 247 278 **123**
    56 **124** 42 **125** 140 141
    127 29 **128** 16 205 **130**
    43 132 135 **133** 214 **138**
    132
  Bethiah **117** 192 193

NYE *cont'd*
  125 253
  Bethiah (Blackwell) **117**
    193 300
  Betsey **127** 71 73
  Betsey (Ellis) **121** 38
  Betty (Ellis) **122** 59
  Braddock **51** 224 **119** 32
  Buel **68** 337
  Caleb **99** 59 **117** 193 **124**
    52 **125** 131 253 **128** 303
    144 25-27
  Caroline **62** 21 **122** 295
  Caroline M. **78** 206
  Caroline Mellen **89** 12
  Caroline Tobey **81** 469
    83 111
  Catherine **121** 131
  Catherine (Sturges)
    118 207
  Celia **120** 251
  Celia (Tobey) (Ellis) **120**
    101 **121** 225
  Charles **127** 113 **133** 296
  Charles Henry **96** 51
  Charlotte **72** 205
  Charlotte J. **68** 337
  Chester **61** 90 **86** 54
  Chester Fairbanks **76** 91
  Chloe (Gifford) **133** 213
  Christiana **116** 105
  Christopher **133** 296
  Clarissa **127** 29 **128** 205
  Clarissa (Gibbs) **123** 219
  Clark C. **126** 155
  Content **115** 273 **120** 288
    124 52 53
  Cordelia **140** 310
  Corissa **128** 205
  Cornelius **91** 93 **118** 207
    140 231
  Crocker **57** 412
  Daniel Butler **127** 113
  David **61** 88 90 192 389
    62 88 **68** 106 **120** 283
    121 40 **124** 219 **127** 29
    134 239
  Deborah **55** 224 **57** 34
    116 104 **117** 187 189
    121 37 38 **125** 249 **134**
    239
  Deborah (Blackwell)
    117 189
  Deborah (Crowell)
    123 214
  Deborah (Ellis) **121** 38
  Deborah (Nye) **134** 239
  Deborah (Perry) **99** 59
  Deborah (Tobey) **119** 36
    121 225 **128** 15 **130** 135
  Deborah B. **119** 191
  Deborah Lazell **89** 12
  Delia **115** 258
  Dolly **68** 337
  Dolly (Shortridge)
    128 205
  Dorcas **119** 32
  Dorothy **86** 54
  Dorothy (Bryant) **118**
    278 279

NYE *cont'd*
  Dorothy (Shortridge)
    128 205
  Ebenezer **57** 410-413 **65**
    225 **67** 116 **68** 106 **72**
    115 **99** 59 **117** 193 **119**
    36 167 **120** 247 250 **122**
    259 **123** 56 **128** 15 252
    130 132 135 **144** 102
    103
  Edmund **113** 119
  Edward John **76** 91
  Eleanor (Ellis) **120** 116
  Electa **62** 129
  Elihu **120** 251 **133** 135
  Elijah **61** 90 191 196 **62** 375
    67 122 **68** 337
  Elisha **68** 320 **104** 206 **123**
    219 **125** 220
  Eliza **124** 257
  Eliza Ann (Chase) **88** 119
  Eliza Frances **89** 12
  Eliza R. **84** 214
  Elizabeth **67** 115 **72** 205 **77**
    lxiv **102** 141 **113** 115
    121 37 38 **125** 292 **126**
    193 **127** 113 **130** 43
  Elizabeth (Atwood) **99** 59
  Elizabeth (Bodfish)
    125 249
  Elizabeth (Bonum)
    117 193
  Elizabeth (Bryant) **130** 43
  Elizabeth (Ellis) **120** 279
    121 38
  Elizabeth (Handy)
    126 104
  Elizabeth (Holmes)
    121 38
  Elizabeth (Wood) **144** 25
    26
  Elizabeth Fearing **120** 251
  Ella **69** 140
  Ellen (Green) **89** 26
  Elnathan **130** 130
  Emma Hollister **86** 54
  Esther **113** 115
  Esther (Shed) **99** 59
  Etta (Towsand) **140** 310
  Eunice **68** 337 **111** 115
    122 131 **125** 247
  Eunice (Handy) **125** 249
  Eunice (Hardy) **89** 12
  Everett **84** 48
  Everett Irving **65** xxxv
  Experience **118** 202 **123** 62
    139
  F. **91** 331
  Fannie **127** 113
  Fannie (Fish) **130** 132
  Fanny Polly **76** 91
  Florania **61** 196
  Frances **83** 366
  Frederick F. **69** 140
  G. H. **113** 21
  George **62** 19 **65** 377 378
    66 24 **117** 192 193 **120**
    156
  George Bonum **117** 193
    300 **125** 253 **126** 104
  George H. **115** 285 **117**

NYE *cont'd*
302 **119** 29 265 **123** 56
125 140 141
George Henry **63** 114
George Hyatt **118** 276
George Warren **100** 191
George Washington
76 91
H. E.G. **53** 382
Hannah **53** 207 **57** 39 **58**
55 **61** 191 293 388 **86**
162 **114** 136 316 **117**
189 308 **118** 207 **119** 29
32 37 **120** 101 **123** 219
124 45 53 **127** 112 113
130 132 **133** 136 **138**
216
Hannah (Butler) **123** 219
127 113
Hannah (Fuller)
(Chipman) **123** 268
Hannah (Gibbs) **123** 218
130 132
Hannah (Lazell) **89** 12
Hannah (Nye) **117** 189
Hannah B. **120** 248
Harriet **113** 116
Harriet A. **122** 215
Harriet M. **83** 366
Helen Louisa **89** 12
Helen Mar **69** xxxv
Hezekiah **72** 205 206
Honor **61** 88 90 192 389 **62**
88 380
Horace **62** 19 22
Hoxie **122** 215
Ichabod **65** 220 **99** 289 **117**
193 **120** 97 278 **123** 300
Iram **120** 116
Isaac **118** 207 276 **120** 279
127 29 **128** 217 **136** 249
Isaiah **62** 382
Jabez **117** 308
James **127** 29 **128** 217
James Monroe **128** 205
Jane **57** 36 158
Jemima **122** 138
Jemima (Tupper) **99** 126
133 55
Jerusha **72** 205
Joanna **118** 207 **119** 29
Joanna (Gibbs) **123** 218
130 132
John **57** 413 **59** 410 **62** 132
99 59 **100** 191 **117** 192
193 **119** 32 **120** 99 247
123 218 **128** 16 249 294
130 43 132 135 **133** 136
296 **134** 61 **138** 216
John Capen **68** 320
John H **83** 366 **91** 331
John Hyde **60** 202
John P. **62** 61
John Philips **125** 249
John Porter **127** 29
128 205
John Ruggles **57** 413
John T. **62** 24
John Wight **76** 90 91
Jonathan **55** 224 **56** 400 **62**
22 133 **99** 59 126 **117**

NYE *cont'd*
189 193 **120** 97 278 279
121 37 38 152 **122** 59
131 263 **123** 268 **125**
140 141 **127** 29 **128** 205
133 55 **145** 352
Joseph **62** 19 **65** 220 **67**
120 **93** 263 **118** 206 207
276 **119** 29 264 **120** 193
279 **121** 38 **122** 138 **124**
216 **126** 155 **127** 28 29
128 205
Joseph Warren **128** 205
Joshua **113** 249 **117** 189
120 250 251 **123** 219
135 160 **137** 363
Josiah **113** 115
Katharine **81** 469
Katharine (Tupper) **99** 59
119 262 **123** 56
Katharine E. Watson
120 154
Keziah **58** 56 **62** 383
Lavinia (Gifford) **130** 132
134 61
Lemuel **117** 189 **118** 276
126 60 193
Lemuel B. **123** 268
Levi **116** 193 **120** 89 91
Lewis **66** 24
Lois **61** 89 190 193 195 **62**
299 **86** 162 **120** 102
Lois (West) **138** 216
Lot **117** 189
Louise **113** 249
Love (Gifford) **130** 136
Lucretia **115** 284
Lucretia (Mehurin)
136 249
Lucretia (Perry) **115** 285
Lucretia Northrop **76** 91
Lucy **123** 214 **133** 296
Lucy (Kingsbury)
115 285
Luther **62** 20
Lydia **106** 147 **113** 20 **115**
190 **116** 195 **123** 65
Lydia (Jenkins) **117** 189
Marah **67** 119
Marcy **113** 116
Maria **118** 207 209 276
127 113
Maria (Bourne) **116** 105
118 276 278 279 **120**
101 **121** 38 122 199 **123**
273 **127** 113 **128** 16 17
133 296
Mariah **118** 277 278
133 296
Mariette **76** 90 91
Marshall **108** 166
Marshall Bridgeman
89 26
Martha **119** 32
Martha (Bourne) **119** 32
Martha Perry **115** 285
Mary **56** 400 **57** 412 **61** 90
191 **62** 375 **67** 119 120
219 **69** 140 **76** 90 91 **77**
50 **81** 469 **83** 487 **99** 59
111 29 **113** 119 **118** 207

NYE *cont'd*
278 279 **119** 36 **121** 225
123 210 **124** 52 **127** 29
135 48 **138** 130 132 133
144 28
Mary (Bodfish) **127** 29
128 205
Mary (Dillingham)
127 28
Mary (Freeman) **125** 131
Mary (Nye) **113** 119
Mary (Perry) (Ellis)
115 192
Mary (Snow) **127** 29
128 205
Mary (Swift) **130** 132
Mary (Yost) **111** 30
Mary Alida **76** 91
Mary Ann **120** 250 **127** 29
Mary Dimmock **126** 60
Mary Eliza **76** 90 91
Mary Green **142** 23 346
Mary Polly (Dimmock)
126 60
Mehitable **60** 146 **118** 276
Mehitable (Bourne)
118 206
Meletiah **62** 89 193 378
68 106 **86** 162 **125** 134
Melvin Gilmore **140** 310
Mercy **99** 59 **113** 115 **119**
262 **120** 97 278 **121** 37
38 152 **122** 57 **123** 216
273 **125** 140 141
Mercy (Bursley) **113** 115
Mercy (Ellis) **121** 38
Mercy Bursley (Parker)
113 115
Milletiah **57** 411
Minerva (Tupper) **99** 289
Moses **59** 258 **130** 132
133 213
Nabby **127** 29
Nancy **116** 199
Nathan **87** 232 **89** 12 **99** 59
100 191 **113** 40 **115** 277
285 **118** 202 278 279
123 219 **124** 48 52 **125**
249 **127** 110 113 **128** 16
133 135
Nathan Lazell **89** 12
Nathaniel **113** 32 **120** 101
121 225 **133** 296
Nathaniel F. **61** xxxv
Nelson **76** 91
Obed Butler **127** 113
Oliver **87** 13 **103** 93
Parker **113** 115
Patience **55** 224 **116** 193
118 202 **120** 278
Patience (Bassett) **116** 193
Patience (Burgess) **99** 59
Patience (Percival)
118 202
Patty (Bourne) **119** 32
Peleg **130** 43
Phebe **67** 115-118 120 216
68 337 **120** 279 **121** 152
122 59 **126** 196
Phebe (Gifford) (Noble)
130 135

NYE *cont'd*
Philena Darwen **120** 251
Philip **64** 348 **117** 192 193
Polly **61** 89 **68** 337
Prince **122** 263 **130** 132
Prince Mavrocatero
 96 51
Priscilla Brown (Arey)
 87 13 **103** 93
Prudence M. **95** 173
Prudy **61** 192
R. Glen **120** 234
R. Glen (Mrs.) **120** 154
Rachel **113** 249
Rachel (Thayer) **125** 220
Rebecca **113** 19 20 115
 117 302 **122** 259 **128** 16
 17 **133** 296
Rebecca (Crocker)
 126 193
Rebecca (Freeman)
 117 189
Rebecca (Parker) **113** 21
 117
Remember **125** 150 **128**
 15 **130** 135
Reuben **130** 132
Rhoda **59** 258
Russell **88** 119 **123** 93
Ruth **126** 60
Sabra **121** 38 **122** 198
Sally **61** 193 **62** 193 **68** 106
 111 117 **133** 297
Sally (Carver) **89** 36
Sally (Clark) **126** 155
Sally (Pearson) **128** 205
Samuel **72** 205 206 **118**
 207 276 **121** 129 137
 123 214 273 **126** 104
 226 **127** 28 29 **128** 205
 144 102
Samuel H. **125** 141
Sarah **60** 146 **67** 118 **72** 206
 86 162 **92** 192 **113** 38
 119 **117** 192 **120** 101
 279 **121** 225 265 **125**
 131 253 **127** 110
Sarah (Blackwell) **117**
 192 193
Sarah (Crowell) **123** 219
Sarah (Freeman) **120** 279
Sarah (Gibbs) **99** 59
 123 56
Sarah (Handy) **117** 193
 125 253
Sarah (Jenkins) **117** 189
 118 276
Sarah (Pease) **130** 132
Sarah Ann (Bancroft)
 96 51
Sarah Delia (Gibbs)
 123 268
Seth **60** 146 **117** 193
Seth Freeman **89** 36
Shubal **68** 106 **125** 193
 133 135
Silas **67** 123 **105** 278
Simeon **57** 412 413 **58** 55
 56
Solomon **61** 89 190 193
 195 293 **62** 193 299 **86**

NYE *cont'd*
 162
Sophia **133** 296
Stephen **52** 128 **57** 39
 116 29 105 **118** 278 279
 120 101 250 **121** 38 **122**
 198 **125** 249 **127** 113
 128 14 16 17 217 **133**
 296
Sukey **140** 143
Susan **59** 410 **68** 106 **72**
 206 **113** 249
Susan (Lazell) **89** 12
Susan (Phinney) **115** 285
Susan E. **122** 215 299
Susan Hinckley **113** 306
Susan Lazell **89** 12
Susanna **123** 268
Sylvania **68** 106
Sylvanus **68** 106 **113** 21
 117
Sylvia Hathaway **64** lxix
Sylvina **134** 239
Tamar **59** 410
Temperance **113** 116
 118 207
Temperance (Crocker)
 117 308
Thankful **60** 146 **127** 110
 138 217
Thankful (Gifford)
 133 214
Thankful (Goodspeed)
 122 138
Thankful (Hinckley)
 (Hatch) **116** 157
Thomas **57** 34 **111** 117 **115**
 192 **117** 189 **125** 185
 127 29
Timothy **57** 410 **67** 117
 105 278 **125** 131
Walter Brigham (Mrs.)
 77 155 **78** 206
Wanda **120** 156
Warren **123** 218 **130** 132
 140 310
Wealthy **68** 337
Wilbur Sturtevant
 124 129
William **62** 18 21 **89** 12
 121 37 38 **122** 143 **125**
 249 **133** 296
William Atkinson (Mrs.)
 83 124 233
William Eaton **76** 91
Willis **120** 156
Willis R. **120** 156
Winthrop **62** 23
Zerviah **83** 487 **123** 140
NYES Sijntje **128** 164
NYLANDER
 Jane C. **148** 184-186
Nyle *see* Niles
NYNEACRES **80** 360
NYQUIST Edna **108** 201
NYRY Irene **91** 48
NYSTROM Anton **85** 169
 Caroline **85** 433
 Maria **85** 169

Oak *see* Oakes
Oakeley *see* Oakley
OAKERMAN
 Margaret **78** 72
OAKES —— **53** 271 **56** 106
 121 208
 — Capt. **69** 13
 — Mr. **51** 47
 Abigail **51** 299
 Abigail (Tripe) **96** 144
 Abigail Rogers (Haskell)
 86 340
 Alice **61** 299
 Amelia H. **60** lxiv
 Augusta Jane **106** 232
 B. L. (Mrs.) **99** 50
 Benjamin **60** 114
 Bradford **97** 19
 Byron K. **75** 15
 Caleb **107** 258
 Catherine V. **90** 112
 Charles **84** 40
 Charles H. **76** 214
 Charlotte **63** 253 **79** 55
 90 112
 Comfort **81** 249
 Cynthia Boynton **134** 149
 Daniel **147** 367
 David **56** 255 **61** 98 **76** 214
 83 60 **91** 387
 David C. **75** 41
 David M. **91** 201
 Dinah (Rich) **84** 40
 Edna May **90** 360
 Edward **77** 272 **129** 366
 136 46
 Edward Everett **99** 154
 100 117
 Eliza **140** 129
 Elizabeth **51** 299 **65** 45 **66**
 269 **93** 93 **95** 254 **100**
 296 **103** 46 **119** 125 **147**
 367
 Elshe **119** 125
 Elvira Margaret **97** 158
 105 125
 Emily **75** 15
 Esther **78** 72
 Eunice (Aldrich) **140** 129
 Fannie M. **69** 206
 Finette **75** 41
 Francis **79** 50
 Francis G. **81** 249
 Francis James (Mrs.) **84**
 341 **85** 197
 Garret **119** 125
 George **52** 322
 Grace **86** 340 **88** 338
 Hannah **51** 299 **77** 281 **82**
 282 295
 Henrietta **79** 157
 Henry **60** lxiv **79** 157
 Henry Edward **98** 48
 Henry Lebbeus **60** 114
 61 208
 Horatio N. **76** 50
 Jacob **111** 320 321
 James **77** 231 **108** 164
 128 160
 John **60** 114 **86** 134 **95** 199
 96 144 **116** 160 163 **145**

OAKES *cont'd*
353
Jonathan **51** 299 **91** 263
Josiah **81** 87 **87** 399 **90** 112
   129 366 375
Julia **147** 367
Julia Maria **113** 252
Lavinia (Law) **97** 19
Lawson Walker **103** 120
Lebbeus **60** 114
Levi **134** 149
Lucy Ann **75** 41
Lusannah **78** 71
Lydia **51** 299 **91** 190
   134 149
Lydice **122** 80
Mabel E. **114** 78
Margaret **76** 214 **100** 296
Maria **51** 299
Maria Cecilia **81** 249
Martha **119** 125
Martha R. **79** 55 **90** 112
Mary **51** 299 **60** lxiv **108**
   164 **114** 133
Mary (Blunt) **86** 134
Mary (Fitz Randolph)
   98 48
Mary (Groves) **134** 149
Mary (Smith) **135** 251
Mary Ella (Philbrick)
   90 360
Mary Jane **75** 41
Mindwell **121** 254
Minnie Elmira **75** 41
Nabby (Tripe) **95** 199
Nathan (Mrs.) **114** 78
Nathaniel **60** 114 **61** 208
   63 220 226
O. M. **91** 331
Ora **61** 208 **62** xxxvii
Pamela A. **93** 240
Pamelia A. **123** 151
Pemela **90** 387
Rachel (Egree) **129** 366
Richard **60** 400
Sally **56** 255 **125** 219
Samuel **82** 282 295
   128 160
Sarah **51** 299 **61** 153 **103** 46
Sarah (Montgomery)
   128 160
Sarah (Wheler) **91** 263
Seth **75** 15
Silas **58** 373
Silence (Wilcutt) **129** 366
Sophia M. **91** 387
Susan **126** 67
Susanna (Sayward) **89** 69
Sylvanus **58** 373
Thankful **77** 33
Thomas **51** 299 **61** 98 **66**
   269 **92** 46 **119** 125 **132**
   86 **135** 251
Thomas Fletcher **86** 340
Uriah **63** 253 **92** 49 **129**
   366 **140** 129
Urian **66** 269 **95** 102 **101**
   265 **104** 260
Walter Danville **90** 360
William **51** 259 **63** 26 **89**
   69 **100** 224

OAKEY Sally Williams
   68 103
William F. **68** 103
OAKHAM
Elizabeth **51** 465
OAKINGTON —— **61** 207
OAKLEY — Mrs. **127** 16
Abigail **69** 238 **145** 246
   146 385
Ann Elizabeth **69** 38
Annie **83** 208
Clara J. **69** 38
David **69** 239
Ed (Mrs.) **89** 95
Elizabeth **145** 246
Elizabeth (Smith) **146** 385
Gilbard **69** 238
Jane (Marakel) **89** 95
Jeremiah **68** 171 **69** 238
   239
John **62** 244 **78** 406
Martin **89** 95
Mary **76** 123 **96** 294
Michael **76** 123
Miles **108** 288
Patience (Sayles) **113** 324
Penelope **89** 95
Richard **59** 109 **89** 95
   146 385
Robert **68** 264
Sarah **69** 238 **131** 131
Sophronia Ryerson
   (Wheeler) **83** 208
Thomas **106** 295
Timothy **83** 208
William **128** 127
William T. **69** 38
Wilmot **113** 324
OAKMAN —— **53** 444
Betty **129** 165
Constant **89** 42
Deborah **60** 176
Deborah (Turner) **129** 165
Elizabeth **57** 402 **59** 137
   61 373
Hatch **66** 34
Isaac **105** 276
Israel **59** 135
Marilla **116** 62
Mary **52** 364
Melzar Turner **126** 226
Nanne **53** 124
Nicholas **53** 124
Olive **88** 392
Samuel **57** 402 **59** 75 135
   137 **60** 176 **61** 373 **81**
   310 **129** 165
Tobias **59** 75 **105** 281
Welthea (Carver) **89** 42
Oaks *see* Oakes
Oalds *see* Olds
OANACO Sachem of the
   Mohicans **87** 157
OANEE David **65** 376
Oarcut *see* Orcutt
OARE Matthew **94** 336
OARLEY Fanny **78** 301
OATEI Richard **112** 253
Oates *see* Otis
OATFORD Isoll **70** 283
OATHOUT Julia **81** 40

Oatis *see* Otis
OATLEY —— **99** 232
Anna Blanche **76** xxxix
Benedict **128** 129
Harry J. **113** 309 **116** 155
   117 156 **118** 166 244
   120 156 **121** 156
Harry J. (Mrs.) **119** 155
Jonathan **113** 309 **118** 244
Joseph **66** 29 **128** 129
Joshua **118** 244
Richard **94** 268
Samuel **127** 8
OATMAN
—— **61** 101 **76** 146
Albert Daniel **107** 226
Ann (Terrill) **133** 156
Avis A. **115** 297
Benjamin **115** 296 **116** 66
Benjamin D. **115** 296
Betsey **115** 296
Caroline **76** lxvii
Caroline Blanchard
   76 lxvii
Clarissa (Beebe) **89** 320
Daniel **115** 296
David **115** 296
Dyer **89** 320
Edwin George **89** 320
Electy **115** 296
Eliakim **133** 156
Elisha **75** 185 **76** 143
Floyd W. **116** 66
Frances Eveline **115** 296
Frederick LaSelle **89** 320
George **116** 66 **133** 156
Gertrude Ellen **89** 320
Gile W. **116** 117
Hannah **75** 185 186
Harvey **115** 296
Hester Ann **115** 296
John W. **115** 296
Joseph **133** 156
Juliaett **115** 296
Laura **115** 296
Lodice **115** 296 **116** 117
Lucinda **116** 117
Lucy (Stoddard) **133** 156
Martha **115** 297
Mary **115** 296
Myra **107** 226
Ophelia Adelaide (Lazell)
   (Hotchkiss) **89** 320
Oscar **115** 296
Phebe **106** 63 **115** 296
Phebe B. **115** 296
Philenda **116** 115
Ruth **115** 296
Samuel **75** 185 186 **76**
   141-143 145 149
Sarah **115** 296
Selden B. **115** 296
Selden M **116** 115
Thomas J. **116** 66
Truelove **70** 110
William Clift **76** lxvii
Oats *see* Otis
Oattley *see* Oatley
O'BANION
Alice Elizabeth **107** 135

O'BANNON
  Catherine **110** 65
  John **83** 62
O'BARRY
  Teague **148** 331 339
OBBINS Thomas **101** 270
Obdike *see* Opdycke
OBE Agnes **104** 248
  Andrew **104** 248
  John **104** 248
  Peter **67** 137 232 233
  Thomas **51** 126
O'BEACAN —— **57** 330
OBEAR
  — Capt. **141** 147
  Aram **85** 374
  Elizabeth (Romer) **85** 374
  Ephraim **119** 20
  Hannah M. **85** 372 373
  James B. **85** 375
  Jane Ann (Benedick)
    85 374
  Joseph W. **85** 376
  L. A. **55** 356 **64** 232
  Lydia B. **85** 373
  Mark A. **85** 374
  Martha (Leonard) **85** 375
    376
  Mary J. **85** 377 378
  Matilda J. (Leonard)
    85 376
  William **85** 378
OBELEY
  John Peter **63** 344
OBENDORF —— **92** 288
OBER —— **56** 388
  — Mr. **56** 251
  Abigail **89** 371
  Abigail (Pitman) **86** 65
  Ann **83** 484
  Anna **81** 485
  Anne **112** 33
  Benjamin **125** 102
  Betsey (Waide) **125** 102
  Catherine **125** 105
  David **56** 251
  Ellen (Kenney) **85** 378
  Hannah **56** 251 257
  Hezekiah **56** 389
  Isaac **55** 425 **56** 251
  J. Hambleton **107** 70
  John Hambleton (Mrs.)
    93 92
  Kendall **56** 258
  Lydia **56** 258 **111** 184
  Maria Frances **103** 73
  Mary **90** 193 **111** 110
  Rebecca **86** 65
  Richard **66** 113-115 123
  Sally **56** 258
  Samuel **54** 437 **55** 59 60
    429 430 **56** 251 258 388
    389
  Sarah **86** 65
  Thomas **86** 65
  William **56** 251
OBERHOLZER
  E. **115** 104
  Emil **110** 321
  Jacob **86** 352
OBERLIN Lulu **98** 146

OBERSHAW
  Louise **99** 47
OBERT Mary Elizabeth
  103 138
OBEY
  Barton **66** 220 222 302
  Elizabeth **66** 142 148 150
    154 210 220 222 302 303
  Jenny **66** 148 154
  Molly **66** 220
  Nathan **66** 210
  Peter **66** 148 150 154 210
    302 303
  Peterson **66** 222
OBIN Mary Jane **145** 140
OBINSON John **101** 274
OBITS
  John Michael **60** 188
OBORNE Edith **51** 349
  Elizabeth **89** 394
  Henry **51** 349
  Jane **51** 349
  Richard **51** 349
OBRE Henry **104** 72
  Robert **52** 349 350
OBREY Martha **83** 22 26
O'BRIEN Princes of
  Thomond **145** 368
O'BRIEN
  —— **58** 323 **72** 184
  — Rev. Fr. **66** 21
  Abigail **65** 257 **99** 192
  Abigail (Tupper) **99** 191
  Adam **62** 325
  Alice (Buckly) **128** 177
  Andrew **118** 46 57
  Ann **61** 134
  Anna **65** 257
  Anthony **115** 214
  Archibald **62** 244
  Bridget **95** 286
  Catherine **77** 188 **107** 48
  Chester J. **83** 124 233
  Chester James **87** 174
  Cordelia **66** 111
  Cynthia **99** 192
  Daniel **65** 257
  Dorothy Cutler (Dole)
    112 150
  Dorothy Dole **112** 150
  Edward **118** 156
  Eliza Maria **91** 291
  Elizabeth (McMurray)
    123 319
  Elizabeth (Pope) **99** 192
  Ellen **77** xci **87** 198 **89** 56
  Esther **128** 91
  Fidelia **99** 121
  Fidelia (Kendrick)
    100 242
  Francenia Bradford
    (Stewart) **112** 144
  Frances Hope **111** 148
  Frances Nelson (Rogers)
    111 148
  Frank **112** 150
  Franklin P. **108** 271
  George Clifford **123** 319
  George McCormick
    108 271
  Gideon **99** 191 192

O'BRIEN *cont'd*
  Hannah **89** 119 **94** 247
    99 192
  Harriet E. **84** 353
  Hugh **125** 43 **139** 12 193
  Isaac **118** 46
  James **99** 121 **100** 242
  Jeremiah **57** 122 **63** 270
    94 247 **99** 192 **113** 156
  Joanna **99** 192
  John **60** 349 **61** 133 **65** 257
    77 188 **99** 121 192 **100**
    25 27 **101** 271 **112** 144
    128 177 **140** 121
  John Bernard **70** xlv
    71 xxxvii
  John J. **73** 318 **74** xxv
    92 92 147
  Josephine **92** 359
  Julia (Coleman) **95** 286
  Kenneth (Mrs.) **84** 333
  Louise J. **84** 348
  Lydia **115** 38
  Lyman **113** 156 157
  M. J. **104** 290
  Mabel Maud **77** 57
  Mabel Stewart **68** xxxv
    74 xxvii **112** 71
  Margaret **85** 456
  Margery **65** 257
  Maria **110** 129
  Martha **65** 257 **99** 192
  Mary **61** 134 **66** 109 **74** 107
    86 310 **99** 192 **108** 187
    118 46 **145** 155
  Mary (Keen) **99** 191
  Mary (Lincoln) **99** 192
    125 287
  Mary (McManus) **128** 177
  Mary (Norton) **128** 211
  Mary Ann **69** 32
  Mary Jane **83** 233 **113** 156
  Mary Louise **84** 348 349
  Mary Margaret **83** 436
    437
  Matthew **72** 182 **128** 211
  May Ann Curtis **84** 219
  Michael J. **75** 241 **81** 241
    82 386 **90** 165 **95** 401
    107 19 **144** 361 **148** 332
    334
  Michael Morgan **110** 129
  Morgan Joseph **89** 132
  Morris **99** 191
  Nancy Bradbury **94** 247
  Nathan Henry (Mrs.)
    98 147
  Ninnie **117** 39
  Oliver **65** 257
  Patrick **62** 251 **128** 177
  Peter **91** 331
  Rebecca **99** 192
  Rhoda (Vail) **140** 121
  Richard **114** 316
  Richard Sylvester **77** 57
  Robert E. **111** 148
  Robert Lincoln **65** 292
    66 xxxv **85** 235 **86** 191
    90 211 **95** 350 **99** 265
  Ruth **94** 247
  Sarah **100** 27

O'BRIEN *cont'd*
Thomas **62** 251 **139** 207
Thomas J. **75** xxvi 76
Thomas Leland **112** 144
William **60** 24 **65** 257 **66** 307 **95** 286 **99** 192 **125** 287
William H. **84** 348
William J. **78** 160
William L. H. **79** 56
Zelda Polk **78** 160
Katharine (Mackay) **84** 333
Mary Ann Curtis **84** 219
OBYE Robert **51** 127
O'BYRNE
Roscoe C. (Mrs.) **93** 209
O'CAIN
Joseph **125** 104
Nabby (Kimball) **125** 104
O'CALLAGHAN Edmund
Bailey **95** 19 20 **121** 175 **124** 101 **145** 23 **148** 41
Henry Davis **117** 201
Jeremiah **116** 186 187
Mary Elizabeth **117** 201
O'CALLAHAN
Thomas **104** 234
O'CARROLL
Daniel **60** 24
Richard **60** 24
OCCLESTON
Lydia **80** 144
W. B. **80** 144
OCCOM
Dolothy **144** 222
Sampson **54** 231 **84** 168 **144** 222 **148** 294
OCCUISH Lucia **79** 76
Lydia **79** 76
Philip **79** 76
Sarah **79** 76
Occum *see* Occom
OCHELTREE
Martha **111** 210
OCHERBLOOM
John B. **77** 313
OCHS —— **143** 167
William John (Mrs.) **85** 197
OCHTERLONEY
—— **57** 120
Alexander **55** 147 **56** 189-193 **95** 25 **118** 173
Ann **56** 192 195
Anna **56** 192
Barbara **56** 191
Bethiah **56** 192
Catherine **56** 193
Charles **56** 193
Charles Metcalf **56** 194 **95** 25
David **55** 147 **56** 187 189 192-194 **57** 120 341 **95** 25
David Ferguson **56** 194 **58** xlv
Elizabeth **56** 189 191-193
Gilbert **56** 191 193 **95** 25
Helen **56** 192

OCHTERLONEY *cont'd*
Isabell **56** 191 192
James **56** 190-193
Jane **56** 193
Johanne **56** 190
John **56** 190-192 194 195
Katharine **55** 147 **56** 191 193
Katharine (Tyler) **95** 25
Margaret **56** 191 192
Maria **56** 193
Mariote **56** 190
Mary **56** 192
Mary Ann **56** 192
Matty **56** 192
Peter **56** 192
Roderick Peregrine **56** 194 **95** 25
Sarah **56** 194
T. H. **56** 195
Turpin **56** 189
Walter **56** 189 190
William **56** 190 191 195
Ocington *see* Ockington
OCKERBLAD Ethel Maude (Williams) **101** 126
OCKERMAN
Alfred B. **68** 239
Charity **133** 218
OCKERSHANSON
John **62** 244
OCKHAM —— **51** 116
OCKINGTON ——
(Phillips) **140** 235
Benjamin **65** 370 **79** 40
Betsey **57** 261
Cressy **57** 262
Crissea **55** 398
David **55** 392 **57** 146 261 262 374
Elizabeth **55** 392 **56** 35
Hannah **56** 31 38
John **56** 143 266 **57** 151 261
Lydia **56** 37
Mary **55** 392 **57** 145
Mary Ann **75** 199
Matthews **56** 266
Matthias **57** 25
Samuel **141** 38
Sarah **54** 18
Susanna **55** 262 **56** 32 **57** 30 147
Thomas **55** 392 **56** 141 143 266 268 **57** 30 145-147 150 151
William **56** 31 **57** 374
OCKLETON
Abigail **56** 37
OCKLEY Eleanor **51** 277
O'CLERY
Cucogry **121** 233
Ocom *see* Occom
O'CONNELL —— **58** cv
Anne Elizabeth **94** 27
Brendan Adrian **98** 77
Conleith **98** 77
D. T. **98** 76
Daniel **139** 205
Daniel Finbar **98** 77
Daniel Theodore **94** 139
Diarmuid **98** 77

O'CONNELL *cont'd*
Elizabeth **98** 76
Elizabeth (O'connell) **98** 76
Eve Weaver **106** 158
Frederick Patrick **98** 77
J. D. **51** 244
James **98** 76
John Thomas Lenahan **98** 77
Joseph Francis **97** 148 158 163 **98** 76 77
Katharine (Condon) **94** 27
Kevin **98** 77
Leila **98** 77
Marisita **98** 77
Marisita R. (Lanahan) **98** 77
Mary **83** 433 437
Meta **98** 77
P. A. **87** 385
Philip J. **56** xxxii
Thomas **94** 27
William (Cardinal) **136** 345
William Henry **132** 256 **137** 57 **139** 193
O'CONNOR Anna **76** 21
Annie M. **64** 126
Biddy **61** 134
Cecilia **70** 120 **115** 134
Charles **59** lxv **62** 320
Charles James (Mrs.) **86** 220
Daniel **75** 260
David B. **76** 21
Edward **64** 126
Hettie C. **84** 466
Jennie Stokes **76** 21
Jeremiah Joseph **95** 286
John **61** 134 **93** 299
Joseph **83** 437 **84** 20
Julia **95** 286
Lula Price **95** 400
Margaret **64** 126
Martin **116** 187
Mary (Purcell) **95** 286
Mary Ann **75** 260
Maurice **57** 204
Norreys Jephson **92** 305
Peter **100** 191
Rose (Spizaker) **83** 437 **84** 20
Rosona (Goodman) **116** 187
Sarah **57** 206
Sarah Elizabeth **57** 204
Julia (Hainer) **86** 220
OCONORTE
Harry **110** 166
O'COURT Henry **110** 162
OCTOR
Mehitable Hacket **91** 300
ODAIN Mary **88** 283
ODAM John **90** 87
O'DANIELS Mehitable (Gilbert) **137** 77
Patrick **137** 77
ODART Jeanne **109** 187

O'DAY
John Raphael **94** 139
ODBER Odberre
Alice **67** 260 **72** 186 189
  88 396
John **63** 33 **67** 260
Robert **63** 33 **67** 260
  72 188
ODDE Eliza A. **73** 192
Maria A. **73** 199
ODDENSELL
Thomas **148** 10
ODDING
Margaret **113** 101
Sarah **67** 157 **87** 51 **88** 296
  105 5
ODELL — Dr. **73** 204
Abigail **106** 294
Abigail (Barton) **106** 294
Almira **83** 342
Anna **122** 287
Anne Elliott **117** 76
Artemus **78** 124
Arthur Lee (Mrs.) **117** 76
Benjamin G. **88** 343
Betsey **61** 378
Bignell **94** 293
Caroline **89** 239
Clary (Gregory) **145** 156
Deborah **137** 37
Ebenezer **61** 236
Elizabeth **53** 462 **58** 319 **61**
  378 **119** 115 195 199
  127 88
Elizabeth Anna **137** 283
Emery A. **90** 305
Eunice **69** 377 378 **119**
  115 195 199
Frances Ann **78** 126
Freeman **130** 50
George **73** 206
George C. D. **107** 8
Hannah **61** 243 **106** 175
Hannah (Chase) **88** 122
Hannah E. **91** 231
Isabella **72** 216
Jacob **78** 126 **127** 159
  137 283
James **60** 91 **66** 36 **73** 74 75
  89 239 **108** 168 249
Jane **107** 51
Jeanette (Main) **137** 283
Jerome **88** 122
Joanna (Walker) **137** 37
John **60** 91 **106** 175 303
  119 195 199 **137** 37 40
John Walker **145** 156
Jonathan **106** 180 **130** 26
  27 29 **132** 325
Joseph **90** 305
Laura Folger **114** 21
Lucena **146** 368
Luther **61** 378
Margaret **78** 418
Maria **78** 124
Mary **53** 462 **65** 355 **73** 65
  127 159
Nancy (Jones) **89** 239
Perrin **114** 21
Polly **61** 379

ODELL cont'd
Priscilla (Messinger)
  134 332
Rebecca **60** 91
Regnold **134** 332
Richard **61** 65 **91** 231
  106 170
Rignell **91** 354
Samuel **69** 378 **91** 354
  106 294 **137** 37 **144** 235
Sara Lascelles **94** 139
Sarah **61** 236 **69** 378
  132 325
Sarah E. (Dennis) **88** 343
Sarah M. **81** 301
Sena **61** 380
Susanna **61** 239
Temperance (Dickinson)
  119 195 199
Thomas **65** 355 **73** 65
Ursula **60** 91
William **60** 91 **69** 378
  137 37 **144** 239 240
ODEN Benjamin **73** 152
  268 278
Catherine **73** 273
Eleanor **73** 154
Ellen **73** 276
Hannah Sophia **73** 267
Maria West **73** 267
Martha **73** 145
Michael **73** 221
Sarah Biggs **73** 138
Sophia Margaret **73** 278
Susanna **73** 148
ODER John **82** 60
ODIAME —— **54** 219
Henry **67** 368
Joan **54** 218
Odierne see Odiorne
ODIL George **128** 299
ODIN —— **53** 264 266
  55 117
— Mrs. **92** 134
Ann Francis **91** 270
Charlotte **87** 69
Elizabeth **91** 270 **100** 30
Esther **78** 178 **100** 237
Esther (Kettell) **91** 270
  100 304
Esther Kettell **107** 70
Harriet Louise **91** 270
Isabella (Redman) **92** 134
John **91** 269 270 **100** 26 27
  29 30 32 237 297 304
  101 270 273 **140** 244
Margaret **91** 269 270 **100**
  26 27 29 30 32 300 303
  101 270
Margaret (Sherman) **91**
  270 **100** 297
Timothy Cutler **91** 270
  100 32
ODINGSELLE
Thomas **107** 47
ODIORNE Odiorn
  —— **54** 219 **58** 231 **140** 55
— Miss **83** 308
___ (Cunningham)
  140 55
Abby Josephine **79** 14

ODIORNE cont'd
Abigail **67** 272 **83** 36
  97 265
Ann **81** 432
Augustus **73** 189
Augustus W. **73** 193
Augustus Walbach **64**
  lvii **95** 357
Benjamin **67** 272 **82** 50 283
  295
Catherine **53** 358
Daniel **54** 446 **97** 265 266
  300
Dinah **83** 36
Dorcas **126** 143
Ebenezer **53** 358 **55** 424 **58**
  231 **59** 56 59 **67** 110 **81**
  448
Edgar B. **83** 437 **84** 21
Elisha **97** 267
Eliza **81** 432 **82** 50
Elizabeth **58** 231 **81** 448 **82**
  50 282 295 **99** 247
Elizabeth Cunningham
  67 110
Elizabeth W. (Trefethen)
  83 437 **84** 21
Flora **83** 308
George **81** 448
Henry **76** 317
Henry M. **78** 181
Isabella (Redman) **92** 134
James **92** 315
James Creighton **58** 231
Jane **81** 432
John **58** 231 **67** 272 **81**
  432 448 **90** 56 **105** 112
  113
Joseph **58** 231 **73** 189 **79**
  14 **81** 448
Joseph M. **113** 163
Joseph S. **84** 31
Jotham **60** 195 **82** 295 299
  94 354 **106** 266 **125** 218
Kate N. **83** 298 300 **87** 90
Katharine **58** 231 235 **64**
  lvii **82** 51
Katharine Norrie **95** 357
Lizzie **73** 195
Lucy **97** 270
Lydia **67** 272
Mary **58** 231 **60** 195 **78** 302
  81 432 448 **82** 51 282
  283 295 299 **93** 121
Mary (Amerige) **90** 56
Mary E. **83** 181 185
Mary R. **73** 193 **84** 31
Mary Rider **64** lvii
Mary Rider (Nutter)
  95 357
Mehitable **60** 195 **63** lxiii
Nabby **82** 51
Nancy **95** 272
Nanny **82** 51
Nathaniel **81** 432 448
  82 50 51
Nicholas **119** 17
Norrie **95** 357
Philip **81** 432
Richard **78** 313
Robert **82** 50 **97** 265 266

ODIORNE cont'd
Sally **82** 51
Samuel **63** 174 **65** 257 **82** 50 51 290 295
Sanpeire **65** 257
Sarah **58** 231 **59** 56 **78** 309 **82** 290 295
Sarah Barrett **55** 424 **67** 110
Sarah C. **97** 266
Stephen **54** 219
Temperance **63** 174
Thomas **58** 231 **65** 220 **82** 51 **145** 361
Thomas H. **83** 308
William **63** lxiii **97** 266
William H. (Mrs.) **92** 134
ODLAND Lewis **91** 55
Lillie May (Hannum) **91** 55
ODLIN see also Audley
—— **92** 269
— Mr. **66** 304
— Rev. Mr. **67** 88
Abigail **103** 272
Anna **140** 312
Augustus **112** 241
Charles Cushing **61** 218
Dudley **65** 220
Elisha **104** 242
Elizabeth H. **91** 394
Everett L. **91** 394
Florence Ella **91** 394
Hannah **140** 312
Henry **51** 124
James Edwin **71** 294
John **55** 340 341 **67** 61 **69** 91 **82** 315 316 **87** 399 **92** 269 270 279 **140** 312 **144** 6
Lydia **103** 272
Margaret **140** 312
Martha **67** 22
Mary **100** 295
Mary (Wilson) **92** 279
Sarah **55** 340 **92** 270
Thomas J. **91** 394
Thomas Jefferson **112** 241
William **96** 93
Woodbridge **82** 315 316 **107** 313
ODOM John **105** 279
Mary A. Virginia (Jones) **101** 80
Miles Irwin **101** 80
Samuel S. **114** 264
O'DONALD
Mabel **72** 160
O'DONNELL Alexander (Mrs.) **87** 192
Anne **101** 321
Anthony **60** 160
Columbus **86** 336
Eleanora **86** 336
Ellen **93** 220
Ferderagh **112** 284
James Edward (Mrs.) **107** 134
Richard **78** 313

O'DONNELL cont'd
Marie Josephine (Hartford)(Makaroff) **94** 137
Mary **60** 27
Mary Elizabeth **82** 396
Mary Ellen **93** 220
Ralph **140** 231
Eleonora **86** 336
Eleonora (Pascault) **86** 336
O'Donnovan see O'Donovan
O'DONOHUE
Florince **109** 106
Lucy (Moseley) **109** 106
Willoughby **76** xxxvii
O'DONOVAN
John **116** 280
121 233 234
Michael **60** 24
O'DOWD Ellen **116** 187
O'DRISCOLL Elizabeth Rose **145** 195
O'DUYER Thomas **60** 24
ODY Ann **82** 492
Nattie Lureen **82** 492
William B. **82** 492
OEHLER —— **60** lxiv
OEIAE Hannah **82** 206
John **82** 206
Mary **82** 206
OELRICHS Blanche (DeLoosey) **136** 310 315
Blanche Marie Louise **136** 310
Charles DeLoosey **136** 315
Charles May **136** 310 315
Henry Ferdinand **136** 310
Julia Matilda (May) **136** 310
Marjorie Frances Marion **136** 315
Marjorie Ramsey (Turnbull) **136** 315
OESTERLIN Pauline (Johnson) **148** 186
OETTINGEN Elizabeth (Princess of) **77** 94
O'FARRELL
D. J. **139** 214
J. **78** 112
OFFELEY Thomas **52** 114
OFFEN John **66** 180 **141** 217
OFFENCED
John **126** 180
OFFENSAND
Anna **126** 180
OFFERTON Patrick de **103** 199 283
OFFING Margaret **62** 303
OFFLEY David **144** 147
OFFORD Rhoda **115** 121
William **115** 121
O'FLAHERTY
Catherine **125** 218
Maria **82** 177
Thomas **82** 177
O'FLANIGAN Jo **71** 117

O'FLAVIN
Thomas **118** 54 57
OGALDE
Transito **109** 288
OGBORN
Elizabeth **60** 290
Francis **60** 291
John **60** 290
William **60** 290 291
OGDEN —— **53** 460 **56** 214 **137** 311
— Capt. **75** 320
— Mr. **56** 251
Abigail **51** 508 **70** 36 **119** 181 182 **134** 255 334
Abigail (Hammond) **122** 160
Abraham **97** 119 **119** 179 **144** 323
Albe S. **69** 366
Alida Gouverneur **54** xciii **81** 477
Ann **79** 163
Anna **119** 192
Anna (Head) **97** 119
Anna (Tidd) **103** 309
Anna Belle **97** 119
Anna S. (Barker) **86** 98
Anne **69** 44 370
Benjamin Stratton **70** 191
Bethuel **69** 44
Caroline Hone (Callender) **144** 323
Catherine **73** 149
Charles **103** 309
Clyde **97** 119
Cornelia Ann **90** 391
Dale A. **97** 119
David **56** 297 **60** 21 **68** 171 **69** 237 **70** 39 41 **122** 160
David A. **105** 152
David B. **119** 192
Donald Clyde **97** 119
Dorothy Mabel **97** 119
Ebenezer **69** 44 233 **70** 34
Edmund **69** 44 375 377 378
Edmund Whitehead **84** 106 190
Edward **70** xl **134** 334 **144** 323
Eleanor **69** 170
Eleanor Elizabeth (Quintard) **109** 261
Eleanor H. **72** 106
Elias Dayton **109** 261
Eliza Ann **68** xxxv **74** xxviii
Elizabeth **69** 237 370
Elizabeth Ida **108** 225
Elizabeth Jane Harriet **94** 51
Ellen **70** 38
Elnora S. **66** 51
Erskine D. **72** 106
Esther **68** 294 **69** 134
Eunice **69** 44 366 378
Fanny (Waddell) **103** 309
Fred Paul **97** 119
George **87** 292
George (Mrs.) **87** 291 297

OGDEN *cont'd*
88 173
George A. 84 86
Grace Elizabeth 105 129
Hannah 112 142
Helen May 97 119
Hezekiah 68 294 69 44 134
Huldah 69 366
Humphrey 69 370
Isaac C. 94 282
Jacob 79 162 163
Jane 68 177 69 237
Jerusha 79 154
Jesse 69 44
Joanna 55 201
John 68 171 174 287 292 69
  44 376 70 40 42 43 73
  142 81 477 83 448 462
  84 9 87 292 94 304 119
  200
John Cosins 75 187
John E. 77 179
John Robert 108 225
John W. 86 98
Jonathan 106 92 136 309
Joseph 68 173 69 44 237
  370 375 70 39
Joseph Crawford (Mrs.)
  102 124
Josiah 119 116
Katheryne 84 9
Katheryne (Bradford)
  83 462
Lancelot 83 449 462 84 9
Lavina 134 334
Louis Henry (Mrs.)
  109 130
Louis Mansfield (Mrs.)
  84 208
Louise R. 77 179
Lydia (Cole) 103 309
Mabel 69 240
Magdalen (Van Norden)
  109 261
Malvina Belle 136 309
Mary 68 174 287 69 44
  237 240 375-378 70 40
  75 187 92 85
Mary Ann 75 lxxxi
Mary D. 119 13
Mary Elizabeth (Gorham)
  136 309
Mary Hone 70 xl
Molly 68 292 69 366 70 34
Moses 68 292 69 44 366
  70 34
Nancy 70 191 81 495
Obadiah 69 44 375
Pamelia (Britton) 97 119
Parthania 128 281
Peter Kemble 109 261
Rachel 82 514
Rebecca 101 335
Rebecca (Edwards)
  105 152
Rhoda 69 240
Richard 83 449 462 84 9
  94 51
Robert 73 136 82 188
  83 462
Rosannah 84 86

OGDEN *cont'd*
Ruranna 69 134
Ruth 69 233 70 34
Samuel 68 171 69 44 240
  378 70 41 103 309 119
  192
Sarah 56 297 69 44 370 375
  72 320 94 51 105 58 59
  152
Sarah (Harris) 105 58 59
Sarah F. 87 65
Sturges 69 237
Thomas 105 58
Ursula 83 462
William 83 449 462 84 9
OGEL —— 143 202
Ogelby *see* Ogleby
OGEN Mary 83 64
OGENS Robert 143 257
OGIER Amy 121 230
  Catherine 63 22 121 230
  Charlotte 63 22
  Elizabeth Martin 121 230
  George 62 322
  Jane 121 230
  John 63 22 121 230
  Lewis 63 22
  Lois McNeil 118 166
  Louis 121 230
  Louise 121 231
  Lucy 63 22
  Marc 121 231
  Mary 63 22
  Peter 63 23
  Pierre 121 230 231
  Thomas 63 22 121 230
  William 121 230
Ogilby *see* Ogleby
OGILVIE
  Amelia Willett 86 102
  Charles Lawrence (Mrs.)
    94 139
  Claude (Mrs.) 104 145
  Duncan 62 301
  Helma Moseley 84 111
    190
  J. S. 61 101
  John (Mrs.) 90 224
  Robert 62 244
  William 113 4 11 13
OGLANDER —— 59 142
  Eleanor 52 261
  Francis 52 266
  George 52 261 262 266
  Jane 52 261
  John 52 261 262 265 266
  Mary 52 261
  Oliver 52 265 266
  William 52 261 265 266
    268 53 12
OGLE Alex 128 172
  Barbara 104 274 275
  Barbara (Fenwick)
    104 275
  Benjamin 63 17
  Betty Lou 109 130
  Constance 104 273
  Dorothy 104 274
  Elizabeth 73 278 104 274
    122 320

OGLE *cont'd*
  Elizabeth (Bartlett)
    106 143
  Emma R. 128 171
  Gawen 104 272 273
  Gertrude 69 323
  Henderson 69 323
  Henry 132 46
  John 101 72 104 271-275
  Joseph 54 xxxix
  Kenneth Neil 106 143
  Lancelot 104 274
  Leah 69 323
  Mabel 104 274
  Margaret 104 274
  Margaret (Errington)
    132 46
  Mary 67 67 104 274
  Phillis 104 269 274 275
  Ralph 104 274
  Richard 67 67
  Robert 104 271-273
  Serra Seata 128 267
  William 104 272 274
OGLEBY —— 145 25
  Henry 51 115
  James 110 274
  John 64 345
  Margaret 71 xlv 137 281
  Robert 65 45
OGLES
  Elizabeth 57 220
  John 57 220
Oglesbee *see* Ogleby
OGLETHORPE
  James Edward 107 47
OGLETREE
  Amanda 82 281
  Louis Edmund 82 281
  Shirley Winifred 82 281
  Turner Watson 82 281
OGLI John 143 201
O'GRADY
  Bolton Waller 145 368
  Edith Faith 145 368
  Elizabeth Caroline
    145 368
  George John 145 368
  John de Courcy 145 368
  Standish Fitzwaller
    145 368
OGSBURY
  Alexander 118 328
  David 81 273
  Maria 81 273
O'HAMILL Peter 61 139
O'HARA
  Arietta 92 177
  Arthur D. 92 177
  Barnard 92 172 177
  Charlotte 92 177
  Charlotte (Briggs)
    92 172 177
  Edward 61 268
  Helen Pet 97 132
  Henry 60 349 61 133
  James 61 268
  John 66 306
  Louisa (Mayham) 97 132
  Mary Jane 89 120
  Michael 61 268

O'HARA *cont'd*
Samuel **97** 132
O'HARE
George Thomas **66** 37
O'HEA
Matthew **116** 250 251
O'HEARN
Catherine A. **100** 12
William **100** 12
OHESTROM
George L. **103** 313
O'HIGGINS
Ambrosio **109** 283
Bernardo **109** 283
OHIO John **73** 147
OHLEN
Henry George **64** 323
OHLER Clara Paine **60** 189
61 204 **67** xxxii 190
126 251
OHLSON William **64** 114
OHRN
Dorothy **82** 282 295
OHURA John **91** 202
OJEDA Horacio Thayer
109 290
Luis Thayer **60** 104 **62**
xxxvii **65** xxxv **88** 209
306 **89** 305 **92** 97 **109**
290
Tomas Thayer **61** 399 **62**
xxxvii **63** 209 **65** 305
109 290
O'KEEFE Eleanor Lucinda
87 190
Elizabeth **113** 316
Okeley *see* Oakley
OKELL — Miss **94** 337
George **65** 34
O'KELLEY Charity (Pease)
87 132 316 322
David **108** 239 **128** 210 260
Deliverance **87** 327
Elizabeth **128** 210 **129** 379
Jeremiah **87** 132
Joseph **87** 323
Sarah **87** 323 324 **124** 239
125 10
Stephen **87** 131
Thankful (Chase) **87** 131
Okely *see* Oakley
OKEN
Christopher **83** 318
OKESTON
Alexander **119** 98
Andrew **119** 98
OKILL — Mrs. **73** 36
O'Killey *see* O'Kelley
Okley *see* Oakley
OKOVER
Philipp de **92** 67
OLAFSDOTTER
Ellen **128** 170
OLAPSTON Bernard
Whitelaw **114** 153
OLAS Robert **91** 331
OLAY
Pelayo Garcia de
113 228
OLBEE John **73** 147
OLCOTT —— **54** 125 56

OLCOTT *cont'd*
162 **78** 383 **118** 13 18 26
116 125 126 212 **119** 43
127 211 295 **120** 123 133
— Capt. **56** 385
— Mr. **54** 199 **85** 37
Abigail **52** 79 308 **62** 11 **71**
162 **148** 30
Agnes **81** 44
Alfred **83** 366
Almira S. **84** 86
Ann **52** 308
Anna M. **88** 95 96
Anne **52** 79
Benoni **53** 448
Betsey **59** 99 **83** 366
Betty **54** 200 202 292 **60** 80
Bulkley **52** 183 **54** 202
57 269
Caroline **56** 254
Damaris **52** 183 308 418
58 196 **59** 413 **60** 200
83 161
Daniel **52** 79 310 **79** 158
David **66** 41
Derocis **83** 366
Dorcas **52** 416 417 **60** 79
204
Eleanor **71** 274
Eli **79** 164
Elias **52** 310 **54** 199 200 202
290 291 293 294 300 **55**
429 **56** 249 387 **132** 113
Elihu Smith **85** 169
Elisha **118** 27 29
Elizabeth **52** 419 **56** 249
84 86
Ellen E. Risley **85** 315
Emeline **84** 87
Emeline (McClure) **98** 80
Emerson E. **85** 169
Emma Marvin **98** 80
Eunice **52** 79 183 184 308
310 408 **54** 123 130 **70**
54 **81** 85
Eusebia **56** 249
Ezekiel **52** 416 417 **58** 196
197 **59** 415 **60** 73 76 200
83 366 **84** 87
F. O. **81** 44
Frank L. **85** 169
George H. **85** 169
Hannah **52** 408 **56** 249
147 58
Hannah (Pitkin) **147** 58
Harriet N. **84** 87
Harriet Winifred **81** 44
Harry E. **85** 169
Horatio **59** 97 414
Isaac **85** 169
Isaac I. **85** 315
James **52** 307 309 310 418
53 447
Jane Adams **85** 169
Jedediah **71** 79 160-162 273
274 279 302 305 **72** 30
John **52** 416 **56** 249 **58** 403
59 95 97 99 413-415 **60**
80 262 263 **64** 81 82 **79**
386 **81** 83 **83** 366 **105**
193 194 **143** 321 **148** 27

OLCOTT *cont'd*
34 189
John H. **74** 91
John H. (Mrs.) **74** 90
75 243 246
John T. **84** 86 87
Jonathan **52** 79
Joseph **81** 85
Josiah **72** 37
Julia **84** 87
Leslie **85** 169
Louise C. Tracy **85** 169
Lucy **54** 292
Margaret **52** 307 418
54 257
Maria Isabel **74** 91 **75** 246
Martha **57** 269 **101** 250
Mary **52** 419 **62** 85 **64** 81-
83 **79** 386 **80** 424 **83** 100
105 193 194 **143** 321
148 30
Mary (Blackleach) (Welles)
148 25 27-29 34 39 189
Mary Louisa Beatrice
98 147
Michael **79** 166
Nathaniel **120** 60 **147** 58
Parthenia **54** 293
Patty **56** 256 **58** 403 **59** 95
97 113 **60** 80 **83** 366
Peletiah Mills **56** 163
83 161
Penelope **72** 37
Persia **84** 87
Persis **60** 200
Peter **52** 183 **53** 449 **54**
253-257 **56** 163 352 **71**
273 305 **83** 161
Queria J. Bidwell **85** 169
R. H. **102** 79
Rachel **79** 386 **148** 30
Robert Henry (Mrs.)
102 124
Roswell **54** 255 **71** 274
Samuel **58** 194 **148** 30
Sarah **52** 307-310 418 **54**
256 **56** 352 **66** 41 **71** 79
160 279 302 **72** 30 **78**
383 **83** 161
Sibyl **54** 200 202 293
56 249 387
Simeon **53** 449 **54** 202
56 391
Sophia **125** 217
Sophronia L. **130** 51
Susanna **71** 161
Thomas **58** 202 **62** 11 **64**
82 **78** 383 **80** 424 **83** 100
89 175 **98** 80 **105** 247
143 321 **145** 323 **148**
189
Thomas Chandler **54** 200
Timothy **52** 183 184 308
310 408 419 420 **54** 200
202 292 **56** 249 390 **83**
100
Titus **52** 183 308 418 **53**
448 **59** 213 **83** 161 **84** 87
William **58** 194
Old *see* Olds
Oldag *see* Aldrich

Oldage *see* Aldrich
OLDAKER William **64** 219
OLDE John W. **145** 156
OLDEN
 Charles Smith **52** 384
 William **113** 285 **136** 54
OLDENBERG
 Gladys **92** 231
OLDENBURG Henry **124**
 100 **144** 213
OLDER Faith **135** 73
OLDERMAN
 William **122** 38
OLDERSHAW
 Alvin H. **68** 337
 Fred A. **68** 337
 John **51** 85
 Rose B. **68** 337
OLDFATHER
 Henry **66** 191
 William A. **70** 194
OLDFIELD Adam **65** 47
 David **76** 57
 Frances **64** 340
 Francis **112** 38
 John **112** 38 **127** 7 **128** 134
 O. B. **91** 331
 Samuel **127** 175 **128** 108
 Susan (Bressey) **112** 38
 Thomas **93** 383 386 387
OLDHAM —— **61** 92 **89**
 280 **119** 255
 — Mr. **91** 288 **94** 348
 Anna **70** 363
 Bethiah **70** 353
 Caleb **58** 387
 David **53** 430
 Deborah **53** 430
 Desire **58** 171
 Edith **137** 40
 Elizabeth **57** 182
 Esther **107** 130
 George **64** 160
 Grace **57** 179
 Hannah **57** 179 **107** 306
 120 260 **133** 192 193
 136 34
 Hannah (Ford) **119** 255
 Hannah (Keen) **133** 193
 Harriet Eleanor **67** xxxv
 Harriet Eleanor Holden
 90 127
 Henry **117** 292
 Isaac **57** 180 **133** 193
 John **53** 112 **54** 147 **55** 157
 71 123 **80** 97 **86** 92 **89**
 175-177 280 281 375 **91**
 286 **93** 358 **96** 272 274
 367 **97** 345 **98** 58 60 **105**
 162 **127** 7 **142** 110-112
 John (Mrs.) **91** 286
 Jonathan **61** 173
 Joseph **55** 277 **57** 86
 Joshua **57** 320 398 400 **58**
 175 **60** 188
 Lucretia **53** 112 **85** 363 **89**
 279 280 **90** 152 **91** 286
 93 358 **95** 130 **110** 229
 111 242 **142** 111
 Lydia **57** 183
 Lydia (Silvester) **86** 92

OLDHAM *cont'd*
 Margaret **53** 379
 Margery **64** 86
 Martha **76** 73
 Mary **57** 86 320 **71** 265
 85 260
 Mehitable **57** 398 400
 58 175
 Mercy **57** 398 **58** 171
 Patience **59** 138 **61** 173
 Philippa (Sowter)
 111 242
 Ralph **82** 189
 Richard **64** 86 **76** 73
 Ruth **55** 277 278 **57** 182
 Samuel **100** 130 **107** 306
 Sarah **57** 178 180
 Susanna **117** 292
 Thomas **57** 86 178-180
 182 183 320 398 **58** 171
 59 138 **89** 281
 William **111** 242
Oldich *see* Aldrich
OLDING — Mr. **71** 142
OLDIS —— **52** 46
OLDMAN
 Elizabeth **106** 44
 Nancy **132** 243
OLDMANES Mary **69** 249
 Timothy **69** 249
OLDMIXON —— **53** 289
OLDNIXON
 Eleanor **100** 222
Oldridge *see* Aldrich
OLDROOF —— **59** 416
OLDS —— **60** 315 **120** 303
 137 46
 — Mr. **52** 79
 Abigail **119** 259 **137** 45
 140 294
 Abigail (Barnes) **105** 66
 Abigail (Bond) **137** 25
 Abigail (Handchit) **90** 167
 Albert **84** 57
 Almon **120** 42
 Amanda (Rich) **84** 57
 Amasa Minley **78** 128
 Amos **90** 167
 Anna R. **141** 144
 Arabella Cook **76** 99
 Barnius **137** 25
 Benjamin **52** 79 **89** 182
 Bernice Estelle **105** 66
 Caroline Jones **90** 385
 Christian F. **61** 346
 Clarissa **120** 40
 Comfort **105** 66
 Daniel **90** 384 385
 David **68** 290 **69** 133
 Dexter **90** 385
 Edson Baldwin **80** 335
 81 222 **89** 121 182 **90**
 141 167 **120** 40
 Edward A. **75** 157
 Edward Allen **76** xxi
 88 88 172
 Eli **120** 40
 Elias **84** 57
 Eliza **120** 40
 Eliza P. **88** 340
 Elizabeth (Lamb) **123** 264

OLDS *cont'd*
 Elizabeth (Walker) **105** 66
 Ella (Knapp) **90** 167
 Elsie **90** 167
 Emily **120** 45
 Evelyn **89** 182
 Frank **84** 57
 Fred O. **108** 237
 George **90** 167
 George Stoughton
 90 167
 Gladys **105** 125
 Gladys Marguerite
 105 66
 Handford **69** 133
 Hanford **90** 167
 Hannah **69** 133 **71** 279
 120 45
 Hannah (Ford) **120** 45
 Hannah (Hanford) **105** 66
 Harriet Trussell **123** 125
 Henry **120** 42
 Henry (Mrs.) **85** 425
 Horace **60** 315
 James **64** 323 **90** 385
 Jane J. **125** 180
 Jason **105** 65 **120** 38 40 41
 Jennie Irene **93** 283
 Jeremiah **90** 384
 John **54** 83 **63** 234 346
 89 182
 John Preston **76** 100
 Joseph **89** 182
 Kingsley **90** 385
 Lavilla (Stoughton)
 90 167
 Lephe **78** 128
 Levi **120** 42 45
 Lilla Marion (Lazell)
 89 225
 Lois **90** 384 385
 Lois (Stanley) **90** 384
 Lucy **52** 79
 Luke **84** 57
 Maria A. **120** 42
 Marian **89** 182
 Mark Lafayette **89** 182
 Martin **90** 167 385
 Mary Ann (Kent) **90** 167
 Mary Porter **76** 100
 Matilda **90** 385
 Matilda (Ford) **105** 65
 120 40
 Mercy **93** 365
 Merton D. **89** 225
 Metta Ursula
 (Woodward) **105** 66
 Nathan **120** 42
 Nathaniel **110** 37 **120** 45
 Nelson **120** 42
 Nelson Horatio **93** 283
 147 69
 Orvilla **60** 315
 Persis (Rice) **105** 65 **119**
 259 **120** 39 40 **137** 45
 Pliny **120** 40
 Pliny Fiske **105** 65
 Ransom Eli **100** 108 **105**
 65 66 68 125 131 319
 Rebecca **60** 315
 Richard **60** 128

OLDS *cont'd*
Robert **89** 182 **90** 167 **105**
  66 **123** 264 **145** 324
Roxana **120** 39
Roxcellana **54** 83
Ruth R. **86** 289
Sabra **120** 42 45
Sally (Avery) **110** 37
Sally M. (Carpenter)
  120 42
Samuel **90** 167 **105** 65
  119 259 **120** 39 40 **137**
  45
Sarah **69** 133
Sarah (Whipple) **105** 65
Sarah Jane **110** 37
Sheldon **120** 42
Silas **120** 38 40
Submit **121** 226
Susanna **120** 41
Susanna (Ford) **120** 42
William **105** 66
Zenas **120** 42
OLDSON
Elizabeth **77** 218
James **62** 382
OLDUFF
Charles C. **116** 207
Freddie **116** 207
Laura A. **116** 207
OLDYE — **57** 409
O'LEARY
Frances **69** 31
Nellie **136** 325
OLEBEARE Susie (Trower)
  (Buchanan) **117** 121
OLEMBERY
Daniel **143** 257
OLEN Anthony **70** 231
John **100** 191
John W. **100** 191
Louise **100** 255
Mary **70** 231
OLENDORF
Betsey **115** 109 118
Conrad Henry **115** 110
Cornelia **115** 118
Lossia Ann **115** 118
Mary **115** 110
Mary Ann **115** 118
Peter **115** 118
OLESTER Rebecca **83** 76
OLFELDE — **51** 353
OLIASON Melvin
  Clarence (Mrs.)
  106 126
OLIER Charles **115** 296
OLIFF — Mr. **57** 316
OLIN Abigail **75** 15 **108** 83
Alice Townsend **92** 77
Ann **87** 337
Anna **84** 209
Arvin **135** 6
Asa **135** 6
Benjamin **60** 124
Bernice Eva (Bixby)
  86 363
Betsey (Green) **135** 6 9
Charles Clifford **86** 363
Ellen F. **75** 15
Elsie Townsend **92** 77

OLIN *cont'd*
Emma Amelia **89** 315
Ezra **135** 6 7 9 10
Fannie **89** 315
Frank **135** 6
Frank James **86** 363
George S. **89** 315
Gideon H. **75** 15
Gladys (Chubb) **86** 363
Hannah **75** 15
Henry **75** 15 **129** 60
John **84** 210 **128** 134
Jonathan **129** 67
Mary R. (Cadwell) **135** 6
Paris **76** 264
Peleg **129** 271
Phineas **55** 179
Rebecca **93** 332
Roxana **75** 15
Sally **60** 124 **87** 337
Sophia **76** 264
Stephen Henry **92** 77
William M. **51** 91 **94** 219
Zipporah **55** 179
OLIND Joyce **113** 210
OLINGER Alice Josephine
  80 158
Benjamin **80** 158
Edna Lucille **80** 158
Elizabeth **80** 158
Lora Park **80** 158
Mark Burnside **80** 158
Park Cranston **80** 158
OLIPHANT
Andrew **71** 59 61
Anna **65** 220
David **51** 93 **65** 220
  107 192
Duncan **70** 285
Elizabeth **105** 51
Ernest R. (Mrs.) **95** 289
Guy Campbell **94** 89
Henry D. **67** 305
James **65** 244 **122** 104
  127 143
Jeannette **89** 132
Lawrence **94** 89
Lucy (Cowin) **94** 89
Mary C. Simms **113** 161
Mary Coulter (Campbell)
  94 89
Mary Eliza **115** 38
Mary Welch **94** 89
Nelson B. **94** 89
Nelson B. (Mrs.) **93** 138
  94 89 126 145
Nina (Jones) **95** 289
Phebe **140** 176
Samuel Duncan **94** 89
Samuel Grant **70** 285
Walter **122** 267
OLISON Albert **78** 190
OLIVE
Elizabeth (Barber)
  125 101
Ida S. **104** 47
James Kelly **78** 362
Jessie May **104** 47
Joyce **113** 210
Judith **54** 218
Margaret **54** 218 **135** 250

OLIVE *cont'd*
Myrtle Iona **104** 47
Nathaniel **104** 242
Rowland **54** 218
Stephen **104** 47
Virginia Ann Frances
  78 362 **80** 440
OLIVER — **54** 29 **58** 323
  81 179 **102** 286 **110** 178
  120 207 **121** 61 67 302
  122 65 306 **131** 270 272
  140 231 **144** 16
— Capt. **94** 319
— Dr. **84** 362
— Judge **51** 483 **84** 251
  262 **85** 8
— Mr. **84** 251
— Mrs. **52** 117 **76** 202
— Sect. **84** 154 156 158 267
____ (Johonnot) **140** 159
A. **145** 61
Abby J. B. **77** 147
Abigail **54** 101 102 **75** 204
  112 152 **147** 76
Abigail (Boardman)
  84 363
Abigail (Bryant) **137** 325
Abigail (Thompson)
  140 231
Agnes (Campbell)
  147 185
Albert E. **96** 161
Albert Edward **111** 60
Alexander **65** 220 **91** 206
  94 95 **100** 65
Alice **142** 237
Alice Armena **97** 159
Alice Maud **87** 111
Amy (Fane) **97** 381 382
Andrew **52** 228 **53** 73 **54**
  lxiii-lxv **55** 291 293 **57**
  280 388 **58** lvi 68 **67**
  108 **69** 112 **71** 102 150
  75 204 **76** 202 **84** 153
  169 171 269 360-363 373
  377 **91** 93 401 **95** 147
  103 276 **113** 318 **115**
  156 **121** 40 248 **130** 198-
  207 **132** 30 285 **136** 280
  281
Andrew C. (Mrs.) **121** 157
Ann (MacCartney)
  100 243
Anna **57** 192
Anna (Richardson)
  100 132
Anna Maria **96** 186
Anne **130** 196 206
Anson Place **100** 87
Anthoine **75** lxxxv **77** 290
Benjamin **59** 369
Benjamin Lynde **130** 204
  207
Bethiah **71** 147 260 **84** 269
Betsey **84** 361 **116** 135
  136 128
Betty **56** 265
Beverly Margaret **105** 220
Blanche Brooke **97** 382
Brattle **96** 325
Bridget **70** 66

OLIVER *cont'd*
Brinley Sylvester **130**
  203 207 **144** 266
Campbell **80** 27
Caroline **64** 155
Catherine **78** 414 **111** 94
  125 100
Cecil Duval **105** 220
Cecil Duval (Mrs.) **103**
  120 **105** 118 133 220 221
Cecil William **105** 220
Celia Sabina (Martin-
  Holloway) **97** 382
Charles **91** 246
Charles L. **83** 430 437
Charles Langford
  97 381 382
Charlotte **73** 50
Cordis **137** 219
Cornelius **73** 144
Cromwell **56** 37 265
Cuthbert Hanson **97** 382
Daniel **51** 91 **52** 228 **54**
  lxiv **55** 293 **63** 377 **64**
  157 **66** 364 **67** 108 **68**
  230 233 234 236 309 **91**
  93 **92** 59 **98** 351 **105** 195
  113 220 **115** 156 **118**
  313 **120** 283 **121** 248
  130 198 204 206 207
  131 178 182 **140** 231
  144 167
David **79** 44 **86** 293 **119** 17
  140 231 **147** 185
Ebenezer **85** 124 125 **94** 68
  125 101 **140** 159 231
Edward **97** 381 **99** 26 **100**
  243 **140** 231
Edward Brattle **84** 153
  107 313 **140** 231
Edwin **112** 165 **123** 222
Eleanor **81** 491
Elizabeth **51** 133 265 **55**
  293 **56** 37 **66** 84 **69** 112
  116 **73** 261 **76** 205 **83**
  488 **84** 155 156 251 **111**
  94 **115** 320 **125** 100 105
  139 61 **147** 76 185
Elizabeth (Belcher) **130**
  198 206
Elizabeth (Brattle) **130** 206
Elizabeth (Newdigate)
  130 196 206
Elizabeth (Rowlan)
  130 206
Elizabeth (Wittum)
  114 49
Elizabeth Shaw **94** 140
Emily **98** 351
Ephraim **147** 76
Esther P. **126** 207
Eugene **114** 265
Evelina Frances **81** 205
Fitch Edward **61** 148 **130**
  204 207
Floretta (Owen) **91** 246
Forbes **57** 192
Forbes H. **90** 57
Frances **80** 26
Frances (Brooke) **97** 382
Frances F. **73** 272

OLIVER *cont'd*
Frances Sophia (Doolittle)
  90 57
Francis **55** 97 **93** 385
Francis Johonnot **136** 309
  140 159 231
Frank L. **103** 269
Frederick Lansing **111** 77
G. L. **111** 129 130
Gamaliel W. **73** 50
George **80** 26 **115** 252
George Francis **100** 112
Glenn **117** 314
Glenn William (Mrs.)
  108 135 **117** 314 **121** 74
Grizell **52** 228 **84** 154
Guy Marriott **97** 382
Hangerford **130** 70
Hannah **63** 376 **64** 75 **66**
  359 360 **85** 388 **114** 293
  115 136 140 141
Hannah (Cowes) **85** 388
Hannah Francis **68** 230
  113 220 **144** 167
Harriet **91** 246
Harry Duval **105** 220
Helen Mae (Smith) **100** 87
Henry **55** 97 **63** 255
Henry Kemble **63** 114
Isabella (Langford)
  97 382
Jacob **63** 377 **64** 76 **66** 363
  77 lxxii **105** 277
James **54** 101 102 **60** 129
  65 132 **66** 370 **67** xxxii
  87 316 **99** 102 **102** 180
  110 178 **111** 94 **112** 286
  114 48 49 **116** 89 **120** 77
  130 196 206 **137** 325
  144 13
James Harrison **64** xxxi
Jane **63** 377 **64** 157 **66** 364
Jo. **69** 108
Joan **53** 376 **98** 117
Joanna **53** 376 **67** 105
  116 298
Joanna Tilestone **92** 59
John **51** 45 133 **53** 376 **54**
  159 **55** 97 **56** 86 **59** 406
  60 356 **64** 221 **65** 239
  66 37 **67** 105 **70** 247 **76**
  186 260 **85** 388 **86** 398
  94 70 **99** 26 **110** 178
  114 130 **119** 20 **130** 196
  206 **144** 6 32
Jonathan **64** 155 **112** 164
  165 324
Jordan **139** 287
Joseph **58** 142 **140** 231
Joseph B. **54** 101
Jotham **115** 307
Joyce **113** 210
Judy **102** 36
Kitty Langford **97** 381
  382
Lancit **92** 47
Leonora Anna **84** 191
Levin **73** 278
Lilian Hays **118** 247
Lois Opal **108** 135
Louisa **81** 257

OLIVER *cont'd*
Love (Frye) **130** 201
Lucy (Silvester) **86** 293
Lucy E. (Winslow) **90** 107
Luther T. **103** 269
Lydia **53** 462 **80** 25 27
  125 222
Lydia (Brown) **106** 148
Lydia (Ellis) **122** 198
Lydia (Wyer) (Keith)
  106 148
Lydia Crosby **77** lxxii
Magdalene **94** 193 **108**
  225 **121** 25
Manuel **118** 152
Marcy **84** 362
Margaret **66** 319 **84** 158
  362 363 **100** 233 **130**
  206 **144** 168
Margaret (MacIntyre)
  111 129
Margaret Virginia
  (Thompson) **105** 220
Margery E. **80** 28
Marguerite **77** 290 **88** 397
  93 374 **97** 91
Martha **53** 9 10 **55** 146 **64**
  185 **67** 107 **73** 136 **80** 26
Martha (Skelis) **105** 220
Martha Vere (Brown)
  97 382
Mary **52** 228 **55** 291 293
  58 219 **59** 369 **68** 309
  69 112 **71** 147 150 **72**
  xxxvi **73** 262 **76** 186 260
  78 68 **84** 153 **85** 8 **92** 47
  93 ix 403 **97** 277 **100** 233
  238 **102** 140 **111** 23 94
  114 49 **125** 100 288 **144**
  167
Mary (Bradeen) **111** 94
Mary (Clark) **130** 199 206
Mary (Fitch) **130** 198 207
Mary (Johonnot) **140** 231
Mary (Langford) **97** 382
Mary (Lynde) **130** 202 207
Mary (Sanford) **103** 276
  130 198 203 207
Mary (Silvester) **86** 293
Mary Abigail **77** lxxii
Mary Alsop **136** 309
Mary Ann H. **90** 43
Mary Bentley **51** 367
Mary Caroline (Alsop)
  136 309
Mary E. **79** 37
Mary Lynde **136** 329
Mary M. **68** 257
Mary Robinson (Pulling)
  130 204 207
Matthew **64** 320
Mercy **80** 25 **127** 158
Mercy (Bradstreet)
  130 206
Mercy G. **88** 286
Michael **90** 42
Nancy Sims **109** 309
Narcissus **78** 51
Nathaniel **57** 275 **60** 29
  63 258 **64** 185 **67** 107
  71 147 260 **87** 399 **96**

OLIVER *cont'd*
325 **123** 191 **130** 206
131 182
Nellie **74** 92
Nellie Augusta **78** 206
Nichola **142** 237
Nicholas B. **107** 43
Otis **122** 198
Ozina H. **91** 331
Palmer F. **91** 331
Parker **86** 292
Patience **86** 293
Patience (Silvester)
86 292
Peter **51** 132 133 **52** 228
54 lxiv **57** 280 388 **65**
220 **67** 108 **69** 112 **71** 59
102 **75** lxvi **84** 262 373
377 **87** 399 **96** 325 **99** 79
242 **107** 313 **111** 15 **119**
272 **121** 248 **126** 226
129 103 **130** 26 196 198-
200 202-207 **131** 182
134 110 242 **136** 280
140 69
Polly **65** 359
Priscilla **147** 76
Priscilla Gray **125** 104
136 79
R W (Mrs.) **77** 322
Rachel **90** 109
Rebecca **63** 377 **64** 76 **66**
363 **106** 148
Rebecca (Belknap) **88** 338
Rebecca (Bradish) **106** 148
Rebecca (Chase) **87** 316
Rhoda **73** 151
Richard **63** 244 **97** 381
119 17
Richard Henry **105** 220
Richard Langford **97** 382
Robert **58** 119 **65** 220 **66**
319 **79** 46 **81** 490 **84** 156
160 **91** 206 **100** 238 **110**
178 **111** 23 **142** 34
Robert William (Mrs.)
78 206
Royal **90** 107
Russell E. **88** 338
Sally **84** 267
Sally (Hutchinson) **84**
262 **130** 204 206
Samuel **63** 376 **64** 75 **66**
360 **125** 44
Sarah **51** 133 **54** 101 419 **67**
107 **68** 234 **73** 50 **76** 244
80 25 **99** 26 **130** 204 207
144 167
Sarah (Babbidge) **144** 167
Sarah (Newdigate) **130**
196 206
Sarah (Pynchon) **130** 204
207 **136** 329
Sarah Ann (Robertson)
90 42
Sarah E. (Gray) **83** 430 437
Sarah F. **88** 341
Sarah S. **79** 51
Sibyl **139** 287 **147** 9
Silence (Bates) **112** 164
Sophia **80** 26

OLIVER *cont'd*
Sukey (Johonnot) **85** 125
Susan **88** 334 **117** 253
Susan Lawrence (Mason)
130 204 207
Susan May (Avis) **106** 148
Susanna **51** 463 **54** 101
102 **68** 236 **78** 301 **92** 59
144 167
Susanna (Cook) **115** 307
Susanna (Honeywell)
130 203 207
T. **101** 273
Temperance P. **80** 26
Thankful **57** 192
Thomas **52** 228 421 **54**
lxiv **64** 109 184 **65** xix
71 259 **72** xxxvi **84** 352
377 378 **86** 293 **91** 93 **97**
381 382 **106** 148 **112**
152 **113** 210 **116** 111
130 196 198 206 **131**
108 **134** 189
Thomas Fitch **54** lxiv
130 203 204 207 **136**
329
Thomasin (Jackson)
144 32
Vere Fane Martin **97** 382
Vere Langford **63** 301
69 xxxiv **78** 222 **82** 258
90 128 **97** 148 159 381
382 **112** 272 **144** 156
Virginia Tucker **121** 157
Wadsworth **80** 26
Walter **139** 287 **147** 9
Warren **100** 132
William **53** 2 10 **57** 192
59 369 **60** 27 356 **65** 170
80 26 **92** 59 60 **100** 233
238 **107** 313 **125** 36 **128**
265 **148** 56
William Albert (Mrs.)
109 130
William B. **73** 50
William H. P. **91** 401
William Hutchinson
Pynchon **85** 197
William M. **77** 147
William Pitts **92** 59
William Pynchon **130**
205 207
William Sanford **51** 463
130 203 207
Willy **73** 277
OLIVÉRA
Diego **100** 325
Maria Estefana **100** 325
OLIVERT
Submit **58** 300
Thomas **58** 300
OLIVEY Bridget **79** 94
OLIVIA Cornelia **95** 285
OLIVIER Marguerite **53**
459 465 **88** 397 **97** 91
OLKERSON Elizabeth
(Faulkner) **132** 40
OLKESSON
James **132** 40
OLLARD Anne **54** 91
Elizabeth **54** 91

OLLERHEAD
Will **64** 341
OLLYN Jane **79** 311
OLMES Thomas **147** 23
OLMSETTER
Hannah **62** 365
OLMSTEAD —— **63** 372
93 357 **94** 121 **96** 370
119 207
— Mr. **71** 118
A. T. **102** 318
Aaron **79** 164
Aaron F. **79** 162
Abigail **58** 319 **59** 357 359
60 211 **80** 417
Adelia **72** liii
Adosha **80** 428
Agnes **65** 284 **80** 115
Alma Leonora **72** liii
Almira **136** 324
Alonson **72** liii
Alpa **71** 122
Alvin Soule **76** 87
Ann **79** 154 **80** 115
Anna **59** 357 **74** 178 **81** 51
136 329
Anne **52** 40 **59** 359 360 **65**
284 **68** 290 **69** 134
Annie **96** 161
Ashbel **81** 269
Ashburn **76** 146 151
Austin M. **84** 87
Bathsheba **100** 260
Benjamin **100** 260 **136** 325
Bertha **85** 158
Betsey **59** 359 360
Bradley H. **76** 87
Catherine (Van Schaick)
100 260
Charles **59** 360
Charlotte **97** 123
Charlotte L. **79** 151 164
Charlotte Law (Hull)
136 325
Clarissa **76** 87
Content (Pitkin) **136** 325
Cordelia **82** 454
Dameras **100** 260
Daniel **59** 357-359 **69** 43
70 39 **71** 281
David **52** 309 **59** 358 359
61 96 202 218 **69** 43 60
76 143 **94** 121
Deborah **59** 357
Denison **54** cxx 136
Didamia (Chase) **88** 27
Dorcas **58** 319
Dorothy **80** 418 428
120 95
Ebenezer **104** 262
Eleazer **59** 359 **69** 43 375
Elias **76** 268
Elihu **81** 418
Elijah **54** 257-259 **55** 35 36
56 163 353 **59** 359 **69** 43
83 161
Elizabeth **51** 331 **59** 356-
358 **72** 219 **79** 154 157
81 83 **94** 121
Emma Pamela **94** 195
Erastus **54** 257 **71** 54

OLMSTEAD *cont'd*

Esther **59** 360 **69** 60
Eunice **59** 356 357 **76** 89
Frances **79** 151
Frances Flowers **136** 324
Frances M. **69** 170
Francis Caldwell **98** 345
Frederick L. **91** 188
Frederick Law **59** xxxi
  xxxiii xliv **62** 111 **79**
  406 **80** 65 **92** 195 **136**
  325
Frederick Law (Mrs.)
  84 99
Gardner **59** 358
George **88** 118 **118** 217
George Arthur **77** 182
George T. **113** 287
George Tyler **81** 196
Gertrude E. **92** 230
Gideon **101** 146
Grace **59** 359
Hannah **52** 183 **58** 319 **59**
  357-360 **72** 219
Hannah (Marsh) **136** 325
  329 330
Hannah (Meakins)
  136 325
Hannah Boudinot (Field)
  113 287
Harper C. **98** 345
Harry **55** 35
Henry Higgins **92** 231
Henry King **67** 191
Herman **92** 230
I. M. **91** 331
Ichabod **59** 358 **80** 428
Ida **90** 350
Ina May **92** 230
Israel **58** 319
J. **80** 63
J. A. **76** 270
Jabez **58** 319 **60** 189 211
  119 79
James **58** 319 **59** 355-360
  64 73 **67** 191 **72** 216 219
  80 131-133 **81** 51 **93**
  357 358 **94** 67 **95** 387 **96**
  280 **98** 94
Jane **59** 357
Jane Brigham **81** 196
Jemima **68** 173
Jeremiah **58** 319
Jesse **59** 359 **69** 43
Job **104** 262
John **52** 308 **59** 355-360
  65 284 **66** 311 **68** 173
  69 43 375 **79** 151 154
  155 164 **80** 418 428 **85**
  158 **104** 262 **136** 325
John (Mrs.) **79** 406
John B. **80** 428
John Hull **97** 123
Jonathan **80** 418 **81** 51
  136 325
Joseph **52** 183 308 309 **53**
  447 **54** 258 **59** 356 **72**
  219 **79** 143-146 151 172
  136 325 329 330
Joshua **60** 331
Julius A. **81** 418

OLMSTEAD *cont'd*

Justice **59** 358
Kneeland **71** 120
LeGrand **76** 87 89
Levi **100** 260
Lewis **59** 360
Lewis B. **80** 428
Lona Esther **92** 230
Louisa A. **76** 87
Lucretia **76** 89
Lucy L. **82** 454
Luke **88** 27
Lydia **59** 357 360
Lydia H. **84** 87
M. Lynde **80** 66
Margaret **52** 418
Marillus **59** 359
Martha **52** 183 308 309 419
  58 319
Mary **59** 356-358 360 **66**
  311 **76** 87 143 268 **77**
  182 **80** 418 **82** 454 455
  118 143 **136** 316 326
Mary (Higgins) **92** 231
Mary Ann **79** 155
Mary Ann (Bull) **85** 158
Mary Bond **84** 459
Mary C. **59** xiii xxxi xxxiii
Mary Cleveland **97** 123
Mary E. **82** 454
Mary Eliza **82** 454
Mary J. **71** 119
Mary L. **79** 164
Mercy **80** 428
Merrick **69** 170
Michael **79** 169 **82** 454 455
Mindwell **59** 359 **69** 43
  375
Moses **58** 319
N. H. **125** 44
Nancy (Chase) **88** 118
Nancy (Judd) **136** 324
Naomi **85** 426 **136** 330
Nathan **59** 356 357 359 360
  113 163
Nehemiah **59** 355
Nellie **83** 231
Nicholas **59** 355 356 **60**
  189 **72** 219 **80** 418 **89**
  175
Noah **59** 359
Nona **81** 196
Norwood Wendell
  92 231
Olive **80** 428
Oliver **80** 428
Owen P. **79** 151
Palladia **65** 285
Phebe **59** 356 358 360 **69**
  134 **91** 245
Polly **59** 359 **71** 53 **76** 270
Polly E. **76** 87 89
Prudence **58** 319
Rachel **59** 359 **71** 281
Rachel (Fitz Randolph)
  98 345
Raymond Lee **92** 231
Rebecca **59** 357
Rebecca Elaine **92** 231
Reuben **59** 358 360 **68** 290
  69 134

OLMSTEAD *cont'd*

Rhoda **94** 121
Richard **51** 330 **59** 355-360
  60 189 **64** 83 **67** 191 **71**
  111 **89** 175 **129** 354
Robert Irving **92** 231
Roger **125** 43
Roger Allen **92** 231
Roswell **81** 418
Rufus Keeler **59** 360
Ruth **81** 51 269 **121** 251
Samuel **59** 356 357 359 360
  80 417 418 428 **81** 268
Sarah **55** 36 **56** 353 **58** 319
  59 355 357-359 **69** 43
  375 **71** 122 **72** 216 **80**
  417 **81** 268 **83** 161 **89**
  246
Sarah (Chase) **88** 118
Seth **59** 360
Silence **58** 319
Small **59** 359
Soule **76** 87
Stanley Lawrence **92** 231
Statira **81** 269
Stephen **52** 418 **59** 359 360
  69 134
Susanna **80** 418 **81** 418
  98 94
Sylvanus **59** 358
Thankful **58** 319 **60** 211
Thomas **144** 49
Timothy **76** 87 89
Timothy Allen **76** 87
Victor Herrick **92** 231
Waldo **71** 52 53 119
Walter **54** 259 **71** 53
Warren **82** 455
Wendell A. **92** 231
Wileman **88** 118
William **60** 302 **76** 145
  80 418
William Henry **92** 230
William Manly **94** 121
Zilpha **100** 260
OLNEY —— **55** 153 **57** 343
  59 236
Abbalena **100** 333 334
  111 133
Abigail **146** 348
Amelia Ann **70** 209
Amos **128** 218
Amy **138** 135
Ann **70** 209
Anthony **135** 200 **138** 135
Asa **138** 135
Augustus **97** 119
Austis **133** 309
Benjamin **82** 179
Bristol **127** 307
Burrill A. **89** 94
Caroline **77** 179
Caroline (Poole) **97** 119
Catherine **62** xxxvii
Catherine H. **89** 390
Christopher **65** 220 255
  127 227
Coggeshall **65** 220 **102**
  235 **138** 320
Cynthia **80** 170

OLNEY *cont'd*
Cynthia Diantha (Bensley)
  93 205
Cythera Diantha
  (Benchley) **142** 381
Dana Bensley **142** 381
Davis **89** 94
Deborah **127** 307 **138** 135
Elisha **142** 12 14
Elizabeth **138** 135
Elizabeth (Chase) (Stone)
  87 315
Elizabeth (Crandell)
  138 135
Ellen J. **105** 82
Ellen Warner **59** 236
Elvira (Ely) **89** 94
Emily (Head) **97** 119
Emor **138** 135
Epenetus **89** 94
Eseck **138** 135
Ezekiel **68** 337 338 **100** 334
  111 133
Frances **140** 181
Frederick **70** 155 156
Freelove **60** 175
G. F. **70** 155
George **97** 119 **127** 307
George Edward **97** 119
George H. **52** 379
George Rufus Atwill
  70 209
Giles Herbert **70** 156
Hallelujah **80** 78
Harriet Minerva
  (Howland) **100** 291
Helen Adel **142** 381
Hopkins **138** 135
Hortensia M. **82** 397
Ira **77** 179
Isaac **71** 203 **110** 33
James **80** 78 **100** 334
  138 135
James D. **97** 119
James H. **142** 381 **144** 320
Jane **100** 334
Jane Meggs **82** 180
Jenne (File) **144** 320
Jennie Amelia **142** 381
Jeremiah **63** 84 **65** 220 **79**
  351 **80** 86 **100** 333 334
  102 235
Jesse **100** 334
Jessie M. **70** 155
John **89** 94 **128** 58
Joseph **128** 58 **138** 135
  142 177
LaFayette **93** 205
LaFayette Washington
  142 381
Lydia **68** 337 338 **100** 334
Lydia (Brown) **100** 334
Lydia (Packard) **110** 33
Marcy **138** 135
Mary **80** 171 **82** 179 **100**
  334 **138** 135
Mary (Callender) **144**
  319 320
Mary (Whipple) **89** 94
Nabby **63** 84
Nancy (Davis) **89** 94

OLNEY *cont'd*
Nathan **142** 381
Nedebiah **80** 183 **89** 94
Olive (Rowe) **89** 94
Olive S. **70** 155 156
Oliver **100** 334
Oliver B. **70** 155
Pardon **138** 135
Parres **138** 135
Peter **142** 381
Phebe **78** 303
Rachel (Coggeshall)
  89 94
Rhoda **81** 387
Rhodea **138** 135
Richard **51** 363 **52** 483 **79**
  239 **127** 228 **144** 320
Roscoe George **100** 291
Sally (Brown) **142** 381
Sally Ann **100** 334
Samuel **54** 170 **138** 135
  144 319 320
Samuel J. **142** 381
Sandra (Sutphin) **147** 91
Sarah **54** 170 **80** 171 174
  82 179
Sarah (Scott) **138** 320
Sibyl **80** 184 **110** 33
Simeon **80** 171 **127** 226
Stephen **87** 315 **102** 235
  128 58 **138** 320
Susan **144** 320
Susan (Brown) **89** 94
Susanna **63** 84 **80** 85 86
  100 333
Thomas **51** 359 **53** 62 **60**
  169 173 **68** 211 **87** 272
  278 279 **136** 216 **140**
  181 **142** 282 381 **143** 28
  144 320
William **70** 178 224 **100**
  334 **142** 381
OLORENSHAW
J. R. **141** 34
OLP Harriet Dowling
  97 396
OLPHEN
Simon Laurens van
  128 166
OLSEN
Agnes Mary **96** 286
Amanda **101** 123
Ann Mary **76** 275
Berta Ethel Young **98** 147
Fred C. (Mrs.) **103** 120
Hilda Matilda **69** 204
Lina **77** 190
Rachel Boice **98** 147
OLSEY George **72** 57
Tillimah **127** 307
OLSON
Albert F. (Mrs.) **86** 114
  87 306
Anders **128** 173
Andrew **114** 66
Borghild Lindevig
  114 157
Carin **128** 262
Chae Ok Hee **139** 220
Chersten (Yohnson)
  128 173

OLSON *cont'd*
Clara M. **128** 262
Daniel **128** 170
Einar Valentine **139** 220
Ellen (Olafsdotter)
  128 170
Ernest Sivereen (Mrs.)
  108 135 238
Hannah **92** 229
Harold **124** 262
Harriet **114** 66
James Edward **109** 130
Jean Edith **139** 220
Jennie **92** 229
Lillian Edith **108** 135
Oskar **85** 169
Susan W. **126** 205
Virginia Amelia (Fracker)
  (Jones) **124** 262
Virginia H. **145** 74
OLVERD — Mrs. **121** 302
OLVERSON
David **59** 194
Olyphant *see* Oliphant
O'MAHONIE
Dierman **139** 3
O'MALLEY
— Lady **112** 184
Aileen **95** 250 251
Austin **95** 251
Eveleen (McGinty) **95** 251
Thomas Francis **81** 108
  222
OMAN Charles **145** 12
Deborah **115** 269 270
Elizabeth **115** 269 270
Henry **127** 9
John W. **122** 296
Jonathan **130** 43
Mary G. **122** 296 **125** 173
Nelson **125** 30
Peter **115** 269 270
Remembrance (Gifford)
  130 43
Susanna (Savery) **115**
  269 270
William **122** 212
OMANS Desire **124** 79
O'MARA Philip **73** 224
OMBE Winifred (Rossiter)
  111 236
OMBLER Anne **93** 26
Elizabeth **93** 12 16 25 26 28
Elizabeth (Colman) **93** 31
Elizabeth (Gibbon)
  93 25 31
Frances **93** 31
Francis **93** 27
Isabell **93** 26 27
Jane **93** 26 27 31
John **93** 12 16 25 26 28 31
  36
Margery **93** 26-31
Margery (Gibbon) **93** 23
  26 29 30 40
Susanna **93** 25
Thomas **93** 25 26 30
William **93** 23 25-31 39
OMEALY —— **110** 129
Michel **110** 130

O'MEARA Maria / May
    (Meade) **100** 260
    Stephen **100** 260
O'MELVENY
    Philadelphia Borden
    (Miller) **87** 379
OMERTON Thomas **52** 259
OMLER Elizabeth (Colman)
    93 25
OMOHOINE Tege **139** 3
OMOHUNDRO
    Malvern Hill **106** 158
OMOND Betsey (Twist)
    125 215
    Henry **125** 215
Omsby *see* Ormsby
ONALE John **119** 21
ONASSIS Aristotle Socra-
    tes **139** 221
    Jacqueline Lee (Bouvier)
    (Kennedy) **139** 221
ONATIVIA Elizabeth
    (Coolidge) (Crosby)
    93 88
ONCHARD John **65** 235
ONDERDONK
    — Bp. **107** 175
    Adaline (Hide) **96** 228
    Elizabeth Carter **87** 57
    John Remsen **87** 57
    Robert **77** 152
    Samuel **96** 228
    Sarah J. **77** 152
O'NEIL O'Neal O'Neall
    —— **51** 125
    Ada M. (Bailey) **83** 422 437
    Agnes **86** 360
    Ann **68** 221
    Anne (Murphy) **86** 360
    Annie **89** 227
    Arthur **61** 137 349
    Bernard **73** 141
    Betsey **127** 269
    Charles F. **128** 177
    Con **112** 290
    Duncan **62** 332
    Elizabeth **68** 228 **73** 268
        75 13
    Elsie M. **68** 153
    Emelia **61** 352
    Esther **68** 224
    Florence L. **115** 280
    Florence Louise **105** 126
    Francis **61** 352
    Gertrude Francis **83** 437
        84 24
    Grace **127** 269
    Henry **60** 162 **68** 220 221
        224 226 228
    James **113** 25 26
    Jane **60** 162
    Jency Alexander **78** 43
    Joanna **85** 440
    John **68** 226 **70** 121 **73** 265
        100 191 **115** 134 **118**
        166 **127** 270 **145** 350
    John Belton **117** 133
    John Franklin **78** 43
    Joseph A. F. **92** 209
    July **127** 269
    Lydia **126** 67

O'NEIL *cont'd*
    Margaret **91** 52
    Mark **60** 162
    Marolia **127** 269
    Martha Augusta **78** 43
    Mary **54** 324 **58** 82 **113** 25
        127 270
    Mary Prudence **78** 43
    Nancy **127** 270
    Nancy Lucinda **78** 43
    Nannie **118** 166
    Nathaniel **73** 150
    Robert James **78** 43
    Samuel **127** 270
    Sarah **68** 220
    Teresa **105** 129
    Theodore **73** 273
    Thomas **73** 268 **113** 25
    William **73** 269 **86** 360
        89 227 **127** 269 270
    William H. **83** 422 437
    William McGee **78** 43
ONEVELLER Iva **96** 130
Oney *see* Olney
ONFRE Anne **67** 20 187
ONG Onge
    —— **98** 67
    Bernice **124** 262
    Eugene Walter **62** xxxvii
    Francis **85** 140
    Jacob **51** 68
    Sarah **51** 448 **94** 283
        121 160
    Simon **124** 262
    Susan (Chandler) **85** 140
ONGER
    Mary Wallace **77** 46
ONGLEY Samuel **94** 346
O'Nile *see* O'Neil
ONION Abigail **62** 188
    Albert **62** 188
    Anne **58** 150
    Asa Fisher **121** 159
    Benjamin **95** 203
    Deborah (Woodcock)
        95 203
    John **59** 88
    Jonathan **58** 150
    Mary **87** 92
    Robert **68** 264
    Samuel **101** 162
    Sarah **95** 203
ONKES Sachem **89** 177
ONLEY Idonis **145** 15
    John **145** 15
ONSLOW Arthur **51** 133
        134 139 140 252
    Denzil **51** 134 139 140 403
    Elizabeth **51** 139 140
    Foot **51** 139 140
    Fulke **96** 23
    Henry **51** 139 140
    Jane **51** 134
    Joseph **54** 148 149
    Katharine **51** 139 140
    Margery **76** 309
    Mary **51** 139 140 403
    Mary (Whetenall) (Scott)
        96 23
    Richard **51** 139 140
    Rose **51** 140

ONSLOW *cont'd*
    Sarah **51** 139
    Thomas **51** 139 140 **76** 309
ONSMAN Thomas **62** 323
ONTHANK
    — Mrs. **85** 444
    Arthur Heath **113** 242
        114 78 157 **115** 237 **116**
        233
    Curtis **137** 331
    Mary Ann (Bryant)
        137 331
    Ruth **85** 444
ONUX —— **54** 265
ONWIN John **62** 244
Onyan *see* Onion
OOTHOUT
    Abraham **73** 130
    Isaac C. **86** 21
    Marcia (Hanks) **86** 21
    Margaret **73** 129
OPDYCK Obdike - *see also*
    Updike
    Catherine (Smith)
        136 177
    Gysbert **136** 177
    Margaret **125** 107
OPECHANCANOUGH
    123 255
OPIE Edward **94** 396
    Helen **94** 396
    Hierome Lindsay **94** 397
    Joan **61** 187
    John **94** 396
    Lindsay **94** 396
    Sarah **94** 396
    Susanna **83** 347 **94** 396
    Thomas **55** 334 **94** 395-397
    William **55** 338 **113** 161
        120 315
OPLAND Nicholas **83** 318
OPP
    Charles E. **98** 341
    Rebecca (Fitz Randolph)
        98 341
OPPEL
    Catherine Margaret
        117 202
OPPENHEIMER
    Francis **107** 160
Oppie *see* Opie
OPSON —— **119** 50
ORAGEHEAD Mary **65** 45
ORAM Agnes **52** 45
    Daniel **100** 300
    Elizabeth (Hacey) **100** 300
    Joanna **63** 314
    John **71** 314
ORANGE — Prince of **54**
        304 **60** 31
ORB Ruth Young **102** 156
ORBALL Susan **52** 116
ORBELL Thomas **63** 285
ORBER Mary **90** 193
ORBERRY Sarah **73** 194
    Stephen C. **73** 194
ORBIE
    Mary / Molly **134** 337
ORCHARD Ann **89** 188
    Richard **104** 19 20
    Robert **68** 340

ORCHARD *cont'd*
Sarah **79** 438
T. **55** 223
Thomas **93** 383 387
Orcot *see* Orcutt
ORCUR James **66** 41
Mary **66** 41
ORCUTT —— **53** 379 **56**
283 287 **57** 251 **59** 70 **61**
374 **92** 256 **104** 62 **108**
281 **109** 255 **110** 209
295
— Mrs. **67** 216
Aaron **104** 184
Abbie M. (Turner) **123** 68
Abigail **86** 116 **104** 58
109 200
Abigail Berry **92** 256
Abigail Redman **104** 184
Adaline **102** 152
Allin **104** 291
Alonzo E. **84** 87
Amos **104** 184
Andrew **57** 179 **114** 303
121 283
Angeline **114** 303
Ann **78** 67 **108** 279 **109** 15
Annah **104** 291
Annah M. **110** 295
Arabel (Needham)
110 117
Arthur A. **84** 87
Basset **67** 215
Benjamin **54** 405 **57** 183
58 266 **114** 303 **136** 117
Bertha Jane **110** 209
Bethiah **67** 120
Betsey **104** 58 61 291
Betsey H. **104** 58
Caleb **67** 120 215 219 **68**
338 **113** 106 **136** 24
Caroline **104** 184
Caroline Sabrina **72** 147
Carrie Brooks **72** 147
Charles **108** 277 **110** 209
115 296
Charles L. **84** 87
Charles W. **110** 111 206
Chauncey **110** 117
Chester **115** 296
Chloe **67** 120
Chloe (Parker) **113** 106
Daisy L. **84** 87
David **83** 394 **105** 278
136 24
Deborah **57** 319
Deborah (Pratt) **120** 47
Desire **104** 134
Diademmia (Mason)
104 58
Dorothy **67** 118
Edith Melana **78** 242
Edna (Grindle) **110** 111
206
Eleanor **67** 120 123
Elijah **114** 303
Eliza P. **125** 220
Elizabeth **96** 52 **108** 277
114 303
Elizabeth (Clewley)
114 303

ORCUTT *cont'd*
Elmer E. **110** 209
Elsy Norah Augusta
109 255
Emerson **59** 312 **90** 87 **105**
278 **114** 303 **119** 254
Ephraim **92** 256
Erasmus **136** 117
Esther **104** 291
Eunice **67** 120 **119** 189
Frank **72** 147
Fred Walton **110** 209
Freelove **67** 118 119
George **96** 52
George W. **111** 327
Georgia **110** 209
Georgie **110** 306
Gertrude May **110** 117
Hannah **57** 181 **59** 108 312
78 311 **120** 47
Hannah (Clewley)
114 303
Hannah M. **110** 295
Harrison **115** 296
Harvey **110** 117
Hattie **110** 209
Helen Amanda **109** 256
Helen Cilicia **109** 255
Henry W. **84** 87
Hiram **108** 277
Horace **102** 152
Huldah **129** 151 376
Ichabod **119** 24 **136** 117
Irania **67** 116
Jacob **104** 61 183 290 291
105 210
James **66** 34 **104** 291 **109**
112 200 255 256 **110** 105
Jane **59** 108 **122** 240
Jane Ann **114** 303
Jane E. **84** 87
Jared **67** 123
Jennie Eliza **72** 147
John **57** 180 **104** 58 183 291
Joseph **57** 181 **119** 24
120 47
Josephine E. **96** 52
Katharine **67** 119
Keziah **54** 405
Lemuel **67** 118-120
Levi **104** 291 **125** 287
Love **67** 222
Lucinda **97** 224
Lucy **104** 183 **114** 303
Lucy (Black) **104** 61
Lucy A. (Etheridge)
111 327
Lucy Ann **108** 281
Lydia **58** 266 **108** 281
Malachi **104** 62 184 **105**
210 **108** 277 280 281 284
110 206
Mandana Brown **110** 209
Margaret S. **108** 277
Martha **57** 180
Mary **57** 181 **67** 219 **88** 263
125 288 **136** 117
Mary (Burrell) **119** 24
Mary (York) **109** 112 200
Mary Ann (Billings)
110 117

ORCUTT *cont'd*
Mary E. **84** 87
Mary Eleanor **109** 256
Mary Etta **115** 205
Mary Lewis **78** 206
Mary W. **114** 303
Matilda **104** 184 **108** 281
Matilda (Marks) **108** 284
Matilda R. **110** 295
May Ann **84** 87
Mehitable **67** 120
Melana **78** 242
Mercy (Pratt) **129** 376
Micah **140** 60 326
Millicent **119** 256
Millicent (Richards)
119 24
Minnie E. **110** 295
Mira **110** 209
Nancy **92** 257 **94** 379
Nancy (Clewley) **114** 303
Nathan **120** 47 **148** 147
Nelson W. **110** 295
Olive **114** 303
Orpha E. **78** 242
Orran **78** 242
Peter **137** 183
Phebe **148** 147
Philip Dana **91** 178 **92** 142
Polly **102** 152
Prudence **104** 184 **108** 277
Rebecca **67** 218 **108** 277
110 111 112
Reginald (Mrs.) **102** 144
Roxe **67** 120
Ruth **87** 105
Ruth (Black) **110** 206
Ruth (Ford) **120** 47
Sally **104** 184
Sally H. (Davis) **125** 287
Samuel **51** 221 363 **54** 321
65 155-159 **66** 330 **75**
175 **79** 55 **92** 256 257 **94**
379 **115** 296 **120** 51 **122**
16 **129** 376 **137** 183 **144**
337 **145** 72 241
Samuel G. **104** 184
Sarah **83** 394 **136** 117
Sarah (Mehurin) **136** 117
Simeon **67** 116
Solomon **67** 116 118-120
219
Susan **108** 277
Susanna **67** 116
Susanna (Bates) **137** 183
Tabitha **56** 202
Thankful **113** 38
Theode **67** 118
Thomas **57** 181 401
110 213
Thomas H. **108** 281
110 295
Warren **116** 66
William **57** 179-181 183
319 **59** 108 **115** 296
William A. **84** 87
William C. **84** 87
William Dana **64** 334 **92**
267 **141** 137
William Dana (Mrs.) **78**
108 206

ORCUTT *cont'd*
William Howard **72** 147
William W. **84** 87
ORD Ann **128** 170
James **58** 346
John **58** 346
Josephine **83** 427 437
Mary **58** 346
Ordaway *see* Ordway
ORDERICUS
Vitalis **79** 369 370
Ordiorne *see* Odiorne
ORDRONAUX John **51** 230
52 401 **62** 213 **65** 384
ORDWAY —— **58** 326
109 14 **119** 59
Abiel **68** 334
Abigail **123** 93
Abigail (Bond) **146** 334
148 310
Abigail (Merrill) **86** 227
Abner **53** 360
Alice Sarah (Fitts) **86** 227
Amanda J. **74** 208
Anna **148** 310
Anne (Emery) **86** 227
148 310
Benjamin **52** 428
Betsey (Stockbridge)
135 128
Caroline Greenleaf
(Foote) **86** 227
Charles **109** 14 15 199 201
Cora F. **68** 334
Daniel **148** 310
Daniel Leighton **86** 227
David **86** 227 **134** 217
Delia P. **68** 334
Donna Florence **89** 117
Edward **148** 310
Edwin **74** 208
Effie L. **68** 334
Elizabeth A. **109** 201
Elizabeth Rich (Chester)
84 297
Esther **140** 210
Frederick **109** 201
Georgianna **67** 353 **68**
334 **109** 201
Giles **92** 321
Grace **74** 208
Grace Frances **90** 136
Hananiah **86** 227
Hannah (Newton) **88** 284
Harriet **89** 118
Herbert Ingersoll **61**
xxxvii **86** 110 205 227
Isaiah **148** 310
Jacob **58** 122 **148** 310
James **51** 77 **53** 360 **58** 269
60 189 **70** 203 **86** 227
89 377 **148** 310
Jeanne Francoise **148** 310
Jennie **74** 208
Joanna **148** 310
John **123** 146
John C. **53** 360 **58** xlv
60 189
John F. **68** 334
John Morse **64** 102
Jonathan **52** 26 **131** 157

ORDWAY *cont'd*
Joshua **134** 217
Lillian M. **68** 334
Lois (Patten) **86** 227
Louisa **68** 334
Lydia **52** 26
Lydia (Harwood) **131** 157
Marilla H. **118** 131
Martha (Piper) **135** 128
Mary **58** 122 **70** 203 **90** 54
104 26 **109** 201 311 **126**
306
Mary (Emery) **86** 227
Mary (Peters) **135** 128
Mary (Wood) **148** 310
Mary Frances **109** 201
Moses **88** 284 **90** 114
Nathan **109** 311
Nathaniel **86** 227
Nehemiah **57** 114 **121** 248
Nehemiah George **62** 113
Patience **57** 114
Priscilla **86** 227
Profinda R. **90** 114
Rachel **148** 310
Rebecca **52** 428
Rebecca (Wright) **148** 310
Ruhamah French **83** 478
Samuel **53** 338 **89** 117
Samuel Blanchard **144**
138 **145** 174 **147** 211
148 310 342 372
Samuel H. **135** 128
Sarah **53** 360 **57** 114 **58** 269
Sarah (Hale) **86** 227
Stephen **134** 216
Susan **90** 114
Thomas **58** 260
Walter **74** 208
Warren **84** 297 **86** 227
Wilbert **74** 208
William **135** 128
Winifred **74** 208
O'REARDON
Catherine **59** 256
O'REILLY
Bernard **85** 115
John Boyle **52** 403 **65** 4
198 **139** 204
Mary **85** 115
Mary Boyle **72** 158 **73** xvii
Vincent F. **76** 160 **77** 242
Vincent Fleming **79** 226
Vincent J. **73** 242 **75** 161
OREN Charles **140** 136
Sarah A. (Howland)
140 136
ORENBRIDGE Alice (Fogg)
(Scott) **96** 22
Robert **96** 22
ORESBY Thomas **51** 283
ORFF Ella M. **74** 30
John **73** 185
Lydia **74** 30
Margery **73** 185
Nicholas **74** 30
Simon **61** 376
Syvilla **61** 376
ORFFOR Arthur **87** 44
Rachell (Fyske) **87** 44

ORFIELD Matthias Nord-
berg **70** 194
ORGAN David **110** 129
Eliza Condon **55** 136
Isaac **55** 136 **111** 321
Mary **140** 231
Thomas **111** 321
O'RIAN John **145** 54
Molly **145** 54
ORIELL James **84** 153
O'RION William **117** 275
ORKINS
Anna F. **122** 218
James **122** 217
Nancy **122** 217
ORKIRD John **63** 244
ORLANDINI Mary
Frothingham **82** 365
Vittorio **82** 365
Orm *see* Orme
ORMAND Henry **79** 49
ORME Orm Ormes
Adrian L. **100** 112
Amelia (Gaines) **85** 54
Ann **73** 144
Annah (Gaines) **85** 54
Anne **56** 87
Dan **85** 54
Elizabeth **51** 135
Elizabeth (Phillips)
110 277
F. H. **57** 328
George Naylor **73** 269
John **110** 277
Jonathan **85** 54
Moses **73** 141 219
Rhoda **128** 269
Sabina **73** 138
Sibyl **121** 92
ORMEROD —— **51** 85
George **72** 131 **112** 43
141 99 104 **142** 240 **147**
235
John T. **117** 295
Ormes *see* Orme
Ormesbee *see* Ormsbee
ORMESHAW Anne **61** 386
ORMESON John **147** 165
Ormeston *see* Ormiston
ORMINDEN
George **91** 331
ORMISTON John **94** 339
Mary **129** 51
Sarah A. **129** 51
W. J. **89** 209
ORMOND Butler James
(Earl of) **76** 311
Eleanor (Countess of)
95 395
Joseph **63** 16
Thomas **64** 317
ORMSBEE Ormesbee
Ormsbie Ormsby
Abigail (Flint) **104** 262
Abigail (Perry) **116** 38
Ann **51** 170
Arba **104** 262
Charity (Fisher) **126** 269
Christopher **99** 66
Daniel **98** 247
Ebenezer J. **135** 306

ORMSBEE *cont'd*
Elijah **116** 38
Elizabeth **70** 31
Elizabeth (Kingsbury)
99 66
Elizabeth (Young)
104 262
Ephraim **71** 203 **86** 383
Esther **98** 242 **146** 339
Ezra **70** 31 **99** 66 **129** 276
Francis G. **120** 236
Grace **63** 79
Grace (Martin) **98** 242
Hannah **126** 269
Hopestill **138** 26 27
Huldah **121** 256
Isaac **87** 315
Isaiah **96** 260
Israel **126** 269 **138** 26
J. L. **62** xxxvii
Jabez **98** 240 **126** 269 **138**
25 26 28 30
Jacob **96** 254 260 **97** 320 **98**
238 **99** 94 96 **129** 379
138 24 25
Jane (Ripley) **99** 66
Jemima **71** 203
Jeremiah **138** 24 28
Joanna (Tupper) **99** 66
John **62** 350 **63** 79 **71** 203
97 319 **98** 242 321 **99** 96
103 60 **125** 263
Jonathan **98** 325 329
Joseph **104** 118 262
Joshua **79** 266 **98** 321
99 66
Keziah **79** 266
Lephe **114** 289
Lydia **71** 203
Lydia R. **71** 38
Mary **96** 260 **97** 105 320
98 247 **104** 118
Mary (Perrin) **96** 260
Mehitable **124** 72
Patience (Chase) **87** 315
Phebe **110** 160
Polly (Wilson) **135** 305
Rebecca **98** 236
Richard **96** 260
Robert **51** 126 **60** 26
Rufus **104** 262
Ruth **71** 203 **86** 383 **87** 263
98 247
Samuel **138** 30
Sarah **96** 260 **99** 66
Sarah R. (Hunt) **90** 376
Stephen **71** 203
Thomas **63** 331 333 **91** 64
97 319 **127** 221 **139** 42
45 **146** 339
Timothy **104** 262
Tryphena **71** 203
William **99** 66
William H. **90** 376
ORMSBURY
Catherine **87** 329
Ormsby *see* Ormsbee
ORMSKIRK
James **68** 351
ORMSTED Elizabeth
(Moore) **94** 121

ORMSTED *cont'd*
Rhoda **94** 121
Ormston *see* Ormiston
Orn *see* Orne
ORNBERG V. **111** 100
ORNE *see also* Horne
—— **54** cv **55** 406 **140** 151
—— (Little) **140** 163
Abbie Ingalls **97** 358
Alfred Augustus **88** 332
Alice **54** 421
Almira C. (Johnson)
90 56
Ann **53** 345
Anna **52** 425 **100** 250
103 222
Anne **81** 466
Azor **90** 87 **97** 7
Caroline (Dodge) **88** 332
Catherine (Cushing)
140 56
Charlotte **88** 368 **108** 123
Christian (Bridge) **84** 381
Eliza **54** 421
Elizabeth **80** 27 28 **99** 252
George **66** 35
Hannah **67** lvii
Henry **75** 66 **140** 163
James **54** 388 **80** 28
John **53** 345 79 38 **97** 358
100 241 **145** 296
Joseph **104** 242 **105** 160
121 248
Joseph T. **90** 56
Joshua **54** 414 **66** 35 **108**
164 **118** 283 **121** 248
Josiah **54** 421
Lois **76** 203
Lucinda D. **79** 166
Lucretia (Bourne) **118** 283
Mahala **80** 28
Martha (Lackey) **100** 241
145 296
Martha H. **90** 92
Mary **65** 220
Nancy **127** 59
Polly **147** 259
Polly (Leavitt) **84** 381
Ralph Leroy **87** 174
Sally **147** 259
Samuel **107** 313
Sarah **54** 388 **124** 62 **145**
294 296 298
Sarah Ingalls (Morse)
97 358
Timothy **76** 203 **104** 287
126 226
William **80** 27
ORNO Mary **54** 393
Rebeca **54** 393
Simon **54** 393
ORON Hannah **81** 388
ORONO Joseph **143** 17
OROSZ Irma Adelaide
(Favreau) **88** 194 195
Josef A. (Mrs.) **88** 194
O'ROURKE Annie Maria
Frances **88** 297
Michael **88** 297
Annie Maria Frances
88 297

O'ROURKE *cont'd*
Margaret Caroline
(Drury) **88** 297
ORPE Joan **80** 93
ORPED
Thomas **71** 311 316
ORPEN
Anne **74** 282 **75** 140
Goddard Henry **116** 280
Hester **101** 21 22
Hester Heywood (Lewis)
101 21
Isaac **100** 191
John **101** 21 22
John Barnard **100** 191
Rhoda **100** 191
Orpin *see* Orpen
ORPWOOD John **62** 243
Orpyn *see* Orpen
ORR —— **53** 467
— Mrs. **60** 349
Abigail (Richardson)
98 365
Abigail Eldridge **69** 256
Alexander **60** 349 **93** 398
100 63
Alice **93** 365
Andrew **82** 413
Ann **73** 195
Arthur **93** 365
Arthur (Mrs.) **75** xxiii 65
93 82 139 364
Arthur C. (Mrs.) **112** 324
Betsey **89** 352
Charles **64** 327
Daniel **140** 231
David **73** 205 **81** 148
Deborah **105** 209
Dorothy **56** 258
Eleanor Noyes **93** 365
Elizabeth **98** 198
Elizabeth P. **125** 177
Elizabeth Polly **66** 86
Emma (Farvis / Jarvis)
83 432 437
Emma (Jarvis) **83** 432
Euphema **104** 96
Fannie **137** 47
Florence Ione **71** xxiii
Frances B. **81** 148
Fred **91** 357
George E. **83** 432 437
George Noyes **93** 365
Gershom **66** 86
Hannah **81** 432
Hannah P. **66** 86
Hanson **98** 198
Harriet **73** 205
Harriet Emily **81** 148 149
Hector **66** lxviii
Helen **84** 31
Henry C. **69** 256
Hugh **56** 252
James **104** 96 97 **120** 45
Jane **81** 432 **104** 103
John **56** 258 **66** 35 **81** 432
86 265 **98** 198 **113** 84
119 22
Joseph **119** 21
Joseph D. **104** 97
Joshua **119** 21

ORR cont'd
Lucy **120** 45 **137** 47
Lussanah **137** 47
Margaret **99** 120 122 **101**
  161 **104** 97 **117** 246
Margaret Dorman **104** 97
Martha **87** 59
Martha Jane **81** 148 149
Mary **79** 287 **81** 148 432
  98 198
Mary Ann **82** 397
Mary Jane **89** 30 **104** 97
Mary Lincoln **95** 297
  96 156
Matthew **56** 252
Melon **98** 198
Minnie **117** 128
Nancy **117** 40
Nathan B. **73** 205
Nathan Bacon **81** 148 149
Peggy **56** 256
Philip **117** 40
Rachel **55** 399
Richard **99** 120 122 **100**
  295 **101** 161
Robert **104** 96 103
Robert Clement **93** 365
S. H. **125** 177
Sadie I. L. **83** 423 437
Sally **56** 257
Sarah **125** 177
Susanna **137** 47
Susanna (Brown) **100** 295
Sylvan (Mrs.) **101** 125
Thomas **55** 399
W. G. **54** 113
Warren H. **109** 239
William **98** 365
William J. **104** 103
ORRAGE George **64** 318
ORRALL
  Blanche **69** 267
  Charles E. **69** 267
  Julia **69** 267
ORRELL Alex **65** 171
  Alice A. **82** 356
  Frederick W. **82** 356
  Gertrude A. **82** 356
  James **82** 356
  Mabel A. **82** 356
  Mary A. **82** 356
  Robert **113** 71
  William **75** xxiii 64 **81** 238
  82 245 356
ORREN Catherine **61** 281
ORRIDGE
  Elizabeth Breeze
  100 310
ORRIS Abigail **54** 350
  106 30
  Experience **54** 350 **106** 30
ORROK ____ (Piemont)
  140 236
  Alexander **140** 236
  Elizabeth Ellen **105** 129
  George Alexander (Mrs.)
  105 129
Orsborn see Osborn
Orsburne see Osborn
ORSBYE Thomas **70** 245
ORSEOLO Pietro **106** 54

ORSMENT Anna **61** 344
  John **61** 344 346
  Margarette **61** 343
  Nancy **61** 346
ORSWELL
  Adeline Melville
  74 lxx
  George Burbank **74** lxx
  Harriet Beetle **74** lxx
  Irene **117** 212
Ortan see Orton
ORTEGA
  José Vicente **100** 325
  Rafaela **100** 325
  Rafaela Louisa **100** 325
ORTEL Augustus F. **120**
  140 215
  Sarah A. (Adams) **120**
  140 215
ORTH Betty Floje
  (Hannum) **91** 51
  Florence Gloninger
  86 197
  Franklin L. **91** 51
  Jacob **113** 152
  Louise Eugenia **113** 152
  Sibilla (Hoffman) **113** 152
ORTIS Frank **91** 331
ORTIZ Alexia DuPont **95**
  84 144
  Alice Eugenie **80** 205
  81 457
  Alice Eugenie (DuPont)
  95 83 **98** 25 **104** 40
  Eve Hermine (Skarga)
  95 84
  Julien **81** 457 **95** 84
  Julien (Mrs.) **80** 205 **84**
  186 **95** 75 83 144 149
  Marguerite Du Pont **94**
  137 **95** 84 144
  Phillipe **95** 84
ORTON ____ **67** 230
  Abigail **124** 221
  Abigail (Jackson) **124** 7
  Angeline C. **82** 128
  Anne **70** 77
  Azariah **124** 7 13
  Beulah **124** 9
  Beulah (Rockwood) **124** 9
  Darius **124** 7
  Dorothy **94** 322
  Edward **51** 94 97 **59** xliv
  120 **60** xxxvi **124** 6
  Elizabeth **76** 60
  Giles de **98** 274
  Hannah **124** 221
  Hepzibah (Buell) **124** 14
  Huldah **124** 14
  Jemima **124** 7
  Joan de **98** 274
  John **124** 221 **147** 168
  Joseph **124** 221
  Luther **124** 221
  Mary (Davis) **124** 12 13
  Mary Hoit **121** 76
  Matilda **124** 221
  Myron **89** 96 **121** 76
  O. W. (Mrs.) **100** 112
  Remember **124** 221

ORTON cont'd
  Remember (Landers)
  124 221
  Rhoda **124** 8
  Robert de **98** 274
  Robert Groves **82** 128
  Sally **84** 319
  Sarah (Atwood) **124** 6
  Thankful **124** 221
  Thomas **51** 94 **114** 189 **124**
  5 6 9 14 **147** 168
  Vashti (Jackson) **124** 7
  William **114** 189
  William Henry **114** 189
ORVIN Maxwell Clayton
  (Mrs.) **99** 148
ORVIS ____ **93** ix
  Amy Alvira (Waste)
  113 159
  Arthur Emerton **93** 373
  Calvin Henry **113** 159
  Edwin Waitstill **90** 137 **92**
  97 **93** 372 **94** 80 144
  Elihu **93** 372
  Francis Wayland **70** 285
  93 372
  George **70** 285 **93** 372
  Homer Waitstill **93** 373
  Joseph Upham **93** 372
  Mary **142** 333
  Polly **61** 274
  Samuel **93** 372
  Schuyler Adams **93** 373
  Waitstill **93** 372
  Warner Dayton **93** 373
  William **93** 372
ORWELL Edward **80** 352
  81 92
ORWIG George **103** 236
  Gottfried **103** 236
  John **103** 236
  Mary Eliz. **103** 236
  Temperance **83** 330
OSAN Alfred **91** 331
OSBALDESTON
  ____ Bp. **52** 59
  Catherine **95** 169
  Jane **139** 231
  John **139** 231
  Judith **52** 139
  Lambert **52** 139
OSBORN Osborne
  Osburn Osburne
  Oseburn
  ____ **51** 264 **53** 268 **54** 344
  55 229 **56** 214 **60** 189
  62 101 **66** 357 **75** 284
  76 151 **80** 223 **98** 22
  101 55 **121** 301 **135** 337
  136 38 **139** 317 **140** 53
  69
  ____ Capt. **59** 396
  ____ Mr. **52** 134 **91** 173
  ____ Mrs. **104** 21 **115** 20
  ____ Widow **127** 13
  A. **61** 34
  Aaron **114** 151 152
  Abel **69** 232
  Abiel **55** 291
  Abigail **55** 206 **57** 67 **59**
  409 **68** 298 **69** 376 **71**

OSBORN *cont'd*
278 **72** 312 **76** 244 **108**
169 **111** 292 **114** 233
145 146
Abigail (Brown) **121** 52
Abigail (Chase) **87** 137
Abigail (Simpson)
114 232
Abigail (Stockbridge)
139 317
Abigail E. **90** 342
Abraham **54** 208 343 **55**
206 **64** 324
Abraham Allen **139** 317
Addison **61** 24 25
Adelia **92** 172
Agnes **141** 239 240
Agnes S. **109** 189
Alexander **76** 68 71 **116** 66
133 235
Alexander Perry **90** 75
Alice **82** 51
Almira **59** 407 **88** 81
114 233
Alonzo F. **81** 291
Alpheus **131** 157
Alvin **73** 218
Amelia **70** 37
Amos **57** 67 **59** 172 **67** 52
108 314 **125** 29
Amy **108** 314
Andrew **78** 264
Angeline D. **89** 39
Ann **71** 6 **73** 279 **83** 40 **91**
159 **105** 313 **112** 251
114 233 **118** 148
Ann (Wilbore) **113** 97
Ann Augusta **114** 233
Ann E. **118** 148
Anna **57** 67 **59** 410 **73** 224
114 233
Anna (Nicholson)
(Fairchild) **106** 109
Annis **54** 343 **141** 240
Archie Clifton **114** 233
Arodyne **76** 271
Aseneth A. **118** 148
Benjamin **55** 208 **70** 122
115 41 128
Benjamin H. **118** 148
Bert Paul **81** 108 222
Betsey **97** 216 **114** 152 233
Betsey (Lee) **139** 318
Betty F. **82** 17
Beulah **59** 72
Bezaleel **55** 207
Burton S. **82** 376
Byrle **87** 208
Byrle Jacob **89** 81 132
Caleb **57** 67
Candace Fidelia **114** 152
Caroline **115** 21
Caroline A. **106** 109
Caroline E. **82** 376
Caroline Frances **77** 186
Catherine **100** 315
Catherine (Gifford)
132 299
Catherine Macauley
(Barber) **133** 306
140 231

OSBORN *cont'd*
Charles **68** 246 **69** 273
72 182
Charles D. (Mrs.) **76** lii
Charles Devens **94** 139
116 73
Charles E. **73** 272
Charles H. **79** 52
Charles S. **81** 291
Chester **123** 19
Clarissa **114** 233
Clay **118** 152
Comfort **76** 146
Cornelius **54** 428 **55** 86
Cynthia **130** 156
D. Boone **118** 77
Daniel **54** 307 308 428 **55**
202 203 206 **60** 77 **68**
246 **69** 376 **73** 47 **75** 195
80 69 **114** 272
David **55** 203 206 **59** 394
68 171 176 291 **69** 232
70 42 **100** 302 **106** 109
115 125 129
Deborah **54** 308 343
55 203
Dennis **73** 145 228
Donald Lewis **125** 295
Dorcas (Follens) **100** 302
Dorothy **53** 461 **59** 394
97 100 **118** 258
Ebenezer **61** 57 **76** 142
148 151
Edith **76** lii
Edward **66** 357 **76** 271
Edward Clarence **114** 233
Effie Gertrude **114** 233
Eleanor **70** 34 **88** 15 **107**
184 185 **139** 291 292 294
Eleanor (Southwick)
113 81
Eleazer Samuel **124** 79
Elial Lyman **114** 152
Elias **104** 262
Elijah **114** 233 **136** 79
Elisha **55** 203 206
Eliza **61** 57 **68** 246 **69** 272
315 **73** 272 **118** 148
Eliza (Goodwin) **126** 141
Eliza Allen **69** 274
Eliza E. **114** 233
Eliza Elmira **69** 274
Eliza G. **118** 148
Eliza Jane **100** 210
Elizabeth **52** 233 **54** 305
307 308 428 **55** 202 203
206-208 **56** 73 **59** 71 **61**
57 **66** 56 **67** 52 128 **68**
246 298 **69** 47 **70** 33 39
73 261 271 **75** 177 **76** 68
71 134 **79** 52 **81** 291 **84**
165 **90** 278 **108** 215 **111**
43 **116** 61 **118** 148 **125**
180 **128** 312
Elizabeth (Culmar)
88 282
Elizabeth (Myrick) (Paine)
108 212
Elizabeth (Walker)
137 181
Elizabeth A. **117** 134

OSBORN *cont'd*
Elizabeth Hanson **73** lviii
Elnathan **115** 21 23
Emily **89** 382 **114** 151
Enos **75** 193 **76** 145 **136** 79
Ephraim **68** 294 **69** 47 **70**
38 **106** 197 **111** 39
Esther **54** 203 323 324 **55**
203 **72** 257 268 **73** 147
Esther (Steevens) **129** 22
Eunice **69** 232 **83** 60
Evva **107** 135
Experience **75** 192 **102** 59
Experience (Scudder)
(Hopkins) **102** 58 59
Ezekiel **71** 278 **100** 210
Fannie Warren **98** 362
Farrand **107** 226
Fides **141** 27-29
Frances Lanier **82** 433
Francis **73** 136 **97** 121
Francis Augustus **69** 192
Fred **100** 210
Freelove Amy **68** 278
Gardner **119** 158 **121** 158
George **54** 284 285 **59** 407
66 171 **85** 138 **86** 464
91 331 **126** 141 **136** 37
140 231
George F. **82** 133
George Francis **82** 496
George Jerry **65** 255 **94**
357 **137** 181
George S. **121** 146 **122** 232
Grace **69** 377
Grizzel **69** 377
Halewise **109** 19
Hannah **51** 69 **54** 208 308
428 **55** 386 **57** 67 **59** 396
60 77 **61** 323 **68** 172 286
298 **69** 47 376 **77** 129 **79**
449 **97** 182 **100** 302 **113**
297 **114** 233
Hannah (Clough) **114** 233
Hannah (Reed) **125** 242
Hannah C. **114** 233
Hannah W. **77** 153
Happy D. **69** 232
Harmony Cushman
(Phillips) **124** 79
Harriet (Paine) **131** 157
Harriet A. **81** 291
Harriet Louisa **69** 274
Harvey **92** 172 **132** 299
Helen Putnam **82** 496
Henry **55** 206 **59** 206 299
301 408 **97** 216 **129** 22
142 53
Henry Chisholm **90** 137
Henry Clay **80** 32 **118** 148
Henry Fairfield **74** xxv
156 **90** 74 75 81 139
Hezekiah **115** 123
Hiram **75** 192
Hitty **57** 67
Homer **115** 23
Howard H. **116** 66
Hugh **54** 285 **60** 331
116 66
Hur **139** 317
Isaac **55** 206 **139** 317

OSBORN *cont'd*
Isabel (Jones) **131** 157
Isabella **135** 73
Jacob **55** 206 **57** 67 **114** 232
  233 **139** 317
Jacobus **87** 208
James **55** 372 **57** lv **58** 145
  61 347 **65** 257 338 **76**
  244 **82** 293 295 **83** 13 **87**
  206 208 **116** 66
James Jerry **82** 51
James S. **69** 272
Jane **54** 308 428 **55** 86 **61**
  347 **97** 330 **114** 151
Jane (Curtis) **97** 330
Jane (Munter) **139** 324
Jane T. **97** 216
Jared **68** 278
Jason H. (Mrs.) **83** 116
Jason W. **118** 148
Jean **55** 203 **77** 140 **133** 235
Jedediah **55** 203 206 279
  139 317
Jehiel **67** 223
Jer: **123** 192
Jeremiah **54** 302 428 429
  55 202 203 206 **59** 71 **62**
  182 **64** 26 **71** 6 **75** 195
  81 125 129
Jeremy **67** 45 **70** 249 255
Jerry **95** 28
Jerusha **115** 41
Jesse B. **139** 295
Jessie Bartlett **83** 116
Joan **54** 343 **141** 239
Joanna **55** 202
Joanna Gaylord **123** 20
John **54** 284 285 343 **55** 109
  206 208 291 **57** 280 **58**
  68 145 **68** 246 **73** 149
  264 272 **77** 239 **79** 162
  83 40 60 61 **84** 152 153
  165 256 363 **100** 15 **104**
  242 **106** 109 **109** 19 **111**
  43 292 **112** 251 **113** 97
  116 67 **117** 87 **118** 258
  128 105 **132** 30 **133** 309
  134 221 **139** 324 **140** 41
  231 **141** 27 29 **148** 236
  238
John Frederic (Mrs.)
  85 197
John Hammond **107** 226
John Husband **78** 221
John L. **69** 274
John S. **105** 284
John Simpson **114** 233
John William **98** 147
Jonathan **54** 307 308 **55**
  203 206 207 **59** 72 **111**
  43 292
Jonathan P. **114** 233
Joseph **54** 208 306 308 428
  55 202 203 206-208 **59**
  396 **67** 45 46 **68** 172 286
  298 **69** 374 **70** 249 251
  255 **73** 230 **74** 65 **75** 177
  195 **105** 59 **114** 233 **118**
  148
Joseph D. **118** 148
Joseph H. **118** 148

OSBORN *cont'd*
Joseph P. **60** 275
Josephine Adams **90** 75
Josephine H. (Noyes)
  100 231
Joshua **73** 269 **114** 233
Josiah **55** 203
Judith **67** 45 **70** 249 255
Juliana **54** 428 **115** 21
Kate Hamilton **71** 95
Katharine **53** 415 **92** 152
  94 146 **95** 152
Keziah **59** 207 409-411
Lemuel **104** 262 **134** 174
Lena **116** 66
Leslie Kelley **79** 135
Levi **69** 232
Lewis **54** 208
Linny **73** 145
Lois **70** 38 **111** 292
Lorinda **82** 376
Louisa **69** 273
Louisa L. **68** 246
Lucinda **115** 21
Lucinda B. (Stoning)
  139 295
Lucretia (Perry) **90** 75
Lucy **68** 246 **114** 104
Lucy (Bassett) **125** 217
Lucy A. (Marston)
  114 233
Lucy J. **115** 126
Lucy Webster **79** 135
Lydia **58** 145 **59** 299 **80** 32
  84 363 **89** 385 **140** 41
Lydia (Kelley) **104** 262
Lydia Burnham **57** lv
Lyman **61** 24 **84** 141
Mabel **70** 34
Margaret **61** 347 **77** 129
  79 449
Margaret (Fowler)
  (Osgood) (Rowell)
  (Coleman) **109** 244
  138 129
Margaret Dillon (Paine)
  97 121
Martha **59** 396 **114** 233
  123 115
Martha Lavinia **79** 132
Martha Scott **145** 376
Mary **51** 408 **54** 169 208
  302 306 307 428 **55** 202-
  204 206 **59** 267 410 411
  62 38 **65** 257 338 **66** 357
  68 294 **69** 47 232 **70** 38
  71 6 **73** 262 **75** 139 195
  79 135 **83** 40 85 96 **102**
  105 **103** 308 **106** 109
  111 147 278 **112** 43 **114**
  200 **115** 42 **117** 106 **135**
  338 **139** 291-293 317
  144 5
Mary (Clark) **107** 185
  139 291
Mary (Frost) **134** 221
Mary (Madden) **125** 290
Mary (Richmond)
  114 151

OSBORN *cont'd*
Mary (Stanborough)
  (Edwards) (Horsing-
  ton) **141** 40
Mary A. **57** lv
Mary Ann **69** 206 **114**
  151 152
Mary B. **69** 272
Mary Eliza **97** 69
Mary Ingersoll **76** lvi
Mary J. **114** 233
Mary Jane **88** 342
Mary O. **71** 12
Matilda Mahala **111** 240
Matthew **55** 203
Mattie Augusta **114** 233
Mehitable **57** 67 **111** 292
Mehitable (Maltby)
  111 292
Mercy **59** 411
Micajah **114** 233
Michael **54** 284
Miles G. **111** 40
Milly (Walkup) (Willis)
  114 272
Milton **89** 384
Mindwell **68** 176 291 **69**
  232 **98** 349
Minott A. **107** 79
Moses **68** 245 246 **69** 77
  272 **73** 47
Mumford **125** 244
N. Myron **124** 79
Nancy **55** 372 **65** 257 338
  83 13 **111** 43 292
Nancy (Lord) **83** 13
Naomi **75** 193
Nathan **68** 289 298 **69** 377
Nathan Henry Clough
  114 233
Nathaniel **88** 282
Nelly **61** 25
Nelson **114** 151
Nicholas **76** 59
Noah **69** 232 **115** 42
Obadiah **61** 25
Obedience **75** 195
Oliva **106** 109
Olive **59** 299 **68** 298 **82** 51
  124 276
Oliver **69** 233
Olivia (Tillinghast) **125**
  244 **137** 363
P. E. **92** 399
Patience **62** 284 **69** 92
Paul **87** 137
Peleg **54** 284 285 **136** 38
Percy E. **86** 464 465
Persis **82** 293 295
Persis Joslyn **84** 61
Peter **68** 291 292 298 **69**
  233 **70** 33 38 39 **74** 69
Phebe **54** 428 **69** 272 **80**
  223 **136** 79
Phebe W. **68** 245
Polly **59** 172 **137** 282
Polly (Bentley) **114** 152
Polly (Lewis) **111** 240
Priscilla **124** 298
Prudence **54** 273
Rachel **61** 167

OSBORN *cont'd*
Rebecca **67** 51 223 **73** 47
82 496 **122** 39
Recompense **54** 213
Reginald Augustus
97 121
Reuben **70** 34
Rheumilla (Ashley)
114 151
Richard **81** 321 **83** 61 **89**
175 **90** 74 **98** 22 **113** 81
123 19 20 22 **131** 157
Richard H. **118** 169
Rilla **76** 148
Ritchard **123** 23
Robert **67** 46 **70** 249 **98** 93
107 62
Roswell **107** 226
Roswell John **107** 226
Roy Wallace **69** xxxv
Russell **106** 109
Ruth **55** 203 279 **68** 245
246 **73** 47
Ruth A. **116** 67
Ruth O. **118** 148
Sally **108** 166 **115** 21 23
Sally Bennett **134** 220
Samuel **54** 169 **55** 206 **57**
228 **59** 207 408-411 **67**
366 **97** 330 **102** 59 **104**
262 **107** 185 **113** 81 **121**
41 42 **126** 236 **127** 159
139 291 292
Samuel C. **114** 233
Sarah **55** 203 205 291 369
370 **68** 292 298 **69** 232
233 376 **70** 42 65 66 **73**
227 271 278 **75** 192 **76**
146 **78** 234 264 **80** 223
83 60 **86** 85 **91** 159 **93**
ix 182 403 **106** 109 **114**
104 233 **118** 143 148
123 262 **136** 37
Sarah (Gates) (Whitcomb)
121 52
Sarah (Parsons) **148** 238
Sarah Elizabeth **77** 182
Sarah L. **116** 67
Sarah Lang **69** 274
Seba **76** 151
Sena **76** 151
Seth **70** 34
Sheldon **76** 151
Sherman **81** 291
Silas **111** 43
Solomon **115** 41
Stephan **125** 46
Stephen B. **61** 25
Subella **135** 73
Susan **59** 408 **61** 25
Susan Maria **95** 313
Susanna **111** 117
Susie Foster **84** 31
Tabitha **85** 96
Temperance **111** 80
Thomas **54** 196 203 284
285 306 308 343 428 **55**
86 201-203 **67** 175 **75**
195 **76** 134 145 146 **77**
72 128 **78** 58 **89** 174 **109**
244 **118** 148 **121** 52 **138**

OSBORN *cont'd*
129 **140** 231 **143** 214
Thomas D. **118** 148
Thomas Watts **63** 27
Usley **73** 147
Viola Irene (Fisher)
101 124
Virginia Reed (Sturges)
90 74
Virginia Sturges **90** 75
W. **75** 139
W. E. **83** 371
Weaver **127** 217
Will E. **95** 208
Will Eli **84** 190 **107** 68
138 226
William **54** 285 305 **55** 87
202 205 386 **57** 218 **77**
129 **79** 449 **81** 129 **97**
297 **113** 81 **118** 148 169
127 12 **135** 77 **141** 27
William E. **125** 217
William Frederick **71** 12
William H. **54** 283 **64** 330
118 148
William Henry **90** 74
William J. **116** 67
William Lyman **107** 226
William W. **125** 242
Woodbury **107** 313
Wyman **125** 290
Zariah **55** 203
Zebedee **55** 203 206
OSBREY
Celia Anna **77** 181
OSBURG
Catherine **69** 328
Osburn *see* Osborn
OSBURY William **139** 231
OSCAR II King of
Sweden **136** 311
OSCAR
Helena **65** 133
Osebern *see* Osborn
OSER Marian Estelle
(Edison) **88** 73
Oscar (Mrs.) **88** 73
OSEVILLE
Sewel de **96** 42 47 48
OSGOOD —— **55** 275 **58**
236 **74** 96 310 **76** 210 **92**
133 269 276 277 282 311
103 258 **109** 113 **121**
302 **140** 69 251 **145** 159
— Capt. **58** 167 **70** 9
148 145
— Dr. **92** 131 253 260
— Mr. **54** 396
— Mrs. **109** 154
— Rev. Dr. **94** 377
— Rev. Mr. **92** 133
Aaron **87** 93 94 **113** 30 37
125 219
Aaron B. **87** 93 94
Abbie M. **87** 93 94
Abby C. **87** 94
Abby S. **74** 307
Abel **57** 410 411
Abigail **54** 101 393 **55** 52
61 345 **79** 399 **93** 46
137 324 **144** 142

OSGOOD *cont'd*
Abigail (Carlisle) **116**
304 305
Abigail C. **87** 94
Abraham **55** 391 **65** 248
92 277 320 **103** 258
Addie Maria **96** 228
Albert G. **107** 154
Alice (Pearson) **97** 130
Ambrose **125** 38
Ann **52** 428
Anna **68** 261 **92** 273 **125** 54
Anna F. **74** 96
Annie Eloise **74** 307
Annie M. B. **87** 93
Annie Manonia **96** 228
Apphia **52** 432
Apphia (Pillsbury)
134 335
Arathusa **58** 56
Arletta Holmes **74** 96
Aron **87** 94
Asahel **58** 56 57
Augusta Ellen **74** 307
Augusta Lenora **74** 309
Augustus Newton
74 307 309
Bailey **87** 93 94
Beatrice A. **74** 309
Belle **69** 165
Belle M. **123** 72
Benjamin **51** 495 **66** 34
140 69
Benjamin S. **99** 115
Betsey **87** 94
Betsey (Colby) **87** 94
Betsey B. **73** 286
Beulah D. **74** 309
Blanche **74** 309
Blanche Adell **74** 307
Calvin **58** 58
Carlton Augustus **74** 310
Caroline Elizabeth **83** 471
Caroline L. **74** 309
Catherine **96** 228
Catherine (Masters)
125 218
Cecil W. **74** 309
Charles **81** 339 **134** 335
137 362
Charlotte **77** lxix
Charlotte (Adams)
106 151
Charlotte (Cannoll) **90** 46
Charlotte Emeline **77**
lxviii lxix **100** 316 **106**
151
Christopher **55** 52 **61** 226
68 197 **74** 302 306 **78** 42
88 298 **89** 260 **93** 45 46
104 317 **109** 244 **119**
234 **138** 129
Clara **96** 228 **97** 134
Consuelo Irene **74** 310
Dana (Mrs.) **85** 197
Daniel **74** 302 **91** 331
David **51** 463 **53** 456 **56**
246 **84** 121 **92** 320 **113**
34 **126** 142 226
David A. **83** 298 300
Deborah **69** 332 **119** 235

OSGOOD *cont'd*
134 230
Deborah (Poor) 106 151
Desire 74 306 78 42
Dorcas (Ballard) 99 115
Dorcas Ann Collins
  (Osgood) 87 94
E. B. 87 93
Ebenezer 61 43 88 286
Edward 116 50
Edward B. 87 93 94
Edward Everett 74 310
Edward Holyoke (Mrs.)
  85 197
Edward L. (Mrs.) 78 292
Eleanor Bagley 89 386
Eleanor T. 92 315
Elisa 80 218 81 339
Elisha 96 227
Eliza (Hide) 96 228
Eliza Smart 89 383
Eliza White 60 xxxviii
Elizabeth 59 58 61 237 71
  260 74 96 78 42 93 87
  93 92 292
Elizabeth (Bayley) 87 94
Elizabeth (Felt) 88 298
Elizabeth Ann 87 94
Elizabeth Bayley 87 95
Elizabeth E. (Cheswell)
  87 94
Elizabeth Lawrence
  (Burling) 88 298
Elsie Loraine 74 310
Elsie Reamer 74 310
Emeline (Ingraham)
  88 339
Emily 74 309
Enoch 58 124 109 111
  128 278
Enoch W. 87 93 94
Ephraim 79 399
Ernest L. 74 309
Esther 128 285
Ethel 74 310
Eugene S. 74 309
Eunice 58 57 133 154 320
Eva Florence 74 302
Ezekiel 74 302 306 78 42
Florence A. 74 309
Francis C. 87 93 94
Frank 96 228
Frank G. 87 93
Frank Hines 81 107 219
  89 121 181 90 140
Frank Storey 79 192
Fred S. 74 309
Fred W. 87 93 94
Frederic L. 60 185
Frederic Larned 81 339
Frederick Stoddard
  74 310
Gamaliel B. 125 217
Gardner 58 57
George 86 148 118 128
George D. E. 87 94
George Henry 96 228
George Richmond
  116 50
George S. 74 309
Georgie Bell 74 302

OSGOOD *cont'd*
Geraldine (Bancroft)
  97 130
Grace B. 87 93
Gretchen 80 209 92 196
II. L. 107 16 108 9
Hamilton 62 113 92 196
Hamilton (Mrs.) 85 197
Hannah 51 462 93 45 98
  78 125 221 128 285
Hannah (Ayer) 88 298
Hannah (Babbidge)
  88 298
Hannah (Belknap) 93 45
  46
Hannah (Buttolph) 88 298
Hannah (Dulgar) 126 142
Hannah (Smith) 108 278
Hannah T. 78 292
Harland B. 74 309
Harold K. 74 309
Harriet Ann 74 302
Harriet L. 88 335 103 44
Hasen 92 270
Helen 97 130 131
Helen E. (Marr) 83 300
Henrietta 113 34 41
Henry 52 427 53 168
Holland W. 103 46
Hooker 89 181
Horace 74 96 95 53
Horace C. 87 93
Horace N. 74 96
Hosea 128 285
Howard Lincoln 74 310
Isaac 61 244 77 lxix 106
  151 110 317 116 304
  305 119 234 235 136 77
Isaac Smith 74 205 302 306
  307 78 41 42
Ivan E. 74 309
J. B.F. 145 219
J. R. 55 20
Jacob 81 380 113 41
James 54 101 392-394 56
  63 65 108 91 93 92 273
  124 60 125 155 137 324
  147 85
James B. 87 94 99 115
James Erskine 74 96
James H. 90 46
Jane L. (Norton) 109 111
Jeanne 124 194
Jennie 103 71
Jennie M. (Grace) 83 298
  300
Joel 113 34
John 58 236 74 306 75 322
  78 42 84 358 88 298 89
  181 91 331 94 197 95 16
  18 101 224 104 242 106
  151 107 156 119 234
  235 125 152 128 278
  285 134 216
John A. 97 130
John E. L. 89 302
John Felt 88 298
John Fiske 54 394 85 118
John Fiske (Mrs.) 85 118
John H. 74 309
John S. 73 116 91 331

OSGOOD *cont'd*
Jonathan 108 278
Joseph 58 56 210 74 309
  78 231 99 115 104 129
  107 313 134 335 137
  362
Joseph (Merrill) 87 94
Joseph H. 125 218
Joseph Otis 59 58
Joseph S. 88 339
Joseph W. 99 115
Joshua Bailey 144 266
Joshua Wright 84 320
Josiah 61 237 95 15 16
Josiah (Mrs.) 93 322
Judith 85 39
Katharine Curtis 78 206
  88 298 89 80 136
Katharine Rochester
  Montgomery 93 98
Kenneth L. 74 309
Lemuel 57 414 58 56-58
Lenora G. 74 309
Lewis C. 89 181
Lois Frances 74 308 78
  41 42 98 185
Lois Hibbert 74 302 306
  78 41 42
Lois W. 87 94
Louis E. 87 93
Louis Edward 74 310
Lovicey (Leighton)
  99 115
Lovicey S. 99 115
Lucinda 87 93 94
Lucinda (Osgood) 87 93
  94
Lucy 64 150 74 96
Lucy Eunice 84 319 320
Lura 86 197
Luther Edward 74 307
Lydia 57 414 63 290 67
  375 108 251 321 113 34
Malcolm W. 74 309
Manasseh 58 56-58
Margaret 92 196 95 15
Margaret (Fowler) 109
  244 138 129
Margaret (Love) 134 335
  137 362
Margaret Chapin 89 181
Margery 68 197
Maria 78 231
Maria Thomson
  (Vaughan) 93 322
Martha 74 205 306
Martha B. 74 309
Martha Blowers 92 133
  94 159
Mary 54 cxxxviii 58 57
  59 288 67 375 74 306
  76 xxxvi 78 42 89 260
  302 90 311 92 128 93
  322 94 159 95 15 99 115
  119 234 235 148 145
Mary (Bancroft) 97 130
Mary (Clement) 106 151
  107 156
Mary (Clements) 88 298
Mary (Cursell) 88 286
Mary (Duran) 136 77

OSGOOD *cont'd*
Mary (Foster) **100** 302
Mary (Merrit) **84** 121
Mary (Shepard) **88** 298
Mary (Stevens) **94** 197
  100 60 **103** 224
Mary Ann **84** 61 121 303
  116 50
Mary Beckford (Archer)
  83 471
Mary Elizabeth **74** 96
Mary Elizabeth (Russell)
  84 320
Mary L. **89** 181
Mary Smith **74** 307
Mary Snow (Weeks)
  105 110
Matilda **87** 94
May (Bancroft) **97** 130
Maynard L. **74** 309
Mehitable **55** lxxix **107** 4
Mehitable Peters **74** 307
Mercy **57** 410
Mildred Carolyn **74** 310
Molly **52** 435 **58** 124
Moses W. **59** 288
Myra **87** 94
Myra L. **74** 309
Myra N. (Wilson) **87** 93
  94
Nancy **58** 56
Nancy (Sweetser) **125** 219
Nancy B. **87** 93 94
Nathan **89** 302
Nathaniel **88** 298
Nathaniel Ward **83** 471
Nehemiah **60** 44
Nettie P. (Brown) **87** 94
Newton I. **74** 309
Olive Bernice **74** 310
Pamelia **140** 156
Pauline **74** 96
Peter **57** 278 280 **66** 317
  68 196 **92** 126 128 133
  93 322 **94** 377 **102** 191
  106 151 **119** 234 235
Phebe **74** 309
Phebe P. **123** 151
Philip **52** 432 **53** 168
Phillips Endecott **94** 279
  95 138 142 159 312 **96**
  161 173 **97** 171 211 **98**
  139 **99** 69 143 210 211
Phineas **74** 306 **78** 42
Polly (Duran) **136** 77
Priscilla Le Fevre **74** 309
Rebecca **95** 16
Rebecca (Knapp) **134** 335
  137 362
Rebecca Taylor (Pickman)
  106 151
Reuben **92** 311 323
Reuben H. **92** 269
Rhoda **52** 427 **53** 168
Richard **58** 142 **136** 34
Robert **91** 202
Roxana **74** 302
Rufus Warren **74** 308 309
Ruth **51** 463 **68** 332 **108** 92
  128 278 **137** 325
Sally **61** 379 **133** 282

OSGOOD *cont'd*
Sally (Wentworth)
  125 217
Samuel **52** 428 **55** xc xci
  65 53 **78** 415 **92** 277 **96**
  228 **104** 129 **107** 156
  124 225 226 **128** 278
  285
Samuel B. **83** 300
Sarah **51** 463 **54** 101 393
  394 396 **60** 60 **61** 226 **65**
  381 **106** 151 **107** 156
  109 52 **125** 223
Sarah (Fiske) **137** 324
Sarah (Johnson) **106** 151
Sarah (Redington)
  109 113
Sarah (Tibbetts) **99** 115
  116
Sarah Morgan (Adams)
  138 34
Sarah Priscilla **74** 307
Sarah Smith **81** 339
Sarah T. **99** 115
Sewall Mason **62** 207
Silas R. **91** 331
Solomon Parker **89** 181
Sophia (Young) **124** 60
Stephen **89** 181 **99** 115
  100 302
Stephen B. **99** 115
Susan E. **87** 93 94
Susan E. (Billings) **94** 56
Susan Kittredge **55** xc
Susanna **57** 414 **85** 39
Sylvia **58** 58
Thomas **85** 39 **113** 30 37
Thomas Herbert (Mrs.)
  100 112
Thomas L. **74** 96
Thomas Scott **74** 302
Timothy **106** 151 **119** 234
  235
Timothy C. **87** 94
Uriah **58** 56
Valerin A. (Earle) **103** 46
Waite (McIntire) (Manson
  123 72
Warren Decoto **74** 310
William **54** cxxxviii **68**
  261 **74** 306 **78** 42 93 **88**
  298 **89** 181 91 93 **94** 56
  95 16 **105** 110 **119** 234
William C. **138** 34
William Jarvis **74** 310
William M. **78** 418
Willis Howard **74** 302
Winthrop Bancroft
  97 130
O'SHAUGHNESSY
Ignatius Aloysius
  101 121
O'SHAW
Jane **82** 285 295
John **94** 354
Joseph **82** 285 295
OSIER Amy **120** 142
Carrie May **74** 92
Consider **51** 160 **56** 74
  141 337 342
Hester **74** 92

OSIER *cont'd*
Hiram R. **74** 92
Lydia **126** 263
Margaret E. **74** 92
Mary **141** 342
Thomas **106** 109
William **120** 142
OSKAMP —— **93** ix
William S. P. **93** 278
OSKANGE —— **93** ix
OSLAND Elizabeth **71** 146
  152 153 259
Esther **71** 259
Hannah **71** 146 259 260
Humphrey **71** 146 259
John **71** 146 152 153 258
  259
Jonathan **71** 259
Lydia **71** 153 260 351
Mary **71** 259
Mary (Silvester) **86** 289
Mehitable **71** 259
Sally **86** 286
Samuel **86** 289
Sarah **71** 146 152 153 258-
  260
Temperance **71** 259
Thankful **71** 152 259
OSLEGER Henry **147** 286
OSLER A. May **101** 336
  Alfred Clarkson **117** 205
  Ellen Free (Pickton)
    145 311
  Featherstone Lake
    145 311
  Grace Linzee (Revere)
    (Gross) **145** 311
  Nellie **117** 205
  William **145** 311
OSLIN Fannie **146** 390
OSLINGTON
  Robert **100** 73
OSMERS M. **122** 239
OSMOND Richard **51** 348
OSMORE Stephen **65** 182
OSMOTHERLEY
  Gilbert de **96** 311
  Isabella **72** 61
OSMUN Martha **55** 379
OSMUNDERLAW
  Joan **98** 272
  William **98** 272
OSNEY Robert **145** 111
OSSANDON Joseph
    Daniel Frost **109** 287
  Manuela Carolina
    Haviland **109** 289
  Maria Felisa **109** 285 288
  Paula **109** 285 287
  Teresa Gregoria
    Edwards **109** 286
OSSMENT John **67** 343
OSSON Squire **143** 17
OSTEILLI — de **120** 230
OSTELER
  Elizabeth **68** 324
  Mary **68** 326
OSTER Clarence (Mrs.)
  129 396
OSTERBURG
  Henry B. F. **83** 437

OSTERBURG *cont'd*
  Lillian Clara **83** 437
  Nelson E. **68** 386
OSTERHOUT
  Ann **122** 296
  Rosa M. (Chase) **133** 70
  Schuyler **133** 70
OSTERMAN Louis Henry
    (Mrs.) **109** 131
OSTERN Albert **91** 331
OSTERVALD ——— **116** 150
OSTIGUY
  Edward J. **145** 139
  Elsie May (Denno)
    145 139
  Mary **145** 139
  Wolfred **145** 139
OSTLEN ——— **54** 212
OSTLERS ——— **54** 212
OSTRANDER ——— **123** 100
  Aggie **116** 118
  Alice **77** 44
  Aurelia (Allen) **90** 376
  Earl **92** 172
  Elizabeth **70** 121 **115** 134
  Emeline **114** 307
  Ervilla B. **92** 172
  Frances F. **92** 172
  George W. **87** 259
  Hiram **90** 376
  Ida M. **92** 172
  James **115** 134
  James S. **77** 44
  M. A. **116** 118
  Myra L. **92** 172
  Polly **115** 134
  Rensselaer S. **116** 118
  Rosie May **116** 118
  Sarah Albina (Chase)
    87 259
  Solomon **76** 266
  William **114** 307
OSTREVANT Anselm
    Ribemonot de (Count)
    96 316 317
OSTROM
  Alonzo Smith **90** 172
  Charles **90** 55
  Emeline **115** 121
  Esther **106** 304
  Flossie **81** 44
  Floyd **81** 44
  Frank **81** 44
  Guy **81** 44
  Hannah **106** 304
  Jane Augusta (Sharpe)
    90 172
  Jennie Eloise **89** 131 **90**
    118 172 **91** 147
  Jenny C. **81** 44
  Laura (Sweet) **90** 172
  Lydia (Cornwall) **90** 172
  Mary W. **69** 167
  Nina V. **81** 44
  Sarah (Prescott) **90** 55
  Smith **90** 172
  Zebulon **90** 172
O'SULLIVAN Cuogora
    McDonough **57** 62
  Joan **63** lxiii
  Mary **63** lxiii

O'SULLIVAN *cont'd*
  Owen **63** lxiii
  Philip **63** lxiii
OSUT
  — Miss **133** 306 309
OSWALD
  Alexander **132** 303
  John C. **104** 92
  Susanna **95** 14
OSWELL Adam **88** 332
  Elizabeth **99** 283
  John **99** 283
  Sylvia (Niles) **88** 332
Osyer *see* Osier
Otes *see* Otis
Oteway *see* Otway
OTEY
  James H. **77** 253 259
OTHEMAN
  Anthony **78** 74
  Hannah **78** 300
OTHER
  Walter Fitz **96** 38 43
OTIS ——— **59** 326 **83** 195 **92**
    253 346 353 **93** 59 65 **95**
    44 45 **97** 5 **121** 41 **131**
    275 279 **138** 172 **140**
    232
  — Dr. **60** 65 180 181
  — Maj. **63** 54
  — Mr. **57** 228 **63** 56 **65**
    370 **79** 407
  ___ (Bordman) **140** 42
  ___ (Coffin) **140** 232
  ___ (Foster) **140** 142
  ___ (Smith) **140** 246
  Abigail **51** 329 **60** 384 **61**
    173 **71** 57 **76** 28 29 36
    92 132 243 249 256 344
    93 316 **94** 156 **120** 198
  Abigail K. **76** 38
  Abigail Tilden **61** 176 288
  Abijah **60** 337
  Addie (Gawn) (Lazell)
    89 310
  Adeline Prudence **92** 256
  Albert Boyd **52** 9-12 152
    291
  Alice Dexter **82** 479
  Alline **78** 188
  Allyne **140** 232
  Almena A. **95** 375
  Almira **76** 39
  Amos **51** 208 328 329 **52**
    187 206 357 358 **54** 168
    169 174 **57** 17-20 **59** 91
    60 113 **68** 209 **95** 42 **99**
    49 **101** 148 **103** 32 37
    111 174 **112** 191 196-
    198 261 **113** 18 20 168
    251 **114** 82 **117** 181 **118**
    83 85 86 89 198-200 207
    208 211 213 282 284 **120**
    95 119 **123** 130
  Ann **93** 59 **98** 134
  Anna **146** 360
  Anne **94** 186
  Asahel **82** 478
  Barnabas **118** 129 130
  Bethiah **81** 162
  Betsey **60** 335 **61** 173

OTIS *cont'd*
  Blanche **76** lxxxi
  Brian **90** 66 197 198
    124 255
  Catherine Waters **92** 353
  Chandler **72** 307
  Charles **120** 200
  Charles E. **95** 375
  Charles Gilbert **72** 308
  Charlie A. **89** 294
  Charlotte **76** 30
  Charlotte (Freeman)
    88 283
  Christine **51** 504
  Clara **70** 202
  Clarissa **70** 202
  Cordelia Swift **72** 308
  Cushing **61** 173 174 288
  David **52** 9 **87** 124 **88** 355
    99 201-203 **118** 129 130
  David P. **89** 250
  Deborah **57** 400 **58** 265
    387 389 390 **59** 76 78
    135 137 309 311 **60** 176
    129 250 264 265
  Deborah (Jacob) **129** 170
  Delia **70** 202
  Demarus (Huntley)
    101 148
  Desire **105** 86 **129** 266
  Dority (Joyce) **100** 150
  Dorothy **52** 76 **118** 127-
    130
  Edward D. **78** 187
  Eliza **76** 36
  Eliza M. **52** 9 **96** 391
  Elizabeth **52** 81 **70** 327 **82**
    478 **89** 397 **90** 66 197 **92**
    17 20 21 **118** 128 129
    124 255 **143** 136
  Elizabeth (Gray) **84** 167
  Elizabeth (Grene) **124** 255
  Elizabeth (Little) **118** 129
  Elizabeth (Wade) **129** 170
  Elizabeth H. H. **125** 245
  Elizabeth Lewis **92** 17
  Elmira (Kenny) **95** 375
  Elwell S. **92** 82
  Emily (Marshall) **140** 232
  Emma Angeanette **63** 117
  Ensign **129** 154 166 251
    260 263 265 266 373 **134**
    141
  Ephraim **57** 402 403 **59**
    136 **60** 335 337 **63** 299
    71 62 **118** 313 **129** 374
  Erwin J. **119** 238 316
  Esther **70** 229
  Eva L. **89** 294
  Everett B. **83** 437
  Frances Emmaline **72** 308
  Frank H. **89** 294
  G. W. **92** 249 256 344 346
    94 42 156 158 159 162
  G. W. (Mrs.) **92** 252
  Galen **140** 253
  George **51** 329 **129** 377
  George H. **89** 294
  George Holman **72** 307
  George W. **92** 132 243 **93**
    59 65 316 **140** 246

OTIS *cont'd*
George Washington **92**
126 **94** 377
Georgianna E. (Noble)
95 375
Geraldine (Fitz Randolph)
98 128
H. G. **78** 188 **83** 195 **91** 331
H. N. **59** 326
Hampton J. **98** 128
Hannah **58** 174 176 **59** 78
60 335 **76** 39 **88** 287 **93**
192 **113** 163 **130** 178
140 231
Hannah (Clapp) **120** 55
Hannah (Cushing)
129 166
Hannah (Ensign) **129** 166
Hannah Barker **92** 344
346 **94** 158
Hannah C. **68** 203
Hannah L. **94** 42
Harriet **54** 317 **76** 36
Harriet E. **89** 250
Harriet N. **79** 80
Harrison Gray **55** 162 **61**
109 **66** 99 **71** 100 **90** 104
92 16 **97** 5 **99** 24 **129** 93
139 6 **140** 42 142 232
324
Helen **80** 111
Henry **51** 329
Horatio N. **118** 128
Hulda (Hills) **91** 197
Ida J. **89** 294
Isaac **57** 400 403 **58** 265 387
389 390 **59** 76 78 135
137 139 309 311 **60** 176
80 181 **107** 313 **120** 71
129 170 386
James **51** 328 475-477 **52**
76 **54** 99 **55** 162 **59** 135
137 **70** 100 **71** 288 **76**
321 **80** 310 **82** 478 **84**
156 158 162 163 165 248
249 252 254 258 269 **93**
65 **105** 86 **107** 74 **110**
317 **112** 197 **113** 114
117 292 **118** 127-130
120 71 **125** 223 **129** 102
375 **130** 31 32 200 201
131 76 272 **132** 34 124
134 104 **136** 281 284
140 232
James Alleyne Gardner
120 71
James S. **89** 294
Jane **51** 329 **52** 9 **83** 22 26
93 59
Jane (Turner) **134** 141
Jefferson **95** 375
Joanna **76** 38 **96** 351
Joanna (Chase) **87** 53
Joanna (Gardner) **125** 223
Joanna (Tilden) **140** 253
Job **71** 57 61 **120** 197 198
134 136 **135** 36
John **51** 328 329 **52** 10 76
191 **57** 65 **60** 384 **76** 28
81 162 **82** 478 479 **84**
168 **87** 399 **100** 150 **105**

OTIS *cont'd*
86 **109** 7 **112** 258 **113** 43
115 **118** 128 196 **119**
238 **120** 55 **121** 18 103
104 106 110 212 **127** 116
128 259 261 **129** 222
130 6 10 **134** 141 **143**
134 136 346
John D. **79** 80
John Thatcher **57** 273
John Turner **79** 80
Jonathan **118** 129 130
Jonathan Mayhew **84** 271
92 21
Joseph **52** 76 **81** 162 **82**
478 **91** 197 **94** 186 **116** 7
118 127-130 **129** 170
130 7
Joseph E. **89** 294
Joshua **76** 28 29 41 **92** 249
126 226 **129** 260 265
377
Josiah **58** 265 389
Joyce **98** 215
Judith **76** 34
Julia Ann **89** 250
Katharine **51** 329
Lorenzo **88** 283
Louisa **57** 273 **88** 355
Louisa W. **89** 294
Love **76** 28
Lucius B. **76** lxxix
Lucy **52** 76 **55** 277 278 **60**
338 **70** 100 **95** 291
Lucy E. (Newton) **83** 437
Lucy Lucretia **57** 292
Lusanna **121** 236
Lydia **58** 174 **76** 31
Mabel **118** 129 130
Marcy (Bacon) **121** 212
Margaret **60** 384 **82** 479
131 25
Margaretta Adams **82** 479
Margaretta Graves
Jackson **82** 478
Mariah **118** 128
Mariah (Goodwin)
113 266
Marian **57** 292 **72** 308
Martha (Gates) **121** 257
Mary **51** 329 **52** 76 191 358
53 207 **55** 449 **60** 337
339 384 **71** 57 **72** 307 **73**
90 **75** 124 **76** 28 **81** 150
84 163 **89** 193 **92** 132
94 156 **105** 86 **118** 281
121 103 **136** 79 **140** 232
Mary (Barker) **129** 373
Mary (Jacob) **143** 136
Mary (Little) **120** 197
Mary (Thaxter) **129** 377
Mary Elizabeth **72** 308
Mary Louise **92** 82
Mary T. **134** 298
Maud **120** 259
Melinda **76** 36
Melissa **85** 377
Mercy **51** 329 **55** 167 **97**
277 **118** 129 130 **129**
169 170 **135** 112-114

OTIS *cont'd*
144 233
Mercy (Little) **129** 170
135 36
Nabby **59** 311
Nancy **51** 329 **78** 379
99 201 203
Nathaniel **58** 174 176 **60**
384 **82** 478 **118** 129 130
119 261 **121** 257 **123** 62
127 23
Nathaniel Walter **118** 128
Nicholas **59** 193 **76** 34 36
87 53 **96** 351 **98** 215
Noah **129** 373 378
O. B. **68** 203
Olive **118** 130
Pamelia **57** 292
Patience (Sherman)
100 150
Paul **55** 277 **60** 338 339
Penelope **60** 339
Peter **105** 86
Phebe **72** 307
Phebe (Burbanks) **90** 104
Phebe (Cushing) **129** 373
Philena Lomira **57** 292
Priscilla **120** 198 200
135 36
Rachel **57** 403 **59** 136 63
299 **71** 62 **94** 186 **118**
128
Rachel (Hersey) **129** 374
Rebecca **118** 128 **126** 191
Rebecca F. **76** 41
Richard **70** 185 **78** 379 **98**
135 215 **107** 267
Robert **78** 379
Rosamond Fay **82** 479
Rose **58** lxxxvi **59** 326 **98**
135 **107** 267
Rose (Stoughton) **98** 135
Ruth **80** 181 **129** 263 **135**
36 39 40
Sally **51** 329 **55** 277 **76** 28
116 139
Sally (Foster) **140** 232
Sally Thaxter **92** 243
94 159
Samuel **52** 9 **76** 31 **100** 150
105 86
Samuel A. **85** 122
Samuel Allen **84** 167 271
92 17
Samuel Allyne **92** 16 20
21 **94** 294 **118** 313 **140**
232
Samuel Allyne (Mrs.)
97 5
Sarah **52** 76 **104** 54 **115** 113
116 129 **119** 251 **120** 55
197 199 200 **126** 257
137 51
Sarah (Harris) **129** 374
Sarah (Tudor) **131** 76
Sarah A. **80** 310
Sarah Ann **76** 41
Sarah Grace **70** 202
Sarah P. **76** 40
Seth Kellogg **57** 292
Sewell **95** 51

OTIS *cont'd*
Shuah **70** 185
Shubael **57** 292 **118** 129
130
Solomon **51** 329 362 **91** 94
130 130
Sophia Frances **57** 292
Stanley Lyman (Mrs.) **76**
lxxxi
Stephen **52** 76 **59** 76 **70**
202 **72** 307 **99** 201 **122**
21 **129** 163 166 170 254
Susan **63** 299 **76** 28
Susan S. **94** 162
Susan Sophia (Munroe)
92 252
Susanna **71** 62 63
Temperance (Hinckley)
113 115
Thankful **100** 150 **105** 86
Theodore **54** 317 **120** 71
Thomas **59** 139 309
120 259
Walter B. K. **76** 40
Walter Joseph **75** xxiii 63
82 122 245 478 479
Whitman B. **89** 294
William **58** 390 **70** 202
89 310 **118** 128-130
William (Mrs.) **95** 54
William A. **62** 386 **79** 450
118 127 128 130 **143**
136
William C. **91** 331
William Foster **140** 232
William Gardner **120** 71
OTLAND M. **91** 331
OTLEY
Adam **68** 195 **70** 183
Charles **100** 31
Elizabeth **70** 183
Mary Judith **100** 31
Susanna **100** 31
OTNESS George Louis
(Mrs.) **87** 174
O'TOOLE —— **59** 117
Barbara E. **108** 271
Mary **92** 223
Peter (Mrs.) **122** 100
OTRINGHAM
Manser de **114** 218
Peter de **114** 218
Richard de **114** 218
Stephen de **114** 218
Walo de **114** 218
OTSIQUETE
Peter **140** 69
OTTERSEN Hannah **120** 5
OTTERTON Richard
(Duke of) **68** 47
OTTERY Rudy **148** 294
Will **148** 294
Ottes *see* Otis
OTTO IV Holy Roman
Emperor **140** 221
OTTO Anna **72** 299
Eliza Corning **93** 189
George **72** 299
John **93** 189
Julie Helen **146** 384 387
Mary **72** 299

OTTY Elizabeth
Crookshank **77** lxvi
Henry Phipps **77** xlvi
Hetty **77** xlvi
OTWAY Eleanor **73** 226
Henry **67** 252
Joanna **82** 57
John **81** 490
Richard **82** 57
Samuel **138** 92
Thomas **54** 92
OUBERKIRK
Margaret **129** 85
OUBY Margery **148** 112
OUDERKERK
Isaac **70** 262
OUELLET
Fernand **145** 129
Ouerall *see* Overall
Oueratt *see* Overatt
Ouerton *see* Overton
OUIJADA
Aureliano **109** 284
OUINETTE Betty **143** 8
Louise / Lisette
(Robichaux) **143** 8
Madeleine (Maisonnat)
143 8
Ould *see* Olds
Ouldfield *see* Oldfield
Ouldham *see* Oldham
OULDRINGE
Edward **63** 281
OULTE Richard **52** 244
OULTON — Miss **53** 392
Ann **53** 391 392
Charles Frederic **82** 174
Deborah **53** 391 **76** 204
Elizabeth **53** 391
Hannah **53** 391 392
Jane **53** 392
Jennie **82** 174
John **52** 219 **53** 391 392
57 275 **67** 213 **82** 174
Julia **82** 174
Lucy **53** 391 392
Mary **53** 392
Samson B. **108** 216
Sarah **53** 392
OUSAMEQUIN **53** 320
OUSPENSKY
Nina **98** 152
OUTERBRIDGE
Albert A. **90** 284
Nancy Elizabeth **105** 160
OUTHAUS Robert **89** 96
OUTHWAITE Charles
William (Mrs.) **84**
105 190
OUTING
John **71** 30 231
Richard **56** 275
OUTLAW
Alvin (Mrs.) **113** 160
Andrew **112** 29
Doris C. **113** 160
Rex Clyde (Mrs.) **105** 129
OUTLEY
Helen May **93** 218
Jonathan Stickney **93** 218

OUTLEY *cont'd*
Mary (McDermott)
93 218
OUTMAN Maria **83** 67
OUTMER William **64** 53
OUTOUT
Catherine **95** 368
Henry **95** 368
Hettie (Van Bergen)
95 368
OUTRAM
Eliza **76** xxxviii
OUTRED John **66** 358
Matthew **66** 358
William **66** 358
OUTRY Joan **66** 245 256
OUTS —— **143** 202
OUTT Dolly **72** 294
James Franklin **72** 294
John **72** 294
Minnie May **72** 294
Phebe Eliza **72** 294
Outterbridge *see*
Outerbridge
OUTTRIM
Eva Fryer **86** 170
John E. **86** 170
Lettie J. Balch **85** 315
Mary Belle **85** 315
Mary J. Emely **85** 315
Thomas **85** 315
Thomas J. **85** 315
OUTWATER
Mary A. **73** lxii
OVEALE John **83** 316
OVELL Nathaniel **75** 222
OVENDEN
Elizabeth **137** 302
John **101** 50 **137** 302
Mary **137** 302
OVENTEN — Mr. **83** 36
Jane **83** 36
Over *see* Overy
OVERACKER
Amy (Barton) **107** 57
Anna J. (Giffin) **104** 103
Barton **107** 57
Cyrus Perkins **94** 201 202
Delilah (Perkins) **94** 202
Delilah P. **94** 202
Edward M. **94** 201
Harriet (Todd) **94** 202
Harvey M. **94** 201 202
James F. **94** 201 202
John H. **94** 201 202
Lucinda M. (Todd) **94** 202
Martha M. **94** 201
Martin M. **94** 201 202
Mary **107** 57
Milton B. **94** 201 202
Minnie L. **94** 201
Robert (Bowers) **94** 202
Sarah H. (Mitchell)
94 201 202
William F. **94** 201 202
William Randolph
107 57
OVERALL Nicholas **83** 74
OVERATT —— **51** 128
OVERBECK
Daniel **106** 8

OVERBECK *cont'd*
Ruth Ann **118** 250
OVERBEEK
Elizabeth (Hals) **106** 8
OVERBEY Ann **89** 95
Ann (Yanvey) **89** 95
Ann Celestia **89** 96
Cornelia Caroline **89** 96
Emma **89** 96
Mary **89** 95 96
Mary (Marvin) **89** 150
Mary Adeline **89** 95
Mildred **89** 95
Minerva **89** 95
Narcissa **89** 96
Peter **89** 95
Polly P. (Pool) **89** 95
Rebecca Alice **89** 96
Robert Camillus **89** 96
Robert Yancey **89** 95 96
Rosalie **89** 95
Sarah Eugenia **89** 96
Zachariah **89** 95
OVERBURY Mary **74** 140
Walter **74** 140
Overe *see* Overy
OVEREND
Jonathan **68** 338
Mary Ann **68** 338
William H. **68** 338
OVERHOLSER
Alonzo Berton **86** 198
OVERING
—— **57** 325 **63** 54
Charlotte M. **57** 335
Elizabeth **57** 418
George **57** 335
Henrietta **57** 335 418 419
Henry **57** 335 418
Henry J. **127** 143
Mary **60** 347
Mary Juliana **57** 418
Robert **57** 418 419
OVERINS —— **101** 51
OVERLAND Robert (Mrs.)
130 72 315
OVERLEESE
Hazel **104** 145
Ruhlin (Mrs.) **104** 145
OVERLOCK
— Mrs. **117** 171
Gardiner **73** 174
Gertrude B. **83** 423 437
Godfrey **73** 174 **117** 171
Lydia **73** 174
Olive **73** 174
Sally **73** 174
OVERLOOK
Eliza **68** 254
OVERMAN Mildred Ann
(Pennell) **117** 319
OVERMEYER
Gladys Foster **80** 98
OVEROEKER Sarah Harris
(Mitchell) **89** 15
OVERPECK
Alemeth E. **109** 306
Destie Faye **109** 306
OVERSTREET
Edwin **69** 260
Elizabeth **76** 121

OVERSTREET *cont'd*
Josephine Martha **69** 260
Thomas **76** 116
Virginia Washington
121 316
William **76** 116 121
OVERTON — Mr. **80** 409
Alethea **53** 78
Barbara **112** 151
Dorothy **76** 79
Dymocke **76** 79
Edward **76** 79
Elizabeth (Waters)
112 151
Henry **59** 324
Isaac **53** 78
Jane **82** 423
John **51** 350 **53** 75
John H. **91** 331
Joseph **68** 79
Katharine **76** 79
Mary **106** 65 66
Nathaniel **53** 78
Ralph A. (Mrs.) **123** 155
Robert **145** 111
Thomas **68** 64
Valentine **128** 22
Wahnetta H. **142** 374
William **100** 258 **112** 151
OVERTURF Alzina M.
(Sheldon) **97** 208
Jesse R. **97** 208
John Lake **97** 208
N. F. **97** 209
OVERY Over Overye
Hannah **104** 47
Harry **74** 135
Henry **104** 47 **112** 26 44
Joan **109** 91
Ioanna **51** 289
Warren A. **78** 400
OVEY
Elizabeth **61** 393
John **61** 393
Samuel **61** 343
Thomas **61** 393
OVIATT Abigail (Harris)
142 342 343
Amy **124** 187
Esther **62** 97
Eunice **142** 343
Freelove **75** 184
George Herman **107** 134
John **62** 97 **75** 184 **142** 343
Keziah (Plumb) **142** 342
Lydia **54** 386
Samuel **142** 342 343
Sarah (Cooke) (Preston)
142 343
Susanna **75** 184
Thalia **62** 97
Thomas **54** 386 **62** 82
142 342
Truman D. **142** 342
OVID **56** 342 343
OVINGTON Edward
Judson **62** lvii
Jeannette Maria **62** lvii
Maria Newman **62** lvii
Marian E. **114** 319 321
OVITT Ada **75** 15 16

OVITT *cont'd*
Charles **130** 50
Charles F. **75** 15
Christian **130** 50
Davis **74** 168
Dennis S. **75** 15
Diannia **74** 168
Eddie Daniel **75** 15
Edgar D. **75** 15
Electa **74** 171
Eliphalet **74** 171
Ella **75** 15
Ella L. **75** 15
Fairzina A. **130** 47
Homer **75** 16
Jane A. **75** 99
John **75** 15
Lydia **75** 15
Martha **130** 53
Mary **74** 168 **75** 15
Matilda E. **75** 15
Mildred Sarah **75** 15
Orpha A. **74** 171
Reuben C. **74** 312 **75** 15
Richard **75** 16
Owane *see* Owen
OWANECO
133 103 104 113
Owayne *see* Owen
OWBRICC John **93** 29
OWEN Owane Owayne
Owens
—— **51** 354 **55** 229 **56** 326
91 246 **96** 63 69
— Dr. **53** 297 **54** 43 **81** 127
— Mr. **71** 136 **96** 64
— Mrs. **71** 119 **113** 37
Aaron **83** 42 43 55
Abby **83** 45
Abby B. **70** 336
Abdon **83** 53 60
Abel **83** 49 **91** 239-244
Abiah **83** 51
Abigail **58** 342 **83** 40 41
45 49 54 58 67 201 **91**
243
Abigail (Leach) **131** 199
Abijah **83** 59
Abner **83** 41 46
Abraham **83** 59 60 67
Abram **83** 52 53
Absalom **83** 47
Adelbert **91** 245
Affiah **89** 399
Agnes Jeanette (Cargill)
117 260
Alanson **91** 242
Albert J. **83** 437 **84** 24
Albert Perley **83** 69
Albertus **91** 246
Alfred **83** 63
Alice **83** 51 **91** 246
Alice M. **89** 399
Allen **91** 246
Almon **91** 246
Almond **91** 241-243
Almyra **83** 58
Alson **91** 244 246
Altamira **83** 56
Alvan **83** 45 46

OWEN *cont'd*
Amanda L. (Wilcox)
  89 242
Amariah A. **123** 11
Amasa **83** 57 58 60-63 68-
  70 **86** 461 462
Ambrose **83** 50
Amelia **62** 127
Amelia Metta **80** 155
Amos **83** 44 45 **91** 239 240
  146 357
Amy **83** 41
Andrew **83** 54 **91** 246
Ann **64** 202 338 **83** 39 42
  44 46 47 50 62 63
Ann (Petty) **123** 260
Anna **83** 59 **91** 241 243 246
Anna Maria (Wright)
  107 117
Anne **55** 413 **83** 41 45 53
  54 **94** 330
Anne (Lady) **94** 253
Anne Eliza **91** 242
Anne F. **70** 322
Anning **83** 56
Anson **91** 243
Armenia **91** 245
Asahel **83** 44 52-54 59
  121 160
Augustus Holdridge
  91 240
Azubah **83** 51
Barbara **120** 317
Barbara (Montgomery)
  112 299
Bathsheba **83** 49 58
Benajah **83** 51 67
Benjamin **52** 437 **59** 274
  63 87 **83** 40 47 63 **91**
  244 245 331 **133** 259
  145 43
Benjamin F. **71** 119
Benson **91** 242
Bert **83** 68
Betsey **83** 58
Betsey (Davis) **91** 244
Caleb **83** 42 43
Calphurnia **91** 247
Candice **83** 56
Carmi **83** 59
Carrie (Charleston)
  89 289
Carrie O. **91** 243
Catherine **83** 51 **96** 70
  102 168
Catherine (Copeland)
  91 246
Catherine Maria
  (Sanderson) (Blake)
  128 122
Cecil Janette **80** 155
Charles **54** 189 **83** 66
  89 399
Charles Hunter **83** 59
Charles LeRoy **91** 246
Charles M. **65** 9
Charles N. **70** 322
Charlotte **83** 50 **91** 241
Charlotte (Gleason)
  91 242
Chauncey **83** 59

OWEN *cont'd*
Cheney **83** 59
Chloe **83** 51 54 55
Chloe (Hatch) **91** 243
Christiana **83** 43
Christine Towne
  (Stocker) **89** 289
Clarence **91** 242
Clarence Rice **104** 145
Clarissa **83** 59
Clayton Ransom **91** 246
Clinton **91** 246
Coburn S. **89** 399
Constantia V. **91** 247
Cotton **58** 342
Cranston Lucius **80** 155
Cynthia **83** 47
Cyrus **63** 87
D. M. **115** 79
Daniel **83** 36 39 40 42 43 47
  49 58 59 62 70 **89** 288
  125 87 **128** 58
Daniel Perry **89** 288 400
David **55** 233 **73** 263 **74**
  102 **83** 45-47 54 57 **94**
  253 330 **121** 187 **146**
  357
David Allen **118** 75
Deborah **73** lv **83** 44 45
  58 59 **138** 212
Deborah (Holdridge)
  91 240
Deidamia **83** 50
Delilah **83** 62 63 70
Deliverance **83** 39 **136** 59
Della **83** 54
Desire **83** 45
Donnell M. **115** 150
Donnell MacClure
  107 239
Dorcas (Williams)
  125 303
Doris (Woodbury) **83**
  437 **84** 24
Dorothy **83** 45 51
E. **91** 331
Eben **83** 180 185
Ebenezer **58** 342 **83** 39 58
Edson **91** 242
Edward **83** 53 59 60
Edward H. **65** 9
Edward Hezekiah **83** 55
  56
Edward Jason **83** 56
Eleanor (Kentfield)
  102 239
Eleanor Ann **83** 67
Eleazer **83** 49 56-58 61
Electa **83** 50
Elijah **83** 44 45 50 52 58 59
  62 63 70 **91** 239 240 243
Elijah Hunter **96** 161
Eliphalet **83** 49 50 54
Eliza **54** 421 **91** 242
Eliza Ann **83** 64 66
  91 244 245
Eliza Anna **91** 244
Eliza Josephine **78** 247
Eliza Katharine **89** 193
Elizabeth **72** xxxii **73** 225
  74 102 **83** 40 41 43-45

OWEN *cont'd*
  56 58 60 **88** 121 **89** 193
  91 239-241 **93** 203 **101**
  10 **125** 87
Elizabeth (Abbott) **91** 240
Elizabeth B. **83** 56
Elizabeth S. M. **73** 268
Ella **83** 58
Ella (Templeton) **91** 242
Ellen **65** 165
Ellen (Canfield) **102** 239
Ellen Austin **78** 247
Ellen Esther **89** 400
Ellen S. (Bird) **123** 309
Elmer Ellsworth **80** 155
Elvan **72** 36
Emeline E. (Ingalls)
  89 399
Emily **83** 67 **89** 399
  115 122
Emily Ann Bradlee
  78 247
Emily Bliss **89** 289
Emily D. **89** 399
Emily Winchester **78** 247
Emma (Bense) **89** 399
Emma Amelia **83** 69
  86 462
Ephraim **66** 80
Erastus **83** 59 **89** 242
Esther **59** 370 **68** 245 **70**
  322 **83** 41-43 46 47 50 54
  55 58 66 **89** 288 400
Eunice **83** 43 45 49-51 54
  62-64 66 70 **85** 47
Eunice (Waters) **146** 357
Eunice Rowena **83** 69
  86 462
Evan **64** 259 343 344
Experience **83** 49
F. A. **70** 191
Fanny **83** 56
Fanny Flossia **78** 176
Florence L. **89** 399
Floretta **91** 246
Frances Ellen **83** 66
Francis **80** 155
Francis Marion **91** 244
Frank **83** 66
Franklin Dodge **89** 400
Frederick **83** 54 **89** 399
Frederick Langdon
  89 399
George **71** 173 **73** 143 **83**
  51 63 **91** 246 **95** 22
George C. **83** 51
George H. **83** 59
George Hodges **89** 288
Guy **146** 357
H. C. **89** 289 399 400
Hannah **52** 437 **71** 188 279
  83 41 45 48 49 51 52 54
  55 58 59 67 **89** 193 377
  91 240 **115** 218
Hannah Maria **91** 241 243
Hannah Stanwood
  74 107
Hans Christian **89** 289
  90 137
Harriet **70** 322 **83** 66
Harriet (Mosher) **91** 246

OWEN *cont'd*
Harriet Lucille (Penrose) **117** 206
Harriet Murich (Doane) **89** 288
Harry T. **146** 357
Harvey **83** 58 59
Haven **91** 331
Helen **83** 67
Henrietta **83** 64
Henry **64** 338 **83** 59 66
Henry Wilson **84** 190 232
Hepsabeth (Callender) **145** 43
Hezekiah **83** 55 56
Hiram **83** 58
Homer W. **91** 244
Howard **51** 244
Hugh **64** 202 257 **96** 70
Huldah **83** 49 50 58
I. W. **91** 331
Ida A. **83** 66
Ira **89** 288 **91** 245
Ira Marilo **91** 246
Irene **83** 46 48 50
Isaac **63** 329 **83** 40-45 51 63 67 **91** 239 240
Isaac Milton **83** 51
Isabelle **83** 65
Isador **91** 246
Israel **70** 322 336
J. B. (Mrs.) **122** 154
J. P. **91** 331
Jacob **83** 62 65 70
James **55** 83 **62** 325 **63** 16 **83** 46 47 49 58 62 63 68
James Alfred **117** 260
James Davie **83** 67
James Hodges **89** 289
James Marshall **107** 134 **109** 309 310 **110** 63
James Monroe **109** 309
Jane **83** 68 **85** 465 **134** 254
Jane (Bodwell) (Deary) **86** 462
Jane Augusta **83** 56
Jane Strong **100** 326
Jason **83** 59 **131** 199
Jedediah **83** 43
Jemima **54** 170 **83** 43 49-51 58
Jennie **91** 244
Jenny **74** 102
Jerusha **83** 51 57 58 **126** 64 79
Jesse **100** 88
Joab **83** 51
Joel **83** 43 53 54 59
Johanna **83** 47
John **55** 332 **58** 300 342 **59** 360 **64** 161 163 **73** 138 **74** 102 **78** 247 **83** 39-41 43 45 53-55 62 63 67 70 412 **85** 56 **86** 460 **87** 97 **89** 288 305 399 **91** 94 239 240 245 **94** 253 330 331 **95** 400 **112** 125 287 299 **116** 7 **117** 206 **123** 95 309 **128** 134 **146** 357
John B. **83** 57
John Calvin **83** 55

OWEN *cont'd*
John Jason **83** 55 56
John Richard (Mrs.) **84** 190
John Vaughton **78** 247
John Wallace **78** 176
Jonas **98** 96
Jonathan **83** 45-47 56 57 61 **91** 239 240 243 **125** 303 **138** 212
Joseph **54** 170 **58** 342 **59** 274 **73** 140 148 **83** 40 42-44 46-50 53 57 59-62 64 66 67 70 **93** 180 **99** 192 193 **102** 151
Josephine **89** 289 **91** 243
Joshua **83** 42 43 49 50 **107** 267 **115** 150
Josiah **83** 40 41 44 45 54 58 **118** 267
Joyce Dice **121** 317
Judith **102** 124
Julia **83** 59
Julius **83** 50
Julius Lawrence **89** 399
Keziah **83** 46 50 51 55 56 58
Laura **82** 17 **83** 67 **84** 301 **89** 399
Laura Ann **83** 67
Lavinia (Davison) **102** 239
Lavinia B. **83** 56
Lemuel Dowe **89** 400
Leonard **83** 49 50 58
LeRoy **91** 244
Lettie **74** 102
Levi S. **128** 122
Lewis **90** 109 **91** 241 **125** 303
Lewis Stiles **91** 242
Lillian **91** 242
Lois **83** 45 50 53 54 56 57
Lois (Post) **146** 357
Lois (Rounds) **91** 244
Loisa **91** 245
Lola **91** 245
Lorinda **83** 67 **91** 244
Louisa **83** 68 **91** 242 245
Louisa Jane (Munroe) **100** 88
Louise **146** 357
Louise E. (Braun) **89** 289
Lovina **146** 357
Lovina (Davison) **91** 242
Lovina Adell **91** 248
Lovina Sophronia **91** 242
Lucretia **83** 51 59
Lucy **68** 246 **70** 322 **74** 102 **83** 47 58 **91** 241 242 246 **92** 189
Lucy (Allen) **91** 244
Lucy Ann **89** 399
Luella A. **117** 244 245 256
Lusina **83** 49
Lydia **60** 77 **83** 45 46 48 49 51 54 58 59 **89** 288
Lydia (Perry) **89** 288
Lydia (Rich) **83** 412
Lydia Anna (Babcock) **91** 244
Lydia Perry **89** 399

OWEN *cont'd*
Mahala **98** 298
Margaret **72** 293 **74** 102 **81** 362 **83** 47 49-51 **89** 289 **132** 243
Margaret E. (Newell) **112** 22
Maria **83** 58 63 67 68 **91** 242
Maria Louisa **91** 242
Marilo Harrison **91** 246
Marilo Pitt **91** 246
Martha **56** 306 **83** 43-45 54 65-68 **91** 239 246 **126** 67
Martha J. **70** 322
Mary **58** 342 **59** 90 274 360 363 **74** 102 **83** 40-47 49-51 53-55 57-59 62 67 **91** 246 **95** 23 **98** 186 **99** 66 **111** 63 **112** 100 **146** 357
Mary (Bell) **91** 242
Mary (Bohun) **94** 330
Mary (Coulter) **91** 245
Mary (Ruttenburg) **110** 47
Mary (Youngs) **146** 357
Mary A. **91** 244
Mary Ann **91** 245 **99** 193
Mary Butler **83** 67
Mary Elizabeth **91** 242
Mary Elizabeth (Hodges) **89** 289
Mary Frances (Bridgeman) **89** 400
Mary G. **65** 9
Mary Grace **93** 180
Mary Isabella **78** 247
Mary W. (Dole) **83** 180 185
Maryette **133** 38
Matthew **113** 211
Mattie (Flint) **91** 246
Mehitable **133** 259
Mehitable (Nash) **91** 240
Mehitable (Savel) **133** 259
Melissa **83** 66
Mercy **83** 45 46 48
Meroe J. **116** 84
Milanda **83** 67
Mildred Ruth **108** 134
Millard Fillmore **89** 399
Miner **89** 288
Minerva (Dowe) **89** 400
Miriam **83** 43 50 58 59
Miriam Loraine **89** 289
Molly **83** 45 50 **146** 357
Moses **83** 42 43 48
Myra **83** 68
N **52** 31
Nancy **77** 134 135 **83** 59 63 **91** 39 **112** 22
Nancy J. (Coburn) **89** 399
Naomi **83** 50
Nathan **102** 239
Nathaniel **59** 90 274 360 363 **63** 282 **68** 245 246 **70** 322 336 **72** 36 38 **83** 40 41 45 46 55 57 58 **91**

OWEN *cont'd*
242 **105** 199
Nellie **83** 67 69
Nelson **91** 244 245
Nelson A. **91** 244
Nellie H. **84** 111
Noah **83** 44 53 54
Nomah **83** 54
Nora **91** 245
Obadiah **83** 40 43 44
Olive **83** 50
Oliver **83** 57 59 61
Olivia **88** 277
Orilla **83** 59
Orvil Ives **83** 68 69 **86** 462
Parintha **91** 248
Parnah **83** 54
Patience **83** 50 52 53 56
57 61
Patience (Rose) **121** 160
Peggy **74** 102 **83** 47 51 54
Pelatiah **83** 59
Phebe **68** 245 246 **70** 322
336 **83** 50 **91** 243
Phebe (Klock) **91** 246
Phebe R. **70** 322
Philip **74** 107
Phyllis E. **124** 320
Polly **83** 54 58 62 63 70
146 357
Polly (Dyer) **91** 246
Priscilla **83** 43 58
Rachel **63** 339 **70** 322 **74**
102 **83** 40 41 47 50 51 53
54
Rainer **83** 54 58
Ralf H. **100** 326
Ralph **83** 58
Ralph Dornfeld **95** 400 **99**
148 **100** 327 **146** 357
Ransom Ezra **91** 246
Ray **122** 287
Rebecca **58** 342 **64** 249 **71**
188 **83** 39 40 44-47 52 60
66 67 **91** 239 243 **93** 391
101 159 **115** 139
Rebecca (Chandler)
89 399
Rebecca (Dayrell) **95** 22
Rebecca (Tilden) **91** 239
Rebecca (Walden) **105** 80
Reed **109** 310
Rhoda **83** 50 59
Rice **96** 357
Richard **63** 20 **64** 161 165
344 **72** xxxii **87** 97 **101**
12 **115** 150 **144** 46
Robert **64** 261 **80** 68 **83** 66
101 6 82 90
Robert Carter **91** 242
Robert Dale **80** 68
Robert P. **72** 275
Robert Wallace **83** 69
86 462
Roderick **83** 58 **91** 241 242
102 239
Roderick Mandred
91 242
Roger **52** 252
Roger Leonard **83** 56
Rosetta **83** 55

OWEN *cont'd*
Ruth **83** 43 46 47 50 55
99 192
Ruth (Heath) **99** 192
Sabra **83** 45 49 51
Sabrina **83** 67
Sally **52** 341 **69** 373 **83** 58
68 **91** 242
Sally (Seely) **91** 243
Sally E. **83** 63
Salmon **91** 243
Samuel **54** 172 **74** 102 **83**
39 43 50 51 **105** 80 **123**
260
Samuel Tine **118** 75
Samuel W. **70** 322
Sarah **58** 342 **80** 155 **83** 40
41 43 44 50 51 54 57 59
60 62-66 70 **127** 69 **128**
122 **140** 232 **141** 5
Sarah (Dennis) **91** 246
Sarah (Grover) **91** 242
Sarah (Ingalls) **89** 399
Sarah Abigail **83** 69
Sarah Brown **65** 9
Sarah Harriet **71** 69
Sarah Seymour **83** 56
Seth **83** 51
Seth Calvin **83** 51
Sewell **70** 322
Shem **83** 59
Sibyl **83** 49
Silas **83** 44 54 59 **91** 243
Simeon **83** 45
Solomon **83** 57 61 62 70
91 241-244 **105** 80 **128**
58
Sophia **83** 55
Sophia M. **146** 357
Sophronia **76** 48 **91** 245
Spencer **83** 66
Stearns P. **91** 248
Susan **120** 42
Susan (Keys) **126** 209
Susan Bowne **74** 102
Susanna **74** 102 **83** 44
Sylvanus **83** 54
Tabitha **83** 43
Tabitha (Farr) **91** 244
Talbut **83** 45 **146** 357
Thaddeus **83** 49
Thalia **83** 54
Theodore **91** 245 246
Theodosia **91** 245
Theresa **83** 55 69
Thomas **55** 413 **64** 162
337 345 **73** 217 **83** 39 47
128 58 **132** 243
Thomas M. **67** 95
Thomas McAdory
54 113 132
Thursey **83** 60
Timothy **83** 49 58 **89** 288
399 400
Ursula **83** 60
Uzziel **83** 53 54
Washington **73** 231 **83** 68
91 244-246
Wealthy **83** 67
Wilbur **83** 66
Willard **83** 58

OWEN *cont'd*
William **52** 251 **59** 274
64 257 **74** 102 **79** 40 **83**
39 56 58 61 **91** 243 **93**
300 **103** 185 **112** 22 100
148 53
William Arthur **83** 39 69
217 **84** 190 **86** 463 **91**
239
William C. **83** 66
William Dana **83** 58
William Doane **89** 289
William Henry **83** 69
89 289
William Henry Bradford
89 288
William Mostyn **71** 69
William S. **126** 209
Willis **91** 243
Zaphira **89** 399
Zelma **83** 68
Zerviah **63** 339 **83** 51 54
OWERY Mary **65** 45
Owfield *see* Oldfield
OWGAN Margery **102** 7
Owing *see* Owen
Owins *see* Owen
OWLES John **64** 243
Margaret **144** 129
Thomas **144** 129
OWLEY Elizabeth **56** 198
71 167 169 **111** 315
John **71** 169
OWN Mary **95** 23
OWNER John **140** 232
OWNESTEADE
— Mrs. **53** 11
Owns *see* Owen
OWSLEY Edward **63** 160
Joan **59** 296
William **59** 295 **63** 160
OWSTE Josias **76** 225
William **76** 225 226
Owting *see* Outing
OWTON Edward **71** 316
Goodder **71** 316
Jedediah **71** 316
Joan **71** 316
John **71** 316
Ox *see* Oxx
OXENBRIDGE —— **54**
cxxxix **56** 41 320 **121**
196
Ann **56** 40
Clement **53** 117 118
Daniel **53** 116-118 **108** 178
Elizabeth **66** 63
Frances (Woodward)
95 258
Goddard **56** 40
Henry **95** 257 258
John **52** 139 **53** 116 118
54 97 342 **59** 325 **95** 107
258 **103** 41 **108** 178 **112**
169 **133** 278 **134** 183
140 112
Susanna **59** 325
Susanna (Parris) **140** 112
Theodora **85** 149 **95** 258
108 178
Thomas **56** 40

OXENBRIDGE *cont'd*
William **56** 40
OXENDEN Ann **69** 352
Henry **76** 67
Mary **120** 243
OXENSTIERNA
Axel (Count) **103** 252
OXFORD
— Earl of **53** 434
Edward de Vere (Earl of)
87 32
Eliza Ann **73** 193 **81** 148
Elizabeth D. **81** 148
Hannah **126** 64
James Decoster **88** 282
Jane **97** 144
John **81** 148 **82** 51
John de Vere (Earl of)
87 32
Rufus **73** 193
Rufus Kittredge **81** 148
Sarah **82** 51 423
Sylvia (Leonard) **88** 282
William **82** 512
Oxinbridge *see*
Oxenbridge
Oxinden *see* Oxenden
OXLEY Elizabeth **98** 53
OXNALL —— **64** 56
OXNARD Edward **53** 87
54 379 382 **64** 191 **82**
287 295 **125** 23
Mary **53** 87 **82** 287 295
Mary Ann **54** 379
Thomas **57** 280 388 **58** 68
W. F. **91** 331
OXX — Mr. **62** 284
Benjamin **120** 5 8
Betsey **120** 8
Celinda P. **122** 300
Elizabeth **120** 8
George **129** 382
Mary **120** 8
Prudence **120** 8
Prudence (West) **120** 5
Samuel **127** 17
Sarah S. **125** 179
OYARZUM
Ines Sanchez **109** 285
OYLE Frederick **63** 25
OYRMEERS
William **73** 230
OYSTEAD John **62** 155
Lucy **62** 155
OYSTERBANK
Isaac **68** 171
OYXMAN
Jeremiah **101** 271
Ozer *see* Osier
OZIAS Antoine **98** 370

PABIJAN
Walenty **117** 295
Pabodie *see* Peabody
PABST Anna Catherine
(Smith) **112** 322 **113** 80
322 **114** 318 **118** 77 166
120 317
Walter (Mrs.) **118** 166
Pabworth *see* Papworth

PACA
Elizabeth **73** 222
William **64** 275
PACCHE William **93** 77
PACE Fred **123** 113
Henry **60** 399
Jackson **80** 161
John **100** 143
Mary **80** 161 **100** 143
Millie **117** 51
Nancy A. **80** 161
Nelly **117** 51
Sarah (Belyea) **123** 113
Paceio *see* De Paceio
PACH John **97** 266
Susanna **97** 146
Thomas **60** 286
PACHEING
Joseph **79** 108
PACHETTE
Symone **143** 198
PACHEURY
Joseph **79** 108
PACHT Ann **111** 165 246
PACINO
Rosemarie **124** 262
PACK Packe Pake
Alice Gertrude (Hatch)
111 149
Ann **63** 21 **84** 306 **102** 108
Anne **52** 108
Arthur Newton **91** 369
Beate Lowis **62** 245
Benjamin **117** 16
Beulah Frances **91** 369
Charles Lathrop **84** 108
185 **85** 113 **91** 368 **92** 90
148 **111** 149 **112** 262
115 276 **116** 102 **118**
202
Christopher **51** 219 220
71 26
Eleanor (Isham) **97** 99
Eliza **98** 349
Frances Brewster
(Farnum) **98** 350
George **98** 350
George Willis **91** 368
98 350
Georgia Beatty (Fuller)
111 149
Harriet **91** 368
Joan Beatty **111** 149
Job **98** 350
John **117** 16 18
Margaret **104** 146
Maria (Lathrop) **98** 350
Mary **75** xxiii **94** 278 **95**
148 **98** 350
Maxine (Wells) **111** 149
Phillote (Greene) **98** 350
Polly **111** 149
Randolph Greene **84**
110 185 **91** 368 **111** 140
149
Thomas **75** 292
Vere (Mrs.) **97** 99
Virginia Lathrop **111** 149
Vivian **99** 148

PACKARD Packhard
—— **59** 325 **86** 17 **98**
314 **105** 116 **118** 91 **122**
64
— Capt. **59** 30 **95** 51
— Dr. **96** 84
— Mr. **86** 34
— Mrs. **79** 401
A. **124** 225
A. K. **108** 260
Abbie Ann **79** 271
Abby Frances **75** 128
Abel **119** 118 187 **126**
120
Abiel **63** lx **100** 337
Abiezer **124** 226 **128** 285
137 41
Abigail **132** 114
Abigail (Pettengill)
137 46
Abner **61** 44
Abraham **123** 22
Adam **119** 187 **126** 120
Agnes **69** 261
Albert **91** 331
Alden **137** 77
Alpheus Spring **73** xxxiii
Amanda **86** 383
Amasa **119** 259 **137** 45
Amy (Hughes) **128** 174
An. **124** 226
Andrew Jackson **106** 144
Anna **88** 154
Arabella G. (Macker)
89 242
Artemisa **145** 160
Azubah **86** 384
Barnabas **119** 183 184 255
Bartimeus **119** 184
Beniah **87** 235 239
Benjamin **66** 279
Beryl **104** 132
Beryl Lucile **104** 144
Bessie C. **89** 67
Bethiah **101** 176 **122** 27
Bethuel **70** 168
Betsey **63** 95 **75** 128
145 160
Betsey A. **76** 272
Betsey Eliza Walsh
105 116
Betty **86** 15 **88** 54 154 **113**
34 38
C. M. **108** 260
Carlos **128** 174
Caroline **75** 128
Caroline C. **108** 260
Cetey **90** 90
Charity **137** 77
Charles **73** xxxii xxxiii
107 68
Charles Foster **75** 128
Charles Henry **75** 128
Charles M. **53** 251
54 xxxix
Charlotte Mellen
73 xxxiii
Content **119** 253
Cyrus **91** 331 **119** 184
123 21
Cyrus (Mrs.) **95** 51

PACKARD *cont'd*
Daniel **145** 354
Daniel Webster **79** 271
David **141** 296
David Andrew **75** 128
Deborah **104** 164 **126** 251
Deborah Marsh **100** 191
Dora (Strout) **98** 314
Dorothy **53** 246
E. L. **98** 314
Edward **108** 260
Edward Newman **51** 243
  68 xxx **73** xxix xxxii
  xxxiii
Eldena (Elden) **106** 144
Eleazer **137** 35
Elijah **101** 32 **113** 318
Eliphaz **52** 454
Elizabeth **85** 370 **86** 384 **89**
  233 **127** 94 **128** 174 **138**
  220
Elizabeth (Carver) **88** 226
Elizabeth (Edson) **101** 176
Ellen J. **75** 129
Ephraim **137** 77
Ermina (Hanks) **86** 17
Ernest G. **92** 221
Esther **74** 88 **126** 120
Esther (Porter) **119** 118
Eunice (Hume) **119** 184
F. A. (Mrs.) **83** 114
Fred C. **79** 34
Frederick A. **59** lxxii
Frederick A. (Mrs.) **89** 306
George **51** 159 **92** 221 **96**
  84 **136** 23
George Foster **75** 128
George W. **74** 92
Georgianna M. **78** 87
Grace K. **82** 273
H. **76** 272
Hannah **52** 208 **88** 67 **119**
  252 256 **124** 226 **128**
  285
Harriet Julia **107** 68
Hattie Newell **82** 273
Hepzibah **71** 115 121
Herbert Winslow **75** 128
Hezekiah **66** 102 **73** xxxiii
Ichabod **136** 23
Isaac **61** 43 **79** 271 **82** 273
  89 233 **124** 225 **128** 285
Israel **88** 67
Jabez R. **86** 383
Jacob **73** xxxiii
Jael **59** 108
James **60** 42 **73** 195 **84** 31
James Lowell **105** 116
James Ward **118** 245
James Willard **89** 67
Janette **55** lxxx
Jemima **88** 67
Jennet **88** 67
Jennet (Gibbs) **112** 155
Jerusha (Perry) **116** 195
Joel S. **89** 242
John **75** 128 **85** 155 **86** 383
  119 183 **133** 233
John Ford **119** 184
John L. **75** 128
Jonathan **105** 290 **136** 23

PACKARD *cont'd*
Joseph **51** 159 160 **58** 107
Juda **88** 54
Judith (Winslow) **133** 233
Julia Etta (Wood) **107** 68
Laura (Bryant) **89** 233
Lemuel **96** 275
Lilian (Pike) **106** 144
Lois **86** 383
Louisa (Hartshorn)
  125 218
Louisa Ann (Porter)
  101 32
Louisa H. **75** 212
Lucinda (Ford) **119** 259
  137 45
Lucinda (Hartshorn)
  125 218
Lucinda (Stetson) (Lazell)
  89 15
Lucy **78** 89 **86** 383
Lucy A. **74** 92
Lurana **52** 341
Luther **119** 253
Lydia **59** 107 **75** 249 **110**
  33 **136** 23
Lydia (Thompson) **119**
  183 184
M. Alice (Cary) **89** 67
Manuela **91** 331
Maria **86** 383
Maria (Briggs) **126** 120
Marquis de Lafayette
  105 116 **147** 69
Martha **134** 172 **136** 118
Martha (Butler) **116** 67
Martha (Edson) **137** 45
Mary **59** lxxii **60** 42 **93** 217
  100 336 **128** 285 **136** 23
Mary (Edson) **136** 23
Mary (Holbrook) **137** 41
Mary (Nash) **119** 184
Mary A. **81** 259
Mary Ann **69** 261 **126** 64
Mary Elizabeth **73** xxxiii
Mary Frances **73** 195
Mary Hooker **59** lxxii
Mary K. **79** 34
Mary Reynolds **133** 123
Matthew **145** 165
Melzer **127** 226
Mercy (Alden) **137** 35
Micha **125** 218
Molly **119** 184
Morton de Lifyat **105** 116
Nathan **88** 36
Nathaniel **59** 107
Nehemiah **88** 54 154 **91**
  331 **145** 160
Olive **85** 229 **119** 252 **141**
  52-54
Olive (Sturges) **87** 235
  239
Orrin Weatherbee
  112 155
Otis **105** 116
Pardon **116** 195
Peris (Howard) **137** 77
Philander **119** 184
Philip **89** 15 **137** 45
Polly **87** 232 235 **88** 54

PACKARD *cont'd*
Polly (Hill) **119** 184
Pollycarpus **119** 184
Prentice **128** 285
Prudence **112** 155
Rachel **113** 34 41
Rachel (Niles) **85** 155
Rebecca **59** 260 383 **70** 168
  136 23
Rebecca Prentiss **73** xxxii
Rhodes **127** 302
Robert Morton (Mrs.)
  98 147 **100** 177
Roscoe Milliken **106** 144
Roscoe Milliken (Mrs.)
  106 116 126 130 144
Roswell **112** 155
Roxana **74** 92
Roxanna Bradford
  (Briggs) **126** 272
Ruth **90** 370
Ruth (Nash) **119** 184
Sally **119** 252 **137** 78
Samuel **51** 159 **59** 107 108
  63 lx **73** xxxii **88** 226
  100 177 **101** 176 **128**
  285
Samuel O. **74** 88
Sarah **63** lx **70** 168 **93** 161
  100 337 **102** 85 **113** 38
  137 78
Sarah (Ames) **100** 337
Sarah (Ford) **119** 183
Sarah E. **59** 30
Sarah Estella **75** 128
Sarah W. **86** 125
Sibyl Dunbar **75** 128
Simeon **119** 252
Solomon **73** xxxii
Stephen **88** 54 **126** 272
Stephen M. **116** 67
Susan Malinday **105** 116
Susan Perkins **75** 128
Susanna **100** 336
Sylvanus **75** 128
Sylvanus Cook **75** 128
Thomas **105** 280
Thomas J. **58** 107
Thurley Maxine **103** 118
  104 141
Timothy **70** 168 **113** 34 38
Vernora **105** 116
Vesuvia **105** 116
Walter Cushman **75** 128
William **59** 260 383
  118 245
William Kaldwell
  105 116
William White **75** 128
Winslow **113** 34 41
Winthrop **107** 19
Zaccheus **63** lx **73** xxxii
  137 35
Zadock **93** 161
Packe *see* Pack
PACKER Paker
—— **80** 34
— Mr. **82** 295 301
Abby Leah **90** 167
Amos Victor **110** 116
Asa **92** 270

PACKER *cont'd*
Bersheba **90** 367
Betsey F. **125** 109
Daniel **90** 167
Edward **61** 81
Eleanor **108** 274-276
Elizabeth **134** 91
Elizabeth (Lingle)
  110 116
Fredericka **110** 149
Isaac Mitchell **110** 116
James **63** 16
John **53** 238 **64** 24 **91** 400
  92 270
Lucretia **85** 332
Martha **82** 295 296
Mary **67** 286
Mary Caroline (Young)
  110 116
Mary E. **84** 31
Nancy **82** 295 301
Nancy Clark **82** 235
Philip **104** 240 **108** 274
Prudence **61** 81
Rebecca (Jones) **108** 274
Rhoda **108** 275 276
Samuel **51** 44
Samuel Jones **108** 274 276
Sennaca **82** 295 301
Thomas **82** 295 296 **91** 94
Warren M. **108** 319
Warren Melvin **104** 240
  105 129 **110** 116
William **127** 223
PACKINGTON
  Pakington
  Packyngton
Ann **57** 317
Edward **57** 316
Eleanor **74** 270
Elizabeth **104** 175
Humphrey **57** 317
Joanna **110** 248
John **57** 316 **104** 174 175
  110 246 248
Joyce **110** 248
Margaret **110** 248
Nicholas **57** 316
William **57** 316
PACKMAN Pakeman
Samuel **113** 5
Thomas **52** 126
PACWOOD
Thomas **78** 67
PACY
Eustace de **119** 96
Roger de **119** 96
William de **119** 96
Paddack *see* Paddock
Paddick *see* Paddock
PADDIVATT
John **94** 338
Mary **94** 338
PADDLEFORD Padelford
Edward **70** liv **80** 100
  122 48
Elizabeth **80** 100
Elizabeth Louisa **70** liv
  80 100
Esther **133** 283
Hannah **59** 87 159 271 **65**

PADDLEFORD *cont'd*
381 **106** 149
Jonathan **59** 87 159 **80** 100
Marion **66** lii **70** liv **78**
  215 **80** 100
Mary **51** 457 **99** 72
Peleg **122** 48
Philip **80** 100
Ruth Russell **92** 146
Sarah **122** 48
Sarah (Briggs) **122** 48
Sarah (Clapp) **122** 48
Sarah Wild **59** 90 271
Seth **123** 43
Susanna Heyden **59** 90
  271
PADDOCK Paddack
  Paddick Paddoch
  Padducke Padock
—— **139** 49
— Miss **81** 297
Aaron **100** 191
Abby Sanborn **108** 134
  113 233
Abial **81** 297
Abigail **100** 191
Adino **84** 159 167 358
  108 183
Albert Halleck **111** 151
Albert William **111** 151
Alice **54** 180 **102** 229
  104 314
Alice (Alden) **135** 251
Ann **100** 191
Ann (Jones) **143** 124
Anna **51** 165
Anthony **122** 244
Augusta **66** 21
Barnabas **100** 191
Bathsheba **123** 80
Benjamin **100** 191
Bethiah **80** 270 **106** 160
Betsey **122** 244
Beulah McLeyne
  (Muhleman) **111** 151
Charles Coffin **100** 191
Cordelia S. (Halleck)
  111 151
Daniel **98** 135 **100** 191
David **100** 191
David S. **100** 191
Deborah (Fenton)
  111 151
Ebenezer **135** 251
Edward **100** 191
Edwin Loveland **106** 258
Eliza **68** 246 **69** 78
Elizabeth **123** 80
Elizabeth (Mayo) **123** 80
Ernest Moorhead **89** 132
Esther **81** 270
Eunice **63** 88 **100** 54
  117 192
Eunice Coomer **81** 298
Fluvia A. **81** 61 270
Francis **68** 246
Frederic Gove **81** 308
George **100** 191 **111** 172
Gorham **100** 191
Hannah **81** 297 306 **139** 41
  142 273

PADDOCK *cont'd*
Hannah (Jones) **143** 124
Hannah (Thomas) **122** 51
Hannah Hall **64** xxi xxxii
Harriet Annie **84** 302
Helen Cordelia
  (Waterman) **111** 151
Henry **87** 260 **111** 151
Henry Augustus **81** 308
Hepzibah (Barnard)
  98 135
Ichabod **81** 297 **100** 189
  114 120 **128** 300
Ira Alden **81** 298
James **65** 374 375 **70** 31
  137 8
Jane **114** 212
Jemima **100** 191
Jenny Dewey **58** 324
  59 xliv
Joanna **86** 104 **128** 193
Joannah (Faunce) **114** 120
John **61** 159 **97** 326 **100**
  191 **102** 52 **108** 183 **139**
  49 **142** 274 **143** 124
Joseph **53** 349 **81** 61 270
  298 **123** 80
Joseph (Mrs.) **81** 270
Judah **54** 180 **80** 270 **100**
  191 **135** 251
Keziah **81** 297 **103** 306
Keziah (Case) **135** 251
Laban **100** 191
Laura A. **77** 177
Leah **51** 161
Lewis Slote **112** 317
Louisa **81** 61 270
Lovisa **81** 270
Lucretia **100** 159
Lucy **100** 191
Lydia **89** 12
Lydia (Snelling) **108** 183
Lydia Clark **100** 191
Margaret **123** 80
Margaretta Lawrence
  112 317
Martha (Hopkins) (Lewis)
  102 52
Martha (Washburn)
  128 193
Mary **68** 246 **81** 298 **100**
  50 191 **142** 274
Mary Elizabeth **81** 308
Mary Elizabeth (Addams)
  112 317
Mary Huntington
  112 317
May **132** 190
Millicent **81** 307
Obadiah **145** 352
Obed **100** 191
Ora Farnsworth **81** 304
  307 308
Paul **51** 165 **100** 159
Peregrine **80** 269 270
Peter **100** 50 54
Polly (Sheare) **111** 151
Priscilla **51** 48
Rebecca (Thatcher)
  108 183
Reliance **53** 349

PADDOCK *cont'd*
Reuben **135** 251
Robert **81** 297
Ruhama (Marshall)
  122 244
Ruth **86** 23
Ruth Frances **102** 124
S. A. **81** 298
Sally **81** 297 304
Samuel **81** 61
Sarah **81** 307 308 **100** 191
Sarah (Cogan) **111** 172
Sarah (Rickard) **111** 172
Sarah M. **81** 270
Seth **51** 161 **100** 191
Sidney **81** 297
Stephen **81** 297 307 **100**
  191 **131** 219
Susan (Chase) **87** 260
Susanna **52** 273
Temperance **80** 269 270
Thankful **81** 294 297 306
  307 **82** 273 **120** 189
Thomas **81** 297
Thomas Jefferson **81** 298
Wealthy **81** 298
William **81** 270 294 296
  297 306 307 **100** 191
  111 151
William Coleman
  100 191
William R. **81** 270 **111** 151
William Spooner **81** 298
William Waterman **91**
  142 **111** 151 309
Zachariah **81** 297 **128** 193
  141 210
PADDON
Adeline **93** 66 116
Charles Frederic **93** 116
Eleanor **148** 119
Ellen **93** 66
John **93** 66 116
Robert **148** 119 120
Padducke *see* Paddock
PADDY Pady
  —— **51** 266
Elizabeth **70** 254
John **73** 268
Robert **73** 272
Samuel **70** 250 254
William **95** 48 **119** 15
Padelford *see* Paddleford
PADEN Betsey **76** 277
George **76** 277
PADFIELD Timothy **144**
  245 246 261 263
PADGETT Padget
Benedict **73** 150
Dora Adele **121** 157
Elizabeth **73** 273
James **73** 272
Joseph **73** 146 262
Josias **73** 222
Matilda **73** 276
Rebecca **73** 144
Sarah **73** 147 273
Theodore **73** 263
Thomas **73** 277
William **98** 70
PADINALL John **51** 262

PADISILL
Cynthia **119** 40
PADLEY
George M. **80** 151
Grace Alberta **80** 151
Helen Artemisia **80** 151
Joan **114** 224 226
Karl Robert **80** 151
Ralph Cranston **80** 151
Robert H. **80** 151
Susan E. **80** 151
PADMAN Eliza **73** 192
Eliza Ann **73** 200
William **73** 192 199 200
PADMORE J. **62** 330
Jos **65** 20
PADNALL
Margaret **51** 265
Thomas **51** 265
Padock *see* Paddock
Pady *see* Paddy
PAEDTS Jacob **68** 183
PAFFORD Paffard
Frederic C. (Mrs.) **74** liv
Lottie Isabel **78** 47
Marion **78** 47
Theresa **78** 47
William **114** 193
PAFRY John **63** 284
PAGE Paige
  —— **53** 350 **57** 121 229
  314 **60** 107 **62** 134 **68**
  270 **70** 143 **71** 124 **76** 88
  88 246 **91** 257 **92** 312
  313 322 356 **95** 349 **106**
  321 **112** 204 212 **144** 13
  145 48 162
  — Capt. **110** 27
  — Dr. **90** 35 **145** 52
  — Lieut. **85** 19
  — Mr. **62** 21 **80** 61 **81** 31
  — Mrs. **62** 157 158 **71** 45
  — Widow **58** 29 **82** 327
  ___ (Dodges) **83** 417
  ___ (Wabosky) **105** 32
A. B. **65** 382
A. G. **75** 16
Aabrus **127** 222
Aaron **112** 235 **145** 349
Abacuc **76** 288
Abby R. **52** 303
Abel **57** 204 205
Abiel **132** 38
Abigail **52** 430 **55** 313 **56**
  44 **58** 43 **59** 284 **65** 219
  82 318 510 **86** 22 **92** 320
  94 392 **100** 258 **102** 303
  109 59 **113** 38 **114** 295
  124 204 **125** 99 **128** 278
  285 **138** 112 **146** 335
Abigail Bates **82** 346
Abigail Jane **109** 251
Abijah **126** 134 **147** 260
Abraham **91** 256 **93** 193
  107 100
Adam **53** 202
Addie **84** 119
Adelaide Helen **58** lxxii
Adelaide M. L. **89** 383
Adelle (Gates) **97** 129
Agnes **52** 247

PAGE *cont'd*
Agnes P. (Warden)
  86 155
Alfred **67** 273 **74** xliii **77** li
Alfred Baylies **57** 111 **60**
  xxxvi 314 **62** 211
Alice **52** 247 **78** 202 **97** 218
  114 105 108
Allan Pierpont **81** 478
Allison Francis **96** 394
Almena (Baker) **89** 288
Almira S. (Kimball)
  112 235
Alpheus **99** 201
Alvin R. **105** 158
Alzina Jane **79** 125
Amitta P. **75** 16
Amity **74** 154 170 **75** 16 18
Amos **60** 56 **70** 81 **112** 235
Ann **54** 196 **66** 183 **73** 151
  101 243 244
Ann (Flood) **90** 334 **91** 26
Ann (Smith) **126** 208
Ann Eliza (Nash) **89** 94
Ann Maria **124** 204
Anna **58** lxxii 47 **62** 70
  159 161 **64** 16 **67** 107
  108 **70** 81 **72** 261 **79** 245
  92 106 **97** 218 **105** 30 31
  133 54
Anna G. **71** 45
Anna Louise **88** 170
Anna M. **124** 204
Anna Winter **71** xxii **89**
  170 190 **93** 83 143 193
Anne **77** li **90** 195 264
  101 243 245
Anne L. **95** 178
Annie (Warner) **103** 167
Annie C. **124** 260
Arthur Wilson **96** 395
Asa **92** 128 130 247 **105** 66
  118 94 95
Asahel **113** 33 40
Asenath Gault **62** 77
Augustus O. **100** 258
Bailey **105** 283
Benjamin **55** 389 **62** 257
  65 298 348 **66** 33 **69** 302
  79 37 89 **90** 247 **105** 29
  283 **112** 235 **121** 17 **125**
  220 **127** 132 **140** 232
  145 349
Benjamin F. **78** 414
Betsey **59** 287 **62** 77 **74** 175
  75 16 **76** 87 **77** 312 **92**
  315 **105** 32 **117** 280
Betsey (Rich) **83** 412
Betsey Elliot (Soule) **75** 16
  76 87 88 **112** 235
Betty **51** 464 **52** 428 **53** 281
  57 204 **58** 44 **61** 393
  105 202
Blinn Stevens **100** 309
Brackett **92** 322
Bridget **76** 288
C. A. (Mrs.) **82** 114
C. H. **91** 331
C. R. **79** 329
Caleb **66** 113 123
Caleb A. **122** 231

PAGE *cont'd*
Caleb F. **99** 201
Calvin **58** lxxii **84** 31 **88** 276 **123** 70
Calvin D. **57** 229 **58** 99
Calvin G. **58** lxxiii
Carl Ellston **102** 124
Caroline **85** 98 **89** 185
Carroll Smalley **64** xxxiii
Catherine **52** 431 **77** 313 **92** 130 247 **94** 39 **101** 243
Catherine (Shapleigh) **95** 274
Catherine Augusta **77** 186
Catherine Frances (Raboteau) **96** 394
Charles **75** 198 **92** 311 **124** 225 **128** 278 285
Charles D. **65** 155
Charles Henry **86** 155
Charles L. **112** 234
Charles Lewis **112** 235
Charles Nash **66** 287
Charles S. **86** 155
Charlotte **88** 281 **92** 276 **107** 208
Charlotte (Briggs) **128** 277
Charlotte A. **105** 158
Chris. **105** 303
Christian **68** 263 270
Christian (Parmenter) **147** 379
Christopher **53** 378 **58** 138 **62** 76 **101** 243-245 **124** 204 **136** 143
Cicely **66** 181 182
Clara **76** 87 **103** 49
Clara E. **74** xliii
Clara P. **72** 275
Clarinda **52** 302
Clarissa **105** 32
Clarissa Ann **92** 279
Clarissa Payson **72** 275
Clavin Gates **58** lxxii
Comfort **73** 49 **81** 249
Cora **89** 85
Cora A. **75** 16
Cora Alice **91** 52
Cornelius **110** 223 **121** 22 **146** 317
Curtis C. **112** 233
Cynthia **66** 25
Cyrus **64** 46 **75** 5 **92** 191 **105** 66
D. D. **91** 331
Dan **112** 47
Dana Bristol **62** 367
Daniel **52** 435 **53** 283 **58** 43 65 297 298 **69** 122 255 **72** 206 256 270 **73** 48 49 135 **92** 320 365 **97** 218 **101** 242 245 **105** 26 28 29 31 283 303 **117** 280 **128** 58 **145** 356
Daniel H. **81** 291
Daniel M. **56** 29
David **53** 277 **58** 34 35 **65** 297 298 348 **72** 270 **74**

PAGE *cont'd*
256 **105** 28 29 289 **124** 246 **127** 132 133
Deborah **125** 112
Deborah (Bassett) **125** 12
Deborah (Rogers) **147** 360
Deborah (Slocum) **125** 217
Delia **136** 341 342
Delilla (Blinn) **100** 309
Deliverance **74** 248 266 **82** 322 **115** 61
Della M. **108** 65
Dollie (Wheeler) **109** 251 252
Dolly Emeline **62** 158
Dorcas (Cole) (Dogget) **127** 117
Doris Elizabeth (Arey) **87** 107
Dorothy **51** 461 **66** 151
E. Stillman **75** 16
E. W. **91** 331
Ebenezer **63** 75 **105** 27
Ed **146** 378
Edmund **66** 181 182
Edson **57** 204
Edward **63** 174 **75** 222 **80** 289 **93** 104 **101** 243-245 **140** 258
Edward Langley **81** 478
Edward M. **91** 331
Edward Payson **99** 201
Edward Stevens **75** ix xxiii **80** 195 **81** 232 477 478
Eleanor **52** 429 **58** 45
Eleanor A. **69** 255
Eli **70** 215 296 297 **79** 246 **126** 162
Elina **82** 92
Elisha **58** 33 **128** 285
Eliza **74** 314 **105** 32
Eliza (Coy) **105** 66
Eliza (Read) **100** 258
Eliza (Woodman) **91** 17
Eliza Ann **62** 367
Eliza M. **77** 235
Eliza W. (Bigelow) **103** 167
Elizabeth **51** 460 463 **52** 247 **54** 196 399 **57** 204 205 **58** 17 **62** 257 **63** 76 **64** 185 **65** 297 298 **67** 107 253 **73** 49 **75** 198 **77** 316 **81** 170 **91** 259 **92** 274 **94** 161 **97** 224 **100** 258 **101** 242 245 **103** 167 **105** 26-31 **109** 251 **115** 150 **125** 97 **146** 331
Elizabeth (Drake) **104** 115
Elizabeth (Redington) **109** 164
Elizabeth Bispham **88** 168
Elizabeth Clough **110** 223
Elizabeth E. **100** 258
Elizabeth M. **69** 257
Elizabeth W. **112** 225
Ellen J. **118** 92
Elsey **62** 73

PAGE *cont'd*
Elvira **113** 36
Emily **62** 367
Emily Adeline **81** 477
Emily Almira **74** 304
Emily Frances (De Bacon) **107** 153
Emily H. **77** 147
Emma **80** 208 **90** 358 359 **97** 218
Emma Coe **79** 186
Emma Victoria (Durrell) (Barker) **134** 277
Emory (Lamb) **101** 245 **105** 26
Enoch **52** 430 434 **53** 279-281 **60** 44 **72** 256 270 **73** 48 **105** 283
Enos **65** 348
Enos C. **112** 235
Ephraim **52** 429 **127** 93
Esther **55** 404 **56** 199
Esther (Lawrence) **126** 135
Esther (Whittemore) **91** 263 **107** 100
Esther Elizabeth **91** 257
Eunice **74** 317 **75** 16 **76** 87 89 **114** 182
Eunice (Bancroft) **95** 371 **97** 218 **103** 63
Eunice (McFarland) **114** 182
Eunice W. **124** 204
Experience **105** 27
Ezekiel **91** 256 **93** 193
F. M. **95** 243
Faith **61** 188 **64** 187 **65** 297 **80** 94
Faith (Dunster) **101** 245 **105** 26 154
Fanny Stowbridge **133** 322
Florence Ruth **92** 290
Florence Shepard **107** 153
Florence Wentworth (Lathrop) **136** 325
Foster **74** 170 **75** 16 **76** 87
Frances **66** 180
Frances E. **77** 175
Frances Sheldon **82** 346
Francis **51** 61 **54** 196 **66** 182 183 **141** 120 127 **142** 266
Frank **89** 105
Frank B. **97** 129
Frank Copeland **96** 395
G. **91** 331
G. A. **75** 16
Gardiner **74** 175 **75** 16 **76** 87
Gemima (Flood) **91** 22
George **71** 124 126 **73** 268 **89** 382 **90** 330 334 **91** 22 26 **93** 299 **97** 129 **123** 89
George H. **77** 175
George Reuben **100** 309
George Shepard **107** 153
George Stevens **74** xxv 78 **100** 232 309 **101** 127
George T. **92** 106

PAGE *cont'd*
Georgia **58** lxxii
Grace B. **97** 129
Grace Kimball **112** 235
Gustas **70** 307
H. N. **66** 33
Hall **58** 237
Hannah **51** 462 **52** 429 431
  55 404 **57** 204 205 **58** 42
  45 181 **63** 74 177 **66** 183
  70 79 **71** 263 **72** 270 **73**
  48 **75** 198 **88** 246 **92** 289
  101 243 245 **105** 27 30
  31 **112** 138 235 **136** 271
  141 120 **142** 258
Hannah (Clerk) **90** 247
Hannah (Nudd) **142** 266
Hannah (Starr) **106** 211
Hannah E. **127** 132
Hannah J. **118** 329
Hannah L. **88** 279
Harold Poore **112** 235
Harriet **62** 367
Harriet Ann **88** 246
Harriet Fidelia **75** 5
  92 191
Harriet Jane **62** 77
Harriet Louisa **59** xliv
Harriet N. **72** 270
Harriette Story (White)
  76 211 **80** 329 **89** 268
  269
Harrison Perry **93** 193
Harry **133** 121
Havell **51** 414
Hazel **101** 122
Helen Lee (Little) **92** 108
  95 213
Henrietta **62** 367
Henry **58** 46 124 **66** 181-
  183 **126** 142 **141** 115
  127
Henry A. **103** 167
Henry Alexander **77** 186
Henry C. **89** 288
Henry Charles **86** 155
Hollis Bowman **58** lvii
  lxxii lxxiii
Huldah (Drew / Drury)
  136 268
Ichabod **67** 50
Ina Mabel (Cole) **86** 155
Ira **97** 218 **103** 63
Ira E. **118** 92
Ira R. **118** 92
Ira S. **118** 92
Isaac **91** 257 **105** 277
Isaiah **72** 264 **95** 274
J. **114** 195
Jabez **58** 44
Jackson **70** 307
Jacob **92** 106
James **57** 204 **58** lxxii **66**
  181 **69** 122 124 252 **70**
  304 305 **76** 38 **91** 17 **92**
  356 **94** 40 **100** 147 **103**
  167 **105** 278 **125** 12 31
  126 162
James A. **103** 167
James Goddard **72** 264
James R. **67** 21

PAGE *cont'd*
James Warner **103** 167
James William **89** 269
Jane **52** 431 **127** 132 133
Jane S. **74** 175
Jasper G. **123** 225
Jeannie **67** 21
Jemima (Flood) **90** 330
Jennette A. **69** 258
Jeremiah **58** 30 35 **64** 16
  69 5 77 lxiv **92** 311 313
  322 **104** 115 **105** 25 30-
  32
Jesse **74** 167 **127** 132 133
  134 294 **147** 178
Jesse Lougee **118** 95
Joan **69** 252 **101** 243-245
Joan (Cowper) **101** 242
Joanna **51** 464 **62** 60 **63** 76
  96 75 **136** 143
Joanna (Freeman) **111** 29
Joanna Wales **128** 278
Job **92** 276 320
Joel R. **134** 277
John **51** 42 **52** 247 **53** 280
  378 **55** 382 383 401 **56**
  44 55 56 150-152 **58**
  lxxii 41 44 121 **59** 283 **61**
  186 188 **62** lxxiv 159 **63**
  74 **65** 20 238 297 298 **66**
  187 **67** 249 **69** 5 9 216
  250 252 303 308 **70** 17
  72 264 **73** 80 **75** li 12
  290 **79** 43 82 80 94 **81**
  170 **82** 59 **83** 417 **86** 348
  349 **90** 195 196 263 264
  91 200 **93** 231 **101** 242-
  245 **105** 26 27 29 31 66
  154 **108** 65 **109** l 250
  251 **112** 50 234 235 **116**
  152 **121** 14 248 **125** 97
  288 **126** 135 **133** 322
  140 232 **146** 317 335
John A. **103** 166
John B. **69** 258
John H. **135** 79
John J. **74** 304
John M. **69** 160
John O. **88** 246
Johnson **91** 331
Jonas **69** 126 214 **70** 144
  219 304 **92** 279
Jonathan **55** 404 **58** 30 **59**
  284 **64** 39 **65** 297 298 **77**
  lxxxi **87** 335 **105** 27-29
  114 105 **127** 93 **146** 335
Jonathan Geer **86** 22
Joseph **58** 30 32 **65** 297 298
  71 45 **81** 170 **82** 172
  105 27-29 154 277 **113**
  33 40 **121** 20 **126** 162
  128 58
Joseph Kimball **146** 335
Joseph Wright **58** 42
Joshua **51** 461 **62** 70-73 75
  77 157 158 161 **114** 105
  134 294
Josiah **146** 335
Josie **97** 218
Judah **105** 202
Judith **53** 277 **69** 255

PAGE *cont'd*
Judith (Worthen) **93** 193
  107 100
Judith J. **118** 92
Julia **76** 88
Julia Little **88** 15
Julia May **133** 121
Juliet Parker **81** 478
Kate **78** 103
Katharine **96** 395 **101** 243-
  245
Keziah **113** 33 40
Keziah (Stockbridge)
  134 294
L. B. **75** 16
L. R. **108** 28 **112** 66
Laban **92** 311 312 315 324
Lazarus **67** 253
Leah **58** 285
Lemuel **51** 464 **127** 93
Levi **72** 43 **100** 309
Levina **72** 270
Lewis **112** 235
Lewis B. **100** 258
Lillis **133** 322
Linda M. (Poore) **112** 235
Lois **58** 47 **92** 116
Lois Green **105** 65
Lois Tanner (Green) **105**
  65 **114** 154
Lory **71** 203
Louisa **97** 378
Louisa (Rich) (Dickey)
  84 60
Louise Constance **69**
  xxxv **97** 187
Lovina **67** 273
Lowell Briggs **100** 309
Lucinda **67** 279 **84** 328
Lucinda Wheelock **62** 190
Lucius Hubbard **62** 190
Lucius R. **147** 127 **148**
  241 258
Lucius Robinson **51** 228
  363 385 **52** 297-307 337
  375 486 **53** 216 242 254
  455 **55** 442 443 **56** 75-78
  80 **57** 110 111 **58** 316 **59**
  109 242 **60** 231 **61**
  xxxvii **64** 333 **65** 11 **71**
  284 **80** 133 **93** 358 **95**
  388 **99** 8 14 **100** 128 **115**
  192 **116** 33 200 **122** 35
  124 30 102 **125** 66 **141**
  385 **142** 52 **145** 61
Lucretia **74** 93
Lucy **52** 303 **56** 44 **66** 180
  183 **70** 327 **71** 203 **82**
  264 **109** 151
Lucy (Lougee) **118** 95
Lucy (Montgomery)
  90 49
Lucy (Ward) **141** 115 120
  121 127 322
Lucy Jenkins (Hopkins)
  103 166
Lucy M. **76** 38
Lucy Maria (Draper)
  94 24
Lucy P. (Bancroft) **97** 129
Lucy Preston **54** 150

PAGE *cont'd*
Lucy S. **89** 288
Lues **126** 277
Luther **83** 412 **103** 166
Lydia **56** 41 **57** 205 **67** 31
  70 80 **72** 270 **75** 16 **91**
  257 **105** 31 **113** 38 **124**
  204 **133** 322
Lydia (Bixby) **109** 164
Lydia (Kimball) **92** 320
Lydia (Pattee) **146** 335
Lydia B. **127** 132
Lydia N. **109** 271
M. Josie **81** 291
Major **92** 106
Marcia (Eldredge) **105** 66
Marcy **113** 155
Margaret **51** 61 **52** 247
  66 180-183 **109** 162 163
  141 120 322 323
Margaret (Goodwin)
  141 122 125-127
Margaret (Rule) **108** 180
Margery **69** 252 **109** 271
Margret (Rule) **108** 180
Maria (Mills) **108** 65
Maria (Tibbetts) **100** 147
Maria Betsey **76** 87
Maria E. **113** 36 42
Marie **90** 195 264 **101** 243
Marilla **127** 93
Marion **52** 247
Marion (Luce) **97** 187
Mark Stephen **92** 403
Martha **58** 81 **62** 161 **65**
  298 **66** 181 182 **69** 118
  215 **74** 256 **78** 71 **105** 27-
  29 **141** 126
Martha (Crosby) **105** 30
Martha (Endicott) **105** 31
Martha (Holland) (Pierce)
  105 27
Martha (Ruggles) **88** 276
Martha M. **53** 233 **95** 238
  318
Mary 31 **52** 297 430 **53**
  279-281 **55** 344 **56** 29
  57 204 **58** 41 45 **59** 189
  63 76 **64** 16 39 **66** 183
  67 li 348 **68** 99 **69** 5 140
  143 160 **71** 126 **72** 256
  267 270 **73** 153 223 **74**
  167 **75** 198 **76** 37 87 **77**
  228 **78** 179 **79** 89 **81** 170
  291 **83** 146 185 187 **84**
  222 **86** 71 **98** 186 **101**
  102 242 245 **104** 115
  105 26 27 30 31 261 262
  108 164 **112** 138 **114**
  105 **121** 18 181 **124** 204
  125 97 **128** 285 **141** 120
  121 223 **146** 335
Mary (Fanning) **125** 288
Mary (Fowler) **105** 31
Mary (Hall) **125** 108
Mary (Hussey) **141** 120
Mary (Kent) **146** 335
Mary (Penniman) **91** 310
Mary (Pinder) **105** 32
Mary (Porter) **133** 121
Mary (Sawtell) **126** 134

PAGE *cont'd*
Mary A. **69** 258 **134** 277
Mary Alta **78** 331
Mary Ann **74** 167 **75** 16
  76 98
Mary Cushing **81** 478
Mary Cutter **96** 30
Mary E. **92** 106
Mary Elizabeth **68** 203
Mary Ellen **62** 367
Mary Foster **124** 204
Mary Gertrude **67** li
Mary H. **83** 425 437
Mary Jane **82** 172 **112** 235
Mary Jane (Larabee)
  86 155
Mary Josephine **87** 113
Mary Mann **87** 295
Mason **97** 218
Maurice Eurelma (Mrs.)
  80 208
Mavran **75** 51
May Alta **79** 203 **105** 66
  69 133
Mercy **59** 283
Meribah **51** 61
Meribah (Smith) **141** 120
Merrian **59** 283
Mildred **105** 27
Miriam **63** 174
Molly **53** 279 **58** 42 **126**
  135 162
Moses **56** 262 **59** 283 **87**
  237 **105** 283 **106** 153
  147 260
Myra **65** lix
Myra Louise **112** 234 235
Nabby **53** 283
Nancy **62** 75 **68** 95 **101** 226
  104 181 **105** 32
Nancy (Colby) **112** 234
Nancy (Davis) **92** 324
Nancy (Gifford) **133** 53
Nancy J. **118** 92
Nancy Jenness **91** 389
Nancy Osgood **83** 174 195
Nathan **55** 368 **93** 218
  105 31
Nathaniel **51** 460 **52** 297
  53 374 378 **55** 401 **56** 41
  44 99 **58** lxxii **62** 60 72
  63 75 **64** 46 **65** 297 298
  354 **79** 125 **82** 346 **93**
  231 **105** 28 29 **133** 53
Nicholas **52** 372 **64** 185
  67 107 108 **68** 180 **69**
  287 **70** 191 **148** 33
Nina **58** lxxii
Norman B. **87** 107
Octavia **147** 360
Octavius A. **66** 33
Olive (Chamberlain)
  137 280
Olive (Hanks) **86** 22
Oliver **70** 295 299 302 307
Onesephris **121** 15
Orvis **133** 322
Overy **59** 326
Pamelia **72** 206
Patience **127** 92 93
Patience (Chase) **87** 335

PAGE *cont'd*
Patty **105** 31
Patty (Dodge) **83** 417
Pauline Stevens **100** 309
Peace (Hanson) **90** 329
  91 18
Peter **57** 205 **93** 398 **100** 63
  114 105
Phebe **58** 17 **62** lxxiv **65**
  354 **69** 250 252 **75** li **79**
  82 **86** 349 **101** 242 245
  103 140 **105** 26 **109** 250-
  252 **140** 129 **146** 335
Phebe (Paine) **101** 245
  105 26
Phebe C. **73** 47
Phebe Cobb **72** 264 272
Phebe N. **140** 129
Philinda **58** lxxii
Philip **57** 313 **96** 30
Phineas **58** 46 **69** 9 12 119
  214 221 222 303 **70** 217
  218 **76** 87 **78** 309
Polly **59** 283 **87** 228 235
Priscilla **89** 180 **126** 162
  127 117 132
Priscilla (Stephens)
  126 162
Priscilla Elvira **113** 42
Pritchard **66** 25
Putnam (Elizabeth)
  105 31
Rachel **54** cxvii **55** 401
  79 89 **127** 93
Rachel (Blanchard)
  (Converse) (Fitch)
  93 231
Rachel (Perrin) **105** 66
Ralph **137** 280
Ralph Walter **96** 395
Rebecca **53** 378 **65** 313 **66**
  182 183 **68** 260 **75** 198
  84 363 **88** 246 **103** 62
  105 32 **115** 75 **141** 120
  127
Rebecca (Putnam) **104**
  181 **105** 31
Rebecca S. **77** li
Reed / Reid **75** 16
Reuben **58** 46 **70** 80
  85 333
Richard **66** 259 **80** 290
  101 243 **103** 7 **113** 58
Richard Chapin **93** 138
Robert **51** 61 **52** 247 **66**
  168 180-183 287 **68** 262
  69 342 **75** 51 **78** 111 **90**
  263 264 **95** 52 **101** 243-
  245 **105** 26 **109** 163 **141**
  114 115 120 122 125-127
  313 322 323 **147** 379
Rodney G. **91** 198 388
Rodney Gerald **96** 161
Rosa B. **103** 48
Rosanna (Coe) (Maltby)
  112 50
Rowland Buckle **88** 170
Ruby **74** 209
Ruby Walker **124** 260
Rufus **74** 93
Ruhamah **53** 378 **102** 162

PAGE *cont'd*
Ruth **58** 342 **62** lxxiv **64**
  123 **66** 151 **67** 50 **71** 221
  72 256 264 **73** 48 **90** 247
  93 218 **95** 194 **109** 164
  111 157 **113** 231
Ruth (Doliber) (Atkins)
  105 29 **111** 157
Ruth (Shute) **92** 311
Ruth Gertrude **112** 235
Ruth Johnson **93** 184
S. **134** 277
Sally **62** 71 **92** 128 **105** 32
  126 118
Sally (Clowe) **125** 220
Sally (Lougee) **118** 94
Sally (Noyes) **140** 129
Sally (Parker) **90** 90
Sally W. **74** 170
Sam **112** 123
Sampson **90** 49
Samuel **58** 140 234 **60** 40
  62 137 **63** 76 **65** 297 298
  67 li 273 **72** 256 264 275
  73 47 **74** 209 **91** 257-
  259 263 264 **92** 274 **93**
  193 398 **100** 63 **101** 226
  242 245 **104** 181 **105** 26-
  32 **107** 100 **111** 157 158
  113 39 **136** 268 **145** 356
Samuel C. **124** 260
Samuel Perkins **91** 389
Sarah **51** 464 465 **52** 435 **53**
  281 283 378 **54** 196 **56**
  41 44 **58** 42 45 124 234
  59 189 283 **61** 153 **62**
  137 161 367 **65** 297 298
  72 270 **73** 48 **84** 446 **85**
  333 **91** 51 258 **105** 27-29
  31 **114** 105 **121** 24 **123**
  89 **126** 107 **137** 183 **146**
  335
Sarah (Andrew) **105** 30
Sarah (Cumings) **91** 264
Sarah (Eaton) **124** 240
Sarah (Holland) (Pierce)
  105 27
Sarah (Lawrence) **105** 27
Sarah (Linsley) **123** 89
Sarah (Moulton) **92** 365
Sarah (Parker) **90** 90
Sarah (Robbins) **93** 193
Sarah (Sanborn) **85** 333
Sarah (Webster) **134** 294
Sarah B. (Jenness) **135** 79
Sarah B. (Wiggins)
  135 79
Sarah Crocker **58** lxxii
Sarah Ellen (Goodwin)
  139 145
Sarah Jane **72** 270
Sarah M. **81** 291
Sarah Melinda **69** 140
Sarah W. **91** 237
Sarah Worthen **76** 19
Seneca **75** 16
Sherman **115** 108
Sherman Daniel **74** 209
Shubael **58** 36 140
Sibyl **57** 205 **91** 296
Simeon **54** 399 **58** 42

PAGE *cont'd*
69 213 215
Simon **51** 462 **57** 204 205
  65 348 **70** 218 **105** 30
Solomon **58** 34 **66** 151
  99 79 **105** 66
Sophia A. **118** 92
Sophia B. **89** 382
Sophia Candace (Stevens)
  100 309
Sophronia **115** 285
Stella Jane **92** 231
Stephen **58** 138 **105** 277
  124 240 **125** 217 **126**
  162 **127** 117 **140** 129
Stephen Benson **81** 477
Stillman **75** 16
Stillman Elisha **76** 87 88
Sukey **87** 235 238
Susan **82** 490 **101** 243-245
Susan (Tole) **126** 142
Susan C. (Souther)
  122 231
Susan Elvira **75** 5
Susan Elvira (Hall) **92** 191
Susan Haskell **58** lxxii
Susan Ross (Hopkins)
  103 166
Susanna **55** 401 **62** 60 73
  65 298 **66** 98 180 183
  103 68 314 **105** 30 229
  141 120 **147** 260
Susanna (Lane) **93** 231
Susanna (Lawrence)
  105 29
Susanna (Syckerling)
  101 243 245
Sylvia **71** 50 **79** 246
Syrene **81** 31
Tabitha **90** 359
Tamar **55** 404
Thaddeus **53** 378 **62** 160
Thankful **56** 262
Thankful (Watson)
  92 403
Thankful M. **82** 172
Theodate **98** 57
Theodate (Drake) **91** 389
Thirza (Hopkins) **103** 167
Thomas **53** 378 **58** 29 32
  42-45 47 **61** 199 **62** 70
  158 161 **63** 74 **65** 298 **66**
  182 183 **67** 348 **70** 220
  78 71 **90** 329 **91** 18 **94**
  334 **100** 309 **105** 28 29
  76 202 262 **109** 164 271
  117 132 **129** 385 **140**
  232 258 326 **141** 120 127
Thomas Nelson **105** 82
  136 325
Timothy **52** 297 **53** 378
  56 75 77 **113** 38 39 **140**
  299
Timothy E. **91** 200
Timothy Stillman **75** 16
Tinnie (Eddy) **89** 105
Tirzah **94** 40
Uriam **82** 318
Vashti **67** 273
Virgil **65** 348
Virlinda **73** 150

PAGE *cont'd*
Walter **70** 214 **97** 129
Walter Bond **54** 150
Walter Gilman **53** 456
  59 xxxiv 104
Walter Hines **89** 43
  96 394
Walter Hines (Mrs.) **77**
  155 **78** 202 **96** 292 394
  97 161
Warren **69** 140
Warren Adams **92** 106
Wealthy **76** 37
Webster **58** 46
Willa Alice (Wilson) **96**
  394 **97** 161
Willard **69** 140
William **52** 247 **54** 289
  57 315 **58** 142 **59** 189
  61 393 **62** 70 73 157 161
  251 **65** 297 298 **68** 73
  370 **69** 252 283 **70** 251
  71 203 **76** 235 **82** 346
  84 60 **90** 90 **91** 91 **92**
  247 323 **97** 239 **100** 309
  101 244 **102** 235 **105** 28
  29 281 **111** 84 **113** 37 39
  118 95 **123** 249 **125** 108
  128 58 **140** 232 **142** 159
  146 335 **147** 360
William Cobb **72** 264
William Lawrence (Mrs.)
  114 154
William N. **139** 145
William Putnam **105** 32
Willis Rix **97** 187
Worthington **75** 16
Zachariah **65** 298 **105** 29
Zeruiah **72** 256 264 **73** 47
  83 491
PAGEL Rush **109** 80
PAGERIE Josephine
  Tascher de la **103** 252
PAGET Pagett Pagget
  —— **112** 204
  — Mr. **52** 257
  Ann **148** 135
  Anthony **64** 287
  Betsey **125** 177
  Charles **80** 389
  George **87** 242
  James **54** 452
  John **105** 189
  Katharine **72** 60 **74** 145
  Lewis **91** 331
  Margaret **64** 287
  Mary (Chase) (Hathaway)
    87 242
  Rebecca **127** 227
  Richard **120** 225
PAGLES John F. **100** 76
PAGRAM William **65** 35
Pagrave De *see* Palgrave
Pagrave *see* Palgrave
Paien *see* Paine
Paige *see* Page
Paighn *see* Paine
PAILHES Frances **78** 409
PAILLE Narcisse **111** 50
PAILLEY Simone **76** 215

PAILLIER Mary Jane
(Grant) **111** 50
PAINE Paien Paighn Pain
Payne Peine
—— **62** 237 **75** 37 229 **83**
405 **85** 274 **86** 349 **97**
138 **99** 231 **103** 29 **121**
203 **127** 319 **144** 17
— Capt. **52** 187 **59** 412
79 253
— Lieut. **123** 191
— Mr. **62** 182 **63** 56 **98** 86
139 34 47
— Mrs. **139** 47
— Widow **64** 348 **71** 142
— **97** 121
____ (Rich) **83** 405
A. Solomon **70** 156
Aaron **56** 141 290 **57** 150
59 363
Aaron H. **76** 92
Abiah **107** 252
Abiel **75** 305
Abigail **51** 464 **52** 219 **54**
88 **58** 195 **59** 64 **61** 203
65 352 **81** 432 457 **86**
308 447 **92** 55 **96** 69 **100**
163 **102** 51 **120** 256 **123**
119 **125** 13
Abigail (Bacon) **138** 36
Abigail (Butts) **112** 145
Abigail (James) **126** 251
Abigail (Strange) **88** 122
Abigail N. **116** 207
Abraham **53** 129 **64** 192
73 116
Absalom **136** 130
Achsa **65** 42
Adolphus **58** 197 401
Agnes **69** 250 251 **79** 82-84
83 366 **102** 192
Albert Bigelow **77** 163
Albert W. **79** 84 **146** 379
Alden **87** 248
Alexander **143** 292-296
Alfred **97** 137
Alfred Barton **85** 456
Alice **65** 291 **69** 251 252
75 230 232 **79** 82 83 386
89 207 **91** 230 **103** 144
139 306 **143** 295 296
Alice (Borden) **84** 78
Alice (Boyd) **97** 139
Alice (Clarke) **143** 294-296
Alice (Mayo) **102** 47
Alice (Parker) **143** 299 301
Alice Leona **82** 396
Alice M. **97** 396
Alice Margaret **97** 139
Alice W. **60** lvii
Allen **76** 267 **88** 125
Allin **56** 93
Allsup **53** 174 325
Almira **59** 208 **60** 202
69 206
Almira E. **76** 276
Alpha **138** 126
Alpheus **62** 84
Alsop **103** 144
Alta M. (Ackler) **97** 139
Althea **83** 481

PAINE *cont'd*
Amanda (Kellogg)
103 144
Amanda M. (Cargill)
117 260
Amaziah **88** 304
Ambrose **69** 252 **79** 83
Amie **87** 264
Amos **58** cii **66** 303
143 291
Amy Angeline **77** 51
Angeline (Vedder) **97** 136
Angeline Eliza **97** 137
Ann **52** 223 **55** 392 **56** 181
62 183 **65** 291 **69** 55 229
252 **79** 82 83 **114** 89 91
128
Ann (Chase) **88** 125
Ann Chickering **144** 357
Ann Hathaway **98** 86
103 222
Ann M. **97** 136
Ann Maria **57** 294
Anna **53** 358 **55** 395 **56** 93
146 266 **59** 269 **62** 84 **69**
252 **83** 88 **92** 54 **97** 137
138 125 **146** 378-380
Anna D. (Sands) **83** 88
85 422 **105** 254
Anna E. (Towne) **93** 188
Anna Virginia (Quintard)
109 260
Anna Woolson **109** 146
Anne **55** 265 **69** 251 252 **70**
157 **110** 59 **114** 47 128
146 379
Anne (Chickering) **143**
301 302
Anne (Donahue) **97** 138
Anne (Hurin) **136** 130
Annis **69** 325
Anthony **64** 221 **66** 37 **76**
129 **78** 153 **143** 292-294
147 71 330
Arnold **138** 119 125
Arthur B. **58** 205 **60** 183
Arthur E. **83** 427 437
Asenath (Higgins)
123 117
Augustine **63** 86
Augustus Wellington
109 260
Barbara **56** 91
Barnabas **83** 269 276 394
113 154
Barnet D. **97** 138
Barney **126** 142
Bartholomew **79** 83
Bathsheba **83** 87 88
Bathsheba (Rathbone)
85 420 421 **105** 266
Benajah **58** 194 **59** 97-100
414 **60** 204
Benjamin **53** 440 **56** 93 94
59 193 273 361 **63** 132
64 31 **66** 150 **74** 65 **79**
387 **87** 265 **97** 134 135
320 326 **128** 60 **143** 301
302 **146** 348
Bennet (Freeman) **102** 47
126 84

PAINE *cont'd*
Bennett **80** 11
Bethania P. (Pratt) **126** 204
Bethiah **60** 384 **61** 203 204
81 331 **86** 349 **140** 232
Bethiah (Sweetser) **86** 349
Bethiah (Thatcher) **98** 85
102 47
Bethiah (Washburn)
99 168
Betsey **60** 265 **82** 19 **84** 39
119 **97** 135 136 **104** 302
Betsey (Hopkins) **104** 300
Betsey (Rich) **84** 119
Betsey Ann **77** lxxvi
Betty **58** 196 **60** 78 **83** 266
270 366
Betty (Chase) **87** 140
Beulah **79** 201
Brent **59** 208 209
Brenton **59** 415 **60** 73 74
77 265 **83** 366 **123** 160
Brewster **97** 136 137
Bridget **74** 65
Brintnal **60** 199
Bushnel **57** 290
Byron L. **97** 139
Caleb **138** 126 **143** 294-297
Calphernia (Devoe)
97 139
Calvin Lee (Mrs.) **128** 160
Carlos Grant **97** 138 139
Caroline (Allen) **97** 138
Caroline M. (Bancroft)
97 71
Caroline Matilda (Barton)
107 211
Carrie A. **97** 136
Catherine **65** 291 352 **79**
387 **109** 303 **140** 234
Catherine (Grimes)
97 136
Cecily **143** 292-294
Cecily (Turnor) **143** 292-
294
Celia (Doolittle) **97** 136
Charity **136** 130
Charles **59** 99 **60** lvii **61**
109 **78** 403 **81** 331 **98** 85
Charles Alden **97** 135 139
Charles Cushing **67** 191
81 331 **97** 121 **98** 85
Charles D. **97** 139
Charles E. **94** 401
Charles Eaton **82** 176
Charles Henry **83** 366
Charles Jackson **76** 207
81 331 **97** 121
Charles T. **64** 192
Charles Thomas **67** xxxii
Charlotte **59** 288 **78** 165
93 365
Charlotte (Mann) **103** 144
Charlotte Caroline **97** 138
Charlotte Jackson **97** 121
Chester **74** 65 **97** 135 136
Chester (Mrs.) **97** 140
Chloe (Chase) **88** 119
Chloe (Thayer) **109** 260
Christopher G. **78** 305
Clara **97** 137 140

PAINE *cont'd*
Clarence Sumner (Mrs.)
  80 333 **95** 147
Clarinda **97** 137
Clarissa **97** 135 136 **123**
  121 124
Clarissa S. **91** 78 **97** 137
Clement **108** 54
Cora (Lewis) **97** 139
Cora Matilda **61** 207
Cora Matilda (Patty)
  62 xxxvii
Cordelia Ayer **65** xxxvi
Cornelius B. **97** 137
Cynthia **83** 88
Cynthia (Osborn) **130** 156
Cynthia Lucretia **57** 291
Cyra (Colburn) **97** 396
Cyrenius **136** 363
D. W. **123** 309
Damaris **60** 77 **83** 366
Dan **53** 441 **56** 94 **143** 295-
  299
Daniel **57** 261 290 **58** cii
  69 252 **70** 228 **83** 263
  97 135 **109** 299 **115** 62
  116 130 **143** 291
Daniel B. **97** 137
Darius **77** 229
David **60** 189 **61** 203 204
  64 227 67 52 **68** 144 **70**
  345 346 **78** 264 **126** 251
  139 119
Davis **135** 77
Debby **59** 97
Deborah **53** 403 **56** 93 **59**
  89 275 284 361 362 364
  60 80 **81** 351 **83** 366 **85**
  429
Deborah (Sherman)
  123 120
Deborah H. (Hopkins)
  104 301
Delia P. (Hinckley) **103** 27
Delight **57** 291
Deliverance **84** 53 118
Delos S. **97** 140 396
Dewitt Clinton **97** 138
Dexter Chauncey **57** 291
Dolly **57** 294
Donald H. **97** 396
Dorcas **83** 254 **102** 47 **112**
  195 **143** 340 344
Dorcas G. (Raynes) **118**
  154 155
Dorothy **69** 250 252 **79**
  82 83 **80** 137 **96** 380 **139**
  306
Dorothy (Raynsford)
  101 169 **139** 306 **143**
  302 **145** 263
Dorothy Ann **97** 396
Dorothy Bowen **77**
  lxxxviii
Earl D. **97** 136
Earl Judson **97** 136
Ebenezer **51** 36 **56** 93 **57**
  257 259 290-292 **62** 204
  92 56 **102** 51 **139** 304
Ebenezer H. **89** 256
Eda **82** 176

PAINE *cont'd*
Edith **90** 179
Edith Maude (Johnson)
  97 121
Edmund **52** 144 **65** 291
Edna (Baldwin) **97** 396
Edna Kittura **97** 74
Edward **51** 394 **58** 142
  196 197 400 401 **59** 209
  213 **60** 73 78 205 **79** 83
  83 88 366 **84** 263 **86** 349
  87 360 **95** 66 **99** 122
  100 242 **101** 169 **120** 81
  131 131 **135** 232 **140**
  146 234 **143** 295 298
Edward F. **101** 116 **102**
  119 **105** 68 124
Edward Lathrop **101** 169
Edward T. **70** 370
Edward W. **140** 230 234
Edwin M. **107** 211
Elbridge **119** 185
Eleanor (Fought) **87** 231
  235
Eleanor (Ross) **101** 169
Eleazar **58** 194
Electa Ann **86** 371
Electa Ann (Warner)
  86 371
Elias **85** 386 **126** 204
Elihu **71** 269
Elijah **57** 290 **59** 416 **60** 74
  79 298 **83** 366 **84** 87
Elisha **52** 219 223 **55** 205
  63 85 **70** 156 157 175
  177 222 345 **71** 151 **83**
  266 **102** 47 57
Eliza **74** 84 **82** 176 **83** 432
  85 419 **93** 372 **97** 71 140
  104 12
Eliza (Wycoff) **97** 136
Eliza G. **78** 305
Eliza Jane (Myrick)
  102 260
Elizabeth **51** 394 420 **53**
  414 **59** 154 **60** 129 **61**
  262 264 **65** 120 290 291
  66 357 **67** 159 372 **69**
  250-252 **70** 222 **71** 269
  75 256 **78** 206 **79** 82 83
  387 **83** 86-88 270 **85** 420
  86 230 349 **94** 175 **98** 12
  99 122 **101** 169 **102** 51
  104 217 **105** 266 **106** 83
  87 **109** 36 **111** 239 **112**
  227 **114** 134 **115** 308
  118 254 **126** 39 **128** 38
  132 88 **140** 52 232 **143**
  253 294-296 301 302 **145**
  263
Elizabeth (Guraine)
  100 242
Elizabeth (Hubbard)
  128 39
Elizabeth (MacNichol)
  (Conant) **85** 222
Elizabeth (Myrick)
  108 212
Elizabeth (Reiner)
  111 239

PAINE *cont'd*
Elizabeth (Shepherd)
  118 255
Elizabeth (Thatcher)
  83 263
Elizabeth (Weeks)
  103 144
Elizabeth (Williams)
  (McCarthy) **105**
  178 265
Elizabeth Louise **97** 139
Elizabeth Mason **98** 86
  103 222
Elizabeth Osborn Myrick
  67 190
Elizabeth P. **90** 57
Elkanah **83** 266 **84** 45
  102 57
Elkanah K. **123** 124
Elkanah W. **123** 121
Ellen **59** 154 155 158 269
  270 **90** 341 **130** 72
Ellen (Veasie) **86** 459
Elmer Dewitt **97** 138
Elnathan M. **124** 35
Eloise Richards **57** xxv
Elsie **97** 138
Elvira **57** 292
Emeline R. **75** 37
Emerson **114** 286
Emily **57** 359 **82** 176 **86**
  196 **94** 382 392
Emily (Phelps) **97** 136
Emily M. **84** 102
Emma Almira **101** 167
Ephraim **55** 263 265 **57**
  23 257 259 260
Erva Winston **88** 189
Estelle **84** 31
Esther **97** 135 136 **127** 281
Esther Humphrey **77**
  lxxxviii
Esther Orne **59** 333
Ethel Lyman **78** 205
Etta M. **116** 67
Eunice **59** 209 **60** 74 80
  65 42 **74** 65 **77** 315 **81**
  331 **83** 366 **137** 327
Eunice (Treat) **98** 85
Eva May **97** 140
Eva St. Clair **85** 456
Everett **72** xx **74** xxviii
  80 216 **81** 350 351
Experience **59** 393
Ezekiel **82** 19
Ezekiel Dexter Smith
  82 19
Ezra **103** 144
F. Estella **92** 341
Fanny **125** 181
Fanny Amanda **97** 139
Fanny Cabot (Jackson)
  81 331 **97** 121 **98** 85
Flora **82** 473 **85** 103
Florence Josephine
  (Cross) **83** 427 437
Frances **69** 251
Frances Amelia **134** 255
Frances Loretta (Averill)
  97 139
Francis **63** 350 **106** 153

PAINE *cont'd*
Francis Cabot **97** 122
Francis Ward **77** lxxxviii
Frank Cabot **97** 122
Frank Earl **82** 176
Frank Inez **97** 139
Fred **91** 331
Fred E. **97** 136
Frederic William **59** 333
Frederick **97** 137
Gamaliel S. **84** 39
George **63** 344 **71** 124 **79** 83 **140** 232 **143** 291-299
George Lyman (Mrs.) **85** 197
George M. **113** 266 **119** 66
George Milton **101** 169
George Moore **119** 278 **120** 215 **121** 70 **122** 73 232 311 **123** 72-74 150-153
George Q. (Mrs.) **98** 147
George R. **90** 33
George Sturgis **63** 114
George T. **51** 243 **67** 299-301
George Taylor **58** lv cii
Georgia May **85** 456
Georgina **97** 122
Gertie **82** 176
Gideon **103** 160 **146** 348
Giles **79** 83
Gladys **97** 140
Gladys G. **97** 396
Gleta **70** 156
Glover **59** 158
Grace **65** 290 291 **101** 291
Grace (Colvell) **101** 292
Grace Jerusha **97** 140 396
Grant **97** 137
Gyra (Colburn) **97** 396
H. Vearle **95** 147
H. W. **102** 260
Hannah **51** 36 **52** 422 **53** 441 **54** 88 225 **56** 94 **57** 76 **58** 77 **59** 153 271 284 **60** 43 77 **61** 203 **63** 85 **66** 301 **70** 157 **83** 215 **93** ix 284 403 **96** 281 **97** 135 **102** 51 **103** 92 **104** 214 **105** 103 147 **106** 306 **109** 4 **110** 48 **111** 225 **113** 47 **119** 125 **136** 130 **139** 306 **143** 43 44 49 128 **146** 377-383
Hannah (Bass) **107** 219 **113** 101
Hannah (Bressey) **112** 43
Hannah (Higgins) **102** 47
Hannah (Hills) **123** 160
Hannah (Hopkins) **102** 51
Hannah (Pearce) **144** 202
Hannah (Tenney) **116** 130
Hannah (Thayer) **125** 223
Hannah Hathaway (Perry) **98** 85
Hannah Maria (Barton) **107** 210
Hannah N. (Crosby) **123** 204

PAINE *cont'd*
Hapsey **123** 119
Harmon **97** 137
Harmon W. **93** 188
Harold J. **97** 396
Harold Lewis **97** 139
Harriet **59** 98 208 333 **76** 210 **99** 122 **112** 145 **131** 157
Harriet Banks (Gould) **103** 144
Harriet Dowling (Olp) **97** 396
Harriet G. **97** 139
Harriet Hatch **77** lxxv lxxvi
Harriet M. (Lowell) **97** 140 396
Harriet S. **77** 179
Harrison **97** 137
Harry Clay **64** xxxii
Harry Francis **69** xxxv
Harry Morse **100** 252
Hazen Wheeler **82** 176
Helen **81** 331 **84** 44 **97** 121
Helen A. **97** 396
Helen Harriet **97** 139
Helen Sumner **97** 121
Helen Vera **79** 324 **80** 207 **81** 351
Henry **59** 97 **65** 352 **66** 302 **67** 33 **81** 351 **82** 176 **83** 266 269 403 **84** 39 **101** 291 **102** 262 **140** 232
Henry B. **82** 473
Henry Clay **62** xxxvii 107
Henry D. **143** 301
Henry E. **84** 87
Henry T. **138** 332
Henry W. **75** lxxiii **80** 439
Hepzibah (Parker) **135** 77
Hester **67** 53
Hiram **85** 456 **109** 260
Hitty **52** 82
Horace Marshfield **83** 130 **103** 144
Howard B. **97** 396
Howell Sherman **105** 129
Hugh **83** 266
Huldah **67** 52 376 **84** 117 **92** 54
Huldah (Rich) **83** 270
Inez L. **97** 139
Irene I. **57** lxiii
Isaac **94** 59 **127** 308
Isabella **125** 287
Isabella Taylor **85** 456
J. A. **97** 136
J. J. **138** 125
J. Lemuel **70** 156
J. T. **91** 230 231
Ja **70** 296
Jabez **107** 94 **128** 38 39
Jacob **92** 56
James **54** xcvii **55** 112 **56** 93 **57** 290 **59** 97 364 **60** 384 **63** 276 **67** 325 **68** 180 **81** 331 **97** 135 136 **98** 85 **102** 47
James Bertrand **54** xcvii
James D. **104** 301

PAINE *cont'd*
James E. **94** 59
James H. **140** 232
James Henry **63** 314
James L. **59** lxxxi
James Leonard **109** 146
James Leonard (Mrs.) **85** 190 **108** 218 **109** 133 146
Jane **52** 203 **65** 42 290 291 **69** 251 **78** 407 **79** 82 **97** 139 **101** 253 **106** 308 **114** 133 **115** 308
Jane (Filer) **97** 138 139
Jane (Gallyon) **99** 60
Jay **138** 121
Jeanie **97** 122
Jedediah **97** 136 138 139
Jeffrey **69** 251
Jemima (Alsop) **103** 144
Jere **82** 211
Jeremiah **74** 305
Jeremiah Goodwin **91** 230
Jerusha **59** 98 **60** 199 204 **74** 65 **93** 301 **97** 135 136 140
Jerusha (Rich) **83** 266
Jerusha (Swift) **97** 135 139
Jesse **104** 300 **138** 117 118
Jessie Aurelia (Kimberly) **101** 169
Joan **65** 176 291 **69** 251 **79** 83 84
Joanna **83** 402 **121** 141
Job **57** 76
Joel **58** 197 400 **59** 213 **83** 366
John **51** 396 420 421 **52** 208 416 **53** 172 334 414 **54** 88 214 **55** 392 **56** 39 91 93 144 266 268 290-292 **57** 22 23 153 261 **58** 77 194 195 **59** 89 98 208 275 286 361 362 364 **60** 74 77 129 265 **62** 351 **63** 85 **64** 31 52 **65** 41 290 291 **66** 149 302 303 **68** 85 148 **69** 251 **70** 92 191 **78** 258 **79** 82-84 386 **80** 11 77 137 **81** 130 351 432 **83** 84-88 366 **84** 150 **85** 279-281 285 347 420-423 **86** 76 330 400 **91** 10 **92** 51 52 54 58 59 **93** 93 **95** 218 254 **96** 282 380 **97** 135 136 140 320 325 **98** 12 **102** 47 92 93 **103** 144 **105** 178 234 254 263 265 266 **109** 299 **110** 192 **116** 226 **124** 97 103 **125** 41 **126** 84 **127** 115 **128** 51 **134** 67 **136** 211 **138** 118 125 **143** 291-296 299-302 **146** 378 379 382 **147** 333
John Adams **109** 146
John Alsop **103** 144
John Bryant **97** 121
John Bryant (Mrs.) **77** 237 **78** 206

PAINE *cont'd*
John Elgie (Mrs.) **108** 135
John H. **120** 104
John Howard **54** 248 **85**
  353 **100** 232
John K. **87** 126
John L. **97** 139 140
John Orlebar **141** 107
  142 157
John Sands **85** 422
John Shearer **109** 146
John T. **91** 230 231
Jonathan **54** 88 **59** 285
  102 261
Joseph **58** 142 **59** 270 275
  67 52 53 375 **73** 116 **83**
  269 394 **87** 140 **88** 304
  92 54 97 **102** 47 **119** 20
  130 156 **136** 363 **145**
  297
Joseph P. **117** 260
Joseph Polly **130** 236
Joseph W. **84** 132
Josephine B. **85** 456
Joshua **56** 37 **62** 274 **83**
  88 266 **85** 347 **123** 120
Joshua S. **123** 203
Josiah **51** 207 208 **54** 87
  60 189 **62** 202-204 **63**
  175 **79** 286 291 296 **80**
  120 **102** 46 49-51 59 60
  107 274 **108** 54 124 **119**
  267 268 **120** 104 105 107-
  109 **125** 7 12 **126** 82 **127**
  102
Josias **58** 196
Judith **69** 251 **138** 118
Judith (Lathrop) **101** 169
Judy **69** 252
Julia **73** 287 **76** 207
Julia (Bryant) **97** 121
Julia (Rich) **84** 132
Julia Ann **97** 137
Julia Bryant **97** 121
Julia Lee **97** 121
Juliana **59** 100
Junius Edward (Mrs.)
  100 112
Kallop **143** 296 297
Kate Fisher (Lazell)
  89 116
Katharine **65** 290
Kathleen Joye **117** 126
Kathleen Susan **97** 396
Keziah **57** 290-292 **105** 110
Larry W. **97** 396
Laura B. (Rutherford)
  117 126
Laura Jane **82** 176
Lawrence **65** 291 **69** 252
Lawson **97** 136
Lemuel **83** 266
Leonard **68** 73 **87** 228 235
Leone **97** 138 140
Leonora Rebecca **81** 351
Lester **74** 65
Lettie May **97** 138
Lewis L. **104** 301
Lila Williams **82** 19
Lodice **60** 200
Lois **60** 79 **74** 305

PAINE *cont'd*
Lois (Kinney) **101** 169
Lois Cobb **74** 305
Lorenzo **97** 136
Louisa Delight **57** 291
Louise Frazer **97** 121
Louise Mason **58** cii
Louise Rue **78** 206
Louise Rue (Frazer)
  97 121
Low **65** 120 **147** 69
Lucinda **76** 268
Lucius F. **97** 136
Lucy **60** 80 **63** 85 **73** 226
  82 268 **84** 39
Lucy (Stouring) **97** 138
Lucy G. **97** 137
Lucy Paine (Fales) **99** 168
Lury (Brewster) **97** 137
Luther **70** 346 **135** 201
Luvania **123** 121
Lydia **53** 174 440 **56** 94
  58 195 **59** 156 158 284
  60 204 **67** 373 **68** 144
  69 206 **70** 346 **83** 88 **97**
  137 **137** 148 149 **142**
  197
Lydia (Frothingham)
  126 141
Lydia Williams (Lyman)
  90 179
Lyman **57** 359
Lyman Kinny **57** 291
Lyman May **70** 191
M. E. **91** 231
Mabel **67** 375
Mabel C. **97** 139
Mara Octavia **93** 188
Marcy **105** 266 **116** 207
  126 84
Margaret **63** 276 **65** 290
  291 **68** 193 **69** 24 25 **79**
  73 82 83 **80** 404 **83** 87
  88 **86** 76 **87** 264 **105** 164
  266 **108** 136 **114** 153
  132 39 **138** 120 **143** 291-
  294 300 396-398
Margaret Dillon **97** 121
Margaret Tewksbury
  81 350 351
Margaret Woolson
  109 146
Margery **54** 87 88 **79** 83
  87 264
Maria **57** 190 **136** 130
Maria Antoinette **140** 232
Maria Otis **82** 19
Marian **65** 291
Mariana **79** 387
Mariette E. **76** 92
Marion **75** 230 232
Marion E. (Langdon)
  123 309
Marion Thurber **81** 351
Marjory H. **97** 396
Marlborough **83** 88
Marshall John **87** 174
Martha **54** 214 **56** 91 **65**
  290 291 **74** 65 **79** 83 **81**
  273 351 **84** 126 **85** 225
  104 143 **138** 117 **140** 69

PAINE *cont'd*
Martha (Hook) **111** 239
Martha (Wheeler) **101** 169
Martha Augusta **82** 176
Martha E. (Filkins) **97** 138
Martha Lee (Gilmor)
  103 144
Mary **51** 396 **52** 219 **53**
  129 172 413 440 **55** 260
  265 **56** 94 **57** 19 22 143
  58 77 **59** 88 89 158 208
  269-274 284 361 363 **65**
  290 291 **66** 335 **67** 34
  372 **69** 252 **70** 157 **73**
  116 **74** 65 84 **75** 247 **79**
  73 388 **80** 21 77 **81** 87
  414 **83** 85 86 88 269 270
  366 **84** 35 53 132 **85** 92
  419 421 **92** 54 **93** 93 **97**
  136 **100** 254 **102** 47 **103**
  24 144 **104** 218 268 **105**
  234 266 **107** 112 **108**
  304 **114** 130 **116** 138
  117 142 **126** 96 **134** 67
  138 125 **139** 306 **140**
  232 234 **143** 302 **147**
  333
Mary (Allen) **102** 51
Mary (Booth) **103** 144
Mary (Clarke) **85** 419 421
  104 12
Mary (Folger) **103** 144
Mary (Golden) **97** 138
Mary (Gookin) **109** 299
Mary (Parker) **134** 67
Mary (Pierce) **109** 4
Mary (Purington) **83**
  276 394 **102** 261 **113**
  154
Mary (Rich) **83** 266 269
  403 **84** 132
Mary (Shute) **139** 304
Mary (Snow) **98** 85 **102** 47
  106 306 **143** 344
Mary (Vickery) **83** 402
Mary (Wells) **138** 322
Mary (Woolson) **109** 146
Mary A. **81** 414 **119** 282
Mary A. (Landers)
  124 266
Mary Ann **65** 291 **79** 387
  85 422
Mary Ann (Hopkins)
  104 301
Mary Ann Landers **121**
  155 **124** 266
Mary Anna Lee **97** 121
Mary C. **97** 136
Mary E. **84** 120 **92** 341
Mary E. G. **91** 230
Mary Elizabeth (Payne)
  88 189
Mary L. (Barton) **85** 456
Mary Louisa **91** 231
Mary M. (Mack) **90** 106
Mary O. **121** 309
Mary Ruth **83** 230
Mary S. (Trafton) **119**
  281 285
Mary Webster **81** 353
Matilda **136** 130

PAINE *cont'd*
Matthew **69** 252
Maude Adelle **97** 140
Maurice **136** 130
Mehitable **52** 82 **59** 272
 67 372 **70** 228 **126** 95
Mehitable (Kirk) **126** 208
Mehitable (Whittemore)
 108 171 **126** 96
Mehitable P. (Knowles)
 123 121 124
Menatha B. **97** 396
Mercy **83** 84 86 276 394
 95 254 **123** 119
Mercy (Hopkins) **102** 262
Micah S. **123** 204
Miller **51** 204
Minerva (Hatch) **123** 204
Miriam Alathea **102** 124
Monroe Emmons **57** 359
Mortimer Seymour
 86 371
Moses **52** 416 437 **54** 87 88
 56 93 **57** 260 **59** 89 270
 271 273 274 361 363 **61**
 203 **64** lxvi **65** 187 290
 80 39 **97** 134 **106** 17 18
 109 4 **121** 203 **139** 298
N. Emmons **61** xxxv
Nabby **59** 97
Nancy **56** 92 **57** 19 **58** 401
 60 200 **83** 88 **85** 422
Nancy (Littlefield) **86** 76
 330 **105** 263
Nancy (Moore) **116** 222
Nancy (Sweet) (Burdick)
 97 139
Nath. **99** 96
Nathan **80** 103 207 **101**
 114 169 **102** 127 **123**
 120 **128** 60
Nathan A. **97** 140
Nathaniel **52** 95 102 **53**
 269 367 **54** xxxvii **56**
 xxxi **57** xxxi **58** xliii **59**
 xlii 393 **60** xxxiv 369 **61**
 xxxiii 104 106 262 **62**
 182 **63** 132 227 332 **64**
 26 31 **72** 248 **77** 51 **83**
 88 **87** 231 235 257 **88**
 304 **92** 52 **96** 259 261
 347 **97** 319-321 325 326
 98 325 **101** 169 **102** 51
 105 290 **123** 287 **124**
 163 177 **127** 163 **139** 27
 49 306 **143** 299-302 **145**
 263 **146** 378 **148** 325
Nathaniel Emmons **66** lii
 83 130 255 **90** 127 **103**
 79 126 144
Nathaniel Sewall **113** 266
Neal H. **117** 126
Neele (Adcocke) **143** 298-
 300
Nehemiah **56** 92
Nellie (Boyd) **97** 139
Nellie Elgiva **85** 456
Nelly **61** 277
Nettie Elmira **85** 456
Nicholas **65** 290 291 **67** 34
 102 47

PAINE *cont'd*
Niobe (Adcocke) **143** 299
 300
Noah **57** 290 294 **63** 85 86
 67 372
Ola **78** 321
Olive **70** 157
Olive D. **97** 138
Olive M. **113** 266
Olive M. (Swett) **119** 66
Olive Nickerson **91** 41
Oliver **82** 473 **97** 137
 119 287
Oliver Brewster **97** 137
Oliver P. **90** 106
Oril (Nelson) **99** 168
Paschal **93** 117 **94** 156
Patience **79** 293
Patience (Freeman)
 102 51
Patience (Sparrow)
 102 47
Patty (Hovey) **101** 169
Peggy **85** 347
Penelope **67** 376
Persey **63** 86
Peter **65** 290 291 **75** 229
 230 232 **84** 78 **103** 144
 116 207
Phebe **53** 174 325 **54** 88
 57 257 **62** lxxiv **63** 175
 69 250-252 **75** li **79** 82
 80 17 **83** 394 **88** 118 **90**
 163 **101** 242 245 **102**
 261 **105** 26 **107** 274 **108**
 54
Phebe (Moore) **103** 144
Phebe (Rich) **83** 394
Phebe (Stone) **108** 124
Philander Alonzo **97** 138
Philenda **84** 87
Philip **87** 140 **127** 303
Phillippe (Strange)
 87 140
Pierce **140** 232
Pleasance **143** 295 296
Pletise **118** 261
Polly **56** 290 291 **59** 97 285
 70 157 226 **78** 264 **83**
 366 **94** 59 **110** 211
Polly (Dana) **97** 136
Polly (Paine) **94** 59
Polly Ann (Sherman) **76**
 92 **97** 396
Priscilla **70** 157
Rachel **57** 390 **65** 42 **74** 65
 100 239
Rachel (Chase) **87** 248
Rachel (Hopkins)
 (Young) **105** 101
Ralph **55** 221
Ralph D. **81** 370
Rebecca **52** 219 **54** 214 **56**
 38 93 94 144 **57** 153 **78**
 421 **79** 102 387 **83** 269
 84 127 **107** 36 **108** 118
 140 146 **143** 299 301
 302 **144** 357 **146** 348
Rebecca (Amory) **120** 81
Rebecca (Coan) **104** 301
Rebecca (Dart) **126** 256

PAINE *cont'd*
Rebecca (Doane) **102** 47
Rebecca (Knowles) **123**
 121 124
Rebecca (Rich) **83** 269
 84 45
Rector **107** 210
Reliance (Young) **102** 57
René Evans (Mrs.) **78** 332
 79 201 **102** 218 **103** 124
Reuben **97** 136
Rex **97** 139
Rhoda **65** 41 **141** 356
Richard **59** 326 **62** 326 **66**
 188 **69** 251 252 360 **76**
 68 **79** 82-84 **102** 192
 103 183 184
Richard Cushing **98** 86
 103 222
Robert **52** 203 **56** 181 **65**
 290 291 **79** 82 83 **81** 351
 85 32 **96** 282 **111** 239
 131 189 **143** 219
Robert Harold **97** 396
Robert Treat **51** 499 **54**
 lxxxiii **67** xxviii 191 325
 75 xxxix **78** 417 **81** 331
 84 234 378 **85** 28 188 **90**
 179 **95** 100 **98** 85 89 149
 103 222 **113** 8 318 **130**
 164 166 167 174 **140** 232
Robert Treat (Mrs.) **77**
 156 **78** 206 **85** 190 222
 103 218 222 **104** 148
Robert Woolson **109** 146
Roger **79** 82
Roger Lee **97** 121
Rosanna (Cottle) **87** 228
 235
Rose **76** 129 **78** 153 **79** 82
 86 411 **143** 300
Ross W. **97** 396
Roswell **59** 97-100 **60** 263
 83 366 **147** 179
Rowena **88** 380
Roxalana **58** 196 **83** 366
Royall **129** 382
Rufus **52** 415
Ruth **55** 262 **56** 39 **70** 222
 73 116 **83** 276 **87** 139
 93 117 **94** 156 **97** 138
 103 152 222 **109** 299
 113 154 **116** 141 **123**
 120 **124** 34 35 **125** 14
Ruth (Cabot) **98** 86
 103 222
Ruth (Leworthy) **97** 139
Ruth (Perrin) **96** 266
Ruth (Phelps) **97** 137
Ruth Ann **87** 284
Ruth Cabot **103** 73
Ruth Felton (Ward) **77**
 lxxxviii **91** 208
Ruth Sargent **77** lxxxviii
S. White **90** 341
S. Wirt **89** 207
Sabina **103** 160
Sabra (Ridley) **126** 142
Sally **56** 257 **57** 290 **59** 97
 208 286 **81** 331 **83** 366
 123 120 **132** 104 **140**

PAINE *cont'd*
235
Sally (Dana) **97** 137
Sally (Filkins) **97** 138
Sally Amanda **97** 138
Sally M. **83** 366
Sally Skinner **83** 366
Salome May (Brigham)
97 121
Samuel **51** 464 **55** 265 **58**
cii **59** 88 269 270 272 273
67 373 **73** 116 **81** 432
83 266 **84** 132 **85** 124
86 398 **96** 266 **97** 135
319 **106** 109 **107** 36 **116**
222 **126** 95 226 **140** 232
143 291 301 302 **145**
160
Samuel E. **119** 281 285
Samuel Eaton **82** 176
Samuel Thomas **102** 51
Sarah **52** 416 437 **53** 334
414 441 **55** 222 263 **56**
93 94 **58** 402 **59** 99 274
60 199 203 205 265 **61**
262 **65** 42 **66** 149 188
303 **67** 372 373 375 **69**
252 360 **70** 92 **71** 269 **73**
116 218 **79** 387 **80** 11 **82**
292 295 **83** 266 270 366
84 39 52 **85** 456 **86** 101
349 447 **92** 267 **99** 256
108 181 **109** 299 **112**
103 **114** 292 **120** 79 254
123 204 **126** 95 **138** 121
139 306 **140** 234 **141** 5
143 301 302 **146** 378
380
Sarah (Carver) **88** 220
118 103
Sarah (Chase) (Young)
87 257
Sarah (Cobb) **98** 85
Sarah (Parker) **146** 378-
380
Sarah (Rich) **84** 39
Sarah (Winslow) **87** 153
Sarah Adelaide (Fenton)
97 396
Sarah Ann **97** 137
Sarah Brown **136** 328
Sarah C. **77** 237
Sarah Cushing **67** 191
78 206 **79** 212 **81** 331
97 121
Sarah J. **84** 130
Sarah M. **109** 98 99
Sarah R. **84** 39
Sarah S. (Smith) **90** 104
Sarah Sumner **81** 331
Sarah Sumner (Cushing)
98 85
Scholastica **54** 214
Semantha (Rice) **97** 138
Seth **53** 441 **56** 93 94 **59**
362 **67** 372 375 **73** 116
74 65 **89** 207 **97** 134-
140 396 **105** 101 **123**
121 124 **145** 349
Seth B. **97** 137
Seth Jedediah **97** 139

PAINE *cont'd*
Sibyl **70** 346
Sibyl (Hethersett)
(Palgrave) **102** 93
Sidna **58** 402
Sidney Borden **143** 291
Sidney Lake **143** 291
144 357
Sidney Small **143** 291
Silas **88** 119
Simeon **128** 60
Simonds **61** 44
Solomon **55** 222 **63** 368
65 381 **70** 157 346 **71**
269 **83** 270 **88** 220 **118**
103
Sophia **89** 256
Sophia E. **89** 352
Sophia Field **58** cii
Stephen **52** 414 415 **53**
358 403 441 449 **54**
xcvii **56** 93 94 291 **57**
290 **58** cii 194-196 **59**
87 156 158 213 269 270
275 414 **60** 204 **61** 203
62 183 231 **63** 79 127
132 360 **64** 31 **65** 175
176 192 290 **66** 187 **67**
372 **68** 324 325 **69** 24 25
229 **74** 65 **77** lxxxviii
78 308 **82** 19 **83** 161 366
86 349 **91** 94 **92** 49 54
267 **96** 259 **97** 36 134
135 255 310 316-318 326
327 **98** 166 174 175 236
99 98 104 105 233 235
236 **101** 169 **103** 152
107 219 **108** 171 **110** 46
112 153 **113** 101 **124**
177 **126** 95 96 **128** 58 60
139 27 49 306 **143** 291
295 298-302 364 **144** 357
Stephen Reed **97** 74
Stillman **112** 145
Stowell L. **75** 37
Str. **99** 96 98
Submit **67** 52 **78** 264
Sullivan **65** 42
Sumner **97** 121
Susan **69** 251 **79** 83
123 118
Susan E. **81** 414
Susanna **56** 269 270 290
66 150 **75** 302 **83** 86 87
95 66
Susanna (Bancroft) **95** 66
Susanna (Beale) **131** 189
Susanna (George)
(Arnold) **105** 266
Susanna (Mitchell)
(Arnold) **105** 164
Sylvanus **83** 270 **124** 34 35
T. L. **78** 321
Tabitha **65** 290 **97** 308
Thankful **72** 115 **83** 266
103 29 **125** 14 **138** 33
Thankful (Hopkins)
102 57
Thankful (White) **102** 51
Thankful W. **105** 103
Thatcher **83** 270

PAINE *cont'd*
Theophilus **55** 69
Theresa **102** 286
Thomas **51** 205 **53** 414 **54**
37 87 88 **55** 112 **56** 38
141 144 146 **57** 14 35 93
150 153 257 **58** 406 **59**
64 **60** 189 310 **62** 325 **64**
219 **65** 290 291 304 367
66 188 **68** 69 69 103 251
252 **74** 65 **79** 82-84 102
80 352 **81** 271 331 **82**
462 463 **83** 84-88 130
255 270 402 **84** 36 119
91 94 **95** 254 **97** 88 135-
137 139 140 **98** 85 **100**
252 **101** 186 **102** 47 **103**
144 145 **105** 164 178 182
265 266 **106** 306 **109**
299 303 **110** 59 **112** 43
103 **116** 141 **123** 117
127 93 **130** 180 192 **134**
254 **143** 291-296 299 341
344 **144** 202
Thomas Almiren **97** 138
Thomas M. **125** 223
Thomas Monroe **97** 138
Tilla **56** 93
Timothy **58** 197 401 **60**
202 **72** 115 **84** 377 **113**
318 **140** 235
Tobias **53** 302 **87** 153
106 33
Tomison **100** 293
Tyler **138** 118
Urania **52** 208 **84** 445
Victor Jacob **89** 116
Virginia Marie (Low)
97 122
Virginia Semmes **88** 189
Waite **83** 88
Walter **58** cii **79** 83 **138** 36
143 291
Walter Cabot **98** 86
103 222
Ward L. **97** 396
Welcome **81** 273
Welcome L. **97** 140 396
Wells **97** 136
Wheatin **88** 304
William **52** 165 421 422
55 141 **56** 184 237-239
57 190 275 **58** 194 **59**
333 60 23 80 **63** 16 27
65 116 290 291 **66** 37 **69**
206 250-252 **70** 222 **71**
172 173 339 **74** 280 **76**
210 **77** 272 **79** 73 82-84
387 **80** 137 **81** 122 130
82 156 **83** 88 **85** 420 **89**
334 90 104 **91** 13 **95** 388
96 279-282 374 380 **97**
138 **101** 242 245 **103**
152 183-185 **105** 26 75
106 83 315 **110** 293 294
118 154 155 255 261
123 81 **124** 97 **126** 141
226 256 **129** 103 **131**
178 181 **136** 363 **138**
121 **140** 234 **141** 189
143 33 **146** 378 379

PAINE *cont'd*
William A. **67** l
William Alfred **91** 208
William Alfred (Mrs.) **77** lxxxviii
William B. **89** 352
William Bainbridge Blackler **81** 350 351
William Cushing **98** 85
William Dana **97** 138
William E. **140** 234
William Elisha **77** lxxvi
William Fitz **59** 333
William Gould **103** 144
William H. **81** 414 **97** 138
William Henry **59** 412
William Henry Fitzhugh **88** 189
William Howard **58** cii
William Littlefield **74** 84 **79** 73 **83** 88 **85** 419-421 **86** 76 **104** 12
William Wirt **58** cii
Yanache **122** 319
Yanache (Ayers) **122** 319
Zerviah **52** 223 **97** 135 137
Zillah **51** 204
Zoe Emeline **54** xcvii
PAINEL
Beatrice **100** 306
PAINT James **59** 300
Mary **59** 300
PAINTARD
Anthony **129** 43
Jonathan **129** 41
PAINTER Panter Paynter Peyntor
—— **70** 264 **143** 202
—— (Rodney) **106** 47
Abby **68** 282
Abby Victoria **68** 279
Abiah **68** 277
Abigail **68** 278-280
Adelaide Elizabeth **68** 282
Alexis **68** 281
Alice **84** 276 278
Amelia **68** 281
Amy **68** 278 280 **69** 60
Angelina **68** 281
Azariah **68** 280
Betsey **68** 283
Betty **68** 278
Caroline **68** 282
Catherine **68** 281
Chester **68** 282
Chloe **68** 282
Cynthia **68** 281
Deborah **68** 282
Deliverance **68** 275-277 280 281
Deliverance Lamberton **68** 280 281
Edward **68** 282
Edward Wright **68** 282
Elisha **68** 277 **73** 11 **114** 184
Elizabeth **68** 273 276 277 282 **69** 54 **73** 11
Elizabeth P. **68** 282
Elizabeth W. **68** 280
Elkanah **68** 276

PAINTER *cont'd*
Emily M. **68** 281
Esther **68** 276
Eunice **68** 282
Fannie C. **68** 282
Flora **68** 281
Florence McMahon **68** 282
Freelove **68** 278 280
Gamaliel **68** 277-279
Grace **51** 288 **61** 199 **68** 282
Hannah **68** 277 280 **73** 11
Harry **68** 281
Henry **51** 309 **94** 267 336 **111** 11 **114** 87 **145** 77
Henry McMahon **68** 282
Henry Noble **68** 281
Henry Wheeler **68** 281 282
Herman M. **58** 283
Hugh **68** 282
Jemima **68** 275
Joanna **68** 282
John **68** 282 283
Joseph **68** 277-282 **69** 60
Joseph Alexis **68** 281
Julia Ann **59** lxix
Julia Maria **68** 281
Julia McMahon **68** 282
Katharine **68** 273
Lamberton **68** 277 278 280 281
Laura **68** 282
Lot **68** 282
Louise Lockwood **68** 282
Lucina **68** 282
Lucius **68** 281
Lydia **68** 277
Lyman **68** 280 281
Mabel **68** 280 281
Margaret **68** 274-276 **69** 51-53 **71** 16
Maria **68** 281
Martha **68** 274
Mary **56** 361 **61** 199 **68** 276-278 282 **78** 263
Mary L. **66** l
Mercy **68** 273 274 276 280 284 **69** 51-53 59 **71** 16 **123** 261
Nicholas **84** 277 278 280
Polly **68** 280
Priscilla **51** 309
Rachel **68** 276
Rebecca **68** 275-278
Robert **68** 282
Rosey **68** 283
Rowland Gardiner (Mrs.) **106** 47
Ruth M. **58** 283
Sally **68** 283
Samuel **68** 278-282
Sarah **68** 277 280 282 **116** 231
Sarah M. **68** 281
Shubael **68** 273-278 280-282 284 285 **69** 51-53 **71** 16 **73** 11
Sidney **68** 281 282 **119** 101 **120** 230 **121** 234

PAINTER *cont'd*
Susanna **68** 282
Thalia Abigail **68** 282
Thalia Maria (McMahon) **68** 281
Thomas **51** 355 **65** 94 **68** 273-278 280-282 285 **69** 52-54 **73** 11 **114** 184 **147** 166
Thomas Alexis **68** 282
Thomas Welcher **68** 282
Urania **68** 281
Ursula **68** 278 279
Victoria **68** 278 279
Walter **68** 281
William **61** 199 **68** 273 281 282 **74** 274 **86** 415
William Le **80** 381
Zillah **68** 280
PAINTIN William **62** 332
PAINTS Samuel **59** 404
PAIO
Antonio Joze de S. **79** 44
Pairtree *see* Peartree
PAJOT Leon **56** 95
Pake *see* Pack
Pakeman *see* Packman
Paker *see* Packer
Pakington *see* Packington
Pakyngton *see* Packington
PALACHE
Eunice Shapleigh (Underwood) **96** 28
John Garber **96** 28
Josephine Cronkhite **96** 28
Lucy Baldwin **96** 28
PALAERE
William **143** 257
PALAN Dorcas **124** 154
PALEN Ida **101** 79
PALET Jane **66** 219
Joseph **66** 219
Nathaniel **66** 219
PALEY William **68** 23
PALFRAMAN
Arthur **51** 123
Elizabeth **51** 123
Robert **51** 124
PALFREY Palfray Pelfrey
—— **54** cxlvi **56** 221
— Mr. **82** 64 **84** 152 **92** 354
Adelaide Eliza **52** 384
B. C. **91** 200
Edward **63** 37
Eleanor **81** 321 **82** 64
Elizabeth **77** 129 **79** 449
Elizabeth Mason **142** 147
Esther **125** 108
Francis Winthrop **54** lxix
George W. **77** 49
H. S. (Mrs.) **83** 370
Hannah **59** 81 83 **67** 173 **125** 100 **133** 309 310 **142** 148
Hannah (Tappen) **142** 145
Henry Cruger **142** 147
Henry Sterling (Mrs.) **84** 190

PALFREY *cont'd*
Ida (Raynes) **83** 301
Jane **114** 23
Joan **63** 40 **78** 144
John **53** 242-244 **63** 37 40
77 311 **114** 23 **142** 146
147
John Gorham **52** 381 384
53 45 **64** lx **67** 148 **68**
22 **69** 157 158 **99** 8 **104**
92 **142** 145
Jonathan **142** 145
Lydia **92** 224
Lydia (Cazneau) **142** 136
146
Margaret **55** 417 **77** 129
79 449 **112** 240
Martha **53** 242 243 **96** 74
101 225 **104** 289
Martha (Crowninshield)
(Gale) **104** 289
Mary **142** 147
Mary Sturgis (Gorham)
142 147
Nancy **142** 147
Peter **53** 44 47 **54** lxviii
59 83 **67** 173 **142** 145
Polly **125** 103
Rebecca **53** 242-244 **77** 311
81 461 **142** 138
Richard **66** 36
Sarah **77** 49
Suckey **142** 146
Susanna **142** 146
Susanna (Cazneau) **142**
133 145 146
T. **84** 152
Thomas **77** 129 **79** 449 **84**
152 **104** 289 **142** 145
Walter **77** 129 **79** 449
Warwick **61** 220
William **78** 144 **84** 152
249 268 **85** 20 21 **130** 34
142 133 136 144-146
William W. **83** 301 **84** 31
PALGRAVE De Palgrave
Pagrave Palgrove
Agnes **102** 98
Alice (Gunton) **102** 92 95
Amy (Patrick) **102** 96
Ann **67** 298 **69** 159 **96** 238
102 87 89 91 98
Anna **102** 87 88 97
Anne **97** 12 13 **102** 88 92-
96 98 **103** 102 **131** 132
Anne (Glemham) 287
102 92 95 **103** 102 287
Anne (Sturmer) **102** 92
94 312
Arabella **102** 98
Benjamin **102** 89 97
Bethiah **102** 88 98
Bridget **102** 92
Clement **89** 74 **102** 91-93
95
Dorothy **102** 92
Edward **102** 88 90-92 96 97
Eleanor **102** 92 93 95
Elizabeth **102** 87-90 92 93
95-97 **103** 287 **105** 243
Frances **102** 92 93 95

PALGRAVE *cont'd*
118 260
Francis **116** 171 **142** 235
145 5
Gregory **102** 91-93 96
Hannah **102** 89 90 97
Henry **102** 91-95 **103** 102
287
James **102** 92 93 95
Jeremy **102** 88 90
Joan **102** 89 92
Joan (Harris) **102** 88 89
John **69** 159 **96** 238 **102**
88 90-95 98 312
Katharine **102** 96
Katharine (Pegion)
102 93
Lydia **102** 88 89 98
Margaret **102** 92-94 96 98
99 2
Margaret (Herward) **102**
92 94
Margaret (Yelverton)
102 92 95
Margery **102** 92
Margery (Read) **102** 92 95
Martha **102** 96
Martha (Lynford) **102** 96
Mary **69** 159 **77** 273 **102**
87 90 92 96-98
Mary (Maverick) **96** 238
102 98
Mary (Seefold / Sefowle)
102 93 96
Pamela **142** 253
Philip **102** 96
Rebecca **102** 88 98
Richard **67** 297 298 **69**
159 352 **96** 238 **97** 12
102 87-90 96 97 118 312
103 102 112 113 287 295
105 163 243 **107** 269
116 23 **131** 19 132 **141**
101
Robert **102** 92 93 96
Sarah **67** 298 **69** 352 **97** 12
99 104 **102** 87 90 97 **105**
163
Sibyl (Hethersett) **102** 92
93
Susan **102** 92
Thomas **102** 89-93 95
Vrsula **102** 92
Walter **102** 92 96
William **102** 92 96
PALICK Sarah **128** 97
PALISTER Joseph **63** 135
PALIZZOLO
Richard **84** 451
PALLA Hiram **91** 331
PALLANT
Edward **75** 293
Samuel **57** 218
PALLETTE Pallet Pallett
Edward Marshall **94** 210
95 210 **96** 210 **97** 302
James **64** 19
William **115** 57
PALLIER Mary Jane (Dam)
111 50

PALLIES
Betsey **78** 417
Francis **125** 221
Rebecca (Bodge) **125** 221
PALLIN — Mrs. **65** 369
PALM Mary Ann
(Hendrick) (Deming)
129 50
Palmar *see* Palmer
PALMAS John **66** 62
Thomas **66** 62
PALMER Palmar Palmere
Pamer
—— **51** 255 **52** 125 137
53 266 320 **54** lvii 344
55 217 **57** 420 **58** 324
405 **59** lxxxvi **60** 102
182 **66** 132 **67** 297 **69**
200 **72** 177 217 **82** 413
85 151 **92** 286 **112** 264
117 15 17 **123** 96 **124**
255 **136** 211
— Capt. **82** 413
— Gen. **95** 235
— Mr. **53** 44 **54** 43 **57** 378
60 59 **78** 363 **81** 448 **82**
51
— Mrs. **51** 109 **119** 138
— Prof. **56** 15
____ (Hall) **87** 358
A. H. **71** 355 **93** 214
A. T. **91** 331
Aaron **131** 219 **135** 55
Aaron Sanford **119** 202
Abbie Easton (Greene)
100 169
Abial **148** 152
Abiel **148** 152
Abigail **60** 124 **63** 183 367
64 28 **68** 260 **69** 258 **70**
107 109 110 **71** 203 **86**
291 384 **103** 300 **117**
300 **126** 65 **137** 282 **142**
394
Abigail (Chaple) **125** 291
Abigail (Church) **123** 189
Abigail (Kimberly)
102 110
Abigail (Lazell) **88** 261
360
Abigail (Veesy) **125** 105
Abraham **53** 46 **99** 231
127 114 **131** 6 9 10 12
19 131 **137** 282
Abram **74** 26
Adelaide I. **117** 286
Alden **98** 354
Alem **88** 177
Alexander H. **129** 47 49 50
Alfred G. **115** 171
Alfred Neobold **53** 83 272
Alice **58** 172
Alice Eugenia **108** 135
Alice Freeman **98** 185
99 170
Alice J. T. **117** 285
Alice Lucinda **70** 156
Almira **124**
Alphaus **117** 17
Amanda **75** 319
Amasa **71** 203 **88** 261

PALMER *cont'd*
Amaziah **115** 261
Ambrose **62** 147 **69** 343
  141 320 324 **147** 137
Amelia **71** 204 **92** 117
Amelia Wales **70** 107
Ammi **102** 110
Amos **54** 82 **115** 24 26 110
  128 294 299 **142** 376
Amy **70** 113 **73** 298
Amy (Blodget) (Whitney)
  (Lawrence) **138** 37
Amy Wait **132** 211
Andrew **81** 164 **139** 313
Andrew Jackson **96** 129
Angelica L. **90** 85
Angeline Eliza **81** 365 366
Ann **52** 223 **58** 168 390 **59**
  77 **65** 355 **68** 260 **69** 284
  285 **81** 448 **113** 282 **115**
  262 **125** 102
Ann (Field) **113** 282
Ann (Sanborn) **98** 184
Ann E. **78** 311
Anna **57** 403 **58** 90 172 262
  59 77 78 135 139 210
  314 **60** 265 **68** 260 261
  70 106 110 **75** 319 **105**
  105 **148** 152
Anna (Brown) **98** 184
Anna (Jones) **124** 154
Anna (Richardson)
  100 131
Anna (Shepard) **130** 53
Anna Lilian **105** 316
Anna Loomis **84** 87
Anna Louise **64** xlvii
Anna S. **129** 50
Anne **51** 61 118 **58** 36 173
  265 **70** 113 **92** 32 **121**
  188
Anne Rowland (Folsom)
  112 146
Annie **77** 291
Annie Gertrude **90** 203
Annie Lila (Lazell) **89** 117
Annie Naoma **81** 365
Annie W. (Brown) **90** 204
Annie Wildes **68** 262
Annis **98** 354 **115** 14
Anthony **72** 206
Appia **111** 305 306
Ariel **63** 367
Arthur Edwin **81** 43
Arvilla **117** 285
Asa **70** 113 **71** 204 **81** 164
  171 **86** 390
Asher C. **112** 146
Audrey **51** 172
Auria **71** 283
Aurinda K. **89** 112
Barbara **104** 174 175
  105 184
Barnabas **64** lxii **66** 313
Barnabas H. **74** 264
Barton **107** 58
Bathsheba **85** 151
Ben **70** 194
Ben G. **125** 175
Benajah **144** 42
Benjamin **59** 308 314 **61**

PALMER *cont'd*
  119 **62** 350 **63** 78 **64** 218
  68 260 **70** 71 **71** 38 **115**
  171 172 **117** 16 17 **132**
  243 **136** 271 325 **145**
  353
Bertha **77** 291
Bertha Bruce **70** 287 369
Bessie C. **102** 152
Bethiah **65** 353
Bethiah (Holmes) **142** 166
Bethiah (Mowrey) **105** 257
Betsey **60** 353 **68** 260 **72**
  172 **74** 264 **86** 390
Betsey (Stetson) **120** 239
Betsey Jane **66** 51
Betty **70** 81
Bezaleel **57** 403 **58** 87 **59**
  78 135 139 308 314 **60**
  179 181 **124** 154 **132**
  243
Bracket **95** 37
Bracket (Mrs.) **83** 152
Bridget **80** 97 **81** 170
  106 292
Bridget (Clark?) (Baxter)
  106 292
C. B.F. **123** 100 101
Caleb **107** 58
Calvin **144** 315
Caroline (Frances) **68** 261
  90 203 204
Caroline (White) **107** 209
Caroline C. **89** 392
Caroline Emma **68** 262
Caroline Frances (Bacon)
  98 184
Caroline Jennie **90** 203
  204
Carrie Emma **90** 203 204
Catherine **56** 39 **57** 371
  81 51 **88** 15 **103** 160
  114 191 **115** 160
Catherine (Marion)
  114 191
Catherine Chauncy
  (Rawson) **127** 101
Charles **83** 375
Charles A. **90** 85
Charles B. **89** 392
Charles Bunker **100** 191
Charles Dana **64** 102
Charles E. **123** 99
Charles E. (Mrs.) **123** 99
Charles H. **129** 49
Charles Henry **119** 202
Charles J. **56** 111 329 **59**
  119 **60** 218 **65** 12 16 **90**
  204
Charles James **68** xxxii
  262 **90** 203
Charles John **102** 88
Charles W. **68** 154 **129** 49
Charlotte **65** 21
Charlton **136** 284
Chauncey **102** 152
Cherry **63** 341
Christopher **58** 31 34 35
  68 259-261 **69** 284 **95**
  218-220 **98** 184 **137** 282
  142 176

PALMER *cont'd*
Clara **69** 140 **89** 392
Clara (Wells) **94** 247
Claracy **70** 110
Clarence Foster **95** 147
Clarinda W. **115** 171
Clarissa **63** 378 **64** 374 **92**
  220 **115** 24 26 110
Clement **94** 189 **97** 3 **144**
  35 37
Content **81** 166
Contentment **140** 135
Cornelia Agnes **81** 365
  366
Cornelia Congdon **66**
  lxvii **71** xlix
Damaris **55** 184
Daniel **53** 164 **61** 300 **81**
  164 **86** 390 **122** 38 39
David **60** 353 **72** 283 **80**
  130 **81** 166 **113** 282 284
David Ervine **81** 365 366
David S. **68** 261
David Shepherd **75** 319
Deborah **58** 172 **68** 260
  87 66 **107** 209 **115** 258
  137 155
Deborah (Deck) **109** 192
Deborah (Gifford)
  137 155
Deborah (Wilbor)
  137 155
Della **114** 61
Delos Manzer **81** 365
Denison **81** 164 **142** 175
Derentine (LaFetra)
  129 49
Desire **81** 165 167 **136** 318
Dewitt **115** 258
Dolly **70** 179 224 232
Dorcas (Cole) **86** 66
Dorothy (Jackson) **144** 37
Dorothy Eaton **120** 156
E. H. **129** 49
E. Mary **91** 250
Eben **73** 228
Ebenezer **81** 165 **90** 85
Edith **115** 261
Edward **65** 236 353 **67** 78
  68 259 260 **81** 165 **90** 85
  92 27 **120** 24 **141** 322
Edward Augustus **72** xx
Edward C. (Mrs.) **120** 156
Edward Dorr Griffin
  85 434
Edward Francis **68** 262 **90**
  203 204
Edward Howland **66** 51
Edward Humphries
  85 434
Edward James Barnes
  90 203
Edward True **66** 51
Elbridge Gerry **136** 271
Eleanor (Squire) **123** 95
Eleanor N. **123** 95 305
Eleazer **86** 390
Eleazer Jewett **86** 390
Elezer **115** 296
Eliakim **58** 70 **81** 165
  99 79

PALMER *cont'd*
Elias **81** 159 **113** 282 **114**
  61 **138** 37 **142** 174 175
Elijah **81** 165 **98** 354
  147 258
Eliot **59** 210-212 416
  84 86 87
Elisha **58** 262 **70** 113
Elisha (Silvester) **86** 291
Eliza (Gifford) **138** 217
Eliza A. **70** 156
Eliza M. **83** 95
Elizabeth **51** 256 **52** 56 115
  53 19 **54** 53 **58** 87 182
  60 333 **61** 287 **62** 256
  350 **68** 260 **69** 200 **70** 73
  81 **71** 280 318 **73** 229 **80**
  428 **86** 390 **89** 312 **90** 84
  92 23 **102** 300 **105** 214
  108 111 **110** 66 **112** 264
  113 282 **114** 280 **115**
  262 **117** 272 **119** 35 **121**
  20 **122** 38 39 **130** 210
  131 296 **136** 310
Elizabeth (Caldwell)
  85 434
Elizabeth (Dunton)
  116 67
Elizabeth (Field) **113** 282
Elizabeth (Griswold)
  114 169
Elizabeth (Hobson) **90** 84
Elizabeth (Hodgkins)
  85 434
Elizabeth (Kendrick)
  97 39
Elizabeth (Kenrick)
  105 199
Elizabeth (Mortimer)
  132 244
Elizabeth (Noble) **95** 37
Elizabeth (Palmer) **89** 312
Elizabeth (Phillips)
  120 80
Elizabeth (Simmons)
  125 175 179 180
Elizabeth (Sturtevant)
  112 264 **123** 239
Elizabeth (Wilbore)
  123 40
Elizabeth A. **68** 154
Elizabeth C. **90** 116
Elizabeth Hartwell **86** 49
  54
Elizabeth R. (Simmons)
  126 21
Elizabeth S. **70** 156
Elkanah **116** 215 **127** 221
  129 341
Ella (Hinman) **123** 101
Ella J. **69** 204
Ellen **75** 319
Ellen Douglas (Keyes)
  132 243
Elliot **60** 265
Elmer Ellsworth **129** 49
Elnathan **57** 398 **58** 172
  84 424 **136** 32
Elva Mildred **81** 43
Emeline **123** 10
Emeline Frances **105** 239

PALMER *cont'd*
  240
Emily **126** 183 **142** 376
Emily (Godfrey) **127** 101
Emma **70** 113 **92** 64 **111**
  134 **117** 285
Emma A. **123** 100
Emma Elizabeth (Luce)
  96 129
Emma Frances **112** 143
Enoch **68** 261 **75** 319
Ephraim **58** 265 **59** 389
  63 378 **64** 375 **106** 302
Erastus Dow **77** 57 **85** 90
Ernest Allison **82** 382
  83 233
Esther **70** 106 107 **91** 265
Esther (Avery) **136** 271
Esther (Randall) **142** 174
  175
Ethel **81** 166
Eunice **81** 166
Eunice Ripley **57** 199
Eva E. **96** 129
Eva P. **97** 219
Experience **58** 86 **59** 311
Ezekiel **58** 172 **72** 30 171
Ezekiel John **104** 63
Ezra **84** 105 190 **85** 434 **86**
  108 204 **148** 152
Ezra Lasell **89** 312
Falle G. **115** 261
Fanny **60** 352
Fanny Breese **77** 57 **85** 90
Fanny Lathrop **70** 156
Fidelia **70** 156
Fidelia Isabel **70** 156
Flewelling **126** 144
Flora **72** 104 **81** 366 **85** 169
Florence (Wright) **116** 67
Florence B. **83** 437 **84** 22
Foster **103** 300
Foster McCrum **120** 76
  77 148
Foster S. **103** 300
Frances **51** 118 **147** 31
Frances D. **77** 297
Frances E. **83** 180 185
Frances Hunt (Johnson)
  79 337 **90** 204
Frances Maria **75** lx 319
Francis **147** 154
Frank **52** 271 **55** 176
  116 67
Frank A. **89** 117
Fred Albert **68** 26
Fred T. **91** 331
Frederic Niles **132** 243
Frederick A. **80** 428
Frederick Tobey **68** 262
  90 203 204
Freeman M. **97** 158
George **56** 275 **81** 51 166
  91 244 **105** 257 277 **127**
  101 **137** 282 **138** 37 **142**
  176
George D. **91** 40
George H. **71** 355
George Herbert **76** lxii
George Milton **81** 365
  366

PALMER *cont'd*
George Monroe **68** 262
  90 203 204
George W. **68** 261 **70** 156
George Washington
  75 319
Gershom **81** 166 **105** 199
  137 282
Gertrude **114** 61
Gertrude M. **81** 43
Gertrude S. **68** 262
Gideon **75** lx **100** 169
  115 261 **125** 175 179
  180 **126** 21
Gilbert **102** 99 **128** 175
Grace **51** 309 310 **55** 448
  68 259 **69** 284 **78** 85 **81**
  165 **90** 70 **96** 267 **101**
  270 **131** 130 131
Gwendolyn (Hart)
  (Fargo) **92** 194
Hannah **53** 165 **68** 260 **70**
  106 113 **71** 38 280 **75**
  319 **81** 159 **82** 413 **88** 18
  85 **94** 87 **97** 39 **98** 172
  104 10 **105** 257 **109** 192
  115 261 263 **116** 124
  121 19 **122** 215 296 **131**
  219 **132** 122 **137** 153
  154 **142** 174
Hannah (Eells) **114** 61
  136 325
Hannah (Holbrook)
  90 51
Hannah (Palmer) **142** 174
Hannah (Swift) **129** 49
Hannah C. **96** 128
Hannah Carr (Greene)
  144 315
Harlena R. **123** 223
Harriet **59** 211 **70** 204 **75**
  126 **90** 52
Harriet L. **73** 116
Harvey **101** 94 **105** 105
Helen **90** 204 **129** 50
Helen Augusta **72** 206
  112 146
Helen Elizabeth **90** 203
Helen LaMar **109** 131
Helen M. **68** 262
Helena Mary Ray **85** 117
Henrietta **61** 142 300
Henrietta (Bracey)
  136 271
Henrietta T. (Johnson)
  108 315
Henry **51** 275 **71** 318 **90** 84
  93 171 108 315 **119** 17
Henry L. **70** 156
Henry Osgood **68** 261
  75 319
Henry Pollard **85** 117
Henry Robinson **63** 308
Herbert C. **116** 124
Hester Ann (Billings)
  98 54
Hester Ann (Fitz
  Randolph) **98** 54
Hetty **125** 292
Hezekiah Hayden **75** 306
Hiram **136** 271

PALMER *cont'd*
Horace W. (Mrs.) **121** 77
Horace Wilbur **81** 497
  121 77
Horatio **59** 212 **79** 52
Horatio Nelson **145** 161
Hoyt **76** 48
Huldah **59** 135 **60** 181
  81 164
Huldah (Whitney) **138** 37
Humphrey **141** 335
I. **54** 99 **92** 286
I. W. **91** 331
Ichabod **104** 265 **115** 14
  142 174
Ichabod Betts **115** 24
Ida May **81** 43
Inez Evelyn **121** 144
Isaac **59** 311 353 **62** 147
  83 22 26 **115** 260 **123** 40
Isaac Newton **119** 202
Isabel Charlotte **123** 305
Isabella **112** 312
Isabella (Stopham)
  112 312
Isaiah **53** 164 **77** 151
Israel I. **72** 104
Israel J. **85** 169
J. **113** 73
J. C. **129** 50
J. Porter (Mrs.) **84** 349
  85 184
Jacob C. **129** 49
Jacob Peabody **77** 291
James **59** 289 **64** 108 **68**
  261 **75** 319 **83** 67 **98** 54
  120 283
James B. **70** 156
James M. **90** 203 204
James Monroe **68** 203
  261 382 **75** 319 **98** 184
Jane **51** 118 **55** 168 **58** 83
  59 137 314 389 **60** 62 63
  66 176 179 **113** 284 **114**
  137 **123** 98
Jared **123** 125 126 **126** 234
Jason Haven **57** 373
Jedediah **60** 352 **70** 106
  107
Jehiel **71** 164
Jemima **53** 164 **81** 166
Jennie C. **68** 262 **90** 204
Jennie C. (Geisler) **90** 204
  98 184
Jennie Carolyn **98** 184
Jennie Vennettie (La Sell)
  89 312
Jeremiah **68** 260 **88** 334
Jerusha **81** 448 **82** 295 298
  106 80 **111** 80
Jerusha (Saxton) **136** 325
Jesse **60** 124 **70** 107 109 110
Jesse A. **116** 124
Jessie Fearing **75** lxi
Jessie Fearing
  (Richmond) **100** 168
Jo **123** 189
Joan **81** 371 **90** 186 **94** 189
  97 3
Joanna **54** 82 **59** 221 **68**
  260 **85** 333

PALMER *cont'd*
Joanna (Webster) **98** 184
Job **86** 384 **95** 204 **107** 313
  112 265
John **51** 109 170 398 404 **52**
  124 125 **54** 417 **55** 168
  57 399 **58** 90 168 173 **61**
  287 374 **63** 231 **65** 26
  190 246 **66** 258 364 **70**
  73 81 **71** 124 **72** 115 **73**
  229 264 **75** lx **78** 301 **82**
  27 51 **85** 259 260 **86** 390
  95 320 **100** 169 276 **106**
  174 175 177 292 **107** 153
  110 317 **113** 72 273 **115**
  262 **118** 45 46 57 **119** 17
  125 105 **129** 49 **131** 10
  132 **132** 243 **135** 56 276
  141 325 **144** 11 12 37
  251 **145** 353 **147** 258
John A. **129** 49
John Adams **81** 365 366
John B. **116** 50 67
John C. **122** 296 **129** 49
John Earl **81** 365 366
John H. **70** 156
John Jacob **52** 27
John Perley **66** 51
John S. **116** 121 **125** 175
John Simmons **75** xxv lx
  lxi **100** 103 168 169 **101**
  127
John Winas **89** 312
Jonah **53** 129 **64** 28 **97** 39
  319 326 **98** 174 **99** 96
  105 199 **114** 169 **123**
  187
Jonathan **54** 53 **62** 33 **64**
  lxii **65** 355 **68** 260 261
  71 76 163 164 280 283
  72 30 175 **75** 318 319 **98**
  184 **105** 287 **125** 221
  142 167
Jonathan D. **116** 215
Jonathan Hilliard **136** 79
Jonathan P. **68** 261
Jonathan Prescott **75** 319
Joseph **57** 371 **58** 30 83 168
  182 **59** 137 311 314 389
  60 62 63 66 176 179 **63**
  187 **64** 217 **68** 259 260
  70 106 113 156 **79** 180
  81 166 448 **84** 268 **88**
  261 360 **91** 353 **92** 23 **95**
  235 **99** 13 **102** 315 **106**
  173 **107** 58 **112** 264 **113**
  272 318 **115** 261 263
  116 67 **118** 285 **119** 35
  126 215 **127** 221 **128** 17
  134 130 **138** 227 **140**
  183 **142** 166 175 376
Joseph (Mrs.) **91** 353
Joseph Andrus **70** 110
Joseph B. **97** 222
Joseph P. **95** 235
Joseph Pears **91** 353 **92**
  23 27 117 119 **126** 226
Joseph Porter (Mrs.) **102**
  124 **107** 125
Joseph Rawson **127** 101
Josephine **70** 156

PALMER *cont'd*
Joshua **58** 173 **60** 62 **107**
  58 **124** 154
Josiah **121** 16
Josiah C. **83** 468
Judith **68** 261 **75** 319 **85**
  426 **135** 48
Judith (Littlefield) **136** 79
Julia **71** 356
Julius **73** 318 **74** xxv **75**
  xxv xxxiii lx lxi **100** 168
  169 **101** 127
Kate Frances **91** 40
Keturah **102** 228
Keziah **124** 15
L. D.P. **118** 131
Laura **83** 67 **117** 285
Laura (Brown) **123** 52
Laura L. **75** 319
Laura Richmond **75** lxi
Lavinia **130** 49
Lawton **87** 358 **128** 303
Lemuel **81** 165 **127** 221
  137 155 **148** 152
Lettie Alzada **99** 146
Lettie L. **123** 97
Levi **80** 428
Lewis **107** 58
Lewis A. **68** 261
Lewis Augustus **75** 319
Lewis Nathaniel **107** 209
Libbie **70** 156
Lizzie Ella **71** xxiv
Lois **68** 261 **75** 319 **81** 171
  107 209
Loring **115** 170
Lot **100** 191
Lottie S. **123** 100
Louisa **70** 156
Louisa (Gale) **85** 434
Louisa C. **81** 51
Louisa Folsom **64** xlvii
Love **68** 261 **81** 448
  82 290 295
Lowell Mason **60** 102
Lucia **120** 239
Lucia E. **77** 176
Lucie **129** 50
Lucinda (Cleveland)
  142 376
Lucius **120** 239 **136** 271
Lucretia **81** 165 **136** 331
Lucy G. **71** 38
Luke **60** 62
Lydia **53** 56 **60** 62 352 **63**
  378 **64** 375 **68** 251 **81**
  366 **98** 354 **101** 94 **115**
  169 261 262 296 **122** 105
  126 234 **132** 212 **135**
  320 **146** 368
Lydia (Dennis) **132** 244
Lydia (Waterman)
  124 154
Lydia Howard **72** 206
Lydia R. **71** 38
M. A. **129** 50
M. J. **71** 355 **129** 47
Madeleine L. **78** 447
Mae Estelle **85** 191
Mager Alfred **89** 312
Maranda Delia **119** 202

PALMER *cont'd*
Marenda **101** 94
Margaret **64** lxii **75** 319
  90 63 65 **127** 100
Margaret A. **77** 151
Maria **75** 319 **90** 84 **101** 94
  112 139
Maria Louise **74** xlvi
Mariah **136** 271
Marian W. (Brackett)
  98 184
Marion Prescott **90** 203
  98 184
Martha **51** 310 **55** 376 **60**
  179 **63** 367 **68** 259 261
  69 284 285 **75** 79 **83** 17
  86 224 **112** 226 **114** 169
Martha (Church) **148** 278
Martha A. **68** 261 **75** 319
Martha H. **117** 286
Martha Jane **70** 204
Marvin **142** 174 175
Marvin (Palmer) **142** 175
Mary **51** 320 397-399 **54**
  417 **55** 434 **57** 399 **58** 90
  168 173 **59** 66 311 314
  60 63 255 **61** 358 **63** 377
  64 76 **66** 362 **68** 260 **70**
  107 113 230 **71** 176 **75**
  158 **80** 180 434 **81** 46
  159 165 366 448 **83** 36
  200 **85** 97 **86** 390 390 58
  100 299 **104** 62 **112** 265
  324 **113** 282 **115** 14 260
  262 **134** 143 **135** 338
  148 185
Mary (Bickford) **136** 271
Mary (Holmes) **142** 170
  174
Mary (Kidder) **90** 51
Mary (Primmer) **90** 204
Mary (Sawdy) (Wetherall)
  148 152
Mary A. (Hammond)
  89 392
Mary A. (Johnson) **129** 49
Mary Albina **119** 202
Mary Ann **88** 395
Mary Ann (Hanson)
  68 26
Mary Ann Wentworth
  94 246
Mary B. **68** 154
Mary E. **74** 26 **75** 319
  130 53
Mary E. (Norton) **116** 67
Mary Ellen **83** 468
Mary F. **68** 261 **75** 319
Mary J. **64** 155
Mary Jane **77** 57
Mary Jane (Seamans)
  85 90
Mary L. **97** 356
Mary N. (Niles) **132** 243
Mary Place **94** 246
Mary S. **129** 49
Mary Submit **81** 365 366
Mary Tilton **61** xxxvii
  62 382 **70** 186 **71** 187
  93 391
Mary Townsend **59** 210

PALMER *cont'd*
Mary V. **91** 303
Mason S. **64** 131 **67** 358
Matilda **90** 84 85
Matilda Eliza **145** 195
Maywood E. **123** 223
Mehitable **60** 146 **70** 156
  100 137
Mehitable (Dibble)
  105 105
Mehitable H. **66** 274
Mercy **57** 398 **58** 172 **103**
  300 **112** 264
Mercy (Clarke) **136** 32
Mercy (Parker) **112** 264
Messenger **144** 44
Micah **55** 183 184
Michael **51** 398 404 **55** 183
  112 35 **122** 38
Mildred Carey **92** 41
Miles J. **129** 50
Miriam (Moulton) **83** 468
Miriam (Whiting) **104** 63
Molly **68** 261 **75** 319
Moses **52** 478 **75** lx **80** 194
  89 251 **100** 169 **105** 211
  126 234
Moses P. **66** lxx
Nabby **70** 110
Nancy **59** 289 **60** 352 353
  81 366 **136** 271
Nancy (Child) **93** 214
Nancy (Warner) **119** 202
Nancy Cooper **94** 39
Naomi **81** 365 366
Nathan **81** 164 **122** 320
  136 271
Nathan Billings **122** 320
Nathan Grandville
  119 202
Nathaniel **59** 78 **64** 325
  81 165 **132** 243 **145** 161
Nathaniel Gates **81** 365
  366
Nehemiah **71** 280 **81** 164
  116 7 **136** 325 **139** 314
  142 376
Nellie A. **74** 88
Nellie M. (Watson) **90** 204
Nellie Morse **121** 77
Nicholas **57** 332 **89** 174
Noah **105** 214
Novella L. **134** 278
Noyes F. **55** 448
Obed Nye **115** 170
Olive **63** 272 **115** 44
Ophelia Almira **85** 225
Orlan **100** 131
Orrin **70** 156
Othniel **137** 282
Ozias **72** 37
Pamela **86** 84
Pamelia **71** 203
Pardon B. **70** 156
Pasco **67** 107
Patience **58** 90 **70** 71 **86**
  120 **106** 303 **132** 211
  212
Paul **52** 368
Peggy **83** 22 26
Peggy (Bushong) **83** 22

PALMER *cont'd*
Phebe **55** 154 **81** 164-166
  134 239
Phebe (Broughton)
  104 265
Philander **120** 239
Phyllis **82** 51
Polly **63** 172 **74** 258 **80** 434
  81 188 **84** 352 **91** 197
  142 342
Polly (McIntosh) **120** 239
Potter **136** 90 325
Prince **58** 390
Priscilla **86** 384 **124** 154
Priscilla (Chesebrough)
  136 325
Prudence **116** 215
Prudence (Holmes)
  142 167
R. R. **102** 256
Rachel **63** 89 **68** 260 **70** 72
Rachel I. **117** 286
Ralph **55** 434 435
Ralph Abbott **81** 43
Rebecca **53** 57 **61** 271 **62**
  147 **68** 260 **74** xlvi **75**
  319 **112** 261 **126** 105
Rebecca (Brightman)
  137 153
Rebecca (Field) **113** 284
Rebecca (Potter) **136** 325
Rebecca (Short) **131** 132
Rescomb **127** 221
Reuben **115** 75
Rhoda **130** 54
Richard **75** lx **100** 137 169
  111 87 **115** 261 **125** 180
  127 221 **128** 137 **146**
  320 **147** 24
Richard Simmons
  100 169
Richmond **125** 36
Robert **69** 343 **81** 170 **112**
  312 **141** 322 **147** 258
Roger **94** 267 **121** 188
Rosanna **81** 51
Rosanna (Barton) **107** 58
Rose **70** 156
Roxana **81** 51
Ruby **147** 258
Ruhamah **81** 177
Russel **137** 282
Ruth **58** 168 **68** 260 **72** 115
  78 28 **89** 237 **94** 62 **115**
  263
S. **55** 395 **123** 95
Sabra **81** 165
Salina (Deitze) **129** 47 50
Sally **53** 163 **70** 232
Sally M. (Peabody)
  125 175
Salome (Smith) **122** 320
Samuel **51** 61 **58** 33 137
  168 172 173 262 265 390
  59 77 **62** 256 **68** 260 261
  69 362 **70** 105-107 113
  71 38 176 **72** 37 **80** 434
  81 46 **86** 66 **90** 51 **97**
  319 **98** 174 184 **99** 79
  105 **100** 137 **102** 99 **112**
  200 262 264 324 **113** 109

PALMER *cont'd*
282 **121** 13 **124** 51 211
212 **125** 93 **128** 258 259
261 **129** 227 **136** 325
Samuel Adams **70** 156
Samuel Harding **66** 51
Samuel P. **116** 124
Sanford **81** 165
Sarah **51** 268 **53** 19 20 164
58 33 81 172 **59** 248 **60**
179 182 239 **64** lxii **68**
260 261 **69** 200 **70** 113
179 224 **72** 280 283 **75**
319 **77** 149 **82** 51 **83** 41
88 78 **95** 246 **96** 159 303
97 3 **102** 99 **106** 303
107 160 **113** 272 273
115 262 **127** 148 **129** 49
50 **132** 244 **136** 32 **144**
36 37 316 **145** 161
Sarah (Mayhew) (Allen)
113 109
Sarah (Morgan) **95** 204
Sarah (Niles) **85** 151
Sarah (Pettigrew) **94** 189
97 3 **144** 37
Sarah (Trussell) **123** 126
Sarah Ann **60** 334 **95** 203
204 **129** 50
Sarah Ann (Ward) **126** 144
Sarah B. **111** 301 306
Sarah Eames **57** 372
Sarah Elizabeth **70** 156
Sarah F. **70** 156
Sarah Jane **81** 366
Sarah M. **70** 156
Sarah Margaret **68** 26
Sarah P. **91** 385
Sarah W. **70** 156 **115** 170
Scott **81** 43
Seneca **82** 51
Seth **70** 113 **109** 192
Sheldon **138** 217
Sibyl **69** 204 **144** 44
Sidney **116** 124
Simeon **115** 169 261 262
132 244 **142** 398
Simon P. **68** 261
Simon Prescott **75** 319
Sinclair B. **107** 153
Socrates **123** 92 305
Solomon **137** 282
Sophia **61** 119 **92** 119
94 246
Sophia Briggs **69** xlviii
Sophie L. **129** 47
Statira (Canfield) **129** 49
Stephen **53** 33 250 **55** 258
56 39 **57** 370-375 **64**
319 **68** 260 261 **70** 72 **75**
319 **78** 178 186 **94** 246
98 354 **136** 225 226
Stephen O. **116** 67
Stephen Wallis **81** 365 366
Stevens Gould **64** xlvii
Submit **98** 354
Sukey (Blackston) **84** 424
Susan **63** 378 **64** 375 **92** li
62
Susan (Caldwell) **126** 205
Susan (Oliver) **88** 334

PALMER *cont'd*
Susan (Porter) **97** 222
Susanna **68** 260 **115** 258
262 **116** 50 121
Susanna (Everson) **90** 85
Susanna (Hilton) **95** 219
98 184
Susanna (Whitaker)
125 221
Sylvester **73** 298 **132** 211
137 153
Tabitha **104** 265
Tamor **107** 58
Thaddeus **70** 156
Thankful **118** 285
Theresa **90** 114
Thomas **51** 255 256 **52** 27
219 **53** 19 20 391 **57** 279
280 388 **58** 69 173 **65**
235 239 248 **69** 343 **70**
106 113 156 **74** 237 **81**
448 **82** 27 51 413 **84** 250
377 **85** 434 **90** 51 85 **94**
339 **103** 9 **110** 160 **111**
278 **112** 244 264 **115**
127 258 262 **120** 239
121 248 **125** 125 291
127 17 221 **131** 178 189
190 **136** 325 **137** 155
148 152
Thomas B. **125** 33
Thomas K. **77** 149
Thomas W. **115** 171
Timothy **69** 204 **70** 107
83 41
Tirzah Strong **84** 87
Trueworthy **59** 221 **68** 260
261 **75** 318 319 **98** 184
Truman Marshall **81** 365
366
Uriah **59** 210 **84** 87
Velma **96** 161 **99** 145
117 71
Victoria Melinda **81** 43
Vincent **53** 19 20
Virgil M. **73** 116
Vose **81** 167
W. O. (Mrs.) **83** 233 247
Waldo Savage **68** 26
Wallie **129** 50
Walter **53** 129 **55** 448 **60**
102 **70** 179 224 **71** 38
134 138 141 142 288 **74**
xlvi **81** 164 166 **99** 228-
230 232 235 **108** 107 108
131 9 19 132 **137** 282
142 376
Warren Sherman **66** 51
Warren W. **122** 215
Wealthy **81** 165 **83** 67
90 366
Wellington G. **92** 41
Wells **85** 169
Wilbour **116** 124
William **51** 118 309-311 **52**
319 320 **53** 19 20 **57** 100
199 **60** 189 352 355 **63**
231 **66** 364 **68** 259-261
69 94 284 285 342 344
345 **71** 311 312 **75** lx 79
80 158 318 319 **85** 434

PALMER *cont'd*
87 48 **90** 63 65 84 85 **91**
331 **98** 167 184 **100** 15
168 169 **107** 209 **108**
107 108 **113** 204 282
115 26 **116** 50 **120** 239
121 77 **130** 53 **136** 271
284 **144** 254 **148** 152
William A. **63** 272 **79** 42
William Choate **68** 26
William H. **71** 38 **129** 49
William Lincoln **56** xxxii
57 xxxiii **59** xlii lxviii
221 331 352 **60** xxxiv
188 189 209 218 314 316
354 355 **61** vii xxxiii 92
96 202 306 359 **62** vii
xxiii xxxv 111 383 **63**
vii 96 **64** vii xxix **66**
xlviii **67** xxx **68** vii xxx
204 206 259 262 382 **69**
xxxi 94 **70** 188 287 71
188 **72** 79 **75** 80 160 319
79 337 **84** 462 **87** 91 **90**
125 203 204 302 **93** 391
95 393 **98** 137 184 **99**
151
William Prescott **75** 319
Willie A. **129** 49
Willie N. **70** 156
Willis F. **117** 286
Wilson **136** 271
Wood **144** 46
Zaidee **85** 434
Zernah **102** 99
Ziba **122** 215 296
Zipporah **70** 113 **81** 166
PALMER-SANBORN
Samborne Stukely
53 264
Palmere *see* Palmer
PALMERSTON Henry
John Temple
(Viscount) **77** lii
Henry Temple (Lord)
69 lxii
PALMERTON
Benjamin **89** 320
Jane **133** 322
Joshua **133** 322
Martha Ann **89** 320
Nancy (Coulson) **89** 320
PALMES Andrew **65** 379
87 399
Ann **99** 240
Dorothy **78** 375
Edward **65** 379 **86** 262
133 112 113
Elizabeth **99** 240
Francis **100** 142
Guy **65** 379 **67** 71
Henry **81** 57
Jonathan **99** 240
Julia F. **116** 259
Lucy **65** 379
Mary **81** 46 **100** 140
Mehitable **100** 141 142
102 29
Richard **100** 141 142
102 29
Samuel **78** 375 **81** 46

PALMES *cont'd*
Sarah **65** 379
Susanna **99** 240
William **99** 229
PALMETER Palmeteer
Palmiter Palmitter
—— **87** 323
Albert Enoch **115** 114
Annvanetta **75** 34
Chase **104** 76
Darwin **75** 34
Ebenezer **116** 7
Elijah **87** 322
Elizabeth **104** 76
Ellen **75** 34
Elmira A. **71** liv
Elnathan **104** 76
Ephraim **115** 114 117
Fannie **75** 34
Hannah **104** 76
Harley E. **75** 34
Harrison Otis **115** 117
Henry Baber **115** 114
Jonathan **116** 7
Joseph **128** 302
Judith **132** 164
Mary **115** 114
Mary Elizabeth **115** 114
Mercy (Chase) (Dean)
87 323
Nancy (Chase) **87** 322
Nathan **104** 76
Paul **128** 302
Phebe Maria **75** 34
Polly **115** 117
Rosabel **75** 34
Russell **75** 34
Susanna (Sanford) **104** 76
Waity **104** 76
Washington **135** 52
PALMGREN
Abby W. **125** 245
Palmiter *see* Palmeter
Palmitter *see* Palmeter
PALMOUNTAIN
Bennet **140** 136
Jenifer **140** 136
Ruth (Howland) **140** 136
PALOSKI Sarah (Jacobs)
125 107 108
William **125** 108
PALOUBET Harriet Frary
(Hanks) **86** 17
Louis **86** 17
PALPERNAN
Aaron **62** 242
PALRIM John **62** 247
PALSERY William **51** 435
PALSFORDE
Edward **114** 86
Palsgrave *see* Palgrave
Palsists *see* Paltsits
PALTEN
Anna Shields **115** 114
Aurelia **115** 114
George **115** 114
Jannet Anderson **115** 114
John **115** 114
Miranda Howard **115** 114
Robert **64** 350

PALTSITS Palsists
—— **58** 218
Victor Hugo **52** 311 **53**
147 **58** 102 **60** 218 **61**
xxxv **62** xxxvii **64** xxxii
97 **65** xxxv 202 305 **66** l
105 239 **107** 162 **147** 70
PAMALICH
Bennony **59** 311
Patience **59** 311
PAMANT Bridget (Reade)
147 378
John **147** 378
Rose **147** 378
Pamer *see* Palmer
PAMIL John **143** 257
PAMISH Abram **61** 310
Hannah **61** 310
PAMMER Anney **141** 353
PAMPE Frederick **63** 16
PAMPHLET
Ann **76** 61 75
Elizabeth **76** 60 61 75
John **76** 60 75
Margaret **76** 60 75
Mary **76** 60 75
PAMPILLO Joan **63** 333
Peter **63** 333
PAMPMUMITTI 127 20
PAMPYON
William **120** 244
PAMWITT
Elizabeth **64** 346
PANCEMONT
— Baron de **110** 133
Panckhurst *see* Pankhurst
PANCOAST George E. **83**
437 **84** 20
Letitia **89** 62
Madeline (Spencer) **83**
437 **84** 20
Sallie (Smythe) **145** 315
Sarah **76** xxxiv
Sarah Abbott **81** 102
William **113** 281
PANDEL Martin **64** 115
PANDO Mary **57** 400
PANDOR John **112** 190
Panell *see* Pannell
PANETIN — Judge **55** 57
PANG L. M. **91** 331
PANGBORN Pangbarn
Pangburn
—— **76** 152
Abbie Laura **89** 92
Amanda M. (Barton)
107 294
Anna **89** 91
Anna Jane **89** 92
Anna May **91** 248
Beebee **89** 91
Bennet **76** 152
Betsey (Farrington) **89** 92
Betsey Jane **106** 73
Clifford Francis **91** 248
David **89** 91
David Knapp **89** 92
DeForest Grant **91** 249
Elnora Parintha **91** 248
Eva Alberta **91** 248
Fern Belle **91** 249

PANGBORN *cont'd*
Floy (Campbell) **91** 248
Francis Albertus **91** 248
Frederick Ransom **91** 248
Harriet Amanda **91** 248
Lovina Adell (Owen)
91 248
Lucy **89** 91
Martha **99** 116 **100** 144
Mary Elizabeth **89** 92
May (Bowering) **91** 248
Naomi **89** 91
Orin Darius **91** 248
Peter **107** 294
Philena **100** 88
Solomon **99** 116
Susan (Knapp) **89** 91
Thyrza Farrington **89** 92
Walter **91** 249
Zebina Knapp **89** 91
Zerah **89** 91
Ziba **89** 91
PANGMAN —— **76** 174
PANIK
Diedama **105** 222 223
PANILLO Warren **62** 196
PANKENHAM-WALSH
W. B. **103** 41
PANKHURST Panckhurst
Elizabeth **55** 217
Francis **64** 320
PANKRATZ
Mary Evelyn **117** 129
PANMAURE
Geoffrey de **106** 280
Maud **106** 280
PANMURE
— Earl of **56** 195
PANNELL Panell Pannil
Pannill
Eliza **77** 290
Frances **69** lxxii
John **68** 263
Margaret **84** 46
Samuel **77** 191
Samuel Weisiger (Mrs.)
91 294
Sarah Barr (Egleston)
91 294
Thomas **57** 220 **64** 53
PANTEN Thomas **143** 202
Panter *see* Painter
PANTHER
Richard **110** 195
Thomas Evertsz **143** 203
PANTLIND
Frederick Z. **101** 318
J. Boyd **101** 318
J. Boyd (Mrs.) **80** 195 207
101 24 129 318
Jessie **80** 207
Jessie (Aldrich) **101** 318
Katharine **103** 119
PANTON —— **143** 202
— Lieut. **84** 258 259
Ellen **133** 302 **147** 62
Henry **53** 13
PANTRY James **95** 255
96 371
John **53** 87 **59** 343 **93** 357
Margaret **89** 177 **93** 357

PANTRY *cont'd*
358
Margaret (Weyborne)
95 133 255 **96** 370
Mary **53** 87 **54** 134 **59** 343
93 357
Thomas **93** 357 **95** 255
96 371
William **87** 273 **89** 173
175 177 **93** 356-358 **94**
66 67 **95** 133 255 387 **96**
280 370 371
William (Mrs.) **96** 380
PAOLI Paschal **60** xvi
Philip A. **86** 170
PAON Charles **131** 95
Edward **131** 95
Thomas **131** 95
PAPASIAN
Bertha S. **75** xviii
PAPATHAKES
Louisa (Miles) **90** 45
Patro **90** 45
PAPAZIAN Bertha S. (Mrs.)
74 156
PAPE T. **68** 384 **69** xxxii **78**
387-389 **81** 136 **94** 269
97 196 **98** 32
Thomas **106** 126
PAPENFUSE
Edward **145** 27
PAPETOO —— **54** 385
PAPILLON Papillion
Papillons
Abigail **124** 178 180
Abigail (Carpenter)
124 177
Abigail (Newton)
(Carpenter) **124**
177 182
Alexander F. W. **124** 165
Benjamin **124** 162 165 166
Bridget **124** 173-175
135 26
Bridget (Bosworth) **124**
172 174 **135** 26
Bridget (Pecker) **124** 174
Catherine **124** 168
Ebenezer **124** 162 164 165
172 174-176
Elizabeth **124** 169 171
Esther **124** 175 180
Esther (Bosworth)
124 176
Joan **123** 191 **124** 161-166
John **124** 162 164 165 172
173 175 176
Josiah Collins **124** 165
Katharine **124** 166 169-
172 181
Martha **100** 243 **124** 169
172
Mary **124** 161 165 170-172
Mercy **124** 172
Molly **124** 172
Obadiah **124** 164 165 175
176
Peter **123** 191 **124** 161-172
175 176 178 180-182
Rebecca (Bosworth) **124**
179 180

PAPILLON *cont'd*
Samuel **124** 162 165 172
Susanna (Hersent)
124 165
Thomas **124** 165
PAPLYE James **121** 204
PAPMONIT
Simon **118** 203
PAPPOON Elizabeth **55**
315 **61** 398 **73** 313 **83** 10
Hannah **73** 313 **74** 41 193
Mary **73** 308 313
Philip **73** 313 **74** 182
Rhoda **73** 311
Richard **61** 398
PAPWORTH Pabworth
—— **57** 418
John Woody **117** 31
Richard **84** 78
Robert **97** 176
William **97** 176
PAQUIN
Joseph Trefflee **117**
138 **118** 67
Par *see* Parr
PARADA Maria **77** 255
PARADIS Lex **145** 377
Marie (Berard) **143** 12
Marie (Nolin) **143** 12
Paul **143** 12
Pierre **143** 12
Sophie (Robichaux)
143 12
Veronique **143** 12
PARADISE Ann **67** 302
Elizabeth **51** 350
Frances **76** 64 67
Thomas **51** 350
PARAGE Thomas **109** 24
PARASCHOS
George T. **64** lvii
Lucinda E. **84** 31
PARASSER Henry **77** 230
PARCE Petor **127** 310
PARCELL Parcells Parcels
Ellison **113** 213
Frances C. **68** 122
Henry **87** 341
Lavinia **68** 122
Peace B. (Chase) **87** 341
Susan **83** 301
PARCHEN —— **66** 311
PARCHER — Mrs. **83** 36
Betty **95** 88
Ivory **88** 369 **90** 337 **91** 25
Jennie **96** 178
John **90** 247 248
Lydia **90** 230 250 **91** 30 119
Polly (Gubtail) **90** 248
Rachel **90** 326 **91** 17
Rhoda Burleigh (Philpot)
88 369 **90** 337 **91** 25
Robert **90** 227 245
Sally (Brown) **90** 247
Samuel **82** 295 302
Sarah **82** 295 302
Sarah (Straw) **90** 227 245
PARCHIER
Gaufrid **79** 370
Parcker *see* Parker
Parckhurst *see* Parkhurst

PARCUS Solomon **118** 218
PARDA Andrew **106** 109
Charles **106** 109
Lydia **106** 109
PARDEE —— **115** 79
A. O. (Mrs.) **105** 79 80
Aaron **91** 206
Abigail **57** 264 **59** 169 **75**
309 **124** 187
Abigail (Brockett)
124 187
Alfred Orville (Mrs.)
102 124
Anna Maria (Robison) **90**
187 **107** 113
Anstice (Cox) **86** 229
90 187
Anthony **81** 322 **86** 229
230 **90** 187
Ariovistus **90** 187 **107** 113
Benjamin **66** 201
Bessie **71** xxiii **74** xxviii
90 117 187 **91** 146
Betsey (Horn) **90** 187
Calvin **90** 187
Charles Albert **81** 456
Clarissa **112** 48
Daniel **54** 26 **78** 263 **86**
230 **140** 121
Daniel W. **86** 366
David **86** 230
Dorothy Dwight (Porter)
101 251
Ebenezer **66** 201
Eliphalet **56** 287
Eliza (Platt) **90** 187
Elizabeth **102** 65
Elizabeth (Payne) **86** 230
Elizabeth (Stainbrook)
86 230
Elizabeth (Yale) **90** 187
Elvira Mary **81** 455
Enos **75** 308
Esther (Vail) **140** 121
Esther Mary **81** 456
Ettie Augusta **81** 456
George **57** 135 **60** 189 **61**
118 **75** 309 **77** 240 **81**
131 455 **86** 229 230 **90**
187
Hannah **75** 309
Harold E. B. (Mrs.)
101 251
Harvey Sabin **81** 456
Jesse **86** 230
Jesse Homan **75** ix xxiii
86 229 230 237 **87** 176
John **66** 189 **81** 130 **90** 187
105 79 **124** 187
John Henry **86** 229 230
John Howard **104** 145
Joseph **57** 264 **75** 309 **81**
455 **86** 230 **90** 187
Joseph Harvey **81** 455
Josiah **59** 169 **81** 455
Julia Ann (Homan)
86 229 230
Katharine (Lane) **90** 187
Luther **107** 57
Lydia **54** 26 **78** 263
Lydia (Potter) **86** 230

PARDEE cont'd
Lyman **82** 455
Maray W. **90** 68
Martha **58** 180
Martha (Miles) **86** 230
Mary **56** 287 **58** 283 **66**
 202 205 327 **97** 189
Mary Imboden
 (MacClung) **86** 230
Mary L. **82** 455
Mercy **61** 118
Miranda **132** 77
Moses **66** 202 205
Phebe (Woodruff) **86** 230
Rachel **66** 329
Rachel (Johnson) **90** 187
Rebecca (Wheaton)
 131 75
Rebecca C. (Richmond)
 105 79
Samuel **66** 329
Sarah **57** 135 **66** 201
Sarah (Jenks) **107** 57
Sarah L. **78** 246
Thomas **90** 187
Walter Stone **74** 158 **75**
 xxvi **81** 109 232 455
Weltheon (Cook) **90** 187
PARDO DE TAVERA
 T. H. **58** 328
PARDON William **63** 41
PARDONNER William
 Stanley **80** 334 **81** 219
 92 136 **93** 140
PARDUE Edith **100** 198
PARDY Enos **83** 67
 Mommoth **144** 42
 Sabrina **83** 67
Pare see Parr
PAREL James Ignatius
 (Mrs.) **83** 233 247
PAREMER Peremer
 Joseph **91** 266
 Rebecca (Meeles) **91** 266
PARENT Anna **60** 20
 Carlos **110** 129
 Esther **64** 319
 Francis **123** 98
 Francisco **110** 129
 Frank (Mrs.) **123** 224
 H. F. (Mrs.) **123** 225
 J. L. **123** 97
 Juana **110** 129
 Julia **123** 225
 T. P. **64** 319
 William **60** 20
PAREPINT —— **121** 35
Pares see Paris
PARES James **148** 320
Pareson see Pearson
PARETT John **148** 117
Pareus see Paris
PARFITT Mercy (Kinney)
 108 211
 Thomas **108** 211
PARGELLIS
 Allen McCrory **88** 383
 Elizabeth Scribner (Allen)
 88 383
 Katharine Lucy **88** 383
 Margaret Ann **88** 383

PARGELLIS cont'd
Stanley **97** 394 **99** 178
 101 279
Stanley G. **104** 175
Stanley McCrory **88** 383
PARGITER —— **52** 135
 Amy **93** 391-393 **98** 36
 Cecily **98** 36
 Christopher **93** 392
 Elizabeth **67** 45 **70** 249
 George **104** 112 113
 James **104** 113
 John **52** 133
 Robert **93** 393
PARHAM Agnes **51** 354
 Alice **78** 47
 James **51** 354
 Joan **51** 354
 William H. **92** 208
PARIFIE Gravill **64** 336
Parinton see Purinton
PARIS Pares Pareus
 Parise Parris Parys
 —— **53** 18 **112** 159
 — Judge **145** 52 53
 A. **112** 158
 Abigail **122** 22
 Agnis **114** 234
 Albion Keith **51** 499
 59 238
 Alexander **124** 114
 Amos **66** 107
 Ann **112** 158
 Benjamin **62** 326 **122** 26
 Benton **65** 136
 Caleb **72** 17 26
 Clarke Mattison (Mrs.)
 93 138
 Columbia **111** 70
 Columbia (Rawson)
 111 70
 David **63** 144 **65** 248 **129**
 283 287
 Deborah **98** 363 **100** 324
 Delphina Keith **111** 70
 Dorothy **93** 195 **137** 48
 253
 Edward Lowden **111** 70
 Elbridge **66** 108
 Elizabeth **58** 246 **74** 71 75
 93 166 **112** 158
 Elizabeth (Blanchard)
 98 363
 Elizabeth (Bonney) **136** 41
 Elizabeth (Wylkys)
 113 240
 Elkanah **72** 23
 Eula (Jennison) **93** 138
 Experience **111** 70
 Experience (Lowden)
 111 70
 Francis **66** 36
 George **66** 107 108
 George Morrison **66** 107
 Grace **72** 17 23 26 **122** 22
 23
 Grace (Record) **122** 21 22
 136 32
 Hannah **55** 188 **66** 105 108
 72 23

PARIS cont'd
Hannah Hinton Lilly
 66 107
Helen Delphina **111** 70
Hepzibah (Hill) **116** 295
Ida **65** 136
Ione **114** 234
John **51** 448 **54** 149 **63** 364
 65 136 **66** 106 **67** 366
 70 245 **96** 361 **112** 158
 159 **114** 234 **131** 132
 140 103-108 110-113
 143 34
Josiah **111** 70
Judith **92** 32
Katharine **114** 234
Leonard **65** 136
Louisa **66** 107
Margaret **66** 108 **114** 234
Marie **112** 158 159
Martin **81** 313 **112** 158 159
Mary **51** 308 448 **65** 136
 66 106 **98** 363
Mary (Crispe) **98** 363
Mary Pauline **65** 136
Matthew **95** 302 397 **106**
 280 281
Mercy **55** 188 **98** 363
Noyes **91** 94
Olin **78** 136
Percival Josiah **111** 70
Peter **71** 75 **74** 71
Phebe **72** 17
Rachel **124** 266 275
Rebecca **112** 158 159
Richard **110** 157 **112** 158
 159
Robert **51** 308 **55** 188 **93**
 165 166 **98** 363
Samuel **61** 71 **63** 364 **69** 7
 93 195 **105** 196 197 **112**
 158 159 **137** 244 252 253
 138 325 **140** 112 113
Sarah **112** 158 159
Seborne **51** 308
Susan **112** 158 159
T. C. **57** 240
Thankful **72** 17
Thomas **63** 364 **80** 352 **112**
 158 159 **114** 235 **122** 21
 22 **136** 32 **140** 107 111
 112
Virgil Delphini **111** 70
Virgil K. **111** 70
William **79** 372 **110** 194
 116 295 **147** 251 252
William Cobb **66** 107
PARISH Parrish
 —— **59** lxv **87** 334
 112 159
 A. **113** 240
 A. G. **110** 122
 Aaron **63** 372
 Abigail **63** 365 366 368 370
 99 298
 Abraham **63** 369-372
 Achsah **88** 117
 Adelina M. **63** 372
 Albert Elisha **57** 360
 Alice **63** 370 **127** 298
 Alice Roberts **85** 199

PARISH *cont'd*
Alonzo Nelson **117** 71
Althea **63** 370 372
Amanda **63** 370 371
Amos Wells **63** 372
Andrew **63** 368 **70** 107
Ann **113** 240
Anna **63** 370 **68** lxvii
Anne **88** 204
Anne (Martin) **112** 158 159
Anne (Mountford) **112** 159
Annie **63** 367 370
Annis **63** 372
Archippus **63** 367 370 372
Ariel **63** 370 371 **68** lxvii
Artemisia **63** 372 373
Asa **63** 366 369 371 372
Asahel **63** 370
Azariah **63** 366
Benjamin **51** 224 **63** 364 366 **71** 204
Bethiah **53** 288 **63** 366
Betsey (Chase) **87** 334
Caroline **63** 370
Caroline E. **63** 370
Celia **80** 158
Charles **63** 372 **103** 160
Chester **63** 369 373
Chloe B. **57** 361
Clarissa **63** 368
Clark W. **84** 43
Cook **88** 121
Cynthia **63** 369 370
Cyprian **63** 369
Dan **63** 369 **70** 317
Daniel **63** 366 369 372 **70** 314 **103** 311 **143** 256
Deborah **63** 366 368
Desire **63** 373
Desire (Smith) **110** 229
Dillwyn **80** 450
Dinah **63** 368
Dorothy **63** 365 368 371
Drusilla **63** 89
E. M. **117** 156 315 **118** 166
Earl Thomas **78** 42
Ebenezer **63** 368 371 **70** 310 312
Edith May (Winch) **96** 305
Edward Codman (Mrs.) **103** 311 **104** 141 **117** 148
Edwin **78** 42
Elijah **51** 71 **63** 368 370 371 **70** 177
Eliphaz **63** 368 371
Elisha **57** 360 **63** 368 **85** 411
Eliza **63** 373
Eliza M. **63** 370 **72** 206
Elizabeth **63** 365 368 370 373 **70** 107 **113** 240
Elizabeth (Tibbetts) **100** 144
Elizabeth Hubbard (Wainwright) **103** 311
Elvira **57** 361
Emma White **66** lii **68** xliii lxvii

PARISH *cont'd*
Ephraim **63** 365 369
Erastus **63** 372
Esther **63** 367
Eunice **51** 71 **63** 368 371 **70** 177
Eunice Cora **80** 242
Evans **63** 373
Freelove (Dodge) **103** 311
Freelove (Powell) **103** 311
Freeman **63** 370
Gates D. **84** 43
George **84** 43
Gertrude (Needham) **110** 122
Gordon **57** 361
Gould P. **63** 372
Grace **82** 195 **85** 188 **103** 311 **104** 65 147
Hannah **63** 292 294 295 364 366 369-372
Hannah (Jewell) **110** 229 **112** 159 **113** 240
Hannah Arvilla **57** 361
Harris Franklin **63** 372
Henry **103** 311
Horatio Nelson **63** 373
Irena **63** 369
Isaac **63** 365 367 369-372 **71** 204
Jacob **63** 369 **103** 311
Jacob Kimball **63** 369 372
James **84** 43
James Green **63** 372
James Scott **96** 305
Jasper **63** 369 372
Jemima **63** 370
Jeremiah **63** 370 **72** 206
Jerusha **53** 288 **63** 366 367 369 **72** 305
Jesse **63** 370 372
Joanna **103** 88
Joel **63** 365
John **60** 314 **63** 364-372 **64** 92 **71** 204 **85** 455 **87** 141 **93** 208 **110** 229 **113** 240 241 **131** 132
John C. **63** 370 **76** 160 **77** 161
John Carl **68** lxvii
John D. **84** 43
John F. **108** 318
John Ford **81** 108 222
John Riley **63** 372
Joseph **63** 366 **80** 450
Judith **63** 368
Julia **63** 373 **78** 42
Keziah **63** 368 371
Lemuel **63** 368 370 372 **110** 229
Leonard Woods **68** lxvii
Loomis **63** 372
Lora **63** 372
Lucy **63** 368 369 371-373
Lucy (Harris) **110** 229
Lucy Jewett **63** 371
Lydia **63** 364 366 368 370 372 **70** 107 **72** 206
Lydia Maria **95** 372
Mabel **68** lxvii
Mabel R. (Winch) **110** 229

PARISH *cont'd*
Mahala Smith **108** 318
Margaret **63** 367 **71** 204
Maria **63** 372
Marie **113** 240 241
Marion **63** 371
Martin **82** 22
Mary **51** 224 **53** 288 **60** 314 **63** 364-372 **82** 85 **110** 229 **136** 311
Mary (Mountford) (Banks) **112** 158 159
Mary (Rood) **110** 229
Mary (Wattell) **110** 229
Mary Ann (Harris) **103** 311
Mary Ellace (Rodgers) (Bennett) **120** 16
Mary Jeanette (McNulty) **110** 229
Matilda **63** 370 372
Matthew **103** 311
Mehitable **63** 368 370 372
Mehitable Melody **63** 372
Mercy **53** 154 **108** 4
Mila Mangrum **78** 42
Miles **84** 43
Miranda Forrest **63** 373
Nancy **63** 371 **84** 43
Nathan **63** 369 372 **120** 16
Nathaniel **63** 365 366 368 371
Nehemiah **63** 365 366
Obadiah **63** 370
Oliver **63** 367 369 371 **70** 313
Orpha (Rich) **84** 43
Orrin **63** 372
Patricia Jane **78** 43
Patty **63** 370
Phebe **63** 369 372
Philomela **51** 71 **63** 371 **70** 177 228
Pluma M. **81** 414
Polly **63** 371
Rachel **63** 365
Rebecca **63** 365 366 368 **127** 229
Reuben **63** 89
Richard **68** 79
Robert Ariel **68** lxvii
Roswell **63** 364 368 370-373 **64** xxxii 92 **89** 132 **93** 208 **110** 221 229
Roxalana **63** 372
Rufus **63** 370
Rufus P. **59** 370
Ruth **63** 366 368
Sally **63** 370
Samuel **63** 364 365 367 368 370-372 **110** 229 **113** 240
Sarah **63** 365 369 371
Sarah Ann **63** 373
Sarah Ann (Chase) **88** 121
Sarah Isabelle **62** 366
Solomon **63** 365 368
Sophia **63** 372
Sophia S. **85** 411
Stephen **63** 369
Susan **112** 159

PARISH *cont'd*
Susanna **63** 367 368
Sylvia **63** 368
Tamar **63** 369
Tammy **63** 370
Tamson **63** 366
Thomas **63** 364 **113** 240
Townsend **103** 311
Tyler Morse **63** 372
W. D. **105** 188
Watson **84** 43
Wealthian **63** 370
William **53** 288 **63** 365
  366 368 369 371
Zachariah **100** 144
Zebulon **63** 367 369 371
Zeruiah (Townsend)
  103 311
Zerviah **63** 370
Zerviah (Smith) **110** 229
PARK Parke Parks
  —— **58** 22 309 **59** 111 **60**
  403 **62** 306 **69** 164 **70**
  109 **74** 96 **96** viii **98**
  359 **101** 51 **109** 75 **121**
  206 **130** 69 314 **133** 263
  136 336 **141** 100 303
  307
— Mr. **142** 274
— Rev. Mr. **66** 248
— Widow **71** 135 140
____ (Austin) **140** 34
____ (Durrell) **140** 62
Abel **70** 151
Abiah (Hickox) **136** 316
Abigail **56** 11 **62** 230 **63**
  366 **66** 239 **81** 29 358 **97**
  49 **101** 107 **105** 33
Abigail (Greene) **136** 361
Abigail (Trowbridge)
  91 265
Abigail (Whitman)
  130 69
Ada **85** 292
Admire **59** 255
Agnes **55** xxxii **124** 252
Albert **116** 120
Alertta Emily **70** 225
Alexander **79** 4
Alice **70** 315 **71** 40 **82** 99
  136 313
Alice (Chaplin) **136** 102
  335
Alice (Freeman)
  (Thompson) **136** 86
  102 **141** 105
Allen **116** 120
Almerin **116** 120
Amanda **114** 303
Amasa **79** 38
Amelia (Rising) **85** 291
Amelia L. **84** 420
Amity (Cady) **136** 316
Amos **55** 177
Amy **63** 366 **146** 374
Andrew J. **132** 326
Anna **70** 229 **79** 3 4 **81** 28
  29 **144** 218
Anna (Killam) **136** 313
Anna Maria **56** 13
Anne **55** 437

PARK *cont'd*
Anthony **70** 224
Archibald **130** 314
Artemisia **63** 373
Arthur **65** 192 **77** 82
Arthur M. **111** 303 306
Asa **57** 289 **70** 312 **80** 45 **81**
  174 **115** 296 **116** 67
Ashly **57** 289
Avery D. **101** 235
Barbara **106** 109
Barzilla Miles **122** 320
Benajah **63** 366
Benjamin **73** 160 **118** 268
  271 **120** 177
Benjamin Franklin
  74 96 97
Benjamin K. **139** 257
Betsey **90** 363 **100** 330
  125 108
Betsey Leeds **78** 379
Beulah **78** 19
Beulah Anne **101** 252 253
Burton Miner **94** 87
C. W. **60** 189
Calvin **56** 11 **76** 53
Calvin Chapin **74** 96 97
Caroline **134** 91
Caroline (Durrell)
  134 149
Caroline (Goodnow)
  130 69
Carrie Belle **82** 381 **83** 233
Carrie G. **116** 120
Catherine **79** 5 **90** 53
Catherine (Clark) **126** 209
Catherine E. **86** 17
Charity (Stout) **86** 287
Charles **116** 120 **130** 314
Charles A. **116** 67
Charles Edwards **64** 184
  65 xix **76** 163 164 167 **77**
  89 **78** 119 332 **79** 194 **81**
  3 247 **82** 271 **85** 183 **88**
  160 **89** 128 **92** 199 **93**
  132 136 **98** 290 **106** 220
  117 71
Charles H. **115** 296
Charles Stuart **79** 5
Charles W. **78** 197
Charles Wellman **64**
  xxxiii **85** 107 205 219
Chloe J. (Brayton) **115** 296
Christabel **70** 177 **71** 40
Content **116** 119
Cynthia **52** 223 **70** 231
Cyrenius **76** 242
Cyrus **128** 121
Dan B. (Mrs.) **122** 160
Daniel **98** 359 **136** 316
David **56** 255 **80** 158 **85**
  219 **122** 320
David P. **70** 156
Deborah **58** 204 **81** 160
  136 325
Deborah (Geere) **94** 87
Delight **72** 221
Dolly **70** 231
Dorothea (Schmidt)
  98 179
Dorothy **53** 238 287 **54** 39

PARK *cont'd*
  136 99 323
Dorothy (Thompson)
  94 87 **136** 101
Dorothy Christena
  98 179
Douglas **70** 230 **71** 135
  140
E. K. **116** 120
Edith Laura **94** 283
Edward **59** 112 **60** 403 **61**
  43 **68** 231 235
Edward A. **93** 301
Edward D. **132** 326
Edwards Amasa **53** 381
  54 447 **55** xliii 123 **56**
  xx xxii lxxvii 11-17 89
  220 **57** 130 132 **58** 108
  60 lxxvi **94** 197
Elcy (Counery) **88** 279
Eleanor **79** 11
Eleanor Robertson
  89 315
Eleazer **69** 246
Elias **70** 179 224 225 314 **71**
  143 **94** 87
Elijah **70** 156 223
Elisha **71** 40 137-139 **108**
  98 **132** 240 **136** 316 **140**
  34
Elisha Foster **120** 319
  132 326
Eliza **80** 443 **116** 119
  132 240
Eliza Ann **83** 178 185
Elizabeth **52** 224 **55** 177 **67**
  279 **68** 231 **69** 246 **70**
  226 **81** 29 160 **86** 194
  342 **92** 89 **101** 235 **116**
  120 216 **127** 273 **136**
  316
Elizabeth (Bucknam)
  85 219
Elizabeth (Gollop)
  115 152
Elizabeth (Hastings)
  (Billings) **85** 219
Elizabeth (Ogle) **122** 320
Elizabeth Augusta
  (Carter) **85** 219
Elizabeth Bigelow **79** 3 6
Elizabeth C. **132** 326
Ella Maria (Leach) **132** 240
Ellen **122** 320
Ellen Elizabeth (James)
  136 316
Elora L. **115** 296
Emeline **98** 359
Emma **70** 156 **116** 120
Emma F. **70** 156
Emma Florence **95** 146
Emma L. **70** 156
Enid Hathaway **111** 322
Ephraim **78** 314 **144** 221
Ernest **89** 237
Esther (Hannum) **90** 260
Esther (Ranney) **136** 316
Eunice **70** 231
Experience **63** 88
Ezekiel **136** 313
F. S. **62** 306 **78** 337

PARK *cont'd*
Frances Elizabeth **89** 20
Francis **124** 253
Francis Robert **72** xx **90**
130 **94** 86 126 144
Frank E. **53** 182
Frank Sylvester **54** 356 **59**
111 **60** 189 403 **61**
xxxiii xxxvii **62** xxxv
63 304 **64** xxix **65** 192
67 385 **68** xxx **76** 242
319 **77** 82 160 325 **79** 7
88 209 **89** 97 **90** 125
147 117
Frederick Willard **51** 89
90 92 235 373 374 379
52 94 147 283 393-395
483 **53** 134 138 139 141
151 255 259 260 263 272
356 364-372 454 455 457
458 **54** xxvi xxx 112
113 117 119 123 126 133
228-233 240 358-367 371
375 454-458 460 **55** xxi
113 228 349 447 **56** 97
211 325 412 **57** 117 228
337 420 **58** 97 207 322
408 **59** 113 223 332 420
60 99 212 317 403 **61** 98
206 300 314
Freelove **70** 110 179 198
224 225
Fridley **74** 96
G. Elton **65** 304
Gaylord **94** 87
George **67** 35 **143** 261
George B. **70** 156
George Bruner **104** 36
George Elton **66** 1
George L. **84** 31
George W. **117** 295
Gertrude Newton
(Chambers) **136** 316
Gilbert L. **132** 326
Goodnow **130** 69
Granville **85** 219
Gussie **128** 94
Guy James **136** 316
Halsey **76** 319
Hannah **52** 74 **56** 400 **63**
366 **70** 156 **81** 158 358
87 159 **116** 120 **120** 165
128 217 **136** 310
Hannah (Frink) **136** 325
Hannah (Witter) **136** 310
Hannah Anne **75** lxxxi
Hannah Avory **106** 109
Harmon O. **115** 296
Harold G. **116** 67
Harriet **66** 108 **70** 156
Helen **115** 291
Henry Bamford **118** 78
Hester **67** 35
Hezekiah **81** 174
Hiram **70** 224 **120** 319
132 326
Huldah (Burt) **94** 87
Irene **57** 273
Isaac **70** 311 312 **109** 271
126 209
Isabel Beecher **74** 97

PARK *cont'd*
Isabel Erskine **74** 97
Isabella E. **70** 156
James **61** 268 **79** 3 4 **81** 28
29 **94** 87 **113** 88 **127** 275
278
Jane (Bordwyn) **124** 77
Jane (Slocum) **94** 87
Jane Henry (Wellman)
85 219
Jane M. **116** 120
Janet **79** 3 4
Jared **100** 330
Jean **79** 4
Jemmy **56** 152
Jennie (Woodell) **116** 67
Jeremiah **94** 87
Jerusha **55** 177 **63** 366
68 231
Joan **124** 253
Job **71** 137
Joel **78** 337 **120** 319
132 326
John **52** 74 **58** 204 **60** 403
70 10 110 **76** 53 **79** 3 4
81 28 29 358 361 **82** 59
87 156 157 159 **101** 235
105 279 **106** 109 **116**
120 **124** 250 252-254
128 217 **129** 58 237 **130**
314 **136** 102 323 **139**
103 252 257 **144** 218
John A. **110** 210
John C. **76** 53 **106** 109
140 62
John Calvin **74** 96
John Gray **79** 3 5 6 11
John M. **132** 240
Jonah **63** 366
Jonathan **56** 400 **77** 281
91 265
Joseph **73** 160 **76** 272 **85**
219 **90** 363 **91** 94 **133**
263 **136** 316 361 **142**
175 **147** 113
Josephine **141** 54
Josephine (Rogers)
89 237
Joshua **63** 365 **110** 28
Josiah **77** 280 **78** 19 **84** 87
95 285 **140** 232
Katharine Dorrance
107 132
Kennedy Delyle **83** 125
233
Kitura Taylor **80** 158
Konah (Bush) **126** 170
Laban **127** 80
Lawrence **57** xxxv **61**
xxxiii **62** vi 98 **63** vi 304
64 vii **65** vii **66** vii
xlviii **67** vii 198 309 **68**
vii xxx 18 119 **69** vii 94
70 vii **71** vii **72** vii **75**
xvii **76** 197 **79** 3 4 6-10
212 **81** 28 120 **96** 321
144 348
Leeanna **122** 320
Leighton **57** xlvi
Leonard **85** 219
Leonard Wellman **85** 219

PARK *cont'd*
Levi **63** 366 **90** 260
Lora **80** 45
Lora Howard **80** 45
Loren C. **84** 420
Louise (Draper) **115** 296
Lucinda (Brayton) **116** 67
Lucretia **70** 227
Lucy **56** 400 401 **70** 223
71 40 **77** 30 **81** 361 **94**
198 **135** 158 **136** 313
Lucy (Bancroft) **95** 285
Lucy (Donahe) **111** 303
306
Lucy B. **77** 177
Lulu I. **117** 295
Luther **93** 115
Lydia **63** 366 **70** 226 **78**
379 **79** 246 **95** 172
Lydia Amelia **100** 315
Lyman **94** 87
M. J. **116** 120
Margaret **56** 37 **67** 372
69 164 **79** 4 **81** 29 **136**
102
Margaret (Stewart)
147 117
Margaret Alice **78** 175
Maria **74** 96 97 **79** 5
Maria (Deming) **109** 271
Maria Davis **79** 7 11
Martha **54** 39 **57** 205 **71**
258 259 266 268 **81** 29
88 85 **97** 81 **101** 51 271
122 320 **136** 312 316-
318 320 323 328 329
Martha (Chaplin) **94** 87
136 102 335
Martha (Holgrave) **136**
309 312 314 316-318 321
331 332 334
Martha Bessac (Frear)
85 220
Martha Billings **81** 174
Mary **51** 421 **56** 44 255 **67**
373 **70** 110 198 227 **76**
272 **81** 29 358 **87** 56 **92**
389 **101** 235 **116** 120
123 112 **124** 216 **127**
201 275 **130** 314 **132** 95
136 316
Mary (Allyn) **136** 310
Mary (Church) **118** 271
Mary (Edwards) (Church)
120 177
Mary (Eveleth) (Rust)
135 30
Mary (MacDonald)
130 314
Mary (Mann) **116** 120
Mary (Sanderson)
128 121
Mary (Witter) **136** 323
Mary Ann **70** 156 **96** 189
Mary B. (Nowell) **126** 66
Mary E. **92** 168
Mary Jane **82** 279
Matilda **80** 158 **84** 415
Matthew **65** 220 370 **79** 47
140 232
Mercy (Safford) **136** 313

PARK *cont'd*
Millie **78** 175
Molly **127** 201 273 274
Moses **57** 386 **71** 40 136
Moses Sanford **120** 319
132 326
Myron **133** 24
Nancy **66** 109 **79** 5 **128** 96
177
Nathan **56** 11 **126** 170
130 314
Nathan Grier **113** 242
115 154 228 **117** 76 **122**
42 **143** 302 338
Nathan Grier (Mrs.) **88** 86
Nathaniel **52** 468 **62** 230
136 313 316
Nehemiah **70** 315 316 **71**
37 40 136 **147** 117
Nell **81** 221
Norman **70** 156
Olive Jane **134** 332
Oliver **71** 138
Olmsted **91** 331
Orilla B. **136** 312
Oscar F. **115** 296
Patience **70** 229
Patrick **118** 269
Paul **70** 107 **119** 317 **135** 30
Perme **64** 155
Persis **88** 212
Peter **59** 112 **60** 403 **63** 366
Phebe **55** 177 **116** 118
144 221
Polly **56** 257 **59** 110
Prentice **70** 231
Prince **55** 179
Rachel **63** 365 **71** 40
Rachel (Leffingwell)
94 87
Ransalear **57** 289
Rebecca **54** 400 **59** 255 **70**
229 **114** 181 **127** 275
278 **132** 108 114
Rebecca (Hemmingway)
114 181
Richard **53** 113 114 **56** 11
60 189 **63** 304 **74** 241
75 lxxxi **78** 268 **113** 55
Richards **85** 219
Robert **51** 268 **54** 39 **55**
177 **59** 112 **60** 189 403
70 226 **81** 160 **94** 87
104 201 **113** 88 **115** 152
118 268 269 271 **119**
237 **121** 237 **127** 80 **136**
86 102 335 **147** 109 113
Robert Hall **74** 97
Robert William **94** 86 87
Roger **65** 239
Rosanna **57** 205 **81** 28
Roswell **81** 160 **94** 228
Roxana **106** 109
Roxanna B. (Nichols)
85 219
Ruby Rilla **107** 131
Ruel **63** 373
Ruhama (Fuller) **94** 87
Russell **98** 179 **101** 235
Ruth **56** 11 **70** 232 **122** 320
Sally **70** 230 **71** 37 **116** 120

PARK *cont'd*
127 274
Sally (Cushing) **125** 218
Sally (McDowell) **132** 326
Samuel **70** 315 **71** 40 **128**
94 **130** 69
Sarah **52** 427 **53** 113 **55** 177
56 11 **68** 231 235 **70** 109
151 160 **77** 281 **78** 19
422 **84** 87 **93** 115 **94** 47
114 181 **122** 320 **147** 67
Sarah (Geer) **136** 313 316
Sarah (Gibbs) **85** 219
Sarah (Gifford) **129** 236
237
Sarah (Hemmingway)
114 181
Sarah (Jackson) **88** 284
Sarah (Sprague) **94** 283
Sarah A. **121** 145 **122** 146
Sarah Hoyt Brown **120** 77
Sarah J. **132** 326
Sarah Jane (McDowell)
120 319
Sarah Violetta (Gaylord)
94 86
Sibyl **70** 229 **71** 37 40
Silas **130** 69
Simon **71** 137
Solomon **101** 48 **116** 111
Sophia **66** 110
Stephen **101** 51
Stuart James **79** 3-5
Submit **52** 468
Susan **88** 285
Susan (Wild) **88** 277
Susanna **55** 177 **116** 120
Susanna (Vannoy) **109** 75
Susanna F. **70** 156
Suzanna (Cooley) **110** 28
Sylvia Ann **76** 25
Thaddeus **56** 257
Thaddeus D. **81** 275
Thankful **77** 280
Theedy **111** 150 151
Theoda **85** 223 **136** 309 314
316 318 321 331 332 334
Thirza **86** 290
Thomas **53** 113 238 **54** 39
55 177 **57** 205 **64** 343
70 217 **79** 3 4 **81** 28 29
358 **87** 157 **94** 87 **132**
108 114 **136** 101 310
139 103 257 **141** 299
Thomas B. **88** 279 284
Thomas Eldon **122** 320
Thomas Lawrence
Motley **79** 11
Timothy **70** 232 **71** 135
78 379 **116** 118 120
Umberzinda **122** 320
Virgil Hickox **136** 316
W. M. **97** 59
Warham **65** 81 **108** 98 99
144 266
William **54** 39 **62** 95 **63**
304 366 **66** 109 **70** 177
224 311 315 **71** 40 **77**
228 **79** 3 4 7 **81** 28 29
158 **84** 430 **85** 291 455
97 11 **106** 109 **116** 120

PARK *cont'd*
124 77 253 **127** 201 273
274 **136** 102 309 312 314
316-318 321 325 331 332
334 **137** 88 **142** 114 118
143 258 **144** 222
William C. **88** 277
William Driver **62** 314
William E. **55** lxxviii
William Henry **94** 283
William J. **116** 67
William M. **101** 235
Zachariah **122** 320
Zebulon **70** 229 **71** 136
136 313
PARKER Parcker
—— **51** 357 491 494 **53**
233 248 267 **54** 232 343
344 **55** 116 350 **56** 185
57 262 337 **60** 189 212
64 55 **75** 136 **76** 230 **91**
265 **92** 11 17 281 314
323 350 354 357 **93** 60
61 63 **94** 221 **96** viii 302
100 16 174 192 239 **105**
29 325 **106** 16 **108** 214
109 42 **111** 29 **113** 170
174 183 250 **114** 7 **122**
59 **124** 247 **136** 188 **138**
41 **140** 69 233 235 245
248 253 **144** 324 **145**
173
— Capt. **70** 301 **112** 204
— Col. **85** 21
— Dr. **69** 211 213 216 222
70 12 20 302 308 **83** 150
— Mr. **55** 409 **63** 373 **65**
362 **66** 279 **67** 24 175 **70**
214 **80** 302 **86** 44 **92** 11
131 41 **142** 143 363
— Mrs. **62** 130 **69** 10
83 195
— Rev. **133** 306 309
— Rev. Dr. **98** 279 280
— Rev. Mr. **62** 277
— Widow **65** 360 **70** 19
125 78
—— (Cutler) **140** 56 233
—— (Hall) **140** 150
—— (Hanks) **86** 19
—— (Powell) **140** 237
—— (Sears ?) **113** 176
—— (Townsend) **140** 232
—— (Ward) **94** 357
—— (Whiting) **113** 172
A. **91** 331
A. Deloss **100** 174
A. G. **60** 189
Aaron **58** 373 **63** 257 260 **64** 79
74 lxv **95** 279 **113** 15 112
Abbie M. (Nicholas)
86 366
Abby L. (Fogg) **83** 180
185
Abby O. **114** 8
Abby S. **114** 8
Abel **63** 194 257 260 **64** 79
67 118-120 122 **69** 12 16
118-120 126 **74** xlv
Abiah **57** 22
Abial **110** 61

PARKER *cont'd*
Abiel **55** 260 **56** 257 **67** 218
Abigail **51** 448 **54** 387 388
  55 263 376 **56** 255 **57**
  103 107 205 **60** 158 **61**
  73 **62** 156 **63** 319 320 **64**
  39 43 144 **66** 329 **67** 217
  69 8 10-13 17 118 119
  223 300 **73** 285 **75** 212
  78 400 **81** 150 **83** 17 **87**
  358 **95** 280 **102** 200 **105**
  160 203 **110** 61 **111** 95
  112 199 259-261 **113** 15
  16 18-21 24 113 116 120
  169 170 172 181 182 250
  257 260 **114** 14 136 **120**
  239 **121** 24 **122** 132 **124**
  52 108 **128** 211 **133** 136
Abigail (Bancroft) **94** 314
Abigail (Barss) **127** 279
Abigail (Bond) **113** 108
Abigail (Bryant) (Eaton)
  137 325
Abigail (Butler) **127** 112
Abigail (Coggeshall)
  113 259
Abigail (Hall) **133** 291
Abigail (Hewes) **113** 171
Abigail (Holmes) **124**
  108 109
Abigail (Lakin) **126** 15
Abigail (Loring) **113** 169
Abigail (Lumbert)
  112 200
Abigail (Mackintire)
  104 132
Abigail (Nason) **83** 17
Abigail (Pope) **113** 261
Abigail (Sawtell) **126** 8
Abigail (Swift) **133** 291
Abigail (Tobey) **113** 259
Abigail Gorham **113** 250
Abigail Hart (Parkman)
  91 215
Abigail Holmes **124** 109
Abigail Needham
  (Andrews) **110** 36
Abigail Prescott **69** 217
  70 21 23 137 140-142
  144 300
Abijah **64** 145 **69** 122 123
  218 **70** 137 297 **115** 44
  125 288
Abney **64** 86
Abraham **51** 447 448 **54** 58
  55 443 **63** 257 **64** 79 **74**
  xlv **85** 445 **88** 347 349
  353 **99** 334 **103** 320 **104**
  47 **112** 154 **135** 340 341
Achsah **56** 142 **57** 151
Achsah (Handy) **114** 9 10
  126 104
Ada R. **54** 388 389
Adaline **58** lvi 389 **113** 118
Adaline M. (Wilson)
  89 196
Adeline **113** 250
Affia **105** 311
Agnes **52** 66 **65** 63 **91** 263
Agnes (Gyle) **113** 104
Albert J. **80** 30

PARKER *cont'd*
Albin Kendall **78** 332
  79 203
Alexander **58** 170 **64** 361
  366 **83** 62 **100** 174 **102**
  276 **104** 47 **124** 109
Alexander A. **114** 137
Alford **88** 146
Alfred (Mrs.) **103** 312
Alice **60** 286 **64** 37 149 341
  70 66 **76** 227 230 **97** 158
  112 133 152 193-195 197
  143 299 301 **144** 360
Alice (Sawyer) **111** 139
Alice Bright **95** 305
Allen **114** 11
Alma **70** 208 **72** 308
Almena W. **85** 429 430
Almira **113** 120 250
Almira (Roberts) **121** 142
Almira (Warren) **114** 13
Almira Sophronia
  113 120
Alpheus Brown **72** 308
Alton Brooks **79** 137
  81 340
Alton Brooks (Mrs.) **77**
  322 **78** 206
Alverde H. **97** 128
Alvin Afflick **86** 223
Alvin Afflick (Mrs.) **75**
  xxiii 65 **86** 202 223 236
Alvin Hallett **86** 223
Alvin Mercer **86** 223
Amanda **58** 283
Amelia **115** 25 108 **145** 134
Amelia Day **78** 206
Americus V. **124** 36-41
Ammi I. **123** 51
Amory **74** 151 **75** 17
Amos **58** 58 **74** 153 **75** 32
  83 397 **115** 190 **121** 142
Amos E. **75** 16 17
Amos Rich **83** 397
Amy (Baldwin) **93** 288
Andrew **56** 287 288 **84** 100
  112 122
Andrew Johnson **64** 208
Angeline (Mason) **111** 80
Ann **54** 346 388 **69** 156 **73**
  285 289 291 **76** 263 **81**
  495 **82** 51 **87** 203 **88** 282
  91 141 **93** 364 **96** 234
  400 **113** 108 **114** 135
  121 142 **146** 371 372
  379 **148** 142
Ann (Pendergast)
  132 275
Ann (Rogers) **127** 210
Ann Eliza **78** 298 **81** 243
Ann Maria (Martin)
  126 65
Ann Mary **83** 174
Ann Sophia **66** 106
Anna **55** 259 263 **57** 147 **61**
  72 **75** 17 136 **77** 297 **80**
  330 **82** 51 **87** 259 **88** 347
  100 174 **105** 203 **106**
  316 **113** 181 182 **114** 8
  135-138 **117** 319 **121**
  142 **124** 109 **126** 6 9

PARKER *cont'd*
Anna (Bragg) **131** 73
Anna (Hardey) **91** 265
Anna (Hix) **124** 109
Anna (Marchant) **114** 12
Anna (Plummer) **121** 142
Anna (Porter) **106** 316
Anna (Upham) **114** 7
Anna Augusta (Elliott)
  84 101
Anna Lane **106** 316
Anna Laura **97** 74
Anna Louise (Crocker)
  113 254
Anna Tucker **77** 297
Anna Virginia **121** 156
Anna W. **75** 17
Anna Whitney **63** 258
Anne **55** 264 **64** 43 **85** 455
  87 203 **88** 80 **93** 364 370
  99 384 **113** 176
Anne (Handy) **114** 10
Anne (Quincy) **102** 304
Anne (Rust) **102** 304
Anne (Tucker) **136** 321
Anne Avery **113** 257 259
Anne Sophia **113** 256
Annie **62** 63
Annie (Thompson)
  101 339
Annie C. **75** xxiii
Annie Catherine
  (Bloodgood) **86** 223
Annis **122** 250
Annis (Gyle) **113** 104
Anselm **113** 178 **114** 137
  138
Anson Beach **105** 61
Anstress **113** 113
Apphia **105** 311 **113** 183
Arabella **114** 8
Archilas **62** 328
Arethusa **67** 119
Arthur G. **77** 176
Arthur L. **114** 10
Arvilla **134** 58
Asa **62** 63 **76** 263 **85** 10 **92**
  273 280 323 **109** 58 213
Asa S. **78** 299
Asenath **76** 97 **81** 57
Ashael Eliakim **89** 313
Augusta **75** 17
Augusta Cornelia **72** 308
Augusta M. **105** 115
Augustin **83** 359
Augustus **53** 71 **56** xiii
  xli li 1 **78** 428 **86** 343
Augustus G. **66** l 94
Aurelia **114** 10
Austen **141** 133 134
Averick **113** 258 259
Averick (Standish) **93** 186
  113 258
Avery **58** 369 **113** 21-23
  170-172 259
Avery Fortune **113** 261
Avis Miriam **83** 427 437
Azricam **68** 202 203 **69** 155
  96 233
B. **136** 57
Barbara **141** 133

PARKER *cont'd*

Barbara (Elseley) **94** 221
Barbara Neville **92** 210
Barnabas **68** 169 **105** 203
  113 181 **114** 8 9 **145** 361
Bartlett **113** 172
Bathsheba **65** 355 **114** 101
Bathsheba (Robie)
  112 153
Bathsheba (Smith)
  114 101
Beatrice **76** 230 **80** 302
Becca **106** 184
Belinda **75** 96
Belle A. **78** 44
Benjamin **51** 448 **54** 293
  56 37 254 **59** 107 151 **61**
  33 **63** 173 **64** 37 **67** 240
  241 **69** 363 **71** 130 **72**
  251 **75** 32 **79** 144 442 **80**
  130 **82** 51 **84** 261 **88** 146
  90 233 253 **91** 206 231
  272 **94** 95 **97** 142 **98** 335
  100 65 **105** 86 **106** 182
  107 313 **108** 301 **109**
  213 **112** 153 194 196 197
  264 265 **113** 107 108 111
  177 182 183 249 253 **114**
  5 11 12 135 136 138 **120**
  247 **126** 8 97 **127** 54 56
  201 202 204 210 279 **128**
  207 209 **130** 131
Benjamin Franklin **54**
  151 **64** 233 **117** 317 **118**
  215
Benjamin G. **76** 36
Benjamin Keith **113** 253
Benjamin Marston **113**
  252 253
Bernice Louise **102** 124
Bethiah **61** 251 356 **78** 428
  113 15 105 112 177 **114**
  12 137
Bethiah (Bassett) **113** 104
  105 **128** 207
Bethiah (Crowell) **114** 12
Bethiah (Swift) **114** 137
Bethuel **72** 99
Betsey **59** 107 **66** 276 **69**
  213 **70** 23 **75** 16 **76** 87
  80 130 **90** 259 **95** 372
  100 191 **106** 185 **113**
  113 120 181 183 260 261
  114 7 10 11 **125** 288 **128**
  178 180 183 **140** 131
Betsey (Brown) **128** 211
Betsey (Hinckley) **113** 178
  114 137
Betsey (Johnson)
  (Perkins) **113** 113
Betsey (Manning) **88** 330
Betsey (Walker) **90** 229
  248
Betsey C. **114** 137
Betsey D. **113** 20
Betsey Davis **113** 168
Betsey Hubbell **101** 233
  235
Betsey Summes **62** 153
Betty **67** 219 **69** 244 **113**
  22-24 172-174 **114** 137

PARKER *cont'd*

Betty (Johnson) **113** 174
Beulah **56** 34
Bradstreet **68** 206
Bridget **64** 208 **77** lxxxv
Bridget (Bosworth)
  (Papillon) **135** 26
Caleb **97** 214 **109** 212
  126 124
Calvin **111** 80 **114** 10
  126 104
Calvin C. **107** 211
Calvin L. **115** 296
Calvin Thomas **114** 14
Candace Augusta **89** 21
Capen **126** 276
Cardee **54** 443
Carlus **115** 54
Caroline **113** 119 120 249
  257
Caroline (Durrell)
  134 149
Caroline (Harding)
  103 44
Caroline A. **53** 233
Caroline Amelia **55** 350
Caroline D. (Pollard)
  99 334
Caroline H. (Raynes)
  117 230
Caroline L. **85** 445
Caroline M. (Keith)
  113 253
Caroline Nelson **91** 203
  113 314
Carrie **54** 389
Carrie Edda (Newcomb)
  112 153
Catherine **113** 15 113 **124**
  52 **133** 73
Catherine (Raynes)
  117 228
Charity **58** 170 **111** 287
Charity (Soule) **113** 256
Charity G. **97** 232
Charity G. (Littlefield)
  97 18 238
Charity Soule **113** 256 257
Charles **65** 36 **70** xxxv **75**
  32 **86** 19 **96** 330 **97** 127
  104 47 **114** 7 136 **115**
  296 **140** 233
Charles A. **114** 10
Charles C. **114** 137
Charles E. **55** 424 **106** 316
Charles E. C. **114** 136 137
Charles F. **85** 445 **100** 191
  114 7
Charles Francis **112** 258
Charles Hamilton
  106 162
Charles Hamilton (Mrs.)
  107 134
Charles Henry **145** 313
Charles L. **92** 341 **109** 16
Charles Parsons **92** 312
Charles Schoff **70** xxxvi
Charles W. **85** 445 **110** 302
Charles W. L. **109** 16
Charles Wallingford **64**
  xxxiii **70** xxvii xxxv

PARKER *cont'd*

xxxvi
Charles Wesley **114** 10
Charles Willie **85** 445
Charlotte **128** 39
Charlotte (Jenkins)
  113 178
Charlotte Alida (Willis)
  84 101
Charlotte Amelia (Clark)
  113 252
Chase **88** 347
Chauncey **101** 235
Chloe **113** 106
Christian **66** 252
Clara **86** 198
Clara Emily (Barton)
  107 211
Clara Maud **101** 125
Clara V. **63** 258
Clarence Walter **102** 124
  105 61 68 132
Claribel (Merchant)
  85 292
Clarissa (Stafford) **90** 49
Clarissa Goves (Kelley)
  145 307
Clarissa M. (Shepard)
  124 41
Clark **125** 294
Clement **113** 125 195 **119**
  144 **147** 259
Clementina Augusta
  137 327
Clementine **121** 142
Clitheroe Mason **96** 296
Clorida Ann (Bearse)
  113 254
Clyde Harrison **81** 222
  237
Colburn **82** 51
Collins **137** 327 337
Comfort **124** 109
Corilla **134** 58
Cornelia Asenath **82** 16
Cortland (Mrs.) **85** 330
Cortlandt **105** 129
Corydon **134** 58
Cosbi B. **60** li
Cuff **82** 51
Cuthbert **127** 11
Cynthia **99** 54 **113** 250
  114 7
Cynthia (Fish) **113** 250
Cynthia Anna
  (Wallingford) **84** 101
Cynthia E. S. **114** 7
Cyrene T. **54** 389
Cyrus **115** 18
D. **91** 331
Dana **75** 17 **97** 128
Daniel **54** 445 **69** 222 299
  300 305 **70** 14-18 21-23
  137 139 141-145 212 296
  297 307 **79** 442 **91** 94 **97**
  131 269 **106** 101 **109**
  213 **112** 194-198 257 258
  260-265 **113** 17-19 21-24
  104 105 114-116 119 168
  169 171 172 174 182 249
  261 **114** 9 10 **126** 192

PARKER *cont'd*
128 207 144 266
Daniel G. 76 42
Daniel H. 85 445
Daniel Henry 114 138
Daniel Pinkney 92 250
343 93 59 63 320 94 47
163 140 323
David 56 318 57 144 62
202 68 217 69 297 70 14
17-20 23 116-119 167
168 181 183 250-254 128
180 181 135 160 137
363 140 233
David Johnson 59 280
David L. 75 xcii
David Lewis 114 8
Davison 129 51
Dean Huntington 96 296
Deborah 54 58 55 404 56
38 64 43 145 149 74 3
91 81 93 187 105 86
113 110 176 249 250
128 209
Deborah (Black) 113 251
Deborah (Crowell) 113
102 109 110 128 208 209
Deborah (Lester) 113 176
Deborah Young 113 252
Delia (Curtis) 91 385
Delia (Lord) 89 24
Deliverance 55 407 56 270
68 169 246 69 182 273
93 232 233 108 91 121
25
Deliverance (Dodge)
84 100
Deliverance (Jenkins)
114 9
Deliverance J. 69 182
Della (Abbott) 96 330
Desire 61 340 80 130 105
88 203 113 18-20 106
111 122 167 181 182 114
10 124 69 126 97 161
127 201 128 114
Desire (Davis) 113 19
166 168 119 125 124 69
128 211
Desire (Freeman) 113 18
20 106 255 124 69 128
211
DeWitt 100 174
Dewitt Lansing 82 16
Dinah 67 87 88
Dolla 61 246
Dominicus 88 347
Dorcas 58 373
Dorcas (Monroe) 84 100
Doris 74 301
Doris Cranston 80 30
Dorothy 55 347 56 37 76
227 230 92 362
Dorothy Leighton
(Dutton) 110 229
Dorothy Little 105 115
Dorothy Mills 112 238
Dorothy R. 109 109
Dorus (Graves) 113 183
Duke 61 395
Dydimus 56 137

PARKER *cont'd*
E. F. 91 331
E. G. (Miss) 84 335
E. W. 132 165
Eben A. 109 15 16
Eben P. 109 15 16
Ebenezer 56 144 57 153
205 260 65 357 67 87 88
78 123 81 150 471 84
100 94 63 319 103 192
105 86-88 309 112 200
265 113 17 18 109-111
118-121 179-182 128
208 209 137 238
Ebenezer Fitch 113 262
Ebenezer Francis 102 304
Edith 63 257 260 86 198
91 59 92 162 93 136 153
292 99 334 100 44 115
Edith Bancroft 97 128
Edith Ellen 82 271
Edmund 59 86 280 75 32
97 395
Edmund Nye 113 120
Edna (Hardy) 99 334
Edward 54 21 22 389 57
105 60 290 66 328 81
130 109 281 113 250
127 279 129 50
Edward Cooke 114 136
Edward E. 63 108
Edward Ernest 54 389
Edward Everett 64 231
Edward G. 71 42
Edward Hazen 92 357
Edward L. 117 244 245 250
124 241 248
Edward Ludlow 63 xxxiii
65 xxi 74 xxviii 80 102
217 81 471
Edward Lutwyche
64 229 231
Edward Melville 98 213
Edward Parry 94 357
Edwin 88 17 121 142
Edwin P. 63 306
Edwin Pond 58 107 118
107 273 119 91 148 25
Edwin R. (Mrs.) 105 124
Edwin Roscoe (Mrs.)
95 147
Elbridge 73 182
Elbridge G. 59 107
Elbridge George 134 149
Elbridge Gerry 73 101
Eleanor 61 393 113 118
251
Eleanor (Post) 146 371
Eleanor (Whittemore)
108 163
Eleanor Stanley 59 xlviii
65 xxi 90 125 102 61 127
304
Eleanor Whitemore
55 396
Eleazer 63 295 64 34 67
87 88 106 96
Eli 90 163
Eliakim 120 17
Elial 81 57
Elias 71 358 93 304 100 66

PARKER *cont'd*
Elijah 52 417 98 105 110
241 124 108 109
Eliphalet 60 76 267 268
397 398 61 33
Eliphalet C. 59 211
Eliphaz 125 173
Elisha 58 174 65 319 360
70 138 74 151 173 75 16
17 104 47 105 89 309-
311 106 182 112 192-
194 196 200 257 265 113
17 18 23 111 112 117 118
171 183 184 252 260 261
114 11 12 115 119 124
108 109 126 97 276 128
209-211 132 240
Eliza 82 176 295 102 301
113 120 257 116 211
Eliza (Bancroft) 97 127
Eliza (Sheppard) 126 66
Eliza (Wilcox) 123 307
Eliza Ann 83 480 85 445
Eliza Davis 113 122 167
168
Eliza Dennet 81 395
Elizabeth 51 273 447 52
487 54 22 388 392 55
170 260 393 443 56 143
287 288 57 147 223 257
60 311 61 203 245 63 30
170 175 65 124 167 298
319 66 107 67 217 321
70 24 73 181 221 74 294
296 77 275 82 51 284
295 83 25 26 85 399 88
146 278 347 90 168 169
259 92 172 94 318 105
28 310 109 39 55 279
281 110 61 225 111 83
90 132 112 121-123 113
23 24 107 176 183 256
259 114 12 14 135 136
138 121 165 265 128
206 208 210 133 124 306
309 135 340 137 238
332 336 337 140 69
Elizabeth (Baker) 114 12
Elizabeth (Bartlett)
113 260
Elizabeth (Blossom)
128 206
Elizabeth (Bridges)
93 291
Elizabeth (Brown) 84 100
Elizabeth (Calthorpe)
109 275-277 279 280
Elizabeth (Crowell)
114 11
Elizabeth (Gray) 85 330
Elizabeth (Hall) 113 172
Elizabeth (Hinckley)
112 192
Elizabeth (Kelley) 128 210
Elizabeth (Longe) 104 38
Elizabeth (Macy) 113 252
Elizabeth (O'Kelley)
128 210
Elizabeth (Page) 105 28 29
Elizabeth (Phillips) 97 57
Elizabeth (Smith) 114 135

PARKER *cont'd*
128 208
Elizabeth (Steele) 97 128
Elizabeth (Wright)
148 145
Elizabeth A. 97 127
Elizabeth Ann 54 389
113 262 127 279
Elizabeth C. 113 254
Elizabeth Clapp (Stone)
102 304
Elizabeth FitzRandolph
98 335
Elizabeth G. (Brown)
113 251
Elizabeth Gardiner
(Clark) 113 252
Elizabeth Grace 128 211
Elizabeth H. 85 445
Elizabeth Helen 74 301
Elizabeth Johnson 64 42
Elizabeth Lyman 63 258
85 192
Elizabeth M. 113 250
Elizabeth Stebbins 66 l
192
Ella Maria 67 xxxiv 306
Ellen 54 389 61 393
100 174
Ellen C. (Sawyer) 121 177
Ellen Miranda (Bates)
112 153
Elmina Augusta 145 158
Elmira 113 250
Elnathan 113 111 182
Elva C. 92 341
Elverton 113 181
Elvira 133 124
Emeline 92 172 97 81
Emeline (Finch) 92 172
Emeline (Howland) 113
118 250
Emeline (Wilson) 112 153
Emeline Finch 92 172
Emeline Perkins 105 115
Emerson 108 306
Emily 86 442 93 256
Emily C. 59 107
Emily E. 68 246
Emily Elizabeth 69 182
273
Emily H. 113 254
Emily Richardson
(Coller) 84 100
Emily Taylor 93 63 94 163
Emma F. 75 16
Emme 53 347 69 11 117
118 120 124 126 127 213
70 295
Emmet 90 378
Enoch 65 363 104 242
Enos 57 412 106 160
Ephraim 69 334 83 359
85 430 94 224 109 212
213 113 178 114 137
174 137 240
Erastus 67 353
Erastus Otis 114 10
Ernest Wellesley (Mrs.)
103 120
Esther 51 447 448 56 36

PARKER *cont'd*
57 102 75 32 89 89 126
122 134 335 141 192
Esther (Holt) 113 261
Esther (Niblow) 129 52
Esther (Silvester) 86 89
Esther Damon 75 248
Ethel C. 130 55
Ethel Winnifred 109 130
Etta 97 349
Etta Mary (Robertson)
89 313
Etta May (Maskers)
85 411
Eulia 76 97
Eunice 52 417 55 265 58
51 63 326 64 42 211 67
87 72 99 74 173 75 17
93 343 101 80 113 121
122 177 114 135 115
306 128 211
Eunice (Brainard) 128 208
Eunice (Doane) 113 176
177 128 208
Eunice (Hinckley)
113 121
Eunice (Jordan) 128 210
Eunice Ann (Rogers)
120 15
Eunice Hinckley 113
121-123 167
Eunice M. 74 173
Eunice W. 75 16
Eva 121 142
Experience 67 118 217 80
130 112 261 113 15 114
122 114 10 134 135 124
216 127 126 142 40-43
45 47 50
Experience (Cooke)
114 136
Experience (Nickerson)
113 15 114 124 52 216
Ezekiel 78 139 115 195
Ezekiel Hersey 113 117
168 251 256
Ezra 60 li 64 156 157
144 215
Ezra Jesse 64 lxx
Ezra Jordan 128 211
F. D. 75 17
Family 147 259
Fanny (Sanford) 114 137
Fanny M. 75 17
Fear 113 106 107 175
119 38
Fearnot 68 202 203 69 155
96 234
Ferdinand A. 113 254
Flavel 72 308
Flora 82 51
Florella Augusta 104 315
Florence 93 255 116 76
Fondall Alexander
107 234
Frances 54 389 65 375 69
99 74 83 77 194 113 175
114 138
Frances Ann 69 99
Frances Eliza (Bills)
125 291

PARKER *cont'd*
Frances Marion 82 175
Francis 99 257 113 134
127 279
Francis C. 113 253 254
Francis E. 51 30 62 280
84 31
Francis Edward 82 423
Francis Jewett 63 xiv
lxviii 193 194 257-260 64
xliii lxx 79 95 330 65 309
93 61
Francis Shaw 128 211
Francis Vose 58 xxxvii
xlv 63 258
Francis W. 108 306
Frank 85 445 90 378
Frank Laselle 89 24
Franklin 65 133 100 174
Frederic Leon 54 389
Frederick 75 17 113 118
178 179 250 259 114 6 7
137 128 212
Frederick Elton 113 254
Frederick Wesley 53 372
64 vii 65 v vii xiv xx
66 v vii 67 v 68 ix xxi
78 215 298 299
Freelove 127 305
Freelove (Lovey)
(Meacham) 114 12
Freeman 66 102 103 106
107 74 96 113 18-21 117
166 167 252 255 119 125
124 69
G. 92 172
Gamaliel 56 287 288
Gara Mabel 84 191
Gardner 57 412 89 196
George 65 63 67 286 68
169 246 69 182 273 74
83 77 194 84 100 92 172
101 29 104 3 105 267
113 108 178 251 114 9
137 140 233
George A. 79 141
George Alanson 93 291
292
George F. 91 44 126 245
246
George Henry 69 182
85 445
George Moore 58 373
George S. 114 137
George Sewell 73 290
George Swinnerton
(Mrs.) 85 197
George T. 84 31
George W. 64 213 85 445
88 343 115 25 54 134
224
George Webster 89 313
Gertrude Codman 63 258
Gertrude E. 85 292 129 51
Gideon 57 355 59 275 277
135 100 124
Gladice Rice 71 42
Gookin 93 116
Gordon 129 51
Grace 62 95 84 446
109 230

PARKER *cont'd*
Grace (Covell) **116** 67
Grace (Matthews) **86** 44
Grace Alberta **89** 313
Grace Badger **97** 157 **103** 78 125
Grace E. **124** 259
Greenlief **63** 374 375
Grosvenor **113** 262
Gurdon Saltonstall **74** xlvi
H. **91** 331
Hananiah **70** xxxv **81** 471 **84** 100
Hannah **51** 448 **52** 82 **54** 23 388 **55** 396 **56** 31 37 144 **57** 22 26 102 152 370 **60** li 72 194 **61** 379 **63** 374 **65** 36 **66** 269 **68** 169 **72** 251 316 **74** 208 **78** 123 428 **81** 121 125 **83** 167 **85** 233 **92** 114 301 375 **93** 167 **94** 319 **100** 28 **101** 304 **104** 261 **105** 86 **106** 96 **107** 289 **109** 233 **110** 61 **111** 79 191 **112** 194 196 197 199 257 261 263 265 **113** 18-21 105 107 108 111 112 117 121 167 168 174 175 177-180 250 255 256 261 **114** 5 6 8 9 50 135 137 138 **117** 226 **125** 294 **126** 8 12 13 97 106 290 **127** 223 **128** 209 **147** 74
Hannah (Ashley) **124** 109
Hannah (Bumpas) **112** 197
Hannah (Carson) **87** 228 205
Hannah (Chadwick) **113** 112
Hannah (Chase) **99** 334
Hannah (Crosby) **113** 116
Hannah (Davis) **114** 136 **128** 207
Hannah (Dyer) **113** 183 184 **128** 209 210
Hannah (Earl) **113** 171
Hannah (Ewer) **114** 137
Hannah (Fish) **125** 173
Hannah (Gearfield) **97** 214
Hannah (Green) **94** 319
Hannah (Harthan) **135** 341
Hannah (Hathorn) **99** 334
Hannah (Kendall) **94** 221
Hannah (Knock) **90** 233 253
Hannah (Lewis) **114** 135
Hannah (Nye) **114** 136 137
Hannah (Stone) **113** 174
Hannah (Whittemore) **106** 96
Hannah C. **114** 8
Hannah D. **113** 120
Hannah Durkee (Kinney) **108** 301
Hannah Hodges **114** 11

PARKER *cont'd*
Hannah Mariah (Kenney) **108** 214
Hannah N. **114** 6
Hannah Octavia **73** 182
Hannah Patch **58** 373
Hannah R. **73** 101
Hannah S. **76** 36
Hannah Stephens **113** 260
Harmony **113** 22 24
Harriet **59** 211 **78** 123 **106** 109 **113** 116 **114** 137 **129** 51
Harriet (Eldredge) **114** 14
Harriet B. **114** 137
Harriet Brooks (Meriam) **84** 100
Harriet F. **57** 337 **58** xlv
Harriet Felton **93** 292
Harriet Maria **86** 366
Harriet Newell (Felton) **93** 291
Harriet Philetta **111** 167
Harriet S. **113** 254
Harriet Stillman **113** 252
Harriet Wolcott **145** 313
Harvey Drury **72** li
Hathbuck **127** 11
Hattie **54** 389
Hattie May **71** 42
Haven **93** 292
Haven (Mrs.) **94** 145 **99** 154
Helen **84** 101 **89** 230 **92** 320 **105** 127 **115** 291
Helen (James) **91** 216
Helen E. (Fitch) **114** 13
Helen Elizabeth **73** 276
Helen Field (Bidwell) **106** 162
Helen Maria (Vannevar) **113** 253
Heman **114** 12
Henrietta **69** 124 212 295 299 304 307 **70** 9 11 14 15 18 22-24 137 138
Henrietta Hewitt (Fitz Randolph) **98** 335
Henry **58** 236 61 393 **73** 270 **85** 135 268 **88** 386 **92** 354 **95** 186 **99** 297 **104** 262 **109** 276 279 281 **113** 175 176 249 261 **114** 138 **121** 142 **125** 294 **137** 78
Henry A. **57** 417
Henry Ainsworth **74** xxxvii xlv
Henry Avery **113** 171
Henry Bacon **113** 249
Henry Langdon **96** 296
Henry Mandeville **73** 182
Henry Matthews **112** 258
Henry Middleton **67** 321
Henry Seabury **74** xlvi
Henry T. **93** 255 256
Henry Tuke **93** 59
Henry W. **114** 137
Henry Ward **114** 8
Henry Webster **114** 13
Hepzibah **102** 158 **110** 277

PARKER *cont'd*
113 15 114 **114** 135 **123** 134 **135** 77
Hepzibah (Davis) **114** 7
Hepzibah Swan (Sears) **114** 12
Herbert **84** 106 190 **93** 276 291 **94** 143 **98** 290
Herbert C. (Mrs.) **121** 159
Herbert S. **84** 101
Herman **70** xxxvi
Hester **54** 389 **61** 393
Hincker **147** 259
Hincker (Mrs.) **147** 259
Hiram **134** 58
Hiram B. **116** 211
Hitty **113** 249
Hollis **75** 17
Honor **61** 256
Hope **54** 22 23
Horace **83** 180 185 **92** 311
Horatio Newton **95** 97
Howes **114** 11 12
Howes Crowell **114** 12
Hulda Nash (Potter) **114** 6
Huldah **54** 389 **74** 252
Huldah (Emery) **112** 153 **121** 79
Ichabod **79** 37
Ida Laura **133** 154 320
Ida W. M. **65** 133
Ingerson **64** 155
Ira **113** 257 **121** 142
Isaac **51** 447 **55** 443 **56** 359 **57** 412 **63** 194 257 258 260 261 **64** 79 **68** 22 **69** 11 **70** 262 **74** xlv **77** lxxxv **78** 180 286 **91** 269 **92** 350 354 357 **93** 61 63 **94** 42 **100** 191 **107** 313 **108** 243 **109** 213 113 106 107 175 261 **114** 135 **124** 108 **127** 112 **135** 205 **140** 150 232
Isaac Henry **113** 262
Isaac Hinckley **114** 136
Isaac M. **92** 312
Isaac T. **61** 384 **92** 320
Isabel Hopewell Hayden (Mason) **96** 296
Isabel Morgan **81** 111 222
Isabel Morgan (Cady) **96** 296 **97** 161
Isabella **92** 350 **100** 335
Isabelle (Russell) **102** 304
Isadore A. **113** 254
Isaiah **76** 155 156 **106** 182 **107** 107 289 291 292 **108** 110 **109** 43 **113** 18-21 166-169 183 249 251 256 **114** 10-12 136
Isaiah B. **97** 18 238
Israel **121** 142
Ithamar **111** 167
Izetta N. **85** 445
J. **63** 375 **65** 360 **136** 136
J. Chase **121** 177
J. Fred **76** 160
J. L. **55** 443
Jabez **105** 86 203 309 310

PARKER *cont'd*
106 101 102 **113** 111
181 **125** 249
Jacob **51** 447 **52** 66 359 **57**
23 151 256 **62** 94 **63** 246
69 222 **78** 178 **79** 295
97 125 **100** 335 **102** 158
105 86-89 **106** 182-185
107 291 **112** 265 **113**
111 134 182 183 256 **114**
8 11 12 **127** 310 **131** 189
Jael **60** 397 398
James **51** 51 447 **52** 340
53 433 **55** 443 **56** 37 265
57 205 **58** 51 **60** 198 344
369 **63** 319-23 137-146
210-219 294-308 **77** 297
78 44 448 **79** 353 **81** 471
86 19 293 **88** 146 **93** 398
96 233 **99** 310 **100** 63
101 244 **102** 60 **104** 38
88 **105** 207 **108** 161 **112**
197 198 259 **113** 17 18
119-121 253 254 **116** 76
157 **121** 248 **122** 292
126 9 **127** 310 **128** 211
129 50 **131** 110 **135** 220
136 45 46 321 **140** 233
James Alexander **82** 16
James Andrew **106** 316
James Bowdoin **113** 172
James F. **110** 36
James G. **97** 391
James Goodrich **81** 472
James Grace **128** 211
James H. **111** 139
James Henegar **109** 230
James Henry **113** 253
James M. **77** 151
James Phillips **84** 173
85 197
James Swain **81** 471
James T. **114** 136
James W. **128** 94
Jane **53** 248 **60** 387 **61** 245
69 126 213 **92** 81 **100**
174 **112** 153 194-196 258
113 257 **114** 9 **121** 24
142 **126** 97
Jane (Hinds) **114** 10
Jane (Main) **111** 127
Jane (Palmer) **114** 137
Jane (Parrot) **84** 100
Jane A. (Brockway) **78** 367
Jane Delzell (Mercer)
86 223
Jane H. **129** 52
Jane Linwood **80** 30
Jane Standish **93** 185 186
113 259
Jane Thompson **69** 36
Jane Williams **113** 254
Janine Louise **84** 209
Jared **60** 76
Jeanette **108** 306
Jeanette Belle (Hinchliff)
108 306
Jedediah **82** 332 **83** 148
Jedidiah **58** 283 **118** 313
Jeduthan **79** 141
Jefferson **64** 117

PARKER *cont'd*
Jemima **55** 264 392
Jennie **90** 378
Jennie (Bearse) **113** 254
Jennie (Hodgdon)
(Willard) **145** 306
Jeremiah **55** 260 **57** 24 **68**
217 **99** 310 **124** 109 **134**
57 58
Jerome **66** 252
Jerome Wesley **78** 298
Jerusha **90** 259 **113** 15 16
22-24 113 172 176 177
257 **114** 13 135 **124** 216
217 222
Jerusha (Lord) **114** 12
Jerusha (Penfield) **109** 34
128 208
Jerusha (Wentworth)
126 276
Jesse **88** 146 **100** 191 **113**
15 16 112-114 **114** 134-
136 **124** 52
Jessie **129** 51
Jessie M. **115** 54
Jim **84** 352
Joan **60** 357 **61** 258 393
66 253
Joanna **57** 266 **61** 393 **63**
250 251 **64** 145 156 **75**
147 **78** 295 **104** 47 59
182
Job **99** 79 **112** 200 **113** 16
108 177 178 **114** 6 135
138 **124** 217 **129** 234
Joel **51** 32 53 156 **55** 51 199
60 228 **106** 316
John **52** 66 236 **54** 22 23
388 449 **55** 443 **56** 36
265 **57** 23 24 26 102 **58**
373 **59** 387 **60** 287 289
61 169 203 393 **62** 94
127 **63** 29 50 **64** 20 86
145 262 **65** 355 358 **66**
252 **68** 202 **69** 16 155
215 300 301 304-307 **70**
xxxv 9 11 12 14 16 69 138
141 143-146 216 219 **71**
173 **72** 251 **73** 101 **74**
lvi **75** 242 **77** 147 **78** 295
401 **79** 413 **81** 131 **82** 51
182 **84** 100 **85** 238 292
87 157 **89** 334 **92** 50 **93**
291 **94** 221 357 **96** 101
233 **97** 57 327 328 **98**
268 **99** 310 **103** 173 **104**
47 97 **109** 212 **110** 56 61
111 95 **112** 153 177 264
113 106 107 174-177 180
262 **114** 135 **119** 16 17
38 **120** 52 **123** 265 **127**
309 **128** 45-47 208 **131**
41 108-111 **136** 45 **137**
332 **140** 55 141 232 233
245 251 253 **141** 217-219
142 11 **144** 360 **145** 111
146 335 **147** 38 75 77 82
84
John A. **116** 67 **137** 158
John Avery **93** 186 **113**
23 169 170 173 258 259

PARKER *cont'd*
261 **128** 212 **135** 312
John Brooks **73** 101 181
John Cotton **113** 179
John D. **66** lxix **125** 291
John Dalling **82** 423
John Flagg **54** 389
John H. **73** 287 290
John Hatch **114** 6
John Henry **113** 262
John Hinckley **114** 137
John Increase **81** 395
John J. **113** 261
John L. **61** lix
John Lord **57** xxxv **64**
xlvii 330
John M. **54** 388 **110** 302
John Milton Grosvenor
83 203
John Peckins **113** 171
John Sturges **109** 16 **113**
118 167-169
John Tappan **89** 24
John W. **134** 58
Jonas **57** 205 **66** 101 **69** 9-
13 15 17 118 120-123
126 127 211-218 220 222
223 296-300 302-307 **70**
10 11 13 14 20 22 24 142
144 214 215 217 304 305
308 **85** 10 **98** 296
Jonas S. **83** 359
Jonathan **51** 49 **55** 259 264
56 142 144 146 266 269
57 147-149 151 153 253
260 **65** 36 **67** 122 219 **72**
251 **75** 32 **78** 186 **85** 10
87 228 235 **92** 124 279
94 220 221 **95** 279 **99** 79
310 **100** 192 **105** 209
309 **109** 212 **112** 259-
261 **114** 8-10 **120** 278
121 248 **122** 59 **126** 104
144 222 **146** 371
Jordan **128** 211 **147** 76
Joseph **51** 448 **57** 412-414
60 60 **61** 345 379 **63** 30
64 144 **66** 269 **70** 69 77
74 313 **75** 17 **80** 125 **85**
399 **92** 311 316 318 376
93 60 288 291 343 **94**
314 **97** 125 **100** 191 192
104 62 133 182 **105** 87
109 213 **112** 122 123
194 196 199 200 257 263-
265 **113** 19 22-24 106-
108 110 115 116 174-176
179-181 249 250 261 **114**
7 9 **115** 296 **116** 157 119
38 **121** 142 **125** 41 **126** 6
8 213 **127** 226 **128** 209
210 257 **129** 37 **134** 57
58
Joseph Avery **113** 257
Joseph Barss **127** 279
Joseph Brooks Blood-
good **86** 223
Joseph E. **129** 51
Joseph Ford **113** 167 255
124 69
Joseph H. **75** 96

PARKER *cont'd*
Joseph P. **104** 59 133
Joseph Patch **58** 373
Joseph R. **114** 7
Joseph Rush **128** 212
Josephine **68** 153
Josephine Victoria **83** 359
Joshua **56** 142 144 **57** 148
149 151 152 413 **58** 170
61 120 **87** 399 **103** 43
113 16 117 118 251 324
117 16 **137** 253
Joshua Dyer **114** 137
Joshua H. **100** 191
Josiah **51** 447 **55** 260 **56**
143 266 267 **57** 22 23
151 252 253 257 **60** 158
62 153 **65** 360 **69** 12 **70**
xxxv **77** 275 **87** 399 **126**
6 7 **137** 78
Josiah Crocker **113** 249
Josiah R. **103** 44
Josie (Carnahan) **128** 94
Judith **58** 387 **94** 220
Judith (Bancroft) **94** 220
221
Judith J. (Gardner)
113 251
Julia Ann **114** 137 **120** 250
Julia Bryant **97** 391
Julia Maria (Stevens)
85 102
Juliet **97** 349
Katharine **57** 26 **67** 286
353 **83** 203 **91** 111 **114**
136 **141** 133
Katharine Roxana **55** xci
Katharine Vose **93** 292
Katy **56** 266 **57** 253
Kendall **61** 245 246 **62** 25
63 250 **72** 251 **87** 126
Keziah **67** 118-120 218 **78**
428 **101** 261 **108** 262
113 174 261 **114** 11
Keziah C. **113** 249
Knowles **80** 130 **114** 10
L. H. **57** xxxiii
Laura **64** 208 **69** 36
Laura Mason **80** 163
Laura Wolcott (Jackson)
145 313
Laurence H. **106** 77
112 154
Laurence Houghton
105 129 **115** 66
Lavina M. **77** 176
Lavinah **56** 34
Lawrence C. **114** 8
Leafe **70** 295 307
Leander M. **60** 158
Leila **85** 324
Lemuel **69** 218 295
115 127
Leona Lydia **89** 313
Leonard **56** 255 **69** 8 **70**
297 **71** 358
Leonard Fletcher **68** 112
Leonard Moody **69** 304
70 141-146 213-220 295-
300 308
Leroy **60** 158

PARKER *cont'd*
Leslie (Nalle) **87** 174
Letitia H. **73** 287
Levi **69** 10 118 123 212 299
70 213 **75** 96 **93** 398
100 63 **122** 160 **123** 160
133 124
Levi Judson **101** 339
Lewis **113** 178 **114** 137 157
134 58 **143** 257
Lewis Frederick **114** 138
Life **139** 257
Lillian P. (McClarty)
116 67
Linus **120** 52
Lizzie Gertrude (Croft)
89 313
Loae **97** 128
Lois **64** 156 **73** 291 **117** 93
Lola (Hunt) **126** 70
Lora **111** 134 136
Lorenzo **88** 330
Louisa Experience
127 279
Louise (Bearse) **113** 253
Love (Marchant) **113** 178
Lovey **69** 117 217 299 306
307 **70** 9 11 14 15 18 20
21
Lovina E. **75** 18
Luceba (Reed) **124** 69
Lucelia J. **97** 127 128
Lucia M. (Smith) **121** 177
Lucilla P. **94** 47
Lucilla Pinckney **92** 250
Lucinda **55** 199 **58** 373 **74**
153 **96** 333
Lucinda M. **125** 53
Lucretia **52** 340 **93** 342 343
Lucretia Green **92** 316
Lucy **66** 108 318 **79** 202
83 359 **86** 343 347 **87**
179 **93** 256 **94** 92 **109** 16
113 175 260 **114** 6 82
Lucy (Bennett) **113** 261
Lucy (Childs) **113** 249
Lucy (Dunbar) **113** 256
114 138
Lucy (Prior) **85** 430
Lucy (Robinson) **115** 190
Lucy (Smallwood)
113 251
Lucy (Taber) **113** 261
Lucy A. **93** 255
Lucy E. **91** 237
Lucy Ellen **82** 16
Lucy Elmira **94** 196
Lucy G. (Crocker) **113** 249
Lucy Jane **81** 150
Lucy S. (Andrews) **110** 36
Luke **61** 393
Luther **57** 205 **70** 213 **76**
46 **128** 211
Luther L. **86** 89
Lydia **51** 448 **54** 22 23 392
55 260 264 443 **56** 31 32
37 39 44 359 **57** 85 149
225 **61** 245 392 **63** 294
325 **70** 77 **73** 101 **75** 32
81 27 **84** 440 **93** 116 **94**
47 318 **95** 279 **97** 15 **100**

PARKER *cont'd*
191 **108** 291 **110** 61 223
113 16-18 21-24 109 171
179 181 261 **117** 93 **142**
304
Lydia (Bartlett) **113** 21 23
Lydia (Cobb) **112** 199
Lydia (Haskell) **113** 180
181
Lydia (Jenkins) **114** 10
Lydia (Nutting) **93** 232
126 14
Lydia (Parker) **113** 18 23
24
Lydia (Thayer) **89** 313
Lydia A. **73** 101
Lydia A. (Kimball) **126** 70
Lydia A. (Lothrop) **88** 343
Lydia Ann **120** 16
Lydia Bowes **60** 198 **69**
302 **70** 137 197-199 215-
217 219 300
Lydia Church **113** 24 261
Lydia Foss (Goodwin)
96 338
Lydia Mary **63** 50
Lydia N. **114** 137
Lydia P. **114** 8
Lydia Peck **60** 158
Lydia S. **101** 235
M. S. **127** 115
Mabel **105** 61
Mahala **114** 138 **132** 190
Mansfield **92** 172 **147** 70
Marcia C. **89** 381
Marcia F. (Lewis) **114** 7
Marcia O. C. (Durrell)
133 124
Marcus Torrey **114** 13
Marcy **113** 105 110 116 **125**
247 **128** 208
Marcy (Ellis) **113** 257
Margaret **52** 426 **54** 389
62 95 **66** 107 173 **71** 243
78 66 **81** 89 **104** 47 **109**
16 **110** 23 25 **113** 256
125 59 **126** 6 **131** 108
Margaret (Adams)
121 142
Margaret (Sheafe)
(Stratton) **125** 59
Margaretta **121** 178
Margery **63** 175 **115** 306
Maria **101** 168
Maria (Hildreth) **83** 203
Maria (Phinney) **113** 254
Maria Ann (Eldridge)
113 249
Maria Louise **113** 254
Maria Williams **113** 257
Miriam **71** 117
Marianne **113** 119
Marilla (Shaw) **134** 57 58
Marion D. **83** 437 **84** 19
Mark **99** 284
Martha **51** 448 465 **56** 184
57 83 105 152 **67** 286 **70**
359 **78** 402 **80** 130 **92**
317 370 **93** 254 **94** 47
113 109 **114** 9 10 135
121 142 **126** 97 108 **127**

PARKER *cont'd*
126 202 279 **128** 114
132 41
Martha (Carver) **88** 230
Martha (Knowles) **102** 60
114 10 **126** 283
Martha (Lasell) **88** 366
89 24
Martha (Lewis) **114** 11
Martha (Livermore)
99 334
Martha (Lovell) **114** 9
126 104
Martha (Mayhew) **113** 108
109 **114** 7 8 135
Martha (Stiles) **110** 241
Martha (Wellington)
87 291
Martha Addie **81** 387
82 178
Martha Ann (Briggs)
126 276
Martha Jeanette **89** 24
Martha W. **94** 162
Martha Wellington **87**
290 291 **93** 252
Mary **51** 308 447 463 **52**
359 **54** 22 23 58 316 388
389 403 443 **55** 392 424
443 **56** 30 37 38 146 **57**
30 83 102 148 253 **58** 86
59 149 280 387 **61** 169
246 256 **62** 25 65 94 95
132 202 **63** 29 174 258
295 323 **64** 34 208 213
65 124 **67** 4 **68** 153 202
69 155 334 **70** xxxvi 68
73 142 **74** xlv xlvi 83
312 313 **75** 32 **77** 194 **78**
448 **79** 141 442 **80** 130
82 51 **85** 233 331 399
445 **88** 347 349 **91** 215
259 **92** 250 343 376 **93**
59 63 180 320 **96** 234 **99**
284 **100** 191 315-18 21
24 105 107 110-112 116
119 134 170-172 174 179
258 259 285 324 **114** 7
10 135 136 **115** 296 **117**
159 **120** 95 **121** 142 **123**
240 **124** 52 69 216 222
272 **126** 97 290 **127** 54
56 201 202 204 210 319
129 46 **131** 110 234 **134**
57 67 **136** 166 **137** 332
333 **140** 129 **141** 194
142 356
Mary (Briggs) **126** 212
Mary (Bumpas) **112** 197
Mary (Burbank) **127** 56
?04
Mary (Chase) **113** 324
Mary (Collins) **100** 328
Mary (Corey) **144** 360
Mary (Danforth) **141** 218
Mary (Fletcher) **91** 263
Mary (Ford) (Freeman)
113 254 **119** 125 **124** 69
Mary (Frost) (Williams)
113 178
Mary (Gorham) **113** 182

PARKER *cont'd*
Mary (Grosvenor)
113 261
Mary (Hawes) **113** 17
Mary (Haynes) **85** 445
Mary (Howland) **113** 258
Mary (Jenkins) **112** 199
Mary (Joyce) (Gorham)
112 196
Mary (Kemp) **112** 241
Mary (Kibbey) **123** 265
Mary (Lord) **89** 24
Mary (Lumbert) **112** 257-
259 265
Mary (Maverick) **96** 233
Mary (Norton) (O'Brien)
128 211
Mary (Pope?) (Poulter)
141 217 218 222 224
Mary (Rogers) (Gookin)
112 153
Mary (Sawtell) **126** 8
Mary (Shaw) **112** 153
Mary (Smith) **109** 230
113 121
Mary (Snow) **113** 182
Mary (Swett) **94** 63
Mary (Tobey) **113** 170 171
Mary (Warner) **94** 63
136 314
Mary (Williams) **103** 43
Mary (Woodcock)
128 206
Mary A. **69** 275 **89** 181
106 109
Mary A. (Smith) **114** 12
Mary A. Johnson **86** 240
Mary A. P. **64** 155
Mary Ainsworth **93** 63
Mary Ann **57** 205 **64** 155
73 182 **114** 138 **121** 142
128 178 181 183
Mary Ann (Bursey)
113 250
Mary Ann (Johnson)
113 257
Mary Ann W. **85** 445
Mary Benham **55** 51
Mary Bradford (Standish)
113 256
Mary Bradley (Beetle)
84 101
Mary C. **79** 144
Mary Carney **93** 292
Mary Carney (Vose)
93 292
Mary D. **92** 75
Mary Deborah **105** 115
Mary Delano (Knowles)
113 257
Mary E. **79** 147 **114** 136
Mary Elice **120** 17
Mary Elizabeth **78** 428
113 262
Mary Elizabeth (Baker)
86 343
Mary Elizabeth (England)
105 61
Mary Elizabeth (Gifford)
138 210
Mary Ellen **113** 117 169

PARKER *cont'd*
256 **136** 321
Mary Esther **85** 445
Mary Esther (Nutter)
85 445
Mary F. **71** 42
Mary Frances **54** 151
Mary Francine **113** 261
Mary G. **72** 253
Mary Hale **69** liv
Mary Hildreth **70** xxxv
Mary J. **76** 42
Mary Jane **70** xxxvi **82** 20
120 154
Mary L. **73** 101
Mary Lee **97** 391
Mary M. **114** 137
Mary Newell **89** 14
145 306
Mary Nye **113** 120
Mary Polly (Briggs)
126 213
Mary S. **78** 429
Mary Sanford **114** 7
128 212
Mary Scollay **56** li
Mary Shearer **85** 191
Mary Walker **81** 472
Mary Ward **78** 138 139
Mason Good **55** xxxv
Matilda **75** 16 17 **125** 222
Matilda Augusta
(Wadleigh) **134** 224
Matthew **53** 82 **55** 101 **61**
245 **71** 244 **114** 6 **146**
369 371
Matthew Stanley **102** 304
Mattie E. E. **124** 99
May Lillian **89** 313
Mehitable **52** 360 **55** 259
57 23 **93** 215 **94** 221
110 56 61 **113** 106-108
116-118 168 175 250 **114**
11 44 136
Mehitable (Bancroft)
94 221
Mehitable (Crocker)
113 249
Mehitable (Hall) (Bassett)
113 116
Mehitable (Lewis) **114** 11
Mehitable (Lovell)
106 160
Mehitable (Smith)
114 136
Mehitable W. **115** 161
Melvina (Bancroft) **97** 128
Melzar Torrey **114** 14
Mercy **57** 148 **72** 220 **110**
61 **112** 200 262 264 **113**
109 115 119 120 175 254
257 **114** 7 12 135 **128**
208
Mercy (Bursley) **113** 175
128 210
Mercy (Crosby) **113** 17
Mercy (Davis) **114** 134
123 134 **128** 207
Mercy (Ellis) **113** 170
122 131
Mercy (Handy) **114** 8

PARKER *cont'd*
125 249
Mercy (Jenkins) **113** 115
Mercy (Vickery) **143** 342
Mercy (Whetstone)
112 264
Mercy (Whiston) **112** 264
Mercy Bursley **113** 115
249
Mercy C. **114** 7
Mercy Crowell **128** 212
Mercy Maria **113** 254 257
Meriam **146** 349
Merritt **88** 111
Merville Josiah **60** 158
Mettie Bethiah **89** 313
Michael Atkins **114** 136
Mighill **105** 209
Mildred Blodgett **78** 299
Miles **57** 85 **58** 87
Milton **55** xci **70** 299
Milton D. **97** 128
Minerva **74** 172
Minerva E. **74** 173 **75** 102
Minnie **82** 182
Minnie A. (Searles)
126 70
Miriam **58** 86
Miriam (Chase) **113** 17
Molly **71** 357 **72** 220 **106**
182 184 **112** 263 **113** 22
23 171 172 174 183 **141**
194
Molly (Sears) (Hallet)
114 5
Morgiana Heath
70 xxxvi
Moses **51** 448 **55** 443 **56** 38
59 352-354 **63** 257 **64**
79 **69** 192 288 **74** xlv
108 93 **113** 112 **116** 67
125 59 **126** 97
Moses Greeley **60** xxxvi
65 xxxiii xxxvii **66** vi
68 xxx **72** xxx lx 251-
253 **73** xiv **74** xiv
Myra Emily **102** 124
Myrtle Janet **80** 208
Nahum **54** 387-389 **55** 116
Nancy **55** 396 **57** 260 **60**
344 **64** 117 **88** 146 **106**
102 **109** 58 **114** 7 9 10
136
Nancy (Bunker) **121** 142
Nancy (Cutler) **85** 126
Nancy (Frisbee) **123** 235
Nancy (Greenwood)
125 294
Nancy Abigail **77** lxxxiv
Nancy Maria **72** li
Nancy R. **114** 7 **128** 212
Nancy Shaw **128** 211
Nathan **53** 454 **57** 29 414
78 42 303 **82** 28 416 423
83 21 30 36 **93** 232 **94**
317 **100** 151 191 **109**
212 **112** 212 **113** 4 108
117 118 178 179 252 **114**
137 138 **116** 299 **137**
325
Nathan Jenkins **114** 138

PARKER *cont'd*
Nathaniel **52** 82 **55** 376
56 1 **57** 27 **58** 86 **62** 72
63 325-327 **69** liv 99 **78**
298 428 **82** 51 **83** 17 **92**
314 **94** 318 **104** 193 **110**
161 **111** 83 283 **113** 15
16 112 114 175 **114** 135
116 157 **125** 96 **126** 14
148 145 147
Nathaniel Stone **114** 136
Nehemiah **67** 217 **71** 358
112 259 263 **113** 21 104
105 119 121 253 261 **121**
248 **128** 207 **131** 73
Nehemiah A. **145** 362
Neil James **94** 139 **116**
157 235 **117** 80 **121** 156
Nellie **124** 192
Nellie Elizabeth **78** 299
Nellie May **89** 235
Nicholas **97** 37 **127** 140
143 26
Noah **51** 40 41 **54** 445 **57**
22 **63** 170 175 **82** 51 284
295 413 **94** 357 **108** 163
113 178 **114** 137
Noble **114** 10
Norman **104** 47
Obadiah **71** 357 358 **78** 298
Obed C. **113** 252
Octavia (Thacher) **113** 249
Olive **58** 373 **83** 359 **88** 279
91 30 35 **97** 228 **112** 241
115 19
Olive (Depuy) **90** 378
Olive (Garrett) **113** 252
Olive Black **113** 252
Olive Garrett **113** 252 253
Olive L. **113** 254
Olive Ringe **94** 357
Oliver **57** 225 **67** 4 87 **69**
302 **104** 132 **105** 209
210 281 **113** 169 170 256
122 58
Oliver H. **121** 177
Orpha **115** 18
Orre **110** 36
Osgood **70** 298
P. Hildreth **60** 189 206
Pamelia (Leighton)
128 211
Pamelia N. **70** 21
Pamelia S. **67** 353
Parette **113** 260 261
Parette Louise (Perrure)
113 260
Parnel **57** 307 308 **61** 120
Parnel (Gray) **106** 16 **131**
131 **138** 41
Patience **57** 83 **61** 256
104 47 **105** 86 222 **112**
192-194 197-199 259-261
113 18-20 110 **124** 109
125 130 **128** 207
Patience (Cobb) **112** 191
192 194 195 259
Patience (Pearson)
124 319
Patience (Russell) **114** 199
Patty **78** 417 **80** 130 **114**

PARKER *cont'd*
10 11
Patty (Silvester) **86** 293
Paul **65** 250 **127** 307
Peace **112** 197 198
Pearl **116** 157 **117** 93
Pearl Hildreth **59** xlviii
60 xxxiv **61** xii xxi
xxxiii 197 **62** vii xxii
xxviii xxxv **63** vii xxii
64 vii xxi xxix **65** vii
xxiii xxxiii **66** vii **67** vii
68 viii xxii **69** viii xxiv
Pearpoint **145** 348
Percival O. **73** 182
Peregrine **68** 268
Permelia (Leighton)
128 211
Permilla **114** 13
Persis **114** 136
Peter **57** 152 **62** 53 **64** 208
68 111 **70** xxxv **72** 251
85 124 **93** 165 **103** 149
108 92 **110** 202 **111** 271
117 16 **123** 171 **127** 307
129 44 67 **140** 233 **143**
342 **145** 239 **148** 65
Peter John Joseph
113 261
Phebe **54** 392 **56** 137 **75** 32
79 141 **83** 167 **88** 146
95 280 **109** 16 **113** 16
122 58 **128** 211 **137** 78
Phebe (Ellis) **113** 256
122 58
Phebe (Gardiner) **113** 16
Phebe (Shaw) **134** 57
Phebe Dole **113** 251
Phebe Ellis **113** 257
Phebe Jeanette **89** 24
Phebe Ware **67** 3 4
Phebe Wise **105** 115
Philip **54** 389 **109** 282
Phineas **67** 87 **69** 12 120
121 123 212 213 218 219
221 297 299 **70** 13 14 17
18 20 137 213 216-218
295 307 **78** 298 **93** 398
100 63 **106** 264 **112** 241
119 21
Polly **55** 51 **104** 47 59 **113**
120 172 179 180 **114** 11
115 127 **123** 117 **125**
100 **140** 129
Polly (Briggs) **126** 213
Polly (Grace) **128** 211
Polly (Lumbert)
(Whitford) **114** 10
Polly (Sherman) **113** 259
Polly Gray **113** 257
Polly Stephens **113** 259
Polycarpus **113** 24 169 170
257 **114** 216 **122** 131
Poppola (Foster) **134** 58
Prince **105** 203 **113** 181
114 8 12 **125** 249
Priscilla **55** 265 **86** 461 **105**
86 **112** 197 198 **114** 11
Priscilla (Torrey) **114** 13
Prudence **99** 310 **112** 197-
200 **113** 111 **114** 14 135

PARKER *cont'd*
128 211
Prudence (Atwood) **113**
 111 **128** 209
Prudence (Hatch) **114** 135
Prudence (Phelps) **122** 80
R. **54** 387
R. H. (Mrs.) **78** 426
Rachel **54** 293 **56** 254 **58** 86
 87 170 174 **61** 380 **63**
 246 247 **91** 17 **111** 167
 113 16 **126** 15
Rachel (Coburn) **133** 123
Rachel (Field) **114** 13
Rachel (Gorham) **113** 16
 178
Rachel (Nye) **113** 249
Rachel (Parker) **111** 167
Rachel F. (Hall) **91** 231
Rachel Jane **86** 150
Ralph **53** 237 **65** 376 **66** 20
 72 316
Ralph B. **92** 341
Rea (Mrs.) **87** 174
Reba **104** 97
Rebecca **56** 1 **63** 292 **66**
 102 104 106 107 328 **67**
 87 88 **74** 96 **77** 147 228
 78 309 428 **79** 295 442
 82 24 **92** 17 **95** 63 **104**
 189 **105** 87 309 **106** 184
 112 259 261 265 **113** 18
 19 21 105-107 111 112
 115-117 175 183 296 **114**
 6 7 138 **124** 17 **125** 254
 128 211 **133** 291 **141**
 218
Rebecca (Bancroft) **95** 279
Rebecca (Freeman) **113** 19
 106 **119** 38
Rebecca (Hatch) **114** 6
Rebecca (Jenkins) **113** 262
Rebecca (Lumbert)
 112 265
Rebecca (Newhall)
 137 238
Rebecca (Noble) **94** 357
Rebecca (Rice) **113** 255
Rebecca (Sandford) **114** 6
Rebecca (Tobey) **113** 111
Rebecca D. **66** 111
Rebecca Damon **69** liv
Rebecca Davis **74** 96
Rebecca Desire **66** 106
 113 256
Rebecca Sanford **128** 212
Reginald Seabury **74** xlvi
 117 72
Relief **69** 307 **74** 313 **75**
 16 17 **125** 43
Remember **62** 94 **114** 138
 131 110
Remember (Weeks)
 114 138
Retire Hathorn **99** 334
Reuben **63** 74 **75** 32 **111**
 134 **140** 129 **145** 307
Rhoda **57** 256 **69** 213 295
 307 **70** 15 21 23 24 138
 80 130 **114** 10 **127** 210
Rhoda (Collins) **127** 210

PARKER *cont'd*
Rhoda Billings **65** 36
Richard **57** 298 **61** 392 **69**
 156 **70** 59 **76** 50 **96** 234
 111 14 **146** 378 379 381
 147 171 **148** 142
Richard Douglas **110** 229
Richard Douglas (Mrs.)
 105 317 **106** 126 **110**
 220 229
Robert **52** 66 **53** 248 **54**
 388 389 **56** 184 **59** 57 **61**
 393 **62** 96 **63** 343 **64** 149
 67 217 **76** 94 **85** 411 **88**
 278 **89** 175 **92** 81 **99** 321
 322 **100** 28 **105** 115 **112**
 190-195 197 199 200 257
 258 262 264 265 **113** 15
 20 104 119 166 249 250
 114 5 14 134 **120** 16 **124**
 69 **128** 206 **132** 275 **136**
 45
Robert Andrew **113** 253
Robert Butcher **87** 174
Robert F. **56** 25 **100** 192
Robert Morgan **96** 296
Robert Rice **83** 174 195
Robert Whipple **54** 388
 389
Rosannah **86** 222
Roscoe G. **73** 182
Rose **51** 448 **55** 443 **61** 393
Ross **70** xxxvi
Rossiter **113** 179
Roy **146** 385
Ruby **133** 124
Rudy **133** 124
Rufus **72** 220
Rufus Hill **128** 211
Russell J. **59** xliv
Ruth **54** 388 **57** 24 146 **58**
 170 373 **62** 65 **64** lvi **69**
 x **70** 140 **72** 283 **82** 423
 88 349 **89** 184 **97** 125
 102 158 **105** 87 **113** 21
 23 110 169 170 259 **114**
 6 **131** 234 **134** 216
Ruth (Avery) **113** 21 169
 260
Ruth (Bancroft) **94** 224
Ruth (Bryant) **137** 327 337
Ruth (Coffin) **113** 179
Ruth (Hammond) **114** 6
Ruth (Rich) **83** 397
Ruth F. **83** 26 27
Ruth L. **83** 21 26
Ruth L. (Brewster) **83** 21
Sabrina **60** 158
Sally **55** 397 **58** 373 **60**
 267 268 **70** 295 **75** 16 17
 90 90 **91** 111 **104** 47
 105 242 **113** 259 **128**
 211 **136** 314
Sally (Dyer) **114** 136
Sally (Kilburn) **125** 288
Sally Davis **113** 249 250
Sally M. **114** 136 137
Sampson **71** 357 **133** 123
Samuel **54** cxliii 316 388
 55 260 **56** 31 **57** 26 27
 29 30 144-149 **61** 72 73

PARKER *cont'd*
 256 **63** 257 319 320 323
 64 lxx 79 **67** 16 **69** 106
 298 **71** 358 **73** 273 **74**
 xlv 252 **76** 46 **78** 72 **80**
 130 **82** 423 **83** 21 26 **85**
 126 399 **90** 49 **94** 220
 320 **95** 280 **97** 127 **104**
 47 **105** 290 **111** 117 **112**
 122 153 194 195 197 258
 259 263 **113** 18-20 106
 108 121 122 167 175 183
 254 255 **114** 10 12 136
 115 18 19 **116** 157 **117**
 228 230 **119** 125 **121** 79
 142 156 248 **122** 80 **124**
 69 **125** 38 **126** 15 226
 127 279 **131** 234 **138**
 210 **140** 56 232 233 **145**
 38 355
Samuel (Mrs.) **121** 79
Samuel Boardman **74** 301
Samuel C. **94** 63
Samuel D. **69** 109
Samuel Dunn **140** 233 237
Samuel Franklin **102** 235
Samuel Handy **54** 388
 82 423
Samuel Jenkins **144** 324
Samuel Joel **114** 13
Samuel Sewall **69** 36
Samuel Woodbury **69** 36
Sarah **51** 448 **53** 248 **54** 388
 56 1 36 142 **57** 151 205
 58 241 **59** 57 60 198 **61**
 169 237 384 **62** 70 94 95
 156 **63** 173 246 258 375
 64 145 313 317 **67** 87 69
 8 11 124 126 213 222 224
 294 297 299 301 304 **70**
 79 357 **71** 130 **73** 265
 291 **75** 32 **77** 275 287 **78**
 295 428 **82** 295 301 **88**
 146 347 **90** 90 185 **91** 81
 237 262 263 **92** 281 **93**
 187 **94** 42 121 122 317
 393 **95** 191 **97** 131 **100**
 301 **102** 158 104 47 **105**
 86 203 309 310 **106** 101
 102 **108** 187 **109** 220
 110 61 307 **112** 177 192
 194-197 200 265 **113** 15
 18 108-110 112-114 119
 120 168 169 172 181 249
 256 257 259 **114** 6 7 9 10
 44 135-138 **116** 157 **119**
 189 **121** 142 **122** 292
 123 10 **124** 51 52 **125**
 135 141 **126** 60 138 **128**
 211 **129** 47 50 52 **131**
 110 **136** 273 **141** 189
 144 215 **146** 378-380
Sarah (Blood) **125** 294
Sarah (Chandler) (Cleves)
 (Stevens) **96** 302
Sarah (Farwell) **137** 78
Sarah (Faunce) (Jackson)
 113 257 **114** 216
Sarah (Fitch) **113** 262
Sarah (Green) **110** 61
Sarah (Hallett) **113** 181

PARKER *cont'd*
Sarah (Holmes) **124** 108
Sarah (Ireson) **122** 292
Sarah (James) **112** 191
Sarah (Landers) **113** 112
Sarah (Lawrence) **114** 135
    125 135
Sarah (Messer) **122** 80
Sarah (Morse) **128** 180 181
Sarah (Newmarch)
    112 153
Sarah (Nye) **113** 119
Sarah (Parker) **97** 131
Sarah (Pitcher) **113** 118
Sarah (Richardson) **89**
    213 **122** 160 **123** 160
Sarah (Ruggles) **148** 65
Sarah (Smith) **113** 256
Sarah (Sturges) **113** 19
    166-168 256
Sarah (Thacher) **113** 261
Sarah (Verin) **131** 110
Sarah (Whitney) **84** 100
Sarah (Willard) **92** 280
Sarah (Wooley) **140** 129
Sarah (Wright) **134** 57 58
Sarah A. **79** 141 **114** 138
    120 249
Sarah Abigail **85** 196
    118 159
Sarah Ann **61** 384 **83** 359
    114 6
Sarah Ann (Moore)
    92 320
Sarah C. **114** 138
Sarah E. **120** 249
Sarah Eliza **109** 16 **110** 302
Sarah Elizabeth **98** 335
Sarah Goodrich **97** 391
Sarah J. **54** cxliii **113** 254
Sarah Jane **64** lxx **85** 445
    93 288 **100** 174 **126** 245
Sarah Jane (Munroe)
    126 246
Sarah Jay (Bogardus)
    107 234
Sarah Lawrence **125** 135
Sarah Leah **81** 472
Sarah Lewis **113** 178 251
Sarah Louisa **77** 151
Sarah M. (Chase) **88** 17
Sarah Maria **55** 423 **85** 102
    96 85
Sarah Melville **78** 286 **83**
    487 **108** 241 243
Sarah Nye **113** 120
Sarah O. **73** 194
Sarah R. **66** 112
Sarah Rebecca **59** lxxxiii
Sarah Rice **66** 106 **113**
    255 256
Sarah S. **54** 388 **120** 249
Sarh **114** 138
Sarh Maria **96** 85
Scarborough **145** 355
Sears T. **113** 171
Seth **57** 280 **112** 264 **113**
    108 109 115 116 118 179
    250 **128** 259 **129** 37 **144**
    266
Seth Doane **113** 176 177

PARKER *cont'd*
Sherman **54** 389
Sherrille Ellen (Lazell)
    89 313
Shubael **89** 313
Sibyl **55** 266 **57** 149 **61** 300
    63 324 325 **69** 118 120
    212 217 297 **75** 32 **147**
    74
Silas **73** 281 282 **75** 32 **82**
    51 **100** 191 192 **104** 262
    113 15-17 114 251 **114**
    135 **124** 217
Silence **113** 260
Silence (Soule) **113** 259
Simeon **62** 158 **67** 4
    110 23
Simon **83** 375 **88** 146
Snow **80** 130 **113** 182 **114**
    10 **126** 97 **127** 126 279
    128 114
Solomon **57** 145 **71** 117
    115 25 108 **126** 116 **147**
    74
Solomon Park **56** 34
Sophia **57** 205 **58** 373 **76**
    94 **88** 341 **91** 387 **97** 128
    214 **109** 58 **113** 253
Sophia (Baker) **124** 63
Sophia (Cotton) **113** 179
Sophia (Gifford) **135** 316
Sophia (Marston) **113** 252
Sophia (Munroe) **88** 278
Sophia (Tupper)
    (Prentice) **99** 297
Sophia B. (Crocker)
    113 254
Sophia M. **76** 94
Sophia Marston **113** 253
Sophia White **58** 373
Sophronia **114** 14
Sophronia (Green)
    113 120
Sophronia (Hinckley)
    113 120
Squire **116** 211
Stacy **114** 9
Stanley **54** 151
Stanley Brampton **74**
    xlvi **77** xxix 78 **81** 90
    120 **91** 59 **120** 147
Stanley Devereux **74** 301
Stanley Vincent **74** 301
Stanton Crocker **112** 258
    113 251
Stata **111** 187
Stata A. **111** 123
Stephen **52** 66 **54** 392 **62**
    17 129 **64** 232 **67** 174 **71**
    357 358 **74** 120 **82** 51
    295 **85** 124 **99** 79 **100**
    328 **110** 277 **113** 257
Submit **64** 39
Sumner E. **75** 16
Susan **56** 45 **82** 423 **83** 36
    113 257 **114** 199 **125** 53
    74 **133** 123
Susan (Cousins) **110** 23
Susan (Cross) **113** 262
Susan (Pickering)
    116 299

PARKER *cont'd*
Susan (Woodbridge)
    126 68
Susan Augusta **81** 471
Susan D. **80** 28
Susan E. C. **114** 137
Susan E. E. **114** 136 137
Susan M. (Winkley)
    114 13
Susan O. **123** 234
Susan P. **73** 286 290
Susan Pickering **82** 423
    83 36
Susan S. (Bodfish)
    (Howland) **113** 252
Susanna **54** 388 **56** 287
    288 318 **61** 120 **62** 25 **63**
    170 175 **66** 85 **70** 152 **73**
    289 **74** 120 243 **89** 213
    214 269 **94** 386 **96** 84
    110 61 **113** 108 **114** 44
    136 138
Susanna (Bisbee) **113** 257
Susanna (Bradford) (Ellis)
    113 259 **122** 59
Susanna (Devereaux)
    110 277
Susanna (Gardiner)
    113 179
Susanna (Haffords)
    113 261
Susanna (Swift) **114** 6
Susanna S. **114** 7
Susanna Sanford **128** 212
Susie **61** 256
Susy (Bancroft) **95** 279
    97 127
Sylvanus **90** 229 248 **105**
    309 **109** 34 42 **112** 264
    113 108 177 179 183
    114 6 12 135 136 138
    123 138 **128** 208 **130**
    131
Sylvanus T. **114** 6
Sylvester **86** 254 **135** 316
Tabitha **51** 447 **113** 114
Tabitha (Gill) **113** 114
Temperance **105** 310 **107**
    107 **113** 20 106 107 116
    168 175 182 250-252 **114**
    11 136 **128** 208
Temperance (Crocker)
    112 261
Temperance (Matthews)
    114 10
Temperance (Parker)
    113 168 250
Temperance Hathaway
    113 254
Temperance Hathaway
    (Crocker) **113** 254
Tempy **107** 289 291 292
    108 110 **114** 11
Thaddeus **59** 280 **113** 22-
    24 170 172 173
Thankful **51** 51 **55** 263
    56 31 **85** 330 **105** 86 115
    309-311 **112** 200 265
    113 105 109 110 183
Thankful (Bigelow)
    114 174

PARKER *cont'd*
Thankful (Downs)
  112 260
Thankful (Gray) **128** 209
Thankful (Marchant)
  113 183 **128** 210
Thankful (Snow) **104** 57
  58
Theodore **54** lxxvi cxlix
  58 112 **61** xlviii liv lv
  63 xlvi **67** 307 **72** 251 **78**
  242 **85** 238 **102** 319
Theodore Edson **72** 253
Thirza (Chase) **88** 111
Thirza (Crocker) **113** 18
Thomas **51** 447 **52** 66 487
  53 36 450 **54** 117 **56** 1
  57 388 **58** 236 237 308
  60 158 189 285 310 **61**
  245 393 **62** 65 94 156 **63**
  160 **64** 189 **65** 167 **67**
  286 **68** 69 202 **69** 18 155
  362 **70** xxxv **72** 251 **73**
  145 **78** 298 306 428 **81**
  471 **84** 100 **86** 343 **91** 94
  215 237 254 257 259 263
  331 **96** 234 **100** 292 **102**
  194 **105** 86 **106** 183 **112**
  153 192 194 196 199 200
  241 264 **113** 15 16 111-
  114 119 182 183 **114** 12
  13 134-136 **116** 157 **119**
  16 17 20 172 **124** 51 52
  216 **125** 93 **126** 60 97
  100 **127** 210 279 **128**
  210 **129** 37 **131** 110 **134**
  335 **140** 233 **147** 348
Thomas Archibald
  128 211
Thomas Ervine **100** 174
Thomas M. **85** 445
Thomas Rice **66** 106
  113 256
Thomas Valentine **62** 392
Timothy **52** 426 **56** 1 143
  57 151 **58** 373 **78** 428
  86 350 **112** 264 **113** 15-
  17 107 108 114 119 120
  176 178 262 **114** 6 7 134
  135 137 **128** 208
Timothy Tyler **58** 373
Titus **72** 220
Triphena **114** 12
Trueworthy **105** 210
Tryphena **64** 144
Tryphosa Colton **113**
  255 256
Tryphosa Colton
  (Freeman) **113** 254
Uriel Crocker **113** 250
Velina (Lovell) **113** 253
Verrin **131** 110
Violet **82** 51
W. **123** 307
W. G. **101** 233 235
W. R. **75** 16
W. R. (Mrs.) **122** 248
W. S. **71** 95
W. W. **120** 221 222
Wallace **76** 97 **121** 142
Walter **98** 335

PARKER *cont'd*
Walter (Mrs.) **98** 335
Walter Edward **84** 100 109
  194
Walter Huntington
  89 132
Walter Smith **54** 389
  73 227
Ward Mayhew **113** 179
  114 7 8
Ward Ralph **89** 313
Warren S. **65** 193
Warren Samuel **66** 1
  112 153
Weston **76** 285
Whiting **113** 173 174
Whitner Roland (Mrs.)
  101 125
William **51** 45 308 463 468
  54 270 388 **55** 83 423 **56**
  337 **57** 24 83 85 257 **58**
  86 87 170 174 **60** 28 195
  290 311 358 **61** 393 **62**
  244 246 326 **63** 29 30
  174 **65** 232 66 34 **69** 11
  217 **70** 59 **76** 155 156
  190 **81** 471 **82** 51 295
  301 **83** 174 195 **84** 31 **85**
  102 **87** 291 **89** 175 213
  91 385 **92** 17 **93** 60 252
  254 **94** 47 63 **100** 192
  102 304 **104** 57 58 90
  105 115 222 **107** 216
  109 213 233 281 **112**
  153 190 **113** 15 16 108
  112 114 119 169 **114** 134
  136 138 **115** 315 **116**
  111 **120** 52 111 **121** 141
  142 **123** 134 **124** 109
  125 78 92 93 96 **128** 207
  211 **129** 52 381 **136** 314
  141 202 **142** 52 **143** 299
William (Mrs.) **83** 195
  85 121
William Ainsworth **74**
  xlv xlvi
William Alderman
  112 237
William Almon **106** 316
William Amory **94** 139
William B. **113** 254
William Bennett **83** 25 26
William Briard **54** 389
William Cranston **80** 30
William Crowell **114** 6
William D. **124** 63
William E. **113** 249
William Edward **113** 250
William Fatar **82** 51
William Gray **113** 257
William H. **62** 394 **100** 191
  106 109 **113** 169 256
William Huntington
  96 296
William Huntington
  (Mrs.) **81** 222 **96** 293
William J. **92** 319
William Lincoln
  61 xxxvii
William P. **109** 199
William Perkins **105** 115

PARKER *cont'd*
William Prentiss **56** li
  68 xix 104 **78** 216 428
  429 **86** 343
William S. **64** 155
William Sewall **89** 24
William Thornton **64** 62
  66 1 192 **68** xxxii 206 **69**
  xxxii 192 288 385
William Wilson **120** 15
Willie **129** 41
Winifred **114** 9
Winslow **64** 39 **69** 222 223
Yelverton **113** 110 **128**
  209 210
Zachariah **63** 295 **133** 291
Zacheus **113** 171 260
Zadock **70** 145
Zalmund **113** 181
Zechaus **121** 24
Zella (Noble) **95** 186
Zelveton **105** 86 **113** 110
Zeruiah (Stanley) **102** 304
Zerviah **54** 201 **56** 253
  125 92
Zerviah Stanley **60** 195
  94 357
PARKERSON
  Varnie **60** 77
Parkes *see* Park & Parkess
PARKESS Parkes Parkis
  —— **121** 206
  Aaron **102** 152
  Albert T. **102** 152
  Betsey **90** 363 **125** 108
  Catherine **102** 152
  David **102** 152
  Edgar **102** 152
  Elizabeth (Danks) **90** 363
  Gardner **125** 34
  Goodwin E. **102** 152
  Hannah **148** 348
  Joseph **51** 307 448
  Lewis **102** 152
  Lewis Cass **102** 152
  Lucy **102** 152
  Lydia **102** 152
  Marshall **125** 218
  Marvin A. **102** 152
  Mary **51** 448
  Nathan **102** 152
  Polly **102** 152
  Rebecca **51** 307
  Sarah **102** 152
PARKHILL Parkill
  Anne **136** 323
  James **99** 305 **126** 141
  Lovisa (Tupper) **99** 305
  Nancy (Parsons) **126** 141
  S. J. **51** 91 **58** 208
PARKHURST Parckhurst
  —— **68** 372 **70** 179 **92** 252
    100 293 **119** 159 **120**
    318 **136** 145 **145** 239
  — Lieut. **70** 310
  — Widow **71** 134 138
    139 141 143
  Abigail **67** 372 374 **68** 373
    70 176 **73** 84 116 **121**
    168 **123** 240
  Abigail (Garfield) **127** 189

PARKHURST *cont'd*
Abigail (Morse) **121** 169
Agnes **68** 374
Albert **91** 104
Alexis **142** 384 385
Alice **68** 374 **110** 3 4
Amelia **63** 275
Amos **55** 393
Anna **112** 131
Anne **52** 137 **68** 374
  112 131
Anthony **68** 375
Ben **128** 232 233
Benjamin **68** 371 372 **110** 4
  128 232
Betsey **52** 456 **66** 126
Betsey (Cook) **125** 103
C. D. **58** 317
Caesar **70** 316 **71** 138
Caleb **68** 372
Calvin **70** 181
Caroline S. S. **75** 99
Catherine **113** 136
Charles A. **78** 305
Charles Austin **92** 133 244
Charles D. **59** xliv **63** 100
Charles Dyer **104** 189
  135 60 **144** 309 **147** 36
  38 41 42
Charlotte (Davis) **128** 232
Chastina Eliza Buck **110** 4
  128 232
Christopher **68** 374
Clara Burnham **58** xlviii
  90 125 **100** 101 312 **101**
  128
Clara P. **57** 192
Cordelia **124** 160
Cordelia (James) **124** 160
Cynthia **113** 222
Cynthia E. (Capron)
  128 232
D. S. **73** 116
Daniel **64** 41 **68** 372
  144 216
Daniel Bowe **110** 3 4 **128**
  232 233
Darius **73** 116
David **113** 222
Deborah **68** 371-373
Dorothy **70** 315
Ebenezer **61** 304
Edward **73** 117 **94** 393
Elbridge **84** 60
Eliza Ann **77** 175
Elizabeth **61** 248 **66** 126
  138 **68** 371-374
Elizabeth Adelaide
  100 312
Elizaette **61** 345
Ella S. **94** 52
Ellen **52** 137
Ephraim **64** 312
Esther **70** 229 **124** 319
Eunice **128** 233 **144** 221
Eunice D. **128** 232 233
Eva (Currier) (Alexander)
  94 393
Fanny **74** 172 **75** 17
Frederic Hale **75** 173
George **53** 302 **63** 289 **68**

PARKHURST *cont'd*
370-374 **69** 69 **110** 4
  128 233 **134** 336 **137** 76
Gertrude **52** 138
Hannah **62** 122 127 **68** 372
  70 179 228 313
Hannah L. **73** 117
Harriet **128** 232 233
Hejoitthan **71** 140
Helen **52** 137 **68** 374
Henry **52** 137 138 **68** 375
  92 341
Hugh **100** 312
Isaac **78** 413 **113** 136
Jabez **52** 227 **70** 156 317
  71 42
James **68** 375 **108** 166
Jane **113** 222
Job **70** 179 **71** 140
Joel **74** 172
John **52** 137 **62** 324 **67**
  372 375 **68** 372-375 **70**
  180 314 **73** 116 117 **104**
  118 **121** 169 **127** 189
John A. **73** 117
John L. **72** 275
Joseph **62** 71 **68** 370-373
  70 179-181 221 **110** 4
  121 317 **128** 232
Joshua **68** 372
Josiah **61** 218 **66** 126
Jotham **63** 275
Judah **70** 177 181
Judith **70** 179 180
Judith Thomas (Parsons)
  100 312
Julia E. **73** 117
Juliana G. **128** 232 233
Katharine **144** 216
Keziah (Nason) **128** 232
  233
Lemuel **70** 312 **71** 139
Lincoln **77** 175
Llewellyn A. **142** 385
Louisa **94** 204
Louisa (Rich) (Dickey)
  (Page) **84** 60
Lucia (Tracy) **128** 232 233
Lucy **52** 227 **70** 229
Lydia **55** 392 **92** 133 244
  94 378
Lydia (Bigelow) **113** 136
M. A **137** 219
Margaret M. (Benchley)
  142 384 385
Maria **61** 345
Martha **67** 375 **68** 372 **73**
  117 **106** 308 **108** 169
  144 221
Martha (Whittemore)
  108 166
Mary **52** 137 **55** 393 **68** 371-
  373 **70** 176 180 181 221
  229 **73** 117 **85** 322 **93**
  168 **100** 309 **110** 4 **121**
  317 **127** 189 **128** 232
Mary P. **73** 117
Mehitable **70** 156
Mercy **64** 41 **68** 372
  113 136

PARKHURST *cont'd*
Minerva (Tenney) (Lee)
  120 318
Nancy **61** 248
Nancy (Ganson) **128** 232
Nathaniel **52** 137 138
  144 221
Nicholas **68** 374
Noah **144** 218
Olive **52** 138
Oliver **66** 126 **68** 374
Patt **144** 221
Perce **71** 143
Persis G. **72** 275
Phebe **68** 370-373 **69** 69
  104 118 **128** 232
Phebe (Day) **128** 232 233
Phebe (Pierce) **104** 118
Phineas **70** 314 317
Phyrilla **73** 117
Rachel **124** 15
Rachel Lucinda (Putnam)
  91 104
Ralph **68** 375
Rebecca **90** 48
Rebecca (Getchell) **137** 76
Reuben **70** 181
Rhoda **62** 71
Richard **68** 374 375
Robbins **92** 252
Robert **52** 137 138 **68** 374
  375
Roland **57** 192
Ruth **113** 33 40
Ruth Cushing (Silvester)
  86 126
Sally **70** 228 **71** 42 **134** 336
  141 8
Samuel **66** 126 **68** 372 373
  70 179 180 314 315 **71**
  139 **111** 117 **125** 103
  144 221
Sarah **62** 122 125 **64** 312 **67**
  375 **68** 372-374 **70** 221
  313 **78** 411 **110** 4 **112**
  226
Sarah (Ball) **136** 145
Sarah (Parsons) **100** 312
Sarah (Shepard) **128** 232
Sarah Maria **78** 347
Sarah W. **92** 341
Silas **92** 133 244 252 **94** 378
Simeon S. **73** 117
Simon **68** 374
Sophia H. **69** 138
Stephen **70** 229 **110** 4
  128 232 233
Stephen H. **128** 232
Susanna **68** 370-372
  81 311
Tabitha **63** 289
Thamar **68** 374
Thomas **52** 137 138 **68** 375
  72 159
Timothy **70** 228 **71** 142
Wellington E. **66** 289
William **68** 374 **86** 126
  100 312 **113** 33 **136** 145
William Pitt **100** 312
Winnifrid C. **107** 159
Parkill *see* Parkhill

PARKIN Parkins
Charles **105** 22 **109** 280
  142 4
Dorothy (Gosnold)
  (Forthe) **105** 11
Edward **115** 57
Gresham **105** 11
John **83** 444 445 **93** 29
Leroy Edward **84** 105 190
Mary **141** 332
Richard **83** 444 **84** 13
William **83** 444 445 **84** 13
  109 79
PARKINSON —— **53** 246
— Mr. **64** 26
Anne Outram **76** xxxviii
Caroline North
  (Bowman) **96** 79
Christopher **65** 45
Daniel **84** 351
George Washington
  88 394
Gertrude **76** xxxix
Grace E. Chandler **117** 92
Hannah **51** 82
Jane **76** xxxviii
John **64** 221 **76** xxxi
  xxxviii
John Webb **84** 350 351
Margaret Ann **88** 394
  103 68
Mary **76** xxxviii
Nanny **64** 55
Rebecca (Ross) **88** 394
Richard **63** 307
Robert **65** 45
William **76** xxxviii **84** 351
William Dwight (Mrs.)
  96 79
Parkis *see* Parkess
PARKMAN —— **54** 111 **62**
128 **76** 281 **140** 40 245
249 **145** 233
— Dr. **90** 35
— Mr. **53** 247 **86** 34-36
— Mrs. **79** 233
— Rev. Mr. **77** 19
____ (Hall) **140** 233
____ (Mason) **140** 233
____ (McDonough)
  140 233
____ (Powell) **140** 238
____ (Rand) **140** 233
____ (Tilden) **140** 253
Abigail **55** 322 327 **138**
134 **140** 233
Abigail Hart **91** 215
Alexander **55** 322 **138** 133
Anna **78** 299
Anne Augusta **93** 287 403
Antonia (Vega) **138** 133
Breck **55** 322
Bridget **55** 322 327 **131**
107 **134** 301
Caroline (Hall) **94** 386
Caroline Hall **94** 386
Catherine (Scollay)
  140 244
Catherine Alla **63** 197
Catherine Scollay **77** 296
Daniel **140** 233 245 253

PARKMAN *cont'd*
Deliverance **55** 322 **131**
106 107 **135** 23
Dorcas (Bowes) **110** 47
Eben **55** 322
Ebenezer **54** 120 **55** 322 **63**
196 **78** 14 131 **91** 94 **137**
144 145 **138** 133 172
  144 340 **148** 185
Edward **62** 21
Elias **55** 321-323 327 **57**
389 **63** 196 197 **73** 241
  107 313 **131** 107 **134**
301 **137** 323 **138** 133
134 **140** 233
Eliza **140** 233
Elizabeth **55** 322 323 **100**
28 301 **101** 271 **110** 47
  137 322 324 **138** 134
  140 233
Elizabeth (Adams)
  138 134
Elizabeth (Weld) **137** 323
Elizabeth Willard **79** 96
97 **81** 98 **83** 116
Esther **55** 322
Felipe **138** 133
Francis **51** 11 13 16 18 90
245 **52** 453 477 **53** 90
361 **54** lxxxiii **55** lxx
lxxi 93 323 **56** 320 **60** 1
77 67 296 **94** 386 **109**
239 **123** 15 **124** 31 **140**
139 233 244
George **63** lii **140** 233 258
George Francis **79** 8
Hannah **55** 322 **77** 232
Henry **62** 131
John **55** 322 323 **100** 28
  101 271 **114** 182 **138**
134 **140** 233
John A. **79** 36
John McGee **63** 197
Joseph Hunter **63** 197
Lucy **55** 322
Lydia **55** 322
Lydia (Proctor) **140** 233
Maria R. **63** 196 197
Maria R. Hunter **63** 197
Martha **55** 322
Mary **55** 322 **58** 305
  138 134
Mary A. **79** 38
Mary Jane **78** 416
Mehitable (Waite) **131** 107
Migail **55** 322
Nathaniel **55** 322
Rebecca **55** 322
Robert Breck **138** 133
S. A. **100** 213
Sally (Shaw) **84** 362
Samuel **55** 322 **65** li **79**
41 96 **84** 252 362 **100**
192 303 **110** 47 **138** 133
  140 40 233 238
Samuel Breck **55** 322
Sarah **55** 321-323 **65** li **67**
374 **79** 96 **135** 23 **138**
134
Sarah (Shaw) **100** 303
Sarah (Verin) **131** 107

PARKMAN *cont'd*
  135 23
Sophia **102** 226
Susan **65** li
Susanna **55** 322 **57** 363
  138 134
Tabitha **55** 322
Thomas **55** 322
William **55** 322 323 **63** 196
  100 28 **101** 271 **105** 286
  106 122 **138** 133 134
  139 312 **140** 233
William Elias **63** 197
PARKS alias GOFFE
Joanna **144** 219
Parks *see* Park
PARLE Mary **127** 269
Rebecca **127** 269
Thomas **127** 269
PARLEE
Hannah **145** 256
Mary A. **74** 176
Parlen *see* Parlin
PARLER Emeline **97** 81
PARLIER
Elizabeth **130** 314
PARLIMENT
William **127** 8
PARLIN Parlen
Aaron **95** 61
Abel **84** 324 **103** 300
Almina **76** 271
Amos **62** 33
Amos F. **103** 236
Anne **54** 51
Clemena (Steward)
  103 236
Daniel **57** 413
David **62** 33 **63** 289
  114 269
Ebenezer **145** 357
Eleazer **97** 395
Elizabeth (Goodridge)
  84 324
Emily Euna **75** 17
Ephraim **103** 236
Etta May **75** 17
Evaline (Leadbetter)
  103 236
Frances **89** 382
Frank Edson **54** xli **67**
189 302 **68** xxx **69** xxxi
  75 17 **80** 113 **84** 181
  114 269
Hannah **52** 398
Hannah (Kimball)
  133 124
Hattie Emeroy **75** 17
Hephzibah **54** 53
Horace Eugene **133** 124
Isaac N. **124** 204
John **54** 53 **62** 33
Jonas **97** 395
Joseph **62** 33
Josiah **62** 33
Lemuel **57** 413
Lucy **103** 236
Lydia **103** 300 **114** 269
Margaret **54** 53
Martha (Bancroft) **95** 61

PARLIN *cont'd*
Mary Blanchard (Durrell)
133 124
Mary Bourne (Perry)
116 195
Nathan **97** 395
Nicholas **67** 189 302
114 269
Phebe (Waters) **114** 269
Robinson Shattuck
68 xxxv
Sarah **63** 289 **108** 84
Sibyl W. **103** 235
Silas **103** 301
Smyrna **116** 195
Sumner **133** 124
PARLINGTON
George **144** 164
PARLOR Martha **61** 335
PARLOW
Abigail **134** 331
Elizabeth (Gibbs) **111** 67
Jesse **100** 185
Joanna **111** 67
John **64** 227
Martha **54** 102 103
Phebe **100** 185
Thomas **111** 67 **120** 279
Parmalee *see* Parmelee
PARMAN Charles **64** 55
Parmantier *see* Parmentier
PARMELEE Parmalee
Parmele Parmeley
Parmelle Parmely
—— **53** 379 **54** 275 **116** 40
123 90 **127** 80
— Rev. Mr. **60** 266
Aaron **53** 410 411 **56** 263
Abel **53** 409
Abigail **53** 313 407 408 410
58 281 361 362 **59** 64
102 105
Abigail (Kimberly)
102 105
Abner C. **91** 382 **92** 206
Abraham **53** 408 410 **61**
285 **102** 107
Achsa **53** 57 409
Alice (Maury) **88** 170
Alice Morris (Butler)
105 52
Ambrose **53** 409
Andrew **53** 409
Ann **53** 407 409 410 **57** 90
89 63 **106** 149
Anna **52** 467 **53** 406-409
55 152 **58** 300 **125** 136
Anna (Handy) **125** 137
Anna (Ward) (Rossiter)
125 136
Anna Louisa (Langen-
bacher) **89** 233
Anne **53** 408
Annie E. **118** 293
Annis (Fowler) **125** 137
Archelaus **53** 409 **58** 361-
363 **59** 62 **61** 27
Asaph **53** 407 **123** 96
Asaph (Mrs.) **123** 96
Ashbel **78** 129
Ashley **77** 147

PARMELEE *cont'd*
Barbara **53** 407
Benjamin **53** 407-409
Betsey **71** 122
Betty **53** 409
Beulah **53** 408
Beulah (Miller) **126** 53
Bryan **53** 407
Caleb **53** 406 407 **62** 147
70 70 **124** 190
Camp **53** 410
Caroline **57** 90
Caroline L. **77** 52
Caroline M. **83** 390
Catherine **58** 304
Charity **81** 57
Charles **53** 407 410 **105** 52
Charles A. **74** 157
Charles Arthur **75** xxvi
Charles M. **118** 293
Charles Roome **105** 52
Charlotte (Johnson)
125 137
Charlotte May **72** 296
Chloe **53** 408 411
Clotilda **57** 139
Cybele **53** 409
Cynthia **56** 59
Daniel **53** 313 407 410
58 300
David **53** 407 **55** 152 **58**
362 **59** 255 **126** 53
Deborah **53** 407 **66** 310
Delia Selden (Hart) **91**
382 383 **92** 206
Dencey **77** 52
Desire **53** 407 **70** 80 **123** 89
Desire (Barnes) **123** 90
Diana P. **77** 149
Dorothy **53** 407 409
Ebenezer **52** 467 **53** 408
Edward **104** 124
Eleazer **54** 352
Eli **57** 139 **58** 363 **128** 9
Elias **57** 90
Eliphaz **53** 410
Elisha **118** 293 **125** 255
Elizabeth **53** 406 408-410
57 134 **58** 282 **59** 62 65
61 25 28 29 **62** 384 **70**
70 **81** 130 **94** 283
Elizabeth (Foote) **124** 190
Else **53** 407
Emelie Frances **105** 52
Emma **76** 276
Esther **53** 406 409
Eunice **56** 59 **59** 47
126 109
Evelyn M. (Kettles)
105 52
Ezra **53** 210 406 **57** 90
Fannaye Louise **89** 233
George I. **60** 189
Gertrude **94** 137
Gilbert **77** 148
Grace M. (McClelland)
105 52
Grace Maime **105** 52
H. Sophia **77** 149
Hannah **53** 404 406-410
54 352 353 **56** 59 134

PARMELEE *cont'd*
264 **57** 87 **59** 62 **71** 8 **77**
52 **81** 130
Hannah (Kimberly)
102 107
Hannah (Spear) **119** 124
Harriet **72** 296 **77** 147
Harriet Newman (Hall)
113 298
Helen **60** 189
Helen Livingstone
105 52
Henry **105** 52
Henry Butler **105** 52
Henry Gilbert Woodruff
105 52
Hezekiah **53** 409 410 **59** 46
Hiel **53** 406 **56** 59
Honor **53** 406
Huldah **53** 410 **61** 287
Isaac **53** 406 408 410 **57** 92
58 362 **61** 29 **62** 384
James **53** 408 410 **118** 293
James (Mrs.) **88** 170
James Sanford **89** 233
Jane **52** 468 **58** 363
Jane A. **80** 111
Jared **53** 407 **61** 28
Jeanne **53** 407
Jedidiah **53** 409
Jeliel **53** 407 409
Jemima **53** 210 408 **62** 147
70 70
Jennette **53** 409
Jeremiah **53** 409 **58** 359
Jerusha **53** 408 410
Job **53** 406 409
Joel **53** 57 406 410 **58** 362
John **52** 468 **53** 405-411
54 270 353 **56** 134 **57**
134 **58** 281 362 363 **60**
189 **61** 25 **62** 384 **81** 130
Jonathan **53** 407
Joseph **53** 407 408 **58** 303
304 361 362 **59** 64 67 **61**
287 **102** 105 **126** 53
Joshua **53** 406 407 **57** 90
Josiah **53** 314 406 408 409
61 27
Julia **61** 27
Julia A. **118** 293
Leah **59** 64 **61** 285
Lemuel **53** 406
Levi **53** 410
Linus **126** 53
Livingstone **105** 52
Lois **53** 411
Loraine **61** 285
Lucretia **53** 408 **59** 64
61 29
Lucy **53** 407 410 411 **57** 90
78 129
Lulu **118** 293
Lumas **58** 362
Luther **58** 304
Lydia **53** 406 408 409 **59** 61-
63 **126** 52
Lyman L. **77** 149
Mabel **53** 410 **58** 361
Maria **53** 57

PARMELEE *cont'd*
Maria Augusta (Lougee)
  118 293
Mariah A. **118** 294
Mark **53** 410
Martha **53** 409
Mary **52** 469 **53** 406-410 **55**
  154 **56** 263 **59** 64 67 **62**
  138 **70** 70 **97** 123 **118**
  293 **124** 190
Mary (Chittenden) **126** 53
Mary (Deming) **126** 53
Mary E. **77** 148
Mary Elizabeth **136** 319
Mary Malinda **102** 230
Mehitable **53** 410
Melvin Benjamin **83** 390
Mercy **53** 410
Mercy (Hopkins) **104** 124
Mereb **53** 407 **59** 64
Miles **53** 409
Mina **61** 27
Mindwell **53** 411
Miriam **58** 361-363 **59** 62
  61 27
Moses **53** 410
Myron Newell **118** 292-
  294
Nathan **53** 409
Nathaniel **53** 406 408 409
  81 130
Nehemiah **53** 406
Noah **53** 409
Obedience **58** 303 304 **59**
  65 **61** 29
Olive **58** 363
Oliver **53** 407 **111** 132
P. **55** 287
Pamela **53** 314
Paninab **53** 409
Parnell (Handy) **126** 53
Patience **53** 407 **59** 255
Phebe **63** 339
Philander **83** 100
Philo **53** 409
Phineas **53** 408-410 **81** 57
Polly **79** 136 **126** 91
Priscilla **53** 406
Priscilla (Handy) **126** 53
Prudence **81** 57
Rachel **53** 407 409 410
  61 28
Rebecca **53** 406-408 411
  58 361 **106** 63
Reuben **53** 408 **59** 61-63
  61 27 285 **72** 296
Rhoda **53** 407 410 **54** 275
  58 301 **59** 64 **125** 137
Rosamund **53** 410
Rosanna **53** 410
Roxanna **126** 53
Roxy (Stanley) **118** 293
Rufus **53** 407
Ruth **53** 408-410 **56** 157
  159 **125** 137
Samuel **53** 407-410 **56** 263
  58 362 **62** 138 **81** 57
  126 53
Sarah **53** 406 411 **56** 263 **57**
  92 137 **58** 362 **59** 46 63
  64 **61** 27 285

PARMELEE *cont'd*
Sarah (Bishop) **126** 53
Sibyl **57** 90
Sibylla **53** 407
Silas **53** 411 **59** 64 **61** 285
Simeon **53** 410
Sophia **63** 269
Stephen **53** 406 409
Susan **77** 149
Susanna **53** 407
Temperance **53** 409
  58 359
Thankful **57** 90
Thomas **53** 410
Timothy **53** 407 **77** 52
Timothy L. P. **77** 52
Truman **113** 298
William **53** 408 **55** 154
  56 159 264
Willis Glenn **69** xxxv
PARMENTER Parmantier
  Parmiter Permenter
  Perminter
—— **53** 299 **56** 106 **66** 174
— Widow **66** 174 **68** 267
___ (Winch) **120** 269
Abel **61** 120 **116** 236
Abigail **57** 368 **61** 120
Abigail (Brewer) **91** 214
  96 189
Abijah **58** 373
Adam **61** 120
Adria **68** 266
Agnes **66** 173 175 **68** 266
  267 270
Agnes (Bayford)
  (Chandler) (Dane) **85**
  142 143 **96** 302 **147** 380
  381
Alice **66** 173 174 **68** 262
  263 265 266 270 271 273
  91 212 **147** 378 379
Alpheus **73** 257
Alvan **73** 257
Amos **116** 236
Amy **66** 174 175 **68** 263
  265 266 271 272 **91** 214
  147 379 382
Ann **66** 168 174 175
  68 265 270
Ann Elizabeth **92** 351
Anna **61** 120 **66** 174 175
Anna J. **95** 238
Anne **66** 108 173-175 **68**
  266 270 273
Annis **68** 262 **91** 213
  96 302
Asahel **61** 120 **73** 257
Audrey **68** 264 266 270
Barbara **66** 173 174
Bathsheba **58** 373
Benjamin **59** 158 **68** 272
  91 211 214 **96** 189
Betsey **58** 373
Bridget **63** 281 **68** 272 **91**
  213 **96** 189 **143** 329 **147**
  380-382
Caleb **126** 38
Caroline **69** 266
Catherine Hephzibah
  (Hartshorn) **95** 237

PARMENTER *cont'd*
Charles **58** 373 **96** 190
Charles O. **65** 15 16
Christian **68** 262 267 270
  147 379
Clifford A. **116** 230 236
Conscience **68** 265 271
Curtis H. **95** 238
Dana **114** 200
Danforth **70** 336
Daniel **66** 168-176 **116** 236
David **61** 120 **91** 214
  96 189
Deborah (Thayer)
  (Rockwood) (Gates)
  120 269 270
Delia Henrietta **95** 238
Deliverance **114** 200
Dorcas (Aikens) **99** 292
Dorothy **68** 266
Ebenezer **61** 120 121 **114**
  273 274
Edith **68** 265 266 269 270
Edmund **61** 120
Edward **68** 262-264 266
  267 270 **147** 380
Edward (Mrs.) **147** 380
Elihu **73** 257
Elizabeth **55** 259 **66** 173
  176 **68** 262-267 270-272
  91 190 **95** 348 **103** 161
  147 379 380
Elizabeth (Lovering)
  114 200
Elizabeth (Mott / Mote)
  (Purchas) **147** 379
Elizabeth Thompson
  91 216
Esther **61** 120 **66** 173 175
Esther French **70** 336
Eunice **58** 373
Ezra **91** 214 216 **140** 165
  233 329
Family **147** 377
Fanny **92** 192
Florence Frances Babbitt
  (Dawley) **96** 189
  113 306
Frances **137** 259
Freeman **61** 120
George **58** 377 378 **68**
  262-267 269-272 **91** 212
  114 200 **147** 377-381
George Washington
  91 216
Guillaume de **134** 254
Hannah **58** 373 **59** 269 **66**
  168-170 173-176 **67** 209
Hannah (Dana) **137** 258
Harriet **69** 266 **114** 200
Hattie May **54** 151
Helen (James) **91** 211
Helen Earl **113** 306
Helen Fisher **91** 217
Helen Francis (Bartlett)
  96 190 **97** 158 **113** 306
Henrietta **95** 237
Henry **68** 264-266 268 270
  96 190
Henry Earl **67** xxxiv **68**
  vii xxi **69** xxxi **70** v vii

PARMENTER *cont'd*
x **71** vii xi **74** xxviii 13
90 127 **96** 149 189 **97**
160 **113** 306
Henry Earl (Mrs.) **97** 158
113 232 306
Hester **66** 169 175
Horace Wellington
54 151
Isaiah **53** 249
Jacob **91** 266
James **61** 120 **68** 266 270
92 351 **96** 189
James Parker **64** xxxiv
65 xx **66** vi **67** vi xx
xxii **68** vii xix xxi 300
69 vii xiv **70** vii viii
xiv xv **71** vii viii xvi
xviii **72** vii viii xv 77
73 vii viii x xv **74** vii
viii xvi 160 **75** vii viii
xv **76** vii viii xv **77** vii
viii xx 79 **78** 109 195 219
220 **79** 190 215 216 **80**
200 221 222 **81** 211 235
236 **82** 221 222 225 248-
250 252 382 383 **83** 216
218 220 244 245 370 **84**
174 177 203 205 **85** 177
179 212 214 346 **86** 185
188 212-214 **87** 162 168
186-188 297 **88** 161 162
183 184 300 **89** 122 124
125 144-146 166 167 **90**
119 122 126 148-150 294
91 127 129-131 133 155
177 211 214 217 218 221
92 138-140 149 **95** 308
Jane **68** 263 265 272
Jason **73** 257 **141** 15
Jedidiah **96** 365
Jennie Hester **95** 238
Jeremiah **96** 189 190
113 306
Joan **68** 262 263 266 269
270 272 **147** 379
Joel **95** 237 **114** 198 200
John **58** 373 **60** 358 63
280 281 **65** 230 **66** 167-
176 **68** 263-272 278 **85**
143 **91** 211-214 **96** 189
302 **116** 230 236 **134**
254 **143** 329 330 **147**
315 326 377-382
John Robert (Mrs.)
104 145
Jonas **96** 189
Jonas Willis **114** 200
Jonathan **137** 258
Joseph **58** 373 **59** 87 157
158 269 **61** 120 **66** 168-
170 172-176 **68** 265 266
270 272 **69** 266 **70** 336
105 199 **116** 236
Joshua **120** 269
Katharine **68** 262 265 267
270 **147** 379
Lawson **73** 257
Leah **66** 176
Levi **58** 373
Lois **87** 195

PARMENTER *cont'd*
Lucinda **114** 200 **125** 289
Lydia **53** 249 **55** 260 **68**
272 **114** 182
Lydia (Earl) **96** 190
Margaret **68** 264 265 267
271 **91** 212 **147** 381
Margery **68** 264 271 **91**
212 **96** 189 **147** 377
Margery (Garrold)
147 380
Maria H. **92** 351
Marie **68** 266
Marie (Usher alias Clarke)
147 380
Martha **66** 173 175 **68** 266
270
Martin **66** 173 176
Martin Luther **95** 237
Mary **56** lxxv **58** 373 **59**
158 269 **61** 120 **66** 169
170 173-176 **68** 264 270-
272 278 **75** 37 **81** 197 **84**
111 **91** 212 213 **114** 200
126 6 38 **147** 378 380
381
Mary (Carter) **96** 189
Mary (Hadley) **91** 266
Mary (Osborne) **114** 200
Mary (Parker) **91** 215
Mary (Spring) **137** 258
Mary (Tower) **91** 214
Mary Elizabeth **54** 151
Mary Elizabeth (Adams)
113 306
Mary Fisher **91** 217 221
114 77
Matilda **73** 257
Millicent **61** 120
Nahum **61** 120 **114** 198-
200
Nathan **99** 292
Nathaniel **68** 265 270
Nicholas **68** 267 269
147 377
O. B. **91** 331
Oliver Tisdel **61** 120
Opal Grace **103** 117
Persis **61** 120
Peter **59** 420 **66** 173 174
Philena (Haynes) **114** 200
Philip **67** 209
Polly **99** 292
Priscilla **66** 173-175
Ralph Franklin (Mrs.)
84 190
Rebecca **61** 120 **66** 174 176
76 86 **137** 259
Reuben **116** 236
Reuel **73** 257
Richard **68** 262 263 265 267
269 270 **147** 377 379
Robert **59** 87 365 **66** 168-
177 **68** 262-273 **91** 211
212 **147** 378-380
Robert Potter **116** 236
Roxy **70** 336
Ruth **136** 304
Sally **61** 120
Sally (Haynes) **114** 200
Sally S. **61** 120

PARMENTER *cont'd*
Samuel **66** 168 173-175
68 265 266 272 **91** 214
Sarah **59** 157 **61** 120 121 **66**
173-175 **68** 264-266 270-
272 **91** 212 **147** 380
Sarah (Richardson)
126 38
Sibyl **58** 373 **114** 180
Silence (Maverick) **96** 365
Stephen **120** 270
Sukey (Brown) **96** 190
Susan **61** 341 **68** 262 265
270 **114** 200
Susanna **61** 120 **114** 197
198 **137** 259
Susanna (Bryant) **137** 258
Susanna (Willis) **114**
197-199
Tamisen (Rice) **91** 214
96 189
Thomas **68** 264-267 269
270 272 **80** 352 **147** 377
Ursula **68** 264 271 **91** 212
147 380
Warren **61** 120 **114** 200
Waty **73** 257
William **66** 173 174 **68** 262-
271 273 **91** 212 215 216
96 189 **147** 377-381
William Ellison **91** 211
216 217 221
William George **91** 217
221
Zenas **114** 200
Zibah (Willis) **114** 273 274
PARMER Jane **52** 232
PARMISTER
Orrin **147** 274
Paulina Elzura (Stone)
147 274
Parnal *see* Parnell
PARNECK William **53** 433
PARNELL Parnal Parnel
——— **53** 35 **84** 314
Abigail **113** 30
Albertus Jenkins (Mrs.)
80 333 **81** 222
Alice M. **91** 138 **92** 95
100 106
Alice Maud (Miner)
112 143
Catherine **109** 72
Charles Sumner **112** 143
Charles Sumner (Mrs.)
95 147 **100** 109 **112** 71
143 144
Fearnot **68** 203 **69** 155
Fearnot (Parker) **96** 234
Francis **69** 360
Hannah **85** 322
Henry **52** 487
Joan **55** 434
John **56** 376 **68** 203 **69** 155
94 262 **96** 234
Jonas **54** 192 193
Josias **55** 434
Margaret **81** 190
Martha **60** 346
Mary **103** 84
Maude **81** 222

PARNELL *cont'd*
Rebecca **106** 63
Sarah **106** 150
Thomas **103** 84 **119** 17
William **107** 214
PARO Margaret **145** 139
PAROAL Betsey **90** 248
PAROT — Ensign **130** 281
PARR Par Pare Parre
— Mr. **64** 158 **65** 171
Agnes **96** 107
Albert C. **94** 164
Alice **101** 13
Catherine **104** 112
Cora (Shumaker) **94** 164
Elisa Jane (Sloan) **86** 368
Elizabeth **145** 20
Elizabeth (James) **126** 256
128 20
Ezekiel **64** 165 252 **65** 167
171
Flora (Pennell) **117** 319
Hannah (Burroughs)
111 273
Harriet Brooks **86** 368
James Robinson **86** 368
Jane L. **64** 155
John **52** 472 **64** 79 **117** 5 7
8 10-12 **126** 256 **128** 20
Joseph **64** 254 **65** 166
Katharine **68** 112 **114** 56
58
Nathaniel **65** 236
Richard **52** 355 **129** 107
117
Samuel **111** 273
Sarah (Reeves) **94** 164
Susan Josephine **77** 221
Thomas **94** 164
William **82** 191 **94** 200 335
98 28 **108** 178 **114** 57
PARRAN Alexander **135**
100 101
Elizabeth (Eveleth)
135 101
Sarah Elizabeth **84** 96
Sarah Eveleth **84** 95
135 100
PARRASITE
Belinda **54** 148
Parrat *see* Parrott
Parratt *see* Parrott
PARRECK John **61** 199
Parret *see* Parrott
Parrett *see* Parrott
Parrey *see* Parry
Parrie *see* Parry
Parris *see* Paris
Parrish *see* Parish
PARROTT Parrat Parratt
Parret Parrett
—— **76** 69 **112** 35
— Widow **84** 152
Alice May **80** 245
Benjamin **52** 451 **62** 244
84 152
Bryant **57** 280 388
Charles **77** 184
Christopher **73** 139
Clarissa (Rice) **90** 43
Daniel **73** 117

PARROTT *cont'd*
Deborah **82** 296 301
Edward **54** 388
Elizabeth **60** 54 **73** 146 **79**
250 253 **84** 212 **87** 74 77
105 230 **111** 119 121
145 262
Elizabeth (Varney) **86** 229
Elizabeth G. (Larrabee)
88 336
Ellen **54** 388
Enoch **54** 388 389
Enoch Greenleaf **54** 388
Francis **93** 41-43 **105** 230
109 230
George William **117** 77
Greenleaf **54** 388
Hannah **54** 388 **84** 127
Henry **76** 56
James **60** 54 **88** 336
James Brackett **54** 388
Jane **84** 100
Jean **76** 56 69
Joan **84** 290
Joan (Gunne) **84** 290
John **60** 54 **61** 92 **80** 245
82 296 301 **90** 43
John F. **54** 388
John P. **54** 388
Jonathan **60** 54
Joseph **112** 32
Judith **79** 250 253 **87** 74
76 77
Lucinda **73** 117
Margaret **111** 119
Martha **54** 388
Mary **54** 388 **60** 54 **109** 230
Mercy **105** 230
Nettie Frances **77** 184
Patty **60** 54
Peter Pierce **54** 388
Rachel **80** 245
Raufe **112** 35
Rebecca **52** 451 **140** 233
Richard **111** 119
Robert **51** 298 **52** 69
Robert Parker **54** 388
Ruth **60** 54
Sarah **60** 54 **129** 256
Sarah P. **54** 388 389
Simon **79** 250 253 **87** 74 77
145 262 **147** 336
Susan **54** 388
Susanna **54** 388
Thomas **65** 236
William **54** 388
PARROTTIN
Nancy B. **100** 192
William **100** 192
PARROW Julia **123** 225
PARRY Parrey Parrie
Parrys Pary - *see also*
Peary & Perry
— Capt. **82** 51
— Mrs. **83** 195
Abel **65** 361
Abigail **82** 51
Ann **91** 188
Anna Lewis **82** 51
Antinetta **125** 294
Benjamin **98** 44

PARRY *cont'd*
Betsey L. **145** 155
Caleb **114** 187
Carmita de Salm **99** 51
Catherine **141** 353
David **93** 300
Edward **93** 300 **104** 175
Egartha **136** 36
Elizabeth **82** 51
George **51** 356
Hannah **82** 51
Henry **64** 337 **93** 300
136 36
Holland **91** 331 332
Jane (Paxon) **98** 44
John **63** 220 **76** 224
John G. **114** 187
John J. **82** 155
John Lewis **82** 51
Martha Kelley **95** 275
Mary **82** 51 **100** 297 **136** 36
Muriel **53** 115
Oliver **98** 44
Oliver Randolph **99** 51
Oliver Randolph (Mrs.)
98 342
Peggy **82** 51
Peter **98** 406
Rachel (Fitz Randolph)
98 44
Richard **82** 51
Richard Randolph **99** 50
Richmond **82** 51
Robert **93** 300
Samuel **82** 51
Sarah **82** 51 **93** 300
Thomas **85** 17 **97** 176
William **65** 48
PARSE Sarah (Holland) 27
105 27
PARSELL John **65** 374
Sarah **65** 374 375
PARSET John **65** 238
Parsevall *see* Percival
PARSHALL
DeWitt **133** 21 36
Israel **54** 459
James **54** 458 459
James Clark **52** 286 288
376 **54** 458 **55** xxxii **58**
xlv 100 **60** 82
Lena Belle **104** 47
Rhoda (Gifford)
(Clements) (Smith)
(Lyman) **138** 211
Susan **133** 21 36
William K. **138** 211
PARSHLEY
Betsey **76** 32
Drusilla **69** 333
Elizabeth **69** 259
Emeline S. **76** 41
Hannah E. **76** 42
Hattie J. **76** 44
John **69** 259 **76** 32
John L. **76** 39
John W. **76** 38
Maria **76** 39
Mary **69** 259 **76** 32
Mary A. **76** 38
Mary Ann **67** 351 **76** 41

PARSHLEY *cont'd*
Marybee **76** 32
Olive **114** 180
Sarah M. **76** 41
Thomas **76** 32
Parsivall *see* Percival
PARSLEY Parsle
Agnes **65** 351 **81** 432
Henry **85** 82
John **63** 344 **81** 432
Richard **51** 46 **65** 351
PARSLOW Frances
(Hawes) **84** 338
Helen L. (Goodwin)
83 430 437
Thomas **84** 338
William A. **83** 430 437
PARSONS Parson Person
Persons Persone
Persones
—— **54** 137 388 **56** 114
214 **59** 113 **72** 180 **74**
222 **78** 57 **83** 36 301 **118**
8 9 15 18 23 25 27 29 108-
110 112 116-118 124 126
220 221 224 228 229 304
119 45 51 52 54-59 124
128-132 135 139 140 208-
213 217-220 **222** 290 292-
300 302 304-307 **120** 58
59 62 123 124 127 128
130 131 133 134 203 205-
211 214 294-297 299 300-
302 **122** 63 65 67 68 115-
119 121 123 222 224 225
227 303 305 306 309 **145**
48
— Capt. **59** 38 **93** 166 **99**
306 **101** 152 200 **137**
257
— Col. **101** 147 152 200
131 41
— Dr. **79** 306
— Mr. **60** 262 263 **80** 30
84 146 267
— Mrs. **94** 222 **118** 24 28
29 120 305 **119** 51 130
140 208 215 218 222 291
293 295 298 299 305 307
120 62 124-126 130 133
203 205 210-212 300 301
303 **122** 63 223
— Rev. Mr. **62** 277
— Widow **64** 181
A. **92** 173
Aaron **145** 29
Aaron S. **122** 108
Abby **120** 220
Abiah **71** 272 **72** 99
Abigail **55** 202 315 **57** 290
59 81 **60** 308 360 **61** 238
71 163 302 **75** 45 **77** 209
82 501-503 **83** 11 148
90 91 **97** 343 **112** 219
117 143 **123** 260 261
136 331 **142** 249 **148**
218 221 223-225 228-230
353 357
Abigail (Ball) **136** 326
Abigail (Beal) **118** 154 155

PARSONS *cont'd*
Abigail (Blaisdell)
111 229
Abigail (Blunt) **83** 11
Abigail (Childs) **113** 267
Abigail (Haskell) **135** 24
105 **142** 249
Abigail (Littlefield)
123 74
Abigail (Phelps) **148** 225
Abigail (Younglove)
102 145 **142** 248
Abigail A. (Littlefield)
120 138
Abigail F. (Blunt) **91** 231
Abigail Frost **76** lxxxix xc
82 503
Abijah **88** 12
Achsah **57** 291 292 295 **68**
338 **94** 280 **136** 333
Ada (Robinson) **83** 301
Addison B. **92** 173
Adelaide I. **81** 408
Adelia A. (Cleaves)
102 145
Agnes Amelia **79** 349
Albert Elmer **89** 233
Albert Ross **55** 450 **56**
xxxii **143** 104 148 221
Albert Tallman **89** 233
Alberta (Wharf) **102** 145
Albion A. **122** 71
Albion E. **119** 283 285
Alice **87** 285
Alice (Colles) **143** 106 112
Alice (Crossing?) **142**
247 248
Alice Lorraine **110** 142
Allen **91** 331 **102** 145
Almeda **93** 295 **113** 267
119 225 226
Almira **85** 169 **145** 29 30
Alonzo **113** 267
Altha **122** 108
Amanda **122** 108
Amelia **83** 472
Amos **109** 214
Andrew J. **120** 223
Andrew Jackson **113** 267
Angie Matilda (Lazell)
89 233
Ann **99** 125 **110** 142 **116** 43
125 222
Ann (Osborn) **105** 313
Ann E. **61** 346
Ann G. **80** 424
Ann Mary **119** 143
Ann W. **72** 49
Anna **53** 250 278 **62** 85 **71**
162 277 **72** 32 168 **73**
257 **118** 37 **119** 57 **147**
183
Anna (Utley) **88** 376
Anna W. **72** 106
Anna Webster **72** 95
Anne **52** 430 **53** 278 **71** 79
83 279 282 **72** 43 178
111 254 **115** 141 **143**
106 112
Anthony **148** 242
Arthur Daniel **72** 98

PARSONS *cont'd*
Arthur Jeffrey **59** 339
Augusta M. **92** 286
Augusta S. **126** 67
Avis **143** 106 116
B. F. **66** 112
Barlow **65** 228
Barnabas **73** 225
Benjamin **53** 378 **66** 210
224 225 295 297 **82** 282
296 **123** 260 261 297
136 324 **143** 101-104
106 108 110 111 115 365
148 215 216 218 219 221-
223 360
Benjamin Franklin **74** 96
Bethiah **145** 324 **148** 228-
233 355
Betsey **55** 373 **62** 85 **72** 46
48 104 **83** 13 **97** 367 377
Betsey (Perkins) **117** 226
227
Betsey (Rogers) **84** 366
Betsey (Trafton) **117** 139
Birney Cleaves **90** 137
102 113 129 145
Bishop **72** 45 96 181
Bishop Case **72** 89 **102** 181
Bray Underwood **112** 105
C. **92** 173 **101** 328
C. C. **142** 246
C. V. **123** 235 236
Caleb **60** 264 **83** 359
Calvin **55** 126
Caroline **79** 159 **113** 267
133 302
Caroline (Lathrop)
133 302
Caroline (Russell) **95** 353
Caroline A. **119** 287
Caroline Mellen (Nye)
89 12
Carrie **128** 265
Catherine **119** 138 294
120 293 **143** 105
Chadwell **71** 281 307
Chandler **72** 91
Charles **54** 371 **116** 141
302 **119** 156 **122** 122
125 104 293
Charles Chauncey
140 233
Charles D. **55** xxxii
Charles F. **91** 388
Charles Hazlitt **108** 224
Charles Hazlitt (Mrs.) **89**
132 **108** 63 139 224
Charles Henry **92** 85
Charles Lathrop **57** 236
58 xlv
Charles Moody **112** 106
Charles O. **101** 328
Charles Sumner **54** xxxix
56 xxxii
Charlotte **112** 106 **116**
300 301
Chester **119** 216
Chloe **68** 338 **94** 382
114 307
Chloe (Cox) **101** 328
Chloe Weston **68** 338

PARSONS *cont'd*
Christian **110** 57 178
Christian (Vynt) **143** 116
Christopher **57** 292 **143**
  106 112 114 115
Clara Ellen **72** xx
Clarence V. **123** 236
Clarissa **65** 138 **79** 155
Clark H. **105** 73
Claudius Dwight **72** 96
Clementina (Janes)
  94 289
Cornelia (Gage) **108** 224
Cornelia A. **68** 338
Cornelia Smith **72** 50
Cynthia **57** 291
Cyrus T. **105** 73
Daniel **54** 371 **68** 338 **72**
  93 94 **116** 262 **143** 113
  114
Daniel Chester **58** xlviii
Daniel Jacobs **91** 82
Daniel Latimer **72** 44 88
  95 96
Daniel Smith **61** 193
David **54** 134 **56** 318 **60**
  393 **65** 138 **79** 161 **81**
  397 **87** 399 **99** 80 **107** 93
  111 254 **115** 225 **118**
  108 126 217 235 **119** 129
  216 **126** 226 **148** 220
David (Mrs.) **118** 108
Deborah **55** 202 **66** 78
Deborah (Blaisdell)
  117 143
Dora E. (King) **120** 223
Dorcas **56** 318 **79** 157
Doris Cranston **80** 142
Dorothy **66** 258 **67** 217
  68 338 **82** 292 296 **119**
  57 138 294 **144** 330 331
  338
Dorothy (Colt) (Sparks)
  144 324 330 **145** 324
  330 331 338
Dorothy Rosamund
  103 120
Dydia **118** 119
E. **98** 208
E. E. (Mrs.) **84** 339 **85** 197
E. T. **79** 167
Eben **51** 152 **52** 186 **65** liv
  94 312 **122** 66 117 122
Eben Ezery **87** 303
Ebenezer **53** 277 **78** 180 **87**
  303 **101** 43 **121** 66 **123**
  32 262 **136** 324 325 **140**
  233 **142** 249 **148** 219
  223-226 228 230 232 233
  235-237 345 348 352-357
  359
Ebenezer Greenleaf **89** 12
Edgerton (Mrs.) **86** 198
Edmund **125** 222
Edward **94** 289 **106** 153
  121 248 **138** 225
Edward F. **53** 250
Edward Rutherin **72** 94
Edward S. **63** xxii
Edward Smith **92** 86
  136 325

PARSONS *cont'd*
Edwin **101** 328
Eleanor **142** 246 248
Eleanor Roy **85** 199
Electa **72** 45 91 103
Electa (Frary) **136** 324
Eli **79** 225
Elihu **110** 58 178 179 **111**
  229 254 **112** 219 **117**
  139 **118** 154 155 **136**
  325 **148** 37
Elijah **62** 379 **81** 51 **84** 366
Elisha **117** 164 169
Elisha (Mrs.) **117** 169
Eliza **72** 100 **97** 377 **112**
  106 **119** 69 **122** 122
Eliza (Demarq) **89** 233
Eliza A. **80** 310
Eliza Ann **126** 205
Elizabeth **52** 427 **53** 166
  167 **54** 388 **55** 202 206
  56 318 319 **60** 311 **61**
  346 **63** 370 **70** 151 **71**
  155 300 **81** 51 **82** 503 **85**
  94 **90** 91 **91** 388 **105** 222
  108 64 88 224 **110** 58
  178 179 **112** 225 305
  114 44 **119** 122 **123** 297
  135 24 98 100 **136** 313
  326 **137** 116 **142** 246-
  249 **143** 160 **145** 29 **148**
  357
Elizabeth (Andrews)
  142 249
Elizabeth (Bradstreet)
  124 319
Elizabeth (Cooke) **143**
  108 **148** 219
Elizabeth (Dunbar)
  148 352
Elizabeth (Geiles) **142**
  247-249
Elizabeth (Hardy)
  (Garlick) **148** 345 346
Elizabeth (Honeywood)
  148 220
Elizabeth (Jones) **89** 132
  108 224
Elizabeth (Silvester) **86** 89
Elizabeth (Strong) **90** 189
  95 353 **136** 313 324-326
  331 333 **143** 109 **148**
  218 219 359
Elizabeth (Usher) **132** 270
Elizabeth (Wadhams)
  91 388
Elizabeth Alden **65** 138
Elizabeth Challis **85** 190
Elizabeth Scott **65** 138
Elizabeth U. **117** 140
Elizabth **108** 64
Ella (Greenfield) **91** 82
Ella Frances **91** 82
Emeline (Sewall) **120** 64
  67
Emily **96** 389 **101** 328
Emily Collins **69** 210
Emily F. (Ellis) **117** 164
Emily M. **68** 338
Emma (Hunkins) **101** 329
Enoch **56** 318 **65** 220

PARSONS *cont'd*
Ephraim **61** 195 **62** 195
  111 229 **115** 213
Erastus J. **101** 329
Esther **54** 203 **57** 213 **110**
  160 **118** 20 123 **122** 108
  148 218 221
Esther (Badger) **125** 222
Esther (Chase) **88** 12
Esther Rosetta (Smith)
  92 85
Eunice **55** 154 **56** 319 **57**
  295 **72** 101 **94** 192 **118**
  28 110 125 231 **119** 283
  121 58 **145** 29 30
Eunice Philena **72** 93
Evaline **119** 62
Evelina **94** 85
Everett **68** 203
Everline **93** 294
Experience **120** 63
Ezra **60** 308 **77** 209
F. **98** 208
Fannie Denison **80** 142
Fanny E. **83** 381
Fitzroy **72** 50
Fitzroy (Mrs.) **72** 50
Fitzroy Brainard **72** 96
Florence (Nourse)
  102 145
Frances **55** 373 **63** 176 **82**
  503 **83** 14
Frances (Usher) **91** 230
Frances C. **79** 152
Frances Usher **132** 270
Francis **65** 138 **75** 162 **79**
  155 **80** 63
Francis W. **78** 316
Frank **63** 114 **108** 224
Frank Henry **66** l 96 **67**
  xxxiv **90** 127 **92** 85 92
  150 198
Fred Russell **89** 233
Frederick T. **88** 87 165 **90**
  294 **91** 137 139
George **55** 141 **101** 328
George Ayer (Mrs.) **109**
  127 **114** 80
George Berkley **148** 237
George Henry **85** 169
George Howland **110** 142
George P. **85** 169
Georgianna F. **123** 74
Gerald James **110** 238
  143 101 365 **145** 29 **147**
  148 **148** 215 218 345
Gertie L. **101** 328
Gertrude **101** 328
Gideon **120** 45
Gladys Marie **89** 233
Goody **148** 229
Gorham **52** 186 **124** 28
  132 325 **140** 233
Gurdon **72** 50
Gustavus **69** 210
Halstead Cushing **89** 342
Hannah **55** 200 201 **57** 290
  68 338 **71** 81 85 164 165
  279 281 305 **72** 99 **86** 18
  87 302 **88** 81 **92** 89 **100**
  267 **108** 246 **110** 58 **111**

PARSONS *cont'd*
229 **112** 218 **114** 128
115 137 **119** 130 140
297 306 **123** 261 **136**
314 **148** 218 221 238 348
Hannah (Cooley) **123** 265
148 225
Hannah (Gray) **101** 65
Hannah (Hitchcock)
148 224
Hannah (Parkes) **148** 348
Hannah (Parsons)
108 246
Hannah (Waitt) **96** 55
Hannah (Younglove)
142 248
Harriet **57** 295 **65** 138 **98**
208 **101** 328
Harriet A. **123** 94
Harriet Eddy **84** 185 **95**
353 357 **96** 87 163
Harriet Electa (Morton)
90 189 **95** 353 357
Harry Elmer **89** 233
Harvey N. **101** 329
Harvy **104** 47
Hattie L. **123** 233
Hattie R. (Miner) **89** 254
Hazel **108** 224
Hector **101** 328
Helen (Carpenter)
110 231
Helen L. (Boynton)
(Wells) **94** 139
Henrietta H. (Farnsworth)
90 115
Henry **55** 90 200 **56** 74 **73**
xxxv **85** 316 **97** 209 **101**
328 **112** 284 **148** 218
221 360
Henry A. **89** 254
Henry I **91** 388
Henry Martyn **89** 342
Henry S. **85** 316 **91** 98
Henry Wood **93** 256
Henry Woolcot **72** 91
Herbert Collins **83** 123
233
Hester **148** 221
Hezekiah **71** 75 79 83 85
158-164 272 276 277 279
282 295 299 300 307 **72**
32 34 43 46 50 87-89 98
99 103 169 172 178 179
79 157 **123** 265 **148** 223
225
Hezekiah Wheeler **72** 93
Hial **79** 349
Hiram **101** 329
Hitty **61** 194
Horace **101** 328
Horace Holly **113** 267
Horatio A. **83** 151
Howard Uriah **89** 233
Hugh **65** 382 **143** 102-104
148 216
Huldah **60** 150
Ignatius **125** 42 44
Isaac **90** 189 **95** 353 **111**
254 **136** 333 **142** 245
Isabel (Grant) **132** 325

PARSONS *cont'd*
Isabell **119** 66 **142** 246
247 249
Isabella **66** 224 305 **119** 64
Isabella (Haines) **142** 248
Israel **94** 313 **96** 55 **107** 93
J. **96** 303
J. D. **83** 36 195
J. Lester (Mrs.) **94** 139
J. P. **80** 424
Jacob **108** 246 **142** 246 248
James **71** 81 155 165 271
273 274 281 305 **72** 31
33 **73** 142 257 **90** 91 **102**
145 **116** 137 **137** 141
142 245-249 **143** 106
115 116
James Adrian **80** 142
James Coleman **73** 257
James Davis **115** 240
124 319
James Edward **113** 302
James Graham (Mrs.)
86 198
James Seton **101** 65
James W. **68** 338
Jane **78** 57 60 62
Jane (Cross) **101** 328 329
Jane Chester **65** 138
Jane F. (Junkins) **122** 71
Janet (Sampson) **89** 342
Jason **57** 295
Jeffrey **53** 28 **102** 145 **112**
225 **142** 245-249
Jemima **56** 319 **135** 24
105 106 **142** 36
Jemima (Nelson)
(Bennett) (Todd)
142 249
Jemima (Phillips) **116** 134
Jeremiah **142** 249
Jerry **101** 328
Jerusha **61** 182 184 **116** 130
Jerusha (Sayward)
112 304
Jna. **117** 170
Joan **66** 256
Joann **92** 106
Joanna **66** 297 **77** 209
Joanna Oram **93** 310
Joanna S. **119** 61
Joel **60** 393
John **53** 168 **54** 203 **55** 86
89 90 202 205-207 **56**
319 **64** 15 **66** 148 150
153 155 210 224 258 **68**
195 **69** 147 **71** 84 85 155-
158 160 161 274 299 300
302 303 **72** 49 **74** 190 **76**
xc 47 53 **77** 209 **78** 60 62
82 503 **84** 285 **90** 248
91 231 **93** 256 **94** 217
95 194 **97** 268 367 377
105 313 **108** 88 **110** 57
58 160 167 178 179 317
111 229 230 254 **112**
219 **114** 130 **115** 222
223 **116** 134 138 142
117 140 169 **118** 166
120 140 **121** 144 303
305 306 **122** 312 313

PARSONS *cont'd*
123 151 152 233 **142**
246-249 **143** 62 113 114
145 324 330 **148** 119
217-219 223 228 230 235
236 345 351 352 355-357
John A. **79** 225 **124** 62
John C. **91** 388
John Caldwell **65** 138
80 63
John G. **68** 338
John K. **88** 114
John Keep **72** 96
John Spencer **120** 45
John U. **87** 206
John W. **84** 31
Jonathan **53** 39 **56** 319 **58**
300 **74** 128 **76** 135 137
77 202 209 **82** 284 296
101 328 329 **102** 145
143 101 102 **145** 29 **148**
215 218-220 345
Jonathan I. **72** 96 104
Jonathan Trumbull
72 45 87
Joseph **51** 50 **53** 276 **54**
371 **55** 450 **59** 56 **60** 189
66 78 157 158 265 312
67 217-219 **68** 338 **73**
224 **76** lxxxix xc **82** 501
90 158 189 **91** 94 **95** 353
97 146 209 273 **105** 302
110 58 179 **111** 4 230
254 **112** 104 218 304
113 127 **114** 134 **115** 60
211 **116** 111 129 133 141
132 270 **136** 313 324-
326 331 333 **143** 101-104
106 111 114 115 119 365
145 29 351 **148** 215-219
221-223 225 228 230 237
345 359 360
Joseph (Mrs.) **97** 273
Joseph A. **102** 145
Joseph P. **91** 231
Joshua **65** 221 **92** 348
Josiah **55** 86 **90** 189 **92** 85
110 58 111 254 **112** 305
115 213 **118** 186 **119**
228 229 276 **136** 333
142 36
Jotham **92** 85
Judith **56** 318 **122** 122
Judith Thomas **100** 312
Julius L. **68** 338
Justin **136** 324
Katharine **72** 46 **143** 106
116 117
Katharine McKinlay **100**
103 **101** 65 129
Kendall **141** 299
Kendig **91** 331
Keziah **123** 126
L. **72** 98
L. B. **105** 302
Lamas **101** 328
Lamira **72** 89
Langdon B. **59** 423
141 141
Langdon Brown **60**
xxxvi **64** 233 **68** 251

PARSONS *cont'd*
Laura (Ford) **120** 45
Laura Esther **122** 108
Laura Melissa **82** 404
Laurence **90** 89
Lavinia **72** 47 102
Lavinia B. Mann **85** 316
Lemuel **57** 290-293 295
Levi **54** 371 **104** 47 **145** 29
  30
Lewis Baldwin **54** xxxix
  369 371 **55** xxxii **61**
  xxxv **63** 207 **91** 388
Lewis Green **54** 371
  81 291
Lidiah (Stanwood)
  102 145
Linus E. **91** 388
Lizzie **71** 276 **123** 151
Lois **77** 209 **83** 359 **85** 460
  461 **94** 313 314
Lois (Bancroft) (Willey)
  94 313 314
Lora **113** 302
Lorania **61** 193
Louis B. **54** 369
Louis P. **84** 31
Louisa **98** 208 **125** 290
Louisa (Hines) **101** 329
Louisa (McIntire) **119**
  283 285
Lovey **91** 231
Lovice **72** 102
Lovisa **72** 88 **98** 208
  101 328
Lovy (Brock) **90** 248
  95 194
Lucetta **68** 338
Lucina **57** 290
Lucina (Strong) **90** 189
  95 353 **136** 333
Lucinda **112** 105 **119** 69
Lucretia **75** lxvii **136** 324
Lucy **57** 268 **66** 148 224 225
  295 297 305 **71** 161 **77**
  209 **86** 297 **89** 342 **112**
  219 **116** 138 **125** 73 **132**
  325 **139** 57
Lucy (Bradbury) **132** 270
Lucy (Dwelley) **125** 104
Lucy (Weeks) **112** 218
Lucy Ann **51** 152 **57** 295
  64 203
Lucy L. **120** 140 **123** 151
  152
Luther **79** 160
Lydia **57** 208 **61** 174 **78**
  182 **82** 284 296 **116** 135
  118 118 **119** 135 **121** 65
  148 345-347
Lydia (Brown) **143** 108
  114 **148** 226 227 229 230
Lydia (Haskell) **142** 249
Lydia (Whittemore)
  108 88
Lydia D. **93** 294 **118** 317
Lydia G. **68** 338
M. Antoinette **93** 256
M. J. **83** 381
Mabel **71** 281 307

PARSONS *cont'd*
Mabel Howard (Randall)
  92 86
Mabel R. **91** 388
Malina **76** 272
Marcy **148** 228 230 347 348
Margaret **81** 153 **98** 208
  101 328 **118** 119 **142**
  246-248 **143** 105
Margaret (Hoskins) **143**
  106 111-114 117 365 **148**
  216 222 226
Margaret (Kelsey) **101** 66
Margaret (Marshfield)
  123 262 **148** 224
Margaret Wellington
  114 80
Margery **143** 113-115 117
Maria **57** 293 **125** 218
Maria (Huntley) **101** 148
Maria Antoinette **93** 256
Maria McKown **74** 96
Mariah (Tripp) **118** 318
Marshfield **77** 209 **78** 380
Martha **62** 84 **71** 160 278
  279 282 **81** 432 **82** 296
  299 **89** 18 **145** 29 30
Martha (Bootman)
  102 145
Martha (Fernald) **116** 302
Martha Kingsley **94** 289
Martha Sophia **72** 96
Mary **52** 186 **53** 250 **54** 434
  55 84 89 202 206 373 **56**
  58 **57** 268 **61** 193 **62** 330
  63 168 **64** 72 **65** 138 **66**
  146 148 150 153 155 210
  224 312 **67** 218 219 **68**
  338 **72** 45 **76** 137 **81** 51
  432 **83** 14 **90** 158 **91** 231
  93 295 **94** 382 **98** 348
  101 201 328 **109** 150
  110 178 179 **112** 104
  115 219 **117** 140 **123**
  261 262 **125** 294 **134** 92
  142 246 248 **143** 62 106
  114 115 117 **148** 217 218
  220 221 223 225 349 353
  356 357
Mary (Anderson) **128** 269
Mary (Ashley) **123** 265
Mary (Baker) **90** 189
Mary (Bliss) **90** 189 **95** 353
  143 115 **148** 216
Mary (Clark) **148** 219
Mary (Cross) **101** 329
Mary (Higgens) **112** 104
  115 60
Mary (Howe) **102** 145
Mary (Lewis) **143** 102
Mary (May) **125** 293
Mary (Stebbins) **136** 325
Mary A. **51** 240 **58** xlv **77**
  148 **118** 196
Mary Abigail **77** 296
Mary Ann **73** 257 **125** 292
  126 206
Mary Ann (Ely) **101** 201
Mary Augusta (Ingersoll)
  136 325
Mary B. **119** 279

PARSONS *cont'd*
Mary Bissell **72** 87
Mary Bowne **110** 142
Mary C. **72** 104
Mary C. (Chandler)
  124 62
Mary E. **101** 329
Mary Eliza **72** 96
Mary Elizabeth **81** 347
Mary Elizabeth (Butler)
  113 302
Mary Elizabeth (Chase)
  88 114
Mary Hooker **65** 138
Mary J. (Williams)
  101 329
Mary Morton **90** 189 201
  91 146
May C. **101** 329
May Ethel **85** 312 316
Mehitable **65** 221 **77** 209
Melicent **81** 51
Melissa **138** 218
Melvina (Doten) **124** 39
Mercy **71** 271 **110** 178
  120 45 **148** 230 347-350
Mercy (Stebbins) **136** 325
Miles G. **81** 408
Milton Alanson **101** 125
Mindwell (Edwards)
  108 64
Miriam **86** 341 **101** 43
  111 254 **115** 221
Miriam (Preble) **111** 254
Moses **65** liv **107** 313 **114**
  307 **121** 248 **127** 115
  136 326 **142** 245
Myrtle A. **81** 408
Nancy **63** 46 169 **90** 90
  113 127 **115** 303 **126**
  141
Nathan Nelson **72** 87 104
Nathaniel **63** 174 **97** 143
  111 254 **112** 105 106
  113 267 **115** 221 116
  222 **119** 67 144 **135** 24
  98 105 **142** 249
Nehemiah **65** 221
Nellie A. **101** 329
Noah **108** 64
Obadiah **65** 221 **126** 226
Olive **71** 158 299 **118** 243
  119 144 **123** 73
Olive (Greenleaf) **92** 85
Olive May **122** 108
Oliver **71** 158 **72** 33
Oren **145** 29
P. **79** 305
Pamelia **61** 294
Pamelia F. **91** 231
Patience **124** 319
Patty **145** 29 30
Paul **95** 51
Pauline (Laing) **91** 388
Pelatiah **71** 77 159 161
  277 300 **72** 41 43 88 89
  91 93 94 173 175
Pelatiah Lorenzo **72** 93
Pene **120** 129 208
Percy Allen **71** xxiii
Peter **57** 295

PARSONS *cont'd*
Phebe **55** 86 90 205 206
  77 209 **78** 380 **118** 18
Phebe (Fernald) **123** 152
  233
Phebe M. (Allen) **119** 228
  229 276
Philadelphia **56** 259
Philip **51** 152 **53** 250
  148 216
Phillis (Hills) **145** 330
  148 356
Philo **54** 371
Phineas **90** 189 **95** 353
Pliny D. **91** 331
Polly **57** 291 **89** 229 **116**
  298 **119** 218
Priscilla **56** 207
Prudence **119** 140
Puah **55** 202 **84** 211
R. **101** 328
Rachel **110** 178 **142** 246-
  248
Rachel R. (Robinson)
  90 91
Rebecca **60** 393
Rebecca (Allen) **116** 222
Rebecca (Sheldon)
  136 325
Rees **110** 169
Reginald Bemis **110** 142
Reginald H. **75** xxiii
Reginald Hascall **110**
  135 142
Reginald M. **74** 157
Rena Cornelia **108** 224
Rhoda **60** 101 **105** 313
Rhoda (Taylor) **148** 219
Rhoda (Tyler) **136** 314
Richard **66** 150 **78** 60 62
  82 292 296 **101** 201 **113**
  190 **143** 205 **148** 216
Robert **54** 434 **55** 202 207
  81 130 **109** 131 **114** 238
  118 166 **142** 246 247
  249 **143** 103
Robert C. **91** 388
Robert Ogden (Mrs.)
  104 145 324
Roxa **71** 77 277
Roxy **72** 41 43 101
Rufus **68** 338
Ruth **71** 85 281 **72** 46 103
  89 362 **110** 58
Ruth (Wilson) **110** 179
Sally **61** 295 **63** 174 **90** 89
  96 55 **104** 47 **112** 106
  116 142 **117** 226 227
  118 125 126 231 **119** 57
  140 208 296 305 **120** 125
  126 **121** 67 **142** 246-248
Sally (Bragdon) **117** 140
Sally (Jameson) **90** 89
Sally (Underwood)
  112 105
Sally H. (Child) **90** 44
Salome **120** 212 **121** 98
  297 **122** 63
Samuel **54** 433 **55** 89 200-
  202 207 **56** 74 319 **57**
  213 268 **61** 193-195 238

PARSONS *cont'd*
293-296 **62** 195 **66** 155
  224 295 **81** 432 448 **90**
  189 **94** 314 361 **95** 353
  97 367 **99** 80 **100** 192
  108 37 **110** 142 **111** 229
  112 218 **115** 141 **116** 7
  224 **117** 143 **122** 108
  123 74 **136** 314 **143** 102
  108 **145** 351 **148** 218
  219 223 224 226 228 230
  232-235 345 350 352-355
  357 359 360
Samuel Augustus
  110 231
Samuel Bowne **110** 142
Samuel H. **77** 209 **99** 8
  101 309
Samuel Holden **64** 359
  362 368 **65** 59-62 139-
  144 146-150 220-227 **70**
  186 **118** 313 **143** 102
Samuel O. **117** 226 227
Samuel Odiorn **112** 105
  116 138
Samuel S. **120** 138
Sarah **52** 427 **53** 166-168
  276 277 378 **54** 432 **56**
  319 **74** 252 **82** 502 **87**
  302 **90** 89 **92** 55 **96** 55
  97 261 **98** 82 208 **100**
  312 **101** 328 108 37 246
  250 **111** 229 **112** 219
  305 **123** 260 262 265
  125 101 288 **126** 142
  133 285 **136** 325 **148**
  223 237 238 353 356-358
Sarah (Clark) **148** 219
Sarah (Dare) **148** 235
Sarah (Davis) **116** 262
Sarah (Edwards) **136** 325
Sarah (Heald) (Leanard)
  123 260 **143** 115 **148**
  222
Sarah (Jameson) **90** 89
Sarah (Keep) **148** 223
Sarah (Keepe) **123** 261
Sarah (Killeran) **90** 91
Sarah (Lane) **102** 145
Sarah (Norton) **142** 248
Sarah (Powers) **123** 297
Sarah (Sewall) **92** 85
  112 305
Sarah (Sheldon) **90** 189 **95**
  353 **136** 333
Sarah (Vinson) **102** 145
  142 245 248
Sarah (Vore) **143** 108 115
  148 222
Sarah D. **121** 297
Sarah Frances **74** 96
Sarah Jane **66** 112 **74** 96
  91 388
Sarah Johnson (Adams)
  89 342
Sarah Russell **80** 30
Seth **54** 432 **55** 84 200 202
  205
Seth F. **101** 329
Shaber **117** 168
Shubel **62** 85

PARSONS *cont'd*
Sibyl **110** 36
Sile **71** 156
Simeon **75** 303 **118** 217
Simon **55** 154
Solomon **71** 161 **90** 44
Sophia **72** 45 102 **123** 150
  232
Sophia W. **119** 143
Sophronia **110** 66
Sophronia N. **117** 163
Starr **123** 297
Stephen **53** 278 **82** 296 299
  93 310 **112** 305
Susan **68** 203 **72** 44 **91** 184
  119 148 150-152 236 312
  120 56 146 150-152 231
  233 310 **121** 75 149-151
  122 107
Susan A. (Beebe) **101** 329
Susan Camilla **72** 93
Susan Elizabeth **58** xlviii
  65 xlv
Susanna **51** 465 **55** 374
  56 319 **63** 176 **65** liv **66**
  148 **82** 282 296 503 **83**
  14 **110** 179 **111** 254 **115**
  225 **116** 141
Susanna (Witham) **119**
  67 144
Susey **61** 296
Sydenham Clark **90** 189
  95 353 357
Sylvester **62** 84
Sylvia **72** 102
T. **122** 226
Talcott **136** 325
Thadious Sobeski
  113 267
Thankful **71** 280
Theodocius **100** 192
Theodore **116** 224 **120** 64
  67 **144** 266
Theophilus **51** 236 **53** 371
  60 228 **65** liv 370 **76**
  321 **79** 229 **122** 122 308
  126 226 **140** 233 247
  142 245
Thomas **52** 430 **53** 250 278
  56 207 **57** 208 **64** 97 226
  68 338 **71** 160 161 301
  77 209 **79** 152 168 225
  81 448 **89** 174 **101** 148
  112 104 304 **116** 235
  117 86 88 **124** 39 302
  132 270 **143** 105-108
  111 112 114 **148** 215 216
  226-228 230 231 235-238
  345 346 352 355-357
Thomas G. **77** 209
Thomas J. **68** 43
Thomas William **51** 446
  105 83
Thurston **57** 99
Timothy **56** 58 **86** 89 **94**
  314 **111** 254 **118** 318
  122 108 **145** 360
Trumbull **72** 46
Tryphena **71** 277 **72** 43
  102
Usher **53** 361 **59** 109 **61**

PARSONS *cont'd*
202 222 **64** 191 **67** 300
74 222 **77** 63 **96** 253 **99**
9 **106** 156 **112** 79 **137**
347
Virginia J. **118** 76
Vivian G. **81** 408
W. **121** 65
W. Hazen **101** 329
W. W. **128** 93 95 174
Walter **147** 86
Wealthea **71** 277
Wealthian **72** 43 102
Wealthian Amelia **72** 94
Wealthy A. **72** 49
Wil. **53** 166
William **52** 421 427 **53** 166-
168 276 277 **55** 141 315
57 268 **65** 221 **72** 45 **74**
222 **76** xc **77** 209 **79** 167
81 448 489 **82** 501-503
83 11 148 **90** 91 **91** 231
92 286 **94** 68 **101** 328
104 242 **117** 170 **120**
294 301 **121** 60 66 **122**
66 226 308 **123** 265 **140**
233 **142** 245 **143** 104-
107 111-114 116-118
148 215 216 222 226 348
355 356
William C. **91** 388
William Decatur **75** 241
William E. **90** 115
William K. **72** 47
William Kelsey **72** 91
William R. **84** 31
William S. **101** 328 329
William Sherman **98** 208
William U. **91** 231
William Usher **66** 369
William W. **65** 220
William Webster **71** 276
72 101
Williams **122** 121
Willis S. **142** 245 249
Woodbridge **111** 117
145 365
Zilpha **57** 293
PARTCH
Angene L. **123** 222
Carleton **123** 222
Clayton W. **123** 223
Ella **123** 224
F. M. **123** 223
Florence (Hathorn)
123 100
Martha E. **123** 99
Mattie **123** 224
Sarah (Winslow) **123** 223
William H. **123** 100 222
PARTE John **143** 204
William **64** 344 **65** 45 166
PARTEE Hannah **125** 228
PARTELO Partelou
Partelow Partlo
Partlow
Abigail **147** 346
Abigail (Main) **143** 363
Alice Blake (Hopkins)
86 462
Ann **123** 254

PARTELO *cont'd*
Annise / Ann (Brown)
147 346
Augusta **98** 348
David K. **86** 462
John **109** 313 **147** 340 346
Nancy **109** 313
Partidge *see* Partridge
Partige *see* Partridge
PARTINGTON
Hugh **64** 159
Mary **70** 123 **115** 129
Partlo *see* Partelo
Partlow *see* Partelo
PARTMAN David **97** 395
PARTON

— Capt. **51** 44 **144** 344
— Col. **101** 238 **118** 23
122 118
— Lieut. **119** 218 **120** 127
295
— Mr. **82** 296 301 **83** 308
90 155 **95** 43
— Mrs. **76** 50 **82** 413 **83**
308 **84** 257 **117** 168 **119**
293 **120** 123 **121** 98 **122**
115
____ (Lyman) **121** 58
Aaron **57** 58 392
Abel **57** 184 189 190 **62** 371
63 93 95
Abiel **57** 51
Abigail **57** 53 55-57 185-
189 191 192 225 283-285
287 392 393 395 **58** 339
63 95 **67** 81 **73** 91 **81**
432 448 **109** 208 **135** 41
Abigail (Dwight) **84** 458
136 330
Abigail Ann **63** 94
Abigail Harding **57** 285
287
Abram **73** 91
Achsa **63** 94
Adam **57** 188 190 282 283
Addison Bliss **57** 396
Adeline **57** 284-286 **58** 373
63 94
Adin **63** 95
Adrial **57** 286
Albert **57** 396
Albert Adams **57** 287
Albert H. **57** 288
Albert R. **74** 31
Albert W. **73** 91
Alden **54** 362 **63** 94

PARTRIDGE *cont'd*
Alford A. B. **98** 259
Alfred **57** 393 395
Alice **82** 51
Allen **57** 285 397
Alma **63** 94
Almira **57** 391
Almond **57** 287
Alpheus Snow **57** 189
Alvin **57** 286
Alvin Adams **57** 192
Amanda **57** 286 390
Amanda P. **57** 396
Amariah **57** 56 283
Amelia Maria **87** 194
Amorette **57** 390
nos **57** 184 189 393 395
396 **58** 316 317 **98** 104
104 103 **117** 172
nos (Mrs.) **117** 172
nos Coolidge **57** 282
nos Dennison **57** 396
ndrew **63** 95 **86** 176
105 181
nn **81** 448 **82** 27
nn (Pacht / Pate)
111 165 246
nn A. **76** 271
nn Augusta **142** 296
nn R. (Jipson) **117** 164
nna **57** 54 187 192 282
283 390 391 **63** 91 92 **82**
292 296
Anna (Williams) **136** 334
Anna M. E. **57** 192
Anne **57** 55 57 58 186 282
Apollos **57** 396
Arabella Maria **94** 23
Arathusa **57** 190 192
Arial **57** 191
Artemas **63** 95
Artemas Lee **104** 103
Asa **57** 54 56 58 186 282 283
285 391 394 **58** 373 **63**
93
Asa Bates **57** 296 **98** 94
Asa Cheney **57** 391
Asa Fairbanks **63** 94
Asahel **57** 284 **58** 373
Asenath **57** 286 394
Athina **57** 394
Augusta M. **57** 288
Austin **57** 284
Azubah **57** 57 187 189 287
Bathsheba **57** 186 393 394
Bellamy **91** 208
Benjamin **57** 52 53 58 391-
393 **82** 51 52 286 296 **85**
365
Benjamin Franklin **57**
188-190 **104** 103
Benjamin Richardson
57 394
Benoni **57** 52 55 58 186-
188 190
Bernard **63** 94 95
Bethiah **57** 56
Betsey **57** 188 190 192 286
390 393 **63** 94 95 **68** 248
75 103 **84** 424
Betsey A. **63** 94

PARTRIDGE *cont'd*
Betty **57** 58 391
Beulah **57** 190
Blanche Estelle **85** 197
Bradford Chase **57** 284
C. (Wing) **128** 265
C. Edward **63** 95
Caleb **57** 53
Calvin **85** 365
Caroline **57** 189 192 282
283 285 286 391 **63** 95
Caroline H. **98** 198
Cata **57** 393 394
Catherine **57** 185-189 287
393 **58** 374 **63** 95 **142**
391
Catherine Adams **57** 394
Catherine Cushing
57 284
Celia **90** 95 **127** 129 130
Celia (Groves) **127** 129
Charles **57** 190 394 **63** 94
94 366 **105** 13 19 21
Charles A. **57** 285
Charles Billings **57** 395
Charles D. **63** 95
Charles E. **98** 198
Charles Franklin **57** 391
Charlotte **57** 188 190 192
285 390 391 394 395 **63**
94 **90** 95 **127** 130
Chloe **57** 56 57 282 393 396
63 94
Christopher **63** 142
Clara B. **74** 31
Clara Frances **74** 30
Clara P. **57** 192
Clarissa **57** 190 191 393
397 **63** 95
Clarissa Prentiss **57** 285
Clark **57** 188 287 **105** 280
Claude E. **98** 259
Clementine **57** 286
Cornelia B. **57** 288
Cotton **84** 458 **120** 302
121 97 **136** 330
Curtis **57** 389
Cynthia **57** 283 284
Cyrus **57** 286 395 **63** 95
Cyrus A. **98** 198
Cyrus W. **57** 395
Dana **57** 393 394
Daniel **57** 184 187 286
105 213
Daniel Bullen **63** 94
Daniel W. **57** 395
David **57** 53 55 184 187 188
191 394-397 **58** 374 **98**
198 251 **105** 280 **142** 67
390
David Sanford **57** 393
Deborah **57** 51 52 282 287
392 **63** 91-94 **83** 485
120 265 266
Dexter Fay **63** 95
Diadama **57** 286
Dinah Holbrook **57** 393
Dolly **57** 283
Dorcas **63** 94
Dornida **57** 393
Dorothy **57** 192 **82** 51

PARTRIDGE *cont'd*
E. **63** 95
Eben **57** 396
Ebenezer **57** 53 184
Ebenezer Henry **74** 30
Eda / Ede **57** 56 288 393
Edeann **63** 95
Editha **63** 95
Edmund **81** 448
Edmund James **57** 287
Edson **57** 393
Edward **57** 395 **63** 91-95
117 170 **136** 334 **141**
189
Edward Emerson **57** 395
Edward F. **63** 95
Edward Lasell **73** 317 **74**
xxv **84** 458 **85** 106 187
202
Edward Martin **57** 396
Edwin **63** 95
Edwin F. **57** 285
Edwin Orlando **57** 396
Elbridge Gerry **57** 287
Eleazer **57** 51 52 56-58 184
192 284 285 288 389-394
63 90 300
Electa **57** 191 284
Eli **57** 55 187-190
Elias **57** 284 **63** 95
Elias Anson **57** 285
Elias Chase **57** 284
Elibeus **63** 94
Elihu **57** 190
Elijah **57** 188 **61** 262
Elijah Fairbanks **57** 392
Elisha **57** 57 288 395 **63**
91 93 94
Eliza **57** 191 286 **63** 94
Eliza (Croker) **131** 74
Eliza I. **72** 107
Eliza Jane **57** 285
Eliza Phipps **57** 192
Elizabeth **55** 393 **57** 32 52-
58 184 185 188 282 287
392 394-397 416 417 **58**
238-240 **60** 246 **63** 92 93
95 **67** 201 **74** 31 314 **79**
47 **86** 442 **91** 180 **94** 175
118 204 **124** 319
Elizabeth (Hubbart)
84 257
Elizabeth (Randsted)
100 297
Elizabeth Ann **57** 391
Elkanah **57** 189
Ella **117** 170
Ellen C. **57** 396
Ellen Julina **128** 265
Ellen R. **117** 165
Ellis **57** 394 395
Elmira **57** 392 396 **63** 95
Elmira Diantha **57** 285
Elsie **92** 46
Emeline **57** 284 395 396
Emeline L. **98** 198
Emerency **57** 393
Emily **57** 395
Emily A. **91** 387
Emily Dow **136** 334
Emma **57** 186 187

PARTRIDGE *cont'd*
Emma A. **63** 95
Emmons **57** 380
Enoch **57** 286
Ephraim **63** 91-93
Erastus **57** 395
Ermina **57** 286
Esther **57** 54 184 286 395
58 373 374 **118** 303
Eugene A. **104** 103
Eunice **57** 57 58 187 188
286
Evangeline **104** 103
Evelyn **57** 192
Experience **57** 51 186 189
391 393
Ezekiel **57** 287 390
Ezra **57** 57 192 288
Fanny **57** 283 389 **79** 121
Faustina **63** 95
Finette **63** 285
Frances **57** 389 **63** 283
Frances H. **98** 251
Francis **84** 31
Francis Adams **63** 94
Frank **63** 94 95 **74** 31
Frank Harvey **57** 50
Frank Reuben **95** 339
Fred Albert **74** 31
Frederick **63** 95
Freelove **57** 190
Freeman **58** 64-66 **117** 166
Freeman (Mrs.) **117** 171
George **53** 285 **55** 112 **60**
142 189 **63** 94 **70** 96 **85**
365 **90** 155 **93** 96 **94** 241
121 238 **143** 337
George A. **57** 192
George Brown **57** 285
George C. **56** 20
George Fairbanks **74** 82
George H. **104** 93 **111** 246
George Henry **70** 96
George Homer **57** xxxv
50 184 281 389 **58** xliii
209 **59** xlii **63** 90 205
64 xxix **77** xxvii **90** 125
96 154 **104** 103
George Ithamar **57** 285
George Job **57** 393
George W. **63** 95
George Wakeman **57** 191
George Warren **93** 345
Gertrude Edwards
(Dwight) **84** 459
Gordon **117** 168
Grace **63** 94
Grace (Silvester) **85** 365
Grata **57** 390
Greenwood **63** 95
H. **63** 95
H. P. **127** 130
H. W. **63** 388
Hallowell **90** 95 **127** 130
Hannah **57** 51-53 56-58
185 189 192 282 283 285
286 288 390 392 396 397
58 60 **63** 91 92 94 95 **82**
27 51 **126** 212 **142** 67

PARTRIDGE *cont'd*
Hannah (Foster)
  (Bradford) (Stubbs)
  143 337
Hannah (Lyman) **84** 458
  136 330
Hannah (Seabury)
  143 337
Hannah B. **57** 393
Hannah L. **63** 95
Harding **58** 58 **142** 67
Harriet **57** 286 390 392
Harriet Keith **57** 285
Harriet Maria **57** 285
Harrison **63** 94
Helen F. **63** 95
Helen Maria **57** 296
Henrietta **57** 285
Henry **54** 190 **57** 57 283
  389
Henry (Mrs.) **117** 171
Henry Clark **74** 31
Herman **57** 390
Hervey **57** 390
Hezekiah **111** 165 246
Hiram **57** 286 288 **63** 94
  73 91
Hiram Cheney **57** 391
Hiram French **57** 391
Horace **57** 284 393 **85** 92
Horace Green **57** 395
Hugh **83** 316
Huldah **57** 56 **58** 239
Ichabod **57** 185
Ira **57** 189
Irene Richardson **57** 394
Isaac **57** 191 284 **85** 365
  90 95 **127** 129 130
Isabella **57** 288
Ithamar **57** 285
Jabez **57** 56 282
Jacob **57** 191 **68** 248 **74** 31
Jairus **57** 391
James **57** 52 55 56 283 284
  286-288 **63** 94
James Erskine **74** 30
James Harvey **104** 103
James Henry **57** 284
James Lester **63** 94
James Madison **57** 192
James Oliver **57** 189
James Rice **57** 192
James Seth Harding
  57 287
James W. **74** 30
Jane **63** 93 **68** 189 **73** 91
Jane Elizabeth **74** 30
Jane Y. **68** 247
Jasper **57** 56 191
Jemima **57** 283
Jemima (Bidwell) **136** 334
Jemima A. **57** 394
Jerome **73** 91
Jerusha **57** 190 288
Jesse **57** 184 186 187 394
  395 **58** 374
Joanna **57** 287 393 395
  98 219
Job **57** 52 53 57 58 287 390
  392 393 **62** 381
Joel **57** 56 57 287 393

PARTRIDGE *cont'd*
Joel Gilbert **57** 287
John **51** 45 **53** 285 444 **54**
  345 **57** 50-58 184-192
  281-288 389-398 **58** 209
  316 **63** 90 91 95 283 **68**
  338 **76** 50 **81** 432 **82** 51
  85 31 365 **86** 6 **87** 399
  90 87 **95** 224 **105** 213
  112 35 **113** 49 **142** 81
  143 337
John Franklin **57** 192
John H. **98** 196 251 298
John Wesley **57** 286
John Wheeler **57** 285
Jonas **57** 191 393
Jonas A. **111** 138
Jonas Rice **57** 192
Jonathan **54** 351 **57** 52 55
  56 191 192 281-283 **58**
  239 240 **81** 432 **82** 27
Jonathan Kendall **57** 389
Joseph **57** 52 53 55 58 186-
  189 393 394 396 **58** 238
  63 91 92 **73** 91 185
Joseph A. **98** 251 **117** 164
Joseph Lyman **84** 458
Joseph Reed **74** 31
Joseph Rockwood **57** 282
Joseph Warren **57** 189
Josephine **77** 190
Joshua **57** 53 185 282 396
  397
Josiah **63** 91 92 **117** 171
Jotham **57** 187
Judith **57** 286 **63** 94
Judith H. **57** 395
Julia **57** 285 390
Julia A. **80** 192 **89** 252
Julia A. B. **57** 391
Julia Ann **57** 285 394 395
Julia P. **57** 296
Julia Porter (Norton)
  98 94
Juliette Richardson
  57 285
Julius Lincoln **74** 31
Katharine **57** 187
Katharine (Seldon)
  111 165
Kendrick **57** 393
Keziah **57** 54 56 58 188
  191 192 285 394 395 **58**
  238 239 **61** 262 **63** 95
L'Orient **57** 282
L. **63** 95
Lafayette **63** 95
Laura Adele **104** 103
Laura J. **63** 94
Lavernia **57** 189
Lavina **63** 95
Lavina R. **57** 396
Lavinia **57** 288
Leah **57** 188
Learned **57** 56
Leila **63** 94
Leonard **57** 191
Leonard Pond **57** 392
Levi **57** 58 284 390 391 393
  71 359 **113** 224
Lewis **57** 286 394-396

PARTRIDGE *cont'd*
Lewis Chapin **131** 74
Liberty **57** 393
Linda A. (Moore) **117** 166
Loenza **57** 283
Lois **57** 56 58 284-286 391
  392 **142** 67
Lois Rockwood **57** 285
Louisa **57** 192 283 286 391
Louise Elmira **57** 396
Lovet **57** 56 283
Lucetta A. **57** 288
Lucina **57** 396
Lucinda **57** 286 392 396
  73 91
Lucinda E. **57** 396
Lucius **57** 391
Lucretia **52** 228 **57** 189 286
  63 93 94 **74** 31 **85** 365
  99 123
Lucy **57** 390 394 395 **63** 95
Lucy A. **57** 390
Lucy Ann **57** 284
Lucy G. **57** 188
Lurinda **57** 395
Luther Lee **104** 103
Lydia **53** 285 **57** 56 57 186
  191 283 390 395 **63** 91-
  94 **68** 338 **71** 359 **73** 91
  90 77 281
Lydia (Adams) **113** 224
Lydia (Clisbee) **136** 334
Lydia Rebecca **57** 395
Lydia Sanford **57** 287
Lydiette **57** 394
Lyman **57** 189 190 395
M. J. **98** 259
Mabel **120** 265
Magdalen **57** 51 54
Malachi **57** 56 284
Maranda **127** 130
Margaret **57** 50 **112** 147
Margaret (Cook) **84** 458
  136 330
Margery **57** 50 51 **63** 90
  73 91 176
Maria **57** 190 286 **90** 47
Maria Antoinette **57** 287
Maria Jane **88** 293
Marietta **63** 95
Marinda **57** 395
Martha **57** 55 391 **90** 95
  127 130
Martha (Williams)
  136 334
Martha Ann (Stratton)
  85 92
Martin **57** 286
Mary **53** 285 444 **57** 51 52
  54 56 57 184 187 189-
  191 281-285 287 288 389-
  394 396 **58** 28 **63** 91-95
  65 73 **67** 81 **69** 112 **73**
  91 **78** 316 **81** 432 448 **82**
  27 286 296 **90** 95 **94** 175
  120 265 **121** 53 **127** 130
  142 391
Mary (Alden) **85** 365
Mary (Brewster) **85** 365
Mary (Cotton)(Atwater)
  84 458

PARTRIDGE *cont'd*
Mary (Smith) **84** 458
Mary Adeline **57** 287
Mary Ann **57** 396 397 **63** 94 **117** 172
Mary B. **57** 282
Mary Bassett **57** 285
Mary Carolyn (Kempton) **95** 339
Mary Clark **57** 285
Mary E. **74** 31
Mary G. **57** 285
Mary H. **104** 103
Mary Hall **57** 192
Mary J. **98** 251
Mary Jane **57** 192 **63** 94
Mary L. **57** 190
Mary R. **57** 285 287
Mary S. **63** 94
Mason **57** 286
Matilda **57** 397
Maynard **57** 390
Mehitable **57** 53 55 189 190 285 287 391 397 **61** 140 **62** lxxiii **63** 93 **129** 368
Mehitable (Crow) **84** 458
Melatiah **57** 191 288 396 **58** 316 317 **63** 92
Melinda **57** 286
Melissa **57** 283 **63** 95
Mercy **57** 58 184 191
Merril **57** 391
Micah **57** 186
Micajah Reed **57** 192
Milcah **57** 392
Milo **57** 284
Miner **88** 119
Miranda **90** 95 **127** 130
Miriam **55** 262 **57** 190 283 397 **63** 91 94 95 **75** 20
Moors **57** 286
Moses **57** 55 187 190 282 393 **145** 348
Moses Maynard **57** 395
Nabby **57** 188
Nancy **57** 186 187 192 284 285 389 392 394 **58** 59 374 **63** 44 **142** 67
Nancy (Chase) **88** 119
Nancy J. (Everett) **111** 138
Naomi **57** 392
Nathan **57** 56 57 186 187 285 288 **63** 93 95
Nathaniel **57** 187 190 282 **63** 91-94 **82** 413 **128** 265
Nathaniel H. **57** 287
Nehemiah **67** 81 **81** 432 448 **86** 72 **105** 262
Nellie C. **121** 307 **122** 150
Nellie Rosalle **85** 92
Nicholas **52** 241 **86** 434
Noah **88** 293
Olcott Osborn **64** xxxii
Olive **57** 191 391 **63** 92-95
Oliver **63** 95 388 **84** 248 **129** 211 214 326 327 **136** 334 **140** 269
Ora **57** 189

PARTRIDGE *cont'd*
Oran **57** 282
Orson **57** 286
Otis **57** 390
Ozias **57** 284 **58** 374
Pamelia **119** 51 **120** 127
Pascha **69** 84
Patty **57** 192 **82** 52
Pearl **57** 396
Pedee **57** 391
Pedee Alvira **57** 391
Peggy **57** 395
Peggy A. **57** 397
Persis **57** 189 286
Peter **57** 53 57 58 184
Phebe **57** 53 54 58 282 286
Philena **57** 191 286
Philip **57** 394
Phineas **57** 285
Phylette **57** 385
Polly **57** 187-189 192 284 285 396 **70** 228
Polly Robinson **63** 95
Preserved **57** 55 186 187
Priah **57** 284
Prindle **57** 286
Priscilla **57** 397 **63** 91 **82** 296 301
Property **127** 130 **147** 68
Prudence H. **57** 192
Prusia **57** 189
Rachel **53** 356 **57** 51 53 58 187-190 288 390 393 395 **63** 92 **73** 238 **104** 103 **128** 24
Rachel Melinda **57** 396
Ralph **57** 416 417 **94** 175 241 **95** 47
Raphael **104** 103
Rebecca **57** 186 187 395 **84** 162 **98** 251
Remembrance **57** 287
Reuben **57** 56 184 281 282 286 396 **63** 95
Reuben L. **57** 286
Rhoda **57** 56 58 184 185 187 282 283 391-393 396 397
Rhode **113** 224
Richard **80** 371-375
Robert **78** 72 **140** 233 326
Robert A. **80** 192 **89** 252
Robert Leander **80** 192 **89** 252
Rosina **57** 187
Roxanna **57** 287 395
Rufus **57** 395
Rufus H. **104** 103
Rufus Harvey **57** 190
Ruth **57** 55 57 188 282 284 390 63 91 92 **85** 365 **91** 80 **95** 339
Ruth S. **57** 392
S. H. **120** 305
S. O. **98** 259
Sabra / Sabria **57** 391 392 397 **62** 371
Sally **58** 58 **63** 95 **104** 103
Sally Harvey **104** 103
Salmon **57** 284
Salome **58** 317

PARTRIDGE *cont'd*
Samantha **57** 393 **127** 130
Samuel **55** 343 393 **57** 51 53-55 184-188 191 395-397 **58** 316 374 **62** lxxiii **63** 299 388 **81** 448 **84** 154 162 257 379 458 **100** 297 **101** 155 239 283 289 105 213 **112** 235 **120** 297 **129** 204 210 **136** 330 **140** 233 **141** 196 199 201 331
Samuel H. **120** 219-221 224 306-308 **121** 72 73 146
Samuel J. **57** 189
Samuel Smith **57** 390
Sanford S. **72** 107
Sarah **53** 285 **54** 351 **57** 52 54 55 57 58 188 189 191 282-285 287 288 392 395 **60** 142 63 90-95 **67** 81 **69** 173 **81** 432 448 **82** 293 296 302 **85** 365 **86** 225 **90** 56 **94** 355 **123** 93 **127** 66 **136** 274
Sarah A. **57** 391 **117** 164
Sarah Abigail **57** 284
Sarah Ann **57** 287
Sarah Brackett **76** xliii
Sarah G. **57** 284
Sarah Nourse **57** 192
Sarah Putnam **57** 285
Sarah Reed **74** 30
Sarah Whiting **69** 269
Seavey William **63** 94
Seneca **57** 282
Seth **57** 55 58 184 187 394 **63** 92 93 95 **90** 95 **127** 130
Seth Clapp **57** 395 **58** 374
Sheffield **57** 188
Silas **57** 56 191 282 **63** 93 **68** 338 **69** 84
Silas B. **63** 95
Silas Emerson **63** 95
Silas Witt **57** 395
Silence **57** 53 184 188 285
Simeon **57** 58 190 284 391 394 **63** 93 94
Simon Peter **57** 394
Sophia **57** 191 **118** 25 28
Sophronia **57** 190
Sophronia (Prindle) (Sprague) **88** 293
Sophronia M. (Graham) **57** 394
Sophronia N. (Morse) **57** 392
Stephen **57** 52 56 57 186 283 286
Stillman **57** 286
Submit **57** 393 **113** 48
Submit (Jones) **113** 49
Sukey **57** 389
Susan J. **57** 390
Susan Johnson **57** 394
Susan P. **63** 95
Susan S. **93** 195
Susanna **57** 284 288
Sylvander **57** 396

Thomas **54** 46 **55** 262 **57**
55 191 **65** 287 **69** 269 **86**
176 **105** 213 **119** 22
Thomas Jefferson **57** 192
Timothy **57** 55 187 188
58 58-60 **142** 67
Truman **90** 95 **127** 130
Truman Edward (Mrs.)
103 120
Tryphena **57** 285
Tryphosa **60** 142
Unity **57** 390
Untimely **57** 287 **147** 69
Urania **57** 187
Uriah **57** 286
Vernon David Barron
57 396
Versilda **57** 288
Vesta **57** 397
W. **92** 271
Waitstill **57** 287 393
Wallace **63** 94
Warren **57** 390 397 **93** 345
Warren Clapp **57** 395
Welcome Pratt **63** 94
Willard **57** 389 **63** 94
William **51** 44 **53** 356 **54**
345 **57** 50 51 191 192
282 287 397 **63** 90-95
205 283 **67** 81 **68** 81 189
69 360 361 363 **73** 238
81 432 448 **82** 27 51 413
84 458 **85** 31 **92** 270
104 32 **106** 265 **136** 334
William A. **57** 288 **63** 95
William Henry **93** 345
William Penn **74** 30
William Robinson **63** 95
Willis **63** 94
Wilson **117** 172
Winfield Scott **57** 288
104 103
Winslow **57** 189
Worthy **57** 286
Zachariah **57** 51-54 184
394 **58** 373 374
Ziba **57** 391
Zibiah **63** 94
Zibiah Nelson (Willson)
84 458
Zillah **57** 188
Zipporah **57** 187 284
Zoniah **57** 191
PARVIN
Eleanor **117** 68
Frances **117** 60

/IN *cont'd*
)mas **117** 60
/IS James **112** 287
/YE
rcissus **100** 220
see Parry
/NTON
nry **53** 256
see Paris
l *see* Paschall
ll *see* Paschall
:AULT
onora **86** 336
:HALL Pascal Pascall
.'aschal
—— **53** 460
— Mr. **82** 52
Alexander **84** 306
Andrew **71** 242 **84** 308
309 313 314
Ann P. (Gibson) **84** 99
Clare **84** 309 314
Edward Earey **81** 222 237
Elizabeth **84** 308 309 313
314
Elizabeth (Lake) **84** 313
314
Francis **84** 36
Garrard **103** 10
Jacob C. **92** 209
John **71** 243 **84** 306
John J. (Mrs.) **118** 326
Joshua Rich **84** 36
Mackie **98** 353
Margery **71** 243
Mary A. **84** 99
Philippa **71** 242
Phillis **82** 52
Rosa Lee Price **118** 326
Sarah **84** 36
Sarah Dyer (Rich) **84** 36
Thomas **84** 308 309 314
Thomas J. **84** 99
PASCO Pascoe Pasko
Aaron **100** 175
Abel **132** 243
Abel Ambrose **132** 244
Alfred **100** 89
Caroline **111** 189
Elizabeth (Thompson)
100 89
Ezra **73** 104
Fluvia **79** 156
Jonathan **101** 256
Jonna **100** 175
Mary **99** 282
Mary (Odlin) **100** 295
Meribah **100** 175
Michael **99** 282 **100** 295
P. Adaline **101** 256
Phebe **101** 256
Phebe Eaton **101** 256
Robert **85** 128
Salina E. **101** 256
Sarah **132** 243
Steven **99** 282
W. W. **107** 16 17
PASE William **64** 320
PASELE
Philippa **109** 31
Robert **109** 31

PASELE *cont'd*
Thomas **109** 21 22
PASHAW Harriet **115** 120
PASHLEY Passhley
Anne **109** 31
Elizabeth **96** 22
George **117** 9 11 16 17
Isabel Peckham **99** 76
John **96** 22
William **63** 346
PASHO
Ruth **90** 56 **141** 141
PASK John W. **74** 28
Sarah Frances **74** 28
Pasko *see* Pasco
PASKS John **85** 455
PASKYN Geurard **103** 18
PASLEW
Elizabeth **116** 170
Robert **116** 170
PASLEY Cicely **113** 63
Eliza **84** 317
Gilbert **84** 317
Pasmore *see* Passmore
Pason *see* Payson
PASONS
Didymus **61** 240
Sally **61** 240
PASS Sarah **115** 78
PASSACONAWAY **94** 347
PASSAGE Adam **120** 20
Anna **120** 20
C. S. **120** 20
Emiline **120** 20
Henry **120** 20
Polly C. **120** 20
PASSAMAN
Elizabeth **65** 70
PASSANAUTON
Samuel **70** 66
PASSENGER
Andrew M. **77** 319
Sarah **78** 419
Passhley *see* Pashley
PASSIG
Henry Edgar **108** 74
Mary (Hook) **108** 72
Sarah (Hook) **108** 74
Passimore *see* Passmore
PASSINGIAM
John **95** 322
PASSMAN
Catherine **114** 187
PASSMORE Pasmore
Passimore
Anna **60** 298
Charles Sumner (Mrs.)
77 237 **78** 206
Comstock **138** 117
Elizabeth **82** 51
G. H. (Mrs.) **114** 162
Hunter W. **114** 162
John **82** 51
Joseph **141** 351
Martain **141** 351
Mary **60** 298 **82** 51 413
Mary (Whittemore)
106 269
Nancy **82** 51
Roger **101** 273
Susie **78** 206

PASSMORE *cont'd*
Thankful **141** 351
Thomas **60** 298 **82** 51
106 269
PASSOW —— **54** 439
PASTE —— **80** 406
PASTEUR Allan E. (Mrs.)
124 313
Margaret Pearce **124** 313
PASTON De Paston
—— **57** 316
Dorothy **120** 243
George **72** 135 137
John **98** 275 276 **102** 94 244
247 252 **103** 103 **120**
243
Margaret **102** 94
Susanna **72** 135 137 138
William **102** 93 **141** 318-
320
PASTORIUS
Francis Daniel **63** 306
86 266
PASTRE Pastree
— Mrs. **101** 271
John **101** 272
Margaret **63** 382 **142** 127
PASTURE Bessie **77** 251
PATCH Abijah **125** 287
Abraham **71** 169 **78** 302
Agnes **71** 167 169
Ann **62** 44
Anna **61** 166 **62** 48 **86** 67
Anna (Cole) **86** 67
Anne **71** 167 168
Aurelia P. **122** 217
Austin Chase **111** 314 315
B. **61** 333
Barzilia **56** 198 199
Bathsheba **89** 110
Benjamin **62** 42 44 45 **82**
91 **86** 63
Bethiah **98** 181
Betsey Jane **134** 92
Charity **86** 67
Charity (Taylor) **86** 67
Charles Endicott **71** xxiii
Charles H. **123** 71 236
Christian **71** 167 168
Christiana **54** 224
Cynthia **56** 198
Daniel **62** 46
David **61** 344 **122** 217
Desire **56** 198
Ebenezer **126** 136
Edith **56** 61 62 198 346 **71**
166 167 169
Edmund **71** 166-169
Edward Carton **82** 382
83 233
Eleanor (Files) **94** 139
Electa **56** 198
Eliza **88** 330 **120** 72 73
Elizabeth **53** 460 **54** 224 **56**
198 **61** 333 **62** 41 44 **71**
166-170 **100** 72 **108** 234
111 315
Elizabeth (Call) **123** 236
Elizabeth (Owley) **111** 315
Elizabeth (Woodberry)
111 315

PATCH *cont'd*
Ephraim **56** 198 199 **58** cix
61 334 **62** 39 **67** 376
Eric Cyrus (Mrs.) **94** 139
106 123 **115** 151
Esther **62** 44
Eunice **56** 198 **61** 203 **62**
42 **71** 169
Ezra **56** 198
Fortune **71** 166-168
Frances **71** 166-168
Francis **71** 167 168
George Washington
119 284 **120** 219 220
122 73 **123** 151 233 236
Hannah **61** 242 **62** 41 **63**
175 **71** 168 170 **96** 342
97 237 261 **100** 72 252
108 234
Hannah (Moore) **89** 110
Hannah (Woodbury)
100 72 **108** 234 **111** 315
Henry **89** 110 **111** 315
Hepzibah **97** 354
Isaac **56** 61 62 198 199 346
61 242 **62** 35 47
Ivory **90** 331
Jacob **64** 146
James **63** 175 **71** 167-170
86 64 **100** 72 252 **108**
234 **111** 315
Jane **71** 167 168
Joan **60** 285 **71** 166-169
Joanna (Knowlton) **86** 67
John **55** 254 **65** 257 **71**
166-170 **111** 315
John H. **123** 233
Jonathan **62** 42
Joseph **111** 315
Joseph A. **121** 306
Josiah **113** 31 39
Lois **113** 31 32 39
Lucida **56** 198
Lucy **56** 198
Lucy A. (Gowen) **123** 71
236
Luther **56** 198
Lydia **56** 198 **69** 244 **82** 91
Mabel Louise (Batchelder)
111 314
Margerie **62** 47
Maria (Sargent) **90** 331
Martha **61** 333 **62** 47
Martha S. (Blaisdell)
121 306
Mary **56** 198 **61** 230 331
332 334 338 **62** 39 45 **71**
166-170 **81** 485 **83** 484
89 371 **94** 389 **100** 72
108 234 **109** 116 **135** 44
Mary (Brown) **111** 315
Mary (Cole) **86** 64
Mary (Dodge) **111** 315
Mary Augusta **74** 238
Miriam **62** 46
Molly **86** 67
Nathan **62** 40
Nicholas **54** 224 **56** 198
199 **71** 166-170 **100** 72
108 234 **111** 315 **122**
315

PATCH *cont'd*
Olive **56** 198
Olive (Moore) **120** 219
220 **122** 73 **123** 151 233
Patience S. (Tobey)
123 233
Penelope **56** 198 **63** 98
67 376
Peter **83** 23 26 27
Priscilla **86** 63
Prudence **122** 217
R. B. **119** 239 240
Rebecca **56** 198 199 **64** 146
Reuben **125** 43
Richard **71** 166-169 **86** 67
Robert **86** 67
Robert Charles (Mrs.)
102 124
Roland Harrison **106** 126
111 314 **112** 72
Rosamond Helen
(Seagrave) **111** 315
Roxanna **123** 151
Russell B. **122** 315 **124** 72
Ruth **58** lxxx **60** 53 **61** 333
62 47 **64** 311 **112** 226
126 136
Sabrina **56** 199
Sally **133** 282
Sally (Woodbury)
(Knowlton) **111** 315
Samuel **56** 198
Sarah **56** 61 198 346 **61**
332-334 337 **62** 40 45-47
63 176 **71** 167 169 **99**
324
Sarah (Babcock) **86** 64
Sarah (Balch) **100** 252
111 315
Sarah (Gardiner) **100** 72
Sarah (Wright) **126** 136
Sarah A. (Webber)
119 284
Sarah E. **122** 73
Serena W. **126** 144
Simon **61** 333 335 **62** 35 46
47
Stephen **60** 53 **61** 333 334
62 34 41 43 44 46-48
Susan **82** 465
Susanna (Whitney)
125 287
Thomas **56** 198 199 **61**
166 331-334 **62** 34 **71**
166 169 170
Timothy **61** 333 **62** 34 41
42 44 46 47
William **71** 166-169 **86** 67
PATCHEN Patchin
Patching
—— **76** 173 **97** 126
— Mr. **52** 107
Aaron D. **54** 354
Almus P. **89** 112
Anson S. **145** 74
Betsey **114** 180
Betsey (Curtis) **114** 180
Chloe **54** 354
Daniel **115** 112
David Thorpe **110** 113
Elizabeth **65** 186 187

PATCHEN cont'd
75 225
Grace (Bancroft) **97** 126
Harriet (De Golyer)
90 378
Hiram **90** 378
Isaac **60** 399
Jeremiah **60** 331
Joanna **115** 112
John **65** 187
Joseph **60** 189 **65** 186 187
75 220 225 **85** 143
Lucy **115** 112
Lydia **60** 189
Lydia M. **54** 225
Mary Abby **110** 113
Philinda **54** 354
Robert **110** 113
Sally **109** 264
Thaddeus **54** 354
Zebulon **127** 92
PATCHET Patchett
— Mr. **72** 133
Henry **119** 247
Katharine **120** 23
Katharine (Watson)
120 23
Robert **120** 23 24
Patchin see Patchen
Patching see Patchen
PATCK L. C. **91** 201
Leonard **91** 201
PATE —— **62** 284
Ann **111** 165 246
Charles B. **91** 331
Ellen **128** 177
J. **128** 177
Jane **77** 221
Mary **99** 120
Priscilla **71** 62
Richard **54** 334 **99** 120
Robert **71** 62
True **147** 180
Vernal Ruth **100** 113
William **51** 133 **78** 272
PATEE Eliza **89** 296
Mary **89** 296
Sarah (Beack) **88** 330
Trew **147** 179
Patefield see Patfield
PATEK Dorcas **56** 319
PATENAUDE
Charles S. A. **86** 312
Gladys Albertine **86** 312
Marie (Demers) **86** 312
PATENDEN
Alice **51** 257
Anne **51** 257
Dorothy **51** 257 261
Harry **51** 257
Henry **51** 257 261
Joan **51** 257
John **51** 257 261 **66** 345
Margaret **51** 257
Mary **51** 257 261
Philip **51** 261
Thomas **51** 257 261
PATERLANGE
John **64** 214
Paterson see Patterson
Pateshall see Patteshall

PATEY Eleanor **54** 420
Elizabeth **97** 320
Mary **54** 420
Philip **54** 420
Thomas **97** 320
PATFIELD Patefield
John **95** 131
Mary **87** 377
PATIE William **147** 179
PATIENCE John **65** 46
Patishall see Patteshall
PATMER
John de **71** 238
Margaret de **71** 238
Philip de **71** 238
Sarah de **71** 238
PATMORE
Richard **63** 240
Thomas **59** 21
PATON
Jane Earle **72** xlix
Mary **54** 375
Thomas **143** 201
PATRICK Partrick Patricke
—— **62** 130 **129** 87
— Capt. **53** 45 47-49
89 176 279
— Dr. **53** 297
— Mr. **142** 112
A. T. **117** 120
Albert T. **82** 475
Alexander Judson **100** 93
Alfaretta (Monroe) **100** 93
Alvin **80** 236
Amy **72** 283 **102** 96
Anna **100** 175
Asa **144** 39
Benoni **72** 284
Bertha Belle (Ritchey)
100 93
Bethiah (Fellow?) **144** 39
Charles **111** 203 **145** 165
Christopher **64** 259
Daniel **89** 173 174 280
95 130
David **106** 267
Dinah **75** 302
Ebenezer **147** 114 116
Eleanor **63** 238
Elizabeth (Campbell)
147 115 116
Elizabeth (Dickens)
86 181
Elizabeth (Rogers) **129** 87
147 111 112 114
Elizabeth M. **100** 93
Ellen **144** 39
Emily **67** 280
F. E. **82** 430 441
George Sutton **55** 351
56 xxxii
Halsey **144** 39
Hannah **72** 284
Hannah P. (Leavitt) **120**
140 215
Harriet **116** 310
Harrison Wells **100** 94
Henry Johnson **64** 102
Herman F. **100** 94
Isabella (Stranahan)
147 114

PATRICK cont'd
Jacob **129** 87 **147** 108 113-
115
Jane **62** 171 **72** 283
Janet (Rogers) **129** 87
Jared **144** 39
Jarrob **91** 331
Jeremiah Gile **82** 510
John **63** 363 **100** 175 **111**
202 203 **144** 39 **147** 111
112 114-116
Johnson **75** 127
Joseph H. **147** 262 264
Joseph W. **137** 29
Laura Ann (Daniels)
100 85
Lena Blanche (Smith)
100 94
Leslie E. **80** 236
Lewis Seaman **58** 72-74
76-81 **61** 405 **62** xxxvii
Lois (Buell) **147** 116
Lucy (Wheeler) **147** 116
Lydia **147** 114 115
Margaret **101** 174
Maria L. **54** cxlv
Mary **75** 127 **137** 29
147 112
Mary (Dixon) **147** 115
Mary (Phillips) **147** 116
Mary D. **82** 430 441
Mary M. (Rutherford)
117 120
Matthew **129** 87 **147** 109
111-116
Nancy **62** 171
Nancy (Nelson) **147** 116
Peter **86** 181
Polly (Bond) **137** 29
Reuben **69** 334
Richard **144** 39
Robert **111** 202 **147** 114
116
Rogers **129** 87
Sally **76** 30
Samuel **72** 283 **144** 102
Samuel J. **100** 93
Sarah **82** 510
Sarah (Ensign) **147** 116
Sarah C. **80** 236
Stephen **144** 39 46
Susan **90** 42
Thankful (Hewit) **147** 115
Theodore F. **100** 85
Thomas **142** 208 **147** 112
Thomas R. **145** 365
W. M. **120** 140 215
William **62** 171 **65** 237
93 398 **100** 63 **102** 96
111 203 **147** 112 114-
116
William E. (Mrs.) **71** lxvi
Zerua (Rogers) **129** 87
Zuruah (Maxwell?)
147 115
Patridge see Partridge
PATRIGH Thomas **55** 379
66 166
Patrison see Patterson
PATSYLL Rose **148** 162
Walter **148** 162

PATT
Elizabeth W. **117** 239
Emily L. **77** 181
Henry W. **77** 181
PATTAH Susanna **75** 189
PATTAN Betsey (Brown)
  84 463
Nancy **84** 463
Polly **84** 463
PATTANE Lavina **84** 463
Patte *see* Pattee
PATTED Ares **113** 283
Richard **113** 283
Thomas **113** 283
PATTEE Patte Pattey
  Pattie Patty
——— **147** 181
___ (Sargent) **146** 333
  147 178
Abigail **70** 197 **123** 240
  146 324 326-329 333 335
  339 **147** 78 80 84 85 177
  183 184
Abigail (Ames) **146** 331
  147 174 175
Abigail (Elliot) **146** 331
  147 174 175
Abigail (Emerson) **146**
  325 334 **147** 177
Abigail (Saunders)
  147 176
Agnes Campbell **147** 186
Alexander **147** 178
Alice **146** 331
Almira **147** 186
Alonzo H. **90** 287
Amelia **147** 180
Anna **109** 251 **147** 77
Anna (Putnam) **147** 80
  186
Antiope **147** 79
Arthur **147** 75
Arthur S. **147** 75
Asa **146** 315 328 329 **147**
  73 80-83 85 174 176
Asa Dustin **146** 333 **147**
  178 181
Azubah (Low) **147** 185
Belinda (Johnson)
  147 180
Benjamin **135** 122 **146**
  320 321 325-327 333-335
  147 73-75 177 185
Benjamin Walker **147** 84
Betsey **111** 43 **147** 83 180
Betsey (Eastman) **147** 86
Betsey (Mallon) **147** 176
Betty **146** 328 329
Caroline **147** 184
Caroline (Fay) **147** 182
Carter **147** 175
Catherine **147** 76
Charles **147** 176
Charles Goodhue **147** 184
Charlotte (Briant) **147** 178
Clarissa (Thomas) **147** 84
Collins **147** 76 187
Cora Matilda **61** 207
  62 xxxvii
Cynthia **147** 187
Cyrus **146** 315 **147** 73 174

PATTEE *cont'd*
Daniel **147** 82 83 187
Daniel Collins **147** 80 186
David **146** 327 **147** 80 84
  187
Day Emerson **147** 86
Dillie **147** 175
Dorcas (Emerson)
  147 176
Dorcas (Savory) **109** 251
  146 323 330 331
Dorothy / Dolly (Austin)
  147 176
Dummer **147** 83
Ebenezer **146** 327 336
  147 77 79
Edmund **147** 175
Edward **146** 332 333
  147 176
Eleanor Tracy **66** lii **77**
  xxxvi lxxxviii lxxxix
Elias **147** 178-180
Eliphalet **109** 251 **146** 323
  330 331 **147** 174 176
Elizabeth **111** 116 **146**
  323 325 **147** 74 76 85
  185 186
Elizabeth (Howard)
  147 76
Elizabeth (Lindsey) **146**
  327 **147** 75
Elizabeth (Oliver) **147** 76
  185
Elizabeth (Prince) **146**
  321 324
Elizabeth (Scribner) **146**
  323 327-329
Elizabeth (Turner)
  147 175
Elizabeth Stead **95** 354
Elizabeth / Betsey **147** 78
Esther **138** 322
Eunice (Sargent) **147** 83
Experience / Speda
  147 182
Ezekiel **146** 326 327 **147** 73-
  76 78 186
Ezepheneiah **146** 328
Fanny (Knapp) **147** 86
Frank Hargrave
  77 lxxxix
Fred Lewis **57** 342
George **147** 175 181
George W. **147** 185
Georgianna Eliza **81** 150
Hannah **51** 319 **109** 251
  146 320 321 328 329 331
  333 **147** 83-86 178 187
Hannah (Clements)
  147 83
Hannah (Corliss) **146** 333
  147 181
Hannah (Dow) **146** 329
  147 80 82
Hannah (Eaton) **146** 333
  147 176
Hannah (Emerson)
  147 176
Hannah (Gordon) **146**
  333 **147** 180
Hannah (Rollins) **146** 323

PATTEE *cont'd*
Hannah Corliss **147** 182
Hannah Standley **147** 181
Harriet (Gibbs) **147** 181
Harriet Amanda (Lewis)
  147 182
Harrison **146** 315 **147** 73
  174
Hope **147** 178 180
Huldah (Daws) **147** 74
Humphrey **146** 320 325
James **147** 74 80 83 181 187
James Paul **146** 332 333
  147 180 182
Jane **88** 9 **146** 335 **147** 78
Jane (Foss) (Pierce) **146**
  333 **147** 183
Jane (Sewall) (McDaniel)
  147 186
Jane (Stuard) **146** 326 335
  336
Jedediah **109** 251
Jedeh **147** 86
Jemima **146** 321
Jenny **147** 78
Jerediah **146** 300 329-331
  147 85 86
Jeremiah **146** 321 326 335
  147 76 185 186
Joanna **109** 251 **146** 331
  147 86 187
John **88** 330 **146** 315 320
  322 323 328 329 333 335
  147 73 76 81 83-85 174
  178 180 183 184 186
John Calvin **147** 184
Jonathan **109** 251 **146** 331
  147 175
Joseph **147** 84 187
Joseph Gile **147** 178
Josephine **146** 315 **147** 73
  174
Judah **147** 80
Judith **147** 187
Judith (Barnard) **147** 83
Laban **147** 182
Lavinia **147** 86
Letitia **62** 31
Linwood Melvin **117** 235
  121 80 **146** 316
Lithgow **147** 74 75
Loami **146** 333 **147** 179
  181 182
Lois **109** 251 **146** 331
Lora J. **90** 287
Louisa **147** 175
Lovina **147** 187
Lucinda **147** 186
Lucinda (Goodhue) **146**
  333 **147** 183 184
Lucy **147** 80 177 187
Lucy (Collins) **146** 327
  147 80
Ludamia **147** 178
Lydia **146** 335 **147** 177 181
Lydia (Saunders) **147** 176
Margaret **146** 336 **147** 78
  79 180
Margaret (Howard) **146**
  327 **147** 73 75
Margaret H. **147** 185

PATTEE *cont'd*
Maria **147** 186
Mariam **109** 251
Martha **135** 340 **147** 84
Mary **100** 243 **109** 251
　146 325 326 331-333 336
　147 77 83 84 176 178
　183-185 187
Mary (Blake) **95** 354
Mary (Clark) **146** 323 332
Mary (Davis) **147** 83
Mary (Hadley) **146** 329
　147 83
Mary (Low) **147** 185
Mary (North) (McKechnie)
　146 327 **147** 80
Mary (Potter) **147** 185
Mary (Stinson) **146** 327
　147 77
Mary (Wells) **147** 84
Mary (Wightman)
　147 182
Mary Ada **147** 182
Mary Ann (Bixby)
　147 187
Mary B. (Robie) **147** 84
Mary E. **147** 185
Mary Frances (Brooks)
　90 287
Mary N. **147** 185
Mehitable **74** 250 **147** 83
Mehitable (Jewett) **147**
　81-83
Mercy **146** 319-321
Meriell **146** 328 329
Miranda **147** 76 186
Miriam **146** 333 **147** 176
　181
Molly **109** 251 **146** 331 **147**
　77 84
Molly (Pattee) **147** 84
Moody **147** 176
Moors **147** 181
Moses **74** 250 **146** 321
　147 83 84
Nancy **147** 185
Nancy (Bliss) **147** 175
Nancy (Chapman)
　147 184
Olive Ann (Gilman)
　147 187
Olive Cordelia **147** 182
Parker **147** 186
Parthenia **147** 79
Patience **146** 327 335
　147 79
Patience (Collins) **146** 321
　325
Patty (Fox) **147** 181
Patty (Perkins) **147** 181
Perthena **111** 116
Peter **60** 189 **117** 235 **146**
　315-325 327-330 332 333
　335 **147** 73 84 174 177
　183
Phebe **146** 334 **147** 177
Phebe (Gordon) **146** 333
　147 177 178
Philemon **147** 80 187
Philena **147** 186

PATTEE *cont'd*
Philena (Goodhue)
　147 184
Philena (Marsh) **147** 178
Polly **147** 83 176
Polly (Merrill Jackman)
　147 84
Polly (Wells) **147** 84
Prince **146** 325
Priscilla **147** 182
Priscilla (Corliss) **146** 333
　147 182
Priscilla (Oliver) **147** 76
Rachel **111** 118 **147** 79 186
Rachel (McCobb) **147** 185
Rebecca **147** 80 182
Rebecca (Burbank) **146**
　333 **147** 183
Rebecca (Ferrin) **147** 84
Rebecca (Sewall) **146** 335
Relief **147** 79 187
Relief (Curtis) **147** 80 187
Rhoda **146** 328 329
Richard **62** 31 **131** 77 **146**
　315 319-323 327-330 332
　333 **147** 73 84 174 176
　177 180 181
Robert **143** 214
Rodney **91** 200
Rosilla **147** 187
Ruth **147** 83
Ruth (Douglas) **147** 187
Sally **147** 83 86 185 187
Sally (Pierce) **147** 182
Sally Ann (Lovell)
　147 180
Salome **147** 187
Salome (Pattee) **147** 187
Samuel **146** 320 321 324
　325 327 333 335 **147** 74
　75 80 184 185 187
Sarah **146** 323 325 326
　147 74 80 86 175 182
　187
Sarah (Beck) **146** 333
　147 183
Sarah (Gill) **146** 316 319
　320
Sarah (Moulton) **147** 178
Sarah (Sewall)
　(McPhettrage) **147** 185
Sarah (Watkins) **146** 331
　147 174 175
Savory **147** 86 175
Selding **147** 177
Seth **109** 251 **146** 320 322
　323 327 328 330-332 **147**
　86 174 175
Sibyl (Parker) **147** 74
Silas Whitney **147** 181
Sophrona **147** 181
Stephen **147** 176 184
Stephen Burbank **147** 184
Sukey **147** 176
Sumner **147** 186
Susan **147** 83
Susan M. (Clark?) **147** 186
Susanna **146** 320 323 328
　329 **147** 83 84 176-178
　185
Susanna (Beale) **123** 240

PATTEE *cont'd*
　131 177 **146** 320-322
Susanna (Corliss) **146** 332
　147 175
Susanna (North) (Hadley)
　146 317
Tamson (Trachey) **147** 86
Thomas **147** 175 184
True **147** 178 180
William **146** 323 332 333
　147 74 178-180 185
William Harrison
　147 182
William S. **60** 93 281 313
　95 354 **147** 187
William Samuel **64** 333
William Sewall **65** 12 16
　147 185
Zephaniah **146** 328 **147** 84
PATTELUCE
Jonthan **127** 304
PATTEN —— **61** 98 **100**
　192 **112** 99
— Capt. **92** 15
— Miss **103** 169
— Mr. **67** 335 **86** 44
— Mrs. **87** 277 278
Abigail **51** 462 **62** 26 **71**
　346 **76** 104 106 110 179
　181 183 184 **100** 296
　107 198 **126** 41 42
Abigail (Makepeace)
　90 72
Abigail M. **91** 28 34
Acter / Actor **66** 106
　99 323
Adelaide **78** 325
Albert Reynolds Soule
　76 95
Alex **112** 283
Alice E. **79** 103
Ann Eliza **78** 46
Anna **66** 339 **79** 102
Anna (Hopkins) **103** 173
Anna Morton **68** lxxviii
Anna Thayer **68** lxxviii
Anne **66** 338 **106** 231
Anne Crosby **91** 84
　105 63
Annie M. **142** 370
Apphia **75** 253
Archbell **112** 286
Artemas Spofford
　58 xciv
Augusta Eugenie **76** 95
Azubah (Willis) **114** 270
Barbara **82** 394 **101** 273
Bertha A. **101** 261
Betsey **84** 464 **125** 106
Betsey (Bradford) **101** 305
Betsey (Clough) **85** 6
Betty **107** 196
Bradley Merrill **82** 394
Bradley Merrill (Mrs.)
　91 297
Caroline M. **81** 349
Caroline Olive **89** 120
Catherine **81** 40
Catherine Lane **79** 102
Catherine M. **123** 153
Charles **140** 234

PATTEN *cont'd*
Charles C. **86** 318
Charles L. **109** 318
Chesley **83** 144
Christian **148** 319 322
323 325
Clarence Wesley **83** 123
233 **89** 81 **90** 210 **91** 158
210 **92** 92 93 158 161
210 **93** 128 151 153 **94**
152 **95** 159 **96** 151 152
101 261-263 **102** 61 129
Cornelia Gray **123** 79
Cyrena (Shelley) **90** 72
Daniel **133** 324
Daniel Warren **90** 72
David **56** 21 349 **89** 246
112 286
David F. **103** 169
David G. **89** 246
David S. **83** 143 146
Deborah **55** 80 **145** 357
Dixey **107** 270
Dorcas **52** 128 129 140 142
E. B. **63** 206
Eady (Gifford) **137** 161
Edward **95** 166 **148** 323
Elisha **75** 54
Elizabeth **52** 129 142 **74**
211 **75** 119 **76** 180 **79** 40
86 318 449 456 **87** 271
276 **97** 93 **118** 132 **143**
215 **148** 323
Elizabeth (Trinder)
148 323
Elizabeth Howe (Heustis)
90 72
Elizabeth Josephine
(De Poyen) **91** 84
105 63
Elizabeth Nelson (Pratt)
95 165
Ella **84** 181 **90** 80
Ella Elizabeth **90** 72 142
Ellen (Swasey) **89** 120
Ellen Boyle **79** 103
Emeline **82** 202
Emeline / Emma (Barnes)
111 137
Emily Gertrude **58** xciv
Emma Frances **78** 46
Esther **90** 233 **96** 89 90
Eunice **96** 89 90 **108** 190
140 234
Fanny **84** 464
Florence **107** 194
Frances **89** 246
Frank Walter **83** 435 438
Frank William **101** 261
Franklin R. **83** 143
Frederick C. **85** 169
Freeman **104** 126
G. J. **80** 57
George **119** 26
George Ferguson **82** 491
George J. **79** 167
George W. **111** 137
George Washington
109 226
Hannah **61** 119 **82** 491 **84**
464 **107** 196 307 **108**

PATTEN *cont'd*
124 **126** 209
Hannah (Hurlbut)
125 238
Hannah (Sloper) **109** 12
109
Hannah Hamlin (Quin-
tard) (Crow) **109** 263
Hannah T. **83** 381
Hannah Thomas **82** 491
95 290
Hans **75** 107 **76** 104 106
110 112 179 181 183 184
196 258 **87** 206 **115** 227
Harriet **115** 125
Harriette Elizabeth
(Bailey) **101** 261
Harrison **84** 464
Hector **66** 106
Helen Rowe **98** 146
Henry **75** 253
Henry H. **109** 263
Henry J. **82** 386
Hugh **65** 169
Isaac **63** 75
James **75** 106 **85** 114 **95**
166 400 **107** 195 197-201
270 273 **108** 54 121 **111**
202 212 **144** 9
James A. **82** 386
James A. (Mrs.) **89** 209
James Littlefield **76** 110
Jane **71** 216 217 **75** 106-
108 118-120 **76** 179 **93**
112 **137** 360
Jane Elizabeth **97** 384
Jane Hunnewell
68 lxxviii
Jane / Jean (Manahan)
90 388
Jemima **92** 49
Jennie **95** 75 151
Jennie M. **69** 261 **81** 238
82 237 386
Jennie Maria **95** 165
Jeremiah **76** 104 **79** 54
Jerusha **85** 411
Jessie Florence **78** 354
Jessie Rose **65** xxxvii
Joan **86** 456 **87** 271
Joanna **76** 112 **115** 127
John **59** 21 **61** 135 **71** 216
75 51 108 **82** 202 **84** 463
464 **85** 6 **86** 456 457 **87**
271 275 276 724 **89** 14
90 72 **92** 49 **96** 89 90 **97**
395 **100** 140 **103** 300
105 290 **107** 194 201
273 **108** 121 **109** 12 109
115 126 **125** 204
John (Mrs.) **85** 121
John Reynolds **76** 95
John Williams **75** xxiii 65
79 102 201 212 **80** 216
81 474
Johnson Harman **76** 103
Jonathan **85** 124
Joseph **76** 106 **97** 395 **101**
261 **115** 125 **122** 293
125 214
Joshua **100** 192 **108** 190

PATTEN *cont'd*
Julian **84** 464
Justine **86** 456 457
Justine (Pyke) **87** 272 274
276 **96** 278
Keziah (Parker) **101** 261
Lavinia **84** 463
Lewis **90** 388
Lizzie **124** 149
Lois **86** 227
Louise **81** 383
Lovina **84** 464
Lovisa **115** 128
Lucretia **68** 330
Lucy **61** 119 **83** 143
126 207
Lydia **76** 184
Lydia (Whiting) **133** 324
M. L. **91** 331
Marcia L. / S. **83** 143
Margaret **78** 242 **82** 284
296 **90** 369 **108** 242
Martha **75** 118
Martha (Nesbitt) **95** 166
Mary **51** 304 **66** 109 **71** 219
78 303 **79** 102 103 **86**
233 **92** 15 **93** 261 **96** 89
90 **107** 199 **123** 172 **125**
181 **126** 20 **139** 306
Mary (Bell) **101** 261
Mary (Dickey) **101** 251
Mary (Hayden) **125** 214
Mary (Robertson) **95** 166
Mary (Stone) **104** 126
Mary A. **79** 152 307
Mary Ann **109** 263
Mary F. **54** 151
Mary French **79** 103
Mary Low **69** 261
Mary S. **104** 126
Matilda (Metz) **109** 226
Matthew **63** 293 **71** 219
74 100 **75** 51 54 **123** 8
15
Maud **82** 202
Medad **61** 119
Mehitable **58** 123 **61** 119
65 8 **108** 227
Miriam **79** 102
Molly **107** 200
Nancy **55** 81 **66** 106 **74** 18
84 463 464 **106** 320 **107**
240
Nathaniel **66** 338 339 **67**
121 **68** 338 79 170 309
80 136 **86** 456 457 **87**
270-276 278 279 **90** 72
91 331 **93** 261 263 **95**
135 **96** 278 **98** 131 **101**
273 **124** 20 **133** 309 **144**
102
Nathaniel (Mrs.) **87** 275
Neil **109** 74
Nevada Estelle **109** 226
Nina Lillian (McConnell)
83 435 438
Noah **109** 263
Peter **52** 312
Pickering **81** 383
Polly **62** 64 **84** 463 464
111 116

PATTEN *cont'd*
Priscilla **75** 312 314 **76**
  103 258 **140** 234
Priscilla (Harmon) **115** 59
Rachel **63** 175 **96** 89 90 **107**
  197 200 273 **108** 124
Rebecca **56** 370 **59** 143
  79 102
Rebecca (Adams) **90** 72
Richard **83** 145
Robert **52** 128 142 **55** 141
  73 41 **76** 112 **107** 195
  196 198 200 270 273 **112**
  286
Robert Francis **78** 46
Roland de **96** 116
Rufus **66** 106 **114** 270
Ruth **56** 349 **66** 338 **68** 338
  79 168 **80** 61 65
Sadie Smathers **109** 239
Sally **79** 102
Sally (Burt) **133** 306
Sally S. **97** 15
Samie **103** 173
Samuel **55** 80 **91** 331 **101**
  261 **103** 300
Sarah **59** 245 **73** 194 **75** 120
  86 456 **87** 271 272 **96** 90
  100 243 **107** 195 196
  198-201 270 273 **137** 334
Sarah (Pomeroy) **90** 72
Sarah (Stone) **108** 121
  144 9
Sarah (Weisell/Wiswall)
  96 89 **108** 121
Sarah B. **66** 112
Sarah E. **73** 41
Sarah Stone **137** 183
Sarah W. **81** 474
Seth William **85** 411
Sibyl W. **84** 419
Stephen **91** 84 **105** 63
Susan **66** 339 **81** 383
  96 89 90
Susan Wheeler **58** xciv
Susanna **74** 100 **75** 314
  108 190 **115** 127
Susanna (Goold) **108** 190
Temperance (Bourne)
  119 26
Thankful (Hopkins)
  103 169
Thankful (Matthews)
  (Joslyn) **86** 44
Thomas **51** 304 462 **52** 141
  59 245 **69** 261 **75** 106
  76 104 **79** 102 **86** 456
  457 **87** 271 272 274-276
  92 49 **96** 89 90 **97** 119
  112 287 **136** 48 **140** 234
W. A. **120** 139
William **52** 129 142 **58** 123
  61 98 **63** 103 **66** 109 **71**
  218 **75** 106-108 118-120
  312 314 **76** 103 258 **78**
  354 **79** 56 102 103 168
  80 63 66 **82** 202 **84** 266
  437 **86** 318 **87** 272 **89**
  120 174 **90** 72 **95** 165
  166 **105** 277 290 **107**
  270 **112** 74 **115** 59 **116**

PATTEN *cont'd*
  111 **119** 71 **123** 172 **125**
  238 **136** 45
William A. **122** 149
William C. **68** 44
William E. **101** 261
William J. **125** 238
William S. **68** lxxviii
Winifred (Hornbuckell)
  148 323
Pattengill *see* Pettingill
PATTENSON Pattinson
Alice **113** 65
Brian **113** 65
John **66** 69
Richard **112** 190
Roger **66** 68 69
Thomas **61** 270 **113** 65
PATTERSON Paterson
  Patrison Patteson
  Pattison
  —— **53** 267 **56** 106 210
  58 97 **62** 289 **70** 217 264
  86 399 **98** 54 **133** 297
  298 **145** 159 164 167
  — Baby **111** 220
  — Capt. **87** 37
  — Gen. **99** 288 **115** 276
  — Mr. **76** 145
  — Mrs. **69** 118 **70** 138
  79 152
  ____ (Mansfield) **140** 35
A. B. (Mrs.) **110** 80
Abigail **66** 109 **82** 291 296
Abigail (Barton) **107** 297
Actor P. **93** 298
Ada M. **91** 105
Adam **61** 266 **73** 257
  105 285
Adelaide M. **86** 356
Agnes **125** 289
Alexander **64** 211 **76** 53
Alexander Bybee (Mrs.)
  99 148 **114** 70
Alfred (Mrs.) **82** 219 237
Alice **86** 369
Alice (Errington) **132** 48
  49
Alice E. **81** 253
Alice L. **95** 284
Alice Maynard **74** liii
Alonzo **64** 211
Amos **128** 301
Andrew **59** 244 245 **60** 189
  83 138 **105** 290 **125** 58
Ann **78** 327 **87** 282 **88** 339
  89 398 **110** 227 **117** 163
Ann (McBride) **92** 172
Ann Graham **113** 163
Ann Mae **92** 172
Anna **54** 291 **64** lxi 93 **73**
  258 **127** 117 **144** 236-
  238 **145** 310
Anna (Chisholm) **127** 117
Anne **54** 199 293
Ansel **136** 78
Arthur F. **81** 253
Arthur Willis **92** 146
Asa **57** 411
Assana (Coffin) **90** 49
Ayers **56** 172

PATTERSON *cont'd*
Benjamin **54** 199 **56** 253
Betsey **61** 238 239 **66** 109
Betty **57** 411 **73** 257
Betty Lee **108** 134
Beulah **53** 216
Bingham **137** 160 161
Bradford **107** 300
Bradley Hawkes **111** 163
Bridget **65** 233
Bridget (Dowd) **93** 371
Calista **66** 107
Calvin S. **73** 258
Caroline **105** 107
Caroline Elizabeth **64** 211
Carrie Bel **82** 237
Charity G. (Parker)
  97 232
Charley **117** 171
Charlotte **66** 107 **84** 319
Clarissa **66** 107 **73** 258
Cora **87** 175
Cordelia **87** 380
D. W. **53** 265 **113** 76
D. Williams **52** 371 **57** 19
Danforth **57** 411
Daniel **91** 105 **109** 12 203
Daniel W. **52** 456
David **53** 216 **57** 411 412
  61 242 **86** 355 **104** 80
David Nelson **64** 209
David Williams **64** 93
  71 101
Dorcas **55** 295 **88** 310
Doris A. **109** 69
E. J. **54** 450
E. L. **91** 331
E. P. **128** 96
Ebenezer **54** 199 291 293
  61 240
Edith (Gifford) **137** 160
  161
Edmund **97** 232
Edward **89** 174 **139** 137
Eleanor (Porter) **112** 94
Elias **83** 417
Elisha **117** 167
Elisha Parkhurst **66** 108
Eliza **61** 135 **106** 308
Eliza (Mayo) **126** 141
Eliza B. **122** 296
Elizabeth **54** 199 **56** 253 **59**
  244 245 **76** 136 **78** 189
  83 138 417 **95** 294 **103**
  72 **126** 209
Elizabeth (Call) **86** 355
Elizabeth (Errington)
  132 48
Elizabeth (Mackey)
  125 109
Elizabeth (Pearson)
  86 355
Elizabeth H. **66** 111
Elizabeth Holmes
  71 xxxix
Elizabeth P. **86** 256
Ella Frances (Gifford)
  133 297 298
Ellen **94** 101
Emily C. **122** 296
Emily Jane **56** 172

PATTERSON *cont'd*
Enoch **53** 216
Ernest Otis **99** 31
Ernest Otis (Mrs.) **99** 31
Escaville **96** 129
Eugenia **90** 351
Eunice **88** 372
Everett W. **74** liii
Faith (Chamberlain) **139** 128 137 **142** 352
Fanny **61** 243 **125** 101
Fanny A. **73** 258
Frances **110** 54
Frances Virginia (Taylor) **135** 79
Frances W. **92** 172
Francis **87** 55
Francis J. **86** 356
Frank J. **98** 267
Frank Miner **75** xxiii 65 **93** 371 **94** 79 141
George **61** 135 **73** 258 **132** 48 49
George E. **92** 172
George Herbert **62** 394
George R. **73** 258
George W. **125** 40
George Washington **68** 385 **110** 319
George William **64** 210
Gertrude **93** 372
Gordon W. **114** 217
Grace E. **85** 353
Graham **116** 82
Hannah **53** 247 **64** 211 **91** 293
Harriet **57** 205 **70** 20 **103** 281 **109** 203
Harriet (Stover) **109** 12
Harriet Frances (Barrett) **99** 30 31
Harriet N. **86** 307
Helen Gilman **111** 163
Helen Gornet **103** 120
Henry **128** 264
Herbert **64** 254 256
Hezekiah **57** 205 **69** 13 127 214 215 301 **70** 11-13 18 139 145 304
Hinsi **128** 96
Hiram **119** 79
Hugh **106** 236
Hutchinson **57** 412
Ida A. (Kelley) **92** 172
Inez E. **92** 172
Isaac **104** 262
Isabelle Bernice **107** 134
J. R. (Mrs.) **116** 235
J. W. **140** 35
Jackson **91** 331
Jacob **57** 410-412
James **59** 243-245 **61** 268 **64** 93 **65** 221 **66** 103 105 107-109 **70** 9 **73** 258 **76** 136 **83** 417 **84** 319 **86** 355 **105** 284 **112** 276 **125** 109 **141** 250
James Lindley (Mrs.) **80** 102 208
James T. **69** 36
James W. **92** 172 **103** 281

PATTERSON *cont'd*
Jane **64** 227 **70** 11 **73** 258 **76** xxxviii **87** 55 **91** 231 **112** 94 **123** 10 11
Jane (Anderson) **87** 195
Janet Dayton **86** 359
Jean **73** 258
Jefferson **87** 56 **98** 267 **99** 145
Jehiel **119** 79
Jehu **135** 79
Jenny **73** 257
Joanna **59** 245
John **51** 70 **53** 137 **54** 162-164 **57** 205 410-412 **59** 245 **60** 385 **61** 135 240 **62** 243 **65** 77-79 81 109 110 113 233 254 255 257-259 261 262 333 336-338 340 341 **69** 126 215 216 218 287 297 300 303-307 **70** 10 13 15-21 220 **71** 130 **77** 48 **87** 55 **91** 206 **92** 172 **93** 371 **105** 283 **107** 297 **116** 111 **127** 117 **145** 353
John A. **122** 72 233
John B. **72** 275
John Henry **58** xlv 107 **59** xlviii
John Mitchell **88** 304
John N. **98** 267
John R. **81** 253
John S. **128** 173
John Stuart **113** 244
John Thomas **87** 56
Jonathan **59** 245 **63** 135
Joseph **59** 245 **71** 147 **140** 234
Josephine (Cushman) **128** 264
Joshua **119** 79
Julia **93** 372
Julia (Corcoran) **93** 371
Julia (Johnston) **87** 56
Julia (Shaw) **98** 266 267
Julia Agnes **81** 253
Julia Ann **64** 210 **88** 339
Julia Perrine (Shaw) **99** 67 150
Juliana **64** 210
Katharine Marie **82** 407
Katharine O. **99** 31
Kirby William **108** 35
Laura Jane (Call) **86** 355
Lemuel **69** 221 222 295
Lemuel (Mrs.) **69** 222
Levi **87** 195 **119** 79
Levina Jane **61** 359
Lewis **61** 145
Linda **105** 221
Louami **119** 79
Louisa Marguerite (Dayton) **86** 359
Lucina (Colton) **136** 78
Lucy **57** 205 410 **86** 399
Lucy (Arey) **86** 399
Lucy (Chisholm) (Briggs) **127** 117
Lucy Ann **52** 456

PATTERSON *cont'd*
Luther Clairbourn (Mrs.) **83** 217 **84** 190
Lydia **56** 37
M. B. **91** 331
Mabel (Prior) **87** 56
Margaret **57** 412 **71** 220 **87** 55 **93** 372 **100** 248 **115** 121
Margaret K. **97** 210
Margaret Strout **77** 48
Maria **64** 209
Martha **61** 240 **73** 258 **91** 77 **105** 111
Martha (Clifford) **83** 417
Martha Alice (Prior) **87** 56
Martha Alverda **96** 28
Martin **105** 284
Martin J. **93** 372
Mary **53** 216 **59** 245 **60** 385 **61** 379 **62** 170 **64** 211 **80** 208 **81** 198 **85** 87 96 **92** 53 **95** 282 355 **101** 122 **134** 90
Mary (Thomas) **87** 55 56
Mary A. Bonner **90** 207
Mary Ann **112** 140 **115** 119
Mary C. (Billings) **98** 54
Mary C. (Fitz Randolph) **98** 54
Mary E. (Bowden) **122** 72 233
Mary Elizabeth **103** 72
Mary F. **112** 140
Mary Jane **69** 36
Mary M. **82** 237 **91** 57
Mary Mathilda **91** 77 147
Mary Newbold **97** 387
Mary P. **98** 267
Matha Alverda **96** 28
Matthew **61** 135 **133** 235
Mattie E. **128** 96
May Frances **81** 219
Mercy **71** 147
Mercy Elizabeth **66** 107
Meta Alice (Bancroft) **96** 129
Molly **110** 29
Moses **54** 199
Moses N. **78** 302
N. **124** 41
Nancy Jane **87** 195
Naomi **73** 257
Nathaniel **105** 284
Nicholas **69** 301
Norman **119** 317
Norman George **95** 147 **116** 82
Olivia E. **128** 264
Oscar **119** 79
Patrick John **93** 371
Patty **66** 110
Paul **66** 108
Peggy **73** 258
Peirce **90** 49
Peter **122** 296 **145** 366
Phebe **119** 79
Polly **61** 239 242 **111** 117
Prince **78** 186

PATTERSON *cont'd*
R. E. **91** 331
Rachel **65** 44
Ralph **121** 105
Rebecca **57** 410 **59** 243-245 **89** 62
Rhoda **127** 56
Robert **58** 107 **61** 266 **71** 133 **74** 165 **80** 106 207 **84** 263 437 **87** 55 56 71 177 **91** 77 **105** 284 **112** 94 **123** 10 **126** 96 **132** 48
Robert Clarke **122** 296
Rohna May **91** 105
Ross E. **99** 31
Ruth **140** 304 305
Sally **55** 406 **61** 240 **73** 258 **81** 198
Samuel **54** 291 **61** 137 **62** 169 **66** 110 **69** 296 **83** 419 421 **105** 290 **126** 141
Samuel D. **73** 258
Samuel F. **60** xxxvi
Samuel White **95** 400
Sarah **61** 380 **65** 37 **80** 64 **83** 138 **92** 289 **125** 40 **133** 235 **134** 329
Sarah Ann **128** 92
Sarah Elizabeth (Cox) **120** 15
Sarah Jane **115** 231
Sarah Jane (Annesley) **91** 77
Selenda **73** 258
Seth **86** 355 356
Sewal **91** 331
Silas **120** 15
Sl___ **128** 174
Sophia **121** 263
Stuart **98** 267
Susan (Barton) **107** 300
Susan Bowman **64** 211
Susanna **61** 239 **77** 48 **127** 56 117 119
Susanna (Bruce) **141** 250
Susanna (Miller) **123** 10
Susanna Smith **54** 293
Thomas **64** 115 254 **65** 233 **73** 104 **76** 240 **81** 198 **82** 52 **91** 77 **127** 56 117 119
Thomas Norton **73** 104
William **61** 239 **63** 19 346 **65** 22 **73** 138 **86** 355 **90** 87 **91** 331 **92** 172 **105** 284 285 **121** 248 **132** 48 **143** 258 **144** 237
William D. **55** 359 **56** xxxii **61** 107 **62** lvi **117** 254 **131** 248
William Davis **59** v xvi xlviii **60** v xiv **61** v xiii **62** v xv **63** v xv **64** v xiii **65** v vii xiii **66** v vii xxviii 102 **67** vii xiii **68** viii **69** viii **70** viii **71** viii **72** viii **73** viii **74** viii 162 **75** viii **76** viii 322 **77** viii 82 326 **78** 220 **79** 114 216 **80** 222

PATTERSON *cont'd*
81 236 366 **82** 251 **83** 246 414 **84** 205 **85** 214 **86** 108 205 355-359 **93** 308
William Donald (Mrs.) **80** 332 **81** 219 **114** 141
William Prior **87** 56
William T. **91** 331
Zacheus **111** 244
Zana M. (Cole) **92** 172
PATTESHALL Pateshall Patishall Pattishall
— Mrs. **65** 363
Abigail **72** 155 156
Ann **72** 156 157
Edmund **72** 153-156 **119** 17
Edward **72** 154 156
Elizabeth **72** 157
Frances **72** 156-158 246 **145** 292 293
Jane **72** 156 157
John **72** 154 155
Margaret **72** 156 157 **84** 362
Martha **72** 153-157
Mary **72** 154-157
Richard **72** 154-157 **84** 256 **104** 242
Robert **57** 389 **72** 154-158 **119** 20 **145** 293
Samuel **72** 154 155 157
William **72** 154 155
Patteson *see* Patterson
Pattey *see* Pattee
Pattie *see* Pattee
PATTING
Abigail M. **91** 28 34
PATTIS Betsey (De Golyer) **90** 378
Solomon **90** 378
Pattishall *see* Patteshall
Pattison *see* Patterson
PATTISS John **127** 305
PATTON Beatrice Banning (Ayer) **136** 325
Eliphalet Warner **127** 135
Frank Edward **127** 135
George Smith **136** 325
Harriet Jane (Price) **97** 119
Isaac **144** 103
Jane (Thompson) **112** 99
Jane Elizabeth **97** 384
Joseph **60** 243
Ledora Ann (Griswold) **127** 134
Louise **127** 135
Mary **86** 233
Nancy **107** 240
Nellie Louise **127** 135
Rachel (Vannoy) **109** 74
Robert **64** 348
Robert Bridges **54** 439
Samuel **60** 243
William W. **144** 121
Patty *see* Pattee
PATY Asenath **75** 127
Bertha Estelle **82** 22
Ephraim **82** 22

PATY *cont'd*
Ephraim Tabor **82** 22
Jane (Ellis) **122** 58
Sarah **82** 22
William **122** 58
PATYNDEN
William **84** 72
Pau *see* De Pau
PAUCHACHUX Sam **63** 231
PAUGUS
—— **63** 291 **104** 205
Antonie **111** 89
Johann (Cogan) **111** 89
PAUL Paull
— Capt. **110** 278 281
____ (Kingsbury) **112** 216
Abiah (Harmon) **90** 227
Abigail **55** lxxx **58** 146 256 **63** 170 **74** 40 **75** 148 **97** 142 **111** 95
Abigail (Talbott) **104** 244
Albert **95** 274
Alice (Paine) **103** 144
Alice Phebe **81** 44
Alice S. **119** 225
Almira **60** liv **65** 112 **128** 278
Althea (Tobey) **101** 226
Amos **55** 252 349
Amy **115** 63
Ann **58** 146 **60** 195 **75** 148
Anna **58** 146
Anna Holmes **113** 297
Anna L. **126** 220
Annie Carter **110** 281
Arza Walter **100** 112
Atlanta **85** 444
Augusta N. **89** 286
Augustus **97** 142
Barbara Frances (Billings) **107** 131
Barsheba **95** 274 **97** 146
Basheba **95** 274
Bathsheba (Weare) **115** 141
Bela **54** cxlviii
Benjamin **55** 376 **65** 190 **69** 256 **83** 17 **87** 139
Benjamin Mason **74** 40
Betsey **63** 271
Betsey (Chase) **87** 255
Betsey Maria **67** li
Burlington **76** 22 **113** 195 **121** 310
Caroline **95** 275 **119** 225
Carroll (Mrs.) **85** 338
Catherine **55** lxxix lxxx
Catherine (Waterhouse) **125** 215
Charles **55** lxxix lxxx **73** 195 **90** 322 **91** 231
Charles Henry (Mrs.) **103** 144
Charlotte **116** 40
Christopher **71** 314 320
Clarissa **57** 140
Daniel **54** 409 **74** 40 **96** 234 **125** 221
David **74** 40 **90** 322 323
Doddridge **121** 178
Dorcas **95** 331 **97** 274

PAUL *cont'd*
Dorcas (Shapleigh)
  95 269
Dorothy **82** 296 297
  133 192
Dorothy (Walker)
  133 192
E. **65** 190
Ebenezer **55** lxxx **60** 38
  75 148
Edmund **74** 40
Edna Florence **96** 179
Edward A. **101** 226
Edward Joy **56** xxxii
  69 287
Edwin **119** 224
Eleanor Ellicot **108** 187
Eliza Ann **96** 191 **119** 145
  228
Elizabeth **55** 374 **63** 168 **66**
  269 **75** 148 **83** 15 **92** 104
  379 **96** 234 **97** 271 **136**
  313
Elizabeth (Phillips) **110**
  278 281
Elizabeth (Weeks) **119**
  144 145 228
Elizabeth Duffield (Neil)
  108 187
Elizabeth Maxwell **70** 96
Emma Louza (Junkins)
  113 195 **121** 310
Esther **57** 26
Evalina (McIntire)
  119 224
Florence **83** 230
Fount Frank (Mrs.)
  103 120
Frank **55** 1
Frank (Mrs.) **84** 219
Franklin **90** 322
Fulton **55** xliii lxxix lxxx
George **78** 241
Gertrude Rose
  (Shapleigh) **95** 275
Hannah **55** lxxx **58** 146
  74 263 **75** 148 **85** 443
  95 79 **106** 193 **116** 131
  126 307
Hannah (Fisher) **113** 297
Hannah (Hambleton)
  111 95
Hannah (Kingsbury)
  115 65
Hannah (Nowell) **119** 146
Hannah K. **97** 268
Hattie Belle **89** 317
Haven Tilton **83** 438
  84 23
Helen McGaw (Longyear)
  85 338
Heloise Inez (Whittier)
  83 438 **84** 23
Henry **54** cxlviii **97** 272
  119 68 144-146 156 228
Hortensia M. **82** 397
Hugh **95** 269 **97** 274
Ida F. **91** 394
Iddo K. **124** 38
Isaac **74** 40 **75** 148 **141** 6
J. Byron **84** 31

PAUL *cont'd*
J. Frank **122** 72 234
Jacob **55** 69
James **97** 142 274 300
  146 322
James Balfour **79** 57 61
  105 170 **108** 174 **117**
  234 **121** 233 **122** 271
James Ira **125** 301
Jane **69** 256 **108** 303
  119 228
Jane R. **113** 265
Janette **55** lxxx
Jeffery **82** 296 297
Jemima Crocker **101** 226
Jennie **78** 241
Jeremiah **55** 252 **87** 206
  90 227 **95** 275 329 **97**
  146 270 **111** 95 **115** 136
  139 307 **116** 136 **119**
  224 **122** 72 234 **133** 47
Joan **71** 314 320
Joel **66** 269
John **54** 409 **64** 32 **66** 269
  71 314 318 320 **83** 22 26
  105 290 **106** 194 **133**
  192 **148** 336
John F. **119** 146
Joseph **55** 254 **95** 269 **97**
  272 **116** 296 **128** 278
Joseph Barnett (Mrs.)
  105 129
Joshua **103** 276 **113** 265
Josiah **74** 40 **116** 297
Joth'a **62** 289
Katharine **69** 157 **71** 318
  320
Katharine (Maverick)
  96 234
Katharine Choate **69** 287
Laura A. **129** 45
Leone **99** 146
Leonora M. **90** 303
Lester H. **93** 109
Lewis A. **91** 394
Lois **91** 231
Lydia **55** 376 **57** 141 **66**
  269 **69** 256 **83** 17 **87** 326
  90 185 **106** 194 **115** 140
  148 334
Lydia (Hodsdon) **83** 17
Lydia (Linscot) **115** 136
Lydia Permelia (Manzer)
  89 317
Margaret **57** 25 **72** 232 237
  79 178
Margaret C. **69** 318 **91** 394
Margeretta **55** lxxx
Margery **54** 219 **55** lxxix
  75 142
Maria (Gravenberg)
  125 301
Maria Elizabeth **110** 281
Marietta Dennett **76** 22
Martha **86** 296
Martha Dresser **102** 150
Mary **54** cxlviii **55** lxxx
  58 256 295 **63** 187 **72**
  232 **73** 203 **75** 145 148
  154 **76** 22 **78** 314 **79** 253
  82 296 302 **87** 75 **95** 329

PAUL *cont'd*
  96 191 **115** 59 61 227
  116 139 277 297 300
  127 12 **136** 341
Mary (Harwood) **87** 77
Mary (Leavitt) **95** 275
Mary (McIntire) **97** 272
Mary A. **69** 256
Mary Ann **83** 22 26 **90** 50
  119 280 281
Mary Ann (English)
  83 22
Mary E. **80** 45
Mary Elizabeth **95** 276
Mary Ellen **110** 281
Mary H. B. **91** 394
Mary Jordan (Frost)
  95 269
Mary L. **116** 304
Mary Louise **109** 226
Mary Stiles **54** xlvii cxlvii
Mehitable **71** 259
Mercy **57** 79
Moses **58** 295 **74** 40 129
  181 185 **92** 104 **95** 269
  97 146 **116** 296
Moses (Mrs.) **95** 269
Moses Newbury **95** 275
Nancy **60** 195
Nancy (McIntire) **119** 68
Nancy R. **90** 105
Nathaniel **60** 195
Noah **82** 296 302 **91** 394
Noah S. **69** 318 **91** 394
Oglesby **93** 296
Olive **55** 314 **83** 10 **126** 209
  83 15
Patience **55** 374 **74** 40 129
  83 15
Patience (Smith) **119** 224
Peter **53** 264 **104** 244
Phebe **77** 294 **90** 322
  134 278
Phineas **55** lxxx
Pliney **90** 322
Polly Rial **125** 223
Priscilla **75** 146 **91** 185
Rachel **75** 152 **91** 394
Richard **54** 97 219 **55** lxxix
  60 liv **71** 314 320 **75** 142
Robert **57** 25 26 **71** 259
  111 219 220
Roby (Williston) (Walker)
  (Bullock) **120** 5 9
Rodolphus **113** 53
Rosamond F. **73** 195
Roscoe G. **91** 394
Rosetta (Rogers) **121** 178
Roswell **91** 394
Rush **54** 213
Ruth **65** 190
Ruth (Dyer) **65** 190
Ruth Woodford **105** 126
S. Nellie (Gillan) **122** 72
  234
S. Rodman **108** 187
Sally **90** 322 **116** 135 **118**
  154 155
Sally (Smith) **125** 221
Sally Rogers (Shapleigh)
  95 274
Samuel **55** lxxx **58** 256 **60**

PAUL *cont'd*
  liv **74** 40 **75** 148 **97** 269
    328 **112** 216 **113** 297
    115 65 225 **128** 278 285
    141 6
  Samuel Walter **89** 317
  Sarah **51** 461 **106** 194 **112**
    164 **142** 21 **148** 334
  Sarah (Sanford) **103** 276
  Sarah J. **97** 266
  Sarah Rebecca **75** 251
  Sarahan **97** 273
  Seth **87** 255
  Sidney **90** 322
  Sophia **78** 30 **117** 140
  Stephen **55** 249 252 **69** 157
    96 234 **97** 145 **115** 141
  Susan **91** 394
  Susan E. (Sanborn)
    124 38
  Susan Jane **113** 265
  Susanna **78** 22
  Susanna Brumbaugh
    119 156
  Susie May **91** 394
  Thomas **62** 169 **72** 232
    82 397 **125** 215 **146**
    322
  Timothy **63** 168
  Vesta E. **91** 394
  Vienna **90** 322
  Vienna Veazie **78** 241
  Wealthy (Chase) **87** 139
  William **54** cl **61** 43 **63**
    162 187 327 **71** 314 320
    72 228 **75** 148 **76** 50 **79**
    253 **81** 44 **87** 75 77 **91**
    394 **95** 269 **97** 273 328
    329 **126** 220 **127** 223
  William Nelson **82** 397
  Winifred Blanche **82** 397
  Zebedee **120** 9
PAULDING
  Hiram **54** 362
  James **107** 213
  Julia **79** 329
  Sarah Ann (Barton)
    107 213
PAULER
  Gylua **96** 139 141
PAULET
  Ada **84** 347 348
  Ada L. (Smith) **84** 347 348
  Henry Monmouth
    Basing **84** 347
  Maude **84** 347 349
  Victor **84** 347
  Vincent **84** 348
  William **118** 256
  William Victor **84** 347 348
PAULEY Lulu May **104** 145
  105 69 133
PAULI Paulli
  —— **143** 259
  Philip **137** 306
PAULK *see also* Polk
  Abigail **111** 306
  Ammi **72** 115 116
  Belinda **72** 115
  Chauncy **72** 115
  David **72** 115

PAULK *cont'd*
  Diana **111** 306
  Diana (Wheeler) **111** 306
  Edwin **72** 116
  Eliakim **72** 116
  Elisha **72** 116
  Ephraim **72** 116
  Erastus **72** 116
  Esther **72** 115 116 **132** 76
  Esther Emeline **72** 116
  Eunice **72** 116
  Grace **72** 116
  John **72** 116 **111** 306
  Jonathan **132** 76
  Julius **72** 116
  Keziah **72** 116
  Margaret S. **72** 115
  Martha **111** 306
  Micajah **132** 76
  Miranda **72** 116
  Nathan **111** 306
  Rebecca (Stearns) **132** 76
  Ruth **132** 76
  Sarah **72** 115 116
  Uriah **132** 76
  Zachariah **132** 76
Paull *see* Paul
Paulli *see* Pauli
PAULLIN
  Charles Oscar **64** 65
  Louise Elizabeth **109** 129
PAULMANN
  Edward **85** 316
  Elizabeth Weber **85** 316
PAULSEN Karen **86** 94
  Kenneth S. **141** 362 **142**
    397 **145** 175 177 **147** 89
    192 284 **148** 81 83 189
    372
  Marion Wildi **120** 156
PAULSON
  Alice M. **69** 259
  Caroline **69** 259
  James **65** 120
  John A. **69** 259
  Samuel **69** 259
PAULUS —— **56** 15
PAULY George Adolph
  (Mrs.) **103** 120
PAUNCEFOTE Pauncefoote
  Jane **110** 232 **111** 162
  Richard **110** 232 **111** 162
PAUNSFORD
  Isott (March) **86** 83
  Thomas **86** 83
PAUPMUNNUCK **118** 88
  203
PAUSTOSS
  George **144** 348 354
PAVER Pavar
  William **53** 109 **59** 52
PAVEY —— **51** 355
PAVIE Roger **103** 201
PAVIER Daniel **51** 460
  Deborah **51** 461 466
  Elizabeth **51** 460
  Hannah **51** 463
  Josiah **51** 463
  Lucy **51** 462
  Noyes **51** 462
  Samuel **51** 461

PAVIOTT John **93** 385
PAVY Sarah **61** 67
PAVYS
  John **86** 414 **87** 369
PAWLE Joan **63** 37
PAWLETT Pawlette
  Ames **82** 307
  Hugh **80** 361
PAWLING
  Albert **111** 161
  Alonzo **98** 73
  Andrew **70** 337 338
  Eunice (Porter) (Bird)
    (Stanton) **111** 161
PAWLYN Thomas **80** 359
PAWSEY
  Martha **85** 316
  Walter **85** 316
PAWSON James **52** 353
PAXSON Paxon
  Amos **90** 345
  Henry **90** 345
  Jane **98** 44
  Margaret Lucille
    (Hannum) **90** 345
  Ruth **98** 44
PAXTON Adeline **69** 32
  Alexis R. **54** 375
  Bright **107** 211
  Charles **57** 280 **61** 257 **84**
    250 253 262 **136** 283
    140 249
  Charlotte G. **144** 116
  Eleanor (Hays) **112** 92
  Eliza **69** 31
  Elizabeth **69** 31
  Ella **69** 32
  Ella Frances **106** 144
  Ellen **69** 332
  Emeline (Barton) **107** 211
  Faith **67** 201
  George **69** 332
  Georgie V. **69** 32
  Ida C. **69** 32
  Jane G. **69** 32
  John **72** 15
  John Franklin **69** 32
  Joseph Henry **69** 32
  Joseph R. **54** 375
  Lotta A. **69** 32
  Louisa **125** 289
  Mary **68** 96 **72** 15 **112** 92
  Mary Ann F. **88** 331
  Mary Elizabeth **69** 32
  Mary Elkins **78** 204
  Sarah Cavendish **54** 375
  Sarah Pettit (Burke)
    106 144
  Sue **99** 145
  Susanna **84** 262
  Thomas **69** 31 **112** 17
  Thomas Chase **69** 32
  Wentworth **67** 201
  William **68** 96 **69** 31 332
    106 144 **112** 92
PAY —— **92** 403
  Eleanor Pilcher **75** 40
    92 193
  William **92** 193
PAYAN Oliver **72** 180
Paybody *see* Peabody

PAYE Henry **76** 223
PAYEN-PAYNE James
Bertrand **54** xcvii
PAYENS Hugh de **62** lxxv
PAYLING John **52** 27
Payn *see* Paine
Payne *see* Paine
PAYNEL Paynell
Christian **110** 185
Elizabeth **79** 367 368
Fulk **110** 185
Julius **110** 185
Thomas **79** 367 368 **94** 207
Paynter *see* Painter
PAYSON Pason
—— **60** liv **119** 49
— Capt. **119** 49 50
— Mrs. **119** 49 50
— Rev. Mr. **62** 277
Abigail **83** 108 **142** 63
Adela Louise **80** 442
Adelaide Eliza **52** 384
Adolphus **96** 50
Alice **95** 81
Alma **104** 234
Ann **68** 220 225 319 **84** 372
100 138
Ann (Robinson) **95** 81
Ann Carroll **95** 81
Ann Jane **80** 67
Ann Louisa **69** lviii
Ann Louise (Shipman)
87 292 **95** 81
Ann Maria (Robinson)
87 292
Anna **68** 167 **70** 46 272
72 275
Anne **107** 98
Anne Jane **79** 157
Anne R. **93** 255
Anne Rowe **93** 255 **94** 163
Asa **71** 343
Bathsheba **67** 314
Betsey **72** 275
C. **91** 331
Calvin B. **104** 234
Caroline (Bancroft) **96** 50
Charles **87** 292 **95** 81
Charles Henry **81** 107 219
87 292 297 **88** 173
Charles Shipman **95** 82
Charles Shipman (Mrs.)
82 474
Clarissa **92** 128
Cynthia **73** 113
Daniel **57** 389
Daniel M. **90** 91
David **72** 275
Edith St. Claire **79** 203
Edmund **67** 371
Edward **52** 384 **54** 31 58
25 **60** 38 **69** lviii lix **72**
275 **73** 117 **87** 292 **95** 81
148 46
Edwin **80** 442
Eleanor **87** 292
Eliphalet **72** 275
Elisha **106** 206
Eliza **72** 277
Elizabeth **52** 197 **68** 219 **71**
343 **73** 117 **86** 342 **113**

PAYSON *cont'd*
297 **130** 276 **148** 57
Elizabeth (Dowell) **148**
45 46 57
Emily **78** 408
Ephraim **60** 38 **68** 167 **89**
119 **107** 253 **130** 211
Esther **67** 376
Fanny Lithgow **85** 197
George **54** 172 **57** 141 **60**
38 39 **68** 225 319 **86** 458
91 331
George A. **93** 255
George Edward **64** xxxii
68 xxxii
Gilbert R. **81** 109 214
Gilbert Russell **52** 384
Giles **52** 197 198 **148** 45
46 57
Grata (Payson) **87** 292
95 81
H. E. (Mrs.) **78** 447
H. M. **91** 331
Hannah **73** 117 **82** 467
Hannah (Wentworth)
89 119
Hannah Gilbert **52** 384
Harriet (Watton) **104** 234
Henry **60** 38
Henry R. **91** 331
Herbert **86** 198 **95** 75 81 82
151
Herbert (Mrs.) **96** 161
103 79 125
Horace Edwin (Mrs.)
79 203
I. P. **79** 157
J. P. **80** 67
J. Phillips **127** 133
Jacob **73** 117
James **52** 384
Jane M. (Wallace) **90** 91
Joan **82** 474
Joan (Webb) **148** 57
Joanna **86** 458
John **61** 43 **67** 373 **69** lviii
73 117 **121** 248
John Brown **95** 82
John Fenno **68** 319
John H. **73** 113
Jonathan **60** 38 39 **68** 219
222 **70** 46 157 **72** 275 **84**
372 **92** 24 25 **96** 49
Joseph **60** 38 **69** lviii **78**
10 **140** 234 328
Judith **67** 374 **68** 167
Judith (Clapp) **107** 253
130 211
Keziah (Bullen) (Morse)
87 292 **95** 81
Lawrence **148** 57
Margaret (Lewis) **90** 89
Margaret (Merrill) **87** 292
Marion (Brown) **103** 67
Mary **72** 275 **75** 146 204
83 471 **90** 89 **92** 24 25
95 355 **108** 181 **110** 223
Mary (Bale) **86** 458
Mary (Eliot) **87** 292 **95** 81
Mary (Phillips) **87** 292
95 81 **108** 181

PAYSON *cont'd*
Mary Frances **75** 248
Mary S. **78** 399
Mehitable **78** 10
Melatiah **55** 343
Mildred Amanda **109** 128
Nancy **72** 275
Nathan **95** 19
Olcott Sprigg **95** 82
Patty **57** 389
Peggy (Lewis) **90** 89
Penelope Ann **54** 31 **69**
lviii lix
Phillips **52** 64 384 **63** 389
391 **69** lviii **87** 292 **91**
94 **95** 81 **116** 111
Phillips M. **87** 292
Polly (Carter) **131** 235
Priscilla **56** 307 **70** 157
Prudence **54** 213
Relief **92** 128 **94** 377
Sally **90** 92
Sally (Robinson) **90** 90
Sally Carroll (Brown)
95 81 **96** 161
Samuel **52** 384 **62** 275 **68**
167 225 229 231 233 **69**
lviii **87** 292 **90** 89 90 **91**
90 94 **92** 128 **94** 377 **95**
81 **108** 181 **118** 313 **130**
211 **140** 234
Samuel Russell **52** 383
384
Sarah **52** 198 424 **67** 373 **73**
117 **78** 19 **80** 23 **89** 119
92 108 **96** 49 **98** 338
108 181 **142** 137
Sarah (Noyes) **130** 211
Sarah H. **91** 90
Seth **69** lviii **87** 292 **95** 81
Silas **72** 275
Silence **73** 117
Susanna **75** 40 **107** 253
Swift **52** 384 **63** 92 **65** 39
141 344
Sylvanus **58** 142
Thankful **58** 25 **67** 371 373
73 117
Thomas **67** 314
Waitstill **86** 458
William **68** 233 **75** 40
William Lincoln **106** 126
116 145-147 228 307
117 74 151 152
William Martin **69** lix
PAYTON Emily **136** 362
Frances Elizabeth **136** 362
George Washington
136 362
Hannah Jane **136** 362
Jemima (Dimmitt)
136 362
John Wesley **136** 362
Mary **123** 122
Mary Ann **136** 362
Rebecca **136** 362
Sarah **134** 173
William **136** 362
PAYZANT
Abigail **127** 272
Abigail (Tupper) **99** 297

PAYZANT cont'd
Anna **127** 272 **128** 116
Anna (Dexter) **127** 272
Augustus **128** 117
Benjamin **127** 272
Charles **128** 117
Cynthia **127** 272
Elizabeth **127** 272 **128** 34
117
George **127** 272
Hannah (Freeman)
128 28
Henry **99** 297 **127** 272
128 116
Henry Alline **127** 272
James **127** 272
John **59** 94 **126** 100 **127**
50 55 56 123 201-203
206 208 267 269 271-273
276 **128** 28 30 31 33-37
113 115-117
Joseph **128** 28 117
Lavinia **120** 17
Lewis **128** 117
Marion M. **115** 318
Mary **127** 272 **128** 28 34
117
Mary (Crowell) **128** 117
Mary Ann **127** 272 **128**
116 117
Nathan **127** 272
Sarah **120** 13
Sarah Young **120** 13
Stephen Octavius **127** 56
Thomas **128** 117
William **120** 13 17
PAZE Harriet **92** 291
PE-AHM-E-SQUEET
68 xx 104 **70** 181 **71** xxi
Peabodie see Peabody
PEABODY Pabodie
Paybody Peabodie
—— **53** 149 **57** 121 **58**
323 328 **60** 189 **62** 260
69 124 **70** 18 **102** 84
136 211 **140** 234
— Col. **59** 36 **77** 46 **109** 57
— Mr. **63** 230
— Mrs. **83** 308
— Rev. Mr. **85** 462
A. **91** 331
A. P. **68** 38 41
Abigail **52** 57 **109** 233
Alexander **122** 215
Alice (Carleton) **109** 230
Alice Ruth **119** 76
Almira **61** 383
Amasa **96** 334
Andrew Preston **51** 100
53 454 **83** 168 174 177
189 **84** 31
Ann **117** 97
Anna **117** 96
Anna True **95** 295
Anne **122** 213
Asa **92** 197 **105** 283
Asa F. **147** 370
Augusta Jay (Balch)
(Neilson) **83** 488
Augustus (Mrs.) **93** 323
Benjamin **59** 23 **95** 113

PEABODY cont'd
96 190 **125** 181 **127** 8
Betsey **90** 54
Betsey G. **55** lvii
Betsey Gooch **97** 303
134 280
Betty (Alden) **115** 169
Caleb **122** 213 215
Caroline **122** 215
Caroline Emily **106** 225
Caroline Eustis **83** 174
Catherine (Friend)
125 182
Catherine (Kimball)
106 225
Catherine E. **98** 270
Catherine Elizabeth **77**
300 **84** 327 **88** 397 **93**
290 **94** 87
Catherine Langdon
83 174
Charles **59** 424
Charlotte **86** 299 **109** 230
Charlotte (Allen) **107** 224
Clara (Endicott) **83** 488
Clara Elizabeth **97** 67
Clarissa (Endicott) **91** 87
93 290
Daisy Isabel **91** 143
Daniel **68** 163 **120** 239
122 160 **123** 160 **129**
231
David **85** 39
Deborah **74** 302 **117** 96
Dexter **88** 339
Dorcas (Sweet) **117** 98
Dorothy (Perkins) **83** 488
Dorothy (Tooley) **117** 98
Douglas Cairnes **85** 316
Easton **115** 180
Ebenezer **82** 52 **91** 206
Edwin **125** 182
Eleanor **113** 36
Eleanor (Gay) (Child)
105 79
Eliza **87** 203 **93** 378 **96** 334
125 215
Eliza Endicott **92** 393 **93**
290 **98** 270 **106** 144
Eliza Smith **92** 392
Elizabeth **52** 54 57 **53** 198
55 124 **60** 144 189 **62**
174 **65** 103 **66** 318 319
76 lxxxv **82** 82 **90** 106
102 86 **110** 44 **115** 263
117 96 97 **128** 42 **135**
264
Elizabeth (Alden) **128** 213
134 120
Elizabeth (Cole) **128** 42
Elizabeth (Reed) **147** 258
Elizabeth (Smith) **83** 488
Elizabeth Ann **118** 170
Elizabeth Copley **76** 211
Elizabeth P. **74** xxv
Elizabeth Putnam **76** xxix
lxxxv lxxxvi
Elizabeth Smith **85** 3 4
Ellen **69** 260 **91** 56 86 87
112 228
Ellen Derby **81** 11

PEABODY cont'd
Ellen Langdon **83** 174
Elvira (Canfield) **92** 197
Elvira (Wentworth)
134 280
Endicott **76** 211
Enos **122** 215
Ephraim **51** 232 **81** 11
109 51 52 **127** 304
Eunice **83** 332 333 **85** 322
122 214 215
Ezekiel **94** 63
Fanny **76** 211 **103** 73
116 255
Frances **94** 106
Frances (Bourne) **118** 283
Francis **51** 305 306 **52** 404
56 320 **58** lxxvii **60** 189
61 227 **64** 195 **72** 156
76 lxxxv 210 211 **83** 488
89 269 **90** 308 309 **92**
197 **109** 114 **146** 329
147 84
Francis (Mrs.) **84** 341 **85**
190 **89** 215 268 **90** 79
140
Francis Bolles **62** 213
Francis G. **62** 212
Francis Greenwood **76** 1
81 11
Franklin Merriam **84** 240
Frederick Forrest **88** 78
G. **140** 244
George **52** 393 **54** 381 **55**
366 **57** 232 59 xii xxvi
235 339 **61** 320 **64** 195
69 5 **83** 488 **84** 240 **91**
56 87 **93** 290 **97** 378 **99**
92 **108** 158
George A. **74** 157 **122** 213
George Augustus **75**
xxiii **82** 232 **83** 488 **84**
107 184 194 **91** 86 145
George E. **125** 182
George Foster **73** 317 **74**
xxv **87** 166 **92** 197 294
93 139
George Henry **92** 197
George Lee **76** 211
Gertrude **76** 211
Giles B. **122** 215
Grace **60** 189
Hannah **52** 56 **55** 269 **59**
lxxix **61** 242 **67** 358 **70**
327 **96** 190 **110** 32 34
113 306 **117** 97 **134** 173
137 239
Hannah (Hale) **92** 197
109 52
Hannah (Redington)
109 51
Hannah Woodcock
95 176
Harold (Mrs.) **85** 197
96 85
Harriet E. **86** 364
Helen **76** 211
Helen Townsend **83** 174
Henry Clay **59** xlviii
Henry W. **54** xcvii
Hope **68** 163 **120** 239

PEABODY *cont'd*
Ichabod **123** 133
Isaac **51** 306 **61** 227 **76**
  lxxxv **83** 488 **109** 114
Isabel **52** 54 **101** 296
Isaiah **96** 330
Jacob **61** 226 **107** 313
  118 170
James **91** 331 **92** 341 **108**
  188 **122** 215
James Bishop **136** 261
James Charles **67** xxxiv
James Charles (Mrs.) **77**
  162 **82** 122 237
Jane **71** 147 **88** 83 **117** 96
Jane S. (Campbel) **88** 339
Jane Wilkinson **89** 30
Jeremiah **106** 225 **125** 181
Jerusha **52** 57
Jerusha (Starr) **91** 73
Jerusha Pride (Bolles)
  97 67
Joanna **82** 52 287 296
John **52** 54 57 **64** 195 **90**
  310 **94** 241 **101** 296 **109**
  230 **115** 262 **117** 96-98
  122 41 212 214 215 **127**
  12 142 **134** 216 280 **136**
  186
John Endicott **76** 211
John Perley **95** 295
John W. **125** 181
Joseph **66** 318 319 **70** 160
  76 lxxxv **83** 488 **101** 224
  117 98 156 **122** 215
Joseph Augustus **85** 4
Judith **52** 57 **115** 263
Judy **131** 234
Katrina (Nichols) (Trask)
  92 198
Laura (Abbott) **96** 330
Laura (Bancroft) **96** 330
Lester Fields (Mrs.)
  83 122 233
Lionell H. **122** 213
Louisa (Putnam) **85** 4
Louise **82** 237
Lucy **80** 177
Lydia **52** 57 **62** 174 **93** 286
  97 387 **122** 215
Margaret **90** 352
Margaret (Knight) **83** 488
Maria **63** 88 **64** 209
Maria Ladd **83** 174
Marian (Lawrence) **96** 85
Marianne Cabot **76** 210
Marianne Cabot (Lee)
  89 269
Martha **52** 55 **59** 23 **76**
  lxxxv 210 **89** 269 **106**
  223 **136** 333
Martha Endicott **76** 211
Martha P. **76** 211
Mary **52** 54 57 **57** 186 187
  58 lxxvii **62** 260 **70** 160
  72 156 **90** 308 309 **94** 63
  109 312 **122** 215 **125**
  104
Mary (Bancroft) **95** 113
Mary (Foster) **90** 309 310
Mary (Gaines) **85** 39

PEABODY *cont'd*
Mary (Goodhue) **94** 63
Mary (Prentice) **92** 197
Mary (Rogers) **117** 98
Mary C. **140** 244
Mary R. **83** 184 185 **86** 151
Mary Rantoul **83** 174
Mattie **91** 56
Mehitable **79** 40 **82** 52
Mercy **52** 55 366 **60** 144
  65 103
Michael E. **122** 214
Miranda (Goddard)
  93 323
Miriam (Fisher) **108** 188
Molly (Hildrick) **137** 361
Moses **61** 237
Nancy **61** 243 **122** 215
Nancy B. **86** 364
Nathan **140** 234 **145** 357
Nathaniel **51** 306 **90** 310
Nicholas **122** 215
O. W. **97** 52
Oliver **63** 186 **67** 139 **91** 94
  110 317 **118** 283 **125** 97
  132 281 282 284 285 287
  288 **144** 266
Peleg **59** 258
Phebe **122** 215
Phebe Ann **122** 213
Philadelphia **61** 226 227
  109 114
Phineas **70** 18 **105** 79
  113 36
Priscilla **52** 55 57 **101** 296
  110 44 **128** 213
Rachel **88** 77 **120** 73
Rachel (Hunting) **96** 190
Rebecca **52** 56 57 **97** 191
  117 97 **134** 120
Rhoda (Runnels) **96** 334
Richard **67** 358 **92** 197
  145 355
Robert Ephraim **107** 224
Robert Rantoul **83** 174
Robert S. **61** 403
Rosamond **76** 211 **89** 269
Rosamond (Lawrence)
  89 215 268 269 **90** 140
Rose **68** 163 **120** 239 **122**
  160 **123** 160
Rose (Gifford) **129** 231
Ruth **52** 56 439 **94** 393
  108 92 **110** 47 **130** 289
Ruth (Buckley) **92** 197
Ruth (Cole) **128** 42
Ruth (Kimball) **92** 197
Ruth (Osgood) **108** 92
Sally **59** 258 **67** 358
Sally M. **125** 175
Samuel **137** 361
Samuel Endicott **64** 102
  76 210 **89** 269
Sarah **52** 55 55 264 **58**
  lxxiii **61** 237 **82** 52 **83**
  333 **122** 211 214 **133** 43
Sarah (Bowles) **125** 242
Sarah (Estes) **83** 488
Sarah Abbie (True) **95** 295
Sarah Ann **76** lii **96** 190
Sarah H. **92** 341

PEABODY *cont'd*
Sarah Hazard **86** 345
Sarah Maria (Garcelon)
  147 370
Sarissa T. **115** 180
Selim Hobart **64** 195 **117**
  96 98
Sibyl (Boston) **125** 181
Sophia **106** 38
Stephen **59** 44 **65** 336 339
  340 **97** 67 **109** 52 **126**
  226
Susan (Waite) **125** 181
Susan P. **79** 54
Susanna **81** 388 **105** 220
Sylvia **89** 269
Temperance (Pearse)
  (Gibbs) **123** 133
Thomas **64** 195 **69** 12 297
  70 15 **108** 92 **122** 213
  214 **125** 242 **128** 42
Thomas R. **125** 242
William **51** 431 **52** 54 57
  362 **53** 114 **55** 124 **59**
  147 **62** 174 **64** 195 **65**
  103 358 **67** 358 **91** 73 **92**
  197 **94** 241 **95** 132 **97**
  311 **102** 86 **109** 51 233
  110 44 47 **115** 169 263
  122 211 213 **128** 213
  131 234 **134** 120 **145**
  355
William B. **122** 213
William Henry **92** 197
Peace *see* Pease
PEACH Pecche Peche Peech
  —— **141** 97 108
Adam **73** 232
Alice **54** 277 278 **74** 119
  148 313
Amy **57** 334
Anna **128** 28
Anne **52** 253
Arthur **96** 252
Ebenezer **73** 286 290
Elizabeth **54** 278 **127** 206
  209
Elizabeth (Convery)
  100 303
Emma **54** 278 **74** 116 119
George **54** 277
Hannah **54** 278 **60** 239
  74 119
Jacob **128** 28
John **54** 276-279 **58** 142
  60 239 **73** 261 **74** 119
  113 63 **127** 206 209 **134**
  254 **148** 313
Joseph **73** 226 264
Lucy **73** 135 267
Lydia **99** 129 **127** 206
Margerie **54** 278
Mary **54** 278 279 **73** 226
  74 119 **127** 209 **148** 313
Mary Ann **73** 276
Richard **63** 165
Robert Westly **54** 276
Samuel **73** 277
Sarah **54** 279 **73** 228 284
  291 **74** 119
Thomas **54** 277-279

PEACH cont'd
Thomasin **54** 105
William **54** 105 277-279 **74**
119 **100** 303
PEACHAM Henry **116** 310
PEACHY Peachee Peachey
Peachie
— Mr. **66** 169
John **111** 281
Mary **51** 216 309 **67** 364
Samuel **51** 309
Thomas **111** 269 270 281
William **51** 216 **111** 269
281 **143** 328
PEACOCK Pecock
Agnes **84** 429
Arthur **69** 202
Catherine **70** xl
Deborah **53** 18 **97** 186
Edmund **99** 320
Edward **58** xlix **60** xxxix
61 xxxvii **62** xl **63**
xxxiv **64** xxxiv **65**
xxxvii **66** liii **67** xxxv
68 xxxvi **69** xxxvi **70**
xxvii xl xli **99** 320
Edward Shaw **70** xl
Eliza **69** 202
Elizabeth **53** 17 18 **64** 221
Emily Sophia **80** 40
Francis **117** 290
Fred **82** 173
George **73** 267
Hannah **73** 226
Hannah (Whittemore)
107 37
Henry B. **80** 140
Hyla Holden **80** 40
James **100** 40
Jane **117** 290
Jane Elizabeth **80** 140
John **53** 17 18 **64** 221 **74**
272 **117** 290
Judith **53** 18
Lucy Ann **70** xli
Manly Smallwood **108**
277 **147** 69
Margaret Isabelle **102** 68
Marguerite **80** 140
Mary **59** 245
Mary (Kittredge) **107** 37
Mary Ann **80** 40 **104** 219
Minnie Bell **82** 173
Rhoda Ann (Hunt)
108 277
Richard **54** 157
Robert **53** 17 18 **64** 115
80 322
Samuel **99** 314 **105** 196
107 37
Sarah **96** 386 **117** 290
Sarah (Tibbetts) **100** 40
Thomas **107** 37
Thomas Richard **80** 140
William **73** 153 **91** 331
99 314
PEAD Peade
—— **54** 95
John **67** 368
Sarah **67** 368
Thomas **67** 368

PEAD cont'd
William **54** 347 **140** 104
PEAIRS C. A. **110** 157
PEAK Peake Peakes
Peaks Peek
—— **122** 277 **133** 322
— Mr. **95** 133
Adeline M. **90** 48
Alice **60** 43 **61** 132
Amos S. **89** 299
Amy S. (Chase) **88** 123
Anna Wing **80** 141
Annatie **52** 475
Arumissia **123** 308
Augustus **88** 123
Bathsheba **79** 37
Benjamin **86** 384 **89** 299
Bessie (Robinson)
106 225
Bethiah **84** 454
Catherine **78** 416
Charles H. **89** 298
Charlotte H. (Brewster)
89 298
Christian **90** 361 **109** 196
Christopher **51** 166
Daniel **99** 26 28 **101** 50
Dorcas **51** 166
Dorcas Bishop (Clark)
85 232
Eleazer **129** 163 170
134 141
Elizabeth **72** 61 **74** 145 **86**
384 **95** 175 **99** 283 **112**
152 **113** 305 **114** 292
115 152
Elizabeth (Symes) **135** 160
136 80
Elizabeth I. **122** 185
Emily **89** 299
Ephraim **51** 166
F. **58** 286
Frederick Robinson
106 225
George **54** 277
Hannah **51** 166 **89** 362
Hannah (Cudworth)
129 170
Hannah Cloues **126** 207
Israel **60** 43 **129** 168
Jan **52** 475
Jerusha (Hopkins) **103** 88
John **67** 362 **99** 25 26 28
119 **113** 63 **125** 289
John Cloues **85** 232
John Clough **80** 141
Jonathan **51** 166 **112** 152
113 305
Joseph **51** 166 **73** 273
99 25
Judith **56** 99
Lydia (Cowing) **129** 168
Margaret Cunningham
(Cuthell) **106** 225
107 70
Marie **52** 475
Marsha **98** 364
Martha **64** 254
Mary **99** 119
Mary (Brown) **126** 205
Mary Ann (Chase) **88** 123

PEAK cont'd
Mary Frances **85** 231 232
Mary L. **89** 298
Mercy **140** 234
Pamela **78** 182
Philip **126** 205
Philipia **60** 43 **108** 183
129 168
Priscilla (Turner) **129** 170
134 141
Priscilla Bird (Chamber-
lain) **125** 289
Rachel (Merritt) **134** 141
Ralph **125** 106
Ralph E. **147** 79
Ralph Ernest **87** 97
Rhoda **126** 167
Russell Joseph (Mrs.)
103 120 **118** 170
Sally **103** 316 **125** 104
Samuel **89** 298 **99** 283
103 316
Samuel E. **89** 298
Sarah **51** 166 **78** 311 **99** 25
26 28 119
Sarah (Doane) **125** 106
Sarah (French) **113** 305
Sarah A. **89** 299
Sarah Hoxie **80** 141
Susan J. **89** 298
Taylor **103** 88
Thomas **69** 67 **90** 361 **139**
305 **140** 234 **148** 142
Warren L. **88** 123
William **51** 133 **54** 278
60 189 **78** 71 401 **106**
225 **129** 170 **134** 141
William Woodhouse **72**
xx **106** 222 225 **107** 70
137
William Woodman **74**
xxviii **90** 130
Willie Stewart **89** 298
PEAKEN John **81** 130
Peakes see Peak
Peaks see Peak
PEAKSTONE
Eleanor **65** 246
PEALE Peal Peel Peele
Peelle
Abigail R. **87** 377
Albert Lee (Mrs.) **102** 124
Anna C. **68** 29
Arthur L. **93** 219
Blanche **52** 271
Charles Wilson **52** 291
53 419 **68** 29
Edna Ann (Russell)
96 161
Edward **61** 279
Elizabeth **103** 167
Ethelred **52** 121
Helen **93** 219
Hiltetje **106** 304
Jane Appleton **110** 279
John **59** 327 **64** 226 **65** 233
91 332
Leonard **101** 4 81
Leslie Adam (Mrs.)
96 161
Lydia (Robinson) **113** 286

PEALE *cont'd*
Margaret (Appleton)
110 279
Margaret Mason **110** 279
Mary **113** 286
Oswald **113** 286
Robert **51** 145 **59** 345
60 225
Samuel **59** 327
Stanton Judkins **67** 385
68 xxxii
Willard **110** 279
William Lawson **58** xlv
William Lawson (Mrs.)
81 242
PEAPES Nicholas **52** 319
PEAR Peare
Allen **65** 257
Betsey **65** 257
Joseph **91** 45
Lovey **65** 257
Lucinda **91** 45
Mary **65** 257 **91** 45
William Hesseltine
88 170
Pearce *see* Pierce
Pearcy *see* Percy
PEARD Jane (Naziter)
71 126
Richard **71** 124 126
PEARDON Alice **97** 130
Peare *see* Pear
PEARICK
Ann (Molton) **125** 221
Martin Gustif **125** 221
PEARL Pearle
—— **52** 248 **54** 367
Abiah **76** 28
Abigail **67** 349 **69** 334
Abigail (Goves) **83** 417
Achsah **59** 97 **60** 264
Ahira Eldredge **51** 51
69 341
Alice **55** 230
Ann **51** 51
Ann Elizabeth **51** 51
Anna **59** 99 **63** 46 **67** 220
68 338 **69** 334 335
Austin **51** 51 **67** 221 **68**
338 **69** 82
Bertie Stedman **84** 87
Betsey **59** 99
Caroline **51** 51
Caroline Bethiah **51** 52
Caroline E. **69** 334
Chloe **67** 220 **68** 338
Chloe C. **68** 338
Chloe Cordelia **51** 52
Clara W. **84** 87
Clark A. **51** 51
Clark Ahira **69** 341
Cyril **59** 96 210 414 **83** 366
Cyrus **67** 221
David L. **63** 46 **69** 334
Deborah **59** 210 **60** 75 266
67 349 **83** 366 367
Deborah Young **67** 349
Desire **69** 334
Dinah **51** 50 74 **54** 287 **67**
115 117 216 **68** 338
Dyer **63** 46 **69** 334

PEARL *cont'd*
Eddie B. **84** 87
Edward **51** 51 **69** 334 335
Elam **59** 210 **83** 367 **84** 87
Eleanor **99** 53
Elijah C. **51** 51 **69** 82
Elijah Crocker **67** 220
Elizabeth **51** 50 **54** 287 **58**
401 **60** 200 **63** 46 **68** 251
69 334 **76** 29
Ella Jennette **69** 334
Ellen C. **69** 334
Emeline **63** 46
Eunice **58** 403 **59** 99 211
414 **83** 366
Frederick **63** 46 **69** 334
335
George **69** 334 **133** 155
George A. **51** 51
George Austin **69** 341
George G. **69** 82
George Gray **51** 51
George Washington
67 349
Georgie David **69** 334
Hannah **67** 218 220
Hannah B. **68** 251
Harrison Warren (Mrs.)
102 124
Henry M. **84** 87
Hepzibah **69** 335
Isabella **51** 51
Isabella M. **69** 341
Jane **117** 80
Jennette **69** 334
John **54** 287 **55** 230 **59** 99
210 **60** 264 **67** 349 382
83 367 **98** 66 **133** 155
141 35
John II. **67** 349
John M. **59** 100 **83** 367
John Marshal **58** 197
Joseph **67** 349 **68** 251
Joseph H. **67** 349
Joshua **58** 197 400-403 **59**
96 97 99 210 211 413 414
60 74 75 205 266 **83** 366
367
Julana **51** 52
Laura **63** 46
Lavinia J. **83** 367
Levina **66** 340
Lodicea **59** 100
Lois **51** 52 74 **54** 287 288
68 338 **69** 82
Louis **67** 220
Lucinda **63** 46 **69** 335
Lucius **51** 51
Lucy **92** 285
Lucy Keep **84** 87
Lydia **58** 402 **60** 201 **76** 30
Mabel E. **51** 51
Marcus **51** 51
Martha A. Marcy **69** 341
Mary **51** 51 **59** 210 **67** 348
349 **83** 366 **98** 65 66
Mary (Tibbetts) **98** 66
Mary A. **67** 349
Mary Elizabeth **67** 349
Mary G. **84** 87
Mary Jane **51** 51 **90** 109

PEARL *cont'd*
Mary Jennette **69** 335
Mehitable (Hall) **133** 155
Mercy **67** 123 218
Nancy **63** 46
Nancy T. **51** 51 **69** 341
Nathaniel H. **67** 349
Nicholas **67** 349
Norman **51** 51
Oliver **67** 121-123 216 218
220 221
Orrin **63** 46
Phebe **67** 117 **112** 225
Polly **51** 51 **59** 96 **69** 335
Ralph **63** 46
Raymond (Mrs.) **95** 147
Rebecca **52** 385
Richard **69** 335
Roxana **63** 46 **69** 335
Rufus **69** 334 335 **79** 157
133 155
Rufus K. **68** 251
Ruth **80** 24 25
Sally **60** 199
Samuel M. **83** 367
Sarah **59** 210 **63** 46 **66** 340
67 115 349 **69** 335 **76** 36
80 310
Sarah (Perry) **99** 125
116 43
Sarah Ann **67** 349
Simeon **80** 24 **83** 417
Solomon **67** 349
Sophronia **51** 51 **68** 338
69 82
Susan (Strutt) **141** 35
Sylvester **63** 46
Thomas **67** 382
Timothy **51** 50 74 **54** 287
58 197 **60** 199 **67** 115
122 177 217 218 220 221
68 338 **69** 82 **99** 125
116 43
Walter **58** 403 **59** 210 413
67 216 220 **83** 367
William **66** 340 **67** 381 382
74 70
William Henry **67** 349
William M. **84** 87
Pearlee *see* Perley
Pearly *see* Perley
PEARMAIN
Barbara **75** lv
John Duncan **75** lv
Nancy Douglas (Brush)
119 5
William Robert **119** 5
PEARMAN Lydia **78** 346
Price **78** 346
PEARNE Henry **99** 80
Mary **82** 413
Nancy **82** 413
Phebe **82** 289 296
Richard **99** 80
William **82** 289 296
PEARS —— **60** 57
Emma (Danforth) **88** 191
John **147** 243 244
PEARSALL Elizabeth
Parrish **84** 188
Nathaniel **66** 166

PEARSALL *cont'd*
Phebe **98** 47
Pearse *see* Pierce
PEARSON Pareson
   Pearsons Peirsoin
   Peirson Pierceson
   Pierson Piersons
— **51** 420 **53** 43 **56** 214
   61 314 **77** 262 **92** 247
   94 403 **105** 197 **130** 232
   136 53
— Mr. **65** 128 **80** 302
   83 195
— Mrs. **71** 116 **79** 408 **83**
   419 **144** 156
___ (Bond) **140** 41
A. **91** 332
A. F. Scott **124** 254
Aaron **104** 47
Abel Lawrence **75** 1
Abiah **57** 264
Abiel **63** 170 **115** 304
Abigail **51** 461 **54** lvii 384
   55 154 **56** 262 **58** 124
   59 lxx **75** 89 **88** 331 **111**
   292 **115** 240 **120** 260
Abigail (Clark) **104** 191
Abigail (Crowell) **127** 126
Abigail (Gates) **120** 260
Abigail (Parish) **99** 298
Abigail (Tupper) **99** 298
Abigail (Wells) **133** 310
Abigail Bromfield **145** 68
Abijah **99** 298 **101** 207
Abraham **51** 222 **54** 384
   55 151 202 **59** 45 **60** 21
   61 339 **68** 206 **75** 182
   78 261 287 **81** 457 **104**
   47 191 **108** 36 152
Addie (Noyes) **133** 47
Addison **82** 177
Adelaide **83** 200 **96** 167
Agnes **77** 188
Agnes Mary (Brown)
   97 359
Albert Waring **74** 158
   75 xxvi
Alexander Cudworth
   92 247
Alfred **97** 359
Alfred Kittredge **109** 131
Alice **75** 18 **94** 110 112
   97 130
Alice L. (Barron) **104** 262
Almira **78** 369 386
Almira (Huntley) **101** 207
Altha **100** 109
Amanda Emily (Edwards)
   (Callender) **145** 41
Amos **75** 18 **83** 184 185
   84 31 **125** 215
Amy **84** 141 **123** 83
Amy (Barnes) **123** 83
Ann **55** 153 **65** 246
Ann (Wyeth) (Taylor)
   95 361
Anna **65** 354 **75** 17
Anne **78** 207 **143** 301
Anne M. (Langley) **83** 183
   185
Anner (Davis) **89** 291

PEARSON *cont'd*
Annie **75** 17
Annie Olive **96** 333
Anthony **103** 184 **128** 269
Archie **104** 103
Armida **75** 28
Armida Kellogg **75** 17
Arthur F. **94** 167
Ascenath (Spencer)
   130 232
Augustus **97** 5
Bartholomew **57** 351
   76 136
Benjamin **89** 291 **97** 209
Bernice **118** 248
Betsey **66** 109 **74** 170 312
   75 18 25 **86** 318
C. H. **98** 251
Caroline **83** 23 26
Caroline (Gerrish) **83** 23
Caroline Lucy (Taylor)
   111 312
Cassie V. (Warren)
   104 106
Catherine **68** 150
Catherine (Godfrey)
   127 101
Catherine DeFord
   (Davenport) **97** 5
Catherine Whitaker
   72 xx
Charles **75** 17 18
Charles Edward **75** 17 18
Charles F. **75** 17
Charles Henry **82** 254 **83**
   200 236
Charles J. **88** 24
Charles Lawrence **69** 287
   70 xix 191 **75** xxxv l
Charles Lewis **77** 262
Charlotte (Matthews)
   125 215
Charlotte Eliza **104** 48
Charlotte Ross (Jeffrey)
   104 310
Christena M. (Peterson)
   128 98
Christopher **63** 244
Clara Clyde **77** 262
Clara H. **103** 70
Clarence F. **83** 426 438
Clark G. **104** 47
Cora **86** 198 **111** 310 312
Corydon **82** 399
Crispin **87** 5
Cynthia (Hardwick) **121**
   79 **122** 320
Darius **119** 182 **137** 36
David **53** 38 39 394 **65** 221
   66 207 **80** 434 **86** 461
   89 384 **105** 60 **145** 67
Deborah **97** 262
Delia **83** 214
Diana **127** 126
Direxa **83** 200
Dodo **52** 325
Dole **51** 465
Dolice **51** 115
Dorcas **58** 122 **61** 398
Dorcas (Bailey) **88** 275
E. N. **53** 264

PEARSON *cont'd*
Earl F. (Mrs.) **83** 484
Earl Linfield **107** 157
Ebenezer **83** 26 28 **146** 277
Edmund **121** 79 **122** 320
Edward **62** 199
Edward Augustus **145** 68
Edward N. **51** 375 **54** 236
   67 57
Eli **76** 146 153
Elijah **128** 269
Eliphalet **61** 103 **144** 266
   145 67
Eliza **104** 47
Eliza Ann (Bradley)
   88 330
Eliza Jane **102** 302
Eliza Porter **92** 126
Elizabeth **52** 372 **53** 394 **55**
   202 204 **58** 310 **66** 321
   80 434 **81** 457 **82** 267
   399 **86** 355 **89** 291
   104 191 **109** 221
Elizabeth (Farnham)
   120 64
Elizabeth (Hoyt) **97** 262
Elizabeth (Williams)
   125 302
Elizabeth A. **77** 150
Ella **100** 197
Ellen **65** 171
Ellen D. (Daily) **133** 33
Ellis **82** 267
Emily **75** li
Emily Pauline **83** 424 438
Emma **61** 378
Emma J. **75** 17
Emma M. **75** 28 **77** 262
Enoch **60** 298
Ephraim **58** 362 363 **59** 65
   123 83
Esther **63** 345 **66** 328
Esther (Furnas) **97** 209
Eunice **60** 298 **104** 47
Eunice (Kitchell) **119** 182
Eunice Floyd **94** 167
Fanny **104** 163
Frances **99** 118 **101** 52
Frances Caroline **101** 207
Francis **127** 126
Gardner Whitman **68** 207
George **51** 115 **63** 31 **95**
   361 **127** 126
George D. **136** 242
George Henry **62** 113
George M. **97** 209
George Washington
   77 262
Georgianna (Rogers)
   94 167
Greenfield Harris **102** 302
Greenfield Harris (Mrs.)
   86 198 **100** 232 **101** 129
   102 302
H. **91** 332
Hannah **57** 89 **58** 122 **69**
   57 **78** 261 **80** 434 **83** 26
   28 **85** 94 348 **88** 9 **94**
   316
Hannah (Pillsbury)
   127 101

PEARSON *cont'd*
Harmon **134** 90
Harriet **75** 1
Harriet Newell **109** 58
  133 119
Harris **97** 359
Harry **92** 125
Harry H. **110** 128
Harvey F. **104** 103
Helen Beatrice **88** 24
Helen Maria (Pierson)
  104 310
Helen Standish (Bowman)
  83 484
Henry **55** 154 200 **57** 389
  65 298 **105** 60 **123** 83
  128 269
Henry Bromfield **145** 68
Henry Clay **101** 207
Henry Lewis **104** 310
Henry Willis **77** 262
Hepzibah **61** 354 **103** 145
Hepzibah (Jones) **111** 312
Herbert Henry **82** 399
Hiram **75** 17 18 **104** 262
Hiram G. **75** 17 18 28
Ida Florence **77** 262
Isaac Green **140** 41
Isabel **56** 191 **94** 101
James **56** 195 **57** 261 88
  330 **111** 270 286 **132** 40
  136 242
James B. **83** 185
James H. **83** 183 185
Jane **53** 38 39 **67** 167 169
  73 14 **75** 17 18 **77** 32
  262 **89** 384 **108** 250
Jane C. (Tompkins) **75** 17
  104 103
Joanna **51** 465
Joanna (Cooper) **123** 83
Job **55** 203 204
John **51** 130 **52** 371 372
  56 86 317 **61** 398 **65** 90
  236 68 74 **77** 210 **82** 267
  83 16 **88** 275 338 **91** 332
  96 75 **99** 298 327 **104**
  163 **107** 161 **109** 221
  111 312 **114** 184 **125**
  302 **145** 106
John Adams **82** 177
John B. **55** 342
John C. **64** 377 **68** 273
  69 50
John Calder **69** 200
John Derby **92** 247
John Hale **77** 262
John Keeling **69** 200
John M. **52** 376 **65** 90
John Mills **127** 101
John Percival **101** 207
John Perley **52** 372
  127 101
John W. **133** 119
Jonathan **71** 96 **73** 161 **76**
  135 136 **120** 260 **127**
  126 **136** 259
Joseph **52** 372 **63** 346 **118**
  313 **123** 83 **141** 112
Josephine **72** 206
Judith **75** 262

PEARSON *cont'd*
Judith (Atkinson) **97** 5
Julia **72** 206 **78** 205
Julia M. **72** 206
Kate Ashley **82** 267
Kate J. (Plumer) **83** 185
Kendall **53** 40 **88** 282 **111**
  312 **121** 168
Keziah (Danforth)
  (Richardson) **104** 128
L. B. **53** 43
Lawrence Brown **97** 359
Leonard W. **79** 39
Leroy Morris **77** 262
Libbie **104** 103
Lois **61** 354 **66** 207
Louler (Newton) **83** 200
Lu M. **75** 17
Lucinda **130** 232
Luke H. **134** 255
Lydia **53** 40 **56** 360 **78** 97
Lydia (Boardman)
  111 312
Lydia (Pike) (Jacques)
  121 168
Lyman A. **72** 206
Mallie E. **109** 266
Mamie **82** 109
Margaret **55** 191 **61** 267
  81 330 **123** 106
Margaret (Underwood)
  88 282
Margaret Bromfield
  145 68
Margaret White **76** 213
Maria **70** 69 **135** 50
Maria (Hurin) **136** 242
Marie Edgar (Black) **94** 25
Martha **55** 203 375 **76** 135
  82 295 296 **83** 16
Martha (Hodsdon) **83** 16
Mary **52** 325 **59** 45 **60** 298
  61 354 398 **63** 170 **70** 69
  78 313 **82** 177 **89** 384
  93 326 **101** 201 **123** 83
  134 92 **135** 78
Mary (Cooper) **123** 83
Mary (Little) **94** 65 **97** 5
Mary (Minter) **128** 269
Mary (Patterson) **134** 90
Mary (Small) **83** 200
Mary (Wilson) **111** 312
Mary A. **136** 242
Mary Ann **77** 187 **101** 207
Mary Ann (Stewart)
  134 255
Mary Creemer **78** 440
Mary E. **77** 148
Mary Elizabeth
  (McFarland) **145** 68
Mary Emma **77** 262
Mary Frances **69** 200
Mary G. **79** 147
Mary Holyoke **145** 68
Mary Keeling **69** 200
Mary N. **88** 283
Mary Simpson **92** 247
Mary Susan **78** 173
Mattie Ellis **102** 302
Maud Emma **75** 17
Maud S. **75** 18

PEARSON *cont'd*
Maybelle L. (Coleman)
  83 426 438
Mehitable **51** 462 **55** 198
Melinda **111** 116
Melissa E. **72** 206
Melvina (Doten) **124** 39
Michael **120** 64
Miranda (Huntley)
  101 207
Molly **58** 363
Moses **61** 354 **111** 312
  130 232 **134** 216
Myra Flora (Titus)
  102 302
Nancy **57** 285
Nancy (Swany) **128** 269
Nancy Miranda **101** 207
Naomi **97** 359
Nathan **61** 354 **72** 206 **84**
  141 **111** 182 184 312
Nathaniel **66** 264 **83** 23 26
Nella Jane **73** 319 **74** xxx
Nellie H. (Fernald) **98** 251
Newton **72** 206
Nicholas **56** 86 **63** 345
Obadiah **65** 221
Olive **91** 266
Olive (Tibbetts) **88** 338
  99 327
P. F. **104** 103
Parnel **78** 369
Patience **124** 319
Peter **78** 369 386 387 **100**
  269 **101** 207
Phebe **55** 169 **136** 267
Phebe Elizabeth **101** 207
Philip **84** 31
Philip Coombs **97** 5
Phylinda **82** 176
Pliny **104** 106
Polly (Adams) **115** 304
Priscilla **132** 40
Priscilla (Holyoke)
  145 68
Priscilla (Jackson) **132** 40
Rachel **69** 57
Ralph E. **92** 401 **103** 158
Rebecca **82** 398 **111** 286
Reuben Rogers **101** 207
Richard **52** 372 **54** 216 **63**
  285 65 45
Robert **92** 71 72
Robert Henry **82** 109
Roger **91** 285
Ruey M. (Webster) **94** 139
Ruth **52** 371 372
Ruth Elizabeth **77** 262
Sally **104** 47 **128** 205
Sally (Powell) **133** 119
Samuel **52** 372 56 360 **58**
  362 **75** li **83** 200 **86** 318
  104 127 128 **109** 214
  123 83
Samuel (Mrs.) **117** 168
Sarah **51** 222 **52** 372 **55** 32
  151 **59** 65 **60** 332 **61** 356
  66 167 75 102 182 **76**
  137 **78** 261 **82** 109 **85**
  430 **89** 291 **94** 317 **99**
  118 **101** 52 **105** 60 **128**

PEARSON *cont'd*
181
Sarah (Bromfield) **145** 67
Sarah (Cram) **111** 312
Sarah (Danforth) **145** 67
Sarah Ann (Moore)
83 214
Sarah Croom **77** 252
Sarah Elizabeth **101** 207
Sarah Green **82** 399
Sarah Jackson **94** 65 **97** 5
Sarah Jane **82** 178
Sarah Jane (Libby) **97** 359
Seth **75** 18
Silas **83** 214 **94** 65 **97** 5
Solon **80** 434
Stephen **61** 398 **66** 328
69 57 **75** 182 **76** 137
Submit **58** 362 363 **59** 65
Susan **109** 166
Susan E. **84** 31
Susan E. (Miller) **83** 184
185
Susanna **75** 182 **78** 287
104 191 **108** 36
Susanna (Wyman)
111 312
Svan Yahn / Swan John
128 98
Tabitha **137** 239 328
Tabitha (Kendall) **111** 312
Theodore Carlton (Mrs.)
106 126
Theophilus **55** 201 **105** 60
Thomas **58** 69 **64** 113 **65**
44 232 **70** 69 **97** 262 **99**
118 **101** 52 **133** 309 **148**
116
Thomas B. **72** 206
Walter **77** 262
Walter Washington
77 262
William **52** 107 **53** 434
55 202 **61** 356 **63** 244
78 405 **89** 291 **92** 125
126 247 **94** 107 **136** 242
145 41
William Augustus
111 312
William E. **75** 17 **122** 320
William Gardner **105** 152
William H. **67** 307 **75** 18
William Lear (Mrs.)
94 139
Zebedee **55** 202
PEART Clara A. **132** 324
PEARTON John **55** 375
PEARTREE Pairtree
Bartholomew **103** 10
Katharine **99** 26 **100** 296
William **106** 293
PEARY Peery - *see also*
Perry
Betsey **76** 31
James **74** 180 183 **85** 353
Keziah **74** 180 183
Lovina **93** 355
Robert E. **62** lv
Smith **76** 31
Susanna **74** 42

PEASE Peace
—— **52** 231 **60** 151 377
379 **61** 84 **62** 353 **64** 191
75 191 **110** 34 **119** 122
121 65 **123** 27 **129** 188
— Capt. **62** 357 **78** 350
— Dea. **56** 386
— Mrs. **127** 138 139
A. U. **128** 175
Aaron **120** 52
Abiah **52** 232 **53** 105 108
59 308 409 411 **104** 74-
76 **122** 165
Abigail **52** 369 371 **59**
259 409 410 **61** 283 **62**
86 196 **89** 380 **119** 120-
122 **124** 187
Abigail (Ford) **119** 122
137 35
Abigail Ferguson **68** 309
Abijah **145** 361
Abishai **59** 197 199 261
86 439 **100** 192
Abner **59** 405 **115** 40
Abraham **52** 231 **60** 380
100 192 300
Achsanna **89** 318 **105** 153
Ada Armstrong **79** 121
Albert S. **70** 287
Albion Parsons **67** xxxiv
Alexander **59** 298 **100** 192
Alfred W. **73** 41
Almira **118** 237
Ama **56** 254
Ambrose **89** 380
Amy (French) **85** 48
98 349
Andrew **147** 244 245
Ann **60** 380-382 **61** 87 388
62 86 297 **125** 173 243
126 25
Ann (Pollock) **128** 175
Anna **52** 233 **53** 105 107 **59**
299 307 409 411 **61** 84
62 87 **75** 191 **86** 402
120 52
Anne **59** 207 307
Anne (Butler) **86** 402
Anne (Cummings) **98**
349 **145** 240
Annie F. **83** 438
Archibald **61** 85
Asa **135** 77
Asenath **137** 35
Bart **59** 305
Bartlett **59** 401 **119** 286
Barzillai **52** 368 370
Bathsheba **59** 410 **72** 206
Benjamin **52** 369 **53** 104
105 **59** 207 299 303 304
306-308 409 411 **86** 394
395 402 **111** 134
Bethiah **86** 394
Betsey **59** 409 **84** 137
109 228
Beulah **60** 208
Billy Fisher **56** 249
C. R. **71** 355
Caleb **115** 124
Calista S. **72** 206
Calvin **60** 377

PEASE *cont'd*
Carlos **79** 309
Charity **60** 380 **62** 297 **87**
132 316 322
Charles **59** 299 **88** 116
Charles A. (Mrs.) **86** 198
Charles F. **143** 21
Charles Fordom **77** 180
Charles Franklin **135** 251
Charlie N. **85** 411
Christopher **70** 151
Clarissa **85** 411 416 **115** 33
Clement **59** 203
Coffin **100** 192
Comfort **65** 257
Corinthia D. **64** 252
Cummings **103** 82
Cynthia M. **72** 206
Daniel **59** 307
Daniel H. **116** 123
Darius **61** 391
David **59** 306 **61** 389 **86**
394 **103** 82 **125** 302
Deborah **52** 371 **53** 106
108 **59** 306
Deborah L. **85** 411
Desire **59** 306
Dorcas **59** 409 **98** 349
Dorothy **136** 166
Ebenezer **118** 206
Edmund **55** 49
Elam **73** 41
Eleanor **89** 380
Elijah **89** 380 381
Eliza **98** 298
Elizabeth **54** 107 **59** 198
199 202 258 264 379-383
409 **80** 412 **107** 186 **111**
90 **119** 122 **147** 375
Elizabeth (Thomas)
107 186
Elizabeth (Warner) **85** 44
Ella G. S. **53** 372 **58** 207
Ellen **135** 251
Enoch **59** 300
Ephraim **52** 231 370 371
53 106 **58** 142 **59** 205
308 380 **120** 52
Esther **118** 237 238
Esther (Butler) **118** 237
Eunice **59** 303
Eunice (Brown) **135** 77
Experience **56** 249
Ezekiel **89** 380
Fanny **59** 301
Fordham **59** 302 406
Fortunatus **59** 198-200 257
262-264 378-380 **100**
192 **130** 289
Francis **59** 404 **72** 228
85 411
Frank **59** 407
Frederick Rich **71** 355
Freeman **59** 204
Gamaliel **73** 272
George **59** 205 **85** 411
George Corlis **59** 207
George S. (Mrs.) **108** 135
George Washington
59 300
Gertrude S. **61** 98

PEASE *cont'd*
Gilson F. **85** 411
Green **52** 28
Hancy **85** 411
Hannah **51** 198 **52** 231
233 371 **55** 49 **59** 207
261 303 304 307 410 **86**
395 **89** 380 **90** 353 **110**
66 **118** 237 **135** 77
Hannah (Bearsman)
100 300
Hannah (Jenkins) **86** 395
Hannah (Parker) **114** 138
Hannah (Warriner)
123 262
Hannah P. **119** 286
Harriet **118** 237 238
Harriet Johnson **77** 180
Harriet M. **51** 196 199 **52**
230 233 368 369 371 **53**
102 107 130 **59** 202 204
207 297 306 400 409
Harriet Marshall **55** 111
112
Harrison **59** 204
Harry **85** 411 **118** 237
Havilla **105** 205
Helen **60** 200 **72** 310
Henry **54** 149 **85** 411
91 332
Hepzibah **59** 409 **60** 380
381 **62** 86 **87** 12
Hepzibah (Ripley) **86** 395
Hiram **129** 188
Horace **118** 237
Hoziah **119** 122
Huldah **95** 365
I. M. **75** xxiii 64
Ira **99** 294
Isaac **84** 137 141 **85** 48 **98**
349 **107** 186 187
Isaac D. **52** 233
Isaac M. **93** 277 **94** 141
98 349
Jacob **54** 290-295 297-299
55 429 **56** 249 388
James **51** 198 **55** 316 **83** 12
118 237 **119** 121 122
189 **128** 96
James R. **85** 411
Jane **53** 108 **59** 308 409
Jarvis **114** 138
Jean **86** 394
Jean (Arey) **86** 394
Jedidah **60** 382 **62** 87
123 133
Jemima **53** 108 **59** 409 **72**
206 **89** 381 **115** 124
Jemima (Markham)
89 380
Jeremiah **51** 198 **59** 379
381 383 384
Jerusha **53** 107 **59** 299 409
61 85 388 **62** 295 **103** 82
Jerusha Spencer **103** 82
Jesse **59** 401 406-408
Jillon **119** 122
Joan **86** 394
Joanna **108** 74
Joel **119** 122 **137** 35
John **51** 152 **52** 231 **53**

PEASE *cont'd*
104 105 **54** 107 217 **59**
204 207 261 299 304 307
407 409-411 **60** 380 **61**
84 **63** 287 **80** 412 **86** 393
395 **98** 349 **100** 261 **101**
74 **102** 181 188 **110** 34
119 122 **127** 141 **145**
240
John C. **85** 156
John Chauncey **55** 118
64 204
John Harper **52** 370 **53**
104 **59** 203 204 **100** 192
Jonathan **52** 368-370 **53**
108 **59** 302 307 **60** 208
Joseph **52** 231 232 **59** 204
207 411 **119** 122 **133**
134 **143** 17 **145** 352
Josiah **53** 104 **132** 76
Judith **111** 240 241
Judith (Parrott) **87** 74 76
77
Juliet **85** 411
Katharine **67** 211
Keturah **53** 108
Keziah **55** 316 **59** 409 410
83 12 **119** 122
Keziah (Sullivan) **83** 12
Kingston **127** 13
Laura **64** 209 **68** 257
118 237
Lavinia **59** 38
Leander Ferdinand
86 439
Lemuel **52** 231 **53** 103 **60**
377 379 **61** 84 87 **62** 378
118 237-239
Leonard **61** 85
Levi **70** 124 **79** 161 **115** 129
140 234
Lillie Maria **85** 191 **86**
110 205 438
Lois **101** 74
Louis A. **79** 121
Love **52** 370 371 **53** 103
59 409 **147** 70
Lovicy **115** 33
Lovisa **54** 292 **56** 254
115 40
Lovisa (Meacham)
119 122
Lucy **64** 150 **70** 124 **72** 147
88 293 **135** 77
Lucy (Adams) **98** 349
Lucy Valentine **129** 188
Lurana **85** 48 **119** 190
Lydia **52** 233 **53** 103 **59**
409 410 **61** 84 87 **89** 380
97 376 **105** 149
Lydia (Nutting) **132** 76
Lydia Amanda (Lake)
86 439
M. Inez **128** 175
Mabel **85** 44
Mabel A. **123** 226
Margaret **51** 152 **61** 391
80 414 **87** 12 **111** 134
119 122
Marie **98** 349
Marshall **59** 299 304

PEASE *cont'd*
Martha **52** 233 **59** 408
106 92
Martha (Willett) **87** 76
Martin **128** 175
Mary **51** 152 **52** 371 **53**
104 108 **55** 429 **56** 249
388 **59** 206 207 261 410
411 **73** 213 **77** 276 **81**
476 **88** 289 **106** 91 92
119 189 **126** 25 99 **140**
234
Mary (Abbe) **119** 122 189
Mary (Bunker) **100** 192
Mary (Handy) **126** 61
Mary (Terry) **120** 52
Mary Ball (Johnson)
86 240
Mary E. **85** 411
Mary Inez **128** 175
Mary Rebecca **90** 354
Matilda **71** 355
Matthew **59** 406 410
100 192
Mattie **135** 251
Mehitable **53** 107 **59** 307
409 **69** 62 **85** 44
Mel. **52** 368
Melatiah **52** 371 **53** 106
59 404 408 **86** 395
Merchant A. **91** 384
Merrick **98** 349
Mindwell (Osborn)
98 349
Molly **59** 407
Nancy **59** 383 **61** 87
Nancy B. **67** 280 282
Nancy T. **85** 411
Naomi **60** 377
Naomi Griswold (Niles)
85 156
Nathan **59** 306 410 **89** 318
105 149
Nathaniel **51** 198 **52** 371
59 199 200 258 264 378-
383 410
Nellie C. (Wentworth)
91 384
Noah **59** 204 207 301 303
Norman N. **85** 411 416
Obadiah **52** 370 **59** 207 299
404 **89** 380
Obed **52** 231
Onesiphorus **126** 61
Ora **135** 251
Otis **117** 78
Otis C. **72** 206
P. E. **71** 355
Patience **145** 79
Patty **145** 79
Peggy **86** 401
Persis **59** 257
Peter **52** 369 **59** 206 298
300 306 403 409 **60** 377
380-382 **61** 84 87 388 **62**
86 87 297 **100** 192 **115**
35
Phebe **86** 439
Phila **73** 41
Philena **132** 165
Philo **98** 349

PEASE *cont'd*
Polly **59** 201 **61** 389 **78** 350 **118** 237
Polly (Collins) **89** 318
Priam **59** 404
Prince **52** 232 **59** 306 **125** 31
Priscilla (Fish) **125** 302
Prudence **59** 258 **79** 309
R. Joanna **108** 74
Rachel **59** 204 207 404
Rachel (Hall) **98** 349
Rebecca **52** 369 **59** 307 **70** 151 **90** 334
Rebecca Folger **100** 192
Reuben **52** 370
Reuben O. **71** 355
Rhoann **61** 85
Rhoda **54** 291 **56** 253 **61** 389 **62** 89 **89** 380
Richard L. **51** 196 198 **52** 233 **122** 193
Robert **86** 394 **98** 349 **123** 262
Robert H. **76** 50
Robertus **59** 203
Roscius M. **71** 355
Rose **59** 257 263 264 380
Rose (Gifford) **130** 289
Rosetta B. **72** 204
Roxana **64** 252
Rufus **72** 206
Ruhamah **59** 204
Russel S. **84** 87
Ruth **51** 55
Ruth (Briggs) **126** 61
Sabra **121** 318
Sabra Diadamia **89** 230
Salathiel **59** 299
Salinda **70** 151
Sally **59** 258 **65** 134 **66** 207 **111** 311
Sally (Allen) **98** 349
Salmon **71** 355
Samuel **60** 378 380 **61** 389 **62** 89 90 **65** 257 **70** 124 151 **85** 44 **105** 205 **106** 91 92 **115** 129 **145** 361
Sarah **51** 57 **52** 231 **53** 106 **54** 107 **59** 197 199 204 205 207 298 299 302 306 307 410 **60** 151 **61** 85 **62** 298 **65** 353 **71** 84 **77** 229 **84** 141 **103** 82 **115** 41 206 **130** 132 289
Sarah (Tupper) **99** 294
Sarah A. **91** 332
Sarah Ann (Chase) **88** 116
Seba **59** 203
Serena **59** 204
Seth **53** 104 **59** 204 205 298 **69** 194
Sherburn J. **72** 206
Simon **62** 289 **67** 211 **87** 75-77
Sophia **56** 30 **93** 58 **125** 240
Sprowel **59** 205
Stephen **52** 230 **53** 103-106 **59** 409 **145** 353
Sukey **59** 380

PEASE *cont'd*
Susan **78** 129
Susanna **59** 207 259 307 409 **89** 380
Sylvanus **52** 370
Thankful **59** 204 297 308 **86** 395 402 **122** 192
Theodore **79** 157
Theodore Calvin **73** 161
Theophilus **118** 280 **126** 58 61
Thomas **52** 230 231 **53** 105 108 **59** 200 203 205 299 409 410 **64** 209 **68** 82 **69** 91
Tilton **119** 122
Timothy **59** 301 **78** 183 **140** 234 327 **145** 353
Tristram **52** 370 **59** 304
Valentine **53** 106 **59** 406 **61** 145
Van **135** 251
Verne Seth **67** 385 **68** xxxii
Walter **73** 213
Watson G. **85** 411
William **59** 205 207 **60** 379 **69** 82 **85** 411 **87** 74-77
William H. **85** 411
Willie K. **116** 123
Zachariah **53** 103 104 106 **59** 407 410 **97** 293
Zepary (Coy) **119** 122
Zioran **101** 74
PEASEFULL
Susanna **100** 303
PEASLEE Peaseley
Peasely Peasley
—— **53** 459 **56** 210 **60** 107 **73** 191 **111** 234
— Mr. **82** 450
Abiah **53** 465
Abigail **59** 225 **73** 46
Agnes **69** 261
Alfred D. **139** 295
Alice **53** 464 465
Almena Melissa **69** 261
Amos **98** 66
Ann **90** 55
Anna **69** 178 **72** 259
Betsey **73** 99
Betsey Ann (Blood) **124** 63
Caroline Elizabeth **140** 131
Charles Henry **67** 100
Ebenezer **53** 465
Elijah **139** 292
Eliza **90** 393
Elizabeth **53** 163 464 **60** 286 **111** 237
Elizabeth (Tibbetts) (Austin) **98** 66
Emma Blanche **69** 261
Enoch **72** 259 **75** 7 10 11 **87** 206
Esther (Goodale) **139** 292
Freeman **117** 170
George **79** 167
Hannah **69** 178 **85** 93
Hugh **82** 444 450

PEASLEE *cont'd*
Huldah **139** 295
Isaac **58** 125
Jacob **90** 114
James **58** 385 **69** 261
James Carr **107** 227
Jane **93** 373
Jedediah **73** 46
John **53** 465
John B. **56** xxxii
Jonathan **73** 99 **106** 300
Joseph **53** 464 **60** 189 **69** 178 **110** 66 **130** 311 **146** 318
Judith **53** 465
Judith (Choate) **140** 131
Leonard **69** 261
Leonard C. **69** 261
Louisa B. (Stoning) **139** 295
Louisa Southard (Green) **107** 227
Lucinda Maria **79** 152
Lucy **58** 385
Lucy A. (Copeland) **90** 114
Lydia **146** 322
Maria A. **90** 109
Mark W. R. **124** 63
Martha **69** 178 **117** 281
Martin **137** 382
Mary **53** 163 464 465 **58** 125 **69** 178 **73** 46 99 **82** 444 450 **115** 31
Mary (Trask) **130** 311
Mary A. **94** 392
Mary Agnes **69** 261
Mary Ann **69** 261
Mary Ann (Currier) **137** 283
Mary Emily **69** 261
Matilda Annis **107** 227
Micajah **140** 131
Moses **53** 163 **69** 178
Moses C. **93** 246
Myles **73** 99
Nabby **73** 95
Nathaniel **53** 465 **109** 162 **146** 322
Patience **69** 178
Richard **60** 286
Robert **53** 464
Ruth **53** 464 465 **72** 256 **110** 66
Sally **66** 23
Sally (Stanton) **111** 161
Sarah **53** 464 465 **72** 255 **73** 89 191 **109** 162 **125** 155
Susanna **73** 98 **84** 423
Thomas **69** 178
Timothy **73** 46 **117** 281
Washington **73** 99
William **69** 178 261 **82** 444 450
Zaccheus **66** 23 **111** 161
PEASON
Joan **79** 411 430
John **79** 411 430
PEASTER James Rhorer (Mrs.) **108** 135

PEAT Peate Peet Peets
—— **54** 367
Alice R. **67** 20
Amelia L. **109** 271
Annie (Olmstead) **96** 161
Bathsheba **144** 336
Benjamin **111** 192
Benjamin H. **118** 150
Dinah **78** 261
Elnathan **144** 49
Emily Jane **85** 326 **109** 223
Eunice **135** 317
George **67** 20
Georgianna Mary (Slade) **95** 291
Harriet N. **111** 192
Harvey H. **79** 168
Helen L. **109** 271
Hiram **116** 67
James **69** 378
Jane **109** 223
Joan **51** 280 **72** 134 **108** 156
John **86** 464 **104** 316 **144** 45
Joseph **65** 228 **92** 172
Joshua **117** 70
Katharine **73** xxxii
Lemuel Hiram **108** 135
Louisa **111** 192
Margaret M. **79** 168
Martha J. **118** 150
Mary **51** 279 **108** 156
Mary (Galpin) **144** 49
Mary (Penrose) **117** 70
Mary (Symonds) **108** 156
Mortimer S. (Mrs.) **96** 161
Olive Woolworth **73** xxxii
Phebe **98** 281
Rebecca A. **116** 67
Sarah **66** 209 **69** 378 **79** 56 **102** 105
Silas **109** 271
Slade (Mrs.) **95** 291
Stephen D. **51** 243 **56** 94
Stephen Denison **73** xxix xxxii
Susanna **100** 299
Thomas **51** 280
William **64** 19 **66** 209 **72** 134 136
William Edward **104** 316 **105** 129
William F. **118** 150
William H. **109** 271
PEATIASON
Ellen **64** 253
PEATMAN David **123** 107
PEATON
Catherine **141** 30
Catherine (Channon) **141** 30
Joan (Channon) **141** 30
Sarah **141** 30
Tobias **141** 30
PEAVER Euphemia Coffrin **96** 159
PEAVEY Peavy Pevey Pevy
—— **58** 253
Abel **58** 249

PEAVEY cont'd
Abigail **59** 289 **90** 237
Abigail C. **76** 34
Abigail Chesley **91** 369
Anna **73** 65
Anna M. **76** 35
Benjamin **73** 63
Bessie **65** 313
Betsey **76** 32
Betsey N. **76** 36
Charles **77** 262
Charles Adams (Mrs.) **89** 132
Dorcas Elizabeth **90** 395
Edward **58** 249
Elizabeth **82** 296 298 299
Emily **69** 258
Eskar **65** 313
Hannah **76** 30 36
Hannah Edna Isabelle **69** 258
Henry W. **117** 163
Hopley Y. **73** 197
Hudson **91** 369 **132** 75
Jane **77** 262
Jeremiah **90** 395
John **76** 43 **82** 27 52 296 299 **121** 93
John D. **69** 258
John N. **77** 148
John S. **59** 288
Joseph **76** 30 **82** 502 **83** 153
Joshua **73** 64
Leroy Deering **82** 125 237
Louisa (Fitch) **90** 395
Lydia **76** 33 **96** 144 338
Mabelle (Swift) **89** 132
Madeline (Brown) **132** 75
Margaret Louise **111** 315
Mary **76** 29 43 **81** 432
Maud **86** 311
Mehitable **81** 448 **82** 285 296
Nathaniel **58** 250 **82** 52
Olive N. **77** 148
Patience **116** 84
Paul Henry **69** 258
Priscilla **82** 283 296
Rebecca (Hodgkins) **97** 18 238
Sally **59** 288
Samuel **82** 52
Sarah **65** 355 **73** 191 **81** 448 **82** 52 **97** 237
Sarah (Knowlton) **117** 163
Sarah Ann **76** 35
Sarah C. **68** 203
Thatcher **97** 18 225 238
William **81** 262 **82** 283 296
PEAY Ann **120** 319
Betsey **117** 319
Mildred Ann **117** 319 **121** 80
PEBBLES Aden **72** 206
Archibald **62** 85
Jean **132** 197
Patrick **132** 197
Sally **62** 85
Pecche *see* Peach

Peche *see* Peach
PECHELL
Augustus **55** xlvii
Blanche **55** xlvii xlviii
Caroline Mary **55** xlvii
Hervey Charles **55** xliv xlvii xlviii
Horace Robert **55** xlvii
Jacob **55** xlvii
Jean Horace **55** xlvii
John **79** 171
Paul **55** xlvii
Pierre **55** xlvii
Samuel **55** xlvii
PECK Pecke Pek Peks
—— **53** 174 **54** 273 387 **55** 415 **57** 310 **58** 218 **71** 16 **72** 170 **86** 384 **88** 317 **89** 18 330 **91** 9 **103** 1 **121** 11 14 82 87 109 **137** 257 **138** 124 220 **139** 44
— Capt. **57** 162 **64** 31 **98** 171 236
— Dea. **81** 126
— Judge **55** 297
— Mr. **57** 229 **62** 180 **84** 153
— Mrs. **62** 284 **115** 113 114 **122** 224
—— (Leeke) **91** 9
—— (Melgrave) **89** 329
Aaron **88** 108 139 **123** 27 **128** 132
Abi **92** 172
Abigail **54** 273 **63** 90 **71** 6 **97** 254 **101** 169 **105** 58 **121** 84 **126** 175
Abigail (Hitchcock) **84** 214
Abigail (Preston) **97** 257
Abigail (Woodruff) **121** 87
Abraham **73** 258 **121** 78 **129** 386
Agnes **90** 195 264
Albert E. **101** 205
Alice **90** 61 62 65 195 264
Alice (Burwell) **103** 230
Alonzo C. **90** 115
Alonzo W. **101** 94
Alpheus **77** 152
Alva **121** 80
Alvin **109** 271
Amanda L. **92** 172
Amarillis **103** 230
Ambrose **86** 384
Amelia **92** 172
Amos **77** 241
Amy **77** 209 **88** 139
Andrew **107** 72
Ann **58** 374 **82** 461 **90** 265 266 **101** 80 **111** 319 320 **115** 164 **116** 78 **121** 85 86 **138** 278
Ann (Andrews) (Camp) **121** 85
Ann (Ford) **103** 230
Ann (Foster) **121** 85 87
Ann Eliza **81** 247
Anna **60** 80 **78** 251 **109** 65 **121** 86

PECK *cont'd*
Anna (Glazier) **120** 160
Anna L. (Bristol) **85** 227
Anna Tasker **79** 331
Anne **57** 318 **70** 76 **89** 328
338 339 **90** 60 61 65 263
91 14 15 282 283 285 **93**
177 **103** 225 **105** 179
124 250
Annie Barker (Earle)
87 377 378
Annie Gardner **97** 120
Ansel **101** 152
Arathusa (Bullard) **121** 78
Arethusa **73** 258
Ariel **129** 386
Arthur **92** 172
Arthur Francis Searing
90 137 **97** 149 189 **98**
151
Arthur Francis Searing
(Mrs.) **81** 338 **98** 147
Arthur J. **92** 172
Arza Canfield **103** 230
Asa **101** 169
Asahel **73** 14
Asenath **78** 251 **101** 206
Asenath (Huntley)
101 206
Augusta **61** 77 **77** 209
Augustus **77** 209
Austin **86** 233
Azubah **77** 209 210
Barbara L. **105** 53
Bathsheba **133** 293
Bayard Livingstone
105 53
Bela **81** 169
Belle **81** 369 **94** 137
Benajah **121** 85 87
Benjamin **59** 169 **61** 398
72 17 114 **77** 209 **80** 188
189 **81** 169 **86** 384 **87**
259 **89** 244 246 **97** 116
252-254 **98** 239 **116** 7
121 82 83 89 90
Benjamin S. **121** 90 91
Bethiah **86** 383 384
Betsey **76** 277 **78** 369
Betsey Ann **101** 204
Betsey L. **101** 235
Betty **97** 254
Bradford **113** 295
Brenda Vance de Vere
(Morrison) **97** 190
Bridget **91** 355-358 361 362
92 73
Bridget (Sayer) **91** 356
C. L. **125** 254
Calvin **73** 258 **101** 204
Calvin D. **120** 160
Calvin H. **101** 204
Camfar **128** 268
Candace **60** 402
Caroline **101** 206
Caroline (Cornell) **97** 189
Caroline H. **101** 204
Carrie Althea **112** 140 141
Catherine **78** 369 **109** 192
Catherine (Hawley)
90 115

PECK *cont'd*
Catherine (Peck) **109** 192
Charaldine **101** 205
Charles **61** 77 **84** 213 214
87 378 **121** 81 85 87-91
123 224
Charles (Mrs.) **123** 224
Charles Edmund **75**
xxiii 65 **85** 176 227 **86**
193 200 **107** 136
Charles L. **77** 209 **78** 369
Charles Manley **87** 377
378
Charles W. **69** 82
Charlotte **57** 79 **81** 169
Charlotte (Dodge)
120 160
Chauncey E. **147** 127
Clara **61** 398
Clarissa **69** 82
Comfort **97** 252
Cynthia **115** 113 114
Cyrus **72** 17
Dale La Varr **108** 135
Dan **77** 209 **101** 152
Daniel **78** 375 **81** 57 266
98 323 **126** 167
Darius **78** 369 **86** 384
David **63** 89 **73** 266 **80** 181
98 288 **126** 142
David M. **78** 251 **101** 206
Deborah **54** 387 **77** 209
109 192 **114** 288 **121** 88
90
Deborah (Sweetland)
97 253
Deborah (Wildman)
121 87
Deborah T. **101** 204
Delia **70** 202
Deliverance (Bosworth)
97 257 **101** 169
Deliverance (May)
133 293
Desire (Loomis) **120** 160
Dorcas **78** 369 **121** 91
Dorothy **90** 61 264 **91** 363
121 80
Dorothy (Bacon) **91** 363
E. **117** 18
Eb. **145** 126
Ebenezer **59** 69 **66** 328 **84**
87 **86** 384 **98** 237 239
245 328 330 **121** 86 87
122 39 **125** 88 **145** 126
Edmund **85** 227
Edward **71** 151
Edward C. **101** 152
Edward How **58** 374
Edwin **100** 107
Eleanor **81** 321 **91** 284
Eleazer **59** 68 352 **81** 128
121 81 83-90 **127** 223
Eli R. **82** 379
Eliakim **92** 172 **121** 85 87
90
Elias **63** 86 **80** 189 **89** 247
110 69
Eliazur **93** 308 **121** 82 84
Elihu **127** 228
Elijah **69** 200 **70** 76 77 **78**

PECK *cont'd*
252 **113** 52 **140** 234
Elisha **61** 77 **63** 85 **69** 335
77 209 **78** 375 **79** 154
98 323 **101** 204 235
Eliza **80** 65
Eliza (Walker) **126** 142
Eliza Jane **88** 81
Elizabeth **52** 215 **57** 162 **58**
283 **59** 69 356 **66** 327 **71**
249 **77** 209 **78** 251 252
81 128 169 **86** 384 **90** 60
61 63-65 263 264 **91** 284
363 **92** 84 169 **93** 373 **96**
347 **97** 38 116 252 253
100 9 175 **101** 152 200
105 53 58 **110** 69 143
113 227 **121** 19 82-85
126 176 **140** 234
Elizabeth (Anderson)
87 378
Elizabeth (Carpenter) **97**
38 253
Elizabeth (Caulkins) **101**
144 200
Elizabeth (Ford) (Culver)
121 84
Elizabeth (Green) **104** 89
Elizabeth (Moore) **105** 58
Elizabeth (Smith) **97** 38
114
Elizabeth (Throop) **87** 378
Elizabeth (Woodruff)
121 87
Elizabeth Beebe **77** 209
Elizabeth C. **78** 369
Elizabeth Ellison
(Stackpoole) **103** 230
Elizabeth Hibbard **83** 472
Elizabeth Stuart (Butler)
105 53
Ella (Keil) **128** 268
Ellen **91** 360 361 363
Ellen (Babbs) **91** 284 363
Ellen R. **101** 94
Ellis **101** 169
Elly (Godard) **128** 268
Emanuel **79** 331
Emily **79** 202
Emma A. **128** 174
Epaphroditus **60** 405
61 xxxv
Esther **53** 174 **56** 139 **59**
168 169 **67** 384 **71** 6 **77**
209 **121** 87
Eugene **101** 94
Eunice **63** 88 **69** 82 **86** 384
Eunice W. **69** 82
Experience **63** 88
Ezekiel Y. **81** 57 266
Ezra **80** 189 **89** 247
Ezra M. **77** 209
Faith **52** 215 **67** 206 **136**
312 315 324 325
Fannie M. **69** 206
Fanny **65** 362 **67** lvi
Fernando **85** 297
Fila (Bryant) **137** 257
Flora A. **117** 216
Florence P. (Peck)
103 230

PECK *cont'd*
Florence Peirce **115** 234
Florence Winn
(Underhill) **93** 85
Frances **53** 174 **90** 60
Francis **90** 264 372 373
94 176
Frank G. **113** 295
Frank G. (Mrs.) **113** 59
294
Frank Merton (Mrs.)
93 85
Franklin G. **85** 316
Frederic **80** 65
Frederick Stanhope **89**
132 327 **90** 58 194 263
371 **91** 7 134 136 282
355 **92** 71 **93** 176 359 **94**
71 **97** 302 **98** 91 210 **101**
114 169 170 178 **102** 128
Frederick Stanhope (Mrs.)
77 322 **78** 206
Freelove (St. John)
109 271
Friendly **125** 37 **147** 70
G. D. **107** 72
George **69** 82 **72** 17 **111**
319 **129** 386 **142** 187
285
George Gibbs **121** 80
George Henry **58** 374
George R. **54** 373 **78** 251
Gertrude H. **92** 225
Gideon **86** 384 **121** 85 87
Glendola Amos **118** 247
Grace **121** 91
Grace Frances **106** 306
Hallock J. **123** 225
Hannah **51** 224 **57** 79 159
327 **66** 328 **69** 200 **70** 76
77 **75** 177 **78** 264 369 **86**
384 **96** 350 351 353 **97**
29 30 115 116 251 252
257 **105** 79 **121** 19 85 87
140 128
Hannah (Peck) **97** 251
Hannah (Pettis) **97** 116
Hannah M. **117** 216
Harriet **73** 258 **79** 331 **81**
169 **100** 290 **101** 94
Harriet E. **69** 82
Harriet H. **92** 225
Harriet Jane **78** 345
Harvey **134** 90
Helen **65** 125 **68** 158 **86**
233 452 **89** 328 **91** 284
285 363 **101** 170 **109**
271
Helen (Babbs) **87** 377 **91**
284 355
Helen Aline Smith **90** 131
Helen M. **82** 379 455
109 170
Henry **60** 71 **66** 327 **69** 94
81 130 169 266 368 **84**
214 **85** 227 **89** 333 334
91 9 **103** 230 **121** 81-83
Henry T. **66** 93
Hepzibah **61** 77 **78** 252
113 52
Hezekiah **97** 319

PECK *cont'd*
Hopestill **80** 181
Horace M. **77** 178
Horatio **88** 17
Hubbard C. **128** 268
Huldah **63** 86
Huldah (Keeler) **103** 230
I. Heyward **102** 80 **105** 152
Ira Ballou **54** xliv **55**
xxxix **56** xxxviii **57**
xxxix **58** lii **59** liii **60**
xliv **61** xlii **62** xlvi
lxxxviii **63** lxxvii **79**
244 **87** 278 **89** 329-332
90 58 59 62 198 372 373
91 283 284 355 **93** 176
94 169 **121** 81
Irena **63** 89 **86** 384
Isaac **65** 125
Isaac Heyward **100** 112
114 139
Isabell **90** 60 65
Israel **62** 350 351 **96** 347
348 350 351 353 **97** 23
25 27 29 38 40 114-116
252-254 257 320 325 **98**
322 328 329 **100** 9 **121**
16 19 **125** 37 **139** 49
Jabez **97** 116
Jacob **72** 17
Jael **120** 145
James **56** 139 **69** 82 **71** 6
80 272 **110** 143 **125** 33
144 43
Jane **65** 125 **79** 154 **90** 62
66 197 198
Janie (Bodes) **103** 230
Jasper **78** 251 **90** 265
Jathniel **96** 353 **97** 37 114
257 319 **98** 239
Jean **81** 338
Jedediah **78** 252 **113** 52
Jedidiah W. **101** 204
Jemima **54** 174 **77** 209
Jeremiah **55** 214 **58** 79 **63**
275 **84** 214 **85** 227 **97**
189 **109** 65 **110** 69
Jerreb **73** 258
Jerusha **78** 375 **81** 57 **85**
431 **97** 116 **137** 39
Jerusha Ann **81** 57
Jesse **78** 251 **101** 206
Jesse Marvin **101** 206
Joan **66** 327 **89** 338 339
90 60 64 **91** 13 14 282
121 83
Joan (Waters) **89** 338 339
91 15
Joanna **55** 214 **73** 258
90 61 62
Joanna (Kitchell) **85** 227
97 189 **109** 65
John **53** 174 **59** 168 **61** 77
78 **62** 350 **63** 79 84 90
71 6 **73** 223 258 **79** 331
82 461 **84** 153 **85** 17 **87**
377 **89** 329 330 332 335
338 339 **90** 58-66 194-
198 263-268 371-373 **91**
13-15 282 283 363 **93**
177 361 **94** 68 168-170

PECK *cont'd*
97 314 316-318 326 **98**
167 169 170 175 236 248
99 95 96 **103** 230 **105**
179 **121** 120 248 **123** 44
134 90 **143** 45
John A. **78** 251 **103** 230
John Carter **79** 331
John E. **76** 53
John P. **77** 179 **92** 225
John Smith **101** 206
John Steele **87** 378
Jonathan **57** 159 **86** 384 **87**
378 **97** 189 **120** 160 **129**
381
Jonathan Kenyon **112** 140
Jonathan Richard **97** 189
Joseph **51** 224 **53** 174 **58**
237 **59** 169 **60** 80 63 88
64 27 **65** 125 **77** 209 210
78 251 263 345 **81** 130
133 134 169 **84** 214 86
384 **89** 327-333 335 **90**
58 59 122 194 198 263
371-373 **91** 7 10 134 136
282 284 285 355 360 361
92 71 142 **93** 176 359 **94**
71 **95** 130 **96** 254 347 **97**
38 114-116 252-254 257
316 319 326 **98** 167 238
324 327 329 **99** 96 232
233 **101** 169 206 **103**
230 **106** 259 **120** 160
121 81-83 113-115 122
126 **123** 29 **139** 130 132
Josephine Middleton **117**
311 314 **123** 86 **142** 176
Joshua **64** 23
Judith **110** 4 **121** 255
Judith (Smith) **97** 257
101 169
Julia (Roberts) **84** 214
Julia A. (Fayerweather)
145 242 247
Julia Elizabeth (Gager)
117 239
Julia M. (Randall) **128** 174
Juliette (Gleason) **120** 160
June (Jenyver) **111** 319
Katharine **61** 77 **89** 334
335 **90** 60 61 263 **91** 9
Keziah **108** 162 **140** 69
Keziah (Barnes) **101** 169
Langton **90** 266
Laurence Freeman **85** 227
86 193 **106** 221 **107** 136
Lavina **109** 271
Lawrence **81** 321
Leander Remington
101 169
Lebbeus **61** 78
Leila M. **68** 124
Lemuel **101** 152 **134** 90
Levi **70** 76 **72** 17
Lewis **127** 302
Lois **78** 251
Lora (Rising) (Huff)
85 297
Loring **129** 381
Louisa **73** 258 **89** 238
92 172

PECK *cont'd*
Louisa A. **77** 152
Louise Manette **105** 127
Louise Parrott **90** 305
Lovice **101** 144
Lovila **73** 258
Lovina (Huntley) **101** 152
Lucien **81** 57
Lucille Marguerite **84** 214
Lucinda **82** 379
Lucretia **53** 174 **101** 204
Lucretia Short
    (Remington) **101** 169
Lucy **72** 17 **77** 211 **78** 251
    86 384 **89** 22 **121** 90 91
Lucy B. **77** 149
Luther **63** 86 **78** 252
Lydia **57** 159 **61** 78 **67**
    130 230 **78** 263 **80** 189
    81 169 **89** 247 **96** 347
    97 114 116 **121** 87 91
Lydia (Fenn) **121** 87
Lydia (Hotchkiss) **134** 90
Lydia (Lines) **84** 214
Lydia A. **101** 206
Lydia J. **125** 53
Lydia Rose **77** 185
Lyman **101** 152 **121** 126
M. A. (Mrs.) **144** 121
Mabel Rodney (Steele)
    87 378
Mahala **70** 77
Marcus **80** 272
Marcy **97** 116
Margaret **82** 461 **89** 338
    339 **90** 60 61 65 263 266
    91 13-15 282 283 **96** 347
    97 114 116 **110** 143 **120**
    5
Margery **89** 334 **91** 9
Margery (Hitchcock)
    (Munson) **121** 85
Maria **114** 184
Maria (Gilmer) **114** 184
Maria O. **81** 266
Marian (Briggs) **92** 172
Marie **72** 17
Mariette **134** 90
Marinda **56** 170
Martha **53** 174 **57** 318 **60**
    303 **67** 51 **69** 82 **70** 74
    86 384 **91** 359-361 **93**
    308 **121** 85
Martha Ann (Chase)
    84 214
Marvin **69** 82
Mary **53** 410 **59** 68 169 **61**
    78 **65** 125 **68** 158 69 335
    72 184 **73** 258 **77** 209
    78 251 **86** 96 384 **92** 163
    172 **96** 346 347 349 352
    353 **97** 22 23 25-30 34 37
    39 40 42 104 114-117
    251 255 258 259 **121**
    85 87 **127** 201 **129** 261
    137 257
Mary (Beach) **84** 214
Mary (Bronson) **121** 87
Mary (Bunnell) **121** 84
Mary (Camp) **103** 230
Mary (Girvan) **85** 227

PECK *cont'd*
Mary (Goold) **143** 45
Mary (Hawkes) **86** 233
Mary (Johnson) **85** 227
Mary (Kinsley) **87** 378
Mary (Pardee) **97** 189
Mary (Sanford) **121** 91
Mary (Sperry) **121** 83
Mary A. **77** 179
Mary Alice **110** 68 69
Mary B. (Curtis) **145** 244
Mary E. **77** 178 **123** 224
Mary Elizabeth (Munson)
    84 214
Mary Etta **71** 16 **110** 231
Mary Frances (Deuel)
    106 306
Mary G. **57** 285
Mary I. **69** 82
Mary Lilian **95** 147
Mary Louise (Briggs)
    (Clark) **126** 126
Mary Rothwell
    (Burlingame) **78** 206
    101 170
Mary S. **61** 78
Mary Stark (Searle)
    112 140
Mary Virginia **96** 74
Maryon **93** 360
Mather **77** 209 210
Matilda **73** 258
Matilda (Lombard)
    113 295
Matthew **78** 251 **107** 73
May R. **125** 240
Mehitable **61** 78 **71** 14 **78**
    369 **121** 85 87
Mehitable (Blackman)
    97 189
Melissa **72** 17
Mercy **58** 79
Minerva (Tupper)
    (Grinnell) **99** 306
Molly **63** 89 **97** 254
    109 264
Moses **56** 139 **73** 258
    140 234
Myrtilla Mead **97** 390
Nabby **73** 14
Nancy **77** 210 **86** 154
    134 90
Nancy Louisa **89** 238
Nath **121** 198
Nathan **96** 269 **98** 326 **99**
    306 **121** 89 90
Nathaniel **56** 362 **62** 351
    77 210 211 **78** 251 **95**
    130 **97** 189 257 320 325
    101 169 **121** 14 84 85 89
    90 **139** 49 142 394
Nelepha **127** 222
Nellie M. **68** 158
Nelson Thomas **106** 126
Nicho **99** 94-96
Nicholas **52** 246 **54** 174
    62 346 350 **63** 78 79 83
    127 130 151 232 **64** 28
    87 378 **89** 331 **90** 60 66
    194-197 264-268 372 373
    91 3 63 285 355-363 **92**

PECK *cont'd*
71-73 **93** 176 177 **96** 253
    259 346-348 350 351 354
    97 23 25 27 29 40 114-
    116 251-254 314 316-318
    98 171 322
Noah **98** 322 324
Norman Van Nearing
    82 234 353
Olive **89** 338 339 **91** 14 15
    282 283 **98** 288 **101** 204
    235
Oliver **78** 251
Orin Miller **77** 210
Orrin H. **126** 126
Parilla **108** 172
Patience **61** 398 **72** 17 **97**
    41 **121** 89-91
Patience (Bosworth)
    97 41
Patience (Chase) **87** 259
Patience (Turner) **123** 44
Patronella **89** 285
Paul **60** 303 **70** 76 **105** 79
Peddy **100** 57
Peggy **97** 252 254
Peleg **57** 162 **87** 378
    128 49
Peninah **67** 230
Percey **63** 86
Persis L. **99** 306
Peter **78** 252 **113** 52
Peter Lord **101** 206
Phebe **86** 384
Phebe (Mason) **87** 378
Phebe K. **84** 87
Phile (Bryant) **137** 257
Philena **92** 165
Philip **87** 254
Philura **64** 206
Phineas **86** 384
Polly **101** 152
Polly (Martin) **87** 378
Prudence **111** 319 320
Prudence (Brewster)
    124 251
Prudence (Clapp) **121** 110
R. S. **57** 342
Rachel **52** 246 **60** 71 **63** 151
    67 53 **70** 76 **80** 189 **89**
    247 **91** 355 358-361 363
    92 73 **97** 251 **133** 307
    309
Rachel (Bowers) (Chase)
    88 108
Rachel (Lambert) **103** 230
Rachel (Yonge) **91** 355
    363
Rachel Wilson **88** 22
Ralph **68** 158 **90** 373
Rebecca **60** 71 **61** 77 **63** 90
    81 369 **86** 96 **87** 390 **97**
    254 **99** 306 **131** 125
Rebecca (Brown) **97** 116
Rebecca (Carver) **88** 317
Rebecca (Clark) **87** 378
    101 169
Reginald E. **90** 402
    103 230
Reliance **63** 275
Rhoda **57** 162 **63** 88 **69** 200

PECK *cont'd*
72 217 87 328 125 271
126 167
Rhumah (Huntley)
101 204
Richard 63 28 65 125 78
251 89 330 90 59-65 194-
197 263-268 371-373 91
283 285 355 92 172 93
177 360 124 255
Roba 69 82
Robert 57 310 318 65 125
87 377 89 327-329 331-
335 337-339 90 58-61 64
195 198 265-267-10 12-
15 136 282-286 355 363
92 71 72 142 93 176-178
359-361 94 72 73 101
169 106 259 107 268
110 69 111 319 320 124
251 138 80 99 139 132
142 119 351
Robert Carter 79 331
Robert Earle 87 378
Robert Halford 83 371
84 190 86 346 87 178
377
Robert Jeremiah 81 364
82 237 84 109 197 213
Robert M. 52 303 58 374
Rodney Halford 87 378
Rose 65 125
Rosemary 87 378
Rubaniah 77 210
Ruth 72 17 78 433 87 174
378 121 88 90 135 77
Ruth (Ferris) 85 227
97 189
Ruth (Peck) 121 90
S. Allyn 89 327 90 58 194
263 371 91 7 282 355 92
71 93 176 359 94 71
S. P. 107 72
Saba 120 8
Saba (Lincoln) 120 5
Sally 63 85 78 190 80 272
Sally Levine 111 116
Samuel 53 410 56 288 62
183 236 237 346-348 63
127 332 333 64 31 206
68 374 71 249 73 258
77 209 210 78 369 84
214 85 227 87 321 91
285 360 361 363 92 172
96 259 262 263 265-267
353 97 29 115 189 251
252 314 316-318 98 238
99 96 98 101 107 109
192 110 69 116 7 121 11
19 84 85 87 129 64 138
30 143 45
Samuel A. 145 247
Samuel I. 100 175
Samuel J. 128 174
Samuel T. 92 172
Sarah 54 174 60 79 62 183
66 201 67 373 70 76 71
8 76 53 77 209 210 78
137 251 80 181 188 189
81 121 87 321 89 244
247 92 172 109 192 112

PECK *cont'd*
76 113 52 118 135 121
85 91 123 123 225 130
235 132 300 134 90 137
331
Sarah (Alling) 84 214
121 83
Sarah (Cable) 85 227
Sarah (Chase) 87 254
88 17
Sarah (Hill) 101 169
Sarah (Hopkins) (Cole)
121 85
Sarah (Jenks) 87 321
Sarah (King) 121 85
Sarah (Marsh) 100 9
Sarah (Plumb) 87 328
Sarah (Smith) 97 257
Sarah C. 125 177
Sarah Elizabeth (Searing)
97 189
Sarah Gould (Cannon)
101 169
Sarah Walton 61 78
Seba 120 8
Seril 86 383 384
Shirley Allyn 103 230
Shubael 57 79
Silas 101 144 152 200 116 7
Simon 63 86 88 121 109-
111
Solomon 92 172 101 169
Sophia 64 206 80 65
Stephen 77 209 96 347 350
97 25 114 116 252-254
98 329 104 89 121 84 85
Susan 84 41
Susan (Gifford) 138 220
Susan Amanda 77 179
Susanna 61 288 67 225
77 210
Susanna (Collyer) 121 85
Susanna (Heron) 121 91
Tabitha 78 252 113 52
Thankful 56 288
Theodore D. 81 266
Theodore S. 51 387
145 138
Theodosia (Lockwood)
97 189
Thomas 52 215 56 79 69
82 70 76 71 92 87 378
89 329 330 338 339 90
59 60 194 265 266 372
733 91 14 15 282 283
285 355 93 177 111 319
121 86 89-91 128 55
129 381 133 293
Thomas Bellows 53 142
54 197 289 435 55 xxxii
58 425 56 xxxii 98 248
321 384 396 57 xxxiii
117 125 58 xlv 267 59
332 60 xxxix 61 xxxvii
62 lxxxvii 63 lxxvi 101
108 109 114 29
Thomas H. 84 260 261
Thomas Handasyd 51
372 56 189 82 461 462
85 128 92 84
Thomas J. 77 185

PECK *cont'd*
Timothy 67 230 78 369
84 214 87 328 121 86
Truman 100 175
Ursel Dawn (Harris)
113 294
V. G. 54 174
Virginia 110 56
W. E. 91 332
W. J. 120 160
W. W. 76 277
Ward 68 158
William 54 24 59 194 65
221 71 288 77 209 210
78 252 81 122 125-127
130-132 169 85 227 90
60 264 372 373 91 14
355 358 359 361-363 92
73 94 169 97 189 102
235 110 69 111 319 121
81-83 124 254 128 72
134 90 143 45
William A. 117 216
127 140
William C. 101 94
William E. 101 204
William H. 68 158
William Henry 82 123
237 103 79 126 230
William L. 68 158 78 369
William S. 101 94
William Ward 106 306
Willie M. 110 257
Willson 110 68 69
Winchester 97 116
Zebulon 121 86 87
PECK-MORRILL
Miriam 58 100
Peckam *see* Peckham
Pecke *see* Peck
PECKELL Joseph 84 137
PECKEN Israel 111 208
PECKER Peker
—— 58 218 326 105 182
— Capt. 83 84
Abigail 69 104 110
Anna 111 233
Betsey 96 53
Bridget 124 174
Bridget (Bosworth)
(Papillon) 124 174
135 26
Daniel 57 389 58 69 85
127 124 174
Frank Stetson 91 367
Frank Stetson (Mrs.) 85
197 91 367 92 91 151
Hannah 58 84
Hannah (Dalton) 136 322
James 58 100 67 312 70
195 84 381 93 398 100
63 142 102 29 110 317
124 169 171 174 136
109 322 140 234 324
146 317
Jeremiah 70 195 90 87 92
285 118 313
John 70 195 110 317 111
233 124 174
Jonathan Eastman 58 xvi
59 v xvi 60 v xiv 61 v

PECKER cont'd
  xiii xxxiii **62** v xv **63** v
    xv **64** v xiii **65** v xiii **66**
    184 **70** xxvii lviii 195
    196
  Katharine (Papillon)
    124 169
  Mary **66** 100 **97** 358 **124**
    174 175
  Mary E. **92** 285
  Mary Lang **70** 195
  Mary Lena (Robinson)
    92 151
  Miriam **58** 100
  Nancy **100** 142
  Peter **143** 261
  Rachel **67** 312
  Rachel (Noble) **84** 381
    140 234
  Ruth (Kimball) **92** 280
  Seth Eastman **91** 367
  Susanna **100** 142 **102** 29
  Susanna (Cogswell)
    136 322
Peckett see Pickett
PECKHAM Peckam
  Peckum Pekham
  —— **75** 279 **91** 171 **127** 79
    135 51 **136** 211
  — Mrs. **62** 352
  A. Laneen **122** 105
  Aaron **57** 162
  Abbie G. **115** 170
  Abby C. **125** 176
  Abby Jane **74** 65
  Abby M. **125** 176
  Abel **57** 37 160 **128** 221
  Abigail **57** 36 39 159 160
    162 **120** 190
  Abigail (Martin) **126** 21
  Abner **125** 177 178
  Abraham **115** 177 **122**
    212 214 296 300
  Abraham T. **125** 173
  Alanson **57** 158 **122** 211
    296 300
  Alanson W. **116** 56
  Alfred **122** 212 **125** 182
  Alfred G. **126** 21
  Alice **122** 295
  Alice Ann (Bean) **125** 182
  Almira **122** 255
  Almy **57** 34 39
  Amos **88** 30
  Amy **55** 74 **57** 37 160 161
  Amy S. **100** 329
  Ann **57** 33 35 37 39 157
    122 102 296
  Ann (Hovey) **123** 39
  Ann M. **122** 300
  Anna **57** 157 158
  Anne **57** 35 36 154 160 **70**
    129 131 **122** 102 212
  Annie B. **125** 177
  Anson Wheeler **109** 223
  Anthony **57** 154
  Asa **122** 300
  Augusta Brown **115** 176
  Augustus **57** 161 **80** 256
    122 297
  Avis **57** 154 160

PECKHAM cont'd
  Barbara **57** 33 36 157 158
    122 102 104 129 211
  Barbara (Rider) **125** 181
  Barbara M. **125** 181
  Barbary (Davis) **122** 129
  Barber **104** 12 **105** 270
    128 129
  Barker **116** 48
  Bathsheba **57** 35
  Benedick **122** 102
  Benedict **57** 158 **125** 237
    240 **126** 21 **128** 131
  Benjamin **57** 33 35 36 155-
    159 **60** 189 **67** 287 **83** 86
    102 19 206 **105** 216 **109**
    223 **115** 180 **118** 65 **122**
    102 104 **125** 238 **127** 15
    143 **128** 126 **137** 155
  Benjamin L. **79** 348
  Benjamin Layton **102** 235
  Benjamin T. **125** 245
  Benjamin W. H. **122** 300
  Benoni **127** 9
  Bethiah **57** 36 157 160
  Bethiah (Gifford) **129** 34
  Byron J. **60** 189
  C. C. **125** 182
  Caleb **57** 37 158 159 161
    117 186
  Catalina Whittier **99** 76
  Catherine **57** 158
  Catherine Davis (Torrey)
    94 84
  Charles **57** 158 163 **122**
    211 297
  Charles B. **126** 21
  Charles H. **117** 215
  Charles J. **83** 438 **84** 20
  Charlotte S. **125** 180
  Christopher V. **125** 178
  Clara **122** 297
  Clemence **55** 390
  Clement **57** 32 34 36 39
    157 158 162 **122** 102
  Comfort **57** 155 **122** 103
  Content **57** 33-35 38 161
  Content Rathbone
    109 223
  Cynthia **57** 161 162
    122 214
  Cynthia (Barker) **125** 180
    237
  Cynthia A. **122** 300
  Cyrus **125** 180 241
  Cyrus B. **125** 240
  Daniel **57** 32 33 35 37 160
    63 198 **122** 104 107 **127**
    143 **128** 220
  David **57** 37 159 **97** 38
    117 186 **125** 247 248
    126 61 62
  Deborah **57** 32 34 36 38
    156 157 161
  Desire **57** 156
  Desire (Watson) **109** 223
  Dinah **57** 33-35 39 **69** 92
  Dora **117** 208
  Dora L. (Durrell)
    (Warner) **133** 123
  Dorcas **57** 37 38 156 157

PECKHAM cont'd
  122 102 104 297 300
  Dorothy **57** 37 159
  Dorothy (Robinson)
    117 186
  Ebenezer **57** 37
  Edgar Spencer **116** 121
  Edmund R. **104** 12
  Edward J. **117** 212 **122** 300
  Edward Smith **122** 104
    124 320
  Edward T. **122** 296
  Eleanor **57** 31 32 34 **63** 198
  Elisha **57** 38 160 **86** 124
    122 104 297 **127** 142
  Eliza **122** 212 214 296
  Eliza (Chace) **126** 20
  Eliza (Tompkins) **115** 180
  Eliza Amelia **122** 296
  Eliza B. **115** 175
  Eliza B. (Tilley) **125** 238
  Eliza D. **125** 177
  Eliza M. **80** 256
  Elizabeth **57** 32-36 38 39
    154-162 **70** 128 131 **75**
    224 **94** 84 **105** 216 **118**
    65 **122** 102-104 **123** 39
    125 174 247 **135** 53 **144**
    309
  Elizabeth (Dunham)
    125 177
  Elizabeth (Handy) **125**
    248 **126** 62
  Elizabeth (Smith) **124** 320
  Elizabeth (Weeden)
    123 40
  Elizabeth (Westcott)
    105 270
  Elizabeth (Whitman)
    125 245
  Elizabeth A. **122** 296
  Elizabeth Clarke
    Chapman **57** 37
  Elizabeth D. (Silvester)
    86 124
  Elizabeth S. **125** 182 183
  Ella Comstock **57** 326
  Ellen **57** 161
  Ellis **120** 191
  Elma Barker **116** 121
  Enos **57** 39 **123** 39 **127** 142
  Erasmus K. **125** 176 244
  Esther **57** 157 161 **63** 43
  Esther Sarah **122** 296
  Ethel Anson (Steel)
    109 223
  Eudora S. **117** 212
  Eunice **57** 38 39 158 159
  Eunice (Clark) **120** 100
  Felix **57** 161
  Felix A. **122** 300
  Fenner H. (Mrs.) **78** 106
  Fenner Harris **94** 84
  Francis L. **80** 257
  Frederick A. **122** 300
  Freelove **57** 38 **123** 40
  Freelove Sophia **125** 245
  G. Barker **125** 180
  George **57** 38 39 162 163
    59 27 **70** 131 **95** 366
    123 39 **127** 217

PECKHAM *cont'd*
George H. **102** 215 **117** 220 **128** 127
George Hazard **57** 156
Hannah Ann **104** 244
Harriet G. **125** 175
Harriet Gardner **125** 179
Isabelle **95** 336
Jean **107** 228
Jeremiah **147** 348
John **147** 344
Louisa (Sisson) **125** 237 **126** 20
Lucinda **115** 177
Lucy **57** 156 **115** 177
Lucy (Morgan) **95** 366
Lucy Ann **74** 65
Lucy T. **74** 65
Lydia **57** 32 34 37 39 154 159 161 **117** 186 **122** 104 105 211 214 296 **123** 39 **126** 248 **147** 333 344 345 351
Lydia (Barnaby) (Simmons) **123** 39
Lydia Eliza **122** 300
Mabel Elizabeth **80** 166
Marcy **120** 190
Margaret **57** 35 36 154 158 162 **74** 76
Margaret A. (Middleburger) (Stuyvesant) **109** 223
Margaret S. **122** 300
Maria (Burgess) **88** 30
Martha **57** 154 157 **122** 298
Martha G. (Coit) **125** 176
Martin V. B. **125** 182
Mary **56** 92 **57** 31-39 154-163 **63** 198 **75** 279 **83** 86 **95** 342 **106** 211 **122** 101 102 104 212 **123** 38 39 **124** 48 **125** 239 242 252 **126** 248 **147** 344
Mary (Carr) **102** 206
Mary (Fales) **120** 6
Mary (Greene) **109** 223
Mary (Hazard) **109** 223
Mary (Hull) **105** 241
Mary (Kingsley) **123** 39
Mary (Landers) **124** 48
Mary (Norton) **125** 244
Mary (Spooner) **117** 186
Mary (Turner) **123** 38 39
Mary (York) **129** 34
Mary A. **78** 106
Mary Anne (Sheffield) **104** 12
Mary B. **77** 45 **115** 172 **116** 195 **125** 176
Mary Elizabeth **76** xxxvii
Mary Emily **80** 329
Mary G. (Oman) **125** 173
Mary Louise (Chesebrough) **109** 223
Mary M. (Chase) **88** 118
Mary Perry (Watson) **95** 337
Mary V. **80** 272
Mary W. **109** 193
Mary Wells **74** 65

PECKHAM *cont'd*
Mary Wythe **99** 148
Mercy **57** 39 155 156 161 162 **69** 92 **111** 30 **131** 138
Mercy (Ellis) **120** 100 190
Mercy (Manchester) (Brown) **102** 19
Mercy (Smith) **94** 84
Mevus **128** 129
Minerva **115** 117
Mordecai **120** 191
Nancy **57** 39 **100** 329 **122** 211 **123** 39
Nancy (Hatch) **122** 189
Naomi **57** 36 158 **122** 101 106
Nathaniel **57** 159
Nathaniel C. **115** 170 **125** 245
Nattie **115** 170
Nye **57** 158
Oliver **116** 121
Pardon G. **115** 171
Patience **57** 35 155 156 162 **122** 104 211
Patience York **57** 177
Peckham **123** 39
Peleg **57** 33 35 36 154-156 160 161 **83** 86 **109** 223 **115** 170 177 **122** 104 **124** 320 **125** 245 **127** 142
Penelope **57** 34 39
Perry M. **125** 176 238
Peter **57** 159 160
Phebe **57** 32 34 38 39 158 160 161 **79** 256 **80** 258 **122** 100 101 104
Phebe C. **117** 217
Phila (Braman) **125** 245
Philip **57** 32 33 36 39 158 159 **63** 198 **117** 186 **120** 100 **122** 102 **125** 248 **127** 302
Philip Mason **122** 214
Prince **57** 39 162
Priority **125** 34
Priscilla **116** 56 121
Prudence **57** 158 162
R. A. (Wyatt) **125** 182
Rachel **57** 33 35 36 112 155 **125** 173
Rachel A. **116** 121
Rachel S. (Barker) **125** 177 178
Raymond **84** 87
Rebecca **57** 32 39 160-163 **125** 180 **126** 22
Rebecca (Sawdy) **148** 159
Rebecca Ann **122** 300
Restcom **122** 212 214
Reuben **57** 32 35 154 155 **69** 91
Rheba Sherman **116** 121
Rhoda **57** 154 158
Rhoda (Sawdy) **148** 156
Richard **56** 126 **57** 36 38 157 161 **70** 59 **122** 104 **127** 143 308
Richard S. **126** 20

PECKHAM *cont'd*
Robert **57** 37 158 159 **117** 186 **120** 6
Robert Congdon **57** 156
Robert L. **115** 175
Roger **74** 76
Rufus **57** 155
Russell G. **125** 237 **126** 20
Ruth **57** 34-37 154-159 **79** 348 **117** 186 **122** 102 104 212 214 **125** 38 182 **127** 8
Ruth (Peckham) **117** 186
Ruth E. **122** 300
Ruth T. **125** 242
S. F. **60** 186
Sabina (Dewey) **125** 180
Sally **57** 159
Samuel **57** 34 38 39 154 159-161 **122** 100 101 189 **123** 40 41 **125** 176 **127** 142 143 216 **148** 156 159 269
Samuel L. **125** 180
Sarah **57** 32 33 35-39 154-156 158-162 **67** 287 **80** 81 **102** 206 211 214 218 **117** 186 **120** 100 **122** 104 106 211 **123** 39 **125** 238 **126** 25
Sarah (Allan) **125** 176
Sarah (Boss) **94** 84
Sarah (Newport) **109** 223
Sarah (Phillips) **125** 176
Sarah (Sheffield) **104** 12
Sarah (Sunderland) **129** 34
Sarah (Tripp) **125** 238
Sarah A. **115** 170 **117** 215 **122** 300
Sarah Allan **125** 176
Sarah B. H. **122** 300
Sarah Elizabeth **74** 65
Sarah F. **115** 170
Sarah J. **125** 245
Sarah L. A. **116** 121
Seth **57** 38 161 **94** 84 **128** 55
Silas **57** 39 162 **122** 212 **123** 39 41 **127** 144
Simeon **74** 65
Stanton **125** 176
Stephen **56** 92 **57** 32 34 36 38 39 157 158 161 162 **60** 275 **63** 198 **94** 84 **97** 311 **122** 102 106 **127** 142 150 **128** 50 127 **129** 236 335
Stephen Farnum **56** 210 **57** 31 154 **60** 168 189 279 318 **61** xxxv **109** 193 195 **120** 100
Susan (Champlin) **125** 178
Susan B. **125** 175
Susan T. **122** 297
Susanna **57** 32 33 36 39 156 157 160-162 **100** 329 **111** 79
Susanna (Thornton) **94** 84

PECKHAM *cont'd*
Tabitha **57** 37 159 **108** 76
Tabitha (Howland)
  (Carey) **108** 76 **117** 186
Thankful **57** 37 159
  120 191
Thankful (Ellis) **117** 186
  120 100 190
Thankful T. **57** 162
Theodore D. **122** 300
Thomas **57** 32 33 36 37 39
  155 158-160 162 **63** 198
  80 81 **85** 418 **96** 11 **125**
  248 **127** 144 **143** 221
Thomas Hazard **57** 156
Timothy **57** 32 33 35 36
  155-157 159 **63** 198 **66**
  26 **67** 287 **69** 91 **83** 86
  125 180 241 **128** 127
  128
Uriah **57** 33
Virtue **57** 36 157 158
  122 104
W. **125** 40
W. P. **125** 182
W. W. **125** 182
Wait **57** 33 35
Walton Hazard **109** 223
Walton Middleburger
  109 223
Welthian **57** 160
Wheeler Hazard **57** 155
  74 xxv 78 **109** 61 133
  223
Wilbor **116** 121
William **55** 74 **57** 32-34
  36-39 156 157 159-162
  63 43 198 **80** 258 **115**
  117 **120** 100 **122** 101
  102 104 105 211 212 214
  296 **127** 142 302 **128**
  126
William Augustus **122**
  296 297
William F. **122** 296 300
William G. **115** 170
William M. **126** 22
William Nash **115** 117
William Sweet **57** 157
William Tweed **117** 220
Winifred **74** 71 76
Zerviah **57** 161
Zilpha **57** 156
Zoa (Mann / Mason)
  125 180 241
PECKINS Peckings
Alexander **126** 210
David **109** 183
Leonard **109** 182
Mary **126** 210
Mary Ann (Randell)
  109 183
Sally (Briggs) **126** 210
Vashty (Randell) **109** 182
PECKMAN Hannah **85** 418
PECKOVER Alexander **117**
  202 203
Alexandrina **117** 203
Anna Jane **117** 203
Elizabeth (Sharples)
  117 202

PECKOVER *cont'd*
Elizabeth Josephine
  117 202
PECKRELL
Richard **73** 138
Peckum *see* Peckham
PECLAIRE Jack **78** 190
Pecock *see* Peacock
PEDDER
Constance May **92** 364
Joseph **126** 205
Laura Green **104** 92
Lydia (Ridley) **126** 205
Stanley **92** 364
William **63** 143
PEDDEY James **101** 14
PEDDOR James W. **77** 317
PEDEHALE
Joan **115** 249
John **115** 249
Pederick *see* Pedrick
PEDIGO
Lee (Mrs.) **108** 135
PEDIGROVE
William **100** 140
PEDIN William **62** 170
PEDINGTON
Abraham **109** 49
Benjamin **109** 49
Margaret **109** 49
PEDRICK Pederick
Alice Abbott **95** 237
Benjamin **128** 27
Elizabeth (Booth) **108** 320
Hugh **108** 320
John **134** 254
Josiah **66** 229
Katharine F. **85** 191
Lydia **128** 27
Mary **128** 27
Mary Elizabeth **90** 47
Mehitable **74** 211 **75** lxxix
Phebe **108** 320
Phebe (Borton) **108** 320
Phebe (Butcher) (Bates)
  108 320
Rebecca **128** 27
Rebecca Ann **128** 27
Robert **128** 27
Robert C. **128** 27
Samuel **128** 27
Sarah **74** 206
Sarah E. **66** 229
Shadick **128** 27
Silas **128** 27
Susanna **128** 27
Thomas **108** 320
William **108** 320
William R. **128** 27
PEDRO I King of Castile
  148 140
PEDUZZI — Mr. **83** 308
Emily P. **83** 308
Florence Sullivan **83** 299
  301 **98** 182
PEDWISE Mary (Sullivan)
  114 180
PEEBBES Ann **62** 170
Annabella **62** 170
John **62** 170
Margaret **62** 170

PEEBBES *cont'd*
Mary Jane **62** 170
Sarah **62** 170
PEEBLES Ellsworth
Gledhill (Mrs.) **91** 142
  106 79 **116** 236 **119** 75
Hugh **63** 244
Jane **110** 224
John **116** 236
Leslie A. **119** 75
Patrick **119** 75
Reuben **106** 79
Rhoda (Gilbert) **147** 127
Robert **119** 75
Seth **147** 127
Thelma **119** 75
Thelma Rebecca (Larsen)
  91 142
Peech *see* Peach
Peek *see* Peak
PEEKINS Annie **82** 430
Peel *see* Peale
Peele *see* Peale
PEELER John **125** 222
Margaret (Gould)
  125 222
Maria **117** 318
Peelle *see* Peale
PEELS Robert **140** 69
Peeples *see* Peoples
Peerce *see* Pierce
Peery *see* Pearyse
PEESO Esther **86** 25
John **86** 25
Mehitable (Ward) **86** 25
Peet *see* Peat
Peeters *see* Peters
Peets *see* Peat
PEEVER Peevers
Alice **67** liii
William **67** 137
PEEVEY Joseph **74** 185
PEFFER Helen **91** 47
PEGEN Martha **77** 230
PEGG Pegge
Caroline **84** 217
Catherine **121** 188
Elizabeth **84** 217
Elizabeth (Pegg) **84** 217
Francis **127** 175
Mary **129** 53
Samuel **52** 351
William **84** 217
PEGGIE Robert **96** 321
Peggram *see* Pegram
PEGIN John **58** 142
Joshua **58** 142
PEGION
Katharine **102** 93
Thomas **102** 93
PEGLER John **60** 291
PEGRAM Peggram Pegrom
Elizabeth **114** 15 16
Elizabeth M. **114** 17
Lucy Binns (Cargill)
  117 257
Mary **114** 15
Polly **114** 16
Robert Baker **117** 257
Sarah **66** 178 **69** 27 **86** 325
PEIFFER John **98** 233

PEIFFER *cont'd*
  Mary Magdalene **98** 233
PEIGNE Norah (Goldsmith)
  (Craig) (Moon)
  104 311
PEILE —— **67** 71 73
  J. **106** 234
  John **145** 113
Peilsephor *see* Pulsifer
PEIME Mary **53** 112
Peine *see* Paine
Peinter *see* Painter
PEION Joan **138** 5 6
  Roger **138** 5
PEIR Joseph **56** 348
Peirce *see* Pierce
Peircey *see* Percy
Peircy *see* Percy
PEIRE
  Sarah (Kynde) **126** 18
  William **126** 18
Peirpoint *see* Pierpont
Peirsoin *see* Pearson
Peirson *see* Pearson
Pek *see* Peck
Peker *see* Pecker
Pekerell *see* Pickerill
Pekeryng *see* Pickering
Pekham *see* Peckham
Peks *see* Peck
Pelfrey *see* Palfrey
PELHAM —— **62** 357 **92**
  14 **145** 114
  — Mr. **144** 158
  Arabella **69** 352
  Arabella (Williams)
  105 178
  Charles **81** 98
  Edward **69** 346-348 352
  96 347 **104** 223 **105** 178
  122 102
  Eleanor **145** 106
  Elizabeth **65** 86 **69** 346
  96 347
  Elizabeth (Bosville)
  121 26
  Freelove **69** 352 **96** 347
  Helena **81** 98 **140** 55
  Henry **57** 343 **69** 106 109
  Henry (Mrs.) **122** 175
  Herbert **65** 86 87 **69** 352
  82 154 **105** 178 **121** 26
  29 **122** 175 177
  Herbert (Mrs.) **121** 26 29
  Hermione **69** 352
  Jane / Joan (Mead) **139**
  234 235
  John **59** 194
  Joseph **115** 130
  Lydia **125** 216
  Martha (Coffin) **100** 192
  Mary **64** 317 **140** 146
  Matha (Bee) **126** 286
  Penelope **60** 29 **121** 29
  Peter **71** 104 **100** 192
  Sally (Sworthow) **125** 219
  Sarah **126** 286
  Thomas **61** 199 279 **92** 14
  125 219 **139** 234
  William **60** 358 **64** 317
  145 106

PELHAM-HOLLES
  Thomas **130** 91
PELICAN Robert **83** 392
PELING George **65** 48
  Richard **65** 48
PELIOTT Marie **95** 169
PELISSERO Candace Can-
  field **104** 232
  Deborah (Spaulding)
  104 232
PELKEY John **98** 259
  Mary Jane **111** 139
  Sarah J. **98** 259
  William C. **69** 386
PELL —— **51** 115 **52** 124
  53 302 303 **54** 191 192
  412 **58** 324 **117** 17
  — Mr. **89** 176
  Abigail (Taylor) **144** 19
  Adelia Duane **83** 201 202
  Allison H. **82** 436
  Anne **66** 342 **127** 80
  Bathsheba **87** 283
  Benjamin **100** 192
  Caroline Eliza
  Townsend (Hyatt) **93**
  379 **104** 220
  Edward **57** 389 **99** 80 **111**
  231 **112** 107 **114** 131
  121 128 **144** 18 164
  Eleanor **105** 230
  Elizabeth (Van Tuyl)
  127 80
  Ellen **94** 104 **105** 230
  127 80
  Ellen Dortch **82** 436
  Howland **54** xxxix **89** 176
  Jerusha **82** 290 296
  Jerusha (Harmon) **111**
  231 **114** 131
  John **65** 177 **66** 342 **82** 154
  83 49 **89** 176 **92** 369 **94**
  172 **118** 326
  John Harmon **111** 231
  John Howard Gibbs
  93 379
  John Howland **93** 379
  104 220
  Joseph **127** 80
  Joshua **117** 4 5 9 12 16
  Josiah **57** 321
  Lucy **51** 447
  Maria Louisa
  (Brinckerhoff) **83** 202
  Marie **82** 369
  Mary **58** 28 **94** 172 **106** 228
  Mary (Maynard) **94** 172
  Mary Howland **104** 220
  Oladina **51** 320
  Phebe **60** 197
  Rebecca **92** 55
  Richard **101** 244
  Robert Livingston
  83 202
  Robert Thompson
  93 379
  Sallue **125** 49
  Sarah **111** 231 **112** 107
  115 136
  Sarah (Clarke) **144** 18

PELL *cont'd*
  Sarah Gibbs (Thompson)
  85 226 **87** 172 **93** 379
  Stephen **65** 177
  Stephen Hyatt Pelham **86**
  347 **87** 170 **93** 379
  Stephen Hyatt Pelham
  (Mrs.) **85** 226 **87** 172 **93**
  379 **94** 79 141
  Susanna **92** 51 55 **94** 329
  Thomas **57** 197 **89** 176 **96**
  278 **107** 121 **118** 75
  William **92** 51 55 **127** 80
PELLAN Mary **66** 71 75
PELLAND John **66** 69
PELLATTE Pellat
  Anne **51** 309 312 **66** 326
  Francis **51** 413
  Mary **51** 448
  Thomas **51** 448
PELLEN Mary **51** 413
  Thomas **51** 413
PELLERIN
  Charles **143** 6
  Etienne **143** 6
  Jeanne (Savoye) **143** 6
  Madeleine (Robichaux)
  143 6
PELLET Pellett
  Amasa **70** 346
  David **80** 192 **89** 252
  Edward **83** 100
  Eunice **53** 444
  Feles **85** 64
  Hannah **71** 348
  Jesse **70** 346
  Mary **71** 244
  Orra **80** 192 **89** 252
  Patience **83** 100
  Phyllis **68** 144
  Roger **70** 346
  Rosetta **63** 345
  Samuel **85** 40
  Susanna **65** 372
  Thomas **67** 37 39 **71** 244
  85 64
PELLETREAU
  Jane **114** 315
  William S. **66** 167 **100** 332
  107 250 **108** 15 **123** 85
  124 185
PELLEW
  Henry Edward **112** 248
PELLISER Guillermo
  Thayer **109** 291
PELLOND
  Adam **65** 174 175
  George **65** 323
PELLOW Mary A. **89** 197
PELLYROVE
  Harrison R. **91** 332
PELOUBET
  Francis N. **73** xliv
  Louise **73** 161
PELOUZE —— **83** 297
  ____ (Collens) **83** 301
  Sophia **126** 206
PELSUE Ruth **97** 215
PELT Hannah **147** 260
PELTE Sarah **140** 234

PELTIER Charles Alanson
124 65
Maria (Reed) **124** 65
Morris **125** 290
Phebe (Tillock) **125** 290
Pierre Denoyer **124** 65
PELTON
—— **65** 63 **123** 95
— Mr. **81** 167
A. L. **128** 151
Abner **109** 34
Andrew Ezra **119** 309
Ann (Penfield) **109** 34
Anna **81** 167 **109** 34
Annis H. **126** 296
Asahel **109** 34
Augustus Griswold
128 151
Austin **80** 64
Azubah **109** 34
Buell Barnes **128** 151
Charity **54** 213
Chauncey **109** 37
Clarissa **79** 402 407
Dorothy (Bagley) **109** 34
Earl Lyman **113** 147
Ebenezer **53** 233
Ebenezer Brown **109** 36
Edward Wallace **107** 74
Elias **128** 151
Elizabeth **96** 80 **109** 34
116 207
Elizabeth (Doane) **109** 34
Elizabeth Ann (Penfield)
109 36
Elizabeth Anne **58** 316
Ellsworth **128** 151
Emma A. **128** 151
Fanny **109** 37
Frances **109** 37
Hannah **53** 233 **128** 151
Hannah (Stiles) **109** 34
Hannah Annis **126** 296
128 151
Hannah Hathaway
(Axtell) **87** 292
Harriet N. **128** 151
Harvey **128** 151
Hatsiel **109** 34
Hezekiah **87** 292 **109** 36
Hiram Shaw **119** 309
Horace **116** 207
Hudah **116** 207
Ithamar **80** 16 **128** 151
Jemima **147** 52
Jesse **109** 37 **128** 151
Joanna **119** 309
Joanna (Pine) **119** 309
John **65** 50 **80** 64 **109** 34
116 207 **128** 151
John Isaac **119** 309
Johnson **109** 37
Jonathan **109** 34
Joseph **109** 34
Josiah **128** 151
Julia **109** 37
Julia (King) **113** 65
Julia A. **102** 152
Julia Ann **119** 309
Julia M. (Bird) **123** 95
Julius **128** 151

PELTON *cont'd*
Lily May **119** 309
Lucian Roberts **128** 151
Lucinda (Bidwell) **109** 34
Lucy **109** 37
Lucy (Barnes) **109** 34
Lydia **128** 151
Lysander Julius **128** 151
Marietta Pratt **87** 291 292
Martha Thomas (Corwin)
107 74
Mary **128** 151
Mary (Shepard) **109** 34
Mary D. **128** 151
Nabby (Ranney) **109** 34
Orrin **60** 202 **85** 411
Ovelia Jane **119** 309
Phebe (Hurlbut) **109** 37
Phebe (Penfield) **109** 37
Philena Sally **128** 151
Polly **109** 37
Prudence Augusta
(Penfield) **109** 36
Rachel (Penfield) **109** 37
Reuel **109** 34
Ruth **109** 37
Sally **109** 36
Samuel **64** 26 **79** 388 **123**
192 193 **128** 151
Sanford **109** 37
Sarah **60** 202 **109** 34
125 302
Sarah (Bidwell) **109** 34
Stephen **116** 207
Susanna **116** 207
Thomas A. **113** 65
V. **102** 152
Warren **116** 207
Winthrop Folsom
128 151
Zenas **128** 151
Zilpha **128** 151
PELTZ Pelz
Elizabeth M. **104** 311
Philip **103** 158
W. L.L. **103** 158 **104** 321
PEMBER —— **144** 171
Agnes (Way) (Harris)
111 146
Anne **89** 17
Azel **86** 384
Bethiah J. **86** 384
Bethiah T. **70** 44
Carolyn (Winchell)
111 146
Celeste Brown **111** 146
Elijah **118** 176
Elisha **84** 87
Emmett R. **111** 146 147
Frances A. **86** 384
Frederick **111** 147
Grace Esther **101** 126
Hannah (Cross) **118** 176
Harriet H. **86** 384
Huldah **118** 176
Irene (Wood) **111** 147
Jacob **86** 384
John **86** 384 **93** 305 **111**
146 147
Julia F. **86** 384
Lucius G. **86** 384

PEMBER *cont'd*
Lucretia (Bill) **111** 147
Lydia **86** 384
Mary **86** 384
Mary (Hyde) **111** 147
Percy S. King **84** 87
Philaster **86** 384
Russel **111** 147
Sarah Polly (Stevens)
111 147
Sibyl **64** 125 **109** 309
Sibyl Bissell **109** 308
Stephen **64** 125 **109** 309
Theodocia **86** 384
Thomas **86** 384 **111** 146
Weltha **64** 125
Willard G. **86** 384
William **79** 79
PEMBERICK
Ruth **100** 241
PEMBERTON Pemerton
—— **53** 460 **99** 26
— Mr **58** 26
— Mr. **55** 145-149 **143** 48
— Rev. Mr. **92** 16
Alice **51** 128 129 **54** 214
60 126 **67** 90 **78** 272 274
97 174 177 178 **131** 132
Amanda Ellen **85** 195
Ann (Powell) **84** 255
Anne **54** 214 **97** 175
Annie M. **117** 286
Benjamin **54** 195 214 **57**
415 **60** 239 **130** 91 **140**
173
Bridget **54** 214
Catherine **78** 272 **97** 174
Catherine (Stokes) **97** 174
Charles **64** 217
Constance Emily **76** 18
Cyman **54** 214
Cyprian **51** 128 129
Deborah **54** 214 **62** 261
Ebenezer **55** 307 446 **61** 51
67 212 214 **84** 157 168
250 255 264 **85** 130 91
94 **114** 297 **121** 248 **144**
164
Edward **62** 243
Elizabeth **54** 195 214 **71** 60
78 274 **117** 289 **136** 322
143 141 148 150 151
Frances **78** 274
Francis **78** 274 **97** 174
George **99** 26 **101** 161
117 34
Grace **54** 214
Hannah **54** 214 **73** 238
84 264
James **54** 214 **99** 242 **104**
242 **106** 31 **117** 286 **131**
10 132 **142** 114 **143** 148
151
Joanna **70** 226
John **54** 214 **67** 91 **78** 274
97 175 286 **117** 286 294
142 114 **143** 148 150
151
Joseph **54** 195 214 **89** 397
Katharine **67** 91
Katharine (Angell) **97** 175

PEMBERTON *cont'd*
  Margaret **142** 114
  Marie **142** 114
  Mary **54** 195 **80** 23 **84** 156
    157 **99** 26
  Mary Grace **117** 294
  Mary Jane **117** 294
  Mathie **54** 214
  Matthew **54** 214
  Matthias **54** 195 214
  Paul **54** 195 214 **131** 10
  R. **97** 174
  Ralph **78** 274 **97** 174
    107 192
  Raphael **97** 175
  Rebecca **84** 250
  Richard **51** 129 **54** 214
    143 151
  Robert **65** 160 **78** 272-274
    97 174 **105** 243 **106** 21
  Roger **67** 91 **78** 272-274 **97**
    174 175 177 178
  Samuel **110** 317 **147** 343
  Sarah **51** 221 **88** 170 **89** 396
    397 **91** 267 **117** 35 **142**
    114
  Sarah (Rutherford) **117** 34
  Stephen **117** 34 35
  Susan (Glover) **105** 243
    106 21
  Susanna **51** 302 **60** 239
  Tecla **78** 274
  Thomas **62** 244 **73** 238 **78**
    303 **83** 322 **94** 168 169
    101 163 **117** 289 **143**
    151
  William **54** 214 **127** 143
    143 151
PEMBROKE —— **51** 285
  52 264 **53** 301 302 **56**
    197
  — Earl of **53** 35
  John **65** 32
  John de Hastings (Earl of)
    96 39
  Philip (Earl of) **92** 182
  William Herbert (Earl of)
    59 141
  William Marshall (Earl of)
    75 62
PEMBROOK
  Ralph (Mrs.) **108** 135
Pemerton *see* Pemberton
Pemfield *see* Penfield
PEMIS Aaron **120** 27
PEMMINGTON
  Elizabeth **138** 129
Pen *see* Penn
PENAL Joseph **91** 332
PENBERRY John **64** 254
PENCE
  John **65** 192 **67** 384
  Kingsley Adolphus **65**
    192 **67** 384 **68** xxxii
  La Fayette Stiles **51** 507
  Monroe Conger **117** 77
  Sophia **125** 183
PENCER Hannah **88** 286
Pencheon *see* Pynchon
PENCILLE Arthur Merle
  (Mrs.) **98** 147

PEND Stephen **137** 302
PENDALL Pendal
  Asahel **52** 311
  Elisha **52** 308
  Elizabeth **52** 307 **59** 414
    60 205
  James **58** 195 **60** 202
  John **52** 307 308 310 311
    410
  Jonathan **52** 410
  Lucy **52** 310
  Matthias **58** 195
  Mehitable **58** 195
Pendar *see* Pender
PENDARVIS
  Elizabeth **99** 73
PENDELL
  Anna (Hodges) **100** 88
  Elizabeth **92** 172
  Huldah **110** 149 **137** 151
  M. L. **92** 172
  Oliver **100** 88
  Sarah A. **100** 88
  Selome (Rogers) **127** 57
  William **127** 57
PENDER Pendar
  Almira **90** 112
  George L. **90** 112
  Lydia **57** 211
  Maria L. (McConnell)
    90 112
  Nathaniel **57** 211
  Seamus **121** 233
  Simon **90** 112
Pendergast *see*
    Prendergast
Pendergrass *see*
    Prendergast
PENDERSON
  John **56** 134 136
PENDERY
  Joyce S. **148** 297
PENDEXTER Alfred **73** 192
    87 344
  Aliab **71** 129
  Barsheba **71** 212 222
  Deborah **71** 129 131 211
    212
  Edmund **87** 121
  Edward **87** 344 345
  Frances **87** 344
  Hannah **71** 222
  Henry **71** 129 131 211 212
    219 **90** 228 246
  Jacob J. **87** 344 345
  John **82** 291 294 296
  Martha **82** 291 296 **87** 344
  Mary **71** 129 **87** 344 345
    98 216
  Mary E. **87** 344
  Mary T. **87** 344
  Paul **71** 131 220
  Peggy **83** 36
  Phebe **73** 192
  Polly (Watson) **90** 228 246
  Rachel **71** 131 221
  Sarah **82** 294 296 414
  Sibley **71** 212 223
  Temperance **87** 345
  Thankful Relief **71** 211
    222 **147** 68

PENDEXTER *cont'd*
  Thomas **87** 345
Pendgrass *see* Prendergast
PENDLEBURY —— **105** 96
  Dorothy **127** 263
  Mary **100** 235 **127** 263
  Nicholas **127** 263
PENDLETON —— **55** 350
  105 284 **117** 169
  — Mrs. **71** 124
  A. B. (Mrs.) **103** 155
  Adele Orville **75** 255
  Alcey Ann (Winston)
    112 151
  Alonzo **117** 170
  Amelia (Babcock) **90** 366
  Amos **107** 225 **128** 221
  Andrew **66** 112
  Andrew Lewis (Mrs.)
    102 124
  Ann **81** 159
  Anna Pierce **92** 184
  Azubah (Arey) **87** 9
  B. F. **84** 463
  Benajah **142** 174
  Benjamin **101** 301 303
    104 165 **128** 221
  Benjamin Franklin
    107 225
  Berilla **119** 201
  Brian **58** 107 **59** 420 **60**
    189 358 **71** 124 **81** 104
    90 365 **95** 182 **101** 303
    306 307 **105** 224 **107**
    225 **109** 228 **143** 362
  Catherine **57** 228
  Catherine Thornton
    104 165
  Charlotte **126** 68
  Chrisantin **101** 307
  Clara Amelia (Thorpe)
    107 225
  Clarinda Huntington
    95 163 164
  Cynthia **64** 120
  Darias **91** 332
  Deborah **53** 312
  Dodge **105** 209
  Dorothy **117** 97 **143** 362
  E. H. **101** 299 306 307
  Edmond **112** 89
  Elden F. **117** 167
  Eleanor **90** 366 **107** 225
  Elizabeth (Strother)
    104 165
  Ellen Fitz **87** 296 **88** 167
    90 365 **91** 57 144
  Elliott Hunt **62** 202
  Else **89** 231
  Emily **86** 241
  Enoch Burrows **90** 365
    366
  Ephraim Wood **84** 58
  Esther **77** 39
  Everett Hall **59** 420 **60** 189
    103 320 **104** 246 **117** 97
    143 362
  Frances **81** 104
  Frances Abby **81** 103 104
    95 177
  Frederick Starr **85** 188

PENDLETON *cont'd*
106 222 **107** 131 136
225 **111** 145
Freelove **104** 9
George **117** 168
George (Mrs.) **117** 168
George W. **117** 163
Godfrey **64** 246
Godfride **141** 119
Green **105** 279
Hannah **107** 225
Hannah (Goodenow)
90 366
Hannah M. (Eaton)
117 164
Harriet Chapman **90** 367
Harris **107** 225
Henry **105** 285 **112** 151
J. H. **103** 172
Jabez **81** 463
James **68** 180 **90** 366 **107**
225 **128** 222 **143** 362
James H. **117** 163
James Munroe **90** 367
James Thorpe **107** 225
Jane (Henderson) **90** 91
Jeremiah **128** 298
John **63** 377 **64** 76 **66** 362
77 40 **90** 91 **105** 209
128 221 **134** 332
John B. **91** 332
John H. **103** 172
Jonathan **105** 209
Joseph **81** 104 **90** 366 **105**
209 **107** 225 **117** 170
128 222
Joshua **105** 209 **128** 221
Juddy **77** 230
Judy (Cook) **125** 104
Julia **143** 56
Katharine Brinley
Huntington (King)
95 164
Keturah **77** 45 54
Laura **107** 225 **111** 145
Lavina (Pattane) **84** 463
Leander **87** 7 **88** 328
Lois **77** 40 **95** 177 **101** 298
301-303
Lois (Burdick) **101** 301
Lucinda (Carver) **88** 325
Lucinda C. **124** 39
Lucinda P. **124** 38 39
Lucy **142** 175
Lydia **81** 463 **105** 223 224
286
Lydia (Burrows) **107** 225
Margaret **105** 100
Margaret (Thompson)
117 163
Marion **107** 225
Martha (Hopkins)
103 172
Martha (Kenyon) **107** 225
Mary **77** 45 **81** 104 **88** 325
107 225 **143** 362
Mary (McDowell)
(Chesebrough) **90** 366
Mary Ette (Chapman)
90 365 366
Mary J. (Ward) **117** 163

PENDLETON *cont'd*
Mary Jane (Cook) **107** 225
Mary Josephine (Carver)
87 7 **88** 328 **109** 7
Mary T. **66** 112
Maud Louise (Brown)
107 225
Mehitable (Gardner)
134 332
Nancy **81** 104 **95** 176
Nathan **77** 39 **90** 87 366
128 221
Nathaniel **105** 285
Nestor **125** 104 108
Nettie C. (Harding)
117 167
Oliver **105** 209
Patience (Potts) **90** 366
107 225
Peleg **90** 87 **105** 279
128 220
Phebe (Cole) **90** 366
Phebe (Hawkins) **125** 108
Phineas **81** 104 **88** 326
Priscilla **84** 58
Rebecca **81** 463 **88** 119
Rhoda **77** 39
Rosina **125** 72
Ruby J. **117** 170
Ruth **107** 225
Samuel **63** 350 **105** 209
128 220
Sarah **77** 40 **91** 250 **107** 80
128 220
Sarah Adelaide **102** 228
Sarah Madison **112** 151
Simeon **128** 220
Statira (Rich) **84** 58
Stephen **105** 209
Susan **63** 377 **64** 76 **66** 362
Susan Amelia **86** 443
Susan Strachan **77** 254
Sylvester B. **117** 164
Sylvina **134** 222
Thankful **111** 224
Thomas **88** 325
Urias **87** 9
Wealthy (Carver) **88** 326
William **77** 45 **84** 58 **90**
366 **95** 176 **105** 100 209
107 225 **128** 221
William Kimbrough
95 164
William N. **53** 256
PENDLEY Mary F. **68** 100
PENDOCK John **60** 285
PENDRE
Patience **65** 103
Prudence **65** 103
Solomon **65** 103
PENDREY Alfred Lowell
(Mrs.) **108** 135
Pendrgrass *see*
Prendergast
PENDY William **133** 192
Penell *see* Pennell
PENFIELD Pemfield
_____ (Buller) **109** 35
Abel **109** 36
Abigail **55** 152 **101** 75
Abigail (Pratt) **109** 37

PENFIELD *cont'd*
Abishai **109** 35
Alfred Counselman
109 38
Amos **109** 35
Ann **109** 33 34
Ann (Butler) **109** 38 229
Ann (Cornwell) **109** 33
229
Anne **101** 75-77 **109** 35
122 13 18
Ansel **109** 35
Asahel **109** 35 38
Asenath **109** 35
Augustine **109** 229
Azubah (Thomas) **109** 34
Belinda (Norton) **109** 36
Benjamin **92** 291 **101** 76
109 34
Caroline **106** 109
Caroline (Chandler)
122 13
Caroline E. **122** 13
Clarissa **109** 37
Clarissa (Savage) **109** 36
Cornelia Sterrett **83** 232
92 136 291 **93** 142
Daniel **58** 362 **106** 109
109 36
David **92** 291 **109** 33
Deborah (Kilbourn) **109**
38 229
Dorinda **109** 37
Edward Augustus **109** 36
Edward P. **106** 109
Edyth **103** 119 **106** 123
107 68 137
Elizabeth **56** 186 **58** 75 80
109 35
Elizabeth (Andrews)
109 35
Elizabeth (Bulkley) **92** 291
Elizabeth (Payne) **109** 36
Elizabeth (Shephard)
109 35
Elizabeth (Williams)
109 38
Elizabeth Ann **109** 36
Ellen (Burr) **92** 291
Emeline (Babcock) **109** 36
Emily Matilda **109** 38
Esther **58** 362 363 **59** 62-64
109 35
F. B. **122** 18
Fanny **109** 37
Florence Louise (Bentz)
109 38 228 **120** 77
Frederic Cortland **109** 36
George Henry **109** 36
Hannah **58** 76 80 **94** 284
109 36
Harold William **106** 126
108 228 **109** 38 216 228
Harold William (Mrs.)
108 228 **120** 77
Harriet **109** 36
Helen Dean (Clingan)
92 291 292
Henrietta (Allen) **92** 291
Henrietta Achsah
(Dwight) **109** 228

PENFIELD *cont'd*
Hepzibah **109** 35
Hepzibah Melissa
  (McNary) **109** 38
Hester **58** 363
Hiram Augustus **109** 38
Horace **109** 36
Horace E. **106** 109 **122** 13
  18
Huldah **55** 33
Ira Kilbourn **109** 38
Isaac **58** 76 80 301 302 362
  363 **59** 62-64 **60** 396 398
James **92** 291
Jane (Stewart) **109** 38
Jemima (Hurlbut) **109** 37
Jeremiah **109** 34 38
Jerusha **109** 34 **128** 208
Jerusha (Brewer) **109** 34
Jesse **109** 37
Joanna (Cook) **109** 34
John **85** 411 **101** 76 77
  109 32-34 37 38 229
Jonathan **109** 33 35-38 229
Josephine **85** 411
Josiah **125** 35
Julia Isabelle **85** 411
Louisa D. **106** 109
Louise Martha **109** 229
Lucia **109** 36
Lucinda Norton **109** 37
Lucy **109** 36
Lucy (Wilcox) **109** 38
Lydia **62** 84
Lydia (Knowles) **109** 34
Maria **85** 411
Mary **55** 33 **58** 80 **101** 75-
  77 **109** 34
Mary (Allen) **92** 291
Mary (Bowers) **109** 34
Mary (Lewis) **92** 291 **101**
  75 **109** 32 229
Mary Selina (Bucking-
  ham) **109** 229
Matson Clinton **92** 291
Molly **59** 62
Nelson **109** 35
Norris **144** 272
Oliver **109** 36
Pauline (Russell) **109** 36
Penelope (Eddy) **109** 34
Peter **55** 33 **92** 291
Phebe **109** 37
Pina **59** 62
Prudence **109** 35
Prudence (Dixon) **109** 36
Prudence Augusta **109** 36
Rachel **109** 37
Raymond Stanley **93** 138
Rebecca **101** 75 77
Rollin S. **106** 109
Russell **109** 37
Ruth **109** 37 38
Ruth (Stocking) **109** 37
  229
Ruth Almira (Wilcox)
  109 38
Ruth Maria **109** 36
Sally **109** 35
Samuel **55** 152 **58** 80 **81**
  239 **92** 291 **101** 75-77

PENFIELD *cont'd*
108 228 **109** 32 34 36 37
  229 **120** 77 **122** 18 **123**
  192
Samuel Lewis **61** 109
Sarah **59** 63 **101** 76 **109** 36
  125 35
Sarah (Hall) **109** 37
Sarah Ann **106** 109
Sarah Parmelee (McNary)
  109 38
Silence **109** 33 34
Simeon **109** 33-35
Sophia (Young) **109** 36
Stephen **101** 77 **109** 33 34
Susan Ames **109** 38
Thomas **73** 151 **101** 76
Vienna **109** 36 37
William **60** 396 **62** 84 **85**
  411 **109** 32
William Augustine **109**
  228 229
William Henry **92** 291
William Walter **109** 36
Zebulon **109** 36
PENFOLD Penfolde
  Penifold
Eda **82** 176
Joan **61** 117
John **61** 117
Thomas **65** 240
William **82** 176
PENGELLEY Pengelly
  Penguilly
—— **62** 207
Abigail (Crandall)
  125 242
Mary **72** 221
Susan A. **125** 242
William **125** 242
PENGNET —— **55** xci
Pengra *see* Pingry
Pengry *see* Pingry
Penguilly *see* Pengelley
PENHALLOW Penhalow
—— **58** 233 **83** 195
— Capt. **97** 104
— Mrs. **83** 195 308
A. J. (Mrs.) **83** 308
Abigail **76** 244
Andrew J. **83** 174 **84** 31
Andrew Jackson **83** 422
  438
Anne **76** 243 244
Anthony Wibond **82** 52
Arthur Shurburne **62** vii
Augustus C. **83** 195
Augustus Cheever **82** 423
Benjamin **76** 244 **82** 423
  83 195 **91** 94
Benjamin (Mrs.) **83** 195
Benjamin Hunking
  82 423
Catherine A. M. **84** 31
Chamond **76** 243
Charles **83** 195
Charles Lowell **83** 174
Charles Pearce **82** 423
Charles Sherburne **59**
  vii liii **60** vii xxiv xxxiv
  xliv lxii 118 206 211 316

PENHALLOW *cont'd*
61 vii xx xliii 97 197 204
  312 **62** xxi 100 204 **63**
  vii xx **64** vii xix **65** vii
  xx **66** vii xxxvii **67** vii
  xxi **68** vii xx xxi **69** vii
  xv xxxi **70** vii xv xxvi
  90 **71** vii xvii xviii
  xxxiii 88 **72** xv xxviii 77
  73 v xi 319 **74** 77 78 **76**
  xxx xc 243 245 246
Clara Wendell **83** 174
D. P. **54** 401
Daniel Pearce **54** 402
David **83** 174
David Pearse **83** 185 189
David Peirce **83** 174
Deblois Peirce **83** 174
Dunlap Pearce **54** 402
Eliza J. **83** 302
Elizabeth **67** 107 **76** 244
Elizabeth J. **83** 301
Elizabeth Joy **83** 174
Elizabeth Warner Pitts
  76 244 245
Ellen M. **84** 31
Eugene **83** 174
Eveline Blunt **76** 246
Hannah **58** 233 **60** 195
Hannah Austin **83** 174
Harriet **76** 244
Harriet Louise **83** 174
Harriet P. **83** 174
Helen Olcott **76** 246
Huldah (Canfield)
  134 333
Hunking **76** 244 **82** 423
  83 36
Hunking (Mrs.) **82** 423
Jane Smith **76** 246
John **56** 238 **58** lxvii **60**
  218 **67** 107 **76** 243-245
  82 52 **83** 174 **96** 223 224
  106 268
John Huntington Coffin
  76 246
Julia Maria **82** 423 **83** 174
Louise **83** 308
Louise Harrison **76** 246
Lucy E. **82** 423
Lucy H. **83** 195
Lucy Hart **82** 423
Lydia **58** 227
M. **82** 423
M. Ellen (Aspinwall) **83**
  422 438
Maranda **134** 333
Margaret **83** 174 195
Margaret Scott **82** 423
Maria Louise **83** 174 299
  301
Mary **55** 294 **73** 239
  76 243 244
Mary (Cutt) **96** 380
Mary F. (Yeaton) **83** 185
  189
Mary King **76** 246
Mary P. **83** 174
Mary Warner **76** 246
Nathan **134** 333
O. W. **83** 308

PENHALLOW *cont'd*
Oliver **83** 174
Oliver Wendell **82** 423
  83 174 195
Pearce Wentworth **76**
  243-246 **82** 423
Phebe **55** 294 **73** 239
Polly **140** 34
Richard **76** 243 **134** 333
Richard Collings **82** 423
Richard Wibird **106** 268
Samuel **51** 44 **55** 294 **58**
  227 233 **64** 98 **69** 361 **73**
  239 **76** 243 244 **83** 36 **86**
  268 **95** 265 **96** 380 **102**
  74 **106** 265
Sarah **76** 244
Sarah Almira **54** 402
Susan **82** 423
Susan Purcell **83** 174 298
  301
PENHULBURY
Ellys **82** 338
PENIALE
Dorothy **65** 289
John **65** 289
Penifold *see* Penfold
Peniman *see* Penniman
PENINGE Anne **59** 398
Penington *see* Pennington
PENKELL Peter **65** 50
PENKVIL Penkivil
John **113** 220
Martha (Jones) **113** 220
PENLAND
Mary (Casey) **101** 338
PENLEY Penly
—— **112** 173
Almon L. **73** 235
Augusta S. **73** 235
Elmira **86** 300
PENN Pen Penne
—— **51** 125 **54** 373
  55 116 131
— Gov. **108** 274
Agnes **54** 336 338 **141** 26
Alice **54** 335-337
Ann **54** 325 328 333 336
  338
Anna **54** 330
Anne **54** 325 328 337 338
Bartholomew **54** 327
  55 332
Catherine **54** 325 327
Christian **54** 325 327 334
  105 180
Christiana **54** 332
Dennis **54** 325 332 333
Edith **54** 337
Edward **73** 275
Edward Lloyd **73** 277
Eleanor **54** 325 327-330
  338
Elizabeth **54** 325 328 330
  334 337 338 **91** 180
George **54** 325 327-330
  333-335
Giles **54** 325-329 333 334
Gulielma **54** 331
Gulielma Maria **54** 325
  330-332 335

PENN *cont'd*
Hannah **54** 325 331-333
  66 282 **102** 177 **113** 163
Hannah Margareta
  54 325 332
Hanson **73** 279
Harry **54** 336
Henry **54** 325 328 334 337
James **52** 64 **54** 327 **55** 333
  93 164 **102** 177-179 **111**
  14 15
Jane **54** 328 336 337
Janet **54** 330
Joan **54** 325 326 328 330
  335-338
John **52** 102 **54** 325 327 332
  335-338 **55** 332 **145** 109
Joseph **54** 327
Juliana **54** 325 332
Letitia **54** 325
Margaret **54** 325 331-336
  56 204
Margery **54** 325 328
Marie **54** 325 333
Martha **51** 255 **54** 325 328
  331
Mary **54** 325 331-333 336
  337 **88** 281
Matthew **54** 338
Nancy **125** 102
Rachel **54** 325 327
Ralph **54** 337
Richard **54** 325 330 332
  334-336 339 **129** 141 142
Robert **54** 335 336 338
Roger **54** 325 326
Samuel **64** 227
Sarah **54** 325 333 **66** 351
Sarah Elizabeth **78** 325
Springett **54** 325 331
Stephen **54** 338
Susan **54** 330
Susanna **54** 325 333 338
Thomas **54** 325 330-332
  336 339 **148** 109
Walter **51** 351
William **51** 72 **52** 32 382
  54 237 325-338 **55** 335
  56 204 **58** 109 **59** lix **61**
  403 **62** 94 **63** 109 306 **64**
  376 **67** 306 **69** 356 **71**
  360 369 **88** 306 **93** 385
  99 68 82 143 250 **101**
  165 **102** 156 **106** 166
  110 224 251 **117** 274-
  279 **122** 180 **123** 257
  131 5 132 **141** 26 **145** 25
  148 40
Penna *see* De Penna
Pennaman *see* Penniman
PENNANT John **64** 257
Penne *see* Penn
PENNEFEATHER Eliza
  (Montgomery)
  112 301
PENNELL Penell Pennel
  Pennil Penniel
  ____ (Preston?) **120** 319
Aaron Edgecombe
  131 239
Abraham **73** 258

PENNELL *cont'd*
Agnes **74** 106
Agnes (Trefry) **131** 157
Andrew **73** 258
Ann (Peay) **120** 319
Archibald **73** 258
Arethusa (Whitney)
  131 239
Austin Peay **117** 319 **120**
  319 **121** 80
Betsey (Gaines) **85** 49
Catherine M. **125** 177
Charles Whials **131** 239
Clement **145** 44
Deborah **71** 126 **74** 106
Edgar Oscar **131** 239
Eleanor **73** 258
Elizabeth **100** 227
Ella A. **100** 86
Esther **73** 258
Eunice (Currier) **97** 231
Evelyn **117** 319
Flora **117** 319
George Neill **120** 319
  121 80
Hannah **68** 96 **71** 216
  73 258
Hannah P. **131** 239
Isaac **73** 258
Isaac E. **131** 239
Jacob **74** 106
James **73** 258
John **73** 258 **85** 49 **117** 319
Joseph Austin **117** 319
Joseph Preston **117** 319
  120 319 **121** 80
Laura A. **131** 239
Leah Isabel **100** 112
Lucy **58** 339
Margaret **117** 265
Mary **71** 126 **73** 258
  117 319
Matthew **131** 157
Mildred **120** 319 **121** 80
Mildred (Turner) **120** 319
Mildred Ann **117** 319
Mildred Ann (Peay)
  121 80
Moses **73** 258
Rachel **71** 131 **73** 258
Rebecca **105** 33
Robert **73** 258
Robert Brown **95** 147
Samuel **97** 231
Sarah **71** 125 **73** 258
Shirley **89** 381
Susanna **71** 126
Thomas **58** 339 **71** 216 217
  74 106
Walter **71** 124-126
Walter Otis **91** 142 **92** 204
William **94** 247
William Austin **117** 319
William Henry **131** 239
William Lee **117** 319 **120**
  319 **121** 80
Pennepacker *see*
  Pennypacker
PENNEWELL
Sarah **114** 44
Penney *see* Penny

Penniel *see* Pennell
Pennifield *see* Penfield
Pennil *see* Pennell
PENNIMAN Peniman
  Pennaman
  —— **56** 328 **62** 205 **70** 22
    23 109 143 **92** 245 257
    349
  — Col. **62** 17 18 130
  — Mr. **52** 124 **70** 138
  — Mrs. **62** 24 **93** 301
  Abigail **59** 155 365 **92** 131
    119 112
  Abigail (Butterfield)
    125 101
  Albert **92** 257
  Albert B. **92** 108 115
  Albert Swan **92** 128
  Alice **59** 290
  Alice S. **69** 137
  Amos **77** 236 **92** 126-128
    131 245 257 349 **93** 70
    94 376
  Ann (Jenks) **95** 349
  Anna **59** 287
  Anna (Chase) **87** 340
  Atherton **125** 101
  Barsillia **93** 301
  Betsey **61** 174
  Betsey (Mayo) **123** 120 124
  Caty Greenleaf **59** 287
  Chiron **95** 349
  Daniel **57** 392 **78** 184 405
    123 120 124
  Deborah **57** 392 **59** 155
    158
  Dorcas **60** 43
  Elias **95** 349
  Eliza Ann **82** 182 409
  Elizabeth **59** 88 90 157-
    159 270 271 273 **66** 176
    125 181 **144** 223
  Elizabeth (Parmenter)
    95 348
  Elizabeth J. **88** 286
  Ellen **59** 155
  Esther **55** 263
  Eunice **60** 43
  Evelina **92** 131
  Ezra **60** 43
  G. W. **52** 376
  George R. **77** 232
  George Wallace **54** xli
    55 439 **56** xxi
  George Washington **82**
    182 409
  Georgiana G. **55** 423
  Hannah **59** 153 157 158
    107 263
  Harden **140** 69
  Harriet M. **88** 282
  Henry H. **60** 40
  Hulda (Wheelock) **58** 95
  Huldah (White) **95** 348
    349
  Ida B. (Jutte) (Walther)
    95 349
  Jabez **62** 205
  Jacob **99** 192
  James **51** 70 171 **52** 23 **59**
    91 155 158 273 365 **62**

PENNIMAN *cont'd*
  132 **78** 310 **95** 348 **99** 80
  232 **107** 69 236 **109** 228
    113 145 **119** 112
  James A. **91** 199
  James Lanman **95** 348 349
  John **59** 156 157 **92** 262 263
  John A. **90** 46
  John M. **59** 287
  Jonathan **59** 156 159 287
  Joseph **53** 346 **59** 87 88 153
    154 156-158 271 **63** 76
    70 182 **91** 94 **105** 196
    107 219 **116** 79 **121** 248
  Joseph H. **87** 340
  Josiah **55** 263 **59** 157 158
  Josiah Harmar **75** xxv 65
    95 297 348 **96** 164
  Judith **70** 109
  Julia Ann (Blue) **90** 46
  Kate L. **82** 182 409
  Lois **82** 21
  Lucy **62** 24
  Lucy S. **77** 229
  Lucy Swan **92** 126
  Lydia **51** 70
  Lydia (Eliot) **95** 348 **107**
    69 236
  Margaret **140** 235
  Maria Davis (Hoomer)
    95 348
  Marian Chandler
    (Lanman) **95** 349
  Martha Anna (Eaton)
    (Sayward) 108
  Mary **51** 232 **56** lxxi **57**
    392 **91** 310 **93** 301 **119**
    112
  Mary (Farnum) **95** 348
  Mary (O'Brien) **99** 192
  Mary Brewer **88** 77
  Mary Suttin **125** 216
  Maryan **62** 23
  Maude Louise **82** 409
  Mildred I. (Basford)
    83 422 438
  Moses **59** 157 **100** 295
  Nancy **59** 285
  Nathan **57** 392 **59** 270
    95 348
  Newell W. **83** 422 438
  Obadiah **95** 349
  Olive (Whipple) **95** 349
  Peter **56** 84 **58** 95
  Priscilla **59** 287
  Rebecca (Edmond)
    100 295
  Ruth **60** 42 **78** 73 **135** 39 40
  Ruth (Stetson) **135** 39 40
  Samuel **59** 87 88 90 155-
    159 270 271 273 **66** 176
    95 348 **105** 196
  Sarah **59** 154 **86** 341
    107 219
  Sarah (Bass) (Stone)
    107 219
  Thomas **85** 371 **108** 85
  Thomas Jefferson **55** 423
  Waiting **59** 88
  William **59** 87 365 **62** 21
    140 235

PENNIMAN *cont'd*
  William Wood **82** 182 409
PENNINGTON
  Penington
  Penyngton
  —— **53** 460 **54** 332
  — Mr. **143** 326
  Adaline E. (Hodge)
    83 182 185
  Alice **54** 342
  Asenath **115** 130
  Catherine **98** 228
  Daniel **54** 342
  Edmund **111** 241
  Edward **107** 267 **117** 277
  Elizabeth **96** 107
  Elizabeth Anderson **96** 72
  Elizabeth Ann (Stirling)
    96 72
  Ellen P. **120** 154
  Ephraim **81** 130
  Frances (Palgrave) **102**
    92 95
  Isaac **54** 342
  Jacob **98** 228
  Jennie May **84** 191
  John **64** 342 **65** 234 **94** 277
    115 57
  John H. **83** 182 185
  Josiah **96** 72
  Judith **54** 342
  Kenneth **111** 153 241
  Lydia Ann **113** 309
  Marcella **86** 437
  Robert **54** 342 **134** 29
  Samuel Hayes **61** 315
  Sarah **63** 31
  Sarah (Fitz Randolph)
    98 53
  Thomas **98** 53
  William **57** 317 **102** 92 95
PENNO Lydia R. **125** 238
PENNOCK
  Adonijah **57** 287
  Ann **79** 357 **80** 51
  Betsey **57** 287
  Daniel **138** 104
  Fannie Blodgett **82** 180
  Hannah **104** 103
  James **76** 133
  Jonathan Clark **82** 180
  Lewis **104** 103
  Mary R. **57** 287
  Maud Josephine **82** 180
  Peter **76** 133
  William **138** 104
PENNOD Bob **116** 152
PENNOT John **117** 212
PENNOYER Pennoyre
  Penoyar Penoyer
  Abigail **72** 215 **108** 290
  Adelia **103** 153
  Caroline **103** 153
  Charles Huntington **77**
    xxix 79 **104** 141 **118** 68
  Christina (Powers)
    107 302
  Daniel **103** 153
  Daniel C. **103** 153
  Elizabeth **106** 171 **108**
    288-290

PENNOYER *cont'd*
Elizabeth (Scofield)
  108 288
Frances Tracy (Morgan)
  97 341
Gould S. **103** 153
Hanford **103** 153
James **120** 92
Jonathan **107** 302
Lucy (Perry) **116** 104
Lydia (Knapp) **108** 290
Martha **71** 244 **83** 261
  108 287 289 290
Martha (Josselyn) **108** 287
Mary **108** 289 290
Mary (Gifford) **130** 42
Mary Faull **78** 171
Nancy **107** 302
Paul G. (Mrs.) **97** 341
Paul Geddes **84** 339
  85 188
Reuben **108** 294 **130** 42
Robert **108** 287-290
Rose (Hobson) **108** 287
Sally **80** 272
Sally (Church) **103** 153
Sallyann **103** 153
Samuel **108** 287 294
Thomas **108** 288-290
Truman **116** 104
Wedworth Clark **78** 171
William **71** 244 **108** 287-
  290 **134** 27
PENNSLEY
Nathaniel **91** 332
PENNY Penney Penye
  —— **103** 264
  — Mr. **142** 135
A. J. **99** 133
Abigail **75** 110-112 119
  311-313 **76** 114 195 252
  257 261 **93** 246 **115** 216
Abigail (Nason) **95** 191
Abraham **75** 110 **76** 103
Ada **76** 103 179 180
Addie **92** 341
Allan **79** 414
Andrew J. **93** 246
Annis **92** 185
Arioch W. **93** 245
Arthur J. **93** 246
Barnarde **110** 194 **147** 251
Benjamin **76** 103 **87** 207
Betsey **76** 252
Bridge **110** 194
Bridget **84** 290
Charles **65** 23 **91** 332 **94** 30
Christiana **76** 252
Cicely **83** 352 354 **90** 190
Daniel **75** 110 **76** 104 258
  87 206
David **75** 137
Dorothy **77** 75
Ebenezer **75** 311
Edmund **54** 166 **101** 101
Edwin Stanton **99** 133
Eli **75** 112 **76** 110
Elizabeth (Rand) **125** 58
  59
Esther L. **92** 341
Frances **95** 191

PENNY *cont'd*
Freeman **92** 341
Gabriel **143** 262
George **76** 114 252 261
  145 349
Giles **63** 162
Hannah **101** 101 103 **106**
  234 **118** 170
Hannah (Bodge) **101** 101
Hannah (Porter) **108** 183
Henry **69** 359 361 **83** 352
  354 355 **85** 316 **88** 255
  256
Huldah **93** 245
Ida J. **93** 246
Isaac **78** 410
J. W. **99** 133
James **91** 332 **95** 191
Jane **79** 414 **83** 355
Japheth **94** 30
Joanna **75** 119 **76** 179 192
John **62** 330 **75** 110 311 312
  76 103 104 106 107 109
  114 195 **77** 75 **105** 163
  106 234 125 58 **145** 364
Johnson **76** 104
Jonathan **76** 109 **145** 349
Joseph **76** 103
Joseph H. **93** 245
Josiah **93** 245
Laury **96** 134
Lydia **63** 255
Lydia (Nason) **95** 191
Margaret **75** 137
Maria **92** 185
Mary **56** 91 **74** 213 225 256
  75 45 **82** 211 **83** 55
Mary J. **93** 245
Nehemiah Gray **75** 111
Olivea **76** 104 258
Pelatiah **74** 256 **75** 312
Phebe A. **94** 30
Rachel **55** 373 **83** 14
Rachel (Abbot) **83** 14
Rufus **93** 245
Salathiel **75** 312 **145** 362
Samuel **65** 126
Sarah **75** 311 312 **76** 103
  104 106 107 109 110 195
  260 **85** 316
Sarah J. **93** 246
Simon **114** 182
Stephen **76** 107
Susanna **95** 88
Thomas **55** 373 **75** 45 46
  110-112 119 311-313 **76**
  103 106 179 180 195 257
  83 14 **93** 245 **110** 194
  147 251 252
Thomas (Mrs.) **99** 170
Timothy **142** 146
William **110** 194 **147** 251
  252
PENNYNGE
Arthur **75** 292
PENNYPACKER
Pennepacker
Morton **93** 306
Samuel Whitaker **53** 378
  63 306 **96** 181
Samuel Whittier **55** 237

PENOW Peter **127** 305
Penoyar *see* Pennoyer
Penoyer *see* Pennoyer
PENRICE John **52** 312
  Joseph **83** 375
PENROD Annie **84** 239
PENROSE Penros
  —— **58** 209
  —— (Neale) **116** 248
Abel **117** 67
Abigail **116** 245 **117** 60 67
Abigail (Barker) **117** 112
Abigail (Cadwallader)
  117 69
Abigail (Foulke) **117** 68
Abraham **117** 68
Abraham Devonsher
  117 64
Adelaide **117** 112
Adella Delilah **117** 202
Agnes Finlayson
  (McKechnie) **117** 199
Aimstiss (Weffe) **116** 240
Albert **117** 109 111
Alexander **117** 112
Alexander Jeremy
  Peckover **117** 207
Alexander Peckover
  Doyle **117** 203 206
Alfred Ernest **117** 198
Alice **116** 239-245
Alice (Chambers) **116** 241
Alice (Horton) **117** 116
Alice (Raw) **116** 245
Alison Mary **117** 205
Amos **117** 69
Angela Priscilla
  Elizabeth **117** 207
Ann **116** 240 252 **117** 58
  61 65-67 69 110 196
Ann (Goff) **117** 64
Ann (Inglefield) **116** 254
Ann (Roberts) **117** 66
Ann (Till) **117** 59
Ann (Wiley) **117** 60
Ann Agnes (Lillingstone)
  117 114
Ann Elizabeth (Swickard)
  117 110
Ann Isobel (Noel)
  117 207
Ann Margaret **117** 203
Anna **116** 247 **117** 112
Anna (Beale) **117** 57
Anna (Crew) **117** 111
Anna (Russell) **116** 247
Anna (Slater) **117** 112
Anna Eliza **117** 108
Anna Hallowell **116** 239
Anne **116** 240 241 244 246-
  248 253 **117** 57 63 64 70
  107 108
Anne (Cooper) **116** 254
Anne (Doyle) **117** 70
Anne (Hunter) **117** 58
Anne (Robinson) **117** 108
Anne (Storye) **116** 245
Anne (Thacker) **117** 112
Anne Rosemary
  (Nicholson) **117** 205
Anne Shannon **117** 112

PENROSE *cont'd*
Annie (Barton) **117** 203
Annie (Bowles) **117** 198
Annie Charlotte (McNeill)
  117 200
Annie Elizabeth **117** 204
Annie Floy **117** 202
Annie Myrtle **117** 202
Anthony William
  Roland **117** 207
Arthur Cruden **117** 115
Arthur Edward Doyle
  117 198 203
Arthur John **117** 115
Barbara Coghill **117** 205
Barclay **117** 110
Barker Thacker **117** 112
Bartholomew **116** 237
  117 198
Beatrice (Quickly) **117** 204
Beatrix Willie **117** 201
Benjamin **116** 251 **117** 59
  66 68
Bernard Edmund **117**
  203 207
Bertha (Rackham) **117** 203
Bertha Gwendolen
  (Baker) **117** 206
Bessie Holly (Boyd)
  117 206
Beth Lenore (Littrell)
  117 206
Boies **78** 90 **95** 97 **116** 237
Bridget **117** 107 109 195
Bridget (Welsted) **117** 64
Casey Ann (Barnes)
  117 115
Catherine **116** 238 248
Catherine (Davis) **116** 248
Charles **117** 110 111
  130 234
Charles Bingham **58** 209
  59 xliv
Charles Cooper **117** 113
Charlotte **117** 58 112
Charlotte (Harmon)
  117 112
Christopher **116** 252 253
  117 58
Clarence Rupert **117** 203
Clarkson T. **117** 110
Constance Monica
  117 200
Cooper **116** 250 251 254
  117 62 63 107 113 114
  200
Daniel **116** 246 249 254
  117 62 70
Daniel Dalbey **117** 116
David **117** 65 66
David Hugh **117** 205
Deborah (Pike) **117** 65
Della (Murray) **117** 206
Denis **116** 238
Derrick Roch **117** 205
Desmond James **117** 205
Devonsher George
  117 108
Diana **117** 112
Dinah **117** 112
Donald Leroy **117** 206

PENROSE *cont'd*
Donald William Henry
  117 108
Dora (Trumbell) **117** 112
Dorothy **116** 240 241 244
  248 254
Edith Florence (Preston)
  117 204
Edward **54** 340 **116** 240-
  242 244 **117** 112 198
Edward A. **117** 203
Edward Alick **117** 115
Edward Henry **117** 112
Edward John McNeill
  117 200
Edward Rawdon **117**
  114 201
Edward Samuel **117** 115
Edward Victor **117** 203
Edwin **117** 109
Eleanor **116** 243 **117** 66
Eleanor (Parvin) **117** 68
Eleanor Mary **117** 206
Eleanor Maud Charlotte
  117 201
Eliza **117** 110
Eliza Jane **117** 112
Elizabeth **116** 238 241 243-
  245 248 251 **117** 57 58
  60 62-64 60 70 107 110-
  112 114 207
Elizabeth (Beale) **117** 57
Elizabeth (Dennis) **117** 62
Elizabeth (Duckett)
  117 57
Elizabeth (Fawcett) **116**
  244 248
Elizabeth (Gilbert)
  117 112
Elizabeth (Shannon)
  117 70
Elizabeth (Sparrow)
  117 108
Elizabeth (Tomlinson)
  117 69
Elizabeth (Watherston)
  117 114
Elizabeth (Wilson)
  116 242
Elizabeth Constance
  117 204
Elizabeth E. **117** 198
Elizabeth Harriet Anne
  Agnes **117** 115
Elizabeth Josephine
  (Peckover) **117** 202
Elizabeth Josephine
  Doyle **117** 198
Elizabeth Lee (Miller)
  117 207
Elizabeth W. Tait **117** 115
Ella **117** 116
Ella Prendergast
  (Triscott) **117** 113
Ellen **117** 69 207
Elvira **117** 111
Emily Kathleen **117** 115
Emlen G. **117** 111
Emma **117** 116
Enoch **117** 67
Ephraim **117** 69

PENROSE *cont'd*
Eric Robert **117** 203
Esther **116** 243
Esther (Tomlinson)
  117 67
Ethel Charlotte (Coghill)
  117 199
Ethel Mary Judith York
  117 200
Euphemia B. **117** 116
Evalina **117** 116
Evaline M. **117** 203
Evan **117** 67
Evelyn Cooper **117** 200
  205
Evelyn Hunter (Jones)
  117 199
Everard **117** 68 109 195
Faith (Tattersall) **116** 244
  245
Fanny (Crawford)
  117 112
Florence Jane **117** 204
Frances Alice (Sandford)
  117 115
Frances Amelia **117** 115
Frances Anne **117** 107
Frances Anne Henrietta
  117 114
Frances Constance
  (Smyth) (Saxon)
  117 206
Frances Elizabeth **117** 112
Frances Henrietta Ing-
  ham **117** 204
Frances Isabel Susan
  Eleanor **117** 201
Frances Matilda (Austen)
  117 113
Francis **116** 251 254 **117** 57
  62 64 70 112
Francis Randall **117** 64
Francis Sinclair **117** 199
Frank B. **117** 111
Freda Irene Mary
  (Hayward) **117** 203
Frederick **117** 112
Frederick George **117**
  112 198
Gainor **117** 68
George **116** 251 **117** 57
  58 64 65 70 106 112 198
George Cooper **117** 112
George Devonsher
  117 108
George H. **116** 237
George Pike **117** 65
George Randall **117** 63
  108
George Richard **117** 203
George Rooke **117** 70
  112 199
George Washington
  117 116
Georgiana Isabella
  (Keane) **117** 114
Geraldine **117** 107
Geraldine Frances
  Louisa **117** 113
Geraldine Patricia
  117 204

PENROSE *cont'd*
Gertrude **117** 107 113
Gertrude (Lunham)
  117 203
Grace **116** 248 **117** 62
Grace (Davis) **116** 254
Gwendolen **117** 203
Hannah **117** 61 62 65 66
  69 70 110 111 116
Hannah (Hicks) **117** 108
Hannah (Jarrett) **117** 68
Hannah (Thacker) **117** 62
Hannah M. (Lightfoot)
  117 111
Hannah S. **117** 110
Hannah Smith **59** lxxvii
Harriet (Hardy) **117** 113
Harriet Lucille **117** 206
Harry Jefferson **117** 202
  206
Harry Whitney **117** 206
Helen Rae **117** 206
Helena (Townsend)
  117 114
Henrietta **117** 107
Henrietta Charlotte
  (Clark) **117** 199
Henrietta Mary (Tibbs)
  117 201
Henry **116** 239 **117** 64
  108 112
Henry Barton **117** 203
Henry Francis Keane
  117 114
Henry Herbert **117** 115
Henry Joseph **117** 112
  198 203
Henry Walter **117** 198 203
Herbert Frederick
  117 198
Hester **116** 241 243
Hester (Gollock) **117** 107
Hilda Lovett (Robertson)
  117 114
Honor Ashley Pettitot
  117 200
Inez Maxine (Whitney)
  117 206
Irene **117** 203
Irene Hester (Smith)
  117 115
Isaac **117** 60-62 68 69 109
Isaac C. **117** 111
Isabel (Byarley) **117** 207
Isabel (Wilford) **117** 199
Isabel Montserrat (Nevill)
  117 201
Isabella **117** 62
Isaiah **117** 65
Israel **117** 66
J. Denis **116** 248 **117** 64
Jacob **116** 251 **117** 64 108
  111
Jacob Hibbs **117** 70
James **117** 63 64 69 70 106
  110 111
James Bernard Killigrew
  117 207
James Doyle **117** 112 198
  202

PENROSE *cont'd*
James Doyle (Mrs.)
  117 203
James Edward **117** 63
  113 199
James Godfrey **117** 205
James Good **117** 204
James Henry Brabazon
  117 113
James Ronald **116** 238
  240 248 253 254 **117** 59
  64 198 203
James Steadman **117** 202
James William Edward
  117 107
Jane **116** 242-244 246 **117**
  57 58 61 66 67 111 112
  116
Jane Isabel (Malone)
  117 198
Jane P. **117** 116
Janet **83** 345
Janet Elizabeth **117** 203
Janet Katharine **117** 205
Jason **117** 70 110
Jean **116** 248 **117** 203
Jennie E. (Stoddard)
  117 111
Jesse **117** 59 68 109 110
Joan **116** 242 **117** 203
Joan Catherine **117** 205
Johanna Anna **116** 255
John **116** 238-245 247 248
  251 253 254 **117** 57 59
  61-64 66 67 69 70 106
  107 198
John Addison **117** 112
John Albert **117** 202
John Anne **116** 255
John Barnes **117** 116
John Barton **117** 203
John D. **117** 111
John Denis FitzGerald
  117 205
John Dennis **117** 107 113
  199
John Ernest **117** 115
John Hughes **117** 111
John Pim **116** 254 **117** 64
  108
John Samuel Sandford
  117 115
John T. **117** 198
John Trevenan **117** 114
  200
John Ware Edgar **117** 204
Jonathan **117** 59 65-67 207
Joscelin Hugh **117** 205
Joscelyn Denis **116** 238
  250 **117** 63 200 204
Joseph **116** 251-253 **117**
  59 60 66-70 110 111 197
  201
Joseph Jacob **117** 70
Joseph Pike **117** 65
Judith **116** 242
Judith Joan **117** 205
Katharine **116** 244 245
Katharine (Lournedale)
  116 244

PENROSE *cont'd*
Katharine Ellen (Forsyth)
  117 205
Katharine Harriet
  (Thackwell) **117** 201
Katharine St. Aubyn
  117 200
Kenneth Kitson **117** 203
Keziah (Speakman)
  117 67
Laura **117** 202
Laura (Power) **117** 205
Lavinia **117** 109 110
Lewis **117** 196 197 202
Lewis Edwin **117** 202 206
Lindley **117** 111
Lionel Sharples **117** 203
  207
Louisa **117** 107
Louisa Josephine Pettitot
  117 114 199
Louisa Pettitot
  (Fitzgerald) **117** 107
Louise (Hyde) **117** 114
Lucy Barrington **117** 199
Lydia **117** 116
M. J. **117** 198
Mabel (Wigginton)
  117 198
Mabel Frances **117** 115
Mahlon **117** 70 110
Margaret **116** 245 252
  253 255 **117** 57 61 64 67-
  69 106 110
Margaret (Godfrey)
  116 249
Margaret (Jamison)
  117 66
Margaret (Leathes)
  117 207
Margaret (Leedes)
  116 240
Margaret (Lonsdale)
  116 239
Margaret (Pim) **117** 108
Margaret (Randall)
  117 64
Margaret (Wright) **117** 61
Margaret Manliffe
  117 198
Margaret Maria **117** 57
  108
Maria **117** 62 64 108 116
Maria (Clendenon)
  117 110
Maria Teresa **117** 64
Marian (Marshall)
  117 203
Marion Annette
  Georgina **117** 108
Marion Elizabeth (Cooke)
  117 108
Mark **116** 239 **117** 109
Martha **116** 243 **117** 65-67
  109
Martha (Edwards) **117** 67
Martha (Harmer) **117** 110
Martha (James) **117** 65
Mary **116** 240-243 247 248
  251-254 **117** 57 59-61 64-
  70 106 107 110 111 207

PENROSE *cont'd*
Mary (Chaytor) **116** 252
Mary (Gilbert) **117** 110 111
Mary (Grattan) **117** 198
Mary (Hall) **116** 248
Mary (Hartzell) **117** 66
Mary (Hawkes) **117** 64 107
Mary (Heacock) **117** 59
Mary (Martin) **117** 62
Mary (Molloy) **117** 108
Mary (Neale) **117** 62
Mary (Osborne) **117** 106
Mary (Randall) **117** 63
Mary (Roberts) **117** 67
Mary (Spencer) **117** 109
Mary (Strawn) **117** 196
Mary Anne **117** 106
Mary Barbara **117** 202
Mary Elizabeth **117** 107 113 202
Mary Elizabeth (Lewis) **117** 201
Mary Esme Violet **117** 200
Mary Geraldine Harriet **117** 201
Mary Gertrude (Dunne) **117** 108
Mary Gladys **117** 206
Mary Jane **117** 116
Mary Jane (Naylor) **117** 111
Mary Jane (Schroeder) **117** 198
Mary Josephine **117** 203
Mary L. **117** 116 198
Mary Pike **117** 65
Maryly B. **144** 362
Matilda **117** 70
Matilda Sophia Georgina **117** 113
Matthew **116** 240 241 243 **117** 207
Maud Beatrice (Kitson) **117** 203
Maye **117** 114
Meribah **117** 110
Mildred (Worthington) **117** 111
Miraetta **117** 197
Morris **117** 68
Myra **117** 197
N. R. **117** 116
Nathan **117** 67 108 109 115 116
Nathan Linville **117** 110
Nathan R. **117** 115
Nathaniel **116** 245
Nellie (Osler) **117** 205
Nevill Coghill **117** 200 205
Nicholas **116** 239 240
Nicholas James Dennis **117** 205
Olive (Thompson) **117** 202
Oliver **117** 207
Oliver J. **117** 110

PENROSE *cont'd*
Olivia (Thompson) **117** 197
Osborn **117** 110
Patricia Mary Alice **117** 114
Patrick Edwin **117** 203
Pearl Ines **117** 199
Phebe **116** 253 254 **117** 59-61 65 66 68 69
Phebe Rebecca (Jones) **117** 202
Philip **116** 239 240 242 244
Phyllis Mary **117** 200
Rachel **117** 67 109 110
Rachel (Fratt) **117** 68
Rachel (Hillman) **117** 67
Rachel (Nevins) **117** 64
Rachel Ann **117** 110
Raymond James **117** 203
Rebecca **116** 251 **117** 2 58 61
Rebecca (Ball) **117** 67
Rebecca (Farmer) **117** 110
Rebecca (Thomas) **117** 62
Rebecca Lelia **117** 198
Rene (Wilson) **117** 203
Rhoda **117** 110
Richard **116** 239-241 243 245 249 251 252 254 **117** 59 61 62 70 110
Richard Lewis **117** 206
Robert **116** 240 241 243 245-249 251-253 **117** 58 60-62 64-66 68 109 110 113
Robert Cooper **117** 114
Robert FitzGerald **117** 114
Robert Samuel **117** 112
Robert Tait **117** 115
Robert Uniacke FitzGerald **117** 107 113
Robert William **116** 250 251 **117** 108 115 198 203
Robert William Edward **117** 201
Roger John **117** 207
Roland Algernon **117** 203 207
Rory Desmond Fane **117** 205
Rosemary Geraldine **117** 206
Rosemary Ruth **117** 205
Ruth Esme **117** 204 205
Samuel **116** 249-251 254 **117** 57 59 63 64 66-69 106-108 112 114 198 207
Samuel George **117** 108
Samuel Neale **117** 62 70 106 112
Sarah **117** 57 59 60 62-70 106 109-111
Sarah (Dalbey) **117** 116
Sarah (Edgar) **117** 198
Sarah (Evans) **117** 62
Sarah (Hibbs) **117** 69
Sarah (Roberts) **117** 67
Sarah (Starr) **117** 68
Sarah (Welstead) **117** 114

PENROSE *cont'd*
Sarah (Wiley) **117** 59
Sarah Ann **117** 70
Sarah Anne (Cooke) **117** 108
Sarah Eliza **117** 112 198
Sarah Elizabeth **117** 107 111 115
Sarah Elizabeth (Cleckner) **117** 202
Sarah Jane **117** 204
Sheila Margaret **117** 207
Shirley Victoria **117** 207
Sibyl (Woodhead) **117** 203
Spencer **89** 132
Steadman **116** 253 **117** 109 195 196
Steadman (Mrs.) **117** 196
Susan **117** 205
Susan (Pim) **116** 254
Susan A. (Wood) **117** 110
Susan Alice **117** 115
Susan Ann **117** 116
Susan Ella **117** 114
Susanna **117** 61 68
Susanna (Foulke) **117** 66
Susanne **117** 64
Sylvia Alice (Green) **117** 200
Sylvia Janet **117** 200
Tacy **117** 109
Thomas **116** 237 239-242 244 **117** 57 61 62 64 67 69 70 110 112
Thomasine (Whincop) (Vaux) **116** 245
Valentine Andree (Boue) **117** 207
Valeria C. **69** 201
Virgil Clare **117** 206
Washington Hicks **117** 109 116
Weston Boyd **117** 206
William **116** 239-241 243-247 249-251 253 254 **117** 57 59-69 106-110 114 197
William C. **117** 198
William Dennis **117** 206
William Edward **117** 63
William H. **117** 110
William Henry **117** 64 106 108 114 204
William Oscar **117** 202
William Robert **117** 115 201
William W. **117** 111
William Watherston **117** 115
Zoe Louise (Becher) **117** 205
PENROSE-FITZGERALD
Cecil Mary (Goldie-Scott) **117** 204
Cecil Philippa Uniacke **117** 204
Charles Bryan **117** 199
Charles Cooper **117** 199
Edward Uniacke **117** 199

PENROSE-FITZGER'D *cont'd*
Elizabeth (Hewson)
  117 199
Elizabeth Constance
  117 204
Eugenie Beatrice
  Gwendoline Allport
  (Howard) **117** 204
Geraldine Patricia
  117 204
Henrietta (Hewson)
  117 199
Herbert James Cooper
  117 199
James Henry Brabazon
  117 199
Jane (Codrington)
  117 199
John Uniacke **117** 199 204
Laura Frances **117** 199
Louisa Josephine
  Pettitot (Penrose) **117**
  114 199
Mabel Frances Warne
  (Tower) **117** 204
Mary Elizabeth **117** 199
Maurice John **117** 199
Michael John Robert
  117 204
Nesta Fanny Harriet
  117 199
Nuala Mary (Cassidy)
  117 204
Robert Francis Uniacke
  117 199 204
Robert Uniacke **117** 199
Romayne **117** 204
Sarah **117** 199
Timothy Michael **117** 204
PENROSE-THACKWELL
Eleanor Maud
  Charlotte **117** 201
Geoffrey Joseph Elliott
  117 201
Marjory Helen Florence
  117 201
Mary Geraldine Harriet
  117 201
William John Rawson
  117 201
PENROSE-WELSTEAD
Eleanor Grace
  (Fleming) **117** 205
Frank Philip **117** 201
Gertrude Eugenie
  (Perfect) **117** 206
Harry Hugh **117** 201
Iris **117** 201
Mary Elizabeth
  (O'Callaghan) **117** 201
Reginald Hugh **117** 206
Samuel **117** 201
Samuel Quayle **117** 201
  205
Samuel Richard **117** 205
PENRY —— **55** 298
Ann **64** 342
John **74** 320
PENT Anthony **122** 195
Archibald **122** 195
Betsey **122** 195

PENT *cont'd*
Deborah / Debsey (Ripley)
  122 195
Francis **122** 195
James **122** 195
Mary **122** 195
Mary (Stewart) **122** 195
Samuel **122** 195
PENTARD
Anne Francoise **92** 184
PENTFIELD
Elizabeth **117** 174
PENTICOST Pentecost
Ernest H. **77** 325
Joanna (Larkin) **131** 132
John **131** 132
PENTLAND —— **143** 366
Bethiah (Cushing) **88** 285
Charlotte M. **89** 13
Clement N. **88** 285
John **112** 291
PENTLEY Joseph **91** 201
PENTLOW Thomas **54** 95
PENTON Edward **138** 98
Elizabeth **148** 63
Frank **66** 232
Samuel H. H. **66** 232
Thomas **148** 63
PENTRES Thomas **83** 322
PENUEL
Anne (Barton) **84** 402
Walter **84** 402
Peny *see* Penny
Penye *see* Penny
Penyngton *see*
  Pennington
PEOPLES Peeples
Alice Catherine **82** 278
Caroline Lucille **102** 65
Daniel Francis **82** 278
Ellen (White) **131** 88
Ethel Emma **103** 141 **104**
  142 **119** 149
George Leonard **82** 278
  409
Hannah **82** 278 409
Maria Cunningham
  71 67
Mary Ellen **131** 88 89
William **109** 318 **131** 88
PEPAU John **75** 18
Joseph E. **75** 18
Nettie **75** 18
Sloma **75** 18
PEPELSHAM
Martha **96** 20
Peper *see* Pepper
Peperell *see* Pepperell
PEPIN
Edward Oscar **80** 250
Ella **80** 250
Marie Charlotte **110** 132
Marie Josephe **110** 132
Roger **96** 313
Ruth **80** 250
PEPLOW Richard **65** 117
PEPOON Daniel **94** 400
James **140** 235
Lucretia **78** 26
Mary **140** 235

PEPPER Peper Pepor
—— **57** 384 **58** 207
  146 261
Abigail **80** 22 265 **123** 118
Alice **58** 163 **80** 23
Allen Polk **78** 160
Anna Fitzhugh **78** 160
Anna Lee **78** 160
Ashbel **62** 131 133
Benjamin **65** 357
Bethiah **80** 22
Bethiah (Freeman)
  123 117
Betsey (Burke) **126** 68
Carlton D. **114** 238
Charles Hovey **81** 67
Charlotte A. **105** 104
Daniel **80** 22 **123** 117
Edward **57** 384
Elbridge **101** 214
Eleanor **88** 281
Elijah **62** 19
Elizabeth **67** 371 **72** 141 **80**
  20 **106** 227
Elizabeth (Johnson) **106**
  227 **146** 275
Foster **62** 24 **110** 114
Francis **100** 236
Hannah **80** 22 **123** 118
Henry **62** 129 132 133
Isaac **83** 262
Jacob **62** 17 22 128
John **57** 100 **100** 236
Joseph **62** 19 **65** 25 **80** 20
  22 23 **113** 114
Louisa **100** 236
Lovina **86** 17
Lucy **65** 357
Malona **137** 29
Marmaduke **84** 75
Mary **57** 384 **83** 81 **123** 118
Mary Ann **128** 266
Mehitable **123** 119
Mercy **80** 122 **114** 3
  123 117
Nancy **133** 219
Pliny **62** 23 132
Rebecca **61** 92 **80** 20
Robert **80** 39 **106** 23 227
  146 275
Sally **81** 272 **123** 117
Salome (Needham)
  110 114
Samuel A. **78** 160
Samuel Alexander **78** 160
Sarah **51** 204 **65** 357
Sarah (Bruce) **125** 215
Sarah P. **125** 222
Solomon **80** 265 **125** 215
William **63** 36 **76** 235
  139 61
Zelda Fontain **78** 160
Zilpha **80** 22 23 **123** 118
PEPPERELL Peperell
  Pepperill Pepperrell
—— **54** xix 460 **61** 314
  62 208
— Col. **54** 408
— Gen. **97** 106-108
— Lady **52** 270 **55** 254
  63 173

PEPPERELL *cont'd*
Algernon **106** 156
Andrew **51** 104 **52** 221
  63 173 **96** 91 **110** 317
  130 86 88 103 104
Christopher **55** 105
Edith **55** 105
Elizabeth **61** 202 **130** 92 93
  131 44
Elizabeth (Royall) **61** 202
  84 253 **106** 156 **131** 44
Margery **53** 124 **61** 222
  106 264
Mary **53** 196 361 **55** liii
  58 231 **61** 222 **95** 26
  104 77 **137** 346
Mary (Hirst) **130** 88 104
  106
Mary (Lady) **85** 120
Mary Ann **63** 173
Miriam **56** 193 **95** 24 **130**
  87 89
Robert **55** 104 105
William **51** 104 256 502
  52 186 187 221 270 382
  53 361 362 453 **54** 408
  410 **55** liii 66-70 104 **56**
  52 53 193 **57** lxvii 214
  215 280 **58** 70 231 **59** 56
  57 108 109 192 **61** 202
  222 **67** 105 385 **70** 8 **72**
  83-85 **75** 82 86 **76** 242
  77 59 63-65 68 69 71 95-
  103 **81** 98 **82** 153 **84** 147
  253 377 **85** 299 461 **86**
  139 **95** 25 26 **96** 91 **97**
  93 **104** 245 252-258 320
  106 156 264 266-269
  108 22 237 **112** 79 **114**
  249 **116** 4 **125** 23 **130** 83-
  106 265 **131** 44 **137** 345-
  347 **144** 339
William Royall **106** 156
PEPPERLO Pepperlow
Eve **62** 371
Hannah **141** 356
Pepperrell *see* Pepperell
PEPPETT Robert **67** 335
PEPPITT Martha **88** 343
PEPYS
Elizabeth **104** 34
Judith **104** 34
Mary **104** 34
Mary (Gosnold) **104** 34
Richard **104** 34 36
Samuel **52** 13 **56** 204 **80**
  447 **95** 214
Walter Courtenay
  106 238
PEQUOT Rudy **148** 284
PERA James **64** 155
Meribah **64** 155
PERATT Philippa **144** 32
PERCE Polly **111** 116
PERCEHAY
Isabel 17 **103** 17
Perceval *see* Percival
Percey *see* Percy
PERCH Eleanor **101** 91
Eleanor (Sherrer) **101** 91
George **101** 91

PERCH *cont'd*
John **101** 901
Judith (Marshall) **101** 91
Katharine **101** 91
Thomas **101** 91
PERCHARD
Clement **88** 254
Mabel (Gavey) **88** 254
PERCHE
Alice de **105** 37
Geoffrey de **105** 37
Harmon de **105** 37
PERCHES William **65** 24
PERCIVAL Parsevall
  Parsivall Perceval
  Percivall Percyvall
  Persevell
—— **123** 52
Abigail **118** 202
Abigail (Robinson)
  139 299
Alden **123** 308
Alexander **67** 18
Alice **76** 279 284 293 **82**
  192 342 **94** 78
Anne **85** 389
Anne E. **67** 18
Annis (Carter) (Fettiplace)
  123 249 251
Annis Goodhu **74** 239 240
Arabella (Chase) **88** 117
Ashur **61** 397
Augustus **102** 285
Bathsheba **118** 202
Caroline **52** 446
Charlte **61** 397
Christopher **76** 284 293
  94 78
Daniel **74** 239
David Crowell (Mrs.)
  94 139
Dorothy **80** 424 **126** 91
Dyer **61** 397
Edmund **123** 249
Elizabeth **82** 192 **95** 343
  118 202 **139** 299 **141**
  251
Elizabeth (Cowles) **123** 52
Elmer **61** 397 **69** 271
Emeline **74** 239
Foster Glenn **105** 129
Franklin **113** 250
Frederick **102** 288
George P. **61** 397
Gladys Spencer
  (Burckhardt) **92** 146
Gorden **74** 239
Hannah **80** 424 **118** 202
Hannah Alger **74** 239 240
Harper **61** 397
Harriet M. **80** 424
Harriette E. (Williamson)
  94 139
Harry Farlam (Mrs.) **92**
  146 162 **93** 153 **94** 155
Helen **106** 142
Helen Jane **80** 424
Henry M. **102** 286
Hezekiah W. **80** 424
Jacob **74** 239
James **80** 119 **118** 201 202

PERCIVAL *cont'd*
  130 10 **139** 299 **141** 251
  252 254
James Gates **72** 84
Jamys **110** 191
Jane Anne **67** 18
Jeremiah **61** 397
John **61** 397 **63** 12 **65** 129
  170 **71** 24 **74** 239 **76** 279
  293 **80** 424 **82** 385 **118**
  201 202 **128** 257 258
  139 299 **141** 251
Judith **52** 259 260 **74** 239
Lavina **120** 41
Lavina (Ford) **120** 41
Lois **68** 332
Lucy Wing **69** 271
Luella **102** 286
Lydia (Fuller) **118** 202
Lydia S. **61** 397
Margaret **80** 424 **85** 389
Margaret (Lyne) **123** 249
Mary **61** 397 398 **80** 424
  118 201 202 **130** 10 **139**
  297 299 **141** 251
Mary (Bourne) **118** 201
  139 299
Mary (Raynsford)
  (Bassett) **118** 201 **139**
  297 299 **141** 251
Mary Kelly **98** 351
Naomi **61** 397
Nathaniel **88** 117
Patience **118** 202
Phebe **80** 424
Philip **123** 251
Prudence **74** 239
Rizpah **61** 397
Roxana (Ayres) **123** 308
Sally **61** 397
Sally Davis (Parker)
  113 250
Sarah **118** 202
Sarah Maria **61** 397
Susan **74** 239
Thomas **61** 397 398
Whitmore **74** 239
PERCUT —— **140** 235
PERCY De Percy Pearcy
  Peircey Peircy Percey
  Percye Persey Piercy
  Purcy
—— **76** 70 **140** 32
— Earl **85** 19 **98** 204
  125 64
— Lord **85** 9
Abigail **142** 344
Agnes **106** 285-289
Alexander **120** 170 172-174
Alice **67** 285
Arnold **142** 241
Arthur **119** 21
Catherine **73** 225
Elena **106** 286-288
Elizabeth **66** 192 **82** 89 **99**
  119 **108** 176 **112** 301
Ernald **142** 241
G. **59** 181 **105** 18
George **105** 21 **106** 260
  123 255
Hannah **100** 295

PERCY *cont'd*
Harriet **144** 108
Harry Stapleton (Mrs.)
82 122 237
Henry **105** 21 **106** 286-289
108 176 177 **112** 284
301 **114** 227
Henry Lord **95** 204
Hugh (Earl) **56** 417
Isabel **142** 241
James **55** 314 **82** 328 331
83 9 **125** 43
Jane **86** 293
Joan **141** 26 **142** 227 241
242 244
Joan (Foliot) **142** 227 241
John **142** 241
Julia A. **86** 292
Katharine **108** 177
Libbie M. A. **111** 299
Love **55** 314 **82** 328 331
83 9
Love (Butler) **83** 9
Margaret **76** 57 70 **120** 170
172 174
Margery **141** 26
Martha Ann **93** 95
Mary **86** 222 **99** 120
Mary J. **93** 95
Miriam **92** 110
Nicholas **54** 182 **142** 241
Peter **116** 174
Richard **86** 415 **99** 117
119 120 **101** 161 **106**
280
Robert **112** 284
Ruth **82** 237
S. V.R. **115** 296
Sarah **55** 313 **83** 9 **125** 109
Stephen **67** 345 **82** 328
Thomas **71** 239 **119** 21 **123**
249 **135** 84 **141** 26
Walter **106** 286 287
William **77** 318 **106** 285-
289 **142** 241
William P. **66** 34
PERCY-SMITH
H. K. **94** 93
PERCYHAY
Isabel **102** 7
Percyvall *see* Percival
PERDRIAU Leslie Harold
121 316
Ralph J. **121** 316
PERDUE
Robert Hartley **82** 123
237 **83** 384
Robert Willingham
(Mrs.) **108** 135 **120** 318
William **83** 384
PERE Richard **67** 365
PERECE Thomas **63** 40
PEREIRA
Antonia **125** 216
Antony Joseph **126** 209
H. P.E. **112** 272 **113** 87
Marian (Fargue) **125** 216
Phebe **120** 149
Sarah A. (Bacon) **126** 209
Perem *see* Perham
Peremer *see* Paremer

PEREN Aaron **97** 66
Abraham **64** 28 **97** 317 319
John **97** 317 319
Sarah Roselle **97** 66
PERERA Caroline (Thacher)
103 69
Gino Lorenzo **103** 69
Gino Lorenzo (Mrs.) **85**
190 **101** 249 **102** 127
103 69
Guido R. **103** 69
PERET
Georgiana **77** 153
Jules **77** 153
PERETT John **67** 330
PEREZ Carmen **90** 363
PERFECT
George **117** 206
George Barham (Mrs.)
102 124
Gertrude Eugenie
117 206
Hazel Lavinia **99** 149
Olivia **108** 151
Thomas William
Chamberlain **108** 151
PERHAM Perem Perhum
—— **55** 350
— Gov. **98** 107
— Sgt. **136** 139
— Widow **99** 96
___ (Wyman) **91** 262
Abby M. **77** 176
Abraham **96** 257 **99** 94 96
98
Adeline **73** 180
Betsey **73** 96
Bette **91** 262
Caroline **73** 180
Charles **91** 261
Charles O. **95** 117
Daniel **91** 261
Darius **73** 96
Dorcas **73** 96
Dorothy **71** 261 262 270
Edmund S. **73** 180
Edythe **103** 115
Eli Rogers **94** 119
Elighah **91** 258
Eliza Ann **94** 119
Elizabeth **91** 256 261
Elizabeth (Pollard) **91** 266
Emerency **57** 393
Enoch **73** 96
Esther **94** 119
Hannah **55** 264 **57** 106 **71**
262 **91** 255 258 259 **94**
118
Hannah (Wyman) **91** 262
Henry S. **62** 204
Isaac **121** 93
Jacob **55** 264 **57** 106
James **71** 262
Jane **73** 96 100 179 **94** 118
114 146 147
Jesse Rogers **94** 118
Joanna **73** 96
John **51** 493 **71** 262 **73** 96
179 180 **91** 255 256 258
259 262 **99** 96
Jonathan **71** 262 **91** 256

PERHAM *cont'd*
260-262 266 **123** 281
Jonn **91** 256-258
Joseph **61** 304 **71** 261 262
270 **91** 256
Katharine **91** 261
Leander **73** 180
Luce **91** 255
Lydia **71** 262 **73** 179
Lydia Ann **73** 180
Lydia Towne (Bancroft)
95 117
Martha Allen **94** 119
Mary **73** 96
Mary Abigail **94** 119
Mercy **91** 260
Orpha **135** 130
Peter **70** 145 **94** 118 119
Polly **61** 343
Rachel **91** 259
Roxana **73** 180
Ruth (Merrill) **91** 267
Sally **73** 96 **94** 118 119
Sally (Rogers) **94** 118
Samuel **58** 236 **73** 96
Sarah **51** 493
Sarah Ann **73** 179
Sarah Augusta **94** 119
Sibyl **91** 262
Sidney **61** 322
Stephen **73** 179
Susanna **71** 262
Thais **73** 96 **79** 11
William **91** 257 262 267
94 118
Zibiah **94** 118
PERIAM
Fannie (Jube) **96** 73
Helen Jube **96** 73
Joseph **96** 73
PERIEN Marie **75** 218
PERIESEL John **65** 169
PERIEW
Gilbert **65** 173
James **65** 173
Perigoe *see* Perrigo
PERIGORD
— Comte de **75** 68
PERIMAR
Richard **83** 313
Roger **83** 313
Perin *see* Perrin
PERINCHEF
— Widow **76** 237
Perine *see* Perrin
Perit *see* Perritt
PERITON
Isabel de **106** 290
Thomas **106** 290
PERKEL Abbie **101** 123
PERKENSEN
John D. **77** 217
Martha Jane **77** 217
Sophia Caroline **77** 217
Thomas **77** 217
PERKILL George **71** 116
PERKINS Parkins
—— **54** 129 **55** 449 **56** 63
58 29 **59** 227 **60** 107 **62**
206 284 **66** 359 **68** 93 **71**
66 **75** 104 **76** 107 108

PERKINS *cont'd*
110 114 182 186 189 251
254 259-261 **78** 386 **85**
154 **89** 41 **92** 17 258 346
352 355 **93** 59 62 109
115 249 339 **95** 54 **98** 63
67 **99** 88-90 221 **101** 56
84 **104** 263 323 **109** 114
110 22 **116** 194 **122** 80
290 **123** 223 **129** 316
140 235
— Capt. **97** 110 **107** 238
134 300
— Col. **133** 309 310
— Dr. **85** 460
— Maj. **66** 359
— Miss **84** 31 **90** 384
— Mr. **71** 137 141 **80** 60
177 **83** 416 **93** 301 **94**
162 **148** 111
— Mrs. **62** 45 **76** 228 **83**
308 **127** 14
— Rev. Mr. **60** 180
— Widow **58** 33 **81** 432
84 153 **105** 212
____ (Adams) **112** 106
____ (Appleton) **140** 32
235
____ (Call) **140** 48
____ (Higginson) **140** 153
____ (Pope) **140** 237
____ (Rogers) **84** 374
A. **129** 49
A. A. **59** 73
A. L. **89** 352
Aaron **60** 191 **69** 144
116 294
Abby B. **80** 186 **89** 255
Abby Melissa **90** 283
Abiel **107** 197 **108** 60 188
Abigail **67** 54 **73** 306 **76** 30
36 109 219 255 **78** 386
88 369 **89** 207 **98** 63
104 165 **108** 61 **112** 106
115 58 **116** 302 303 **119**
144 **124** 65 **126** 85 168
127 207
Abigail (Collins) **127** 123
Abigail (Cook) **126** 86
Abigail (Hill) **108** 189
Abigail (Roberts) **98** 63
Abigail (Simpson)
114 294
Abigail (Wardwell) **112**
23 **114** 132
Abigail R. **69** 143
Abijah **85** 411
Abner **107** 195 **108** 60 61
123 **110** 288 **114** 293
116 220 **118** 318 319
140 293 **141** 151
Abraham **51** 58 **53** 143
54 354 **62** 119 121 **67**
286 **75** 112 **78** 386 **85**
146 **88** 225 **97** 357 **105**
211 212 **111** 270 281 282
285 **116** 7 **128** 222 **135**
25
Abraham E. **78** 386
108 265
Abram **58** 156

PERKINS *cont'd*
Abram E. **78** 386
Ada **81** 249
Ada M. **110** 109
Ada May (Jackson) **86** 370
Ada R. **92** 341
Adaline **119** 225 **123** 152
Adaline (Havemeyer)
111 147
Addie M. (Hutchins) **93**
240 **123** 235
Adelbert L. **93** 240
Adeline **54** cxxiii
Adeline Adams **83** 213
214
Adeline Mary **74** 303
Agnes **67** 253 256 **95** 324
Albert **97** 229 233 **123** 149
Albert B. **110** 109
Alcott **119** 229
Aldrich W. **130** 55
Alexander J. **110** 22
Alfonso **125** 150
Alice **76** 30 224 225 229
107 272 274 **108** 54-56
58-60 **112** 139
Alice (Leach) **119** 67
Alice (Low) **96** 144 336
Alice (Stone) **108** 123
Alice A. **110** 303
Alice B. **73** 187 188
Alice E. **110** 215
Alice L. **73** 187
Alice P. **98** 193
Alma I. **92** 341
Almeda G. **119** 62
Almira **128** 173
Almira J. (Tibbetts)
110 26
Almira M. **88** 338
Almon Ernest **73** 81
Alphonso W. **81** 249
Alta (Appleby) **119** 226
Alvin **93** 249
Amanda (Hawes) **109**
200 201
Amasa **122** 290
Ambrose **66** 220 222 224
299 305
Amelia (Cook) **123** 51
Amos **100** 175 **104** 183 **108**
285 **109** 112 271 **110**
207 **125** 43 **126** 86 **127**
160
Amos G. **92** 341
Amos J. **109** 112
Amy L. **102** 151 158 **104** 80
107 157 **109** 80
Amy Louise **93** 138
109 127
Amy M. **111** 187
Amy Melissa **86** 198
Andrew **107** 201 275 **108**
55 56 59 60 188
Andrew J. **90** 387 **93** 109
110 **120** 66 **123** 150 234
Angelina **92** 324 325 328
341
Ann **75** 179 **80** 177 **94** 42
98 63 **111** 285 **134** 87
Ann Augusta **105** 222

PERKINS *cont'd*
Ann E. **68** 160
Ann M. **93** 339
Ann Martha **147** 60
Ann P. (Drew) **111** 137
Ann Townsend **92** 258
Anna **53** 164 **61** 35 336 337
62 37 **66** 18 **75** 54 111
119 179 **76** 182 189 255
78 386 **82** 360 **83** 59 93
339 **98** 134 **107** 272 **108**
61 123 **115** 227 **116** 302
119 253 **120** 257
Anna (Bracy) **123** 149
Anna (Coon) **127** 34
Anna (Littlefield) **110** 174
Anna D. T. **78** 73
Anna M. **109** 112
Anna Minot (Weld)
103 76
Anna P. **147** 60
Annah **110** 216
Anne **61** 65 **66** 147 159 213
67 256 **74** 130 180 **76**
225 227 228 230 **97** 382
Anne Elizabeth **84** 192
Anne Maynard **136** 312
Annie **75** 267
Annie Abigail **82** 399
Annie M. **92** 341
Annie M. (Wilson)
121 145
Anson **136** 247
Anthony **136** 90 325
Arad **122** 80
Arthur **109** 271
Arthur Marion **91** 142
Arthur T. **93** 240 332
Arthur W. **107** 157
Asa **76** 35 **99** 293 **118** 189
120 257 **126** 86
Asenath **97** 222
Augusta **133** 119
Augusta Lincoln **93** 115
Augustus **94** 385
Augustus T. **99** 15
Augustus Thorndike **67**
10 11 **69** 385
Azariah **66** 18
B. J. **75** 18
Barbara **56** 309 **127** 229
Barbara Cooper
(Higginson) **92** 84
Barten **66** 149
Bathshua **76** 228 231
Beamsley **60** 52
Beatrice **76** 224 225 228-
230
Benjamin **51** 466 **52** 432
59 73 **65** 15 **66** 18 **70**
222 **73** 187 188 **75** 18
105 278 **107** 196 201
108 56 124 **109** 197 232
136 271
Benjamin Gay **104** 183
Bertha L. **123** 235
Bethiah (Baker) (Kingsley)
94 385 **136** 311
Bethiana **100** 175
Betsey **56** 250 256 **67** 226
70 230 **74** 170 312 **75** 18

PERKINS *cont'd*
25 **76** 223 230 254 **83**
416 **84** 368 **86** 91 **89** 112
92 20 **108** 56 **117** 226
227 **118** 170
Betsey (Johnson) **113** 113
Betsey A. **60** 297
Betsey C. **98** 197
Betty **53** 164 **63** 175 **66** 295
74 228 **76** 106 181 196
258 **88** 155 **107** 201 **108**
124 **120** 257 **124** 65
Bradbury **112** 106
Bradbury P. **93** 249 339
Brayton M. **109** 204
Brenton **102** 210 **127** 16
Brooks Selina (Daniels)
90 347
Caleb **80** 182 **100** 175
Calista **136** 247
Callie K. **98** 251
Carlos **125** 150
Caroline **71** 66 **75** 18 **82**
399 **106** 309 **108** 192
Carrie **69** 208 **93** 249
Catherine **74** 295 **76** 225
136 328
Catherine (Chase) **88** 121
Catherine (Pitkin)
136 328
Catherine Callender
(Amory) **120** 84
Celestine M. **60** 297
Cephas **137** 26
Charity **113** 140 **120** 266
132 74 **138** 322
Charity (Perkins) **138** 322
Charles **62** 366 **81** 248 **89**
105 **93** 238 240 **119** 279
Charles A. **109** 271
Charles Allen **125** 150
Charles Almon **82** 252
83 233 **84** 238
Charles C. **51** 103 **106** 305
Charles E. **72** 6 **75** xliii
89 112 **92** 341
Charles Elliott **62** 113
Charles Ely **81** 392
Charles F. **92** 341 342
Charles F. M. **98** 251
Charles Floyd **75** 316
77 xxix
Charles Gilman **69** 145
Charles H. **109** 112
110 215
Charles Huff **108** 56
Charles L. **93** 240 **123** 235
Charles M. **90** 387 **92** 341
342
Charles N. **110** 215
Charles Stoke (Mrs.)
89 132
Charles W. **81** 249 **106** 117
Charlotte **69** 255 **86** 384
126 143 169 **136** 247
140 235
Charlotte (Snowman)
117 140 141
Charlotte L. (Elizabeth)
108 265

PERKINS *cont'd*
Charlotte Sophia
(Woodbridge) **136** 311
Chesley **75** 312
Clara Bartlett (George)
103 76
Clara J. **90** 303
Clara Leonora **82** 472
Clarence A. **92** 341
Clarence E. **92** 341
Clarence Oakley **101** 65
Clarissa **108** 57 **109** 271
Clarissa A. **68** 93
Clarissa S. **119** 281
Clary S. **90** 387
Clella Lester **103** 120
Comfort **76** 189
Cora Amanda **110** 215
Cora E. **92** 341 342
Cordelia **82** 18
Cordelia Lowell **93** 62
Cornelia Leonard
136 322
Cynthia C. (Lazell)
(Thompson) **89** 120
Cynthia Evelyn **73** 188
Cynthia P. **75** 36
Cyrus **108** 60 **141** 151
Cyrus G. **89** 389
D. W. **66** 369 **67** xxxii
93 109
Daisy V. **92** 341
Damaris **75** 179
Damaris (Robinson)
94 385
Daniel **51** 440 **55** 45 **60**
191 **63** 377 **64** 374 **66**
365 **67** 56 **76** 103 **91** 94
95 55 56 **101** 74 **105** 211
212 **107** 200 201 272-274
108 54 56 57 121 123
191 **109** 200 201 **113**
318 **115** 216 **127** 123
Daniel C. **66** 24 **93** 109
Daniel L. **68** 204
Daniel W. **90** 302 **92** 341
93 109
Darius **76** 39
David **68** 160 **75** 309 **97** 16
128 224 **131** 74 **145** 351
147 178
David B. **68** 160
David G. **85** 158 **141** 151
David L. **111** 306 **115** 116
David Page **64** 211
David W. **70** 191
Deborah **66** 299 **74** 263
76 35 **78** 386 **104** 183
107 271 **109** 112 **112** 23
261-263 **115** 138 **118**
189 **122** 134 **124** 65 **127**
160
Deborah (Bennett) **112**
263 **124** 231
Deborah (Browning)
86 339
Deborah (Lazell) **88** 362
108 121
DeForest H. **110** 215
Delilah **94** 201 202
Deliverance **75** 309

PERKINS *cont'd*
Dona Maria Francoise
(de Bourbon) **125** 150
Dorcas **71** 17
Dorinda (Mason) **110** 22
Dorothy **65** 352 **83** 211
488 **98** 63 **109** 12
Dorothy Reba **89** 352
Dow W. **121** 154 **122** 80
125 150
Drusilla **124** 65
Dyer **86** 384 **136** 311
E. N. **93** 109
Eaton H. (Mrs.) **107** 130
Eben **109** 112
Ebenezer **83** 418 **87** 83 **89**
112 **100** 340 **101** 65 **107**
195 275 **108** 55 57 58 60
128 296 **129** 64
Ebenezer Hovey **108** 57
Edgar **92** 45
Edith (Carver) **89** 41
Edmond (Mrs.) **95** 50
Edmund **53** 302 **57** 415
84 152 **92** 84 **106** 261
107 98 **134** 138
Edmund H. **126** 205
Edna **78** 284
Edna Elethier **90** 347
Edna N. (Wardwell)
117 166
Edward **62** 359 **66** 153
295 306 **75** 179 309 **76**
227-229 231 232 **79** 165
82 296 301 **94** 385 **125**
43 150
Edward A. **90** 387 **94** 116
Edward Augustus **81** 392
Edward Cranch **59** xlviii
65 xx **75** xxxvi xliii **92**
84 85
Edward Henry **94** 385
Edward Lorenzo **75** 18 19
Edward M. **122** 71 231
123 149
Edwin Lorenzo **75** 19
Effie **92** 341
Elben **109** 112
Elbridge C. **92** 322
Elcy **94** 116
Elcy (Sawyer) **90** 387
Elcy J. **90** 387
Elcy S. **90** 387
Eleanor **67** 55 **88** 289
98 63
Elias **76** 139-142 **127** 307
136 322
Elias J. **120** 136
Elijah **77** 81
Eliphal **80** 448
Eliphalet **53** 282 **105** 290
107 201 **108** 123 **132**
268 **133** 44
Elise **123** 235
Elisha **60** 49 **67** 127 **70**
177 178 222 223 316 **71**
134 **76** 107 109 185 191
194 **85** 237 238 **86** 442
112 106 **114** 293 **115** 59
132 267 **133** 44 **136** 331
Elisha B. **140** 237

PERKINS *cont'd*
Eliza **70** 363 **79** 155 **81** 392
    82 24 **90** 387 **100** 175
    250 **103** 222 **108** 192
    109 271 **116** 304 305
    118 320 329 **119** 280
Eliza (Cobb) **140** 235
Eliza A. **90** 303 **110** 24
Eliza Ann **111** 187
Eliza Ann (Hannum)
    90 347
Eliza J. **90** 387
Eliza M. **73** 258
Eliza Seymour **57** xliv
Eliza T. **83** 26 28
Eliza Thomas **81** 382
    82 24
Elizabeth **51** 466 **52** 432 **53**
    338 **55** 269 344 **60** 94 **61**
    333 338 356 **62** 34 **65** li
    66 142 145 149 152 153
    155 211 213 215 257 301
    67 55 **70** 197 223 **73** 135
    224 **75** 111 118-122 215
    311 **76** 109 185 194 212
    223-225 228-232 **77** 81
    235 **78** 302 386 **79** 193
    83 507 510 **90** 100 **92** 50
    93 261 **95** 284 **98** 63
    101 74 **104** 183 **107** 195
    108 61 123 282 **109** 271
    111 92 **114** 50 **115** 63
    116 138 **119** 108 **120**
    256 257 **122** 71 232 **125**
    93 **126** 168 **127** 207 273
    128 34 **135** 25 27 **140**
    153 165 293 **143** 348
Elizabeth (Ault) **98** 58
Elizabeth (Bell) **118** 318
Elizabeth (Bradbury)
    112 106 **115** 59
Elizabeth (Bushnell) **94**
    385 **136** 311
Elizabeth (Eveleth)
    134 305
Elizabeth (French)
    120 256
Elizabeth (James) **127** 34
Elizabeth (Knapp) **97** 357
Elizabeth (Loomer) **126**
    86 178
Elizabeth (Newent)
    101 65
Elizabeth (Peck) **92** 84
Elizabeth (Rogers)
    100 304
Elizabeth (Sawbridge)
    94 385
Elizabeth (Staples)
    117 141
Elizabeth (Stone) **108** 123
Elizabeth (Thomas)
    127 273
Elizabeth (Westcott)
    127 160
Elizabeth (Young)
    (Headley) **126** 168
Elizabeth Bishop **94** 386
Elizabeth C. **75** 101 **83** 20
Elizabeth H. **101** 235
Elizabeth Jane **81** 249

PERKINS *cont'd*
Elizabeth Julia **81** 393
Elizabeth Rogers **136** 311
Elizabeth S. (Wood)
    83 301 303
Elizabeth T. (Winn)
    93 240
Elizabeth Vinton **79** 183
Elizabeth W. **109** 254
Elizzabeth (Bell) **118** 319
Ella **75** 15
Ella (Lazell) **89** 112
Ella F. **92** 325
Ella M. **92** 324
Ellen Augusta **76** lvi
    110 231
Ellen Christina **81** 392
Ellen M. **89** 37
Elliott **92** 85
Elsie **80** 182 **94** 117
    123 235
Elsie (Sawyer) **123** 152
Elsie J. **123** 151 233
Elsie L. **123** 150
Elsie S. **90** 387
Elvira **136** 247
Emeline (Gould) **106** 305
Emeline Marla **95** 328
Emily **75** 18 **78** 249 **79** 151
    82 359 360 **84** 325 **122**
    230 **123** 74 **136** 247
Emily A. **90** 387
Emily B. **64** lxi
Emily H. **65** 313
Emily N. **121** 310
Emily T. **120** 217
Emma (Fitzgerald)
    123 73
Emma (Jones) **110** 22
Emma (Ramsdell) **123** 73
Emma A. **93** 240 **120** 305
Emma F. **110** 215
Emma Maude **69** 200
Enoch **63** 379 **79** 166 **80** 56
    82 360 **95** 50
Enoch (Mrs.) **95** 50
Enoch P. **80** 60
Ephraim **82** 296 299 **98** 63
    107 196-198 201 270-
    273 **108** 190
Eri **83** 24 26
Estelle Ruth **111** 245
Esther **55** 268 312 344 **61**
    240 **62** 37 **66** 24 **74** 196
    227 **75** 179 **78** 260 **82**
    510 **108** 122 192 **136**
    247
Esther (Blanchard) **103** 76
Esther (Frothingham)
    92 84
Esther (Perkins) **108** 122
Eugenia E. **92** 341
Eugenia E. (Lord) **92** 341
Eunice **66** 159 **67** 127 277
    75 179 **78** 260 **83** 416
    107 272 274 275 **108** 54-
    60 122 **111** 306 **115** 116
    120 140 215 **126** 168
Eunice (Bancroft) **95** 113
Eunice (Davis) **108** 188
Eunice (Ellis) **121** 132

PERKINS *cont'd*
Eunice (Millar) **108** 188
Eunice (Parsons) **119** 283
Eunice (Thompson)
    108 123
Eva N. (Clark) **90** 303
Evelyn Edith (Duncan)
    96 161
Everett **92** 341
Experience (Holmes)
    100 340
Ezra **89** 20
F. B. **53** 372
F. Everett **92** 341
F. Wainwright (Mrs.)
    89 132
Fanny **73** 177
Fanny P. **147** 60
Flora H. **82** 175
Flora J. **92** 341
Florence **69** 143
Florence Clinton **69** 200
Florence H. **148** 274
Forest **69** 143
Frances **76** 224 225 227-
    231 **98** 63
Frances (Corlew) **130** 52
Frances (Sturgill /
    Sturgis) **122** 80
Frances Emeline **106** 305
Frances M. **73** 195 **93** 240
Francis **76** 223 225-227 230
    134 305
Francis Asbury **117** 77
Francis C. **93** 250 **109** 204
Francis W. **78** 386
Frank E. (Mrs.) **74** 158
Frank Elmer (Mrs.) **75**
    xxvi **76** 223 227 **77** xx
    79 192
Frank H. **93** 240
Frank S. **74** 242
Franklin **93** 123
Franklin (Mrs.) **92** 344
Franklin Elwood **102** 72
Fred E. **93** 240
Fred J. **110** 215
Frederick E. **93** 240
G. **61** 35
Gaius **141** 151
George **66** 149 152 153
    155 211 213 215 225 302
    70 223 **71** 223-225 227
    228 230 **87** 206 **93** 240
    102 155 **105** 212 **107**
    201 272 273 **108** 54 **109**
    271 **112** 139 **113** 113
    119 67 147 224 **120** 137
    133 216
George A. **120** 257 258
George Batcheller
    59 xlviii
George H. **120** 308
George Hamilton **103** 76
George Irwin **81** 392
George Otis **109** 112
George R. **73** 258
George W. **82** 24 **85** 64
    107 128
George Walbridge (Mrs.)
    84 110 185 **115** 66

PERKINS *cont'd*
George Walpey **66** 295
Georgia A. **98** 251
Georgia Everett **85** 193
Gideon **61** 31 **124** 65
Gilbert Brooks **82** 472
Gilman **93** 339 **119** 228
Gladys **74** 295
Gladys A. **92** 341
Godfrey **62** 288
Gooch **93** 250
Gordon **122** 80
Grace **134** 137
Grace (Thaxter) **134** 138
Granville **119** 224 **122** 72
    123 149
H. G. Otis **98** 251
Hamilton Eliot **103** 76
Hannah **51** 179 464 **60** 49
    52 191 **62** 28 35 46 **66**
    262 **69** 255 **75** 119 154
    76 29 139 **78** 284 386 **79**
    53 **88** 366 **92** 341 **93** 249
    339 **94** 116 **95** 55 **98** 63
    251 **100** 312 **107** 200
    201 272 273 **108** 56 58
    60 122 189 265 **109** 271
    113 31 39 **117** 143 144
    118 187 **120** 265 **121**
    318 **124** 65 231 **132** 121
    122 **134** 154 **135** 123
    136 309 317 324 332
Hannah (Beamsley)
    135 25
Hannah (Bishop) **136**
    324 328 329
Hannah (Cookery)
    143 348
Hannah (Gardner)
    141 151
Hannah (Gates) **101** 65
    120 265
Hannah (Hawes) **109** 112
Hannah (Littlefield)
    119 228
Hannah (Longe)
    (Cockery) **104** 38
Hannah (Oliver) **114** 293
Hannah (Page) **136** 271
Hannah (Safford) **101** 65
Hannah (Sampson)
    124 231
Hannah (Spencer)
    110 288
Hannah (Stone) **108** 121
Hannah (Sturtevant)
    126 205
Hannah (Tibbets) **98** 63
Hannah (Trowbridge)
    103 76
Hannah (Welch) **119** 279
    123 73 149
Hannah (West) **101** 65
Hannah M. **92** 341
Hannah Maria (Griffin)
    126 204
Hannah O. **89** 201
Hannah Saul **92** 15
Hannah Snow **66** lxiii
Harold **74** 295
Harriet **74** 153 **75** 18 **76** 36

PERKINS *cont'd*
    81 392 **85** 411 **108** 59 60
Harriet Emeroy **75** 18
Harriet Marilla **62** 366
Harriet Seavey (Marden)
    107 309
Harrington **76** 228 229
    232
Harrison G. **98** 251
Harry **93** 240
Harry Frederick **110** 296
Harry T. **92** 341
Harvey **100** 175 **110** 215
Harvey C. **109** 271
Hattie N. **83** 301 303
Helen (Viele) **112** 139
Helen Louise **82** 181
Helen Virginia (Anthony)
    136 325
Helevetia Orr **93** 365
Henri E. **110** 109
Henrietta **106** 231
Henrietta Maria **62** 366
Henry **60** 244 **70** 223 **74**
    260 **78** 100 **80** 186 89
    255 **94** 385 **130** 42 **134**
    137 138 **136** 331
Henry A. **79** 156
Henry Clay **81** 392
Henry Esban **76** 320
Henry Olin **101** 65
Henry Phelps **136** 325
Henry R. **80** 186 **89** 255
Henry W. **80** 186 **89** 255
Hepzibah **88** 316
Hipsibeth (Dean) **128** 34
Hiram **88** 121 **93** 240 **118**
    320 **119** 68
Hiram N. **93** 249
Hollis **93** 249
Horace **74** 303
Horace Bean **93** 123
Houghton **92** 15 17 18 20
    93 261 **94** 294
Huldah **107** 196-198 201
    270-273
Huldah (Williams) **101** 65
Ida **95** 188
Ida E. **92** 341
Ida F. **98** 251
Ida May **75** 18 19
Ignatius **73** 258
Irenia **62** 31
Isaac **75** 112 **79** 193 **93** 339
    105 211 212 **107** 272
    108 282 **110** 288 296
    115 211 216 **122** 80 **124**
    79 **132** 89 **145** 353
Isaac T. **75** 18
Isabel **93** 249
Isabel M. **93** 249
Isabel Weld **103** 76 79
    116 126
Isabella **81** 249 **108** 56 192
Isaiah S. **90** 387 **92** 341 342
    120 307 **123** 152
Isaiah W. **90** 303
Israel **68** 155
Ithiel **75** 179 **78** 260
Ivory **108** 54
Izetta Bell **110** 215

PERKINS *cont'd*
J. **61** 333 **66** 365 **70** 187
    91 332
J. H. **89** 352
Jabez **60** 191 **62** 190 **74** 252
    122 80
Jacob **59** lxxi **60** 49 **75**
    110 111 113 114 118 119
    76 108-110 114 189 257
    259 **80** 113 **85** 237 **86** 16
    87 206 **92** 322 **93** 339
    94 64 385 **102** 72 **103**
    236 **107** 195 **108** 54 61
    110 172 174 **111** 92 270-
    272 **115** 212 216 221
    126 168 **137** 184
James **54** xcviii xcix **58**
    29 233 **74** 261 **75** 18 **77**
    320 **78** 371 **79** 155 **81**
    432 **84** 364 368 **85** 128
    88 155 **91** 332 **92** 84
    100 302 **105** 210 **107**
    195 197 201 270 **108** 56
    58 60 124 **116** 135 **125**
    101 **140** 69 235
James A. **75** 18
James C. **75** 18
James Croswell **81** 108
    222
James E. **92** 341 342
James F. **91** 332
James H. **73** 258
James Handasyd **75** xliii
    92 84 85
James Hovey **107** 198
James M. **79** 47 **92** 327 341
James Monroe **92** 352
James Ripley Osgood
    136 325
James S. **111** 187
Jane **62** 127 **76** 227 228 231
    93 240 337 **95** 55 110
    288 **115** 59 **118** 189 **128**
    174 **133** 46
Jane (Lunt) **110** 288
Jane (Pool) **119** 67
Jane (Powers) **119** 229
Jane (Robinson) **95** 56
Jane M. **68** 160
Jane R. (Houghteling)
    89 389
Jane Richards **60** 270
Jane Sedgwick (Watson)
    75 xliii **92** 84
Jane Sigourney **93** 59
Janet **77** 182
Janet Esselstyn (Rane)
    136 325
Japheth **93** 339
Jaraz **122** 80
Jeanie Lawrence **109** 232
Jedediah **76** 261 **90** 303
    387 **93** 109 **94** 116 **116**
    301 **119** 225
Jedediah M. **90** 303
Jedidiah **115** 218 220
    116 295
Jemima **109** 149 **136** 316
Jenny **107** 201
Jere **109** 112
Jere (Mrs.) **109** 112

PERKINS *cont'd*
  Jerediah **66** 262 263
  Jeremiah **60** 191 **66** 264
    76 104 **92** 341 342 **108**
    286 **109** 14 112 **116** 295
  Jeremiah W. **104** 183
  Jerome **104** 183 **108** 285
  Jerusha **101** 56
  Jesse **117** 140 141
  Joan **76** 225 227 228 230
  Joanna **60** 191 **66** 211 297
    74 252 **89** 207 **140** 235
  Joanna (Burnham)
    136 322
  Joel **112** 106
  Joel H. **90** 303 **93** 109
  Johan **93** 390
  Johanna **93** 390
  John **51** 179 **53** 44 146 **55**
    344 **56** 207 309 335 **59**
    lxxi **61** 331 336-338 **62**
    45 47 **63** 376 377 **64** 76
    374 **66** 24 25 198 312
    360 365 **70** 197 **71** 17 **73**
    232 **74** 170 263 **75** 111
    118-122 179 241 311 **76**
    106 181 191 193 219 223
    225 227-230 232 258 **82**
    332 **88** 362 **92** 341 342
    93 398 **94** 117 385 **95** 51
    53 **97** 31 **98** 63 **100** 63
    101 65 235 **105** 209 **107**
    197 271 275 **108** 56-58
    121 123 189 **110** 288
    111 281 **114** 129 **115**
    140 **120** 257 258 **121**
    132 **122** 80 **123** 73 **125**
    29 94 **126** 86 168 **127**
    273 307 **132** 267 **136**
    311 **138** 322 **141** 151
    147 58
  John (Mrs.) **95** 51
  John A. **66** 24 **69** 144 **74**
    154 312 **75** 18
  John B. **110** 26 109
  John Bradbury **76** 107
  John C. T. **110** 109
  John Carroll **91** 306 **95** 98
  John Carroll (Mrs.) **84**
    182 **85** 184
  John Douglas **70** 222
    109 204
  John Forbes **75** xliii
    83 426 438
  John Forbes (Mrs.) **85** 197
  John Hawkins **76** 140
  John Hovey **108** 58
  John Isaac **94** 386
  John K. **109** 112
  John M. **80** 186 **89** 255
  John S. **75** 18 25 **88** 276
    92 256 258 346 352 355
    93 59 62 115
  John Sullivan **92** 256
    93 323
  John T. **113** 33
  John W. **111** 306 **126** 204
  John William **86** 370
  Jonas **55** 240
  Jonathan **51** 63 **52** 429 **53**
    281 **66** 147 215 298 **74**

PERKINS *cont'd*
    264 **75** 82 **87** 207 **93** 249
    107 313 **108** 56 **116** 131
    119 67 **145** 353
  Jonathan C. **69** 255
  Jonathan Tay **92** 355
  Joseph **51** 462 **53** 212 **56**
    84 **59** lxxi **60** 297 **62** 28
    66 156 262 **74** 261 **75**
    110 311 **82** 175 **93** 249
    94 385 **95** 54 **98** 63 **105**
    209 **107** 198 271 272 274
    108 54 55 122 123 **110**
    283 **112** 23 **114** 132 **115**
    211 225 **116** 128 **118**
    330 **122** 80 **123** 51 **128**
    126 **136** 311 312 322 324
    328 331 **140** 294
  Joseph E. **104** 183
  Joseph F. **81** 249
  Joseph Hart **92** 341
  Joseph Jewett **81** 392 393
  Joseph W. **110** 22
  Joseph Woodbridge
    81 249
  Josephine Evans (Welsh)
    109 232
  Joshua **65** 352 **98** 63 **107**
    197 **108** 56 **116** 7 **124** 65
    231
  Joshua Newton **127** 273
  Josiah **76** 182 **90** 231 251
    108 223 **112** 261-263
    124 231
  Jotham **95** 54
  Joyce **70** 222
  Judith **55** lvii **60** 49 **67**
    272 280 **92** 48 **97** 303
    118 91 **127** 123 **132** 267
    268
  Judith (Gates) **94** 385
    101 65
  Judith M. **93** 240
  Julia A. (Glenn) **120** 308
  Julia A. (Lothrop) **120** 307
  Julia Amelia **82** 175
  Julia E. **98** 251
  Julia F. **92** 341
  Juliette (Emery) **122** 71
    231
  Julius Augustus **81** 392
  Julius Frank **110** 22
  Katharine **76** 223-226 228
    230 231 **85** 238
  Katharine (Towne)
    85 237
  Keturah **135** 18
  Keziah (Huff) **108** 192
  L. Annie **62** xxxix
  L. H. **103** 299
  La Fayette **87** 233
  Lanora F. **76** 39
  Larissa **73** 258
  Laura **70** 197 **136** 247
  Laura A. **85** 64 **123** 73
  Laura E. **145** 313
  Laura Ellen **69** 144
  Lawrence A. **93** 240
  Leah **58** 137
  Leander H. **85** 169
  Lemuel **98** 63 **119** 21

PERKINS *cont'd*
    132 122
  Leonora M. **93** 109
  Leonora M. (Paul) **90** 303
  Levi **122** 80
  Levi H. **90** 303 **93** 109
  Lewis W. **93** 339
  Lighteral **122** 80
  Lilla **100** 212
  Lilla B. **92** 341
  Lillie M. **92** 341
  Lizzie **70** 364 **75** 18 98
  Lizzie (Parsons) **123** 151
  Lizzie T. **93** 240
  Loice (Loomis) **120** 257
  Lois **75** 189
  Lois C. **124** 231
  Lothrop **124** 65
  Louisa **82** 181
  Louisa A. **75** 18
  Louisa Catherine (Adams)
    92 85
  Louisa Elizabeth **81** 393
  Louisa Minerva **81** 392
  Louise **81** 248 249
  Louise Childs **96** 158
    100 232 **101** 65 129
  Louise S. (Fisher) **107** 157
  Love **66** 147 298 306 **68**
    261 **75** 315
  Lovey **65** 257
  Lovina E. **75** 18
  Lua **93** 240
  Lucinda **140** 294
  Lucius M. **110** 299
  Lucius Marcus **110** 22
  Lucretia **84** 87
  Lucretia Deming **76** lxiv
  Lucretia Shaw
    (Woodbridge) **136** 322
  Lucy **60** 191 **63** 341 **65** 257
    66 24 **75** 122 **76** 186 **77**
    51 **80** 177 **86** 16 303 **92**
    80 **93** 250 **95** 374 **107**
    270 **108** 123 **112** 106
    115 141 **116** 139 **117**
    141 **122** 80 290 **126** 168
    127 273
  Lucy (Adams) **114** 293
  Lucy (Dorman) **108** 190
  Lucy (Fitch) **86** 16
  Lucy (Huntington)
    94 385
  Lucy E. **93** 109
  Lucy M. **119** 277
  Lucy Maria **75** xxvi
  Lucy S. **90** 387 **119** 282
  Lucy Y. (Hill) **97** 229 233
  Luke **62** 42 **104** 38 **124** 65
    143 348 **148** 145
  Lulu Isabelle **69** 144
  Lura Bell **86** 370
  Luther **93** 250 **98** 193 196
    251 **108** 56 192 **119** 283
  Luther S. **92** 342
  Lydia **53** 297 402 **59** 72
    62 190 **73** 188 **75** 18 118
    121 179 **76** 31 179 180
    93 249 250 **107** 195 201
    108 60 124 **110** 174 **115**
    212 220 **117** 224 **124** 79

PERKINS *cont'd*
  126 196 **128** 254 **133** 46
Lydia (Moore) **116** 300
Lydia (Stover) **110** 174
Lydia A. **122** 72 310
Lydia L. **73** 188
Lydia Whitman **86** 442
M. **78** 371 **98** 251
Mabel **69** 160
Madeline **74** 295
Mae (Eddy) **89** 105
Mae (Rosback) **89** 132
Mahala **62** 28
Manley **82** 181
Manlius Rand **75** 18 19
Manning **110** 303
Manning Ellis **109** 204
Mansfield **70** 191
Marcus **79** 183
Marcy **115** 294
Margaret **54** xcviii **58**
  xcix **67** 286 **126** 64 **128**
  172
Margaret (Lusk) **135** 250
Margaret (Olive) **135** 250
Margaret Forbes **75** lxxxi
Margery **63** 170 175
Maria **68** 93 155 **75** 18 **82**
  179 **89** 112 **90** 47
Maria (Bodwell) **120** 137
Maria B. **104** 141 **117** 148
Maria L. **117** 230
Maria S. **126** 24
Mariam L. **92** 342
Mariam N. (Chase)
  (Norton) **123** 152
Marian **63** 379
Marian (Griswold)
  136 322
Marian Dorcas **92** 45
Mariann **96** 333
Marietta J. (Niles) **85** 158
Marion Nicholas (Mrs.)
  96 161
Mark **51** 495 **56** 208 **76** 114
  113 140 **116** 294
Mark D. **62** 28
Marrilla Harriet **81** 392
Martha **51** 465 **56** 208 **62**
  35 42 **63** 377 **64** 374 **66**
  203 365 **67** 56 **72** 287 **82**
  295 296 **95** 211 **98** 63
  100 311 **124** 65 **130** 313
Martha (Lamson) **88** 276
Martha (Morgan) **94** 385
  136 311 312 322 324 328
Martha Ann **81** 392
Martha Ann (Weare) **90**
  387 **120** 66 **123** 150 234
Marvel **127** 34
Mary **51** 462 **53** 212 **54** xci
  55 169 268 **56** 208 **58**
  319 **60** 49 **61** 227 331
  333 338 357 **62** 40 44 **63**
  377 **64** 212 374 **67** 4 53
  68 155 **69** 159 **70** 222
  73 181 229 **74** 260 261
  75 17 120 179 215 **76**
  189 228 229 231 232 255
  78 386 402 **79** 73 155 **80**
  177 **81** 98 392 **82** 296

PERKINS *cont'd*
  301 **83** 301 **88** 320 365
  90 215 **92** 48 256 341 **93**
  323 **94** 64 **96** 238 **98** 63
  107 195 201 270 273 275
  108 56 57 60 121 122
  188 192 223 296 **110** 22
  112 23 179 **113** 209 **114**
  128 **115** 137 138 **116**
  222 **118** 240 242 **122** 49
  126 168 **132** 268 **133** 44
  134 330 **136** 312 324
  139 303 **141** 151 **143**
  213 **144** 268 269 **147**
  348
Mary (Bushnell) **136** 322
  331
Mary (Carver) **88** 225
Mary (Cook) **120** 257
Mary (Coolidge) **83** 426
  438
Mary (Dorman) **108** 191
Mary (Eglin) **94** 385
Mary (Eveleth) **134** 305
Mary (Farris) **134** 138
Mary (Ford) **119** 184
Mary (Hatch) **118** 320
Mary (Johnson) **121** 132
Mary (Lazell) **88** 362
Mary (Niles) **85** 154
Mary (Perkins) **133** 44
Mary (Pratt) **88** 320
Mary (Redington)
  109 114
Mary (Scribner) **90** 231
Mary (Shaw) **89** 255
Mary (Shays) **140** 293
  141 151
Mary (Stone) **108** 123
Mary (Tasker) **98** 63
Mary (Washburn) **88** 316
Mary (Wildes) **132** 268
Mary A. **124** 62
Mary Ann **81** 392 **83** 24 26
  89 260
Mary Asenath **75** 18
Mary Cornelia (Childs)
  101 65
Mary E. **92** 342 **120** 309
Mary Elizabeth **109** 271
Mary Ella **92** 342 355
Mary Eloise (Giddings)
  101 65
Mary Emma **69** 145
  116 185
Mary Frances **59** lxxi
  69 200
Mary G. **113** 117
Mary Hooker **59** lxxii
Mary J. **92** 341 342 **109**
  112 204
Mary Jane **97** 357 **108** 222
  119 65
Mary Jane (Wells) **93** 240
Mary L. **98** 193 251
Mary Lathrop **81** 392
Mary Melissa **64** 211
Mary O. **92** 325 **93** 240
  121 308
Mary R. **129** 49
Mary S. **73** 258 **75** 103 104

PERKINS *cont'd*
  92 342
Mary Shaw **80** 186 **89** 255
Mary T. **123** 74
Mary Tay **92** 256
Mary Teruty **74** 153
Mary White **115** 116
Mary Woodbridge
  136 331
Matthew **59** lxxi **66** 159
  76 110 251 255 **117** 141
  119 287 **136** 324 328
  329
Maude M. **92** 342
Maywood E. (Palmer)
  123 223
Mehitable **55** 373 **59** 283
  68 160 **75** 309 **76** 181
  83 13 **102** 210 212 213
Mehitable (Carr) **102** 210
Mehitable (Emmons)
  97 16
Mela **51** 179
Melinda E. **75** 36
Melvina S. **92** 342
Mercy **66** 225 295 297 306
  67 56 **82** 292 296 **87** 83
  104 183
Mercy H. **109** 112
Merritt Greenwood **68**
  xxxv **74** xxviii **90** 128
Micajah **119** 226
Mildred **108** 134
Minerva **59** 73
Minerva Mercy **81** 392
Minnie Belle **100** 113
Miriam **52** 429 **109** 204
  122 80
Miriam (Mills) **109** 111
Miriam Mason **93** 375
Miriann **96** 333
Molly **66** 222 **74** 225 **77**
  266 **107** 201 **108** 54 124
Molly (Lassel) **108** 121
Molly (Scribner) **90** 251
Morris W. **110** 215
Moses **58** 33 139 **70** 300 **90**
  387 **92** 341 342 **93** 51 55
  337 **94** 116 117 **101** 65
  116 294 **123** 152
Moses S. **92** 341 342
Myron A. **90** 387 **92** 342
N. **105** 211
Nabby **76** 254 **133** 309 310
Nahum **76** 251 **93** 249
Nahum F. **94** 34 36
Naman **87** 206
Nancy **58** 233 **65** 257 **116**
  303 **120** 220 222
Nancy (Adams) **119** 68
Nancy (Coon) **127** 34
Nancy (Hughes) **130** 55
Nancy (Littlefield)
  116 301
Nancy (Russell) **86** 442
Nancy (Stevens) **90** 387
Nancy A. **93** 240
Nancy E. **117** 164
Nancy L. **76** 44
Nancy M. **92** 342
Nannie B. **110** 303

PERKINS *cont'd*
Nathan **72** 30-33 35 87 92
  75 160 **79** 165 **136** 328
Nathaniel **61** 227 **67** 280
  71 226 **74** 256 **76** 36 **89**
  112 **93** 339 **98** 63 **104**
  183 242 **105** 114 **109**
  111 204 **114** 294 **115**
  220 **127** 160 **128** 125
  133 120 **135** 250
Ned Allen **76** 142
Nella M. **74** 170
Nettie Eliza **110** 296
Newman **75** 315 **76** 102
  103 114 180 182 189 191
  258 **110** 172 **127** 34 **128**
  296
Nicholas **76** 223 224 229
  230 **111** 153
Nicholas T. **78** 51
Nickerson **110** 22
Noah **76** 114 **89** 207 **92** 341
Norman Frost **68** 160
Norton **93** 249
Norton (Mrs.) **86** 198
O. **129** 49
Octa **100** 175
Olive **68** 95 **70** 223 **74** 264
  75 82 118 **76** 189 **88** 335
  93 250 **97** 228 **108** 282
  115 136 **116** 142 **136** 25
Olive (Manley) **120** 257
Olive (Young) **123** 149
Olive B. (Young) **119** 224
Olive H. **89** 299
Olive N. (Smith) **107** 157
Oliver **60** 297 **101** 65 **108**
  55 **109** 271 **120** 265
Oliver M. **117** 166
Orren **69** 200
P. **92** 342
Palfrey **99** 224
Pamela **74** 33 88
Pamelia A. (Oaks) **90** 387
  93 240 **94** 117 **123** 151
Patty **147** 181
Paul **66** 366 **71** 326 **76** 36
  92 324 325 328 341 **98**
  63
Paulina (Swett) **119** 277
  278
Peggy **74** 264
Pelatiah **64** 181 **66** 159 **75**
  311 **76** 186 254 260 **115**
  218 **119** 277 278
Percy R. **92** 342
Perley H. **92** 342
Permelia M. **94** 36
Persis **63** 376 379 **64** 76
  66 360 **119** 277
Peter **104** 263
Phebe **60** 244 **62** 289 **66**
  156 **75** 112-114 120 311
  312 **76** 104 179 181 195
  85 237 238 **91** 179 **107**
  195 **108** 54 58 190 **115**
  140 **120** 257 **122** 80 **126**
  178
Phebe (Perkins) **115** 140
Phebe Catherine **81** 392
Phebe Jarvis **109** 204

PERKINS *cont'd*
Phila **116** 222
Philip **51** 179 **78** 300
  81 408
Philip Lufkin **110** 299
Philomela **76** 181
Phineas **61** 34 **120** 182
Plaisted Hill **108** 61
Polly **63** 170 **70** 227 **74** 261
  82 180 **83** 418 **88** 155
  93 339 **108** 56 **115** 304
  120 47 **140** 293 **141** 151
Polly (Huff) **88** 362
  108 123
Polly (Shay) **141** 151
Priscilla **66** 262 302 **108** 57
  124 295
Prudence **109** 112 **124** 251
Prudence (Blodgett) **108**
  286 **109** 14
Prudence May **110** 215
R. Hamilton **83** 301 303
Rachel **67** 53 **73** 140 **74** 130
  108 223
Rachel E. **85** 169
Rachel M. **128** 172
Ranford **71** 139
Ransom A. **109** 271
Rebecca **59** 73 **61** 335 **62**
  37 **66** 18 **71** 17 **73** 261
  76 227-229 231 232 **77**
  233 235 **95** 53 **112** 262
  124 65
Rebecca (Gray) **130** 42
Rebecca (Parker)
  (Lothrop) (Hatch) **112**
  259 261
Rebecca (Perry) **116** 194
Rebecca (Tupper) **99** 293
Remember (Woodman)
  96 360
Reuben **75** 189 **90** 347
Reuben Melville **90** 347
Rhasa P. **121** 145
Rhoda **53** 164
Rhoda Elizabeth **147** 220
  221
Rhoda Keith **55** 240
Richard **53** 302 **66** 155
  225 295 297 **75** 215 **76**
  31 227 **82** 292 296 **91**
  332 **92** 48 **111** 320 **113**
  318 **116** 298 300
Richard S. **111** 147
Robert **66** 35 **76** 223 224
  229 230 **120** 256 257
  125 93 94 **135** 102
Robert H. **111** 137
Robert P. **75** 18
Roger **75** 179 **126** 168
Roger E. **61** 240
Roger Eliot **103** 76
Rose L. **69** 145
Rosella **75** 18
Roselle C. **83** 498 **84** 87
Royal S. **136** 247
Rufus **71** 53 **99** 303 **101** 65
  107 157
Rufus Adams **83** 214
Rufus L. **57** 200
Rufus Lyman **107** 157

PERKINS *cont'd*
Russell **111** 187
Russell W. **84** 87
Ruth **60** 297 **66** 263 **67** 51
  104 183 **107** 272 274
  108 54 55 **110** 212 215
  112 23 **136** 247
Ruth (Grindle) **110** 215
Ruth (McHuron) **136** 247
Ruth (Wakefield) **108** 122
Ruth Grindle **110** 215
Ruth M. **98** 251
Ruthy (Lunt) **116** 221
S. Isabella **68** 204
Sabrina **59** 240
Sally **56** 250 **61** 240 **70** 230
  74 256 **75** 36 308 **87** 123
  92 19 **93** 249 339 **94** 295
  140 69
Sally (Bond) **137** 26
Sally (Elliot) **140** 139
Sally (Lord) **108** 189
Sally (Paine) **140** 235
Sally (Stevens) **117** 141
Sally P. (Upton) **116** 255
Salome **93** 339
Sampson **124** 65
Samuel **59** lxxi **65** 354 **66**
  312 **73** 195 222 **74** 33 75
  75 **76** 228 229 232 **81**
  392 **82** 296 **88** 362 **92** 19
  94 295 **98** 63 **101** 65
  107 272 **110** 128 **115**
  224 **116** 221 **119** 21 **120**
  257 **126** 86 **127** 307 308
  140 48
Samuel Clarke **58** xlix
  59 xxxix lvii lxxi lxxii
Samuel G. **65** 221 **140** 153
Samuel Gardner **63** 207
  92 84
Samuel Goff **92** 346
Samuel Huntington
  59 lxxi
Samuel J. **123** 234
Samuel Jorden **115** 223
Samuel M. **93** 249
Samuel R. **89** 299
Samuel Ransom **81** 392
Samuel S. **90** 387 **93** 238
  240 **94** 117
Samuel W. **86** 384
Sands **128** 125
Sarah **51** 63 464 **53** 281 282
  56 62 207 319 **58** 92 394
  60 49 52 191 **61** 35 **62**
  36 **65** 351 **66** 149 152
  220 222 224 295 299 306
  67 127 **70** 178 222 223
  73 264 **74** 23 33 88 212
  214 219 225 227 228 248
  255 267 **75** 110 118 179
  315 **76** 102 103 114 180
  182 189 228 229 231 232
  257 **79** 156 193 **81** 167
  82 296 299 301 332 **85**
  238 **88** 226 **89** 36 293 **93**
  123 249 **95** 86 **100** 175
  107 196 197 201 270 275
  305 309 **108** 58 61 124
  188 189 192 **110** 141

PERKINS *cont'd*
111 285 115 59 212 120
256-258 124 65 133 44
140 235 147 58
Sarah (Cossens) 90 183
Sarah (Cox) 140 293
Sarah (Douglas) 136 331
Sarah (Homes) 100 302
Sarah (Hurd) 132 89
Sarah (Jewett) 120 256
Sarah (Lazell) 89 20
Sarah (Perkins) 95 86
108 124
Sarah (Taylor) 125 101
Sarah (Wallis) 85 238
Sarah A. 74 312 96 203
Sarah Ann 76 35 94 162
Sarah Ann (Bean) 92 344
Sarah B. 87 83
Sarah C. 84 87
Sarah Cabell 78 164
Sarah E. 90 303 93 109
121 307 122 151
Sarah E. (Haley) 90 303
387 119 225
Sarah E. (Welch) 120 136
Sarah Elliott 63 207
Sarah H. 75 xliii
Sarah Jane 98 251
Sarah L. 108 279
Sarah L. (Kimball)
123 149
Sarah M. 93 109
Sarah Maria 69 200
Sarah P. 79 37
Sarah Peck (Fisher)
111 187
Sarah S. 144 108
Sarh Hunt (Elliott) 92 84
Seabury 125 38
Seth 66 24 67 55 108 58
Seth B. 78 386
Sharks 66 157
Sheldon 125 42
Shubael 84 87
Sidney 92 341
Silas 99 303 108 58
Simeon 75 126 80 121 129
102 60 116 6 12 13 126
94 168 127 54 207 273
128 34 133 304
Simeon Leonard 126 169
128 34
Simon 108 59
Solomon 74 255 95 86
98 63
Sophia 113 33 38 119 225
Sophia (Donnell) 119
147 224
Sparks 75 112-114 120
311 312 76 104 179 181
191 193 105 211 110
174 115 216
Spencer 110 288 115 215
Stella L. (Burnham)
136 325
Stephen 74 219 225 227
228 248 267 82 332 107
272 274 108 54-56 58 60
123 122 80 134 305
Stover 66 312 105 209

PERKINS *cont'd*
117 141 119 279 123 73
149
Sukey 116 301 302
Suky Maria 108 58
Susan 63 377 64 374 66
365 76 38 95 51
Susan Alitha 60 297
Susan C. 73 258
Susan E. 93 240 116 185
119 279
Susan E. (Perkins)
119 279
Susan G. 83 424 438
Susan M. 93 240
Susan T. 69 144
Susan Y. 121 303 122 312
Susan Z. 120 137
Susanna 51 179 461 59
187 60 198 297 66 298
70 229 73 227 82 289
296 87 286 90 249 100
340 107 197 198 108 55
123 188 116 129 130
136 329 140 69 235
Susanna (Dutton) 101 65
Susanna (Hudson)
(Howlett) 92 84
Susanna (Wiswal)
108 123
Susy G. 83 424 438
Sylvania 125 31
Sylvester Miller 81 392
Sylvia 136 257
Sylvia (Tupper) 99 303
107 157
T. 67 62 95 51
T. A. 52 379
T. N. 124 33 34
Tabitha 115 309
Tabitha (Anderson)
122 80
Tabitha (Niles) 85 146
Tabitha (Washburn)
113 140
Thaddeus 76 109 108 56
Thankful B. 88 336
Theodate (Boston)
119 287
Theodosia 76 185
Thomas 51 44 57 280 58
69 61 65 335 62 35 44
46 47 206 66 149 152
224 302 67 53 59 76 223-
231 78 260 85 238 88
316 320 362 95 328 96
144 336 360 98 63 134
220 107 196-198 271 274
309 108 56 121-123 188
116 177 120 256 257
126 86 178 132 117 118
267 268 133 44 140 32
235 293 145 64
Thomas A. 63 392 65 101
Thomas Allen 68 xxxii
210 72 250 80 113 103
237
Thomas C. 72 6 79 155
Thomas H. 54 xcix 140
69 139 249
Thomas Handasyd 56 lii

PERKINS *cont'd*
76 212 82 461 105 179
106 309
Thomas N. (Mrs.) 70 xl
Thomas Nelson 75 xliii
80 186 84 106 190 89
255 92 84 85 92 151
Thomas Shaw 136 322
Timothy 51 179 78 284
98 63 103 76 121 154
122 80
Titus 52 77
Tobijah 56 207
Toby 76 228 229 232
Tristram Jordan 108 58
True 51 464 53 282
Trueworth 53 281
Tryphena 76 141
Ursula C. 92 339 341 342
Valentine 129 316
Vivienue 93 109
W. 89 120 98 251
W. A. 91 332
W. P. 77 51
W. W. 77 266
Walter 92 127 93 240
Walter M. 93 240
Warren G. 93 339
Warren H. 76 44
Warwick 93 339
Washington 123 73
Wealthian 66 302
Wentworth 93 249
Wesley P. 136 247
Wilhelmenna 92 342
William 53 164 255 55 268
58 394 65 257 66 149
67 51 70 315 73 134 188
74 130 151 75 lxxxvi 18
36 76 102 223 225 227-
232 78 97 79 96 158 87
206 92 15 93 250 95 50
98 58 100 192 107 272
108 59 280 282 109 255
256 110 23 111 206 210
111 187 116 139 255
117 169 118 313 120 84
121 132 125 94 128 126
130 52 124 134 183 147
46
William B. 73 188
William Clarke 90 347
William E. 94 117
William Eaton 92 322
William H. 74 153 75 18
85 169 90 387 93 240
94 117 123 151
William Herbert 75 19
William Huntington 72
xx 90 130 94 385 95 73
150
William Lee 84 374 100
304 144 162
William M. 98 251
William N. 109 112
William Robertson (Mrs.)
108 135
William S. 98 93
William Titcomb 70 191
William Wallace 93 339
Williams 65 354

PERKINS *cont'd*
  Willie (Bond) **88** 362
  Willie L. **147** 60
  Winefred F. (Norton)
    123 234
  Winfred R. **93** 240
  Yolande (Vandeveer)
    89 132
  Youngs **79** 73
  Zaccheus **95** 113 **124** 295
  Zebulon **85** 237 **127** 123
  Zephaniah **119** 184
  Zilpha **59** 210 **60** 266
PERKINSON
  Andrew **135** 248
  Ann **135** 248
  Annie Maria **135** 248
  James **135** 248
  John **65** 45 **135** 248
  Mary **135** 248
  Richard **65** 45 **135** 248
  Robert **65** 45
PERKLE James **64** 114
PERKS
  Martha **99** 25 27
  Stephen **99** 25 27
  Susanna **99** 27
PERLEY Pearlee Pearly
    Perlee Perly
  —— **55** 267 269 270 **61**
    100 **74** 315
  — Rev. Mr. **62** 276
  Alfred H. **109** 71
  Alfred Howard **96** 161
    208 **118** 79
  Allan **60** 190 **62** 206 **83** 332
  Allen **57** 283 **83** 333
  Amos **108** 220
  Ann E. **89** 381
  Anna Porter **127** 129
  Annette **75** 19
  Augusta L. **103** 47
  Clara Elizabeth **74** lxii
    105 61
  Cyrus **82** 180
  David **57** 283
  Dolly Ann **76** lxx
  Dora Prescott **74** lxii
  Eleanor Spofford **83** 333
  Elizabeth **96** 377
  Ellen **117** 169
  Enoch **145** 162
  Eunice (Peabody) **83** 332
    333
  Fanny **75** 19
  Frances **96** 377
  Hannah **99** 168 **108** 220
    119 240
  Hannah (Coker) **83** 333
  Harriet Hood (Spofford)
    83 333
  Helen May **82** 180
  Hepzibah **109** 52
  Humphrey **83** 332 333
  Isaac **96** 377
  Jeremiah **109** 52
  John **60** 193 **83** 222 333
    85 85 **109** 183
  John Langdon **74** lxii
  Joshua **145** 360
  Juda **57** 283

PERLEY *cont'd*
  Lizzie **64** 213
  Lois **121** 169
  Louisa **75** 19
  M. V.B. **60** 190 **102** 73
  Maranda (Perry) **109** 183
  Martha **62** 206 **88** 195
  Martha (Fowler) **83** 333
  Martin Van Buren **61**
    xxxv 100
  Mary A. **121** 310
  Mehitable (Dwinells)
    83 333
  Moses **75** 19
  Nathaniel M. **125** 36
  Orpha C. **69** 327
  Permela **96** 146
  Priscilla **125** 107
  Rebecca **96** 400
  Richard Hood **83** 333
  Ruth **51** 461
  Sally **60** 193
  Samuel **51** 460-466
    121 248
  Sarah (Osgood) **109** 52
  Sarah P. **74** 315
  Sidney **59** xlii **60** 206 **61**
    xix **62** 51 **64** 333 376 **68**
    xxx 207 **73** 160 **77** xxv
    159 78 338 79 196 450
    80 204 **81** 114 215 **82**
    231 **83** 124 222 237 332
    98 361 **109** 47 **111** 130
    114 262 **115** 241 244
    122 41 **123** 172 **124** 101
    103 **142** 110 **144** 373
    146 318 **148** 9
  Stephen **83** 333
  Susan **82** 180
  Susan H. **60** 193
  Thomas **82** 180 **109** 52
  •Timothy **83** 333
  Zenas **89** 381
PERLIER Jean **96** 208
Perly *see* Perley
Permenter *see* Parmenter
PERMILLION
  Susanna **73** 264
Perminter *see* Parmenter
PERMIT Hannah **58** 18
  Mary **58** 16
PERNA Lydia **126** 183
PERNAL Benjamin **55** 68
PERNAN Rosanna **56** 319
PERNAY Honorine Julia
    Elizabeth de **112** 247
PERNE John **100** 217
  Katharine **100** 217
  Rachel **61** 128 **100** 216 217
    103 186
  Rachel (Greene) **100** 217
  Richard **100** 216 217
PERNELL Lucy **127** 207
PERNETTE
  Eliza Georgina
    128 115
  Maria **128** 115
  Michael **128** 115
PERNEY Thomas **142** 257
PERNOLL J. W. **91** 332

PERO
  Elizabeth (Weaver)
    123 308
  Harriet Rosilla **123** 309
  Louis **123** 308
PERONNEAU
  Ann Motte **119** 194
  Mary **91** 76
  Mary (Hutson) **119** 195
    137 37
PEROT
  Elliston **53** 460
  Francis **53** 460
  Henry **138** 10
  John **53** 460 **121** 187
  Thomas **121** 190
PEROTT Grace **68** 49
Perpont *see* Pierpont
PERPOUND Peter **93** 80
PERRAM John **51** 308
  Lydia **51** 308
PERRAULT
  Joseph Francois
    54 360
PERRELL
  Mary Ajen **112** 316
Perren *see* Perrin
PERRERS Agnes **119** 99
Perrey *see* Perry
PERRIAM Mary **100** 240
PERRIELLO
  Henry Alfred **102** 124
    105 230 **106** 129
PERRIER Anne Francoise
    110 133
  Jean Hypolite **110** 133
  Pierre **110** 133
  Thereze Adele **110** 133
PERRIGO Perigoe
    Porrigoo
  —— **137** 362
  Ann **76** 270
  Elizabeth **141** 196
  H. S. **123** 100
  H. S. (Mrs.) **123** 100
  Henrietta (Silvester)
    86 131
  James **65** 40 **141** 196
  Joel **86** 131
  Laura **123** 100
  Mary **99** 26 **100** 240
  Rachel **88** 63
  Robert **128** 294
  S. F. **123** 100
  Waitstill **141** 196
PERRILL
  Margaret **105** 147
  Maria (Breedlove)
    105 147
  Nathan **105** 147
PERRIMAN Perryman
    Poryman
  Dorothy **111** 54
  Henry **64** 222
  Nicholas **51** 468 **61** 360
  Peter **66** 35
  Rebecca **136** 301
  Richard **52** 111 **64** 22
    71 28
  Walter Lewis (Mrs.)
    106 126

PERRIMAN *cont'd*
William **142** 366
PERRIMAN-AMSDEN
Frances **58** 126
PERRIN Perin Perine
Perren Perrine
Perring
—— **92** 355 358 **93** 61 63
116 **133** 119
— Goodman **96** 258
— Mr. **55** 432
— Widow **75** 228 **96** 251
Aaron **59** 210 212 **60** 201
266
Abel **122** 17
Abigail **96** 263 270
Abigail (Carpenter)
96 263
Abra **96** 264
Abraham **62** 236 237 347-
349 **73** 117 **96** 249-251
254-256 259-262 264-268
Abram **96** 259
Albert **91** 201
Albert S. **93** 216
Alice **104** 103
Ann **62** 236 **96** 257 265
Anna **60** 264 **83** 359 **96** 257
259 264
Anne **96** 266 267
Anquetil du **99** 138
100 106
Arthur **55** xxxv
Asahel **83** 359
Asia **96** 270
Augustine Josephine
Sophie **110** 129
Augustus **92** 353 355 358
93 61 63 116 **94** 39 **140**
167
Augustus Williams
92 353
Benjamin David **104** 103
Betsey **83** 359
Calvin **96** 270
Catherine (McLean)
126 292
Charles **69** 124 125 214
216 218 221 224 295 306
307 **70** 143 213 **83** 359
120 142
Charles R. **121** 30
Chloe **96** 270
Daniel **60** 190 **62** 347 **65**
94 **96** 262-264 270 **98**
266 322
Daniel Ide **96** 270
David **62** 347 **63** 126 **96**
259 262 264 **104** 103
David Child **93** 61
Dorothy **71** 270 **87** 126
Edna Elethier (Perkins)
90 347
Edward **96** 270
Elizabeth **52** 77 **53** 335 336
96 251 255 263 266 267
269 270
Elizabeth (Lyon) **96** 270
Emily T. **83** 359
Emory A. **80** 35
Esther Maria **104** 124

PERRIN *cont'd*
Evelyn Marie (Requist)
109 130
Ezra **96** 269 270
Franklin **93** 116
George **93** 63
Glover **96** 256 257 270
121 30
Hadlock **93** 214
Hannah **96** 257 259 264
270
Harriet **92** 353 358 **94** 39
Helen Jube **96** 73
Henry **81** 297 **106** 169
Henry Harry (Mrs.)
100 112
Hepzibah (Williams)
121 30
Howland Delano **55** 227
60 190 **65** xxxv 94
Huldah **96** 270
Isaac **96** 256 265-267
Jacob **96** 267 270
James **96** 270
Jane (Whittemore)
(Carlile) **106** 270
Jeremiah **60** 77
Jesse **96** 269 270 **98** 320 330
Joanna **52** 77
John **55** 224 **62** 236 346-
349 **63** 140 **81** 297 **95**
299 **96** 251 254-265 267-
270 **98** 167 168 267 **106**
270 **121** 30 31 34 **144**
100
Joseph **52** 77 **71** 270 **77**
73 132 **96** 73 270
Jude **123** 11
Lemuel **96** 270 **121** 30
Lois **59** 210 **60** 201
Louise Jeanette **80** 35
Lucetta (McIntosh) **123** 11
Lucy **83** 4 **96** 270
Lucy (Durrell) **133** 119
Lydia **96** 264 270
Margaret **71** 269 **73** 117
Marian **59** 210
Mariet **59** 210
Martha **96** 263 **108** 244
Martha (Nash) **96** 270
Martha Ann **80** 40 48
Mary **55** 224 **62** 347 **77** 73
132 **84** 224 **96** 256 259-
264 **98** 266 **136** 314 **143**
155
Mary (Polley) **96** 260
Mehitable **58** 54 **62** 346
347 **96** 262 263 267
Molly **73** 117 **96** 270
Nancy **96** 270
Nancy (Burr) **96** 270
Nathaniel **96** 263 264
Noah **52** 77 **62** 347 **73** 117
96 263 264
Patience **96** 263
Patience (Walker) **96** 263
Payson Harrington
92 355
Perez **78** 189
Polly **92** 314 **96** 260 270
Rachel **93** 325 **96** 269 270

PERRIN *cont'd*
105 66 **121** 34-36
Rachel (Ide) **95** 299
96 269 270
Rachel (Rice) **121** 30 33 34
Rebecca **96** 266
Ruth **96** 250 265 266 **144**
100 103-105 356
Ruth (Cosset) **144** 100
Sally **81** 297
Samuel **62** 347 **71** 269 **73**
117 **96** 256 262-264 270
98 321
Sarah **62** 236 346 347 **63** 90
81 297 **95** 299 **96** 249
255 256 263 265-267 270
107 295
Sarah (Eddy) **96** 267
Sarah (Hunt) **96** 264
Sarah (Vorhees) **98** 267
Sarah (Walker) **96** 255
256 264
Sarah Roselle **59** 212
97 66
Solomon **60** 264 **83** 359
Solomon Lavalette
59 210
Stanley E. **121** 29 56
125 138
Stanley Ernest **144** 100
Stephen **81** 297 **144** 100
356
Stephen Child **92** 353
Susan **79** 39
Susanna **62** 347 **67** 372
96 262-264 267
Susanna (Gye) **96** 266
Thankful **81** 297 **96** 263
Thomas **53** 335 336
144 100
Timothy **96** 269 270
W. H. **117** 132
Wesley Ellis **90** 347
William **104** 103
William Davison **89** 401
90 305 **91** 210 306
PERRINGTON
W. H. **91** 332
PERRIS Thomas **63** 352
William **107** 83
PERRISH Mary **83** 155
PERRITT Perit
Anna Rumsey **58** lxxxix
Anthony **109** 190
Elizabeth (Quintard)
109 190
John W. **58** lxxxix
Margaretta **58** lxxxix
Margaretta D. **81** 202
Peter **93** 213 **109** 190
PERRONS
Esther Maria **112** 78
PERRURE Parette Louise
113 260
PERRY Perrey Pery Perye
—— **51** 12 **52** 480 **53** 55
252 **54** 72 **56** 102 249 **57**
239 **60** 337 **61** 317 375
401 **62** 387 **70** 298 **76**
171 **78** 140 **79** 301 **83** 36
85 294 **88** 22 **99** 104

PERRY *cont'd*
103 191 **105** 325 **116** 44
105 106 **123** 92 **130** 72
156 **136** 165 **138** 7
— Capt. **121** 136
— Comdr. **117** 257
— Dr. **56** 249
— Mr. **63** 187 **65** 179 368
74 186
— Mrs. **81** 299 **83** 195 308
103 193
— Rev. Mr. **60** 202 205
— Widow **76** 174
____ (Parmalee) **116** 40
A. E. **119** 70
Abby (Webber) **119** 280
Abel **54** lxxxiii **77** 292
102 235
Abiel **58** 261 **130** 72
Abigail **57** 323 **69** 134 **81**
293 **110** 33 35 **115** 184
185 192 193 198 273-275
277 **116** 31-33 36 38 40
42-44 102 106 107 195
196 200 **119** 27 **120** 160
123 215 **125** 103 104
134 335 **135** 304 **144**
318
Abigail (Batchelder)
116 192
Abigail (Bourne) **116** 105
119 28
Abigail (Damon) **115**
183 184 187 188 273 **126**
280
Abigail (Dyer) **87** 230 235
Abigail (Gibbs) **116** 195
119 27 **123** 216
Abigail (Hammond)
115 192 **116** 32
Abigail (Nasson) **90** 245
Abigail (Presbury)
115 192
Abigail (Spooner)
116 198
Abigail (Tupper) **99** 125
Abigail (Williams) **126** 24
Abigail Gibbs **116** 195
Abigail H. (Wing)
116 107
Abigail Thacher **123** 216
Abijah **76** 136 **98** 221
Ablena (Buck) **116** 38
Abner **54** 70 **58** 84 263 374
59 389 392 **76** 172 **82**
470 **110** 114 **115** 98 99
194 **116** 34 36 37 201
122 319 **123** 67
Abraham **115** 275 277
116 102 103 107 **124**
243 **132** 21
Achsah **86** 402 **116** 193 194
Achsah Ann **126** 215
Adah **116** 202 203
Adah (Shepardson)
116 202
Adam **136** 38
Adelaide **74** 31
Adelija T. **116** 200
Alanson **116** 39 103 204
Alexander **62** 322 **116** 107

PERRY *cont'd*
Alexander James **90** 75
Alexina (Carver) **89** 42
Alfred **116** 43
Alice **69** 275 **88** 59 126
115 269 **116** 192
Alice (Chase) **88** 126
Alice H. (Houghton)
116 202
Alice Weston (Cone)
84 454
Almerin **121** 80
Almon **116** 39
Alonzo **116** 204
Alsada I. (Donaldson)
83 427 438
Alvin Earl **99** 148
Amanda **116** 40 204
Amos **51** 230 **52** 378 396
53 262 367 **54** 245-252
461 **57** 323 402 **58** 263
267 389 390 **59** 76 78
136 139 312 **90** 51 **92**
323 **129** 66
Amy **97** 36 **116** 192
Amy A. **110** 114
An: **99** 96
Anda **116** 191
Andrew **76** 147 **116** 203
204 **122** 290 319
Angeline **122** 255
Ann **62** 247 **73** 177 **97** 335
115 289 **132** 21
Ann (Booth) **115** 281
Ann (Clemons) **116** 203
Ann (Newman) **132** 21 22
Ann (Parsons) **99** 125
116 43
Ann (Snow) **116** 43
Ann (Ward) **126** 21
Ann Eliza (Gould) **121** 80
Anna **62** 85 **63** 294 **75** 179
93 229 **106** 211 **113** 143
115 190 191 195 271 272
279 288 289 **116** 28 29
35 39 40 42 108 203 **121**
264 265 **122** 259 **126**
254
Anna (Bliss) **116** 37
Anna (Clemons) **116** 203
Anna (Downer) **116** 39
Anna (Perry) **115** 271
116 29
Anna (Saunders) **115**
190 191 289 **127** 254
Anna (Seeley) **116** 36
Anna (Snow) **99** 125
Anna Melissa **116** 204
Anna Nye **116** 105
Anne F. **145** 154
Anne Isabel **84** 190
Annes (Peerce) **132** 21
146 268
Annie **110** 114
Annie Estelle **83** 308
Annie F. (Pease) **83** 438
Annie Perthina **82** 395
Anselm **134** 254
Anson **116** 38
Anson Luce **116** 200 260
Anthony **98** 167 172

PERRY *cont'd*
99 238
Apolos **103** 196
Appa **88** 59
Arba **63** 86
Artemisia **116** 204
Arthur **75** 179 **87** 21 **96**
323 **115** 96 182 184 185
274 275 289 **116** 101 103
104 107 **125** 191 234 235
129 228 **130** 287 **132**
298 299
Arthur Clark **116** 200
Arthur Dunton **71** xxiii
74 xxviii **88** 185 **89** 147
90 129 151 **91** 157 **92**
161 **97** 79 161 187
Arthur Dunton (Mrs.)
74 xxviii **120** 146
Arthur Latham **57** 239
65 19 **67** 379 **95** 121
Asa **113** 31
Asa T. **83** 438
Asahel **116** 40 **141** 197 333
Asaph **116** 36
Asenath **89** 118 **116** 39
Asenath (Lambert)
116 198
Augustus **116** 199
Augustus B. **78** 293
Azariah Hawley **76** 147
Azor **115** 198 **116** 39 40
Azubah **61** 121
Barnabas **58** 88 **122** 51
Barsheba **115** 286 **116** 106
Bathsheba **115** 286 287 **116**
41 106 107 198
Bathsheba (Gibbs) **115**
286 **116** 106 **119** 27 28
30 **123** 139
Bathsheba (Gould)
116 201
Bathsheba (Perry) **115** 287
116 106
Belinda **116** 196 197
Benjamin **57** 321 400 **58** 83
84 170 172 174 261 263
267 390 **59** 75 79 312
391 **60** 176 **67** 286 **70**
xxxv **82** 470 **90** 245 **92**
36 **99** 65 125 **115** 87 90-
92 98 99 188 193-197
272 275 279 **116** 33 43
105 **120** 115 **121** 266
123 133 207 **128** 128
129 370
Benjamin F. **77** 149
Benjamin Fessenden **97**
187 **116** 198
Benjamin Franklin
116 41
Benjamin Freeman
116 200
Bertha Clarke **108** 135
Bessie Lillian **82** 395
Bethiah **83** 291 **115** 93 182
Bethiah (Tupper) **99** 60
115 182
Bethuel **87** 230 235 **116** 28
Betsey **76** 30 **103** 270 **116**
36 38 39 107 198 199 203

PERRY *cont'd*
126 65
Betsey (Bowen) **116** 204
Betsey (Corliss) **116** 105
Betsey (Dotey) **116** 192
Betsey (Ellis) **116** 105
121 266
Betsey (Fessenden)
116 200
Betsey (Gridley) **88** 283
Betta **88** 59
Betty **115** 272
Beulah (Benjamin)
116 102
Beulah (Kellogg) **116** 33
Blanche Thorne **84** 209
Bliss **64** 296
Bridget **143** 329
Brunette **116** 204
C. J.A. **116** 315
C. M.B. **118** 164
Calbraith Bourn **68** 111
Caleb **76** 135-137 140 145
147 150 153 172 174 **115**
188-190 277 283 284 **116**
193 **122** 260 **125** 235
Calvin **115** 284 285
116 194
Candace T. (Hubbard)
89 266
Carlton H. **79** 157
Caroline **57** 90 **82** 508
Caroline (Bryant) **116** 199
Caroline C. (Eaton)
85 381
Caroline Slidell **81** 339
340 **101** 323
Carroll **81** 110 214 **82** 124
230 **84** 235 **85** 182
Catherine 36 **61** 121 **92** 36
104 103 **108** 308 **115**
276 **116** 43
Catherine (Gifford) **115**
274-276 **129** 228 **130**
287 **132** 298 299
Catherine (Perry) **116** 43
Catherine (Sloane) **99** 125
116 43
Caty **115** 275
Celia **108** 239 **116** 28
117 310
Charles **82** 330 **89** 42 **96**
286 **116** 106 200
Charles Adelbert **81** 108
222 **82** 126 247 470 **83**
100
Charles Chamberlain
56 249
Charles French **89** 70
Charles French (Mrs.)
89 70 137 190
Charles Hartshorn
116 202
Charles Howes **116** 195
Charles J. **104** 284
Charles Robert **122** 319
Charles Smith **73** 263
Charlotte (Paul) **116** 40
Charlotte A. **125** 236
Chester **62** 85 **99** 125
116 43

PERRY *cont'd*
Chipman C. **119** 280
Chloe **115** 275 276 288
116 39 40 202
Chloe C. (Emlott) **116** 260
Christiana **60** 339 **86** 64
116 101 106 107
Christiana (Cushman)
97 187
Christiana (Nye) **116** 105
Christiana (Perry) **116**
101 107
Christopher Grant
125 178
Christophers Raymond
70 xxxv
Clara **63** lv **116** 40
Clara Estelle **107** 69
Clara Harmon **109** 130
Clarinda B. **81** 276 283
Clarinda D. **69** 367
Clarissa Arvilla
(Blanchard) **116** 201
Comfort **78** 262
Comfort (Bates) **96** 286
Constant **114** 182
Content **116** 104
Content (Crocker)
116 104
Cornelius A. **84** 209
Corydon M. **76** 277
Cyrene **116** 40
Cyrus **58** 374 **116** 37 204
D. B. **52** 149
Daniel **55** 431 **56** 251 **67**
178 **115** 188 190 282-285
287 **116** 101 191-193
119 27 **121** 134 **125** 271
Daniel B. **72** lvi
Daniel F. **76** 38
David **57** 321 **62** 394 **76**
140 150 **96** 185 **110** 80
115 184 185 191 198 269
278 288 289 **116** 37 38
41 203 **122** 206 319 **123**
270 **125** 175 191
David Barnes **101** 318
David Barnes (Mrs.) **84**
106 190 **99** 69 152 **101**
318
David Charles **76** 173
David G. **123** 306
David Shepherd **94** 125
David Sinclair **101** 318
Davis **116** 106
Dawes **110** 121
Deborah **57** 281 **83** 212
98 76 **99** 59 **100** 192
106 19 **107** 228 **113** 305
115 86 87 90 97 182 192-
194 269 **116** 31 44 102
105 107 **118** 201 **120**
273 **124** 50 **125** 235 **128**
247 **129** 30 31 224 **132**
293
Deborah (Ivery) **113** 305
Deborah (Johnson)
115 193
Deborah (Landers) **115**
273 274 **116** 44 **124** 53
Deborah (Oman) **115** 269

PERRY *cont'd*
Deborah R. (Eaton)
85 378
Deidamia **122** 206
Delia (Bourne) **116** 107
Deliverance **84** 54 **115**
286 287 **116** 41 106 107
119 27
Deliverance (Bourne)
115 287 **116** 107
Deliverance (Gross)
116 41
Desire **115** 186 278 279
Desire (Handy) **115** 185
125 128
Desire (Needham) **110** 30
Diadema **116** 103
Diadema (Bacon) **116** 201
Diana **116** 41
Diantha **116** 201
Diman **88** 59
Dinah **115** 98 194
Dinah (Swift) **99** 65 **115**
98 **123** 133
Dolly **92** 313
Dolly (Wilson) **115** 285
Dorcas **57** 156 **58** 374 **93**
214 **126** 254 **133** 156
Dorcas (Fowler) **130** 72
Dorcas (Newhall) **136** 165
Dorothy **68** 97 **131** 169
173
Dorothy (Powell) **131**
170 174
Dorothy Thelma **101** 318
Downer **116** 39 204
Duncan **116** 199
Dwight Ruggles **116** 200
Dyar **63** 86
E. A. **82** 182 409
Ebenezer **70** 34 **91** 260 **115**
91 93 97 181 182 191 192
268-271 **116** 28-31 33
198 200 **118** 279 **119**
273 **121** 138 **123** 207
125 190 191 **130** 4
Edgar **112** 13 14
Edith M. **83** 384
Edmond **125** 191
Edmund **115** 93 181 182
268 269 **116** 41
Edna **116** 40
Edna M. **117** 292
Edward **64** 166 **70** xxxv
73 134 **82** 215 **108** 76
301 **115** 86 88 89 273
119 171 **124** 50 **127** 11
250 **128** 217 243 247 248
129 30 31 33 **142** 364
Edward (Mrs.) **82** 215
Edward Cornelius **80**
106 208 **83** 100
Edward Hale **89** 70
Edwards **130** 14
Edwin W. **72** 300
Edyth Evolin **72** 300
Elbridge **58** 346
Eldad **99** 60 **115** 182
Eleanor **68** 292 **90** 339
116 42 **120** 115 116
Eleanor (Ellis) **115** 271

PERRY *cont'd*
120 116 121 264
Eleanor Gray (Bodine)
87 59
Eleazer 115 283
Eli 87 8
Eliakim 99 65 115 98 99
193-198 116 39 40
Elias 134 254
Elijah 54 245 65 363 91 260
115 95 96 182 185 187-
190 273 275 277 282 284
286 288 116 100 107 192
196 197 119 28 120 115
123 139 125 191
Eliphael (Smith) 124 50
Eliphaz 116 34 201
Elisha 73 225 115 95-97
182 186 190 191 272 279
287-289 116 42 104 105
196 119 27 28 120 273
121 134 139 122 261
123 140 127 254 132
293
Elisha G. 88 283
Elisha Hewitt 130 232
Elishua 125 234
Eliz. 116 203
Eliza 69 34 81 432 82 52
89 23 116 202 203 126
181 130 72
Eliza (Faunce) 116 102
Eliza (Green) 126 64
Eliza A. 116 107
Eliza A. (Liscomb)
135 159
Elizabeth 51 463 56 398 57
90 322 391 412 58 86
308 59 79 134 137 139
63 86 67 286 68 105 72
216 74 65 76 172 80 447
87 246 92 36 98 172 99
253 100 237 106 16 18
108 301 109 160 113 30
115 90 94 97 184 185
187 191 192 198 270 272
277 279 280 116 29 32
36 38 39 42 43 103 105-
109 198 199 202 203 122
102 125 234 129 369
134 173 135 44 138 7
141 361 143 329
Elizabeth (Adams)
116 204
Elizabeth (Bennet)
125 219
Elizabeth (Bourne) 116
27 195 119 27
Elizabeth (Bowen)
116 204
Elizabeth (Bryant) 129 369
Elizabeth (Buck) 116 38
Elizabeth (Burges) 115 86
124 50
Elizabeth (Crow) 125 235
Elizabeth (Dotey) 116 192
Elizabeth (Dunham)
122 319
Elizabeth (Ellis) 116 105
121 266

PERRY *cont'd*
Elizabeth (Fessenden)
116 200
Elizabeth (Freeman) 115
192 116 32
Elizabeth (Gray) 115 279
117 313
Elizabeth (Green) 90 58
116 197
Elizabeth (Harding)
116 204
Elizabeth (Lobdell) 133
192 143 348
Elizabeth (Oman) 115 270
Elizabeth (Rowe) 105 315
Elizabeth (Tallman)
(Taber) 116 198
Elizabeth (Tippetts)
98 221
Elizabeth (Trask) 116 42
Elizabeth (Tupper) 99 289
Elizabeth (Valentine)
108 239
Elizabeth (Williamson)
115 94 125 128 131 126
279 280 127 254
Elizabeth A. 73 273 79 157
Elizabeth Agnes 82 470
Elizabeth Ann (Bayard)
116 103
Elizabeth Bartlett 116 193
Elizabeth Cornelia (Hall)
101 318
Elizabeth L. 115 54
Elizabeth Lejee 89 70
Elizabeth M. 125 174
Elizlabeth (Burges)
124 50
Elkanah 116 33
Ellen 69 367
Ellen Maria 72 lvi
Ellis 115 279 287 116 105-
107
Emelia Alice 116 204
Emeline 115 284
Emeline (Frisbie) 116 107
Emily 78 207 104 103
Emily A. 77 149
Emma 104 103
Enoch 103 256
Ephraim 58 374 62 370
Ephraim Cutler 58 374
Erasmus 73 276
Esther 55 74 63 288 68 105
69 130 70 37 73 137
115 96 284 285 116 41
125 183
Esther (Gates) 115 284
120 268
Esther (Marvin) 116 40
Esther (Taber) 115 96
Esther (Tinkham) 116 192
Esther Arnold 82 470
Ethel 130 234
Eunice 56 43 68 292 69
130 367 81 293 116 36
44
Eunice (Center) 90 51
Eunice (Clothier) 116 201
Eunice (White) 116 36
Eunice (Witherell) 136 40

PERRY *cont'd*
Evelina 115 300
Evelyn Sophronia 69 34
Everett 96 331
Everett E. 92 342
Experience 115 96 120 268
125 131 126 280
Experience (Blackwell)
116 28 117 305 141 58
Experience (Williamson)
125 131
Experience Taft 116 202
Ezekiel 75 180 115 198
116 39
Ezra 60 190 77 xlv 82 470
99 60 109 160 114 71
229 115 86-88 90 91 93-
96 98 181 182 186 187
191 268 270-273 280 281
116 27 100 103 108 191
117 313 118 209 119
164 120 101 123 132
124 50 58 132 171 298
134 254
Fannie 116 39
Fannie (Barnes) 99 125
116 43
Fanny 116 36
Fanny (Gibbs) 123 270
Fanny (Sergeant) 125 178
Fear 115 192 279 116 104
107
Ferdinand D. 135 159
Flora Elizabeth (Belcher)
110 121
Flora H. 82 175
Florence May 102 124
Frances 90 245 103 46
116 36 39
Frances (Gibbs) 123 270
Francis 73 223 131 100 102
103
Francis F. 136 165
Frank 72 295
Franklin 116 199
Franklin R. 81 276 283
Frederick 116 203
Frederick A. 117 292
Freelove 115 92 93
Freeman 70 xxxv 115 288
116 32 197 199 200 128
125
Freeman Allen 115 286
116 196
Freeman L. 87 21
G. E. 83 100
Gad 88 59
Gardner Braman 89 70
Gates 103 45
George 62 321 368 84 152
91 332 96 331 110 80
114 182 116 38 109 122
319 126 24 254 127 141
George Adelbert 115 86
George Buchman 136 165
George C. 109 80
George Cary 116 203
George Covington
108 135
George H. 117 294

PERRY *cont'd*
George Ingraham
   116 199
George Leonard **136** 165
George Lyman **93** 251
George Milton **116** 108
   109
George Nelson **116** 201
George Talbot **116** 109
George W. **95** 246 **110** 80
   122 290
George Warren **110** 70
George Williams **116** 202
Georgianna **78** 220
   79 216
Georgianna West
   (Graves) **55** xxxv **84**
   181 **89** 70 137
Gideon **78** 262
Gilbert **91** 332 **115** 287 288
   116 197
Gilbert E. **121** 80
Godfrey **127** 148
Gould Henry **121** 80
Grace **70** 37 **77** xxviii **81**
   40 **103** 193
Grace A. E. **122** 319
Hannah **56** 30 258 **57** 323
   59 78 396 **63** 86 174 **64**
   156 **70** 166 **87** 383 **115**
   86 92 93 188-192 195
   277 278 285-287 289 **116**
   28 34 37 38 41 100 101
   104 106 108 191 192 195
   197 202 **117** 305 **119** 28
   31 **120** 116 **123** 65 131
   207 **124** 50 **125** 191 **126**
   23 **128** 13 **134** 291
Hannah (Baker) **116** 42
Hannah (Blish) **115** 277
   283
Hannah (Damon) **115** 184
   187 **123** 139 **126** 280
Hannah (Ellis) **122** 257
   261
Hannah (Floyd)
   (Whittemore) **108** 92
Hannah (Fountain)
   (Sherwood) **115** 288
Hannah (Hemeon) **116** 42
Hannah (Leland) **105** 314
Hannah (Phinney)
   116 101
Hannah (Savary) **115** 94
Hannah (Sherwin)
   115 278
Hannah (Stoddard)
   116 36
Hannah (Upton) **116** 201
Hannah (Wood) **116** 194
Hannah (Yeomans)
   116 35
Hannah C. **115** 54
Hannah Cornish **116** 198
Hannah E. **115** 54
Hannah Hathaway **98** 85
Hannah M. **76** 43
Hannah T. (Baker)
   130 232
Hannah Wisewell **68** 321
Harold G. **118** 164

PERRY *cont'd*
Harriet **75** 254 **85** 294
   116 199 202 203 **122**
   319
Harriet (Bancroft) **96** 331
Harriet (Howes) **116** 194
Harriet A. **122** 319
Harriet Arline **116** 204
Harriet Comfort **96** 286
Harriet Howes **116** 195
Harriet Jennie (Davis)
   136 165
Harvey **116** 202
Hattie Louise (Keeney)
   97 81
Helen **70** xxxv
Helen E. **54** 251
Helena **116** 108
Heman **115** 284 285 **116**
   102 195 196
Heman Gibbs **116** 195
   123 216
Henrietta **116** 202
Henrietta Maria
   Sparhawk **58** 62
Henry **58** 88 **64** 163 **114**
   182 **116** 108 109 **134**
   254
Henry Gardner **61** 121
Henry M. **85** 378 381
Henry Nelson **116** 203
Henry Sullivan **68** 301
Hepzibah **116** 39 **133** 156
Hepzibah (Ladd) **115** 197
Hester **63** 128
Hester (Kennicut)
   116 203
Hiram **110** 80 **116** 109 201
Hitty Jane **82** 52
Hix **116** 44
Horace **110** 80
Horatio **103** 266
Horatio Nelson **89** 265
Howard Bowdoin **67**
   xxxiv 285
Howard E. **75** xxiii 64 **99**
   140 **100** 108 114
Howland **93** 300
Hugh **73** 261 272 277 **93**
   300 **148** 32
Hugh G. **106** 80
Huldah **60** 339 **73** 234 **93**
   215 **131** 57
Hylon N. **82** 470
I's **117** 318
Ichabod **59** 99 **60** 199 **69**
   130 **93** 344 **99** 60 125
   115 182 183 270 **116** 29
   43 **128** 261
Isaac **57** 323 400 **58** 390
   59 139 **63** 344 **64** 156
   104 103 **110** 80 **116** 33
   192 **130** 72 **132** 21
Isabel **87** 248
Isabella Hunt **70** lvii
Isaiah **115** 192
Israel **81** 293 **86** 126 **116** 40
Jabez **116** 101 107
Jabez Downer **116** 39 203
Jacob **115** 95 96 189
James **52** 15 **57** 181 **58** 87

PERRY *cont'd*
   63 86 **67** 287 **79** 40 **82**
   330 **95** 194 **97** 187 **100**
   156 192 **108** 239 **110** 80
   114 191 **115** 191 197
   272 276 282 **116** 29 36
   37 105 192 198 202 203
   120 117 **125** 38 **133** 156
James DeWolf **82** 385
James H. **69** 34
James Leonard **116** 203
Jane **54** 194 **60** 199 **71** 130
   81 340 **113** 31 38 **116**
   105 **117** 292
Jane (Cash) (Verin)
   131 102
Jane (Hobart) **119** 251
Jane (Weeks) **116** 105
Jane B. **136** 165
Janine Louise (Parker)
   84 209
Janne **116** 105
Jasiel **98** 323 330 **99** 98 108
Jemima **55** 393 **79** 149 **89**
   380 **109** 160 **115** 187
   116 100 101 107 192
Jemima (Benson) **116** 192
Jemima (Swift) **115** 190
   116 100 107 196
Jennie M. (Pettit) **98** 362
   104 233
Jeremiah **57** 323 **127** 148
   137 148
Jerusha **57** 323 413 **115** 194
   116 32 195 200 **123** 216
Jerusha (Hapgood)
   88 283
Jesse **59** 324 **81** 175
   140 235
Jireh **116** 31 199
Joan **73** 20 29
Joanna **70** 119 **115** 95 194
   276 287 **116** 33 196 197
   202 **126** 280 **129** 228
   132 299
Joanna (Gibbs) **115** 194
   123 67
Job **74** 31
Joel **69** 367 **115** 54
Johannah **115** 187 275
John **51** 166 167 **52** 245
   54 195 245 **56** 74 **57** 183
   58 159 **59** 194 396 **60**
   362 **61** 121 334 342 **62**
   lviii **63** 220 226 **64** 109
   67 300 **69** 275 **70** 263
   264 **71** 30 225 **73** 227 **76**
   141 174 **81** 432 **82** 52
   206 **83** 36 195 **85** 262
   272-275 **87** 249 **90** 114
   91 386 **94** 74 **99** 125 309
   105 205 **106** 92 93 **109**
   271 **110** 155 **113** 30 37
   115 87 90 91 94 95 183-
   191 273-275 277 279 283
   285-289 **116** 29 42 44
   100-102 104-107 192 195
   196 198 **118** 280 **119** 27
   28 30 262 **120** 101 **121**
   134 **123** 139 **124** 48 **125**
   40 128 131 191 **126** 279

PERRY *cont'd*
127 141 149 254 **128**
128 217 **132** 21 22 298
141 59 **146** 268 **148** 271
John B. **90** 58
John Cornish **116** 198
John E. **109** 271
John Francis **65** 230
John Frank **54** xli **61** 218
62 lviii lix 1
John H. **60** 320 **115** 296
John M. **73** 194
John Magray **116** 43
John T. **51** 227 **53** 247 **54**
xxxix
John Taylor **53** 257
John W. **122** 319
Jonah **58** 92
Jonathan **59** 312 **100** 192
108 92 **115** 269 **116** 41
128 126
Jonathan F. **117** 292
Jonathan Pratt **116** 203
Joseph **56** 382 383 **58** 240
242 387 **59** 134 390 **60**
61 204 **69** 130 **70** 40 **72**
29 **76** 136 170 172 **88**
283 **91** 266 332 **97** 292
99 125 **113** 30 37 39 **115**
93 183 194 271 272 **116**
36 42 43 111 **121** 139
127 17 **130** 155 **133** 192
141 199 201
Joseph Hartshorn **116**
34 202
Josephine **85** 294
Josephine (Adams) **90** 75
Josephine (Rising)
85 294
Josephine M. **114** 288
Joshua **57** 156 **73** 147 **115**
188-190 281 282 **122** 211
Josiah **51** 189 190 **54** 70-
76 164-167 **82** 470 **83**
378 **98** 105 **99** 65 108
115 98 99 193-198 **116**
33-35 201 202
Josiah W. **93** 344
Judah **115** 269 **116** 41
Judith (Barrows) **116** 196
Judith (Phippen) **131** 132
Judith (Savery) **115** 181
123 207
Julia **122** 261
Julia A. **103** 46
Julia Ann **130** 72
Julinus **116** 201
Justus **115** 284 285 **116** 194
Karl **75** 19
Katharine **64** 159
Katharine Lucile **72** 295
Keziah **58** 86 **63** 86 **72** 287
88 364 **116** 38
Keziah (Root) **115** 278
Kimball **116** 193 **125** 188
251 **130** 135
L. **58** 62
Laura **76** 153
Laurel Catherine **116** 33
Lavinia **116** 38
Leafy **94** 125

PERRY *cont'd*
Lelia Eunice **89** 118
Lemuel **115** 273 274 **116**
44 101
Leonard **116** 37 43 199
202 203
Leonard Baltelle **97** 81
Leslie A. **82** 470
Lever **88** 59
Levi **73** 222 **88** 153 **115** 272
116 43
Lewis **104** 103 **110** 80
116 107
Lewis (Mrs.) **89** 56
Libbie M. **111** 306
Lincoln **67** 380
Lizzie M. **104** 284
Lloyd **116** 204
Lois **116** 29 31 108
Lois (Belding) **116** 108
Lois (Benedict) **116** 108
Lois (Collins) **116** 41
Lorinda (Harris) **116** 203
Louisa **58** 57 **100** 280 **115**
287 **116** 196 197
Louisa (Phinney) **116** 197
Louisa Beebe **73** xxxiv
Louise Constance (Paige)
69 xxxv **74** xxviii **90**
128 **97** 187 **120** 146
Louise R. **116** 201
Love **82** 330
Lovisa (Reynolds) **123**
92 306
Lucinda **88** 192 **116** 37 40
Lucretia **77** 229 **90** 75 **115**
285 **116** 194 204
Lucretia (Kenyon)
116 203
Lucy **61** 121 **63** 76 **99** 125
115 278 283 **116** 30 38-
40 43 104 201
Lucy (Root) **110** 118
Lucy Ann **82** 275
Lucy Augusta **95** 246
Luke **65** 47 **94** 125 **115**
284 285 **116** 194
Lurana Nancy (Clark)
116 104
Lusanda **60** 61
Lusanna **59** 137
Luther **110** 80 **115** 284 285
116 194
Lydia **59** 77 **70** 299 **89** 288
104 103 **108** 247 **109**
160 **115** 187 194 197 278
282 286 **116** 27 28 35 36
39 42 44 196 198 **119** 27
120 101 **126** 120 **141** 59
Lydia (Badcock) **116** 44
Lydia (Bourne) **115** 272
116 27 196 **117** 310 **118**
276 **119** 28
Lydia (Hathaway) **116** 105
Lydia (House) **116** 34 35
Lydia (Kellogg) **99** 125
116 43
Lydia (Kinney) **108** 301
Lydia (Nason) **95** 194
Lydia (Snyder) **116** 204
Lydia (Swift) **116** 107

PERRY *cont'd*
Lydia (Tinkham) **116** 42
Lydia Swift **122** 261
Lyman **93** 251 **94** 161
116 104
Lynn **85** 353
M. A. **101** 74
M. C. **101** 323
Mabel **75** 19
Major Lewis **115** 288
Malvina (Wilson) **89** 265
Manassah **115** 43 194
Maranda **109** 183 **116** 40
Marcus Lafeyette **110** 80
Marcy **133** 156
Marcy (Taft) **116** 202
Margaret **62** 65 **80** 236
81 432 **115** 86 93 **124** 45
46 50
Margaret (Bacon) **90** 114
Margaret B. (Allen)
115 283
Margaret Lawrie
(Hubbell) **89** 56
Maria **74** 31 **115** 191
Marian (Lincoln) (Bogert)
89 266
Marianne Moseley
70 xxxv
Marion **96** 331
Marion (Bague) **116** 36
Marion L. **87** 21
Marsden Jasiel **73** 317 **74**
xxv **89** 265 266 283 **90**
139
Marshall **78** 265
Marshall Sears **58** 62
116 200
Marsylvia **110** 114
Martha **70** 34 **75** 180 **92**
351 **99** 60 **115** 182 183
190 191 284-287 **116** 29
102 103 196 **119** 30
Martha (Dewey) **99** 125
116 43
Martha (Frost) **116** 194
Martha (Niles) **85** 150
Martha (Perry) (Gibbs)
116 102 196
Martha (Tupper) **115** 191
117 305 **118** 276 **121**
135
Martha Ann **89** 263
Martha E. (Jones) **103** 45
Martha Olivia **116** 194
Martha R. (Kingsbury)
116 202
Marty **92** 351
Marvin **116** 40
Mary **53** 55 **54** 245 **57** 156
182 281 391 **58** 87 374
389 **61** 342 **66** 13 **68** 192
197 317 **69** 130 275 328
378 **70** 33 38 **71** 133 **73**
144 **76** 277 77 xliv xlv
78 140 246 **81** 274 **82**
215 296 298 **85** 219 **89**
372 **92** 351 **94** 39 **96** 260
98 24 **100** 237 **104** 313
106 93 **108** 213 214 317
109 160 **115** 86 92 93 97

PERRY *cont'd*
182-185 187 190-193 195
196 272 274-276 278 282
286 **116** 28 31 32 34 35
38 40-42 44 102 103 192
194-196 200 201 **117** 305
310 **118** 206 **119** 26 251
120 274 **121** 135 136
123 207 208 **124** 50 58
125 190-192 **128** 247
132 20 22 **137** 41 **146**
268
Mary (Bissell) **116** 101
Mary (Brown) **116** 34
Mary (Bumpas) **116** 41
125 191
Mary (Clark) (Noftsger)
116 232
Mary (Cornish) **116** 198
Mary (Fenton) **116** 194
Mary (Freeman) **115** 86
129 30
Mary (Hammond) **116** 43
Mary (Hartshorne)
116 34
Mary (Haven) (Edwards)
116 194
Mary (Hill) **116** 39
Mary (Kinsley) **115** 194
Mary (Perry) **116** 102 196
Mary (Salmon) **116** 197
Mary (Spicer) **125** 53
Mary (Stone) **115** 281
Mary (Swift) **115** 182 190
116 102 195 **141** 59
Mary (Tucker) **115** 96
Mary (Upham) **116** 201
Mary (Wallbridge)
116 201
Mary (Williams) **116** 35
36
Mary A. (Judson) **122** 319
Mary A. (Smith) **126** 65
Mary Almeda **108** 132
Mary Ann **70** xxxv **75** 189
116 39 43
Mary Ann (Crowell)
116 107
Mary Ann (Dennis)
116 107
Mary Augusta **78** 293
Mary B. (Peckham)
116 195
Mary Bourne **116** 195
Mary Carlton (Johnson)
95 246
Mary E. (Federhen)
90 114
Mary J. **68** 97
Mary Julany **134** 254
Mary Langdon **67** 380
Mary Lawrence **116** 193
Mary Lee (Barnard)
95 172
Mary Neal **92** 323
Mary Nicholls **116** 202
Mary Philena **82** 395
Mary Wealthy **96** 185
Matthew Calbraith **77** 301
81 340
Maude Blaisdell **80** 209

PERRY *cont'd*
Maude Marion **98** 362
104 233
May Louise **97** 81
Mehitable **90** 245 **109** 160
115 186 187 195-197
116 36
Mehitable (Eliot) **106** 18
131 174
Mehitable (Fish) **120** 101
Mehitable (Leonard)
(Willis) **115** 196
Mehitable (Perry) **90** 245
Meletiah **116** 193
Melinda **115** 300
Melissa **116** 39
Mercy **57** 156 **115** 92 97
98 279 **116** 29 32 193
136 267
Mercy (Atwood) **116** 200
Mercy (Blish) **116** 193
Mercy (Borden) **116** 199
Mercy (Cobb) **116** 41
Mercy (Doty) **116** 41
123 270
Mercy (Freeman) **116** 31
Mercy (Handy) **116** 41
125 191
Mercy (Phinney) **116** 101
107
Mercy (Robbins) **116** 42
Mercy (Smith) **116** 43
Meribah **115** 98 181
123 133
Micah **98** 359
Micajah **59** 219
Michael **59** 219 **131** 169
170 173 174
Milla **115** 288
Miller **116** 204
Minnie **72** 300
Mirah **114** 182
Miranda **116** 191
Miranda (Hurd) **122** 319
Miriam **51** 164 **133** 156
Miriam (Stratton)
120 117
Molly **69** 367 **116** 34 35
197
Molly (Lovejoy) **91** 266
Molly (Salmon) **116** 197
Moses **57** 281 **113** 305
115 183 186 271 272
116 41 43 **120** 116 **121**
133 264 **124** 218
Nabby **79** 38
Nancy **58** 374 **63** 274 **76**
150 **88** 153 **110** 80 116
105 106 200 224 **126** 209
Nancy (Bowman) **126** 145
Nancy (Gay) **96** 185
Nancy (Nye) **116** 199
Nancy (Ruggles) **116** 200
Nancy (Spoor) **116** 204
Nancy (Wentworth)
126 64
Nancy A. **62** 368
Nancy Mariah (Reynolds)
116 204
Nancy Teresa **116** 204
Nathan **68** 292 **69** 130 367

PERRY *cont'd*
83 378 **111** 183 **115** 92
95 97 191 193 **116** 28 32
33 105 107 200 **117** 305
118 276 **120** 116 **121**
135 **123** 138 **131** 30
Nathaniel **56** 74 **96** 260
265 **97** 36 319 **98** 172
322 324 **99** 287 **105** 207
115 98 99 193 194 **116**
33 35-37 42 107-109 **130**
274 **138** 29
Nathaniel Green **116** 38
Nathaniel Mallory
116 204
Nehemiah **78** 405 **116** 36
Nicholas **104** 20
Noah **119** 251 **136** 37 40
O. H. **78** 293
Oaks **103** 256 266
Obadiah **55** 187 **61** 121
63 86 294 **79** 149 **91** 266
115 281 **116** 108 109
Olive **76** 153 **82** 215 **103** 63
116 33 136 38
Olive (Win) **91** 266
Oliver **57** 391
Oliver A. **110** 114
Oliver Hazard **54** 110 **56**
xxxii xxxiv **66** 368 369
67 xxx 184 385 **70** xxvii
xxxv **79** 158 **98** 290 **125**
178
Orange **116** 204
Ozias **115** 198 **116** 40 41
Pamela **78** 265
Patience **99** 60 **115** 92-94
182 183 189 268 281 282
116 41 **123** 207 **126** 268
Patience (Butterworth)
97 36
Patience (Lucas) **115** 281
Patience (Nye) **116** 193
Patience (Pierce) **126** 268
Patience (Randall)
115 268
Patience Pierce **126** 268
Patty **116** 29 103 198
Paul **60** 40 **131** 57
Peleg **58** 174
Penelope **88** 59 **115** 288
Percy **115** 194
Peter **69** 134 **128** 219
Phebe **115** 275-277 **116** 33
34 38 104 193 203
Phebe (Bartlett) **116** 193
Phebe (Cramphorne)
132 22
Phebe (Marshall) **116** 201
Philena (Hayden) **116** 103
Philip **115** 195 **116** 34 35
Philip Fletcher **103** 46
Philippa **115** 198 **116** 39
Philo **76** 136
Phineas **115** 189 190 281
284 285 **116** 195 **119** 27
120 268 **127** 217
Pierce **127** 148
Polly **63** 86 **116** 38 40 103
192 194 201 **119** 251
134 63 **137** 41

PERRY *cont'd*
Polly (Cormish) **97** 187
Polly (Fenton) **116** 194
Polly (Merrill) **90** 245
Polly (Upham) **116** 201
Polly (Williams) **116** 35
  36
Polly Ann **121** 80
Prence **115** 271 **116** 41
Prince **84** 54 **115** 183 286
  116 102 107 196
Priscilla **58** 267 **60** 177 **87**
  52 129 **115** 287 288
Priscilla (Andrews)
  115 287
Priscilla (Muxham)
  116 41
Prudence **131** 76 **143** 60 61
  164
Rachel **52** 222 **59** 390 **73**
  136 **76** 136 174 **115** 271
  116 33 108 204 **133** 56
Rachel (Allen) **115** 272
Rachel (Boyden) **116** 33
Rachel (Gifford) **116** 107
Rachel (Mallory) **116** 204
Rachel (Miller) **116** 204
Rachel (Rice) **120** 80
  136 77
Rachel (Wing) **115** 278
Ralph **68** 91 **82** 395
Rebecca **51** 166 167 **56** 251
  70 264 **77** xlv **87** 235
  238 **94** 284 **99** 60 334
  100 241 **115** 92 93 97
  182 183 186 194 269 271
  272 283 **116** 28 33 38 41
  42 192 194 **120** 116 **121**
  264 **130** 18
Rebecca (Atkinson)
  115 285
Rebecca (Bailey)
  (Greenwood) **116** 38
Rebecca (Bliss) **116** 38
Rebecca (Browne) **131** 30
Rebecca (Ellis) **116** 102
  122 261
Rebecca (Freeman) **99** 60
  115 91-93 97 **124** 58
  126 280
Rebecca (Josselyn)
  133 192
Rebecca (Sears) **134** 254
Rebecca G. **125** 293
Rebecca M. (Needham)
  110 114
Relief **115** 282
Remember **99** 65 194
  115 90 91 184 185 195-
  198 272 278 280 **120** 101
  130 274
Remembrance **115** 87 91
  98 99
Rest **128** 247 **129** 224
Reuben **99** 125 126 289
  110 30 **116** 40 **122** 257
Rhobe (Smith) **116** 202
Rhoda **115** 272 **116** 202
  129 166
Rhoda (Bumpas) **99** 125
  115 93 272

PERRY *cont'd*
Rhoda (Crocker) **116** 191
Rhoda (Griggs) **116** 204
Richard **59** 219 **82** 470 **86**
  415 **115** 289 **116** 34 201
  125 36 **131** 10 132 **135**
  230
Richard (Mrs.) **104** 145
Richard A. **73** 271 276
Rival Tyler **135** 339
Robert **64** 314 **85** 150
Rosa **87** 21
Rose (Spooner) **116** 198
Rowland **115** 194 **116** 33
  34 202
Rowland Briggs **116** 43
Roxa **116** 34
Roxanna **116** 34
Roxanna (Hutchinson)
  116 38
Roxanna M. **101** 257
Roxay **116** 34
Ruby **58** 346 **129** 370
Ruby L. **87** 21
Rufus **78** 386 **115** 196 270
  273 **116** 35 42
Ruhama **110** 30 **115** 289
Russell **69** 34
Russell Chester **72** 92
Ruth **57** 100 102 **58** 83
  170 172 174 261 263 267
  389 390 **59** 75 76 78 79
  136 139 312 **60** 175 176
  87 137 **100** 156 **115** 191
  194 275 276 **116** 38 41
  104 203 **120** 117 **127** 31
  129 228 **132** 298 299
Ruth (Downer) **116** 38
Ruth (Phillips) **115** 194
Ruth (Wilder) **125** 175
S. M. Gibbs **116** 105
Sabina **116** 40
Sabra **81** 175
Sabra Oceania (Wicker)
  87 8 **109** 8
Sadie **116** 40
Safford **116** 39
Salathiel **115** 269 **116** 41
  123 270
Salina A. **81** 252
Sally **59** 279 **60** 199 **79** 301
  81 494 **95** 317 **116** 32
  192 198 201 202 **122** 211
  136 77
Sally (Wiley) **103** 45
Samantha **116** 201
Samira **114** 15 16
Samuel **54** lxxxiii 245 **55**
  393 **57** 320 **58** 170 **59**
  137 139 **62** 237 **63** 80 89
  67 287 **68** 105 170 175
  69 130 275 376 **70** 33 38
  39 **71** 204 **76** 171 **83** 379
  85 150 **90** 245 **91** 331
  332 **98** 326 **99** 94 104
  125 309 **100** 156 **104**
  103 **105** 315 **108** 213
  110 121 114 182 **115** 87
  90-93 96 97 183 191-193
  197 269 270 272 273 **116**
  30 31 35 36 43 44 103

PERRY *cont'd*
  198-200 **117** 16 **118** 207
  276 **125** 190 **127** 86 **128**
  128 217 248 **129** 369
  130 211 **134** 254 **136** 38
  40 **138** 25-28 30 **143** 60
  144 41 **147** 347
Samuel B. **126** 145
Samuel Savory **115** 182
Samuel Taft **116** 202
Sanders **115** 288
Sara Abbott Woods
  52 292
Sarah **58** 159 **59** 389 392 **60**
  362 **63** 89 131 **66** 77 **67**
  287 **68** 28 175 301 315
  69 130 134 376 **70** 33-36
  39 **71** 204 **73** 151 226 **81**
  432 **82** 91 **83** 164 **85** 150
  87 249 **89** 296 297 **96**
  260 **98** 171 **99** 125 **100**
  156 **113** 30 **115** 87 88 90
  97 183 191 198 269 271-
  273 282 **116** 29 30 32 35
  37 40-44 103 104 198
  201 202 **124** 50 51 **125**
  271 **127** 25 86
Sarah (Arey) **87** 21
Sarah (Benson) **116** 202
Sarah (Blackwell) **116** 28
  117 304
Sarah (Browne) **89** 70
Sarah (Bumpas) **115** 181
  123 207 **125** 190 191
Sarah (Carpenter) **98** 172
Sarah (Crocker) **115** 282
Sarah (Dennis) **116** 42
Sarah (Dexter) **97** 187
  116 29
Sarah (Ditson) **109** 183
Sarah (Doane) **130** 72
Sarah (Freeman) **115** 97
  116 104
Sarah (Gifford) **115** 270
  116 29 **128** 261
Sarah (Howard) **116** 41
Sarah (Hudson) **116** 200
Sarah (Joy) **115** 197
Sarah (Kellogg) **93** 251
  94 161
Sarah (Leonard) **115** 183
  118 276 **125** 190
Sarah (Perry) **116** 42
Sarah A. (White) **54**
  lxxxiv **116** 201
Sarah Augusta **70** xxxv
Sarah B. **73** 194
Sarah Jane (Dunton)
  97 187
Sarah Marie (Greene)
  127 86
Saunders **115** 288
Seth **51** 190 **53** 193 195 **57**
  411-413 **58** 62 **96** 323
  324 **99** 125 **102** 178 **106**
  18 19 **115** 97-99 182 191-
  194 198 272 273 281 **116**
  27-29 31-33 38 43 44 200
  203 **117** 310 **118** 276
  121 135 **125** 234 235
  131 169 170 173 174

PERRY *cont'd*
145 259
Seth Harden **116** 39 203
Sheldon **125** 219
Sherman **104** 103
Silas **110** 114 **114** 280 **115**
184 185 273-275 277 278
116 101 102 **117** 16 **122**
261 **124** 53
Simeon **59** 389 390 **62** 370
116 37 **128** 127 217
Solomon **115** 191 279
287-289 **116** 101 107 197
Solon **103** 45
Sophia **116** 192
Sophronia **116** 43 198 203
Sophronia (Gifford) **116**
193 **125** 188 251 **130**
134 135
Sophronia (Phinney)
116 197
Squire **116** 201
Stephen **54** lxxxiii **82**
296 298 **97** 187 **115** 192
193 273 **116** 29 32 33
106 192 198 200 **117** 192
126 21 **128** 129
Stephen A. **109** 160
Stephen B. **126** 21
Stephen Kingsbury
(Mrs.) **84** 454
Surviah (Safford) **116** 39
Susan **71** 204 **97** 383 **99**
125 **105** 314 **116** 43 **130**
72
Susan (Crosby) **116** 101
107
Susan (Lawrence) **116** 192
Susan (Porter) **116** 42
Susan B. (Hopkins)
116 202
Susan C. **100** 227
Susan C. (Ingraham)
116 199
Susan Crosby **116** 107
Susan Marston (Jones)
116 105
Susanna **57** 181 284 322
67 286 **87** 249 337 341
88 59 **100** 192 **115** 99
182 272 278 279 **116** 30
31 43 **120** 115
Susanna (Benson) **116** 41
Susanna (Ellis) **115** 278
120 116
Susanna (Magray) **116** 43
Susanna (Sheafe) **125** 65
Susanna (Swift) **116** 30
Susanna (Tupper) **99** 125
116 43
Susanna (Washburn)
116 33
Susanne **87** 337
Suzanne **130** 156
Sylvania **115** 278
Sylvanus **65** 221 **115** 198
286 287 **116** 37 38 195
119 27 **123** 216
Sylvester **126** 268
Sylvia **69** 263 **110** 114
116 104 191 194

PERRY *cont'd*
Sylvia (Clapp) **116** 199
Sylvina **115** 278
Sylvina N. (Berry) **91** 386
T. S. **56** 204 412
Tabitha **57** 320
Tamor **116** 103
Temperance **115** 278 **116**
104 194
Temperance (Hatch)
116 102
Thaddeus **70** 37 **116** 199
Thaddeus A. **121** 80
Thankful **115** 283 **118**
207 276 **141** 355
Thankful (Blish) **115** 277
283
Thankful (Bourne) **115**
272 **118** 207 276
Thankful (Munson)
116 203
Thankful (Tyler) **135** 339
Theodore M. **98** 362
Theodore Marion
104 233
Thomas **56** 398 **57** 180-
183 320 321 **58** 57 **61** 43
44 **63** 86 **64** 163 **66** 77
68 315 317 319 321 **71**
22 **73** 234 263 **88** 59 **100**
237 **108** 301 **109** 160
115 97 187 191-193 272
273 279 280 284 285 **116**
27-29 42 108 109 198
117 4 13 16 304 305 313
120 113 **121** 135 **125** 41
Thomas Alson **116** 198
Thomas Crosby **115** 87 88
91 94 96-98 182 183 188
190-192 272 274 277 283
285 287 **116** 27-29 44
101 102 104 107 193 195
198 200 **119** 166 172
122 257 259 261
Thomas N. **116** 108 109
Thomas Park **93** 251
Thomas T. **109** 183
Timothy **115** 95 96 185 186
191 278 279 287 **116** 101
105 106 **118** 279 **120**
115-117 **121** 133 135
125 128 132 **135** 339
141 355 **142** 58 **144** 221
Tryphena (Spooner)
116 44
Tuba **116** 40
Varnum **68** 97
Veda **100** 110
Vinal R. **87** 21
Waitstill **116** 109
Walter **69** 367 **134** 254
Walter C. **125** 53
Washington **116** 39
Wilfred P. **83** 427 438
William **51** 463 **57** 182
319 323 **58** 86 **59** 76 77
134 312 **61** 44 **66** 33 37
67 100 **68** 91 315 **73** 221
74 65 **76** 136 **78** 407 **81**
232 274 **82** 91 215 508
85 262 **90** 114 **93** 398

PERRY *cont'd*
99 125 **100** 63 192 **104**
103 **105** 314 315 **115**
271 277 279 284 285 287
116 36 42 43 104 106
192 194 **130** 211 **133**
192 **138** 7 **143** 329 348
144 41 **147** 381
William Bliss **116** 38 203
William Gilman **67** 386
William Graves **89** 70 82
128
William Graves (Mrs.) **85**
197 **87** 59
William H. **135** 159
William Hayne **57** xxxiii
232
William Henry Tenni-
son **125** 65
William Hudson **116** 200
William M. **87** 21
William Sobie (Mrs.) **80**
102 209 **119** 149
William Stevens **52** 291
53 382 **54** lxxxiii
lxxxiv
Wilma Jeanette **99** 146
Winifred (Clark) **116** 32
Winslow **115** 195 196
116 35 **119** 320 **120** 80
136 77
Winthrop **110** 114
Winthrop Irving **62** xl
85 197 **114** 141
Wolverton **144** 41
Wyman **116** 201
Yelverton **76** 141 145 147
150 153 **125** 235
Zachariah **115** 183-185
189 273 277 278 283 **116**
104
Zacheus **116** 105
Zeba C. **75** 254
Zebedee Cushman **97** 187
Zechariah **115** 277
Zenas **116** 28
Zerviah **116** 36 37
Zerviah (Safford) **116** 39
Zerviah (Wetherill)
116 36
Zillah **59** 75 **129** 251
Zilpha **116** 34 43
Perryman *see* Perriman
PERSALL — Mr. **55** 432
Perse *see* Pierce
Persevell *see* Percival
PERSEVERE
Mary **139** 298
Persey *see* Percy
PERSHING Helen Francis
(Warren) **136** 326
Henry A. **85** 353
John J. **111** 3
John Joseph **76** 23 **136** 326
PERSHO Lucinda **126** 278
PERSIS
Elizabeth **113** 158
PERSKE
Betty Joan **136** 311
PERSMYTHE
John **107** 216

PERSMYTHE *cont'd*
 Tabitha **107** 216
Person *see* Parsons
Persone *see* Parsons
Persones *see* Parsons
PERSONIUS
 Gilbert **125** 53
 Mary E. (Buck) **125** 53
PERSONNEAU
 Ann Motte **119** 194
 Arthur **119** 194
Persons *see* Parsons
PERT Alice **74** 137
 George **74** 137
 Helen P. **74** 302
 Margery **74** 137
 William **73** 68 **74** 302
PERTH Andrew **77** 81
PERTHULLS
 James **111** 202
PERTOIS
 Jean Baptiste **110** 128
 Marie Anne **110** 128
PERTRE John **93** 76
 Robert **92** 384
 William **93** 78
PERTZ Mary (Turner)
 126 142
 Nickals **126** 142
PERTZOFF Constance
 (Cunningham) **85** 103
 Constantin A. (Mrs.)
 98 270
 Olga (Monks) **98** 270
 Vladimir Alexander
 (Mrs.) **85** 103
PERVERE Everett
 Whitfield **99** 148
 Nancy **58** 18
 Phebe **58** 18
 Richard **58** 18
PERVORSE
 Albert **133** 73
 Daniel **133** 73
 Everett Henry **133** 73
PERWICKE Perwich
 Alice **71** 174 **75** 135
 Thomas **71** 174 **75** 135
Pery *see* Perry
Peryman *see* Perriman
PERYSSON
 William **80** 381
PESALE
 Adam de (Sir) **101** 89
 Margaret de **101** 89
PESCHIER
 — Mme **64** 322
 John **64** 322
PESCOD Joseph **65** 232
PESEY Ella M. **80** 52
PESIN Hugh **80** 351
PESKETT Hugh **141** 23
PESLIE
 Elizabeth **60** 286
PESON Joanna **105** 260
PESSE John **59** 173 174
PESSICUS **97** 345 **98** 20
PESTALOZZI —— **62** 389
 Heinrich **135** 261 262
PESTER
 William **148** 67 75

Pet *see* Pett
PETCHE Thomas **72** 55 56
PETCHEL
 George L. **89** 110
 Isabel (Lazell) **89** 110
 James Addison **89** 110
PETCHEY Anne **51** 282
 Edward **51** 282
 Joan **51** 282
 John **51** 282
 Samuel **83** 74
 William **51** 282
PETE Jediah **147** 85
Petel *see* Pettel
PETER FERDINAND
 Archduke **77** 93
PETER THE CRUEL King
 of Castile and
 Leon **75** 318
PETER THE GREAT
 of Russia **52** 345
PETER Hugh **148** 10
PETERGRO
 Abigail **60** 298
PETERKIN
 Alexander **65** 246
 George William **109** 309
PETERS Peter Petre Petters
 —— **57** 336 **58** 100 **63** 362
 99 202 **130** 95
 — Capt. **69** 381
 — Lord **79** 152
 — Mr. **95** 47
 A. B. **113** 87
 Abbie M. **75** 19
 Abigail **79** 155
 Ada E. **85** 169
 Adam **58** 346
 Adeline M. (Elder) **86** 331
 Agnes **117** 188
 Alberta (Preston) **88** 170
 Alberta Louise **90** 137
 Alexander Abercrombie
 51 104 **67** 290 **140** 235
 325
 Alvah H. **64** 142
 Alvin **99** 116
 Amelia **138** 116
 Amelia Kelley **85** 169
 Amy **74** 203
 Andrew **58** 100 249 **59**
 lxxxiv **65** 221 **69** 34 **80**
 419 **83** 470 **91** 94 **148**
 143 144
 Andrew James (Mrs.)
 85 197
 Ann **54** 340 **114** 76
 Anna **52** 314
 Anna (White) **104** 263
 Annabelle **99** 116
 Anson **68** 158
 Arabella (Butler) **108** 187
 Aravester **69** 34
 Barbara **102** 66
 Bethiah **55** 224
 Betsey **122** 288
 Betty **70** 228
 C. A. **98** 97 **100** 338
 105 318
 C. J. **72** 164
 Charles **51** 93 96 **69** 34

PETERS *cont'd*
 Daniel **97** 352
 Deborah (Burchard)
 134 88
 Dorcas (Howland)
 100 289
 Dorothy **83** 45
 E. B. **54** lix
 Ebenezer **79** 245
 Edith B. **110** 160
 Edith Robena **108** 304
 Edmund Frank **58** 100
 Edward **88** 284
 Edward McClure **57** 336
 58 100 **59** 223 **60** 83 87
 276
 Eleanor Bradley **54** 339
 58 xlv 100 **70** 95
 Eliza (Rich) (Lytle) **84** 125
 Elizabeth **54** 340 **74** 117 **77**
 40 **85** 76 **114** 76 **148** 143-
 145 361
 Ellen **90** 111
 Elmer Leslie (Mrs.)
 101 125
 Emily **68** 158
 Emma (Fitz Randolph)
 99 38
 Emma A. **68** 158
 Eunice **79** 247
 Evelina Louisa **77** 143
 F. I. **123** 159
 Fannie E. **59** lxxxvi
 Fanny **142** 63
 Fidelia **85** 169
 Florence Ann **75** 250
 Fortin **62** 123
 Francis **82** 283 296
 Frank H. **98** 345
 George **64** 251 **124** 207
 George Boddie **77** 143
 George S. **83** 100
 Georgianna (Snelling)
 108 187
 Gertrude **54** lix
 Gertrude C. **54** lix
 Gertrude E. **75** 19
 Gilbert **58** 100
 Goodsil **75** 21
 Goodsil B. **75** 19
 Hannah **55** 179
 Hannah (Laha) **125** 100
 Hannah (Martin) **125** 108
 Hannah Owen **72** 216
 Harry Twyford **86** 331
 Helen **76** 91 **99** 116 146
 135 235
 Hugh **54** 43 44 339 340 **59**
 lxviii **63** 311 **71** 102 **72**
 224 **74** 115 117-119 **79**
 168 **80** 60 **84** 304 316 **87**
 271 **98** 68 **99** 20 **114** 76
 129 15 247 **135** 87 289
 140 184
 Ian **148** 286
 Ireta **89** 132
 Isabel **96** 179
 Israel **79** 247
 James **134** 88
 James Arthur **77** 143

PETERS *cont'd*
James Baldwin **75** 250
Jane **114** 76
Jane (Steves) **111** 137
Jenny **64** 251
Job **83** 18
Joel C. **85** 169
Johan **87** 60
John **54** 340 **55** 250 376
    58 100 **59** lxxxiv **65** 25
    70 315 **84** 125 **86** 217
    247 **97** 352 **114** 76 180
    125 100 **140** 105 106
    141 28
John A. **56** liii
John Andrew **59** lvi
    lxxxiv
John Charles **108** 187
John P. **59** lxxxviii
    62 lxxiii
John Punnett **54** xxxix
John R. **90** 106
John S. **85** 169
John Samuel **73** 137
John Yale **122** 112
Jonathan **142** 63
Joseph **76** 91 **83** 45 **112**
    193 **134** 88
Joseph Godfrey **108** 187
Josephine (Gemmel)
    86 331
Justinian **99** 38
Kenira **66** 17
Keziah **114** 169
Lavinia (Brown) **88** 284
Leah **108** 79
Lewis **100** 289 **122** 288
Lois **60** 351
Lovice Margaret **64** 251
Lucy **137** 78
Lucy (Brown) **90** 106
Lydia **104** 21-23 **110** 65
    124 207
Lydia (Bliss) **104** 21 263
Lydia (Phelps) **104** 21
Macdonald (Mrs.)
    101 326
Madison C. **65** 102
Margaret **65** 349 **87** 287
    104 118
Mark **128** 57
Martha **79** 245 **81** 152
Martha G. (Snow) **99** 116
Martin Hunter **108** 304
Martin Luther **90** 57
Mary **54** 340 **55** 376 **64** 152
    71 73 **74** 203 **83** 18 **93**
    281 **107** 187 **114** 76 **134**
    88
Mary (Dyer) (Cushing)
    97 352
Mary (Haggens) **83** 18
Mary (Payne) **108** 304
Mary (Rogers) **104** 263
Mary (Sherman) **93** 62
Mary Ann **59** lxxxvi
Mary Elizabeth **77** 188
    83 470
Mary F. **108** 277
Mary J. **75** 19

PETERS *cont'd*
Mary Jane (Thompson)
    93 281
Mary M. **85** 169
Mehitable **79** 245
Mercy **63** 275
Minnie **64** 251
Nancy S. **126** 206
Nathan **60** 351
Olive **58** 346
Phebe **56** 306 307 **97** 352
Phebe (Billings) **97** 352
Philena **137** 78
Philippe **143** 261
Preston (Mrs.) **88** 170 **90**
    152 **91** 158
Rachel 217 **98** 221 **125** 217
Richard **76** 90 91 **93** 281
    110 88
Richard D. **54** lix
Rolla **66** 36
Rosina **75** 21
Sadie (Watson) **98** 345
Sally **59** lxxxiv
Sally (Jordan) **83** 470
Salmon **76** 91
Samuel **52** 295 **62** 371
    85 169
Samuel T. **73** 316 **74** xxv
    76 xxix xc
Samuel Twyford **86** 331
Sarah **54** 340 **67** 290 **69** 34
    92 **76** 90 **82** 283 296 **92**
    276 **114** 76 180 **134** 88
Sarah (Wells) **134** 88
Sarah A. (Wright) **85** 169
Sarah Ann (Reed) **90** 57
Sarah Welford **78** 445
Stephen **64** 251
Susan E. **122** 288
Susan Hamilton **71** 73
Thankful **70** 227
Thelma **101** 126
Theophilus **111** 137
Thomas **54** 339 340 **114** 76
Thomas NcNeal **77** 143
Thurston C. **54** 339
Virginia Cary **80** 195
    81 222
Weintie **66** 16 17
William **64** 316 **65** 47 **74**
    203 **141** 23
William Cowper **54** lix
William D. **85** 169
William M. **54** lix
William Richmond **54**
    xxxix 339
William S. **85** 169
Willis **122** 112
PETERSDR
Stina Kajsa **128** 170
Petersen *see* Peterson
PETERSFIELD
Mary (Price) **148** 18
PETERSHAM
— Mr. **54** 30
PETERSON Petersen
    Petterson
—— **60** 182 **62** 284 **83** 308
— Capt. **91** 273
— Mr. **65** 369

PETERSON *cont'd*
— Mrs. **84** 31 **127** 138
A. Frederick **121** 303
A. H. Dumont **125** 182
A. M. **91** 332
Abbot **85** 197
Abby **70** 357
Abigail **70** 163 168 267
    349 351 354 **81** 379 **120**
    189 **125** 72
Abigail (Whittemore)
    107 260
Abigail F. **70** 352
Abigail M. **70** 357
Abigail Soule **70** 357
Abigail W. **70** 355
Abraham **70** 165 266
    145 355
Achsah **70** 359
Ada Bell Trowbridge
    70 191
Adelaide **107** 158 318
Adeline **70** 352 355 363
Adeline A. **70** 363
Adeline Eliza **65** 39
Adeline P. **70** 363
Adrianna **70** 355
Africa **70** 353
Alander **70** 268
Alexander **106** 86
Alfred **70** 355 **99** 49
Algernon Asaph **70** 364
Alice **70** 164 166
Alice (Brown) **85** 216
Alice Luella **89** 20
Alida (Anderson) **128** 170
Allen **70** 353
Alma Amelia **70** 365
Almina **70** 358
Almira **70** 364
Almira Stetson **70** 364
Alonzo F. **70** 362
Alvah **70** 351 **81** 383
Amanthis **70** 353
Amasa **70** 166
Amelia Annie **81** 383
Amelia Meigs **70** 352
Amherst **70** 353 358
Andrew **125** 290
Angeline **70** 355
Ann **70** 362
Ann L. **70** 360
Ann W. **70** 354
Anna **70** 166 350
Anna (Lauson) **128** 174
Anna C. (Bergren)
    128 174
Anna C. (Lawson) **128** 96
Anna Emery **70** 365
Anne **70** 163 350 354
Anne E. **70** 356
Anne J. **70** 361
Anne W. **70** 352
Annie **81** 383
Antoinette **70** 360
Arbella **84** 94
Arthur **70** 360
Asaph **70** 364
Asaph Torrey **70** 364
Athina W. **70** 355
August **128** 174

PETERSON *cont'd*
Augusta **70** 354
Augusta E. **70** 360
Augustus Briggs **70** 359
Barzilla A. **70** 355
Benjamin **70** 162-166 266
    353 355 364 **124** 123
Benjamin Franklin
    70 364
Bethiah **70** 266 353
Betsey **70** 267 268 349 350
    352 360 361 364 **112** 318
Betsey Ann **70** 359
Betsey Bates **70** 364
Betsey Thomas **70** 357
Beulah **70** 351
Bion **70** 360
Bodil Marie **109** 231
Briggs **70** 353 359
Briggs Ruggles **81** 383
C. Stewart **100** 80
Caleb B. **70** 352
Calvin **70** 358
Carnalas **70** 266
Caroline **70** 161 357 359
    128 174
Caroline (Cutter) **125** 182
Caroline Ford **119** 254
Caroline M. **70** 352
Carrie **70** 358
Catherine **78** 399 **125** 103
    294
Catherine (Oliver)
    125 100
Catherine Kimball **70** 357
Charles **70** 267 351 356
    128 170
Charles A. **70** 361
Charles B. **96** 287
Charles F. **104** 79
Charles H. **70** 363
Charles Henry **70** 357
Charles Robert **70** 364
Charles Sprague **70** 358
    364
Charles Theodore **77** 182
Charlotte **70** 350 360
    73 259
Chloe **70** 360
Christena M. **128** 98
Clarence Stewart **115** 319
    147 175
Clarice **86** 105
Clark **70** 351 356 357
Clark R. **70** 362
Constant Sampson
    70 352
Content **70** 167
Cora **70** 352
Cornelia **70** 352
Cornelia A. **70** 360
Cynthia **70** 360 364 **73** 259
Daniel **70** 162 164 266 267
    353 359
Daniel A. **70** 359
Daniel B. **70** 360
Daniel Cowing **70** 358
Daniel P. **70** 353
Daniel Porter **70** 357
David **70** 162 163 167
David Lewis **70** 357

PETERSON *cont'd*
Davis **124** 123
Deborah **70** 164 166 352
    356-358
Deborah Clark **70** 356 357
Deborah Hall **70** 352 358
Deborah S. **70** 354
Deborah W. **70** 354
Delia S. **70** 361
Don Collins **85** 197
Dorcas **70** 167 353 **114** 278
Dorothy **70** 353
Edgar D. **70** 363
Edward **96** 12 **125** 182
Edward Bates **70** 365
Edwin **70** 354
Edwin J. **84** 31
Edwin P. **70** 362
Elbridge **70** 365
Eleanor H. **70** 364
Elias **89** 20
Elijah **70** 168 349 354 360
    361 **82** 275 **107** 260
Elisha **70** 350 355 362
Eliza **70** 357 **78** 397
Eliza Ann **70** 363
Eliza E. **70** 361
Eliza Jane **70** 357
Elizabeth **55** 316 **70** 162
    168 266 353 357 361 364
    83 12
Elizabeth (Clarke) **127** 88
Elizabeth (Howland)
    (Whittemore) **107** 260
Elizabeth (Jillison) **83** 12
Elizabeth Amelia **70** 364
Elizabeth W. **70** 352
Ella **70** 352
Ellen M. **70** 361
Ellen Maria **70** 359
Ellen Mehitable **70** 364
Ellen W. **70** 359
Ellis **70** 357 359
Elmore **104** 245
Emeline T. **70** 356
Emily **70** 364
Emily Bates **70** 364
Emma **70** 352 363
Emma L. **70** 361
Emmons A. **70** 360
Ephraim **70** 166
Ernest C. **70** 362
Esaias **70** 350 355 362 363
Ethel Mary (Crate)
    83 426 438
Eudora **70** 361
Eudora Bradford **82** 275
Eugene T. **123** 373
Eveline (Bates) **70** 364
Everett E. **70** 361
Faith **70** 164
Fannie **70** 360
Fannie Belle **83** 301
Fannie E. **70** 364
Fanny **73** 259
Fanny (Bell) **125** 291
Florence Hepp **104** 245
Forrest Hand **81** 383
Francis **70** 358
Francis A. **70** 358
Frank **70** 360

PETERSON *cont'd*
Frank L. **130** 55
Frank Lloyd **70** 359
Franklin **70** 364
Freddie **70** 359
Frederick **70** 350 355 363
Frederick Carl **83** 426 438
George **70** 267 351-354 358
    360 362 363
George Edward **70** 365
George F. **70** 352 361 363
George G. **70** 364
George H. **70** 359
George M. **70** 363
George O. **70** 360
George P. **70** 352 355 358
    363
George Soule **70** 357
George W. **70** 352 359 364
Gerry **89** 20
Gilbert M. **70** 359
Hannah **70** 163 165-167
    266 268 352 353 355 359
    125 101 **128** 96 **130** 237
Hannah B. **70** 352 364
Hannah Hayward **70** 359
Hannah P. **70** 166
Hannah W. **70** 351
Harlow **70** 360 **73** 259
Harriet **70** 362
Harriet Augustus **70** 364
Harriet M. **112** 318
Harriet S. (Kimball)
    90 108
Henrietta **70** 361 **125** 245
Henrietta C. **70** 357
Henry **51** 343 **70** 353 354
    356 357 **77** 210 **90** 55
Henry A. **70** 355
Henry O. **70** 362
Henry Ray **70** 362
Hepzibah **56** 36
Herbert **70** 359
Herbert Austin **70** 365
Hewitt **70** 267
Hiram **70** 352
Hope **70** 167 353
Hopestill **65** 103 **70** 164
    75 125
Horace **70** 362
Howard Bigelow **85** 217
Hyrum J. (Mrs.) **106** 126
Ichabod **70** 167 350 351
    356 363 **127** 88
Ichabod B. **70** 357
Ichabod W. **70** 354 361
Ichabod Wadsworth
    70 350
Ida **128** 175 263
Ida Bella (Bigelow) **85** 217
Isaac **70** 162-166 **124** 123
Isaac W. **70** 356
Isabella Maria **70** 362 363
Jabez **70** 349 354 360 361
Jabez Porter **70** 361
Jacob **70** 163 165 266 267
    353
Jacob Joseph Sumner
    84 180 **85** 108 203 216
Jael **70** 163-165 167 **141** 297
James **66** 37 **70** 267 351

PETERSON *cont'd*
352 358
James Bates **70** 364
James Hall **70** 359
James Holman **117** 237
Jane **70** 350 354 360 **81** 383
Jane W. **70** 352
Jemima **70** 358 **131** 73
　132 74 165 **135** 336 **136**
　80 **137** 78
Jennet **70** 267
Jerome R. **89** 20
Jerusha **70** 353 354
Jerusha M. **70** 357
Joanna **70** 349 351 **81** 383
Joanna (Lemeree) **126** 206
Joel **70** 349
John **64** 192 **66** 35 **70** 161-
　168 266-268 349-364 **85**
　49 **124** 123 **126** 206 219
John Butler **70** 352
John Clark **70** 357
John J. **70** 358
John James **70** 358
John Parker **70** 353
John T. **70** 359
Joie **70** 358
Jonathan **70** 162-164 166-
　168 266-268 349-364 **73**
　259 **86** 7 10 **114** 278 **124**
　123
Joseph **70** 162 163 165
　166 266 353 359 **85** 216
　124 123
Josephine **70** 357 359 360
　363
Joshua **70** 168 351 358 363
Josiah C. **70** 356 357
Judah **70** 349 354 361
Judith **70** 351
Julia **70** 352 357 359 363
Julia (Carnahan) **128** 174
Julia Ann **70** 365
Julia Ann T. **70** 360
Julia L. **70** 360
Julius **70** 359
Julius G. **143** 170
Kathrina **51** 343
Lambert **110** 88-91
Lars Jacob (Mrs.) **91** 142
Laura **70** 351 363
Laura A. **70** 362
Laura Clark **70** 357
Laura Peterson **81** 383
Laurelia **70** 362
Lavina **70** 360
Lawrence **70** 363
Lemuel **70** 167
Levi **70** 267
Levina **70** 360
Lewis **70** 267 350 354 356
　359 360 **100** 287
Lily A. **70** 360
Lizzie **70** 364
Lois **70** 353 360 **73** 259
Lois (Sturtevant) **114** 278
Loring **70** 350
Louantha **70** 360
Louis **70** 353
Louisa C. **70** 356
Louise **81** 383 **121** 160

PETERSON *cont'd*
Lovina **73** 259
Lucas **125** 220
Lucia Parthenia (Lazell)
　89 20
Lucius A. **70** 361
Lucy **70** 267 351 354 357
　362
Lucy Ann **70** 355
Lucy Edwin **70** 360
Lucy G. **70** 357
Lucy Warren **70** 354
Luella **70** 362
Luke **70** 350
Lurania **70** 167
Lusa **70** 167
Luther **70** 168 350 356 364
　81 383
Lydia **70** 164-168 350 352
　355 357 358 363
Lydia A. **70** 355
Lydia Ann **70** 358
Lydia Clark **70** 357
Lydia Curtis **70** 364
Lydia H. **70** 363
Lydia Howland **70** 364
Lydia J. **70** 352
Lydia Jane (Howard)
　85 216
Mahala A. **70** 354
Marcia **70** 355 **81** 383
Margaret A. G. **81** 383
Maria **70** 350 352
Maria L. **70** 358
Marshall **70** 351 356
　81 383
Marshall Alden **70** 356
Martha **70** 162 358 359
　124 123
Martha D. **70** 361
Martha George **70** 361
Martin **70** 355 362
Mary **56** 37 **70** 162-165
　168 266 350 353 355 358
　360 362 **73** 259 **74** 11 **95**
　355 **124** 123 **127** 16
Mary (Soule) **124** 123
Mary A. **70** 361 363
Mary Ann **70** 166
Mary Annie **77** 182
Mary C. **70** 356
Mary Catherine **81** 383
Mary D. **70** 361 **99** 49
Mary E. **70** 361
Mary H. **70** 360
Mary Jane **70** 362
Mary L. **70** 363
Mary Porter **70** 360
Mary T. **70** 352
Mary T. (Call) **90** 55
Mary Wakefield **70** 352
Matilda **70** 357
Matilda W. **70** 358
Mehitable **70** 351 354
Mehitable Hunt **70** 364
Mehitable P. **70** 354
Mehitable Weston **70** 361
Mercy **70** 163 166
Mildred Johanna
　(Nyborg) **91** 142

PETERSON *cont'd*
Minnie J. (Bigelow)
　89 132
Mira **70** 362
Myra D. **86** 105
Nancy **70** 267 268 355 **89**
　20 **93** 270
Nancy (Clark) **89** 20
Nancy Brown **65** 39
Nancy D. **70** 359
Nancy S. (Norton)
　121 303
Nathan **70** 167 **128** 124
Nathaniel **70** 268
Nehemiah **70** 168 350 355
　362 363
Nels **128** 96
Nelson **70** 360 **73** 259
　128 174
Nicholas **55** 316 **83** 12
　85 216
Olaf A. **117** 286
Olive **70** 268 360 **73** 259
Olive Chaffin **120** 314
Orphan **60** 182 **70** 164
Oscar **70** 363 **128** 170
Oscar R. **70** 362
Otis **70** 354 355 363
Packard **70** 350
Parker **70** 364
Patience **70** 167 266
Pelham Bonney **81** 383
Penelope C. **70** 361
Perez **70** 350 **112** 318 319
Perez P. **112** 318
Peter **88** 283 **119** 21
　125 100
Phebe **70** 353 359 361
Phebe L. **106** 126
Polly **70** 268
Polly (Robinson) **88** 283
Princess **70** 350
Priscilla **70** 162 164 350
　81 383 **112** 318 319
Priscilla N. **112** 318
Rachel T. **70** 357
Ray **70** 362
Rebecca **70** 163 168 266
　350 355 **81** 298 **124** 123
Rebecca (Lambord)
　126 65
Reuben **70** 161 164 168
　349-352 354-364 **81** 298
　107 260
Rhoda **70** 167 360
Rhoda H. (Brown)
　140 265
Rhoda M. **73** 259
Roxana L. **70** 357
Ruth **60** 248 **70** 166 167
　362
Ruth C. **70** 356
Ruth Holmes **70** 358
Ruth Merrit **96** 287
Sally **70** 267 268 351 354
　356 364 365 **112** 319
Sally (Miller) **125** 220
Sally Turner **70** 355
Samuel **70** 168 352 358 364
Samuel Clark **70** 357
Samuel H. **140** 265

PETERSON *cont'd*
Samuel Soule **70** 351 356
    363
Sanford **70** 362
Sarah **70** 163 165 167 168
    266 267 349 350 353 354
    357 359 **78** 422 **81** 298
    127 88
Sarah (Goddard) **91** 273
Sarah A. **93** 270
Sarah Alden **70** 356
Sarah Allyn **70** 363
Sarah B. **70** 361
Sarah C. **70** 363
Sarah E. **112** 318 319
Sarah George **70** 354
Sarah H. **70** 350
Sarah Jane **70** 356
Sarah M. **70** 361
Sarah Merritt **82** 275
Sarah Oldham **70** 364
Sarah R. **70** 359
Selah **70** 268 350
Seth **70** 352 358 364
Seth Clark **70** 357
Seth Turner **70** 358
Sidney **70** 357
Silas Noyes **70** 364
Silvina **70** 350
Simeon W. **70** 362
Sophia **70** 350 351 356
    121 263
Sophia (Briggs) **126** 219
Sophia A. **70** 357
Sophia Anne **70** 356
Sophia L. **70** 352
Stella (Gifford) **96** 287
Stephen **70** 352 359
Stephen Douglas **89** 20
Stephen F. **70** 359
Stillman **70** 352
Susanna **70** 165 352 **81**
    310 312 382
Sylvanus **70** 167 266 267
    353 360 **73** 259
Sylvester Holmes **70** 357
Sylvia **70** 351 356
Sylvia Lola (Read)
    109 131
Thaddeus **70** 168 350 355
Thankful **70** 356
Thomas **70** 166 351 352
    356 363
Thomas Whittemore **70**
    168 352 359
Timothy **90** 108
Turner **70** 163 167 268
Valeda C. **130** 55
Waldo **70** 363
Walter **70** 362 363
Walter Scott **70** 359
Warren **70** 365
Washington **70** 364
Wealthea **70** 267 364
Weldon (Mrs.) **107** 134
Wentworth **70** 363
Whittemore **70** 350 354
Wilbur F. **70** 361
Wilford C. (Mrs.) **107** 134
William **70** 168 267 352
    356 358 359 **83** 36 **93**

PETERSON *cont'd*
    270 **101** 56 **111** 117 **128**
    174
William Bradford **70** 359
William Curtis **70** 358
William Edward (Mrs.)
    100 112
William Essom (Mrs.)
    89 132
William F. (Mrs.) **119** 158
William Henry **65** 39
William Otis **70** 363
William P. **70** 360
Zephaniah **70** 362
Zephaniah Sanger Cross-
    man **70** 355
Zilpah **70** 167
PETFIELD Pettfield
Deborah **66** 324
Elizabeth **51** 309 **66** 324
John **66** 325
Judith **51** 309 **66** 324 325
Matthew **66** 324 325
Richard **51** 309 **66** 324
Susan **51** 309 **66** 324
William **51** 309 **66** 324 325
PETFORD Lydia (Mitchell)
    90 299
William **90** 299
Petgro *see* Pettigrew
Petgrow *see* Pettigrew
PETHER Mary **62** 253
PETHERICK
Mary **60** 239
Petigrew *see* Pettigrew
Petigrow *see* Pettigrew
Petigru *see* Pettigrew
PETIN Margaret **73** 97
Petipas *see* Pettitpas
Petit *see* Pettit
PETITE
Elizabeth (Finney)
    (Cooper) **148** 319
PETITOT
Denis **143** 5
Marie (Robichaux) **143** 5
Petitt *see* Pettit
PETLEY
Agnes **51** 389 404
Alicia (Brampton) **51** 389
Ann **51** 402
Anthony **51** 403
Christiana (Philpot)
    51 389 404
Isabella **51** 389
John **51** 389 404
Juliana (de Trouemer)
    51 389 404
Ralph **51** 392 402
Richard **51** 389 404
Thomas **51** 389
PETO Petoe
Ann **110** 165
Florence **94** 306
Henry **59** 418
Sidracke **59** 418
PETOWNONOWIT   54 264
PETRE *see also* Peters
William (Lord) **147** 244
    245 250-252

PETRIE
— Major **145** 65
— Prof. **80** 5
A. P. **128** 263
Aaron **104** 97
Absalom **104** 21 263
Adam **104** 97
Alexiana **128** 263
Alexina **128** 263
Andrew **104** 21 263
Andrew B. **104** 21
Anna **104** 263
Barbara **104** 97
Elizabeth **104** 97
Emily **104** 104
Emogene **104** 104
Ervy **104** 104
George **104** 104
George M. **104** 104
Hannah (Hall) **128** 263
Jacob **142** 189
John **104** 21 97 263
John I. **104** 97
Joseph **104** 97
Joseph Howard **104** 263
Lewis R. **104** 104
Lydia **104** 22 23
Margaret **104** 97 118
Mary (Whitbread) **145** 65
Mary A. **104** 97
Melvin V. **104** 97
Thelma **101** 126
Thomas S. **128** 263
William **104** 97
William H. **104** 97
PETROSKY C. Matt (Mrs.)
    107 134
PETT Pet
Elizabeth **51** 349
John **75** 228
Richard **65** 179
Sarah **65** 353
Thomas **51** 349
PETTA John **147** 180
PETTAWE Thomas **56** 402
Pette *see* Pettee
Pettebone *see* Pettibone
PETTEE Pette Pettey
    Pettie Petty
— Mr. **56** 386
Abiel **130** 213
Abigail **55** 266
Abigail (Jenkins)
    (Caswell) **92** 189
Abner **58** 149
Abraham **146** 316
Ann **83** 39 **123** 260
Ann Lydia (Gott) **92** 189
Anna **65** 42 43 **87** 303
    123 260
Annie Folsom **85** 192 **92**
    151 189 199
Artemisa M. **122** 288
Betsey **125** 218
Caroline **102** 25
Catherine **58** 149
Charles **146** 315
Charles Seneca **92** 189
Charlotte **72** lvi
Christian **53** 328
Clary **122** 111

PETTEE *cont'd*
Curtis **115** 52
Cynthia **59** 374 **105** 216
Daniel **93** 344 **105** 216
Deborah G. **115** 171
Deric **146** 316
E. H. **122** 288
Ebenezer **58** 149 **87** 54 129
  129 341
Edward **147** 176
Eleanor **122** 288
Eliezor **105** 75
Elisha **115** 52
Elizabeth 378 **56** 255 **65** 41
  78 182 **92** 378
Elizabeth Chase (Folsom)
  92 189
Esther **146** 316
Eunice **53** 413 415
Frank **107** 134
Fred **122** 289
Fred O. **122** 289
G. W. **122** 288
George **75** 258 **105** 216
George W. **122** 289
Gerald McKinney
  117 132
Grace **122** 289
Grace (Maverick) **97** 59
Grace M. **122** 289
Harriet **113** 141 **122** 288
Harrison T. **122** 289
Henry **146** 315
Hester **52** 116
Hiram H. **122** 288
Hosea B. **122** 288
Howard (Mrs.) **108** 135
Isaac **146** 316
J. G. **122** 289
James **53** 328 **65** 41 **87** 53
  303 **119** 20 **122** 111 **123**
  261
James Harvy **142** 60
Jemima **131** 56
Joanna **58** 149
Job **87** 303
John **52** 116 126 **63** 237
  68 240 **83** 39 **123** 263
  146 315
John Julius **122** 290
John T. **115** 176
John Tyler **61** 218
Joseph **58** 150 **98** 105 **105**
  75 **128** 217
Judith **146** 316
Julia S. **115** 176
Julius A. **115** 171
Julius F. **122** 289
Louisa **94** 53
Lucinda **80** 29
Lucy (Owen) **92** 189
Mabel O. **71** xxxviii
Marie (Du Prie) **146** 316
Mary **53** 328 **58** 149 150
  68 240 **92** 377 **122** 111
  288 **123** 262 **131** 56 57
Mary (Lawton) **123** 261
Mary (Taylor) **123** 263
Mary A. **106** 320 **122** 288
Mary Ann **78** 37
Mary Pierce **77** 185

PETTEE *cont'd*
Nancy **65** 43 **77** 266
Nanny **65** 42
Nathan **65** 42 43
Nellie **65** 41 **122** 289
Oliver **65** 41 **93** 162
Otis **97** 59
Patience (Chase) (Wilcox)
  87 54 129
Pierre **146** 316
Polly **115** 52
Rebecca **58** 149
Robert **83** 449
Ruth **113** 132
Sally **109** 69
Samuel **65** 41 **92** 189
Sarah **58** 150 **75** 258 **77** 178
  103 64 **105** 216 **146** 316
Seneca **92** 189
Simon **92** 189
Solomon **56** 255
Stephen **140** 69
Susan **111** 271
Susanne **146** 316
Tabitha **87** 53
Tabitha (Chase) **87** 53
Thomas **65** 42 43 **141** 333
Warren Chester **77** 185
William **92** 189 **146** 315
  316
William S. **93** 349
Zepheniah **147** 85
Pettegrew *see* Pettigrew
Pettegrow *see* Pettigrew
PETTEL Petel
—— **101** 270
Elizabeth **101** 247
Rachel **100** 241
Sary **101** 163
Pettengill *see* Pettingell
Petters *see* Peters
Petterson *see* Peterson
Pettes *see* Pettis
Pettet *see* Pettit
Pettey *see* Pettee
Pettfield *see* Petfield
PETTIBONE Pettebone
  Pettybone
—— **122** 118 120
Abel **72** 39 175
Abigail **102** 309 **122** 42 43
Abijah **72** 38
Abraham **51** 103 **81** 408
  137 11
Alexander **137** 11
Anna **72** 316
Arthur Dudley **75** xxiii 64
  111 309 310
Betsey **72** 316
Bishop **72** 89
Caroline M. (Swetland)
  85 225
Catherine **83** 55
Charlotte **123** 47
Chauncey **137** 11
Chloe **83** 52
Daniel **71** 81 165 271-273
  276 281 **72** 42 89 101 **85**
  56
Deborah (Bissell) **85** 225
Dorinda **83** 55

PETTIBONE *cont'd*
Dorothy **123** 46 47
Dudley **72** 39 **111** 311
Ebenezer **121** 91
Eli **76** 155
Elizabeth **72** 176 **81** 408
  111 240
Elizabeth (Thrall) **111** 240
Eunice (Gaines) (Graham)
  85 56
Fanny **83** 55
Hannah **72** 42 180 **83** 55
Harlow **83** 55
Harriet **72** 89 102
Helen Folger **111** 311
Huldah (Williams) **85** 225
Isaac **123** 47
Isabel A. **82** 376
Jacob **72** 5
Jean Provost (Folger)
  111 311
Jennie **72** 5
Jerusha **81** 408
John **71** 272 **83** 55 **85** 225
  91 400 **112** 127 **122** 42
  125 35
John L. **105** 73
Jonathan **72** 38 **83** 55
Joseph **72** 172
Kate Swetland **84** 185 **85**
  108 202 225
Levi **71** 271
Lucina **72** 39
Lucy **72** 172 **83** 55
Lurannah **72** 5
Lydia **72** 42 100
Margaret **72** 101
Marian Pease (Norton)
  111 311
Martha **72** 38 **83** 55
Martha (Payne) **85** 225
Noah **85** 225
Norman **81** 408 **137** 11
Oliver **85** 225
Oziah **100** 7
Payne **85** 225
Polly **72** 39
Rhoda **72** 101
Roderick **81** 408
Rosanna **72** 100
Roxy **72** 42 89 100
S. N. **82** 376
Samuel **71** 276 **81** 408 409
  83 55 **85** 46 **111** 240
  122 37 39 **142** 341
Sarah **71** 81 273 281 **72** 172
  105 225 **122** 42
Sarah (Eggleston) **85** 225
Stephen **85** 225
Susanna Lorinda **72** 319
Theodora **137** 11
Theophilus **137** 11
Ursula **81** 286
Virgil **83** 55
Zeruah (Howe) **121** 91
Pettice *see* Pettis
Pettie *see* Pettee

PETTIGREW Petgro
Petgrow Petigrew
Petigrow Petigru
Pettegrew Pettegrow
Petygrewe
—— **53** 134 **65** 178
— Mr. **55** 452
— Mrs. **83** 308
Abby M. **120** 68
Amanda M. **83** 301 303
Anne **63** 168
Elizabeth **121** 303
Elsie **82** 296 300
Francis **54** 409 **144** 37
Frank **73** 189 202
George **78** 74
Helen **81** 106
James **83** 26 27
John **55** 251 253 **84** 75 **97**
267 **116** 131
Joseph **97** 270
Joseph (Mrs.) **97** 270
Mary **82** 290 296 **83** 26 27
95 246
Mary Ann (Forsaith) **83**
180 185
Mary Elizabeth **83** 232
Mercy **102** 239
Nicholas **144** 37
Rhoda **87** 148
Robert **81** 106
Samuel **55** 251 253 **63** 168
144 37
Sarah **94** 189 **97** 3 **114** 294
144 37
Sophia Errett **81** 106
Thomas **82** 296 300
William **82** 290 296
83 180 185
PETTINGER
Ruth **108** 310
PETTINGILL Pattengill
Pettengill Pettingale
Pettingall Pettingell
Pettingil Pettinil
—— **73** 193
— Rev. **114** 7
A. S. **91** 332
Abigail **51** 464 **58** 17 **128**
285 **137** 46
Akerman **52** 373
Albert A. **81** 250
Alma Elizabeth 230 **92** 230
Althea A. **71** 48
Amy **112** 154
Andrew Haskell **119** 156
Angeline **73** 235
Anna **94** 64
Anne (Moulton) **141** 322
147 143
Bathsheba **55** 196 197
Benjamin **58** 125
Betsey **91** 182
Charles F. **112** 59
Charles Ireland **79** 103
203 **95** 213
Curtis E. **64** 119
Cutting **55** 197 **83** 259
Daniel **73** 235
Deborah **52** 373 **69** 36
73 235

PETTINGILL *cont'd*
Edwin C. **64** 119
Eleanor **71** 192
Eliphalet **64** 119 **143** 18
Eliza **125** 293
Elizabeth **55** 196 **64** 119
Elizabeth Colley **113** 301
Elizabeth Garcelon **94**
140 **96** 158
Ephraim **92** 320
Esther **86** 390
Ethan **73** 235
Evelyn Muriel **92** 230
Frank Hervey **66** lii **71**
287 **73** 322 **77** 162 **81**
109 231 **83** 259 260
George W. **64** 119
George William **92** 230
Hannah **107** 253 254
114 184
Hannah (Burbank) **91** 267
Hannah (Dean) **114** 184
Harriet **64** 119
Harriet E. **112** 59
Helen Olmsted **92** 230
Henrietta **64** 119
Horatio **112** 59
Ina Adelaide 230 **92** 230
Irving Wolford (Mrs.)
94 188
Isaac **78** 335
Jacob **111** 107
James **126** 206
James C. **62** 122 127
Jane **64** 119
Joanna **53** 37
John **78** 111 **81** 448 **91** 267
92 322 **141** 322 **147** 143
John H. **128** 212
John M. **116** 261 **119** 156
John Mason **124** 203 303
John W. **84** 321
Jonathan **128** 285 **137** 46
Joseph **65** 114 262 **83** 259
94 95 **100** 65
Joseph Wesley **92** 226
Judith **116** 261 263 274
Julia V. **112** 56 59
Laura Ann **69** 326
Laura K. **114** 315 **118** 182
120 71 **125** 72
Laura Keziah **104** 145
106 123 **116** 72 **119** 150
156 242 **121** 150 151 235
313 **122** 208 **123** 68 147
221 **124** 84 146 264
Lavinia **73** 193
Lemuel **86** 390
Lewis **112** 59
Lona Esther (Olmsted)
230 **92** 230
Lucile (Kroger) **94** 188
Lucretia **122** 279
Lydia **58** 125 **125** 223
126 273
Lydia (Briggs) **126** 272
273
Lydia Hale **97** 357
Margaret **124** 295
Martha **111** 107
Martha (Coates) **111** 107

PETTINGILL *cont'd*
Mary **51** 466 **80** 439 **106**
226 **124** 289 **147** 143
Mary Agnes **83** 260
Mary Ann **92** 322
Mary Ann (Batterton)
126 206
Mary Ann (Shapleigh)
95 273
Matilda **64** 119
Matthew **53** 36 37 **83** 259
111 107
Maud 226 **92** 226
Moses **81** 448 **125** 39
Nancy **117** 140
Nathaniel **56** 74 **83** 259
Nathaniel Henry **83** 259
Nicholas **53** 122 **111** 107
Oliver H. **73** 235
Rachel **126** 271
Raymond R. **92** 230
Rebecca Sanford (Parker)
114 7 **128** 212
Reuel **126** 272 273
Richard **53** 37 **55** 192 194
60 190 **71** 287 **83** 259
113 301
Roy Vernon **92** 230
S. **112** 59
Sally (Grover) **112** 57 59
Sampson **69** 326
Samuel **55** 196 **95** 273
Sarah **53** 36 37 **58** 16 **69**
326 **90** 51
Sarah Adda **81** 250
Sarah Ann **112** 144
Silas **91** 206
Stephen **91** 332 **125** 43
Tabitha **53** 122
Tabitha (March) **111** 107
Thankful **112** 59
Timothy **134** 216
U. L. **91** 332
William **112** 57 59
William Flavel **112** 59
Zema Mae (Schwab) 230
92 230
PETTINGTON D. **91** 332
Pettinill *see* Pettingill
Pettipace *see* Pettitpas
PETTIS Pettes Pettice Pettys
—— **63** 55
Abiel **105** 235
Amy (Newhouse) **122** 91
Benjamin **56** 129
Betsey **79** 44
Eliza **95** 333
Elizabeth **86** 384 **131** 55 56
Frances Beatrice (Chellis)
122 91
Georgiana **77** 187
Hannah **90** 113 **97** 116
105 235
Harriet Fracker **122** 91
Helen Gordon **122** 91
Henry **122** 89 91
Henry B. **122** 87
Henry Bass **122** 91
James **74** 65 **127** 309
Jehiel **86** 384
John **58** 237 **63** 52 **90** 113

PETTIS *cont'd*
John Henry **77** 187
Joseph **56** 129
Lydia (Hoar) **142** 20
Maria Woodward **122** 91
Mary **131** 138
Mary (Domett) **122** 91
Mary (Gifford) **129** 337
Mary Dwight **122** 91
Mary Woodward **122** 91
Nathan **129** 337
Nathaniel **128** 294
Nellie Gordon **122** 87
Norman William **107** 134
Peter **86** 384
Polly **105** 235
Reuben Wellington **72** 290
Ruth **72** 290
Sabra Emeline **72** 290
Sabria **86** 384
Samuel **122** 91
Sarah **81** 191 **126** 20 **134** 313
Sarah (Porter) **122** 91
Sarah Ann **90** 54
Solomon **72** 290
Stephen **59** 222
Temperance **74** 65
William **128** 300 **134** 313
PETTISHALL Margaret **111** 154 **114** 74
Thomas **111** 154 **114** 74
PETTIT Petit Pettet Pettitt Pettyt Pettytt
—— **70** 210 **140** 120
— Lt. **117** 33
A. J. **92** 173
Adlington **100** 141
Alice **69** 19 **82** 235
Alice Emily **70** 210
Andrew **92** 173
Ann **100** 135
Annis **113** 283
Bethiah **75** 177
Caroline **92** 173
Carrie D. (Nuttman) **104** 309
Catherine **101** 71
Charles **68** 209
Charlotte J. **92** 173
Cyryacke **67** 174
Eliada **76** 138
Elizabeth **106** 67 **113** 282
Elizabeth E. **126** 45
Ella (Keel) **104** 309
Emis **113** 283
Esther **100** 141
Esther (Barton) **140** 120
Frank H. **92** 173
Frederick Robinson **100** 245
Frederick Robinson (Mrs.) **87** 375 **100** 44 114
George H. **92** 173
H. **92** 173
Hezekiah **92** 173 174
Hezekiah P. **92** 173
Hila J. **92** 173
J. P. **65** 129

PETTIT *cont'd*
James **113** 280
James Henry **92** 173
Jean **106** 67
Jean Louis **136** 106
Jennie M. **98** 362 **104** 233
John **98** 123 **100** 135 **113** 204
John Cooke **60** 399
John Gilbert **65** 230
John Samuel **51** 464
Joseph Nuttman **104** 309 **105** 129
Lottie J. **92** 173
Louisa **92** 174
Lydia **92** 166
Lydia Ann **100** 245
Lydia Crosby (Wallis) **87** 172 375 **100** 245
Lydia Wallis **100** 245
M. R. **92** 173
Margaret **68** 241
Mary **51** 464 **72** 215
Mary E. **92** 173
Mary Rosalia (Hogaboom) **92** 173
Mary Wilhelmina **104** 309
Naomi **92** 173 174
Nathaniel **113** 204
Nicholas **65** 230
Rachel L. (Cox) **92** 173
Rebecca **127** 100
Rebecca E. **126** 45 **127** 100
Richard **69** 19 **113** 283
Robert **100** 141
Ruth **84** 234 **85** 197
Sally Ann (Van Valkenburgh) **92** 173
Samuel **76** 138
Sarah **100** 141 **107** 50
Silas F. **92** 173
Thomas **69** 357 **94** 339 **113** 283
Wealthy May **86** 361
William Lindley **104** 309
William Lindley (Mrs.) **101** 125 **104** 309 **105** 68 132
William Warren **92** 172 173
PETTITPAS Petipas Pettipace
Catherine (Bugaret) **143** 5
Claude **143** 5
Elizabeth **143** 7
Geoffrey **123** 242
Henriette **143** 5
William **83** 320 329
Pettitt *see* Pettit
PETTS —— **70** 140
— Lieut. **70** 142
Bathsheba **64** 145
John **64** 145 **81** 38 **136** 266
Lemuel **64** 146
Lillian E. **82** 274
Milly **64** 146
Nancy Maria **81** 38
Relief **81** 38
Rose (Elliott) **97** 133
William **97** 133

Petty *see* Pettee
Pettybone *see* Pettibone
PETTYFACE
Jonathan **127** 17
Rebecca **127** 9
Pettys *see* Pettis
Pettyt *see* Pettit
Pettytt *see* Pettit
PETTYWATT Petywat
John **57** 219
Thomas **64** 57
PETULA William **51** 398
PETWELL
James **93** 173
John **93** 223
Robert **93** 173 175 223 226
Rose **93** 223
Thomas **93** 223
Petygrewe *see* Pettigrew
PETYN James **111** 197
Petyngrewe *see* Pettigrew
PETYVER John **86** 423
Petywat *see* Pettywatt
Pevare *see* Pevear
PEVE John **73** 73
PEVEAR Pevare Pevere Piveyer
—— **84** 37
Alma **81** 254
Bert **83** 437 438
Caroline Hanscom **89** 186 187
Edward **89** 187
Ella (Nealey) **83** 437 438
Euphemia Coffrin **96** 159
Everett (Mrs.) **74** xl
Mary **87** 26
Olive Tellow Verde (Hanscom) **89** 187
Samuel **65** 235
Sarah D. (Rich) (Comey) **84** 37
PEVERELL Peverel
— Widow **81** 491
Henry **109** 22 28 29
John **79** 370
Maud **105** 37
Richard **92** 385 **93** 75 **94** 77 231
Thomas **109** 22 28 29
William **94** 206 **105** 37 **107** 123 **119** 95
PEVERLY Peverelly
—— **82** 414
Abby Jane **81** 254
Abigail **58** 297 **81** 142 147 149 259 432 **82** 284 296
Abigail Minerva **81** 252
Adeline Louise **81** 250
Albert **73** 200 **81** 149
Alice **81** 261
Alice Justine **81** 250
Almira **81** 254 257
Almira Jay **81** 155
Ann **81** 138 141 143 145 146 261 448
Ann A. **81** 149
Ann Constance **81** 259
Ann Elizabeth **81** 146 **100** 39

PEVERLY *cont'd*
Anna Card **81** 142
Arthur Freeman **81** 252
Arthur Tilden **81** 259
Benjamin **81** 146 147 155
256
Benjamin Cotton **81** 147
Benjamin Henderson
81 257
Betsey **81** 150 259
Betty **81** 262
Caroline E. **81** 256
Catherine **81** 147 152
Catherine H. **81** 259
Charles **79** 46 **81** 254 259
Charles Arthur **81** 252
Charles George **81** 255
Charles Kimball **81** 256
Charles Lewis **81** 250
Charles Taylor **81** 254
Charles Thomas **81** 252
Charlotte Ann **81** 251
Clara **81** 255
Clarissa Bartlett (Powers)
81 255
Clarissa Ursula **81** 255
256
Costella L. **81** 251
Deliverance **81** 140 432
Dexter Dana **81** 256
Dexter T. **81** 253
Dolly **81** 259
Donald L. **81** 259
Dorothy Louise **81** 252
Eben B. **81** 256
Eben Turk **81** 248
Edith O. **81** 259
Edward Blake **81** 255
Edward Everett **81** 257
Effie **81** 252
Ethe Florence **81** 256
Eliza **81** 151
Eliza D. **81** 148
Eliza E. **81** 155
Eliza J. **81** 149
Eliza Jane **81** 251
Eliza K. **81** 259 260 **84** 345
Eliza M. **81** 253
Elizabeth **58** 297 **81** 138
141 142 145 146 149 150
248 257 260 262 432 **82**
52
Elizabeth B. **81** 259
Elizabeth Ellen **81** 258
Elizabeth Jane **81** 149
Elizabeth Kinsman
81 142
Elizabeth Louise **81** 258
Elizabeth Mary **81** 256
Elizabeth T. **81** 257
Ellen **81** 258 259
Emily Belle **81** 253
Emily Gilchrist **81** 257
Emma Alice **81** 252
Ephraim Powers **81** 255
Ernest Tilden **81** 259
Etta Isabel **81** 257
Evelyn S. **81** 258
Everett **81** 155
Florence **81** 252
Florence Belle **81** 252

PEVERLY *cont'd*
Florence May **81** 253
Frances **81** 260
Frances Ann **81** 249
Frances E. **81** 259
Frances Jane **81** 254
Frances L. **81** 259
Frances Leland **81** 253
Frank **81** 254
Frederick **81** 260
Freeman **81** 149 250
Freeman Herbert **81** 252
Freeman Webster **81** 252
George **73** 204 **81** 141
143 145 147-149 248 260
432 **82** 52
George Dow **81** 255
George Washington **81**
151 254
Georgianna **81** 255
Grace **81** 140
Hannah **81** 148 150 152
154 255 260 496 497 **86**
148
Hannah (Henderson)
86 148
Hannah L. **81** 251
Harriet **73** 197 **81** 149 151
Harriet Eliza **81** 254
Harry Everett **81** 257
Harry Loomis **81** 258
Harry R. **81** 259
Helen **81** 155 257
Helen M. **81** 147
Henrietta **81** 259
Henry **81** 261
Hiram **81** 261
Horace Emery **81** 253
Horace Loomis **81** 258
Howard A. **81** 253
Ida **81** 257
Ida May **81** 254
Ida Reed **81** 258
Isabella S. **81** 248
James **81** 146 147 262
James Burnside **81** 256
James Carr **81** 257
James Henry **81** 255
James Horace **81** 252
James Walker **81** 257
Jane **73** 192 **81** 139 252
258 259
Jane (Walford) **94** 353
Jane Colbath **81** 250
Jeremiah **81** 140 147 152
Joanna **73** 201 **81** 142 148
154 256 261
John **81** 138-143 146 150
261 262 432
John Sanborn **81** 141
146 150 254 255 262
John W. **81** 149
John Wilton **81** 252
Joseph **81** 147 152 255 496
86 60 148
Joseph Orin **81** 256
Judith **81** 253
Julia **81** 155 257
Julia Agnes **81** 253
Katharine B. **81** 153 **86** 153
154

PEVERLY *cont'd*
Katy **81** 261
Kinsman **73** 197 200 **81**
142 149 448 **82** 284 296
Lazarus **81** 139 140
Lenore **81** 256
Leola Foster **81** 255
Leonora May **81** 255
Lois **81** 248
Louisa **81** 257
Louisa F. **81** 255
Louise **81** 248
Lucy Jane **81** 150 254
Lura Edith **81** 253
Lydia U. **81** 258
Margaret **81** 261 262
Maria T. **81** 257
Marianna B. **81** 258
Martha **81** 139 253 **94** 353
Martha B. **81** 259
Mary **58** 297 **81** 139 142-
144 250 257 260-262
Mary Ann **81** 251
Mary E. **81** 257
Mary Elizabeth **81** 252 253
Mary Ellen **81** 251 255
Mary Louisa **81** 248
Mary S. **81** 150
Mary Sophronia **81** 250
Minnie Belle **81** 253
Moses **81** 260
Nancy **81** 151
Nathaniel **58** 297 **81** 138
140-142 146 149 150 253
260 432
Nellie Mary **81** 255
Olive Augusta **81** 256
Otis Bolster **81** 256
Pauline **81** 257
Persis **81** 255-257
Peter **81** 262
Rachel **81** 141
Raymond **81** 253
Richard **81** 258 259
Robert **73** 192 **81** 149 249
262
Robert H. **81** 258
Robert Ham **81** 259
Rosanna **81** 256
Ruby Woodworth **81** 254
Rufus **81** 149
Rufus Alonzo **81** 250
Sally **81** 261 262
Samuel **81** 140 141 262
Samuel Carr **81** 257
Sarah **81** 139 140 145 149-
151 261 262 **82** 52 **111**
46
Sarah Adda (Brown)
81 250
Sarah Ann **81** 147
Sarah Anna **81** 254
Sarah Elizabeth **81** 253
Sarah Miles **81** 251
Sarah Sanborn **81** 150
Saul **81** 262
Sumner D. **81** 257
Susan Francis **81** 252
Susanna **81** 144 256 257
260 **82** 52
Temperance **81** 141 145

PEVERLY *cont'd*
Thomas **58** 297 **81** 138-
140 142 147 150 154 155
248 252 258 496 **82** 130
84 345 **86** 60 **88** 299 **94**
353
Thomas Davis **81** 259
Thomas Ham **81** 259
Walter **81** 258
William **58** 297 **73** 201 202
81 141-143 147 149 248
262 448
William A. **81** 248
William Davis **81** 259
William Edward **81** 252
William James **81** 248
Pevey *see* Peavey
PEVIS — Mr. **72** 133
Pevy *see* Peavey
PEW *see also* De Pew
Abigail (Grover) **87** 285
Alice (Huntington)
87 286
Alice (Parsons) **87** 285
Althea Huntington
87 286
Caroline Fidelia (Calkins)
124 313
Catherine Whipple
87 286
Drusilla Florence **78** 355
Hannah Jane **94** 82
Harriet Winchester
87 286
Harriet Winchester
(Presson) **87** 285
Hyrum William **124** 313
John **87** 285
Mary **72** 15 **110** 55
Mary (Garsoe) **116** 258
Mary Huntington **87** 286
Paul **116** 258
Sarah Knutsford (Tarr)
87 285
William **87** 285 **124** 313
William Andrews **84**
340 353 466 **85** 197 **87**
204 285 **88** 175
Pewsey *see* Pusey
PEX — **103** 13
PEYER Susanna **54** 50
PEYERDEN John **64** 227
Peygotte *see* Piggott
PEYNE Barnarde **147** 252
Peyntor *see* Painter
PEYNTREE
Hannah **80** 304
John **64** 73 **80** 131 304
Margaret **64** 73 **80** 131
Mary **64** 73 **80** 131
William **64** 73 **80** 131-134
136 **90** 154
PEYSER — **83** 308
— Mr. **56** 21
Albert Lowe **84** 31
Benjamin Davis **54** 130
241 372 460 **55** 131 239
Elise **83** 428 438
Eliza E. **84** 31
Henry **84** 31
Lawrence G. **83** 438 **84** 19

PEYSER *cont'd*
May (Shillaber) **83** 438
84 19
Mildred **83** 438 **84** 24
Samuel G. **84** 31
Peyster *see* De Peyster
PEYTO
Alice de **102** 312
John de **102** 312
Mary **53** 11
Stephen **53** 11
Thomas **53** 11
William **53** 11
PEYTON — **109** 75
— Col. **52** 470
Alice Victory **71** xxiii
Elizabeth (Vannoy)
109 75
Jessie Caroline **79** 132
Katharine Holly **117** 123
Margaret **117** 122
Robert **122** 7
William **91** 332
PEYVEN Abigail (Nason)
95 189
Francis **95** 189
PFAELZER Blanche Bell
(Walker) **88** 170
Franklin Theobald (Mrs.)
88 170
PFAU A. H. **86** 318
C. A. **86** 318
Carrie Belle **86** 318
Herman **86** 318
PFEIFFER Pfeffer
Anna (Fullerton) **99** 45
Anna Marguerite **99** 45
Charles **85** 316
Francis Joseph **54** 126 128
George **85** 316
George W. **92** 115
Gustavus Adolphus **84**
110 186 **110** 63
Gustavus Adolphus
(Mrs.) **80** 105 207
110 63
Jacob **85** 316
John **99** 45
Louise **80** 207
Margaretha **85** 316
Mary **85** 316
Milton John **81** 40
Nellie Grace **81** 40
Ortmar **85** 316
Raymond L. (Mrs.)
115 238
William **85** 316
William Frederick **92** 115
PFEIL — **148** 183
PFISTER
Eliza von **76** 54
William H. von **76** 54
PFIZENMAYER Mason
(Mrs.) **85** 112 **91** 208
PFIZER
Charles **96** 389
Fannie **96** 389
PFLUEGER
A. C. **81** 291
C. A. **81** 291
J. F. **81** 291

PFLUEGER *cont'd*
Otto Henry (Mrs.)
104 145
PHAGE Joan (Giddings)
135 280 281
Joan (Purrier) **135** 280 281
Robert **135** 278-282
Thomas **135** 278 282
William **135** 282
PHAGINS
Joseph E. **88** 339
Sarah L. (Titcomb) **88** 339
PHAILL
William P. **79** 40
PHAIN Francis **65** 117
PHAIR — **54** lxxx
— Mrs. **123** 305
Edward Francis **123** 305
Eliza Ann **123** 305
Henry William **123** 305
John Preston **123** 305
Mary **123** 94
R. **52** 319
Sarah Jane **123** 305
Phalen *see* Phelan
PHALINGS
Mary A. **75** lxxxiv
PHAN Anthony **111** 320
PHANTON S. **68** 46
PHANTRAY
Helenora **77** 186
Moses **77** 186
PHARES Pharez Pharis
Abigail **80** 153 154 **103** 91
105 306
Zacharias **56** 126
PHARO Phebe **83** 26 29
William **83** 26 29
PHAROD Joseph **143** 258
PHASLAY John **90** 66
PHAUP Benjamin **63** 352
Phayre *see* Phair
PHEARS Betsey **91** 261
Humphery **91** 261
Polly **91** 261
PHEARSON
Mary Dennis **88** 340
PHEASANT
Samuel **63** 19
PHEATT David **85** 112
PHELAN Phalen Phelen
Phelon
— **63** 340
Clarence W. **88** 128
Edward **91** 206 **94** 95
100 65
Eleanor (Knowles) **88** 128
Emily **63** 340
Fally (Hoisington)
141 51
Harold R. **109** 158
Hester **53** 417
James **88** 128 **131** 90
James Joseph (Mrs.)
88 170
Johannah **101** 270
Johannah (Sulavan)
100 298
John **91** 206 **100** 298 **114**
182 **119** 21 126 **141** 51
Louise (Dugas) **131** 90

PHELAN *cont'd*
Mabel (McGaffee) **88** 170
Maria Louisa **88** 338
Nicholas **114** 182
Patrick **91** 206 **94** 95
100 65
Priscilla (Ford) (Morris)
119 126
Sarah Jane (Knowles)
88 128
Stephen **78** 314
Timothy **63** 238
William **88** 128
PHELPS Phelpes
—— **53** 238 **56** 327 **57** 338
58 199 **59** 236 **72** 31 **85**
449 **92** 251 346 **103** 174
118 23 306 315 **119** 55
302 **120** 123 128 203 298
121 98 **122** 120 122 123
224 225 302 307 **126** 269
— Miss **71** 77
— Mr. **79** 403
— Mrs. **51** 321 **72** 179
123 310
— Prof. **62** 52
A. H. **62** 187
Aaron **71** 76 77 161-164
272 273 **72** 30 166 170
111 192
Abel **69** 213 215 220 300
303 304 **70** 11 14 92 298
Abiel Smith **100** 77
Abigail **62** 188 **71** 81 **72**
307 **74** 65 66 **81** 83 **83**
41 **88** 74 **103** 141 **108** 65
124 60 **136** 319 **148** 225
Abigail (Eno) **105** 150
Abigail (Fairfield)
121 159
Abigail (Griswold)
102 309
Abigail (Pettebone) **102**
309 **122** 42 43
Abigail (Post) **146** 366
Abigail (Stebbins)
148 225
Abitha **146** 358 359
Abner **71** 161 **72** 174 **99** 8
Abram **85** 169
Achsa **139** 94
Achsah (Mansfield)
124 10
Achsah L. (Hoar) **134** 117
Adna **139** 94 98 257
Adosha Williams **86** 318
Alexander **102** 309
104 263
Alfred E. **85** 316
Alice **56** 307 **83** 257 **109** 73
Almira M. **109** 271
Alvah Nelson **78** 355
Alvan P. **81** 57
Ama **72** 102
Amanda **109** 73
Amoret **72** 116
Amos **61** 242 **122** 41 42
Andrew C. **81** 57
Angie Margaret **60** 45
Ann **71** 83 282 **73** 14 **79**
154 **89** 15

PHELPS *cont'd*
Ann S. **95** 367
Ann S. (Risley) **85** 316
Anna **57** 269 **60** 79 **61** 389
71 274 **79** 321 **91** 242
136 314
Anna (Lincoln) **114** 103
Anna Theresa (Fitch)
113 298
Anne **93** 182 **136** 333 **147**
154 161
Anne A. **72** 104
Anson Greene **68** lxvii
82 195 **90** 174 **95** 356
Anstis **62** 187 **121** 61
Anthony **130** 304
Anthony William Coo-
per **125** 165 **133** 85
145 367
Apama **126** 306
Arvilla (Webster) **111**
187 189
Asa **83** 44 **85** 152
Asabel **60** 205
Augusta **100** 77
Augustus **72** 307
Austin **72** 39 **83** 55
Avah **80** 57
Azariah **83** 51
Azubah **71** 273 **81** 57 **83** 51
Barnet **146** 364 365
Barney Smith **100** 77
Barsheba **71** 274
Bathsheba **56** 243
Becky **121** 300
Bela C. **81** 57
Benajah **62** 295 **106** 109
107 181
Benjamin **73** 220 **81** 414
109 73 **130** 304
Betsey **72** 116 **85** 169 449
109 271 **119** 301 304
306 307 **120** 58 60-63
123-129 131-134 203-214
294-304 **121** 57-69 95-
100 297-303 **147** 63
Betsey (Stewart) **95** 367
Betsey B. **81** 270
Betsey Law **73** 14
Betty **119** 49 128 129 136
138 294 300 303 304 306
120 58 207 303
Bildad **72** 36
Bishop **72** 44 93 94 102
Buley **81** 57
Caleb **71** 278
Carolina **58** 401
Caroline **64** 379 **68** lxvii
76 47 53
Caroline Alexandra
105 150
Caroline Augusta
114 232
Caroline Eliza **84** 102
Caroline Lord **70** xlix
Catherine **72** 232 **80** 57
83 44
Celestia **83** 20
Charity **71** 165 272 303
Charles **60** 394 395 **61** 34
62 187 188 **71** 77 78 83

PHELPS *cont'd*
156 158 159 161 162 274
275 278 282 307 309 **72**
40 170 180 **84** 243 291
114 103 **118** 3 4 6 21 28
109-112 114-127 217-222
225 231-234 236 298-306
308 **119** 43 45-48 50 51
53 55 57 127 131 133-
137 139 205-208 210-223
289-307 **120** 57-63 123-
135 203-214 293-304
121 57-69 95-100 296-
303 **122** 62-69 115-120
122 123 220-227 302-309
123 27 32 **129** 213 214
216
Charles (Mrs.) **118** 229 230
234 **120** 57
Charles B. **54** lxxiii
Charles Goodrich **114** 232
Charles Henry **114** 232
136 332
Charles J. **76** 86
Charles P. **123** 23 **140** 159
Charles R. **83** 431 438
Charles Shepherd **72** 81
Charles William **136** 332
Charlotte **79** 21 **81** 61 270
Charlotte (Wilcox) **98** 340
Charlotte Lenora **83** 55
Chester **71** 277 **126** 25
Clarissa **70** 92 **80** 62
Clarissa Orton **72** 307
Clinton A. **130** 304
Clinton Leandrew
130 304
Cornelius **71** 81 165 273
274 303 **72** 31 39 170
116 7 **122** 80
Cynthia **76** 85 **78** 236
80 130
Cynthia Lee **133** 232
Damaris **71** 277 **122** 42
Damaris (Gilman)
105 150
Daniel **60** 331 **70** 92
71 163
David **55** 390 **74** 65 **81** 57
83 44 **102** 309 **108** 239
109 308 **122** 41-43 **126**
144
Deborah **139** 94
Delia **79** 152
Desire **127** 258
Dolly **118** 109-120
Dolly Ann **81** 57
Dorcas A. **81** 57
Dorothy **62** 187 188 **68** 97
87 202 **102** 309 **118** 109-
111 115 **123** 263
Dorothy (Ingersoll)
123 259
Dudley Ames **109** 261
E. L. **80** 62
Ebenezer **61** 139 **76** 85
86 90
Edward **56** 242 **58** 199 **60**
313 314 **61** 74 **69** 1 **72**
103 **75** 306 **81** 433 **100**
77 245 **104** 163 **122** 221-

PHELPS *cont'd*
223 225 307 **123** 23 **126**
14 **130** 304
Edward John **80** 4
Edwin **109** 271
Eleanor **136** 332
Eleazer W. **66** 41
Elihu **71** 273 **83** 44
Elijah **74** 65 66
Elisha **72** 170 **83** 55
112 125
Elisha Pitt **83** 55
Eliza **62** 187
Eliza (Ayres) **84** 102
Eliza (Houghton) **84** 243
291
Elizabeth **54** 181 222 **61**
287 **64** 248 **66** 41 **67** 374
72 116 232 **73** 275 **74** 65
78 401 **81** 414 **85** 169
90 276 **109** 310 **122** 42
123 27 **126** 25
Elizabeth (Abbott)
108 251
Elizabeth (Adams) **104**
163 **130** 304
Elizabeth (Ames) **109** 261
Elizabeth (Eno) **102** 309
Elizabeth (Hungerford)
105 150
Elizabeth (Porter) **118** 3
71 108 217 297 **119** 43
90 127 205 289 **120** 57
123 203 293 **121** 57 95
296 **122** 62 115 220 302
309 **123** 16 **129** 213 **148**
185
Elizabeth Georgiana **86**
198 **99** 69 152 **100** 245
Elizabeth Gray **92** 343
Elizabeth Whiting **119** 44
Elizabeth Woodbridge
90 174 **95** 356
Elizer W. **144** 103
Ellen (Gunne) **84** 287 289
290
Ellen Ada **82** 101 102
Ellen Maria (Sheffield)
102 309
Elnathan **79** 321
Emelia **66** 41
Emily **72** 93 **97** 136
Emily L. **73** 38
Enoch **83** 40 41
Ephraim **83** 44 **100** 332
101 105
Erastus **72** 87
Erastus Hibbard **60** xxxvi
45 214 **61** xxxv
Esther **74** 65 **81** 270 414
Etta **80** 51
Eulina **71** 273
Eunice **60** 394 395 **62** 187
71 77 277 **72** 41 99 101
172 **120** 209 **121** 57
Eunice Maryette **72** 94
Eveline (Silvester) **86** 90
Experience **118** 115
119 206
Ezekiel **123** 311
Fanny **83** 55 **84** 243 291

PHELPS *cont'd*
133 233
Floral A. (Henry) **83** 431
438
Fluvia **79** 156
Frances **71** 45
Frances Henriette (Fitz
Randolph) **98** 340
Francis **64** lvi **104** 163
134 117
Franklin Stiles **54** lxxiii
George **61** 139 **73** 14 **75** 35
103 174 **113** 298 **123**
259
George A. (Mrs.) **78** 99
George Alexander **84** 102
George Bishop **72** 94
George Dwight **93** 204
98 340
George Henry **62** xl
69 xliii l
George M. **114** 315
George N. **78** 375 **81** 61
Gilbert A. **130** 304
Grant **81** 39
Guy **106** 109
Hannah **54** 222 **59** lxxix
317 **61** 242 243 **67** 374
70 92 **71** 78 156 204 278
281 309 **74** 65 **97** 91 **115**
278 **122** 42 **123** 263 264
146 374 147 60
Hannah (Dane) **104** 163
Hannah (Newton)
102 309
Hannah (Olcott)
(Hubbard) (Post)
147 58
Hannah Elizabeth **103** 174
Harriet **69** l **81** 270
Harriet (Denio) **100** 245
Harriet Augusta (Ayers)
93 204
Harriet Burr **78** 99
Harriet Melissa (Denio)
100 245
Heepah Rosetta **83** 55
Helen **71** 51
Helen Louisa **64** 379
68 lxviii
Helen M. **88** 343
Henry **111** 178 **114** 231
Henry A. **90** 32
Henry Roger **69** l
Henry Seymour **114** 232
Herbert L. **109** 271
Hezekiah **70** 92 **115** 34
Hiram Goodwin **72** 87
Hiram Soule **76** 86
Huldah (Dean) **130** 233
Huldah (Lillie) **126** 306
Humphrey **72** 232
Ichabod **147** 58
Isaac **61** 139 **65** 373 **71** 278
72 36 38
Isaac Newton **68** lxvii
lxviii
Isabel **56** 246
Isabel S. (Griswold)
85 316
Israel **71** 272

PHELPS *cont'd*
Iva **82** 382
J. H. **64** 236
Jabez A. **81** 57
Jacob **70** 141 304 **71** 81
165 272-274 276 303 309
72 33 174 175 **123** 259
James **54** lxxiii **61** 287 **66**
336 **83** 41
James Franklin **54** lxxiii
Jane Pelletreau (Lewis)
114 315
Jarvis **123** 292
Jason **69** 62
Jemima (Post) **146** 366
Jeremiah **122** 80
Jerome **100** 77
Jerusha **72** 316 **76** 85 **122**
67 223
Jerusha (Nash) **105** 150
Jesse **73** 220 230
Joab **71** 162 **72** 99 167
Joel **76** 85 **105** 150 **126** 306
130 233
John **56** 243 **58** 374 401
60 202 **61** 241 **62** 187
63 179 **64** 107 **66** 41 **71**
56 **72** 116 **73** 14 278 **75**
303 **78** 129 **83** 41 **84** 281
86 318 **91** 240 **100** 245
104 163 **109** 73 **113** 31
118 221 306 **119** 43 130
120 169 204 268 299
121 46 47 **122** 42 117
123 308 **123** 265
John B. **104** 163
John Case **52** 96
John H. **111** 187 189
John J. **80** 104 207
John Jay **82** 102 **102** 308
309 **103** 77 124
John L. **72** 206
John R. **60** 266
John Samuel **54** lxxiii
John Wolcott **96** 71
Johnny **120** 57
Jonathan **61** 243 **83** 44
Jonathan Russell **100** 77
Joseph **59** 317 67 375 **71**
204 **74** 65 66 **80** 285 446
81 57 **84** 289 290 **92** 346
100 277 **102** 309 **108**
251 **112** 127 **122** 41 42
147 154 161
Joseph Brown **104** 162
163
Josephine May **73** xx **90**
131 **104** 135 149 162 163
Josephus **81** 61
Joshua **54** 222 **61** 345
76 47 53
Josiah **72** 36 **83** 41 **101** 157
109 73 **124** 60
Josiah C. **74** 66
Judith **74** 66
Julia (Ayres) **104** 163
Julia Eliza **66** 41
Juniette **123** 94
Juniette (Cook) **123** 92
306
Keziah **72** 99 167 **74** 66

PHELPS *cont'd*
122 42
Lamittea 72 103
Laura Roselle 83 55
Lavina E. 103 47
Lavinia 73 14
Lemuel 115 126 123 311
312
Levi 61 74
Levi Whiting 100 77
Levina 94 400
Liberty 81 409
Lois 57 212 71 154 78 129
88 199
Louis 100 77
Louisa 56 308
Lovina 78 375
Loyal 123 92 94
Loyal O. 123 306
Lucinda 146 364
Lucretia Lathrop
(Armour) 104 162
Lucy 62 187 70 76 71 156
281 72 36 88 172 75 35
90 339 119 127
Lucy Ann 89 15
Luther 85 449
Lydia 57 268 67 375 72
291 74 66 81 414 104 21
265 108 251 112 324
123 309 126 14
Lydia (Morey) 104 263
265
Lydia (Nutting) (Parker)
126 14
Lydia (Osgood) 108 251
Lydia Ann W. 100 77
Lydia Ann Whiting
100 77
Mabel Addie (Smith)
130 304
Marc Tully Cicero
136 271
Margaret 53 239 71 87
Margaret (Dewey) 122 80
Margaret (Gillett) 101 49
Margery Willard 69 l
Marie Frost 69 l
Martha 61 74 71 277 278
83 55 109 267
Martin 118 217 119 211
120 298 121 60
Mary 56 242 243 58 199
59 317 64 188 66 41 70
92 71 278 73 14 78 98
186 375 434 81 433 83
40 41 44 90 160 93 204
100 77 104 263 110 241
122 42 124 80 136 145
145 331
Mary (Ayers) 93 204
Mary (Booth) 136 332
Mary (Brown) 104 163
Mary (Case) 122 41 42
Mary (Chase) 102 309
Mary (Colburn) 139 94
Mary (Collier) 122 42
Mary (Eller) 109 73
Mary (Griswold) 105 150
Mary (Jagger) 100 332
101 105

PHELPS *cont'd*
Mary (Newell) 100 77
125 215
Mary A. (Farnham)
130 304
Mary Ann 72 206 81 270
Mary Delilah 81 39
Mary E. Moyer 85 316
Mary Elizabeth 54 lxxiii
Mary Fordham 114 232
Mary Howell (Fordham)
114 231
Mary Jane Lippitt 116 155
Mary M. (Hoar) 134 117
Mary Maria 78 375
Mary Newell 100 77
Mary Octava (Eller)
109 73
Mary Wilson (Smith)
136 332
Matilda 122 122
Matthew 72 316 118 315
Melissa A. 86 318
Melissa Almira 69 l
Methew 123 48
Methew (Mrs.) 123 48
Miles 81 270
Mindwell 71 278
Mirilla 60 80
Morris 109 271
Morrison 133 231
Moses Porter 118 121
119 293
Nabby 72 102 118 110
118 120 121 126 233
Nancy 119 220
Nancy (Eaton) 125 218
Nancy M. 69 258
Naomi 71 278 279 74 65
118 15
Nash David 105 150
Nathan 61 242 71 164 72
168 125 218
Nathaniel 64 248 72 116
119 298 147 154 161
Nicholas 106 39 111 178
Niles 81 270
Noadiah 71 78 87 153 278
297
Noah 123 299
Noah Amherst 79 152 98
340 101 239
Norman 104 263
Octavia 127 58
Ogden 81 61
Ogden N. 81 61 270
Ola 108 135
Olive 81 414
Oliver 56 307 61 391 71
77 159 277 72 41 87 88
102 172 73 14 78 236 81
414
Oliver C. 72 103
Oliver Leicester 73 14
Oliver Seymour 148 225
Olivia (Egleston) 90 174
95 356
Orice 78 375
Patty 71 275 307 118 109
Paulina 60 45
Pene 118 117-120 123 124

PHELPS *cont'd*
126 218 220-222 224 225
227 230 233-236 297 298
301-307 119 43 47-59
127-134 136-140 205 206
Peter 61 74 100 77 125 215
Phares 72 38
Phebe 60 157 66 41 72 316
75 210 81 414 107 226
123 50 306
Phebe (Holt) 104 163
Philo 70 92
Philo A. 85 316
Philo F. 85 169 316 318
Phineas 105 150
Pliny M. 109 271
Polly 61 391 71 162
111 192
Porter 118 229 230 297
299 300 119 46 49 53 54
56 59 127-129 131-133
139 205 206 208 209 211
216-220 289 292 294-298
300-307 120 57-63 123
125-127 129 132 135 203-
207 209 211 212 294 295
298 301 121 57 65 67 96-
98 122 65 305
Priscilla 59 lxxix
Priscilla B. 57 205
Prudence 122 80
Prudence (Phelps) 122 80
Rachel 72 116 83 40 41
Rachel Badgeley 82 102
Rachel Badgeley
(Phinney) 102 309
Ralph Rowley 109 261
Rebecca 54 lxxiii 72 100
89 180 105 252
Rhoda 62 125 71 158 281
85 152 113 298
Rhoda (Harris) 100 245
Rhoda (Spencer) 126 144
Rhoda Barker 54 402
Rhoda L. 69 62
Richard 54 90 95 367
Robert 69 l 130 304
Robert Fordham 114 232
Robert H. 81 61
Roger 69 l 133 232
Roger Edward 105 129
Rosanna Clarinda 83 55
Rose 102 309
Rose Janet (Hutchinson)
102 309
Rosetta 83 55
Roswell 78 375
Royal 122 117 119 221 223
Rufus C. 78 375
Ruth 56 78 57 272 60 397
62 374 66 41 70 78 83
43 85 322 86 233 97 137
105 150 108 239 115
123 118 315
Ruth (Andrews) 126 14
Ruth (Barber) 105 150
Ruth (Phelps) 105 150
Ruth (Ward) 108 239
109 308
S. S. 128 174 269
Sally 60 371 61 240 241

PHELPS *cont'd*
72 103 **118** 306 **121** 299
300 302 303 **122** 66 115
117 120-123 220 221 224-
226 307
Sally (Briggs) **126** 269
Salmon **79** 154
Samuel **59** lxxix **60** 397 **61**
240 **71** 51 **72** 36 **78** 375
83 40 41 **100** 245 **104**
163 263 265 **105** 150
108 65 **118** 245 **130** 304
147 154 161
Samuel S. **71** 45
Samuel Shethar **71** 56
Samuel Tiffany **78** 375
Sarah **61** 242 **63** 335 **65** 373
71 204 **72** 319 **74** 65 66
79 321 **81** 414 **83** 44 **96**
325 **122** 42 307
Sarah (Case) **122** 41 42
Sarah (Chandler) **104** 163
Sarah (Farnsworth)
104 163
Sarah (Frazell) **128** 174
Sarah (Gillett) **100** 277
Sarah (Griswold) **108** 65
Sarah (Pettebone) **122** 42
Sarah C. **81** 57
Sarah Letitia (Quintard)
109 261
Sarah Maria **68** lxviii
Sarah T. **78** 375
Sewall **72** 39 **79** 51 **92** 125
251 343 346 **94** 376
Shadrach **83** 41
Sherman S. **85** 316
Shubael **71** 87 301
Silas **74** 65
Silas Nelson **78** 375
Silas O. **81** 61
Simeon Dustin **100** 245
Simeon Larkin **100** 245
Sl--- (Patterson) **128** 174
Solomon **118** 22 111 117
125 126 217 222 226 229
230 232 306 307 **119** 45
48 50 52-54 132 135 137
138 140 206 208 209 216
217 220 222 290 300 301
304 305 **120** 59 **121** 248
Sophia Emilia Lyon
(Linsley) **136** 326
Sorti **128** 174
Stephen **140** 295 301
145 162
Stephen B. **78** 413
Stephen Rice **69** 1
Stephen Richardson
92 251
Stephen S. **128** 174
Stuard **57** 205
Submit **74** 66
Susan Haskell **58** 374
Susan Story **78** 355
Susanna **58** 374 **61** 139
72 30 **118** 63 **120** 169
170
Susanna (Farley) **136** 145
Susanna (Gates) **120** 169
170

PHELPS *cont'd*
Susanna A. **72** 105
Susanna Tucker **75** 205
Susie P. **57** 205
Sylvanus Dryden **136** 326
Sylvester P. **81** 57
Sylvia Adelia **72** 87
Sylvia Lorinda **83** 55
Temperance **81** 57
Thankful **57** 272 **63** 179
118 307
Thankful (Hitchcock)
123 265
Thanks **122** 42 **147** 68
Theodora **78** 445
Theodorah (Wheelock)
104 263
Theodosia **72** 36
Thirza **124** 280
Thomas **53** 239 **64** 321 **71**
76 87 154 **73** 14 **79** 440
Thomas Treadway **60** 394
Thomas W. **81** 409
Tim **120** 300 **121** 61
Timothy **62** 187 188 **69** 9
11 215 **81** 83 **100** 276
101 49 **104** 163 **105** 150
118 109 111 118 126 217
223 228 230 233 299 307
119 48 49 53 127 132-
134 205 206 209-212 218
289 296 302 **120** 57 58
63
Tirzah **72** 174
Tryphena **72** 36 **83** 41
Ursula **71** 282
Uzziel **56** 308
Virginia **136** 295
Walter **73** 263 **79** 408
Willard Schetky **54** lxxiii
William **51** 496 **57** 272
60 190 **61** 389 **69** 1 **70**
xlix **71** 277 **72** 226 **73**
277 **78** 98 **82** 102 **102**
309 **104** 263 308 **105**
150 **109** 311 **118** 245
121 159 **130** 304 **147**
150 154 161 **148** 225
William Addison **116** 155
William B. **126** 25
William C. **117** 38
William D. **75** 205
William F. **136** 145
William Henry **109** 310
William Lyon **98** 97 250
136 326
William Walter **58** 324
325 **59** xl **102** 308 309
Winslow **69** 121
Wyllis **79** 156
Zelotes **72** 175
Zipporah **62** 187 188
Phelypson *see* Philipson
Phenix *see* Phoenix
PHENNYNGE
Margaret **84** 307 312
Margaret (Lake) **84** 313
PHENY Hugh M. **91** 332
PHEPOE Mary (Whitfield)
125 101
Richard **125** 101

PHEPOL Mary **65** 30
PHEREY Alexander **56**
143 144 146 148 266 **57**
152 153 254 255
Elizabeth **56** 144 **57** 153
Jane **56** 148 **57** 255
Mary **56** 146 **57** 254
PHERIN
Alpheus **58** 125
Margaret **58** 125
PHERSON John **129** 369
PHETTEPLACE Phettiplace
Abraham **88** 30
Alaxa (Barrows) **110** 117
Benjamin **128** 60
Caroline Lucretia **51** 232
Charlotte Alaxa **110** 117
Christopher **129** 75 77
Dorcas **138** 119
Eber **54** 251
Eliakim **128** 60
Elizabeth Anastasia
54 251
Ezekiel **128** 60
Francis **129** 77
Hosea **128** 60
Jane C. (Chase) **88** 30
Job **128** 60
John **128** 60
Jonathan **128** 60
Mary **87** 260
Mary (Brown) **129** 77
Parnell (Cole) (Ward) **129**
75 77
Philip **54** 251 **126** 29 **129**
75 77
Resolved **128** 60
Ruth **138** 125
Samuel **128** 60
Sarah **87** 261
Smith **110** 117
Waite **54** 251
Walter **126** 29 **129** 75 77
PHICKET
Margaret **65** 354
Sarah **65** 355
PHILBRICK Felbregg
Felbrigg Filbrigge
Philbrook Philbrooke
Philbrooks Philbruck
—— **58** 32 35 36 138 **60**
107 **92** 272
— Mr. **83** 308
— Mrs. **83** 308
— Widow **105** 206
Abiah **65** 351
Abigail **59** 37 **88** 372 **90**
329 **99** 323
Adda Francis (Shaw)
142 370
Addie F. **142** 370
Adelaide (Huggins)
123 73
Alban R. **75** 254
Albert F. **74** 32
Alice (Badlam)
(Sanderson) **141** 142
Alice M. (Shapleigh)
95 275
Allen **74** 32
Almira (Leach) **119** 229

PHILBRICK *cont'd*
Anita L. **92** 225
Ann **65** 352
Anna **116** 271
Anna (Jones) **112** 312
Anne **56** 305
Anne (Knopp) **147** 315
  318 326
Annie **87** 8
Annie Maria **122** 72 73 310
Apphia **58** 339
Barnabas **88** 326
Benjamin **109** 184 **124** 41
  141 142
Benjamin Elden **142** 370
Bethiah **65** 353
Betsey **61** 376 **103** 236
  111 44 113
Beulah Rogers **70** 330
Caleb **58** 394
Charity (Grant) **88** 371
Charles **111** 44 113 117
Charles C. **123** 73
Charles G. **77** 148
Charles O. **123** 73
Clarinda **124** 63
Clarinda (Fuller) **124** 62
Clarissa **119** 67 **123** 153
Daniel **111** 95 **115** 135
  116 131 136 **119** 229
  147 267 269
David **59** 37 **111** 95
Deborah **65** 351
Deborah P. **70** 331
Diadamia (Lazell) **88** 363
Donald Lockey **116** 90
  117 149 151 231 312
  118 69 160 161 246 324
  119 72 150 151 236 312
  120 56 150 151 233 310
  121 75 150 151
Dorinda **81** 254
Dorothy **54** 443 **65** 352
  95 38 **111** 44
E. A. (Miss) **84** 31
Edward **92** 272 284
Edwin **68** 155
Elisha **88** 372 **122** 80
Eliza (Ayers) **120** 67 70
Eliza M. **77** 148
Elizabeth **58** 19 46 **65** 352
  108 258 **129** 384
Elizabeth (Knopp) **108**
  257 **147** 317 318 327
Elizabeth (Maddocks)
  124 41
Elizabeth Ann **57** 391
  83 174
Ellen L. (Beedle) **122** 71
  231
Emma **69** 330
Emma E. **84** 464
Emma Lora **70** 330
Enoch **74** 32
Ephraim **112** 105
Esther **98** 61
Eunice **61** 249
F. C. **68** xxxii
Fannie **99** 113
Frank B. **142** 370
Frank J. **95** 38

PHILBRICK *cont'd*
Frederick Bacon **62** 113
George A. **90** 45
George Crossfield
  70 330 336
George Dary **103** 120
Georgiana A. **75** 254
Georgianna **84** 31
Guy **95** 275
H. A. **101** 213
Hannah **51** 63 **58** 34 36
  65 351 **76** 19 **97** 185
  108 256 **109** 161 **111**
  239
Hannah (Tandy) **124** 63
Hannah S. **70** 330 334 336
  104 214
Harriet **78** 294
Herbert Shaw **142** 370
Isaac **68** 260
Isabella **92** 386
James **51** 63 **105** 290 **120**
  67 70 **124** 60 63
Jeannette Tuttle **82** 115
Jeda: **125** 92
Jedidiah **58** 44-46
Job **119** 21
Joel **105** 206
John **51** 45 **56** 410 **58** 19
  339 **65** 352 355 **67** 78 **92**
  211 225 **109** 161 **111** 95
  147 315 318 326
John C. **83** 308
Jonathan **54** 443 **56** 29 **65**
  352 **88** 372 **111** 44 95
  112 312 **114** 49 **115** 65
  119 21
Joseph **57** 391 **58** 30 33 139
  70 334 336 **73** 127 **75** 9
  10 **88** 363 371 **105** 209
  107 227 **124** 62
Joshua **58** 35
Josiah **58** 35 44 **70** 330
  334 336
Josiah H. **68** 97
Jotham Sewall **111** 113
Julietta P. **70** 336
Karl Russell **102** 124 **110**
  137 **111** 141 142 **112** 70
  134 135 222 314 **113** 61
  148 149 233 293 **114** 70
  140 142 228 309 **115** 68
  145 146 229 313 **116** 73
  144 145 227 306 **117** 73
Kate Alice **82** 363
Lois H. (Hardy) **121** 178
Lucy **88** 372 **124** 61
Lucy Noble **111** 113
Lucy Thomas (Carver)
  88 326
Lydia **74** 32 **87** 109 **111** 95
  115 215
Lydia (Linscot) **111** 95
Lydice (Oaks) **122** 80
Marcia C. (Higgins) **147**
  267 269
Maria **68** 155 **88** 372
Martha **56** 305 **108** 258
  111 116 **112** 105
Mary **58** 45 394 **65** 351 355
  68 97 260 **71** 133 **83** 202

PHILBRICK *cont'd*
  88 371 **89** 382 **91** 32 78
  108 258
Mary (Lazell) **88** 363 371
Mary (Todd) **116** 131
Mary Adeline (Nutting)
  90 45
Mary Ann **134** 87
Mary E. **120** 65 67
Mary Eliza **70** 336
  77 xxviii
Mary Ella **90** 360
Mayo Hesseltine **127** 320
Mehitable **51** 464
Michael **94** 362
Milton **111** 113
Minerva **147** 267 269
N. P. **56** 21
Nabby **111** 116
Nancy **56** 29
Nancy B. **57** 391
Nathan **58** 138 **104** 214
Nathaniel **145** 356
Oliver Blunt **141** 142
Olivia (Varrell) **119** 276
  123 73
Patty **111** 44
Penelope **63** 169 **111** 95
  115 135 304
Phebe **88** 372 **107** 227
Phebe (Lazell) **88** 372
Polly **111** 44 113 **124** 60
Polly (Randall) (Varrell)
  141 142
Priscilla **65** 355 **71** 130
R. E. **147** 269
Robert **87** 225 235 **111** 44
  113
Robert Tuftin **65** 355
Ruel W. **122** 80
Ruhamah **88** 371
Ruth (Sherburn) **124** 60
Sabina **65** 352
Sally **76** 43 **92** 211 **111** 113
  115 304 **125** 289
Sally (Durgin) **92** 284
Sally (Sherburne) **104** 214
Samuel **82** 363
Samuel Johnson **111** 113
Sarah **58** 46 **59** 37 **63** 169
  70 334 336 **89** 382 **112**
  312 **147** 326
Sarah (Abbot) **87** 225 235
Sarah (Fowles) **88** 372
Sarah (Marden) **92** 211
Sarah (Stover) **115** 135
Sarah Austin (Jenkins)
  95 38
Sarah C. **68** 97
Sarah S. **103** 236
Seth Pitts **111** 113
Simon **109** 315
Sophronia **111** 113
Thomas **51** 62 **56** 305 **65**
  351 **109** 315 **111** 113
  147 315 317 318 327
Truman **121** 178
Walter **51** 45
William **51** 45 **88** 363 371
  91 332 **92** 382 387 **105**
  209 **119** 21 276 **122** 73

PHILBRICK cont'd
123 73
William H. 122 71 231
PHILEY
Sarah A. 110 311
PHILIP II King of Spain
59 235 143 291 146 318
PHILIP of Macedon 54 262
PHILIP Pometacom 94
346 347
PHILIP Sachem of the
Wampanoag 51 62 76
84 97 100 175 230 237
294 295 297 379 454 52
33 76 145 190 214 449
53 43 192 194 201 310
317-321 341-344 346 347
350 381 406 431 463 54
lxxx 235 262 264 266 286
404 55 xlv 70 73 75 161
302 324 443 452 56
lxviii 276 297 358 365
366 369 381 409 57 lii
lix 20 120 345 408 58
lxxxi cxiii 22 24 50 52
110 159 165 305 59
lxxxii cvi 53 161 231 246
342 60 lvi 29 99 129 130
132 139 173-175 61 70
71 212 213 258 62 lxxv
58 168 67 199 89 281 94
346 347 103 215 136
178 143 301 144 61 211-
214 292 357 145 77 78
195 211 258
PHILIPEAU
Anthony 65 230
Philipot see Philpot
Philipott see Philpot
PHILIPPA of Hainault
148 140
PHILIPPA Queen of
England 104 270
141 94
PHILIPPE Count of
Flanders 88 99 102
Philips see Phillips
Philipse see Phillips
PHILIPSON Phelypson
Phillipson
Ann 104 107
John 104 107
Mary A. 63 197
Mary E. 90 94
PHILL Richard 66 254
Phillebrown see
Fillebrown
PHILLEO
Bonaparte 143 59
Eliza (Benchley) 143 58 59
Enoch 143 59
Gertrude Estelle 143 59
Hart Benton 143 59
Helen Marr 143 59
John 143 59
Julia Cornelia 143 59
Marian Braidfoot 143 59
Samuel 143 59
Sarah (Agard) 143 59
Sarah Cornelia 143 59

PHILLEO cont'd
Sarah Maria Louise
143 59
Phillepot see Philpot
PHILLETT Mary 104 18
PHILLIBERT
John 127 32
PHILLIMORE
—— 52 86 96 99 61 38
Abigail 62 42
Ebenezer 62 41
Jane 69 xlvii
John 62 42
W. 114 124
W. H.P. 97 101
W. P. 69 xlvi 90 402
W. P.A. 101 264
William Phillimore
Watts 51 233 388 506
509 53 260 263 266 356
357 54 xxxvii 229 55
xxx 232 239 56 212 213
57 xxxi 342 58 349 59 49
54 215 333 60 xxxiv 84
87 221 354 61 394 62
100 63 100 204 64 xxix
85 186 65 xxxiii 73 84
89 202 380 66 87 68 65
66 69 70 72 75 76 78 79
109 69 xliv xlvi 70 117
71 32 317 72 185 228
231 232 237 117 244
119 8 122 276 145 266
PHILLIPPE
Elizabeth D. 87 174
PHILLIPS Philips Phillipp
—— 52 143 56 350 57 415
58 101 199 59 xxx 243
60 104 61 315 62 280
290 65 53 357 70 141 75
102 79 256 82 52 88 266
92 13 101 94 118 20 219
222 120 11 121 17 127
141 129 316 130 88 133
72 135 139 136 37 138
279 140 235 236
— Capt. 92 54 102 33
— Col. 97 5
— Goodman 68 195
— Gov. 54 377 116 12
— Mr. 51 277 54 59 62
273 66 280 80 85 83 90
88 308 92 53
— Mrs. 62 284 285
120 205
— Widow 71 134 139
_____ (Bracy) 123 149
_____ (Gifford) 135 139
_____ (Sargent) 110 276
_____ (Stanley) 94 174
_____ (Tilden) 140 235
A. 78 34
A. V. 89 401 96 401
A. W. 55 226
Aaron 111 305 115 108 114
128 60
Abbie 92 342
Abbie M. 115 199
Abbott Lawrence 110 280
Abby (Atwood) 123 201
Abiah 136 39

PHILLIPS cont'd
Abial 72 216
Abiezer 125 90
Abigail 51 196 52 228 53
10 55 148 400 66 101 67
374 70 223 228 73 238
81 293 82 27 52 84 260
85 132 86 10 88 307 91
296 372 103 141 105
196 229 110 277 115
301 116 139 190 117
308 118 303 120 31 123
219 127 32 128 116 140
239 143 233 144 343
Abigail (Baldwin)
98 282 360
Abigail (Dresser) 88 307
Abigail (Gould) 137 361
Abigail (Hathaway)
110 225
Abigail (Sloan) 125 220
Abigail Ames 89 15
Abigail Bromfield
112 318
Abigail Salisbury 55 362
Abraham 60 162 127 307
129 316
Achsah 70 201
Adah M. 95 331
Adaline 115 108
Adam 128 60
Addie F. 125 54
Addie May 82 268
Adele Marguerite 110 280
281
Adele Rebecca (Budlong)
(Herbert) 110 280
Adolph 106 4
Agnes 70 312
Ahiza 87 256
Albert (Mrs.) 102 79
Albert Alexander 81 338
Albert Ira 101 125
Albert M. 144 342
Alexander Van Cleve 59
xlviii 74 xxviii 90 125
98 161 203 204 99 69
163 100 102 124 125
101 138 139 102 138
103 135 111 61 148
Alice 51 191 52 319 54 214
80 85 111 148 120 230
143 230
Alice (Brown) 143 232
Alice (Fish) 143 226 229
230
Alice (Owen) 91 246
Alice Willetta 81 339
Alma Janet (Sherman)
99 167
Almira 81 338 109 253 115
285 119 288
Almira (Boston) 119 69
Alphia (Chalmers)
111 117
Alvah 62 273
Alvina 102 79
Amanda 71 38 115 108
Amanda Autentia 115 114
Amanda Malvina 89 387
Amaziah 60 155

PHILLIPS *cont'd*
Amelia **111** 306
Amelia (Ross) (Curit)
  (Hamilton) **134** 332
Amity (Harris) **129** 316
Amos M. **78** 359
Amy **87** 247
Amy Angeline **95** 347
Anderson **78** 308
Andrew **54** 351 **101** 9
  128 60
Andrew Brown **115** 108
Andrew F. **85** 120
Andrew Fanuel **99** 117
Andrew M. **88** 341
Ann **59** 366 367 **64** 227 **71**
  99 **87** 191 **101** 50 **108**
  181 **115** 108 **116** 79 **122**
  101 **138** 279 **143** 227
  231 233
Ann (Sears) **108** 181
Ann (Tyler) **143** 232
Ann (White) **110** 276
Ann Barbara **133** 217 218
Ann / Nancy (Maverick)
  97 57
Anna **54** 222 **69** 89 **71** 40
  77 lxiii **91** 246 **93** 349
  120 266 **135** 40
Anna (Gibson) **125** 217
Anna Doris (Mills)
  111 148
Anna E. **52** 151
Anna Goddard **82** 119
Anna James **128** 116
Anna Maria (Yates)
  83 345
Anna Pingree (Wheat-
  land) **110** 280
Annabel **110** 277
Annah (Collins) **143** 232
Anne **52** 319 **54** 402 403 **70**
  259 **73** 239 **122** 105 **143**
  232
Anne (Gates) **120** 266
Anne (Hill) **88** 115
Anne E. **77** 152
Annie Maria **77** 222
Anstice **51** 424
Araminta Anna **79** 128
Ardella **79** 121
Arthur **72** 61
Arthur Cyrus **92** 363
Arthur Leighton **92** 363
Arthur Milo **100** 193
Asa **70** 177 223 226 232 **71**
  138 140 **111** 117 **113** 33
  40
Asa E. **70** xxxvii
Asa Mitchell **89** 15
Asenath (Averill) **117**
  143 144
Augustine Louise **80** 168
Aurelia **89** 102
Avice (Briggs) **127** 63
Avis **110** 107
Ayer **71** 40 133
Barbara **57** 33 36 **143** 221
  231-233
Bathsheba **57** 363 **64** 35
  70 223 **71** 39

PHILLIPS *cont'd*
Bathsheba (Godfrey)
  127 46
Benjamin **55** 417 **57** 86
  60 347 **78** 373 **84** 152
  168 **90** 97 **94** 319 **99** 119
  101 163 **110** 277 **112**
  240 **136** 36 **140** 69
Benjamin John **109** 79
Bertha **80** 168
Bertha Elnora **100** 193
Bessie L. **100** 193
Bethiah **58** 199
Bethiah (Kedal) **110** 277
Bethiah (Lazell) (Mitchell)
  89 15
Betsey **114** 183 **117** 141
Betsey (Benton) **114** 183
Betsey (Clark) **109** 184
Betsey A. S. (Eli) **88** 341
Betty **89** 387 **133** 322
Bial **75** 199
Blanche **65** 135
Blaney **88** 221 **136** 41
Bloomfield **91** 332
Bridget **56** 409 410 **79** 249
  80 140 **90** 225 **103** 212
  213 **113** 74
Bridget (Bosworth)
  113 278
Bridget (Hutchinson)
  (Sanford) **103** 211
Caleb **59** 194 **100** 296
  128 53
Calvin G. **75** 19
Calvin Tilden **68** xxvii
Camila **98** 343
Caroline **80** 168 **83** 345
Caroline R. (Quimby)
  121 69
Caroline S. **142** 376
Carrie (Hartwell) **144** 108
Carrie W. (Meader) **93**
  113 **121** 145
Catherine **80** 178 **82** 268
  88 111 **110** 280 **143** 233
Catherine Prowde (Lewis)
  101 10
Charles **70** 223 **71** 38 142
  79 107 **85** 310 316
Charles A. **79** 107
Charles Abbot **108** 271
Charles Appleton
  110 280
Charles C. **121** 69
Charles H. **79** 107 **85** 316
Charles J. **145** 114
Charles Perkins **115** 114
Charles White **89** 387
Charlotte **144** 108
Charlotte B. **120** 66 67
Charlotte Foxcroft **95** 147
  97 163
Chloe (Chase) **87** 256
Chris. **128** 132
Christian **68** 60 102 **69** 92
Christian (Wadsworth)
  136 41
Christiana (Barker) **143**
  221-223 225 366
Christina **111** 305

PHILLIPS *cont'd*
Christopher **52** 318 319
  58 199 **60** lxxii **80** 81
  110 276 **116** 79 **136** 37
  40 **138** 279
Clara H. **95** 147
Clarinda M. **85** 316
Clarissa (Sawyer) **116**
  303 305
Clarissa F. **70** 158
Clifford Smith **98** 264
Content **79** 121
Cora Elizabeth **65** 135
Coral Alfred **100** 193
Cornelius **81** 432
Crystal F. **100** 193
Cynthia **102** 24 **127** 122
Cynthia (Wait) **108** 160
Cyrus **89** 387 **111** 79 165
Dan: John **58** 69
Daniel **51** 181 **71** 40 143
  88 307 **115** 263
Daniel H. **79** 107
Daniel L. **79** 194 **120** 271
Darius **70** 223 315 **79** 392
David **81** 338 **89** 387 **92** 15
  98 53 **102** 243 **117** 16
  127 122 206 267 312
  128 60 116
David C. **108** 271
David Everett **57** xxxiii
  125 **58** xlv
Deborah **54** 421 **57** 66 66
  101 **70** 313 **71** 129 219
  97 387 **103** 211 **111** 94
  122 25 **147** 185
Deborah (Murch) **111** 94
  114 47
Deborah Frances **87** 384
Deborah Southworth
  109 242
Desire **127** 258
Desire (Ryder) **127** 259
Dianna **115** 263
Dolly (Trafton) **116** 300
Dorcas **70** 232 **93** 107 **107**
  77 **110** 278
Dorcas (Woodbridge)
  110 278
Dorothy **66** 252 **111** 148
Dorothy (Boyer) **116** 79
E. **59** 179
Ebenezer **110** 225 **124** 17
Ebenezer Humphrey **60**
  lxxii **82** 113
Ebenezer Morgan **60**
  lxxii **82** 113
Ebenezer Sanborn
  69 xxxvi
Edgar Blondel (Mrs.) **84**
  106 190
Edith **95** 379
Edith Henrietta **81** 339
Edna A. **93** 113
Edward **55** 362 **58** 199 **66**
  264 353 355 **77** 152 **81**
  433 **101** 9 10 **111** 306
  123 149 **127** 308 **140**
  235 236 **147** 17 18
Edward C. **119** 281 282
Edward H. **123** 149

PHILLIPS *cont'd*
Edward Mendenhall
80 168
Edward Woodbridge
110 280
Effie Pearl **100** 193
Eleazer **98** 203 **105** 196
Elijah **82** 119
Elijah Brigham **60** xlvii
lxxii lxxiii **82** 113
Elisha **73** 117 **127** 311
Elisha P. **71** 38
Eliza **55** 424 **63** 373 **79** 107
125 288
Eliza A. **70** 156
Eliza Caroline (Morgan)
98 264
Elizabeth **52** 162 **53** 106 **59**
188 **61** 68 **62** 345 **63** 81
298 **65** 354 **70** 353 **71** 93
72 61 **73** 238 239 **74** 209
76 79 **78** 303 **80** 178 **81**
432 **92** 54 **94** 273 **97** 57
99 119 **103** 216 **108** 66
110 276-278 281 **111**
306 **116** 271 273 **117** 49
120 80 **127** 8 **128** 298
133 308 309 **135** 340
143 222-224 226 228 233
144 159 161 342
Elizabeth (Blowers)
144 342
Elizabeth (Chase) **88** 7
Elizabeth (Clarke) **127** 32
Elizabeth (Elkins) **110** 278
Elizabeth (Emerson)
110 278
Elizabeth (Fairchild) **143**
226 232 233
Elizabeth (Fitz Randolph)
98 53
Elizabeth (Lee) **100** 303
Elizabeth (Mills) **119** 180
Elizabeth (Owen) **101** 10
Elizabeth (Oxley) **98** 53
Elizabeth (Parker)
110 225
Elizabeth (Pierce) **110** 279
Elizabeth (Weldon)
110 276
Elizabeth A. **79** 107
Elizabeth D. **87** 174
Elizabeth Griste **110** 279
Elizabeth Palmer **120** 80
Elizabeth Payzant **128** 116
Elkanah **79** 121
Elmer Isaac (Mrs.) **96** 74
Elvira **62** 273
Emily (Aldrich) **100** 193
Emily Blagden **63** lii
Emily J. **75** 19
Emily Marina (Monroe)
100 193
Emma (Penrose) **117** 116
Ephraim **110** 277 **121** 165
127 63
Esak **132** 144
Esquire **120** 266
Essie Delta **100** 193
Estelle **70** xxxvii
Esther **70** 225

PHILLIPS *cont'd*
Esther (Hunt) **109** 184
Esther (Whittemore)
108 83
Ethel **65** 135
Ethel Warner **80** 168
Etta (Ellsworth) 363
92 363
Eugene Ellsworth **92** 363
Eunice **88** 30
Eva **98** 146 **106** 4
Eva A. May **79** 107
Eva Doraine **120** 147
Evalina Jane **89** 387
Ezekiel **127** 308
Ezra **108** 83
F. H. **66** 86
Fadey **127** 122 206
Faith **51** 472 **67** 214 **69** 253
87 154 **144** 348
Fannie **82** 119
Fannie J. **103** 47
Fanny **89** 387
Fanny Hitchcock **105** 129
Florence **78** 34
Florence Elizabeth **82** 113
Frances A. **85** 316
Frances E. **92** 342
Frances Malona **79** 120
Frances Marion **78** 359
Francis **52** 351
Frank **91** 246
Frank C. **82** 403
Frank Irving **71** 42
Frank M. **114** 157
Franklin T. **91** 332
Frederick **52** 313 **84** 109
190 **93** 401 **100** 107 **106**
4 **107** 120
Freelove **73** 117 **79** 351
120 5
Gaius **136** 34
Gamaliel **132** 164
Genevieve **91** 246
George **52** 318 **55** 108 **58**
199 **60** lxxii 190 348 **63**
23 **64** 377 **65** 257 **69** 157
76 53 **81** 338 **82** 113 **83**
291 **85** 114 **88** 307 **91**
310 **96** 236 **97** 393 **109**
225 **110** 276-278 281
117 226 **119** 180 **120**
167 **144** 342
George (Mrs.) **110** 276
George A. **93** 113
George Davis **71** 42
George E. **93** 107
George H. **71** 38 **93** 113
111 80 **112** 75 **121** 145
George Nelson **92** 363
George W. **63** lii **67** 19
75 19
George William **110** 279
George Young **89** 15
Georgianna Willard
(Pierce) **109** 187
Gertrude Eleana **100** 112
Gideon **111** 80
Gilbert Anthony **63** 114
Gillam **58** 69 **67** 212 213
374 **84** 267 **99** 117

PHILLIPS *cont'd*
Gladys Elizabeth **98** 147
Grace **57** 86 **85** 198
Hager **125** 176
Hannah **53** 393 **54** cxxx
55 108 **57** 86 104 331 **59**
243 **61** 393 **63** li 84 189
67 198 201 212 214 **69**
356 357 **73** 238 239 **75**
199 303 **79** 261 392 **83**
36 167 291 **91** 310 **93**
159 **99** 281 **110** 277 **126**
259 **127** 11 267 **133** 309
142 382 **143** 233
Hannah (Burt) **87** 384
Hannah (Fry) (Cranston)
143 227
Hannah (Morse) **89** 102
Hannah (Prior) **126** 263
136 35
Hannah (Ramsdell)
126 263
Hannah (Salter) **106** 21
Hannah (Sanford) (Bailey)
103 272 **104** 75
Hannah (Sayward)
119 144
Happy (Bassett) **125** 10
Harmony Cushman
124 79
Harold N. **92** 342
Harriet **71** 40 **92** 27
Harriet (Percy)
(Chamberlain) **144** 108
Harriet Irene **82** 403
Harriet Jane **118** 242
Harriet M. **98** 264
Harrison **100** 193
Harry **90** 97
Harvey **71** 38 **90** 260
Henrietta **66** xxi
Henrietta Alice **81** 339
Henry **51** 114 **54** lviii **55**
108 **64** 181 **67** 209 212
73 239 **91** 94 **92** 54 **98**
53 **105** 196 **116** 133 134
119 69
Henry A. **58** 200 407 **59**
417 **61** 307 308 **63** 201
Henry Ayling **59** xlviii
64 377 **70** 288 **80** 334
81 231 **82** 113
Henry B. **143** 221
Henry Bethune (Mrs.)
86 198
Henry Byron **70** xix **74**
xxv **79** 211 **80** 112 113
81 196 338 339 **90** 36
Henry M. **54** lix
Henry W. **134** 332
Hepzibah **110** 277 280
Hepzibah (Bassett) **125** 10
Hepzibah (Parker)
110 277
Hezekiah **113** 82
Hiram G. **71** 42
Hope **122** 101
Hope (Fish) **143** 226 229
231
Hopestill (Babbitt)
110 225

PHILLIPS *cont'd*
Hugh L. (Mrs.) **120** 76
Hugo **101** 10
Ira B. **80** 249
Irene (Cook) **108** 271
Isaac **70** 353 **80** 168 **92** 11
    13 15 18 22 27 **94** 294
    132 145
Isabella Louisa **79** 203
Israel **62** 273 **88** 115 **129**
    316 **143** 222 226 230-232
Ivers C. **90** 37
J. E. **69** 341
J. Leonard **71** 38
Jack **128** 215
Jacob **87** 6 **127** 307
Jairus **126** 272
James **53** 275 **54** cxiii **59**
    219 **62** 236 345 **63** 81 **64**
    227 **71** 135 140 **84** 153
    89 387 388 **92** 18 **97** 328
    329 **102** 31 **110** 225 **122**
    101 105 **123** 318 **125**
    217 **127** 14 307 **129** 65
    140 235 **143** 222 225
    226 229 231 232 **146** 348
James Boyd **95** 401
James Conelly **100** 304
James Duncan **59** 323 **60**
    xxiii **70** 181 **71** xxi **83**
    248 **84** 112 114 182 186
    88 210 **91** 402 **92** 98
    100 233 **101** 119 **102** 78
    104 321 **106** 39 317 **107**
    158 **109** 62 133 225 **110**
    276 280
James Henry Harrison
    89 387 388
James J. **107** 293
James Jones **127** 267 **128**
    116 117
James Putt **133** 72
James R. **123** 150 151
James Thompson **120** 80
Jamson **83** 167
Jane **51** 122 61 68 **77** 236
    87 321 **112** 296
Jane (Adams) **125** 102
Jane Appleton **110** 279
Jane Appleton (Peele)
    110 279
Jane Elizabeth (Young)
    110 279
Jane L. **75** 19
Jane Peele **110** 279
Jane Rumming **89** 387
Janet (Whitcomb) **95** 347
Janet DeBlois **99** 167
Jasper W. **144** 108
Jedediah **63** 94 **110** 228
Jemima **116** 134
Jennett (Young) **89** 15
Jennie (Fitz Randolph)
    98 345
Jenny (Beard) **102** 36
Jeremiah **62** 290 356 **68**
    304 **80** 178 **128** 60 **143**
    233
Jerusha **67** 286 **113** 156
    119 48 49 53 56 58 130
    136 139 140 293 **120** 296

PHILLIPS *cont'd*
    144 342
Jesse **127** 122
Jesse C. **71** 38
Jesse Simeon **79** 128
Joan **51** 424 **66** 355 **71** 245
Joanna **73** 36 **83** 331 **90**
    289 **111** 79 165 **134** 298
    137 239
Job **127** 14 **146** 348
John **51** 210 507 508 **52** 151
    164 246 451 **55** 145 147
    56 243 **57** 36 86 280 388
    389 **58** 70 199 **59** 366
    411 **61** 68 69 **62** 273 301
    64 223 **65** 232 **66** 37 **68**
    62 73 315 **69** 253 **70**
    xlix 259 264 **71** 129 136
    73 239 **75** 221 **77** 239
    79 107 161 339 **80** 83
    315 316 **81** 74 433 **82** 52
    119 **84** 154 156 158 161
    167 **87** 153 154 326 332
    88 7 **89** 15 324 **90** 97 **95**
    68 **96** 273 **97** 12 **99** 281
    101 162 102 36 **104** 242
    105 278 **107** 313 **110** 19
    276 317 **111** 79 94 148
    165 299 301 305 306 **114**
    47 **119** 141 **120** 5 **122**
    101 **123** 202 **126** 144
    127 32 115 312 **128** 58
    299 **129** 211 **132** 91 **136**
    35 **138** 97 104 **140** 235
    143 222 226 229 230 233
    366 **144** 107 108 **145**
    312 **147** 118
John Bunyan **120** 80
John C. **55** 20 **60** 40
John Capen **68** 320
John Cranston **80** 168
John E. **119** 67
John G. **62** 312
John Goddard **64** 202 **81**
    109 230 **82** 119
John H. **92** 342
John King **82** 119
John Lillie **140** 235
John Marshall **102** 279
    106 233 **112** 176 **145**
    292
John Marshall (Mrs.)
    84 444
John Mills **111** 148
John Mortimer **127** 88
John Otterson **99** 148
    119 149
John Van Cleve **111** 148
John W. **79** 107
John Wesley **79** 107
John Woodward **72** 303
Jonas **119** 180 **127** 122
Jonathan **51** 68 **56** 347 350
    57 104 **60** lxxii **82** 113
    268 **83** 167 **98** 288 **109**
    225 **110** 276 277 280 281
    121 92 **127** 267 **128** 116
    117 **140** 235 236
Joseph **58** 407 **60** lxxii **64**
    35 **65** 357 **66** 36 **67** 286
    81 338 **82** 113 **83** 167

PHILLIPS *cont'd*
    91 269 271 **103** 272 **104**
    75 **106** 197 **110** 225 **111**
    79 165 **128** 60 **142** 278
    143 233
Joseph C. **126** 22
Joseph I. **98** 264
Joseph Lanson **79** 107
Joseph Lewis **94** 139 **95**
    75 151 **98** 264
Josephine Marie **98** 148
Joshua **54** 222
Josiah **65** 135 **143** 232
Jubaetta (Lazell) **89** 324
Judith **111** 301 306 **127** 32
    144 107
Judith (Randall) **144** 107
Julia **90** 260 **111** 306
    144 108
Julia Ann (Dean) **144** 100
    107 108
Julia Maria **145** 316
Katharine **52** 319 **101** 9 10
Katharine (Wells) **100** 304
Katharine Edith (Falley)
    108 271
Katharine Sherman
    99 167
L. B. **129** 316
Lamont O. **93** 107
Lavina H. **93** 107
Leah **70** 227
Lebbeus Rude **82** 119
Lemuel M. **77** 222
Lenthall **137** 361
Lenthier **125** 220
Leo F. **102** 228
Leo F. (Mrs.) **84** 190 **102**
    219 228 **103** 124
Leona Myrtle (Robbins)
    100 193
Lewis **113** 82 **132** 164
Lewis A. **93** 107
Lillian V. R. **69** 341
Lillie **140** 235
Linus Austin **111** 79 165
Linwood A. **93** 113
Lizzie (Chase) **87** 332
Lloyd C. **92** 342
Lois (Browning)
    (Hawkins) **116** 79
Louisa **54** 222 **126** 145
Louisa (Bayard) **98** 264
Louisa A. (Emerson)
    119 67
Louisa B. **98** 264
Lowes **83** 167
Lowrie **83** 167
Lucie (Mayo-Smith)
    92 390
Lucinda **59** 411
Lucretia **54** 85
Lucy **55** 147 **56** 245 **71** 40
Luke **127** 307 **138** 121
Lulu **77** 262
Lura **70** 226
Lurana **53** 230
Lydia **59** 366 **60** 155 **68**
    312 **69** 245 **75** 19 **86** 121
    87 107 **93** 107 **98** 203
    102 191 **110** 228 278

PHILLIPS *cont'd*
115 79 **127** 122 206 259
143 230
Lydia (Rand) **110** 278
Lydia F. **75** 19
M. Irving **111** 306
M. Kate **79** 107
Mabel E. **92** 342
Mabel Elizabeth
(Bancroft) **96** 328 329
Maggie **83** 438 **84** 19
Major **109** 184
Mandana **111** 306
Marcia **120** 41 **137** 46
Marcia Bowdish **120** 76
Margaret **55** 145 **65** 8 **72**
137 **78** 169 **79** 107 **83**
231 438 **84** 328 **89** 223
110 220 **115** 167 **140**
235
Margaret (Duncan) **109**
225 **110** 280
Margaret (Palfrey)
(Cunningham)
112 240
Margaret (Rathbun) **116**
79 **138** 279 284
Margaret Ann **110** 225
Margaret Ann (Terry)
110 225
Margaret Mason (Peele)
110 279
Margaret Peele **110** 279
Margaret Seymour
99 167
Margaret Tewksbury
81 350 351
Margaret Wendell
145 312
Margery **72** 134 137
Maria B. **71** 42
Maria Rebecca **60** lxxiii
82 113
Marie **96** 129
Martha **52** 319 **64** 189
Martha (Barton) **107** 293
Martha Anne **78** 49
Martha Churchman
80 168
Martha Robeson **85** 197
Martin **55** 196 **72** 116
101 94
Mary **52** 319 **53** 275 356
54 cxiii 403 **55** 147 346
424 **56** 243 410 **58** 199
261 **61** 302 **62** xxi **63** 94
343 **65** 257 338 373 **66**
101 67 209 212 286 **69**
34 357 **70** 177 223 226
227 311 **71** 38-40 **72** 116
73 152 238 239 **75** lxxvi
76 66 67 72 **77** 145 313
79 107 **80** 81 **81** 104 433
82 52 403 **83** 90 167 **87**
292 **88** 312 **89** 392 **92**
342 **93** 266 **94** 310 **95** 81
99 117 **100** 183 240 **101**
9 **105** 147 **107** 293 **108**
181 **110** 225 277 278
111 306 **112** 183 **115**
108 114 167 **116** 79 **119**

PHILLIPS *cont'd*
104 108 180 190 **121** 259
122 102 **123** 230 **125** 14
133 229 **138** 279-281
141 5 **142** 384 **147** 116
Mary (Bennet) **110** 277
Mary (Bracy) **119** 144
Mary (Bullen) **110** 228
Mary (Burrill) **123** 318
Mary (Buttolph) **144** 342
Mary (Byles) **111** 148
Mary (Eames) **136** 39
Mary (Henckly) **100** 296
Mary (Houghton)
131 131
Mary (Hunt) **121** 165
Mary (Jacobs) **117** 228
Mary (Phillips) **138** 279
Mary (Randall) **141** 5
Mary (Sheldon) **84** 168
Mary (Smalley) **125** 10
Mary A. **79** 107
Mary Ann **59** 366 **71** 38
111 306 **115** 108 **144**
108
Mary Ann (Payzant) **128**
116 117
Mary Anne **79** 107
Mary Bishop (Cushman)
124 79
Mary Boardman **110** 279
Mary E. (Freebody) **125**
243 244
Mary E. (Thompson)
123 149
Mary Elizabeth **72** xxxv
79 107 **89** 387
Mary Elizabeth (Rex)
110 225
Mary Hodges
(Boardman) **110** 279
Mary J. **92** 342
Mary Nightingale **82** 119
Mary P. **98** 264
Mary S. **79** 107
Mary W. **85** 316
Mary Williams **82** 119
Matthew **127** 122 206
Maud **106** 126
May **101** 94
May Alice (Chapman)
102 228
May C. **83** 249
May Catherine Charlotte
96 161
Mehala **71** 36
Mehitable **59** 374 **67** 209
111 306 **128** 116 **133** 42
Mehitable (Jones) **127** 267
Mehitable (Mores)
123 202
Mehitable Frances Davis
(Congdon) **127** 88
Melinda (Hannum)
90 260
Mercy **63** 169 **65** 257 338
75 302 **110** 281 **115** 228
121 259 125 14 **143** 232
Mercy (Hunt) **121** 165
Meriam (Mason) **84** 379

PHILLIPS *cont'd*
Merrick / Merritt F.
144 108
Metta Frances (Hubbard)
84 444
Mial **143** 222 233
Micah **83** 167 **109** 184
Michael **73** 117 **81** 338
100 303 **143** 221 225
226 228 229 231 232
Mildred A. (Van Slyck)
100 193
Mildred Elaine **92** 363
Miles **68** 108 109
Minnie May **100** 193
Miriam **52** 451 **54** 351 **64**
181 **96** 335
Miriam (Mason) **112** 318
Montague **100** 107
Moses **66** 101 **83** 61
Myrtle **80** 249 **91** 246
Myrtle Iva **100** 193
N. C. (Mrs.) **102** 159
Nabby **55** 61 **118** 21 23
Nancy **83** 195 **88** 22 **92** 54
97 57 **125** 107
Nancy (Hathaway)
(Brewster) **120** 5
Nannie Jenckes (Borden)
109 225 **110** 280
Nat **71** 36
Nathan **75** 19 **89** 102 **90** 88
127 46
Nathaniel **71** 138 **78** 414
97 57 **110** 277 **120** 6
127 307 **140** 235
Nehemiah **66** 101
Nellie Ann (Hoxsie)
127 88
Nelson **100** 193
Nelson Chancellor (Mrs.)
95 147
Nelson L. **71** 38
Nicholas **52** 319 **53** 393
54 cxxx **55** 108 **57** 331
63 298 **73** 238 239 **82**
119 **93** 266 **106** 21 **119**
112 123 124 **141** 5
Nightingale **82** 119
Noah **112** 75
Norton **65** 257 338 **66**
262 311 312 **116** 303 305
Norton Woodbridge **54**
403 **115** 219
Obadiah **110** 277
Oker **125** 10
Olive **71** 40 **75** 19 **111** 301
306 **138** 121
Olive (Babcock) **111** 299
Ordelia **108** 199
Otis **95** 347
Otis L. **93** 107
P. Lee **51** 246 **52** 400 **54**
375 462 **56** 114
Pamelia (Ross) (Curit)
(Hamilton) **134** 332
Patience **66** 101 **79** 256
125 17 **143** 231 232
Patrick **60** 347
Peggy **140** 53
Peletiah **108** 160

PHILLIPS *cont'd*
Peter **62** 359 363 **65** 221
   128 131 **142** 19 **143** 222
   227 **144** 107 108
Phebe **79** 37 107 **103** 212
   125 14 **127** 10 **143** 233
   144 108
Phebe (Cahoon) **126** 22
Phebe (Ford) (Arnold)
   119 180
Phebe C. **126** 22
Philander **62** 273
Philip **82** 119
Philip Lee **59** 235 **64** 200
   67 96 **69** 194 **76** 82
Phillipa **68** 62
Phyllis **113** 81 82
Pitts **53** 230
Polly **71** 38 **83** 167 **89** 236
   97 57 **111** 79 165 **118** 21
   140 248
Priscilla **92** 22 **128** 166
Priscilla (Fletcher) **128**
   162 163
Prudence **67** 376 **83** 167
   120 167
Prudence (Gates) **120** 167
Rachel **58** 256 261 **69** 92 **79**
   92 **129** 366
Rachel (Chadwick) **124** 17
Rachel (Gale) **124** 17
Rachel (Koch) **133** 218
Rachel Frue **132** 164
Ralph **112** 296
Randall **51** 424
Raymond E. **69** 341
Rebecca **57** 36 **72** 17 216
   108 180 **113** 82 **120** 80
   274 **121** 229 **122** 261
   123 273 **127** 206 **143**
   227
Rebecca (Lewin) **127** 206
Rebecca (Snelling)
   108 180
Rebecca Capen **59** 374
Rebecca Chalkley (Lewis)
   98 264
Rebecca Jones **128** 116
Rebecca Kimball **109** 187
Rebecca L. **98** 264
Rebecca M. **79** 107
Rebecca Williams **120** 80
Reuben **124** 79 **128** 60
Rhoda **70** 353 **73** 117 **113**
   33 40 **132** 145
Richard **52** 264 **59** 188 **68**
   102 **72** 134 137 **82** 119
   99 281 **108** 160 180 **119**
   104 108 110 **126** 272
   128 130 134 **133** 218
   136 34 **143** 221 226 227
   230 233 **146** 348
Richard Bates **111** 148
Rienzi **65** 135
Roazel **71** 140
Robert **63** 39 **65** 135
   82 423
Robert N. **83** 345
Robert Rensselaer
   102 124
Robert Titus **84** 109 191

PHILLIPS *cont'd*
   111 148
Roger **101** 9 **147** 30
Roger Sherman **99** 167
Roland **62** 285 354
Rosina **86** 303
Roswell **93** 107
Rowland **62** 353 **143** 233
Roxy (Bancroft) **95** 68
Roysil **83** 167
Rufus **62** 273 **75** 19
Ruth **58** 407 **66** 280 **70** 227
   73 239 **110** 277 278 281
   111 79 148 165 **115** 194
   142 135 **144** 108
Ruth (Bonney) **126** 272
Ruth (Dunbar) **111** 79 165
Ruth (Pitts) **108** 160
Ruth Rawson **115** 108
S. A. **89** 388
Sabra **71** 38
Sabrina **70** 227
Sadie M. **93** 113
Sally **85** 126 **111** 79 165
   120 132 **122** 200 **140**
   235 236
Salome (Nickerson)
   (Girdley) **127** 122
Samuel **54** 415 **57** 363 **59**
   374 **64** 118 **65** 233 **67**
   201 209 212 214 363 **69**
   lviii **71** 38 204 **73** 151 **75**
   19 **80** 178 **81** 433 **82** 52
   87 399 **95** 207 **97** 57
   102 185 **103** 211 **104**
   242 **105** 75 288 **106** 17
   108 180 **110** 276 277
   281 **111** 79 165 **115** 164-
   166 **116** 79 119 180 **126**
   226 **127** 140 **128** 53 132
   296 305 **138** 279 284
   140 235 **143** 262 **144** 16
   342
Samuel B. **79** 107
Samuel M. **140** 235
Samuel Maverick **59** 374
Sarah **53** 275 **54** cxiii **57**
   104 **58** 374 **59** 188 **61** 35
   63 94 **65** 232 **70** 266 **71**
   129 219 **73** 151 238 **80**
   83 **83** 484 **84** 167 **88** 82
   89 387 **92** 11 **97** 57 **98**
   282 **103** 211 **106** 21 **110**
   277 278 **119** 68 **120** 6
   125 176 **126** 64 **127** 206
   128 307 **133** 306 **142**
   376 **143** 226 230
Sarah (Appleton) **110** 276
Sarah (Arey) (Cahoon)
   87 6
Sarah (Beck) **133** 306
Sarah (Bull) **110** 278
Sarah (Carver) **88** 221
Sarah (Holland) **110** 277
Sarah (Lathe) **124** 17
Sarah (Stedman)
   (Brackett) (Alcock)
   (Graves) **97** 12
Sarah (White) **89** 387
Sarah A. **93** 107
Sarah A. (Bracey) **119** 281

PHILLIPS *cont'd*
   282
Sarah Ann **62** 122 **89** 387
Sarah Ann (Sanborn)
   126 144
Sarah F. **70** 156
Sarah Hurd (Walley)
   132 91
Sarah J. **85** 316
Sarah K. (Madden) **98** 288
Sarah S. (Perkins) **144** 108
Seth **96** 63 65 **100** 11
   111 306
Sibyl (Pearce) **110** 225
Sidney **123** 201
Silas **144** 108
Silas Terry **110** 225
Silence (Briggs) **126** 272
Simon **142** 376
Smalley **125** 10
Solomon Wilson **132** 164
Sophia **76** 264 **77** 235
Southard **111** 117
Squire **120** 266
Stanley Cooper **81** 339
Stephen **64** 20 **73** 220
   109 225 315 **110** 277-
   280 **127** 259 **128** 58
Stephen C. **109** 225
Stephen Clarendon
   110 279
Stephen Henry **52** 102
   486 **84** 441 **109** 225 **110**
   279 280
Stephen Willard **110** 280
Stewart Nelson **92** 363
Submit **75** 302
Susan **70** 262 **89** 29
   134 209
Susan (Dean) **110** 225
Susan (Dubois) **96** 74
Susan (Kegrice) **133** 72
Susan A. **116** 259
Susan Amy **88** 115
Susan C. **73** 276
Susan G. **125** 238 239
Susan J. **93** 107
Susanna **74** 202 **102** 31
   110 277 281 **122** 101
   132 191 **143** 226 230
   144 127
Susanna (Stanley)
   131 132
Susanna Capen **68** 311
Susanna E. **79** 107
Susanna Heath **82** 119
Tamasin **111** 94
Temperance (Osborn)
   111 80
Temperance (Stone)
   111 80
Temple **51** 196
Temra **111** 306
Thankful **124** 239
Thankful (Chase) **87** 326
Thankful (Pearce) **116** 79
Theoda (Weare) **117** 226
Theodore **92** 326 342
   117 228
Theodore H. **92** 342
Theophilus **58** 199 200 **60**

PHILLIPS *cont'd*
  lxxii **82** 113 **110** 277 **111**
  148 **114** 230
  Thirza **70** 223
  Thomas **51** 196 **52** 321 **54**
    42 **55** 141 **56** 316 **57** 240
    58 261 **60** 39 **61** 43 **64**
    370 **65** 288 **66** xxi 254
    67 239 331 **68** 311 312
    315 320 **69** 356 357 **73**
    238 **79** 92 **80** 81 **82** 119
    84 71 **96** 65 **108** 278 280
    110 195 **111** 148 **112**
    278 285 **116** 300 **117**
    143 144 **119** 17 **127** 88
    128 131 278 **134** 203
    135 136 **136** 39 **143** 230
    232
  Thomas W. **67** 19
  Thomas Walley **69** 89
  Thomas Wharton **99** 167
  Thomas Wharton (Mrs.)
    85 188 **99** 140 167 **100**
    114
  Thompson **65** 373
  Timothy **70** 67 **77** 313 **92**
    54 **106** 199
  Trafton **93** 107
  Turner **92** 11 **140** 235
  Ulrich Bonnell (Mrs.)
    92 390
  Valeria P. **65** 135
  Viola Allen **103** 120
  Virginia **98** 147
  Vrederick **106** 4
  W. **91** 332
  W. C. **91** 332
  W. T. **98** 345
  Waite **80** 104 207
  Walter B. **82** 114
  Walter Fiske **109** 187
  Walter Mason **110** 280
  Wealthy **71** 36
  Wendell **54** 419 **55** lxxviii
    56 338 **59** lxxvii 345 **61**
    liv lv **62** 309 **64** 296 **66**
    369 **71** 295 **73** 1 **75** 215
    79 231 **132** 83 91
  Wilfrid Maurice **110** 74
  Willard **63** 13
  Willard L. **65** 135
  Willard Peele **110** 279
  Willard Quincy **84** 31
  William **52** 162 267 **53** 10
    54 115 **55** 145 300 **56**
    409 410 **59** 411 **60** 366
    61 35 68 **63** 17 **64** 321
    65 48 66 37 **67** 335 **71**
    124 **74** 271 **77** 239 **79**
    165 248 249 261 **80** 140
    84 260 359 364 374 379
    85 122 132 **89** 175 **90**
    225 **91** 332 **94** 69 174 **95**
    127 182 183 **97** 57 **98** 40
    101 9 **103** 211-213 **108**
    181 **110** 225 276 278 281
    112 318 **117** 116 **119** 17
    120 280 **125** 102 243 **126**
    259 263 **127** 149 **128**
    130 **129** 316 **131** 132
    133 309 **136** 35 37 **140**

PHILLIPS *cont'd*
    235 236 239 325 **143** 221
    222 225 227-233 262 366
    145 362
  William A. **96** 328
  William Bower **68** 303
  William Commons
    80 168
  William Leverett
    56 xxxiv
  William M. **65** 135
  William Morgan **98** 264
  William R. **79** 107 **125** 244
  William S. **82** 268
  William Stoddard **87** 384
  William Stought **120** 80
  William Titus **111** 148
  Zachariah **56** 410 **112** 160
  Zachary **95** 133
  Zavan **136** 40
  Zilpha **54** 80
  Zorobabel **110** 276
Phillipson *see* Philipson
PHILLIS
  Dinah 220 **125** 220
  Jane Elizabeth (Young)
    110 279
  John **99** 25 26 28
  Sarah **99** 25 26 28
  William **99** 26
Phillport *see* Philpot
Phillpot *see* Philpot
PHILOON
  Mehitable **124** 153
PHILPE Joan **115** 250
PHILPOT Philipot
    Philipott Phillepot
    Phillport Phillpot
    Philpots Philpott
    Philpott
  —— **53** 93 **58** 371 **65** 332
    76 71
  — Widow **84** 77
  Abbie Lassell **88** 369 370
  Abigail **74** 48 129
  Abigail (Emons) **95** 194
  Alexander **73** 230
  Ann **70** 249
  Ann Perkins **74** 34
  Benjamin **74** 34
  Betty **74** 35
  Charlotte **82** 283 296
  Christiana **51** 389 404
  Deborah **74** 257
  Dorothy **70** 249 254
  Elias **74** 195
  Elizabeth **66** 72
  Francis **82** 283 296
  George **70** 249
  Hannah **90** 330 **91** 20 **107**
    200 273
  Hannah (Lassell) **88** 369
    90 230 251
  Henry **70** 249
  Hiram **88** 369 **90** 329
    91 19
  Isaac **88** 369 **90** 230 248 251
    95 194 **98** 296
  James **74** 34
  John **55** 112 **67** 46 **70** 249
    250 **71** 176 **74** 35 41 130

PHILPOT *cont'd*
    76 223 **89** 330 **94** 346
    101 3 **110** 201 240 **117**
    29 **137** 142 **142** 229 **147**
    6
  Lillian May **98** 147
  Lydia (Tibbetts) **88** 369
    98 296
  Margaret **76** 71
  Mary **70** 249 **74** 48
  Mary (Hooper) **88** 369
    90 329 **91** 19
  Mercy **74** 35
  Molly **74** 34
  Moses **74** 35 257
  Nabby **74** 41
  Nabby (Emmons) **90** 248
  Nancy **58** 371
  Peter **67** 45 46 **70** 249
  Rachel **74** 41 49 130
  Rhoda B. **90** 337 **91** 25
  Rhoda Burleigh **88** 369
  Richard **74** 35
  Ruth **73** 305 **74** 34 35 40 **90**
    229 247 **92** 115
  Ruth (Nutter) **88** 369
  Ruth B. / H. (Nutter)
    91 28 34
  Sarah **70** 249 250 **73** 311
    74 41
  Sarah Rollins **103** 44
  Seth **88** 369 **91** 28 34
  Susan **128** 108
  Thomas **51** 389 404 **52** 234
    67 45 46 **70** 249 **144** 147
  William **56** 410 **69** 254
    70 249 **88** 369 **98** 296
PHINEA John **145** 365
Phiney *see* Phinney
PHINION John **112** 195
PHINISA John **69** 14
PHINNER E. **110** 234
  H. **110** 234
PHINNEY Phiney - *see also*
  Finney
  —— **71** 50 **109** 41 42 **145**
    49 55 56 162 163 165 168
    170
  — Col. **145** 54
  Aaron **70** 32
  Abigail **142** 38
  Abigail (Bishop) **148** 324
  Abigail (Blish) **116** 101
    102 197
  Abigail (Bourne) **115** 287
  Abner **120** 247 251
  Abraham **132** 298
  Alice **51** 223 **114** 161
  Almira Bernice **106** 241
    242
  Alvin **99** 123
  Ancel **130** 41
  Anna **148** 319
  Anna (Thomas) **106** 243
  Asa **120** 247
  Asenath **120** 247
  Augustus **88** 246
  Barnabas **120** 101 **130** 41
  Benjamin **130** 41
  Betsey **99** 123
  Betsey B. **79** 33

PHINNEY *cont'd*
Calvin **130** 41
Charles **78** 417 **120** 250
Charles Franklin Alvin
    92 223
Charles Freeman **110** 150
Charles Willis **109** 122
Charles Wills **84** 106 191
Charlotte (Sandals)
    99 123
Chloe **84** 330
Christian **106** 243
Christian (Patten) **148** 319
Clement **88** 246
Content (Fish) **124** 274
Daniel **70** 26
Daniel M. **101** 216
Daniel P. **79** 355
David **53** 207 **118** 201
Deborah (Gifford) **120**
    101 **130** 41
Ebenezer **120** 249 250
Edmund **52** 291 **64** 129
    131 132 327 **65** 79 82
    109 110 112 115 255 258-
    260 262 264 334 335 337
    338 340 **78** 426 **83** 411
    412
Elias **64** 328
Elihu **124** 21
Elijah **70** 327
Elisha **70** 31 32 157
    129 379
Elisha (Tobey) **99** 123
Elisha B. **116** 197
Eliza **79** 355
Eliza K. **70** 26
Elizabeth **55** 78 **57** 187 **61**
    342 **78** 445 **82** 284 287
    96 398 **105** 63 **148** 326
Elizabeth (Durland)
    106 243
Elizabeth (Kenney)
    108 117
Ernest E. **92** 223
F. D. **87** 208
Florence (Voorhees)
    94 139
Francis **116** 28
Frank Douglas **81** 108
    222
Frank Douglas (Mrs.)
    94 139
Frederic E. **70** 157
Freelove **124** 282 283
George Morrison **92** 223
Hannah **70** 32 **75** 152 **99**
    123 **115** 287 **116** 101
    126 145 **142** 202
Hannah (Perry) **116** 101
    197 **119** 31
Heman **115** 287
Henry **124** 21
Howard **82** 125 236
Huldah (Gifford) **132** 298
Inglis **106** 242 243
Isaac **106** 243
Isabella M. **70** 157
Jabez **116** 102 193 197
    119 31
Jacob M. **88** 246

PHINNEY *cont'd*
James **142** 38 **145** 164
Jemima **70** 32
Jeremiah **120** 5
Jirah **99** 123
Joanna **70** 32
John **64** 20 **78** 445 **79** 442
    85 364 **87** 208 **106** 243
    116 101 102 197 **130** 41
    142 37 **145** 164 **148** 318
    319 324
Jonathan **51** 223 **70** 32
    120 247
Jos: **123** 192
Joseph **142** 202
Josiah **55** 78 **99** 123
Julaan **110** 150
Levi **106** 243
Lot **106** 243
Louisa **116** 197
Louisa (Perry) **116** 197
Louise **119** 40
Love **120** 247 248
Lucy **110** 150
Lucy E. **120** 250
Lydia **110** 150 151
Lydia A. W. **70** 157
Lydia B. **115** 86 181 268
    283 **116** 27 100 191 **117**
    180 295 **118** 83 197 275
    119 26 161 260 **120** 26
    97 113 187 272 **121** 37
    127 224 260 **122** 51 131
    196 254 **123** 54 129 205
    266 **124** 42 70 146 209
    126 103 279 291 **127**
    108 178 193 250 **141** 57
Margarita **148** 318
Maria **113** 254
Martha **145** 164
Mary **78** 445 **87** 123 **88** 316
    114 161 **120** 249-251
Mary (Allen) **148** 323
Mary (Pope) **118** 201
Mary (Rogers) **106** 243
Mary Allen **109** 156
    148 322
Mary Ann **115** 287 **119** 31
Matilda (Craig) **106** 242
    243
Matthew **142** 38
Maude (Brower) **87** 77
Mehitable **85** 219 **126** 191
Mehitable (Smith) **99** 123
Mercy **70** 32 **116** 101 107
Miriam **145** 164
Molly **114** 161
Nathan **70** 32 **79** 246
Nathaniel **99** 123 **120** 247
Olive **120** 247
Pamelia (Tobey) **99** 123
Patience **96** 178
Patty **110** 150
Persis (Bourne) **119** 36
Peter **120** 247
Phebe **81** 471
Philip **119** 36 **120** 247
Polly **120** 247
Prince **124** 274
Rachel Badgeley **82** 102
    102 309

PHINNEY *cont'd*
Rebecca **70** 32 **85** 364 **119**
    31 **120** 248 **142** 202
Rebecca (Griffith) **108** 117
Rebecca (Tobey) **99** 123
Reliance **120** 247
Reliance (Goodspeed)
    106 243
Robert **82** 36
Ruth **88** 246
Ruth (Gates) **106** 243
Ruth (Silvester) (Cooke)
    (Ring) **85** 364
Ruth Maria **88** 246
S. B. **119** 35
Sally **110** 150 151
Sally (Meserve) **99** 123
Samuel **99** 123 **118** 285
    145 164
Sarah **53** 207 380 **58** 340 **78**
    445 **79** 442 **88** 246 **110**
    150 151
Sarah (Lumbert) **106** 243
Sarah Berry **110** 150
Sarah E. (Farley) **101** 216
Sarah L. **120** 248
Seth **58** 340
Sisley **148** 319
Sophronia **116** 197
Squire Zenas **110** 150
Stephen **142** 202
Susan **110** 150 **115** 285
    120 250
Susan (Meserve) **99** 123
Susanna **120** 247 **142** 38
    202 **145** 164
Sylvanus **130** 41
Tabitha **124** 274
Temperance (Tobey)
    99 123
Terzah **120** 248
Thankful **110** 150 151
Thankful (Tupper)
    99 123
Thomas **106** 243 **124** 282
Thomas Russell **110** 150
Urana **79** 246
William **70** 157 **120** 247
William Henry **110** 150
William P. **120** 250
Zaccheus **130** 41
Zenas **110** 150 151
PHIPP Joan **148** 73
Phippany *see* Phippen
PHIPPAY — Widow **96** 321
PHIPPEN Phippany
    Phippeny Phippeney
    Phippin Phipponey
    —— **102** 190
Abigail **77** 41
Amos R. **81** 291
Anne (Cook) **131** 236
Damaris **68** 58
David **82** 152 **131** 236
    139 129 **142** 360 **143**
    338
Ebenezer **140** 69
Eliza **81** 291
Eliza H. (Howard)
    126 142
Elizabeth **66** 87 **77** 41 **142**

PHIPPEN *cont'd*
354 360 **143** 340
Eunice **72** 102
Gamaliel **143** 251 252
George **81** 291 **142** 354
360
George D. **53** 52 **71** 101
Harriet Maria **85** 221
Henry **72** 102
James **142** 278 354
James H. **77** 41 **81** 291
Joanna (Chamberlain)
142 354
Joseph **63** 382 **66** 87 **68** 58
121 14 15 **139** 131
Joshua **126** 142
Judah **66** 87
Judith **57** 353 **66** 87 **131**
124 132 **148** 239 361
Mary **121** 15
Nancy (Cook) **131** 236
Rebecca **143** 131 250-252
338 339 343
Rebecca Maria **90** 289
Robert **77** 41
Sarah **142** 360 **143** 338
Sarah (Purchase) **143** 251
252
Sarah E. **79** 218
Susanna **61** 204
William **66** 87
Phippeny *see* Phippen
Phippin *see* Phippen
Phipponey *see* Phippen
PHIPPS Phippes Phips
—— **56** 51 **69** 297
— Capt. **58** 228 232
— Gov. **94** 360
— Mr. **66** 12 **91** 354
A. M. **61** 202
Aaron B. **81** 311
Abigail **91** 354 **107** 256
Ada (Kent) **87** 174
Adeline Osgood **77** 186
Almira **89** 228
Alzina **103** 175
Anna **93** 280
Anne **57** 55
Arrold **131** 26
Asa H. **101** 35 **103** 175
Blanche Beatrice **103** 180
Caroline May **103** 175
Caroline Steele **93** 121
Charles **66** 101 **69** 125
Clara **86** 308
Constantine **60** 60 61
67 94
Cora Adelaide **88** 169
David **110** 317
Dorcas (Harriman)
86 308
Edson Sumner **103** 175
180
Edwin L. **81** 481
Eleanor **63** 153
Elisha **86** 308
Elizabeth **52** 199 **58** 242 **76**
202 **96** 365 **100** 242 **102**
29
Elizabeth (King) **87** 38
Elizabeth (Wood) **123** 231

PHIPPS *cont'd*
Elizabeth Loomis
(Fairchild) **86** 308
Elizabeth S. **81** 311
Elzina **103** 175
Elzina S. (Fisher) **101** 35
Emily **86** 362
Emily Lydia **86** 361
Emma **51** 302
Esther **55** 344
Frances Bowman
77 xxix 78
Francis **60** 60 61
G. **145** 126
George **63** 174
George Lucas **103** 175
H. R. **66** 1 191 **67** xxxii 94
Hannah **51** 445 **81** 433
125 107
Hattie H. **110** 48
Herman Horace **103** 175
Humphrey **53** 20
Ivan Dexter **103** 175
J. W. **87** 346
James **60** 61 **73** 237
104 177
James M. **86** 308 361
James S. **86** 308
Jemina (Sawtell) **126** 15
Jennie Elzina **103** 175
Jesse **87** 38
Joan **80** 297 **148** 74
John **57** 55 **60** 61 **61** 66
65 376 **79** 225 **139** 237
John Miller **103** 120
Joseph **56** 237 **89** 71
107 255
Joseph Gardner (Mrs.)
87 174
Joshua B. **72** 275
Katharine **51** 302
Laura Ann (Briggs)
126 220
Laura Olivia **103** 175
Lawrence Cowle **89** 132
Lawrence Cowle (Mrs.)
80 335 **81** 219
Lida F. **103** 180
Linnie Inez **103** 175
Lois (Burrill) **89** 71
Lucy **93** 121 **94** 158
Lucy Adelaide **93** 121
Lucy J. **81** 481
Lydia Ann **77** 183
Lydia G. (Wheeler)
86 308 361
Malissa (Furlong) **91** 386
Margaret **81** 219 **104** 177
Marie (Raynsford)
139 237
Mary **52** 199 337 **73** 237
75 144 **78** 12 **81** 433 **86**
148 **89** 71 **91** 270 **107**
255 **130** 264
Mary (Kettell) **107** 255
Mary Catherine **81** 383
Mary Clark **57** 285
Mary E. **81** 311
Mary Elizabeth **75** lvii
Mary Jane **68** 99
Mary N. **51** 446

PHIPPS *cont'd*
Mary Newell **87** 38
Maurice Asa **103** 175
Mehitable **51** 461
Miriam **63** 174
Nancy W. **116** 260
Nathan **126** 220
Nicholas **57** 44
Persis **93** 216
Polly (Adams) **126** 220
Rebecca **76** 202
Rhoda (Beverstock)
125 217
Richard **125** 217
Roger **80** 297
Rufus D. **91** 386
Samuel **51** 302 **65** 376 **70**
67 **78** 303 **91** 270 **96** 280
107 256 **123** 231
Sarah **76** 312 **78** 12 **108** 28
Sarah Walter **126** 205
Solomon **52** 199 337 **54**
166 **56** 82 236 237 **75**
144 **78** 12 **123** 231
Spencer **63** 189 267 **76** 202
77 305 **84** 165 **87** 399
119 19 **130** 105 264
Spencer (Mrs.) **84** 165
Submit **118** 126
Susan F. **72** 275
Susanna **91** 270
Sylvester **126** 220
Thomas **51** 44 **54** 387 **60**
61 **64** 227 **69** 362 364 **81**
433 **93** 121 106 265 **118**
313 **125** 92 **140** 171
Thomas G. **93** 121 **94** 158
Walter Bowen (Mrs.)
77 xxix
William **51** 181 **52** 15 52
53 389 421 **53** 202 204
244 56 216 343 **57** 55
285 **58** 125 127 **60** 61 67
61 152 **67** 205 207 298
68 99 **69** 361 **71** 102 **72**
85 **73** 237 **75** 145 **81** 79
88 295 **90** 292 **96** 323
97 257 **99** 80 307 **104**
177 **106** 147 **112** 12 244
113 318 **116** 8 **119** 18 19
263 273 **121** 279 **126** 15
129 204 **130** 264-266
131 274 **133** 100 **137**
240 **142** 120 **143** 348
William K. **51** 445 **81** 383
87 38
PHISTERER Frederick **64**
69 **108** 8
PHITHIAN Thomas **64** 339
PHOEBUS John **86** 221
Mary Ann (Jones) **86** 221
Mary Jane **86** 221
PHOENIX Phenix
— Mrs. **79** 299
Alexander **79** 152
Cyrus **101** 33
Daniel **119** 192
Eliza Waldron **104** 235
George **98** 336
Mary **63** 173
Mercy **63** 174

PHOENIX *cont'd*
    Richard **63** 173
    S. Whitney **145** 71 144
    Sarah **79** 152
    Sarah (Fitz Randolph)
        98 336
    Thomas **73** 152
    William **63** 174
PHRONE Anne **71** 318 320
PHYLER Abigail **72** 34
    Lucy **72** 34
PHYLLIS Dinah **125** 220
PHYLYKE John **84** 75
PHYSICK
    Charles **64** 341
    Elizabeth (Emlen) **98** 125
    Ellen **64** 341
    Philip Syng **98** 125
    Sarah Emlen **98** 125
    Thomas **64** 341
    William **64** 341
PIALO R. **91** 332
PIATT Abner **87** 376
    Annie M. (Murphy)
        87 376
    Carrie Althea (Peck) **112**
        140 141
    Don Lyle **79** 275
    Elizabeth (Cline) **87** 376
    Emily **87** 376
    Emily Frances **112** 148
    Frances (Van Vliet)
        (Wycoff) **112** 141
    Francis Hammond
        112 141
    Grace Bella **79** 275
    Hannah (Brady) **87** 376
    Jane (Williamson) **87** 376
        112 141
    John **60** 190 **87** 376
        112 141
    Joseph Wood **112** 140 141
    Josephine Althea **112** 141
    Lois J. (Keast) **112** 141
    Marion Adele Haskins
        (Sheppard) **112** 141
    Marion Sheppard
        112 141
    Mary (Brady) **112** 141
    Mary Searle **112** 141
    Rebecca Heston
        McClintoch **112** 141
    Rebecca Hestor
        (McClintoch) **112** 141
    Ruth Peck **112** 141
    William **87** 376 **112** 141
    William McKinney **98**
        147 **112** 73 140 141
PIBELLS Isabel **112** 280
PIBUS Margaret **72** 63
Piccard *see* Pickard
PICCOPE   **68** 353 360
        363 366 367
PICHE Eleanor **106** 143
PICHEL Thourot **112** 239
PICHETTE Adele Emelie
        Stephanie **111** 52
    Joseph Eduoard **111** 52
    Marie Leocadie Lemaitre
        (Auger) **111** 52
PICHNAIL Anne **63** 173

PICHNAIL *cont'd*
    Nelson **63** 173
PICHOT Ralf **109** 24
Pick *see* Picke
PICKARD Piccard Pycard
    ——— **140** 149
    — Mrs. **93** 19
    Andrew B. **76** 269
    Anna (Holland) **84** 426
    Burham **105** 298
    Carl **97** 126
    Charlotte L. (Pulver)
        97 126
    David **84** 426
    Edgar L. **105** 298
    Elizabeth **58** 269
    Elizabeth (Culverwell)
        148 113
    Emma C. **123** 79
    Frances **94** 101
    Francis J. **62** 324
    Georgia **112** 316
    Homer **85** 296
    Jane **93** 167
    Jane (Crosby) **119** 248
    Janneta (Cleaver) **85** 296
    John **76** 60 **119** 244 248
    Jonathan **83** 138 **120** 79
    Joseph **117** 171
    Mark **52** 14 **140** 149
    Mary **52** 14 **78** 421 **83** 138
    Mary (Kilbourne) **120** 79
    Mary Lovell **52** 14 **53** 152
    Miriam J. **52** 74
    Nicholas **115** 254 **148** 113
        114
    Polly **83** 138
    R. Jane **76** 269
    William **65** 326 **92** 382
    Winfred J. **105** 298
PICKAS
    Alice **52** 128 129
    Judith **52** 129
PICKAVER — Dr. **51** 355
PICKE Alice **111** 8
    Eliam **52** 66
    Elizabeth **52** 66
    Richard **52** 66
    Stephen **52** 66
    William **146** 269
Pickel *see* Pickles
Pickels *see* Pickles
Pickeman *see* Pickman
PICKENS Picken
    ——— **53** 134
    Andrew **63** 196 197 **78** 171
    Ann **63** 196
    Betsey **115** 295
    Catherine **63** 196
    Edith **121** 55
    Eliza Ann (Chase) **88** 23
    Ellen **112** 31
    Evelyn Sarah **78** 171
    Ezekiel **63** 196
    James **88** 23
    Jane **63** 196
    Joanna (Roundsville)
        126 217
    John Henderson **78** 171
    Joseph **63** 196
    Katharine **63** 196

PICKENS *cont'd*
    Louise Milliken **100** 113
    Lucy **87** 3
    Margaret **63** 196
    Mary **63** 196
    Matilda **126** 217
    Matilda (Briggs) **126** 217
    Monroe **106** 78
    Rebecca **63** 196 **87** 3
    Samuel **126** 217
    Silas **100** 214 215
    Thomas **101** 254
PICKERILL Pekerell
    Pickrell
    Alethea Comegys Worth
        (Sharp) **102** 71
    Dennis **102** 71
    Eleanor **73** 266
    Francis Byers **102** 71
    Helen Irene **77** 302 **79** 202
        80 207 **102** 62 71 128
    Henry **73** 137
    Richard **67** 169 **73** 137
    Samuel **102** 71 **104** 80
    William **73** 228
    William Feport **102** 71
PICKERING Pickeringe
    Pickern Pekerynge
    ——— **54** xvii cv **56** 404
        57 219 **58** 249 250 **67** 75
        73 192 **82** 414 **87** 248
        113 263 **119** 42 **129** 188
    — Dea. **76** 204
    — Goodman **94** 218
    — Mr. **52** 404 **67** 202
    — Mrs. **53** 11
    ——— (Goddard) **140** 145
    A. M. **73** 192
    A. Rosamond **73** 195
    Abby **73** 190 **84** 31
    Abigail **73** 192 200 203
        76 32 **81** 433 **82** 52 296-
        298 423 **132** 276
    Abigail (Chase) **87** 128
        247
    Abigail (Durrell) **132** 275
    Abigail (Meserve)
        132 275
    Abigail M. **83** 26 28
    Absalom **58** 253 **73** 198
    Alice **66** 125 **101** 82
    Alma **73** 190
    Alvin Gee **73** 202
    Amanda **73** 189 203
    Ann (McKlish) **125** 244
    Ann E. **73** 203
    Ann Jos. **73** 202
    Ann W. **83** 36
    Ann Wentworth **82** 423
    Anna **73** 206 **81** 144 145
    Anna Olivia **73** 200
    Annie Goddard **55** 134
    Anthony **124** 301 **132** 275
        276
    Arthur **140** 321
    Asenath **63** 274
    Bathia **114** 74
    Bening **125** 244
    Benjamin **73** 203 205
        113 135
    Betsey **73** 196 **132** 276

PICKERING *cont'd*
Betsey Wentworth **82** 52
Bilzey **73** 279
Catherine **73** 197
Catherine C. (Stetson)
  91 386
Charles **73** 206
Charles G. **84** 31
Charles N. **73** 189
Charlotte **73** 206
Christian **81** 448
Daniel **82** 52 **105** 207
Daniel N. **73** 201 202
  83 21 26
Deborah **73** 191 **81** 433
Deborah C. **73** 192
Delia **73** 190
Dorothy **81** 448 **82** 295
  296
E. W. **82** 423
Edward **87** 128 247 **128**
  288 289
Eleanor **97** 203
Eleanor M. **73** 194
Eliza **73** 191
Eliza C. **125** 244
Elizabeth **55** 137 **58** 296 **64**
  13 **65** 214 **70** lvi **73** 192
  193 **81** 433 448 **82** 283
  296 **83** 21 26 **84** 327 **93**
  290 **97** 203 **98** 270 **129**
  188 **145** 109
Elizabeth (Appleton)
  83 21
Elizabeth (Boland)
  129 188
Elizabeth (Flanders)
  132 276
Elizabeth (Smart) **132** 275
Elizabeth (Tufts) **132** 275
Elizabeth (Winslow)
  140 321
Elizabeth F. **73** 201
Elizabeth Jane **73** 193 204
Elizabeth Sheafe **82** 423
  83 36
Elizabeth W. **82** 423
  83 26 27
Elizabeth Wentworth
  82 423
Ellen **112** 31
Ellen R. **95** 271
Ellen Rogers **96** 35
Ephraim **73** 189-192 194
  206 **82** 284 297 **83** 182
  185 **97** 203
Esther **93** 343
Frances **64** 340 **82** 52
  83 36
Frances M. **73** 195
Frank T. **73** 189 190 193
  201 **83** 179 185
Frank Tuscan **81** 149
Gee **73** 191 195 206
George **66** 12 **132** 276
George Wallace **73** 190
Georgiana **73** 195
Gilbert **73** 197 204
Gilman S. **73** 206
H. W. **140** 145
Hannah **65** 354 **66** 125 **73**

PICKERING *cont'd*
  194 198 **82** 52 286 296
  83 22 26 **92** 285
Hannah (Chase) **87** 248
Hannah J. **73** 190
Harriet Winslow **66** 12
Henry **82** 52
Henry Goddard **61** 209
  62 xxxvii
Henry Smith **73** 200
Isaac **82** 52
J. K. (Mrs.) **83** 308
J. S. **83** 36
J. S. (Mrs.) **83** 195
Jacob Sheafe **82** 52 423
  83 26 27 195
James **64** 340 **73** 190 191
  195 198 199 202 203 206
  132 275
James Alfred **73** 189 193
James C. **73** 194 203 205
Jane **76** 40 **138** 124 **145**
  103 104 107-109
Jemima **82** 52
John **51** 43-45 **52** 289 290
  425 **54** 182 **55** 134 56
  367 **58** 249 296 **64** 13 15
  66 125 **68** 81 **69** 360 361
  71 23 73 198 200 203 **76**
  lx 203 310 **81** 433 **82** 52
  283 286 296 298 414 **92**
  285 **94** 355 **106** 316 **107**
  188 **111** 316 **118** 313
  121 248 **125** 92 **128** 288
  129 188 **132** 275
John A. **73** 189 190 203
John A. K. **73** 204
John Andrew **73** 201 204
John Edward **73** 190
John F. **91** 386
John Gee **73** 194 204
John Gilman **73** 204
John J. **84** 31
John Jacob **82** 423
John K. **83** 195
John Knight **55** 134
  73 204
John Lowel **73** 189 190
  192 200 203-206
Joseph **73** 192 201 202 **76**
  41 **97** 203
Joseph T. **73** 197
Joseph Warren **73** 190 191
  195 201
Josephine **73** 193
Josephine E. (Barton) **83**
  178 185
Joshua B. **73** 189 193 202
  204
Judith **73** 203
Laura **81** 252
Levina **93** 343
Lois **76** 203
Loring **73** 192 **80** 335 **81**
  219 **114** 68
Lucia **74** 206
Lucretia **73** 195 **82** 52 **113**
  263 **116** 142
Lucy Maria **55** 134 **83** 174
Luther C. **73** 189
Lydia **73** 191 192 197 199

PICKERING *cont'd*
  81 448 **82** 284 297 **83** 25
  26
M. A.L. **73** 191
Manthano **95** 271 **96** 35
Marcy **113** 135
Margaret **73** 189 192
  89 108
Margaret E. **73** 194
Margaret F. (Weeks) **83**
  185 187 188
Maria **66** 12 **136** 327
Maria D. (Horne) **83** 182
  185
Martha **65** 352 **67** 310 **81**
  149 **97** 203
Martha Ann **83** 26 28
Martha P. **73** 203
Martha S. **73** 205
Mary **58** 296 **60** 292 **64** 13
  68 81 **73** 189-191 196
  197 203 205 **76** lx **82**
  290 292 296 **96** 33 **106**
  265 **123** 160 **128** 288
Mary (Nutter) **132** 275
Mary (Stubbs) **128** 288
  289
Mary Ann **132** 276
Mary E. **73** 194
Mary Elizabeth Langdon
  83 174
Mary Emily **73** 194
Mary G. **76** 41
Mary Gee **73** 192
Mary J. **69** 142 **73** 192
Mary M. **83** 426 438
Mary Paul **73** 189 194
Mary Susette **73** 190
Mary W. **73** 190
Mattie **81** 448
Mehitable **65** 353 **73** 191
  192 197 198 **82** 288 296
  97 203 **100** 42
Mehitable (Weeks) **97** 203
Michael **59** 175
Molly (Jones) **113** 135
Nancy **73** 199
Nathaniel **76** 40
Nehemiah **58** 253 **73** 193
  197 199 203 205
Nellie **73** 191
Nicholas **73** 200 **82** 292
  296 **132** 276
Nicholas D. **83** 26 28
Olive **63** 276 **73** 189 194
  313 **83** 23 26 **132** 276
Oliver O. **73** 195
Peperel **82** 52
Peter **63** 276
Phebe **63** 276 **73** 192
Phebe (Chase) **88** 110
Polly **73** 198 201
Rachel Wakefield
  (Durrell) **132** 275
Rebecca Russell (Lowell)
  84 327
Rebecca W. **78** 207
Rhoda Davis (Libby) **95**
  271 **96** 35
Richard **55** 134 **58** 253 **73**
  197 205 **145** 107

PICKERING cont'd
Richard L. **73** 193 **83** 178 185
Robert H. **73** 189
Rosamond **73** 201 202
Rowland **145** 109
Ruth **73** 191 198 202 **93** 343
Ruth (Benson) **111** 315 316
S. A. **73** 192
Sally **73** 202 204
Sally Q. **73** 190 195
Samuel **58** 296 **63** 28 **67** 310 **82** 52 **93** 343 **105** 207 208
Samuel A. **75** xxiii xxx 65
Sarah **52** 289 290 425 **58** 296 **73** 189 **76** 203 210 **81** 433 **82** 52 **90** 67 **97** 203
Sarah (Thing) **90** 237 **138** 321
Sarah E. **73** 190
Sarah M. **68** 204 **73** 189
Sarah T. **84** 31
Simeon **63** 274
Simon **93** 343
Sincere **128** 288
Sophia **73** 191 195 **83** 26 28
Sophia Eleanora Gertrude (DeWitt) **73** 189 193 **81** 149 **83** 179 185
Stephen **73** 199 **82** 288 296
Suky **82** 52
Susan **116** 299
Susan E. **73** 193
Susan M. **73** 189
T. A. **68** 204
T. A.H. **78** 317
Temperance **59** 288 **73** 200 **95** 265 **102** 74
Theodore **73** 191
Theophilus **91** 94 **135** 28 29
Thomas **51** 45 **55** 134 **58** 253 **64** 336 **68** 81 82 **69** 360 361 **73** 191 194 196-199 201 203 **81** 149 433 448 **82** 52 **83** 25 26 **106** 265 **111** 321 **132** 276 **145** 109
Thomas J. **88** 110
Thomas L. **73** 192 **83** 185 188
Timothy **51** 36 **54** 123 **61** 226 **68** 17 **74** 206 **76** lx **79** 166 229 **99** 16 **101** 221 **121** 248 **130** 279 **139** 121
Valentine **58** 253 **73** 191 198
William **56** 87 **58** 253 **64** 340 **73** 195 205 262 **79** 46 **82** 52 **90** 237 **93** 75 **102** 190 **138** 321 **140** 321
William C. **73** 189
William P. **73** 197

PICKERING cont'd
William Pepperell **82** 52
William Sheafe **82** 423
Winthrop **73** 205
Pickern see Pickering
PICKERNAIL Pickernal Pickernale Pickernel Pickernell Pickernelle
— Mrs. **97** 266
Amos **117** 229
Betty **116** 127
Esther **97** 270
Hannah (Junkins) **117** 143
James **54** 445 **97** 146 266 **116** 133
Joseph **97** 142
Mary (Seymoure) **115** 214
Molly **116** 129
Richard **117** 143
Sarah **82** 288 296
Susan (McDaniel) **117** 229
William **115** 214
PICKETT Peckett Picket Pickitt
—— **54** lxxix **73** 247 **88** 376 **90** 346 **128** 312 **143** 202
— Mr. **71** 136 139 140 **83** 308
Abercy **115** 119
Abigail **71** 112 **72** 210
Alice May (Hannum) **90** 346
Alonzo **128** 312
Amy Kate **100** 112
Angelo Campbell **86** 198
Anna **88** 157
Annis **88** 157 **145** 169
Antoinette Erpercia **68** xxxv
Benjamin **59** 412 **60** 79 **83** 367 **128** 312
Betty **88** 156
Bridget **90** 106
Catherine Whitaker **72** xx
Charles R. **84** 31
Daniel **91** 332
Dorcas **88** 156 **145** 169
Dorces **88** 157
Dorothy **54** 419 **73** 247
Ebenezer **72** 211
Edna Stanley **104** 78
Edward **63** 136
Elizabeth **72** 211 **109** 259
Elizabeth (Benedict) **109** 259
Esther **59** 412 **60** 79 **83** 367
Ezra **109** 259
George **145** 169
George Dennes **88** 157
George Edward **64** 69 **70** 193
Giles **63** 137 **104** 262
Grace **59** 359
Hannah **72** 210 **88** 156 **125** 218 **145** 169
Harriet **88** 156 **90** 164
J. H. **61** 95
Jacob **72** 210

PICKETT cont'd
James **63** 137 **65** 249 **77** 222
John **53** 113 283 **63** 137 **66** 113 **72** 210 **82** 296 297 **104** 87 262 **115** 100
Joseph **84** 137 **100** 237
Josiah **62** 213
Laura **128** 312
Lucy **88** 156
Margaret **63** 137 **72** 210 **100** 237 **104** 116
Mary **63** 137 **104** 87
Mary Ann **145** 169
Mary Eliza **77** 222
Maryan **88** 157
Mercy **66** 284 285 **93** 369 **97** 192 **115** 99 119
Mercy (Abercy) **115** 119
Nancy **77** 222
Nathaniel **88** 156
Orrin **128** 312
Oscar **128** 312
Polly **108** 320
Robert **84** 146 **128** 312
Ruth **53** 113 **66** 284
Sarah **53** 379 **82** 296 297
Sarah Ann **126** 143
Tabitha **88** 375
Tabitha (Lazell) **88** 376
Thomas **71** 112 **72** 210
William **54** 419 421 **63** 137 **88** 156 157 **100** 237 **104** 262 **145** 169
William P. **84** 31
William Sanford **77** 222
Pickeworth see Pickworth
PICKFORD
— Mr. **54** 194
A. M. **56** 92
Alice **55** 338
Alice Tolman **69** lxviii
Anna Maria **56** xxxiv 318 **57** xxxii 337 417 **58** xliii **60** xxxiv 62 281 372 384 **63** 98 **69** xliii lxvii
Charles Jarvis **69** lxviii
Elizabeth **69** lxviii
Emily **62** 374
Grace **55** 338
James **55** 337 338
Jedidiah **55** 334 337 338
John **55** 334 338
John Kay Livermore **62** 374 **69** lxviii
Jonathan **55** 338
Mary **54** 194
Priscilla **55** 338
Samuel **55** 334 338
Thomas **55** 334 338
Pickitt see Pickett
Pickle see Pickles
PICKLER Fanny **63** 145
Grace **63** 145
Mary **63** 145
Nancy **63** 145
Sarah **63** 145
PICKLES Pickel Pickels Pickle
—— **78** 232
— Mr. **57** 179

PICKLES *cont'd*
— Rev. **83** 416
Alice **57** 323 401 **70** 257
  142 272
Baltes **68** 124
David **58** 86
Elizabeth Kase **68** 124
Elsie **57** 323
Eunice **57** 178
Jonah **57** 86
Jonas **57** 178 **70** 256 257
Lydia **57** 179 **70** 257
Margaret **89** 227
Mary **57** 321 **60** 153
Mary Holcombe **68** 124
Mercy **70** 257
Michael **67** 175
Miriam **57** 322 323 **58** 86
Nathan **57** 178 321 323
  401-403 **58** 86 **60** 176
  70 257
Rose V. **123** 235
Thomas **60** 153
William **105** 287
PICKMAN Pickeman
  Pickmans
—— **82** 414 **120** 206
— Capt. **66** 122
Abigail **67** 370
Anstis (Derby) **87** 68
B. T. **140** 236
Benjamin **67** 370 **77** 131
  83 130 **84** 365 **87** 68
  101 224 **118** 313 **139**
  298
Benjamin T. **140** 247
Dudley Leavitt **95** 153
Elizabeth **77** 131
Hannah **51** 407
Hannah (Smith) **140** 247
John **51** 407 **59** 173 **77** 131
Jonathan **82** 414
Martha **87** 68
Mary **77** 131
Rebecca Taylor **106** 151
William **51** 288 **67** 370
  125 23 **140** 236
PICKMER
Elizabeth **75** 140
Robert **75** 140
PICKMORE
— Mr. **52** 112
John **52** 112
Thomas **52** 112
PICKNY Michael **63** 243
Pickrell *see* Pickerill
PICKS Elizabeth **83** 76
Pickton *see* Picton
PICKUP Ellen **89** 259
Susan **89** 259
PICKWICK
Harold Curtis **108** 129
  117 316 **130** 312
Harold Curtis (Mrs.) **80**
  102 209 **106** 122 **108**
  129
Hazel **80** 209
Hazel Ash **117** 316
PICKWORTH Pickeworth
Abigail (Elithorp) **113** 43
Alan de **80** 379

PICKWORTH *cont'd*
Ann **56** 345
Hannah **56** 345
John **56** 345 **113** 43
Joseph **113** 43
Mary **108** 164
Rachel **83** 214
Ruth **56** 345
PICNE Milton **123** 313
PICO Isabella **78** 186
John **101** 52
Joshua **78** 267 300 **140** 236
  145 33
Maria **88** 337
Mary **78** 270
Sarah **78** 267 270
Sarah Presbury (West)
  (Callender) **145** 33
Picoat *see* Picot
PICOLET Jules Emanuel
  Arthur **86** 266
PICORNELL Jean Bta
  Mariano **110** 130
PICOT Picoat
Agnes (Shaw) **119** 62
Joseph **119** 67
Martha E. **121** 73
Mary **122** 73
Mary A. **123** 153
Mary Ann (Shaw) **119** 229
Nicholas **119** 62
Sarah F. **121** 72
Thankful (Shaw) **119** 67
PICQUART —— **105** 182
— Capt. **83** 84
PICQUINY
Agnes de **106** 279
PICROFTE
Thomas **82** 187 334
PICTET —— **67** 101
PICTON Pickton
Ellen Free **145** 311
PIDAL
Menendez **103** 153
Ramon Menendez **117**
  94 96
PIDDOCK
Charles A. **103** 48
Gertrude P. (Farnsworth)
  103 48
PIDGE
Abigail **66** 138 139
Anna Elizabeth **132** 242
Clarissa **66** 140
Comfort **66** 139
Daniel **66** 138
Eliza **66** 139
John **66** 139 140
Josiah **66** 138
Keziah **66** 136
Lucinda (Briggs) **132** 242
Martha **63** 91
Nabby **66** 138-140
Pelemon **132** 242
Polly Massy **66** 140
William Love **66** 139
PIDGELEY
Patience **66** 155

PIDGEON Pidgin Pigeon
  Piggan Piggen
  Piggeon Pydgeon
Alexander **51** 372
Ann **55** 415 **61** 393
Charles Felton **61** xxxv
Daniel **127** 83 84
David **134** 228 230
Deborah Annis (Chase)
  88 114
Edward **52** 262
Edward Dumaresq **100**
  135 **101** 274
Elizabeth **102** 146
George **69** 113
Henry **58** 64 69 **77** 228 **99**
  26 121 **100** 134 240 **101**
  55 274
Jane **78** 315 **100** 30 32 134
  135 **101** 274 **122** 83
Jane (Dumaresq) **100** 298
John **55** 415 **65** 365 **77** 231
  85 127 **99** 26 **100** 30 32
  134 135 298 **101** 274
  102 35 36 **122** 83
Matthew **61** 393
Patience **85** 127 **99** 121
  100 30 **122** 83
Roger Warren **105** 129
Sarah (Nesbitt) **129** 188
Stephen **88** 114
Thomas **58** 142 **143** 293
Walter **99** 26 121 **101** 55
Walter (Staekey) **100** 240
William **67** 355 **101** 51
  113 271
PIE Eleanor **72** 232
John **72** 232
PIEMONT Hannah
  (Crosby) **100** 300
John **77** 314 **100** 300
  140 236
PIER Arthur Stanwood
  89 306
Betsey (Mills) **123** 90
Fordyce **123** 309
John Thomas **90** 53
Kate H. **70** 95
Lucy **123** 96
Mary Ann **122** 216
Mary Ann (Stanley) **90** 53
Orrin **122** 216
Phebe **123** 304
Phebe (Phelps) **123** 50 304
Reinelle (Plimpton)
  109 69
Samuel Matthew Phelps
  123 304
Thomas **70** 95 **113** 79
William S. **109** 69
PIERCE Pearce Pearse
  Peirce Pers Perse
—— **51** 13 **53** 128 137
  297 385 431 **55** 116 351
  56 12 **57** lxiii 337 **60** x
  107 154 **68** 42 **73** 259 **76**
  235 **81** 449-12 29 113
  122 211 **123** 92 **128** 313
  131 23 **136** 211 **138** 284
  140 69 236
— Capt. **83** 195

PIERCE *cont'd*
— Col. **77** 292
— Dr. **93** 61
— Miss **83** 195
— Mr. **53** 198 **57** 222 378
  62 133 275 387 **66** 22 **82**
  296 298 **83** 376 **92** 349
— Mrs. **62** 362 **79** 409 **83**
  36 **94** 57 **103** 299 **118**
  302 305 **119** 55 130 296
  120 58 129 130 210 293
  295 299 **121** 61 95 **123**
  17
— Rev. Dr. **85** 460
— Rev. Mr. **92** 127
— Widow **71** 137
A. (Mrs.) **78** 293
A. R. **91** 332
A. W. **108** 72
Abel **56** 410 **58** 374 **66** 10
  98 355
Abel Bonaparte **66** 10
Abiah **51** 74 **119** 103 104
Abial **91** 97
Abiel **115** 282
Abigail **51** 74 304 466 **57**
  359 **58** 129 133 **59** 82 85
  154 **61** 396 **64** 34 **68** 236
  70 163 **71** 255 **75** 149
  199 **76** 30 **78** 286 **80** 255
  82 52 89 296 300 **83** 49
  88 152 **91** 373 **93** 231
  94 61 **97** 261 **98** 221
  108 243 **109** 160 240
  110 160 **113** 32 34 41
  299 **121** 117 **125** 62 **127**
  186 **137** 154 **138** 117
Abigail (Bailey) **129** 167
Abigail (Blanchard)
  93 231
Abigail (Brooks) **86** 364
Abigail (Brown) **94** 61
  97 260
Abigail (Comee) **89** 99
  113 299
Abigail (Harrington)
  127 186
Abigail (Long) **104** 39
Abigail (Parks) **97** 49
Abigail (Sanderson)
  127 185
Abigail (Tisick) **90** 53
Abigail (Tucker) (Chase)
  87 128
Abigail (Vinton) **85** 110
Abigail (Winslow)
  125 221
Abigail B. (Kendall)
  126 141
Abigail C. **88** 244
Abijah **53** 198 **103** 308
  114 197
Abijah Hoar **53** 198
Abner **69** 306 **70** 12 17 19
  88 110 **134** 252
Abraham **62** lxxiv **64** 188
  68 232 **70** 163 **94** 241
  113 38 39 163 231 **124**
  18 **127** 186 **128** 4
Abram **55** 91
Ada Hortense **57** 350

PIERCE *cont'd*
97 184
Addie Isabelle (Bond)
  89 263
Adelbert O. **68** 94
Adele (Duteau) **113** 299
Adeline **105** 224
Adelle J. (Conn) **87** 88
Agnes **65** 327 329 **66** 69
  81 291
Albert **82** 270
Albert F. **51** 377
Albert K. **90** 107
Alexander **61** 43 **68** 315
Alexander F. **117** 210
Alexander S. **117** 210
Alfred **101** 68
Alice **66** 69 74 75 **74** 215
  128 285
Alice (Cunningham)
  93 116
Allan E. **97** 49
Almira (Cole) **124** 18
Almira Nourse **75** 260
Althea Electa
  (Spreadbury)
  (Vancore) **86** 364
Amanda E. **77** 179
Amanda G. **117** 210
Amanda M. **116** 123
Amanda Mason (Chase)
  88 27
Amelia Maria (Hannum)
  90 259
Amity **67** 94
Amity (Fessenden) **89**
  100 **111** 160
Amos **113** 39 **124** 18
  144 223
Amy **89** 108 **127** 121
Amy A. **118** 190
Amy P. **117** 209
Ancilla **81** 321
Andrew **86** 78 **110** 283
  114 127 **145** 28
Angelina **98** 359
Ann **51** 74 **55** 146 **58** 404
  59 284 **61** 323 **68** 217
  73 139 **81** 448 **105** 268
  110 283 **111** 71 **121** 117
  126 144 **133** 187 **136** 79
Ann B. **115** 171
Ann E. **116** 46
Ann Eliza **96** 92
Ann Frances (Hardon)
  88 299
Ann Jane **69** 34
Ann Jenckes (Vose)
  (Lewis) **120** 7
Ann Maria (Chase) **87** 250
Ann Sarah **74** 14
Ann Stocker **60** 195
Ann T. **84** 31
Ann W. **117** 210
Anna **51** 49 **53** 128 **56** 318
  61 238 **74** 243 **78** 406
  86 133 134 142 143 **90**
  290 **91** 373 **93** 231 **120** 5
  126 217 **127** 288
Anna (Hathaway) **122** 198
Anna (Hodgkins) **97** 260

PIERCE *cont'd*
Anna (Sanderson)
  127 289
Anna A. **131** 237
Anna Carey **120** 5
Anna Lydia **89** 99 100
Anna Lydia (Pierce) **89** 99
Anna Maria (Billings)
  94 56
Anna Statia (Carroll)
  145 27
Anne **56** 255 **68** 310 **77** 194
  97 261 **104** 4 **111** 256
  112 43
Annes **132** 21 **146** 268
Anney **128** 303
Annie **88** 133
Annie (Bancroft) **97** 127
Annie (Kendig) **97** 127
Annie Elizabeth **96** 33 53
Annie G. **77** 56
Annie L. **84** 31
Annie L. (Sise) **83** 301 302
Annie Lawton **80** 225
Annie M. **69** 315
Anson **76** 177
Anthony **55** 443 **89** 99
  100 264 **111** 71 158 **113**
  299
Antoinette Louise
  (Bancroft) **97** 127
Antrace **115** 174 **116** 46
Apama **70** 179
Arthur **69** 166 **78** 334
Arthur E. **93** 48
Arthur Wilson **83** 244
Arthur Winslow **59** xlviii
  61 xxxiii **64** v xiii **65** v
  66 v **67** viii xiii xxx **68**
  vii **69** vii **70** vii **71** vii
  72 vii **73** vii **74** vii **77**
  75 v vii xi **76** v vi **77** v
  vi viii **78** 192 193 339 **79**
  105 **81** 109 **82** 221 249
  84 204 85 177 **89** 99 137
  190 **90** 122
Arthur Winslow (Mrs.)
  77 322 **78** 206 **89** 101
Asa **57** 291-293 **87** 341
  115 234 **141** 11
Ashbel Fenton **89** 264
Atkins **116** 256
Aubrey Roger **92** 294
Augusta Shapleigh
  95 325
Augustus **93** 61 **94** 43
Augustus C. **92** 319
Azriakim **73** 213 **129** 63
  138 25-29 31
Bailey **78** 333
Barbara **75** lv **89** 99
Barnum B. **69** 335
Bartlett **114** 285
Basil Charles (Mrs.)
  88 299
Bela **92** 294
Belinda **98** 355
Benjamin **51** 74 **54** 86 286
  55 374 **57** lviii 318 355
  58 381 **59** 247 284 **60** 40
  61 238 **65** 275 280 **68**

PIERCE *cont'd*

317 **73** 268 272 **74** 41 **75**
259 **78** 333 **80** 135 136
255 **82** 314 **83** 15 223 **85**
10 **90** 231 234 238 241
249 **91** 332 **92** 293 **96**
279 **102** 79 237 **107** 96
111 71 **116** 46 124 **118**
329 **124** 80 **125** 62 102
241 243 **127** 186 **129** 60
164 167 269 363 368 369
136 34 248 325 **138** 115
117 **139** 105 **141** 7 11 16
144 215 216 218 219 221
145 27 28 296
Benjamin Clark **115** 179
Benjamin Osgood **78** 287
Benjamin S. **116** 46
Benjamin Ward **145** 28
Benoni **127** 228
Bethiah **55** 91 **62** 66 **76** 244
113 34 41 **140** 262
Betsey **70** 349 **78** 333 **80**
146 **88** 24 32 **94** 55 **99**
133 **106** 223 **124** 18 **148**
274
Betsey (Chase) **87** 256
Betsey (Cheever) **85** 130
Betsey (Field) **103** 308
Betsey (McKay) **124** 80
Betsey H. (Horton)
123 199
Bettina **64** xlvii
Betty **70** 31 226 **91** 373
Blount Coleman **122** 126
Borradill **70** 228
Bradford Hendrick **67**
xxxiv **74** xxviii **90** 127
113 59 231
Bridget **55** 62 64 **136** 306
Bridget (Bryant) (Brown)
(Butman) **137** 337
Bukey **78** 333
Caesar **71** 133
Caleb **60** 189 **74** 65 **78** 333
87 325 **129** 167
Caleb S. **138** 322
Calista **87** 7
Calvin **103** 299 **115** 123
129 262 265 **138** 322
Candace **60** 402
Carlos Thornton **92** 146
Caroline **57** 291-293 **62**
lxxi **76** xlv **78** 316 334
Caroline Augusta **78** 293
Caroline Frances (Hersey)
92 356
Caroline Lucina **78** 202
101 114 **102** 127 142
Caroline Lucinda **102** 142
Caroline M. **92** 165
Carrie G. **92** 62
Catherine **62** lxxi 130 **78**
334 **82** 52 **103** 161 **111**
80 **112** 297 **120** 5
Catherine (Beeman)
84 447
Catherine (Boyd) **112** 297
Catherine Wilson **97** 127
Cecilia Walker **122** 125
126

PIERCE *cont'd*

Celia Ann (Gorton) **138**
281 282
Chalmers Addison
95 147
Charity **56** 79 **78** 333 **84**
428 **129** 167
Charity (Howard) **129**
269 369
Charles **69** 30 **73** 139 **76** 43
86 232 **96** 344 **110** 317
111 80 **115** 320 **125** 100
128 41
Charles D. **91** 332
Charles F. **64** 331
Charles Frederic **77** 187
Charles H. **92** 293 294
116 123
Charles Henry **75** 248 **78**
334 428
Charles J. **88** 244
Charles M. **77** 179
Charles Morgan **57** 360
Charles Sanders **136** 325
Charles Sprague **80** 334
81 222 **92** 293 295 **93**
143
Charles Stephen **88** 24
Charlotte **58** 347 **68** 318
73 213 **81** 291
Charlotte A. **87** 7 **88** 328
109 7
Charlotte Ann **86** 345
Chartley **88** 124 125
Chauncey **88** 24
Chester **62** 131
Chester (Mrs.) **120** 41-43
Chloe **88** 127
Chloe (Chase) **87** 258
Choice Mason **96** 18
Christopher **66** 72
128 215
Christopher Columbus
57 360
Clara **69** 38 **76** 155
Clara May **89** 116
Clarence E. **60** 89 279
80 225
Clarence Frost **90** 137
Clarissa **91** 373
Clarissa (Williams)
92 294
Clarissa Baldwin **57** 358
Clarke **125** 34
Clementina B. **67** 358 359
Clothier **51** 74 **87** 258 **88**
27 107 **137** 149
Comfort (Chase) **88** 27
Comfort M. **116** 46
Constance (Heffenger)
83 431 438
Constant **87** 338
Cordelia **68** 158
Cornelius C. **74** 14
Curtis **74** 41
Cynthia **115** 174
Cynthia R. B. **116** 125
Cyrus **95** 357
Czarina (Dexter) **126** 208
Damaris **104** 263
Damaris (Swift) **104** 263

PIERCE *cont'd*

Daniel **51** 472 **53** 239 **60**
190 **61** 396 **63** 168 170
64 34 **68** 219 311 **70** 7
349 **71** 143 222 **74** 42
129 **81** 448 449 **82** 52
320 413 **88** 244 **89** 100
275 **96** 33 **97** 144 260
274 **99** 80 **102** 235 **103**
308 **111** 70-72 80 **112** 59
113 39 **115** 320 **118** 330
121 52 **124** 97 **125** 93 95
127 115 186 225 **128**
304 **129** 54 62 **148** 148
David **51** 74 **55** 91 402 **60**
40 **62** 66 **63** 273 **64** 85
65 221 **73** 259 **74** 261
76 244 **87** 251 341 **89**
115 **90** 88 **97** 395 **111**
321 **120** 167 **140** 69
David N. **62** 129
Dean **87** 256
Deborah **51** 74 **54** 286 **57**
282 **61** 74 **73** 270 **102** 12
103 298
Deborah (Arey) **87** 7
Deborah (Chase) **88** 109
Deborah (Wood) **89** 264
Delia **136** 79
Deliverance **60** 247 **63** 152
Desire **116** 123
Desire (Case) **144** 305
Dexter Daniel **77** 185
Dilley **144** 224
Dilly (Ford) **119** 256
Dolly **74** 261
Dorcas **99** 58 **140** 236
Dorothy (Pike) **121** 164
Drusilla **73** 138
Duty J. **125** 236
E. W. **53** 431 **57** xxii **111**
176 245 **123** 44
Earl **124** 80
Ebenezer **51** 74 **56** 79 **57**
lxii **59** 146 148 **60** 39 350
68 222 **71** 157 165 299
303 **82** 319 **84** 415 **89**
108 **129** 63
Ebenezer Munroe **89** 100
Ebenezer W. **104** 5 **111**
159 **119** 109 **144** 212
Ebenezer Weaver **57** xlii
lxii **64** 327 **65** 151 **87**
209 **99** 14
Edgar (Mrs.) **92** 356
Edith **83** 233
Edith B. **83** 435 438
Edith Evelyn **134** 280
Edith M. **69** 30
Edmund **74** 42
Edward **51** 94 98 370 **53**
185 **68** 229 232 312 **73**
144 **103** 308 **129** 55
Edward Allen (Mrs.)
100 112
Edward D. (Mrs.) **77** 323
78 206
Edward Huguenin **85**
197 **87** 386 **88** 87 175
Edward L. **55** 224
Edward Lillie **54** xli **63**

PIERCE *cont'd*
xxi **75** xxv 155 **84** 181
90 124 **96** 154 **110** 63
Edward Peter **113** 299
Edward Rumford **92** 319
Edwin P. **116** 123
Edwin W. **102** 288
Edwin Willis **87** 174 **89**
264 283 **90** 141
Elbridge **57** 252
Elbridge Bancroft **97** 127
Elbridge G. **84** 31
Elbridge Gerry **56** 75 79
93 85 **132** 220
Eleanor **75** 205 **82** 270
108 225 **115** 178
Eleanor H. D. **109** 78
Eli **108** 240
Eliakim **56** 33
Elias **123** 232
Elias D. (Mrs.) **103** 155
Elihu **123** 25 26 28 29
Elijah **78** 333 **116** 123
144 224
Eliphal T. **115** 172
Eliphalet **73** 259 **104** 244
Elisha **51** 74 **57** 282
Eliza **69** 315 **82** 296 299
87 104 **88** 152 248 **123**
232 **132** 75
Eliza (Brewster) **96** 390
Eliza (Hathaway) **134** 204
205
Eliza (Lear) **124** 62
Eliza (Smith) **97** 222
Eliza (Young) **138** 322
Eliza A. **115** 177 **116** 124
125
Eliza C. **107** 202
Eliza Jane **75** 205 **77** 188
Eliza O. **90** 336 **91** 25
Eliza Oliver **90** 241
Eliza P. **69** 315
Eliza S. **51** 369
Eliza Shattuck **93** 61
Elizabeth **51** 55 74 299 304
52 81 **54** 222 286 **55** 315
402 443 **56** 33 79 255
319 **57** 111 223 **59** 148
289 **60** 158 **61** 153 **62**
272 **63** 253 **66** 69 146
147 298 299 305 316 **67**
13 105 246 **68** 234 **70**
225 309 310 **73** 147 148
264 306 **74** 229 **75** 199
76 220 222 **78** 69 187
308 309 416 **79** 35 439
80 28 **81** 448 449 **82** 52
89 94 206 208 217 290
296 315 **83** 10 **87** 300 **89**
99 **92** 244 **93** 232 263
325 **94** 378 **97** 333 **98**
359 **99** 253 **100** 69 238
101 72 **103** 298 **106** 94
107 27 **110** 279 283 **111**
70 71 158-160 194 **114**
129 **116** 79 80 **121** 250
125 25 27 **127** 10 186
221 **131** 207 **133** 322
136 58 **137** 149 **144** 223
145 27

PIERCE *cont'd*
Elizabeth (Bollom)
100 304
Elizabeth (Bowers)
120 167
Elizabeth (Chase) **87** 338
Elizabeth (Chever) **92** 12
Elizabeth (Clark) **125** 104
Elizabeth (Cole) **106** 94
Elizabeth (Fessenden)
141 11
Elizabeth (Gifford)
134 312
Elizabeth (Hanks) **86** ⌐
Elizabeth (Hubbard) **87** 7
Elizabeth (Newcomb)
(Morton) **99** 192
Elizabeth (Oliver) **125** 100
Elizabeth (Pappoon)
83 10
Elizabeth (Pierce)
(Whittemore) (Foster)
106 94
Elizabeth (Rand) **107** 253
Elizabeth (Smith) **89** 99
93 231 **111** 70 **113** 299
Elizabeth (Southard)
102 142
Elizabeth (Wheeler)
104 244
Elizabeth (Wilcox) **92** 294
Elizabeth Ann **76** 272
Elizabeth Brown **62** lxxv
Elizabeth Carroll **93** 85
132 220
Elizabeth D. **53** 207
Elizabeth H. **88** 337
Elizabeth M **145** 296
Elizabeth Margaret
(Cooper) (Wolcott)
(Spooner) **97** 49
Elizabeth Tolman **68** 316
Elizabth (Bowers) **120** 166
Elkanah **117** 90
Ellen **62** lxxiv lxxv
Ellen A. (Dodge) **89** 241
Ellen Brown **84** 447
Ellen Maria (Bliven)
77 185
Ellen Maria Theresa **66**
lxxv **75** lv **81** 346
Elmira **96** 126
Elmira A. **98** 79
Elmore Allen **63** 301 **67**
302 **68** xxxii
Elsie **78** 339 **108** 76
111 321
Emeline Adams **113** 231
Emily **142** 186
Emily (Dame) **104** 263
Emily Aurelia (Hannum)
90 340
Emily F. **83** 179 185
Emily Jane **78** 334
Emily Olive **90** 241
Emily R. **117** 210
Emily Ruth **89** 265
Emma **69** 34 **80** 236
Emma Frances **87** 63
Emma Julia **109** 118
Enoch E. **98** 359

PIERCE *cont'd*
Enoch F. **69** 143
Ephraim **51** 74 **58** 133 **64**
31 **69** 321 **73** 213 **108**
243 **111** 321 **129** 379
130 290 **138** 25 27-29
Erasmus **140** 236
Erasta G. / J. **119** 257
Erastus **57** 360
Erastus Lake **86** 198
Eriakim **64** 31
Ermina (Merriam)
113 231
Ernest M. **69** 30
Esther **53** 197 300 **57** 355
62 151 **70** 227 **73** 3 **74**
260 **82** 315 **83** 293 **87**
246 **97** 260 **144** 221
Esther (Hazard) **125** 241
243
Esther B. **69** 335
Esther Henrietta **105** 148
Etta **75** 260
Eunice **57** 361 **68** 310 **70**
229 230 **71** 204 **77** 319
127 186
Eunice (Brown) **127** 190
Eunice (Sanderson)
127 186
Eunice B. (Derby) **88** 381
97 229 233
Eunice D. (Fuller) **124** 18
Evelina Lewis (Brown)
111 241
Eveline Griggs
(McCurdy) **113** 231
Exercise **94** 106
Experience **60** 158 **79** 90
Ezekiel **70** 310 **86** 142
111 70 **126** 141
Ezra **88** 24
Ezra Sanford **102** 142
F. B. **52** 52 53
F. C. **56** 409 **61** 395 **99** 309
114 206
F. Horatio **116** 53
Fanny **131** 157
Feroline Walley **79** 409
85 460 **95** 170
Florence Ethel **86** 200
Foster **84** 447
Frances **82** 270 **102** 26
Frances (Judkins) **134** 280
Frances M. **84** 31
Frances Mary **134** 150 180
Frances Priscilla **62** lxxv
Frances Temple (Cordis)
136 79
Francis **51** 397 **57** 293 **74**
179 **81** 291 449 **124** 11
Francis M. **75** 205
Francis Marshall **57** 361
Frank A. **116** 46
Frank N. **116** 125
Frankie **116** 123
Franklin **53** 157 **54** 453
57 293 **72** lv **77** 270 **84**
132 **86** 364 **118** 329 **136**
67 167 **146** 274
Frederick **89** 263 **113** 231
Frederick Beech **54** xxxix

PIERCE *cont'd*
  111 159
  Frederick Clifton **51** 93
    96 **52** 278 285 287 **54**
    109 123 124 **56** 98 **64**
    185 335 **84** 427 **86** 406
    91 373 **98** 362 **111** 70 71
    158 160 **113** 197-199 203
    211 212 **114** 96 **124** 18
    125 25 **144** 305 324 **148**
    309
  Frederick Emery **69** xxxv
    90 128
  Frederick Newton
    62 lxxv
  G. Frederick (Mrs.) **82**
    220 221 **83** 227
  G. G. **78** 339
  Gardiner **57** lxiii
  Gardiner M. **116** 124
  George **58** 230 **61** 74 **62** 76
    63 343 **66** 33 **68** 237 315
    69 10 12 **75** 202 **77** 56
    81 449 **82** 52 296 300 **88**
    109 381 **91** 373 **93** 232
    97 229 233 **111** 80 194
    115 320 **125** 290 **128**
    250 293 **138** 281 282
    141 11
  George (Mrs.) **92** 134
  George A. **75** 205
  George A. O. (Mrs.)
    93 116
  George Albert **78** 334
    82 270
  George Augustus
    105 148
  George B. **89** 241
  George Francis **75** 260
  George H. **125** 243
  George Hartwell **113** 231
  George L. (Mrs.) **85** 184
  George W. **116** 52 124
  George Washington
    124 18
  George Willis **89** 264 265
  Georgianna Virginia
    (Brown) **95** 325
  Georgianna Willard
    109 187
  Geraldine **92** 294
  Giles **66** 27 28 **125** 238
    127 221 **129** 54 **137** 154
    144 305
  Godfrey **116** 46
  Grace Estelle **69** 30
  Grace M. **68** 386
  Green **100** 238 304 **140** 234
  H. B. **121** 30
  H. C. **111** 158
  Hall **76** 39
  Hannah **52** 52 **57** 102 **59**
    247 **62** lxxiv 151 **64** 146
    152 **67** 206 **68** 226 229
    315 **69** 38 **73** 67 90 259
    74 65 66 262 **75** 205 259
    78 414 **81** 303 449 **82** 89
    283 296 **87** 7 **88** 119 120
    332 **90** 228 **93** 232 275
    97 261 **100** 31 **104** 47
    108 83 **111** 80 **113** 33 40

PIERCE *cont'd*
  115 282 **116** 256 **128** 41
    186 187 190 191 **134** 252
    136 304-306 **141** 11 **144**
    202
  Hannah (Badlam) **141** 7
    11 16
  Hannah (Bowers) **125** 62
  Hannah (Briggs) **88** 119
    125 127
  Hannah (Brown) **113** 231
  Hannah (Choate) **99** 294
  Hannah (Johnson) **124** 11
  Hannah (Lewis) **124** 18
  Hannah (Lopez) **126** 141
  Hannah (Mason) **128** 41
  Hannah (Munroe) **89** 264
  Hannah (Smith) **92** 294
  Hannah C. **88** 244
  Hannah Clapp **78** 102
  Hannah D. **77** 151
  Hannah Elizabeth **75** 205
  Hannah Francis **93** 275
  Hannah Jane **78** 334
    82 270
  Hannah P. **100** 167
  Hannah Phillips **116** 53
  Hannah Pitts **86** 452
  Hannah S. **115** 259
    116 124
  Hardy **80** 111 **93** 398
    100 63
  Harlan Ashley **57** 359
  Harold Fisher **85** 197
  Harriet **57** 292 **76** 244 **78**
    397 **84** 31 **90** 50 **92** 244
    128 278
  Harriet (Bass) **125** 236
  Harriet Green (Carver)
    87 7 **88** 328 **109** 7
  Harriet Maria **78** 334
  Harriet Pitts **83** 209 **86**
    232 452 **100** 167
  Harris **128** 278
  Harry R. **80** 102 209
  Harvey Cushman **91** 97
    100 112 **111** 159 **141** 11
  Hattie **79** 131
  Hattie Langley **77** 187
  Hayward **62** lxxi **78** 333
    334 **82** 270 **129** 152 155
    161-167 169 170 250-253
    256 260 262 265 269 365
  Helen (Spencer) **124** 18
  Helen F. **91** 108
  Helen Grace (Adams)
    113 231
  Henry **88** 109 **97** 49 260
    111 159
  Henry Alexander **57** 361
  Henry Augustus **75** 260
  Henry B. **52** 483
  Henry L. **71** xliii **79** 236
  Henry Lillie **51** 369 370
  Henry Ward **145** 27 28
  Hephzibah **115** 234
  Hepzibah **110** 283 **144** 215
  Hepzibah (Lord) **96** 344
  Herbert **128** 5
  Herbert Benjamin **96** 161
  Hester (Spencer) **123** 262

PIERCE *cont'd*
  Hilkiah **88** 119 125 127
  Hiram **69** 30
  Holden W. **83** 301 303
  Hope **116** 256
  Hopestill (Hollaway)
    104 25
  Horatio **87** 7
  Howard Richards (Mrs.)
    106 126
  Hugh **64** 337 **101** 12
  Humphrey **115** 233 234
  I. **91** 332
  Ichabod **96** 63 64 **115** 174
    116 46
  Ichabod B. **115** 171
  Ida Estelle **57** lxiii
  Irene T. **57** lxiii
  Isaac **56** 90 **57** 265 **58** 347
    68 227 **84** 153 **87** 128
    250 **88** 285 **93** 398 **100**
    63 **101** 72 **115** 178 **124**
    17 18 **127** 186 289 **128**
    41 126 **137** 248 **140** 236
    144 223
  Isaac B. **116** 53
  Isaac Newton **59** xlviii
    62 xlix lxxiv lxxv
  Isaac Withington **75** 248
  Isabel **51** 223 **62** lxxiv
    105 246 **108** 166
  Isabel (Chase) **87** 335
  Isabel (Witherspoon)
    113 231
  Isabella **145** 27
  Isabelle V. **78** 206
  Israel **63** 379 **74** 41 **81** 303
    82 211 316 319 **114** 291
    127 304 **128** 38
  Israel Andrew **115** 234
  J. F. **93** 48
  J. Gilbert **78** 197
  Jacob **55** 443 **59** 280 **74** 31
    89 99 **124** 11 12 **132** 113
  Jacob Willard **58** xciii
  Jael **51** 74 **87** 129
  James **52** 52 **54** 166 **55** 443
    57 111 223 60 39 **67** 246
    68 220 317 **69** 315 **75**
    248 259 **82** 216 **100** 31
    277 **103** 303 **104** 263
    111 80 **115** 174 177 320
    128 304 **141** 11
  James Bradford **90** 364
  James C. **69** 315
  James F. **105** 124 **116** 123
  James Goodright **134** 335
  James H. **90** 333 **115** 296
  James Hamilton **90** 241
  James L. **125** 33
  James Luther **88** 27
  James Mills **58** 217
  James Morgan **83** 233
  James N. **116** 125
  James P. **116** 46
  James R. **96** 206 208 **97**
    207 **100** 327 **103** 150
    104 21 114 262 **105** 154
    111 80
  James Ralph **94** 139
  James W. **94** 56

PIERCE *cont'd*
Jane **53** 375 **73** 139 229 **78**
333 334 **111** 80 **115** 296
116 123
Jane (Carr) **114** 127
Jane (Foss) **146** 333
147 183
Jane (Hayward) **129** 164
Jane (M'Kaye) **111** 80
Jane (McCoy) **104** 263
Jane B. **75** 199
Jane E. **75** 205
Jane S. **87** 7
Jean **73** 259
Jemima (Whittemore)
107 253
Jennie (Hopkins) **103** 308
Jerathmeel **51** 300 **63** 253
132 89
Jerediah **104** 263 **111** 80
Jeremiah **82** 52 **91** 373
104 39
Jeremiah W. **80** 224 225
Jerusha **57** 318 **81** 449
Jesse **51** 369 **94** 247 **103**
235 297 **124** 17 18 **128**
285
Jessie Landreth Osgood
92 146
Joan **111** 206 208
Joanna **57** lxii **88** 280
114 290 **115** 282
Joanna (Bartlett) **96** 33
Joanna (French) **145** 28
Joanna (Gerrish) **97** 260
Joanna (Horton) **88** 24
Joanne **115** 282
Job **129** 54 **138** 31
Joel **69** 38
Johan **86** 78
John **51** 74 223 **52** 449 **53**
216 375 **54** 409 **55** 311
315 443 **56** 126 **57** 67 **59**
149 154 **60** 39 40 307 **61**
323 324 326 **62** xc 305
306 **63** lxxix **64** lx **65**
45 **66** 35 37 69 187 **67**
147-153 **68** 216 217 219
220 222 224 226 227 233
236 238 310 312 313 315
317 318 320 **69** 121 124
221 **70** 179 226 315 **73**
147 150 224 259 264 314
74 25 **75** 149 **76** 30 37
220-222-224 375 **97** 312
98 239 **99** 9 **100** 63 **102**
97 **103** 297 **104** 4 **105**
113 211 246 279 280 **108**
7 **109** 160 240 **110** 160
234 **111** 65 70-72 80 158-
160 **113** 291 292 299
114 117 165 **115** 234
320 **123** 260 **124** 313
125 25 27 290 **127** 221
128 135 304 **129** 53 **134**
252 **140** 69 236 **141** 11
31 **142** 20 22 **144** 255
147 243
John (Mrs.) **79** 409
John A. **90** 259

PIERCE *cont'd*
John Appleton Prentiss
75 lxxx **89** 100
John B. **109** 160 240 **110**
160 234 314 **111** 72 160
142 186
John Burney **78** 447 **79**
203 **113** 59 299
John C. **117** 210
John D. **76** 37 **91** 382
92 206
John Dorr **92** 256
John Flavel **68** 312
John Frank **117** 218
John Gerrish **74** 216
John Howard **104** 145
John L. **73** 277 **74** 66
John Morgan **83** 126
John Randolph **104** 263
John T. **115** 172 174
John Webb **125** 290
John Winslow **89** 99 100
Johnson **81** 449
Jonas **68** 312 **75** lxxx **83**
166 168 **89** 99 100 263
111 70 **113** 299 **121** 92
93 **127** 190 289
Jonas (Mrs.) **121** 92
Jonathan **51** 74 **60** 39 40
62 272 273 **65** 221 68
216 310 311 313 315 318
69 13 **78** 333 **81** 448 **93**
231 **105** 300 **108** 166
111 70 **120** 193 264 **125**
220 **129** 269 369 370
134 205 **143** 348 **144**
219 **147** 281
Jonathan D. **116** 53
Jonathan E. **115** 178
Jonathan Pelton **62** 272
Joseph **55** 443 **66** 26 28
70 31 **74** 41 **82** 52 317
413 **84** 358 **87** 7 388 **89**
99 264 **91** 373 **92** 54 **93**
398 **94** 44 **96** 126 **99** 58
192 **100** 63 **101** 72 **106**
268 **111** 71 72 **113** 299
115 234 320 **116** 125
121 52 **123** 199 201 **127**
115 185 **137** 337 **138** 25
29 31 **140** 236 **144** 201
220 221 224
Joseph B. **116** 125
Joseph H. **92** 256 **140** 236
Joseph Hardy **136** 79
Joseph M. **126** 206
Joseph W. **83** 301 302
Josephine **75** 205
Josephine Ada Hortense
82 270
Joshua **51** 45 467 468 472
59 315 **67** 105 68 94 69
301 **73** 145 **74** 261 **94**
356 **97** 260 **104** 25 **121**
164 **124** 18 **127** 186 **128**
134 **138** 31 **141** 11 16
Joshua B. **103** 304
Joshua Kent **100** 238
Joshua Winslow **83** 431
438
Josiah **51** 238 **64** 131 **97**

PIERCE *cont'd*
293 **103** 303 **104** 242
111 241 **118** 20 117 220
125 223 290
Josiah Gale **124** 18
Josiah S. **115** 172 174
Judith **59** 280 **78** 333 **89** 99
122 198 **128** 313
Judith (Bailey) **129** 164
Judith (Clark) **87** 388
Judith S. **90** 57
Julia **78** 334
Julia (Lougee) **118** 192
Julia A. **116** 122 123
Julia A. (Swan) **138** 322
Julian **66** 72
Juliet **57** 291
June **124** 18
Justus **54** 271
Kate Lucy **57** xxxv **88**
376 378 383 **96** 154 **99**
68 153
Katharine **82** 270
Katharine (Reed) **103** 235
Keziah **70** 84
Keziah (Wheeler) **107** 71
Langdon (Mrs.) **109** 78
Langworthy **66** 28
128 132
Laura **136** 79
Laura J. **76** 43
Lavinia **72** 105
Lawrance **128** 132
Lemuel **60** 39 **68** 224 320
71 134 139 **74** 41 **118**
329
Lena Rose (Webber)
92 294
Letitia **73** 217
Levi **54** 317 **66** 11 **115** 234
121 177 **124** 62 80 **140**
57
Leviah (Chase) **87** 325
Levina Eliza **98** 359
Lewis **60** 40 **68** 317
75 199 260
Lewis Franklin **75** 260
Liberty **98** 359
Lillian **98** 10
Lily **141** 11
Linda **66** 243
Lizzie E. **75** 100
Loenza Abigail **57** 360
Lois **68** 317 **71** 157 158
278 281 **128** 119
London **127** 148
Lorraine McElroy **122**
161 167 **123** 189
Louis **71** 298
Louis K. **116** 53
Louisa **69** 321 **82** 270 **115**
320 **119** 257
Louisa (Chase) **87** 341
Louisa (Wyman) **123** 319
Louisa B. **80** 255
Louisa B. (Chase) **88** 107
Louisa L. **60** 103
Louisa R. **142** 186
Lucia (Burgess) **136** 248
Lucilla **78** 334
Lucinda **58** 381 **68** 330 **90**

PIERCE *cont'd*
241 **119** 65
Lucinda (Buckman)
  89 264
Lucinda (Chase) **88** 109
Lucretia **126** 212
Lucretia Ann **87** 388
Lucy **66** 13 **68** 319 **70** 122
  227 **73** 213 **83** 489 **97**
  293 **115** 134 174 **116** 46
Lucy (Graves) **110** 234
  113 299
Lucy B. **116** 46
Lucy B. (Appleton) **90** 333
Luella P. **69** 30
Luman O. **91** 332
Luther **72** 105 **78** 333 **103**
  297 **115** 296 320 **116**
  123 **122** 47
Lydia **51** 74 **63** 337 **66** 128
  70 226 355 **74** 249 **75**
  248 **76** 157 **77** 230 **81**
  449 **82** 52 **84** 415 **87** 337
  89 59 **92** 359 **98** 359
  107 71 72 **113** 31 38 **115**
  320 **121** 244 **124** 18 **125**
  216 290 **137** 361 **144**
  198 201 202 224
Lydia (Chadwick) **124** 17
Lydia (Chase) **87** 341
  88 11 110
Lydia (Farrar) **113** 231
Lydia (Fernside) **144** 201
Lydia (Frances) **125** 220
Lydia (Gale) **124** 17
Lydia (Hartwell) **134** 252
Lydia (Hersey) **137** 149
Lydia (Howland) **134** 335
Lydia (Morgan) **123** 260
Lydia (Perry) **115** 282
Lydia (Prentiss) **89** 100
Lydia (Sheppard) **92** 294
Lydia (Williams) **97** 260
Lydia H. (Bancroft)
  124 18
Lydia J. **68** 94
Lydia Paine (Ray) **78** 206
  89 101
Lydlia (Gale) **124** 17
Lyman J. **87** 88
M. A. **125** 244
Maggie N. (Hunt)
  122 126
Mahala **80** 28
Marcia **74** 312 **136** 79
Marcus **102** 288
Marcy A. **138** 281
Margaret **56** 410 **60** 350
  67 105 **73** 140 **74** 28 **80**
  357-360 363 **81** 323 **82**
  64 **92** 34 **111** 159 **115**
  296 **129** 55 **147** 243 244
Margaret (Eldered)
  (Bullock) **138** 284
Margaret (Gates) **121** 52
Margaret (Law) **91** 263
Margaret (Slater) **89** 108
Margaret (Ward) **145** 27
  28
Margaret Barton **89** 265

PIERCE *cont'd*
Margaret Knicker-
  bocker (Clark) **85** 194
Margaret R. **77** 178
Margaret Williamson
  82 270
Margery **131** 27 **133** 187
Maria **71** 204 **76** lxxvii
  94 44 **116** 46 **135** 318
Maria Abbot (Williams)
  89 264
Maria C. **116** 46
Maria Louisa (Chase)
  89 263
Marian **78** 334
Marie Adele **113** 299
Marietta **75** xxxvi lxxx
Marilla **69** 30
Marion Williams **80** 208
  83 371 383 **84** 186 **85**
  214 **86** 214 **101** 24 68
  128
Mark W. **96** 227
Marley **59** 289
Marmaduke **75** 223 225
Marshall **57** 358-361 **111**
  194 **118** 192
Martha **51** 74 **52** 450 **55**
  312 **56** 31 36 **57** 318 **58**
  129 **59** 280 **82** 52 509 **84**
  428 **89** 99 **101** 72 **115**
  234 **124** 11 18 **138** 322
Martha (Adams) **129** 363
Martha (Beale) **95** 357
Martha (Freeman)
  (Hopkins) **104** 218
Martha (Gifford) **130** 290
Martha (Gilman) **102** 79
Martha (Godding)
  127 186
Martha (Graves) **124** 17
  127 186
Martha (Holland) **105** 27
Martha (Nutting) **138** 322
Martha (Rich) **83** 401
Martha Learned (Locke)
  84 452
Martha Richardson
  (Williams) **101** 68
Martha S. **73** 259
Martha S. (Bunting)
  116 256
Martin **87** 256 **107** 71
  120 7 11
Mary **51** 49 74 299 304 **54**
  271 286 **55** 311 312 376
  443 **57** 282 353 355 358
  359 **58** 230 **59** 146 148
  149 247 **60** 195 247 **62**
  lxxiv 272 **63** 37 46 250
  379 **64** lvii 14 **66** 13 134
  269 **68** 158 313 **70** 31
  176 225 232 **73** 145 259
  74 34 41 **75** 199 202 223
  259 **76** 177 77 194 **78** 67
  294 301 334 **79** 50 **81**
  432 449 **82** 89 94 208
  294 296 509 **83** 18 36
  161 **86** 222 **87** 90 **88** 32
  338 **91** 373 **92** 244 **93**
  231 **94** 55 **95** 357 **96** 385

PIERCE *cont'd*
  97 146 **100** 69 164 242
  101 274 **102** 21 **106** 70
  109 4 306 **110** 283 **111**
  65 228 232 **114** 127 **115**
  42 179 **116** 46 **120** 193
  122 126 **125** 25 218 **126**
  22 204 **127** 253 **128** 134
  135 **131** 211 **133** 264
  137 337 **140** 69 **143** 348
  144 221 **145** 27 28
Mary (Adams) **127** 289
Mary (Bale) **110** 283
Mary (Bancroft) **103** 64
Mary (Booth) **129** 363
Mary (Burney) **113** 299
Mary (Chadwick) **124** 11
Mary (Chase) **87** 251
Mary (Curtis) **114** 291 292
Mary (Dickens) **125** 290
Mary (Ellis) **120** 193
Mary (Gates) **120** 264
Mary (Hanks) (Young)
  86 24
Mary (Lobdell) **143** 348
Mary (Miriam) **125** 290
Mary (Proctor) **113** 231
Mary (Sanders) **127** 252
Mary (Starr) **94** 244
Mary (Stowe) **84** 415
Mary (Stowell) **125** 223
Mary (Tallman) **85** 73
  111 65
Mary (Underwood)
  89 100
Mary (White) **83** 301 303
Mary (Whitney) **108** 243
Mary A. **69** 143
Mary Adaline (Thrasher)
  90 364
Mary Agatha (Day)
  (Greeley) **75** lv **94** 139
Mary Ame **75** lxxx
Mary Ann **78** 334 **111** 194
  118 318 **119** 144
Mary Ann (Chase) **88** 117
Mary Ann (Etheridge)
  125 290
Mary Anne (Locke)
  89 100
Mary B. **58** cxiii **87** 300
  301
Mary C. **91** 40
Mary Cone (Pitkin)
  134 150
Mary D. **117** 285
Mary Dennis **126** 65
Mary E. **80** 223 225
Mary Eliza **87** 18
Mary Elizabeth **78** 428
  83 181 185 **96** 390 **136**
  79
Mary Ellen **66** lxxv **74**
  lxviii **81** 346 **89** 115
Mary Elmira **87** 7
Mary Emma **69** 143
Mary Esther **97** 77
Mary F. **78** 197
Mary Frances **51** 377 **54**
  xxxix **55** 357 **56** xxxii
  114 **74** 25 **75** 248

PIERCE *cont'd*

Mary Hunter **125** 239
Mary J. **68** 94
Mary K. (Stevens) **90** 107
Mary L. **74** 31 **97** 223
Mary M. **74** 31
Mary Mackie **110** 225
Mary Messer **93** 61 **94** 43
Mary Moody **111** 228
Mary S. **122** 128
Mary Smith (West) **122** 126
Mary Whiting **75** 248
Maryann **140** 69
Mather **62** 20
Matthias **81** 291
May **109** 148
Mehitable **58** 230 **82** 94 **115** 234
Mehitable (Bolter) **133** 261 262
Mehitable (Carver) **103** 308
Melinda **69** 321 **73** 213
Melissa **75** 260
Melvin Webster **68** xxxv
Melvina King (Weld) **104** 263
Mercy **63** 184 **111** 194 **121** 12
Mercy (Gates) **121** 52
Mercy (Nelson) **121** 177
Mercy (Rouse) (Schreech) **137** 154
Mial **87** 335 **138** 27-29 31
Michael **51** 74 **53** 201 204 343 **55** 73 **56** 409 **76** xlvi 155 **77** 49 **84** 352 **101** 68 **119** 104 **121** 114 **127** 147 **129** 37 165 **133** 187
Miel **115** 296
Mildred Pomeroy (Midgley) **96** 288
Miranda **83** 470 **116** 53
Miriam **56** 90 **119** 130
Miriam Badlam **105** 129 **141** 6
Molly **68** 238 **73** 259 **74** 251 **76** 37 **82** 217 **88** 152
Morris **73** 259 **96** 61 63
Moses **94** 61 244 **97** 260 **115** 320
Moses C. **103** 302
Murphy **88** 262
Myra Belva **101** 123
Nabby **58** 347
Nancy **54** 317 **77** 49 **82** 296 298 **88** 11 **111** 241 **115** 174 **117** 169 **121** 92 **136** 248
Nancy Abigail **78** 334
Nancy G. **96** 92
Nancy James **116** 219
Nancy S. (Peters) **126** 206
Nancy Valeria **78** 334
Nancy W. **79** 49
Naphthale **60** 38
Nathan **58** 374 **68** 158 **76** 155-157 **87** 335 336 **88** 117 **90** 53 **112** 128 **126**

PIERCE *cont'd*

216 **128** 217 **138** 29 31
Nathaniel **58** 131 **60** 307 **70** 312 **82** 413 **83** 401 **85** 124 130 455 **100** 167 329 **105** 214 278 **106** 94 **115** 179 259 **125** 93 94 **127** 221 **129** 381 383
Nathaniel (Mrs.) **92** 12
Nathaniel W. **116** 125
Nehemiah **70** 226 **86** 7 **92** 294 **106** 30 **136** 32 34
Nellie **147** 82
Nellie Theodora (Trowbridge) **87** 386
Nicholas **77** 317 **115** 320 **133** 261 262 **140** 236 328
Obadiah **51** 74 **88** 23
Olive **60** 103 **63** 269 **71** 282 **82** 94 **124** 80
Olive Lee **88** 13
Oliver **65** 79 **66** 12 **69** 30 **83** 161 **94** 55 **111** 80 **121** 223 **122** 126 128 **142** 37
Oliver M. (Mrs.) **84** 452
Oliver V. **116** 125
Orpha **103** 305
Palo Alto **123** 44
Pardon **60** 145 **129** 63
Parker Hall **75** 205
Parkman Dexter **75** lv
Patience **57** 67 **61** 323 324 **66** 58 **68** 318 **100** 329 **107** 320 **124** 80 **126** 268 **136** 248
Patience (Dobson) **87** 129
Patty **78** 180 **90** 241 **124** 18 **125** 107
Patty (Freeman) (Hopkins) **104** 218
Patty (Hamilton) **90** 231 249
Peace **55** 374 **83** 15
Peace (Thompson) **83** 15
Pelatiah **74** 262
Peleg **117** 210
Peleg F. **59** 221 222 **66** 26 **103** 208
Percy **93** 48
Perry **69** 275
Persis **51** 74 **75** 178 **88** 13 24 **121** 18 **127** 121
Persis (Rich) **84** 132
Peter **60** 195 **65** 327 329 **66** 58 298 **103** 298 **111** 159 **113** 299
Phebe **52** 52 53 101 **58** 131 **70** 226 309 **80** 225 **88** 23 **91** 373 **101** 250 **104** 118 **105** 215 **115** 172 174 **116** 125 **125** 88
Philip **85** 169 **87** 7 **88** 328 **129** 54
Philip D. **77** 178
Phineas **71** 134
Polly **62** 84 **73** 259 **84** 373 **108** 227 **111** 116 **133** 264 **136** 141 **140** 236 **144** 223 **145** 28

PIERCE *cont'd*

Polly (Brown) **125** 102
Polly Adams **79** 325 **80** 209
Portsmouth **82** 296 298
Preserved **129** 55
Priscilla **70** 228 **82** 315 **127** 221 **128** 278
Proctor **62** lxxv 271 272 **94** 62 **113** 36 38 39
Prudence **124** 80
R. **51** 226
R. Andrew **142** 388 **148** 295
Rachel **73** 150 259 **123** 97
Rachel (Francis) (Relfe) **145** 27
Ralph **122** 47
Raymond Oren **84** 31
Rebecca **51** 300 **52** 449 **57** 111 223 **63** 253 **73** 143 **87** 7 **88** 283 **106** 80 **109** 160 **113** 163 **137** 248
Rebecca (Chase) **87** 335
Rebecca (Hoar) (Snell) **142** 20
Rebecca (Hurd) **132** 89
Rebecca Ann **88** 284
Remembrance **127** 159
Reuben **119** 256
Rhoda **71** 160 282
Rhoda (Atwood) **123** 201
Richard **60** 402 **66** 69 75 **67** 151 152 370 **70** 367 **73** 274 **82** 208 **84** 427-429 431 433 **86** 415 **91** 94 **92** 297 **97** 207 **104** 84 **105** 213 215 **111** 159 **113** 290 291 **119** 17 19 **120** 193 **123** 192 **125** 185 **127** 221 **136** 216 **144** 305
Richard A. **73** 147
Richard D. **116** 315 **119** 78 **144** 5 255 **145** 259 **148** 10 67
Richard Donald **95** 147 **120** 148 **127** 257
Richard N. **76** 275
Right **116** 46
Robert **57** 351 353 **58** 404 **61** 323 **64** 225 **73** 259 **75** lv **84** 428 **86** 424 **87** 218 **89** 263 **96** 288 **99** 133 **111** 159 160
Robert Cutts **69** 197
Robert F. Y. **55** 125
Robert J. **90** 37
Robert T. **115** 171
Robert Weldon **134** 280
Robert Willard **82** 270
Roby **70** 31
Roger **72** 227
Roger Newton **94** 62
Romilla **122** 48
Rosamond **88** 82
Rosamond (Williams) **113** 299
Rosamond Williams **111** 160 **113** 299
Roscoe **62** xxxvii **68** xxxv

PIERCE *cont'd*
89 263 283 90 141
Roswell 88 110
Roswell G. 73 213
Rouse 116 46 127 221
Roxa 51 193 128 278
Roxana Taft 75 270
Roy Harvey 100 180
Rozilla (Rogers) 123 92
Rufus 78 421 96 390
138 322
Rufus W. 138 322
Ruth 51 74 59 146 62
lxxiv 71 161 282 86 348
87 286 88 244 89 275
102 267 124 80 141 339
Ruth (Bishop) 111 71
Ruth (Paige) 113 231
Ruth (Steele) 89 264
Ruth S. 90 328
Ruth Sargent 90 241
Sabin 73 259
Sally 57 293 66 11-13 69
275 76 33 39 84 370 90
241 92 171 103 235 297
105 300 112 59 113 33
40 115 320 125 108 215
216 126 205 128 38 41
147 182
Sally (Homer) 138 322
Sally (Joslin) 124 18
Sally (Rowe) 126 66
Sally (Sanderson) 128 41
Salome 115 320
Sampson 62 128
Samuel 51 74 53 73 54 287
59 82 60 39 40 158 62
lxxiv 272 332 64 371 66
12 13 68 216 217 230
232 234 236 237 239 310
315 317 70 31 71 84 157-
161 165 278 298 299 303
306 73 259 75 224 77
236 82 52 83 36 87 246
88 152 91 373 100 277
105 113 107 253 111 70
71 113 32 38 231 120
299 123 18 319 124 80
125 88 221 127 147 185
252 129 277 131 23 140
236 143 348
Samuel A. 88 244
Samuel B. 60 40
Samuel Blake 68 313
Samuel D. 73 259
Samuel G. 117 210
Samuel Henry 69 34
Samuel Shove 80 224 225
Samuel Shove (Mrs.)
80 223
Samuel Stillman 66 lxxv
75 lv 81 346
Sarah 51 302 466 55 91 56
38 57 67 265 361 58 210
211 374 59 287 60 361
61 323 62 66 272 63 46
64 xlvii 65 298 68 216
217 236 318 73 231 314
74 185 75 199 224 260
76 38 155 157 80 224 81
302 82 94 208 258 282

PIERCE *cont'd*
296 301 84 417 85 169
86 26 87 22 246 88 193
90 333 97 261 103 235
104 25 108 113 166 110
283 111 160 194 321
115 234 282 116 46 120
7 11 121 250 127 186
221 129 56 130 132 144
302 305
Sarah (Andrews) 115 233
234
Sarah (Blood) 137 248
Sarah (Champlin) 125 238
Sarah (Coffin) 97 260
Sarah (Flanders) 124 18
Sarah (Gates) (Earle)
121 223
Sarah (Gorham) 93 85
132 220
Sarah (Holland) 105 27
Sarah (Keyne) 108 114
Sarah (Lynch) 145 28
Sarah (Plummer) 89 115
Sarah (Read) 112 128
Sarah (Sanderson) 128 41
Sarah (Waste) 113 158
Sarah (West) 124 80
Sarah A. 78 184
Sarah Ann 115 174
Sarah C. (Champlin)
125 238
Sarah Celina 87 82
Sarah E. 92 341 93 48
Sarah G. 117 210
Sarah Hazard (Peabody)
86 345
Sarah Hunt (Mills)
136 325
Sarah Jane 56 79
Sarah M. (Sprague)
92 293 294
Sarah Martha 78 428
Sarah P. 117 210
Sarah W. 75 205
Seraph Amanda 69 166
Serena (Dexter) 135 158
Seth 59 315 86 294 95 365
115 282 128 278 285
Sewall 74 28
Shepard 134 150
Sibyl 51 74 110 225
Sibyl (Chase) 88 110
Silas 64 146 71 204 73 259
78 333 334 83 166 91
206 94 95 97 127 98 359
100 65 122 198 126 141
137 337
Silas Franklin 78 334
Silas H. 140 252
Simon 97 222 395
Smith 66 27
Solomon 67 94 69 124 125
75 lxxx 85 10 89 99 101
111 160
Sophia 73 267
Sophia (Anderson)
113 299
Sophia (Hersey) 92 134
Sophia (Redman) 92 134
Sophia M. 57 360

PIERCE *cont'd*
Stella Emma 90 364
Stella Louise 75 lv
Stephen 51 447 60 371
62 272 66 146 298 299
67 246 70 227 74 41 86
345 88 152 107 253 111
159 127 221 129 55 141
11
Sumner 53 207
Susan 63 254 74 263 87 7
88 23 105 300 121 93
125 238
Susan (Halstat) 125 290
Susan (Ross) 88 285
Susan (Write) 84 428 429
Susan B. (Lougee)
118 192
Susan Josephine (Barton)
89 265
Susan L. 63 273
Susan M. 84 31
Susanna 52 227 53 198
300 60 145 159 62 lxxv
271 66 10 68 317 71 159
282 76 222 82 206 84
431 87 314 89 55 95 110
101 72 113 36 38 115
178 179
Susanna (Chase) 87 256
Susanna (Newton) 94 62
Susanna (Wright) 84 431
Sylvester 70 232 71 133
139 141 128 132
Sylvia (Chase) 87 336
Tabitha 51 447 60 154
Tamsen 71 249
Tamzine H. 76 37
Temperance 56 170 123
133 129 235
Temperance (Kirby)
128 250
Teresa 113 5
Thankful 53 198 116 79
124 12
Theodocia 71 51
Thomas 51 299 447 52 81
53 94 54 222 286 55 333
443 56 318 57 351 60 39
247 62 151 63 37 68 222
316-320 70 58 59 228 73
143 266 269 74 41 81
432 448 449 82 52 316
86 349 88 152 248 96
208 105 205 224 106 94
111 159 115 172 296
127 121 128 304 129
254 363 383 131 207
136 167 140 236
Thomas C. 56 21
Thomas Clinton (Mrs.)
88 191
Thomas Dean 77 239
Thomas Raymond
59 xlviii
Timothy 67 13 70 173 309
71 140 74 66 118 270
127 16
Truman 90 340
Ursula 81 449
Val 115 174 116 124 125

PIERCE *cont'd*
Varney **113** 38 39
Vassar **75** lv
Vaynor **104** 47
Versilda **57** 288
Virginia **75** lv
Waitstill **113** 35
Waldo **62** lxxi **78** 333 334
Waldo Paine **82** 270
Waldo T. **57** 350
Waldo Treat **78** 334
Wallace Lincoln **73** 317
74 xxv **75** xxxiii lv
Wallace Lincoln (Mrs.)
94 139
Walter **125** 241
Walworth **75** lv
Warren **113** 31 38 231
Warren W. **57** 359
Warren Worthington
57 291
Wealthy **88** 127
Webb Nicholson **87** 386
Westermon **82** 290 296
Wheeler **138** 25 27-29
Wilkinson **91** 332
Will **83** 36
Willard **52** 227 **71** 135
William **51** 70 **52** 372 **55**
xix 107 **60** 39 247 **62**
lxxiv lxxv 301 **63** 140 **64**
115 **65** 44 46 221 **66** 69
187 299 **67** 246 354 356
357 **69** 363 **70** 293 316
71 133 143 **73** 259 **75**
205 **76** 38 **77** 233 274 **79**
439 440 **80** 28 **81** 321
432 **82** 94 206 208 315
86 424 **87** 272 **88** 152
89 177 **91** 124 **93** 231
275 **95** 47 129 210 390
96 208 **97** 233 267 **98** 67
102 182 **105** 112 **108**
114 **110** 283 **111** 159
175 228 232 256 **114** 83
86 117 **115** 178 234 282
123 262 **125** 104 **129** 56
61 381 **134** 313 **135** 218
140 236 **142** 113 **143** 26
145 27 28
William F. (Mrs.) **96** 191
William Frederick **77** 188
William H. **88** 248 **117** 209
William Haskell **88** 152
William Henry **75** 205
95 325
William Howard **97** 127
William Leach **115** 320
William M. **109** 131
115 320
Wilmot Grant **84** 109 190
Winfield **80** 146
Winslow S. **78** 338
Wright **116** 46 122 123
127 221
Wyat Wright **57** 359
Zachariah **115** 320
Zebulon **73** 259 **91** 263
Zilpah **78** 401
Zilpah (Adams) **94** 62
Zipporah **55** 320 345

PIERCE *cont'd*
Zoa **124** 18
Zurishaddai **58** 129 **59** 85
Pierceson *see* Pearson
Piercy *see* Percy
PIERITZ Carl Fredrick
(Mrs.) **84** 342 **85** 197
PIERMAINE
Anne **54** 196
David **54** 196
Elizabeth **54** 196
John **54** 196
Keziah **54** 196
William **54** 196
PIERPONT Peirpont
Perpont Pierpoint
Pierrepont
—— **97** 270 **118** 306
— Dr. **97** 273
Abiah M. **75** 93
Abigail **75** 89-91
Adeline **75** 95
Alfred **75** 95
Alice C. **75** 96
Alice S. **83** 25 26
Alice V. D. **112** 74
Almira **75** 95
Ammi Miles **75** 94
Andrew **75** 95
Ann **75** 93
Anna **75** 94
Anna Marie (Jay) **125** 238
Anne **75** 89
Annis **75** 91
Asahel **75** 93
Austin **75** 93
Azubah **75** 92
Bede **75** 92 94 96
Bede Eliza **75** 96
Bela **75** 96
Belina **75** 94 96
Benjamin **55** 390 **56** 287
75 89 90 92 96 **140** 236
Bethiah **75** 91 94
Betsey **75** 96
Betsey Loiza **75** 96
Byard Andrew **75** 95
Byard Barnes **75** 95
Caleb **134** 337
Caroline S. **75** 98
Celia A. **75** 96
Charles Joseph **75** 93
Charles Thomas **75** 95
Charlotte **75** 96
Chloe **75** 93
Chloe Maria **75** 93
Clorana **75** 93
Cornelia Rosette **75** 95
Croswell E. **75** 96
Daniel **75** 91 94
Daniel Hobart **75** 94
Daniel Lorenzo **75** 96
David **75** 96
Delia **75** 96
Delia Maria **75** 93
Dennis **75** 93
Desdemona **75** 93
Dorothy **75** 90
Ebenezer **58** 27 **75** 91
91 94
Edward **75** 95 97 98

PIERPONT *cont'd*
Eli **75** 91
Eliada **75** 92
Elias **75** 94
Elias Richard **75** 94
Eliza **75** 95 **100** 258
Elizabeth **55** 420 **61** 285 **75**
90-92 94 **97** 125 **100** 258
Ella J. **75** 96
Ellen Adelia **75** 96
Ellen Maria **75** 93
Elmon **75** 98
Emilia **75** 95
Emily **75** 93
Emily Cordelia **75** 93
Emily Jane **75** 93
Emily Jennet **75** 93
Emily Montague **81** 477
Enos Augustus **75** 93
Enos Austin **75** 93
Esther **75** 92-94 97
Esther Maria **75** 96
Eunetia **75** 95
Eunice **75** 92 95-98
Evelyn **61** 285 **89** 23
Ezra **75** 91 92
Ezra Alonzo **75** 93
Ezra Stiles **75** 93
Fanny T. **75** 94
Frances Ann **75** 93
Frances Edwards **89** 23
Franklin W. **75** 96
George **75** 94 96
George Rufus **75** 94
Giles **75** 90 92 97
Grace **75** 94 95
Guy **75** 98
Hannah **69** 57 **75** 90-93
95-97 **84** 224 **105** 156
Hannah Rebecca **75** 95
Harriet **75** 93 94
Harriet A. **75** 94
Harriet Ann **75** 96
Harriet B. **75** 94
Harriet Loisa **75** 93
Harriet Maria **75** 93
Harriet P. **71** 74
Helen M. **75** 98
Henry E. **125** 238
Henry L. **75** 94
Henry Stiles **75** 93
Hezekiah **67** 302 **75** 89 90
92
Hezekiah Beers **117** 315
Horace **75** 95
Isaac **75** 92
James **60** lxii **61** 285 **67**
302 70 349 **75** 89-92 95
81 129 **128** 66 **133** 110
James Edward **75** 93
James H. **83** 25 26
James N. **75** 96
Jane A. **75** 93
Jane M. **75** 94
Jared **75** 94 96
Jared Le Grand **75** 94
Jason **75** 96
Jerusha **75** 98
Joel **69** 57 **75** 92 96 97
John **52** 154 **54** 378 **58**
112 114 **61** xlviii **65**

PIERPONT *cont'd*
221 **70** 349 **75** xx 67 89
92 95 **89** 168 **99** 12 **104**
311 **124** 149 **136** 318
John Russell **75** 95
Jonathan **91** 94 **97** 125
Joseph **75** 89-91 93 94
Joseph E. **75** 93
Julia Eliza **75** 95
Julia Jay **125** 238
Juliet **97** 341 **101** 167 **104**
310 311 **136** 318 323
Laura **75** 98
Lavinia **75** 96
Lena **75** 98
Leonard **75** 94 95
Lewis **75** 97
Lois **61** 285 **75** 93 96
Loiza **75** 96
Louann **75** 95
Lucas Alonzo **75** 94
Lucinda **75** 92 95 97
Lucy **75** 92-94 97
Lucy Sabrina **75** 93
Luther **75** 93
Lydia **75** 89 91 93
Lydia R. **75** 96
Mabel **75** 91
Margaret **70** 349
Margaretta **75** 97 98
Maria C. **75** 93
Martha **75** 95
Martha A. **75** 96
Mary **75** 89 90 92-94 **94**
315 **104** 311
Mary (Ruggles) **146** 277
Mary Anna **75** 93
Mary Cornelia **75** 96
Mary E. **75** 96
Mary Elizabeth **75** 97
Mary Selina **75** 93
Mary Sheldon (Lord)
136 318
Maryette **75** 96
Mehitable **75** 92 96
Mercy **75** 95
Mercy Elvira **75** 95
Merritt **75** 96
Merritt Sackett **75** 94 96
Miles **75** 96
Munson **75** 97
Nancy **75** 94 95
Nancy Jennet **75** 93
Nathalie Elizabeth **71** liii
Noyes **75** 95 96
Pauline **74** 30
Peter **109** 23
Philemon **75** 92 96
Polly **75** 95
Reuel **75** 96
Rhoda **61** 285
Rhoda (Collins) **89** 23
Robert **55** 420 **61** 285
112 213
Rosetta E. **75** 97
Roxana **75** 91
Rufus **75** 94
Russell **75** 91 94
Ruth **75** 92 95
S. C. **74** 30
Sala **75** 96

PIERPONT *cont'd*
Sally **75** 93 94
Sally Rosetta **75** 94
Samuel **75** 89-91 **77** 202
210
Sarah **56** 287 **58** 27 **59** 15
75 89-92 96 97 **87** 208
99 311 **103** 141
Sarah Ann **75** 93 94
Sarah Eliza **75** 96
Sarah Jennette **75** 95
Sarah Mehitable **75** 96
Sarah Miles **75** 94
Sarah Minerva **75** 93
Seabury **75** 93
Selina **75** 93
Seth Low **71** liii
Sophia H. **104** 70
Sophronia L. **75** 94
Susan E. **75** 93
Susanna **75** 92 96
Sylvia **75** 98
Thankful **70** 349 **75** 89
Theodore **75** 91
Theodosia **75** 91
Theron G. **75** 98
Thomas **75** 92 94 95 **91** 94
99 311
Watson T. **75** 98
William Henry **75** 93
William Seabury **75** 93
Zerah **75** 92 98
PIERREFUE Alain
Dedons de **80** 99
Elizabeth de **80** 99
Pierrepont *see* Pierpont
PIERRON Anna Grace
(Jarvis) **81** 222 **85** 436
Hannah Ann (Hammond)
85 436
Henry Joseph **85** 436
Henry Joseph (Mrs.) **81**
111 222 **85** 436 **86** 108
205
Julien Pierre **85** 436
Muriel **85** 436
Pierson *see* Pearson
Piersons *see* Pearson
PIETY Sarah **77** 136
PIFER George Henry (Mrs.)
106 126
Pigeon *see* Pidgeon
PIGFORD Rosa **82** 431
PIGG
Albert Milton **95** 147
Alice **55** 302 **81** 130
Margaret **59** 392
Robert **55** 302 **59** 392
81 126 130
Thomas **58** 21
Piggan *see* Pidgeon
Piggen *see* Pidgeon
Piggeon *see* Pidgeon
PIGGOTT Peygotte
Piggot Pigot Pigott
Pygott
—— **88** 269 **118** 253 259
Catherine (Murtagh)
92 115
Elizabeth **53** 83 **119** 314
Elizabeth (Fiske) **88** 269

PIGGOTT *cont'd*
Elizabeth (Giffard)
118 251
Florence **54** 191
Humphrey **52** 132
Johan **86** 412
John **65** 69 **83** 72
Letitia **108** 215
Ralph **115** 57
Robert H. **92** 115
Thomas **53** 83 **54** 191 **118**
252 **119** 314
Thomas E. **92** 115
Wiburga **74** 136
William **56** 273 **76** 279
PIGMAN
Eliza Ann **83** 64 66
Joshua **83** 66
Simpson **83** 66
PIGNOLET
Joachim **65** 231
Pigot *see* Piggott
Pigott *see* Piggott
PIGSLEY Pigslee
Benjamin **121** 128
Elizabeth **121** 127
Robert **57** 64 66
Sarah **57** 65 66
Willam **115** 128
PIKCOT Nancy **74** 263
PIKE Pyke
—— **51** 347 **53** 266 **58** 101
60 107 212 **61** 206 **72**
182 **121** 176
— Ensign **59** 352
— Lieut. **51** 59
— Mr. **51** 60 **66** 304
82 208
— Rev. Mr. **66** 275
— Widow **77** 32
A. Ullilla **91** 382
Aaron **114** 207
Abby (Wood) **91** 113
Abigail **51** 442 **52** 429 **57**
335 **71** 263 **73** 310 **74**
250 **78** 306 **79** 46 **82** 213
87 38 **121** 166 167 169
176
Abigail (Gould) **121** 169
Abigail (Parkhurst)
121 168
Abigail (Sawtell) **126** 137
Abigail H. **67** 282
Abraham **91** 381
Ada Mae (Bishop) **86** 302
Adelaide Arvilla **82** 108
109
Agnes **66** 261
Agnes Evelyn **86** 305
Albert **106** 144 **130** 236
Albert Leonard **86** 305
Alfred **78** 47
Alfred J. **121** 176
Alice **66** 258 260 **141** 131
Almira C. **68** 203
Almira W. **67** 282
Amasa **53** 76
Amos **63** 170 **70** 156 **74**
217 **82** 86
Ann **91** 381 **121** 162 172
Ann E. **125** 175 183

PIKE *cont'd*
  Ann Eliza **100** 204
  Ann M. **122** 217
  Ann Maria **88** 344
  Anna **63** 84 **91** 381
  Anna Augusta **91** 382
  Anna Maria Blanchard
    92 112
  Anna Tonge **68** 122
  Anne **66** 258-260 **74** 48
    121 175
  Anne (Bennett) **121** 174
  Annia A. **91** 381
  Annie Miller **82** 272
  Annis **77** 31
  Ardella A. **79** 31
  Asenath **93** 103
  Asenath H. **93** 103
  Austin Franklin **72** lv
  Avis **66** 260
  Benjamin **61** 236 **66** 34
    91 206 **94** 95 **98** 104 105
    100 65 **106** 144 **113** 172
    121 164 168 170 172 173
  Bertha J. (Russell) **121** 182
  Bethiah (Brinley) **114** 207
  Betsey **58** 20 **90** 328 **94** 50
    102 155 **114** 207 **121**
    169 **133** 323
  Betsey (Pike) **90** 328
  Betsey Maria **86** 149
  Betty **73** 310 **74** 48 250
    121 174
  Bridget **66** 257-259
  C. **91** 332
  Caleb **121** 173 174
  Carl Olson **86** 302
  Carleton **94** 139
  Caroline **72** 275 **134** 89
  Caroline Frances **68** 122
  Catherine **66** 259 260 **87**
    272 277 278
  Cemantha Almira (Smith)
    86 149 150
  Charles D. **134** 277
  Charles Lockwood
    91 382
  Charlotte T. (Wyman)
    86 302
  Christopher **72** 275
  Clarke **57** 188
  Clifford Llewellyn
    61 xxxv
  Comfort **94** 186
  Conant **87** 277 278
  Constance Harrison
    82 109
  Cynthia **70** xxxv
  Cyprian **51** 189
  Daniel **67** 281 282 **73** 310
    74 48 **82** 109 **87** 234 237
    240 241 **121** 168 169 173
  David **56** 254 **57** 190 **71**
    263 **77** 25 **91** 125 **92** 112
    121 176 **127** 187 **133**
    323
  David B. **81** 51
  David C. **81** 51
  Deborah **66** 275 **81** 154
    82 109 **86** 303 **117** 65
  Deborah (Smith) **86** 146

PIKE *cont'd*
  148 303
  Deliverance **84** 53 118
    104 302
  Deliverance (Paine)
    84 53 118
  Dorcas **52** 341 **88** 281
  Dorothy **66** 99 258 260
    97 261 **121** 162 164 167
    168
  Dorothy (Day) **106** 144
    121 161
  Dorothy (Tenney)
    121 170
  Douglas Parker **86** 302
  Dudley **58** 342 **99** 56
  Ebenezer **71** 262 270 **77**
    25-28 31 **81** 493
  Edmund **66** 257 258
  Edmund Noyes **89** 70
  Edward **51** 285 **76** 21
    128 265
  Edwin Bertram **75** ix xxiv
    80 334 **81** 217 230 **82**
    108 109
  Edwin Burbank **82** 108
    109
  Edwin R. **90** 116
  Egbert **81** 51
  Eldora Arvilla **81** 496 **86**
    71 149
  Eleanor **55** 310 **66** 260 261
    81 491 **82** 76
  Elias **90** 229 248 **121** 167
    173-175 **133** 323
  Elias W. **121** 177
  Elijah **71** 263 **89** 106
  Elisha **75** 308 **82** 215
  Eliza (Thing) **91** 33
  Eliza N. (Dodge) **90** 116
  Elizabeth **66** 257-260 **71**
    263 **72** 275 **81** 154 **93**
    103 **109** 67 **111** 29 **121**
    162 164 169 170 172-175
    125 241 **126** 78 **136** 50
  Elizabeth (Andrews)
    104 177
  Elizabeth (Atkinson)
    121 171
  Elizabeth (Bloomfield)
    121 171
  Elizabeth (Blossom) (Fitz-
    Randolph) **97** 276
    121 162
  Elizabeth (Fellows)
    121 171
  Elizabeth (Frazee) **121** 170
  Elizabeth (Moody)
    90 227 244
  Elizabeth (Parker)
    121 165
  Elizabeth (Stephens)
    121 174
  Elizabeth (Vogle) **126** 204
  Elizabeth (Woodman)
    121 172 173
  Elizabeth F. **93** 103
  Elizabeth H. **87** 351
  Elizabeth M. **67** 282
  Ella **94** 168
  Ella E. **67** 282 **69** 136

PIKE *cont'd*
  Ella Frances (Paxton)
    106 144
  Ellen **66** 259
  Elmeda L. **103** 45
  Emma (Chace) **91** 25
  Emma A. **121** 180
  Emma S. (Purington)
    121 180
  Enoch **121** 173
  Ephraim **77** 26
  Esther **61** 236 **121** 244
    147 183
  Esther (Atkins) **121** 244
  Ethel Melora **92** 147
    115 66
  Etta F. **121** 180
  Eunice **82** 207 297 302 **90**
    231 247 **121** 175
  Eunice (Chase) **90** 336
  Eva M. **143** 164
  Evaline (Denning)
    128 265
  Ezekiel **67** 281 **69** 136
  Ezra G. **121** 180
  Frances A. **76** 21
  Francis **51** 466 **121** 174
    133 323
  Francis W. **91** 382
  Francis William **91** 382
  Freelove **56** 385 **57** 190
  George **58** 342 **65** 293
    121 241 242 244 **133**
    323
  George B. **93** 103
  Gershom **121** 169
  Gilman **90** 254
  Grace **121** 171
  Grace (Trumbull) **121** 171
  Hannah **51** 466 **58** 19 342
    71 262 263 270 271 **74**
    48 **81** 273 **82** 414 **87** 272
    277-279 **88** 272 **97** 358
    98 130 **102** 105 **121** 162-
    166 169 170 173 174
  Hannah (Gilman) **121** 172
  Hannah (Kimberly)
    (Lyon) **102** 105
  Hannah (Moodey)
    121 174
  Hannah (Rich) (Hopkins)
    83 402
  Hannah (Smith) **121** 168
  Hannah E. **93** 103 **133** 41
  Harriet **74** 318 **95** 35
  Harriet (Hodge)
    (Rosebrook) **86** 302
  Harriet Newhall **82** 272
  Harwood **81** 154 **86** 148
    150 305
  Henry **58** 342 **66** 258 260
    261
  Herbert **134** 277
  Hester **65** 293 **121** 171 242
  Hester (Bunn) **121** 165
  Hope **53** 164 **121** 173 174
    715
  Hopestill (Hoyt) **121** 173
  Hopey **90** 230 252
  Hugh **58** 20 **121** 172
  Humphrey **121** 174

PIKE *cont'd*
Isaac **82** 109
Isereny **88** 153
Israel **88** 153 **121** 162 174
Jacob **58** 342 **77** 23 24 31
121 174 175
James **53** 122 **60** 190 **61** 43
62 27 **66** 261 **68** 44 **71**
262 263 270 271 **73** 310
74 48 193 **82** 76 86 91
326 **91** 94 **121** 169 170
173 174 **127** 187 **128**
278 **140** 69
James G. **81** 51
James Massure **86** 149
James S. **121** 176
Jane **63** 172 **66** 260 **70** 198
77 24 **82** 213 214 **121**
170
Jane S. **88** 336
Janet **121** 170
Janet (Forman) **121** 170
Jarvis **70** 157 **71** 263
Jeannette **82** 423
Jemima **121** 176
Jennet **121** 170
Jephthah **75** 304
Jereal **112** 223
Jeremiah **61** 247 **72** 275
133 323
Jerusha **128** 278
Joan **66** 258-261
Joanna **58** 342 **110** 59 **121**
168 169 175
Joanna (Allen) **121** 173
Joanna (Webber) **106** 144
121 169
Johanna Anna (Penrose)
116 255
John **53** 38 **57** 335 **58** 341
63 84 **66** 123 257-261
67 82 **70** 262 **71** 261 262
349 **73** 310 **74** 48 182 **75**
113 304 **82** 73 74 89 97
98 108 212 215 285 297
312 **83** 402 **88** 276 **90**
228 246 **91** 381 **92** 102
97 276 **98** 64 132 136
215 **99** 336 **100** 254 **106**
144 **107** 161 **112** 223
121 161-170 172-176
124 96 253 **125** 180 238
127 187 **136** 50
John C. **68** 203
John D. **66** 36
John M. **91** 381 382
John Q. **66** 83
Jonah **66** 260
Jonas **51** 189
Jonathan **71** 263 270 **90**
335 **93** 166
Joseph **62** 360 **66** 36 **71**
263 270 **74** 48 **82** 109 **90**
227 244 **91** 33 **100** 254
106 144 **121** 162-168
170 175 176 **126** 137
127 11
Joseph Addison **86** 149
305
Joseph Coffin **121** 173
Joseph Savage **68** 122

PIKE *cont'd*
Josephine Winfred
68 122
Joshua **59** 59 **121** 166 167
171-173
Judith **53** 38 **121** 168 175
Judith (Knight) (Noyes)
121 169
Justine **87** 272 274 276
96 278
Katharine **66** 260
Keturah **121** 175
Keziah **133** 323
Laura A. **67** 282
Lavinia **68** 122
Leander B. **134** 277
Lemira Avis **77** 186
Leonard **75** 305 **84** 53 118
Lilian **106** 116 126 130 144
Lillia **91** 382
Lois **90** 315 **91** 16 **121** 169
175 **138** 321
Lois (Moody) **90** 228 246
Lois (Perley) **121** 169
Lois (Tenney) **121** 170
Loren **81** 273
Louisa **86** 146
Lucian M. **132** 220
Lucinda (Dodge) **86** 149
Lucy **133** 323 **136** 80
Luther **56** 257 **133** 323
Luther M. **67** 282 **69** 136
Lydia **61** 237 **72** 275 **92**
196 **121** 168 169 176
Lydia (Brown) **121** 173
Lydia (Coffin) (Little)
121 168
Lydia (Drury) **121** 168
Mamie **82** 109
Marcy **121** 165
Margaret **66** 258 **121** 167
170
Margaret (Cutts) **121** 171
Margaret E. (Hilton)
134 277
Margaret F. **103** 47
Margery **66** 258 261
Mariah **78** 47
Martha **58** 341 **66** 258 **67**
282 **74** 48 **82** 322 **121**
174
Martha (Emery) **138** 321
Martha (Goldwire)
121 163
Martha (Tappan) **121** 169
Martha Augusta **81** 389
Mary **55** 313 **58** 50 342 **66**
89 257 260 261 **73** 310
75 113 121 **77** 23 **82** 205
215 511 **88** 275 **89** 70 **90**
239 314 335 **91** 24 381
382 **95** 86 87 **106** 70 **117**
57 **121** 162-167 169 171-
175 **125** 179 **126** 145
127 186 187 **138** 321
147 37 43
Mary (Cole) **86** 302
Mary (Dunwell) **125** 238
Mary (Eames) **121** 168
Mary (Follinsby) **121** 167
Mary (French) **121** 2 174

PIKE *cont'd*
Mary (Holton) **91** 381
Mary (Hook) **121** 174
Mary (Hunt) (Phillips)
121 165
Mary (Newell) **89** 106
Mary (Pike) **90** 239 314
121 172
Mary (Sanderson)
127 187
Mary (Turvell) **121** 162
Mary A. **76** 21
Mary Aliza **91** 381
Mary Ann **77** 184
Mary Ann (Hamilton)
106 144
Mary Augusta (Durrell)
(Andrews) **134** 276 277
Mary Cotton **58** 342
Mary D. **123** 123
Mary F. (Purington)
121 177
Mary Graves **89** 70
Mary S. **82** 359
Matilda **86** 146
Mattie Catherine **78** 47
Mehitable **113** 300
Melinda **81** 154 496
Melinda (Cole) **86** 71
148-150 305
Mercy **84** 53 **121** 166
169
Miami S. (Russell) **91**
381
Mildred Estella **104** 145
Molly **74** 193
Moody **90** 234 235
Moses **53** 124 **63** 175 **82**
109 **90** 245 **97** 261 293
121 164 167 169 172 173
175 176
N. **68** 140
Nancy **67** 278
Nancy (Trafton) **90** 335
Nancy (Trask) **88** 276
Nanne / Nanny **121** 173
Nathan **77** 30 **94** 50
Nathaniel **58** 50 **74** 48 **81**
154 **86** 146 **121** 166 167
169 171 172 176
Nellie A. **67** 282
Nicholas **65** 225 **66** 258
73 310 **74** 48 **87** 351
121 169 **125** 23
Noah Thorp **68** 122
Noah Webster **68** 122
Norris **138** 321
Olive **63** 171
Olive Estella **103** 122
Onesiphorus **127** 187
Pamela (Beardsley)
133 323
Pamelia **58** lxxxvii
Patience **55** 374 **82** 205 215
83 15
Patty **82** 285 297
Penelope **121** 165
Perley **121** 169
Persis **94** 50
Phebe **124** 45

PIKE *cont'd*
Phebe (Varney) (Tibbetts) **99** 56
Philena Robinson **90** 193
Philip **66** 258 **75** 113 121 **107** 194 **144** 201
Philomene Loretta **80** 208
Polly **57** 188 **63** 175 **81** 154 **86** 302 **138** 321
Polly (Thing) **90** 245
Randolph L. **93** 103
Rebecca **55** 400 **56** 254 **75** 121 **82** 312 **98** 364
Rhoda **62** 27
Rhoda (Emery) **91** 31
Richard **52** 154 **66** 258-260 **90** 336 **91** 25 **104** 177 **116** 255
Robert **52** 253 **53** 264 **54** 364 **58** 342 **63** 35 **66** 89 257-259 **81** 154 **86** 146 148 303 392 **87** 272 277-279 **95** 218 219 233 **97** 261 **121** 161-164 166 167 170-172 174 175 **124** 96 291 **143** 141
Robert E. **104** 104
Rosina **86** 146
Roxanna **89** 106
Ruel R. **86** 302
Ruth **71** 263 270 **121** 162 163 **133** 323
Ruth G. **121** 178
Sally **56** 257 **63** 170 177 **76** 263 **114** 207
Sally (Fiske) **90** 234 235
Sally (Townsend) (Emery) **100** 147
Sally Vincent **57** 335
Samuel **55** 310 **74** 48 **77** 30 **121** 167 169 174 **133** 323
Samuel H. **93** 103 104
Sarah **53** 122 **61** 237 **66** 274 **67** 281 **69** 136 **71** 261-263 **73** 310 **74** 48 **79** 292 **82** 97 98 **83** 36 **85** 97 **90** 214 **95** 86 87 351 **121** 161 163-165 167 169-175 260 **136** 50
Sarah (Andrews) **106** 144
Sarah (Eaton) **121** 173
Sarah (French) **121** 174
Sarah (Gilman) **121** 169
Sarah (Little) **106** 144 **121** 169
Sarah (Moody) **121** 166 169
Sarah (Mulliken) **121** 173
Sarah (Parker) **113** 172
Sarah (Sanders) **121** 163
Sarah (Stout) **121** 165
Sarah (Thing) **90** 245
Sarah (Thompson) **121** 175
Sarah (Townsend) **121** 174
Sarah A. **81** 51 **87** 351
Sarah E. **67** 282 **69** 136
Sarah Fellows **89** 70

PIKE *cont'd*
Sarah Frances Mabie **68** 122
Sarah Young **77** 180
Satura Dole (Wadley) **132** 220
Sewall **133** 323
Sherman L. **121** 182
Silas **121** 174
Simeon W. **125** 180
Simon **66** 259 260
Solomon **71** 263 **121** 167 172 176
Sumner C. **134** 277
Susan (Day) **91** 125
Susan Charlotte **68** 122
Susan Potter **86** 149
Susanna **53** 38 124 **74** 251 **75** 305 **99** 72 **121** 168 175
Susanna (Barry) **132** 41
Susanna (Bean) **90** 229 248
Susanna (Cole) **86** 146
Susanna (Day) **90** 254
Susanna (Kingsbury) **106** 144 **121** 164
Susanna (March) **121** 173
Susanna (Worcester) **97** 261 **121** 167
Susanna S. **81** 51
Suse **74** 224
Thankful **88** 153
Theodore **121** 172
Thomas **52** 253 429 **53** 38 **54** xci **57** 335 **58** 342 **66** 257-261 **68** 175 **74** 227 **82** 88 205 207 213-215 314 322 329 **102** 105 **106** 144 **107** 161 **121** 162-166 169 171 **124** 61 **126** 204
Thomas Delaware **82** 272
Thorpe **66** 259-261
Timothy **55** 400 **57** 335 **63** 177 **78** 404 **90** 245 328 **91** 113 **121** 167 170 172-174 **140** 236
Torrey **118** 61
Violet Plumadore **104** 104
Walter **66** 258 **87** 272 **104** 104
William **58** 342 **66** 257-261 **72** 275 **87** 272 **90** 239 314 **91** 31 **118** 313 **121** 166 171 173 174 **127** 9 223 **132** 41 **138** 321
William Henry **77** 186
William O. **134** 276 277
William Thomas **81** 496 **86** 71 149 150
William Wallace **86** 302
Yron **106** 144
Zaceriah **145** 353
Zadock **86** 146
Zebulon **121** 165 170
Zebulon M. **51** 500 501
PIKUZINSKI
Eunice B. **130** 314
PILBEAME James **99** 242

PILCHE Robert **69** 343
PILCHER James **60** 190
James Evelyn **60** 190
John **68** 186
Joseph **105** 87
Nicholas **67** 251
Susanna **75** 40 **92** 193
PILCORNE Joan **81** 491
Walter **81** 489
Pile *see* Pyle
PILEBEAME ―― **97** 320
PILES Ann **73** 225
Charles **73** 228
Elizabeth **73** 146 266 **108** 79
Francis **73** 220
Henry **73** 137
Hilleary **73** 219
Jemima **73** 147
Leonora **73** 135
Lucy W. **88** 330
Mary **73** 140
Richard **73** 261 272
Thomas **53** 32
Zachariah **73** 228
PILET Elizabeth **106** 35
PILGRIM Pilgrym
―― **54** 29
Adeline **81** 57
David R. **81** 53
Dorcas **81** 53 57
Elizabeth **110** 70
John **51** 353
Lydia **81** 57
Sarah **66** 178 **69** 27 **86** 325
Thomas **81** 53 57
PILKE Juddy **78** 419
PILKERTON
Honora **144** 348 354
PILKINGTON Pilkinton
Abigail **60** 128
Agnes **64** 258
Alice **95** 5
Arthur **95** 5
Deborah **55** 377
Esther **52** 311
Faith **60** 128
Henry W. **120** 85
James **55** 377
John **64** 258 **95** 6
Lora **68** 342
Mark **60** 127 128
Martha **52** 311
Mary **60** 128 **108** 181
Maryann Fellows (Amory) **120** 85
Mercy **60** 128
Robert **95** 5 7
Roger **68** 342
Sarah **60** 128
Thomas **52** 311
William **64** 258 **80** 90
PILKINHORN
John **100** 139
Pilkinton *see* Pilkington
PILL Pille
Francis **98** 41
Joan (Washington) **98** 41
Mary (Chauncy) **120** 245
Richard **120** 244
Thomas **76** 115

PILLAR Pillars
— Mrs. **82** 414
Charles **65** 236
Elizabeth (Amme) **90** 390
   114 51
Margaret **72** 297
Thomas **90** 390 **114** 51
PILLATH
Louisa **81** 257
Mary **81** 258
Samuel **81** 258
Pille *see* Pill
PILLESTON
Richard **85** 135
PILLOW J. M. **92** 285
Mimi Polk **78** 161
Narcissa **78** 164
William B. **78** 161
Pillsbery *see* Pilsbury
PILMORE Joseph **79** 163
   107 234
PILNO H. Dela **115** 23
John M. **115** 23
PILOT Andrew **132** 326
Anna Maria (Luce) **88** 375
Elijah **132** 326
Elizabeth (Nicholson)
   132 40
John **88** 375 **132** 40
William **56** lxvii
PILOTTI Edward Francis
   102 227
Edward Francis (Mrs.)
   102 227 **103** 120
Pilsbery *see* Pilsbury
PILSBURY Pilsbery
   Pillsbury
—— **52** 397 399 **91** 349
   350 **92** 17 **136** 90
— Mr. **92** 12
— Mrs. **91** 352
Abby Mary **66** 277 **74** 308
Abel **64** 157
Abigail **64** 75 157 **66** 276
   277 **91** 353 **92** 19 **125**
   100 **126** 204
Abigail (Rolf) **85** 233
Adella **140** 130
Albert E. **57** 341 342
Albert Enoch **57** xxxiii
   58 xlv **72** xx **74** xxviii
   82 382 **83** 229 **85** 202
   233 235
Alpha I. **76** 33
Alphonso C. **67** 353
Amos **97** 141
Andrew Jackson **66** 274
Anna **66** 274
Anna (Smith) **85** 233
Annie **67** 353
Annie Bell **74** 302
Apphia **63** 373 **64** 156 157
   66 276 279 **134** 335
Asenath C. **67** 353
Bertha A. (Barron) **134** 330
Betsey **64** 156 **66** 276
   108 243
Caleb **64** 75 157 **67** 353
Caleb Grant **67** 353
Calvin **66** 276
Caroline **66** 274

PILSBURY *cont'd*
Charles **100** 299
Charles Stinson **92** 400
   102 4 **112** 151 **113** 70
   136 326 **141** 19 313 **143**
   99 213 **144** 359 **148** 311
Charles Stinson (Mrs.)
   74 xxviii **104** 73 **112** 150
   151 **114** 75
Christiana **66** 277 **74** 302
Clara Sophia **66** 276
Daniel **64** 75 157 **65** 254
   261 342 **93** 398 **100** 63
   134 216
David **53** 162 **65** 77 80 82
   66 276 **90** 47
David B. **53** 140 **66** 275
David G. **64** 156
David Jaques **66** 275
Deborah **54** cxxxviii **94**
   197 **100** 60 **103** 224 **107**
   236
Dolly **55** xcii
Dorothy **53** 140 **64** 157
Dorothy (Crosby) **85** 233
Edmund **66** 276
Edward Payson **66** 275
Eleanor (Bellows) **112** 151
Eliza **76** 34
Eliza Ann **66** 274
Eliza D. **84** 31
Elizabeth **52** 433 **53** 162 **55**
   316 **64** 157 **66** 274-277
   76 lxvi **79** 49 **83** 12 **91**
   349 **92** 21 **100** 30
Elizabeth (Davis) **97** 264
   353
Elizabeth (Joy) **83** 12
Elizabeth (Mooney)
   85 234
Elizabeth Dinsmore **57**
   122 **85** 233 234
Elizabeth Jane **66** 274
Elsie **63** 379 **66** 276
Elsie Greenwood **85** 198
Elsie M. **68** 153
Emma G. **68** 153
Enoch **64** 156 **66** 274 276
   97 264 353
Enoch H. **76** 34
Experience **64** 157
Ezra **64** 75 **134** 216
Frank **68** 153
George A. **66** 276 277
George Alfred **122** 94
George E. **134** 330
George L. **66** 276
George Larrabe **64** 75
George Melville **74** 302
George T. **92** 323
Gilbert **66** 274
Hannah **64** 157 **92** 17
   127 101
Hannah (Godfrey)
   127 101
Hannah Maria **66** 275
Harriet **73** 192 **128** 119
Harriet (Newell) **90** 47
Harriet A. **66** 276 277
Harriet Ann **74** 302
Harriet Newell **66** 274

PILSBURY *cont'd*
Harry M. (Mrs.) **104** 316
Helen P. **66** 277
Helen Pendleton
   (Winston) **72** xx **90**
   130 **92** 400 **103** 80 114
   107 238 **112** 150 **136**
   326
Helen Winston **112** 151
Henry M. **77** 176
Horace D. **76** lxvi
Increase **64** 157
Isaac Newton **67** 353
Israel **66** 363
Jackson **66** 274
Jacob **64** 157
James Edward **64** 156 **66**
   276 277
James K. **67** 353
Jane **126** 65
Job **64** 75 157 **77** 35
John **53** 279 280 **63** 374
   64 156 157 **66** 274-276
   97 264 353 **100** 30
John C. **63** 379
John Calvin **64** 156 **66** 275
   276
John Hale **66** 275
John L. **78** 301
John M. **74** 302
John Sargent **92** 400 **102**
   4 **113** 70 **141** 19 313 **143**
   99 213 **144** 359 **148** 311
Joseph **54** 409 **64** 157
Joseph Hopkins **66** 275
Joseph Huckins **67** 353
Joshua **64** 157 **91** 353
Josiah **64** 75 157 **66** 276
Josiah Dixon **64** 75 **66** 276
Josiah Webster **57** 122
   66 274 **85** 233
Judith **64** 157 **75** 272
Julia Maria **74** 302
Katharine **64** 157 **77** 35
Katharine Stevens
   112 151
Keith **64** 75 **66** 276
Lois **74** 302
Louisa Fuller (Johnson)
   (Wheeler) **85** 234
Lucretia A. **64** 156
Lucretia Ann **63** 374
   66 274
Lucretia Smith **85** 198
Lucy **66** 275 **87** 110
Lucy (Brown) **97** 264 353
Lucy Ann **66** 275
Lucy M. **87** 20
Lydia **64** 157 **73** 192
Margaret **76** 33
Maria A. **66** 276
Maria Abigail **63** 375
   74 302
Maria E. **67** 353
Martha **66** 275
Martha Ann **66** 274
Martha E. **66** 275
Martin Luther **66** 275
Mary **64** 157 **66** 274 **80** 116
   91 350 **92** 15 **97** 353
   103 317 **110** 205

PILSBURY *cont'd*
Mary (Palmer) **100** 299
Mary (Parker) **85** 233
Mary Abigail **66** 277
Mary Ann **88** 333
Mary Ann (Stinson)
  112 151
Mary Jane **64** 156 **66** 274
  276 277
Mary Lee **64** 75
Mary R. **74** 302
Mary Smith **66** 274
Mary Stinson **112** 151
Mary Susan **66** 276
Mehitable H. **66** 274
Molly **53** 164
Moses **63** 373 375 376 **64**
  75 157 **66** 274-277 **85**
  233 305 **103** 317 **134**
  216
Moses Foster **66** 274
Moses Hale **66** 275
Moses Henry **66** 275
Nancy **67** 353
Nathan **64** 157 **66** 276 365
Nathan B. **67** 353
Nathan H. **73** 185
Nathaniel Emmons
  66 275
Nellie **74** xxviii
Oliver **64** 156 **66** 274 276
  277 **85** 233
Pamelia S. **67** 353
Parker **57** 122 **63** 373 **64**
  156 **66** 274 276 277 280
  85 233
Parker K. **66** 276 277
Parker Kimball **74** 302
Parker Webster **85** 234
Paul **64** 156 **66** 274 276
Phebe **63** 373 374 **64** 156
  66 276
Phebe Wood **64** 155
  66 276
Philip W. **110** 157
Philip Winston **112** 151
  136 326
Phineas **63** 373-378 **64** 75
  154-157 374 **66** 274-280
  359-365 **74** 302 **114** 146
Priscilla **103** 317
Rebecca **77** 313
Rhoda **53** 162
Sally **63** 378 **64** 156 374
  66 274 276
Sally C. (Hawks) **114** 146
Samuel **53** 164 **64** 156 **66**
  274 276 **78** 190 **92** 13 15
  17 19 21
Sarah **64** 75 156 157 **66**
  274 276 280
Sarah (Dickenson) **85** 233
Sarah D. **64** 155
Sarah Eliza **66** 277
Sarah Elizabeth **66** 276
Sarah H. **66** 275
Sarah Hall **66** 277
Sarah Jane **66** 275
Sarah Jewett **66** 275 276
Sophia **77** 176
Stephen **55** 316 **83** 12

PILSBURY *cont'd*
Susan **64** 157 **66** 276 365
Susanna **53** 163 279 280
  64 157 **67** 343 **91** 352
  135 76
Susanna (Worth) **85** 233
Tappan Persons **66** 274
Thankful **64** 157
Thomas **53** 162 **91** 350
  352 353 **104** 263
Thomas Green **64** 156
  66 276 277
Thomas Moor **64** 75
Thomas Joor **66** 276
Timothy Pike **53** 279
William **53** 140 **64** 157
  66 276 **85** 233 **103** 317
  104 316 **134** 216
William H. **119** 69
William Henry **66** 274
William O. **91** 332
William Tennent **66** 275
Zenelda E. **64** 75 **66** 276
PILSON
Elizabeth **128** 263
PILTES
Robert **69** 344 345
PILTOUN John **79** 63
Pim *see* Pym
PIMAN Isaac **127** 303
PIME Mary **94** 189
PIMER Elizabeth **52** 200
PIMLATT Ann **54** 194
Pimm *see* Pym
PIMONT Jean Grenelle
  (Lord of) **90** 69
PIMPE Anne **96** 21 22
  Elizabeth (Pashley) **96** 22
PIMPLE I. W. **91** 332
PIN Joan **141** 29
  Odard du **95** 123
PINCE Benjamin **110** 265
Pincheon *see* Pynchon
Pinchin *see* Pynchon
Pinchon *see* Pynchon
Pinckham *see* Pinkham
PINCKNEY
  De Pinckney Pinkeny
  Pinkney Pynkeny
  ——— **53** 134 **62** 205 353
  101 55 **137** 344
— Capt. **62** 284
— Mr. **144** 158
— Mrs. **144** 159
C. C. **137** 344
Charles **68** 240 **79** 16 **133**
  232 **137** 344 **142** 198
  144 156 158
Charles Cotesworth **79**
  163 **100** 277 278
Denise de **102** 41 44
Eda de **96** 45
Elise **144** 156
Eliza (Lucas) **144** 156 158
  159
Elizabeth **79** 16
Frances **144** 321
Frances Sayre **104** 220
Gilbert de **101** 293 294
Hawise de **101** 293
Irvin R. (Mrs.) **117** 159

PINCKNEY *cont'd*
John **95** 321 322 **99** 118
  101 55 161
John (Mrs.) **85** 120
Louisa C. **108** 301
Margaret **108** 302
Mary **99** 118
Mary Esther **79** 16
Phebe V. (Hopkins)
  104 220
Rebecca (Cook) **133** 232
Robert **143** 105
Robert de **102** 41 44
  122 266
Thomas **68** 240 **100** 278
  106 177 **137** 344
William **79** 160 **91** 178
William de **101** 294
PINCOCK John **63** 25
Pincon *see* Pynchon
PINDAR Pinder Pindir
  Pindor Pynder
— Mr. **83** 308
Alice **114** 226
Anne **68** 74
George **65** 29
Hannah **90** 193
Harriet E. **83** 438 **84** 21
Henry **138** 129
J. **73** 76
Joanna **83** 107 **87** 194 **90**
  170 **138** 129
John **96** 227 **114** 226
Katharine **53** 338
Martha **131** 48
Martin **51** 420
Mary **105** 32 **138** 129
  148 181
Moses **56** 83
Paul **51** 417 **52** 129
Richard **76** 59
Sarah **88** 283
Thomas **55** 341 **65** 240
  83 445
William **68** 74 **125** 30 34
PINDELL
Philip **73** 148 221
Rinaldo **73** 266
Thomas **73** 272
Pinder *see* Pindar
Pindir *see* Pindar
Pindor *see* Pindar
PINE Pyne
  ——— **51** 288 **54** 195 338
Aaron **116** 32
Anne **65** 291
Charles **94** 189
Elizabeth **141** 194 **147** 189
George S. **57** 226
James **55** 299
Jermyn **52** 109
Joanna **119** 309
John **81** 492
John B. **51** 373
Julia Evelyne **103** 69
L. G. **108** 70 **148** 252
Leslie Gilbert **121** 148
Lorana (Chase) **87** 325
Mary **52** 108 **88** 285 **94** 189
  126 287
Peter **87** 325

PINE *cont'd*
Priscilla (Nickerson)
 126 287
Rachel **135** 79
Robert Edge **59** 335
Seth **58** 142
Thomas **112** 249
William **81** 490
PINEDA
Joseph Mary **110** 131
PINEL
Blanche M. (Winn) **83**
 438 **84** 23
William E. **83** 438 **84** 23
Pineo *see* Pinneo
PINES Mary **79** 287
PINGEL
Martha M. **103** 80
PINGREE Pengra
 Pengry Pingrey
 Pingry
Aaron **142** 52-55
Agnes **95** 2
Agnes (Noble) (Pingree)
 95 186
Almon **90** 302
Anna (Jewett) **127** 289
Arthur **95** 187
Camella E. (Chase) **90** 302
Charles **90** 302
Charles C. **103** 47
David Edwin **107** 134
Dolly **121** 79
Edward **95** 186
Eliza Ann (Chase) **88** 111
Faith (Jowett) **94** 107
Gladys Adelia **107** 135
Herbert **95** 187
Hezekiah S. **90** 386
Isabel (Sargent) **103** 47
Iva **95** 187
Jane **58** 269
Jane (Bancroft) **95** 113
Job **98** 221
John **85** 387 **94** 107
Lena **95** 187
Lydia **63** 379
Maria **110** 280
Mary **79** 136 **90** 386
Mary (Sanderson)
 127 289
Mary E. (Kempton)
 103 48
Michael **63** 379
Miranda **118** 321
Moses **94** 107
Rachel (Tippetts) **98** 221
Samuel **119** 319
Sarah **105** 316 **109** 229
Solomon **88** 111
Stephen **95** 113 **127** 289
Thomas P. **60** lxxiii
Walter **95** 186
Walter E. **103** 48
PINHEE Rebecca **109** 250
PINION Abigail **59** 167
 102 107
Elizabeth **54** 322
Experience **66** 206
Mercy **54** 322
Nicholas **54** 322 **81** 130

PINION *cont'd*
Thomas **54** 322
PINK Edward **64** 321
W. Duncombe **51** 286
Pinkeny *see* Pinckney
PINKERTON Pinkertown
Eleanor **96** 167
Eliza (Carnahan) **128** 263
Ida (Lewis) **94** 139
Jean **65** 85
John **63** 202
Marie Antonette **128** 263
Nancy L. (Dilley) **128** 91
Samuel Stanhope Smith
 63 202 **64** 377
Samuel Walter (Mrs.) **94**
 139 **118** 68
William E. **128** 263
William W. **128** 91
PINKHAM Pinckham
—— **98** 216 220 **143** 369
— Widow **105** 285
A. **91** 332
Abiel **100** 277
Abigail **51** 163 **58** lxxxvi
 59 39 **67** 181 **68** 243 **69**
 72 **73** 307 **98** 135 223
Abigail (Lamos) **98** 223
Abigail (Tibbetts) **98** 135
 222 **100** 35
Abijah **67** 181 **98** 136
Abisha **100** 277
Albert **70** 318 328 330 335
Alden S. **69** 274
Alexander **100** 277
Alfred **147** 270
Alfred Kennard **69** 180
Alfred Tennyson **69** 309
Alice **91** 25 30
Allen Gardner **69** 309
Allen W. **69** 316
Amy (Woodworth)
 134 293
Andrew **111** 288 289
Ann (Starbuck) **98** 135
Anna **51** 162
Anna Maria **69** 274
Anne **67** 181 **69** 71 **98** 135
Anstress G. **68** 247 **69** 309
Aroline Chase **76** xli
Barnabas **51** 56 **99** 127
 128 291
Benjamin **98** 223
Betsey **58** lxxxvi
Betsey (Hill) **90** 330
Caroline Chase **76** xli
Caroline H. **69** 180
Catherine (Dame) **113** 311
Catherine F. **68** 248
Catherine Way (Jenks)
 89 109
Celia **100** 277
Charles **68** 247 **87** 343
Charles G. **68** 247 **69** 309
Charles H. **89** 299
Charles Melvin **69** 316
Charles P. **91** 118
Charles Sumner **69** 309
Cyrus F. **113** 311
Daniel **98** 223 **100** 152
 153 277 **114** 180 **136**

PINKHAM *cont'd*
326
David **69** 72
David Coffin **100** 277
Deborah **51** 162 **108** 215
Dorothy **68** 247
Dovall **98** 223
Edith **69** 316
Edmund **98** 223
Edward Albert **70** 330
Edward Everett **69** 309
Elias **69** 274
Elijah **68** 243 **70** 318 **98** 223
Eliza Brackitt **70** 318 329
 334
Eliza M. **77** 148
Elizabeth **51** 56 **72** 268 **73**
 50 **87** 343 **98** 223 **100**
 225 **103** 312
Elizabeth (Allen) **102** 187
Elizabeth (Tripe) **98** 223
Elizabeth Ann **73** 50
Elizabeth Jones **70** 330
Ellen J. (Olney) **105** 82
Elvira **116** 183
Elvira Mitchell (Huff)
 116 183
Emily (Grant) **116** 179
Enoch **98** 223
Eri **103** 43
Ernest Percy **58** lxxxvii
Etta M. **147** 364
Eunice **100** 277
Eunice (Tuttle) **98** 223
Eunice W. **89** 299
Fanny **69** 274
Franklin **70** 330 **95** 54
George **114** 231
George C. **100** 278
George Franklin **105** 82
George H. **76** 34
George S. **69** 274
Hannah (Young) **98** 223
Harriet A. (Leavitt) **91** 118
Henry **100** 278
Henry K. **69** 274
Henry Morris **89** 109
 105 129
Henry Wilson **69** 309
Hepzibah **51** 164 **69** 72
 100 278
Herbert W. **60** 355
Hezekiah **61** 134 **100** 278
Horace A. **91** 119
Isaac **76** xli **136** 326
James M. **147** 364
James Parnel **69** 180
Janvrin Fisher **69** 282
Jason **100** 35
Jedida **51** 162
Jemima **100** 278
Jennie J. **98** 251
John **58** lxxxvi **68** 243 **69**
 71 72 171 **70** 318 334
 335 **90** 330 **98** 135 222
 223 **100** 278
John F. **147** 361
John Franklin **70** 318
John Howard **69** 309
John Warren **69** 274
Jonathan **100** 277 278

PINKHAM *cont'd*
Joseph **58** lv lxxxvi
 lxxxvii **98** 223
Joseph G. **69** 274
Joseph H. **87** 344
Judith (Tibbetts) **98** 220
Judson A. **116** 183
Leila May **105** 82
Lois A. **147** 364
Loretta Ann (Rogers)
 147 361
Lozette **69** 282
Lucinda **69** 180
Lucy Abbie **64** xxxiii
Lucy Ann Lazell (Guild)
 89 109
Lydia **76** xli **147** 270
Lydia (Coffin) **108** 214
 215
Lydia (Ham) **98** 223
Lydia (Sanborn) **147** 364
Lydia Estes (Mrs.) **136** 326
Marcus F. **97** 207
Margaret **99** 127 **120** 102
Martha **92** 364 **98** 300
Martha I. **89** 299
Mary **68** 243 **69** 171 **70**
 318 334 335 **87** 343 **100**
 152 153 **128** 291 **134**
 293
Mary (Jones) **99** 127
Mary A. **89** 299
Mary Ann **70** 318
Mary B. **69** 180
Mary Elizabeth **69** 180
Mary Eloise **87** 174
Mary Susan (Jones)
 103 43
Matilda **108** 191
Matthew **89** 109
Mellen J. **89** 299
Mercy **59** 39
Miriam (Gould) **98** 223
Nabby (Hawkes) **136** 326
Nancy (Davis) **98** 223
Nancy (Taber) **91** 119
Nancy H. **70** 328 330 335
Nathaniel **134** 293
Nicholas **73** 50 **98** 223
Nicholas A. **73** 50
Obed **100** 278
Orlando Cunningham
 92 362
Otis **58** lxxxvi **74** 183 **98**
 135 222 223
Parnel **108** 214
Patience **76** 34
Paul **67** 181 **98** 135
Peggy **100** 184 278
Peggy (Slade) **100** 278
Petey **51** 56
Phebe **58** lxxxvi **69** 180 **98**
 223 **103** 312
Phebe (Tebbets) **98** 135
 222
Phebe A. **69** 316
Priscilla **51** 56
Priscilla (Gardner)
 128 291
Rachel **67** 181

PINKHAM *cont'd*
Raymond Dirwood
 98 251
Rebecca **69** 71 **100** 278
Rebecca A. **147** 364
Reuben **92** 362 **98** 135
 111 289
Reuben Gardner **100** 278
Rhoda **100** 284
Richard **58** lxxxvi **97** 207
 98 223 **100** 278 284 **108**
 214 215 **116** 179 183
Rose **58** lxxxvi **98** 135 223
Rose (Austin) **98** 135
Rose (Otis) **98** 135
Ruth **63** 271 **69** 71
Sally **58** lxxxvi **87** 229 235
 114 180
Samuel **67** 181 **89** 299 **98**
 135 223 **105** 114
Sarah **59** 39 **67** 181 **73** 307
 83 416 **89** 299 **98** 136
 146 223 **99** 54
Sarah (Tibbets) **98** 216
Sarah (Young) **98** 223
Sarah Vail **55** 225
Shubael **100** 278
Sibyl H. **73** 50
Silas **116** 179
Stephen **59** 39
Susan Vincent **92** 77
Susanna (Canney) **98** 135
Thomas **67** 181 **69** 180 **89**
 299 **102** 187
Thomas Coleman **70** 318
Thomas Edward **69** 180
Timothy **67** 181
Tristram **92** 102 365 **100**
 278 **125** 95
W. F. **98** 251
Walter **69** 71
Willard S. **92** 109
William C. **100** 278
William E. **70** 318
William Fulton **98** 251
William S. **69** 274
Zephaniah **70** 264
Zerviah **51** 162
Pinkney *see* Pinckney
PINKNOTTEL
 — Mr. **71** 135
PINKS John **58** 56
 John Chapin **126** 134
 Mary (Sawtell) **126** 134
 Nancy **58** 56
 Sarah **58** 56
PINKSTON Pinkstone
 —— **117** 13-15 17
 Fleming **117** 4 16
 Sarah **64** 256
PINNEGAR
 — Mrs. **62** 355
 John **127** 11
 Mary **127** 10
PINNELL
 Audrey Albee **146** 386
 Henry Edward **64** xxxii
PINNEO Pineo
 Ann (Huntley) **101** 203
 Annie Evelyn **127** 129
 Austin L. **120** 78

PINNEO *cont'd*
B. **84** 236
Caroline **88** 38
David Sampson **101** 203
Edith Caroline **127** 129
Grace **127** 129
Henry Addison **127** 129
Hiram **85** 349
James **60** 731 **85** 349
 133 322
Jonathan **52** 453
Lewis **98** 338
Luke **120** 13
Mary **52** 453 **85** 349
Mary (Fitz Randolph)
 98 338
Mary Isabel **127** 129
Priscilla (Newcomb)
 133 322
Rosanna (Smith) **85** 349
Sally **85** 349
Sally (Bryant) **85** 349
Sarah **133** 322
Susanna (Killam) **120** 13
PINNER Pynner
 — Mr. **73** 196
 — Mrs. **83** 318
 Edmund **57** 317
 Elizabeth **52** 108
 John **74** 134 **75** 291
 114 192
 Nicholas **112** 296
 Sarah **74** 134
 Thomas **80** 388 389
PINNEY Pinny Pinnye
 Pynney
 —— **60** 67 **61** 336
 Abraham **71** 279 **72** 36
 144 356
 Agnes **63** 41 42
 Alexander **63** 36 39 41 42
 Alice **63** 36
 Almon **71** 49 51 52
 Almon W. **71** 120
 Angeline **83** 360
 Ann **87** 147 **102** 306
 Anne **63** 37
 Anthony **63** 36
 Beatrice **63** 42
 Benjamin **72** 115
 Bridget **63** 41 42
 Carlos E. **85** 169
 Caroline M. **96** 203
 Catherine **63** 42
 Charles Almon **71** 52
 Charles C. **96** 203
 Chloe **72** 101 **83** 51
 Daniel **66** 41
 Ebenezer **72** 206
 Edmund **59** 328 **63** 36 37
 39-42
 Eleazer **60** 78 362
 Elizabeth **63** 37 38 40 41
 Ellen **96** 203
 Ellen Agnes **52** 328
 Elma J. (Sherwood)
 119 309
 Esther **83** 359 360
 Esther Maria **83** 360
 Eunice **60** 78
 Evelyn **85** 160

PINNEY cont'd
Frances B. **83** 360
George **72** 232
Grace **63** 41
Grace De W. 53 **105** 53
Henry H. **119** 309
Hester **63** 37 40
Horatio **87** 147
Humphrey **59** 328 **63** 38-41 **81** 122 **100** 220 **145** 77 **147** 158
Isaac **66** 41 **72** 37
Jane **59** 328
Joan **59** 328 **63** 36-41 **72** 232
John **59** 328 **63** 36-42 **82** 307 **100** 220
John B. **52** 328
Jonathan **72** 36
Katie C. **93** 48
Lorinda **71** 49
Louise T. **93** 48
Lucretia **71** 279
Lurana **71** 52 120
Martha **66** 41
Mary **52** 418 **71** 120 **112** 125 **136** 333
Mary (Hull) **100** 220
Maude **96** 160 **147** 148 253
Nancy J. **72** 206
Nancy R. **72** 206
Nathaniel **148** 356
Nicholas **63** 37 38 40 41
Oliver **71** 51
Pamelia **60** 362
Parthesy **63** 40
Peter **63** 37
Priscilla **77** 303
Protesia **63** 41
Prudence **63** 40
Ralph L. **93** 48
Richard **63** 37 38 40 42 **64** 322
Roger **63** 37 40 42
Romanta **83** 359 360
Roswell **96** 203
Rozana **60** 199
Ruth **72** 100
Sabra **83** 51
Sally (Woodbury) **87** 147
Salome **72** 37
Sarah **59** 328 **63** 37 38 40 41 **71** 279 **72** 101 **86** 17
Sarah A. **119** 308
Sophia L. **72** 106
Susanna **63** 37 40 **66** 41 **72** 115
Thankful **72** 115
Thomas **63** 37 39 41 42 **134** 303 304 **135** 23
William **63** 36-38 40 42 **71** 53 54
PINNING Pynning
—— **51** 389
Daniel **147** 31
PINNOCK Pynnock
Dorcas (Titus) **114** 172
Isaac **114** 172
John **101** 268
Pinny see Pinney
Pinnye see Pinney

PINOTEAU Hervé (Baron)
133 85 **145** 368
Hervé Baron **117** 269 271
PINSON Pinsen Pinsent
— Mrs. **51** 412
Ann **72** 232 238
Dorothy **79** 414
Elizabeth (White) **133** 193
Henry **66** 164 165
John **62** 327
Margery **66** 165
Mary **111** 106
Simon **79** 414
Thomas **87** 118 **111** 106 **133** 193
William **53** 29
PINTARD
John **72** xviii 76 **107** 17
John L. **68** 242
Sarah **68** 242
PINTE Joseph **63** 26
PINTNER Dora **108** 140
PINTO Ann **73** 94
F. Mendes **110** 275
Mary Ann **73** 94 182
Samuel **73** 94
PIO Agnes (Williams) **83** 438 **84** 23
Harry L. **83** 438 **84** 23
PIODA John B. **55** 237
PIPARD —— **141** 108
Ralph **75** 130 131
PIPE Pype
— Capt. **64** 363
Alice (Jenney) **118** 201
John I. **91** 332
Peter **91** 328
Thankful (Dillingham) **118** 201
Thomas **87** 219
PIPER —— **53** 360 **54** 109 238 **62** 36 **78** 347
— Mr. **62** 197
Abigail **56** 42 **59** 290 **61** 274 **97** 370 **100** 70 71 **135** 128
Abigail (Goodens) **125** 108
Abigail (Haines) **91** 394
Abigail C. **73** 206
Abigail Haines **91** 394
Adeline **75** 259
Albert G. **52** 85
Alfreda **111** 113
Alice **61** 333 337 **62** 41 **68** 188
Anna **111** 41
Anna Dumont **75** lxxxii
Anne **69** 19
Anne Palfrey **66** 3 9 **76** 215
Anne Taggard **66** 3 **76** 215
Annie Belle (Dame) (Crowell) **92** 203
Artemas **87** 232 235
Asa **68** 100 **92** 107 **97** 370
Azekah **111** 113
Benjamin **62** 39 **73** 64 **100** 71 **135** 128
Blanche Telula **80** 209

PIPER cont'd
Caleb **109** 80
Caroline A. **76** 177
Caroline H. **91** 394
Caty **109** 80
Charles **92** 203 **115** 38
Charles A. **91** 394
Charles W. **91** 394 **100** 71
Clark **91** 392 394
Comfort **100** 70 71 **135** 128
Daniel **105** 289
David **71** 54 **105** 290
Dennis B. **75** 259
Dolly **59** 289
Dorcas B. **96** 75
Dorothy **109** 80
Ebenezer **109** 80
Ebenezer H. **76** 177
Elba **69** 142
Eleanor **51** 186
Eley **59** 290
Elisha **68** 332 **105** 289
Eliza A. **91** 394
Eliza Jane **69** 142
Elizabeth **71** 116 **76** 177
Elizabeth Bridge **66** 3
Elizabeth Mary **147** 230
Ella Wayman **81** 43
Emily Elizabeth **78** 347
Erastus B. **91** 394
Frances **62** 31
Francis **76** 42 **125** 108
Frank (Mrs.) **79** 324 **80** 209
Fred S. **56** 330 **57** xxxiii **64** xxxii **67** 306
Fred Smith **68** xxxii **70** 193 **73** 161 **89** 305
George **69** 142
George A. **91** 394
George F. **64** 44
George Henry **54** 115
George W. **100** 71
Gretchen **83** 110
Hannah **95** 338 **100** 70 **135** 128
Hannah (Goss) **135** 128
Hannah (Stockbridge) **100** 70 **135** 126 128
Hannah J. **124** 41
Hannah M. **76** 42
Harold L. **91** 394
Harriet **78** 180 **83** 22 26 **100** 71
Harriet (Carter) **83** 22
Helen A. **91** 394
Helkiah **88** 119
Henrietta M. (Weare) **119** 287
Henry M. **91** 394
Ida M. **91** 394
Israel **97** 370
James **59** 289 **100** 71 **121** 223
James A. **97** 370
James Monroe **119** 308 309
Jane **91** 394
Jane (Doe) **111** 117
Jason **100** 71

PIPER *cont'd*
Jason E. **100** 71
Jean **65** 353 **135** 127
Jennie **91** 394
Joel **109** 80
John **61** 242 **62** 45 **65** 353
 73 67 69 73 **100** 70 **111**
 41 113 **135** 128
John B. **91** 332
John Gill **69** 244
John H. **92** 115
Jonathan **62** 41 42 44 45
 66 3 **73** 71
Joseph **56** 42 **66** 3 **111** 117
Joseph P. **91** 394
Josiah **62** 42 **68** 332
Kathy **109** 80
Keziah **109** 80
Laura A. **76** 177
Lauretta **100** 71
Lenora Betsey (Sherwood)
 119 308 309
Lois **100** 71
Lois (Rowell) **100** 71
Louisa C. **100** 71
Lucy A. **124** 62
Lydia **61** 332 334 **62** 36
 109 79
M. (Stevens) **90** 325
Marcia **87** 392 **91** 296 297
Margaret **73** 227 **75** 259
Margaret A. **68** 332
Margery **116** 315
Martha **100** 71 **135** 128
Mary **59** 283 **68** 332 **71** 116
 76 177 **93** 286 386 **97**
 370
Mary (Hammond)
 87 232 235
Mary (Stevens) **92** 115
Mary A. **83** 110
Mary C. (Foss) **91** 392 394
Mary E. **83** 178 185 **91** 394
Mary Elizabeth **66** 3
Mary Elmira (Cole)
 86 365
Mary J. **69** 142
May (Gordon) **123** 224
Merrick **73** 75 76 **91** 297
Molly **100** 70 **135** 128
Moses **69** 142 **83** 22 26
 140 236
Myra Susan **92** 203
N. **65** 375
Nancy **59** 290 **97** 370
Nathan **73** 64 **100** 70 71
 340 **135** 128
Nathaniel **54** 240 **62** 39 41
 66 3 **73** 64 **89** 305 **100**
 70 71 **125** 93 **135** 128
Nathaniel E. **119** 287
Noah **73** 75
Nora Anna **84** 192
Olive (Kezar) **86** 365
Patience **62** 39
Patty **100** 71
Pelatiah **92** 115 **97** 370
Pelatiah A. **90** 325
Phebe **61** 242 **109** 80
Pliny **75** 259
Prudence **74** 295

PIPER *cont'd*
Rachel **69** 142 **100** 71
 135 128
Ralph Crosby **66** 3
Rebecca **59** civ
Richard **69** 19
Sally **64** 205 **111** 41 113
 114 179
Sally (Currier) **135** 128
Samuel **59** 290 **62** 39 **73**
 64-66 75 76 **91** 332 **100**
 71 **116** 76 **118** 101 195
 135 128
Samuel J. **91** 394
Samuel Park **78** 347
Sarah **62** 36 44 **65** 352 **73**
 206 **100** 70 **135** 128
Sarah (Pierce) **103** 235
Sarah J. **91** 394
Sawyer **109** 80
Sewell W. **100** 71
Silas **71** 48 116 117
Simon **103** 235
Solomon **66** 3
Sophronia **68** 97 **111** 113
Stephen **73** 64 67 68 75 206
 97 370
Suel W. **100** 71
Susanna **59** 284 **67** 182
 73 206
Tabitha **73** 206 **107** 236
 237
Thomas **62** 38 **67** 182 **69**
 19 **73** 75 76 **86** 365 **100**
 70 71 **107** 236 237 **135**
 128
William **51** 356 **76** 177
 86 365
William Bridge **66** 3
William H. **83** 110
William T. **52** 377
William Taggard **53** 452
 54 v vii xxii xxiii 110
 220 221 **55** xiv xv 221
 57 vi **58** xvii **59** v vi
 xxiii xlii **60** v vi xvii **61**
 xiv xvi **62** xiv **64** vi **65**
 vi **66** lix lxxxvi 4-9 **76**
 215
PIPES Clement **115** 79
John **115** 79 240 **136** 127
Jonathan **63** 138
Joseph **115** 79
Stephen **115** 79
William **63** 138 **115** 79
Windsor **115** 240
PIPOON
Abigail **100** 141
John **100** 141
Mary **100** 141
PIPPLE
William **58** 397 398
PIRE Leonora (Howard)
 123 309
PIRKINS Mary **141** 332
PIRONE
Tertulliano **136** 345
PIRRITTE
David A. **69** 33
Eliza **69** 33
Eliza A. **69** 33

PIRRITTE *cont'd*
Isaac N. **69** 33
John **69** 33
John N. **69** 33
Lucy M. **69** 33
Mary E. **69** 33
William **69** 33
William A. **69** 33
PIRRUN G. R. **129** 397
PISCATORE
Johann **124** 312
PISCO Abigail **91** 263
PISEAN Polly **63** 49
PISHAM Alice **84** 74
PISHON Almira **69** 182
Eunice **111** 42
Hiram **69** 182
Pit *see* Pitts
PITCAIRN —— **56** 342
— Maj. **85** 9
PITCHER —— **52** 254 **60**
 190 **99** 125 282 285 **101**
 163 **117** 16
— Mr. **58** 174
Abigail **76** 132 **100** 28
Abigail (Chase) **87** 335
Abigail (Tupper) (Perry)
 99 125
Abner **91** 38
Andrew **55** liv **96** 76 **109**
 234 **132** 326 **136** 184
Asa **76** 132
Barnard **81** 322
C. Norwood **64** xxxii
Catherine **60** 284
Claude Meek **97** 158
David **75** 305 **99** 285
Edmund **60** 284
Edward **142** 61
Electa **82** 272
Elijah **132** 326
Elizabeth **60** 283 **100** 296
 105 222 223
Ernest **100** 26
Experience **55** liv **96** 76
 113 134
Experience (Jones)
 113 135
Ezra **113** 135
Frances **143** 346 347
George **105** 285 **125** 33
Gurdon **86** 390
Hannah **56** 208 **75** 154
Henry **106** 306
Hugh **81** 322
Isaac **87** 335
Isabella **60** 295
Jacob **100** 28
James **119** 75
Jennet **86** 390
John **75** 154 **99** 282 **105**
 223 **128** 50 **129** 55
John Ernest **99** 209 282
 285 **100** 28 **101** 163
Jonathan **86** 385 **128** 54
Joseph **58** 172 175 **66** 35
Lemuel **117** 239
Lewis **105** 286
Louise **77** 254
Lucy (Hannum) **91** 38
Lydia **58** 175 **99** 209

PITCHER *cont'd*
Margaret **58** 404 **104** 314
Mary **52** 451 **112** 181 **113**
  118 **125** 222 **126** 80
Mary (Dolbeare) **112** 181
Mary Ann **90** 56
Mehitable **86** 385
Mercy **58** 172 175
Molly **86** 384 **91** 306
Moses **112** 181 **113** 118
  117 11 16
Nabby **125** 105
Nancy **57** 187
Nathaniel **57** 226 **87** 399
  113 135
Nazareth **106** 306
Olive **61** 43
Raphael Chase (Mrs.) **99**
  148 **109** 234
Rebecca **86** 390
Rebecca (Brown) **105** 222
Reuben **55** 69
Ruth **51** 465 **134** 116
  142 24
Samuel **51** 465 **76** 132
Sarah **99** 254 **113** 118
Sargent (Mrs.) **117** 239
Stephen **60** 295 **116** 222
Susan **130** 291
Thomas **60** 284 **100** 26
Ursula **60** 287
William **52** 254 **55** 69 **60**
  287 **81** 196
Zerviah (Booth) **113** 135
PITCHWALL
Abu **100** 243
PITHARD Amos **111** 117
PITHOUD Philip
  Augustus **65** 230
PITILEE Daniel **112** 291
PITIMY Hannah **62** 370
PITKIN
—— **119** 132 **122** 221
— Col. **118** 304 **119** 127
  206
— Mr. **66** 163
— Mrs. **79** 405 **118** 24 25
  219 231
Aaron **103** 62
Albert P. **66** 161
Alice Woodruff **96** 129
  130
Amy **136** 333
Amy (Moore) **136** 333
Ann **129** 211
Anna **54** 258 **82** 360 **98** 94
  118 3 230
Anne **66** 162
Annie **68** 26
Ashbel **72** 288
Betty **119** 207
Billy **118** 110 **119** 208 211
Caleb **59** 268
Calvin **52** 418 **79** 160
Caroline **122** 186
Caroline (Hand) **122** 186
Catherine **136** 328
Chloe (Norton) **98** 94
Clarissa **79** 152
Content **136** 325
Cynthia **83** 162

PITKIN *cont'd*
Daniel **98** 94
David **54** 84
Deborah **59** 268
Dorothy **72** 317
Edward **79** 152 **82** 455
Edward H. **122** 185
Eleazur **136** 333
Eli **136** 333
Elisha **119** 45
Elizabeth **52** 412 **53** 447 **54**
  80 82 **55** 442 **66** 161 163
  79 317 **118** 3 **129** 211
  136 313 328
Ella **76** 19
Emele **120** 295
Emily (Norton) **98** 94
Ephepras **122** 221
Epp. **118** 230
Eppa **118** 118 **119** 207 219
  302 **121** 62
Eppa (Mrs.) **119** 208 302
Eppephoras **118** 122
Eunice **52** 417
Ezra **122** 302
Fanny **79** 151
Fidelia M. (James)
  136 333
Fidelia Maria **80** 247
Florence Terry **80** 247
Frances **79** 405 **80** 62
Francis **66** 162 163
Frederick Walker **80** 247
  136 333
George **66** 162 163 **79** 151
  118 110 **119** 207 222
  137 256
Gilbert Stanley **96** 130
Hannah **79** 153 **147** 58
Hannah Miller (Torrey)
  136 333
Harry **122** 186
Horace L. **79** 160
J. O. **79** 156
Jane **66** 161 163
Jerusha **54** 254 **79** 317
  119 207
Joan **66** 161 163
John **66** 161-163 **118** 24
  118 119 217 219 **119** 207
  222 229
Joseph **79** 153
Joshua **122** 186
Julia **103** 62
Kate Cheney (Hudson)
  96 130
Leonard **58** 403
Lucy **54** 253
Lucy M. **79** 156
Lydia **122** 212
Maria B. **53** 398
Martha **52** 409-412 414-
  416 418 **53** 448 **54** 82 **60**
  376 **61** 180 181 **66** 160-
  163 **79** 317 **83** 100 **85**
  426 **90** 358 **104** 250 251
  105 234
Mary (Hatch) **99** 125
Mary Ann **79** 156
Mary Cone **134** 150
Mary H. **79** 152

PITKIN *cont'd*
Mary Yale **90** 136
Mehitable (Cone) **136** 333
Minerva **122** 186
Minerva (Hand) **122** 186
Minnie E. **76** 19
Nabby **119** 208
Nathaniel **118** 3 **129** 211
Osmyn **98** 94
Owen **58** 403
Ozias **67** 89
Paul **52** 416 **58** 403 **60** 203
Phebe **122** 105
Polly **54** 84
Rebecca **52** 415
Rhoda **54** 258 **56** 353
Richard **52** 417 **54** 258
  118 118 122 **119** 215
Robert **66** 161
Robert James **136** 333
Roger **66** 160-163
S. L. **79** 156
Samuel **52** 410 411 **54** 259
  56 163 **79** 310 405 **80** 62
  83 100
Samuel (Mrs.) **80** 62
Sarah **55** 442 **66** 163 **118** 3
  129 205 **136** 326
Susanna (Stanley) **98** 94
Theodocia **61** 398
Theodore **119** 207
Thomas **52** 309 409-412
  414-416 418 **53** 447 449
  54 253 254 **56** 162 163
  352 **64** 323 **83** 100 **99**
  125
Thomas White **52** 409 **54**
  257 258
Timothy **82** 360
W. F. **83** 162
White **54** 259 **56** 353
William **55** 442 **66** 160-163
  76 19 **79** 317 **82** 360 **83**
  59 **85** 34 36 **87** 174 **89**
  396 **105** 247 **107** 69 **118**
  26 **129** 205 206 **142** 333
PITLER John **125** 216
Juley (McClannan /
  Claret) **125** 216
PITMAN Pittman Pittmann
—— **55** 437 **67** 132-134 **83**
  36 **118** 238 **140** 230
— Dea. **62** 284
— Mr. **62** 290
— Mrs. **83** 36 195
—— (Tebbets) **98** 136
Abigail **86** 65 **96** 227
  132 242
Adeline Mary (Hinsdale)
  113 227
Alice **51** 348
Almira **78** 202
Almira (Hollander)
  94 195
Ann **73** 311 **78** 294
Ann (Bennett) **125** 175
Anna **94** 123 124
Barnabas Palmer **94** 124
Benjamin **62** 356 **63** 57
  71 288 **81** 433 **94** 123
  195 196 **100** 278 **111** 57

PITMAN *cont'd*
113 227 116 42 120 6
125 236 289 127 221
Benjamin Franklin
94 195
Benjamin Franklin (Mrs.)
77 321 78 202 94 127
143 195
Betsey 76 36 133 121
Bridget 55 437
Charles 82 52 113 227
Charlotte 75 266 94 125
Charlotte (Thoms) 94 125
Cornelius 94 123
David 76 36
Dorcas 82 287 297
Dorothy 83 22 26 88 337
Dorothy (Card) 83 22
Edson 94 125
Eliza 81 433 125 177
Eliza A. 126 24
Eliza Trafton 94 124
Elizabeth 51 45 54 312 81
141 142 449 82 52 125
180 126 145 136 49
Elizabeth (Bolles) 132 242
Elizabeth (Perry) 116 43
Elizabeth (Reynolds)
113 227
Elizabeth (Spiller)
135 105
Elizabeth Grace 102 123
113 59 227
Elizabeth H. 125 179
Ellen Harrod 75 266
Ezekiel 81 141 82 52 282
297
Francis 98 136
Frederick 54 312
Frederick Cobbe 54 309
311 312 84 466
George B. 126 24
George H. 75 266
George L. 75 266
Grace M. 141 244 250
H. Minot 89 97 94 304 105
54 106 50 108 179 291
113 242 119 154 121
235 123 169 142 39
Hannah 78 187 91 369 94
124 99 294
Harold Minot 93 138
Harry A. 54 309 312
145 262
Harry Anderson 84 466
Henry 71 288 113 227
Henry Warren 94 125
Howard Mason 103 120
Ira 94 124
Isaac 125 183 242
Isabel 94 125
Isabel (Beal) 94 125
Isanna 72 246
Izah 94 125
James 67 62 63 117 186
125 173 127 15
Joanna 55 437
John 51 348 55 437 66 37
70 263 71 288 81 449
82 52 93 382 385 387 94
125 174 111 55 113 227

PITMAN *cont'd*
116 42 125 173 175 126
24 127 11 139 133 252
144 344 147 339
Jonathan 80 304 93 385
387
Joseph 62 127 81 449 82
52 94 124 116 43 124
275 127 216
Josiah 81 433
Kenooli (Hoohilu) 94 195
Leonard Thoms 94 125
Lucinda Sernia Roach
133 72
Lucy Ann 124 190
Lucy Morton (Kent)
113 227
Lulu Isabelle 69 144
Lydia 54 309 311 312
87 283
Lydia (Barker) 125 183
242
Lydia (Perry) 116 42
Lydia Greenleaf 94 125
Mark 81 433 449 82 52 83
22 26 94 123-125
Mark Gleason 94 123 125
Mary 75 47 49 81 449 82
52 90 192 111 56 124
275
Mary (Handy) 125 137
Mary (Saunders) 113 227
Mary (Usher) 120 6
Mary (Wardwell) 113 227
Mary A. 69 144
Mary Ann 88 15
Mary Ann (Carter)
125 236
Mary Elizabeth 100 278
Mary Smith 94 125
Moses 62 94 127 144
Nancy (Bennett) 125 173
126 24
Olive 108 190
Olive Gibbs 82 52
Oren C. 69 144
Peleg 113 227 127 15
Polly 89 84
Rachel Hall 125 174 240
Rachel Hull 125 240
Rebecca 78 310
Rebecca (Cary) 113 227
Remember 62 94
Robert 54 312
Robert C. 125 236
Roxana 138 282
Ruth 133 252
Sally 94 123 124
Sally (Richardson)
125 289
Sally (Stilphen) 94 123
124
Samuel 113 227
Sanders 127 228
Sarah 81 449 82 282 297
Sarah (Spooner) 117 186
Saunders 65 221
Sequal 82 52
Sukey 94 123
Susanna 67 276 72 246
Tabitha 98 136

PITMAN *cont'd*
Temperance 80 304
Theodore Baldwin 94 196
Theophilus Topham
71 288
Thomas 54 277 278
127 224
Thomas Cobbe 54 312
William 51 45 54 312 55
83 64 113 66 36 77 75
78 111 98 136 116 43
William C. 100 278
William D. 69 144
Zachariah 89 83
PITMANN James 115 57
PITMORE — Widow 127 14
PITNER J. 91 332
Paul Jerome (Mrs.) 81 354
Ruby Hortense 81 354
PITNEY James 58 cxi 95
135 101 73
Sarah 58 cxi 101 73
PITRE
Angelique 143 7 9
Claude 143 9
Marie (Comeau) 143 9
PITSNER Simon 94 340
PITSON Hannah 144 202
PITSOR Wilson 76 275
Pitt *see* Pitts
PITTAM
Abiah M. 68 255
Adeline 68 255
Cecilia R. 68 255
Clementine D. 68 255
Edward 68 255
Elizabeth 68 255
Ellen 68 255
James H. 68 255
Mary E. 68 255
Miriam S. 68 255
Orville A. 68 255
Samuel E. 68 255
Pittard *see* Pitterd
Pitte *see* Pittey
Pittee *see* Pittey
PITTENGER
George L. 104 80
PITTERD Pittard
____ (Cogan) 110 195
Agnes 128 153 154
Elizabeth 63 36
Elizabeth (Lavor) 110 195
John 110 195 261 262
William 110 195 262
Pittes *see* Pitts
PITTEY Pittee Pitty
Elizabeth 61 51
Hanna L. 90 42
James 119 112 123 124
Joseph 61 51
Marcy 102 149
Mary 61 51
Nathaniel 93 154
Ruth 119 12
Samuel 61 51
Thomas 54 88
Pittinggell *see* Pettingill
Pittis *see* Pitts
Pittman *see* Pitman
Pittmann *see* Pitman

PITTOCKE Elizabeth **67**
39 40 44
William **67** 38-40 44
PITTRO
Joseph **82** 283 297
Mary **82** 283 297
PITTS Pit Pitt Pitte Pittes
Pittis
——— **70** 22 **92** 357 **93** 63
104 175 **121** 270
— Capt. **145** 293
— Widow **138** 119
Aaron **90** 229 247
Abby (Chase) **88** 16
Abiah **111** 44
Abial **111** 44 113
Abial Hiram **111** 44
Alice **62** 232 233 **148** 72
Alice (Pinkham) **91** 25 30
Almira (Chase) **91** 119 123
Anastasia (Clary) **86** 221
Ann **90** 67 **113** 45 **125** 272
143 129
Anna **121** 17 **129** 49 51
Anna G. **122** 217
Anne (Cary) **125** 272
Asenath M. **101** 95
Augusta S. (Parsons)
126 67
Azubah **111** 44
Benjamin **90** 252 320 326
91 17 **100** 69
Beswick **86** 221
Betsey **111** 113
Betsey (Trask) **87** 236 240
Calvin Waide **111** 113
Catherine **72** 244
Charles **78** 183
Charles Lendell **92** 256
Christopher **55** 334
Deborah **54** 417 418 **121**
24 192
Delia **122** 217
Dorcas **89** 103
Ebenezer **62** 232 233 **63**
129 **121** 267 **142** 19
Edmond **90** 318 **121** 215
Edmund **90** 229 250 **95**
199 **113** 45 **143** 129
Eliza **75** 38 **88** 286 **90** 318
330 **91** 22
Eliza Jane **93** 124
Elizabeth **52** 114 **54** 417
418 **55** 405 **58** 69 **84** 271
91 81 **113** 45 **119** 33
121 20 194 **143** 126 129
130 343
Elizabeth (Bowdoin) **86**
221 **114** 252
Elizabeth (Brightman)
123 39
Elizabeth (Hoskins)
125 272
Elizabeth (Lindell) **86** 221
Elizabeth (Peckham)
123 39
Elizabeth Warner **55** 406
Emeline **90** 43 **125** 245
Emily **55** 405
Emily (Shattuck) **125** 223
Eseck **138** 119

PITTS *cont'd*
F. S. **122** 217
Frances **125** 241
Francis Henry **92** 356
Fred **122** 217
Freelove **100** 69
Friend **82** 382 **83** 233 **86**
109 204 221
George **81** 492 **123** 39
George M. **109** 271
Gilbert D. **96** 328
Hannah **66** 125 **67** 286
90 318
Hannah (Hamilton) **90**
229 250 **95** 199
Hannah (Low) **90** 246
Hanover **88** 16
Harriet **86** 232 **90** 337
Harriet (Briggs) **126** 268
Henry **81** 92 **88** 27 **93** 176
125 272
Hepzibah **90** 318 326
91 18
Ichabod **87** 236 240
Ignatious **127** 226
Ireney **63** 88
Isaac **121** 18 203
J. Angeline **109** 271
James **55** 405 **57** 280 388
58 69 **63** 85 **65** 32 **84**
258 271 357 **85** 118 **86**
221 **91** 94 **104** 242 **107**
100 **114** 252 263 **119** 20
33 314 **131** 189 270
James Lendall **55** 406
James R. **101** 95
Jane **93** 124
Jeremiah **63** 86-88 **118** 140
121 106 199
Joanna **51** 466
Johanna **83** 167
John **55** 315 **61** 279 **66**
125 126 **68** 180 181 **81**
93 **83** 10 167 **85** 122 128
86 221 **118** 313 **119** 34
121 103 201 **122** 217
127 228 **134** 196 **138**
321 **141** 30 **147** 27
John Avery **111** 44
John K. **101** 94 95 **109** 271
John M. **76** 268
Joseph **116** 7 **126** 268
Judah **90** 320
Judith **55** 315 **83** 10 90
239 314 **138** 321
Judith (Wood) **83** 10
Katinka (Utt) **86** 221
Lendall **55** 405 **85** 124 **92**
356 357 **93** 63 **94** 40
Louisa **70** xxxii
Lucinda G. **91** 120 124
Lucy Hellen **101** 95
Luke **90** 321
Margaret **80** 353
Margaret Birney **107** 238
Margery **144** 54
Martha **125** 215
Martha (Lord) **138** 321
Mary **51** 455 **52** 16 **59** 247
60 239 **62** 232 233 **83**
167 **90** 327 **91** 18 **100**

PITTS *cont'd*
241 298 **113** 45 **121** 14
15 193 267 **125** 211 272
126 41 164
Mary (Derby) **86** 221
Mary Ann **76** 268
Mary Jane (Bancroft)
96 328
Mary Jane (Phoebus)
86 221
Mary Lovina **101** 94
Matilda **118** 140
Maud **63** lxiv **131** 6 208
Mehitable (Bishop)
124 79
Mehitable (Scribner) **90**
334 **91** 24
Meliora **81** 316
Molly **90** 227 244
Moses **90** 230 246 320 321
Nancy (Brooks) **86** 221
Nario C. (Hall) **96** 328
Nathan **61** 279
Nathaniel **90** 321 **91** 119
123
Olive **111** 44
Orlando **92** 357 **94** 160
Parthia **111** 44
Percey **63** 87
Perly **63** 87
Peter **51** 455 **52** 16 **60** 313
62 232 63 129 **97** 328
329 **125** 79 83 **131** 237
Polly **90** 321 **111** 117
121 266
Polly (Knight) **90** 326
91 17
Rachel **63** 86
Rebecca **52** 106 114
Richard **93** 124
Robert **51** 435
Rufus **128** 53
Ruth **90** 254 **108** 160
Ruth (Philpot) **90** 229 247
Sally **63** 86 **90** 320
Sally (Hamilton) **90** 230
246
Samuel **51** 466 **60** 313 **62**
232 233 **63** 86 129 **69**
112 **83** 167 **97** 329 **124**
79
Sarah **62** 233 **63** 129 **72** 244
275 317 **83** 167 **90** 229
248 **94** 40 **101** 94 95 **109**
271 **121** 12 114
Sarah (Archer) **96** 70
Sarah (Warren) **90** 252
Sarah Barney (Chase)
88 27
Sarah Eliza **93** 63
Sarah L. **96** 129
Simeon **90** 321
Simeon H. **90** 334 **91** 24
25 30
Stephen **65** 30
Susanna **63** 89 **90** 228 246
102 180
Sylvanus **100** 278
Thankful **59** 196 201
Thomas **67** 286 **79** 412 **81**
321 **83** 167 **84** 258 **90**

PITTS *cont'd*
246 **99** 80 **126** 164
William **52** 114 **54** 417 418
55 405 **59** 247 **60** xvi
239 **63** lxiv **65** 22 **72**
244 275 **79** 313 **81** 92 **84**
155 **86** 221 **94** 60 **102**
180 **103** 15 **121** 27 **123** 6
125 223 **132** 33 **145** 348
William (Earl of
Chatham) **129** 145
Willie **122** 217
PITTSBURY
Abin **91** 332
PITTWINE Alice **52** 66
Pitty *see* Pittey
PITZER
Andrew Baker **102** 165
Beatrice (Batten) **102** 165
Emma **83** 65
Mabel **102** 165
Mary Belle (Sharpe)
102 165
Rachel (Marshall) **102** 165
PIUS X Pope **59** 338
132 254
Piveyer *see* Pevear
PIXE Anne **51** 260
George **51** 260
PIXLEY Abigail (Clark)
90 160
Clara **76** 177
David **54** 163
Electa **85** 223 **111** 151
Elizabeth (Hannum)
90 160
Jonah **90** 160
Jonathan **53** 314 **115** 14
Joseph **90** 160
Lebbeus **115** 14
Linda J. **117** 238
Lydia **137** 36
Lydia (Dibble) **123** 264
Mabel **53** 314 **115** 14
Malinda **136** 327
Martin W. **76** 177
Mary **53** 314
Mary J. **76** 177
Polly **66** 23
Raymond H. **130** 47
Samuel **76** 177
Sarah **123** 260
Tho **123** 264
Violet E. **130** 47
William **115** 128
PIXSTON Pixton
Alice **141** 116 118
Alice (Warde) **141** 118
Daniel **147** 143
Elizabeth **141** 118
Elizabeth (Moulton) **141**
322 **147** 143
Johane **141** 118
John **141** 117 118 322
147 143
Nicholas **141** 118
Thomas **141** 117-119
William **141** 118 **147** 143
PLACE Plaise Playse
— Mr. **71** 137
— Mrs. **82** 414

PLACE *cont'd*
Abigail **76** 27
Alice **65** 214
Alice (Tempest) **93** 11 35
96 107 **114** 52
Amos **65** 257
Anne **63** 173
Benajah **127** 308
Charles **83** 298 301
Christopher **93** 35 **114** 52
Christopher P. **70** 157
Clarissa (Durrell) (Green)
133 120
Daniel **119** 69 **120** 68
David **65** 78 80 112 258 342
95 374 **99** 244 245
Dorothy **73** 198 **91** 365
Eddie **84** 87
Eliza B. **127** 198
Elizabeth **82** 290 297 **125**
301 **128** 224
Emily Y. **76** 42
Enoch **76** 27 28 44 **85** 112
87 268 **96** 227 **100** 229
118 185 187 196 **127**
308
Enos **65** 257 **73** 198
Esther Frances **61** 80
George **95** 54
Hannah **65** 257
Hannah (Cole) **122** 245
Hannah (Walker) **145** 265
Henry **117** 289
J. **59** 181
James **62** 325
Jesse **146** 349
John **60** 190 **66** 232 **73** 198
82 290 297 **85** 112 **95** 53
John M. **80** 310
John S. **127** 33
Joseph **65** 214
Keturah **66** 232
Lucy **135** 128
M. D. **85** 112
Marbury **122** 242 245 246
248
Margaret **64** 260
Margaret (Stafford)
122 246
Martha Jane **73** 198
Mary **53** 450 **74** 26 **146** 349
Mary (James) **127** 33
Mary (Welch) **119** 69
120 68
Mary Esther **70** 157
Mary H. **68** 203
Mary Locke **93** 48
Miriam **53** 384 450
Myra (Edgerly) **83** 298
301
Myron Darling **83** 371
84 191 **102** 62 129
Nancy **117** 289
Nancy (Slate) **110** 31
111 135
Nathan **127** 309
Nicodemus **53** 450
Olive S. (Cox) (Benchley)
142 376
Pamelia **80** 310
Peter **96** 273 **128** 60

PLACE *cont'd*
Phebe **73** 127 **80** 310
Philip **129** 55
Polly **65** 257
Rhobe (Luther) **138** 45
Richard **80** 310
Robert **93** 15
Robert K. **133** 120
Rufus **127** 308
Ruth **108** 299
Sally **80** 310
Samuel **53** 450
Sarah **80** 310 **128** 224
Silas **65** 257
Simeon **65** 257 **128** 60
Solomon F. **142** 376
Stephen **127** 308
Thomas **110** 31 **111** 135
122 245 246 **129** 55
William **80** 310 **93** 15
116 226 **117** 289
PLACETHES Mary
(Stewart) **105** 80
Nicholas **105** 80
PLACEWAY Plaisceway
Plaseay Plaseway
Mary **126** 96
Mary (Leigh) **94** 60
Mehitable (Hamilton)
(Godfrey) **126** 96
127 40
Robert **126** 96 **127** 40
William **94** 60
PLACIDE Della Marie
Louise du Guay du
116 236
PLAINE Anna **53** 406
William **53** 406
PLAINFIELD
Eunice **56** 270
Plaisceway *see* Placeway
Plaise *see* Place
Plaiseay *see* Placeway
PLAISTED Plaistedd
Plaisteed Plaisterd
Plastard
—— **55** 405 **83** 308
— Col. **59** 147 **95** 362
Abigail **82** 325
Adaline (Perkins) **119** 225
123 152
Addie **122** 72 300 310
Almira S. **67** 274 284
Amanda **67** 273 274
Ann J. (Fuller) **123** 73 150
Ann L. **123** 150
Anne **67** 188 **74** 49 125
Anne L. (Roberts) **120** 309
121 70 **123** 150
Annie T. (Bagley) **123** 152
Benaiah D. **67** 273
Benjamin Browne
144 266
Benjamin Small **99** 201
Benning Moulton **67** 183
68 151 **69** 331
Betsey **74** 257
Betsey (Colcord) **90** 237
238
Betsey (Littlefield) **117**
141 142

PLAISTED *cont'd*
Byron **99** 202
Caroline Virginia **67** 281
Catherine B. **68** 153
Celia Louvan **69** 144
Charles **123** 152
Charles H. **67** 274
Charles W. **122** 71 232
Chester **68** 153
Clara F. (Garey) **123** 73
Cyrus C. **68** 153
D. Jane (Merrifield)
  120 306
Daniel **67** 188 **74** 49
Deborah **117** 223 224
Dora J. **67** 281
Dorothy **88** 355 **99** 200
Ebenezer **116** 305 **118** 154
  120 309 **121** 70
Ebenezer P. **83** 150
Edward **120** 223 224
Elisha **54** 408 **63** 266 **73**
  198 199 **82** 77-80 85 86
  88 90 91 94 213-215 218
  328 **83** 153 195 **95** 267
  106 229
Eliza Jane **67** 277
Elizabeth **55** 312 **68** 153 **73**
  199 **82** 91 510 **95** 267
  268 **100** 169 **106** 229
Ellen **69** 169
Ellen M. **121** 72
Elvira (Littlefield) **83** 183
  185
Emily (Norman) **120** 138
Emily A. **120** 65
Emma S. **121** 306
Ernest **91** 245
Eugene **94** 113
Eunice **55** 405 **67** 277
Ford **67** 188
Frances **99** 202 203
Frances Adeline **67** 281
Frances Olivia **59** 240 241
Francis **116** 134 **119** 146
  285
Francis H. **123** 73
Frank Curtis **67** 281
George **118** 242
George F. **109** 297 305
  113 193 **114** 45 **119** 61
  147 **120** 306
George P. **73** 201
George Walton **82** 330
H. M. **76** 320
Hannah **65** 216 **67** 183
  188 277 **68** 97 **73** 314 **74**
  41 129 **82** 77 78 85 86 88
  314 328 **88** 355 356 **95**
  86 **99** 199-202
Hannah (Moulton) **115**
  306 **119** 226 228 **123**
  153
Hannah (Wheelwright)
  95 267 **106** 229
Hannah E. (Bracy) **120** 224
  304 **123** 234
Hannah H. **73** 193
Hannah R. **67** 183
Hannah Robertson **68** 97
Henry **123** 149

PLAISTED *cont'd*
Henry Fillmore **68** 153
Hiram **67** 183 **68** 97
Horace **91** 245
Horace Lyman **67** 274
Howard W. **93** 48 **123** 234
Ichabod **51** 45 46 **58** 235
  82 74 331 **107** 187 **110**
  317 **124** 289 290 **139**
  290
James **82** 80 211 217 314
  319 322 325 328 **83** 153
  109 297 **111** 19 **115** 306
  117 222 **119** 288 **120** 64
James H. **67** 274 284
James W. **83** 183 185
Jane **55** 313 375 **82** 328
  330 331 511 **83** 16
John **51** 44 **74** 251 **82** 322
  88 356 **99** 201-203 **115**
  60 218 307 **142** 304
John F. **120** 224 304
  123 234
John H. **123** 73 150
Jonathan K. **119** 225
  123 152
Joseph **67** 277 **90** 237 238
  111 19 **112** 214 **114** 46
  119 226 228 279 280
  122 72 **123** 153
Joshua **82** 77
Judith **67** 183 188 277
  73 314
Judith P. **67** 281
Julia A. **121** 307 **122** 150
Julia Ann **120** 216 217
Laura **67** 273
Levi **82** 218
Lois **67** 277 **68** 151
Lorinda (Woodruff)
  91 245
Louis Sumner **67** 281
Lovilla E. **67** 273
Lucy (Lewis) **118** 242
Lulu B. **93** 48
Lulu B. (Morrison)
  123 234
Lydia **109** 297 **123** 149
  142 304
Lydia A. **120** 305 **123** 150
  153
Lydia R. (Goodwin) **121**
  69 70
Lyman **120** 138
Maran **99** 202
Margery **67** 273 277
Marietta (Young) **122** 71
  232
Martha **74** 251 **131** 233
Martha A. **119** 288
Martha G. **67** 274 **68** 152
  161
Mary **51** 46 **55** 316 **58** 235
  67 278 280 **69** 145 **82** 79
  317 322 **83** 12 150 152
  85 299 **97** 266 **115** 223
  307 **124** 290
Mary (Brooks) **118** 154
Mary (Craige) **114** 46
Mary (Nowell) **115** 60

PLAISTED *cont'd*
Mary (Preble) (Craigs)
  111 19
Mary (Smith) **116** 305
Mary A. **123** 153
Mary Ann **67** 274 **68** 155
  119 64 **120** 223 224
Mary Ann (Plaisted) **120**
  223 224
Mary Ellen **67** 281
Mary Malvinah **99** 203
Mary N. **67** 281
Mary S. **63** 94
Matilda K. (Seavey)
  119 285
Mehitable **82** 85 **86** 440
  93 287
Mercy **118** 240 316
Myron **91** 245
Nancy **67** 183 273 281 284
  68 155 161
Naomi **67** 188 **74** 49 181
  120 218
Naomi (Ramsdell) **119**
  288 **120** 64
Olife **109** 297
Olive **67** 188 **73** 201 314
Olive (Austin) (Roberts)
  123 150
Olive Jane **120** 223 224
Oren C. **67** 273 281
Paulina (Ramsdell) **119**
  279 280
Phebe **67** 183 274 **68** 151
  88 355
Rhoda **117** 142
Ricker **67** 277
Robert Andress **99** 203
Roger **59** 116 240 241
  67 188
Ruby **69** 144
Sabrina **59** 240
Sally **55** 375 **83** 16
Sally (Littlefield) **117** 222
Samuel **67** 183 188 273
  274 277 281 284 **68** 155
  161 **73** 314 **82** 88 **88** 355
  91 94 **99** 199 **116** 305
  117 141 142 **131** 233
Samuel Pomery **59** 240
Samuel S. **69** 144
Sarah **67** 277 278 **82** 217
  317 319 328 **99** 202 **111**
  19 **112** 214 **114** 291 **116**
  127
Sarah Ada **120** 308
Sarah Ann **120** 307
Sarah B. **67** 281
Sarah E. **67** 274
Sarah H. **67** 274
Sarah J. **122** 71
Shipwe **82** 217
Sidney G. **121** 69 70
Simon **88** 355 356 **99** 199-
  203
Stephen **67** 277 **68** 153
Susan (Grant) **119** 146
Susan E. **120** 217
Susan Elizabeth **59** 241
Susan K. **119** 226 **123** 150
Susan M. **67** 274 **68** 161

PLAISTED *cont'd*
Thankful **99** 202 203
Will **82** 322
William **55** 313 **67** 183
188 277 278 **68** 97 **69**
144 **73** 314 **74** 49 125
181 185 187 188 **82** 90
325 328 330 331 511 **91**
245 **98** 217
PLAISTER John **55** 338
Simon **87** 122
Plaisterd *see* Plaisted
PLAISTRIDGE Harriet
Amelia **78** 244
Joseph **78** 244
PLAMPIN William **64** 348
350 351
PLANCHE J. R. **118** 172
123 373
PLANK De Plank
Anna (Whiting) **104** 63
Henry Peter **104** 63
Nicholas de **84** 135
PLANNER Philip **128** 108
PLANT Plante
—— **130** 314
Abraham **58** 180
Annie **80** 156
Betsey **146** 372
Elizabeth **71** 73
Eugene **130** 314
Francis W. **60** 187
Hannah **62** 147
Hannah (Wheadon)
124 187
Harriet M. **85** 341
Harry P. **124** 197
Jane / Jennie Houghton
(Fracker) **124** 197
John **62** 147 **91** 332
Lois **54** 177
Peggy **58** 182
Samuel **54** 177 **71** 73
Solomon **95** 19
Tamar **58** 180
Theresa M. **117** 291
PLANTAGENET
Anne **148** 139 140
Anne (Mortimer) **148** 140
Arthur **103** 7 **121** 187
Cecily (Neville) **148** 140
Edmund **141** 94
Edward **104** 270
Elizabeth **108** 172
Joan **148** 255
Philippa **108** 176
Richard **121** 187 190
148 140
PLANTAIN
Jane R. **90** 106
Plante *see* Plant
PLANTIN — Mr. **83** 52
Patience **83** 52 53
PLANTS — Mr. **54** 419
PLANTY Louis Barnabe
110 132
Sebastien Marie **110** 132
Plaseway *see* Placeway
PLASSE
Phebe **51** 406 407
William **51** 401 406 407

PLASSE *cont'd*
107 49
Plastard *see* Plaisted
PLASTER
Dorcas **82** 294 297
Roger **82** 294 297
PLASTRAGE
John **71** 339
Plat *see* Platt
PLATEN
Evelina **114** 190
Mary **80** 248
PLATER George **140** 69
Margaret **73** 267
PLATFOOT
Robert **112** 187
PLATNER
Eliza **115** 114
Eve **115** 114
Hannah **115** 114
Jacob **115** 114
Jacob M. **115** 114
Lucia **115** 114
Maria **115** 114
Mercia **115** 114
Nancy McNamee **115** 114
Peter **115** 114
Polly **115** 114
William **115** 114
PLATO COMICUS **57** 42
PLATO **59** 131 **60** lxi
135 261
PLATT Plat Plats Platte
Platts
—— **53** 137 **61** 317 **91** 174
Abby Jennette (Bullard)
89 22
Abel **69** 377 **141** 301
Abigail **101** 209
Abigail (Sawtell) **126** 135
Amos **126** 102
Ann **61** 67 **96** 297
Anna **109** 311
Aphia **52** 79
Augustus **88** 27
Benjamin Keen **116** 187
Beulah (Bancroft) **96** 331
C. M. **58** 319
Charles **117** 156 **119** 155
Charles Grander **115** 108
Cynthia (Jones) **147** 55
Daniel **115** 26 108
David **116** 187 188
David Rittenhouse **116**
187 188
E. S.W. **101** 216
Ebenezer **56** 258 **73** 213
147 49
Edith G. Russell **78** 205
Edward **61** 67
Edwin **73** 213
Eleanor **116** 187 188
Eliza **75** 268 **90** 187
Elizabeth **52** 432 **62** 219 **63**
195 **108** 290 **109** 185
Elizabeth (Scudder) **107**
302 **108** 223
Elizabeth (Skinner)
91 142
Ella **77** 190
Elsie (Chase) **88** 27

PLATT *cont'd*
Emerson Harlow **115** 26
Emily M. **71** 12
Frances **76** 93
Francis **61** 67
Frank Elbert (Mrs.)
91 142
Fred **96** 332 **108** 290
G. Lewis **126** 102
George **96** 331
George F. **96** 331
George Wood **75** 268
Grace **96** 331 332
Grace Ann **65** 134
Gwen (Mrs.) **122** 320
Hannah **54** 384 **57** 92 **66**
232 **75** lxxxi **86** 102 **96**
382
Hannah (Lane) **147** 55
Hannah M. **76** 43
Harriet **65** 135
Helen Maria **110** 71
Henry **61** 67
Herman Eugene **77** 190
Hezekiah D. **65** 134
Hiram **89** 22
Homer **52** 79
Huldah **56** 257
Isaac **78** 397 **126** 102
Isaac L. **108** 223
Isaac Stephen **108** 222 223
Israel **73** 207 213 **107** 302
108 223
Jacob **66** 232
Jacob L. **108** 223
James **52** 79 **58** 319 **60** 331
65 171 **76** 27
Jane **65** 171 **116** 187
Jane Wallace **82** 237 **108**
63 139 222
Janet Judson **70** xli
Jenny **56** 258
Jeremiah **65** 221
Jesse **94** 305 **111** 293
126 102
Jesse Keen **116** 187
John **52** 79 **54** 384 **59** 356
60 190 **61** 67 **63** 353
144 242
John K. **76** 43
Jonas **126** 102
Jonas Keen **116** 187 188
Jonathan **116** 187 188
Jonathan J. **116** 187
Jonathan Jarmin **116** 188
Jos. **66** 232 **144** 42
Joseph **62** 219 **126** 135
Josiah **55** 108 **56** 361
Lavina R. **57** 396
Letitia **116** 187 188
Letitia (Gilman) **116** 187
Levi **52** 79
Lucy **73** 213
Lucy Etta (Fitz Randolph)
98 232
Lydia **95** 116
Mabel **96** 331
Malora **52** 79
Maria Roshore **75** 268
Martha **65** 171
Martha D. **73** 215

PLATT *cont'd*
Mary **55** 108 **58** 319 **60** 192
61 67 **64** 94 **65** 165 **95** 8
Mary E. **76** 41
Mary H. **125** 54 545
Mary Jane (Redfield)
108 222
Mehitable **56** 361 **107** 152
Mercy **69** 377
Moses **107** 152 **116** 187
Newton **102** 112
Obadiah **126** 102 **147** 55
Ophelia **52** 79
Phebe **86** 446
Philippa (Andrews) (Felt)
148 134
Rachel **116** 187
Rachel (Martindale)
116 187
Randle **65** 48 167
Rebecca **66** 232 **116** 187
188 **127** 8
Rebecca (Keen) **116** 187
Richard **65** 57 58 221 **66**
232 **108** 222 **117** 156
Ruany **73** 213
Ruth **148** 37
Sally **76** 27 **108** 245
Samuel **107** 152 **148** 134
Sarah **52** 79 **55** 108 **61** 381
80 109 **107** 152 **116** 187
126 102 **128** 237 **147** 55
Sarah M. **121** 178
Sophia (Kimberly)
102 112
Stephen **108** 223
Susan **76** 32 **126** 64
Susan D. **76** 40
Tabitha **116** 187
Thomas **61** 67 **63** 83 347
Thomas Collier **91** 101
Timothy **126** 102
Washington **121** 237
Wealthy Jane **65** 135
Willard **65** 134
William **98** 232 **125** 35 36
Zebulon **126** 102
Zilla **107** 302
PLATTER
Lawrence **70** 264
Platts *see* Platt
PLATZ Elizabeth **56** 360
PLAUDEN John **75** 138
PLAUNCHE
Elizabeth de la **103** 294
James de la **131** 101
William de la **103** 294
PLAUT
W. Gunther **114** 160
PLAXTON
Elizabeth **93** 22
PLAYCE —— **52** 237
PLAYER Pleyer
Carita **77** 259
Drusilla **67** 260
Eva Frank **77** 258
George Polk **77** 258
James Yeatman **77** 258
John **76** 56
Lucile N. **77** 258
Sally Hilliard **77** 259

PLAYER *cont'd*
Simon **67** 261
Susan Polk **77** 258
Susan Spratt **77** 258
Susan Trezevant **77** ?58
Thomas Trezevant **77** 259
PLAYFOOTE
Robert **52** 136
PLAYFORD —— **136** 154
Mary **142** 5
PLAYLE Thomas **84** 308
PLAYNE
William **106** 86 315
Plays De *see* De Plays
Playse *see* Place
PLEASANTON Pleasington
Davis (Mrs.) **106** 45
Deborah (Luff) **106** 45
Francis **76** 225
John **106** 45 49
Sarah **106** 45
PLEASANTS —— **55** 272
— Mr. **51** 21 156
Frederick (Mrs.) **89** 388
389
J. Hall **86** 466 **87** 400 **89**
210 **90** 210 **92** 98 **93** 306
94 402 **95** 306 **96** 402
98 98 370 **100** 259
Jacob Hall **74** 82
Nancy **94** 363
PLEASE Ruth **66** 231
William **66** 231
Pleasington *see* Pleasanton
PLEDEN John **63** 235
PLEDGE Mary **65** 129
PLEDGERD
John **63** 358 **68** 324
PLESANCE
Audrey **68** 324
Marable **59** 399
PLESSETIS
Hugh de **139** 285
PLESSETO
Richard de **79** 372
PLESSEY Ela (Malmains)
de **140** 222 223
Hugh de **140** 223
John de **140** 223
Margery de **140** 223
Robert de **140** 222 223
PLESTCHEEFF
Guendolen (Carkeek)
86 222
Theodore (Mrs.) **86** 222
PLEYDELL Oliver **54** 218
Pleyer *see* Player
PLIMPTON De Plimpton
Plumpton Plympton
—— **61** 121
Abigail **53** 348 **58** 346 **61**
261 **79** 38
Albert **109** 69
Amos **62** 370
Amy (Stratton) **94** 50 298
Anne (Pond) **103** 220
Anthonye **86** 424
Asahel **84** 357
Augustus **93** 62 64 **94** 44
Augustus Mandlebert
93 64

PLIMPTON *cont'd*
Benjamin **62** 372
Betsey **61** 121
Calvin Snow **109** 69
Caroline L. (Bacall) **109** 69
Charles G. **103** 120
Charlotte **55** 418
David **103** 220
Doris A. (Patterson)
109 69
Ebenezer **61** 121
Edna (Taylor) **89** 263
Elias **92** 376
Elijah **109** 69
Eliza (Morse) **109** 69
Elizabeth **52** 125 **84** 55 90
360 **104** 97
Elizabeth (Fisher) **58** 346
103 220 **109** 69
Esther **58** 346 **64** 17
Ezekiel **58** 346 **64** 371
Fanny **61** 121
Frances Amelia **71** xxiv
90 130 **103** 218 220 **104**
149
Frank **104** 97
Frederick **51** 189
George **58** 346 **114** 223
George H. **56** 220
George Porter **58** 346
George Washington
62 113
Gershom **51** 189
Hadassah **87** 293
Hannah **56** 382 **57** 396 **58**
346 **94** 44 **124** 187
Hannah (Richardson)
103 220
Harriet Amelia (Adams)
103 220
Henry **56** 37 **57** 103 **61** 121
79 95 **103** 220
Henry R. **103** 220
Huldah (Lovell) **109** 69
Irene (Snow) **109** 69
Isabella **114** 222
James **51** 189 **91** 332 **94**
50 298 **109** 69
James Leonard **103** 220
Jane **61** 261 **63** 93 **66** 235
Jane (Damon) **103** 220
109 69
Jeremiah **146** 349
John **57** 51 **58** 346 **66** 235
84 55 **85** 334 **97** 11 **103**
220 **109** 69
Joseph **58** 318 **63** 91 93
136 167
Katharine **114** 223
Leonard **103** 220
Lettice **51** 112
Louisa **61** 121
Louise Edna **89** 263
Martha E. **84** 55
Mary **53** 346 348 **58** 346
63 91 **66** 235 **94** 50 298
Mary (Morse) **58** 318
136 167
Mary (Pond) **109** 69
Mary (Smith) **103** 220
Matilda Fiske **85** 334

PLIMPTON *cont'd*
  Mehitable **56** 37 **57** 103
  Millicent (Fiske) **85** 334
  Moses **89** 263
  Nathan **57** 260 **58** 346
    106 271
  Olive **79** 95
  Peter **61** 121 261
  Priscilla **56** 39 **63** 91
  Reinelle **109** 69
  Richard **52** 125 **114** 223
    116 174
  Robert **114** 55 223 226
  Ruth **57** 368 **58** 346 **61** 121
  Sallay (Pettee) **109** 69
  Samantha (Partridge)
    127 130
  Sarah (Wright) **103** 220
  Sarah Bullard **58** 346
  Sarah Turner (Lane)
    103 220
  Seth D. **68** 239
  Simon **58** 346
  Stephen Wardwell **109** 69
  Susanna **61** 121
  Susanna (Draper) **109** 69
  Susanna Ruggles **79** 95
  Theodore Albert **109** 69
  Theodore Barnel **88** 170
    109 61 69 134
  Thomas **52** 37 **53** 348 **61**
    121 **86** 417 **87** 220
  Thomas R. **61** 121
  Wales **58** 346 **62** 372
  Walter Scott **58** 346
  Warren **127** 130
  William **64** 352 **114** 55
    222 223 226
PLINK Maria Dolores
    112 298
PLINLY Thomas **72** 198
PLINY **59** 183
PLOANT Osmond **53** 15
    77 111
Plomer *see* Plummer
Plommer *see* Plummer
PLOOIJ Daniel **119** 162
    143 196 **144** 24
PLOPPER Mary G.
    (Thompson) **100** 89
  Riley G. **100** 89
PLOTINUS **135** 261
PLOTT Robert **52** 31 32
PLOUGHTON
  Alexander **64** 110
PLOWDEN
  Edmund **53** 302
  Mary **74** 139
PLOWE
  Elizabeth **59** 326
  John **59** 326
PLOWGWRYGH
  Thomas **71** 326
PLOWMAN
  Jonathan **65** 44
PLUEARD Lloyd Edward
    (Mrs.) **105** 129
PLUGH Byron **111** 326
  Diana (Hilylerll)
    (Kirtland) **111** 326
  John **111** 326

PLUGH *cont'd*
  Margaret (Sible) **111** 326
Plum *see* Plumb
PLUMADORE
  Anna Keys **104** 104
  Israel **104** 104
PLUMB Plum Plumbe
    Plumbes
    —— **59** 167 **60** 343
    — Dea. **126** 255
    — Mr. **72** 171 176
  A. H. **68** 126
  Abigail (Bassett) **126** 232
  Albert **56** 17
  Albert H. **55** 123 **75** 160
  Albert Hale **62** 214
  Amariah **115** 109
  Andrew **66** 341
  Anna **69** 32 **76** 147
  Caleb **100** 7
  Catherine **72** 320
  Charity **75** 196 **78** 262
  Clarina **81** 188
  Daron **128** 18
  David **76** 141
  Dorcas **89** 60 **93** ix 403
  Dorothy **104** 162
  Edwin **72** 180
  Eleanor **100** 7
  Eleanor (Welch) **100** 7
  Elizabeth **53** 87 **70** 76
    81 268
  Esther **100** 13
  Esther H. (Sumner)
    116 260
  Eunice **68** 275 **71** 17 **76**
    148 **81** 266
  Evelyn Howland **82** 485
  Ezra **70** 76
  Geneva Julia **97** 159
  George **81** 266
  Grace **81** 167
  Green **77** 13 **81** 268
  Ichabod **72** 320
  Ida Aline (Jones) **111** 306
  Isaac **72** 182 **115** 112
    126 232
  Jared **76** 134 143 145 147
    170
  John **52** 248 **53** 87 **66** 181
    71 17 **89** 175 **107** 268
    111 4 **126** 256 **128** 20
    148 15
  John Huckins **69** 32
  John M. **69** 32
  Joseph **76** 142
  Joseph C. **116** 260
  Joshua **76** 140
  Keziah **71** 17 **142** 342
  Lewis W. **73** 225
  Louise **69** 32
  Lydia **59** 167
  Margaret **81** 268
  Marquis L. **100** 10
  Mary **52** 249 **75** 189 **76** 145
  Mary B. **69** 32
  May **72** 176
  Nancy (Clark) **100** 10
  Nathaniel **114** 192
  Noah **69** 32
  O. L. **111** 306

PLUMB *cont'd*
  Peter **108** 23
  Robert **54** 384
  Ruth **54** 384 **60** 343 **76** 143
  Samuel **55** 257 **76** 134
    140-142 144-146 148 170
    81 167
  Sarah **76** 144 145 **87** 328 **97**
    84 **136** 310
  Sarah Charlotte **115** 109
  Stephen **52** 248 249
    115 110
  Susan **71** 19
  Susanna **75** 196 **115** 109
  Sylvia **115** 112
  Thankful **55** 257
  Thomas **55** 214 **98** 122
  Verda May **98** 147
  Waiting **54** 213
  William **52** 248 **64** 343
  William D. **92** 109
  William D. (Mrs.) **82** 485
  Zuriel **76** 145 146
PLUMBACK
  Henry **77** 319
Plumber *see* Plummer
PLUMBLY Plumbley
    Plumely Plumley
    —— **122** 223 **123** 27
    — Mr. **71** 117 119
  Abigail **104** 114 115
  Anna **60** 80 **123** 49 53
  Anna (Goodrich) **123** 53
  Benjamin **60** 80
  Daniel **130** 233
  Elizabeth **51** 114
  F. S. **123** 306
  Frances Smith **123** 306
  Fred **71** 119
  Fred Loomis **123** 306
  Frederick Smith **123** 95
    227
  Horatio **71** 121 **123** 52 227
  Horatio Clark **123** 306
  Isabel **51** 392
  Lodice **123** 51
  Lovisa **123** 304
  Miriam (Fletcher) **130** 233
  Richard **51** 115
  Sally **125** 221
  Sarah **76** 79 **123** 96 306
    137 50
PLUME — Dr. **60** 92
  Edmund **112** 253
  Elizabeth **113** 98
  Elizabeth (Purchas) **112**
    112 **113** 98
  Irene Louise **101** 321
  John **113** 98
  Mary **112** 112 **113** 98
  Robert **112** 112 253 **113** 98
  Thomas **62** 165
  W. Beach **60** 82
Plumer *see* Plummer
Plumley *see* Plumbly
PLUMMER Plumber
    Plumer
    —— **58** 394 **60** xxix **73**
    315 **95** 50 **103** 259 260
    113 126 **148** 57
  — Dr. **56** 319

PLUMMER cont'd
— Gov. **83** 195
— Mr. **70** 187 **74** 180
 83 195
— Mrs. **83** 195 **103** 193
 ___ (Jones) **100** 146
Ababella Johnson **83** 476
Abel **55** 313 **82** 510
Abiezer **73** 220 **118** 215
Abigail **61** 378 **62** 155 **74**
 34 **85** 65 **142** 209 **145**
 166
Abigail (Tibbetts) **98** 294
Abner **72** 275
Abraham **68** 33-39 134 135
 103 261 263 266 268
Agnes **54** 347
Ai **103** 190 193 256 260
 262 265 269
Albert **61** 318 **64** 330
Alice **66** 360
Almira **76** 39
Alvan **103** 260
Alvin **59** xliv 116
Ann **52** 364 **58** xcviii **69**
 284 **85** 65 **92** 292 **116**
 300 301 **123** 230
Ann (Wood) **123** 230
Ann H. **73** 264
Anna **56** 319 **63** 177 **65** 311
 72 265 **73** 126 **121** 142
Anna Laura **87** 174
Anne **74** 194 **85** 57 **131** 126
Anne Lockwood **85** 64
Arabella Johnson **83** 476
Asa **109** 166
Avery **87** 391 **91** 364
Bart **83** 301 302
Benjamin **62** 155 **74** 93
 75 49 50 **103** 265 **109**
 307 **113** 225 **117** 256
Benjamin L. **103** 267
Betsey **73** 97 **78** 73 **84** 424
 103 262 264 **126** 65
Betsey (Cargill) **117** 256
Betsey (Plummer) **84** 424
Betsey C. **68** 39
Bezor **118** 215
Bryce T. **125** 142
C. Lemuel **101** 214
Cager **118** 215
Calestra **133** 265
Caroline **103** 264
Catherine **83** 26 27
 122 296
Charles A. **122** 296
Charles Avery **87** 391
 91 364
Charles Avery (Mrs.) **87**
 391 **88** 87 176 **91** 364
Charles Henry **122** 296
Converse F. **83** 179 185
D. **83** 300
Daniel **63** 177 **72** 265 **74**
 185 194 **84** 424 **103** 196
 259 **111** 202 **121** 142
 133 155
David **87** 298 **91** 332 **112**
 24 **119** 240
David O. **103** 268 270
Deborah **64** 157 **92** 196

PLUMMER cont'd
Dorothy **53** 39
E. K. **80** 127
Ebenezer **74** 194 **85** 64 65
Eleanor Jane **69** 255
Elisha **85** 65
Eliza **91** 231
Eliza (Adams) **91** 231
Eliza A. **68** 332
Eliza A. (Griffin) **83** 181
 185
Eliza Adams **91** 231
Elizabeth **54** 347 348 **60**
 140 **65** 135 **66** 186 **80**
 310 **84** 331 **85** 64 65 **87**
 298 300 **103** 190 262
 115 220 **134** 112 **148** 58
Elizabeth (Hodgdon)
 87 391
Elizabeth (Norris) **133** 285
Elizabeth (Yate) **118** 215
Elizabeth B. **103** 263
Ellen (Tarlton) **83** 301 302
Ellen A. **103** 268
Ellen T. **84** 31
Ellice **63** 376 **64** 76
Elmira M. **147** 370
Enoch **74** 34
Ephraim **74** 179 194
 121 142
Esther **73** 94 **103** 266
Fanny **96** 77
Frances **103** 266
Frances Bennoch **105** 225
Frances Leland (Cushing)
 89 341
Francis **54** lxx 347 **59** 116
 117 **60** 190 **69** 284 285
 73 160 **76** 39
Frank **75** 259
Franklin **91** 231
Frederick **122** 296
George **54** lxx **69** 255 **85**
 57 64 65 **117** 281 **118**
 330 **119** 80 240 **120** 160
 134 134
George E. **75** 258
George W. **69** 255 **118** 330
 119 80
Gershom **74** 34 194
Gideon **103** 194
Gilbert **91** 332
Hannah **69** 259 **73** 95 **74**
 34 195 **75** 50 **83** 22 26
 116 128 **133** 155 **142**
 209
Hannah (Gifford) **134** 134
Hannah (Moody) **114** 294
Hannah Harmon
 (Moulton) **94** 65
Hannah Matilda **83** 116
Hannah Woodbridge
 94 65
Harriet **94** 363 **103** 265
Harriet Leola (Dame)
 89 386
Hazen Mitchell **105** 225
Henry **58** 122 **122** 296
Hiram **91** 231
Howard C. **83** 438 **84** 23
Isaac **85** 65

PLUMMER cont'd
Izetta **83** 27
Jacob **61** 378
James **63** 376 377 **64** 76
 66 360 362 **95** 50 **103**
 194 **117** 144 222 **127**
 158
Jane **73** 97
Jane (Patterson) **91** 231
Jane Ann Morris (Dixon)
 83 179 185
Jason **103** 261 264 266
Jeremiah **103** 190 196 258
Jerome **115** 79
Jesse **61** 381 **103** 196
Joan **54** 347
Joanna **58** 122
John **54** 347 348 **56** 182
 63 168 **65** 240 **72** 265
 73 97 139 142 265 **74**
 127 194 **75** 10 **80** 310 **83**
 26 27 **91** 231 **115** 320
 116 164 **118** 215 **142** 43
 144 29 143 **145** 239 365
 147 158
John C. **134** 224
John H. **83** 20
Jonathan **54** lxx
Joseph **85** 64 **97** 200
Josephine **118** 330 **119** 80
Joshua **103** 254 256 259 262
 115 218 **144** 266
Josiah **73** 97
Judith **58** 125 **74** 34
Judith M. **114** 161
Julia **91** 231
Julia Morton **56** xxxii **57**
 xxxiii
Kate J. **83** 185
Kemp **59** 234 340
Lillian **75** 259
Lizzie B. (Hunnewill)
 103 270
Louisa J. **61** 378
Lucy (Perkins) **115** 141
Lydia **63** 168 **69** 282 **74** 38
 80 310 **93** 365
Lydia Augusta (Durrell)
 134 224
Lydia Emily Jane
 (Billings) **96** 180
Macajah **118** 215
Major **103** 266 268
Margaret **54** 347 **108** 233
 148 47
Margaret F. **83** 174
Margaret Jane (Gookin)
 83 181 185
Martha **103** 263
Martha (Farnham)
 127 158
Mary **54** 347 **55** 178 313
 59 287 **63** 377 **64** 76 **66**
 362 **68** 332 **72** 275 **82**
 510 **84** 216 **91** 231 **93**
 219 **97** 75 **103** 269 **108**
 164 **113** 126 225 **116**
 130
Mary (Redington)
 109 166
Mary Ann **75** 258 **97** 268

PLUMMER *cont'd*
122 296
Mary Ann (Bedel) **117**
144 222
Mary B. **62** 155
Mary E. **53** 467
Mary E. (Whitten) **83** 438
84 23
Mary Elizabeth **83** 174
Mary J. **68** 152
Mary Little (Leigh) **94** 65
Mary Locke **109** 307
May Agnes (Lobdell)
105 225
Mercy **74** 194
Mordecai **73** 231
Moses **74** 195 **103** 189
254 265 **115** 141
Nancy **90** 327 **94** 363
Nathan **147** 258
Nathaniel **116** 157
Nicholas **54** 345 **147** 236
Nicholas (Mrs.) **147** 236
Norman R. **86** 384
Olive **103** 270
Ophelia **73** 181
Parker **59** 287
Philip **73** 278
Polly **54** lxx **84** 424 **96** 338
108 164
Rachel **122** 296
Rebecca **67** 276
Reuben **74** 34
Richard **53** 20 **54** 347
74 194
Richard Page **94** 65
Riel **120** 160
Robert **111** 202
Royal **120** 160
Ruth **64** 157 **89** 60 386
112 24 **114** 294
Sally **61** 381 **96** 248
114 320
Sampson **103** 267
Samuel **98** 294 **100** 146
114 294 **126** 226 **143** 42
Sarah **69** 255 **73** 229 **74** 34
37 **75** 49 **81** 257 **89** 115
103 258
Sarah (Wentworth)
133 155
Sarah D. **117** 281
Sarah E. **91** 231
Sarah Hale (Rockwood)
68 xxxv **87** 391 **88** 176
Sarah S. (Kelley) **125** 142
Silas **94** 65
Solomon **73** 97
Susan E. **74** 94
Susanna **99** 111 **100** 146
Theodore **122** 296
Thomas **54** 348 **115** 79
118 215
Thomas Fox **94** 65
Timothy **73** 97
Warren **73** 97
Washington **73** 97
83 181 185
William **51** 229 **53** 467
58 313 **67** 239 **70** 7 **79**
89 83 181 185 195 **89**

PLUMMER *cont'd*
386 **92** 396 **96** 180 **99** 8
103 262 263 269 **142**
209 **145** 165
William I. **137** 219
William Thompson
89 341
William Warren **61** 378
Plumpton De *see* Plimpton
Plumpton *see* Plimpton
PLUMSTED
A. G. **91** 332
Anne **68** 148
Clement **98** 202 **107** 191
PLUNCE William **67** 332
PLUNKETT Plunket
—— **62** 247
Charles H. **57** 358-360
Charles Taylor **62** 113
Emily Wells **57** 359
George Taylor **57** 360
Gertrude **77** 255
Henry **57** 358
Katharine Frances
117 199
Lovisa (Brown) **136** 165
Lucinda **85** 115
Mary Robinson **57** 358
Mary W. **57** 358 359
Nancy **57** 360
Nancy T. **57** 361
Oliver **61** 269 **85** 115
Thomas **62** 301
Thomas Kittredge **57** 359
PLURDY David **76** 53
PLUSH Aaron **61** 391
Roxy **61** 391
PLUYMERT Ann **65** 136
PLYE William **140** 69
PLYER C. W. **51** 361
PLYMOUTH —— **59** 418
Other Hickman (Earl of)
96 70
Plympton *see* Plimpton
Poage *see* Pogue
POAK Poake
Alice **71** 224
Anna **71** 220 222
Ephraim **75** 107 116
John **71** 223
Margaret **75** 107 116
Miriam **75** 116
Sarah **71** 223
Thomas **75** 107
POBANZ Ann **92** 116
POCAHONTAS
Princess **59** 178
123 256
POCHIN Thomas **71** 318
POCKNET Ann **114** 182
POCOCK Pococke Powcock
Ann (Cary) **100** 297
Catherine Clark **60** lxvii
Charles **100** 297
Cordine **59** 155
Elizabeth **85** 422 423
Elizabeth (Dickens) **86**
178 **105** 266
Elizabeth (Rose) (Clarke)
85 422
George **60** lxvii

POCOCK *cont'd*
Jean G. **82** 101
John **63** 78 **67** 149 151 153
71 322 **82** 462 **85** 422
86 178 **105** 266
Mary **71** 322
Mary (Cole) (Almy)
105 266
Peleg **85** 421
Robert **51** 288
Rosina Rose **105** 252
Sarah **72** 197
Sibyl **85** 423
William **65** 238
PODANN
Friedrich **85** 169
PODDY —— **54** 190
PODGER
Katharine **110** 262
PODMARE William **64** 350
PODMORE F. **113** 87
PODVIN John **63** 239
PODYER
John **121** 17 18
Mary **121** 17
Mehitable **121** 17 18
POE —— **52** 278
Adam **53** 357
Agnes **53** 357
Charles **53** 357
David **75** 252
Edgar Allan **69** lxvii
Elizabeth **53** 357
George **53** 357
George Jacob **53** 357
Jane **53** 357
Joseph Miles **75** 252
Mary Caroline **75** 252
Ruth **53** 357
POEHLER
Alvin Henry **86** 361
Elizabeth (Frankenfeld)
86 361
Eugenia Louise (Cole)
86 361
Gladys Eugenia **86** 361
Henry **86** 361
Josephine Annette (Allen)
86 361
Kenneth Cole **86** 361
Marjorie **86** 361
POELKING
Henry **111** 54
Virginia (Dame) **111** 54
POERSCHEKE
Johan **106** 207
POFFENBARGER Livia
Nye (Simpson) **62** 308
64 xxxii 99
POFFORD
Ann (Sherman) **59** 399
John **59** 399
POGHILL
Robert de **115** 249
POGNIT Samuel **65** 358
POGUE Poage
Anne **93** 177
Bill **145** 270
John **93** 177 **111** 202 206
145 270
John Marshall **145** 270

POGUE *cont'd*
John Wilbur **145** 270
Lloyd Welch **145** 270
Robert **93** 177
Thomas **93** 177
POHL Gunther E. **107** 15
165 **108** 15
POHLMAN Annie **81** 288
Frederick W. **81** 291
Louisa **81** 291
POIGNAND —— **140** 38
POINCY Jane Mary
Sebastian Zepherine
Javain de **73** 231
POINDEXTER Poingdestre
Ann **106** 65
Edouard **88** 254
Elizabeth **88** 255
Marie **88** 254
Thomas **88** 255 256
POINSETT —— **110** 131
Elisha **77** 319
Peter **110** 133
POINTER Poynter
Elizabeth **86** 414
Elizabeth (Fiske) **87** 369
John **53** 18
Mary **55** 219
Michaell **83** 327
Nicholas **55** 219
William **86** 414 **87** 369
POINTING
Elizabeth **57** 332 333
Philip **124** 146
POINTZ Poyntz
—— **141** 103
— Capt. **52** 29
Hugh **115** 149
POIRET Jeanne **97** 73
POIRIER Simon **131** 90
POIS —— **52** 202
POISAL — Rev. **108** 231
POISSON Edward **143** 306
148 41
Elizabeth (Harris)
(Wheeler) (Nesbitt)
143 306
James **143** 306 323 324
POITOU
Roger de **106** 283
POKANOKETT
Alexander **54** 262-264
POKE Edward **112** 286
POLACEK Joseph Adam
(Mrs.) **108** 135
POLAERE
William **143** 257
POLAND Polland
—— **102** 15
— Judge **55** 297
Abigail **62** 38
Abner **126** 141
Benjamin **59** xcii **145** 167
Bethiah **61** 335 337 **62** 38
Caroline **100** 146
Catherine **114** 185 **128** 175
Clara **89** 315
Dolly **56** 293
Dorcas **145** 44
Eliza Maud (Chrisman)
89 315

POLAND *cont'd*
Elizabeth **61** 332 335 337
62 38 **86** 133 136
Elizabeth (Aborn) **108** 163
Hannah (Welch) **125** 223
Jacob **108** 163
James B. **89** 349 352
John **56** 293 **62** 41 **114** 185
Jonas Richardson **56** 293
Joseph **62** 40 **74** 92 **125**
223 **128** 266
Josiah **89** 315
Longstreet **114** 185
Lucina (Baker) **126** 141
Martha E. **89** 352
Mary **62** 45 **74** 19 92
108 163
Mary Reed **100** 319
Moses **145** 44
Nancy **74** 20
Nathaniel **62** 43
Orville Swett **85** 197
86 110 212
Peter B. **114** 185
Rebecca **128** 266
S. **62** 41
Samuel **61** 332 337 **62** 38
40 43 45 **133** 74
Sarah **62** 39 **96** 286
Seward **83** 375
Susan (Deeds) **128** 266
Thomas **83** 375
William **114** 185
Polard *see* Pollard
POLCHET
Marie Celestine
110 132
POLDEN
Cicely **79** 413 432
Nicholas **61** 279
William **79** 413 432
POLE Catherine de la
103 290
Elizabeth **60** 96 **141** 27
Margaret **105** 21
Martha (Gregson)
128 107
Michael de la **103** 290 291
Richard **59** 174 **105** 21
128 107
Samuel **127** 307
William **124** 306 **141** 27 99
William de la **103** 290
POLECHIO
Joseph **126** 245 246
Sophia B. (Munroe) **126**
245 246
POLEMBO Moses **63** 343
POLEN Mary **98** 84 894
POLER Nemiah **127** 310
Robert **127** 312
POLERECZKY
Francis **66** 106
John **66** 105 106
Lucy **66** 106 109
Nancy **66** 105
POLES Azor **59** 290
Roxanna **59** 290
POLET Thomas **147** 165
POLEY *see also* Polly
—— **102** 251

POLEY *cont'd*
Agnes **102** 247
Agnes (Whetehill)
102 247
Anthony **102** 247
Elizabeth **80** 368
George **102** 247
Jacob **102** 31
John **102** 247 248 **105** 11
Mary **102** 31
Micajah **105** 76
Richard **102** 247
Robert **113** 95 96
Roger **109** 23
Thomas **102** 247
Ursula (Gilbert) 11 **105** 11
William **80** 368
POLHEMUS Polhemius
Anna **67** 303 **96** 294
Ella Groat **77** lxxxix
Johannes Theodorus
105 152
POLITZER Adam **82** 344
POLK Polke
—— **56** 210
Aaron Gordon **78** 175
Abby **78** 325
Abigail **77** 220
Ada Clarissa **78** 50
Ada Lee **78** 170
Ada Octavia **78** 169
Ada Thressia **78** 50
Addie Blanche **78** 325
Adelaide **78** 49
Adelaide E. (Roe) **78** 168
Adelaide Elizabeth **78** 169
Alabama **78** 321
Albert **77** 143
Albert Clark **78** 173
Albert McNeal **78** 326
Alexander Hamilton **77**
215 257 **78** 166
Alfred **77** 218 220 266 **78**
38 44 320
Alfred Irvin **78** 47
Alfred Pascal **78** 320
Alfred Sapington **78** 38
Alice **78** 159 170
Alice Irene **78** 173
Alice L. **77** 266
Alice Ophelia **78** 172
Alice Potter **78** 168
Allen **78** 323
Allen Campbell **78** 172
Allen Jones **77** 252
78 159 160
Allie Elizabeth **78** 325
Alma **78** 174
Almeda **78** 45 319
Almonte Lee **78** 36
Alpha **78** 321
Alphonso **77** 139
Althea **77** 267
Alva **78** 172
Amanda **78** 264 266
Amanda Elizabeth **78** 173
Amanda M. **77** 264
Amanda Pauline **77** 263
Amy Daisy **78** 173
Anderson **78** 37 318 319
Andrew **77** 137 218

POLK *cont'd*
Andrew Jackson **77** 216 259
Andrew Tyler **77** 268 **78** 174
Angelina **77** 143
Ann **77** 134 135
Ann Eliza **77** 226
Ann Elizabeth **77** 267 268
Anna **77** 135 **78** 319
Anna Clark **78** 160
Anna Elizabeth **78** 49
Anna Leah **77** 259
Anna Lee **78** 160
Anna Louise **78** 319
Anne **77** 253
Anne Leroy **78** 166
Anne Patterson **78** 327
Annie **78** 50 170 319 323
Annie Blanche **78** 175
Annie Cecil **78** 170
Annie Laurie **78** 173
Annie May **78** 175
Annie McNeal **78** 171
Annie Penn **78** 325
Annie Sperry **78** 327
Annie T. **78** 163
Antoinette Van Leer **77** 259
Archibald Yoll **78** 175
Argyle Foster **78** 176
Armour Cantrell **78** 165
Atlas Erving **78** 47 329
Augusta **78** 38
Belinda G. **78** 48
Bell Virginia **78** 325
Belle **77** 261 **78** 330
Benigna **77** 145
Benigna Jane **78** 174
Benjamin **77** 219 220 **78** 45
Benjamin Carlo **78** 36
Benjamin D. A. **77** 219 268
Benjamin F. **77** 269 **78** 320
Benjamin Franklin **78** 38 176 321 322
Benjamin Rufus **77** 270 **78** 176
Bertha **78** 177
Bertie **78** 324
Bessie **77** 140 **78** 164 321 330
Bessie Isadora Alice **78** 320
Bessie Lee **78** 177
Bessie Olga **78** 322
Bessie Western **78** 173
Betsey **77** 136
Bettie Ann **78** 175
Betty **77** 136
Betty Georgiana **78** 36
Beverly Porter **78** 38
Birdie Douglas **78** 47
Blanche **78** 162 165
Blanche Rebecca **78** 325
Brantly **78** 173
Burt **78** 38
Cadwallader Long **77** 252 **78** 163
Caldona **78** 319
Campbell **78** 172
Caroline **77** 225 259 **78**

POLK *cont'd*
45 161 163 172
Caroline James **78** 170
Caroline Lafayette **78** 170
Carra Lee **78** 173
Carry May **78** 163
Catherine B. **78** 174
Charles **74** 308 **77** 133-136 138-140 216-218 220 **78** 33 34
Charles Arnold **78** 174
Charles Bingley **77** 260 **78** 169 170
Charles Clark **77** 217 261 262 **78** 173
Charles Eaton **78** 324
Charles Edwin **77** 226
Charles Grandison **77** 264 **78** 174
Charles H. **77** 139
Charles Isaac **77** 266 267
Charles James **77** 216 261
Charles Junius **77** 216
Charles King **77** 270
Charles Loyd **78** 174
Charles Marion **77** 263 **78** 173
Charles Martin **78** 164
Charles Michael **78** 173
Charles N. **78** 45
Charles Perry **77** 145 226
Charles Shelby **77** 218 263
Charles Taliaferro **77** 261
Charles Thomas **77** 264 **78** 174
Charles Wesley **77** 267
Charles Wessen **78** 174
Charlotte **78** 165
Charlotte H. **78** 166
Charlotte Patricia **78** 166
Christian **77** 136
Christine Hance **78** 176
Clara **77** 226
Clara Allison **78** 327
Clara Bills **78** 172
Clarence **78** 170
Clarissa **77** 143 224
Clarissa Adeline **77** 220
Clark Fitzhugh **78** 160
Claud **78** 321
Cleora Lawrence **78** 163
Clifford Allen **78** 322
Clyde **78** 45
Cora **78** 320
Cora Ann / Anna **78** 47 175
Corinne Lucile **78** 173
Cornelia **77** 226
Cornelia Jane **77** 262
Cornelia Lowry **78** 163
Cumberland **77** 220 **78** 37-39 319 323
Curren Whitthorne **78** 177
Currie **78** 45
Currie Young **78** 45
Cynthia **77** 216 **78** 164
Cynthia Cornelia **78** 172
Cynthia Martin **78** 164
Cynthia Springs **77** 218 **78** 33

POLK *cont'd*
Daisy **78** 165 328
Daisy Cantrell **78** 166
Daisy Ellen **78** 166
David **77** 134-136 **78** 320
David Taylor **78** 319
Deborah **77** 136 138 217
Delilah **77** 136
Della **78** 322
Dessie **78** 177
Dicy **77** 137
Dora **78** 175
Dora J. **78** 321
Dora Marie **78** 327
Dorcas Lear **78** 175
Dorothy Kitchine **77** 260
Douglas **78** 174
Dovie Jane **78** 323
Dow **77** 261
Drew Smith **77** 267
Drusilla **77** 270
Duke **78** 321
Edmond **77** 136 **124** 79
Edna **77** 269 **78** 324
Edward **78** 175
Edward Marshall **78** 326
Edward McNeal **78** 326
Edward Monroe **78** 328
Edward Winfield **78** 163
Edwin Fitzhugh **77** 145
Edwin Moore **78** 163
Effie **78** 48 174
Eleanor **74** 308 **77** 139 140 217 **78** 37 319
Eleanor Frances **78** 326
Eleanor Margaret **78** 175
Elias Rector **78** 43
Elise Warren **78** 171
Elisha **91** 332
Eliza **78** 318
Eliza Eastin **77** 254
Eliza Tannahill **78** 49
Elizabeth **77** 135-137 142 218 219 223 264 **78** 36 38 44 48 172 175 323
Elizabeth Adline **78** 325
Elizabeth Allen **77** 264
Elizabeth Ann **77** 269
Elizabeth Devereux **77** 257
Elizabeth Emily **78** 174
Elizabeth Hazylin **78** 170
Elizabeth Jane **78** 51
Elizabeth Jerome **78** 34
Elizabeth Kinchin **78** 46
Elizabeth Parmelia **78** 50
Elizabeth Sturgis **78** 168
Ella **78** 159 170 173
Ella Baillio **78** 159
Ella Martha **78** 169
Ella Wood **78** 34
Ella Word **77** 267
Ellen **77** 226 **78** 37 319
Ellen Harrell **78** 166
Ellen Matilda **77** 226
Ellie **78** 51
Ellis Rivere **78** 163
Elmer E. **77** 270
Elmer Scott **78** 327
Elva Dee **78** 320
Elva Lona **78** 177

POLK *cont'd*
Elvira Juliette **77** 255
Emeline **77** 266
Emeline Winifred **78** 36
Emily **77** 250 **78** 166 173 177
Emily B. **77** 265
Emily Donelson **77** 254
Emily Hamilton **78** 166
Emma **78** 169
Emma Augusta **78** 319
Emma Grier **78** 162
Emma Lou **78** 325
Emma Louise **78** 173 325
Emma M. **77** 262
Emma Octavia **77** 260
Emma Thomas **78** 48
Emmit Brit **78** 322
Ephraim **77** 134 135
Erasmus **78** 36
Esther **77** 138 **78** 43 168
Ethel **78** 320
Eugene **78** 47
Eugene Le Noir **78** 169
Eugenia **77** 145 226 **78** 35
Eunice **78** 326
Eunice Ophelia **78** 48 327
Euola **78** 161
Eva **78** 324
Eva Bills **78** 327
Eva Jane **78** 176
Eva Josephine **78** 321
Eva May **78** 321
Evan Shelby **77** 219 269 **78** 34
Evelina McNeal **78** 326 327
Evelyn **78** 37 330
Evelyn Sarah **78** 171
Evie **78** 174
Ezekiel **74** 308 **77** 133 137-141 145 214 217 219 220 262 **78** 39 325 **133** 235
Fanny **78** 45 176
Fanny Douglas **78** 47
Fanny Elizabeth **78** 176 177
Fanny Tabitha **78** 51
Fessonia **78** 36
Florence **78** 50 324
Florence Helen **78** 177
Floyd Idella **78** 323
Frances A. **77** 255
Frances Anne **77** 254
Frances Devereux **77** 257
Frances J. **77** 261
Frances L. **78** 175
Frances Letitia **78** 173
Francis Devereux **78** 166
Frank **77** 266 **78** 323
Frank Devereux **78** 166
Frank Lyon **78** 167 168 322
Frankie **78** 175
Franklin **77** 269
Franklin Armstead **77** 219 269 **78** 36 177
Franklin Ezekiel **77** 223
George Beach **78** 166
George Brevard Mecklenburg **77** 258

POLK *cont'd*
George Clark **78** 173
George Donnell **78** 163
George Marion **78** 324
George R. **78** 47
George W. **77** 139
George Washington **77** 133 138 139 216 217 253 255 258 **78** 164 165 168 169 329
Georgia **77** 263
Gilbert **77** 250 **78** 173
Gladys **78** 175
Gloria Adell **78** 324
Grace **78** 45 329
Greenfield Quarles **78** 163
Griselda **77** 213 **78** 161
Griselda Gilchrist **77** 251
Griselda Houston **78** 160
Hamilton R. **78** 166
Hannah **77** 137 217 **78** 320
Hannah Elizabeth **77** 262
Harding **78** 168
Harris **78** 323 324
Harrison Jackson **78** 165
Harry K. **77** 267 **78** 34
Henrietta B. **77** 264
Henry **77** 135 **78** 38 319
Henry Atlas **78** 47
Henry C. **77** 264
Henry Clay **78** 37 319
Henry Dickson **78** 319
Henry M. **77** 139
Horace Moore **77** 260 **78** 171 172
Hortense **78** 322
Ida A. **78** 166
Ida Florence **78** 177
Iola **78** 50
Iredell D. **77** 267
Irene **78** 170
Irene Deborah **77** 217
Irene Florence **78** 47
Irvin **78** 48
Irving Kenneth **78** 174
Isaac Carlo **78** 34
Isaac Hilliard **77** 259 **78** 169
Isaac Shelby **77** 218
Isabel **78** 162
Isabel Grier **78** 162
Isabella **77** 266
Isadora **78** 320
Isam Walker **78** 320
Jack **78** 322
James **77** 134-136 138 139 220 **78** 38 39 48
James Anderson **78** 44 323
James Cecil **78** 170
James D. **78** 45
James E. **77** 264
James Elbert **78** 330
James Franklin **78** 330
James H. **78** 36
James Hilliard **77** 258 **78** 168
James Irvin **77** 220 **78** 46 47 325
James Knox **62** 191 **63** 158

POLK *cont'd*
66 95 **74** 308 **77** 133 142 221 222 224 226 250 262 264 270 **78** 37 38 44-46 48 49 163 176 177 323 325 326 **111** 50 **133** 235 **136** 67
James Lafayette **78** 175
James Martin Sylvester **78** 321
James Monroe **78** 51 327
James Moore **77** 269
James Potter **78** 168
James V. **77** 267
James Vernon Noah **78** 172
Jane **77** 134-136 218 221 250 266 269 **78** 37 164 319 320
Jane Elizabeth **77** 261
Jane Jackson **78** 165
Jane Margaret **77** 269
Jane Maria **77** 222
Janie **78** 45
Janie Frances **78** 320
Javita **78** 323
Jency **77** 219 220 **78** 37 38
Jency Alexander **78** 43
Jennie **78** 328
Jesse Newton **78** 324
Jessie **78** 177
Jessie Irene **78** 170
Jessie Lee Forest **77** 266
Jewel **78** 320
Jimmie Belle **77** 262
Joanna **77** 134
Job **77** 137
John **74** 308 **77** 134 135 137-140 142 143 218 219 264 268 269 **78** 33 48 51 169
John A. **77** 217
John Crofford **78** 174
John D. **77** 267
John De Kalb **78** 36
John Edward **78** 325
John Fleming **78** 168
John Floyd **78** 319
John Hale **77** 262
John Hawkins **77** 215
John Horace **78** 171
John Houston **78** 171 327
John Jackson **77** 226 **78** 49 50
John Kenneth **77** 267
John Lee **77** 223 **78** 321
John Lewallen **78** 321 322
John McGowan **78** 50
John Metcalfe **78** 168
John P. **77** 139
John R. **77** 264
John Shelby **77** 270 **78** 175
John Simmons **78** 174
John Thaddeus **77** 269
John Wesley **78** 330
John Wilson **78** 47
Johnnie **78** 177
Jonathan **98** 278
Jones **78** 322
Joseph **74** 308 **77** 134 135 **78** 174

POLK *cont'd*
Josephine Elizabeth
  78 173
Josiah L. **78** 45
Judge **78** 328
Julia **78** 43
Julia Anne **78** 51
Julia Bell **78** 173
Kate **77** 264 269 **78** 320
Kate Jackson **78** 165
Kate Lillian **78** 170
Katharine **77** 257 **78** 328
Katie **77** 263 **78** 174
Kelsey Hibbler **78** 326
Keziah **77** 138
Knox Sylvester **78** 177
Lalla **78** 38 230
Lamar **78** 159
Laura **78** 38 321
Laura Ann **78** 175
Laura Ellen **78** 320
Laura Emmeons **78** 173
Laura Jane **78** 323
Laura Lee **78** 50
Laura Prudence **78** 327
Laura T. **78** 48
Laura Weston **77** 223 224
Laurentine S. **77** 266
Lavinia Boncille **78** 173
Lavinia C. **78** 160
Lawrence **78** 319
Lawrence Norton **78** 326
Lecie Amelia **78** 47
Lecie Norwood **77** 221
Lee **78** 38
Leland Thomas **78** 174
Lelia **78** 175
Lena **78** 173
Lena Elizabeth **78** 174
Lena May **78** 324
Leonidas **74** 308 **77** 133
  215 253 255-257 259 **78**
  38 164 166 167 327
Leonidas Charles **78** 166
Leonidas Napoleon
  78 170
Leonidas Tennessee
  78 48
Leonora Maude **78** 170
Leontine Adele **78** 166
Levi **78** 220
Lewis Bradbury **78** 169
Lewis Gilbert **78** 173
Lewis Reynolds **78** 174
Lila M. **78** 45
Lilla Belle **78** 173
Lillian **78** 324
Lillie **78** 322
Linda **78** 323
Lizzie **78** 38
Lois **78** 177
Lois M. **78** 330
Lona Elizabeth **78** 177
Lonzy Frances **77** 270
Lottie **78** 163 320
Lottie Isabel **78** 47
Louie Cerf **78** 329
Louis Christian **78** 329
Louis James **78** 322
Louis Shelby **78** 323
Louis Taylor **78** 43 322

POLK *cont'd*
Louisa **77** 144 226 **78** 174
Louisa Blount **77** 221
Louisa Jane **78** 43
Louise **78** 49
Louise Adeline **78** 46 329
Lucia **77** 257
Lucille **78** 163
Lucille Quarles **78** 163
Lucinda **78** 39 50 319
Lucinda Davis **77** 215
Lucius **77** 256 269
Lucius B. **77** 269
Lucius Benjamin **78** 335
Lucius Eugene **77** 215 252
  78 161-164
Lucius Josephus **78** 174
Lucius Junius **77** 215 252
  255 259 **78** 165 166
Lucius Leonard **78** 47 329
Lucretia **74** 308 **78** 39 40
  98 184 185
Lucy **78** 174
Lucy Blount **78** 48
Lucy Eugenia **78** 48
Lucy Fairfax **78** 49
Lucy Narcissa **78** 320
Lucy Nicholson **78** 170
Lucy Prudence **78** 320
Lucie Gertrude **77** 267
Lula Ella **78** 51
Lula Gilmer **78** 170
Lula Iza **78** 328
Lulu **78** 163
Lydia **78** 321
Lydia Blanche **78** 328
Lydia Eliza **77** 223 224
Mabel **77** 259 **78** 38
Madeleine Tasker **78** 161
Mae **78** 320
Magdalen (Tasker) **77**
  134 135 **78** 166
Magdalene **74** 308
Maggie **77** 266 269
Maggie McCorkle **78** 325
Mamie **77** 267 **78** 173
Margaret **77** 136 138 139
  217 218 **78** 33 45 166
  169 171
Margaret A. **78** 166
Margaret Alice **78** 175
Margaret Ann **78** 174
Margaret Benigna **77** 264
  78 174
Margaret Catherine
  77 267
Margaret Douglas **78** 325
Margaret Emma **77** 261
Margaret Ethel **78** 166
Margaret Jane **77** 269
Margaret Olivia **78** 34
Margaret R. **77** 268 269
Margaret Ruth **78** 175
Margaret Viana **77** 263
Margaret Wendell **78** 166
Maria **78** 166
Maria H. **78** 329
Marie **78** 323
Marie H. **78** 167 329
Marion Deveux **78** 170
Marjorie **78** 48 323

POLK *cont'd*
Marshall Alexander **78** 43
Marshall T. **77** 143
Marshall Tate **77** 223 **78**
  48 326 327
Marshall Wesley **78** 172
Martha **77** 135 138 139
  218 220 264 **78** 319 320
  322
Martha Ann **77** 263 264
  78 46
Martha Hicks **77** 261
Martha Isabelle **78** 322
Martha Jane **77** 270
Martha Rebecca **77** 261
Martha Robinson **78** 44
Martha Washington
  77 139
Marvin **78** 48
Mary **77** 135-138 140 143
  216 217 261 262 267 269
  78 33 45 48 160 174 177
  324 327
Mary (Fultz) **124** 79
Mary A. **110** 297
Mary Abigail **78** 46
Mary Adelaide **77** 250
Mary Adeline **110** 306
Mary Alice **78** 319
Mary Ann **77** 252 260 264
  78 37 44 174
Mary Bell **78** 38
Mary Brown **77** 215 253
Mary Caroline **78** 50
Mary Cynthia **77** 267
Mary Delphine **78** 164
Mary Demoville **78** 168
Mary E. **77** 261
Mary Eliza **78** 36 37 171
  176
Mary Elizabeth **77** 269 270
  78 169 171 175 322 324
Mary Ellen **77** 262
Mary Eloise **77** 250 **78** 159
Mary Frances **78** 177 326
Mary Gertrude **78** 168
Mary Helen **78** 330
Mary Hurt **78** 48
Mary Jane **78** 45
Mary Jones **77** 252
Mary L. **78** 48
Mary Lenora **78** 177
Mary Lizinska Brown
  78 172
Mary Louisa **78** 172
Mary Louise **78** 48
Mary Marvin **78** 173
Mary Murfree **78** 258
Mary Ophelia **77** 269
  78 170
Mary Rebecca **78** 161-163
Mary Rebecca A. **77** 216
  251
Mary S. **77** 139
Mary Susan **78** 173
Mary Tasker **78** 49
Mary Virginia **78** 166
Mary W. **77** 220
Mary Walton **78** 170
Mary Wilson **77** 220 225
  78 326

POLK *cont'd*
Mary Winslow (Wilson)
  133 235
Matilda **78** 319
Matilda Golden **77** 141
  219
Matilda Jane **78** 175
Matta **78** 51
Matthew **77** 269
Mattie **78** 328
Mattie Catherine **78** 47
Mattie E. **77** 266
Mattie J. **78** 330
Mattie Lena **78** 323
Mattie Virginia **78** 175
Maud **78** 321
May Lillian **78** 170
Melissa Jane **77** 262
Melvina **77** 219
Michael **77** 138 216 **78** 172
Michael Sanders **77** 262
  78 173
Milbry Catherine **78** 169
Minerva Josephine
  78 169
Minnie **77** 218 **78** 48 172
  322 323
Minnie Eveline **78** 324
Minnie Louise **78** 177
Minnie Murphy **78** 48
Minnie Pearl **78** 320 323
Miranda Ann **78** 325
Miriam Bessie **78** 173
Mitchell Alfred **78** 45 324
Mitchell Anderson **78** 37
Mittie **78** 173
Mollie **77** 269 **78** 330
Myrtle **78** 38
Nancy **77** 134 135 219 263
  265 266 **78** 33 38 39 323
Nancy Katharine **78** 47
Nannie **78** 164 325
Naomi Tate **77** 223
Narcissa Augusta **78** 173
Ned **78** 320
Nellie **78** 175
Nellie Jane **78** 322
Nellie White **78** 325
Nettie **78** 322
Newton Napoleon **77** 260
  78 170 172
Nichols Beach **78** 166
Nora **78** 45 174
Octavia **77** 145
Octavia Rowena **77** 145
Oleta Mae **78** 322
Olga **78** 173
Olivia **78** 51
Olivia Marbury **77** 225
Olivia Mary **77** 143
Olivia Winston (Sharpe)
  (Scott) **78** 326
Ollie **77** 270
Opal Frances **78** 177
Ophelia Clarissa **77** 223
Ophelia Elizabeth Hines
  78 36
Ophelia Jane **78** 171 175
Ophelia Wilson **78** 172
Oscar Bowles **78** 50

POLK *cont'd*
Oscar Maximilian **101**
  121 **103** 78 123
Owen **78** 324
Pascal **78** 320
Patsy **77** 137
Patty **77** 227
Pauline **77** 145 **78** 322
Pearl **78** 324 328
Pearl Margaret **78** 50
Peggy **77** 138 220
Penelope **78** 319
Perrion Young **78** 324
Perry **77** 226 227
Phebe **77** 139 261
Philemon Hawkins
  77 216
Philopena **77** 138
Polly **77** 140
Porter Grier **78** 162
Priscilla **77** 134 135 220
  78 171
Priscilla McNeal **78** 171
Prudence **77** 220 **78** 37 38
  43 319
Prudence Ann **78** 321
Prudence McNeal **78** 327
Rachel Marie **78** 327
Ralph Bingley **78** 170
Ranzy **78** 320
Rebecca **77** 218 219 254
  259 260
Rebecca Evaline **78** 159
Rebecca Novaline **78** 37
Richard **77** 220 250
Richard Edward **78** 47
Richard Tyler **78** 44 45
Richard Watson **78** 47
Riley Madison **78** 324
Robert **74** 308 **77** 133-135
  219 **78** 38 320 329
Robert Bruce **77** 270
Robert Evender **78** 177
Robert Franklin **78** 325
Robert Green **77** 269
Robert Hicks **78** 47
Robert Hill **78** 327
Robert Le Noir **78** 170
Robert Lee **78** 44 45 177
Robin Ap Allen **78** 329
Rosa **78** 45 324
Rose Ella **78** 321
Rose Etta **78** 324
Rose La Valle **78** 328
Rose Mary **78** 324
Roxana **78** 48
Roy Alonzo **78** 330
Rufus Eugene **78** 164
Rufus Julius **77** 252
  78 164
Rufus King **77** 215 253
  258 **78** 161 162 169
Rufus Walter **78** 163
Sallie **78** 325
Sallie Ann **78** 37
Sallie Hawkins **77** 258
Sallie L. **78** 258
Sally Abigail **78** 48
Sally Clymer **78** 170
Sally Hilliard **78** 169
Sally Moore **77** 215

POLK *cont'd*
  78 161
Samuel **77** 141 142 221
  78 45 48
Samuel Clarence **78** 175
Samuel McNeal **78** 171
Samuel Singleton **78** 323
Samuel T. **78** 45
Samuel Walker **77** 227
Samuel Wilson **77** 223
Samuel Wistar **78** 328
Sarah **77** 135 136 213 216
  221 **78** 38 39 51 170 319
  323
Sarah Ardella **78** 177
Sarah Delaney **78** 37 319
Sarah E. **77** 263 **78** 164
Sarah Elizabeth **78** 46
Sarah Ella **78** 170
Sarah Evelyn **77** 262
Sarah Glass **78** 163
Sarah H. **77** 257
Sarah Henrietta **77** 261
Sarah Irene **78** 44
Sarah Isabella **77** 268
Sarah Isham **77** 260
Sarah Jane **78** 320 321
Sarah John **78** 169
Sarah Moore **77** 215
  78 161 162
Sarah Rachel **77** 253
Sarah Roach **77** 226
Sarah Robina **77** 269
Serena Devereux **78** 168
Shelby **77** 137 140
Silas Gelaspy **77** 267
Sophia **77** 140 226
Sophia Lulu **78** 174
Stella **78** 320 328
Stella Maud **78** 320
Sue Louise **78** 163
Susan **77** 136 **78** 48 319
Susan Elizabeth **77** 261
Susan Huntington
  78 160
Susan R. **77** 257
Susan Rebecca **77** 255
Susan Spratt **77** 216 258
Susan Williams **78** 322
Susanna **77** 137 139 216
Susanna Amelia
  Caroline **77** 221
Sylvester **78** 38 319
Sylvester Walker **78** 37
  320
Sylvester Wilkes **78** 321
Tabitha **77** 139
Tabitha Josephine **77** 262
Tasker **78** 49
Taylor **77** 140 219 220 **78**
  37 319
Texana **78** 319
Thelma Maud **78** 174
Theresa **78** 50 328
Theresa Carruth **78** 177
Thomas **74** 308 **77** 133
  136-138 141 218 220 250
  78 43 319
Thomas Allison **78** 327
Thomas Benjamin **78** 46
  325

POLK *cont'd*
Thomas Calvin **77** 269
Thomas Emmett **78** 328
Thomas Gilchrist **77** 215
250 252 **78** 160
Thomas Hamilton **78** 174
Thomas Independence
77 216 260 **78** 172
Thomas James **77** 261
Thomas Jefferson **77** 221
78 48
Thomas Julian **78** 170
Thomas Lucius **78** 325
Thomas Luton **78** 325
Thomas Marlborough
77 226 **78** 50
Thomas Marshall **77** 261
78 172
Thomas Polk **78** 170
Thomas Richard **77** 260
78 170 171
Thomas Trammell **78** 322
Thomas Walker **78** 320
Thomas Wilson **78** 327
Thressia (Bowles) **78** 49
Thurston **78** 170
Tillie **78** 45
Trannie **78** 330
Travis Wayne **78** 324
Tyler Vernon **78** 175
Van Leer **77** 260
Verlie **78** 174
Victoria **77** 265-267 **78** 320
Viola Catherine **77** 269
Viola Tranquilla **77** 270
Virginia Adeline **78** 48
Virginia Gibson **78** 326
Virginia Green **78** 50
Walter Earl **78** 174
Walter Marcus **78** 173
Warren **78** 324
Wayne **78** 323
Will **78** 48
William **74** 308 **77** 133-139
141 213 220 221 250 254
78 36 38 159 160 174
William Alexander
78 51 328
William Alfred **77** 268
William Allen **77** 264
William Arthur **78** 170
328
William C. **77** 266
William Cartez **78** 324
William Charles **77** 264
78 174 324
William D. **78** 50
William Eddings **78** 174
William Epps **78** 49
William Ezekiel **78** 47
William Franklin **78** 322
William Hale **77** 263
William Harrison **77** 133
William Hawkins **77**
223 259 **78** 48 49
William Henry **78** 324
William I. **77** 266
William Jackson **78** 43
William Julius **77** 215
216 251 **78** 161 163 164
William Knox **77** 218 266

POLK *cont'd*
78 325
William Lee **78** 164
William Long **78** 175
William McNeal **78** 327
William Mecklenburg
77 257 **78** 166
William Port **78** 45
William Rufus **78** 176
William S. **77** 139
William Tannahill **78** 49
William Vincent **77** 269
78 175
William Wilson **77** 142
143 223 **78** 50 328
William Wood **77** 227
Willie **78** 50
Willie May **78** 163
Wilma **78** 50
Wilmoth Elizabeth
78 325
Wilport Alfred **78** 45
Winifred **77** 137
Winnie Elizabeth **78** 45
Wylie Amanda **78** 170
Yettie **78** 324
Young C. **78** 45
Zilpha **78** 323
POLKINGHAM
Prudence **86** 222
POLKINGHORN Polkinhorn
Frank **125** 150
Frank A. **119** 252
J. H. **67** 384
POLKINGTON
Jennie **78** 354
Polkinhorn *see*
Polkinghorn
POLL Eunice I. **95** 51
Pollack *see* Pollock
Polland *see* Poland
POLLARD Pollards Polard
—— **51** 503 **89** 352 **100**
278 **110** 263 **119** 127
140 258
— Mr. **62** 131 134 **70** 22
— Mrs. **83** 381
Abel **78** 425 **91** 260
Abigail **56** 172 **78** 425 **91**
257 260 266 **111** 43 **115**
196
Abigail Whitacy **91** 260
Achsah **90** 283 **114** 199
Agnis (Robbins) **105** 77
Albert **90** 53
Alexander **100** 278
Alice **93** 325
Allura N. **89** 352
Amarillus (Sawyer)
113 224
Amos **91** 258-260 264
Amos F. **125** 293
Ann **62** 384 **65** 167
Ann Elizabeth **118** 294
Ann Elizabeth (Lougee)
118 293
Anna W. **64** 127
Anne **111** 264
Annie Virginia **118** 293
Asa **100** 208
Asa R. **100** 208

POLLARD *cont'd*
Asaph Abijah **56** 172
Asenath **76** 14
Barton **111** 43
Benjamin **57** 280 **58** 69
59 280 **62** 384 **67** 211
85 5 **132** 27 **144** 220
Benjamin Ryland **118**
293 295
Benjamin William **118**
294 295
Bethiah (Lyon) **91** 263
Betty **63** 76
Caroline D. **99** 334
Caroline M. (Bell) **83** 178
185
Carrie A. **100** 214
Catherine **91** 258
Charles **94** 27
Clara Augusta **86** 194
Clinton James **113** 224
Cumings **91** 259
Curtis **56** 169 172
David G. **98** 255 259
Dionisia (Hedworth)
111 263 264
Dorcas **91** 259 **100** 149
Dorothy **63** 74
E. J. **98** 255
Ebenezer **78** 425 **91** 257-
260
Edith **94** 27
Eleanor (Emmons)
97 221
Eliza **111** 43
Eliza (Jordan) **90** 104
Eliza A. **63** 269
Eliza Ann **78** 425
Elizabeth **53** 302 **68** 333 **91**
266 **100** 214
Elizabeth (Harvey)
125 293
Elizabeth (Win) **91** 263
Elizabeth Ann Taylor
(Johnston) **118** 293
Elizabeth W. **125** 293
Ella F. **100** 214
Elvira Harding **118** 295
Emery **98** 255
Emily F. **100** 214
Erastus Abiathar **122** 79
F. H. **141** 99
F. W. **56** 23
Francis **79** 39 **105** 76 77
Frank L. **56** 213
Frankie **85** 316
Frederick **105** 76 77
111 150
Frederick William **92** 115
George **53** 302
George Edward **78** 216
425
George Wyatt **118** 295
Hannah **53** 302 **58** 166 **62**
155 **134** 64 **142** 303
Hannah (Hills) **113** 224
Helen **66** 227
Henry Dearbone **111** 43
Ida L. (Chandler) **98** 255
259
Irene **68** 333

POLLARD *cont'd*
Isaac **78** 405 **92** 252
Isaac F. **92** 115
Jabez **52** 386
Jacob O. **98** 255
James **63** 75 **97** 221 **113** 223 224
James B. **77** 104
James Martin **125** 104
Jane **62** 157 161 **66** 111
Jane Ann (Whitney) **113** 223
Jennie (Durant) **94** 27
Jeremiah **103** 152
Joanna **59** 280
John **53** 302 **55** 141 **62** 232 233 346 **80** 244 **89** 38 **91** 256 258 260-263 266 **97** 330 **100** 17 **110** 273 **125** 84
John Joyce **118** 295
John P. **89** 352
Jonathan **58** 123 **142** 303 **144** 151
Joseph **68** 333 **71** 357 359 **85** 316 **91** 256 261 263 **113** 224
Joshua H. **90** 104
Josie A. **121** 182
Katharine **51** 262
Lance **91** 260
Laura **56** 172
Levi **100** 210
Lewis C. **100** 208
Lilla G. **100** 208
Louisa **56** 172 **68** 333
Lucy **56** 169 172
Lucy Gordon **84** 188 **111** 150
Luke **56** 172
Luther **78** 425
Lydia (Stetson) **125** 104
Margaret **60** 153 **67** 211
Margaret (Alld) **92** 316
Margaret Barton (Pierce) **89** 265
Margaret Nelson (Dam) 115
Marian Edna **100** 110 **113** 223 233
Marqus Quintius Cen Cinatus **111** 43 **147** 69
Martin **78** 415
Mary **52** 386 **58** 319 **59** 280 **62** 161 **78** 425 **80** 244 **92** 252 **93** 320 **111** 43 **124** 278
Mary (Ball) **107** 224
Mary (Cogan) **110** 273
Mary (Landers) **124** 278
Mary E. **78** 426 **79** 54 **85** 316
Mary Elvira **118** 294
Mary J. **92** 293
Matthew **53** 302
Maurice **80** 334 **81** 222
Maurice J. **105** 77 **110** 309 **115** 237 **119** 317
May J. **98** 255
Mehitable **91** 259
Melvina M. **100** 210

POLLARD *cont'd*
Mercy **136** 360
Miriam (Grele) **91** 264
Molly **91** 254 260 261
Nancy **66** 110
Nathaniel **59** 280
Nic. **63** 363
Obed **62** 74
Olive **63** 76 **125** 214
Olive (Ingals) **91** 267
Oliver **62** 76
Ora **100** 215
Peggy **85** 5
Peggy Savage **91** 266
Peter **53** 302 **100** 278
Phebe (Carver) **89** 38
Philip **111** 43
Polly **62** 161 **124** 277
Portor **66** 111
Priscilla Estelle **92** 116
Rachel **91** 264 267 **100** 208
Ralph Burton (Mrs.) **103** 120
Randolf Albion **92** 115
Relief **81** 38
Rhoda **87** 226 236
Rhode (Partridge) **113** 224
Richard **109** 286
Riddie **118** 294
Robert **111** 263 264
Roger **51** 262
Rowland Collins (Mrs.) **89** 265
Ruth **56** 172 **71** 357 359
Ruth (Burge) **113** 224
Sadie **80** 244
Sally **64** 43 **91** 261
Samuel **91** 255 259 **92** 316 **115** 196
Sarah **56** 172 **58** 123 **62** 384 **63** 75 **78** 425 **91** 256
Sarah (Farmer) **113** 224
Sarah (Gould) **91** 266
Sarah (Locke) **137** 73
Sarah (Whittemore) **108** 92
Sarah Ann **117** 209
Sarah Jane **118** 295
Solomon **91** 262 **147** 84
Stephen **56** 213 **57** xxxiii
Stephen Curtis **56** 172
Susan (Anderson) **90** 53
Susan Francis **92** 252
Susanna **63** 269 **91** 258 259
Theodore Nelson **92** 115
Thomas **56** 213 **71** 233 **78** 425 **91** 254 255 267 **113** 224 **118** 295
Thomas W. (Mrs.) **118** 295
Thomas Wyatt **118** 292-294
Timothy **108** 92
Uriah A. **83** 178 185
Warren Wales **56** 172
Wealthy **121** 258
William **51** 234 **55** 234 **56** 213 413 **59** 338 **62** 329 384 **63** 269 **64** 341

POLLARD *cont'd*
99 239 **100** 214 215 **103** 152 185 **111** 263 **143** 257
William Frederick **92** 252
POLLARD-LOWSLEY
Anne Pamela **117** 200
Herbert de Lisle **117** 200
John Inglis Penrose **117** 200
Sylvia Janet (Penrose) **117** 200
Sylvia Marion (Lind) **117** 200
Sylvia Patricia **117** 200
Pollards *see* Pollard
Polle *see* Polly
POLLEN —— **62** 286
POLLER
Mary A. **71** xxxviii
POLLES Jane **62** 236
Joseph **143** 260
POLLETT Pollet
Hugh **82** 188
Marie **52** 313 314
Martha **77** 135
Richard **112** 188
Robert **64** 165
Thomas **77** 134 135
Polley *see* Polly
POLLICOT
Francis **83** 319
POLLISON
Rachel **106** 150
POLLISTER —— **103** 191
POLLOCK Pollack Polock
—— **140** 43
— Gov. **99** 219
— Miss **79** 306
— Mr. **63** 54
— Mrs. **63** 53
Abigail **127** 6
Agnes **87** 199
Albert Edward **144** 316
Alexander **128** 175
Allan **140** 43
Ann **128** 175
Ann (Wallace) **128** 175
Charles **128** 58
Charlotte **62** 301
Edward **75** 292
Eliza **92** 36
Elmira **75** 258
Emily W. (Wilson) **144** 312 316
Erastus **132** 306
Erwin H. **110** 101
Frances **77** 255
Frederick **147** 8
George **118** 313
Helen Mary **82** 235
Henry **128** 57
James **75** 258
James G. (Mrs.) **106** 160
James Herbert **144** 316
James W. **144** 312 316
Jane Wilson **144** 309 312
Jeremiah Wilson **133** 23
Joseph **77** 134
Lydia E. **144** 316
Magdalen **77** 134

POLLOCK *cont'd*
Margaret H. **146** 387
Margaret L. **128** 171
Mark (Mrs.) **116** 314
Martha **88** 190 **105** 67
Mary **69** 380
Mary (Torrey) **144** 301
302
Mary (Wilson) **144** 299
302 311
Mary Ann **144** 311
Mary Inez (Pease) **128** 175
Mary Knowles (Wilson)
144 311 316
Mary Louisa **77** 148
Nancy **126** 22
Polly **116** 314
Robert **66** 28 **69** 380 **77**
134 **78** 329 **80** 55 **144**
309 312
Robert Bruce **144** 316
Robert M. **77** 148
Sarah **109** 149
Sarah Knowles **144** 312
Thomas **77** 255
William **112** 17 **144** 299
302
William W. **128** 175
William Wilson **69** 380
144 301 302
Wilson **62** 357
Zephaniah **77** 135
POLLY Polley Pollye Poly
Abigail **97** 42 **100** 239
112 59 **146** 278
Adam **64** 139
Agnes **67** 262
Ann W. **94** 393
Asbond **83** 60
Bethiah **78** 428
Dorcas **79** 400
Ebenezer **79** 400
Edmond **62** 214
Elnathan **57** 74
Ephraim **83** 60
Hannah **81** 97 **94** 393 **96**
260 **101** 324 **130** 235
148 176
Hiram **148** 176
Jacob **100** 142 234 236 239
140 329
James Henry **148** 176
Jane **96** 261 266 267 **125**
108 **148** 176
Jane (Metcalf) (Walker)
96 261
Jemima **92** 49
John **62** 59 348 **78** 428 **92**
48 49 **96** 260-262
Jonathan **130** 235 236
Joseph **79** 400
Lucy **115** 159
Lyman **112** 59
Margaret **148** 176
Mary **62** 59 **79** 400 **96** 260
100 234 236 239
Matthew **115** 159 **130** 235
Nathaniel **92** 49 55
Patience **67** 371
Priscilla **62** 59 **69** 90
Rebecca **57** 74 **62** 346

POLLY *cont'd*
96 263 267
Robert **112** 188 189
Sally (Ridgeway)
(Stutson) **140** 237
Samuel **62** 59 **92** 60
Sarah **67** 371 **92** 55 56
96 260
Simeon **78** 190 **140** 237
Thomas **94** 393
Thursey **83** 60
William **74** 268 **85** 10
William G. **148** 176
POLLYFOOT
Thomas **112** 188
POLLYTT Wyllm **147** 165
POLNER Almon **91** 384
Julia E. (Scolley) **91** 384
POLO Marco **58** ci
Polock *see* Pollock
Polson *see* Poulson
POLSTED Henry **94** 336
Thomas **135** 224 234
POLTUR Edmund **83** 319
POLWHELE —— **52** 344
Poly *see* Polly
POMBAL
— Marqueses de **92** 97
POMER George P. (Mrs.)
102 285
POMERANTZ
Sidney I. **107** 249
POMEROY Pomeray
Pomery Pommeraye
Pomroy Pomry
Pumroy
—— **118** 9 218 **119** 209
302 **120** 295 **121** 96 **122**
223 **123** 21
— Col. **110** 32 **118** 24
— Dr. **52** 277 **53** 247
— Mr. **60** 205
— Mrs. **123** 19
— Widow **67** 261 262
—— (Donaldson) **94** 49
Aaron **57** 272 **90** 160
Abigail **57** 208-213 269-
271 273 **63** 179 **72** 214
217 221 **85** 50 **116** 282
118 220
Abigail (Remington)
136 321
Abigail (Wheeler)
136 309
Abishai **57** 269
Abner **57** 272 **90** 256 257
Achsah **136** 321 327
Adino **57** 268
Agnes **68** 53-56
Alanson **137** 78
Albert A. **64** xxxii 89 93 **65**
xxxv **66** 91 **116** 282 **143**
113 **148** 226
Albert Alonzo **67** xxxii
191
Alice **68** 49 50 54 **98** 259
Amanda **96** 287
Amasa **57** 273
Andrew **100** 299
Ann **57** 268
Anna **57** 270 272 273 **68** 53

POMEROY *cont'd*
90 160 257 258 **108** 248
Anna (Bush) **89** 266
Anna (Ellis) **122** 65
Anne **57** 268 **68** 53 56
Annis **68** 53
Ariette (Farley) **103** 87
Asa **57** 271 **72** 217 221
Asahel **57** 269 273 **65** 221
121 302
Ashbel Strong **133** 22
Augustus Wheelock
57 271
Bathsheba **57** 213 272
Benjamin **57** 268 270 271
58 300 **72** 214 **119** 21
136 309
Bette **54** 83
Billy **144** 325
Bishop **115** 128
Brenton C. (Mrs.) **81** 217
82 107 **116** 227
Bridget (Hannaford)
(Chapin) **83** 354
Caleb **57** 208 210-212 272
273 **71** li **88** 198 **89** 266
101 45
Calvin **137** 78
Caroline **103** 87
Catherine **57** 209 210
Catherine Boyer **77** 297
Charles **57** 273
Charles V. **122** 130
Charlotte Eliza **91** 44
Chloe **57** 272
Clarissa **77** 297
Daisy Esther **95** 148
Damaris **57** 273
Daniel **57** 212 213 269 271
72 217 **74** 66 **95** 65
Daniel Eleazer **88** 170
Daniel W. **103** 87
David **71** li
Deborah **57** 273 **75** 304
Deborah (Foster) **102** 197
Deborah Jane Spaulding
71 xxxv li
Dinah **57** 273 **67** 261
Dolly **119** 213
Dorcas **57** 273
Dorothy **57** 268 **136** 331
Ealema **57** 272
Ebenezer **57** 209-213 268-
270 272 **89** 266 **90** 255
123 17 18 **136** 309 331
137 78
Edward **67** 261
Eldad **57** 208 210 212 213
272 273 **71** li **89** 266
Eleanor **57** 213 270 272 292
68 47 53 **108** 45
Eleanor (Lyman) **101** 288
Eleazar **57** 268 **136** 309
Eleazar Wheelock **57** 271
Eliakim **57** 209 212 271
72 214 **85** 50 **136** 321
Elihu **56** 307 **57** 271 273
114 182
Elijah **57** 213 271 272
Elisha **57** 212 272 273 **71** li
Elizabeth **54** 152 **57** 209-

POMEROY *cont'd*
213 270 271 **65** 351 **67**
261 **68** 53 **72** 217 221
119 50
Elizabeth (Callender)
  144 325
Elizabeth (Hunt) **136** 331
Elizabeth (Strickland)
  88 199
Elizabeth Leitch (Watson)
  89 266
Ellen L. **133** 22
Eltweed **57** 208-213 268-
  273 **58** 100 **59** 215 **60**
  190 **64** 89 93 **67** 191 261
  262 **68** 47 55 56 **70** 55
  71 li **72** 214 217 **88** 198
  89 266 **143** 108 111 114
  147 158 **148** 226 227
  229 230
Emeline **101** 34
Emma B. **62** 381
Enos **57** 272
Epaphras **57** 271
Esther **57** 210 213 268
  72 100
Ethan **57** 213
Ethel **89** 314
Ethel Josephine (Braman)
  83 473
Eunice **57** 213 268-272 **72**
  319 **90** 337 **118** 125 126
  218 221 222 225 229 232
  297 **119** 43 52 214 **136**
  331 360
Experience **57** 208 209
  213 270 272 273 **72** 214
  91 99 **136** 310 321 325
Experience (Woodward)
  136 309 310 315 318 321
  328 331
F. **100** 305
Fanny S. **87** 383
Francis **60** 132
Frederick **79** 159
Freedom **57** 272
Geoffrey de la **145** 4 5
George E. **61** xxxv
George Eltweed **60** 404
Gershom **57** 272
Gideon **71** li
Hannah **57** 208-213 269-
  273 **71** 112 **72** 213 214
  217 **90** 160
Hannah (Hannum)
  90 160
Hannah (Seymour) **136**
  309 321
Hannah (Trumbull)
  136 321
Hannah Cooper **86** 245
Heman **57** 213
Henry **67** 261 262 **68** 47
  48 51 53-56
Henry de la **145** 4 5
Hepzibah **57** 208 210 212
  271
Hepzibah (Baker) **89** 266
Hiram Sterling **57** xxxv
Hopkins Chillingsworth
  103 87

POMEROY *cont'd*
Horace B. (Mrs.) **83** 473
Huldah **57** 273 **90** 254
Irene **57** 273
Isaac **57** 213 270 273 **71** li
  75 306
Isabel **57** 273
Isabella C. (Low) **87** 383
J. N. **75** 19
Jabez B. **103** 87
Jabez Davis **103** 87
Jacob **57** 272 273
Jane (Chipman) **103** 87
Jemima **57** 273
Jerusha **57** 269 270 **123** 136
Jesse **116** 282
Joan **79** 414
Joanna **57** 212 268 **67** 261
  112 145
Joel **57** 272
John **57** 209-211 213 271
  273 **68** 47 53 **72** 217 221
  80 399 **98** 259 **102** 197
  105 290 **136** 310
John N. **58** lxiii
John S. **83** 100
Jonah **57** 211
Jonathan **57** 268 271
Jonathan Law **57** 289
  69 367
Joseph **57** 208 209 211
  213 270 271 273 **61** 140
  71 112 **72** 213 214 217
  105 210 291 **136** 309
  321 **148** 229
Joshua **57** 209 210 212 213
  71 li **88** 199
Joshua B. **98** 259
Josiah **57** 268 270 271 292
  293 **90** 349 **101** 333 **136**
  331
Julius **88** 199
Julius Clark **88** 198 199
Justin **57** 270
Justus **88** 199
Katharine Adams **81** 217
  82 107
Kent L. (Mrs.) **119** 319
Keziah **57** 273
L. K. **125** 42
Lavinia **57** 271
Lawrena **57** 273
Lemuel **54** 83 **57** 210 269
  90 257
Leona **75** 19
Leonard **76** 316
Lilly (Maxwell) **89** 266
Lois **57** 212 268
Lois (Phelps) **88** 199
Lorency **137** 78
Louis Sherrill **103** 87
Louisa **57** 269 273
Lucina **72** 217
Lucius R. **100** 209
Lucy **57** 268 273 **75** 306
  78 73 **89** 267 **137** 78
Lucy (Bemis) **89** 266
Lucy (Bowen) **144** 325
Lucy (Wyeth) **89** 267
Lucy F. **78** 181
Lucy Sophia **79** 272

POMEROY *cont'd*
Lurana **57** 273
Lydia **56** 307 **57** 208 209
  211 212 268 271
Lydia (Ashley) **136** 331
Lydia (Brown) (Parsons)
  143 108 114 **148** 226
  227 229 230
Lynne **102** 124
Margaret **68** 53
Margery **59** 215 **67** 261
Margery (Rockett) **88** 198
  89 266
Margery (Wilkins)
  100 299
Maria **79** 151
Maria (Clark) **88** 199
Martha **57** 269 272
Martin K. **83** 147
Mary **57** 208-213 268-272
  59 215 **60** 303 **67** 261
  68 52 **72** 217 221 **90** 256
  136 309
Mary (French) **90** 256
Mary (Hunt) **136** 309
Mary A. (Featherly)
  133 22
Mary Ann **71** li **75** 19
  106 310
Mary C. (Dean) **103** 87
Mary E. (Byrne) **103** 87
Mary Fuller **106** 227
Mary L. **75** 19
Mary Lorinda (Bement)
  88 198 199
Mary Wyllys **136** 309
Matilda (Ralegh) **145** 4 5
Medad **57** 208 209 211-
  213 268-271 **60** 303 **72**
  214 217 **88** 95 **89** 266
  136 309 310 315 318 321
  328 331 **141** 15 **143** 119
Mehitable **57** 209 **136** 315
Mercy **57** 210 211 213 270
  273 **90** 258
Mildred **96** 288
Mindwell **57** 209 212 213
  271 **80** 399 **119** 53
Mindwell (Lyman)
  136 331
Mindwell (Sheldon)
  136 310
Miriam **57** 269 272
Morris **137** 78
Myron **103** 87
Nancy **133** 263 264
Nancy Maria (Carrier)
  122 130
Naomi **74** 66
Nathaniel **57** 211 212 271
  72 214 217 221
Nellie **100** 209
Nettie Maria **88** 198
Nettie May **81** 220 **88** 160
  89 136
Noah **57** 210-213 271 273
  63 179 **72** 214 **136** 321
Norton **103** 87
Olive **106** 212
Oliver **57** 213
Orpha **109** 226

POMEROY *cont'd*
Orpha L. **103** 87
Pamela **75** 306
Phebe **57** 269 270 272 273
  79 404 **80** 62
Phebe (Coleman)
  (Hannum) **90** 349
Phebe (Hopkins) **103** 87
Phila **139** 108
Phineas **57** 270
Phineas Ashley **54** 152
Pliny **57** 269
Polly **94** 285 **119** 213
Priscilla **57** 213 272 273
Prudence **57** 271
Quartus **57** 269 **120** 123
  210 **121** 299 **122** 116
Rachel **57** 211-213 269 272
  273 **90** 255 **106** 212
Rachel (Searle) **89** 266
  90 255
Ralph **57** 271
Rebecca Rossignol
  76 169
Repent **57** 210
Rhoda **57** 270 273
Richard **58** 249 **67** 261 **68**
  47-49 52-56 **70** 55 **89**
  266 **143** 114 **148** 226
Richard Watson **75** xxiv
  64 **89** 266 267 283 **90**
  139
Ruth **57** 271 272 292 293
  115 128
Ruth (Thayer) **101** 333
Sabra **75** 307
Samuel **55** 109 **57** 209
  210 212 213 271-273 **71**
  li **88** 199 **90** 160
Samuel French **90** 160
Samuel Wyllis **77** 297
Sarah **57** 209-213 268-272
  293 **58** 311 **61** 142 **68**
  176 **69** 367 **85** 50 **90** 72
Sarah (King) **136** 309 331
Sarah (Sheldon) **85** 50
  136 321
Sarah (Wait) **89** 266
Sarah C. **103** 87
Seth **57** 212 268 270 **60**
  211 404 **61** 142 **68** 170
  176 291 **69** 367 379 **77**
  59 64 66 **116** 111 **130**
  217 **136** 309 **137** 114
  147 122
Shammah **57** 268
Sibyl **57** 269
Silas **57** 272
Silence (Brown) **88** 199
Simeon **57** 211-213 271
Solomon **57** 272
Sophia **109** 105
Stephen **57** 213 **75** 306
  118 18
Susanna **57** 212 269 271
  63 184 **72** 214 217
Temperance **57** 273
Thankful **57** 209 212 270
  272 273 **61** 140 **72** 214
  129 368 **136** 318 328
Theodora **60** 132

POMEROY *cont'd*
Theodore Medad **89** 266
Theodore S. **87** 383
Thomas **54** 196 **68** 48 51
  53 54
Thomas M. **79** 272
Thomasine **68** 53
Timothy **57** 269 272 273
  89 266
Titus **57** 213 273
Violatia **137** 78
Violatia (Thayer) **137** 78
Walter **137** 78
Walter Herman **98** 259
William **57** 270 **105** 289
  115 127 **144** 325
William F. **78** 302
POMFRET Pomphret
—— **112** 29
— Earl of **54** 325 332
Elizabeth 101 **65** 212 **88**
  196 **89** 192 **92** 101 **98** 65
  111 45
Elizabeth (Allen) (Von
  Kronenshelt) **102** 189
Hannah **117** 288
Husanna **111** 45
John **117** 288
John E. **97** 394 **124** 103
Margaret **117** 289
Mary **117** 288
Richard **127** 263
Richarde **127** 168
Rose **92** 101 **111** 45
Thomas **56** 86 **102** 189
  104 287
William **65** 212 **92** 101 102
  111 45
POMFREY William **65** 118
POMHAM Sachem **87** 265
POMMER
Sibyl **82** 125 237
Pommeraye *see* Pomeroy
POMPEY
Ezekiel **100** 287
George **100** 278
John **100** 278 287
Nancy **108** 264
Rosanna **100** 287
Sally **100** 278
Samuel **100** 278
Sherman Lee **117** 75
  119 73
Pomphret *see* Pomfret
POMPILLO
— Widow **123** 191 193
POMPIMUET **127** 24
POMYEA Peter **129** 43
PONARD Benjamin **119** 20
PONAY George **63** 239
POND
—— **57** 56 **99** 314
— Capt. **98** 104
— Maj. **98** 106
— Mr. **60** 264 **71** 116
Abia **114** 303
Abial (Blake) **115** 161
Abigail **57** 392 **70** 70 **88** 84
Abigail (Heath) **115** 161
Abigail (Shepard) **102**
  303 **115** 161

POND *cont'd*
Abijah **143** 14
Abner **142** 68
Abner French **75** 258
Abraham **54** 348
Addie Amelia **89** 316
Alvira M. **142** 74
Amos **102** 303
Ann **142** 162 163
Anna **57** 54
Anna A. (Hutchings) **83**
  432 438
Anne **54** 348 **103** 220
Arba **141** 336
Arthur A. **117** 285
Asa **57** 394
Barbara A. (Koons)
  115 162
Benjamin **57** 56 392
Catherine **91** 293
Charlotte E. **69** 37
Chloe Adeline (Upham)
  85 341
Cynthia (Clewley)
  114 303
Cynthia Deacon **115** 162
Dan **77** 92
Daniel **58** 159 412 **74** xlix
  99 314 **102** 303 **110** 317
  115 161
David **141** 190 192
Deborah (Howes) **115** 161
Desire **142** 74
Dinah **57** 397
Dorcas **63** 94
E. D. **91** 332
Ebenezer **143** 14
Eli **58** 239
Elias Cornelius **85** 341
Elijah **115** 161 **141** 195
Elijah Parker **115** 161
Eliphalet **63** 187 188 192
  262
Elisha **98** 104
Eliza J. (Bancroft) **97** 134
Elizabeth **63** 188 **98** 344 **99**
  314 **141** 192 **142** 162
  164
Ellen **142** 162-164
Ellen (Hanks) **86** 16
Ellen J. **122** 91
Emma (Williams) **115** 161
Enoch **67** 215 221 **142** 74
Ephraim **115** 161 **116** 84
  130 213
Ermenell **54** 348
Ezekiel **65** 375
Florence Louisa **86** 198
Frances **142** 161 164
Frances (Floyer) **100** 300
Frances L. (Moore) **90** 48
Francis **142** 162
Franklin Amos **102** 303
Fred E. **83** 432 438
George E. **75** lxiii
George Kimball **69** xxxv
  90 128 **101** 25 130 **102**
  303
Georgia H. **117** 285
Gideon **55** 171 **98** 104
Handel **63** 214 **76** lviii

POND *cont'd*
Hannah **58** 159 **136** 362
Hannah (Fisher) **130** 213
Harlow S. **95** 188
Harriet **103** 269
Harriet (Sweetsir) **103** 269
Harriet F. **93** 394
Harriet Hunt **83** 101
Hartwell **107** 68 129
Harvey **95** 188
Hattie Dinsmore
  (Kimball) **102** 303
Helen Amanda (Sanborn)
  95 188
Helen Melville **103** 120
Henry **97** 134
Herbert **103** 269
Hezekiah **57** 392
Horace **108** 269
Huldah **58** 239 **141** 336
Ichabod **57** 56 392 **102** 303
  142 80
Increase **141** 336
Increase S. **91** 332
Irene Richardson **57** 394
Isabel **142** 164
Israel **63** 94
J. Alanson **54** 127
J. Almeron **54** xxxix
Jacob **115** 161 **142** 76
Jennie Adeline **85** 341
Jeremiah **141** 356
Joanna **57** 54
Joanna (Lawrence)
  102 303
Job **136** 362
John **54** 348 **56** 74 **58** 412
  83 313 **136** 362 **142** 159
  162-164
John V. **103** 265
Jonas **56** 31 **77** 320
Jonathan **98** 104 **102** 303
Joseph **141** 195 196 347
Joshua **63** 187 **98** 104 105
Josiah **70** 70 **143** 309
Keziah **90** 76
Leon Y. **91** 400
Levi Merrill **84** 87
Lois **53** 55 **57** 56 392 ·
  143 309
Lucinda **140** 170
Lucretia **57** 394
Lydia **56** 373 **100** 299 **130**
  281 **141** 139
Mabel **77** 92
Mary **56** 31 **75** 147 **109** 69
  116 84
Mary (Garfield) **102** 303
Mary (Smith) **115** 161
Mary ---delia **142** 74
Mary Ann **103** 64
Mary Lovett **75** 258
Mary Snow **72** 310
Mehitable W. (Parker)
  115 161
Mene Mene Tekel
  Upharsin **77** 11
Mercy (Daniels) **120** 122
Michal (Man) **130** 213
Milcah **57** 56 392

POND *cont'd*
Milcah (Farrington)
  102 303
Milla Hartwell (Temple)
  115 161
Mindwell **54** 213
Miriam **54** 50 **58** 357
Nancy **79** 43
Nathan **126** 277
Nathan G. **51** 72 **54** 224
  56 93 209 **57** 114 334 **58**
  94 **59** 105 220
Nathaniel **139** 308 **148**
  235 266
Olive Margaret
  (Thompson) **102** 303
Oliver **114** 301 302 **130** 213
  218 281 282 **131** 41 43-
  45 49
Partridge **57** 394
Philip **58** 180 **83** 101
Philister **102** 303
Preston **115** 161
Prudence **140** 144
Rachel **55** 395 **121** 78
Rachel (Fuller) **148** 266
Reuben **141** 338 350
Rhoda (Howard) **102** 303
Robert **56** lxvi **57** 54 91
  400 **102** 303 **142** 80
Robert W. **117** 160
Ruth **105** 125
Ruth (Shaw) **89** 316
Samuel **55** 395 **58** 357 **77**
  11 **86** 16 **98** 344 **123** 88
  141 192 **148** 227
Sarah **57** 392 **123** 88
  136 317
Sarah (Fales) **115** 161
Sarah Annis **54** 127
Sarah Rebecca **126** 220
Sarah Sumner **75** 258
Sarah W. **84** 56
Selma Ellis **67** vii **68** vi
  xxxv **69** vi **70** vi xiii **71**
  vi xv
Seth **89** 316 **100** 300
Stephen **55** 171 172 174
  175
Stillman **91** 400
Susanna **54** 348 **72** 175
Susanna (Webster)
  98 344
Thankful **58** 145 180
  75 147
Thankful (Thomson)
  102 303
Thomas **142** 162
Thomas Temple **99** 139
  148 162 **100** 124 **101**
  138 **102** 115 117 137
  103 110 134 **104** 137-
  140 **111** 141-144 **112** 70
  134-137 222 314 **113** 61
  148-151 233 234 293 **114**
  70 140 142-144 228 309
  310 **115** 68 145-149 161-
  163 229 **116** 72
Timothy **113** 318 **141** 197
  142 81
Walter Rice **115** 161

POND *cont'd*
William **54** 348 **59** 106
  75 147 **90** 48 **115** 161
  142 162 164
Zaccheus **56** 74
Ponderson *see* Punderson
PONETT Thomas **65** 177
PONG Charles **131** 95
  Edward **131** 95
  Thomas **131** 95
PONS Thomas **140** 237
PONSLIN William **125** 31
PONSOLD
  Alice de **76** 298-300
  Stephen de **76** 298 300
  Thomas de **76** 299
PONSONBY
  — Lord **125** 64
  Eleanor Ann **126** 204
  Sarah **73** 221
  William Carr **125** 64
PONTBRIAND
  Benoit **145** 130
PONTEY Beatrice
  Grosvenor (Hadfield)
  103 71
PONTHIER
  Elizabeth de **76** lxxiii
PONTIUS
  H. G. (Mrs.) **125** 97
PONTON Richard **106** 173
  175 177
PONTUS GLASS
  Mary **52** 364
PONTUS Hannah **82** 118
  90 72 **111** 172
  Mary **111** 178
  William **111** 178 **120** 280
  Wybra (Hansen) **111** 178
POOD Agnes **83** 71
POOK Pooke
  Abigail **78** 70
  Mary **79** 49
  Mary Ann **144** 222
  William **77** 316 **140** 237
  142 290
Pool *see* Poole
POOLAM
  Mary **75** 281 289
  Robert **75** 281 289
POOLE Pool Pooll
  —— **53** 385 **55** 19 **56** 114
  232 **59** 202 **60** 212 **123**
  95
  — Capt. **85** 258 **137** 245
  — Mr. **57** 187 **63** 82 327
  64 26 **79** 301
  — Mrs. **51** 251 **101** 161
  Abigail **70** 361 **88** 51 53
  248 **96** 298
  Abigail (Hayward)
  125 291
  Abijah Rogers Nurse
  Chase **110** 160
  Agnes **71** 241
  Alexis **110** 223
  Alice **67** 118
  Almy (Chase) **87** 139
  Amai **69** 82
  Amos **120** 42
  Amy **120** 41

POOLE *cont'd*
Ann Maria **88** 335
Anna **67** 121 **88** 366 **91** 265
  115 127
Anna (Ford) (Pratt)
  120 42
Anne **67** 118 **71** 241
Anne (Bancroft) **94** 318
Annie Maria **71** xlix
Asa **88** 53
Bathsheba **59** 258 378
Benjamin **55** 292 294 **59**
  200 **61** 109 **64** 186 **67**
  115
Benjamin Fletcher **85** 436
Bethiah **55** 292
Betsey **70** 360
Bridget **55** 290-292
Bridget (Fitch) **137** 244
Caleb **137** 141
Calvin **67** 120
Caroline **97** 119
Catherine **69** 275
Cecily **123** 256
Charles Henry **54** 226
Charlotte M. **82** 19
Clara Augusta **84** 191
Clarissa **126** 221
Clarissa (Hill) **95** 56
Cora Jane **89** 234
Daniel **59** 223 **60** 190 **67**
  119 120 218
David **70** 361 **88** 51
David de Sola **107** 19
Deborah **67** 118-120 **69** 82
DeWitt Clinton **93** 401
  122 91
Ebenezer **125** 90 **137** 139-
  141
Edmund **147** 321
Edmund Duval **54** 237
  55 xxxii **78** 447 **79** 203
Edward **54** 226 **59** 221
  223 328 **60** 190 **63** 41 **85**
  250
Edwin Bartlett **95** 53
Effie **108** 136
Eldora Mindwell **100** 109
  110 220 223
Elisha **115** 33
Eliza Sprigg **108** 231 233
Elizabeth **51** 408 **55** 292 **59**
  328 **61** 280 **70** 284 **77**
  313 **78** 404 **94** 398 **95** 56
  96 400 **97** 328 **110** 78
  113 134 **130** 316 **141** 33
  142 358 **143** 41 46 334
  147 252 253
Elizabeth Dinsmoor
  (Pillsbury) **85** 234
Elizabeth Frost **111** 316
Ella / Ellen Maria **82** 19
Ellsworth W. (Mrs.)
  85 234
Emily Alfaretta **82** 19
Enos **142** 206
Ephraim **59** 201 259 380-
  384
Esther **55** 292 **67** 100
  77 138
Eunice (Gates) **125** 287

POOLE *cont'd*
Eunice (Green) **126** 80
Eunice (Lazell) **88** 365
Eunice I. **95** 51
Experience **53** 394
Fitch **51** 408 **84** 266
  111 316
Frances Merritt **82** 19
Francis **137** 141
Francis Herbert **82** 253
  83 230
Frederick Arthur **82** 122
  130 237 **86** 262
Galen **77** 180 **88** 331
Geffery **105** 17
George B. (Mrs.) **94** 194
George Sanger **61** 406
Georgianna 40 **92** 40
Granville Church **70** 361
H. **65** 34
H. F. **100** 208
Hannah **65** 121 **88** 51
  119 119
Hannah (Nichols) **136** 145
Harriet **142** 206
Harriet (Andrews) **88** 331
Henry **59** 223 **60** 190 **107**
  48 **123** 256
Henry C. **91** 202
Herbert Armstrong **89**
  132 **98** 88 **109** 184 257
  145 145
Hester M. (Hunt) **123** 95
Hiram **134** 336
Isaac **119** 117 **125** 90 291
  127 158 **136** 25
Jacob **119** 254
James **88** 365
Jane **52** 185 **119** 67
Jane (Bailey) **89** 234
Jane Bailey (Lazell) **89** 234
Jason B. **115** 126
Jemima **53** 30
Jessamine **142** 303
Job **142** 206
John **53** 30 **54** 226 **59** 223
  60 190 **61** 280 **62** 235
  63 127 **64** 188 **67** 115
  217 **69** 82 83 **73** 144 231
  82 19 130 **93** 299 **94** 398
  97 328 329 **100** 139 **104**
  128 **108** 76 **110** 223 **113**
  286 289 **127** 223 **137**
  141 242 **143** 41
John C. **91** 332
John Hudson **93** 401
  122 81
John W. **84** 296
Jonathan **55** 290-292 **63**
  266 **69** 275 **78** 281 **79**
  321 **94** 219 221 318 398
  399 **95** 109 **100** 81 **106**
  153 **108** 25 **109** 214 **110**
  223 **137** 141 242 244
  142 358 **143** 40 41
Joseph **51** 160 **53** 394 **59**
  221 328 **110** 160 **119**
  117 119 **142** 206
Joseph Russell **118** 323
Joshua **72** 275 **88** 53 **95**
  51 53 56

POOLE *cont'd*
Judith **55** 291 292 **79** 321
  94 397-399 **142** 358 **143**
  40-42
Judith (Jacobs) **94** 219
Julia V. **79** 16
Keith B. **123** 242
Lilly Blackwell (Lundy)
  101 79
Lizzie S. **77** 180
Lois **57** 368 **67** 120
Lorraine Seville **84** 296
Lott **110** 223
Lucinda **59** 259 381-384
  88 53
Lucius M. **66** xxv
Lucy **75** 35
Lydia **82** 19
Lydia (Cox) **89** 234
Margaret **71** 32 245 **94** 398
  110 223 **143** 41
Margaret (Parmenter)
  147 381
Maria **122** 87
Maria (McNeil) **134** 336
Maria Woodward (Pettes)
  122 91
Marion Simmons (Rowe)
  94 194
Mark **119** 283
Marl **119** 283
Martha **77** 276 283 **115** 121
Mary **55** 292 **59** 197 221
  67 119 217 **69** 82 83 **79**
  321 **94** 398 **97** 94 **102**
  277 **110** 223 **119** 257
  142 206
Mary (Leman) **95** 109
  137 242
Mary Ann (Poor) **111** 316
Mary L. (Stover) **119** 283
Matthew **59** 201 **60** 190
Maybel (Moses) **83** 436
  438
Mehitable **55** 292 294
  118 96
Minnie A. Lewis **90** 305
Murray Edward **54** 226
  55 345 348 **58** xlv 101
  59 221 223 328 419 **60**
  84 88 96 188 190 274 **63**
  306 **64** xxxii **65** xxxv
  96 **71** 369 **75** xvii **79**
  192
Nabby **88** 51
Nahum **77** 56
Nancy Fitch **70** 346
Nancy H. **147** 383
Nathan Morton **89** 234
Nathaniel **52** 185
Nathaniel Albert **82** 19
Nicholas **88** 366
Olive (Cleaveland)
  127 158
Oliver **67** 119 **126** 260 262
Patrick **60** 190
Penelope Rowe **77** 185
Periam **61** 280
Peter **59** 223 **60** 190
Phebe **67** 119
Polly **59** 201 259 380 **88**

POOLE *cont'd*
51 53 **104** 127 128
Polly P. **89** 95
Rachel **93** 267
Rachel (Knopp) **147** 320
321
Rebecca **55** 292 **142** 303
Rebecca (Washburn)
136 25
Rebecca Spalding
(Eastham) **85** 436
Rebecca Thomas **77** 56
Return **77** 283
Richard **53** 238 **96** 182
105 17 **140** 15 **147** 381
Robert **59** 223 **60** 190
68 264
Rowland **107** 48
Ruth **59** 221 **119** 119
Ruth (Ford) **119** 112 119
Sally (Yates) **100** 81
Samuel **55** 292 **59** 221 223
60 190 **63** 330 **65** 357
88 51 248 **89** 234 **115**
127 **119** 119 183
Samuel Hale **100** 68 81
Samuel Porter **88** 51
Samuel S. **83** 436 438
Samuel Sheldon **96** 49
126 226
Sarah **55** 294 **59** 328 **63** 41
67 122 **85** 229 250 **91** 79
94 219 398 **95** 109 **96** 49
100 296 **108** 308 **110**
223 **119** 183 **126** 260
262 **137** 239 242
Sarah (Farley) **136** 145
Sarah (Field) **113** 286
Sarah (Nash) **119** 119 183
Sarah (Ramsdell) **126** 262
Sarah (Solart) **144** 358
Sarah (Warren) **126** 80
Silas **110** 223
Simeon **86** 461
Stephen **137** 141
Stephen P. **89** 95
Susan **142** 206
Susan E. **100** 208
Susan Rebecca **85** 436
Susan Woodward **100**
68 81
Susanna **78** 309 **137** 325
Sylvanus **125** 287
Temperance **67** 119 120
218
Thomas **71** 241 **79** 166 **87**
139 **137** 241 245 **142**
303
Timothy **67** 118-122 **69** 82
125 81 **137** 244 258 329
W. F. **59** 79
Wellington **54** xxxix
Wendell **82** 19
William **52** 185 **55** 292
57 368 **59** 197 199 223
258 378 **60** 190 **61** 280
82 155 **88** 53 **94** 398
102 277 **107** 48 **110** 78
115 249 252 **136** 145
141 33 102 **143** 41 **147**
252 253

POOLE *cont'd*
William F. **52** 282
William Frederick **65** 276
William Henry **77** 185
Zachariah **55** 292
Zeria **108** 76
Zurviah **67** 217
POOLER Allyn **66** 136
Feno **89** 383
John **89** 383
Levi **103** 81
Lucy (Owen) **91** 246
POOLEY Agnes
(Coningsby) **102** 9
Agnes (Wheathill) **102** 7
Alice (Rockhill) **102** 7
Elizabeth **114** 73
John **64** lii **102** 7 9
Mercy **64** lii
Thomas **102** 7
Pooll *see* Poole
POORE Poore Pore
——— **51** 186 **54** 127 **62** 55
66 43 **79** 278 **111** 107
— Capt. **99** 285 **135** 106
— Col. **95** 375
— Gen. **55** 320
Abigail **53** 38 **100** 238
103 310
Abigail (Hale) **106** 225
Abraham **55** lxxix
Agnes Blake **57** xxxiii
Albert **52** 395 **55** xxxv
xliii lxxix
Alfred **53** 43 **54** xxxvii
58 xlviii **59** xlii **60**
xxxix **61** xxxvii **62**
xlviii lxxvii lxxix 51-55
Alfred Easton **112** 142
Alice **93** 87
Alonzo Stephen **88** 302
303
Amelia Titcomb **111** 107
Amos **140** 21
Ann Maria **88** 335
Anna Easton **112** 142
Anna Louise (Easton)
112 142
Anne **52** 430
Arthur G. **106** 225
Beatrice (Kimball)
125 161
Ben. Perley **51** 236 **90** 4
93 87
Benjamin **106** 225
Bethiah **136** 362
Bethiah (West) **136** 362
Betsey **88** 302 303
Caroline Emily (Peabody)
106 225
Catherine **63** 257
Charles **104** 97
Charles Lane **112** 142
Charles Lane (Mrs.) **85**
188 **112** 71 142
Charles V. **83** 178 185
Charlotte (White) **87** 294
Christopher **148** 62
Clarence Henry (Mrs.)
77 322 **78** 206
Clarence Milton **94** 392

POORE *cont'd*
Dandridge **111** 239
Daniel **53** 37 **54** 129 **55**
lxxix **89** 65 **106** 232 **107**
4 **111** 107
Daniel Morrill **88** 302
David **93** 398 **100** 63
111 107
David Coats **111** 107
David Morrill **88** 303
Deborah **106** 151 **119** 234
Ebenezer **58** 124
Ebenezer Parson **88** 302
303
Edith (Adams) **106** 225
Edward Alson **90** 374
92 96
Edward E. **72** xx **90** 130
106 116 130 224 225
Edward Eli **112** 142
Edward Eri **106** 224 225
Edwina Ward **112** 142
Eliphalet **88** 302
Eliza (Munroe) **107** 5
Elizabeth **55** lxxix **83** 261
466 **88** 302 303 **99** 285
100 238 **104** 97 **106** 232
Elizabeth (Felt) **106** 225
Elizabeth (Searle) **139** 55
Elizabeth (Welch) **88** 337
Elizabeth Hill **104** 97
Ellen Frances **87** 294
Emeline Cynthia **79** 278
Enoch **56** xxii 88 333 **58**
210 **60** 311 **65** 77 256 **68**
261 **77** 46 **94** 355 **98** 299
110 233 **136** 362
Eva **110** 222
Fannie **123** 126
Francis **74** 274 275 **75** 137
Frederick **104** 97
George **88** 302 303
Hannah **52** 430 **53** 38 **91**
86 **103** 310
Harriet Little **88** 302
Harry **125** 161
Henry **53** 38 **106** 225
Henry William **61** xxxvii
Hepsabath **88** 302
James **55** lxxix **145** 348
James Hobart **79** 278
James P. **93** 48
Jane Wallace **88** 302
Janet (Sheppard) **112** 142
Jennie (Emerson) **107** 5
Jeremiah **106** 225
Jesse **62** 51 **88** 302
Joanna (Carr) **106** 225
Job **88** 302
John **52** 430 **54** 129 **58** 268
62 55 **88** 302 **106** 225
John Alfred **59** xxvi **66** xx
John Sheppard **112** 142
Jonathan **146** 330 **147** 86
Joseph **55** lxxix **88** 302 303
106 225 **107** 4
Laura **83** 350
Lelia Margaret **108** 136
Leslie G. **104** 104
Leverett **107** 4 5
Linda M. **112** 235

POORE *cont'd*
Louise Ward **104** 97
Lucy Tucker (Gupton)
   111 239
Luke **66** 298
Luther **105** 287
Lydia **88** 302
Malvina A. (Bennett) **83**
   178 185
Margaret **88** 303
Margaret (Bailey) **88** 302
Marion **106** 225
Martha **106** 232 **107** 5
Mary **53** 36 37 **55** lxxix
   197 **58** 268 **62** 26 **88** 286
   302 **96** 400 **100** 25 246
   103 310
Mary (Abbott) **107** 4
Mary (Adams) **107** 4
Mary (Coates) **111** 107
Mary (Farnum) **106** 232
   107 4
Mary (Little) **88** 302
Mary Adelaide **78** 206
Mary E. **104** 97
Mary Susanna **95** 170 171
Mary Wellington (Law)
   106 224 **112** 142
Mattie H. **107** 3 4
Maude Gertrude
   (Mudgett) **94** 392
Mehitable **55** lxxix
Mehitable (Osgood)
   107 4
Micajah **88** 337
Mildred Ann **111** 239
Millecet (Titcomb)
   136 362
Molly **66** 298
Moses **87** 294 **88** 302 303
Nellie R. **93** 48
Noyes **88** 302
Patty **140** 21
Paul **55** 198
Polly **88** 302
Priscilla **59** lxxix **89** 65
Prudence **74** 275 **75** 137
Rebecca **59** 93
Robert **111** 107 **119** 21
Rose Wilkinson **119** 318
Ruth **55** 198 **88** 302
   106 225
Ruth (Poor) **106** 225
Sally **62** 51 **79** 15 **88** 302
   303 **137** 335
Sally (Little) **88** 302
Samuel **54** 129 **88** 302 303
   106 225
Sarah **58** 124 **66** 298 **88** 302
Sarah (Reed) **107** 4
Sarah Elizabeth **88** 302
Stephen **88** 302 303
Susan **55** lxxix
Susanna Bundy (Brown)
   95 171
Susie (Grimes) **106** 225
Sylvanus **95** 171
Tamison **90** 393
Thomas **55** lxxix **66** 321
   107 4

POORE *cont'd*
Thomas L. **88** 302
Tristam **111** 107
Virginia (Dodge) **93** 87
Virginia Sargent **99** 256
   101 121
Walter **124** 202
Washington Jefferson
   106 225
William **82** 92 **100** 238
   148 62
POORING
Mary Juliana **62** 199
POORMAN
Barbary **114** 185
Barbary (Burns) **114** 185
Elizabeth Ellmaker
   113 163
Loretta **96** 129
Minnie Loretta **96** 129
POOTINGTON
— Mr. **83** 446
POOTMAN
Elizabeth **108** 309
Mary **114** 186
POPE Pop
—— **56** 56 **57** 127 162
   331 416 **58** 406 **59** 109
   61 100 **62** 18 22 **92** 248
   253 259 346 356 **93** 48
   102 283 **132** 295 **140**
   149 237 **145** 164
— Capt. **91** 160
— Gen. **54** 145
— Mrs. **145** 247
——— (Bourne) **118** 201
——— (Russell) **140** 243
A. **109** 268
Abbey E. **89** 352
Abbie A. **93** 48
Abby **64** lxvi
Abby Russell **68** 118
Abigail **60** 359 **68** 217 **98**
   187 **100** 166 **113** 261
   114 138 **118** 202 **119** 31
   123 59 **127** 112 **128** 285
Abigail (Gifford) **132** 295
Abigail Hubbard
   (Goodwin) **133** 43
Adam **110** 123
Addie A. **93** 48
Adela Clarissa **77** 144
Agnes **51** 391
Ahrend **91** 184 **93** 183
Ahrend Christian John
   91 184 **92** 91 146 151 **93**
   183
Ahrend Christian John
   (Mrs.) **81** 108 222 **91**
   129 183 **92** 150 **93** 183
Albert Augustus **55**
   xxxiv **64** xliii lxvi
Albert Linder **64** lxvi
Alexander **51** 140 **69** 106
   77 15 **100** 218 **128** 178
   131 175 **143** 337
Alfred A. **105** 147
Alice **75** 225
Alice (Freeman) **124** 46
Alice (Jenney) **118** 201
Alice Eliza **73** xl

POPE *cont'd*
Alice Warren **66** xxxvi 83
Almira **115** 113 114
Alton **69** 180 **73** 49
   105 147
Amanda M. C. (Schadt)
   93 183
Amasa (West) **118** 202
Amelia **73** 148
Amelia Eliza **96** 161
Angelia **69** 312
Ann **68** 228 245 **70** 275 **73**
   219 **79** 319
Ann Rogers **70** 333
Anna **60** 67 **113** 213
   128 285
Anna Elizabeth **72** xliii
Annabel **54** 342
Anne **77** 253 **94** 251
   105 314
Anne (Fallowell) **148** 317
   323
Anne (Finney) **148** 318
Anne (Stubbs) **143** 335
Anson Waterman **72** 94
Arthur **65** lxv
Arthur Wilson **69** 312
Asa **62** 19 **104** 47 48
   109 271
Augustus II. **78** 304
Augustus R. **94** 160
   140 243
Augustus Russell **84** 219
   92 356
Aurora Ann **115** 111
Azor **128** 285
Bathsheba **115** 286 **118** 202
   123 137-139
Beatrix **79** 394
Belinda **82** 180
Benjamin **128** 312
Bertha (McIntosh) **123** 13
Bethiah **68** 244 **69** 173 176
   271
Betsey **125** 102 **128** 285
Betsey Jones (Talbot)
   83 410
C. H. **95** 127 **112** 66 **114**
   116 **115** 256
Catherine **78** 422 **103** 229
Catherine Ann **115** 113
   114
Charity **73** 136
Charles **64** lxvi **123** 172
Charles A. **93** 48
Charles E. **93** 48
Charles Edward **92** 248
Charles H. **51** 93 378 407
   53 140 364 451 **56** 213
   413 **58** 21 72 **69** 312 **82**
   180 **100** 222 **103** 98 **113**
   111 **120** 101 **124** 103
   131 252 **144** 25 147
Charles Henry **52** 285
   286 290 **53** 25 **54** xxix l
   lxxxiii 357 358 460 **55**
   xxx 181 280 449 **56** xxxi
   57 xxxii **59** xv lxxx **60**
   48 61 249 250 324 357
   61 37 55 100 **62** xxv
   lxxxv 184 303 387 388

POPE *cont'd*
390 **63** lxxiv 147 201
363 **64** xxix 85 195 **65**
85 195 296 319 331 380
66 87 92 125 351 368
369 **67** 77 78 191 302
363 **68** xxx 67 82 181
190 **69** xxxi lxxii 157
158 270 **70** 192 369 **71**
94 257 288 321 **72** 80
160 **73** xxviii xl **74** 309
75 225 226 **78** 107 **98**
164 99 173 **104** 91 **115**
244 **117** 96 **118** 139 **141**
219 **142** 121 **143** 133
254 337 338 346 **144** 119
145 323 **146** 276 334
147 327 **148** 67 69 323
340 341
Charles Linder **64** lxvi
Charles O. **93** 48
Chester H. **93** 183
Clara **69** 312
Clara H. **69** 316
Colmore **73** 228
Content **69** 173 314
Content W. **69** 311 **70** 336
Cynthia Ann **106** 65
Cyrus Waterman **72** 94
Daniel **127** 112
Daniel Butler **127** 112
Daniel S. **69** 270
Daniel Stewart **113** 296
Deborah **99** 61 **108** 225
   116 104 **118** 201 212
   120 202 **122** 55 **123** 274
   118 201
Deborah (Perry) **115** 90
   118 201
Dominicus **93** 48 **108** 191
Dryden **72** 94 **147** 70
Ebenezer **53** 73 **60** 359 **61**
132 **68** 166 217 220 222
223 225 228 244-246 **69**
173 271 **70** 333 **78** 414
88 10 **93** 73
Edith J. **69** 314
Edith M. **70** 337
Edmund **68** 228 **128** 312
Edmund L. **123** 13
Edward **115** 25 **116** 199
   121 248 **125** 184 **140** 39
Edward W. **69** 311 314
   70 336
Edwin **74** xxxix
Edwin E. **91** 332
Edwina Abigail (Avery)
   104 310
Eleanor **131** 130 207
Eleazer **55** 330
Elijah **53** 73 **68** 165 166
216 217 220 228 229 231
311 313 314 380 **69** 173
181 **70** 333 **76** xliii **105**
147 **128** 278 285 **143**
335
Eliphalet Stickney
   115 111
Elisha **113** 109 **118** 203
Eliza **66** 90
Eliza Ann (Goodwin)
   133 43

POPE *cont'd*
Elizabeth **64** lxvi **73** 218
269 **99** 192 **104** 282 **105**
314 **106** 243 **111** 187
   118 201 **123** 63 **127** 112
Elizabeth (Bourne) **118**
201 202
Elizabeth (Brockett)
   139 236
Elizabeth (Handley)
   106 243
Elizabeth (Johnson)
   105 314
Elizabeth Leach **73** xl
Ella Rebecca **69** 312
Ellen Eliza **82** 180
Emma **80** 353 364
Enos **56** 201
Ephraim **99** 239
Esther **69** 181 182
Esther B. **68** 246
Esther Bartlett **69** 173
Eunice **73** xl
Everett **109** 271
Ezra **92** 240 **93** 48 **127** 15
F. J. **51** 105 116 **62** xxii **79**
410 411 430
Fannie L. (Shaw) **113** 221
Frances D. **77** 297
Frances Emily (Whipple)
   105 147
Francis **82** 180 **100** 219
Frank H. **69** 187 **70** xvii
Franklin Leonard **71** 369
Fred **69** 314
Frederick **58** 244 **64** lxvi
   73 xl **128** 278 279 285
   143 337
Freelove **72** 45 **100** 219
   122 100 **147** 69
George H. **69** 270 312 316
George W. **104** 310
Georgia W. **104** 310
Georgina **139** 236
Gershom **98** 359 **115** 111-
114
Hannah **52** 227 229 **60** 246
   68 216 380 **69** 181 **72**
171 **74** 42 197 **86** 15 **88**
33 **98** 359 **101** 279 **113**
306 **115** 90 111 **118** 201
202 119 29 **140** 237 **143**
337 **148** 317 323
Hannah (Bourne) **84** 219
   118 202 **123** 137
Hannah (Sturtevant)
   113 109
Hariette Frances **105** 147
Harold Linder **64** lxvi
Harriet **73** xl
Harriet Amanda **85** 425
426
Harriet Zerviah **78** 106
Harvey **109** 271
Helen Augusta **74** 301
Henry **98** 289
Henry A. **93** 48 49 **123** 225
Henry F. **84** 110 186
Henry Francis **105** 69
131 147
Henry W. **69** lxxii

POPE *cont'd*
Hepzibah **68** 245 **69** 173
Hester (Netherton)
   105 314
Hezekiah **68** 244 247 **69**
76 173 270 311 312
Humphrey **73** 143
Ida Florence **69** lxxii
Irving H. **93** 48
Isaac **87** 207 **92** 339 **93** 48
49 **97** 311 **113** 170 **115**
310 **124** 46 **142** 390
Ivory **93** 48
Jacob **69** 180 **73** 50
James **69** 173 310 314 **70**
336 **73** xl **100** 219 **128**
279 285 **143** 337
James M. **98** 147
James Raymer **72** 94
Jane **75** 225
Jane (Brown) **105** 314
Jennie S. **93** 48
Jennie Standley **96** 328
Jerusha (Taylor) **128** 312
Jerusha (Tobey) **118** 201
   128 230
Joan **51** 389 **67** 47
Joanna **124** 46 **128** 285
John **51** 175 **58** 406 **60** 295
   62 331 **64** lxvi 69 321
   68 166 220 **69** 180 **72** 94
   73 xl 49 50 **75** 221 225
226 **76** 206 **77** 144 **79**
394 **84** 219 **105** 147 314
   118 201 202 **119** 29 264
   125 127 **127** 112 **128**
259 278 **139** 236 **140**
237
John Collins **105** 147
John H. **93** 48
John Lang **105** 147
John S. **93** 48 49
Jonathan Adams **85** 426
Jos. **113** 33
Joseph **73** 148 273 **84** 364
   104 282 **105** 147 **126**
226 **140** 237
Joseph H. **111** 302 306
Joseph Henry **127** 112
Joshua **90** 38
Julia Ann **109** 271
Justinian **128** 285
Lavina M. **73** 50
Lazarus **128** 285
Lemuel **77** xxv **79** 196 **80**
204 **81** 215 **82** 231 **84**
109 195 219 **92** 248 253
259 346 356 **93** 322 **94**
291 **115** 90 **125** 193 **127**
112 **128** 278 **140** 243
Letitia **69** 312
Lewis **113** 175
Linder **64** lxvi
Lizzie F. **69** 312
Lloyd W. **111** 187
Lois **79** 37 **119** 28 29
Lucelia Angleine (Butters)
   84 219
Lucinda **94** 58
Lucretia **143** 337
Lucy **105** 314 **118** 280

POPE *cont'd*
Lucy (Bourne) **119** 31
123 217
Lucy Ann (Meacham)
84 219
Lucy Ellen **83** 215
Luin **62** 130
Luther **128** 285
Lydia **68** 166 **69** 180 **73**
49 50 **77** 287
Lydia (Cotton) **113** 109
M. **109** 268
Marcus **109** 271
Margaret **51** 175 **73** 223
75 225 **82** 291 297 **110**
123
Margaret Roberts **64** lxvi
Marguerite (Jones)
113 296
Maria A. **109** 268
Maria H. **94** 93
Marie **66** 180 **141** 217
Marie Augusta (Busch)
91 184 **93** 183
Marie E. **109** 271
Marion Dora **69** 314
Marjorie (Hart) **111** 168
Mary **67** 376 **68** 165 217
222 **75** xlii **76** xx **93** 48
49 **94** 55 **97** 273 **100** 219
111 187 **115** 262 **118**
201 202 **123** 42 60 **127**
112 **128** 278 285 **133** 43
141 217-219 222 224 385
Mary (Butler) **84** 219
127 112
Mary (Sissons) **105** 314
Mary (Tarbox) **133** 43
Mary A. **109** 269 271
Mary Ann **109** 271
Mary E. **68** 247
Mary Elizabeth **69** 182 270
311 **105** 314
Mary H. **93** 49
Mary Hill **93** 48
Mary Linder **64** lxvi
Mary Shaw **109** 127
Mary Wallis (Tucker) **83**
301 303
Matthew **58** 406
Mehitable **128** 230
Mercy **127** 112
Mercy (Swift) **84** 219 **118**
202 **119** 29 **127** 112
Meribah B. **109** 271
Micajah **83** 301 303 **94** 58
128 278 279
Michael **55** 337 **79** 424
Milly **128** 285
Miranda H. **93** 48
Nancy **128** 279
Nancy W. **93** 48
Nathan **75** 225
Nathaniel **73** 228 **90** 209
105 314 **113** 63
Nathaniel N. **79** 52
Nellie **69** 204
Nellie Buckingham
74 xxxix
Nellie F. **79** 279
Nettie Mayne **111** 129 187

POPE *cont'd*
Niran Bates **73** xl
Olive **72** 94 **93** 48
Parkes Lord **133** 43
Paschal Paoli **140** 42 237
Patience **75** 225 **118** 203
Patty **68** 313
Penelope (Edwards)
105 314
Perry **109** 271
Phebe **68** 165 166 246 **69**
173 **70** 333 **76** xliii **126**
33
Phebe (Spooner) **123** 63
Phebe P. **70** 328
Phebe W. **69** 310
Polly **68** 314 **71** 343 **104**
47 48
Polly (Harmon) **115** 310
Polly A. **104** 47
Priscilla **73** 278
Rachel **59** 154 364 **60** 359
68 220 231 **110** 226 **143**
337
Rachel (Neale) **143** 337
Ralph **59** 154 364 **64** lxvi
68 223 **73** xl **93** 73 **128**
279 285 **143** 337
Rebecca **57** 162 **59** 207 308
68 244 247 **69** 76 173
311 312 **101** 253 **143**
337
Rebecca (Stubbs) **143** 337
Rebecca S. **69** 270
Richard **51** 391 **54** 409
67 362
Richard A. **93** 48
Robert **66** 244 **76** 150 **84**
435 **105** 147 **140** 237
Roger W. (Mrs.) **111** 168
Rufus **128** 279 285
Russell H. **86** 464
Russell H. (Mrs.) **145** 242
243 **146** 383 384
Ruth **125** 108
Ruth (Thayer) **84** 364
S. P. **91** 332
Sabina **94** 93
Sabrina (Daily) **111** 302
306
Sally **93** 48
Sally (Tarbox) **108** 191
Sally Belknap **93** 322
Sally Belknap (Russell)
84 219
Sally Loring **68** 311
Salome **123** 219
Samuel **55** 330 **57** 280 **68**
165 225 **72** 45 94 **105**
147 **133** 43
Samuel Marden **69** 312
Samuel P. **111** 187
Samuel Ward **143** 337
Samuel Warren **83** 410
Sarah **51** 301 **52** 225 **68** 166
244-246 **69** 174 271 273
72 264 **100** 219 **105** 147
107 242 **113** 170 **115** 25
118 201
Sarah (Chase) **88** 10
Sarah (Eldredge) **94** 299

POPE *cont'd*
Sarah (Jenney) **84** 219
127 94
Sarah Chase **69** 173
Sarah H. **93** 48
Sarah Jane **109** 271
Sarah Rogers (Collins)
105 147
Sarah Russell **92** 253
Sarah Taber **69** 181
Sarah W. **125** 294
Seth **57** 34 **61** 105 **62** 181
63 128 **84** 219 **97** 311
109 271 **111** 29 **115** 90
262 **118** 201 202 **123**
137 **125** 185 **127** 112
128 230
Sherebiah **68** 229
Sibyl **72** 264 **73** 125
Susan **139** 294
Susan Louise **81** 222
Susan Louise (Wonson)
(Brown) **91** 183 **92** 150
93 183
Susanna **78** 426 **79** 394
127 94 **128** 285
Susie M. **93** 49
Tabitha **76** xliii **102** 64
Temperance (Parker)
113 175
Thankful **51** 175 **123** 216
Thankful (Dillingham)
118 201
Thankful Y. **57** 162
Theodate **61** 211 **73** 49
Theodosia **93** 49
Theresa Ann (Smith)
105 314
Thomas **54** 345 367 **60** 67
64 344 **71** 369 **72** xliii
78 426 **80** 362 **84** 219
85 455 **86** 464 **89** 174
93 305 **106** 243 **113** 306
118 201 280 **119** 31 **123**
82 217 **127** 94 112 **133**
188 **148** 317 318 323
Thomas Butler **92** 259
Timothy **115** 111
Vesty **128** 285
Virgil **72** 94
Virginia B. **117** 76
Wallace B. **93** 49
Walter **131** 207
Walter Henry **69** 312
Ward **124** 226 **128** 285 286
Willard **74** 238 **75** xxiv
108 126 **109** 127 132
113 221 222
Willard B. **113** 221
William **51** 109 **57** 328
64 223 **77** 287 **92** 68 **93**
49 70 **100** 218 **105** 314
109 271 **128** 279 286
143 337
William A. **93** 49
William F. **61** 109
William Richards **115** 25
Wilson **94** 299
Worden **105** 314
POPEJOY Grace **107** 135
POPENOE Paul **70** 192

POPHAM
Edward **100** 222
Elizabeth (Daniels)
112 227
Frances **96** 295
George **62** 12 **66** x **122** 5
John **82** 61 **123** 247
Letitia **100** 222
Louise Ann **112** 227
Samuel **73** 144
Sarah Elizabeth **111** 53
William **112** 227
POPIL Stephen **129** 57
POPKIN Popkins
—— **122** 66
Joanetta V. H. **79** 48
John **91** 349-351 **93** 304
97 45 **100** 66 **105** 55
John S. **140** 237
John Snelling **81** 7
Mary **91** 349-351
Rebecca **77** 316
Rebecca (Snelling) **105** 55
Stephen **91** 351
Thomas **91** 350 **140** 237
Pople *see* Popple
POPLETT
Elizabeth **64** 316
Poppel *see* Popple
POPPINO
H. E. (Mrs.) **111** 325
POPPLE Pople Poppel
—— **129** 316
Adonijah Lazell **89** 23
Agnes (Cogan) **111** 90
Derias **98** 355
Dorcas **129** 316
Edward **111** 90
Eli **98** 355
Elvira **89** 23
George **128** 303
Hannah **98** 355
Hiram **98** 355
John **92** 69 **128** 301
129 316
Mary **98** 355
William **128** 300 **129** 316
POPPLESTONE
Gideon **128** 294
William **128** 224 295
POPPLETON
Samuel **60** 355
POPULWELL —— **57** 315
PORCH Andrew **77** 81
Elizabeth **100** 299
PORCHER
Annie Robert **77** 267
Esther P. **109** 296
John W. **77** 268
Joseph H. **77** 267
Margaret Isabella **77** 268
Martha (DuBose) **91** 293
PORDAGE
Edward **139** 322
Samuel **89** 74 75
Pore *see* Poore
PORHOEST
Alix de **119** 98
Eudon de **119** 98
PORKINS
Edna Elethier **90** 347

PORKWOOD
Thomas **60** 284
PORMORT Pormont
Anne **53** 71
Elizabeth **95** 135
George **53** 71
Philemon **53** 302 **68** 79 80
95 135 **96** 368
Susan **68** 79 **96** 368
Susanna **68** 80
Thomas **53** 302
PORREDGE Adam **67** 176
Alice **67** 173 174 179
Arthur **67** 176
Barbara **67** 174 179
Caleb **67** 174 179
Edward **67** 169 170 172
175-179
Elizabeth **67** 174-176 179
180
Gabriel **67** 176 179
Henry **67** 170 172 175-177
179 180
Joan **67** 173 174 176 179
John **67** 171 173-176 179
Joseph **67** 174 178 179
Joshua **67** 177 178
Katharine **67** 178 179
Lawrence **67** 174 179
Margaret **67** 174-176 179
Richard **67** 173-176 178
179
Robert **67** 173 174 176 179
Rose **67** 174 179
Sampson **67** 174 179
Stephen **67** 173-176 179
Susan **67** 171 175-177 180
77 ci **86** 334 **87** 211 **139**
324
Thomas **67** 173 174 177-
179 **87** 211
Thomasine **67** 175 180
William **67** 173 174 176
179
PORRIER Simon **131** 90
PORRITT
Elizabeth A. **68** 154
Francis **68** 154
Mary **68** 154
William **68** 154
PORTAGE Portige
—— **82** 414
Hannah **114** 252
PORTE
Marie de la **95** 83
Rosamond **111** 128
Porteous *see* Porteus*
PORTER —— **52** 118 122
354 **54** 246 441 **55** 443
56 12 **57** 138 **59** 421 **62**
206 **70** 302 **72** 57 **84** 312
148 65
— Capt. **57** 54 **118** 125 126
217 218 220-223 **120** 123
129-131 134 203 302 303
121 57-63 65
— Col. **74** 308 **77** 134
118 230 234 297 298 300
301 303-306 **119** 43-45
48-56 58 59 127 128 131-
133 135-137 139 205-208

PORTER *cont'd*
211-215 217-223 291-294
120 131 206 211 213 214
293 295 302 **121** 59 60
62 64-68 96 98-100 298
300 302 **122** 63 64 66 68
69 115 116 118 119 121-
123 220 221 223 225-227
305 **144** 102
— Dr. **61** 286 **92** 58 117
134
— Gen. **119** 294-307 **120**
57-63 123-126 129 131-
133 135 205 206 208 209
213 214 294-301 **122** 303
304 307 308 **123** 18
— Lieut. **62** 41
— Maj. **118** 219 220 229
234 298-302 304 305 307
119 45-47 49 51-57 59
127-133 135 137-140 206-
211 213 214 217-219 221-
223 290-299 **120** 59 63
134 **121** 298 299 301
122 62 63 65 68 69 116
117 119 220 221 223 225
— Miss **71** 45 **74** 64
101 170
— Mr. **55** 79 **64** 161 **72** 87
92 122 129
— Mrs. **71** 48 **94** 40 **99**
184 **118** 15 22 27 110
112 113 116 118 120 121
123 124 222 224 225 229
302 307 **119** 49 56-58
138 206 210-212 215 218
219 222 294 305 307 **120**
59 293 300 **121** 66 68
100 **122** 63-69 117 120
223 304 308
— Rev. Dr. **92** 244 258
— Rev. Mr. **92** 125 128
— Sgt. **53** 50
— Widow **67** 263
—— (Cowan) **91** 108
—— (Hubbard) **122** 223
—— (Lake) **84** 312
—— (Williams) **121** 61
Aaron **53** 456 **59** 11 **71** 225
82 362 **87** 399 **106** 215
129 205 206 **136** 313
145 164
Abby **134** 293
Abby P. **121** 309
Abel **53** 128 **83** 162
Abial (Early) **101** 100
Abigail **51** 408 465 **58** 133
67 259 **79** 169 269 276
387 **87** 134 **102** 304 **105**
79 **110** 141 **119** 118 **123**
239 **124** 6 **128** 177
Abigail (Arnold) **136** 314
Abigail (Evans) **134** 293
Abigail (Phillips) **144** 343
Abigail (Williams) **129**
211 **136** 314 318
Abigail Barstow **82** 22
Abigail H. (Whaples)
85 170
Abigail S. **132** 163
Abigail Voter **123** 239

PORTER *cont'd*
Abner **119** 118
Abraham **51** 278 **90** 45
  120 16
Adaline **111** 300 **130** 71
Adam **53** 246 **102** 223 **103**
  280 **119** 118 187 **121**
  248
Adelaide (Bently) **120** 16
Adelaide (Hart) **97** 91
Adelia B. **77** 153
Adeline **75** 18
Adrian **146** 274 **148** 48 49
  51 57
Agnes **146** 267 **148** 48 49
  51 56
Albert **69** 207
Albert Coolidge **102** 221
Albert F. **120** 17
Albert Henry **103** 280
Alexander **66** 31
Alexander Sylvanus **66** l
  lxxvii **70** xxviii li lii
Alfredo **109** 290
Algernon Sydney
  136 326
Aline (Kilham) **103** 74
Allen **55** 284
Almira **82** 119
Almira (Dexter) **97** 184
Almira Loring (Gardner)
  88 391
Alonzo **123** 11
Alvin **82** 22
Amanda F. **111** 325
Ambrose **55** 436 **81** 298
Amelia (Eaton) **120** 17
Amos **65** 221 374 **66** 21
  89 207 **91** 197
Amy **101** 70
Amy (Brewer) (Gaines)
  85 45
Amy (Colt) **100** 337
Andrew **134** 336
Andrew Tyler **86** 155
Ann **52** 308 **67** 259 **83** 78
  83 282 **102** 223 **148** 48
Ann (Pitkin) **129** 211
Ann Field **61** 350
Anna **52** 438 **55** 23 24 27-
  29 **61** 96 **67** 259 **75** 153
  78 203 **104** 143 **105** 79
  106 316 **118** 14 22 27 28
  108 109 114 115 119 121-
  123 231 299 304
Anna (Colton) **129** 205
Anna (Hall) **106** 316
Anna (Pitkin) **98** 94
Anna Estelle (Barnard)
  84 457
Anna Guernsey **68** xxxv
Annah **83** 139
Anne **51** 260 412 413 **64**
  341 **71** 277 **86** 433 **98** 94
  148 45
Anne (Elliot) **148** 46 50-52
Annie **76** lv
Annie (Nichols) **138** 287
Annie Gardner **84** 189
  88 89 176 391

PORTER *cont'd*
Annie Metcalf (Dwight)
  101 250
Annis **148** 48 49 51
Annis E. **86** 170
Arazina S. **85** 65
Arthur **51** 413
Asa **62** 74 **67** 210 **114** 182
  121 248 **127** 115 **137** 9
  11
Asa Bingham **55** 285
Asa Spaulding **98** 350
Asahel **51** 465 **58** 133
  97 220
Ashton Everett **82** 22
Athalia (Tharp) **136** 29
Augusta **136** 310
Augusta A. (Holmes)
  85 169
Augustus **73** 13 **91** 401
Augustus Granger (Mrs.)
  96 386
Basheba **102** 221
Bathsheba (Reed) **112** 146
Beatrice Robbins **83** 436
  438
Benjamin **58** 204 **59** 421
  61 96 202 203 218 **62** 37
  67 259 **76** liv **77** 239 **82**
  362 **84** 414 421 **88** 125
  137 391 **101** 250 **121** 12
  123 17 **142** 197 **145** 354
Benjamin Curtis (Mrs.)
  94 139
Benjamin J. **142** 197
Benjamin Jones **91** 206
  94 95 **100** 65
Berta **109** 290
Bertha Abigail **79** 20
Bethiah **82** 22
Betsey **92** 58 **97** 220 **122**
  118 **134** 293
Betty **108** 160 **118** 14 29
  118 119 122-124 231 233
  299
Billy **93** 398 **100** 63
C. B. **91** 332
Carlos **109** 290
Carlos Emilio **109** 290
Carlos Oscar **109** 290
Caroline **85** 170 **114** 321
  123 20
Caroline (Hammond)
  126 209
Caroline (Head) **114** 321
Caroline (Silsby) **93** 366
Caroline M. **76** 271
Caroline Williams **123** 18
Carter (Mrs.) **120** 160
Catalina (de los Saldivia)
  109 290
Catherine **66** 31 **135** 103
Catherine (Bryant)
  137 331
Catherine L. **90** 105
Catherine Mary **69** 202
Charles **52** 122 **123** 26 27
Charles B. **79** 269
Charles B. (Mrs.) **79** 276
Charles Burnham **63** 394
Charles S. **86** 170

PORTER *cont'd*
Charles W. **85** 316
Charlotte **102** 226
Charlotte Nash **57** 294
Chloe **52** 184
Clara A. **101** 213
Clara Abbie **82** 22
Clara Thurston **81** 104
  85 187 **95** 137 176 **96**
  163
Clarissa **80** 62
Clarissa Harlow **96** 395
Concurrence **80** 13
Content **91** 85
Cora S. **65** 10
Cordelia Noble **57** 293
Cornelia **79** 153 **102** 144
Cuthbert **67** 370
Cynthia **62** 84
Cyrus **65** 10 **71** 115 **82** 348
Daniel **51** 222 **52** 308 **55**
  12 **79** 160 168 **101** 14
  105 5 **120** 15 **134** 336
Daniel Pomeroy **96** 395
David **54** 85 **57** 205 **58** xcii
  62 46 **72** 37 **76** 271 **79**
  153 165 387 **85** 169 **109**
  290 **118** 16 26 216 230
  119 252 **120** 15 90 **134**
  293
David C. **79** 333
David Dixon **109** 290
David George **109** 290
David P. **79** 169
Deborah **53** 246 **55** 33 **61**
  96 **75** 263 **78** 264 **148** 52
  53
Deborah (Gannett)
  119 118
Deborah (Shaw) **119** 118
Deborah G. **100** 337
Delia Dwight **123** 30
Denison A. **85** 169
DeWitt C. **85** 316
Diadema **86** 17
Dora **84** 189
Dorcas **87** 17
Dorothy **66** 21
Dorothy Dwight **101** 251
Dyzory **71** 107 108 **72** 209
E. **120** 90
E. Zachariah **111** 325
Ebenezer **62** 46 **65** 221 **79**
  169 **106** 206 **120** 205
Edgar Joshua **82** 22
Edith **91** 108
Edmund **57** 99 **102** 24
Edmund Williams **85** 230
Edna **54** 84 **55** 283 **56** 354
Edna (Bingham) **126** 305
Edna Margaret **96** 160
Edward **77** 203 210 **79** 20
  97 11 **99** 184 **100** 30
  101 100 272 **146** 267
  148 45 46 50-52 57 61 65
Edward Clark **91** 399
Edward G. **52** 290 291
  124 166 **126** 245
Edward Griffin **53** 147
  254 361 364 452 453 **54**
  v xx xxiv xxxvii cx

PORTER *cont'd*
cxxxv cxlvi 11 110 120
130 131 202 220 222 241
456 **55** ix xv xxx xxxvi
xliii xcvi 11-22 **56** 193
417 **60** lxxvi **63** xl **64**
90 131 **70** xi **75** 69 **99**
184 185
Edwin A. **79** 333
Elbridge **57** 205
Eleanor **63** lix **112** 94
Eleanor (Detin) **134** 293
Eleanor Hodgman
68 304
Eleazer **51** 408 **55** 442 **56**
83 **67** 259 **93** 398 **98** 94
100 63 **118** 3 4 17-23 25
26 28 29 108 110 112-
115 117 120 121 123 **119**
48 59 133 208 214 218
222 223 295 298 299 **120**
60 124 127 129-132 135
203-206 210 212 214 294-
296 298 301 **121** 64 66
122 227 303 **123** 17 19
20 23 25 **129** 202 203
205-216 **136** 326
Eleazer (Mrs.) **118** 120
Eleazer Williams **123** 17
136 326
Elector **60** 394
Eli **115** 119
Elias **75** 263 **100** 19
134 293
Elijah **104** 263 **114** 227
Eliot Furness **91** 399
Eliot Furness (Mrs.)
103 74
Eliphalet **54** 441 **92** 117
Elisha **64** 250 **71** 87 **85**
169 173 **94** 319 **103** 64
104 195 **114** 182 **118** 4
23 25-28 123 126 225
226 **121** 96 248 **129** 211
213-216 **137** 26 124 **140**
299 **144** 343
Elisha LeRoy **85** 169
Elishema **60** 397
Elitia **66** 31
Eliza **73** 117 118 **122** 223
123 23 24
Eliza (Vredenburgh)
109 185
Eliza Ann **82** 23
Eliza Storrs (Williams)
98 350
Eliza Thayer **82** 362
Eliza Wilcox **65** 10
Elizabeth **51** 408 413 420
54 lxix **58** 133-6 71 108
217 297 299 **119** 43 90
127 205 289 **120** 16 57
123 203 293 **121** 57 95
296 **122** 62 115 220 302
309 **123** 16 20 **125** 237
129 213 **146** 267 274
148 45 46 48-50 52 53 57
65 185
Elizabeth (Allott) **146** 274
148 48-50 56 57
Elizabeth (Bass) **100** 300

PORTER *cont'd*
Elizabeth (Farwell)
113 101
Elizabeth (Hawkins) **108**
95 **148** 53
Elizabeth (Leonard)
119 118
Elizabeth (Netcher)
125 176
Elizabeth (Pitkin) **118** 3
129 211
Elizabeth (White) **88** 343
Elizabeth Augusta **120** 15
Elizabeth C. **142** 284 285
Elizabeth Clapp **88** 200
Elizabeth Frances **82** 22
Elizabeth L. **142** 197
Elizabeth Lane **109** 131
Elizabeth S. **70** lii
Ella Graves **65** 10
Ellen **65** 50 **134** 293
Ellen M. Griswold **85** 316
Elmera **91** 332
Emeline **102** 221 **114** 202
Emerson **132** 270
Emilia (Mosso) **109** 290
Emiline Brown **85** 170
Emily (Bancroft) **95** 279
Emily M. **85** 170
Emma **78** 162
Emma (Ensign) **102** 227
Emma Elizabeth **67** 323
Emma L. **65** 10
Enos **85** 170
Epaphras **63** lix
Esther **52** 308 **82** 348 **112**
146 **114** 215 **119** 118
Esther (Fenton) **114** 161
Esther (Ford) **119** 118
Esther (Jackson) **89** 134
90 68
Esther L. (Smith) **90** 105
Ethel F. **85** 316
Eunice **56** 307 **58** 204 **71**
277 **100** 295 **111** 117
161
Experience **55** 343 **107** 182
136 314 318
Fairfield Wadsworth
91 399
Fanny **85** 169
Fanny W. **85** 170
Fanny Woodbury **73** 118
Fidelia Carrier **85** 316
Fitz-John **55** 134 **69** lxxiv
Flora McDonald **65** 10
Florence Elizabeth
105 127
Florinda **128** 271
Fordyce **57** 294
Frances **55** 436 **145** 308
Frances D. **83** 300 301
Frances Helena **102** 221
Frances L. **123** 128
Frances R. **70** lii
Frances Wentworth
70 lii
Francis **58** 204 **61** 199
Frank Farrington **93** 366
Frank Farrington (Mrs.)
93 126 141 366

PORTER *cont'd*
Frederick **100** 29 31
101 272
Frederick Wadsworth
93 366
George **54** cxxi **76** liv **82**
348 **84** 306 311 312 **95**
279 **109** 290 **116** 42 **117**
315 **133** 230
George A. **79** 333
George Albert **82** 22
George D. **85** 170
George E. **88** 343
George Epaphras **63** lix
George French **73** 316
74 xxv **81** 363 **82** 245
362
George L. **142** 285
George Langdon **65** 10
George Plummer **85** 316
George Shepard **60** xxxvi
16 121 321 **61** xxxiii
xxxvii **62** xxxv **63** xliv
lix lx 207 **64** 102
George W. **85** 465
Georgia (Miller) **142** 285
Georgiana **82** 22
Gertrude Louisa
(Copeland) **97** 162 184
Gertrude Peacock
(Wright) **96** 386
Gideon **79** 333 **86** 390
Ginger 30 **67** 259 **105** 30
123 185 **141** 227
Grace **51** 309-311 313-315
68 259 **69** 202 284 **77**
272 **80** 402
Guillermo **109** 290
H. C. **80** 70
H. E.V. **64** 192
H. G. **110** 185
H. S. **85** 169
Hannah **51** 222 **53** 128 **55**
23 **56** 35 **57** 80 **60** 43 **62**
48 **71** 299 **74** 134 **87** 63
95 78 **98** 282 360 **101**
100 103 **103** 56 **106** 193
108 183 113 101 **119**
118 **120** 320 **134** 293
148 52 53
Hannah (Burrell) **133** 230
Hannah (Church) **125** 52
Hannah (Dodge) **88** 195
391
Hannah (Peck) **105** 79
Hannah (Smith) **88** 195
Hannah (Stanley) **129**
199-201
Hannah Curtis **73** 118
Harold Everett **73** xx
Harold F. Jr. **142** 361 368
Harriet **76** 12 **79** 333 **83**
493 **88** 284 **89** 11 **93** 369
103 280
Harriet (Newell) **90** 45
Harriet E. **79** 333
Harriet L. **91** 89
Harriet M. **85** 161
Hattie E. **65** 10
Hattie J. **86** 170
Haynes L. **79** 152

PORTER *cont'd*
Helen **82** 348 **90** 68 **94** 139
Helen M **124** 193
Helen M. **124** 193
Henrietta **57** 200 **98** 350
Henry **51** 413 **142** 284
Henry C. **79** 153
Henry Hobart **84** 108 186
101 248 250 251 **102**
127
Henry Homes **82** 362
Henry K. (Mrs.) **83** 371
Henry Kirke **75** xxiv 64
76 xxviii liv
Henry Knox **97** 184
Henry Knox (Mrs.) **84**
190 **97** 79 162 184
Henry Martin **65** 10
Henry Smith **85** 170
Henry Whittier **97** 184
Hepzibah **67** 259
Herbert Gleason **103** 120
104 159 **106** 222 **107**
138
Herodias (Long) (Hicks)
(Gardiner) **105** 258
Hester **119** 118
Hester (Ford) **119** 118
Hezekiah **55** 12 343 **61** 144
88 227 **129** 200 201 **134**
336
Horace **55** 424
Howard Augustus **77** 186
Hubert Elmer Volney
63 xxxiii
Hugh **60** 27 **101** 34
102 223
Hulda **142** 344
Huldah **59** 41 **79** 333
142 344
Huldah (Chase) **87** 333
Huntington **67** 355
102 275
Ida May **82** 22
Increase **85** 148
Ira **87** 333
Isaac **66** 34
Isaac Adams **76** liv
Israel **51** 408 **58** 133 **67** 259
121 15 **123** 185 **140** 237
J. **91** 332
J. W. **52** 77 373 **54** 226
Jabez **75** 148 **92** 58 **110** 317
140 237
Jacob **119** 118 **120** 45
140 237
James **52** 310 **55** 12 27 28
56 318 **57** 293-296 **61**
347 **73** 117 118 **77** 150
79 332 333 **82** 348 **87**
232 236 **102** 221 **106**
316 **109** 185 **118** 235
134 336 **142** 344
James Edmund **102** 221
James Foster **91** 399
James H. **142** 284
James Jackson **90** 68
James Otis **70** lii
James P. **69** 202
James R. **69** 202
Jane **51** 413 420 **57** 138 **65**
163 **88** 115 **97** 131 **102**

PORTER *cont'd*
223 **114** 301
Jane (Chase) **88** 125
Jane Augusta **57** 205
Jane Marie **85** 170
Jane P. **142** 284 285
Jane Smith **76** 246
Jeanette (Mitchell)
145 272
Jennie **101** 213
Jennie Henderson **84** 352
142 342
Jeremiah **91** 332
Jerusha **67** 375 **105** 79
129 206
Jessie **142** 284 285
Jessie Alice (Woods) **68**
xxxv **70** viii **71** viii **72**
viii **73** viii **74** viii
xxviii **75** viii **76** viii **77**
viii xxii **78** 220 **79** 216
80 222 **81** 214 236 **90**
128 **93** 141 366
Joan **51** 278 **148** 51
Joanna **51** 222 **58** 182
110 142
Joanna (Cooke) **129** 201
205 **136** 313 318 321 326
334
Job **52** 309
Joel **85** 170 **103** 56
John **51** 411-413 420 **52**
122 461 **53** 11-13 **55** 11
12 23 24 27-29 33 221
323 **56** 84 **58** 133 **59** 173
60 311 372 **61** 335 **62** 35
43 44 46 47 206 **63** lix
64 192 257 **66** 31 **67** 259
68 144 **75** 263 306 **76**
liv 12 **79** 221 **80** 434 **82**
348 362 **84** 253 306 311
312 352 **88** 195 391 **91**
305 **92** 180 **93** 398 **96**
248-52
John Addison **79** 333
John B. **96** 146
John C. **86** 390
John Foster **91** 399
John Kirkland **70** li
John L. **114** 202
John Lovering **66** 21
John Lyman **68** xxxv **77**
325 **146** 338
John T. **85** 65
Jonathan **62** 44 **66** 315 **70**
li **118** 17 109 176 **119** 292
296 **120** 62 128 133 203
204 **123** 18 **125** 276 **133**
230
Joseph **55** 240 **60** 43 **62** 70
65 10 **67** 259 **70** li **71**
86 87 155 299 300 **78**
400 **82** 348 **103** 56 **105**
282 **121** 11 **128** 286 **148**
53
Joseph Scovil (Mrs.)
84 457
Joseph T. **77** 153
Joseph W. **52** 162 163 **54**
108 **55** 222 **59** 161 **79**
192 **131** 250

PORTER *cont'd*
Joseph Whitcomb **51** 223
53 392 393 **55** 240
Josephine Bonaparte
(Carpenter) (Cole) **86**
155 311
Joshua **79** 162 **108** 160
124 12 **125** 48
Josiah **58** 133 **75** 263
Judith **54** ciii **81** 469
Julia **98** 94
Julia Ann **97** 20 238
Julia Ann Maria **84** 421
Julia Climena **57** 296
Julia Maria **91** 237
Julia Maria (Wright)
91 237
Julia S. **79** 333 **85** 170
Juliet **62** 306 **65** xxii xxxvi
66 xxxviii **67** xxii **68**
xxi **70** xv **71** xviii **88**
174 195 202
Julius Wilcox **65** 10
Katharine (Cooke)
(Brehm) **97** 81
Katharine (Delano)
101 251
Katharine Clinton **69** 202
Katharine Delano **101** 251
Katrina **98** 10
Kenneth Wiggins **92** 97
Keziah **85** 170
Keziah (Murphy) **96** 146
Laurinda **57** 293-296
Laurinda Bridgeman
57 295
Lavina (Bailey) **101** 32
Lavinia **73** 13 **120** 15
Leslie C. **85** 316
Levi **61** 96
Lillie Gertrude **82** 22
Lily **77** 266
Lois **74** 103 **92** 186
Lois (Gragg) **88** 195
Lois (Shaw) **119** 118
Lois A. **81** 104
Lois Abigail (Shute)
95 176 177
Lois Eastman **123** 21
Loranda **69** 207
Louisa **85** 170
Louisa Ann **101** 32
Louise **97** 184
Lovisa **88** 321
Lucetta (McIntosh)
(Perrin) **123** 11
Lucina (Benchley) **142** 283
284 **143** 64
Lucinda **79** 152 **103** 171
Lucinda S. **72** 206
Lucius Stratton (Mrs.)
98 147
Lucretia **63** lix **74** 66
100 337
Lucretia Bushnell **65** 303
Lucretia C. **100** 337
Lucretia Colt **123** 28
Lucy **57** 205 **61** 96 **76** 134
82 362 **84** 355 **85** 148
97 73 **109** 290
Lucy Anne **66** 21

PORTER *cont'd*
Lucy E. **91** 237
Lucy Lee **57** 205
Luther **83** 162 **104** 263
Lydia **56** 318 **61** 331 **62**
　35 47 **78** 263 **86** 230 **95**
　211 **104** 118 **148** 49
Lydia (Gould) **96** 395
Lydia (Herrick) **88** 195
　391
Lydia (Tarbox) **104** 118
Lydia Brainard **80** 14
Mabel **54** 84 **115** 78
Magdalene **74** 308 **77** 134
Mamie Teresa **93** 138
　101 249 **102** 128 227
Margaret **70** 355 **71** 174
　72 60 **74** 146 **75** 135 **79**
　333 **94** 187 **105** 258
Margaret (Ford) **119** 94
Margaret (Goodman
　alias Manne) **148** 59
Margaret (Odding)
　113 101
Margaret (Plomer)
　148 47
Margaret Seton **101** 251
Margery **79** 332 333
Maria **77** 150 **109** 290
Maria Luz Camus (Galeas)
　109 290
Mariana (Wilkinson)
　109 290
Marion K. **95** 317
Mark **80** 364
Martha **51** 411 **57** 199 **58**
　204 **60** 372 **62** 206
Martha (Olcott) **101** 250
Martha (Perley) **88** 195
Martha (Ruggles) **92** 117
Martha A. (Snell) **100** 337
Martha Alice Dodge
　85 316
Martha Elizabeth **82** 348
Martha Elizabeth
　(Samson) **90** 68
Martin **91** 108 **109** 290
　143 258
Mary **51** 413 420 **52** 121
　122 **54** cxi 85 **55** 23 27-
　29 **56** 47 **59** 11 **61** 144
　62 39 **67** 259 **69** 352 **71**
　278 **72** 240 **76** 12 **77** 279
　79 156 **85** 169 343 **86** 89
　88 284 **90** 292 **91** 266
　92 58 **96** 332 **98** 355 **99**
　122 **100** 31 248 **101** 250
　272 **102** 65 **105** 147 149
　108 69 **110** 143 **112** 165
　115 121 **119** 110 118
　123 23 **133** 121 230 **136**
　318 319 321 325 333 **142**
　197 **145** 72 **148** 49 51-53
Mary (Clapp) **88** 200
Mary (Cobb) **119** 118
Mary (Nash) **119** 118 119
Mary (Niles) **85** 148
Mary (Norton) **119** 118
　137 35
Mary (Robinson) **113** 66

PORTER *cont'd*
Mary (Stockbridge)
　134 292
Mary (Whittier) **88** 391
Mary (Woodford)
　136 311
Mary A. **79** 333 **80** 62
Mary Ann **85** 170
Mary Ann (Brown)
　88 195
Mary Aurelia **69** 202
Mary Brown **65** 10
Mary Chatfield (Clark)
　94 139
Mary D. (Saunders)
　88 336
Mary Dennison **98** 84
Mary Duick **73** 118
Mary E. **117** 164
Mary Frances (Ditson)
　101 251
Mary H. (Staples) **117** 167
Mary Jane Virginia
　(Swaim) **136** 326
Mary Lawrence **65** 303
Mary Maurine **101** 125
Mary Moore **55** 424
Mary O. **70** lii
Mary Olive **65** 10
Mary Otis **70** lii
Mary Provost **70** li
Mary S. (Kelley) **133** 230
Mary S. (Laighton)
　83 299 301
Mary Stetson **55** 240
Mary W. **83** 101 **94** 204
Matilda C. **69** 206
Matthew **108** 183
Maud **95** 323
Maud F. **65** 10
Mehitable **61** 144 **62** 38
　67 210 259 **71** 279 **129**
　206 207 **136** 321
Mehitable (Clark) **96** 248
Mehitable M. (Sprague)
　101 34
Melvina **77** 219
Merah **89** 207
Mercy **119** 93
Mercy (Carver) **119** 94
Mercy (Clarke) **115** 61
Mercy (Hamblen) **123** 136
Micah **76** 12 **125** 202 **134**
　292 293
Milla **85** 161 **128** 286
Mima **82** 363
Minerva E. **65** 10
Molly **63** 75
Molly (Ford) **119** 252
Monina G. **83** 299 301
Moses **65** 303 **70** 113 **76**
　liv **82** 362 **93** 398 **100** 63
　337 **118** 3 4 23 **120** 61
　123 127 128 133 206 213
　293 297 **121** 59-61 64 68
　297-299 302 303 **122** 63
　65 67-69 115 116 118
　120 122 123 220 222 223
　226 227 302-305 307-309
　123 17 19 20 25 27 28 30
　129 211

PORTER *cont'd*
Nabby **118** 217
Nancy **88** 9 **105** 221
Nancy (French) **126** 67
Nancy (Pendleton) **95** 176
Nancy (Warriner) **102** 227
Nancy Ann **86** 390
Nancy Foster **91** 399
Nathan **75** 307 **83** 162
　102 227 **128** 301
Nathaniel **55** 23 27 33 **65**
　145 **67** 259 **85** 170 **125**
　112 **126** 226
Nehemiah **60** 177 181 **62**
　37 **70** 278 331 **88** 195
　110 317 **121** 265 **134**
　293
Nicholas **92** 180 181 **112**
　146 **114** 215
Nina **65** 10
Nina Malinda (Leavitt)
　102 227
Noah **53** 134 **57** lxi **76** 12
　77 239 **88** 335 **118** 269
　119 118 **134** 293
Octa **55** 284 **126** 305
Olinda **85** 170
Olive D. **91** 36
Olive Louisa **85** 170
Oliver **97** 91
Olmsted **85** 169
Orin **55** 283
Othniel **62** 84
Ottilia (de la Barrera)
　109 290
Pamela **110** 66 67
Pamela (Barton) **84** 414
　421 **88** 391
Pamelia **123** 18
Patience **125** 289 **131** 293
Patience Taber **70** 331
Patty Williams (Ruggles)
　92 117
Paulina **85** 170
Pauline **59** 11 **82** 362
Peggy **121** 99 **122** 223
　125 103
Peter **65** 374
Phebe **75** 148 **99** 300
　123 126
Phebe Ann **120** 16
Phebe Clarissa **76** liv
Phebe Henrietta **69** 206
Phebe Levina **102** 144
Philip K. **88** 318
Philo **61** 96
Pierce **88** 195
Pierpont **121** 64 98 300
　122 66 302 **123** 19 21 22
　24
Polly **52** 225 **55** 12 **92** 58
　118 13-25 27-29 108-110
　114 306 **123** 18
Polly (Ford) **119** 252
Preston Buell (Mrs.)
　97 81
Priscilla **58** 204
Prudence **80** 434
Prudence (West) **120** 88
　133 322
Rachel **94** 384 **99** 300 **128**

PORTER *cont'd*
264 **136** 308 313
Rachel (Reed) **119** 118
Raphael **123** 136
Rebecca **55** 27 28 **62** 78
  79 162 **104** 189 **106** 149
Rebecca (Francis) **88** 335
Rebecca (Storey) **132** 270
Rebecca Seton (Maitland)
  101 250
Reuben **134** 293
Rhoda **129** 170
Rhoda (Gore)
  (Remington) **148** 50
  52 61 64 65
Rhoda (Sage) **106** 215
Rhoda J. **79** 192
Rhoda Josepha **55** 240
Rhoda Keith **55** 240
Ricardo **109** 290
Richard **51** 413 420 **53** 12
  13 **55** 438 **65** 163 **70** li
  75 263 **76** 12 **92** 318
  134 293
Richard King **88** 200
Robert **51** 260 **81** 104 **83**
  139 **95** 176 **105** 280 **136**
  29 **148** 47 51 58 59 65
Roger **51** 309-311 315 **60**
  59 **68** 259 **69** 284 **80** 402
Rosamond **111** 12 128 187
Rosanna **61** 96 203
Rose **55** 12 24 27 28
Rosemond **111** 187
Royal Francis **55** 13
Royal Hervey **61** 322
Royal Loomis **55** 12 13
  99 184
Rubie (Hastings) **87** 232
  236
Rufus King **67** 323 **82** 362
Russell A. **91** 305
Russell Woods **93** 366
Ruth **60** 392 394 **67** 259
  75 148 **76** 132 **103** 223
  121 265 **125** 220 **129**
  206 **136** 311 334
Ruth (Ford) (Pool) (Reed)
  119 112 119
Ruth (Foster) **88** 391
Ruth (Whitman) **134** 293
Ruth Coffin (Worth)
  136 326
Ruth Wadsworth
  (Furness) **91** 399
S. Jennie **101** 213
Sadie E. **97** 91
Sally **61** 286 **70** 113 **118**
  223 225 299 **119** 48 49
  53 56-58 212 **122** 221
  225 **123** 19 24 **125** 215
Sally (Carver) **88** 318
Sally (Jones) **134** 293
Sally (Parkhurst) **134** 336
Sally (Webster) **91** 197
Sally S. (Dolbeare) **126** 67
Samuel **52** 184 308 310
  53 50 **54** 84 **55** 12 24 27
  28 283-285 343 **56** 36
  354 **61** 335 **62** 35 44 46-
  48 206 **65** 356 **67** 259 **71**

PORTER *cont'd*
155 **74** 66 **76** liv **77** 279
  82 362 **83** 162 **88** 195
  391 **99** 80 **114** 157 **118** 3
  18 27 302 **119** 48 58 108
  118 119 130 139 291 298
  304 **120** 57 88 89 92 95
  204 208 297 299 301 **121**
  58 248 298 **122** 116 **123**
  18 20 22-25 28 **126** 305
  129 198-212 **133** 322
  134 293 336 **136** 313
  318 321 326 334
Samuel Doak **114** 157
Samuel Phillips **123** 22
  25 28
Sanford **102** 227
Sanford Marius **102** 227
Sarah **52** 184 309 **53** 448 **55**
  24 27 28 442 **57** 213 385
  60 151 **61** 333 **62** 41 65
  303 **67** 259 **70** 331 **75** 33
  263 320 **79** 154 **80** 69 **83**
  162 **86** 390 **93** 369 **96**
  378 **104** 179 **105** 79 **106**
  206 **110** 227 **118** 4 **122**
  18 91 **123** 47 **129** 206
  211 **133** 230 **136** 314
  331 **146** 366
Sarah (Carver) **88** 227
Sarah (Cobb) (Hunt)
  119 118
Sarah (Hart) **136** 313
Sarah (Josselyn) **119** 108
Sarah (Keyes) **136** 326
Sarah (Pitkin) **129** 205
  136 326
Sarah (Skinner) **120** 95
Sarah (Tompkins) **77** 186
Sarah (Tyler) **88** 391
Sarah (Westwood)
  136 313
Sarah A. **78** 184
Sarah Ann **55** 13 **57** 205
  93 324
Sarah C. **79** 153 **134** 89
  142 295
Sarah J. **101** 213
Sarah Jane **75** 264
Sarah Jewet **123** 20
Seth **119** 118
Seward **90** 105
Sharon (Bates) **134** 293
Sibyl **52** 309
Sidney **123** 17 **136** 326
Simeon **54** 84 **123** 312
Smith **114** 161
Solomon **79** 159 162
Sophia **123** 19
Stephen **51** 424 **65** 145
  72 37 **75** 306 **120** 16
Sukey **85** 170 **122** 221
Susan **51** 413 420 **53** 13
  65 10 **81** 466 **82** 348 **97**
  222 **116** 42 **148** 49 51
Susan (Hay) (Dudley)
  116 42
Susan Ida **65** 10
Susan Stimpson (Tidd)
  94 40
Susanna **63** 15 **101** 101

PORTER *cont'd*
103 **128** 50 **136** 313 319
Susanna (Edwards) **129**
  211 **136** 326
Susanna (Sewall) **129** 205
  136 313
Susanna (West) **102** 227
Sylvanus **70** li
Sylvia **57** 205
T. H. **128** 116
Thankful (Fullerton)
  126 208
Thankful (Smith) **124** 12
Theoda **136** 318
Theodore C. **54** lxvi
Theodore Woolsey
  123 20
Thomas **53** 12 13 **55** 390
  57 80 213 **60** 372 **68** 149
  70 li **100** 300 **104** 263
  108 69 **115** 61 **117** 46
  119 83 84 **122** 11 **125** 84
  176 **136** 311 318 **145**
  272
Thomas Andrew **120** 16
Thomas J. **88** 336
Thomas Whittier **88** 391
  97 184
Timothy **76** 132 134 **95**
  176 **102** 227
Timothy Dwight **123** 18
Tryphena **83** 162
Tyler **86** 311 **88** 391
Tyler Copeland **97** 184
Valentine Mott **59** 338
Victoria **105** 35
W. Arthur **89** 306
W. D. **77** 266
Wade T. **117** 315
Walden **91** 237
Walter C. **65** 10
Wareham **79** 162
Wealthy **81** 298
Wealthy (Manchester)
  102 24
Weston **76** 286
Whitworth **113** 12
Willard **57** 205
William **52** 122 **55** 343
  58 133 **60** 392 394 **61** 33
  62 76 **64** 165 262 **65** 163
  66 31 **67** 259 **71** 174 **75**
  135 148 **76** liv 50 **79**
  333 **85** 161 **94** 68 **95** 177
  103 25 **106** 316 **108** 95
  109 290 **115** 119 **123** 17-
  21 23 25-27 29 30 **134**
  293 **140** 237 **143** 261
  148 45 46 48-52
William Bates **75** 263
William David **109** 290
William Foster **82** 22
William H. **86** 170 **117** 167
William Henry **73** 316
  74 xxv **75** 263 **81** 230
  237 **82** 347 348 **90** 68
  101 32
William Henry (Mrs.)
  84 108 186 **89** 79 134 **90**
  68
William Rogers **55** 13

PORTER *cont'd*
William S. **59** 318
William Smith **51** 333
William Stevens **82** 22
William Sydney **136** 326
William T. **86** 170
William Trowbridge **82**
348 **90** 68
William Wallace **85** 65
Zerah **71** 118
Zilpha Esther **86** 311
PORTERFIELD
Alexander **79** 328
137 306
Archibald Shearer **79** 328
Eliza **74** 22
Elizabeth Shearer **79** 328
Fanny **86** 301
Hannah **79** 328
John **111** 219
Margaret **74** 22
Margaret Eliza **74** 22
Robert **74** 22
Sarah **111** 215 217-219
William **74** 22 **116** 11
PORTES
Richard le **98** 113
PORTEUS Porteous
—— **143** 366
Beatrice Grosvenor
(Hadfield) (Pontey)
103 71
Betsey **107** 240 **112** 164
Euphemia **107** 240
Euphemia (Brunton)
112 164
Jessie **104** 234
Louisa Maria (Lynn)
103 70
Robert **51** 372 **136** 87
Ruby Sylvia **103** 71
Samuel **112** 164
Simon **65** 244
Thomas **103** 70
Thomas Cruddas **68**
xxxiii 339 **69** xxxi 94 **76**
159 **80** 449 **87** 149 150
90 128 **94** 209 **103** 70 71
77 122
Wilfrid Beilby **103** 71
PORTHESY Jane **59** 328
Portige *see* Portage
PORTINGALL
Alice **81** 491
Christopher **113** 77
PORTINGTON
De Portyngton
Portington
Agnes **116** 167 168 171
Alasia **116** 173
Alice **116** 166 169 171 175
Charlotte (Graves) **88** 282
Cicily **116** 168
Edmund **116** 167 168 172
173
Edward **116** 168
Eleanor **116** 175
Elena **116** 169 173
Elizabeth **94** 14 **116** 169
170 173-175

PORTINGTON *cont'd*
Elizabeth (Paslew)
116 170
Ellen **116** 168 169 173 174
George **116** 170
Isabel **116** 169
Joan **116** 166
John **94** 14 18 **116** 166-
169 172-176
Julian **116** 174 175
Julian (Lisle) **116** 169
Juliana **116** 173
Margaret **116** 167 173 175
Margaret (Ermyn)
116 169
Margery **116** 166
Maud **116** 169
Nicholas **116** 167 170 173
175
Odo **116** 166
Otwell **116** 170
Peter **116** 167 171 174
Richard **116** 166 169 170
173-175
Robert **116** 166 167 169
170 172 173 175
Roger **88** 282
Thomas **116** 166-171 173-
176
William **116** 166 170 172
PORTLAND
— Duke of **124** 102
Charles Weston (Earl of)
74 139
Cora Ella **91** 233
Dorothy **90** 181
Francis Weston (Earl of)
74 73
Jerome Weston (Earl of)
74 139
Richard Weston (Earl of)
74 69 70 134-136 138 **79**
248
Thomas Weston (Earl of)
74 139
William Bentinck (Earl of)
74 139
PORTLOCK Nancy (Lester)
125 217
William **125** 217
PORTMAN
Cristina **111** 84
Elizabeth **113** 221
Grace **113** 221
Henry **80** 361
John **113** 221
Robert **142** 161
Walter **111** 84
William **110** 197 **113** 221
PORTRIDGE
Elizabeth **91** 180
PORTRYFF
Elizabeth **137** 294
PORTSMOUTH —— **59** 194
PORTWAYE
Edmund **84** 307
Portyngton *see*
Portington
PORY
Eleanor **52** 122 126
Elizabeth **52** 119 122 125

PORY *cont'd*
126
Helen **52** 126
Jane **52** 126
John **52** 122 125 126 **118**
145 146
Katharine **52** 126
Mary **52** 122 125 126
Robert **52** 122 125 126
Thomas **52** 122 125 126
POSEY John **52** 461
Sabre **117** 34
POSIDIPPUS 57 42
POSSE Edward **66** 358
Maria Eleanora
Haroldsdotter **111** 100
POSSON Cornelius
Franklin **83** 249 **84** 191
POST Poste
—— **53** 137 465 **57** 236
60 147 **91** 174 **146** 357
— Mr. **62** 84 **91** 174
— Mrs. **62** 197 **91** 174
123 310
Aaron **69** 332 **70** 92 **104**
263 **111** 297 **146** 360
374 **147** 63
Abel **146** 368
Abel P. **147** 60
Abigail **54** 81 **62** 178 240
146 360 363 366 372 373
147 58 59
Abigail (Abbey) **147** 61
Abigail (Dean) **146** 363
147 384
Abigail (Denison)
(Williams) **147** 63
Abigail (Lay) **146** 370
Abigail (Loomis) **147** 57
Abigail (Willcocks)
146 372
Abigail (Williams)
146 370
Abitha **146** 359
Abitha (Phelps) **146** 358
359
Abner **59** 132 **62** 333 **146**
371 372
Abraham **62** 333 **63** 196
124 186 **146** 356 357
361 363 365-368 371 373
375 387 **147** 49 61-63
383 **148** 18
Abram **63** 196
Absalom **54** 354
Acmon **147** 54
Adin **147** 53
Adosha **57** 289 290
Adosha (Kellog) **146** 359
Alanson **88** 27
Albert Warner **147** 60
Alpha H. **147** 54
Alson Hoyt **146** 363
Amanda **111** 312
Amy **146** 364 365 **147** 56
Amy Adeline **147** 56
Ancel Bassett **113** 296
Ancel Bassett (Mrs.) **112**
73 **113** 295
Andrus **86** 19
Ann **60** 344 **146** 263 363-

POST *cont'd*
365 372 373
Ann (Parker) **146** 371 372
Ann (Post) **146** 263 363
Ann (Terry) **146** 362
Anna **54** 354 **62** 121 127
  146 362
Anna (Cheeseman)
  146 359
Anna (Clark) **147** 50
Anna (Jones) **146** 370
Anna (Terry) **147** 383 384
Anna P. (Bissell) **147** 60
Anne **146** 360 363-365
  369-373 365 / **147** 50 53
  384
Anne (Gladden) **147** 50
Anne (Hunte) **147** 62
Ansel K. **147** 55
Asa **146** 375
Asa D. **78** 372
Ashbel **146** 370 **147** 63
Augustus **146** 364 365
Azubah (Chapman)
  147 54
Bela **146** 364 **147** 54
Benjamin **146** 360 **147** 50
  52 53 384
Benjamin Franklin
  147 52
Beriah **52** 416 **146** 357
Bethiah (Higgins)
  146 374
Betsey **62** 84 **85** 411
  146 375
Betsey (Atwater) **133** 302
Betsey (Church) **146** 375
Betsey (Fuller) **146** 359
Betsey (Phelps) **147** 63
Betsey (Plant) **146** 372
Betsey Ann E. **85** 411
Betsey Gordon (Strong)
  146 364 365
Bissell E. **147** 60
Calvin G. **147** 55
Caroline (McEwen)
  146 363
Caroline (Parsons)
  133 302
Caroline Cushman
  (Lathrop) **133** 302
  136 326
Carrie A. **86** 54
Catherine **62** 240
Catherine A. (Kennedy)
  147 61
Charity **146** 368
Charity (Lewis) **146** 374
Charles **146** 364 365 **147**
  50 53 54
Charles Alfred (Mrs.)
  147 62
Charles Rollin **133** 302
  136 326
Charles William **118** 166
  133 302 **136** 90 326
Chauncy Jones **147** 56
Chloe **62** 240 **146** 370 376
  147 51
Chloe (Chapman)
  146 369

POST *cont'd*
Chloe (Dee) **147** 53
Christopher **146** 367 373
  375
Christopher Columbus
  146 375
Clarissa **146** 361
Clarissa (Brown) **147** 60
Clarissa (Fobes) **146** 363
Clarissa (Way) **146** 365
Clarissa (Wright) **146** 364
Comfort **54** 81
Comfort (Coleman)
  (Goodrich) **147** 63
Comfort (Goodrich)
  146 228
Cornelia **62** 240
Cornelius **62** 265 **147** 54
Cynthia **111** 62 **147** 54
Cynthia (Fuller) **146** 365
Cynthia (Pratt) **147** 51
Dan **143** 63 64 **146** 372
Dan Lane **147** 55
Daniel **56** 359 **104** 263
  146 360
Daniel H. **54** 354
Daniel Hazeltine **55** xxxii
Darius **146** 362 363
  147 384
David **54** 83 **146** 370 374
  147 50 51 59
David Warner **147** 60
Deborah **147** 51 59 61
Deborah (Chapman)
  147 52 53
Deborah (Curtice) **147**
  58 59
Deborah (Skinner)
  (Tarbox) **147** 58 60
Deborah (Ward) **147** 51
Delilah M. (Brown)
  147 61
Dencey **147** 52
Deney **62** 240
Dense (Lay) **146** 370
Desire (Eaton) **146** 356
  357
Destoma **147** 58
Diana **146** 370
Dinah **146** 360 371
Dinah (Brown) **104** 263
  146 357
Diodate **54** 85 **147** 60
Don E. **146** 368 **147** 61 62
Donald E. **89** 400 **147** 61
  63
Dorothy **147** 59 60
Dorothy / Dolly (Birdsey)
  147 52
Dudley **146** 364
Dudley Barber **146** 365
Dwight **146** 364
Ebenezer **147** 50
Eldad **56** 306 **104** 119 263
  146 357-360 **147** 63
Eleanor **146** 371 372
  147 59
Eleazur Colton **146** 375
Electra M. (Spencer)
  147 50
Elihu **146** 364

POST *cont'd*
Elijah **147** 60 384
Eliza **86** 54
Eliza (Denison) **147** 54
Eliza (Hollester) **147** 60
Elizabeth **52** 411 **59** 67 71
  168 **66** 330 345 350-352
  72 206 **84** 171 **126** 5
  146 357 359 362 368 372
  374 **147** 383 384
Elizabeth (Barnes) **124**
  186 **146** 366 367 **147** 61
Elizabeth (Bissell) **146** 362
Elizabeth (Buckingham)
  147 51
Elizabeth (Clark) **106** 243
  147 383
Elizabeth (Culver) **146**
  357 358
Elizabeth (Forbes) **147** 61
Elizabeth (Fuller) **146** 359
Elizabeth (Knowles)
  147 58
Elizabeth (Maltby) **111**
  297 **146** 360 **147** 63
Elizabeth (White) **146** 370
Elizabeth Cornelia
  146 375
Elizabeth G. **69** 332
Ella **89** 290
Ella Letitia (Merriweather)
  133 302 **136** 326
Ellen (Panton) **133** 302
Ely **146** 368
Emily **113** 296 **146** 364
Emily F. **86** 54
Emily H. **66** 227
Enoch **146** 372 373
Ephraim **147** 56 58
Erastus **146** 364 365
Esther **52** 311 **53** 405 **146**
  357 361-363 **147** 54 60
  384
Esther (Lawrence) **147** 53
Esther (Meeker) **133** 302
  146 367
Esther (Skinner) **147** 60
Eunice (Gibbs) **146** 368
Experience **146** 363
Ezekiel **147** 58 60
Ezekiel Augustus **147**
  59-61
Ezekiel Lavius **147** 61
Ezra **146** 370 **147** 63
Faith W. **66** 227
Fanny **147** 51
Fanny Amelia (Chapman)
  147 54
Flavius Augustus **147** 61
Flora **147** 53
Flora (Hill) **147** 53
Florence (Dean) (Crumb)
  91 143
Frances Marie **105** 128
Frank R. **63** 301
Frederick J. **147** 63
George **147** 50 53
George H. **51** 77
George S. **86** 54
George Washington
  146 375 **147** 58

POST *cont'd*
Georgia **68** lxiv
Gideon **52** 182-184 309-
311 408 409 **53** 447 **146**
356 361 362 **147** 383 384
Gordon **147** 57
Gracieuse **131** 93
Gracie / Grove **147** 56
Halpah (Hoskins) **147** 53
Hannah **52** 182 410 **56** 306
61 389 **62** 84 **70** 92 **104**
118 119 263 **107** 54 **146**
357-360 362 368 374 375
147 49 50 55 56 59 384
Hannah (Barnes) **146** 367
373
Hannah (Calkins)
146 363
Hannah (Case) **104** 119
263
Hannah (Cass) **146** 359
147 63
Hannah (Gear) **147** 60 61
Hannah (Johnson)
133 302
Hannah (Olcott)
(Hubbard) **147** 58
Hannah (Phelps) (Buttles)
146 374
Hannah (Whittlesey)
147 49
Hannah L. **147** 55
Hannah Lencey **147** 61
Harley **147** 60
Harriet **57** 360 **85** 411
147 53
Harriet E. **68** lxiv
Harriet Marilla **147** 61
Harriet Terry **66** 227
Harriet W. **66** 227 **79** 154
Harrison **68** 95
Helen M. **86** 54
Henrietta (Seldon)
(Welch) **147** 61
Henrietta Minerva **147** 61
Henrietta S. (Welch)
86 170
Henry **146** 370 371 **147**
53 54 58 60
Henry Lay **62** 240
Hepsibah (Pratt) **147** 52
Hester **146** 374
Hester (Tooker) **147** 52
Hezekiah **146** 376 **147** 49
50
Hiram **104** 263
Hoyt **63** 207
Hudson **147** 52
Huldah **146** 367 368
I. B. **147** 55
Ichabod **57** 289 290 360
146 359 **147** 60
Isaac **147** 50 54 55
Isaiah **146** 369-371
Isiah **147** 63
Israel **146** 360 364 365
Jacob **146** 361
James **63** 196 **65** 221 **146**
375 376 **147** 49 55 56 58
384
Jared Wilson **146** 375

POST *cont'd*
Jazaniah **52** 184 **72** 206
146 362
Jedediah **86** 54 **146** 370
147 57-60
Jedediah G. **86** 170
Jedediah Gear **147** 61
Jedidiah **54** 83 **61** 389 **62**
178 240
Jemima **127** 199 **146** 366
Jemima (Hurd) **146** 374
Jemima (Pelton) **147** 52
Jeremiah **60** 190 **146** 359
361
Jeremiah K. **146** 375
147 55
Jerusha **146** 370 **147** 383
Jerusha (Pratt) **146** 371
Jesse **146** 368
Jimmy **147** 55 56
Joanna **66** 351
Joel **146** 358 360 361
147 55
John **54** 81 **62** 240 **66** 351
146 360 367-370 373
147 57 60 63
John D. **75** 95 **85** 411 **86** 54
John H. **86** 54 **147** 60
John Henry **86** 54 **147** 60
John J. **106** 249 **107** 84 86
John Samuel **147** 61
Jonathan **147** 50 52
Jordan **54** 81 **146** 363 **147**
56-58 63
Joseph **52** 310 **55** 39 **56**
356 **146** 363 368 373 374
Joseph Herbert **68** lxiv
Joseph Otis **146** 360
Joshua **146** 369 370 **147** 63
Josiah **146** 374
Joy **147** 51
Julia **147** 54 60
Julia (Stephens) **146** 375
Julia Ann **147** 55
Julianna (Post) **146** 375
147 55
Katharine **57** 250 **59** 133
63 196
Keturah **147** 55 56 61
Keturah (Jones) **147** 55
Keziah **146** 368
Keziah (Jones) **146** 368
Kitty **86** 54
Laura (Sage) **147** 50
Leah **83** 233
Leander **57** 289
Leilia (Young) **133** 302
Levi **52** 309 **146** 362 **147** 51
384
Levina (Jones) **146** 364
Levy **146** 363 **147** 384
Lewis **146** 375
Linda **146** 371
Lois **52** 310 **60** 147 **83** 45
146 356 357
Louann **75** 95
Louisa **146** 363 375 **147** 53
Louisa (West) **147** 60
Lucena (Odell) **146** 368
Lucinda (Bower) **146** 368
Lucinda (Hanks) **86** 19

POST *cont'd*
Lucinda (Phelps) **146** 364
Lucretia **146** 374 **147** 51
Lucretia (Post) **146** 374
147 51
Lucy **57** 290 **146** 361 365
374 **147** 50 53 54
Lucy (Bissell) **146** 364 365
Lucy (Buckingham)
147 51
Lucy (Denison) **147** 51
Lucy (McKall) **146** 360 361
Lucy (Rollo) **146** 359
Lucy (Warner) **146** 368
Lucy O. **55** 52
Lydia **52** 183 **57** 289 **62**
240 **146** 359 362 368-370
372 373
Lydia (Buckland) (Brown)
(Lord) (Dunk) **147** 62
148 18
Lydia (Bushnell) **146** 369
Lydia (Doane) **146** 371
Lydia (Palmer) **146** 368
Lydia (Tremain) **147** 63
Mabel **147** 50 53
Major **146** 368
Margaret **60** 150 **147** 54
Margery **146** 367
Maria **79** 156
Marjorie **78** 205
Marjorie Merriweather
133 302 **136** 323 326
Martha **54** 83 **147** 60
Martha (Mead) **133** 302
Martha (Warner) **147** 59
Mary **52** 182 184 309-311
409 419 **53** 447 **54** 81 **56**
162 **59** 132 **62** 176 265
333 **63** 196 **66** 73 351 **68**
95 **104** 263 **146** 356 357
360 362 363 372 373 376
147 62 384
Mary (Barber) **146** 363
Mary (Chase) **146** 361 362
Mary (Clark) **146** 375 376
Mary (Colt) **147** 50 384
Mary (Denison) **146** 374
Mary (Downer) **146** 356
357
Mary (Gardner) **146** 365
Mary (Hartford) **146** 365
Mary (Holcomb) **146** 375
Mary (Hull) **147** 54
Mary (Pratt) **146** 360
Mary (Taylor) **146** 357
Mary (Thompson)
146 360
Mary Ann **86** 19 **147** 60
Mary Ann (Spencer)
146 375
Mary D. (Chase) **88** 27
Mary E. **66** 228
Mary M. **66** 228
Mary / Molly **147** 51
Maud Wilson (Barnes)
113 295
Mehitable **146** 376 **147** 58
Mehitable (Curtice)
147 56
Mehitable (Jones) **133** 302

POST *cont'd*
  146 367
  Melinda (Woodruff)
    147 58
  Melissa 147 53
  Mercy 52 409 146 362 363
  Mercy (McEwen) 146 363
  Mercy (Pratt) 146 372
  Millisent 147 58
  Milton 57 289
  Mima 146 374
  Mindwell 146 360
  Mindwell (Hurd) 146 374
  Molly 146 362 372 373
  Molly (Dee) 146 370
    147 63
  Molly (Stannard) (Jones)
    146 370
  Moses 146 368
  Nancy 106 243 143 63
    147 383
  Nancy (Ford) 146 359
  Nancy F. 78 372
  Nathan 146 367-369 373
    374 147 384
  Nathaniel 146 371 372
  Noah 124 160 146 368
  Noah P. 147 55
  Olive 146 362 147 52
  Oliver 52 408 146 362 363
    147 384
  Otis 57 289
  Pamela 54 85
  Pamelia (Birge) 147 60
  Pardon 146 375
  Parnal 146 365
  Patience 54 83
  Patience (Strictland)
    (Cone) 147 59
  Patricia 113 296
  Persia 146 365
  Peter 146 357 360
  Phebe 146 364-366 368
    374 375 147 55 56 384
  Phebe (Lay) 146 363
    147 63
  Phineas 56 307 146 363-
    365 374 147 55
  Polly 108 45 147 53 54
  Polly (Hammond)
    146 359
  Polly (Stevens) 146 370
  Polly M. (Aria) (Conklin)
    147 53
  Polly Septima 146 366
  Prudence 147 58
  Rachel 146 362 366 147 55
  Rachel (Ford) 146 359
  Ralph 146 365
  Rebecca 66 351 352 146
    367 368 372 373
  Rebecca (Ackley) 147 56
  Rebecca (Bason) 133 302
  Rebecca (Stevens) 133 302
  Rebina 147 53
  Rebina (Hull) 147 52 53
  Rene 114 184
  Reuben 147 50-52
  Richard 62 240 66 345
    350-352 79 154 147 62
  Richard B. 66 227

POST *cont'd*
  Roswell 133 302 146 366-
    368
  Roxy Ann 142 284 143
    63-65 67
  Russel 104 263 147 50
  Russell 146 360 147 52
  Ruth 56 158 146 360
    147 55
  Ruth (Morris) 147 54
  Ruth (Spencer) 146 372
  Ruth (Walker) 146 360
  Ruth M. (Ferguson)
    147 61
  Saba (Redfield) 147 49
  Sala 147 51
  Sally 62 241 147 55
  Sally (Bushnell) 147 53
  Sally (Ingraham) 146 375
  Sally (Sumner) 147 60
  Sally Ann 55 257
  Sally M. 147 55
  Sally S. (Boon) 146 375
  Samuel 62 240 146 359
    147 61
  Sarah 56 359 59 410 411 95
    163 103 221 146 360
    361 375 147 55 383 384
  Sarah (Buckingham)
    147 51
  Sarah (Bushnell) 146 360
    361
  Sarah (Chapman) 146 375
  Sarah (Fenning) 147 63
  Sarah (Gilbert) 146 364
  Sarah (Larnard) 146 368
  Sarah (Platts) 147 55
  Sarah (Tubs) 147 384
  Sarah R. 147 60
  Sarilla L. 72 206
  Sibyl 56 307 104 263 146
    360 364 366 147 59 60
    384
  Sibyl (Barber) 146 364
  Sibyl (Hudson) 147 52
  Sibyl (Huntington)
    146 365
  Silas Holcomb 146 375
  Simeon 147 50 52 54
  Sophia 147 59
  Sophia F. (Bill) 147 56
  Sophia J. (Foote) 147 61
  Sophronia 147 56
  Stephen 52 310 311 409-
    411 416 53 448 54 81 56
    162 63 196 207 89 400
    91 173 174 106 243 133
    302 146 356 357 361 363-
    366 368 371 373 375 376
    147 49 62 63 383
  Submit 146 363
  Submit (Hoyt) 146 363
  Susanna 66 351
  Sylvester 147 52
  Sylvia 147 56
  Tabitha 147 55 56
  Tamar 147 56
  Tamar (Jones) 147 56
  Tempe 146 372
  Temperance 62 240 146
    369-371

POST *cont'd*
  Temperance (Bushnell)
    146 371
  Thankful 146 372
  Thankful (Wells) 147 58
  Thomas 66 350-352 104
    263 126 5 135 299 146
    356-359 361 362 364 365
    147 59 60
  Truman 133 302
  Urania 146 374 147 55
  Urania (Post) 147 55
  Ward 147 51
  Watson 143 64
  Wealthy 147 54 55
  Wealthy (Hurd) 146 375
  William 62 84 68 114 69
    332 85 411 133 302 146
    367 368 147 62
  William Abner 146 364
  William Glenn (Mrs.)
    91 143
  William W. 86 54
  Woolcott 62 240
  Wright 66 228
  Zinah 146 370 371
POSTAN M. M. 112 322
Poste *see* Post
POSTEL Mary 100 109
POSTHOUS John 64 257
POSTLE
  Elizabeth 87 394
POSTLEIGH
  Hannah 138 211
POSTLES —— 106 49
POSTLETHWAITE
  Gwalter 94 179
  Mary 86 370
POSTON
  Christian 73 149
  Estella W. 84 191
  Henry T. (Mrs.) 84 106
    191
  Jane 73 263
  John 65 50
  John Hamill 114 158
  John Stone 73 223
  Sarah 116 273
  Simeon 90 88
  William 73 223
POTBERY Mary 113 49
    143 129
POTE
  Ferdinand C. 84 122
  Hannah 66 48
  Lilla Hamblen (Rich)
    84 122
  Olive Titcomb 110 152
  Richard 55 101
  Samuel 66 48
  William 66 113 70 261 264
Poter *see* Potter
POTERIE
  Claude de la 140 237
POTHIER Aram J. 139 12
POTIER DE LA
  MORANDIERE
    Francois 107 268
    Henri Alain Gabriel
      107 268

POTMETURE
Benony **115** 195
Pots *see* Potts
Pottel *see* Pottle
Pottell *see* Pottle
POTTER alias FINBUS
Jane **52** 247 248
POTTER Poter Pottor
—— **51** 91 **56** 106 333 **57**
  337 **58** 318 **71** 32 **73** 302
  85 150 **92** 272 319 323
  98 367 **114** 6 **117** 14
  118 18 **120** 203 **137** 183
  146 332
— Col. **142** 282
— Lieut. **85** 17
— Mr. **71** 142 **74** 287 **84**
  152 **90** 35
— Mrs. **59** 77 **62** 59 **63**
  56 58 **71** 117
—— (Hall) **87** 358
—— (Tallman) **85** 74
Aaron **54** 25 26 **129** 237
Abbie J. (Perry) **85** 170
Abby **134** 313
Abby (Carr) **126** 24
Abby S. **126** 21
Abednego **128** 51
Abel **54** 26 **129** 63
Abigail **54** 24-26 **56** 289
  60 72 **62** 45 **63** 153 **66**
  198 **69** 275 **71** 9 **104** 47
  115 264 **128** 233
Abijah **81** 154 **86** 149 151
Abner **135** 52 312
Ada **68** 158
Adeline G. **132** 295
Agnes Lura **116** 285
Albert **52** 379
Albert E. **148** 180
Albert N. **148** 180
Albert R. **120** 305
Alden **125** 293
Alexander **119** 21
Alfred **125** 245
Alfred Claghorn **51** 385
  58 107
Alfred Warren **88** 126
Alice **51** 407 **67** 173 179
  73 301 302 **104** 76 **122**
  212 **127** 31 **136** 309
Alice (Bass) **125** 217
Alice (Brown) **126** 22 25
Alice Hitty **95** 315
Allen Gifford **134** 129
Allis Lucretia (Williams)
  106 313
Allis Williams **106** 314
Almira **75** 95
Alonzo **77** lxvii lxviii
Aloren D. **116** 285
Amanda C. **117** 212
Ambrose **93** 112
Amelia **72** xx
Amorette **57** 390
Amos **54** 25 **140** 237
Amy **101** 70
Ann **54** 26 **63** 157 **70** 121
  76 lxviii **88** 332 **110** 27
  115 134
Ann (Fish) **125** 244

POTTER *cont'd*
Ann Elizabeth **112** 319
Ann Mary (Handley) **83**
  181 185
Anna **54** 23 26 **104** 46 47
  130 136 **134** 313
Anna Gates **75** 34
Anna Maria
  (Cunningham) **86** 450
Anne **63** 35 **67** 287 **74** 66
  101 310
Anne Urquhart **77** lxviii
  98 186
Annie M. **148** 180
Anstis Greene **125** 284
Anthony **73** xlvi **86** 140
  385 **88** 279 **92** 269 272
  313 **109** 307 **111** 317
  128 52 **138** 285 289 **148**
  311
Apphia **134** 313
Archer R. **123** 225
Arthur C. **148** 180
Arthur E. **116** 285
Asa **92** 283
Asahel **113** 78
Bartholomew **69** 275
  72 146
Belle **130** 47
Benjamin **58** 35 **61** 271
  67 286 **73** 104 **74** 202
  76 273 **83** 87 **87** 252 **88**
  137 **105** 164 217 266
  111 225 **135** 53
Benjamin A. **73** 104
Bertha **123** 224
Bertha R. **75** 19
Bethuel **75** 19
Betsey **92** 275 **102** 17 **144**
  348 354
Betsey (Hewitt) **136** 362
Betsey Rundlett **97** 128
Better **60** 379
Beulah **126** 240-242
Boston **67** 287
Burtie **116** 285
C. A. **93** 349 351
C. E. **105** 303
C. V. **93** 302
Caleb **112** 59 **127** 308 **128**
  49 54 303
Calista (Gifford) **135** 51
  52
Caroline **62** 134
Caroline Judith **86** 307
Catherine **91** 350 **132** 215
  146 336
Celia Ann (Taylor)
  116 259
Cesar **128** 128
Champlin **115** 264 **131**
  294 296
Chandler E. **118** 39
  146 328
Chandler Eastman **63** 296
  64 133 191
Charles **80** 448 **91** 332
  116 259 **126** 22 **127** 308
  146 336
Charles Alfred **93** 350 351
Charles E. **116** 285

POTTER *cont'd*
Charles Edward **67** 92
  80 448 **116** 79
Charles F. **117** 212
Charles Francis **51** 84
Charles H. **117** 212
Charles Milton **95** 315
Charles Wenzel **95** 316
Charlotte (Worden)
  85 289
Chauncy **75** 19
Cheeny **60** 95
Chloe **86** 170 **113** 33 40
Christian **51** 348
Christiana **97** 192 **125** 16
Christie Ann **116** 115
Christina **97** 192
Christopher **128** 125
Clarissa **60** 77 **70** 232
Clarkson Augustus
  (Mrs.) **86** 198 **106** 123
  114 68
Clarkson Nott **77** lxviii
Cora **77** lxviii
Cornelius **116** 115
Crystal **105** 128
Cynthia (Howard)
  135 252
Cynthia Caroline **134** 129
Cyrus E. **116** 285
Cyrus Q. **116** 285
Daisy Lucille **85** 297
Daisy V. **123** 225
Daniel **54** 25 26 **79** 274
  92 275
Daniel Merrit **134** 129
David **54** 25 26 **56** 45 **61**
  191 **68** 158 **69** 275 **73**
  xlvi **88** 7 **92** 275 **102** 77
  105 320 **106** 80 **109** 307
  130 47 **146** 336 **148** 311
David Anthony (Mrs.)
  107 134
Deborah **54** 24 **67** 286
Deborah (Chase) **88** 126
Deett **101** 95
Deliverance **131** 234
Dennis **60** 380
Dexter **78** 247
Dianah (Colvin) **113** 77 78
Dinah **59** 29
Dinah (Gifford) **131** 52
Dolly **75** 19 20
Donald Williams **106** 314
Dorcas **54** 25 26 **80** 262
Dorcas G. **69** 275 **72** 146
Dorothy **54** 26 **74** 169
Dorothy Elizabeth
  106 125
Ebenezer **95** 315 **97** 293
  125 23
Eddison / Edson E.
  116 285
Edmund **111** 315
Edward **51** 348 **54** 26 **60**
  379-381 383 **61** 88 190
  191 358 **62** 87 375 **80**
  448 **86** 170 **91** 348-350
  352 **93** 302 **105** 217 **112**
  323 **116** 187
Edward E. **85** 170

POTTER *cont'd*
Edward Tuckerman **77** lxviii
Edwin **91** 201
Edwin D. **75** 20
Edwin Tower **86** 150
Elam **53** 176 **54** 25
Elam O. **79** 165
Eleanor **115** 39
Eleanor (Lewis) **127** 35
Eleanor (Piche) **106** 143
Electy **104** 47
Elihu **125** 29
Eliphalet Nott **77** lxviii
Elisa (Freeland) **125** 109
Elisha **128** 126
Elisha R. **99** 9 **138** 283
Eliza **75** 95 **77** 151
Eliza (Coolidge) **88** 279
Eliza (Freeland) **125** 109
Eliza Greenwood **95** 316
Eliza J. **75** 19
Eliza L. **75** 19
Eliza Maria **145** 304
Elizabeth **51** 222 313 **54**
  21-26 **56** 278 282 **58** 76
  80 **62** 37 **63** 35 246 **67**
  286 **69** 335 **85** 220 **87**
  258 **88** 330 **91** 3 348-350
  352 **101** 310 **108** 227
  116 157 **122** 215 **124**
  294 **131** 33 51 207 **146**
  336
Elizabeth (Bodge) **101** 100
Elizabeth (Carpenter)
  112 323
Elizabeth (Gifford) **134**
  129 **135** 53
Elizabeth (McLaughlin)
  137 183
Elizabeth (Stokes)
  113 102
Elizabeth (Stone) **148** 311
Elizabeth (Vaughn) **105**
  320 **106** 80
Elizabeth (Whipple)
  86 140 141
Elizabeth Ann (Knowles)
  88 137
Elizabeth E. A. **92** 283
Elizabeth Ellen **81** 258
Elizabeth Lydia **86** 150
Elizabeth Maria **81** 258
Elizabeth R. **125** 242
Elizabeth Sturgis **78** 168
Ellen E. **75** 19
Ellen L. **116** 62
Ellis David **106** 314
Ellsworth S. **116** 285
Elvina (Freeland) **125** 109
Emily **83** 185 188
Emily Graff (Spooner)
  95 250
Enos **54** 25 26
Epheraim **147** 38
Ephraim **86** 450 **92** 275
  130 136 **136** 301 **147** 39
Ervin D. **148** 180
Esther **54** 25 26 **116** 57
Esther (Gifford) **137** 161
Esther (Harwood) **90** 260

POTTER *cont'd*
Eugenia **100** 90
Eunice **54** 26 **129** 67
Evelyn **117** 43
Evelyn (Arnold) **94** 139
Ezekiel **129** 64
Ezra **54** 26 **57** 161 **128** 50
F. H. **75** 19
Fanny **70** 201 **80** 260
Finette **109** 271
Flora E. **148** 180
Frances **54** 23 **66** 308
  125 241
Frances G. (Wakefield)
  88 285
Frances Jane **79** 16
Frances Juliet **80** 448
Frances R. **103** 226
Frank **117** 219
Freddie **112** 59
Frederick E. **84** 31
Frederick S. **134** 313
Freelove **134** 123 **135** 52
Freeman Thomas **86** 150
George **91** 242 **101** 95
  128 220 **129** 61 66 **134**
  210 **136** 217
George Benjamin (Mrs.)
  94 139
George II. **125** 242
George Levi **85** 289
George Martin **86** 450
George Shepard **64** 102
George W. **117** 212
Georgia A. (King)
  83 433 438
Gideon **54** 25 **56** 285 **58** 75
  76 80
Gilbert **76** lxviii **111** 293
  128 53
Hannah **54** 20-26 **56** 277
  278 **75** 19 20 **84** 458 **85**
  337 **91** 352 **92** 58 **102** 16
  104 47 **120** 317 **131** 33
  142 333
Hannah (Brown) **111** 225
Hannah (Chase) **87** 258
Hannah (Dodge) **86** 366
Hannah (Luce) **98** 367
Hannah F. (Spicer) **85** 289
Hannah N. (Parker) **114** 6
Harriet **91** 108 **122** 296
Harriet (Prescott) **85** 289
Harriet Maria **113** 286
Harriette **91** 108
Hazel Park **120** 77
Helen A. **69** 275
Helen L. **69** 275
Henrietta (Adams) **85** 225
Henry **58** 374 **73** 300 **88** 35
  36 **115** 174 **127** 13 **128**
  127 **134** 179
Henry A. **85** 170
Henry Austin **51** 84
Henry B. **126** 25
Henry Clay **95** 250
Henry Codman **77** lxviii
Henry David **106** 313
Henry Leman **85** 289
Hepzibah **100** 278 **129** 237

POTTER *cont'd*
Hepzibah (Gelson)
  126 241
Herbert W. **83** 433 438
Hitty (Wenzel) **95** 315 316
Holder **58** 369
Hope **54** 24 26 **81** 130
Hopestill **54** 173 **129** 237
Horatio **64** lxv **71** liii **77**
  lxviii **78** 439
Hosea **54** 25
Howard **77** lxvii lxviii
Hugh **123** 97 100
Hulda Nash **114** 6
Humphrey **110** 27
  129 345
Humphrey R. **69** 202
Hunnemon **83** 181 185
Ichabod **67** 286 287 **98** 24
  105 256 **127** 144 **128** 51
  128 129 64 **144** 296
Irene **117** 212
Isaac **83** 36
Isabel **52** 247
Isabel Elizabeth **77** 183
Israel **86** 450
Israel R. **66** 96
Iva Orlena **86** 151
J. **92** 275
J. A. **91** 332
J. H. **81** 38
J. W. **91** 332
Jabez **125** 245
Jabez Turner **75** 95
Jacob **56** 289 **92** 323 **100** 41
James **54** 24-26 **67** 287 **78**
  168 **81** 258 **106** 143 **115**
  75 **117** 9 16 **119** 21 **122**
  215 **127** 143 **128** 58 217
  129 63 **131** 56 **134** 204
  146 193 194 **147** 193
  194
James Addison **136** 309
James Brown **73** 316 **74**
  xxv **77** xxxv lxvii lxviii
James C. **85** 170
Jane **58** 374 **80** 448 **106** 143
  146 336
Jane (Burlingame) **87** 269
Jane (Carpenter) **137** 180
Jane (Frances) **125** 293
Jane P. **100** 335
Jared **103** 236
Jedediah **147** 85
Jemima **54** 173
Jennie **75** 19
Jennie L. **148** 180
Jennie Louise (Besio)
  138 289
Jenny **92** 272
Jeremiah **80** 178
Jeremiah Niles **85** 150
Jeremiah P. **146** 336
Jerusha **61** 190 **62** 375
Jesse **56** 131 **127** 35 **129** 65
Jessey **128** 58
Joanah **148** 311
Joanna **131** 134 **135** 45
Joanna (Wilbore) **113** 102
Joanna (Wood) **148** 311
Joanna T. **77** 179

POTTER *cont'd*
Job **54** 25 **102** 10 **115** 75
Joel **54** 25 26 **70** 78
John **54** 20-26 **56** 278 **57**
    220 **58** 74 80 374 **59** 24
    60 95 **61** 88 **63** 328 **66**
    198 **70** 78 **73** xlvi **75**
    227 **76** 122 **81** 122 128-
    131 133 **86** 140 141 **87**
    269 **95** 92 **102** 16 **109**
    196 **110** 241 **112** 48 **115**
    75 **118** 270 **120** 159 318
    124 160 **126** 54 **127** 312
    128 128 **129** 237 **131**
    207 **143** 300 **144** 294
    296 **146** 336
John Chamberlin **75** 19
John Church **95** 315
John L. **109** 271
John L. (Mrs.) **91** 209
John N. **125** 174 242
    126 22
John O. **125** 244
John Salisbury **138** 289
John W. **72** 321 **86** 390
Jonah **54** 25
Jonathan **128** 303 **135** 252
Jorge **127** 223
Joseph **54** 23-26 **77** lxvii
    81 130 **86** 450 **105** 277
    106 153 **109** 307 **110**
    241 **112** 324 **127** 305
    128 52 **129** 57 **131** 52
    142 333
Joseph B. **136** 362 **137** 180
Joseph G. **72** 321
Joseph Seabury **117** 219
Josephine Orma **89** 30
Josephine Wood **80** 141
Josiah **86** 450 **102** 10 **128**
    55 **129** 62
Josway **126** 24
Judith **67** 286
Judith (Clark) **138** 279
Julia (Carr) (Sawdy) **148**
    275 276
Julia Baxter **113** 65
Julia M. **75** 19
Julia W. **72** 107
Julian **55** 184
Julian C. **85** 170
Justus Miles **86** 366
Katharine Haines **89** 291
Keziah **69** 275
L. L. **91** 332
Laura **109** 267 271
Laura Ann **76** 273
Laura Maria **134** 129
Laurana **81** 153
Lemuel **54** 25
Leonard **81** 154 **86** 149
Lettie L. (Palmer) **123** 97
Levi **85** 289
Levi Baxter **95** 315
Levi Frank **95** 316
Levi Lemont **136** 362
Lewis **112** 59 **145** 353
Lillian M. **85** 170
Lillian May **117** 219
Littece **104** 47
Lizzie J. **93** 112

POTTER *cont'd*
Lois **54** 25
Lois (Guernsey) **112** 324
Lorana **86** 152
Loren D. **116** 285
Louisa (Barteaux) **86** 450
Louisa Phebe **86** 366
Louise **103** 66 **111** 323
Louise May **85** 195 **86** 450
    87 71 179
Lovina Mehitable
    (Rowell) **86** 150
Lucilla Train **95** 315
Lucinda **78** 247
Lucinda L. **85** 170
Lucretia A. (Potter)
    85 289
Lucy **60** 95 **67** 287 **86** 93
    97 73
Lucy (Tilden) **88** 330
Lucy E. **127** 35
Lucy Maria **81** 38
Lucy V. **117** 284
Luis J. **104** 47
Luke **74** 150 **85** 31
Luthan **134** 313
Luther A. **116** 285
Luther F. **79** 5
Luther S. **72** 107
Luthera Negus (Gould)
    85 289
Luthun **72** 321
Lydia **54** 24 26 173 **59** 105
    61 271 **70** 78 **81** 154 **86**
    230 **92** 310 **112** 227 **116**
    76
Lydia (Chase) **87** 245
Lydia (Devol) **131** 56
Lydia (Rowell) **86** 149
Lydia (Thomas) **112** 227
Lydia Gardiner (Eldred)
    138 281 285
Lydia Haley **138** 285 289
Mabel **54** 26
Mahala Shaw **130** 47
Margaret **67** 287 **72** 305
    83 87 **98** 24 **99** 115 **146**
    336
Margaret (Gifford) **126**
    54 **129** 236 237
Margaret (Helme) **98** 24
Margaret (Paine) **105**
    164 266
Margaret J. **73** 213
Margaret Malvina **69** 202
Margaret S. (Tibbetts)
    100 41
Maria **77** 178 **127** 55
Maria Louisa (Owen)
    91 242
Marie **69** 275
Marion Elizabeth **95** 315
Mark Louis **109** 307
Martha **54** 26 **58** 374 **75** 95
    76 273 **144** 296
Martha (Dresser) **111** 317
Martha (Hall) **86** 450
Martha (Hazard) **98** 24
    144 296
Martha (Yeomans) **125**
    174 242 **126** 22

POTTER *cont'd*
Martha Ann (Rutherford)
    117 43
Martha J. (Wood) **95** 316
Martha Jane **101** 95
Martha Jane (Knott)
    86 150
Mary **53** 338 **54** 23-26 **55**
    lxv **57** 154 **58** 318 374 **59**
    31 168 **61** 271 **63** 155 **66**
    198 308 **67** 286 **73** 213
    75 29 **77** lxviii **87** 269
    92 269 **94** 286 95 368
    98 24 355 **100** 335 **102**
    16 **105** 147 **109** 195 **113**
    102 **115** 75 167 **116** 51
    199 **123** 240 **125** 236
    126 54 **127** 304 **128** 307
    129 237 **136** 301 **144**
    296 **146** 336 **147** 185
Mary (Adcocke) **143** 300
Mary (Arnold) **102** 16
Mary (Briggs) **126** 210
    211
Mary (Call) **125** 245
Mary (Casey) **116** 79
    138 279
Mary (Chase) **87** 252 **88** 7
    20
Mary (Farnsworth)
    86 450
Mary (Pattee) **146** 336
Mary (Rathbun) **116** 79
    138 279
Mary A. (Lyon) **116** 259
Mary Ann **77** 187
Mary Ann (Farmer)
    126 207
Mary Anna **134** 210
Mary C. **148** 180
Mary Douglas **105** 53
Mary E. **125** 243 244
Mary Edith **86** 150
Mary Ellen **117** 43
Mary Emily **95** 250
Mary Helen **95** 316
Mary Jane **71** liii
Mary L. **112** 324 **113** 65
Mary Lincoln **103** 120
Mary Louie **75** xxi **110** 63
Mary Louisa **77** lxvii
Mary Louise **109** 307
Mary M. **93** 112
Mary Miller (Denio)
    136 309
Mary R. (Peabody) **86** 151
Mary Scudder (Butler)
    105 53
Mattie C. **83** 296 301
Maud **119** 317
Maurice Ray **80** 102 209
Mechi **54** 25
Mehitable **54** 25
Melinda Carr **77** lxxvi
Melvin **116** 285
Mercy **54** 25 26 **62** 40
    111 315
Mercy (Burlingame)
    138 285
Mercy (Manchester)
    102 10

POTTER *cont'd*
Mercy (Quarles) **111** 315
Merritt **135** 51 52
Merton Henry **86** 150
Meschek **128** 51
Milton Baxter **95** 315
Mingo **128** 128
Moriah **123** 240
Moses **54** 25
Murray Anthony (Mrs.)
 84 341 **85** 197
Nancy **126** 22 **146** 336
 148 279
Nancy Maria **71** lxiv
Naomi E. **86** 366
Nathan **54** 25
Nathaniel **54** 23 24 26 **56**
 282 **61** 336 337 **62** 45 **66**
 308 **67** 286 **68** 384 **81**
 130 **87** 267 **101** 310 **112**
 227 **113** 102 **116** 111
 128 250 **132** 214 **134**
 239 **136** 217 **142** 333
 147 347
Nellie **79** 120
Nelson (Mrs.) **120** 77
Nicholas **51** 407 **86** 450
 110 241
Norman **86** 150
Octavia **75** 19
Olive **86** 390
Omah Byron **148** 175
Omah O. **148** 175
Orvilla **75** 19
Orvillus **75** 20
Osman **87** 245
Pamela **73** xlv
Pardon **88** 320
Patience **80** 448 **135** 53
Patience (Macomber)
 135 52
Patience G. **134** 313
Patience G. (Hoyt) **97** 128
Peace **129** 237
Peleg **59** 27 **122** 214
Perley **88** 285
Peter **79** 165 **127** 308
Peter Corbett **85** 289
Phebe **54** 24-26 **58** 74 **59**
 24 27 **86** 390 **103** 316
 119 196 **126** 194 **127** 34
 129 64 **142** 333
Phebe (Arnold) (Greene)
 109 196
Phebe (Chase) **87** 325
Phianes **127** 305
Phiannia **104** 47
Philemon **54** 25
Philena R. **69** 275
Philip **69** 275 **128** 51
 148 279
Phineas **54** 25
Piana **144** 324
Polly **122** 129
Prince **87** 258 **135** 45
Prudence **103** 110 **104** 139
R. L. **75** 19
Rabah **86** 222
Rachel **97** 337
Rauffe **56** 85
Rebecca **54** 24 **56** 72 **67**

POTTER *cont'd*
 285 **69** 275 **81** 130 **90**
 301 **110** 27 **128** 250 **136**
 325
Restcome **137** 161
Reuben **127** 223 305
Rhoda **54** 25 **70** 78 **131** 56
Rhoda (Carver) **88** 320
Richard **92** 310 315
 110 274
Rillie (Reynolds) **112** 59
Robert **58** 200 **63** 246 **64**
 59 **67** 286 **73** xlv **86** 450
 87 360 **88** 20 36 43 **98**
 19 20 22 **115** 167 **116** 79
 127 7 **128** 49 125 294
 136 217 **138** 279
Robert Brown **77** lxviii
Roby **70** 230
Roena **75** 20
Rouse **56** 124 **62** 287 **98** 24
 122 212 **126** 25 **127** 307
 128 128
Rouse T. **126** 22
Rowena Rising (Corbet)
 85 289 **136** 362
Ruphus **127** 302
Ruth **61** 271 398 **67** 286
 69 275 **73** 213 **74** 201
 202 **84** 221 **101** 310 **111**
 225 226 317
Ruth (Clarke) **134** 210
Ruth (Driver) **86** 450
Ruth (Dunton) **148** 311
Ruth (Manchester)
 101 310
Ruthie (Walker) **102** 290
Sabrina **101** 95 **109** 271
Sally **75** 303 **104** 47
 125 243
Sally H. **86** 385
Samuel **54** 21-26 **56** 72 278
 58 80 **66** 30 **73** xlvi **74**
 66 **81** 122 131 **109** 307
 116 76 **118** 195 **119** 115
 128 51 60 **133** 69 **135** 45
 144 296 **148** 311
Samuel F. **75** 95
Samuel G. **92** 319
Samuel H. **74** 66
Samuel J. **67** 287 **144** 309
Sarah **54** 24-26 **58** 200 **60**
 95 379-381 383 **61** 88
 388 **62** 87 378 **67** 286 **84**
 96 **85** 150 **86** 134 141 **88**
 43 133 135 **89** 20 **97** 331
 101 95 **105** 256 **112** 59
 143 **125** 175 **127** 89 **128**
 217 **142** 333 **144** 296
Sarah (Brenton) **133** 69
Sarah (Fellows) **86** 140
 141
Sarah (Niles) **85** 150
Sarah (Robinson) **105** 256
Sarah (Snipe) **146** 336
Sarah (Wilson) **144** 293-
 295
Sarah (Witt) **86** 450
Sarah (Woodmansee)
 147 39
Sarah F. **77** 56

POTTER *cont'd*
Sarah H. **64** lxix
Sarah Jennie (Church)
 95 315
Sarah Lilly **73** xxviii xlv
Sarah N. **125** 176
Sarah Wall (Salisbury)
 138 289
Selea (Griffeth) **129** 237
Seth E. **117** 212
Sibyl **54** 25 **56** 45
Silas **69** 335 **74** 169 **75** 19
 20
Silas J. **75** 19 20
Simeon **127** 308
Sophia A. (Carr) **125** 244
Sophia Elizabeth **115** 174
Sprague **128** 58
Stafford **104** 47
Stella Grace (Marsh)
 95 316
Stephen **54** 24 25 **87** 358
 125 244 **127** 5 **128** 54
 128 303 **129** 67
Stephen Nye **59** 29
Susan **69** 275 **81** 154 **86**
 149 **90** 113
Susan (Cole) **86** 149
Susan Haven **95** 316
Susan L. **116** 258
Susanna **54** 26 **67** 286 **69**
 335 **85** 221 **115** 167 **126**
 249 **144** 296
Susanna (Brigham)
 95 315
Susanna Stewart **146** 336
Sylvester **128** 52
Temperance (Weeks)
 134 239
Thankful **54** 25 26 **114** 319
Thetis (Teriel) **116** 187
Thomas **53** 338 **54** 25 **61**
 190 271 **63** 143 **67** 174
 179 286 **75** 19 20 **90** 301
 91 201 **97** 128 **98** 24
 100 278 **101** 95 **105** 214
 109 271 **115** 75 167 **127**
 146 308 **128** 51 52 127
 128 **129** 237 **148** 311
Thomas Benjamin **61** 271
Thomas Webster **77** 183
Tibudah (Hayden) **86** 450
Timothy **54** 25 **87** 325
 131 51 52
Titus **54** 25
V. W. **77** 151
Vesta A. **68** 158
Walter **60** 383 **62** 87
 117 43
Warren B. **62** lviii lix
 78 227
Waterman **60** 77 **70** 232
Will **102** 290
William **54** 20-24 26 **56**
 278 **57** 156 **65** 154 223
 66 308 **67** 263 **73** xlv
 xlvi 213 **81** 122 128 130
 86 390 **92** 272 **98** 24 **99**
 231 **100** 289 335 **101**
 100 310 **102** 235 **109**
 307 **115** 164 **116** 79 160

POTTER *cont'd*
161 164 **125** 109 217
126 25 207 241 **127** 7
305 **128** 54 125 127 293
129 275 **130** 136 **138**
279 285 **142** 187 333
144 231 **146** 336
William A. **73** 213
William Armstrong
138 285 289
William B. **69** 275
William Columbus (Mrs.)
107 134
William E. **88** 330
William H. **135** 53
William I. **116** 259
William J. **73** 213 **82** 271
William W. **85** 225
111 323
William Y. **125** 174
Willis **104** 46 47
Winfield Scott **60** 87
105 53
Winifred Eleanor
(Durham) **95** 315
Winsor **128** 58
Woodbury Hastings
146 336
Zane **117** 43
Zerviah **57** 161 **126** 216
Zuriel **128** 53
POTTERF Casper **98** 370
POTTEY Potty
George **142** 366
Robert **103** 11
POTTHOFF
Mary **129** 189
POTTIFER
William **62** 301
POTTINGER Don **108** 70
James **64** 219
Robert **73** 145
Thomas **84** 438
POTTLE Pottel Pottell
Abigail **88** 247 **111** 23
Abigail (Cane) **111** 23
114 48
Anne **111** 23
Azariah **86** 89
Bemsley **97** 203
Benjamin **73** 70 **135** 127
Christopher **111** 23
114 48
Daniel **105** 287 **111** 23
David **66** 110 **111** 23
115 139
Eleanor (Pickering)
97 203
Elizabeth **66** 103 **74** 94 95
111 23
Frances **125** 288
Hannah **126** 145
Henry **73** 69 74
Jean (Piper) **135** 127
John **102** 16
Joseph **111** 23
Judith P. **67** 282
Lucy (Silvester) **86** 89
Martha (Stockbridge)
135 126
Mary **102** 16 **111** 23

POTTLE *cont'd*
Nicholas **64** 243
Rachel **51** 462
Rebecca **111** 23
Richard **99** 57
S. B. **72** 275
Samuel **73** 74 **111** 23
135 127
Sarah **66** 110
Simon **73** 65 67 77
Thomas **125** 36
William **51** 462 **73** 66 **88**
247 **111** 23
POTTON William **109** 236
Pottor *see* Potter
POTTS Pots Pott
—— **58** 321 **98** 346
— Judge **127** 57
— Mr. **57** 228
___ (Cogan) **111** 169
Alfred (Mrs.) **102** 125
Alice (Croadsdale) **89** 53
Amanda **77** 266
Ann **132** 73
Ann (Rush) **89** 53
Annie E. **117** 295
Catherine Agnes (Fitz
Randolph) **98** 347
Charles **101** 51
Cleland **78** 170
Daniel **89** 53
David **57** 339 **89** 53
Edgar Nelson **77** 260
Edmund **56** 404
Elizabeth **89** 91 **100** 134
101 51 273
F. F. **77** 260
Fanny **98** 295
Florence Henrietta **86** 196
George A. **98** 347
Horace B. **77** 260
James **89** 53 54 **117** 295
Jane **77** 218
Jemima **121** 551
John **77** 218 **89** 335 **111**
198 **133** 265
John J. **77** 260
Joseph **56** 123
Judge **127** 57
Kate **77** 266
Lafayette Brown **78** 170
Laura **77** 266
Louis Maxwell **89** 54
Lucy **77** 260
Margaret (Carter) **89** 53
Margaretta Sherman
136 334
Mary (Fitz Randolph)
98 346
Mary (Miller) **89** 54
Mary Ann **77** 260
Mary Octavia **77** 260
Mary Ophelia **78** 170
Missoni **77** 218
Mitchell Miller **89** 54
Parthena (Mallery)
133 265
Patience **90** 366 **107** 225
Pauline **78** 170
Reuben Claude **89** 54
Richard **123** 256

POTTS *cont'd*
Ruth **100** 134 **101** 273
Ruth (Cutler) **100** 299
Samuel **89** 53
Sarah **101** 271 **125** 241
144 348 354
Sarah (Goonough)
100 296
Sarah (Smith) **127** 57
Sarah (Wessell) **89** 53
Sumner Aiken **77** 260
Thomas **77** 260 **99** 51 **100**
134 296 299 **101** 273
Thomas (Mrs.) **99** 51
Thomas Jefferson **89** 53
Thomas Maxwell **57** 339
58 xlv **64** xxix **84** 179
89 53 81 134 **117** 240
Thomas Pliny **89** 54
Timothy **111** 169 170
Van H. **77** 266
Walter **60** 243
William **66** 37 **80** 88
107 225
William Baker **89** 54
William John **52** 94 101
57 339
William N. **77** 260
Potty *see* Pottey
POTWIN Potwine
— Mr. **52** 416 **60** 203
— Rev. Mr. **72** 32
Abigail **73** 11
Ashel Steele **62** 188
Aurora Hatch **62** 188
David **73** 10 11
Dorothy **62** 188
Dorothy Williams **62** 188
Edward **80** 69
Elizabeth **73** 11
Eunice **73** 10 11
George **62** 188 **73** 10 11
George Seymour **62** 188
Hannah **80** 69
Henry Wolcott **62** 188
Imogene **62** 188
Israel **80** 69
Jane Grey **62** 188
John **73** 10 11
John Stoughton **62** 188
Joseph Root Williams
62 188
Lydia **85** 329
Mary **80** 69
Mary Ann **62** 188
Rachel **73** 10
S. A. **79** 169
Stephen **79** 169 **80** 69
Thomas **79** 162 **80** 69
120 12
William Wheeler **62** 188
POTZER Clarinda
(Hulbert) **126** 182
Mary (Cook) **126** 182
POUCHARD
Catherine **66** 106
Daniel **66** 107
Elizabeth **66** 105
Freeman Richmond
66 107
George **66** 103 105-107

POUCHARD cont'd
James **66** 106
Joanna **66** 106
Joanna C. **66** 111
Mary **66** 106-108
Nancy **66** 109
Nancy Mary **66** 106
Peter **66** 103 105
Robert **66** 106
Sally **66** 107
Sarah **66** 108
POUCHEE Ruth **54** 353
POUCHER J. W. **111** 75
POUGH John **94** 177
POULETT Robert **67** 343
POULL John **66** 62
POULSON Polson
—— **93** 4
Alexander **69** 37
Archer **65** 87
Catherine **69** 37
Emma C. G. **69** 37
George **116** 171
Janet **108** 135
Laurence W. (Mrs.)
113 232
Maud **85** 196
Tessie Iva **117** 130
POULSSON
Emilie **57** 231
POULTENEY
John **142** 231
POULTER Pulter
— Goodman **141** 216
Abiel **141** 222
Abigail **111** 160 **141** 225
Anthony **52** 242
Benoni **141** 220 222
Bertha M. (Arey) **87** 111
Christopher **141** 217
Edmund **83** 319
Edward **141** 215 **145** 110
Eliot **141** 223 224
Elizabeth **58** 129 **66** 180 **77**
272 **111** 160 **141** 215
216 218-220 225 226
Elizabeth (Coolidge?)
141 224 225
Hannah **141** 220-223 225
226
Hannah (Hammond)
141 222
John **66** 180 **111** 160 **141**
215-222 224 385
Jonathan **58** 129 **111** 160
141 220 221 224-227
Joseph **141** 221
Katharine **141** 224
Margaret **52** 242
Margerie **141** 217
Marie **66** 180 **141** 216
Mary **66** 180 **141** 215-218
220 225 226 385 **145** 110
Mary (Pope?) **141** 217-
219 222 224 385
Rachel **66** 180 **131** 33 **141**
220 221 225 227
Rachel (Eliot) **111** 160
141 219
Robert W. **87** 111
Samuel **64** 226

POULTER cont'd
Sarah **141** 222-224
Submit **58** 129 **141** 225
227
Thomas **141** 215
POULTNEY Pulteney
Edward **106** 86
POULTON John **110** 274
POUNAL Mary **125** 292
POUND Pounde Pounds
Pownde
—— **86** 249
Andrew **141** 30
Arthur **90** 306
Betsey **119** 259 **137** 45
Edward **63** 18 235 **81** 321
Elijah **98** 229
Emme **81** 321
Jacob **101** 269
John **81** 321
Laura B. **68** 114
Margaret **69** 68
Rachel (Kinsey) **98** 229
Sarah **86** 78 248 **98** 229
Sarah (Marche) **86** 249
Susanna **64** 257
Thomas **81** 321
William **81** 321
Pouning see Powning
POUNTEIS Anne **54** 342
Jacob **54** 342
POUNTNEY
William **86** 464 **87** 400
POUPARD
Marguerite **68** 27
POUPARDIN —— **107** 276
POUPART Jeanne **94** 167
POURE
Isabel le **95** 124
Walhamet le **95** 124
POUSLAND
Edward **105** 299 300
Edward A. **105** 299 300
Frederic Graham (Mrs.)
84 234 **85** 197 **115** 67
Grace **105** 299
Hannah **105** 299 300
125 293
POUSSIN Gustave
Adolphe **120** 85
Maryann Fellows
(Amory) (Pilkington)
120 85
POVEY —— (Bressey)
112 30
Catherine **95** 169
James **64** 227
John **112** 29 30
Roger **112** 30
William **112** 30
Pow see Powe
POWAHATAN 123 255
132 13
POWDELL Martin **51** 298
POWDERKIRK
Isaac **70** 262
POWDERLY T. V. **53** 134
POWE Pow
— Elder **63** 375
Albert S. **51** 51
Arthur T. **88** 134

POWE cont'd
Jane (Knowles) **88** 134
Mabel E. **51** 51
Robert **100** 338
Thomas **88** 134
POWELL Powel Powhell -
see also Howell
—— **103** 187 **148** 82
— Capt. **77** 108
— Elder **95** 107
— Gen. **74** 286 292
— Mr. **71** 116 **95** 101 102
— Mrs. **65** 63 **71** 48
83 308
____ (Gardner) **140** 237
A. W. **71** 355
Abigail **74** 37 **89** 74 **131**
169 174
Abigail (Bedle) **89** 79
131 173 174
Abigail (Collins) **89** 79
Alice **54** 337 **107** 133
Alvin W. **71** 355
Amanda M. **71** 355
Andrew **52** 251
Angelica Talcott (Devens)
84 211
Angerona (Erickson)
84 211
Angerona Erickson **82**
237 **84** 112 197 211
Ann **56** 112 **65** 237 **73** 227
84 165 255
Ann (Adamson) **84** 211
Ann (Dummer) **84** 165
Anna **89** 24
Anne **70** 151 **76** 309
Benjamin **92** 273 275 278
Betsey **71** 355
Betsey (Bradley) **92** 278
Bradford **70** 151
Bryan Bonnell **98** 75
C. **54** 282
C. Percy **115** 238
Calvin **70** 151 **115** 313
Caroline **134** 43
Caroline Emily
(Hepburn) **106** 312
Carrie V. (Twambley)
120 220
Catherine S. **71** 355
Charles Chester Andrew
103 120
Charles F. **83** 308
Charles Frederic **116** 115
Charles McLane **120** 220
121 147 **122** 147
Charles Thuillier **118** 81
Charlotte **71** 55
Christine C. **141** 151
Cora Leslie **99** 269 **118** 81
David **52** 28 **99** 27 120
Deborah **122** 240
Dorothy **65** 354 **131** 170
174
E. **60** 352
E. S. **71** 355 356
Edmond **112** 92
Edward **52** 251 **139** 322
Edwin **134** 43 44
Eleanor **68** 256

POWELL *cont'd*
Eleazer **52** 414
Elijah **52** 185 **71** 355
Eliza **60** 353
Eliza (Baker) **100** 12
Elizabeth **52** 309 **86** 348
349 **89** 93 **123** 50 **131**
174 207
Elizabeth (Heath) **146** 263
Elizabeth (Munter)
139 322
Elizabeth (Porter) **98** 75
Ellen J. **121** 310 **122** 231
Ellen M. (Ridley / Ripley)
121 147 **122** 147
Ellen Maria Beverly
(Fuller) **118** 81
Ellen May (Williams)
100 12
Emily Higby **98** 75
Esther **133** 234
F. **71** 55
Felix **83** 53
Francis **52** 251 **92** 283
Francis K. **92** 284
Francis Washburn **134** 43
Frank **77** 265
Freelove **103** 311
Garston **73** 266
George **89** 93 **116** 156
117 158 **118** 168
George E. **92** 206
George G. **73** 268
Hannah **81** 130 **99** 27 120
Hannah (Riddell) **111** 278
Henrietta **134** 37
Henrietta (Howells) **134**
42 43
Henrietta Beasley **134** 43
Henry **64** 259
Henry Charles **134** 43
Horatio **70** 151
Hugh **64** 160
Huldah **71** 355
Inez J. **68** 258
Isaac **79** 146 **100** 12
Isaac Newton (Mrs.) **80**
334 **81** 222
Isabel (Clark) **119** 214
Isabella (Ware) **100** 242
J. W. **52** 104
Jacob **111** 283
James **64** 21 107 **91** 332
98 208 **104** 97
Jane **108** 239 **116** 118
Jane Prynn (Maddick)
118 81
Jennet **115** 312 313
Jeremiah **53** 10 **60** 366
119 20 **127** 115 **144** 154
145 66
Jeremy **84** 377
Joan **53** 96
John **52** 414 **63** 18 **65** 247
70 151 **84** 83 152 153
165 255 **89** 24 **91** 332 **92**
278 **99** 118 **110** 167 **134**
43
John T. **60** 47 **116** 118
John Wesley **51** 510
Jonathan **140** 237

POWELL *cont'd*
Joseph **62** 249 **73** 232
134 43
Josephine **115** 320 **134** 43
Josephine Victoria
(Hewitt) **89** 93 **92** 206
Julia C. **71** 355
Julia Eliza (Morhous) **96**
162 **98** 75
Julia M. **75** xxiv
Katharine Julia **98** 126
Keys B. **76** 32 **92** 284
118 196
Leonidas Hudson (Mrs.)
85 197
Lois **52** 309
Lon H. (Mrs.) **84** 173 **100**
61 **106** 239
Louie Gertrude **81** 222
Louisa **134** 43
Lucy **70** 151 **128** 80
Luther **70** 151
Lydia **62** 328 **76** 32
Lydia (Lougee) **118** 196
M. E. **69** 290
Mabel **71** 355
Margaret **70** 115 **131** 174
Margaret Benigna **77** 265
Margaret T. **104** 97
Martha **130** 155 **135** 76
Martha (Montgomery)
112 294
Martin **106** 312
Mary **55** 51 **64** 224 **70** 151
75 270 271 **88** 341 **92**
245 **93** 319 **109** 221 222
110 167 **131** 173 174
Mary (Osborne) **111** 278
Mary (Weeks) **92** 284
Mary Ann **79** 146
Mary Beatrix **54** 197
Mary de Veaux **98** 264
Mary E. **75** 241 **120** 215
Mary Edith (Johnson)
98 126
Mary Eliza **120** 140
Mary Elizabeth **109** 219
Mary Jane **134** 43 44
Mate Gaylord **84** 191
Matthew **145** 538
Maude **109** 73
Michael **63** 280 282 **89** 74
79 **95** 100 **131** 173 174
Minerva A. **71** 355
Moses **123** 22
Nicholas **93** 385
Oliver **100** 223
Olivia (Guiness) **84** 211
P. C. **71** 356
Paulina **71** 355
Penelope **65** 21
Perry Edwards **100** 112
Peter **92** 273
Peter Malaput **118** 81
Philemon **114** 165
Polly **116** 65
Priscilla **66** 198 **133** 320
134 85
Rachel **52** 414
Rebecca **75** 182
Reuben **71** 355 356

POWELL *cont'd*
Richard **52** 251 **62** 321
110 167
Robert **52** 251 **64** 261 **76**
309 **77** 76 **146** 263
Robert William **54** 197
Robonnia **134** 171
Rowland **70** 151
Sally **115** 312 **133** 119
Sally (Mead) **115** 313
Samuel **53** 459 **71** 355
111 283
Samuel D. **115** 320
Samuel Willing Hare
98 126
Sarah **53** 10 **65** 122 **100** 303
114 181 **131** 170 173
174 **133** 320 **134** 85 **138**
14
Sarah (Bromfield) **145** 66
Sarah (Gustin) **114** 181
Sarah (Mead) **115** 313
Sarah Peters **62** 366
Snelling **101** 164
Stella M. **60** 47
Stephen Alonzo **96** 158
98 75
Stephen Alonzo (Mrs.)
75 xxiv 65 **95** 297 **96**
158 162 **98** 75
Stephen Henry **98** 75
Sue Louise **78** 163
Sumner Chilton **106** 126
107 67 129 **113** 76 **117**
238 **118** 322 **128** 238
Susan **53** 20 **87** 229 236
Susan Maria **79** 146
Susanna Snelling
101 164
Terciah **59** 222 **61** 271
Thomas **52** 251 **64** 16 225
66 198 **71** 124 **81** 130
96 357 **110** 167 **133** 320
134 37 85 **140** 237 **143**
102
Thomas Howells **134** 43
Thomas Joseph **134** 37
42 43
Trueman **52** 185 309
Vavasor **54** 43
Violet **97** 78 154
W. C. **109** 295
Wallace D. **100** 12
Walter **111** 278
William **51** 417 **62** 328
73 145 **76** 286 **78** 74 **84**
211 **93** 385 **100** 242 **104**
97 **105** 71 **131** 207 **134**
29 42 43 **140** 235 237
145 125 126
William C. **71** 356
William Devens **84** 211
William Dummer **56** 112
William E. **71** 356
William H. **107** 90 **116** 115
William Henry **64** 63 69
134 43
William Hopton **54** 197
William Howells **134** 43
William John **84** 211
William L. **92** 284

POWELL *cont'd*
William N. **71** 356
William Ogden **70** 191
William P. **86** 241
William S. **117** 158 **124**
  103 **145** 143
Willis McDonald **98** 75
POWERS —— **52** 474 **54**
  336 **99** 121 **101** 260 **117**
  15 17 **119** 137 **147** 127
— Mrs. **83** 308 **101** 247
  270
Aaron **123** 286
Aaron R. **103** 46
Abigail **61** 378 **72** 283
  123 297 **134** 336
Abigail (Smith) **123** 297
Abigail S. **123** 200
Abijah **147** 263 265
Ada A. **85** 341
Addison **111** 137
Adeline **123** 294
Agnes Theresa (Mehand)
  123 234
Alexander **131** 77
Alfred **123** 284 285 289-
  292 295 297 298
Alfred S. **123** 298
Alice **54** 336
Alice E. **84** 120
Allen A. **123** 298
Almira **75** 20 **123** 284 285
  292
Almira (Russell) **123** 292
Almond M. **123** 298
Amos **126** 307
Amos H. **123** 280
Amy **88** 138
Andrew **65** 239
Ann **54** 223 **88** 138 **99** 121
Ann (Smith) **100** 240
Ann Maria **127** 278
Anna **61** 250 **77** 33
Anne **52** 250 251
Anny **127** 225
Anthony **52** 250
Arma **103** 81
Arrabel (Wheeler)
  123 281
Arthur **72** 28
Arthur J. **93** 240
Asa **123** 280-286 289-291
  293 295 297 298
Aurilla **141** 46
Avis **123** 298
Avis (Cooley) **123** 298
Azubah **123** 281 287-289
Azubah (Wheeler)
  123 281
Battercy **78** 307
Benjamin M. **118** 247
Benjamin N. **95** 96
Bethiah **58** 83 **59** 139
  123 270
Betsey **57** 192 **79** 79 **96** 127
  123 289 290 292
Betsey (Cory) **148** 160
Betsey (Curtis) **111** 137
Betty **66** 225
Blanche **101** 124
Bridget **68** 328

POWERS *cont'd*
Calvin **59** 313
Cameron **114** 64
Carrie A. **123** 294
Carrie L. **110** 54
Catherine **80** 27
Charles **123** 293 294 **147**
  124 128
Charles D. **123** 291
Charles E. **123** 294
Charles S. **123** 294
Charlotte **78** 180 **134** 336
Charlotte (Green) **99** 299
Chester **123** 284 289-292
  294 295
Christina **107** 302
Christopher **78** 310
Clarissa Bartlett **81** 255
Content **80** 26
David **91** 332 **98** 105 **100**
  298 301 **123** 280-282
Deborah **72** 28
Deborah (Ball) **139** 109
Delia Agnes **120** 239
Diana (Nash) **123** 288
Edith Lorraine **72** xx
Edmund **68** 78 **134** 336
Edward **55** 402 **61** 287 **88**
  279 **115** 133 **120** 14 **140**
  238 **142** 109
Edward R. **79** 49
Eleanor **100** 240
Eleanor (Power) **100** 240
Elijah **64** 312
Eliza **147** 128
Elizabeth **66** 294 **73** 273 **78**
  416 **79** 79 **80** 171 **83** 477
  99 283 **102** 29 **120** 14
  123 292 295 296 **127**
  278
Elizabeth (Gates) **121** 260
Elizabeth (Hinds) **123** 286
Elizabeth (Kidder)
  141 221
Elizabeth (Pattee) **147** 185
Elizabeth (Proctor) **103** 46
Elizabeth (Robbins)
  123 280
Elizabeth (Warner)
  123 295
Elizabeth R. **123** 294
Elizabeth / Betty (Cooley)
  147 128
Emeline **123** 298
Emily (Owen) **89** 399
Emily W. **123** 297
Emmaette A. (Smart)
  121 180
Enoch **100** 178
Ephraim **51** 495 **81** 255
  141 221
Esther **57** 192 **93** 390
  112 155
Eunice **57** 205 **64** 153
Eveline **123** 100
Fannie **93** 353
Frances **100** 144
Frances (Eager) **123** 288
Frances (Patterson)
  110 54
Francis **75** 137 **123** 298

POWERS *cont'd*
Frank C. **110** 54
Franklin E. **147** 128
Franklin R. **123** 293 294
Frederick **123** 298
Frederick W. **110** 54
George **123** 296 297
George H. **75** 20
George P. (Mrs.) **102** 285
George Whitefield **64** 330
Gertrude Bradford **110** 54
Gideon **57** 284 **67** 273
  141 221
Guy **131** 77
H. Hale **103** 120
Hale **105** 210
Hannah **54** 223 **57** 303 **59**
  67 **61** 250 **67** 273 **72** 21
  283 **80** 27 **109** 226 **136**
  79 362 **141** 221
Hannah (Pratt) **129** 316
  136 79
Harriet **69** 166 **78** 190
  120 14 **123** 290 292 293
  295 **125** 223
Harriet (Sloan) **123** 292
Harriet M. (Plant) **85** 341
Harriet Newall **95** 327
Harrison Gray Otis **123**
  292 295 924
Hattie (Noyes) **131** 77
Helen Greenwood
  67 xxxv
Henrietta **75** 20
Henry **61** 250 **123** 291
  293 296 297
Henry J. **121** 180
Hiram **61** 215
Hope **80** 171 172 **142** 13
Hopestill **74** 134
Huldah (Daws) **147** 185
Ichabod **126** 255 **128** 19
  134 336
Ida A. **85** 341
Ira **75** 20
Ira F. **128** 94
Isaac **97** 395 **140** 296 299
  141 221 224
Isabel **110** 54
Isabel (Wheeler) **123** 281
J. L. **123** 295
Jacob **78** 69 **80** 27
James **69** 211 **76** 267
James A. **79** 45
James L. **123** 290-293 295
James M. **123** 295
James Madison **106** 126
Jane **73** 100 **74** 134 **119** 229
Jane (Gaines) **85** 41
Jefferson **123** 293
Jennettea (Hoar) **134** 117
Jerahmeel **55** 271 **121** 47
Jeremiah **123** 206 **147** 128
Jerusha **123** 282
Jesse **123** 280 282
Jessie C. **123** 294
Jester **123** 294
Joanna A. **88** 330
Johanna (Gay) **93** 390
John **54** 97 223 **55** 434 **77**
  33 **78** 401 **79** 55 **88** 138

POWERS *cont'd*
95 327 99 283 123 280
281 284 287-291 295 127
278 135 28 140 300 147
185
John L. 79 80
John W. (Mrs.) 112 165
324
Jonas 144 215
Jonathan 54 223 57 303 62
38 64 42 211 105 211
141 221
Joseph 63 371 134 336
Joshua 79 79
Josiah 123 281
Julia 61 287 123 296
Julia Maria (Wolcott)
123 297
Kate 128 97
Laura 117 205
Lee L. 65 lv
Lettie E. 75 21
Leveret Jerahmeel 57 205
Levi 64 153
Levina 123 284 285 294
295
Lilian D. 60 323 61 108
215
Linnie Elizabeth 104 146
Lois 55 402 69 211 123
289-291 297
Lois (Felton) 123 289
Loren R. 85 341
Lottie 103 173
Louetta H. 115 160
Louis 123 289 290
Louisa 91 55
Luce 141 221
Lucinda 123 282
Lucius 147 128
Lucy 54 223 64 211 126
56 143
Lucy G. 96 135
Lucy J. (Jones) 123 295
Luke 66 146 221 223 225
294 296
Luther 80 27
Lydia 53 437 59 139
134 336
Lydia (Rice) 88 279
Lydia Hermione 99 255
Lyman 123 298
Marcia 147 128
Margaret 100 136 301
112 309 127 278
Margaret (Rhodes)
100 301
Margaret M. 125 38
Mariah 123 281
Martha 88 138 123 296
129 316 136 79 142 291
Martha (Glazier) 123 281
Martha (Hilton) 131 77
Martha A. 123 296
Martha Ann (Graves)
123 297
Martha M. 73 188
Mary 51 447 62 360 74 170
78 361 412 80 27 81 161
89 289 91 263 100 303
109 183 123 234 281

POWERS *cont'd*
282 285 287-290 126 215
140 131 141 221 142
334
Mary (Bauke) 123 280
Mary (Carrain) 100 304
Mary (Linnehan) 100 298
Mary (Poulter) (Winship)
141 220
Mary (Wheeler) 123 290
Mary Ann 79 20 80 88 138
Mary Levinah 92 293
Mary M. 79 80
Mary S. 119 203
Matthew 127 278
Mehitable 79 79
Mercy 80 28 171 94 43
Meriam (Wheeler)
123 283
Milton 123 288
Minnie T. (Jennings)
110 54
Miriam 61 341
Molly 66 296
Moriah 83 396
Morris 101 272
Nahum 123 281
Nancy 63 371 86 156
Nancy (Sawyer) 126 307
Nancy Jane (Burns)
128 94
Nancy M. (Fish) 123 294
Nathaniel 57 192
Nellie R. 123 294
Nicholas 53 437 58 83 59
139 65 221 67 137 74
134 80 171 85 41 98 287
99 121 100 240 127 228
134 336
Noah 123 288
O. B. 69 166
Obed 54 cxiv
Olive 81 255
Orrin S. 73 188
Patrick 100 136
Patrick Henry (Mrs.)
107 134
Permelia 123 288
Peter 62 276 74 170 75 20
116 111 134 117 139
101
Peter T. 79 19 20
Phebe 98 287 123 287
Phebe (Haskins) (Briggs)
123 285-287
Polly 64 153 123 291
Prescot 105 207
Proctor 123 284 289-293
295 296 298
Prudence 75 137
R. F. 77 151
Rachel 80 27 91 82
Rebecca 64 42 87 122 90
345 123 281 289 291-293
296
Rebecca (Reed) 111 246
123 293
Rebecca (Wheeler)
123 281
Rebecca D. 123 297

POWERS *cont'd*
Rebecca Dean (Willard)
123 296 297
Resina 123 284 285
Resinah (Wheeler)
123 282
Reuben 123 280-283 285
286 289 293-295 297 298
Rhoda C. 77 151
Richard 66 221
Robert 80 26 117 205 123
280 281 284 285 288 289
291 292
Robert Sanders 66 223
Rodney 123 296
Rodney M. 123 298
Roswell 123 284 289-292
297 298
S. 91 332
S. E. 93 240
Sally 74 170 260 75 20 79
79 127 298
Samuel 123 289 291 292
295-298 128 126 134
336
Samuel E. 123 298
Samuel Leland 80 114
82 134
Sarah 57 284 64 312 66 146
221 223 225 294 296 77
316 101 272 123 294
297 127 298
Sarah (Beeks) 101 260
Sarah (Eveleth) 135 28
Sarah (Lamb) 123 294
Sarah (Leonard) 110 54
Sarah C. 75 20
Sarah E. (Baker) 123 295
Sarah W. 123 296
Sibyl 114 276
Silence 147 128
Silence (Rogers) 147 124
128
Sophronia A. (Smith)
123 298
Stephen 56 397 112 309
123 280-282 285-288
293
Sula 54 cxiv
Susan 86 19
Susan (Barker) 134 336
Susan M. 123 298 133 320
Susanna 64 211 100 136
Susanna (Collins)
(Taylor) 127 278
Sylvester 126 255 128 19
T. L. 123 298
Tamison 137 29
Theodore 123 298
Theodore Lyman 123 298
Theresa 68 328
Thomas 59 194 72 21 73
220 276 94 42 100 240
304 101 247 117 11 16
123 286 287 293 129
316 134 336 136 79 140
238 299
Thomas (Mrs.) 94 42
Thomas J. 111 246 123 287
289 293 294

POWERS *cont'd*
 Thomas Jefferson **123**
  287 289 293 294
 Titus **125** 44
 Trial (Shepard) **120** 312
  123 280 **141** 221 **147** 68
 Tryphena **123** 285 **141** 221
 Uranah **123** 283
 Ursula **123** 294
 W. H. **93** 240
 Walter **51** 447 **59** 313 **70**
  262 **99** 299 **118** 97 194
  120 312 **123** 234 280-
  282 285 286 289 293-295
  297 298 **134** 336 **141**
  221
 Wealthy **126** 255 **128** 19
 Webster **148** 160
 Wilbur H. **89** 399
 William **61** 350 **64** 111
  65 118 **72** 283 **76** 53
  112 809 **120** 312 **121**
  260 **123** 280-282 285 286
  289 293-295 297 298 **125**
  44 **139** 109 141 337
 William H. **110** 54
 William L. **123** 291
 William LaForest **123** 295
 William T. **110** 51
 Williams **125** 29
 Wright **123** 291 296 297
 Zacharias **54** 337
POWERSCOURT
 — Lord **103** 288
Powhatan *see* Powahatan
Powhell *see* Powell
POWICK Powicke
 —— **106** 275
 Frederick Maurice **106** 57
  119 101
POWICKE
 F. Maurice **148** 255
Powis *see* Powys
POWLAND
 Anstice **102** 190
 James **102** 190
POWLESS Purcell R. (Mrs.)
  86 198
POWLETT
 — Lady **52** 262
 Nassau (Lord) **105** 187
  106 76
 Richard **52** 262
 William **118** 251
POWLEY —— **108** 203
 Edward B. **119** 99
POWNALL Pownal Pownell
 — Gov. **104** 245 **114** 298
  301 **117** 251
 Ann **86** 367
 Esther **82** 282 297
 Hannah **113** 240
 John **77** 313 **144** 220 221
 Mary (Brown) **140** 46
 Sylvanus **82** 282 297
 T. **104** 79
 Thomas **52** 221 **56** 48 **57**
  237 347 **58** 141 142 **60**
  110 **63** 189 191 **73** 149
  84 154 **90** 85 **97** 5 **107**
  45 **116** 8 **129** 104 213

POWNALL *cont'd*
  130 25 30 31 34 105 106
  131 269 273 **132** 33 124
  136 280 281 290
Pownde *see* Pound
Pownell *see* Pownall
POWNEY
 Henry **67** 249 251
 Joan **67** 256 **95** 324
 Richard **67** 249 256
 William **67** 250 251
POWNING Pouning
 Daniel **51** 65
 Henry **102** 178 **106** 19
  111 14
 Kimball Colby (Mrs.)
  119 79 **122** 208 **123** 221
  124 265 **125** 212
POWNSETT Jane **83** 76
 William **83** 76
POWTER
 Elizabeth **113** 296
POWYS Powis
 Jonas de **101** 5
 Marian **94** 145
 Roger de **101** 5
POYAS Elizabeth Ann
  114 191
POYEN DE ST. SAUVEUR
 Joseph Rochemont de
  108 35
POYEN Elizabeth
 Josephine de **91** 84
 Joseph Rochemont de
  91 85
POYNGES Edward **102** 248
POYNINGS
 Agnes **148** 255
 John **109** 31
 Michael **148** 255
POYNTELL William **65** 30
Poynter *see* Pointer
POYNTON Hannah **96** 57
 Judith **60** 290
 William **65** 234
Poyntz *see* Pointz
POYSER Thomas **111** 91
 Trothe (Cogan) **111** 91
POYTE Barbara **55** 335
 John **55** 335
POYTHER Martha **99** 112
POYTON James **64** 216
PRAAL Antje (Staats)
  113 279
 Arent **113** 279
 Elizabeth **113** 279
PRACE John **100** 261
PRADOX Mary **125** 216
PRAED W. M. **56** 68
PRAGER Adolph **76** 20
 Catherine **110** 322
 Elizabeth **76** 20
PRAHL Elise Marie
  (Ellebye) **113** 307
 Jessie (Moeser) (Farley)
  113 308
 Karen **113** 308
 Marthe (Weissgreber)
  113 308
 Samuel Christian **113** 307
 Theodore **86** 198 **113** 232

PRAHL *cont'd*
  307
PRAKLE
 Hannah **51** 269 271
 Vincent **51** 269 271
PRALL Edwin Theodore
  104 69
 Helen Ames **78** 206
 Henrietta **73** xlviii **83** 487
  95 76
 Rachel Ware (Thomson)
  104 69
 William **104** 69
 William (Mrs.) **77** 322 **78**
  206 **104** 67-69 149
PRAN Betsey **59** 210 **60** 265
PRANG
 Jonas Louis **82** 494
 Louis **63** 394 **82** 494
 Louis (Mrs.) **75** x xxiv
 Mary Amelia **82** 126 245
  493 494
 Mary Dana **75** xxiv
 Rosa **82** 494
 Rosina **82** 494
PRANKER Mary **59** 377
PRAR Jeru **60** 313
Prat *see* Pratt
PRATHER
 Benjamin **73** 141 231
 Derry **73** 231
 Eleanor **73** 273
 Emily **97** 397
 James **73** 152
 Joseph **73** 140
 Josiah **73** 230
 Malinda **83** 68
 Margaret **73** 265
 Mary **85** 197
 Massey **73** 141
 Miranda **73** 275
 Rachel **73** 262
 Rebecca **73** 230
 Ruth **73** 231
 Thomas **73** 272
 William **73** 231
 Zachariah **73** 135
PRATT Prat
 —— **65** 85 361 382 **128**
  238 **129** 316
 — Dr. **51** 169 **97** 395
 — Mr. **57** 228 229 **62** 18
  80 126
 — Mrs. **70** 145
 — Rev. Mr. **124** 148
 — Sgt. **121** 198
 — Widow **70** 216
 ____ (Beamont) **126** 254
 ____ (Davis) **123** 184
 ____ (Eaton) **140** 138
 ____ (Williams) **140** 263
 A. **91** 332
 Aaron **126** 215 **129** 377
 Aaron G. **114** 66
 Abbie **110** 118
 Abbie Anna **69** 309 **99** 58
 Abial **72** 201 **111** 113
 Abigail **53** 34 228 **58** 87
  385 **63** 251 **65** 7 **66** 315
  316 **79** 153 179 **84** 411
  96 363 **109** 37 **116** 20

PRATT *cont'd*

202 **134** 331
Abigail (Bancroft)
(Hartshorn) **94** 223
Abigail (Shepard)
137 283
Abigail (Stowers) **93** 189
Abigail (Wilcott) **111** 226
Abigail Cook **65** 8
Abigail Fenno **78** 124
Abigail H. **55** xci
Abigail S. **81** 51
Abijah **65** 42
Abner **89** 94 **90** 298 **118** 20
Abraham **78** 136 **97** 25
131 207 **143** 35-37
Abram **143** 36
Adoniram **66** 316
Agnes **76** 123 127 **78** 206
94 338 **110** 73
Albertina **89** 37
Alexander **105** 11
Alexis **65** lxiv
Alfred Stuart **87** 174
Alice **94** 268
Alice Doyle Sherring
110 67
Alice Ellerton **55** xcii
Almira **116** 58
Alonzo Rufus **69** 309
Alpheus **116** 79 80 **135** 76
Amanda (Hinds) **90** 107
Amarilla **72** 98
Amasa **64** 211 **127** 308
Amelia Isabel (Steel)
86 94
Amos **70** 263 **83** 472
Amy **71** 18 **120** 42
Andrew **88** 340
Angelina (Burt) **92** 195
Ann **51** 177 **55** 222 **89** 60
111 226
Ann (Bolton) **88** 373
Anna **53** 108 **56** 38 **57** 26
73 7 **76** 224 **98** 359 **116**
79 **120** 41
Anna (Carver) (Richards)
88 217 218 **119** 14 24 25
94 **142** 271
Anna (Ford) **120** 42
Anna Laura Mason **98** 96
Anna Maria Bailey **69** 309
Anna Sephira **116** 80
Anne **54** lxxxiii **70** liv
83 201
Anne Elizabeth **70** 200
Anne Maria **124** 28
Anne Weeks (Thayer)
83 472
Annes **122** 133
Annie Currier **60** xxxviii
Annie Louise (Martin)
133 322
Annie Weston **53** 355
Annis **98** 359 **113** 256
122 58 133
Ansel **53** 395
Arazina **85** 170
Arthur W. **96** 332
Asa **56** 146 **57** 254 **66** 316
111 40 41 117 **116** 79

PRATT *cont'd*

126 204 **133** 123 **145**
350
Asa T. **82** 21
Asaph **147** 365
Aurelia Ann **96** 77 78
Azubah **62** 368
B. H. **91** 332
Barnabas **116** 79
Bathsheba **55** 112 **136** 25
137 181
Beatrice **76** 224
Bela **58** 59
Bela Lyon **63** 110 **89** 249
Bela Lyon (Mrs.) **85** 197
Bellona **89** 94 **90** 298
Benajah **88** 259 262 263
Benannuel **55** 393 **56** 145
57 253
Benjamin **51** 192 **53** 228
58 59 **62** 199 **63** 276 **82**
21 **84** 147 **88** 264 **92** 58
98 96 **99** 72 73 **107** 313
110 309 **136** 25 117 **142**
271 **147** 62 365 366
Benjamin A. **145** 358
Benjamin C. **86** 124
Bethania P. **126** 204
Bethiah **111** 40 117 **126** 262
127 64 **136** 25 117 118
Bethiah (Flood) **133** 123
Bethiah (Keith) **136** 25
Bethiah (Tower) **129** 377
Betsey **56** 355 **64** 147 **68**
310 319 **75** 103 **78** 136
83 162 **100** 278 **111** 40
117
Betty (Pearce) **91** 373
Beulah **81** 88 89
C. **76** 53
Caleb **78** 68 **81** 88 **109** 68
69 **125** 222 **132** 26 327
Caleb S. **90** 105
Calvin **72** 275
Calvin William Edwin
82 169 170
Caroline **83** 388 **109** 68
Caroline Pamelia **54** 151
Carrie Maria **54** 151
Cassius Montgomery
Clay **86** 300
Catherine **76** 92 **90** 43
Catherine (Seaver) **88** 279
Catherine M. **120** 42
Celia **89** 275
Celia Ann **89** 275
Chandler Mason **89** 322
Charity **55** 259 **57** 24 58
240 **98** 356
Charles **76** 53 **77** 146 **85**
114 **96** 298 **147** 364-366
Charles E. **97** 201 202
Charles Edward **97** 202
Charles H. **51** 364 **52** 99
Charles Harmon **65** 8
Charles M. **71** 14
Charles Mayo **99** 73
Charles S. **54** 151
Charles Thayer **82** 125 237
83 238 248 472
Charlie E. **81** 283

PRATT *cont'd*

Charlotte **89** 352 **93** 195
Chester Mayo **67** xxxiv
90 127 **99** 68 72 73 152
Chloe (Hawes) **134** 331
Chloe (Richards) **136** 25
Clara Sophia **66** 276
Clarence E. **81** 283
Clarissa **64** 212 **116** 212
Clarissa A. **75** 103
Cora Louise (Aulls)
114 66
Cornelia **79** 153
Cornelia Bailey **88** 85
Cynthia **61** 343 **92** 375
147 51
Cynthia Frances **122** 53
Cyrus **53** 34 **56** 33 148 **57**
255 **88** 281
Cyrus M. **64** 155 **66** 276
D. S. **54** 151
Daniel **54** 406 **55** 171 **56**
265 269 **57** 23 24 26 28
30 **60** 42 **61** 354 **76** 53
77 315 **85** 65 **89** 257 **97**
127 **98** 356 **109** 68 214
111 226 **122** 50 **134** 331
Daniel Ford **92** 195
Daniel Lincoln **120** 42
Daniel Miles **86** 94
Daniel T. **69** 309
Daniel Taber **69** 269
97 202
David **55** 13 **58** 120 **60** 39
61 43 **67** 32 **68** 319 320
76 266 **77** 315 **79** 179
83 472 **85** 170 **87** 228
236 **109** 151 **111** 41 **125**
293 **142** 271 **145** 358
David Brainerd **98** 359
David Upham **83** 472
David Wolcott **59** 211
Deborah **55** 260 **56** 33 269
57 23 24 **58** 59 87 **77**
280 **120** 47
Deborah (Lazell) **88** 264
Deborah Isabel (Nelson)
95 166
Dexter **64** 102
Dolly **56** 258
Dolphus **78** 127
Dorcas **60** 392
Dorcas (Rowan) **88** 276
Dorothy **59** 329 419
145 168
Dorray **77** 312
E. **116** 212
Eben **57** 206 **63** 273
Ebenezer **55** 259 **56** 146 **57**
24 254 **58** 240 **63** 246 **69**
221-224 294 295 297 298
300-304 306 307 **70** 9 13
14 138 143 **72** 201 **78**
418 **92** 49 **111** 113 117
124 27 28 **132** 40 **145**
358
Ebenezer (Mrs.) **69** 222
Edgar Oliver **82** 273
Edith Josephine **94** 138
Edmund **86** 300
Edmund R. **54** 151

PRATT *cont'd*
Edward **69** 175 221 301
303 **90** 32 **94** 223 **98** 356
359
Edward Ellerton **55** xlii
xci xcii
Edward H. C. **91** 332
Edward L. **97** 202
Edward Leander **78** 332
79 203
Edward Little **69** 269
97 202
Egbert **128** 180
Eleanor **73** 139
Eleanor (Trevalley)
126 205
Eleanor Maria **65** 8
Eleazer **82** 21 **119** 273
120 120
Eleazer F. **51** 364 **78** 421
Eleazer Franklin **52** 96
99 101 **122** 50
Electa (Tyler) **128** 180
Electa M. **82** 100 101
Eliab **89** 352
Elias **96** 363
Elijah **55** 263 **56** 148 **66** 316
Elisha **98** 359 **118** 166
Elisha B. **88** 340
Elisha L. **88** 127
Elisha P. **74** 151 **75** 20
Elisha S. **55** 109
Eliza **72** 103 **76** 268 **78** 307
89 94
Eliza (Perry) **116** 203
Eliza A. (Ford) **137** 51
Eliza Ann **77** 175
Eliza B. **125** 243
Eliza Brackett **92** 254
Eliza Ellen **122** 53
Eliza M. **58** 239
Eliza Maria **78** 3
Eliza Wing **69** 269 **97** 202
Elizabeth **51** 299 304 305
54 222 **56** 37 142 270 **57**
23 397 **58** 120 **60** 246 **65**
7 **75** 20 143 **78** 307 **80**
318 324 **81** 85 **85** 170 **89**
15 **91** 182 **92** 53 58 261
93 183 **94** 328 **96** 363
108 223 245 **111** 41 293
113 133 223 **116** 19 **121**
244 **122** 52 53 **124** 28
126 37 65 **132** 270 **136**
311 **142** 254
Elizabeth (Bancroft)
96 137
Elizabeth (Bate) **110** 309
Elizabeth (Collins)
136 271
Elizabeth (Edmonds)
132 39
Elizabeth (Ellis) **122** 53
Elizabeth (Fracker) **124** 28
Elizabeth (Gurney) **120** 47
Elizabeth (Perry) **116** 203
Elizabeth (Pratt) **124** 28
Elizabeth Ann **116** 115
Elizabeth Brown **65** 8
Elizabeth G. (Adams)
88 335

PRATT *cont'd*
Elizabeth Harriet **76** 92
Elizabeth J. **98** 207
Elizabeth Jane **98** 207
Elizabeth Nelson **95** 165
166
Elizabeth R. **90** 111
Elizabeth T. **86** 85
Ella **106** 311
Ellen **81** 283
Ellen Augusta **87** 289
Ellen Louise Post **86** 54
Emeline A. **120** 42
Emerett O. **96** 126
Emily **56** 171 **79** 202 **86**
108 204 **100** 244 245
Emily Matilda **65** 8
Emma (Pullen) **128** 94
Emmons **106** 311
Enoch **51** 98 **66** 103 **123**
123 159 **126** 111
Ephraim **55** 263 **56** 148
57 258 **60** 363 **65** 357
359 366 **81** 88 **90** 111
144 217
Ephraim R. **88** 335
Esther **57** 161 **58** 240 **60**
167 **72** 98 **75** 306 308 **89**
19 224
Esther (Bancroft) **95** 110
Esther Victoria (Cole)
86 300
Eunice **51** 178 **57** 206 **76**
86 **100** 329
Everett **95** 344
Experience **119** 22 **126** 213
Ezra **90** 88
Florence Amy (Lane)
124 192
Florence Livingston **84**
191 232
Floyd **92** 48
Forbes **64** 212
Frances Louise **124** 191
Francis **105** 14
Francis G. **119** 14
Francis N. **95** 377
Francis S. **52** 99
Frank **95** 377
Frank W. **73** xxx
Franklin **54** 91 **56** 417
76 92
Franklin Nathan **85** 197
Franklin S. **51** 364
Frederick B. **85** 114
Frederick H. **63** xlvi
Frederick S. **96** 30
Frederick Theodore
87 174
Frederick Wolsey **97** 121
George **55** xci **64** 111 **86**
54 **89** 249 **91** 332 **141**
242 **144** 224 **145** 358
George A. **133** 322
George C. **123** 92 306
George N. **124** 191
George Nathaniel
124 192
George R. **81** 283
George W. **123** 304

PRATT *cont'd*
George Woodman **73**
319 **74** xxx
Georgianna (Folie)
97 201
Georgianna Folie **97** 203
Gertrude **89** 249
Gill **59** 194
Grace **144** 142
Gratia (Briggs) **126** 124
H. H. **128** 267
Hannah **51** 388 **53** 87 402
55 398 **56** 32 **57** 24-26
146 206 **58** 59 346 **59** 95
328 **60** 363 **78** 411 417
79 47 **81** 88 **88** 276 **89**
246 257 **93** 67 **96** 364
111 113 **113** 135 **119**
123 125 74 **129** 165 316
136 79 **137** 283 **142** 271
Hannah (Chase) **88** 127
Hannah (Felton) **136** 79
Hannah (Hill) **125** 292
Hannah (Jones) **113** 135
Hannah (Whitcomb)
129 165
Hannah A. **89** 247
Hannah A. (Brown)
89 247
Hannah Sprague **82** 21
Hannah Sweet **124** 28
Hannah T. **69** 316 **97** 201
Hannah Taber **97** 202 203
Harden De Valson (Mrs.)
77 237 **78** 206
Harold **86** 300
Harold Gleason **83** 472
Harriet **65** 8 **96** 332
Harriet (Bancroft) **96** 332
Harriet (Wilkinson)
86 94
Harriet Edna **54** 151
Harriet M. **89** 244
Harry **79** 402
Harvey **120** 42
Harvey B. **120** 42
Harvey Hunter **74** xxx
84 354 **133** 94
Harvey W. **130** 315
Helen **69** 329
Helen (Lugarda) **89** 249
Helen Amelia **93** 188 189
Helen Choate **55** xcii
Helen Folsom **96** 298
Helen Louisa **82** 273
Helen Lugarda **89** 249
Henrietta Hamblin
92 195
Henry **54** 345 **56** 265 **57**
24-26 28 **60** lxxiii **78**
147 **113** 229 **126** 277
Henry Leprellet **77** 185
Hepzibah **55** 266 **92** 266
147 5
Hepzibah (Bancroft)
(Cook) **94** 314
Hepzibah (Cook) **91** 266
Honor **136** 41
Horatio N. **120** 42
Huldah **88** 225 **89** 44
Huldah (Ford) **120** 42 47

PRATT *cont'd*
Humphrey **65** 221 **96** 364 **104** 193
I. **91** 332
Ichabod **86** 295
Ira **91** 332
Isaac **105** 76 **109** 213 **113** 33 40
Isaac Cary **69** 309
Isaac Reed **81** 342
Isabel (Curry) **113** 229
Isabella **140** 173
Isabella Sprague **82** 21
Issachar **57** 145
J. C.G. (Mrs.) **88** 395
J. Lockwood (Mrs.) **106** 50
Jabez **53** 354 **58** 89
Jackson **98** 228
Jacob **65** 365 **66** 315 316 **122** 207
Jaenette M. **116** 212
James **56** 408 **58** 239 **71** 132 211 **78** 417 **79** 158 **100** 329 **111** 40 117 **125** 222 **143** 36
James A. **100** 329
James Albert **100** 329
James Franklin **76** 92
James Maxey **86** 198
James S. **91** 332
James T. **79** 153
James Timothy **65** 8
James W. **78** 124
Jane **85** 156 **126** 67 **131** 207
Jane (Charter) **143** 36
Jane E. **76** 53
Jane Moody **69** 269 **97** 202
Jane R. **78** 356
Jared **60** 392
Jarvis **70** 262
Jean Charlotte **102** 124
Jedediah **88** 239 249 **98** 251 **127** 308
Jemima **55** 261 **56** 143 147 268 **57** 254 255 **62** 175 238
Jennet **98** 356
Jennie **97** 201 202
Jennie Almira May **82** 169
Jeremiah **56** 38 **57** 24 259 397 **63** 94 **74** 150 **75** 20 103 **88** 373 **98** 356
Jerusha **57** 265 **85** 170 **115** 127 **146** 371
Jesse **65** 41 42 **66** 316 **89** 235
Joan **101** 242 **110** 309
Joanna **92** 53
Job **104** 104
Joel **113** 142
John **53** 87 224 401 **54** 334 458 459 **56** 69 **57** 206 **58** 346 59 387 **61** 244 358 **62** 168 **63** 225 257 **65** 7 221 **66** 332 **68** 310 **69** 124 **76** 224 **78** 310 79 162 401 **80** 318 320 324 **86** 416 **91** 266 **92** 53 250 254 261 **94** 268 314 **96**

PRATT *cont'd*
363 364 **97** 25 **100** 17 **107** 66 **109** 68 **113** 223 **115** 9 **122** 50 52 53 320 **123** 160 **124** 28 **125** 74 171 175 215 **127** 311 **128** 98 **129** 377 **132** 41 **136** 25 117 **140** 261 **141** 242
John A. **65** 1 **88** 85 **90** 370
John Cooper **65** 8
John F. **143** 17
John Frank **53** 354 355 **54** 131
John Sherring **110** 67
John Taber **69** 269 309 **97** 202
John Teele (Mrs.) **77** 323 **78** 206 **88** 170
John Wilks **73** 230
Jonah **111** 41
Jonathan **56** 1 266 268 **57** 252 324 **58** 87-89 **62** 352 **63** 323 **69** 212 **70** 10 20 139 **77** 280 **84** 409 **88** 27 **93** 68 **108** 223 **111** 289 293 **129** 165 **142** 271
Joseph **55** 82 222 **77** 314 **88** 218 259 279 **91** 332 **92** 53 58 60 **100** 278 **110** 309 **113** 135 **119** 22-25 94 **124** 28 **126** 141 **129** 316 **136** 26 79 **142** 271
Joseph H. **69** 316 **97** 201 202
Joseph Hersey **95** 147 **110** 308 309 **111** 60
Joseph Howland **69** 269 **97** 201 202
Joseph N. **97** 202
Joseph Newell **97** 202
Joshua **79** 443 **80** 189 **89** 246 247 **136** 36 40
Josiah **65** 40 **113** 48 132 **125** 74 **136** 25 **144** 218
Jude **108** 245
Judith **82** 170
Julia **65** lxiv
Julia Adelaide **67** xxxiv
Julia Ann (Draper) (Lazell) **89** 322
Juliana **77** 185
Julius L. R. **90** 107
Kate Amelia (Gleason) **83** 472
Katharine (Gosnold) **105** 11
Katharine Chase **96** 30
Keziah **104** 104
Laban **58** 59
Laura-Ann **90** 111
Lawrence Arthur (Mrs.) **108** 135
Lemuel **55** 260 398 **56** 142-145 148 267 268 **57** 24 151 152 252-255 257
Leonard **56** 143 267 **57** 152
Lester **58** 385 **128** 180
Lester A. **122** 320 **123** 160
Lester Amos **122** 95
Levi **89** 15 **116** 79 **136** 25

PRATT *cont'd*
Lewis **88** 277
Liberty **136** 363
Lillian Elizabeth **94** 138
Lodisa **110** 115
Loea **61** 381
Lois **55** 263 265 394 **60** 363 **82** 21 **144** 217
Lot **116** 115 211
Louisa **53** 405 **88** 239
Louise Miller (Johnson) **87** 216
Lovina **78** 128
Lucelia B. **74** 174
Lucia **79** 300
Lucina **78** 127
Lucinda **125** 37
Lucy **55** 393 **61** 381 **73** 148 **79** 56 **80** 126 **85** 65 **103** 220
Lucy (Covell) **96** 78
Lucy (Lazell) **89** 15
Luther **72** 103 **79** 300
Luther Leslie (Mrs.) **100** 112
Lydia **55** 260 394 **57** 30 257 **63** 274 **66** 316 **75** 200 **84** 409 **88** 16 **92** 48 58 **96** 364 **116** 79 **126** 215 **136** 26 27
Lydia (Harlow) **110** 309
Lydia (Leonard) **136** 26
Lydia (Lynde) **83** 472
Lydia (Mixer) **116** 80
Lydia (Mower) (Breed) **122** 53
Lydia (Tully) **96** 364
Lydia (White) **119** 111
Lydia Caroline **79** 123
Lydia H. **72** 275
Mahala **103** 235
Manoah **85** 170
Margaret **57** 324 **58** 87-89 **71** 211 216 **83** 472 **96** 363
Margaret (Crockett) **90** 113
Margaret (Felton) **129** 316
Margaret (Maverick) **96** 363 **97** 25
Margery **58** 246
Maria **66** 25 **145** 379
Maria Ann **95** 344
Marion **86** 94
Marrell **66** 19
Martha **56** 146 270 **57** 28 254 **58** 87 **66** 25 **69** 175 **75** 247 **78** 189 **133** 123 **136** 25 **137** 361
Martha (Lazell) **88** 259
Martha (Mahurin) **136** 25 117
Martha Cary **73** xxx
Martha E. **69** 269 316 **97** 202 203
Martha Ellen (Fracker) **124** 191
Martha Eunice (Hanson) **97** 201 202
Martha Jane **90** 369 370

PRATT *cont'd*
Martin **58** 59 **75** 258
 136 25
Martin Van Buren **99** 72
 73 **110** 308 309
Mary **53** 401 **55** 44 **56** 247
 383 **57** 28 **58** 89 **59** 371
 61 244 358 **63** 247 **66**
 316 332 **69** 269 **71** 259
 76 123 127 **77** 230 **78** 20
 67 **79** 56 179 **85** 170 **86**
 295 **88** 320 **89** 235 **95**
 294 **96** 363 **98** 356 **105**
 64 **110** 146 **111** 41 **116**
 79 115 211 **119** 111 **122**
 50 51 53 **123** 190 304
 305 **125** 292 **126** 83 145
 128 238 **136** 25 37 41
 143 36 **146** 360 **147** 49
Mary (Barker) **122** 50
Mary (Brommet) **125** 104
Mary (Cobb) **122** 58
Mary (Davis) (Lewis)
 123 190
Mary (Davis)(Lewis)
 109 68
Mary (Floyd) **109** 68
 112 42
Mary (Hathaway) **136** 25
Mary (King) **110** 309
Mary (Lash) **109** 68
Mary (Latham) **108** 223
Mary (Lazell) **88** 258 259
Mary (Post) (Bull) **147** 62
Mary (Priest) **122** 51
Mary (Rhodes) **89** 235
Mary (Rogers) (Keezer)
 147 364 365
Mary (Smith) **123** 92
Mary (Taber) **97** 201
Mary (Whitcomb)
 129 377
Mary A. **98** 251
Mary A. (Carroll) **95** 377
Mary A. (Smith) **123** 306
Mary Agnes **82** 21
Mary Alice **54** 151
Mary Ann **98** 359 **125** 244
Mary Ann (Gould) **87** 91
Mary Anna **132** 327
Mary B. **89** 37
Mary Barton **113** 224
Mary Dennis (Phearson)
 88 340
Mary Emily **122** 53
Mary Foster **75** lxix
Mary G. (Alden) **86** 300
Mary H. **124** 142
Mary Helen (Richardson)
 96 298
Mary J. **142** 370
Mary K. **84** 87
Mary King **59** 209
Mary Louise **65** 8
Mary Macdonald (Booma)
 128 180
Mary R. (Roulstone)
 94 45
Mary Seymour **71** 14
Mary Smith **123** 304
Mary Taber **97** 202

PRATT *cont'd*
Mary V. **69** 309
Mary W. **75** 242
Mason D. **98** 96
Matthew **52** 78 **59** 328 **97**
 25 **98** 97 **99** 72 **110** 309
 119 14 **136** 271
Maverick **96** 364
May (Brooks) **109** 68
Mehitable **52** 83 **58** 346
 60 43 **79** 90 **136** 117
Mehitable (Davis) **132** 41
Melatiah **81** 89 **119** 172
Melvin **100** 329
Mercy **57** 28 **63** 276 **82** 21
 105 320 **129** 376 **146**
 372
Mercy (Doty) **98** 356
Merriel P. (Lincoln)
 90 105
Mildred Irene (Noble)
 95 377
Minot Whittlesey **89** 249
Miriam **63** 94 **75** 20 **85** 170
Miriam Foster **55** xcii
Molly **55** lxv **119** 253
Moses **55** 261 **56** 143 146
 268 269 **57** 26 254 255
 98 105
Myra **116** 66
Nabby **54** 85 **56** 354 **60** 43
 72 275 **80** 189 **89** 247
Nahum **116** 203
Nancy **86** 92
Nancy (Degraves)
 126 141
Nancy (Moore) **124** 28
Nancy (Slocum) **88** 281
Nancy G. **94** 65
Nancy M. **75** 258
Nancy Sharkey (Stuart)
 86 94
Nathan **56** 258 **69** 269 309
 73 7 **79** 56 **95** 57 **97** 201
 202 **142** 271
Nathaniel **66** 316 **72** 98
 95 110 **116** 79 **122** 58
 125 44 **126** 217
Nehemiah **52** 453 **65** 348
 136 25
Noah **57** 24 **59** 354 **141** 355
 145 358
Noah W. **56** 171
Norton **93** 302
Obed **66** 316
Olive **52** 453 **56** 38 **68** 320
 124 29 **136** 25
Olive (Perkins) **136** 25
Oliver **57** 24 **65** 357 358
Oramel Whittlesey **89** 249
Orlen **135** 76
Orlin **116** 79
Orpah **72** 318 **98** 359
Orpha **98** 359
Othniel **58** 88 **147** 364
Ozias **109** 37
Pamona (Atkins) **109** 69
Parmenas **90** 38
Patience **58** 87
Patience (Chase) **88** 27
Patty **53** 34

PRATT *cont'd*
Patty (Chase) **87** 228 236
Paul **57** 257 **140** 138
 145 358
Percival **143** 36
Permelia (Woodcock)
 (Dimick) **136** 363
Persis **106** 227
Persis (Hayden) **124** 239
Peter **79** 386 **96** 126 **122**
 50 51
Peter (Mrs.) **94** 45
Phebe **61** 44 **66** 315 **97** 202
 116 79 **119** 187
Phebe Ann **69** 269 **97** 202
Phebe Cary **69** 309
Phebe P. **68** lxv
Phebe W. **64** 155
Phebe Wood **66** 276
Philenda **111** 41
Philip **71** 259
Philota **60** 392
Phineas **51** 364 **52** 96 99
 101 **79** 443 **82** 19 **90** 112
 113 **93** 232 **122** 50 51
Pitkin **86** 94
Polly **58** 59 **75** 308 **111** 41
 226 **137** 335 **147** 366
Polly (Bancroft) **95** 57
Pomona (Atkins) **109** 68
Porter **78** 375
Preston Powell **114** 66
Priscilla **53** 210 211 384
 73 221 **87** 283 **126** 204
Priscilla (Pratt) **126** 204
Priscilla (Sears) **106** 311
Prudence **58** 241 **147** 63
Prudence (Handy)
 126 110
Rachel **58** 89 **63** 246 323 **64**
 372 **81** 51 **92** 58 375 **93**
 270 271 **145** 168
Rachel (Floyd) **132** 40
Rachel Emma (Fitz
 Randolph) **98** 228
Rebecca **57** 397 **66** 320 **71**
 259 **88** 239 249 **92** 59 **93**
 85 **98** 251 **109** 151 **121**
 264 **126** 129 **143** 36
Rebecca (Chandler)
 109 151
Rebecca (Hanna) **130** 315
Rebecca Adams (Dyer)
 110 308
Rebecca Ellis (Silvester)
 86 124
Reuben King **59** 211
Rhoda (Whittemore)
 108 245
Rhoda Elizabeth **99** 73
Richard **53** 401 **55** 124 132
 62 168 **81** 51 **83** 472 **98**
 359 **107** 66 **109** 68 **148**
 334
Richard Henry **98** 96
Robert **51** 118 **81** 88 **90** 37
 113 132
Robert Henry **86** 300
Robert K. **90** 37
Roger **105** 13
Rosamond **110** 309

PRATT *cont'd*
Rosamond (Thomson)
  110 309
Rose Eleanor **113** 229
Roswell **104** 104
Roxanna **58** 386
Roy Perley (Mrs.) **99** 148
  108 158 **120** 147
Russell **145** 168
Ruth **52** 453 **61** 354 **63** 247
  78 66 **96** 363 **100** 298
  111 225 **125** 74
Ruth (Lawson) **88** 277
Ruth Sears **78** 206
Ruth Sears (Baker) **88** 170
Ruthy **125** 290
S. Marius **96** 137
Sally **55** 396 **63** 256 **64** 211
  88 239 **92** 58 **98** 251
  100 329 **110** 113 **136** 25
Sally (Willis) **125** 222
Sally Brown **55** 199
Samuel **55** 173 175 266
  56 142 408 **57** 151 **58** 59
  59 209-212 328 **60** 43
  201 **61** 43 **65** 365 **75** 157
  76 xxi **78** 302 402 **86** 94
  108 202 **87** 91 **92** 58 **104**
  193 **109** 213 **116** 212
  119 111 **122** 50 **124** 28
  239 **125** 38 **126** 36 205
  128 53 **142** 271 **144** 222
  148 263
Samuel B. **89** 275
Sarah **54** 406 **55** 259 260
  263 266 396 **56** 38 **57** 24
  53 258 259 **59** 387 **60** 42
  201 264 **61** 344 358 **62**
  200 374 **65** 1 **66** 316 **77**
  146 **78** 411 **80** 434 **84**
  157 **86** 25 **87** 95 **89** 358
  90 112 113 **93** 195 **98**
  251 **101** 103 **103** 227
  104 188 **109** 184 **113** 48
  119 14 **122** 50 51 **125**
  171 **126** 206 275 276
  128 98 **132** 41 **141** 141
  142 271
Sarah (Bailey) **88** 85
  90 370
Sarah (Benson) **110** 309
  119 24 **142** 271
Sarah (Bush) **125** 175
Sarah (Drowne) **122** 320
  123 160
Sarah (Gale) **84** 409
Sarah (Hunt) **97** 25 **119** 14
Sarah (Jones) **113** 48 142
  223
Sarah (Judkins) **110** 309
  142 271
Sarah (Kingman) **110** 309
  136 25 117
Sarah (Rogers) **125** 215
Sarah (Upham) **83** 472
Sarah A. **90** 112
Sarah Ann **55** 13 **82** 19
  90 43
Sarah B. **63** 273
Sarah Elizabeth **97** 201-
  203

PRATT *cont'd*
Sarah Frances **81** 342
Sarah Jones **113** 223
Sarah Joy **99** 73
Sarah Louise **65** 1
Sarah Oakman **82** 19
Sarah P. (Pepper) **125** 222
Sarah Temple **78** 356
Sarah V. (Whittlesey)
  89 249
Sarah V. Whittlesey
  89 249
Sarah Whiting **69** 269
  97 202
Sarah Williams **81** 342
Sarie M. **89** 246
Seba **147** 364
Seth **56** 37 **57** 254 **105** 283
Sibyl **56** 37 **57** 24
Silas **55** 13 **57** 25 **65** 348
  125 74
Silence **56** 400
Simeon **57** 147 **144** 216
Simon Newcomb **95** 166
Solomon **55** 172 **63** 274
  70 12 **93** 67 **96** 78 **142**
  271
Sophia **53** 354 **110** 37
Sophronia Wells **82** 273
Stephen **92** 58 **111** 40
  144 272
Steven **128** 94
Stillman **67** 359 **96** 332
Susan B. (Sharp) **88** 340
Susan F. **74** 174 **75** 20
Susan M. **84** 87
Susan Sharp **100** 317
Susanna **60** 201 **73** 10 **88**
  373 **92** 53 **96** 364 **100**
  312 **105** 307 **119** 24 **122**
  50 51 **136** 25
Susanna (Keith) **110** 309
Susanna (Richards)
  119 24
Susanna (Simmons)
  129 377
Susanna Smith **123** 305
Susanna Willard **59** 210
Susie Warren **89** 249
Sylvanus **125** 171 175
  126 110
Sylvester **80** 434
Sylvia Mayo **110** 309
Tabitha **56** 38
Tamsin **58** 239
Thaddeus **145** 168
Thankful **53** 228 379
Thankful (Ellis) **122** 207
Thankful Payne (Atkins)
  95 344
Theodore Cary **73** xxx
Theresa (Winsor) **97** 121
Thomas **51** 304 364 **63** 247
  64 186 **66** 187 315 **73**
  221 225 **78** 411 **79** 56 **83**
  472 **88** 276 **92** 48 53 57
  58 **107** 98 105 **109** 68
  117 156 **123** 190 **127**
  140 **132** 39 42
Thomas B. **125** 104
Thomas Dennie **110** 309

PRATT *cont'd*
Thomas F. **124** 28
Timothy **55** 199 **56** 147
  57 255 **83** 367 **109** 213
Ulysses **65** lxiv
Ursula **105** 13
Ursula (Gosnold) **105** 14
Ursula (Nunn) **141** 241
Walter **76** 123 127 **80** 320
  108 51 **147** 366 368
Walter Merriam **83** 122
  230 **86** 242 **95** 138 159
  96 173 **97** 171 398 **98**
  139 140 162 **99** 69 164
  100 102 124-126 **101**
  115 138-140 **102** 115 137
  138-140 **107** 66 126 127
  145-147 **108** 127 128
  110 137 **111** 141 142
  112 70 134 135 222 314
  113 61 148 149 233 293
  114 70 140 142 228 309
  115 68 145 146 229 313
  116 73 144 145 227 306
  117 73 149 151 231 312
  118 69 160 161 246 324
  119 72 150 151 236 312
  120 56 150 151 233 310
  121 75 150 151
Walter Merriam (Mrs.)
  103 120 **104** 160 **105**
  144 **106** 100
Walter Stewart **54** 151
Walter W. **54** 458
Wealthy **76** 266
Welcome O. **74** 174 **75** 20
Whitcomb **120** 47
William **53** 228 **54** 222 459
  57 258 **63** 247 **66** 316
  70 200 **75** 143 **79** 123
  81 88 **85** 170 **89** 175 **90**
  88 **93** 189 **94** 338 **97** 202
  99 73 **102** 235 **104** 188
  110 309 **112** 146 **119**
  123 **132** 26 27 **136** 271
  140 42 263 **148** 121
William B. **82** 170
William F. **120** 42
William Frederick
  116 203
William H. **82** 21
William Henry **90** 113
  92 250
William Henry Harrison
  124 191
William Selden **59** 212
William Taber **69** 269
William Veazie **87** 216
William W. **71** 18
Winifred (Race) **86** 300
Zadock **65** 348 **79** 87
Zebedee **89** 275
Zebediah **56** 38 266 270
  57 24 30 145-147
Zebulon Keith **110** 309
Zebulon King **99** 73
Zechariah **65** 7
Zephaniah **81** 51 **126** 276
  137 283 **147** 63
Zibia **96** 400
Zipporah **126** 217

PRATT *cont'd*
Zoa (Sessions) **136** 25
PRAWOKR ?
Maude **94** 12
PRAY —— **57** 224 **62** 93
  83 308 **99** 54 **145** 53
— Dea. **97** 293
— Mrs. **71** 48 **83** 308
A. W. **62** 201
Abby **94** 189
Abigail **55** 316 **57** 385 **74**
  256 264 **83** 12
Abraham **74** 261
Abram **92** 114
Addie E. **85** 381
Adeline A. (Tibbetts)
  99 54
Alexander **82** 317
Alfred Arnold **85** 325
  109 223
Alice **55** 280 **61** 256 **63** 173
  74 254
Alice Emery **92** 114
Allen S. **62** 201
Amelia (Goodrich) **141** 48
Ann **73** 314 **82** 315
Ann Carroll **92** 114
Anna **55** 316 **74** 265 **83** 13
  99 325
Anne **55** 374 **63** 167 **74** 186
  83 15
Annie Walker **83** 174
Arthur Harwood **83** 479
Beatrice Wardwell **83** 479
Benjamin **78** 314
Benjamin S. **77** 56
Betsey **65** 258 **74** 261 262
  265 **78** 345
Bion **96** 203
Caroline F. **69** 37
Cecilia **85** 325 **109** 223
Chadbourn **74** 262
Charles **63** 178 **74** 260 **83**
  76 **148** 169
Charles E. **91** 332
Charles Farquhar **83** 295
Clarissa **85** 372 373
Daniel **82** 315 **83** 479
  129 385
David **127** 309
Dorcas **74** 257 262
Dorothy **55** 280 281 **60**
  285 **74** 215 250 **82** 315
Ebenezer **61** 256 **68** 106
Edmund **74** 197 219
Eleanor (Wheelock)
  88 279
Eliphalet **74** 251 254
  82 317
Eliu **97** 145
Eliza (Caswell) **85** 325
  109 223
Eliza Olive **83** 174 308
Elizabeth **55** 280 313 **57**
  224 **74** 248 **82** 511 **96**
  340 **102** 310 **143** 49
Elizabeth Gertrude
  (Wardwell) **83** 479
Elizabeth P. S. **83** 174
Elizabeth S. **83** 301 303
Ellen L. **83** 185

PRAY *cont'd*
Ellicee **90** 235
Ellis **74** 189
Elsie Chapman **83** 479
  84 105 186
Emma S. (Barnard) **83** 296
  301
Ephraim **55** 280 281
  57 76 224
Eunice **73** 193 313
Experience **73** 313 **74** 213
  248 **82** 95 206 208 210
  214
Ezra **100** 37
F. C. **91** 392
Frances Motley **77** 56
Francis W. **122** 92
Georgiana **89** 113
Hannah **55** 280 281 **113** 48
  143 128
Hannah (Tibbetts) **100** 37
Harriet **68** 106
Helen B. **84** 31
Helen Chamberlin **83** 479
Helen Lugarda **85** 197
Hiram **69** 37 **74** 223
Hugh **127** 308
Isaac **69** 282
Isaiah **73** 200
J. E. S. **68** 131
J. L. **60** 190
James **82** 317
James Foster Shores
  83 174
James Sturgis **56** xxxiv
  77 56
Jane **82** 214
Jane M. (Bartlett) **89** 113
Joanna **55** 280 281 **74** 249
  252 261 264 **82** 317 320
Joanna (Dowman)
  130 231
John **55** 280 281 **57** 224
  63 167 **74** 186 197 212
  213 218 **80** 76 82 **82** 96
  206 208 210 214 218 288
  297 317 320 **128** 60 **130**
  231 **141** 48 342 **146** 349
John F. **122** 92
John H. **88** 279
John Lansing **58** lxv
John S. **84** 31
Jonathan **127** 308
Joseph **54** 98 **55** 280 281
  315 373 **57** 385 **63** 168
  74 42 186 223 256 257
  82 207 208 315 **83** 10 14
  111 24 **127** 310 **129** 383
Joshua **61** 256 **66** 109 **74**
  197 213 218-220 **82** 79
  214
Julia **73** 195
Julia A. **84** 32
L. Ellen **83** 181 185
Levi **74** 263
Lewis G. **93** 60
Lloyd W. D. **92** 114
Louise H. **108** 320
Love **74** 42 249 **82** 317
  147 70
Lucy **83** 308

PRAY *cont'd*
Lucy Maria **83** 175 181 185
Lydia **57** 385 **60** 41
Lydia H. **73** 193
Margaret **69** 37 **74** 252
Margaret W. **83** 185 186
Mark Wentworth **89** 113
Martha **55** 280 311 **74** 248
  82 85 208 **111** 24 **114** 48
Mary **55** 280 315 373 **63**
  168 **74** 186 214 223 251
  256 **81** 142 **82** 79 96 **83**
  10 14 24 27 **90** 325 **96**
  191 **114** 302 **124** 49 **127**
  255
Mary (Hight) **83** 14
Mary (Libby) **83** 10
Mary A. **82** 350
Mary C. **84** 32
Maude E. (Sanborn)
  96 203
Mayhew **73** 201
Mehitable **55** 316 **69** 283
  83 12
Mehitable (Libbey) **83** 12
Meribah **74** 249
Miriam **55** 280 **82** 95
Molly **74** 261 **82** 317
Moses **63** 178 **74** 189 252
  260 **82** 207 **92** 114
Moses Frank **92** 114
Nabby **74** 262
Nathan **82** 218
Nathan Aldin **92** 114
Nathaniel **55** 316 **61** 256
  74 220 **83** 12
Nellie **70** x
Nellie A. **83** 297 301
Nellie May (Chamberlain)
  56 xxxiv **59** vii **60** vii
  61 vii **62** vii **63** vii **64**
  vii **65** vii **66** vii **83** 238
  248 479
Olive **91** 33
Patience **69** 282
Pelatiah **74** 261
Peter **55** 280 **63** 172 **74**
  252 258 **82** 315 317 **84**
  32 **145** 361
Phebe **63** 174
Polly **63** 172 177 **74** 258
  259 261
Quinton **55** 280 **57** 224
  60 190
Rachel **63** 178 **74** 38 249
  260 **82** 315
Rachel Arabel **92** 114
Ralph Marble (Mrs.)
  100 112
Richard **52** 211 **55** 280 **80**
  76 **99** 238
Robert **142** 62
Rosa (Torres) **89** 113
Ruth **57** 224 **82** 288 297
Sally **63** 178 **65** 258 **74**
  256 259 260
Samuel **55** 280 281 313
  61 256 **65** 258 **74** 197
  215 218 256 262 **82** 207
  208 315 317 320 323 511
  83 195 296 301 **97** 145

PRAY *cont'd*
Sarah **63** 83 173 **66** 109 **74** 197 214 218-220 250 252 253 255 **80** 76 82 **82** 320
Sarah (Lander) **93** 60
Sarah Ann **83** 185 188
Sarah E. **84** 32
Sarah Elizabeth **92** 114
Sarah Lander **93** 60
Sibyl **57** 76
Stephen **74** 249 255 **82** 210
Susan **92** 225
Susanna **73** 284 **74** 261
Temperance **83** 36
Thankful **81** 87
Theodorah **126** 206
Thomas **65** 258 **90** 37
Thomas Oliver **83** 479
Vesta W. (Flagg) **91** 392
William **74** 249 **81** 87 **82** 317 409
William F. **83** 174 175
William Peirce **83** 175
PRAYTOR Eleanor **144** 32
PREASE Elizabeth **63** 76
PREASEY
Challis **53** 162
Sarah **53** 162
Preast *see* Priest
PREBLE Prebbel Prebel Prebles Prible Pribble
—— **113** 266
— Commodore **55** 93
— Sgt. **58** 236
Abby **68** 19
Abigail **66** 156 **98** 299 **109** 297 **110** 286 **112** 306 **114** 47 **115** 136 **116** 133 **119** 68
Abigail (Beatea) **112** 305
Abraham **51** 264 **54** 403 408 **57** 83 **59** 307 **65** 331 **74** 70 **76** 318 **98** 105 **109** 297 299 **110** 19 95-97 174 176 178 284 **111** 19 232 **112** 24 **114** 44 47 134 **115** 62
Abram **95** 182 **109** 297 **124** 150 151
Ada P. (Lilly) **91** 388
Adeline **124** 149
Albert B. **123** 233
Alberta W. **123** 233
Alexander **112** 24
Andrew **68** 19 **119** 284 285
Anna **54** 403 **110** 59 **117** 143
Anne **54** 402 403 **114** 128
Anne (Payne) **110** 59 **114** 47 128
Archie **74** 93
Asenath (Bassett) **125** 12
Augusta E. **121** 144 146
Azubah **124** 150
Azubah M. **124** 150
Benjamin **66** 159 **75** 51 52 **109** 298 **110** 283 286 **111** 98 **114** 46 **115** 137 **116** 135 **143** 18
Bethiah **110** 58 **111** 230 **114** 131

PREBLE *cont'd*
Caleb **109** 299 **110** 95 **111** 254 **112** 101 **115** 59
Caroline M. **119** 285 286
Caroline Matilda **68** 19
Charles D. **120** 304 **122** 310
Charles S. **68** 19 **119** 228
Clarissa **80** 28
David **110** 95 176 **112** 24 25 **115** 58 63 225 **116** 140
Deborah **110** 176 **115** 215
Deborah (Turner) **118** 320
Dorcas **112** 25
Dorothy (McIntire) **112** 24 **114** 291
E. H. **80** 127
Eben **120** 82
Ebenezer **54** 98 **80** 29 **109** 299 **110** 97 178 284 **115** 59 **116** 295
Edward **55** 251 253 **72** 84 **109** 297 **110** 96 178 **114** 293 **115** 220 **120** 82
Edward P. **57** xxxiii
Elaine **92** 230
Eleanor **63** 169 **115** 227
Elias **82** 290 297
Elizabeth **110** 58 176 **111** 25 233 **114** 129 131 **118** 240 242
Elizabeth (Grant) **119** 285
Elizabeth (Welch) **90** 230 251
Ellen Frances **84** 114
Emeline Wall **82** 280
Emily G. (Varrell) **120** 304 **122** 310
Emma F. (Rogers) **121** 144 146
Esaias **66** 262 **110** 289 **112** 217 **116** 220
Esther **112** 25
Eunice **59** 303
Flora Abby **74** 92
Francis **112** 306 **118** 320
Fred **92** 230
George **118** 242 317 **124** 149
George Henry **64** 66 **70** 293 **75** 166 **77** 101 **99** 14
Glover B. **83** 428 438
Grace Estelle **82** 280
Hannah **82** 297 **104** 122 **109** 297 **110** 58 95 96 176 283 286 288 **111** 97 254 **112** 25 **114** 125 132 134 295 **115** 225 **117** 140 141 **121** 307 **122** 151
Hannah (Preble) **114** 134
Hannah (Simpson) **110** 178
Hannah (Weare) **110** 288
Hannah (Welsh) **110** 176
Hannah (Young) **110** 286 **114** 46
Hannah M. **119** 283
Harriet **116** 140
Hattie **68** 19

PREBLE *cont'd*
Hattie F. **83** 437 438
Henry **138** 322
Hepzibah **66** 156 **109** 299 **110** 95 97 176 289 **115** 138
Humility **109** 297 **110** 96 **111** 232 **114** 129
Isabella (Stewart) **118** 242 317
James **116** 136
James G. **84** 32
James Orne **68** 19
Jane **66** 156 **112** 24
Janey **112** 306
Janna (Gullison) **116** 222
Jedediah **63** 266 **64** 14 128 **75** 110 112 113 **110** 286 **114** 126 **116** 137 222
Jedidiah **60** 111 **90** 88 **109** 158 **114** 129
Jellison **143** 18
Jemima **59** 284 **109** 301 **110** 95 **112** 101 **114** 133
Jere **66** 262
Jeremiah **120** 67
Joanna **117** 228 230
Joanna (Bane) **115** 137
Joel **112** 24
John **58** 340 **75** 110 **83** 385 **90** 230 251 **109** 298 **110** 283 286 **112** 101 103 **114** 46 **115** 219
Jonathan **80** 28 **109** 299 **110** 176 284 **125** 12
Joseph **55** 57 **66** 78 156 312 313 **110** 58 59 97 176 177 **111** 97 230 233 254 **112** 25 **113** 124 **114** 47 **115** 136 220 **116** 131 **118** 243 317
Joseph H. **121** 144 146
Joshua **125** 28
Josiah **120** 68
Judah **109** 298
Judith **65** 331 **110** 283 **111** 98 **114** 47
Julia **68** 19 **119** 146
Julia Ann (Card) **120** 67
Kadmiel **112** 306 **125** 33
Lavina **116** 300
Lavinia **112** 306 **116** 301
Lilla **92** 226
Lillie E. (Dow) **83** 428 438
Loisa **68** 19
Louise **68** 19
Lucinda (Harper) **122** 192
Lydia **66** 262 **82** 290 297 **110** 95 286 288 **112** 103 217 **115** 62 309 **119** 224
Lydia (Ingraham) **112** 217
Lydia (Leavitt) **118** 243 317
Mariam **97** 266 **114** 131 134
Martha **75** 110 112 113
Martha (Junkins) **114** 126
Martha (Moulton) **115** 59
Mary **72** 84 **80** 29 **97** 272 **109** 297 299 **110** 58 96 174 177 **111** 19 **114** 50

PREBLE *cont'd*
  125 129 **120** 82
Mary (Avery) **120** 68
Mary (Bragdon) **110** 96
Mary (Junkins) **112** 25
  115 63
Mary (Moulton) **112** 25
  115 58
Mary (Preble) **110** 96
Mary Ann **119** 143
Mary E. **68** 19
Mary Elizabeth (Grant)
  119 284
Mary Jane (Bridges)
  119 145
Mercy **110** 286 **115** 63
  119 62
Meriam **109** 299 **110** 96
Miranda **119** 277 287
Miriam **110** 59 **111** 254
  112 101 **114** 131
Miriam (Harmon) **112**
  101 **115** 59
Nancy **124** 150 151
Nancy G. **119** 279 280
Nancy G. (Tucker)
  116 225
Nancy N. **123** 149
Nathaniel **57** 83 **109** 297
  110 96 178 **114** 291
Nehemiah **110** 58 **114** 132
Obadiah **112** 306
Olive **92** 222 **112** 306 **113**
  266 **116** 301 302 304 305
Olive (Bowden) **138** 322
Oliver **66** 262
Patty **116** 294
Paul **110** 95 96 **112** 24
  114 291
Peter **110** 288 **112** 305
  115 212
Phebe **110** 288
Phila (Perkins) **116** 222
Polly **97** 266
Priscilla **57** 66
Rachel **109** 301
Rachel (Maine) **109** 301
Rebecca (Harvey) **110** 284
Rhoda **115** 226
Ruth **116** 224
Ruth Estella **106** 125
Sally Ann **68** 19
Samuel **55** 57 **63** 297 **66**
  156 264 **68** 19 **75** 112
  109 299 **110** 289 **113** 28
  124 **114** 47 **115** 227 **116**
  222 296
Samuel Edward **82** 280
Samuel Washington
  68 19
Sarah **55** 57 **58** 340 **66** 78
  312 313 **68** 19 **90** 390
  110 176 289 **112** 217
  113 124 **114** 51 **115** 60
  116 130 131 137
Sarah (Muchmore)
  110 289
Sarah (Preble) **116** 137
Sarah (Wilder) **123** 233
Sarah A. **120** 140
Statira **116** 294

PREBLE *cont'd*
Stephen **109** 301 **110** 288
  112 306 **116** 137
Stephen A. **84** 32
Susan **68** 19
Susan (Barnard) **119** 228
Susan H. (Cox) **124** 149
Susan J. **120** 140 **123** 74
  151 234
Susan Jane **118** 154 155
  120 215
Susanna **63** 297 **68** 19
  109 297 **110** 96 178 **115**
  138 **116** 297 **117** 143
Susanna (Remick) **113** 28
Susanna (Sayward)
  110 96
Susetta **74** 93
Tabitha **110** 286 **115** 60
  227
Theodore **112** 25
Theodosia **112** 217
  115 308
Thomas **112** 24
Timothy **110** 59 **112** 101
Turner **143** 18
Welden P. **91** 388
William **75** 113 **112** 24
  119 145
William P. **51** 144
William Pitt **116** 225
Zebulon **110** 176 **111** 25
PREDDEN Richard **94** 268
PREDDETH Ann **139** 141
  Christian **139** 141
  James **139** 141
PREDEN
  George W. **55** 199
  Mary S. **55** 199
  Sarah S. **55** 199
PREELY Charles **82** 414
PREEM Joseph **65** 168
  Thomas **65** 174
Preestley *see* Priestly
PREFUME
  Carmetta **104** 104
  Charles **104** 104
  Hazel (Van Valkenburg)
  104 104
PREISCH Anna
  Margaretta **104** 78
PREISSNER Christina
  Elizabeth **138** 229
  Henrick George **138** 229
  John Adam **138** 229
Preist De *see* Priest
Preist *see* Priest
Prence *see* Prince
PRENDERGAST
  De Prendergast
  Pendergast
  Pendergrass
  Pendgrass Pendrgrass
  — Dr. **87** 331
  — Miss **98** 83
  Ann **54** 388 **58** 297 **132** 275
  Betsey **132** 275 **135** 129
  Bridget **58** 297 **100** 27
  Catherine **75** lxxxix **98** 82
  Daniel **97** 236
  Deborah **132** 275

PRENDERGAST *cont'd*
  Deborah (Durrell) **132**
  275 **135** 129
  Edmund **58** 297
  Edward **100** 27 **122** 283
  Gerald de **110** 185
  Hannah (Emerson)
  132 275
  James **132** 275
  James Maurice **72** xx **75**
  xxxvi lxxxix **98** 83
  Jane **58** 297 **65** 353 **132** 275
  Jane (Cotton) **132** 275
  Jeffrey **75** lxxxix **98** 82 83
  John **56** 74 **58** 297 **128** 285
  132 275 **135** 129
  Julia Catherine **94** 139
  98 82 87 152
  Lois (Emerson) **132** 275
  M. S. **72** 250
  Margaret **58** 297
  Mary **69** 38
  Mary (Williams) **132** 275
  Mary de **110** 185
  Nicholas **132** 275
  Olive **97** 236 **128** 285
  Penelope (Chase) **87** 331
  Polly **132** 275
  Rachel **132** 275
  Ruby **116** 256
  Sarah **132** 275
  Solomon **58** 297
  Stephen **58** 297 **65** 353
  132 275
  Theodore **97** 236
  Thomas **100** 27
  Thomasyne **122** 283
PRENFORT
  Abby **125** 241
PRENTICE Prentis
  Prentiss Prentys
  Printice
  ——— **53** 248 **92** 55 133
  120 301
  — Capt. **63** 83 **77** 67 101
  99 109 **118** 266
  — Judge **76** 272
  — Mr. **55** 442 **66** 137
  67 380
  A. LaRoy **71** 42
  Abigail **66** 137 **78** 428 **81**
  164 172 **95** 80 128 155
  Abigail Adams **62** lv
  Ada Spencer **89** 131
  Alonzo Tyng **86** 226
  Amasa **90** 55
  Amelia **116** 316
  Amos **81** 164
  Angeline **70** 123 **115** 129
  Ann (Kendall) (Cook)
  126 113
  Ann (Peasley) **90** 55
  Ann Eliza **92** 349
  Ann Lucretia **115** 112
  Anna **71** 346 **83** 101
  Anne **81** 360
  Appleton **140** 238
  Artemas **81** 126
  Asa **81** 164 **83** 101
  Asahel Barrett **83** 233 247
  Augusta **128** 36

PRENTICE *cont'd*
Benjamin **78** 307
Bethiah **71** 346
Betsey **81** 171
Caleb **55** 149 **73** 84 **77** 315
  84 260 **108** 28 **121** 248
  128 214
Caroline **79** 77
Catherine **115** 112
Catherine B. **83** 101
Catherine Phelps **62** 190
Channing **70** 122 **115** 130
Charles E. **66** lxiii
Charles Henry **75** 247
Charles Morris **82** 423
Charlotte **126** 143
Chauncey **79** 77
Christina (Thompson)
  88 337
Clarissa **82** 472
Daniel **81** 166 172 **143** 24
David **81** 172
Deborah **60** 305 **61** 79 342
  147 272
Delight **99** 297 **127** 272
Dorothy **81** 164 **109** 306
Ebenezer **77** 232 317
  81 164
Edward **55** xxxii **71** 146
  76 225 226 **147** 37
Edwin Dwight **82** 472
Elilzabeth (Rand) **108** 28
Eliza **82** 423
Elizabeth **56** lviii **61** 260
  76 226 **78** 308 429 **81**
  164 **85** 95 **96** 82 **125** 66
  281 **129** 367 **130** 214
  143 24
Elizabeth (Briggs)
  125 281
Elizabeth (Drury) **126** 113
Elizabeth (Fosdick)
  143 24
Elizabeth (Phillips)
  144 342
Elizabeth (Rand) **130** 214
Elizabeth (White) **143** 24
Elizabeth (Whittemore)
  (Brooks) **108** 246
Elizabeth Paine **82** 423
Elizabeth S. (Severance)
  (Allen) **98** 185
Ellen **62** lxxiv lxxv **75** 247
Ellen Atwood **84** 456
  97 90
Ellen Pierce **75** 247
Elsie **62** lvi
Emeline (Rockwell)
  86 226
Emily (Bonney) **84** 328
Emma **84** 328
Ephraim **70** 229 **115** 131
Esther **75** 209 **80** 97 **81** 164
Esther (Green) (Muzzy)
  (Whittemore) **107** 28
Eunice **79** 79 **127** 272
  128 36
Eunice W. **71** 42
F. F. **84** 455
Flora Isabel **79** 137
Frances Maria **75** lx

PRENTICE *cont'd*
Francis Fleury **98** 185
Francis Fleury (Mrs.) **85**
  188 **98** 185 248 **99** 150
George M. **75** 247
George W. **81** 252 **98** 355
Grace **81** 164
Hannah **56** 33 389 **59** 80
  81 **66** 137 **71** 146 149 **78**
  73 **98** 354
Hannah (Minor) **126** 255
Harris **99** 297 **128** 36
Helen **62** lxxiv **75** 247
Helen (Whittemore)
  108 249
Henry **60** 358 **62** liv lvi
  63 **75** 67 326 **73** 84 85
  76 226 **78** 190 429 **82**
  500 **98** 354 **108** 28 253
  254 **125** 66 **130** 178 214
  140 238 **143** 24 **144** 342
Henry Bowdoin **126** 113
Henry E. **62** liv lv
Henry James **90** 56
Henry Josiah **98** 355
Henry Mellen **60** xxxviii
  61 xlv **62** l liv lvi **65** 1
Hepzibah **125** 66
J. **61** 145
James **59** 80 81 **67** 172 **71**
  349 **81** 174 **84** 328 **88**
  205 **92** 133 249 **121** 248
  126 113 **140** 238
James H. **88** 337
James Henry **88** 205
  92 249
James Mackay **92** 347
Jane **81** 252
Jane Atwood (Russell)
  84 456 **97** 90
Jesse **81** 164
Joanna **130** 178
John **60** 368 **61** 260 **62** 93
  64 348 350 **67** 336 **71**
  146 346 **80** 97 **81** 164 **94**
  316 **99** 8 **101** 144 **109** 55
  123 170 **125** 23 **126** 113
  255 256 **128** 18 21 **129**
  367 **137** 97
John A. **98** 355
John Brewster **62** 190
John H. **115** 112
John M. **88** 205 **92** 347 349
  94 39
John P. **88** 285
John Thomas **88** 205
  92 347
Jonas **62** lxxiv **65** 221 **75**
  247 **81** 164 166 171 **108**
  249 **145** 126
Jonas Whittemore **75** 247
Jonathan **77** 20 **131** 75
Jonathan Cooper **108** 251
Joseph **60** 352
Joshua **78** 429 **81** 164
  107 313
Joyce **76** 226
Juba **116** 316
Julia A. **62** lvi
Julia Matilda Gardner
  92 133

PRENTICE *cont'd*
Keziah **77** 284
Laroy **71** 42
Laure **115** 131
Leslie **62** lvi
Louise M. **81** 252
Lucinda **70** 335 **81** 171
Lucretia **81** 171
Lucretia (Holmes) **142**
  168 169
Lucy Young **62** 116
Lydia **75** 247 **89** 100 **93** 89
  108 28
Lydia (Whittemore)
  108 28
Lydia Ann **98** 355
Lydia Caroline **75** 247
Maria **79** 39
Maria Woodward
  (Baldwin) **95** 343
Marion Louise **62** xl lvi
  65 xliv xlix l
Martha **81** 166
Mary **61** 260 **70** 120 229
  73 85 **75** 209 **78** 429 **81**
  164 166 172 177 **88** 264
  92 56 197 **115** 134 **116**
  115 **130** 178
Mary (Bulman) **114** 293
Mary (Scollay) **140** 244
Mary (Whittemore)
  108 251
Mary Alice **82** 472
Mary Ann Elizabeth
  (Russell) **93** 62
Mary Ann Paine **82** 423
Mary Elizabeth **77** 180
Mary Hart **73** 83-85
Mary Josephine **86** 226
Mary Martha **115** 112
Mehitable **82** 332 500
Mehitable (Spencer)
  115 137
Nancy **81** 171 **88** 341
  126 113
Nancy Kendall **126** 113
Nathan **81** 166 **82** 332 500
  115 137 **118** 313
Nathaniel **62** lxxv **91** 94
  125 289
Nathaniel A. **82** 423
Oliver **115** 122 **127** 272
  128 36
Pamela **73** 84
Patience **78** 99 **105** 221
Phebe **81** 164 171 **98** 354
Polly **81** 164
Rachel **85** 390 392
Rebecca **59** 252 **71** 146 149
  81 164 171 174 **109** 55
  128 214
Rebecca (Foster) **100** 11
Richard **143** 24
Robert **57** 29 259
Ruth Teal **92** 56
Sally **60** 352 **81** 171
Sally (Cambell) **125** 289
Sally (Chalmar) **125** 289
Samuel **78** 304 **81** 164 171
  83 378 **126** 226 **142** 169
Samuel Blake **84** 456

PRENTICE *cont'd*
97 90
Samuel O. **61** 79
Samuel T. **79** 137
Sarah **70** 335 **71** 146 149
75 215
Sarah (Jones) **123** 170
Sarah (Sawtell) **126** 12
Sarah Abigail **75** 247
Sarah Esther **137** 281
Sarah Mackay **88** 205 **92**
347 349 **94** 39
Sarah Mackay (Hunt)
88 205
Sarah Richards (Jewett)
90 56
Shubal **115** 133
Smith **86** 239
Solomon **78** 66 429 **99** 80
108 247 **124** 17 **125** 66
126 12 **141** 10
Sophia **78** 306 **88** 205
Sophia (Gould) **88** 285
Sophia (Tupper) **99** 297
128 36
Sophie **126** 113
Stephen **75** 209 **79** 79 **92**
55 56
Susan **58** lxxii **59** 80 81
67 172 336 **78** 304
Susan Y. **79** 52
Susanna **59** 82
Susanna O. **88** 332
Sylvester **115** 131
Tabitha (Leland)
124 17
Thaddeus **97** 395
Thomas **56** 39 370 **59** 252
60 132 **61** 258 **62** liv
371 **64** 139 **70** 120 **71**
146 149 349 **76** 226 **78**
428 429 **81** 164 166 171
85 455 **99** 80 102 103
107 28 **114** 293 **115**
103 132 **125** 23 **140** 244
143 24
Truman **98** 355
Valentine **56** lviii **70** 335
Walter **100** 17 18
William **63** 74 **64** 138 **76**
226 **78** 186 429 **82** 332
85 125
William K. (Mrs.) **95** 343
William Kelly **101** 258
William L. **98** 355
William Parker **101** 258
Zelotes **116** 115
PREO
Mary (Ranco) **136** 268
Peter **136** 268
PRESBREY Presbee
Presberry Presbery
Presbey Presbury
Presby
—— **57** 338 **71** 124
— Mr. **81** 433
Abby Leonard **76** xlviii
Abigail **92** 278 **115** 192
Allen **59** 32
Ann Jane **126** 276
Annie (Newland) **126** 276

PRESBREY *cont'd*
Arthur Sumner **117** 292
Catherine (Miller) **90** 57
Deborah **60** 143
Deborah (Skiffe) **115** 192
Edward **132** 119
Edward Hyde **76** xlviii
Erastus **133** 283
Eusebia **118** 328
Harriet **59** 32 33
Helen Hyde **76** xlviii
James **128** 286
John **71** 124 **76** xlviii
78 267
John Oliver **76** xlviii
Joseph **53** 437
Joseph Waite **73** xx
Josiah **126** 276
Lewis **125** 36
Lucy Ann (Batchelder)
133 283
Mary **53** 437 **59** 32 **60** 143
81 433
Mary G. (Chellis) **124** 62
Mary Jane **59** lxxvi
107 224
Mason D. **124** 62
May Dean **59** 33
Oliver Hyde **76** xlviii
Oliver Stetson **73** xx **76**
xxx xlviii
Parthenia **81** 433
Sarah **78** 266 267
Sarah Maria **76** xlviii
Seth **59** 32
Simeon **128** 286
Stephen **60** 143 **90** 57
115 192 **132** 119
Usebe **118** 328
William **76** xlviii
William Hyde **76** xlviii
PRESCH Henry **85** 71 114
PRESCOTT Prescot
—— **51** 13 **56** 221 **57** 281
337 **58** 323 **61** 303 **62**
xxviii **68** 98 **69** 300 **70**
299 **83** 195 **92** 320 **117**
13 19 **119** 217 **120** 208
145 45 171 233
— Capt. **58** 136
— Col. **85** 18 **95** 64
— Gen. **85** 129 **137** 310
— Mr. **125** 29
— Mrs. **83** 36
— Rev. **101** 221
____ (Amory) **140** 32
Aaron **94** 26
Abba Maria Wood **66** 128
Abel **85** 10 **100** 27 **106** 264
Abigail **51** 247 462 **53** 398
64 39 43 **82** 498 **100** 27
147 258
Abigail (Cargill) **117** 256
Abigail (Hale) **136** 326
Abigail (Marston)
113 302
Abigail B. **140** 253
Abijah **69** 295
Abraham **92** 320 **132** 275
Agnes **113** 71
Albert Hussey **94** 248

PRESCOTT *cont'd*
Alexander **113** 71
Alfred **94** 248
Alice **52** 428 **80** 222 **81**
222 236 **113** 70 71
Alice Durgin (Chase) **92**
137 **112** 226
Almira **68** 332
Alvah Rowe **66** 1
Ann **87** 229 236
Anna E. **69** 309
Anne Elizabeth
(O'Connell) **94** 27
Arthur Thompson
68 xxxv
Benjamin **53** 196 300 **54**
414 **56** 71 399 **57** 67 **61**
223 **82** 53 **83** 36 **87** 399
97 309 **100** 27 **101** 206
222 **104** 77 **107** 313 **113**
318 **139** 288
Benjamin Franklin
70 196
Benjamin T. **73** 193
Bethiah **61** 342
Betsey (Whittier) **113** 303
Betsey H. **74** lxxii
Bridget **113** 71
Caesar **64** 46
Calvin Stockbridge
113 303
Carlos Herbert **94** 27
Caroline D. C. **66** 112
Carrie J. **69** 137
Catherine **94** 248
Catherine Bradbury
71 190
Catherine Greene
(Hickling) **136** 326
Catherine L. (Clough)
88 329
Catherine Larkin **71** 190
Cecilie **113** 70 71
Charles F. **70** 319
Charles Herbert **94** 249
Charles Jones **71** 190
Charles Smith **104** 161
162
Cicely **113** 71
Comfort **67** 284
Cora Elma **74** lxxii
Cynthia **72** 259
David **59** 285 **126** 156
Dorcas (Dyke) **126** 66
Dorothy **53** 196 300 **83**
338 **99** 299 **106** 212 **136**
135
Drusilla Arvilla **109** 130
Eben Greenleaf **94** 249
Ebenezer **61** 304 **69** 189
77 23
Ebenezer Clough **71** 190
Edith **56** xliv
Edmund **69** 309
Edmund P. **70** 319
Edward **54** 197 **71** 190 **88**
277 282 329
Edward Franklin **113**
302 303
Edward Payson **94** 249
Eleanor **90** 225 **112** 226

PRESCOTT *cont'd*
Elene **113** 70
Eliphalet **59** 290
Elisha **104** 162
Eliza G. (Brackett) **95** 333
Elizabeth **53** 196 300 **54**
  cxxxviii **55** 136 **58** 124
  61 223 **69** 189 **72** 259
  73 49 **76** 211 **78** 423 **84**
  294 **100** 60 **103** 224 **108**
  312 **113** 71
Elizabeth (Brown) **131**
  31 202
Elizabeth (Higginson)
  104 77
Elizabeth (Mayhew)
  113 303
Elizabeth (Redington)
  109 50
Elizabeth Ann **72** 259
Ella Grace **69** 318
Ellen **113** 71
Elwin J. **69** 137
Emeline P. **94** 248
Emerson B. **94** 248
Emily **90** 50
Emily Ann (Woods)
  94 26
Emily Blanche **94** 27
Emily D. **69** 204
Emma Adella **94** 26
Emma Elizabeth (Frye)
  113 302
Esther **94** 249
Esther H. **73** 193
Etta May (Smith) **94** 26
Evelyn J. **69** 317
Experience (Huntley)
  101 206
Frances Lear **82** 423
Fred Elmer **94** 249
G. W. **91** 332
George **65** 261
George H. **65** 308
George Lincoln **66** 128
George W. **95** 333
George Washington **63**
  114 **82** 423 **83** 36 **95** 333
Georgiana Maud **94** 26
Grace **113** 71
Grace L. **98** 259 260
H. A. **64** 120
H. M.B. **58** 97
Hannah **70** 123 **92** 307 308
  115 129 **124** 152 **147**
  258
Hannah (Batchelder)
  113 302
Harriet **66** 111 **71** 61
  85 289
Harriet Gertrude **78** 206
Harriet Maria **94** 248
Helen **113** 71
Helen M. (Blount) **51** 77
  52 285 288 **58** xlv **97** 53
  54
Henry **61** 223 **64** 162 **65** 29
  83 36 **94** 248 **101** 222
  105 112 **113** 71
Henry Eugene **94** 26
Henry Kellogg **94** 26

PRESCOTT *cont'd*
Henry Martin **94** 248
Hope **53** 164
Huldah Elmira **72** 259
Huldah Jane **94** 248
Isaiah **69** 204
Israel **74** lxxii **94** 249
James **51** 61 **54** 99 **65** 78 79
  112 335 339 **66** 127 **70**
  211 217-219 301 **104** 162
  113 71 302 **115** 77 318
  121 48 **128** 121 **132** 275
  135 34
Jane **58** 234 **113** 71
Jane (Pendergast) **132** 275
Jed **59** 423
Jedediah **51** 463 **113** 302
Jeremiah **58** 234
Jesse **83** 143 145 **132** 275
  138 108
Joanna **69** 189 **79** 245
Joanna Abbott (Fitts)
  104 161
John **51** 124 **53** 190 196 300
  58 19 **60** 318 **61** 304 **64**
  94 161 252 **67** 280 **69**
  189 **71** 256 **73** 193 199
  76 lxxvi **78** 282 **79** 245
  82 101 **83** 195 **85** 455
  86 349 **92** 307 **93** 231
  95 8 **99** 80 **100** 27 **105**
  286 **107** 232 **108** 225
  112 238 **113** 70 71 302
  115 77 318 **125** 223 **129**
  349 **132** 275
John Melville **94** 248
Jonas **105** 224 **108** 243
  126 6 **143** 330
Jonathan **53** 193 196 300
  54 45 **55** 136 **68** 261 **78**
  423 **79** 398 **100** 81 **102**
  33 **110** 219 **131** 32 **142**
  73
Joseph **53** 398 **68** 332 **77**
  23 **78** 401 **93** 304 **100** 66
  105 287 **117** 9 16 **125** 30
  92
Joseph F. **69** 137
Josephine Winnifred
  94 27
Joshua **133** 287 **147** 258
Josiah **69** 268 **72** 259 **73** 49
Josiah A. **69** 316 317
Josiah Albert **72** 259
Josie Fitts **85** 197 **104** 135
  149 161
Judith **90** 70
Judith (Johnson) **132** 275
Lavinah **66** 110
Lucinda **67** 280
Lucius M. **94** 249
Lucretia **94** 249
Lucy **70** 122 **79** 50 **83** 331
  89 269 **90** 289 **115** 130
Lucy (Beaverstock)
  125 223
Lucy Ada (Jewett) **120** 75
  126 49
Lucy Oliver **83** 487
Lydia **68** 261 332 **75** lvii
Lyman W. **94** 249

PRESCOTT *cont'd*
Margaret **60** 28 **113** 71
Margaret A. F. **73** 193
Maria **66** 128 **84** 32
Marian **94** 137 **113** 147
Marion **113** 302
Martha **52** 434 **60** 28 **61**
  304 **68** 261 **69** 189 **71**
  256 **94** 248
Martha E. **94** 248
Martha Elizabeth **94** 249
Martha Lovejoy (Russell)
  113 303
Mary **53** 163 196 300 347
  55 376 **61** 73 74 222 223
  304 **64** 94 **70** 323 **78** 286
  82 423 **83** 18 **85** 455 **87**
  227 236 **95** 8 **100** 168
  102 33 **107** 232 **108** 243
  126 136 143
Mary (Boulter) **113** 302
Mary (Loker) **108** 243
  143 330
Mary (Pepperill) (Frost)
  (Colman) **104** 77
Mary (Pierce) **83** 18
Mary (Platt) **95** 8
Mary Adeline **82** 53
Mary Ann **67** 282 283
  68 159
Mary Clough **71** 190
Mary D. **67** 284
Mary E. **103** 312 **118** 132
Mary Emily (Cate)
  112 226
Mary Grafton Newmarch
  82 423
Melschack **94** 249
Mercy **53** 196 300
Mercy (Gibbs) **61** 223
  104 77
Meshech **148** 169
Mina (Jones) **88** 282
Moses Greenleaf **94** 248
Myra Sophia **95** 333
Nancy **147** 258
Olive **109** 128
Oliver **78** 72 **95** 364
  113 318
Orianna Maria **95** 333
Patience B. **90** 105
Persis (Hubbard) **94** 26
Peter **68** 364 **99** 80 **109** 50
  131 189
Phebe W. **69** 316
Phebe Worth **69** 268
Polly **59** 285
Rachel **69** 189 **117** 256
Rachel R. **59** 290
Ralph **113** 70 71
Rebecca **51** 61 **53** 196 300
  55 136 **58** 19 **59** lxiv **66**
  111 **84** 451 **86** 224 **100**
  254
Rebecca Jane **72** 259 266
  73 49
Rebecca P. **126** 206
Reform **86** 142
Reuben **52** 428
Richard **68** 353 366 **113** 7-9
  71

PRESCOTT *cont'd*
Robert Sedgwick **90** 225
  112 226
Robert Smith **104** 162
Roger **113** 71
Rufus **67** 284 **94** 249
Rufus Harrison **94** 249
Ruth **59** 284
Ruth (Smith) **136** 273
Sally **83** 143 **89** 365 **114**
  173 **142** 296
Samuel **53** 163 164 **55** 376
  83 18 **85** 354 **105** 286
  113 302 303 **131** 31 **132**
  275 **136** 273
Samuel Cate **91** 141 **112**
  226 **116** 227
Samuel Cate (Mrs.) **76**
  169 **80** 334 **81** 222 **83**
  230 **89** 147 **90** 151 225
  91 158 **92** 159 **93** 151
  99 266 267 **112** 133 226
Samuel Chase **90** 225
  112 226
Samuel Melcher **90** 225
  112 226
Samuel Potter **131** 202
Sarah **51** 463 **58** lxxxv **61**
  304 **64** 37 **69** 189 **73** 199
  90 55 **95** 294
Sarah (Dearborn) **138** 108
Sarah (Dumont) **126** 156
Sarah (Hayward) **86** 349
Sarah (Woodbury) **88** 277
Sarah Ann **71** 190
Sarah P. **69** 137
Sarah Worcester **79** 99
Sewell **117** 256
Silvena **72** 259
Simeon **104** 162
Simon Blake **94** 249
Sophronia **131** 31 202-204
Sophronia Potter **131** 30
  33
Stephen **66** 110 **78** 313
  94 249 **117** 256
Stephen Alfred **72** 259
Susan (Amory) **120** 83
Susan Edes **94** 249
Susanna **78** 184 **94** 315
  95 64
Sylvena **69** 316
Tappan **94** 248
Thomas **64** 252 **113** 71
Timothy **66** 128
Tryphonia (Wilbur)
  87 236 241
Vastil **79** 398
Warren **66** 111
Washington Lafayette
  71 190
Watson D. **83** 143
William **51** 102 503 **55** 368
  59 lxxv **63** 194 **64** 64
  202 **65** 82 107 111-113
  254 256-258 261-264 334
  335 337-339 **66** 128 181
  317 **68** 159 332 **69** 9 126
  212 219 224 **70** 15 19 **73**
  85 **76** lxv **77** 292 **81** 28
  87 236 241 **120** 83 **130**

PRESCOTT *cont'd*
  216 217 **131** 48 **136** 138
  326 **139** 101 **140** 183
  242
William Benjamin **98** 147
William H. **52** 388 **94** 248
  99 24 **140** 32
William Henry **62** 214
William Hickling **56** xliv
  59 235 236 **79** 232 **136**
  90 326
William Pepperell **71** 61
Worrall Dumont **107** 153
  120 75 **121** 236 **124** 312
Zulema **67** 280
Zulema Webster **90** 274
PRESCY Chase **105** 207
John **105** 208
Paul **105** 208
PRESENT William **55** 67
PRESERT
  Jonathan **112** 122
PRESGRAUE
  Alice **63** 283
PRESHAW
  Elizabeth **61** 342
PRESHO Abi **53** 437
Almira **54** 17
Anna **51** 224 **53** 437
Asa **54** 16
Billings Whitfield **53** 437
Clarissa **53** 437
Damaris **53** 437
Daniel **54** 17
Drusilla **53** 437
Ebenezer **54** 16
Elijah Williams **53** 437
Elizabeth **51** 290 **53** 437
Ezra **54** 17
Hannah **53** 437
Hosea **53** 437
Isaac **54** 17
James **51** 224 **54** 16
Joseph **53** 437
Laban **53** 437
Laura **54** 16
Luin **53** 437
Malinda **53** 437
Orpha **51** 292 **54** 16
Peter **53** 437
Phebe **53** 437
Polly **51** 290 **53** 437
Ruth Forbes **54** 17
Sally **53** 437
Samson **53** 437
Sarah **53** 437
Sullivan **54** 16
Varanes **53** 437
Vison **53** 437
William Henry **54** 17
Zadock **51** 292 **54** 16 17
PRESLEY —— **53** 13
John **69** 35
Sanford **73** 154
PRESMARCH
  Reynald de **99** 277
Preson *see* Preston
PRESSEL Willis Reid (Mrs.)
  104 145
PRESSER Elise **77** 252
  Theodore **77** 252

PRESSETT John **62** 332
PRESSEY Pressy
  —— **60** 107
Edwin Sidney **86** 371
Elbridge **110** 23 107
Fidelia **75** 254
Fidora **75** 254
Georgiana A. **75** 254
Hannah **58** 124
Helen Maria **75** 254
Hezekiah **52** 435
John **53** 162 **66** 34
John Friend **76** 19
Jonathan **75** 254
Lovilla **75** 254
Luella Winifred (Cole)
  86 371
Marietta **110** 107
Martha **53** 162
Mary **58** 123 **82** 211
  116 264
Moses **66** 108
Nancy (Gray) **110** 23
Olive **88** 330
Orrie Belle (Little) **86** 371
Park **72** 245 **73** xvii **80** 106
  81 214 **106** 116 121
Sarah F. **110** 107
Sidney Leavitt **86** 371
Stella Torney **76** 19
Susanna **66** 108
Tanizen **52** 435
Presson *see* Preston
Pressy *see* Pressey Presy
PRESTAGE John **115** 57
Prestewoode *see*
  Prestwood
PRESTHOLDT
  Harriet Alice **90** 169
PRESTIDGE
  Roger **65** 168
  Thom **65** 165
PRESTLAND Ann / Anne
  71 175 **75** 138
John **71** 175
PRESTON Preson Presson
  —— **57** 120 **62** 50 **86** 23
  120 319
  — Capt. **84** 264 267 **111**
  291 293
  — Dr. **51** 288 **62** 158 160
  71 359 **123** 164
  — Major **92** 312
  — Mrs. **83** 150 151 153
A. P. **68** 130
Aaron **56** 83
Abel **128** 254
Abigail **52** 310 **56** 318 **58**
  52 **62** 50 **66** 331 **68** 216
  75 145 **97** 257
Abigail (Eaton) **127** 136
Abigail (Maltby) **112** 45
Abigail (Sargent) **84** 95
Abigail (Thomas) **108** 291
Abigail E. **112** 45
Abraham **51** 288
Abylene **54** 201 **56** 253
Ada Estelle (Mason)
  102 303
Albert B. **51** 51
Alberta **88** 170

PRESTON *cont'd*
Alexander **54** 218
Alfred **68** xliii **84** 95
Alice **83** 432
Alice Briggs (Bryant) **134** 254
Alice de **96** 107
Alice Roberts (Parrish) **85** 199
Almira **69** 83
Amabel de **96** 107 122 123 320
Amariah **62** 75 **65** 382 **119** 122
Amos **69** 83 **119** 122
Amy (Knowlton) **86** 134
Andrew Jackson **75** 214
Andrew Peabody **83** 175 311 **84** 32
Ann H. (Sanford) **108** 196
Ann Maria **75** 205
Ann Withington **75** 214
Anna **59** 285 **69** 335 **119** 122
Anna (Hayward / Howard) **119** 122
Anna R. **83** 195
Anna Rantoul **83** 175
Annie **84** 239
Apphia **69** 318
Arthur John **117** 204
Asa **71** 117 **112** 45
Austin **67** 221
Bathsheba **69** 335
Bathsheba (Snow) **136** 19
Bebe **68** 220 **75** 145
Belle **54** 59 **84** 239 **143** 343
Benham **112** 45
Benjamin **66** 130 **69** 335 **119** 188 **134** 254 **136** 20
Bethiah **54** 199 **56** 253 **66** 131
Betsey T. **84** 88
Betty Louise Foster **118** 326
Buel **112** 45
Burtren D. **51** 51
Calvin **67** 118 **119** 188
Candace **112** 45
Caroline **51** 51
Caroline (Winchester) **87** 285
Caroline Matilda **78** 232
Catherine **103** 89
Charles Edward **75** 214
Charles H. **55** 344 **60** 190
Chloe **119** 188 **123** 176
Chloe (Hanks) (Doty) **86** 23
Christopher **68** 91
Clarence R. **84** 172
Clarence R. (Mrs.) **85** 197
Clarissa **69** 335
Colburn **54** 200 290 292 **58** 273
Cyprian **90** 186
Daniel **54** 292 **63** 83 **65** 63-66 **67** 118 **68** 218 221 **75** 145 199 **85** 17 **119** 188
Darius **67** 116-119 121

PRESTON *cont'd*
122 217 219 **69** 83
David **54** 290 **56** 82 385 **59** 285 **70** 119 **115** 128
David Christie **66** xlviii lii **67** 384 **68** xxx **84** 455
David Christie (Mrs.) **85** 204
Deborah **86** 334
Deborah (Holt) **119** 188
Dinah **119** 121 188
Dinah (Ford) **119** 188
Dorcas (Brown) **134** 254
Dorothy **65** 382
E. F. **123** 224
E. F. (Mrs.) **123** 224
Edith Florence **117** 204
Edith Spear (Garcelon) (Dennis) **84** 174 454
Edward **53** 73 **55** 445 **58** 73 **60** 39 **63** 279 **64** 22 **65** 64 **68** 217-219 221- 224 232 320 **75** 204 214 **81** 121 128 **83** 323 327 **120** 159 **121** 83
Edward M. **57** xxxiii 120
Edward V. **51** 51
Elbridge **62** 160
Eleanor **54** 199 200 290 292 297 **55** 429 **56** 388 **109** 26
Elisha **68** 318
Elisha H. **75** 205
Eliza **69** 335 **80** 247
Eliza Lorence **87** 286
Elizabeth **55** 299 445 **56** 81 **63** 376 **64** 76 **65** 63 66 **66** 131 360 **70** 241 **75** 145 **86** 134 **100** 296
Elizabeth (Hart) (Bacon) **119** 122
Elizabeth (Penrose) **116** 245
Elizabeth (Warren) **119** 122
Elizabeth White **83** 311
Ella Maria **83** 175
Elma Smythe **90** 186
Emeline **123** 14
Emma **78** 292
Erneburga de **96** 320
Estelle R. **51** 51
Esther (Cummins) **119** 188
Esther (Eaton) **119** 122
Esther P. **109** 271
Eugene **147** 334
Eugene D. **66** 92 **81** 213
Eugene Dyre **145** 265
Eunice **67** 122 **72** 116
Everett B. **51** 51
Fannie E. **104** 97
Fanny **144** 38
Fear G. **69** 83
Fidelia **75** 254
Florinda **67** 221
Frances **51** 288
Frank **134** 254
Frank Mortimer **83** 311
Fred **134** 254
Frederick **128** 311

PRESTON *cont'd*
George **62** 249 **68** 223
George E. **51** 51
George Rogers **52** 282 **78** 232
Gertrude Mary (Knight) **117** 204
H. **91** 332
H. L. **65** 382
Hackeliah **102** 102 **142** 343
Hannah **56** 80 82 **59** 73 **62** 70 158 161 **67** 116- 119 219 **69** 83 266 **83** 480 **107** 70
Hannah (Smith) **119** 122
Harriet **75** 214
Harriet Winchester **87** 285
Harris **112** 45
Helen Mason **100** 110 **102** 62 128 303
Henry **63** 84 **79** 149
Henry S. **69** 83
Hester **52** 123 125
Hovey **119** 122
Howard **134** 254
Howard Willis **69** xxxv **148** 150
Isaac **52** 123 125 **66** 130 **69** 266 **91** 240 243
Isabel **96** 314
Jacob **119** 122
James **52** 370 **56** 254 **63** 376 **64** 76 **66** 360 **95** 118 **97** 218
James Harry **75** 162 242
Jane (Owen) **134** 254
Jareb **119** 122
Jerusha **69** 83
Jesse M. **69** 335
Jessie **78** 292 **83** 311
Joan **75** 281 289
Joanna **55** 369 370
Joanna (Chapin) **128** 311
John **56** 80 81 **58** 397 **60** 39 **63** 279 **65** 64 **66** 113 123 124 **68** 224 318 320 **71** 358 **81** 433 449 **95** 364 **101** 271 **104** 263 **106** 146 **109** 163 **119** 121 122 **130** 107 **140** 238 **141** 230
Jonas **66** 35
Jonathan **51** 45 **65** lvi
Jonathan S. **123** 307
Joseph **52** 310 408 **70** 123 **102** 102 **115** 130
Joshua **51** 51 **56** 82 **67** 119 221 222 **69** 83 **87** 286
Judya **119** 122
Julia E. **112** 45
Julia M. (Flemming) **123** 307
Junia **119** 122
Justina H. **51** 51
Kenneth **108** 236 **109** 157 **110** 155 **111** 164 **112** 162
Kenneth B. **113** 161 **114** 157 **115** 156

PRESTON *cont'd*
Kenneth Bruce **110** 239
Laura **112** 45
Laura Guthrie (Curtis) **100** 338
Lawrence de **79** 366 368
Leonard J. **78** 232
Leonard Jarvis **87** 285
Levi **56** 83 **58** 52 **66** 131 **69** 335
Lida Margaret **84** 190
Lucius **123** 14
Lucretia **69** 335
Lucy **56** 139 **68** 232 **69** 140 **95** 363
Lucy (Devotion) (West) **119** 122
Lydia **91** 385
Mabel (McAfee) **84** 185
Margaret **63** 279
Margaret Anne (Christie) **84** 455
Margaret M. **69** 266
Margery **69** 252
Maria **63** 89 **75** 214
Maria L. (Salter) **83** 185 186
Maria S. **69** 335 **84** 32
Maria Salter **83** 175
Martha **69** 83 **94** 326 **100** 297 **101** 271
Mary **52** 408 **54** 218 **60** 193 **61** 388 **63** 279 **65** 64 66 **66** 129 131 **67** 49 374 **68** 217 219 **74** 186 **75** 145 199 204 214 **81** 126 433 **109** 67 **118** 259 **119** 121 122 **123** 12 **137** 259
Mary (Aldrich) **119** 122
Mary (Ford) **119** 122
Mary (Redington) **109** 163
Mary (Seabrook) **102** 102
Mary A. **104** 97
Mary A. (Moore) **84** 95
Mary Ann (Walker) **119** 122
Mary Belle (Munroe) **100** 93
Mary Desire **110** 33
Mary E. **85** 291
Mary Elizabeth **133** 124
Mary Ellen **75** 214
Mary H. **65** lvi
Mary Hamilton (Stockwell) **90** 186
Mary L. **85** 197
Mary M. **103** 89
Mary T. **91** 374
Mary W. **69** 319
Medinah **119** 122
Medine **69** 335 **119** 122
Mehitable **56** 199 **132** 73
Meribah (Slocum) **128** 254
Mersilvia **78** 364
Mina (Rich) **84** 40
Miner **84** 88
Molly **63** 89 **74** 184
Moses **56** 83
Nancy **70** 191

PRESTON *cont'd*
Nathan **124** 299
Nathaniel Cogswell **71** 138
Nellie A. **83** 301
Nellie E. **83** 299 301
Nicholas **75** 281 283 287 289
Noble D. **108** 196
Oliver **84** 40
Orrin **69** 83
Otis **65** 382
Patience (Gould) **119** 122
Patrick **95** 304
Patty **69** 83
Peter **76** 47 **84** 426
Phebe **101** 179
Phebe (Barney) **119** 122 **137** 35
Philatheta (Bibbens) **119** 188
Philip **56** 81
Polly (Winslow) **84** 426
Priscilla (Randall) **84** 95
Quartus **69** 83
Rachel **71** 11
Rachel (Lloyd) **107** 70
Randall **84** 95
Rebecca **52** 370 **70** 69 **71** 358 **75** 214 **123** 185 **135** 51
Rebecca (Farrar) **95** 364
Rebecca (Holt) **123** 14
Remember **53** 73 **68** 216-218 220 222 **75** 145 **140** 238
Richard **63** 279 **81** 433 **95** 304
Richard de **96** 107 110 111 114 115 122 123 312 319 320
Robert **81** 131
Robert Hall **105** 129
Roger **56** 80 **57** 120 **60** 190 **79** 421 **90** 308
Rosa Clemen **112** 45
Roswell **57** 120
Ruhamah **62** 75
Sabra L. **112** 45
Sally **56** 254 **67** 221 **95** 118 **97** 218
Sally (Clark) **140** 238
Sally (Dawson) (Forbes) **108** 164
Samuel **56** 139 **68** 218 **71** 358 **107** 70 **108** 291
Sarah **63** 84 **65** 64 **66** 129 **67** 117 118 221 222 **68** 217 **79** 149 **84** 94 **89** 232 **100** 241 **106** 146 **124** 299 **136** 274 **140** 238
Sarah (Cooke) **142** 343
Sarah (Eastman) **119** 122 **137** 35
Sarah (Hayward) **119** 122
Sarah (Wilson) **119** 122
Sarah Augusta **69** xlix
Sarah Augusta (Wyman) **87** 286
Sarah Eleanor Frances **75** 214

PRESTON *cont'd*
Sarah Elizabeth (Parran) **84** 96
Sarah Eveleth (Parran) **84** 95
Shubael **69** 335 **70** 241
Silas **110** 33
Solomon **69** 335
Sophronia **131** 29 33
Stephen Lewis **84** 455
Susan **51** 288
Susanna **65** 382 **69** 335 **72** 116
Susanna (Aldrich) **119** 122
Susanna (Stone) **84** 95
Susanna (Wood) **119** 122
Sylvanus **54** 200
Sylvester T. **69** 83
T. **57** 343
Tamar **63** 369
Thankful **67** 53
Theodore **72** 116
Thomas **56** 80 **63** 279 **64** 341 **65** 169 **84** 267 373 **104** 97
Timothy **71** 11
Tiras **119** 122
Titus **67** 53
Vinton Wingate **102** 303
Virginia **86** 154
W. R. **83** 308
Walter **134** 254
Warren **62** 75 160
Washington **92** 312
William **51** 288 **54** 21 **55** 299 445 **56** 318 **62** 360 **64** 338 **65** 63 64 66 67 **67** 118 374 **68** 92 **69** 254 **74** 184 186 **75** 280 **81** 126 **84** 95 **89** 305 **102** 102 **111** 213 **116** 245 **118** 259 **122** 80 **127** 136 **135** 100 **145** 358
William B. **78** 264
William Bowker **65** xxxv
William E. **75** 254 **94** 101
William Gibbons **58** xliii **65** xliv lvi
William Henry **83** 175
William Peabody **83** 311
William R. **83** 175 185 186
Wilson **119** 122
Wynne **100** 93
Zephaniah **63** 89
Zera **119** 122
PRESTWICH
James **70** 244
Joseph **70** 244
Susan **70** 244
Thomas **82** 188
PRESTWOOD Prestewoode
—— **110** 198
Cuthbert **93** 18
PRESWICKE
Roger **65** 48
Presy *see* Pressey Presy
PRETCH Charles **115** 133
PRETLOW
Elizabeth **97** 334

PRETTEY Henry **147** 29
PRETTYMAN Prittyman
— Mr. **52** 124
Joanna B. **128** 263
PREVET James **78** 55
PREVITE-ORTON
——— **110** 41-43
PREVOST
  Elizabeth **115** 111
  Emily Theodosia **115** 111
  George W. **115** 111
  Harriet E. **102** 152
  Julius S. **102** 152
  Phebe **121** 183
  Richard **53** 417
PREW George **116** 258
  Matilda (Gravlin) **116** 258
  Nelson J. **130** 54
  Sarah L. **130** 54
Pribble *see* Preble
Prible *see* Preble
PRICE Pricce Pryce
  ——— **51** 262 **52** 397 **55** 229
    59 265 **92** 273 318 **101**
    271 **114** 302 **124** 103
    140 238
— Gen. **78** 327
— Maj. **120** 126
— Mr. **62** 284
— Mrs. **63** 56 **127** 138
— Widow **69** 375
  ——— (Avery) **140** 34
  ——— (Hall) **140** 150 238
  Abigail **52** 371 **68** 292 **69**
    236 **89** 291
  Alexander **111** 145
  Alice **102** 175
  Alice Lillian **111** 187
  Alice P. (Welch) **111** 18
    187
  Amanda **54** 171
  Amanda M. **77** 180
  Amarilla **114** 180
  Amos Jonas **89** 313
  Amy **114** 180
  Amy (Covell) **114** 180
  Amy A. **77** 181
  Anderson **79** 329
  Angelia S. (Hood) **88** 344
  Ann **92** 202 **105** 80 **115**
    10
  Ann (Moore) **98** 349
  Ann Maria **82** 477
  Anna **106** 43 **128** 268
  Anna (Cooper) **92** 201
  Anna Black **78** 326
  Anna Maria **92** 201
  Anne **65** 291 **139** 139
  Anne (Wood)
    139 139-141
  Anne McDowell **102** 66
  Annie **87** 194
  Annie Leavenworth
    92 200 202
  Antoinette **79** 329
  B. H. **91** 332
  Bathsheba **70** 227
  Belle Charlotte (Bancroft)
    97 126
  Benjamin **123** 133
  Benoni **129** 274

PRICE *cont'd*
  Bertha Wilson **109** 239
  Betsey **69** 369 **92** 22
  Beulah **79** 201 **102** 218
    103 124
  Byron C. **111** 187 189
  Caroline (Everett) **88** 338
  Caroline Brooks (Ward)
    96 390
  Carrie Ernestine **117** 160
  Carrie L. **117** 160
  Catherine **97** 126
  Catherine Frances **92** 201
  Charles **92** 27
  Charles Edward **92** 201
  Charles Stuart **79** 329
  Christina **92** 201
  Christina Elizabeth
    92 201
  Christine **102** 166
  Christopher **89** 62
  Clarence (Mrs.) **84** 186
    231 **104** 65 147
  Clarina **69** 364
  Clark Monroe (Mrs.)
    94 83
  Clarky Nunnery **118** 326
  Cromwell **112** 289
  Crummal **61** 388
  D. Otis **117** 160
  Daniel **68** 294 **69** 132 237
  David **68** 171 177 292 294
    378 **69** 364 375 **70** 39
  Deborah **123** 133
  Deborah (Gibbs) **123** 133
  Dorothy **133** 99
  Ebenezer **64** 228 **68** 292
    378 **69** 236 **105** 284 **114**
    301
  Edward **62** 246 **92** 200 201
    94 276 **127** 303
  Elihu **89** 291
  Eliza **83** 432 438 **86** 288
  Elizabeth **52** 371 **66** 258 **70**
    37 **80** 244 **92** 19 **114** 126
    130 289 **131** 107 **135**
    339 **139** 139 **143** 138
    348 **146** 385
  Elizabeth (Bull) **100** 243
  Elizabeth (Cromwell) **143**
    340 343 348
  Elizabeth (Geiger) **89** 62
  Elizabeth (Johnson)
    98 348
  Elizabeth (Robinson)
    127 111
  Elizabeth (White) **98** 348
    349
  Elizabeth Ann **83** 511
    125 99
  Elizabeth Anne **92** 201
  Elizabeth Jane (McGraw)
    146 387
  Ellen **69** 364
  Ellura Frances (Lazell)
    89 313
  Emanuel **77** 180
  Emma Theodora **86** 196
    91 299 **92** 150 **98** 348
    349
  Ethel **91** 394

PRICE *cont'd*
  Eunice **68** 293 **69** 369 378
    70 36
  Everett Warren **92** 202
  Ezekiel **53** 179 **77** 313 **84**
    168 **92** 16 18 19 21 22 27
    94 295 **140** 34 148 238
    323 **144** 232
  F. H. **91** 202
  Fanny B. **77** 268
  FitzJames **55** 424 **140** 238
  Frances **68** 227 **78** 72
  Francis **53** 73
  Fred James **82** 272
  Frederick **73** 224
  Frederick Leavenworth
    92 202
  Frederick Ponsonby
    92 202
  G. **62** 109
  George **62** 84
  George (Mrs.) **81** 106
  George B. **115** 131
  George F. **64** 69
  George H. **117** 160
  George Michener **98** 348
    349
  George P. **116** 257
  George W. **52** 371
  Gertrude Sarah **92** 201
  Gold **69** 369
  Grace **121** 89
  Grace (Peck) **121** 91
  Grace Agnes **79** 203
  Grace E. **117** 160
  Gurnet **101** 54
  H. E. **111** 192
  Hannah **68** 294 378 **69**
    132 237 **70** 36 **110** 48
    111 187 **131** 107 **133**
    323 **134** 45
  Hannah (Chase) **87** 328
  Hannah Catherine **98** 359
  Hannah Davis **107** 211
  Hannah Jane **98** 359
  Hanoia **61** 352
  Harriet Jane **97** 119
  Henrietta Florence (Jay)
    94 83
  Henry **54** cxliii 191 **84** 154
    88 337 338 **94** 61 **140**
    238
  Henry Yelverton **125** 235
  Herman **92** 318
  Hester **68** 378 **70** 33
  Hezekiah **68** 293 378 **69**
    369 **70** 36
  Howell **115** 9
  Hugh **64** 216
  Huldah **69** 364
  Hurd **69** 236 **121** 89 91
  Isaac **114** 192 **123** 133
  Isabella Hughes **79** 329
  Ivie **77** xxix
  J. **91** 332
  J. Lampton **78** 290
  Jacob **88** 278
  Jacob T. B. **52** 371
  James **73** 137 **92** 201 **93**
    206 **118** 326 **140** 150
    238

PRICE *cont'd*
James Grandison (Mrs.)
  105 129
James H. **77** 181
James J. **92** 201 202
James John **92** 200
Jane **102** 168 175
Jerusha **61** 388
Jessie Christina **80** 244
Joan **66** 258 **102** 171-175
  107 268 **140** 181
Joanna **52** 371 **102** 175
John **53** 266 **54** 191 **57** 314
  59 109 **61** 135 **62** 250
  64 31 165 **65** 127 **66** 258
  84 456 **87** 328 **91** 394
  102 171-176 **106** 83 **115**
  10 178 **127** 111 139
John Avery **92** 21
John B. **80** 244
John Edward (Mrs.)
  105 129
John Robinson **92** 201
Jonathan **128** 268
Jonne **102** 171
Joseph **52** 371 **59** 327 **92**
  201 **93** 206
Joseph H. **114** 183
Joylieffe **61** 48
Keziah **79** 319
L. H. **111** 192
LaRue (Anderson)
  105 129
Lemuel **68** 175 286 287 378
  69 374 377
Lillian C. (Merrow)
  84 456
Lois **92** 201 202
Lucy (Eaton) **116** 257
Lucy Jane **102** 168
Lydia **69** 377
Lyman **97** 126
Mabel Josephine (Custer)
  (Fracker) **124** 259
Margaret **102** 171 172
  174 175
Margaret (Murphey)
  125 175
Maria Margaret **140** 238
Marian C. **118** 132
Mark Cordier (Mrs.) **77**
  xxix 77
Marshall L. **142** 382
Martha **115** 178
Martha W. **113** 145
Mary **56** 35 **64** 31 137 **67**
  219 **68** 286 293 378 **69**
  369 374 **70** 37 **73** 141
  231 274 **84** 99 **91** 394 **93**
  180 **96** 397 **105** 52 **115**
  169 178 **120** 250 **123**
  133 **148** 18
Mary (Marplehead) **93**
  206 **127** 185
Mary (Michener) **98** 349
Mary (Montgomery)
  112 289
Mary (Parsons) **98** 348
Mary Ann **92** 200 **98** 148
Mary Bell **78** 290
Mary Demming **92** 18

PRICE *cont'd*
Mary Jane (Benchley)
  (Cornwall) **142** 382
Mary L. **84** 456
Mary Pearl Brown **95** 400
Mary Thomas **81** 457
Matthew **92** 201 **127** 111
  129 274
Mattie Jane **82** 272
Maud Alice **82** 272
Maude Maranda **77** 323
  78 206
Mordecai **98** 348
Myra **98** 349
Myra Agnes (Kelsey) **98**
  348 349
Naomi **69** 132 **70** 38
Nathan **68** 378
Nathaniel **52** 371 **62** 322
  70 227
Nicholas **52** 318
Oliver **123** 133
Paul **114** 5
Penelope **62** 84
Peter **98** 359 **111** 187
Pheba A. (Russell) **128** 92
Phebe **86** 339 **99** 37
  123 133
Phebe (Coates) **98** 349
Phebe (Gibbs) **123** 133
Polly **84** 154 **140** 148
Polly X. **85** 170
Rachel **68** 294 **92** 305
Ralph **109** 271
Rebecca **61** 48 **68** 292 **69**
  364 **70** 39 75
Reuben **70** 75
Reynold Knox **98** 349
Rice **65** 119
Richard **54** 96 **61** 145 **65**
  291 **73** 142 **98** 349 **106**
  83 **110** 310 **124** 95 **143**
  343 348
Richard Annesley **92** 201
Richard W. **142** 4
Richarda **92** 200
Richarda Lois **92** 201
Robert **64** 337 **97** 126
Robert Tottenham
  92 201 202
Roger **61** 112 **62** 199 **67**
  288 **71** 59 **100** 243 **125**
  235 **144** 166
Rosamund (Ingalls)
  111 145
Rose **92** 201
Rosina Eleanor **92** 201
Roswell **67** 219
Ruth **92** 18 19 21 22
Ruth (Avery) **84** 168
  140 238
S. (Kislow) **128** 268
Sally (Jackson) **88** 278
Samuel **65** 118 **68** 175 378
  69 132 **70** 37 38 **76** 52
  85 170 **98** 349 **129** 63
Sarah **52** 371 **63** 90 **64** 12
  68 175 287 378 **69** 132
  379 **70** 37 **138** 211
Sarah (Chadwick) **127** 111
Sarah Ann **89** 62

PRICE *cont'd*
Seth **68** 293 378 **69** 369
  123 133
Simeon **92** 273 312
  123 133
Sophia Maria (Beatty) **92**
  201 202
Sophia Richarda **92** 202
Stephen **92** 201
Sterling **77** 142
Susanna **55** 424 **115** 79
  123 133 **126** 191
Theodore **139** 139 140
Thomas **52** 31 **55** 83 **56** 35
  57 94 **61** 352 **63** 241 **64**
  107 **66** 258 **70** 57 **82** 385
  98 348 **102** 175 **127** 138
Thomas Brooke (Mrs.)
  96 390
Towson **79** 329
V. C. **124** 259
Violet Hallett **103** 237
Wa: **53** 51
Walter **63** 362 **68** 196 **102**
  190 **131** 107 **139** 139
Walter A. **88** 344
Warren **123** 133
Warren Beatty **92** 202
William **52** 393 **54** 171
  58 64 69 **60** 399 **61** 112
  62 323 **84** 269 **91** 206
  93 206 385 **94** 95 **100** 65
  117 160 **123** 133 **125**
  175 **127** 185 221 **136**
  262
William Gladding **54** 171
William J. **117** 160
William W. **128** 92
Worthy **111** 187 **147** 68
Zalmon **69** 364
Zelma Wells **116** 233
  117 238 **118** 327 **119** 76
Prichard *see* Pritchard
Pricherd *see* Pritchard
Prichet *see* Pritchett
PRICKE Mary **69** 249
  Timothy **69** 249
PRICKER John **64** 325
PRICKETT
  Allan **93** 23 37
  Ann **108** 275
  Ann (Chambers) **93** 23 37
  Ann Eliza **114** 185
  Elizabeth **93** 37
  George Washington
    113 153
  Julia Ann (McKee)
    113 153
  Mary Ethelinda **113** 153
  Nathaniel **83** 321
  William **93** 37
PRIDDLE
  Elizabeth **143** 155
PRIDE Abigail **60** 124
  Absalom **77** 43
  Elijah **70** 109 113
  Eliphaz **57** 334
  Elisha **118** 40 46 48
  Elizabeth **84** 403
  Elizabeth (Bond) **137** 20
  Eunice **57** 187

PRIDE *cont'd*
Experience (Whittemore) **127** 204
Frank **86** 130
Hannah **55** 179
Herbert **70** 201
Huldah **77** 43
Ira **127** 204
Jane **62** 95
John **62** 95 **70** 105 **116** 149 **119** 18
Joseph **116** 7 **137** 20
Lucy (Silvester) **86** 130
Margaretta **132** 164
Mary **70** 201 **93** 371 **127** 204
Micajah **116** 7
Miria 215 **125** 215
Polly **77** 43 52
Robert **60** 124
Ruth **57** 334
Sally **60** 124
Sarah **102** 239
Susanna **86** 66
William **57** 187 **60** 124 **62** 95 **70** 105 **116** 7 **127** 204
Zipporah **55** 179 **70** 109 113
PRIDEAUX Prydeaux
Bridget **61** 40 41
Edmund **100** 216
Humfrey **142** 366
John **63** 190
Nicholas **61** 40 41
William **51** 287 **55** 101
Pridget *see* Pritchett
PRIDMORE
Elizabeth **97** 279
PRIE Mary B. **125** 243
Prier *see* Prior
Priesley *see* Priestly
PRIEST De Preist Preast
—— **69** 315 **82** 52 414 **83** 36 **93** 122 251 255 **130** 69
— de **60** 318
— Mr. **57** 228
— Widow **83** 36
Aaron **73** 104
Abigail **64** 7 **79** 396 **109** 65
Abraham **65** 66 **125** 219
Adelie **124** 203
Adeline H. **124** 203
Albert Wallace **93** 122
Alice Lucinda **56** 206 **78** 330 **79** 201 **82** 251 **83** 246 254 **84** 111 186 205 **85** 214 **86** 214 **87** 188 **93** 207 **98** 364 **100** 272 331 **101** 43 153 237 283 **102** 74 237 **104** 198 **108** 217 **109** 65 127 133
Allen **69** 315
Alonzo **93** 255
Andrew **90** 112
Ann **61** 250
Anna **79** 396
Annie M. **69** 315
B. C. **100** 207
Benjamin **69** 124 301 **70** 9

PRIEST *cont'd*
10 **124** 203
Betsey F. **76** 37
Caldona **78** 319
Catherine Brewer (Marcan) **113** 295
Charles F. **61** 344
Chloe **66** 339
Clara **100** 207
Damaris **79** 396
Daniel **58** 374
Deborah **82** 290 297
Deborah (Tupper) **99** 291
Degory **103** 297 **111** 320 **122** 51 **124** 111 **141** 204 **142** 359 **143** 203
Deliverance **52** 438 **60** 285 **84** 327 **90** 369 **126** 305
Dwight Edward **109** 65 127 **120** 232
Dwight Solomon **109** 65
Eldora **100** 207
Eliza **83** 23 27
Elizabeth **65** 66 **92** 307 308 **93** 206 **100** 298 **127** 185
Elizabeth (Buford) **111** 121
Elizabeth (Cogan) **110** 194
Elizabeth Katharine Whitford **51** 444
Ellen Mabel (Langford) **59** xlviii **90** 125 **113** 295
Ellen Marean **113** 295
Elliot (Mrs.) **99** 168
Ephraim **134** 117
Ernest **69** 315
Esther (Brown) **95** 315
Eunice Maria **81** 38
Ewina **93** 251
Francis **61** 249 **82** 52 53
Frank Bigelow **59** xlviii **74** xxviii **90** 125
Gabriel **76** 50 **109** 65
George **93** 122
George Eaton **113** 295
George Wesley **113** 295
George Wesley (Mrs.) **112** 220 **113** 295
Georgiana **93** 251
Hannah **73** 204 **77** 295 **78** 408 **93** 206 207 **114** 184 **127** 185 **130** 69 **133** 323
Hannah (Hager) **93** 207 **127** 185
Harriet Elizabeth **65** xxxvii
Hattie **100** 207
Henry **69** 315
Hephzibah **79** 396
Holman **104** 131
Hugh **111** 320
Huldah (Wells) **125** 219
Jacob **61** 250 **88** 335 **90** 112
James **53** 25 **65** 63 66 **77** 295 **93** 206 207 **115** 57 **127** 185 **141** 300
Jeremiah **69** 246 **109** 65
Jerome **124** 206
Joel **93** 122 251 255
Joel Henry **93** 122

PRIEST *cont'd*
John **61** 250 **66** 339 **70** 302 **73** 204 **79** 396 398 **82** 52 **109** 65 **114** 184
John Fox **113** 295
John Sylvester **113** 295
Jonathan **79** 396 **99** 291
Joseph **65** 238 **69** 302 **93** 206 207 **115** 57 **127** 185
Josiah **92** 306 **144** 215
Josiah Stedman **93** 122
Katharine **111** 121
Katharine Langford **113** 295
Leah **59** 159
Leon A. **124** 207
Levi **58** 374
Louisa **66** 12
Louisa (Hoar) **124** 207
Lucy **124** 203 **127** 295
Lucy Amands **124** 203
Lydia **93** 206
Mabel **124** 207
Margaret **81** 449
Maria **79** 396
Martha **64** lvii
Martha de **60** 318
Mary **61** 250 **73** 204 **79** 396 398 **81** 449 **122** 51
Mary (Bacon) **109** 66
Mary (Gum) **109** 66
Mary (Whitney) **109** 66
Mary Ann (East) **88** 335
Mary E. **73** 194
Mary Ella **95** 315
Mary Wallace (Whittier) **113** 295
Micah **95** 315
Michael Leslie **82** 53
Nancy **61** 249 250 **88** 279
Nathan **83** 36 **109** 65
Orrin Allen (Mrs.) **101** 125 **108** 131
Paris **100** 207
Peggy **66** 339
Pelatiah **76** 37
Peter **111** 320
Philip **71** 261
Priscilla **140** 128 129 132
Rachel **79** 396
Rachel (Garfield) **109** 65
Richard **81** 449
Robert **78** 319
Roger **110** 194
Ruth Hall **101** 125 **108** 131
Sally **81** 37 **82** 53 **90** 112 **124** 203
Sally (Hoar) **134** 118
Sarah **61** 250 359 **82** 27 **110** 182 **124** 203 **128** 161 **141** 204 **142** 359
Sarah (Hoar) **134** 117 118
Sarah Ann (Edwards) **90** 112
Susan **124** 203
Susan Mandana (Caldwell) **109** 65
Susanna **69** 246
T. **82** 414
Thomas **82** 52 53
Walter **93** 255

PRIEST cont'd
  Wilbur N. **81** 38
  William **59** 159 **82** 52 53
    290 297 **111** 121 **119**
    316
PRIESTLY Preestley
  Priesley Priestley
  Abigail **125** 104
  Alice **61** 65
  Amy **61** 65
  James **116** 289
  John **61** 65 **113** 268
  Jonathan **64** 254
  Joseph **51** 231
  Mary (Fairman) **113** 268
  Richard **61** 65
  Thomas **113** 268
  William **61** 65
PRIESTMAN
  Amy V. **69** 262
  Joan **63** 35
  John **69** 262
  Martha **69** 262
  Robert William (Mrs.)
    85 197
PRIGG Prigge
  Ann (Cook) **100** ?41
  Judith **101** 51
  Mary **52** 120
  Samuel **100** 241 **101** 51
PRIGGER Edward Reuben
  (Mrs.) **87** 174 **107** 223
  108 140
  Laura A. **105** 79
  Laura Ann (Wilbraham)
    87 174 **107** 223
PRIHERCH Thomas **55** 434
PRIL Sara Anthonetta de
  93 189
PRIMATE Josiah **67** 72
PRIME — Col. **89** 34
  Alexander **63** 178 **74** 259
  Alfred Cox (Mrs.) **96** 27
  Ann **107** 152
  Apphia **63** 178 **74** 259
  Betsey **59** 289
  Charlotte Wilkins **82** 195
  Cornelia **82** 195 **86** 342
  Cornelia (Sands) **107** 152
  Edward **82** 195
  Elizabeth **74** 38 262
  Elizabeth (Swett) **114** 127
  Emily **82** 370
  Frederick **86** 198 **107** 68
    138 152
  Grant **123** 48
  Hiram **59** 289
  Horace **123** 91
  James **74** 185 189 262
  John **123** 96
  John (Mrs.) **123** 96
  John H. **76** 274
  Joseph **74** 185 189 **91** 272
    132 271
  Joshua **82** 195 **107** 152
  Laurette De Tousard
    (Coxe) **107** 152
  Lewis **99** 327
  Lydia **74** 185 189
  Lydia (Hare) **107** 152
  Mark **63** 178 **74** 259 **82** 195

PRIME cont'd
  370 **93** 33 **98** 298 **107**
  152 **114** 127
  Martha **104** 162
  Mary **97** 133
  Mary (Tibbetts) **99** 327
  Mary C. **74** xxv
  Mary Catherine **81** 109
    230 **82** 195
  Mary Gardiner (Curtis)
    107 152
  Mehitable (Platts) **107** 152
  Natalie **102** 227
  Nathaniel **82** 195 370
    107 152
  Olive **63** 176 **74** 259
  Pamelia (Doud) **123** 50
  Penelope **63** 71
  Ralph Earl **57** 340
  Rebecca **74** 261
  Ruby Belle (Hill) **97** 158
    102 227
  Sally **63** 178 **74** 259
  Sally (Tibbetts) **98** 298
  Samuel **82** 195 **107** 152
  Sarah **140** 210
  Sarah (Jewett) **107** 152
  Sarah (Platts) **107** 152
  Stephanie **102** 227 **103** 120
  Stephen LeRoy **102** 227
  Stephen LeRoy (Mrs.)
    97 158 **102** 62 129 227
  Sylvester Gardiner
    107 152
  Temple **53** 458 461 **54**
    xxxix 458 **55** xxxii **114**
    263-265
PRIMMER Mary **90** 204
PRIMROSE Prymrose
  Alexander **118** 50 54-57
  Edith **79** 414
  Edward **81** 94
  George **79** 414
  J. S. **64** xxxii
  Quentin Le **137** 362
  William **65** 21 27 **118** 54
Prinale see Prindle
PRINCE Prence
  —— **54** ccxcix 381 **56** 335
    58 153 **61** 59 98 **62** 284
    389 **65** 276 **66** 29 **74** 201
    92 13 351 **93** 251 252
    255 **114** 118 **115** 101
    136 34 **140** 60 238 254
  — Gov. **95** 45 103 108
  — Mr. **66** 114
  Abbie Kinsley (Norman)
    108 150
  Abby **55** lviii
  Abel **67** 129
  Abiel **61** 236
  Abigail **67** 159 206 **92** 17
    140 69 238
  Abigail (Chapman)
    143 253
  Abigail (Kimball) **108** 150
  Abigail G. (Reed) **98** 207
  Adam **143** 247
  Agatha Manetta **106** 125
  Agnes **143** 247
  Agnes (Gordon) **140** 238

PRINCE cont'd
  Agnes Gordon **93** 123
  Albert Gordon **92** 257
  Alice **52** 339 **123** 251 **142**
    350 **143** 253
  Alice (Honor) **108** 150 **143**
    248 250
  Alice Florence **79** 34
  Alpheus **114** 176
  Amanda J. **103** 161
  Amelia **93** 123
  Andrew Henshaw **92** 28
  Ann **65** 187 **108** 150
  Ann R. **125** 217
  Anna **51** 114 **61** 237
  Anna (Hobart) (Barstow)
    143 248 249 252
  Anna McCarthy **92** 118
  Anna S. C. **122** 299
  Anna Storer **77** 297
  Anne **68** lxxi
  Apphia **59** 217
  Apphia (Quicke)
    (Freeman) **97** 393
  Arlon Polsey (Mrs.)
    102 125
  Arminda B. (Clark)
    123 10
  Bathsheba (Snow) **136** 34
  Benjamin **85** 363 **99** 299
    121 24 **142** 207 **143** 248
    253
  Benjamin Clarke **92** 27
  Bernard Henry **93** 255
  Betsey **61** 380 **84** 364
    93 262
  Betsey (Cutler) **84** 382
  Betsey F. (Higgins)
    123 203
  Betty **93** 262
  Caleb **84** 153 **143** 253
  Caroline **92** 122 250 257
    344 351 **93** 252 **108** 150
  Caroline (Prince) **92** 122
    108 150
  Catherine **100** 278
  Charles **81** 409 **91** 332
  Charles A. **140** 156 238
  Charles Albert **55** xcii
  Charles Henry **92** 351
  Charlesia M. **83** 301
  Charlotte G. **122** 295
  Christopher **52** 200 **68**
    227 **92** 13 14 **126** 256
    128 20
  Clara H. **117** 134
  Cora B. (Mitchell) **83** 436
    438
  Crissa **136** 33
  D. C. (Mrs.) **103** 239
  Daniel McCarthy **92** 26
  David **92** 284 **97** 395 **106**
    71 **143** 253
  David Chandler (Mrs.)
    98 147
  David M. **83** 178 185
  Deborah **84** 250 **89** 109
    323 **106** 230 **121** 107
    201
  Deborah (Fuller) **108** 150
  Edson **123** 10

PRINCE *cont'd*
Edward **60** 190
Elisha **143** 253
Eliza (Watson) **88** 289 290
Eliza E. **81** 409
Elizabeth **63** lv **66** 338 **67**
  159 **88** 363 **91** 351 353
  354 **92** 17 27 28 **121** 13
  137 **126** 280 **129** 36 38
  140 238 **143** 135 249
  250 **146** 321 324
Elizabeth (Allen) **108** 150
Elizabeth (Cutler) **140** 238
Elizabeth (Gould) **143** 253
Elizabeth (Harraden)
  146 324
Elizabeth (Paine) **143** 253
  145 263
Elizabeth (Starr) **96** 378
Elizabeth (Tolderbury)
  143 247 248
Elizabeth (Woodin) **88**
  363 **121** 138
Elmira **137** 182
Enoch **143** 253
Ethel (Jaques) **96** 161
Eugene DeFersey **88** 289
Eugene Mitchell **88** 290
Eunice **142** 207
Experience **142** 272 360
  143 250
F. O. **56** 339
Fanny **61** 378 **67** 129
Frances (Davis) **140** 58
Francis **51** 144
Frank A. **52** 97
Frederic O. **93** 255
Frederick **114** 185 **123** 122
Frederick H. **55** lviii
Frederick Henry **75** xxiv
  64 **107** 125 **108** 137 150
Frederick Octavius **55**
  xcii **73** xxxvi **108** 150
George **61** 380 **100** 278
  143 247
George Ingersoll **140**
  156 238
Gertrude **122** 299
Gordon **73** xxxvi **93** 255
Gordon Chickering **73**
  xxxvi
Grace Thurber (Cilley)
  (Tibbetts) **89** 109
Guy Salisbury **88** 290
Hannah **79** 293 **95** 48 **102**
  49 **123** 11 13 14 **142** 36
  147 362
Hannah (Rogers) **140** 210
Harold Sherman (Mrs.)
  96 161
Harriet **145** 255
Hattie (Sutton) **83** 438
  84 20
Heavy **67** 159
Helen (Friedenthal)
  108 151
Helen (Levy) **108** 151
Helen Choate **55** xcii
Helen Ricker **99** 57
Helen Susan **73** xxxvi

PRINCE *cont'd*
Helen Susan (Henry)
  108 150
Hezekiah **106** 230 **131** 247
Hezekiah Blanchard **91**
  353 **92** 26
Honour **54** 406 **143** 253
Howard L. **61** 98
Isaac **61** 374 **67** 158 **85** 363
  121 104 **142** 121 **143** 48
  248 249 251 253 254 **146**
  324
Isabella (Hunt) **143** 247
Jacob **143** 253
James **79** 159 **85** 363 **91**
  332 **92** 12 122 128 **94**
  297 **108** 150 **123** 203
  140 238 **143** 252 253
James Moulton **114** 176
Jane **60** 239 **79** 292 442
  102 47 **106** 229
Jane (Callender) **144** 201
Jane Hayston **57** liii
Jerusha (Tupper) **99** 299
Joanna **143** 139 251
Joanna (Morton) **143**
  250 251
Job **84** 364 382 **85** 363 **91**
  353 354 **92** 12 13 16 17
  26-28 117 121 **93** 262
  108 150 **121** 20 **140** 69
  238 **142** 143 **143** 248
  249 251 252
John **52** 314 **53** 172 **61** 98
  67 14 158 **85** 363 **88** 58
  363 **92** 13 **100** 149 **106**
  230 **108** 150 **117** 8 **119**
  75 **121** 10 275 **123** 10
  139 131 133 **142** 115-
  118 272 350 360 **143** 247-
  250 338 340 **146** 324
John A. **116** 260
John B. **143** 247
John Rogers **80** 333 **81**
  219 **88** 160 289 290 **89**
  135
John Tucker **57** 121
Jonathan **88** 58 **140** 210
Joseph **57** 281 388 **66** 338
  82 325 **96** 378 **105** 206
  208 **121** 15 **123** 10 **141**
  356 **143** 139 248-251 253
Joseph Freeman **123** 10
Josiah **143** 252
Judith **51** 224 **53** 427
Juliana (Doddington)
  143 247
Katharine **51** 114
Kimball **108** 150
L. M. **121** 80
Laura Augusta **81** 203
Lebenon **122** 295
Lida Cox **108** 160
Lillian **73** xxix xxxvi
Lillian Chickering
  63 xxxiii
Lois Lucy **88** 290
Louisa Gordon **122** 299
  301
Louise M. **143** 247
Lucy (Colfax) **126** 256

PRINCE *cont'd*
  128 20
Lydia **75** 126 **125** 108
  143 251
M. C. **91** 332
M. O. **91** 332
Martha **77** 313 **114** 185
  118 212 **121** 18 **129** 38
  143 249 251 255
Martha (Barstow) **118** 212
  143 252
Martha W. **85** 322
Mary **52** 200 **53** 30 **59** 217
  67 158 **71** 167 168 **74**
  200 **92** 14 **99** 65 **100** 133
  106 39 232 **121** 22 120
  195 **136** 314 **143** 43 48
  252 253
Mary (Ashley) **143** 253
Mary (Charnock)
  (Greenwood) **143** 253
Mary (Collier) **126** 280
Mary (Howes) **100** 320
Mary (Moulton) **114** 176
Mary (Mussey) **123** 11
Mary (Townsend)
  143 253
Mary (Turner) **143** 48
  253 254
Mary Ann Rogers
  83 183 185
Mary H. (McIntosh)
  123 10
Mary Ivis **92** 26
Maude Elizabeth
  (Mitchell) **88** 290
Mehitable **143** 252
Mercy **60** 239 **79** 295 **122**
  293 **136** 34 **143** 251
Mercy (Hinckley) **143**
  252 253 **144** 226
Morris M. **83** 438 **84** 20
Morton (Mrs.) **84** 342
  85 197
Morton Peabody **94** 139
Nancy **88** 331 **114** 3 **133**
  309 310
Nancy M. (Marcy) **116** 260
Nathan **91** 94 **143** 252
Norman **73** xxxvi **108** 150
Onner **53** 265 267 **113** 139
  143 253
Orpha Matilda (Bebee)
  88 289 290
Patience **53** 111 **59** 217
Patience (Brewster) **114** 3
  115 91 **126** 280
Paul **53** 372
Phebe (Fuller) **106** 71
Phebe (Lincoln) **123** 122
Phebe (Symonds) **108** 85
Phena **61** 236
Polly **61** 379
Rachel **86** 232 **100** 167
Rebecca **54** 386 **87** 381 **92**
  117 **113** 134 **115** 91 92
  126 280 **134** 144 **142** 36
  272 **143** 250 252
Rebecca (Phippen)
  (Baldwin) **143** 251 252
Rebecca (Vickery) **142** 272

PRINCE *cont'd*
  360 **143** 250
  Rebecca Langdon **93** 251
  Reliance **53** 172
  Reliance (Fuller) **143** 250
  Rhoda **88** 58
  Richard **70** 262 **143** 247
  Richard Nourse **88** 290
  Robert **60** 190 **108** 85
  Ruth **85** 363 **143** 253
  Ruth (Turner) **85** 363 **98**
    211 **108** 150 **143** 254
  Sally **61** 241 **78** 178
    141 356
  Sally Dunn **92** 121
  Samuel **60** 239 **78** 407 **92**
    13 16 **108** 151 **113** 44
    118 212 **119** 269 **121** 22
    138 **123** 61 62 **128** 305
    140 156 238 **142** 124
    358 **143** 122 137 249 251-
    253
  Sarah **59** 217 218 **61** 200 **68**
    227 **84** 270 **88** 58 **106** 71
    108 85 **113** 17 **121** 24
    103 **141** 356 **142** 207
    143 252
  Sarah (Ingersoll) **140**
    156 238
  Sarah (Lincoln) **143** 253
  Sarah (Wyatt) **123** 10
  Sarah Ann (Smith) **123** 10
  Sarah J. (Titus) **114** 176
  Sarah Jane (Clark) **123** 10
  Sewell H. **83** 436 438
  Sidney S. **108** 151
  Solomon **123** 11
  Susan (Buxton) **83** 178
    185
  Susan Lyman **122** 299
  Sylvester **136** 33 34
  T. **90** 375
  T. J. **92** 351
  Tabbie **122** 281
  Tabitha **81** 409
  Theodore **75** 157 **76** xxi
    107 223 **108** 138 151
  Thomas **51** 49 76 **52** 13
    102 297 360 **53** 30 111
    112 318 320 322 393 427
    54 lxxxiii 235 263 367
    55 70 128 129 167 294
    56 308 **57** 197 **58** 316
    59 141 178-180 185 186
    217 **60** 35 320 **61** xlviii
    148 161-163 328 **62** 2 91
    65 381 **66** 357 **67** lx 108
    69 lx 107 158 **71** 167 168
    73 xli **74** 299 320 **76**
    lxvii **77** xlv **78** 95 450
    79 292 410 **80** 135 304
    81 203 **84** 250 270 **85**
    363 **87** 48 399 **89** 174
    177 **90** 154 **92** 26 117
    118 **93** 99 **94** 296 **95** 42
    44 46 102 130 **97** 316
    393 **99** 15 **100** 320 **101**
    68 **107** 313 **108** 150 **112**
    258 **113** 15 17 **114** 3 **115**
    87 91 93 181 **118** 84 287
    119 15 16 19 75 **121** 108

PRINCE *cont'd*
  193 **122** 293 **124** 286
  127 41 **130** 43 **134** 301
  143 45 247-249 252 254
  144 152 160 165 226 233
  266 **145** 203 204 219 226
  146 324
  Thomas (Mrs.) **92** 122
  Thomas I. **92** 250
  Thomas J. **92** 257 344
    94 379
  Thomas James **92** 250
  W. **91** 332
  William **92** 344 **100** 133
    101 274 **114** 185 **125** 33
    144 201
  William E. **91** 332 **122**
    299 301
  William Edgar **77** 297
  William G. **93** 123 251 252
  William Gordon **92** 128
  William Wood **108** 150
PRINCESS
  Nancy (Ware) **125** 101
  Nicholas **125** 101
PRINCETON
  Caster **91** 332
PRINCIPALL
  Mr. **52** 69
PRINDERSON
  Sylvia **60** 352
PRINDLE *see also* Pringle
  ——— **61** 101
  Abigail **75** 188 **78** 260
  Abraham **114** 184
  Alexander **61** 101
  Asa **77** 153
  Caroline **75** 310
  Catherine **77** 153
  Charles **75** 310 **77** 81
  Charles Day **104** 162
  Currence **102** 108
  Cyrus **114** 184
  Deborah (Booth) **142**
    334-336
  Ebenezer **102** 105
  Elizabeth (Hubby)
    102 105
  Emily (Dean) **104** 162
  Flavia (Horsford) **71** 356
    104 162
  Frank **80** 35 264
  Franklin **80** 264
  Franklin C. **60** 190 **61** 101
  George **71** 356
  George William **104** 162
  Gideon **71** 356 **104** 162
  Hannah **78** 260
  Harris M. **71** 356
  Jabez **75** 186
  Jennie Maria (Byington)
    104 162
  Joanna (Wheeler) **116** 115
  John **78** 260 **104** 162
    142 335
  Joseph **102** 105
  Lazarus **116** 115
  Lester Marsh **71** xxiv 353
    74 xxviii **90** 130 **104** 66
    148 162
  Lois (Marsh) **104** 162

PRINDLE *cont'd*
  Mark **71** 356 **104** 162
    147 179
  Martha (Prime) **104** 162
  Mary **57** 265
  Mercy **108** 84
  Olwen (Williams)
    104 162
  Paul W. **107** 54 **110** 239
    116 82 **119** 243 **120** 21
    24 225 **121** 157 **127** 167
    260 **145** 74
  Robert Hinsdale **104** 162
  Ruth **61** 183
  Ruth S. **60** 190
  Samuel **104** 162
  Sarah **102** 105
  Sarah (Kimberly) **102** 105
  Sarah Amelia **80** 35
  Sophronia **88** 293
  Susanna **75** 186
  Walman **114** 184
  Wenas **114** 184
  William **60** 190 **61** 101
    70 264 **104** 162
  Zalmon **61** 101
PRINE N. J. **91** 332
PRINET M. **99** 274 278
PRING Pringe
  Anna **109** 132
  Elizabeth **55** 333
  Martin **57** 347 **87** 271
    96 276
PRINGLE *see also* Prindle
  ——— **53** 134 **59** 331
  ——— (Mrs.) **144** 158
  Abraham Marks **76** 140
  Alexander Bullions
    87 284
  Alys Puffer (Scott)
    (Anthony) (Van Clef)
    93 281
  Amasa **115** 15-17 20 115
  Andrew **118** 49 **125** 259
  Artemas **115** 15
  Betsey **76** 146 **94** 280
  Betty **76** 142
  Clarry **115** 15
  Daniel Huse **115** 115
  David **65** 85
  Ebenezer **76** 140-146 148
    150
  Eliot Victor (Mrs.) **93** 281
  Enos **76** 140-144
  Esther **115** 15-17 20
  Eunice **115** 15 17 21 25 26
    115
  Ezbon **115** 15-17 19 21 25
    26
  Florence Eleanor **87** 284
  Franklin C. **59** 331
  George **62** 328
  Hannah **115** 16
  Harace **115** 15
  Harriet **115** 17
  Homer **115** 16
  J. F. **51** 88 89
  James **64** 224
  James Harvey **115** 21
  James R. **64** 335
  James R. (Mrs.) **72** xx

PRINGLE cont'd
John **62** 301 **64** 19 **65** 130
76 145 151 **84** 141 **112**
302 **115** 15 16 26 109
Jonathan **76** 133
Joseph **59** 171 **76** 140 141
Josiah **76** 143
Julia Ann (Laughlin)
87 284
Lewis **76** 144
Lois **76** 141
Lucy **76** 140 **115** 16 19
Luella (Houghton)
96 161
Mary **59** 171 **76** 145
127 124
Mildred **97** 183
Mordecai **76** 142 144
Norman **72** 318
Olive **115** 26
Orpheus **115** 17
Patience **115** 15 16 21 26
109
Ralph (Mrs.) **96** 161
Richard **76** 148
Robert **127** 124
Sally **76** 145
Sarah **72** 318
Sarah Jane (Hartman)
125 259
Sophia **115** 16
Sophronia **115** 20
William **59** 331
Zalmon **59** 331
PRINGLEY
William **63** 348
PRINGRIDAY
Mary **123** 260
PRINOCH
Jonathan **63** 234
PRINT John **64** 21
Printice see Prentice
PRIOLEAU —— **53** 457
Catherine (Cordes)
119 194
Elizabeth **119** 194
Hext **93** 291
John Cordes **119** 194
Mary Magdelan **119** 194
Providence Hext **93** 291
Samuel **119** 194
PRIOR Prier Pryer Pryor
—— **53** 307 **77** 143
Alice **141** 358
Allen **70** 356
Allyn **71** 276
Amanthis **70** 353
Ann **125** 302 **127** 159
Ann (Barney) **125** 239
Anna Elizabeth **80** 154
Anne **79** 406 **80** 64
Benjamin **64** 22 **70** 179 224
227 315 354 **71** 135 136
126 262
Benjamin F. **138** 213
Bethiah **70** 266
Bethiah (Allen) **136** 35
Bethiah (Pratt) **126** 262
Charles **125** 239
Christiana **70** 356 359
Daniel **57** 85 **70** 257

PRIOR cont'd
Deborah **126** 41
Ebenezer **60** 307
Edith **126** 20
Edmund **52** 312
Elias **126** 259
Eliza **91** 42
Elizabeth **67** 287 **80** 241 **97**
284 285 **113** 272
Ella Nieda **83** 340
Emily (Whitwell) **87** 56
Emily Jane (Barber)
83 340
Eunice **70** 224 **135** 338
Geoffrey **105** 39
George **79** 155 306
Hannah **79** 155 **87** 376 **110**
146 **126** 259 263 **136** 35
Hannah (Dillaway)
141 20
Hannah Hayward **70** 359
Hannah M. **77** 177
Harriet **60** 307
Humphry **148** 348
I. **63** 363
James **55** 141 **95** 134 **110**
146 **117** 16
Jane Vermilye **67** 18
Joan **54** 195
John **59** 326 **64** 159 **67** 18
69 114 **70** 231 **71** 142
80 64 **81** 134 **123** 261
125 239 **126** 259 262
136 35
John E. **70** 285
John Eben **71** xxiv 33 133
Jonathan **125** 239
Joseph **70** 266 **95** 134
Katharine **65** 50
Keziah **77** 138
Louisa **69** 114
Louisa M. **122** 217
Lucy **70** 179 224 **85** 430
Lydia **99** 148
Lydia (Osier) **126** 263
Mabel **87** 56
Martha **76** 271
Martha Alice **87** 56
Martha D. **125** 240
Martha S. **77** 189
Mary **54** 195 **60** 307 **70** 257
74 134 **127** 94
Mary (Geare) **123** 261
Matthew **74** 134
May **70** 231
Mercy **126** 259
Mercy (Delano) **126** 259
262
Nancy (Barney) **125** 239
Nathaniel **126** 259 262
Olive **71** 136
Olivia Mary **77** 143
Pamelia Wells **71** 276
Patience **99** 54
Peggy **114** 181
Peggy (King) **114** 181
Peter **64** 160
Ruth **70** 231 **83** 406 **126**
259 263 **133** 289
Ruth (Gifford) **138** 213
Sally **70** 354

PRIOR cont'd
Sarah **67** 18 **69** 114 **70** 353
354 **74** 134 **92** 389 **125**
239 243 **147** 263 265
Seth Franklin **83** 340
Sophia **69** 114
Sophia Anne **70** 356
Susanna **110** 146
Sylvanus **70** 356 359
Tabitha **70** 227
Walter **64** 222
Watkin **64** 160
William **64** 164 **67** 287
70 353 **87** 56 **93** 178
103 289 **127** 140 **141**
117
William A. **76** 271
PRIOUX Nicholas **65** 230
PRISCELEY
Simon **84** 306
PRISCIAN —— **57** 41 42
PRISSE William **76** 116
PRITCHARD Prichard
Pricherd
—— **92** 311 **145** 46 166
— Goodman **123** 259
— Mrs. **106** 296
— Rev. Mr. **82** 441
A. H. (Mrs.) **77** 325
A. M. **100** 338
Abigail (Tower) **129** 375
Abraham **108** 181
Ada Thressia **78** 50
Alice **57** 134 **119** 320
Amy **64** 342
Anna **100** 278
Archibald **76** 137
Armstead Mead **66** 369
67 xxxii
Atlanto **99** 280
Azariah **76** 139 140 142
144 145
Barnard **126** 143
Benjamin **63** 276
David **76** 137
Elizabeth **66** 332 **100** 303
123 261
Elizabeth (Allyn) **123** 261
Elizabeth (Davis) **123** 262
Elizabeth (Gragg)
126 143
Ely **99** 280
Emma F. **124** 228
Eunice **65** 10 **76** 139
Frances **119** 320
Gail **78** 206
George **66** 332 **85** 424
Gilman **95** 351 **126** 40
Gilman (Mrs.) **95** 297 350
96 164
Gladys (Rising) **85** 295
Hannah **69** lxxiv
Hannah (Snelling)
108 181
Harold **85** 295
Harry Dudley (Mrs.)
78 109 206
Harvey **65** 10 **123** 96
Helen (Vila) **95** 351
Hugh **53** 235 237 **97** 264
J. L. **119** 320

PRITCHARD *cont'd*
J. M. **82** 376
Jacob L. **104** 78 **108** 318
James **65** 182
James Gilman **92** 285
Jennie Creesy **98** 178
Jeremiah **92** 285 311
95 351
Jerusha **123** 96
Joan **78** 324 **119** 320
John **78** 142 **129** 375
John Clyde **98** 178
John Franklin (Mrs.)
108 135
John Jones **80** 333 **81** 219
96 87 163 **98** 178
Josephine (Spencer) (Gay)
90 130 **95** 350 **96** 164
K. A. **52** 77 **58** 79
Kate Strandbury **108** 222
Katharine A. **72** 322
144 61
Lavinia E. **65** 10
Leaverit **76** 173
Lillice **63** 276
Lottie M. (Creesy) **98** 178
Lucy **78** 142
Lydia **99** 280
Margaret J. (Jones) **98** 178
Marmara **76** 145
Martha **78** 142
Mary **78** 324 326 **79** 35 **93**
262 **99** 280 **106** 296 **123**
259
Mary (Briggs) **126** 40
Miriam Carol **98** 178
Nath **123** 259
Nathaniel **123** 262
Nathaniel Riddick **78** 50
Oliver **129** 375
Polly **75** 310
R. H. **82** 376
Ralph **76** 142 144
Rebecca **61** 140
Rebecca (Taylor) **123** 263
Richard **54** 354 **129** 375
Roger **57** 134 **108** 318
119 320
Roy H. (Mrs.) **111** 246
112 320
Samuel **99** 280
Sarah **74** 251 **91** 385
Susanna (Huntley)
101 203
Thomas **53** 186 **55** 334 **64**
159 **65** 110 337 **93** 385
398 **100** 63 **101** 203
Thomas D. **98** 178
Virginia Gibson **78** 326
W. G. **78** 326
Wesley Kolb (Mrs.)
109 131
William **66** 369 **94** 273
99 280 **100** 278 **123** 261
263
William Blue **78** 324
Willie J. **82** 376
PRITCHETT Prichet
Pridget Pritchet
— Mrs. **108** 160
Andrew **64** 337

PRITCHETT *cont'd*
Attalanty **92** 56 57
Esther **61** 310
John **56** 207 **64** 161
John C. **77** 269
Mary **122** 100
P. **122** 19
Sally **125** 101
Sarah **56** 207 **63** 205
Sarah Robina **77** 269
Prittyman *see* Prettyman
PRITZKER Lee **117** 315
PROAL Sally **90** 229
PROBARDS —— **61** 307
Bathsheba **58** 16
PROBART Hazel Bee **100**
112 **105** 125 **120** 232
PROBEE Edward **52** 134
62 96
Elizabeth **52** 133 134 **62** 96
Matthew **52** 134 **61** 393
62 96
PROBST
Agnes Thayer **61** 95
Jacob Philip **84** 238
PROCTOR Prockter
Procter
—— **58** 305 **68** 300 **70** 20
— Capt. **135** 99
— Col. **65** 369
— Lieut. **58** 236
— Mr. **145** 34
Aaron **100** 207
Aaron M. **76** 271
Abel **51** 408 **75** 172
103 223
Abel Harrison **51** 409
Abel Johnson **51** 409
Abigail **51** 409 **52** 435 **71**
128 129 131 211 212
Abigail (Burroughs)
140 47
Abigail A. **107** 317
Agnes Eliza (Adams)
86 152
Alexander **86** 152
Alley **73** 229
Alpheus **85** 87
Ann **73** 268 **117** 92
Anne Louise (White)
85 437
Anthony **104** 281
Augustua **51** 409
Barbara Austin **110** 231
Benjamin **51** 408-410 **60**
208 209 **66** 37 **70** 69 **71**
211 221 **84** 326 **91** 264
103 223 **107** 187 **117** 92
Benjamin F. **117** 92
Bethiah (Hardey) **91** 264
Betsey **70** 211 **126** 207
Bettey **83** 168
Caleb **113** 24
Charles **69** 114 **88** 230
Charles Anderson **76** lvi
110 231
Charles Anderson (Mrs.)
85 197 **97** 150 163 171
110 221 231
Charles Marden **114** 69
Charlotte (Hudson) **85** 87

PROCTOR *cont'd*
Cynthia (Hopkins)
85 436
Cyrus **85** 436
David Redfield **62** 113
Deborah **51** 409 410 **97** 21
Dorothy **51** 447
Ebenezer **117** 92
Ede (Carver) **88** 230
Edith **51** 362
Edward **51** 372 **71** 128
129 131 211 212 **78** 189
417 **84** 326 358 369 379
92 117 **96** 325 **97** 297
108 240 **140** 69 238 239
Edward Otis **65** 304
Eleanor **73** 219 **85** 87
Eli **117** 282
Elijah **64** 312
Eliza **83** 147
Elizabeth **51** 409 410 **61**
150 **70** 66 68 **84** 405 **94**
40 **100** 303 **103** 46 223
108 240 **126** 207
Elizabeth (Cock) **108** 240
Elizabeth (Johnson)
114 290
Elizabeth (Singer) **84** 326
Elizabeth Mason **57** 199
Ellen Augusta **76** lvi
Ellen Osborn **51** 409
Ellen T. **96** 200
Ellenor **85** 87
Elmira (Bartlett) **101** 281
Emma Esther (Howe)
103 223
Esther **51** 448 **64** 312 **103**
224 **104** 265
Eunice (Bound) **84** 267
Evan **132** 77 164 244 326
133 73 234 323 **134** 90
Ezekiel **62** 158
Fanny **58** 124
Frances **67** 278
Frances Ingersoll **76** lvi
110 231
Francis **57** 199 **73** 276
Fred F. **74** xxv 78 **84** 173
Frederick Freeman
85 87 201
George **51** 362 **97** 297
George Burroughs **90** 58
George Burroughs (Mrs.)
85 197
George Pond **84** 191 232
Georgena E. (Mills) **85** 87
Grace (Hopkins) **110**
221 231
Grace Amanda **94** 140
H. **78** 70
Hannah **51** 409 **56** 41 47
58 18 **63** 300 **71** 131
100 207 **108** 240 **125**
106 **140** 37 239
Hannah (Harwood) **85** 87
Hannah (Slocum) (Bokes)
120 5
Hannah (Wildes) **108** 192
Harriet Elizabeth (Glazier)
90 58
Harrison E. **117** 92

PROCTOR *cont'd*
Henrietta **85** 87
Henry **64** 338
Henry H. **97** 187
Henry Harrison **59** xlviii
  76 xxix lvi **110** 231
Hittie A. **121** 180
Ida E. **69** 260
Ips **117** 92
Isaac **92** 317 **101** 281 **120** 5
Isaac Knight **63** 314
Israel **51** 448
Israel F. Evans **92** 317
J. **70** 214
James **51** 448 **67** 278
James Henry **124** 192
Jane **53** 266 **78** 412 **133**
  308 309
Jane (Hildreth) **85** 87 436
  132 326
Jean (Goodwin) **110** 281
Jennet **83** 442
Joan Stevens **67** 278
Joel **145** 349
John **51** 408-410 **56** 341
  344 **57** 281 **58** 306 **59**
  229 **60** 208 209 **66** 284
  285 **67** 316 **70** 66 68 103
  71 128 212 **73** 270 **76**
  219 **84** 265 267 326 367
  405 **85** 436 **92** 117 **97**
  297 **98** 219 **103** 223 224
  107 185 **108** 189 240
  112 121 181 **134** 303
  135 282 285 286 **140**
  239
John Henry **69** 260
John W. **76** lvi
Johnson **51** 408 410
  103 223
Jonathan **52** 434 **95** 120
  107 186
Joseph **51** 408 409 **57** 388
  69 260 **71** 211 **108** 192
Joseph H. **79** 147
Julia P. **74** 25
Katharine **97** 297
Katherin **97** 297
Lavinia **89** 69
Leonard **53** 267
Levi **83** 167
Lucien B. **107** 10
Lucretia **66** 284 **69** 260
Lucy **92** 77 **131** 30
Lucy Ann (Tufts) **85** 87
Lydia **51** 408 410 **55** 430
  56 256 **66** 285 **78** 416
  140 233
Lydia (Waters) **103** 223
Lydia P. **75** 172
Lydia Porter (Emerson)
  103 223
Lydia Susan (Fracker)
  124 192
Margaret **51** 448 **55** 434
  69 114 **97** 297
Margaret (Fitz Randolph)
  97 297
Maria (Fash) **84** 326
Marie **135** 285
Martha **51** 409 **52** 434

PROCTOR *cont'd*
  103 223
Martha (Harper) **135** 285
Mary **51** 408-410 448 **59**
  245 **60** 208 **62** lxxiv **78**
  308 **85** 437 **88** 230 **92**
  114 **95** 294 **110** 281 **113**
  231 **117** 282 **125** 294
  127 228 **128** 121 **132**
  106
Mary (Ashfield) **108** 240
Mary (Byam) **85** 436
Mary (Patterson) **85** 87
Mary (Tibbetts) **98** 219
Mary (Whittredge)
  103 223
Mary C. (Hiler) **88** 338
Mary E. **117** 282 **124** 40
Mary Elizabeth **124** 40
Mary Ingersoll **76** lvi
Mehitable **51** 409
Mehitable Cummings **75**
  172 **99** 187
Molly **56** 47
Mortimer Robinson
  66 369
Moses **85** 436
Nancy Elizabeth **79** 147
Nancy R. **125** 290
Nathan **55** 430 **56** 388
Nathan Putnam (Mrs.)
  85 197
Nellie (Parker) **124** 192
Nicholson B. **88** 338
Nina M. **84** 124
Obediah **108** 240 **131** 235
Olive **117** 92
Peter **56** 47 **59** 245 **85** 87
Priscilla **60** 208
Prudence **51** 408
Rachel **108** 240 **131** 235
  144 198
Rebecca **61** 343 **82** 496
Rebecca (Foster) **85** 87
Redfield **53** 267
Richard **108** 240 **144** 198
Robert **53** 264 266 **57** 416
  85 87 436 437 **131** 317
  132 77 164 244 326 **133**
  73 234 323 **134** 90
Roger **104** 281
Ruth (Porter) (Rae)
  103 223
Sally **56** 257 **83** 167
Samuel **58** 27 **71** 131 **78**
  111 **83** 167 **84** 326 **108**
  240 **114** 290 **136** 261
  140 69 238
Sarah **51** 308 408 409 **53**
  264 377 **56** lxv **57** 416
  60 208 **61** 249 **64** 312
  69 114 115 **83** 167 **117**
  22 **123** 318 **131** 155 **136**
  129
Sarah (Greenough)
  84 326
Sarah Ann Emerson
  51 409
Sarah Jane **76** 271
Sarah Parks **69** lxxvi

PROCTOR *cont'd*
Sibyl (Farnsworth)
  85 436
Simeon **85** 87
Simon **128** 121
Stephen **107** 182
Susan **113** 24
Susan Rebecca (Pool)
  85 436
Susanna **78** 403 **84** 265
  117 92
Susanna (Burnham)
  108 189
Susanna (Langdon)
  84 326
Sylvester **51** 408
Thirzah (Smith) **86** 152
Thomas **58** 124 **67** 278 **85**
  436 **110** 281
Thomas Emerson **51** 409
  59 xlvi **64** 303 **90** 125
  103 217 223 224 **104**
  148
Thomas Redfield **53** 267
Thomas White **85** 437
Thomas William **69** xxxv
  85 436 **86** 108 205
Thorndike **56** 201 **58** 18
  60 209 70 69 **91** 202 203
Vouletti Theresa (Singer)
  84 326
W. B. **140** 43
W. L. **52** 85 **53** 264 266 **60**
  85 184
Willard **71** 212
William **98** 39
William A. **54** cxxxvii
William Fash **84** 326
William H. **124** 192
William H. (Mrs.) **91** 400
William Lawrence **53**
  264 266 267 **84** xxxix
William Martin **86** 152
William Ross **67** xxxiv
  80 207 **84** 235 326 **85**
  203
PRODDON Sally **103** 171
PROFFIT Profit Profitt
Caleb **128** 53
Elizabeth **55** 438 **120** 244
John **55** 438 **120** 244
Walter **128** 53
PROGERS Thomas **63** 18
PROLE Henry **92** 119
PRONAY Alwine
  Friederike (Von
  Volborth) **122** 179
Andrew **122** 180
PRONG Susanna **98** 128
PROOM William **62** 331
PROPER David R. **116** 150
  121 78
Elizabeth (Haight)
  120 238
Johanes Joseph **116** 150
Sally **134** 63
William **120** 238
PROPST Alice **118** 329
PROSCH
Charles **64** 292
Christiana **64** 292

PROSCH cont'd
Susan 64 292
Thomas Wickham 64 292
65 xxxv
William 64 292
PROSSER Prossor
Alice V. 80 234
Amanda 72 106
Ann 112 239
Arnold 74 xlvi
Bridget 58 312
Charles Smith 58 xlv
Cornelia Ann 80 234
Desire 80 144
Elizabeth 147 231
Esther 80 144 145
Harriet N. 72 106
Ichabod 128 300
Isaac 80 144 145 234
James L. 72 106 182
John 72 183 74 xlvi
John Kenyon 74 xlvi
Levi 72 106
Louise Snow 63 xxxiv
74 xxxvii xlvi 79 247 80
263
Maria Louise 74 xlvi
77 186
Martha 91 250
Roger 58 312
Safety 80 145
PROTTS Carrie 81 41
George 81 41
Prouce see Prowse
PROUD Proude Prowd
Prowde
—— 55 96 103 9
— Widow 127 14
Agnes 101 10
Alice 101 8 9 11
Allen 101 10
Amie 122 100
Andrew 101 11
Catherine 101 8-10
Eleanor 101 8
Elizabeth 101 9 10
Ellen 101 7-9
Ellen (Lewis) 101 8
George 101 7-11 15
Hannah 76 204
Joan 101 7 8 10
Johan 101 7
John 62 355 54 325
129 55
Katharine 101 9
Lewis 101 7-10
Marie 101 8 9
Mary 54 325 101 10
Phebe 80 81
Richard 101 8-11
Robert 80 81 101 10
Roger 101 9 10
Samuel 127 303
Thomas 76 238 239 101 9
10
William 64 20 101 9 10
127 306
PROUDEN John 54 330
PROUDFIT
Alexander 66 94

PROUDFOOT
John 64 226
Lewis C. 114 265
PROUDLOW
Pemberton 65 50
Prous see Prowse
Prouse see Prowse
PROUST Charlotte
(Gaudfray) 128 179
Claude 128 179
PROUT Proute Proutt
—— 62 167
Abigail 67 206 103 262
Agnes 55 103 104 106
Alice 55 97 99-101
Alison 55 100
Andrew 55 97
Baptist 55 102
Beatyn 55 97
Benjamin 55 106
Betsey 103 268
Blanche 55 97
Bridget 55 100 104
C. 66 124
Christian 55 104
David 55 101
Deborah 55 106
Dennis 55 104
Dominicus J. 89 357 358
Dominicus Jordan
103 265
Ebenezer 55 106 66 113
117 67 206 78 67 86 349
350
Edward 57 324
Eleanor 55 101
Elizabeth 52 276 480 55
97 99 100 104 106 57
324 67 206
Elizabeth (Wheeler)
86 349 350
Emme 55 100
Eunice 55 96 100 102 106
Ezekiel 103 256 268 269
Francis 55 97
George 55 101 104
George H. 103 267
Grace 55 98 101 106
Gregory 55 98
Griffey 55 103
Hannah 55 97 67 206
Henry 55 98
Hugh 55 96 97 99-103 106
Jacob 100 278
Jane 55 99 100 278
Joan 55 96 97 99-104 106
John 55 97-100 102-106
103 193 260 262
John W. 103 263
Jordan 103 256 261
Joseph 55 97 106 67 206
86 350 103 256
Louisa J. 89 357
Love 55 106 67 309
Lydia 67 206
Margaret 55 106
Margery 55 98
Maria 91 180
Martin 55 101
Mary 55 97-100 102-106
67 206 122 113 124 31

PROUT cont'd
Mary S. E. 89 358
Matthew 55 97
Michael 55 98
Nicholas 55 97 98
Patience 62 370
Phillipe 55 100 103 106
Priscilla 55 100
Radulph 55 97
Richard 55 97-100 102
104 106
Samuel 55 106
Sarah 55 99 106
Susan 55 96 100 103 106
89 357 358
Susanna 55 102 106
T. M. 85 170
Thomas 55 96-100 103
104 106
Thomasyn 55 97
Timothy 55 96 100-106
142 230 231 239 58 202
67 206 110 317 117 12
17
Walter 55 100
William 55 96 98-106
Wilmote 55 97
Zachariah 55 106
PROUTY
Abigail 59 140 141
Adam 58 266
Addie M. 92 205
Agnes 89 106
Alfred 66 24
Alfred W. 59 417
Arnold 66 24
Asa 93 65
Benjamin 59 144
Caleb 58 266
Charles 59 417
Christopher C. 75 20
Cynthia 59 417
Damaris 60 179 182
David 58 266 60 179 338
61 59
Deborah 59 312
Dwight 93 124 94 159
Dwight Mortimer 59
xlviii 65 vii 66 vii l 68
liii
Dwight Mortimer (Mrs.)
68 liii 69 x
Ebenezer 94 56
Edward 57 399 58 85 87 89
90 169 171 173 175 59
138 140 312 314 388 391
Eleanor 59 78
Elijah 59 417
Elijah W. H. 59 417
Elisha 58 173 59 417
85 369
Eliza B. 59 417
Elizabeth 58 85 87 89 90
169 171 173 175 266 389
59 75 77 78 135 312 60
175
Emma I. / L. 103 48
Ethie Bigelow (Linder)
68 xxxv 69 v vi 70 xii
Eunice 57 403 58 169 59
417 84 411 85 366

PROUTY *cont'd*
Florence Newell **96** 306
Francis D. **59** 417
Frederick Elon Thomas
103 158
Hannah **58** 171 **59** 417
Hannah D. **59** 417
Hattie **75** 20
Horace **87** 88
Isaac **58** 266 389 **59** 75 77
135 **60** 179 182 **126** 260
262
Jacob **58** 266
James **58** 87 **59** 77 417
Jane (Conn) **87** 88
Jemima **58** 84 **59** 312
60 176
Job **58** 266
John **58** 90 266 **59** 144
66 24
Johnson **59** 144
Jonathan **58** 170 **59** 312
60 181
Lemuel D. **59** 417
Lettice **60** 179
Lewis Isaac **65** xxxv **92**
147 **103** 158
Lorenzo **75** 205
Lucy **108** 86
Lucy Withington **75** 205
Lusannah **59** 312 **60** 63
Lydia **59** 417 **60** 338
Lydia C. **59** 417
Margaret **58** 169 **59** 310
Marion Elizabeth **144** 119
Martha **85** 368
Martha (Silvester) **85** 369
Mary **58** 175 **94** 56
Mary Caroline **93** 65
Mary Elizabeth (Miles)
144 119
Mary Ruggles **94** 159
Nehemiah **59** 310 **60** 179
181 182
Phebe **93** 380
Polly A. **59** 417
Priscilla **60** 182 **126** 260
Priscilla (Ramsdell) **126**
260 262
Rebecca **59** 138 140 312
314 388 391 **60** 176
Richard **58** 89 **59** 312 **65**
195 **103** 158
Roswell **66** 24
Ruth **59** 75
Salmon **59** 417
Sarah **59** 388 **128** 96
Sarah A. **75** 20
Sarah B. **59** 417
Sarah R. **88** 337
Schuyler **144** 119
Simon **59** 417
Sophia **59** 417
Susanna **59** 391
William **58** 84 169 **59** 312
417 **60** 63 176 179
William C. **75** 20
PROUUE Ian G. **110** 84
Susanne **110** 84
PROVAN Mary Elizabeth
(Ketchum) **109** 186

PROVAN *cont'd*
William Bruce **109** 186
PROVENCHE
J. H. **84** 32
PROVENDER Provinder
Elizabeth **90** 390 **111** 92 95
114 51
Isaac **109** 296 **111** 92 95
John **93** 385
Jonathan **84** 405 406
Miriam **91** 262
Prudence **114** 294
Sarah **107** 100
PROVIN
Waitstill **113** 41
PROVINCE John **84** 153
Sarah **78** 403
Provinder *see* Provender
PROVO
Chestleton **75** 20
Harriet **74** 171
Paul **75** 20
Rosa **75** 20
PROVOST Provoost
— Bp. **115** 14
— Rev. **133** 309
— Rev. Bp. **133** 308
Andrew J. **107** 78
David **51** 335
Helena **133** 235
Peter **53** 417
William **133** 235
PROW — Mrs. **83** 36
Prowd *see* Proud
Prowde *see* Proud
PROWN
Jules David **120** 236
PROWSE Prouce Prous
Prouse
—— **57** 65
— Mr. **82** 414
Agnis **144** 36
Ann **82** 53
Daniel **82** 53
Dorothy **82** 53
Elizabeth **59** 297 **82** 292
297 **83** 36
Jane **115** 251
Jane (Bayntun) **115** 251
Joan (Radford) **115** 251
John **59** 297 **115** 249-251
Lawrence **59** 297
Martha (Peabody) **89** 269
Mary **82** 53 **115** 251 **122**
282 283
Maud (Cruwys) **115** 251
Montague W. W. (Mrs.)
89 269
Nancy **83** 36
Nicholas **115** 250 251
of Chagford **141** 99
of Chevithoren in
Tiverton **141** 99
Richard **59** 297
Roger **81** 322 **115** 250 251
Thomas **82** 53 292 297 414
115 250 251
William **115** 251 253
142 366

PROXMIRE
Edward William
136 326
Elsie (Rockefeller)
136 326
PRUDDEN Pruden
Abigail **84** 64 65 67
137 280
Caroline **145** 306
Caroline (Gulliver)
145 306
Elizabeth **84** 62-64 67 68
Grace **54** 385 **84** 67
Grace (Judson) **84** 64
Hannah **54** 107 385
Henry J. **56** 221
Israel R. **145** 306
Joanna **51** 495 **56** 206 221
61 164 **84** 63 64 67 **97**
84
Joanna (Boyse) **84** 63 64
Joanna Willet **84** 63
John **51** 495 **53** 127 **54** 385
84 62-67
Lillian E. **56** 221 **84** 63
Mary **54** 385 **79** 354 **84** 64
67
Mildred **84** 64 65 67
N. **60** 265
Peter **53** 127 **56** 221 **61** 164
81 133 **84** 62-64 67 68
93 197
S. B. **79** 354
Samuel **54** 385 **84** 64-66 68
Sarah **84** 64 65 67
Sibyl **79** 160
Theodore Philander
57 xxxiii
William **105** 290
PRUE Robert **55** 336
Prueitt *see* Pruitt
PRUELLE
Elmire **142** 63
Joseph **142** 63
Jules **142** 63
Julierme **142** 63
Louis Augustin **142** 63
Manette **142** 63
PRUESS
Charles August **73** 261
PRUESSING
Elizabeth **91** 306
PRUITT Prueitt Pruett
—— **55** 96
Alice Josephine **111** 315
Docia Melvina (Nelson)
104 233
Frances H. **116** 308
Francis **116** 308
Ivan Philip **104** 233
PRUMME Robert **75** 282
PRUST
Elizabeth **100** 29
William **100** 29
PRUTRAND
I. L. **91** 332
PRUTZMANN
Margaret **83** 477
PRUYN Anna **74** xxv
Anna Martha (Williams)
93 368

PRUYN *cont'd*
  Carrie Dean **144** 112
  Carrie Marion (Dean)
    144 119
  Edward Lansing **93** 368
  Frederic **93** 368
  Jane Anne (Lansing)
    93 368
  John V. L. **53** 118
  Magdalena **110** 158
  Marianna B. **82** 478
  Minott C. **144** 119
  Robert Clarence **93** 368
  Robert Clarence (Mrs.)
    74 xxv 156 **93** 368 **94** 79
    141
  Robert Dunbar **93** 368
  Robert Hewson **93** 368
  Ruth Williams **93** 368
Pryce *see* Price
Prydeaux *see* Prideaux
PRYDNEY Stephen **68** 182
Pryer *see* Prior
PRYIBIL Helen (Porter)
    (Davisson) **90** 68
    94 139
  Paul **90** 68 **94** 139
PRYK Robert **103** 289
PRYKINTON
  Robert **102** 242
PRYKKE Edward **54** 289
PRYMAROLE
  John **100** 21
Prymrose *see* Primrose
PRYNNE John **91** 11 12
  William **136** 148
PRYNTE Matthew **89** 338
PRYON Susanna **77** 216
Pryor *see* Prior
PRYTHERCH
  Richard **112** 173
PSILLY
  Elizabeth **126** 65
PTOLEMY VII **75** 318
PTOLEMY VIII **75** 318
PTOLEMY
  Norman **123** 85
  Phebe (Barnes) **123** 85
PUACHACHUX
  Sam **63** 231
PUALE
  Agnes (Bett) **92** 297
  John **92** 297 298
PUALL Elizabeth (Phillips)
    110 278
PUAUX Frank **114** 260
PUBLICOVER Charlotte
    (Fleet) **125** 260
  Edward **125** 260
  Martin **118** 53
Puckerdge *see* Puckridge
PUCKETT Clemmie **77** 263
PUCKINS Thomas **111** 203
PUCKLE William **51** 125
PUCKMORE Ann **51** 187
PUCKRIDGE Puckerdge
  John **54** 345
  Moses **64** 320
PUDDIFULT
  John **68** 179

PUDDINGTON
  ____ (Barnes) **84** 402
  John **84** 402
  Mary **88** 123
PUDDOCK
  Priscilla **85** 423
PUDEFORD Jane **63** 20
PUDNEY Hannah **119** 13
  John **61** 151 **72** 224 **119** 13
  Judith **61** 151
  Mary **61** 151
  Mary (Jones) **119** 13
  William **83** 71
PUDSEY — Bp. **103** 282
PUE Jonathan **112** 180
PUETTE
  Frances H. **116** 308
PUFFER —— **57** 337 **58**
    224 **59** 90 161 **61** 98 **92**
    312
  — Mr. **141** 343
  — Mrs. **141** 343
  Aaron **126** 206
  Abigail **61** 121 **64** 370
    75 200
  Abigail (Smith) **114** 199
  Abigail Prentice **73** lvi
  Arhoah (Pollard) **114** 199
  Alvin Davis **93** 281
  Amos **121** 92
  Azubah **114** 199
  Bathsheba **86** 54
  Benjamin **59** 157 **141** 343
  Bradley **114** 195 196
  Chandler **111** 291
  Chenery **114** 199 278
  Chloe **57** 396
  Daniel **61** 121 122 **114** 42
    110
  Dorothy **61** 122
  Dorothy (Haynes)
    114 194
  Ebenezer **59** 364 **61** 121
    122
  Eliza **79** 277
  Elizabeth A. **103** 45
  Elizabeth Ann **79** 277
  Ella Frances **74** xxv **93**
    82 140 281
  Emily **114** 195
  Emily Maria **61** 121
  Ephraim **114** 105
  Esther **71** 257 **141** 190
  Farwell **114** 195
  George **56** lxv **60** 190 **61**
    98 **70** 191 **114** 195 **141**
    199
  Hannah **52** 450 **60** 360 **61**
    121 **75** 146
  Isaac **61** 122
  Jabez **59** 91 155 156 363-
    365 **61** 121 122 **114** 40
    97 102
  Jabish **59** 156
  James **52** 450 **59** 91 153
    156 363 364 **61** 122 **64**
    370
  Jemima **114** 273
  Jemima (Taft) **114** 273
  Jepthah **114** 199
  Jerusha **61** 122

PUFFER *cont'd*
  Jesse **114** 195
  Joanna **61** 122
  Joel **92** 315
  John **60** 359 **61** 122 **75** 264
    86 460 **114** 198 199
  Jonathan **54** 52 **61** 122 **62**
    33 **114** 273
  Joseph **59** 363 **114** 33
    141 192
  Josiah **114** 199
  Laomi **114** 195
  Laura Adna **61** 121 122
  Lois **54** 52
  Loring William **53** 246
    59 xlii **60** 190 **61** xxxiii
    65 xxii xxxiii **67** xxx
  Louisa (Davis) **114** 195
  Louise **128** 40
  Lucy Thomas (Alden)
    114 199
  Luther **61** 122
  Marcy **61** 122
  Martha **59** 88 363
  Mary **54** 52 **59** 91 153 155
    363-365 **60** 359 **61** 122
    75 211 **85** 329 **103** 139
    114 195 **141** 199
  Mary (Balcom) **114** 42
  Mary (Glode) **92** 316
  Mary (Read) **114** 33
  Mary Ann **61** 122
  Mary Jane **55** xxxv
  Matthias **52** 196 **59** 157
    71 257
  Miriam **103** 150
  Molly **141** 199
  Molly (Stratton) **114** 275
  Moses Hastings **79** 277
  Nancy **114** 195
  Nancy (Walker) **112** 148
  Nancy (Warren) **114** 199
  Nathan **61** 122 **69** 244
  Olive **75** 264 **114** 199
  Olive (Rice) **114** 199
  Otis **114** 199
  Patience (Tolman) **86** 460
  Persis **114** 275
  Phebe **141** 199
  Phineas **61** 122 **114** 275
  Polly (Brown) **92** 315
  Prentiss **114** 195
  Rachel **59** 90 154
  Rebecca **75** 209 **105** 226
    114 42
  Rebecca (Balcom) **114** 42
  Rebecca (Willis) **114** 42
  Reuben **112** 148 **114** 195
  Richard **59** 269 **128** 40
  Roxa **114** 195
  Ruth **58** 239 **59** 269 **64** 370
    75 149 **114** 197 198
  Ruth (Willis) **114** 197-199
    278
  Sabre Ann **86** 54
  Samuel **59** 365 **61** 121 122
    114 195 199
  Sarah **61** 16 122 **93** 270 **114**
    194 195
  Sarah (Willis) **114** 195
  Sereno Samuel **61** 122

PUFFER cont'd
Seth **86** 460 **114** 199
Silas **61** 16 122 **114** 195
Silence **75** 264
Simon **61** 121
Sophia **136** 236
Sophia Elizabeth **112** 148
Susan (Parker) **114** 199
Susanna **114** 271
Thankful **61** 122
Theodorah (Pray) **126** 206
Thomas **61** 122 **92** 312 316
Timothy **141** 199
Timothy M. **86** 54
Tisdal **141** 199
Warren **92** 318
William **59** 269 **141** 199 347
PUGH Alice **98** 345
Ann **65** 47
Clara Ann **117** 123
David **117** 123
David Edgar (Mrs.) **99** 148
Gladys **117** 123
Hanson **98** 344
James **98** 344
Jane (Penrose) **117** 66
Jonathan **143** 257
Jonathan A. **98** 344
Leroy David **117** 123
Margaret **51** 370
Maria (Fitz Randolph) **98** 344
Marie (Rutherford) **117** 123
Mary **98** 345 **133** 266
Ophelia **98** 345
R. A. (Mrs.) **117** 80
Randolph **98** 345
Samuel **117** 66
William **51** 370
PUGIN Welby **60** 58
PUGLISI
Michael J. **146** 318
PUGN Polly **66** 109
PUGSLEY Pugsly
Abigail **82** 323 **95** 31 246
Abraham **74** 252 **116** 273
Albert G. **104** 285
Darius P. **91** 332
Edward **95** 248
Emma (Small) **95** 248
Eunice **91** 121
Eva Small **95** 248
Francis **116** 142
Hannah A. **104** 284 285
Jane **66** 336
John **74** 248 **82** 323
Lydia **87** 126
Martha **116** 273
Mary **74** 248
Matthew **106** 291
Mattie J. **104** 284
Molloy **87** 124
Moses W. **104** 284 285
Richard **93** 383 387
Ruth B. **83** 422 438
Susanna **74** 252
PUGSON Henry **97** 297
PUISANTE John **52** 253

PUISET
— Bp. **103** 283 285
Hugh du **97** 244 **100** 307
PUITTI Elise **95** 163
PULASKI — Count **54** 52
Pulcifer see Pulsifer
PULE Phebe **127** 222
PULFORD Joan **139** 287
Richard **65** 299
PULHAM
Margery **87** 217
Thomas **87** 217 218
PULIT Thomas **147** 165
PULLEN Pullayne
Pulleyn Pulling
Pullings
——— **140** 49
— Mrs. **67** 362
Abel **52** 39 **60** 331
Ann **100** 25
Anne **97** 35 36 254
Annis **84** 271 **91** 397 **100** 141 143 **102** 30
Benjamin King **77** 261
Betsey (Chase) **87** 228 236
Desire **52** 39
Edward **99** 285 **100** 32 **101** 247
Elias **128** 175
Emma **128** 94
Eunice **97** 256
George **91** 332
Hattie L. **128** 97
James **97** 256 **100** 28 **128** 97 **141** 195
Jane **97** 255 256
Joan **112** 185 186 **113** 103
Joan (Wilbore) (Faction) **113** 103
John **58** 64 69 **76** 219 **81** 342 **84** 271 **97** 256 **99** 120 204 207 280 282 285 **100** 26 28 32 138 140 141 143 234 236 241 **101** 54 247 **102** 29 30 **112** 187 **143** 33 34
Jonas **145** 362
Joseph H. **56** 91
Josiah **100** 26
Larnard **87** 229 236
Loftus **111** 206
Lydia **87** 256
Maggie **128** 175
Margaret **97** 254
Margaret (Boroughs) **128** 97
Martha **97** 256 **99** 120 204 207 **100** 26 28 **101** 54 271
Martha (Mountjoy) **100** 241
Mary **97** 255 **99** 204 285 **100** 303 **141** 195
Mary (Cowan) **87** 229 236
Mary (Tucker) **97** 35 254 255
Mary Robinson **130** 204 207
Matthew **126** 121
Minerva Anner **77** 261
Minnie Fisher **77** 261

PULLEN cont'd
Molly **97** 256
Nicholas **96** 353 **97** 25 27 35 42 254-256
Nooma **97** 255
Nooma (Bucklin) **97** 255
Oliver **97** 256
Ralph **94** 4
Rebecca (Hayward) **126** 121
Richard **60** 284 **97** 254 **99** 280 **122** 83
Robert **100** 25 **102** 30
Sally **100** 234 **102** 30
Sarah **78** 66 315 **97** 254 256 **100** 234 236 **102** 30
Stephen **97** 256
Susan (Cunningham) **128** 175
Susanna **121** 199
Sylvia **87** 228 236
Thomas **60** 283 **63** 344
William **87** 228 236 **97** 255 256 **135** 234
PULLER Myles **101** 85
Sarah **52** 140
PULLEY Edward **65** 234
Emma Anna **110** 75
Mary Winton **106** 126
Pulleyn see Pullen
PULLIAM
Joel L. **78** 49
Tymoxena **78** 49
Pulling see Pullen
Pullings see Pullen
PULLMAN Pullmon
Pulman
Elizabeth **115** 296
Fidelia **59** 326
George **56** 114
George Mortimer **81** 246 **141** 107
George Mortimer (Mrs.) **106** 235 **141** 107
Henry **128** 298
James **95** 26 **100** 241
John **129** 58
Mary **114** 44
Mary (Tippen) **100** 241
Nathaniel **115** 296 **129** 58
Ruth **55** 179
Updike **55** 179
William **59** 326
PULSE Puls
——— **88** 375
Dorcus (Munnon) **97** 293
Frederick **97** 293
PULSIFER Peilsephor
Pulcifer Pulsipher
——— **60** xxix
— Mrs. **55** 429
Abbie S. **89** 352
Abel **69** 107
Abiel **57** 388
Abigail **60** 198 **98** 311 312
Ada B. **98** 311
Addie **98** 311
Addison G. **98** 311
Allen C. **89** 352
Alphonso N. **98** 311
Angelia **98** 311 312

PULSIFER cont'd
Ann L. **89** 352
Anna **53** 254 **56** 259 **58** 274
Annie G. **89** 352
Apphia (Jenkins) **98** 311 312
Apphia J. **98** 311 312
Arvilla Eliza (Bancroft) **96** 132
Benedict **51** 408 **53** 254 **60** lv **142** 54
Benjamin **98** 259 261 263 311 312 **133** 281
Betsey **62** 159 **88** 69 **98** 311 312
Betsey (Dwelee) **125** 101
Betsey W. **88** 241
Bickford **52** 104 **53** 254 **60** 198 **109** 155
Calvin F. **98** 259
Caroline A. **89** 352
Charles **85** 170
Charles E. **98** 259
Charles H. **89** 352
Charles Weaver **55** 63
Christiana **98** 312
Christiana (Chandler) **98** 261 312
Cornelia Lucretia (Boardman) **60** xxix xxxvi
Cushman R. **88** 241
D. **55** 59
D. B. **98** 259
Dana **55** 63
David **52** 104 **53** 254 450 **54** 295 438 **55** 61 63 425- 429 **56** 249-251 387 389 391-393 **58** 272 **66** xvii **79** 51 **88** 68 233 **99** 10 16 **109** 155 **144** 293 **145** 214 222 **147** 324 **148** 12
David Henry **74** 30
Deborah **98** 313 314
Diantha B. **98** 259
Dorcas **98** 312
Dorcas (Ford) **98** 263 312
Ebenezer **54** 294 **56** 254 387 **125** 101
Elias **56** 251
Eliza **98** 259
Elizabeth **56** 253 259 387 388 **78** 307
Elizabeth Aspinwall **69** li
Elizabeth D. **103** 44
Elizabeth H. **98** 312
Elizabeth J. **86** 55
Elizabeth Stowell **54** 295 **55** 63
Ella M. **98** 312
Ellen L. **86** 55
Ellen N. **98** 312
Elnora **87** 110
Elva (Heap) **89** 133
Elvin D. **98** 312
Elvira **55** 63
Emaline **86** 55
Emily **86** 54 55
Emily Jane **103** 46
Emma L. **98** 259
Ephraim **88** 69 241

PULSIFER cont'd
98 311 312
Ethel **89** 352
Ethel L. **89** 352
Eunice (Rich) **84** 303
F. A. **89** 352
Fobis C. **98** 259
Frank A. **89** 352
Franklin Elijah **96** 132
Fred Lovell **68** 160
Freelove **86** 55
Freeman **85** 411
George Henry **55** 63
Haley **88** 241
Hannah **53** 254 **88** 68 69 233
Helen W. **98** 312
Herbert F. **89** 352
Horace E. **98** 259
Howard E. **98** 259
Hudson **86** 55
Huldah **85** 411
I. D. **91** 332
Irena **56** 259
Isaac **98** 311 312
Isaac M. **98** 312
J. D. **91** 332
Jared **86** 54 55
Jemima **56** 257
Joanna **56** 389
John **55** 430 **56** 259 386 393 **58** 272
John A. **86** 55
John C. **98** 312
John E. **86** 55
John R. **98** 311 312
John S. **53** 254
John T. **88** 241
Jonathan **53** 254 **83** 130 **88** 69 **98** 312
Joseph **62** 71 **85** 411 **87** 110 **98** 311
Joseph S. **98** 311 312
Laura **55** 63
Laura Ann **85** 170
Lewis **55** 63
Lois Ann **89** 355
Lucinda **85** 170
Lucy **55** 61 **56** 249 **88** 241
Magor **85** 411
Marcus W. **98** 312
Margaret L. **89** 352
Martha A. **85** 163
Martha V. **98** 311 312
Mary **98** 312
Mary (Bean) **133** 281
Mary Ida **68** 160
Mary R. **98** 312
Mehitable **88** 241
N. G.H. **91** 332
Nabba **88** 152
Nabby **60** 198
Nancy **83** 130 **89** 352 **98** 312
Nancy B. (Osgood) **87** 94
Nathan **87** 94
Nathaniel **54** 291 **89** 352 355
Nehemiah **68** 160
Nehemiah Alva **88** 233
Nettie N. **87** 94

PULSIFER cont'd
Olive **98** 314
Oliver **56** 257
Patty **56** 251
Pauline **74** 30
Phebe **88** 233
Phebe A. **118** 131
Philena **55** 61 **56** 250 389
Pitt P. **89** 352
Polly **56** 256 **88** 69
Priscilla **54** 295 **55** 429 **56** 249 251 388
Rachel **88** 69
Rebecca **55** 63 **56** 389 **103** 44
Rebecca A. **89** 352
Rebecca T. **89** 352
Rhena **56** 249
Robert **62** 159
Rubie A. **89** 352
S. G. **98** 259
Sally **55** 61 63 **56** 258
Samuel **56** 258 **88** 152
Samuel G. **98** 259
Samuel Woods **54** 295 **55** 63
Sarah **52** 104 **53** 254 **56** 318 69 107 **98** 263 312
Sarah A. **86** 55
Sarah F. **87** 110
Sarah H. **98** 312 314
Seve **88** 152
Solomon **56** 259 **58** 274 **88** 68 233 **98** 312
Sophia **89** 352
Sophronia **133** 281
Susan **125** 221
Susan Nichols **122** 114
Susanna **51** 407 **53** 254 **100** 240
Sylvester **85** 170 411 **86** 55
Thomas **140** 239
Timothy D. **88** 241
Unity **54** 294 **56** 254
Victoria **89** 352
William **84** 303 **98** 314
William D. **98** 314
William E. **83** 130
William H. **53** 254
William Henry **60** xlvii lv
Wilson **88** 241
Winfield S. **98** 259
PULSOM
Catherine **133** 320
Catherine (Bean) **133** 320
Catherine A. **133** 230
Rhoda Ann **133** 230
Pulteney see Poultney
Pulter see Poulter
PULTZ Polly **95** 339
PULVER Annie **107** 208
Belle Charlotte **97** 77 126
Charity (Barton) **107** 58
Charlotte L. **97** 126
Clara A. **97** 126
Gordon Ward **97** 126
Henrietta **107** 301
James Madison **107** 58
Maye Louise (Bancroft) **97** 126

PULVER cont'd
  Wilhelmus **107** 58
PUMHAM Chief **99** 103
PUMPELLY Pumpely
  Pumphilly
  Amélie Sibyl Huntington
    79 319
  Betsey **109** 182
  Betty **136** 36
  Elise **79** 319
  Eliza Frances **79** 319
  Hannah **79** 317
  John **79** 317 **136** 36
  Margarita **79** 319 **85** 198
  Mary Hollenback **79** 317
  Raphael **65** xxi **66** xxxvii
    67 xxii **68** xxi **69** xv **71**
    xviii **78** 216 **79** 317 318
  Raphael Welles **79** 319
  William **79** 317
PUMPHREY Pumphy
  Ann **73** 136
  Elizabeth **73** 279
  James **73** 147 277
  John **61** 136
  Lloyd **73** 272
  Margaret **73** 136
  Rachel **73** 220
  Richard **73** 147
  Sarah **73** 220
  William **73** 153 270
  William E. **73** 265 274
Pumroy see Pomeroy
PUNCH Terence M. **145**
  176 177
PUNCHARD Abigail **51**
  407 **75** 309
  Benjamin **107** 183 185
  Betsey **75** 310
  Edward Oscar **68** xxxv
    72 xxxi li lii
  Emma **72** lii
  George **54** lxxvii
  Hannah **75** 309
  Jeremy **86** 432
  John **72** li **86** 427 432 **87**
    44 **88** 143
  Julia Arabelle **72** lii
  Margaret **86** 432
  Margaret (Fiske) **87** 44
    88 143
  Mary **75** 309 310 **76** 131
    86 432
  Mehitable **75** 309
  Nancy Maria **72** li
  Phebe **75** 310
  Samuel **72** li
  Sarah **75** 309
  Thomas **72** li
  William **51** 407 **72** li **75**
    309 310 **76** 131 132
  William de **145** 7
PUNCHARDON
  —— **145** 8 12
  Ermengard **145** 5
  John **145** 5 6
  Mabel **145** 5-7
  William **145** 6 13
PUNCHON
  Amy (Wyllys) **141** 98

PUNDERSON Ponderson
  —— **54** 23
  — Rev. Mr. **62** 277
  Damaris **52** 325
  Ephraim **60** 18
  Hannah **81** 130 **136** 327
  John **52** 325 **54** 225 **81**
    122 124 130
  Lydia **66** 202 **85** 336
  Margaret **81** 130
  Mary **67** 126
  Prudence **60** 18
  Rhoda **54** 225
  Sarah **66** 207
  Thomas **66** 202 **67** 126
PUNTER Giles **52** 68
  Peter **67** 62
PUNY David **145** 357
PUPPLETT
  Richard **64** 139
Purcas see Purchase
PURCELL Purcel
  Alice **79** 123
  Bridget **93** 371
  Charles **85** 290
  Clara Winslow **74** 300
  Gervaise **74** 301
  Helen Augusta **74** 301
  Hugh Devereux **74** 301
  Hugh Gervaise **74** 301
  John Edwin **97** 208
  Margaret **71** 69
  Marion **85** 290
  Martha S. **125** 177
  Mary **95** 286
  Matilda Helen
    (Morehouse) **132** 243
  Nicholas **64** 224
  Penina (Crawford)
    85 290
  Phebe **127** 319
  Richard **132** 243
  Sarah A. **68** 151
  Sarah M. **68** 151
  Thomas **68** 151
  Virginia (Crawford)
    85 290
  William **73** 227
PURCHASE Purcas
  Purchas Purchis
  Purkas
  Aquila **100** 222
  Caleb **102** 32
  Elizabeth **56** 69 **63** 32 **85**
    147 **112** 112 **113** 98 **122**
    36 40
  Elizabeth (Andrews)
    (Pike) **104** 177
  Elizabeth (Mott / Mote)
    147 379
  Francis **147** 379
  George **76** 229 231 **122** 33
  Joan **91** 112 **95** 354
    100 222
  John **54** 404 **85** 147 **147**
    249 250
  Mary **54** 404 **76** 229 231
    85 147
  Oliver **65** 187 **100** 222
  Rose **147** 379
  Samuel **59** 181 182 **66** xv

PURCHASE cont'd
  76 231
  Sarah **55** 305 **143** 251 252
  Thomas **61** 278 279 **66** 180
    88 389 **95** 321 **101** 18
    104 177 **119** 16 **141** 217
  William **147** 379
PURCIPHER
  David **67** 373
  Elizabeth **67** 373
Purcy see Percy
PURDEN Alice **83** 210
  John **97** 326
PURDY Purdie
  —— **53** 418 **55** 383
  Aaron **93** 398 **100** 63
  Abraham **103** 305
  Alexander **82** 174
  Amy (Requa) **103** 305
  Andrew S. **133** 264
  Archilaus **123** 109
  Charles A. **87** 107
  Charlotte **87** 283
  Charlotte Ann **82** 174
  Clarissa (Bolter) **133** 264
  Doris B. **87** 107
  Dorman Steele **90** 137
  Ebenezer **90** 382
  Elijah **142** 348 349
  Elizabeth **123** 110
  Emily Cecilia **82** 174
  Evelyn Mary **79** 105 203
  Ezekiel **125** 40
  Frances Elizabeth
    (Harrison) **90** 382
  Francis **52** 83
  Gabriel **60** 190
  George Jacob (Mrs.)
    102 125
  Glorianna **89** 259
  Hannah (Fowler) **103** 305
  Henry **115** 125
  Hugh **82** 174
  Isabel Townsend **93** 137
  Jafrey **143** 214
  James E. **85** 197
  Jemima **123** 109
  Jesse **121** 318
  Jessie Whitmore Patten
    62 207 388
  John **82** 174
  Julia **72** 308
  Katharine Jerome **78** 205
  Lewis **103** 305
  Lizzie **100** 201
  Lulu May Alida **83** 234
  Margaret **82** 174
  Margaret Maria **82** 174
  Mary **52** 83
  Mary (Leboyteaux)
    101 321
  Mary Ann **82** 174
  Mary Jane **82** 277
  Millie (Sisson) **87** 107
  Polly (Chase) **87** 334
  Rachel **123** 110
  Sarah Jane **82** 174
  Sarah W. **109** 192
  Stephen **87** 334
  Susan **121** 318
  Tamar (Harris) **142** 348

PURDY *cont'd*
349
Thomas **65** 244
Udavilla **108** 211
William Alexander
82 174
William T. H. **60** 279
62 xxxvii
PUREFOY
Alice **142** 228
Alice (Denton) **142** 227
229 232 233 244
Anne **66** 341-343 **120** 240
Anne (Fettiplace) **123** 254
139 283 **142** 229 233
Edward **66** 343 **123** 254
142 227 229 233 244
Galfridus **142** 228
Isabel (Brome) **142** 232
233 244
John **65** 189 **66** 342 **142**
227 229 232 244
Magdaleine **102** 153
Margaret (Chetwynd)
142 229-231
Margaret (Knightley)
142 229 230 232
Margaret (Shirford) **142**
228-230
Marger (Moton) **142** 229
232 238
Marian (Ayot) **142** 227 229
232 237 238
Mary **65** 189 **66** 342 343
123 254 **139** 283 **140**
219 **142** 227 229 233
Nicholas **142** 227 229 232
233 244
Philip **142** 227-230 232
234 237 244
Richard **66** 342
Thomas **142** 230
William **66** 343 **142** 227-
232 237 238
PURELLIO Camlin **65** 22
PURFIELD Alicia **60** 348
PURGALL —— **52** 241
PURGE Richard **100** 17
PURINTON Parinton
Purringeton
Purrington Purrinton
—— **60** 107
Abel **125** 35
Abigail **51** 463
Abigail (Farnham)
103 235
Alexander **102** 224
Alice Isadora **108** 309
Amasa **70** 360
Amos **88** 157
Andrew Jackson **102** 224
Anna **57** 67 **73** 126
Benajah **72** 262
Bethany (Chase) **88** 23
Betsey **59** 289 **88** 157
99 132
Betsey J. **121** 178
C. A. **87** 347
Charles B. **89** 384
Chase **72** 112
Clarke **88** 23 **126** 216

PURINTON *cont'd*
Clinton J. **121** 179
Daniel **102** 224 **130** 288
David **68** 167
Eben **121** 178
Elizabeth **72** 260
Elizabeth (Walker) **93** 280
Emma S. **121** 180
Eugene T. **121** 179
Francis O. **88** 47
Francis S. **99** 326
Franklin **89** 382
George **132** 120
George C. **55** xxxii
121 179
Georgietta C. **121** 182
Gideon **103** 235
Hannah (Whittemore)
108 92
Hezekiah **54** 88 **108** 92
Hulda M. **87** 347
Huldah **72** 262 267
Isabella N. (Stockbridge)
134 295
Isaiah **125** 29
Jacob K. **73** 50
James **59** 289 **88** 157
Jennie Walker **93** 279 280
Jesse **70** 360
Jessie M. **69** 317
John **72** 262 **75** 7 9 **87** 122
102 224 **132** 120 121
John T. **59** 289
Jonathan **89** 382
Joshua **52** 80 **132** 120 268
134 295
Lavine **88** 157
Lucile **137** 218
Luella J. (Gregg) **121** 179
Lydia **72** 112
Lydia (Gifford) **130** 288
Margaret **102** 224
Maria (Chase) **88** 23
Maria E. **102** 224
Marsilla **121** 177
Mary **52** 80 **59** 289 **70** 360
73 50 **83** 276 394 **102**
261 **113** 154
Mary Ann **88** 157
Mary F. **121** 177
Melissa **102** 224
Mercy **124** 63
Micajah **73** 50
Minnie M. **69** 317
Molly **90** 228 245
Moses (Mrs.) **123** 224
Nathaniel **91** 332
Patience **99** 63
Peace **72** 262
Phebe **68** 167
Philip F. **112** 72
Priscilla **99** 325 326
Rachel **99** 125
Rhoda **70** 360
Robert **88** 157 **99** 132
Rose E. (Messer) **121** 179
Ruth **68** 167 **72** 112
Ruth G. (Pike) **121** 178
Ruth H. **72** 112
Sabrina (Boardman)
123 176

PURINTON *cont'd*
Sarah **88** 7 16 **103** 155
126 216
Susan (Tibbetts) **99** 326
Susie (French) **121** 179
Thankful **63** 268
Thomas **96** 60 **123** 174 176
William **73** 126 **75** 9-11
88 157 **111** 8
Winslow **88** 157
Woodbury Bryant **93** 280
Zaceus **130** 288
Purkas *see* Purkiss
Purkett *see* Purkitt
Purkines *see* Perkins
PURKISS Purkas
Elizabeth **51** 221 **68** 271
Francis **68** 263 271
George **51** 221
James **51** 221
John **89** 175
Rose **68** 271
Sarah **51** 221
Thomas **68** 263 265
PURKITT Purkett
Clarissa **93** 89
Eunice (Wright) **137** 181
George **137** 181
Henry **137** 181
John Henry **88** 335
Rebecca (Hadley) **88** 335
PURLAND William **84** 308
PURLE William **51** 124
PURLEN
Abigail **60** 286
Elizabeth **60** 286
John **60** 285
PURMORT
Amelia **104** 104
C. H. **52** 278 376
Callista Viola **104** 104
Charles H. **62** 206
Charles Hiram **62** xxxvii
Elias **52** 376
Eliza I. (Smith) **123** 99
Hannah (Woods)
(Moulton) **141** 329
Ira M. **104** 103
James **123** 99
Jasper A. **104** 104
John **52** 376
Joseph **52** 376 **58** 297
141 329
Judith **58** 297
Lazarus **52** 376
Nathaniel Harwood
81 108 222
Philemon **58** 297 **62** 206
Richard **104** 104
Sarah **104** 104
Theopolus B. **104** 104
Theron A. **104** 103
PURNELL
Elizabeth **59** lix
John **123** 257
Mary **123** 257
Nicholas **60** 284
PURNETT Rachel **73** 137
PURPETT John **94** 369
PURPLE
Alice A. **80** 424

PURPLE *cont'd*
Clesson L. **111** 306
D. C. **111** 306
Daniel **81** 269
Edson C. **111** 306
Edward **55** 236
Elijah B. **80** 424
Ezra **109** 34
Hannah **111** 306
Hannah (Higgins) **126** 87
James **126** 87
John **61** 237
Josiah **111** 306 **126** 87
Josiah DeWitt **111** 306
Julia **126** 87
Liva **126** 87
Luba **111** 306
Lucy **111** 306
Lydia **80** 424 **126** 87
Martha **126** 87
Martha (Cook) **126** 87
Mary (Penfield) **109** 34
Mehitable **126** 87
Nathaniel **126** 87
Phila **126** 87
Polly **126** 87
Ruth **106** 217 **107** 160
   126 87
Samuel **80** 424
Samuel S. **80** 424
Samuel Smith **55** 236
PURRIER Alice **55** 378
Annes **135** 280
Catherine **55** 378
Isabel (Tilbrooke) **135**
   279 280
Joan **135** 279-283
John **135** 280
Mary **55** 378 379
Ralph **135** 275
Robert **135** 280
Sarah **55** 378 379
Thomas **135** 275 278-281
   283 284
William **55** 378 **135** 275
   280
Purringeton *see* Purinton
Purrington *see* Purinton
Purrinton *see* Purinton
PURRIS William **111** 204
PURRY —— **83** 36
Mary **83** 27 29
St. Patrick **83** 27 29 **147** 69
PURSE George **69** 15
PURSELL
Christiana **108** 155
William McClain (Mrs.)
   101 125
PURSER James **63** 143
Thomas **52** 134
PURSEY John **111** 171
PURSLEY
Ann Elizabeth **118** 295
Miriam **115** 213
Peter **114** 189
Purves *see* Purvis
PURVEY Anne **74** 131
John **74** 69 131
Robert **74** 69
William **74** 69 131

PURVIANCE
Samuel **130** 174
PURVIS Purves
Edna Cleora **78** 109 206
Harriet **81** 42
Jay **81** 42
John Coleman **109** 131
Peter **63** 143
PURY Anne **139** 230
PUSE Anna **69** 253
Richard **69** 253
PUSEY Pewsey Puzey
—— **53** 460
— Mr. **80** 52
Francis **52** 262
Nathan M. **108** 219
Pennock **58** 106
Phebe **80** 54
Rebecca **52** 113
S. Florence **80** 52
PUSHARD
Elizabeth **88** 277 377
PUSHEE
Abigail **118** 330
Alice Markham **84** 329
Charles **84** 101
Daniel **118** 330
Eliza Arnold (Hunt)
   84 101 329
Elizabeth **118** 330
Emma Jean (Rowley)
   84 101
Gabriel **84** 101 **118** 330
George Durant **81** 217
   84 101 234 235 329 **85**
   187 201
George Horton **84** 234
   329 **85** 187
Henrietta **69** 256
James M. **69** 256
Jeanne **84** 101
John **84** 101 **118** 330
John Clark **84** 101 329
John E. **73** 318 **74** xxv
John Edward **80** 102 216
   81 217 **84** 101 329 **85**
   201
Jonas **64** 147
Lillian (Horton) **84** 329
Lucy (Blodgett) **84** 101
Lydia **64** 147
Mary **118** 330
Mary A. **69** 256
Nathan **118** 330
Persis (Durant) **84** 101
Rosanna (Clark) **84** 101
Roy Edward **84** 101
Ruth **118** 330
Sarah **118** 330
Sarah (Williams) **84** 101
PUSHOR
George Prescott
   89 114
Lizzie Amanda (Norris)
   89 114
PUSLEY Caleb **52** 429
Margaret **90** 381
Sarah **52** 429
PUSSELL Rebecca **73** 140
PUTE
Frank I. **121** 180

PUTE *cont'd*
Lizzie T. (Trow) **121** 180
PUTNAM Putenham
Putman Putname
—— **53** 463 **56** 100 **60** 126
   62 307 388 **86** 44 **93** 253
   133 154 **145** 44 160 170
   171
— Capt. **70** 301 **94** 284
— Gen. **85** 16-19 117 **86**
   37 38 40 **99** 288 **117** 319
   121 140
— Mr. **82** 419
— Mrs. **62** 129 130
— Prof. **54** 128
Aaron **73** 118 **113** 38 39
   116 111 **145** 62 65 **146**
   384
Aaron H. **78** 397
Abby Devereux (Putnam)
   90 193
Abigail **51** 408 **55** 52 **56**
   401 **78** 307 **142** 186 187
   189-191 193 194
Abraham **104** 104
Adelaide **94** 136
Adelaide Martha
   (Edmands) **87** 381
Adeline (Josselyn) **88** 287
Agnes **78** 151 **108** 111-113
Alfred **69** 5
Alfred Barron **93** 118
Alfred P. **55** 450 **56** xxxii
Alfred Porter **60** 225
Alice **83** 308 **107** 215 **108**
   112 113
Alice Bruce **85** 101
Allen **54** cx **65** 221 **105** 32
Alonzo S. **64** 154
Amelia Mary (Earhart)
   136 315
Amos **86** 44 **113** 30 31 33
   37 38 40 **139** 290
Amy **108** 110
Amy (Knowlton)
   (Presson) **86** 134
Andrew **62** 265 268 269
   64 378 **105** 31 **116** 233
Ann **55** 324 **58** 127
Ann Maria **86** 229
Anna **86** 134 **147** 80 186
Anna Cabot **93** 251
Anna Louise **91** 290
Anna Scott **79** 25
Anne **72** 101 280 281
   108 111
Anne (Holyoke) **147** 21
Annes **108** 111
Annie M. (Salter) **83** 301
Annie Walker **79** 25
Ansel G. **88** 341
Archelaus **90** 193 **91** 94
   121 248
Asa **56** 82 **108** 240
Augusta A. **126** 220
Bartholomew **53** 231
   64 13
Beatrice **64** xxxii
Benajah **125** 275
Benjamin **55** 111 **63** 75
   90 193 **136** 144 **144** 266

PUTNAM *cont'd*
Benjamin A. **76** 53 **107** 73
Benjamin F. **83** 26 27
Beriah (Mrs.) **73** 118
Bethiah Scarborough
 (Gleason) **99** 289
Betsey **70** 230 **109** 221
 113 38
C. A **81** 347
C. A. **58** cx
C. F. **111** 157
Caleb **104** 263 **125** 116
Caroline (Bryant) **88** 331
Caroline Campbell
 68 250
Carolyn Electa **90** 193
Carolyn Rosalie
 Richards (Haines)
 90 193
Catherine (Hunt) **136** 315
Charles F. **105** 154
Charles Freeman **116** 145
 117 152 **118** 162 **119**
 152 **120** 152
Charles G. **93** 251 253
 94 161
Charles Pickering **93** 253
Charlie **118** 329
Clara Adella **79** 119
Daniel **55** 419 **61** 261 **73**
 280 281 **83** 167 **86** 229
 91 94 **113** 38 39 **120** 49
 140 55
David **55** 52 **62** 269 **70** 230
 93 398 **100** 63 **114** 177
David F. **130** 234
Delia F. (Chandler) **88** 341
Deliverance **78** 296
Dorothy **67** xlviii
Dorothy (Prescott) **99** 299
Dorothy Pino (Dowse)
 83 213
Dummer **113** 41
Eben **51** 94 95 98-100 222
 227 **52** 54 80 113 246 **53**
 198 260 262 270 **54**
 xxxvii 232 460 **55** xxx
 116 448 **56** xxxi 100 **57**
 xxxii 115 227 **58** xliii
 126 **59** xlii **60** xxxiv
 190 **62** xxxv 307 388 **64**
 xxix **65** 85 **67** xxx **70**
 xlvii **71** 314 315 **74** 159
 306 **75** 217 240 **76** xv 54
 82 **77** xx 292 **78** 42 **79**
 107 108 112 196 **80** 204
 81 216 240 **82** 231 **83**
 514 **84** 179 **87** 161 380
 392 **88** 92 173 **89** 7 **92**
 366 367 370 **108** 111
 109 208 **119** 234 **135** 75
 142 186 **144** 9
Eben Fiske Appleton
 87 382
Ebenezer **64** 13 **87** 381 **107**
 187 313 **126** 226
Edith **108** 112 113
Edmond **78** 150
Edward **76** 95 **108** 111
 114 169 **142** 186
Edwin **65** 221 **83** 310

PUTNAM *cont'd*
Elijah **109** 55 **125** 23
Elijah Braman **85** 101
Elisha **55** 319 **86** 44 **136**
 109 **142** 186
Eliza **57** 357
Eliza (Page) **105** 32
Eliza G. **81** 97
Eliza Matilda **54** cx
Elizabeth **55** lxxxi 111 **63**
 74 **64** 12 13 **72** 284 **76**
 lxxxv **79** 151 **83** 488 **84**
 327 **91** 86 **93** 251 290 **98**
 270 **104** 104 181 **105** 31
 108 309 **119** 79 **125** 116
Elizabeth (Appleton)
 87 381
Elizabeth (Fiske) **87** 381
Elizabeth (Hale) **86** 229
Elizabeth (Hutchinson)
 90 193
Elizabeth (Putnam) **84**
 327 **93** 290 **105** 31
Elizabeth (Richardson)
 104 128
Elizabeth Cabot **70** lv
 89 60
Elizabeth Pierce **76** 95
Ella **104** 93
Ellen **108** 110
Elmeda L. (Pike) **103** 45
Eloisa **57** 359
Emily Maria **84** 192
Emma **128** 143
Engeland **104** 104
Enoch **65** 80
Erastus **108** 240
Ernest C. **103** 120
Ernest H. **104** 97
Esther **61** 333 338
Eunice **55** 48 **86** 44 **124** 16
Ezra **112** 212
Fannie L. (Fernald)
 123 233
Fanny **81** 256
Flora **57** 361
Flora Merinda **57** 360
Flora Minerva **57** 359
Florence (Tucker) **87** 382
Frances (Faulkner)
 136 315
Francis **134** 292
Franklin Delano (Mrs.)
 83 213
Frederic **57** 290
Frederic Lawrence **87** 382
Frederick Ward **71** 96
 87 381
Freeman **93** 219
G. **54** 231
G. P. **52** 387 **53** 137 **54** 121
 55 xxviii **56** 217 **58** xli
 100 102 **59** 233 **62**
 xxxiii 111
G. W.S. **122** 231 **123** 72
George **54** 316 **60** 226 **79**
 308 **83** 384 **107** 215
George E. B. **60** xxxvi
George G. **69** 8
George Haven **78** 113
George J. **55** 111

PUTNAM *cont'd*
George Jacob **65** vii
George N. **59** xliv
George Palmer **51** 10 18
 239 373 **136** 315
George W. **68** 250 **91** 104
 119 284
George W. S. **120** 140
 123 232
George Washington
 119 279
Georgiana **100** 110
 109 127
Georgina Lowell **93** 122
H. **116** 151
Hannah **52** 220 227 **53** 231
 55 111 242 **56** 80 **64** 12
 13 **66** 126 **83** 111 **86** 44
 96 57 **97** 379
Hannah (Marble) **86** 44
Hannah (Pindar) **90** 193
Hannah (Roberts) **90** 193
Hara **65** 222
Harriet **83** 475 **93** 252
Harriet (Upham) **83** 475
Helen (Kirby) **107** 73
Helen H. **71** xxiii
Helen K. **76** 53
Henry **57** 290 295 296 357-
 360 **78** 148 **85** 10 **108**
 110 **136** 316
Henry Dwight **57** 296
Herbert **93** 305
Hiram **78** 335
Horace **108** 240
Hugh **76** 116 **108** 111
Huldah **86** 32 44 **93** 84
 104 118
Idonea **108** 112 113
Isabella **113** 38
Israel **51** 503 **52** 76 220 227
 53 365 54 118 378 388
 55 242 359 450 **56** 80
 320 370 **58** 271 272 **60**
 324 408 **61** 232 **65** 19
 222 **67** 369 68 144 **76**
 241 **77** lxi **78** 13 26 113
 79 317 80 274 **81** 296
 83 111 167 **85** 53 **94** 228
 95 19 **99** 289 **100** 59
 101 326 104 181 **105** 31
 108 240 **109** 52 118 **129**
 372 373 **130** 217 **131** 45
 136 144 336 **137** 122
Jacob **93** 293 295 **113** 36 38
James **57** 361 **62** 307 **77**
 239 **87** 381 **97** 286 **104**
 128 **113** 318 **144** 266
James B. **103** 45
James Jackson (Mrs.) **84**
 342 **85** 197
James Josiah **82** 20
Jan **62** 388
Jane **108** 110
Jean **94** 49
Jennie **82** 237
Jere S. **118** 155
Jeremiah S. **113** 124
 117 230
Jesse **51** 201 **55** lxxxi **140**
 44 239

PUTNAM cont'd
Jethro **56** 82 **65** 141 222
Joan **78** 150 **108** 112 113
Joanna (Leland) **134** 292
Jocten **128** 58
Johannes **62** 388
John **52** 227 **53** 50 51 **55**
111 **57** 200 292 359-361
60 190 **62** 307 388 **64** 13
68 211 **79** 25 **82** 154 443
86 127 **87** 381 **88** 287
90 193 **96** 365 **103** 113
104 263 264 **105** 153
107 215 **108** 110-113
113 38 39 **119** 174 175
134 116 118 **142** 186
147 21
John Bishop **136** 315
John Jay **53** 459 **54** xxxix
57 xxxiii 124
John M. **92** 313
John P. **93** 252
John Pickering **83** 475
John W. **79** 119
Jonas **62** 72
Jonas P. **62** 160
Jonathan **63** 73 76 **68** 196
86 44 **139** 290
Joseph **52** 227 **64** 12 13
113 39
Joseph N. **118** 131
Joseph P. **122** 314
Joshua **56** 80 **113** 30 35-38
41
Judith **119** 175
Julia **57** 295 **93** 219
Julia Louise **81** 481
Katharine Lawrence
108 132
Katharine Scobey **142** 3
Keturah **133** 71
Laura **69** 320 **78** 335 336
Laura Ann **78** 335
Lefe Ann **64** 154
Levi **106** 208
Lizzie Frances **82** 20
Louisa **85** 4
Louise **100** 204
Lucia **113** 36 38 41
Lucinda **68** 250 **91** 104
117 160
Lucy **62** 76 265 **104** 264
Lucy (Brooks) **93** 293
Lucy (Redington) **109** 55
Lucy D. **62** 160
Luella 362 **92** 362
Lydia **51** 408 **55** 319 320
75 303 **88** 138 **99** 299
Mabel Elmina **57** 359
Margaret (Goodspeed)
105 153
Margaret (Scollay) **87** 381
Margaret Adelaide **87** 382
Margaret Vryling **90** 193
Maria Louisa **136** 310
Maria Louise **108** 240
Martha **55** 419 **57** 290 295
296 357 358 **91** 86 **96** 73
99 289
Martha Ann **55** lxxxi
57 296

PUTNAM cont'd
Martha Page **69** 5 **99** 87
Mary **51** 301 409 **57** 290
61 301 384 **63** 75 **64** 12
13 **67** 369 **69** 5 **71** 259
76 xli **93** 257 321 **99** 253
104 118 **109** 148 **113** 36
38 41
Mary (Baker) **134** 116 118
Mary (Fix) **90** 193
Mary (Gibbs) **142** 186
Mary (Hawkes) **136** 315
Mary (Herrick) **86** 127
Mary (Kimball) **126** 220
Mary (Orber) **90** 193
Mary (Page) 31 **105** 31
Mary (Taggart) **108** 240
Mary (Verin) **131** 107
Mary Ann **89** 38 **94** 157
Mary Farnham **86** 127
Mary H. **123** 232 **124** 62
Mary Hannah **113** 124
Mary Hurd **98** 5
Mary Jane **82** 20
Mary R. **84** 32
Mary T. S. **93** 118 122
Mary Taggart **108** 239
Mary Trail Spence
(Lowell) **92** 251
Mary Upham **93** 252
Matilda S. **119** 61
Maud **95** 125 **108** 111
Mehitable **60** 193 **64** 12 13
90 193 **143** 161
Mehitable (Putnam)
90 193
Melvina P. **78** 336
Mildred **91** 109
Mildred Hazel **91** 49
Milton **92** 313
Miriam **86** 337
Molly **52** 227 **56** 47
Mona Ilene **107** 133
Moses **109** 57 **118** 313
Nancy **83** 26 27 **134** 292
Nancy Corinne **109** 130
Nathan **69** 373 **85** 11
Nathaniel **51** 301 **53** 50
56 82 **90** 193
Nehemiah **86** 44 **127** 80
Nicholas **105** 153
Olive (Barron) **104** 263
Oliver **53** 364
Ophelia Maria **57** 359
Perley **85** 10 **105** 31
Persis (Rice) **99** 289
Peter **132** 242
Phebe **83** 480 **99** 129
141 152
Phebe (Deacon) **119** 175
Philip **72** 101
Philura **57** 290 292
Polly **61** 301 **108** 320 **113**
38 **134** 116
Polly (Peckett?) **108** 320
Polly (Titus) **114** 177
Primas **69** 223
Priscilla **113** 35 **119** 175
Priscilla (Gould) **119** 175
147 21

PUTNAM cont'd
Priscilla (Putnam)
119 175
Prudence (Johnson)
132 242
R. **89** 38
Rachel **56** 80 **83** 147
Rachel Lucinda **91** 104
Read H. **118** 75 326
119 174
Rebecca **64** 12 13 **73** 118
104 181 **105** 31 **113** 38
131 157
Rebecca (Farley) **136** 144
Rebecca (Prince) **87** 381
Relief **61** 261
Richard **78** 151 **108** 111
Robert **108** 110
Robert Mitchell (Mrs.)
122 208 **123** 221 **124**
264
Rufus **53** 456 **55** 319 **56** 81
64 361 **65** 59 60 62 139-
146 149 150 220-225 229-
231 259 260 335 339 **67**
95 **72** 292 **79** 161 **85** 353
86 32 37 44 461 **99** 289
100 278 **113** 14 **117** 91
122 164 203 **123** 286
140 294 295 298 **141**
211 **142** 186 300
Ruth **51** 373 **62** 307
113 124
Ruth (Hathorne) **87** 381
Ruth (Thompson)
117 230
Ruth (Thornton) **117** 230
118 155
Ruth (Wilkins) **85** 53
Sally **75** 308 **113** 38 **128**
143 **134** 118
Samuel **61** 301 **71** 259 **82**
497 **91** 199 **94** 157 **96** 57
365 **113** 36 39 41 **114** 39
Samuel H. **62** 75 160
Samuel R. **92** 251 **93** 118
122 257
Samuel R. (Mrs.) **92** 251
Sarah **52** 220 **56** 370 **63** 73
64 12 13 **82** 497 **83** 214
87 381 **94** 157 **106** 143
108 112 113
Sarah (Bacon) **136** 336
Sarah (Brocklebank)
97 286
Sarah (Gooll) **82** 497
96 57
Sarah (Hewitt) **137** 361
Sarah (Hutchinson) **136**
144 336
Sarah (James) **87** 381
Sarah (Maverick) **96** 365
Sarah (Page) **105** 31
Sarah Maria (Rockwood)
126 220
Seraph **57** 358
Sewall **64** 233
Silas **119** 160
Sophia **57** 290
Sophia (Marshall) **122** 314
Stella Bertha **109** 129

PUTNAM cont'd
119 74
Stephen **62** 268 **86** 44
109 57 **142** 186
Submit **75** 308
Sumner **113** 36
Susan Elizabeth
(Thompson) **119**
279 284
Susan Emma **85** 101
Susanna **86** 44 **127** 80
Susanna (Fuller) **86** 44
Tabitha G. **133** 54
Tamar **96** 285
Tarrant **93** 398 **100** 63
105 31 **121** 248
Terissa **113** 33 40
Thankful **61** 261
Theresa **107** 124 **108** 129
Thomas **52** 227 **55** 324
326 327 448 **62** 388 **67**
369 **78** 148 296 **90** 193
108 94 110 112 113 **131**
107 **142** 186 **147** 21
Timothy **137** 361
Tryphena J. (Remick)
120 140 **123** 232 233
Uzial **113** 30 37 38
Victorine (Haven)
136 315
W. P. **99** 289
Walter **57** 360
Wiley **91** 332
William **64** 12 13 **68** 250
86 40 **92** 50 **99** 299 **105**
31 **108** 110-113
William Allen **75** xxiv 65
90 193 200 **91** 141 144
120 147
William B. **88** 331 **104** 264
William De **103** 286
William Henry Harrison
54 197 **57** 359
William Lowell **93** 257
William R. **65** 222
William S. **123** 233
Woolcot Deforest **57** 357
Zilpah **75** 305
PUTNEY Putne
—— **92** 275
A. E. **91** 201
Anna Cordelia **76** lxxxix
Ardelia **76** lxxxix
Benjamin **134** 174
David **134** 174
Eleazer **120** 319
Ellis **134** 174
Ellsworth **75** 271
Etta W. **121** 180
George Henry **76** lxxxix
Gideon **73** 104
Harriet Ann **92** 318
Harvey **120** 319
James **134** 174 **137** 327
John **92** 313 318 **117** 313
Jonathan **105** 283
Laura A. **103** 47
Lewis **134** 174
Lyman T. **126** 269
Maria (Smith) **120** 319
Minnie **94** 26

PUTNEY cont'd
Orinda (Briggs) **126** 269
Pearl Blatchley **103** 119
Polly **95** 348
Rebecca **134** 174
Rhoda **92** 313
Richard **134** 174
Robert E. **120** 319
Roxana **114** 183
Roxana (Hall) **114** 183
Sally **75** 271
Samuel **91** 332
Sarah **134** 174
Sarah (Green) (Bryant)
137 327
Shadrack **91** 333
Susan **68** 157
W. R. **91** 333
Willis P. **117** 313
PUTT —— **61** 310
Andrew **93** 298
Eliza **61** 309
Henry **61** 309
PUTTENHAM
De Puttenham - see
also Putnam
—— **95** 405
Agnes **102** 192
Alice **102** 192 193
Alina **102** 193 194 312
Aline **102** 42 45
Charles Freeman **102** 125
Christian **76** 116
Denise (de Pinkeny)
102 44
Eben **102** 39 40 118 193 194
George **102** 43
Henry **102** 43 194 195
Israel **102** 73
John **95** 126 **102** 39 40 42
44 45 192 193 195
Katharine **102** 43
M. **102** 41
Margaret **102** 194
Margery **102** 194
Maud **95** 124 125 127 **102**
40 43 44 192
Nicholas **102** 39 40 43
Payn **95** 123
Ralf **102** 41 44
Richard **95** 126 **102** 39-44
192 195
Robert **102** 40 42 43 192
194 195
Roger **95** 126 **102** 42 45
192-194 312
William **95** 123-125 **102** 39
40 42-45 192 194 195
PUTTON William **131** 101
PUTTUM Abraham **100**
133 134 136 137 **101** 276
Elizabeth **100** 137 **101** 276
Michael **100** 134
William **100** 133
PUY Anna Estelle de
85 197
Puzey see Pusey
PYATT Jane **119** 181
PYBERN Mary **95** 288
Pycard see Pickard
PYCKE Joan **139** 233

PYCKENDEN
Joan **67** 162
John **67** 167
Thomas **67** 167
PYCOMBE
Edward **70** 125 126
Grace **70** 125 126
PYCROFT —— **56** 301
PYD John **120** 21
Pydgeon see Pidgeon
PYE —— **52** 127 140 **54**
325 335 **55** 437
— Lady **52** 114
Ann **98** 122 **118** 55 **125** 259
261
Ann (Taylor) **125** 198
Catherine (Pye) **125** 198
Catherine (Walters)
125 258
Charles **73** 145 **118** 46
125 198 258
Dorcas **98** 122 123
Edward **98** 119 121 122
Elizabeth **98** 122 **125** 261
Elizabeth Ann **125** 198
Esther **98** 122
George **54** 289 **98** 122
Hannah **64** 373
Henry **98** 121 122 **118** 57
Hester **52** 109 115 116
98 122
Jam **64** 256 **147** 70
John **58** 397 **64** 227 373
83 73 292 **98** 122 123
Leonard **118** 46 **125** 258
Margaret **98** 122 123
Margaret (McDiarmid)
125 259
Mary **64** 344 373 **98** 122
Mary Ann **125** 198
Nancy (Taylor) **125** 194
195 247 257
R. F. **145** 369
Robert **52** 122
Susan **98** 122 123
Thomas **86** 414 **98** 122 **118**
41-43 45 46 48 53 **125**
194 195 198 257 259
Thomas Edward **125** 195
Walter **52** 109 114 116
William Lenard **125** 194
PYERS John **80** 361
Margaret **80** 361 362
Mildred **65** 323
Peter **65** 323 324
Richard **65** 323
PYET Ann **139** 143
William **139** 143
PYGAN
Alexander **104** 188
Jane **104** 83
PYGARE ____ (Beamont)
126 254
PYGEWELL John **92** 383
Pygott see Piggott
Pyke see Pike
PYLDREN-DUMMER
—— **55** 361
PYLE Pile
—— **51** 283 **52** 113 258
Alice **80** 52

PYLE *cont'd*
Ann Pennock **80** 51
Bessie **80** 51
Edward **80** 52
Eliza (Hutchings) **126** 205
Ella **80** 52
Ella Frances **80** 52
Ella M. **80** 52
Ellis Wilkinson **80** 52
Emma **80** 51
Fletcher (Mrs.) **88** 292
Hannah **80** 51 **107** 70
Hannah Mary **80** 51
Hazel Mildred (Fletcher)
   88 292
Henry **147** 252 253
Howard **65** 94
Jane **110** 270
John **126** 205
Lizzie M. **80** 52
Lucy W. **88** 330
Lydia Emma **80** 52
Marshall J. **80** 51
Pennock **80** 52
Philena C. **80** 52
Samuel **80** 51
Samuel Simon **80** 52
Sarah Elizabeth **80** 51
William Cranston **80** 51
PYLER Mercy **100** 242
PYLES James L. **118** 248
PYLSTONE
Agnes **107** 215
Richard **107** 215
William **107** 215
Winifred **107** 215
PYM Pim Pimm Pymm
   Pymmes
—— **60** 213
Anne **90** 349
John **57** 280 **64** 189 **81** 488
Margaret **117** 108
Margaret (Penrose)
   117 57
Mary **100** 30
Rachel **117** 64
Rauffe **56** 85
Rebecca **100** 30
Samuel **117** 57 108
Susan **116** 254
Thomas **100** 30
PYMAN Joyce **52** 266
Pymm *see* Pym
Pymmes *see* Pym
PYMPE
Anne **96** 7 21-23
Anne / Amy **141** 107
Elizabeth **102** 8 247
Elizabeth (Whetehill)
   102 8 9 247
Henry **102** 248
John **102** 245 247
Reginald **96** 22 23
Reignolde **102** 247
William **102** 8 9 247 248
Pyncheon *see* Pynchon
PYNCHEPOLE
Roger **110** 124

PYNCHON Pencheon
   Pincheon Pinchin
   Pinchon Pincin
   Pincon Pyncheon
—— **58** 411 **62** 167 **101** 45
   117 13 15-18 **138** 233
   143 111
— Dr. **54** 64
Abner **129** 258
Agatha **60** 177-179
Agatha (Hammond)
   129 168
Amy **53** 220 222 377
Amy (Wyllys) **94** 387
Ann **64** 250 **74** 140 **143** 109
Anne (Andrew) **147** 21
Anne (Taylor) **129** 168
Bathsheba (Taylor) **94** 387
   123 265
Beatrice **94** 387
Betty **136** 38
Catherine **58** 37
Catherine (Brewer)
   136 329
Catherine (Sewall)
   136 329
Daniel **94** 387
Dorothy **74** 138 140 **82** 66
Edward **55** 450 **74** 69 70
   131 138 140 **95** 16 **101**
   160
Elizabeth **57** 178 **74** 138
   82 384
Esther (Billings) **94** 387
Frances **74** 140 **87** 224
Frances (Brett) **94** 387
Frances (Smith)
   (Sandford) **143** 109
Frandes Amanda (Tift)
   94 387
George M. **73** 318 **74** xxv
George Mallory **94** 387
   95 73 149
Hannah (Cowing)
   129 258
Harriette **95** 16
Joanna **57** 179
John **51** 97 **53** 220 222 377
   59 220 **63** 299 **65** 371
   382 **74** 69 140 **75** 237 **87**
   224 **94** 349 387 **101** 158
   123 258 265 **129** 200
   201 204 **133** 165 167 168
   171 175 176 **137** 267 268
   140 103 185 186 **143**
   103 109 **145** 78 **148** 36
   42 216 218 222
Joseph **58** 37 **84** 168 170
   272 377-9 12 16 **126** 51
Joseph C. **51** 94
Joseph Flint (Mrs.) **85** 197
Judith **60** 178
Louisa **57** 269
Lucy (Harris) **94** 387
Margaret **53** 220 **97** 283
Margaret (Hubbard)
   94 387
Mary **57** 180 **60** 178 **81** 101
   84 168 377 **87** 302 **108**
   307 **123** 258 **147** 21

PYNCHON *cont'd*
Mary A. (Lahm) (Leary)
   94 387
Nathan **121** 248
Philip **135** 225 232 **143** 29
Richard **97** 283
Rose **74** 138 140
Sarah **55** 153 **57** 180 398 **58**
   37 169 **60** 175 303 **68**
   150 **130** 204 207 **136**
   329
Sarah (Bliss) **94** 387
Sarah (Stockbridge)
   134 143
Simeon **60** 178 179
Simon **82** 66
Thomas **55** 153 **57** 178-
   180 398 **58** 169 **60** 177-
   179 **82** 384 **85** 259 **87** 84
   91 401 **129** 157 168
Walter **64** 250
William **51** 97 **54** civ
   cxliii 235 **55** 157 450 **59**
   lxix 220 233 **72** 190 **74**
   138 140 **75** 236 **76** 170
   81 101 **82** 151 **87** 224
   94 348 349 387 **99** 229
   101 288 289 **104** 250
   110 317 **113** 5 **129** 200
   210 **130** 204 **133** 164-
   166 168 **134** 82 **136** 329
   137 267 **138** 234 **140**
   185 **143** 101 103 104 109
   110 **147** 21 154 **148** 185
   216-218 228 359 360
William (Mrs.) **143** 109
   110
William Hyde (Mrs.)
   101 125
William Trask **95** 16
Pynder *see* Pindar
Pyne *see* Pine
PYNELL —— **67** 344
Pynkeny *see* Pinckney
PYNKERNELL John **93** 79
   171 173 174 226
Pynner *see* Pinner
Pynney *see* Pinney
Pynnock *see* Pinnock
Pynnynge *see* Pinning
PYNSBURY
Annable **54** 280
Pype *see* Pipe
Pyper *see* Piper
PYWALL Ellen **65** 320
Goddard **65** 320
PYX —— **103** 18

Qua *see* Quay
QUABRIGG
Ancelm de **109** 18
Joan de **109** 18
QUACHATASETT
Quachassett
Quachattasett
Quackassett
Sachem of Manomet
   115 88 **118** 85 86 **127**
   20 23

QUACKENBUSH
  Quackenbos
  Quackenbosh
  Quackenboss
  Quackinbush
  Quakenbosch
  Quakenbush
  Quaquinbush
  Ququinbush
  —— **57** 236 **70** 262
  Abraham **81** 99
  Adonijah Schuyler **81** 99
  Alexander **82** 390
  Armetje **81** 99
  Claesje Jacobs van **81** 99
  Clarissa **110** 30
  Emma **89** 325
  Gerritt Van Schaick
    89 325
  Hannah Abigail (Bayeux)
    89 325
  Heither **70** 262
  Helen **81** 99
  Isaac **70** 263
  Jacob **70** 263
  James **81** 99
  Julia H. **94** 399
  Leah **81** 99
  Lena **81** 99
  Margaret **61** 277
  Maritje **81** 99
  Martha **70** 263
  Mary **70** 262
  Oscar Myron (Mrs.) **94**
    304 **95** 147
  Pieter **81** 99 **106** 14
  Reynier Van **81** 99
  Sophia **81** 99
  Susantje **81** 99
QUAIFE
  Milo Milton **66** 95
  Quail see Quayle
QUAIN
  Helen **85** 429
  William Henry **108** 135
QUAKELY
  Charles **82** 53
  George **82** 53
  John **82** 53
  Quakenbosch see
    Quackenbush
  Quakenbush see
    Quackenbush
  Quale see Quayle
  Quamby see Quimby
QUANOPIN **96** 192
QUANTIN —— **58** 103
  Peter **66** 35
QUARITCH Bernard **52**
  481 **56** 112 **57** 237 **59**
  liv 51 122 **60** 110 **108 63**
  110 **65** 97 **66** xii xiii 98
  67 98 **68** 114 **72** 82 **76**
  322 **77** 162 **78** 338
QUARKER
  Hannah (Hill) **90** 104
  Thomas Jefferson **90** 104
QUARKEY
  Hannah (Bash) **132** 38
  Lever **132** 38

QUARLES Elizabeth **74**
  211 **86** 449
  Francis **56** 182 **62** 35 **74**
  140 **86** 449 **111** 72
  Hattie **93** 138
  James **111** 72
  Jemima **62** 36
  Joanna **56** 182 **111** 72 **112**
  159 **113** 241
  John **62** 37 38
  Lois **62** 40
  Lucille **78** 163
  Martha **62** 39
  Mary **61** 333 335
  Mercy **62** 35 43 **111** 315
  Nancy (Kenniston)
    86 449
  R. **61** 335
  Robert **74** 140
  Robert T. **113** 242
  Samuel **65** 339
  Sarah **62** 38
  Susan **74** 140
  William **62** 43 **107** 47
QUARRYER
  Charles **64** 262
QUARRYNDON
  Bennet **82** 443
QUARTERMAN
  Anne **95** 16
  Joseph **95** 16
  Mary Jemima **95** 16
  Robert **95** 16 18
  Sarah E. (Sanford) **95** 16
  Thomas **95** 16
QUARTERMAYNS
  Quatremain
  —— **136** 102 **141** 98
  Richard **139** 229
QUASH Quas Quache
  Andrew **59** 294
  Christopher **68** 59
  Clarissa (Freeman)
    91 198
  James **91** 198
  John **98** 121
  Samuel **70** 264
  Vroth **68** 59
QUASON John **119** 267
QUASSINGTON
  Quassyngton
  Qwassington
  Henry de **132** 45
  Isabel de **132** 45
  Quatremain see
    Quartermayns
QUATTAQUANHIM
  145 341
QUAY Qua
  —— **59** 113
  Anna (Norton) **116** 67
  Charles W. **115** 296
  Emily (Waller) **115** 296
  George R. **116** 67
  John **115** 296
  Lucy A. **116** 67
  Margaret E. **128** 160
  Mary E. **116** 67
  Norton D. **116** 67
  Olivia **116** 58
  Polly **116** 120

QUAY cont'd
  Robert **116** 120
QUAYLE Quail Quale
  Alexandros Jack **76** 81
  Ann **93** 299
  Iris St. John **102** 125
  James **76** 81
  John **93** 299
  Margaret **105** 226
  Maud C. **76** 81
  Oliver A. **60** 109
  Papie Lee **76** 81
  Patrick **93** 299
QUEALY John **88** 187
  Margaret (Fennell)
    88 187
  Patrick John **80** 333 **81**
    220 **88** 89 172 187
  Susie **88** 187
  Susie (Quealey) **88** 187
QUEAR Joe **118** 144
  Minerva **118** 144
QUEAVY Charity **60** 80
  Solomon **60** 80
QUEEKMAN
  Samuel **63** 52
QUEEN Qween
  Ann **73** 264
  Edward **115** 315 **125** 261
  Eleazer N. **78** 401
  Henrietta **73** 146
  John **73** 268
  Mary **73** 224
  Mary (Dickson) **115** 315
    125 261
  Nicholas L. **73** 227
  Samuel **115** 211
QUEENEY E. J. **129** 47
  L. L. **129** 47
  Lutie **129** 47
QUEENYARD
  Sally **125** 103
QUEKARD
  Michael **143** 257
QUEN Richard **94** 263
  Quenci see Quincy
QUENNELL
  Peter **104** 175
QUERALL William **80** 89
QUEREAU E. C. (Mrs.) **73**
  xxxiii
  Querk see Quirk
QUERNEBIE
  George **57** 317
QUERTON Emma
  (Hastings) de **96** 41 **97**
  200 201
QUESTED
  Dorothy **65** 315 317
QUESTEL
  Nicholas **65** 230
QUESTRAUW
  Jan **143** 205
QUETTEVILLE
  Jeanne de **88** 255
  William de **54** 330
QUEXIN John **81** 131
QUEYNT
  William **141** 228 230
QUICK Quicke Quyke
  —— **83** 278

QUICK *cont'd*
Alice **84** 157
Apphia **97** 393
Arthur Craig **97** 397
Bethiah (Rich) **83** 278
Dorothy **81** 106
Elizabeth **57** 64 **68** 331
Gertrude **81** 106
James **99** 319
Jane **68** 331
Jasper **68** 331
Jennie E. **130** 48
Joe **84** 271
Mabel Emily (Bancroft) **96** 289
Mary **80** 141 **84** 152
Robert O. **96** 289
Virginia **96** 289
William **97** 393 **131** 16 207 **143** 261
Willma **125** 303
QUICKE Apphia **97** 393
QUICKLY
Beatrice **117** 204
QUIFFE
Remy Thierry **65** 230
QUIGG Daniel **58** 237
Ethel Gwynna (Murray) **76** xxi **89** 57
Jane (Townsend) **89** 57
John Bolton **89** 57
Lemuel Ely **89** 57
Lemuel Ely (Mrs.) **75** 316 **76** xxi **89** 57 82 135
Murray Townsend **89** 57
QUIGGIN
Ellen K. **79** 130
QUIGGLE Quigle
Bertha Maria **108** 134 **114** 309
Harriet C. **100** 147
Mildred **104** 143
QUIGLEY Quigly
Eleanor Elizabeth **84** 210 **89** 373
Electa (Hannum) **90** 257
Elizabeth **100** 297
James **90** 257
Jane **106** 68
Jennie **94** 287
John **65** 222
Mary **80** 146
Thomas Quinn **97** 158
William Henry (Mrs.) **97** 158
QUIJADA
Aureliano **109** 285
Bernardino **109** 285
Clorinda (Burr) **109** 285
Jose Bernardino **109** 285
Roberto **109** 285
QUILL —— **100** 278
Catherine H. **98** 251
Emeline E. **98** 251
Francis **98** 251
Joseph Antonio **100** 278
QUILLAN
Daniel **108** 214
Mary Elizabeth (Kenney) **108** 214
Michael **60** 24

QUILLEN
Elizabeth **124** 305
Greenberry **124** 305
Nancy S. (Hilton) **124** 305
QUILTER
— Widow **68** 189 190
Anna **68** 189 190
Dorothy **68** 190
Edward **68** 189
Elizabeth **68** 189 190
Frances **68** 190
Jane **68** 189
John **68** 189 190
Joseph **68** 190
Mark **68** 189
Mary **68** 189 190
Rebecca **68** 190
Sarah **68** 190
Simon **68** 189 190
Thamar **68** 189 190
QUILTY
Ralph G. **116** 187
QUIMBY Quamby
Quimbey Quimbie
Quimbly
—— **89** 383
— Mr. **52** 264
— Mrs. **52** 264
Aaron **58** 41 43 44
Abel **120** 319
Abigail **52** 435 **58** 44 **120** 319
Almira (Phillips) **119** 288
Amos **146** 258
Ann P. (Averill) **91** 388
Anna **67** 353
Anthony **53** 10 11
Audry **53** 10
Benjamin **52** 428
Betsey **120** 319
Caroline R. **121** 69
Catherine **58** 124
Daniel **58** 43
David **58** 42-44
Dennis **108** 281 286 **109** 14
Dira **62** 73
Dolly **58** 44 **147** 258
Dorcas **105** 252
E. F. **91** 333
Edward **52** 268 **53** 11-13 **120** 319
Eliflet **145** 355
Elihu Thayer **63** lxi
Elisha **58** 43
Elizabeth **52** 428 **53** 10 11 **58** 42 **63** 266 **71** 260 261 **108** 281 **109** 254 **114** 182
Elizabeth (Darby) **108** 286 **109** 14
Enoch **147** 258
Esther **119** 61 63 **122** 73
Eunice **58** 124
Fred E. **88** 210
Frederick B. **117** 228
George H. **89** 383
Hannah **58** 46 125 **120** 319
Hannah (Whittemore) **108** 244
Hannah Colby **112** 76

QUIMBY *cont'd*
Helen Harriet (Towne) **97** 139
Henry **53** 11 **58** 43
Hubbard **86** 290
Ira **147** 258
Ira B. **120** 69
Jacob **147** 258
Jane **52** 268 **53** 10-13
Jemima **58** 43 **84** 96
Jeremiah **58** 42 43 121 **83** 20
Jesse **59** 289
Jethro **71** 260 261
Joanna **58** 41 **116** 264
John **53** 10 11 **58** 42 45 124 **60** 274 **71** 260 261 **80** 310 **125** 96 **145** 356
John J. **91** 388
Jonathan **145** 356
Jonathan H. **119** 61 288
Joseph **147** 258
Joshua **140** 130
Judith **58** 43
Katharine **53** 10
Lucy **52** 268 **58** 42 43
Lucy A. (Raynes) **120** 69
Lydia (Silvester) **86** 290
Mandana **83** 20
Mandana (Goodwin) **83** 20
Martha **53** 163 **147** 258
Martha A. (Howland) **140** 130
Mary **58** 43 44 121 124 **59** 289 **71** 260
Mary (Moulton) **117** 228
Mary A. **72** 106
Mary B. (Johnson) **136** 78
Mary Jane **119** 282 283
Mehitable **108** 244
Mehitable (Kenison) **140** 130
Miriam **58** 121
Molly **58** 122
Moses **58** 42-44 **120** 319
Moses A. **140** 130
Parthena **108** 281
Patience **147** 258
Paul **58** 42
Philip **63** 266
Polly **116** 304 305 **118** 242 318 **120** 319
Rebecca **62** 73 **116** 136
Rhoda **58** 42 43
Robert **53** 10 11 **71** 260
Rose **132** 277
Ruth **83** 18 **119** 62
Sally **86** 19
Sally Ann **119** 143
Salma Davis **136** 78
Samuel **52** 428 **58** 42-46 **83** 382 **108** 244 **120** 319 **145** 357
Sarah **58** 42 43 124 **88** 24 **104** 119 120 **120** 319
Sarah (Morrill) **120** 319
Sarah A. **83** 254
Sarah Ann **137** 281
Sarah J. **80** 310
Simpson **147** 258

QUIMBY *cont'd*
Susan **120** 319
Susy **58** 43
Theodosia (Moulton) **119** 61
Thomas **53** 11 **58** 44
Timothy **58** 46
Tirzah J. **79** 142
Wentworth **97** 274 **116** 226
William **58** 42
William H. **97** 139
QUIMLING Jane **78** 179
Quin *see* Quinn
QUINBY Quinbey
—— **57** 232 **60** 107 **61** 314 **62** 208 **73** 315 **74** 180
Aaron **113** 287
Adelaide Sophronia **81** 221 **92** 292 295 **93** 142 **109** 311
Alice **101** 63
Ann **74** 191
Ann (Plummer) **92** 292
Anne **73** 315 **78** 94
Azubah **57** 187
Benjamin **60** 44 **65** 94 **73** 315 **74** 187 190 191 **92** 292
Benjamin Wentworth **74** 40
Betsey **74** 187
Candace Ellen **78** 96
Carl Noyes **65** xxxv
Charlotte Angela (Bartels) **124** 148
Edward **65** 163
Eliphalet **55** 67
Elizabeth **78** 93
Elizabeth (Betts) **101** 63
Elizabeth (Cornell) **113** 287
Elizabeth (Jones) **92** 292
Elizabeth (Osgood) **92** 292
Erasmus Collins **80** 335 **81** 220 **100** 44 116 **101** 63
Eunice **74** 40 **78** 94 95
Florence Adelaide **78** 96
Fred E. **66** 52
Frederick Augustus **124** 148
George Washington **92** 292 **109** 311
Henry Brewer **78** 93 94
Henry Cole **60** 274 **61** 314 **62** xxxv 107 208 390 **74** xxviii **77** xxxvii **78** 93 95 96 **102** 6
Henry Cole (Mrs.) **86** 198
Isaac **65** 94 **77** 164 **125** 33
Jacob **73** 315 **74** 35 40 186 191
Jane **65** 163
Jane Elizabeth **61** 314 **78** 94 95
Jesse B. **101** 63
John **66** 89 **74** 41 **78** 94 95
Jonathan **65** 94
Joseph **57** 187 **73** 315 **78**

QUINBY *cont'd*
94 **92** 292
Lucy Ann (Corliss) **92** 292
Lydia **57** 186 **74** 35 187 190
Lydia (Clements) **92** 292
M. Octavia **78** 93 94
Maria Coffin **78** 96
Marietta **66** 52
Mary **78** 94 **113** 287
Moses **73** 315 **78** 94
Nancy **74** 187
Nathan **57** 187 **73** 315
Phebe **77** 163 164
Rachel **78** 94
Rachel (Morrill) **92** 292
Rebecca **74** 41
Robert **60** 274 **65** 94 **78** 93 94 **92** 292
Rosina **57** 187
Ruth **55** 376
Samuel **60** 44
Silas E. **65** 94 382
Simeon **73** 315
Tamzine **74** 40
Thomas **61** 314 **78** 94 95
William **78** 93 **92** 292
William Emory **62** 394
QUINCE
Richard **52** 169 171
QUINCY De Quincy Quenci Quincey Quinsey
—— **53** 291 **55** 361 **56** 344 **59** 227 **92** 16 **112** 64 **121** 207 210 **140** 239
— Mr. **59** 87
— Mrs. **121** 285
____ (Atkins) **140** 33
Abby Adams **51** 37
Abigail **55** 148
Abigail (Atkins) **83** 204 **89** 362
Abigail (Phillips) **84** 260 **140** 239
Albert **105** 235
Alice **92** 32
Ann **72** 201 **84** 165 **99** 199
Ann (Huske) **84** 165
Anna **59** 155 **134** 138
Anne **92** 32 **99** 198 **102** 304
Anne (Palmer) **92** 32
Ascelina **112** 63
Catherine **130** 173 174
Charles Frederick **105** 236
Daniel **53** 299 300 **72** 201 **106** 17 **121** 210 276
Dolly **85** 24
Dorothy **52** 268 **53** 190 **54** 419 451 **55** 21 **56** 258 **59** 363-365 **61** 198 **89** 362 **97** 6 **103** 75 **130** 168 173-176 178
Dorothy (Flynt) **53** 190 **83** 204 **106** 307
Dorothy Clement **93** 86
Edmund **53** 190 296 299 300 378 **54** 419 57 281 388 **59** 158 363-365 **61** 198 **67** 208 **76** lxiv **78** 423 **83** 204 **84** 152 165

QUINCY *cont'd*
249 255 261 262 **85** 24 **91** 94 **92** 30-32 **93** 260 **94** 47 **99** 230 **101** 276 277 334 **103** 209 **105** 236 **106** 147 307 **110** 217 218 **116** 111 **119** 20 **121** 285 **130** 168 173 **131** 165 166 168-170 189
Edmund (Mrs.) **92** 250
Edward **58** 69
Elena **108** 174
Eliza **78** 397 **99** 198 **105** 235
Eliza Susan **65** 200
Elizabeth **51** 37 303 **53** 299 300 **54** 419 451 **59** 88 158 365 **74** 203 **84** 261 262 **92** 31 32 **98** 183 **106** 307 **121** 210
Elizabeth (Gookin) (Eliot) **83** 204 **131** 169
Elizabeth (Norton) **134** 138
Elizabeth (Wendell) **83** 204 **84** 261
Elizabeth Ann (Williams) **83** 204 **89** 362 **93** 191
Elmira **105** 235
Esther **59** 364
Eunice **84** 156
Experience **53** 299 300 **59** 154 **121** 281
F. J. **76** 46
Fanny Huntington **78** 205
Geoffrey **92** 31
George **91** 333 **92** 32
George H. **105** 235
George Washington **105** 235
Hannah **53** 299 300 **92** 14 **105** 235
Hannah (Sturgis) **145** 69
Henry **84** 367 **92** 31
Hilon **105** 235
Horatio Gates **105** 235 236
Jacob **76** lxiv **83** 204 **99** 198 199 **116** 111
Joan **92** 31
Joanna **53** 299 300 378 **59** 87 **67** 208 **78** 423 **92** 32 **121** 104 206 **131** 166
Joanna (Hoar) **110** 217 **131** 165 166 168-170
John **51** 303 **53** 299 300 **59** 158 **64** 95 **84** 252 **85** 26 **87** 399 **92** 31 32 **94** 293 **134** 138 **140** 175 176 178
John Temple **105** 235
John W. **140** 33
John Williams **76** lxiv **83** 204 **89** 362
Joseph **84** 379
Josiah **51** 25 37 369 476 **53** 10 183 **54** 247 252 **55** 147 148 **56** 337 57 281 **58** xc 69 **59** 125 **60** 308 **63** lii **64** lx **67** 184 **73** 1 **75** lxxxix **76** 220 **77**

QUINCY *cont'd*
lxxxiii **78** 103 397 **80**
135 **82** 480 483 **84** 147
260 261 379 **99** 9 24 80
105 42 **121** 248 **129** 136
130 24 29 **131** 189 272
132 34 **136** 292 **140** 150
172-174 239 **145** 69 205
227
Judith **53** 299 300 **59** 87
131 165 166 168-170
Judith (Pares) **92** 32
Julia (Child) **83** 203
Julia Child (Bradford)
83 204
Julia Frances **105** 235
Lucilla Pinkney (Parker)
92 250 **94** 47
Lucretia Deming **76** lxiv
Lucy **51** 303
Margaret (de Beaumont)
(Countess) **112** 61
Margaret (de Beaumont)
Countess **112** 61
Martha **53** 299 300
Mary **51** 37 **53** 299 300 **59**
158 **67** 208 **82** 297 298
105 235 **125** 215 **131**
168 169
Mary Ann **105** 235 236
Mary Apthorp **51** 369 **82**
480 **89** 371
Mary H. **58** 412
Mary Jane **82** 480
Mary Perkins **55** 361 367
56 109 **71** 289 **76** xxx
lxiv **77** xii **99** 183
Matilda **112** 64 65
Matilda (St. Liz) (Clare)
112 62
Mehitable **84** 249 **101** 276
277
Mehitable (Temple)
84 249
Norton **57** 281 **58** 69 **94**
293 **107** 313 **138** 227
140 171 176
Orabella (Ness) **112** 63
Polly **84** 367 **105** 235 236
133 308 309
Polly (Pettis) **105** 235
Pomp **84** 267
Richard **92** 31
Robert **92** 31 **101** 277 **112**
61 63-65
Robert Hancock **105** 235
Roger **79** 61 **108** 174
111 200
Rose (Thurlbie) **92** 32
Ruth **53** 299 300 **101** 334
121 270
Saher **102** 297 **105** 236
108 174 **112** 61-65
Samuel **51** 37 **67** 114 **92** 14
16 **94** 294 **116** 111
Sarah **105** 236
Simon **112** 64
Thomas **64** xlvi **92** 16 31
32
Thomas Burnham **105**
235 236

QUINCY *cont'd*
Thomas Dennie **77** xxv
79 196 **80** 204 **81** 215
82 231 254 **83** 203 204
222 236
Walter **92** 31
William **92** 31 32
William Adair **105** 235
William P. **78** 412
QUINER
Samuel **110** 281
William **78** 70
QUINEY —— **56** 342
Adrian **128** 136
Joanna (Hoar) **101** 334
Richard **128** 136
QUINLAN
Ann Tasker **79** 331
Francis J. **78** 114
Hugh **79** 331
John **62** 301
Mary **60** 24
Tasker Carter **79** 331
QUINLAND Anne **99** 209
QUINLEY Quinly
Lucretia (Skarriot) **126**
256 **128** 20
Thomas **126** 256 **128** 20
QUINLON
Angeline **86** 55
Harriet A. **86** 55
William **86** 55
Quinly *see* Quinley
QUINMAN
Isabella K. **74** 25
James **102** 31
Mary **102** 31
QUINN Quin
—— **106** 321
Eliza (Bates) **90** 55
Elizabeth Lucy **106** 64
Ellen (Cummiskey)
139 197
Gertrude Veronica **97** 389
Helen Wells **101** 164
Hillrie Marshall **89** 323
Hugh **75** 305
James **105** 206
Jane **89** 40
John **83** 224
Kate (Darden) **89** 323
Katharine Lester
(DeMille) **113** 306
Louisa **84** 32
Lucy (Carver) **89** 40
Mary (Dickson) **115** 315
Mary Jane **83** 224
Maud **80** 152
Miles S. (Mrs.) **118** 75
119 155
Molly **100** 54
Nancy **125** 220
Nicholas **90** 55
Patrick **131** 87
Sally **83** 409
Samuel **89** 40
Thomas **62** 81 **73** 153
93 299
Thomas C. **67** xxxii
W. Johnson **107** 9

QUINNAM
Caroline T. **113** 237
James **72** 276 **100** 235 303
Mary **72** 276 **100** 235
Mary (Forester) **100** 303
Quinsey *see* Quincy
QUINT
—— **73** 194 **82**
290 297 316
— Mr. **83** 36
Abigail **74** 215 217 225
Alonzo Hall **51** 67 228 **54**
453 **55** 245 247 **58** 248
392 **61** 201 **64** 329 **66** 82
67 82 84 **75** 159 **99** 14
124 287 292 293 303
Anna **74** 264
Benjamin **73** 205
Betsey **73** 204
Clarissa **73** 192
Daniel **74** 251 254
David **74** 253 **82** 323
Dorothy **74** 250
Eliza **73** 194 202 **82** 317
Eliza A. **68** 99
Elizabeth **55** 312 **74** 250
254 **82** 210 326 510
Esther **74** 253 **82** 320
George W. **91** 199
Hannah **55** 312 **74** 225
253 256 **82** 502 509
Hannah Abigail **68** 99
Isabella S. **77** 50
Jane O. T. **73** 202
Joan R. **120** 68
John **55** 312 **58** 249 **74**
217 254 **82** 316 320 321
323 326 502 509
John A. W. **73** 194
John Andrew **73** 203
Joseph **68** 99 **73** 194 202
204 **74** 250 **82** 314
Joshua **74** 215 217 225 256
82 314 317 321 324 328
502
Luther **103** 300
Lydia **82** 502
Margaret **65** 354
Mary **65** 355 **73** 196 **74** 253
Molly **74** 254
Nabby **82** 502
Nancy J. **91** 121
Polly **73** 196
Rachel **82** 502
Rebecca **73** 194 203
Sally **74** 254
Sarah F. **73** 193
Thomas **65** 354
William **74** 264 **82** 210
321 328 **145** 348
William Goodwin **73** 205
QUINTARD Abraham
109 185 190 192
Adah Louise **109** 263
Adele Sophia (Hughes)
(Rudd) **109** 261
Adeline **109** 261
Ann **109** 259
Ann Elizabeth **109** 261 263
Ann Mary (Jocelyn)
109 262

QUINTARD *cont'd*
Anna Virginia **109** 260
Anne **109** 193
Anson **109** 257 259 263
Antoinette **109** 192
Betsey **109** 257
Caroline **109** 259
Caroline Louise
  (Gilliland) **109** 263
Catherine D. **109** 261
Charles **109** 193 259 264
Charles Augustus
  109 265
Charles Edward **109** 261
Charles Henry **109** 264
Charles Morris **109** 258
Charles R. **109** 261
Charles Todd **109** 260
Charles Van Rensselaer
  109 261
Charlotte (Dodge)
  109 192
Chauncey Thomas
  109 263
Clarissa **109** 190
Clarissa (Grant) **109** 262
Clarissa (Hoyt) (Shaw)
  109 260 **145** 145
Cornelia (Bowman)
  109 192
Cornelia Chloe (Clark)
  109 264
Cyrus Beach **109** 264
Daniel Dodge **109** 193
  261
Daniel Lockwood
  109 265
Deborah **109** 192
Deborah (Knapp) (King)
  109 187
Deborah Palmer **109** 192
Dena (Johnson) **109** 261
Edward Augustus
  109 260
Edwin Lewis **109** 264
Effie C. (Johnson) **109** 261
Eleanor Elizabeth **109** 261
Eli Sanford **109** 263
Eliza Catherine (Hand)
  109 260
Eliza Jane **109** 258
Elizabeth **109** 190 193 259
Elizabeth (Byington)
  109 264
Elizabeth (Davis) **109** 265
Elizabeth (De Mille)
  109 190
Elizabeth (Ford) **109** 262
Elizabeth (Pickett)
  109 259
Elizabeth (Whitney)
  109 263
Emeline Maria **109** 264
Emma Adelaide **109** 263
Esther Betts (Gregory)
  109 265
Esther Maria (Church)
  109 265
Eunice B. (Hoyt) **109** 262
Evert **109** 190 258 259 263
Fanny **109** 190

QUINTARD *cont'd*
Frances **77** 251
Francis Edmond **109** 264
Francis Egbert **109** 262
Francis Elizabeth
  (Morgan) **109** 260
Francis Walter **109** 261
Frederick A. **109** 263
Frederick Francis **109** 265
George **109** 259 265
George Franklin **109** 265
George W. **109** 263
George William **109** 260
Hannah **109** 186 188 258
  261 **145** 150
Hannah (Knapp) **109** 185
Hannah (Palmer) **109** 192
Hannah (Raymond)
  109 258
Hannah (Warren) **109** 263
Hannah Elizabeth **109** 192
  259
Hannah Hamlin **109** 263
Harriet Emeline **109** 262
Harriet Maria (Allen)
  109 264
Helen (Ray) **109** 265
Helen Rebecca **109** 263
Henry **109** 259
Henry Ferris **109** 261
Henry Harrison **109** 258
  262
Isaac **60** 274 **109** 184 185
  187 188 190 192 259 260
  145 145
Isaac Burroughs **109** 190
Isaac Edwin **109** 261
Isabelle (Chapelle)
  109 261
Jacques **109** 188
James **109** 188 257 262
James A. **109** 262
James Bradley **109** 264
James D. **109** 265
James H. **109** 190 257
James Hamilton **109** 262
Jane **109** 188
Jane M. (Bennett) **109** 262
Jeanne **109** 188
Jeanne (Baillereau)
  109 187
Jeanne (Fumé) **109** 184
John Addison **109** 260
John Cotton **109** 262
John H. **109** 262
John Henry **109** 265
Josephine (Brady) **109** 265
Josephine (Moore)
  (Atkinson) **109** 263
Joshua Ferris **109** 259
Julia A (Byxbee) **109** 265
Julia Maria **109** 262
Laticia (Humphrey)
  109 265
Lewis J. **109** 192
Lucretia **109** 262
Lucretia (Burroughs)
  109 188
Lucy (Ford) **109** 260
Lucy Cordelia **109** 261
Lucy Holmes **109** 260

QUINTARD *cont'd*
Lydia **109** 189
Lydia Ensign (Treat)
  109 264
Madaline Felicity
  (Watkins) **109** 265
Margaret **109** 262
Maria **109** 258
Maria (Ferris) **109** 192
Maria (Jelleff) **109** 264
Maria (Lockwood)
  109 265
Maria Louisa **109** 192
Maria Mercy (Whiting)
  (St. John) **109** 263
Marie **109** 184 188
Marie Anne **109** 185
Martha Elizabeth **109** 265
Mary **109** 185 188 190 193
Mary (Chapman) **109** 265
Mary (Dingee) **109** 257
Mary (Knapp) **109** 192
Mary (Shepard) **109** 265
Mary (Skiddy) **109** 260
Mary (Stevens) **109** 263
Mary Amelia **109** 262
Mary Amelia (Waterbury)
  109 260
Mary Augusta **109** 257
Mary Bogardus (Berry)
  109 265
Mary Clarissa **109** 260
Mary Eleanor P. (Harvey)
  109 261
Mary Elizabeth **109** 264
  265
Mary Emelia **109** 262
Mary Frances **109** 263 265
Mary Jane **109** 262
Mary Jane (Adams)
  109 259
Mary Jane (Campbell)
  109 261
Mary Jane (Ferris)
  109 261
Mary Louisa **109** 260
Mary Matilda (Gillespie)
  109 260
Matilda (Lounsbury)
  109 264
Morris Read **109** 258 263
Orestes Penthilus **109** 262
Peggy **109** 189
Peter **109** 187 188 190
Peter De Mille **109** 192
  260
Pierre **109** 185 187 188
Polly **109** 191 257
Polly (Dingee) **109** 257
Polly (Sanford) **109** 263
Rebecca **109** 191 257
Robert Palmer **109** 192
Ruth (Stevens) **109** 190
Sally (Chichester) **109** 262
Sally (Hilliard) **109** 257
Sarah **109** 257
Sarah (Peck) **109** 192
Sarah (Raymond) **109** 257
Sarah Ann **109** 265
Sarah Ann (Canfield)
  109 264

QUINTARD cont'd
Sarah Clark (Smith)
109 262
Sarah Deborah **109** 262
Sarah Elizabeth **109** 263
Sarah Elizabeth (Boyd)
109 260
Sarah Esther **109** 264
Sarah Knapp **109** 192
Sarah Letitia **109** 261
Seth Palmer **109** 192 259
Susan **109** 259
Susan Ann **109** 259
Susan Letitia (Ferris)
109 259
Sylvester **109** 265
Walter Chichester
109 262
William **109** 257
William A. **109** 257
William Curtis **109** 264
William Knapp **109** 193
261
William Lewis **109** 264
William Martin **109** 265
William Seth **109** 192

QUINTARD cont'd
William T. **109** 261
QUINTILIAN —— **56** 14
QUINTON
James **123** 108
Sarah (Belyea) **123** 108
QUINTRELL —— **110** 198
QUINTUS
Curtius Rufus **51** 9
Horatius Flaccus **52** 332
QUINTYNE
Henry **139** 141
QUIQUEQUANCHETT
54 264
QUIRK Querk
Christian **144** 159
Christian (Fayerweather)
(Simpson) **144** 16 165
340 **145** 66
Galer (Mrs.) **120** 319
James **64** 128 **144** 16 153
John **99** 301
Mary Elizabeth **64** 128
Mildred Richardson
120 313

QUIRK cont'd
Phebe (Tupper) (Fitz
Randolph) **99** 300 301
QUISENBERRY
Anderson Chenault
51 380 **55** 116 **56** xxxii
Andrew C. **55** xxxii
John **51** 382
Willye **105** 128
QUIVEY
Maurice Burdett **80**
333 **81** 220 **109** 308 **110**
63
Reuben **109** 308
QUIXLE John **108** 253
QUOMINE Sarah **54** 82
QUONYEAR Elizabeth
(Hare) **100** 243
Philip **100** 243
Ququinbush see
Quackenbush
Qusamequen see
Ousamequen
Quyke see Quick
Qwassington see
Quassington